W9-BTD-486

R00404

CHICAGO PUBLIC LIBRARY
NORTH AUSTIN

R0040449715

E
185.96
.D53   Dictionary of
1982   American Negro
              biography

Chicago Public Library

C
P L

REFERENCE

Form 178 rev. 1-94

NORTH AUSTIN BRANCH
5724 W. NORTH AVE.
CHICAGO, ILLINOIS 60639

REFERENCE

© THE BAKER & TAYLOR CO.

Dictionary of American Negro Biography

EDITED BY

Rayford W. Logan

AND

Michael R. Winston

W · W · NORTON & COMPANY

NEW YORK · LONDON

Copyright © 1982 by Rayford W. Logan and Michael R. Winston. *All rights reserved.* Published simultaneously in Canada by George J. McLeod Limited, Toronto. Printed in the United States of America.

The text of this book is composed in photocomposition Roma. Display type is set in Baker Signet. Manufacturing is by the Haddon Craftsmen. Book design by Marjorie J. Flock.

Library of Congress Cataloging in Publication Data
Logan, Rayford Whittingham
  Dictionary of American Negro biograghy.
  1. Afro-Americans—Biography. I. Winston,
Michael R., 1941– II. Title.
E185.96L6 1982   920'.009296073 [B]   81-9629
                                         AACR2

ISBN 0-393-01513-0

W. W. Norton & Company, Inc., 500 Fifth Avenue, New York, N Y 10110
W. W. Norton & Company Ltd., 37 great Russell Street, London WCIB 3NU

2 3 4 5 6 7 8 9 0

Contributors

Richard H. Abbott
Aldrich W. Adkins
O. Rudolph Aggrey
Wilbert H. Ahern
Ann Alexander
Raymond Pace Alexander
Samuel W. Allen
William L. Andrews
Frank Angelo
Herbert Aptheker
Howard D. Asbury
Sheldon Avery
Houston A. Baker, Jr.
Robert L. Baker
Richard Bardolph
Evelyn Brooks Barnett
Roy P. Basler
Franck Bayard
James A. Bayton
Silvio A. Bedini
Bernard W. Bell
Jewel H. Bell
Donnie D. Bellamy
Jacqueline de S. Bernard
David W. Bishop
Helen M. Blackburn
Allison Blakely
John W. Blassingame
Donald Bogle
L. Venchael Booth
Ernest B. Boynton, Jr.
Robert H. Brisbane
Sherman Briscoe
Fawn Brodie
Claudette Brown
Penelope L. Bullock
Andrew Buni
Mary Cable
Ocania Chalk
Hal S. Chase
Marcus B. Christian
Benjamin F. Clark
John Henrik Clarke
Mae P. Claytor
Anna B. Coles
Clarence G. Contee, Sr.
E. David Cronon
Barry A. Crouch
Maceo Crenshaw Dailey, Jr.

Chandler Davidson
Aldeen L. Davis
Arthur P. Davis
Clarice Winn Davis
Edwin Adams Davis
Russell H. Davis
David W. Dean
Irene Diggs
Tom W. Dillard
John A. Dittmer
Melvin Dixon
Charles E. Donegan
David C. Driskell
Ernest Dunbar
Alice A. Dunnigan
G. Franklin Edwards
Robert J. Ege
Joellyn Pryce El-Bashir
James A. Emanuel
Michel Fabre
W. Edward Farrison
Elton C. Fax
Harold W. Felton
Louis H. Fenderson
Henry J. Ferry
Louis Filler
Mary M. Fisher
John E. Fleming
Albert S. Foley, S.J.
Philip S. Foner
Stephen R. Fox
John Hope Franklin
Samuel L. Gandy
Larry Gara
Mary F. Germond
Carol V. R. George
Al-Tony Gilmore
Peter Goldman
Lorenz Graham
Daniel Savage Gray
Constance McLaughlin Green
Marcia M. Greenlee
Grace Towns Hamliton
James E. Haney
John C. Harlan
Louis R. Harlan
Conrad K. Harper
Charles W. Harris
Janette Hoston Harris

Robert L. Harris, Jr.
Hugh Hawkins
Dorothy Drinkard-Hawkshawe
J. Carleton Hayden
Robert C. Hayden
Nancy Gordon Heinl
James H. M. Henderson
Reginald F. Hildebrand
Thomas Holt
John Holway
Alton Hornsby, Jr.
Gossie Harold Hudson
Mary G. Hundley
Jean Blackwell Hutson
Sylvia M. Jacobs
Felix James
Martin D. Jenkins
Charles Johnson, Jr.
Clifton H. Johnson
George T. Johnson
Clifton R. Jones
James T. Jones
R. Frank Jones
Vernon E. Jordan, Jr.
Ernest Kaiser
Melvin D. Kennedy
J. Scott Kennedy
Judith M. Kerr
William J. Kimball
Aaron E. Klein
Theodore Kornweibel
Aaron Kramer
Kenneth L. Kusmer
Lester C. Lamon
Peggy Lamson
Rudolph W. Lapp
Julia B. Laroche
Vera Brodsky Lawrence
Delores Leffall
Lasalle D. Leffall, Jr.
Raymond LeMieux
Dominique-Rene de Lerma
Frank R. Levstik
Eugene Levy
David Levering Lewis
Harold O. Lewis
Inabel B. Lindsay
Rayford W. Logan
Joseph Logsdon

John Lovell, Jr.
Maurice A. Lubin
Irwin M. Marcus
John F. Marszalek
Robert E. Martin
Marcia M. Matthews
Grace Rushings Maxwell
August Meier
Walter M. Merrill
Carroll L. Miller
Jeanne-Marie Miller
Richard B. Moore
Edward Morrow
Vivian F. McBrier
Dorothea Olga McCants, D.C.
Richard P. McCormick
Doris E. McGinty
Robert G. McGuire III
William S. McKinney, Jr.
James M. McPherson
Paul McStallworth
Lois Jones Pierre-Noël
Earl Ofari
M. Brent Oldham
Otto H. Olsen
Charles Edwards O'Neill
Carl R. Osthaus
Nell Irvin Painter
Carol Page
Freddie L. Parker
Cassandra Smith-Parker
Guichard Parris
Thomas D. Pawley
Jane H. Pease
William H. Pease
Huel D. Perkins
Glenn O. I. Phillips
Betty L. Plummer
Dorothy B. Porter
Kenneth Wiggins Porter
Charlotte S. Price

Samuel D. Procter
Benjamin Quarles
Arnold Rampersad
Bernice Johnson Reagon
Saunders Redding
Anne Cooke Reid
George W. Reid
C. Peter Ripley
Aubrey Robinson, Jr.
William H. Robinson
Carole Cleaver Rodman
William Warren Rogers
Roger Rosenblatt
Elliot Rudwick
Sadie Daniel St. Clair
Doris E. Saunders
W. Sherman Savage
Frank N. Schubert
Gunther Schuller
Loren Schweninger
Roland B. Scott
Otey M. Scruggs
Samuel L. Shapiro
George Shepperson
J. Reuben Sheeler
Joan R. Sherman
J. C. Simpson
Donald L. Singer
Glenda Diane Smith
Robert P. Smith
William D. Smith
Raymond Smock
Raymond Smyke
Geneva Southall
Eileen Southern
James G. Spady
Dorothy Sterling
Philip Sterling
Earl P. Stover
Sterling Stuckey
Edward F. Sweat

Arnold H. Taylor
James E. Teele
Roslyn Terborg-Penn
Betty Thomas
Deborah Willis-Thomas
Emma Lou Thornbrough
Elvena Tillman
George B. Tindall
Sidney Tobin
E. Berkeley Tompkins
Eleanor W. Traylor
William J. Trent, Jr.
James D. Tyms
Constance Porter Uzelac
Bonita Valien
Preston Valien
Charles Vincent
Betty Volk
Daniel Walden
Hanes Walton, Jr.
Adelaide James Ward
Charlotte C. Watkins
Francis P. Weisenburger
Nancy Weiss
Roger Weiss
Ernest R. Welch
Elaine C. Wells
Charles H. Wesley
Earle H. West
Hollie I. West
John W. Wideman
Roy Wilkins
Edward B. Williams
Lorraine A. Williams
Robin W. Winks
Michael R. Winston
John B. Wiseman
Stanton L. Wormley, Jr.
Walker D. Wyman
M. Wharton Young

Introduction

Despite the existence of an extensive biographical literature about American Negroes, there has long been a need for a comprehensive biographical dictionary based on scholarly research. This volume has been prepared to help meet that need. Its aims are quite different from many of the earlier collective biographies in this field. Some of them, quite understandably, were undertaken for a variety of related social purposes: to "defend" the Negro against charges of inferiority by compilation of the achievements of outstanding individuals, to inspire youth by the examples of Negro "heroes and heroines," or present to the general public significant episodes in Negro history through the popular medium of biography. Better known early efforts of this kind were William Wells Brown's *The Black Man: His Antecedents, His Genius, and His Achievements* (1863), William J. Simmons's *Men of Mark: Eminent, Progressive and Rising* (1887), Monroe A. Majors's *Noted Negro Women, Their Triumphs and Activities* (1893), John W. Cromwell's *The Negro in American History: Men and Women Eminent in the Evolution of the American of African Descent* (1914), and Benjamin G. Brawley's *Negro Builders and Heroes* (1937). There have also been useful collected biographical guides to living persons, such as *Who's Who of the Colored Race: A General Biographical Dictionary of Men and Women of African Descent* (1915) and *Who's Who in Colored America: A Biographical Dictionary of Notable Living Persons of African Descent in America* (1927–1950).

With the remarkable growth of scholarly interest in Negro history in the last thirty years, significant advances have been made in the depth and quality of full-length biographies of historically important individuals. That collective biography was also receiving more scholarly attention was indicated by the publication in 1959 of *The Negro Vanguard* by Richard Bardolph, who stated in the introduction that his study was "not a compilation of success stories," but an attempt to identify "the most celebrated Negro Americans in the country's past." The standard scholarly biographical dictionaries have also included sketches of outstanding Negroes. The twenty volumes of the *Dictionary of American Biography (DAB)* include 81 Negroes, and four *Supplements* (the last in 1974) covering the period through 1950, add 39, for a total of 120. *Notable American Women, 1607–1950, A Biographical Dictionary (NAW)* includes forty-one Negro women. While all of these more scholarly efforts have repre-

sented an improvement in the availability of authoritative accounts of historically significant American Negroes, the relatively small number is clearly insufficient to meet the need for an accurate, carefully researched, comprehensive compilation.

We decided not to include living persons because of the obvious problems involved in assessing the historical significance of careers still in progress, and the difficulty of attempting to update entries continually prior to publication. It was decided that January 1, 1970, would be the latest reasonable cut-off date for several reasons. One is the fact that this date permits a better perspective of the individual's career in light of a reexamination, frequently a revision, of the events in which the individual participated. Second, additional information about the individual often changes an evaluation of his career. Third, some necessary documentary materials are not discovered, not accessible, not processed by archives until several years, or longer, after death. Even in the case of several individuals included in the *DANB*, discovery of and access to new materials and interpretations necessitated revision of some entries.

One of the most difficult editorial problems was development of criteria for inclusion. This was made all the more complex by the realization that the criteria could not be held constant for all historical periods. Thus achievements that were notable in the colonial period would in many cases be less so a hundred years later. It was a significant achievement for Jupiter Hammon and Phillis Wheatley merely to be published poets in the eighteenth century, but by the early twentieth century the standard is necessarily higher. There are similar examples in science and public affairs.

It should be pointed out that "fame" was not an important criterion. Many of the persons included in the *DANB* were largely unknown to the white public of their day, but they played significant roles in the separate life Negroes lived as a result of segregation. Opportunity is a source of career choice as well as achievement, and in those decades when Negroes were barred from participation in public life as elected officials, or economic life as entrepreneurs, and so forth, the energies of many gifted people were channeled to professions and occupations that could be sustained within the Negro community and its institutions, notably Negro churches, schools, and fraternal organizations. Thus there are, for certain periods, probably a higher percentage of clergymen and educators than would be found in the *Dictionary of American Biography.* Another consequence of race relations in the United States has been the emphasis often placed on the "the first" Negroes to enter fields formerly closed to them by law or custom. The editors have not given heavy weight to "firsts"; in many cases there are dozens or more "firsts," all of whom may have believed they enjoyed this "distinction" simply because they were ignorant of the others and the frequent absence of any clear record. As research progressed on this project, such firsts not only multiplied rather spectacularly in the hopelessly confused case of the "first Negro woman physician" but also of the "first Negro college graduate."

Many individuals included were not "national figures," but major influences in their region or local community. Some of these entries are also important as illustrations of the broad participation of Negroes in the development of the United States. Examples would be the Negro cowboys, Indian fighters, explorers, whaling captains, soldiers, and architects included. Obviously "importance" as a frontiersman will be judged differently from eminence as a lawyer or novelist. In all of these matters the editors were guided by the test of historical *significance,* more than eminence or achievement per se. What is significant will vary with changes in social and political circumstances from one period to another.

The length of entries alone should not be regarded by readers as a reflection of the editors' judgment of the significance of an individual. For many individuals, particularly in the earlier periods, reliable information is frequently unavailable or spotty. In other cases, when an individual might have been important historically, but has been relatively neglected, more explanation and background were required.

A work of this kind is not possible without the active cooperation of many persons. The editors have been particularly fortunate in receiving the assistance of many scholars, librarians, archivists, and experts in a variety of fields. Although it is impossible to name all of them, we wish especially to acknowledge the help of Dr. Dorothy B. Porter Wesley, curator emeritus of the Moorland-Spingarn Collection, Howard University; Dr. Kenneth Wiggins Porter, professor emeritus, University of Oregon; Dr. Benjamin Quarles, professor emeritus, Morgan State University; Dr. Charles H. Wesley, execu-

tive director emeritus, the Association for the Study of Afro-American Life and History, Washington, D.C.; Mrs. Amelia K. Bucksley, librarian, Keenland Library, Keenland Race Course, Lexington, Ky.; Dr. W. Montague Cobb, former editor, *Journal of the National Medical Association;* Prof. August Meier, Kent State University, Kent, Ohio; James de T. Abajian, California Historical Society; Elton C. Fax, painter and art critic, Long Island, N.Y.; Edward Tripp, editor-in-chief, Yale University Press; Ernest Kaiser, bibliographer, Schomburg Center for Research in Black Culture, New York City; James P. Johnson, chief librarian, and Ms. Betty Culpepper, Dr. Doris Hull, Mrs. Charlynn Pyne, and Mrs. Janet Sims-Wood, reference librarians, Moorland-Spingarn Research Center, Howard University; Dr. Elsie M. Lewis, professor emeritus, Hunter College of the City University of New York; Dr. Eileen Southern, professor of music, York College of the City University of New York; Prof. John Hope Franklin, past president, American Historical Association; Dr. Arthur P. Davis, university professor, Howard University.

This project was initiated in 1970. After Dr. Winston was appointed director of the Moorland-Spingarn Research Center at Howard University in 1973, Dr. Logan bore the heaviest burden of maintaining a voluminous correspondence with contributors and also writing a number of entries originally planned as joint articles.

The editors acknowledge with gratitude the support of a university-sponsored research grant from the Office of the Vice-President for Academic Affairs at Howard University.

We express grateful appreciation also to the staff of the Moorland-Spingarn Research Center, especially the staff of the Research Department, the Manuscript Division, the Reference Department, the Photography Department, the Photoduplication Department, and the Prints and Photographs Department.

We acknowledge warm thanks to Mrs. Mary Duarte, Mrs. Pat Lumpkin, and Mrs. Myrtle Grosvenor for typing correspondence and the manuscript for this reference work; to Frederick E. Bidgood for his thorough copyediting of the manuscript; and to the production staff at W. W. Norton & Company.

RAYFORD W. LOGAN
MICHAEL R. WINSTON

ABBREVIATIONS

AHR	American Historical Review
DAB	Dictionary of American Biography
JNE	Journal of Negro Education
JNH	Journal of Negro History
JNMA	Journal of the National Medical Association
NAW	Notable American Women
NHB	Negro History Bulletin

Dictionary of American Negro Biography

⇒⟩⟨⟨⇐

ABBOTT, ROBERT SENGSTACKE (1870–1940), newspaper editor and publisher. Born at Frederica, St. Simon's Island, Ga., Abbott was the first son and second child of former slave parents, Thomas and Flora (Butler) Abbott. His stepfather, John Hermann Henry Sengstacke, aroused his interest in the cause of Negro rights. Young Abbott studied at Beach Institute in Savannah, Claflin University in Orangeburg, S.C., and learned the printer's trade (1892–1896) at Hampton Institute. He received his LL.B. degree from Kent College of Law, Chicago (1898). During his study there he adopted his stepfather's surname as his middle name. He practiced law in Gary, Ind., Topeka, Kans., and returned to Chicago in 1903. On May 6, 1905, with a total capital of twenty-five cents, he founded the *Chicago Defender,* which he brashly called "The World's Greatest Weekly." By the time of his death in 1940 he had made it the most widely circulated Negro weekly. On Sept. 18, 1918, he married a widow, Helen Thornton Morrison. Following their divorce in June 1933, he married in August 1934 Edna Rose Brown Denison, the mother of five adult children and the widow of Col. Franklin M. Denison who had commanded the Eighth Illinois (370th) Infantry Regiment during World War I. Abbott had contracted tuberculosis in 1932 and died of Bright's disease in Chicago on Feb. 29, 1940. His body lay in state at his mansion, 4742 South Parkway (now Martin Luther King Drive). Funeral services, conducted by the Rev. Joseph Evans and the Rev. Archibald Carey, Jr., were held at Metropolitan Community Church, and he was buried in Lincoln Cemetery, Chicago. He was survived by his widow, by John Herman Henry Sengstacke (the son of his half-brother Alexander Sengstacke), his principal beneficiary who succeeded him as editor and publisher of the *Defender,* and by two nephews.

Abbott's choice of journalism as a career resulted, according to one account, because he had been told that he was too dark to be successful in Chicago's courts, and according to another version because he failed to pass the Illinois bar and failed to develop a remunerative law practice. When Abbott began peddling the four-page *Defender* from door to door between 29th and 35th on State Street, he was editor, business manager, and entire staff, and his office was the kitchen of Henrietta Lee's apartment on State Street where he took his lodging. Financial support and columns written by friends kept the paper going, and circulation increased through sales in barbershops, churches, and poolrooms, which were likewise a source of local news.

The editorial creed in 1907 was to fight against "segregation, discrimination, disfranchisement . . ." and it "pledge[d] itself to fight against these evils until they have been removed." The paper gained circulation also by using a masthead so similar to that of William Randolph Hearst's *Chicago Evening American* that Abbott had to change the masthead to prevent suit for infringement of copyright.

It was, however, the mass migration of Negroes from the South during World War I that gave the *Defender* national prominence. In 1915 it boldly inaugurated a new slogan in response to the increasing incidence of lynching: "If you must die, take at least one with you." For months after this appeared in the paper, it was not permitted on sale in many towns and cities outside of Chicago. On Jan. 8, 1916, the slogan was simplified to "An eye for an eye."

After discouraging migration in early 1916, the paper's banner headline on Jan. 6, 1917, asserted: "Millions to Leave South." The effect was reciprocal: the paper's strident style, set by Abbott, became the bible of many seeking "The Promised Land," and the rapidly burgeoning Negro population in Chicago increased circulation to some 230,000.

To many migrants, "The Promised Land" soon became a cruel hoax despite aid given by Negro churches and the Chicago Urban League. Some migrants did not possess the necessary skills for jobs and many older Chicago Negroes resented their "intrusion." The *Defender* published a list of "A Few Do's and Don't's" to improve the public conduct and raise the cultural level of the rural Negroes.

Pent-up anger over jobs, housing, and politics were basic causes of the Chicago Race Riot of July 1919, one of several during what James Weldon Johnson called "The Red Summer"—red not because of Communist involvement but because of the flames that enveloped the scenes of race riots. The fighting, which began as the result of the stoning and subsequent drowning of a young Negro who was bathing on a "white" beach on Lake Michigan, spread to other parts of the city as whites invaded Negro sections and Negroes fought whites caught in the black sections. Perceiving the growing tensions between Negroes and whites in Chicago, Abbott, Jesse Binga, the leading Negro banker, and other leaders had tried in vain in 1917 to work out a program with the Chicago Real Estate Board acceptable to whites and blacks. The report in the *Chicago Tribune* of April 10, 1917, that the Negro community leaders were "anxious to confine themselves to their own community life, social affairs, and business" and "did not want to live in the same block with whites" was denounced by the leaders in the *Chicago Defender* as a deliberate misquote (April 21, 1917).

On the other hand, the *Defender* unwillingly supported the role of Negroes as strikebreakers against the exclusionary AFL trade unions. Abbott's newspaper also publicized the bombing of Negro homes in white neighborhoods. Between July 1, 1917, and March 1, 1921, there were fifty-eight bombings of Negro-owned or -rented homes, including the home of Jesse Binga and that of the actor Richard B. Harrison in November 1918. The *Defender* frequently criticized police inaction in these cases, as well as stories of brutality by "white skunk officers." Abbott's support of William H. ("Big Bill") Thompson, Republican mayor, infuriated Irish-Americans because of his anti-Catholicism. The return of the old 8th Illinois to Chicago in February 1919 was featured, as was that of the old 15th New York to New York City. The *Defender* perceived its role as spokesman for and advisor to the Negro community; as such it stimulated a sense of unity and gave voice to many of the outrages that would not have been documented had the *Defender* not printed the Negro point of view.

The *Defender* gave exhaustive coverage to the five days of rioting, and Oscar de Priest, first Negro elected to Chicago's City Council, became a folk hero when he went into the stockyards, a stronghold of the rioting Irish community, and brought black workers out to safety. Abbott was named a member of the Chicago Commission on Race Relations, which published in 1922 the frequently cited *The Negro in Chicago*. Abbott concurred in the commission's findings even when the black press was taken to task for overreacting.

One of the most difficult problems that confronted Abbott as well as other Negro leaders was the establishment of the segregated Colored Officers Training Camp at Fort Des Moines, Iowa, in June 1917. W. E. B. Du Bois criticized the *Defender* and some other Negro newspapers for opposing the camp, stating in brief that the choice was between a segregated camp or no camp (*The Crisis*, April 1917, pp. 270–71). "Abbott fell in line" (Redding, *The Lonesome Road* [1959], p. 217) when he saw clearly that the only way in which black college-trained men could be commissioned officers was to accede to a separate training camp.

In 1919 the *Defender* vigorously opposed Marcus Garvey's Universal Negro Improvement Association, denouncing Garvey consistently and warning *Defender* readers not to be taken in by his promises. On Jan. 15, 1923, Abbott, along with John E. Nail, William Pickens, Chandler Owen, Robert W. Bagnall, and three other prominent Negro leaders, urged the U.S. attorney-general to "vigorously and speedily push the government's case against Marcus Garvey for using the mails to defraud" (Edmund David Cronon, *Black Moses: The Story of Marcus Garvey, . . .* [1955], pp. 75–76, 110–11). The *Defender* pushed for the Dyer Anti-Lynching Bill (1922), and urged defeat of the confirmation of John J. Parker to the U.S. Supreme Court by using both news and editorial columns to highlight the issues involved in the 1930 appointment. Although nominally an independent in politics, Abbott was generally in the Republican camp and backed Oscar de Priest, a Republican and the first Negro to be elected (1928) to Congress after the departure of George H. White in 1901. Abbott supported the Chicago Urban League campaign in 1928–1931 for upgrading and employment of black workers in white-owned and -operated services located within the Negro community. When pressure from white advertisers became severe, the *Chicago Defender* and the Urban League turned the fight over to the militant *Chicago Whip*, edited by Joseph Bibb.

In 1939 Abbott lent his name to the National Urban League's Committee of 100 for Negro Workers to "engage in an active, aggressive fight in behalf of the Negro worker to the end that he shall have fair and just opportunities to earn a living wage and to participate in the recovery program under the New Deal" (Nancy J. Weiss, *The National Urban League, 1910–1940* [1974], p. 285).

In addition to serving as president and treasurer of the Robert Abbott Publishing Company (1905–1940), which also published the short-lived *Abbott's Monthly*, Abbott was a board member of the Wabash Avenue branch of the Chicago YMCA (1923–1933), a life member of the Chicago Art Institute, the Chicago Historical Society, and the Chicago Field Museum, national president of the Hampton Alumni Association, a donor to the Chicago Civic Opera, a member of the Ancient Order of Foresters, a Thirty-third Degree Mason, a member of the Appomattox Club and of the Lincoln Memorial Congregational Church.

Basic facts are in *Who's Who in America* (1938–1939). Roi Ottley's *The Lonely Warrior: The Life and Times of Robert S. Abbott* (1955) is a favorable biography. *Anyplace But Here* (1966), by Arna Bontemps and Jack Conroy, has many useful references, and Saunders Redding's *The Lonesome Road* (1958) vividly portrays the man and his times. *Race Riot: Chicago in the Red Summer of 1919*, by William M. Tuttle, Jr. (1970), is the best source for the role of Abbott and the *Defender*. Obituaries were published in the *New York Herald-Tribune*, the *New York Times* (March 1, 1940), the *Norfolk Journal and Guide* (March 9, 1940), and the *Chicago Defender* (March 29, 1940). The sketch in *DAB* (Supplement 2 [1958], 11:2–4), by Armstead S. Pride, exaggerated when it concluded that " 'the dean of Negro publishers' . . . had taken rank alongside such figures of his race as Frederick Douglass, Booker T. Washington, and W. E. B. Du Bois." The best source is, of course, the *Chicago Defender*, complete files of which are at the present office (2400 S. Michigan Ave., Chicago, IL 60616), and on 16-mm microfilm in many colleges and universities. The Robert S. Abbott Papers are in the *Chicago Defender* archives under the personal supervision of John Sengstacke, president and publisher, Sengstacke Publications, and the Robert S. Abbott Publishing Company, Inc. — DORIS E. SAUNDERS

ABRAHAM (Seminole busk-name: **"SOHANAC"** or **"SOUANAKKE TUSTENUKLE"**), (c. 1790 to after 1870), principal interpreter and counsellor to Seminole head chief Micanopy and principal Seminole Negro chief (c. 1825–1845). A full-blooded Negro, of large and powerful stature but with a "cast" in his right eye, he was in youth a slave, probably a household servant, to Dr. Sierra of Pensacola, and was probably one of the Negroes whom the British, after their occupation of the city in July 1814, recruited under the promise of freedom and land, and later employed in building a fort—British Post or the Negro Fort—on the Apalachicola. If so, after the destruction in July 1816, he was among the refugees who settled among King Bowlegs's Seminole on the Suwanee and were dislodged by Andrew Jackson's invasion of Florida in 1818. By the early 1820s he was living in Micanopy's Negro town of Pilaklikaha and in 1825–1826 accompanied the head chief on a delegation to Washington, D.C., receiving his "freedom" as a reward for his "many and faithful services and great merits."

Abraham witnessed as interpreter the Seminole "removal treaty" of Payne's Landing (May 9, 1832), and accompanied a Seminole delegation to the Indian Territory, where (March 28, 1833) he witnessed the Treaty of Fort Gibson whereby the delegation illegally agreed, for the Seminole Nation, to remove from Florida. However, although during the next couple of years he publicly confined himself to interpreting at various councils at which the Seminole agent insisted on removal, secretly he was encouraging Micanopy to resist, and was active both in instigating the plantation slaves of the region to assist the Indians and Negroes in such resistance and in laying in a supply of ammunition.

When hostilities finally broke out on Dec. 28, 1835, Abraham was prominent in most of the actions in the Withlacoochee region. However, he was always ready to negotiate and on Jan. 31, 1837, after a serious defeat in the Big Cypress, he agreed to discuss terms of peace with Gen. T. S. Jesup. On March 6, largely through his diplomatic skill, the general and the principal Seminole chiefs agreed to the Treaty of Camp Dade whereby the Seminole agreed to leave Florida on the condition, as they understood it, that their Negro "slaves" and allies should accompany them.

Unfortunately, General Jesup yielded to pressure for the return of the most recent runaway slaves, and most of the Seminole who had "come in" left the emigration camp and resumed hostilities. Abraham and his family, however, remained prisoners, and under the threat of hanging and the promise of freedom, the Negro chief thereafter worked for peace. He persuaded Micanopy to surrender, and working through the head chief brought about the surrender of other chiefs. Apparently, however, he did this with the understanding that the principles of the Camp Dade treaty would actually be carried out. By the late spring of 1838 nearly all the hostile Indians and Negroes had surrendered or been captured, and on Feb. 25, 1839, Abraham was shipped west.

Abraham greatly impressed all the numerous officers who reported on the Seminole War. Whether friendly or hostile, they agreed on his intelligence, described him as "obviously a great man." His importance in mustering Seminole resistance to removal, and in bringing about peace on as favorable terms to the Indians and Negroes as could reasonably be expected, can hardly be doubted.

Abraham's subsequent life was anticlimactic. In 1845 he was removed as official interpreter at the Seminole subagency on the charge of habitual intoxication. Joshua R. Giddings's portrayal of him (*The Exiles of Florida* [1858], pp. 333–37) as co-leader with Wild Cat of a migration of Seminole Indians and Negroes to Mexico is fictitious. In 1852, however, he served as interpreter on a delegation to Billy Bowlegs, the principal Seminole chief still in Florida, whom he accompanied to Washington and New York; the chief, however, refused to emigrate. Abraham thereafter sank into obscurity, although he was long remembered as an able and prosperous cattle raiser. He presumably survived the viscissitudes of the Civil War, since late in 1870 he was reportedly still living on Little River. By his wife Hagar, Abraham had at least two sons, Renty and Washington, and one daughter.

All that is presently known about Abraham is presented in Kenneth W. Porter's *The Negro on the American Frontier* (1971, pp. 294–338).

— KENNETH WIGGINS PORTER

ADAMS, HENRY (1843– ?), grass-roots political organizer, president of the Committee and the Colonization Council of north Louisiana (1870–1880), and erroneously considered a leader of the Exodus to Kansas of 1879 with Benjamin "Pap" Singleton.

Henry Adams had worked toward Afro-American emigration to Liberia for several years when the millennarian Exodus to Kansas overwhelmed him and his organization, the Colonization Council. Appearing before a U.S. grand jury and at a New Orleans meeting on the Exodus, Adams established the reputation which brought him to the attention of the U.S. Senate committee on the Exodus. In his testimony to that committee, he revealed the existence of an underground, grass-roots emigration movement in Louisiana, Texas, and Mississippi which claimed nearly 100,000 adherents. Adams's evidence formed the core of the committee's minority report, and since 1880 his name has been intimately associated with the Exodus to Kansas of 1879. Yet he neither migrated to Kansas nor left the South.

Born in Georgia and taken to Louisiana in 1850, Henry Adams early exhibited special talents. He began faith healing as a child, and that gift, together with his enterprising independence, assured him economic self-sufficiency, even before his emancipation in 1865.

Immediately after the Civil War he earned money peddling along the roads of Caddo Parish, La., but joined the U.S. Army to escape the unrelenting slaughter of freed people by local whites. Adams served in the 80th Volunteers, the 39th Infantry, and the 25th Infantry. He learned to read and write in the army. Returning to Shreveport after his discharge in 1869, he found that southern whites considered him and other ex-soldiers corrupting influences; Negro soldiers threatened the precarious and abusive social order by reading contracts to the freed people and explaining their new civil rights. In the face of persistent political and economic oppression, the ex-soldiers banded together in a secret intelligence organization in 1870, which they called simply "the Committee."

Between 1870 and 1874 the Committee included about 500 men, of whom about 150 traveled across the countryside, working on equal footing with the freed people of north Louisiana and adjacent portions of Mississippi and Texas. Although the Committee was not overtly political, its members acted as local organizers, encouraging the Negro Republican electorate. Henry Adams voted for the first time in 1870 and made his first public speeches in that campaign. Meanwhile he continued faith healing, which reinforced his public influence. In 1873 he sat on Shreveport's grand jury and the following year served as president of the Shreveport Republican Club, the "mother club" of Caddo Parish.

The violence which had convulsed Caddo Parish time and again since the Civil War resumed in 1874, moving the Committee to send petitions to Pres. Ulysses S. Grant and to Congress. Toward the end of the year, the 7th Cavalry occupied the area and reestablished a modicum of order. Nonetheless, irregularities marred the elections, in which Adams acted as a U.S. supervisor of elections at Tom Bayou. The 7th Cavalry stayed at Shreveport during 1875, and Adams worked as a scout during the first part of the year. Traveling widely, he discovered the same oppression in other Gulf states that he had witnessed in Caddo Parish.

For the Committee, this period between 1874 and 1876 saw a transition from reconnaissance to advocacy. Adams took an emigrationist position, convinced that neither the state of Louisiana nor the United States intended protecting the lives or rights of freed people. However, not all Committee members were prepared to emigrate to Liberia immediately, and the majority decided to participate in the elections of 1876 and 1878. At the same time, they proselytized for emigration to Liberia under the aegis of the American Colonization Society. Henry Adams canvassed in both bloody campaigns, and late in 1878 he was subpoenaed to testify before the U.S. grand jury in New Orleans concerning the recent election cases. He and the other witnesses remained exiles in New Orleans, for white opposition to their appearances before the U.S. grand jury prevented their returning home.

Adams spent the rest of his life in New Orleans, where he resumed his Liberian emigration work. When the millennarian Exodus to Kansas of the spring of 1879 overtook him and the Colonization Council (as the Committee had been called since 1876), Adams headed a committee on transportation which grew out of a mass meeting. He operated out of New Orleans and did not go to Kansas.

After the Exodus, Henry Adams found himself progressively eased out of Liberian activities by respectable "New South" Negroes. The Liberian interest in New Orleans modified during the early 1880s from a mass emigration movement to a philanthropic "civilizing" mission. Adams dropped out of sight in 1884. Having long favored emigration of Afro-Americans to Africa, he had supported the millennarian Exodus to Kansas of 1879, welcoming any avenue of escape from the South as a crucial first step.

The only source on Henry Adams in print is the *Report and Testimony of the Select Committee of the United States Senate to Investigate the Causes of the Removal of the Negroes . . .* (46th Cong., 2nd sess., Senate Report 693, Washington [1880], 2:101–214).

— NELL IRVIN PAINTER

ADAMS, J[OHN] Q[UINCY] (1848–1922), editor and civil rights leader. Adams was born in Louisville, Ky., on May 4, 1848, to free parents, the Rev. Henry and Margaret (Corbin) Adams. His father was a prominent clergyman of the community, having founded the Fifth Street Baptist Church in Louisville and served it for thirty-three years. J. Q. Adams attended schools in Louisville, Wisconsin, and Ohio, and graduated from Oberlin College. After college he participated in the reconstruction of Arkansas. Cooperating with his uncle, Joseph C. Corbin, superintendent of public instruction during the Baxter administration, Adams moved from schoolteacher to engrossing clerk of the state Senate. After Republicans lost control of the state in 1874, Adams returned to Louisville. There, besides teaching and holding appointive office, he began his lifelong profession with the publication, in 1879, of the *Bulletin,* a weekly newspaper.

By 1886, however, he decided that he had no future in the South and moved to St. Paul. He joined the staff of the *Western Appeal,* a Negro-owned and -edited weekly, and within a year assumed control of it. Until his death in 1922, he spoke to and for the Afro-American (his term) community through the *Appeal.* During these years he held appointive office (bailiff of the municipal court, 1896–1902), was active in the Republican party, and played a leading role in the Minnesota Protective and Industrial League, the NAACP, and the Equal Rights League. In 1892 he married Ella B. Smith of St. Paul; they had four children.

Adams's first editorial in the *Western Appeal* expressed the message of his career: "Unity among us is desired but not isolation from those around us. We are Negroes, but we are also Americans" (March 5, 1887). He would later change the appellation to Afro-American, but continued to call for race pride and equality of opportunity. Those "negroes" who would settle for segregated institutions came under fire from the *Appeal.* Adams was an early critic of the Tuskegee machine. Under his guidance, the *Appeal* consistently condemned segregation by any level of government and criticized the failure of national administrations of both parties to protect the rights of all citizens. At the same time he called for "more race love; the tie of racehood should bind us as the tie of brotherhood."

On Sept. 3, 1922, Adams was struck and killed by an automobile. Although seventy-four, he had continued to be active in civic affairs and to edit the *Appeal.* Nor had his message weakened. He was willing to question his lifelong Republicanism in the face of President Harding's acquiescence to segregation and lynching.

The most detailed account of J. Q. Adams's life is the obituary in the *Appeal* (Sept. 9 and 16, 1922; these issues of the paper also reprint selected editorials by him). Earl Spangler's *The Negro in Minnesota* (1961) analyzes his editorials and places him in the context of his community. — WILBERT H. AHERN

ADAMS, NUMA P[OMPILIUS] G[ARFIELD] (1885–
1940), physician, educator, dean of medical school.
Adams was born in Delaplane, Fauquier County, Va.
Under the guidance of his grandmother, Mrs. Amanda
Adams, a highly respected midwife who had delivered
hundreds of Negro and white babies, he started his own
collection of herbs reputed to be of medicinal value. His
mother was Martha E. Mathews; the name of his father
is unknown. He received his early education in a country school taught and operated by his uncle, Henry
Adams. In 1898 the family moved to Steelton, Pa.,
where the Rev. Henry Howard Summers, a Howard
University graduate, befriended the shy country boy as
though he were his son. Graduating from the high
school with honors in 1905, Numa served as a substitute teacher (1905–1906) and as a seventh-grade
teacher in the public schools of Carlisle, Pa. (1906–
1907). He received a B.A. degree, *summa cum laude,*
from Howard University (1911), and in the following
year an M.A. in chemistry from Columbia University.
He had served as an assistant in chemistry in the Preparatory Department of Howard University (1909–1910)
and as a student assistant in the College of Liberal Arts
(1910–1911). He rose from instructor to associate professor and head of the Department of Chemistry, Howard University (1912–1919), serving in 1918–1919 as
head of the department. He entered Rush Medical College, Chicago, in the spring quarter of 1920, received
a certificate for completion of the four years work in
December 1923, and was granted his M.D. degree
upon completion of his internship at St. Louis City Hospital No. 2 (later Homer G. Phillips Hospital) in 1924.
He practiced medicine and surgery in Chicago (1925 to
1929). There he was assistant medical director of the
Victory Life Insurance Company and from 1927 to
1929 an instructor in neurology and psychiatry in the
Provident School of Nursing. On June 4, 1929, he became the first Negro dean of Howard University Medical School. He died on Aug. 29, 1940, in Billings Hospital, Chicago, a "martyr" to the difficulties he had
encountered as dean of the medical school.

Adams became dean at a crucial period in the history
of Negro colleges of medicine. Abraham Flexner's
seminal report on *Medical Education in the United
States and Canada* (1910) had urged the need for fewer
and better medical schools. Five of the seven Negro
medical schools were "in no position to make any contribution of value" to the training of Negro physicians.
Meharry, and especially Howard, were the only two
deemed adequate. But Howard required the support of
the federal government. The medical school, however,
had difficulty in raising its own endowment fund and
money for a new Medical School Building. On April 3,
1925, the Executive Committee of Howard University's
Board of Trustees approved as the site for a new building land owned by the university south of W Street NW.
The congressional appropriation for 1926 had allocated
$370,000 for the construction of the building and the
General Education Board committed itself to an appropriation of $60,000 toward the additional cost of the
building if the medical school had collected $130,000
pledged during the medical school's campaign for
equipment. Through the unremitting efforts of William

C. McNeill (Howard, 1904), secretary and a longtime
member of the faculty of the medical school, the
pledges were collected and the new medical building
was opened in 1927.

The appointment of Dean Adams came two years
after Mordecai W. Johnson became the first Negro president of Howard University. W. Montague Cobb, who
served as an instructor in embryology (1928–1929) and
was on the faculty of the medical school from 1932
until his retirement in 1974, concluded in January 1951
that President Johnson's decision to appoint a Negro
dean "made possible for the first time assumption of top
responsibility in a medical school by a Negro and paved
the way for the accession by Negro physicians to full
responsibility for progress and operation of an institution primarily for their development. White physicians
who subsequently joined the staff have had to do so in
a spirit of coequal collaboration devoid of the old attitude of benevolent paternalism" ("Numa P. G. Adams,
M.D., 1885–1940," *JNMA*, Jan. 1951, pp. 43–52).

As dean, Adams undertook herculean tasks: the reorganization of the curriculum on a more rational basis;
establishment of the primacy of the medical school in
the teaching functions of Freedmen's Hospital, recruiting capable young physicians, securing superior postgraduate training for them, and assuring them salaries
competitive with the income of physicians in private
practice; improvement of the selection of a higher caliber of students, of their clinical instruction and morale
as well as that of the faculty. Dr. Cobb concluded that,
despite many obstacles, Adams achieved a large measure of success.

The long struggle "destroyed" him, for he had "neither the gift nor the inclination" to participate in the
politics of administration. And he no longer had time for
playing music as he had done in a band, called the Lyric
Orchestra, in order to pay his way through medical
school, support his wife, the former Osceola Macarthy
whom he had married in 1915, and their three-year-old
son. Even trips with his wife to his beloved Delaplane
and plans to build a home there did not provide the
necessary surcease for his troubled mind. He died on
Aug. 29, 1940, of pneumonia in Billings Hospital, Chicago, following an operation there. Private rites were
held on Aug. 30, and the body was cremated and interred at Graceland Cemetery, Chicago. He was survived by his mother, his wife Osceola Macarthy Adams,
a former actress and teacher of drama at Bennett College, Greensboro, N.C., and a son Charles.

In addition to Dr. Cobb's article in the *JNMA* (Jan.
1951, pp. 43–52) and tributes in following pages by his
colleagues, the obituary in the *Baltimore Afro-American* contains valuable information. — RAYFORD W. LOGAN

"NIGGER ADD" [OLD ADD, OLD NEGRO AD]
(fl. 1889–c. 1906), rider, roper, and range boss. "Nigger
Add" was widely acknowledged as "one of the best
cow-hands on Pecos River" (Thorp), "the most noted
Negro cowboy that ever 'topped off' a horse" (Haley),
and "the most famous Negro cowpuncher of the Old
West" (Whitlock).

According to Haley he had "drifted up from the
Guadalupe bottoms" of southeast Texas "to the high

plains''; other accounts say that he had been ''raised'' by the famous cattleman George W. Littlefield (Jones) with whom he had been ''since Emancipation days'' (Whitlock). In any case he apparently worked virtually his entire active life for various Littlefield outfits, particularly the LFD brand, first in the Texas Panhandle and later in eastern New Mexico.

While some ''top hands,'' white and Negro, were noted as riders or bronco busters, Add was almost equally distinguished in both roles. Stocky and strongly built, with such powerful hands that he reputedly could ''practically twist the hide off'' a horse, he would walk into a corral of bad broncos, get any of them by the ear and nose, smother him down, lead him out of the bunch, and ''take the sap out of him''—''topping off'' several outlaw horses of a morning. His personal ''mount'' was always made up of the worst horses in the outfit, that no one else could, or wanted to, handle. Reputedly, he was thrown but once in his life.

As a roper he specialized in the probably unique feat of roping on foot. He would tie a rope around his hips, work up to a horse in a corral or even open pasture, rope him around the neck as he dashed by at full speed, and then, when the ordinary man would have been dragged to death, Add, by a combination of skill and sheer strength, would flatten the animal out.

Add could tell, almost at a glance, what a horse's capacities were, and by looking him in the eye, what he was thinking. He was a ''dictionary on earmarks and brands'' and was widely popular among cattlemen from Toyah, Tex., to Las Vegas, N.Mex. All these capacities would not necessarily, because of the racial problem, have added up to his ever being more than a particularly highly thought of and skillful cowhand. His boss, however, was a man of independent mind and at least by 1889 Nigger Add was range boss of the LFD outfit, a position unique for a Negro in the Southwest, however able. But Add ''worked South Texas colored hands almost entirely''; any exceptions were probably Mexicans. He seemed to have worked out well as a range boss, and when he married, whenever it was, his many friends among the ranchers of the region were each so anxious to give him and his wife a particularly impressive present that he received no fewer than nineteen stoves and ranges! In 1899 he received literary immortality of a sort when N. Howard (''Jack'') Thorp made him the hero of a poem in Negro dialect, ''Whose Old Cow?'' (*Songs of the Cowboys,* 1st ed., Encina, N.Mex., 1908; 2d ed., Boston, 1921; 3rd. ed., edited by Austin E. and Alta S. Fife and Naunie Gardner, New York, 1966).

However, by the end of the century Add had passed his prime. He was, for whatever reasons, no longer range boss but merely an unusually able and responsible top hand, and it also seems probable that by this time the virulent East Texas racism was strongly influencing even the New Mexico cattle country. Some white cowboys in other outfits, although admitting that he was ''a good roper and rider,'' resented his status as ''a privileged character'' and his occasional assumption of authority. Such ill-feeling reached a climax about 1899 when Add was at a neighboring ranch and, finding the water bucket empty, presumed to drink from the hose

attached to the water tank, whereupon one of the wagon bosses struck him on the back of the neck with a wagon yoke and ''knocked him cold.'' Although a man of powerful frame, who shortly before at a dance in Carlsbad had knocked out a ''town Negro'' at a single blow, Add, when he came to, took no action, but mounted his horse and headed for home.

During the earliest years of the twentieth century Add was still a prominent member of the LFD outfit. Although ''too old and crippled up'' to take an active part in dealing with the young unbroken horses, he was still highly thought of for his horse savvy, and neophyte cowboys appreciated his concern for their welfare. One of them was particularly impressed by his ability to give appropriate names to each of the 120 horses broken during a particular season (Whitlock). And although no longer a bad-bronc rider, his prowess as a roper remained unimpaired, including his ability to rope on foot. One of his most memorable roping feats was performed in 1906, in Roswell, N.Mex., when a milk-wagon team ran away. Old Add double-half-hitched one end of his rope to the saddle horn, built a big loop in the other, roped both horses as they dashed by, and then threw the slack over the wagon, as if it were an outlaw steer, and ''stacked the whole shebang in the middle of the street''!

''There was never a Littlefield horse too rough for Add to handle,'' runs J. Evett Haley's obituary, ''never a Littlefield trail too long for him to ride. He rode until he was so crippled with rheumatism that he could not get on a horse; and then, like a man whose work is well done, he lay down on his bed and died. . . .'' But despite Add's cow-country fame we do not know even such elementary facts about him as the dates of his birth and death, or his surname. According to Whitlock he was ''known only as Old Negro [*sic*] Add.''

J. Evetts Haley's *George W. Littlefield, Texan* (1943) is the principal authority for Add as rider and roper, but N. Howard (Jack) Thorp's *Songs of the Cowboys* (1921; also 1966, edited by Austin E. and Alta S. Fife and Naunie Gardner) and ''Banjo in the Cow Camps'' (*Atlantic Monthly,* Aug. 1940) are indispensable, particularly for his position as range boss. Matt Ennis Jones's *Fiddlefooted* (1966) tells with considerable racist glee of Add's difficulties with white cowboys, while Vivian H. Whitlock's *Cowboy Life on the Llano Estacado* (1970) treats his later years with sympathy and respect. — KENNETH WIGGINS PORTER

ADGER, ROBERT MARA (1837–1910), bibliophile, political activist, businessman. One of thirteen children, Adger was born in Charleston, S.C. His paternal grandmother, Lucy Adger, was a New York free Negro. In 1810 she paid a visit to relatives in Charleston and they were sold into slavery. Three decades later, following legal proceedings instituted by the Philadelphia Society of Friends, they were released. Lucy's son, Robert Adger, married a full-blooded Indian, Mary Ann Morong. In 1848 the small family, which included a young son, Robert Mara, moved to Philadelphia. Adger Sr. first secured employment as a waiter in the Old Merchant's Hotel. Later he was employed as a nurse and while working in that capacity industriously saved enough funds to open a furniture business. He was active in numerous activities and was a founder of the Benjamin Banneker Institute.

Robert Mara received his early training at the Bird School, one of the early Negro educational institutions in the United States. During his teenage years he worked in his father's furniture stores, which had expanded from one in 1850 to three by 1858. Serving as a manager provided him with the business experience which he later found valuable as director of the Philadelphia Building and Loan Association. Adger's business acumen contributed largely to the success of this pioneering Negro mortgage company. This was during a period when Negroes were denied access to new jobs in the expanding factory system, while simultaneously being replaced by white semiskilled laborers arriving in larger numbers. Adger witnessed a repressive racial climate which forced 38 percent of Negro skilled artisans to give up their trades. Believing that conditions would worsen if the Civil War was won by the Confederacy, Adger joined the Black Enlistment Committee, assisting in recruiting colored men to fight on the side of the Union Army.

In 1860 he also organized the Fraternal Society, a group of refugees from South Carolina interested in gaining equal rights. Adger and other members of this organization worked collectively with Negroes from other social-political groups on many issues pertaining to equal rights. Four years later the National Convention of Colored Men met in Syracuse, N.Y. Their agenda included an even wider scope: promoting educational opportunities, encouraging sound morality, practicing economic restraints, organizing politically for their equal rights that would assure a well-ordered and dignified life. Delegates returning to Philadelphia and other parts of Pennsylvania moved toward the creation of the Pennsylvania Equal Rights League, which held its first state conference in Harrisburg (Feb. 8–10, 1865). Adger was a delegate from the Banneker Institute. Two of his young associates in this institution were elected secretaries of the league's organization: Jacob C. White, pioneer Negro educator and principal of the Vaux School; and Octavius V. Catto, a highly reputable young principal of the Institute for Colored Youth, who was later murdered for his political activities. Adger presented a motion for Daniel Williams, father of the famed heart surgeon Daniel Hale Williams of Hollidaysburg, Pa., to address the convention. Another of Adger's many contributions to the convention was an adopted resolution urging "our young colored men to organize among themselves institutions tending to their intellectual and moral elevation." He and Catto also fought for passage of a resolution which would assure Negro teachers for Negro schools. The excellence of the staff at the Institute for Colored Youth had convinced Adger and Catto of the qualified Negro teacher's intrinsic merit. This belief was given even greater credence when Adger watched his brother William, a graduate of the Institute for Colored Youth, become the first Negro graduate of the University of Pennsylvania (1879).

During his intensely active career Adger married Lucy Davidson and reared a family of several children. Mrs. Adger had previously performed with the famed opera singer Elizabeth Taylor Greenfield. Her background and willingness to assist greatly aided Adger in his activities. At no time was this better demonstrated than when he organized the Afro-American Historical Society (Oct. 25, 1897). Adger had amassed a considerable collection of rare books and pamphlets on the "black Nation" and antislavery agitation. In 1894 he printed *A Portion of a Catalogue of Rare Books and Pamphlets,* offering his collection for sale. Three years later he decided to keep the materials, donating them to the Home for Aged and Infirm Colored Persons founded by Stephen Smith, a wealthy Negro businessman. In organizing the Historical Society, Adger was maintaining a tradition of preserving materials which dated back to the activities of the Reading Room Society, the first known organized Negro library (1828). Adger's last years were spent building up this organization to ensure future generations a base on which to build. He died on June 10, 1910, of a heart attack; funeral services were held in his last residence, 1115 Lombard St., and he was buried in Merion Cemetery, Merion, Pa. He was survived by four sons, numerous grandchildren, and other relatives.

There is one readily available published source on Robert Mara Adger's life, James G. Spady's "The Afro-American Historical Society: The Nucleus of Black Bibliophiles, 1897–1923" (*NHB,* June/July 1974, pp. 255–56). His papers (filed under Code No. 209954, Household I.D. #1095, Document 32, Philadelphia Social History Project, University of Pennsylvania) provide solid information. — JAMES G. SPADY

ALBERT, OCTAVIA VICTORIA ROGERS (1853–c. 1890), author. Born in Oglethorpe, Macon County, Ga., on Dec. 24, 1853, Mrs. Albert is best known for her religious activities in the Methodist church and for her published slave narratives. Very little information remains of her private life and nothing is known of her early family life except that she was born a slave. Following emancipation, Octavia attended Atlanta University where she was trained as a teacher. Upon leaving Atlanta, she taught school in Montezuma, Ga. In 1873 she met A. E. P. Albert, who was an instructor at the school in which she taught, and on Oct. 21 of the following year the two were married. Mrs. Albert soon gave birth to their only daughter, Laura T. Albert.

While in Oglethorpe, Octavia attended the African Methodist Episcopal church. Under the ministry of Bishop Henry M. Turner, Mrs. Albert dedicated her life to Christ and joined the A.M.E. church. In 1877 her husband was ordained a minister in the Methodist Episcopal church. Mrs. Albert converted to her husband's faith and was baptized by him in 1888 in Houma, La.

Mrs. Albert is best remembered for her book *The House of Bondage* (1890), published posthumously by her husband and daughter. The book consists of seven slave narratives collected by Mrs. Albert after she and her family moved to Louisiana. The narratives add considerably to the historiography of slavery. Mrs. Albert, a former slave herself, recorded them some fifteen years after the end of slavery.

Mrs. Albert does not indicate her methodology, but from what she does say, it would appear that she recorded the narratives from informal conversations with her informants. She does not attempt to relate the narratives in dialect form, but does include such phrases as, "La, me, child!" for added emphasis. The idea for the title of the book probably came from a number of references to slavery as bondage. One informant saw similarities between the "children of Israel in Egypt in bondage" and Negro Americans in slavery. After considering the tales of woe as told by the former slaves, the title is indeed an appropriate one.

The dominant character in *The House of Bondage* is Charlotte Brooks, a former slave separated from her family in Virginia and sold to a planter in Louisiana. Aunt Charlotte, as she was affectionately called, told of how other slaves were separated from their families. During the Cotton Centennial Exposition of 1884, Mrs. Albert witnessed the reunion of Aunt Jane and her son Coleman Lee, who, according to Aunt Charlotte, had been sold and taken to Texas as a child.

Contrary to recent scholarship on comparative slavery, the former slaves viewed slavery under Catholicism as much harsher than slavery under Protestantism. All the informants agree that slavery was harsh, but those who had experienced slavery in predominantly Protestant states positively concluded that slavery in Louisiana was more cruel.

The narratives are vivid accounts of the barbarous treatment accorded the slaves and show how anonymous men and women endured not only slavery but also the continued suffering the elderly encountered after slavery when they were no longer capable of making a livelihood. Mrs. Albert also records the progress the freedmen made during the Reconstruction period. One informant, Uncle Cephus, is not as precise on details, but is generally correct in noting the active participation of men he knew in the reconstruction of various state governments following the war.

The House of Bondage is a valuable account of slavery in the words of those who endured. Mrs. Albert succeeded in portraying slavery as it was by recording the narratives of those who suffered under its heavy yoke. —JOHN E. FLEMING

ALDRIDGE, IRA FREDERICK (1807?–1867), actor. Considered to have been one of the greatest Shakespearean tragedians of his time and one of the famous actors of the European theater (he was called the "African Roscius"), Aldridge was born in New York City, probably on July 24, 1807, the son of Daniel Aldridge, a straw vendor and a lay preacher. Little is known of his mother except that she was born in North Carolina and died when Aldridge was a child. He attended the African Free School in New York City and may have studied later at the University of Glasgow in Scotland.

Aldridge showed an early interest in the theater. A minor job enabled him to observe from behind the scenes the action on the stage of the Chatham Theater in New York City. He received some acting experience in the African Theater in New York. The role of Rolla in August von Kotzebue's *Pizarro* is perhaps the first that Aldridge played with that group.

Around 1824 he left New York for England, shipping as a steward on the same boat as James Wallack and becoming his personal attendant. Aldridge had established a relationship with Henry and James Wallack, brothers and actors, who often appeared together in New York theaters. There have been varying accounts of the early life of Ira Aldridge, but those of his later life coincide.

Of these varying accounts of Aldridge's life, the most often repeated is that he was born in Senegal to royalty, and that his forefathers were princes of the Fulah tribe. A missionary is said to have converted Aldridge's father in order that he might civilize his countrymen. Eventually the father was brought to America by the missionary and sent to Schenectady College. He became a minister of the gospel. After an opposing chief died, he returned to his country, but civil war broke out again and Aldridge's father was defeated. During the first month of the arrival of Aldridge's parents in Africa, Ira was born. Nine years elapsed before the family migrated to America, where the father resumed his ministerial duties.

Still another version of his beginnings is that Aldridge was born in Maryland, where he was a carpenter before he became an actor.

Documents support, however, that on Oct. 10, 1825, Aldridge opened at the Royal Coburg, London, in *The Revolt of Surinam, or A Slave's Revenge,* an adaptation of Thomas Southerne's *Oroonoko.* During this same engagement he played in Thomas Morton's *The Ethiopian, or the Quadroon of the Mango Grove (The Slave),* followed by *The Libertine Defeated, or African Ingratitude,* H. M. Milner's *The Negro's Curse, or The Foulah Son,* originally written for Aldridge, and J. H. Amherst's *The Death of Christophe, King of Hayti.* This engagement is his first with top billing in London. Immediately following his appearance at the Coburg, he filled an engagement at the Theatre Royal, Brighton, his first provincial engagement where he played Oroonoko and later Othello. In 1827 he toured the provinces, appearing in such places as Sheffield, Halifax, Manchester, Newcastle, Edinburgh, Lancaster, Liverpool, and Sunderland. His basic repertoire was Shakespeare's *Othello,* Southerne's *Oroonoko,* Morton's *The Slave,* Mathew Gregory Lewis's *The Castle Spectre,* Isaac Bickerstaff's *The Padlock,* and Edward Young's *The Revenge.*

In 1831 the paths of Ira Aldridge and Edmund Kean, one of the outstanding actors of his time, crossed in Dublin, and Aldridge won the commendation of Kean. There is no evidence, however, that the two actors ever played together despite frequent statements to the contrary. But in Belfast in 1829, Charles Kean, the son of Edmund Kean, did appear as Iago to Aldridge's Othello, and Aldridge played Aboan to Kean's Oroonoko.

In 1833 Aldridge made his debut at the Theatre Royal, Covent Garden, London, in the role of Othello. It was in this appearance that he is referred to as "Mr. Aldridge (A Native of Senegal) known by the appellation of The African Roscius." From then on he was known as "The Celebrated African Roscius, Mr. Ira Aldridge" or "The Celebrated African Tragedian" or just "The African Roscius." Between 1831 and 1833 the name "Keene," the stage name used during his early years, was dropped.

In 1852 Aldridge went on his first continental tour.

The plays in which he appeared were often given in the mother tongue of the audience, with the exception of his own role. Among his large repertoire as an actor were the roles of Mungo, Othello, Macbeth, Shylock, Lear, and Richard III. And after more than a century of neglect he restored *Titus Andronicus* and won distinction playing Aaron the Moor. He was acclaimed for his acting in England, but especially on the continent was he accorded unqualified recognition.

Some contemporary critics thought Aldridge a novelty and expressed doubt that a man of African birth could interpret Shakespeare. Many critics, however, called Aldridge an actor of genius. A Viennese critic wrote as follows: "Ira Aldridge is without doubt the greatest actor that has ever been seen in Europe. . . . It may well be doubted whether Shakespeare himself had ever dreamed for his masterpiece, *Othello,* an interpretation so masterly, so truly perfect." The *Preussische Zeitung,* carried the following appraisal: "After this Othello it would be anticlimax to have to see an ordinary Othello again. . . . A Negro from Africa's Western Coast had to come to show me the real Othello, the great, one and only, the most beautiful male artist that one can imagine" (Herbert Marshall and Mildred Stock, *Ira Aldridge: The Negro Tragedian,* 1958).

Aldridge has been described as tall, well built, noble, and graceful. James McCune Smith, one of his contemporaries, wrote that Aldridge's complexion was black and his hair woolly. As he grew older, he became a little stocky.

His first wife, Margaret, an English woman, died at the age of sixty-six, on March 25, 1864. On April 20, 1865, Aldridge married Amanda Pauline von Brandt, who was born in Sweden. Although she is listed on their marriage certificate as the daughter of a baron of Sweden, there is no evidence to support this claim.

In 1863 Aldridge became a citizen of Great Britain. While on a tour in Poland, he died in Lodz on Aug. 7, 1867. He left some property, among which was Luranah Villa, the family home in upper Norwood, near London. At the time of his death he was making arrangements for a long-delayed American tour. He never returned to the United States, not even to Baltimore, as some biographers have claimed.

During his lifetime Aldridge received many tokens of the highest esteem. On Dec. 2, 1827, he received his first state recognition when the government of the Republic of Haiti honored him as "the first man of colour in the theatre" with a commission in the Army of Haiti, in the 17th Regiment of of Grenadiers, and aide-de-camp to the president of Haiti. Other honors include the following: member of the Prussian Academy of Arts and Sciences, and holder of the society's Large Gold Medal (First Class) presented by Frederick William IV, at Berlin (Jan. 25, 1853); recipient of the White Cross of Switzerland, *"Pour la Mérite"* (Berne, 1854); member of the Imperial and Archducal Institution of "Our Lady of the Manger" (Pesth, Hungary, 1856); Knight of the Royal Saxon Ernestinischen House Order and recipient of the Verdienst Medal of the Order, in Gold (presented on Jan. 31, 1858, by Duke Bernhard, reigning sovereign of Saxe-Meiningen); member of the National Dramatic Conservatoire of Hungary (Pesth, March 2, 1858); cor-

responding member of the Royal Bohemian Conservatoire of Prague (Sept. 1858); honorary member of the Imperial Academy of Beaux Arts, St. Petersburg, and holder of the Imperial Jubilee de Tolstoy Medal (St. Petersburg, Dec. 19, 1858); member of the Russian Hofversamlung of Riga (Oct. 14, 1859). Around 1854 the Grand Cross of the Order of Leopold was presented to Aldridge by the Emperor of Austria. In addition, he was made a member of the Associate Order of Nobles, Highest State Honour, Bessarabia (Herbert Marshall and Mildred Stock, *Ira Aldridge: The Negro Tragedian,* 1958). In 1928 James Weldon Johnson, at the request of the committees organized for the purpose of rebuilding the Shakespeare Memorial Theatre at Stratford-upon-Avon, helped to raise $1000 from Negro Americans for the endowment of an Ira Aldridge Memorial Chair in the theater (James Weldon Johnson, *Black Manhattan,* 1930; the chair is located in the fourth row of the stalls in the theater at Stratford-upon-Avon). At Howard University in Washington, D.C., the Ira Aldridge Theatre is named in honor of this great actor.

An excellent full-length biography of Ira Aldridge is Herbert Marshall and Mildred Stock's *Ira Aldridge: The Negro Tragedian* (1958). In addition to presenting data about Aldridge's life, this work gives information about the dramatic works in which he appeared as well as significant critical reviews of these performances. Other works offering brief comments on his life are: Edith J. R. Isaacs's *The Negro in the American Theatre* (1947), James Weldon Johnson's *Black Manhattan* (1930), and Loften Mitchell's *Black Drama* (1967). There is a very short sketch by Arthur Hornblow in *DAB* (1:160–61).

— JEANNE-MARIE MILLER

ALEXANDER, JOHN H[ANKS] (1864–1894), army officer. Alexander was born in Helena, Ark., the son of slave parents. Details of his early life are unknown but in 1882 he enrolled as a freshman at Ohio's Oberlin College. He did well academically and was described by one of his professors as having "very rare ability as a student." In May 1883 he was tendered an appointment as alternate to the U.S. Military Academy from the 14th Congressional District of Ohio. He made the highest score on the academic part of the examination but was made an alternate because another candidate (the son of Chief Justice Morrison Waite) scored better on the physical. Friends who were skeptical of the military medical evaluation that Alexander was "pigeon breasted" (Ransom, p. 34) held parties in Oberlin and Cleveland and raised enough money to send him to West Point anyway. When the young Waite failed his entrance examination, Alexander received his chance, passed the examination, and was admitted.

While at the academy Alexander continued to display his academic ability. During his four years, despite white ostracism, he ranked 16th out of 100, 26th of 70, 45th of 67, and graduated 32nd of 64. He showed particular talent for languages, ranking (in his first year) fourth in English and seventh in Spanish. His high number of demerits throughout his academic career for the usual cadet deficiencies pulled down his class rank. Twice he was placed in close arrest, once for skating on the frozen Hudson River.

Upon his graduation from the Military Academy in 1887, Alexander was commissioned a second lieutenant and reported to the all-Negro 9th Cavalry Regiment at Fort Robinson, Neb. When he arrived, he found there was no vacancy for him because of the delay in the promotion of another second lieutenant. After an exchange of several letters between Washington and the West (and with Alexander worrying about his pay), Washington ordered him kept on and utilized "where his services are needed."

During the next seven years except for leaves of absence and a brief temporary-duty assignment training an all-Negro North Carolina unit in conjunction with the 1891 Southern Inter-State Exposition, Alexander stayed with the 9th Cavalry. During this period he was stationed at Fort Robinson; Fort Washakie, Wyo.; and Fort DuChesne, Utah. Among other tasks he ran a post commisary and conducted prisoners to Omaha. During his off-duty hours he read, mostly military biographies and texts. His efficiency reports were good, one of his commanders writing: "I look upon this officer as one of the best that I have ever met except at times a little frivilous." In October 1893 Alexander became eligible for promotion to first lieutenant by passing a long physical and military examination.

As early as October 1887 interest was expressed in the possibility of having Alexander serve as an instructor of military science in a Negro college. At this early date Booker T. Washington requested Alexander's services for his Tuskegee Institute. He was told that, according to regulations, an officer first had to serve three years with a regiment. Besides, Alabama already had its quota of college-assigned officers. In 1892 and continuing for the next two years, the Rev. S. T. Mitchell, the president of Wilberforce University in Ohio, attempted to acquire Alexander's services for such a task. He was told that Ohio already had its quota of officers. When Congress increased the number of officers available for such duty, Mitchell's persistent efforts with the War Department and other politicians paid off. On Jan. 6, 1894, Alexander was detailed as professor of military science and tactics at Wilberforce University. He had just begun his tour of duty when, on March 26, 1894, he died of a heart attack in Springfield, Ohio. He was interred in Xenia, Ohio.

Since he outranked the later famous Charles Young by two years, and since he was highly regarded and a man of ability, John H. Alexander might well have been the ranking Negro officer in World War I had he lived.

There is no study of Lieutenant Alexander. There are a few materials available in the National Archives and the Archives of the U.S. Military Academy. Scattered information is available in Roverdy C. Ransom's *The Pilgrimage of Harriet Ransom's Son* (n.d.) and William S. Scarborough's *A Tribute to Colonel Charles Young* (n.d.). — JOHN F. MARZALEK, JR.

ALLAIN, THÉOPHILE T. (1846–1917), businessman and politician. Allain was born on Oct. 1, 1846, on a plantation in the Parish of West Baton Rouge, La., owned by a wealthy white man, Sosthene Allain. Like some other slaveholders, he made one of his slaves, "a pretty brown woman," his mistress. Although a "col-

ored creole," Théophile, their son who bore the improbable nickname of "Souloque" (the black dictator of Haiti), accompanied his father on trips to the North and to Europe. In 1856 Sosthene Allain sent for his son to join him in France, where he witnessed the christening of the prince imperial at Notre-Dame. They journeyed also to Spain and England. Returning to the United States in 1859, he entered school under a Professor Abadie in New Orleans. In 1868 he was enrolled in a private school in New Brunswick, N.J. He owned a grocery business in West Baton Rouge Parish, where he opened schools for Negroes and whites in 1869. For many years he was the owner of a large plantation in Iberville, said to embrace 790 acres worth $15,000, worked by thirty-five laborers, that produced 7000 hogsheads of sugar, 4000 gallons of molasses, and other produce worth $14,400 in 1870. Both as a planter and as an exporter, he was held in high esteem by some of the leading commercial men of the South.

In 1872 he began a political career that lasted until 1890, further evidence that Reconstruction did not come to an end in 1877. In 1882, the Republican Executive and Financial Committee and other organizations sent him as one of two spokesmen to urge action by the federal government to improve the levees of the Mississippi River. On April 18, 1882, he made a lengthy speech on the subject to the House Committee on Commerce. Like many other appeals even to the present time, his address resulted in little improvement. There is not much information about his later life: he is said to have lost his plantation because of indebtedness, and to have moved to Chicago in the early part of the twentieth century.

As a member of the Louisiana House of Representatives from the 14th District, in 1874 he helped obtain the passage of the Funding Act, which made the state liable for an annual interest on its funded debt. Outside the legislature he supported the abortive unification effort of 1873, designed to remove race as an issue in Reconstruction politics in Louisiana. After two terms in the House, Allain represented the 14th District in the state Senate (1876–1880), even though the last of the federal troops were withdrawn in 1877. He served again in the House from 1881 to 1890.

One of his more significant acts was his co-sponsorship, as a member of the Louisiana Constitutional Convention (1879) of legislation that resulted in the establishment of an institution "for the education of persons of color." Three colleges or universities (all largely elementary and high schools)—Leland, Straight, and New Orleans—110 been established in the city of New Orleans in 1869. In 1886 (Simmons, p. 228) he introduced a bill in the state legislature for an appropriation of $20,000 (of which $14,000 was authorized) for the purpose of erecting buildings of "Southern University" in New Orleans, later moved to Scotlandville. In a speech at the laying of the cornerstone, he said: "I look forward to a period not far distant, when Louisiana will be able to have a white and a colored school-house dotting every nook and corner in the State of our birth, the home of our choice, with a public sentiment advocating for high and low, for white and colored popular education." In 1887 he proposed to the Farmers'

State Association a resolution to recommend the passage by the legislature of an industrial school for colored people. He succeeded in having the four institutions in the city of New Orleans (Leland, Straight, New Orleans, and Southern) designated as repositories of public records.

Allain was a man of considerable learning and an effective speaker. His address to the House Committee on Commerce is a valuable source for the economy of Louisiana, the need for levees and the obligation of the federal government to fulfill that obligation. In one of his more eloquent paragraphs he stated: "We form, in the relations we have alluded to, no inconsiderable portion of the United States, and our welfare is materially injured by the trespass of the river, and when we observe Congress recognizing the loud and just clamor raised against the imprisonment abroad of American citizens, and dealing with the the [sic] question as suits a free republic; when we see the interest taken in projects to check the influx of Chinese, even to the practical abrogation of a solemn treaty with China, without the consent of 'the other party'; when we see Congress undertaking the laudable, if gigantic, task of even regulating the polygamists of Utah; when we see, last, but not least, the beneficent propositions seriously made by a revered Senator to provide for the education of the aboriginal Indians of our country, and I reflect that the warrant and the authority for the accomplishment of these diversified objects, and that these all are regarded as *duties* of the United States Government, I wonder whether the *interests* of a million of people in Louisiana, a people who feel that by every just and patriotic consideration should—are entitled to have their 'welfare' considered by the government to the extent we are seeking."

He was a fine example of those "Colored Creoles" of Louisiana, speaking French fluently. Although his family of six children were Catholic, they attended Straight University, a nondenominational school.

Some facts about his life are uncertain. His wife, the former Aline Coleman, possessed some properties of her own according to tax records. Although Alice Dunbar-Nelson stated that he moved to Chicago ("People of Color in Louisiana, Part III," *JNH*), evidence that he lived there is lacking. Masonic records in New Orleans state that a "Brother T. T. Allain," with a wife named Aline, died there on Feb. 2, 1917. His wife received the customary $300 paid to the widow of a member who was active at the time of his death.

The biography in William J. Simmons's *Men of Mark . . .* (1887, pp. 208–30), was probably written by Allain. There are brief references in John W. Blassingame's *Black New Orleans* (1973), which is indispensable for background information. His career as a legislator is recorded in the Louisiana *House Journal* and *Senate Journal* (1872–1890, passim). His financial status is found in Iberville Parish Tax Assessment Rolls for 1870–1890 (Iberville Parish Courthouse, Port Allen, La.), and West Baton Rouge Parish Tax Assessment Rolls for 1873 (West Baton Rouge Parish Courthouse, Port Allen). Additional information is in the New Orleans *Semi-Weekly Louisiana* (1870s and 1880s, passim). Also valuable are the William Pitt Kellogg Papers, De-

partment of Archives and Manuscripts, Louisiana State University, Baton Rouge. Some information about his Masonic activities is in *Proceedings of the M. W. Eureka Lodge A.E. and A.M. of Louisiana* (privately published), in the possession of John Lewis, PH Mason, Baton Rouge. — CHARLES VINCENT

ALLEN, MACON B. (1816–1894), lawyer. The exact details about the early life of Allen are somewhat mysterious. He was born, probably a free person, during the pioneer days of Indiana in 1816. By the early 1840s he was well established as a businessman in Portland, Me. Through the efforts of white liberals, Allen attempted to gain admittance to the bar in Maine in 1844. On his first attempt, when he was introduced into the courthouse by Gen. Samuel Fessenden, he was rejected because it was alleged that he was not a citizen. On the second effort in the same year, he passed a rigorous examination on the law and was admitted, thus becoming the "first" licensed Negro attorney in the United States.

Since there were few Negroes in Maine, Allen chose to begin the practice of law in Boston. On May 3, 1845, he was admitted to the Suffolk County, Mass., bar. He was the first Negro so recognized in Massachusetts, which by this time was well known for the antislavery work of William Lloyd Garrison and Negro abolitionists, notably William C. Nell and Robert Morris. He became a justice of the peace by 1848, and continued to practice law in Massachusetts until the start of Radical Reconstruction in the South. It is difficult to determine precisely when Allen settled in Charleston, S.C., but he was there by the end of 1870.

While some of the other Negro lawyers in Boston entered local politics and were elected to the Massachusetts legislature and to various borough councils, Allen obviously felt that his legal skills and experience would be more useful in the South where the vast majority of the Negroes were located. He became a member of the law firm of William J. Whipper, Robert Brown Elliott, and Macon B. Allen. Whipper and Elliott were elected members of the South Carolina legislature; Elliott was elected to Congress in 1870 and 1872. Allen also attempted to gain political office as a Republican. Although he was very capable, his bid to become the secretary of state for South Carolina in 1872 was abortive. However, in the next year the death of the incumbent of a minor judgeship enabled Allen to be elected as a judge of the Inferior Court. He was thus one of the first Negro judges in the United States (Mifflin W. Gibbs of Little Rock, Ark., was another Negro judge elected in 1873). The selection of Allen led the *Charleston Courier,* a white newspaper, to advocate the elimination of the position. When Allen completed his term as judge, he resumed his law practice in Charleston and continued in politics for several years.

Not much is known of his career after the late 1870s. On Oct. 10, 1894, Judge Macon B. Allen died in Washington, D.C. He was then seventy-eight years old. His widow and his son, Arthur W., survived him; he was buried from St. Mark's Episcopal Church. His death marked a fifty-year period during which Negro lawyers had established themselves as capable advocates of the rights of Negroes and others.

There is little information about Allen. Some data are in the *Liberator* and in Charleston newspapers. There is information in William C. Nell's *The Colored Patriots of the American Revolution* (1855) and in Wilson Armistead's *A Tribute for the Negro* (1848). The best documented source is by Charles Sumner Brown, "The Genesis of the Negro Lawyers in New England" (*NHB*, April 1959, pp. 147–52). — CLARENCE G. CONTEE, SR.

ALLEN, RICHARD (1760–1831), abolitionist and founder of the Free African Society and the African Methodist Episcopal church. Allen was born in Philadelphia on Feb. 14, 1760, of slave parents owned by Benjamin Chew who served as attorney-general and chief justice of the High Court of Errors and Appeals. Chew was a kindly master, and according to Allen treated his slaves well. About 1767 there was a decline in Chew's law practice, and the Allen family—father, mother, and four children—were sold to the Stockley family who owned a plantation near Dover, Del. Allen lived and worked there until he was twenty years of age. Methodist preachers were very active in this area and Allen joined the Methodist Society with the permission of his master. He taught himself to read and write, and soon began to head the meetings.

Shortly thereafter it was proposed by Allen's owner that he and his brother could have the opportunity of purchasing their freedom for $2000 in Continental money or £60 in gold and silver currency. Allen began to work as a day laborer, brick maker, and teamster, converted his master, purchased his freedom, and returned to Philadelphia.

As a wagon driver during the Revolutionary War, he preached at regular stops. After the end of the war, he preached in Delaware, West Jersey, and eastern Pennsylvania. It is probable that he attended (Dec. 1784) the first organizing Conference of American Methodism. Rejecting an offer by Bishop Francis Asbury to travel in the South with him but not mingle with slaves, Allen continued to ride and preach on his own. In 1786 he returned to Philadelphia where he met Absalom Jones and began to hold prayer meetings for Negroes. The Methodist elder in charge assigned him to preach at the 5 A.M. meeting. His proposal to build a separate place of worship was widely debated. While the debate over a separate church continued, in November the officials of the St. George's Methodist Episcopal Church pulled Allen, Absalom Jones, and William White from their knees during prayer. The Negro members walked out of the church in a body. With the help of Jones, Allen organized on April 12, 1787, the independent Free African Society, the first such body in the United States. Allen and Jones were "overseers" of this beneficial and mutual aid society. After its articles of association were adopted on May 17, 1787, it encouraged the organization of other Free African Societies in Newport, Boston, and New York. In addition to extending mutual aid, they forbade drunkenness, disorderly conduct, and loose marriage ties. Allen and Jones denounced slavery, and the Free African Society of Philadelphia also urged the abolition of slavery. It issued a plan for "The African Church," a nondenominational body. With the assistance notably of Benjamin Rush, the church was orga-

nized on July 7, 1791. Toward the end of 1792 the Free African Society decided to build a church. When a severe yellow fever epidemic in 1793 interrupted the construction, Allen and Jones organized the colored community to serve as nurses and undertakers. They successfully refuted allegations of charging exorbitant rates and cheating.

When the plague ended, Allen and Jones resumed plans to build a church. Working as a master shoemaker with journeymen and apprentices in his employ, he saved enough money to buy a lot and hauled an old blacksmith shop to the site where carpenters repaired it. On July 17, 1794, it became the Bethel Church. Since a majority of the congregation opposed affiliation with the Methodist church because it persecuted Negroes, most voted to affiliate with the Episcopal church under Jones. Allen then formed the first African Methodist Episcopal congregation. In 1799 Bishop Francis Asbury ordained Allen as a deacon, and he later became an elder. Between 1799 and 1816 other A.M.E. congregations were established in Baltimore, Wilmington, and other cities; by the latter date these congregations were prepared to form a separate denomination. Allen, Daniel Coker, and others met in Philadelphia on April 9, 1816, and established the African Methodist Episcopal church. On April 11, 1816, Jones helped to consecrate Allen as the first bishop of the African Methodist Episcopal church.

Meanwhile, in 1795 Allen had opened a day school for sixty pupils, and in 1804 he organized a "Society of Free People of Color for Promoting the Instruction and School Education of Children of African Descent." When George Washington died, the *Philadelphia Gazette* published Allen's Bethel sermon in which he stressed Washington's belated uneasiness about slavery as a sin. In 1799 and 1800 Jones and Allen led the colored community in petitioning the state legislature for the immediate abolition of slavery. In 1800 they sent a similar petition to Congress. In 1809 they founded the Society for the Suppression of Vice and Immorality. They also began a short-lived insurance company. During the War of 1812, Allen, Jones, and James Forten led 2500 Negroes in building adequate defenses for Philadelphia. In January 1817 Allen worked with Jones and Forten to organize a convention of 3000 colored men who vigorously condemned the newly formed American Colonization Society. He supported the antislavery societies in Philadelphia, and in 1827 aided *Freedom's Journal,* the first Negro newspaper in the United States.

On Nov. 2, 1827, his letter to the editor of *Freedom's Journal* eloquently expressed his continued opposition to colonization in Liberia and elsewhere in Africa. The large number of "poor ignorant Africans" in the United States were not capable of converting, civilizing, or Christianizing "heathen" in Africa. Slaveholders wished to send free people of color away from the United States because they might inspire slaves to seek freedom. Foreign immigrants were encouraged to come to the United States while Negroes, who had tilled the soil before their arrival, were being forced to leave. He concluded the letter: "This land which we have watered with our tears our blood, is now our mother country; & we are well satisfied to stay where wisdom abounds, & the gospel is free." Allen played a leading role in the organization (Nov. 30, 1830) of the "American Society of Free Persons of Colour, for improving their Condition in the United States; for Purchasing Lands; and for the Establishing of a Settlement in the Province of Upper Canada." Allen was elected president and William Whipper corresponding secretary. An address to the "Free People of Colour of these United States" explained the reasons for the stated purposes, and a call, signed by Allen, was issued for the "First Annual Convention of the People of Colour" in 1830 to implement the purposes. The conventions, which met periodically prior to the Civil War (and were resumed after its close), were opposed by some leading Negroes who deemed the measures and the convention movement itself unsound.

Allen was married to a young woman named Sara who had been born in Isle of Wight County, Va., in 1764. They were married in Philadelphia when she was a young woman. She was his devoted wife and he "an affectionate husband [and] a tender father." She died in Philadelphia on July 16, 1849, at the home of her daughter, Mrs. Anna Adams (Hallie Q. Brown, *Homespun Heroines and Other Women of Distinction* [1926], pp. 11–12). They had four sons—Richard Jr., Peter, John, and James—and another daughter Sarah. Allen and his wife were buried in 1901 in Bethel African Methodist Episcopal Church, Sixth and Lombard Streets, Philadelphia.

Allen's greatness was acknowledged by contemporaries and posterity. Churches commemorated his name as did the Allen Christian Endeavor Society and Allen University in Columbia, S.C. On June 12, 1876, there was formally dedicated in Fairmont Park, Philadelphia, a monument to him, which may have been the first erected to Negroes by other Negroes. Among those present were Mifflin W. Gibbs, Henry McNeal Turner, Benjamin T. Tanner, Robert Brown Elliott, John M. Langston, and Norris Wright Cuney.

The most comprehensive biography is the 1969 edition of *Richard Allen: Apostle of Freedom,* by Charles H. Wesley. Also indispensable is *Segregated Sabbaths: Richard Allen and the Emergence of Independent Black Churches 1760–1840* by Carol V. R. George (1973). There is a very short sketch by Carter G. Woodson in *DAB* (1:204–5). — CHARLES H. WESLEY

ALLENSWORTH, ALLEN (1842–1914), businessman, chaplain, educator, and town founder. Born to slave parents, Phyllis and Levi Allensworth, in Louisville, Ky., on April 7, 1842, Allensworth successfully escaped from his master in 1862 on his third attempt. He joined the 44th Illinois Infantry's hospital corps as a civilian nurse and saw action in the 1862 campaign through Nashville. Then he worked on a hospital ship before enlisting in the navy in April 1863. He served on the gunboats *Queen City, Tawah,* and *Pittsburgh,* and rose to the rank of chief petty officer.

After a short, profitable venture as a restaurateur in St. Louis where he operated two restaurants, he studied at Ely Normal School, which the Freedmen's Bureau had established at Louisville. He taught in a Freedmen's Bureau school in Christmasville, Ky., in 1868, and was ordained to the Baptist ministry in Louisville three years later. While ministering to several Kentucky congregations, he worked as financial agent of the General Association of the Colored Baptists in Kentucky, superintendent of Sunday schools of the state Baptist convention, and missionary for the American Baptist Publication Society in Philadelphia. He was chosen a Republican elector from Kentucky in 1880, and attended Republican national conventions as a delegate in 1880 and 1884. In 1884 he made a lecture tour of New England and served the Joy Street Baptist Church of Boston for four months while the congregation looked for a permanent minister. Later that year he moved to the Union Baptist Church in Cincinnati, Ohio. He left in 1886 to accept a commission from Pres. Grover Cleveland as a chaplain of the 24th Infantry, a Negro regiment.

He began his military career at Fort Supply, Indian Territory, and later served at posts in New Mexico, Arizona, Utah, and Montana. During his army career, he became well known for his efforts as an educator. He established separate school programs for enlisted men and children, in which a different subject, such as grammar or arithmetic, was emphasized each day. This system, which he devised while at Fort Bayard, N. Mex., was widely copied by chaplains throughout the army. In recognition of his status as an educator, the National Education Association invited him to address its Toronto convention in 1891. He spoke on "The History and Progress of Education in the U.S. Army," tracing the army's growing recognition of the importance of formal learning.

During the Spanish-American War he was assigned to detached duty as a recruiter in Louisville. He rejoined the 24th Infantry for service in the Philippine Insurrection. During his three years in the islands, as his biographer Charles Alexander notes, Allensworth directly confronted the paradox of Afro-American soldiers, relegated to a second-class status at home, risking their lives to suppress the Filipino struggle for independence.

When Allensworth retired in 1906, he was the senior chaplain in the army. On his departure from the service he was promoted to lieutenant-colonel, the highest rank held by a Negro until Charles Young's promotion to colonel during World War I. The chaplain moved to Los Angeles and organized a company (1908) to aid Negroes who desired to migrate to California. The company sold lots in the new town of Allensworth, Tulare County, which was about halfway between Los Angeles and San Francisco. The community grew rapidly to nearly two hundred families. Its citizens engaged in farming, dairying, and mercantile pursuits. In only six years the town grew to be a market center for the surrounding area, and included a hotel, post office, and railroad station. One resident, Oscar Over, who had served as a lieutenant in a Kansas regiment during the Spanish-American War, became California's first Negro justice of the peace in 1914. The town began to decline in a decade, partly because of Allensworth's untimely death on Sept. 14, 1914, after being struck by a motorcycle. The growing scarcity of water, the souring of the soil in the largely agricultural community, and better opportunities in the San Francisco Bay Area shipyards also contributed to its demise. The site of the town has been designated Allensworth State Historical Park by the state of California.

Allensworth married Josephine Leavell of Bowling Green, Ky., in 1877. She continued to live in Allensworth after his death. Their two daughters, Eva and Nella, married Harrie Skanks and L. M. Blodgett, respectively.

There is one full-length biography of Allensworth. Charles Alexander's *Battles and Victories of Allen Allensworth* (1914) quotes extensively from military documents and is useful for all phases of his career. A short biographical sketch in William J. Simmons's *Men of Mark: Eminent, Progressive, and Rising* (1887) deals mainly with his years as a civilian minister. Delilah L. Beasley's *Negro Trail Blazers of California* (1919) and the *New York Times* (Oct. 22, 1972) contain good supplementary materials on the town of Allensworth.

— FRANK N. SCHUBERT

ANDERSON, CHARLES WILLIAM (1866–1938), government official. Born in Oxford, Ohio, on April 28, 1866 (the 1870 manuscript census indicates Tennessee), the son of Charles W. and Serena Anderson, he attended public schools in Oxford and Middleton, and after graduation received further training at the Spencerian Business College in Cleveland and the Berlitz School of Languages in Worcester, Mass. Anderson went to New York City in the late 1880s and was appointed United States gauger in the Second District of New York, serving until 1893. For the next two years (1893–1895) he was private secretary to the state treasurer of New York, and in the latter year succeeded to the position of chief clerk of the state treasury, which he held until 1898. From 1898 until 1905 Anderson was supervisor of accounts for the New York State Racing Commission. In 1905 Pres. Theodore Roosevelt appointed him collector of internal revenue for the Second District in New York City, where he remained until his termination by Woodrow Wilson ten years later. Anderson moved back into state office as supervising agent of the Agricultural Department until 1922, when Warren G. Harding appointed him collector of internal revenue for the Third District of New York City. He retired in 1934 because of ill health, after serving under six presidents as collector of internal revenue for the Second and Third Districts.

From Anderson's first arrival in Manhattan in 1886, his rise among New York City Negroes was meteoric. He immediately became active in Republican politics and canvassed the predominantly Negro wards. As a result of his activities he was elected president of the Young Men's Colored Republican Club of New York County and awarded the gauger position in the Internal Revenue section of the Second District. Later, he was for ten terms a member of the New York State Republican Committee (for a number of years he was the only Negro) and a delegate at large to three Republican national conventions. Anderson was undoubtedly the most prominent Negro Republican in the state, and the *New York Age* commented, "You just can't think of Republicanism in New York without remembering Charlie Anderson."

Anderson's most significant friendship began in the latter 1890s when he aligned himself with Booker T. Washington. From then until Washington's death in 1915 the two were inseparable allies. In a letter in 1904 Anderson indicated his unswerving loyalty to the "Tuskegee Wizard": "I am not easily frightened," he asserted, "and when I believe in a man, no opposition which may be made to him can swerve me by so much as a hair's breadth." It was partially through Washington's influence that Anderson was appointed collector of internal revenue (his district encompassed Wall Street) in 1905. By then, however, Anderson had already established his credentials as a superb politician and an outstanding administrator. Moreover, Roosevelt needed to appoint a Negro to a major office in the North to offset the controversy over William D. Crum's selection as collector of customs in Charleston, S.C. Anderson was the last Negro appointed to office by Roosevelt.

Anderson's friendship was extremely important to Washington because the New Yorker kept a careful watch on those opposed to the Tuskegeean's philosophy and planted spies in their organizations. He continually fought Negro Democrats as well as William E. B. Du Bois and others, who seemed to be threatening his or Washington's position of influence. To him, they were visionaries and dreamers. Anderson summed up his philosophy when he wrote to Emmett J. Scott (Washington's private secretary) in 1905: "We do not belong to that group to whom nothing is desirable but the impossible. Some of us are trying to provide opportunities for members of the race." Accordingly, he provided numerous positions and better paying jobs for New York's Negroes. In short, Anderson was dedicated to what could be done at the moment, and to the proposition that through proving oneself now, the future would take care of itself.

There can be little doubt that in the late nineteenth and early twentieth centuries Charles W. Anderson was one of the most important Negro politicians of either party in the North. He was largely responsible for the New York Civil Rights Law of 1895. Essentially a self-made man, he was cool and brilliant, worked mostly behind the scenes, and seldom miscalculated political situations. Moreover, Anderson was suave and affable, his charm and wit serving him well in many instances. Anderson, of course, owed much to the influence of Booker T. Washington, but he had already established himself in New York when Washington emerged as the race leader. Through persistent attention to detail and organization, Anderson rose to his eminent position as a pillar of the New York Negro community. James Weldon Johnson wrote in *Along This Way*, "I regarded him as being, beyond any doubt, the very ablest Negro politician."

Unfortunately, there is no major collection of Charles W. Anderson's papers; at least none has been discovered. There are, however, certain sources which may profitably be consulted. In the Schomburg Collection in the New York Public Library and the Collis P. Huntington Memorial Library at Hampton Institute are two clipping files dealing specifically with Anderson. In the Manuscript Division of the Library of Congress there are hundreds of Anderson letters in the Booker T. Washington Papers, and many more in the Theodore Roosevelt, William Howard Taft, and Carter G. Woodson Papers. The two most important and interpretive biographical sketches are in Gilbert Osofsky's *Harlem: The Making of a Ghetto, Negro New York, 1890–1930* (1966) and August Meier's *Negro Thought in America, 1880–1915: Racial Ideologies in the Age of Booker T. Washington* (1963). — BARRY A. CROUCH

ANDERSON, OSBORNE PERRY (1830–1871), one of John Brown's men at Harpers Ferry. Born in Pennsylvania of free parents, he attended Oberlin College and as a young man worked as a printer. His education and skill made him valuable to John Brown, whom he met in Chatham, Ontario, in the spring of 1858. He was the only member of the party who took part in the heaviest of the fighting and escaped. He lived to give the only eyewitness account of the raid in his book, *A Voice From Harper's Ferry* (1861).

At Chatham, Ontario, Brown set up an organization of white and colored men who wanted to take direct action against slavery. Ex-slaves who had settled in Canada and free Negroes from the United States met with Brown and his men who had shared in the fighting in Kansas. Anderson served as recording secretary at some of the sessions. When he returned to Oberlin he was fully committed to Brown's cause. He arrived in Virginia a few weeks before Brown made his strike. His book describes the conditions on the farm which Brown had rented five miles from Harpers Ferry. Supplies and fighting equipment were accumulated there, while men were being secretly assembled and trained.

On the morning of Sunday, Oct. 16, 1859, John Brown assembled his twenty-one men for worship. Five of them were Negroes. Anderson later wrote: "He read a chapter from the Bible, applicable to the condition of slaves, and our duty as their brethren, and then offered up a fervent prayer to God to assist in the liberation of the bondmen in that slaveholding land. The services were impressive." The final orders were given in the afternoon. Each man knew his part. The march began after eight o'clock that night. The town was taken by surprise, the armory, the arsenal, and the rifle works seized. Anderson assisted in the capture of Col. Lewis Washington, a leading citizen and relative of George Washington.

Anderson and Albert Hazlett had been ordered to hold a station on the wall at the arsenal. When they saw that Brown, with a small number of fighters in the engine house, was completely surrounded and overwhelmed by the local militia and armed citizens, they found a way out by escaping to the river. After a series of contacts with pursuers, Hazlett was captured but Anderson reached friends in Pennsylvania who moved him farther north to Canada. A year later Anderson visited the grave of John Brown in North Elba, N.Y.

He served as a noncommissioned officer in the Union Army during the Civil War, and died in Washington, D.C., in 1871.

Anderson's book *A Voice from Harper's Ferry,* long out of print, was reprinted in 1975 by World View Publishers, New York. W. E. B. Du Bois quoted from it in his *John Brown* (1909), which gives a detailed account of the Chatham meeting and of the raid at Harpers Ferry. Jules Abels's *Man on Fire, John Brown and the Cause of Liberty* (1971) has a brief passage about Anderson's career after 1861. — LORENZ GRAHAM

ANDERSON, WILLIAM T. (1859–1934), clergyman, chaplain, and physician. He was born a slave in Seguin near San Antonio, Tex., on Aug. 20, 1859. He and his mother fled eastward to Galveston during the Civil War. In his childhood in Galveston, he joined the Texas Conference of the African Methodist Episcopal church, which sent him to Wilberforce University for three years. An Ohio benefactor, Stephen Watson, who was vice-president of the London Exchange Bank of Madison County, financed the remainder of his education: Anderson received a Theology Certificate from Howard University in 1886 and graduated from the Homeopathic Medical College of Cleveland in 1888. In the next decade he served as pastor for A.M.E. congregations in Urbana, Lima, Toledo, and Cleveland, Ohio. His Cleveland church, St. John's, was the largest A.M.E. congregation in the state. Anderson was appointed to the chaplaincy of the 10th Cavalry, U.S. Army, with the rank of captain, by Pres. William McKinley on Aug. 16, 1897.

Anderson joined the 10th Cavalry at its Fort Assinniboine, Mont., headquarters in November 1897, less than six months before the Spanish-American War. The regiment departed for the Chickamauga staging area in April 1898 to prepare for the invasion of Cuba, but Anderson remained behind at Assinniboine, perhaps one of the first Negro officers to command an American military post. On July 25, 1898, he joined the 10th Cavalry near Santiago, Cuba. Within one day after his arrival in Cuba, Anderson used his medical training in attending fourteen members of the regiment who were suffering from fever and dysentery. Sgt. Horace W. Bivins credited him with saving his life. Anderson and the regiment spent the months immediately after the brief conflict at camps along the Gulf Coast of Alabama and Texas. During this time Anderson joined in the writing of *Under Fire with the Tenth Cavalry* (1899 and 1969), with Herschel Cashin, recorder in the United States Land Office at Huntsville, Ala., writer Charles Alexander, and two men of the 10th Cavalry, surgeon Arthur M. Brown and Sgt. Horace Bivins. The book told the story of the heroism of Negro soldiers in the Cuban campaign, largely through the eyewitness accounts of both commissioned officers and enlisted men.

In mid-1899, Anderson and his regiment returned to Manzanillo, Cuba, where they served as part of the army of occupation until April 1902. The chaplain spent the next five years at Fort Mackintosh, Tex., and in the Pine Ridge country of Nebraska. During the years in Cuba and Nebraska he helped the enlisted men organize a regimental YMCA, a forum through which they could discuss race issues and manage their own affairs. In April 1907 Anderson's regiment was transferred to Fort William McKinley, near Manila in the Philippines. He was promoted to major in August of that year, only days after meeting the requirement of ten years' service. While at McKinley, he commanded the U.S. Morgue located in Manila. Shortly after he returned to the

United States and Fort Ethan Allen, Vt., on Jan. 10, 1910, he was retired for a disability caused by a fever he had contracted in Cuba in 1898.

He returned to his home at Wilberforce, and his job as accountant and secretary to the bishop in the Third Episcopal District. In September 1916 he became the minister of Warren Chapel in Toledo, a church he had briefly served in 1896–1897. He resigned in September 1918 to offer his services to the Quartermaster Corps of the army. However, World War I ended only a few weeks later, and Anderson retired to Cleveland. In the following spring, he led a drive for funds for the defense of Dr. Bundy, who had been accused of murder during the East St. Louis, Ill., riot of 1917. When he died at his home in Cleveland on Aug. 21, 1934, he was one day over eighty-five. An early American Legion post was named for him in the Cleveland area. The chaplain's wife, Sada J. Anderson, was also active in the A.M.E. church and held several offices in the Women's Parent Mite Missionary Society.

The weekly *Cleveland Gazette* reported Anderson's activities throughout his career. Other good sources of biographical information include the book he co-authored and his official monthly reports as chaplain, which are on file in the records of the adjutant-general, National Archives. There is no published biography of Anderson. Details of Anderson's career after the war can be gleaned from his grave registration record filed with the State Archives at the Ohio Historical Society, and obituaries appearing in the *Cleveland Plain Dealer* (Aug. 23, 1934) and the *Cleveland Gazette* (Aug. 25, 1934). — FRANK N. SCHUBERT *and* FRANK R. LEVSTIK

ANTOINE, CAESAR CARPETIER (1836–1921), army

officer, politician, businessman, and editor. Antoine was born in New Orleans in 1836, the son of a veteran of the War of 1812 who had fought the British at the Battle of New Orleans. Antoine's mother was a native of the West Indies and the daughter of an African chief, whose parents were taken as slaves from the shores of Africa. On his father's side (so the story goes), his grandmother Rose Antoine was a remarkable woman who purchased her freedom and acquired a small fortune through her work as a midwife.

Caesar C. Antoine spent his childhood in New Orleans and attended private schools. He was fluent in both French and English. After graduating he entered one of the few occupations open to Negroes in the antebellum South—the barber trade. After federal troops captured Baton Rouge in 1862, he organized a colored company known subsequently as Company I, 7th Louisiana Colored Regiment (Corps d'Afrique). As captain of the company he served in minor engagements until the end of the Civil War. He moved to Shreveport, where he established a family grocery business, but his native shrewdness and general community support impelled him to enter politics. He was elected a delegate to the Louisiana Constitutional Convention of 1867–1868, one of the two southern states (South Carolina was the other) that had a majority of Negroes. He advocated an extensive Bill of Rights, tax reforms, and a petition to Congress requesting the extension of the Freedmen's Bureau.

In the first legislative session after the Constitution was adopted, Antoine served as state senator from Caddo Parish (1868–1872). He was assigned to the Senate committees on commerce and manufactures, and education. As a friend of public education he led in the fight for state support of education. He was later appointed to the School Board of Caddo Parish (1875). Perhaps his biggest triumph in politics was his election as lieutenant-governor of Louisiana (1872–1876). Thus he holds the distinction of being one of three Negroes elected to this position in Louisiana (the others were Oscar J. Dunn and P. B. S. Pinchback). Again, in 1876, he was renominated for the position of lieutenant-governor on the Republican ticket with Stephen B. Packard as governor. But when federal troops were withdrawn in 1877, the government which Packard established toppled.

Antoine was a man of noted financial ability. During Reconstruction he invested in railroad and lottery stocks, and raised several race horses. One notable event was the match in 1871 for a $100 purse between his horse Nellie and another horse. He was president in 1880 of the Cosmopolitan Life Insurance Company, a co-partner with Pinchback in both a cotton factorage, and the *New Orleans Louisianian,* a semiweekly, from Dec. 25, 1870, to April 27, 1872; other businesses in New Orleans were also backed or invested in by Antoine separately. Before he died in September 1921, he had purchased a small plantation in Caddo Parish, owned several city lots, and a $1300 residence.

Little is known about him after 1887 except that he was vice-president of the New Orleans Comité des Citoyens, including Rodolphe L. Desdunes. Formed in 1890 by free people of color, it worked to wage legal battle against discrimination and to create public sentiment unfavorable to those injustices. On Feb. 5, 1892, the Comité des Citoyens reported $2276.25 collected toward a fund to test the constitutionality of the 1890 Jim Crow law. The committee engaged Homer Plessy to test the public accommodations provision of the law, an action that resulted in the famous case *Plessy v. Ferguson* (1896), in which the U.S. Supreme Court for the first time upheld the doctrine of "separate but equal." The committee was also unsuccessful in its attempt to have the law forbidding intermarriage declared unconstitutional.

Biographical information about Antoine is based primarily on the sketch in William J. Simmons's *Men of Mark. . . .* (1887, pp. 1132–34), probably written by Antoine. John W. Blassingame's *Black New Orleans 1860–1880* (1973) gives valuable additional information against the background of the city's colorful life. See *Our People and Our History,* the translation with editing by Sister Dorothea Olga McCants (1973, pp. 141–48) of Rodolphe Lucien Desdunes's *Nos Hommes et Notre Histoire* (1911) for the Comité des Citoyens.
— CHARLES VINCENT

ARMISTEAD, JAMES [LAFAYETTE] (1760–1832),
Afro-American spy in the services of General Lafayette during the American War for Independence. He had been the slave of William Armistead of New Kent County, Va., before being granted permission by his

master in March 1781 to serve with General Lafayette. By July 7, 1781, he was able to infiltrate the headquarters of Gen. Charles Cornwallis, ostensibly as a servant hired to spy on the Americans but in reality a patriot who spied on the British. Although his birth and early childhood remain in obscurity, he is remembered for his written intelligence reports relative to the Yorktown campaign which ended the Revolutionary War. In the spring of 1781 Cornwallis had moved his British forces from the Carolinas into Virginia, quartering near Portsmouth, and practically controlled the Old Dominion. Lafayette quartered near Richmond at New Kent County Court House and Williamsburg, with American forces half the size of those of the British. These circumstances necessitated intelligence reports of enemy movements, equipment, and personnel.

On July 13, 1781, General Washington sent instructions to Lafayette to strengthen his forces and to keep him informed of Cornwallis's future positions, equipment, and military personnel. Lafayette sent several spies into Cornwallis's camp, but none was able to make reliable reports until the messages from Armistead were received on July 31, 1781. Lafayette's letter to Washington reveals not only intelligence reports on Cornwallis but also the ability of Armistead: "A correspondant of mine, servant to Lord Cornwallis, writes on the 26th of July at Portsmouth, and says . . . the greatest part of the army is embarked. There is in Hampton Road one 50 guns ship, and two six and thirty guns frigats . . . 18 sloop loaded with horses. There remain but nine vessels in Portsmouth. . . . There is a large quantity of Negroes . . . but no vessels it seems to take them off." This information was enough for Lafayette to suggest to Washington that if a French fleet entered Hampton Roads, the British army would be trapped.

Probably the most significant military information Armistead sent to Lafayette was related in the Aug. 25, 1781, letter to Washington: "I have got some intelligences by way of this servant I have mentioned. . . . I hear that they begin fortifying at York. . . . The works at Gloster are finished—They consist of some redoubts across Gloster Neck and a battery of 18 pieces. . . . The enemy have 60 sails of vessels into York River.

"There is an amazing quantity of Negroes. . . . In a word this part affords the greatest number of regulars and the only active Army to attak [sic]."

The value of Armistead's reports is stated in the following certificate by Lafayette: "This is to certify that the bearer by the name of James has done essential services to me while I had the honour to command in this State. His intelligences from the enemy's camp were industriously collected and more faithfully delivered. He properly acquitted himself with some important communications I gave him and appears to be entitled to every reward his situation can admit of. Done under my hand, Richmond, November 21st, 1784. La-Fayette."

It was the quality of Armistead's reports that led American and French commanders to station a French fleet in Chesapeake Bay, thus forcing the surrender of Cornwallis. After his surrender he "was shocked to find in the Frenchman's headquarters a Negro he had hired to spy on the Americans."

The Virginia legislature granted Armistead his freedom in 1786 because of his services as a spy. (Special enactment was necessary because Armistead did not qualify for emancipation under the Act of 1783 for slave-soldiers: he was a slave-spy.) In 1816 he bought forty acres of land nine miles south of New Kent County, and reared a large family there. In 1819 the Virginia legislature granted him an annual pension of $40. His signal postwar honor came when Lafayette greeted him personally in Richmond upon his return to America in 1824.

The best documents of the activities of James Armistead are in Louis Gottschalk (ed.), *The Letters of Lafayette to Washington* (1944). Luther Porter Jackson's *Virginia Negro Sailors and Seamen in the Revolutionary War* (1944) includes a brief account.

— DAVID W. BISHOP

ARNETT, BENJAMIN WILLIAM (1838–1906), seventeenth bishop of the African Methodist Episcopal (A.M.E.) church. He was born in Brownsville, Pa., the grandson of Samuel J. and Mary Louise Arnett, who made him "eight parts Negro, six parts Scotch, one part Indian, and one part Irish" (Robert R. Wright Jr., *The Bishops of the A.M.E. Church* [1963], p. 79). His father, Benjamin Sr., purchased the first lot on which to build an A.M.E. church in Brownsville. Benjamin Jr., who was baptized when he was six months old, was educated in a one-room school near Brownsville taught by his father's brother, Ephram Arnett. He worked as a wagon boy, assisting in loading and unloading wagons, on steamboats on the Ohio, the Mississippi, and adjacent waters, and waiting tables in hotels. A tumor on his leg caused an amputation in March 1858. He received a teacher's certificate on Dec. 19, 1863, and was for a period the first and only colored teacher in Fayette County, Pa. He taught and served as a principal in Washington, D.C., for ten months (1864–1865), then returned to Brownsville and taught there until 1867.

He joined the A.M.E. church in February 1856 and was licensed to preach on March 30, 1865, at the Baltimore Annual Conference at Washington, D.C. His first appointment was at Walnut Hills in Cincinnati (April 19, 1867); he was ordained a deacon (April 30, 1868) at Columbus, and as an elder by Bishop Daniel A. Payne (May 12, 1870) at Xenia, Ohio. He filled the following appointments in Ohio: Walnut Hills (1867–1869); Toledo (1870–1872); Allen Temple, Cincinnati (1873–1875); St. Paul A.M.E. Church, Urbana (1876–1877); St. Paul A.M.E. Church, Columbus (1878–1879).

Arnett was a delegate from the Ohio Annual Conference to the General Conference in 1872, assistant secretary in 1876, and general secretary in 1880. He was elected the financial secretary of the General Conference in 1880, held at St. Louis, Mo., and reelected in 1884 in Baltimore. At the General Conference of 1888 he was elected bishop on the first ballot. After his election to the bishopric he served the Seventh Episcopal District, South Carolina (1888–1892); the Fourth Episcopal District composed of Indiana, Illinois, Iowa, and northwestern states (1892–1900); the Third Episcopal District of Ohio, California, and Pittsburgh (1900–

1904); and the First Episcopal District (1904–1906).

Arnett was active as a Republican. In Syracuse, N.Y., on Oct. 4, 1864, he joined the National Equal Rights League of which Frederick Douglass was president. He was a member of the Equal Rights Convention held at Cleveland (John M. Langston, president), and secretary of the convention held at Washington, D.C., in December 1866. He was chaplain of the Republican State Convention of Ohio in 1880 and acted as chaplain of the Ohio legislature (1879). At Toledo in 1872 he was foreman of an otherwise all-white jury. He was chaplain of the National Republic Convention at St. Louis, Mo., in 1896.

In 1886 he was elected to the Ohio legislature by a margin of eight votes to represent Greene County, and helped draft the bill abolishing the state's "Black Laws." While a member of the Ohio legislature he met Maj. William McKinley, Jr., with whom he formed a lasting friendship. He presented McKinley, on behalf of the A.M.E. church, the Bible upon which he took his oath as president (March 4, 1897). During President McKinley's administration (1897–1901) he was said to be "the powerful individual Negro at the White House."

Arnett's connection with fraternal societies began with the organization of the Sons of Hannibal at Brownsville, Pa., in August 1859. In 1864 he organized the Faith and Hope League of Equal Rights at Brownsville, Washington, Uniontown, Monongahela City, Allegheny, and Pittsburgh, Pa. In June 1865 he organized the Grand United Order of Odd Fellows at Brownsville, Pa., and later organized lodges of this order at Toledo, Walnut Hills, and Urbana, Ohio; and Covington and Harrodsburg, Ky. He was a member of Corinthian Lodge of Free and Accepted Masons at Cincinnati, and was grand orator of the Grand Lodge in 1879. A member of the Ohio State Sunday School Convention in 1878, he was elected by the Sunday School Union of Ohio to represent it at the Robert Raikes Centennial in London in 1880. The Inter-Denominational Sunday School Union of South Carolina sent him as a delegate to the World's Convention in London (July 2, 1889). He was elected one of the vice-presidents of the International Sunday School Convention, holding this office until 1893.

Arnett was an outstanding orator and delivered speeches before many audiences: the Republican State Convention of Denver, Colo. (1886); the Centennial Celebration of the First Settlement of the Northwest Territory at Marietta, Ohio (1888); commencement addresses at Wilberforce University (June 19, 1877) and Claflin College, Orangeburg, S.C. (1889); an address to the Grand Army of the Republic in Chicago in August 1900. He often brought his audiences to their feet, handkerchiefs waving in the air in the wildest demonstration.

He held offices in many organizations: secretary of the Bishop's Council, A.M.E. church; trustee of the Archaeological and Historical Society of Ohio; vice-president of the Anti-Saloon League of America; trustee of Wilberforce University; director of Payne Theological Seminary at Wilberforce, Ohio; trustee of the United Society of Christian Endeavors; trustee and vice-president of the Normal and Industrial Board at Wilberforce University; a member of the Executive Committee of the National Sociological Society and life member of the National Negro Business League of the United States.

He married Mary Louisa Gordon on May 25, 1858. From this union seven children were born, five boys and two girls. Two of his sons, Benjamin William Jr. and Henry Y. Arnett, became ministers. Benjamin was a chaplain in the Spanish-American War, later president of Edward Waters College and Allen University. Henry Y. Arnett became a pastor and presiding elder in the Philadelphia and Delaware conferences.

During Arnett's assignment to the Third Episcopal District he established a home at Wilberforce University on a beautiful estate of some ten acres. This home was known as "Tawawa Chimney Corner" and was located near the old Indian Tawawa Springs. In this cultural setting the Arnett home became a social center for many of the intellectuals of the day.

He collected a large library of Negro literature and upon his death the library was sold. Some of the rare and out-of-print volumes went to the scholar W. E. B. Du Bois, some to Fisk University Library and to the book collector Arthur A. Schomburg. A few remained at Wilberforce University.

Arnett died of uremic poisoning on Oct. 9, 1906, at Wilberforce University. His funeral, attended by almost 1300 mourners, was held in Galloway Hall, where the principal address was delivered by Bishop Henry McNeal Turner. He was buried in Tarbox Cemetery just outside Wilberforce. He was survived by his wife, Mary Louise Gordon Arnett, five sons, and two daughters.

The principal source is the Horatio Alger–type biography by Lucretia H. Newman Coleman, *Poor Ben: A Study of Real Life* (1890). A short sketch is in Richard R. Wright, Jr.'s *The Bishops of the African Methodist Episcopal Church* (1963, pp. 78–82). Some early information is also in George F. Robinson, *History of Greene County, Ohio* (1902). Obituaries were published in the *New York Times* (Oct. 9, 1906, p. 7) and the *Cleveland Gazette* (Oct. 20, 1906, p. 1). The Arnett Papers are in the Carnegie Library of Wilberforce University.

— MARY M. FISHER

ATTUCKS, CRISPUS (1750?–1770), the first man to fall in the historic Boston Massacre. Attucks was a muscular mulatto, with some combination of African and Natick Indian blood. Little else about him can be proved beyond doubt, although it is highly probable that he had at one time been a slave of Deacon William Brown of Framingham, Mass., his birthplace, and that he had escaped in November 1750 at the age of twenty-seven. As a free man he had followed the sea, serving on whaleships. The spotlight fell upon him on March 5, 1770, when he met his death at the hands of British soldiers stationed in Boston.

However obscure his origins, Attucks played a prominent role in the proceedings of that fateful night. Carrying a cordwood stick, he was, according to the court testimony of James Bailey, the leader of the noisy, shouting crowd that confronted the British soldiers stationed at the Custom House on King Street. Pressing forward, the jeering crowd began to pelt the soldiers with snow and ice. Growing bolder, one of the demonstrators—Attucks, according to slave Andrew, an eyewitness—struck at one of the grenadiers. Losing their poise, the soldiers fired into the crowd and five civilians were killed. The shooting ended quickly but its effects were far-reaching. There, on the streets of Boston, lay the martyrs of the coming revolution.

Of the five men who lost their lives, Crispus Attucks had special points of distinction. He would be the first to die, being "killed instantly," in the words of the *Boston Gazette and Country Journal* for March 12, 1770. In the trial of the British soldiers, Attucks overshadowed by far any of the other victims. The bill of indictment which the court brought against the soldiers devoted its major attention to Attucks, presenting his name first and separately from the others and charging that he had been assaulted "with force and arms, feloniously, willfully, and of malice aforethought." As if taking his cue from the plaintiffs, in his defense of the British soldiers John Adams likewise chose to focus on Attucks. It was Attucks, charged counsel Adams, who had formed the assaulting party; it was Attucks who had taken hold of the grenadier's bayonet and knocked him down; and it was Attucks "to whose mad behavior, in all probability, the dreadful carnage of that night is chiefly ascribed."

The name of Attucks lived on after the Revolutionary War. During the antebellum period colored military companies took the name of Attucks Guards. From 1858 to 1870 Boston Negroes held a Crispus Attucks Day annually, and in 1888 they succeeded in getting the city and state authorities to erect a Crispus Attucks monument on the Boston Common.

Reference to Attucks by his contemporaries may be found in Frederic Kidder's *History of the Boston Massacre* (1870), which reproduces much of the court testimony. Hiller B. Zobel's scholarly and readable work *The Boston Massacre* (1970) indicates something of the difficulty of reaching hard and fast conclusions about the event itself and the roles of the individual participants. The very short article in *DAB* (1 [1927], Part 1:415) by Edmund Kimball Alden, by dwelling unduly on the problem of the racial identity of Attucks practically ignores the significance of the massacre in stirring up anti-British sentiment, the significant role of Attucks in the massacre, and the symbolic importance of an Attucks, particularly to Afro-Americans.

— BENJAMIN QUARLES

AUGUSTA, ALEXANDER THOMAS (1825–1890), surgeon, medical school professor, and practicing physician. Born free in Norfolk, Va., on March 8, 1825, Augusta learned to read a little because Daniel Payne, later a bishop of the African Methodist Episcopal church, taught the boy secretly, since Virginia law at that time forbade teaching any Negro to read. After serving an apprenticeship to a local barber, young Augusta made his way to Baltimore where, while earning a living as a journeyman barber, he took tutoring lessons that helped him acquire an elementary knowledge of medicine. From Baltimore he moved to Philadelphia in hopes of enrolling in the medical school of the University of Pennsylvania. Although the school refused to let him matriculate, Prof. William Gibson took an interest in the personable young Negro and arranged to have Augusta study in his office.

On Jan. 12, 1847, Augusta married Mary O. Burgoin, of Huguenot descent, in Baltimore. Shortly thereafter, still driven by ambition to become a doctor, he went to California in pursuit of money for his medical education. Although success there failed to gain him admission to a medical school in the United States, Trinity Medical College of the University of Toronto accepted him in 1850, and in 1856 awarded him a Bachelor of Medicine degree. Torontoans manifestly recognized his competence, for he took charge of the city hospital and then of an industrial school, in addition to conducting a private practice. Despite those opportunities, he left for the West Indies before 1860, returned to Baltimore in 1861, and in October 1862 sought in Washington a post in the army's volunteer medical service.

Augusta's unique place in American history dates from April 1863, when he received a medical commission with the rank of major as surgeon of colored troops, U.S. Army, thereby becoming not only the first of eight Negro physicians to obtain a commission but also the highest ranking Negro officer in an army whose commanders had long hesitated over enlisting any Negro troops. Assigned initially to the 7th U.S. Colored Infantry at Camp Stanton, Md., Major Augusta was soon transferred, apparently because two white officers at the camp complained to President Lincoln at the "degradation" of being subordinate to a Negro officer. His next post was in Washington as head of what came to be known as Freedmen's Hospital. That winter he and another Negro officer, both attired in full military regalia, braved the possible embarrassments of attending a White House soirée; President Lincoln greeted them with marked cordiality. During most of 1864 he served as medical examiner of Negro recruits in Benedict, S.C., and Baltimore, where the army paymaster at first refused to pay him more than seven dollars a month, the figure allotted Negro enlisted men. He spent 1865 and much of 1866 in the Department of the South. In March 1865 he was breveted lieutenant-colonel, U.S. Volunteers, for meritorious service, the first Negro to attain that rank. During his lengthy tour of duty as head of a hospital in Savannah, "medical gentlemen of the first eminence in that city . . . often came to his hospital to observe cases interesting to the profession, and to join with him in uncommon surgical operations." Upon his discharge in October 1866 he returned to Washington to open a private practice.

Two years later Augusta attained further distinction: the recently organized Medical Department of Howard University elected him to its faculty as a demonstrator of anatomy. The first Negro to be offered a faculty position in any American medical school, for the next nine years he held a succession of professorships in anatomy and for several years served also on the Freedmen's Hospital staff and as lecturer on dermatology. Yet in 1869, his already notable record notwithstanding, he and two new Negro associates on the Howard faculty were refused admission to the Medical Society of the District of Columbia, a rejection which troubled Augusta chiefly because he correctly foresaw that it would impede the careers of younger Negro physicians for years to come.

Generosity of spirit, dedication to his profession, and a cultivated mind always marked the quiet, slender, handsome Alexander Augusta. When hard times resulting from the Panic of 1873 struck the Howard Medical Department in 1873, its faculty voted to remit all student tuition, but only Augusta and two others were willing to reinforce that decision by taking severe cuts in salary; the others resigned. Augusta left the university in 1877 to devote himself to private practice in Washington. He died at his residence, 1319 L St. NW, on Dec. 21, 1890, and his funeral was held at St. John's Episcopal Church, Lafayette Square, on Dec. 24. He was buried in Arlington National Cemetery.

Augusta's career is most fully portrayed in Daniel Smith Lamb's *Howard University Medical Department . . . A Historical, Biographical and Statistical Memoir* (1900) and W. Montague Cobb's "Alexander Thomas Augusta" (*JNMA*, July 1952, pp. 327–29). See also Notes from the Anderson R. Abbott Papers at the Toronto Public Library deposited in the Moorland-Spingarn Research Center, Howard University, and House Executive Document 315 (41st Cong., 2nd sess., pp. 250–51). — CONSTANCE MCLAUGHLIN GREEN

BAGNALL, ROBERT WELLINGTON (1884–1943), clergyman and NAACP official. Bagnall was born into middle-class circumstances in Norfolk, Va., the son of an Episcopal priest, the Rev. Robert and Sophronia Harrison Bagnall. Educated at Bishop Payne Divinity School, Va., he was ordained a priest of the Episcopal church in 1903 and served pastorates in Pennsylvania, Maryland, and Ohio. In 1911 he moved to St. Matthew's Church in Detroit where he built up membership and finances and abolished the rented pew system. In addition, although it was not a working-class congregation, the church began to orient itself toward the problems of adjustment of the increasing stream of migrants from the South.

Church prominence catapulted Bagnall into civil rights leadership. In 1911 he joined a local protest group and soon reorganized it as an NAACP branch. He spearheaded efforts to persuade the Ford Motor Company to hire more Negro workers, the successful fight against Jim Crow schools in Ypsilanti, and a campaign against police maltreatment in Detroit; he also worked for the passage of the Michigan Civil Rights Bill. In 1918, having gained a reputation as a skillful organizer and forceful orator, Bagnall was appointed an NAACP district organizer, founding twenty-five new chapters in Michigan and Ohio and stimulating the campaign for a civil rights bill in the latter state within the next two years.

In 1921 the NAACP hired Bagnall as full-time director of branches to relieve James Weldon Johnson of some of his traveling and fieldwork responsibilities. During the next twelve years Bagnall reorganized the branch system, weeding out moribund units, strengthening those that could be saved and encouraging them particularly in their local efforts against school segregation. The branches raised 75 percent of the association's revenues and much of the credit for their enthusiasm

was due to Bagnall and William Pickens. Bagnall traveled over 10,000 miles yearly, attended over a hundred meetings, and delivered a similar number of addresses, spending at least 100 days in the field; his job was one of the most grueling in the NAACP.

Bagnall, like Pickens and the Rev. George Frazier Miller, could serve the NAACP yet be compatible with the more radical *Messenger* circle, although neither Bagnall nor Pickens had agreed with A. Philip Randolph's and Chandler Owen's opposition to the World War. In 1920 Bagnall became the first executive officer of the Friends of Negro Freedom, a civil rights group sponsored by the *Messenger*. He wrote for the magazine, serving on its staff from 1923 to 1926, and joined wholeheartedly in its campaign to get Marcus Garvey deported. It was Bagnall who penned the most famous caricature of the West Indian organizer. In an article in the *Messenger* (March 1923, p. 38) Bagnall wrote that Garvey was "a Jamaican Negro of unmixed stock, squat, stocky, fat, and sleek, with protruding jaws, and heavy jowls, small bright piglike eyes and rather bulldog like face." Bagnall wrote also in the *New York Times* (Aug. 21, 1922) that he opposed Garvey's Back to Africa movement on the grounds that it was "impractical, visionary, and ridiculous," and asserted that "Garvey must go, because like Judas Iscariot, he sold himself for thirty pieces of silver" in order to curry favor with the hated Klan (E. David Cronon, *Black Moses*, p. 107). On Jan. 15, 1923, Bagnall was one of a "Committee of Eight" (along with Robert S. Abbott, William Pickens, and Chandler Owen) who sent an open letter to Attorney-General Harry M. Daugherty in which they bitterly accused Garvey of demagoguery, arousing ill feeling between the races, mismanagement, and inciting to violence; they urged Daugherty to proceed expeditiously with the trial of Garvey on charges of using the mails to defraud (*Negro World* supplement, Feb. 6, 1923). Garvey retaliated by alleging that Bagnall had run a "bluevein church" in Detroit before being dismissed for immorality (in fact, Bagnall had been exonerated in court and by his church superiors in 1919 of the charges of misconduct). In 1926 Bagnall requested the local branches of the NAACP to collect signatures and send them to William Monroe Trotter who, through the *Guardian* and his National Equal Rights League, had launched an antisegregation drive (Stephen R. Fox, *The Guardian of Boston: William Monroe Trotter* [1970], p. 257).

By 1930 the NAACP was in financial difficulty and staff salaries were a large item; some cutbacks seemed essential. Walter White urged that Bagnall be let go because, he charged, Bagnall was not bringing in sufficient revenue. After a year of internal dissension White persuaded the NAACP board and at the end of 1931 Bagnall left. It was a cruel reward for dedicated service, although he was tiring of the exhausting pace of his duties.

Bagnall accepted the pastorate of St. Thomas's Episcopal Church in Philadelphia. Always a builder, he liquidated the stagnant church's debt and put new esprit into its congregation. This was his life for the last eleven years; he was not particularly active in the local NAACP branch. He died and was buried in Philadelphia.

Bagnall was a man of broad knowledge, writing widely in periodicals, notably *The Crisis,* and nationally known as an orator. His power was not that of a golden tongue, but the ability to marshall solid facts. An outgoing, charming man, he and his wife were bons vivants. It was not piety that made an impression, but the breadth of his social conscience. His impact on NAACP branches was significant: he could spark them to action when they seemed incapable of doing it themselves. From their perspective he was perhaps the most indispensable executive in the association. The NAACP could not exist without strong branches, and they needed expert encouragement. Bagnall had the needed touch.

There is no full-length biography of Bagnall. An obituary was published in *The Crisis* (Nov. 1943, pp. 334, 347). See also Walter White's *A Man Called White* (1948, reprint 1969). For a fuller treatment, the NAACP Papers in the Library of Congress are indispensable.

— THEODORE KORNWEIBEL

BAKER, EDWARD LEE, JR. (1865–1913), soldier. Born on Dec. 28, 1865, in a California-bound freight wagon on the North Platte River in present-day Laramie County, Wyo., his father French, his mother a Negro American, Baker enlisted in the army at Cincinnati on July 27, 1882, and served as an enlisted man and officer for twenty-eight years, in the American West, Cuba, and the Philippines.

His first assignment was to the 9th Cavalry at Fort Riley, Kans. He remained with the regiment for five years and participated in the efforts to restrain "Sooners" who sought to claim Oklahoma homesteads before the official opening of the territory. In 1887 he joined the 10th Cavalry at Santa Fe, N. Mex. During the next ten years he was stationed at Arizona and Montana posts. In 1892 he was promoted first to regimental quartermaster sergeant and then sergeant major, the highest enlisted rank.

In April 1898 he and the 10th Cavalry moved to Chickamauga, Ga., to prepare for war with Spain. Baker participated in the battles at Las Guasimas on June 24 and at San Juan Hill on July 1. Prior to the assault on San Juan, in which the 10th Cavalry rescued Col. Leonard Wood's 1st Volunteer Infantry or "Rough Riders," Baker lay on the bank of the San Juan River seeking cover from enemy fire. A comrade fell wounded into the river and Sergeant Major Baker dove into the stream to save the foundering soldier. In spite of heavy fire, including one projectile which Baker claimed "passed so close as to cause me to feel the heat," he successfully completed the rescue. He was awarded the Congressional Medal of Honor for this daring act. Later in the day, while participating in the assault, Baker himself was wounded twice by flying shrapnel.

When his regiment returned in August, Baker was commissioned a first lieutenant in the 10th Volunteer Infantry, a Negro regiment which was disbanded in early 1899. Then he received command of a company of the Negro 49th Infantry, with the rank of captain. He served in the Philippine Insurrection, south of Manila at Pasay and later in northern Luzon at Claveria. His remarkable record as a company commander received notice in several contemporary periodicals. Not one of his 100 men ever faced a military court or even reported sick. As the *Army and Navy Journal* noted in a 1900 issue, this achievement was "unprecedented in the annals of any regiment."

In June 1901 the 49th Infantry was mustered out in San Francisco. Six months later, Baker returned to the Philippines as a second lieutenant of Philippine Scouts, an organization of Filipino soldiers with American officers. He was promoted to first lieutenant in 1906 and captain in 1908, and remained with the Scouts until October 1909. He returned to the United States as post quartermaster sergeant of Fort McDowell, Cal., and retired on Jan. 12, 1910. He died of an intestinal disease at Letterman General Hospital, San Francisco, on Aug. 26, 1913.

Baker married Mary Prince Hawley in Santa Fe on July 31, 1887. Their five children—Edward Lee, Eugenia Sheridan, Myrtle May, Gwendolyn James, and Dexter Murat—were all born at frontier posts. His widow lived in Los Angeles until her death in 1950.

Baker wrote a short diary of his service in the Cuban campaign, which was published in Theophilus G. Steward's *The Colored Regulars in the U.S. Army* (1899, 1969). He also compiled a "Roster of Non-Commissioned Officers of the 10th U.S. Cavalry with some Regimental Reminiscences" (1897). This pamphlet, which is on file in the records of the Adjutant-General's Office, National Archives, narrates several significant encounters with Indians during the 10th Cavalry's frontier service. — FRANK N. SCHUBERT

BALDWIN, MARIA LOUISE (1856–1922), educator and community worker. The daughter of Peter L. and Mary E. (Blake) Baldwin, Maria was born in Cambridge, Mass., the eldest of three children. Her father, an emigrant from Haiti, was employed for many years as a letter carrier in Boston; her mother was from Baltimore.

Maria Baldwin was educated in the public schools of Cambridge. In June 1881 she graduated from the Cambridge Teachers' Training School and immediately began her career as a teacher in Chestertown, Md. The following year she was appointed a primary-grade teacher at the Agassiz Grammar School, Cambridge, Mass., where she taught all grades from the first to the seventh. Her success as an educator led to her appointment in 1889 as principal of Agassiz School. In April 1915 this school was torn down and in October construction was completed on a larger building partially planned by Maria Baldwin. It opened with twelve teachers and five hundred students of whom 98 percent were white. The improved facilities and enriched educational program required a position of master for the new school rather than principal. Baldwin was appointed master, becoming the only Negro and one of only two women to hold this important position in Cambridge.

"Mollie" Baldwin, as she was affectionately called, did not confine her activities to the classroom or to her office, but extended them to the community where she was a driving force in several organizations. For a number of years she was president of the League of Women for Community Service which she helped organize, a member of the Twentieth Century Club of Boston, the Cantabrigia Club, the Council of the Robert Gould Shaw House Association, the Omar Circle, the Teachers' Association, and the Boston Ethical Society. Baldwin served as secretary of the Boston Banneker Club, a scholarly literary society organized in 1874 during the period Archibald Grimké was its president. At her Prospect Street home Baldwin held weekly reading classes for Negro students attending Harvard University, one of whom was W. E. B. Du Bois. He later recalled how "she grew on us all. Her poise commanded greater and greater respect. Her courage—her splendid, quiet courage astonished us, and so she came to larger life and accomplishment. She fought domestic troubles and the bitter never-ending insults of race difference. But she emerged always the quiet, well-bred lady, the fine and lovely woman" (*The Crisis,* April 1922, pp. 248–49).

Baldwin, a forceful lecturer, spoke throughout the country on notable individuals like Lincoln, Grant, Jefferson, Madison, and Washington, and on subjects such as women's suffrage, poetry, and history. She was frequently called upon to address Teachers' Associations throughout New England. She was the first woman to give the annual George Washington's Birthday Memorial Address held in 1879 at Brooklyn Institute, choosing as her subject "The Life and Service of Harriet Beecher Stowe." Numerous papers which she read at the Banneker Literary Society meetings indicated her broad knowledge of literary and historical subjects. As secretary of this organization, she published in the *Hub* detailed summaries of the discussions.

Maria Baldwin expanded her knowledge by enrolling in courses at Harvard University, Boston University, and other institutions, and shared it with teachers whom she taught in summer school classes held at Hampton Institute, Va., and the Institute for Colored Youth in Cheyney, Pa.

The Rev. Charles Gordon Ames, minister of the Church of the Disciples in Boston, influenced Baldwin to become a member in 1907. She spoke at many of the meetings of the society, "contributing her own gifts of enlightened and persuasive speech."

The high esteem in which Maria Baldwin was held is reflected in the fact that among her associates and close friends were educators and intellectuals including Alice Freeman Palmer, Edward Everett Hale, William Monroe Trotter, Ednah D. Chaney, Archibald Grimké, Thomas Wentworth Higginson, Elizabeth Cary Agassiz, Julia Ward Howe, Josephine St. Pierre Ruffin, and Charles W. Eliot (the former president of Harvard who once said that Maria Baldwin was the best teacher in New England).

Baldwin died of a heart attack on Jan. 9, 1922, just after she had addressed the members of the Council of the Robert Gould Shaw House Association meeting in the Copley-Square Hotel. Funeral services were held at the Arlington Street Church on Jan. 12. Her ashes were buried in Forest Hill Cemetery, Boston. She was survived by a sister, Alice Gertrude Baldwin, a teacher in Wilmington, Del., and a brother, Lewis F. Baldwin, a graduate of Harvard and a practicing lawyer in the West.

After her death, many tributes were paid to "Master"

Baldwin. The Class of 1922 of Agassiz School unveiled a memorial tablet. A scholarship was established in her memory, and the auditorium of the Agassiz School was named Baldwin Hall. The Maria L. Baldwin Memorial Library was dedicated on Dec. 24, 1923, at the League of Women for Community Service (she was its president at the time of her death). On April 25, 1950, a dormitory for women at Howard University was named Maria Baldwin Hall.

The example Baldwin set led to the appointment of other young Negro women to positions in the schools of New England. A former pupil who was deeply impressed by her said: "Miss Baldwin was a magnet for children's hearts, drawing them after her into the way of beauty and goodness and peace. . . . She was the very personification of dignity and calm strength, of vision and inspiration and tireless patience, of kindness and affectionate humor, of restfulness and harmony."

Two perceptive biographical sketches are by Dorothy B. Porter: "Maria Baldwin" (*NAW* [1971], 1:86–88) and "Maria Baldwin, 1856–1922" (*JNE,* Winter 1952, pp. 94–96, which has a comprehensive bibliography). See also League of Women for Community Service, *Souvenir Program of the Dedication of the Maria L. Baldwin Memorial Library* (Dec. 20, 1923). Of many tributes and obituary statements those in the *Southern Workman* (March 1922) and *Boston Evening Transcript* (Jan. 10, 11, 17, and March 18, 1922) are representative. Miss Baldwin published an article, "The Changing Ideal of Progress," in the *Southern Workman* (Jan. 1900). — DOROTHY B. PORTER

BANNEKER, BENJAMIN (1731–1806), self–taught amateur mathematician and astronomer. He assisted in the survey of the Federal Territory in 1791, and calculated ephemerides for almanacs for the years 1792 through 1797, which were published and widely distributed.

Banneker was born on Nov. 9, 1731, near the Patapsco River in Baltimore County, Md. His father was a freed Negro slave named Robert, and his mother was Mary Banneky, the daughter of Bannka (or Banneka), a freed Negro slave, and an indentured Englishwoman named Molly Welsh. After fulfilling her servitude, Molly had established a small tobacco farm in the area and purchased two slaves to help her with her work. Subsequently, after giving each of them their freedom, she married one of them, Bannka, who claimed to have been an African prince.

Having no surname of his own, Banneker's father, Robert, took his wife's surname at the time of their marriage. He was industrious and managed to purchase first a 25-acre lot and then a 100-acre farm with his savings. He built his own log house, cleared the fields, and planted them in tobacco. It was on this farm that Banneker grew up as a boy, and spent the remainder of his life. His grandmother taught him reading and writing with a Bible she had imported from England. He attended a nearby country school for several seasons but received no further formal education. He enjoyed reading, and with such few books as he could borrow or occasionally purchase, he taught himself in literature, history, and mathematics during the leisure hours after work on his father's farm.

Banneker had a natural gift for mathematics, and even as a boy he collected and created mathematical puzzles. At the age of about twenty-one he constructed a successful striking clock without ever having seen one, although he had examined a pocket watch. He undertook the project primarily as a mathematical challenge, calculating the proper ratio of the gears and wheels, and then carving them from wood with a pocket knife. The clock operated for more than forty years, until the time of his death, and was a subject of considerable interest throughout the entire region.

Robert Banneky died in 1759 and thereafter Benjamin continued to work the farm, living with his mother and three sisters. One by one his sisters married and left home to settle in the vicinity. After his mother's death, sometime after 1775, Banneker continued to live alone, his housekeeping needs attended by his sisters who visited him frequently. His life was lived almost totally on his farm, remote from community life and potential persecution because of his color.

The event that most affected Banneker's life occurred about 1771, when five Ellicott brothers, Quakers from Bucks County, Pa., purchased a large tract of land adjoining his farm and developed it into a major center for the production of wheat and the milling of flour. Within several years they formed the industrious community of Ellicott's Lower Mills, with flour mills, saw mills, an iron foundry, and a general store, and successfully revolutionized the economy of the region. As a frequent visitor to the mills, he met his new neighbors. He was befriended by George Ellicott, the young son of one of the founding brothers, who had an interest in the sciences, and from whom he derived his first interest in astronomy after observing astronomical presentations made by George at the Mills. In 1789 Ellicott loaned Banneker several of his texts on astronomy as well as instruments, and an old table on which he could study. Without further assistance or guidance Banneker taught himself in astronomy from the texts at hand. He learned to calculate an ephemeris and to make projections for lunar and solar eclipses, working by trial and error until he had mastered the subject. He compiled an ephemeris for the year 1791 to be incorporated into an almanac, and although he submitted it to several printers it was not published. Meanwhile he continued his self-studies and learned how to use astronomical and surveying instruments.

It was quite by coincidence that during this period Banneker came to the attention of the surveyor Maj. Andrew Ellicott, George Ellicott's cousin. At the beginning of 1791 President Washington appointed Major Ellicott to undertake the survey of a ten-mile square known as the Federal Territory (now the District of Columbia) in which a new national capital was to be established. Ellicott had been engaged with his two younger brothers on a survey in New York, and he left the project in their hands in order to begin the new one. He experienced difficulty in finding an assistant competent to assist him in the use of scientific apparatus. During a visit to the mills en route to the Territory, he learned from George Ellicott about Banneker and his recently acquired skills. Ellicott arranged for Banneker to accompany him to the Federal Territory to work as his scien-

tific assistant for a short period until his brothers could join him. Banneker was almost sixty years of age at this time, and chronically unwell, so that we was unable to work in the field. They arrived and began work early in February 1791, with Banneker assisting Ellicott in the observatory tent, making and recording astronomical observations, maintaining the field astronomical clock, and compiling other data as required by the surveyor as the project progressed. At the end of April, after the base lines and initial boundaries had been established, Ellicott's brothers arrived to assist him and Banneker returned to his farm.

Banneker's experiences in the field made him more interested than ever in astronomy, and after his return to the farm he calculated an ephemeris for the following year. Through George Ellicott and his family it was brought to the attention of the Pennsylvania and Maryland abolition societies. With their sponsorship and support, it was published in Baltimore by the printers Goddard & Angell as *Benjamin Banneker's Pennsylvania, Delaware, Maryland and Virginia Almanack and Ephemeris, for the Year of Our Lord, 1792; Being Bissextile, or Leap-Year, and the Sixteenth Year of American Independence, which commenced July 4, 1776.*

Shortly before its publication, Banneker sent a manuscript copy of his ephemeris to Thomas Jefferson, then secretary of state, with a covering letter urging the abolition of slavery of the Negro, a situation which he compared to the former enslavement of the American colonies by the British Crown. Jefferson acknowledged Banneker's letter and enclosure and forwarded the manuscript to the Marquis de Condorcet, secretary of the Académie des Sciences in Paris, as an example of a unique achievement by a black man. The manuscript arrived on the eve of the French Revolution, and if received, was not acknowledged by the marquis, nor was it presented to the academy. The exchange of letters between Banneker and Jefferson was published as a separate pamphlet through the offices of the abolition societies at the same time that the almanac appeared, and received wide publicity, which helped the almanac's distribution. The two letters were subsequently reprinted in Banneker's published almanac for 1793, which also included "A Plan for an Office of Peace" originally prepared by Dr. Benjamin Rush.

The first almanac featured a biographical sketch by Sen. James McHenry, who described Banneker's station and achievements as new evidence in support of the arguments against Negro slavery. "I consider this Negro as a fresh proof that the powers of the mind are disconnected with the colour of the skin," he wrote. The almanac sold in great numbers and was issued in a second edition by the original printer and in another edition by the printer William Young of Philadelphia.

Encouraged by his success and the prospect of calculating future almanacs, Banneker retired from his tobacco farming to devote all of his time to his studies. His increasing poor health was a major factor in this decision. Furthermore, he was a man of few needs, and he supplemented his income by the occasional sale of parcels of land of his 100-acre farm, and he anticipated a continuing modest income from the almanacs he would calculate in the future, assured by the success of the first one. His ephemeris for the year 1793 was published by Goddard and Angell and in separate editions by printers in Philadelphia. The almanacs published for the following four years enjoyed continued success, and a total of at least twenty-nine separate editions of his almanacs was published during this six-year period with a wide distribution in the United States and in Great Britain as well. The publication of Banneker's almanacs terminated with the issue for 1797, probably as a result of diminishing interest in the abolition movement. Nonetheless, he continued to compute the ephemerides for almanacs each year until 1804.

Although the published almanacs bore Banneker's name, he provided only the ephemeris and the projections for the eclipses. The literary and supplementary content was furnished by the printer. Nonetheless, Banneker became interested in writing and during this period produced several short pieces which he described as "dreams" and which appear to be fantasies. At the same time he continued to collect mathematical puzzles, but none of these materials was incorporated in the published almanacs. Banneker also occasionally wrote brief accounts of natural phenomena that occurred about him, such as storms, bees, cicadas, and similar subjects. Throughout most of his life Banneker also suffered from an inclination to drink, which had been kept under rigid control by his mother while she lived.

During the final period of his life he visited frequently at Ellicott's Lower Mills and became a familiar figure in the Ellicott Store, where he discussed dominant topics of the times with the Ellicotts and others. Although not affiliated with any denomination, Banneker was a deeply religious man all his life. He attended services of various denominations when ministers and speakers came to the region, and favored the Society of Friends, frequently attending meetings in Elkridge Landing and at the Friends Meeting House in Ellicott's Lower Mills. Throughout his life he was greatly respected by all who knew him. He was described as being of a complexion "not jet black, but decidedly negro," and having "a most benign and thoughtful expression. A fine head of white hair surmounted his unusually broad and ample forehead, whilst the lower part of his face was slender and sloping towards the chin. His figure was perfectly erect, showing no inclination to stoop as he advanced in years. His raiment was always scrupulously neat; that for summer wear, being of unbleached linen, was beautifully washed and ironed by his sisters. . . . In cold weather he dressed in light colored cloth, a fine drab broadcloth constituting his attire when he designed appearing in his best style."

Others who knew him noted that "He was very precise in conversation and exhibited deep reflection. His deportment . . . was perfectly upright and correct, and he seemed to be acquainted with everything of importance that was passing in the country."

During the final years that Banneker lived alone in his log house, pursuing his reading, calculating ephemerides, and producing occasional pieces of original writing, he cooked for himself, and was assisted by a young boy, the grandson of an old schoolmate. Two of his sisters lived nearby and saw to his housekeeping needs.

He died on Oct. 9, 1806, a month short of his seventy-fifth birthday. It was a Sunday, and on that morning he had gone for a walk on his farm. He met an acquaintance and while they chatted he felt suddenly unwell. He returned to his house and retired to his bed. A short time later he was dead. He was buried two days later in the family burial plot on his farm. While the burial was in progress, with the members of his family in attendance, his house caught fire and burned to the ground with all its contents before help could be summoned. Most of his possessions, including his clock, his books, and his writings, were destroyed. Fortunately he had left instructions prior to his death that all the books, instruments, and the old table which had been loaned to him by George Ellicott were to be returned to the lender after his death. Prior to the funeral a nephew had collected the materials mentioned and delivered them in a wagon to George Ellicott's home. Among the memorabilia that were preserved were Banneker's commonplace book in which he made entries of his accounts as well as some astronomical notes, and his manuscript astronomical journal. The latter was the original compilation of all his astronomical calculations for each of the ephemerides he had calculated, with scattered personal notes and household accounts. These manuscript materials, a selection of the borrowed scientific works from which he taught himself, a few of his pieces of creative writing, the original manuscript of his ephermeris for the first almanac of 1792, and a number of his letters are all that have survived to the present time.

The publication of his almanacs brought international acknowledgment to Banneker, derived primarily from such an unusual achievement by a colored man. Modern studies have confirmed that he was an extremely accomplished natural mathematician and his ephemerides compared favorably with those compiled for the same years by the outstanding men of science of his time.

The exact site of Banneker's house and of his grave in the little nineteenth-century town of Oella, Md., have been lost and can no longer be identified. In 1845 Bishop Daniel Alexander Payne of the Bethel Church of the African Methodist Episcopal church in Baltimore attempted to raise funds to erect a monument over Banneker's grave, but was unsuccessful. In 1852 Moses Sheppard, the Baltimore philanthropist, discovered Banneker's astronomical manuscript journal in the Maryland Historical Society and had lithographic copies made of the drafts therein of the Banneker-Jefferson correspondence, which he distributed widely. Banneker was again memorialized in 1854 when a "Young Man's Mutual Instruction Society" for colored youth of the city, founded in Philadelphia in 1852, was renamed the "Banneker Institute." A marker was erected at the Westchester Elementary School in Oella, Md., in February 1954. In 1970, Banneker Circle, adjoining L'Enfant Plaza in Washington, D.C., was named in his honor.

During the century and a half that followed Banneker's death his memory was kept alive by writers who described his achievements as the first Negro American man of science. During that period more than a hundred books, periodical articles, or newspaper accounts have included mention of Banneker, ranging from brief references to several extensive biographical sketches. The first of these was several reprints of Senator McHenry's biographical sketch which appeared in various periodicals in 1792, and references in works relating to Thomas Jefferson's position on slavery.

The most important published works relating to Banneker are three biographical sketches of varying lengths based on contemporary sources. The first is a "Memoir of Benjamin Banneker, Read Before the Historical Society of Maryland" by John H. B. Latrobe (*Maryland Colonization Journal*, n.s., 2, no. 23, [1845]: 353–64); *A Sketch of the Life of Benjamin Banneker; From Notes Taken in 1836. Read by J. Saurin Norris Before the Maryland Historical Society, October 5, 1854;* and Martha E. Tyson's *Banneker, The Afric-American Astronomer. From the Posthumous Papers of Martha E. Tyson. Edited by Her Daughter* (1884). The two last named accounts were based on the personal recollections of Martha Ellicott Tyson, daughter of George Ellicott, who had compiled data about Banneker from those who had known him in his lifetime while they still lived. All subsequent biographical sketches about Banneker have been based on one or another of the foregoing. The first book-length work about Banneker was a novelized biography for children written by Shirley Graham, entitled *Your Most Humble Servant* (1949). The most comprehensive study of Banneker's life and work to date is *The Life of Benjamin Banneker* by Silvio A. Bedini (1972). This work is based on a review of all previously published references as well as a detailed study of his surviving manuscript astronomical journal and commonplace book, letters and literary manuscripts, the records of the Pennsylvania and Maryland abolition societies, and a scientific analysis of his calculation of ephemerides. This work in particular has confirmed that Banneker was born with a natural gift for the sciences and mathematics in particular, and that his self-studies had made him extremely competent in astronomical studies. Without the limitations of opportunity due primarily to regional location and the state of the sciences in his time, Banneker would undoubtedly have emerged as a far more important figure in early American science. — SILVIO A. BEDINI

BANNISTER, EDWARD MITCHELL (1828–1901), painter. He was born in 1828, the son of Edward Bannister of Barbados and Hannah Alexander Bannister, a native of St. Andrews in New Brunswick, Canada. At the age of six his father died. He was afforded a grammar school education in his home and thus received a better education than other persons of his origin. His mother died when he was still young and he suffered, therefore, a severe handicap in his struggle to rise in his chosen field. It was necessary for him to live with Harris Hatch, a lawyer of his hometown. There he exercised his talent copying from engravings in the old family Bible and from two faded family portraits. These drawings were found reproduced on barn doors, fences, and any sort of surface he could find to substitute for materials which he did not have. His education broadened and he became proficient in discussing art and literature

from which he gained inspiration to do the work which was to gain him renown.

It is said that he was challenged to an art career by a statement he read in the *New York Herald Tribune* in 1867, that the Negro seems to have an appreciation of art while being manifestly unable to produce it. Throughout his career he was determined to disprove this statement.

He had an idealistic poet's view of life enriched by a deeply rooted love for woods and water, envisioned by landscape painting. These qualities established him as one of the first Negroes to earn recognition as an American regional painter of importance.

As a young man he went to Boston where he received commissions for paintings. Here on the seacoast he shipped on vessels engaged in the coastal trade and served as a cook on a coaster. This early experience developed within him a love for nature and a liking for the sea.

John Nelson Arnold, a personal friend and author of *Art and Artists in Rhode Island,* says that after Bannister came to Boston (probably in 1850) he learned to make solar prints, which he developed into a prosperous business and thus gained leisure to sketch and paint scenes in and around the city of Boston. By 1854 he had produced his first commissioned painting, *The Ship Outward Bound.*

About 1855–1856 he married Christiana Cartreaux, a Narragansett Indian born in North Kingstown, R.I., in 1822. She worked in Boston as a wigmaker and hairdresser. She was a highly spirited personality and a great inspiration to her husband. Her ties with the abolitionist movement and her involvement in the politics of Boston, which concerned the welfare of the Negro soldiers, are recorded with praise in manuscripts of the Rhode Island Historical Society.

Bannister's move to Rhode Island in 1871 was indeed prompted by his love for yachting, for Narragansett Bay and Newport Harbor were a "yachtsman's paradise."

Even though Bannister derived much from nature as a landscapist and a painter of poetic realism, Arnold said he studied at Lowell Institute, and finally had lessons in anatomy and painting under Dr. William Rimmer, the famous sculptor and lecturer. Unlike his colleague Robert Duncanson, who left America to study in Scotland and Italy, Bannister refused all opportunities offered him for study abroad. According to James Porter, his paintings were exhibited in the Boston Art Club, and he helped found in his own studio in 1873 the Providence Art Club, which later became the Rhode Island School of Design.

Four years after Duncanson died in 1872, Bannister achieved great fame as the recipient of the gold medal in the Philadelphia Centennial Exhibition of 1876 for his huge landscape *Under the Oaks.* It was exhibited in the group representing Massachusetts artists. Associated with his receiving the award is the following story: When the artist presented himself for the award, the gallery guards insulted him by asking him what he was doing there. When he told them he was the winner of the award, the judges attempted to reconsider the decision, but the other contestants, being men of honor, proclaimed that if the decision was changed because of the race of the artist they would withdraw in protest and announce the injustice to the whole world. As a result the decision stood. The painting was sold to James Duffe of New York for $1500, a good price in those days for a living American painter. It was a meritorious work, painted in the manner of the Hudson River School, and received the following contemporary notice: "E. M. Bannister of this city whose picture, Under the Oaks, was spoken of in these columns some weeks ago has had an offer for it by a Boston party with the understanding that it is to go to the Centennial Art Gallery" (*Providence Star,* April 24, 1876).

This success was followed by a series of recognitions, three more medals, and several honors and commissions.

Bannister was a regular participant in the exhibitions of the Boston Art Club and a close associate and studio companion of Martin Milmore (sculptor), William E. Norton (marine painter), and Edward Lord Weeks (a painter of East Indian figure subjects who shared his Boston studio).

He is well represented by sixteen paintings in the museum of the Rhode Island School of Design where students having a flair for landscape and marine painting find them valuable for study purposes. Others are in the collections of Atlanta University, the Howard University Gallery of Art, and the Providence Art Club. Fourteen works donated by C. William Miller along with a small collection of works by Negro American artists, made possible through a grant from the American Federation of Arts, form the nucleus of a collection at the Museum of African Art (316 A St. NE, Washington, D.C.).

Among the chief works are *After the Storm, Sabin Point, Narragansett Bay, The Ship Outward Bound,* and *Dusk,* all inspired by nature rather than racial subjects which were not popular at that time.

Among collectors of his work are Isaac C. Bates, Mrs. Eliza G. Radeke, H. A. Tillinghast, all residents of Rhode Island, affiliated with the Museum of Art, Rhode Island School of Design. These works were included in the Memorial Exhibition of some 101 paintings, drawings, and watercolors arranged by the Art Club only five months after his death as a testimony to the great affection they had for their colleague who had stimulated and inspired a visual culture in the struggling community of Providence during the last quarter of the nineteenth century.

Of paramount importance were the acclamations of his work by his ardent friend William Alden Brown, who rated him high and consistently kept his name bright. Over sixty years he collected some of the best of Bannister's pictures and contributed to Negro art history valuable facts related to his career.

The sensitive and poetic realism of Bannister's work is justly expressed in John Nelson Arnold's statement: "He looked at nature with a poet's feeling. Skies, rocks, fields were all absorbed and distilled through his soul and projected upon the canvas with a virile force and a poetic beauty."

In the opinion of Professor Porter: "His technic, though original was never inadequate to the feeling of the artist except, perhaps, in his old age, when his infir-

mities made his work increasingly fumbling in character and hurried in effect" (*Modern Negro Art* [1943], p. 56).

Bannister became faint on Jan. 9, 1901, in the Elmwood Avenue Baptist Church, Providence, R.I., where he had just offered prayer, and died suddenly of heart failure in an anteroom. Funeral services were held in the church on Jan. 12, and he was interred in North Burial Ground, Providence. The gravesite was marked by a monument of a rough natural stone about eight feet high, bearing on its face a palette and inscribed with his name.

In addition to the sources mentioned in the text, see the obituary in the *Providence Journal* (Jan. 11, 1901, p. 8) and the article by John S. Brown, Jr., in *The Crisis* (Nov. 1933, p. 248). — LOIS JONES PIERRE-NOËL

BARBADOES, JAMES G. (c. 1796–1841), abolitionist and colonizationist. His name may have been derived from the island of Barbados, West Indies, a market for the sale of slaves since the seventeenth century. Nothing is known regarding his place of birth, his early life, or his education. In 1830 his name appears in Boston on a list of free Negro heads of families; at that time he was living with three other members of the family. His infant son named for William Lloyd Garrison, whose radical abolitionism Barbadoes greatly admired, died in 1832. During the 1830s Barbadoes kept a barbershop and rented rooms in Boston, as can be seen in advertisements published in Garrison's abolitionist paper *The Liberator.* Toward the end of the decade he and his family accompanied a group of Negroes to Jamaica, where they planned to settle. Owing to the alleged dishonesty of the local proprietors, the venture proved a failure for the entire group. For the Barbadoes family the move to Jamaica was a disaster. Two children and, subsequently, on June 22, 1841, Barbadoes himself died of "West India fever" (*The Liberator,* Aug. 6, 1841).

Other facts known of James G. Barbadoes and his important work as a Negro leader and abolitionist are sporadic and incomplete. He was an energetic member of the Massachusetts General Colored Association (founded in Boston in 1826). He was a delegate to the Convention of the People of Color in Philadelphia in 1831. Two years later he was a founder of the American Anti-Slavery Society and a signer of that organization's Declaration of Sentiments; he also served on the society's board of managers. In May 1834 he was a member of the committee of arrangements for the annual meeting of the New England Anti-Slavery Society. At that meeting he urged support of Garrison and *The Liberator,* and he described the persecution faced by his seaman brother Robert H. Barbadoes. Robert had been kidnapped in New Orleans, jailed, chained, and held incommunicado for five months until he was finally released through the efforts of many supporters, including a free Negro named Peter Smith, his parents in Boston, and the governor of Massachusetts (*The Liberator,* June 7, 1834).

During 1839–1840 Barbadoes played a significant role in an antislavery schism. Conservative elements were revolting against Garrison's radical principles of universal reform, the crucial issue being women's rights. In *The Liberator* there is evidence of Barbadoes's continuing support for Garrison and the established organizations. He and other Negroes signed a strongly worded pro-Garrison statement that appeared April 3, 1840, and in the issue of Sept. 11 Barbadoes was one of three signers of a letter to Garrison, welcoming him home from England and asking him to attend a meeting of colored citizens who wished to express their loyal support. Such support was, at least in part, responsible for Garrison's success in maintaining control of both the Massachusetts and the American Anti-Slavery Societies; the dissidents withdrew and formed new societies.

Although Barbadoes was undoubtedly one of the leaders among the free Negroes in Boston during the first half of the nineteenth century, little documentation survives. Garrison referred to Barbadoes a number of times in his letters and wrote one letter to him and two other Negroes, Thomas Cole and J. T. Hilton (see Walter M. Merrill and Louis Ruchames, eds., *The Letters of William Lloyd Garrison . . .* [1971], Vols. 1 and 2). He can be observed obliquely in a few secondary sources like Herbert Aptheker (ed.), *A New Documentary History of the Negro People in the United States* (1965–1966) and Charles H. Wesley's *Neglected History, Essays in Negro-American History* (1965).

— WALTER M. MERRILL

BARBER, J[ESSE] MAX (1878?–1949), journalist, dentist, and civil rights leader. Born in Blackstock, S.C., to ex-slave parents, Jesse Max and Susan (Crawford) Barber, young Barber, working his way through school, completed the teachers course of study at Benedict College, Columbia, S.C. Then in 1903 he earned the bachelor's degree from Virginia Union University, Richmond, where he was president of the Literary Society and student editor of the *University Journal.*

After a few months of teaching in Charleston, Barber accepted the offer of Austin N. Jenkins, a white publisher, and went to Atlanta to assist in establishing a new periodical, the *Voice of the Negro.* In the first two issues, January and February 1904, Barber was designated managing editor. The editor was John Wesley Edward Bowen, a professor at Gammon Theological Seminary and later president of that institution. With the March number, both Bowen and Barber were listed as the editors. Barber eventually became, in fact, the principal editor. The *Voice of the Negro* developed into a first-class journal, a unique publication edited by Negroes in the South and a leading Negro magazine in the United States. Supported by the financial and publishing resources of J. L. Nichols and Company, and its successor, Hertel, Jenkins and Company, the periodical sustained regular monthly publication from January 1904 until September 1906, when it became a casualty of the race riot which occurred in Atlanta in that month.

Following his involvement in charges and countercharges concerning the immediate cause of the riot, Barber relocated the periodical in Chicago and became the sole editor. It survived there for only a year, from October 1906 to October 1907. (With the November 1906 issue the title was changed to *The Voice.*) Controlling stock in the publishing company was acquired

by the journalist T. Thomas Fortune. No issues were published by Fortune, and Barber severed his connections with the periodical. For a brief period Barber edited a weekly newspaper, the *Chicago Conservator.*

During these years in journalism Barber was an outspoken critic of racial injustice. He advocated political activity and the use of the ballot as the means toward first-class citizenship for Negroes. Barber associated himself with those movements and individuals regarded in his day as the militant vanguard of the struggle for civil rights. He was among the twenty-nine persons who responded to W. E. B. Du Bois's call to establish the "radical" Niagara Movement in 1905. (Formed to combat "conservative" policies of Booker T. Washington, the Niagara Movement was a forerunner of the NAACP.) Barber was one of the sponsors of the Georgia Equal Rights Convention of 1906. When the National Negro Political League was organized in Philadelphia in 1908 by William Monroe Trotter, Alexander Walters, and J. Milton Waldron, Barber delivered an address at one of the sessions. He attended the National Negro Conference which convened in New York City in 1909, which set the stage for the founding of the NAACP. At this time he was also in close contact with John E. Milholland, president of the Constitutional League. Milholland had suggested that Barber edit a publication for the organization, but this plan was dropped because Du Bois was preparing to launch *The Crisis* magazine for the NAACP. Although there is no indication that Barber was actively involved with *The Crisis,* he was listed in the magazine as a contributing editor during the first three years of publication.

In 1909, seeking a more secure means of livelihood than journalism had offered, Barber enrolled in the Philadelphia Dental School (of Temple University). Upon graduation in 1912 he opened his dental office in Philadelphia. That same year he married Hattie B. Taylor, a teacher in the public schools. A few years after her death, he married Elizabeth B. Miller, also a schoolteacher. Barber continued to participate in civil rights activities. He worked with the NAACP, serving as president and as executive committee member in the Philadelphia branch for several years, and as a member of the National Board of Directors during the early 1920s.

Barber had a great interest in commemorating the life and deeds of the abolitionist John Brown. Beginning in 1922, under the leadership of Barber and T. Spotuas Burwell, annual pilgrimages were made to John Brown's grave in North Elba, N.Y. The John Brown Memorial Association was formed to raise funds for a monument honoring Brown. In 1935 this goal was achieved and Barber, the perennial president of the association, gave the dedication address at the unveiling of the statue in North Elba. After this accomplishment, Barber became less and less involved in public activity. He continued to practice dentistry in Philadelphia, where he died in September 1949, nine months after the death of his second wife.

J. Max Barber, however, had made his major contribution many decades before his death, in the editorship of the *Voice of the Negro* and *The Voice* during the four years from 1904 to 1907 while he was a young man still in his twenties. During the Atlanta period of publication the issues averaged from forty-eight to seventy-two pages of commendable literary quality, presented in pleasing typography, extensively illustrated, and supplemented with a large number of advertisements. Circulation figures reported for the magazine ranged from 3000 for the initial number to 15,000 in 1906.

The most prolific contributors to the *Voice of the Negro* were William Pickens, William S. Scarborough, Kelly Miller, W. E. B. Du Bois, and Mary Church Terrell. Other frequent writers were Fannie Barrier Williams, John E. Bruce, T. Thomas Fortune, and Pauline E. Hopkins. Several articles in the *Voice of the Negro* dealt with colored peoples in Haiti, the Philippines, and other parts of the world. Fiction was not a prominent feature, but poetry appeared often, especially from William Stanley Braithwaite, James D. Corrothers, and Benjamin G. Brawley. Throughout the issues of the periodical, illustrations, political cartoons, and other artwork were contributed by young Negro artists to whom the periodical gave encouragement. Among them were John Henry Adams of Atlanta and William E. Scott of Chicago. Book reviews were included, and many articles related to art, literature, and science. Current news events were reported regularly, and articles were published frequently on the achievements and organized activities of Negro women. During 1905 and 1906 the periodical served as a medium of communication for the Niagara Movement.

In this periodical, major attention was given to the political, educational, economic, and social status of the Negro, particularly in the South but also elsewhere in the United States and other parts of the world. J. Max Barber, in his first editorial in the January 1904 issue of the *Voice of the Negro,* had written prophetically when he had stated: ''It shall be our object to keep the magazine abreast with the progress of the times. We want to make it a force of race elevation. We want it to be more than a mere magazine. We expect to make of it current and sociological history so accurately given and so vividly portrayed that it will become a kind of documentation for the coming generations.''

The principal sources are: William Pickens, ''Jesse Max Barber'' (*Voice* 3 [Nov. 1906]: 483–88; *Who's Who of the Colored Race, 1915* (p. 19); *Philadelphia Independent* (Oct. 1, 1949); *Philadelphia Tribune* (Sept. 24 and Oct. 4, 1949); Penelope L. Bullock, ''Profile of a Periodical: The 'Voice of the Negro,' '' (*Atlanta Historical Bulletin* 21 [Spring 1977]: 95–114; Abby Arthur Johnson and Ronald M. Johnson, ''Away from Accommodation: Radical Editors and Protest Journalism, 1900–1910'' (*JNH* 62 [Oct. 1977]: 325–38; Louis R. Harlan, ''Booker T. Washington and the *Voice of the Negro,* 1904–1907'' (*Journal of Southern History* 45 [Feb. 1979]; 45–62; Abby Arthur Johnson and Ronald M. Johnson, *Propaganda and Aesthetics: The Literary Politics of Afro-American Magazines in the Twentieth Century* (1979, pp. 1–29). See also Penelope Bullock, *The Afro-American Periodical Press, 1837–1909* (1981, pp. 66–275 passim). — PENELOPE L. BULLOCK

BARÈS, BASILE (1846–c. 1910), pianist, music teacher, and composer. The names of parents are unknown.

When very young, Barès began work at the large music store of J. A. Périer on Royal Street. Whether or not he was related to this white merchant, the *New Orleans Tribune,* noted organ of the free colored group, frequently referred to him as ''Basile Périer.'' Basile Barès is often referred to as a self-made musician and composer since, unlike many of his musical contemporaries, he never attended recognized conservatories. Like most of them, however, he studied music under some of the leading white instructors of his day. Basile was clearly a musical prodigy and he began to show evidence of this while still in his teens. He began his musical studies under Eugène Prevost, a prominent musician who had formerly directed the orchestras of the Orleans Theater and the famed French Opera of New Orleans. He later studied harmony and composition under Master Pedigram. He was at one time one of the two saxophone players in the city, but most of his compositions were written for the piano.

Barès learned the trade of piano tuner while working at Périer's and became proficient in this pursuit, which helped give him an overall knowledge of the instrument he had chosen as a part of his life's work. His employer sent him to Paris on several business missions as a representative of the firm. On a visit to Paris in 1867 he remained four months during which he gave many public performances on the piano. When Edmond Dédé, the famous violinist, composer, and orchestra leader, visited New Orleans in 1893 for a series of concerts, he selected Barès to accompany him on the piano. Composer/piano-players like Eugène Macarty and Barès probably set the style of piano playing at fashionable *soirées,* and it was this fashion—later followed by piano-player/composers like ''Jelly Roll'' Morton and others—that was adopted by the ''madames'' of Basin Street and other ''goodtime houses'' in which jazz and ragtime later originated.

Barès's ability as a pianist and composer was held in very high esteem by the composers of his day, both white and black. Many prominently placed white musicians sought his services for difficult orchestrations in vaudeville and opera; in sub rosa manner, Rodolphe Desdunes tells how on one occasion Barès composed what ''a renowned artist'' of New York called the perfect ballet—not knowing that the Negro who stood before him was the creator of it. According to Desdunes, ''Unfortunately, the color of his skin overshadowed his genius each time he was near triumph.'' Prominent white musicians, he continued, ''used his talents and took advantage of his kindness and his zeal, but when it was time to recognize his services or honor his talents, those who had been his judges and who had proof of his valor and of his good will remained silent. The conspiracy of silence was unforgivable. People who employed him, who extended him an invitation, who requested his performances were so filled with prejudice toward his race, that they said not a word of praise or even gave the slightest mark or sign of appreciation, not even a little publicity.'' Desdunes ends his stinging indictment of prejudice with this final summation: ''It was against the principles of Louisiana to let a man of color know that his work was better than that of a white man.''

Barès maintained a fast pace of productivity. Roughly speaking, he probably wrote each year what people of today would call a "hit song." He composed many dance numbers for a city that loved to dance, and many of his pieces became so popular that he entitled one of his dances "Basile's Galop." More of his compositions are available today than those of any other Negro composer of his era. Beginning with his "Grand Polka des Chausseurs, à pied de la Louisiane," written in 1860 when he was only fourteen, his numerous compositions run the gamut of polkas, waltzes, quadrilles, and mazurkas to his "Exhibition Waltz," published in 1884 when he was thirty-eight. He had six or more publishers, all in New Orleans, his favorite being A. E. Blackmar who issued many of the "elegant and much admired compositions by the well-known Creole Pianist." His *Variétés du Carnaval,* a collection of five short dances published by Louis Grunewald in 1875, carries the notation: "OP:23." His "Mamie Waltz," published by Junius Hart in 1880 has "OP. 27." No exact figure can be given as to the number of his compositions. Sometimes in public performances he played selections whose titles have not been found among his published works. In 1866, when he was twenty, the beauty and romance of Creole life burst upon him and he published during that year "La Belle Créole," "La Coquette," "La Course," and "Les Folies du Carnaval." On the night of May 10, 1865, at a brilliant concert in the Orleans Theater, his playing of two of his own numbers, "The Magic Belles" and "The Fusées Musicales," "held the house in rapture." He died in New Orleans about 1910, leaving a son and three daughters.

Brief sketches are in Rodolphe Desdunes's *Nos Hommes et Notre Histoire* (1911) and various issues of *La Tribune de la Nouvelle-Orleans.* For original scores of New Orleans Negro music, see the Howard-Tilton Library of Tulane University and the Marcus Christian Collection of the Earl Long Library, University of New Orleans. One piece is in James Monroe Trotter's *Music and Some Highly Musical People* (1878). For background, see John W. Blassingame's *Black New Orleans, 1660–1880* (1973) and Herbert Sterkx's *The Free Negro in Ante-Bellum Louisiana* (1972).

— MARCUS B. CHRISTIAN

BARNETT, CLAUDE A[LBERT] (1889–1967), founder of the Associated Negro Press. Born in Sanford, Fla., the son of William Barnett and Celena Anderson, Claude was one year old when he went to live with his maternal grandparents in Mattoon, Ill., where he received his early training. He later attended school at Tuscola, Ill., where he lived with an aunt. He also attended Douglass Elementary School in Chicago and the Lille Boys House in Knoxville, Tenn. He received his high school education at Oak Park High School in Chicago. He entered Tuskegee Institute in Alabama in 1904, graduating in 1906 when he was awarded the highest certificate that Tuskegee Institute afforded at that time. He returned to Chicago where he lived with an aunt and worked in the post office. As a postal clerk Barnett had the opportunity to read large numbers of magazines and newspapers. He found such trade journals as *Printers Ink* and *Editor and Publisher*

so interesting and inspiring that he decided to make advertising and journalism his career.

He entered the field of advertising in 1913 when he produced, with the aid of a photo reproduction expert, a series of portraits of famous Negroes for exhibition and sale at the Chicago Exposition. Out of this venture a mail-order business was established for the distribution of Negro portraits. Later Barnett joined with several other enterprising young men to form a cosmetic business, the Kashmir Chemical Company, and became its advertising manager.

Resigning his post office job, Barnett set out on a cross-country trip from Chicago to California stopping in several cities to sell his pictures and the company's products. In every town he visited the Negro newspaper office if one existed, hoping to interest more newspapers in selling him advertising space. He soon discovered that publishers were more interested in getting news items from across the nation than in his advertising proposition. Out of this discovery grew the idea of creating a press service to supply national news to Negro newspapers around the country.

The Kashmir board of directors, upon Barnett's recommendation, provided funds needed to translate the idea into reality; thus the Associated Negro Press was born in 1919. It began by exchanging national news releases to publishers for advertising space; soon they began to subscribe for the ANP service. For a minimum fee of $25 a week, ANP would mail out to subscribers a packet of original stories two or three times a week. This material was collected, edited, and assembled by a seven-member staff located at 3531 South Parkway in Chicago. The material was supplied by a number of stringers located in leading cities around the United States and some foreign countries. A special news service for African news was produced by ANP in both French and English. Before long the Associated Negro Press won a reputation as a reliable news service. At the height of its operation it supplied copy to nearly 200 newspapers or 95 percent of the Negro press. At the time of its termination in 1967, ANP was still servicing 112 newspapers.

Barnett maintained a close relationship with his alma mater, serving on the Tuskegee Board of Trustees for almost twenty years before retiring in 1965. He also served as a member of the board of directors of the Supreme Liberty Life Insurance Company, Chicago, for more than twenty years and as advertising advisor for the Poro Beauty College. His interest in the health field led him to accept a post as president of the board of directors of Provident Hospital in Chicago (1938–1942), and later as a member of the board of governors of the American Red Cross during the time of the controversy over the segregation of blood donated by Negroes and whites for use by the armed forces during World War II. During that same period Barnett, in cooperation with a few other Negro publishers, succeeded in getting some Negro newsmen accredited as war correspondents and sent overseas in order to get firsthand information on the racial situation in the military.

Barnett's interest in the plight of the southern Negro farmer was aroused by George Washington Carver during his early days at Tuskegee. Observing the conditions under which tenant farmers and sharecroppers had to live and work, he concluded that these farmers needed an opportunity to own a piece of land and adequate credit to develop it, and he sought to do something about this. His offer to serve as a consultant to the Department of Agriculture was accepted in 1930, a position he held under three secretaries, Henry A. Wallace, Claude R. Wickard, and Charles F. Brannon. He advised the agriculture secretaries on means of assisting Negro farmers throughout the United States. When Ezra Taft Benson became secretary of agriculture in 1953, he declared that Negro consultants were no longer needed or wanted: Barnett and his co-worker, Frederick D. Patterson, president of Tuskegee, were terminated. He was a member of the board of directors of the Liberia Company, New York City; the Chicago chapter and the National Red Cross; the Phelps-Stokes Fund, New York City; President Truman's Committee for the Physically Handicapped; a life member of the Art Institute of Chicago. He was a chevalier, Order of Honor and Merit, Republic of Haiti, and commander, Star of Africa, Liberia.

On June 24, 1934, Barnett was married to Etta Moten, a well-known actress, singer, and radio personality. They traveled widely together in Europe, Africa, and the West Indies, and became exponents of African art in the United States.

In spite of Claude Barnett's varied interests and activities, both professional and social, the Associated Negro Press service continued to operate efficiently until his death on Aug. 2, 1967. He died of a cerebral hemorrhage at his home, 3619 Street, South Park, Chicago. Funeral services were held in Quinn Chapel, A.M.E. church, Chicago, on Aug. 5, and he was buried in Oaks Cemetery. He was survived by his widow and three daughters.

Basic facts are in *Who's Who in America.* Obituaries are in the *New York Times,* the *New York Herald Tribune,* and the *Chicago Defender* (Aug. 1967). See also the Vertical File, Moorland-Spingarn Research Center, Howard University. — ALICE A. DUNNIGAN

WELLS-BARNETT, IDA BELL (1862–1931), journalist,
lecturer, and civil rights leader. The oldest of four boys and four girls, she was born on July 6, 1862, in Holly Springs, Miss., of slave parents. Her mother, Lizzie Bell, the child of a slave mother and an Indian father, had come from Virginia. She married James Wells, who had learned carpentering from Miss Bell's master. After emancipation they continued to work for him as carpenter and cook.

She was educated at Rust University, a high school and industrial school for freedmen established in Holly Springs in 1866. After the death of her parents and three of their children in a yellow fever epidemic, Miss Wells began teaching in a rural school at $25 a month, when she was fourteen. From 1884 to 1891 she taught in a rural school near Memphis and in Memphis, and attended summer classes for one year at Fisk University in Nashville. Because of her militancy—she refused to accept a seat in a Jim Crow car and carried an unsuccessful suit to the Tennessee Supreme Court in 1887, and criticized, under the pen name of "Iola," the inade-

quate schools for Negroes—the Memphis school board dismissed her in 1891.

She bought a one-third interest in a Negro newspaper, the *Memphis Free Speech,* and became half-owner in 1892. On March 9 of that year she denounced in the newspaper the lynching of three of her friends, accused of raping three white women when actually they were competing with white storekeepers. She urged Memphis Negroes to migrate to the West, urged them to boycott streetcars, investigated other lynchings, and reported her findings. On May 27, 1882, while she was in Philadelphia and New York, a mob destroyed the offices of the *Memphis Free Speech.*

After serving briefly on the *New York Age* of T. Thomas Fortune, who helped her secure lecture engagements for her crusade against lynching, she became nationally known. Fortune also put her in touch with Catherine Impey, a leading figure in the English Anti-Caste Society. Of her two visits to England in 1893 and 1894, one British clergyman said that nothing since *Uncle Tom's Cabin* had aroused public opinion as much as her antilynching crusade. In 1893 she edited a pamphlet protesting the virtual exclusion of Negroes from the World's Columbian Exposition in Chicago. Another pamphlet, *A Red Record* (1895), with a preface by Frederick Douglass, gave a statistical record of three years of lynchings and their causes, and urged churches and organizations like the YWCA and the WCTU to join the antilynching crusade.

On June 27, 1895, Wells was married to Ferdinand Lee Barnett, a Negro lawyer and editor of the *Chicago Conservator.* They had four children: Charles A., Herman K., Ida B. Wells, and Alfreda, who became Mrs. Duster and published her mother's autobiography with the title *Crusade for Justice* (1970).

Mrs. Wells-Barnett was a member of a delegation that called on President McKinley to demand action in the case of a Negro postmaster who had been lynched in South Carolina. As early as 1893 she had organized, in Chicago, a Negro woman's club. Its example led to the formation of many other colored women's clubs and to their amalgamation with the Federation of Colored Women's Clubs. As lifelong president of the Ida B. Wells Club, she founded the Negro Fellowship League, for several years a social center with reading rooms and a dormitory for Negro men and helped them find work. Aided by her husband, she served as a probation officer (1913–1916) for the Chicago municipal court. Following the race riot in East St. Louis, Ill., in 1918, she went there to seek legal aid for the Negro victims. In a letter to the *Chicago Tribune* (July 7, 1919) she urged the city to "set the wheels of justice in motion before it was too late" to prevent a similar explosion. But the city took no action and one of the bloodiest race riots in the history of the nation up to that time soon followed.

Mrs. Wells-Barnett usually supported W. E. B. Du Bois in his opposition to the accommodationist policies of Booker T. Washington. At the March 1898 meeting of the National Afro-American League in Rochester, N.Y., she was elected secretary of its successor, the National Afro-American Council, a forerunner of the NAACP. At the December 1898 meeting of the council in Washington, D.C., she denounced mob violence in the North and South, criticized President McKinley for his indifference to the rights of Negroes, called for a reduction of southern representatives in the House, and opposed U.S. imperialism. She was elected secretary of the council, and served until 1902 when Booker T. Washington gained control. When Fortune and Bishop Alexander Walters, president of the council, called for a meeting to take place in September 1905, Wells-Barnett denounced the action as an attempt to weaken the Niagara Movement which Du Bois and other adversaries of Washington had launched in June.

She attended the meeting of the Niagara Movement in August 1906. As chairman of the Anti-Lynching League, she was one of two Negro women (Mary Church Terrell was the other) who signed "The Call" on Feb. 12, 1909, the centennial of Abraham Lincoln's birth, for a meeting "To Discuss Means for Securing Political and Civil Equality for the Negro." She, Terrell, and Maria Baldwin were members of the Committee of Forty formed in New York City (May 31 and June 1, 1909) which led to the founding of the NAACP on May 12, 1910. As a member of the Executive Committee, also organized in 1910, she became inactive after 1912 because she believed that her active participation was to be limited to the development of the Chicago branch of the NAACP.

She then devoted most of her time to promoting suffrage for women. She founded the Alpha Suffrage Club of Chicago, said to be the first Negro woman suffrage organization. She marched in the famous suffrage parade in Washington, D.C., on the eve of Woodrow Wilson's first inaugural in 1913, and led her club members in the parade (June 1916) of some 5000 suffragists to demand that the Republican party include a suffrage plank in its platform. She had supported Taft in the 1912 campaign and accompanied William Monroe Trotter when in the fall of 1913 he led a delegation of his National Independent Political League to obtain a statement by President Wilson of his views on segregation. She and Trotter spoke for the group. She was one of eleven Negroes chosen by a group of 250 Negroes in Washington, D.C., in December 1918 to represent them at the Versailles Peace Conference. They were denied passports, and only Trotter was able to go to France. She worked with Jane Addams in a successful attempt to block the setting up of separate schools for Negroes in Chicago. By the time of Wells-Barnett's death in 1931, the great increase in Chicago's Negro population and the increased neighborhood segregation had begun the resegregation of public schools. She was for many years a director of the Cook County League of Women's Clubs. She died in Chicago of uremia on March 25, 1931, and was buried there in Oakwood Cemetery.

The principal source is her autobiography, edited by her daughter Alfreda Duster as *Crusade for Justice* (1970). For her activities with the NAACP, see Charles Flint Kellogg's *NAACP, A History of the National Association for the Advancement of Colored People*, Volume 1, *1909–1920* (1967, pp. 22, 26, 29, 45 n.67, 77 n.1, 92, 124). Stephen R. Fox's *The Guardian of Boston: William Monroe Trotter* (1970, pp. 168, 175, 223) is the source for her associations with Trotter.

Eleanor Flexner has written the best brief summary, with bibliography, in *NAW* (1971, 3:565–67).

— RAYFORD W. LOGAN

BARRETT, JANIE PORTER (1865–1948), social welfare leader. Barrett was born in Athens, Ga., the daughter of former slaves. Until she was fifteen she lived with her mother, Julia Porter, who was employed in Athens as a housekeeper and seamstress by a Mrs. Skinner of New York. She entered Hampton Institute, Va., in 1880, was graduated in 1884, taught for a year among sharecroppers in Dawson, Ga., and then at Lucy Craft Laney's Haines Normal and Industrial Institute in Augusta, Ga. From 1886 to 1889 she taught night classes at Hampton Institute. On Oct. 31, 1889, she married Harris Barrett of the Hampton business staff. They had four children: May Porter, Harris, Julia Louise, and Catherine. She founded the Locust Street Social Settlement in October, the first in Virginia and one of the first in the nation (Catherine Ferguson had begun hers in New York in 1814). In 1908 she became the first president of the Virginia State Federation of Colored Women's Clubs. Six years later the federation purchased a 147-acre farm in Peake (also known as Peakes Turnout, Va.), where she was at first secretary of the board of trustees of the Virginia Industrial School for Colored Girls, and the resident superintendent from 1914 until her retirement in 1941. She died on Aug. 27, 1948, in Hampton of diabetes mellitus and arteriosclerosis. She was buried at Elmerton Cemetery in Hampton. In 1950 the Virginia Industrial School for Colored Girls was renamed the Janie Porter Barrett School for Girls.

At the time the school was founded in 1914 white residents in the community opposed its establishment, but by the late 1920s most of these residents accepted it because of its obvious success. State appropriations, contributions by northern philanthropists, and advice by social welfare experts had helped to develop "a moral hospital where each girl is studied and given individual treatment" (Sadie I. Daniel, *Women Builders* [1931], p. 68). Most important, however, was Barrett's firm, motherly personality and concept of the institute's goals. She encouraged what is today called "student participation" and a successful parole program. One visitor, with built-in prejudices against industrial education and somewhat fearful of "wayward girls" in what some persons referred to as a "reform school," recognized the value of an eighth-grade elementary education combined with vocational education which prepared the graduates for useful employment and the decorum of the girls, especially those girls who waited on table. The well-tended campus and cottage contributed to the positive atmosphere. It was no wonder, then, that the Russell Sage Foundation in the early 1920s placed the school among the top five institutions of its kind in the nation. In 1929 Barrett received a William E. Harmon Award for Distinguished Achievement among Negroes. The Virginia Industrial School for Colored Girls was an important factor in winning respect for Negroes not only in its community but also through its reputation in a wider area. Barrett helped achieve this respect by emphasizing biracial support for the school, and by her membership on the executive board of the Richmond Urban League and the Southern Commission on Interracial Cooperation. At the same time she maintained her affiliation with the colored community and was active in the National Association of Colored Women, serving for four years as chairman of its executive board.

The best short sketches of Barrett are by Letitia Brown in the *DAB, Supplement Four, 1946–1950* (1974), and by Sadie Daniel St. Clair in *NAW* (1971, 1:96–97). St. Clair's sketch was based in part on her *Women Builders* (1931) and Mary Ovington's *Portraits in Color* (1927). For the later period, especially valuable is Winone R. Hall's "Janie Porter Barrett, Her Life and Contributions to Social Welfare in Va." (M.A. thesis, Howard University, 1954). — RAYFORD W. LOGAN

BASSETT, EBENEZER DON CARLOS (1833–1908), educator and diplomat. Born at Litchfield, Conn., on Oct. 16, 1833, the son of Tobias Bassett, a mulatto, and Susan (Gregory) Bassett, an Indian of the Shagticoke branch of the Pequot tribe, Bassett attended the Wesleyan Academy at Wilbraham, Mass., and graduated with honors from the Connecticut State Normal School. While principal of a high school in New Haven, Conn., he continued his studies at Yale College, where he seems to have been held in wide respect. From 1857 to 1869 Bassett was principal of the Institute for Colored Youth in Philadelphia, a school founded by Quakers for "the education of Colored Youth in school learning and to prepare them to become teachers." In addition to his duties as principal, Bassett taught mathematics, natural sciences, and classics, and acted as school librarian. The mayor of Philadelphia referred to the school, under Bassett's management, as "widely known and unquestionably the foremost institution of its kind in the country." Bassett also gave a series of evening lectures on chemistry and natural philosophy. In 1855 Bassett married Eliza Park; they had three sons and two daughters.

In 1869 Pres. Ulysses S. Grant appointed Bassett U.S. minister to Haiti and the Dominican Republic, thus giving the United States its first Negro diplomat. Letters on file in the National Archives urging Bassett's appointment came from many prominent citizens, including twelve of his Yale professors, and show clearly the high esteem in which he was held. His study of French at Yale, later perfected in Haiti, and his acquisition of a knowledge of Creole helped establish a real understanding of the country and its people.

The eight years Bassett spent in Port-au-Prince would have been a challenge to any diplomat. The persistent attempt of the Grant administration to annex the Dominican Republic, or at least to obtain a naval base there, created fears of similar designs on Haiti, where diplomatic probes for a coaling station at Môle St. Nicolas affronted Haitian nationalism. No overt attempt was made during Bassett's mission. He was accredited to the government of four different presidents, one of whom was shot summarily, one who made a forced and hurried escape from the country, and one who was for many months a political refugee in the American minister's residence. Bassett handled all difficulties with a calm and tact that earned him the admiration of his diplomatic colleagues and of members of the Haitian government alike. For a few years he was the dean of the diplomatic corps and was elected in 1875 to the presidency of the exclusive "Cercle de Port-au-Prince." Frederick Douglass later wrote that Secretary of State Hamilton Fish had told him that "he wished one-half of his ministers abroad performed their duties as well as Mr. Bassett" (*Life and Times of Frederick Douglass . . .* [1962 ed.], p. 417).

After his resignation in 1877, in accordance with custom when a new president took office, Bassett and his family returned to New Haven. From 1879 to 1888 Bassett served as consul-general for Haiti in New York, with the office located at 22 State Street. When Frederick Douglass was appointed American minister to Haiti and the Dominican Republic in 1889, Bassett offered his services as secretary and interpreter to an old friend and they were accepted. At a salary of $850 a year, he served as Douglass's interpreter during the crucial abortive negotiations (1891) for cession of Môle St. Nicolas.

In the early 1900s Bassett was again in the employ of Haiti at the consul-general's office in New York and corresponded with Booker T. Washington with a view to sending young Haitian scholarship winners to Tuskegee Institute. During these latter years Bassett wrote *A Handbook on Haiti* for the Pan American Union. Although it does not bear his name, his meticulous style is readily identifiable.

Bassett's last years were spent with his family in Philadelphia, where they resided at 2121 North 29th Street. He had been in ill health frequently after leaving Haiti in 1879, probably due to malaria or dengue, or both. In his last letter to Frederick Douglass (Jan. 18, 1894) he wrote of a heart condition and "an annoying affection of my eyes which are never in good trim." This letter was also a reply to a dunning note from Douglass asking payment of a loan and stating, without proof, that he had learned that Bassett had accepted $6000 from Pres. Florvil Hyppolite of Haiti to influence Douglass's decisions as minister. In any event, Bassett died poor and obscure in Philadelphia, where he was buried.

A surviving picture in the National Archives shows Bassett as a handsome, square-cut man with a receding hairline and twirling mustaches. Persons who recalled both Bassett and his best known son, Ulysses S. G. Bassett (who taught at Dunbar High School in Washington, D.C.), state that his dignified bearing was reminiscent of that of his father.

The most complete source is Nancy Gordon Heinl's "America's First Black Diplomat" (*Foreign Service Journal,* Aug. 1973, pp. 20–22). Diplomatic correspondence from Haiti in the National Archives and letters from Bassett to Frederick Douglass in the Frederick Douglass Papers, Manuscript Division, Library of Congress, are the best unpublished sources. Rayford W. Logan's *The Diplomatic Relations of the United States with Haiti, 1776–1891* (1941) is the source for this subject. — NANCY GORDON HEINL

BATSON, FLORA (FLORA BATSON BERGEN) (1864–1906), internationally famous singer of ballads whose prominence and whose soprano-baritone range caused her to be known as the "double-voiced queen of song." She was born on April 16, 1864, in Washington, D.C., but at the age of three she was taken by her widowed mother, Mary A. Batson, to live in Providence, R.I. She never received formal training as a singer, although her powerful voice attracted attention as early as her ninth year when she began singing in church choirs of Providence. Beginning in 1878 she was hired to perform for the benefit of Storer College in Harpers Ferry, W.Va. At the end of two years she was offered tuition-free education there but chose to continue her singing career in order to provide support for her mother. There followed a three-year engagement with Peoples' Church of Boston, and from 1883 to 1885 a series of appearances with Thomas N. Doutney and other temperance advocates. These appearances included a European tour and climaxed in a temperance revival in New York City at which Flora Batson sang on ninety-six consecutive nights. The song which she made famous was "Six Feet of Earth Makes Us All One Size."

The turning point in her career came in 1885 when she met Col. John Bergen, a white concert manager who had made his reputation as a promoter of Negro performers. Batson became the leading singer of the Bergen Star Concerts, making her first major appearance in Steinway Hall in New York City on Dec. 8, 1885, with Adelaide Smith, Sam Lucas, and the Walker Male Quartet. By the end of 1887 she had achieved national fame.

Flora Batson and John Bergen were married in December 1887. The interracial marriage caused much comment and created some problems; nonetheless the marriage endured and the professional association was mutually beneficial. Until the time of his death, Bergen remained his wife's concert manager and promoted her as the star of his productions. Her success enabled Bergen, who had been partly dependent for financial support on his collaboration with Negro churches, to achieve more security as a concert manager. With her husband, she triumphantly toured all sections of the United States, including the South, and gave several concerts in British Columbia. She performed before large audiences and received rave notices throughout her concert tours.

Sometime after the death of her husband, she formed a team with Gerard Millar, Negro basso, who also acted as her manager. She engaged in extensive tours of the United States and twice traveled around the world, singing before the crowned heads of Europe as well as the rulers of the Far East. Vaudeville and musical comedy had meanwhile become favored forms of entertainment with the result that Batson was less in demand. She might have turned with profit to the more popular styles, but according to Millar (*Life, Travels, and Works of Miss Flora Batson,* p. 31), her intense religious feeling caused her to prefer church work and benefit concerts for charitable organizations. She was beginning to develop as an elocutionist, and just before she died was reported to be in the process of learning the poem "The Black Man's Plea" to recite in the next production of Millar's sketch "The Klansman's Confession." Although no longer at the zenith of her career, Batson still pos-

sessed at the end of her life the power to move an audience. Her last concert was given at Philadelphia's Bethel A.M.E. Church to a standing-room audience. She died suddenly two days later in Philadelphia on Dec. 1, 1906.

Flora Batson's career began to expand at a time when Madame Marie Selika, a formally trained coloratura, had won a secure place as the leading Negro prima donna in the United States and abroad. Nellie Brown Mitchell, a younger singer of operatic arias and ballads, was at the height of her popularity. Batson replaced Nellie Mitchell as the leading performer of the Bergen Star Concerts and eventually rivaled Madame Selika in her appeal to American and foreign audiences. The qualities most often cited as the basis for Batson's great success were the sweetness of her voice, her astounding range, and her ability to elicit the most enthusiastic emotional response from her audiences. She occasionally sang excerpts from Coleridge-Taylor's *Hiawatha Trilogy* (after 1898) and Verdi's *La Traviata* in which she demonstrated the range of her voice, but audiences most frequently requested the popular ballads of the day such as "The Last Rose of Summer," "The Cows Are in the Corn," and "The Ship of Fire." Standing ovations and numerous encores were commonplace at her concerts, and audiences of different cities vied with one another to demonstrate their affection for her. At the close of the Bergen Star Concert in Philadelphia on Dec. 15, 1887, Batson was presented with a magnificent crown of solid gold set with precious stones and was crowned "Queen of Song." In January 1888 the audience at Steinway Hall in New York followed suit with a diamond crown and a necklace; in February 1888 the citizens of Providence presented her with diamond earrings; and in 1890 a diamond breast pin, ear drips, and a ring were given to her by admirers in Pittsburgh. In pictures subsequent to 1887 Flora Batson is always shown wearing a crown and some other part of the jewelry.

Honors were heaped upon her in foreign countries also. En route to her first tour in New Zealand, she stopped at Honolulu where a performance of the Batson team brought her to the attention of Queen Liliuokalani. After a triumph in New Zealand there followed a nine-week engagement in Sydney, Australia. The return trip included visits with royalty in the Samoan Islands. On her next overseas tour Batson accepted Queen Liliuokalani's invitation to appear for an eleven-week engagement at the queen's private theater in Honolulu, and went on to give concerts in Ireland, Scotland, Wales, and England, where Queen Victoria presented to her a vase in recognition of her artistry. She sang a program in South Africa in honor of Paul Kruger, president of the Union of South Africa, and in Rome for Pope Leo XIII. Her travels also included India, Fiji, China, and Japan.

During the years spanned by Batson's career, it was the practice to present several performers at a single concert, for it was extremely difficult for a Negro performer to achieve success as a solo act. That she was singled out for individual recognition is a tribute to the qualities of her vocal talent. One contemporaneous writer (*The World,* Nov. 13, 1887) considered her to be "the greatest female ballad singer the Negro race has thus far produced."

Gerard Millar's *Life, Travel, and Works of Miss Flora Batson, Deceased Queen of Song* (n.d.) is a personal tribute which affords insight into Batson's character and gives some facts concerning her career. See also "In Retrospect: Black Prima Donnas of the Nineteenth Century" (*The Black Perspective in Music* 7, no. 1, pp. 95–106). — DORIS E. MCGINTY

BEASLEY, DELILAH ISONTIUM (1871–1934), journalist and historian. Beasley was born in Cincinnati, and wrote for several newspapers during a career which began at the age of twelve, from the black *Cleveland Gazette* to the white *Oakland* (California) *Tribune.* Her only book, *The Negro Trail Blazers of California* . . . (1919), was a pioneer effort to chronicle the role of Negroes in the Far West. In addition to writing, Beasley was a civil rights activist, who strove to end use of the defamatory words "darky" and "nigger" by American newspapers.

Within three years of her first work for the *Cleveland Gazette,* she began writing regular columns for the Sunday edition of the *Cincinnati Enquirer.* Her nascent career in journalism was disrupted shortly thereafter, however, when both of her parents died. She then found employment as a maid for the family of a Cincinnati judge, but she soon left to go to Chicago, where she trained as a masseuse. Then she moved to Springfield, Ohio, where she plied that trade. She also took courses in other branches of physical therapy, including hydrotherapy, gymnastics, and diagnosis. On completing her training, she became head operator in a bath house at a family resort in Michigan.

During her years in Springfield she began her intensive researches into the history of Afro-Americans, increasingly focusing on the early years in the Far West. Friends urged her to move to California where she might better pursue this work, and she did so about 1910, as nurse to a former therapy patient who had moved to Berkeley. She continued her studies in California and planned to present her findings in a series of lectures. A friend, the Rev. David R. Wallace of Oakland, heard her first talk, "My City of Inspiration—San Francisco," and convinced her to write a book devoted to Negro pioneers of the West.

While she laid the groundwork for *The Negro Trail Blazers of California,* Beasley also resumed her career as a newspaper writer. In 1915 she wrote a series of articles for the *Oakland Tribune,* partly to counteract the effects of the movie *Birth of a Nation,* through publicity for the Panama-Pacific Exposition exhibits created by Negroes as well as prominent Negro visitors to the exposition. She wrote for the *Tribune* at least until 1925, contributing a regular column, "Activities Among Negroes," to the Sunday edition. She also conducted her campaign against the labels "darky" and "nigger" through the *Tribune,* and convinced many editors in the San Francisco area and elsewhere to discontinue use of the contemptuous terms.

Beasley achieved considerable success as a reporter for the *Tribune.* She represented the paper and the Alameda County League of Colored Women Voters at the National Convention of Women Voters in Richmond, Va., in 1925. She was the only Negro woman with press credentials at the conference. Later in the same year she represented the *Tribune* at the quinquennial meeting of the International Council of Women at Washington, D.C., as the only reporter from a West Coast paper.

Still, her book is her major achievement. She devoted much of her time over eight years to the compilation of data. Despite her complete lack of formal training, Beasley made a remarkably thorough search of records dealing with her subject. Working primarily at the University of California's Bancroft Library and the State Archives at Sacramento, she examined newspapers, land, hospital, and poor-farm records, Assembly and Senate journals, and legal reports and statutes. She also conducted numerous interviews. Three well-known California scholars—Charles Chapman, Herbert Priestley, and Theodore Hittell—aided and encouraged her in her research.

The book was finally completed and published in 1919. The author divided the volume into three parts. The first dealt with Spanish exploration and settlement, slavery, and the period of statehood. The second focused on the earliest Negro settlers, notably the miners, and their struggle for civil rights. The third described turn-of-the-century conditions. The emphasis throughout the book, consistent with Beasley's own times, was on property accumulation as the key to improving the overall position of Afro-Americans. Thus the book highlights the limited but real achievements of the small middle class and its institutions. Some of her judgments would be considered naïve by most modern scholars. For example, her view of the opponents of slavery as animated particularly by humanitarian considerations has been challenged by a large number of historians, such as Eugene Berwanger in his *The Frontier Against Slavery* (1967).

These defects are minor in an overall consideration of her work. Beasley called attention to the great contributions of Negroes to the development of California from the days of Estevanico to the early years of the twentieth century. Her book traces the lives of Negro merchants, soldiers, poets, and educators and the community institutions they and others created. As Jack D. Forbes commented in his handbook *Afro-Americans in the Far West* (1970), Beasley's book "illustrates in an impressive way the manner in which California Negroes had overcome hurdles and had achieved prominence in many areas of California life." Moreover, years before professional scholars turned to the Afro-American experience in the West, this untrained amateur showed the way into the source material and created a volume which is itself now a basic part of the body of documents dealing with that experience.

The most recent source is Richard N. Dillon's *Humbugs and Heroes: A Gallery of California Pioneers* (1970); also useful is Elizabeth Lindsay Davis's *Lifting as They Climb* (1933, pp. 107, 188–95), which has a foreword by Beasley. Her book is now easily available in 1968 and 1969 reprint, and contains a modest amount of biographical information in the preface. Her article, "Slavery in California," is in *JNH* (Jan. 1918, pp.

33–34), and "California Freedom Papers," which she and Monroe N. Work collected, are in the same *JNH* issue (pp. 45–54). Information about her activities in the League of Women Voters is found in its minutes, correspondence, and printed materials, deposited in the California Historical Society Library, San Francisco. Carter G. Woodson wrote a devastating review of *The Negro Trail Blazers* in the *JNH* (Jan. 1920, pp. 128–29).

— FRANK N. SCHUBERT

BEAVERS, LOUISE (1902–1962), motion picture actress. She was born in Cincinnati but was brought up and educated in Pasadena, Calif., where she graduated from Pasadena High School. The details of her life before 1928 when she began her movie career include two versions, both offered by Miss Beavers herself. One version is in an interview in the *Philadelphia Tribune* (March 14, 1935). Beavers said: "I was eleven years old when I moved to California with my parents. I went to Pasadena High School and graduated from there, and with sixteen other girls presented amateur plays until at one of these performances, I was approached by a spotter from the Universal Pictures Company and given a screen test which I passed. . . . At first, I was making preparations to enter nursing. This was in 1927 and from that time on I have been portraying various characters of Negro servants and maids on the screen until the time I made 'Imitation of Life.' "

The other version appears in an article written by Beavers for *Negro Digest* (Dec. 1949, pp. 20–22) called "My Biggest Break." She wrote: "It was back in 1927 and I was a concert singer then, believe it or not. I was looking for my first break in the music business. But I wasn't making much headway. . . . I walked past the Philharmonic Auditorium in Los Angeles, my home, and saw a small sign telling about an amateur contest that was going to be held the following week. Acting on impulse, I went to the box office and asked for an application. As I was filling it out, I stopped and laughed at myself. What was a concert singer doing in an amateur show? Shows like that are for comedians and singers and dancers—but not for concert people interested in classical music. But I had been getting nowhere, and in desperation, I finished the form and signed my name with a flourish, 'Louise Beavers, concert singer.' " Beavers appeared on that amateur show and sang a song called "Pal of My Old Cradle Days." She continued: "I didn't win or even get honorable mention in the contest but three days later the telephone at home rang, and it was Charles Butler, the movie agent at Central Casting in Hollywood. He told me, 'Miss Beavers, I watched you in that amateur contest the other night, I believe you can do a job I have here at Universal studios. It's the movie "Uncle Tom's Cabin" and I recommended you to the producers.' I got the part and have been in movies ever since."

Generally, sources which tell of her early years follow the former version in which sixteen girls called "the Lady Minstrels" organized, produced, and staged a show each year from 1923 to 1926. Whether Universal Studios summoned her from an amateur show put on by "the Lady Minstrels" or from the one she described in "My Biggest Break" is a matter of conjecture, but it is with the original *Uncle Tom's Cabin* of 1927, a silent picture starring James B. Lowe, that the movie career of Louise Beavers began.

From 1928 when she appeared in her first "talking pictures," RKO-Pathé's *Geraldine*, and Universal Artists' *Glad Rag Doll*, she worked in motion pictures regularly until 1960 when she replaced the deceased Hattie McDaniel on the CBS radio and television series "Beulah," a domestic comedy which ran five nights a week, Monday through Friday, until 1962. The motion picture role which earned Beavers both fame and criticism was Delilah in Universal Studios' *Imitation of Life*, a movie based on Fannie Hurst's novel. Beavers plays the long-suffering yet understanding mother of a beautiful and rebellious daughter (played by Fredi Washington) who resents her limited opportunities as a Negro even though she is white of skin. Delilah is also the lifelong friend, business partner, and servant to a white woman (played by Claudette Colbert) whose life intertwines with her own. On the one hand the role brought Beavers praise reviews from critics, which may be summarized in the one by Jimmie Fidler, widely known commentator and reviewer of the time: "I also lament the fact that the motion picture industry has not set aside racial prejudice in naming actresses. I don't see how it is possible to overlook the magnificent portrayal of Negro actress, Louise Beavers who played the mother in 'Imitation of Life.' If the industry chooses to ignore Miss Beavers' performance, please let this reporter . . . tender a special award of praise to Louise Beavers for the finest performance of 1934." On the other hand the part drew an equal amount of criticism from those who felt that the role was yet another image of a stereotype, that the thesis of the entire picture made the dubious if not outrageous point that all light-skinned Negroes want is to pass over into a trouble-free white world, and that here was another clear example of the genuine ability of Negro actors and actresses being wasted on mediocre material. Nevertheless, for Beavers the film was the vehicle by which her career in motion pictures became guaranteed. Her more than 100 featured roles include the following: *Coquette* (Universal Artists, 1929), *Wall Street* (Columbia, 1929), *She Couldn't Say No* (Warner Brothers, 1930), *Ladies of the Big House* (Paramount, 1932), *Imitation of Life* (Universal, 1934), *The Last Gangster* (MGM, 1937), *Brother Rat* (Warner Brothers, 1938), *Made for Each Other* (United Artists, 1939), *Belle Starr* (Fox, 1941), *Mr. Blandings Builds His Dream House* (RKO, 1948), *The Jackie Robinson Story* (Eagle and Lion, 1950), *The Goddess* (Carnegie Productions, 1958), and *The Facts of Life* (United Artists, 1960).

Louise Beavers, in private life Mrs. LeRoy Moore, died of diabetes at Cedars of Lebanon Hospital in Los Angeles on Oct. 26, 1962, having recently completed a nightclub engagement at the Congo Room in Las Vegas with Mae West, a colleague and friend of many years. She was survived by her husband.

In addition to the references mentioned in the text, see the vertical files on "Louise Beavers" in the Schomburg Center for Research in Black Culture and the Lincoln Center Library and Museum of the Performing Arts of the New York Public Library, which contain articles, reviews, and obituaries in several newspapers. See also Michael Valenti's "Portrait of a Stereotype" (*The Realist,* Aug. 1963, p. 1), *Ebony* (Nov. 1954, pp. 103–106), *Sepia Records* (July 1954, pp. 28–29), Peter Noble's *The Negro in Film: Literature of the Cinema* (1970), Donald Bogle's *Toms, Coons, Mulattoes, Mammies and Bucks: An Interpretive History of Blacks in American Films* (1973), Thomas Cripps's *Slow Fade to Black: The Negro in American Film, 1900–1942* (1977) and his *Black Film as Genre* (1979). Records of screen appearances are found in *International Motion Picture Almanac, American Movie Reference Book,* and Shuster's *Motion Picture Reference.*

— ELEANOR W. TRAYLOR

BECHET, SIDNEY (1897?–1959), soprano saxophonist, clarinetist, and composer. The son of Homer and Josephine (Mitchell) Bechet, he was born in New Orleans and started playing the clarinet at the age of six. Within a few years he came under the tutelage of George Bacquet, one of the leading clarinetists of that first generation of Creole musicians who effected the change from the concert and marching band tradition to a kind of early, elementary jazz. Thus Bechet developed at precisely the time when jazz, as an improvised music, was in its very beginnings. He began playing professionally in his early teens, working with most of the famous bands or orchestras of New Orleans: Freddie Keppard, Buddy Petit, Jack Carey, John Robichaux, the Eagle Band, and later King Oliver's Olympia Band.

This rich apprenticeship enabled Bechet to venture forth from New Orleans, work in 1918 in Chicago, thence on to New York, and finally to Europe with Will Marion Cook's 41-piece Southern Syncopated Orchestra. It was in appearances in London with the latter group that Bechet came to the attention of Ernest Ansermet, the Swiss conductor who had premiered Stravinsky's *Histoire du Soldat* a few years earlier and who from time to time reported on the European musical scene for the Swiss periodical *Revue romande.* Ansermet praised Bechet for the virtuosity and fervor of his playing and quite unequivocally called him "an artist of genius." This marked the first time that a Negro jazz musician received serious recognition from a distinguished white "classical" musician.

In the early 1920s Bechet returned to New York, in the meantime virtually abandoning the clarinet for the soprano saxophone. Bechet's first recordings were with Clarence Williams's Blue Five in 1924–1925, a series of performances now justly celebrated as being among the most significant of the 1920s. After a brief stint with Duke Ellington's Orchestra, Bechet returned to Paris in the famous *Revue nègre* starring Josephine Baker. On this European visit, tours took Bechet to most of the capitals of Europe, including Moscow. In 1928 he joined Noble Sissle's band in Paris, with whom he played for a decade except for a spate of recordings (with the great New Orleans cornetist Tommy Ladnier under the name of the New Orleans Feetwarmers) and a year away from music as the owner of a tailor shop in Harlem.

For the next ten years Bechet remained mostly in New York, gathering around him other fine musicians, including, in addition to Ladnier, the trombonists Vic Dickenson and J. C. Higginbotham, and the drummer Sid Catlett. In 1949 Bechet finally settled permanently in France, where he became in the last years of his life a celebrated national figure, popular as both a musician and a beloved music hall entertainer. He died of cancer of the throat and stomach at his home in Garches, a suburb of Paris. At his bedside were one of his oldest friends, Mezz Mezzrow, and members of his family. He was survived by his second wife, the former Elizabeth Ziegler whom he had married in 1951 after divorcing Louise Crawford, and Daniel, a son by his second wife. His age was officially listed as sixty-two but intimate friends said he was "pushing heavily" seventy.

Bechet was an outstanding representative of the New Orleans tradition and, like Louis Armstrong, was one of its major soloists and creative figures. He was the master of a highly ornamental style, very well suited to the embellishment and obbligato role of the clarinet in New Orleans–style collective improvisation. He was also a profoundly moving player of the blues, as exemplified by his recordings of the late 1930s and early 1940s (for example, "Weary Blues," "Really the Blues," "Blues in Thirds," "Blue Horizon"). His improvisational style is marked by remarkable rhythmic invention and fluidity, apparently free from the prevailing beat, yet never without a strong inner sense of swing.

Bechet played with intense throat vibrato, which is particularly pronounced in his soprano saxophone playing. It is not merely a decorative characteristic of his tone, but functions as an integral part of his ornamental style, i.e., the vibrato on sustained notes is a corollary to the runs and arpeggios in moving passages. Thus Bechet's playing is never without momentum, never without a propulsive inner energy which, in turn, is not merely the result of digital virtuosity, but a quality embedded in the very essence of his tone and timbre.

One of the supreme melodists of jazz and of its most eloquent soloists, Bechet exercized a strong influence on Johnny Hodges. But his influence on other saxophonists was insignificant, primarily because Bechet played the saxophone more in the manner of a New Orleans clarinet style than the more idiomatic saxophone styles developed by Coleman Hawkins, Ben Webster, and Lester Young.

Bechet was the composer of a number of fine tunes, notably "Viper Head," "Blackstick," "Delta Mood," and "Petite Fleur," which became an international hit. "Treat It Gentle" (1960) is based on tapes recorded and edited by Joan Reid, Desmond Flower, John Ciardi, and others. See obituaries in the *Los Angeles Weekly* (May 23, 1959) and the *Washington Daily News. Le Monde* (Paris) gave his age as sixty-eight but gave no details about his funeral or interment (May 15, 1959, p. 12).

— GUNTHER SCHULLER

BECKWOURTH, JAMES PIERSON [BECKWITH] (1798–1866), explorer, trader, scout, and trapper. Beckwourth was born in Fredericksburg, Va., on April 6, 1798, the third of thirteen children. Narratives of his life, based largely on his autobiography, are still subjects of controversy (as are those of Buffalo Bill, for example).

The following account is believed to be as valid as others.

Beckwourth's father, a white man, had served in the Revolutionary War; his mother, a Negro, was perhaps a slave. When he was a child the family settled some twelve miles below St. Charles on the Missouri River. After four years of schooling he was apprenticed to a blacksmith. He ran away to New Orleans, but unable to find employment and refusing to accept racial discrimination, he signed up as a scout for the second and third expeditions (1823 and 1824) of Gen. William Henry Ashley's Rocky Mountain Fur Company. For the next thirteen years he worked as a "mountain man," becoming a legendary figure like Kit Carson. He was accepted by Indian tribes, the Blackfoot and later the Crow. In 1837 he declared he was tired of the "savage life" and lived for a few years in St. Louis. He served in the Second (or Western) Seminole War, which ended in 1842. Before the end of the war he built and operated trading posts for William Sublette, Louis Vasquez, and the Bent brothers in the area of the headwaters of the Arkansas and South Platte Rivers. In 1840 Beckwourth established his own post in St. Fernandez (Taos) and later in Pueblo de Angels (Los Angeles). He fought in the California revolution against Mexico (1846) and in the War with Mexico (1846–1848), serving as guide and dispatch carrier for Gen. Stephen Kearny. In 1848 Beckwourth became the chief scout for the exploring expedition of Gen. John Charles Frémont. While on this expedition he discovered a pass in the Sierra Nevada Mountains between the Feather and Truckee Rivers in California which became part of a major emigrant route to California. Though it was later named the Beckwourth Pass, this most notable achievement of his career is strenuously denied by some writers.

In 1866 his fame as a friend of Indians led the government to ask him to visit the Crow in an effort to keep them neutral. According to his own account, he had been a chief of the Crow, had Indian wives, and participated in their wars with other Indians. His success in maintaining the preeminence of the Crow was due to his objections to the use of whiskey, which had brought ruin to many Indian tribes. He boasted that he had "saved more life and property than a whole regiment of United States regulars could have done at the same time." The boast was not entirely unjustified.

The facts of his death are as inconclusive as those of Esteban's. The Crow wanted Beckwourth to stay with them, lead them, and restore them to their former greatness. When he refused, they honored him as one of their greatest chiefs with a farewell repast. But the Crow were determined to have him—alive if possible, but if not, dead. They poisoned him so that his body and his powerful medicine would remain in their land.

Beckwourth was a man of "great legs," who could travel enormous distances with astounding rapidity and certainty. He gained new information about Indian tribes, geography, and climate which was of great importance to future explorers of the West. He has been referred to as "fabulous" and his adventurous life characterized as "daring, desperate and marvelous," as "unbelievable in many respects, but true." He occupies a secure place in American heroic mythology as well as in the history of the exploration of the American West.

Harold W. Felton's *Jim Beckwourth, Negro Mountain Man* (1966) contains a selective bibliography. See also Nolie Mumey's *James Pierson Beckwourth, 1856–1866* (1957). Beckwourth's autobiography was recorded at his dictation by Thomas D. Bonner (ed.), *The Life and Adventures of James P. Beckwourth, Mountaineer, Scout, and Pioneer, and Chief of the Crow Nation of Indians, With Illustrations* (1856), republished as *The Life and Adventures of James P. Beckwourth* (1969) with an introduction by William Loren Katz. A large photograph appears on page 80 of Bil Gilbert's *The Old West, The Trailblazers* (1973). The very brief article by Harrison Clifford Dale in *DAB, Part One* (1927, 1:122), concluded that apart from Beckwourth's egotism, his account was "singularly reliable." On the other hand the well-known historian, Prof. Kenneth Wiggins Porter, in his review essay "On Jim Beckwourth" (*Journal of Ethnic Studies,* Fall 1973, pp. 78–85), concluded: "That he survived the vicissitudes of mountain life for over forty years is in itself sufficient evidence of his ability and endurance. But under the pressure of a tragic racial situation he felt a compulsion to exaggerate his importance and status that the reality was largely buried under the weighty mass of these exaggerations" (p. 83). — HAROLD W. FELTON

BELL, GEORGE (1761–1843), educator. Bell was born a slave and lived as such in Virginia. His freedom was purchased by his wife Sophia Browning for $400 with money she earned secretly by selling produce from her garden. He in turn purchased her freedom. Two sons were bought from their slave owners a few years later, but the Bell family was unable to free a daughter named Margaret. Their first free-born child, Harriet, was born in 1803. The family lived in Washington, D.C., where Bell worked as a carpenter.

Bell's enduring contribution is in the foundation he established for the education for Negroes in Washington, D.C. The municipal government of the City of Washington authorized the establishment of public schools for whites in 1804, and in 1806 public education of white children was begun with the opening of two school buildings. There was no provision for the education of Negroes. The census for the City of Washington at this time showed 494 free Negroes. In 1807 George Bell, the principal activist in this endeavor, with two other free Negroes, Nicholas Franklin and Moses Liverpool, built the first school for Negro children. None of these men could read or write. They had only recently left their status as slaves in Virginia and had come to respect the importance of education.

Bell School, as it was called, was a one-story, frame schoolhouse, erected in the southeastern section of the city. A white teacher, Mr. Lowe, was hired. The difficulties in supporting the school forced its closing, and the building was used later as a private dwelling. Although the Bell School was of brief duration, its influence in establishing the precedent for the education of Negroes was significant.

Bell joined with other free Negroes in a second effort to educate the free Negro children in the City of Washington, and they organized the Resolute Beneficial Society for this purpose. On Aug. 29, 1818, this society announced in the *National Intelligencer* the opening of a new school "for the reception of children of free people of color, and others that ladies or gentlemen think proper to send, to be instructed in reading, writing, arithmetic, English grammar, or other branches of education, applicable to their capacities. . . ." The newspaper article expressed confidence that free Negro families would either send their children to the new school or support it financially. The society offered the use of the school building to the Sunday schools in the "Eastern District" of the city. It was also stated that an evening school was to begin in October 1818. The announcement was signed by the officers of the society, with Bell signing as the treasurer of the organization.

This new school was housed in the old Bell School's building. The first teacher was a Mr. Pierpont of Massachusetts, who after several years was succeeded by John Adams, the first male Negro teacher in the District of Columbia. The average attendance at the school was between sixty-five and seventy students, and the school was successful for several years. After Adams left the school, the building became the home of one of Bell's sons.

Bell died in 1843 at the age of eighty-two and his wife some years later at age eighty-six. His great legacy can be seen when it is noted that no provision for public education of Negro children in the nation's capital was made prior to the abolition of slavery in 1862. Nevertheless, the number of private schools increased in number and widened in scope of learning so that at the outbreak of the Civil War, when the Negro population of school age was 3172, it is estimated that 1200 were in school. Public schools for Negroes in the District of Columbia were established by Congress in 1864.

Information about George Bell may be found in M. B. Goodwin's *History of Schools for the Colored Population in the District of Columbia* (1871), Marie Perry's "The Development of Education of the Negro in the District of Columbia, 1807–1864" (master's thesis, Howard University, 1937), and James Storum's "The Colored Public Schools of Washington, Their Origin, Growth, and Present Condition" (*A.M.E. Church Review* 5, Jan. 1889). — ELAINE C. WELLS

BELL, JAMES MADISON (1826–1902), artisan, poet, orator, and politician. Born in Gallipolis, Ohio, Bell moved to Cincinnati in 1842 where he learned from his brother-in-law the plasterer's and brickmason's trades. Here he also gained his basic education in a private school connected with Oberlin College. In Cincinnati he married Louisiana Sanderline, and in 1854 he moved with his family to Chatham, Canada, where he remained until 1860. It appears that he wrote his first poetry in Canada. While in Canada he became friends with John Brown. Brown was his guest, and Bell aided him in raising funds for Brown's enterprises on behalf of Negroes, including the raid at Harpers Ferry in 1859.

In 1860 Bell moved to California and remained there until at least the end of 1865. He continued at his plasterer's and brickmason's trade in San Francisco while producing more poetry and giving public readings for Negro audiences. He was an active member of the

A.M.E. church and was involved in nearly every public ceremonial event conducted by the Negro civic and church organizations of San Francisco.

Bell delivered a poem there (Aug. 1, 1862) at the grand festival to commemorate the emancipation of the slaves in the District of Columbia and in the British West Indies. He composed and read an Emancipation Day poem, "The Day and the War" (Jan. 1, 1864), dedicated to John Brown for the celebration of that event. He was a member of the Fourth California Colored Convention which took place in Sacramento in October 1865. This was probably Bell's last public activity in California. On leaving the West, he wrote "Valedictory on Leaving San Francisco, California," which was considered one of his best poems (N. I. White and W. C. Jackson, *An Anthology of Verse by American Negroes* [1924], p. 215).

In late 1865 or early 1866 Bell returned to Canada where he rejoined his family and shortly afterward took them to Toledo, Ohio. He made Toledo his home while continuing to write poetry, give public readings, and practice his artisan trades. In 1872 Bell was elected a delegate from Lucas County to the state Republican convention. From there he was elected a delegate at large to the Republican National Convention that renominated Ulysses S. Grant. In 1888 Bell wrote one of his last political poems, dedicated to the candidacy of Republican Benjamin Harrison. Beyond this date, little is known of Bell's career.

Prof. Sterling Brown wrote, with respect to "The Day and the War," that Bell "must have felt deeply on these subjects, but his rendering is cold and lifeless because so conventional." He quoted three lines: "And we today reiterate/ With warmth of heart and depth of soul/ God bless America's magistrate!" Brown added: "This needs only to be placed beside the folk lyric: 'And before I'd be a slave/ I'd be buried in my grave/ And go home to my Lord and be free!' for telling contrast" (*Negro Poetry and Fiction*, 1937, p. 10).

A brief biography is in Benjamin Griffith Brawley's *The Negro Genius* . . . (1937, 1966). *The Poetical Works of James Madison Bell*, a volume of 208 pages (published in Lansing, Mich., c. 1901), has a biographical sketch by Benjamin W. Arnett. — RUDOLPH M. LAPP

BELL, PHILIP ALEXANDER (1809–1889), editor, publisher, and abolitionist. Nothing is known about Bell's early life. He first came into prominence on Jan. 25, 1831, as secretary of a group of "colored citizens" of New York City which opposed the organization of a Colonization Society of New York City. A little more than two years later (April 20, 1833) he was recorded as one of the directors of the Phoenix Society and Auxiliary Ward Associations of New York City. This interracial organization had for its object the promotion of the improvement of "the coloured people in Morals, Literature, and the Mechanic Arts."

Bell was medium-sized, of dark-complexion, gentlemanly in deportment, and with artistic tastes, particularly in the drama. He was a well-known attendant of Negro conventions, and a member of the American Anti-Slavery Society. At its meetings he made impressive appearances, thanks to his "fine powers of analysis and a vivid imagination" (Charles H. Wesley, "The Negroes in New York in the Emancipation Movement," *JNH* 24 [Jan. 1939]: 65ff). Bell urged Negro self-help programs, rejecting William Lloyd Garrison's criticism of them as "exclusive." Bell's policy was to denounce segregation in churches and schools, and also to oppose colonizationists. At the same time he believed Garrison's program involving such "nonessentials" as woman's rights did not help the Negro community or the abolitionist cause. Garrison's *Liberator* (Oct. 6, 1837) printed a protest by J. B. Cutler, a leader in the Boston Negro community, reproving Bell for his unwillingness to publish correspondence exposing differences among abolitionists.

In January 1837 he began publishing in New York the *Weekly Advocate,* edited by Samuel E. Cornish. The *Advocate,* the second Negro newspaper (*Freedom's Journal,* in 1827, was the first), continued publication only to March 4, 1837, when it became the *Colored American,* also a weekly. Cornish had retired as editor of the *Advocate,* and Bell edited the *Colored American* until 1839; the latter, under the editorial management of Charles Bennett Ray, ceased publication in 1842. They favored support of the Liberty party as a feasible means of ending slavery. They also challenged the constitutionality of the state law requiring a property qualification only for Negroes in order to vote. In 1839 Bell and others forced the resignation of David Ruggles as secretary of the New York Vigilance Committee because of his alleged financial irregularities.

Bell's other activities are unknown until he moved to San Francisco in 1857. There, in 1862, he joined William H. Carter as editor of the *Pacific Appeal,* a lively, six-column weekly which reported developments affecting Negroes in both the East and the West. Bell's last venture in journalism was the *Elevator,* first issued in San Francisco on April 18, 1865 (another *Elevator* was first published in Albany, N.Y. in 1842). Bell's *Elevator* was later absorbed into *Mirror of the Times,* founded in 1855. In 1880 he became doorkeeper of the California Senate. He is said to have died destitute on April 24, 1889 (I. Garland Penn, *The Afro-American Press and Its Editors* [1891], p. 33).

The basic reference on Bell is Philip Michael Montesano's *Philip Alexander Bell: San Francisco Black Community Politician of the 1860's* (mimeographed copy, n.d.), in the San Francisco Public Library. An earlier sketch is in William Wells Brown's *The Rising Sun . . .* (1874). *The Address and Constitution of the Phoenix Society and The Auxiliary Ward Associations* is in *Early Negro Writing 1760–1837, Selected and Introduced by Dorothy Porter* (1971, pp. 141–45); *Resolutions of the People of Color* is in in ibid. (pp. 281–85). — LOUIS FILLER

BENJAMIN, R[OBERT] C[HARLES] O['HARA] (1855–1900), politician, teacher, lawyer, lecturer, author, and journalist. He was born, according to his own account, on the island of St. Kitts in the British West Indies, but it is difficult to establish how much of this account is fact. It is possible that he was sent to England at age eleven and was taught by a private tutor. The librarian of Trinity College, Oxford, states, however, that no R.

C. O. Benjamin name appears on the college's books at any time during the nineteenth century. The following summary of his career is based also almost entirely on his autobiographical statements.

He traveled for two years through several of the islands of the East Indies which now comprise Indonesia. After returning to England, he migrated to New York City in April 1869, then shipped as a cabin boy for a six-month cruise to Venezuela, Curaçao, and other West Indian islands. From the fall of 1869 to 1877 he worked in New York City and became a naturalized U.S. citizen about 1875. He taught in several southern cities, studied law, and was admitted to the bar in Tennessee (Jan. 1880). A group of Alabama politicians tried unsuccessfully to have him nominated for Congress from the 9th Congressional District. He declined an appointment by Pres. Benjamin Harrison to a consulship to Haiti. He practiced law, published and edited several newspapers, lectured, and wrote pamphlets until sometime after 1894.

His years in New York City (1869–1877) reflected his varied career. He was acquainted with Henry Highland Garnett, one of the best known abolitionists. His introduction to journalism came with his employment as a salesman and office worker during several months for the *New York Star* and later as city editor for the *Progressive American,* founded on Aug. 15, 1871, by John J. Freeman. He helped organize clubs and spoke in support of Rutherford B. Hayes during the presidential campaign of 1876. He was rewarded by appointment as a letter carrier, but found the work too laborious and after nine months moved to the South.

Here, too, his activities embraced many fields. He taught school in several Kentucky counties, in Alabama, and in Arkansas. He practiced law in some twelve states and published and edited the *Negro American,* said to have championed ably the cause of Negroes. His travels in the South made him acquainted with conditions that formed the basis for several of his pamphlets. He also lectured to large audiences in Canada during 1886.

He continued his peripatetic career in journalism by publishing and editing the *Colored Citizen* in Pittsburgh, Pa.; the *Chronicle,* in Evansville, Ind.; and as corresponding editor of the *Nashville Free Lance,* where he wrote under the *nom de plume* of Cicero. He went to California sometime before 1888, where he was one of the editors of the *Los Angeles Observer.* He was best known for his editing of the *San Francisco Sentinel,* beginning 1890, which had as its motto "My race first, and my friends next." In the *Sentinel* he repeatedly denounced lynching and other outrages in the South. Benjamin was also the only Negro local editor for a white newspaper, the *Los Angeles Daily Sun.* In addition he practiced law for clients of both races, and lectured in several Pacific Coast cities, including Portland, Ore. Little is known about him until he was murdered in October 1900 (*Seattle Republican,* Oct. 19, 1900, p. 3). According to this account he was shot by southern Democrats for registering colored voters while editor of the *Lexington* (Kentucky) *Democrat.*

Although many details of Benjamin's life are undocumented, his writings have survived. He wrote several essays: *Future of the American Negro, The South and*

Its People, and *Africa, the Hope of the Negro;* two works of fiction: *The Boy Doctor* and *The Adventures of Obediah Kuff;* a book of poetry, *Poetic Gems* (1883); and *Don't; a Book for Girls* (1891). His lecture in Portland, Ore., to an A.M.E. Zion church, *The Negro Problem and Its Solution,* was also published in 1891.

In addition he wrote *Historical Chart of the Colored Race* (n.d.) and *History of the British West Indies* (n.d.) and three books: *The Life of Toussaint L'Ouverture . . . with a Historical Survey of Santo Domingo* (1888), to inspire Negro youth to "follow the glorious footsteps of the noble descendants of Africa, our Fatherland." His experiences in the South, where he was assaulted by whites on at least three occasions, formed part of the basis for his *Southern Outrages: A Statistical Record of Lawless Doings* (1894). This compilation from newspapers and other sources of reports of lynchings and other kinds of physical abuse was one of the first of its kind.

Benjamin's Pocket History of the American Negro: A Story of Thirty-One Years from 1863 to 1894 (published in Providence, R.I., 1894), had as its theme "History furnishes no example of emancipation under circumstances so unfavorable as that of the American Negro" (p. 5). It praised the progress Negroes had made in education, the professions, literature, the churches; stated that the Patent Office had granted Negroes more than 200 patents since 1863; and decried the failure to recognize the Negro's contributions to the development of agriculture and industry. It mentioned the painter Edwin M. Bannister and the sculptor Edmonia Lewis, and quoted Antonín Dvořak's praise of Negro folksongs. The book also listed the wealth of Negroes by states, and emphasized progress in industry and politics. It closed with an optimistic belief in the future of the American Negro and the possibility of his carrying "the blessings of Christian civilization to that dark continent" of Africa (p. 20). Though little known, this *Pocket History* may have brought encouragement during the gloomy years of the late nineteenth century.

A virtually unknown publication of Benjamin's was his essay "Los Negros Americanos," on pages 135–42 of Rafael Serra y Montalvo's *Ensayos Políticos,* published at New York in 1899.

The principal source of generally accepted accounts of Benjamin's career is the sketch, most probably written by Benjamin himself, in William J. Simmons's *Men of Mark . . .* (1887, pp. 991–94). Contemporary newspaper clippings in I. Garland Penn's *The Afro-American Press and Its Editors* (1891, pp. 320–24) support statements that he was editor of the *Negro American* and the *San Francisco Sentinel.* Copies of the *Observer* and the *Sentinel* are in, notably, the Bancroft Library, University of California, Berkeley. — ARNOLD H. TAYLOR

BERRY, EDWIN C. (1854–1931), businessman. Berry was born in Oberlin, Ohio, on Dec. 10, 1854, the son of free parents born in Gallia County, Ohio. In 1856 his family moved to Athens County, Ohio, where Edwin was to remain for the rest of his life. While in Athens County, Berry attended Albany Enterprise Academy, one of the earliest educational institutions in the United States conceived, owned, and operated by Negroes. The Berry family took in boarders, two of whom were

to gain fame in their own right, namely Milton M. Holland, Congressional Medal of Honor winner, and his brother, William, Texas legislator and educator.

Berry first found employment in Athens, manufacturing bricks for the state mental hospital being constructed in town. In 1868 he secured work in a local restaurant where he apprenticed himself as a cook for five years. On Oct. 18, 1877, Berry married Mattie Madra of Pomeroy, Ohio, the daughter of slave parents. The following year, with financial aid from a friend, he opened his own restaurant in Athens. The restaurant prospered and during the next fourteen years Berry moved his establishment several times to keep pace with the increase in business.

A participant in Republican party activities in southeastern Ohio, Berry actively sought a clerkship in state government during the summer of 1889. However, his support of the Joseph Foraker wing of the Ohio Republican party left him without a job prospect after the party's defeat in the gubernatorial election. The only offices he held were several terms on the Wilberforce University Board of Trustees during the early decades of the twentieth century.

In 1892 Berry erected a twenty-room hotel on property adjoining his restaurant, placing him in debt to the amount of $9000. A farmer friend furnished the money and took a mortgage on the building. The Hotel Berry quickly prospered and several additions were made to the structure. At the time of Berry's retirement in 1921 the hotel had expanded to fifty-five rooms, with its owner gaining the reputation of being the most successful Negro small city hotel operator in the United States. The reputation of the Hotel Berry came to be based on the fine meals served there and the extra attention lavished on the customers. Berry is reputed to be the first hotelkeeper in the United States to put needle, thread, buttons, and cologne in the rooms. Each room also came equipped with a clothes closet. G. F. Richings observed that Berry's patrons were all white and that he was the only Negro in the nation who operated a first-class hotel patronized by white people.

Berry kept quite active in philanthropic work among the race in Ohio. A member of the Baptist denomination, he was largely responsible for the construction and financing of the Mount Zion Baptist Church in Athens, Ohio. He participated in the work of the church on both the state and local level, serving as superintendent of the church Sunday school, church clerk, officer, and delegate and speaker at the Ohio Baptist Convention for nearly a half century. His church affiliation brought him to be a zealous supporter of temperance in the Negro community.

On March 12, 1931, Berry died in Athens, leaving an estate of $55,000. In an editorial written several weeks after Berry's death, Harry C. Smith, editor of the *Cleveland Gazette,* eulogized him as "the leading and best Afro-American businessman in the last quarter of a century."

No single biography exists on Edwin C. Berry. The most complete account of his life is contained in an essay written on the Negro community in Athens County by the Federal Writer's Project and maintained in the State Archives at the Ohio Historical Society. His political activities can be traced in the Charles L. Kurtz and George A. Myers Papers at the Ohio Historical Society. The published *Minutes of the Ohio Baptist Convention* document his role in the religious life of Ohio. Berry's business activities receive mention in G. F. Richings's *Evidences of Progress Among Colored People* (1901), and in the *Cleveland Gazette* (March 21 and 28, 1931). Berry's participation in the activities of the community is mentioned in the pages of the *Athens Messenger.* — FRANK R. LEVSTIK

BETHUNE, MARY JANE MCLEOD (1875–1955), educator, civil rights leader, advisor to presidents, and government official. She was born July 10, 1875, in Mayesville, S.C., the fifteenth child of former slaves, Samuel and Patsy McLeod. Since she was one of their first children born free, her family struggled to send her to the local Presbyterian Mission School for Negroes. Through scholarships and jobs she attended Scotia Seminary (now Barber-Scotia College) in Concord, N.C., and Moody Bible Institute in Chicago. Upon graduation from Moody in 1895 she returned south to teach, first at Haines Institute in Augusta, Ga., and then in Sumter, S.C. In Sumter she met and married a fellow teacher, Albertus Bethune. The following year (1898) their only son, Albert McLeod Bethune, was born. In 1899 Mrs. Bethune taught in the Palatka (Florida) Mission School. After four years of work, she moved on to Daytona Beach, Fla., where in 1904 she founded the Daytona Normal and Industrial School (now Bethune-Cookman College).

Her herculean struggle to build this school over the next two decades brought her to national attention. In 1920 she became a vice-president of the National Urban League. She also served two terms as president of the National Association of Colored Women (1924–1928). Beginning with the Coolidge administration, she served as counsellor and advisor on Negro education and general problems of minority groups to five successive presidents. Her participation in this capacity reached its zenith during the administration of Franklin D. Roosevelt. In 1935 she founded the National Council of Negro Women (NCNW) as an umbrella organization of Negro women organizations. Under the New Deal's National Youth Administration (NYA), Bethune served as director of the Division of Minority Affairs from 1936 to 1943. In 1945 as special representative of the State Department she attended the conference in San Francisco which established the United Nations. She was also special assistant to the secretary of war (1945) for the selection of candidates for the Women's Army Corps (WAC), established as the Women's Army Auxiliary Corps in 1942. From 1945 to her death in 1955 she was one of the more influential women in the United States. She died of a heart attack at her home in Daytona Beach on May 18, 1955. Funeral services were held in Bethune-Cookman Auditorium, where the eulogy was delivered by Howard Thurman. She was buried on the campus. She was survived by a son Albert, a grandson, a granddaughter, and five great-grandchildren, all of Dayton Beach.

Among her many awards were the Spingarn Medal from the NAACP (1935), the Medal of Honor and Merit from the République d'Haïti (1949), the Star of Africa from the Republic of Liberia (1952), the Frances Drexel Award for Distinguished Service (1937), and the Thomas Jefferson Award (1942) for outstanding leadership. She was the recipient of numerous honorary degrees. Her death, just prior to her eightieth birthday, brought to a close an intense and unrelenting struggle for Negro progress and opportunity that spanned some sixty years.

The McLeod family, poor by national standards, were the symbol of stability and unity in the Negro community of Mayesville. Deciding against migration at the end of slavery, Samuel and Patsy McLeod gathered together their surviving fourteen children (some having been sold to neighboring plantations) and grandmother Sophia and struggled to buy land for a small farm. This tightly knit Methodist family fashioned, as far as their material resources allowed, a life that reflected highly set goals. Their priorities of securing land, storing food for harder times, and sharing with those less fortunate soon included an education for Mary Jane.

As a child, Mary McLeod was keenly aware of the differences between the comforts of the more affluent white family for whom her mother worked and the more barren realities of her home. Education, especially reading, became a key to this great gap in her early years because of an incident she experienced with the white daughter of that family. One day while playing, Mary picked up a book that was snatched by her white playmate who explained that since Negroes could not read, the book was not for her. To this child, reading then became the symbol of such differences between whites and Negroes as houses with windows and log cabins without them. Education remained high on her list of necessities for eliminating the gaps between Negroes and whites, although as her world widened she added many others, including political organizations, pride in oneself, faith, and skilled use of power.

The resources of the family were galvanized to send her to the local school. After she completed her studies there, her teacher, Emma Wilson, found a patron for her in a Mary Crissmon, a white Quaker schoolteacher from Denver, Colo., to finance her education at Scotia Seminary and the Moody Bible Institute, where she planned to become a missionary. When she finished in 1895 she was unable to gain placement as a missionary in Africa. At the age of twenty she was teaching school at Haines Institute in Augusta, Ga., under Lucy Laney. It was Laney who showed McLeod that there was an essential mission to be carried out among Negroes in the United States that was as worthy as a comparable one in Africa.

In 1897, while teaching at the Kindall Institute in Sumter, she married Albertus Bethune. When their son was only six months old, Mrs. Bethune accepted a teaching position in Palatka, Fla. After the reorganization of the Palatka Mission School, she was attracted by the problems and needs of the Negro workers building the railroad in Florida. In 1904 she and her son joined them in Daytona Beach, Fla. The Daytona Normal and Industrial School for Negro Girls was started the same year with the sum of $1.50. Within two years this school had grown to 250 students and included boys in the student body.

Bethune saw the school as the center of the community and thereby responsible to the entire Negro community. This philosophy, guiding her work over the next twenty years, led her to have a day and night school; a curriculum that included the development of the mind, hands, and heart through an integrated academic, vocational, and religious program; the organization of a series of mission schools serviced by her students in the turpentine camps surrounding Daytona Beach. She organized a hospital for Daytona Negroes after her students were refused service in the white hospital; her singing group visited jails as well as the local hotels; and in 1920 she organized the local Negro community to vote for municipal services in face of overt hostility from the local Ku Klux Klan.

The needs of the community soon demanded a larger campus, and in 1907, on the city dump nicknamed "Hell's Hole," the first building was completed on the new campus. Faith Hall and other buildings followed. Of her efforts to buy land for the campus, she wrote: "I have learned already that one of my important jobs was to be a good beggar; I rang doorbells and tackled cold prospects without a lead. I wrote articles for whoever would print them, distributed leaflets, rode interminable miles of dusty roads on my old bicycle, invaded churches, clubs, lodges, chambers of commerce. If a prospect refused to make a contribution I would say "thank you for your time." No matter how deep my hurt, I always smiled. I refused to be discouraged, for neither God nor man could use a discouraged soul."

These efforts brought her and the school lifelong friends among the affluent visitors who vacationed in Daytona. The major contributors were James M. Gamble of Procter and Gamble Enterprises and Thomas H. White of the White Sewing Machine Company. The needs of the school led her to travel in search of funds and support. Her work brought her much-needed support from the Negro leaders of the day such as Booker T. Washington and Mary Church Terrell of the National Association of Colored Women.

After serving on the National Child Welfare Commission during the Coolidge and Hoover administrations, she came to Washington in 1935 as a special advisor on minority affairs under the Roosevelt administration. By 1936 she had become the director of the Division of Negro Affairs in the NYA, and one of the few Negroes in the country who had personal access to the president. In her role as director, Bethune traveled the country inspecting the various projects set up to serve the needs of youth during the Depression. She was also able to influence the expenditure of NYA funds for such Negro institutions as Bethune-Cookman College.

The New Deal period provided fertile ground for national organizations. In 1935 Bethune organized the National Council of Negro Women in keeping with her theory that such a coalition would provide a more powerful platform from which to be heard. Following the same strategy, in August 1936 she called together Negroes holding various positions in the Roosevelt administration to her home to plan ways to secure the

Negro's fair share of the New Deal. This group became known as the Black Cabinet, and was the foundation of two national conferences organized by Bethune, and supported by the NYA, to explore Negro problems and solutions further. The "Blue Book" was the result of the first conference on civil liberties, held in January 1937. It was Bethune's task to deliver this report to the president; although the response to this statement of Negro concerns was slight, it remained a testimony of Bethune's efforts at effecting change and opportunity for her people. Her influence was particularly strong because of her personal friendship with Mrs. Eleanor Roosevelt.

With the United States entry into World War II, Mrs. Bethune pledged the support of the NCNW and saw the first Negroes hired in the National Defense plants who had been trained in the NYA centers. Although she supported the national effort, she never allowed it to be construed that she supported segregation in the armed forces, especially in the training of the Women's Auxiliary Army Corps at Fort Des Moines, Iowa (1917).

After the NYA ceased on Aug. 3, 1943, Bethune continued her work as an advocate of her people, though ill health had forced her to give up the presidency of Bethune-Cookman College in 1942. She missed no opportunity to make a point in the name of dignity and respect due every human being. She was widely known for not answering to "Mary," or "Auntie," or any of the other names commonly used to refer to Negro women. During a stay at Johns Hopkins hospital for a sinus operation in 1940, she demanded that two Negro doctors be allowed to observe the operation, a first for Johns Hopkins. Her doctors were among the many whites who were reprimanded for not addressing her properly as "Mrs. Bethune." Bethune developed a flair for dress, characterized by long capes, velvets, jewelry, and a cane that she said she carried for "swank." A big woman who made an impressive figure, she used it and her superb oratorical ability to influence audiences, especially in the United States. Of herself she said many times, "Look at me, I am Black, I am beautiful."

In the latter years of her life she continued to travel, against the wishes of her doctor, and to publish her views, with the assistance of Constance Daniels, in newspaper columns in the *Chicago Defender* and the *Pittsburgh Courier*. Her theories and philosophy were published in several anthologies, notably chapters in *What the Negro Wants* (1944) edited by Rayford W. Logan, and *Thirteen Americans, Their Spiritual Autobiographies* (1953) edited by Louis Finkelstein. In these efforts Bethune's image of herself as a missionary for her people, and all mankind less fortunate and shackled by racial and economic discrimination, was prominent. In her "Last Will and Testament" (first published in *Ebony*, Aug. 1955, again in Sept. 1963, and for a third time in Nov. 1973) she emphasized several essentials for the forward movement of her people. Self-respect, pride, and love for oneself as a Negro were among the gifts she left to her "children." On her death, Mrs. William Thomas Mason, then president of the NCNW, said: "She built innumerable bridges between the races through her depth of understanding of the problems of the Negro people and the ideals of America." The *Pittsburgh Courier* ended its tribute to her with these words: "The accident of color made her Negro and she ennobled the word." On the ninety-ninth anniversary of her birth, a bronze statue commemorating her leadership was unveiled in Lincoln Park, Washington, D.C. It was the first statue in honor of any woman and of any Negro in a public park in the nation's capital.

A more thorough treatment of Mrs. Bethune's life is in the following biographies: Catherine Owens Peare's *Mary McLeod Bethune* (1951), Rackham Holt's *Mary McLeod Bethune, a Biography* (1964), and Emma Gelders Sterne's *Mary McLeod Bethune* (1957). There is an obituary in *JNH,* probably written by William M. Brewer (Oct. 1955, pp. 393–95). Bethune kept a diary for most of her productive years and her papers are in the memorial erected for her on the Bethune-Cookman campus in Daytona Beach, Fla. — BERNICE REAGON

BETHUNE, THOMAS GREENE [BLIND TOM] (1849–1908), composer-pianist. Born a slave within a few miles of Columbus, Ga., the twentieth child of Charity Wiggins, the blind Thomas was included as a bargain when Col. James Bethune, a Columbus lawyer-journalist, purchased his parents in 1850. From infancy he manifested an extraordinary fondness for musical sounds and showed exceptional retentive skills. Said to have demonstrated musical genius before he was two, by his fourth year he was being exhibited as the "musical marvel" of the Bethune plantation and publicly presented by his owner at age eight throughout Georgia. Soon after Tom was hired out for three years to Perry Oliver, a Savannah tobacco planter, who promoted him in concerts throughout the United States. With the outbreak of the Civil War nonsouthern engagements were cancelled, and Tom was returned to Colonel Bethune who used his slave's talents to benefit the Confederacy throughout the war. In 1864 Bethune "persuaded" Tom's parents to have him appointed Tom's guardian, thereby continuing to profit from Tom's talents. Immediately following the war, Tabbs Gross (a Negro) challenged in a Cincinnati court (July 25, 1865) the "agreement" by which Tom was placed under guardianship that was almost tantamount to slavery. The Bethunes made several fortunes on Tom, beginning with an 1866 European tour that netted $100,000. Concert appearances continued throughout his lifetime in major concert halls and on the vaudeville circuit.

After years of travel with Colonel Bethune, Tom's guardianship was taken over by the colonel's son, John G. Bethune, who until his death in 1883 doubled as Tom's manager. By the terms of his will, the guardianship went to his widow, Eliza Bethune. In 1893 Eliza married attorney Albert Lerche of Hoboken, N.J. A legal attempt by Colonel Bethune to get Tom from his daughter-in-law failed. Tom spent his last fifteen years in Hoboken under management of the Lerches. An effort by Tom's mother during these years to get her son back was unsuccessful. Until her death in 1902 Charity Wiggins expressed resentment of those who "stole" Tom from her. Despite exploitation until a few months before his death from apoplexy (June 13, 1908), Tom reportedly died penniless. He was buried in Brooklyn, N.Y.,

as Thomas Wiggins. Twenty years later his remains were taken to Columbus, Ga., where a marker was erected near his burial site by the Georgia Historical Society.

Although blind from birth, Tom composed over 100 piano and vocal compositions from age five. Included among his repertory were works by Bach, Beethoven, Chopin, Liszt, Thalberg, and other European masters. He also exhibited technical skill by improvising on operatic airs and contemporary ballads. His original compositions reflect pianistic and theoretical practices of the nineteenth century, being primarily parlor waltzes, marches, and mazurkas, or descriptive-type works such as "The Rainstorm," "Cascade," "The Music Box," and "The Battle of Manassas." Reputable testimonies offer documentation about Tom's ability to perform difficult selections almost flawlessly after one hearing, sing and recite poetry or prose in several languages, duplicate phonetically lengthy orations by noted statesmen, and reproduce sounds of nature, machinery, and various musical instruments. He also performed reasonably well on the cornet, showed remarkable vocal ability, and wrote poetry. Contemporary accounts reveal many astonishing feats, such as the rendition of three tunes simultaneously in several keys, ability to play equally well standing or with his back to the keyboard, perform either part of a duet upon one hearing, and successfully pass the most complicated and technical public examinations routinely given throughout his life by prominent musicians, physiologists, and other scientific skeptics. The commonly described "idiocy" of Tom was in part due to certain childish and animal-like stage mannerisms he enacted which his managers shrewdly cultivated in order to create the myth that Tom's genius was due to occult practices.

Contrary to advertisements that Tom was a "natural untaught" pianist, he did receive informal instruction throughout his career. Colonel Bethune's wife and daughters were all accomplished musicians who aided Tom's early musical development, while an Atlanta music teacher, W. P. Howard, accompanied the Bethunes as Tom's musical tutor when they exhibited Tom in Europe. However, most of Tom's instruction was sporadic since his managers usually hired teachers from the locales where Tom performed. In order to increase his repertory (said to number over 700 pieces), professionals were hired to play for him. A rigid practice schedule (extending sometimes to eight hours) accounts for his exceptional keyboard dexterity.

Tom's reputation was so widespread that in 1860 he performed for foreign dignitaries and before President Buchanan in Washington, D.C.; so impressed was the piano manufacturer William Knabe by Tom's Baltimore appearance that year that he presented the ten-year-old pianist a grand piano. Immortalized by poets and literary personages, Tom has remained one of the prodigies and musical wonders.

Music and Some Highly Musical People, by James Monroe Trotter (5th ed., 1879, pp. 141–69), is a principal source. The *Columbus* (Georgia) *Magazine* (July 11, 1941) contains many eyewitness accounts in this special commemorative issue. See also *The Marvelous Musical Prodigy, Blind Tom, the Negro Boy Pianist,* by an unknown author (1867?). The most recent publications are Geneva Southall's "Blind Tom: A Misrepresented and Neglected Composer-Pianist" (*Black Perspectives in Music,* May 1975, pp. 141–59), and her *Blind Tom: The Post-Civil War Enslavement of a Black Musical Genius* (1979). — GENEVA SOUTHALL

BIBB, HENRY WALTON (1815–1854), author, editor, and separatist. One of the seven children of Mildred Jackson, Bibb was born a slave on the Shelby County, Ky., plantation of Willard Gatewood on May 10, 1815. His father was state Sen. James Bibb. Whatever its impact on others, bondage did not crush the Bibbs. Mildred Jackson married a free Negro riverboatman who signed an agreement with her owner to purchase her, but the planter reneged. As a young man Bibb saw his brothers and sisters sold away one by one. Consequently, when he married in the 1830s he began contemplating ways to obtain his freedom. After a slave trader forced his wife to become a prostitute, Bibb's search for freedom grew more intense. He was such an incorrigible slave that he had six different owners and tried to escape six times. Whenever he was successful he returned to try to help members of his family escape. Finally realizing the impossibility of rescuing his widely scattered family, Henry escaped to Detroit in 1842. An extremely intelligent man, Bibb attended the school conducted by the Rev. William C. Monroe for about three weeks.

From 1842 to 1844 Bibb lectured extensively on antislavery and campaigned for the Liberty party in Michigan. For the next six years he lectured from Michigan to Pennsylvania, and joined Frederick Douglass and William Wells Brown as one of the most effective antislavery speakers. A master of humor and pathos, Bibb impressed on his audiences all of the contradictions inherent in slavery. In one report of a lecture he gave, a journalist declared that the audience "cheered, clapped, stamped, laughed, and wept, by turns." During his lecture tour Bibb met Mary Miles of Boston and in June 1848 he married her. A year later he published one of the most reliable of the slave autobiographies, *Narrative of the Life and Adventures of Henry Bibb, An American Slave* (1849).

Shortly after the appearance of Bibb's narrative, Congress passed the Fugitive Slave Act. Bibb's reaction was typical of many fugitive slaves: "If there is no alternative but to go back to slavery, or die contending for liberty, then death is far preferable." To avoid the possibility of both reenslavement and death, Bibb and his wife fled west to Canada. They quickly became leaders of the Canadian Negro community of more than 30,000 persons, and helped to establish a school, a Methodist church, and educational, temperance, and antislavery societies in Sandwich, Chatham, and Windsor, Ontario. In January 1851 Bibb established Canada's first Negro newspaper, the *Voice of the Fugitive.* In the *Voice* Bibb urged fugitive slaves and free Negroes to come to Canada and led the fight for emigration between 1851 and 1854. He also greeted fugitives when they arrived, interviewed them, and published their stories in the *Voice.* The most important of these events occurred in August 1852, when Henry's brothers—John, Lewis, and

Granville—successfully escaped from bondage and joined him and his mother.

Pursuing his goal of establishing Canada as a haven for oppressed American Negroes, in January 1852 Bibb joined with Josiah Henson and white philanthropists in Michigan to purchase 2000 acres of land and establish the Refugee Home Society near Windsor. The *Voice of the Fugitive* quickly became the organ of the emigrationists: Martin Delany was a regular correspondent and James Theodore Holly eventually became a co-editor of the paper. Bibb was the organizer and president of the North American Convention of Colored People which met in September 1851 and condemned the American Colonization Society, the Fugitive Slave Act, and formed an early pan-African society, the American Continental and West India League, to unite free Negroes. Before his death at thirty-nine in the summer of 1854, Henry Bibb had made a permanent impression on his times.

The principal source is Henry Bibb's *Narrative of the Life and Adventures of Henry Bibb, An American Slave* (1849). Interpretations and facts about his life are in Floyd J. Miller's *The Search for a Black Nationality: Black Colonization and Emigration, 1787–1863* (1975), Roger W. Hite's "Voice of a Fugitive: Henry Bibb and Ante-bellum Black Separatism" (*Journal of Black Studies* 4 [March 1974]: 269–84), and Fred Landon's "Henry Bibb, a Colonizer" (*JNH* 5 [Oct. 1920]: 437–47). A background analysis is John W. Blassingame's *The Slave Community, Plantation Life in the Antebellum South* (1972). — JOHN W. BLASSINGAME

BILLY, alias WILL, also WILLIAM (? – ?), subject of a notable case of alleged treason during the American Revolution. Like many slaves prior to the Revolution, he left no records. His life is interesting less because of what he did than what was done to him. A mulatto slave belonging to John Tayloe, Richmond County, Va., he was condemned to death by the Court of Oyer and Terminer, Prince William County, on May 8, 1781, for allegedly seizing an armed vessel, along with others, and "feloniously and traitorously" waging war against Virginia. Two justices of the court, Henry Lee and William Carr, in a dissenting opinion (May 11, 1781), stated that since Billy was a slave and not a citizen, he owed no allegiance and could not, therefore, be guilty of treason. In addition there was no positive proof that he had gone voluntarily on board the vessel. On the contrary, Billy had offered proof that he was taken to the boat against his will and that he had never aided the enemy of his own free will. Accepting the belief of Mann Page (May 13, 1781), one of the executors of Colonel Tayloe, Gov. Thomas Jefferson of Virginia responded that a reprieve to June 30 would be signed. Apparently by joint resolution of the Virginia House and Senate (June 14, 1781) the reprieve was granted. In view of the fact that many slaves had defected to the British, the judgment bespeaks a latent sense of justice in a slaveholding state and adds to the ambiguity about Jefferson's views on slavery.

This interesting case is documented in Julian P. Boyd and others (eds.), *The Papers of Thomas Jefferson* (1952, 5:640–43). — RAYFORD W. LOGAN

BINGA, JESSE (1865–1950), banker and realtor. Binga was born in Detroit, the youngest of ten children. His father, William W. Binga, a barber, was born in 1817 in Amherstburg, Ontario; his mother, Adelphia Lewis, became the owner of a considerable amount of property near Rochester, N.Y. After Jesse left high school in his third year, he collected rent for his mother. She also found employment for him in the law offices of a Negro, Thomas Crisup. He roamed through the West, opening a barbershop (he had learned the trade from his father) in Tacoma and Seattle, and working in a barbershop in Oakland, Calif. He worked his way east as a Pullman porter, buying and selling at a handsome profit lots recently opened on a former Indian reservation near Pocatello, Idaho. After a meteoric career as realtor and banker in Chicago after 1893, he was imprisoned for embezzlement in 1933. Upon his release in 1938 he lived quietly and died penniless on June 13, 1950.

Taking advantage of the booming real estate market, his shrewd business calculation, driving personality, and a certain amount of luck made him by 1907 one of the most prosperous colored real estate dealers in Chicago. He opened his office first at 3331 South State St. By 1926 he owned more frontage on State Street south of 12th Street than any other person. In order to expand the Negro real estate market, he opened white neighborhoods to colored settlement despite strong white opposition. Gradually he moved into banking, in 1908 opening a private bank and in 1921 the Binga State Bank. The Chicago Negro community encouraged his state bank with praise and, more important, with deposits, which rose in the first three years from $300,000 to $1,153,000. Binga viewed his bank as an example of thrift and business enterprise as well as a necessary financial service providing a happy medium between the large white banks of the Loop, too often discriminatory and discourteous, and the ubiquitous loan sharks. Because of his financial success and leadership ability, Binga became a South Side booster and an esteemed philanthropist. In 1912 he married Eudora Johnson, who provided him with a substantial dowry and social prestige. Climaxing his career in 1929, Binga, by now almost a legendary hero of colored Chicago, erected the Binga Arcade Building, an impressive five-story building and ballroom on the corner of 35th and South State Streets. Neither the bombing of his real estate office nor of his home during and after the "Red Summer" of 1919 (the name given to the race riots by James Weldon Johnson) had deterred him from helping the burgeoning Negro population from acquiring homes in Chicago's South Side.

Then, in 1930, the Binga State Bank collapsed and brought tragedy to Chicago's Negro community. Just as Binga had climbed to the heights of success largely through the expansion of the Negro population and real estate market, so the decrease in migration and the collapse of that market resulted in his ruin. The Binga State Bank held an excessive number of first mortgage real estate loans. Yet the country's general economic collapse was not solely responsible for the failure (every neighborhood bank outside the Loop also closed), for Binga had made many unwise financial decisions and had engaged in illegal activities. When the bank was examined in 1930, the capital stock and surplus were gone and there was a shortage in assets over liabilities of over $500,000. The state bank examiner concluded that the institution had been conducted in an illegal, fraudulent, and unsafe manner. Binga lost a personal fortune estimated at $400,000 and many working-class Negroes lost their hard-earned savings. After a first trial resulted in a hung jury, Binga was convicted in 1933 of embezzling $22,000 and sentenced to ten years in the Illinois State Penitentiary.

While certain elements had always criticized Binga for his imperious nature, hard-driving personality, and rent-gouging policies, many blacks sympathized with his plight. People seemed to associate his imprisonment with the collapse of his bank and not with the embezzlement, and felt that he was harshly and unjustly punished. Leading citizens organized a petition drive to obtain his freedom; after serving three years, he was released in 1938 and worked as a handyman at St. Anselm's Catholic Church, to spend his remaining years quietly. On June 14, 1950, the *Chicago Herald-American* recognized his death in a one-sentence summary of his career: "Jesse Binga, who rose from a laborer to a millionaire and a power on Chicago's South Side . . . died penniless yesterday in St. Luke's Hospital."

Four days earlier, feeble and worn by old age, he had been stricken on the stairway of the home of his nephew, Albert Roberts, and fallen over the bannisters. He died of head and shoulder injuries on June 13, 1950. A rosary was recited at the Major and Miller Funeral Home on June 19 and a requiem mass at St. Anselm's Catholic Church the next day, with burial in Oakwood Cemetery (*Chicago Defender*, June 24, 1950, pp. 1, 2).

The early career of Binga is developed in Inez V. Cantey's "Jesse Binga, The Story of a Life" (*The Crisis*, Dec. 1927, pp. 329, 350–52). Abram L. Harris's *The Negro as Capitalist* (1936) traces his rise and decline, as does Carl R. Osthaus's "The Rise and Fall of Jesse Binga, Black Banker" (*JNH*, Jan. 1973, pp. 39–60). Details about his entire life are in David M. Katzman, *DAB, Supplement Four, 1946–1950* (1974, pp. 82–84); it has a comprehensive bibliography. — CARL R. OSTHAUS

BIVINS, HORACE W. (1862–1937), soldier and author. Bivins was born on May 8, 1862, on the eastern shore of Chesapeake Bay at Pungoteague, Accomack County, Va. His parents, Severn S. and Elizabeth Bivins, were farmers and he worked with them during his childhood. His father financed the first church and schoolhouse built on Virginia's eastern shore, in 1862. Bivins enrolled at Hampton Institute in June 1885. He studied briefly there and at Wayland Seminary in Washington, D.C., before enlisting in the 10th Cavalry in November 1887. He joined the regiment at Fort Grant, Arizona Territory, in time to participate in the final phases of the Apache Wars.

Bivins saw action in the Cuban campaign of 1898, and was commended for conspicuous bravery as operator of a Hotchkiss mountain gun in the battle for Santiago. He was promoted to squadron sergeant major in November 1900. In the summer of 1901 he commanded a detachment at La Granga, on Samar Island in the Philippines, where he led patrols in pursuit of insurrectionists. In one month, July 1901, these forays entailed over 650 miles of marches. During July he received an appointment as ordnance sergeant, and left the 10th Cavalry to accept the new post in December. He served in this capacity at posts in Montana, the Philippines, California, Wyoming, New York, and Vermont, before he retired to a home he had established in Billings, Mont. His wife, Claudia Bivins, was active in the Colored Women's Club of Montana, where she was reported as having raised more money for scholarships than any other woman.

When World War I began, Bivins offered to organize a regiment of volunteers in his native Virginia. The government declined the offer but commissioned Bivins a captain of infantry. He spent six months on active duty at Camp Dix, N.J., in 1918, and then returned to his Montana residence.

Bivins was a remarkable marksman, one of the best in the army. He won several medals in military competition, placing sixth with the pistol in the combined Departments of Dakota and Colorado in 1892, and second the following year. In 1894 he won the gold first-place medals with both revolver and carbine. He represented the Department of Dakota in the 1894 army-wide carbine competition at Fort Sheridan, near Chicago, and won first place with a near-perfect score. As late as 1910 he still qualified as an expert marksman. In a short book in praise of Negro troops in Cuba, one Afro-American author called Bivins "Marksman of the Army" (Miles Lynk, *The Black Troopers,* p. 31). His exploits brought an offer to travel with Buffalo Bill Cody's Wild West Show, which he turned down to return to Hampton on furlough in December 1897. He was at Hampton when the United States declared war on Spain in the spring of 1898.

On July 1, 1898, the same day on which men of Bivins's regiment successfully stormed San Juan Hill, Bivins was a member of a three-man Hotchkiss crew. The other two men were wounded early in the day, and Bivins operated the weapon alone, in spite of heavy enemy fire and a slight head wound: "I was stunned for five minutes but soon forgot that I had been hurt" (Willard B. Gatewood, ed., *"Smoked Yankees" and the Struggle for Empire* [1971], p. 49). His courage won him national fame. The semiofficial *Army and Navy Journal* chronicled his deeds, as did several Negro newspapers. One of these, the *Indianapolis Freeman,* called him "a character worthy of the emulation of every young man of the Negro race." W. E. B. Du Bois also took note of his career in an article in *The Crisis* (May 1930).

Shortly after he returned from Cuba, Bivins cooperated in the writing of *Under Fire with the Tenth Cavalry* (1899, reprint 1969), a narrative of the heroism of the Negro regulars in Cuba. His thirty-page recollection of the Cuban campaign is one of the several eyewitness accounts in the volume he compiled with United States Land Office recorder Herschel Cashin and other Negroes: writer Charles Alexander, and two 10th Cavalry comrades, Chaplain William T. Anderson and Surgeon Arthur M. Brown.

The best single source of biographical data is Bivins's autobiographical sketch in *Under Fire with the Tenth Cavalry.* Newspapers and military records in the National Archives, particularly the Descriptive Book of the Tenth's Non-Commissioned Staff and the records of the Adjutant-General's Office, provide the best supplemental information. — FRANK N. SCHUBERT

BLAND, JAMES A. (1854–1911), composer and minstrel entertainer. He was born in Flushing, a section of Queens, New York City. His mother was born of free parents in Wilmington, Del. His father, Allen Bland, also a free-born Negro, had attended a school in Charleston, S.C., taught by Daniel Alexander Payne, later bishop of the African Methodist Episcopal church and founder of Wilberforce University. Allen Bland studied in the Oberlin College preparatory department and graduated from Wilberforce University. While serving as the first Negro examiner in the U.S. Patent Office, Washington, D.C., he enrolled in the Howard University Law Department, beginning in 1867. James Bland graduated from high school in Washington and studied briefly at Howard University where his father hoped he would earn a professional degree, but he was more interested in music than in an academic profession. While studying at Howard he heard the spirituals and other folk songs performed by ex-slaves working on the campus. He taught himself to play the banjo, played in hotels and private clubs, and began composing. He met several musicians, especially John Philip Sousa, then a violinist in a music hall and from 1880 to 1892 conductor of the famous U.S. Marine Band. Sousa, best known for his "The Stars and Stripes Forever," used band arrangements of some of Bland's songs.

James Bland began his notable career in the late 1870s as a member of the first successful all-Negro company, the Georgia Minstrels, organized in 1865 by Charles Hicks, a Negro. In 1843 Dan Emmett, the white man who wrote the song "Dixie," had headed the first blackface minstrels to appear in a regular theater. A quartet of white men, the Virginia Minstrels, they portrayed the plantation life of Negroes, as did many of their white successors. When Negroes began to organize their minstrel shows, they followed the general pattern of the white minstrels, even to blackening their faces with enormous red lips, and using similar slapstick jokes and gestures, comic patter-songs, and stylized dances. But they introduced such dances as the jig, the buck and wing, and stop-time, along with a monologue. Shortly after 1865 Billy Kersands and Sam Lucas, two talented Negro entertainers, headed the Georgia Minstrels, then known as Callender's Original and Georgia Minstrels. James Bland joined them and other Negroes after Jack Haverly bought the Callender Minstrels in 1878. In that year Bland published his best known song, "Carry Me Back to Old Virginny," which he had written while visiting the parents of Mamie Friend, who became his wife. She helped him with many of his lyrics, especially the poem which became the song "You Could Have Been True."

Haverly developed the troupe into a huge show, the Minstrel Carnival of Genuine Colored Minstrels, which played in Niblo's Garden, New York City (March 29 to May 8, 1879). After playing in Brooklyn and on the Pacific Coast, the troupe went to England in 1881. By that time the intimate minstrel show with two end men, Mr. Bones and Mr. Sambo, was enlarged into an extravaganza stage production. In July 1881 Haverly's Mastodon Minstrels played in London's His Majesty's Theatre. A London review stated: "When the curtain went up on opening night it disclosed on the stage about 65 real Negroes, both male and female, ranging in shades of complexions from the coal black Negro to the light brown mulatto or octoroon. They were all ages. . . . 16 corner men in all, eight bones and eight tambourines, twenty dancers and a banjo orchestra. James Bland introduced to this country . . . *Oh, Dem Golden Slippers.*" This song had already sold 100,000 copies by 1880. His other best known songs were "In the Evening by the Moonlight" and "In the Morning by the Bright Light."

Haverly's show left England late in 1881 to return in 1884 for another short season. James Bland remained in Europe from 1881 until 1901, with occasional trips back home. He did not like the huge stage show with parades and nightclub scenes. His intimate song and banjo style earned him the billing "The Idol of the Music Halls." He lived in a fashionable apartment, hired a booking agent, wore suits from the finest tailors in the most tasteful style, was honored by a command performance before Queen Victoria and the Prince of Wales. He performed in Scotland, Germany, and other countries. Hans Wunderlich, Sousa's cornet soloist, said that only three American composers were known in Germany: Sousa, Bland, and Stephen C. Foster, best known for his "My Old Kentucky Home."

Bland returned destitute to Washington, D.C., in 1910. He found none of his old friends, who thirty years before had included writers, musicians, prize-fighters, actors, clergymen, and politicians. Pennsylvania Avenue had been his "Broadway" where he had been known as "Melody Man." A boyhood friend, William Silence, made a desk available to Bland in his law office. Bland wrote a musical *The Sporting Girl,* two acts and eighteen songs, which he sold for $250. And that was the end of his composing. Vaudeville had replaced minstrelsy.

In 1911 he went to Philadelphia where he tried to join a troupe playing in Market Street, but he had lost his spirit. In March 1911 he caught cold and died alone and without friends of tuberculosis at 1012 Wood St., Philadelphia, on May 5, 1911. He was buried in Merion Cemetery, Bala-Cynwyd, Pa. He had two sisters, Mrs. Irene Bland Jurix and Mrs. Mary James. According to Mrs. James, he lost touch with them after he began to achieve success.

When Virginia in 1940 adopted "Carry Me Back to Old Virginny" as its official state song, few knew that its composer was a Negro. "Oh, Dem Golden Slippers" was used as the theme song of the Mummers' Annual New Year's Day parade in Philadelphia. The opening bars of "In the Evening by the Moonlight" are identical, note for note, to the opening of the chorus of "There's a Long, Long Trail a-Winding," one of the most popular songs of American troops in France during World War I. Other melodies of his, notably "The Missouri Hound Dog," have been used as campaign songs, and in background music for movies, radio and television shows.

James Weldon Johnson observed that of Bland's long list of songs, the four best known "at least possess the qualities that entitle him to a place in the front rank of American song-writers" (*Black Manhattan* [1940], p. 113).

In July 1939 Kelly Miller, Sr., of Howard University wrote an article for *Etude,* "The Negro 'Stephen Foster' —James A. Bland." James Francis Cooke, formerly editor of *Etude,* became interested in searching out the composer of the newly adopted state song of Virginia. His search led him to Dr. Miller and so to the grave of the composer. The tombstone was erected that at last told the story: "James A. Bland/ Oct. 22, 1854 – May 6, 1911/ Negro Composer Who Wrote/ 'Carry Me Back to Old Virginny'/ and 600 Other Songs/ Erected and Dedicated by/ Lions Clubs of Virginia/ July 15, 1946."

In 1944 Charles Haywood of Queens College presented a lecture to the Flushing Historical Society; "James A. Bland, Prince of the Colored Songwriters," published by that society under the title *Famous Men of Flushing.* The same author compiled, edited, and arranged *The James A. Bland Album of Outstanding Songs: A Collection for Voice and Piano* (1946). A narrative biography, *A Song in His Heart,* was written by John J. Daly (1951). Also valuable is Eileen Southern's *The Music of Black Americans: A History* (1971, esp. pp. 259–67, 270, 353, 309). Many of Bland's songs are in the Library of Congress. Kelly Miller and John J. Daly, relying on the Philadelphia Bureau of Statistics, give May 5 as the date of his death.

— RAYMOND LEMIEUX

BLEDSOE, JULE [JULIUS, JULES] (1898–1943), singer and actor. He was born in Waco, Tex., on Dec. 29, 1898. His maternal grandfather was the Rev. Stephen H. Cobb, noted for his singing voice. His father, Henry B., sang tenor, and his mother, Jessie Cobb Bledsoe, was a soprano soloist for whom the young Bledsoe played piano accompaniments during his adolescent years. His mother heard him singing nursery songs at age two. At age five he sang solos in a church concert, and was in demand as a soloist until the age of fifteen when he stopped singing "until my voice lost the squeaks and sudden bass notes." At age eight he began the study of piano, which added to his versatility as a musician.

He completed the preparatory course at Central Texas College and went to Bishop College, Marshall, Tex., where he continued his academic and musical education studying piano, harmony, and music history, to graduate with a B.A. degree in 1918. He began graduate study at Virginia Union University, Richmond, Va., and served in the Students Army Training Corps until discharged in 1919. He entered the Medical School of Columbia University where he also continued his study of languages and music, including private lessons in voice. Maud Cuney-Hare reports (p. 359) that Bledsoe sang for her at that time. She was "deeply impressed at the virile quality of his voice and his intelligent interpretation." He studied voice with Claude Warford, Parisotti, and Lazar Samoiloff. His friends and teachers urged him to undertake a concert career. Among those friends were James Weldon and J. Rosamond Johnson and many other musicians.

Bledsoe's debut in Aeolian Hall, New York City (April 21, 1924), was under the concert management of Sol Hurok. The review by W. J. Henderson in the *New York Sun* was enthusiastic for the quality of voice and for the scholarship in languages, musicianship, and style, but stated, "Mr. Bledsoe's art is not yet complete." Bledsoe's answer was reported later in the *Boston Chronicle* (June 1, 1929): "Success to me means work and more work. Because I have done this part well doesn't make me sit back and stop working. To the contrary, it makes me work harder."

The initial success of his debut was followed immediately by favorable reviews of many concerts: *New York Times* (Dec. 7, 1924)—"The singer's diction, least clear in English, still lags behind his dramatic intelligence and remarkable hushed tones of a natural beauty rare on the professional stage"; *Amsterdam News* (Oct. 17, 1925) —"He sang a concert in Town Hall including songs in six languages and spirituals by J. Rosamond Johnson with the composer at the piano"; *Boston Chronicle* (Jan. 10, 1926)—"This baritone really has a superb voice, without a rough patch in it, and in some respects the finest baritone we have heard in these parts in many a year." The reviewer also mentioned "poor diction."

Bledsoe returned to New York (June 16, 1926) after an extended concert tour of thirteen states culminating in a concert in the City Auditorium of Dallas, Tex., where he received an ovation.

Bledsoe, of a dark complexion, strikingly handsome, a tall, well-formed figure, was a natural for the stage. His first dramatic role was in the opera *Deep River* (1926) with Rose McClendon, Charlotte Wallace Murray, and Frank Harrison. "His singing in the voodoo scene was one of the highest spots in the opera" (James Weldon Johnson, *Black Manhattan* [1930, 1969], p. 207). This was probably the first opera in America to include a racially mixed cast. Bledsoe said later: "I contend that the only way to better race relations is by more contacts of the race with Negro artists. . . . A beauty is often hidden by dark skin and un-Caucasian features."

Two months after the closing of *Deep River,* Bledsoe was starred in Paul Green's *In Abraham's Bosom* (Dec. 28, 1926) in Provincetown, with two white and ten colored players, including Rose McClendon, Abbie Mitchell, and Frank Wilson. "It was closer and truer to actual Negro life and probed deeper into it than any drama of the kind that had yet been produced" (*Black Manhattan,* p. 207). It won the Pulitzer Prize in 1927.

Bledsoe sang (1927) the world première of James Welson Johnson's *Creation,* set to music by Gruenberg and performed with the Boston Symphony under Serge Koussevitzky.

Florenz Ziegfeld offered Bledsoe the role of Jo in *Show Boat* in 1927. The artist created the interpretation of the song "Ole Man River," giving a new personal character and tragic significance to the Mississippi, and a living personality to the stevedore who was "tired of living and scared of dying." Theater-goers were quoted as returning again and again to hear Bledsoe sing that song, which he said he had sung 1000 times by 1929, and later, toward the end of his life, that he had sung

it 18,000 times. Bledsoe also starred in the motion picture *Show Boat* in 1929.

Bledsoe returned to his favorite medium, the concert stage. In 1928 Herman Deories, music critic for the *Chicago Evening American,* reported, "Julius (Jules) Bledsoe, Negro baritone is a baritoned twin to Roland Hayes. His recital program at Kimball Hall last night was a demonstration of superlative musical culture."

On Jan. 27, 1929, the *New York Age* reported that Bledsoe's role of Amonasro, with Lisa Roma as Aïda, "marked the first occasion in New York City . . . when a Negro singer had portrayed, in costume and with lighting effects and support of the Philharmonic Symphony Orchestra, a character from grand opera with a singer of the other race enacting the supporting role." On April 18, 1931, the *Age* reported, "Jules Bledsoe sang his only New York recital . . . at Carnegie Hall, displaying a ripened art and natural vocalism."

On June 25, 1931, Bledsoe sang his first concert in Paris, reported to the *New York Age* by Clarence Cameron White, who was working on his opera *Ouango:* "Bledsoe certainly captured a musical Paris tonight. I have never seen a finer ovation. He sang numbers in Italian, French, German and English, including spirituals by himself and Mr. White, and of course 'Old Man River.'" He sang also on an extended tour of Europe.

A review in the *New York World Telegram* (July 11, 1932) of Bledsoe's performance at the Municipal Stadium, Cleveland, stated that he "is the greatest Amonasro in the World." If the New York Metropolitan Opera did not have him sing that role, L'Africain, Otello, and whatever other Negro roles the following year, "it will be asininity downright criminal." In October 1932 he won renewed acclaim for his role in *Show Boat,* broadcast Thursdays at 9 P.M. E.S.T. over a coast-to-coast network.

He was equally acclaimed for the title role in the opera *Emperor Jones,* which he first sang in November 1934 before an enthusiastic audience of 5000 in the Hippodrome, New York City, and later throughout the United States and Europe. He also sang in Vichy, France, the title role of *Boris Godunoff* and Mephistopheles in *Faust.* It was during this period that Maud Cuney-Hare wrote: "While it is true that Bledsoe has no superior as a vocal recital artist, he is the most versatile Negro singer on the stage today" (*Negro Musicians and Their Music* [1936], p. 358).

He was a deeply religious man who said: "I feel that the prayers of my mother and my aunt, both of whom are still living in Texas, are responsible for all that I may have accomplished" (*Afro-American,* Aug. 13, 1932). He was possessed of a keen sense of humor, illustrated in the remark he made to a judge who asked him to sing "Old Man River" as he gave him a suspended sentence for speeding: "That may give you a reason to fine me anyway." He died on July 14, 1943, in Hollywood, Calif., of a cerebral hemorrhage.

Newspaper items in the vertical file of the Schomburg Research Center, New York City, provided valuable information to supplement the references cited in the text. There is a photograph in Maud Cuney-Hare, facing p. 360. — RAYMOND LEMIEUX

BLYDEN, EDWARD WILMOT (1832–1912), scholar, diplomat, journalist, and educator. Born on Aug. 3, 1832, in St. Thomas, West Indies, of free, literate parents of Ibo descent, Romeo a tailor and Judith a schoolteacher, he was only ten when his family went to Venezuela for two years. Back in St. Thomas in 1844, his precocious literary and linguistic talents were aided by a white American pastor who encouraged Blyden's ambition to enter the Christian ministry and took him to the United States in May 1850 for further education. Denied entry to American theological colleges because of his race, Blyden accepted the offer by the New York Colonization Society of a passage to Liberia where he could study at the new Alexander High School in Monrovia, and reached there on Jan. 26, 1851. Although he received his only formal education at this high school, he became a recognized scholar. By 1858 he had become principal of the school, was ordained a Presbyterian minister, and had revealed his promise as a champion of his race by becoming editor of *Liberia Herald* and by publishing the first of many pamphlets, *A Voice from Bleeding Africa* (1856), in which he attacked slavery and praised the achievements and potentialities of the black man.

During the next fifty years, in addition to heavy literary labors and rigorous lecture tours at home and abroad, Blyden held many important offices in Liberia, notably as professor of classics (1862–1871) and president of Liberia College (1880–1884); secretary of state (1864–1866) and minister of the interior (1880–1882), minister to Britain (1877–1878 and 1892), and minister plenipotentiary to London and Paris (1905) over Liberia's disputed northern boundary. From 1896 to 1897 Blyden acted for the British government in Lagos as agent for native affairs. After unsuccessfully contesting the Liberian presidential elections in 1885, he moved to Sierra Leone where he taught, wrote, and for five years ((1901–1906) was director of Mohammedan education. In 1909 he underwent an operation for an aneurysm on the knee at the Royal Southern Hospital in Liverpool and was hospitalized for fifteen weeks. He died in Freetown on Feb. 7, 1912. His funeral was attended by large numbers of Christians and Moslems. Moslem men bore his coffin from his residence at Rawdon Street to the graveyard at the race course, while in the procession schoolchildren marched from all the Moslem schools in the city. It was reported that memorial services were held throughout English-speaking West Africa (Lynch, pp. 245–46).

Between 1850 and 1896 Blyden visited the United States eight times, for a total of about three years. After his unhappy introduction to America in 1850, the road back was made easier for him by his friendship with the Afro-American divine Alexander Crummell, his colleague in Liberia who wrote an introduction to Blyden's second pamphlet *A Vindication of the African Race* (1857). They were commissioned by the Liberian government in March 1861 to travel to Britain and America to interest philanthropists in Liberian education, and in March 1862 to go to the United States to encourage Negroes to return to their African fatherland. Although Crummell became disillusioned with this idea in the 1870s, his views influenced Blyden who believed throughout his adult life that the American Negro had an important part to play in the colonization and "redemption" of Africa.

His hopes, however, waned during the dark days of Reconstruction. Advocating a policy of racial accommodation similar to Booker T. Washington's, Blyden declared during his last visit to America in 1895, "The Negro problem must be solved here or it will appear in Africa in a new form." But he never gave up his hopes for an eventual Negro American exodus to Africa. His active support for the African repatriation scheme of the American Colonization Society which, as in the pre-Civil War days, was disliked by many American Negroes as a white man's attempt to divert attention from conditions in the United States, caused some Negroes to distrust Blyden. Furthermore, although he was greatly respected by Afro-Americans of his time because of the esteem in which he was held by notable men of different races and classes and for his scholarly defense of Negroes everywhere, Blyden's tactlessness and his antimulatto bias did not endear him to all. He was also severely criticized for his advocacy of polygamy as a natural expression of the African personality, culture, and social conditions. Some critics accused him of espousing a convenient philosophy to rationalize his personal conduct. "Some considered that he engaged in polygamy because of his long and intimate relationship with Anna Erskine, a pretty black school teacher from Louisiana, while he was legally married to Sarah Yates, member of a wealthy mulatto family whom he married in 1856 at the age of twenty-five and who bore him three children." Their life together was all the more difficult because she did not share his stringent and long-term denunciation of "mongrelized" mulattoes. He was further criticized for naming his paper, published in Sierra Leone, *The Negro*. He defended the name on the ground that "it is intended to represent and defend the interests of that peculiar type of humanity known as 'the Negro,' with all its affiliated and collateral branches whether on this continent or elsewhere" (Andrew Billingsley, "Edward Blyden: Apostle of Blackness," *The Black Scholar,* Dec. 1970, pp. 4, 9, 11). Yet soon after Blyden's death, W. E. B. Du Bois indicated his attraction for many Afro-Americans when he called him "prophet of the renaissance of the Negro race."

Blyden's views are summed up in his influential book *Christianity, Islam and the Negro Race* (1887), in which he demonstrated the appeal of Islam for colored men, and in his pamphlet *African Life and Customs* (1908), which has been called "the first important attempt at a sociological analysis of African society as a whole."

Essential documents for Blyden's biography are provided in Edith Molden's *Blyden of Liberia* (1966). Hollis Lynch's *Edward Wilmot Blyden: Pan-Negro Patriot* (1967) and *Black Spokesman: Selected Published Writings of Edward Wilmot Blyden* (1971) are valuable for the appreciation of his life and influence. An excellent brief sketch, with photographs, is "Edward Wilmot Blyden, 1832–1912," by Henry S. Wilson in *Abroad in America: Visitors to the New Nation, 1776–1914,* edited by Marc Pachter and Frances Stevenson Wein (1976). — GEORGE SHEPPERSON

BOLIVAR, WILLIAM CARL (1849–1914), bibliophile, journalist, and historical researcher. The eldest son of George and Elizabeth LeCount Proctor Bolivar, he was born in Philadelphia on April 18, 1849. His grandfather was mustered into a battalion of troops in the Old State House Square during the War of 1812, a contingent raised by James Forten, an early abolitionist and sailmaker. James LeCount, Bolivar's maternal grandfather, kept the Delaware House at Second and Race Streets for nearly a century before 1855. William's father, George, a sailmaker in Forten's loft, succeeded the latter in business following his death in 1842. The growth of steam vessels, however, soon made this business less profitable, and Bolivar went into the tobacco business, which enabled him to provide his family a comfortable living. William Carl was educated at the old Bird School and the Institute for Colored Youth (now Cheyney State College). Ebenezer D. Bassett, the first Negro U.S. diplomat and former minister to Haiti, was his principal. In later years Bolivar came under the tutelage of Fanny J. Coppin, early educator and author of *Hints on Teaching,* written with Bolivar's assistance. For a brief period following the Civil War, Bolivar worked in the War Department, Washington, D.C. In 1866 he returned to Philadelphia and worked for John Ashhurst & Co., a banking firm, where he remained until his death.

During the eighteenth and nineteenth centuries the Negro community of Philadelphia served as a model for other similarly populated areas in terms of cultural, religious, and economic development. It was the most heavily populated northern Negro community. In 1838 when *A Register of Trades of Colored People in the City of Philadelphia and Districts* was published, there were 656 persons engaged in fifty-seven different occupations. Eighty Beneficial Societies had been established and Philadelphia was considered the hub of progressive literacy, underground railroad, and abolitionist movements. At an early age, following his family tradition, Bolivar joined the Benjamin Banneker Institute, a literary-political organization founded in 1853. This institution was responsible for preserving records of early Negro history, as well as instilling in young Bolivar an early desire to be a bibliophile. In 1867 he joined the Pythian Baseball Club, serving as player, publicist, and organizer for nearly three decades. Bolivar was instrumental in founding the Mutual Baseball League, consisting of East Coast teams. During this same period Bolivar began a lifetime interest in ferreting out the hidden facts of the Negro historical past. It is in this area, as a researcher, collector, and lecturer, that he made his most solid contribution.

In 1892 Bolivar began publishing articles on Negro, United States, Pennsylvania, and Philadelphia history in the *Philadelphia Tribune,* a new weekly newspaper. He chose the lively and descriptive pen name "Pencil Pusher" to give a special identification to his column. His articles were written in a clear, informative narrative style. Frequently, bits of wit and satire would appear but they were tempered by his strong bent toward accuracy in historical data. As a writer of historical columns and as a lecturer Bolivar was careful to be as precise as possible in presenting a large body of heretofore unknown information. Having come from a family whose genealogical history predated the American Revolution, his interest is not surprising. In October 1897 he served as an organizer of the Afro-American Historical Society (AAHS), a worthy precursor of the twentieth-century Association for the Study of Negro Life and History founded by Carter G. Woodson and others in 1915. As a historian Bolivar is best represented in a paper delivered before the membership of the AAHS on "The History of the Institute of Colored Youth." His dedication in building this organization coupled with his reputation as a bibliophile clearly pioneered in establishing a nucleus of Negro bibliophiles. During the years 1903–1907 Bolivar was director of the Department of Negro History at Downingtown Industrial and Agricultural School, Downingtown, Pa. Here he pioneered in teaching Negro history to a doubting audience. In 1908 his booklet, *A Brief History of St. Thomas P. E. Church,* appeared. Four years later he was elected a corresponding member of the Negro Society for Historical Research, Yonkers, N.Y. Arthur A. Schomburg and John E. (Bruce Grit) Bruce were co-founders, both having been impressed with Bolivar's work.

Bolivar became one of the active bibliophiles of the nineteenth and twentieth centuries. His collection of rare Africana, Americana, and Lincolniana was probably one of the more valuable at that time. Many knew him as "Uncle Billie" and gained self-pride by listening to Bolivar's historical accounts. He also served as co-editor, along with Daniel A. Murray, of the unpublished *Murray's Historical and Biographical Encyclopedia.* Murray was also a conscientious bibliophile and staff member of the Library of Congress for forty years.

In April 1914 a group of Bolivar's friends gave him a surprise birthday party and presented a 3000-entry catalogue of his collection. Bolivar died at his home shortly thereafter, on Nov. 12, 1914. His funeral was well attended. The eulogy, by Archdeacon Henry L. Phillips, was a fitting tribute for this relatively unknown bibliophile, historian, journalist, and organizer of historical societies.

There is no full-length biography of Bolivar. Two publications give historical accounts of Bolivar's life: Henry L. Phillips's *William Carl Bolivar: A Eulogy* (1914) and James G. Spady's "The Afro-American Historical Society: The Nucleus of Black Bibliophiles, 1897–1923" (*NHB,* June/July 1974). Both contain an excellent photograph of Bolivar. — JAMES G. SPADY

BOUCHET, EDWARD ALEXANDER (1852–1918), educator. He was born in New Haven, Conn., on Sept. 15, 1852, the son of William Francis and Susan (Cooley) Bouchet. William Francis Bouchet had migrated from Charleston, S.C., in 1824 as the valet of the father of Judge A. Heaton Robinson of New Haven and was said to be "prominent" in New Haven's Negro community, serving as a deacon of the Temple Street Church, the oldest Negro church in the city. Edward attended the New Haven High School (1866–1868) and graduated from the Hopkins Grammar School (1870) as valedictorian of his class.

Bouchet entered Yale College in 1870. He was the first of his race to graduate from Yale College, in 1874. On the basis of his outstanding academic record he was elected to Phi Beta Kappa. Although Bouchet was elected to Phi Beta Kappa along with other members of the Yale class of 1874, the election did not take place until 1884, when the Yale chapter was reorganized after thirteen years of inactivity. Because of this circumstance, Bouchet was not, as frequently stated, the first Negro to be elected to Phi Beta Kappa. (George Washington Henderson, elected in 1877 at the University of Vermont, was actually first.) Bouchet continued study at Yale as a graduate student in physics, and wrote a doctoral dissertation on "Measuring Refractive Indices." Awarded the Ph.D in physics in 1876, Bouchet was the first American Negro to earn a doctorate from an American university.

Upon graduation from Yale, Bouchet began his career as a teacher of physics and chemistry for twenty-six years at the Institute for Colored Youth, a Quaker institution in Philadelphia that had earned a reputation for high academic standards since its founding in 1837. When the institute's college preparatory program was discontinued in 1902 at the height of the Du Bois–Washington controversy over industrial vs. collegiate education, Bouchet resigned. The school was moved to Cheyney, Pa., where it was initially a vocational and teacher-training institution; decades later it became Cheyney State College.

From l902 to 1903 Bouchet was a science teacher at the Sumner High School in St. Louis, Mo., where a high quality college preparatory program was maintained. He then served successively as business manager of the Provident Hospital, St. Louis (1903–1904), and U.S. inspector of customs at the Louisiana Purchase Exposition (1904–1905). From 1905 to 1908 Bouchet was director of academics at St. Paul's Normal and Industrial School in Lawrenceville, Va. He was appointed principal of the Lincoln High School, Gallipolis, Ohio, in 1908 and served for five years, until he joined the faculty of Bishop College in Marshall, Texas. Forced by illness to retire from college teaching in 1916, Bouchet returned to New Haven, where he died on Oct. 28, 1918. He never married.

Information on Bouchet is scarce. See Frank Lincoln Mather's *Who's Who of the Colored Race* (1915), p. 31; Harry Washington Greene's, *Holders of Doctorates Among American Negroes* (1946), pp. 140, 145; Herman R. Branson's, "The Negro Scientist: His Sociological Background, His Record of Achievement, and His Potential," in Julius H. Taylor, ed., *The Negro in Science* (1955), p. 5; Phi Beta Kappa, *The Key Reporter* (Spring 1969), p. 8; and Howard University Chapter of Phi Beta Kappa, "Black Americans in the Natural Sciences and the Professions: A Memorial Symposium in Honor of Edward Bouchet" (1975) in the Moorland-Spingarn Research Center vertical file. Especially useful is Yale University's *Biographical Record of the Class of 1874* Part 4, 1874–1909 (1912), and Part 5, 1909–1919 (1919). — MICHAEL R. WINSTON

BOUSFIELD, MIDIAN OTHELLO (1885–1948), physician, insurance executive, and army officer. The son of William Hayman and Cornelia Gilbert Bousfield, he was born in Tipton, Mo. He received an A.B. degree from the University of Kansas in 1907 and in 1909 an M.D. degree from Northwestern University School of Medicine. He interned at Freedmen's Hospital in Washington, D.C. In 1911 he went to Brazil with the intention of practicing there, but disillusioned with the lack of opportunities, he prospected for a short time and then returned to the United States. He worked on the railroad for a year as a barber and porter in order to secure sufficient funds to equip his medical office and to marry Maudelle Brown in 1914. They made their home in Chicago, where he began his practice. Bousfield was school health officer and school tuberculosis physician from 1914 until 1916. In the following years he was consultant to the U.S. Children's Bureau as well as the Chicago Board of Health. In 1934 he served as president of the National Medical Association. Appointed director of the Negro Health Division of the Rosenwald Fund in 1939, he supported the National Association of Colored Graduate Nurses and supervised contributions to Negro medical colleges. A member of the planning committee for the 1940 White House Conference on Children in a Democracy, he served on two subgroups, Children in Racial and Ethnic Minorities, and Public Health and Medical Care. In 1945 he pointed out that there were southern states where at least 20 percent of the Negro population died without a doctor during their last illness. In all, he was a member of advisory committees to more than thirty national, state, and local governmental agencies. He was also a member of the board of Provident Hospital, Chicago, for more than twenty-five years.

During World War II he organized and subsequently became commanding officer of the 1000-bed Station Hospital Number One at Fort Huachuca, Ariz., the first U.S. Army hospital to be staffed entirely by Negro physicians. In the face of criticism against a segregated hospital, he pointed out the lack of an alternative. Bousfield, who retired from the army in 1945, was the first Negro colonel in the Army Medical Corps. He was especially active in promoting work against tuberculosis. He is credited with being responsible for Negro physicians' becoming members of state boards of health.

An incorporator of Liberty Life Insurance Company, Bousfield served the company between 1921 and 1929 as member of the board of directors, medical examiner, vice-president, medical director, and president. After the 1929 merger that created Supreme Liberty Life Insurance Company, he was chairman of the executive committee, vice-president, and medical director, retaining the later two offices until the time of his death. He died of a heart attack at his home, 9323 South Michigan Ave., Chicago; funeral services were held at St. Edmund's Episcopal Church, and he was survived by his widow, Maudelle, principal of Wendell Phillips High School, and a daughter, Mrs. Maudelle Evans.

Articles written by Bousfield include "Major Health Problems of the Negro" (*National Conference of Social Work, Proceedings,* June 1933); "Reaching the Negro Community" (*American Journal of Public Health,* March 1934); "The Home and the Health Education Program" (*JNE,* July 1937); and "An Account of Physicians of Color in the United States" (*Bulletin of History of Medicine,* Jan. 1945).

The best source is the article by Peter Marshall Murray, "Midian O. Bousfield, M.D., 1885–1948" (*JNMA*, May, 1948, p. 120), and an obituary in the *Chicago Daily News* (Feb. 17, 1948, p. 20).

— ADELAIDE JAMES WARD

BOUTELLE, FRAZIER AUGUSTUS (1840–1924), army officer and conservationist. Born on Sept. 12, 1840, in Troy, N.Y., he was the son of James Boutelle from Fitchburg, Mass., and Emeline Lamb Boutelle. He began his army career in 1861 as a member of the Ira Harris Cavalry, subsequently designated as the 5th New York Cavalry Regiment. After serving as quartermaster sergeant, he was commissioned a second lieutenant on Nov. 5, 1862. Participating in the Gettysburg campaign, Boutelle was injured on June 30, 1863, when he fell from his horse during a charge at Hanover, Pa. Consequently, he was assigned to First Brigade, 3rd Cavalry Division, on Jan. 17, 1864, as an ambulance officer. Boutelle did not return to his regiment until he reenlisted in the army in 1864 and he remained with the regiment until he was discharged with the rank of captain on July 10, 1865.

When the U.S. Army was expanded in 1866, Boutelle enlisted in the 1st Cavalry Regiment. Attaining first the rank of sergeant major, he accepted a commission as a second lieutenant on May 8, 1869. Participating in several Indian campaigns, he made his most significant contribution during the Modoc Indian War. For his coolness, gallantry, and efficient service in the engagement at Lost River, Ore., against the Modocs, who were under the command of Captain Jack (Kintpuash), he was awarded the rank of brevet first lieutenant. Boutelle continued to exemplify the high principles of the military service. Therefore on July 1, 1890, Gen. John M. Schofield recommended him for brevet major.

Boutelle served as the regimental adjutant, as a recruiter, and as an inspector of National Guard organizations before he was assigned as the commander of Company K, 1st Cavalry Regiment. It was in this position that he was subsequently appointed as the superintendent of Yellowstone National Park in Wyoming. With his command he not only fought forest fires and prevented hunters from slaughtering the animals which roamed throughout the park area, but he improved the methods of reducing the hazardous conditions which contributed to fires and established regulations which curtailed the activities of hunting expeditions composed of Europeans and easterners who killed animals only for sport. Cognizant of the value of the park's natural resources, he implemented policies which preserved the forests, maintained roads, and established flood-control methods. More significantly, he established a program of not only restocked fishing areas but also stocking streams and rivers which had heretofore been barren or where fish had died because of harmful parasites. Coordinating his activities with Marshall McDonald, commissioner of the U.S. Commission of Fish and Fisheries, he carried out a program that proved to be extremely successful and discovered a formula to eliminate the parasites. This policy was duplicated by other federal superintendents. Additionally, Boutelle agreed to support the National Zoological Park by providing animals from Yellowstone National Park.

Officially Boutelle retired from the army on Aug. 27, 1895; however, he was already serving as the adjutant-general of the Oregon National Guard. Appointed by Gov. John H. McGraw and promoted to the rank of brigadier general, he became the first appointed adjutant-general because his predecessors were all elected officials. Immediately upon assuming his duties he discovered that the guard regulations were unnecessarily burdensome and caused the officers to submit organizational returns which varied in form. Therefore a study was initiated which resulted in a complete revision of the system. A new military code which simplified and standardized reporting procedures was instituted and the Board of Military Auditors was reorganized, thereby ensuring maximum efficiency. Boutelle terminated his services as adjutant-general on Jan. 13, 1897. Advanced to colonel on the U.S. Army Retired List, he served as an army recruiter from Aug. 1, 1905, to Sept. 20, 1918, thus terminating a military career which spanned a period of fifty years.

He married Mary Adolphine Augusto Haydon on Oct. 12, 1873, at Vancouver, Wash. Their son, Henry Moss Boutelle, born on June 17, 1875, in Vancouver, was commissioned a second lieutenant on July 9, 1898. Assigned to Battery H, Third Battalion, 3rd U.S. Artillery Regiment in Manila, Philippines, Henry Boutelle served as the adjutant and the quartermaster of his battalion before he volunteered for a special assignment which consisted of commanding a company of Macabebe Scouts. This assignment was not completed because he was ambushed by insurgents near Aliago and subsequently died on Nov. 2, 1899.

Colonel Boutelle died at the family residence, 2540 34th Ave. South, Seattle, on Feb. 12, 1924. Funeral services were held at the parlor of Bonney Watson Co., and he was survived by his widow, Mary H. Boutelle.

References pertaining to Boutelle's military career are located in the National Archives, Washington, D.C. Among the most significant are the Records of the Adjutant-General, Record Group 94, and the Records of the National Park Service, Record Group 79. For his National Guard experiences, consult the *Sixth Biennial Report of the Adjutant General of the State of Washington, 1895–1896*. His obituary was in the *Seattle Post-Intelligencer* (Feb. 14, 1924, p. 15).

— CHARLES JOHNSON, JR.

BOWEN, JOHN WESLEY EDWARD (1855–1933), Methodist clergyman, denominational official, and educator. He was born in New Orleans on Dec. 3, 1855, the son of Edward and Rose (Simon) Bowen. Edward Bowen, a carpenter, had removed from Maryland to New Orleans, where he was snared into slavery and held in bondage until he purchased his own freedom, and subsequently that of his wife and of his son John, then three years old. Edward Bowen later served in the Union Army during the Civil War.

Themselves more than ordinarily intelligent, industrious, and ambitious, the newly freed parents quickly recognized their son's gifts and directed him in early childhood to the best education that their means and circumstances placed within their reach. They enrolled him in New Orleans University, established for Negroes by the Methodist Episcopal church, and there his basic education was attained, from the first grade up through the bachelor's degree (1878), which he achieved with the institution's first graduating class.

Young Bowen early determined upon the ministry as a career. After a four-year interval (1878–1882) as a teacher of ancient languages at Central Tennessee College (formerly Walden University), he entered the School of Theology of Boston University, where he earned the degree of Bachelor of Sacred Theology in 1885. Two years later the same institution granted him the degree of Doctor of Philosophy, the second Ph.D. degree to be earned by a Negro in America. Later, Gammon Seminary, of Atlanta, Ga., made him its first recipient of the honorary degree of Doctor of Divinity. Meanwhile, in 1886 he had married Ariel S. Hedges of Baltimore; they had four children.

During the three years he spent as a theological student at Boston University (1882–1885) Bowen labored as pastor of a local church, and from 1888 to 1892 he ministered to congregations in Newark, Baltimore, and Washington, serving also, while in Baltimore, as professor of church history at Morgan College, and while in Washington as professor of Hebrew at Howard University (1890–1891).

These were the years when the movement of the first generation of highly trained Negro clergymen into the Methodist Episcopal ministry precipitated a struggle over the representation of these churchmen in the Methodist Episcopal organizational structure, and raised the question of the precise relationship of Negro congregations to the denomination at large. Several decades later the controversy was uneasily resolved by the creation, in 1939, of the church's "Central Jurisdiction," which, with the gradual dismantling of formal segregation in the United States, was abandoned in 1968.

As early as the 1896 General Conference of the Methodist Episcopal church, Bowen was an unsuccessful candidate for the office of bishop, but it was not until the early 1920s that two Negro clergymen, Robert Elijah Jones and Matthew Wesley Clair, were elevated to the episcopacy. In 1892 Bowen became a field secretary for his denomination's Missionary Board, but a year later he was called by Gammon Theological Seminary to its chair of historical theology. The first Negro to attain a regular professorship at Gammon, he succeeded William Henry Crawford, who had resigned to become president of Allegheny College. Bowen continued in his post at Gammon until 1932, when he became professor emeritus, having held also the office of president of the seminary from 1906 to 1910, and thereafter until his retirement the office of vice-president.

Widely respected in Methodist circles as a seminary professor, he won an extensive reputation as a lecturer and pulpit orator of great power and eloquence. He was, for his day, an outspoken critic of racial discrimination, and an exemplar of Negro intellectuals who were pioneers in the categorical affirmation of the equal mental and moral endowments of all men, regardless of race. In addition to pressing for the full and equal assimilation of Negro clergymen in the Methodist establishment, he was especially active in opposing segregation in public transportation, and in the crusade to provide Negro youth with a fully developed system of public high schools in Atlanta.

During his four decades at Gammon he was identified with numerous religious and social enterprises looking to the welfare and advancement of Negro Americans. For a time he was co-editor of the *Voice of the Negro,* and later, of *The Negro,* a periodical which was regarded at the time as the most widely circulated journal then published wholly by Negroes. In 1895 he was chief organizer of a widely noticed three-day "Conference on Africa," which was loosely related to the famous Cotton States Exposition held that year in Atlanta. On another occasion he directed an important convention of young people associated with the Negro section of the Methodist church's Epworth League. Both of these conferences issued substantial volumes of published addresses and proceedings. During 1892–1900 he served as a member of the national Epworth League's Board of Control.

His own Annual Conference delegated him to successive General Conferences of the church, and at three of these assemblies (1896, 1900, 1904) he received a large vote for the episcopacy, in acknowledgement of his standing as the most distinguished Negro clergyman of the Methodist Episcopal church. In the early 1920s, however, when the first Negro bishops of the denomination were elected, he was passed over in favor of younger men. In 1891 and 1901, respectively, he represented the Methodist Episcopal connection in the Ecumenical Conferences of Washington and London.

A Chautauqua lecturer, and a member of the American Historical Association, Bowen was the author of *An Appeal for Negro Bishops, but no Separation* (1912), and of a series entitled *National Sermons* (1892?–1902?). He was also an editor of *Africa and the American Negro . . . Addresses and Proceedings of the Congress on Africa . . . in Connection with the Cotton States . . . Exposition, Dec. 13–15, 1895;* and co-editor, with I. Garland Penn, of *The United Negro . . . Addresses and Proceedings [of] the Negro Young People's Christian and Educational Congress . . . 1902.*

Bowen and his wife were the parents of four children, one of whom, John W. E. Bowen, Jr., a graduate of Phillips Exeter, Wesleyan University, and Harvard, became, like his father, a prominent figure in the Methodist Episcopal church. Bowen's first wife died in 1904 while visiting the World's Fair in St. Louis. In 1906 he married Irene L. Smallwood, who survived him. Bowen himself died on July 20, 1933, the last of his New Orleans University graduating class, and the school's oldest alumnus. He was survived by his widow, a son John W. E. Jr., and two daughters, Irene and Mrs. Juanita Dix.

This sketch is based in part on an extensive interview with J. W. E. Bowen, Jr., on May 26, 1957, in Greensboro, N.C. Basic information is in *Who's Who in America* (1926), and the *National Cyclopedia of American Biography* (1917, 14:361). A perceptive evaluation is J. R. Van Pelt's "John Wesley Edward Bowen" (*JNH,* April 1934, pp. 217–21). — RICHARD BARDOLPH

BOWERS, THOMAS J. (1836–1885?), musician. He was born in Philadelphia, Pa. An outstanding young tenor in the mid-nineteenth century, he was compared favorably with the leading world tenors of that day. He was consistently called "Mario," "the colored Mario," "the American Mario," or "the Indian Mario" after the renowned Italian tenor Conte di Candia Mario.

His father was the warden of St. Thomas's Episcopal Church in Philadelphia, where sacred music was sung as early as 1800. His first music teacher was his pianist brother John, whom he succeeded as the organist at the church. His youngest sister Sara Sedgwicke Bowers also became a fine singer. Several bands, including the Frank Johnson band, eagerly sought his services. It was his outstanding singing, however, that won him public acclaim. His vocal training was received under the tutelage of the famous soprano Elizabeth Taylor Greenfield, popularly known as the "Black Swan." Greenfield sang with her own troupe of Negro opera singers, and following a successful tour of London added Bowers to her group. They appeared in Philadelphia, the Midwest, New York, and Canada. His appearance in Philadelphia at Sanson Street Hall in 1854 won approval by the Philadelphia music critics for his light, clear, sweet voice. The midwestern tour was a musical and social success. The acclaim of both Bowers and Greenfield was enhanced by the color of their skin, and many who came out of curiosity to see, remained entranced by what they heard.

Bowers, in addition to his widely acclaimed ability as a musician and an opera singer, was also widely known as a champion of human rights. He would not perform if Negroes were either barred from the concert halls or forced to occupy segregated seats. For instance, he created a disturbance in Hamilton, Ontario, Canada, in 1855 when he refused to sing until an attempt to segregate six colored patrons was stopped. Moreover he was dedicated to the idea of proving to the general public that Negroes were capable of the same level of performance of classical music as anyone else. This attitude did not win friends for him among those music critics who felt that a Negro artist should show humility on the stage. One critic wrote that if Thomas had more modesty, both in dress and demeanor, his voice might entitle him to some credit for his concerts. He further wrote that Bowers's self-esteem was very highly developed and that, despite his claims of Indian origin, he was known among the "boot-black" fraternity from Philadelphia and had been in the choir in one of the African churches for years past.

Despite these types of articles, the music critic of the *Daily Pennsylvanian* commented on Feb. 9, 1854, that Bowers had a naturally superior voice, far better than many of the principal tenors who had been engaged for star opera troupes. Other newspapers of the day, including the *Boston Journal,* shared this opinion. Some of the remarks were as follows: "a voice of wonderful power and beauty"; "second to none of our celebrated opera singers"; "The colored Mario's voice is unequalled by any of the great operatic performers."

The best source is *Music and Some Highly Musical People* (1881) by James Monroe Trotter, who knew Bowers personally. An unpublished manuscript by Arthur Labrew (Baton Rouge, 1974) is the most recent useful study. — ALDRICH W. ADKINS

BOWLES, EVA D[EL VAKIA] (1875–1943), pioneer social worker and YWCA administrator. She was born on Jan. 24, 1875, in Albany, Athens County, Ohio, the daughter of John Hawes and Mary Jane (Porter) Bowles. Her paternal grandfather, the Rev. John Randolph Bowles, was said to be the first Negro teacher to receive a salary from the public school fund in Ohio. During the Civil War he served as chaplain of the 55th Massachusetts Regiment. Her father was the first Negro schoolteacher-principal in Marietta, Ohio. When he discovered that his all-Negro school was the only segregated school in the area, and that it was kept open just to give him a position, he resigned, even though he had no other job in prospect. He subsequently became one of the first Negro railway postal clerks in Ohio, perhaps in the nation.

Although born in Athens, Eva Bowles was reared in Columbus, Ohio. She attended the public schools of that city and in later life continued her education at Ohio State and Columbia Universities. Given the best musical preparation that her community afforded, Bowles was initially trained to teach music to the blind. Her first position, however, was at Chandler Normal School, an American Missionary Association institution in Lexington, Ky. Carrying on the pioneering tradition of her family, she was the first Negro teacher at Chandler. Bowles later taught at St. Augustine's School (later, College) in Raleigh, N.C., and at St. Paul's Normal and Industrial Institute, Lawrenceville, Va.

In 1906 Bowles was called to New York to head a project for Negro women which had been inaugurated by a few churchwomen under the auspices of the YWCA. This early effort eventually became the 137th Street Branch YWCA, for many years the largest Negro branch in the country. As director of this project, Bowles became, to use her term, the first "employed" Negro YWCA secretary in America.

After two years in New York (1906–1908), Bowles was called back to Columbus to become the first Negro caseworker in the Associated Charities of that city. Because of her outstanding work for that organization she was asked to return to New York in 1913, this time to join the staff of the National Board of the YWCA. She was put in charge of the YWCA's work in the cities for Negro girls and women, a position she held, along with others, until her retirement.

In 1917 Bowles was appointed head of the Colored Work Committee of the YWCA's War Work Council and given an appropriation of $200,000 to use in bettering the recreational opportunities of Negro girls and women who were entering industry, most of them for the first time. With this objective in mind, she set up numerous recreational facilities in industrial centers throughout the nation and in communities near army camps. In this project, she was able to call to her assistance, both as full-time workers and as lecturers, an impressive number of outstanding Negro women. Among this group were May Belcher, Crystal Bird, Sara W. Brown, Myra H. Colson, Ruth Anna Fisher, Josephine Pinyon, Ionia Whipper, and Cordella A. Winn.

As a special part of her war project Bowles established fifteen hostess houses in various army camps. The house at Camp Upton in New York so impressed Theodore Roosevelt that he assigned $4000 of his Nobel Peace Prize to be used under Bowles's direction.

In her report on the accomplishments of the Colored Work Committee of the War Work Council, Bowles stated that the war had given colored women the opportunity to prove their ability for leadership. "The time is past for white leadership for colored people. As white and colored women, we must understand each other, we must think and plan together for upon all of us rests the responsibility of the girlhood of our nation" (*The Work of Colored Women* [1919?], p. 132). She did not want an all-black YWCA, and she fought vigorously against those forces within the association seeking to create a permanent "colored department." On the other hand she did not want an organization in which all of the decisions were made by a white leadership. Her objective was what she called "branch relationship," which in essence meant that Negro women should share fully and equally in all activities of the YWCA, whether as members or workers (*The Work of Colored Women*, pp. 7–8).

Bowles believed that the YWCA was "the pioneer in interracial experimentation" (*New York World,* June 8, 1930) and she wanted it to carry on in that tradition. She presented her position on many Negro and white college campuses throughout the nation, at many regional YWCA conferences, and to numerous local boards of city branches. Although by no means "militant," Bowles believed strongly in the principles adumbrated in her 1919 report, and when she felt that the National Board's 1932 reorganization plan would diminish "participation of Negroes in the policy making" of the association, she resigned in protest, though far from retirement age. A short feature article in the *Woman's Press* (July 1932) stated that "she had the vision of a truly interracial movement in the Y.W.C.A. and has never deviated from it."

After leaving the YWCA, Bowles worked for a short while as an executive of the National Colored Merchants Association (CMA stores). During the 1940 presidential campaign she was a Harlem organizer for the Wendell Willkie Republicans. From January 1934 to June 1935 she served as acting secretary of the West End Branch of the Cincinnati YWCA.

Eva D. Bowles died of cancer in Richmond, Va., on June 14, 1943, while on a visit to her niece, Mrs. Arthur P. Davis, and she was buried in the Bowles family plot, in Columbus, Ohio.

The most recent published account is the sketch by Jean Blackwell Hutson in the *NAW* (1971, 1:214–15). For the World War I years, *The Work of Colored Women* (1919?), compiled by Jane Olcott Walters, is the best source. The Moorland-Springarn Research Center, Howard University, has a mimeographed copy of "Colored Work 1907–1920," which gives *inter alia* an account of Bowles's early years in the YWCA. A carbon copy of her letter of resignation from the National Board of the YWCA, dated April 1, 1932, is in the possession of the contributor. The records in the office of the National Board of the YWCA, New York City, contain Bowles's official reports. Articles by Miss Bowles include: "The Colored Girls in Our Midst" (*Association Monthly,* Dec. 1917), "Race Relations in the Light of Social Research" (*Woman's Press,* Feb. 1929), "Negro Girls in Clerical Occupations" (ibid., July 1929), and "The Y.W.C.A. and Racial Understanding" (ibid., Sept. 1929). There is a short obituary in *Woman's Press* (Sept. 1943). — CLARICE WINN DAVIS

BOYD, HENRY ALLEN (1876–1959), publisher, church leader, and banker. The son of Richard Henry Boyd and Hattie Moore, Henry Allen Boyd was born in Grimes County, Tex.,on April 15, 1876, and grew up in San Antonio. During the early 1870s his father, a former slave and Texas cowboy, received the call to the ministry and launched a successful career as minister, church promoter, and race entrepreneur. More than any of his eight brothers and sisters, Henry Allen identified with his father's aggressive concern for race achievement and personal initiative. While still in his teens the younger Boyd attained a clerkship in the San Antonio post office (the first Negro to hold such a position), and he held this post until he moved his wife and young daughter to Nashville, Tenn., just before the turn of century. Nashville remained his residence until his death in 1959.

Richard Henry Boyd had become active in the politics and home mission work of the National Baptist Convention, and in 1896 he attained the office of secretary of the denomination's Home Mission Board. In this same year the elder Boyd parlayed a long-standing friendship with certain officials of the Southern Baptist Convention into the founding of a publishing firm in Nashville for national Baptist literature. Shortly after the National Baptist Publishing Board became operational in 1896, Henry Allen Boyd joined his father as a man "Friday." Neither father nor son had extensive formal education, but the two Boyds served as catalysts for Nashville's Negro community. Richard Henry provided much of the early entrepreneurial initiative and financial backing, but Henry Allen managed, nurtured, and carried a variety of colored business, educational, and church ventures to fruition. The younger Boyd joined his father as an ordained Baptist minister in 1904 and proceeded to combine successfully his business talents with a deep sense of Christian devotion and race pride.

The success of the National Baptist Publishing Board inspired both pride in the hearts of the Boyds and jealousy within the political ranks of the denomination. Part of the resulting dispute centered in the clear intent of Richard Henry Boyd to elevate his son to the position of heir-apparent. Religious conflict ended in the courts, and the Boyds emerged as legal owners of the publishing facilities. The convention divided in 1915, and after his father's death in 1922 Henry Allen Boyd guided the business through several expansions as it became an influential force among twentieth-century publishers of religious material.

Henry Allen Boyd's personal impact, however, probably stemmed more from his race consciousness and his business success than from his church activities. Even the National Baptist Publishing Board made a dual contribution: as a business enterprise it stimulated as much race pride as it did religious devotion. Within the Publishing Board's physical plant were two other reasonably successful business ventures. The National Baptist Church Supply Company made and sold pews, benches, and other church furniture, and the National Negro Doll Company produced black dolls and marketed them nationwide. The father initiated these concerns, but it fell to the son to manage and promote them. Henry Allen Boyd once remarked that "when you see a Negro doll in the arms of a Negro child then you know that the child is being taught a lesson in race pride and race development which will not result in race suicide" (*Nashville Globe,* Sept. 26, 1913). It was therefore a combination of race pride and business ethic which pushed Boyd to expand his economic horizons.

In 1905, when the Nashville Negro community had launched a streetcar boycott in protest against newly imposed Jim Crow laws, Richard Henry Boyd financed, and Henry Allen Boyd managed, the publication of a new Negro newspaper, the *Nashville Globe,* Utilizing the printing facilities and expertise of the Publishing Board, the younger Boyd generated a well-edited and issue-oriented paper which was published weekly for over forty years and spearheaded a multitude of local and statewide race reforms and campaigns. A contemporary later recalled that "he had various titles, but H. A. Boyd was the *Globe.*" Boyd also served as an early organizer and corresponding secretary of the National Negro Press Association.

One of Henry Allen Boyd's major civic campaigns involved the creation of a state-supported college for Negroes in Tennessee. His efforts, both personally and through the *Globe,* were instrumental not only in lobbying for the creation in 1911 of the Tennessee Agricultural and Industrial State Normal School (now Tennessee State University), but also in securing its location in Nashville and in lending support to its early administrators, notably William Jasper Hale. His interest in higher education for Negro Americans would also lead him to trusteeships at both Meharry Medical College and Fisk University.

Heavily influenced by his father's example, Henry Allen Boyd occupied an important position on the cutting edge of black capitalism. In 1903 Richard Henry Boyd founded the One Cent Savings Bank and Trust Company (now the Citizens Savings Bank and Trust Company), and Henry Allen took over direction of the enterprise after his father's death. Following very conservative business practices, Boyd pulled the bank through the Depression years, while most of the country's Negro banking institutions closed their doors. Financial conservatism did not mean inaction. Boyd invested widely in Negro business enterprises, buying initial stock in, among others, a Jacksonville, Fla., real estate project, Atlanta's Standard Life Insurance Company, and the Supreme Liberty Life Insurance Company of Chicago. Boyd served as a longtime director and emeritus director of the latter firm.

As a driving force, race pride played perhaps the most important role in Henry Allen Boyd's multifaceted career.

After ill health for several years and two major opera-

tions, he died of pneumonia on May 28, 1959, at Hubbard Hospital, Nashville. His funeral was held on June 3 at Mount Olive Baptist Church and he was buried in Greenwood Cemetery. He was survived by a daughter, two sisters, and a brother (*Nashville Banner,* May 28, 1959, p. 10, and May 29, p. 6; *Pittsburgh Courier* [national edition] June 6, p. 1).

For the early history of the National Baptist Publishing Board, see Richard H. Boyd's *A History of the National Baptist Publishing Board. The Why, How, When, Where and By Whom It Was Established* (1915). One of the best sources for his activities is the *Nashville Globe.* See also Lester C. Lamon's *Black Tennesseans, 1900–1930* (1977). — LESTER C. LAMON

BOYD, RICHARD HENRY [born Dick Gray] (1843–1922), Baptist leader, publisher, banker, and manufacturer. Boyd was born into slavery as Dick Gray on the Gray family plantation in Nexubee County, Miss., in March 1843. His mother, Indiana Dixon, was born in Richmond, Va., sold to slave traders about 1840, carried to Mississippi, and then acquired by the Gray plantation. In all she gave birth to seven boys and three girls. In 1849 the Gray family left Mississippi and reestablished themselves in Washington County, Tex., near the town of Branham. During the Civil War some members of the family joined the Confederate forces and had Dick accompany them. The plantation owner and two of his sons were killed near Chattanooga, but Dick and the youngest son survived and returned to Texas, whereupon the slave was given the responsibility of managing the plantation.

When Emancipation went into effect Gray successively became a cotton trader, cowboy, and then a sawmill hand. In 1867 he dropped the name by which he had been known as a slave and became Richard Henry Boyd. After Emancipation Boyd attempted to equip himself with a rudimentary education using *Webster's Old Blue Black Speller* and *McGuffey's First Reader.* The year 1869 was momentous for Boyd. During that year he entered Bishop College in Marshall, Tex., became a Baptist preacher, and married Hattie Moore. Although he did not remain in college long enough to graduate, he did have a long and influential career as a Baptist leader, and his marriage, which lasted for the duration of his life, resulted in nine children.

In 1870 Boyd organized the first Negro Baptist Association in Texas, starting with only six churches. He pastored and organized churches in Waverly, Old Danville, Navasota, Crockett, Palestine, and San Antonio during the twenty-six years of his ministry in the state. He was selected to represent Texas Baptists at the Centennial Exposition in 1876. He served as secretary of home missions of the National Baptist Convention from 1896 until 1914. While serving in that capacity he was credited with having fostered the development of four Panamanian churches during the years when the canal was being constructed. Boyd held the positions of secretary and treasurer of the National Baptist Publishing Board from 1896 until 1922. He also was a delegate to the World Baptist Alliance meeting in London in 1905.

In 1896 Boyd moved to Nashville and founded the

National Baptist Publishing Board. In 1912 the physical plant of the Publishing Board was valued at over $350,-000. During the first eighteen years of its existence it issued over 128 million periodicals. Boyd was also one of the organizers of the Citizens Savings Bank and Trust Company of Nashville, and served as its first president from 1904 until 1922. In 1906 he became the first president of the Nashville Globe Publishing Company which issued a newspaper called the *Nashville Globe.* Boyd also founded the National Negro Doll Company which began distribution of Negro dolls in 1911. He was a life member of the National Negro Business League.

In 1909, at the request of the National Baptist Convention, Boyd compiled a small volume entitled *The Separate or "Jim Crow" Car Laws or Legislative Enactments of Fourteen Southern States.* In his introduction to this compendium of "Jim Crow" legislation, Boyd stressed that it was "the imperative duty of every Negro" to make legal protests whenever the separate accommodations provided for them were not "equal," as was required by law. In addition to that book, he authored or edited fourteen others for the Baptist denomination. Among them were *Baptist Catechism and Doctrine* (1899), *The National Baptist Pastor's Guide* (1900), and *National Baptist Commentary* (1904).

In 1915 Boyd became embroiled in a controversy over whether the National Baptist Convention should have become an incorporated body. Those opposing incorporation were known as the "Boyd faction." They feared that such a change would have altered the traditional voluntary nature of Baptist associations by giving the convention legal control over all the organizations and property that were identified with it. That was a particularly ominous prospect for Boyd, who had established the National Baptist Publishing Board largely through his own initiative and with his own funds. The conflict resulted in the formation of two Baptist conventions, one incorporated and the other unincorporated. Boyd and the Publishing Board were, of course, part of the latter group. Following the split, the incorporated convention initiated an unsuccessful legal battle to wrest control of the Publishing Board from Boyd's group.

Boyd suffered a cerebral hemorrhage and stroke on Saturday, Aug. 19, 1922. He died at his home in Nashville on Wednesday, Aug. 23, at 8:30 P.M. At midnight on Sunday, Aug. 26, the Thirty-second Degree Masons, of which he was a member, held fraternal rites for him at the Mount Olive Baptist Church, the same church in which the inaugural meeting of the National Baptist Publishing Board had taken place thirty-six years earlier. A larger service was held the next day at the Ryman Auditorium. According to a report appearing in the *Chicago Defender,* approximately 6000 people were in attendance. Interment took place at the Greenwood Cemetery in Nashville.

Boyd was survived by his widow, Hattie Moore Boyd; three daughters, Annie B. Hall, Lula B. Landers, and Mattie B. Johnson; and by two sons, Theophilus Bartholomew Boyd and Henry Allen Boyd. Also surviving were three of Boyd's sisters and four brothers.

Henry Allen Boyd succeeded his father as secretary-treasurer of the Publishing Board, and following his own death in May 1959, supervision of the business was passed on to his nephew, Theophilus B. Boyd, Jr.

The best source for information on Boyd's involvement in the development of the National Baptist Publishing Board is his *A Story of the National Baptist Publishing Board* (1915). A shorter, heavily illustrated description of the Publishing Board with some biographical information can be found in W. N. Hartshorn's *An Era of Progress and Promise 1863–1910* (1912, pp. 73–76). Fairly good biographical sketches appear in the *Chicago Defender* (Sept. 2, 1922, pp. 1 and 2), *Nashville Banner* (Aug. 24, 1922, p. 7), and Samuel W. Bacote's *Who's Who Among the Colored Baptists of the United States* (1912, pp. 73–76). A balanced account of the 1915 split in the ranks of National Baptists can be found in "The Baptist Controversy" (*The Crisis* 11 [April 1916]: 314–16). An account of the event that is hostile to Boyd's position can be found in Lewis G. Jordan's *Negro Baptist History U.S.A. 1750–1930* (1930, pp. 127–36).

— REGINALD F. HILDEBRAND

BRAGG, GEORGE FREEMAN, JR. (1863–1940), Episcopal priest, civil rights leader, editor, and author. The son of George Freeman and Mary Bragg, he was born on Jan. 25, 1863, in Warrenton, N.C. Two years later the family moved to Petersburg, Va., where they joined his paternal grandmother, Caroline Wiley Bragg, who had been the house slave of an Episcopal rector. Before she died at the age of eighty-six, she saw four of her sons join three other Negro vestrymen in founding St. Stephen's Church for Negroes in Petersburg (1867). George's father was a junior warden and his mother was highly respected by the white people of Petersburg. George Jr., who had been baptized in Immanuel Episcopal Church in Warrenton, studied in the elementary school in Petersburg and St. Stephen's Parish and Normal School. He delivered newspapers and won the favorable attention of John Hampden Chamberlayne, editor of the *Petersburg Index* who employed him as a valet. In 1879 he entered the Theological School for Negroes in Petersburg, a branch of the Virginia Theological Seminary in Alexandria, Va. He was suspended the next year because the rector, a former Confederate officer, adjudged Bragg "not humble enough." His suspension was probably due also to his campaigning for the "radical" Readjuster party, which greatly increased taxes on corporate wealth and rewarded him with several minor positions.

After a serious case of typhoid fever in 1883, Bragg taught school in Staunton, Va., continued his theological studies under private tutors, and after a change of rectors, in 1885 reentered the theological school, which was renamed in 1886 the Bishop (John) Payne Divinity School. On Jan. 12, 1887, he was ordained a deacon. On Sept. 20, 1887, he married Nellie Hill, who became the mother of their four children. He was ordained a priest on Dec. 19, 1888, in St. Luke's Church, Norfolk. He increased the size of the congregation, built a church and rectory, and repaired the school. He founded the Industrial School for Colored Girls and opened the Holy Innocents Mission, later renamed

Grace Church. He also opened a mission in Portsmouth, renamed the St. James Mission after he became (1891) rector of St. James Church in Baltimore. During these fruitful years he served also as one of the state's curators of the Hampton Normal and Industrial Institute, as well as chaplain of the second battalion of Colored Militia and secretary of the National Colored Association.

He became rector of the declining St. James Church in Baltimore on Nov. 17, 1891. Its sixty-nine communicants were worshipping in rented quarters and financially dependent on the bishop. Within a few years Bragg made the parish self-supporting, purchased a rectory and a lot, and built a new church. By 1931 the church numbered 500 communicants and gave $1000 annually to charities. More than twenty men entered the ministry through his influence. After nearly forty-nine years as rector, he died after a very brief illness on March 12, 1940. His funeral was held on March 15 at St. James Protestant Episcopal Church, Arlington and Lafayette Avenues, Baltimore.

Bragg was an active leader in Negro social and educational movements. In 1884 he was an honorary commissioner of the New Orleans Exposition. His work in Norfolk helped to prepare the way for William Alpheus Hunton to become the first colored YMCA general secretary. His major achievement in Baltimore was the founding in 1899 of the Maryland Home for Friendless Colored Children. His philosophy of child welfare, advanced for his time, insisted on a homelike atmosphere, kept routine to a minimum, and placed boys in foster homes at the age of twelve or thirteen. In 1912 the home was moved to a farm near Catonsville, Md. Bragg was also a member of the board of the House of Reformation for Colored Boys at Cheltenham, Md. He was an associate of Booker T. Washington, and worked covertly with him to defeat disfranchisement in Maryland. He also led the fight to have Negro teachers appointed in Negro schools in Baltimore. In 1905, however, he became a supporter of William E. B. Du Bois in the Niagara Movement, which opposed the conservative policies of Booker T. Washington and was a forerunner of the NAACP.

Bragg believed that Negro "Manhood and Freedom" would be best promoted by understanding and cooperation by the best of both races. By the "best" he meant educated, refined, moral, and economically productive persons. The Episcopal church, he believed, was the leading national institution where such interaction between races occurred. He therefore vigorously denounced racial discrimination within the church, especially the exclusion of Negroes from church synods. When he realized that segregation was being accomplished by diocesan action, he became the chief advocate of a Negro missionary district under a Negro bishop. He constantly urged white Episcopal authorities to actualize their catholic principles and his Negro colleagues to become self-supporting. Their lack of militancy, he said, was due to dependence on bishops for their salaries.

Bragg never became a bishop. When Bishop James Theodore Holly died in 1911, the U.S. minister to Haiti petitioned the bishops for Bragg's appointment to suc-

ceed Holly; however they selected a white clergyman. Again in 1917 when the Diocese of Arkansas decided to elect a Negro suffragan bishop, Bragg was not chosen although he seems to have been the preference of the Negro clergy of the diocese.

Bragg edited and published with his own press a newspaper during his adult life. He taught typesetting to his own sons and other young men who worked with him, such as Benjamin G. Brawley. For four years, beginning in 1882, he published the *Lancet,* one of the first Negro weeklies in Virginia. He disposed of it and in 1886 founded the *Afro-American Churchman* which became the *Church Advocate.* Shortly after coming to Baltimore he began the *Ledger,* which later merged with the *Afro-American,* purchased in 1896 by his parishioner, John H. Murphy, Sr. For a while he also published a monthly, the *Maryland Home.* He was at one time secretary of the National Colored Press Association.

Bragg was a pioneer writer on the history of Negro Episcopalians and Negro Marylanders. He published more than twenty historical pamphlets, including *The Story of the First of the Blacks, The Pathfinder, Absalom Jones, 1746–1818* (1929). His major work, *The History of the Afro-American Group of the Episcopal Church* (1922), is still the only book on that subject.

Much biographical information is scattered throughout his writings, especially *A Bond-Slave of Christ: Entering the Ministry Under Great Difficulties* (1912) and *The Colored Harvest of the Old Virginia Diocese* (1901). See also the *Baltimore Afro-American* (Jan. 9, 1937; March 16, 1940; and March 23, 1940). Mildred Louise McGlotten's "Rev. George Freeman Bragg, A Negro Pioneer in Social Welfare" (M.A. thesis, Howard University, 1948) is indispensable. There are obituaries in *JNH* (July 1940, pp. 399–400) and the *Baltimore News-Post* (March 12, 1940, p. 26).

— J. CARLETON HAYDEN

BRAITHWAITE, WILLIAM STANLEY BEAUMONT (1878–1962), poet and anthologist. Braithwaite was born in Boston, where he spent most of his life. His father, William Smith Braithwaite, a native of British Guiana, could boast a distinguished background of English, French, and Creole Negro ancestry. He had studied medicine in England, where he apparently ran through a "considerable legacy" from his French grandmother, but did not attain a degree. When he migrated to Boston in the early 1870s he found employment as a physician's assistant. In 1875 he married Emma DeWolfe, the eldest of the three illegitimate near-white daughters of a mulatto ex-slave who had made her way north immediately after the Civil War. William Stanley was the second of the five children of this marriage. So long as the father lived, the children were taught at home and taught not only the lessons from the standard primers of the period: they were taught French, for instance; they learned the ritual of the Church of England; and they were trained in the tea-time manners of an upper-class British family. If little "Willie" (as the family called him) seemed to make small use of these lessons then, he was nevertheless strongly influenced by his father, and especially—though to a gradually lessening degree as time passed—by his father's attitudes about race, which in the first place had led the older Braithwaite to seek a wife "with no distinquishable [Negro] racial features or characteristics," and in the second place, to count only whites—and these "some of the most eminent citizens of Boston"—among his friends. The father was quite frankly a cultural and social snob. He had no faith in the American system of public education, and on the written testimony of his son, "did not believe that any children were good enough to associate with his own." But when the father died in 1884, he left the family destitute. One child, a girl, had died in infancy, and of the four remaining, Eva was only nine, Willie seven, Arthur two, and Rosie one. Immediately following her husband's death, the widow went to work as a domestic; later she filled the house with lodgers. Eva and Willy were sent to public school. In the course of the next five years William Stanley advanced from kindergarten through grammar school—a fact that suggests a sharper than average intelligence—and there his formal education ended.

Times were desperate for the Braithwaite family, and Willie, though not yet thirteen, was sensitive to the economic struggle his mother could not win alone. He abandoned his hope of finishing high school and going on to Harvard. His still childishly vague ambitions hung suspended in the obscurity of the uncertain future. He quit school and took full-time employment. Referring to this period of his life many years later, Braithwaite wrote, "The brief past of my existence was suddenly loaded with something precious that was beyond enjoyment or possession, and what beckoned ahead was confused and menacing. Out of the confusion and menace, I had to shape a destiny." (*Phylon,* 1941).

His destiny began to take shape almost by accident and certainly by virtue of the confluence of intellectual and spiritual resources he did not even know he possessed. After two or three years as errand boy and porter in several commercial establishments, at the age of sixteen he found employment in the press rooms of Ginn and Company, Publishers. He was hired as an errand boy again, and at first, as with earlier jobs, the wage was everything. But gradually his curiosity and a sense of wonder grew. He watched the compositors setting type from "manuscript"—a word that was new to him, as was indeed much of the language of the publishing trade; the machines flicking off sheet after sheet of printed matter; the women bent over desks scarcely lifting their eyes from the "proof sheets," which it was his job to carry to the editorial offices several blocks away. What were these lines of printed words about? He began to read in snatches of curiosity, and the superintendent of the composing rooms encouraged him and lent him new-bound books, mostly high school and college texts. He read history, folklore, mythology, geography. When he was invited to accept an apprenticeship as a compositor, he grasped the opportunity. His interest in books had developed "into a passion," and his readily acquired skill as a compositor was enhanced by his passion.

The desire to write struck suddenly. "The morning I stood by that window before my case [of type] waiting for copy," he was to state in his autobiography, "I did not know it was a day of annunciation, and that my spirit would magnify the Lord for making me a chosen vessel!" The copy came and he was setting the first line of John Keats's "Ode on a Grecian Urn," when the poem "broke upon both my sense and spirit with the flush of a sunrise," and with an "instantaneous transformation" he wandered into a world of "magical beauty." It was a world he was to inhabit and to invite others to share for nearly all of the remaining sixty years of his life.

His career in that world did not begin at once. It is true that he began writing poetry immediately, but these early poems were, as it were, private maps for identifying and exploring this new universe and for finding his own direction in it. He showed these poems to no one. He stayed on as a compositor for Ginn and Company for several more years, during the latter days of which he began submitting occasional pieces—poems and critical essays—to newspapers and other periodical publications. None of his work could be racially identified, and since in his particular case being Negro had had little influence on either his personal or professional life, there was no reason why it should be. His poems played on the traditional romantic and mystical themes of nineteenth-century British verse and employed the traditional forms and meters. In 1904 he published his first volume, *Lyrics of Life and Love,* but only after guaranteeing the cost of printing. He literally sold the small volume from door to door. Four years later his second book of verse, *The House of Falling Leaves,* was published in the conventional way.

By this time his name was familiar in literary circles. Critical essays and occasional poems had appeared in the *Atlantic Monthly,* the *North American Review,* and *Scribner's,* and he had edited *The Book of Elizabethan Verse* (1906) and *The Book of Georgian Verse* (1908). *The Book of Restoration Verse* was published in 1909. But Braithwaite was to be best known and most admired for the yearly anthologies of magazine verse which he edited from 1913 to 1939, with a selection and an anthology for 1958 and 1959. The early work of several important American poets, including Carl Sandburg, Edgar Lee Masters, and Vachel Lindsay, was brought to wider attention through these volumes. An editorial in the *Boston Transcript* for Nov. 30, 1915, said that he had helped readers as well as poets to understand poetry. "One is guilty of no extravagance in saying that the poets we have—and they may take their place with their peers in any country—and the gathering of deference we pay them, are created largely out of the stubborn self-effacing enthusiasm of this one man. In a sense their distinction is his own. In a sense he has himself written their poetry."

Widely honored by the white literary community, Braithwaite was claimed by Negroes as their own, and in 1918 he was awarded the Spingarn Medal for outstanding achievement by an American Negro, and Talledega College and Atlanta University conferred honorary degrees on him (1918). In 1935 he accepted a professorship in creative literature at Atlanta University, where he remained until 1945. Three years later, Coward McCann published his *Selected Poems.*

Braithwaite died at his home, 409 Edgecombe Ave.,

New York City, on June 8, 1962, after a brief illness. He was survived by his widow, Emma Kelly Braithwaite, three daughters, four sons, four grandchildren, and two great-grandchildren. Funeral services were held at St. Luke's Protestant Episcopal Church, Convent Avenue and West 141st Street, on June 12.

There is no adequate biography and no extensive critical treatment of Braithwaite's work. His uncompleted autobiography, entitled *The House Under Arcturus* and published in three parts in *Phylon* in 1941, is no more than a series of anecdotes and sketches strung loosely together on a thread of subjective observations. Benjamin Brawley devotes seven brief pages to Braithwaite in *The Negro in Literature and Art* (1918) and one page to him in *Negro Builders and Heroes* (1937). "The Twentieth Century's Greatest Negro Anthologist," by Fronzell Spellman in *NHB* (vol. 26, 1963) and Phillip Butcher's "William Stanley Braithwaite's Southern Exposure: Resume and Revelation" in the *Southern Literary Journal* (vol. 3, Spring 1971) suggest the extent to which Braithwaite has been so undeservedly neglected. See also the obituary in the *New York Times* (June 9, 1962, p. 25).

— SAUNDERS REDDING

BRAWLEY, BENJAMIN GRIFFITH (1882–1939), college professor, dean, and author. The second son of Edward McKnight Brawley and Margaret Dickerson Brawley, he was born in Columbia, S.C., where his father taught at Benedict College and pastored a Baptist church. The family moved several times, and although Benjamin attended schools in Nashville, Tenn., and Petersburg, Va., he was later to feel that his principal teachers before high school were his parents. At the age of thirteen he entered the preparatory department of Atlanta Baptist (in 1913 renamed Morehouse) College, and was graduated with a baccalaureate degree in 1901. After one year of teaching in a rural one-room school in Georgetown, Fla., he was appointed an instructor in English and Latin at his alma mater. His summers were spent in study until 1907, when he received a second A.B. degree from the University of Chicago; and in 1908, after a full residential year, an M.A. from Harvard. Then he was promoted to professor of English at Atlanta Baptist College, where he remained until 1910 when he accepted a similar rank at Howard University. In 1911 he was named a member of a newly appointed committee of the faculty of the College of Liberal Arts to supervise the work of candidates for the degree of master of arts (Walter Dyson, *Howard University . . .* [1941], p. 181). On July 20, 1912, he married Hilda Damaris Prowd; they had no children. But Atlanta Baptist wanted him back, and in 1912 he returned as professor of English and dean of the college, a dual post he held until 1920. In that year he was persuaded to undertake an educational survey of Liberia. Six months later he returned to the United States, stood for ordination in the Baptist church, and in 1921 became the pastor of the Messiah Baptist congregation in Brockton, Mass. Finding it impossible to minister according to the dictates of his social and religious conscience, he resigned the following year and went back to college teaching, this time at Shaw University, a Bap-

tist institution in Raleigh, N.C., where his aged father was teaching theology, and there he stayed until 1931, when Howard University invited him to rejoin its faculty, where he remained for the rest of his life.

The invitation from Howard was in recognition of his reputation as a scholar, a master teacher, and an occasional poet. It was a reputation that Brawley had nurtured and guarded with some care. On the strength of it, but without arrogance or vanity, in 1927 he had declined the Harmon Foundation's second-place award for excellence in education. Many who had had him as a teacher believed that he deserved first place, and his scholarly output seemed to support their judgment. Since 1913 when he published *A Short History of the American Negro,* he had been producing steadily. Historical essays, social commentaries, and book reviews had appeared under his signature in *The Dial,* in *Lippincott's Magazine,* in the *Springfield Republican, The Bookman,* the *Harvard Monthly,* and the *Sewanee Review,* among others, with commendable frequency since 1916. Although the subject matter of most of these pieces, and of several books which came later, and of the lectures he delivered under the auspices of the Society of Friends at a number of white colleges, was Negro History, culture, and biography, he did not neglect English literature. He published *A Short History of the English Drama* in 1921, *A New Survey of English Literature* in 1925, and a textbook manual for teachers entitled *Freshman Year English* in 1929. *A History of the English Hymn* was to follow in 1932. Some of his books on English literature, and especially the *New Survey,* were adopted as texts in several institutions of higher learning, and were recommended reading in others.

Brawley's principal concerns, however, were the intellectual and social development of his people, popularizing the substantive facts of the Negro experience in the United States, and appealing to white America's sense of justice and truth. He worked as hard to enlighten the white audience as to inspire the black. All of his major works had this emphasis and so did his six booklets of poems, though to a lesser degree. His verse is ignored now, but *The Negro in Literature and Art,* first published in 1918, was revised and republished as *The Negro Genius* in 1937, and has been twice reprinted. *Paul Laurence Dunbar: Poet of his People* (1936) is still an excellent biography of that important poet, and *A Social History of the American Negro* (1921) was, in 1971, still important and authoritative enough to be reissued.

Excluding his book reviews, of which there were many, and his six booklets of poems, Benjamin Brawley wrote twenty-three scholarly articles, including several in the *Dictionary of American Biography,* and seventeen books, a half dozen of which many reputable scholars consider "standard."

He died on Feb. 1, 1939, after a brief illness following a stroke at his home, 1201 Harvard St. NW in Washington, D.C. He was survived by his widow, Hilda Prowd Brawley, two sisters, three brothers, two nieces, and one nephew. Funeral services were held at the 19th Street Baptist Church on Feb. 6. Walter H. Brooks presided and delivered the eulogy; Benjamin Mays, dean of the School of Religion, Howard University, also spoke. All campus activities at Howard University were suspended for the day. Interment was in Lincoln Memorial Cemetery, Suitland, Md.

The best sources of information are the *National Cyclopedia of American Biography,* the *North Carolina Historical Review* (vol. 34), and John W. Parker's memoir in *Phylon* (vol. 10, no. 1). See obituaries in the *New York Times* (Feb. 7, 1939, p. 19) and the *Afro-American* (Feb. 11, 1939). — SAUNDERS REDDING

BRAWLEY, EDWARD MCKNIGHT (1851–1923), minister and college president. Brawley was born of free parents, James M. and Ann L. Brawley, in Charleston, S.C. Until he was nine he attended a private school taught by an elderly lady. When he was ten his parents sent him to Philadelphia where he studied for three years in grammar schools and at the Institute for Colored Youth until 1866. He was apprenticed to a barber in Charleston from 1866 to 1869, worked as a journeyman in Philadelphia for a few months, and in the fall of 1870 entered Howard University in Washington, D.C., its first full-time theology student. Three months later, determined on a college career, he transferred to Bucknell University, Lewisburg, Pa., in January 1871. When he graduated in 1875, Bucknell's first Negro student, he was ordained a minister by a council vote of the white Baptist church in Lewisburg where he had been preparing.

Commissioned to do missionary work by the American Baptist Publication Society, Brawley's first assignment was to organize Sunday schools in South Carolina in every association. When formed into a state convention in 1877, there were as many Sunday schools as churches. He also raised funds for Benedict College, where he taught. As he wrote much later in *The Negro Baptist Pulpit* (1890), "The great need . . . of our colored churches is instruction in our denominational principles." The people "need to understand fully *why* they are Baptists."

In October 1883, partly because of ill health, Brawley accepted the position of president of the Alabama Baptist Normal and Theological School; within a year, as a result of his efforts, the school was renamed Selma University. Meanwhile, in January 1877 he had married Mary W. Warrick, who had received a normal school certificate from Howard University in 1876. At the end of 1877 both wife and child were dead. In December 1879 he married Margaret Dickerson, by whom he had four children. He received his M.A. degree from Bucknell in 1878 and an honorary Doctor of Divinity degree from the State University, Louisville, Ky., in 1885. When his second wife's health failed, he moved back to South Carolina as president of Morris College, which he had helped to found. From 1912 to 1920 he served as minister at the White Rock Baptist Church in Durham, N.C. The last three years of his life were as professor of Old Testament history and evangelism at Shaw University in Raleigh. When he died on Jan. 13, 1923, his funeral was attended, *The Crisis* reported, by "a great concourse of people at White Rock Baptist Church."

In addition to being a persuasive and successful minister, Brawley was an energetic and exceedingly fine speaker and writer. Author of a textbook on evangelism, *Sin and Salvation* (rev. ed., 1927), he edited the *Baptist Tribune,* a weekly denominational organ, and *The Evangel,* a monthly pamphlet. His most important editorial work, *The Negro Baptist Pulpit* (1890), was a collection of twenty-eight sermons and papers, four of which he wrote. Many of his own sermons and papers were published separately. Always he showed his interest in the relationship between education, religion, and morality. In a commencement address "Our Schools and Our Students," delivered in 1889 at Roger Williams University, Nashville, Tenn., he said, "We need a membership prepared by grace and education that will be able to take hold and do their duty. . . . We seek not the training of the head only, but, ever and above that, we seek the culture of the soul."

In *The Negro Baptist Pulpit* Brawley developed an assimilationist thesis that is still very controversial. Looking at the helping hands of America's white Christians, he felt that the opportunities offered to "colored Baptists" were intended to develop Negroes "into American Christians. An *American* Christianity, not a race or sectional one, was the aim." In short, the Negro "must be made a citizen, an American citizen, a Christian American citizen—nothing less."

In retrospect, Edward Brawley can be appreciated for his challenging mind, his successful missionary and evangelical work, his accomplishments at Selma College and Morris College, and his sermons and papers. As he wrote in 1889, and the words sum up his work and belief, "we are amazed at the wonderful change, and with the most profound thanksgiving we are led to exclaim, 'what hath God wrought.' " His son, Benjamin Brawley, wrote that his father, "possessor of an unusually logical mind, was known for years as an outstanding scholar of his denomination, and especially excelled as a teacher of preachers and a writer of Church and Sunday School literature."

The major source for his early career is William J. Simmons's *Men of Mark . . .* (1887, pp. 908–13). For his later career, see *The Crisis* (Dec. 1920, p. 75, and May 1923, p. 31). — DANIEL WALDEN

BROOKS, ARTHUR (1861–1926), employee of presidents and army officer. Born on Nov. 25, 1861, in Port Royal, Va., to William and Elizabeth Hall Brooks, he arrived in the District of Columbia at an early age and was later employed as a laborer until he applied for employment in the federal government. Brooks served in several positions but the most significant was as the custodian for the Executive Mansion. Simultaneously, he was actively involved in military activities. Enlisting in the National Guard, Brooks subsequently commanded the 1st Separate Battalion from 1897 until he retired in 1912. He was also appointed as the instructor for the colored high school cadets of Washington, D.C. Praised for his keen sense of devotion and loyalty, he was a member of the White House staff until his death on Sept. 7, 1926.

Brooks's military career began in the Washington Cadet Corps under Capt. Christian A. Fleetwood. Serving as a first lieutenant in Company A, he was promoted to captain when his company was reorganized into the 6th Battalion of the District of Columbia Militia on July 2, 1887. When this battalion was subsequently redesignated as the 7th Battalion on April 22, 1889, and as the 1st Separate Battalion in 1891, he continued as the commander of Company A until Dec. 10, 1897, whereupon he was selected as the battalion commander, with the rank of major. Brooks held this position until he retired on July 15, 1912, and was immediately promoted to the rank of lieutenant-colonel on the National Guard Retired List. For his continuous service in the National Guard he was awarded a gold medal for twenty-five years of militia service.

Brooks did not participate in any military engagements during his service with the National Guard. Although recommended for the command of a colored regiment during the Spanish-American War, he was not selected for any military duties. His command was mobilized briefly in 1898, however, but none of its personnel were utilized for the war effort. Aside from the annual ceremonies performed by his battalion, the most prominent event for him was the presidential inauguration parade. Participating in several of them, Brooks was also selected as a member of the subcommittee for colored visitors during the inauguration of Theodore Roosevelt in 1905.

Brooks succeeded Major Fleetwood as the instructor of the colored high school cadets on Oct. 15, 1888. Analogous to the 1st Separate Battalion, the Cadets established themselves as participants in the inaugural parades under Brooks. Reorganized and furnished the necessary arms and equipment under legislation enacted by Congress, the Cadets were impressive in their first inaugural parade on March 4, 1893. Brooks remained instructor of the Cadets until Nov. 30, 1918, when he obtained a special leave of absence in order to accompany Woodrow Wilson to Europe. Some of the cadets trained by him, notably Charles H. Houston and Campbell C. Johnson, won commissions after completion of training at Fort Des Moines, Iowa (June–Oct. 1917).

Brooks's civilian endeavors were as impressive as his military accomplishments. Employed by the federal government in Washington, D.C., as a stabler in the Quartermaster Department on Jan. 27, 1881, he was subsequently accepted as an assistant messenger in the War Department on Dec. 13, 1881. Functioning in this capacity until March 5, 1885, Brooks was promoted to messenger during the administration of Grover Cleveland. He also served as the doorkeeper for the secretary of war, and on July 1, 1899, he was appointed foreman of the laborers. Receiving annually $1000, he eventually became the chief messenger in the War Department.

Former Secretary of War William H. Taft was obviously impressed by his performance on duty, both as the chief messenger in the department and as the commander of the 1st Separate Battalion. Immediately upon his inauguration on March 4, 1909, he selected Brooks as the doorkeeper for the White House. During his tenure at the White House, which extended over a period of seventeen years, Brooks utilized his knowledge of the military to effect a sartorial censorship over the presidential household. Recognized as an authority on dress for all occasions, he quickly became the presidential valet in addition to his other duties. This intimate contact naturally exposed him to the private life of the presidential families, but he never imparted even the most trivial information concerning the occupants of the White House. Consequently, high officials not only confided in him but they also respected his keen judgment of men.

Each president from Taft to Calvin Coolidge recognized Brooks's professional demeanor. Undoubtedly, it was Brooks's loyalty that partially influenced President Wilson's decision to utilize the 1st Separate Battalion in the defense of the capital in 1917, and to take Brooks to Paris during the peace negotiations of 1919. Performing as a clerk custodian (March 26, 1911), with an annual salary of $1400, Brooks became a bonded official at the White House when he was appointed as the custodian of the Executive Mansion in July 1924 by President Coolidge.

It was while serving as the custodian of the executive property, which included the presidential plates, that his services were terminated. Suffering from a heart ailment, he had accompanied the presidential party to the President Coolidge's summer camp at White Pine, N.Y. Physically weakened by a heart attack which forced his return to Washington on July 23, 1926, he never recovered from its effects and died at his home, 1302 S St. NW, on Sept. 7, 1926. Among those paying tribute to him was President Coolidge, who regarded him as one of the finest men in Washington. Brooks was survived by his wife Lula Joy Brooks, his daughter Florence, who was married to James Waters of the Howard University Law School, a grandson Arthur Brooks, and three brothers. His funeral was held at St. Mary's Protestant Episcopal Church where he had been a vestryman for more than thirty years, with interment in Harmony Cemetery.

The most important information on Brooks is located in organizational records of the National Guard in the District of Columbia National Guard Armory; in the contemporary issues of the *Washington Bee,* the *Washington Evening Star,* and the *Washington Post;* in the Christian A. Fleetwood Papers in the Manuscript Division of the Library of Congress, and in the Department of Commerce and Labor, Bureau of the Census, *Official Register, Persons in the Civil, Military and Naval Service of the United States* and *List of Vessels, 1909–1926.* See also his obituary in the *Washington Evening Star* (Sept. 8, 1926, p. 9).

— CHARLES JOHNSON, JR.

BROOKS, WALTER HENDERSON (1851–1945), clergyman, temperance leader, and poet. Born in Richmond, Va., he was the fifth of nine surviving (of twelve) slave children of Albert R. Brooks and Lucy Goode, who had married on Feb. 2, 1839. His paternal grandmother, Peggy Henderson, was of "pure African stock"; family records do not give this information about Judith Goode, the mother of Lucy Goode, but a photograph in the possession of the family shows that Lucy Goode "looked like a white woman." Albert R. Brooks was first a fieldhand, then a hired servant in a

Richmond tobacco factory. Hiring himself out, he owned an "eating-house business," then started a livery stable. With the money thus earned he purchased his wife's freedom in 1862, but he and the children were not freed until 1865. Dr. Brooks often recalled in his sermons the sale in Richmond of one of his sisters. Taught in his youth by his father, who had learned to read and write and had accumulated a sizable library, including Milton's *Paradise Lost,* in 1866 he entered the preparatory school of Lincoln University (Pennsylvania) and graduated with a B.A. in 1872 and a B.D. in 1873. He professed his Christian faith in 1867 and became, along with Archibald Grimké, an elder of the Ashmun Presbyterian Church, which had been organized at Lincoln University in 1868. Probably because his mother had been a member of the First Baptist (later the First African Baptist) Church in Richmond, he was baptized in 1873 in this church by the Rev. James H. Holmes. Shortly thereafter he became a clerk in the Richmond post office and married the pastor's daughter, Eva Holmes. He resigned his clerkship to accept appointment by the American Baptist Publication Society of Philadelphia as Sunday school missionary for Virginia. Formally ordained by the First African Baptist Church, he was licensed to preach on Dec. 24, 1876. From April 1877 to October 1880 he was pastor of the Second African Baptist Church of Richmond. He then went to Louisiana as a Sunday school missionary for the American Baptist Publication Society. On Nov. 12, 1882, he became pastor of the 19th Street Baptist Church, Washington, D.C., where he remained until his death in 1945. The church, which was organized in August 1839, was rebuilt in April 1871 (that building was razed in 1975–1976). After the death of his first wife in 1912, he married Mrs. Florence H. Swann in 1915.

Dr. Brooks (LL.D., Lincoln University, 1929, and D.D., Howard University, 1944) had a notable career as a leader in the temperance cause and pastor of the 19th Street Baptist Church. From 1875 to 1882 he was chaplain of the Anti-Saloon League of the District of Columbia. On the occasion of his eightieth birthday, Francis J. Grimké stated that no one he knew had "spoken more strongly or fearlessly in favor of temperance and against the liquor traffic." Brooks's eloquent sermons depicting the evils of drunkenness contributed to the sobriety of the members of his congregation.

His poems mirrored his religious beliefs, notably "Christ the Burden-Bearer," "Why Jesus Died," "God so Loved the World," "Abiding in Christ," and "Trust in God." The final stanza of this last poem, written Oct. 18, 1932, conveys his basic Christian faith: "Dear Lord, my soul with rapture fill,/ My lips with songs of praise to Thee:/ A present help art Thou, my Lord,/ My hope for all eternity."

Church services were well organized and decorous (although a few older members "became happy" and voiced their happiness). Brooks is remembered for his influence in urging an exemplary life and in preaching scholarly sermons. For more than sixty years Brooks dignified the pulpit and promoted the art of respectability among the members of the congregation.

He denounced not only drunkenness but gambling, fornication, and adultery; he opposed strenuously even

dancing. But he also preached and practiced the social gospel. One of his longest poems (1908), "Africa," questioned whether other parts of the world "be subdued/ to Jesus, Prince of Glory/ And Africa Alone/ Cling to her idols hoary?/ No, let the Truth be known." On the occasion of the fiftieth anniversary of a wedding, another poem pointed out that a couple possessed no fortune but was happy because they possessed a home and a bank account. This poem was published in a colored newspaper, the *Washington Tribune* (June 1930).

A collection was taken regularly for missions, support for which was voiced in a poem "Our Missions," published in the *Mission Herald* (March 1932). An acrostic poem, "The Teacher," (March 15, 1932), to Romain Brown, extolled the profession and urged: "Never shirk one single duty:/ Earn your honors, earn your rest." In "Security" (Oct. 10 and 17, 1932), he urged goodwill, the avoidance of "malice" and "bitterness of spirit." An example of psychology in religion is found in "Be Strong and of Good Courage" (Oct. 9, 1932): "Tax your intellects to fulness:/ Face your problems:/ Leave them not unsolved, to others."

The Sunday school had a library of both religious and secular books. Secular speakers, including Neval H. Thomas, occasionally gave lectures in the Sunday school room, located on the first floor. Declamations by young members also broadened the uses of this room. The National Association of Colored Women was founded (1896) at a meeting in the church.

During the programs commemorating the 100th anniversary of the organization of the church (1939), singers included Madam Lillian Evanti and R. Todd Duncan, who had created the role of Porgy in *Porgy and Bess* (1935). A selection was given by the Washington Concert Orchestra; the Sunday school presented *Saul of Tarsus,* under the direction of the WPA Recreational Project. Guest speakers included Carter G. Woodson; Garnet C. Wilkinson, first assistant superintendent of the D.C. public schools; and Robert P. Daniel, president of Shaw University.

Two clubs were particularly active. The Widow's Mite brought solace and aid to the bereaved. The Helping Hand Club was founded in December 1907; its motto was "It is more blessed to give than to receive" and its theme song was "Scatter Sunshine." Funds raised by nominal dues, rummage sales, and "Miles of Dimes" enabled the club to distribute some $20,000 between 1907 and 1947. Special projects involved visits to St. Elizabeth's Hospital for the mentally ill, dinners at the Stoddard Baptist Home for the elderly and for other old folks and shut-ins (The Helping Hand Club, *The History of the Helping Hand Club of the Nineteenth Street Baptist Church,* 1948).

Brooks gave further evidence of his interest in education and social conditions by his association with John W. Cromwell in the Virginia Historical and Literary Society, as first vice-president under Cromwell of the Bethel Literary and Historical Association in Washington; by serving as a trustee of Nannie H. Burrough's National Training School for Women and Girls and the Stoddard Baptist Home for the elderly in Washington, and of the Virginia Theological Seminary and College,

Lynchburg, Va.; and as a member of the National Baptist Foreign Mission Board, Philadelphia. For many years he was honored by Lincoln University as its oldest living alumnus; in 1935 he was a key figure in the university's nationwide drive to raise $400,000, to which he personally contributed $1000. He wrote several magazine articles, the most important of which were "The Evolution of the Negro Baptist Church" (*JNH,* Jan. 1922) and "The Priority of the Silver Bluff Church and Its Promoters" (*JNH,* April 1922).

Of the nine children by his first wife, Ottie (who married R. L. Jones of Charleston, W.V.), Julia, and Albert were teachers in the District of Columbia public schools; Julia taught English and Spanish (1916–1922) and served as assistant principal of Dunbar High School (1922–1948). As dean of girls, she handled the problems of more than a thousand girls, women teachers, and the entire school; twice she was appointed acting principal (Mary Gibson Hundley, *The Dunbar Story 1870–1955,* 1965). Albert, after serving as a teacher, became principal of Garnet-Patterson Junior High School and was active in the Association for the Study of Negro Life and History, serving as editor of the *Negro History Bulletin* (Jan. 1952–April 1964). Their careers are indicative of those of many of the predominantly middle-class members of 19th Street Baptist Church.

Shortly before 1932 a writer in the *Southern Workman* stated: "Dr. Brooks is a man of deep convictions and keen intellect, and is known throughout the land for his deeply spiritual sermons. Tall, stalwart, strong, he has ever been a good minister of Jesus Christ."

He died of natural causes, and after funeral services in the 19th Street Baptist Church, was buried in Lincoln Memorial Cemetery, Suitland, Md., beside other members of his family.

A brief biographical sketch of Brooks is in his *Original Poems* (1932). The pamphlet, *One Hundredth Anniversary of the Nineteenth Street Baptist Church, 1839–1939; the Fifty-Seventh Anniversary of Rev. Walter H. Brooks, 1882–1939* (1939), contains a valuable history of the church, a sketch of Brooks's life, and several photographs of him as a boy, youth, young man, and at age eighty-eight. The pamphlet also gives brief histories and photographs of several of the church clubs. His granddaughter, Evelyn Brooks Barnett, made available "Some Additional Comments" and a mimeographed "History of the Brooks Family Written by Rev. W. H. Brooks in 1930," with additions by a daughter of Brooks, Antoinette Mitchell. An obituary was published in the *Washington Evening Star* (July 8, 1945) and in *JNH* (Oct. 1945, pp. 459–61). The vertical file, Moorland-Springarn Research Center, Howard University, contains a letter from Pres. Franklin D. Roosevelt to Dr. Brooks (Nov. 2, 1938), which extended hearty congratulations on the completion of his fifty-six years as pastor of the 19th Street Baptist Church and as a "leader" of his race. — RAYFORD W. LOGAN

BROWN, ARTHUR MCKIMMON (1867–1939), surgeon and army civilian employee. The son of Winfield Scott and Jane M. Brown, he was born in Raleigh, N.C. on Nov. 9, 1867. His grandmother, who was one of the first public school teachers in Raleigh, and his parents were concerned that he be educated. Enrolled first in the public school system, he attended Shaw University for two years before returning to the public school system at age fourteen. In 1884 he won a scholarship to Lincoln University in Pennsylvania where he excelled as a student and won the Silver Leaf Glee Club Award. Brown earned an A.B. from Lincoln University in 1888. In the same year he matriculated at the University of Michigan where he studied medicine, serving in the capacity of a medical assistant. He received his M.D. from the institution in 1891; the only member of his class who applied to take the examination of the Medical Board of Alabama, he passed an exceedingly rigid examination.

Brown began his practice in the mining town of Bessemer, Ala., then practiced in Chicago and Cleveland before he established himself as a surgeon in Birmingham, Ala., in 1894, where he engaged also in business and civic activities. His interest in the People's Drug Store made it a very lucrative enterprise in 1895. Additionally, he served as chairman of the Alabama Prison Improvement Board; director of the Alabama Penny Saving Bank; surgeon in the Provident and John C. Hall Hospitals in Birmingham; a member of the surgical staff at the Andrew Memorial Hospital in Tuskegee, Ala.

During the Spanish-American War, Brown was determined to serve in the U.S. Army. Organizing a company of infantry in Birmingham, he offered the services of the group to the governor; however, it was never activated. But the surgeon-general, George M. Sternberg, commissioned Brown a first lieutenant (July 21, 1898) and appointed him as surgeon for an immune regiment in Santiago, Cuba. Upon his arrival Brown was assigned to the U.S. 10th Cavalry. According to Herschel Cashin (*Under Fire with the Tenth Cavalry,* c. 1899), Brown was the only Negro surgeon who served in Cuba, and he also commanded the regiment from Aug. 12 to Oct. 8, 1898. Returning with the regiment to the United States as an acting assistant surgeon and assigned to duty at Huntsville, Ala., he was ordered to proceed with the regiment to Fort McIntosh, Tex., on Jan. 20, 1899. Discharged in April 1899 at Laredo, he was later denied a pension for his services rendered during the war. The director of pensions, who rejected his pension claim on Jan. 22, 1930, stated that Brown was appointed as a contract surgeon in the army from July 22, 1898, to March 8, 1899. Therefore, he was neither a commissioned officer nor an enlisted man in the military service of the United States, but a civilian employee.

Brown was first married to Mamie Lou Coleman from Atlanta, Ga. on June 5, 1895, in Cleveland, Ohio. After her death on Feb. 8, 1903, he married Mamie Nellie Adams of Brimingham on Sept. 27, 1905. Brown, who died on Dec. 4, 1939, was survived by his wife and his children, Arthur, Herald, Walter, and Majorie.

Biographical data about Brown are contained in Herschel Cashin's *Under Fire with the Tenth Cavalry* (c. 1899) and Clement Richardson's *The National Cyclopedia of the Colored Race* (1919). His pension records in the National Archives contain valuable information concerning his military service and genealogy. Brief accounts of his military career are also located within records of the Adjutant-General's Office, Record

Group 94, in the National Archives, Washington, D.C.
— CHARLES JOHNSON, JR.

BROWN, CHARLOTTE HAWKINS (1883–1961), educator, founder of Palmer Memorial Institute, advocate of civil and women's rights. She was born in rural Henderson, Vance County, N.C. According to her later recollections, her slave grandmother, Rebecca Hawkins, was a descendant of the English navigator John D. Hawkins, whose children became prominent slaveholders and traders in Vance County. The fair-skinned, blue-eyed Rebecca, a house maid, married a plantation fieldhand, Mingo Hawkins. Charlotte Hawkins's mother, Caroline Frances Hawkins, was born to this union. Little is known of her father, Edmund H. Hight, a brick mason, who had apparently not married her mother and had separated from the family by the time that Charlotte was born. Both parents had once lived with a part of the white Hawkins family on an adjoining plantation; mother and daughter used the name Hawkins rather than Hight.

One of Charlotte Hawkins's earliest memories was of moving to Boston when she was about seven years old, by wagon on the first leg of the journey, then by train to Norfolk, Va., and finally on a boat to Massachusetts. With her were her mother, brother, and several young aunts. The era, she noted, was one of steady migration in that section of North Carolina for Negroes who regarded Boston as the mecca for "progressive" members of her race.

More comfortable living conditions were available in New England, made possible in part by the financial support afforded by the young girl's stepfather, whom she did not identify. The new environment also nurtured the ideals and friendships which determined her direction in later years. Beginning with her public school education, Charlotte developed the self-confidence and talent for performing in public which subsequently made her an outstanding lecturer. She was chosen graduation speaker of the Allston Allison Grammar School in Cambridge. Before she was twelve she had started a small kindergarten department in the Sunday school of the local Union Baptist Church. At the Cambridge English High and Latin School, the principal became one of her lifetime supporters. She developed her talents in the arts by painting portraits of her fellow students as well as by taking private lessons in art, music, and drama. The entire span of years of her early education, as she later recalled, was singularly free of segregated activities and racial prejudice.

Since her practical mother was unsympathetic to her daughter's original desire for an education at Radcliffe College, Charlotte entered the Massachusetts State Normal School at Salem to prepare for a career in teaching. Although at that time public school teaching in the state did not require a normal school diploma, Charlotte Hawkins, both then and later, sought the fullest educational development.

The occasion for her enrollment at the normal school was fortuitous. It resulted from a casual meeting between the high school senior and Alice Freeman Palmer, who became her closest mentor and benefactor. Mrs. Palmer had been the second president (1881–

1887) of Wellesley College, Wellesley, Mass., and was then a member of the state board of education. She was also the wife of Harvard University professor George Herbert Palmer. Mrs. Palmer interceded to assure the financial assistance which Charlotte Hawkins needed at this stage of her life.

Another chance meeting resulted in the young woman's receiving her first teaching post. While on a train when she was commuting between Boston and Salem, she met the field secretary of the Women's Division of the American Missionary Association. After receiving permission to leave Salem Normal in October 1901, a year earlier than her class, Charlotte Hawkins accepted a position as a missionary teacher in North Carolina. Then eighteen years old, she began her career at Bethany Institute, McLeansville, near Greensboro, where her $30-a-month salary was frequently used to buy clothes for her young Negro pupils. When lack of funds forced the AMA to close the school at the end of that year, Charlotte Hawkins went back to Cambridge with a vision of returning to North Carolina and starting a school of her own. She later wrote that the people who needed what she had to give lived in the land of segregated ideals. She therefore vowed to help break down walls of segregation in American life.

She devoted the remainder of her life to this goal. At the same time she continued to broaden her own education. In addition to receiving the Salem Normal diploma (1901), she studied during the summer and some regular terms at Harvard University (1901, 1909); Simmons College, Boston (1921); and at Temple University, Philadelphia. She was awarded several honorary degrees, including master of arts degrees from Livingstone College (1921) and North Carolina State College; LL.D. degrees from Wilberforce University, Wilberforce, Ohio (1938), and Lincoln University, Oxford, Pa. (1937); and an Ed.D. degree from Howard University, Washington, D.C. (1944). She was also elected an honorary member of the Wellesley College Alumnae Association (April 1944).

Charlotte Hawkins Brown, who married Edmund S. Brown in 1911, started Palmer Memorial Institute in 1902, remained as president until 1952, and then as financial director until 1955. At first consisting of a ramshackle church as a schoolhouse, with a log cabin as the president's home and the dormitory, it eventually encompassed 300-odd acres at Sedalia, ten miles from Greensboro. Brown credited Booker T. Washington and especially his wife, Margaret M. Washington, an educator in her own right and a prominent clubwoman, with sparking her interest and determination to found the institute. This influence is borne out by the language of the charter which cited as the principal objective, teaching the colored race improved methods of agricultural and industrial pursuits.

In 1909 Brown was one of the organizers of the North Carolina State Federation of Negro Women's Clubs. In 1915 she became the federation's second president, and remained in office until 1936. One of the club's programs to which she contributed was the purchase and maintenance of the Efland Home for Wayward Girls, located in Orange County, N.C., the only facility at the time for these girls. This home is now continued under the supervision of the North Carolina Department of Youth Development with state funds. Brown was also instrumental in the founding of the Colored Orphanage at Oxford, N.C.

Brown acknowledged her greatest inspiration as that which she received from her mother. The choice of a career and the courage to sustain her were instilled, she recounted, through the examples set by her contemporaries Maria L. Baldwin (1856–1922) and Lucy Laney (1853–1933), women who overcame race prejudice and other handicaps in order to maintain successful schools. In the early years, she faced the hostility of the surrounding white community which feared, she later recalled, that a northern-educated woman would infuse "social equality" in the minds of her young pupils. Brown named the school for her early benefactor, Alice Freeman Palmer, who died shortly before the opening. Mrs. Palmer had not only encouraged her after hearing of the proposal, but had also called on wealthy friends to contribute funds to start the institute.

Charlotte Hawkins Brown's accomplishments were intricately tied to the history of Palmer Memorial. Although the institute was forced to close in 1971 because of financial difficulties, its prestige as one of the oldest Negro preparatory schools in the United States to that date bears testimony to the founder's ingenuity and perseverance as an administrator and fundraiser. Not unusual for its day, Palmer began with elementary, high school, and junior college instruction. The upper division consisted of both academic and cultural courses. The cultural emphasis stemmed from Brown's belief that gentility and mannerliness would bring greater respect and opportunity for Negroes. She also thought that interracial contacts should be part of the education of Negro youth. These associations within a cultural environment, she once stated, enhanced "race pride, mutual respect, sympathetic understanding, and interracial goodwill." To this end she sponsored exchange programs with the North Carolina State College for Women at Greensboro, as well as other educational and social activities. She considered her campus as one of the first public interracial meeting places in North Carolina.

Brown personally solicited most of Palmer's financial support. In the first years she raised money by singing and reciting at Massachusetts summer resorts. She received funds and contacts from northern supporters such as the educators George Herbert Palmer and Charles W. Eliot; banker and philanthropist Galen S. Stone; Seth Low, president of Columbia University and later mayor of New York City; and from her friend Madame C. J. Walker, millionaire producer of beauty products for Negroes. In the South contributions came from both Negro and white benefactors. Beginning in 1924 the AMA shared responsibility for Palmer's financial support, based on the condition that Brown obtain additional money for buildings and expenses. The president met these conditions by raising a $250,000 permanent endowment. At the time of its closing the institute was valued at $1.3 million.

Palmer's emphasis on cultural education led to Brown's wide reputation as a "social dictator." This was enhanced by her incorporation of the teachings and practices at Palmer in a volume, *The Correct Thing to Do, Say, to Wear* (1941). This book influenced many youths in public and private schools throughout the nation. Dedicated to the well-being of all youth, she also started the movement to establish the State Training School for Negro Girls in Rocky Mount, N.C.

Charlotte Hawkins Brown was an ardent civil rights advocate who prided herself on being ejected frequently from Pullman berths and seats on southern routes. Occasionally she instituted lawsuits because of discriminatory incidents during her travels, winning at least one case, in 1920. Equally adamant against condoning discrimination in the North, she refused to use freight elevators in the customary fashion in such places as New York City. Brown was an outspoken foe of lynching at a time when this was a dangerous position to take in the South, once averring publicly that colored women were insulted by white men a thousand times more than the opposite.

Following her deep desire to promote better relations between the races, Brown was one of the founders of the Commission on Interracial Cooperation (1919), to help reduce tension after World War I, the forerunner of the Southern Regional Council (1943). As a prominent clubwoman her major influence was to promote interracial movements, with a more radical and uncompromising stance than her contemporaries, Josephine St. Pierre Ruffin, Mary McLeod Bethune, and Margaret M. Washington. Brown held high positions in both North Carolina and national organizations, notably as president of the Federation of Women's Clubs of North Carolina and as a vice-president of the National Association of Colored Women.

Because of her many interests and wide travels throughout Europe and the United States, she was in great demand as a speaker on both northern and southern platforms. During World War II one of the first Negroes to be appointed to the North Carolina Council of Defense, she served as a consultant to the secretary of war on hostesses and recreation camps; she was a member of the Executive Committee of the Home Nursing Council of the American Red Cross; and was an American delegate to the International Congress of Women, Memphis, Tenn. (Oct. 8, 1920). She was one of the seven educators honored by the Board of Education of North Carolina in its "Hall of Fame." Alpha Kappa Alpha Sorority, Inc., presented to the Association for the Study of Afro-American History a bronze marker honoring her at the sorority's Boulé in the Waldorf Astoria Hotel, New York City (July 18–22, 1976).

Brown wrote many articles and short stories, including *Mammy: An Appeal to the Heart of the South* (1919). Although she had no children of her own, she reared six children of relatives, including her niece, Maria Cole, wife of Nat "King" Cole. She died in a hospital in Greensboro on Jan. 11, 1961.

The most reliable and informative sources on Brown's life are manuscripts and newspaper clippings in the Schlesinger Library, Radcliffe College, and the Schomburg Collection, New York Public Library. Copies of her books are in the Moorland-Spingarn Research Center, Howard University. See also *Who's Who in America.* A recent biography is Constance H. Marteena's *The Lengthening Shadow of a Woman: A Biography of Charlotte Hawkins Brown* (1977).

— ELVENA TILLMAN

BROWN, HALLIE QUINN (1845?–1949), teacher, elocutionist, and civil rights leader. She was born in Pittsburgh, Pa., on March 10, 1845(?), the fifth of six children of former slaves, Thomas Arthur and Frances Jane (Scroggins) Brown. Because of the mother's poor health, the family moved to a farm in Chatham, Ontario, Canada, when Hallie was still a small child. Her early education was acquired there (1864–1870). It was from this farm that she was sent to Wilberforce University, an African Methodist Episcopal church institution in Wilberforce, Ohio. Later the family established residence in Wilberforce and erected a home, Homewood Cottage. She was graduated from that institution with a B.S. degree in 1873. Brown studied also in the Chautauqua Lecture School, graduating in 1886 after several years of summer school.

Brown's first teaching position was on a plantation in South Carolina, where she taught children from various plantations. She also taught adults, particularly the aged, to read their Bibles. Later she took charge of a school on the Sonora Plantation in Mississippi. She also held a teaching position in the city public schools of Yazoo, Miss., and Columbia, S.C. From 1885 to 1887 Brown served as dean of Allen University in Columbia, taught school in Dayton, Ohio (1887–1891), where she also headed a night school for adult migrants from the South. During 1892–1893 she was lady principal (dean of women) of Tuskegee Institute, and then accepted appointment as professor of elocution at Wilberforce University.

While teaching in the public schools of Dayton Brown had met a Professor Robertson of the Boston School of Oratory, enrolled in a course which he taught —the Art of Speech and Oratory—and after completing the course, was launched on her career as an elocutionist. Soon she was in demand as a speaker in New York, Philadelphia, and other cities. Bishop Daniel A. Payne, whose teachings greatly inspired Miss Brown, sponsored a southern speaking tour for her and she appeared in the large cities of North Carolina, Georgia, Alabama, Louisiana, Arkansas, and other states. When Pres. Benjamin F. Lee of Wilberforce University formed the Wilberforce (later Stewart) Concert Company, Brown became a member as reader and traveled with the group for four seasons.

In 1894 Brown made her first of several European trips. This one extended over a period of six years, during which she lectured and recited in the major cities of Great Britain. In 1895 she spoke at the World's Women's Christian Temperance Union in London. On July 7, 1899, she was entertained by Queen Victoria at tea in Windsor Castle. She spoke at an entertainment of the then Princess of Wales, later Queen of England. During Queen Victoria's jubilee year Brown was the guest of the lord mayor of London. This same year she attended the International Conference of Women in London. While on this first trip abroad Brown was asked to seek funds for Wilberforce University, as she was also when she returned to Europe in 1910, as a repre-

sentative of the Women's Parent Missionary Society of the A.M.E. church to the World Missionary Conference held in Edinburgh, Scotland, June 14–23. Out of her efforts came Emery Hall, a dormitory on the campus of Wilberforce University, named for the mother of Mrs. E. Julia Emery, a London philanthropist.

Again appointed professor of elocution at Wilberforce (1900–1903), travel and speaking engagements limited her teaching until 1906 when she filled the position on a full-time basis. After her European travels she spent many years as instructor in the English Department and was a member of the Board of Trustees of Wilberforce University. Until a few years before her death Brown taught a Sunday school class of college students.

Brown began her espousal of women's suffrage when, as a student, she heard Susan B. Anthony speak at Wilberforce. It is quite likely that she began her later crusade for women's rights in 1900 when she requested the A.M.E. church to elect her to the office of secretary of education. She did not win the appointment but continued to fight for equal rights for women. She traveled extensively pleading for full citizenship for women, and was an ardent, unrelenting supporter of civil rights for Negroes. As early as May 1925, during the All-American Musical Festival of the International Council of Women meeting in the Washington Auditorium in Washington, D.C., she delivered a scathing speech against discrimination shown in the seating of Negroes at the event. Brown declared in her protest that unless the proposed policy of segregation was changed, she would withdraw the part of the program to be performed by Negroes. Included in this program were the Hampton Glee Club and Choir directed by Robert Nathaniel Dett, and the Howard University Glee Club and Choral Society directed by Roy W. Tibbs. Brown stated: "This is a gathering of women of the world here and color finds no place in it." As a result of this speech, two hundred Negro entertainers refused to take part in the program and the Negro audience left the auditorium.

Brown was president of the National Association of Colored Women (1920–1924), president of the Ohio State Federation of Women's Clubs (1905–1912), founder and chairman of the Scholarship Fund of the National Association of Colored Women. It was during her administration that the National Association of Colored Women provided for the maintenance of the home of Frederick Douglass in Washington, D.C.

Brown died in Wilberforce on Sept. 16, 1949, of coronary thrombosis and was buried in the family plot in nearby Massie's Creek Cemetery.

The published writings of Hallie Q. Brown include *Bits and Odds, A Choice Selection of Recitations* (n.d.), *Our Women: Past, Present and Future* (n.d.), *Tales My Father Told* (1925), *Pen Pictures of Pioneers of Wilberforce* (1937), and a dramatization of the Rev. P. A. Nichols's *Trouble in Turkeytrot Church* (privately printed, 1917). Her *Homespun Heroines and Other Women of Distinction* (1926) is a source of much valuable information.

Information on Miss Brown is in the following sources: "Hallie Quinn Brown" by Charles H. Wesley (*NAW* [1971], 1:253–54); Ruth Neely's *Women of*

Ohio; A Record of Their Achievements in the History of the State (1939, 1: 237–38), Effie Lee Newsome's "Miss Hallie Q. Brown, Lecturer and Reciter" (unpublished essay, April 17, 1942) and her "The Significance of Hallie Q. Brown's Closing Days" (unpublished essay, Sept. 1949), George F. Robinson's *History of Greene County Ohio* (1902), Mollie E. Dunlap's "A Biographical Sketch of Hallie Quinn Brown" (Central State University *Alumni Journal,* June 1963), and Annjennette Sophie McFarlin's "Hallie Quinn Brown—Black Elocutionist, 1845(?)–1949" (Ph.D. dissertation, Washington State University, 1975). Her unpublished papers, lectures, correspondence, and other memorabilia are in the Hallie Q. Brown Memorial Library of Central State University. — GEORGE T. JOHNSON

BROWN, JESSE LEROY (1926–1950), naval aviator. When his plane went down in flames over Korea on Dec. 4, 1950, Ensign Brown became the first Negro American naval officer to lose his life in combat. He was also America's first Negro naval aviator. The son of John Brown and his wife, he was born in Hattiesburg, Miss., on Oct. 13, 1926. He graduated from Eureka High School in 1944 and attended the College of Engineering at Ohio State University (Oct. 1944 to March 1947; Office of the Registrar to Rayford W. Logan). On July 8, 1946, he enlisted in the U.S. Naval Reserve and the following spring was appointed as an aviation cadet and ordered to navy preflight school at Ottumwa, Iowa. Continuing his flight training at Pensacola, Fla., he became Ensign Brown and won his wings on Oct. 21, 1948, despite some racial discrimination.

He was assigned to Fighter Squadron 32, Atlantic Fleet, at Norfolk, Va., and on Jan. 4, 1949, embarked with his squadron on the U.S.S. *Leyte.* In October 1950 the *Leyte* joined the Seventh Fleet in combat off the northeast coast of Korea. Brown flew twenty missions from that time until he was shot down on Dec. 4, 1950. He and Lt. (J.G.) Thomas J. Hudner were flying close support for Marines fighting near the Chosin Reservoir. Brown's plane was hit by enemy gunfire and crashed. Hudner crash-landed his plane in an attempt to save Brown who was trapped alive in the wreckage, but to no avail.

Brown had been awarded the Air Medal and the Korean Service Medal; posthumously he was awarded the Purple Heart and Distinguished Flying Cross. His citation read: "For heroism and extraordinary achievement in aerial flight. . . . His exceptional courage, airmanship and devotion to duty in the face of great danger reflect the highest credit upon Ensign Brown and the United States Naval Service. He gallantly gave his life for his country."

Brown left a widow, a Eureka High School classmate whom he had secretly married while in flight school, and a daughter.

On Saturday, March 18, 1972, the first ship of the U.S. Navy to be named in honor of a Negro naval officer, the U.S.S. *Jesse L. Brown* (DE-1089), an ocean escort ship, was launched at the Avondale Shipyards, Westwege, La. Mrs. Gilbert W. Thorne, Brown's widow, served as sponsor of the ship, and his daughter, Mrs. Terence Knight, as matron of honor when the ship

was commissioned at the Boston Naval Shipyard, during Negro History Week on Feb. 17, 1973. Capt. Thomas J. Hudner, who was awarded the Congressional Medal of Honor for his attempt to rescue Brown, was the principal speaker, and Rear Admiral Samuel Gravely Jr., the first Negro to earn flag rank in the navy, was present.

An article in the *Washington Post* (Feb. 19, 1973, p. B1) gives essential details, a photograph of the destroyer escort, and of the personalities attending the commissioning. — NANCY GORDON HEINL

BROWN, JOHN MIFFLIN (1817–1893), teacher and eleventh bishop of the African Methodist Episcopal (A.M.E.) church. Born in Cantwell's Bridge (now called Odessa), New Castle County, Del., he lived there until he was ten years of age and then moved to Wilmington, Del. During his stay in Wilmington he lived with the family of William A. Seals, a Quaker. In Cantwell's Bridge he had attended a private white school and the Sunday school. In Wilmington he first attended the Presbyterian Sunday school, where all Negroes were relegated to the gallery. He disliked this and united with a Roman Catholic Sunday school, where he was received kindly. At the end of his stay in Wilmington, an older sister who lived in Philadelphia brought him to that city, where he found a home with a Dr. Emerson and attorney Henry Chester. They continued his instruction in the rudiments of education along with the precepts of a Christian life, and he attended St. Thomas Colored Protestant Episcopal Church until 1835. He united with Bethel A.M.E. Church in Philadelphia in January 1836. From 1835 to 1837 he studied with Frederick H. Hinton who taught him barbering. He attended school briefly in Poughkeepsie, N.Y., and worked at his trade there and in New York City until 1838. In the fall of 1838 he entered the Wesleyan Academy at Wilbraham, Mass., remaining there two years preparing for college. In 1840 he suffered ill health and returned to Philadelphia to recuperate, studied (1841–1842) at Oberlin College, Oberlin, Ohio, and at a school in Detroit (1844), and after the death of the pastor of the A.M.E. church in that city, assumed the pastorate as acting pastor from 1844 to 1847.

In September 1849 he united with the Ohio Conference and was assigned to Columbus, Ohio, where he preached three years and was then appointed principal of the Union Seminary, which was combined with Wilberforce University in 1855. Union Seminary was located fourteen miles from Columbus, but never enjoyed much success since better schools supported by state funds existed in Columbus. The seminary lingered until Wilberforce University became the property of the A.M.E. church and then by a vote of the Ohio Annual Conference it was abolished and the property ordered sold for the benefit of Wilberforce University. The agents appointed to sell the 180 acres on which the school was located allowed this valuable property to be sold with little profit to Wilberforce University. During Brown's administration the enrollment of Union Seminary increased from three pupils to one hundred. But his efforts to raise money for the erection of a new building met with little success.

In August 1852 he was appointed to Allen Station, Pittsburgh from the Ohio Conference; in 1853 Bishop Daniel A. Payne appointed him to the mission in New Orleans, which also consisted of Morris Brown Mission. He built Morris Brown Chapel and another chapel, each at a cost of $3000. He remained in New Orleans for a period of five years but grew weary of the persecution and imprisonment he suffered for allowing slaves to attend his church. He requested Bishop Payne to relieve him of this assignment, and in April 1857 was transferred to Asbury Chapel, Louisville, Ky. In May 1858 he was assigned to Bethel Church, Baltimore, remaining in that charge three years. Here he was very successful; the church was remodeled at a cost of $5000 and some 700 members added to the church roster. He served the Ebenezer Church of Baltimore from 1861 to 1863, when he was sent to Brite A.M.E. Church and given the responsibility of organizing A.M.E. churches in Virginia and North Carolina. In 1864 he was elected corresponding secretary of the Parent Home and Foreign Missionary Society of the A.M.E. church and was instrumental in raising $10,000 to assist in establishing schools and churches in the South.

The General Conference of the A.M.E. church met in Washington, D.C., in May 1868, at which time John Mifflin Brown was elected and consecrated the eleventh bishop of the A.M.E. church. He was first assigned to the South Carolina District which he served until 1872. He organized the Alabama Conference of the A.M.E. church on July 25, 1868, in Selma, Ala. He also organized Payne Institute in 1871, which later became Allen University at Columbia, S.C. In 1876 he planned the school which in later years grew into Paul Quinn College at Waco, Tex. He organized the West Texas, South Arkansas, West Tennessee, and Columbia, S.C., conferences, serving as an organizer from 1872 to 1876. He assisted Bishop Ward in organizing the North Georgia Conference in 1872. Brown served the Third District, consisting of the Baltimore, Virginia, and North and South Carolina conferences, from 1876 to 1880. His next assignment was to the First District, consisting of Philadelphia, New York, New Jersey, and the New England conferences (1880–1884); then he was assigned to the Fourth District, composed of Missouri, Kansas, Illinois, Iowa, South Kansas, North Missouri, and California (1884–1888); and then a part of the Fourth District, including the Indiana, Illinois, Michigan, and Iowa conferences (1888–1892).

He was married to Mary L. Lewis of Louisville, Ky., on Feb. 13, 1852. From this union eight children were born, four of whom completed courses in higher education (John Jr., the eldest, finished medical school at Howard University in 1881, and became a practicing physician in Kansas City, Mo.; William L. graduated from the college department of Howard with class honors, A.B. in 1880, M.A. in 1891, and was a public school administrator in Morristown, N.J., and in the West; Daniel entered the ministry; Mamie L. attended Howard but graduated from Miner Teachers College, accepting a teaching position in the public school system in Washington, D.C.). Mrs. Brown was the bishop's constant companion in his various travels, and labored with him in the A.M.E. church. The bishop was cultured, scholarly, a fluent speaker, writer, and popular with all classes. Brown died at his home, 1424 Rhode Island Ave. N.W., Washington, D.C., on March 16, 1893, after an illness of about two weeks. His funeral was held on March 20 at Metropolitan A.M.E. Church and he was buried at Graceland Cemetery (Woodlawn). He was survived by his widow, Mary Lewis Brown, and seven children.

His memory survives through the many chapels named for him. Brown Chapels have been established at Pittsburgh and Oil City, Pa.; Washington, D.C.; Joliet, Ill.; Brazil, Ind.; Ypsilanti, Mich.; Selma, Ala.; McMinnville, Fayette, and Union City, Tenn.; Houston, Tex.; Clarendon and Helena, Ark.; Columbus and Fort Gaines, Ga.; Tulsa, Okla.; Cameron, Greenwood, Scranton, Sumpter, and Columbia, S.C.; Cincinnati, Ohio; Kansas City, Topeka, Nicodemus, Parsons, and Ossawatomi, Kans.; and Popular Bluff and Boone Terre, Mo.;

The basic sources are William J. Simmons's *Men of Mark . . .* (1887, pp. 1113–18; reprint 1970), Richard R. Wright, Jr.'s *The Bishops of the African Methodist Episcopal Church* (1963, pp. 111–14), and Dorothy E. Hoover's *A Layman Looks with Love at Her Church* (1970). — MARY M. FISHER

BROWN, MORRIS (1770–1849), second bishop of the African Methodist Episcopal (A.M.E.) church. Born in Charleston, S.C. of mixed parentage, Brown was ordained a deacon in 1817 and an elder in 1818, and consecrated bishop in 1828. He left his native state in 1822 in the aftermath of the Denmark Vesey plot, and took up residence in the Philadelphia area. A pious, simple, and industrious man, Brown presided over the A.M.E. church during a period when it experienced significant growth. Incapacitated by a stroke in 1844, he died at home in Philadelphia on May 19, 1849.

Brown spent his formative years in Charleston, and although little is known of his early life, the evidence indicates that at a comparatively early age he identified himself as a free person. A self-educated man, he was converted to Methodism sometime during his youth, and subsequently secured a license to preach. He supported himself by working as a boot- and shoemaker, allocating some of his slim resources to those slaves who appealed to him for financial assistance to purchase their freedom. He was reportedly imprisoned for a year because of his activities on behalf of slaves. One of those he helped was the Africa-born Marcus Brown, who responded to Morris's kindness by presumably adopting his name and then following him into the A.M.E. church. While still in Charleston, Morris Brown often spoke to small groups of free Negroes and sometimes, usually on Saturday nights, he was able to preach to slaves living on plantations in the area. As a result of such efforts, he and Marcus were able to gather enough people to form the nucleus for a church. By 1816, the year in which the A.M.E. church formally established its identity as a separate religious denomination apart from the predominantly white Methodist church, Brown was able to list approximately 1400 people in his congregation. No one from the Charleston church was able to attend the organizing General Conference of the church in Philadelphia, largely because of the difficulties free Negroes faced when attempting to travel in the South, but the group registered its support for the undertaking and asked to be considered a branch of the new denomination.

The congregation in Charleston grew rapidly, probably reaching 2000 by 1822, and its leader was invited to participate in denominational affairs. Brown apparently accepted the risks involved in traveling, because he attended important functions, such as annual and general conferences, and served on the committee appointed in 1819 to examine the case of Daniel Coker, one of the A.M.E. founders who had been expelled. He also continued to attend to his secular work in order to support himself and his family.

In 1822 Brown left Charleston permanently and settled in the Philadelphia area. State legislators in South Carolina suspected that he had been involved in the Vesey plot, and although they could find no conclusive evidence to support their suspicions, they accused him of being a co-conspirator because Vesey allegedly used the local church to hold secret meetings. Brown quickly left the area, and subsequent state laws forced the church to close.

Once established in the North, Brown became more actively involved in the affairs of the denomination. In 1826 he was appointed to minister to the churches on the Bristol Circuit, in Bucks County, Pa., and on occasion he was asked to serve as an assistant to the aging founder of the A.M.E. church, Bishop Richard Allen. On May 25, 1828, Brown was elected a bishop in Bethel A.M.E. Church in Philadelphia, continuing to serve as Allen's associate until 1831 when the older man died and Brown succeeded him.

Allen had brought the church through its early years of development and hard times: Brown guided it through a period of growth and maturation. During Brown's tenure in the episcopacy, the denomination established branches in thirteen states, adding new congregations in places as distant from Philadelphia as Illinois, Indiana, Kentucky, and Missouri. The bishop traveled extensively, attending or presiding over conference sessions in widely scattered areas. On one such trip, to attend the meeting of the A.M.E. conference in Toronto, he suffered a crippling stroke, which impaired his speech and mental faculties. During periods of lucidity he attended to church business, but for much of the last five years of his life he was confined to his home. He died at his residence on Queen Street in Philadelphia on May 9, 1849, leaving his widow, Maria, and six children, one of whom, Morris Jr., became a well-known musician in Philadelphia. His will bequeathed a small estate to his widow and children. Funeral services were held at his home on May 14.

According to one of his successors, Bishop Daniel A. Payne, Brown was a good preacher but not a great one, with an appealing style that was simple and direct. A physically impressive man—over six feet tall and with a heavy build—he was reportedly able to attract people because of his piety and his ability to keep "abreast of the age."

Brief biographical accounts are found in Richard R. Wright, Jr.'s *The Bishops of the African Methodist Episcopal Church* (1963, pp. 111–18), Daniel A. Payne's *History of the African Methodist Episcopal Church* (1891, passim), and Carol V. R. George's *Segregated Sabbaths, Richard Allen and the Rise of Independent Black Churches, 1760–1840* (1973). There is a short article by Carter G. Woodson in *DAB* (2, Part 1:145–46). An obituary by D. A. Payne appeared in the *Philadelphia Public Ledger & Daily Transcript* (May 12, 1849, p. 2). — CAROL V. R. GEORGE

BROWN, SOLOMON G. (1829–1903?), scientific technician and lecturer. Born on Feb. 14, 1829, near Boundary and 14th Streets NW in Washington, D.C., he was the fourth of six children born to Isaac and Rachel Brown, both free. His father died in 1833 leaving his mother and siblings facing heavy debt. The father's property, taken in 1834 to settle the debts, left the family poor and homeless. As a child Solomon was not able to acquire a formal education, since there were very few schools for Negroes in Washington at that time. He worked in the Washington, D.C., post office with Samuel F. B. Morse, and for the Smithsonian Institution (1852 to about 1903).

At fifteen years of age Brown started working under the assistant postmaster in the Washington, D.C., post office. He was assigned to assist Joseph Henry and Samuel F. B. Morse in the installation of the first Morse magnetic telegraph system between Washington and Baltimore. Morse had invented the electromagnetic telegraph system during the 1830s, but was not able to generate funding to try it out over a long distance until 1843, when Congress appropriated $30,000 to test the system. Between March 1844 and the middle of May 1844, wires on poles were run between Washington and Baltimore. Brown provided important aid in the installation. On May 24, 1844, the first formal message was transmitted over the wires, a distance of forty miles between the two cities, using the dot-and-dash alphabet known as the Morse Code. From this time on the success of the electric telegraph in the United States was assured. Solomon Brown played a significant role as a technician in this historic scientific event. He continued to work for Morse and Joseph Henry, and in 1845 assumed a position as a battery tender with the newly formed Morse Telegraph Company. Brown's association with Morse and his associates sparked his interest in and increased his knowledge of scientific matters. After service with Morse he went on to positions as an assistant packer in the laboratory of Gillman and Brothers, chemical manufacturers.

In February 1852 Brown took a position in the foreign exchange division of the new Smithsonian Institution. Joseph Henry, an electrical engineer and experimenter who worked with Morse, was secretary of the institution. In his first position Brown was paid $24 a month for "services in the museum." By 1864 he had become a museum assistant at $60 a month. In 1869 he worked as the registrar in charge of transportation, registry, and storage of animal specimens and materials received by the institution. Correspondence between Brown and Joseph Henry and Spencer F. Baird (the first two secretaries of the Smithsonian Institution) indicates that

Brown was indispensable to both men in the operation of the national museum from at least 1855 to 1870. According to Brown's account, he prepared nearly all of the illustrations used for the scientific lectures presented at the Smithsonian Institution until 1887. A document from the Archives of the Smithsonian Institution stated that he "performed duties in almost all sections of the S I" with the "official title—Packer." His duties were "General miscel[laneous] and packing in the Exchange Bu[reau]" under "Mr. Winlock, Curator of Exchanges."

Brown's long years of association with the Smithsonian Institution provided him with a vast amount of knowledge about natural history. He was a frequent lecturer before adult groups and scientific societies in Baltimore, Alexandria, and Washington. His first public lecture, on the characteristics and social habits of insects, was given in early 1855 before the Young People's Club at the Israel A.M.E. Church in Washington. His lectures were illustrated and he received requests to speak to many groups. Some of his topics were "Geology," "Telegraph," "Embryo Plants," "Food," and "Minerals." His first lecture on "Geology" was presented before the Annual Conference of the African Methodist Episcopal church in Baltimore in April 1863. He discussed descriptive, theoretical, and practical geology.

Brown also volunteered in a number of civic and educational programs: as a trustee of Wilberforce University; a trustee of the 15th Street Presbyterian Church, Washington; superintendent of the North Washington Mission Sunday School; and an active member of the Freedmen's Relief Association after the Civil War. In 1866 he was elected president of the National Union League; in 1871, to the legislature for the District of Columbia, to which he was twice reelected. Other civic positions held were executive committee member of the Emancipation Monument Erectors, director of the Industrial Savings and Building Association of Washington, D.C., and Washington correspondent to the *Anglo-African Christian Recorder*.

Most of the information about Brown is in William J. Simmons's *Men of Mark . . .* (1887; reprinted 1970). Although this article was probably written by Brown himself, as were most of the other articles in *Men of Mark,* his employment at the Smithsonian Institution from at least 1852 to 1903, "according to other sources," is confirmed in most details by a letter from James A. Steed, assistant archivist, Smithsonian Institution Archives (Aug. 21, 1974), and a photocopy of his employment record. There are copies of the correspondence between Brown, Spencer Baird, and Joseph Henry in the Smithsonian Institution. For Brown's "departmental appointment," see Constance McLaughlin Green's *The Secret City . . .* (1967, p. 43).

— ROBERT C. HAYDEN

BROWN, WILLIAM WELLS (c. 1814–1884), abolitionist, author, and reformer. Brown was born a slave on the plantation of John Young, a physician, near Lexington, Ky. His mother, Elizabeth, owned by Young, was an attractive mulatto who bore seven children of whom Brown was one of the youngest, if not the youngest. His father, according to Elizabeth, was George Higgins, a first cousin of Young's. In 1816 Young moved to Missouri, taking with him his slaves, including Elizabeth and her children, and his other movable property. Brown spent his first twenty years mainly in St. Louis and its vicinity as the property of three owners in succession. At various times during those years he was a house servant, a servant in St. Louis taverns, a handyboy in Elijah P. Lovejoy's printing office, a factotum on Mississippi River steamboats, a fieldhand, an assistant in Young's medical office, and a handyman for James Walker, a notorious Missouri slave trader with whom he made three trips to the New Orleans slave markets. In Young's office he acquired a lifelong interest in the practice of medicine, and in the taverns he learned to dislike intoxicants and drunkards and was thereby inspired to become a temperance reformer. His multifarious experiences as a slave familiarized him with many departments of the "peculiar institution."

On Jan. 1, 1834, Brown escaped from slavery in Cincinnati. He had gone there as a servant with Enoch Price, his last owner, who was a St. Louis commission merchant and steamboat owner. Enroute from Cincinnati to Canada, Brown was befriended in central Ohio by a Quaker, Wells Brown. Upon the Quaker's suggestion he added the Quaker's name to William, the first name he had in slavery, and thus acquired a middle name and a surname. Instead of going to Canada he settled in Cleveland, began working diligently and educating himself, married Elizabeth Schooner of Cleveland late in the summer of 1834, and began rearing a family. The Browns became the parents of three daughters. The first of these died in infancy; the other two grew into womanhood, and the younger of the two, Josephine, became her father's first biographer. After two years in Cleveland, Brown moved his family to Buffalo, N.Y., where he maintained his home for nine years before moving to Farmington, a village near Rochester, N.Y., in 1845. In the meantime, as an employee on Lake Erie steamers he became an expert conductor on the Underground Railroad who consistently safeguarded his passengers by way of both Buffalo and Detroit to freedom in Canada. In seven months in 1842, for instance, he conveyed sixty-nine fugitive slaves to Canada. He was also active in a temperance society in Buffalo, in whose meetings he gained some knowledge of parliamentary procedure and experience in public speaking. Whether consciously or unconsciously, he was thus preparing himself for the work he was soon to begin. In the fall of 1843 he became a lecturing agent for the Western New York Anti-Slavery Society and continued as such for almost four years, holding antislavery meetings in many places in Ohio as well as in New York. Early in May 1847 he and his wife Elizabeth separated, and he took custody of their two daughters. Having been engaged by the Massachusetts Anti-Slavery Society to lecture in New England, he first went to Boston in the same month, and with the exception of five years he spent abroad, he made his home in that city or its vicinity for the remainder of his life. During the next two years, in close association with William Lloyd Garrison, Wendell Phillips, and other great abolitionists, he became prominent as an agent of both the Massachusetts and the American Anti-Slavery Societies.

In July 1849 Brown went abroad on a twofold mission—to represent the American Peace Society at the International Peace Congress in Paris, and to win continued British support for the antislavery crusade in the United States. At the Peace Congress, which convened late in August, he was cordially welcomed by such liberals as Victor Hugo, Alexis de Tocqueville, and Richard Cobden. On the last day of the meeting he spoke briefly against American slavery as a constant state of war between slaveholders and slaves. From September 1849 to September 1854 he remained in Great Britain, where he traveled more than 25,000 miles and delivered more than a thousand antislavery lectures. One reason for the prolongation of his sojourn abroad was the enactment of the stringent new Fugitive Slave Act of 1850, which immediately made it impossible for him to return to the United States unless he wanted to risk being arrested and reenslaved, for he had never been legally manumitted. His freedom having been purchased by friends in England in the spring of 1854, however, he returned to the United States in the following September and continued his antislavery activities until the Civil War ended. While Brown was abroad, Elizabeth Brown died in Buffalo. In 1860 Brown married Annie Elizabeth Gray (1835–1902) of Cambridgeport. They became the parents of two children, neither of whom lived beyond early childhood. When the Union Army was opened to Negroes in 1863, with Frederick Douglass and others Brown recruited Negro enlistees in Massachusetts, New York, Pennsylvania, and New Jersey for the Massachusetts 54th Regiment.

After the war, having studied medicine privately and as an apprentice, Brown became a practicing physician. He devoted much of his time, nevertheless, to lyceum lecturing, writing, and the promotion of temperance until his death. A man of medium stature, Brown was possessed of extraordinary intelligence, a wholesome sense of humor, and a pleasing personality. From the facts concerning his parentage and numerous references of his time to his complexion, it appears that he could easily have passed for a white man, but he deliberately avoided doing so lest he compromise his integrity.

Although suffering from a tumor of the bladder, he continued his activities and died at his home in Chelsea, a suburb of Boston, on Nov. 6, 1884. He was survived by his second wife, Annie Elizabeth Brown, and two daughters. After a private service in his home, public funeral services were held at the A.M.E. Zion Church on North Russell Street in Boston on Nov. 9. Among the speakers was Lewis Hayden, a well-known abolitionist. He was buried in Range 31, Grave 7, Cambridge Cemetery, some distance southwest of Harvard Square.

The first of the more than a dozen books and pamphlets Brown wrote was his *Narrative of William W. Brown, A Fugitive Slave, Written by Himself* (1847). A forceful antislavery argument, this slave autobiography went through four American editions totaling 10,000 copies in two years and five British editions with slightly different titles in the next four years. In 1852 Brown published in London *Three Years in Europe; Or, Places I Have Seen and People I Have Met.* In addition to being interesting in itself, this volume is noteworthy because in it Brown pioneered as an American Negro writer of a book of travels. A revised but hardly improved version of this work was published in Boston in 1855 with the title *The American Fugitive in Europe: Sketches of Places and People Abroad.* Brown's *Clotel; Or, The President's Daughter: A Narrative of Slave Life in the United States,* published in London in 1853, is generally considered the first novel by an American Negro. The president in the story was Thomas Jefferson, who had been repeatedly accused of begetting children by Sally Hemings, a slave concubine, and later forgetting them. This version of *Clotel* was not published in America until 1969. Meanwhile Brown published three different if no better versions of it—*Miralda; Or, The Beautiful Quadroon: A Romance of American Slavery, Founded on Fact* (a serial, New York, 1860–1861); *Clotelle: A Tale of the Southern States* (1864); and *Clotelle; Or, The Colored Heroine: A Tale of the Southern States* (1867). By the spring of 1856 Brown had written an antislavery drama in three acts entitled *Experience; Or, How to Give a Northern Man a Backbone.* He read this drama occasionally to deeply interested audiences but seems never to have published it. Before the end of 1856 he wrote another antislavery drama in five acts entitled *The Escape; Or, A Leap for Freedom.* After reading this drama on many occasions, he published it in Boston in 1858. This work thus became the first drama to be published by an American Negro.

Although Brown was not a scholarly historian, he wrote four historical works in which he contributed notably to the preservation of Negro history. His first two historical works were *St. Domingo: Its Revolutions and its Patriots* (1855) and *The Black Man, His Antecedents, His Genius, and His Achievements* (1863 et seq.). Brown's next historical work was *The Negro in the American Rebellion: His Heroism and His Fidelity* (1867). In this work he proved himself a pioneer in writing the military history of the American Negro. Others had previously written sketches of the parts Negroes had played in the American Revolution and the War of 1812, but Brown's was at once the first attempt to write a history of the Negro's part in the Civil War and the first attempt to bring together in one work the history of the Negro's part in all three of these wars. Brown's fourth, and most comprehensive, historical work was *The Rising Son; Or, The Antecedents and Advancement of the Colored Race* (1874). In this volume Brown repeated much of what he had included in his previous historical writing. Together with the several editions of *The Black Man,* this work contains biographical sketches of 110 "representative" Negro men and women, many of whom might have been forgotten if they had not been thus commemorated. Brown's last book was *My Southern Home: Or, The South and Its People* (1880). This work consists of reminiscences of slavery and a reflective and critical account of a tour Brown had made of several erstwhile slave states during the winter of 1879–1880.

In addition to the fourth American edition of Brown's *Narrative,* see the following: Josephine Brown's *Biogra-*

phy of an American Bondman, By His Daughter (1856), William Edward Farrison's *William Wells Brown: Author and Reformer* (1969), William Wells Brown's *Clotel; Or, The President's Daughter: A Narrative of Slave Life in the United States,* with an introduction and notes by William Edward Farrison (1969), and his *The Negro in the American Rebellion: His Heroism and His Fidelity,* introduced and annotated by William Edward Farrison (1971). There is a very brief sketch by Carter G. Woodson in *DAB* (2, Part 1:161).

— WILLIAM EDWARD FARRISON

BROWNE, HUGH M. (1851–1923), educator, civil rights leader, and inventor. Born in Washington, D.C., in June 1851 to John Browne and Elizabeth Wormley, he thus had family connections among the most prominent free Negroes in Washington. His maternal aunt, Mary Wormley, established a school for free Negroes in 1832, and other members of the Wormley family owned a boarding house patronized by the Washington political elite. His paternal aunt, Mary Browne Syphax, was married to William Syphax, who had a position in the Office of the Secretary of the Interior and who was a member of the Board of Trustees of the colored public schools of Washington. Browne was educated in the schools of Washington, D.C., and received his B.A. from Howard University in 1875 and his M.A. in 1878. In 1878 he also received a B.D. from Princeton Theological Seminary and was ordained in the Presbyterian church. After graduation from Princeton, he studied in Germany and Scotland for two years. For a short time after his return from Europe he was pastor of Shiloh Presbyterian Church in New York City. In August 1883 he arrived in Liberia to begin an eighteen-month appointment as professor of intellectual and moral philosophy at Liberia College. He returned to the United States and from 1886 to 1898 taught physics at the Colored Preparatory and M Street High School in Washington. From 1898 to 1901 he taught at Hampton Institute, then spent one year as principal of the Colored High School in Baltimore. In 1902 he became the principal of the Institute for Colored Youth in Philadelphia, and remained there until 1913 when he retired. He returned to Germany to study vocational education, after which he became an "educational engineer" or consultant in Washington. Shortly before his appointment in Philadelphia he married a widow, Julia Shadd Purnell, a member of another Washington family prominent in education, whose sister, Marion Shadd, was supervising principal of the Eleventh Division of the school system. Browne died on Oct. 30, 1923. The District of Columbia Board of Education has recognized his contribution to the field of education by naming a school for him, as well as one for his sister-in-law.

Browne was an educator who had a strongly developed philosophy which tied together the development of mind and body, academic and industrial training, and theory and practice. This philosophy was based on his analysis of the cognitive process and on his belief that the efficient management of public affairs necessitated that people be trained in schools to do the jobs they expected to begin after graduation. In addition to his well-articulated, systematic body of thought about the

nature and purpose of the educative process, he believed that the education of Negro children must be geared to their specific needs. In a letter to Booker T. Washington, Browne stated that the Negro child had a peculiar heritage and lived, moved, and had his being in peculiar conditions which his education must take into account. He stated that it was harmful to attempt to fit Negro children into curricula developed for children of a different heritage, environment, and condition. This particular viewpoint represented the coupling of his general educational philosophy with his overriding concern for the development and advancement of the Negro race. His main tenet was that the purpose of education was to impart to the student the ability to adapt general concepts to the peculiarities of a specific environment in order to solve problems presented by that environment. He felt that this kind of education for Negroes was the only way to develop the independence necessary to escape political and economic control by whites. His interest in Negro education was manifested as early as his student days at Princeton when he brought pressure on the authorities there to provide previously neglected public education for Negroes in the area.

His lifelong pattern of remolding and revising educational systems was begun during his stay in Liberia. Although political problems within the College of Liberia caused by Principal Edward Wilmot Blyden's distrust of the Afro-American "mulattoes" Browne and T. McCants Stewart, and by Blyden's problems with the Liberian government, prevented Browne from teaching, he did submit to the Liberia College Board of Trustees a plan for the educational and administrative reorganization of the college. When he returned to Washington to teach, he introduced and developed student experimentation in physics and taught the students to make their own scientific apparatus. This wedding of theory with practice was considered a revolutionary innovation.

When he went to Hampton Institute he inaugurated a summer training session for teachers to give them skills in this educational methodology. Following this pattern of innovation, he reorganized and united the Colored High School and Training School in Baltimore and placed the work of the school under its first colored faculty. In 1902 he was asked to head the Institute for Colored Youth in Philadelphia. He convinced the management board of the school, who were members of the Society of Friends, to move the school from Philadelphia to Cheyney, Pa., and to develop it into a normal school which would correlate academic and industrial education. He also devised the plan for the reorganization and removal to Cheyney of the Shelter Orphan Asylum of Philadelphia to become a practice school for the normal school. He further developed his summer sessions which attracted teachers from all over the South. Browne left Cheyney in 1913 because he felt that the board of managers was unwilling to allocate or raise the funds for teachers and equipment which he felt necessary for the welfare of the school. He returned to Washington where he proposed scientific management of schools and vocational education.

In addition to his educational activities, Browne was

active in other areas. He was the secretary of the Committee of Twelve from 1904 to 1913. This committee was the outgrowth of a Carnegie Hall meeting of Negro leaders earlier that year which was aimed at mitigating the effects of the division between Booker T. Washington and W. E. B. Du Bois. Du Bois originally belonged to the committee but dropped out because he felt that Carnegie's financial support of the group gave Washington a controlling hand in its activities. Washington, Browne, Archibald Grimké, Kelly Miller, Charles Anderson, T. Thomas Fortune, Dr. E. C. Morris, J. W. E. Bowen, Charles Chesnutt, Bishop G. W. Clinton, and H. T. Kealing remained as members. The major activity of this group was to publish or republish statements by Negroes and whites which were aimed at enlightening the public in general and the white southern public in particular about the Negro and his rightful place in American society. The committee ceased to function shortly after Carnegie ended his financial support. Although Browne was the secretary of the committee (which was indeed dominated by Washington), although Browne's educational philosophy was similar to Washington's, and although Browne was disdainful of Du Bois because he perceived him as floundering rather than settling down on this earth and making "an honest effort to subdue it," Browne was no political and educational lackey of Washington. His educational philosophy was original and more scientifically developed than Washington's, he asserted his own points of view to Washington, and often declined requests from Washington to meet with him or to gather information on rival groups. In fact, his correlation of academic and industrial education was one answer to part of the Du Bois–Washington dispute.

Browne's bent for innovation also led him to invention. Among his inventions, some of which were patented, was a device (patented on April 28, 1908) to govern the position of dampers in a furnace in order to regulate the draft.

Data about Browne are not found in any one book, and many standard works do not mention him. Information for this article was obtained from materials in the Moorland-Spingarn Research Center at Howard University, including Theressa Wilson Brown's "Biographical Sketches of Individuals After Whom Schools in Divisions 10–13 Have Been Named"; the Booker T. Washington Papers in the Library of Congress; Hollis Lynch's *Edward Wilmot Blyden . . .* (1967); newspapers and magazines of the period; and an interview with a member of Browne's family. A letter from Diane Girvin (archives assistant, Princeton University) to Rayford W. Logan (June 5, 1975) confirms the statement that Hugh M. Browne was a member of the Princeton Theological Seminary class of 1878. — ROBERT G. MCGUIRE III

BRUCE, BLANCHE KELSO (1841–1898), teacher, planter, politician, second Negro U.S. senator from Mississippi. Bruce was born a slave near Farmville, Prince Edward County, Va. The youngest of eleven children of Polly, a slave owned by Pettus Perkinson, he showed his mixed ancestry. Bruce took his surname from the man who had owned Polly and her ten children before Blanche was born. When his wife died, Perkinson (between 1844 and 1850) took his slaves from Virginia to Missouri and back, then to Mississippi and again to Missouri. Blanche—the origins of his feminine name are not known—received his early education from the tutor of young William Perkinson. Bruce worked as a hand in a tobacco field and a factory, and studied the printing trade until the outbreak of the Civil War. One of his brothers later recalled that the young slaves "were well fed, seldom punished . . . [and] enjoyed life in the factories very much."

Blanche nevertheless sought escape from slavery by running away to the free state of Kansas. In Lawrence he opened the first elementary school in the state for Negroes, taught in it, and received additional tutoring from a minister. After Missouri emancipated the slaves in January 1865, he returned there, taught school, and worked as a printer's apprentice in Hannibal. He studied for a few months at Oberlin College until his money ran out and then worked for two years as a porter on a Mississippi riverboat, the *Columbia,* running between St. Louis and Council Bluffs, Iowa. A speech in Memphis, by John Lusk Alcorn, later Republican governor of Mississippi, convinced Bruce that Mississippi was a land of opportunity.

Soon after his arrival in February 1869, Bruce was made supervisor of elections in Tallahatchie County. In 1870 he went to Jackson, the state capital, where he was elected sergeant-at-arms of the Senate. Later he was elected sheriff and tax assessor of Bolivar County, and made his home in Floreyville. In addition to serving as sheriff for two terms, he was also superintendent of education and a member of the Floreyville Board of Aldermen. Profiting from his fees as sheriff, he built a house and paid $950 for a 640-acre plantation which its owner had lost during the Civil War.

In 1874 the state legislature elected him to the U.S. Senate, the second Negro from the state to serve in that office. Whereas Hiram R. Revels had served only from Feb. 25, 1870, to March 3, 1871, Bruce served a full term (1875–1881). He was register of the treasury (1881–1885) under Republican presidents Garfield and Arthur, recorder of deeds for the District of Columbia during the administration of President Harrison (1889–1893), and was appointed register of the treasury again by President McKinley in 1897. In ill health for several years, he died of a kidney ailment on March 17, 1898. He was buried in Woodlawn Cemetery, Suitland, Md., the final resting place of many prominent Negroes. He was survived by his widow, the former Josephine B. Wilson of Cleveland, whom he had married on June 24, 1878, and their only son, eighteen-year-old Roscoe Conkling Bruce who later graduated Phi Beta Kappa from Harvard University and became assistant superintendent for colored schools in the District of Columbia.

Blanche K. Bruce owed his fame and fortune partly to his education, ambition, and support of better opportunities for Negroes, and partly to his affiliation with the Republican party. He won election to the U.S. Senate the year before white Democrats "redeemed" Mississippi by a combination of force and fraud. A successful and wealthy planter in Mississippi, he had support for his election to the Senate from Gov. Adelbert Ames and also from James Hill, a successful colored "carpetbagger'' businessman who likewise found favor among influential whites and large numbers of Negroes. When Sen. James L. Alcorn, whom Bruce had opposed for governor in 1873, refused, contrary to long-established custom, to escort the newly elected senator to his seat, Sen. Roscoe Conkling of New York saved Bruce and the Senate from embarrassment. Conkling helped Bruce win appointments after he left the Senate.

Although Bruce occasionally declined to follow the party line, his record in the Senate won him Republican support and Democratic opposition for his appointments after 1881. Bruce voted with the Democrats to seat L. Q. C. Lamar to succeed Alcorn (whose term expired on March 4, 1877). Against the wishes of Sen. John Sherman and President Hayes, Bruce voted for the Bland-Allison Act (1878), to provide for the limited coinage of silver. Since inflation was generally opposed by property owners like Bruce, reasons for his vote must be conjectured. Easily understandable, however, was his unsuccessful opposition to the Chinese Exclusion Act of 1878, which he explained as an expression of sympathy for one downtrodden race by another.

As the only Negro senator at that time, and for two years the only Negro in Congress, Bruce considered himself a spokesman for his race throughout the country, and repeatedly spoke and voted on their behalf. His maiden speech (March 3, 1876) was an unsuccessful appeal for P. B. S. Pinchback and the Negro voters who chose the legislature that elected him to the Senate. The first bill he introduced called for the desegregation of the U.S. Army; and at various times he tried to get bounty money for Negro soldiers and sailors, to support Negro industrial education, to investigate the brutal hazing of Johnson C. Whittaker, a Negro cadet at West Point. He opposed migration to Liberia but supported in vain appropriations to aid Negro migrants during the "Great Exodus," the movement in the late 1870s from the South, especially to Kansas. All of the above proposals, in the indifferent or hostile atmosphere of the Hayes administration, were defeated.

Bruce's most positive accomplishment for the freedmen, and his most constructive work in the Senate, was his role in winding up the affairs of the bankrupt Freedmen's Savings and Trust Company. Because it was chartered by Congress and advertised as a nonprofit institution, many ex-slaves confided their first earnings to it; at its height the bank had 70,000 depositors and over $57 million in deposits. But venality, incompetence, and reckless loans forced it to close in 1874; it seemed that salaries, attorneys' fees, and other expenses would eat up all the remaining funds. The Democratic Senate named Bruce head of an investigating committee in 1879, and his report, issued a year later, was a crisp indictment which named the guilty and advised a speedy winding-up of the bank's affairs. Bruce's recommendations, embodied in Senate Bill 711, were followed, and the depositors managed to get three-fifths of their money back. His handling of the complicated problem was an impressive performance, which fittingly closed out his senatorial term.

Bruce's political survival after the end of his senatorial term in 1881 depended exclusively on presidential patronage. Although he and his political allies could no

longer hope to win elections in Mississippi, they continued to control the state's delegation to the Republican national conventions; their votes, added to those of the other southern skeleton delegations, were an essential element in winning a contested nomination. And in the November elections, while they could not hope to carry Mississippi, they might tip the balance in closely contested northern states. Bruce was exceedingly skillful in playing the difficult game of representing a despised minority, most of whom were disfranchised; down to the end of his life, as long as there was a Republican in the White House he held a lucrative federal job in Washington.

Bruce and his wife enjoyed the good life of elite Negroes during late-nineteenth-century Washington. He owned some 3000 acres of Delta land, made speeches for fees of $100 to $150, and operated a successful investment, claims, insurance, and real estate agency in the capital. As recorder of deeds, he collected $1.50 per transaction, hired as many clerks as he pleased, paid them as little as he could, and pocketed the surplus, less some judicious campaign contributions. Bruce, graceful, polished, and self-assured, was well built, with broad shoulders and a large head. One of the most perceptive writers of the period wrote: "His complexion is café-au-lait, and his slightly curly hair is well brushed. He dresses well, and he is as intelligent and polite a gentleman as you will find in Washington." Mrs. Bruce "has Caucasian features, large, beautiful eyes, a somewhat brunette complexion, and long, slightly waved hair. Her form is slender and shapely, and she dresses in elegant taste. She is well educated and said to be an intellectual" (Frank G. Carpenter, Carp's Washington [1960], p. 245).

In 1883 and probably later, however, the color line in "white society" was for the most part rigidly drawn against the Bruces and other prominent Negroes. Bruce did serve as a member of the Board of Trustees of Howard University (1894–1898), which awarded him an honorary LL.D. in 1893.

Bruce's "tireless zeal" and "unconquerable ambition," noted by a perceptive obituary writer, carried him from slavery to the U.S. Senate. His ability as an orator, businessman, and politician is particularly remarkable when it is remembered that he had been a slave, and a field slave at that, and that he had to struggle all his life against the persistent, pervasive, and often ferocious racism of the dominant white majority. Bruce, like Booker T. Washington, believed that the dominant white majority would continue to control American society, and that compromise and persuasion, patience, and education were the Negro's best hope. He rejected armed uprising as suicidal and emigration to Liberia as impractical; he insisted instead that the Negro was "an integral element" in American society, and that he would and should continue to make "slow and painful" progress toward equality. If he agreed with his brother Henry that "Freedom has been sweet indeed to the ex-bondsman, . . . one glorious harvest of good things" even among the trials of the 1890s, it must be remembered that they were measuring Negro progress from the benchmark of slavery. Bruce eschewed violence in thought, speech, and action, preferring instead moderation, compromise, elections, and maneuvering. It is obvious that he achieved far more for himself and his friends than he did for the great mass of southern Negroes. But he did provide the image of an honorable, competent, reasonable man, a good senator, and a more than competent bureaucrat-politician. In the racist society of the United States in the last three decades of the nineteenth century, there was perhaps not much more that he could have done.

The *Charleston News and Courier* had stated on Jan. 10, 1881, that Bruce was equal in ability to the average cabinet officer of the day and bore a higher character, personally and officially, than 90 percent of the candidates for prominent positions. Since Frederick Douglass had died in 1895, "the Negro race felt that it was indeed bereft. And the feeling among the whites was that Bruce had discharged his duties as well as they could have been done by anyone with his preparation, overshadowed by the partisanship of those troublous years" (Samuel Denny Smith, *The Negro in Congress, 1870–1901* [1940], p. 41).

The sketch by Carter G. Woodson in *DAB* (2, Part 1 180–81) is reasonable and fair. A memoir by Bruce's brother Henry K. Bruce (*The New Man,* 2d ed. 1969) is the best source for Blanche's early life, and the *Washington Bee* covered the last decades of his public career. In addition, see Maurine Christopher's *America's Black Congressmen* (1971, pp. 15–24). Background information is in Vernon Lane Wharton's *The Negro in Mississippi, 1865–1890* (1947, especially pp. 160–61, 169, 175, 236, and 270), and Constance McLaughlin Green's *The Secret City: A History of Race Relations in the Nation's Capital* (1967, especially pp. 122, 126, 129, 140, 189, 196, and 211). The only full-length biography is an unpublished doctoral dissertation by Sadie Daniel St. Clair, "The National Career of Blanche K. Bruce" (New York University, 1947).

— SAMUEL L. SHAPIRO

BRUCE, JOHN EDWARD [BRUCE GRIT] (1856–1924), journalist and historian. He was born in Piscataway, Md., on Feb. 22, 1856. His father, Robert Bruce, and his mother, Martha Allen (Clark) Bruce, were slaves. When John was three years old his father was sold and sent to Georgia, never to be heard from again. His mother's master, Maj. Harvey Griffin, let her cook and sell pies and coffee to the Marines at nearby Fort Washington, aided by her mother. She also set up a secondhand clothing trade with the old clothes from the Marines. Her master received one-half of the money.

The slave child John knew about the auction block for children and about slaves escaping to freedom or being liberated. John and his mother were freed in 1860 by marching along with the Union soldiers from Maryland into Washington, where she found her cousin Busie Patterson. There his mother worked as a domestic and John grew up. He attended a public school in Stratford, Conn., when his mother was there with a family employer, and had public and private instruction in Washington, D.C., including a three-month course at Howard University. His formal education was minor, for he was largely self-educated.

In 1874 Bruce secured a job as a general helper in the *New York Times* Washington correspondent's office. The young journalist founded the *Argus,* a weekly newspaper in Washington, D.C., in 1879, the *Sunday Item* in 1880, and the *Washington Grit* in 1884. Bruce was editor of the *Republican* of Norfolk, Va., in 1882; assistant editor and business manager of the *Commonwealth* of Baltimore, Md., in 1884; and associate editor of *Howard's American Magazine* from 1896 to 1901. Around 1874 he began to write as a correspondent for Negro newspapers. Over the years he wrote for more than twenty Negro papers, and many of his articles appeared in such white newspapers as the *Boston Transcript,* the *Washington Evening Star,* the *New York Times,* the *St. Louis Globe-Democrat,* the *Buffalo Express,* and the *Sunday Republican* of Washington, D.C. His articles also appeared in several Negro publications in England, Jamaica, the West Indies, and in West and South Africa. "Bruce Grit" became his famous column head in the *Gazette* of Cleveland and the *New York Age* in 1884. Around 1900 Bruce moved from Washington, D.C., to Albany, N.Y., and later to New York City and Yonkers. He founded (with Charles W. Anderson) the *Chronicle* of New York City in 1897 and the *Weekly Standard* of Yonkers, in 1908. He also edited the *Masonic Quarterly* in New York City.

Bruce married Lucy Pinkwood, a contralto, of Washington, D.C. They were childless and she presumably died before his second marriage to Florence A. Bishop of Cleveland on Sept. 10, 1895. There was one daughter from this union, Mrs. Olive Bruce Miller of Asbury Park, N.J., and New York City, who died on Jan. 20, 1943, and three surviving grandchildren: Onnie K. Miller, Mrs. Agnes B. Conway, and Edwin L. Miller of New York City.

Bruce's writings did not always keep him solvent, so he held a job for most of his adult life with the Port of New York Authority. He retired in 1922 and died on Aug. 7, 1924, at Bellevue Hospital, New York City, at the age of sixty-seven. Funeral services were held on Aug. 10 at Liberty Hall, 120 West 138th St. Marcus Garvey gave one of the eulogies, and an honor guard was furnished from Garvey's Legion. Services were conducted by representatives of the Prince Hall F.&A.M. Many of the mourners were delegates attending the Fourth Convention of Garvey's Universal Negro Improvement Association. Bruce's wife survived him.

Bruce was a very popular speaker. He published two books—*Short Biographical Sketches of Eminent Negro Men and Women in Europe and the United States* (1910) and *The Awakening of Hezekiah Jones* (1916), a story—and many pamphlets such as *The Blot on the Escutcheon, Concentration of Energy, The Blood Red Record, The Making of a Race, A Tribute for the Negro Soldier,* and *Tracts for the People.* The voluminous Bruce Papers in the Schomburg Center for Research in Black Culture, New York Public Library, contain about 1300 of his letters, articles, speeches, unpublished manuscripts, programs, and scrapbooks.

A brilliant militant writer for the Negro press on many Negro problems, personalities, and history for half a century, Bruce worked with T. Thomas Fortune in the Afro-American League and the Afro-American Council in the 1890s. With Arthur A. Schomburg and others he organized the Negro Society for Historical Research in 1911. Bruce emphasized separate economic development or self-help, race pride, and solidarity during this period of frequent lynchings and severe proscription of Negroes. But he also agitated for political and civil rights for Negroes and hoped that World War I would usher in democracy for them. Disillusioned by the many race riots and lynchings in 1919 after he had supported World War I, Bruce criticized, then zealously joined Marcus Garvey's Universal Negro Improvement Association, and as contributing editor, wrote columns for the *Negro World* and the *Daily Negro Times,* the association's newspapers. He looked to Africa as the rightful home of the black man. The UNIA held three memorial services for him when he died. A book of selections from his writings was published in 1971 and renewed scholarly interest in Garvey has brought Bruce to the fore again. The John Edward Bruce Day Care Centers in Brooklyn, N.Y., were named for him in June 1972.

Additional material on Bruce may be found in *The Selected Writings of John Edward Bruce, Militant Black Journalist* (1971) edited by Peter Gilbert; *Calendar of the Manuscripts in the Schomburg Collection of Negro Literature and History* compiled by the Historical Records Survey, Work Projects Administration, New York City (1942, 1970); *The Afro-American Press and Its Editors* (1891, pp. 344–47; 1969) by I. Garland Penn; *Who's Who of the Colored Race* (1915); the *Negro World* (Aug. 16, 1924); the *New York Age* (Aug. 16, 1924); and Ralph L. Crowder's "John Edward Bruce: Pioneer Black Nationalist" (*Afro-Americans in New York Life and History* 2, no. 2, July 1978) and his "Self-Taught Street Scholars" (*Black Collegian* 9, no. 3, Jan.–Feb. 1979). — ERNEST KAISER

BRYAN, ANDREW (1737–1812), clergyman. Born a slave at Goose Creek, S.C., about sixteen miles from Charleston, he was brought to Savannah, Ga., where he was converted to Christianity by another pioneer Negro preacher, Andrew Liele. Bryan first began by public exhortations and prayer meetings at Brampton, Ga. Some nine months after Liele left Savannah following the failure of the French attack on the city in October 1779, Bryan began to preach to both Negroes and whites. Since his influence upon slaves was viewed at first as salutary, he was permitted to build a rough building on the land of Edward Davis at Yamacraw. Some slaveholders, however, fearful of his influence over the slaves, prevented Bryan and his followers from holding frequent meetings and drove them into the swamps. With the aid of his brother Sampson, he held his group together until the Rev. Abraham Marshall of Kioke baptized forty-five additional members, organized them as a church on Jan. 20, 1788, and ordained Andrew Bryan as a Baptist preacher. On the day before, Marshall had written Bryan: "This is to certify, that the Ethiopian Church of Jesus Christ at Savannah, have called their beloved Andrew to the work of the ministry. We have examined into his qualifications, and believing it to be the will of the great head of the church, we have appointed him to preach the Gospel, and to administer the ordinances, as God in his providence may call" (*The Annual Baptist Register, 1780–1801,* p. 367).

This increased influence led to growing fears of a servile insurrection, aggravated by news of the slave uprising in Saint-Domingue. Patrols whipped, arrested, and punished the worshipers even when they had passes. When Andrew Bryan refused to discontinue his work, he, his brother Sampson, and two of his first deacons were so "inhumanly cut and their backs were so lacerated that their blood ran down to the earth as they, with uplifted hands, cried unto the Lord; but Bryan in the midst of his torture, declared that he rejoiced not only to be scourged but would freely suffer death for the cause of Jesus Christ" (ibid., p. 366). Andrew and Sampson Bryan were imprisoned and dispossessed of their meeting house. Sympathetic white preachers condemned the barbarous treatment, and Jonathan Bryan, the master of Andrew and Sampson, obtained a hearing before the Inferior Court of Chatham County, which ordered their release. Despite renewed persecution, Andrew Bryan continued his preaching in a barn on Jonathan Bryan's plantation. Influential white friends and Bryan's communicants raised funds with which his first church was built in 1794 on a lot in Savannah. Shortly thereafter Jonathan Bryan died and the heirs permitted Andrew Bryan to purchase his freedom for £50, and to purchase a lot and build a house near the rough building he and Sampson had previously constructed. The church soon numbered 700 members.

Bryan's concept of the ministry far exceeded his time and period. He recognized the limitations of one's capacity to serve and proceeded to establish new churches when his immediate church grew too large. He consequently organized the Second African Baptist Church of Savannah and installed Henry Francis, slave of Col. Leroy Hammond, as pastor. Here again ability triumphed and Francis's freedom was purchased by some white men who wanted to see him devote all his time to his chosen work. Following continuous progress and growth, Bryan again divided his church and organized the Third African Baptist Church in another part of the city. From this church workers went to other cities, including Augusta, where a flourishing church was established.

When he died in 1812, the (white) Savannah Baptist Association paid tribute to "his extensively useful and amazingly luminous course in the lively exercise of faith and in the joyful hope of a happy immortality" (quoted by Carter G. Woodson, *The History of the Negro Church,* 2nd ed. [1921], p. 53). Andrew Bryan was one of the pioneer founders of Baptist churches in the United States.

His nephew, Andrew Marshall, succeeded him and enjoyed a long ministry until the insurrection of Nat Turner in 1831 led to the enactment of laws circumscribing the activities of Negro preachers.

The principal source is *The Baptist Annual Register, 1780–1801.* A perceptive summary is in Woodson's *The History of the Negro Church* (1921), and Miles Mark Fisher's *A Short History of the Baptist Denomination* (1933). See also John Rippon's *Baptist Register* (1791, passim). — L. VENCHAEL BOOTH

BURCH, CHARLES EATON (1891–1948), educator and literary scholar. Burch was born on July 14, 1891, in Bermuda. His early education was in the elementary and secondary schools of Bermuda and his advanced training in the United States, at Wilberforce University (B.A., 1914), Columbia University (M.A., 1918), and Ohio State University (Ph.D., 1933). He taught in the academic department of Tuskegee Institute in 1916–1917, and from 1918 to 1921 at Wilberforce, as instructor in English. In 1921 he was appointed to the faculty of Howard University, where he served, successively, as assistant professor (1921–1924), associate professor (1924–1936), and professor of English, and as acting head and (from 1933) head of the Department of English until his death on March 23, 1948. In addition to his work as a Defoe scholar, Burch made two major contributions to Howard University. In the early 1920s he introduced the course "Poetry and Prose of Negro Life," one of the first in an American university devoted to Negro literature. During the fifteen-year period when he was head of the Department of English he strengthened it significantly by recruiting several prominent scholars as well as many other able teachers.

Burch's published scholarship was widely known and influential. He was a specialist in the field of eighteenth-century English literature and an authority on the life and works of Daniel Defoe. His essays on Defoe's literary reputation were pioneer studies, which have remained the standard account, and his published research on Defoe's life and writings has been incorporated in the work of all subsequent biographers and bibliographers.

Early essays on a variety of subjects (listed by Mitchell) included articles on Paul Laurence Dunbar, the subject of Burch's master's thesis at Columbia University ("A Survey of the Life and Poetry of Paul Laurence Dunbar"). Foreshadowing his later, major interest, an essay on Defore, "Daniel Defoe's Views on Education," was first published in 1922 in the Howard University Record, revised for the London Quarterly Review in 1930, and ultimately resumed for an expanded study, still in draft at the time of his death.

A year of sabbatical leave from Howard (1927–1928) was spent at Edinburgh University where he studied with H. J. C. Grierson. His primary interest at the time was in Defoe's literary relationships. His research during that year at the National Library of Scotland produced a series of articles dealing with Defoe's life in Scotland, particularly his activities in connection with the Union, and established Defoe's authorship of hitherto unattributed pamphlets and periodical writings: "An Equivalent for Daniel Defoe" (Modern Language Notes, 44 [June 1929]: 378); "Defoe's Connections with the Edinburgh Courant" (Review of English Studies 5 [Oct. 1929]: 437–40); "Attacks on Defoe in Union Pamphlets" (Review of English Studies 6 [July 1930]: 318–19); and "Wodrow's List of Defoe's Pamphlets on the Union" (Modern Philology 28 [Aug. 1930]: 99–100).

Two essays on Defoe's literary relationships were related to his doctoral dissertation at Ohio State University, "The English Reputation of Daniel Defoe": British Criticism of Defoe as a Novelist 1719–1860" and "Defoe's British Reputation 1869–1894" (Englische Studien 67 [1932]: 178–98, and 68 [1934]: 410–23).

(A third article, extending the account to 1931, appears to have been accepted by the same journal but never printed.) A later article, "Notes on the Contemporary Popularity of Defoe's Review" (Philological Quarterly, 16 [April 1937]: 210–13), supplied evidence of the contemporary reputation of Defoe's periodical in London. An important essay, "The Moral Elements in Defoe's Fiction" (London Quarterly and Holborn Review, 162 [April 1937]: 207–13), focused on Defoe's character and personality and has continued to influence Defoe's biographers.

A return to Scotland in 1938 for a six-month period, for research at the National Library of Scotland and in the archives of Edinburgh University, led to further biographical and bibliographical discoveries which were published in the form of articles over the next decade. "Defoe and the Edinburgh Society for the Reformation of Manners" (Review of English Studies 16 [July 1940]: 306–12), "Benjamin Defore at Edinburgh University, 1710–1711" (Philological Quarterly 19 [Oct. 1940]: 343–48), and "Defoe and His Northern Printers" (Publications of the Modern Language Association of America 60 [March 1945]: 121–28), explored Defoe's life in Scotland; and there were further attributions in a series of published findings: "The Authorship of A Scots Poem (1707)" (Philological Quarterly 22 [Jan. 1943]: 51–57), "An Unassigned Defoe Pamphlet in the Defoe-Clark Controversy" and " 'A Discourse concerning the Union': An Unrecorded Defoe Pamphlet?" (Notes and Queries 188 [May 5, June 16, 1945]: 185–87, 244–46), "Defoe's First Seasonable Warning (1706)" (Review of English Studies 21 [Oct. 1945]: 322–26), and "Defoe's 'Some Reply to Mr. Hodges and Some other Authors' " and "The Authorship of 'A Letter concerning Trade from several Scots Gentlemen that are Merchants in London,' etc. (1706)" (Notes and Queries 193 [Feb. 21, March 6, 1948]: 72–74, 101–03). Posthumously published articles on Defoe and on Tobias Smollett were included in the American Peoples Encyclopedia, first published in 1948.

At the time of his death he was engaged in two major book-length projects: a biography of Defoe and an edition of Defoe's pamphlets on the Union, for which about half the material had been collected.

He was married to Willa Carter Mayer (1893–1953). Willa Burch was professor of education at Miner Teachers College, a supervisory official of the public schools of the District of Columbia, and the author of Clinical Practices in Public School Education (1944).

Burch died of a heart attack in Stamford, Conn. Funeral services were held in Rankin Memorial Chapel, Howard University, on March 26, where Mordecai W. Johnson, president of the university, delivered the eulogy. Burial was in Lincoln Memorial Cemetery, Suitland, Md. He was survived by his mother, Helena Burch of St. Georges, Bermuda, his widow, and three brothers. The English Department of Howard University established in 1949 the Charles Eaton Burch Memorial Lectures, which have continued annually. The speakers have been distinguished scholars.

Burch's collected correspondence and papers are in the Moorland-Spingarn Research Center of Howard University. His writings are listed in the Cambridge Bib-

liography of English Literature and *New Cambridge Bibliography of English Literature,* and in Velma McLin Mitchell's "Charles Eaton Burch: A Scholar and His Library" (*College Language Association Journal* 16 [1973]: 369–76), a portion of her "The Charles Eaton Burch Collection in Founders Library" (Howard University), which also catalogued Burch's library before its dispersal. Brief biographical accounts are in the *Directory of American Scholars* (1942), in obituary notices in the *Washington Star* and *Washington Post* (March 25, 27, 1948), and in "Charles Eaton Burch, Who Treads an Unbeaten Path" by Verna Arvey (*Opportunity* 20 [1942]: 245–46).

— CHARLOTTE CRAWFORD WATKINS

BURLEIGH, HARRY T[HACKER] (1866–1949), singer, composer, and arranger. The younger of two sons of Harry T. and Elizabeth (Waters) Burleigh, he was born in Erie, Pa. His maternal grandfather, Hamilton Waters, had been a slave in Somerset County, Md. Sustaining eye injuries as the result of a whipping, and discarded by his Maryland owners, he managed to escape to Erie, where he reared his family. Blind in his old age and employed as a town crier, he was often led about by his grandson. The boy's parents worked hard for the meagre existence they were permitted to earn. Elizabeth Burleigh, a college graduate and a natural singer, had been trained to teach but racist attitudes denied her the right to practice her profession in Pennsylvania. To earn a living she was obliged to perform the menial chores of a custodian in Erie's Public School No. 1, the very school in which she should have been teaching. Her son Harry often recalled how, led by his mother, he, his father, and his brother Reginald would harmonize as they jointly swept and dusted the classrooms.

Young Burleigh's first music lessons were given him by his mother, and the desire to be a musician settled upon him early in life. Still, he learned not to shrink from manual labor. He was only twelve when he and his brother began to earn a little money as lamp lighters in Erie's First Ward. They rose at four in the morning to extinguish the old-fashioned oil street lamps and Harry Burleigh often sang as he went about his work. Later in the morning before school, he was still singing as he delivered the *Erie Dispatch* to subscribers on his route. He soon became a chorister in Erie's St. Paul's Cathedral and a soloist in the choirs of that city's Park Presbyterian and First Presbyterian churches. In his desire to hear fine music he would often slip undetected into the Park Opera House to listen to the celebrated singers who performed there. By the time he graduated from the Erie high school, he was certain he wanted to be a professional musician.

Burleigh was twenty-four when he won a scholarship to study at the National Conservatory of Music in New York City. There he met Frances MacDowell, the mother of composer Edward MacDowell. As registrar of the conservatory, Mrs. MacDowell, impressed by the talent and manner of the young Negro singer, extended herself to help him. She quickly introduced him to the great Czech composer Anton Dvořak, who was then the director of the conservatory. A close and lasting

friendship was kindled between the two men, and continued to glow during Dvořak's sojourn in America. During his four years at the conservatory, Burleigh worked alternately as teacher, orchestra percussionist, and orchestra librarian. One summer he worked as a waiter in a Saratoga, N.Y., hotel. The following summer he returned to Saratoga as baritone soloist in the Episcopal church.

Meanwhile, in 1894 he entered the competition for a baritone soloist at Saint George's (all-white) Protestant Episcopal Church in New York City. His tryout performance topped those of fifty-nine white entrants. And although not everyone in the church was initially enthusiastic about his presence there, Burleigh, with the support of Dr. Rainsford, the rector, remained at Saint George's for the next half century. One year after joining the choir at St. George's, Burleigh sang his first solo there. It was Fauré's *The Palms,* and he sang it thereafter for fifty-two consecutive Palm Sundays.

In 1898 he married Louise Alston and the following year their son, Alston Waters Burleigh, was born. The child was a year old when Burleigh again broke precedent by joining the choir at New York's Temple Emanu-El, one of the world's largest synagogues. With his ability to sing not only in Hebrew but in Italian, Latin, French, and German as well, he remained there from 1900 until 1925.

It was in 1898, when the baritone singer was thirty-two years old, that he began his career as a songwriter. For the next thirty-seven years he carried on his work in that medium even as he performed on the concert stage. In 1898, too, he briefly performed in vaudeville, with Bert Williams and George Walker.

Although Burleigh, unlike his contemporary Will Marion Cook, did not restrict himself to the use of the Negro theme, his love and respect for that theme were evident in his earliest works and certainly in the later arrangements for which he is well known. Childhood contact with ex-slave grandfather Waters had left its impression and the young Burleigh had been liberally exposed at home to spirituals and other slave songs. As early as 1901 he transcribed a group of plantation tunes for piano and violin. In 1905 he did more of them, and five years later he transcribed an edition of Negro melodies composed by Stephen Foster. With these as a beginning Burleigh moved into more ambitious attempts. "The Young Warrior" (1914), his most extensive song, was followed in 1915 by "The Prayer" and "Ethiopia Saluting the Colors." These were followed by the sentimental "Little Mother of Mine" (1917), "In the Great Somewhere" (1919), and "Just You" (1921). John McCormick and Ernestine Schumann-Heink were among the popular singers who performed Burleigh's songs of that period. And a contemporary critic and composer, A. Walter Kramer, wrote in *Musical America* (March 17, 1919): "Mr. Burleigh's songs are continually becoming finer and finer. Each new one is bigger and more original than the last."

But it was Burleigh's 1916 and 1917 arrangements of the spiritual "Deep River" that established a new era in music. They were the first known arrangements of a Negro spiritual for solo voice with an independent piano accompaniment. With "Weepin' Mary," "Bye

An' Bye,'' and "You May Bury Me in the Eas' '' (1917)
Burleigh was quickly hailed as a pioneer and an authority. In 1917 he won the Spingarn Medal, the first musician to do so. He was awarded an honorary M.A. degree from Atlanta University and a D.Mus. degree from
Howard University in 1918 and 1920, respectively, and
the Harmon Award in 1930.

Burleigh continued arranging spirituals through 1935:
"My Lord What a Morning" (1918), "There Is a Balm
in Gilead" (1919), "Were You There?" and "Every
Time I Feel de Spirit" (1924), "Joshua Fit de Battle of
Jericho" (1935). At the same time he was doing his own
versions of such English, Swedish, and Scottish folk
tunes as "Some Rival Has Stolen My True Love Away"
(1934), "The Dove and the Lily" (1927), and "Ho-Ro:
My Nut Brown Maiden" (1930). In 1941, as he approached his seventy-fifth birthday, the American Society of Composers, Authors, and Publishers named him
a member of its board of directors. Among his protégés
were Roland Hayes, Paul Robeson, and Marian Anderson.

As a concert singer, Burleigh performed on stages all
across the United States, and in Europe where he sang
for heads of state. His impressive list of published works
includes ninety songs, two groups of songs, a group of
plantation melodies, forty-nine solo arrangements of
Negro spirituals, fifty choral works, and a dozen miscellaneous works.

Burleigh died on Sept. 12, 1949, at Stamford Hall, a
private convalescent home in Stamford, Conn., where
he had been ill for two years. Funeral services, attended
by almost 2000, were held in St. George's Church, 207
East 16th St., New York City, with burial in Mount Hope
Cemetery, Hastings, N.Y. Among the honorary pallbearers were Hall Johnson, Noble Sissle, Eubie Blake,
and Clarence Cameron White. He was survived by his
son Alston W. Burleigh (who died in Washington, D.C.,
on Nov. 27, 1977), and his grandson, Harry T. Burleigh
II. The burial was private.

Ellsworth Janifer's "H. T. Burleigh Ten Years Later"
(*Phylon,* Summer 1960) is a warm tribute. Maud
Cuney-Hare's *Negro Musicians and Their Music*
(1936, passim) has valuable comments, as does Henry
Lee's "Swing Low, Sweet Chariot" (*Coronet,* July
1947). Most significant are Eileen Southern's biographical sketch in *The Music of Black Americans: A History*
(1971, pp. 284–87, with comments passim) and *DAB,
Supplement Four* (1974, pp. 125–26). The Burleigh
Collection of magazine articles is in the Schomburg
Center for Research in Black Culture, New York City.
See the obituary in the *New York Times* (Sept. 13,
1949, p. 13) and the *New York Herald Tribune* (Sept.
18, 1949, p. 22). There is a marker near his birthplace
in Erie. — ELTON C. FAX

BURNS, ANTHONY (1834–1862), fugitive slave and
clergyman. Born in Stafford County, Va., Burns grew up
in slavery. From the age of seven he was hired out by
his master, Col. Charles Suttle; Burns later recalled that
the only wage he ever received from Suttle was a Christmas gift of twelve and a half cents at the end of every
year. As a child he managed to persuade some white
children to teach him to read, and at ten he experienced

a conversion to the Baptist faith. He preached to his
fellow slaves while in his teens, and began to dream of
escaping to the North. At twenty, having been hired out
to a Richmond mill owner, he hid away on board a ship
where he had a friend, and landed safely in Massachusetts in February 1854.

Arriving in Boston, Burns found a job in a downtown
clothing store and tried to keep his presence there a
secret. But on May 24, while walking home from work,
he was seized by a deputy marshal, carried to the U.S.
Court House, and confronted by his master. Anguished
and unnerved, "a piteous object," Burns was at first
unwilling to contest his case lest he suffer for it upon his
return to slavery. But the next day, after conferring with
his minister, the Rev. Leonard A. Grimes, he agreed to
do so.

For the next nine days Boston was in an uproar over
this attempt to enforce the Fugitive Slave Act of 1850.
Suttle had to be protected by a guard of southern students enrolled at Harvard, and troops were brought in
from Rhode Island, New Hampshire, and New York.
Wendell Phillips and Theodore Parker addressed an
angry protest meeting at Faneuil Hall, and a group of
Boston Negroes with white supporters made an unsuccessful attack on the courthouse in which a special
policeman was killed. Several days later the Reverend
Grimes's parishioners, with the aid of a State Street
businessman, raised the $1200 Suttle demanded for
Burns's freedom, but the sale was prevented by the U.S.
district attorney for political reasons.

Burns's hearing before a U.S. commissioner was brief
and one-sided; the best efforts of his lawyer, Richard H.
Dana, Jr., were of no avail. Denied the writ of *habeas
corpus,* bail, a jury trial, the right to testify in his own
behalf, and the right to appeal, Burns was turned over
to his master on June 2 for immediate return to Virginia.
State and federal troops and the entire Boston militia of
1500 men were needed to escort Burns through the
angry crowds and aboard a Treasury Department revenue cutter; the cost to the United States was over $100,-
000. Although a hundred-gun salute was fired at Alexandria, "in honor of the triumph of the law," the
Richmond Examiner complained that the manner of
Burns's return was "a mockery and an insult. . . . A few
more such victories, and the South is undone." No
other fugitive slave was ever returned from Massachusetts.

Back in Virginia, Burns was confined in the Richmond
slave jail for five months, his hands and feet so tightly
chained that his manacles wore through to the bone.
Having proved his point by recovering his slave from
abolitionist Boston, Suttle was anxious to dispose of
him. Public feeling against Burns in Virginia prevented
a direct sale to the North, so Suttle sold him instead to
a speculating North Carolina slave trader for $910. He
was then bought and freed for $1300 and expenses, the
money raised by the Reverend Grimes and his parishioners in 1855.

After his return to freedom, Burns briefly lectured for
antislavery societies, and then enrolled in the preparatory division of Oberlin College to complete his education. Turning down a contract offered to him by P. T.
Barnum and requests for more lecture tours, he pre-

ferred to study theology at Oberlin and at Fairmont Theological Seminary in Cincinnati. After ordination as a minister, he took charge of a Baptist church in Indianapolis in 1860. Later that year he became pastor of Zion Baptist Church in St. Catherine's, Ontario, where he preached to a congregation of former fugitives like himself. He died in Canada in 1862, at the age of twenty-eight, his health undermined by his sufferings as a slave. An early biography is C. E. Stevens's *Anthony Burns, A History* (1856). A modern treatment is *The Fugitive Slave Law and Anthony Burns: A Problem in Law Enforcement* by Jane H. Pease and William H. Pease (1975). There is a very brief sketch in *DAB* (new ed., 3:308) by Marie A. Kasten. — SAMUEL L. SHAPIRO

BURROUGHS, NANNIE (1879–1961), educator, civil rights advocate, and religious leader. She was born in Orange, Va., the daughter of John and Jennie (Poindexter) Burroughs. In 1883 she moved with her mother to Washington, D.C., where she was educated through the high school level. Employed in Louisville, Ky., during the years 1900–1909, Miss Burroughs worked as bookkeeper and editorial secretary of the Foreign Mission Board of the National Baptist Convention. In Louisville she organized a women's industrial club which conducted domestic science and secretarial courses. Nannie Burroughs was one of the founders of the Woman's Convention, auxiliary to the National Baptist Convention U.S.A., Inc., and served efficiently as its corresponding secretary from 1900 to 1947 and as its president from 1948 until 1961. Her childhood dream of establishing an industrial school for girls resulted in her mobilizing the energies of the Woman's Convention to build such an institution. On Oct. 19, 1909, the National Training School for Women and Girls opened at 50th and Grant Sts., NE, Washington, D.C. with Nannie Burroughs as president. By the end of the first year the school had enrolled thirty-one students. Twenty-five years later it boasted of more than 2000 women trained at the high school and junior college level. Housed in the campus dormitory, the girls came from all over the United States, Africa, and the Caribbean. Burroughs emphasized the training of spiritual character and thus dubbed her school the "School of the 3 B's— the Bible, bath, and broom" as tools for racial advancement. In 1934 the school was renamed the National Trades and Professional School for Women. Although closed for a short time during the Depression of the 1930s, the school continued to operate until Burroughs' death in 1961. In 1964 the board of trustees abandoned the old tradeschool curriculum and reestablished it as the Nannie Helen Burroughs School for students of elementary school age.

Her empathy for the Negro working woman was expressed through her participation in the club movement among colored women during the early decades of the twentieth century. In addition to her outstanding contribution to the National Association of Colored Women, Burroughs also founded the National Association of Wage Earners in order to attract public attention to the plight of Negro women. Its national board included Nannie Burroughs as president, along with other well-known clubwomen, Mary McCleod Bethune as vice-president, and Richmond, Va., banker Maggie L. Walker as treasurer. The women concentrated more on educational forums of public interest than on activities of a trade-unionist nature.

A staunch advocate of racial pride and heritage, Burroughs was a life member of the Association for the Study of Negro Life and History. At the Twelfth Annual Meeting of the association, held in Pittsburgh in 1927, she shared the platform on the last day with Carter G. Woodson and Alain Locke. Her paper, "The Social Value of Negro History," was described in the *Journal of Negro History* (Jan. 1928) as follows: "By a forceful address Miss Nannie Burroughs emphasized the duty the Negro owes to himself to learn his own story and the duty the white man owes to himself to learn of the spiritual strivings . . . of a despised but not an inferior people." Burroughs, along with other clubwomen, worked zealously to memorialize the home of Frederick Douglass in Anacostia, D.C., which was officially dedicated by them on Aug. 12, 1922. She was also a staunch supporter of the religious and secular programs sponsored by the Rev. Walter H. Brooks and the 19th Street Baptist Church in Washington, D.C.   .

The writings of Nannie Burroughs reflect both strong religious convictions and the belief in racial self-help and self-reliance. In her article "Not Color But Character" (*The Voice,* July 1904), she chastised black women who failed to appreciate their natural beauty. In an article in the *Southern Workman* (July 1927), "With All Thy Getting," Burroughs prophetically wrote: "No race is richer in soul quality and color than the Negro. Some day he will realize it and glorify them. He will popularize black." Motivated by a strong belief in God, she felt that racial equality was an ethical priority—a spiritual mandate from heaven. She denounced segregation and also such concepts as individualism and race deliverers. In a Feb. 17, 1934, *Afro-American* article, "Nannie Burroughs Says Hound Dogs Are Kicked But Not Bulldogs," she told Negroes to use "ballots and dollars" to fight racism instead of "wasting time begging the white race for mercy." In 1944 the Baptist Woman's Auxiliary began publication of a quarterly journal entitled *The Worker* under the editorship of Miss Burroughs. Other writings of a religious nature are her *Making Your Community Christian* (n.d.) and *Words of Light and Life Found Here and There* (1948).

She died of natural causes in Washington, D.C. Funeral services were held in the 19th Street Baptist Church, Washington, D.C., with interment in Lincoln Memorial Cemetery, Suitland, Md. There were no immediate survivors.

Published biographical material related to the life of Nannie Burroughs includes Sadie I. Daniel's *Women Builders* (1931), Earl L. Harrison's *The Dream and the Dreamer* (1956), and William Pickens's *Nannie Burroughs and the School of the 3B's* (1921). Also dealing with Burroughs's efforts to form a school and her ideas within her social milieu is Evelyn Brooks Barnett's "Nannie Burroughs and the Education of Black Women" (in Sharon Harley and Rosalyn Terbourg-Penn, eds., *The Afro-American Woman,* (1978). Her obituary in the *Washington Post* (May 21, 1961, p. B6, and May 22, 1961, p. B8) is also of interest. The most comprehensive collection of materials related to her life and activities can be found in the Nannie H. Burroughs Papers in the Library of Congress.

— EVELYN BROOKS BARNETT

BUSH, GEORGE WASHINGTON (1790?–1863), entrepreneur. Bush was probably born in Pennsylvania, but moved to Tennessee with his family while still young. Little is known of his life before 1812 when, during the War of 1812, he fought under Andrew Jackson in the Battle of New Orleans. Following his military service he worked for fur-trading companies. He worked first for a Frenchman named Robidoux, whose headquarters were in St. Louis, and later for the Hudson's Bay Company. Sometime in the 1820s, while in the employ of the Hudson's Bay Company, he traveled to the Pacific Coast.

Upon his return to Missouri he settled in Clay County where he married Isabella James in 1831 and raised a family of five sons. His stock-raising, farming, and nursery business made him a wealthy man. In the spring of 1844 when he agreed to join a party of white Missourians headed west, he was the wealthiest member of the group and the only one with previous knowledge of the West. Through his generosity several of his poor neighbors were able to join the party with wagons and teams he had purchased for them. The Bush party reached the Dalles in the Oregon Territory in the late fall of 1844. Although a white man, Michael T. Simmons, was elected to head the group, Bush's presence and guidance, as well as his continued financial support of members of the party, were indispensable to the success of the venture.

Ironically, the discrimination that George Bush hoped to escape by leaving Missouri was firmly established in the Oregon Territory when he arrived. Largely through the efforts of white emigrants from slave states, an amendment to the provisional government's organic code had been passed in the summer of 1844 which forbade Negroes to settle in the territory. Bush and his family were forced to settle north of the Columbia River in the Puget Sound region, which was then British territory. American settlers anywhere north of the Columbia River were actively discouraged by the Hudson's Bay Company which represented the British government, and it often refused to sell the settlers supplies in order to enforce its control. Because George Bush had friends among the French Canadians in the region from his previous trip west, and had also previously worked for the Hudson's Bay Company, he and his party were able to cross the Columbia River and settle where other American emigrants had been excluded. Bush was on excellent terms with the Indians too, and the whites in his company benefited accordingly.

Once the party had reached the Puget Sound region, Bush took up a donation claim of 640 acres, which became known as Bush Prairie, four miles south of Olympia. He started a farm and soon became the main supplier of fruit, vegetables, and grain to newcomers in the area. Although he was often the only person in the region with food to sell, he never took advantage of the situation by raising his prices beyond a fair amount. Because of Bush's integrity and his refusal to exploit his

position to the harm of others, he saved many lives during a period of virtual famine in the winter of 1852.

In 1846 the Hudson's Bay Company moved its headquarters to Victoria on Vancouver Island, Canada, and the United States–Canadian border was fixed at 49° N. This brought Bush's property within the Oregon Territory and the racist provisions of the provisional government's organic law. Even though his property was in jeopardy, Bush nevertheless continued to work his farm and lend his support to the economic development of his community. He helped construct the first saw and grist mill, and purchased a fanning mill which he allowed other grain farmers to use.

When in 1853 the Washington Territory was declared separate from the Oregon Territory, Bush's white friends, to whom he had devoted long and faithful assistance, belatedly decided to use their influence to have Congress grant Bush title to his land. Their efforts proved successful and in 1855, eight years before his death, George Bush was granted title to his property. George Washington Bush died in 1863.

Jalmar Johnson's *Builders of the Northwest* (1966) has a perceptive chapter on George Washington Bush and Oregon. Secondary sources are numerous but for the most part lack solid documentation. Perhaps the best of these are Ezra Meeker's *The Busy Life of Eighty-Five Years of Ezra Meeker* (1916), Ruby El Hult's article "The Saga of George W. Bush" (in *This Land Around Us: A Treasury of Pacific Northwest Writing* edited by Ellis Lucia, 1969), the Oregon Pioneer Association's *Transactions of the Fifteenth Annual Reunion* (1887), and Mrs. George Blankenship's *Early History of Thurston County* (1914). The Memorial to the Legislative Assembly, Washington, is in the *House of Representatives, Journal . . . First Session . . . begun February 27, 1854* (1855), pp. 157–58. The congressional bill of Feb. 7, 1855, granting Bush 640 acres of land is in the *Congressional Globe* (33rd Cong., 2d sess., 1855). The *Index to the First Federal Census: Territory of Washington* (1860, 1972, p. 212) shows Bush as a head of a household. — MARCIA M. GREENLEE

BUSH, JOHN EDWARD (1856?–1916), fraternal official, Republican politician, and businessman. Born a slave in Moscow, Tenn., he knew little of his father but a photograph shows that his father was probably white. At the end of the Civil War, Bush, his mother, brothers, and sisters were abandoned in Little Rock where they had been taken in 1862 to avoid the approaching Union Army. He became an orphan at the age of seven and lived a beggar's existence for a time. He became a brick molder, made his way through Capitol High School in 1876, and immediately became a teacher in the school. During 1878–1879 he was principal of the Negro public school in Hot Springs, Ark. In 1879 Bush married Cora Winfrey, daughter of Solomon Winfrey of Little Rock, one of that city's old and respected families. They had four children—Stella, John E. Jr., Chester, and Aldridge —all of whom were active in the Mosaic Templars of America, of which their father was a co-founder.

Besides teaching, Bush engaged in several other professions. He served as a railway mail clerk for a time, and in 1898 was appointed receiver of the U.S. Land

Office in Little Rock, a post he held until the Wilson administration. Bush assisted in the establishment of the Negro Capitol City Savings Bank, and served as vice-president. He also invested heavily in real estate.

It was his interest in Negro business that brought Bush into contact with Booker T. Washington. Bush became an active participant in Washington's "Tuskegee Machine," serving for a time as vice-president of the National Negro Business League. On several occasions Bush called upon his friend at Tuskegee to assist him in his political problems. For example, in 1906 Bush used Washington's patronage powers to win reappointment from President Roosevelt as receiver of the Little Rock Land Office; Bush also had the support of many white leaders in Arkansas.

It was in the area of partisan politics and civil rights that Bush exerted his most powerful influence. As early as 1883 he was active in Pulaski County Republican affairs. He was closely aligned with the party faction headed by former Reconstruction governor Powell Clayton. From 1890 until his death Bush found himself constantly fighting the "lily white" forces in the state Republican organization. In 1890 he overcame white opposition to win the party nomination for Pulaski County chancery clerk. In 1905 he helped organize the Fred Douglass Club, a Negro Republican patronage-lobbying group. By 1914 Bush was being mentioned as a possible gubernatorial candidate of disgruntled Negro Republicans.

In the area of civil rights for Negroes, Bush was a leader in opposing the 1891 Arkansas separate-coach proposal. In 1898 he worked for the placement of Negroes in governmental service in Arkansas. Bush particularly opposed the efforts of the racist governor, Jeff Davis, to segregate school taxes in Arkansas.

When not involved in governmental service or politics, Bush spent much of his time in fraternal activities. In 1882 he and Chester W. Keatts organized the Mosaic Templars of America. Bush served the fraternity in a number of capacities, including editor of the *Mosaic Guide* newspaper. By the time of his death the fraternity had 80,000 members in twenty-six states and several foreign nations. In February 1916 he suffered a stroke, never returned to his office, and died on Dec. 11, 1916. He was buried in an impressive Mosaic Vermont granite mausoleum in Little Rock.

The most thorough and scholarly historical account of Bush is C. Calvin Smith's "John E. Bush of Arkansas, 1890–1910" (*Ozark Historical Review* 2 [Spring 1973]: 48–59). A laudatory sketch is in A. E. Bush and P. L. Dorman (eds.), *History of the Mosaic Templars of America, Its Founders, and Officials* (1924, pp. 19–114), with a photograph and a commencement address at Tuskegee Institute (n.d.). — TOM W. DILLARD

BUSH, WILLIAM OWEN (1832–1907), Washington state pioneer, master farmer, and legislator. Bush was born in Clay County, Mo., on July 4, 1832, the oldest son of George Washington Bush and his wife Isabella James, born in Tennessee of German ancestry. The Bush family left Missouri in 1844 for the Oregon Territory and in 1845 settled at what became known as Bush Prairie, a few miles south of present-day Olympia,

Washington, where George Bush won esteem as a progressive, innovative, and generous farmer. William Bush, on May 26, 1859, in Marion County, Ore., married Mandana Smith Kimsey, daughter of Dr. J. Smith and Nancy Scott Wisdom Smith, and the widow (1858) of Duff Kimsey, who had been born in Howard County, Mo., on June 1, 1826, and had crossed to Oregon with her husband and parents in 1847. They had three children: George O., who died in infancy, and John Shotwell and Mandana Isabella, who lived to maturity and married. His wife died in 1899.

William Bush followed in his father's footsteps as a master farmer. He bought a farm on Mound Prairie, where he lived until 1870 when he moved to a part of his late father's donation claim. He exhibited Puget Sound products at the Centennial Exposition in Philadelphia in 1876 and won a gold medal for his wheat. In 1879 he was reported as raising oats eight feet high and in 1880 was president of the Washington Industrial Association. In 1893 he was sent to the Columbian Exposition at Chicago, in charge of the Thurston County exhibit. He was elected in 1889 to Washington's first state legislature, and was reelected for a second term.

A photograph of William Bush (c. 1889) does not at all suggest Negro ancestry, and some of his descendants assert that his grandfather Matthew Bush was a native of India without African ancestry; however, all contemporaries of his father—and indeed George Bush himself—regarded that pioneer as a mulatto.

The principal authority on William Bush is the Rev. Harvey K. Himes's *An Illustrated History of the State of Washington* (1893), which should be supplemented by newspaper references in Hazel E. Mills (ed.), *The Negro in the State of Washington, 1788–1969: A Bibliography* . . . (1970), and by Bush genealogies in the Washington State Library. — KENNETH WIGGINS PORTER

BUTLER, THOMAS C. (1865–1905), army officer. Born in Baltimore, Md., Butler studied for the priesthood at a Jesuit college in Annapolis, but went to sea before completing his preparation. After an 1887 shipwreck off Cape Hatteras, N.C., he enlisted in the 9th Cavalry and served with that unit at Forts McKinney, Wyo., and Robinson, Neb. During the Sioux campaign of 1890–1891 he participated in the rescue of the 7th Cavalry from a Sioux trap at Drexel Mission on the Pine Ridge reservation. In 1895 he transferred to the 25th Infantry, then in Montana, and remained in that regiment through the Cuban campaign of 1898. After the war, Butler served as a commissioned officer with volunteer infantry in the Philippine Insurrection. When his regiment was mustered out of service in 1901, he remained in Manila, where he died in June 1905. He was buried in Arlington National Cemetery with military honors two months later.

During the battle for Santiago, Cuba, on July 1, 1898, the 25th Infantry attacked the Spanish garrison on El Caney, a key hill northeast of the city. After a hard fight, the Negro infantrymen drove the defenders out of the blockhouse on the crest of the hill. Butler, then a private in H Company, and Pvt. J. H. Jones of D Company, were the first Americans into the small stone fort. Butler seized the Spanish flag but was forced to surrender it by a white man dressed like an officer, perhaps correspondent James Creelman. Butler managed to tear off and hide a corner of the trophy.

After the war Butler was awarded a commission as second lieutenant in the 9th Infantry, U.S. Volunteers. The regiment was disbanded in 1899, and he joined one of the new regiments organized for service in the Philippine Insurrection. Gen. Nelson Miles recommended Butler for a captaincy, but there were no vacancies at that grade. He joined F. Company of the 49th Infantry as a first lieutenant and company executive officer. After a short tour of recruiting duty in Baltimore, he joined the regiment at Jefferson Barracks, Mo., for the journey to Manila. On two occasions his bravery and leadership brought official recognition from his regimental commander, Col. William H. Beck. On May 29, 1900, at Cabangan Nuevo on Luzon, he and seventeen men withstood an attack by nearly 250 of the enemy, killed twenty, and captured over one hundred weapons. Colonel Beck praised Butler in a regimental order for the "great courage" with which he repulsed the attack after a "hot and continuous fight" of over two hours. He was also commended in regimental orders for his leadership on Aug. 12, 1900, when he single-handedly disarmed one insurgent soldier and killed another with his pistol, while his men dispatched four more of the enemy.

W. Hilary Coston's *The Spanish-American War Volunteer* (1899) contains a useful biographical sketch of Butler. Other good sources of information are the army enlistment registers and the books of the 49th Infantry, in the National Archives. The seizure and theft of the El Caney flag stirred some controversy in military circles. John H. Nankivell's *The History of the Twenty-fifth Regiment United States Infantry* (1927, 1972) contains substantial contemporary comment on the matter.

— FRANK N. SCHUBERT

CAESAR, JOHN (? –1837), insurrectionist. The principal Negro of King Phillip (Emathla or Imala), the head chief of the St. Johns River Indians and the second chief (after Micanopy) of the Seminole nation, Caesar was next to Micanopy's chief Negro Abraham in his influence among the Indian-Negroes and Indians of Florida. Caesar on the eve of the Seminole War was a rather old man who had either been born among the Indians or had lived with them most of his life. He had a wife on one of the St. Johns River plantations, and with Abraham visited these plantations and arranged with the principal slaves to revolt whenever the Seminole began open resistance to the U.S. government's attempt to remove them. Late in December 1835 Philip and John Caesar with their Indians and Indian-Negroes attacked the St. Johns River plantations and were joined by hundreds of slaves.

Caesar was at the siege of Fort Izard on the Withlacoochee early in 1836, perhaps as a representative of the St. Johns River hostiles to Micanopy's Seminole, and on March 6 was a negotiator, with Osceola, Abraham, and others, at a conference with Gen. E. P. Gaines. Caesar then dropped out of sight for nearly a year, but when Gen. T. S. Jesup late in 1836 began an aggressive campaign which drove Micanopy's and Osceola's hos-

tiles eastward toward Philip's territory, he organized a guerrilla campaign against plantations in the St. Augustine vicinity, using primarily recent runaways. On the night of Jan. 17, 1837, he was interrupted in a horse-stealing raid, and surprised in camp the following night; Caesar and two other Negroes were killed.

Caesar was, however, even more effective in death than in life. The discovery that runaway slaves were raiding so close to St. Augustine and were in communication with some of its Negro residents produced general alarm. General Jesup was led to recognize the importance of conciliating the Seminole Negro element, lest a general slave insurrection result. Although the Treaty of Fort Dade (March 6, 1837), whereby the Seminole agreed to emigrate on condition of protection for their Negro "slaves" and allies, was speedily violated, in the long run all Indian-Negroes and runaways who agreed to surrender were permitted to go west.

John Caesar, by his rousing of the plantation slaves at the beginning of the war and by his attempt, abortive though it was, to employ such runaways in guerrilla activities near St. Augustine, was largely responsible for a policy which meant freedom for numerous Negroes who otherwise would have been reenslaved.

For a more detailed discussion of John Caesar's life and role, see Kenneth W. Porter, *The Negro on the American Frontier* (1971, pp. 338–57).

— KENNETH WIGGINS PORTER

CAIN, RICHARD HARVEY (1825–1887), clergyman and South Carolina congressman. Cain was born free in Greenbrier County, Va., the son of a Cherokee Indian mother and an African father. In 1831 his parents moved to Ohio where the boy received a limited education, first in Portsmouth, then in Cincinnati, before signing on the steamboat service on the Ohio River. At the age of sixteen he was converted to the Methodist Episcopal church while continuing to work on the riverboats. But three years later he became a full-fledged clergyman when he was ordained and licensed to preach in Hannibal, Mo. He soon became dissatisfied with conditions in the M.E. church, returned to Cincinnati, and joined the African Methodist Episcopal church. In 1859 he was ordained a deacon, but realizing that he needed more formal education, in 1860 he enrolled as a student at Wilberforce University. In 1861 he was sent to the New York Conference and had charge of an important Brooklyn pulpit for four years. In 1862 he was ordained an elder by Bishop Daniel A. Payne in Washington, D.C.

He was transferred to the South Carolina Conference in 1865 at the close of the Civil War and sent to Charleston to stimulate religious activity among the freedmen. His principal mission was to rebuild and reorganize the huge Emanuel Church which had been closed since 1822 when Denmark Vesey was thought to have laid plans for his famous insurrection within the sanctuary of the church. Emanuel Church was not segregated; anyone except former slaveholders was permitted to join, and under Cain's guidance over 3000 persons soon became members.

Cain promptly became active in secular matters as

well, as he was quickly drawn into the vortex of political life in which his race was for the first time playing a vital role. A few months after his arrival in Charleston he made an important speech at the Colored People's Convention held in Zion Church, a gathering which marked the first concerted action of the newly emerging Negro leadership. By the fall of 1866 he had become editor of the *South Carolina Leader,* the first newspaper to be published by Negroes in the state after the war. Within two years this became the *Missionary Record,* and Cain remained its editor throughout its effective life, which lasted until 1872. He was a man of great energy and enthusiasm, a splendid organizer, ambitious for himself and for his race. Under his aegis the *Missionary Record* became increasingly critical of the white carpetbaggers whose often arrogant attitude toward the Negro Cain considered more of a threat than the out-and-out enmity of the native whites.

He became a delegate to the 1868 Constitutional Convention at which universal manhood suffrage was for the first time embodied in the state constitution. At the convention he was a leader in trying to obtain land for the freedmen, recognizing that the popular slogan "forty acres and a mule" symbolized their passionate desire to "own the land which for so long owned them."

Following the convention he was elected to represent Charleston in the state Senate. After one term there he ran, and was defeated, for alderman in Charleston. Shortly thereafter "Daddy" Cain, as he was referred to, became involved in an ambitious real estate venture. He contracted to buy 3000 acres of land, subdivided the area, named it Lincolnville, and sold twenty-five lots before the previous owners foreclosed because he had failed to make the promised payments. A brief scandal followed, but he was not indicted at the time and was, in fact, elected to the U.S. House of Representatives shortly afterward (1872).

As a member of the 43rd Congress he made notable speeches (as did all the other Negro congressmen) in favor of civil rights. His oration on Jan. 10, 1874, was less scholarly and received less acclaim than did that of his South Carolina colleague, Robert Brown Elliott. But Cain's pungent rhetoric, at times spiced with wry humor, was a strong defense of his embattled race ("Mr. Speaker, I had supposed the cruel war as over," he began), with an eloquent demand for their liberty and equality, and adamant opposition to colonization. In the second session he outraged opponents when he hoped the time would come "when there should be no white, no black . . . but one common brotherhood, going forward forever in the progress of nations."

He did not stand for reelection in 1874 but was again elected in 1876 to the 45th Congress. During this session he introduced an important bill calling for money from the sale of public lands to be set apart for education. He also put forward several petitions for a constitutional amendment favoring women's suffrage and a measure to establish a mail and steamship line between the United States and Liberia. None of these was passed.

Cain served out his term in Congress after Reconstruction came to an end in 1877. His post-Reconstruc-

tion career was far more successful than that of most of the other southern Negro politicians. He left South Carolina in 1880, having been elected fourteenth bishop of the A.M.E. church and assigned to Louisiana and Texas. In that capacity he helped found Paul Quinn College in Waco, Tex., and became its second president. In 1880 he returned to his post as bishop, presiding over the New York, New Jersey, New England, and Philadelphia district. He died in Washington, D.C., on Jan. 18, 1887.

Marie Le Baron, a newspaper correspondent in Washington, wrote a sketch of him for the *St. Louis Globe* (reprinted in the *National Republican,* April 16, 1874) in which she referred to his "peculiar expression," his long arms, and the fact that some of his detractors called him the "Darwinian Link." Yet she was impressed by his "fervid eloquence," his wit, his sardonic humor, and his dramatic power.

The *American Baptist* (Feb. 5, 1887) praised the "priceless legacy" he had left young men, especially to those of the A.M.E. church.

A contemporary account is in William J. Simmons's *Men of Mark . . .* (1887, pp. 87–96); a favorable chapter in Maurine Christopher's *America's Black Congressmen* (1971, pp. 87–96), and unfavorable comments in Samuel Denny Smith's *The Negro in Congress, 1870–1901* (1940, passim). The brief sketch by Carter G. Woodson in *DAB* (Part 1 [new ed.], 2:403–4), asserted that "he was generally referred to, even by his enemies, as an upright and honest man who deserved the good will of all citizens." Useful references are in *After Slavery* by Joel Williamson (1965) and *The Glorious Failure, Black Congressman Robert Brown Elliott and the Reconstruction of South Carolina* (1973) by Peggy Lamson. — PEGGY LAMSON

CALIVER, AMBROSE (1894–1962), teacher, college administrator, and public servant. He was born in Saltsville, Va., on Feb. 25, 1894, the son of Ambrose and Cora (Saunders) Caliver. His intellectual ability, academic background, and sense of professional responsibility contributed to his important place in American education. His elementary and secondary education in the public schools of Virginia and Knoxville, Tenn., was followed by collegiate work at Knoxville College, from which he received a B.A. in 1915. Five years later the University of Wisconsin awarded him an M.A. (1920), and in 1930 his Ph.D. degree was received from Columbia University.

His professional experiences began as a high school principal in Rockwood, Tenn. (1916), and as an assistant principal of Douglass High School in El Paso, Tex. His first appointment in higher education came at Fisk University (1917) where he was asked to develop a program of training in manual arts, an area in which he had especial interest in view of his opinion that the complete education of the individual involved learning to work with one's hands. His progress through the academic ranks at Fisk was rapid; within ten years he became the first Negro dean of the university (1927). His earlier administrative positions at Fisk included publicity director (1925) and dean of the scholastic department (1926).

In 1930 Caliver was appointed to a new position in

the Office of Education, specialist in Negro education. He was a moving force in the opening of the government cafeteria in the Department of Interior to Negroes, and in the elimination of the lowercase "n" in the spelling of Negro. His courage, tact, and perseverance garnered financial and professional support for the many projects in which he was interested.

Caliver's numerous research activities included surveys of pressing educational problems, new programs, bulletins on special phases of Negro education, and bibliographies. His important publications include *Bibliography on Education of the Negro, Comprising Publications from January, 1928 to December, 1930* (1931); *Background Study of Negro College Students, Rural Elementary Education Among Negroes under Jeanes Supervising Teachers* (1933); *The Education of Negro Teachers* (1933); *Secondary Education for Negroes* (1933); *Availability of Education to Negroes in Rural Communities* (1936); *Fundamentals in the Education of Negroes* (1935); and *Vocational and Educational Guidance of Negroes* (1938). In 1945 Caliver noted that his office had published nineteen bulletins, ten leaflets, pamphlets, or mimeographed circulars, and thirty-six articles during its fifteen years of existence.

Caliver's activities extended beyond his publications, for his recommendations resulted in the establishment of the National Advisory Committee on the Education of Negroes (1930–1950), the convening of the National Conference on Fundamental Problems in the Education of Negroes (1934), the National Survey of the Vocational and Educational Guidance of Negroes (1935–1938), and the National Survey of the Higher Education of Negroes (1939–1942). Other major efforts were directed toward adult education and the eradication of illiteracy. His designation in 1946 as director of the Project for Literacy Education resulted in significant developments in adult education: (1) a determination of the extent of illiteracy and the need for adult education; (2) the preparation of instructional materials adapted to adult needs; and (3) the training of teachers for adults with literacy below the fourth-grade level. Workshops were held throughout the United States and a special program developed for the army through which 86 percent of the trainees considered illiterate were brought up to the fourth-grade level.

As Caliver moved up in the Office of Education to specialist in the higher education of Negroes (1946), assistant to the U.S. commissioner of education (1950), and chief of the Adult Education Section of the Office of Education (1955), he became increasingly involved in national and international activities, including his appointments as a consultant to the U.S. Displaced Persons Commission (1949), advisor to the United Nations Special Committee on Non-Self-Governing Territories (1950), and a member of the Survey Staff of Education in the Virgin Islands (1950), of the committee to explore federal participation in the development of community colleges (1951), the U.S. Delegation to the Inter-American Cultural Council (1951), and consultant to the National Commission on Literacy Education of the Adult Education Association (1955).

His devotion to adult education and his numerous efforts in this field had a significant impact on the national scene. He was in demand as a consultant, speaker, and adviser. Adult education had become his primary concern; his contributions and leadership in adult education were recognized in his election to the presidency of the Adult Education Association of the United States in 1961.

The outstanding contributions made by Caliver to American education, and especially to adult education, were in part a by-product of his mature personality. His ability to have persons and groups of divergent backgrounds and concerns understand their mutual problems and resolve conflict made him a distinguished leader.

Caliver married Everly Rosalie Rucker in December 1916. He died of a heart attack after a long illness at his home, 1210 Lamont St., NW, Washington, D.C., on Jan. 29, 1962. Funeral services were held on Feb. 2 at Lincoln Temple Congregational Church, 11th and R Sts. NW, with interment in Lincoln Memorial Cemetery, Suitland, Md. He was survived by his widow, his daughter Jewell (Mrs. Richard Terrell), a sister, brother, two grandchildren, and his son-in-law.

The best study is Walter G. Daniel's and John B. Holden's *Ambrose Caliver, Educator and Civil Servant* (1966). See also Theresa Wilkins's "Ambrose Caliver: Distinguished Civil Servant" (*JNH,* Spring 1962, pp. 212–214). See the obituaries in the *Washington Evening Star* (Jan. 29, 1962) and the *Washington Post* (Feb. 2, 1962). — CARROLL L. MILLER

CALLIOUX [CAILLOUX], ANDRÉ (1820?–1863), cigar maker, soldier, and hero of Port Hudson. In many ways a unique Louisianian on the eve of the Civil War, Callioux was a free man in a state which held as slaves thousands of his race. He was a superb horseman, boxer, and athlete, skills which were largely reserved for upper-class whites in antebellum southern society. He proudly boasted of being the blackest man in New Orleans, a city whose free black population had a caste system based on color. Callioux was a skilled, educated, and erudite member of the Cresent City's black Creole society.

When secession and civil war came to Louisiana, Callioux and 440 other New Orleans free Negroes raised and equipped a regiment for Confederate service. What motivated Callioux and his comrades is unclear. One officer later claimed that he had joined because of threats by the New Orleans police. However true that may have been, it is also true that many members of the regiment had property to protect and economic reasons for maintaining stability in southern society.

Whatever the impetus, Callioux and his regiment were accepted for service by the Confederate governor of Louisiana. But when New Orleans fell to the Union forces of Brig. Gen. Benjamin F. Butler in April 1862, Callioux and the Native Guard Regiment elected to remain in the city rather than evacuate the area with the rest of the Confederate forces. That passive act tends to suggest that Callioux and the Native Guard members were more intent on protecting the gains they had made in society than on serving the Confederacy. Within a few weeks after Butler's arrival, and after some hesitation, the Native Guard was mustered into federal service.

Callioux was a captain in the 1st Regiment Louisiana Native Guard. But Callioux and his comrades in the four colored units were not accepted as line soldiers either by Butler or by his replacement in Louisiana, Brig. Gen. Nathaniel P. Banks. Both federal officers used Callioux and his men as garrison troops or for guarding roads and rail lines. It was widely believed in both North and South that Negroes lacked the qualities necessary for combat soldiers.

By May 1863 Callioux and the members of the Native Guard regiments were eager to destroy the myth of Negro inferiority as soldiers, eager to take their place as line soldiers in a war which was increasingly becoming one of abolition, eager to respond through action to the question "Will they fight?" Their opportunity came at Port Hudson, La., a high-walled and well-garrisoned Confederate strong point strategic to the control of the Mississippi River. Federal gunboats were able to silence the rebel batteries but were unable to force the surrender of the fort. That would come only with costly ground assaults.

Despite the military hazards, or perhaps because of them, Callioux and his fellow officers of the Native Guard requested that their regiments be given lead positions in the assault on Port Hudson. The request was granted, and the 1st and 3rd Louisiana Native Guard Regiments assaulted the works in the early morning of May 27, 1863. Throughout the morning and into the afternoon the Negro troops made six distinct assaults on the Confederate works, suffering heavy losses. During the final assault of the day, Callioux was seen leading his men with sword in hand while the other arm hung at his side with a wound above the elbow. He was killed by a direct artillery hit.

Callioux lay where he fell until July 9 when the fort surrendered. Once his body was recovered, it was taken home to New Orleans for a hero's burial. His funeral was described as "the most extraordinary local event that has ever been seen within our borders." His flag-draped coffin lay in state where Negroes and whites paid homage while members of the regiment paced silently as guards. On the day of the funeral the route from the church to the cemetery was lined with crowds of Negroes; no fewer than thirty-seven Creole social and economic societies were represented.

Callioux was one of many, black and white, who died in the American Civil War, but for Louisiana Negroes his death had special meaning. At Port Hudson Callioux repeatedly displayed the courage and soldierly qualities which skeptics asserted blacks did not possess. The question of whether or not Negroes would fight was largely answered after Port Hudson. Moreover, with Callioux's death black Americans could look to the articulate, educated, and gentlemanly Callioux as a national hero, as a symbol of courage.

For sources on Callioux, see Donald Everett's "Ben Butler and the Louisiana Guards, 1861–1862" (*Journal of Southern History,* 1967), Mary F. Berry's "Negro Troops in Blue and Gray: The Louisiana Native Guards" (*Louisiana History,* 1967), Peter Ripley's "Black, Blue and Gray: Slaves and Freedmen in Civil War Louisiana"

(Ph.D. dissertation, Florida State University, 1973). See also *National Anti-Slavery Standard* (June 20 and Aug. 15, 1863); *New York Times* (July 1, 1863).

— C. PETER RIPLEY

CAMPBELL, JAMES EDWIN (1867–1896), poet, educator, and journalist. Born in Pomeroy, Meigs County, Ohio, the son of James and Lethia Stark Campbell, and the youngest of their three children, James attended Pomeroy High School, graduating in 1884. While in school he pursued the Latin and German course which prepared him for the teaching profession. Soon after graduation he found employment in the colored schools of Rutland, Ohio. His success brought the offer of the principalship of the white school in the community, an offer which he refused.

An outstanding public speaker, Campbell stumped the state of Ohio in behalf of the Republican State Executive Committee during the fall of 1887, an activity he continued and expanded to West Virginia during the following year. He became a delegate and secretary to the Meigs County Republican Convention, and later served as a delegate to the 12th District Congressional Convention.

Campbell's literary career traces to 1887, when he became editor of the *West Virginia Enterprise,* published in Kanawha County, W.Va. The same year marked the publication of his first book of poetry, *Driftings and Gleanings.* Two years later, in April 1889, the *A.M.E. Church Review* published his poem "Pariah's Love."

In 1890 he became principal of Langston School in Point Pleasant, W.Va. While principal, he guided the move into a five-story brick structure. The same year a biographical sketch and poem of his appeared in a work titled *Poets of America.* In 1891 Campbell was named the first principal of the West Virginia Collegiate Institute, near Charleston. The earliest state-supported institution of higher education for the Negro in West Virginia, Campbell was able to see it through the formative construction phases and popularize its work throughout the state. Concurrent with the opening of the institute was the establishment of the West Virginia Teachers Association, organized by Negro teachers in the state. Campbell played an active part in the organization, addressing it in 1892 and being named its president in the following year. On Aug. 5, 1891, he married Mary Champ, a graduate of Marietta College and a fellow teacher.

Leaving West Virginia in 1893, Campbell moved to Chicago, obtaining employment on the staff of the *Chicago Times-Herald.* While in the city he met Paul Laurence Dunbar at the Chicago Exposition. Campbell continued to contribute to a number of Chicago newspapers such as the *Chronicle, Record, Inter-Ocean, Tribune,* and *Illustrated Push.* He maintained his interest in poetry by being part of a group which issued the *Four O'Clock Magazine,* a literary publication. The zenith of his literary career came in 1895 with the publication of a book of poems entitled *Echoes from the Cabin and Elsewhere.* The book, which received much critical acclaim, used the Gullah dialect of South Carolina. The publication marked Campbell as one of the earliest Negro poets to write in dialect, making him a precursor of Dunbar. From an artistic point of view Campbell's verse was more representative of the minstrel than the plantation tradition. He was, as James Weldon Johnson notes, "free from the sweetness of the plantation tradition." Campbell's phonetics were primitive and less sophisticated than those of Dunbar, yet they more nearly approached the nuances of dialects of African and West Indies origin. His poetry in literary English was far less effective. Campbell returned to Pomeroy, Ohio, in January 1896 to begin a series of poetry readings in southern Ohio and West Virginia. He died on Jan. 26, 1896, of pneumonia, at his parents' home.

The most complete biographical data on Campbell are in the *Cleveland Gazette* (Jan. 20, 1891) and his obituary in the *Pomeroy Tribune-Telegraph* (Jan. 29, 1896). For his role in education, Carter G. Woodson's *Early Negro Education in West Virginia* (1921) should be consulted. Campbell's poetry can be found in a number of anthologies of Negro poetry published since his death. His acquaintance with Dunbar is documented in Addison Gayle, Jr.'s *Oak and Ivy: A Biography of Paul Laurence Dunbar* (1971). The work *Echoes from the Cabin and Elsewhere* (1895) is found in the collections of the Ohio Historical Society. — FRANK R. LEVSTIK

CAMPBELL, THOMAS MONROE (1883–1956), pioneer in agricultural extension work among the Negro farmers of the South. Campbell was born on Feb. 11, 1883, on a small farm in Elbert County, Ga. His father, William Campbell, was a Methodist preacher and tenant farmer. His mother (whose name is not given in his *The Movable School*) died when he was five years old. Possessing little but the determination to get an education, at the age of fifteen Campbell began his trek to Tuskegee Normal and Industrial Institute in January 1899. Arriving a few months later, he enrolled in the lowest grade of the agricultural course of the school. In his largely autobiographical *The Movable School Goes to the Negro Farmer,* Campbell gives a poignant account of his impoverished childhood, the arduous journey to Tuskegee, and his long struggle to receive an education there. By 1906 he had worked his way through to completion of the agricultural course, and began advanced study in that same year. He did further graduate study at Iowa State College, Ames, Iowa, in the summer of 1910.

As a student at Tuskegee, Campbell was outstanding. Both George Washington Carver, head of the agriculture department, and Tuskegee's principal, Booker T. Washington, commended him on several occasions for his excellent work and for the progress he had made in the agricultural course.

Prior to 1906 all of Tuskegee's extension activities had focused on bringing the uneducated Negro farmers to the institute to learn improved methods of farming. Washington soon realized, however, that there was little hope of advancement for the isolated farmers unless modern agricultural training were carried to their doorsteps. For this purpose, a traveling agricultural school, in the form of a wagon outfitted with farm demonstration equipment, was initiated in May 1906. The wagon,

named the Jesup Agricultural Wagon after its donor, New York philanthropist Morris K. Jesup, was operated by Tuskegee faculty, who proceeded to carry scientific agricultural methods to the farmers in the fields. This was the beginning of agricultural extension work in the South.

In the fall of 1906 Seaman A. Knapp, special agent in charge of farmers' cooperative demonstration work for the U.S. Department of Agriculture (USDA), visited Tuskegee to solicit the support of the institute in establishing a cooperative demonstration program for the Negro farmers of the South. The ensuing agreement provided that the USDA would share, with Tuskegee, the expenses for employing a man to operate the Jesup Wagon, popularly called the "Movable School," and conduct demonstration work in Macon and surrounding counties of the state.

On the recommendations of Washington and Carver, Thomas Campbell was hired on Nov. 12, 1906, and became the first Negro demonstration agent in the United States. Gradually he spread the demonstration work of the Movable School into all areas of Alabama until, in 1909, he was promoted to district agent with the responsibility of supervising and instructing other agents. The Movable School, through the operation of succeeding Macon County demonstration agents, continued functioning until World War II. Meanwhile the idea of the Movable School which Campbell had popularized had spread to Europe, East Asia, India, and Africa.

Campbell advanced rapidly from district agent to field agent (1918), with the seven lower southern states as his territory. As USDA Extension Service field agent, Campbell conferred with state directors of extension on the conduct of cooperative extension work with Negro farmers and farm families in the states of Alabama, Georgia, Florida, Louisiana, Mississippi, Oklahoma, and Texas. He advised and cooperated with state agents in charge of extension work with Negroes in those states in directing the activities of county farm and home agents. He advised the presidents of the land-grant colleges in the seven states regarding the education and training of their students for work as extension agents. He also worked with farm and civic organizations for the purpose of aiding them to direct their efforts along lines of practical help to black farmers, and the general improvement of community and living conditions.

Under his direction county agents fostered the introduction of electricity and water systems into rural areas; they encouraged and aided in the construction and upkeep of modern farmsteads and sanitary toilet facilities; and among other things they preached the importance of gardening, orcharding, crop rotation, and animal care.

Although Campbell was a federal employee, he continued to work closely with Tuskegee Institute, where his headquarters remained throughout his career. It was his work and influence that made Tuskegee Institute the center of Negro agricultural extension work in the Deep South.

While Campbell used his influence to promote the ideas of Booker T. Washington, he probably made his greatest contribution to Negro farmers by continually pressuring the USDA to hire more Negro extension agents and to expand its operations among Negro farmers. By the time of his retirement in 1953, more than 800 Negro extension agents were employed in farm and home demonstration work in the South.

During his career of forty-seven years, Campbell wrote a number of articles which appeared in some of the leading agricultural journals of the nation. *The Movable School Goes to the Negro Farmer* was published by the Tuskegee Institute Press in 1936. His interest was not limited to agriculture. At the time of his death he was engaged in the preparation of a history of extension work in the South, a project sponsored by the Ford Foundation. He was an active member of the Eugene Field Society of the National Association of Authors and Journalists; and in 1936 he began the collection, for possible publication, of Negro folk traditions as told to him by the ex-slaves he met on his rural circuit. He is credited, by the concert singer Roland Hayes with having collected the words and music for the spiritual, "He Never Said a Mumblin' Word," which Hayes sang in a 1923 concert.

Campbell received many honors for his outstanding agricultural extension work. In 1930 he received the Harmon Award for distinguished service in the field of farming and rural life. He was awarded an honorary M.S. degree by Tuskegee Institute in 1936; and in 1947 he received the Length of Service and Superior Service Awards of the USDA. He had been narrator and speaker on NBC and CBS nationwide radio broadcasts on several occasions, and served as consultant in the Southern States War Savings Committee of World War II.

At the request of the General Education Board in 1944, Campbell joined a three-member commission which studied the progress of agriculture and rural education among the peoples of West Africa. For six months he traveled in Liberia, Sierra Leone, Ghana, Nigeria, and the Cameroons, studying the methods used by African farmers in preparing soil, planting, and cultivating crops, visiting experiment stations, and sampling local diets to learn something of African food habits in regard to health and nutrition. Results of the survey were published in *Africa Advancing,* issued by the Friends Press in 1945 and written jointly by Campbell and the other commission members.

At the time of his retirement in 1953 it was said that in terms of years of service, Campbell was the oldest active Extension Service worker in the United States, having devoted his life to the elevation of the standard of living of the rural Negro farmer through promoting the application of scientific principles to farming, through encouraging the farmer to improve and beautify his home and to provide adequate health care for his family, and through stressing the importance of education for his children.

On the campus of Tuskegee Institute there stands a marker commemorating Thomas Monroe Campbell and the beginning of extension work among rural Negro Americans. It was dedicated on Jan. 13, 1952, four years before his death on Feb. 8, 1956.

The most extensive information on Thomas M. Campbell was found in the Thomas Monroe Campbell Papers, Manuscript Collection, Tuskegee Institute Archives, Tuskegee Institute, Ala. Campbell's *The Movable School Goes to the Negro Farmer* was also helpful. The unpublished paper by Allen W. Jones of Auburn University, "Lifting the Veil of Ignorance: Tuskegee Institute's Role in the Education of Black Farmers," gave valuable information on the history of Tuskegee's extension activities and Campbell's role in them.

— JOELLYN PRYCE EL-BASHIR

CARDOZO, FRANCIS L[OUIS] (1837–1903), clergyman, educator, and politician. He was born free in Charleston, S.C., on Feb. 1, 1837, the son of a white economist and journalist, Jacob N. Cardozo, and a half-Negro, half-Indian mother. Between the ages of five and twelve he attended school, then became a carpenter's apprentice for five years and a journeyman for four. At the age of twenty-one, with his savings he left for the University of Glasgow, Scotland. There he studied for four years, and then at Presbyterian seminaries in Edinburgh and London for three years.

About 1864 he became pastor of the Temple Street Congregational Church in New Haven, Conn. A year later, as an agent of the American Missionary Association, he returned to Charleston to be the principal of the Avery Normal Institute. In 1868 he was an influential delegate to the state constitutional convention, called under the Reconstruction acts. In 1868 and 1870 he was elected secretary of state of South Carolina. In 1870 he was also elected state president of the Grand Council of Union Leagues of South Carolina, an organization to ensure Republican votes, and became a director of the Greenville and Columbia Railroad. In 1871–1872 he was professor of Latin at Howard University, but the governor refused to accept his resignation as secretary of state and a deputy served in his absence. In 1872 and 1874 he was elected state treasurer, and claimed to have been reelected in 1876 but relinquished the office on April 11, 1877, with the downfall of the Republican regime. In 1877 he was "recommended by Governor Daniel H. Chamberlain of South Carolina, Frederick Douglass and others for the presidency of Howard University and received two of fourteen votes" (Rayford W. Logan, *Howard University . . .* [1969], p. 83). In 1878 Cardozo secured a position in the Treasury Department at Washington. He served there also as principal of the Colored Preparatory High School (1884–1891) and its successor M Street High School (1891–1896). He married Catherine Rowena Howell of New Haven in 1864; they had four sons and two daughters, one of whom died in infancy. Cardozo died in Washington on July 22, 1903. One of his granddaughters was Eslanda Goode Robeson, and a grandson was William Warrick Cardozo.

As secretary of state in South Carolina, Cardozo in 1872 was given responsibility for the State Land Commission and successfully brought order out of the chaos into which its operations had fallen under a corrupt management. As state treasurer he undertook to achieve the same purpose in state finances generally. In association with Gov. Daniel H. Chamberlain and other reformers, he guarded the state treasury against the manipulations of corruptionists who tried unsuccessfully to remove him in 1875. Despite this, under the Democratic regime in 1877 he was indicted for conspiracy and convicted on the charge of having paid interest on certain bonds fraudulently issued before he took office but identical with others of their type. Cardozo himself was not charged with participation in the fraud and was pardoned before the sentence was executed.

Cardozo's chief contributions as an educator were the founding of Avery Institute in Charleston, his work in planning a state system of public schools when he was chairman of the Committee on Education in the constitutional convention of 1868, his maintenance of high academic standards at the Colored Preparatory High School and M Street High School, and his introduction of business courses there. A business high school in Washington, D.C., opened in 1928, was named in his honor.

Alrutheus A. Taylor's *The Negro in South Carolina during Reconstruction* (1924), Francis B. Simkins's and Robert H. Woody's *South Carolina during Reconstruction* (1932), and Joel L. Williamson's *After Slavery: The Negro in South Carolina During Reconstruction, 1861–1877* (1965), are scholarly studies that include references to Cardozo. The sketch in William J. Simmons's *Men of Mark . . .* (1887) is uncritical.

— GEORGE B. TINDALL

CARDOZO, W[ILLIAM] WARRICK (1905–1962), physician and pioneer investigator of sickle cell anemia. Cardozo was born in Washington, D.C., on April 6, 1905. His father, Francis L. Cardozo, Jr., was a school principal in Washington, D.C., and his grandfather, Francis L. Cardozo, a prominent politician and educator. He received his early education in the public schools of Washington, D.C., and Hampton Institute, Va. He earned his A.B. (1929) and M.D. degrees (1933) from Ohio State University. He was an intern at City Hospital, Cleveland (1933–1934), and a resident in pediatrics at Provident Hospital, Chicago (1934–1935). Then followed a two-year General Education Board fellowship in pediatrics at Children's Memorial Hospital and Provident Hospital. During this period he pursued research on sickle cell anemia with the aid of a grant from the Alpha Phi Alpha fraternity, and published in the *Archives of Internal Medicine* (Oct. 1937) a pioneer study "Immunologic Studies in Sickle Cell Anemia." In 1937 he began private practice in Washington, D.C., and in the same year joined the staff of the Howard University College of Medicine and Freedmen's Hospital as part-time instructor in pediatrics. He was promoted to clinical assistant professor and later to clinical associate professor of pediatrics. Cardozo was certified by the American Board of Pediatrics in 1942 and became a fellow of the American Academy of Pediatrics in 1948. In later years, he concentrated on gastrointestinal disorders in children, working for nearly twenty years in collaboration with R. Kelly Brown at Freedmen's Hospital. In addition to private practice, Cardozo served for twenty-four years as a school medical inspector for the District of Columbia Board of Health. He died suddenly on Aug. 11, 1962, of a heart attack. He was survived by his widow Julia M. Cardozo, a daughter Judy, and five sisters.

Despite intensive research in later years, Cardozo's findings in sickle cell anemia are still valid. He concluded that the disease was largely familial and inherited, following Mendelian Law; that it was found almost exclusively in Negroes or other persons of African descent. He further concluded that not all persons having sickle cells in the blood were anemic, that not all patients died of sickle cell disease per se, and that no successful treatment had been found.

Cardozo, an Episcopalian, was a member of the American Academy of Pediatrics, the Medical Society of the District of Columbia, the Advisory Committee of the District of Columbia Crippled Children's Society, the National Medical Association, and a founder of Alpha Omega Alpha Honorary Society at the Howard University College of Medicine.

Unlike most of his colleagues, he vigorously opposed socialized medicine. In interviews, his medical colleagues remember him as a dedicated amd excellent physician. They recall that his lectures were prepared with meticulous detail.

In addition to "Immunologic Studies in Sickle Cell Anemia," Cardozo was co-author with Katsuji Kato of "Hodgkin's Disease with Terminal Eosinophilia" (*Journal of Pediatrics,* Feb. 1938), and with Roland B. Scott and others of "Growth and Development of Negro Infants. III. Growth During the First Year of Life" (ibid., 1950). — ROLAND B. SCOTT

CARNEY, WILLIAM H. (1840–1908), Civil War veteran and Congressional Medal of Honor winner. Carney was born in Norfolk, Va., the son of Ann and William Carney. His mother, a slave, was freed by her owner upon his death. Carney, who was fourteen years old at the time, then attended for a year a secret school maintained by a local minister. The following year he worked with his father in the coasting trade. In 1856 the elder Carney decided to seek greater freedom and opportunity for his family in the North, and moved with his wife and son to New Bedford, Mass.

In New Bedford young Carney undertook a variety of odd jobs and joined a local church. A man of strong religious conviction, he considered becoming a minister, but the Civil War interrupted his plans. On Feb. 17, 1863, Carney enlisted in the 54th Massachusetts Infantry, the first regiment of colored troops to be raised in the North for the Union Army. He became sergeant in Company C, whose members came mostly from New Bedford. Carney accompanied the 54th Massachusetts to South Carolina, where on July 18, 1863, the regiment spearheaded an assault on Fort Wagner, outside Charleston harbor. The attackers were thrown back with heavy losses, and Carney was among the wounded. His commanding officer cited Carney for bravery, and thirty-seven years later, on May 23, 1900, Congress awarded him a Medal of Honor for the heroism he had displayed during the attack on the fort.

On June 30, 1864, Carney was discharged because of disabilities caused by his wounds. After a brief sojourn in California, he returned to New Bedford, where he served as a mail carrier for thirty-two years. Upon his retirement in 1901 he moved to Boston to take a job as a messenger in the State House. On Nov. 23, 1908, he was injured in an elevator accident and died on Dec. 9. Carney, who was buried in New Bedford, was survived by his wife and daughter. His wife was the first colored woman to graduate from New Bedford High School, and was one of the first colored women to teach in the state's public schools.

Carney's heroism at Fort Wagner earned him lasting fame. During the charge on the fort Carney saw the Union color bearer fall; he immediately seized the flag and carried it to the front of the column. Crossing the ditch that lay under the fort's guns, Carney struggled up the parapet beyond. Struck in the thigh by a bullet, Carney fell to his knees but continued to hold the flag aloft. He knelt there for over an hour, as musket balls and grapeshot flew around him. As the Union troops were forced to fall back under the heavy fire, Carney followed them; creeping on one knee, he was shot twice more before he reached safety. His fellow soldiers cheered as they saw him return with the colors; as he entered the field hospital, exhausted from loss of blood, he was able to say: "Boys, the old flag never touched the ground."

The flag which Carney so zealously guarded was enshrined in the Massachusetts State House after the war, and Carney never tired of telling visiting schoolchildren of the day he held the standard aloft. The Massachusetts veteran was a popular speaker at Memorial Day observances; in 1897 he participated in ceremonies dedicating a monument to the 54th Massachusetts and its commanding officer, Robert G. Shaw. Upon Carney's death the governor of Massachusetts ordered the State House flag flown at half mast, and the chaplain of the state Senate pronounced a eulogy at his funeral.

A letter of Carney's containing some autobiographical information can be found in volume 8 of Frank Moore (ed.), *The Rebellion Record* (1865). Carney's own description of his conduct at Fort Wagner can be found in volume 1 of W. F. Beyer and O. F. Keydel (eds.), *Deeds of Valor* (1906). Several Boston newspapers carried obituaries of Carney; the most informative are in the *Transcript* and the *Globe*.

— RICHARD H. ABBOTT

CARTER, LOUIS A[UGUSTUS] (1876–1941), army chaplain. Born on Feb. 20, 1876, in Auburn, Ala., Carter attended Tuskegee Institute, Tuskegee, Ala. (1895–1897), and Selma University, Selma, Ala. (1897–1900), and although he did not graduate from either institution, he attended the Virginia Union University Theological School, Richmond, Va. (1901–1904), as a special student and graduated from there with a B.D. degree. After his ordination at Auburn in 1899 he served pastorates in Dawkins, Ala. (1899–1900); Orange Court House (1901–1902), Trevilians (1903), and Ashland (1904), Va.; and Knoxville, Tenn. (1905–1910). As pastor of the 1500-member First Baptist Church of Knoxville, he was active in the colored YMCA and was said to have done more to encourage young men to participate in "Y" activities than any other clergyman in that city. Guadalupe College of Texas awarded him a Doctor of Divinity (D.D.) degree in 1907. He married Mary B. Moss, a member of his congregation, in 1909.

Although his popularity and success as a pastor was characterized as "phenomenal," he applied for an appointment as chaplain of one of the four Regular Army Negro regiments with references from two members of the U.S. House of Representatives, the mayor and a former mayor of Knoxville, the president of the East Tennessee Banker's Association, several attorneys, and numerous ministers. In April 1910 he became the eighth Negro pastor to be appointed a Regular Army chaplain and served on continuous active duty for thirty years. He also became the only chaplain to serve with all four Regular Army Negro regiments: the 24th Infantry at Sackett Harbor, Madison Barracks, N.Y. (1910), and Fort Benning, Ga. (1931–1935); the 25th Infantry at Camp Stephen D. Little, Nogales, Ariz. (1921–1931), and Fort Huachuca, Ariz. (1935–1940); the 9th Cavalry at Camp Harry J. Jones, Douglas, Ariz. (1915), and Camp Stotsenburg, Philippine Islands (1916–1921); the 10th Cavalry at Fort Ethan Allen, Vt. (1910–1913), and Fort Huachuca, Ariz. (1913–1915); and the U.S. Army Chaplain School, Fort Leavenworth, Kans. (1924).

Upon entering the army Carter quickly concluded that personal contact with the enlisted men was the key to winning their confidence and respect, and to helping him understand their attitudes, behavior, and problems. He attributed whatever success he had in his army ministry to personal contact—in hospitals and guardhouses, in garrison and the field, in barracks and homes, and at places of recreation and worship. Aside from his traditional chaplain duties he occasionally served as post schoolmaster and librarian. He promoted sports, entertainments such as minstrel and vaudeville shows, literary societies, and debating clubs. He started special programs such as "Letter Writing Week" during the week before Mothers' Day, and "Man's Night" which consisted of a short, spirited, and convincing talk by surgeons, clergymen, other professional men, and businessmen. Moreover, he advanced racial pride and an interest in Negro studies by making *The Crisis* and books about Negro soldiers available in the libraries and by presenting impressive programs during regimental anniversaries that recounted the military successes of the colored soldier on the frontier and in the Philippines, Cuba, and Mexico. He was known by his commanders as a forceful public speaker and preacher who attracted large congregations and as a good influence on the enlisted men.

When the 10th Cavalry moved to Fort Huachuca in 1913 and the troopers were allowed to wear their weapons off the post, one trooper went into a Douglas bar to get a drink and a white cowboy provoked him by making racial slurs. This provocation resulted in a gunfight, and the trooper killed his adversary. Carter went throughout the regiment to raise funds for a good lawyer, and the trooper was freed on the basis of self-defense.

Upon arriving in the Philippines in 1915 the men of the 9th Cavalry in ranks below staff sergeant found no army housing available for their families, but Carter managed to persuade the Camp Stotsenburg commander to set aside an area within the camp for married men to build houses at their own expense. A habitable bamboo hut for two could be built for $200, less if the men did most of the work, but with their low pay they found it difficult to raise the money. Carter again came to their aid by persuading the quartermaster to assume "certain financial responsibilities" outside army regulations for their housing projects, and the men repaid the money in installments. In a few months a village sprang up and was named after its "Patron Saint," Chaplain Carter.

Both Carter and the men of the 25th Infantry admired and supported *The Crisis* for its "manly stand for the advancement of . . . the Negro race," but on one occasion Carter took issue with its editor, W. E. B. Du Bois, who said the United States needed and could get more funds for health, education, and social uplift "by taxing the rich and by spending less for silly battleships and for the salaries of impudent army officers." Carter wrote that the 25th Infantry was "doing as much for the advancement of the Negro race as any University in the country" and that Du Bois was lessening his influence by sponsoring "such pacifist-bolshevik doctrines." Du Bois, of course, had the last word by repeating that battleships were silly and dangerous and by saying most —but not all—army officers were impudent because of their bad attitude toward Negro soldiers during World War I, by admitting his pacifism, and by stating he was a Bolshevik if being one was striving "to organize Industry for public service rather than for private profit." Du Bois also requested Carter's sympathy and the regiment's support for *The Crisis* and the NAACP, "even with this knowledge of my personal aims and attitudes." This apparently ended the exchange.

The army awarded Carter the Mexican Border Service Medal, World War I Victory Medal, and Expert Badge with Pistol Bar, and in 1926 Western University of Kansas awarded him his second D.D. On April 29, 1936, he became the first Regular Army Negro chaplain to be promoted to colonel. Carter Street at Fort Huachuca was also named after him. Upon his retirement in February 1940 he lived briefly in Los Angeles before he moved to Tucson, Ariz., where he died in a Veterans' Hospital on July 16, 1941. He was buried in the Fort Huachuca Cemetery.

The principal sources are: Richard Johnson's "My Life in the Army" (Entry No. 199, Special Bibliographic Series No. 6, Manuscript Holdings of the U.S. Army Military Research Collection, Carlisle, Pa.), *The Crisis* (vol. 34, nos. 5 and 7); interview with Sgt. William P. Banks (Ret.), May 10, 1973, West Point, N.Y.; Louis A. Carter AGO Document File No. 1549808, Record Group 94, National Archives; and Louis A. Carter file, Fort Huachuca Museum, Fort Huachuca.

— EARL P. STOVER

CARVER, GEORGE WASHINGTON (1861?–1943), pioneer in the field of chemurgy, and internationally acclaimed agricultural experimentalist and researcher. Carver was born of slave parents on the plantation of Moses and Susan Carver near Diamond, Mo., around the year 1861. He knew little of his parents for, as one story of his infancy goes, during the last years of the Civil War a band of nightriders kidnapped him and his mother, carrying them into Arkansas after which the mother was never heard of again. According to this version Carver's owner, Moses Carver, sent searchers after them and was able to secure the child after paying a race horse as ransom. This is the story of his infancy as Carver told it.

A slightly different version is given by Booker T. Washington, founder of Tuskegee Institute, in his autobiography *Up From Slavery*. Washington wrote that when the Civil War began and nightriders flourished in Missouri, Moses Carver sent his slaves into Arkansas hoping that they might escape being kidnapped. When the danger was over, Carver went into Arkansas looking for his slaves, but was able to find only the baby. The mother had disappeared entirely from sight or record. Whatever the facts, Carver preferred the narrative as he remembered its having been told him by the Carver family.

At the time of his rescue, Carver was seriously ill with whooping cough. This sickness was the beginning of a long siege of poor health which troubled him for many years. His sickliness, however, gave him freedom from manual labor, and leisure time which he spent in the woods "talking with the flowers." In a short autobiographical sketch, Carver wrote: "From a child I had an inordinate desire for knowledge and especially music, painting, flowers, and the sciences. Day after day, I spent in the woods alone in order to collect my floral beauties, and put them in my little garden I had hidden in the bush not far from the house, as it was considered foolishness in that neighborhood to waste time on flowers. . . . When just a mere tot in short dresses my very soul thirsted for an education. I wanted to know every strange stone, flower, insect, bird or beast. No one could tell me."

Even though slavery had ended after the Civil War, George and his brother James continued to live with the Carvers, their former owners. George, unable to do heavy labor, learned to cook, clean, sew, and launder, valuable skills which helped support him through school. But more important, he learned to read. His only book was "an old Webster's Elementary Spelling Book," and he soon "knew the book by heart."

Eager to learn about "every strange stone, flower, insect, bird, or beast," Carver set off in his early teens for the neighboring town of Neosho, having learned of the existence there of a school for Negro children. This trek set the course of Carver's life for the next ten years or so. Learning what he could at the school in Neosho, Carver wandered about the Midwest, harvesting wheat, cutting wood, working sometimes as a cook, sometimes as a gardener, but attending a school whenever he had the opportunity. He finally completed high school in the town of Minneapolis, Kans.

Carver's interest in plant life continued and broadened from that of observing and collecting plant specimens to nursing scrawny ones back to health, and eventually learning to sketch and paint his "floral beauties." In his late twenties Carver was still determined to get an education. He applied for admission to the small church-supported college, Highland University, in Olathe, Kans. Without an interview, he was duly accepted for admission on the basis of his scholastic record and recommendations, but was refused permission to register upon his arrival at the school.

He continued his wandering across the western plains. In 1886 he became a homesteader on some newly released government land in Kansas. After working the arid land for two years, Carver mortgaged his claim for $300 and started eastward toward Iowa and opened a laundry in Winterset. After some months, friends recognized his desire for education and encouraged him to enroll at Simpson College in Indianola, Iowa, a few miles away. Carver attended Simpson College from 1890 to 1891. There he studied the natural sciences, music, and art. When his art teacher, Etta Budd, discovered his knowledge of flowers and plants and his interest in soils, she wrote to her brother, J. L. Budd, professor of botany at Iowa State Agricultural College, asking him to take Carver on in botany and agriculture. Through this professor, Carver was admitted to Iowa State College at Ames in the spring of 1891.

Concentrating on the study of systematic botany, Carver was guided and inspired by his professors in botany and agriculture: J. L. Budd, Louis Pammell, James C. Wilson (soon to become secretary of agriculture under Presidents McKinley, Theodore Roosevelt, and Taft), and Henry C. Wallace (who became secretary of agriculture for Presidents Harding and Coolidge). The son of the last, Henry A. Wallace (secretary of agriculture to FDR) was in turn guided by Carver, and on one occasion said of him, "It was he [Carver] who introduced me to the mysteries of plant fertilization. . . . [He] deepened my appreciation of plants in a way I could never forget."

At Iowa State, Carver was at the top of his class in scholarship, and excelled in artistic endeavors as well. His combined love of plants and painting won him several prizes for his still-life canvases at the Iowa State Teachers Association art exhibit. One of his four paintings received an honorable mention at the 1893 World's Columbian Exposition in Chicago.

In 1894 Carver was graduated from Iowa State, the first Negro graduate of that institution. His thesis for the bachelor's degree was based on the amaryllis and was entitled "Plants as Modified by Man."

Placing Carver among the most brilliant students he had ever taught, Louis Pammell offered him a position at the college as assistant in the agricultural experiment station. While working in this capacity, Carver was also studying for his master's degree, concentrating on mycology, that branch of botany dealing with fungi. During these years Carver began one of his little-publicized hobbies, collecting fungus specimens with particular reference to those fungi known to be plant parasites. His completed collection consisted of some 20,000 specimens, including several named in his honor. His added skill at hybridization soon won recognition as an authority in both mycology and horticulture. Carver began to be cited in scientific papers, and was invited to lecture throughout Iowa. In 1896 he received the master's degree from Iowa State College.

It was during these years at Iowa State that Carver laid the foundation for his later knowledge of plant chemistry which opened to his genius the wonders of the peanut, sweet potato, soybean, and southern clays.

In the spring of 1896 Booker T. Washington, principal of Tuskegee Normal and Industrial Institute in Alabama, having heard that there was a noted Negro agriculturalist at a school in Iowa, wrote to Carver: "I cannot offer you money, position or fame. The first two you have; the last, from the place you now occupy, you will no doubt achieve. These things I now ask you to give up. I offer you in their place work—hard, hard work—the task of bringing a people from degradation, poverty, and waste to full manhood." Carver replied: "Of course, it has always been the one great ideal of my life to be of the greatest good to the greatest number of 'my people' possible, and to this end I have been preparing myself for these many years; feeling as I do that this line of education is the key to unlock the golden door of freedom to our people."

In October 1896 when Carver, the new head of the institute's Department of Agriculture, arrived at Tuskegee, he was told by Principal Washington, "Your department exists only on paper, Carver, and your laboratory will have to be in your head." With thirteen student helpers, Carver started his job from scratch, fashioning his laboratory equipment from the odds and ends he collected from the campus junkpile: his mortar was a cracked, heavy teacup; his classroom bell was a horseshoe mounted on an iron stand. Reeds made excellent pipettes, and his kerosene lamp doubled as a bunsen burner. He used a flat iron to pulverize, and made his own zinc salts from discarded fruit jar tops.

At the same time that he was luring Carver from Iowa State, Washington was also working to get the Alabama legislature to create a branch agricultural experiment station at Tuskegee Normal School. On Feb. 15, 1897, the act was approved, establishing a "Branch Agricultural Experiment Station and Agricultural School for the colored race" at Tuskegee Normal School. The state agreed to pay $1500 a year for the operation and maintenance of the experiment station and agricultural school. The station and school were directed to advance the interest of scientific agriculture through experimentation, to give "the colored race . . . an opportunity to acquire intelligent practical knowledge of agriculture in all of its branches," and to educate Negro students in scientific agriculture. Carver became the director of the experiment station in 1897.

Carver's task in relation to his new role was plainly evident. In his assessment of the agricultural conditions in the late-nineteenth-century South, Carver said: "The virgin fertility of our Southern soils and the vast amount of unskilled labor have been a curse rather than a blessing to agriculture. This exhaustive system of cultivation, the destruction of forests, the rapid and almost constant decomposition of organic matter, together with the problems of nitrification and denitrification, the multitudinous insects and fungus diseases which are ever increasing with marvelous rapidity year by year make our agricultural problem one requiring more brains than that of the North, East, or West." His objectives were to restore the fertility of the soils of the South debilitated by the one-crop system (usually cotton or tobacco), to encourage the cultivation of a variety of crops, and ultimately to find new commercial uses for them. Always deeply concerned about the plight of his people, Carver was ever aware that this constituted the key to raising the standard of living of the poor, ignorant farmer, black and white.

Carver believed that where the soil was properly cultivated, fertilized scientifically, and crops were selected in accordance to the soil type, the land would be productive. Through the experiment station the use of such commonly available organic wastes as leaves, garbage, paper, grass, and rags, and the occasional growing of a nutrient-restoring crop such as cowpeas, was demonstrated and widely encouraged. Soil analyses were run in his lab, and recommendations were made regarding the proper chemical fertilizers needed to overcome deficiencies. The basic lesson he was constantly trying to teach was the conservation of the earth's natural resources rather than their wasteful exploitation.

Carver made weekend trips in his buggy to rural communities where he gave talks and instructive agricultural demonstrations, showing the farmers and their wives how to improve their conditions. When the Agricultural Farmers' Institute was organized at Tuskegee in 1897, Carver used the opportunity of these monthly meetings to give simple lectures and demonstrations on such subjects as the culture and value of sweet potatoes, practical farm economy, and the value of deep plowing. He frequently took the farmers on a tour of the grounds of the experiment station in order to "stimulate and encourage them."

To further communicate with the farmers of Macon County, Carver started a bulletin in which he began to explain his scientific discoveries and concepts to the semiliterate common people in a language they could read and understand. He was determined that the bulletins be more than theory, insisting upon their being thoroughly practical. In broad divisions the bulletins, numbering forty-four in all published from 1898 to 1942, represented distinct phases of the farmer's problems such as soil building, cotton growing, sweet potato raising, growth of cowpeas, corn raising, wild plum conservation, gardening for the farmer, dairying and dairy products, raising small grain crops, poultry raising, the pickling and curing of meat, home canning of fruits and vegetables, fertilizers, home menus, hog and cattle raising, growing and canning tomatoes, the peanut and how to use it, and the use of native clays.

Another effective means of disseminating to the farmers the agricultural knowledge that Carver was producing at the experiment station came to be known as the "Movable School"—a mule-drawn wagon outfitted with "milk separator and churn, charts on soil building, orcharding, stock raising and most operations pertaining to the farm." Beginning in 1899 Carver and his protégé Thomas M. Campbell, a graduate of Tuskegee, drove the mule and wagon through impoverished farmlands, teaching techniques of raising, improving, and preserving foods. In 1906 Carver's wagon became the Jesup Agricultural Wagon, better equipped with funds given by Morris K. Jesup, a New York philanthropist. The Jesup Wagon and Campbell helped bring agricultural transformation to the South, and the U.S. Department of Agriculture appointed Campbell as agricultural demonstration agent for Macon County. In 1918 the state of Alabama gave a large automobile truck to replace the Jesup Wagon, and by the 1920s Campbell

was in charge of the movable school in seven southern states. In later decades of the century Carver's rural movable school idea and techniques were adopted in China, India, Rhodesia, Albania, and many other countries.

However, it is for his work in creative science that Carver is best known. His first major success was with the peanut, which he advised farmers in Alabama to grow in place of cotton. The boll weevil attack on cotton from the 1890s to the 1910s made this advice especially acceptable, and soon peanuts were the number one crop in a great farming belt that ran from Montgomery to the Florida border. When the increased planting quickly created an oversupply, Carver went to his laboratory to seek additional uses for the new crop. In doing so he was to revolutionize the southern agricultural economy by demonstrating how hundreds of products can be made from peanuts. From the peanut Carver developed 300 different products, including milk, cheese, face powder, butter, shampoo, printer's ink, creosote, vinegar, coffee, salads, soaps, and wood stains. His appearance with specimens before the U.S. House Ways and Means Committee in 1921 was largely instrumental in effecting the highest protective tariff the peanut industry ever enjoyed. This brought worldwide recognition of Carver's work.

In this research Carver was the pioneer in a new science, chemurgy, the industrial utilization of agricultural products—wall board from pine cones, banana stems, and peanut shells; synthetic marble from sawdust; woven rugs from okra stalks. From another southern farm crop, the sweet potato, Carver created 118 products, including rubber; and from the clays of the South he produced pigments for paints. During World War I, a crisis in the dye industry occurred when importation of dyes from Germany was stopped. Called on for help, Carver prepared over 500 dyes from twenty-eight kinds of plants.

When Carver's fame became international, requests arrived from foreign countries for help. For example, Carver responded to the call for assistance in developing a milk supply in regions of Africa where the prevalence of the tsetse fly impeded raising dairy herds. This request was answered through his discovery that a nourishing milk could be made from the peanut which was widely grown in Africa.

Before the development of the Salk and Sabin vaccines for immunization against poliomyelitis there was no preventive for the crippling disease, and the only treatment for those who experienced it was to place their limbs in casts or to apply braces. During the early 1930s Carver began to experiment with the use of massages of the affected limbs, using the peanut oil which he had developed, to restore life and usefulness to the atrophied parts. His work was widely publicized and hundreds of patients were brought to him for treatment. Although no miraculous cures were reported, many patients were helped. More important, his work contributed to the search for other effective methods of restorative treatment.

Over a thirty-year period international recognition was given Carver as botanist and chemurgist. He was elected a fellow of the Royal Society of Arts of Great

Britain in 1916 and awarded the Spingarn Medal in 1923. Carver was the recipient of an honorary Doctor of Science degree from Simpson College in 1928. He was appointed collaborator for the Mycology and Plant Disease Survey, Bureau of Plant Industry, U.S. Department of Agriculture, in 1935. Carver was awarded the Franklin Delano Roosevelt Medal in 1939, and received an honorary doctorate from the University of Rochester in 1941. (In the early 1920s Thomas A. Edison invited Carver to join his staff of highly trained scientists at Menlo Park, N.J. Carver declined the offer. He said that he preferred to remain in the South where he thought he would be of more value to the southern farmer.)

Carver's paintings, as well as his creative research, have received worldwide attention. One of his paintings, *Three Peaches,* done with his fingers and with the pigments he developed from the clays of Alabama, was requested by the Luxembourg Gallery. Less well known is the fact that Carver was awarded three patents: for a process for producing a cosmetic (Jan. 6, 1925); for paint and stain (June 9, 1925); and for a process of producing paints and stains (June 14, 1927; Patricia Carter Ives, "Patent and Trademark Innovations of Black Americans and Women," *Journal of the Patent Office Society,* Feb. 1980, p. 112).

Carver, generally considered by many to be an introvert and mystic of high degree, was little understood during his lifetime. Described by those who knew him as modest and unassuming, yet profound, Carver preferred to live and work alone. Deeply religious, he credited his success in developing new products to divine guidance, and was only cursorily interested in patenting his myriad discoveries. Carver apparently found little pleasure in accumulating material possessions. It is said that he never asked for an increase in salary during his forty-seven years at Tuskegee Institute, and that some of his monthly salary checks went uncashed.

In his later years Carver realized that he would not be able to continue his work much longer. In 1940 he contributed his life's savings, more than $60,000 in all, to the establishment of the George Washington Carver Research Foundation, "dedicated to the progress of humanity through the application of science to the problems of agriculture and industry." During his remaining three years Dr. Carver continued to work in the foundation with the assistance of his young assistant, Austin W. Curtis, publishing his last bulletin (posthumously) with Curtis in February 1943. Its title was, appropriately, "The Peanut."

During the next thirty years the foundation grew from the one-man operation on a meager budget to its current status of a multifaceted research organization with over 100 faculty and staff investigators and an annual operational budget in excess of $5 million. These projects include pure research, training and demonstration, and outreach projects.

Carver died of anemia at Tuskegee Institute on Jan. 5, 1943, and was buried on the campus beside Booker T. Washington. In commemoration, Congress in 1953 authorized the establishment of the George Washington Carver National Monument, a park area located now upon the site of his birth near Diamond, Mo. This was the first federal monument in the United States dedicated to an American Negro. It was officially dedicated on July 17, 1960. The first George Washington Carver commemorative stamp was issued on Jan. 5, 1948, and postmarked at 9:00 A.M. On Nov. 1, 1973, it was announced that George Washington Carver had been the second Negro elected to the New York University Hall of Fame, the first being Tuskegee Institute's founder, Booker T. Washington. The "enshrinement" ceremony was held at Tuskegee Institute on April 23, 1977, with Prof. John Hope Franklin of the University of Chicago as the principal speaker (*New York Times,* April 23, 1977, p. 21).

The two most comprehensive biographies on Carver are Rackham Holt's *George Washington Carver: An American Biography* (1943) and Lawrence Elliott's *George Washington Carver: The Man Who Overcame* (1971). Other useful sources cited are "The Life and Character of George Washington Carver," by Getahun Dilebo (an unpublished paper written for the U.S. Department of the Interior, National Park Service, 1972); "Dr. George Washington Carver, Scientist, Humanitarian and Mystic," by John C. Crighton (*Bulletin of the Missouri Academy of Science* 2, no. 1, 1973); "The George Washington Carver Story," by Samuel P. Massie (*Chemistry* 43, no. 8, 1970); and a short (three-page) autobiographical sketch written in 1922 and located in the Carver Papers at Tuskegee Institute. The article in *DAB Supplement Three, 1941–1945* (1973), by Harold T. Pinkett states that "his endurance of . . . racial indignities without protest or abatement of zeal for service to all was in the tradition of the Tuskegee spirit of patience in race relations, and it doubtless accounted for the praise given by many white religious and civil groups." — JAMES H. M. HENDERSON

CARY [CAREY], LOTT (1780?–1828), Baptist missionary. Born a slave in Charles City County, Va., Cary was the only child of a father who was a Baptist and a mother of no known religious affiliation. Lott's owner, William A. Christian, hired him out as a laborer at the Shockhoe Tobacco Warehouse in Richmond. In 1807, after three years of "profanity and intoxication," he was converted, baptized, and made a member of the First Baptist Church, Richmond. Like most slaves (and many freemen, white and black), Lott could neither read nor write. Like some slaves he learned to read and write from hearing sermons and finding the relevant passages in the Bible. His conversion resulted from a sermon based on John 3:1–13, in which Jesus told Nicodemus: "Except a man be born again, he cannot see the Kingdom of God." Securing a copy of the New Testament, Lott began his self-education in both reading and writing.

His conversion led to better habits which, with the ability to read and write, brought a promotion to skilled laborer in shipping tobacco. He received cash wages and the privilege of selling parcels of tobacco for his own account. In 1813 he purchased his freedom and that of his two children for $850 (information about his wife and children is not available). He was then engaged at a regular salary. In 1813 also he received a license to preach from the First Baptist Church of Richmond. Inspired by the sermons of Luther Rice, a pioneer white Baptist missionary, Cary in 1815 helped to organize the Richmond Baptist Missionary Society.

For a number of years he was a preacher and exhorter, having been ordained about 1815. His interest in Africa was aroused by the publication in 1819 of the *Journal* of exploration of Sierra Leone by Samuel John Mills, Jr., an agent of the American Colonization Society. Mills concluded that he was "every day more convinced of the practicability and expedience of establishing American colonies" in a larger Sierra Leone. The motives of the society, organized in 1817, were mixed, and Cary remained doubtful about them. They included the beliefs that the colonizing abroad of free American Negroes was the only feasible means of ameliorating their plight and of removing potential leaders of slave insurrections. Cary's interest in Africa was further stimulated by the Baptist General Convention and the Richmond African Missionary Society, the latter of which contributed during several years funds for mission work in Africa. On May 1, 1819, Cary was received for service by the Baptist Board of Foreign Missions. He, Colin Teague (Teage), a missionary, and others organized what was to be the first Baptist church in Liberia, with Cary as pastor.

Under the aegis of the American Colonization Society, on Jan. 23, 1821, Cary, Teague, and some twenty-eight colonists and their families sailed in the brig *Nautilus* from Norfolk, Va., for Sierra Leone. After the arrival of other colonists in December 1821, they moved in early 1822 to Cape Mesurado (now Monrovia), to form the nucleus for the Colony of Liberia. Despite the ravages of fever and the hostility of indigenous tribes, Cary founded a church which within three years had some sixty members. By that time he had begun to oppose Jehudi Ashmun, one of the principal white founders of the Colony of Liberia, who had become in effect the principal agent of the American Colonization Society. The colony was in a deplorable and dangerous state: tribes in the interior were threatening to attack the settlement at Cape Mesurado; provisions and ammunition were in short supply; no documents existed to define the limits of the territory that had been purchased; the number of settlers was small; and the finances of the colony were at a low ebb. Cary fought valiantly against the tribes, but in 1823 and 1824 his actions aroused the suspicion of Ashmun. The specific cause of Cary's agitation is not clearly known, but instructions from the society to Ashmun (April 1, 1824) referred to Cary's and others' "disgraceful proceedings." Ashmun was instructed to inform Cary that "in consideration of the sorrow and repentance, expressed by Lot Carey [*sic*] and his former usefulness, . . . we proceed to direct that the mildest punishment be awarded which the circumstances will allow." But any who refused to give up their arms and ammunition and comply with all the other requirements imposed by the agent would be tried *by the agent* and receive punishment, including banishment, if found guilty. On the other hand, the instructions stated: "It is not intended that Lot Carey should be prevented from teaching as a schoolmaster or of taking care of the captured Africans."

An address by the board of managers of the society to the "Citizens of Liberia" (April 1824), suggests a probable cause of the difficulties, namely a virtual mutiny created by Cary and his followers to establish American Negro leadership in the colony. The crucial paragraph stated: "We fear there has been something of a feeling among you of a union and sympathy of coloured against white people. If so, you ought to dismiss it; you yourselves have felt the necessity and urged the importance of having a white agent with you, at least for some time. We shall endeavour always to select the best we can procure. His very situation makes him more impartial than anyone among you can be. Dismiss all unfounded jealousies against him. Be jealous of those only who would seduce you from your duty and who endeavour to sow divisions and excite suspicions among you. Their motives cannot be good, nor their objects justifiable." The lengthy statement ended with the admonition: "[a]nd may God of his infinite goodness and mercy, preserve and protect you, guide you in the path of duty, enable you to lead peaceable and quiet lives in all godliness and honesty, and finally, receive you to himself, through the infinite merits of our Lord Jesus Christ!"

Cary recanted, staunchly supported Ashmun, rendered valuable medical services to the inhabitants, became an acknowledged leader, and in September 1826 was elected vice-agent of the colony. He conferred with the society during a visit to the United States in the fall of 1825. When Ashmun left the colony in March 1828, he placed it in charge of Cary. Cary's administration did not last long, for he died in an explosion on Nov. 10, 1828, while assisting in the defense of the colony.

During that brief period, however, he ordered the jail to be put in "complete order," to have guns and armaments ready, and to get the new settlers on their lands. He concluded a treaty with several tribal kings by which they ceded to the American Colonization Society a territory on the St. Paul's River adjoining the settlement at Millsburg. He continually urged the society to acquire new lands and purchase a vessel to bring provisions from Sierra Leone. One of his other significant actions was a show of force to compel the captain of a Spanish ship, suspected of engaging in the slave trade, to leave the harbor of Cape Mesurado. "Though we did not pretend to attempt suppressing this trade," Cary wrote in his *Journal,* "we would not aid it, and that I allowed him one hour, and one only, to get out of reach of our guns. He was very punctual, and I believe before his hour."

Ralph Randolph Gurley's account of Cary in *Life of Jehudi Ashmun . . .* (1835) described Cary's features and complexion as "altogether African. . . . His words were few, simple, direct, and appropriate. His conversation indicated rapidity and clearness of thought, and an ability to comprehend the great and variously-related principles of religion and government." Another statement by Gurley might well serve as an epitaph for Lott Cary: "It has been well said of Mr. Cary, that 'he was one of nature's noblemen;' had he possessed the advantages of education, few men of his age would have excelled him in knowledge or genius."

Cary's vision of founding an enlightened colony was not achieved, but the founding of the Lott Cary Foreign

Mission in America in 1897 by American Negro Baptists is a fitting memorial to the man and his dream.

The principal sources for Cary's career are the sketch in Ralph Randolph Gurley's *Life of Jehudi Ashmun* . . . (1835); Charles Henry Huberich's *The Political and Legislative History of Liberia* . . . (2 vols. [1947], 1:153, 307–13, 368–74); and Miles Mark Fisher's "Lott Cary, The Colonizing Missionary" (*JNH* vol. 7, pp. 318–48). There is a brief sketch by Benjamin Brawley in *DAB* (2, Part 1 [1929]:555). — JAMES D. TYMS

CASSELL, ALBERT IRVIN (1895–1969), architect, engineer, planner, entrepreneur, and educator. Born in Towson, near Baltimore, Md., the third child of Albert Truman and Charlotte Cassell, young Albert finished his elementary and high school education in Baltimore and received the B.A. degree in architecture from Cornell University in 1919, where he sang in churches to help pay his expenses. His studies had been interrupted by service as a second lieutenant, training officers in the heavy field artillery in the United States and France (1917–1918).

From 1920 to the eve of his death he was one of the more prominent architects and engineers in the United States. He had three wives and children by each of them: Calvin, a son by his first wife, and four children —Charles Irvin, Martha Ann, Alberta Jeanette Charlotte, and Alberta Thomas—by his second wife, the former Martha Ann Mason. On March 3, 1947, he was married to Flora B. McClarty Scroggins, the widow of Dr. Cornelius Scroggins and the mother of two children. Paula Catherine Cassell became the sixth and youngest Cassell to attend Cornell University (class of 1977). After suffering a heart attack, Albert Cassell died in his home in Washington on Nov. 30, 1969. Funeral services were held at the Washington Cathedral on Dec. 3, 1969, with interment in Baltimore National Cemetery on the same day. His wife and six children survived him.

Cassell laid the foundation for a strong Department of Architecture in the School of Applied Science at Howard University when he succeeded William A. Hazel in 1921 as assistant professor and head of the department, after having been appointed a member of the faculty in 1920. As head of the department until 1928 he helped develop the School of Applied Science into the College of Applied Science, which became in 1934 the College of Engineering and Architecture.

Cassell's civilian career as an architect began in 1919 when he and Hazel planned the initial architectural and structural design for five trade buildings at Tuskegee Institute. In 1920 he was an architectural draftsman, designing silk mills and industrial plants in the office of Howard J. Wiegner, Bethlehem, Pa. He and Hazel were the architects for the construction of the Home Economics Building at Howard University (1921).

From 1924 to 1969, singly until 1961 and later in partnership with other architects and engineers, he engaged in architectural practice, appraisals, property acquisition and management, land planning, site planning, creation of large private ventures, and other similar enterprises. In 1924, Cassell designed the gymnasium, armory, and athletic field at Howard. From then until

1938, when the alleged "personal vindictiveness" of Pres. Mordecai W. Johnson terminated his services (Rayford W. Logan, *Howard University: The First Hundred Years, 1867–1967* [1969], p. 339), he largely transformed the physical appearance of the university. He designed the interior and exterior of the College of Medicine Building, and personally supervised almost its entire erection and facilities (1926–1927). During 1929–1932 he made a detailed property acquisition survey and appraisals of 300 parcels of property in the environs of Howard, obtained grants of $900,000 from the General Education Board and the Rosenwald Foundation to acquire such land as was necessary to execute the twenty-year program of physical improvements, and served as the university's agent in securing and managing 107 of the above-mentioned properties. During 1929–1930 he also coordinated with municipal authorities topographical surveys of the university and its environs.

During 1926–1927 he designed the exterior and interior and supervised the construction of three women's dormitories, named for Sojourner Truth, Prudence Crandall (white founder of a school for colored girls in the 1830s), and Mrs. Julia Caldwell Frazier, a distinguished alumna of the university. He was the architect and engineer (1930–1933) for surveys and construction of heat, light, and power requirements of Howard and Freedmen's Hospital, and also for a tunnel system to distribute heat, light, and power in 1932. In that year he was also architect and engineer for the roads over newly built tunnels which were in some cases thirty feet below grade level. During 1929–1932 as head of the Maintenance Department at Howard, he had direct oversight of approximately 120 mechanics of various trades and custodial force in planning and supervising alterations to the Art Gallery and School of Religion buildings.

Three of Cassell's most important landmarks at Howard were the Chemistry Building and Frederick Douglass Memorial Hall, an educational classroom building (both completed in 1935), and Founders Library (1938). For these, as usual he was the architect, the structural designer, and supervisor for the construction and interior facilities. Completed in 1936 under his similar supervision was a new heat, light, and power plant.

Cassell was also the architect and supervisor for the construction and interior facilities of a women's dormitory at Virginia Union University, Richmond, Va. (1923), a Girls' Dormitory and Christian Center (both 1940–1941), armory or Military Science Building (1956–1957), and new men's residence Buildings for Morgan State College, Baltimore. Other buildings for which he similarly served were the Masonic Temple (1930) and Odd Fellows Temple (1932), the Margaret Murray Washington Vocational School Addition (1938), and the James Creek Alley Housing Development (1940–1941), all in Washington, D.C. He was architect and engineer for projects of the Catholic Diocese of Washington and a fire house in Washington. The Odd Fellows Temple (1924–1925), Provident Hospital and Free Dispensary (1927–1928), Sollers' Point War Housing Development in Baltimore (1942), and the George Washington Carver War Housing Building in Arlington, Va. (1942), give further evidence of Cassell's expertise as architect and supervisor.

As senior member of Cassell, Gray, and Sulton, he participated in the construction of an environmental computer control (1963); U.S. Army installation at National Airport; alterations at the Pentagon (1964); Kimball School, Washington, D.C.; and (Cassell and Gray) engineer for St. Paul Baptist Church in Baltimore (1966), an expanded field house for Morgan State College (1967–1968), and an addition to the Birney School in Washington (1968–1969).

At the height of the Cold War, Cassell was the creator and architect (1951–1954) for a proposed bomb shelter under a federal lease-purchase project, costing $192 million, in northwest Washington. The beginning of better relations between the United States and the Soviet Union ended the project.

Cassell's wide-ranging interests included providing work and wider economic opportunities as well as housing for Negroes during the 1932–1935 period of the Depression. With his personal funds he purchased a 380-acre site fronting 3170 feet on Chesapeake Bay, Calvert County, Md. Although the project had the strong support of Secretary of the Interior Harold L. Ickes, political and racial problems prevented its consummation.

On the other hand, Mayfair Mansions, Mayfair Extension Housing Developments, and Mayfair Extension commercial facilities on the site of the old Bennings Racetrack in northeast Washington established Cassell as a successful creator and architect for middle-income Negroes. Out of his own funds he took an option on 624 acres in 1938. Construction of 594 dwelling units was begun on Oct. 15, 1942, and delayed because of the war and other reasons. Between Aug. 1, 1945, and July 4, 1946, the 594 dwellings of Mayfair Mansions were completed at a cost of $4.1 million and fully occupied. From August 1945 through 1952, as 20 percent owner and executive vice-president, Cassell managed these apartments, collecting income in excess of $400,-000 a year, and completed plans for the construction of 513 garden-type apartments and the Mayfair Extension first commercial site. The total projected cost of the entire development was $13 million.

In 1946 the 594 dwelling units received the award in architecture from the Committee on Municipal Art of the Washington Board of Trade with the citation: "In Acknowledgement of the Benefit of Such Supreme Architecture in the City of Washington, D.C." Cassell should be honored also for demonstrating the values of interracial cooperation in his various enterprises, the possibilities of the good life in privately constructed housing, and for setting an example for Negroes in professions from which they had been largely excluded.

Endowed with a prodigious memory, he recognized every instrument in a symphony. Listening to music helped him find solutions to his architectural problems.

Most of the information for this sketch is based on materials provided by Cassell's widow, Flora B. Cassell; particularly valuable was "Experience Record of Albert I. Cassell, Registered Architect," a mimeographed brochure of eleven pages provided by Charles I. Cassell. Also helpful were the obituaries in the *Washington Eve-*

ning Star (Dec. 2, 1969) and the *Washington Afro-American* (Dec. 5, 1969). The voluminous Cassell Papers are deposited in the Moorland-Spingarn Research Center, Founders Library, Howard University.

— RAYFORD W. LOGAN *and* MICHAEL R. WINSTON

CHARLESTON, OSCAR (1896–1954), center fielder, regarded by most authorities as one of the greatest baseball players. The son of Tom and Mary Jeanette Charleston, he was born in Indianapolis. His father was first a jockey and later a construction worker. Oscar attended the public schools in Indianapolis and ran away at age fifteen to join the army. In the Philippines he played ball for the 24th Infantry, ran on the track team, and was the only Negro in the Manila League. Returning in 1915 to Indianapolis he joined the ABCs, one of the best Negro baseball teams of that era. He played center field with the (colored) St. Louis Giants (1920–1924), the Harrisburg Giants (1924–1927), the Philadelphia Hilldales (1927–1930), and the (Pittsburgh) Homestead Grays (1930–1932). Along with most of the Grays, including Josh Gibson, Charleston jumped in 1932 to the rival Pittsburgh Crawfords, where he was manager and first baseman. The "Craws" broke up in 1936, and Charleston, fat and forty, drifted to Toledo as manager of the Toledo Craws and in 1944 to Branch Rickey's Brooklyn Brown Dodgers, a phantom club set up as a cover to sign Jackie Robinson. It was Charleston who urged Rickey to sign another youngster, Roy Campanella, for the Dodgers.

A center fielder, Charleston displayed the grace of Tris Speaker and Joe DiMaggio, the exuberance of Willie Mays. At bat and on the bases he played with the same savage, slashing drive as Ty Cobb. Both were panther fast and played for blood. Both ripped the ball to all fields. But unlike Cobb, Charleston often swung for the fences—and reached them. He was said to have been superior to the more famous Cobb. Fast enough to stand behind second base and outrun the longest line drive, powerful enough to loosen a baseball's cover with one hand, fearless enough to snatch the hood off a Ku Klux Klansman, Charleston, along with Babe Ruth, was one of the most exciting players the game has seen.

Statistics, contemporary evidence, and cherished beliefs establish Charleston as one of the truly great baseball players, regardless of race. "He could hit the ball a mile," St. Louis Cardinal pitcher Dizzy Dean used to say. "He didn't have a weakness. We just threw and hoped like hell he wouldn't get ahold of one and send it out of the park." In one game against the great white pitcher Walter Johnson, Charleston reportedly said, "Mr. Johnson, I've heard about your fast ball, and I'm going to hit it out of here." Charleston struck out the first two times up, then on the third try pulled the ball over the fence to win the game 1–0 for Smokey Joe Williams, a pretty good fastballer himself. Playing with the St. Louis Giants (1920) against the National League Cardinals in a postseason series in segregated Sportsmen's Park, Charleston's homerun won the first game in the tenth inning, 5–4. In 1930 he and Josh Gibson played on the Homestead Grays, considered one of the best teams of all times. In 1931 the Grays won 134 games and lost 10.

Charleston and Satchel Paige played on the Pittsburgh Crawfords, which many authorities consider the greatest Negro baseball team of all time. In the fall of 1932 the "Craws" beat Casey Stengel's all-stars five games out of seven. In 1934 the Craws entered the Negro league playoffs against the New York Cubans. Down three games to one, they had to sweep the last three to take the flag. They won the fifth game, but were losing 6–3 in the sixth game when Charleston hit a three-run homer to tie it. They eventually won, tying the series. In the final game, against lefty Luis Tiant, Sr. (the father of the colorful Red Sox pitcher), the Crawfords were losing again until Josh Gibson smacked a homer to make it 7–6 and Charleston smacked another to tie it. "Cool Papa" Bell knocked in the winning run a moment later and the Craws were champs.

How good was Oscar Charleston? John McGraw of the New York Giants thought he was the best player ever. Some sportswriters called Charleston "the black Ty Cobb." Others disagreed. Cobb, they said, should be known as "the white Charleston." Charleston was the second Negro elected (1976) to the Baseball Hall of Fame, Cooperstown, N.Y. (Josh Gibson had been the first, in 1972).

Charleston and his wife, Jane B., had no children. He died of a heart attack on Oct. 6, 1954, and was buried in Floral Park Cemetery.

Like other great Negro baseball players Charleston helped pave the way for the signing of Jackie Robinson in 1947 by the Brooklyn Dodgers, the first identified American Negro player in the big leagues (several were said to be Afro-Cubans). Some of the players in the Negro National League were seen in action in the league by scouts of the big-league teams. What is more important, they demonstrated equal, sometimes superior, skills in games with the stars of the American League and the National League.

The most recent reliable published source is John Holway's illustrated *Voices from the Great Black Baseball Leagues* (1975), based in large measure on interviews with former players, journalists, and contemporary newspapers. A photograph of Charleston with the Homestead Grays in 1931 is on page 173. The book also contains valuable statistics. Robert W. Peterson's *Only the Ball Was White* (1970), likewise based on interviews and newspapers, has a photograph of Charleston with the Indianapolis ABCs of 1915 (p. 71); as manager of the Pittsburgh Crawfords in 1932 (p. 165); and a single in 1949 (p. 241). — JOHN HOLWAY

CHASE, W[ILLIAM] CALVIN (1854–1921), editor, lawyer, and Republican politician. Born free in Washington, D.C., to William H. Chase, a successful blacksmith, and Lucinda Seaton Chase, a member of one of the finest families of Alexandria, Va., he was the second of six children and the only son. His parents were literate, and their neighborhood, according to the census data of 1860, 1870, and 1880, was integrated and composed largely of artisans and craftsmen.

Chase attended John F. Cook's school which was held in the basement of the nearby 15th Street Presbyterian Church where the Chases were members. He also attended public school, and perhaps the Preparatory

Department at Howard University. He did not attend the college, but later (c. 1883–1884) he attended courses at the Howard Law School. In 1889 Chase was admitted to the bar in both Virginia and the District of Columbia. Thereafter he actively practiced law until his death.

From 1882 to 1921 Chase was editor and proprietor of the *Washington Bee,* one of the most significant colored journals of the era. Chase used the terms "colored" and "Negro" interchangeably but his predominant usage was "colored"; both are used here. As an editor, Chase was known for his talented use of invective, and the *Bee*'s motto, "Honey for Friends, Stings for Enemies," suggests his inclination for *ad hominem* attack and its pragmatic basis. His caustic personality and editorials seriously limited the acclaim which he received in his own time despite a very active career in journalism, politics, and law which was national in scope. The complete files of the *Bee* testify to the fact that week in and week out for forty years Chase and the *Bee* spoke out on the issues which concerned Negroes.

The *Bee* (1882–1922) was a four-page newspaper from 1882 to 1895. Much of its front page was devoted to advertising, and in the early years the remaining space was devoted to items of incidental intelligence. Over time, however, the front page became the location of news about Negroes which was thought to be of national importance. After 1918 the format of the front page included a banner headline. The format of the editorial page remained constant throughout the lifetime of the *Bee,* although it became the fourth page when the *Bee* was expanded to eight pages in 1895. The society page also remained relatively constant in terms of its contents, and always emphasized the coming and going of notable colored Americans to Washington. Notes of fraternal orders were another regular feature of the society page, as well as notes of the colored communities in West Washington and Anacostia. The activities of the various cultural and social clubs such as those of the Bethel Literary and Historical Association and those of the Mu-So-Lit Club were also regularly reported on the *Bee*'s society page. The remaining pages were largely devoted to advertising, which consumed more than 50 percent of the total space in the *Bee.* Moreover, half the advertising featured white-owned businesses, while less than 10 percent featured hair straighteners and bleaching creams. Indeed, the largest advertiser for hair straighteners and skin creams was the white-owned chain of Peoples Drug Stores. After the expansion to eight pages, the *Bee* resorted to the use of "boiler-plate" columns for several of its pages, and very often these ready-made columns appeared more than once. The quality of the *Bee*'s own printing was comparable to its weekly peers despite frequent typographical errors, and over time the *Bee* became increasingly graphic by the publication of cartoons and photographs.

The two issues which consumed most of the space in the *Bee* were those of racism and politics. The *Bee* gave most publicity to the violent aspect of racism inherent in race riots and/or lynchings. For example, in response to the riots in Hemphill, Tex. (July 25, 1908), Coatesville, Pa. (Aug. 9, 1911), East St. Louis, Ill. (July 14,

1917), Washington, D.C. (Aug. 2, 1919), and Chicago (Aug. 23, 1919), the *Bee* incurred the added expense of publishing a cartoon on the front page. In general these cartoons concerning race riots and those pertinent to lynching were unmitigated satires on the indifference of local, state, and federal governments to criminal acts.

In its early years the *Bee* viewed racism as endemic to the Democratic South, but after the defeat of the Federal Elections Bill of 1890 the *Bee* came to view the federal government as increasingly responsible for the existence of racism. It was especially critical of the federal government's treatment of colored soldiers in the Spanish-American War, and it was outraged at the federal government's handling of the Brownsville Affair in 1906 and the so-called riot of Negro troops in Houston, Tex., in 1917. The latter definitely contributed to the *Bee*'s criticism of the federal government concerning enlistment, training, and deployment of colored troops in World War I. However, it did not associate the Houston riot with the one-month extension of the colored officers training camp at Fort Des Moines, Iowa. In fact, through George W. Cabaniss, an influential colored resident of Washington, D.C., the *Bee* (July 14, 1917) received and reprinted several speeches of Brig. Gen. Charles C. Ballou who was in charge of the camp. These speeches not only explained the government's position but denied the implication that the extension was due to inferior ability of the candidates. Moreover, as a result of the conference for Negro editors called in June 1918 by Emmett J. Scott, who served as special assistant to Secretary of War Newton D. Baker, the *Bee* did print Ralph W. Tyler's roseate articles. However, in December 1918 a Tyler article exposed the duplicity and race prejudice rampant in the U.S. Army, and the *Bee* followed this with several articles in January 1919 based on accounts of returned veterans. The *Bee* was equally critical of the federal government's treatment of Negro civilian employees, and it was unrelenting in its criticism of the segregation expanded under Pres. Woodrow Wilson. However, the *Bee,* throughout its career, stalwartly defended segregated schools, claiming that members of the colored race were best qualified to teach their own.

This specific acquiescence to the contrary, the essence of the *Bee* was protest, but it was not, therefore, an ardent advocate of the protest organizations of its era. Chase was instrumental, however, in the efforts which led to the establishment of both the Afro-American League (1887) and its successor, the Afro-American Council (1898), forerunners of the Niagara Movement. But in both instances he opposed the leadership of his journalistic contemporary, T. Thomas Fortune, and consequently contributed to the internecine factionalism which hamstrung both organizations. Chase also opposed W. E. B. Du Bois's leadership of the Niagara Movement (which opposed the conservative policies of Booker T. Washington and was itself a forerunner of the NAACP), primarily on personal grounds, but perhaps because of the competitive threat which the *Horizon* presented to such weekly journals as the *Bee.* Additionally, after 1906 Chase's allegiance to the Tuskegee camp also accounts for the *Bee*'s indifference to the

Niagara Movement. Chase's opposition to Du Bois (often anti-intellectual in tone) persisted and affected the *Bee*'s view of the NAACP. Chase clearly perceived *The Crisis* as a threat to the *Bee* as a principal spokesman for Negro protest, and before 1915 the *Bee* attempted to fan the flames of controversy which existed between Oswald Garrison Villard and Du Bois. After 1915, however, Chase and the *Bee* increasingly promoted the work of the NAACP, perhaps because the association (not *The Crisis*) began the policy of placing articles in the *Bee.* Chase's relationship with Du Bois became more cordial as well, but it was never firm.

Chase first opposed Booker T. Washington for different reasons than he opposed Du Bois. He viewed Washington from 1895 to 1906 as an "accommodating apologist" whereas he viewed Du Bois as a "water-brained theorist." The *Bee* criticized the Atlanta Exposition Address (Sept. 18, 1895) as "a bait of Southern fancy," and the White House dinner in 1901 by President Roosevelt for Booker T. Washington as "the political decapitation dinner." This epithet referred to Chase's charge that Roosevelt and Washington had conspired to eliminate Mark Hanna's political influence with colored Republicans and thereby enhance Roosevelt's chances for the presidential nomination in 1904 by supporting a "lily-white" policy concerning the Republican party in the South and by appointing Washington's allies in the northern states. One of those decapitated was Chase (a Hanna-sponsored delegate in 1900) even though T. Thomas Fortune had effected a détente between Chase and Washington in 1900. Consequently, Chase and the *Bee* continued to sting Washington for the next five years. In 1906, due to financial needs, Chase and the *Bee* entered the Tuskegee camp and both remained there, albeit uneasily, until Washington's death in 1915. The two men were never close personally, but after 1906 the *Bee* promoted Washington, Tuskegee, and the National Negro Business League (founded in 1900) with apparent consistency.

One race organization which Chase and the *Bee* totally ignored was Marcus Garvey's Universal Negro Improvement Association. This is surprising despite the *Bee*'s earlier antipathy to the pro-Africa positions of Edward Blyden and Bishop Henry M. Turner. The *Bee* did not ignore African affairs and it carried several brief accounts of the Pan-African Congress of February 1919 which it received from the Rev. M. W. D. Norman, a Washington, D.C., minister who attended the congress. However, it refrained from publishing any editorial comment regarding the congress.

Chase's political career was more consistent but no less controversial. During most of his life he was a Republican, albeit he was increasingly disaffected from its ranks because of its "lily-whiteism" after 1900. In large measure his disaffection stemmed from his affinity for the so-called Radical Republicans and the fact that his political heroes were Charles Sumner, Thaddeus Stevens, and Benjamin Wade. In short, Chase's political outlook was forged by the Civil War and Reconstruction, and he never moved beyond them. In his lifetime there was ample reason not to do so, for during his tenure as editor of the *Bee* colored Americans, especially in the South, lost most of the civil and political rights they had gained as a result of the "War of Rebellion," as Chase called it. In general, the *Bee* gave more attention to campaigns than issues, but when the issue was suffrage for Negroes the *Bee* was especially attentive. Such was the case regarding its coverage of the Federal Elections Bill of 1890 and the case of *Guinn v. U.S.* concerning the Oklahoma "grandfather clause" in 1915. (This was a device, ruled unconstitutional by the U.S. Supreme Court, which permitted unqualified men to vote if their grandfathers—almost all white—had voted.) To Chase the involvement of Negroes in the political process was the means toward the full expression of their freedom, and consequently the *Bee* was unrelenting in its criticism of the rise of "lily-whiteism" under Theodore Roosevelt. As a consequence too, the *Bee* flirted with the Socialist party in 1904 and again in 1916. Moreover, it championed the cause of the *Messenger* which was attacked in 1919 by the Justice Department in the Palmer Report on "Radicalism and Sedition Among the Negroes as Reflected in Their Publications." Declared the *Bee,* "lynching and burning Negroes, denying them suffrage and discrimination North and South antedates by many years even the first conception of Bolshevism."

As a politician Chase was a pragmatist and as a journalist he was a practical businessman. Both characteristics disqualified him as a radical, but he militantly protested for equal rights with such words as the following: "This much should be remembered by all civilized governments . . . 'the same sun that softens the wax, hardens the clay' . . . and does not it also follow in indisputable language that the injury, oppression, or any attempt at a gradual or indirect extermination of either one of the two great races comprising the American nation, would be the overthrow or downfall of this government?"

On Jan. 28, 1886, Chase married Arabella V. McCabe at a wedding said to be one of the most elaborate in Washington. He died of a heart attack seated in his editorial chair in Washington on Jan. 3, 1921. Funeral services were held in the 15th Street Presbyterian Church and he was buried in the Harmony Cemetery. He was survived by his wife, his daughter Beatriz Lucinda, and his son William Calvin Jr.

At present no published monograph exists concerning W. Calvin Chase or the *Washington Bee.* There is a long biographical sketch of Chase in William J. Simmons's *Men of Mark . . .* (1887, pp. 118–32), with an engraving facing p. 120; and a shorter sketch in I. Garland Penn's *The Afro-American Press and Its Editors* (1891, pp. 287–90). The most extensive study of Chase and the *Bee* is Hal S. Chase's "Honey for Friends, Stings for Enemies: William Calvin Chase and *The Washington Bee,* 1882–1921" (Ph.D. dissertation, University of Pennsylvania, 1973), based primarily on the contents of the *Bee* and the correspondence of W. Calvin Chase located in various manuscript collections and the National Archives. A microfilm copy of the *Bee,* photocopies of Chase correspondence, and Hal Chase's dissertation are available in the Moorland-Spingarn Research Center, Howard University, Washington, D.C.

— HAL S. CHASE

CHAVIS, JOHN (c. 1763–1838), clergyman and teacher. So little is known about his early life that he is said to have been born in either the West Indies or near Oxford in Granville County, N.C. Most sources agree, however, that he lived in Granville County in a locality known as "Reavis Cross Roads." According to George C. Shaw who knew Sarah Young, Chavis's great-granddaughter, the name of his mother was Lottie Chavis, and of his grandmother, Peggy Chavis. The records of later years indicate that he married a woman named Frances. He also had one brother, Anthony, who fought in the American Revolution.

In 1832 Chavis stated that "he was a free born American and saw service in the Revolutionary War." He enlisted with Capt. May Cunnington on Dec. 29, 1778, at the age of fifteen. Both Anthony and John Chavis fought under Washington and Lafayette at Brandywine, at White Plains, N.Y., and at Yorktown, Va.

At the close of the eighteenth century Chavis pursued the regular course of study at Washington Academy, Va., now Washington and Lee University. At Princeton he studied under John Witherspoon, president of the college, and became an able and impressive theologian.

In 1801 the General Assembly of Presbyterians commissioned him as a missionary to slaves, the first Negro in the Presbyterian church prepared for Christian leadership and home missionary tasks. The active ministry of Chavis covers a period of thirty years, 1802–1832. The records of the Hanover Presbytery disclose that he was "riding as a missionary under the direction of the General Assembly" in 1801. After 1807 the name of John Chavis disappeared from the Acts and Proceedings of the General Assembly. But he joined the Orange Presbytery in 1805, and in 1809 received his license. As a minister, Chavis preached to both races—white, free Negroes and slaves—in and out of churches, in homes in North Carolina, Virginia, and Maryland. There is also a strong probability that he preached to whites in white churches.

He was an educator as well as a minister of the gospel. He taught in a school in Fayetteville, N.C., and for two years lived in the counties of Franklin, Wake, and Chatham where he also preached. By 1808 Chavis was principal of his own school. Open to black and white children, he charged blacks $1.75 and whites $2.50. Most of his students were the sons and daughters of prominent white families in North Carolina, among whom the following names stand out: Willie P. Mangum, U.S. senator; Priestly H. Mangum, his brother; Archibald and John Henderson, sons of Chief Justice Henderson; Charles Manly, governor; Abram Rencher, minister to Portugal and governor of New Mexico.

Chavis involved himself vigorously in American politics in the 1820s and 1830s. He labeled himself a Federalist, favored the 1828 protective tariff act, opposed nullification, and bitterly opposed Andrew Jackson. He supported, in fact, aristocracy, training, wealth, and regarded Jackson as a backwoods countryman without benefit of "blood or training." In his frequent letters to Mangum he constantly urged his "sons" (former students) to return to the true doctrine of Washington and Hamilton.

Contending that abolition would add to the woes of his fellow Negroes, Chavis opposed immediate emancipation. He admitted that slavery was evil but that "all that can be done is to make the best of a bad bargain." In 1831 he referred to the Nat Turner slave rebellion as "that abominable insurrection in Southampton." The revolt made it impossible for Chavis to continue both his ministry and his school.

In the summer of 1835 the North Carolina General Assembly deprived him of the franchise. William Gaston, who opposed the action, did not feel that the minister-teacher deserved "an additional mark of degradation fixed upon him solely on account of his color." Gaston failed to impress the General Assembly and Chavis never voted again.

One year before John Chavis died on June 13, 1838, Gales and Son published a pamphlet, *Chavis' Letter Upon the Atonement of Christ.* Costing a mere fifteen cents, the booklet contained nearly 6000 words. Proceeds from the sale added to the support given him and his wife, after his death, by his presbytery. For about half a century the life and works of John Chavis were almost forgotten. Interest in his life was revived chiefly through the efforts of Charles Lee Smith, a prominent educator in North Carolina. A large recreational park and federal housing project in Raleigh, N.C., memorialize Chavis's accomplishments.

John Chavis (1931) is a biography written by George C. Shaw, who knew Chavis's great-granddaughter. John Hope Franklin's *The Free Negro in North Carolina, 1790–1863* (1943) is a scholarly interpretation. Perhaps the best work on Chavis is Edgar W. Knight's "Notes on John Chavis (*North Carolina Historical Review* 7 [1930]: 326–45). Almost all of Chavis's letters are in the Willia P. Mangum Papers, Library of Congress, Duke University, and the University of North Carolina at Chapel Hill. A letter from Diane Girvin, archives assistant, the University Archives, Princeton University, to Rayford W. Logan (June 5, 1975), stated: "According to our records, John Chavis most likely did attend Princeton." There is a brief sketch in *DAB* (2, Part 1:44–45) by James Curtis Ballagh, author of *History of Slavery in Virginia* (1902).

— GOSSIE HAROLD HUDSON

CHEATHAM, HENRY PLUMMER (1857–1935), member of Congress, recorder of deeds, and orphanage superintendent. He was born a slave on Dec. 27, 1857, on a plantation near Henderson, N.C. His mother was at that time a house slave who served as a maid. The formative years of his life as the son of a house slave did not subject him to the rigor and agony of the generally less fortunate field slaves. Moreover he benefited culturally and educationally from this domestic atmosphere. Upon receiving his freedom at the end of the Civil War, he entered a public school in Henderson with an edge on most of his peers. At the age of eighteen Cheatham entered the normal school of Shaw University in Raleigh, N.C., and three years later the college department of the same university. Graduating in 1882 with honors, Cheatham immediately replaced A. B. Hicks, Jr., who died while in office, as principal of the Plymouth Normal School in Plymouth, N.C. With a starting salary of $50 per month, he worked until 1884 along with his first wife, Louise Cherry Cheatham, who taught instrumental music.

In 1885 Cheatham returned to the county of his birth, Vance County, to accept a position as recorder of deeds. Contemporaries describe him as being a distinguished-looking mulatto. Maurine Christopher, in *America's Black Congressmen* (1971), described Cheatham as being a "pleasant unassuming man, with even features and a chiseled profile." With patience, magnanimity, conciliation, and constructive leadership, he gained the respect of both white and black North Carolinians while holding that office.

By 1887 Cheatham was able to read law extensively and would have applied for a license had it not conflicted with his official duties. Shaw University, in further recognition of his talent, conferred upon him the M.A. degree in 1887. With this background Cheatham entered the election as the Republican nominee for the 2nd Congressional District of North Carolina in 1888.

Furnifold Simmons, the white Democratic incumbent, was unable to discover an issue that could divide the Republican majority in the 1888 election. Even though Simmons had selected and successfully obtained legislation beneficial to the Negroes of Craven County, he was astounded at the ease with which Cheatham's demagoguery won Negro support. Cheatham is alleged to have told the Negroes that President Cleveland and Simmons would put them back in slavery because it was too expensive to furnish Negroes both work and wages. Cheatham won the election and was the only Negro member seated in the 51st Congress in December 1889. Nearly one year later he was joined by John Mercer Langston of Virginia and Thomas E. Miller of South Carolina.

Cheatham was officially absent from Congress on four occasions in the first session of the 51st Congress, three of which were due to important business and the fourth due to illness of his wife. During his second term he was granted six official excuses, most of them because of his own poor health.

In the 1890 election the Democrats, after a long debate, finally chose a candidate. Shortly thereafter the candidate became ill, and Cheatham enjoyed an easy victory over James Mewborne, a last-minute substitute. Cheatham was the only Negro in the 52nd Congress.

During both the 51st and 52nd Congresses Cheatham remained cognizant of his responsibility to the constituents of his district. His first act was to introduce a bill (HR 632) to reimburse the depositors of the Freedmen's Savings and Trust Company for losses incurred due to bankruptcy of the company. A second bill introduced the same day (HR 633) called for the erection of a public building at Henderson for the accommodation of the post office and other government buildings. Still, a third and more comprehensive bill (HR 634) was introduced on Dec. 18, 1889. This bill called for federal aid in the establishment and temporary support of common schools in the United States. He hoped that this bipartisan, biracial, and intersectional bill would make it possible for all children to receive an education. With equal enthusiasm he introduced over fourteen other bills, among them a bill fostering a display of Negro history at the Chicago World's Fair and one providing for further compensation to Robert Smalls. Although Cheatham was unsuccessful in getting any legislation enacted, his patience, persistence, and belief in the democratic system remained undaunted.

Even though Cheatham won the Republican nomination in 1894 and 1896, he lost both elections to a white Democrat, Frederick Woodward. These losses were due mainly to dissension among Negroes and Populist party proselytism. In the election of the 55th Congress in 1898, Cheatham lost the Republican nomination to George H. White, his brother-in-law, who represented the 2nd Congressional District until 1901. Cheatham remained in North Carolina until he was appointed recorder of deeds for the District of Columbia by Pres. William McKinley; the Senate confirmed the appointment on May 13, 1897. After four years he returned to North Carolina, and in 1907 he became the superintendent of the colored orphanage at Oxford which had been in existence since 1882. During his tenure at the orphanage (1907–1935) Cheatham transformed many of the campus buildings from wood-frame to brick, increased the farm acreage, and through philanthropic donations erected two buildings. By 1935 the orphanage was accommodating over 195 students.

From his marriage to Louise Cherry he fathered three children, Charlie, Mamie, and Plummer; from his marriage to Laura Joyner, the offspring were Susie, Richard, and James.

For additional information, see Maurine Christopher's *America's Black Congressmen* (1971, pp. 156–59); Helen G. Edmonds's *The Negro and Fusion Politics in North Carolina 1894–1901* (1951, pp. 19, 84, 87), Frenise Logan's *The Negro in North Carolina, 1876–1894* (1964), and Samuel Denny Smith's *The Negro in Congress, 1870–1901* (1940, pp. 121–25, 142–43).

— BENJAMIN F. CLARK

CHESNUTT, CHARLES WADDELL (1858–1932), teacher, lawyer, businessman, and author. He was born on June 20, 1858, on Hudson Street in Cleveland, Ohio, the first child of Andrew Jackson and Ann Maria (Sampson) Chesnutt who met two years previously when both were among a party of free Negroes traveling by wagon train northward in flight from the increasingly severe restrictions imposed on the free colored population of North Carolina. Charles Chesnutt's exposure to the region which would be the locus of his major fiction began in 1866 when his father, who had been serving in the Union Army, decided that his wife and three young sons should leave their home in Cleveland and join him in Fayetteville, N.C.

Growing up in the South during the turbulent Reconstruction period meant constant, personal exposure to the issues left unresolved by the Civil War. At the age of nine Charles had seen a colored man murdered in the streets of Fayetteville. As a pupil, then a teacher, in small country schools he was pained by slavery's legacy of ignorance. He lamented in his journals: "uneducated people are the most bigoted, superstitious, hardest-headed people in the world! These folks downstairs believe in ghosts, luck, horse shoes, cloud-signs, witches, and all other kinds of nonsense, and all the argument in the world couldn't get it out of them." Journal entries from 1871 to 1876 document the growth of an imaginative, romantic sensibility. The death of his mother in 1871 and the necessity of earning a living in rural schools far removed from the rest of his family contributed to the melancholy tone of many of the jottings which date from this period. In Byron, Cowper, Burns, and Dickens, whom he mentions in his letters and diary, Chesnutt found numerous passages which reflected his personal experience of loss and loneliness and perhaps more important he observed how these authors rendered such sentiments into literary form.

But to picture Chesnutt at this stage of his life as simply a homesick young man barely enduring the enforced exile of country teaching is to ignore the streak of stubborn practicality which runs like a vein of iron from adolescence to his mature years. Chesnutt embarked early on a vigorous program of reading and study which eventually would lead to proficiency in Latin, German, French, mathematics, legal stenography, and law. Such a regimen and the self-discipline required to sustain it produced a remarkably talented, competent man who prospered in his teaching career. By the time of his marriage to Susan Perry on June 6, 1878, Charles was dissatisfied with his position as a teacher-administrator in the Howard School at Fayetteville, and planned to resettle in the North where he might practice the legal stenography he had spent countless hours teaching himself.

But a trip to Washington in 1879 failed to produce job opportunities, so Chesnutt returned to Fayetteville and his career in teaching. In spite of being named principal of the state normal school, Chesnutt's ambition and the growing needs of his family caused him to continue seeking opportunities beyond the scope of those available in Fayetteville. Never simply a dreamer, Chesnutt made the goals he set for himself realistic by constant cultivation of his personal resources. With the aid of sympathetic tutors, but largely on his own, Chesnutt acquired all the accoutrements of a man of learning, becoming in the intellectual sphere a model of that self-made man glorified by American society at the turn of the century.

Since he was very much a man of his age, when the notion of writing a book arose in Chesnutt he saw his potential novel not only as an opportunity to improve on the efforts of previous Negro writers, such as William Wells Brown, but also as a means to make his fortune. The example of Judge Albion W. Tourgée was very much in Chesnutt's mind, both because Chesnutt felt himself more familiar with the many sides of southern life than Tourgée and because the white southern Judge had recently sold a novel, *A Fool's Errand,* for $20,000.

A second trip north (1883) seeking employment was successful, and after working a year in New York City on Wall Street as a stenographer and journalist, Chesnutt moved to Cleveland and was joined by his family. A career in legal stenography was combined with law practice after he passed the Ohio bar at the top of his class (1887). His business successes were paralleled by the publication of short stories in the McClure syndicated newspapers and in numerous magazines. Although Chesnutt had broken into print at the age of fourteen with a story serialized in a Fayetteville weekly newspaper, the growing demand for his stories crowned by *Atlantic Monthly*'s acceptance of "The Goophered Grapevine" (1887) and "Po Sandy" (1888) provided the first serious evidence that he had both talent and the potential for earning a living with his pen.

Like one of his characters, Doctor Miller of *The Marrow of Tradition,* Chesnutt while still a young man had achieved high personal stature through demonstrated ability and talent, yet because the real and fictional men were Negro their accomplishments and position cannot be understood without reference to the racist character of American society. Although Chesnutt accepted the standards of civility, of style, and of learning which epitomized the white Anglo-Saxon gentleman-scholar of the turn of the century, and even strove tirelessly to absorb and reflect these values in his own person, he was not unaware of the paradox embodied in his behavior: the irony of acting out "civilized" values while his race, just recently emerged from chattel slavery, continued to be the victims of that "civilization's" irrationality and violence. Because of his brilliance in reading law and his talent for writing fiction Chesnutt was offered first a chance to practice law in Europe so that he might avoid the race issue altogether and later an opportunity to become the private secretary of a prominent American man of letters. What was being offered was the closest approximation of equality available for American Negroes during the Gilded Age: a metaphysical rite of passage which combined voluntary resignation from the Negro race and total identification with a white man or white institution.

Chesnutt accepted neither Judge Samuel E. Williamson's nor George Washington Cable's invitations. Instead he maintained financial independence by energetically cultivating his law and legal stenography practice. Evenings when available were devoted to writing fiction, and in spite of the demands of family life and business Chesnutt was able to compose stories which continued to appear in the best literary magazines, and by 1889 had completed his first novel, *Rena Walden.* This book, which would be much rewritten and eventually published as *The House Behind the Cedars* in 1900, was circulated while in manuscript form among Chesnutt's literary acquaintances, including George Washington Cable and Richard Watson Gilder. Chesnutt was disturbed by what seemed to be the intractability and blindness in regard to matters of race even among these sophisticated readers. Such responses in private and in print were reflections of the kind of bigotry which dominated popular thinking about blacks and whites and ominously foreshadowed the insensitivity of the general reading public to the characters, themes, and perspectives Chesnutt would develop in his later fiction.

In 1891 Chesnutt sent a manuscript to Houghton Mifflin Company in Boston. An accompanying letter summarized what Chesnutt felt would be unique about his collection of stories: "In this case, the infusion of African blood is very small—is not in fact a visible admixture—but it is enough, combined with the fact that the writer was practically brought up in the South, to

give him a knowledge of the people whose description is attempted. These people have never been treated from a closely sympathetic standpoint; they have not had their day in court. Their friends have written of them, and their enemies; but this is, so far as I know, the first instance where a writer with any of their own blood has attempted a literary portrayal of them. If these stories have any merit, I think it is more owing to this new point of view than to any other thing." Mifflin refused to undertake publication, advising him to publish more short pieces, enlarge his reputation, and then submit a collection for reconsideration. By 1897 a cordial relationship with Walter Hines Page, literary editor of the *Atlantic,* and the popular and critical success of his stories encouraged Chesnutt to attempt again to publish a collection of his stories. Another refusal to print his collected stories did not daunt Chesnutt; instead he continued to correspond with Page and Mifflin until a cohesive volume of tales organized around the theme of "conjure" proved acceptable for publication. In the last week of March 1899 seven stories of southern life united by their exploration of Negro folklore and story-telling traditions appeared bearing the title *The Conjure Woman.* The end of the same year saw publication of a second volume of stories, *The Wife of His Youth,* and a commissioned biography, *The Life of Frederick Douglass.*

With these successes behind him and a novel completed and accepted for publication in the forthcoming year, Chesnutt's desire to set up as an author seemed finally realizable. Closing his lucrative business office, for the next two years Chesnutt attempted to support his family solely from savings and his income as a professional author. Two daughters at college, two children still at home, the comfortable standard of living to which the family was accustomed, and the uncertainty of the literary profession conspired to make Chesnutt's decision a difficult one, but the prospects of success and the strength of his ambition made him optimistic: "an elevator boy asked me the other day if it was true that I was going into the 'author business.' I told him 'Yes.'" Unfortunately the sales of his books were not commensurate with the critical acclaim and recognition he was receiving. Though the first novel, *The House Behind the Cedars,* went into four printings between October 1900 and April 1901, its sales together with the income from his other books, freelance journalism, and speaking engagements were proving far from adequate for the needs of his family.

A tour of the southern states in 1901 confirmed for Chesnutt what had been made so brutally apparent in the Wilmington, N.C., massacre of 1898. North Carolina as well as the rest of the South, through violence and legal chicanery, were denying constitutional guarantees to Negro citizens and thereby reestablishing unequivocally the doctrine of white supremacy. Contemplating the possibility of a career in fiction Chesnutt had written in 1880: "If I do write, I shall write for a purpose, and this will inspire me to greater effort. The object of my writings would be not so much the elevation of the colored people as the elevation of the white —for I consider the unjust spirit of caste which is so insidious as to pervade a whole nation and so powerful as to subject a whole race and all connected with it to scorn and social ostracism—I consider this a barrier to the moral progress of the American people; and I would be one of the first to head a determined, organized crusade against it." Twenty years later this resolve would be focused in the writing of *The Marrow of Tradition,* a novel which exposes the tragedy inherent in a society built on self-deception and lies.

But the spirit of social reform and the aesthetic challenge implicit in a new, major work of fiction were combined with at least one other motivating factor as Chesnutt considered his new novel: "Upon its reception will depend in some measure whether I shall write, for the present, any more 'Afro American' novels; for a man must live and consider his family." The publication of *The Marrow of Tradition* (1901) occasioned more controversy than sales, and Chesnutt was forced to return to his Cleveland law and court reporting office.

A renewed, intense involvement with his business affairs did not prevent Chesnutt from writing. In 1905 Doubleday, Page, and Company published *The Colonel's Dream,* a novel in which Chesnutt examined the futility of schemes for the economic regeneration of the South unless those schemes included some plan for moral and ethical reform as well. The novel received less attention than *The Marrow of Tradition* and garnered even fewer sales. *The Colonel's Dream* was Chesnutt's last full-length work to be published during his lifetime.

Five years after the publication of *The Colonel's Dream* Chesnutt collapsed in his Cleveland office and remained unconscious for several days. His recovery was slow, necessitating curtailment of his strenuous schedule. A pleasant summer abroad was the prelude to a lightened round of social, public, and professional engagements. But correspondence with important public figures and writers on the race question indicate the respect with which Chesnutt's views and reputation continued to be held throughout his life.

An attack of appendicitis followed by peritonitis in 1920 left Chesnutt's health permanently impaired. Games of solitaire and crossword puzzles became his favorite pastimes. A renewed interest in writing quickened incidentally by praise of his work by Carl Van Vechten led to the completion of a manuscript *The Quarry,* which was subsequently refused by Knopf in 1928. The next year a new edition of *The Conjure Woman* compensated somewhat for the refusal of his novel, yet the republication of his first book of short stories must have reminded Chesnutt that all of his books had gone out of print.

The Springarn Medal given annually by the NAACP was awarded to Chesnutt in 1928 commemorating his "pioneer work as a literary artist depicting the life and struggles of Americans of Negro descent, and for his long and useful career as scholar, worker and freeman." The year 1931 marked Chesnutt's last published work, an article for the *Colophon* entitled "Post Bellum—Pre Harlem." Looking back over his literary life and the history of Negro writing in general, Chesnutt gave a lucid synopsis of his various books and commented on the ambivalence of his publishers toward the question of his race, especially their withholding of the fact of his Negro ancestry from the general public during the early years of his career.

At 5:30 in the afternoon on Nov. 15, 1932, Charles Chesnutt died at home in his bed surrounded by his wife and their daughters Dorothy K., Ethel P., Helen M., and Edwina J. The simple Episcopal service was held at the home, attended by the president of Western Reserve University, school administrators, his business associates, representatives of the Cleveland Bar Association, and clubs in which he had been active.

Charles Waddell Chesnutt was a brilliant, abundantly gifted man endowed with an inordinate capacity for hard work and self-discipline. Because of his physical appearance he could have chosen to pass for a white man, but because he did not deny his race, he made to American literature, through his fiction and occasional essays, a lasting contribution which helps to define abiding truths about the Afro-American experience.

The fiction of Charles Waddell Chesnutt has suffered from the lack of serious readers and serious critical attention. The period in which the main body of his work was published (1899–1905) was a time when North and South had reconciled their differences over "the Negro problem" and cemented a prosperous, commercial partnership, an epoch that saw the European nations in a mad rush for the resources and cheap labor of the nonwhite world, when the doctrine of white supremacy was the essential ingredient harmonizing the economic, social, and political philosophies that justified the thrust of European industrialized societies toward global control and domination. Given such a period, it is not surprising that the work of a nonwhite author who took as his dominant theme the dehumanizing, destructive consequences of racial prejudice was ignored by the reading public.

The object of the necessarily short description of Chesnutt's major works which follows is not to provide plot summaries but rather to indicate the range and intensity of the thematic elements in his work and to bring into focus those issues, literary and historical, which are raised by Chesnutt's fiction.

The Conjure Woman (1899) is a collection of seven short stories narrated by a white northerner, John, who has bought land in the South and come to live there with his wife Annie. The narrator's black servant Julius Macadoo, known surprisingly as Uncle Julius, seems to be a living relic of the antebellum South, tied to the land, retaining in his manner the bondsman's servility, submissiveness, obedience, and loyalty. Yet his dialect tales framed within the stories of the narrator manage to provide the reader with insights into owner and servant and by analogy into the dynamics of master-slave relationships. Chesnutt notes elsewhere that "each story reveals the old man's ulterior purpose, which as a general thing, is accomplished." The literary rendering of black speech, the incorporation of Afro-American folklore into fiction, the reconsiderations of literary stereotypes, the elaboration of a technique through which Negro viewpoints can be given subtle independence but so as not to offend a predominately white readership—are all essayed in this volume.

The Wife of His Youth (1889) contains nine stories collected over a period of years. Of less interest on some accounts than Chesnutt's first volume, the stories are not structurally or organically related except that, here, the problems of the "color line" are explored without the qualifying frame of Uncle Julius's subtle irony and the supernatural events of the *Conjure Woman*. The problems of people of mixed blood and the nether world they inhabit often is given a sentimental patina by the use of elevated diction and improbably moralistic sentiments. Such moments, however, are balanced with flashes of violence, with subtle, psychological insights and analysis which restore a sense of reality to the situations Chesnutt describes. Since the "moral" or lesson seemingly embodied in many of the stories is a demonstrably simple one, the reader may tend to miss what is complex and demanding in Chesnutt's execution of character and detail.

The House Behind the Cedars (1900) is a much-rewritten first novel whose subject is marriage between blacks and whites. Chesnutt's problem in this novel was a formidable one: to render palatable a situation and a character who is a priori repugnant to the majority of his reading public. Rena Walden, since she is concealing her African ancestry, must prove herself whiter than white. Chesnutt attempts to gain the reader's sympathy by endowing his major character with implausible virtues; further, he attempts to create a tragic situation through a plot too dependent on coincidence and transparent devices. The novel's strengths lie in the treatment of minor characters, in isolated scenes, in the narrator's incidental asides on human nature and the ways of the world.

The Marrow of Tradition (1901) is Chesnutt's finest, most ambitious novel, and perhaps his most significant single work. Spurred by memories of the recent Wilmington massacre (1898) and profoundly depressed by the calculated oppression of American Negroes, Chesnutt creates the fictional town of Wellington so that he can expose the hypocrisy and deception which lead inevitably to bloody confrontations between blacks and whites. Into his panoramic view of Wellington Chesnutt brings a knowledge of politics, economics, history, a sense of class differences, an insight into the motivation of both races. Dr. Miller, into whom Chesnutt projects many of his own characteristics, particularly the ability to achieve a high degree of personal success within a society which stacks the deck against such success, is the central figure of the novel, an admirable man who seems a living example of Du Bois's Talented Tenth, those Negroes who through personal force of character and achievement lead the way for their less fortunate brethren's eventual amalgamation into the mainstream of American life. The novel is full of ironies implicit and explicit, and is in a sense unresolved since Chesnutt holds out no solution for men like Miller or himself. The book is profoundly pessimistic since the individual Negro, no matter how resolutely he proves his equality, is crushed just as utterly as his most ignorant, underprivileged brother once the manichean fury of race war begins. History as a lie and a cage is vividly symbolized in the novel by the self-delusions which underlie the lives of Wellington's citizens. Chesnutt's novel is unique in its insistence on Negro and white complicity in the construction of a false history. His comprehension of national and international politics, stylistic details such as the sustained imagery of disguise and masquerade, the variety of narrative modes ranging from intrusive essay-commentary to naturalistic dialogue, the use of dialect, folk maxims, parodies of newspaper propaganda create a context for examining the question of Negro-ness that is subtle, complex, and suggestive.

The Colonel's Dream (1905), Chesnutt's last published novel, is best seen not as a propaganda piece attacking the system of convict labor but as yet another grappling with the broader problem of, as he once put it, "the elevation of the whites." The colonel who attempts to "save" the decaying town in which he spent his boyhood is a man blessed with intelligence, goodwill, prodigious financial resources, and almost saintly patience. Yet he fails because he underestimates the hold of superstition and tradition in Clarendon. In fact he prefers his "dream" to the reality he sees around him, a reality finally forced on him as it was on Dr. Miller by the death of a son. Economic rebuilding of the South in order to have meaning must coincide with spiritual and moral rebirth, and these latter can begin only by the eradication of those very areas of sanctioned violence and irrationality the colonel avoids disturbing. *The Colonel's Dream* is thinner in narrative invention and complexity of theme than its predecessor, but portrays graphically in a straightforward, engrossing manner the defeat of a man and a region.

One full-length critical biography of Chesnutt exists, Frances R. Keller's *An American Crusade: The Life of Charles Waddell Chesnutt* (1977). The indispensable and highly readable biography, *Charles Waddell Chesnutt: Pioneer of the Color Line* (1952), by his daughter Helen M. Chesnutt, gives a full account of her father's life and is richly documented with selections from his diary and letters. Chesnutt is mentioned in most standard book-length studies of the Negro novel, but the treatment tends to be perfunctory. A careful reading of his fiction should restore his reputation as an accomplished storyteller and significant commentator on American life.

Dean Keller's bibliographical article in *American Literary Realism* (no. 3, Summer 1968) is a good starting point for any serious study. The article mentioned above, "Post Bellum—Pre Harlem," is a valuable commentary by Chesnutt on his own career and is reprinted in Elmer Adler's *Breaking into Print* (1937). Comments of early reviewers including William Dean Howells can be found in the *Atlantic Monthly,* the *North American Review,* and other major literary periodicals at the time of original publication. More recent shorter studies of Chesnutt's importance as a novelist are Samuel Sillen's "Charles Chesnutt: A Pioneer Negro Novelist" (*Masses and Mainstream* 6, Feb. 1953), Russell Ames's "Social Realism in Charles Waddell Chesnutt" (*Phylon* 14, no. 2, 1953), and John Wideman's "Charles Waddell Chesnutt: The Marrow of Tradition" (*The American Scholar,* Winter 1972–73). A longer study is *The Short Fiction of Charles W. Chesnutt,* edited and with an introduction by Sylvia Lyons Render (1974). For the scholar interested in Chesnutt, Mildred Freeney and Mary T. Henry have compiled "A List of Manuscripts, Published Works and Related Items in the Charles Waddell Chesnutt Collection of the Erastus Milo Cravath Memorial Library,'' Fisk University (1954). Much of Chesnutt's published fiction has been made available in paperback reprints. — JOHN W. WIDEMAN

CHESTER, T[HOMAS] MORRIS (1834–1892), educator, recruiter of soldiers, lawyer, and journalist. Chester was born on May 11, 1834, in Harrisburg, Pa., the fourth child of George and Jane Chester. His mother was a former slave who had escaped from Maryland (interview with Chester, *Harrisburg Patriot,* Sept. 13, 1892). In 1851 he began attending Avery College, a trade school in Allegheny, Pa., now part of Pittsburgh. Two years later he went to Monrovia, Liberia, where he enrolled in Alexandria High School. At the end of 1854 he returned to the United States and entered the junior class at Thetford Academy in Thetford, Vt., where he graduated second in the class of 1856. He returned to Liberia in 1857 and became superintendent of an organization which educated those liberated from American slave vessels. He also began publishing a newspaper in 1860, the *Star of Liberia,* and participated in local politics (letters from Chester to Jacob C. White, Moorland-Spingarn Research Center, Howard University). At the same time he was the *New York Herald*'s correspondent in Liberia (''Civil War Reporter,'' *Ebony,* Nov. 1959, an article based on Chester's private papers).

Although he visited the United States earlier, Chester did not move back until the outbreak of the Civil War in early 1861. Later he joined Frederick Douglass and others in recruiting the Negro soldiers who formed the 54th and 55th Massachusetts Volunteer Infantry Regiments in 1863. Chester decided not to enlist after he learned that Negro soldiers would not be allowed to advance beyond the rank of sergeant. In 1864 Chester learned shorthand so that he would be able to preserve for posterity some of the impressive Negro orations he frequently heard. Later in the same year his employment of this skill in writing a report on the proceedings of the A.M.E. church General Conference in Philadelphia earned him a job as a war correspondent for the *Philadelphia Press,* in which his report had appeared. Assigned to follow the Army of the James, under the pen name ''Rollin,'' he reported closely on the war in that sector until its conclusion and was one of the first reporters to enter Richmond after it fell. He wrote his description of the Union Army's victorious entry into the city while seated in Confederate Pres. Jefferson Davis's chair in the capitol (*Press,* April 6, 1865).

At the end of 1866 Chester once again went abroad, this time to Europe on a fundraising mission for the Garnet League of Harrisburg, a freedmen's aid society of which he was corresponding secretary. By the end of 1867 he visited England, Russia, France, Holland, Belgium, some of the German states, Denmark, and Sweden. He was well received in all these countries and had an audience with a number of the kings. In Russia, for example, he accepted an invitation to accompany the tsar on a review of the Imperial Guard, followed by a luncheon with part of the royal family. He spent the winter of 1866–1867 in Russia (despatches from U.S. ministers in St. Petersburg and Copenhagen, Feb. 9, 1867, and April 6, 1868, respectively). Among the

many famous people Chester met during his travels in Europe were the American Negro tragedian Ira Aldridge and Alexander Dumas. Chester remained in Europe for four years, residing primarily in London. There he studied law at the Middle Temple of the Inns of Court, was admitted to the bar in 1870, and practiced in the criminal and civil courts (*Harrisburg Patriot,* Sept. 13, 1892).

In 1871 Chester returned to the United States and settled in New Orleans, where he was admitted to law practice by the State Supreme Court in November 1871. He was a pall bearer (Nov. 1871) at the funeral of Oscar James Dunn, former lieutenant-governor of Louisiana. He became active in Louisiana politics and was a staunch supporter of Gov. W. P. Kellogg (*New York Times,* Sept. 10, 1873, p. 3). In 1873 the latter appointed Chester a brigadier general in the state militia. In 1875 he was appointed division superintendent of public education in a division with seven parishes and in 1876 in a division with thirteen parishes, with both Negro and white students. He held this latter position until the Kellogg administration lost power in 1877. Chester then turned to the federal government for posts. In February 1879 he was appointed a United States courts commissioner in New Orleans and served until January 1880 (records of the General Accounting Office, U.S. National Archives). Continuing his law practice all the while, he gained admittance to practice before the Supreme Courts of the District of Columbia in 1879 and Pennsylvania in 1881. In December of 1882 he was living in Delta, La., when U.S. Attorney-General Benjamin Brewster appointed him as a special assistant to the U.S. attorney for the Eastern District of Texas. There he was given the extremely dangerous task of investigating alleged violations of federal electoral laws through manipulation of Negro votes. In one instance he discovered that the votes for an entire county had been ''spirited away'' (Department of Justice Chronological Files, U.S. National Archives). In 1884 Chester gained a reputation as a ''railroad magnate'' by being elected president of a Negro railroad corporation (*Harrisburg State Journal,* Oct. 18, 1884); however, the corporation did not enjoy much success (William J. Simmons, *Men of Mark . . .* [1887], pp. 675–76). Though traveling widely for various purposes, Chester continued to reside in Louisiana until April of 1892, when, due to an illness, he moved back to his mother's house in Harrisburg. There he died of a heart attack on Sept. 30, 1892.

It would be difficult to imagine a higher degree of involvement in the events of one's time than Chester achieved in his career. At the same time his peripatetic endeavors clearly grew out of a consistent dual purpose: to advance himself and to advance the Negro in general. This goal was a direct outgrowth of his origins, for his parents' home had been a main station of the Underground Railroad (*Harrisburg Patriot,* Sept. 13, 1892). His identification with that background is most clearly articulated in the Civil War columns of ''Rollin.'' Although his highly perceptive reports are comprehensive in their scope, it is obvious that the conduct of the Negro soldiers and the fate of the Negro population are of paramount interest for him. And neither the disappointments of Reconstruction nor his personal achievements exhausted his commitment. In 1879 he was among the organizers of a self-styled "Exodus Convention" in New Orleans, which encouraged consideration of Negro migration to Kansas. In this action Chester was opposing the stand taken by most of the local Negro politicians (William Ivy Hair, *Bourbonism and Agrarian Protest*, 1969). However, his own opinion at the end of his life was that, aside from friction over politics, the South offered the Negro a healthier relationship between the races than the North and was an area where the Negro could gain real power if he purchased land and used it well for profit. In his political views Chester remained a confirmed Republican to the very end. This did not, however, prevent him from concluding that Grover Cleveland as president was "more friendly to colored people than most Republicans in exalted high positions," including Benjamin Harrison. Chester also opposed the Republican position on tariffs because in practice they did not benefit enough colored people (*Harrisburg Patriot*, Sept. 13, 1892).

Chester did not write a major work. Some of his numerous public speeches and writings can be found in the newspapers mentioned above and in other periodicals. One of his speeches has been published under the title *Negro Self-Respect and Pride of the Race* (1869).

— ALLISON BLAKELY

CHILDERS, LULU V[ERE] (1870–1946), musician, founder and director of the School of Music at Howard University. She was born to Alexander and Eliza Butler Childers in Dryridge, Ky., on Feb. 28, 1870. When she was five years old the family settled in Howell, Mich., where she graduated from Howell High School in 1890. She studied voice at the Oberlin Conservatory of Music and received a diploma in 1896. The diploma was replaced by the Bachelor of Music degree in 1906, Oberlin having begun to grant degrees. Childers, considered an outstanding graduate, was honored in 1927 by being elected to membership in the newly established Oberlin chapter of Pi Kappa Lambda, the National Music Honor Society. She pursued her interest in voice by studying privately with Oscar Saenger and William Shakespeare and by making occasional appearances as a contralto soloist.

Despite her promise as a singer, mentioned prominently even as she graduated from high school (*Livingston County Republican*, June 26, 1890), her interests in teaching, choral conducting, and administration determined the direction of her career. In the two years following her graduation (1896–1898), Childers taught in the public schools of Ulrichsville, Ohio, after which she began her career in college teaching and administration at Wiley College in Marshall, Tex. She served as director of the Music Department of Knoxville College in Knoxville, Tenn., from 1900 to 1905, when she developed the choir sufficiently to perform a major choral work with orchestra. Her appointment in 1905 as instructor in methods and music at Howard University coincided with the upgrading of the Music Department to the collegiate level, and she was appointed university director of music and instructor in singing in the following year. To develop the new department she established college-level curricula, hired experienced and

capable instructors, built a University Choral Society of recognized competence, and presented to the community programs of high quality. Under her guidance the department was upgraded to a conservatory in 1912 and to a school of music in 1918. She retired as director of the school of music in 1940 although she remained as acting director until 1942. In 1943 Lulu Childers returned to her home in Howell, Mich., where she died on March 6, 1946.

Childers's contributions to Howard University were officially recognized when the university conferred upon her (June 1942) the honorary degree of Doctor of Music and later named the classroom portion of its Fine Arts Building Lulu Vere Childers Hall (1956). Her portrait, painted by Lois Jones Pierre-Noël, was hung there in 1964.

When Childers became university director of music, instruction was available in only piano and voice. She and C. Beatrice Lewis constituted the entire faculty. Instruction in orchestral instruments and courses in theory, history of music, and music education were gradually added; the two-year course was lengthened to a regular four-year college course; and the number of instructors was increased to eighteen by the time of her retirement. In 1929 a Junior Preparatory Department was established to provide children with a sound background and thus prepare them for advanced studies.

The successful performance in 1907 of Mendelssohn's *Elijah*, the first major choral production of the University Choral Society conducted by Childers, gained for her department recognition and respect in the university community, according to Walter Dyson (*Howard University, The Capstone of Negro Education* [1941], p. 128). In succeeding years she conducted Handel's *Messiah* (1912), Gabriel Pierne's *The Children's Crusade* (1915), and Coleridge-Taylor's *Hiawatha* (1919) using Florence Cole-Talbert, William Simmons, and Roland Hayes as soloists. In addition to performances by the University Choral Society, Childers conducted in Rankin Chapel the Vested Choir in weekly vespers services which became an institution in the cultural life of Washington, D.C. Particularly popular were the special Easter and Christmas programs. Rayford Logan, in *Howard University: The First Hundred Years, 1867–1967* (1969, p. 280), tells of the Christmas service and candlelight procession of 1929, which drew a standing-room-only audience with as many as 400 persons unable to be accommodated. The University Choir sang at the funeral of Col. Charles Young in the Amphitheater of Arlington National Cemetery on June 1, 1923 (*Washington Evening Star*, June 1, 1923).

Under Childer's leadership the university orchestra, the band, the Women's Glee Club, and the Men's Glee Club also brought credit to the university in their public appearances. Howard University president J. Stanley Durkee, in his report for 1922–1923, cited the University Choral Society as "making a new departure in the nature of the Japanese Comic opera *Mikado*"; and in his report for 1924–1925 he referred proudly to his school as "the only institution of the Colored race that ever produced a Symphony orchestra." Gilbert and Sullivan's *Mikado* was the first of four operas produced during Miss Childers's tenure and the only one which she herself produced and directed. In the later productions, *Il Trovatore* (1939), *Faust* (1940), and *I Pagliacci* (1942), Childers directed the University Choral Society augmented by the Men's and Women's Glee Clubs. The University Symphony, supported by members of the National Symphony Orchestra, provided the orchestral assistance. The results were, if not unique on an American campus, certainly unusual at that time. Washington newspaper critics were greatly impressed with the voices and the professional nature of the production. Glenn D. Gunn stated in the *Times-Herald* (May 21, 1939): "The choruses were brilliant, the ballet picturesque, the orchestra competent, though practically unprofessional, and every person in the production, the conductor excepted, a Negro." The conductor was Kai de Vermond, a faculty member.

Of great importance to the community was the concert series through which guest artists and faculty were presented. Childers's prominence was such that she was able to include Marian Anderson in the series. This performance in Washington received international attention because the Rialto Theatre, in which she was to perform, was destroyed by fire, and both the Board of Education of Washington, D.C., and the Daughters of the American Revolution refused the use of their facilities to a Negro performer. Harold Ickes, secretary of the interior, was so chagrined by this blatant racism that he offered the Mall as a concert site. On Easter Sunday 1939, Marian Anderson sang on the steps of the Lincoln Memorial to an integrated audience of over 75,000.

Childers's success seems even more remarkable in view of the fact that very few women were active as choral conductors and administrators in early twentieth-century America. She spent much time in counselling and encouraging her students. She insisted on hard work and high standards of performance for all, most of all for herself. Her striving for perfection and her dedication to the beauty of music had a profound and lasting influence on the Department of Music at Howard University.

A pamphlet, *Semi-Centennial of the School of Music, College of Fine Arts, Howard University, 1914–1964,* contains tributes to Childers and sketches of her life by faculty and alumni who knew her. The two books *Howard University: The First Hundred Years, 1867–1967* (1969), by Rayford W. Logan, and *Howard University; The Capstone of Negro Education* (1941), by Walter Dyson, include many references to Lulu Childers and excellent accounts of music at Howard University.
— DORIS E. MCGINTY

CHURCH, ROBERT REED, SR. (1839–1912), businessman and philanthropist. Church was born a slave in Mississippi on June 18, 1839, the son of a well-to-do white riverboat owner and captain who maintained a close interest in his life for over forty years. When his mother died in 1851, Church's father took him aboard ship (based in Memphis), first as a dishwasher and eventually as a steward responsible for provisioning the vessel's mess. Freed after the Civil War, "Bob" Church still maintained close ties with his father, but he moved swiftly and independently into a very successful business career. His family ties, his sober demeanor, his serious pursuit of business success, and his undenied ability allowed Church to operate rather freely, in a formal way, in Memphis for over fifty years despite a generally hostile racial climate.

Post–Civil War Memphis witnessed violence, opportunity, and confusion. In the Negro communities, especially, the needs and desires of thousands of free migrants from the Mississippi Delta had to be met. During Reconstruction Robert Church took the small savings left over from his slave days and invested it in a saloon and adjoining billiard room. From this beginning Church constantly expanded his business and real estate holdings in the Negro sections of the growing city. His budding career was nearly extinguished by a purposefully aimed bullet during the race rioting in Memphis in 1866, but Church recovered and relentlessly pursued his accumulation of wealth and economic power. He followed a policy of continually buying, never selling, and always exercising close personal supervision over his investments. As the city expanded so did Robert Church; these were the years of the "New South" and the "Gilded Age," and Church demonstrated that such phrases should not be exclusively white in their application.

Although not a man to hoard idle cash, by the mid-1870s Church had accumulated a sizable sum of uncommitted money. Therefore, when repeated yellow fever epidemics threatened to depopulate (by evacuation more than death) Memphis permanently in 1878 and 1879, he was able to invest his money in the now-inexpensive real estate of the diminishing city. Church remained optimistic about Memphis and took the risk, even though the city was reduced to a mere "taxing district" when its charter was revoked by the state. Having invested heavily in the city's future, Church then became a true "founding father" by promoting the community's rebirth—buying Municipal Bond #1 ($1,000) when the city sought to pay off its past debts and regain its charter. Although his action was celebrated for its demonstration of civic devotion, Church knew full well that Memphis's rejuvenation would greatly raise the value of his recently expanded properties in the city.

Because of his slave beginnings and his early business career he lacked much formal education, and yet he moved as easily in local Negro cultured circles as he did in making daily inspections of his Beale Street saloons. Divorced from his first wife, Louisa (Ayers) Church, Church married Anna Wright, a school principal, accomplished pianist, and the first graduate of Le Moyne College. In 1888 he joined his daughter Mary (later Mary Church Terrell, founder of the National Association of Colored Women and wife of Washington's first Negro judge, Robert H. Terrell), in a lengthy tour of Europe. Although a professed southerner and an economic product of the optimistic "New South," Robert Church sought something more for his four children. He provided them with private tutors and northern educations, and he insisted that they maintain positions of dignity and demand respect from both blacks and whites. Beginning with the unusual, especially for Negro southerners, good fortune of financial security,

Church's children attained successful careers in law, civic affairs, politics, and education.

Throughout his own career Church realized the practical necessity of keeping open contacts with the controlling white system, and he therefore eschewed the sensitive field of politics. He did serve as a delegate to the Republican National Convention in 1900 as a McKinley supporter, but it would be his youngest son, Robert R. Church, Jr., who would later draw the family name into political activity. The elder Church preferred to stay out of partisan racial and political affairs. In 1901 he even went so far as to donate $1000 to help finance the official Confederate Reunion held in Memphis. Although he was a man who took great wealth from the Negro community and cooperated with white power, Church also demonstrated a somewhat paternalistic concern for the well-being of his race. Seeing that Negroes were denied entrance into any of the city's public parks, Church developed a park on his own Beale Street property and equipped it with a large auditorium. These facilities served as a site for graduation exercises, political rallies, Negro road shows, and an annual Thanksgiving dinner for the poor, financed totally by Church.

Church's business success had been built on individual drive and personal investment; he was the epitome of the late-nineteenth-century rags-to-riches entrepreneur. Church endorsed no active racial philosophy and yet he regularly preached the wisdom of savings and investment to other Negroes. Partly as an effort to promote these virtues in Memphis's Negro community, but more especially to expand his own financial and real estate network, Robert Church founded the Solvent Savings Bank and Trust Company in 1906. The Solvent Bank was only one of many Negro banking institutions founded in the first twenty years of the twentieth century, but it was among the fastest growing. The institution held deposits in excess of $100,000 by 1912 and had passed the $1-million mark by 1920. Unfortunately for the Solvent Bank and for the Negro Memphis business community, Robert Church did not live to see the institution through the speculative and shaky (fatal in this case) decade of the 1920s. He died after a brief illness on Aug. 2, 1912.

Church's career had been remarkable, and he was reputed to have been the wealthiest Negro in the South. He had played a direct and vital role in the business history of Memphis, he established a much revered name in the city's Negro communities, and he provided the financial security for his children to expand the family's prominence and diversify its role.

Mary Church Terrell's *A Colored Woman in a White World* (1940) and Shields McIlwaine's *Memphis Down in Dixie* (1948) are major sources. A recent, rather laudatory biography is *The Robert Churches of Memphis* (1975) by his daughter Annette E. Church and granddaughter Roberta Church. — LESTER C. LAMON

CHURCH, ROBERT REED, JR. (1885–1952), politician and businessman. The son of Robert R. Sr. and Anna (Wright) Church, Robert Jr. was born on Oct. 26, 1885, in Memphis, Tenn. He spent most of his life in the South, but he was not a typical Negro southerner. Born in his father's thirteen-room mansion staffed by servants, "young Bob" avoided the sense of economic insecurity which plagued most Negroes. His schooling (private tutors, Episcopal parochial classes, and then Oberlin College) and early associations (as a "banker's apprentice" on Wall Street from 1904 to 1907) set him apart from the uncertain swirl of Negro life in Memphis. His business career was that of second-generation manager rather than hard-driving entrepreneur, and he could enjoy the luxury of a semidetached concern for the needs and handicaps of his race.

Little in Church's early activities marked him for more than the heir and administrator of his father's fortune. His lifestyle and social patterns were distinctly upper class; he married Sara P. Johnson of Washington, D.C. (July 26, 1911), had one child, Sara Roberta, developed a passion for bird hunting, and after an "apprenticeship" joined his father's business in 1907 as cashier of the Solvent Savings Bank and Trust Company. In 1909 his father stepped aside and Robert became president of the rapidly growing family-controlled institution. With the death of Robert Sr. in 1912, however, this well-ordered, seemingly prearranged career took a new turn. At the age of twenty-seven the younger Church resigned his position at the bank, slowly removed most of the family holdings and guidance, and became the executor and manager of his father's properties. This was no small task, involving as it did the management of over 300 pieces of real estate, but Church's interest seemed more perfunctory than enthusiastic. He soon revealed a passion for politics, a field his father had preferred to avoid, that came to consume much of his time and resources.

Robert Church's political role developed in full accordance with his station in society. He did not enter the hand-shaking world of the candidate, but instead pursued a position of power and influence in the councils of the Republican party. His political ambitions were not easily fulfilled. The presence of a persistent "lily-white" wing in Tennessee's Republican party had initially challenged Church to action, and it continued its struggle for Negro exclusion throughout his career. Recognizing that the vast majority of potential Republican voters in West Tennessee's 10th District were Negroes, Church set about organizing them into a voting bloc. Utilizing this strength, Church forced his way into party councils. In 1916 he founded and financed the operations of the Lincoln League, which successfully increased the number of registered Negro voters, made respectable showings in local and congressional elections, and won recognition as the "regular" Republican machinery in West Tennessee. Without ostentation Church directed the Lincoln League's activities. He earned a place on the state executive committee, served as a delegate to national conventions, and drew the praise of the party's national heirarchy. Church served on the National Republican Advisory Committee for Negroes in 1916 and sat on the Advisory Committee on Policies and Platform for the 1920 convention. When Warren G. Harding's victory in 1920 returned the Republicans to national power (the party also carried Tennessee for the first time since Reconstruction), Church's active support was rewarded with considerable patronage power. He became one of the most important Negro voices in national Republican politics, and he effectively combined with J. Will Taylor (white) of East Tennessee to control federal appointments in his home state.

Church shunned the public eye, feeling more comfortable in the paternalistic role of patronage dispenser and political strategist. He even rejected many of the traditional rewards of party service, turning down appointments to commissions studying relations with Haiti (1922) and the Virgin Islands (1924). He spent large sums from his personal fortune to finance his travel to political meetings and to support the activities of his local organization, and yet he never expected monetary reward for his actions. Church operated quite consistently from a sense of noblesse oblige.

Robert Church was not insensitive to the needs of less fortunate black Memphians, and he utilized his political influence to ameliorate the local inequalities of the caste system. He "coexisted" with Memphis's white boss, E. H. Crump. Each respected the political power and domain of the other; Crump rarely engaged in race-baiting and harassment of Negro political activities, and Church-influenced federal officials seldom interfered with Crump.

The years of the 1930s were harsh for Robert Church. When the Depression struck, his tenants were especially hard pressed, and real estate taxes became a problem. The Democratic sweep into power in 1932 had damaged much of Church's political power, leaving him vulnerable to his opponents. "Lily-white" Republicans and most southern Democrats had long resented Church's confident participation in Tennessee politics. There were few regrets, therefore, when the city of Memphis claimed Church's property in lieu of a sizable back-tax debt. Although the value of the property far exceeded the tax claims, Church found real estate difficult to sell and had to forfeit. Church left Memphis and moved to Chicago in 1940, where he continued to participate in high Republican circles, but his source of power and influence had been shattered.

In the heyday of his national and state prominence, Church was in great demand. He sat on the boards of directors of several Negro business enterprises (e.g., Standard Life Insurance Company) and also on the national boards of such prominent civic organizations as the NAACP, but he was only occasionally active in their programs. It was normal practice for such businesses and organizations to seek out people of family, economic, or political prominence to adorn their letterheads. Robert Church fulfilled all these qualifications, but he showed little enthusiasm for active involvement in anything beyond politics. In that field he contributed significantly to the racial direction and attitudes of the Republican party from the local level in Memphis to the back rooms of party leadership in Washington. Had death not overtaken him on April 17, 1952, his career might have experienced a significant renewal. He had been one of the earliest and relatively few Negro supporters of Dwight D. Eisenhower for the Republican presidential nomination.

See Clarence L. Kelly's "Robert R. Church, A Negro Tennessean, In Republican State and National Politics from 1912–1932" (M.A. thesis, Tennessee State University, 1954) and George Washington Lee's *Beale Street: Where the Blues Began* (1934).

— LESTER C. LAMON

CINQUE [CINQUE], JOSEPH (c. 1817– ?), leader of the history-making mutiny aboard the Cuban slaveship *Amistad* in the summer of 1839. Cinque—the name is a phonetic approximation of the African *Sing-gbe*—was born in the hinterland of the country now known as Sierra Leone, probably about the year 1817. He was a member of the Mende tribe. As a young man in his early twenties, married and the father of three children, he was captured by slave traders of an enemy tribe and subsequently sold to the Spanish owners of a notorious "slave factory" on the island of Lomboko. A man of unusual strength, fortitude, and judgment, he survived a hellish voyage to Havana in a Portuguese slaver, the *Técora,* during which 50 percent of the "cargo" died.

Because the importation of slaves into Cuba was officially illegal, Cinque and his fellow captives were sold clandestinely and given Spanish Christian names so that it would appear that they had been born in Cuba. José, or Joseph, was the name assigned to Cinque when he and forty-eight other adult males were sold to a Cuban planter called Ruiz. Under cover of night Ruiz placed his slaves aboard a schooner, the *Amistad,* for a short voyage along the Cuban coast. Also sailing was a friend of Ruiz, Pedro Montes, who had bought three little African girls and a boy.

The captives were chained together in the hold by means of iron collars, with the end of the chain secured to the wall. Their rations were scanty and when they begged for more, the mulatto cook gave them to understand by means of sign language that they would soon be slaughtered and salted down as meat for the Spaniards. After that, Cinque said to the others, "We may as well die in trying to be free as be killed and eaten." With the aid of a nail Cinque managed to unfasten the chain from the wall and to separate each man from the next. All except the children then armed themselves with cane-knives, found in the hold, and stole out upon the dark, rainswept deck. Cinque killed the cook with one blow. The captain fought desperately but was soon overwhelmed and killed, while two sailors managed to escape in a lifeboat, eventually bringing news of the mutiny to Havana. Ruiz and Montes were put in irons, but as Montes proved to have some knowledge of navigation, Cinque ordered him to sail the *Amistad* to Africa. Montes managed to hoodwink his captors by sailing a zigzag course, sometimes east but more often northwest, hoping to reach the southern United States. Instead, six weeks later the *Amistad* arrived off the tip of Long Island. While a party of Africans was on shore, seeking supplies, the ship was captured by a U.S. Coast Guard vessel. Cinque tried to escape by leaping overboard, but finally allowed himself to be taken.

The case of the *Amistad* immediately became a *cause célèbre.* Spanish and Cuban authorities demanded the return of ship and cargo, human and otherwise, to Havana, where Cinque and all or most of the others would have been burned at the stake. Pres. Martin Van Buren, known as "the northerner with southern leanings," favored this step; but he found himself vigorously opposed by abolitionists, as well as by many other citizens who believed that the criminals in the case were not Cinque and his fellows but Ruiz and Montes, who were guilty of kidnapping. One who was strongly of this opinion was former Pres. John Qunicy Adams, who, in his seventies, was serving in Congress. When the case eventually reached the Supreme Court in February 1841, Adams agreed to defend the Africans. This he did so persuasively that the Court set them free.

During the eighteen months between the capture of the *Amistad* and the Supreme Court decision, the Africans, or "Amistads," as they had come to be called, were in prison. Theological students and ministers worked with them daily, teaching them English and the principles of Christianity. An "Amistad Committee," headed by prominent abolitionists, hoped to send them back to Africa accompanied by white missionaries, in order to bring Christianity to the "dark continent." After the Supreme Court decision, the "Amistads" helped raise money for this project by appearing at public meetings in New England, New York, and Philadelphia. Cinque, an eloquent speaker, was always the center of attention and remained the unchallenged leader of the group. An area of Farmington, Conn., where they all lived during this period was known for years afterward as Cinque Park.

Perhaps the very qualities that made Cinque a leader prevented him from being a follower; for after the return of the "Amistads" to Sierra Leone in early 1842, he went his own way. For many years nothing was heard of him. Then one day in 1879 an old, emaciated African came to the compound of a mission run by the American Missionary Association (an outgrowth of the Amistad Committee). He said that he was Cinque and that he was dying and wanted to be buried there. Not long after, he was laid to rest among the graves of American missionaries, black and white, whose presence in Africa he had brought about. A missionary who had been born a plantation slave preached at Cinque's grave.

The repository of the American Missionary Association records in New Orleans is named the Amistad Research Center in honor of Cinque's famous exploit.

The name Cinque entered the news again in the 1970s when Donald DeFreeze, the leader of the Symbionese Liberation Army, kidnapper of the newspaper heiress Patricia Hearst, called himself "Cinque" as a symbol of defiance.

A valuable contemporary account is John W. Barber's *A History of the Amistad Captives* (1840). Mary Cable's *Black Odyssey: The Case of the Slave Ship Amistad* (1971) and Edwin Palmer Hoyt's *The Amistad Affair* (1970) give the essential details. Warren Marr II's "Out of Bondage" (*United Church Herald*, 1964) gives a detailed account. See also Roger S. Baldwin's *Argument Before the Supreme Court in the Case of the United States, Appellants, vs. Cinque and others, Africans of the Amistad* (New York, 1841). — MARY CABLE

CLARK, ALEXANDER G. (1826–1891), businessman, leader in church and civil rights activities, lawyer, politician, and diplomat. Clark was born in Washington County, Pa. His father, John Clark, had been freed by his Irish master; his mother, Rebecca (Darnes) Clark, was said to have been a full-blooded African. Alexander received a limited education in Washington County and in Cincinnati, where he was sent in 1839 to live with an uncle. He learned barbering, worked as a bartender on the steamer *George Washington,* and went to Muscatine, Iowa, in May 1842 where he opened a barbershop. He later contracted with steamboats to supply them with wood. Investing his money wisely, he purchased real estate and became a wealthy man. He devoted most of the rest of his life to the African Methodist Episcopal church, Prince Hall Masonry, the Republican party, civil rights movements, and editing the *Chicago Conservator.* He graduated from the University of Iowa Law School in 1884, and opened a law office in Chicago. Appointed by President Benjamin Harrison as minister and consul-general to Liberia (Aug. 8, 1890), he died of fever in Monrovia on May 31, 1891. His remains were brought back to Muscatine where he was accorded a state funeral, attended by many dignitaries. He was buried in Muscatine's Greenwood Cemetery, beside the body of his wife, the former Catherine Guffin whom he had married in 1848, and two children who had died in infancy. Three other children survived them.

Alexander Clark began his notable public career when in 1849 he and three other men founded the local African Methodist Episcopal church in Muscatine. He served it for twenty-five years as trustee, steward, and Sunday school superintendent. He attended the General Conference in St. Louis (March 1880), and served as a lay delegate to the Methodist Ecumenical Conference in London (1881). He and his wife attended the reception given by the lord mayor of London before visiting France and Switzerland.

Meanwhile, he also was active in Masonic circles. He joined Prince Hall Lodge No. 1, St. Louis, in 1851, and in 1868 was elected deputy grand master of the Grand Lodge of Missouri, with jurisdiction extending over six states. After holding other high offices, he organized in 1884 the Hiram Grand Lodge of Iowa and was elected to the Grand East, a larger lodge, for three successive years. Through tact and strong will he combined his lodge with another colored grand lodge into one body known as the United Grand Lodge of Iowa, and served as its president. His eloquence and knowledge of Masonic law and jurisprudence had previously (1877) won the right of concurrent jurisdiction for colored Masonic lodges.

His church and Masonic affiliations probably provided a base for his successful career in politics. He was chairman and spokesman for the committee of the first convention of colored men held in Iowa (1868). His eloquence as a speaker—he became well known as the "Colored Orator of the West"—further contributed to this phase of his career. Some contemporaries considered him second only to Frederick Douglass, who was his friend for forty years, in the ability to convince audiences. Although physical disability prevented him from accepting appointment as sergeant major in the 1st Iowa Colored Volunteer Infantry (1863), he actively engaged in recruiting to the end of the Civil War. He worked hard to get pensions for every honorably discharged soldier and supported such movements as postal telegraphy, women's suffrage, and savings banks. At the 1868 Convention of Colored Men he urged political equality for colored men of Iowa, which was recognized by the state constitution of Dec. 8, 1868.

In 1869 Clark served as one of the vice-presidents of the Republican State Convention of Iowa and was a member of the committee which called upon Pres. Ulysses S. Grant and V.-P. Schuyler Colfax to extend congratulations on behalf of the colored people of the United States. Clark was a delegate-at-large from Iowa to the Republican National Convention in Philadelphia (1872), and an alternate delegate from Iowa to the national convention in Cincinnati. It was this staunch Republicanism which led President Grant to nominate Clark for the post as consul to Aux Cayes, Haiti (1873). He declined this post because of its meager salary, but did accept in 1890 the position of minister and consul-general to Liberia.

During all these years he continued his civil rights activities. When his daughter Susan was refused entry to the Muscatine public schools, Clark sued the school board and carried the case to the Iowa Supreme Court, which ruled that under the state constitution of 1857 and state laws, the public schools were open equally to white and colored pupils of school attendance age. Susan was admitted in 1868 and graduated from high school in 1871 (*Muscatine Evening Journal,* June 24, 1871).

His activities included other issues of the day. In 1876 he represented Iowa at the Centennial Exposition in Philadelphia for the purpose of preparing statistics about Negroes. On Jan. 21, 1880, he wrote an editorial in the *Muscatine Evening Journal* in which he said: "This [Great] Exodus is forced upon our people as a last resort and the only one left." In the *Conservator* he denounced the Supreme Court's decision of 1883 which stated that the Constitution did not prohibit denial by private citizens of public accommodations to Negroes. He also vigorously criticized Pres. Rutherford B. Hayes for his policies of accommodation with the former Confederate states. From December 1882, when he became one of three owners of the *Conservator* (sole owner in 1884), until March 15, 1887, when he sold his interest, he continued the efforts of Richard De Baptiste to make the weekly one of the strongest Negro protest journals of the period. By that time it had a circulation of about 1200. He received recognition at the National Press Association (Atlantic City, 1886), where he was elected treasurer and appointed chairman of the executive committee. He prepared the program for the annual meeting in Louisville (1887), and received such favorable comments by both the white and colored press of the city that he was prevailed upon to continue in office.

Though little known to most historians today, Clark still is remembered with pride by the people of Muscatine. In April 1975 the Clark home was being moved from Third and Chestnut Streets to 211 West Third St. There it was to be refurbished, furnished in the style of Clark's life and opened to the public as a center and museum.

The most recent biographical sketch is "Alexander Clark, A Rediscovered Black Leader," by Marilyn Jackson in *The Iowan* (Spring 1975, pp. 43–49). An earlier study is Leola Nelson Bergmann's "The Negro in Iowa" (*Iowa Journal of History and Politics,* Feb. 1969, pp. 50–53). Though incomplete, George Van Horn's "A Remarkable and Great Example" (*A.M.E. Church Review,* republished in the *Muscatine Weekly Journal,* Jan. 27, 1888, and May 31, 1940) is indispensable. For the lawsuit involving Susan Clark, see *Iowa State Supreme Court Records* (April 14, 1868, 24:267–77). Information about Clark's Masonic activities is in *Phylaxis* (March 1975, p. 64); about his diplomatic career in the article by John Briggs, "Iowa and the Diplomatic Service" (*Iowa Journal of History and Politics,* July 1921, pp. 321–63). The files of the *Muscatine Evening Journal* and the *Muscatine Weekly Journal,* as well as the University of Iowa Alumni Records in Iowa City, are additional sources. A eulogy of Clark is on file in the Muscatine Public Library. There is a photograph of Clark, facing page 1097 and the article about him, in William J. Simmons's *Men of Mark . . .* (1887). The reminiscences of some older inhabitants of Muscatine were also illuminating. A photograph of the Clark home appeared in the *Muscatine Journal* (April 25, 1975).

— ALDEEN L. DAVIS

CLARK, J[OSEPH] S[AMUEL] (1871–1944), university president. He was born in Bienville Parish near Sparta, La., the son of Phillip and Jane Clark. His early education was pursued in the vicinity of his birth through the generous concerns of whites while he maintained his share of the family responsibilities. During 1891–1895 Clark studied in the preparatory department of Coleman College, Gibsland, La., as he worked his way through school. From 1896 to 1901 he attended Leland College in New Orleans, from which he received the B.A. degree in 1901. Prior to attending Leland College he had matriculated at Bishop College in Marshall, Tex., but received no degree. Further degrees included an M.A. degree from Selma University in 1913 and honorary Ph.D. degrees from Leland College (1914) and Arkansas Baptist College (1921). He did postgraduate study at Harvard University and the University of Chicago.

Organizations with which J. S. Clark was identified included the National Association of Colored Teachers (1916–1917); he was a member of the National Survey Committee, composed of seventy-two of the leading educators in the United States (1928–1930); in 1930 he was appointed a member of President Hoover's White House Commission on Child Welfare and Protection, and in 1931 a member of the President's Conference on Home Buildings and Home Ownership. From 1932 to 1943 he was a member of the Commission on Interracial Cooperation, one of the most effective organizations for promoting the advancement of southern Negroes. Clark was also president of the New Capitol Insurance Company of New Orleans (1932–1935). Other organizations include the National Teachers League, the National Urban League, Land-Grant College Presidents Association, and the Louisiana Colored Teachers Association, which he helped to reorganize and later served as its president (1908–1915).

After beginning his career as a schoolteacher, which

took him across the state of Louisiana, in 1901 he was appointed president of Baton Rouge College in Baton Rouge, La., which was supported by the Fourth District Missionary Baptist Association of Louisiana. In 1913 he became the president of Southern University and Agricultural and Mechanical College, the land-grant college in Louisiana for colored citizens. Southern University had been established by the Louisiana State Constitutional Convention in 1879, and recognized by the federal government as a land-grant college under the Second Morrill Act (1890). After an unstable beginning in 1880 in New Orleans, the institution was closed. It began operation again in 1883. During the thirty years in New Orleans the institution had eight presidents and never achieved university status. Legislative Act 118 in 1912 authorized the closing and sale of Southern University in New Orleans and the establishment of the university on a new site. On Sept. 1, 1913, Clark was appointed president of Southern University but given the task of finding a new site, preparing curricula, and recruiting pupils and teachers for the new school. These duties were completed in time to open classes on March 9, 1914. On this date the "new Southern University," located on the banks of the Mississippi seven miles north of the city of Baton Rouge in a small community known as Scotlandville, opened with an enrollment of forty-seven students and nine teachers.

Building goodwill for the reestablishment of a state-supported Negro college in the state of Louisiana and overcoming opposition to the removal of Southern University from New Orleans remain two of Clark's significant achievements. Southern University was a free, publicly supported institution and thereby offered education to the citizenry of New Orleans at a lower cost than Leland and Straight Colleges, which were private. For this reason a group of thirty-eight persons from the Parish of Orleans instituted an unsuccessful suit against the Board of Trustees declaring that Act 118 of 1912 authorizing the changing of the domicile of the state university was unconstitutional and that Southern University should remain in Orleans Parish.

A gift for persuasive oratory and an unswerving commitment to establishing harmony and understanding between races were the attributes which contributed to Clark's success in his new position. Under his leadership the university attained permanence and in the 1960s, during the tenure of his son Felton G. Clark, Southern University was recorded as having the largest enrollment of any publicly supported institution of higher education for Negroes in the United States.

Under J. S. Clark's administration the institution grew physically from a small tract of land and two buildings valued at $100,000 to over 500 acres comprising forty buildings valued at $12 million, employing 139 teachers and a student body of 1500 in 1938 when he retired. The academic program witnessed a similar growth. While initially students could register for elementary school, high school, and teacher-training classes, the normal curriculum of one year was added in 1918, a two-year normal curriculum in 1920, and in 1924 a full college curriculum was offered; specialized studies could also be pursued in home economics, agriculture, and industrial arts. Following the retirement of J. S.

Clark, his son assumed the presidency. During the latter's administration the institution grew into a university encompassing three campuses offering undergraduate, graduate, and professional degrees. When the younger Clark retired in 1969, the university enrolled over 10,-000 students on its campuses, employed a staff of 544 teachers, and the physical plant had reached a value in excess of $60 million.

In 1901 Clark married Octavia Head, the daughter of a Monroe, La., minister. To this union were born two sons—the first died at birth (Oct. 12, 1902); the second was Felton Grandison (born Oct. 13, 1903).

In 1930 J. S. Clark was offered the position of minister to Liberia, which he refused because of his desire to remain in Louisiana.

Known as a "dreamer," J. S. Clark envisioned buildings on the campus as one day having encompassed the entire 500-acre tract and stretching from the Mississippi River on the west to the small community of Scotlandville on the east, some one mile distant. He was personified by neatness, punctuality, courtesy, and discipline, and expended every effort to instill these qualities in the students and faculty members of Southern University. He stressed manual labor as a means of discipline and until 1930 required that every student at the university do one hour per day of nonacademic work. He stressed courtesy as a means of creating genuine goodwill between blacks and whites within Louisiana. Through his extemporaneous speeches and frequent appearances before the students of Southern University he inspired them to become leaders in their respective communities and to work toward creative, positive, human relationships.

Basic facts about Joseph S. Clark are in *Who's Who in Colored America* (1937), edited by Thomas Yenser, an obituary in *JNH* (Jan. 1945, pp. 112–14), and a biography by John Brother Cade entitled, *The Man Christened Josiah Clark, Who, As J. S. Clark Became President of a Louisiana State Land Grant College* (1966). Information about the development of Southern University is based on Ulysses Simpson Lane's "The History of Southern University: 1879–1960" (Ph.D. dissertation, Utah State University, 1969).

— HUEL D. PERKINS

CLARK, PETER HUMPHRIES (c. 1829–1925), educator, civil rights leader, and socialist. He was the grandson of William Clark of the famous Lewis and Clark Expedition. Since his wife and children might be enslaved prior to his return from the expedition, William Clark moved them from the South to Cincinnati. One of his children, Michael Clark, became a respected citizen of Cincinnati. Hence Peter was born a free Negro in Cincinnati in 1829, when white citizens sought through mob violence to remove all Negroes from the city. It is estimated that some 1200 left Cincinnati for Canada. Other riots occurred in 1836 and 1841. Little is known of his father except that he operated one of the best tonsorial parlors in the city. Few if any early educational opportunities were presented Peter in his youth until the Rev. Hiram S. Gilmore opened a high school for Negroes in 1844. Before completion of high school Peter, because of his talents, became an assistant teacher. Meanwhile he assisted runaway slaves on the Underground Railroad. Leaving high school in 1848 and disliking to give service to narrow-minded and conservative whites in his father's shop, he apprenticed himself to a liberal white printer, Thomas Varney, who had connections with Horace Greeley. He worked for Greeley more than a year, and became a schoolteacher when the Ohio legislature passed a law in 1849 permitting Negroes to organize and control their own schools. However, the next year, disgusted with conditions in the city, he started for Africa, traveling as far as New Orleans. By 1852 he was interested in the emigration movement, and in 1853 he became the national secretary of the Colored Convention in Rochester, N.Y. Later in that same year he drafted the constitution for the National Equal Rights League which worked strenuously in behalf of Negroes. In the same year he attended the National Convention of Colored People in Syracuse, N.Y.

In 1856 he became associated with some of the founders of the Republican party and remained a devoted and loyal member until 1872. His wide interests in the national activities of Negroes, along with his Unitarian religious beliefs, brought him into conflict with the school board. He then operated a grocery store, but in 1853 he left it to become editor of the *Herald of Freedom.* In 1856 he was associated with Frederick Douglass in publishing the *North Star.* In 1857 the citizenry of Cincinnati recalled Clark to the public schools. Clark furthered the establishment of public schools in Cincinnati, achieving success in 1865. With the rise of the war fever and the outbreak of the Civil War, Negroes in Cincinnati met to form a home guard. The raids of John Morgan and the successful activities of Confederate troops in Kentucky accelerated home guard organizations. Negro efforts were given a violent reception until Gen. Lewis Wallace and Judge William Martin Dickson eventually eliminated abuse and violent arrests. Negroes were then allowed to establish a voluntary home guard unit. The officers marched them from the mule pen camp, established their headquarters in the city, and designated them as "The Black Brigade" for fatigue duty. Organized on Sept. 2, 1862, they labored without arms from Sept. 3 to Sept. 20, because of white opposition. Upon discharge they were complimented for having "labored faithfully, building miles of roads, rifle pits, magazine areas and clearing acres of land." Seeking to preserve their roll list, reports, and records, they selected Peter Clark as their historian. He wrote *The Black Brigade of Cincinnati,* an official military history, called the "Dickson report."

Clark is best known as an educator. With the addition to the public school system of the Gaines High School, he became its first principal, and he gave it devoted service for thirty years. A biographer stated that the demand for his "students as teachers became so urgent that it was for a time difficult to hold them until graduation, so eager were their parents to have them accept jobs." He served not only as teacher and principal but also as the first colored superintendent. He also served as a trustee of Wilberforce University, and received four of fourteen votes for the presidency of Howard University in 1877 (Rayford W. Logan, *Howard University*

. . . [1969], p. 83). When the Arnett Law was passed in 1887, separate schools were abolished and Negro children attended white schools. Clark was removed in 1887, seemingly on political grounds, and W. H. Parkam became principal of all colored schools.

Prior to his removal Clark also became known as an "agitator." Herbert Gutman, writing in the *Journal of Negro Education,* calls him the first American Negro Socialist. As a member of the Workingmens' party of the United States, he made many speeches in Hamilton County and in Kentucky. In 1875 in an address to the businessmen in Cincinnati he condemned extreme wealth and poverty, attacked the middleman, and called for the support of producer and consumer cooperatives. The next year in speaking to the Cincinnati Workingmens' Society on "Wages, Slavery and Remedy," he held that capital "had to give up some of its assumed selfish rights and give labor its share." He bristled with indignation against the evils of railroad abuses but advised against all violence by the workers. In 1877 the Workingmens' party nominated him for state superintendent of schools in Ohio. This socialist ticket as a whole fared badly, but in Ohio Clark ran well ahead of all other nominees in the fall election.

Prior to this political stand he was recognized as a brilliant orator and organizer. Highly respected for his sincerity, honesty, and principles of public and private life, he was considered important in city, county, state, and national affairs. In 1882 he aided the Democrats in the county and state elections, advocating the "radical" doctrine of "universal suffrage and universal amnesty." Clark and other close friends bolted the Republican party and successfully supported George Hoadley (Democrat) for governor. On the matter of the Black Laws, Hoadley, urged by Clark, advised the legislature that "the existing legal discriminations on account of color are not based on character or conduct and have no relation to mental or moral fitness for civil usefulness, but are rather relics of prejudice which had its origins in slavery. I recommend their total repeal." Clark realized that keen political rivalry between Hoadley (leaving the governorship) and the new governor Joseph B. "Fireball" Foraker would certainly eliminate vestiges of the Black Law in Ohio. In a letter to the *New York Freeman* (March 29, 1887) Clark admitted that such tactics were necessary in national politics.

While principal, Clark married Frances Williams, a music teacher who received her education at Oberlin. They had three highly gifted children. Following his loss of the principalship in 1887, Clark moved to St. Louis where one of his daughters, Mrs. John S. Nesbit, was teaching. He taught at the well-known Sumner High School until he was retired and pensioned by the board of education in 1908. He died at his home, 4581 Garfield Ave., of infirmities due to old age, on June 21, 1925. Funeral services were held at his home, and he was buried in St. Peter's Cemetery. He was survived by his daughter, five grandchildren, and twelve great-grandchildren.

Some good sources on Clark are William Wells Brown's *The Rising Son* (1874); Peter H. Clark's *The Black Brigade of Cincinnati* (1869); Wendell P. Dabney's *Cincinnati's Colored Citizens, Historical, Socio-*

logical and Biographical (1920); William J. Simmons's Men of Mark . . . (1887, pp. 374–83); and Hubert Gutman's "Peter H. Clark: Pioneer Negro Socialist" (JNE, Fall 1965). Significant items are in the following newspapers: the Cincinnati Herald of Freedom (1885); the Cincinnati Commercial (Nov. 27, 1875; June 17 and 26, 1876); and the New York Freeman (March 29, 1867). A highly laudatory obituary in the St. Louis Argus (June 26, 1925) is in the vertical file, Moorland-Spingarn Research Center. — PAUL MCSTALLWORTH

CLARKE, LEWIS G. (1815–1897), abolitionist, lecturer, and author. He was born in Madison County, Ky., the son of a mulatto plantation slave, Letitia (Letty) and her white, Scottish-born husband, Daniel Clarke. Born a slave, Lewis Clarke's lifelong belief in the right to freedom resulted in his own eventual escape and an ensuing personal dedication to the abolitionist cause. Besides repeatedly risking his own freedom to help other runaway slaves, his travels throughout the free states relating his own experiences in bondage influenced many of his listeners to join the fight against slavery. His sincerity and integrity so impressed Harriet Beecher Stowe that she asked to meet him, and arranged for repeated interviews with him in her own home. In her book The Key to Uncle Tom's Cabin (1856) she asserted that the character of George Harris, husband of Eliza in Uncle Tom's Cabin, was based on the personality of Lewis Clarke, and that she had used many incidents from experiences of the Clarke family in the novel that had aroused nationwide indignation and controversy five years earlier.

Clarke's own account of his life as a slave, dictated with his brother Milton's story to abolitionist writer J. C. Lovejoy and published in Boston in 1846, was also influential in the antislavery cause. Entitled Narratives of the Sufferings of Lewis and Milton Clarke, Sons of a Soldier of the Revolution, During a Captivity of More Than Twenty Years Among the Slaveholders of Kentucky, One of the So Called Christian States of North America, it enjoyed a brisk sale at abolitionist gatherings throughout the free states. A few copies are still extant, and the book is one of the few sources of biographical data on Lewis Clarke and his family.

His early childhood in a small cottage on the plantation gave Lewis Clarke the only early taste of family life he was to know. His mother Letty was the daughter of the plantation owner, Samuel Campbell, and one of his own slaves, and she grew up in bondage in her father's household, serving her white half-brothers and half-sisters. At her eventual marriage to Daniel Clarke, a wounded Revolutionary War veteran and a weaver by trade, her father gave his promise that she and any children born to her would be granted freedom by a provision in his will.

The Clarkes and their ten children lived as a family unit until one of Campbell's married daughters, Betsy Campbell Banton, laid claim to the six-year-old Lewis as part of her rightful dowry, and took him to her Lexington home. Here for ten years, abuse, beatings, and cruelty were a daily part of the long hours spent at first as servant to her children, later at the chore of spinning flax and hemp.

In spite of the promise made to Lewis's mother, the death of Samuel Campbell in 1831 brought the Clarke family no nearer to freedom. His will was never found, or was perhaps destroyed by heirs unwilling to relinquish the market value represented by a large slave family. An auction was held and the family members sold to several bidders. In his later years Lewis made many attempts to locate and achieve reunions with his brothers and sisters.

Financial trouble meanwhile had overtaken Lewis's owners, and at sixteen he was sold to a planter, Tom Kennedy, where under the overseer's whip he labored from dawn to dark in the tobacco fields. Here again he was without friends or hope; heat, hunger, thirst, and brutality made life almost intolerable.

At this owner's death a few years later he became the property of Kennedy's son, who found it more profitable to hire out his time. This meant that the slave would board and clothe himself, turning over the balance of his earnings to his master. For Lewis Clarke this was a tantalizing taste of the freedom of which he had long dreamed. He found work splitting rails, and traveled about on horseback selling grass seed. At the death of this master, when rumors reached him that the administrators of the estate planned to sell him in Louisiana, he decided to make his break for freedom. In August 1841 he started north with another slave. Because of Clarke's light skin they hoped to pose as master and body servant. In Uncle Tom's Cabin George Harris used this ruse to escape, but the real-life George Harris had gone only a few miles with his friend when they realized that their inability to read signposts and their awkward manners would give them away. They returned, and two weeks later, Clarke set off alone.

His hazardous journey on foot and by boat, first to the free state of Ohio, then on to Port Stanley, Ontario, was a triumph of courage over fear, weariness, and loneliness. It was loneliness too that shortly afterward prompted his return to Oberlin, Ohio, in search of his brother Milton. Here for the first time in his life he found himself welcomed into a circle of kind friends, black and white. With their aid and encouragement he became a frequent speaker at abolitionist meetings on lecture tours which included nearly all of the free states. His quick wit and intelligence were instrumental in helping many other runaway slaves to obtain their freedom.

Canadian census records show that by 1861 Clarke had returned to Canada, married, and taken residence near Windsor, Ontario. At the death of his wife about 1875 he returned to Oberlin with his children, where he had the satisfaction of seeing several of them educated and on their way to successful careers.

At his death in Lexington, Ky., at the age of eighty-two, his body lay in state in the City Auditorium by order of the governor, to permit his many friends to pay homage to him. He was the first Negro in the state to be so honored. His body was sent to Oberlin for burial, in a grave that remained unmarked and almost forgotten for more than seventy years. A recently placed headstone now identifies him as "the Original George Harris of Harriet Beecher Stowe's Book, Uncle Tom's Cabin."

In addition to the Narrative of the Sufferings of Lewis and Milton Clarke . . . (1846), and Harriet Beecher

Stowe's *The Key to Uncle Tom's Cabin* (1856), the most valuable published sources are Chet Lampson's *The Jefferson Gazette* (1896, 1955), and "A Chat with George Harris" (Chapter 6 of *A Jubilee Volume . . .* [1883], published by Oberlin College). The Department of Public Records and Archives, Toronto, Ontario, Canada, has valuable information in its Private Manuscripts Section. — BETTY VOLK

CLEMENT, RUFUS (EARLY) (1900–1967), university president. Rufus Clement was born in Salisbury, N.C., the son of A.M.E. Bishop George C. and Emma Clarissa (Williams) Clement, who in 1946 was chosen the American Mother of the Year, the first colored woman so honored. He married Pearl Anne Johnson of Sumner, Miss. (1919); they had one child, a daughter Alice (Mrs. Robert P. Foster) of Los Angeles. He earned his B.A. at Livingstone College, Salisbury, N.C. (1919); a B.D. from Garrett Biblical Institute, Evanston, Ill. (1922); an M.A. from Northwestern University, Evanston (1922); and his Ph.D. from Northwestern University (1930).

Clement's first teaching position was as instructor of history at Livingstone College, Salisbury, in 1922. In 1925 at the age of twenty-five he was chosen as dean of the college—one of the youngest academic deans in America. During his tenure as dean Livingstone College received its accreditation from the Southern Association of Colleges and Secondary Schools. While teaching at Livingstone, Clement, an ordained minister, was the pastor of an A.M.E. Zion church at Landis, N.C. He also found time to serve as baseball coach at Livingstone and as a football official of the Colored Intercollegiate Athletic Association (he had been a three-letter athlete at his alma mater).

In 1931 Clement left Livingstone to become the first dean of Lousiville Municipal College, a new educational institution for Negroes affiliated with the University of Louisville. Under his administration, Louisville Municipal College received its first accreditation from the Southern Association of Colleges and Secondary Schools. Clement was an able administrator and an excellent teacher.

In 1929 a major educational reorganization in Atlanta, Ga., brought about the creation of Atlanta University as a graduate school affiliated with several undergraduate institutions in a cooperative plan. Upon the demise of its first president, John Hope, in 1936, Clement was chosen to succeed him. During his administration the Atlanta School of Social Work became the Atlanta University School of Social Work, an integral part of the university. Clark College was moved from South Atlanta to a new campus in close proximity to Atlanta University, near Spelman College, Morehouse College, and Morris Brown College. An Interdenominational Theological Center was organized and also became affiliated with the university. In the graduate school, under Clement's administration the School of Library Science, School of Education, and School of Business Administration were organized. In 1957 Clement was elected an honorary member of Phi Beta Kappa at Brown University. In 1966, *Time* magazine selected Clement as one of the fourteen most influential university presidents in America. *Time* said (Feb. 11, 1966,

pp. 64–65): "Rufus Clement, 65, Atlanta University, a Negro historian with a Ph.D. from Northwestern who had headed his school for 29 years. Clement takes pride in his skill in race and human relations, first, and foreign relations, particularly African, second."

Clement had always been associated with organizations in the South devoted to the improvement of race relations and the abolition of all forms of segregation and discrimination. He was a member of the Council on Inter-racial Cooperation and gave leadership to its political programs. He was identified with efforts to abolish the poll tax and secure voting rights for all citizens. As a consequence there was an increase of political awareness on the part of the Negro citizens of Atlanta. In 1952 Clement announced his candidacy for membership on the board of education. He ran as a member at large and won handily, receiving the largest majority of any candidate. He carried eight of the nine wards, white Atlantans joining black Atlantans in electing the first Negro officeholder in Georgia since 1871. Clement served fourteen years on the board of education. In 1960, while he was a member of the board, he devised a plan for the integration of Atlanta public schools under a federal court decree.

Clement was affiliated with a number of important national organizations. He was a member of the board of directors of the Southern Regional Council, United Nations Association of America, United Negro College Fund, National Science Foundation, and Institute of International Education. He was also a member of the Advisory Council on African Affairs of the State Department. He was chosen by Pres. Lyndon B. Johnson to represent the United States on the occasion of the independence celebration of Malawi in 1964.

While attending a series of meetings with Atlanta University trustees, he died in his room in the Roosevelt Hotel, New York City, on Nov. 7, 1967. Funeral services were held in Sisters Chapel, Spelman College, Atlanta, and at Broadway Temple A.M.E. Zion Church, Louisville, Ky., with burial in Louisville Cemetery. He was survived by his widow and a daughter, Mrs. Robert Foster of Los Angeles and her three children.

The principal printed source is Clarence A. Bacote's *The Story of Atlanta University . . .* (1969, especially pp. 316–30 and 344–82). See the obituary in the *New York Times* (Nov. 11, 1967, p. 46) and the *Atlanta Daily World* (Nov. 8 and 12, 1967).

— WILLIAM J. TRENT, JR.

COBB, JAMES A[DLAI] (1876–1958), lawyer, educator, judge, and civil rights leader. Cobb was born in Arcadia, La., but published biographies give no information about his parents. According to information provided in 1975 by friends in Washington, D.C., who had known him in his later life, his mother was a Beauregard, a member of one of the most prominent white families in Louisiana. If this is true, Cobb's father must have been colored. The Cobb Papers in the Moorland-Spingarn Research Center suggest, however, that his mother may have been Eleanor J. Pond, also a white woman. A sentence in *Howard Magazine* (Jan. 1959, p. 24) stated: "Judge Cobb was orphaned while an infant." His Washington friends state that the next sentence is false: "He obtained his first job at the age of eight, and saved enough money to purchase a pushcart, which was used to peddle fruits and candies through the streets of Shreveport."

According to information supplied by the registrars of Fisk University and Dillard University (April 23 and May 15, 1975, respectively), young Cobb attended Fisk University at some time prior to 1890 and Straight University (now Dillard University) during 1893–1895, leaving at the end of his junior year. At Straight he participated in the Choral Union. Enrolling in the School of Law at Howard University, he received his LL.B. degree in 1899 and his LL.M. in 1900. In addition he was awarded the degree of Bachelor of Pedagogy from the University's Teachers College in 1902.

He was admitted to the bar of the District of Columbia in 1900, and was appointed as special assistant in the Department of Justice in 1907. He practiced law from 1915 to 1926 when he was appointed judge of the Municipal Court for the District of Columbia by Pres. Calvin Coolidge. He had been admitted to the bar of the U.S. Supreme Court in 1917. However, strong recommendations from Emmett J. Scott, formerly confidential advisor to Booker T. Washington, from William H. Lewis, the first Negro assistant attorney-general of the United States, and others failed in 1921 to win nomination of Cobb's appointment to the high court. After the expiration of his term in 1935 he resumed private practice, which he continued until his death in 1958. Meanwhile he had been a member of the faculty of the Howard University Law School from 1916 to 1938, serving also as vice-dean from 1923 to 1929.

As special assistant to the Department of Justice (1907–1915) he is said to have gained a national reputation in prosecuting cases under the Pure Food and Drugs Act enacted in 1906. A staunch Republican, he was a delegate to the 1920 Republican National Convention in Chicago, and an alternate delegate in 1924 in Cleveland. His support was rewarded by appointment as successor to Robert H. Terrell as judge of the Municipal Court of the District of Columbia (1926–1935). Perhaps because of his political affiliation, Pres. Franklin D. Roosevelt did not reappoint him, despite a petition signed by some 100 lawyers representing the Washington and District Bar Associations.

Much of Judge Cobb's career at Howard University was stormy, partly because of continuing controversy with Mordecai W. Johnson who had become president in 1926. Debate continues about the basic reasons for this hostility. Dr. Johnson was a "strong" president; allegations persist that Cobb and Emmett J. Scott conspired to get rid of Johnson. Some persons insist that Johnson acted in the best interests of the university.

In any event, Cobb was replaced by the Board of Trustees on June 4, 1929 by Charles H. Houston as resident vice-dean of the law school. This action followed an exhaustive report by H. C. Horack, secretary of the Association of American Law Schools in 1928, on the steps necessary for the Howard University Law School to receive accreditation. Among other recommendations was one to make the school a day school instead of an evening school. Since Cobb was then serving as judge of the Municipal Court, he obviously

could not give full administrative supervision of a day school. In addition, Houston's academic preparation was superior to that of Cobb—Houston was a Phi Beta Kappa graduate of Amherst College (1915), had received his first degree in Law from Harvard in 1922, where he was for two years a student editor of the *Harvard Law Review,* and had received his law doctorate in 1923. Cobb remained, however, as a part-time member of the faculty (Rayford W. Logan, *Howard University: The First Hundred Years, 1867–1967* [1969], pp. 266–67).

Cobb's services were terminated as of June 30, 1938, by action of the Board of Trustees (the article in the *Howard Magazine,* Jan. 1959, states that he resigned). This termination resulted from undocumented vitriolic reports on Johnson by Prof. Lorenzo D. Turner, Dean Emeritus Kelly Miller, and Cobb. The charges appeared in a special issue of the *Howard University Alumni Journal* (1937–1938) entitled "The Case Against President Johnson." The vote of the Board of Trustees on April 12, 1938, stated that Cobb should be informed that the board's action resulted from his appearance before a congressional committee in opposition to appropriations for the university. An article in the *Baltimore Afro-American* (June 18, 1938) also stated that counsel for Judge Cobb had withdrawn a motion for a preliminary injunction to restrain the university from terminating Cobb's services. According to this article, the university had invoked its right to terminate the services of faculty members when their actions were incompatible with the welfare of the university. Cobb continued his attacks on Johnson, notably when (Nov. 5, 1938) he revived before the House Committee on Un-American Activities accusations that Johnson had at one time advocated Communism.

Although there is no evidence in the Minutes of the Board of Trustees to indicate collusion between Cobb and Scott, Johnson was convinced that such collusion existed (Logan, *Howard University . . .* pp. 338–41). The fact that he succeeded in obtaining a vote of the board on April 12, 1938, to retire Scott as well, to take effect likewise on June 30, 1938, has helped perpetuate the rumor that Scott, Cobb, and others were ringleaders in the abortive attempt to get rid of Johnson. Both remained bitter in their denunciations for many years (personal reminiscences of R.W.L.).

During these stormy years Cobb was recognized as an able constitutional lawyer. He was associate counsel in *Buchanan v. Warley* (1917) in which the U.S. Supreme Court ruled that a Louisville, Ky., ordinance designed to maintain residential segregation was in "direct violation of the fundamental law enacted in the Fourteenth Amendment preventing state interference with property rights except by due process of law" (245 U.S. 60, 80–82). He was less successful as associate counsel in a Washington, D.C., case, *Corrigan v. Buckley* (1926). In that case the Court ruled that restrictive covenants did not fall within the province of the Fifth Amendment, since the action of only private individuals was involved (271 U.S. 323).

But he gained additional renown as associate counsel in the first two Texas primary cases, *Nixon v. Herndon* (1927) and *Nixon v. Condon* (1932). In 1923 Texas had enacted a law prohibiting Negroes from participating in any Democratic party primary election. The U.S. Supreme Court ruled that it would be difficult to imagine "a more direct and obvious infringement" of the Fourteenth Amendment (273 U.S. 536). When Texas sought to circumvent this decision by authorizing each party to prescribe qualifications for its own members, the U.S. Supreme Court declared, in effect, that what the state could not do itself it could not delegate power to others to do (286 U.S. 73, 85).

As senior partner in the most prestigious Washington, D.C., colored law firm, Cobb, (Perry) Howard and (George E. C.) Hayes, 613 F St. NW, beginning 1935, Cobb was recognized as a prominent lawyer in the nation's capital. He served also on the board of many organizations, notably as member of the George Washington Bicentennial Commission (1932); chairman of the D.C. Selective Service Appeals Board; trustee of the Washington Public Library; director of the NAACP, the National Urban League, and the National Council of Christians and Jews. As a member of Epsilon Boulé of Sigma Pi Phi fraternity, composed of some of the most distinguished Negroes in Washington, he is remembered for his unremitting support of the Republican party and condemnation of Howard's Pres. Mordecai W. Johnson.

Nonetheless, Howard University conferred upon him in 1955 the Alumni Achievement Award for distinguished postgraduate service in the field of law. To the astonishment of many who remembered his feuds with Johnson, Cobb bequeathed $300,000 of his $350,000 estate to establish a scholarship fund for needy law students at Howard.

A bachelor, he resided for many years in the home of Mr. and Mrs. George E. C. Hayes, 1732 S St. NW. He died there on Oct. 14, 1958, on the same day that the D.C. Bar Association voted to accept Negro lawyers into membership. Cobb was one of the Negro attorneys who had filed for membership in 1956 (*Washington Post*, Oct. 16, 1958, p. B2). Funeral services were held at Rankin Memorial Chapel, Howard University, on Oct. 17 and burial was private. There were no survivors.

Some basic facts are in *Who's Who in Colored America* (1950), edited by G. James Fleming and Christian E. Burckel. The information about his attendance at Fisk University and Straight University was supplied by the registrars of the institutions on April 23 and May 15, 1975, respectively. Valuable information was obtained by Michael R. Winston in interviews with surviving friends of Cobb and from correspondence in the Scott Papers, made available by the Soper Library, Morgan State College. The Cobb Papers in the Moorland-Spingarn Research Center contain letters urging his reappointment as judge of the Municipal Court, memorabilia, and the unpublished letters from Eleanor J. Pond.
                                                                    — RAYFORD W. LOGAN

COKER, DANIEL [born **ISAAC WRIGHT**] (1780–1846), minister, teacher, writer, activist, and colonizationist. Born in Frederick County or Baltimore County, Md., the son of a white mother Susan Coker, an indentured servant, and a slave father Edward Wright, Daniel

was raised with his white half-brothers, children of his mother's first marriage. He attended the local school as his half-brothers' valet. While still a youth he escaped to New York and changed his name to Daniel Coker on reaching manhood. He met Bishop Asbury, who later ordained him to the Methodist ministry. His return to Baltimore, the center of one of the nation's largest free Negro populations, was made with the utmost secrecy since legally Maryland regarded him as a slave. Through the efforts of friends his freedom was purchased. According to Huberich (2:144) he succeeded in gaining a liberal education.

Freedom gave Coker the opportunity to boldly and courageously articulate views and participate in activities not expected of Negroes. As he became widely known for his teaching and preaching, he became more outspoken against the institution of slavery and the general treatment accorded Negroes. From around 1802 to 1816 he taught in the African School connected with the Sharp Street Church, in Baltimore. From 1816 to 1820 he acted as manager and teacher of the African Bethel School established in Baltimore by the African Methodist Episcopal church.

For a number of years prior to 1816 Coker advocated that Negro Methodists should totally withdraw from the white-controlled Methodist church organization and establish an independent African Methodist church. Unable to gain the support of the majority of the members of the Sharp Street Church, he and other separatists withdrew from the church and formed the African Bethel Church (later known as Bethel A.M.E. Church). Along with others who supported the independent church movement, Coker was invited by Richard Allen to attend the Philadelphia Conference of 1816, which established the African Methodist Episcopal church as a national organization. Coker acted as secretary and was nominated and elected on April 9, 1816, as the first bishop of the African Methodist Episcopal church. Perhaps because of dissension surrounding the question of his light skin color, Coker declined the position and Richard Allen became bishop on April 11, 1816 (Carol V. R. George, *Segregated Sabbaths, Richard Allen and the Rise of Independent Black Churches, 1760–1840* [1937], especially p. 88, n.36).

On April 17, 1818, for reasons unknown, Daniel Coker was expelled from the church, but in 1819 was restored to his ministerial position. He was sent to Africa as a missionary with a subsidy from the Maryland Colonization Society in 1820, a year before Lott Cary. Coker first settled in Liberia. In 1820 when Samuel A. Crozer, the last of the three agents of the society who accompanied Coker, died, the sole responsibility for the emigrants and the care of the property of the society and the government rested on Coker. Since conditions in Liberia were unfavorable, Coker and some emigrants went to the British colony of Sierra Leone, where Gov. Charles MacCarthy, a bitter foe of the slave trade and a supporter of colonization, advised Coker in September 1820 to await instructions from America. Coker's administration terminated on March 8, 1821, when new agents from the American Colonization Society arrived. Coker and his family remained in Sierra Leone when the other emigrants left for Cape Mesurado, Liberia. On a motion by Francis Scott Key, the managers of the ACS resolved unanimously to thank Coker for his "care, attention and prudence in superintending" the affairs of the colony of Liberia "in a time of great difficulty, and danger" and that a present not exceeding $150 be sent to him "as a further expression of their approbation of his conduct." Huberich condemned the society for not appointing Coker to some position of honor and trust in the settlement. It was the first instance of not entrusting power to men of color, a policy that later cost the society the loss of the services of men like John B. Russwurm.

Coker wrote a number of pamphlets, the best known of which was *A Dialogue Between a Virginian and an African Minister* (1810), which, using the Bible as his authority, presented an argument against slavery and its evils. Equally important among his writings is the published part of the *Journal of Daniel Coker, a Descendant of Africa, from the time of Leaving New York in the Ship Elizabeth . . . on a Voyage for Sherbro, in Africa, in Company with Three Agents and about Ninety Persons of Colour . . . With an Appendix* (1820). The published volume contains only Part I. He sent Part II to the American Colonization Society but Charles H. Huberich was unable to find it (1947) in the society's archives (2:110, n.13). Coker hoped that the society would in particular prevent persons who drank from coming to the colony; it was also desirable that some mechanics should come. Coker, who established a church in Freetown, remained there until his death in 1846. Some of his descendants continued to live there.

There are references to Coker in George Freeman Bragg's *Heroes of the Eastern Shore* (1939); Daniel Alexander Payne's *History of the African Methodist Episcopal Church,* edited by the Rev. C. S. Smith (1891), and his *Recollections of Slavery Years* (with the same editor; 1888). There are some minor contradictions in Payne, Charles H. Wesley's *Richard Allen, Apostle of Freedom* (1935), and *The Encyclopedia of the African Methodist Episcopal Church . . .* compiled by Richard R. Wright, Jr. (2d ed., 1948). Charles Henry Huberich's *The Political and Legislative History of Liberia* (2 vols., 1947) is particularly valuable for excerpts from Coker's *Journal* and the Minutes of the ACS about conditions in Liberia. — BETTY THOMAS

COLE, NAT "KING" [NATHANIEL ADAMS] (1919–1965), musician and entertainer.

Cole was born on March 17, 1919, in Montgomery, Ala., one of five children of the Rev. Edward James and Perlina Coles. Encouraged by his musically inclined mother, "the only music teacher" he ever had, he played "Yes, We Have No Bananas" on the piano when he was four years old. When he was five the family moved to Chicago, where his father pastored the True Light Baptist Church, and Nat sang and played the organ. While attending Wendell Phillips High School, he also played the piano in the Rogues of Rhythm, a band led by his brother Eddie. In 1936 Nat played the piano in *Shuffle Along,* an all-Negro musical revue, written and first produced in New York City (1921) by four Negroes, F. E. Miller, Aubrey Lyles, Eubie Blake, and Noble Sissle. By the mid-1930s

Shuffle Along had lost some of its popularity; after closing in Chicago, it folded in Long Beach, Calif., in 1937. By that time Eddie and the Rogues of Rhythm had left the show and Nat had married Nadine Robinson, one of the dancers.

After playing in beer joints in Los Angeles, Nat formed in 1938 a trio with Oscar Moore on guitar and Wesley Prince on string bass. According to legend, which Nat denied, he became known as "King" after a nightclub patron placed a crown on his head. In any event, the entertainers became known as the King Cole Trio. It has been conjectured that Cole dropped the "s" from the family name because his mother had wanted him to be a classical musician and his father had objected to his playing in nightclubs. Although not a great success at first, the trio gradually won popularity in the 1940s with the cafe-society set, especially for Cole's skill at the piano and Moore's at the guitar.

Nat King Cole became one of the more versatile and successful entertainers of his era. He launched his career as a singer in 1943 when he recorded his song "Straighten Up and Fly Right," the text of one of his father's sermons. It was not until 1947, however, that his recording of "The Christmas Song" presaged his fame. In the next few years his recordings sold a million copies each and earned large royalties. Among the most successful were "Nature Boy" (1948), "Mona Lisa" (1949), and "Too Young" (1951). He was also one of the first Negro stars on radio (1948–1949) in a musical show sponsored by Wildroot Cream Oil.

He had divorced his wife and in March 1948 married the widowed Mrs. Maria Ellington (no relation to Duke Ellington). After an elaborate wedding in Harlem, they spent their honeymoon in Mexico.

His royalties enabled him to purchase a twenty-room house with a swimming pool in the exclusive, previously all-white Hancock Park area of Los Angeles. His fame helped overcome the initial hostility of some of the residents.

Delinquent income taxes, amounting to some $150,-000, however, led to a temporary attachment of the home, which he paid off at the rate of $1000 a week. This burden may have contributed to acute ulcers and internal hemorrhaging which caused his collapse while playing an Easter Sunday concert (1953) in Carnegie Hall, New York City. Surgeons had to remove part of his stomach.

Despite the operation, during the next eleven years he developed his remarkable versatility. He starred in seven motion pictures and appeared as guest on television shows. In 1956–1957 he was the first Negro to host a nationwide network television show. It was short-lived because the opposition of many southern white viewers reduced commercial advertising. This hostility had already resulted in an assault (1956) by three white men when he was performing in an integrated show before a segregated audience in Birmingham, Ala.

In the early 1960s he was criticized in several Negro newspapers for not joining other Negro entertainers in the struggle for civil rights. Asserting that it was "both stupid and ridiculous" to criticize prominent Negroes for refusing to participate in the movement in the South, he contributed some $50,000 of funds raised by his concerts to civil rights organizations.

He reached the pinnacle of his fame and fortune in the 1960s. During each of three successive years he earned $500,000 at the Las Vegas Sands Hotel. He also won acclaim in Australia, Europe, and South America. He gave a command performance for Queen Elizabeth II at London's Palladium Theatre and visited "brown babies" in Frankfurt. In Brazil, where he gave charity performances for homeless children and flood victims, he lunched with the president.

In 1962 his recording of "Rambling Rose" and an album by the same title sold a million copies each, as did two other albums, *Love Is the Thing* and *Unforgettable.* He is said to have earned $2.5 million in royalties on the sale of five million copies of recordings for Capital Records and another $1 million for songs published by his firm, Kell-Cole Productions. He added to his fame and increased his wealth by his performances in his own musical revue, *Sights and Sounds.* His first attempt in this medium, *I'm With You,* had failed because of unfavorable reviews but had launched on her career Barbara McNair, who later had her own successful television show. During three years, annual editions of *Sights and Sounds* played in nightclubs, theaters, and on concert stages in some 100 cities.

In mid-December 1964 physicians at St. John's Hospital, Santa Monica, Calif., diagnosed an advanced stage of cancer in almost every vital organ. Cole died there on Feb. 25, 1965, after a three-hour operation for removal of his left lung on Jan. 25. Episcopal funeral rites in St. James's Church, Los Angeles, were attended by members of his family and large numbers of friends. Frank Sinatra, George Burns, Jack Benny, Sammy Davis, Jr., José Ferrer, Peter Lawford, and Eddie ("Rochester") Anderson were among the forty honorary pallbearers. Flags flew at half-mast in the Music Center, Los Angeles; Mrs. Lyndon B. Johnson, among many others, sent flowers.

Nat King Cole was buried in Forest Lawn Memorial Park in Glendale, Calif. He was survived by his widow, four daughters—Carol, Natalie (who later achieved her own notable success as a singer), twins Tomlin and Casey—and an adopted son Kelly, the child of a deceased sister of Mrs. Maria Cole.

Since the late nineteenth century many other Negro entertainers had achieved success on the stage and in movies. Nat King Cole's versatile career helped perpetuate the tradition and pave the way for the larger number of Negro entertainers on the stage, in radio, movies, and television.

In Black and White: Afro-Americans in Print, edited by Mary Mace Spradlin (2d ed., enlarged and rev., 1976), lists several references to Nat King Cole, especially in *Our World* and *Ebony.* The April 1965 issue of *Ebony* has an excellent photographic profile by Louis Robinson (pp. 123–34). He collaborated with Maria Ellington Cole in *Nat King Cole: An Intimate Biography* (1971). — RAYFORD W. LOGAN

COLE, BOB [ROBERT] (1863?–1911), composer, singer, dancer, musician, and actor. He was born in Athens, Ga., the son of devout parents whose father was prominent in politics in the South during Reconstruction. After reputedly graduating from Atlanta University, he went to New York City and found employment as a singer, dancer, musician, composer, actor, and stage manager. He was the playwright and manager at Al Worth's Museum for the All-Star Company, the first Negro stock company. In 1893 he wrote the music for the minstrel show Black Patti's Troubadours, starring Sissieretta Jones ("Black Patti") in songs and operatic selections. During the first year of performance at Proctor's 58th Street Theater, Cole became involved in a salary dispute with the producers, Voelckel and Nolan. Arrested, he protested to the magistrate: "These men have amassed a fortune from the product of my brain; and now they call me a thief; I won't give up." It is not clear whether this incident alienated him from minstrel shows, but he began to plan a play of his own.

In the season of 1898–1900, aided by Billy Johnson, he presented the first all-Negro full-length musical comedy, *A Trip to Coontown,* the first colored show to be organized, produced, and managed by Negroes. "Coon" was considered belittling, almost like "nigger," and Ernest Hogan's All Coons Look Alike to Me (1896), which had won general popularity, caused Hogan and others much unhappiness when the word was separated from the music. *A Trip to Coontown* not only broke away from the minstrel tradition, but it had a plot and some character development as well as songs, dances, and pretty girls.

During the New York race riot of Aug. 15, 1900, a white mob yelled "Get Ernest Hogan and Williams and Walker and Cole and Johnson," but only Hogan and George Walker were in danger of being attacked.

In 1901 Bob Cole teamed with J. Rosamond Johnson and his brother James Weldon Johnson in producing such successful songs that they were dubbed "those ebony Offenbachs." Cole and Johnson, unlike George Walker and Bert Williams, did not include minstrelsy. Cole and the Johnson brothers signed a three-year contract in 1901 with Joseph W. Stern and Company that guaranteed monthly payments to be deducted from their royalties. This may have been the first contract between Negro songwriters and a Tin Pan Alley publisher. Such Broadway stars as May Irwin, Anna Held, Marie Cahill, Fay Templeton, and Lillian Russell popularized such of the team's songs as "The Old Flag Never Touched the Ground," "Under the Bamboo Tree," and "Didn't He Ramble." The trio also wrote music for exclusive Klaw and Erlanger productions—*The Sleeping Beauty* and *Humpty Dumpty.* They gained added fame when their songs were published in the *Ladies' Home Journal.*

After *A Trip to Coontown* the team produced in 1903 *The Evolution of Ragtime: A Musical Suite of Six Songs Tracing and Illustrating Negro Music.* After James Weldon Johnson was appointed U.S. consul in Venezuela in 1906, Cole collaborated with J. Rosamond Johnson. Their *The Shoofly Regiment* (1906) was another landmark in that it presented romantic love between two Negroes despite the stereotype that such romance had to be presented in a minstrel show. Cole and Johnson wrote and appeared in the play at the Bijou Theatre in New York City. Two years later they produced *The Red Moon*. James Weldon Johnson wrote: "Each of these plays was a true operetta with a well-constructed book and a tuneful, well-written score. On these two points, no Negro play has ever equalled *The Red Moon*" (*Black Manhattan* [1930], p. 109). Although the operetta was a financial failure, its influence continued.

Cole died from drowning, which may have been suicide, on Aug. 2, 1941. He had suffered a mental breakdown on the last night of an engagement at the Fifth Avenue Theater, was sent to Bellevue Hospital and then to Manhattan Hospital on Ward's Island, where he remained until July 1. On July 29 he left Amityville, accompanied by his mother, for the Catskills and had been there until he said he was going for a walk. Shortly thereafter word was brought that he had drowned in a nearby creek. His funeral was held on Aug. 6 at the family home, 102 West 136th St., New York City. Among the pallbearers were Bert Williams, John E. Nail, and Lester A. Walton. Interment was in Woodlawn Cemetery. He was survived by his mother and four sisters.

James Weldon Johnson's *Black Manhattan* (1930) and Eileen Southern's *The Music of Black Americans: A History* (1971) give basic information. The obituaries in the *New York Times* (Aug. 5, 1941, p. 7) and the *New York Age* (Aug. 10, 1941) give details about his tragic death. G. H. Taylor, registrar of Atlanta University, wrote on May 21, 1976: "This office has made a thorough search of our files, both undergraduate and graduate, but we do not find Mr. Cole's record."

— RAYFORD W. LOGAN

COLTRANE, JOHN W. [called **TRANE**] (1926–1967), musician. He was born in Hamlet, N.C., on Sept. 23, 1926. Both his grandfathers were ministers. He was the only son of John Robert and Alice Blair Coltrane. His father was a tailor and an amateur musician who played several instruments. When Trane was still a boy the family moved to High Point, a city of 35,000 in the northern part of the state. There he grew up in an atmosphere of religious music—hymns and gospel—of a southern church. He was also influenced until the age of twelve, when his father died, by instruction on several instruments. At William Penn High School, Trane played the E-flat horn, clarinet, and later the alto saxophone in the school band.

After his graduation from high school in 1943, Trane's family moved to Philadelphia, where he studied music at the Granoff Studios and the Ornstein School of Music. He achieved an excellent classical musical education. His professional debut in 1945 as a member of a cocktail quartet was interrupted by his service in a navy band in Hawaii (1945–1947). He gained fame with several of the best known bands in the United States and with his own groups. He was also acclaimed in Japan (1966), France, England, Italy, and Holland. By the time of his death in Huntington, Long Island, N.Y., on July 17, 1967, he was the acknowledged "father" of the avant-garde in jazz.

Coltrane married first Naima Gibbs of Philadelphia in 1955. He dedicated records to her and their daughter Antonia (Seeyda). After his divorce from Naima he married Alice McLeod in Juarez, Mexico, in 1966. They, along with the other children from the first marriage, lived quietly in Deer Park, Long Island, until his death.

Coltrane's jazz style was derived from many influences. At age seventeen he heard a record of Count Basie and Lester Young; in Philadelphia his quartet listened to Charlie Parker and Sidney Bechet and imitated their style in their own performances. After his discharge from the navy in 1947 he played tenor saxophone with Eddie Vinson's Rhythm & Blues Band. His change to tenor from alto in Vinson's band was prompted by the realization that Charlie Parker could not be equalled on alto. He then played tenor with Dizzy Gillespie (1949–1951), Earl Bostic (1952–1953), Johnny Hodges (1953–1954), and Miles Davis (1955–1956). In 1956 he played record dates with Paul Chambers for Jazz West in Los Angeles, and with Miles Davis for Prestige Columbia in New York. "When they first heard me with Miles, they didn't like it," he said.

In 1957 Thelonius Monk invited Trane to join him in the Five Spot in Greenwich Village. Trumpeter Lee Morgan said: "He's the only cat around who doesn't sound a damn bit like Bird. I don't know how Trane plays so many notes so fast and keeps them from running together." Coltrane said: "Musically, my experience with Monk was one of the best things that ever happened to me. At that time, I had begun to try to play faster on the horn. I tried to adopt certain runs he'd make to the saxophone, and I tried to capture his sound, and certain glissandos that he used to play on the horn."

In 1958 Trane recorded with Cecil Taylor (*Coltrane Time*, United Artists). He matured with Miles Davis (1958–1960) and developed into one of the most imitated and influential jazz men (Spellman, in *Evergreen Review*, Feb. 1967).

From 1960 to 1967 Trane played with his own groups, beginning with the first John Coltrane Quartet (pianist McCoy Tyner, drums Elvin Jones, bass Steve Davis, and Coltrane on soprano sax and tenor sax). He recorded *Ascension* with eleven men. His wife Alice played piano in later albums; Jimmy Garrison was on bass from 1961.

In 1965 Trane was voted top tenor saxophonist of the year in the Readers Poll of *Downbeat* magazine, Jazzman of the Year, and *A Love Supreme* the Record of the Year. He went to Chicago for the Jazz Festival with Archie Shepp who recorded his allegiance to John in *Four for Trane* (Impulse A-71), all Coltrane's pieces.

His records reveal other influences. Sun Ra's records and words (Transition, Cambridge, Mass.) were a precursor of John's "to reach for a better world," "to write the sounds I hear," "use notes like words in a sentence, making each series of sounds a separate thought." Trane found a friend in Ravi Shankar, and employed Hindustani modal improvisation in *A Love Supreme* (Impulse A-77). Improvisational meditation and the use of extreme registers, the low growls and other sounds that are not "native" to the saxophone, may be traced to Shankar's sitar, *Music of India* (Angel Records). In *A Love Supreme* one also hears African rhythms and textures, as well as the African talking rhythms which are finally realized by repeating the words in the same rhythm and melody, a technique used by the Ballet African drummers to say "Thank you very much."

Members of Coltrane's band said of him: "There was a love that he emitted that is rare to find"; "There was something sainted about him. There was never any malice. We were like four brothers in the deepest sense of the word"; "Often there was no music. He'd just announce what key we'd be playing in, or that we'd be playing in twelve tones and we'd take it from there"; "He gave you confidence by giving you responsibility. He was a genius" (Ebony, Nov. 1967). On the piano where he composed, and nearby, were a tenor, an alto, and a soprano sax, an Indian sitar, a set of drums, a flute, a bagpipe, a small African horn.

Coltrane lived music as a force for good in the world, incorporated philosophical systems into his music, and at the same time Hindustani and African sound systems into his jazz improvisational theory and style. He was a supreme audile who can be understood readily by audiles, but with difficulty by others.

John Coltrane died of a liver ailment. The funeral service was memorable, in St. Peter's Lutheran Church, New York City, where on July 21, 1967, a thousand friends heard the Albert Ayler Quartet and the Ornette Coleman Quartet.

Acknowledgment is made to the Schomburg Research Center, to John Gensel and J. C. Thomas, to other friends of Trane, to the quoted sources, including the editors of the sleeves of recordings, and the following: Leonard Feather, The Book of Jazz (1957), and J. C. Thomas, Chasin' the Trane: The Music and Mystique of John Coltrane (1975). Other records: Africa/Brass (Impulse A-6); Expression (Impulse A-9120).

There is a photograph on page 110 of Lindsay Patterson's The Negro in Music and Art (1969).

— RAYMOND LEMIEUX

COOK, GEORGE F. T. (1835–1912), superintendent of the Washington, D.C., Negro school system. The son of the Rev. John Francis Cook, a former slave, George F. T. Cook was born in Washington on June 18, 1835. John Cook, one of Washington's most prominent Negroes during the first half of the nineteenth century, operated a school for Negro children, and it was at this school that young George received his early education. Later he studied at Oberlin College, as did his brother, John F. Cook, Jr. In 1855 he returned to Washington, D.C., upon the death of his father, and along with his brother continued the school that John Cook Sr. had conducted until his death. George and John Jr. operated the school until 1867, when it closed.

On May 21, 1862, about five years before the Cook school closed, Congress enacted a law calling for 10 percent of the taxes levied on the property of Negroes to be used for the education of Negro children. After this law had been in effect for two years it became apparent that its provisions were not sufficient to fund the Negro schools. Additional legislation gave a pro-rata share of all municipal school funds to the Negro schools through a Negro Board of Trustees. A superintendent of the Negro school system was also required, and A. E. Newton was appointed and served from 1865 to 1868. In 1868 the Board of Trustees appointed George F. T.

Cook as superintendent of the Colored Public Schools of Washington and Georgetown. The following year (1869) there were fifty teachers in the Negro school system, and an average student attendance of 2532. George F. T. Cook was the superintendent of the Negro school system until 1900, when the system had grown to include 352 teachers and a total of 12,748 students. Furthermore, in that year the school system owned twenty-three buildings and rented three others, making a total of 227 classrooms (John W. Cromwell, The Negro in American History [1914], p. 232).

Cook's term as superintendent was not without its problems. During his first year in office Congress passed a bill abolishing separate management of the two school systems, Negro and white, by repealing the provision establishing a separate Negro Board of Trustees. The Negro community, however, objected to this bill because of the hostility and indifference a white school board might show to the Negro school system. Meetings were held protesting the bill, and these protests caused Pres. Andrew Johnson to shelve it, unsigned.

Cook's ability enabled him to weather a number of organizational changes in the government. In 1873 control of the Negro school system was transferred from the U.S. Department of the Interior to the government of the District of Columbia. The governor at that time, whose duty it was to appoint school officials, reappointed Cook (J. Ormond Wilson, "Eighty Years of the Public Schools of Washington—1805 to 1885," Records of the Columbia Historical Society, 1869). A year later, in 1874, when the territorial government of the District of Columbia was abolished and a system of three commissioners established, Cook was again continued as superintendent. He resigned his position on July 1, 1900, when both the white and Negro schools were placed under the control of a single white superintendent having two assistants, one of whom was to be a Negro in charge of the Negro school system.

George F. T. Cook died after a short illness on Aug. 7, 1912, at the age of seventy-seven. His legacy was the highest quality Negro school system in the United States, and his passing was widely mourned. Funeral services were held on Aug. 10 in the 15th Street Presbyterian Church. Cook had been a member of this church ever since joining it on May 9, 1879, and over the years had given the church liberal financial support. In his eulogy the Rev. Francis J. Grimké stated that Cook "was by instinct a gentleman," and was thoroughly honest, modest, and industrious. Though a man of abundant means, "he was content all his life to live simply." Further, George F. T. Cook was kindly disposed toward others and commanded the respect of his community.

In addition to the works of Cromwell and Wilson cited above, information about George F. T. Cook can also be obtained from The Crisis (Jan. 1913) and Winfield Scott Montgomery's Historical Sketch of the Education for the Colored Race in the District of Columbia, 1805–1907 (1907). — STANTON L. WORMLEY, JR.

COOK, GEORGE WILLIAM (1855–1931), university administrator and civic leader. Cook was born a slave on Jan. 7, 1855, in Winchester, Va., in a family of seven children. When the Union Army captured Winchester in May 1862, the entire Cook family fled as war refugees, traveling north with the troops of General Banks, stopping for a time in Chambersburg, Pa., and settling in Harrisburg. George worked initially as a bootblack, and delivery boy for a newspaper and grocer. He then became a servant in the home of David D. Mumma, a member of the Pennsylvania state legislature, who permitted George to use his fine personal library after working hours. Cook later said the experience of working for this Pennsylvania Dutch family fired his ambition to seek higher education despite formidable obstacles. In 1871 Cook went to New York City to work in the home of a wealthy white family. He met the Rev. Henry Highland Garnet, who advised him to try to further his education at Howard University. Unable to attend because he lacked funds, he secured a position as "general factotum" for a physician. In the course of his work he met George B. Cheever, a classmate of Longfellow and Oliver Wendell Holmes. Impressed by Cook's ambition, Cheever provided financial assistance for one year for him to attend Howard University, where he entered the Preparatory Department in October 1874. Graduating from the Preparatory Department in 1877, Cook entered the College Department and received his B.A. degree as valedictorian of his class (1881). He earned his M.A. at Howard in 1886, an LL.B. in 1898, and an LL.M. in 1899.

In 1881 Cook began his half-century career at Howard University with an appointment as tutor of mathematics and assistant principal of the Normal Department. In 1887 Cook was appointed tutor in mathematics in the College Department, retaining, however, his administrative responsibilities in the Normal Department. Two years later, upon the death of Martha B. Briggs, Cook was made principal of the Normal Department, where he served until 1899. During the later years of Cook's service as principal, the university trustees began to reorganize the Normal Department, for decades one of the largest, but educationally most diffuse, units at Howard. It included elementary, secondary, and some collegiate-level courses, as well as instruction in music, industrial arts, and such commercial subjects as bookkeeping and typing. The trustees wished to deemphasize the "work of lower grade" and establish a professional teachers' college modeled after the successful one founded at Columbia in 1892. In the reorganization Lewis Baxter Moore (Ph.D., Pennsylvania, 1896) was appointed dean of this new school and Cook, who was primarily interested in business education, was appointed dean of the English Department (1899 to 1903) and the English and Commercial Department (1903–1905). From 1902 to 1928 Cook was professor of civics and commercial law. Cook never succeeded in his dream of building a stable business college at Howard University. From 1905 to 1919 the Commercial Department was restricted to offering subjects at the secondary level. When such courses were abolished at Howard in 1919, Cook secured a reprieve for commercial subjects by having them transferred to the new junior college. This proved to be temporary, since the junior college itself was abolished in 1925. Cook was made dean emeritus and a professor in the College of Liberal Arts.

While his efforts as an educator to build a business college at Howard ended in failure, Cook's success as an administrative officer of the university was unmistakable. In 1908 he was appointed business manager and acting secretary, and secretary of the university and the Board of Trustees in 1909. For ten years he was the highest ranking Negro official of Howard University. A sober, steady man, he inspired confidence at Howard as well as in the community.

George W. Cook married Coralie Franklin of Harpers Ferry, W.Va., on Aug. 31, 1899. They were both leaders in the social life of colored Washington and active in many civic organizations. Cook was a friend of Frederick Douglass, John Mercer Langston, Blanche K. Bruce, John R. Lynch, Alexander Crummell, Archibald Grimké, and other well-known Washingtonians of the period. Mrs. Cook was a member of the District of Columbia Board of Education. Cook was president of the Washington Colored Social Settlement, a member of the District of Columbia Board of Charities and appointed by Theodore Roosevelt to the President's Homes Commission to investigate housing conditions in Washington. He was granted sixteen months' leave from the university to establish "a cottage system for dependent colored children" at Blue Plains in Washington.

Cook's most noteworthy civic activity was as a member of the NAACP. A treasurer of the District of Columbia branch from 1912 to 1931, he was elected to the National Board of Directors on Nov. 4, 1914, and served until his death. In connection with his NAACP work he became a friend of Joel Spingarn, and was, with Dean William Pickens of Morgan State College and Dr. George W. Cabaniss of Washington, one of the leaders of the movement to secure a training camp for colored officers during the First World War. He arranged for Spingarn to speak at Howard, and was an important organizer of the Central Committee of Negro College Men, which coordinated the efforts of Negroes to volunteer for officer training. When the War Department claimed that a colored officer's camp was an impossibility because all available facilities were already committed for the training of white officers, Cook, acting on his own, but later supported by a resolution of the Board of Trustees, offered the campus of Howard University for the camp. At the conclusion of the controversy a camp was established at Fort Des Moines, Iowa. In addition a Student Army Training Camp was established at Howard which trained 1786 men. George W. Cook was the official most responsible for the university's prompt and successful response to the war emergency, managing the myriad details of housing, food, supplies, health, and recreation facilities necessary for such a program.

Cook was associated with Howard University for nearly fifty-eight years. He saw it develop from a Freedmen's Bureau experiment to a respected university. He was loyal to the original goals of the founders and first faculty, many of whom he knew personally, including General Howard. His conception of the university is clear in his Charter Day Address on March 2, 1925: "There can be no Howard University without equal rights and highest culture for all, based upon merit and capacity. To be plain, we know of no Negro education. Political rights and civic privileges are accompaniments of citizenship and are therefore part of the warp and woof of Howard University's curricula.'' He was a much beloved figure on the campus. Along with Deans Kelly Miller and Lewis Baxter Moore, Cook was part of the "triumvirate" of Negro leadership at Howard in an era of white presidents. When Cook retired in 1928 after serving under ten presidents, he was elected secretary of the General Alumni Association and served until his death. He was also elected an alumni trustee in 1931 but died before he was able to attend a meeting. He died on Aug. 20, 1931, at Mercy Hospital in Philadelphia after a two-week illness at his summer home in Asbury Park, N.J. His last words were "Tell all the girls and boys who are now in Howard University or have ever been there, that I love them and send word to them to go in the world and make good.'' Funeral Services were held in Andrew Rankin Memorial Chapel at Howard on August 24. Cook was buried in Lincoln Cemetery, Washington, D.C. He was survived by Mrs. Cook and a son, George Jr. In 1940 the university named a men's dormitory in his honor.

For the career of George W. Cook, see Walter Dyson's *Howard University, The Capstone of Negro Education: A History, 1867–1940* (1941) and Rayford W. Logan's *Howard University, The First Hundred Years 1867–1967* (1969). The George W. Cook Papers in the Manuscript Division, Moorland-Spingarn Research Center, contain important biographical data, unpublished speeches and essays. The significant role Cook played in the establishment of the Colored Officers Training Camp at Fort Des Moines is revealed in his correspondence in the Joel E. Spingarn Papers, Moorland-Spingarn Research Center. Cook's activities in the Washington, D.C., branch of the NAACP are reflected in the Archibald H. Grimké Papers at Howard University. — MICHAEL R. WINSTON

COOK, JOHN FRANCIS, SR. (1810?–1855), educational and religious leader in Washington, D.C. John F. Cook, Sr., was probably born in 1810 in Washington. This date is the one most often quoted, and it appears in one of the two family trees found among the Cook Family Papers in the Moorland-Spingarn Research Center of Howard University. The other family tree gives Cook's birth date as 1790, but it should be noted that this second chart contains a number of erroneous dates.

The members of the Cook family in the late 1700s were slaves. Young John was a slave until his sixteenth year, at which time his aunt, Alethia Tanner, who had purchased her own freedom from the proceeds of her vegetable market at Lafayette Square, purchased the Cooks and set them free. Young John was apprenticed to a shoemaker for five years after gaining his freedom in order to pay Mrs. Tanner back.

In 1831 Cook was appointed assistant messenger in the Land Office. His dream, however, was not government service, but education for his people. In his spare time Cook studied in order to realize his ambition to operate a school for free Negro children. In 1834 Cook was able to fulfill that ambition. A dozen years earlier, in 1822, a school had been started by Henry Smothers,

a student of Mary Billings, an Englishwoman who had operated a school in Georgetown. Smothers had erected a building at 14th and H Streets in northwest Washington. He had been succeeded by John W. Prout, who during his incumbency attempted to operate the school as a free school. This experiment failed after two or three years and the school became a tuition school again. In 1834 Cook took charge of the school, which at that time was called the Columbian Institute and which was governed by a Board of Trustees. Cook renamed the school the Union Seminary and began the task of providing education to children of the Negro community. The school was generally well attended, sometimes having as many as one hundred students enrolled. Cook left the school only once, in 1835, on account of the anti-Negro riot, frequently called the "Snow Riot," that caused many of Washington's Negroes to flee the city. The riot destroyed much of the one-room school, and it was not until August 1836 that Cook could return to Washington from his sanctuary in Columbia, Lancaster County, Pa., to reopen his school. Cook may have done some teaching in Columbia, for in the Cook Family Papers there is mention of a letter from Cook to his wife in Washington, D.C., in which he tells her of his pupils. In this letter (Nov. 22, 1835) he speaks of teaching more than seventy students, a number of whom were evidently quite ill-mannered, for he stated, "it takes half of my time to whip them."

Cook was also very much involved in the religious life of Washington's Negro community. After returning from Pennsylvania in 1836 Cook began to study for the ministry. In 1838, according to John W. Cromwell's *The Negro in American History* (1914, pp. 228–229) Cook was a preacher in the Israel A.M.E. Church on South Capitol Street. In the same year he helped organize the Union Bethel Church, which, nearly fifty years later, became the Metropolitan A.M.E. Church. Cook withdrew his membership from Union Bethel Church in 1840 in order to found a Presbyterian church. According to an article in the *Washington Evening Star* (July 3, 1949), Cook became a licentiate in the Presbytery of the District of Columbia on Oct. 11, 1841. On Oct. 27 and Nov. 3, 1841, meetings were held in Cook's schoolhouse by "people of color, members of the several Presbyterian churches and other evangelical churches" who did not "enjoy in our white churches all the privileges that we desire" and who, consequently, resolved to establish a separate Presbyterian church in Washington. Cook and David Carroll were authorized to prepare a constitution and to arrange a subsequent organizational meeting. It was at this meeting (Sunday, Nov. 21, 1841) that the First Colored Presbyterian Church of Washington (later known as the 15th Street Presbyterian Church) was officially organized. Cook was elected pastor, and the church was formally received into the Presbytery of the District of Columbia on May 3, 1842.

Cook prepared for his role as a religious leader. He spent eighteen months studying for the theology examination that the Presbyterian church required of all candidates for ordination. On July 14, 1843, he was ordained and installed in his church. The previous day, July 13, Cook had delivered a sermon at the white

Fourth Presbyterian Church, located at the corner of Ninth Street and Grant Place, between G and H Streets NW, and had been well received by the congregation. Constance McLaughlin Green stated in her *Washington Village and Capital, 1800–1878* (1962, p. 145), that Cook was "Washington's first colored Presbyterian minister." Under his thirteen-year pastorate the church he helped to found grew in size from only a handful of original church-goers to around 120 members.

Aside from helping to establish two of Washington's most important Negro churches, Cook also had the distinction of being one of the original members of the early Ministers' Councils organized by Daniel A. Payne, Bishop of the A.M.E. church.

Cook's activities and interests were not restricted to the fields of education and religion, but encompassed the political sphere as well. He was active in the Negro Convention Movement. Begun in 1830, the movement was composed of free Negroes and was dedicated to bettering the lot of the Negro in the United States. At the third convention, Cook was named the corresponding secretary to the District of Columbia convention, and at the fifth meeting of the national organization he was elected secretary of the convention.

Cook married twice, the first time to Jane Mann, and the second time to Jane Le Count. He had a total of five children: John Jr., George F. T., a third son whose name is unknown, and two daughters whose names are likewise unknown. Because the Cook Family Papers do not reveal exactly when Cook was married to each of his two wives, there is, unfortunately, no way of knowing which children were born to each wife.

Cook died on March 21, 1855. Funeral services were held at the 15th Street Presbyterian Church. Much of what he accomplished and created during his lifetime lived on after his death. The school that he established was continued in different locations by his sons John Jr. and George, until 1867. The Columbian Harmony Cemetery, a cemetery in Washington for free Negroes which Cook also helped found, still exists today in a new location as the National Harmony Memorial Park in Landover, Md. The 15th Street Presbyterian Church has also withstood the passage of time, and has moved from the original site at 15th and H Streets NW to 15th and R Streets NW.

The three principal sources of information regarding John F. Cook, Sr., are the Fiftieth "Anniversary Address" of Francis J. Grimké in *The Works of Francis J. Grimké,* edited by Carter G. Woodson (1942), 1:531–40); George Washington Williams's *History of the Negro Race in America* . . . (1883, 2:187–91); and Letitia W. Brown's *Free Negroes in the District of Columbia 1790–1846* (1972). The article by the Rev. J. T. Kelly, "Rev. John C. Smith, D.D., and Other Pioneer Presbyterian Ministers of Washington" (*Records of the Columbia Historical Society,* vol. 24), deals with John F. Cook, Sr., exclusively. — STANTON L. WORMLEY, JR.

COOK, JOHN FRANCIS, JR. (1833–1910), educator and government official. The older son and namesake of the Rev. John F. Cook, Sr., he was born in Washington, D.C., on Sept. 21, 1833. He attended his father's school, the Union Seminary, which was located on H Street near the corner of 14th Street NW. Later he studied at Oberlin College. He remained at Oberlin until 1855, when he was called home upon his father's death. After he returned to Washington, he and his brother George assumed control of his father's school. John Jr. taught for a brief period in New Orleans until the outbreak of the Civil War, when he returned once again to Washington to help operate his father's school. The two brothers were able to continue the school's operation until 1867, when it closed.

In 1867 John F. Cook, Jr., began his career in government by accepting a clerkship in the office of the collector of taxes in Washington, D.C. At this time there existed in Washington a Board of Aldermen composed of representatives from the various districts of the city. Cook was made a member of that board in 1868. In the same year he was elected registrar of the city (1869, according to Daniel Smith Lamb's *History of the Howard University Medical Department,* 1900). In 1871, when Washington, D.C., became a federal territory, Cook was reappointed to the same office by Gov. Henry D. Cooke.

In 1874 Cook was named collector of taxes for the District of Columbia and remained in this position through the administrations of Presidents Grant, Hayes, Garfield, and Arthur. The election of Grover Cleveland and the accession of the Democratic party led to Cook's resignation on April 30, 1888, for he had been quite active in Republican party politics, having been three times a delegate to the Republican National Convention.

While still serving in the various capacities enumerated above, Cook also held the office of justice of the peace in the District of Columbia from March 24, 1869, to January 28, 1876 (C. S. Bundy, "A History of the Office of Justice of the Peace in the District of Columbia," *Records of the Columbia Historical Society,* vol. 5).

Cook did not end his service to the city and the community with his retirement from the office of collector of taxes. From July 1, 1889, he served as one of the District's juror commissioners, and in November 1892 he became one of the members of the Board of Children's Guardians.

Although he followed a career in government rather than in education, Cook never lost his interest in promoting the benefits of education. When the House of Delegates of the territorial government of the District of Columbia in 1873 barred Negroes from opening a normal school, Cook joined John M. Langston, Charles Purvis, Frederick Douglass, and other Negro leaders in an unsuccessful attempt to have the public schools integrated. He was a member of the Board of Trustees of Howard University for thirty-five years, from 1875 until his death in 1910. In June 1891 Cook was elected a member of the board's executive committee, and occasionally served as its acting chairman. Upon his death he was mourned as "one of the strongest supporters since 1875" of the university (*Howard University Journal,* Jan. 28, 1910). Even after his retirement from government service John F. Cook, Jr., retained an interest in the education of young people, serving as the president of the Samuel Coleridge-Taylor Choral Association and as a member of the District of Columbia Board of Education from its reorganization in 1906 until a few months before his death.

Cook apparently acquired a fair amount of wealth in the later years of his life. The Cook family in Washington had always been well off; in the 1830s, for example, the Cooks had owned land and at least one house in Washington. A clipping found among the Cook Family Papers in the Moorland-Spingarn Research Center, Howard University, throws additional light on the financial standing of the Cooks. The clipping, dated "ca. 1890," from an unnamed newspaper, identified Mrs. John F. Cook, Jr., as the "wife of the wealthy owner of the Langham Hotel Building."

According to the Certificate of Death on file at the Bureau of Vital Statistics in Washington, D.C., Cook died on Jan. 20, 1910, of heart failure. He was buried on Jan. 28 at Harmony Cemetery in Washington, D.C., the cemetery his father was instrumental in founding.

The *Records of the Columbia Historical Society* (vols. 5 and 19) contains valuable information regarding the Cook family. See also John W. Cromwell's *The Negro in American History* (1914, pp. 230–31).

— STANTON L. WORMLEY, JR.

COOK, WILL MARION (1869–1944), violinist, composer, and orchestral director. Cook was born in Washington, D.C., the son of John Hartwell Cook and Isabelle Lewis Cook. Both parents were Oberlin graduates, the father later receiving his LL.B. degree from Howard University in 1871 and serving as professor and dean of the Law Department from 1877 to 1878 (Walter Dyson, *Howard University* . . . [1941], p. 223).

Young Will showed such unusual proclivity for music that his parents sent him to Ohio to live with an aunt as he pursued his studies at the Oberlin Preparatory School Conservatory. He was only thirteen years old. After a year or two at Oberlin he was urged by his violin teacher to continue his studies in Berlin. The boy returned home, gave a concert at the First Congregational Church sponsored by Frederick Douglass and other leading Negroes of Washington, and raised sufficient funds to study abroad for three years. There in Berlin, at age fifteen, the youngster began to study with the celebrated teacher Josef Joachim. For the next nine years under rigorous tutelage he mastered the fundamentals of the violin. With the hope and enthusiasm so typical of youth, Will Cook returned home with every intent of being a concert virtuoso.

For a brief time he studied with the Czech composer, Antonin Dvořák, who was then heading the National Conservatory of Music in New York City. In 1895, at age twenty-six, Cook made his solo debut at New York's Carnegie Hall. The reviews of that concert hailed Will Marion Cook as "the greatest *colored* [italics added] violinist in the world." Young Cook was outraged and momentarily crushed. Why did they have to place such a limitation on his achievement? Deeply stung, he resolved never again to play the violin. At the same time his consciousness was alerted to the exciting possibility of exploiting the genius of purely "Negro expression" in American music. Having carefully studied Dvořák's explorations in that genre, Cook was certain that he, a Negro, had even more to say musically than his Czech teacher. He turned to musical comedy. Collaborating with the poet Paul Laurence Dunbar, in 1898 he wrote the score for Dunbar's *Clorindy, The Origin of the Cake Walk.* That musical, produced by George W. Lederer with forty performers featuring Ernest Hogan, successfully played Broadway's Casino Roof Garden. It also established Cook as a composer and orchestra director of unusual skill and it brought him together with a richly talented teenage girl from Baltimore who sang in the show. She was Abbie Mitchell, who would later become his wife and the mother of their two children, Will Mercer Cook and Marion Cook (who died in New York City in 1950). Will Marion and his wife were later separated.

Other noteworthy musical works of this period were those shows Cook wrote for the comedy team of Bert Williams and George Walker. They were *Bandana Land, In Abyssinia,* and *In Dahomey.* That last show was the biggest hit of the trio, and of its music the *Boston Transcript* reported: "The composer has succeeded in lifting Negro music above the plane of the so-called 'Coon-Song' without destroying the characteristics of the melodies, and he provided a score which is . . . unusually diversified." Other outstanding Cook works of this period were his music for the shows *The Casino Girls, Darkeydom,* and *The Traitor.* His song hits included "Mandy Lou," "Wid De Moon, Moon, Moon," and "Bon Bon Buddy, the Chocolate Drop."

Cook's excellent musical background combined with a drive to create a truly indigenous Negro music was bearing results. Not yet out of his thirties, he was also assembling his own instrumental performing group. It was 1905 when Will Marion Cook's jazz band, using the name "The Memphis Students," appeared at Proctor's 23rd Street Theater in New York City. The band's uniqueness lay in its being a playing, singing, and dancing aggregation making liberal use of strings, reeds, brasses, and drums. Its instrumentalists lent color to their performances by playing one part while singing another. And the overall effect was highlighted by the spectacular gyrations and percussion artistry of its peerless drummer, Buddy Gilmore.

Shortly after 1910 Cook formed his famed New York Syncopated Orchestra with which he toured the nation. This group included several pianos, along with strings, reeds, brasses, and tympany. Moreover it featured a double male quartet, a soprano, and a number of singing instrumentalists. Its repertoire included Viennese waltzes, marches, and the compositions of composers as diverse as Brahms and W. C. Handy. Cook took this orchestra to Europe where it performed as the American Syncopated Orchestra, and featured a young clarinetist named Sidney Bechet.

In the interim the Clef Club was incorporated in New York City in 1910. Its membership comprised the best Negro musicians and entertainers, and from their ranks came the first of several legendary Clef Club Orchestras under the baton of James Reese Europe. Cook composed and arranged for that orchestra, which in 1912 broke "long-hair" precedent by playing New York's Carnegie Hall. On that occasion director Europe persuaded Cook (who had vowed never again to play violin in public) to sit in the violin section. Europe in return promised Cook the anonymity upon which the latter had insisted. But so stirring were Cook's arrangements of his own songs "Swing Along," "Exhortation," and "Rain Song" as to bring the audience out of its seats with cries of "a speech from the composer." Cook was too overcome with the emotions of gratitude to respond with more than a bow. The Carnegie Hall success took the musicians to Europe where, in London, they played a command performance at Buckingham Palace before moving on to Paris and other capital cities.

Back in America, radio's earliest public broadcasting programs demanded live music, and a Clef Club Orchestra directed by Will Marion Cook helped fill the need. Cook was thus able to provide opportunities to other talented performers. Among them were actor Richard Berry Harrison and a young singer named Paul Robeson. After Cook's death W. C. Handy reported: "I had emulated our greatest conductors in the use of the baton, but when I saw Cook conducting the Clef Club of a hundred musicians and singers with no baton; when I saw him set the tempo with the sway of his body and develop perfect crescendos without a baton by the use of his opened and extended palms, he again was my ideal." Similarly Duke Ellington, who often referred to Will Marion as "my conservatory," generously acknowledged his indebtedness in an interview in the *New Yorker* (July 8, 1944). Indeed "Dad" Cook's name is permanently linked with such luminaries of arts and letters as Scott Joplin, Harry T. Burleigh, Hall Johnson, Florenz Ziegfeld, the Schuberts, Countée Cullen, Arna Bontemps, and James Weldon Johnson. The last once wrote of him: "Cook was the most original genius among all the Negro musicians" (*Along This Way* [1933], p. 173).

He had a great interest in Negro history, particularly the career of Frederick Douglass, and in current events. For instance in 1938 he suggested that if Kelly Miller had read Edward Gibbon's *Rise* [*sic*] *and Fall of the Roman Empire,* he would not have supported Franklin D. Roosevelt for a third term (*Black Dispatch,* July 6, 1938).

Will Marion Cook died of cancer at Harlem Hospital, New York City, after an illness of four weeks. Funeral services were held at the Rodney Dade Funeral Home, 2332 Seventh Ave., with interment in Woodlawn Cemetery, Washington, D.C. He was survived by his son Mercer Cook, author and professor of romance languages at Howard University, later ambassador to Niger, Senegal, and the Gambia; and three grandchildren.

Black Manhattan by James Weldon Johnson (1930) is particularly valuable because of the author's appreciation of a contemporary fellow-composer. Loften Mitchell's *Black Drama* . . . (1967) and Tom Fletcher's *100 Years of the Negro in Show Business* (1957) give later perspectives. Valuable information was provided by Dr. Mercer Cook. There is an excellent article in *DAB, Supplement 3, 1941–1945* (pp. 187–88) by Eugene Levy. Obituaries were published in many papers, including the *New York Herald Tribune* and the *New York Times* (July 21, 1944). — ELTON C. FAX

COOPER, ANNA JULIA (1858–1964), educator. Born on Aug. 10, 1858, in Raleigh, N.C., the daughter of a slave, George Washington Haywood, and a free woman, Hannah (Stanley) Haywood, she was educated at St. Augustine's Normal and Collegiate Institute, Raleigh. On June 21, 1877, she married the Rev. George Christopher Cooper, an Episcopal clergyman and professor of Greek, who died two years later. She entered Oberlin College in 1881 and was graduated A.B. (1884) and A.M. (1887). In 1900 at the Pan-African Conference in London she read a paper "The Negro Problem in America" which described as pathetic an America that called itself Christian, and was named a member of the executive committee. Graduate study at La Guilde Internationale, Paris (1911–1912), and Columbia University (1913–1916) prepared her for her doctorate at the University of Paris (1925). Her dissertation, "Le Pélerinage de Charlemagne," a translation of an eleventh-century epic, is a rare college edition. She defended her thesis on the subject of slavery, "L'Attitude de la France à l'égard de l'Esclavage pendant la Révolution," with discussion of slavery and racial equality in America. This subject was probably chosen by her professors because of their interest and Cooper's knowledge. The doctorate was presented to her by representatives of the French Embassy on Dec. 29, 1925, at Howard University, under the auspices of Xi Omega chapter of Alpha Kappa Alpha sorority, of which she was a member.

An educator of rare courage and vision, Cooper was a pioneer in secondary education and civil rights. After student teaching at St. Augustine's Institute (1867–1881) and at Oberlin College (1881–1884), and teaching mathematics, and ancient and modern languages at Wilberforce University and St. Augustine's Institute (1885–1887), she taught thirty-nine years in Washington, D.C., first mathematics, later Latin (1887–1906, 1910–1930) with an interval (1906–1910) at Lincoln University, Mo. As principal of M Street High School (1901–1906) she won its acceptance by northern colleges, demonstrated by scholarships to its students. (Cooper to M.G.H.). Her insistence upon electives and exclusively academic courses provided college preparatory training and a tradition of high standards for almost half a century. M Street High School and Dunbar High School, its successor after 1916, were for many years the only academic high school for Negroes in Washington. Larger numbers of graduates of M Street and Dunbar, until recent years, won honors at more of the best universities in the nation than did Negroes from any other high school in the nation.

When teachers had no sabbatical leave, Cooper dared to go to Paris several times to earn her doctorate at the Sorbonne, at the risk of losing her job. On her return she bought a large home to rear five orphans, her nephew's children, just arrived from the South. Here, amid statues and Roman columns, she was hostess to a French-speaking group of teachers, "Les Amis de la Langue Française," with monthly meetings.

She advocated educational reforms to adjust the curriculum to the students' interests and needs. She protested against colonization and exploitation of the darker races, and pleaded for world peace and brotherhood.

Cooper was president of Frelinghuysen University (1930–1940) and its registrar (1940–1950). This was a group of evening schools for employed colored persons, with collegiate courses, including law and religion, and a volunteer faculty. Classes were held in her home, 201 T St. NW. Her last years were devoted to unsuccessful efforts for its recognition. She died in her sleep at the age of 105 on Feb. 29, 1964.

Cooper was the author of "Le Pèlèrinage de Charlemagne" and "L'Attitude de la France à l'égard de l'Esclavage pendant la Révolution," both in 1925; *Legislative Measures Concerning Slavery in the United States* (1942); and *Equality of Races and the Democratic Movement* (1945). In 1951 she edited *Life and Writings of the Grimké Family* (2 vols. in 1, 1951). She wrote also the words of the Dunbar Alma Mater (1924).

Valuable information is found in her autobiographies: *A Voice from the South by a Black Woman from the South* (1892); *Ten Years of Frelinghuysen, 1930–1941* (1941?); *My Second Decennial: The Third Step, 1941–1952* (n.d.); "The Humor of Teaching" (*The Crisis,* vol. 37). She was also included in *Who's Who in the East 1942–1948* and *Who's Who in the South and Southwest 1954.* Mary Gibson Hundley's *The Dunbar Story 1870–1895* (1965) contains a photograph and brief references to M Street High School, which became Dunbar High School in 1916. See also Louise Daniel Hutchinson's *Anna J. Cooper: A Voice from the South* (1981). — MARY GIBSON HUNDLEY

COOPER, JOHN W[ALCOTT] (1873–1966), pioneer ventriloquist. Cooper was a native of Brooklyn, N.Y. Little is known of his parents except that his father, John Cooper, came from Beaufort, S.C., and his mother, Annie, from Georgia. Both died while their son was still a small boy. The child, meanwhile, received his formal schooling at Professor Dorsey's Institute in downtown Brooklyn. Because of his small stature, young Cooper became an exercise boy at the nearby Sheepshead Bay racetrack. There his attention was initially drawn to ventriloquism by a white practitioner who liked to visit the stables. The ventriloquist, hoping to frighten the exercise boy into believing the horses "talked," would slyly practice his craft around the animals' stalls. But young Cooper, wise to the pranks of track habitués, listened with no fear and with more than casual amusement.

With his keen intelligence, good singing voice, and a flair for showmanship, the lad soon joined a vocal group called "The Southern Jubilee Singers," and continued to dream of a career in ventriloquism. For four years as he trouped with the singers through Canada, New England, and the Middle Atlantic states, he studied and practiced the ventriloquist's deceptive art. Then in 1900, at age twenty-seven, he made his debut with the Richards and Pringles Minstrels.

The time was most opportune. New York City's choice vaudeville stages were being struck by white performers. Their action opened the way for little-known Negro artists whose talents extended beyond traditional singing and dancing into the area of specialty and novelty acts. Ventriloquist Cooper was ready. In addition to playing New York he was engaged in 1901 as a special feature of Rusco and Holland's Big Minstrel Festival, a traveling troupe. John Cooper's immediate success was due in large measure to his inventive mind. Moreover he was made to order for the restrictive demands of vaudeville whose performers rarely had more than ten minutes on stage. In that brief span they had to establish rapport with audiences, display consummate skill, and move quickly into a "wow-finish" climax. In addition, their material had to be "clean" if they hoped to perform in the best theaters. Cooper fulfilled every requirement.

From the very outset he wrote his own material and continued to do so throughout his sixty years as a performer. His earliest skit, "Fun in a Barber Shop," not only created a sensation with audiences everywhere but also won the respect of critics and fellow showmen. In that sketch Cooper appeared as a barber in a shop of his own design occupied by five "customers" and himself. Using no assistants, he rigged his figures with wires and operated them with foot pedals from his position at the barber's chair. One of the figures was wired to "walk unaided" across the stage. And using five different voices along with his own natural voice, Cooper created a scene of completely believable barbershop hilarity. No other ventriloquist had ever equaled that accomplishment. The *Seattle Post Intelligence* in 1902 said: "He introduces five characters, one of which is a mechanical walking figure. He talks in six different voices and within a second's time three distinct voices are heard." And the *Daily Nonpariel* of Council Bluffs, Iowa, called him "The most talented ventriloquist ever seen in this city" (Feb. 2, 1902).

For the next twenty-five years Cooper successfully took his act into the nation's leading vaudeville houses, lodge halls, and private clubs. Although vaudeville grew to the point where it developed its own monopolies, it was destined to wither and die with the advent of sound films, radio, and in the wake of the financial depression of the 1930s.

However, Maj. Edward Bowes, an impresario of the period, provided work for many performers through his weekly radio show, "The Major Bowes Original Amateur Hour." Winners and runners-up, many of them unemployed professionals, subsequently traveled about the country under pseudonyms with the Major Bowes troupes. Cooper, having replaced his barbershop skit with a single figure named Sam, trouped with Major Bowes units under the name of Hezikiah Jones. With America's entry into World War II the sixty-eight-year-old Cooper and his wooden partner Sam toured the United States with the USO camp shows. Their performances took them not only into servicemen's camps and clubs but into veterans hospitals as well. At one point, because of his vast experience, Cooper was called upon in an emergency temporarily to manage the company with which he was traveling. New York City's fashionable East Side nightclubs The Kit Kat and El Morocco, along with the Hotel Lexington, featured Cooper and Sam. The latter, often referred to by his alter ego as the "cousin" of Edgar Bergen's Charley McCarthy, had indeed been carved by Theodore Mack of Chicago who had also carved the McCarthy figure.

Cooper was well known to and highly regarded by his fellow ventriloquists. Among them were Reynard, the Great Lester, the Great Howard, J. W. Winton, and Edgar Bergen. Cooper was once engaged by a magician friend to give lessons in ventriloquism to the magician's young daughter. The girl learned well; she became widely known to television audiences as Shari Lewis. In the late years of his distinguished career, Cooper worked private dates. He was especially fond of entertaining children, which he did with equal gusto in the open wards of New York City's hospitals and in the drawing rooms of wealthy patrons.

John W. Cooper was a member of the Knights of Magic, the International Brotherhood of Ventriloquists, the Negro Actors Guild, and the Colored Vaudeville Benevolent Association.

Upon the death in 1960 of his second wife, Juliana St. Bernard, whom he had married about 1928, he retired from show business at the age of eighty-seven. He died of diseases incident to old age. Funeral services were held at St. Peter Claver's Church, Brooklyn, with interment at St. John's Cemetery of Middle Village, Queens. He was survived by his only daughter, Mrs. Edward Maynard.

For further information, see Tom Fletcher's *100 Years of the Negro in Show Business* (1954) and the papers of John W. Cooper (c/o his daughter, Mrs. Edward Maynard [née Joan Cooper], Brooklyn). —ELTON C. FAX

COPELAND, JOHN ANTHONY, JR. (1836–1859), one of John Brown's men at Harpers Ferry. Born in Raleigh, N.C., of free parents, Copland grew up in Ohio. He was attending Oberlin College when he was jailed for helping a fugitive slave. He and his uncle, Lewis Leary, were recruited for service with John Brown by John Kagi, Brown's most trusted lieutenant. He went to Virginia with his uncle, arriving at the farm near Harpers Ferry in late September 1859. Brown assembled there seventeen white men and five Negroes for his planned attack on the government's gun factories and warehouses at Harpers Ferry. For nearly three weeks Copeland was in hiding with the others at the farm. During that time Brown and the experienced leaders gave the new recruits instructions and some military training.

On Sunday morning, Oct. 16, 1859, Brown assembled his men for worship. He offered a solemn prayer asking God to assist in the liberation of the slaves. Without being told, Copeland knew that the time for action had come. In the afternoon Brown gave his final orders. Three men were to be left at the farm, a rear guard to advance later with supplies. Two others were to capture the lone guard on the bridge leading across the river into the town. Each man was given specific tasks. Copeland was to advance with John Kagi, to seize and hold the rifle factory. The factory was on an island in the rocky and shallow waters of the Shenandoah River. Some of the men were to arouse the slaves in the area and bring them into the service. Slave recruits would be sent to the rifle factory to Copeland and Kagi.

Rain was falling that night when the party started their five-mile march from the farm to the town. They did not talk. They met no one on the road. At the bridge the guard was taken by surprise. Telegraph lines were cut.

The men crossed the river, and moving swiftly, they captured the guards at the armory where heavy military equipment was made and the arsenal where guns and ammunition were stored. Kagi and Copeland went to the rifle factory and captured the watchman. All of this was done without firing a shot. But the town was aroused and the alarm went out. Local citizens, in panic, started firing at the invaders and by morning the local people were joined by militiamen.

Lewis Leary and four newly liberated slaves (whose names are not recorded) were first to arrive to be with Copeland and Kagi at the rifle factory. Others reached the factory later. In the afternoon well-organized militia units were in the town. John Brown was barricaded with most of his party at the armory. The rifle factory came under heavy attack. Some of Kagi's men were killed. The last of them tried to escape by withdrawing across the river, firing as they went. Four of them, including Kagi, were killed. Copeland was taken alive after his gun, wet with river water, would not fire. He was jailed at Charlestown with John Brown and the others who were captured later. While he was held in jail and during his brief trial his courage and bearing won the respect of all who saw him. The prosecuting attorney stated: "From my intercourse with him I regard him as one of the most respectable persons we had. . . . He was a copper-colored Negro, behaved himself with as much firmness as any of them, and with far more dignity. If it had been possible to recommend a pardon for any of them it would have been this man Copeland as I regretted as much if not more, at seeing him executed than any other of the party" (W. E. B. Du Bois, *John Brown* [1909], p. 281).

On Dec. 16, 1859, he was hanged beside Shields Green, whom some called the Emperor. As he went to the scaffold he shouted, "I am dying for freedom. I could not die for a better cause. I had rather die than be a slave."

Osborne P. Anderson's *A Voice From Harpers Ferry* (1861) is the only eyewitness account by one of the participants. W. E. B. Du Bois's *John Brown* (1909) gives details about the raid at Harpers Ferry.

—LORENZ GRAHAM

COPPIN, FANNY MURIEL JACKSON (1837–1913), educator, lecturer, and missionary. Fanny was born a slave in Washington, D.C. Her maternal grandfather saved enough money to buy himself and, subsequently, four of his six children. One of his children, whom he did not buy, was Fanny's mother Lucy. "On account of my birth," wrote Fanny, "my grandfather refused to buy my mother." However, Fanny's Aunt Sarah, who was purchased by Fanny's grandfather, recognized Fanny's potential. Mrs. Sarah Clark went to work for six dollars a month, saved $125, and bought Fanny's freedom. Afterward her Aunt Sarah sent her to New Bedford, Mass., where another aunt lived. There Fanny obtained employment and was able to go to school when she was not working. At age fourteen Fanny went to Newport, R.I., with Elizabeth Orr, an aunt by marriage, who offered Fanny a home and better schooling. Fanny's great sense of independence would not allow her to rely solely on Mrs. Orr. Therefore, she secured employment in the home of George H. Calvert and his wife, Elizabeth Stuart Calvert, the descendants of aristocrats. For a while she took private lessons at the Calvert home under a Mrs. Little for one hour every other afternoon. In her spare time she also took piano lessons in her aunt's home. When the private schooling under Mrs. Little ended, Fanny attended the "public colored school" for a few months in order to prepare herself to take the examination for the Rhode Island State Normal School, in Bristol. Mrs. Calvert did not want Fanny to leave Newport, and Fanny did not want to leave, for the two women had become very close friends. "My life there was most happy," Fanny wrote, "and I never would have left her [Mrs. Calvert], but it was in me to get an education and to teach my people. This idea was deep in my soul. Where it came from I cannot tell. . . . It must have been born in me."

At the Rhode Island State Normal School, under Dana P. Colburn, Fanny's interest in teaching was redoubled. After she completed her studies at the Rhode Island State Normal School, she entered Oberlin College in 1860, with the financial help of her Aunt Sarah and the aid of Bishop Daniel A. Payne of the African Methodist Episcopal church, who gave her a scholarship of nine dollars a year. Oberlin, founded in 1834, admitted female students from the beginning. It was not only the first coeducational college, but it was also the first recognized college to admit Negroes. At Oberlin, Fanny studied Latin, Greek, and mathematics. In addition one of the college professors gave her private lessons in French because it was not part of the curriculum. Fanny had also studied French at the Rhode Island State Normal School. In her junior year at Oberlin (1863), the year of the Emancipation Proclamation and the New York draft riots, which had racial overtones, Fanny was chosen to be a pupil-teacher. It was the custom at Oberlin to employ forty students from the junior and senior classes to teach the preparatory classes, but a Negro student had never before been chosen. Fanny's undertaking was an experiment. She was told that the faculty would not force the students to accept her if they rebelled against her teaching. They did not rebel, "tho there was a little surprise on the faces of some when they came into the class." The class actually increased in number to the extent that it became necessary to divide it. At the insistence of the students Fanny was given both divisions. One of the classes greatly increased in number again, but the faculty decided that Fanny had enough work and that she could not handle another class. In addition to teaching classes Fanny gave private music lessons to sixteen students. During her last year at the college she organized an evening class to teach freedmen, who had come to Ohio from the South, how to read and write. Fanny's achievements at Oberlin included her election as class poet and the presentation of her graduation essay in French.

The year 1865 marked a new beginning not only for Fanny but for the entire nation. The Civil War ended in April and four months later Fanny graduated from Oberlin, thus becoming one of the earliest Negro female college graduates in the country. When she graduated, a job was waiting for her. A year before her gradu-

ation the Institute for Colored Youth, founded by the Society of Friends in Philadelphia in 1837, had requested Oberlin to send them "a colored woman who could teach Greek, Latin, and high mathematics." Fanny was that woman. At the institute, she wrote, "I was given the delightful task of teaching my own people, and how delighted I was to see them mastering Caesar, Virgil, Cicero, Horace and Xenophon's Anabasis." Many distinguished Americans and Europeans often visited the school. On one occasion Gen. O. O. Howard was brought into a class to hear an examination on Virgil. General Howard remarked that "Negroes in trigonometry and the classics might well share the triumphs of their brothers on the battlefield."

The institute's principal, Ebenezer D. Bassett, was appointed U.S. minister to Haiti in 1869 by President Grant. Leadership of the institute fell upon Octavius V. Catto and Fanny Jackson. Catto took charge of the boys' department, and Jackson headed the girls' department. Jackson soon became principal. The change in leadership brought about new dimensions in the institute's program. A growing demand by surrounding states for public school teachers who were trained to teach the three Rs and the social studies convinced her that the time spent on teaching Greek, Latin, and the classics could be better used by providing normal training. A normal school program was initiated, and according to Miss Jackson, "these students became so efficient in their work that they were sought for and engaged to teach long before they finished their course of study." The normal training program consisted of English studies, the theory of teaching, school management, methods, and practice teaching in the Preparatory Department.

The next project that Jackson undertook was the crusade to establish an Industrial Department at the institute, in order to train students who desired a trade. She thought that it was "cruel to make a teacher or a preacher of a man who ought to be a printer or a blacksmith." That was precisely the situation, for few Negroes could find positions as apprentices in industries and businesses, and there were few opportunities for institutional industrial training in the decades following the Civil War. Hampton Institute (1866), Tuskegee Institute (1881), and the Philadelphia Institute for Colored Youth were among the early schools to provide vocational training for young Negroes. The Quaker who gave the first endowment for the founding of the Institute for Colored Youth, Richard Humphreys, stipulated that it should not only teach higher literary studies, but that a Mechanical and Industrial Department, including agriculture, should come within the scope of its work. However it was not until 1879 that the institute, under Jackson's leadership, began its push to establish an Industrial Department. Jackson, with the support of the institute's managers and teachers, began in earnest to raise funds for the establishment of the new department. As field agent she had the responsibility of enlightening communities on the necessity of industrial education. To achieve this goal she gave speeches in Philadelphia and suburban towns, New York, Washington, D.C., and everywhere she could get a sympathetic and attentive audience, which was not difficult for Miss

Jackson, a platform speaker with few equals. Also, in the interest of industrial education she organized a fair in November 1879, initially to raise adequate funds to liquidate the debts of the *Christian Recorder,* a Philadelphia Negro paper which had been started in 1852. The long-range effect of saving the paper, according to Jackson, was "to keep open an honorable vocation to colored men." Individuals representing twenty-four states donated articles and money to the fair. Many of the articles were made by the donors. Needlework, crochet work, worsted work, sculpture, decorated plates, and paintings were among the articles on exhibit and for sale. The fair was a success; it demonstrated the virtues of self-help and collective action, and at the same time, promoted the cause of industrial training.

One of the more personal consequences of the fair was Jackson's introduction to the Rev. Levi J. Coppin, pastor of the Philadelphia Bethel Church, and later bishop of the A.M.E. church. In 1881 they were married in the 19th Street Baptist Church in Washington, D.C., the home of Jackson's aunt, Sarah Clark. Although Levi Coppin wanted his new bride to give up teaching, Mrs. Coppin had a different opinion. "She had a fixed course in life, and stubbornly maintained it until it became a fixed habit," according to her husband. Thus, "the school room habit clung." In addition, Mrs. Coppin was determined to continue her industrial education crusade. After many years of giving speeches and raising funds, the institute expanded its grounds and erected a building for teaching trades to students who desired such training. When the Industrial Department was fully established, young men were taught bricklaying, plastering, carpentry, shoemaking, printing, and tailoring. Women were taught dressmaking, millinery, typing, stenography, and cooking. Men also took classes in the last three subjects.

In an effort to find work for the women students with vocational training, Mrs. Coppin organized an Industrial Exchange. Women exhibited samples of their sewing, millinery, and cooking. Items were displayed at the institute, as well as in churches. Because of racial prejudice, Mrs. Coppin realized that the work of finding jobs for her students was just as important as their training. The work of the institute attracted students from other cities and states. Mrs. Coppin opened her home to some of the women students from out of town; but the number became so great that the Coppins rented a ten-room dwelling next to their home as a dormitory. Those who could not pay board did light housekeeping at the dormitory.

After her marriage, Mrs. Coppin became very active in the A.M.E. church's missionary work. In 1888 foreign missionary societies sent delegates to the Centenary of Missions, held in London. As president of the Women's Home and Foreign Missionary Society of the A.M.E. church, she was elected a delegate to represent the society at that meeting. The London trip was her first abroad. Her participation in the meeting not only manifested her missionary zeal, but it also demonstrated her support of the right of women to use their minds in whatever capacity they could. In recounting her experiences at the meeting, she recalled the speech of a Presbyterian minister who repeatedly told the women that

they should not assume ecclesiastical functions. "This got me riled," reported Mrs. Coppin, "and in reply I tried to make it plain that the Lord God alone gives the limit to the functions of woman's religious work." Mrs. Coppin took the zeal that characterized her teaching into her missionary work. To her, "the spirit of mission work, is the spirit of sharing all we have." She believed that "the greatest of blessings, and the truest happiness is to share all that you have with those who need it." The application of this philosophy could not have been more apparent than it had been in her school work, which came to an end in 1902. The Rev. Levi Coppin was elected a bishop of the A.M.E. church in 1900 and was assigned to Cape Town, South Africa. Mrs. Coppin joined him there on Nov. 30, 1902. In her memoir she wrote that "after having spent thirty-seven years in the school room, laboring to give a correct start in life to the youth that came under my influence, it was indeed, to me, a fortunate incident to finish my active work right in Africa, the home of the ancestors of those whose lives I had endeavored to direct."

While she was in Africa Mrs. Coppin organized temperance and missionary societies at Bethel Institute, the mission house that Bishop Coppin had established before she joined him in the field. In spite of the fact that she had reached her sixty-fifth birthday, she traveled as far as 1360 miles from their headquarters at Cape Town in order to establish missions and to talk with the "native and colored women upon the subjects of righteousness, temperance and the judgment to come."

The Coppins returned to their home in Philadelphia in the spring of 1904. Mrs. Coppin's health began to fail her, and for the next eight years she was practically confined to the house. "Years of constant and strenuous work began to tell on an iron constitution that had responded so faithfully to the call of duty," wrote one eulogist. She died of arteriosclerosis in Philadelphia on Jan. 21, 1913, and was buried in Merion Cemetery.

During the last years of her life she wrote *Reminiscences of School Life, and Hints on Teaching* (1913), an unpretentious, but eloquent autobiography. Bishop Coppin's *Unwritten History* (1913) also briefly portrays her life. In addition, a tribute to her work is found in the *A.M.E. Church Review* (Jan. 1901). See also the article by Leslie H. Fishel, Jr., in *NAW* (1971, 3:383–85). — DOROTHY DRINKARD-HAWKSHAWE

COPPIN, LEVI JENKINS (1848–1924), thirtieth bishop of the African Methodist Episcopal church, editor, and missionary. Coppin was born in Frederick Town, Md., on the Eastern Shore. His parents, Jane Lilly and John Coppin, were free persons; therefore he and his three brothers and three sisters were born free. His mother was a very religious woman who had a profound influence on his life. In addition to giving him religious training, she taught him to read and write. Although it was against a state law before the end of the Civil War to educate Negroes, his mother held classes secretly in her home at night and on Sunday mornings before church. Coppin assisted his mother in this task. As a teenager he had a reputation for being able to read and write, and boys began going to him to have their love letters written. For this service he charged ten cents a letter, and according to Coppin "they gladly paid." Coppin also earned money by working on farms. At age twelve he earned $20 and a suit of clothes for ten months of work, but in 1861, his salary was increased to $32 and a suit of clothes for the same period of work.

Near the close of the Civil War in 1865, Sunday classes for Negroes were openly held at Friendship Church, which in 1866 became part of the A.M.E. church. Coppin became the school's first teacher. Horace Brown, from Baltimore, was its first principal. Friendship Institute, as it was called, was the first school in Cecil County where colored people openly learned to read and write. In January 1866 a regular day school for Negroes was established in the county. Levi studied at the day school for two terms under Sarah Christmas, a certified teacher, and then became a day school teacher. In addition to his day school teaching, he was elected superintendent of the Friendship Sunday School, six months after he had been converted to Christianity in 1865. Thereafter he began to study the Scriptures in earnest. A realization of his limitations, and a burning desire to prepare himself for the "highest and best purpose" in life, motivated him to seek a higher education. The task was not easy without financial means. He went to Philadelphia in February 1869, but did not remain long. In the same year he traveled to Wilmington, Del., where he remained until 1877. Many changes took place in his life while in Wilmington. He cast his first vote at age twenty, as the law allowed citizens to vote "on age," which meant that one was approaching twenty-one, the legal voting age. Coppin favored the Republican party because it made freedom and the vote possible for Negroes. In Wilmington he learned to read music, first under James Crozier, the leader of the Ezion Church choir, then under Peter S. Blake and James A. Anderson. After listening to an insulting sermon by a visiting white minister, he moved his church membership from Ezion to the Bethel A.M.E. Church and became a member of the Bethel choir. When the leader of the latter choir, Josiah Loans, died, Levi was unanimously elected by the members to succeed him. In September 1875 Coppin married his first wife, Martha Grinnage, a Wilmington schoolteacher. This union produced a male child, who died nine months after his birth; Coppin's wife followed the child in death eighteen days later. Thus his first marriage ended after only eighteen months. While in Wilmington, Coppin worked at the brickyard of James Beggs. After a few years he had saved enough money to open a retail flour business with a company of young men— Collins, Coppin & Co. The bitter lesson of experience taught that too much extended credit was unsound business. After the business closed, he taught school at Smyrna, Del.

In the spring of 1877 Coppin entered the ministry from Bethel A.M.E. Church in Wilmington. His first charge was the Philadelphia City Mission, a circuit of missions consisting of the Morris Brown Mission, the St. James Mission, and the Kingsessing or Pascalville Mission. After two years of service and required study Coppin was ordained a deacon at his second conference, and was sent to the Bethel Church in Philadelphia as an assistant to the Rev. George C. Whitfield, who was in poor health. The latter died and Coppin became the temporary pastor. Upon the insistence of Bethel's parishioners and the consent of the Morris Brown Mission, to whom Bishop Daniel A. Payne had promised to return Coppin, his appointment at Bethel was made permanent. At this point Coppin was not a full-fledged minister. The completion of his fourth year in Philadelphia (1881) qualified Coppin to be ordained a minister. In 1881 he was transferred to the Baltimore Conference, where he was pastor of the Baltimore Bethel Church. In the same year he married Fanny Jackson, principal of the Philadelphia Institute for Colored Youth. Coppin remained at the Baltimore Bethel Church until 1884.

At the General Conference of 1884 the *A.M.E. Church Review* had its birth. Benjamin Tucker Tanner, later Bishop Tanner, was its first editor. At this conference, Coppin, at his own request, was appointed to Allen Chapel, a small and self-sustaining church in Philadelphia. The assignment gave him the opportunity to study theology at the Protestant Episcopal Divinity School in West Philadelphia (1884–1887). In 1888 he succeeded Tanner as editor of the *A.M.E. Church Review*. With few funds, he could not pay for articles which appeared in the *Review,* but persons with literary talents were sympathetic and church members contributed their articles gratutitously. Among the many contributors to the *Review* during Coppin's editorship were Bishops Payne, Turner, Campbell, Dickerson, and Ward, Mrs. F. E. W. Harper, Judge D. A. Straker, Prof. W. S. Scarborough, B. K. Bruce, the Rev. J. H. Durant, the Rev. William H. Thomas, Dr. T. G. Steward, T. Thomas Fortune, T. McCants Stewart, and Frederick Douglass. The *Review* served as an important source of information on significant religious, political, economic, and social issues from its inception. Coppin remained editor of the *Review* until 1896, when H. T. Kealing was elected editor at the General Conference of that year. Coppin was a candidate for the bishopric at the 1896 Conference, but he was not elected. Instead, the conference appointed him pastor of the Philadelphia Bethel Church for a second term. His second term expired in 1900, and at the General Conference of 1900 he was again a candidate for bishop. This time he was elected, and was assigned to the Fourteenth District, in Cape Town, South Africa. While in South Africa he organized Bethel Institute, a mission house at Cape Town; and he and his wife Fanny Jackson Coppin traveled far into the interior of Africa to establish missions and to spread the Gospel. His assignment in South Africa ended in 1904 when he and his wife returned to their home in Philadelphia. At the General Conference in 1904 Coppin was assigned to the Seventh Episcopal District, which consisted of South Carolina and Alabama. In 1908 he was assigned to the Second Episcopal District (North Carolina, Virginia, Washington, D.C., and Maryland). In 1912 he was returned to the Second Episcopal District, but before the end of the four-year term he was transferred to the Seventh District.

In January 1913 his second wife died, and once again loneliness and sadness surrounded him. He wrote: "everything about my life seemed so indefinite, uncertain, unreal. . . . I took to smoke. Thank God I did not take to drink." After more than a year of mourning, he married a Baltimore physician, M. Evelyn Thompson, on Aug. 1, 1914. A year and a half later this union resulted in the birth of a daughter, Theodosia.

In 1916 the General Conference assigned him to the Fourth Episcopal District (Kentucky, Indiana, Illinois, Wisconsin, Iowa, Minnesota, North Dakota, South Dakota, and Winnipeg, Dominion of Canada). In 1919 his autobiography, *Unwritten History,* was published. Five years later his lifelong work as a minister came to an end at age seventy-six. He died at his home in Philadelphia.

Information concerning Coppin's life and work can be obtained from his *Unwritten History* (1919) and *Letters from South Africa* (n.d.), and Fanny Jackson Coppin's *Reminiscences of School Life, and Hints on Teaching* (1913). — DOROTHY DRINKARD-HAWKSHAWE

CORBIN, JOSEPH CARTER (1833–1911), government official, journalist, and university president. Corbin, who was to serve as Arkansas state superintendent of public instruction during Reconstruction and later as the founder and president of the first Negro institution of higher education in Arkansas, was born in Chillicothe, Ohio, on March 26, 1833, of free Negro parents, William and Susan Corbin. By attending several small schools he managed to secure a basic education and in 1850 entered the Ohio University of Athens, Ohio. He received his bachelor's degree in 1853 and a master's in 1856. Before receiving his graduate degree Corbin had accepted employment with a Cincinnati bank. Later he taught in a Louisville, Ky., school. During the Civil War Corbin edited a Cincinnati newspaper, the *Colored Citizen.* In 1866 he married Mary Jane Ward. The couple had six children, two of whom survived the father.

Corbin and his family moved to Little Rock, Ark., in 1872 where he accepted employment as a reporter for the Republican party newspaper, the *Daily Republican.* Like many other Negroes of that day, Corbin rose quickly in the ranks of the party and in 1872 he was nominated for state superintendent of public instruction on the ticket of the regular Republican faction. He narrowly defeated the incumbent, Thomas Smith, a white physician who was the nominee of a rival faction. Corbin was unable to complete his term in office because of the success of the "Redeemer" Democrats who assumed power in Arkansas in 1874. He left the state after the return of Democratic rule and accepted a teaching position at the Lincoln Institute, Jefferson City, Mo.

Despite his rather short tenure as superintendent of public instruction, Corbin was instrumental in laying the groundwork for an institution of higher learning for Arkansas Negroes. When the Democrats assumed control of the university they called upon Corbin to return to Arkansas and establish Branch Normal College in Pine Bluff, Ark., a unit of the state university. On Sept. 27, 1875, Corbin opened the school with seven students. A majority of the early students took preparatory work since few had received an adequate education before reaching Corbin's new school. Although constantly plagued by the lack of proper funds and staff, Corbin was able in 1880 to convince the university trustees to

appropriate funds for a permanent building to replace the cramped rented facilities. It was not until 1883 that Corbin was authorized to hire an assistant teacher. By 1893 he had a staff of five.

Despite Corbin's success as an educator he began experiencing harassment from the state legislature. In 1893 Corbin's Republican party affiliation apparently caused his school to be investigated. In April 1893 the legislature recommended that Corbin be fired because of alleged financial and managerial inability. While he was not fired by the university trustees, he was, however, relieved of his managerial responsibilities, which were turned over to the white foreman of the industrial shops, William S. Harris. Finally, in 1902 Corbin's opponents were able to persuade the trustees to dismiss Corbin and replace him with a young Negro educator from Tuskegee Institute, Isaac Fisher. Corbin did not accept his forced retirement gracefully. Rather, he undertook an appeal for reinstatement, which he lost.

After leaving Branch Normal College in 1902, Corbin became principal of Merrill High School in Pine Bluff. During 1902–1903 he served as state president of the Colored Teachers Association. He also kept up his Freemasonry activities and in 1903 led in the building of a large masonic temple in Pine Bluff. Corbin died in Pine Bluff on Jan. 9, 1911, and was buried in Chicago.

Corbin's tenure as head of Branch Normal College has been ably treated in Thomas Rothrock's "Joseph Carter Corbin and Negro Education in the University of Arkansas" (*Arkansas Historical Quarterly* 30 [Winter 1971]: 277–314). Brief references to Corbin may also be found in John Hugh Reynolds's and David Yancey Thomas's *History of the University of Arkansas* (1910) and T. M. Stinnett's and Clara B. Kennan's *All This and Tomorrow Too* (1969). The brief sketch in William J. Simmons's *Men of Mark . . .* (1887, pp. 829–33) contains some undocumented information.

— TOM W. DILLARD

CORNISH, SAMUEL E[LI] (1795–1858), abolitionist and editor. Cornish was born of free parents in Sussex County, Del. Of his youth little is known. In 1815 he went to Philadelphia where he received an elementary education and was trained for the ministry by John Gloucester, pastor of the First African Church, Presbyterian. He was licensed to preach in 1819, and the next year spent six months as a missionary to slaves on Maryland's Eastern Shore. In 1821 he organized the New Demeter Street Presbyterian Church in New York City where he was ordained in 1822 and where he preached until 1828. In 1824 he married Jane Livingston (d. 1844). Their four children were Sarah Matilda (1824–1846), William (1826– ?), Samuel (1828–1838), and Jane Sophia Tappan (1833–1855). Between 1824 and 1846 Cornish labored extensively as an itinerant preacher and missionary to Negroes in the New York City area and also served several parishes. In 1831–1832 he was pastor of Gloucester's Philadelphia church, and in 1843 he ministered to the Negro Presbyterian church in Newark, N.J. In 1845 or 1846 he organized Emmanuel Church in New York City and was its pastor until 1847. After 1833 he considered New York his permanent home. But in 1838, stung by prejudice directed against his children, he moved his family first to Belleville, N.J., and then in 1840 to Newark. In 1845, following his wife's death, he returned to New York. Plagued in his later years by the sickness of his daughter Jane and by his own poor health, Cornish moved to Brooklyn in 1855 and died there on Nov. 6, 1858. He was buried in Greenwood cemetery.

Besides being a clergyman, Cornish twice edited newspapers in New York. With John B. Russwurm in the spring of 1827 he established *Freedom's Journal,* the first Negro newspaper in the United States. After he resigned in September the paper, under Russwurm's sole editorship, declined. In 1829 Cornish revived it as *The Rights of All,* which lasted about a year. Cornish's principal editorial post was with the *Colored American,* successor to the short-lived *Weekly Advocate,* founded in March 1837 by Philip Bell and subsidized briefly by Arthur Tappan. Cornish served either as sole or joint editor until mid-1839, for the first two of the paper's four-year existence.

Cornish also served missionary, antislavery, and other reform causes through various benevolent organizations. Among those in which he held office were the New York African Free Schools (agent, 1827–1829); American Anti-Slavery Society (a founder; executive committee, 1833–1838; agent, 1834, 1837, 1840); New York City Vigilance Committee (executive committee, 1835–1837); American Moral Reform Society (vice-president, 1835–1836); American and Foreign Anti-Slavery Society (executive committee, 1840–1841, 1847–1853); American Bible Society (manager, 1835); Union Missionary Society (manager, 1842); American Missionary Association (a founder; executive committee, 1846–1855; vice-president, 1848–1858). He also helped found the New York Anti-Slavery Society in 1833, was active in the New York City Phoenix Society, a mutual aid and educational group during the 1830s, and participated in the early Convention Movement (1830–1837).

Cornish won lasting recognition by his antislavery activity and his efforts to improve the condition of free Negroes in the North. In whatever he undertook he stressed the efficacy of education, the desirability of cultivating hard work and frugal habits in a rural atmosphere, and the desirability of racial advancement. Convinced that American Negroes must find their future in the United States, in 1840 he wrote with Theodore S. Wright a long pamphlet condemning the American Colonization Society's program, *The Colonization Scheme Considered, in Its Rejection by the Coloured People— in Its Tendency to Uphold Caste—in Its Unfitness for Christianizing and Civilizing the Aborigines of Africa, and for Putting a Stop to the African Slave Trade . . .* (1840).

Such values and aspirations served Cornish well during the 1830s, but even then he was highly critical of much race action. Unhappy with its lack of zeal, he soon broke with the American Moral Reform Society and the Garrisonian multireformism it represented. Opposed to the occasionally illegal methods of David Ruggles, who dominated the New York City Vigilance Committee and directed its aid to fugitive slaves, Cornish also dropped out of its work. When the mood and methods of abolitionism and civil rights efforts changed in the 1840s and 1850s, he disagreed with much in their programs. He had been an active Garrisonian; but as a conservative cleric he was in the late 1830s driven by the American Anti-Slavery Society's anticlericalism into the rival American and Foreign Anti-Slavery Society, whose support of the Liberty party soon alienated him. Similarly, when in the 1840s his younger Negro colleagues moved to exclusive race conventions and political action, Cornish held back as he did subsequently in the 1850s when many supported emigration and intense militance. Sympathetic though Cornish tried to be, he responded within the limits set in the 1830s. Although he had become peripheral by the mid-1840s, his role in Negro abolitionism was of real importance. He tried to bridge factions rather than lead them, and in so doing provided a channel for maximum interchange.

Sources for the study of Cornish's life and thought are limited. Indispensable are the files of *Freedom's Journal, The Rights of All,* and particularly the *Colored American,* in which he developed his most mature ideas. The most recent study of Cornish is Jane H. Pease's and William H. Pease's "The Negro Conservative: Samuel Eli Cornish" (in *Bound with Them in Chains: A Biographical History of the Antislavery Movement* [1972], pp. 140–61). There are numerous references in *They Would Be Free . . .* (1974) by the same authors. —JANE H. PEASE *and* WILLIAM H. PEASE

CORROTHERS, JAMES DAVID (1869–1917), clergyman and poet. He was born in the "Chain Lake Settlement," Calvin, near Cassapolis, Mich., on July 2, 1869. This community in southern Michigan had been originally founded by fugitive slaves and free Negroes. His mother, Maggie (Churchman) Corrothers, was part Negro and part French, and his father, James Richard Corrothers, had a Negro mother. His mother died in childbirth, and the boy was reared in South Haven, Mich., by his paternal grandfather, who was of Indian and Scottish-Irish ancestry. James attended public schools there from 1874 to 1883 and, because he was the only Negro, had to fight white boys to go to school in peace. He worked in lumber camps, sawmills, hotels, sailed the lakes for a season, was a bootblack in a barbershop, coachman, waiter, boxing instructor, and janitor in a newspaper office. Encouraged by Henry D. Lloyd and Frances E. Willard, he attended Northwestern University from 1890 to 1893. He also attended Bennett College, Greensboro, N.C. He worked his way up from a janitor to a "space writer" on the staff of the *Chicago Tribune.* Although newspaper work was Corrothers's first love, the Chicago editors did not feel that the city was ready for a Negro columnist. Although he contributed special articles to the *Record, Daily News,* and *Journal,* his work was often revised and published under the name of a white author.

Discouraged by the bigotry of the newspaper world, he began to see the church as an important factor in the progress of the race. Ordained to the Methodist ministry in 1894, he held pastorates at Bath, N.Y., and Red Bank and Hackensack, N.J. He later joined the Baptist denomination and built and presided over the Union

Baptist Church of South Haven. He also held pastorates in Dowagiac, Mich., and Lexington, Va., preaching occasionally in Washington, D.C. He taught theology and sacred oratory at the Wilbank Institute, served as assistant secretary of the educational board of the National Baptist Convention, and preached at Haverhill, Mass. In 1914 he became a minister in the Presbyterian church and held a pastorate at West Chester, Pa., for several years. He had a reputation as an elocutionist and temperance advocate. An energetic worker, he saved several bankrupt churches and returned to his native state to establish churches in rural areas where Negroes had been denied church participation.

His newspaper sketches were later published as *The Black Cat Club: Negro Humor and Folk-lore* (1902). Although the work was severely criticized and he later regretted its publication, it is nevertheless an important, pioneering book of humorous Negro literature. Corrothers admired Paul Laurence Dunbar's stories and poems because they gave a beauty and new dignity to Negro dialect. Encouraged by Dunbar's success, he began to write dialect poems and a number of them were accepted by newspapers and magazines. *Selected Poems* was published in 1907 and *The Dream and the Song* in 1914, with an introduction by Ray Stannard Baker. One of his best known poems, "The Negro Singer," was written in memory of Dunbar. His autobiography, *In Spite of the Handicap* (1916), reflected not only his own experiences but focused attention on the lifestyle of northern rural Negroes at a time when southern Negroes were the center of national attention. Life in the "wilds" of Michigan, he wrote, was much the same for a black man as for a white man. He grew up "western-style" and differed from his white counterparts in color more than in habits. His speech and ways were those of the white community around him, and this was true of "every colored writer who has attained any particular degree of success in America," especially Phillis Wheatley, Dunbar, W. E. B. Du Bois, and William Stanley Braithwaite. However, as a public man and minister he regretted his lack of early contact with the masses of his race. He had to learn their moods and methods of thought as an observer rather than through intuition.

For over twenty-five years his short stories and poems appeared in many of the country's leading newspapers and magazines, including the *New York Herald, Philadelphia Record, Boston Post,* and *Springfield Republican, Century, Pearson's Magazine,* the *Associated Sunday Magazine,* and *The Crisis.*

He was twice married, first to Fannie Clemens, who bore him two sons, Richard and Willard, and died in 1894. In 1906 he married Rosina B. Harvey, a musician and composer, and the daughter of Lee Roy Harvey of Washington, D.C. They had one son, Henry. Corrothers died in West Chester, Pa., on Feb. 12, 1917.

The best source of information is his autobiography. He was listed in *Who's Who in America 1906–1907.* There is a brief sketch by John Donald Wade in *DAB* (2, Part 2:242). However, an understanding of his struggles and his philosophy can best be attained through a careful reading of his writings.

— CASSANDRA SMITH-PARKER

COSTON, JULIA RINGWOOD (? – ?), publisher and magazine editor. She was born on Ringwood Farm, in Warrenton, Va., and this is apparently the origin of her maiden name. At an early age she was brought to Washington, D.C., where she reached "the highest grade" in the public schools. When her mother's health failed, Julia became the governess in the family of a Union general, and continued her studies. In the spring of 1886 she married William Hilary Coston, then a student at Yale University. Since he had published in 1884 *A Freeman and Yet a Slave,* a pamphlet of eighty-four pages, he may have broadened her formal education. A longer version of the same book was published in Chatham, Ontario (1888), which may suggest that they lived there at the time.

They settled in Cleveland, Ohio, where she began publishing *Ringwood's Afro-American Journal of Fashion* also known as *Ringwood's Home Magazine.* It is not known why she used her maiden name as editor of this monthly magazine, unless it appeared unseemly for the wife of a minister to be engaged in such a "frivolous" undertaking. According to Russell H. Davis, her husband was the pastor of St. Andrew's Church in Cleveland. This may be true despite the fact that Davis erred in accepting a statement that the magazine "was started in 1894" (*Blacks in Cleveland* [1971], p. 203, with a footnote reference to an unpublished master's thesis by Charles J. Storkan, "Cleveland Newspapers, Magazines and Periodicals from its [*sic*] Beginning to 1900," Western Reserve University, 1950, p. 204).

The *Journal* must have begun publication as early as 1892, for Monroe A. Majors included several letters to her, beginning with March of that year (*NAW* [c. 1893], pp. 251–58). Victoria Earle, later Mrs. Matthews, wrote her from 631 Park Row, New York City, on May 22, 1892: "It is so pure, so womanly—positively agreeable in its every feature as reading for private home, instruction and guidance" (ibid., p. 256). This was high praise from another woman journalist. Bishop James Theodore Holly wrote from Port-au-Prince, Haiti, on June 14, 1892: "Strange as the fact may seem to you it will be the first journal of fashion issued in Hayti, and I am proud that the introduction be made by a lady of our race, for none other should have the precedence in a country of independent blacks." And Dr. Majors on June 29, 1892, in Waco, Tex., described it as "pure, yet simple, characterizing the sublime force of education, of woman's prosperity, and portraying staying qualities in the field of journalism" (ibid., pp. 256–57).

The *Philadelphia Recorder* observed: "It is especially designed to be an Afro-American magazine, and is edited in its different departments by colored women, but the pleasing fashion articles, instructive talks with girls and mothers, and witty all-around paragraphs and interesting love stories make Ringwood's *Magazine* a welcome addition to any home, whether its occupants be black or white."

The *Richmond Planet* emphasized that the twelve-page journal, which sold for $1.25 a year, was a "typographical beauty and its matter is nicely compiled and interspersed with cuts dear to the human heart." Besides the latest Parisian fashions of ladies' gowns, etc., "it contains biographical sketches of prominent ladies of the race and young misses," edited by Mary Church Terrell.

Evidence is lacking about Mrs. Coston for the years after 1893. She had two children, Julia R., who was five years old in 1893, and W. H., who was three (Lawrence A. Scruggs, *Women of Distinction: Remarkable in Works and Invincible in Character* [1893], p. 141). Both Majors and Scruggs have drawings of Coston. William Hilary Coston, her husband, published in 1899 the valuable *The Spanish-American War Volunteer; Ninth United States Volunteer Infantry Roster, Biographies, Cuban Sketches.* He also wrote a pamphlet, *The Betrayal of the American Negroes as Citizens, as Soldiers and Sailors by the Republican Party in deference to the people of the Philippine Islands* (n.d.). It has a portrait of him.

Extensive research has failed to find copies of *Ringwood's Afro-American Journal of Fashion.* There is not even an entry in the Library of Congress Union Catalog.

— RAYFORD W. LOGAN

COTTER, JOSEPH SEAMON, SR. (1861–1949), teacher, author, and civic leader. Born on Feb. 2, 1861, in Bardstown, Ky., Cotter was the son of Michael and Martha (Vaughn) Cotter. Martha Vaughn was a slave of mixed Indian, English, and African blood. She was said to have a strong dramatic inclination and a definite will of her own. While she worked, she made up her own plays and stories over the washtub. It is assumed that Joseph received his love of literature and his talent for writing from his mother. Joseph's father was a prominent citizen of Louisville who was married to Martha by common law. It is claimed that Martha named her son for Joseph, the dreamer of biblical stories.

Joseph S. Cotter's formal education was very scant. He attended grammar school through the third grade, but then was forced to leave to help support his mother. He worked at a variety of jobs as a day laborer. He was a teamster, ragpicker, tobacco stemmer, prize fighter, whiskey distiller, and brick hand. Because he was small he was often harassed by the other workers. He was not big or strong enough to fight to gain his dignity, but he won his fellow workers' respect in another way—by telling them stories. When he was twenty-two his desire for knowledge became so great that he enrolled in a Louisville night school at the primary level. At the end of just two sessions, because of his hard work, he was evidently deemed ready to teach. This was to be the beginning of a long career in education.

He taught English literature and composition in Cloverport (1885–1887), conducted a private school (1887–1889), taught at the Western Colored School (1889–1893), was the founder and principal of Paul L. Dunbar School (1893–1911), and from 1911 was the principal of the Coleridge-Taylor School. In 1938, after he had been elected to the Louisville Board of Education to serve as principal and teacher for the fiftieth year, he dedicated his *Collected Poems* to the superintendents, supervisors, and his co-workers in Louisville.

Cotter was not only active in the field of education, but also played a role in the business and social life of Louisville, especially when he felt he could be of help to Negroes. He served as director of the Louisville Colored Orphan's Home Society, belonged to the Negro Educational Association, the NAACP, the Story Tellers League, and the Author's League of America.

But Cotter's major fame lies not in his educational career, but in his own writing. He was a storyteller, a dramatist, and a poet of many moods and styles. His early poems were published in local papers like the *Louisville Courier Journal,* and one poem, "The Tragedy of Pete," won first place in an *Opportunity* prize contest. He went on to publish many books, including *A Rhyming* (1895), *Links of Friendship,* (1899), *Caleb, the Degenerate* (1903), *A White Song and a Black One* (1909), *Negro Tales* (1912), and finally *Collected Poems* (1938).

For an author of such limited schooling Cotter's writing shows tremendous variety. His poetry could be philosophical speculation, racial protest, cultural tales, moral lessons, or simple reflections on people or places. Sterling A. Brown has divided the poetry during the period in which Cotter wrote into three concerns or stylistic tendencies—the dialect tradition to which Dunbar belongs, protest poetry where we find W. E. B. Du Bois, and "literary" because it expressed noble sentiments and was academic and lyrical in nature. Cotter shows some evidence of each style, but is primarily known as one of the first poets of racial concern. He used poetry as protest, yet also as a way to explore human nature and to try to discover just what man is.

A criticism of Cotter's poetry is that it sometimes seems too intellectualized or precise, the rhyming too forced, and the rhythm too pounding. He does seem at times too much the schoolmaster writing poetry, yet he was trying to work with a great many traditions.

The use of dialect was one of his strong points in poem and story. He had an extraordinary ability to capture the sound, wit, and folklore of the people. This is clearly evident in a tale "Kotchin' De Nines," which Cotter states was a story current in Louisville. It is full of the humor and warmth that are typical of many of his tales. But his poetry, largely dedicated to protest, did not often look at the brighter side. Both poetry and tales reflect a great variety. Some are from the African past, some satire, some the tragedies of everyday life, and some fables.

Caleb, the Degenerate, written in blank verse, was his only play. Negro drama at this time was very poorly received, and *Caleb* was considered unactable and was never performed. Yet it was important for its social and philosophical implications. Cotter wrote it as an attempt to reply to Thomas Dixon's attack on Negroes in *The Clansman,* which was published earlier that year. It had extolled the Ku Klux Klan and practically stated that freeing the slaves was a great error.

Cotter married Maria F. Cox of Louisville on July 22, 1891. They had two children, both of whom died of tuberculosis. Before his death at twenty-three, however, Joseph Jr. tried to follow his father's image as a poet and left behind his memorable *The Band of Gideon,* published in 1918.

Detailed biographical information about Cotter is

scarce. The best source is *Negro Poets and Their Poems* by Robert Thomas Kerlin, published in 1923. There is also a brief autobiographical statement in Countée Cullen's *Caroling Dusk* (1927). Other information about Cotter's life can perhaps best be inferred from the stories and poems themselves. — SAMUEL W. ALLEN

COUNCILL, WILLIAM HOOPER (1849–1909), educator and race leader. He was born a slave in Fayetteville, N.C., on July 12, 1849. Five years later his father William escaped to Canada, from where he tried unsuccessfully to obtain the freedom of his family. In 1857 two of Councill's brothers were sold to the Deep South while he, his mother (Mary Jane), and youngest brother were sold at the Richmond slave market to a trader who took them to northern Alabama and sold them to a planter. When Union troops occupied Chattanooga in 1863, the family escaped to Yankee lines. Young William attended a freedmen's school at Stevenson, Ala., for three years (1865–1867), his only formal schooling. For several years he taught in Negro public schools, worked in hotels and restaurants, and studied chemistry, mathematics, and Latin at night. He also read law and was admitted to the Alabama bar in 1883, but never practiced. He was a member of the A.M.E. church and held several church offices. Politically ambitious, Councill was chief enrolling clerk of the Alabama House of Representatives (1872–1874), secretary of a national civil rights convention in 1873, ran unsuccessfully for a seat in the legislature in 1874, and served briefly as receiver at the General Land Office in Alabama (1875).

The latter year saw the first change in Councill's zigzag course between militancy and accommodation. As a reward for becoming a Democrat, the Alabama legislature made him principal of the newly created State Normal and Industrial School at Huntsville. Started in the basement of a Negro church, the school grew steadily, and in the 1880s rivaled Tuskegee as an industrial institute. By flattering and cajoling whites, by appealing to the upper class's sense of paternalism and noblesse oblige, and by proclaiming the Negro's docility and faithfulness as a laborer and domestic servant, Councill went much further than Booker T. Washington in his attempt to curry favor with southern whites. In 1877 he founded the *Huntsville Herald*, which he edited for seven years. In 1885 Councill was charged with raping a twelve-year-old student and shooting at her uncle. Although he was acquitted, Huntsville Negroes, angry with Councill for his accommodationism, used the incident to demand his resignation as principal, and northern philanthropists cited it as a reason for giving money to Tuskegee rather than to Councill's school. In an attempt to regain their confidence, Councill swerved toward militancy in 1887 by bringing suit against a railroad for ejecting him from a first-class coach. Although the Interstate Commerce Commission decided in his favor, the ruling was based on the "separate but equal" principle that opened the floodgates for Jim Crow laws. Nevertheless, Alabama Democrats punished Councill by firing him as principal of Huntsville Normal. He got back into their good graces, however, and was reappointed in 1888.

For the next two decades Councill was publicly more conciliatory and sycophantic than ever. In 1891 he outmaneuvered Booker T. Washington to receive Alabama's share of federal land-grant funds under the second Morrill Act (1890). His school was renamed the Alabama State Agricultural and Mechanical College for Negroes, and moved to a former plantation at Normal, just north of Huntsville, where Councill's office for several years was in a converted slave cabin. Despite repeated efforts Washington failed to get the land-grant funds shifted to Tuskegee, but in 1897 he did win a struggle to get the state agricultural experiment school for Negroes at Tuskegee. Completely overshadowed by Washington after 1895, Councill died at Normal, following a long illness, on April 17, 1909.

Councill's real beliefs about race relations are something of a mystery. During Reconstruction he stood boldly for equal rights. After he turned Democrat in 1875, however, he rarely missed a chance to praise southern whites as the Negro's best friends and to deprecate "social equality." His suit before the ICC in 1887 was only a temporary departure from this stance, and even then he stated his approval of separate facilities for Negroes so long as they were equal. In 1899 Booker T. Washington said that he was reluctant to appear in public with Councill, for he had "the reputation of simply toadying to the Southern white people." Some of Councill's statements certainly merited this description. He celebrated the "love and attachment between the races at the South" and declared that no people were "better suited for domestic and personal service than the Negro." Segregation instead of "a curse is in reality a blessing to the race," he said, because it provided opportunities for colored businessmen, teachers and professionals to work among their own people.

But there is some evidence that such statements were the mask that Councill wore before the white world to get from it all he could. In many ways he exemplified the tragedy of the ambitious Negro who finds all paths blocked save that of sycophancy. And in a remarkable article, "The Future of the Negro" (*Forum*, July 1899), his private bitterness is manifest. Starkly pessimistic about the chances of racial equality in a white man's country, Councill endorsed Bishop Henry M. Turner's ideas of black nationalism and emigration to Africa, where the Negro race could build a powerful nationality free from blighting prejudice.

Basic biographical information can be found in William J. Simmons's *Men of Mark . . .* (1887), pp. 390–93; D. W. Culp (ed.), *Twentieth Century Negro Literature* (1902); Gustav Kobbé's "Once a Slave—Now a Teacher" (*Harper's Weekly*, May 21, 1892); and *Afro-American* (April 24, 1908). Some of Councill's own writings are: *Lamp of Wisdom, or, Race History Illuminated* (1898); "Is There a Negro Problem?" (*Arena*, April 1899); *Negro Development in the South* (1901); and *Bright Side of the Southern Question* (1903). Analyses by modern scholars include Horace Mann Bond's *Negro Education in Alabama* (1939), August Meier's *Negro Thought in America, 1880–1915* (1963), and Louis R. Harlan's *Booker T. Washington* (1972). — JAMES M. MCPHERSON

COUVENT, MADAME BERNARD (1757?–1837), founder of a school for indigent Negro orphans. Little is known of her origin or her parentage, but it is believed she was born in Africa, that she was brought to New Orleans as a slave, that her maiden name was Justine Fervin, and that she received no formal education. She was probably granted her freedom by her master, or it was provided through her husband, Gabriel Bernard Couvent, who at his death left her a substantial legacy, a large portion of which she used to found a Catholic Indigent Orphans' School. This institution was formally opened in 1852, some fifteen years after her death, and is still operating today.

Although there exists no early record relative to Madame Bernard Couvent, she is known to have been held in high esteem by the people of New Orleans who spoke of her with admiration and gratitude. They extolled her piety and charity, and dedicated a plaque to her memory. They honored her for her farsighted ingenuity, for her distinguished qualities of heart and mind, her solid common sense, and for her endless compassion. This compassion Couvent held for all peoples, but particularly for the youth of her race whom she wished to protect from slavery and difficulties in obtaining a livelihood.

There is a story that two free families of color, the Fletchers and the Couvents, lived in the Faubourg Marigny. Both families were Catholics and regular attendants at St. Louis Cathedral. Henry Fletcher and Gabriel Bernard Couvent, carpenters by trade, were close friends and companions. The Couvents had no children. They acquired in time a considerable fortune which Madame Couvent wished to share with underprivileged people. Her chief dream was to found a school to ensure the education of orphans of free colored people, many of whom had white fathers. When Gabriel Bernard Couvent died on May 22, 1829, at the age of seventy-one, he left his entire estate to his widow. Madame Couvent's religious director and lifelong friend of her husband's friend Henry Fletcher was Fr. Constantine Manehault of St. Louis Cathedral. This priest encouraged Couvent to remember the proposed school for orphans in the disposal of her property.

In her will, drafted in 1832, the widow Couvent bequeathed several small houses on the corner of Union and Great Men Streets to be used for the building of her school. Five years later on June 28, 1837, at the age of eighty, the widow Couvent died. The execution of her wishes was seemingly neglected until 1848 when the Society for the Instruction of Indigent Orphans made restitution by a settlement that established a primary school for the colored orphans of the Third District. Shortly afterward free classroom instruction was organized and given to colored children.

The Couvent will stated that the school should be placed under the supervision of the Catholic clergy. The first cleric to fill this role was the Reverend Manehault. Prudence and discretion had to be observed carefully because of the existing tenets among city fathers averse to the operation of a school for free people of color, even under the auspices of the community's leading Catholic church. This continuous prejudice was the major cause of the delay in the inauguration of the Couvent School. It was only through the voluntary risk of safety by those involved in the project and through the cooperation of an organization led by François Lacroix that the Couvent will was finally implemented.

The Couvent School, coeducational and nontuitional, reached out to all children of color with no specific restriction to those living in the Third District of New Orleans. The institution was presided over by five or six instructors teaching in both French and English with separate classes for boys and girls. Parents or guardians who could afford a monthly stipend made a donation. Felicie Cailloux, a highly intelligent colored woman, was the first teacher employed. The program of academic studies included the classics. Special courses were also offered in French and Spanish which concentrated on the works of La Fontaine, Boileau, Fénelon, and Corneille. The Couvent School was considered the best attended in the city.

Among teachers working with Cailloux were Armand Lanusse, who also served as first principal, Paul Trevigne, Samuel Snäer, and Joanni Questy. According to John W. Blassingame in *Black New Orleans, 1860–1880* (1973, p. 108), the instructors at the Couvent School were among the best in their profession.

During the pre–Civil War years the directors obtained gifts for the school from the state legislature and from the city of New Orleans to supplement other donations for maintenance.

All the teachers were colored. All were dedicated. The list of Couvent benefactors included some of the best known Negro leaders of that era, such as Thomy Lafon, Armand Lanusse, Rodolphe L. Desdunes, Aristide Mary, and Paul Trevigne. They gave not only of their money but their time and their talents to the school. And their reward was commensurate with their generosity, for a large number of writers, poets, artists, and leaders went forth from the portals of the Bernard Couvent Institute, or the "Institute Couvent" as it was sometimes called. It was also at times called the St. Louis School.

With the launching of the Reconstruction period most of the city's colored children attended the free public schools with white children. Hence attendance at Bernard Couvent Institute fell off. By 1884 the decline in attendance was so great that the upkeep of the facility seemed in imminent jeopardy. The school was saved from this threatened ruin by the combined efforts of twelve patriotic, community-minded men, including Desdunes. Today the facility once known as the Bernard Couvent School is called Holy Redeemer School and is under the auspices of the Catholic church, directed by the Sisters Servants of the Holy Ghost and Mary Immaculate. It is located on Dauphine Street.

This contribution is based on Rodolphe L. Desdunes's *Nos Hommes et Notre Histoire* (1911), translated and edited as *Our People and Our History* (1973), by Sister Olga Dorothea McCants, D.C. Also of valuable assistance was Charles B. Roussève's *The Negro in Louisiana . . .* (1937). — DOROTHEA OLGA MCCANTS, D.C.

CRAFT, ELLEN (c. 1826–c. 1897), well-known fugitive slave. Craft was born in Clinton, Ga., of her white master father Maj. James Smith and a slave mother, Maria.

When she was eleven years old Ellen was given as a wedding present to the daughter of her mistress who lived in Macon. There she was a favorite house servant, and there too she met another slave, William Craft, who was to become her husband. William suggested running away together, but Ellen was at first reluctant, so instead they asked for and obtained permission to marry. They continued to think of escape, however, and in December 1848 they decided to leave slavery in disguise. William, who was hired out to a cabinetmaker, was able to earn some money for himself which he saved to purchase the necessary disguises and travel fare.

According to the plan, the nearly white Ellen, wearing dark glasses and a muffler to hide her face, would travel as an aged and ailing master with William as the faithful servant. Since Ellen was illiterate and would not be able to sign hotel registers or other documents, she suggested that her arm should be in a sling. She acquired and hid some of her own disguise and sewed the trousers she needed in order to play the part of a master. To cover their flight the Crafts got permission to leave Macon during the Christmas season. They traveled north by train and steamer, encountering few problems until they arrived in Baltimore, the last slave city on their journey. According to Maryland law, a master was required to sign and post a bond for any slave going north. William persuaded the railroad agent that his master desperately needed medical care, and other passengers supported him. On the train they met a free Negro who gave them the address of an abolitionist living in Philadelphia.

After abandoning their disguises and resting briefly in Philadelphia, the Crafts went on to Boston accompanied by William Wells Brown, another former slave and antislavery lecturer. They lived in Boston for two years. There Theodore Parker performed a second marriage ceremony for them. William worked as a cabinetmaker and Ellen studied to become a seamstress. The Crafts were well known in New England and they attended numerous antislavery meetings. All went well until October 1850 when two agents of their masters appeared in Boston with arrest warrants issued under the new and stronger Fugitive Slave Act. With assistance from local abolitionists the Crafts eluded their pursuers and fled the country, going first to Nova Scotia and then to England.

In England abolitionists again befriended the fugitive couple, providing some financial aid and sending them to school. They made several speaking tours with their friend William Wells Brown, and attracted considerable attention as visitors to the Crystal Palace Exhibition of 1851. In England, Ellen found it necessary to quash rumors that she had left William and that she longed to return to the security of slavery. Quite the contrary, she said in a letter published in the abolitionist newspaper, the *Boston Liberator*. Since leaving bondage she had fared much better than she could possibly have anticipated, but even if she had not, she would prefer freedom. She would rather starve in England "a freewoman, than be a slave for the best man that ever breathed upon the American Continent."

The Crafts remained in exile in England until after the Civil War. Their five children were born there: Charles Estlin Phillips, Brougham, William Jr., Ellen, and Alfred. They returned to the United States in 1868, living in Boston for a while, and then moving to Georgia to manage a Southern Industrial School and Labor Enterprise, financed by English and New England abolitionists. It was a combination school and farm where the freedmen studied agriculture part of the day and worked the fields the rest of the time. The project was destroyed by a fire set by the Ku Klux Klan, but a similar venture was later located on the "Woodville" plantation in Bryan County, Ga., which eventually became the Craft family plantation. In the 1890s Mrs. Craft went to live with her daughter Ellen in Charleston, S.C., where she died around 1897. She was buried on the family plantation in Georgia.

Ellen Craft was an imaginative and intelligent woman, devoted to her family, unassuming and industrious, and according to family remembrance, an excellent business woman. As a youth her desire for freedom, combined with William's assurances, conquered her fear of a very dangerous escape-journey. Her ordeal and the courage with which she faced it provided an example and inspiration to many others of her time.

The Crafts recorded their own account of their early lives and escape, publishing it in London in 1860 under the title *Running a Thousand Miles for Freedom, or the Escape of William and Ellen Craft from Slavery*. William Still also included a narrative of the escape and reprinted some pertinent documents in his book *The Underground Rail Road* (1872). Several letters about the Crafts in England, first published in the *Boston Liberator*, are reprinted in *The Mind of the Negro as Reflected in Letters Written During the Crisis, 1800–1860* (1926), edited by Carter G. Woodson. The sketch in *NAW* (1971, 1:396–98) by Larry Gara provides additional bibliographic references. — LARRY GARA

CROGMAN, WILLIAM H[ENRY] (1841–1931), college professor and president, Latin and Greek scholar. Crogman was born in Philipsburg on St. Maartin, Leeward Islands, on May 5, 1841. Little is known of his first few years except that he was never a slave. He was orphaned at twelve, and shortly thereafter was befriended by B. L. Boomer of a New England shipowning family, who took young Crogman to his home in Middleboro, Mass. In 1855, at the age of fourteen, he began an eleven-year career at sea on one of the Boomer ships. During this period he visited many ports in Europe, India, and South America, experiences which had a profound effect on the keenly observant young Crogman.

In 1866 with Boomer's encouragement he began preparations to secure an education. Two years later he entered Pierce Academy in Middleboro, and completed with distinction the four-year course in English, French, and bookkeeping in half the time normally required. His academic prowess so impressed the principal that Crogman was made a special class of one in order that his development would not be hindered by the slower students. Upon graduation in 1868 he was the first Negro teacher of English at Claflin College in Orangeburg, S.C.

In 1870, driven by a desire to achieve a mastery of

Greek and Latin, studies which he had already under-taken on his own, Crogman entered Atlanta University. Here, he completed the classical course with distinction in three rather than four years, to finish as one of the members of that institution's famous first graduating class.

Immediately thereafter he entered upon his long ser-vice at Clark College in Atlanta and at closely related Gammon Theological Seminary. In 1880, and again in 1884 and 1888, he was a lay delegate to the General Conference of the Methodist church, and in 1888 be-came the first Negro to be elected one of its assistant secretaries. In 1892 he was made one of the fifteen members of the University Senate of the Methodist Episcopal church, which determined standards for all Methodist colleges. Also in 1884 he addressed the con-vention of the National Education Association in Madi-son, Wis. In the next year he was elected secretary of the Board of Trustees of Clark College, a post which he retained until 1922. As commissioner for the Cotton States Exposition, held in Atlanta in 1895, Crogman was largely responsible for the large and creditable Negro exhibit that was assembled with great difficulty.

All the while Crogman continued teaching. In 1903 he was elected president of Clark College, then known as Clark University, and served in that capacity until 1910. While by no means an ineffective administrator, he resigned to return to the classroom. Eleven years later he retired and lived quietly in Philadelphia for the last ten years of his life. Meanwhile he had married Lavinia C. Mott, a graduate of Atlanta University, who bore him seven children. On Oct. 16, 1931, at the age of ninety, he preceded his wife in death by one week.

Crogman was a man of keen intellect and intense devotion to education and to his students. His resolute but reasoned convictions won him respect beyond his campus, in other parts of the country, especially in Methodist circles. He made silent but positive protest against the segregation and discrimination prevalent in the South by refusing to ride on the street cars of At-lanta, regardless of the weather, preferring instead to walk the three or four miles from the campus to town and back.

It was as teacher, scholar, writer, and speaker that Crogman distinguished himself. In the great controversy that developed after the 1880s over the primacy of industrial or classical education, especially in the newly founded Negro colleges in the South, he was a firm and frequent exponent of the concept that a "good educa-tion" could be found only in the study of the classics. Yet he was not categorically opposed to industrial or vocational education, which, incidentally, had been eliminated from the Clark curriculum during his presi-dency but which he conceded to be both wise and necessary. He had more than once criticized liberal education for not preparing young men for useful lives. He developed a lifelong friendship and admiration for Booker T. Washington and was a strong supporter of Tuskegee, which he believed had an importance of its own. Nevertheless he was strongly opposed to the large amount of money and energy that was being expended on vocational education to the neglect of liberal college programs in the Negro schools.

Several of Crogman's speeches have been published in his *Talks for the Times* (1896; rev. and enlarged, 1897), which includes an excellent biographical sketch to 1896 by Edward L. Parks. Further biographical details to 1921 are to be found in A. A. McPheeters's *History of Clark College* (1944). Crogman was also co-author with Henry F. Kletzing of one of the early histories of the Negro in America, *Progress of a Race, or the Re-markable Advancement of of the American Negro from the Bondage of Slavery and Poverty to Freedom and Citizenship, Intelligence, Affluence, Honor and Trust,* with an introduction by Booker T. Washington (1897, reprinted by Negro Universities Press, 1969); revised, with J. W. Gibson as co-author, under the title *The Colored American* (1901); revised and enlarged, with J. L. Nichols as co-author, and published under the original title (1920; reprinted in the Arno Press Series *The American Negro, His History and Literature,* 1969). — MELVIN D. KENNEDY

CROMWELL, JOHN WESLEY (1846–1927), editor and historian. Cromwell was born a slave in Ports-mouth, Va., on Sept. 5, 1846, the youngest of the twelve children of Willis Hodges and Elizabeth (Carney) Cromwell. In 1851 Willis Cromwell obtained the free-dom of his family and moved to West Philadelphia where John was admitted to the Preparatory Depart-ment of the Institute for Colored Youth in 1856. Crom-well graduated in 1864 and began his professional ca-reer as a schoolteacher in Columbia, Pa. In 1865 he returned to Virginia and opened a private school at Portsmouth. Shot at, and his school burned to the ground, Cromwell returned to Philadelphia where he was employed by the Baltimore Association for the Moral and Intellectual Improvement of the Colored People. After a short stay in Philadelphia he again re-turned to Virginia as an agent of the American Mission-ary Association, and was assigned to Providence Church, Norfolk County, Va. Cromwell was elected delegate and appointed clerk to the first Republican convention in Richmond (1867). Following a short po-litical career, Cromwell resumed school teaching, working in Withersville, Richmond, and Southhampton, Va. In 1871 he moved to Washington, D.C., and en-tered Howard University Law School from which he graduated in 1874 and was admitted to the bar in the same year. Two years later he organized the *People's Advocate,* a weekly newspaper, in Alexandria and moved it to Washington in 1877. While a student at Howard, Cromwell successfully completed the civil ser-vice examination, and following the conferring of his law degree, was appointed chief examiner of the divi-sion of money orders in the Post Office Department and subsequently register of money order accounts, a posi-tion he held until his retirement in 1885. He was ap-pointed by Blanche K. Bruce as one of the commission-ers to secure exhibits from colored people at the Cotton Exposition in New Orleans, 1895.

Elected president of the Bethel Literary and Historical Association in Washington, D.C. (1881), Cromwell used the organization as an intellectual forum to attract Negroes from across the nation to discuss and debate issues of importance to the race. Besides his literary contributions through the *Advocate,* the Bethel Literary and Historical Association, and secretary of the American Negro Academy, Cromwell was a part of the revived interest in Negro history which inspired Carter G. Woodson and others to organize the Association for the Study of Negro Life and History in 1915. Although he published his most important work, *The Negro in American History* (1914), before the founding of the association, two of his scholarly articles, "The Aftermath of Nat Turner's Insurrection" (1920) and the "First Negro Church in the District of Columbia" (1922), appeared in Woodson's *Journal of Negro History.* Other works by Cromwell included *History of the Bethel Literary and Historical Association* (1896) and "The Challenge of the Disfranchised; A Plea for the Enforcement of the 15th Amendment" (1924). His major work, *The Negro in American History: Men and Women Eminent in the Evolution of the American of African Descent,* published in 1914 by the American Negro Academy, was a creditable work for the time, preceding the first edition of Woodson's *The Negro in Our History* by eight years. Cromwell acknowledged indebtedness for many helpful suggestions from Theophilus G. Steward, T. Thomas Fortune, William C. Bolivar, Daniel A. Murray, and Arthur A. Schomburg. His bibliography included many useful references and a chronology.

Cromwell died at his home, 1439 Swann St. NW, Washington, D.C., on April 14, 1927. Funeral services were held at St. Luke's Protestant Episcopal Church, 15th and Church Streets NW on April 16, with interment in Woodlawn Cemetery. He was survived by his second wife, Annie E. Cromwell (his first wife was the former Lucy McGuinn), four daughters (Otelia, Mary, Lucy, and Mrs. Martha Cromwell Brent), and John W. Jr. Three of the children, Mary, Otelia, and John W. Jr., obtained college educations and taught at M Street (Dunbar after 1916) High School in Washington, D.C., for many years.

While there is no biography or autobiography of John W. Cromwell, information concerning his early career is in William J. Simmons's *Men of Mark . . .* (1887, pp. 898–907). The *People's Advocate* is also an important source for his early economic, political, and social philosophies. The best critical study of Cromwell's economic philosophy as well as his views on many contemporary issues is in August Meier's *Negro Thought in America* (1963). Obituaries are in *JNH* (Oct. 1927, pp. 563–66), and the *Washington Evening Star* (April 15, 1927, p. 9). — JAMES E. HANEY

CROMWELL, OLIVER (1752–1853), soldier in the American Revolution. Born in Columbus, Burlington County, N.J., and said to have been born free, Cromwell worked as a farmer and enlisted in a company attached to the 2nd New Jersey Regiment under the command of Col. Israel Shreve. According to Cromwell's reminiscences, when he said he was 100 years old, he accompanied General Washington when he crossed the Delaware in 1776, fought in the battles of Princeton, Brandywine, Monmouth, and Yorktown. There, he recalled, he saw the last man killed. Regardless of the dependability of his detailed recollections,

his honorable discharge as a private in the Jersey Battalion was signed by Gen. George Washington at his headquarters on June 5, 1783. An endorsement stated that he was "honored with the Badge of Merit for Six Years faithful service." He also received a federal pension of $96 a year. After his discharge he settled on a farm in New Jersey and reared a family of six children. When he died in Burlington, N.J., in January 1853, he was survived by several children, grandchildren, and great-grandchildren.

Most historians have relied on William C. Nell's *The Colored Patriots of the American Revolution* (1855, reprint 1968). Of modern histories Benjamin Quarles's *The Negro in the American Revolution* (1961) is an authoritative source. Another principal source, an article in the *Burlington N.J. Gazette* in the spring of 1852, was a warm tribute based largely on Cromwell's reminiscences. The article is reproduced in Sidney Kaplan's *The Black Presence in the Era of the American Revolution 1770–1800* (1973, p. 47). A reproduction of the discharge is on page 48. — RAYFORD W. LOGAN

CROSSWAITH, FRANK R[UDOLPH] (1892–1965), labor organizer, author, and editor. Born in Frederiksted, Danish West Indies (now the U.S. Virgin Islands), the son of William I. and Anne Eliza Crosswaith, he was educated at the University Preparatory School there and in New York City at the Rand School of Social Sciences. From the 1920s to his death he was one of the most effective organizers of Negro workers in New York City. In 1915 he married Alma E. Besard of Charleston, S.C., who became the mother of their three children: Paul, Morris, and Alethia.

Crosswaith's achievements were all the more remarkable because the discriminatory practices of the American Federation of Labor excluded most Negro workers, skilled and unskilled. More than 50 percent of gainfully occupied Negroes were in domestic and other personal service: servants and laundresses in private homes, waiters, porters, janitors, elevator operators. The migration from the South during World War I intensified the existing competition and antagonisms between Negro and white workers, but at the same time increased stronger class and organization consciousness. In New York City Marcus Garvey and his Universal Negro Improvement Association personified the former, while A. Philip Randolph and Chandler Owen spoke for the "economic radicals" in their magazine *Messenger.* This militancy helped promote the organization in 1925 of the Trade Union Committee for Organizing Negro Workers with the slogan "Union Hours, Union Conditions and Union Wages for the Negro Worker in New York City." Crosswaith, who had already gained recognition by organizing elevator operators, motion-picture operators, mechanics, laundry workers, drugstore clerks, and grocery clerks, was elected executive secretary. But after he discontinued his work in order to become a full-time organizer for the Brotherhood of Sleeping Car Porters, and its affiliated unions neglected to make their payments, the Trade Union Committee for Organizing Negroes ceased to function.

The foundations it had laid were weakened by the

Depression. On the other hand the National Industrial Recovery Act, approved by President Roosevelt on June 16, 1933, improved the lot of some Negro workers in New York City (see especially Charles Lionel Franklin's *The Negro Labor Unionist of New York* [1936], p. 129). Section 7(A) of the act provided, among other things, for the right of employees to organize and bargain collectively through representatives of their own choice, not to be obliged to join a company union but to enjoy the benefits of maximum hours of labor and minimum pay. Crosswaith helped increase Negro membership in at least one local union, but few were in the highest paying crafts.

Another factor in the growing efforts to organize Negro labor workers was the establishment of the Harlem Labor Committee (1934), planned by Crosswaith who at that time was a general organizer of the International Ladies Garment Workers' Union (ILGWU). Elected its chairman, he set as its principal goal working through those AFL trade unions that were seeking to organize Negro workers. To this end the committee planned to carry on campaigns in Negro newspapers and magazines, and to organize labor demonstrations. Crosswaith's adherence to socialism was perhaps responsible for the plan to publish leaflets offsetting the propaganda of Communists. Among the local unions to which Negroes were admitted on an equal basis were those of motion-picture operators, cleaners, dyers and pressers, building services, shoe repairers, cloth, hat, cap, and milliners, laundry workers, and the ILGWU.

Crosswaith also played an important role in the committee's "call" for a meeting in the auditorium of the Renaissance Casino, 138th Street and Seventh Avenue in the heart of Harlem on July 20, 1935. This "first Negro Labor Conference" (ibid., p. 144) was attended by unions representing practically every organized industry or trade in New York City. A. Philip Randolph and Crosswaith were two of the principal speakers. Some of the important resolutions adopted called for the solidarity of black and white labor, the thirty-hour week, condemnation of the failure of the New York state legislature to ratify the child labor amendment, and adoption of a comprehensive amendment to the Constitution of the United States covering practically all the goals of organized labor. Other resolutions urged Negro clergymen and the Negro press to "recognize their responsibilities" in promoting the interests of bona fide unions. The conference congratulated the ILGWU for its "edifying example of labor solidarity" and the Brotherhood of Sleeping Car Porters for its progress toward obtaining a satisfactory contract with the Pullman Company. Out of this conference evolved the Negro Labor Committee, of which Crosswaith soon thereafter became chairman. The committee established an imposing Harlem Labor Center which, Crosswaith said, was to be "the pivotal point from which will emanate all constructive efforts affecting the work-a-day life of Negro labor in Harlem and greater New York." After the American Newspaper Guild was organized in November 1933, nineteen of the first Negro members constituted the entire editorial staff of the *New York Amsterdam News,* a Negro weekly. When they struck the paper instituted a lockout, and in August 1935 the unit

sought a contract for union recognition. The strikers were supported by the public, members of the guild including its president Heywood Broun and white advertisers, and the paper was forced into the hands of a receiver and later sold. The workers were reinstated, a guild shop was established, a five-day forty-hour week, annual vacations of two weeks, dismissal notices of up to three months for ten years' employment, creation of an adjustment committee, and assurances against strikebreaking and discrimination were recognized. Crosswaith felicitated the victors, congratulated the new management for recognizing the right of collective bargaining, and finally "the heroic locked out workers of the editorial department who have written a most creditable new page in the story of Negro labor" (ibid., p. 213).

Crosswaith's dynamic efforts in organizing Negro workers led to his involvement in numerous liberal causes that were being espoused by independent political parties. During the course of his identification with these parties he became known as a socialist. He was a member of the state executive board of the Liberal party and vice-chairman of the American Labor party. He was a lecturer for the Socialist party and the League for Industrial Democracy. As a lecturer for these groups he made tours of college campuses across the country. Bearing the Socialist label, Crosswaith ran unsuccessfully for several public offices: aldermanic president and president of the City Council of New York City, secretary of state and lieutenant-governor of New York state. He was supported in these candidacies for public office by the American Labor party. Mayor Fiorello LaGuardia appointed him to membership on the board of the New York Housing Authority in 1942.

At a meeting in Madison Square Garden on June 16, 1942, attended by some 20,000 persons, Crosswaith said the meeting marked the fact that there was a "new Negro in America who, loyal to the government and determined to give every effort toward winning the war for the democracies, would still be determined and insistent upon gaining the same rights and liberties accorded to other citizens of the country." His own son, who was in Europe, was ready to die for the Stars and Stripes, but, Crosswaith believed, was fighting for these same goals. He closed his remarks by "urging the audience to let nothing blind them to the fact that 'your fate and the fate of your children rests in the lap of the working class' " (*New Jersey Herald,* June 20, 1942).

Less well known than other Negro labor leaders, Crosswaith deserves a full-length biography. He was a member of the committee, along with A. Philip Randolph and others, that made plans for the March on Washington in 1941 culminating in President Roosevelt's Executive Order 8802 (June 25, 1941) and the establishment of the Committee on Fair Employment Practice. Crosswaith served on the New York Housing Authority from 1942 to 1947, was co-author of *True Freedom for Negro and White Workers* and *Discrimination Incorporated.* For twelve years he edited *Negro Labor News.* Called the "Negro Debs" of the labor movement of the 1920s and the 1930s, he exercised perhaps almost as much influence on the development of what was once called "radicalism" as did Eugene V.

Debs. His memory is kept alive by the Negro Labor Center which still exists today.

He died at his home, 55 La Salle St., Chicago, on June 17, 1965. Funeral services were held at St. Martin's Episcopal Church, 230 Lenox Ave., New York City. He was survived by his widow, one son Morris, and his daughter Alethia Davis.

Some basic information is in *Who's Who in Colored America* (1950), edited by G. James Fleming and Christian E. Burckel, and the obituary in the *New York Times* (June 18, 1965, p. 35). Valuable background information is in Jervis Anderson's *A. Philip Randolph, A Biographical Portrait* (1974), and especially in Charles Lionel Franklin's *The Negro Labor Unionists of New York* (1936), and papers in the Schomburg Center for Research in Black Culture, New York City.

— JAMES T. JONES

CRUM, WILLIAM D[EMOS] (1859–1912), Customs collector and diplomat. Crum was born near Orangeburg, S.C., the youngest of seven children. His grandfather, a German, had settled in South Carolina early in the nineteenth century. His father, Darius, owned a sizable plantation; little is known about his African ancestry. He graduated (1875) from the Avery Normal Institute, a school sponsored by the American Missionary Association in Charleston, studied briefly at the then-integrated University of South Carolina and received his M.D. degree at Howard University in 1880. In 1883 he married Ellen Craft, the daughter of Ellen Craft and William Craft, who had escaped from slavery to Boston in 1848. Dr. Crum practiced medicine in Charleston, headed the local hospital for Negroes and served as a trustee of the Avery Normal Institute. In addition to engaging in various business enterprises, he was active in Republican politics. He was a friend of many prominent Negroes, including the former lieutenant-governor of Louisiana, P. B. S. Pinchback, Whitefield McKinlay, a prosperous real estate dealer in Washington, D.C., Harry Smith, editor of the *Cleveland Gazette,* and T. Thomas Fortune, editor of the *New York Age.* Most valuable to him was the political support of Booker T. Washington, who along with McKinlay, Pinchback, T. Thomas Fortune, and other prominent Negro politicians persuaded Pres. Theodore Roosevelt to nominate him in January 1903 for the position of collector of Customs for the port of Charleston. Despite strong opposition by southern senators, he was confirmed in 1905. Booker T. Washington doubted that Crum would be confirmed again after Taft became president in 1909, though Crum had been an able collector of Customs. But Taft did nominate him and the Senate confirmed Crum in 1910 to the traditional "Negro post" of minister resident and consul-general to Liberia. In September 1912 he fell a victim to "African fever" and died in Charleston in November of that year.

Crum's career could be called that of "the tragic mulatto." Although refined and well-to-do, he deemed it expedient to decry "social equality." This attitude helped him gain the support of Booker T. Washington and President Roosevelt, but his political aspirations earned him the disapproval of such fire-eaters as "Pitchfork" Ben Tillman and James Calvin Hemphill of Charleston. White Charlestonians had successfully opposed as early as 1892 Pres. Benjamin Harrison's nomination of Crum as postmaster of Charleston. Although Crum was a delegate to every Republican National Convention from 1884 to 1904, the "Road-to-Reunion" policy of President McKinley and the persistent opposition of many southerners delayed a political appointment for Crum until after Roosevelt became president in September 1901. As a member of the House of Representatives, Hemphill in opposing the Lodge Bill for the federal supervision of federal elections (1890), the so-called Force Bill, had declared: "We know that the honest and intelligent people must either rule it [the nation] or we must leave it; and for myself, gentlemen, in this presence and before the people of the United States and before that God who sits upon the circle of the heavens, in all reverence, but in all earnestness, I swear that we will not leave it." As editor of the *Charleston News and Courier* he relentlessly attacked Crum as soon as Roosevelt announced (November 1902) his intention to nominate Crum as collector of Customs. Although Tillman and Hemphill led the opposition to the nomination, the *New York Times* and the *New York Herald* also opposed the nomination. Because of this bitter opposition the Senate refused for two years to confirm the nomination. Roosevelt had further aroused southern indignation by having Washington as a guest for dinner at the White House in October 1901.

Roosevelt's persistence in giving Crum interim appointments until the Senate confirmed him in 1905 is not easily understood. As C. Vann Woodward has observed: "Simultaneously, or by turns, he [Roosevelt] wooed the mutually hostile Black-and-Tans, Lilywhites, and White Supremacy Democrats" (*Origins of the New South, 1877–1913* [1951], p. 463). By 1905 Roosevelt was speaking in favor of southern traditions and in 1906 he summarily discharged three companies of the 25th Regiment of Infantry on unproven charges of rioting in Brownsville, Tex. It is not surprising then that neither Roosevelt nor Taft, who proclaimed his southern sympathies during a tour of the South in 1909, was willing to support another battle for the confirmation of Crum. Booker T. Washington then prevailed upon Taft in 1910 to nominate him for the post in Liberia.

Crum sought vigorously to aid Liberia in settling the republic's boundary difficulties and financial crises. In 1909, however, Emmett Jay Scott, as one of three commissioners sent to Liberia to assist it in its difficulties, wrote a report that strongly influenced the decision to establish, in effect, a United States protectorate. Under the circumstances Crum's interest and efforts had little beneficial effect.

Basic facts are in *Who's Who in America, 1912–1913* (1912). William B. Gatewood's "William D. Crum, a Negro in Politics" (*JNH* Oct. 1968, pp. 301–20), is the only comprehensive biographical sketch, with abundant references. Additional information and interpretations are those of the contributor. There is a brief discussion, with some new supporting material, in George Sinkler's *The Racial Attitudes of American Presidents from Abraham Lincoln to Theodore Roosevelt* (1971, pp. 362–64, 369). — RAYFORD W. LOGAN

CRUMMELL, ALEXANDER (1819–1898), clergyman, teacher, and missionary. Crummell was born free in New York City. The Negro community in which he grew up believed passionately in "mental and moral improvement" and was fervently committed to the anti-slavery cause. His father, Boston Crummell, had been born in Africa in what later became part of Sierra Leone. His mother was descended from generations of free Negroes. Hardworking, church-going people, they instilled in their children the values of education and service. Crummell attended the African Free School on Mulberry Street in Manhattan, whose alumni came to include such notables as James McCune Smith, Ira Aldridge, Samuel Ringgold Ward, and Henry Highland Garnet. From 1831 to 1835 he was a student in the Canal Street High School, whose directors were Peter Williams and Theodore S. Wright, two of the leading Negro clergymen of the era. In 1835 Crummell, along with Garnet and several other Negro youths, matriculated at the newly opened Noyes Academy in Canaan, N.H. Before they had been there more than a few months neighboring farmers, angered by the boys' presence and their participation in local abolition meetings, dragged the school into a nearby swamp and forced the Negroes to leave. The next year Crummell entered Oneida Institute at Whitesboro, N.Y., from which he graduated in 1839. Headed by "that master-thinker and teacher" Beriah Green, Oneida combined manual labor with the classical curriculum. Run by abolitionists—black and white—these schools provided Crummell with almost as good a public school education as any received by a youth in Jacksonian America.

At an early date Crummell had decided on a career as a minister of the Protestant Episcopal church, a career that was to disclose that the life of a highly talented and ambitious Negro clergyman in an essentially white church would be far from easy. On the advice of his rector, the Rev. Peter Williams of St. Phillip's Church, New York, he applied for admission to General Theological Seminary, New York City, in 1839, only to be rejected on the basis of color. For the next four years he studied privately with several of the leading Episcopal clergymen of Boston and Providence. In 1844, after unsuccessfully attempting to organize a mission church among the Negroes of Providence, Crummell journeyed to Philadelphia, where he was ordained a priest. Refused admission to the Diocese of Pennsylvania as an equal, he returned to New York where he succeeded in organizing a congregation of poor, hardworking Negroes. Unable to raise funds for the construction of a church building, he was encouraged by friends to go to England to solicit support.

Because of his training and reputation as a scholar Crummell was called upon early to play a prominent role in the antislavery crusade and in projects for Negro uplift. He spoke on abolition and on self-help at Negro gatherings. He was active in the Negro Convention Movement. At the Albany Convention in 1840 he drafted the petition to the New York legislature seeking removal of restrictions against Negroes on the right to vote. At the National Convention in Troy, N.Y., in 1847 he worked with Frederick Douglass in considering the best means of abolishing slavery and caste, and he

joined James McCune Smith in recommending the establishment of Negro colleges. Crummell always subordinated such activism to his religious duties, however, and in later years he would articulate the view that concern for politics merely wasted valuable energy that could be more effectively directed toward "mental and moral improvement."

Crummell lived in England from 1848 to 1853, a period he later referred to as one "of grand opportunities, of the richest privileges, of cherished remembrances and of golden light." After spending three years raising money for his church, traveling all over the British Isles preaching and lecturing, he studied in Queen's College, Cambridge, under the patronage of English liberals; he graduated in 1853. When Crummell left England he had received more formal schooling—with one or two exceptions—than any American Negro in the mid-nineteenth century. He also left England a firm believer in the efficacy of British institutions.

Instead of returning to the United States, Crummell went to Liberia as a missionary of the Episcopal church. Never too healthy, he had been advised to seek a warm climate. Furthermore he believed that Liberia would offer a person with his training greater opportunities for service to his race than a United States then in the throes of tightening its repression of Negroes. Dedicated to the redemption of Africa, Crummell became a citizen of the new republic, and along with his close associate Edward Blyden became a formulator and an articulate spokesman of Liberian nationalism.

Although Crummell undertook many activities in Liberia, his church work always came first. He performed his missionary labors in almost every corner of the republic, establishing several churches. From the start he was at odds with many of his missionary colleagues, whom he accused of bringing "the malignant and spiteful caste spirit" from America. In 1858 he became master of Mount Vaughan High School at Cape Palmas, where he threw himself into the work of training a group of future leaders for church and state. Three years later, together with Blyden he was appointed to the faculty of the new Liberia College at Monrovia. He was also frequently called upon to speak at the great celebrations of Liberian national life, and he came to see himself as "a public teacher," counselling love of race and country and above all "moral and political restraint." During the American Civil War, Crummell made three visits to the United States to promote emigration to Liberia among Negroes and to stimulate philanthropic interest in Liberian education. In these efforts he worked closely with the American Colonization Society.

Dismissed from his college post in 1866 over long-standing differences with the school administration, Crummell established his own school, modelling it after Oneida Institute. But before he could begin construction the country was overtaken by political strife between the mulatto ruling group and those who like Pres. Edward Roye were identified with the "pure" blacks. Roye was deposed and murdered, and since Crummell had long opposed color caste, advocating that Liberian society be opened to greater participation by native Africans, his life was threatened and his son jailed. Sick and somewhat disillusioned, he left the country for the last time in 1872. To the end of his life, however, he continued to urge the "christianization and civilization" of Africa by skilled, educated Negroes from all over the world.

Back in the United States, in 1873 he settled in Washington, D.C., and later founded St. Luke's Church. He spent much of the time until his retirement as an active minister in 1894 raising funds to build and enlarge the church. As the senior Negro priest in the Episcopal church, he was looked to by his colleagues and young aspirants to the priesthood for leadership and counsel. In 1883 he called a meeting of Negro clergy and laity to protest the absence of Negro bishops in the church, and from it emerged the Conference of Church Workers among Colored People. In his later years, as disfranchisement and segregation gained across the country, Crummell became a frequent lecturer before Negro audiences, especially on college campuses. Always his message was the same: the need for educated Negroes to lead in the redemption of the race. He spent much time after his retirement considering how best to encourage such leadership. He taught at Howard University from 1895 to 1897. In 1897, the year before his death, he organized the American Negro Academy, whose purpose was to encourage intellectual excellence among the race and to counter the mounting volume of racist propaganda against Negroes. Its membership of forty included, among others, W. E. B. Du Bois, Kelly Miller, and Paul Laurence Dunbar.

Crummell published several books of sermons and addresses: *The Relations and Duties of Free Colored Men in America to Africa* (1861), *The Future of Africa* (1862), *The Greatness of Christ* (1882), and *Africa and America* (1891). Conveying his religious and social thought, these large volumes contained the best of his ripe scholarship. A synthesis of religion, sociology, psychology, history, and philosophy, his thought was directed toward the practical goal of elevating the Negroes of Africa and America. Throughout his long life he held the conviction, shared by many in the Negro community of his youth and strengthened by his own experience, that Negroes the world over were linked as a people by ties of kinship and social experience that transcended class and geography. Whether in Liberia or in the United States, they were the victims of a color caste that led whites to assume arrogantly that they were inherently superior, and more important to Crummell, led Negroes to a crippling belief in their own inferiority. His mission was to change the negative image of blacks in the white and the black mind by encouraging Negroes to work for their own redemption.

Crummell rested his concept of race advancement and his attack on color caste on the Christian ideal of brotherhood, the "answering heart of man responding to the beating heart of his brother." Man best expressed his love of God in service to his fellowman, a perfectionist principle stressed by many antebellum reformers. Although he had a duty to all men, man's first responsibility was to his immediate family and his second was to his race, for, said Crummell, "race feeling, like family feeling, is of divine origin. . . . Indeed, a race *is* a family."

A Christian moralist, Crummell judged nations and peoples, like individuals, by what he fondly referred to as character, "the consummate flower of true religion." The Puritan values of thrift, restraint, honesty, industry, godliness, and philanthropy must be the basis of "a grand moral revolution" that would achieve black liberation, replacing the oppressiveness of inferiority, with a manly sense of superiority. In his view British "civilization" provided the best model for a "new and rising people" like the Liberians and the American Negroes because it contained the proper balance between freedom and restraint.

Work and education, not politics, especially as practiced in Liberia and in the United States in the Gilded Age, Crummell regarded as the principal means of cultivating character. For the Negro masses he recommended the acquisition of trade skills, stressing manual training as much for the moral discipline that theoretically inhered in it as for its material rewards. Of primary importance to him, however, was the education of a leadership class, "scholar-philanthropists" who pursued knowledge not for its own sake but with the intent of putting it to the practical use of solving problems confronting the race. They required an education in the liberal arts. Crummell thus anticipated Booker T. Washington in his emphasis on manual training for the masses, but he also anticipated Du Bois in his fear that ideals were in danger of being sacrificed on the altar of materialism. (Near the end of his life Crummell told a group of Negroes that "He greatly preferred the master idealist [Plato] to his materialist junior Aristotle.")

If difficult to measure with precision, Crummell's influence was nonetheless sizable. He was instrumental in establishment of a tradition of Negro scholarship. There was little consistent, systematic body of scholarly Negro thought before Crummell. Moreover, as much as anyone he was responsible for the precedent of putting scholarship to the service of Negro protest and advancement. Antedating the vogue of scientific or critical method, his scholarship was strongly imbued with a humanistic faith in reason and a deterministic belief in the intervention of God in human affairs. His ideas were a synthesis of several disciplines. A man of eloquence, dignity, and rectitude, he provided inspiration and moral and intellectual guidance to a small but influential minority of concerned Negroes in Liberia and in America. He was a "public teacher" on three continents. As such he played a significant role in determining the perimeters and rhetoric of key issues affecting Negroes: the nature of black leadership, the kind of education best suited to the needs of the race, the efficacy of participation in politics, and the relationship of Afro-Americans to Africa. Du Bois did not greatly exaggerate when he wrote about Crummell: "In another age he might have sat among the elders of the land in purple-bordered toga; in another country mothers might have sung him to the cradles" (*The Souls of Black Folk* [1970 ed.], p. 185).

After the death of his first wife in the 1870s, Crummell married Jennie M. Simpson in New York City on Sept. 28, 1880. He died of "heart disease" at Red Bank, N.J., on Sept. 10, 1898. Funeral services were held in St. Phillip's Church, New York City, where Crummell had begun his church life as an infant, and he was interred in the church's burial grounds. He was survived by his widow.

There are no biographies or extended studies of Crummell. In addition to his works mentioned in the text, see *Alexander Crummell, 1844–1894: The Shades and Lights of a Fifty Years' Ministry* (1894). "Of Alexander Crummell" is one of the more moving essays in Du Bois's *The Souls of Black Folk* (1903). See also Otey M. Scruggs's *We the Children of Africa in This Land: Alexander Crummell* (1972). The scope of his writings is evident in the *Dictionary Catalog of the Jesse E. Moorland Collection of Negro Life and History,* compiled by Dorothy B. Porter (1970, 2:764–66). He is not included in *DAB.* — OTEY M. SCRUGGS

CUFFE, PAUL (1759–1817), wealthy merchant-mariner and humanitarian. Cuffe is best known for his leadership in the early movement for the settlement of Negroes from the United States in Sierra Leone. To the social historian he is significant as a counter to the racial stereotypes in the works of James Fenimore Cooper and others. Paul Cuffe's life was shaped by the sea, a frontier in the sailing-ship era, and by his close association with the Society of Friends. The seventh of ten children and the youngest of four boys, Cuffe was born to a former slave, Cuffe Slocum, and an Indian mother, Ruth Moses. His Massachusetts birthplace, the island of Cuttyhunk (land's end), was opposite New Bedford and so wedded to the sea as to convince him "that commerce furnished to industry more ample rewards than agriculture" (*Freedom's Journal* [New York], March 16, 1827). Paul Cuffe—the family save one, had adopted its father's given name as its surname—spent most of his life in Westport, a sea-oriented Quaker haven in southeastern Massachusetts. Here he was married to Alice Pequit, of his mother's Wampanoag tribe, in 1783; and here, fourteen years later, he purchased a $3500 farm on the East Branch of the Westport River where his six daughters and two sons were to grow up.

In his advance from forecastle to quarterdeck, Cuffe amassed a fortune derived from whaling, coastal shipping, and trade with the Caribbean and Europe. He was not deterred by five unsuccessful ventures in Cuffe-built or -owned vessels in the Buzzards Bay area. Success came after the Revolution. His codfishing in an eighteen-ton ketch earned subsidies under federal acts of 1792 and 1794. Probably the captain and his associates circumvented the Jefferson Embargo of 1807 by trading with Canada along the ill-defined frontier of Maine's Passamaquoddy Bay; Cuffe's vessels cleared for that point after the deadline.

The captain held shares at various times in at least ten vessels, including the schooner *Ranger,* the brig *Hero,* the ship *Alpha,* and his favorite, the brig *Traveller.* These four were built at Westport, between 1795 and 1806 (*Ship Registers of New Bedford, Massachusetts* [1940], 1:8, 147, 268, 310). What this meant in terms of capital investment is hard to estimate. The ten-year-old brig *Traveller,* inventoried for Cuffe's will at $1800, and the ship *Alpha* were offered for sale for $10,000 (*Probate Court,* Taunton, Mass., and Samuel Fisher from Paul Cuffe, April 20, 1815, Cuffe Papers).

In the great commercial expansion of his times Paul

Cuffe could earn up to $50 per ton per year for cargoes (Robert Albion and Jennie Pope, *Sea Lanes in Wartime: The American Experience, 1775–1942* [1942], p. 94). But the record indicates that the sponsorship of leading Quakers and even Quaker doctrine were ingredients in his success. His closest associate was Friend William Rotch, Jr., whose *Letter Book for 1804–1808* (Old Dartmouth Historical Society, New Bedford, pp. 365–66) reveals concern that Paul Cuffe, "Master and owner of the ship *Alpha,*" be given a second opportunity to extend his voyage to Saint Petersburg to load a cargo of hemp and iron. Rotch told the master of the ship *Pacific* to contact Cuffe at Bordeaux and to give him the assignment if he wished it. Members of the society captained Cuffe vessels and shared with him the belief that spiritual and material worlds were inextricably connected and that industry, frugality, and zeal, the essentials for success in the counting house, were pleasing to God and were manifestations of a true Christian. Similarly, God's work was manifest in Cuffe's contract with his Swedish indentured servant Abraham Rodino (Sheldon H. Harris, "Paul Cuffe's White Apprentice," *American Neptune* 23 [July 1963]: 192–96). Another interesting commentary on the captain's status comes from William Rotch's *Letter Book, 1804–1808.* Instructions were issued to "pay Samuel Tobey craftsman for $25 *his owner* [italics added]. Capt. Paul Cuffe will repay me." His wealth and social status, however, did not protect him from racial discrimination in travel and accommodations. As an earnest of his religious zeal Paul Cuffe donated $574.25 in materials toward the nearly $1200 cost of a new Friends Meeting House in Westport. This was done with the same self-sacrifice attendant upon establishing a school on his farm in 1797 for a community unwilling to build one itself.

Paul Cuffe was a pioneer in the struggle for minority rights. The action may have been influenced by debate over a clause of the Massachusetts Constitution of 1778 to withhold the franchise from Negroes and Indians. But in 1780 Paul and his brother John, after refusing to pay their taxes, joined with other Dartmouth Negroes to petition the state, county, and local government to grant relief from the payment of taxes. Although the petitioners complained that many Negroes and Indians had "gone into the wars," their request was rejected. A court decision in 1783 granted them the right to vote.

It was Cuffe's effort to colonize Sierra Leone and Christianize its inhabitants which brought him an international reputation. But there is no satisfactory explanation of what led to this deep interest in Africa and in settling Negroes from the United States in Sierra Leone. Perhaps his formal adherence to the Society of Friends in 1808 was part of a deep religious experience which convinced him that he was God's agent for conversion of Africans. He had the active support of the Westport Friends, of the African Institution in London and Quakers in Philadelphia. There is, however, no evidence of any association with the African Union Society of nearby Newport, R.I.; the society had been established by free Negroes in 1787 and had promoted the idea of a return to Africa in correspondence with the Committee of African Affairs in London (*Correspondence of the African Union Soci-*

ety, Letters 1–3, Jan. 1787, Newport Historical Society, Newport, R.I.).

Paul Cuffe made two trips to Sierra Leone; the first (1810–1812) was exploratory and was broken by a nine-week stay in England; this visit evoked wide attention in the press (*The Times* [London], Aug. 2, 1811, p. 3) and won him the respect and admiration of William Wilberforce and other prominent Englishmen; the stay of three additional months in Sierra Leone convinced the captain of the feasibility of settlement and of the bright prospects of a triangular trade funneled through his personally sponsored Friendly Society.

In 1812 he and his friends marshalled enough pressure to win Cuffe audiences with Secretary of the Treasury Albert Gallatin and Pres. James Madison to restore the Sierra Leone cargo seized from the *Traveller* for violation of laws against trading with the British. And in 1814 the *Annals of the Congress of the United States* (13th Cong., 1st and 2d sess., pp. 569, 570, 601, 861–863, 1265) reported a Memorial from Paul Cuffe requesting a congressional clearance to Africa for ship and cargo; the request was approved by the Senate but rejected by the House.

Thus the second trip to Sierra Leone was delayed until December 1815 when the *Traveller* went to sea with thirty-eight settlers (eighteen adults and twenty children), the nucleus of the planned model community. Paul Cuffe returned home convinced that settlement in Sierra Leone and southern Africa constituted a workable solution to the blind alley in which Negroes of the United States found themselves, provided British trade barriers and shortages of funds could be solved. Before Cuffe's death, James Forten, Richard Allen, and Absalom Jones first gave their tacit or open support to colonization, but a strong popular reaction arose among free Negroes in Philadelphia and elsewhere.

A shipping and business dynasty grew up around Paul Cuffe which lasted for another generation and perpetuated his influence. He entered into a partnership with two sons-in-law, Alexander and Peter Howard, to sell goods from Europe, Asia, and the West Indies. His brother-in-law, Michael Wainer, and the Wainer boys were joint-owners and captains of vessels. Pardon Cook, another son-in-law, became master of vessels owned by other Quakers. Also the strength of the Temperance Movement among New Bedford and Nantucket Negroes may be attributable to the early influence of Paul Cuffe.

Paul Cuffe's Journal, letters, and scrapbook are in the Free Public Library in New Bedford, Mass.; other Cuffe correspondence is located at the Historical Society of Pennsylvania in Philadelphia, the New York Historical Society, and Yale University. *The Liverpool* [England] *Mercury* (Oct. 4 and 11, 1811) contains an interview with Paul Cuffe; this is a major source for the history of his life. The same material appears in New York's *Freedom's Journal* (March 16 and 23, and April 6 and 13, 1827). Also consult Cuffe's work, *A Brief Account of the Settlement and Present Situation of the Colony of Sierra Leone in Africa as Communicated by Paul Cuffe (a Man of Colour) to His Friend in New York* (1812).

General treatments of Paul Cuffe are Sheldon Harris's *Paul Cuffe: Black America and the African Return*

(1972), George Salvador's *Paul Cuffe, the Black Yankee, 1759–1817* (1969), Henry Noble Sherwood's "Paul Cuffe" (*JNH,* vol. 8, April 1923). There is a short article by Benjamin Brawley in *DAB* (3, Part 2:585).

— HAROLD O. LEWIS

CULLEN, COUNTÉE [P.] (1903–1946), poet, novelist, and anthologist. Cullen was born Countée Porter in New York City on May 30, 1903. Very little is known about his early childhood. It is believed that he lived with his maternal grandmother until she died in 1918. He was then adopted by the Rev. and Mrs. Frederick A. Cullen. The Reverend Cullen was the pastor of Salem Methodist Episcopal Church. Under his leadership, Salem became one of the largest and most influential churches in Harlem. The childless Cullens made the young Countée their son in every way they could, giving him all the advantages and, more important, all the affection which a child of their own would have received.

Countée Cullen was educated in the public schools of New York, attending De Witt Clinton for his high school work. At that time Clinton was considered one of the best public secondary schools in the city. Although very few Negroes attended De Witt Clinton, Cullen made an excellent adjustment there. He was vice-president of his senior class, treasurer of the Inter-High School Poetry Society, editor of the *Clinton News,* the school's weekly, chairman of the Senior Publications Committee, and editor of the senior edition of *The Magpie,* the school's literary magazine.

The young Cullen also made an excellent record in scholarship. He was elected to Arista, the scholastic honor society; and when he graduated on Jan. 26, 1922, he received not only general honors but also special honors in Latin, mathematics, English, history, and French as well.

Cullen began writing poetry while in elementary school; during his career at Clinton he began to attract public attention. He won second prize in a contest conducted by the Inter-High School Poetry Society for an entry entitled "In Memory of Lincoln." In the Jan. 1921 issue of *The Magpie,* however, he published the well-known "I Have a Rendezvous with Life," a poem which brought him not only wide acclaim but also a prize in a contest sponsored by the Federation of Women's Clubs.

Cullen did his college work at New York University, showing there the same scholarly excellence he had shown in high school. He was elected to Phi Beta Kappa in 1925, one of only eleven graduates to receive this honor. While in college Cullen also greatly sharpened his poetic techniques and by the time of his graduation was nationally known. In 1923 he won second prize in the Witter Bynner Undergraduate Poetry Contest; in 1924 second prize again, and in 1925 first prize. His 1923 entry was "The Ballad of the Brown Girl," a poem which elicited praise from Harvard's George Lyman Kittredge.

The year 1925 was an exceptionally fruitful period for Cullen. In May of that year he won second prize in the *Opportunity* Literary Contest for his poem "To One Who Said Me Nay." (The first prize went to Langston

Hughes for his "The Weary Blues.") Cullen's entry, "Threnody for a Brown Girl," won the John Reed Memorial Prize awarded in 1925 by the magazine *Poetry.* And in that year Countee Cullen published *Color,* his first and perhaps his best major collection of verse. This was truly an *annus mirabilis* for the young college poet.

After graduating from New York University, where he had prepared in a general way to become a teacher, Cullen went to Harvard where he took his M.A. in 1926. In subsequent years he studied at the Sorbonne, making an excellent record there as a scholar in French literature.

In 1926 Cullen became the assistant editor (under Charles S. Johnson) of *Opportunity,* a position he held for approximately two years. While on the staff he wrote editorials for the periodical and conducted "The Dark Tower," a series of columns/articles which featured many of his book reviews.

The year 1927 was another remarkable period for Cullen. In recognition of his growing significance as a poet he was given the Harmon Foundation Literary Award for that year. He was also given a Guggenheim Fellowship for study abroad. And in 1927 Countee Cullen published *Copper Sun,* his second major collection of poems.

Before leaving America to study abroad on his Guggenheim Fellowship, Cullen took a step which he was later to regret. On April 10, 1928, he married Nina Yolande Du Bois, the daughter of W. E. B. Du Bois. The couple were joined in a highly publicized wedding held in the church of the groom's father. The affair was the major event of the year for Harlem society. It was an unfortunate alliance, however, which lasted only a short while. Yolande Cullen was granted a divorce in Paris in 1930. Countée Cullen contracted a second and a highly successful marriage on Sept. 27, 1940, this time to Ida Mae Roberson, the sister of the then well-known singer Orlando Roberson.

The fact that from 1934 until his early death Cullen was a popular, dedicated, and effective schoolteacher is often overlooked. He taught French and English at Frederick Douglass Junior High School (P.S. 139) in Harlem. In spite of his success as a writer, he seemed to believe that a steady income was a necessity. With the exceptions of Langston Hughes and possibly Wallace Thurman, practically all Harlem Renaissance writers felt that they needed a fixed income from other sources in order to be creative writers.

Cullen died in New York City on Jan. 10, 1946, in Sydenham Hospital. Funeral services were held in Salem Methodist Church, Seventh Avenue and West 129th Street. Interment was in Woodlawn Cemetery. He was survived by his widow, Ida Mae Roberson Cullen, and his father, pastor emeritus of the church.

The major writings of Countée Cullen are contained in ten published volumes. Five of them are collections of his verse: *Color* (1925); *Copper Sun* (1927); *The Black Christ, and Other Poems* (1929); *The Medea, and Some Poems* (1937), primarily a new version of Euripides' classical drama but classed here as a collection because of the "Some Poems"; and *On These I Stand: An Anthology of the Best Poems of Countee Cullen* (1947). Posthumously published, the selection

was made by the poet. He added six new poems. When considering Cullen's major poetry publications, one must add *The Ballad of the Brown Girl: An Old Ballad Retold* (1927).

In 1927 Cullen also edited and published *Caroling Dusk,* one of the outstanding anthologies "of verse by Negro poets" of the Renaissance.

In his later years, the poet published two whimsical and lighthearted volumes: *The Lost Zoo (A Rhyme for the Young, But Not too Young) by Christopher Cat and Countée Cullen* (1940) and *My Lives and How I Lost Them by Christopher Cat in Collaboration with Countee Cullen* (1942).

Cullen's single novel, *One Way to Heaven,* came out in 1932. He collaborated with Arna Bontemps in making the latter's novel, *God Sends Sunday,* first into a play and then into a musical, *St. Louis Woman.* The musical was presented on Broadway in April 1946 and ran for 113 performances.

Countée Cullen wished to be considered a poet and not a *Negro* poet. He wanted to feel that he was not, as an artist, a prisoner of his color; and yet, as he sadly admitted, he found his poetry "of itself treating of the Negro." It is also true that a considerable number of his best poems have racial themes. Cullen, however, rebelled against the pressure of race and after a certain time simply turned away from racial subjects.

Cullen was preeminently a lyric poet, and he wrote about things and themes that lyric poets from the time of the Greeks have emphasized: love (its ecstasy and its heartbreak), the changing faces of nature, the transitoriness of life, the certainty of death, and similar subjects. There are also several special themes which often recur in Cullen's verse. The first of these is the one referred to above—his attitude toward the label "Negro poet." The initial poem in Cullen's first collection of verse, *Color* (1925), is entitled "Yet Do I Marvel." Its theme is driven home in the last couplet. Although God is capable of explaining all things, the persona says: "Yet do I marvel at this curious thing:/ To make a poet black, and bid him sing!"

This poem set the stage for Cullen's many subsequent comments on the same subject. In the Foreword to *Caroling Dusk,* an anthology he edited in 1927, the poet tells his readers that he calls his volume "an anthology by Negro poets" rather than "an anthology of Negro verse." He then adds that he believes that as long as Negroes speak English, their poetry will have more to gain from English and American literature "than from any nebulous atavistic yearnings toward an African inheritance."

Racial poems in each of Cullen's collections are grouped under the rubric "Color." In the first collection there are twenty-three such poems; in *Copper Sun* (1927), the second, there are seven; in *The Black Christ* (1929), the third, there are four, including the long title-poem; and in *The Medea, and Some Poems* (1935), the last collection (not counting *On These I Stand*), only one poem touches on the racial theme and that obliquely. It is therefore fair to say that after 1929, the year he published *The Black Christ,* Countée Cullen tired of racial themes; and he tells us just that in a poem addressed "To Certain Critics": "Then call me traitor if you must," he says to those who felt that he had betrayed the race by his action, "For never shall the clan/ Confine my singing to its ways/ Beyond the ways of man."

A second strain that runs through much of Cullen's racial poems is what may be called the alien-and-exile theme. Used by many of the New Negro poets *inter alia* to glorify Africa, this theme stated or implied that the American Negro is an alien in the United States, an exile from his idyllic homeland. As an exile, he contrasts the harsh, ugly existence in racist America with the free, dignified, and beautiful life his ancestors led in Africa. Africa, of course, for these poets was not an actual place. The "dusky dreamlit" land of their verses is pure fantasy, pure escapist symbol. But the theme was popular, and there are many variations on it in Cullen's lines, particularly those found in *Color* (1925). Perhaps the finest expression of the alien-and-exile theme in New Negro literature is Countee Cullen's "Heritage."

Another subject to which Cullen often returned was his own religious faith. In the sketch of himself that he wrote in the third person for *Caroling Dusk*, he states that "reared in the conservative atmosphere of a Methodist parsonage, Countee Cullen's chief problem has been that of reconciling a Christian upbringing with a pagan inclination." This was written in 1927. Early works of his like "Heritage," "Pagan Prayer," and other poems in *Color* (1925), show this conflict. In *Copper Sun* (also published in 1927), one notes changes in the poet's attitude (assuming here that the speakers in the verse express their creator's opinion). "In spite of Death" and "The Litany of the Dark People" tend to repudiate the pagan stand of his earlier poems. In the next collection, *The Black Christ*, the poet, through his personae, seems to have come full cycle to a Christian position. The title-poem of this work is a strong affirmation of faith, and in another piece, "Counter Mood," the speaker dispels all doubts concerning his belief in the Christian promise.

Still another recurring theme in Countee Cullen's verse is a concern with death and the funereal. His poems contain an unusual number of images of and allusions to death, often in poems that on the surface have nothing to do with man's last enemy. For Cullen, death was several things: an escape for the oppressed, a release from an intolerable or harsh situation, a source of wisdom, and the way to a new world of beauty. Characteristic death poems are found in "A Brown Girl Dead," "The Wise," and "Two Thoughts on Death." Cullen's concern with death also carried over into an apparently serious interest in suicide. "The Shroud of Color," "Suicide Chant," and "Mood" are all suicide poems, and there are others.

In Cullen's first collection of verse there is a section, labeled "Epitaphs," which contains twenty-nine of these pointed burial inscriptions, most of them quatrains with alternate eight- and six-syllable lines. Cullen had great skill in writing these short pieces. He could condense into a few brilliant lines a wealth of humor, of wisdom, and of keen social comment. The best known of these epitaphs are "For a Lady I Know" and "For a Mouthy Woman." Although it is not an epitaph, the poet's now-classic "Incident" has the same condensed

suggestiveness and brilliance found in the burial inscriptions. The little boy, "riding in old Baltimore," who was called "nigger" has become a symbol of the deep hurt that racial slurs cause in children. And the poem itself, with its surface calm and its ironic implications, is representative of the new type of protest verse written by many poets of the New Negro Movement.

His single novel, *One Way to Heaven* (1932), belongs to those works of fiction loosely classified as Harlem-novels. The best known—not necessarily the best —but certainly the most widely read of those novels written by a Negro was Claude McKay's *Home to Harlem*. In his book McKay emphasized the seamier, the more primitive side of Harlem life. Cullen on the other hand delineated two conventional slices of Harlem living: the lower-middle-class, church-affiliated Negroes whom he came to know in his father's church *and* the New Negro "intelligentsia," the segment of Harlem/ New York life to which *he* belonged. McKay seemingly wrote for a public of white readers who were basically interested in the delineation of the Negro as a primitive exotic. More of an inside-the-family novel than McKay's, *One Way to Heaven,* like Fisher's *Walls of Jericho,* brings together two widely separated Harlem worlds and gently satirizes the foibles of each world.

Most contemporary readers of the work enjoyed immensely the good-natured attack on the middle-class world of Constancia Brandon, one of the novel's principal characters. In his description of Constancia's reception, the author laughs at phony black intellectuals, at whites who come to Harlem seeking excitement, at Negro writers who never write anything, and at many other middle-class shortcomings. Cullen's most delightful satirical barbs were launched at those well-to-do Negroes in Harlem who *bought* (and used) titles—lord, duke, lady, countess et al.—from the Marcus Garvey Universal Negro Improvement Association. At the time the Garvey Movement was considered fair game for Negro satirists. Incidentally, several of Cullen's characters, like those in Fisher's work, were well-known Harlem personages easily recognized under fictional names.

One Way to Heaven is not a great novel, but it is a charming and highly readable work. In addition the book makes two significant contributions to Negro fiction: it tells a lot about a segment of Negro life which had not been delineated too often before, that of the big-city Negro church; *and* it is among the first works (*Infants of the Spring* also came out in 1932) to point out some of the shortcomings of the New Negro Renaissance. Countée Cullen, however, did not possess in any great measure a talent for prose fiction. He was essentially a poet.

As is now commonly known, although Cullen was influenced by certain contemporary poets like Edward Arlington Robinson and Edna St. Vincent Millay, his favorite poet was Keats. Cullen adored the romantic writer this side of idolatry; his "To John Keats, Poet. At Springtime" is one of the finest works in praise of Keats found in our language. And this should not surprise us. Writing about himself in *Caroling Dusk,* Cullen makes the following statement: "As a poet he [Cullen] is a rank conservative, loving the measured line and the skillful rhyme; . . . He has said perhaps with a reiteration sickening to some of his friends, that he wishes any merit that may be in his work to flow from it solely as the expression of a poet—with no racial consideration to bolster it up. He is still of the same thought."

Unlike his contemporaries Hughes and Sterling Brown, Countée Cullen did not experiment with blues or jazz forms or with free or blank verse to any appreciable extent, although he was "not blind to the virtues" of those who did. He *was* a conservative, but he handled "the measured line and the skillful rhyme" musically, adroitly, and on occasion brilliantly. Countée Cullen was one of the better American poets of his generation.

For a brief but scholarly life of Cullen, for full and excellent bibliographies, and for critical analyses of some of his poems, see Margaret Perry's *A Bio-Bibliography of Countée P. Cullen 1903–1946* (1971). Blanche E. Ferguson's *Countée Cullen and the Negro Renaissance* (1966) is a very "human" biography which gives many fascinating anecdotes and details concerning the poet's studies, his work as a teacher, his friends and social life here and abroad, his foster parents, and of Harlem and Negro life in general during the first four decades of this century. *Roots of Negro Racial Consciousness, the 1920's: Three Harlem Renaissance Authors* (1964) by Stephen H. Bronz is basically unsympathetic, playing up what Bronz felt was Cullen's "failure to grow as a poet." Jean Wagner's *Black Poets of the United States* . . . (1973) contains sixty-six pages of intense, dynamic, and often brilliant psychological and critical analysis of Cullen as torn personality and as poet. It is the fullest and best documented study of Cullen as a poet yet published. Wagner emphasizes "the great spiritual adventure of a poet named Countee Cullen" rather than the delineation of the poet "mirroring the black soul." There are obituary notices in the *New York Times* (Jan. 10, p. 23, and Jan. 13, 1946, p. 44. — ARTHUR P. DAVIS

CUNEY, NORRIS WRIGHT (1846–1896), politician and businessman. The fourth of eight children of a white man, Col. Philip Cuney, and a slave, Adeline Stuart, Norris was born on Sunnyside Plantation, near Hempstead, Tex. He and the other children lived like free people. In 1856 he and two brothers studied at the Wyle (Wylie?) Street School in Pittsburg, Pa. The outbreak of the Civil War prevented them from attending Oberlin College. Settling in Galveston shortly after the close of the war, Norris Cuney by 1884 was recognized as the leader of the Negro vote in Texas and was the Republican state national committeeman from 1885 to 1896. From 1889 to 1893 he was collector of Customs at Galveston. Six months after his defeat as national committeeman for Texas, Cuney died and was buried in Lake View Cemetery, Galveston (from the obituary of his daughter in the *Houston Informer,* June 23, 1936).

Cuney's rise and fall reflected the shifting pattern of Texas and national politics. From 1867 to 1872 the Republican party was in the majority in Texas and Negroes were so numerous that during that period and for many subsequent years it was called the "nigger party." Even some white Republicans opposed the domination of Negroes and resented Cuney's leadership. In addition Cuney's lack of visible means of support made him vulnerable to attack. Appointed inspector of Customs in Galveston in 1872, he was dismissed for accusing the collector of Customs of prejudice in dispensing patronage. At that time, however, leading white citizens aided him in gaining reinstatement, but he was again dismissed in 1877. In 1874, however, he had been appointed secretary of the state executive committee and in 1876 was a delegate to the Republican National Convention. In 1881 and 1883 he was elected alderman in Galveston. The opposition of white Republicans to Negro leadership became particularly virulent in elections to the state convention and of delegates to the Republican National Convention in 1884. Cuney was nevertheless selected one of the four delegates-at-large to the national convention. At that convention, John R. Lynch served as temporary chairman, Cuney as one of the vice-presidents. Cuney supported the candidacy of James G. Blaine and was named to the committee which officially notified him of his nomination. Following Cuney's return to Galveston, however, a lily-white fusionist movement of Republicans and Democrats gained momentum. Moreover, as early as 1876 some Negroes had begun to support the Democrats, and in 1884 worked for the election of Grover Cleveland. His victory led to fear that Negroes would be reenslaved and temporarily impeded the growth of Democrats. Meanwhile the division between white and Negro Republicans increased.

Cuney's active support in 1888 of Benjamin Harrison led directly to the president's nomination and Senate confirmation of Cuney as collector of Customs at Galveston. His position, which included dispensing patronage, strengthened lily-white opposition and promoted the abortive idea of a separate party. In the Republican state convention of 1890, lily-whites gained control but were defeated in 1892 largely because they doubted their ability to maintain control. At Dallas, the first all-white Republican convention in Texas, elected delegates to the Republican National Convention as well as a separate state ticket. Harrison's support ensured the seating of Cuney's delegation in Minneapolis. But Harrison's defeat and Cleveland's second election undermined Cuney's leadership in Texas. Cuney's endorsement of fusion in 1892 and the support of Populism by some Texas Negroes so weakened Cuney that in 1893 he was removed as collector of Customs. An attempt to unite the lily-whites and the "Black and Tans" at Fort Worth in June 1894 failed, as did a meeting of the regular Republicans.

Cuney's refusal to support Mark Hanna and McKinley in 1896 led to Cuney's downfall. The Republican National Convention in St. Louis nominated McKinley. Cuney's followers joined the Populists on the state level. Within six months Cuney was dead. His leadership fell to William "Gooseneck Bill" McDonald.

Cuney's other interests were perhaps indirectly linked to politics. As a member of the Texas delegation to a national convention of Negroes in Nashville (May 6–9, 1879), he opposed the Great Exodus led by Moses ("Pap") Singleton. Cuney's opposition may have resulted from his belief that the Exodus would diminish the voting power of Negroes in Texas. As one of the founders (1884) of the Colored Teachers' State Association of Texas, he saw in it not only an educational and social but also a political body. But he also gave generous financial assistance to Sidney Woodward who became one of the best known colored tenors of that era.

It is not known how much Cuney's testing in 1893 of the applicability of the recently established Texas law requiring separate coaches to interstate commerce contributed to his downfall. Nor are the results of the suit known. It is also possible that Cuney's support of Negro longshoremen on the Galveston wharves during the 1880s and his lucrative longshoreman business increased white opposition to him.

Cuney's career makes evident that, in Texas as well as in other southern states, Reconstruction did not come to an end in 1877. His political influence was a factor that led to the Democratic white primary in Texas in the early part of the twentieth century. But recollection of it also buttressed the determination of Negroes to continue opposing the Democratic white primary until the Supreme Court overruled it in 1944. Cuney's name is still invoked in Texas as a pioneer for Negro participation in politics.

Cuney was described by a contemporary: "Slender figure, five feet, ten; straight black hair and mustache, black eyes; high cheek bones; a complexion more suggestive of Italy's sunny clime than of any portion of Africa's darkness." He married Adelina Dowdy, who bore him a daughter, Maud, on Feb. 16, 1874. She received an excellent musical education, notably at the New England Conservatory of Music. As Maud Cuney-Hare she gained fame as a concert and lecture pianist, and wrote *Negro Musicians and Their Music* (1936), an indispensable source.

The principal source for Cuney's career is the somewhat eulogistic biography by his daughter Maud Cuney-Hare's *Norris Wright Cuney: A Tribune of the Black People* (1913). His life is more objectively treated in Lawrence D. Wright's *The Negro in Texas, 1874–1900* (1971). — RAYFORD W. LOGAN

CUNEY-HARE, MAUD (1874–1936), pianist, folklorist, lecturer, and author. She was born in Galveston, Tex., the daughter of Norris Wright and Adelina (Dowdy) Cuney. After graduation from the Central High School, Galveston, she received her musical education at the New England Conservatory of Music, Boston, and later under such private instructors as Emil Ludwig, a pupil of Rubinstein, and Edwin Klare, a pupil of Liszt. She then served for a number of years as director of the Deaf, Dumb and Blind Institute of Texas, and at Prairie State College in Prairie View. In 1906 she returned to Boston and married William P. Hare of an old and well-known Boston family. She died there in 1936 and was buried in Galveston in the grave between her father and mother in Lake View Cemetery (*Houston Informer,* June 23, 1936).

Shortly before her death she completed at her home, "Sunnyside," in Squantum, Mass., the manuscript for her book *Negro Musicians and Their Music* (1936). This volume carries the story well beyond *Music and*

Some Highly Musical People by James Monroe Trotter (1878). Chapter 4, "Negro Folk Songs—Religious and Secular," is published in part and with some editorial changes in Lindsay Patterson's *The Negro in Music and Art* (1967).

In the Preface to her book, Cuney-Hare stated: "As an integral part of the nation, the Negro is influenced by the same political institutions; thus we may expect the ultimate result of his musical endeavors to be an art-music which embodies national characteristics exercised upon his soul's expression." Clarence Cameron White, in his Introduction to the book, wrote: "As a concert and lecture-pianist Mrs. Hare has travelled widely and as a folklorist she has collected songs from far off beaten paths in Mexico, the Virgin Islands, Puerto Rico, and Cuba. She was the first to collect and bring to the attention of the American concert public the beauties of New Orleans Creole Music as attested by her *Creole Songs,* published by Carl Fischer and Company of New York City."

Cuney-Hare also contributed articles to *Musical Quarterly, Musical Observer,* the *Christian Science Monitor, Musical America,* and many other magazines and newspapers. For many years she edited the column of music notes for *The Crisis* (some of which are listed in Dorothy Porter, comp., *Dictionary Catalog of the Jesse E. Moorland Collection of Negro Life and History, Howard University, Washington, D.C.* [1970], vol. 4).

Cuney-Hare's *Negro Musicians* consists of fifteen chapters, an Appendix, "African Musical Instruments," an additional section on "Negro Folk Songs," and a valuable bibliography. Numerous illustrations, especially of such hard-to-find contemporary photographs as those of the Fisk Jubilee Singers, Will Marion Cook, Robert Cole and Rosamond Johnson, Flora Batson, Abbie Mitchell, the Coleridge-Taylor Society of Washington (1900), Harriet Gibbs Marshall, E. Azalia Hackley, and Samuel Coleridge-Taylor, make *Negro Musicians* an indispensable source of information. The biographical sketches have been widely used by later writers.

Cuney-Hare also compiled an anthology of poems, *The Message of the Trees . . .* with a foreword by William Stanley Braithwaite (1918). Her *Norris Wright Cuney: A Tribune of the Black People* (1913), although understandably laudatory, is a principal source for the life of her father.

Cuney-Hare established in Boston the Musical Art Studio and promoted there a "Little Theatre" movement among Negroes. Among the plays was her "Antar, Negro Poet of Arabia" (*The Crisis,* June 1924, pp. 64–67, and July 1924, pp. 117–19).

As a recitalist, Cuney-Hare appeared with William Howard Richardson, a noted baritone. One of their most acclaimed performances was a song recital in Boston where he was accompanied by a string quartet from the Boston Symphony Orchestra, with the conductor Arthur Fieldler as viola player and Mrs. Cuney-Hare as accompanist (*Negro Musicians . . . ,* pp. 366–67).

The principal printed source is Clarence Cameron White's Introduction to Cuney-Hare's *Negro Musicians and Their Music.* — RAYFORD W. LOGAN

CURRIN, GREEN JACOB (initials sometimes given as G. I. or G. L., and surname as Curran) (c. 1847 – probably after 1915), Oklahoma's pioneer civil rights advocate and the first and only Negro in its territorial legislature. Born in Tennessee, he came to Kansas (c. 1877) in the great "Exoduster" movement of southern Negroes, and by 1883 was living in Topeka where in 1885 he was a member of the police department (1885 Kansas Census, Shawnee County, Ward 1, p. 63). In 1888 he was the Republican nominee for police judge, but despite the city's Republican majority of 1500, he and two other Negro Republican candidates were defeated (W. H. Chafe, *Journal of Southern History,* vol. 34, Aug. 1968).

This defeat seems to have turned Currin's thoughts from Kansas to Oklahoma. He participated in the great land rush of April 22, 1889, was successful in obtaining a claim in Kingfisher County, and in July was elected vice-president of the Oklahoma Immigration Association of Topeka, which supported the plans of E. P. McCabe for Negro colonization of the Cherokee Strip. He was elected, principally by the votes of white Republicans, to Oklahoma's first territorial legislature, and introduced a civil rights bill which passed the Assembly by an overwhelming majority on Dec. 20, 1890, but was defeated in the Council, or upper house, by a single vote.

Thereafter, as Kaye M. Teall states, "Very little . . . is known" about Currin. During the territorial period he served as a deputy U.S. marshal and as a regent of the Colored Agricultural and Normal University (later Langston University), founded in 1897. In 1910 he was one of the Negroes denied registration under a new state constitutional provision aimed at disfranchising all Negroes while through the "grandfather clause" permitting even illiterate whites to vote. In a suit in the Circuit Court of Appeals in 1915 *(Guinn et al. v. U.S.)* he testified that he had been denied registration although entitled to vote both because he could read and write and because his grandfather Tommy Curran, an Irishman, had voted. Although the U.S. Supreme Court in 1916 found the "grandfather clause" unconstitutional, Oklahoma's white Democratic majority continued for nearly half a century to disfranchise Negro citizens through other devices.

Nothing further is known about Currin after his testimony in 1915, when he was in his late sixties. Two photographs, taken in early middle age and in more advanced years, show him as a bearded man of notably dignified aspect. Currin and his wife Caroline, whom he married in Tennessee (c. 1869), had four sons and three daughters of whom the youngest, a son, died in infancy.

The principal source for Currin's Oklahoma career is Kaye M. Teall's *Black History in Oklahoma* (1971), but other information is in *Kingfisher Panorama* (1957), and in census and land records in the Oklahoma Historical Society. — KENNETH WIGGINS PORTER

CURTIS, AUSTIN MAURICE (1868–1939), surgeon and hospital administrator. One of nine children of Alexander and Eleanora (Smith) Curtis, Austin was born in Raleigh, N.C. Among his teachers in the public schools of Raleigh was Louisa Dona, a northern school ma'am who inspired him to seek a higher education. He attended Lincoln University in Pennsylvania, where he earned the B.A. degree in 1888 and received two honorary degrees: M.A. in 1898 and Sc.D. in 1929. He earned his M.D. degree from Northwestern University in 1891. He spent his summers as a Pullman car porter. For three years after graduation Curtis came under the influence of Dr. Daniel Hale Williams, founder of the Provident Hospital in Chicago and the famous surgeon credited with the first successful operation on the pericardium. He was Williams's first intern and remained as his first assistant and house surgeon at the Provident Hospital in 1897–1898.

When Williams was called to Washington to become the surgeon-in-chief of Freedmen's Hospital in 1894, Curtis continued to practice surgery in Chicago. By 1896 his reputation was such that he became the first Negro to be appointed to the surgical staff of the Cook County Hospital.

When the election of Pres. William McKinley led to the removal of Williams, a Democrat, Curtis (a Republican) was appointed in 1898 as the chief administrative officer at Freedmen's. He was surgeon-in-chief of Freedmen's for only four years, but remained identified with it and the Howard University College of Medicine for the remainder of his life, as professor of surgery at the Howard University School of Medicine, and professor of surgery and head of the department and chief of surgical service at Freedmen's Hospital (Rayford W. Logan, *Howard University: The First Hundred Years, 1867–1967* [1968], p. 123). During his incumbency as surgeon-in-chief he was referred to by the hospital and medical school personnel affectionately as "Pa Curtis" and addressed by all as "Dr. A. M." "Pa Curtis" had mastered not only the art of surgery but also the art of teaching, being most effective at the bedside, on rounds, and in the operating room.

He initiated, and for many years directed, a faculty of surgeons who conducted a six-week postgraduate course for many rural surgeons. He operated before local and state societies in various localities and was the first Negro surgeon to operate in some hospitals, in both the North and South. He was consulting surgeon at Provident Hospital and Richmond Hospital, Richmond, Va. In 1911 he was elected president of the National Medical Association. During World War I he was an army contract surgeon.

He was married to Namahyoka Sockume on May 5, 1888, and the father of four children—three sons, all of whom became physicians: Arthur L., Austin M. Jr., and Merrill H.—and one daughter, Gertrude E. Norris. He was head of the Curtis Private Surgical Sanitarium in Washington, first vice-president of the Prudential Bank in that city, and a director of the Standard Investment Company. One of the colored elite of the nation's capital, he was a member of the Mu-So-Lit Club and Epsilon Boulé, Sigma Pi Phi fraternity. For many years he resided at 1736 U St. NW, with his office at 1939 13th St. NW.

There is an obituary in *JNH* (Oct. 1940, pp. 502–3), probably written by Carter G. Woodson. See also *Who's Who in Colored America* (1937), edited by Thomas Yenser; and William Montague Cobb's "Austin

Maurice Curtis, 1868–1939" (*JNMA*, July 1954, pp. 294–98). Interviews with persons who knew Curtis have also been helpful. He is in the group photograph of some of Washington's most distinguished colored citizens shown in *History of Sigma Pi Phi . . .* by Charles H. Wesley (1954, p. 78). See also Arthur Burroughs Caldwell's *History of the American Negro and His Institutions* (1922, 6:279). — LASALLE D. LEFFALL, JR.

DABNEY, AUSTIN (1760?–1834), soldier. Allegedly the son of a Virginia white woman and a Negro father, Dabney was probably born in North Carolina. Shortly after the outbreak of the American Revolution a man named Richard Aycock brought Austin from North Carolina to Wilkes County, Ga. It was naturally assumed that Austin was a slave. However, when Aycock was ushered into the Georgia Militia, he asked that the young mulatto be permitted to take his place, swearing that the boy was indeed a free person of color, since the law forbade slaves to bear arms for any reason. Austin was placed under the command of Col. Elijah Clarke in the Georgia Militia and assigned to a company headed by a Captain Dabney. The captain soon gave his own surname to the young soldier.

As Austin Dabney prepared to join those American patriots who had vowed to sacrifice fortunes and lives for colonial independence, other Georgians were rallying to obey Lord Cornwallis's order that the property of "all who refuse to take the oath of allegiance to England" be burned and destroyed. At Kettle Creek, on a cold winter day in February 1779, the issue was to be joined. Could the patriots break the Tory domination of northeastern Georgia and halt the Loyalist reign of terror? Understandably the encounter was one of the bloodiest battles fought in Georgia, ending in a decisive patriot victory. All of the patriots except Austin Dabney were free white men. Of all the heroics of the day, none was perhaps greater than that of the young boy, Austin Dabney. During the combat, a rifleball passed through his thigh, crippling him for life and ending a brief but distinguished military adventure.

While convalescing from his combat wound, Dabney was the guest of the Giles Harris family of Wilkes County. Dabney had been taken immediately into the Harris home after being struck, and the Harrises' care probably saved his life. The colored soldier was never to forget the kindness which the family had shown to him. He attached himself to the family as a laborer, friend, and, eventually, benefactor.

In 1786 the Georgia legislature emancipated Dabney by statute to prevent his former "master," Aycock, from seizing him as a slave and reaping benefits from the young soldier's military fame. Then in 1821 the legislature passed a special act granting Dabney a farm of 112 acres of choice land in Walton County. Dabney had been passed over in the Land Lottery of 1819 because Negroes were not permitted to participate in this program designed to encourage settlers in Georgia. The special act, to reward Dabney for his Revolutionary War heroism, was bitterly opposed by many white Georgians. Others, like Stephen Upson of Oglethorpe, who had introduced the measure in the legislature, and Gov. George Gilmer supported Dabney. The governor reminded the opposition of the soldier's "courageous service" to Georgia and chided them for acting in such an "unpatriotic" manner.

During the later years of his life, Dabney became increasingly prosperous, owning a number of fine horses and achieving a reputation as a professional sportsman. When the Harris family moved to Pike County about 1830, Dabney accompanied them. Despite his prosperity and fame, he continued to serve the Harrises and, upon the death of Giles, shared his resources with them. He financed the legal education of Harris's eldest son and underwrote the boy's early practice.

Honored and respected by some of the most notable whites of the day in Georgia, including two governors, Dabney had lived apart from the harsh life which most of his fellow Negroes, slave and free, had to endure. Thus when he died at Zebulon in 1834 it was not surprising that his remains were laid beside those of a white man, Giles Harris, and he was, in the words of Carter G. Woodson, "mourned by all." He was Georgia's only genuine Negro hero of the American Revolutionary War.

W. B. Hartgrove first called attention in recent years to Dabney in "The Negro Soldier in the American Revolution" (*JNH*, April 1916, pp. 110–31). Benjamin Quarles referred to Dabney in *The Negro in the American Revolution* (1961). See also Mrs. Howard H. McCall's *Roster of Revolutionary Soldiers in Georgia* (vol. 3, 1969). For life in Georgia, see George W. Gilmer's *Sketches of Early Settlers of Upper Georgia* (1855) and Edward F. Sweat's "Social Status of the Free Negro in Antebellum Georgia" (*NHB*, March 1958). The grant of land to Dabney is in *Acts of the General Assembly of Georgia* (1821). — ALTON HORNSBY, JR.

DABNEY, WENDELL PHILLIPS (1865–1952), writer, musician, journalist, protest leader, publisher, and man of political influence. Born in Richmond, Va., on Nov. 4, 1865, the son of John and Elizabeth (Foster) Dabney, he progressed through school and experienced racism and prejudice as most Negroes did during that era. It appears that he was an average student who probably was not motivated to study while in school. In his youth he was influenced by his father's political and religious beliefs. His father taught him that Republicans helped Negroes and Democrats did not. His family was semireligious.

Wendell's daily routine consisted of selling newspapers in the afternoon, completing homework in the evening, and learning to play the guitar with his older brother or learning to dance with his sister. He waited on tables during the summer months. Because of racial prejudice, he began to dislike waiting on white people. He believed that whites were enemies and that they viewed Negroes favorably only when they were servants.

During his senior year in Richmond's high school there arose a problem that had been brewing for a number of years, the fact that commencement exercises for Negroes were held in a church while commencement exercises for whites were held in a Richmond theater. Wendell's class decided to rebel. The result of the class discussion was that the Negro graduates would not use the church as the site for the ceremony. Wendell was selected spokesman and therefore had the responsibility to communicate the decision of the class to the principal. His class graduated at the school rather than the church and Wendell was somewhat successful as the class spokesman. About this time he began to realize the value of books and read very often.

He waited on tables again that summer with his father. Upon graduation from high school he was looking forward to earning wages on an annual basis beginning in the fall. Instead he entered Oberlin College. While at Oberlin he was accepted as first violinist at the Oberlin Opera House. He was a good student at Oberlin and was honored by being accepted as a member of the Cademian Literary Society. This experience coupled with his earlier experiences led him to believe that a Negro man could succeed in a white man's world if given an opportunity. He also believed that Negroes should no longer remain silent. Now twenty and having completed his first year at Oberlin, he decided to return home and help his parents by waiting on tables because no other position was available to him. In 1884, however, he secured a job teaching school in Louisa County, sixty-two miles from Richmond, because of his feeling about the degrading effects of waiting on tables. In addition to teaching, he directed a banjo and guitar club in Richmond, and also gave mandolin lessons. In 1890 Dabney established a music school in Boston and taught some students from Harvard. In 1893 he worked with Frederick Douglass on the Emancipation Exhibition for the World's Fair in Chicago.

In 1894 he moved to Cincinnati to settle business affairs for his mother who had been willed the Dumas House. Started in the 1840s, it was the first hotel for Negroes in Ohio and became a station of the Underground Railroad. He converted part of the Dumas House into a gymnasium, the first of its kind in Cincinnati, and rented the other part to organizations for meeting rooms. While there he married Nellie Foster Jackson in August 1897. After their one son died in 1898, they adopted two stepsons.

George Jaberg and Wurlitzer Music Companies published several songs written by Dabney. Later he became interested in politics and decided to give up music. Through the Republican party he was appointed assistant license clerk in Cincinnati. About this time Dabney and his associates founded a political league named for Frederick Douglass, and Dabney was elected president. The Douglass League consistently spoke out against racial injustice, and also tried to educate Negro voters how they should vote. He served as assistant paymaster and head paymaster of the treasury in Cincinnati (1898–1923).

Dabney established a newspaper, *The Union,* on Feb. 13, 1907. Its motto was "For no people can become great without being united, for in union there is strength." Although it had only a few pages, it helped mold public opinion in behalf of Negroes.

He was the first president of the Cincinnati branch of the NAACP and fought against segregated schools. He had acquired much property during his earlier years in Cincinnati, and in 1925 he sold it for a total of $127,-500. In 1923 he published a pamphlet, *The Wolf and the Lamb.* In 1926 he wrote and published a book, *Cincinnati's Colored Citizens,* lauded by both of Cincinnati's major newspapers. In 1927 he wrote and published *Maggie L. Walker: The Woman and Her Work,* and *Chisum's Pilgrimage and Others.* In 1934 he wrote "Slave Risings and Race Riots," an article in *A Negro Anthology,* edited by Nancy Cunard.

He proposed a Public Conduct, Appearance, Industry and Savings Week. In November 1949 he was given a testimonial dinner and birthday party, in recognition of his achievements and in honor of his eighty-fourth birthday, which was attended by over four hundred people. He was also honored at a national convention of Negro publishers in January 1950.

In retrospect his two most notable achievements were editing and publishing *The Union* for approximately forty-five years, and his book *Cincinnati's Colored Citizens. The Union,* manned by Dabney entirely, was respected for its accuracy, candor, sarcastic approach, and wit. *Cincinnati's Colored Citizens* is believed to be the first book in the state of Ohio that discussed the history and achievements of Negro Americans. It is still a valuable source.

In his home Dabney had one of the largest collections of photographs of famous Negroes extant at that time. He knew many contemporary Negro leaders. A man of pungent wit, he could keep several stories going at the same time.

There are few published works about Dabney. J. T. Beaver's *I Want You to Know Wendell Phillips Dabney* (1958) is the most useful. Gail E. Berry's "W. P. Dabney: Leader of the Negro Protest" (M.A. thesis, University of Cincinnati, 1965) is indispensable. There are valuable references in the Cincinnati Historical Society. The last paragraph of the text is based on the reminiscences of Rayford W. Logan. — WILLIAM DAVID SMITH

DAILEY, ULYSSES GRANT (1885–1961), physician, surgeon, author, and editor. Born in Donaldsonville, La., the son of S. Toney Hanna and Missouri (Johnson) Dailey, he attended high school in Fort Worth, Tex., and did his college work at Straight (now Dillard) University in New Orleans. After receiving his M.D. degree from the Northwestern University Medical School in 1906, the youngest and the fifth-ranking member of his class, he served there as assistant demonstrator of anatomy (1906–1908). He was an ambulance surgeon (Chicago Civil Service, 1907–1908), a gynecologist in Provident Hospital, Chicago, founded by Daniel Hale Williams in 1890 (1907–1912), and associate surgeon there (1910–1912). After postgraduate work in Paris and Berlin (1912) he became attending surgeon at Provident (1912–1926), instructor in clinical surgery at Chicago Medical College (1916–1918), and attending surgeon at Fort Dearborn Hospital, Chicago (1920–1926). Meanwhile he continued postgraduate work in London, Paris, and Vienna (1925–1926). In 1926 he founded the Dailey Hospital and Sanitarium in Chicago. From 1926 to 1932 he was surgeon-in-chief at Provident and senior attending surgeon and senior attending surgeon emeritus there from 1932 to 1961.

From 1916 to 1917 Dailey was president of the National Medical Association, editor of its *Journal* (1948 to 1949), and consultant editor until shortly before his death. He wrote more than forty articles for *JNMA*. "The Future of the Negro in Medicine" (July–Sept. 1929, pp. 116–17) observed that while there was need for high-grade general practitioners, more attention should be given to the training of specialists, not only in surgery but in internal medicine, obstetrics, pediatrics, and eye, ear, nose, and throat. In "Proposals with Reference to the Idea of a Negro College of Surgeons" (March 1942, p. 76) he strongly urged tabling "for the time at least" the establishment of a separate (Negro) college of surgeons.

Among his medical articles were "Total Congenital Absence of the Veriform Appendix in Man" (*Surgery, Gynecology and Obstetrics,* Oct. 1910) and "Vasovesiclities Acute Appendix" (*New York Medical Journal and Record,* June 1924). He was a fellow of the American College of Surgeons, the American Medical Association, the International College of Surgeons, the Institute of Medicine of Chicago, and a diplomate of the American Board of Surgery. In 1952 he was elected a member of the International Board of Trustees of the International College of Surgeons.

In addition to his professional activities in the United States Dailey had a great interest in health problems in Haiti. In 1942 he and his wife, the former Eleanor Jane Curtis, a sister of Austin M. Curtis, whom he had married on Feb. 16, 1916, were received with high honor by Haitian officials and by Mr. and Mrs. Nolle Smith, the head of the U.S. Technical Assistance Program. In 1952 Dailey established a chapter of the International College of Surgeons in Karachi, toured Pakistan for the U.S. State Department as a visiting surgeon, lectured and performed several operations. He also visited India. In 1953–1954 he made a second tour for the State Department, including visits to Pakistan, India, Ceylon, the Belgian Congo, Kenya, Uganda, Ghana, Nigeria, Senegal, and Liberia. In 1955 he made a world tour with other surgeons under the auspices of the International College of Surgeons, with stops in Japan, the Philippines, Hong Kong, Thailand, India, Pakistan, Turkey, and Lebanon. He was awarded the honorary D.Sc. degree by Howard University in 1947 and Northwestern University in 1955. Haiti conferred upon him the grade of officer of the National Order of Honor and Merit and made him its honorary consul in Chicago.

There is a brief obituary by W. Montague Cobb in *JNMA* (July 1961, p. 432). Earlier information is in *Who's Who in Colored America* (1950), edited by G. James Fleming and Christian E. Burckel, and an article in *JMNA* (July 1960, pp. 309–10). Dailey is in the group photograph with Charles Victor Roman and others on page 70 of Herbert M. Morais's *The History of the Negro in Medicine* (1967). — RAYFORD W. LOGAN

DANCY, JOHN CAMPBELL, JR. (1888–1968), Detroit Urban League director and community leader. Born in Salisbury, N.C., the son of John C. and Laura G. Dancy, he was greatly influenced by his father who had been born a slave and studied in the Howard University Preparatory Department (1874–1876) at the same time as T. Thomas Fortune, George H. White, George W. Cook, and William D. Crum. The elder Dancy was one of the better known laymen in the A.M.E. Zion church: he edited at Tarboro, N.C., the *North Carolina Sentinel* and during twenty-five years made the *Star of Zion* and the *A.M.E. Zion Quarterly Review* two of the more influential denominational journals among Negroes (1892–1917). He was an ardent advocate of the church's support of Livingstone College, Salisbury, and other higher educational institutions. A staunch Republican, he served as collector of customs at Wilmington, N.C. (1889–1893 and 1897–1901), and as recorder of deeds, Washington, D.C. (1901–1911). In 1898 the elder Dancy was elected a vice-president and a member of the National Afro-American League. In 1907 he, his wife, young John, and his brother Joseph attended a banquet given by Pres. Theodore Roosevelt which young John remembered as the first occasion when a colored family attended a banquet at the White House. If his recollection is correct, it is all the more memorable because little known, and remarkable because of the vituperation heaped upon Roosevelt when he had entertained Booker T. Washington at dinner in 1901.

The father's relative affluence enabled young John to attend private schools in Salisbury until he was fifteen, to spend three years at the Phillips-Exeter Academy (1904–1906), and to graduate from the University of Pennsylvania in 1910 (Betty Schmiedtgen, executive secretary, Phillips-Exeter Academy, to Rayford W. Logan, July 14, 1976).

During the summer he worked, mainly as a waiter on boats on the Great Lakes. He was school principal in Clairmount, W.Va., and in 1911 he became secretary of the Negro YMCA in Norfolk, Va. He recalled the five years he spent there with a special fondness. "There wasn't much chance for colored kids to have any decent recreational outlet in Norfolk at the time so they used to flock to the 'Y.' I've had as many as 500 kids in my care at one time. You know, I went back to Norfolk a couple of years ago and they hadn't forgotten me," Dancy told a reporter in 1954.

After a year as a probation officer in the Children's Court of New York City (1916) he became active in the Urban League and the Big Brother Movement. He went to Detroit in 1918 to succeed Forrester B. Washington as director of the local Urban League.

When he arrived, Detroit like many other northern cities was faced with the problem of large numbers of Negroes arriving from the South. He was convinced that "The Colored [Urban League] worker knows and understands the psychology of the migrant. He has a warm sympathy that cannot and does not carry with one of another race" (Detroit Urban League board minutes, in Nancy J. Weiss, *The National Urban League, 1910–1940* [1974], p. 74). Dancy was quietly determined that the war by which the world was "to be made safe for democracy" bring benefits to Negroes, especially in Detroit. Years later he wrote: "I can remember when I came to Detroit, no one dreamed that one day there would be Negro judges, a Negro councilman and Negro baseball players in the majors. Many doors have been opened to qualified Negroes." What he did not add, of course, was that he personally was responsible in considerable measure for turning the doorknob in hundreds of cases.

Urbane in manner and appearance, quiet in speech, he managed to win the confidence of scores of business and industrial leaders. At one point he was to say: "I've been to these men for hundreds of favors. They have refused me almost nothing. But in all those requests I have never asked anything for myself."

Dancy's achievements were legion. In 1920 he convinced the United Community Services to hire a Negro stenographer, and made national news. She was reported to be the first Negro stenographer in the country to be hired by a white organization. He was instrumental in breaking the "ghetto" pattern that had forced Negroes to live in one small corner of Detroit, and he introduced scores of Negroes to art, music, and his special pride and joy, the Green Pastures Camp, which provided hundreds of children a free camp experience for many summers.

He was a total citizen. He was a member of the Detroit House of Corrections Commission for twenty years and secretary-treasurer of the Parkside Hospital for seventeen. He was a director of the United Community Services, and was active in the Metropolitan Planning Commission, the Board of Education, the American Red Cross, the Governor's Commission on Youth Problems, the Detroit Symphony Orchestra, and the Detroit Round Table of Christians and Jews. He was also president of the Detroit Library Commission. He was to serve forty-two years as the Detroit Urban League's director before he retired on Sept. 30, 1960, when a *Detroit Free Press* editorial stated: "Often berated by those to whom age has not yet brought the wisdom of deliberateness of his pace, Dancy has had possibly the greatest impact of any individual on race relations in Detroit. Others have been momentarily more militant, more dramatic, but none has been more effective." The mayor of Detroit proclaimed "John C. Dancy Day" and more than seven hundred civic leaders attended a dinner to pay tribute to "Mr. Urban League." President Eisenhower, Vice-President Nixon, and Gov. G. Mennen Williams of Michigan sent congratulatory telegrams. In 1963 he was given an annual Amity Day Award by the Women's Division of the American Jewish Congress. On Alumni Day, May 27, 1967, the trustees of the Phillips-Exeter Academy conferred upon him the John Phillips Award, honoring an alumnus "whose life and contributions to the welfare of his community, his country, and mankind exemplify in high degree the nobility of character and usefulness to mankind that John Phillips sought to promote in establishing the Academy."

He died after a lingering illness of nine months in Kirkwood Hospital, Detroit, on Sept. 10, 1968. Funeral services were held on Sept. 14 at John Wesley A.M.E. Zion Church, Beachwood and Moore Place, with burial in Elmwood Cemetery. Among the honorary pallbearers were Gov. George Romney, Whitney Young, Lester Granger and Guichard Parris of the Urban League, Henry Ford II, and Joe Louis. Dancy was preceded in death by his first wife, Maude Bulkley, in 1964. There were no children (*Detroit News,* Sept. 11, 1968, p.

12B). A younger brother, Joseph, had also predeceased him.

Information about Dancy Sr. is in William J. Walls's *The African Methodist Episcopal Zion Church, Reality of the Black Church* (1974, passim). Dancy Jr.'s career in Detroit is based on the Detroit Urban League Papers, Michigan Historical Collections of the University of Michigan, and Detroit daily newspapers. Editorial in the *Detroit Free Press* (Sept. 12, 1960).The Dancy Papers are in the Carnegie Library, Livingstone College, Salisbury, N.C. — FRANK ANGELO

DANDRIDGE, DOROTHY (1922–1965), singer and motion picture actress. She was the second daughter of a Cleveland minister, Cyril Dandridge, and his wife Ruby, a stage entertainer. Shortly after Dorothy's birth, the couple separated. Most of the child's early formative years were spent entertaining on road tours. Billed as "The Wonder Kids," she and an older sister Vivian sang, danced, and performed comedy skits at schools, churches, and social gatherings around the country.

During the 1930s the family abandoned the road-tour circuit to settle in Los Angeles. There her mother Ruby was eventually to make her mark as a successful comedy actress on radio and television. The children, while enrolled in school, also did bit parts in Hollywood films such as in the closing sequence of the Marx Brothers comedy *A Day at the Races* (1937).

In the 1940s, appearing with another colored girl, Etta Jones, and then billed as "The Dandridge Sisters," Dorothy and Vivian toured the country with the Jimmy Lunceford Band. At sixteen Dorothy appeared at the Cotton Club where she met Harold Nicholas of the famed Nicholas Brothers dancing team. The two married and had one child, a brain-damaged daughter, Harolyn. The marriage ended in divorce. In subsequent years Dorothy Dandridge was to say it was the tragedy of her daughter's condition, perhaps more than anything else, which propelled her into her remarkable career.

She always had an interest in developing a film career. That interest was intensified when she appeared in minor roles in *Drums of the Congo* (1942) and *The Hit Parade of 1943.* Her early roles, however, only served to whet her appetite. They failed to satisfy her burning drive and astounding ambitions. At the time, most Negro women in films, such as Hattie McDaniel and Louise Beavers, were confined to servant or "mammy" roles. Dorothy Dandridge hoped to break that mold.

Surprisingly, a trio of low-budget films, *Tarzan's Perils* (1951), *The Harlem Globe-Trotters* (1951), and *Bright Road* (1954), brought her to national attention and gave momentum to her movie career.

While she struggled to establish herself as a dramatic leading lady, Dandridge managed simultaneously to build a highly successful career as a nightclub singer. Appearing at some of the smartest supper clubs in the country, she made her New York debut in 1952 at La Vie En Rose. So successful was her engagement there that she saved the then financially teetering cafe from bankruptcy and became New York's "overnight sensation." Later she was to become one of the first Negro performers to appear at the exclusive Waldorf Astoria.

But it was in 1954 that the Dandridge career reached its apex when she won the much-sought-after title role in Otto Preminger's all-star black spectacle *Carmen Jones.* Appearing opposite Harry Belafonte, Pearl Bailey, Diahann Carroll, and Brock Peters, she was the very embodiment of the capricious, self-destructive flirt. Running her picture on its cover, *Life* wrote: "Of all the divas of grand opera . . . who have decorated the title role of *Carmen* and have in turn been made famous by it, none was ever so decorative or will reach nationwide fame so quickly as the sultry young lady . . . on *Life*'s cover this week." Her performance won her an Academy Award nomination. Although Grace Kelly won the award that year, it was the first time in the history of American motion pictures that a Negro woman had been nominated for an Oscar in a leading role.

Afterward, with the continuing success of her nightclub work and with either cover stories or feature articles on her in *Life, Paris Match, Time, Ebony, Confidential,* and a host of other publications, she emerged as an international personality, the most celebrated and talked about Negro performer working in American films. Sadly, though, her meteoric rise soon diminished, not so much because of its star but because of the period in which she lived.

In the apathetic 1950s the movie business was still a conservative and bigoted industry. Had she been a white actress with such a great success, Dandridge would have been signed to an exclusive studio contract and carefully starred in a series of important films. But as she herself said in her autobiography *Everything and Nothing,* "I was to reach a high and also the beginnings of a decline inevitable for a Negro actress for whom there was no place else to go, no higher or better role to play, no new story available, no chance to play roles meant for white only." It was three years before she again appeared in front of the cameras.

Island in the Sun was the film that marked her return. Centering on the theme of miscegenation, the film cast Dandridge opposite white actor John Justin and Harry Belafonte. It was the first time the interracial love theme had been explored in movies, but even as its producer Darryl F. Zanuck has admitted, the film was weakened by compromise and the studio's fear of offending the large white audience by having interracial segments that were too explicit. Her later films, *The Decks Ran Red* (1958), *Tamango* (1959), and *Malaga* (1962), all touched on the miscegenation theme, but they too failed to deal honestly and intelligently with the subject. Producers were unsure how to cast Dandridge, what her "nationality" or "race" should be in her pictures, and how to handle her love scenes with white actors. The problems in working out an *acceptable* screen image troubled the beautiful actress. One of her most important later roles was as Bess in Preminger's *Porgy and Bess* (1959), another all-star Negro musical extravaganza with Sidney Poitier, Pearl Bailey, and Sammy Davis, Jr.

In the early 1960s Dandridge's career took as disastrous a turn as her stormy personal life. Her second marriage to white restaurant owner Jack Dennison ended in divorce. Later the actress filed for bankruptcy and was forced out of her deluxe Hollywood mansion.

There were few film or nightclub offers, and Dorothy Dandridge found herself an anachronism in a new Hollywood. Finally, in 1965, at the age of forty-one, she was found dead in her Hollywood apartment. After a debate over the exact cause of her death, an autopsy attributed it to an overdose of an antidepressant drug. Funeral services were held in Little Church of the Flowers, Forest Lawn Memorial Park in Glendale, and her body was cremated. She was survived by her mother, Ruby Dandridge, and her divorced husband, Jack Dennison.

The best source is Dorothy Dandridge's and Earl Conrad's *Everything and Nothing: The Dorothy Dandridge Tragedy* (1970). Obituaries appeared in the *New York Times* (Sept. 9, 1965, p. 41; Sept. 11, 1965, p. 27; Oct. 12, 1965, p. 58). — DONALD BOGLE

DART, ISOM [ISHAM, ISAM] (fl. c. 1885–1900), roper, rider, rustler, and rancher. He is remembered principally as a victim of the notorious Tom Horn, hired killer for the big cattle interests, but partly as a fictional character, under the name of Ned Huddleston in an amateurish novel *Outskirt Episodes* (1927), by W. G. Tittsworth, which several writers have taken at face value.

Dart arrived in Brown's Hole, "where Colorado, Wyoming, and Utah corner," sometime in the mid-1880s, possibly with a Texas trail herd. He soon became well known and popular for his horsemanship, skill with a rope, physical strength, elaborate costumes, and good nature. People who knew him declared later that he was "one of the best cowboys ever to mount a horse in the high mesa country," "the best bronc rider that ever threw a leg over a horse," who "could ride any horse on the range" and was "an adept with a rope." One Brown's Hole pioneer summed up: "I have seen all the great riders, but for all-round skill as a cowman, Isam Dart was unexcelled and I never saw his peer."

At first employed as a horse wrangler by the Middlesex Land and Cattle Company, he soon attached himself to the Bassett family, both as ranch hand and as cook, woodcutter, launderer, and general houseman.

Brown's Hole, however, was a noted rustlers' hangout and Dart soon became a member of a band of cattle thieves of whom Elizabeth Bassett was probably the mastermind. He is said to have "rustled more than his share of cattle," for he was an expert with rope and branding iron and the hot wire used in running "hair brands," which looked genuine until the hair grew out. He had homesteaded a little ranch at Summit Springs, which he is said to have stocked with stolen cattle bearing the "wagonwheel brand," which could cover almost any other brand. But a more recent historian thinks that the cattle he rustled were promptly sold and that he stocked his little ranch by capturing wild horses, gentling and training them, and swapping them for cattle, on which he used the I D Bar (ID) brand.

Dart, however, was probably the most amiable and indeed almost innocent rustler who ever altered a brand. His popularity was such that even when, with difficulty, he was arrested, the district attorney usually failed to issue an indictment, and when indicted it proved impossible to convict him. In 1890, although

Dart, with other Brown's Hole residents, was indicted both for arson and for altering the brands on three horses, he broke jail and was never brought to trial. On another occasion, when arrested in Wyoming, the buckboard in which a deputy was bringing him to Rock Springs slipped off a mountain road, seriously injuring the officer—whereupon Isom rescued him, gave him first aid, got the vehicle back on the road and the deputy to a hospital, and quietly surrendered to the sheriff. At the trial the deputy appeared as a character witness and so impressed the jury that in spite of the evidence, the verdict was "not guilty"!

Abhorred by the wealthy cattlemen, Dart was beloved by most Brown's Hole residents. When Josephine Bassett married Jim McKnight and gave birth to two sons, Dart attached himself to her family, as previously to the Bassetts, singing the little boys Negro songs, "putting on shows" for them (so that one of them commented that he would never need to go to a circus since he had one right at home), and as they grew older teaching them riding and roping so that they became superlative rodeo performers—although Dart himself shunned the publicity of such occasions.

Finally, however, early in April 1900 the wealthy ranchowners hired Tom Horn to spy out and eliminate the Brown's Hole rustlers. In June several suspects, including Matt Rash, a Texan whom Horn considered the principal leader, and Dart found on their doors notes ordering them to leave within thirty days, and on July 8 Rash was shot dead in his doorway. Early on the morning of Oct. 3, when Dart stepped out of Jim McKnight's cabin to go on roundup, he too was shot dead. Not until Oct. 21 did Dart's friends dare to return to give his body proper burial.

Thus perished Isam Dart, after, however, having for some fifteen years enjoyed the affection and respect of most Brown's Hole residents as a superlative rider and roper, a good neighbor, and an expert and industrious cattle thief.

John Rolfe Burroughs's *Where the Old West Stayed Young* (1962) is the best researched of several works incidentally dealing with Dart. Other works, more concerned with Tom Horn, are Charles Kelly's *The Outlaw Trail* (1938; rev. ed. 1959), Jay Monaghan's *Last of the Bad Men* (1946), Dean Krakel's *The Saga of Tom Horn* (1954), and—slightest and least trustworthy—Dane Coolidge's "Tom Horn—Scout and Man-Hunter," in *Fighting Men of the West* (1932). A studio portrait of Tom Horn as a well-groomed, two-gun, cowboy-dandy appears in William Loren Katz's *The Black West* (1971), dust-jacket and p. 159). A photograph in Katz (p. 159) and Burroughs (p. 29) portrays him more realistically as the central figure in a group of Brown's Hole cattlemen. — KENNETH WIGGINS PORTER

DAVIS, BENJAMIN J[EFFERSON], SR. (1870–1945),

politician, fraternal organization leader, entrepreneur, and editor. He was born in the little cotton town of Dawson, Ga., on May 27, 1870. His mother, father, and elder brother had been born slaves. With his formal education cut off at the sixth grade, Davis became essentially a self-educated man. He was intelligent, aggressive, and resourceful, and after spending some time

searching for a career he decided to devote his life to journalism and politics. He married Jimmie Willard Porter on Aug. 7, 1898; they had two children, Benjamin Jefferson Jr. and Johnnie Katherine. By the turn of the century Davis had also begun to develop a special interest in a Negro fraternal group known as the District Grand Order of the Odd Fellows. Years later, as its leader, he was to help make the Odd Fellows the wealthiest Negro fraternal organization in the South. In 1903 Davis began publishing a weekly newspaper, the *Independent,* soon known as the most militant Negro newspaper in the Deep South. Unable to obtain advertisements from either Negro or white businesses, the *Independent* existed principally on subscriptions and a subsidy from the Odd Fellows. However, Davis's reputation as a militant editor spread throughout the country. He was ultimately to be elected president of the National Negro Publishers Association.

In 1909 Davis moved with his family from Dawson to Atlanta, where he immersed himself in the affairs of the Odd Fellows. In 1912 under his dynamic leadership the organization built a complex of buildings known as the Odd Fellows Block. It consisted of a modern six-story office building and a two-story office annex, housing a large auditorium which could seat 2000 people. The complex was to become the commercial and professional center of Atlanta's Negro community, and Booker T. Washington pointed to it as the "way out" for the southern Negro.

Throughout his life, however, Davis's first love was politics. Like most Negroes of his time he was a Republican. In Atlanta he became secretary of the Georgia state Republican organization, a post he held for ten years. For nearly twenty-five years he served as state at-large delegate to the Republican National Convention. On the death of his friend and associate Henry Lincoln Johnson in October 1925, Davis moved into a position of real power in the southern wing of the Republican party. Johnson had been serving as a Georgia member of the Republican National Committee. Upon his death Davis succeeded him in the post.

As national committeeman Davis became a patronage boss in Georgia. His approval was required for all federal appointments, including postmaster, postmistress, U.S. district attorney and internal revenue collector. Davis's son, Benjamin Jr., described this period: "I used to view with sardonic pleasure the small time postmasters beating a path to my father's door—perhaps a Southern Klan-minded white seeking favors of a Negro political boss." By 1927 Davis was being recognized as one of the three top Negro leaders of the Republican party in the South. (The other two were Perry Howard of Mississippi and Robert Church, Jr., of Memphis, Tenn.)

These men were, however, not without their detractors. Called "black and tan" Republicans, northern white Republican accused them of being parasites who represented a nonexistent electorate. As early as 1901 Theodore Roosevelt had blasted southern Negro Republicans as a group "who make not the slightest effort to get any popular votes, and who are concerned purely in getting Federal offices and sending to the National Convention delegates whose venality makes them a menace to the party." During the next quarter of a century northern white Republicans continued their efforts to divest the "black and tans" of their power and status in the party.

After winning the Republican nomination for president during the summer of 1928, Herbert Hoover mounted a campaign to drive the Negro leaders out of the party and to replace them with whites. Davis, Howard, Church, and others were accused of representing "rotten boroughs," of wanting an all-Negro Republican party in the South and of selling patronage. Called before a Senate subcommittee investigating patronage conditions in the South, Davis spent a week on the stand denying that he was engaged in the sale of federal offices. Davis was harassed by Hoover's men all through the fall and winter of 1928. In April 1929, a little more than a month after his inauguration as president, Hoover called Davis to Washington and summarily dismissed him from the Republican National Committee.

With the advent of the Depression Davis's Odd Fellows organization found itself in disastrous financial difficulties. Beyond this, his weekly *Independent,* without a subsidy and never able to subsist on subscriptions alone, ceased publication. With it all, however, Davis remained a moderately wealthy man. He had maintained his son in high style while a student at both Amherst College and the Harvard Law School. In 1932 he had set him up in practice in Atlanta. It was Benjamin Jr., on the other hand, who was to cause Davis the greatest shock and disappointment of his life. This was the younger man's decision in 1936 to give up his law practice, join the Communist party, and move to New York to work in the party's headquarters. Relations between the two remained strained for some time. As the younger Davis put it: "Little by little the relations between my father and me took on the character of an armed truce. It was more armed than 'truce' when I abandoned the practice of law in 1936 and entered full time into labor and Communists movements."

Although no longer a member of its national committee and considered *persona non grata* by many of the older white party leaders, Davis Sr. doggedly continued his allegiance to the Republicans. At the party's national convention in 1944 when an attempt was made to unseat southern Negro delegates, Davis arose and said, "For fifty years I have supported the ticket and built the party . . . and now, for the first time, I see the Southern Negro in real jeopardy. . . . My son is now a member of the City Council of New York elected on the Communist ticket. If this convention does not give us a seat, my people and I know where to go." Politically this was to be Davis's swansong. He died of cancer after a long illness in New York's Harlem Hospital on Oct. 28, 1945. He was survived by his son Benjamin J. Jr., his daughter Mrs. Richard M. Carey, two brothers, a granddaughter, and a nephew. Funeral services were held on Nov. 2, 1945, in Friendship Baptist Church, Atlanta, the Rev. Maynard H. Jackson, Sr., officiating. Burial was in Southern Cemetery, Atlanta. — ROBERT H. BRISBANE

DAVIS, BENJAMIN J[EFFERSON], JR. (1903–1964), lawyer and Communist leader. The son of Benjamin J.

Sr. and Jimmie W. (Porter) Davis, he was born in Dawson, Ga., on Sept. 8, 1903. In 1909 the family moved to Atlanta. His father was the founder and editor of the weekly newspaper, the *Independent.* He was also a leader among Negro Republican politicians in the Deep South. Young Davis attended the Morehouse College Academy (a high school then operated by the institution). Graduating in 1920, he spent the next year as a freshman in the college, and in 1921 transferred to Amherst College. Besides playing varsity football and tennis he played the cornet in the band, sang in the glee club, and participated in intercollegiate debating. One of his teammates on the football team was Charles R. Drew, who would later become a medical scientist and earn national fame for his development of the blood bank. Another of Davis's classmates was William H. Hastie, who was to become the first Negro judge named to the U.S. Circuit Court of Appeals. After graduating from Amherst in 1925 Davis entered the Harvard Law School, receiving his LL.B. degree in 1929.

In 1932 Davis began the practice of law in Atlanta and took on a partner, John Geer. In June of that year the young law partners began the defense of youthful Negro Communist, Angelo Herndon. Arrested in Atlanta for leading a protest demonstration, Herndon had been charged with violating a law enacted by the Georgia legislature in 1861 against slave insurrections, amended in 1871 to apply to both white and black "insurrection." Conviction carried the death penalty.

Davis based his defense on the unconstitutionality of the Georgia insurrection statute, the exclusion of Negroes from grand and petit juries, the right of citizens to assemble to petition their government against grievances, and the many other rights denied to ordinary working people. He asserted the right of the workers to organize, to strike, to make their demands, and to nominate candidates of their choice. The prosecution held that the possession of Communist literature was enough to send Angelo to the electric chair. As the trial progressed Davis found the hostility in the courtroom to be almost incredible. The presiding judge turned his back and read newspapers whenever Davis spoke. The prosecutor was permitted to call Davis and his client "nigger" and "darky." At the conclusion of the trial the all-white jury returned a verdict of guilty with a recommendation of mercy. Davis was to say later that "It was the turning point in my life. . . . I considered what I could do . . . that would enable me to hit this thing, this Jim Crow System. I considered that the best thing I could do was to join the Communist Party because that would hurt most of all, and so I did." Herndon was sentenced to from eighteen to twenty years in prison. After a five-year battle the International Labor Defense, with Davis as one of the principal attorneys, won a reversal of the decision.

The Herndon case brought Davis national as well as international renown. In 1935 he gave up his law practice in Atlanta and went to work in the party's headquarters in New York City. He was almost immediately appointed editor of the *Liberator,* the party's periodical directed at Negroes. In 1936 he joined the *Daily Worker,* the organ of the American Communist party, as a writer and music critic. He soon became a power on that paper's managing and editorial board.

In 1942 Davis ran unsuccessfully for congressman-at-large from Manhattan, receiving some 50,000 votes. In 1943 the Rev. Adam Clayton Powell, Jr., who had been elected in 1941 as the first Negro member of the New York City Council, ran for the new seat in Congress awarded to Harlem as a result of a recent reapportionment. Davis decided to run for the City Council post. During the late summer and early fall of 1943 he waged a vigorous campaign. One of his most effective supporters was the renowned singer Paul Robeson. Polling a total of 44,334 votes, Davis was elected to the Council from the borough of Manhattan. Davis specialized in Negro affairs during his first term in the Council. He demanded investigations of such issues as segregated housing, the overcrowding of Harlem hospitals, alleged police brutality, inadequate fire protection in Harlem, and the color bar in major league baseball. Davis's popularity in New York City continued to rise through 1945. Running again in 1945 on the Communist party ticket, Davis along with his colleague Pete Cacchione was again elected to the City Council. This time, however, Davis polled 63,498 votes, some twenty thousand more than he had received in his first election. Davis's first term in the Council was a busy and hectic one. His second term, however, was to be stormy and ultimately tragic. In November of 1946 his friend and confidant Pete Cacchione died of a heart attack, thus robbing Davis of an almost-indispensable ally and supporter in the City Council. There were no City Council elections in 1947. In 1945 a law had been passed extending the term of Council members from two to four years.

In November 1949, when Davis made a bid for a third term in the City Council, he was opposed by Earl Brown, an upcoming Negro politician who had managed to secure the endorsement of the Democratic, Republican, and Liberal parties. The result of the election was disastrous for Davis. He polled only 21,962 votes against 63,030 for Brown. A final ignominy for him was his expulsion by unanimous vote from the City Council in late November 1949. On July 21, 1948, Davis and ten other leaders of the American Communist party had been indicted by a federal grand jury in New York City on the charge of violating the Smith Act of 1940, which made it illegal for anyone to teach or advocate the overthrow of any government in the United States by force, or to organize or join any group teaching such a doctrine. The trial began in District Judge Harold Medina's court on Jan. 20, 1949. On Sept. 23 the jury returned a verdict of guilty. Davis and the other defendants were sentenced to five years in prison and a $10,000 fine. In July 1951 Davis was committed to the federal penitentiary in Terre Haute, Indiana. Released from prison after having served three years and four months, Davis was jailed for another two months in Pittsburgh on contempt charges growing out of his appearance as a witness in one of the many trials of secondary party leaders. However, this was not to be the end of his difficulties with the federal law. On March 15, 1962, he and Gus Hall, the Communist party's "chief spokesman," were indicted in the Federal District Court for failure to register the party as an agent

of the Soviet Union as required by the McCarran Internal Security Act of September 1950. Davis was to die before coming to trial under this indictment.

In the years following his release from prison Davis became an ally of William Z. Foster, the national chairman of the party, in demanding a Stalinist hard-line Communist policy after Premier Nikita Khrushchev of the Soviet Union publicly disclosed the excesses of the Stalin era. Davis and Foster defeated efforts to turn United States Communism to a more moderate national course. Davis also defended the Soviet intervention in Hungary (1956), an event which caused many important persons to leave the party in what they called a grim but painful necessity. In addition to being a member of the national committee and national secretary, Davis had also been chairman of the Harlem region of the Communist party, chairman of its National Commission on Negro affairs, and chairman of the New York State District, the party's largest. Davis died on Aug. 22, 1964, of lung cancer in Beth Israel Hospital, New York City. Funeral services were held at First Corinthian Baptist Church, 1912 W. 116th St., and on Aug. 28 at the Unity Funeral Home. He was survived by his widow, Nina Stanley Davis, whom he had married after his release from prison, a daughter Emily (age six), and a sister, Mrs. Johnnie Carey. He was buried in Kensico Cemetery at Valhalla, Westchester County.

Basic facts are in *Who's Who in Colored America.* The Herndon case was widely reported in the Atlanta dailies and by Herndon in his autobiography, *Let Me Live* (1937, reprinted 1969). Brief references and valuable background are in Wilson Record's *The Negro and the Communist Party* (1951) and William Z. Foster's *The Negro People in American History* (1954). Davis is best revealed in his numerous publications. Some of the more important are: *James W. Ford, What He Is and What He Stands For,* (1936), *The Negro People and the Communist Party* (1943), *The Path of Negro Liberation* (1947), *Why I Am a Communist* (1947), *In Defense of Negro Rights* (1950), and *Must Negro-Americans Wait Another Hundred Years for Freedom? Against Tokenism and Gradualism* (1963). Obituaries were in the *New York Times* (Aug. 24, 1967, p. 27) and the *Worker* (Sept. 1, 1967, p. 3).

— ROBERT H. BRISBANE

DAVIS, HARRY E. (1882–1955), politician, government official, Masonic and civil rights leader, author. Born in Cleveland, the son of J[acob] Henry and Rosalie Dete Davis, he attended Hiram College during 1904–1905, then transferred to Western Reserve University and graduated from its law school with the class of 1908. His entire life was spent in his native city as a thoughtful counselor and attorney, as a member and officer of Masonic bodies (Prince Hall affiliation), an early member and proponent of the National Association for the Advancement of Colored People, of the Association for the Study of Negro Life and History, an ardent worker in the church of his boyhood, and a public servant who devoted himself to advancing his profound belief in democracy.

Davis's public service began with his identification with the Republican party, and he served first in the

Ohio General Assembly as an elected representative of Cuyahoga County in 1921. Three consecutive terms followed. He was selected by the Cleveland City Council as a city civil service commissioner, a position he filled creditably from 1928 to 1934. The experience gained in these public offices resulted in his election as a member of the Cuyahoga County Charter Commission in 1934, where he served under the chairmanship of Harold H. Burton, later an associate justice of the U.S. Supreme Court. Davis maintained an active interest in public affairs and in 1947–1949 he served as a state senator for a two-year period in an office which had not been filled by a Negro for fifty-four years. He was elected again to this position for 1953–1954. For his service in the Ohio General Assembly Davis was characterized by newspapermen as "the best legislator in the state" and "the most able member in a quarter century."

Davis joined a Masonic lodge (PHA) in 1910 and developed an intense and scholarly interest in this fraternal movement; as an avocation he engaged in historical research on the foundation of Negro Masonry in America. The work occupied his interest for more than twenty-five years and resulted in the publication in 1946 of a carefully documented history entitled *A History of Freemasonry Among Negroes in America*. An effective speaker on the subject of Prince Hall Masonry, he was frequently called upon in all parts of the country for this purpose. In 1935 Davis was commissioned as special deputy of foreign relations by the Northern Supreme Council and became an advocate of greater racial understanding within the fraternity of freemasonry through meetings of white and Negro Supreme Councils. In 1951 Davis received the Northern Supreme Council Gold Medal Achievement Award for his untiring and continuous efforts to promote interracial accord within the Masonic fraternity.

With the formation of the NAACP he took an active interest in its program, was one of the early members of the Cleveland branch, and for many years served as an executive committee member. The Ohio State Conference of Branches followed his leadership in the promotion of state fair employment practices legislation. His local service with the NAACP led to his selection as a director of the national organization in 1919, a position he held until his death. In August 1920 he and James Weldon Johnson failed in their attempt to have Republican presidential candidate Harding endorse several civil rights proposals (Eugene Levy, *James Weldon Johnson: Black Leader, Black Voice* [1973], pp. 208–9).

In 1926 he was appointed as the first Negro member of the trustee board of Karamu House, a well-known settlement house established to challenge the black-white racial conflict through the cultural arts. He served this organization also until his death. He was a trustee of the Euclid Avenue Christian Church, which he attended for more than sixty years.

The social, civic, and cultural progress of Negroes in his native city was a source of pride to Davis and he devoted some of his spare time to researching the history of the Negro in Cleveland; he had completed a manuscript on this topic shortly before his death. This work was reorganized and updated by his brother, Russell H. Davis, and published in 1972 under the title *Black Americans in Cleveland*. His occupation with the Masons led him to become a prolific writer of articles on masonry. Among them were *The Cathedral*, a pamphlet published in 1938; *The Scottish Rite in Prince Hall Masonry*, a historical sketch, published as a pamphlet in December 1940; "The Prince Hall Sodality," a series of ten articles on Prince Hall Masonry in the *Pittsburgh Courier* starting with the issue of January 1954; "Documents Relating to Negro Masonry" (*JNH*, April 1935); "Prince Hall Masonry" (*Opportunity*, Feb. 1935, pp. 52, 53, 56; reprinted in Bulletin No. 50, International Masonic Association [L'Association Maçonnique Internationale], Geneva, July–Aug. 1934; reprinted in *Dansk Frimeuren*, Denmark, Oct. 1936); "History of Excelsior Lodge No. 11 (PHA)" (1926); "St. John's Lodge No. 350 of Pennsylvania," an extract from "The Prince Hall Sodality"; "Prince Saunders," a biographical sketch of an early Negro Mason (*NHB*, May 1940).

At the age of eighteen he enlisted in the army, and by the time he left this service in 1917 he had advanced to first lieutenant of Company D, Ninth Battalion, Ohio National Guard. He was a member of the delegation representing the state of Ohio at the funeral in Arlington Cemetery of Col. Charles Young on June 1, 1923 (*Washington Evening Star*, June 1, 1923).

Davis was married to Louise Wormley of Washington, D.C., who died in 1946. No children were born to this union. He was buried in Lakeview Cemetery, Cleveland.

In addition to Russell H. Davis's *Black Americans in Cleveland* (1972), see *Here in Ohio* (Oct. 1947); the *Cleveland Press* (July 14, 1947); the *Cleveland Herald* and the *Cleveland Call and Post* (Sept. 6, 1947).

— RUSSELL H. DAVIS

DAY, THOMAS (c. 1800–1860?), furniture maker. He was born on the British West Indies island of Nevis, the birthplace of Alexander Hamilton (North Carolina *State Magazine*, Feb. 15, 1941) or in the rural portion of Caswell County, N.C., approximately two miles from Milton (Caroline Pell Gunter, *Raleigh News and Observer*, June 30, 1929). The date of his birth is also uncertain: between 1785 and 1795 according to Mrs. Gunter; between 1794 and 1804 according to the U.S. Census for 1830. He became well known in Milton for his beautifully carved chairs, small tables, and footstools made first of walnut and later of mahogany imported from the West Indies. By the time of his death, before the Civil War, he was reputed to be the wealthiest free Negro in his part of the state, with an estate worth about $100,000.

Evidence about his life is, in many respects, uncertain. There appears to be no information about his father; his mother is said to have been given her freedom in North Carolina and to have sent him, at his request, to study woodcarving in Boston and Washington for three years. He then returned to Milton, married a Portuguese woman, and began offering furniture for sale in 1818. Other sources state that he studied in Boston between 1818 and 1823, when he moved to Milton.

His business expanded so rapidly that he worked and lived in the old yellow brick Willow Tavern, located across the street from the town's post office. The 1830 Census stated that there were five persons in his family, including some slaves to whom he taught his craft. In that same year he married Aquilla Wilson, a free woman of color from Halifax, Va., (*Journal of the House of Commons,* General Assembly of North Carolina, Jan. 6, 1830). Day also submitted a petition, initiated by Stephen Dodson and other "citizens of Milton," to grant him exemption from the state law of 1826, effective as of 1827, which prevented free Negroes from migrating into North Carolina without the payment of onerous fines and other penalties imposed on the migrants and their sponsors. The petition, introduced by Thomas M. M. Gehee of Person County, adjacent to Day's Caswell County, protected both Thomas Day and his wife Aquilla. Approved by the General Assembly by a vote of seventy-four to forty, the petition stated that Thomas Day was said to be a man whom whites could trust, for, a slaveowner himself, he would report any disturbances among Negroes.

They had three children, Thomas Jr., Devreaux, and Mary Ann. Both sons learned their father's trade and all three attended Wilbraham Academy, Wilbraham, Mass. An article by W. A. Robinson, great-grandson (or great-grandnephew) of Thomas Day, included photocopies of two letters written by Day to his daughter while at Wilbraham, one dated Nov. 27, 1831, and the other of no specified date. This is only one of the many mysteries of Day's life: Thomas and Aquilla Day were married in 1830. The evidence is clear, however, that at the request of her father to Christian Friedrich Sussdorff of the Moravian church of North Carolina, Mary Ann resided at the house of Sussdorf and studied music with him at Aufseher Collegium, the supervisory board that managed the material and financial interests of the Salem congregation. She was accepted on June 28, 1847, which may mean that she was the first person of color to study at Salem College, of which the Aufseher Collegium was the embryo (Minnie J. Smith, ed., "Minutes of the Aufseher Collegium, 1847, *Records of the Moravians in North Carolina,* 1838–1849). According to this version, Mary Ann did not begin to study at Wilbraham Academy until after harassment at the Aufseher Collegium forced her to leave about 1848. She later married Luke Dorland, the founder of Scotia Seminary in Salisbury, N.C. (now Barber-Scotia College). Thomas Jr. moved to Asheville after the Civil War, later married the first principal of Stevens School in Washington, D.C. (built in 1871), and was murdered in Seattle, Wash., while operating his own business. Devreaux reportedly went to South America, became president of a country, and died of a strange fever (Gunter, *Raleigh News and Observer,* June 30, 1929). How much of this is fact is virtually impossible to determine.

Evidence about his prominence as a craftsman rests primarily on the report of a visitor to Milton in 1929. One of Day's best "masterpieces" was a "magnificent old sideboard" in the dining room of G. G. Donoho, which had been in the family for two or three generations. The Donoho family owned other examples of Day's fine craftsmanship, including a little mahogany sidetable with a marble top, seven little mahogany chairs, and a writing table. Donoho reported that Day's mahogany furniture was scattered all over the state, especially in Durham, Greensboro, Raleigh, Charlotte, Winston-Salem, and Fayetteville. J. M. Fleming, Milton's oldest inhabitant, remembered particularly "the fame and work of that straight-haired West Indian Tom Day." The visitor also reported that W. A. Robinson, a "grandnephew" of Thomas Day and "director of the Secondary Schools and Colleges for Negroes of North Carolina," had sat on the same pew in the Presbyterian church in "which Tom Day was privileged to sit" (Paul Ader, "Article Brings Out New Information about Day Furniture," *Durham Morning Herald,* April 13, 1941).

The career of Thomas Day illustrates that the difficulty of separating fact from fiction of a free Negro in nineteenth-century North Carolina, parallels that of many other individuals. The letters to his daughter reveal him as a deeply religious, fairly well-educated father, prescribing rules of conduct for Mary Ann and Devreaux as "the worst boy I ever had to manage in most of his ways." Thomas Day's wife was still living at the time he wrote the letters.

The most easily available information about Day's life is in "Thomas Day and His Family," by W. A. Robinson and others, (*NHB,* March 1950, pp. 123–26, 140). It is based in large part on the article by Paul Ader and the one by Caroline Pell Gunter, "Negro Cabinet Maker Whose Art is Just Now Receiving Full Recognition for Its Merit" (*Raleigh News and Observer,* June 30, 1929). See also the *North Carolina State Magazine* (Feb. 15, 1941), "Tom Day: He Swapped a Whole Set of Pews for the Privilege of Being Allowed to Sit in Church with Aristocratic White Folks of Milton"; *Journal of the House of Commons,* as well as *Records of the Moravians in North Carolina.* Background information about Thomas Day is in John Hope Franklin's *The Free Negro in North Carolina, 1790–1860* (1943).

— GEORGE W. REID

DAY, WILLIAM HOWARD (1825–1900), abolitionist, editor, printer, educator, and clergyman. Day was born in New York City on Oct. 19, 1825, of well-to-do parents, John and Eliza Day, who sent him first to a private school and then the high school at Northampton, Mass. While there, he became an apt learner and student of printing in the office of the *Northampton Gazette.* In 1842 he was examined in Latin and Greek by the Rev. Beriah Green, president of Whitestown Institute, N.Y. As a result, Day was sent to Oberlin College and was accepted after again passing a stiff examination in Latin, Greek, and algebra. His ability as an exceptional printer made it possible for him to pay his own way through college. In 1847 when he graduated from the college he was said to have been the only Negro in a class of fifty. In 1852 he married Lucy Stanton, who had graduated from the Literary Department (Ladies' Course) in 1850.

After graduation Day moved to Cleveland where he worked for the repeal of the Black Laws of Ohio. In substance there were three main points to this repressive legislation. The first held that the settlement of black or mulatto persons in Ohio was prohibited unless they could show a certificate of freedom and obtain two freeholders to give security for their good behavior and maintenance in the event of becoming a public charge. The second excluded them from common schools. The third held that no black or mulatto could be sworn or allowed to testify in any court in any case where a white person was concerned. The situation provoked Day, on behalf of the free Negro, to call a convention of Negro people of the United States that met in Cleveland in 1848. He was chairman of the group that originated plans for the National Convention of Colored Freemen. This council, with Frederick Douglass as president, was the forerunner to the famous meeting (1853) of free Negroes in Rochester, N.Y. In 1849 Day was elected as the Negro convention delegate to address the members of the Ohio legislature in the halls of the lower chamber. This daring request not only contributed to eventual repeal, but assisted in opening up educational opportunities previously denied to Negro children. Fifteen years before the Fifteenth Amendment, Day became very active in support of those politicians who displayed sympathy with the plight of Negroes.

As the nation experienced strains and stresses in the 1850s, Day increased his activities, convening as many as possible of the living colored veterans of the War of 1812 in Cleveland in 1852. Day was the key orator and it was the first occasion that cannonade salutes were given there to their heroic deeds. In that same year as chairman of the citizens' committee of Cleveland, he paid homage to Louis Kossuth of Hungary, whose statement has been often quoted, "Liberty is one, Despotism is one, the world over." Later in the same year Day led a selected group of citizens to welcome a German liberal, Prof. Gottfried Kinkel, an action which aided in creating stronger bonds of friendship between Germans and Negroes.

Day's expertise in printing paved the way for his assignment as a compositor and editor of the *Cleveland Daily True Democrat* (1851–1852). In 1853 he was selected as editor of the *Aliened American,* a weekly published especially for Negroes, originating from the insistent demands of several state conventions between 1849 and 1852. This paper and its successor, the *People's Exposition,* were strong advocates of the abolition of slavery, and social and political justice for Negroes. In view of his college training, he was appointed in 1854 librarian of the Cleveland Library Association, the forerunner of the city's public library system.

Friends observed that Day gave unstintingly of his time and energies. Observing that his program and schedule affected his health, his physician advised him to retire to a farm. Day went to Canada. By 1856 he was not only seeking to regain his health in a rural area, but was again lending his efforts to the educational development of some 40,000 underground freemen (some of whom he had previously assisted to escape) in the area of the Elgin settlement in Buxton, Canada. To crown his efforts with success he, along with the Rev. William King of Canada, visited England, Ireland, and Scotland and raised $35,000 with which his colleague returned to Canada to build a church and school.

While in Canada, Day printed John Brown's constitution for a new United States that was to be established in the event of the success of the Harpers Ferry venture.

Because of secrecy, just how close Day's connections were to this conspiracy is still not known. In 1858, prior to his departure for England, he was elected by the free Negroes as president of the National Board of Commissioners of Colored People of Canada and the United States. He was thus in a position to sign the official papers authorizing Martin R. Delany (later a major in the U.S. Army in the Civil War) to go to Africa and explore the valley of the Niger. From Ireland, Day wrote Delany in Africa to come home by way of Great Britain. The latter replied that his return had already been arranged direct to America. Later Delany found that direct passage to the United States had been prevented, forcing him to return via England. The fortuitous meeting of Day, Delany, and a Professor Campbell of the Institute for Colored Youth in Philadelphia resulted in the formation of the African Aid Society, whose history extends into the twentieth century. While overseas, Day spoke to and was welcomed by the lord mayor of Dublin, Whitehall Clubs in Great Britain, the Young Men's Christian Association at Hull, various women's organizations, and a large Congregational church at Lincolnshire. Declining a professorship at a classical academy, Day returned home after an absence of five years. He was immediately sought as the featured speaker for the great Emancipation Meeting at Cooper Union, New York City, where he delivered a stirring address. Day was soon assigned to the Freedmen's Aid Association, and became an inspector-general of schools for refugees and freedmen in Maryland and Delaware. He founded 140 schools, hired 150 teachers, and enrolled 7000 students, using churches to encourage enrollment. In 1867 he was ordained a minister in the African Methodist Episcopal Zion church. Like a number of others associated with Reconstruction programs, Day veered into politics. In 1869 in Wilmington, Del., he risked his life by organizing the Negro citizens as voters. He was successful at the end of the year in entirely changing the representation in the lower house, a change for the first time in twenty years.

Day came to Harrisburg, Pa., in 1872, and lived in the Eighth Ward. With his excellent educational background, character, and political affiliation, he became a clerk in the corporation department of the auditor-general's office. In 1875, upon the death of the Rev. James A. Jones, Day was elected general secretary of the General Conference of the A.M.E. Zion church.

Suspended from his office in 1880 for failure to forward the manuscript minutes of the 1878 General Conference, he was reinstated in 1888 in recognition of his faithful services and served "with immense efficiency" until his death on Dec. 3, 1900. In 1878, following a heated political contest, Day was elected to the school board, the first Negro elected to that body in Pennsylvania. He was reelected in 1881 and served as its president from 1891 to 1893, perhaps the first Negro city school board president in any "white" American community. Harrisburg did not elect its second Negro president until 1969.

He was a member of the Grand United Order of Odd Fellows as well as a member of the Masons, representing both York and Scottish rites. At his death on Dec. 3, 1900, he was given the first front-page obituary for a Negro in the *Harrisburg Telegraph:* "By all, he was recognized as one of the leading men of his race." He was buried at the Lincoln Cemetery in Penbrook. The present cemetery in Steelton, near Harrisburg, was named in his honor, with the dedicatory address by W. E. B. Du Bois. A large Harrisburg public housing project is also named in his honor.

Like most sketches in William J. Simmons's *Men of Mark . . .* (1887, pp. 978–84), his is largely autobiographical. The essential facts of his career are in Russell H. Davis's *Black Americans in Cleveland* (1974, pp. 48–53, 60, 62, 68–70, 110) and William J. Walls's *The African Methodist Episcopal Zion Church, Reality of the Black Church* (1974, esp. pp. 167–68, 268–72; there is a photograph on p. 269, and Day's poem, "The Centennial of the A.M.E. Zion Church," is on p. 559). See also W. E. B. Du Bois's "The World of William Howard Day," a manuscript in the State Library, Harrisburg. — PAUL MCSTALLWORTH

DEAN, WILLIAM H., JR. (1910–1952), educator, economist, and United States and United Nations executive. Dean was born on July 6, 1910, in Lynchburg, Va., the only son and the third of four children of the Rev. and Mrs. William Henry Dean, Sr. He spent his early years in Lynchburg, Washington, Baltimore, and Pittsburgh, where his father pastored Methodist churches. Bill, as he was called by his friends even in later life, graduated as valedictorian of his class from Douglass High School, Baltimore, in 1926. Recipient of a scholarship from the Baltimore chapter of the Alpha Phi Alpha fraternity, he was elected to Phi Beta Kappa in his junior year at Bowdoin College and was awarded the B.A. degree *summa cum laude* in 1930. He earned his M.A. (1932) and Ph.D. degrees from Harvard University (1938), both in economics.

From 1933 to 1942 he taught economics and business administration at Atlanta University, serving meanwhile as lecturer in economics during the summer session (1939) at the City College of New York. During his last two years at Atlanta University he was also consultant to the National Resources Planning Board on the location of defense industry. From 1942 to 1944 he was price executive of the Office of Price Administration in the Virgin Islands. After serving as director of the Community Relations Project of the National Urban League (1944–1946), he became acting chief of the United Nations Africa Unit, Division of Economic Stability and Development; in 1949 he was made chief of the unit. In that year he also served as secretary of the United Nations Mission to Haiti and later in that year was appointed administrative officer and second ranking official of a United Nations Mission to Libya. During four months in late 1951 he directed a six-man mission to Italian Somaliland to determine means by which that colony could be made self-supporting. Shortly after his return to the United States he committed suicide on Jan. 8, 1952, in the New York City apartment of his father-in-law, Channing H. Tobias. Funeral rites were held at St. Mark's Methodist Church, New York City, with interment in Woodlawn Cemetery in the Bronx. He was survived by his widow Mary Tobias Dean, whom he had married on Thanksgiving Day 1936, a son Chan-

ning and a daughter Joyce, thirteen and twelve years of age, respectively.

The immediate causes of his death were his concern for the hardships of primitive living conditions in Italian Somaliland, the obstructiveness of the Italian government, and despondency resulting from his concern, whether justified or not, that his mission had been a failure. This concern resulted from one of his most outstanding characteristics—a striving for perfection. He made a straight "A" in all his courses in high school, Bowdoin College, and Harvard University, where he led his class in economics. A contributory cause was racial discrimination which occasionally denied him deserved recognition. At Harvard he was University Scholar (1930–1931), Henry Lee Memorial Fellow (1931–1932), and Edward Austin Fellow (1932–1933). Harvard, however, did not offer him a tutorial post, an honor regularly given the top man in the various disciplines. Ironically, his doctoral dissertation, "The Theory of Geographical Location of Economic Activity," was published by Edward Brothers, Inc., Ann Arbor, Mich. (1938), and used as a text in economics courses at Harvard, as well as at Northwestern University. A second example of racial discrimination was the refusal of the City College of New York and of Queens College to appoint him as a member of the faculty, despite the endorsement of Prof. Frederick W. Taussig of Harvard, Walter White, secretary of the NAACP, and Mayor Fiorello LaGuardia. A letter from Abbot Payson Usher, professor of economics at Harvard to the Board of Higher Education, New York City (Jan. 30, 1939), stated: "Beyond any possible doubt he is the most talented man that has at any time worked under my direction. . . . We deeply regret that special circumstances make it impossible for us to use Dr. Dean here at Harvard. Any institution that can place Dr. Dean on its staff will be indeed fortunate. He is a man of exceptional attainment and promise." His widow, Mary Messner, wrote March 1974, "This turn down was a real heart breaker for Bill" (Messner to R.W.L.). In a letter from Cambridge, Mass., where he was completing work on his doctorate (Oct. 13, 1938), Dean wrote: "Really, Harvard disgusts me more and more. I have been strongly advised here [at Harvard] to go into government service. An institution which will have nothing of me expects me to get a better break from whites elsewhere. Frankly, I don't see what keeps a colored man's courage up. I feel more beat and licked every day. I don't seem to be able to muster up the fortitude to go ahead with the work already well under way" (Dean to R.W.L.). His extraordinary ability to concentrate on whatever task he was performing probably assuaged his bitterness, but it is not inconceivable that it was a factor in the despondency that led to his untimely death.

It is probable, too, that Dean feared that insuperable forces prevented some of his notable achievements as an educator and public servant from bearing full fruit. As associate professor of economics and business administration at Atlanta University (1933–1942), Dean introduced courses in labor economics, bringing to his classes workers from many occupations and sharing with them their on-the-job toil and drudgery. His efforts created improved opportunities for Negro workers in the Bell Aircraft bomber plant in nearby Marietta, Ga. But he was too much of a realist and a perfectionist not to realize that the company and white workers resisted equal opportunity for Negro workers. His expert survey (1942–1946) of thirteen cities for the National Urban League is still a valuable contribution to urban history. But his recommendations, which helped prevent a repetition of the race riots which followed World War I, were defeated by continuing economic and racial factors.

Mission to Haiti (1949), on which he served as secretary of the United Nations technical assistance mission is still one of the best analyses of Haiti's problems of demography, health, production, transport, trade, and finance. Its excellent recommendations, however, produced few beneficial results because of the overwhelming dimensions of the problems and the failure of the United Nations and the United States to provide adequate funds to ameliorate them. On the other hand there is some evidence to support the belief that the mission to Libya in 1950 may have been a contributory factor to the country's independence in the following year. But the mission to Italian Somaliland in 1951 documented the inglorious legacy of colonialism. In brief, even an economist as brilliant as Dean could not destroy the vestiges of racism and colonialism. His legacy is an unremitting attempt to ameliorate them. One endeavor belatedly helped achieve its goal. On July 29, 1942, he proposed a boycott until and unless Negroes were permitted to play on major league baseball teams.

The principal printed source is an article by W. Montague Cobb, "In Memoriam" (*JNMA*, Nov. 1952, pp. 472–73). Intimate details of his life were provided by his widow, Mary Tobias Messner, and papers in the files of Rayford W. Logan. — RAYFORD W. LOGAN

DE BAPTISTE, GEORGE (1814–1875), "conductor" on the Underground Railroad, army recruiter, civil rights leader, politician, and businessman. He was born free in Fredericksburg, Va., the son of William and Eliza De Baptiste. After serving an apprenticeship with a Richmond barber, he traveled for several years throughout the South as valet to a professional gambler. Returning to Fredericksburg, he married Lucinda Lee. They moved in 1838 to Madison, Wis., where he opened a barbershop. Suspected of assisting runaway slaves, he was ordered to comply with a state statute requiring Negroes entering Indiana to post a $500 bond. He retained a leading lawyer and appealed first to the circuit court and then to the state supreme court, which overturned the lower courts on a technicality. Soon afterward De Baptiste became valet to William Henry Harrison, whom he accompanied to Washington when the latter became president in 1841. After Harrison's death on April 4, 1841, De Baptiste returned to barbering in Madison.

Finding whites in Indiana hostile, he migrated about 1846 to the freer atmosphere of Detroit. As a member of a secret Negro abolition society known variously as the Order of the Men of Oppression, the African-American Mysteries, and the Order of Emigration, he became a prime leader in the Underground Railroad. On one occasion, he rescued a runaway slave by leading a mob

in attacking the courthouse. In March 1859 he joined the Rev. William C. Munroe, Dr. Joseph Ferguson, William Lambert, and other Negroes in the Detroit meeting between Frederick Douglass and John Brown to consider the latter's proposed slave uprising. De Baptiste, "the firebrand of the group," urged a terror campaign initiated by blowing up churches throughout the South on an appointed Sunday. During the Civil War De Baptiste was instrumental in recruiting Michigan's colored regiment. He also collected supplies for freedmen's schools in Louisiana. In 1870 he served on Detroit's first Negro jury, was elected a delegate to the local Republican senatorial convention, and played a large role in bringing about the integration of Detroit's public schools.

De Baptiste became one of Detroit's wealthiest Negroes. During his career he operated various businesses: a barbershop, a bakery, a steamship which plied between Detroit and Sandusky, Ohio, and a catering service for the Detroit Boat Club. In 1867 when his real estate holdings were valued at $10,000, he opened a catering service which he expanded in 1872 by purchasing a four-story building which featured a fine restaurant and ice cream parlor. He expanded again in 1874 by developing a suburban pleasure resort in Hamtramck with a restaurant, dancing floors, and tented picnic gardens.

He died on Feb. 25, 1875, of stomach cancer. Survived by his second wife and two of his ten children, he was buried from the Second Baptist Church, Detroit's oldest Negro congregation, of which he was a longstanding member and generous contributor. The *Detroit Post* summed up the import of his life by calling him "a bold, uncompromising advocate of right and justice, a firm friend of the poor and oppressed, and in every station honorable."

De Baptiste is treated in David M. Katzman's *Before the Ghetto: Black Detroit in the Nineteenth Century* (1973) and Frank B. Woodford's *Father Abraham's Children: Michigan Episodes in the Civil War* (1961). Various newspaper references are located in the Detroit Public Library's Burton Historical Collection.

— J. CARLETON HAYDEN

DE BAPTISTE, RICHARD (1831–1901), Baptist clergyman, organizer, and editor. He was born free on Nov. 11, 1831, in Fredericksburg, Va., to Eliza and William De Baptiste, who operated the largest building and contracting business in Fredericksburg. De Baptiste's grandfather, John De Baptiste, a Frenchman, had fought in the Revolutionary War. A brother of George De Baptiste, Richard began his education in a school in his home taught first by a Negro and later by Richard Dillingham, a Scottish-Irish Quaker. When De Baptiste was nine years old his family migrated to Detroit, where he continued his education under the Rev. Samuel H. Davis, pastor of the Second Baptist Church. In 1858 De Baptiste was licensed to preach in that church. Later he attended the University of Chicago.

He was ordained in April 1860 at Mount Pleasant, Ohio, where he pastored the Negro Baptist church and taught school. In January 1863 he was called to Olivet Baptist Church in Chicago, which had only about 100 members. De Baptiste, an impressive preacher, made Olivet a haven for freedmen emigrants, and operated day and evenings schools for them. By 1868 he had increased the membership to 480 and replaced the rented frame church with a brick structure capable of seating 800 and costing $18,000, thereby making Olivet Chicago's largest Negro congregation. When the great Chicago fire of July 14, 1874, completely destroyed the church, De Baptiste built in 1876 an even larger, three-story brick structure.

Although De Baptiste participated freely in white ministerial groups, he became the West's foremost advocate of separate Negro Baptist associations. He put Olivet Church back into the Negro Wood River Baptist Association of Illinois in 1864. Through his leadership Negro Baptist churches in the Midwest and South were organized in the same year into the Northwestern and Southern Baptist Convention. He was a prime leader in uniting this convention with the American Missionary Convention (Aug. 1866) made up of Negro churches in New England to form the Consolidated American Baptist Convention, the first national Negro Baptist association. He served as president almost annually from 1867 to 1873. De Baptiste was a special advocate of his denomination's outreach in the West and Haiti, and actively supported many young ministers.

He was also a champion of race journalism. In 1878 he became editor of the *Conservator,* Chicago's first Negro newspaper. For a while he was corresponding editor of the *St. Louis Monitor* and the *Baptist Herald* of Keokuk, Iowa. He founded in 1884 the *Western Herald,* a short-lived religious journal. He edited Chicago's *Baptist Observor* and was for many years corresponding editor of the Consolidated Convention's *National Monitor* published in Brooklyn, N.Y.

De Baptiste was tall, very fair, and distinguished looking. He married Georgianna Brische of Cincinnati, Ohio, in the fall of 1855; she died on Nov. 2, 1872. He married again in 1885 and his second wife died in April 1886. He had three children.

The failing health of his children and dwindling membership at Olivet led him to resign in December 1881. Thereafter he devoted himself to small churches in the Chicago vicinity. He died on April 21, 1901.

De Baptiste was one of the most outstanding ministers of his denomination, and one of the leading men of Illinois. Through his leadership in building up the Negro Baptist denomination and in the Negro press, he played a significant role in the development of race pride, independent social institutions, and national black leadership.

See William J. Simmons's *Men of Mark . . .* (1887), Fred Hart Williams's "Richard De Baptiste" (*NHB,* May 1959), Mae Bibbs's "Noted Man and Women in Illinois: Richard De Baptiste" (*NHB,* May 1942) and I. Garland Penn's *The Afro-American Press and Its Editors* (1891, pp. 262–64). Two useful unpublished sources are Miles Mark Fisher's "The History of Olivet Baptist Church of Chicago" (M.A. thesis, Graduate Divinity School, University of Chicago, 1922) and Albert Lee Kreiling's "The Making of Racial Identities in the Black Press: A Cultural Analysis of Race Journalism in Chicago, 1878–1929" (Ph.D. dissertation, University of Illinois, 1973). — J. CARLETON HAYDEN

DEBERRY, WILLIAM NELSON (1870–1948), clergyman and community leader. He was born Aug. 29, 1870, in Nashville, Tenn., the son of Caswell and Charlotte (Mayfield) DeBerry, former slaves who were freed following the Civil War. His father, a railroad shop worker, was also a lay preacher in a local Negro Baptist church. William attended public schools in Nashville and enrolled in 1886 at Fisk University. Following his graduation in 1896 with a B.S. degree, he entered Oberlin Theological Seminary, where he earned a B.D. degree in 1899. That same year he married Amanda McKissack, who bore him two daughters, Charlotte Pearl (Mrs. Henry G. Tracy) and Anna Mae (Mrs. Arthur H. Johnson). After his wife's death, he was married in 1943 to Louise Scott.

DeBerry was ordained a Congregationalist minister in 1899, the year he took up the pastorate of St. John's Congregational Church in Springfield, Mass. He developed St. John's from a small congregation of about 100 members into a prominent institution known for its city-wide "institutional activities" or social service program. The church's social service arm, St. John's Institutional Activities, Inc., won national recognition for its originator. Lincoln University awarded him an honorary D.D. in 1914. The following year DeBerry became a trustee of Fisk University, the first alumnus to serve on the board. In 1919 he was elected second assistant moderator of the National Council of Congregational Churches of Christ in America, and in 1925 he became recording secretary of the American Missionary Association, a post to which he was reelected on three successive occasions. The William E. Harmon Foundation in 1928 awarded DeBerry its first prize "for distinguished service in religion among Negroes of the United States" in 1927, and in 1928 the city of Springfield named him the recipient of its William Pynchon Medal "for distinguished public service."

The growing community responsibilities of St. John's Institutional Activities, together with the growing needs of Negroes in the city, suggested the desirability of separating the social service program from the church. At the request of the committee that recommended the creation of an independent, expanded social service agency, DeBerry resigned from his pastorate in 1930 in order to devote full time to social work among Negroes in Springfield. He became executive director of the new Dunbar Community League, Inc., an agency incorporating the work of St. John's Institutional Activities and affiliated with the National Urban League. He retired from the league in 1947 but continued to direct Camp Atwater, a well-known summer camp for colored children in East Brookfield, Mass., which he had founded. He died after an illness of twenty-three months in Springfield Hospital, and was buried in Springfield Cemetery. He was survived by his wife, two daughters, and one brother.

Through St. John's Institutional Activities, DeBerry effectively pioneered social work among blacks in Springfield. The organization enriched the social, recreational, and cultural lives of Negroes in the city through its music department, boys' and girls' clubs, playground, social center for women and girls, and classes in cooking, sewing, and other activities. The agency's professional staff visited colored homes to deal with problems of personal and social adjustment. A free employment service was one step toward improved industrial opportunities. A home for working girls and a housing project involving rental to colored families of houses and apartments owned by St. John's helped meet the ever-present problem of decent, reasonably priced shelter. Camp Atwater enabled hundreds of boys and girls to escape the city each summer.

St. John's Institutional Activities was organized in 1911, the same year that the National Urban League was founded, and its program corresponded closely to the social service work envisioned for blacks in the cities by the new national organization. The league accepted St. John's as a local affiliate in 1917. Incorporated as the nonsectarian Dunbar Community League in 1931 under the sponsorship of the Springfield Community Chest, the organization later became the Urban League of Springfield.

Although best known for his leadership of St. John's and the Dunbar League, DeBerry was "the moving spirit in practically every line of endeavor undertaken" by Negroes in Springfield (Johnson, *Hampden County,* p. 491). He was a director or trustee of a host of religious and secular agencies for social welfare, mutual benefit, and community service. His abilities were recognized in his appointments to state and municipal boards and commissions, where he was often the first of his race to serve in such capacities. He lectured widely on race relations as well as religious themes. Contemporary assessments agree in evaluating him as "by far the most outstanding negro leader in Springfield" (Johnson, *Hampden County,* p. 491), "one of the greatest churchmen of his time" (*JNH,* July 1948, p. 384).

There is no biography of DeBerry, but information concerning his life and career may be found in *The History of St. John's Congregational Church, Springfield, Massachusetts, 1844–1962* (1962); Clifton Johnson's *Hampden County, 1636–1936* (1936); *Who Was Who in America* (1950); *JNH* (July 1948, pp. 384–85); *New York Times* (Jan. 21, 1948); and the daily newspapers of Springfield, especially the *Springfield Republican* (May 29, 1927; July 28, 1930) and the *Springfield Union* (Jan. 21, 1948). — NANCY WEISS

DÉDÉ, EDMOND (1827–1903), New Orleans–born violinist, clarinetist, orchestra leader, and composer. The names of his parents are not known, but they arrived in New Orleans from the French West Indies, probably in 1809. Although he had at first learned to play the clarinet in his youth, it was as a violinist that he was known during the thirty years that he lived in New Orleans. He began the study of this instrument under the guidance of the free Negro musician and teacher Constantin Deberque, one of the conductors of the "Philharmonic Society," an antebellum organization consisting of more than a hundred white and colored musicians of New Orleans. After studying under Deberque, he continued his studies under L. Gabaci, who was at one time head of the St. Charles Theater

Orchestra. With the rise of hostile white public sentiment against the free people of color during 1830–1840, Dédé continued his studies in Mexico, where a number of his compatriots also sought exile. He returned to New Orleans after his Mexican sojourn. Being of an economical turn of mind, he saved the money from his earnings as a cigar-maker; combining this with the financial assistance of admiring friends, he embarked for Europe. Arriving at first in Belgium and finding none of the things he had hoped for, he continued on to Paris where he was soon granted an audition in 1857 and entered the Paris Conservatory of Music. One of his teachers at the conservatory was the famous Jacques Halvey who taught Gounod, and it was thus that Dédé later became an intimate friend of this great composer. His other instructor was the famous teacher of the violin, Jean Delphin Alard. Some years later, after completing his studies at the conservatory, he went to Bordeaux where he became the leader of the L'Alcazar Theater Orchestra, a post he held for twenty-seven years. While there he married the beautiful and accomplished Mlle. Sylvie Leflet on June 19, 1864.

As a master violinist and composer Dédé received many honors from his native city, from France, and elsewhere. Clarence Cameron White named him as one of the five foremost Negroes in the tonal art. Roussève cites his "Valliant Belle Rose Quadrille" (later called, according to James Monroe Trotter, "Le Palmier Overture" as one of his best known pieces. His *Quasimodo Symphony* was presented at the Orleans Theater on the night of May 10, 1865, before a vast audience composed of the leading Negroes of New Orleans and prominent northern whites, with Samuel Snaër, Jr., leading his own orchestra in its production. All of his compositions were considered of the highest order. On a journey to Algeria he wrote his "Le Serment de l'Arabe." Among his other compositions was "Si j'étais lui," and many others that are for the most part unlisted. According to Rodolphe Desdunes, he composed thousands of pieces—"not counting his dances and the ballets distributed over all parts of Europe where he visited or lived." This lavish estimate of Dédé's productivity was probably due not to facts but to the high esteem in which the people of his race held him. Forty-six years after his self-imposed exile his name was still a legend in his native city. Some were fond of recalling his handsome figure, amiable disposition, commanding appearance, and "unmixed Negro blood." The music lovers recalled his mastery of the violin—how while he was still a student in New Orleans his admirers never seemed to grow tired of listening to his peculiarly fine playing of the studies of Kreutzer and the "Seventh Air Varié de Beriot." His staccato and legato were considered an exercise in perfection. Admirers declared that he threw his whole soul into his playing and "meets with no difficulties that he does not easily overcome."

Dédé returned in full measure the high esteem that his compatriots accorded him. He set to music a poem written by Desdunes, entitled "Patriotisme." His visit to New Orleans in 1893 became a triumphal homecoming. The elite of the old free colored class and their descendants flocked to his concerts to hear the aging maestro "charm and captivate his public by the enchantment of his bow," even though he had lost at sea his beloved Cremona and was thus forced to play on an inferior instrument. At one of his concerts the music critic of the *New Orleans Bee (L'Abeille),* accorded him the honor of assisting him. It was said that Dédé had memorized the works of all the great masters, and on this occasion he put his astounding memory to the test by playing "Le Trouvère" without a printed score. The critic was so impressed by this mnemonic feat that he praised the artist in the columns of his newspaper. His own race likewise responded to the genius of its maestro. *La Société des Jeunes Amis,* one of the outstanding Negro organizations of the city, tendered an honorary membership in their exclusive circle. Many members of this group were *passé blancs,* its membership standards being family background, wealth, education, and the ability to speak French. Even their soirée invitations were printed in French; many of their social events were held at the old Masonic Hall (which is still standing on St. Claude Avenue). Among its membership list were the Meinés, Mansions, Vigers, Staes, Josephs, Mathieus, and Perraults. Its invitation list included the beautiful Moore sisters—one of whom later became Mrs. Paul Laurence Dunbar, Alice Dunbar-Nelson.

Although Dédé's concerts were outstanding events in the city of his birth, the golden moments soon tarnished. According to Rousséve, "He found conditions in his native city intolerable" and soon returned to France. He was a member of the Société des Auteurs et Editeurs de Musique and of Auteurs et Compositeurs Dramatiques. A grand opera, *Le Sultan d'Ispahan,* was interrupted by his final illness and remained unfinished. He died in Paris in 1903.

Sources include Maud Cuney-Hare's *Negro Musicians and Their Music* (1936); Rodolphe Desdunes's *Nos Hommes et Notre Histoire* (1911); Charles B. Rousséve's *The Negro in Louisiana* (1937); and various issues of *La Tribune de la Nouvelle-Orleans.* For original scores of New Orleans Negro music, see the Howard-Tilton Library of Tulane University and the Marcus Christian Collection of the Earl Long Library, University of New Orleans. One piece is in James Monroe Trotter's *Music and Some Highly Musical People* (1878). For background, see John W. Blassingame's *Black New Orleans, 1660–1880* (1973) and Herbert Sterkx's *The Free Negro in Ante-Bellum Louisiana* (1972).
— MARCUS B. CHRISTIAN

DE GRASSE, JOHN V[AN SURLY] (1825–1868), physician. Born in New York City, one of several children of George De Grasse, born in Calcutta, and Maria Van Surly of German parentage, he attended private and public schools in New York City until 1840. He then entered the Oneida Institute, N.Y., of which Beriah Green was president. Since Latin was not taught there, he left and entered Aubuk College in Paris, where he spent two years. In 1845 he returned to New York City and commenced the study of medicine with Samuel R. Childs. After two years of patient and diligent study he entered Bowdoin College in Brunswick, Me., where on May 19, 1849, he received his M.D., with honors. Leaving Bowdoin College he went again to Europe and spent considerable time in the hospitals of Paris, travel-

ing at intervals through parts of France, England, Italy, and Switzerland. He returned to America on the ship *Samuel Fox* in the capacity of surgeon. He was married in August 1852.

After practicing medicine in New York City for two years he moved to Boston, which became his home, and continued the practice of medicine. Earning a good reputation in this city by his diligence and skill, he was admitted as a member of the Massachusetts Medical Society on Aug. 24, 1854.

A Boston newspaper of that date stated that it was the first time such an honor had been conferred upon a colored man in Massachusetts at least, and probably in the United States. The honor deserved particular notice because the means by which he had achieved the distinction was creditable to his intelligence and perseverance and because "others of his class may be stimulated to seek an elevation which has hitherto been supposed unattainable by men of color." The Boston medical profession had honored itself "in thus discarding the law of caste and generally acknowledging real merit, without regard to the hue, of the skin." De Grasse was probably "the most accomplished" of the colored pioneers in the postrevolutionary and pre–Civil War days. The prominence given to Phillis Wheatley, Benjamin Banneker, and others would not have attracted an unusual amount of attention if they had been white. De Grasse was not necessarily more gifted than they but "he had the advantages which university training and foreign travels give a man."

De Grasse volunteered his service in the Union Army during the Civil War, and served as assistant surgeon with the 35th U.S. Colored Troops in 1863. He was one of the first eight Negroes to be commissioned a surgeon in the U.S. Army.

Most of the information about De Grasse is in the article in a Boston newspaper, quoted in part in George Washington Williams's *History of the Negro Race in America . . .* (1883, 2:133–34). Herbert M. Morais's *The History of the Negro in Medicine* (1967, p. 38), has a photograph and a reference to his service during the Civil War. Information about his parentage is in S. A. M. Washington's *Thomas Downing: Sketch of His Life and Times* (1910, pp. 7–8). — HOWARD D. ASBURY

DELANY, MARTIN R[OBINSON] (1812–1885), editor, author, physician, abolitionist, black nationalist, colonizationist, and army officer. Delany was born in Charles Town, (W.)Va., on May 6, 1812, the son of Samuel Delany, a slave, and Pati (Peace) Delany, a free colored woman. His grandparents were natives of Africa who had been brought to the United States as slaves: his paternal grandfather was a Mandingo prince, the other a Golah village chieftain. As a small child, he heard tales of their homeland from his grandmother, Graci Peace.

A Yankee peddler taught the five Delany children to read. When their white neighbors discovered this, Pati Delany was threatened with imprisonment. Rather than deprive her children of an education, she took them across the Mason-Dixon line to Chambersburg, Pa., in 1822. Samuel Delany purchased his freedom and joined his family there a year later. Martin continued his elementary education in Chambersburg, and when he was nineteen left home, traveling on foot across the Allegheny Mountains to Pittsburgh. There he attended a night school in the basement of the African Methodist Episcopal church and was tutored at home by a young divinity student. For a short time he studied medicine with a white doctor and became qualified to practice as a cupper, leecher, and bleeder.

In Pittsburgh, where he lived until 1856, Delany quickly became a leader of the growing Negro community. An officer of the Pittsburgh Anti-Slavery Society and an Underground Railroad activist, he also helped to organize literary, temperance, and "moral reform" societies. In 1836 he traveled to Philadelphia and New York as a delegate to a colored convention.

In 1843 Delany married Catherine Richards, granddaughter of Benjamin Richards, a butcher, and reputedly the wealthiest Negro in Pittsburgh. The couple had seven surviving children, born between 1846 and 1864. Delany named his sons after prominent Negroes: Toussaint L'Ouverture, Charles Lenox Remond, Alexander Dumas, Saint Cyprian, Faustin Soulouque, and Rameses Placido. His only daughter was named Ethiopia Halle Delany.

Shortly after his marriage, Delany began publishing in Pittsburgh *The Mystery,* the first Negro newspaper west of the Allegheny Mountains. A four-page weekly devoted to news of the antislavery movement, *The Mystery* reported meetings and social affairs, reprinted speeches, and crusaded for schools for Negro children. Although the newspaper, written in a vigorous if unpolished style, gained wide respect, it folded at the end of 1847 because of lack of financial support. Delany then joined Frederick Douglass as co-editor of the *North Star,* a newspaper started by Douglass in December 1847 in Rochester, N.Y. For the first year and a half Delany toured Ohio, Michigan, and some of the eastern states to gather subscribers and news for the paper. Speaking to antislavery audiences in churches, schools, and farmhouses, he often held three meetings a day, then traveled on horseback at night to keep his next engagement. Although most audiences were friendly, he encountered hostility in rural areas and in one Ohio village barely escaped lynching. His weekly letters to Douglass which appeared in the *North Star* were the first detailed reports on the lives of free Negroes in the Midwest.

The paper could not support two editors and Delany resigned in June 1848 to resume his medical studies under the direction of two of Pittsburgh's most prominent physicians. His applications to Pennsylvania and New York medical schools were rejected, but in November 1850 he was admitted to the medical school of Harvard College. He had attended lectures for less than a month when his fellow students met to protest his presence in their classes. In response to student petitions, the medical faculty, headed by Oliver Wendell Holmes, permitted him to finish the winter term but barred him from further study at Harvard. Since there were no licensing requirements for physicians at that time, he returned home as Dr. Delany and continued to practice medicine throughout his life.

Back in Pittsburgh once more, he organized resist-ance to the Fugitive Slave Act passed in 1850, boldly wresting fugitives from the hands of slave catchers. He worked day and night during a cholera epidemic, and for a year served as principal of the colored school. Nevertheless, at forty Delany was a disappointed man. His dismissal from Harvard and the failure of white abolitionists to protest the expulsion had left scars. Now that the Fugitive Slave Act was threatening the security of every Negro man and woman in the country, he questioned whether they should continue to live in the United States.

His dissatisfactions drove him to New York where, writing tirelessly for a month in a boarding house room, he produced *The Condition, Elevation, Emigration and Destiny of the Colored People of the United States, Politically Considered,* published in Philadelphia in 1852. This first, full-length formulation of black nationalism reported the achievements of black men and women, indicted the abolitionists for their failure to fight consistently for Negroes' integration into American society, and recommended emigration as a solution to discrimination. "We are a nation within a nation," wrote Delany; "We must go from our oppressors." Although he recommended emigration to Central or South America, he included as an appendix a plan for an expedition to Africa.

Condition, Elevation, Emigration was attacked in the white antislavery press and ignored by Frederick Douglass and other Negro editors. Nevertheless, the proposal for a Negro-led emigration movement struck a responsive chord in many Negro communities across the country. In August 1854 he was able to bring more than a hundred men and women to Cleveland for a National Emigration Convention. In his reports to the delegates on "The Political Destiny of the Colored Race" he stressed the need for an independent black nation and predicted that "the great issue" facing the world "will be a question of black and white, and every individual will be called upon for his identity with one or the other." The convention empowered a national board of commissioners headed by Delany to correspond with and visit countries in the American tropics to find a homeland for American Negroes. Delany began by investigating Central America and Hawaii, and he sent a representative to Haiti.

During this period he moved with his family to Chatham, Ontario, Canada, joining more than 10,000 American Negroes who had crossed the border since the passage of the Fugitive Slave Act. Here Delany practiced medicine, lectured, and for the first time in his life cast a vote in the provincial elections. Despite the attractions of his new home, which included an adequate school for his sons, Delany maintained his ties with the antislavery movement in the United States.

Delany was one of John Brown's intermediaries with the Canadian Negro community during the guerrilla leader's 1858 visit to Canada to recruit fighting men. He was an organizer of the secret, largely Negro-attended convention in Chatham for an unspecified region Brown hoped to liberate from the slave-holding South. After the convention Delany continued to correspond with Brown. When the foray was postponed, Delany was traveling in Africa.

When the Emigration Convention met for the third time in August 1858 in Chatham, Delany presented a program for a three-year-long "Topographical, Geological and Geographical Examination of the Valley of the River Niger." The convention officers noted, however, that they were "entirely opposed to any Emigration there as such," although they would not "interfere with the right of the Commissioners to negotiate in their own behalf for territory" for a settlement for American Negroes. In the spring of 1859 Delany and Robert Campbell, a young science teacher, sailed to Africa, and for nine months they traveled in Liberia and the Niger Valley. In Abbeokuta, a city-state in what is now Nigeria, the *alake* (king) signed a treaty with them which granted members of "the African race in America" the right to establish a self-governing colony there.

During an extended visit to England and Scotland on his way home, Delany secured the backing of British officials and businessmen who were interested in expanding trade with Africa. Hailed as an explorer of the then little-known Dark Continent, Delany was invited to address the Royal Geographical Society and the International Statistical Congress. (A dramatic incident at the congress occurred when Lord Henry Brougham, the Congress president and a pioneer in the British antislavery movement, introduced the notables and remarked on the presence of a black man, adding that he hoped that this would not offend George Mifflin Dallas, the United States minister. Dallas, who was seated on the platform, tried to ignore the taunt, but Delany seized the opportunity to respond. Rising to address himself to Prince Albert, consort of Queen Victoria, he thanked Lord Brougham for the recognition and then said, "I assure your Royal Highness and his Lordship that *I am a man.*" His simple affirmation evoked cheers from the assemblage in London. Newspapers in the United States lamented "the public humiliation" of an American minister, and President Buchanan met with his cabinet to consider asking the British government for an apology, but took no action.)

Returning to North America in 1861, after South Carolina had seceded from the Union, Delany wrote his *Official Report of the Niger Valley Exploring Party* (1861), a rambling account of the climate, topography, and resources of western Africa. He traveled for two years in Canada and the United States to sign up settlers for his proposed settlement in Abbeokuta. When lecturing on Africa to white as well as black audiences, he wore a handsomely embroidered African robe and sought to destroy the stereotype of the "African savage."

After Abraham Lincoln issued the Emancipation Proclamation in 1863 and agreed to accept Negro soldiers in the army, Delany became an official recruiter for the Union's Negro military units, first for the Massachusetts 54th Regiment (which his son Toussaint joined) and then for state regiments raised in Rhode Island, Connecticut, and the Midwest. In February 1865 he went to Washington with a plan to arm slaves behind the enemy lines. Following an interview with President Lincoln, he was commissioned as a major in the army, the first Negro field officer of high rank. Sent to Charles-

ton, S.C., he raised two regiments of ex-slaves before the war ended.

Remaining in South Carolina, Delany became a sub-assistant commissioner in the Freedmen's Bureau, assigned to Hilton Head Island. His job included supervising labor contracts, adjudicating disputes between planters and their former slaves, and organizing cotton agencies and schools. His return to civilian life in August 1868 coincided with the beginning of Radical Reconstruction in the South. Leaving his family on the campus of Wilberforce University in Xenia, Ohio, where they had been living since the last years of the war, he rented rooms in Charleston. He became a member of the Republican State Executive Committee and a lieutenant-colonel in the state militia. In 1873 he was appointed customs inspector in Charleston, but resigned to enter the 1874 campaign. In the latter year he was appointed trial justice in Charleston's Third Ward. But younger Negroes were winning power in South Carolina, and although they respected the veteran of the antislavery campaigns, their goals and attitudes often differed from Delany's. By 1874 he had become disenchanted with the course of Reconstruction. Foreseeing its imminent end unless Negroes came to an accommodation with the whites who were determined to "redeem" the state, he ran unsuccessfully for lieutenant-governor with conservative backing from the Honest Government League, and two years later supported the Democrats.

When his Democratic allies failed to keep their promise of equal rights for Negroes, thousands of dispossessed Negro farmers began to leave the South. While some headed for Kansas, others looked toward Africa. In February 1876 Delany was tried on a charge of breach of trust. Gov. Daniel Chamberlain, a Republican, pardoned him on Aug. 30. But Delany, continuing to seek an accommodation with the majority of whites, supported Gen. Wade Hampton, a Democrat, against Chamberlain in his campaign for reelection. During the campaign Delany barely escaped being killed by a mob of angry Negroes. Hampton became governor after the disputed 1876 presidential election and quickly reappointed Delany a trial justice. In 1878 Delany reluctantly supported the Liberian Exodus Joint Stock Exchange Company to carry emigrants to Liberia. A steamship purchased by southern Negroes made two transatlantic trips before its white captain and a Charleston merchant conspired to seize it for debts. Delany led a fight to reclaim the ship, but the lawsuit which dragged through the courts until 1884 was unsuccessful.

While working for the Exodus Company, Delany completed *Principia of Ethnology: The Origin of Races and Color* (1879), a blend of biblical history, archeology, and anthropology. Using the biblical account of the Creation, he traced the descendants of Ham from their settlement in Egypt and Ethiopia to their diffusion through all of Africa. From Egyptian sculpture and hieroglyphics, and from the alphabet of Ethiopia, he demonstrated that "the builders of the pyramids, sculptors of the sphinxes and original god-kings were blacks." Although his work fell far short of present-day standards of scholarship, his emphasis on the role of

Negro peoples in the development of world civilization have later won much wider acceptance.

Still planning to go to Africa as soon as his children were self-supporting, Delany left South Carolina in 1880. After fruitless attempts to obtain a government appointment in Washington, he returned to his family at Wilberforce. He died there on Jan. 24, 1885. He was survived by his widow and six of his children (*Cleveland Gazette,* Feb. 21, 1885, p. 1).

Writer, doctor, self-taught scholar in an era when most Negroes were barred from learned professions, Delany's vigorous personality and inquiring mind often led him to diverge from the mainstream of his contemporaries. It is precisely these qualities, together with his early awareness of his family history, that contributed to his stature as a pioneering black nationalist and Africanist. Although he wielded considerable influence in his day, perhaps his abiding legacy to subsequent generations of American Negroes is the pride of self and of race which moved Frederick Douglass to say: "*I thank God for making me a man, but Delany thanks him for making him a black man.*"

For more than a century the only substantial source of information about Martin R. Delany had been *Life and Public Services of Martin R. Delany* (1868), by Frances Rollins Whipper, who used the pen name Frank A. Rollin. Although it was based on extensive interviews with Delany, the book paid scant attention to the emigration movement, failed to mention Delany's dismissal from Harvard, and gave an account of the John Brown convention in Chatham that differed from all other firsthand reports of the gathering. This adulative and often inaccurate biography has now been supplemented by two full-length, carefully researched books: *Martin R. Delany, The Beginnings of Black Nationalism* by Victor Ullman (1971), and *The Making of an Afro-American: Martin Robinson Delany* by Dorothy Sterling (1971). In addition, a number of Delany's writings have been reprinted. These include *Blake,* a novel of a slave rebellion written in the 1850s (originally published serially in the *Anglo-African* magazine in seven installments in 1859, and published for the first time in book form in 1970) and *The Condition, Elevation, Emigration and Destiny of the Colored People of the United States* (1852, 1968). His *Official Report of the Niger Valley Exploring Party* has been reprinted in *Search for a Place, Black Separatism and Africa* (1860; edited by Howard Bell, 1969), and *The Political Destiny of the Colored Race* may be consulted in *The Ideological Origins of Black Nationalism,* edited by Sterling Stuckey (1972). — DOROTHY STERLING

DELARGE, ROBERT CARLOS (1842–1874), congressman.

Born a light mulatto slave in Aiken, S.C., DeLarge was, on his mother's side, of Haitian descent. He received such education as was then available to Negroes from Wood High School in Charleston, became a tailor, farmer, agent of the Freedmen's Bureau, and Republican politician.

At the 1865 Colored People's Convention, DeLarge was named chairman of the Credentials Committee. The convention adopted his resolution which urged unsuccessfully the establishment of public schools for all.

DeLarge's speeches delighted the crowded evening sessions. The 1867 state convention of the Union Republican party adopted the report of its Platform Committee, chaired by DeLarge, which advocated public schools, abolition of capital punishment, universal suffrage, tax reform, court reorganization, welfare assistance, liberal immigration laws, funds for railroads and canals with contracts to be awarded equitably, popular election for all offices, and the breakup of land monopolies.

A member of three standing committees of the South Carolina Constitutional Convention of 1868, DeLarge participated often in debates. The convention rejected his motions to petition Congress for cessation of "further confiscation of lands and disfranchisement for political offenses" and for removal of political disabilities already imposed. But the convention passed his resolution which asked Congress for a $1-million grant to purchase lands to be sold to the state's land-hungry poor. He favored state-supported public schools, but not mandatory provisions which, he said, could not be enforced. In the 1868 and 1869 sessions of the state legislature DeLarge chaired the Ways and Means Committee and sponsored some railroad legislation. The loquacious Charlestonian argued successfully against a debate-limitation proposal.

A bargain in the spring of 1870 secured the resignation of C. P. Leslie as land commissioner and agreement to name a Negro as his successor. The legislature chose DeLarge. In March 1871 he reported that nearly 2000 small tracts had been sold or would soon be taken over by homeowners who would have eight years to pay for them. DeLarge was implicated in the resulting charges of land fraud.

In the closely contested campaign for Congress in 1870 DeLarge alternately used, and then denied using, the "black man's party" as an issue. With a Negro majority among registered voters in the four-county 2nd Congressional District, DeLarge's rival Republican candidate, Christopher C. Bowen, and the state's leading Republican newspaper condemned the tactic. After the Board of Canvassers declared DeLarge elected, Bowen appealed to Congress. The contest bedeviled DeLarge throughout his tenure in Congress (March 4, 1871 to Jan. 24, 1873). In a speech on the floor of the House (April 6, 1871) he criticized lawlessness by both political parties, condemned Negroes for trusting white carpetbaggers, and urged that ex-Confederates be admitted to political life. He spoke at length in favor of the Fourteenth Amendment. Samuel Denny Smith stated: "This was one of the sanest and most sensible speeches ever delivered by a Negro Congressman" (*The Negro in Congress, 1870–1901* [1940], p. 50). During the second session of Congress, which began on Dec. 4, 1871, DeLarge was engaged in proving his right to keep his seat.

The U.S. House of Representatives on Jan. 24, 1873, after a brief debate that found DeLarge absent and reported sick, accepted its Committee on Election report, based on massive testimony, that fraud and other irregularities had so pervaded the election that neither DeLarge nor Bowen had actually been elected.

Thereafter, DeLarge lived for a while in Columbia, S.C., until he was appointed a Charleston magistrate by

Gov. Robert Scott, a position he held until his death of consumption on Feb. 14, 1874, in Charleston. His funeral was held on Feb. 16 at his late residence, 105 Calhoun St., and he was buried in Brown Fellowship Graveyard. The afternoon of the funeral saw other magistrates' offices in the old city closed in tribute to the young politician. He was survived by his widow and family, which included a daughter, Victoria.

Samuel Denny Smith's *The Negro in Congress, 1870–1901* (1940), adversely critical of most Negroes, praised DeLarge for his speech on April 6, 1871. Maurine Christopher's *America's Black Congressmen* (1971) is neutral and more detailed. See the *Biographical Directory of the American Congress* (1774–1971) and the *Charleston News & Courier* (Feb. 16, 1874, p. 4). — SIDNEY TOBIN

DEPRIEST, OSCAR STANTON (1871–1951), businessman and politician. One of six children, he was born in a cabin to ex-slave parents in Florence, Ala., on March 9, 1871. His father was a teamster and farmer and his mother was a part-time laundress. Constant economic insecurity and periodic lynchings caused the family to migrate to Kansas in 1878 during the "Great Exodus." After grade school Oscar entered Salina Normal School and took a business course for two years. He left home at seventeen, and after knocking around for a year, came to Chicago in 1889. After living precariously for a while DePriest became a painter, decorator, and, later, an independent contractor.

DePriest soon entered politics and became an energetic and resourceful organizer. His service to the party attracted the attention of influential Republican leaders. As a result in 1904, at the age of thirty-three, he was nominated and elected to the Cook County Commission. His record enabled him to win renomination and reelection in 1906. Factionalism, however, led to his defeat in 1908 and prevented him from running for the state legislature. Out of office, DePriest increased his business activity, becoming a successful real estate agent. Rising property values, which accompanied Negro population growth, and wily real estate management enabled him to accumulate considerable wealth. This provided a more substantial base for building his political career.

DePriest's political acumen was demonstrated forcefully in his campaign for the Chicago City Council in 1915. For many months he held meetings, made speeches, and solicited support. Long before the primary he had secured the endorsements of thirty-eight precinct captains, dozens of civic, religious, labor, and professional organizations, as well as many individual party workers and community leaders. This show of strength assured support of the Second Ward Republican organization and Rep. Martin Madden. He was nominated easily and won handily in a race against two white competitors. As the first Negro alderman, DePriest became a significant figure in Chicago politics, a vital part of Mayor William ("Big Bill") Thompson's political machine, and a powerful dispenser of party patronage.

Despite many political misfortunes later, including unstable, controversial alliances, and several unsuc-

cessful campaigns, DePriest refused to give up. Upon the death of Congressman Madden after his nomination in the primary, DePriest became the Republican candidate in the Illinois 3rd Congressional District. He won the November 1928 election and took his seat in the 71st Congress. The first Negro elected to Congress in the twentieth century, and the first from the North, he had risen to power in large measure as a result of the migration of large numbers of Negroes from the South during and after World War I. He served in three Congresses (April 15, 1929 to Jan. 2, 1935).

When Mrs. DePriest accepted the invitation from Mrs. Herbert Hoover to a White House tea, the "incident" caused almost as much furor as had the acceptance by Booker T. Washington to luncheon at the White House with Pres. Theodore Roosevelt in 1901. Although subsiding more quickly, it did not allay white resentment against the first Negro to sit in Congress since 1901. This fact and the Great Depression probably suggested to DePriest that, as a "freshman" in Congress, he should not be unduly active. After his reelection in 1930 despite a Democratic sweep, he introduced a bill (Dec. 1931) threatening to halt organization of the House until he was assured the government would cease job discrimination in the South. The Depression made such assurance impossible.

DePriest's career in Congress produced mixed reactions, especially among colored people. He was roundly condemned for opposing federal aid to the needy. On the other hand he was applauded for speaking in the South despite threats upon his life, for telling Sen. James Heflin of Alabama that he was not big enough physically to prevent DePriest from being served in the Senate restaurant, and for defending the right of Howard University students to eat in the House restaurant. He secured an increase in an appropriation for a Howard University power plant from $240,000 to $460,000. His greatest legislative achievement was passage of his amendment, introduced March 29, 1933, to prohibit discrimination in the Civilian Conservation Corps because of race, color, or creed, and the employment of incarcerated criminals. The Senate approved the bill and President Hoover signed it. He was unsuccessful, however, in three other proposals. A bill which would have permitted transfer of jurisdiction if a defendant believed he could not get a fair trial because of race or religion died in the Judiciary Committee. The same fate met his antilynching bill, introduced Jan. 3, 1934. Unlike the bill introduced by George H. White (1900), DePriest's bill did not make lynching a federal crime. State and local officials found negligent in allowing prisoners to fall into the hands of a mob would be liable to punishment of five years in jail, a fine of $5000, and removal from office. In addition, the county in which the lynching occurred would be required to pay $10,000 to the next of kin of the victim. Although the measure failed in the Judiciary Committee, the concept of county responsibility, supported for example by Gov. Harry Flood Byrd of Virginia, helped reduce the incidence of lynching despite repeated defeats of several bills in Congress. His effort to have Negroes, other than members of Congress, served in the House restaurant was defeated after heated debate (Jan.–March 1934).

DePriest's reputation as a "Red hunter" in condemnation of Communists offset the popularity accruing from his condemnation of the conviction of the "Scotsboro boys," accused of raping two white girls. On the other hand his speech in June 1933, when Mordecai W. Johnson, the first colored president of Howard University, was accused of endorsing Communism, enhanced his reputation to some degree. He stated that he was not trying to defend Johnson, that he believed in the right of free speech, that un-American doctrines should not get federal funds, but that he believed Johnson was not a Communist since he was a Baptist minister. DePriest thus continued his strong opposition to Communism but his speech helped Johnson and Howard University survive the attack (Rayford W. Logan, *Howard University . . .* [1969], pp. 294–95). DePriest's resolution calling for the investigation of Communism in schools died in the House committee.

In the 1934 election DePriest was defeated by a colored Democrat, Arthur W. Mitchell. Not even those measures and activities which had won him support could prevail against his opposition to President Roosevelt's pump-priming proposals and overwhelming Democratic majorities.

He resumed his real estate business in Chicago, was defeated by Mitchell again in 1936, won an election to the Chicago City Council in 1943, and led a fight for fair employment standards until he lost his seat in 1947, partly as a result of an accusation that he supported an unpopular Democratic mayor of Chicago. He was hit by a bus and died on May 12, 1951, of a kidney ailment in Provident Hospital. He was survived by his widow Jessie, their son, and five sisters. Funeral exercises were held on May 15 at Metropolitan Community Church, First and South Parkway, with interment in Graceland Cemetery, Chicago.

The high esteem in which DePriest is still held is evident in the formation of the "DePriest Twelve," some of the most respected Negro citizens of Washington.

The best brief biography is the chapter in Maurine Christopher's *America's Black Congressmen* (1971). His career in Chicago is fully developed in Harold F. Gosnell's *Negro Politicians: The Rise of Negro Politics in Chicago* (1967). The debates about service in the House restaurant are discussed in detail in Kenneth Eugene Mann's "Oscar Stanton DePriest: Persuasive Agent for the Black Masses" (*NHB,* Oct. 1973, pp. 134–37). See also the obituary in the *New York Times* (May 13, 1951, p. 88) and the *Chicago Defender* (May 19, 1951, p. 1). — ROBERT E. MARTIN

DERRICOTTE, JULIETTE [ALINE] (1897–1931), YWCA official and college dean. She was born in Athens, Ga., on April 1, 1897, the fifth child of Isaac Thomas and Laura (Hardwick) Derricotte, and attended the public schools of Athens until 1914. In 1918 she graduated from Talladega College, Talladega, Ala., and received her M.A. degree in religious education from Columbia University in 1927.

Juliette Derricotte learned early the handicap of being a Negro. She wanted desperately to attend the exclusive Lucy Cobb Institute located in her hometown. She voiced her desire to her mother, only to be told that she could not attend this school because it did not accept colored students. This incident was a factor in her efforts to reduce racial discrimination.

At Talladega College she was very active in campus and community activities, especially as a representative of the YWCA in visiting numerous colleges. In many speeches she stressed the need for better relations between Negro and white women.

After graduation from Talladega she enrolled in a summer course at the National YWCA Training School in New York City. Immediately afterward she was appointed traveling secretary of the National Council of the YWCA for various colleges, a position she held for eleven years. She was one of two colored delegates to the World's Student Christian Federation in England in 1924. In 1928 she attended the World's Student Christian Federation in India. Her lecture tour took her to China and Japan before returning to the United States. In 1922 Derricotte was instrumental in the organization of the interracial structure of the National Student Council of the YWCA. Her tireless efforts enabled it to become an effective part of the council, sponsoring many student forums and weekend conferences. Derricotte resigned her position as national student secretary for the YWCA in 1929. From 1929 until 1931 she was the only woman trustee at Talladega College.

Upon her resignation from the YWCA Derricotte became the dean of women at Fisk University, a position she held for approximately three years. On Nov. 6, 1931, while she and three students were en route to her home in Athens, her car collided head-on with that of a white couple in Dalton, Ga. Negroes were not admitted at that time for treatment in the only hospital in that city. Derricotte and her injured companions were given emergency treatment in the office of a white physician and then carried to the home of a Negro woman before being driven several hours later to Walden Hospital in Chattanooga, Tenn. She died there on Nov. 7, 1931.

Howard Thurman, her friend, delivered the eulogy at the funeral in Athens, where interment took place. Juliette Derricotte's many friends and students remembered her as a very sympathetic and understanding person.

References pertaining to Derricotte's life are relatively few. The following citations proved valuable: Marion V. Cuthbert's *Juliette Derricotte* (1933); Mary Jeanness's *Twelve Negro Americans* (1936); W. E. B. Du Bois's "Juliette Derricotte; Dalton, Georgia" (*The Crisis,* March 1932); and Walter White's "The Color Line: Even at Death's Door in the Case of Miss Derricotte" (*New York Herald Tribune,* Dec. 10, 1931).

— DOLORES LEFFALL

DESDUNES, RODOLPHE LUCIEN (1849–1928), historian and community leader. He was born in New Orleans, La., on Nov. 15, 1849, the oldest of several children of Jeremiah and Henrietta Desdunes. His mother was a Cuban and his father a Haitian whose forebears came to New Orleans presumably during the 1791 revolution in Saint-Domingue. Rodolphe Desdunes's education was most probably provided by his parents, his friends, and confreres such as Armand Lanusse and Joanni Questy and attendance at the Bernard Couvent Institute of New Orleans. Both Rodolphe and his poet brother, Pierre A. Desdunes, served as directors of this institute. Desdunes married Mathilde Chaval of Point Coupee Parish and New Orleans. Of this union were born six children, two boys and four girls: Wendell, Daniel, Cortiza, Agens, Lucille, and Jeanne. Their home was at 928 Marais St., New Orleans.

Not inclined toward working on the family's tobacco plantation nor in their cigar factory, Rodolphe Desdunes in 1879 obtained employment as a messenger with the U.S. Customs Service at a salary of $600 a year, which he held until 1894, except for a lapse between 1885 and 1891 because of party differences. In addition Desdunes gave his time and his services to his community of fellow-citizens. He promoted and supported various social, educational, economic, and political movements in the interest of the Creoles of color. With several of his friends he organized in 1890 the Citizens' Committee in New Orleans, known as the Comité des Citoyens, to ensure the protection of Negroes against segregation and disfranchisement. Desdunes stated that this group launched the case of *Plessy v. Ferguson* (Desdunes, *Hommage rendu . . . à Alexandre Aristide Mary* [1893], p. 11).

In 1899 Desdunes was appointed weigher at the customhouse with a salary of $1200 a year on a probationary basis. On Jan. 31, 1900, he received a permanent appointment to this position. All circumstances then seemed to point toward stability, security, happiness, and prosperity for Desdunes and his family. But tragedy struck in 1911. A painful accident arrested his progress toward future promotion in civil service work. While he and four other officers were supervising the unloading of granite in a New Orleans harbor, dust from the stone blew into his eyes and partially blinded him. All medical assistance proved of no avail to Desdunes, and in September 1912 he was forced to resign from his government position.

Rodolphe L. Desdunes had a strong penchant for writing. His chief ambition was to memorialize in either pamphlet or book form the deeds and the accomplishments of his friends and fellow Creoles of color who had contributed to the building of a highly prized culture in the city of his birth. To this end in 1911, even though now afflicted with poor eyesight, he wrote and had published in Montréal, Canada, a work entitled *Nos Hommes et Notre Histoire.* This anthology includes biographical sketches of some fifty noted Creoles of color living in New Orleans during the middle and latter part of the nineteenth century. It also records a number of poems by writers of this group, as well as essays and an account of Reconstruction in Louisiana. The work is a plea for understanding and recognition of the Creole of color. It is written in a wholesome, refreshing style that gives facts and impressions of a man truly dedicated to the people of his race. The translation of Desdunes's work by Sister Dorothea Olga McCants under the title *Our People and Our History* (1973) is prefaced by a valuable Foreword written by the Rev. Charles E. O'Neill, S.J.

Rodolphe L. Desdunes died of cancer of the larynx on Aug. 14, 1928. He is interred in the family tomb in St. Louis Cemetery No. 2, Square 3, New Orleans. His widow Mathilde and six children survived him.

Other writings of Desdunes include his contributions to the post-Reconstruction periodical the *Daily Crusader,* published in New Orleans (1889–1898). Charles Barthélemy Rousseve, in *The Negro in Louisiana* (1937), states that Desdunes wrote regularly in French and in English for the *Daily Crusader.* Desdunes also wrote several pamphlets, including *Hommage rendu à la memoire d'Alexandre Aristide Mary . . . décedé à la Nouvelle Orleans, le 15 mai, 1893, à l'age de 70 ans* and *A Few Words to Dr. DuBois, "With Malice Toward None,"* in which the author challenges any attempt to claim that southern Negroes lacked learning and skills. — DOROTHEA OLGA MCCANTS, D.C.

DETT, R[OBERT] NATHANIEL (1882–1943), music educator, composer, and pianist. He is best known for his choral compositions which use Negro spirituals and folksongs for thematic material and development; and for his piano compositions, most of which are written in the style of nineteenth-century Romanticism.

Dett was born on Oct. 11, 1882, in Drummondsville, Ontario, Canada, a small community which has since become a part of Niagara Falls, Ontario. He was the third son and youngest of four children of Robert Tue and Charlotte (Washington) Dett. Two of the children died at an early age leaving Samuel, the oldest, and Robert Nathaniel. Robert Tue, the father, came from Reisterstown, Md., and Charlotte Washington Dett was born and lived in Drummondsville. Both parents were educated and musical: his father played the piano and guitar; his mother played the piano and sang soprano. Hariett Washington, his maternal grandmother, lived with the Dett family until her death, and it was in her singing that R. Nathaniel first heard the Negro spirituals that were later to influence his musical career.

Dett's father, a railroad porter, spent much time away from home. After leaving the railroad, he operated a hotel in Niagara Falls, Ontario. In 1893 the family moved to Niagara Falls, N.Y., and opened a tourist home which remained in the family until the death of his brother Samuel.

The major influence in Dett's life was his mother who was a forceful, ambitious and idealistic woman. She taught Dett, at an early age, to recite long biblical passages and poems by Tennyson, Longfellow, and Shakespeare. A love for poetry remained with him throughout his life and he considered himself an amateur poet, having published in 1911 a volume of poems, *The Album of the Heart.* He maintained an affectionate and close relationship with his mother until her death in 1937.

Dett was a musically precocious child who played the piano at age three without training. Although his first piano lessons began at age five, serious training did not begin until 1901 when he entered the Halstead Conservatory, Brockport, N.Y. In 1903 he enrolled in a five-year course of study at the Oberlin Conservatory of Music, where he graduated in 1908 with a Bachelor of Music degree in composition and piano.

While a student at Oberlin, Dett heard the Kneisel

Quartet playing a slow movement by Dvořák based on traditional Bohemian airs. He was profoundly moved by this music as he recalled the spirituals which his grandmother had sung through the years. It was this experience that inspired him to utilize the music of his own background, traditional Negro folk melodies, in conventional artforms. This idea was to dominate his creative efforts throughout his life.

His teaching career began at Lane College, Jackson, Tenn. (1908 to 1911); from 1911 to 1913 he taught at the Lincoln Institute, Jefferson City, Mo. It was at Hampton Institute, Va. (1913–1932), that Dett made his most significant contributions. He created the Hampton Choral Union, an organization of community people who worked closely with Hampton Institute; he founded the Musical Arts Society, which presented one of the outstanding college concert programs of the country; he organized and directed the famous Hampton Institute Choir; and he established and directed the School of Music.

On Dec. 27, 1916, Dett married Helen Elise Smith of New York City. An honor graduate of the Institute of Musical Arts, New York City, she was a concert pianist of distinction and one of the directors of the Martin-Smith School of Music in New York. From this marriage were born two daughters: Helen (Hopkins) and Josephine (Breelove).

In 1920 Dett spent the year studying at Harvard University where he won the Bowdoin Prize for his essay "The Emancipation of Negro Music," and the Francis Boot Prize for the best piece of vocal concert music, "Don't Be Weary, Traveler."

Further honors were bestowed upon him. In 1924 he received an honorary Doctor of Music degree from Howard University; in 1926 his alma mater, Oberlin College, conferred upon him the honorary Doctor of Music; and in 1927 he received the Harmon Award for achievement in music.

In spite of strenuous duties at Hampton Institute, Dett studied formally when possible. The University of Pennsylvania, the American Conservatory of Music in Chicago, Columbia University all stimulated new ideas. In 1929 he studied in France under Nadia Boulanger at the Fontainebleau School of Music. After several years of study at the Eastman School of Music, he graduated with a Master of Music degree in composition in 1932. The title of his thesis was "Composition for Chorus and Orchestra." This work was later published as *The Ordering of Moses.* He continued, however, to study composition under Dr. Howard Hanson in 1932–1933 when he permanently left Hampton Institute. He moved to Rochester, N.Y., opened a private studio, organized a Negro community choir, and directed a radio program for Stromberg-Carlsen.

In 1937, after teaching a summer session at Sam Houston College in Texas, he accepted the position of director of music at Bennett College, Greensboro, N.C. Dett resigned from Bennett College in 1942 and with his family returned to Rochester. He joined the USO in 1943 as musical adviser and was sent to Battle Creek, Mich. It was in Battle Creek, on Oct. 2, 1943, that a heart attack which he had suffered in September of that year proved to be fatal. He was buried in Fairview

Cemetery, Niagara Falls, N.Y. He was survived by his widow and two daughters.

As a music educator Dett will be remembered as one who was always concerned about his students, their development and welfare, and as one who presented an image of industry, wisdom, and scholarship for their emulation.

Throughout his professional life Dett devoted some time to concert work. As a pianist he was well trained, possessed a facile technique and expressive touch, and was widely acclaimed as a performer by critics in leading cities in the U.S. and Canada.

National and international fame was bestowed upon Dett as conductor of the Hampton Institute Choir. Reviews of the choir concerts in Carnegie Hall, New York City (1928), Symphony Hall, Boston (1929), the Library of Congress, Washington, D.C. (1930), are all strong in praise. In 1930 he successfully conducted the Hampton Institute Choir in concerts in major concert halls of seven European countries.

Dett was a significant American composer who successfully utilized the Negro spiritual in traditional artforms. His music is dominated by nineteenth-century Romanticism although his later works used some modern techniques. He was a skillful craftsman whose music speaks with clarity, simplicity, and sincerity.

Among his published compositions are five piano suites and eight Bible vignettes; forty or more choral works; two oratorios; twenty-four vocal solos; one violin solo; and two collections of Negro spirituals. His best known works are "Juba" from *In the Bottoms Suite* for piano (1913) and "Listen to the Lambs" for mixed voices (1914).

Vivian F. McBrier's "The Life and Works of R. Nathaniel Dett" (doctoral dissertation, Catholic University of America, 1967) recommends several brief references, especially Dett's autobiographical "From Bell Stand to Throne Room" (*Etude,* Feb. 1934, pp. 78–80). Eileen Southern's *The Music of Black Americans* (1971, pp. 291–93) is informative despite a few inaccuracies. Likewise valuable despite similar inaccuracies are Maud Cuney-Hare's *Negro Musicians and Their Music* (1936, pp. 336–37); volume 2 of *Grove's Dictionary of Music and Musicians* (1954), and *Baker's Biographical Directory of Musicians* (5th ed., 1958, pp. 376–77). See the obituary in the *New York Times* (Oct. 4, 1973, p. 17). Prof. Walter Fisher ranked him with Harry T. Burleigh, Will Marion Cook, and Samuel Coleridge-Taylor (*DAB, Supplement 3* [1973], p. 226).

                                              — VIVIAN F. MCBRIER

DICKERSON, SPENCER C. (1871–1948), physician and army officer. The son of Patrick and Eliza Dickerson, he was born on Dec. 1, 1871, in Austin, Tex. First migrating to Nashville, Tenn., where he taught school, Dickerson continued his education at the University of Chicago. Graduating from that institution with a B.S. in 1897, he enrolled in the Medical School of Northwestern University in 1898 and became, it is said, the first student to complete the two-year program in one year. Completing his studies at the Rush Medical College in 1901, Dickerson served as an intern at Freedmen's Hospital in Washington, D.C. In 1902 he established his medical practice in New Bedford, Mass., and remained there until 1907.

Upon his return to Chicago, Dickerson began an association with the staff of Provident Hospital which continued for more than two generations. Appointed the first Negro pathologist at Provident, he held that position from 1907 to 1912. Serving as an ophthalmologist and as an otolaryngologist from 1920 to 1937, Dickerson not only won the acclaim of the Provident staff and personnel but was was cited in 1946 as a distinguished alumnus by the University of Chicago. During that same year he was awarded the Charles Victor Roman Medal for service in the John A. Andrew Clinical Society, Tuskegee, Ala.

Paralleling his career as a physician were his achievements in the military. Enlisting in the Illinois National Guard as a private in 1914, he was assigned to the Medical Detachment of the 8th Illinois Infantry Regiment. Promoted to the rank of first lieutenant before his regiment assumed its duties on the Mexican border in 1916, he attracted attention because of the efficient manner in which he performed his duties. When his regiment was federalized in 1917 and redesignated as the 370th Infantry Regiment, he was promoted to the rank of captain on April 18, 1918, and served in France. He continued to serve in the National Guard after the termination of the World War, assuming the command of the Medical Department Detachment of the 8th Illinois Regiment. After being promoted to major on July 14, 1926, Dickerson was selected to succeed Col. Otis B. Duncan in 1929. Promoted to colonel on Sept. 9, 1929, Dickerson instituted several innovations which significantly improved the proficiency of the regiment. Under his leadership, and for the first time in the history of the regiment, three officers attended the Fort Benning Infantry School in Georgia. More significantly, he persuaded every officer and more than two-thirds of the enlisted personnel to enroll in the appropriate Army Extension Courses. This success was attributed to Dickerson's quiet but forceful disposition which inspired the confidence of his personnel. He retired from the National Guard on Dec. 1, 1934, with the rank of brigadier general.

Information concerning the career of Dickerson is contained in *JNMA* (vol. 40, July 1948); the Records of the Adjutant-General, Record Group 94, the National Archives, Washington, D.C.; the *Annual Reports of the Adjutant General for Illinois* as well as the contemporary editions of the *Chicago Defender*.

— CHARLES JOHNSON, JR.

DILL, AUGUSTUS GRANVILLE (1881–1956), sociologist, business manager of *The Crisis,* and musician. The son of John Jackson and Elizabeth (Stratton) Dill, he was born in Portsmouth, Ohio. After finishing local schools at the age of seventeen, he taught briefly there. He was a member of the debating team and played the piano in the choir of the original Atlanta University where he graduated (B.A., 1906). He earned a second B.A. at Harvard (1908), and returned to Atlanta to receive his M.A. (also in 1908). A pupil of W. E. B. Du Bois, he took his mentor's place as associate professor of sociology in 1910 when Du Bois left Atlanta to estab-

lish the NAACP's magazine *The Crisis.* In 1913, as that monthly grew, Du Bois persuaded Dill to become its business manager and editorial assistant although he was not a businessman by training or temperament. Du Bois wrote in *Dusk of Dawn* (1940, p. 226) that Dill "gave to the work his utmost devotion and to him was due much of its phenomenal business success." Within three years *The Crisis* was self-supporting, and by 1919 it reached a circulation peak of 104,000. In that same year both men incurred the censure of Attorney-General A. Mitchell Palmer, who charged, inaccurately, that they published a magazine "always antagonistic to the white race and openly defiantly assertive of its own equality and even superiority."

In 1920 while still publishing *The Crisis,* Dill and Du Bois, with the assistance of Jessie Fauset, formed a corporation to publish the *Brownie's Book,* a monthly for Negro children which featured history, current events, literature, and a positive view of their race. No other periodical for colored children then existed. Although filling a great need, and attractively printed, the magazine failed to support itself and folded after two years. Dill's service to *The Crisis* was cut short in 1928 when his personal lifestyle proved embarrassing to the association and Du Bois, although the latter bade him farewell with heartfelt gratitude.

Dill remained in New York City, erratically and at times inadequately supporting himself on the meager returns from a short-lived bookstore, a personal service shop, and private tutoring, all the while pursuing an interest in music. This was his avocation since youth. He had been college organist at Atlanta University and was for many years, on a part-time basis, organist and choir director for John Haynes Holmes's Community Church of New York. An accomplished pianist as well, he accompanied a number of artists in recital and on recordings, including Roland Hayes and Florence Cole-Talbert. From 1910 to the end of his life various other recitals, art exhibitions, and choral productions claimed his services, including Du Bois's *Star of Ethiopia* pageant (1913), for which he directed the music. Dill claimed that New York was the only city in which he felt happy, because of the cultural resources available to him there as well as the relative absence of racial indignities. It was not until four years before his death that ill health persuaded him to move to the family circle in Louisville, Ky.

The association with Du Bois was a major influence in Dill's life. He took over Du Bois's sociology courses at Atlanta while providing Du Bois the opportunity to carry on the Atlanta University publications in absentia; the two edited *The College-Bred Negro* (1911), *The Common School and the Negro American* (1912), *The Negro American Artisan* (1913), and *Morals and Manners Among Negro Americans* (1915). When Du Bois in 1913 practically insisted that Dill come to work on *The Crisis,* he knew his former pupil would sacrifice his academic career. Yet Dill followed willingly, in part out of loyalty, yet also because, while enjoying university life in Atlanta, he had suffered "Jim Crow" indignities and was glad for the opportunity to escape. Temperamentally he was not equipped to endure such insults easily, and he never thereafter regretted leaving the

South. Like Du Bois, Dill relished most the life of the mind; he was even less an activist than his older associate. The two were, however, similar in their cultivation of impeccable English and wearing of immaculate, conservative clothes. Each had considerable respect for the other, although they did not retain a close relationship after their *Crisis* partnership ended.

Dill impressed others as a quiet, cultured man. To Du Bois, "he was by nature and training the sensitive artist and musician rather than the business man." His pupils, especially, remembered his deep interest in young people of talent. Selfless in his use of time, he was devoted to their progress. His most important contribution, however, was his service to the young NAACP and its magazine. He was instrumental in setting *The Crisis* on firm feet, freeing Du Bois from many of the cares of day-to-day operation. This was the only reasonably comfortable niche he could have found in the NAACP, for he was willing to live only part of his life in the political arena. Music, especially, gave him much greater satisfaction.

He died on March 9, 1956, in Louisville. Funeral services were held on March 10 at the Rodgers Funeral Home, 951 South Preston, and his body was cremated. He was survived by his sister, Mary Dill Broadus, with whom he had lived for four years at 827 South Preston (*Louisville Courier-Journal,* March 10, 1956, p. 13).

There is no biography of Dill. The report of the Department of Justice, "Radicalism and Sedition Among Negroes as Reflected in Their Publications," is in *Investigation Activities of Department of Justice* (66th Cong., 1st sess., U.S. Senate Document No. 153, 12 (1919): 161–87). There are brief references in Clarence A. Bacote's *The Story of Atlanta University: A Century of Service, 1865–1965* (1969, pp. 137–38, 211, 214).

— THEODORE KORNWEIBEL

FATHER DIVINE [born **GEORGE BAKER**] (1880?–1965), cult leader. Both his early and last years need documentation. Most of his biographies give the year of his birth as 1880, and the place as Hutchinson Island in the Savannah River (Ga). His parents were poor sharecroppers, and the number of his brothers and sisters is not known accurately. He came to Baltimore probably in 1899, worked as an initerant garden laborer and preached occasionally. He served his apprenticeship as a latter Messiah under St. John the Divine Hickerson, and Samuel Morris who proclaimed himself "the Father Eternal," took the name of Father Jehovia and annointed George Baker as the "Messenger" and "God in the Sonship Degree." In 1914 Baker and a small group of his followers moved to Valdosta, Ga., where he proclaimed himself God.

Found guilty of being a public menace because of his noisy street-corner congregation, but not "crazy" enough to be confined in an asylum, he left Valdosta and made his way north. One of the disciples who accompanied him was Peninah ("Sister Penny"). In Harlem Baker polished his techniques of self-proclaimed godhood under the tutelage of Hickerson, then left him and established his own church on Myrtle Avenue in the Negro section of Brooklyn. He proclaimed himself the only living God, demanded complete loy-

alty of his followers, and forbade sexual relations between even husband and wife. He married Sister Penny, a homely stout woman, and set the example for abstinence from "carnal lust." Penny's free dinners were forerunners of the lavish banquets which later helped to attract large numbers of followers. Baker asserted a black chauvinism and so greatly increased the number of followers that in 1919 he purchased a home in Sayville, Long Island. The deed was signed in the name of Maj. J. Devine and his wife Penny. He gradually became one of the most powerful and controversial American Negroes until his death in 1965.

His Sayville congregation grew slowly from the original twenty disciples in 1919 until the late 1920s when his lavish dinners and recruitment in Harlem of domestic workers for the wealthy residents of Long Island started a rapid increase. At the same time there began a trickle of white converts, a few of whom were wealthy and well educated. In 1930 he formally took the name of Father Divine.

Several factors led to his almost unbelievable rise to power. From the beginning his Peace Mission movement was nondenominational and interracial; it attracted both sexes, illiterate domestics, middle-class and professional workers, a few millionaires, the devout, and the hungry. An incident in 1931 appeared to validate his mystic powers. Some eighty of his followers in Sayville were arrested on a disorderly conduct charge, stemming from a noisy demonstration that turned the white community against him. Father Divine was condemned to prison; four days later the judge dropped dead of a heart attack. Father Divine is reported to have said from his prison cell: "I hated to do it." After his release, a "Monster Glory to Our God" reception at Rockland Palace in Harlem convinced Father Divine that Harlem was the logical place for the expansion of his kingdoms.

The number of Peace Mission Kingdoms, cooperatives, and other business enterprises increased. He became one of the largest landlords in Harlem; he owned restaurants, barbershops, grocery stores, huckster wagons, and a coal business. In the 1930s he acquired on a smaller scale properties in Newark, Jersey City, Bridgeport, and Baltimore. His business and kingdoms expanded to large cities in most parts of the nation, especially in California, and even in Austria, Australia, Sweden, Germany, Switzerland, and England. The full extent of his enormous wealth was not known because he filed no income tax returns and paid no income tax. He claimed twenty million followers; two million may be more accurate.

Harlem was ripe for a new Messiah. In 1925 Marcus Garvey had been sentenced to five years in the penitentiary on a charge of using the mails for fraudulent purposes. W. E. B. Du Bois and the elitist "Talented Tenth" drew their support mainly from middle- and upper-class Negroes. The Great Depression left large numbers of Negroes in Harlem and elsewhere without jobs or much hope, and little faith in the white man's church. Father Divine was the most skillful of the "New Messengers," some of whom had only a small following, a banjo, and a tambourine. Langston Hughes left a memorable picture of these cult leaders in his novel *Tambourines to*

Glory (1958). Father Divine became the main attraction among Harlem cult leaders. The "glorious domain" of his Kingdoms of Peace was expanding. This was the beginning of his triumphant years in Harlem. For him it was truly wonderful. Another incident in the fall of 1933 helped solidify his influence and power.

The people of New York were in the throes of a three-way election battle to decide who would be mayor. Only one of the contesting candidates sought the support of Father Divine and his followers. On Nov. 4, 1933, Father Divine was holding a vespers banquet in the Rockland Palace. To the surprise of all, in walked the candidate, Fiorello LaGuardia. "I came here tonight to ask Father Divine's advice and counsel," he said, "Peace be with you all." Thereafter several candidates sought his endorsement. Although he was not overtly political, he encouraged his followers to register and vote for their own benefit and that of their community. The political structure recognized the potential strength of this voting bloc to such an extent that it even waived the stipulation that people use their given names as they registered to vote, and allowed Father Divine's followers to use such names as "Mother's Delight," "Brother of the Good Faith," and "Sister Who Stood by the Way."

There were other sources of his power. His weekly newspaper, *New Day,* presented contemporary issues as he interpreted them. He gave stimulus and dignity to the lowly, instilled in his followers honesty, good personal habits, dependability in domestic service and other jobs. He provided wholesome meals, without cost to the unemployed or for ten or fifteen cents to others, to followers and visitors in his "kingdoms."

Even skeptics left his meetings, astounded by the chants of "Yes, he God" by the lowly and the well-to-do, black and white. His self-proclaimed "philosophy" was expounded in an interview with Claude McKay (*Nation,* Feb. 6, 1935). Father Divine asserted that if he represented race, creed, color, or nation, he could not be "omnipotent," as he was. Masses, classes, and in time governments would have to recognize this omnipotence. He supported Communists in seeking international peace and the abolition of segregation and discrimination; the Communists were trying to do what he was actually doing. He alone could "give emancipation and liberty." It is difficult to know whether Father Divine believed in his omnipotence. But large numbers in the United States and abroad were "true believers."

His omnipotence was soon shattered on the altars of two subjects that were supposed not to be discussable in his kingdoms—money and sex. It was widely believed, then and later, that big business firms supplied him with large sums for keeping Negroes satisfied with their lot (he did not long espouse Communism) and training capable, tractable domestic servants. About noon on April 20, 1937, two white men entered Headquarters Kingdom at 20 W. 115th St., after a confrontation between Father Divine and "Faithful Mary" over a sum which had been given her. One of the white intruders, a process server, was badly beaten and his companion stabbed. Later that day a police search failed to find Father Divine in New York. An order was issued for his arrest, charging felonious assault. Three of his angels

were held on the same charge. Three days later Father Divine was discovered in one of his kingdoms in Milford, Conn., and brought back to New York. In Los Angeles the same week, John West Hunt, a wealthy white disciple whose cult name was "St. John the Revelation" was arrested under the Mann Act for the interstate transportation for sexual purposes of a young follower named "Miss Delight Jewel." The most serious, and least expected, trouble came when "Faithful Mary," the star angel of the movement, defected after making lurid charges about Father Divine's sex life and alleged blackmailing of his followers.

But, strangely, 1938 found the movement recovering and Father Divine once more in triumph. The wayward angel "Faithful Mary" returned temporarily to the good graces of the kingdom. Father Divine and his followers acquired the Krum Elbow estate and became the neighbors of President Roosevelt in Hyde Park, an event that received almost nationwide publicity.

Not long thereafter, however, his power began to decline. After 1941 he lived in a thirty-two-room Philadelphia mansion on seventy-three acres, the gift of a white disciple, John De Voute. Defying several court orders to pay almost $5000 to an angel who had accused Father Divine of defrauding him, he refused to pay, was found in contempt of court (none of the judges died), and left Harlem forever in order to avoid going to jail. The abandonment of his principal power base, Harlem, further weakened his influence. His marriage in April 1946 to Ednah Rose Ritchings ("Sweet Angel"), a Canadian-born white woman, after the death and "reincarnation" of Penny, provoked scurrilous attacks in the press, both Negro and white, as well as among many of his followers. Wide publicity given to the allegations by Hunt, "The Prodigal Son," that Father Divine was a "hoax" and a court ruling in 1944 that set aside a large bequest by Mary Lyon ("Sweet Dove") on the ground that she had been of unsound mind further tarnished the image of "God."

Father Divine died on Sept. 10, 1965, of arterioscloris and diabetes mellitus. No funeral services were held. The body was to lie in state at Woodmont, the movement's country estate in nearby Conshohocken; burial was to be on the estate and the body was to be preserved until officials of the Peace Mission Movement decided where to build a crypt (*New York Times,* Sept. 11, 1965, p. 1; Sept. 12, pp. 1, 86; Sept. 13, p. 35).

An evaluation of the "Messiah" is difficult. He inculcated good habits among his followers, fed many of them free of charge, and found jobs for them. His "faith healing" is of course subject to skepticism. One visitor who attended a meeting in one of his Harlem "kingdoms" in the late 1930s concluded that Father Divine, among other techniques, exerted a kind of hypnotic spell over his audience. Barely five feet tall, squat, completely bald, "Negroid," he intoned, rhythmically, "Tens, hundreds, thousands, ten thousands, hundred thousands, millions. Tens, hundreds, . . . millions." Although this seemed nonsense to the visitor and his two female college-graduate friends, at the end the true believers were chanting: "Yes, he's God. Yes he's God." Only psychologists may be able to explain Father Divine's power as well as that of his contemporary, Elder

Becton and his "Consecrated Dime," or the sexual vibrations of Aimee Semple McPherson or Sun Myung Moon and his "God Bless America."

How much he pandered to employers and political conservatives is debatable. Thorough research is necessary to determine the disposition of his businesses, including hotels, beauty parlors, and moving firms in the United States and abroad. Most difficult is an assessment of his continuing impact.

John Horshor's *God in a Rolls Royce* (1936) is a classic debunker, as is Robert A. Parker's psychohistory, *The Incredible Messiah: The Deification of Father Divine* (1937). Even more devastating in general is Sara Harris's *Father Divine, Holy Husband* (1953), reprinted with an Afterword as *Father Divine* (1971).

— RAYFORD W. LOGAN

DIXON, GEORGE ["LITTLE CHOCOLATE"] (1870–1908), world champion boxer. Dixon was born in Halifax, Nova Scotia. After attending school for two years there, he moved with his parents when he was eight years old to Boston where he attended public schools and at the age of fourteen secured employment with Elmer Chickering, a well-known photographer. It was through this job that young Dixon had the occasion to witness a boxing match at the Boston Music Hall. Impressed by what he had seen, on the very next day Dixon purchased a book on boxing. He later recalled that it was then that he decided on boxing as a career.

He married when he was fifteen and began fighting in 1886 when he was five feet, three and a half inches tall, and weighed eighty-seven pounds. Because of his brown complexion, he was widely known as "Little Chocolate." His manager, Tom O'Rourke, won recognition for Dixon as bantam-weight champion (118-pound limitation). The title had been declared vacated in 1887. On May 10, 1888, Dixon fought a draw with Tommy Kelly who had laid claim to the vacated title. When Kelly retired, O'Rourke's claim for recognition of Dixon as world champion was recognized.

He established an undisputed claim to the title when he knocked out Nunc Wallace in eighteen rounds in London on June 17, 1890, when he weighed 112 pounds. The *Cleveland Gazette* on Aug. 16, 1890, heralded his return to the United States and declared that he was ready to fight Cal McCarthy. Dixon became the first double titleholder in pugilistic history when he defeated McCarthy in Troy, N.Y., on March 31, 1891, and won the 115-pound featherweight title (a previous fight of seventy rounds in February 1890 had ended in a draw). Dixon knocked out McCarthy in the twenty-second round. He defeated Jack Skelly at New Orleans on Sept. 6, 1892. In 1894 he began touring the country with a vaudeville and athletic company called the George Dixon Specialty Country. By this time he had married the sister of his manager, O'Rourke. Dixon stayed at colored boarding houses while his wife and brother-in-law put up at white hotels.

So numerous were Dixon's fights that no complete official record is available (158 were recorded). Numbering perhaps 500, most took place in theaters and dance halls. He lost his featherweight title to "Terrible Terry" McGovern by a knockout in the eighth round at the Broadway Athletic Club on Jan. 9, 1900. Advancing age—he was almost thirty—and high living brought to an end a memorable career. On Aug. 25, 1900, the *Cleveland Gazette* reported that he had squandered most of almost $100,000 he had won and had only a $6000 house in Boston. After he lost his title he fought for six years and was defeated sixteen times in forty-one bouts.

The *Washington Post* on Jan. 7, 1908, reported in banner headlines: DRINK ENDS DIXON'S LIFE—FORMER HEAVYWEIGHT CHAMPION DIES IN NEW YORK HOSPITAL—WAS THE GREATEST FIGHTER OF HIS TIME AND CHAMPION UNTIL HE MET TERRY MCGOVERN.

Nathaniel Fleischer, boxing authority, wrote: "The darling of the fighters, they called him, and that is what he was to thousands of American fight fans who adored him for his fighting qualities. America has had its fistic heroes—John L. Sullivan, Jim Corbett, Bob Fitzsimmons, Jim Jeffries, Joe Gans . . . Jack Dempsey, Joe Louis among others—but I doubt that there was a pugilist who was as popular during his entire career as was 'Little Chocolate' " (*Black Dynamite* . . . [1938], 3:6).

Dixon died in the alcoholic ward of Bellevue Hospital on Jan. 6, 1908. His body rested for two days in the mainroom of the Longacre Athletic Club, New York City, where it was viewed by thousands of admirers. Sufficient funds were raised for his relatives (not named) in Boston to escort the body to the Mount Hope Cemetery. When plans for a monument over his grave were rejected, McGovern and others used the funds for a watering trough on the west side of New York City.

Dixon made an art of boxing; his perfect timing and skills of punching, blocking, and evading blows placed him far ahead of his boxing era. He is acclaimed as being the founder and first successful exponent of scientific boxing. He was fast, clever, tricky, courageous, a debonair dresser and convivial fellow, but above all he was a showman and widely popular. As testimony to his brilliance in the ring, he was elected to boxing's Hall of Fame in 1956.

There is no full-length biography of George Dixon. His autobiography, published in 1893, is the single best source of information. Brief biographical sketches of Dixon's ring career are contained in A. S. Young's *Negro Firsts in Sports* (1963), Nat Fleischer's *Black Dynamite,* vol. 3, *The Three Colored Aces* . . . (1938), and Ocania Chalk's *Pioneers of Black Sport* (1975), with photographs on page 128. — AL-TONY GILMORE

DORMAN, ISAIAH (? –1876), frontiersman, interpreter, and soldier. Dorman was probably born in slavery, and little is known of his moving into the Indian country. Like others before him he was in all probability an escaped slave avoiding capture by inhabiting the frontier wilderness. Known as "Teat" or the Wasicun Sapa (Black White Man) among the tribes, his affiliation with the Sioux is alluded to in tribal history as early as 1850. Dorman first presented himself at a white settlement in 1865. He was wed to a young woman of Inkpaduta's band of Santee Sioux and had mastered the gutteral and difficult dialect of his chosen friends. He built a log cabin adjacent to Fort Rice, Dakota Territory, near present-day Bismarck, N.D., and supported his wife by cutting wood for the fort. In early fall of 1865 he was hired for that chore by the trading firm of Durfee and Peck.

On Nov. 11, 1865, according to military records, Dorman was hired by Lt. James M. Marshall of the 13th Infantry to carry the mail between Fort Rice and Fort Wadsworth. He made the 360-mile round trip only once that year but his reputation for diligence and dependability was established. Between 1865 and 1876 he rendered valuable service to the army in various capacities, among them a stint as guide and interpreter for the Northern Pacific Railroad survey of 1871. During this period his average earnings from governmental sources were about $60 per month, a goodly sum during those years. On Oct. 19, 1871, the commanding general of the Military Department of the Dakotas, in Special Order No. 149, hired Dorman to serve as post interpreter at Fort Rice at the rate of $75 per month. His skill with the Sioux language and an apparent understanding of the problems of both red and white men helped avert many "incidents" at Fort Rice. An easygoing manner and the strong smoking and chewing tobacco of which he was inordinately fond, and which he readily shared with his Indian friends, brought many of the hostiles to the fort in friendly trading visits.

Dorman's immediate superior was Lt. William Van Horne of the 17th Infantry. In 1872 Van Horne was transferred and Dorman served under Capt. James Wall Scully of the Quartermaster Corps until he served with General Custer and the 7th Cavalry. Custer was noted for his desire to have only the best available in his selection of civilian employees to accompany his expeditions. He knew of Dorman's prowess, and when preparing for the 1876 summer expedition against hostile and recalcitrant Indians, caused Special Order No. 2 (May 14, 1876) to be issued: "The commanding officer Ft. Rice, D.T. [Dakota Territory] will order Isaiah Dorman, Post interpreter to proceed to this post and report for duty to accompany the expedition as Interpreter—During his absence he will still be borne on the rolls of the Post Quartermaster at Fort Rice." Dorman was officially hired as interpreter for the 7th Cavalry by the regimental quartermaster, Lt. Henry J. Nowlan, and assumed duties on May 15, 1876, at the pay rate of $75 per month.

Custer's command arrived at the "Crow's Nest," an Indian landmark about fifteen miles east of the Little Bighorn River on June 25, 1876. It was there that Custer made the controversial division of his command. Dorman, as did most of the civilian employees, accompanied Maj. Marcus A. Reno's battalion of three companies. This arm of the assault crossed the Little Bighorn and executed an abortive attack on the southern perimeter of the hostile village. A skirmish line was formed, but after a few minutes Major Reno ordered a retreat to the timber bordering the west bank of the river. It was at the edge of this timber that, early in the fight, Isaiah Dorman received a fatal chest wound from the rifle of an Indian marksman. Unable to mount or ride a horse, Dorman, with several others, including famed scout "Lonesome Charley" Reynolds, was left to the dubious mercy of the Sioux. Reports as to atrocities committed

upon his body are varied but one enlisted man on the burial detail reported that when Dorman's body was found, it had been stripped, more than a dozen arrows shot into his chest, and a cavalry picket-pin driven through his genitals.

At the time of his demise $102.50 was due him for services during the months of May and June. The money was never rightfully claimed and remains unpaid. In all probability he died without issue. Fort Rice medical records fail to disclose any pregnancy or childbirth in his wife's name.

In his report of the battle Major Reno made the only reference to the color of Isaiah's skin. He also omitted his surname in his casualty report. Someone, at a later date, penciled "Dorman" beside the major's entry. That sparse entry is followed by the words "Killed by Indians."

Roland C. McConnell's "Isaiah Dorman and the Custer Expedition" (*JNH*, July 1948, pp. 344–52) and Robert J. Ege's "Custer's Negro Interpreter" (*Black World*, Feb. 1965, pp. 29–35) give essential details; see also Edward C. Campbell's "Saving the Custer Muster Rolls" (*Military Affairs*, Summer 1946). The following records in the National Archives are essential: Medical History of Fort Rice, 1865–1876; Quartermaster's Reports of Persons and Articles Hired, June 1876, Seventh U.S. Regiment of Cavalry; Register of Claims, 1877 and 1878, vol. 5, Quartermaster General's Office; M.A. Reno Report of Battle of the Little Big Horn . . . , Record Group 94. — ROBERT J. EGE

DOUGLASS, FREDERICK (1817–1895), orator, journalist, reformer, public servant, and often referred to as the "father of the civil rights movement." Douglass was born a slave in Tuckahoe, Md. Sent to Baltimore in 1825 to be a houseboy, he escaped thirteen years later and settled in New Bedford, Mass. A talent for public speaking led him into the organized abolitionist movement as an agent for the Massachusetts Anti-Slavery Society. In 1845 he published his *Narrative of the Life of Frederick Douglass,* the first and most important of three autobiographies. In 1847 he began a career in journalism, publishing and editing a reformist weekly. His spirits were braced by the Civil War, which he viewed as a golden opportunity to strike at slavery. He urged Negroes to join the Union Armies, himself becoming an official recruiter. During the Reconstruction period he resumed his reformist activities, including his demands that Negroes be given the ballot and their full civil rights. A staunch Republican, his party rewarded him with three appointive positions during the closing phases of his career.

The heights to which Douglass rose stood in sharp contrast to his obscure parentage and humble beginnings. Born a slave, Douglass never knew the date of his birth. He assumed that he was born in 1817 and he took February 14 as his birthday because his mother, Harriet Bailey, had referred to him as her valentine. His knowledge of his mother was, in his words, "very scanty." When he was eight or nine his mother died, having worked as a field slave on a plantation twelve miles distant from her son. Douglass's father was an even more shadowy figure, never emerging from anonymity, although Douglass believed that he was white and possibly his master, Aaron Anthony.

Too young to work in the fields, Douglass did odd jobs and ran errands. A favorite companion of his master's son, he seldom felt the whip, suffering more from hunger and cold. In 1825 Douglass was sent to Baltimore, a turning point in his life. Here for eight years he served as a houseboy and an unskilled laborer and learned to read and write. Returned to the plantation in 1832, Douglass was dismayed by the restrictions of rural slavery that contrasted sharply with the more permissive life of the city. He made an attempt to escape, forging passes for himself and four comrades. The attempt was thwarted but instead of being branded on the forehead or sold to the lower South, Douglass was sent back to Baltimore. For the next two years he worked in the shipyards, becoming an expert caulker. Still bent on escaping, he succeeded in September 1838, impersonating a sailor whose papers he borrowed.

Upon his arrival in New York City Douglass had the good fortune to be directed to the secretary of the Negro-run New York Vigilance Committee, David Ruggles, who spent much of his time in assisting runaways. While under Ruggles's roof Douglass was married to Anna Murray, a Marylander whom he had met in Baltimore and who, herself free, had stimulated his desire to liberate himself. After the marriage the newlyweds went to New Bedford, Mass., where Douglass took the name by which he is known to history and where he worked at any job, however menial or low-paid, that became available. Color prejudice prevented Douglass from getting work as a ship caulker, but his race and previous condition of servitude opened to him an unexpected calling—abolitionist.

The organized movement to abolish slavery, which had gained new momentum in the 1830s, counted many Negro men and women among its supporters. Hence it is not surprising that within six months after Douglass arrived in New Bedford he became a regular reader of the militant weekly, the *Liberator,* and an admirer of its outspoken editor, William Lloyd Garrison of Boston. The personification of the uncompromising school of abolitionists, Garrison demanded that the slaves be freed immediately and without compensation to their masters. In August 1841 while attending an abolitionist gathering at Nantucket, Mass., with Garrison present, Douglass was unexpectedly called upon to speak. His words were halting, but as he spoke with feeling of his experiences in slavery the crowd listened attentively. Sensing his platform potentialities, the officers of the Massachusetts Anti-Slavery Society immediately urged him to become one of their agents. Refusing to take "no" for an answer, they prevailed upon Douglass to take a trial appointment of three months.

During the following four years the young ex-slave was one of the prize speakers of the society. Six feet tall and broad-shouldered, he had the build of an athlete. His deep-set eyes were steady and searching. His face was bronze-colored, with a thin line of black chin whiskers set off by a white cravat. He wore his hair long, a thick mass but freshly brushed as a rule and neatly parted on the left.

Often traveling in company with Wendell Phillips, the prince of nineteenth-century orators, Douglass was not slow in developing his own speaking qualities. His voice, a rich and melodious baritone, was a flexible instrument, capable of varying degrees of light and shade. Newspaper editor N. P. Rogers, appraising him four months after he had become an abolitionist lecturer, found "his enunciation quite elegant," adding that "he has wit, argument, sarcasm and pathos."

The content of his addresses added to Douglass as a platform attraction. At first he was content to confine himself to a recital of his experiences in slavery. Gradually he broadened his scope, presenting the standard abolitionist arguments against slavery. But however familiar the theme, a speech by the maturing Douglass was carefully organized and equally reasoned. Although never speaking in public inadequately prepared, Douglass had the ability to think on his feet, particularly in responding to hecklers. Hence it is not surprising that sometimes his listeners wondered whether a man of such eloquence and platform poise could ever have been held in bondage. "People doubted if I had ever been a slave," he wrote in the second of his autobiographies. "They said I did not talk like a slave, look like a slave, nor act like a slave."

To prove that he was not an imposter Douglass published an account of his slave experiences, *Narrative of the Life of Frederick Douglass,* a slim volume of 125 pages, prefaced by letters from Garrison and Phillips. Appearing in May 1845, the book immediately became a bestseller in reformist circles. The work belonged to a distinctive genre, the "heroic fugitive" school of American literature. Designed as a plea for human freedom, the *Narrative* was much like its prototypes in its general approach—a succession of sorrowful stories couched in bitterly indignant tones. Douglass's *Narrative,* however, had special points of merit which would make it a landmark in the literary crusade against slavery.

To begin with, it came from the pen of Douglass himself rather than from that of a ghost-writer, as did many of the slave narratives. Thus by its very authorship it struck at the notion of Negro inferiority. Its literary qualities included pathos, such as in the passages on Douglass's mother; a reflective tone, such as his apostrophe to a ship's putting out to sea; and a sense of objectivity, such as its portrayal of certain all-too-human characteristics of the slaves themselves. The *Narrative,* moreover, had the great asset of credibility, giving specific names of persons and places. Indeed the credibility of his narrative exposed Douglass to the danger of being seized by his former master, now no longer in the dark as to his whereabouts. This sobering possibility gave the final impetus to his plans to tour the British Isles. With his book as a path-breaker he would have new audiences for the abolitionist message.

Arriving at Liverpool in August 1845 Douglass spent twenty-one months in England, Ireland, and Scotland, often traveling alone but sometimes in company with other reformers, British or American. His tour can justly be described as triumphal. As a rule his audiences were large and, even more invariably, sympathetic. The response he evoked against slavery would soon lead a score of other Negro reformers across the Atlantic, repeating his message and giving a new dimension to mid-Victorian humanitarianism. His cordial reception on the public platform was matched in other quarters. His personal treatment at hotels and inns was all he could have wished. He made the acquaintance of Parliamentary leaders Richard Cobden and John Bright, and had a dinner with the renowned abolitionist Thomas Clarkson. The many friends of Douglass raised money to purchase his freedom and upon his mention that he might like to edit a newspaper they gave him a purse of $2175 for the venture. Some of his new friends pleaded with Douglass to send for his wife and four children and take up permanent residence in the British Isles. But Douglass felt that his future was in his native land, to which he owed much—and vice versa.

Upon his return to America in August 1847 Douglass found that his Massachusetts friends, particularly William Lloyd Garrison, were cool toward his idea of starting a newspaper. For a year Douglass heeded their advice. But on Nov. 1, 1847, he moved his family to Rochester, N.Y., where five weeks later he brought out the first issue of the *North Star,* sharing for a time a joint editorship with Martin R. Delany, the founder-editor of the *Pittsburgh Mystery.* "Wielding my pen, as well as my voice" in the service of "my enslaved and oppressed people" was the reason Douglass gave for launching his weekly. Unquestionably, as he himself was quick to note, the publishing of a weekly brought him in much closer contact with the free black community than had been the case when he was an agent of an antislavery society. Upon becoming a journalist Douglass developed a deeper sense of identification with his Negro fellows, never seeking to deny his color or his kind. "Whatever character or capacity you ascribe to us, I am not ashamed to be numbered with this race," he said in May 1853 in an address to the American and Foreign Anti-Slavery Society. "I shall bring the Negro with me," he once wrote in response to an invitation to lecture.

A sense of racial pride led Douglass to advocate group solidarity and economic development and to condemn color prejudice and discrimination. Holding that blacks should unite for their advancement, Douglass inevitably became a major figure in the Colored Convention Movement, to give it the name by which it is known to history. Beginning in 1830 colored leaders throughout the North had held periodic meetings to make clear their attitude on public issues and to take concerted action thereon. At the meeting held in Cleveland in 1848, Douglass was chosen president. A year later Douglass proposed through the columns of the *North Star* that a new organization be formed, bearing the title "The National League" and with the motto "The union of the oppressed for the sake of freedom." The suggestion died aborning. Douglass did not permit his mortification to prevent him from playing an important role in subsequent colored conventions.

It is hardly surprising that Douglass gave much attention to the greatest hurdle facing the colored people in the North—job discrimination. He became one of the leading exponents of vocational education. "We need mechanics as well as ministers," he wrote in "Learn Trades or Starve," one of his most widely quoted editorials. "We must build as well as live in houses; we must make as well as use furniture; we must construct bridges as well as pass over them."

Along with his emphasis on skilled labor, Douglass urged upon his fellow Negroes the standard virtues of middle-class morality—industry, thrift, honesty, and sobriety. The columns of his weekly sometimes read like a black *Poor Richard's Almanac.* But unlike a much later contemporary, Booker T. Washington, with whom he shared many economic viewpoints and character-building ideas, Douglass did not soft-pedal racial discrimination against blacks. He was unceasing in his condemnation of all forms of color prejudice. He challenged Jim Crow head-on, making it a practice to enter public places in which he might be coolly received if not summarily ejected.

Although proud of his color and bitter about discrimination against black people, Douglass was not anti-white. By the time he joined the abolitionists his slavery-days distrust of whites had left him. He viewed whites as individuals, not stereotyping them. Douglass had a host of friends across the color line; perhaps no black leader was as relaxed as he in the presence of whites.

Douglass's broad sense of brotherhood led him to take an active role in reforms that were not primarily Negro-centered, among them temperance and women's rights. In the latter movement he was a pioneer. He was present at the meeting at Seneca Falls, N.Y., in July 1848 which formally inaugurated the women's rights movement in the United States. Besides giving a major address he was prominent in the session-to-session deliberations. He remained a staunch women's righter, a dependable supporter of the great triumvirate, Elizabeth Cady Stanton, Lucretia Mott, and Susan B. Anthony.

A man of many interests, a true reformer in the round, Douglass never forgot, however, that his main target was slavery. He spoke about it, he wrote about it, and he gave money to assist fugitives. His printing shop in Rochester was a station on the Underground Railroad. Over a ten-year span no fewer than 400 runaways found refuge under the Douglass roof, having received "food, shelter, counsel and comfort," before being sped on to nearby Canada.

Douglass shared the general abolitionist hostility to the Fugitive Slave Act of 1850, a measure that denied both the testimony of the alleged runaway and his right to a trial by jury. In the chorus of condemnation that followed, no language was stronger than that of Douglass. He told an audience in Boston's Faneuil Hall that if the law were put into operation the streets of the city would run with blood. He advised a Pittsburgh gathering that the way to make the Fugitive Slave Act a dead letter was to make some dead kidnappers. His weekly carried an editorial, "The True Remedy for the Fugitive Slave Bill," which turned out to be a "good revolver, a steady hand, and a determination to shoot down any man attempting to kidnap."

Many abolitionists, Douglass among them, reasoned that such a monstrosity as a fugitive slave law could never have been passed with the right kind of Congress. For nearly ten years Douglass believed that political action was the best way to strike at slavery. Shortly after moving to Rochester he had become a voting abolition-ist, prepared "to use the terse rhetoric of the ballot box," as he put it. The Liberty party, born in 1840, had practically run its course by the time Douglass became a political activist, but in 1852 Douglass gave his support to its successor, the Free Soil party. In the presidential elections four years later Douglass supported the new Republican party.

Douglass's venture into reform politics was unfruitful, the growing rift between the North and South seeming not to respond to peaceful approaches. The growing sectional polarization was heightened by the Dred Scott decision, which drew the Douglass ire because of its ruling that Negroes were not citizens. The latent violence of the times was further fanned by the John Brown raid in 1859.

Douglass had known Brown since paying him a visit in Springfield, Mass., in 1848. Thereafter the relations between them were cordial. In 1858 Brown spent three weeks at the Douglass home in Rochester, devoting much of his time to a Provisional Constitution which he planned to put into effect after the raid. In August 1858, two months before he struck, Brown met Douglass at Chambersburg, Pa., pleading with him to join the planned raid. Douglass demurred; he would not be numbered among the five Negroes who took part in the Harpers Ferry affair. After Brown was captured, however, Douglass sped to Canada, fearful that he might be seized as an accomplice. Douglass remained abroad for only five months, brought back in May 1860 by the death of his fifth and last child, his especially loved Annie.

If the spring of 1860 was low tide for Douglass, the autumn brought a Republican president, Abraham Lincoln, a development Douglass had predicted. Having also said that he had "little hope of the freedom of the slave by peaceful means," Douglass welcomed the coming of the Civil War. To him, as to other blacks and abolitionists in general, the war quickly became a crusade for freedom, nothing more and certainly nothing less. To this end Douglass called upon the Lincoln administration to recruit Negroes into the Union Army and to free the slaves as a war measure. The cautious Lincoln, his ear to the ground, ignored such advice, and scarcely paid more attention to the subsequent sharp criticism from Douglass and others. But a war, particularly a prolonged war, has realities that could not be ignored. Hence on Jan. 1, 1863, Lincoln issued the Emancipation Proclamation, declaring free the slaves in states still in rebellion and welcoming Negroes into the Union Armies.

The elated Douglass urged Negroes to enlist and himself became a recruiting agent for two colored Massachusetts regiments, his two oldest sons becoming his first signees. After one of his two visits to the White House, Douglass had a conference with Secretary of War Stanton, from which he got the impression that he would be granted an assistant adjutantship. He thereupon announced that he was bringing his journalistic career to a close. This step was not too painful, his paper having fallen on lean days. Since 1851 it had borne his name, *Frederick Douglass' Paper* to 1860, and *Douglass' Monthly* thereafter. However inglorious

its end, the journalistic career of Douglass was notable not only for the causes it espoused but as a symbol of the free press in action, much as its editor's innumerable public addresses symbolized a tradition of equal importance—freedom of speech. Before abandoning journalism Douglass, as it turned out, might better have waited until he had an army commission in his hands. Such a commission never came, Stanton or Lincoln, or both in concert, having come to the conclusion that a commission to a colored man was at that stage too far in advance of public opinion.

Douglass turned again to the lecture platform, his speeches increasingly centering on Negro suffrage. In 1860 he had worked zealously in the vain effort to repeal the New York constitutional requirement that Negro men own $250 worth of real estate before they could vote. In the closing stages of the war, as it became evident that slavery was on its way out, Douglass and other Negro leaders gave their major attention to the suffrage issue. With Douglass in the chair a National Convention of Colored Men, meeting in Syracuse, N.Y., in October 1864, drew up an "Address to the People of the United States," which asserted that the right to vote was the keystone of the arch of human liberty.

With the war over, Douglass claimed that the nation owed a heavy debt to the nearly 200,000 Negroes who had worn the Union blue. This debt could be paid in part, he added, by a national policy of equal suffrage for all. At a White House conference with Andrew Johnson, Lincoln's successor, Douglass and four other colored spokesmen expressed the hope that Negroes would be fully enfranchised throughout the nation. When Johnson argued that black voting might lead to a war of the races, Douglass begged leave to differ, stating that Negro voting lessened the likelihood of racial conflict. Negroes got little from President Johnson in any quarter. But in 1870 the Fifteenth Amendment was ratified, forbidding states to deny the ballot on the grounds of race, color, or previous servitude. Ratification ceremonies were numerous, the largest taking place in Baltimore in mid-May 1870, with Frederick Douglass the orator of the day.

Meanwhile, in September 1870 Douglass became editor of the *New National Era*, a weekly newspaper to "cheer and strengthen [the recently emancipated slaves]." He purchased the paper on Dec. 12, 1870, and published it until September 1874 when he had to relinquish it due to financial losses incurred when the Freedmen's Bank failed.

The politically minded Douglass found a natural home in the Republican party, becoming one of its staunchest supporters. It was the party of the martyred Lincoln, and although Douglass was not one of Lincoln's Negro idolaters, he had felt a sense of personal loss upon his death. Douglass owned Lincoln's walking cane, sent to him by the widowed Mrs. Lincoln. Moreover, the Republican party's claim to having won the war had its weight with Douglass. He was, in addition, always cool to the Democratic party, regarding it not only in terms of "the bloody shirt," but viewing it as the political refuge of the Klan types in the rural South and the black-labor-competitor, working-class whites in the urban centers of the North.

The fidelity of Douglass was not lost upon the Republican party. In March 1877 President Hayes named him marshal of the District of Columbia, and four years later another Republican administration appointed him recorder of deeds for the District of Columbia. Having moved from Rochester to Washington in 1872, Douglass was not personally inconvenienced by these patronage plums. Indeed these federal appointments had a beneficial effect on Douglass, enabling him to escape the rigors of the lecture circuit.

As an officeholder Douglass took his responsibilities seriously, giving short shrift to job-seekers of questionable competence. While in the marshal's office he stated publicly that his subordinates were "honest, capable, industrious, painstaking and faithful," an assertion that nobody challenged, it seems. Himself putting in a full day's work, he insisted that those under him do likewise. The functions of the marshal's office included surveillance of criminals, and for this aspect of the job Douglass had little enthusiasm. But otherwise he found the appointment to his liking, particularly after the first weeks when he had been under fire by some blacks for not resigning when Hayes removed from the office its ceremonial functions on social occasions held at the White House. But the marshal's office retained its highest honorary function, that of escort at a presidential inauguration, accompanying both the outgoing and incoming chief executives. In performance of this duty, Douglass led the impressive march from the Senate chamber to the Capitol rotunda on March 4, 1881, where James A. Garfield took the oath of office.

The new president appointed Douglass recorder of deeds for the District of Columbia, an exchange of posts which he readily accepted. As in the case of Douglass's previous appointment this was a Negro "first." Douglass held the recordership for five years, since Garfield's successor, President Cleveland, did not call for his resignation immediately. Douglass found the recorder's post easily mastered and somewhat routine, "though specific, exacting, and imperative," as he put it.

During his years in the marshal's and recorder's offices Douglass never felt that he had to hold his tongue on public issues. The charge, made by one critic, that "a fat office gagged him" could hardly hold water. Always outspoken, he continued to hit hard at practices which he considered unwise, unjust, or prejudice-ridden. The most prominent Negro of his day, his words carried weight on both sides of the color line.

On no major issue relating to Negroes during the 1870s and 1880s did Douglass fail to state his views, always leaving no doubt as to where he stood. On many issues his stance was predictable. Obviously he would denounce such developments as the suppression of the Negro vote in the South, the leasing out of convicts as laborers, the crop-lien system, and the prevalence of lynching. He railed against the rulings of the Supreme Court, particularly in voiding the Civil Rights Act of 1875: "Oh, for a Supreme Court of the United States which shall be as true to the claims of humanity as the Supreme Court formerly was to the demands of slavery!" Predictably, too, Douglass urged Negroes to support the Cuban insurgents who were struggling to overthrow Spanish rule.

But even on issues which were less clear-cut from a reformist point of view, Douglass did not hesitate to offer his advice. In 1871 he urged Negro Americans to support the Grant administration's efforts to annex Santo Domingo, a position at loggerheads with that of Charles Sumner, the great Senate champion of Negro rights. Later in the decade Douglass vigorously opposed the colored migration to Kansas movement, the "Great Exodus," publicly debating the issue with Richard T. Greener, national secretary of the Emigration Aid Society and the first Negro to be graduated from Harvard College.

During the 1870s and 1880s there was little change in Douglass's long-held economic views of Negro thrift and self-help. Himself moderately well off, his economic orientation was middle class, reflecting something of the acquisitive spirit typical of America's Gilded Age. A believer in self-reliance, Douglass held that the black man's destiny was largely in his own hands, that his white friends could not do for him what he could and should do for himself.

His belief that Negroes should be their own spokesmen did not mean that he favored a policy of "go it alone." In social matters Douglass retained his viewpoint that America was a composite nation and the racial cooperation and amalgamation were the solutions to the color problem. Negroes should become a part of the American community, said Douglass, a component of the "body politic." His belief that a solid and separate Negro minority would tend to polarize black-white relations drew a sharp disapproval from journalist John Edward Bruce: "Mr. Douglass evidently wants to get away from the Negro race, and from the criticism I have heard quite recently of him, he will not meet any armed resistance in his flight."

If a touch of personal pique made Bruce's barb more pointed than the evidence would bear, Douglass himself left no doubt that he did not believe that separation was the way out for the American Negro. His second marriage was an affirmation of this conviction. In January 1884, two years after the death of his first wife, he married Helen Pitts, a white woman of forty-five who had worked in the recorder's office as his secretary. Douglass was fully prepared for the criticism that followed, taking the view that this crowning act of his private life was a concrete demonstration that whites and blacks could live in complete equality under the same roof. Whether Douglass proved anything by his second marriage is conjectural although it certainly could be counted as a congenial union.

In 1886 Douglass, no longer on the federal payroll, took a belated honeymoon. For nearly a year he and Helen traveled throughout Western Europe and the Near East, following the familiar tourist trail in the main. Douglass found the trip stimulating in every way. The famed historic sites inevitably held a deep attraction for an ever-learning, reflective mind such as his. He was also moved by the apparent lack of color prejudice, rejoicing that "I could and did walk the world unquestioned, a man among men."

Shortly after returning home he was approached by

the Republican National Convention to assist the party in the presidential election of 1888. Assigned four key states, he took the stump night and day, despite his seventy years. His reward came when the new chief executive, Benjamin Harrison, appointed him as minister-resident and consul-general to the Republic of Haiti, and chargé d'affaires for the Dominican Republic. Douglass was well received by the Haitians, reflecting their awareness of his long career as a reformer. He proved to be a conscientious official, whether in the performance of routine commercial duties as consul-general or the more ceremonial responsibilities as minister-resident. His first year was relatively calm but in January 1891 he came into the eye of a storm when his government announced its intention to seek a naval lease at Môle St. Nicolas. Douglass favored the lease but, as it turned out, the Haitians did not, politely turning down the offer. Supporters of the project made Douglass the scapegoat, charging that he had been lukewarm in his efforts. Douglass published a lengthy reply but the setback, along with reasons of health, led him to resign in June 1891.

Douglass's five remaining years after his return from Haiti were quiet but far from inactive. He held no federal post and he cut down on his speaking engagements. But he kept busy in writing, corresponding, and accepting the numerous honors that came his way, such as a doctorate of laws from Wilberforce University. Age did not dim his interest in reformist movements. On his last day, Feb. 20, 1895, he had spoken to a meeting of the National Council of Women, held in Washington. That evening he suffered a fatal heart attack. Upon the news of his death one state legislature adjourned for the day out of respect for his memory and four other legislatures adopted resolutions of regret.

He would not be forgotten. Reformers of a later day, particularly Negroes, hailed his name. Sixty years after his death the federal government responded in a number of ways—in purchasing his last home (Anacostia, D.C.) as a national shrine under the National Park Service of the Department of the Interior, in naming a bridge in the nation's capital after him, and in issuing, on Feb. 14, 1967, a twenty-five-cent postage stamp showing his likeness.

Frederick Douglass cast a long shadow because of his sense of humanity and his willingness to battle for his convictions. He is remembered too for his remarkable social insights. No one, for example, pointed out more insistently than he that the status of the Negro was the touchstone of American democracy, its inevitable and ultimate test.

Douglass produced three autobiographies, *Narrative of the Life of Frederick Douglass* (1845), *My Bondage and My Freedom* (1855), three times longer than its predecessor, and *Life and Times of Frederick Douglass* (1881, updated 1892). Of the earlier book-length biographies of Douglass the best is Frederic May Holland's *Frederick Douglass: The Orator* (1891), a clearly written, briskly paced work. In 1948 Benjamin Quarles brought out a full-length volume, *Frederick Douglass*, giving "a balanced account which portrayed him neither as a demi-god or as a demagogue," in the words of Rayford W. Logan in the 1962 Collier Books reprint

of *Life and Times*. In 1964, after bringing out a path-breaking four-volume series, *The Life and Times of Frederick Douglass* (1950–1955), Phillip S. Foner wove together much of the material therein under the title *Frederick Douglass* (1964). A very useful work, this book profited from Foner's professional skills and his extensive research in black and labor history. There is a very brief sketch by William E. B. Du Bois in *DAB* (3:406–7). In 1979 the Yale University Press published the first volume of a projected fourteen-volume edition of *The Frederick Douglass Papers*, edited by John W. Blassingame. — BENJAMIN QUARLES

DOUGLASS, SARAH MAPPS DOUGLASS (1806–1882), teacher and abolitionist. She was born in Philadelphia on Sept. 9, 1806, the daughter of Robert and Grace (Bustill) Douglass. The Bustills were prominent Quakers, her maternal grandfather, Cyril Bustill (1732–1806), having been owner of a bakeshop, a schoolmaster, and an early member of the Free African Society, the first Afro-American benevolent organization. Her mother ran a "Quaker millinery store" next to the family bakery. Her father, perhaps a hairdresser, was one of the founders of the First African Presbyterian Church of Philadelphia.

Privately tutored, she opened a school in Philadelphia for Negro children sometime in the 1820s which the Philadelphia Female Anti-Slavery Society began supporting financially in March 1838. Sarah was then corresponding secretary of the society and attended several abolitionist conventions. Through them she became acquainted with Lucretia Mott, the wife of Robert Purvis, Charlotte Forten (Grimké) and two other daughters of James Forten, a wealthy shipbuilder. More important was the friendship she developed with the white Grimké sisters, Sarah and Angelina, daughters of the Oxford-trained Judge John F. Grimké, a slaveowning justice of the South Carolina Supreme Court. "The girls revolted against the formalism of the Episcopal Church, the shallowness of social life, and the restraints upon education and useful activity for women. They hated the barbarism of slavery and the laws which forbade the education of slaves. Finally, they fled from the stifling environment of the South and went to Philadelphia, where both became Quakers" (Dwight Lowell Dumond, *Anti-Slavery . . . The Crusade for Freedom in America* [1961], pp. 190–91). Not even the Grimké sisters could change the discriminatory practices of the Philadelphia Quakers. They were censured in 1837 for sitting beside Mrs. Douglass and her daughter in the Arch Street Meeting. When Sarah and her mother were among the Negro guests at the wedding of Angelina Grimké and Theodore Weld, a prominent abolitionist, in May 1838, the Philadelphia press condemned it as an intolerable incident of abolitionist "amalgamation practice." Two days later a mob burned down Pennsylvania Hall, the newly built headquarters of the state antislavery society, and set fire to the shelter for colored orphans. This was one of several race riots in Philadelphia: on Aug. 13, 1834, a white mob had wrecked the African Presbyterian church, burned homes, and brutally beaten several Negroes. Similar riots occurred in 1835 and 1842, and in other northern cities during the

1830s and 1840s. Sarah Douglass nonetheless continued to attend Quaker meetings at the Meeting House at Ninth and Spruce Streets.

Accepting enforced segregation, she took charge in 1853 of the girls primary department of the Institute for Colored Youth, a Quaker-supported school in Philadelphia, of which Ebenezer Bassett was principal from 1857 to 1869. She continued until her retirement in 1877 to teach under Fanny Jackson Coppin as principal, introducing scientific subjects such as physiology. The institute, later Cheyney State College, was well known for the number of public school teachers who received their education there. After the Civil War she was vice-chairman of the Women's Pennsylvania Branch of the American Freedmen's Aid Commission. Sarah Douglass's career epitomized the struggle to achieve civil equality, combat a racist society, and train Negroes in segregated institutions. She died in Philadelphia on Sept. 8, 1882. On July 23, 1855, she had married the Rev. William Douglass, a widower, father of several children and rector of St. Thomas Protestant Episcopal Church, who died in 1861.

The best brief biographical sketch is by Gerda Lerner in *NAW* (1971, 1:511–13), which has a comprehensive bibliography. — RAYFORD W. LOGAN

DOWNING, GEORGE T[HOMAS] (1819–1903), businessman and civil rights leader. Born in New York City, the son of Thomas and Rebecca (West) Downing, he attended the old Mulberry Street school in New York City, some of whose students became leaders in the fight for Negro rights. When fourteen years old he organized a literary society with a number of boys of his own age, in which they discussed "live subjects." They adopted a resolution to refrain from celebrating the Fourth of July because in practical terms the Declaration of Independence was to colored Americans "a perfect mockery." His education was completed at Hamilton College in Oneida County, N.Y. Downing's public career began when he was but a youth serving as an agent of the Underground Railroad. In this capacity he helped to spirit away "Little Henry," a slave who was in jail in New York City. He was arrested but released after payment of the slave's value.

On Nov. 24, 1841, he married Serena Leanora De Grasse, the daughter of George De Grasse. (Born in Calcutta, De Grasse came to New York City, became a prosperous landowner, and in 1808 married Maria Van Surley of German parentage. One of their sons, John Van Surley De Grasse, was admitted to the Massachusetts Medical Society in 1854.) Downing delivered one of the addresses of welcome to Louis Kossuth, the Hungarian patriot, on his visit to the United States in 1851. During the agitation over the fugitive slave, Anthony Burns, in Boston (1854), a body of men marching with a banner inscribed "Freedom" were assaulted by the police who captured the banner. Downing rushed into the crowd and after a desperate struggle in which the banner was torn almost to shreds, captured it from the police and amid expressions of admiration returned it to the marchers. He took an active part in organizing the Grand United Order of Odd Fellows, served as grand master for several years, and was a Royal Arch Mason.

From 1857 to 1866 he led the fight that resulted in the abolition of separate publicly supported schools in Rhode Island. He was a spokesman along with Frederick Douglass in urging Pres. Andrew Johnson (Feb. 6, 1866) to adopt a more liberal Reconstruction policy, especially in the South. The delegation also urged Sen. Charles Sumner to support the Fourteenth Amendment. Along with J. Sella Martin, he persuaded Douglass to begin publishing the *New National Era* in Washington (Frederick Douglass, *The Life and Times of Frederick Douglass* [1962 ed.], pp. 382–86, 399). Unlike Douglass, however, at the colored National Labor Convention (1869) he favored a division of support for the Republican and Democratic parties. Senator Sumner, as he lay dying, said to Downing: "Do not let my Civil Rights Bill fail" (C. Edwards Lester, *Life and Public Services of Charles Sumner,* 1874). How much Downing contributed to its passage in 1875 is debatable. He is credited with helping repeal the New York State law requiring Negroes to own $250 worth of property before they could vote, and a similar law in Rhode Island with respect to the Irish of Rhode Island. He also participated in the abolition of Jim Crow cars on the Baltimore and Ohio Railroad, the opening of the Senate gallery to Negroes, the abolition of a nine o'clock curfew in Washington, and the passage (1873) of the public accommodations law in the nation's capital.

In 1883 he broke with the Republicans and supported northern Democrats. In 1891 he again urged a divided vote. He opposed colonization and at the end of his life he predicted that amalgamation of the races was the ultimate solution.

During these active years as one of the effective civil rights leaders, he was also a successful businessman. He became a caterer in New York City in 1842 and established a summer business in Newport, R.I., in 1846. In 1879 he purchased the old Atlantic House, in which the U.S. Naval Academy was located for several years. In 1850 he opened a catering establishment in Providence, while continuing his summer business in Newport. During the fall of 1854 he erected the luxurious Sea Girt Hotel. After it was destroyed by fire on Dec. 15, 1860, with an estimated loss of $40,000, he erected a building on Downing Block, renting the upper part to the federal government for a hospital for the Naval Academy. For twelve years after the Civil War he had charge of the restaurant in the House of Representatives in the Capitol. By 1888 he was a large real estate owner on Bellevue Avenue, Newport, where a street was named in his honor. He was a large donor of funds to secure Touro Park, and took great pride in increasing the architectural beauty and prosperity of Newport.

An editorial in the *Boston Globe* (July 23, 1903) stated: "Probably the foremost colored man in this country expired in the person of George T. Downing of Newport, Rhode Island. His skin fades almost out of sight when it is remembered that he fought not only for his own race but that his purse strings were always open in helping all races who were oppressed." He died after a long illness at his residence on Bellevue Avenue, Newport, on July 21, 1903, and was survived by three sons, three daughters, his brother Peter W., and his nephew

Henry F. Downing. Funeral services were held on July 24 at Emmanuel Church, Newport.

The principal sources are S. A. M. Washington's *George Thomas Downing: Sketch of His Life and Times* (1910); brief references in Irving H. Bartlett's *From Slave to Citizen: The Story of the Negro in Rhode Island* (1954, pp. 53–59) and Richard H. Bayles (ed.), *History of Newport County, Rhode Island* (1888). August Meier's *Negro Thought in America, 1880–1915* (1963) is especially valuable for Downing's political views. See the obituary in the *New York Times* (July 22, 1903, p. 7), *Providence Journal* (July 24, 1903, p. 6), and *Cleveland Gazette* (Aug. 1, 1903, p. 1). — HOWARD D. ASBURY

DOWNING, HENRY F[RANCIS] (1846?–1928), sailor, consul, author, and playwright. Born about 1846 in New York City on Sullivan Street in Lower Manhattan, a son of Henry Downing and Nancy (Collins) Downing, he was the grandson of Thomas Downing, operator of an oyster-selling business and well-known free Negro. He was the nephew of George Thomas Downing, friend of Frederick Douglass and famed politician in New York City and in Providence, R.I. The family maintained the oyster business and a refectory on Broad Street into the 1850s. Henry Francis Downing received enough education to be able to read and to write.

By the time of the Civil War, Downing was still in school. Young Downing, anxious to serve, enlisted in the Union Navy at the Brooklyn Navy Yard on Aug. 25, 1864, beginning his service on board the *North Carolina*. He was transferred to the *Pawtuxet* in December 1864, just in time to see action at the first bombardment and later capture of Fort Fisher, N.C., a key fort in aiding Confederate running of the Union blockade. Although it was recorded that he deserted from the navy on Dec. 15, 1865, it was later explained that his mother went aboard to get Downing to attend the funeral of his stepfather; she kept him ashore, saying that she had gotten his discharge on the ground that he was needed to help her.

After the Civil War, the love of travel led Downing to make a trip around the world. Among the places he visited was Liberia, perhaps because his cousin, Hilary Johnson, was there. Johnson served as president of Liberia (1884–1892). Downing settled in Liberia for three years, during which he lived in the rural areas and served the government as a private secretary to the secretary of state, and in one of the wars of Liberia. He was described at this time as an intelligent, moral, and capable person.

He returned to the United States and enlisted again for a three-year term in the navy. He served from Oct. 25, 1872, until Oct. 28, 1875, most of the time on board the U.S.S. *Hartford* on duty with the Asiatic Squadron. Downing said that he was instrumental in preventing the *Hartford* from being wrecked on the East African coast, and the captain, David Harmony, became his friend and patron as a result of this incident.

Thus Downing had a great deal of experience with Africa by the end of the third quarter of the nineteenth century. When he earned his second discharge from the navy, Downing returned to live and work in New York City. He became a letter carrier, a messenger at the Brooklyn Navy Yard, and a clerk there. On July 8, 1876, Downing was married to Isadora (?) in Williamsburg, N.Y., by the Rev. Jacob Thomas, pastor of Mother A.M.E. Zion Church, New York City. The Census of 1880 said that they had two children, a boy (two) and a girl (three); Downing was then thirty-three years old and working as a waiter, living at 19 Second St.

Downing was not unaware of the political activities of his uncle George Thomas Downing, who was advocating an independent course for Negroes by this time. In the early 1880s Henry Downing became an active supporter of Democrats, including the so-called reformer Grover Cleveland. Downing became widely respected in New York State politics and in 1886–1887 had won such support from Cleveland as well as leading Negroes that he was appointed U.S. consul to Loanda, Angola, Portuguese West Africa. Among those who supported his application were Richard T. Greener and T. McCants Stewart, both leading lawyers. He served from Oct. 1, 1887, until Aug. 18, 1888, when he resigned. In Angola, Downing constantly advocated, albeit unsuccessfully, advantageous trading opportunities for American shipping there; he also failed to obtain an appointment to Liberia or Sierra Leone. He did not view the Africans as "savages," but he felt that Afro-Americans were superior to them.

After his resignation from the consular service, Downing returned to New York politics. Still determined to promote the natural resources of Africa, he attempted to encourage United States business interests in the early 1890s through his management of the "Afro-American Advice Bureau." He was, however, unsuccessful.

On June 30, 1894, Downing married Margarita Doyle, an Irish woman in Boston. The following year they migrated to London where they remained until 1917. In England Downing became a commercial agent for Liberia and for merchants interested in Liberia and other African countries. By the early 1900s he was working for New Cotton Fields, Ltd., an English firm hoping to develop cotton fields in Africa; Downing wrote to Booker T. Washington in 1902 requesting him to send some recent graduates to help. In an interview in London in 1906, Downing claimed that he had been a key person in opening Liberia to Western trade; he also advocated selected migration by American Negroes to develop Liberia.

In the meantime Downing made contacts among the Africans and Afro-Americans in London. He attended the Pan-African Conference of 1900, donating one of the larger sums of money to help finance the meeting, and was appointed to the Executive Committee of the "permanent" Pan-African Association founded at the meeting. He must have met W. E. B. Du Bois and Bishop Alexander Walters, both delegates, and became friends of Samuel Coleridge-Taylor and Duse Mohamed Ali. In 1913 he and Duse Mohamed Ali attended a conference on Africans in London, and in the same year Downing began publishing the first of several plays and novels, one of which was serialized in the *African Times and Orient Review*, Duse Mohamed's monthly for which

Marcus Garvey worked in 1913–1914. By the end of 1914 Downing had published at least six plays for the London stage, none of which dealt directly with race questions.

Apparently Downing had written several plays before 1913, because the title page of *The Shuttlecock, or Israel in Russia,* published in 1913, stated that he had written *The Exiles, The Sinews of War, Human Nature, The Arabian Lovers, Lord Eldred's Other Daughter, Melic Ric, The Statute and the Wasp,* and others. In collaboration with his wife, Margarita, he had also written *Placing Paul's Play* and *Which Should She Have Saved?* Thus at least nine plays were the product of his fertile mind. Just how successful they were is difficult to determine. But the fact that five of them were published by Francis Griffiths indicates that there must have been a reasonable degree of acceptance, success, and profit, since performances of the play required a payment of five guineas in advance.

Just before he left England in 1917 he published a novel, *The American Cavalryman,* about life in Liberia, dedicating it to the two Spingarn brothers, Joel and Arthur. He listed his occupation by this time as a writer. When he came back to live in Harlem in New York City in 1917, Downing at first tried to promote motion pictures. He also wrote about Liberia, publishing *Liberia and Her People* (1925) and *A Short History of Liberia* (n.d.), neither of which was thorough; in *Liberia and Her People* Downing advised on migration to and survival in Liberia, and he probably supported Garvey's Back to Africa Movement in the 1920s. Since he did not make much money, he had to apply for his pension and to go on relief in New York City. On Feb. 19, 1928, Henry F. Downing died of nephritis and arteriosclerosis in Harlem Hospital at the age of eighty-two. Both of the women he had married survived him; of his two children, only his daughter survived.

Valuable information on Downing is in pension and diplomatic files in the National Archives in Washington, D.C. There is some correspondence of Downing in the Grover Cleveland and the Booker T. Washington Papers in the Manuscript Division, Library of Congress.

— CLARENCE G. CONTEE, SR.

DOWNING, LEWIS K[ING] (1896–1967), engineering educator and administrator. He was born in Roanoke, Va., on Jan. 2, 1896, the third son and fourth child of six children of the Rev. Lylburn and Mrs. Charlotte J. (Clinton) Downing. He and the former Morease M. Chisolm (d. June 17, 1969) were married on Dec. 26, 1925, in Charlotte, N.C. To this union were born Charlotte C. (d. Jan. 1, 1973) and Morease M. A quiet and thoughtful man, Downing decided early in life that he was going to be an engineer and prepared himself for his career by earning a B.A. degree in 1916 from Biddle University (later Johnson C. Smith University) where he was a member of the baseball team, a B.S. degree in civil engineering in 1921 from Howard University where he was captain of the football team, a B.S. degree in engineering administration (civil option) from MIT in 1923, and an M.S. degree in engineering (highway transport and traffic control) from the University of Michigan in 1932. He also did postgraduate work at the University of Michigan during the summers of 1939 and 1940.

He returned to Howard University in the fall of 1924 to join the faculty of the School of Applied Science as instructor in civil engineering. In 1926 he was promoted to assistant professor. He became an associate professor in 1930, and in 1938 he was promoted to professor of civil engineering. In 1928 the dean of what had by that time become the College of Applied Science resigned and Downing was appointed acting dean. The College of Applied Science consisted of the departments of architecture, civil engineering, electrical engineering, mechanical engineering, art, and home economics.

The Great Depression brought significant changes in the organization of Howard University. Offerings in engineering and architecture were on the verge of termination because of the college's small enrollment. Downing was able to convince the university that offerings in engineering and architecture should be continued, and in 1934, by trustee action, the name of the college was changed to the School of Engineering and Architecture. Home economics and art were transferred to the College of Liberal Arts. Downing was continued as acting dean of this new school. In 1936 he was named dean of the School of Engineering and Architecture, a post that he held with distinction until his retirement on June 30, 1964.

Downing was a man of vision, courage, and persistence who saw a great future in the fields of engineering and architecture for Negroes when very few were engaged in this work and when opportunities were severely limited. He distinguished himself by his work with professional societies, his publications, the papers that he presented to a wide variety of audiences, and his consulting work. Under his inspiration and leadership, the School of Engineering and Architecture flourished and developed into the second-largest school of Howard University, in spite of many discouragements and obstacles. Downing was firm and unyielding in his convictions even though there were many who tried to persuade him that Negroes would find little acceptance in these fields, and that these programs should be curtailed. The school grew from an enrollment of twenty-five students in engineering and architecture with three graduates at the end of his first year as dean to an enrollment in excess of 700 students in engineering and architecture and a graduating class of ninety-nine in the year he retired. Fortunately, he lived to see his predictions come true.

During his administration as dean all departments of this school became accredited. Student chapters of the American Institute of Architects, the American Society of Civil Engineers, the Institute of Electrical and Electronics Engineers, and the American Society of Mechanical Engineers were established. District of Columbia Alpha chapter of Tau Beta Pi, national engineering honor society, was formed. A new building (96,000 square feet in area) was designed and built to meet the needs of the rapidly growing school. The School of Engineering and Architecture moved into this fully equipped building in September 1952.

Among his publications are "The Negro in the Professions of Engineering and Architecture" (*JNE,* January 1935); "Howard Engineers" (*Howard University Alumni Journal,* 1923); "Some Contributions of Negro Scientists to Progress and Culture" (*The Crisis,* May 1939); and "The Civil Engineer" (*Beta Kappa Chi Bulletin,* June 1943). In addition, he was co-author of the *Howard University Professional Guidance Bulletin,* published by the Howard University School of Engineering and Architecture (1930). He was also editor of the *Yearbook of the National Technical Association* (1936–1937, 1942, and 1948–1949).

Downing was a fellow in the American Society of Civil Engineers and a member of the American Society for Engineering Education, the National Technical Association, the National Society of Professional Engineers, the District of Columbia Society of Professional Engineers, the Washington Academy of Sciences, Beta Kappa Chi Science Honor Society, and Tau Beta Pi. Among the many honors that he received in recognition of his work and achievements were the Johnson C. Smith University "Alumni Award for Distinguished Service in the Field of Engineering Education" (1950) and the Howard University Award, "For Distinguished Post Graduate Achievement in Engineering." He was a member of the District of Columbia Board of Registration for Professional Engineers and a registered civil engineer in Virginia and the District of Columbia.

In recognition of the significant contributions made by Downing in the field of engineering education the Engineering Alumni Association of Howard University established the Lewis K. Downing Scholarship Fund for deserving students in the School of Engineering. The engineering building that was erected during his administration was later named Lewis K. Downing Hall at ceremonies held in the auditorium of this building on April 9, 1974.

Downing suffered a heart attack on Oct. 18, 1967, while driving home from a meeting, and died the next day in Casualty Hospital, Washington, D.C. Funeral services were held at Andrew Rankin Memorial Chapel, Howard University, on Oct. 23 with interment in Lincoln Memorial Cemetery, Suitland, Md. He was survived by his widow, Morease Chisholm Downing, two daughters (Morease M. and Charlotte), a sister (Letitia D. Rose of Roanoke, Va.), and a brother (Gardner Downing of Chicago).

Additional information may be found in *50 Years of Engineering and Architecture—The School of Engineering and Architecture, Howard University, 1910–1960* by Frederick D. Wilkinson; *Who's Who in Engineering* (1959); *Who's Who in America, 1968–69; American Men of Science* (1944); *Leaders in Education* (1948); Annual Reports of the School of Engineering and Architecture, Howard University; *Howard University Magazine* (Jan. 1968, p. 32); and the *Washington Post* (Oct. 20 and 22, 1967). This article is also based on the personal reminiscences of some associates of Downing. — ERNEST R. WELCH

DREW, CHARLES RICHARD (1904–1950), athlete, surgeon, pioneer in the development of blood plasma preservation, and teacher. Drew was born in Washington, D.C., the first son and eldest of five children of

Richard T. and Nora (Burrell) Drew. His father, a high school graduate, generally earned as a carpenter a salary which provided his family with the necessities of life. His mother, well known for her beauty and amiability, was a graduate of Miner Normal School in Washington. Charley, as his friends called him, graduated from the public schools of the District of Columbia, received his B.A. degree from Amherst College (1926) and the M.D. and C.M. (Master of Surgery) degrees from McGill University, Montréal, Canada (1933). He served an externship in the Royal Victoria Hospital and spent two years as intern and resident at Montréal General Hospital. He was appointed instructor in pathology at Howard University (1935–1936) and served a residency in surgery at Freedmen's Hospital, Washington, D.C. (1936–1937). From 1937 to 1938 he was instructor in surgery and assistant surgeon, and then (1938–1940) was a resident in surgery at Presbyterian Hospital, New York City, while a General Education Board fellow in surgery at Columbia University. He received the Med.D.Sc. (Doctor of Medical Science) from Columbia in 1940. He wrote his doctoral dissertation on "Banked Blood" and became supervisor of the blood plasma division of the Blood Transfusion Association of New York City, in charge of collecting blood plasma for the British army. After the fall of France in June 1940 Drew returned to Howard University Medical School as assistant professor of surgery. In February 1941 he was named director of the American Red Cross Blood Bank in New York City and assistant to the director of the National Research Council, which had charge of collecting blood for the U.S. Army and Navy. Since the Red Cross segregated blood by the race of the donors, he resigned and returned to Howard, where in 1942 he became professor and head of the Department of Surgery and chief surgeon of Freedmen's Hospital. From 1944 to 1946 he was chief of staff at the hospital and its medical director (1946–1948). He devoted practically all his time to teaching and surgery. He died after an automobile accident near Burlington, N.C., on April 1, 1950. Funeral services were held on April 5 at Rankin Memorial Chapel, Howard University, with interment on the same day in Lincoln Memorial Cemetery, Suitland, Md.

Charles Drew's career reflected the advantages and disadvantages of gifted Negroes in the first half of the twentieth century. His closely knit family lived in modest circumstances in an area known as "Foggy Bottom" because of the heavy mists from the Potomac River. They were members of the 19th Street Baptist Church, then located at the southwest corner of 19th and I Streets NW. Contemporaries recalled that although Drew was only a nominal Baptist, the "social gospel" preached by the pastor, Walter H. Brooks, greatly influenced his life. He graduated from Stevens Elementary School on Twenty-first Street, between K and L Northwest in 1918. At that time it was one of the better elementary schools in the city. Dunbar High School (M Street High School until 1916), where he graduated in 1922, was still the school which prepared more colored students for college than any other high school in the nation. Williams College and Amherst College were among the Ivy League colleges attended by some of the graduates, many of whom received particular attention from dedicated teachers, some of them graduates of those and other elite institutions of higher learning. He was a four-letter man in sports, and captain, in his senior year, of Company E in the Third Regiment of the (Colored) High School Cadet Corps. He received the James E. Walker Memorial Medal for all-round athletic performance in both his junior and senior years. Drew in 1922 followed in the footsteps of Charles H. Houston (Amherst, 1915) and two of of his schoolmates, William H. Hastie and W. Montague Cobb, who had entered Amherst in 1921.

Drew encountered race prejudice early in life. Not only public schools but also most places of public accommodations in Washington were segregated. At Amherst he was the victim of the discrimination then common at New England colleges and universities. Although in his junior year he received the Thomas W. Ashley Memorial Trophy awarded to the football team's most valuable player, he was not elected captain of the team, as was the custom. Since two other Negroes had been denied captaincies in the two previous years, the "conscience of the college was aroused" and Drew, the highest scorer on the track team, was unanimously elected captain. On graduation he received the Howard Hill Mossman Trophy, "a huge and magnificent cup," as the man who had contributed the most to Amherst in athletics during his four years in college. Drew was chosen for the All Little Three (Amherst, Williams, and Wesleyan) legendary football teams in 1924 and 1925, and in 1925 received an All-America honorable mention as an All Eastern halfback. In the *Saturday Evening Post* (Dec. 6, 1952), Coach D. O. McLaughry termed him "The Best Player I Ever Coached." Despite his outstanding athletic achievements, Drew was not tapped by a group called Scarab (composed of some dozen seniors) as one of the most outstanding juniors on the campus from the standpoint of all-around achievement. The time spent on athletics and waiting table to augment the stipend received from a scholarship prevented him from achieving high grades, although he did score 100 on a chemistry final. At Amherst, as at some other schools, membership in fraternities, from which Negro students were then barred, as well as other subjective factors frequently determined election in these clubs.

Like many other colored youth of the period Drew had to discontinue his studies temporarily to earn an income. During 1926–1928 he coached the football team at Morgan College (later Morgan State University) in Baltimore, lived with his family in Arlington, Va., and during summers was manager of the Francis Junior High School swimming pool in Washington.

Nevertheless he was able to enter McGill University Medical School in 1928 only with the aid of a loan from several of his Amherst classmates (which he later repaid); and he at first waited on table as he had done at Amherst. He had been denied admission to the Howard University School of Medicine because he had not studied English for eight hours at Amherst. Although he continued to excel in sports, his scholarship improved in such subjects as anatomy, chemistry, and biology. With the aid of a scholarship in 1930, he no longer had to work as a waiter, devoted more time to his studies, won the annual prize in neuroanatomy, was elected to Alpha Phi Omega, the medical honorary scholastic fraternity, and in his senior year won the Williams Prize, awarded after competitive examination to the top five men in the graduating class.

His studies at McGill marked a significant turning point in his life, for there he began his research in blood groupings. He continued his research at Columbia University–Presbyterian Hospital (1938–1940) under the direction particularly of John Scudder, director of research. Drew added his own knowledge of similar work in the Soviet Union, in Spain during the civil war of the 1930s, and at Cook County Hospital in Chicago. His experiments in the use of plasma transfusions—blood with the cells removed—and on the Rh factor which, when combined with certain proteins in the blood resulted in serious illness and death, led to his establishment of a fairly successful blood bank. His principal contribution was his presentation of evidence showing the longer life of liquid plasma than of whole blood, which frequently spoiled or was contaminated. The blood banks which he helped develop are generally credited with saving the lives of many British and other wounded at Dunkirk in June 1940. After the Nazi bombings of British cities created a dire new need for blood plasma, Dr. Drew directed large-scale experiments in New York City which considerably reduced the ratio of contamination. In February 1941, when the British need for shipments of plasma decreased, he became director of the American Red Cross Blood Bank in New York City and assistant to the director of the National Research Council, which collected blood for the U.S. Army and Navy. It was the acceptance by the Red Cross of an armed forces unscientific directive that blood be typed according to the race of the donor that led Drew to hold a news conference at which he denounced this grouping. His conclusions were later confirmed by other scientists. In April 1959 Gen. Alfred M. Gruenther, president of the American Red Cross, accepted a portrait of Drew by Betsy Grove Reyneau to be placed in the American Red Cross Building in Washington, D.C.

Although widely known for his contributions as one of the pioneers in the development of blood plasma, Drew's major continuing significance lay in teaching large numbers of Negro students in Howard University Medical School, his training of surgeons, and his authorship or co-authorship of a dozen articles in scientific journals. During the summer of 1949 he was a consultant to the surgeon-general of the U.S. Army as a member of a team of four physicians who toured hospital installations in Occupied Europe to improve the quality of medical care and instruction.

During his relatively brief life—he was only forty-five at the time of his death—he received many well-earned recognitions: diplomate of surgery by the American Board of Surgery, Johns Hopkins University, Baltimore (April 1941); recipient of the Spingarn Medal of the NAACP as the outstanding Negro of the year (1944); the honorary D.Sc. degree from Virginia State College and Amherst College (1945 and 1947, respectively); a fellow of the International College of Surgery (1946). A painting by Alfred C. Laooan was unveiled at the National Institutes of Health on Sept. 9, 1976, when tributes were paid to Drew for his scientific work.

The circumstances of his death epitomized his service to mankind. After performing several operations on March 31, 1950, he acceded to the request of some of his colleagues and students to drive them to Tuskegee, Ala., where he was to deliver the annual lecture at the John A. Andrew Memorial Clinic. He dozed at the wheel and the car ran off the road near Burlington, N.C. He was the only passenger to die as a result of the accident. Conflicting versions to the contrary, Drew received prompt medical attention.

Handsome, six feet tall and solidly erect, Drew was married on Sept. 23, 1939, to (Minnie) Lenore Robbins of Philadelphia. He was survived by his widow and four children—Bebe Roberta, Charlene Rosella, Rhea Sylvia, and Charles Richard Jr.—his mother, a brother Joseph, and two sisters, Nora Drew Gregory and Eva Drew Johnson. Since salaries at Howard University did not permit Drew to accumulate adequate resources for his family, a memorial fund started by his colleagues at Howard and Freedmen's, considerably augmented by a ruling from the insurance division of the federal Social Security administrator, enabled his family to live comfortably.

The major source is "Charles Richard Drew, M.D., 1904–1950," by W. Montague Cobb, M.D. (*JNMA*, July 1950, pp. 239–45), used with the permission of Dr. Cobb. See also Richard Hardwick's *Charles Richard Drew, Pioneer in Blood Research* (1967); Cobb's "Charles Richard Drew—1904–1950" (*NHB*, June 1950); newspaper clippings in the vertical file at the Moorland-Spingarn Research Center, Howard University; and the sketch in *DAB, Supplement 4* (1974, pp. 242–43). Personal reminiscences of those who knew Drew were also valuable. — RAYFORD W. LOGAN

DRURY, THEODORE (c. 1867–c. 1943), tenor, impresario, and organizer of the most extensive early American opera company using Negro performers. According to Jerrold Lytton (as reported by H. S. Fortune in the *Colored American*, June 1900), Drury was born in Kentucky of a musical family and owed his proficiency in acting to Delsarte, his training as a pianist to Katzenstein, and his vocal training to a Professor Howard of New York City. Lytton states further that Drury was well read and able to speak both French and German. Described in contemporary reports as thoroughly trained, elegant, and highly professional in bearing, he was considered by some as the first highly trained male singer of the Negro race.

It was in New York and the New England states that Drury's early performing experience as a tenor took place, often in support of more established singers. Through these appearances his name became known and in 1889 he organized the Drury Comic Opera Company; toward the end of that same year the company was renamed the Theodore Drury Opera Company and gave concerts of operatic selections under the management of G. H. Barrett. An advertisement in 1889 (*New York Age*, Oct. 5) stated that the company owned its costumes, scenery, and decorations, and included fifteen singers, a musical director, and a pianist. Drury continued his solo concert performances when he was not occupied with the opera company. In the 1895–1896 season he toured 100 cities in the United States, giving solo recitals under the management of the Alexander Concert Company.

In 1900, as a singer and director of the Theodore Drury Opera Company, Drury began a series of semi-professional annual presentations of operas in New York, Boston, Providence, and Philadelphia. Given regularly from 1900 to 1910, these performances continued sporadically into the 1930s. In defiance of the strongly entrenched concept that Negroes could not perform in this medium, Drury adhered mainly to the standard grand opera repertory of his day. In the first six years he produced Bizet's *Carmen* (1900 and 1905), Gomez's *Il Guarany* (1901), Gounod's *Faust* (1902), Verdi's *Aïda* (1903), Mascagni's *Cavalleria Rusticana*, and Leoncavallo's *I Pagliacci* (1904). The 1900 *Carmen* was hailed as the first successfully executed performance of its kind (*Colored American*, June 1900): the cast was composed predominantly of Negroes, and the opera was presented in English. The most extensive venture took place in 1906 when Drury advertised a series of eight alternating performances of *Aïda* and *Carmen* from May 28 to June 2 at the 14th Street Theater in New York. The cast numbered thirty-one and featured, in addition to the singers, a Negro ballet dancer named de Forest (*New York Age*). At one point Drury felt sufficiently encouraged by his success to consider building an opera house for members of his race and advertised stock in such a project, but this dream was never realized. He continued appearances in such places as the 14th Street Theater and Lexington Opera Hall in New York, and Infantry Hall and Providence Hall in Providence, R.I.

Drury's proficiency as a pianist enabled him to accompany other singers occasionally, and to give instruction. His piano method, *Piano Playing, Self-Taught: A Simple and Easy Method,* was advertised with an endorsement by E. Azalia Hackley (*New York Age*, Oct. 27, 1904). His interest in voice led to two magazine articles. "The Science of Vocal Culture" (*Colored American*, Jan. 8, 1901, pp. 216–18) is a scientific explanation of basic principles of voice production. A longer article, "The Negro in Classic Music; or Leading Opera, Oratorio, and Concert Singers" (*Colored American*, Sept. 5, 1902, pp. 324–35), reflects Drury's conviction of the importance of musical education for Negroes, along with the industrial education then being strongly advocated by Booker T. Washington. It contains brief sketches of thirty-two currently performing Negro singers, readers, and actors. Drury acted as concert manager for many singers, some of them quite prominent, and he arranged the first joint concert in Boston of the pianist Raymond A. Lawson with the singer and composer Harry T. Burleigh.

Because of the stereotypes ingrained in the minds of white Americans in the wake of the minstrel show, few were willing to consider the Negro in serious roles at the turn of the century. There was no place for Negroes in white opera companies, and the only sustained effort at operatic production among Negroes up to this time had been made by the Colored Opera Company of Washington, D.C. (1872–1873), whose repertory consisted of only one operetta. Hence Drury's endeavor required some breadth of imagination and depth of conviction. His operatic performances were advertised as social affairs and were concluded with supper and dancing to Walter F. Craig's orchestra. The audiences, much like those on opening night at the Metropolitan Opera House, included persons of social prominence.

Lacking financial support, Drury was unable to sustain a stable company of performers and was forced to rely on those musicians who responded to advertisements of rehearsals, no matter the extent of their experience. Nevertheless he was able to feature such well-known Negro singers as Estelle Clough, George Ruffin, Stanley Gilbert, Adolphus Haston, George Taylor, and Franklin Fowler Brown. Drury usually sang a tenor or baritone role; his most popular roles were Mefistofele (Faust) and Pery the Indian Chief in Il Guarany. The accompaniments were provided by either the regular pianist, a guest such as organist Melville Charlton, or an orchestra. At least in one instance Drury's orchestra and its conductor were white. Some Negro newspapers were critical of this (Negro Music Journal, 1903); others spoke positively of the fact that both the cast and the audience were racially mixed. He was later able to organize an all-Negro orchestra. In general the white press, and occasionally the colored press, were patronizing or critical of the artistic results. But those who recognized the difficulty of the undertaking praised Drury's efforts and felt that his vision of Negroes in grand opera was successfully realized.

References to Drury appear in several issues of the New York Age, Colored American, and the Negro Music Journal. His picture is included in Charles Alexander's One Hundred Distinguished Leaders (1899).

— DORIS E. MCGINTY

DU BOIS, WILLIAM EDWARD BURGHARDT

(1868–1963), teacher, author, editor, poet, scholar, Pan-Africanist. Du Bois (pronounced "Du Boyce") was born in Great Barrington, Mass., on Feb. 23, 1868, of French Huguenot, Dutch, and Negro ancestry. His father, Alfred Du Bois, left his mother Mary Silvina Burghardt while Du Bois was still a young lad. She was a descendant of the "Black Burghardts" whose white ancestors had been prominent in the Dutch colonial history of Massachusetts. (The ancestral chart of the Du Bois and Burghardt families is on page 112 of Du Bois's Dusk of Dawn, An Essay toward an Autobiography of a Race Concept, 1940.) Even though his mother struggled to make ends meet, by the time of her death in 1884, Will, as he was then known, was left penniless. He worked as a timekeeper in a local mill and then graduated, the only colored student, from Great Barrington High School in 1884. Encouraged by the school principal, Frank Hosmer, he enrolled, with the aid of a scholarship, at Fisk University, Nashville, Tenn., in the fall of 1885. After graduation with a B.A. degree in 1888, he entered the junior class of Harvard College, assisted by the Price Greenleaf Award of $300. He graduated B.A. cum laude in 1890 and received his M.A. degree in 1891. After two years at the University of Berlin, he completed his dissertation at Harvard and in 1895 received his Ph.D., the first American Negro to receive this degree from Harvard. He taught Latin, Greek, German, and English at Wilberforce University (1895–1897), made a survey of Negroes in Philadelphia (1897), and taught economics and history at the original Atlanta University (1897–1910), where he edited fourteen of his Atlanta University publications. In 1900 he was secretary of the Pan-African Conference in London. He founded the Niagara Movement in 1905 in opposition to the conservative policies of Booker T. Washington, and served as its general secretary until 1909. He founded and edited the magazine Moon in 1906, and was chief founder and editor of a newspaper, Horizon (1907–1910). In 1909–1910 he was one of the original founders and incorporators of the NAACP, and served as its director of publicity and research, a member of its board of directors, and editor of its publication The Crisis (1910–1934). He attended the First Universal Races Congress in England (1911). He founded and edited (1920–1921) The Brownies' Book. In 1923 he was special minister and envoy extraordinary at the inauguration of the president of Liberia. In 1919 he investigated for the NAACP the discriminatory treatment of Negro troops in Europe. In that same year, he was the chief organizer of the First Pan-African Congress (Paris, 1919), the Second (London, Brussels, and Paris, 1921), the Third (London and Lisbon, 1923), and the Fourth (New York City, 1927).

In 1934 he resigned from The Crisis and board of the NAACP and became chairman of the Department of Sociology in the new Atlanta University under Pres. John Hope. He returned (1944) to the NAACP as director of special research, a position which he held until 1948. He was an accredited consultant of the NAACP at the San Francisco Conference which founded the United Nations (1945). In that same year he presided at the Fifth Pan-African Congress, Manchester, England. From 1948 to 1951 he was co-chairman of the Council on African Affairs; helped organize (1949) the Cultural and Scientific Conference for World Peace, New York City, and attended its Peace Congress in Paris and Moscow. He was chairman of the Peace Information Center and unsuccessful Progressive party candidate for United States senator (1950). In 1961 he joined the Communist party of the United States and took up residence in Ghana at the invitation of Pres. Kwame Nkrumah. He became a citizen of Ghana in 1963, died in Accra on Aug. 27, 1963, was honored by a state funeral, and buried in Accra.

On May 12, 1896, he had married Nina Gomer whom he had met in Wilberforce. She bore him two children: Burghardt Gomer, who died some time before 1903 and was buried in Great Barrington; and Nina Yolande (later married briefly to Countée Cullen and then to Arnett Williams), born in 1900 or 1902. After the death of his first wife on July 1, 1950, Du Bois married on Feb. 14, 1951, Shirley Graham, who survived him; they had no children. Du Bois's only granddaughter, Du Bois Williams, was born in 1932.

Du Bois encountered little overt race discrimination in Great Barrington; his record as an athlete and student in school won respect, and there were no fraternities or school dances to create social problems. His mother lived to see him graduate from high school in 1884 and deliver an oration, on "Wendell Phillips." After his mother's death in the fall of 1884 he went to live with an aunt. Soon thereafter he faced the crucial problem of his college education.

He considered nearby Williams College because most of the few high school graduates who went to college enrolled there. His heart, however, was set on Harvard, an unattainable goal at that time because the Great Barrington High School did not meet Harvard admission standards and because he lacked the necessary funds. Despite misgivings about going to the South, in the fall of 1885 he received a scholarship to Fisk University, for he believed that he could help provide leadership for Negroes. Matriculating as a sophomore, he graduated with a B.A. in 1888.

These three years changed much of his outlook on life. He learned firsthand some of the dimensions of the "Negro problem," especially by teaching in rural Tennessee during summer vacations. He began his writing by editing the *Fisk Herald* and became an impassioned orator. At Fisk "a new loyalty and allegiance replaced my Americanism; henceforward I was a Negro" (Du Bois, "My Evolving Program for Negro Freedom" in Rayford W. Logan [ed.], *What the Negro Wants* [1944], p. 36). On the other hand his personal contact with his white professors at Fisk impressed him favorably and their erudition inspired his zeal for scholarship. He became critical of religion and its practices, and declared in his commencement oration that Bismarck had demonstrated the kind of leadership that Negroes needed.

His B.A. degree from Fisk enabled him to enter Harvard College in 1888 as a member of the junior class. He "was happy at Harvard, but for unusual reasons" (*Dusk of Dawn* . . . [1940], p. 34). His three years at Fisk had led him to accept racial segregation; he became acquainted with several colored girls and enjoyed the friendship of a colored classmate, Clement Morgan. He knew only a few white students but he had fortunate personal contact with some of the most eminent professors of that era, especially William James, Josiah Royce, George Palmer, George Santayana, Nathaniel Shaler, and Albert Bushnell Hart. Hart and James in particular influenced him to concentrate on history and other social sciences.

In June 1890 he was one of five students selected to speak at commencement (Clement Morgan was one of the others). He chose "Jefferson Davis" as his subject, "with deliberate intent of facing Harvard and the nation with a discussion of slavery as illustrated in the person of the president of the Confederate States of America." The oration won high praise, notably in an editorial in the *Nation*.

Shortly before his graduation, a classmate astounded Du Bois with the remark that "There's nothing which I am particularly interested in." Writing in 1944 Du Bois recalled that he himself had already planned his life's work. But he felt the need for further preparation. He was Henry Bromsfield Rogers fellow at Harvard, receiving his M.A. in 1891, was reappointed for 1891–1892, and began work on his dissertation, "The Suppression

of the African Slave Trade." When former Pres. Rutherford B. Hayes wrote him that the Slater Fund no longer provided funds for a colored student to pursue graduate study in Europe, Du Bois sent him "a letter that could be described as nothing less than impudent and flatly accused him of bad faith." The letter recounted his graduate record at Harvard and mentioned a paper he had read on the suppression of the slave trade at the annual meeting of the American Historical Association (December 1891). To his surprise he received a fellowship of $750, half grant and half repayable as a loan, with the understanding that it might be renewed.

His two years (1892–1894) as a graduate student at the University of Berlin and a traveler in Germany, Austria, Poland, and Hungary, broadened his knowledge, forced him to rethink the Negro's status, his relationship to it, and to the international aspects of these problems. As at Harvard he studied especially economics, history, and sociology with some eminent teachers and scholars—Gustav Schmoller, Adolph Wagner, and Heinrich Von Treitschke. He became proficient in German, the only foreign language he really mastered, although he boasted that he "could be silent in six languages." On his twenty-fifth birthday (Feb. 23, 1893) he made a long, remarkable entry in his diary. He knew that he was "either a genius or a fool." He planned to "make a name in science, to make a name in literature and thus to raise my race. Or perhaps to raise a visible empire in Africa thro' England, France, or Germany." The desire to raise his race explains, as he wrote in 1944, why he rejected the wish of Dora, a blue-eyed young German woman who wanted to marry him. He told her it would be unfair to bring her to the United States, and besides, he had work to do. In 1944, too, he reflected that as a result of his European experiences, "I became more human; learned the place in life of 'Wine, Women, and Song'; I ceased to hate or suspect people simply because they belonged to one race or color" ("My Evolving Program . . .," p. 42). While he fulfilled for nearly seventy years his vow of doing his work, he did not cease to hate or suspect white people.

Du Bois expressed strong views also about Negroes, especially Booker T. Washington and Marcus Garvey. During almost ten years after Du Bois's return from Europe in 1894, he maintained rather cordial relations with Washington, and gave a balanced assessment of him in *The Souls of Black Folk* (1903). Thereafter the controversy between the two leaders became a major factor in the conflicting aims and methods for improving the status of American Negroes. It is difficult to assess the factors of personalities, views on education, self-help, and politics that embittered the controversy. Most historians are inclined to accept Du Bois's statement that the basic reason for their controversy was Washington's "Tuskegee Machine" which, until Woodrow Wilson's administration, largely controlled political appointments, foundation grants for education, many Negro publications, and opposed such organizations as the Niagara Movement and the NAACP. However, after Washington's death (Nov. 14, 1915) Du Bois's editorial in the December 1915 issue of *The Crisis* was as balanced as had been the essay in *The Souls of Black*

Folk. Du Bois called Washington "the greatest Negro leader since Frederick Douglass, and the most distinguished man, white or black who has come out of the South since the Civil War. . . . On the other hand, in stern justice, we must lay on the soul of this man, a heavy responsibility for the consummation of Negro disfranchisement, the decline of the Negro college and the firmer establishment of color caste in this land."

The feud between Du Bois and Garvey was more bitter than that between Du Bois and Washington. Du Bois called Garvey either a "lunatic or a traitor" and the latter retorted that Du Bois was a "white man's nigger." In *Race First, The Ideological and Organizational Struggles of Marcus Garvey and the Universal Negro Improvement Association* (1976), Tony Martin held Du Bois responsible in part for Garvey's imprisonment and deportation (p. 333).

Du Bois did not permit these controversies during more than twenty years to divert him from the goals that he had set for himself in his diary on Feb. 23, 1893.

In 1896, Longmans, Green and Company published his *The Suppression of the African Slave Trade to the United States of America, 1638–1870,* the first volume of the Harvard Historical Studies. It revealed an extraordinary amount of research in original sources, supported by abundant footnotes, two lengthy appendices, and a bibliography of almost fifteen pages. It is still an indispensable source for the study of this era of "man's inhumanity to man."

Du Bois was one of the founders and a vice-president of the American Negro Academy, organized on March 5, 1897. His "occasional paper," *The Conservation of Races,* published in that year, propounded a dilemma which still plagues many American Negroes. "Am I," he queried, "an American or am I a Negro? Can I be both? Or is it my duty to cease to be a Negro as soon as possible and be an American?" His final answer, of course, was to continue to be a Negro and cease to be an American.

Most of his scholarly works adhered to his oft-repeated prescription of seeking the truth "on the pure assumption that it is worth seeking." *The Philadelphia Negro* (1899) is a painstaking and objective interpretation. Forty-five years after its publication, Gunnar Myrdal and his associates praised it in *An American Dilemma* as a model study of a Negro community.

The Atlanta University Publications were significant contributions to social science. Du Bois did not exaggerate when he wrote in his autobiography, *Dusk of Dawn* (1940): "Between 1896 and 1920 there was no study in America which did not depend in some degree upon the investigations made at Atlanta University; often they were widely quoted and commended."

The Souls of Black Folk (1903) established his reputation as a great American essayist. His temperate essay "Of Mr. Booker T. Washington and Others" is still a model for an adversary's criticism. It also launched the first effective attack on the darling of capitalists who had grasped Washington to their bosom for his accommodationist apostasy at Atlanta (Sept. 18, 1895).

Du Bois's other publications reveal an extraordinary capacity for work and range of interests. His *John Brown* (1909, with additions in 1962) is valuable

largely because of the author's revelation of his passionate support of Brown and Brown's prophecy that his death would not mean the end of the Negro question (p. 403). Du Bois's first novel, *Quest of the Silver Fleece* (1911), is perhaps his best. William Stanley Braithwaite's review compared it favorably with Frank Norris's trilogy on wheat. The little book, *The Negro,* published in 1915, was praised in the perspective of 1970 by the distinguished Africanist, Prof. George Shepperson of the University of Edinburgh, for its place "in the history of ideas on the socio-economic nature of the 'new imperialism.' " *Darkwater: Voices Within the Veil* (1920; also published with the subtitle *The Twentieth Century Completion of "Uncle Tom's Cabin")* contained new versions of previously published articles in the *Atlantic,* the *Independent, The Crisis,* and the *Journal of Race Development.* His *Credo* proclaimed his belief in God, the Negro race, pride of race and lineage, service, the devil and his angels, the Prince of Peace, liberty for all men, the training of children, and finally, patience. Though historically less important than *The Souls of Black Folk,* the essays and poems (including "A Litany at Atlanta," first published in 1906), make the work one of his more significant. By contrast, *The Gift of Black Folk, Negroes in the Making of America* (1924), an exaggerated assertion of the contributions of Negroes to civilization, is one of his least valuable writings. *Dark Princess, A Romance* (1928) is likewise his least successful novel, but the concept of solidarity between Asians and Negroes is less utopian today than in 1928, and the treatment of the workingman and machine politics gives the book additional value.

Du Bois's most controversial book is *Black Reconstruction in America, An Essay Toward a History of the Part which Black Folk Played in the Attempt to Reconstruct Democracy in America, 1860–1880* (1935). It has been criticized for its Marxist views. On the other hand Du Bois was correct in emphasizing the admirable provisions of the Reconstruction conventions and legislatures, particularly the mandatory provisions for the inauguration of free public school systems. Also still valid is *Black Reconstruction's* formerly ignored emphasis on economic problems.

A Pageant in Seven Decades, 1868–1938. An Address Delivered on the Occasion of His Seventieth Birthday at the University Convocation of Atlanta University, Morehouse College, and Spelman College, February 23, 1938 (Atlanta, 1938) is a useful short autobiography. He caused consternation among some in the audience when he said "I have loved wine, women and song." The ceremony was highlighted by the presentations of a bust by Alexander Portnoff.

In *The Revelation of Saint Orgne the Damned,* his commencement address at Fisk University (1938), Saint Orgne (Negro), speaking in parables, climbed the "Seven Heights of Hell to view the Seven Stars of Heaven. The Seven Heights are Birth and Family; School and Learning; the University of Wisdom; the great snow-capped peak of Work; the naked crag of *Right and Wrong;* the rolling hills of the Freedom of Art and Beauty; and at last, the plateau that is the Democracy of Race" (p. 3). Saint Orgne wandered and preached during seven groups of seven years, and Du Bois added his own interpretations of the seven heights which reveal many of his views expressed in *The Crisis* and his other writings.

Black Folk Then and Now: An Essay in the History and Sociology of the Negro Race (1939) incorporated some of the material in *The Negro* and attempted to refute a widespread belief that "the Negro has no future" (p. vii). The volume was inspired in part by the failure of the Phelps-Stokes Fund to obtain additional financial support for a proposed "Encyclopedia of the Negro," one of the great disappointments of Du Bois's life. This support was denied because a white consultant alleged that Du Bois was a "racial chauvinist" (Papers of R.W.L., filed under Phelps-Stokes). Instead of a multivolume encyclopedia, the Phelps-Stokes Fund published the *Encyclopedia of the Negro: Preparatory Volume with Reference Lists and Reports* (1945 and 1946), with Du Bois as the principal editor. Du Bois may have used the volume to help prepare another aborted project, *Encyclopedia Africana,* on which he was working when he died in 1963.

Dusk of Dawn: An Essay Toward an Autobiography of a Race Concept (1940), reprinted 1968) was his first full-length autobiography which used his own life to conclude: "This heritage [of color, slavery, discrimination, and insult] binds together not simply the children of Africa but extends through yellow Asia and into the South Seas. It is this unity that draws me to Africa" (p. 117).

Color and Democracy: Colonies and Peace (1945) expressed the hope that the end of World War II might lead to the liberation of colonies. *The World and Africa: An Inquiry into the Part which Africa Has Played in World History* (1947) reprinted much of the material in *Black Folk Then and Now,* and contended that "America invests in colonies—British, Dutch and French; and colonies are slums used to make a profit from materials and labor" (p. 252). This book is particularly valuable for Du Bois's recollections of the Pan-African Congresses in 1919, 1921, 1923, 1927, and 1945.

In Battle for Peace: The Story of My 83rd Birthday, with comments by Shirley Graham (1952), gives a graphic account principally of his trial and acquittal on the charge of being an "unregistered foreign agent" of the Soviet Union. Some sponsors withdrew from participation in the birthday dinner, but E. Franklin Frazier presided and Paul Robeson "spoke courageously and feelingly" (p. 64). "Of the fifty presidents of Negro colleges, every one of which I had known and visited—and often many times as speaker and adviser—of these only one, Charles Johnson of Fisk University, publicly professed belief in my integrity before the trial; and only one congratulated me after the acquittal" (p. 153).

Arthur P. Davis and Julius Lester, among others, agree that *The Black Flame* trilogy—*The Ordeal of Mansart* (1957); *Mansart Builds a School* (1959); and *Worlds of Color* (1961)—fail as novels in tracing the life of one family from Reconstruction through the 1940s.

Like much of the life and writings of Du Bois, *The Autobiography of W. E. B. Du Bois: A Soliloquy on Viewing My Life from the Last Decade of Its First Century,* edited by Herbert Aptheker (1968), has provoked continuing controversy. The editor asserted that "the manuscript is now published for the first time in the language of its composition and in full. It is published as Dr. Du Bois wrote it; changes have been few and only of a technical nature—correcting a date, completing a name and the like" (p. 5). Some critics continue to challenge this assertion. From a different point of view the volume would be more valuable if the editor had indicated the published and unpublished sources. Scholars have gone through the volume page by page and found the passages taken largely from *Dusk of Dawn,* "My Evolving Program for Negro Freedom," and *A Pageant in Seven Decades.* In many instances the continuity of the passages has been changed, thereby giving a different emphasis, and some passages have been slightly modified. The volume contains a valuable "Selected Bibliography of the Published Writings of W. E. B. Du Bois" and "A Calendar of the Public Life of W. E. B. Du Bois."

Du Bois was not only a great scholar, he was also a prophet and a great leader of protest. For most of his life he was called "An Authentic American Radical." At the second meeting of the Niagara Movement, Harpers Ferry, on Aug. 15, 1906, he made what some consider the most succinct and eloquent demand for what was later called first-class citizenship: "We will not be satisfied to take one jot or tittle less than our full manhood rights. We claim for ourselves every single right that belongs to a free-born American, political, civil and social; and until we get these rights we will never cease to protest and assail the ears of America." Although he changed his goals, his protests deserve high rank among the great American polemics.

In addition to his many books, pamphlets, essays, and articles, the magazine *Moon* (1906), the newspaper *Horizon* (Jan. 1907 to July 1910), and especially *The Crisis,* which he edited from 1910 to 1934, reveal his views on virtually every issue. In November 1909 his editorial in the *Horizon* which he defiantly called "A Radical Newspaper," demanded, first, universal suffrage, including votes for women. The first issue of *The Crisis* in November 1910 stated that its object was "to set forth those facts and arguments which show the danger of race prejudice, particularly as manifested toward colored people." Of the vast number of articles and editorials written by Du Bois, a few are particularly revelatory. Some of his closest friends denounced him for his famous editorial "Close Ranks," in the July 1918 issue. The sentence which evoked the most virulent criticism urged: "Let us while this war lasts, forget our special grievances and close our ranks shoulder to shoulder with our white fellow citizens and the allied nations that are fighting for democracy." Few critics took note of the clause "while this war lasts." Even Du Bois's editorials in the August and September 1918 issues urging protest and reiterating the demand for full manhood rights did not mollify critics. Some accused him of having "sold out" his demand for equal rights in return for the promise of a captaincy in army intelligence. The thunderous protest led the army to withdraw the offer of the commission (Elliott M. Rudwick, *W. E. B. Du Bois: Propagandist of the Negro Protest* [1969], pp. 203–6).

It is probably impossible to determine whether Du Bois wrote his editorial "Returning Soldiers," in the May 1919 issue of *The Crisis,* to offset the lingering criticism. It castigated the United States for lynching and disfranchising Negroes, encouraging their ignorance, stealing from them and insulting them. It ended:

"We return.

"We return from fighting.

"We return fighting.

"Make way for Democracy! We saved it in France, and by the Great Jehovah, we will save it in the United States of America, or know the reason why."

Segregation was the most crucial issue. Like most Negro leaders and some white supporters, Du Bois preferred in 1917 a separate training camp for colored officers at Fort Des Moines, Iowa, rather than no camp. The continuing dilemma about the advantages and disadvantages of segregation led to Du Bois's resignation on July 9, 1934, as editor of *The Crisis* and member of the board of the NAACP. A series of his editorials in *The Crisis,* beginning in January 1934, presented in historical perspective the case for voluntary segregation, from the establishment of separate churches and other institutions at the end of the eighteenth century. He also declared that "As a matter of fact, the Association [NAACP], while it has from time to time discussed the larger aspects of this matter, has taken no general stand and adopted no general philosophy." He answered accusations about his own views by writing: "I am not worried about being inconsistent. What worries me is the Truth. I am talking about conditions in 1934 and not in 1910."

In his letter of resignation he cited particularly the pattern of the board in fighting vigorously against the separate officers training camp at Fort Des Moines and the separate Tuskegee Veterans Hospital and then seeking to make them as efficient as possible. Without responding to the reasons for his resignation, the board accepted it on July 9 with high praise and sincere thanks for his distinguished services and wishing him "all happiness in all that he may now undertake."

Du Bois's economic and social philosophy and programs were as changing as his views on many other subjects. "An Authentic American Radical" at Harpers Ferry (1906), in 1961 he finally became a Communist. In his letter of application (Oct. 1, 1961) for membership in the Communist party of the United States, he reviewed the long and slow path to his commitment. While studying at the University of Berlin (1892–1894) he had attended meetings of the Socialist party and considered himself a Socialist. Following the advice of such leaders in the NAACP as Mary White Ovington, William English Walling, and Charles Edward Russell, he joined the Socialist party in 1911. But because he knew nothing of practical Socialist politics, he urged Negroes to vote for Woodrow Wilson in the campaign of 1912. During the next twenty years he attacked Republicans, Democrats, Socialists, and Communists, largely on racial grounds. His gradual conversion to Communism began with his systematic reading of the works of Karl Marx and other Communist authors during this twenty-year period and was reenforced by his visits to the Soviet Union and other Communist countries in 1926, 1936, 1949, and 1959.

In his letter applying for membership in the Communist party of the U.S.A., as of Oct. 1, 1961, he summarized his changing economic views, asserted that "Capitalism cannot reform itself," and that "Communism—the effort to give all men what they need and to ask of each the best they can contribute—this is the only way of human life."

One of Du Bois's principal contributions was his role as "Father of Pan-Africanism." At the Pan-African Conference in London, July 1900, he urged the "British Nation" to give "the rights of responsible government" to the black colonies of Africa and the West Indies. Evidence is lacking that he meant a cabinet of Africans whose tenure of office depended on a majority of elected Africans in an elected legislature. He also urged respect for the "integrity and independence" of such nations as Abyssinia, Liberia, and Haiti. His "Address to the World" made the famous prophecy that "the problem of the Twentieth Century is the problem of the color line." But the concept of Pan-Africanism had no deep roots and the idea died for a generation (*The World and Africa,* pp. 7–8).

According to reports in the London *Times,* the subject was not discussed, even by Du Bois, at the Races Congress in London, July 1911. In his well-known article "The African Roots of War" (*Atlantic Monthly,* May 1915), Du Bois did not use the words "Pan-African" or "Pan-Africanism." He did, however, assert that "permanent peace" required the extension of the principle of "government by the consent of the governed" among not only the smaller European nations but also among "natives" of Asia, Africa, the Western Indies, and the Negroes of the United States.

Du Bois's demands for self-government evolved during five Pan-African Congresses. At the First (Paris, Feb. 19–21, 1919), one resolution—very probably written by Du Bois—stated that "The Natives of Africa must have the right to participate in the government as fast as their development permits." The Second Pan-African Congress (London, Brussels, and Paris, Aug. 29 to Sept. 6, 1921) did not define self-government and did not use the word "independence," largely because of the opposition in Brussels of Mfumu Paul Panda, a Congolese educated in Belgium from the age of five, and of Blaise Diagne, the first black African elected to the French Chamber of Deputies, opposition repeated by Diagne in Paris.

Interest in Pan-Africanism declined after 1921. Diagne made a statement in Paris which Rayford W. Logan translated as "I am a Frenchman first and a Negro afterward" and resigned as the African leader in France from further participation. Lack of funds was another major factor. Gratien Candace, black deputy from Guadeloupe, Commandant Camille Mortenol (a World War I commander of the aerial defense of Paris), Isaac Béton, a high school teacher, and Rayford W. Logan served as unpaid officers of the Pan-African Association (8 Avenue du Maine, Paris) from 1921 to 1923. The NAACP, which had established a fund of $3000 for the Second Pan-African Congress, was unable because of the postwar depression to continue its support. In addition, domestic problems, particularly lobbying for the Dyer antilynching bill, took precedence over Pan-Africanism.

Resolutions adopted by the London session (1923) of the Third Pan-African Congress emphasized the importance of labor solidarity between white and black labor in England, America, and elsewhere. The resolutions adopted at the Lisbon session, later in 1923, demanded that Africans should have "a voice in their own government" and that the development of Africa should be for "the benefit of Africans, and not merely for the profit of Europeans."

Another Pan-African Congress which Du Bois planned to be held in the West Indies failed because, as Du Bois wrote, "I suspect that colonial powers spiked this plan" (*The World and Africa,* p. 242).

The Fourth Congress in New York City (Aug. 1927) was made possible through the financial support of the Circle of Peace and Foreign Relations under the leadership of Addie W. Hunton and Addie Dickerson. It had the largest attendance, 208 delegates from twenty-two states of the United States and the West Indies, South America, Africa, Germany, and India. The resolutions repeated substantially those adopted at Lisbon, and added withdrawal of the American Marines from Haiti.

A "desperate effort" proposed by Du Bois in 1929 to hold another meeting in North Africa failed because the French government opposed it and the Great Depression made a meeting anywhere virtually impossible.

From 1929 to 1945 Du Bois made little attempt to plan another Pan-African Congress. He spoke, however, vigorously at San Francisco (1945) in favor of changes in the charter of the United Nations to ensure steps toward self-government and independence. In the same year he renewed his active participation in the Pan-African movement.

Du Bois presided at several sessions of the Fifth Pan-African Congress in Manchester, England (Oct. 15–21, 1945), and was elected permanent chairman of the congress and president of the Pan-African Congress. At the first session, Dr. Peter Milliard of British Guiana, president of the Pan-African Federation, said that "the Pan-African Congress was Dr. Du Bois's child." George Padmore, who had organized the meeting and urged Du Bois to attend it, declared at the opening session on October 16 that "he had the great honor of welcoming Dr. William Edward Burghardt Du Bois, the 'father' of Pan-Africanism to the Congress." "The Challenge to the Colonial Powers," which Du Bois probably helped draft, stated: "We demand for Black Africa autonomy and independence." This was the first time that resolutions adopted by a Pan-African Congress demanded independence.

As Du Bois looked at the audience, however, he must have reflected that his role of "Father" would soon end. The valuable brochure edited by George Padmore, *History of the Pan-African Congress* (Manchester, 1945[?], pp. 71–76), did not list a single delegate or organization from the United States. Nineteen delegates came from West Africa, six from East and South Africa, thirty-three from the West Indies, thirty-five (some of them listed under other rubrics) from Great Britain. Eleven were "Fraternal Delegates and Observers." The

NAACP was not listed among the associations that paid fees for delegates.

The Fifth Congress was the high-water mark of Du Bois's influence on Pan-Africanism. During the thirteen ensuing years he was buffeted as he had rarely been before. In 1948 the NAACP dismissed him as director of special research. In 1951 he was indicted as "the agent of a foreign principal," the Soviet Union. Even after he was acquitted, many denounced him as a traitor. The State Department compounded the harassment of the Justice Department by denying him a passport until 1958.

Prosecution and persecution left him little time and energy. He did serve, however (1948–1956), as cochairman of the Council on African Affairs, a private organization which published indispensable information about Africa, and he wrote about Africa in the *National Guardian.* He mentioned Africa frequently in an extensive lecture tour which he and Shirley Graham Du Bois made in 1956.

The independence of Ghana on March 6, 1957, 100 years to the day after the Dred Scott decision, changed Du Bois's demands for independence to warnings against Western neocolonialism and praise of aid by Socialist countries. In his letter to Prime Minister Kwame Nkrumah expressing regret at the refusal of the State Department to issue him and Mrs. Du Bois passports, he advised: "Pan-Africa . . . should avoid subjection to and ownership by foreign capitalists who seek to get rich on African labor and raw material, and should try to build a socialism founded on old African communal life."

Free to travel abroad in the summer of 1958, he made more specific his advice at Tashkent in the Soviet Union. Illness prevented him from attending the First All-African Peoples' Conference in Accra, Ghana, sometimes called the Sixth Pan-African Congress. His "message," delivered by his wife on Dec. 9, 1958, again denounced Western imperialism and neocolonialism. But he mistakenly saw "The whole world, including capitalist countries . . . moving toward Socialism," and naïvely asserted that "acceptance" of aid from Socialist nations such as the Soviet Union and the People's Republic of China "involves no bonds which a free Africa may not safely assume." This naïveté can probably be understood in light of his gradual total commitment in 1961 to Communism.

One specific result of his visits to the Soviet Union was the establishment in 1961, and the opening in 1962, of the Institute of African Affairs. There is little doubt that its goals were the furtherance of Soviet interests rather than promotion of real independence in Black Africa.

At a meeting in Washington on the eve of the March for Jobs and Freedom (Aug. 27, 1963), John O. Killens, James Baldwin, Sidney Poitier, and others were told: "The Old Man died." Killens added that no one had to tell them who "The Old Man" was since they knew he was Du Bois. To some of them, Killens wrote, he was "our patron saint, our teacher and our major prophet" (Introduction by John O. Killens to *An A B C of Color* by W. E. B. Du Bois, . . . [1963], p. 9). By contrast the *American Historical Review* merely reported "he [Du

Bois] had died, thus indicating its own inability or unwillingness to comment on the impact of Du Bois on the field represented by that Journal'' (John Hope Franklin in an address at the Du Bois Memorial in Carnegie Hall, New York City, 1964). On Dec. 28, 1968, however, the American Historical Association made its *amende honorable*. It devoted the opening session to the topic "W. E. B. Du Bois (1860–1963): In Observance of the One Hundredth Anniversary of his Birth."

No predominantly white American university conferred an honorary degree on Du Bois, but several foreign universities did. He received the following honorary degrees from American universities: LL.D. (Howard, 1930), LL.D. (Atlanta, 1938), Litt.D. (Fisk, 1938), L.H.D. (Wilberforce, 1940). He was elected an alumni member of the Fisk University chapter of Phi Beta Kappa in 1958. Only after a bitter struggle did the town of Great Barrington authorize in 1969 a memorial park surrounding the site of the Du Bois family home. As late as 1972 the house was still in woeful disrepair. His son Burghardt was buried in the north side of the Mahaiwe Cemetery located south of Great Barrington on Route 7. There was a separate gravestone in the shape of a cross. No mention was made of the date of the birth (Oct. 2, 1897), in Great Barrington. Yolande Du Bois Williams and Nina Gomer Du Bois were buried in the same plot as the son (Cecilia Adams Gross to R.W.L., Oct. 30, and Nov. 1972). Plans for the removal of Du Bois's remains from Accra to the United States have encountered the same kind of opposition that prevented Shirley Graham Du Bois for several years from coming to the United States. Despite continued local opposition, on May 11, 1976, Secretary of the Interior Thomas S. Kleppe formally designated the Du Bois site in Great Barrington as a national historical landmark. The nomination for justifying the designation stated that "William Edward Burghardt Du Bois . . . is generally recognized as one of the most incisive thinkers and profound scholars of his time."

In addition to the works cited in the text, see *W. E. B. Du Bois: A Profile*, edited by Rayford W. Logan (1971), which contains a brief biography, excerpts from the writings of ten authors, and a long, critical bibliographical note. For his early activities with the NAACP, Mary White Ovington's *The Walls Came Tumbling Down* (1947) and Charles Flint Kellogg's *NAACP, A History of the National Association for the Advancement of Colored People,* volume 1, 1909–1920 (1967) are indispensable. *His Day is Marching On, A Memoir of W. E. B. Du Bois* by Shirley Graham Du Bois (1971) is valuable particularly for his visits to the Soviet Union and China as well as several of his addresses.

Du Bois's great mind is best revealed in his published correspondence and collected works, edited by Herbert Aptheker. *The Correspondence of W. E. B. Du Bois:* volume 1, *Selections 1877–1934* (1973), volume 2, *Selections 1934–1944* (1976), and volume 3, *Selections 1944–1963* (1978), justify the claim that his "interests were all but universal, his productivity and impact monumental." One obvious basis for criticism is the paucity of materials dealing with the Pan-African Congresses of 1919, 1921, 1923, and 1927. In addition, important correspondence between Du Bois and

Blaise Diagne is not included—Diagne is not even listed in the index. A comparison of the *Correspondence* with *The Papers of George Washington, Thomas Jefferson, Alexander Hamilton,* and *James Monroe,* for example, suggests the need for publication of all the correspondence, with additional footnotes. There remains need for a more complete exploration of one of the great minds during the last hundred years. Aptheker's *The Published Writings of W. E. B. Du Bois: An Annotated Bibliography* (1973) is also selective. *The Collected Works of W. E. B. Du Bois,* in forty volumes edited by Aptheker, is being published. The Padmore Research Library on African Affairs in Accra, Ghana, published as No. 4 (April 1964) in its bibliography series the incomplete but valuable *Dr. W. E. B. Du Bois, 1868–1963, A Bibliography*. Also valuable are reminiscences of Du Bois from 1921 to 1945 and materials in the diary and correspondence with Du Bois of Rayford W. Logan. — RAYFORD W. LOGAN and MICHAEL R. WINSTON

DUDLEY, SHERMAN H. (1864–1940), Texas-born singer-comedian, organizer, and promoter, popularly known as S. H. Dudley. Like many southern Negroes who resented being addressed by their first names by whites, Dudley used only his initials in the effort to ward off the insult. And in the tradition of most Negro performers of his day he worked the "medicine show" circuit: talented singers and dancers often began their professional careers as performers hired by itinerant street salesmen of patent medicines. The performances were designed to attract prospective buyers to the hucksters' medicinal wares. Most such entertainers of the South were Negroes, many of them mere boys.

While still in his twenties, Dudley joined the McCabe and Young Minstrels, working as a comic end man who called himself "Hapsy." He followed that stint by teaming with singer and dancer Dude Kelly and performing as a substitute for Sam Lucas at Broadway's Star Theater. So successful was the pair of substitutes that they were booked by Rusco and Holland's Georgia Minstrels through a scout who had seen their performance. Then in 1899 Dudley began to share honors with the great Negro minstrel Billy Kersands, who was the company's star.

It was during this period that a group of Negro showmen, tiring of the caricature of the minstrel and what it was doing to the image of the Negroes, decided they must break the minstrel pattern in American entertainment. Sam T. Jack with his original *Creole Show* of 1890 set the pace. His effort was followed by Bob Cole's *A Trip to Coontown;* Will Marion Cook's and Paul Laurence Dunbar's *Clorindy, The Origin of the Cakewalk;* and S. H. Dudley's *Smart Set* of 1896 with its chorus line of beautiful Negro girls. Those musicals, written by Negroes, made a serious attempt at establishing plot, characterization, and some authentic relevancy to Negro life.

In the early 1900s Dudley went into vaudeville with a mule he had purchased, trained to perform, and decked out in overalls. Dudley and His Mule quickly attained national fame, their bookings extending over a number of years. The obituary in the *Afro-American* for March 16, 1940, stated: "Leading the mule on stage he would engage in conversation with the animal who, seemingly at the right time, would nod his head in approval, conveying to the audience the impression that the mule understood. This act never failed to convulse the house.''

In the interim Dudley, in cooperation with several other Negroes, began to rent, lease, and buy theaters for the purpose of creating their own vaudeville circuit. The group, formed in 1911, was known as Dudley's Theatrical Enterprize, and it occupied offices at 1818 Seventh St. NW, Washington, D.C. The circuit consisted of four theaters, three in Virginia, and one in Washington. Dudley himself owned two of them, and his field agent was a young actor named Leigh Whipper. From this beginning of Dudley's, the larger Theater Owners and Bookers Association (TOBY), with theaters from Philadelphia to Florida, eventually grew. Dudley also organized the Colored Actors Union.

The period during and following World War I saw Dudley emerge as a producer of Negro shows. Along with such Negro producers as the brothers Salem Whitney Tutt and J. Homer Tutt, Irvin C. Miller, and J. Lubrie Hill, Dudley managed to book Negro shows into Negro theaters. His own *Smart Set* productions, revamped to meet current vogues, were always welcome hits with Negro audiences. For more than half a century Dudley functioned not only as a pioneer entertainer but as a pioneer in altering the character of the Negro show as well as a leader in theater ownership.

The chapter on ''Musical Comedy'' in Maud Cuney-Hare's *Negro Musicians and Their Music* (1936) shows Dudley's role in the development of this form of entertainment. See also Tom Fletcher's *100 Years of Negro in Show Business* (1954, pp. 143, 151), and Loften Mitchell's *Black Drama* (1967, pp. 40, 68, 97). Basic information is in the obituary, the *Baltimore Afro-American* (March 16, 1946). — ELTON C. FAX

DUNBAR, PAUL LAURENCE (1872–1906), poet and novelist. The son of Joshua and Matilda Murphy Dunbar, Paul was born in Dayton, Ohio, on June 27, 1872. His father, escaping from slavery in Kentucky, had made his way to Canada. He returned to the States during the Civil War and enlisted in the Massachusetts 55th Regiment. Dunbar's mother, also an ex-slave, was a widow. Formerly married to R. Weeks Murphy, she had two sons by him. After his death she came to Dayton and made her living there as a laundry worker. It was in Dayton that she met and married Joshua Dunbar. From this union there were two children, Paul and Elizabeth, who died when only two years old.

Joshua Dunbar died when Paul was only twelve; Matilda, however, survived her son for many years. A very strong woman, she had a great influence on the poet. Although born and reared in slavery, she could read and write, and she encouraged young Paul in his efforts to become a poet. Along with her husband she supplied their son with firsthand knowledge of life in the South both before and immediately after the war.

Paul Laurence Dunbar's formal education came from the public schools of his native city. At Central High School he was well liked by his teachers and classmates. During his second year he became a member of the school's literary society and wrote for the school paper. In his senior year he was elected president of the society and editor of the paper. The only Negro in the class, Dunbar graduated on June 16, 1891. He wanted to attend college, but there was no money for that purpose. He found a job as elevator operator in the Callahan Building on Main Street in Dayton.

Although the future did not look promising, Dunbar still planned on a writing career and in his free hours tried to prepare himself. During these years he sent poems to newspapers throughout the East and Midwest. Some were printed, others returned. One of his first breaks came in the summer of 1892 when the Western Association of Writers met in Dayton. Through one of his former teachers, Dunbar was invited to deliver a welcome address to the association. Dating his piece on June 27, 1892 (his birthday), Dunbar wrote a rhymed welcome which was well received, and he was made a member of the association.

In 1892 Dunbar collected his verses that had appeared in various newspapers with the intention of publishing them in a volume which he called *Oak and Ivy.* However, it cost $125 to print the book, and the elevator boy-poet had no way to raise such an amount. A white friend (one of many to help the poet throughout his career) ''stood'' for the money. Selling his works to interested riders on his elevator and to others, Dunbar soon repaid the helpful loan.

Shortly after the publication of *Oak and Ivy* (dated 1893) another white friend, a judge, gave the poet a job as messenger in the city's courthouse. Along with the appointment went an opportunity to ''read'' law. In the spring of 1893, however, the Chicago World's Fair was opened; and Dunbar, thinking that there would be better jobs for him in the Exposition city, went there. Opportunities were not as plentiful as he had thought they would be, and Dunbar had a difficult time. Eventually, Frederick Douglass, who was the commissioner in charge of the Haitian Exhibit, made the young poet his clerical assistant and paid him five dollars a week from his own funds. At the World's Fair Dunbar also met Richard B. Harrison, who became a close friend.

Through the help of Dr. H. A. Tobey of Toledo and other white friends whom Tobey brought together, Dunbar was able to publish in 1895 his second collection of verse, *Majors and Minors.* The work contained 148 pages, 86 of them presenting verses in classic or standard English. The other poems were printed under the heading ''Humor and Dialect.'' Although Dunbar thought of his poems in standard English as ''Major,'' critics from the very beginning have tended to change his classification. Modern scholars realize that *Majors and Minors* is a remarkable work, and that it contains some of Dunbar's best poems in both dialect and standard English. As Benjamin Brawley has said: ''Any one who could write these poems was already very nearly if not quite mature'' (*Paul Laurence Dunbar, Poet of His People,* 1936).

Through Dr. Tobey, copies of *Majors and Minors* were sent to two distinguished Americans destined to play important roles in the poet's life. The first of these was Col. Robert G. Ingersoll, the professional atheist of the period; the other was William Dean Howells, the reigning literary critic. In *Harper's Weekly* for June 27, 1896, Howells favorably reviewed *Majors and Minors.* Because it carried an announcement of McKinley's nomination for the presidency, this issue of *Harper's* had an exceptionally wide circulation. The review made Paul Laurence Dunbar famous. It also set the style for most subsequent reviews of Dunbar's works by white critics. Howells, in effect, dismissed Dunbar's standard English poems and emphasized his dialect verse.

On the basis of his new popularity the poet engaged the services of a manager, Maj. James B. Pond (of the then-famous Pond's Bureau). He went on a successful reading tour which was climaxed with an appearance at the fashionable Narragansett Pier. Major Pond secured Dodd, Mead and Company to publish Dunbar's work, and in 1896 this major firm brought out *Lyrics of Lowly Life,* the author's third collection. Dunbar received an advance of $400, and the work became a great popular success.

A large part of the volume's success must be attributed to its famous "Introduction," which was written by Howells. Among other things, the critic said: This "was the first instance of an American negro who had evinced innate distinction in literature. . . . So far as I could remember, Paul Dunbar was the only man of pure African blood and of American civilization to feel the negro life aesthetically and express it lyrically." One may easily argue with the critic's statement, but its result is hardly debatable. Howells's recommendation helped make Paul Laurence Dunbar the most popular Negro writer in America at the time.

Riding the wave of this popularity, Dunbar went to England to give a series of readings. The tour was unsuccessful financially, but while abroad the poet wrote a large portion of his first novel. During his stay in England he also received a letter from Colonel Ingersoll concerning the offer of a position at the Library of Congress. Back in America, Dunbar was hired as an assistant with an annual salary of $720. He worked there for only fifteen months, for by that time he was certain that he could make a living from his literary efforts alone. Publishers were demanding not only poems from Dunbar but prose sketches and novels as well. *Century Magazine, Lippincott's,* and other national periodicals were snatching at anything that came from the pen of this popular Negro writer.

In the May 1898 issue of *Lippincott's,* Dunbar published *The Uncalled,* his first novel. It was reissued the same year in book form. Also in 1898, the poet married Alice Ruth Moore, a poet herself and a schoolteacher. A native of New Orleans, Moore taught in Boston. The wedding took place on March 6, 1898, and the couple moved into a house in Washington, D.C., at 1934 Fourth St. NW, that Dunbar had prepared for his mother earlier in the year. And finally in this fruitful year of 1898, Dunbar published *Folks from Dixie,* a collection of twelve short stories, most of which had already appeared in *Cosmopolitan.*

The years from 1898 until the time of his death were extremely busy ones for the popular writer. Dunbar and his wife entered fully into the social life of the capital, a city to which he was deeply attached. He was called upon to help raise money for Hampton Institute and Tuskegee Institute. He came to know Booker T. Washington, and he wrote Tuskegee's school song. In the meantime the demand for his works increased dramatically. So great was this demand that one publishing company gave Dunbar a retaining fee for the privilege of having a first look at whatever he wrote.

In 1899 Dunbar published *Lyrics of the Hearthside.* He also set out on an extended reading tour which had to be canceled because on May 1 the poet contracted a deep cold which led to pneumonia. He was very seriously ill for several weeks; in fact he never fully recovered from this illness. Several of Dunbar's contemporaries believe that the addiction to drink which plagued his last years was brought on by the serious lung trouble he had. He drank to keep going, and sometimes he drank too much. On one occasion at least he appeared for an important engagement at Northwestern University intoxicated, but this incident was overplayed by the press.

In spite of his worsening condition, Dunbar never stopped producing. He went to Colorado for his health, writing there his second novel, *The Love of Landry* (1900). He also published in that year *The Strength of Gideon and Other Stories.* In addition he wrote two plays (neither of them published) for his friend Richard B. Harrison as well as lyrics and sketches that were set to music by Will Marion Cook.

The hectic tempo continued in the next year. In 1901 Dunbar published *The Fanatics,* a third novel. A fourth, *The Sport of the Gods,* came out in *Lippincott's* in 1901 and in book form in 1902. In 1903 he published *Lyrics of Love and Laughter;* in 1904 *The Heart of Happy Hollow;* and in 1905 *Lyrics of Sunshine and Shadow.*

During 1902 Dunbar and his wife Alice separated. The reasons for this break-up are not known. After the separation the poet left Washington, going first to Chicago and then to Dayton, where he established another home for his mother. He died there on Feb. 9, 1906, in his thirty-fourth year.

Paul Laurence Dunbar was a poet, short-story writer, novelist, writer of articles and dramatic sketches, plays, and lyrics for musical compositions. But he is best known as a writer of dialect verse, and this is as it should be because in this genre he stands supreme. Like Robert Burns, the Scottish poet, Dunbar was not happy over the public's tendency to play down his poems in standard English; he did not want to be judged alone by his "jingle in a broken tongue."

Because he wrote so many different kinds of poetry, Dunbar's verses could be grouped in many fascinating ways; but the simplest is to do as he did in his second volume—divide them into poems written in standard English and poems written in dialect. The first group covers the themes usually found in lyrical poetry: nature, love, joy, sadness, death, the vanity of human effort, and others. These pieces include sentimental, didactic, and derivative works as well as poems of undoubted excellence. Dunbar had a strong melodic and rhythmical talent, and his lines often sing and swing along gloriously. Several of his standard English poems have been favorites among Negroes, particularly those

Negro readers who frowned on dialect verse. Among these hardy perennials are "Ere Sleep Comes Down . . ." "Ode to Ethiopia," "The Poet," "The Colored Soldiers," "Ships That Pass in the Night," and "Sympathy."

Because politically he was an "accommodationist," Dunbar did not write a great deal of protest poetry; however, he did publish a few pieces that spoke out gently against America's treatment of the Negro. Among the works in this vein are "We Wear the Mask" and "The Haunted Oak," an antilynching poem. It should also be noted that Dunbar paid poetic homage to great freedom fighters like Frederick Douglass, Harriet Beecher Stowe, and Robert Gould Shaw.

Taken as a whole, the dialect poetry of Dunbar is his best work. Several of Dunbar's white contemporaries wrote better poems in standard English than he did, but none surpassed him in dialect poetry. Although he had several white forerunners in the field—among them Thomas Nelson Page and Irwin Russell—Dunbar was closer to the material than they were, had more sympathy with his characters, and of course understood them better. Dunbar tended to laugh *with* his humorous fictional folk. All too often white writers tended to laugh *at* them. Unlike the poets of the New Negro Renaissance who used folk material for all human moods, Dunbar was inclined to limit his treatment to humor and pathos. Within these limits, however, he performed brilliantly. The best dialect pieces of Dunbar have become American classics, among them "The Party," "The Corn-Stalk Fiddle," "Little Brown Baby," "When de Co'n Pone's Hot," "When Malindy Sings," "In the Morning," "Signs of the Times," and "An Ante-Bellum Sermon."

Between 1898 and 1904 Dunbar published four collections of short stories: *Folks from Dixie* (1898), *Strength of Gideon . . .* (1900), *In Old Plantation Days* (1903), and *The Heart of Happy Hollow* (1904). The titles of these collections tell the reader what to expect. For the most part Dunbar's short stories are the kind found in the works of Thomas Nelson Page and other southern apologists of the period. The majority of Dunbar's characters are faithful retainers, comical folk preachers, and happy, carefree, dancing, good-eating slaves or peasants. A few of these stories touch on issues of importance—among them two lynching stories, "The Tragedy at Three Forks" and "The Lynching of Jube Benson"—but these are not typical. Dunbar wrote for a living; he therefore had to please a white reading public, North and South, which was not interested in Negro protest. This public had been conditioned to believe that practically all Negroes lived in "Happy Hollow." As an "accommodationist" and as a professional writer, Dunbar gave them what they wanted.

During the years which saw the appearance of these short fiction collections Dunbar also published four novels. The first, *The Uncalled* (1898), deals primarily with the lack of Christianity found in supposedly Christian churches. It also deals with a search for identity on the part of the protagonist, a young minister. The search may have autobiographical overtones because the author at one time considered going into the ministry. The

second, and probably the weakest of the four novels, *The Love of Landry* (1900), is a pale, sentimental love story based on class barriers in white American society. The third work, *The Fanatics* (1901), is an intriguing story of political fanaticism in an Ohio town during the Civil War between two families, one pro-Yankee, the other pro-southern. There are some fascinating Negro minor characters in this novel, but Dunbar was seemingly afraid to develop them adequately because it meant dealing with an ugly race problem.

The author's last novel, *The Sport of the Gods* (1902), is the only one with principal Negro characters. It is different in yet another way: Dunbar describes here a flagrant case of southern injustice perpetrated on an innocent and respectable Negro family. The father, though guilty of no wrong-doing, is sentenced to prison; and the mother, son, and daughter, forced to leave town, move to New York where they go to pieces morally. The fascinating thing about *The Sport of the Gods* is that the author feels strongly that in spite of the inhumanity found in the South, that region is better for the Negro than the big cities of the North, especially New York. The work is interesting in yet another respect: it is probably the first Negro novel to make use of the theatrical and night life of New York, a theme which became popular during the Harlem Renaissance.

Paul Laurence Dunbar lacked both the insights and the techniques required of a first-rate fiction writer. Although his short stories are amusing, they tend to be conventional and surface treatments of characters and customs. The same may be said of his first three novels. *The Sport of the Gods* is by no means a good novel, but it is certainly more convincing than the first three.

Dunbar, however, will survive as a poet, particularly as a dialect poet. In this genre he has few if any peers, and his popularity in the field gives him a unique position in Negro letters. Beloved of the folk who recited his works on all possible occasions and who named their schools and other public buildings for him, Paul Laurence Dunbar was more definitely the "Poet of His People" than any other Negro writer has been.

Not as much biographical and critical work has been done on Paul Laurence Dunbar as he deserves. Perhaps the best single full-length study of the author is Benjamin Brawley's *Paul Laurence Dunbar, Poet of His People* (1936). Brawley states accurately and concisely the facts of Dunbar's life; he gives an excellent bibliographical analysis of the author's overlapping publications; and he makes excellent use of the comments of contemporaries who knew Dunbar personally. Victor Lawson's *Dunbar Critically Examined* (1941) is also a useful work, one which emphasizes the literary backgrounds of Dunbar's creations. The account of Dunbar found in Vernon Loggins's *The Negro Author* (1931) is both scholarly and perceptive. So also are the accounts found in Sterling A. Brown's *The Negro in American Fiction* (1937) and *Negro Poetry and Drama* (1937), particularly the comments in the latter work on Dunbar as a pastoral poet. The original source of much of the extant biographical material on the poet is Lida Keck Wiggins's *The Life and Works of Paul Laurence Dunbar* (1907?). In addition to an old-fashioned, sentimental, but useful biography, the volume contains Dunbar's complete poetical works, a selection of his best short stories, many anecdotes, and other valuable material. *The Complete Poems of Paul Laurence Dunbar,* originally published in 1913, has been reprinted recently in paperback (Apollo Editions A–177). There were published in 1975 the following works on the poet: *A Singer in the Dawn: Reinterpretations of Paul Laurence Dunbar,* an anthology of eleven essays edited by Jay Martin; *The Paul Laurence Dunbar Reader,* edited by Jay Martin and Gossie H. Hudson; *Paul Laurence Dunbar: A Selected Bibliography* by E. W. Metcalf; and an article, "Dunbar as Playwright," by Thomas Pawley (*Black World,* April 26, 1975). — ARTHUR P. DAVIS

DUNCANSON, ROBERT S. (1817–1872), journeyman painter, daguerrotypist, landscape and portrait painter. Duncanson was born somewhere in New York State, his father was a Scotsman and his mother a mulatto. Although born free by the state manumission act of 1785, effective in 1799, Robert like other free Negroes in New York suffered many disabilities. His father therefore took him to Canada, where he received his early education. Duncanson came to Ohio in 1841 or 1842 and lived with his mother at 7338 Hamilton Ave., Mount Healthy, about fifteen miles from Cincinnati. By 1842 he had begun exhibiting in Cincinnati.

Largely self-taught until then (he had also worked as a house painter), his style of landscape painting was greatly influenced by the Hudson River School of painters residing in Cincinnati, especially William L. Sonntag. Between 1845 and 1853 he also painted in Detroit, North Carolina, western Pennsylvania, and New England. In 1853 he went to Europe with Sonntag, bearing a letter of introduction from Nicholas Longworth to the world-famous sculptor Hiram Powers, who had moved from Cincinnati to Italy in 1837. The influence of Powers on Duncanson is unclear. There is reason to believe that this trip, as well as that in 1863, was sponsored by the Anti-Slavery League. Between the two trips he did some of his best paintings, based in part on his visits to Minnesota and Vermont. It is suggested that his second trip to Europe resulted in part from the growing antagonism of many whites opposed to participation in the Civil War. He exhibited in Glasgow and other Scottish cities. One of his best paintings, *Land of the Lotus Eaters,* which he had begun in 1861, won the unstinted praise of the Duchess of Sutherland, Alfred, Lord Tennyson, and critics in art journals. While in Scotland, Duncanson visited many places featured in the novels of Sir Walter Scott and painted some of the scenes he had observed. Six of them were exhibited after his return to Cincinnati in 1867. He made a last visit to Scotland in 1870–1871, possibly with the assistance of the Freedmen's Aid Society. Upon his return he exhibited in Detroit and Cincinnati. In 1872 he died of insanity in Detroit, on Dec. 21, 1872. Whether his mental illness was caused by his experiences as a "Tragic Mulatto," seeking escape from his life as a Negro and being spurned by whites, is debatable in view of the large measure of recognition accorded him in the United States and abroad. A tribute drafted by several leading artists in Cincinnati casts some doubt on the reasons for his mental instability. It read in part: "A devoted hus-

band and father, honored both at home and abroad, an artist who never forgot the kindly word and generous sympathy for the humblest beginner, a genial soul who cherished malice toward none" (quoted by Edward S. Dwight, "Robert S. Duncanson," *NHB,* Dec. 1954, pp. 53–54).

Evaluations of Duncanson's works are restrained. Although he was recognized before his death "as the best landscape painter in the West" (Dwight, p. 54), a recent assessment is as follows: Duncanson's contribution to the history of American art, "while not a major one, is that of a conscientious artist working skillfully and imaginatively within a particular idiom. While not the precursor of a new philosophy, his work within the Hudson River tradition and his sensitive reaction to the beauty of landscape give his painting a very personal poetry" (McElroy, p. 15).

From March 16 to April 30, 1972, the Cincinnati Art Museum sponsored a Centennial Exposition of thirty-five of Duncanson's paintings and portraits. Not included in the exhibition were fifty-four other paintings and portraits; some were not available, the whereabouts of others unknown.

Most biographical sketches of Duncanson are based in large measure on the monograph by James A. Porter, "Robert S. Duncanson, Midwestern Romantic-Realist" (*Art in America,* Oct. 1951). See, for example, "Robert S. Duncanson (1821–1872): A Study of the Artist's Life and Work," by Guy McElroy in Cincinnati Art Museum, *Robert S. Duncanson, A Centennial Exhibition* (1972, pp. 5–15). This handsome brochure, which lists other articles by Edward H. Dwight, director of the Munson-Williams-Proctor Institute, and other sources, has a valuable bibliography, chronology, and list of lenders. Most important are reproductions of thirty-five of his paintings and portraits, and a description and location of each of them. — RAYFORD W. LOGAN

DUNJEE, ROSCOE (1883–1965), editor and civil rights leader. The son of John William and Lydia Ann Dunjee, Roscoe was born in one of the dormitories of Storer College at Harpers Ferry, Jefferson County, W. Va., on June 21, 1883. His father, the Rev. John William Dunjee, a Baptist minister and financial officer for Storer College, also published a six-column hand-set newspaper, the *Harpers Ferry Messenger.* Born a slave, at the age of twenty-seven he escaped to Canada by the Underground Railroad (William Still, *The Underground Railroad from Slavery to Freedom* [1872], pp. 541–47). In this book the name is "Dungy," changed to Dungee and later Dunjee by his father. After some training at Oberlin College, the elder Dunjee was employed by the American Baptist Missionary Society to organize churches in the United States. In the Oklahoma Territory young Roscoe Dunjee obtained most of his formal education at Langston University. By the death of his father, Dunjee was left with his mother, a brother, and a sister to care for, and a $1100 mortgage on a small farm, which afforded the family livelihood for some time. Roscoe Dunjee's father also left a library of 1500 books, which served young Dunjee well for his outstanding role as a civil rights leader in Oklahoma. Founded in 1915, by 1950 his paper *Black Dispatch* claimed circulation in every state of the United States. He continued as editor and publisher until 1965, when it was one of the better Negro papers.

Dunjee wrote long provocative editorials in the *Black Dispatch.* His advice to Negroes in Oklahoma and elsewhere was to try legal means to compel other Americans to abide by their own laws. He attacked the "grandfather clause" which Oklahoma had used to keep Negroes from voting. From 1916 to 1920 he was urging Negro citizens to "demand registrations" and press for penitentiary sentences for those registrars who refused their demands. Using his newspaper to encourage them to vote, he instructed Negro voters on legal procedure to gain registration. Laying the foundation for federal cases, he pointed out that the state district courts might ignore the appeals. In 1920 he wrote: "You will probably not get your relief there. What we want, however, is a record properly drawn with which to go to federal court. We black folk can put some jail birds where they belong this fall if we just follow the election law to the letter."

Roscoe Dunjee was involved with many national movements as well as most of the movements inside the state of Oklahoma. He was a member of the Executive Board of the Association for the Study of Negro Life and History and of its Nation-Wide One Dollar Sustaining Membership Drive; he was a national director of the NAACP and vice-chairman of the Southern Conference for Human Welfare. He organized the Oklahoma Conference of Branches for the NAACP, and the Oklahoma Youth Legislature. His assistance in the organization of the Oklahoma Federation for Constitutional Rights led to his being accused of "subversive activities" and investigation by the Oklahoma legislature's "Little Dies Committee" in 1941. He was one of the organizers of the Oklahoma Commission for Interracial Cooperation. For two years (1926–1928) he was regional director for the Elks' oratorical contests, and for five years he served as president of the Oklahoma State Negro Business League.

During his administration as president of the Oklahoma State Conference of NAACP, Dunjee courageously led the legal fight in the Ada Lois Sipuel case to the Supreme Court of the United States. It was through the Court's decision in *Sipuel* v. *Board of Regents of Universities of Oklahoma* (332 U.S. 631, 1948) that Sipuel and other Negroes were admitted to Oklahoma State University. (Sipuel, as Mrs. Fisher), later became a professor at Langston University.)

Dunjee supported the case of *Hollins* v. *Oklahoma* (295 U.S. 394, 1935), which resulted in the acquittal of Jess Hollins because Negroes had been excluded from the jury by reason of race. In the same year Dunjee financed the Sidney Hawkins *habeas corpus* case and for five hours gave testimony as an expert witness to break down residential segregation in the state. In 1935 Dunjee was given the Award of Merit by the NAACP at its St. Louis Conference.

During World War II Dunjee was elected chairman of the Oklahoma County Council of Defense, Negro Division, and served throughout the conflict. In his latter years he spent time lecturing to many groups. Some of his lectures were published, such as his key-note speech at the National Negro Democratic Association in Chicago, 1940 (in the *Congressional Record*), his address before the Negro land-grant college presidents, also in 1940, and the keynote address before the thirty-second annual session of the NAACP in 1941 at Houston, Tex.

Of all the experiences of his journalistic career, Roscoe Dunjee said, "I think the most exciting . . . was when I went to the lynching scene of George Hughes at Sherman, Texas, and later to the scene of the lynching of Henry Arge, Negro half-wit of Chickasha, Oklahoma. In the latter incident, I took two white men with me and they were slammed in jail on investigation charges. I later, that same day, came back to Oklahoma City, took Moman Pruitt, noted criminal lawyer, back to Chickasha and the night of the same Sunday these white men incarcerated were released."

From 1951 to 1954 Roscoe Dunjee served as president of the National Negro Business League. In 1955 he retired, and his friends and associates held a testimonial dinner in his honor and gave him an expense-paid trip to West Africa. He served as a consultant and lecturer to journalistic and human rights groups until his failing health curtailed his activities from 1961 until his death on March 1, 1965.

The *Black Dispatch* newspaper which he published for fifty years (1915–1965) reflected the life and courage of its editor, and was well known for its editorials. A tireless worker for civil rights, Roscoe Dunjee was involved in practically every such issue in the state of Oklahoma. In 1969 Dunjee was inducted into the Oklahoma Journalists Hall of Fame at Central State University.

Dunjee is best reflected in his writings, especially in the *Black Dispatch,* copies of which are on microfilm in the Oklahoma Historical Society, Oklahoma City. Kaye M. Leall's *Black History in Oklahoma: A Resource Book* (1971) has a brief biographical sketch and a photograph. — J. REUBEN SHEELER

DUNN, OSCAR JAMES (c. 1821–1871), the first Negro lieutenant-governor in the United States. Although he was one of the first Negroes to be elected to a high executive position, details about his ancestry and early life are obscure. Dunn was born in Louisiana, and most accounts say that he was born a slave and that he "emancipated" himself by running away when a boy. However, it is probable that he was the child of a free Negro woman and hence was freeborn. The identity of his father is unknown. The child took the name of Dunn from a mulatto whose wife his mother subsequently became.

His mother kept a lodging house in New Orleans where most of the residents were actors and actresses and musicians. Although the boy had no formal schooling, he apparently learned to read and write and some of the elements of elocution from these theatrical folk. From them he also gained some musical training, becoming a skillful violin player. At an early age he was apprenticed to learn the plasterer's trade, but he appears to have largely abandoned this occupation to become a music teacher, a vocation which he followed until the Civil War. He had a comfortable income and was regarded as one of the leading Negroes in New Orleans.

When Gen. Benjamin F. Butler entered New Orleans, Dunn enlisted in the first regiment of Negro troops raised in Louisiana. He attained a captaincy, the highest rank then open to a Negro. He resigned his commission when an incompetent white was promoted over him to the rank of major. During the war years he began to be active in politics at a time when the Republican party was first being formed in Louisiana. He was appointed by Gen. Phil H. Sheridan as a member of the City Council of New Orleans. In this position he learned more of politics and showed an understanding of civic needs and an interest in public questions which were not always racial in character.

After the adoption of a new state constitution, Henry Clay Warmoth, a youthful white carpetbagger, was elected governor and Dunn was elected lieutenant-governor in April 1868. In this office, which included the task of presiding over the state Senate, Dunn proved to be effective and dignified, and gained a reputation as an eloquent speaker. In contrast to some of his more flamboyant contemporaries, Dunn appears to have been a modest man who did not seek publicity. He was regarded as incorruptible even by his political enemies. During the time he was lieutenant-governor he also served as president of the Board of Police Commissioners of New Orleans. He also worked for the racial integration of the New Orleans public schools in accordance with the provisions of the 1868 constitution. He was a member of the Board of Trustees of Straight University and was Grand Master of the all-Negro Free and Accepted Masons of Louisiana.

He soon became involved in bitter factional strife among Louisiana Republicans. He was a leader in the "customshouse group," which included numerous federal appointees and had the support of President Grant. In the early stages of the internal feuds in the Republican party, P. B. S. Pinchback, the most conspicuous colored politician in Louisiana in this period, was identified with the faction which Dunn opposed. Pinchback continued for a time to cooperate with Warmoth while Dunn was increasingly alienated from him. In furthering his own political ambitions, Warmoth was making a bid for the support of white Democrats. Dunn accused the governor of planning to sell out the interests of the recently enfranchised Negro voters. In the contest Dunn had widespread popular support not only because he championed the rights of Negroes, but because he was a native Louisianan, whereas Warmoth was an outsider. Dunn was also considered, even by whites, as being more honest than the governor.

At the Republican State Convention which met on Aug. 9, 1870, Dunn had the support of a majority of the delegates and was elected presiding officer in a contest with Warmoth. It appeared that he was in a strong position to become the Republican nominee for the governorship in 1872 and perhaps, after that, a U.S. senator. However, his promising career was cut short by his sudden death on Nov. 22, 1871. His death, following a violent illness of only two days, aroused speculation that he might have been a victim of poisoning, although no evidence to confirm this was ever pro-

duced. His untimely end weakened the Republican party and its prospects in Louisiana. He was buried in a private vault in New Orleans, following the established Masonic ritual. Among the pallbearers was T. Morris Chester. Since the body was not exhumed, the truth about the cause of his death is not known.

There is no adequate study of Dunn. An account of his life, probably not entirely accurate, by A. E. Perkins, "James Henri Burch and Oscar James Dunn in Louisiana" (*JNH*, 1943, pp. 321–34), after detailed examination concluded that only circumstantial evidence supported the belief that he had been poisoned. See also Marcus B. Christian's article "The Theory of the Poisoning of Oscar J. Dunn" (*Phylon* 6 [Third Quarter 1945]: 254–66). — EMMA LOU THORNBROUGH

DURHAM [DERHAM], JAMES (1762– ?), physician. The earliest known Negro physician in the United States, James Durham was born a slave on May 1, 1762, in Philadelphia, Pa. Very little is known about Durham's earliest masters except that they taught him the fundamentals of reading and writing as well as a basic knowledge of religious teachings. While Durham was still quite young he became the property of John Kearsley, Jr., a prominent Philadelphia physician, who openly espoused the British cause during the period preceding the Revolutionary crisis. Kearsley employed Durham in the compounding of medicines and in the performance of simple medical duties. At the time of Kearsley's death in 1772 Durham became the property of Gregory West, who had served as an apothecary with the British forces in America.

At the close of the war James Durham became the slave of Roberto Dow, a Scottish physician who had resided in New Orleans since about 1773. Dow employed Durham in the performance of many medical services. On April 2, 1783, Dr. Dow granted Durham his freedom for the sum of 500 pesos.

In 1788 while he was in Philadelphia, Durham made the acquaintance of Benjamin Rush, prominent physician. After his meeting with Durham, Rush wrote a lengthy letter to the Pennsylvania Abolition Society describing Durham's medical abilities. In the letter (later published in the *American Museum,* Jan. 1789), Rush maintained that Durham was well acquainted with the method of treating diseases which were prevalent in the New Orleans area. Moreover, Rush found that the Negro physician was quite familiar with the use of various drugs. He noted that "I expected to have suggested some new medicines but he suggested many more to me." Finally, Rush noted that Durham was fluent in Spanish and French and that he derived approximately $3000 annually from his medical practice. While in Philadelphia, Durham also made the acquaintance of Drs. Redman, Shippen, and Jones, all prominent members of Philadelphia's medical community.

By 1789 Durham had returned to New Orleans and had resumed his medical practice. That same year he sent Rush a paper describing his method for treating putrid sore throat (diphtheria). He claimed that he had found the best method for treating the disease in the New Orleans area. On Aug. 4, 1789, Rush read Durham's paper, "An Account of the Putrid Sore Throat at

New Orleans,'' before the College of Physicians of Philadelphia.

Durham's knowledge of medicine extended beyond his ability to treat only persons stricken with diphtheria. About 1796, when a serious yellow fever epidemic raged in New Orleans, Durham related that of the fifty yellow fever victims who sought his attention only six died and that he lost fewer patients than all the other doctors in the city. During another serious yellow fever epidemic around 1798 in which many persons died, Durham stated that he lost only eleven of the sixty-four patients whom he treated for the disease. He had been successful by combatting the disease with a "decoction of garden sorell and sugar.''

On Aug. 14, 1801, James Durham's medical practice was officially restricted by the commissioners of the Cabildo (city council). They felt that it was necessary to prevent certain persons from practicing medicine in New Orleans since they were not licensed physicians with medical degrees. James Durham was among those persons cited, since he was practicing without a formal medical degree. The commissioners, however, stated that they would permit Durham to treat only diseases of the throat. On Aug. 29, 1801, the commissioners once again warned the unlicensed physicians, including Durham, that they must either abandon their medical practices or be punished.

There is evidence, however, that Durham practiced medicine briefly after 1801. Moreover, this practice was not limited to diseases of the throat. In 1802 he requested that Benjamin Rush send him a pamphlet on kine pock (cowpox) in order that he might determine whether or not they were experiencing a smallpox epidemic in New Orleans. It is almost impossible to determine if James Durham practiced medicine in New Orleans after 1802. His correspondence to Benjamin Rush apparently ceased and his name does not appear in the New Orleans *City Directory* of 1805 as either a resident or a physician. Evidence exists, however, to show that in May 1800 Durham asked Rush if he might be able to earn a living in Philadelphia. He stated that he wished to leave New Orleans. There is no concrete proof that he moved to Philadelphia.

While his name is generally spelled Derham, he used Durham in his letter to Rush.

In addition to Rush's letter in the *American Museum,* the brief sketches in Wilson Armistead's *A Tribute for the Negro* . . . (1848), Lydia Maria Child's *An Appeal* . . . (1833), and Abigail Field Mott's *Biographical Sketches* . . . (1826), pp. 179–88), are the principal sources. — BETTY L. PLUMMER

DURHAM, JOHN STEPHENS (1861–1919), diplomat, lawyer, and journalist. The son of Samuel and Elizabeth Stephens Durham, he was born in Philadelphia on July 18, 1861. The family had been well known in this area for several generations, two of his uncles, Clayton and Jeremiah Durham, having been noted clergymen who helped Bishop Richard Allen found the African Methodist Episcopal (A.M.E.) church in 1816. A mulatto who could have passed for white, Durham studied in the Philadelphia public schools and graduated from the Institute for Colored Youth there in 1876. For five years

he taught in Delaware, New Jersey, and Pennsylvania to help support his widowed mother and family. Then in 1881 he entered Towne Scientific College, a branch of the University of Pennsylvania, graduating with a civil engineering degree in 1888. He decided against pursuing a career in engineering, and studied law privately. During that period he worked as a night superintendent at the Philadelphia post office.

Editor of the university *Journal* during his college days, Durham also worked as a reporter with the *Philadelphia Times.* Later he joined the staff of the *Evening Bulletin,* one of the principal daily newspapers of that time. He received acclaim for his articles on the socioeconomic problems of the colored people and for others on international problems. These led to his appointment as assistant editor of the *Bulletin,* which was backing the Republican party. A Republican, and fluent in French and Spanish, he aspired to a diplomatic career and requested of Secretary of State James Blaine appointment to the post of U.S. consul in the Dominican Republic. Backed by Philadelphia leaders, he was appointed to the post by Pres. Benjamin Harrison on May 20, 1890.

At that time although two independent countries— Haiti and the Dominican Republic—shared the same island, the United States sent only one diplomatic representative to the two. The minister-in-residence was the famous Frederick Douglass, who had become embroiled in an attempt by certain United States interests to purchase Môle St. Nicolas in Haiti and Samaná Bay in the Dominican Republic. Unwilling to become the agent responsible for an action detrimental to Haiti, Douglass resigned in 1891 and was replaced by Durham as minister-in-residence and consul-general to Haiti and chargé d'affaires in the Dominican Republic. Durham was probably more acceptable to Admiral Bancroft Gherardi and shipping magnate William P. Clyde than Douglass had been. During 1891–1892 Durham negotiated with the dictator president Ulises Heureaux of the Dominican Republic for the leasing of Samaná Bay. Although Congress appropriated $250,000 for the first payment, opposition among Dominicans brought the agreement to an end.

The atmosphere, especially in Haiti, was tense and mistrust was high. As a result serious diplomatic activity was difficult. However, Durham, through negotiation, was able to effect indemnity to American citizens who had suffered losses or had had property and goods seized during uprisings in Haiti. When Grover Cleveland became president for the second time in 1893, Durham, as is the custom, tendered his resignation, which was accepted in September of that year.

He returned to Philadelphia and was admitted to the bar. Much in demand as a speaker, he delivered a series of six lectures at Hampton and Tuskegee Institutes. They were later condensed and published under the title *To Teach the Negro History (A Suggestion)* (1897). During this period he also managed a sugar refinery at San Pedro de Macorís in the Dominican Republic. In 1902 he was appointed assistant attorney with the Spanish Treaty Claims Commission in Cuba, remaining in that post until 1905. While there he was named with J. Martin Miller of the Navy Department to evaluate

Conference (1838) in Indianapolis, Early seemed not to encounter much opposition. But in New Orleans where he established a church for free people of color in 1842 (he had presumably become free in Iowa or Illinois), meetings could be held only between sunrise and sunset. Both bond and free met surreptitiously in private homes. Later generations could not "form the least conception of the terrors and disquietudes which the colored people experienced who lived in the slave holding states." Since members of churches called them abolition churches, they were suspected of engaging in Underground Railroad activities. About 1851 he began itinerant work in Jefferson City and St. Joseph, Mo., traveling hundreds of miles on horseback. On the eve of the Civil War, it was dangerous for a Negro to travel in the southern and western states, even with a pass from the chief military officers of the district. In the Shawneetown Circuit of Illinois (1861) he escaped from a mob who thought him a fugitive slave, through the intervention of a friendly magistrate. In addition, cholera epidemics claimed the lives of many church members, in St. Louis in 1866.

His career documents the attendance of ministers at annual conferences and the quadrennial General Conference of the A.M.E. church and the numerous "stations" to which he was assigned, especially in Tennessee. Early almost invariably had to repair buildings, install gas, organize choirs, pay off indebtedness, and calm dissenters. By 1867 in the larger cities "a higher form of church ordinances was developed, and refinement and elegance was attendant in the house of God. . . . The A.M.E. church, as usual, seemed to be the first to lay hold of necessary reforms such as monthly communions, general speaking meetings, the introduction of choirs and organs, lighting their churches with gas, holding religious concerts and Sabbath school exhibitions, and other social gatherings which always accompany an exalted Christianity." At the General Conference in Nashville (May 1872) the "Dollar Money System" went into effect as a law "for all time thereafter." One bishop "recalled the days when he forded rivers, climbed mountains, crossed forests, encountered wild beasts, and faced and fought vindictive mobs, and was called before courts of justice to establish the Church he so much loved."

By 1873 a course of study was introduced for those who wished to join the itinerary on which they had to pass an examination before being admitted. The church also established literary societies, missionary societies, emphasized temperance, especially for ministers, gave much-needed support to such church-affiliated schools, as Wilberforce University, and encouraged subscriptions to the church's organ, the *Christian Recorder*. By 1885 ministers were receiving a competency sufficient to meet all necessary expenses and supply all their needs.

Early was married twice. On June 6, 1843, he married Louisa Carter who bore him eight children, four of whom reached the age of maturity. After her death in 1862, he married in 1867 Sarah J. Woodson of Berlin, Ohio. She was the author of *Life and Labors of Rev. Jordan W. Early* (1894), the source of this biography.

— RAYFORD W. LOGAN

ELDRIDGE, ELLEANOR (1784–1845?), skilled servant and businesswoman. Born in Warwick, R.I., on March 27, 1784, she believed that her paternal grandfather had been born in Zaïre (the ancient and present name of the former Belgian Congo) and had been brought to America on a slave ship. One of his sons, Robin, was Elleanor's father. He and his two brothers had fought in the American Revolution and been promised two hundred acres of land apiece in the Mohawk Valley. Since they received pay in the almost worthless Continental currency, they had been unable to take possession of the land. It is not clear how he was able to purchase a lot and a house in Warwick, where he settled with his wife, Harriet Prophet, whom he had married before entering military service. Elleanor was the last of seven successive daughters, only five of whom lived to mature age.

Elleanor's maternal grandmother was Mary Fuller, a native Indian. By the sale of a part of the land owned by the Fullers, she purchased her slave husband Thomas. She was given her name by Elleanor Baker, daughter of Joseph Baker of Warwick. Despite the opposition of her father, Elleanor began work at an early age washing clothes for the Baker family at twenty-five cents a week. During nearly six years with the family, she became skilled in spinning, plain and ornamental weaving, and arithmetic. From age seventeen to twenty-four she had charge of the dairy farm of Capt. Benjamin Greene at Warwick Neck. The cheeses she made were recognized as of "premium" quality.

Upon the death of her father when she was nineteen, she went 180 miles to Adams, Mass., where her mother's only sister helped her obtain letters of administration for her late father's estate. She returned home, had the estate settled, and returned to work for Captain Greene. On his death in 1812 she went back to Adams where she lived with her sister Lettise, who had been appointed by the Probate Court as guardian for the younger children. The sisters entered into a miscellaneous business of weaving, washing, and soap boiling which enabled Elleanor to purchase a lot and build a house which she rented for $40 a year. After three years she went to live with another sister in Providence, where she remained for most of some twenty years.

By 1822 she had saved enough from her business of whitewashing, papering, and painting, and during the winter months from her wages in private families, hotels, and boarding houses, to save $600. She paid $100 in silver for a lot and began building a house which cost $1700. After this was completed, she built an addition on the east side for herself and one on the west side for an additional tenant. Wishing to purchase two other lots, she borrowed $240 at 10 percent, the note to be renewed annually. She agreed also to purchase another house for $2000 with a down payment of $500, the balance of $1500 to be paid in four years.

While she was on her way to visit her relatives in Adams, it was reported that she had died. The holder of the note for $240 filed an attachment to her property. She promised to pay $100 within a specified time. Because of a cholera epidemic she left for Pomfret, Conn., after caring for many of the sick as nurse and attendant. Before she left, she paid all that was due on the mortgage but not on the $240 note which was to be renewed as long as she paid the interest.

When she returned to Providence, all her property, valued at $4000 had been sold to pay the note of $240. The sale at auction had not been legally advertised and she had not been notified. On the advice of friends she entered a suit for "Trespass and Ejectment" before the Court of Common Pleas in January 1837. Since there was no evidence of advertisement, Elleanor Elldridge was entitled to recover her property after payment of $2700. When her *Memoirs* were first published in 1838, the author (who assisted her in the lawsuit) stated in the Preface: "It is believed that the colored people, generally, will be proud to assist in sustaining one who is both an honor and an ornament to their race" (p. 4). White friends were already assisting. Since a second edition was published in 1845, it may be conjectured that the sum had not been paid. Information about Elleanor Eldridge's death is not available. There were probably no children. The beautiful Elleanor had a very romantic affair with a "cousin" Christopher which seems not to have been consummated.

The *Memoirs of Elleanor Eldridge* was written by Frances Harriet Whipple Greene McDougall (1805–1878). The first edition was published in 1838 in Providence by B. T. Albro, Printer, and the second in 1845. It may be presumed that she was related to Captain Greene. Although stilted in style and abundantly sympathetic to Elleanor Eldridge, the *Memoirs* are probably factually accurate. It is one of the very few narratives of free Negroes. — RAYFORD W. LOGAN

ELLIOTT, ROBERT BROWN (1842–1884), politician, editor, and lawyer. The accepted biographical facts concerning Elliott have come under new scrutiny and appear to be partially if not wholly false. The conventional account stated that he was born in Boston, educated first in Jamaica and then in England where he allegedly graduated from Eton College in 1852. He then read law with a famous barrister before returning to the United States to join the Union Army. However, present-day authorities at Eton deny that Elliott or anyone who fit his description ever attended their college. Furthermore, no record of his birth can be found in Boston, nor is he included in any of several accounts of prominent Negroes living in Boston prior to the Civil War, nor does his name appear on any of the generally complete rosters of colored regiments in the Union Army.

Among conflicting contemporary references to Elliott's antecedents, one brief note in the *Charlestown* (Mass.) *Chronicle* (Feb. 18, 1881) offers the most plausible explanation of his background: Elliott was born and educated in Liverpool, England, where he also learned the printer's trade. He served in the British navy, traveled extensively, and sometime in 1867 arrived in Boston, worked as a typesetter, quickly became a popular member of the "colored literary society," married a handsome mulatto, and then after a few months moved to South Carolina to become an editor of the Republican *South Carolina Leader,* one of the early newspapers published by Negroes. His arrival in South Carolina coincided with the beginning of Reconstruction. Negroes and whites alike were soon to elect

delegates to a state constitutional convention. Along with a handful of other educated Negroes, the brilliant young Elliott was a natural candidate. There is, however, a strong probability that he was not yet an American citizen and therefore not eligible to be elected to any public office. Given this timing and the importance of being a delegate to the constitutional convention, it is not unreasonable to assume that Elliott may have simply conferred citizenship upon himself, invented his Boston birthplace, and added the Eton College and other related biographical details to account for the fact that there were no traces of his antecedents anywhere in the United States until his twenty-fifth year.

At the 1868 constitutional convention where there were forty-five white and seventy-eight Negro delegates, Elliott emerged as a forceful and remarkably prescient leader. He vigorously espoused compulsory education for all children between the ages of six and sixteen, but fought against a poll tax to pay for the cost of this public education because he rightly foresaw it was a measure which could someday be used to disfranchise the Negro. For the same reason he successfully persuaded the convention to adopt universal manhood suffrage as opposed to suffrage qualified by any form of literacy test.

Elected to the state House of Representatives, he played a dynamic role in the Negro-dominated General Assembly; in addition he read law intensively for six months, was admitted to the South Carolina bar in September 1868, and opened the first of his four law offices. In March 1869 he was appointed assistant adjutant-general of the state, in which capacity he was charged with forming and maintaining a state militia (often called the Black Militia) to protect white and black citizens alike from the murderous, fast-growing Ku Klux Klan.

Elliott's belief in the Republican party as the savior and defender of his race was fundamental; as a strong, dedicated party man he served throughout his public career as chairman of the Republican state executive committee.

In 1870, he was elected (along with three other Negroes and one white man from South Carolina) to the U.S. House of Representatives. As a member of the 42nd Congress he made an important speech against an amnesty bill to remove political disabilities from Confederates, and another in support of a proposed bill to punish the Ku Klux Klan and protect Negroes by federal intervention.

In 1873, having lost his bid for the U.S. Senate, he returned to the House of Representatives; on Jan. 6, 1874 he made a brilliant and justly celebrated speech in favor of the Civil Rights Bill, debating and, by all accounts, easily besting Alexander S. Stephens, the ex-vice-president of the Confederacy. A few months later Elliott again won national acclaim for his eulogy of Charles Sumner, delivered at a memorial service in Faneuil Hall, Boston.

At the pinnacle of his career Elliot suddenly resigned from Congress and returned to South Carolina to try to rid the state of the widespread corruption which he recognized was being blamed (often unjustly) on the Negro majority. He became speaker of the House, a position of great influence; unfortunately his efforts were largely frustrated by his conflict with the white Republican governor, Daniel H. Chamberlain, who was also dedicated to reform but whom Elliott mistrusted because of his affinity for the old-line Democrats, the Bourbons, who were determined to degrade the Negro and to return the white man's government to the state. Eventually these white supremacists prevailed.

In the much-contested election of 1876 Elliott was elected attorney-general, but after months of conflict was ousted from office along with all other Republican officeholders when Pres. Rutherford B. Hayes, in accordance with the Compromise of 1877, removed federal troops from South Carolina and Louisiana and agreed to let the southern whites "handle the Negro problem." Thus Reconstruction came virtually to a tragic end.

After his fall from high office Elliott managed to secure a post as a treasury agent. Against increasing odds he continued to try to hold together the sagging state Republican party, but he could not stem the political tide that was leading his race almost to political extinction in the South. Nor could he rise above his own declining fortunes. He died of a final bout of malarial fever, obscure and penniless, survived by his wife Grace, at the age of forty-two.

A biography of Elliott, *The Glorious Failure: Black Congressman Robert Brown Elliott and the Reconstruction in South Carolina* by Peggy Lamson, was published in 1973. A chapter on him is in *American Black Congressmen* by Maurine Christopher (1971).

— PEGGY LAMSON

ELLIS, GEORGE WASHINGTON (1875–1919), lawyer, sociologist, diplomat, and author. Born in Weston, Platte County, Mo., he was the son of George and Amanda Jane (Drace) Ellis. After studying in the Weston elementary schools and the high school in Atchison, Kans., he received his LL.B. degree from the University of Kansas (1893) upon completion of the two-year curriculum and was admitted to the Kansas bar. From 1893 to 1897 he practiced law in Kansas to defray the expenses of four years in the university's collegiate department, receiving his B.A. in 1897. In that same year he moved to New York City where he took a two-year course in the Gunton Institute of Economics and Sociology. After he passed the examination of the U.S. Census Board in 1899, he received an appointment in the Census Division of the Department of the Interior at Washington, D.C., where he remained two years. Here his spare moments were spent in "postgraduate" work in philosophy and psychology in the School of Pedagogy at Howard University. In the routine of his departmental duties he attracted the attention of President Roosevelt, upon whose nomination, confirmed by the Senate, he was in 1902 appointed secretary of the U.S. legation in the Republic of Liberia. He was induced to accept this position chiefly because of the opportunity it afforded him to study the social conditions of the Negro in Africa, a subject in which he had become intensely interested.

The next eight years he spent in Liberia, with Monrovia as his headquarters, but under instructions from Washington he undertook numerous expeditions into the hinterland for the purpose of investigating and reporting on the various tribes of the interior. He studied their ethnological, linguistic, sociological, and economic characteristics, and sent an extensive collection of ethnological specimens to the National Museum in Washington, D.C., after his return.

Although plagued with poor health and numerous frustrations throughout the eight years he spent on the West African coast, Ellis managed to perform his duties as secretary of the Liberian legation remarkably well— so well, in fact, that his reports aided the Department of State in the formation of its policies toward Liberia. Ellis's most important contributions were reports on the problems of Negro migration to Liberia, intertribal wars and the African Chiefs' Peace Conference, and the history of the Anglo- and Franco-Liberian boundary disputes. Primarily through his own efforts Ellis helped to buttress the confidence of the Liberian government in the United States' desire to aid the black republic. However, because Ellis's goals were commensurate with his skills and education, he found his ambitions thwarted by the Department of State's policy of restricting the number of Negroes assigned to diplomatic posts. Although Ellis spent eight years in Liberia, he never rose above the level of legation secretary.

On the nomination of Sir Harry H. Johnson and Dr. J. Scott Ketlie he was elected a fellow of the Royal Geographical Society of Great Britain. He married (Jan. 27, 1906) Clavender L. Sherman, daughter of Robert Sherman, a member of the Liberian government. In 1910 before leaving Liberia, Ellis was decorated knight commander of the Order of African Redemption.

He resigned in 1910 and on his return to the United States opened a law office in Chicago, where he quickly acquired a large and lucrative practice. A good lawyer and excellent speaker, he argued not only in the Illinois courts but also in the U.S. Supreme Court. In 1917 he was elected assistant corporation counsel for the city of Chicago, a position he held until his death. A strong Republican, a good campaign speaker with a thorough knowledge of political issues both national and state, he was frequently heard on the public platform, and wielded much influence in the party councils.

In spite of his legal and political activities, he continued to maintain his interest in sociological work, and wrote several books, pamphlets, and articles. His earliest and most important work was *Negro Culture in West Africa* (1914), a scholarly book which contained evidence that the Vai-speaking people of Liberia had a written language. This is all the more important because as late as 1955 Sir Philip Mitchell stated on page 12 of *Africa Today,* edited by C. Grove Haines, that "their [the indigenous Africans'] languages were unwritten." George H. T. Kimble, on the other hand, wrote in the authoritative *Tropical Africa* (1960, 2:388) that in the opinion of many Liberians, Vai "was one of the very few languages of tropical Africa to be reduced to writing before the time of the 'partition.'" But Kimble did not mention Ellis. Raymond Leslie Buell in his *The Native Problem in Africa* (1928), still considered by many Africanists as in some respects the best book on the subject, wrote: "The Vai people are apparently the only people in Africa who have developed a written language" and cited in a footnote Ellis's *Negro Culture in West Africa* (2:705 and n.2).

Then followed *The Leopard's Claw* (1917), a novel of love and adventure in the West African jungle, and *Negro Achievements in Social Progress* (1915). He was a prolific contributor to scientific and literary periodicals, his articles dealing mainly with the social institutions of the West African and American Negro. He was a contributing editor of the *Journal of Race Development* (Clark University, Worcester, Mass.), in which some of his best studies appeared.

There is no full-length biography of Ellis. His views are best revealed in his publications. His lecture, "International Law as a Factor in Social Progress," given before the Liberian National Bar Association in 1908, revealed a broad knowledge of writers on international law, the development of international pronouncements to promote humanity in war, and plans for international arbitration. In one of his more scholarly articles, "Political Institutions in Liberia" (*American Political Science Review* 5 [May 1911]:213–23), he deplored the country's lack of funds for social and economic development. He also contended that "American capital will find safe and lucrative investment in the development of Liberian natural resources, in which alone lay the ultimate and future foundations of the Liberian state."

It is his articles in the *Journal of Race Development* (forerunner of the *Journal of International Relations* and of *Foreign Affairs*), of which he was a contributing editor (1910–1919), that he best revealed his thinking. His first article (Oct. 1913), "Negro Social Institutions in West Africa," dealt primarily with the Vai, as in his *Negro Culture in West Africa.* "Sociological Appraisement of Liberian Resources" (April 1915) gave exaggerated praise to Liberia as a "Negro democracy"; it optimistically referred to the country as a source of diamonds but showed prescience in extolling the possibility of developing rubber. His "Political and Economic Factors of Liberian Development" in the July 1915 issue presented too roseate a picture, as had his April 1915 article.

His views on the status of the Negro in the United States were ambivalent. "The Negro in the New Democracy" (July 1916) asserted that in Chicago "we are articulating the true American ideals of equality more than other large cities." In April 1918, "The Negro and the War for Democracy" asserted that since Germany was the enemy of democracy, Negroes should remember that every shot fired against that country was a "shot fired against the enemies of democracy and justice everywhere."

But in "Psychology of American Race Prejudice" (Jan. 1915) he criticized prejudice against "Asiatics and blacks," and voiced stronger denunciation in "Psychic Factors in the New American Race Situation" (April 1917). The race question, he wrote, was "like a cancer . . . [which] gnawed at the very vitals of American ideals and institutions." After accusing the South of having nullified the equal protection clause of the Fourteenth Amendment, he posed the trenchant question: "Shall we have the New Slavery founded on race and color or shall we have the New Democracy, where all men and races are in fact free and equal before the law." He answered his own question by asserting in "Liberia in the New Partition of Africa" (Oct. 1918) that after the war "The world will be safe for democracy, Liberia will be safe in West Africa, and the Negro will be safe in the United States."

As these brief summaries show, Ellis is a neglected writer who deserves a full-length biography.

He died after a long illness on Nov. 26, 1919, at his home, 3262 Vernon Ave., Chicago. At his bedside was his sister, Mamie E. Clark. Funeral services were held on Nov. 30 at the Institutional Church and he was buried in Oakwood Cemetery.

In addition to his writings, one should consult the short sketch by H. W. Howard Knott in *DAB* (3, Part 2:104), *Who's Who in America, 1918–1919,* and obituaries in the *New York Times* (Nov. 28, 1919, p. 13), *Chicago Daily Tribune,* (Nov. 28, 1919, p. 21), and the (Chicago) *Broad Ax* (Dec. 6, 1919, p. 2).

— JOHN E. FLEMING *and* RAYFORD W. LOGAN

EQUIANO [GUSTAVUS VASSA] (1745?–1797), author and abolitionist. Born Olaudah Equiano, the son of an East Nigerian tribal chief, probably near Onitsha, he enjoyed a childhood filled with a sense of tribal unity, made particularly happy by his keen memory and understanding. This idyll ended when he was about ten years of age and kidnapped by nearby tribesmen. He passed through several hands and experiences before being brought to white slave traders on the coast. Equiano observed a brutality toward slaves which made him despair during the voyage to the West Indies. He was taken then to Virginia, however, where he was purchased by a lieutenant in the Royal Navy, Michael Henry Pascal, and transported to England, a turn of fortune which began his education and new adventures. Pascal named him for the sixteenth-century Swedish king Gustavus Vasa. While yet on ship Vassa began to learn English, thanks to the kindness of Richard Baker, a young sailor whose death he later mourned. Following his master, he spent a number of years on ship and in ports during which he saw fighting between the British and the French in the Mediterranean and in Canada, where he witnessed the siege of Louisburgh. Meanwhile Pascal's visits to London had made Vassa a favorite of the Misses Guerin, sisters of a friend of Pascal's. They helped Vassa advance his education, and had him baptized in St. Margaret's Church, Westminster, in February 1759.

That summer he was present at a sea battle between the British and French in the Mediterranean, and performed service before and after the event. He was a steward on a number of ships, including the *Aetna* in 1761. Vassa had been promised freedom, and more than earned it; but when he asked for it in England late in 1762, Pascal was angered and sent him to the West Indies to be sold. Good fortune gave Vassa as a new master Robert King, a Philadelphia Quaker and merchant from whom he learned commercial arts and whom he served responsibly in return, traveling between Philadelphia and the West Indies. Although Quakers had discarded slavery within their sect in 1761, King required Vassa to buy his freedom through money earned. Vassa did so by patient trading during voyages in the Caribbean and on the Georgia coast. In 1766 he attained his wish, acquiring his freedom papers. Cruising the islands, collecting rum, sugar, and other goods, Vassa saw that, as limiting as were the terms of his servitude to King, numerous slaves suffered more onerous employment and masters who ranged from inhumane to inhuman. Vassa's dream of abolition was thus aroused and contributed to the inspiration which later produced his autobiography, *Interesting Narrative.*

His journeys from Philadelphia to the Caribbean were replete with adventures. He learned navigation, paying the mate of his vessel for the privilege; Vassa had it in mind that should King prove recreant to their agreement, he might seize the ship and escape. Once he found himself forced to ferry slaves—his "manacled brothers"—to slave markets. At Savannah on one occasion he was set upon by a Dr. Perkins and a ruffian in his service, and solely for reasons of malevolence beaten and left all but dead. Philadelphia, where he sold his goods to Quakers, seemed to him by comparison all but heavenly. When, later in 1785, he embarked on a ship sailing to Philadelphia, he "was very glad to see this favorite old town once more." Quaker emancipation of slaves pleased him further, as did his visit to a free school they had erected for every denomination of Negroes.

Sidney Kaplan's chapter, "Olaudah Equiano," in *The Black Presence in the Era of the American Revolution 1770–1800* (1973, p. 193), holds that Equiano's *Interesting Narrative* ranks with the autobiographies of Benjamin Franklin and Frederick Douglass in interest and execution.

There were eight British editions and one American publication in Vassa's lifetime, ten posthumously, including Dutch and German translations (Paul Edwards, ed. and abridger, *Equiano's Travels* [1967], p. xviii); see also Edward's introduction to his full reprint of the book in Colonial Historical Series (1969). Philip Curtin's *Africa Remembered* (1967) reprints a section of the *Travels,* with additional notes by G. I. Jones. Beatrice J. Fleming's and Marion J. Pryde's *Distinguished Negroes Abroad* (1946) includes a popular account of Vassa, in a book intended for high school use.

— LOUIS FILLER

ESTEBAN, [ESTEVANICO, ESTEBANILLO, ESTEBAN DE DORANTES] (? –1539), pioneer and explorer. A native of Azämor, Morocco, he was probably made captive and Christianized when King Manoel of Portugal took Azämor in 1513. It is not known how he became a slave of the Spaniard Andrés Dorantes, a member of the Spanish expedition of Pánfilo de Narváez which in 1528 attempted to conquer and settle Florida. All but four of the company succumbed to Indian attacks and fever. With Álvar Nuñez Cabeza de Vaca as commander, Dorantes, Esteban, and one other survivor made an almost unbelievable journey of eight years along the northern shores of the Gulf of Mexico, across Texas and Mexico to the Gulf of California, and finally reached Mexico City. Aided perhaps by his color, Esteban won the friendship of the many Indian tribes. He is reported to have been a kind of healer or medicine man. Viceroy Antonio de Mendozo retained Esteban to serve as guide of Fray Marcos de Niza in the search for the fabled seven cities of Cibola. On March 30, 1539, Fray Marcos sent Esteban ahead with some Indians with orders to send back crosses of lengths varying according to the importance of the information gathered. Esteban continued to lead the expedition, sending back messengers. When Fray Marcos arrived within two or three days' march of Cibola, an Indian brought back word that Esteban had been killed.

Esteban's life and death constitute one of the earliest controversies in the history of what is now the United States and Mexico. Scholars disagree about the routes the four survivors followed from Florida to Mexico, and the 1539 expedition. There is agreement, however, that Esteban reached the Zuni region of western New Mexico and discovered the Hawikuh, the first of the Seven Cities of Cibola. The major controversy concerns his "race." Some writers still insist that he was of "Hamitic" stock and therefore not a Negro. This writer, after analysis of sixteenth-century accounts in Spanish, Portuguese, French, German, and English, concluded that these writers considered Esteban a Negro ("Éstevanico, Negro Discoverer of the Southwest," *Phylon* [1940], pp. 305–14). Carroll L. Riley, professor and director of the University Museum, Southern Illinois University at Carbondale, in a recent analysis of the controversy, concluded that Esteban was probably "Black in the sense that we would use the word in modern America. . . . Actually, in modern generic terms I suspect that Esteban was very mixed, as seemed to have been the case with many of these northwest African peoples— but the Spanish insistence on using the word *negro* for him suggests that this mixture must have been well tipped phenotypically on the Negro side" (Riley to Eleanor B. Adams, Feb. 8, 1974).

Some of the comments about Esteban tend to emphasize so-called Negro characteristics. He was arrogant, wore braclets and anklets of bells and feathers, had two greyhounds following him and Indian bearers carrying the loot he had accumulated. The cause of his death is frequently attributed to his insatiable lust for Indian women. Finally, his name is frequently omitted in discussion of the influence of the Niza expedition or the Coronado expedition (1540–1542) which entered the region now known as Arizona, New Mexico, Colorado, Texas, Oklahoma, and Kansas. A final footnote to the career of Esteban is the conclusion that the descriptions of "Cibola" were vastly exaggerated.

The scholarly article "Blacks in the Early Southwest" (*Ethnohistory,* Summer 1972, pp. 247–60), by Carroll L. Riley, discusses Esteban's "race," summarizes some contemporary accounts, and gives a comprehensive bibliography. See also Rayford W. Logan's "Estevanico, Negro Discoverer of the Southwest, A Critical Re-Examination" (*Phylon,* 1940, pp. 305–14) and Richard Robert Wright's "Negro Companions of the Spanish Explorers" (*Phylon,* 1941, pp. 325–33). John Upton Terrell's *Esteban the Black* (1968) contains a bibliography (pp. 147–51). Elizabeth Shepherd's *The Discoveries of Esteban the Black* (1970) has photographs, prints, and maps. — RAYFORD W. LOGAN

EUROPE, JAMES REESE (1881–1919), band leader, composer, violinist, and pianist. He was born in Mobile, Ala., the son of Henry and Lorraine (Saxon) Europe. His family moved to Washington, D.C., where James studied the violin with Enrico Hurlei, assistant director of the U.S. Marine Corps Band. At the age of fourteen James entered a musical contest in which he was defeated by his sister Mary. He also studied theory and instrumentation under Hans Hanke, formerly of the Leipzig Conservatory of Music, and Harry T. Burleigh. In the early 1900s he and another musician, Ford Dabney, moved to New York City where they met other musicians and composers at a hotel run by a colored man, Jimmie Marshall, on West 53rd Street. He found work in various musical shows and in 1906 was the musical director of *The Shoofly Regiment,* a successful production of Bob Cole and J. Rosamond Johnson. Four years later Europe organized the Clef Club, a union comprising many of the best Negro musicians in New York City. This launched him upon a spectacular career in New York and as a lieutenant and director of one of the most famous bands in Europe during World War I. After a triumphal return to New York on Feb. 12, 1919, his dazzling career came to an abrupt end later in the year when, after a concert in Mechanics Hall, Boston, he was stabbed to death by Herbert Wright, a drummer in his band. Europe was buried with full military honors in Arlington National Cemetery.

Europe's Clef Club had its own building, which served as a booking office where orchestras of all sizes and types could be hired virtually day and night. The Clef Club venture was such a success that in 1912 Europe took an orchestra of over 125 Negro musicians to Carnegie Hall. Nothing quite like that had occurred before in New York's musical life, and although critical reactions were mixed, Europe's fame spread throughout the city. Moreover, Europe had stormed a bastion of the white musical establishment and made many members of New York's cultural elite aware of Negro music for the first time. A "Negro Symphony," as it was called, playing in Carnegie Hall—that was a concept and setting that could hardly be disparaged as "primitive" or "lowdown."

With the increased popularity of social dancing in the early teens of the century, Europe established another organization, the Tempo Club, this time offering dance orchestras for hire. This led in 1914 to an association with the famous white dance team of Vernon and Irene Castle. Europe composed new dances for them—notably the turkey trot, the foxtrot, the "Castle Walk," and the "Castle House Walk"—and supplied orchestras for the Castle's dance salons, *thés dansants,* and tours. In late 1914 Europe was offered a Victor recording contract, one of the very first offered a Negro musician.

As a first lieutenant in the 15th New York National Guard Regiment, Europe suffered indignities in the United States.

While the 369th was stationed at Spartanburg, S.C., he was given credit for quelling a riot in late October 1917 after a white man had brutally beaten Drum-Major Noble Sissle.

But he won spectacular fame in Europe. A line officer —army bands at that time were under the command of a band sergeant (Eugene F. Mikell)—he had built the band instrument by instrument and later conducted it on a tour of duty in France. Soon after the arrival of the 15th Regiment at Saint-Nazaire, General Pershing ordered the band detached to entertain troops in leave areas. After playing in several cities and towns, the band arrived at Aix-les-Bains on Feb. 15, 1918. It played not only for troops but also to enthusiastic townspeople there and in nearby Chambéry, the rest station for Negro troops. The band left on March 17 to rejoin the regiment, newly named the 369th, at the front near Givry-en-Argonne. In early September 1918 the band was ordered to Paris for a week of concert duty. It played on Christmas day near Belfort and at Brest on the eve of departure from France (Jan. 31, 1919).

The 369th Infantry Regiment, with Europe and his band of sixty pieces of brass and reed, and a field music section of thirty trumpets and drums at the head, was the first unit of troops to march through the nearly completed Victory Arch in New York City, erected by the city at Madison Square Park on Fifth Avenue and 25th Street. To the surprise of many, "there was no prancing, no showing of teeth, no swank; they marched with a steady stride, and from their battered tin hats eyes that had looked straight at death were kept to the front" (James Weldon Johnson, *Black Manhattan* [1930], p. 236). The regiment continued north to Harlem where it disbanded.

Europe's significance to the musical life of America, and particularly to achievements in Afro-American music, has been unduly neglected by historians. Jazz cognoscenti have overlooked him under the mistaken impression that Europe had no relationship to jazz. White and/or "serious music" historians have disregarded Europe because he was considered no more than a popular entertainer. Thus he has almost always fallen between the proverbial two stools.

Through his Clef and Tempo Club leadership, however, he was the first to bring prestige and some degree of professional order to Negro musicians' lives in New York. Moreover, he established his "symphony" orchestras without compromising the essential character of Negro music. He was remarkably lucid and unequivocal on this question: "We colored people have our own music, that is the product of our souls. It's been created by the sufferings and miseries of our race. Some of the melodies we play were made up by slaves, and others were handed down from the days before we left Africa. We have developed a kind of symphony music that lends itself to the playing of the peculiar compositions of our race" (a newspaper interview quoted in Samuel B. Charters and Leonard Kunstadt, *Jazz: A History of the New York Scene,* 1962).

When Europe turned from this "symphony music" to a frankly more popular dance music (in association with the Castles), he was making a decision in response to a dilemma which Negro musicians had always faced (and still do to some extent today): trained as a "serious" musician, should he pursue a career in "classical" music, in the process compromising or abdicating his Afro-American heritage and risking the disfavor of the public by playing music that Negroes were not expected to touch; or should he turn to a career as a "popular entertainer," in accordance with the role the public expected Negro musicians to perform. Europe chose the latter, bringing to his endeavor not only the skills of his earlier training, but a high sense of integrity regarding the role that Afro-American musical elements played in his music. By these means Europe developed a musical style which exhibited an extraordinary rhythmic excitement and exuberance. It is no wonder that Europe enjoyed a phenomenal success. Indeed, his "syncopated music" almost singlehandedly influenced the musical tastes, the social and leisure life of virtually an entire generation of Americans. The electrifying momentum and rough excitement of Europe's style can fortunately still be heard on his recordings (for Victor and Pathé) which, although hard to find, are worth the search.

Europe's vision of music drew from both his "classical" training and his own ancestral heritage. In both his Society Orchestra and the Hell Fighters Band, he demanded (and got) from his musicians the precision and control associated with "strictly written" music, combined with a new improvisatory freedom and directness. Already present in the best of ragtime, Europe's translation of these elements to the orchestra and the band multiplied the potential musical impact. Symptomatic of the sense of abandon such music could generate are the "breaks" taken by the entire clarinet section of the Hell Fighters Band in Europe's recordings of "That's Got 'Em" and "Clarinet Marmelade."

Europe was, along with "Jelly Roll" Morton, the most important figure in the prehistory of jazz. And like Morton he added new rhythmic dimensions to ragtime and prepared the way, especially in New York and on the East Coast, for the full emergence of jazz. By the end of his life he was enjoying a popular success which can only be described as phenomenal and which was unequalled by any Negro up to that time.

Had he lived, he would have undoubtedly achieved even greater worldwide success and might have gone on to make a counterpart to Morton's Red Hot Peppers or Armstrong's Hot Five recordings. Failing that, he nevertheless was a figure of major significance, for he brought a new dignity to Negro musicians. And as the leader of a kind of Negro musical avant-garde, he gave a new thrust to the development of Afro-American music. He was the real initiator of the Jazz Age and a mentor of countless numbers of Jazz Age musicians.

Europe died in a Boston hospital on May 9, 1919. Funeral services, attended by John Wanamaker, Sr., Maj. Hamilton Fish, Jr., members of the Hell Fighters Band and of the 369th Infantry, of the Hayward Unit of the National League for Womens Service, Masons and Elks, were held at St. Mark's M. E. Church, New York City, on May 13. Harry T. Burleigh sang "Victory." Interment with full military honors was in Arlington National Cemetery. He was survived by his widow, Mrs. Willie Europe, a mother, sister, brother, and other relatives whose names were not given in the *New York Age,* (May 17, 1919, pp. 1 and 6). It is known, however, that his sister, Mary Europe, taught music in the public schools of Washington, D.C.

For Europe's career and significance in the early 1900s, see James Weldon Johnson's *Black Manhattan*

(1930, esp. pp. 119–24). Photographs of the Clef Club Band, Europe conducting (1914); the Clef Club Orchestra (1915); a program of the Tempo Club presenting Mr. and Mrs. Irene Castle (1915); of the Hell Fighters Band marching in France (1918), returning on board ship, (1919), and the parade on Fifth Avenue are in *Harlem on My Mind, Cultural Capital of Black America,* edited by Allon Schoener (1968, pp. 42–43, 46–47). There are other photographs in the best source for his experiences in Europe, Arthur W. Little's *From Harlem to the Rhine, The Story of New York's Colored Volunteers* (1936, betw. pp. 158 and 159, and on pp. 174, 214, 215). Irene Castle's "Jim Europe—a Reminiscence" (*Opportunity,* March 1930, pp. 90–91) is a warm tribute.

— GUNTHER SCHULLER

EVANTI, LILLIAN [MADAME EVANTI, born **Lillian Evans**] (1891–1967), the first colored American woman to sing in opera anywhere in the world, celebrated as a coloratura soprano and later as a lyric soprano. From 1925 she sang in France, Italy, England, Germany, the United States, Brazil, Argentina, Cuba, Haiti, the Dominican Republic, Liberia, Nigeria, and Ghana, until her last trip to Ghana in 1962 to act as toastmistress at the investiture of Pres. Nnamdi Azikiwe. She was hailed as the equal to Galli-Curci, was sent as goodwill ambassador with Toscanini and the NBC Orchestra to Argentina and Brazil in 1940. Her "Himno Panamericano" (1941) was orchestrated and sung daily on Radio Cultura in São Paulo, Brazil. The Baltimore *Afro-American* (Dec. 8, 1967) wrote in her obituary notice, "every major cultural center in the world became familiar with the thrilling versatility of Evanti."

Evanti's father was W[ilson] Bruce Evans, M.D. (Howard University, 1891), who devoted his life to education in Washington, most notably as the organizer and first principal of Armstrong Technical High School. Her mother, the former Anne Brooks, was a teacher of music in the public schools of Washington, D.C.

Lillian's musical talent was manifest early. At age four she sang as the featured soloist at a concert in Friendship Gardens. She began the study of piano at age five and became an accomplished performer as early as her teens. She graduated from Armstrong Technical High School in 1908, from Miner Teachers College, and taught kindergarten in the public schools and was later on the faculty of the college. She received a Bachelor of Music degree from Howard University in 1917.

In 1918 she married her teacher, Roy W. Tibbs, professor of music at Howard University from 1914 until his death in 1944. Evanti died in Washington, survived by their son Thurlow Tibbs. The name Evanti, suggested by Jessie Fauset, is a contraction of the two names Evans and Tibbs.

During the early years Evanti was much in demand for local concerts in the Washington area. She studied voice with Frank LaForge in New York. In 1933 Roland Hayes helped Evanti make contact with Mme Salmon Tan-Harbe who met her in Paris and introduced her to friends. She studied voice with Madame Ritter-Ciampi and acting with M. Gaston Dupins. The pace of these studies (and of her study of French) so exhausted her so that she was compelled to go to Vichy for six months' recuperation. Upon her return to Paris, Madame Salmon arranged an audition for a contract with the Paris Opera, which was ultimately awarded to her for three seasons to begin in the fall of 1925. In March 1925 her debut in the opera *Lakmé* in Nice was acclaimed, and resulted in contracts to sing in various French cities.

When Evanti returned to Washington in the late summer of 1925, an editorial in the *Washington Daily American* heralded the significance of her career. Lillian Evanti, better known as Washington's own Mrs. Lillian Evans Tibbs, deserved the congratulations "of the whole race" on her recent successes abroad in grand opera. Washington was also proud of her, for her picture had appeared on the rotogravure page of one of the white newspapers. But while the capital of the U.S. was basking in her glory, the editorial resented somewhat the fact that no mention was made of her race. "White papers are very careful, always, to indicate the race of a criminal . . . when that criminal is colored, but . . . if something worthwhile has been accomplished the individual is merely an American."

On Oct. 17, 1925, the *Washington Sentinel* also heralded the return of the "Washington girl" who had won laurels with the Paris Opera Company. In a recital on Oct. 17, 1925, at the popular Negro Lincoln Theatre, the report continued, she would sing *Lakmé*, which had received favorable comment in many foreign papers when she made her well-praised debut in Nice.

At International House in New York City (Oct. 23, 1925) patrons and sponsors for her recital included Harry T. Burleigh, Peter Marshall Murray, and other prominent citizens. Her program consisted of songs by Handel, Scarlatti, Rameau, and Bellini, as well as Negro spirituals.

Between 1925 and 1928 Evanti gave performances and studied in Paris, Monte Carlo, Menton, Montpelier, Nîmes, Toulon, Milan, Turin, Palermo, and other cities. Her performance in the title role of *Lakmé* at the Opera Trianon Lyrique in Paris (1927) won an ovation. Another notable performance was in *The Barber of Seville* in Milan (1930). She sang in other operas, gave radio concerts in Paris, and concerts in the salon of Mme Joseph Salmon. Gatti-Casazza, who heard her sing in Italy, invited her to audition for the Metropolitan Opera in 1932; even his influence as director could not overcome the exclusionary racial policy of board members.

On the other hand, on March 20, 1932, she gave a recital at the Belasco Theater, the only prestige stage in Washington which at that time presented a few Negroes to an unsegregated audience. She sang also in Town Hall, New York City (April 3, 1932), and gave a command performance at the White House for Pres. and Mrs. Franklin D. Roosevelt (Feb. 9, 1934). Meanwhile she gave other recitals in Washington, D.C., Kansas City, at Hampton Institute, and in Knoxville, London, Berlin, and Munich. The American concerts were under the well-known management of Arthur Judson.

Evanti won acclaim also in Latin American countries, including Cuba, Haiti, the Dominican Republic, and Venezuela. For her performance in Haiti the government awarded her a diploma and medal with the rank of chevalier, Ordre National de l'Honneur et Mérite. One of the highlights of her career was a tour in Argentina and Brazil (1940) sponsored by the State Department, with Toscanini and the NBC Orchestra (*Washington Post,* May 31, 1940).

Preparatory to the tour she gave a concert of music by Spanish composers in Washington. *La Nación,* one of the leading Latin American newspapers, praised her concert (Sept. 18, 1940) of *lieder* and Negro spirituals arranged by Burleigh and others. She also lectured and gave recitals at colleges and universities (Nestor R. Ortiz Oderigo, *Panorama de la Música Afro-Americana,* 1944).

These Latin American tours inspired her to compose (1941) her "Himno Panamericano." The June 1945 issue of *Newspic* commented that at the Inter-American Conference in Chapultepec Palace, Mexico City, the "Himno" was a significant contribution to Latin American unity. The "Himno" had been translated into Portuguese by Celso Guimares, director of Radio Nacional in Rio de Janeiro, and arranged for grand opera by Radames Grattali. The U.S. Office of Education selected it for a Latin American exhibition.

During World War II Evanti was cited by Gens. Dwight Eisenhower and Mark Clark and by Adm. Chester Nimitz for her concerts at army and navy installations for the entertainment of the men in uniform. Later she was invited by Presidents Eisenhower and Truman to sing at the White House.

Evanti was a founder of the National Negro Opera Company in Washington. This company produced *La Traviata* at Watergate before an audience of over 12,000 people, with Evanti singing Violetta. Glenn Dillard Gunn wrote in the *Times Herald* (Aug. 29, 1943), "She is a coloratura whose vocal gifts and attainments include all the resources of the lyric soprano. Her interpretation was in consequence, both brilliant and sympathetic."

Madame Evanti's last years were spent singing as a lyric soprano, in coaching and teaching voice. Through the 1950s she made several concert tours to Africa where she was decorated for her cultural contributions in Nigeria, Liberia, and Ghana.

Besides the "Himno Panamericano," Evanti wrote a song "Salute to Ghana," which was commissioned by the Voice of America and recorded by the U.S. Army chorus and sent to Ghana for its independence celebration in 1957. Among her other compositions were "On Furlough Mañana," dedicated to soldiers and their sweethearts in World War II, and "Forward March to Victory," dedicated to the United Nations. W. C. Handy published her "23rd Psalm," "My Little Prayer," "Speak to Him Thou," and "Mighty Rapture."

Madame Evanti had a repertoire of twenty-four operas, including *Traviata, Lakmé, Rigoletto, Barber of Seville, Manon, Romeo and Juliette, Bohème, Thaïs, Mireille, Don Pasquale, Sonnambula, Ariadne and Naxos, Carmen, Magic Flute, Rosenkavalier, Die Entführung, Hamlet, Turandot, Dac Christelflein, Lu-Tai-Pe,* and *Coq d'Or.*

This achievement attests Evanti's brilliance, industry, and cultural breadth. Edward Lawson wrote in the *Washington Tribune* (March 29, 1934): "Not only does she sing in five languages, she speaks them fluently." The distinguished critic Olin Downes described her (1935) as "The sensational coloratura soprano." She maintained her own "Columbia Music Bureau" at her home, 1910 Vermont Ave. NW, Washington.

Through the courtesy of her grandson, Thurlow Tibbs, Jr., and the vertical files of the Schomburg Center for Research in Black Culture, New York City, information was made available for this sketch. Obituaries in the *Washington Post* (Dec. 8 and 10, 1967) state that she died on Dec. 6, 1967, at Ruth's Personal Care Home, Washington, D.C., after a long illness. Funeral services were held on Dec. 11 at the McGuire Funeral Home, 1820 9th St., NW, followed by a private interment. She was survived by her son Thurlow and two grandchildren. — RAYMOND LEMIEUX

EVERS, MEDGAR WILEY (1925–1963), civil rights leader. The son of James and Jessie Evers, he was born in Decatur, Miss., the third of four children. His father operated a small farm and supplemented his income by working in a sawmill. His mother, of mixed Indian, white, and Negro parentage, worked as a domestic and took in ironing. He attended a one-room school and later walked twelve miles each way to a school in Newton. After one year in the army during World War II, he returned to work in Mississippi. When he and his brother Charles attempted to vote in 1946, the family was threatened. In the fall of the same year he enrolled in the laboratory school of Alcorn A&M College, from which he graduated in 1952. On Dec. 24, 1951, he married Myrlie Beasley. At the time of his death there were three children, one of whom, Darrell Kenyatta, was named for the leader of the Mau Mau uprising in Kenya.

He joined the NAACP in 1952 and two years later was appointed Mississippi field secretary. His active leadership in the civil rights movement led to his assassination by Byron de la Beckwith on June 12, 1963.

Evers actively sought the enforcement of the U.S. Supreme Court decision of 1954, which declared segregation in public schools unconstitutional. Since Mississippi had one of the most rigid systems of segregation of any southern state, his speeches were considered revolutionary. Equally incendiary in the view of state and local officials were his efforts to encourage Negroes to register to vote. In addition he advocated boycotting white merchants who discriminated against Negro workers and consumers. After the rise to fame of Martin Luther King, Jr., following the 1955 bus boycott in Birmingham, Ala., Evers supported the Southern Christian Leadership Conference. During the Centennial of the Emancipation Proclamation (1963), Negroes renewed demonstrations in favor of fair-employment opportunities, desegregation of public accommodations, and the right to vote. The demands encountered violent reaction, especially in Birmingham on May 3, where police used dogs, electric prods, and high-pressure water hoses on the marchers. The brutality increased the number of demonstrations in many parts of the United States.

When Mississippi Gov. Ross Barnett and Alabama Gov. George Wallace defied federal court orders requiring the admission of Negro students to the universities of Mississippi and Alabama, Pres. John F. Kennedy directed federal marshals to enforce the courts' orders. In a nationwide televised address on June 11, 1963, he stated his intention to seek comprehensive federal legislation to protect the civil rights of Negroes.

Medgar Evers, a symbol of leadership for the protection of those rights, was a natural target for assassination by those who opposed them. Early on the morning of June 13, 1963, he was shot in the back outside his home in Jackson, Miss. His death, which occasioned new demonstrations and violence, was one of the factors that led President Kennedy on June 19, 1963, to ask Congress to enact a comprehensive civil rights law. Evers was buried in Arlington National Cemetery in May 1964.

For Us the Living (1967), by his widow, is the principal source of information. — ROY WILKINS

FAGEN, DAVID (1875–1901?), guerrilla officer. Born in Tampa, Fla., Fagen enlisted in the army on June 4, 1898, at his hometown and was assigned to Company H of the 24th Infantry. Prior to being mustered into the army, Fagen was employed by a phosphate processor. In late January 1899 he was honorably discharged at Fort Douglas, near Salt Lake City, Utah. By this time both of his parents were dead. Fagen reenlisted at Fort McPherson, Ga., on Feb. 12, 1899, and was assigned to Company I of the same regiment. The following June he sailed from San Francisco with the 24th Infantry for the Philippine Islands. For the next few months he fought against the Filipino Insurrectos in central Luzon. On Nov. 17, 1899, he defected to the enemy and served a year and a half as a lieutenant and captain in the Insurrecto forces. Fagen was allegedly killed by a Filipino hunter on Dec. 1, 1901.

The motives which prompted his decision to take up arms against the United States remain somewhat unclear. He was exposed to and probably influenced by the indignation expressed by Negro journalists and fellow Negro soldiers over America's imperialistic adventure in the Philippines. The young soldier may also have recognized the parallels between the Filipino struggle for independence and the American Negro confrontation with racial abuse and discrimination in the United States. Jim Crow attitudes and practices which Negro soldiers encountered in the islands probably added to the disillusionment of carrying the "white man's burden." In addition Fagen's decision to join the Insurrectos was probably influenced by difficulties he had with his military superiors. During his first enlistment he was evidently a model soldier and easily secured permission to reenlist. Moreover, he was promoted to corporal after less than eighteen months of service. Nevertheless, while in the Philippines he was constantly at odds with his white officers and Negro sergeants. He was ordered to do a number of dirty jobs, and reportedly came close to being court-martialed. His three requests for transfer were denied.

Relief from these vexing circumstances came from his erstwhile enemies. The Insurrectos coveted the military skills of American soldiers and promised commissions to defectors. Fagen accepted their offer and on Nov. 17, 1899, left his unit at San Isidro in Nueva Ecija province with the aid of an Insurrecto officer. During the next eighteen months as a guerrilla officer Fagen exhibited a wholehearted commitment to the Filipino revolutionary struggle. His military record indicates that he was a dedicated, cunning, and skilled commander of irregular troops, who earned the plaudits of his subordinates and superiors. The men he led referred to the former corporal from Tampa as "General Fagen," and after less than a year in the Insurrecto army he was promoted to captain by Gen. Urbano Lacuna.

Military censorship obscures his first year as a guerrilla officer, but newspaper and other accounts reveal that from Aug. 30, 1900, to Jan. 17, 1901, Fagen clashed at least eight times with American forces and Filipino auxiliaries. On these occasions he harassed and deftly evaded his former comrades-in-arms. His exploits were particularly irksome to Gen. Frederick Funston, who won prominence for the capture of Filipino leader Emilio Aguinaldo. Funston found Captain Fagen a more agile prey and seems to have regarded the ex-soldier as his personal *bête noire.* Fagen gained added notoriety from spurious press reports issued by the army which claimed that he was brutal toward American prisoners. His reputation spawned other false accounts, including one which alleged that he had boarded a troop ship bound for Los Angeles and had been subsequently captured.

Fagen's career continued until the spring of 1901 when Filipino resistance in central Luzon collapsed. In early May his commander surrendered to Funston. Fagen sought refuge with his Filipino wife in the mountains of Nueva Ecija, where he apparently thought he could lose his identity among the indigenous Negrito population. His former nemesis Funston ensured that Fagen would remain a hunted man. Funston had him branded a bandit and a price of $600 was placed on his head. Nevertheless, he evaded his pursuers for six more months.

In December 1901 a Filipino hunter, Anastacio Bartolomé, claimed that he and some companions had killed Fagen at Dingalan Cove, where the Umiry River flows into the Pacific Ocean in eastern Luzon. The army publicly announced his death, but privately marked the file containing Bartolomé's story "the supposed killing of David Fagen." Therefore it is possible that Fagen lived a long and peaceful life among the Negritos.

For an excellent background analysis, see Willard B. Gatewood, Jr.'s *Black Americans and the White Man's Burden* (1975). It gives a brief account of Fagen (pp. 288–89), and quotes an editorial in the *Indianapolis Freeman* (Dec. 14, 1901): "Fagen was a traitor and died a traitor's death, but he was a man no doubt prompted by honest motives to help a weaker side, and one with which he felt allied by ties that bind." The ideological and racial motives of the few Negro deserters like Fagen inspired a polemical novel by Robert L. Bridgman, *Loyal Traitors,* less than two years after Fagen's death.

Biographical data on Fagen are in the records of the Adjutant-General's Office, National Archives. Details of his Insurrecto career are in the *Manila Times* (1900–1901), and Frederick Funston's *Memories of Two Wars, Cuban and Philippine Experiences* (1911).

— FRANK N. SCHUBERT

FARD, W[ALLACE] D. [W. FARRAD MUHAMMAD, THE PROPHET] (? –1934?), cult leader and founder. There is little authentic information about this mystic, founder of the first Temple of Islam, the members of which were later known as Black Muslims. Reliable facts span only about four years, 1930–1934. By his own undocumented account he was born in Mecca, the son of a wealthy member of the tribe of Koreish to which the Prophet Mohammed belonged. There is no evidence that he was educated somewhere in England or at the University of California (which campus is not specified). Nor is there valid evidence to support the assertion that he was once jailed in California as a narcotics pusher. His disappearance in 1933 or 1934 is also shrouded in mystery.

Even the exact date of his arrival in Detroit is uncertain. Whenever it was, he exploited the woes of Negroes during the Great Depression in much the same manner as did Marcus Garvey on the eve of and during World War I and the immediately succeeding years. He was even closer to the people than was Garvey—a door-to-door peddler of silks and raincoats in the "Paradise Valley" Negro neighborhood of Detroit. That time was propitious for a new cult leader is evident in the career of Prophet Noble Drew Ali, also a Prophet of Islam. He is said to have founded his first temple in New Jersey in 1913 and later in Pittsburgh and Detroit before he went to Chicago in 1925. The circumstances of his death in 1929, like those of Fard in 1933 or 1934, are still obscure.

It is also difficult to determine the extent to which Drew Ali's assertion that American Negroes are of Moorish descent paved the way for similar claims by Fard. In any event, the large number of southern Negroes in Detroit, uprooted and seeking solace in a mystic, quickly gained for Fard a substantial following. His denunciation of "white devils" was buttressed by the "first-to-be-fired" lot of many Detroit Negroes. Some 8000 are said to have become members of his first Temple of Islam.

Fard insisted that they substitute "X" for their last name in order to disavow their slave ancestry. He organized the Fruit of Islam (FOI), a semimilitary organization, a Muslim Girls' Training Corps Class, and a University of Islam, which was largely an elementary and high school. When the Detroit Board of Education sought to compel students at the university to attend public schools, fear of violent resistance impelled the courts to release most of those arrested.

His assertion of divinity, his disloyal attitude toward the United States government, and his infrequent appearances led to a decline in membership before his death. His legacy may be more significant than his achievements. He is said to have exercised great influence over Elijah Muhammad, born Elijah or Robert Poole. When Elijah Muhammad died on Feb. 25, 1975, he was reputed to have been a millionaire, the revered leader of an estimated 50,000 to 70,000 Black Muslim followers. His death occurred on the eve of the annual Saviour's Day observance of Fard's death. The most famous of the Black Muslims were Malcolm X and Muhammad Ali, formerly known as Cassius Clay, the heavyweight champion who refused induction into military service but eventually was allowed to continue his phenomenal boxing career.

The influence of the Black Muslims on American Negroes is as difficult to determine as is that of Marcus Garvey. Their exact number is not known, but like latter-day Garveyites, they constitute a nucleus of Black Nationalists who advocate separatism and a mystical allegiance to "Black Africa." Orthodox Muslims refuse to recognize the Black Muslims.

C. Eric Lincoln's *The Black Muslims in America* (1961) is the principal source for the origins and history of the cult to that date. *Anyplace But Here* by Arna Bontemps and Jack Conroy (1945, 1966) presents perceptive interpretations of Drew Ali, W. D. Fard, and Elijah Muhammad (pp. 205–30). An obituary of Elijah Muhammad in the *Washington Post* (Feb. 26, 1975, pp. A1, A8) and an interpretive comment (p. C9) reveal aspects of Fard's influence. — RAYFORD W. LOGAN

FARLEY, JAMES CONWAY (1854–1910?), photographer. Farley was born to slave parents in Prince Edward County, Va., on Aug. 10, 1854. Following the death of his father, James and his mother moved to Richmond, Va., in 1861, where his mother was a storeroom keeper at the Columbia Hotel. He assisted in making candles, learned to read and write, and attended public schools for three years. After working briefly with a baker he was employed in 1872 in the chemical department of the photographic establishment of C. R. Rees and Company in downtown Richmond. During a number of years after 1875 he set the scene and made photographs for the G. W. Davis Photograph Gallery, also in downtown Richmond on Broad Street. In 1895 he opened his own studio, the Jefferson Fine Arts Gallery, 533 E. Broad St. *(Richmond City Directory)*. For thirty-five years he prospered in a profession which had few colored men. When four white operators in the darkroom of the Davis Gallery demanded that Farley be fired, Davis discharged the four white operators. Despite difficulties with later white employees Farley continued to work with Davis, presumably until he opened his own Jefferson Fine Art Gallery in 1895. On Dec. 10, 1876, he married Rebecca P. Robinson of Amelia County, Va., who bore him seven daughters.

There remains little extant evidence of his work. He received a first prize for his exhibit at the Colored Industrial Fair, Richmond (1884), and a premium at the World Exposition at New Orleans (1885). The only known surviving photograph attributed to him is at the Valentine Museum, 1015 E. Clay St., Richmond. He is said to have photographed many black and white Americans.

A comprehensive biographical sketch is in G. F. Richings's *Evidence of Progress Among Colored People* (pp. 495–96), first published in 1896, which had its twelfth edition in 1905. A shorter version is in W. J. Simmons's *Men of Mark . . .* (1887, pp. 801–04; reprinted 1968). — DEBORAH WILLIS-THOMAS

FAUSET, JESSIE [REDMON] (1885?–1961), novelist, teacher, editor, and poet. The daughter of the Rev. Redmon and Anna (Lehman) Fauset, she was born in Philadelphia, Pa. She came from an old Philadelphia family, the kind known as "OPs" in the Negro society of the period, and this background had a definite influence on her novels. Educated in the public schools of her native city, Fauset took her B.A. at Cornell University in 1905, winning election to Phi Beta Kappa. Her further education included an M.A. from the University of Pennsylvania and study at the Sorbonne.

On Oct. 5, 1906, Fauset was appointed a teacher of Latin and French in the well-known M Street High School in Washington, D.C. (which became in 1916 the equally well-known Dunbar High School). On June 30, 1919, Jessie Fauset resigned from the D.C. public schools and in the same year joined the staff of *The Crisis* as literary editor. After seven active years in this position she gave it up in May 1926 to assume "the less exacting duties" of contributing editor. During her early years with *The Crisis* Fauset also worked with *The Brownies' Book,* a monthly publication for children, (Oct. 1919 to Dec. 1923), at first as literary editor and subsequently as managing editor.

In 1921 Fauset attended the Second Pan-African Congress in London, Brussels, and Paris, and wrote for *The Crisis* (Nov. and Dec. 1921) two valuable articles covering those historic meetings.

After giving up full-time work with *The Crisis,* Fauset returned to teaching, this time in the New York public schools. She taught first in a Harlem junior high school, later moving to the prestigious DeWitt Clinton High School. In later life Jessie Fauset married Herbert Harris, a New York–New Jersey businessman. She died on April 30, 1961, in Philadelphia. The obituary in the *New York Times* (May 3, 1961, p. 37), gave her age as about seventy-six.

The most prolific of the New Negro Renaissance fiction writers, Fauset published during her career four full-length novels: *There Is Confusion* (1924), *Plum Bun* (1929), *The Chinaberry Tree* (1931), and *Comedy: American Style* (1933). All of these works belong to what has been called the "best foot forward" school of Negro writing. They deal almost exclusively with the lives of middle- and upper-class Negroes, and they try to show, among other things, that except for the superficial matter of color the "best" Negroes are in no wise different from the best whites. With this objective in mind, she naturally avoided as much as possible delineation of the lower-class Negro. And for the same reason she made use of the "passing" theme, a theme popular with the writers of the Renaissance.

During the 1960s when many young Negro critics adopted a black nationalistic "line," it became fashionable to dismiss the novels of Jessie Fauset. In all fairness one must admit that she did not possess a great fictional talent, (none of the Renaissance novelists had such a talent, not even Jean Toomer). One must also admit that her insistence on portraying largely the "best" Negroes does result in a one-sided picture. And above all else one must confess that her works, although protesting America's treatment of its Negro minority, do imply an overly optimistic faith in the fulfillment of the American

Dream. And yet in spite of these concessions, one cannot *dismiss* Jessie Fauset. She was a significant novelist of the Renaissance years.

We should also bear in mind that her attitudes with regard to fiction were held by many of the best Negro critics of the day. William Stanley Braithwaite, for example, felt that in *There Is Confusion* Fauset had "created an entirely new milieu in the treatment of the Race in fiction." In this novel, he contended, "Race fiction emerges from the color line and is incorporated into that general and universal art which detaches itself from prejudices of propaganda and stands out the objective vision of artistic creation" (*The Crisis,* Sept. 1924). This is high praise and perhaps not warranted, but it indicates that she was representative. And one should add that whatever her faults, Jessie Fauset gives us a fuller and more sympathetic picture of middle-class life and thought of the period than any other writer, and this is an important contribution.

A poet of some reputation during the New Negro Renaissance, Fauset's lyrics appeared in *The Crisis, The Brownies' Book,* the *New York World,* the *Independent,* and other periodicals. Widely anthologized at the time, her poems are found in most of the Negro collections published just before, during, and just after the Renaissance period. Dealing with the usual subject matter of lyrical verse—the heartbreak of love, nature, and the vagaries of human life—Jessie Fauset's poems have surface facility and polish but lack real depth. Among her best known pieces are "La Vie C'est la Vie," "Noblesse Oblige," "Words! Words!" "Christmas Eve in France," and "Rondeau."

Among Fauset's many critical essays, the best known is "The Gift of Laughter," an article on Negro drama which appears in Alain Locke's *The New Negro, An Interpretation* (1925, pp. 161–67).

During her connection with *The Crisis* and *The Brownies' Book,* Jessie Fauset was a versatile and prolific contributor to both periodicals, furnishing a steady stream of poems, short fiction, reviews, articles, and translations. Her essay subjects ranged from "Notes on the New Books," done with Alain Locke, to sketches on men like Martin R. Delany, Bert Williams, and Henry O. Tanner. Her contributions to these pioneer periodicals showed that she had a disciplined and well-stocked mind.

There are many biographical references to Jessie Fauset throughout New Negro publications, but all of them are very brief and, of course, incomplete. There are also many discrepancies among them, a few caused by Fauset's reluctance to "date" herself.

According to the *Philadelphia Tribune* (May 6, 1961, p. 11) she was seventy-four when she died on April 30, 1961, at her home 1853 N. 17th St., Philadelphia. Funeral services were held on May 3 at the Hobson Reynolds Funeral Home, 2044 Ridge Ave., the Rev. Robert Harris, rector of the Church of the Annunciation, officiating. She was buried in Eden Cemetery. Survivors were two brothers, Arthur Huff Fauset and Redmond Fauset, Jr., and a sister Marion Fauset.

For short critical comments on Jessie Fauset's fiction, see Robert A. Bone's *The Negro Novel in America* (1958), David Littlejohn's *Black on White* (1966), and

Arthur P. Davis's *From the Dark Tower* (1974, pp. 90–94, with photograph facing page 93).

— ARTHUR P. DAVIS

FERGUSON, CATHERINE [KATY] (1779?–1854), pioneer founder of a Sunday school and home for unwed mothers. She was born a slave while her mother was traveling from Virginia to New York City, in which slavery was still permitted. When Katy was seven years old her mother was sold. A kind mistress permitted Katy to attend church services; another sympathetic woman purchased her freedom for $200 when she was sixteen years old. When she was eighteen she married and had two children who died young. Information is lacking about her husband who died before she was twenty. At her home on Warren Street, Manhattan, she instructed black and white children in religious matters. About 1814 a Dr. Mason visited her home on a Sunday and invited her to transfer her school to the basement of his church on Murray Street. Here "she took the children of the streets of New York, white and black, to her empty arms, taught them, found them homes, and . . . established the first modern Sunday School in Manhattan" (W. E. B. Du Bois, *Darkwater* . . . [1920], pp. 177–78). These children, some of them from poorhouses, were said to number forty-eight, twenty of them white, some of them unwed mothers. She thus preceded Ionia Whipper, who founded a school for unwed mothers in Washington, D.C., in 1931.

Katy Ferguson died of cholera in New York City on July 11, 1854. The Katy Ferguson Home for Unwed Mothers was founded in 1920, and was supported by private enterprise.

Brief sketches are in Hallie Quinn Brown (comp.), *Homespun Heroines* . . . (1926), Catherine A. Latimer's "Catherine Ferguson" (*NHB,* Nov. 1941, pp. 38–39), and Wilhelmina S. Robinson's *Historical Negro Biographies* (1969, pp. 79–80). All are probably based on an American Tract Society publication, *Katy Ferguson* (n.d.). — RAYFORD W. LOGAN

FERGUSON, THOMAS JEFFERSON (1830–1887), educator, author, Masonic leader, and politician. Ferguson was born on Sept. 15, 1830, in Essex County, Va., the son of free-born parents of mixed blood. Little is known of his early years, although it is known that by the 1850s he resided in Cincinnati, Ohio. There, Ferguson became an active member of the Masonic order, serving as junior warden of the Cincinnati lodge in 1859 and 1860. During 1859 he moved to Albany, Athens County, Ohio, becoming a landowner and enrolling as a student at the integrated Albany Manual Labor University. Four years later he was a leading figure in the establishment of the Albany Enterprise Academy (Ohio). Ferguson further served on the first board of trustees of the school.

The Enterprise Academy opened its doors to students in 1864, following an appropriation from the Freedmen's Bureau and private gifts from such individuals as Gen. O. O. Howard. During the Civil War and the early days of Reconstruction Ferguson taught in schools in Albany and Middleport, Ohio. In 1866 he taught at a public school in Parkersburg, W.Va.

By the 1870s Ferguson returned to Albany and the "Enterprise Academy" where he served as a faculty member and principal teacher. In addition to his teaching duties he served as a minister to Colored Free Will Baptist congregations in Albany, Kerr's Run, and Pomeroy, Ohio.

An active participant in enlarging educational and political opportunities for Negroes, Ferguson authored a pamphlet entitled *The Education of the Negro or the Hope of the Race* (1872). A staunch Republican, Ferguson won election to the Albany City Council in April 1872. A powerful and effective public speaker, he stumped the counties of southeastern Ohio on behalf of the Republican party. He served as an alternate delegate to the 15th Congressional District Convention, held at Marietta, Ohio, during the summer of 1872. Named to the Committee on Resolutions at the convention, Ferguson made an address decrying the presidential aspirations of Horace Greeley. During the ensuing years he actively campaigned for Republican candidates in the southern regions of Ohio. His connection with the church made him an active participant in the temperance movement in Athens County, and provided a strong support to his political interests.

In August 1879 Ferguson was elected president of the Mass Convention of Colored Voters of Athens County, one of the earliest postwar Negro caucuses in Ohio. His address to the convention urged suffrage, jury duty, colored teachers, aid to candidates who supported Negro issues, and efficient schools. Later that same fall the Republican state executive committee named Ferguson to their speakers bureau. His speaking engagements became statewide and were directed to Negro audiences in various urban areas.

Although an active political campaigner, education of the Negro remained Ferguson's chief personal concern. He headed the Albany Enterprise Academy from the 1870s to the mid-1880s. Numbered among his students was Olivia A. Davidson, the second wife of Booker T. Washington, Milton M. Holland, and other well-known Negroes. Failing health and extensive fire damage to the academy caused Ferguson to resign in 1886. He died on March 30, 1887, after a prolonged bout with pneumonia, and was buried in Albany. No information is available about his marriage, but he left two children, Luella and James.

No biography of Ferguson exists. The most extensive mass of material is in the Ohio University Archives, Athens, Ohio, and includes catalogs, essays, and recollections by local residents of the Albany Enterprise Academy and the subject of this sketch. Ivan Tribe's "Rise and Decline of Private Academies in Albany, Ohio" (*Ohio History*, 1969) places Ferguson and his institution in the proper perspective of Negro education. William H. Parham's *An Official History of the Most Worshipful Grand Lodge Free and Accepted Masons for the State of Ohio* (1906) covers his role in the Masonic order. The most useful sources for tracing Ferguson's life are the newspaper files of the *Athens Messenger, Athens Journal,* and the *Albany Echo.* Carter G. Woodson's *Early Negro Education in West Virginia* (1921) illuminates Ferguson's participation in Negro education. — FRANK R. LEVSTIK

FERRIS, WILLIAM H[ENRY] (1874–1941), author, lecturer, and editor. Born in New Haven, Conn., he was the son of Henry and Sarah A. (Jefferson) Ferris. He graduated from Hillhouse High School, New Haven, in 1891, and from Yale University in 1899. He attended the Harvard University Divinity School (1897–1899) and received his M.A. degree in 1900. In 1901 the *Boston Transcript* published his article on a fire in Jacksonville, Fla.; in 1904 the *Literary Digest* published his article on "Negro Religion." His career revealed many difficulties of some of the "Talented Tenth." He supported William Monroe Trotter and other "radicals" in the early part of the twentieth century, soon severed relations with him, sought the help of Booker T. Washington, temporarily supported W. E. B. Du Bois and the Niagara Movement (founded in 1905 to oppose the conservative policies of Washington), then like T. Thomas Fortune joined the crusade of Marcus Garvey, especially as literary editor of Garvey's *Negro World* (1919–1923). He had previously been editor of *The Champion* in Chicago (1916–1917) and general literary assistant with the A.M.E. Book Concern, Philadelphia (1917–1919); later he was literary editor of *The Spokesman* (1925–1927). Meanwhile he had written his magnum opus, *The African Abroad; or His Evolution in Western Civilization, Tracing His Development under the Caucasian Milieu* (2 vols, 1913).

He died suddenly on Aug. 23, 1941, in obscurity in his room at 10 W. 123rd St., New York City. A committee of his Yale Class (1895) published a notice which said in part: "He was indeed a credit to his university and his country." He was saved from the Potter's Field by a check for $300 from the treasurer of Ferris's class at Yale (obituary in *JNH,* Oct. 1941, p. 550, probably by Carter G. Woodson).

The shifts in Ferris's loyalties reflect in part his education, the dilemmas of many Negro leaders, and Ferris's personality. As a boy he read Douglass's *Life and Times;* as a sophomore at Yale he had been greatly influenced by Thomas Carlyle's *Heroes and Hero Worship,* as a senior by Ralph Waldo Emerson's *Nature and Other Addresses,* and by Carlyle's *Sartor Resartus* in his graduate days. Du Bois's *The Souls of Black Folk* (1903) "came to me as a bolt from the blue. It was rebellion of a fearless soul, the protest of a noble nature against the blighting American caste prejudice" (*The African Abroad,* 1:273).

In 1898 while a student at the Harvard Divinity School he signed the call by Bishop Alexander Walters urging Fortune to hold the meeting of the Afro-American League which became the National Afro-American Council, one of the forerunners of the Niagara Movement and the NAACP. Ferris attended the Louisville meeting of the council in the spring of 1903, when Booker T. Washington and Fortune defeated the "radicals." At this meeting, Ferris caused an uproar by objecting to a huge picture of Washington in the meeting hall until a picture of Joseph C. Price was placed beside it. When he failed in an attempt to obtain a position as a member of the faculty of Howard University (1903–1904), he "spent much of his time freeloading, an embarrassing illustration of the classically educated, unemployed Negro [Booker T.] Washington was always denigrating" (Stephen R. Fox, *The Guardian of Boston, William Monroe Trotter* [1970], p. 109, n.37).

Although Ferris supported Du Bois against Trotter and the Bookerites in the first years of the Niagara Movement (he did not list himself as having attended its meetings), in 1907 he broke with Trotter. Trotter alleged that Ferris owed the *Guardian* $100 and Ferris joined William H. Lewis, Clement G. Morgan, and others in sponsoring a banquet for Du Bois in October 1907. A month later Ferris was seeking to win the favor of Booker T. Washington, perhaps because he realized that Washington and his supporters were undermining the Niagara Movement. But in 1908 he was one of the colored speakers at an interracial dinner of the Cosmopolitan Club that Washington caused to be denounced.

By the time Ferris wrote *The African Abroad* (1913) Washington's power had begun to wane. Portions of the manuscript must have been written some years before publication, for Ferris wrote: "It remains to be seen whether the Niagara Movement, headed by Du Bois will sweep Washington and his theories from the field. This is not a personal fight, but a battle of ideas, a struggle for the supremacy of rival theories" (*The African Abroad,* 1:276–77). Nevertheless Ferris, despite his wordy digressions, attempted to give an objective assessment of Du Bois and Washington; for example: "Du Bois is gifted with a more powerful intellect than Washington, is a more uncompromising idealist, and is a more brilliant writer. . . . But Washington is a more magnetic speaker and more astute politician, a greater humorist, and less of an aristocrat" (ibid.). But Washington was also right in emphasizing the accumulation of property (ibid., pp. 187–88).

While Ferris considered Du Bois greater than Washington, he found a basic weakness in Du Bois. A wordy paragraph asserted that he would have been a greater man if, going back to Father Abraham, he had "championed the idea of the sovereignty of God" (ibid., pp. 274–75).

It is probable that the articles in Garvey's *Negro World* glorifying the histories of the Moorish and Ethiopian empires, the heroism of Toussaint L'Ouverture, Denmark Vesey, Gabriel Prosser, and Nat Turner were written or inspired by Ferris. In any event, his alliance with Garvey is all the more odd because *The African Abroad* contained this passage: "But I must confess that dark and gloomy as is the outlook, at present, cheerless and hopeless as seem our prospects, I look forward to the future with hope" (1:191).

Despite its verbiage and erudite digressions, *The African Abroad* has been a valuable source for later historians. He expressed special indebtedness to John E. Bruce, president, and Arthur Schomburg, secretary, of the Society for Historical Research, and the staff of the Yale University Library.

It would be fascinating to try to trace the extent to which subsequent historians have drawn upon Ferris's volumes. One scholar thought he had discovered Arnold H. L. Heeren's *Historical Researches* (translated from the German, 1838) as evidence that "civilization descended the Nile from 'Negroland' to Egypt" (*The Negro and the Post-War World* [1945], p. 7), but Ferris had already quoted Heeren (1:490–93). Like many

other historians and editors, the editors of this volume have included some individuals whose biographies are found (particularly in volume 2) in *The African Abroad.* On pages 863–66 of Ferris's volume are a brief history of the Negro Society for Historical Research, the rare books in its collection, and a list of its members. Ferris was unwilling to accept claims that Aesop, Terence, Alexander Hamilton, Robert Browning, and Ludwig van Beethoven, or Josephine Beauharnais, for example, were Negroes (2:929–32).

In summary, modern historians and others who read *The African Abroad* by skipping some of its passages will find it a rewarding experience. Several photographs, including those of Ferris, Edward A. Bouchet, the first Negro member of Phi Beta Kappa (Yale, 1874), Alexander Crummell, Josephine St. Pierre Ruffin, William H. Lewis, and many others give added value to the work. An index would have made it more useful.

Basic information about the early life of Ferris is found in *The African Abroad* (especially 1:107–41, 348–57). For his later career, see *Who's Who in Colored America* (1937) and the obituary in *JNH* (Oct. 1941, pp. 549–50). The evaluation of *The African Abroad* is original. — RAYFORD W. LOGAN

FISHER, RUDOLPH (1897–1934), radiologist, author, and musician. The son of the Rev. John W. and Glendora (Williamson) Fisher, he was born in Washington, D.C., on May 9, 1897. Reared in Providence, R.I., where his father was a clergyman, he graduated in 1915 with honors from the city's Classical High School. In 1919 he received a B.A. degree from Brown University with a major in English and biology. He was elected to Phi Beta Kappa, Sigma Xi, and Delta Sigma Rho honor fraternities; he won the Caesar Misch Prize in German and the Carpenter Prize in public speaking. A James Manning Scholar and a Francis Wayland Scholar, he was elected as the class-day orator and the student commencement speaker. In 1920 he received an M.A. degree in biology from Brown University and his M.D. degree on June 6, 1924, from the Howard University Medical School, graduating with highest honors. The same year he married Jane Ryder, a schoolteacher in Washington, D.C. After an internship of one year at Freedmen's Hospital, he became a fellow of the National Research Council at the College of Physicians and Surgeons of Columbia University, specializing in biology for two years. He began the practice of medicine in New York City in 1927 when Harlem was becoming a social and cultural mecca, studied radiology and opened an x-ray laboratory at 2352 Seventh Ave., connected with the x-ray department of the New York Health Department. He served as superintendent of the International Hospital at Seventh Avenue and 138th Street. After three operations, the last on Nov. 21, 1934, he died of cancer on Dec. 26, 1934, in New York City and was buried from the Chapel of Duncan Brothers, 2303 Seventh Ave. He was survived by his widow, an eight-year old son Hugh, a sister Pearl, and a brother Joseph.

"Unembittered, and one of the wittiest of the [Harlem] Renaissance group, Rudolph Fisher was among the first to light up the dark realities of Negro life with humor" (*Cavalcade: Negro American Writings from 1760 to the Present,* edited by Arthur P. Davis and Saunders Redding [1971], p. 337). His first Harlem short story "City of Refuge," written while he was in medical school, was published in *Atlantic Monthly* (Feb. 1925), in that same year in Alain Leroy Locke's *The New Negro, An Interpretation,* and in Foley's *Best Short Stories of 1925.* The central theme expressed in its title and in many of his other writings dealt with an uprooted southern Negro in Harlem. Five other episodes about other southern Negroes in Harlem, "The South Lingers On," were published in the *Survey Graphic* on March 1, 1925, and republished as "Vestiges, Harlem Sketches" in *The New Negro.* "In these simple and uncontrived vignettes he has shown Harlem to be, not the fun city of downtown white thrill seekers, but, actually, a transplanted Southern community, bigger and brassier, of course, but still essentially a slice of the South" (Davis, *From the Dark Tower, Afro-American Writers 1900–1960* [1974], p. 100). He won the Amy Spingarn Prize Contest for his short story "High Yaller," published in *The Crisis* (Oct. and Nov. 1925). Like several of his other short stories it poignantly reveals color prejudice among Negroes. Among his other short stories, the following are particularly noteworthy: "Ringtail" (*Atlantic Monthly,* May 1925), "The Promised Land" (ibid., Jan. 1927), and "Blades of Steel" (ibid., Aug. 1929). The best of his transplanted-southern stories is "Miss Cynthie," which was published originally in the *Story Magazine* (June 1933). "Although Claude McKay and Langston Hughes have written a larger amount of fiction than Fisher, their works lack the controlled intensity, the suggestiveness, the subtlety, and the overall artistry that his short stories have" (*From the Dark Tower,* pp. 100, 101). He also published two children's stories about transplanted southern Negroes: "Ezekiel" and "Ezekiel Learns" in the *Junior Red Cross News* (March 1932 and Feb. 1933, respectively).

Fisher's two novels, *Walls of Jericho* (1928) and *The Conjure Man Dies: A Mystery Tale of Dark Harlem* (1932), give added dimensions to the Harlem scene. *Walls of Jericho* contains authentic Negro slang or jive talk, and folk sayings such as "One jig [Negro] in danger is ev'ry jig in danger." It spoofs interracial do-gooders and the "color line"—a rich white woman talked all evening with a man without knowing that he was a Negro. "Fisher's overall purpose in this novel was to look at Harlem steadily, see it whole and show that Harlemites are like all people—varied and all too human" (*From the Dark Tower,* p. 102).

In *The Conjure Man Dies,* Fisher was perhaps the pioneer among Negroes in writing a detective novel. In addition to such conventional ingredients as red herrings, the least likely suspect, and a team of detectives, *The Conjure Man Dies* reveals Fisher's medical and scientific knowledge in the solution of the crime. Arthur P. Davis commented that Fisher's style in the novels "is clear and uncomplicated"; his "characters talk convincingly and naturally" without using four-letter words and frequent references to sex. Like other "New Negro" authors, he did not portray the "debauched Tenth" as did McKay. "Although Dr. Fisher could easily have played *up* the primitive side of Harlem life, he

preferred to play it *down.* It was part of the price one's dual inheritance demanded" (*From the Dark Tower,* p. 103).

Fisher compiled an unpublished collection of arrangements of Negro spirituals, gave concerts with Paul Robeson, conducting and arranging the music, in and around New York City. He dramatized and staged *The Conjure Man Dies.* It was presented by the Federal Theatre Players at the Lafayette Theater in New York City by a Works Progress Administration unit there and by the Karamu Players in Cleveland, Ohio.

Four unpublished and undated manuscripts, "The Lost Love Blues," "The Lindy Hop," "The Man Who Passed" ("False Face"), and "Across the Airshaft" are in the Brown University Archives.

The best critique is the chapter in Arthur P. Davis's *From the Dark Tower* (1974, pp. 98–103), which recommends Robert A. Bone's *The Negro Novel in America* (1965) and Robert Hemenway's *The Black Novelist* (1970). There is a photograph in Davis's book facing page 101. See also the Introduction to the Arno Press reprint of *The Walls of Jericho* (1968) and Eleanor Claudine Queene's "A Study of Rudolph Fisher's Prose Fiction" (M.A. thesis, Howard University, 1961). Obituaries are in the *New York Times* (Dec. 27, 1934, p. 26) and the *New York Age* (Jan. 5, 1935, p. 3).

— CLAUDETTE BROWN

FLEETWOOD, CHRISTIAN ABRAHAM (1840–1914), editor, army officer, bureaucrat, and musician. Born in Baltimore on July 21, 1840, the son of Charles and Anna Maria Fleetwood, both free persons of color, he received his early education in the home of a wealthy sugar merchant, John C. Brunes and his wife, the latter treating him like her son. He continued his education in the office of the secretary of the Maryland Colonization Society, went briefly to Liberia and Sierra Leone, and graduated in 1860 from Ashmun Institute (later Lincoln University) in Pennsylvania. He and others published briefly the *Lyceum Observer* in Baltimore, said to be the first Negro newspaper in the upper South. When the Civil War disrupted trade with Liberia, he enlisted in the Union Army (Aug. 17, 1863). Honorably discharged on May 4, 1866, he worked as a bookkeeper in Columbus, Ohio, until 1867, and in several minor government positions in the Freedmen's Bank and War Department, Washington, D.C. He organized a battalion of D.C. National Guards and the high school cadet corps in the 1880s.

He died suddenly of heart failure in Washington on Sept. 28, 1914. Funeral services were held at St. Luke's Episcopal Church. Interment was in Harmony Cemetery, Washington, D.C., the First Separate Battalion of D.C. National Guards serving as escort. Among the honorary pallbearers were such prominent Washingtonians as Maj. Arthur Brooks, Daniel Murray, Whitefield McKinlay, and Judge Robert H. Terrell.

The participation by the National Guard, and by Arthur Brooks in particular, was an appropriate recognition of the most significant aspects of Fleetwood's career. Enlisting as a sergeant in Company G, 4th Regiment, U.S. Colored Volunteer Infantry, on Aug. 11, 1863, he was promoted on Aug. 19 to sergeant major.

The regiment, assigned to the 3rd Division, saw service with the 10th, 18th, and 25th Army Corps in campaigns in North Carolina and Virginia. For heroism in the critical battle of Chaffin's Farm on the outskirts of Richmond (Sept. 29, 1864) he was awarded the Congressional Medal of Honor. Although every officer of the regiment sent a petition for him to be commissioned an officer, Secretary of War Edwin Stanton did not recommend appointment.

It was his military career that probably inspired Fleetwood's interest in the Washington colored National Guard and the colored high school cadet corps. A Washington cadet corps, organized and commanded by Capt. D. Graham on June 12, 1880, was expanded into the Sixth Battalion of D.C. National Guards on July 18, 1887, with Fleetwood appointed major and commanding officer. After reorganizations, several Negro battalions were consolidated into the First Separate Battalion in 1891. Passed over as its commanding officer, Fleetwood resigned in 1892. Meanwhile he and Maj. Charles B. Fisher, who had commanded the Fifth Battalion, were instrumental in organizing the Colored High School Cadet Corps of the District of Columbia in 1888. Military science instruction was first offered in the Miner Building, 17th and Church Streets NW, but because of inadequate facilities the cadets drilled at the O Street Armory of the Washington Cadet Corps. Fleetwood, the first instructor of the colored high school cadets, served until 1897, when he was succeeded by Maj. Arthur Brooks. These two officers developed a tradition of military service among young colored men in Washington which led some of them to enlist in World War I and others to be commissioned at the Colored Officers Training Camp in Fort Des Moines, Iowa.

Fleetwood never returned to active duty with any military organization. However, many residents of the District of Columbia recommended that he be appointed as the commander for the 50th U.S. Colored Volunteer Infantry during the Spanish-American War. This request was not seriously considered by the War Department, and the participation of colored soldiers from the District of Columbia was similarly disregarded. It is not known whether Fleetwood's short stature and physical ailments reduced his chances for consideration. His army records state that he was five feet, four and one half inches tall. These records also state that he applied in 1891 for a pension because of "total" deafness in his left ear, the result of "gunshot concussion," and "severe" in his right ear, the result of catarrh contracted while in the army. His application also stated that these ailments prevented him from speaking or singing in public. Other evidence shows that for a number of years he had served as choirmaster of the 15th Street Presbyterian Church, St. Luke's and St. Mary's Protestant Episcopal Churches, as well as the Berean Baptist Church. Supported by the community, including the wives of former presidents (Lucy Webb Hayes and Francis Folsom Cleveland), his musical presentations were extremely successful.

With his wife Sara Iredell, whom he married on Nov. 18, 1869, he led an active social life. Fleetwood was acquainted with most of the prominent Negroes of the period. They frequently visited his residence, and presented him with a testimonial in 1889.

Most references containing material on the career of Fleetwood are in the Fleetwood Papers of the Manuscript Division, Library of Congress. Information concerning his military and militia activities are located in microfilm publication number 929, *Documents Relating to the Military and Naval Service of Blacks Awarded the Congressional Medal of Honor from the Civil War to the Spanish-American War* in the National Archives, Washington, D.C., and the Records of the Adjutant-General's Office, District of Columbia National Guard, respectively. For contemporary accounts of his activities, see the Washington, D.C., newspapers, especially the *Bee* and the *Evening Star*. His speech "The Negro as a Soldier" was published as a pamphlet (1895), and in Alice Dunbar-Nelson (ed.), *Masterpieces of Negro Eloquence* (1914). — CHARLES JOHNSON, JR.

FLEMING, THOMAS WALLACE (1874–1948), businessman, lawyer, newspaper publisher, politician, civil rights leader, and the first Negro city councilman of Cleveland, Ohio. He was born in Mercer, Pa., the son of Thomas W. Sr. and Lavinia Green Fleming. Fleming's father deserted his family and his mother was left with the responsibility of raising Thomas and his two sisters. The fatherless family moved to Pittsburgh and stayed a short time, but later settled in Meadville, Pa., where Thomas was taught the barber trade at age fourteen by a relative. Leaving school to help his mother provide for the family responsibilities, he worked in Ashtabula, Ohio, for a short time but returned to Meadville to take charge of a barbershop and finally purchased his own.

In 1892 Fleming left Meadville for the Chicago World's Fair, stopping in Cleveland to visit a relative and to work as a barber. A year later he formed a partnership and opened a shop in downtown Cleveland. He soon sold his interest to his partner and established his own five-chair shop in the downtown area. However, the burden of business indebtedness and the support of his wife (the former Mary Ingels Thompson) and his first son resulted in failure of his enterprise. The financial support of one of his customers enabled him to open another shop. Soon, through the influence of his customers he secured the barbershop concession in the new Chamber of Commerce Building in the heart of the city's business district. The shop was a success but his ambition led him to study nights at Cleveland Law School, and in 1906 at the age of thirty-two he passed the state bar examination after first completing a high school equivalency test. He then sold his barbershop and entered the practice of law.

Fleming had been well received by the Republican party organization of the city and he participated actively in party matters. He successfully opposed older Negro political leadership in the city, in 1906 was chosen for service on the state executive committee of the party and was placed in charge of organizing the state campaign among Negroes. He sought public office locally and was supported by the party for councilman-at-large in 1907 but was unsuccessful. However, in 1909 he was successful in his quest for the same office and served a two-year term. He is said to have owed his election in large part to Albert D. ("Starlight") Boyd, a notorious Negro racketeer.

The repeated successes of the Democratic party in Cleveland forced Fleming to wait until 1915 when he was elected a city councilman from the populous ward where the Negro vote was concentrated. Fleming's term was again for two years, beginning in January 1916. He was the power behind the Attucks Republican Club, the city's leading Negro political organization which came into being in 1907.

In 1903 he had joined with others to form the Journal Publishing Company which published the weekly *Cleveland Journal*. A strong supporter of Booker T. Washington and vigorous opponent of the "radical" Harry C. Smith, the *Journal* continued publication until the 1920s. In 1907 he was one of the organizers of the Cuyahoga Lodge of Elks (IBPOEW) and became grand legal advisor of the order. Fleming was the organizer and first president of the Cleveland Association of Colored Men, formally established in January 1914 as a branch of the NAACP.

The migration of large numbers of Negroes from the South during and after World War I gave Fleming and other Negroes additional opportunities in business. They formed the Cleveland Realty, Housing, and Investment Company, and by the winter of 1917–1918 owned nearly every apartment building in the section along Central Avenue which was rapidly becoming a Negro area. Elected in 1915 as a councilman from his ward, Fleming helped some Negroes to acquire positions as clerks or assistants to department heads in the city government.

Fleming continued to be elected biennially until 1928 and build up seniority in the city's legislative body. He was a member of the powerful Appropriations and Finance Committee of the council and held the chairmanship of the Fire and Police Committee. In the work of this committee he was accused by a disabled policeman of accepting money in a matter that might come before him as a member of council. A Democratic county prosecutor seized upon the accusation and Fleming was indicted, tried, and convicted. He resigned from the council and, after exhausting all legal appeals, was sent to the Ohio Penitentiary from which he was released in January 1933 after serving thirty months. He was readmitted to the practice of law on Dec. 24, 1934.

In 1936 Fleming suffered a cerebral hemorrhage and in 1937 a fractured hip. Incapacitated, he died in 1948. He left his second wife, Lethia B. Cousins Fleming, whom he had married in 1912 following a divorce from his first wife, Mary Ingels Thompson Fleming, who had borne him three sons.

An ardent admirer of Booker T. Washington's philosophy of self-help and racial solidarity, Fleming also realized the value of Negro institutions as a base of political power, the press, churches, fraternal organizations, the YMCA, the YWCA, and even racketeers. He used them, on the whole, for his own personal aims rather than for the advancement of Negroes in Cleveland and Ohio.

His self-serving manuscript autobiography "My Rise and Persecution" is in the Western Reserve Historical Society, Cleveland. Kenneth L. Kusmer's *A Ghetto Takes Shape: Black Cleveland, 1870–1930* (1976) portrays Fleming in a generally unfavorable way. Russell H. Davis's *Black Americans in Cleveland* (1972) is more charitable. — RUSSELL H. DAVIS

FLETCHER, BEN[JAMIN HARRISON] (1890–1949), radical labor leader. Born in Philadelphia, Pa., Fletcher played a prominent role in the Industrial Workers of the World (IWW), which peaked in the early twentieth century. He devoted most of his attention to the organization of Philadelphia longshoremen while also serving the IWW as a convention delegate and a strike participant. Ben Fletcher spearheaded the organization of the Marine Transport Workers (Local 3) of the IWW. This local union conducted a series of strikes between 1913 and 1916 which resulted in benefits for workers as well as a stronger union. In this period Fletcher also conducted a nationwide petition campaign in behalf of Joe Hill, who became an IWW martyr. As a defendant in a conspiracy case prosecuted by the federal government against leaders of the IWW in 1918, Ben Fletcher received a prison sentence and a fine. His sentence was commuted by Pres. Warren Harding in 1923, and he received a full pardon by Pres. Franklin D. Roosevelt in 1933. Although Fletcher continued his activities in the IWW and Socialist party of America after his release from prison, he never recovered his earlier prominence as a labor leader and a radical. He died at his home, 813 Hancock St. in Brooklyn, N.Y., on July 10, 1949, survived by three sisters and a brother. Funeral services were held at Farlel Funeral Home, 1865 Fulton St. (*Brooklyn Eagle*, July 12, 1949, p. 9).

Most nineteenth-century labor unions denied Negro workers equality with whites. Racism and the fear of cheap labor competition usually proved more decisive than the ideal of labor solidarity. Although the Knights of Labor preached, and to a fairly significant extent practiced, labor solidarity, most labor unions chose another path. The American Federation of Labor and its affiliates retreated from the position of the Knights of Labor as a craft organization. High dues and opposition from white workers limited Negro membership.

The antagonism of organized labor and many other white workers toward Negroes reflected race relations in the early twentieth century. Institutionalized segregation became the national norm. Many Negroes migrated to the cities of the North where they encountered housing and job discrimination as well as greater opportunities for advancement than in the South. The IWW, a small countervailing force, preached and practiced labor solidarity. The organization welcomed all workers regardless of race, creed, and color. Many Negroes joined the IWW, especially Louisiana lumber workers and East Coast longshoremen. Ben Fletcher played a significant role in the organization of Philadelphia longshoremen. Local 3 of the Marine Transport Workers of the IWW provided a rallying point for many longshoremen suffering from a number of grievances. More than 3000 longshoremen struck on May 13, 1913, for higher wages, better working conditions, and union recognition. In the course of the two-week strike IWW organizers and leaders made speeches and workers held mass meetings and parades. The strike settlement featured wage increases and union recognition. By 1916 Local 3 could point to a large membership of almost 3000, additional wage increases, and union control of the docks. Other characteristics also set Local 3 apart from most labor organizations. The monthly rotation of Negro and white chairmen, for example, visibly manifested the racial solidarity of the IWW. By means of a button system which signified membership in good standing, the organization achieved the assets of the closed shop without its liabilities.

The outbreak of World War I placed the IWW on the defensive as employers, "patriots," and the government attempted to suppress the "subversive" IWW. Ben Fletcher received a ten-year sentence from Judge Kennesaw M. Landis in his Chicago trial in 1918. A. Philip Randolph protested Fletcher's imprisonment, which he attributed to Fletcher's efforts to help Negro workers, his collaboration with white workers, and his defense of principle. He demanded Fletcher's release from prison and advised the Negro press to give more recognition to individuals aiding their race.

In an article in the *Messenger,* "Philadelphia Waterfront's Unionism" (June 1923, pp. 740–41), Fletcher condemned the gross indifference of organized labor toward Negroes and its failure to breach the color line. Negroes must be organized, he declared, before organized labor could win significant victories. He advised labor unions to eliminate racial exclusion and enroll Negroes, join them in their struggle for enfranchisement in the South, and utilize Negro organizers and elect Negro officers in a proportion commensurate with their capacity and numbers. He recommended that Negroes establish a national organization to promote their general welfare and demonstrate to whites their power for good and evil.

Fletcher continued his activities in the IWW and the Socialist Party of America after his release from prison in 1923. However, he never regained his former prominence and effectiveness although he continued to disseminate his message of working-class unity until his death in 1949. More than a hundred people, most of them old IWW members, attended his funeral. The funeral ceremony included the reading of a message from Norman Thomas and a eulogy with the following tribute: "Rest, rest old fighter, rest,/ Your noble deeds by memory blest,/ Inspire us all in Freedom's quest,/ Rest, rest old fighter, rest."

Although there are no biographies of Ben Fletcher, two articles provide sources of information about his life. Philip S. Foner's "The IWW and the Black Worker" (*JNH* 55 [Jan. 1970]: 45–64) places Fletcher's activities in the setting of the relationship of Negroes and the IWW. Irwin Marcus's "Benjamin Fletcher: Black Labor Leader" (*NHB*, Oct. 1972, pp. 138–41) presents biographical data about Fletcher as well as a description of his activities as a labor leader and a radical. Background material can be gleaned from Foner's *The Industrial Workers of the World, 1905–1917,* volume 4 of *History of the Labor Movement in the United States* (1925); *We Shall Be All: A History of the Industrial Workers of the World* by Melvyn Dubofsky (1968); and *The Black Worker* by Sterling D. Spero and Abram L. Harris (1931). — IRWIN M. MARCUS

FLEURVILLE [FLORVILLE], WILLIAM DE [BILLY THE BARBER] (c. 1806–1868), businessman and friend of Abraham Lincoln. He was born probably in Cap-Haïtien, Haiti, about 1806. In 1821 the boy's grandmother took him to St. Mary's Convent in Baltimore, Md., where he learned the trade of barbering. Leaving Maryland, he traveled to New Orleans, St. Louis, and Mississippi. In the fall of 1831 he arrived penniless in New Salem, Ill., where Abraham Lincoln befriended him. He introduced De Fleurville to the customers of Rutledge Tavern, Lincoln's boarding house in New Salem, and informed them of the young man's business and need for patronage. This action provided De Fleurville with a substantial number of customers among the boarders. He then went to Springfield, Ill., where he opened (1832) the first barbershop, opposite the post office, and advertised that he had begun his old trade. Sometimes he advertised it in the form of comic prose in both the *Illinois State Journal* and the *Springfield State Journal,* similar to the following: "William Fleurville, the Barber king of the village, announced that he had erected a new barber pole, against which the storms of factions, the hurricanes of the prairies, a common size earthquake, or a runaway team will dash in vain." An advertisement in the *Sangamon Journal* shows De Fleurville at his best, using a current political campaign to boost business: "Times are pregnant with important events. Among them, and not the least is the approaching election. I am personally friendly to all the candidates. No one of them have any reason to fear any opposition. I shall exert myself to secure the election of them all. To effect this object, I would say to them that nothing is so necessary as to have a smooth face. I am adept in making smooth faces. My terms are moderate. I shall rise in price on some after the election."

Billy, a musician of sorts, played the clarinet with John Ives and Amos Camp in the Springfield Artillery military band. "Jack" Hough, the leader of the band, dressed the company in blue with red cuffs, a wide red collar extending down the front of the coat, and tall red plumes waving from their helmets. Billy also played the flute at evening entertainments in various homes.

The story of Abraham Lincoln, among "Billy's" first patrons, and William Florville, as Lincoln referred to him, is one of the more fascinating of Lincoln's friendships. Abe Lincoln, who attracted many customers to "Billy's" shop, usually sat in a barber chair facing a mirror while the barber shaved Lincoln's face and trimmed his hair. The citizens used this shop, where Lincoln sometimes left his law books for days, as the center for debates and camaraderie. The friendship of De Fleurville and Lincoln prompted the *Illinois State Journal* to state that "only two men in Springfield understood Lincoln, his law partner, William H. Herndon, and his barber, William de Fleurville."

Both a confidential friend and attorney in several transactions, Lincoln advised "Billy" on business and legal matters. A shrewd businessman, Billy acquired sizable land holdings with Lincoln's patronage and set up the first clothes-cleaning establishment in Springfield. He also sold a large tract of land for $1000 to a Judge W. Taylor and others. In 1853 Lincoln represented "Billy" in the case of *William Florville v. James*

Allen in an attempt to obtain for the plaintiff clear title to some lots purchased in Bloomington. After winning the case, Lincoln paid taxes on the lots but during the 1860 political campaign neglected to do so. However, on at least two occasions Lincoln instructed two of his close friends, Maj. W. Packard and C. R. Welles, to assume the responsibility.

By this time Billy was looked upon as one of Springfield's leading Negroes. He headed a movement to have established, according to an 1855 law, a school supported by taxes imposed on colored citizens, and paid for the advertisement for a schoolmaster. Although a Catholic, he contributed generously to the charities of various religious groups.

When Lincoln left Springfield for Washington, Billy agreed to take care of the president's property, a promise which he faithfully kept. He also observed Lincoln's career in the White House with interest and wanted "to assist in putting down this infamous Rebellion." After the Emancipation Proclamation became a reality, Billy wrote him: "I and my people feel grateful to you for it" and expressed the hope that "it may be universal in all the slave states." In the same letter Billy called the slave owners "cruel masters who make them work, and fight against the Government," and he hoped for an early end to the rebellion so that the instigators would "receive their just recompense of reward and the People to be at Peace."

Before the end of the war Billy visited Lincoln at the White House. If, as stated, the president considered appointing Billy as minister to Haiti, it did not materialize, and may well not have been considered. On another visit Billy thanked Lincoln for the goodness shown to him and said: "I hope and trust, that you may be chosen for a second term to administer the affairs of this government. . . . The nation will rejoice, the oppressed will shout the name of their deliverer, and generations to come will rise up and call you blessed."

A few years later (1865) the news of Lincoln's assassination reached Springfield. Billy would never be the same. He died on April 3, three years after the end of the Civil War. He had married in Springfield, shortly after his arrival there, the former Phoebe Ann Rountree, born in Glasgow, Ky. (Feb. 4, 1811). They had five children: Samuel H., Alseen, Sineet, Varveel, and William L. Later he adopted a son, Samuel Henry. His funeral was said to be the largest attendance in Springfield, as distinguished black and white citizens crowded the church. Because of his affiliation with the Roman Catholic church, which he had helped establish in Springfield, the family buried him in the Calvary Cemetery. Later Phoebe married Reuben Coleman (May 10, 1873) and continued to reside in Springfield.

Primary sources, in addition to the newspapers mentioned, are scarce. Among them are a letter in the Robert T. Lincoln Papers (Illinois Historical Society) and two letters in Roy P. Basler (ed.), *The Collected Works of Abraham Lincoln,* volumes 2 and 3 (1953). Much about De Fleurville's early life and descendants was learned from an interview with Dr. Wayne Temple, editor-in-chief of the *Lincoln Herald,* who collected information and who knew some of his descendants. A brief biographical sketch in John C. Power's *Early Set-* *tlers of Sangamon County, Illinois* (1876), contains similar information. There is a brief reference to Billy in Carl Sandburg's *Abraham Lincoln: The Prairie Years and the War Years* (1954, p. 170). The best sketch is in *They Knew Lincoln* by John E. Washington (1942).

— GOSSIE HAROLD HUDSON

FLIPPER, HENRY O[SSIAN] (1856–1940), first Negro graduate of West Point, author, and engineer. He was born a slave in Thomasville, Ga., the son of Festus and Isabella Flipper. Festus Flipper was a skilled workman who bought his wife's and his children's freedom. Henry's brothers also became well known: Joseph, a bishop of the African Methodist Episcopal church; Carl, a Georgia college professor; E. H., a Florida physician; and Festus Jr., a Georgia farmer.

Henry O. Flipper attended American Missionary Association schools, including Atlanta University. It was from the latter that he was appointed to the U.S. Military Academy in 1873. He was not the first Negro to attend West Point, but he was the first Negro graduate. In 1877, after four years of white cadet ostracism, Flipper graduated 50th out of a class of 76 and received his commission as second lieutenant. In January 1878 he was assigned to the all-Negro 10th Cavalry Regiment. He served with this unit at Fort Sill in the Indian Territory and at Fort Elliott, Fort Concho, Fort Davis, and Fort Quitman, all in Texas. It was at Fort Davis that he ran into difficulties. At a general court-martial on Nov. 4, 1881, he was accused by his commanding officer, Col. William R. Shafter, of "embezzling funds and conduct unbecoming an officer and gentleman" because of his alleged failure to turn in nearly $4000 in commissary funds. He was found not guilty of the first charge, guilty of the second, and discharged from the army on June 30, 1882.

After his dismissal Flipper remained in the West and for the next half century was engaged in engineering, mining, and surveying work. His fluent Spanish, his skill as an engineer, and his knowledge of law made him a valuable asset to the various companies which employed him. Between 1892 and 1903 he was a special agent of the Department of Justice, in the Court of Private Land Claims. In 1892 he published a book on Spanish laws which helped bring about the return of large tracts of land to their rightful owners and earned him the animosity of Land Grabbers.

When the Spanish-American War began, Flipper offered his services. A congressman and a senator simultaneously introduced bills to restore Flipper to his former rank and give him command of one of the four newly proposed colored regiments. Both bills died in their respective committees, and as it turned out no new Negro regiments were recruited.

Flipper continued working for various mining companies in the West, including the one controlled by Col. William C. "Bill" Greene, one of the area's most famous speculators. It was during this time that he met the general manager of Greene's Chihuahua interest, Albert B. Fall. When Fall became a U.S. senator, he utilized Flipper's reports on the Mexican political situation in his role as chairman of a subcommittee studying the impact of the Mexican Revolution on American economic interests. In 1919 Fall brought Flipper to Washington as a subcommittee translator and interpreter. Fall became secretary of the interior in the Harding administration and made Flipper an assistant. When Fall was found guilty in the Teapot Dome scandal, Flipper, not implicated, left the government and went to work for an oil company in Venezuela from 1923 to 1930. He then moved to Atlanta and lived with his brother Joseph until his death of a heart attack in 1940.

Until his death Flipper insisted that in 1882 he had not been guilty of any wrongdoings and should never have been dismissed from the army. He blamed his dismissal on the prejudice of whites particularly angered over his taking horseback rides with one of the few white women in the area of Fort Davis. As late as the 1920s he continued making official attempts to have his name cleared, but was never successful. On May 3, 1977, however, a bust of Flipper by Helene M. Hemmans was unveiled at West Point by Lt.-Gen. Sidney B. Berry, superintendent of the academy, in the presence of many relatives while two of the academy's four regiments, including Negroes and other minorities, marched in review. Berry stated that Flipper had "become one of the most honored citizens of the nation, a credit to all of its people and its rich diversity." Flipper had been exonerated posthumously by the army in 1976 (*New York Times,* May 4, 1977, p. 42).

Although Flipper had a full life and made an important contribution to the development of the West, he is most remembered as being the first Negro military academy graduate and the author of his autobiography, *The Colored Cadet at West Point* (1878). He also wrote *Negro-Frontiersman; The Western Memoirs of Henry O. Flipper . . .* (edited by Theodore D. Harris, 1963); *Mexico Laws, Statutes, etc.* (1892); *Venezuela Laws, Statutes, etc.* (1925); and, according to W. E. B. Du Bois, *Did a Negro Discover Arizona and New Mexico?* (*The Gift of Black Folk* [1924], p. 43n). During his years in the West he also contributed articles to the *Old Santa Fe* journal and a number of newspapers, one of which, the *Nogales Sunday Herald,* he edited for four months.

There is no book-length study of Henry O. Flipper. His own autobiographical works give a good insight into his life, but leave much unsaid. Sara Dunlap Jackson's Introduction to the 1969 reprint of his *Colored Cadet* and Theodore D. Harris's Introduction to his *Western Memoirs* are helpful, as are Ezra J. Warner's "A Black Man in the Long Gray Line" (*American History Illustrated* 4 [Jan. 1970]:30–38), and William H. Leckie's *The Buffalo Soldiers: A Narrative of the Negro Cavalry in the West* (1967, pp. 225, 237–38).

— JOHN F. MARSZALEK

FLORA, WILLIAM (? –c. 1818), soldier of the American Revolution and businessman. Flora was born free, probably in Portsmouth, Va. On Nov. 7, 1775, Lord Dunmore, governor of Virginia, proclaimed free all Negroes who would serve under the British flag. At the Battle of the Great Bridge, some fifteen miles south of the city of Norfolk, during the winter of 1775–1776, a detachment of Dunmore's army, including some soldiers of his "Ethiopian Regiment," drove back the Patri-

ots and attacked Col. William Woodford's 2nd Virginia Regiment. Among the defenders who repulsed the British was William Flora. Capt. Thomas Nash, who was wounded during the engagement, later wrote: "Flora, a colored man, was the last sentinel that came into the breast work. . . . he did not leave his post until he had fired several times. Billy had to cross a plank to get to the breast work, and had fairly passed over it when he was seen to turn back, and deliberately take up the plank after him, amidst a shower of musket balls. He . . . fired eight times."

At the close of the Revolution Flora returned to Portsmouth and became one of the first Negroes to buy property there. He prospered, and bought the freedom of his slave wife and children. In addition to his real estate holdings he owned (about 1810) six horses, several stage wagons, three two-wheeled riding carriages, three tables, a watch, and other valuable goods. He ran stage wagons out of Portsmouth hauling freight for farmers and merchants, while hiring out his horses and carriages.

Appearing before the Norfolk County Court on April 21, 1818, shortly before his death, he applied as a Revolutionary War veteran for a land grant. Probably supporting his claim with a certificate dated July 16, 1806, attesting his service until the "siege of York" (Yorktown?), he was given by Virginia 100 acres of land.

Recent sources are Luther Porter Jackson's *Virginia Negro Soldiers and Seamen in the Revolutionary War* (1944, pp. 16, 18–19), and Sidney Kaplan's *The Black Presence in the Era of the American Revolution 1770–1800* (1973, pp. 20–21), with a copy of the certificate of his Revolutionary War service on page 20.

— RAYFORD W. LOGAN

FORBES, GEORGE W[ASHINGTON] (1864–1927), lawyer, editor, civil rights leader, and librarian. Forbes was born in Shannon, Miss. His parents, former slaves who had been freed by Lincoln's Emancipation Proclamation, were uneducated but intelligent and deeply religious. As a youth Forbes worked in brickyards and on farms at home. Knowing that he could not get a good education in Mississippi, he left Shannon at about the age of fourteen for Ohio, where he went briefly to Wilberforce University.

It appears that Forbes arrived in the Boston area in the mid-1880s and found friends willing to help him. He saved his money by working at Harvard University and in 1888 enrolled in Amherst College. He worked his way through Amherst, where among his friends were two fellow graduates in 1892, William H. Lewis and William T. S. Jackson. Among those who attended their commencement were W. E. B. Du Bois, a student at Harvard University, and Mrs. Josephine St. Pierre Ruffin, widow of Judge George L. Ruffin. Forbes became a member of the Boston Negro "radicals," who included Archibald H. Grimké, William Monroe Trotter, Butler R. Wilson, and briefly William H. Lewis.

Upon his graduation from Amherst Forbes returned immediately to live the rest of his life in the Boston area. From 1892 until 1897 he served as editor of the weekly *Boston Courant,* the second Negro newspaper in Boston. (The first one had been *The Hub,* edited from 1883 to 1886 by Grimké and Wilson, both attorneys.) Very few issues of the *Boston Courant* exist; among those who published articles in it was Du Bois. This editorial experience helped Forbes to develop a caustic and critical style. He also published some of his poetry during these days, and kept a lifelong interest in creative writing by Negroes. From 1897 to 1901 he was one of the few Negro assistant librarians in the Boston Public Library system, working in the largest branch, the West End Branch in a predominantly Negro neighborhood.

Forbes's major historical significance is based on his early and devastating criticism of the racial ideology of Booker T. Washington. After the *Boston Courant* ceased publication in 1897, Forbes, William H. Scott (a colored clergyman of Woburn, Mass.), and Trotter, members of the Massachusetts Protective Association, discussed the feasibility of establishing another newspaper. Forbes provided the technical expertise and Trotter the "seed money" for the *Guardian.* The first issue appeared on Nov. 9, 1901, and became a relentless foe of Washington. In the beginning Forbes wrote most of the *Guardian*'s editorials—"long, graceful essays crammed with literary allusions" (Stephen R. Fox, *The Guardian of Boston: William Monroe Trotter* [1970], p. 30). Du Bois wrote that "The *Guardian* was bitter, satirical and personal; but it was earnest, and it published facts. It attracted wide attention among colored people; it circulated among them all over the country; it was quoted and discussed. I did not wholly agree with the *Guardian,* and indeed only a few Negroes did, but nearly all read it and were influenced by it" (*Dusk of Dawn . . .* [1940], p. 73).

Forbes remained co-editor of the *Guardian* only until October 1903. At the mid-July 1903 meeting of the Afro-American Council in Louisville, he, Trotter, and other "radicals" had been roundly defeated in a confrontation with T. Thomas Fortune and other supporters of Washington. On July 30, 1903, at the meeting of the Boston branch of the National Negro Business League, Fortune made a derogatory remark about the Boston delegation at the Louisville meeting. Forbes vehemently protested, and Fortune conceded that he was not talking about Forbes. Further confrontation led to the "Boston Riot." Trotter heckled Washington and in October was sentenced to serve thirty days in jail. Two days after Trotter's release, Forbes, alienated by Trotter's combativeness, dissolved the *Guardian* partnership. On Dec. 4, 1903, Forbes filed a petition to have the paper declared bankrupt. Trotter secured enough contributions to prevent Booker T. Washington from purchasing the notes against the paper.

Like many other Negro leaders during this period Forbes vacillated between support of the "radicals" and the "conservatives." Perhaps because of his feud with Trotter, he aligned himself with the "Bookerites" on the Committee of Twelve, an unsuccessful attempt to reconcile the opposing factions. In late 1905 Forbes sent a letter to the *Boston Evening Transcript* opposing, like Washington, the reduction of southern congressional representation. Forbes also refused to attend the "radical"-supported ceremony to mark the centenary of the birth of William Lloyd Garrison on Dec. 10, 1905. But he aligned himself with Du Bois at the last meeting of

the Niagara Movement (Aug. 1907) that Du Bois had organized in 1905 to oppose Washington's conservatism. Moreover, Forbes attended the banquet for Du Bois in October 1907 that Trotter bitterly opposed.

Forbes devoted most of the rest of his life to his work as a librarian. He began research on the history of Negro creative writing and wrote occasionally for a church journal. Among the Jewish population that gradually replaced Negroes in the West End neighborhood he became highly regarded for his knowledge of literature. When he died on March 10, 1927, in Boston, newspapers, especially Yiddish journals, praised his work as librarian.

His wife, Elizabeth Harley Forbes, whom he had married in 1900, survived him. He was buried in Boston, and on the day of the funeral the West End Branch was closed in his honor.

The few sources on Forbes include Stephen R. Fox's *The Guardian of Boston: William Monroe Trotter* (1971, passim); *The Crisis* (July 1927, pp. 151–52); M. Bendor's "A People's Tribune" (*Opportunity,* June 1927, pp. 184–86). His political and racial positions are best revealed in his editorials in the *Guardian.*

— CLARENCE G. CONTEE, SR.

FORD, BARNEY LAUNCELOT (c. 1824–1902), businessman, "conductor" on the Underground Railroad, and political leader. Born a slave in Virginia, Ford escaped to freedom off a Mississippi River steamer on which he had been hired out by his owner, at Quincy, Ill., in 1848. In Chicago he met Henry O. Wagoner; both taught themselves to read and write. Wagoner drew Ford into his work on the Underground Railroad. After gold was discovered in California in 1848, Ford and his wife Julia left for the West Coast by ship to Nicaragua. In late 1851 he opened in Greytown the United States Hotel, a favorite of United States speculators. During a diplomatic dispute with Great Britain in 1854 an American ship bombarded Greytown and destroyed Ford's hotel and most of the city. Ford then went inland to Virgin Bay, where he operated first the Hotel William Walker and then the California Hotel. Richer by some $5000, he opened a livery stable business in Chicago and then struck out for the Colorado gold fields. He was refused passage on a stagecoach in Denver City and worked as a barber on a wagon train. At Mountain City, where he was refused hotel accommodations, he boarded with Aunt Clara Brown. He lost two claims to gold fields by theft, and in 1860 he and five other Negro prospectors were driven from a hill southeast of Breckinridge, Colo., by white men. Because they could not find any gold, they began a legend that Ford had buried the gold in the hill and called it "Nigger Hill." He and Wagoner then opened barbershops, restaurants, and hotels in Denver. He gave financial assistance and food, and found jobs for the escaped or freed slaves who drifted into Colorado during the Civil War. In 1865, after Colorado's proposed constitution prohibited Negro suffrage, Ford took his family back to Chicago. Encouraged by Wagoner, he went to Washington at his own expense to lobby against the bill. Sen. Charles Sumner of Massachusetts led the successful fight for the elimination of the provision by persuading Pres. Andrew Johnson to veto (1867) a new bill providing statehood with white suffrage only. The ratification of the Fifteenth Amendment in 1870 ended this phase of Ford's career.

Returning to Denver, Ford, Wagoner, and others established in Wagoner's home the first adult education classes for Negroes in Colorado. Ford was a member of the Arapahoe County Republican Central Committee and an unsuccessful candidate for the state legislature in 1873.

Meanwhile he had operated a restaurant in Cheyenne, Wyo. (1867–1870), until it was destroyed by fire. In 1875, at the request of the Cheyenne Chamber of Commerce, he opened an elegant hotel there. He boasted in advertisements that the Inter Ocean Hotel was "the largest and Finest Hotel between Omaha and San Francisco." Although Pres. Ulysses Grant stopped there, the resulting publicity did not generate enough business to stave off creditors and Ford had to sell the hotel. In 1880 he moved to San Francisco, rented a lunch counter, and again prospected unsuccessfully for gold. In 1882 he returned to Denver and opened another series of restaurants, absorbed major losses in the depression of the 1890s, and rebuilt his fortune as owner of two barbershops and residential properties.

Ford was the first Negro to serve on a Colorado grand jury and Wagoner the first to serve as deputy sheriff of Arapahoe County. In 1882 Ford and his wife were the first Negroes invited to a dinner of the Colorado Association of Pioneers. After the Supreme Court civil rights decision in 1883, Ford organized a successful drive for a state public accommodations bill prohibiting discrimination (1885).

Julia Ford died of pneumonia in 1899; Ford died three years later after a stroke. They had three children: Louis Napoleon, Sadie, and Frances. Tardy and incomplete recognition of Barney Ford was accorded in 1964 when "Nigger Hill" was renamed "Barney Ford Hill."

Forbes Parkhill's *Mister Barney Ford, A Portrait in Bistre* (1963) is the only full-length biography of Ford. This illustrated book provides a lengthy survey of Ford's adult life but is highly conjectural regarding his youth. William Loren Katz's *The Black West* (1971, pp. 188–94) gives a brief account of Ford's life, with photographs of Ford, his hotels in Cheyenne and Denver, and an advertisement of his People's Restaurant, Denver, reproduced from *The Rocky Mountain News* in 1863. — FRANK N. SCHUBERT

FORD, CORNELIUS EVARTS (1870–c. 1950), businessman. He was born in Jonesboro, Tenn., the son of Mark and Angeline Ford. When he was eleven years old he worked on a farm owned by his grandparents and attended school during the winter months. At about age thirteen he became overseer of a farm owned by a white man, and superintendent of some thirty-five farm hands. After the death of his parents in 1885 he studied for two years at Warner Institute, an American Missionary Association school in Jonesboro. He then moved to Addison, Mich., where during three years he gained his first experience in raising and buying livestock for Fred S. Smith, a cousin of one of his teachers at Warner Institute. He again studied at Warner Institute until

Smith sent for him, and became a trotting race-driving expert. In 1891 he was buying and selling cattle in Michigan, Illinois, New York, and Pennsylvania. In 1903 he became a partner with F. Hart Smith in a joint livestock and shipping business. Four years later he moved to Buffalo where he became one of the leading cattle brokers with a business of more than $1 million a year. He was one of the chief buyers for such large firms as Armour & Company and Cudahy and Company. In 1937 he was elected to the Buffalo Livestock Exchange Board of Directors and in 1945 president of the exchange; he was also a vice-president of the National Livestock Association. During World War II his business was restricted by embargo restrictions on cattle from Canada, but regained thereafter some of its importance.

In 1911 he had married Martha Thompson of Painted Post, N.Y. (deceased before 1950). They had one son, Cornelius Jr. Cornelius Ford Sr. was an assistant treasurer of the Buffalo Urban League, a director of the Michigan YMCA, and during World War I a lieutenant in the Buffalo Police Reserves.

The significance of his career was stated as follows: "Here one finds the rare example of the successful realization of the hope of Booker T. Washington, that farming would lead to other business enterprises. Here, too, is integration in the true sense of the word, namely that the Ford Company functions like any other firm, neither buying from, selling to, nor depending upon a particular racial group. And, finally, the successful integration of the head of the firm into local and national trade associations should serve as an example to Negroes of what can be accomplished, and as an example to American industry of the meaning of industrial democracy" (Robert Kinzer and Edward Sagarin, *The Negro in American Business . . .* [1950], pp. 181–82).

There is no comprehensive biography of Ford. Basic facts are in *Who's Who in Colored America* (7th ed., 1950); additional information is in E. Vincent Suitt's "A Livestock Exchange President" (*Opportunity*, Spring, 1947, pp. 102–03). — RAYFORD W. LOGAN

FORD, GEORGE W. (1847–1939), soldier and cemetery superintendent. He was born on Nov. 23, 1847, in Alexandria, Fairfax County, Va., to free parents, William and Henrietta (Bruce) Ford. With the exception of 1860–1861, when he attended school in New York City, he spent his entire childhood in northern Virginia with his parents, first in Alexandria and after 1857 on a farm adjacent to the Mount Vernon estate. He enlisted in the 10th Cavalry, one of four regiments made up of Negro enlisted men, in September 1867 when the regiment was less than a year old. He saw combat intermittently through his ten years of service against the Commanches and Kiowas of the southern plains, and rose to the rank of first sergeant of L Troop and later to regimental quartermaster sergeant.

After his honorable discharge at Fort Concho, Tex., in September 1877, he worked at several national cemeteries, starting at Arlington and finishing in 1930 after twenty-four years as superintendent of the Camp Butler National Cemetery near Springfield in Sangamon County, Ill. In 1879 he was transferred from the superintendency of the Negro section of the national cemetery at Chattanooga, Tenn., to Beaufort, S.C., where he married Harriett Bythewood, by whom he had eight children. He then worked as superintendent of the burial grounds at Fort Scott, Kans., and Port Hudson, La., before moving to Camp Butler in 1906. He interrupted his career briefly in 1898–1899 to serve as a major and commander of the second battalion of the 23rd Kansas Infantry in the Cuban occupation.

In his later years Ford recalled his frontier service in the cavalry with considerable pride. He claimed in 1937 to be "the only living survivor of the original regiment . . . who marched away toward the Rio Grande, 1,225 strong in 1867" (*Winners of the West,* Feb. 1938). He had every reason to be proud. As a private Ford spent many hard winter days on courier duty between posts in present-day Oklahoma. He recalled that this duty was extremely arduous: "besides fording the icy waters of the Ganadian, the Washita, and Wild Horse, there was also the danger of capture by Indians" (*Winners of the West,* April 1924). He reached high noncommissioned rank in the 10th Cavalry and was commended in orders for heroism during a Kiowa attack on the Wichita Indian Agency at Anadarko, Indian Territory, in August 1874, when L Troop drove the attackers off twice, in a dismounted skirmish on Aug. 22 and in a mounted clash on the following day. Ford survived his many campaigns unscathed, but was wounded in the ankle in 1871 at Fort Sill when a loaded pistol accidentally discharged in his hand while he issued arms to soldiers of the guard.

In 1938 Ford received recognition as the only survivor of the original 10th Cavalry, and his picture was placed on display in the regiment's archives at its Fort Leavenworth, Kans., headquarters. One year later, on June 30, he died of bronchial pneumonia, and was buried at Camp Butler. His wife survived for another nine years.

Ford wrote several letters to *Winners of the West,* a magazine that lobbied for higher pensions for veterans. These are good source material on the early history of the 10th Cavalry as well as Ford's life, and are well known to historians of the Indian wars (e.g., William Leckie, *The Buffalo Soldiers,* 1967; Don Rickey, *Forty Miles a Day on Beans and Hay,* 1963). Ford's Veterans Administration pension file, in the National Archives, also contains much valuable data. In addition a short obituary in *The Crisis* (Oct. 1939, p. 306) has some useful information. — FRANK N. SCHUBERT

FORD [FOURSCHE], JAMES W[ILLIAM] (1893–1957), labor union and Communist leader. The son of Lyman and Nancy Reynolds [Foursche] Ford, he was born in Pratt City, Ala., a suburb of Birmingham. (The family surname at the time of his birth was Foursche; it suddenly became Ford one day when a race-hating cop, questioning the elder Ford, asked, "How do you spell it? Oh, never mind—we'll just make it a name you can pronounce, F–o–r–d.") His father was a poorly paid steelworker in the mills of Pratt City and Ensley; his mother was a domestic. Family and home conditions forced young Ford to go to work at the age of thirteen, first as a railroad gang waterboy, then as a mechanic's

helper, finally as a steamhammer operator, all in the plants of the Tennessee Coal, Iron and Railroad Company, where his father was employed. Early in life Ford learned of the terror and exploitation of Negro people in the South; the lynching of his own grandfather, a railroad worker in Georgia, made an indelible impression on him.

Although his opportunity for education was severely hampered, Ford had an intense interest in learning and was an avid reader. He and his parents viewed education as the channel through which Negroes could hope to improve their condition. Although they could ill afford to send their son to school, the Fords urged James to get the education that had been denied them.

Ford completed high school while working and entered Fisk University at the age of twenty. He became a "leader on campus" and made a brilliant record as athlete and scholar. His fleet-footedness as tailback on the Fisk football team won him the nickname of "Rabbit" Ford; he starred on the baseball and track teams and later played semiprofessional baseball in Chicago. In 1917, before graduating from Fisk, he joined the army to fight in World War I, serving in France with the signal corps as a radio engineer. He advanced to noncommissioned officer and earned the respect of his men. While in France Ford took the initiative in organizing a protest meeting against the actions of a white captain who slandered Negroes, and the captain was soon removed from his command. Ford served with the 86th Brigade of the 92nd Division, which returned to the United States in 1919. Honorably discharged, he returned to Fisk for the first semester 1919–1920 and remained there until he graduated (May 27, 1920), receiving a B.A. degree.

After graduation Ford went to Chicago in search of a job. His proficiency in radio communication led him to seek a position with the federal government. After lengthy negotiations and red tape, his application was rejected for reasons which Ford felt certain were racial. Finally he got a job at the post office as parcel post dispatcher where he worked from 1919 to 1927, joined the postal workers' union, and plunged into the trade-union movement. He soon became known as a militant trade unionist and won the loyalty and admiration of black and white workers. His main targets were the Jim Crow policies of the officials of the postal service and the dictatorial tactics of the bureaucratic union officers. Ford supported the initial organizational steps of the Brotherhood of Sleeping Car Porters, and formed a friendship with A. Philip Randolph, president of the brotherhood; his own Local Union #1 was the first AFL unit to become friendly to the brotherhood. Ford's militant union activities caused complications on his job; he was reportedly framed, and was discharged in 1927.

Ford's experiences in Chicago made a deep impression on him. His early belief that education and self-improvement on the part of the Negro would open doors and facilitate upward mobility was quashed. He became a serious student of the organized labor movement, read the works of Eugene Debs, and developed expertise on the general problems of labor as well as on the particular problems of Negro people. He was convinced that their rights could be won only through a fight "to the bitter end" against the capitalist class. The watchword of his fight was the "unity of the Negro people and the white workers."

Ford joined the Communist party in 1926 through the Trade Union Educational League, led by William Z. Foster, and the American Negro Labor Congress, organized in 1925. In 1927 he was the elected delegate of the Trade Union Educational League to the Fourth World Congress of the International Labor Union in Moscow, and the members of the congress elected him to its executive committee. He was again in Moscow in 1928 to attend the Sixth World Congress of the Communist International. During this trip he traveled extensively in the USSR, observing and studying Soviet society with emphasis on their recognition of the problem of national minorities.

As he became more involved in Communist activities, his base of operations shifted from Chicago to New York City. In 1929 he was arrested for leading a demonstration against the shooting of citizens of Haiti by the U.S. Marines. During the same year he was a delegate to the Second World Congress of the League Against Imperialism, meeting in Frankfurt, Germany, where he delivered a scathing report calling for the unqualified independence of Ethiopia.

Ford worked to develop a spirit of solidarity between the oppressed of the United States and those of other nations. He was one of the first Negro leaders to understand the vital importance of the link between the Negro struggle in America and the great liberation movements of the colonial and semicolonial worlds. Ford became an organizer and leader of Negro workers in Africa, the West Indies, and other areas. For many years he was in charge of the Negro department of the Trade Union Unity League, an American affiliate of the International of Labor Unions he had helped to organize. He also helped organize the American Negro Labor Congress, as well as its successor, the League of Struggle for Negro Rights. He was a prime mover in the organization of the First International Conference of Negro Workers which first met in Hamburg, Germany, in 1930. During this period he made a thorough study of the African colonial question, and in 1931 spoke at Geneva to a conference on African children called by the League of Nations, exposing imperialist colonial policy, to the discomfort and embarrassment of some of the other delegates.

The election campaign of 1932 found Ford back in the United States, where he was nominated for vice-president on the Communist party ticket headed by William Z. Foster. During that year he toured the country, speaking and campaigning in most important urban centers. As a war veteran he participated in the Bonus March of 1932, and was jailed during President Hoover's brutal eviction of veterans from Anacostia Flats.

In July 1933 Ford became leader of the Harlem section of the Communist party. He attended the Seventh World Congress of the Communist International in 1935, where he spoke on the Ethiopian situation and where he was elected a candidate to the executive committee. He was again nominated for vice-president on the Communist party ticket in 1936, and in 1938 was the party's candidate for the U.S. Senate from New York. Ford served as a member of the Political Committee, the National Committee, and the New York State Committee of the Communist party. He was again Communist party candidate for vice-president in 1940.

His political and social views are best articulated in his campaign speeches and writings during the 1930s. He wrote a book, *The Negro and the Democratic Front* (1938), numerous pamphlets and monographs, and was a regular contributor to the *Daily Worker,* the *Communist,* and the *Communist International.*

His views on Negro organizations underwent a substantial change during this period. In 1937 he supported the idea of a "United Front" with the NAACP, the National Negro Congress, the Urban League, and other Negro organizations. This "United Front" attitude contrasted sharply with the earlier Communist castigation of Negro organizations. (Interviews of some of Ford's contemporaries revealed that in the early 1930s he was not against Negro organizations per se, but he was opposed to the leadership of some of these organizations, particularly that of the NAACP.)

James Ford's formula for Negro advancement was to increase the strength of the farmer-labor vote and to organize Negro support for the labor movement, effecting alignments between Negro voters and voting groups of other minorities. In keeping with the Communist position, Ford dealt with "the Negro problem" through a class analysis: Negroes must mobilize with the world proletariat in the international struggle against imperialism. He also addressed other problems: the liberation of Ethiopia, a possible merger of Garveyism and Communism, and amelioration of the plight of workers of South Africa.

In 1940 Ford and Earl Browder, Communist candidates for vice-president and president, ran on a platform which said that "the issue among the American masses is no longer a third term—it is a third party." Ford stated the minimum desires of Negroes as (1) a decent and secure livelihood, (2) human rights, and (3) an equal, honorable, and respectable status in all social life.

Ford remained loyal and active in the Communist party until his death on June 21, 1957. He was survived by his second wife, Mary, three sons (by his first wife), and two granddaughters. Of the many condolences and tributes that came in from many parts of the world at the time of his death, the following tribute appeared in the *Daily Worker* (July 2, 1957), written by the Communist party leader William Z. Foster: "In the death of James W. Ford, the Negro people have lost one of their most active, loyal, and farsighted leaders, and the Communist Party one of its best workers and fighters. Modest to a fault, Jim Ford tended to obscure much of the good work he did in his rich life. But as the years go by his name will stand forth with ever greater luster as one of the major Negro fighters during the past generation of hard and successful struggles by the Negro people."

He had died on June 21 in Beth Israel Hospital, New York City, from natural causes, and was cremated on June 25.

There is no comprehensive biography of Ford. "James W. Ford: A Tribute" (*Political Affairs,* Aug.

1957, pp. 14–29) is valuable though eulogistic. An earlier publication, *Communist Candidate for Vice-President of the United States, James W. Ford, What He Is
and What He Stands For* (1936) was written by Benjamin Davis *(Jr.)* who shared many of Ford's views, set
forth in his *The Negro and the Democratic Front*
(1938). More specialized is *The Negroes in a Soviet
America* by Ford and James Allen (1935), which contains much useful information about Ford. Ford also
wrote numerous brochures and pamphlets, especially
during the 1930s when he was a frequent contributor
to the *Daily Worker*. The Schomburg Center for Research in Black Culture in New York City has an extensive newspaper file. For more critical views, see Wilson
Record's *The Negro and the Communist Party* (1951,
passim). Some details were supplied by his son, Hugh
H. Ford. — CHARLES W. HARRIS

**FORTEN, CHARLOTTE L. [MRS. FRANCIS J.
GRIMKÉ]** (1837–1914), poet, schoolteacher, and diarist. Born in Philadelphia, she was the granddaughter of
James Forten, Sr. (businessman, abolitionist, and champion of Negro rights), the daughter of Mary Wood
Forten and Robert Bridges Forten, who followed in his
father's footsteps in advocating abolition, as did her
aunts, Margaretta, Sarah, and Harriet, as well as her
uncle, James Forten, Jr., and Robert Purvis (who married Harriet Forten). Since Charlotte's father would not
permit her to attend the segregated schools in Philadelphia, she had received her early formal education from
tutors. Her wider education, especially her early interest
in abolition, developed during the years she spent at
Byberry, the "elegant country home" of Purvis, some
fifteen miles from Philadelphia. For her further education her father sent her in 1854 to Salem, Mass., where
she lived with family friends Charles Lenox Remond
and his sister Sarah, also notable abolitionists. There she
met such other renowned abolitionists as William Lloyd
Garrison, William Wells Brown, Wendell Phillips, and
John Greenleaf Whittier.

Charlotte realized that she had to prove her own
intellectual ability. Fortunately, Mary L. Shepard, principal of Higginson Grammar School, shared her interest
in "the cause" and in Charlotte's intellectual development. When she graduated in February 1855, she received thunderous applause for her prize-winning
poem "A Parting Hymn." The acclaim probably resulted also from some astonishment that a colored student could display such talent.

Her graduation from Salem Normal School in July
1856 likewise was a notable event, as was her appointment as a teacher in the Epes Grammar School of
Salem. During her two years there she attended anti-
slavery lectures by the men she had met in Robert
Purvis's home, Ralph Waldo Emerson, Theodore
Parker, and others. She joined the Female Anti-Slavery
Society in September 1855, read constantly, acquired a
knowledge of French and a smattering of German. Her
poems and an essay "Glimpses of New England" received higher praise than they perhaps deserved. When
the death of Charles Remond's wife on Aug. 15, 1856,
left him understandably irritable, Charlotte Forten
moved in December 1867 to the home of another cul-

tured colored family, Israel and Caroline Putman. Her
frail health, which could not surmount her teaching and
studies, did not improve even after a rest at Byberry. In
March 1858 she resigned from her position as teacher
and returned to Philadelphia, consoled probably by the
lavish praise bestowed upon her by the *Salem Register*
and the *National Anti-Slavery Standard*. Despite suffering from "lung fever," she taught briefly at the school
of her aunt, Margaretta Forten, in Philadelphia, and one
summer in Salem.

In October 1862 Charlotte Forten sailed from New
York for Port Royal, St. Helena Island, off the coast of
South Carolina, which Union forces had captured in
November 1861. She arrived shortly after the beginning
of a "social experiment" designed to prove that the
freedmen were as capable of self-improvement as were
whites, and taught there until May 1864. After some
seven years in Philadelphia, she assisted Richard T.
Greener, principal of the Sumner School, in Washington, D.C. (1871–1872). She served as a clerk in the
Treasury Department, joined the 15th Street Presbyterian Church, and on Dec. 19, 1878, married its pastor,
Francis James Grimké, thirteen years her junior. Their
one child, Theodora Cornelia, born in 1880, died in
infancy. Except for three years during the 1880s when
she and her husband lived in Jacksonville, Fla., she
spent the rest of her life in Washington. She died there
of a cerebral embolism, which had kept her bedridden
for thirteen months, on July 23, 1914, and was buried
in Harmony Cemetery in Washington.

Charlotte Forten began keeping a diary in Salem on
May 24, 1854, and closed the Port Royal entry on May
15, 1864. She made occasional entries between November 1885 and July 1892, during her marriage.
Among the more interesting entries in the early years of
her diary (mentioned above) are the following. In June
1857 she was "perfectly sick" of the behavior of some
colored people in Philadelphia, was outraged by the
denial of service or segregation in places of public accommodation. On July 4, 1857, she wrote: "The celebration of this day! What a mockery it is! My soul
sickens of it." (She was voicing views similar to those
of Frederick Douglass and other Negro leaders.) She
exulted over a visit (Aug. 10, 1857) from Whittier. She
could not understand (Nov. 15) Emerson's poem
"Brahma," which was "remarkable only for its utter
obscurity." Most revealing was her entry on Jan. 2,
1858: "I wonder why it is that I have this strange feeling
of not *living out myself* [her italics]. My existence
seems not *full* not expansive enough. . . . What means
this constant restlessness, this longing for—something,
—I know not what?" She became more and more skeptical about spiritualism (Jan. 16), but she did enjoy chess
(Feb. 15).

While these and other entries through Jan. 1, 1860,
deserve reading in their entirety, her most valuable contribution begins with the entry of Oct. 28, 1862, when
her ship was about to land at Hilton Head: "On the
wharf was a motley assemblage,—soldiers, officers,
and 'contrabands' of every hue and size. They were
mostly black, however, and certainly the most dismal
specimens I ever saw." But the singing by Negro boat-
men taking her to St. Helena's Island was "so sweet and

strange and solemn," especially "Roll, Jordan, Roll." She found that "The negroes [*sic*] on the place are very kind and polite" and she thought she would "get on amicably with them." She began teaching on Oct. 31 in a school held in the Baptist church. She soon found the children, many of them "babies," restless and "too young even to learn the alphabet" (Nov. 5). They did enjoy singing "John Brown" and listened attentively while she told them about Toussaint L'Ouverture. On Thanksgiving Day 1862 she thanked God for the "crowd of eager, happy black faces from which the shadows of slavery had forever passed." Gen. Rufus Saxton, commanding the Port Royal region, urged the freedmen to volunteer for military service. Despite occasional boredom, homesickness, fleas (Dec. 14), cold weather, and even snow, she found some rewards. She enjoyed the spontaneous singing of "My Country 'Tis of Thee" after the reading of Lincoln's Emancipation Proclamation on Jan. 1, 1863. The dress parade of the First South Carolina Volunteers (formed after General Saxton's appeal), commanded by Col. Thomas Wentworth Higginson, "was typical of what the race, so long downtrodden and degraded will yet achieve on this Continent." When the regiment was first mustered on Nov. 7, 1862, it was the first official regiment made up of former slaves and "strictly speaking, the first of all the Negro regiments with official military status" (Benjamin Quarles, *The Negro in the Civil War* [1953], p. 119). Among the wives of the noncommissioned officers was Susie King Taylor, laundress, teacher, and nurse. Miss Forten was thrilled by the expedition of the regiment up the St. Mary's River (Feb. 7–8, 1863) and the expulsion of the Confederates from Jacksonville (April 2, 1863). But soon thereafter the regiment was disbanded because of the storm of public protest. In July 1863, after the attack on Fort Wagner, S. C. by the 54th Massachusetts (Colored) Regiment, in which Col. Robert Gould Shaw was killed, Miss Forten went to Beaufort, mended the pantaloons and jackets of the wounded soldiers, and wrote letters for them. By July 26, 1863, she had become so weak that she feared she would be an easy prey to the late summer's fever. A trip by sea to New York, Philadelphia, Byberry, Salem, and Boston, where she visited her friends (July 31 to Oct. 10, 1863), restored her health to some extent. But the small number, four, and the brevity of the entries in her diary after she returned to Hilton Head on Oct. 10, 1863, until May 15, 1864, suggest that she had lost most of the enthusiasm that led her to undertake her mission in October 1862. She left Port Royal in the latter part of May and arrived in New York on June 3.

Miss Forten's diary does not reveal, either, the outcome of the "social experiment" at Port Royal. Although she was in no way responsible, its failure was due primarily to the failure of the federal government to ensure continued possession of land granted the freed slaves after the Civil War and the effective demise of the Freedmen's Bureau by 1872.

Miss Forten enjoyed the friendship of many prominent whites during her mission of eighteen months. One young white man showed a romantic interest in her, but she spurned his advances because "although he is very good and liberal he is still an *American* [her italics], and

w'ld of course never be so insane as to love one of the proscribed race" (May 18, 1863). On the other hand, one would like to know the degree of affection between her and Dr. Seth Rogers, whom she frequently mentioned. Although she cherished her relationships with some of the former slaves, she did not establish a meaningful rapport with most of them.

Her husband Francis idolized her. Lottie, as he called her "was one of the dearest, sweetest, loveliest spirits that ever graced this planet." On the anniversaries of her death, he recorded in his reflections, *Stray Thoughts and Meditations,* his rhapsodic praise to her memory. He did not marry again.

The most extensive printed account of Charlotte Forten's life is in the Introduction to *The Journal of Charlotte Forten,* edited by Ray Allen Billington (1953). Much of the same information is in his sketch in *NAW* (1971, 2:95–97), with some added details from Dorothy Porter, curator emeritus of the Moorland-Spingarn Collection, Howard University. The manuscript diaries were deposited by Mrs. Grimké's friend of many years in Washington, Anna J. Cooper, in what is now the Moorland-Spingarn Research Center.

— RAYFORD W. LOGAN

FORTEN, JAMES [SR.] (1766–1842), businessman, abolitionist, champion of Negro rights, and leader of reform movements. Forten was born in Philadelphia of free Negro parents. According to tradition, his great-grandfather had been brought as a slave from Africa; his grandfather was born a slave but became free. James studied briefly at the school of Anthony Benezet, the famous Quaker abolitionist. After the death of his father he worked in a grocery store to support his mother. At the age of fifteen he volunteered as a powder boy on a Philadelphia privateer, *Royal Louis,* during the Revolutionary War. Captured by a British frigate, he was imprisoned for seven months. He spent a year in England where he talked with such prominent abolitionists as Granville Sharpe. Upon his return to the United States he was apprenticed to Robert Bridges, a sailmaker. He became foreman of the sail loft in 1786, and when Bridges retired in 1798 Forten became owner of the firm. By 1832 he had amassed a fortune of $100,-000 by employing some forty white and colored workers and by inventing a device to handle sails.

Meanwhile he became one of the best known and influential abolitionists of the first half of the nineteenth century, using his personal fortune to promote the cause as well as women's rights, temperance, peace, and equal rights for Negroes. When he died in 1842, his funeral on Feb. 24 was one of the largest in the history of Philadelphia. He was survived by three daughters and two sons. One of them, Robert Bridges Forten, who continued his father's interest in business and abolitionism, was the father of Charlotte Forten.

James Forten, Sr., was a product of his birthplace and his era; he also greatly influenced the events of his age. It was in Philadelphia that Richard Allen, Absalom Jones, and a group of other Negroes were forced to leave St. George's Methodist Church in November 1786; they and others organized Bethel Church less than two years later. On April 12, 1787, they "formed a curious sort of ethical and beneficial brotherhood called the Free African Society. How great a step this was, we of to-day [sic] scarcely realize; we must remind ourselves that it was the first wavering step of a people toward organized social life" (W. E. B. Du Bois, *The Philadelphia Negro: A Social Study* [1899, reprinted 1967], p. 19). Free Negroes had increased in number after Pennsylvania in 1788 prohibited the internal and foreign slave trade, and in 1790 gave the suffrage to free Negro property holders (as well as to white), a right enjoyed in most counties until 1837. In 1789 Quakers formed the Pennsylvania Society for Promoting the Abolition of Slavery, the Relief of Free Negroes Unlawfully Held in Bondage, and for Improving the Condition of the African Race. Benjamin Franklin was its first president.

Forten's decision to become an active abolitionist probably resulted from the overwhelming rejection by Congress (1800) of a petition (of which he was one of the signers) for modification of the Fugitive Slave Act of 1793. He was the author of a pamphlet (1813) which protested against a bill before the Pennsylvania Senate to bar the immigration of free Negroes from other states. Invoking the Declaration of Independence and the Constitution, and asserting that "This is almost the only State in the Union wherein the African race have justly boasted of national liberty and the protection of the laws," he pointed out that the bill required a colored man in Philadelphia to become an informer if he received an out-of-state visitor for only a few days. He envisaged a dire possibility: "The dog is protected and pampered at the board of his master, while the poor African and his descendant, whether a Saint or a felon, is branded with infamy, registered as a slave, and we may expect shortly to find a law to prevent their increase, by taxing them according to numbers, and authorizing the Constables to seize and confine every one who dare to walk the streets without a collar on his neck!" Like Frederick Douglass in his famous oration of July 5, 1852, he denounced the celebration of the Fourth of July: "Is it not wonderful that the day set apart for the festival of liberty, should be abused by the advocates of freedom, in endeavoring to sully what they profess to adore" (the pamphlet may be conveniently consulted in Carter G. Woodson [ed.], *Negro Orators and Their Orations* [1925], esp. pp. 42, 43, 46). His appeal was in vain.

Although most historians have included Forten among the vigorous opponents of colonization, especially since he presided at protest meetings in Philadelphia in 1817, recent research in the Paul Cuffe Papers reveals that he at first expressed his opposition by silence rather than by public statements (see especially the letter from Forten to Cuffe, Philadelphia, Jan. 25, 1817, in Sheldon Harris's *Paul Cuffe Black America and the African Return* [1972], pp. 243–45). It was not until after Cuffe's death in 1817 that Forten in 1819 publicly proclaimed his opposition to colonization. Thereafter he greatly influenced other opponents of colonization, especially at meetings of the Negro Convention, beginning in 1830, and in his activities as an abolitionist.

The Negro Convention made clear the divisiveness among strong-minded Negro leaders about how "to devise ways and means for the bettering of our condition." Forten, for example, endorsed raising funds for a Negro college for training in the skilled trades, and regretted that a donation of $1000 was made to the American Colonization Society rather than to master mechanics for the training of Negro mechanics. Others opposed even the meetings of the National Convention. His opposition to colonization increased as his participation in the crusade for abolition became more effective.

He is, in fact, given credit for convincing William Lloyd Garrison that colonization was evil. By the 1830s his recognized role as a leader enabled him to obtain subscriptions for Garrison's *The Liberator* before it was first published in January 1831. His sizable fortune made him such a generous contributor to *The Liberator* that only Arthur and Lewis Tappan surpassed him. Garrison frequently visited Forten in his spacious home on Lombard Street, Philadelphia. It was there that the American Anti-Slavery Society was organized in 1833, and Forten served on its board of managers while he contributed funds for the support of the society when it was in financial difficulty. At the same time he advocated universal peace and women's rights, founded and served as president of the American Moral Reform Society, a body of Negro men dedicated to the "promotion of Education, Temperance, Economy, and Universal Liberty." He arranged local mass meetings to urge emancipation and equality of the races, and was a delegate to numerous state gatherings, notably one at Harrisburg in 1837 to press for the end of slavery and colonization. When the Pennsylvania state legislature in 1832 again considered measures to restrict the immigration of Negroes and pressed for a more vigorous enforcement of the 1793 Fugitive Slave Act by suggesting the repeal of a Pennsylvania statute requiring a judge to hear all fugitive slave cases, Forten, William Whipper, and Robert Purvis organized a petition drive (January 1832) against the proposals (Herbert Aptheker [ed.], *A Documentary History of the Negro People in the United States* [1951, 1969], 1:129–33). But the U.S. Supreme Court, in *Prigg v. Pennsylvania* (1842), ruled that state officials were not required to assist in the return of fugitives, thus overturning an 1826 Pennsylvania "personal liberty" statute. Forten died at age seventy-six in the same year as *Prigg v. Pennsylvania*. After his funeral in Philadelphia, men and women of both races paid tribute to his memory at a large public gathering. His career inspired many other abolitionists, especially his children, his son-in-law Robert Purvis, and his granddaughter Charlotte Forten.

A full-length biography is Esther M. Doughty's *Forten the Sailmaker, Pioneer, Champion of Negro Rights* (1968). The best brief biography of James Forten, Sr., is in *The Journal of Charlotte Forten,* edited with an introduction and notes by Ray Allen Billington (1953, pp. 6–14). There is also a very brief sketch by Benjamin Brawley in the *DAB* (1928, 1937, 6:536–37).

— RAYFORD W. LOGAN

FORTUNE, AMOS (1710?–1801), tanner and bookbinder. Little is known about his life until he lived as a slave in Boston (1725–1740) with Caleb Copeland and his family. Sold to Ichabod Richardson, a tanner in Woburn, Mass. (1740–1779), he learned the craft, worked off his indentureship in 1770, went into business for himself, and bought a half-acre lot. He saved enough money to buy Lydia Somerset, a crippled slave in 1778. When she died a few months later, he bought and married Violate Baldwin (Nov. 10, 1779). For reasons unknown they moved to Jaffrey, N.H., where he built his own tannery while Violate worked at a loom. He was respected by the white people of the town, although he and the few other colored inhabitants had to sit in a separate pew in the gallery of the church.

By 1789 he had prospered enough to buy a piece of land and build a house on it. He aided less fortunate colored people in Jaffrey, notably Polly Burdoo, who had been supported by the townspeople. He trained black and white apprentices. In 1796, after he had paid three dollars as a founding member of the Social Library, he began binding the books.

When he died in 1801 he left what was then a fairly substantial sum of something less than $800. He bequeathed his estate to Violate, except a few pieces of furniture and a foot-wheel to his adopted daughter Celyndia Fortune. After the death of his widow, the remaining funds were to be used by the village church and for the support of the local school. The cash balance was allowed by the legislature for the consolidated school. In 1928 the town voted to use a part of the income for prizes to be awarded to the boy and girl who won in a public-speaking contest. In 1946 a summer forum was named the Amos Fortune Forum, conducted in the building where he had worshipped and a short distance from the place where he and his wife were buried. Two gravestones were provided for in his will.

The most comprehensive biography is by F. Alexander Magoun, *Amos Fortune's Choice: The Story of a Negro Slave's Struggle for Self-fulfillment* (1964). A more popular account is Elizabeth Yates's *Amos Fortune, Free Man* (1950). There is a short sketch, "Amos and Violate Fortune: First Citizens of New Hampshire," with reproduction of the gravestones, in Sidney Kaplan's *The Black Presence in the Era of the American Revolution, 1770–1800* (1973, pp. 226–27).

— RAYFORD W. LOGAN

FORTUNE, T[IMOTHY] THOMAS (1856–1928), journalist and civil rights leader. Fortune was born to slave parents, Emanuel and Sarah Jane, in Marianna, Jackson County, Fla., on Oct. 3, 1856. His ancestors were a mixture of Negroes, Indians, and whites, among them Thomas Fortune, an Irishman who was his paternal grandfather. Emanuel Fortune, who was elected to the Florida constitutional convention of 1868 and to the lower house of the state legislature, was forced by threats of the Ku Klux Klan to leave Marianna and move to Jacksonville.

Fortune's education in Florida was limited to three sessions in schools sponsored by the Freedmen's Bureau. In Jacksonville he learned the printer's trade, becoming an expert compositor. In 1876 he entered the Preparatory Department of Howard University with the intention of later studying law but lack of money forced him to abandon these plans. While in Washington he worked on the *People's Advocate,* a Negro newspaper. About this time he married Carrie C. Smiley of Jacksonville and returned to Florida. Of five children born to this marriage, two reached adulthood: Jessica, who became Mrs. Aubrey Bowser, and Frederick White, who graduated from Meharry Medical College and practiced medicine in Philadelphia. Fortune and his wife separated in 1906.

In 1879 Fortune moved to New York City, where he found work as a printer. He soon became part owner of a weekly tabloid, *Rumor.* In 1881 the paper became the *Globe* and Fortune its editor. After the *Globe* failed in 1884 Fortune began publication of the *New York Freeman,* of which he was sole owner. In 1887 the *Freeman* became the *New York Age,* with Fortune and Jerome B. Peterson as joint owners. Fortune sold the *Age* to Fred R. Moore in 1907, but it continued publication until 1960. The reputation which the *Age* enjoyed as the leading Negro newspaper rested primarily on Fortune's editorials, which condemned all forms of racial discrimination and uncompromisingly demanded full equality for Negro citizens. Fortune's militancy made him a controversial figure, often criticized in the white press. His economic views, expressed in editorials and in his book *Black and White: Land and Politics in the South* (1884), were tinctured with radicalism of the Henry George variety. Fortune was a political maverick, who denounced the Republican party for its betrayal of southern Negroes and urged Negroes to become politically independent. He briefly supported the Prohibition party in 1887. In 1888 he worked actively for the reelection of Cleveland, but in 1889 returned to the Republican party.

He was the prime mover in the founding in 1890 of the National Afro-American League, which foreshadowed in its objectives and methods civil rights organizations of the twentieth century. The league became defunct in 1893 because of lack of funds and of mass support, as well as the refusal of such leaders as Frederick Douglass, John Mercer Langston, Blanche K. Bruce, and P. B. S. Pinchback to become members. Because of greater need a few years later of a similar organization, Fortune, responding to an appeal by Bishop Alexander Walters and some 150 endorsements, called a conference in Rochester, N.Y., in September 1898 which organized the National Afro-American Council. Many prominent Negroes and Susan B. Anthony were present; conspicuously absent, however, was Booker T. Washington, although he had signed the call for the meeting. At the opening session Fortune voiced a new concern: the fate of Cubans, Filipinos, and Puerto Ricans after the United States' defeat of Spain. Since Fortune, in ill-health, expressed doubt about the viability of a new organization, he resigned as president and Walters was elected in his stead. The National Afro-American Council advocated substantially the same objectives as had the Afro-American League. When the "Declaration of Principles" of the Niagara Movement in 1905 emphasized suffrage and civil rights, Fortune accused W. E. B. Du Bois of copying the platform of the council. Fortune also denounced Du Bois and William Monroe Trotter for their attacks on Booker T. Washington. One basic difference between Fortune and the Niagara Movement was implementation of the second section of the Fourteenth Amendment. Fortune, who converted Booker T. Washington to his view, held that this action tacitly recognized the constitutional right of states to deny the suffrage to Negroes; they preferred legislation based on the Fifteenth Amendment. Controversies between the supporters of Washington and Du Bois at the annual meetings of the council had already weakened it and its last meeting was held in New York in October 1906. The Niagara Movement likewise declined and ceased virtually to function after 1911. Many of its objectives were advocated by the Constitution League in 1905 and by the NAACP, formally organized in 1910. Fortune had resigned from the Afro-American Council in March 1904, but one of his more important legacies was the platform of the league and the council which shaped some of the goals of the NAACP. A less significant legacy was his advocacy of the term "Afro-American" instead of "Negro," a term used by some later spokesmen who opposed both "Negro" and "Black."

The *Age* was never a financial success and Fortune was forced to supplement his income by other writing. During the 1890s he wrote regularly for the *New York Sun.* For several years he wrote editorials for the *Boston Transcript* and did other freelance writing. He persistently but unsuccessfully sought political appointments to ease his chronic financial problems. In 1903 he went to Hawaii and the Philippines to study race and labor conditions as a special agent of the U.S. Treasury Department. After visiting Japan and Hong Kong, he arrived in Manila in February 1903 and remained on the island of Luzon until May. His observations are among the more valuable contemporary reports: southern whites, in disproportionate numbers, were hated by Filipinos; white Americans had illicit unions with Filipino women and left them and their children behind on their return to the United States. His statement that Filipinos showed no race prejudice against discharged American Negro soldiers may not be entirely accurate. He believed that American Negroes might find better opportunities in the Philippines than in the United States. Like many other observers he concluded that the race prejudice of white officials alienated many Filipinos. After his return to the United States he recommended the appointment as governor of the Philippines an American Negro such as Booker T. Washington to conciliate the Filipinos and encourage Negro migration. Nothing, of course, came of his proposal. The trip not only did not improve Fortune's financial situation but caused a recurrence of malaria which he had first contracted in Florida.

At the turn of the century Fortune was probably the best known, most militant, and most articulate race spokesman in the North. Somewhat paradoxically he was also an ally of Booker T. Washington, for whom he was confidant, adviser, publicist, and ghost writer. The relationship between the two men rested on genuine friendship, but Fortune's increasing financial dependence on Washington eroded his political independence. In addition to paying Fortune for ghost writing, Washington loaned him money and subsidized the *Age.*

In 1907 he secretly became a stockholder in the *Age* corporation, although he continued to deny that he had any financial interest in the paper. Fortune disagreed strongly with Washington on some issues and Washington did not control the editorial policy of the *Age,* but Fortune consistently defended Washington against such critics as William Monroe Trotter and W. E. B. Du Bois, and helped him control the Afro-American Council. One of the more dramatic examples of his support of Washington had been his speech on July 30, 1903, at the Columbus Avenue African Methodist Episcopal Zion Church to the Boston branch of the National Negro Business League. Despite heckling by some members of the audience and sneezing resulting from red pepper scattered on the platform, Fortune was able to finish his speech in favor of Washington and deprecation of divisiveness among Negroes. When the audience tried to prevent Washington from speaking, William H. Lewis and Fortune tried in vain to quiet the audience. Only after Trotter, his sister Maude, and a leader of the disturbance were taken away under arrest was Washington permitted to deliver his address. Fortune was condemned by the anti-Washingtonians; he in turn denounced the supporters of Trotter. After the death of Washington on Nov. 14, 1915, Fortune wrote an article in the April 1916 issue of the *A.M.E. Church Review* which reviewed his relationship with Washington and Washington's role as a race leader, and evaluated his own place in history. After working together in the 1890s, Fortune had criticized Washington for his endorsement of Theodore Roosevelt's catering to the South and discharge without honor of three companies of the 25th Infantry following the Brownsville, Tex., riot on Aug. 13, 1906. Fortune further wrote that while Washington had done a great work, it was less significant than that done by Douglass between 1841 and 1880 and that done by Fortune from 1880 to 1904. Fortune also contended that Washington had no further use for him after he had lost his health and sold the *Age* to Fred R. Moore in 1907.

In 1907 Fortune, who had become an alcoholic, suffered a mental breakdown. For several years thereafter he suffered from mental illness, was unable to find permanent employment, and was virtually a derelict. But he regained his health in the last decade of his life. From 1919 until his death he wrote editorials and special columns for the *Norfolk Journal and Guide.* In 1923 he became editor of the *Negro World,* publication of Marcus Garvey's Universal Negro Improvement Association, after Garvey had been sentenced to federal prison. Fortune did not share Garvey's belief in racial separatism but he believed in Garvey's honesty and admired his capacity for leadership.

In early April 1928 Fortune suffered a collapse in New York City. A week later he was taken to Philadelphia by his son, Frederick White Fortune, a surgeon at Mercy Hospital. After a relapse, T. Thomas Fortune died on June 2, 1928. He was survived by his estranged wife Carrie; his daughter Jessie (Mrs. Aubrey Bowser) and their children, and his son.

Fortune was widely eulogized in the Negro press. For instance, Kelly Miller wrote: "After all has been said and done, Timothy Thomas Fortune represented the best journalist that the Negro race has produced in the Western World"; between the decline of Douglass's greatest influence and the rise of Booker T. Washington, Fortune had been the most influential Negro in the United States (*New York Amsterdam News,* June 13, 1928). In her biography, Thornbrough concluded: "When [Claude] McKay urged [in 1919] that Negroes 'nobly die' so that 'the monsters' they defied should be compelled to honor them, and when he declared, 'Like men we'll face the cowardly pack' and die 'fighting back,' he was echoing in verse what Fortune, the Afro-American agitator, had said years before in editorials and speeches" (p. 370).

Emma Lou Thornbrough's *T. Thomas Fortune, Militant Journalist* (1970) is based in large part on the Booker T. Washington Papers, Manuscript Division, Library of Congress, which contain correspondence between Fortune and Washington, Emmett J. Scott, Fred R. Moore, Charles W. Anderson, and others; the T. Thomas Fortune Papers, a private collection in the hands of Fortune's descendants; and the Emmett J. Scott Papers, Soper Library, Morgan State University, Baltimore, Md. Also analyzed were the extant copies of the *New York Globe,* the *New York Freeman,* and the *New York Age.* Although Robert S. Abbott, editor and publisher of the *Chicago Defender,* is the subject of an article in *DAB,* Fortune is not.

— EMMA LOU THORNBROUGH

FOSTER, ANDREW [RUBE] (1879–1930), "The Father of Negro baseball" and a preeminent figure in the history of the Negro leagues. A star pitcher, and a great manager, strategist, and innovator, Foster founded the Chicago American Giants, one of the finest Negro teams, and proposed the first viable Negro league, the Negro National League, in 1919 when Jackie Robinson was one year old. Foster's historic achievement saved Negro baseball. Without it, it is fair to say, there may never have been a Jackie Robinson or a Hank Aaron.

Foster was born in Galveston, Tex., on Sept. 17, 1879, the son of a Methodist minister, and Sarah Foster. He attended school in Galveston and by 1901 had attracted the attention of the Philadelphia Athletics, who were training in the South. That same year he went north with the (Negro) Leland Giants, jumping in 1902 to the Cuban Giants, a misnamed club of American Negroes from Philadelphia. He pitched for a salary of $40 a month plus fifteen cents a meal eating-money, and called himself the best pitcher in the country. He may have been right—that year he won fifty-one games, one of them a 5–2 victory over the A's star pitcher Rube Waddell, and earned his own nickname, Rube, which would follow him throughout his life.

In 1903 Foster joined the rival Cuban X-Giants, also a Philadelphia American team, and that fall they challenged the Philadelphia (Black) Giants to the first modern Negro world series. Foster won four games as the X-Giants took the series, five games to two. The next year he and most of the X-Giants changed sides, joining their former victims, and this time won again, defeating their old team, the X-Giants. Although sick, Foster won two games, one a two-hitter, the other on eighteen strike-outs.

Honus Wagner, the great white shortstop, called Foster "the smoothest pitcher I've ever seen." And John McGraw, manager of the New York Giants, hired Foster to coach Christy Mathewson and the other Giant pitchers. Rube taught them his screwball, which Mathewson would make famous as a "fadeaway." Writing in Sol White's *Black Baseball Guide* of 1906, Foster summed up his philosophy: Even with the bases filled, he counseled, "do not worry. Try to appear jolly and unconcerned. This seems to unnerve [the batters]."

Foster rejoined the Lelands, then in Chicago, in 1907 and led them to forty-eight straight victories. They finished the year with a 110–10 mark. Chicago Cubs manager Frank Chance wistfully called him "the most finished product I've ever seen in the pitcher's box." The Lelands played Chance's Cubs that fall, losing three games, 4–1, 6–5, and 1–0. Foster pitched the second game, his first in three months after being sidelined by a broken leg. The winning run scored in the ninth on a steal of home after Foster thought time had been called. In 1908 Foster broke with the Lelands and formed his own team, the Chicago American Giants. With John Henry Lloyd and Grant "Home Run" Johnson rivaling the Cubs' Johnny Evers and Joe Tinker on the double play, Foster called it his greatest team ever. They won 129 and lost only 6. Three years later they were outdrawing both the Cubs and White Sox at the gate, and Cubs manager Evers turned down a challenge for a rematch on the field. The American Giants traveled in their own private Pullman car with uniforms and equipment that dazzled their opponents. In 1914 they beat the Brooklyn Royals four straight and claimed the Negro championship of the world.

Foster called a historic meeting of Negro club owners in 1919 and organized in 1920 the first Negro league, serving as president until his death in 1930. The league consisted of the American Giants, Kansas City Monarchs, Indianapolis ABCs, Chicago Giants, Detroit Giants, St. Louis Giants, and a team of traveling Cuban all-stars. A formal schedule replaced the barnstorming, mutual raiding was ended, and player salaries increased. Foster probably saved the Negro game.

Foster's own American Giants won the first three pennants (1920–1922). He had a team of "race horses" —Cristobel Torriente, Jimmy Lyons, Jelly Gardner, Bingo DeMoss, Dave Malarcher. Rube designed the hit-and-run bunt for them. A fast man on first could take third when the batter pulled the third baseman off to field a bunt. Sometimes the runner even scored. The Giants made their own breaks and demoralized their foes with their speed, a style later brought into the major leagues by Jackie Robinson, Maury Wills, and Lou Brock. In their park at 79th and Wentworth, Chicago, they played to overflow crowds, including many white fans.

In 1926 tragedy struck suddenly. Midway through the season Foster had a severe mental breakdown and had to be taken to the state insane asylum where he died in 1930, raving about one more championship. He received a mammoth funeral and was buried in Lincoln Cemetery, Chicago. He was survived by his wife Sarah and two children, Earl and Sarah.

"He was a genius," grieved his former outfielder,

George Sweatt. "He had to be—the brainwork he had to do to organize eight teams of Negroes, because they're hard to organize. He was my idol of a man." Third baseman Dave Malarcher added that Foster had turned down a chance to enter white semipro ball. Although he was a leading drawing card, he turned down the offer to stay with the National Negro League until the time finally came when the big leagues would admit Negroes. "The thing for us to do," he said, "was to keep on developing so that when the time did come, we would be ready." The time finally came in 1946, and Jackie Robinson was ready.

John Holway's illustrated *Voices from the Great Black Baseball Leagues* (1975) is based in large measure on interviews with former players, journalists, and contemporary newspapers. The book also contains valuable statistics. Robert W. Peterson's *Only the Ball Was White* (1970), likewise based on interviews and newspapers, has a photograph in civilian clothes (p. 103). See also William Brashler's *Josh: A Life in the Negro Leagues* (1978), Ocania Chalk's *Pioneers of Black Sport* (1974), Edwin Bancroft Henderson's *The Negro in Sports* (1949), and A. S. ("Doc") Young's *Negro Firsts in Sports* (1963). — JOHN HOLWAY

FOSTER, LUTHER HILTON, SR. (1888–1949), college administrator. He was born on May 26, 1888, in Clover, Halifax County, Va., the son of Oliver (a general store merchant) and Mary Elizabeth (Smith) Foster. He attended the public schools of Halifax County, and during boyhood was engaged in part-time farm work and as clerk in his father's store. Following graduation from St. Paul's Institute in Lawrenceville, Va., he taught for one year in the public schools, after which he returned to St. Paul's to serve a three-year apprenticeship in the institute's business office. From 1911 to 1913 he was employed as head bookkeeper at St. Paul's under the supervision of Daniel Crawford Smith, CPA, of New York City, auditor for the institute. Along with serving as college administrator from 1913 until his death in 1949, Luther Hilton Foster, Sr., was a pioneer in educational financial planning and management. He applied much of his attention and expertise to assisting Negro higher educational institutions improve their business operations from 1929 to 1949 as consultant for the General Education Board and the Julius Rosenwald Fund.

It was Foster's work at Virginia State College—where he served as treasurer and business manager (1913–1943), as acting president (1943–1944), and as president from 1944 until his death—that brought him wide acclaim as an astute administrator and financial "wizard." Those who knew and were associated with him at Virginia State characterized Foster as a "person of high integrity and demanding standards, whose passion for work set an outstanding example for faculty and staff as well as students of the college."

Virginia State College was established in 1882, as the direct outgrowth of activities of Negroes in the political history of Virginia. The bill for establishing the school was drawn up and led through the legislature by A. W. Harris, a Negro citizen of Petersburg. Known originally as the Virginia Normal and Collegiate Institute, the school was first under the management and control of

a seven-man Board of Visitors, with James Storum, a graduate of Oberlin College, serving as principal. When Foster went to Virginia State the president was James Hugo Johnston, who died after Foster's first year.

Johnston was succeeded by John M. Gandy, who served as Virginia State's president until 1942. Foster was then asked by the State Board of Education to serve as acting president, and in April 1943 he was appointed to the presidency.

When Foster became associated with the school in 1913 it was a normal school without accreditation. During his thirty-six-year tenure—with extended leaves of absence to pursue further study at the University of Chicago—Virginia State strengthened and expanded its program to offer Bachelor of Arts, Bachelor of Science, and Master of Science degrees, and received full accreditation by the Southern Association of Colleges and Schools. For thirty years as treasurer and business manager of the college Foster had responsibility for all financial operations, including planning for capital additions, preparation and justification of operating and capital expenditures to state officials and other agencies from which funds were secured. While Foster was at Virginia State the plant grew from $285,000 to $5 million in value; the endowment fund increased from zero to $173,000; the operating budget expanded from $36,000 to $1.4 million; and the annual income from public funds increased from $16,500 to $635,000. At the time of Foster's death in 1949 the college had a resident enrollment of 1500 students; the junior college division —established in Norfolk in 1944—enrolled 800 students. In addition, the college offered a number of services to adults in the state through home study and extension courses, workshops, and special institutes.

Despite offers to take positions at other institutions— including Howard University, Hampton Institute, Tuskegee Institute, and Kentucky State College—Foster chose to remain at Virginia State College. He wrote to one of his friends in 1942: "I have remained here because I have been interested in and fond of the work which I have tried to do here. We have had good Boards under which to work during the last 30 years. There has been a growing tendency toward more liberal support of this College, and I have been happy to work under the several Boards and with my associates here looking toward the coming of brighter days and better things. To say that I feel encouraged and rewarded over the results would be expressing it very mildly."

For twenty years—from 1929 until his death—Foster was financial adviser for all Negro institutions which received funds from the General Education Board. He was also a specialist in business administration for the Julius Rosenwald Fund. The board was making modest grants to some of the Negro colleges and needed to be assured that the money would be used with maximum effectiveness in carrying out a carefully developed educational program in each instance. His services as consultant to the General Education Board included visits and evaluations of programs at the colleges, in which he was often joined by board officers such as Jackson Davis and Leo Favrot, as well as by business officers from other Negro colleges.

In Foster's work with Negro colleges to improve their

fiscal operations, the need for better trained business officers was evident to him. He established an internship for college business officers at Virginia State College—with financing from the General Education Board—and a number of promising young men were associated with the program for several months to learn the Virginia State College system and the business management techniques employed so effectively by Foster. Among these persons were James B. Clarke, who became treasurer of Howard University in 1949, and W. A. ("Squat") Hamilton, who became chief business officer at Lincoln University in Missouri.

In 1939 Foster joined with Virginius D. Johnston, treasurer of Howard University, and Don A. Davis, business manager of Hampton Institute, in establishing the Association of Business Officers in Schools for Negroes. He served as the association's first president and as a member of its executive committee until his death. In 1947 he obtained authorization for the establishment of a senior ROTC at Virginia State (Thomas D. Pawley to R.W.L., Feb. 13, 1976).

From 1946 to 1949 Foster was president of the Association of Presidents of Negro Land Grant Colleges; was administrator of the Virginia Graduate Aid Fund for out-of-state study by Negro students; served as a member of the Virginia State Planning Board, the Board of Trustees of Bishop Payne Divinity School in Petersburg and of St. Paul's Institute. He was active in the YMCA, the United Service Organization during World War II, and was a life member of the NAACP. He was also a member of the Masonic order, Alpha Phi Alpha fraternity, Iota Sigma Lambda fraternity, and Sigma Pi Phi fraternity.

An Episcopalian, Foster served as vestryman at St. Stephen's Church in Petersburg, and was a member of the executive board of the Diocese of Southern Virginia, and of the subcommittee, Division of Domestic Missions, National Council of the Protestant Episcopal church.

Foster received honorary Doctor of Laws degrees from Morris Brown College in 1943 and from Virginia Union University the same year. His name was included in the Honor Roll of the *Richmond* (Va.) *Times-Dispatch* in 1942, and in 1944 he was awarded a certificate of merit by Camp Lee, Va., for his community college–army cooperation during World War II.

Foster was married in Hampton, Va., on Sept. 9, 1912, to Daisy Octavia Poole of Surry, Va. She and their three children, Luther Hilton Jr., Virginia Poole, and Mary Allen, survived him. He died of natural causes in Petersburg, Va., on July 6, 1949, and was buried in Blandford Cemetery, Petersburg.

Foster Hall—which houses student activities at Virginia State College—was dedicated on May 5, 1954.

Basic information is in *The National Cyclopedia of American Biography* (1951). This article also used information based on the memorabilia of his son, Luther H. Foster, Jr., then president of Tuskegee Institute.

— RAYFORD W. LOGAN

FOWLER, JOHN W. ("BUD") [JOHN W. JACKSON] (1854?–1919?), probably the first Negro professional baseball player. Fowler was born in Cooperstown, Otsego County, N.Y. There is little evidence about his early life, but it is generally accepted that he learned to play baseball on the old Cooperstown Seminary campus, the perhaps mythical site of the first game. During some twenty-eight years (1872–1900) he played on teams in Alabama, California, Guelph (Ontario, Canada), Colorado, Indiana, Iowa, Louisiana, Massachusetts, Michigan, Minnesota, Mississippi, Nebraska, New Hampshire, New Mexico, New York, Ohio, Pennsylvania, Texas, Vermont, and Wisconsin. His habit of calling other players "Bud" led to the nickname for him.

Beginning with 1872 he was with a team in New Castle, Pa.; until 1895 he was usually the only Negro on otherwise all-white teams. In 1884, for example, he was a member of the Stillwater, Minn., team in the twelve-team Northwestern League. The next year, following the disbanding of Stillwater, he played with the Keokuk, Iowa, team, and in 1886 with Denver of the Western League. He was one of the first Negroes, along with Frank Grant (who was passing as an "Italian") on Binghampton's team in the International League.

Racial prejudice led Fowler and Grant to organize in 1895 in Adrian, Mich., the Page Fence Giants. Other all-Negro teams, the Argyle (Long Island) team and the Philadelphia Orions, had been formed as early as 1885, and in 1887 the League of Colored Baseball Clubs lasted only a month. Several other clubs and leagues were formed in the latter part of the nineteenth century and the early twentieth century. The Page Fence Giants, one of the more prosperous of these teams, traveled in a $20,000 private railroad car for several seasons, playing Negro and also all-white teams.

Like many other players during this era and later, Fowler played more than one position, sometimes in the same game. Primarily a pitcher, he played also in the infield and the outfield.

At the turn of the century Adrian Constantine (Cap) Anson and John Joseph ("Buggsy") McGraw hardened the color line against colored players on white teams while occasionally passing off dark American Negroes as Cubans. There is a hiatus of information about Fowler from 1900 to 1909. On Feb. 25, 1909, the *New York Age* reported (p. 4) that he was "ill and in want" at his sister's home in Frankfort, N.Y. It was believed that he was a "victim of consumption" but x-rays revealed that his illness resulted from an injury in Indianapolis seven years earlier when a collision while sliding into second base broke two of his ribs and damaged his kidneys.

The last available mention of Fowler is in an article by Lester Walton (later U.S. ambassador to Liberia) in the *Age* on April 22, 1909. A baseball game scheduled for April 25 at Meyerrose, Brooklyn, for the benefit of Bud Fowler had been postponed because "the managers of the benefit were unable to get the players together by the date set."

Like many other pioneers, Fowler died in obscurity and is virtually unknown. This sketch is based largely on Ocania Chalk's *Pioneers of Black Sport* (1975). Copiously illustrated, it shows Fowler as a member of the otherwise all-white Keokuk, Iowa, team in 1885.

— OCANIA CHALK

FRANCIS, MILTON A. (1882–1961), specialist in genitourinary diseases (urology). He was born in Washington, D.C., one of four children of the union of John R. Francis, an obstetrician, and Betty Cox, who became an effective member of the District School Board. He became the first Negro specialist in genitourinary diseases. Educated in the public schools of Washington, he received his M.D. from Howard University in 1906. His internship class was the last to be completed in the original Freedmen's Hospital building created by the Freedmen's Bureau under the direction of Gen. O. O. Howard in 1868. A few years later Francis married Emily Beatrice Lewis, a childhood sweetheart.

Immediately after his internship Francis joined the staff of the Freedmen's Hospital's Genitourinary Department, which had been formed the year before under a recent graduate of Johns Hopkins, Harry Fowler. Francis's skill and technique advanced steadily as he observed in the shadow of Fowler, for "he was never accepted by Dr. Fowler as a trainee, apprentice or even as an assistant," Francis stated in an interview.

When Fowler and his staff of white associates and assistants went to the First World War in 1917, the genitourinary service "was abandoned." Only Francis remained. His performance was so acceptable to the staff and embarrassing to Dr. Fowler that he rarely appeared personally after his return from the war. A series of young white assistants were assigned by Fowler to serve in his stead, but they became discouraged by the unique protective tactics of Francis, and each withdrew until T. C. Thompson was brought to the hospital in the fall of 1922 by Fowler and personally given a tour of the outpatient clinic, following which he was escorted to the office of the surgeon-in-chief, William A. Warfield, and introduced as the director of the G.U. Outpatient Clinic. Thompson remained the director of this clinic.

Following an emergency admission in July 1923 when Francis was on vacation, the need for continuous coverage of the inpatient service became apparent. Thereafter this service was shared with Thompson. R. Frank Jones was then invited by Francis to become his assistant.

By 1930, when the College of Medicine at Howard University was reorganized, Francis had lost interest in the surgical aspect of urology. He had delegated his segment of the urologic service to Jones while he pursued his active private office practice.

Dr. and Mrs. Francis presented Roland Hayes and Marian Anderson in separate concerts at Washington, before their first theater audiences. For each, these concerts were musical triumphs and for Hayes his first significant purse.

Francis's life was saddened by the prolonged terminal illness and death of his wife. He married Ethel Murray several years later. She too developed a chronic illness which further depressed him.

Soon after Francis retired from private practice on Aug. 21, 1959, he created with $100,000 in cash the "Milton A. Francis Trust Fund; the income is to aid Medical Students by Loans and Scholarships." This is administered by Howard University. This trust fund was then the largest single gift ever received from a living alumnus of Howard University. Francis bequeathed his entire personal and real property, valued at approximately $200,000, to the trust fund. The contested will resulted in dividing the corpus equally between his widow and the trust fund.

In a state of melancholy and depression, Francis committed suicide on July 22, 1961.

This article is based on "Men of the Month" (*JNMA,* Aug. 1913, p. 173), and personal reminiscences.

— R. FRANK JONES

FRAZIER, E[DWARD] FRANKLIN (1894–1962), educator and sociologist. Frazier was born in Baltimore, Md., on Sept. 24, 1894, one of five children of James H., a bank messenger, and Hattie (Clark) Frazier. His early education was received in the public schools of Baltimore. Following the completion of high school in 1912, he entered the College of Arts and Sciences at Howard University in Washington, D.C., from which he was graduated with honors in 1916. At Howard he demonstrated a proficiency in languages, literature, and mathematics, subjects he later taught at a succession of institutions: mathematics at Tuskegee Institute (1916–1917); English and history at St. Paul's Normal and Industrial School, Lawrenceville, Va. (1917–1918); and French and mathematics in the Baltimore High School (1918–1919).

Frazier's first graduate educational experience and his introduction to sociology as a formal discipline occurred during a year of study (1919–1920) at Clark University, Worcester, Mass., at the conclusion of which he received an M.A. degree in sociology. After spending a year (1920–1921) as a Russell Sage Foundation fellow at the New York School of Social Work (later the Columbia University School of Social Work) and a year of study at the University of Copenhagen as a fellow of the American Scandinavian Foundation, which provided one of the bases for his broader study of peasants, Frazier began a long and distinguished career in teaching and research by accepting an appointment (1922–1927) at Atlanta University which combined the duties of director of the Atlanta University School of Social Work with instructor in sociology at Morehouse College. In 1922 Frazier married Marie Brown of Winton, N.C.

These early professional years witnessed Frazier's publication of a number of articles on the Negro family, the cooperative movement, business enterprise among Negroes, and the role of social work in addressing problems experienced by Negroes. These articles are interesting because they provide insights into Frazier's early preoccupation with race relations, the Negro family, stratification processes, and the development of a Negro middle class, substantive areas which dominated much of his later research investigations and writing.

One of the articles published during this period, "The Pathology of Race Prejudice" (*Forum Magazine,* June 1927), produced such strong reactions among whites in Atlanta that Frazier became the object of a manhunt as soon as the article appeared on the newsstands. He was forced to leave the Atlanta community, thus ending abruptly his association with the Atlanta educational institutions.

It was at this point that Frazier completed his formal

education by spending two years (1927–1929) of study in sociology at the University of Chicago, where he was strongly influenced particularly by the noted sociologist Robert E. Park, and from which he received the Ph.D. degree in sociology in 1931. His dissertation, published in 1932 as *The Negro Family in Chicago,* his first important contribution to the social sciences, was comparable to the classic study *The Philadelphia Negro* published by W. E. B. Du Bois in 1899.

Meanwhile he joined the faculty of Fisk University as research professor of sociology in the Department of Social Sciences where, under the leadership of Charles S. Johnson, a program of research and investigation of Negro life had been initiated. Frazier remained at Fisk until 1934 when he accepted a position at Howard University as professor and head of the Department of Sociology. From 1935 to 1943 he was also director of the program in social work. He was also appointed in 1942 resident fellow of the Library of Congress. Retired as professor emeritus of sociology in 1959, he taught in Howard's Program of African Studies from 1959 and of the Johns Hopkins School of Advanced International Studies in Washington from 1957 to his death in 1962.

Although Frazier played a major role in the establishment and development of schools of social work in two Negro institutions, Howard and Atlanta Universities, his professional identification is with the field of sociology, to which he made significant substantive contributions in the areas of the Negro family and race relations. His classic work *The Negro Family in the United States* (1939) won the Anisfield Award as the most significant contribution to race relations in the year in which it was published. Building on Frazier's earlier studies of the Negro family, this volume furnishes an analysis of the history of the Negro family as it was influenced by slavery and by post-Emancipation experiences, especially the mass migrations to urban centers which began during World War I. It thus provided sociological explanations of the observed variations of Negro families from many normative patterns of American family behavior, and for many of the social problems experienced by Negroes. Thus the larger incidence among Negroes, as compared with whites, of illegitimate births, common-law marriages, female-headed families, and the higher rates of crime, illiteracy, desertion, and poverty were explained in other than genetic terms which heretofore had been used to characterize the Negro as "a defective, dependent and delinquent." It thus also served in part as a countervailing influence to policy decisions in social work and in other areas in which policy determinations in matters affecting the Negro were based on nonsociological explanations.

In analyzing the impact of urbanization on the Negro family, Frazier observed that the large-scale movement of predominantly rural family units to the metropolitan areas during and after World War I produced both personal and social disorganization on an extensive scale. But he viewed this initial reaction to the complexities of urban life as the first phase of a process that would result in a reorganization of individual and family behavior as Negroes adapted to the demands of their new milieu. His study of the Negro community in Chicago demonstrated that great variation in the degree of stability existed from one area to another, and that, in part, these differences were related to variations in the length of family residence in the city and to its socioeconomic status.

Status distinctions among Negroes and the development of the Negro middle class claimed much of Frazier's professional attention. One of his early essays, "Durham: Capital of the Black Middle Class," published in *The New Negro: An Interpretation* (1925), extolled the virtues of the Negro businessman of Durham who had demonstrated over more than a generation the puritan virtues of hard work, thrift, and reverence for educational achievement and morality. Many of these same virtues had been found among the free Negroes whose descendants took pride in their family heritage and traditions. It was the movement of Negroes to cities that provided the basis for marked economic distinctions within the Negro population. Segregated communities in these large urban areas provided support for a growing corps of Negro professionals, a small entrepreneurial group, and a substantial number of clerical and service workers who constituted the backbone of the Negro middle class. Frazier pointed out, however, that the new Negro middle class which emerged with the great migrations lacked many of the stable virtues of the older middle class, represented by free Negroes and their descendants and the businessmen of Durham. The behavior of this class was the subject of Frazier's most controversial book, written in Paris, *Black Bourgeoisie* (French ed., 1955; U.S. ed., 1957).

The contemporary Negro middle class, Frazier wrote, did not develop around the marketplace as did most middle classes, but was made up largely of persons in professional and clerical occupations. The rapid upward mobility of many of its members led to an emphasis on the conspicuous display of newly acquired material goods. The class in effect imitated the values of the American upper class but lacked the substantive basis for much of this behavior. Its interest in education and the arts and its morality in general, quite unlike that of the older middle class, was superficial in character. The class, Frazier stated, lived in a "world of make-believe."

Critical reactions to Frazier's delineation of the behavior of this class came mainly from members of the class itself, who regarded Frazier's analysis as only a partial view. There also were critics who pointed out that the volume had methodological weaknesses, inasmuch as the data on which it was based were not collected in an objective and systematic manner. In the Preface to *The Black Bourgeoisie* (1962 Collier Books Edition, pp. 9–10), Frazier replied: "The critical reviews which appeared in American scholarly journals were concerned for the most part with questions involving methodology and the validity of my conclusions. In some of the more serious journals of opinion there also appeared critical reviews. But even in some of the scholarly reviews as well as in the serious journals of opinion there was either an implicit or explicit criticism that the book exhibited anger or lack of sympathy in its stark objectivity. A leading political analyst said that the book was cruel because if Negroes were happy in their world of make-believe, why should I feel it was my duty to let them know the truth about their real position in the United States? Although it appeared that many whites shared this opinion, there were others who welcomed the book as an explanation of the behavior of middle-class Negroes—behavior which had long puzzled them."

Frazier's sociological studies of race relations served to buttress his personal convictions regarding the dehumanizing effects of racial segregation and discrimination. He was unalterably opposed, both as a social scientist and as a person, to those forces which attempted to maintain segregated community life. He recognized that some Negro groups and organizations had a vested interest in segregation, but that the interests of Negroes were best served by legal and social forces which operate to produce desegregation.

Frazier's belief in the integration of Negroes into American society did not carry with it the idea that Negroes should lose their identity as a minority. He strongly believed that Negroes should insist on all the rights and privileges enjoyed by other American citizens, whether or not they elected to exercise them. As a race-conscious person who supported organizations and programs designed to improve the status of Negroes, his position regarding the relationship of Negroes and other minorities to American society is best described as cultural pluralism. This position is quite different from that imputed to Frazier by some of his critics who asserted that he espoused an assimilationist position with regard to the Negro and other minorities.

The problems of race and race relations, Frazier believed, could best be studied in a broad, comparative framework. His writings included comparisons of race relations and the Negro family in Brazil and in the United States, and the impact of urbanization on African family organization as well as the effects of urbanization on the Negro family in the United States. His framework for the study of race relations is best demonstrated in his *Race and Culture Contacts in the Modern World* (1957), in which he assesses the role of demographic, ecological, economic, social, and political factors in influencing the patterns of behavior which develop on various racial frontiers.

As an intellectual Frazier realized the value of knowledge as a contributor to social change, although it often took a long period for social facts to become diffused. In race relations as well as in the broader area of human relations, myths, stereotypes, and group self-interest often distorted social reality. Racial ideologies frequently served to rationalize the behavior of dominant groups as they engaged in economic and political exploitation of racial minorities. In one of his essays, for example, Frazier pointed out that the sociological theories of early American sociologists served to rationalize the subordinate position assigned the Negro. What was needed, he stated, was a further development of a dynamic theory of race relations which would discard all rationalizations of race prejudice and provide a realistic orientation for the study of changing patterns of race relations in America and in other parts of the world.

In the development of such a theory, Frazier believed Negro social scientists should play a significant role because of their experiences. The study of race relations,

moreover, was for him a respectable specialty which deserved the attention and energies of able social scientists.

Throughout most of his life Frazier was an academic man, devoting most of his time to teaching and research. He understood and valued the role of service organizations and action groups in the promotion of social change, but he reserved a specialized role for the man of knowledge. He did accept two nonacademic assignments which should be noted. In 1935 he became the director of the Mayor's Commission on Conditions in Harlem, to investigate the social and economic conditions responsible for the Harlem riot of March 19, 1935. This assignment lasted for one year; the report was never published. In 1951–1953 he served as the director of the Division of Applied Social Sciences of the United Nations Educational, Scientific, and Cultural Organization in Paris.

In addition to his teaching at Atlanta, Fisk, and Howard, Frazier taught at other colleges and universities on a part-time basis. Included among these were the New York School of Social Work, New York University, the New School for Social Research, Sarah Lawrence College, the University of California at Berkeley, and Carleton College. He lectured widely at universities in this country and abroad.

The last twenty years of Frazier's life were marked by continuing controversies but also by an increasing respect and esteem. He demanded racial integration and equality of opportunity for Negroes, for example, during an era when segregation was the official policy of the government. He won widespread admiration when, during one of the bitter periods of the Cold War, he had the courage to preside at a dinner in New York City in honor of W. E. B. Du Bois, one of his mentors, who had been indicted (although later acquitted) for his activities as the "unregistered agent" of a foreign principal, the Soviet Union.

Despite the controversies in which he was involved, Frazier not only belonged to many sociological professional associations but exercised a leadership role in most of those in which he held membership. He was a founding member and later president of the District of Columbia Sociological Society (1943–1944), president of the Eastern Sociological Society (1944–1945), a vice-president of the African Studies Association, and president of the American Sociological Society (now the American Sociological Association). His election to the presidency of the American Sociological Society in 1948 marked the first time that a Negro had been elected to head a predominantly white national professional association in this country. He was elected in 1955 the first honorary member of Gamma chapter, Phi Beta Kappa, Howard University. He delivered three lectures under Special University Lectures in Sociology at the University of London (May 4, 7, and 8, 1953); a lecture under the Munro Lectureship at the University of Edinburgh (May 12, 1953); and the Sir James G. Frazer Lecture in Social Anthropology at the University of Liverpool (June 26, 1953). Many other honors were bestowed upon Frazier, including honorary LL.D. degrees from Morgan State College (1955) and the University of Edinburgh (1960).

He died in Washington, D.C., on May 17, 1962, of a coronary occlusion. Funeral services were held at the Jarvis Funeral Home in Washington, and his body was cremated. He was survived by his widow.

Since there is no full-length biography of Frazier, published references relate more to his written works than to him as a person. One source is G. Franklin Edwards's chapter on Frazier in *Black Sociologists: Historical and Contemporary Perspectives,* edited by James Blackwell and Morris Janowitz (1974, pp. 85–117). A "Postface" and a "Bibliography" of Frazier's publications by Michael R. Winston are included in the second edition of the French publication *Bourgeoisie Noire* (1969, pp. 217–20). The volume by John H. Bracey, Jr., August Meier, and Elliott Rudwick, *The Black Sociologists: The First Half Century* (1971), includes a discussion of Frazier's works in the "Introduction" (pp. 1–12) and presents four selections from his published works in the section on "In the Park Tradition" (pp. 69–157).

The most helpful material on the educational forces influencing Frazier's decision to become a sociologist and his conception of sociology as an academic discipline, based on a statement prepared and submitted by Frazier, is in Howard Odum's *American Sociology: Sociology in the United States Through 1950* (1951, pp. 233–39). The Frazier Papers are in the Moorland-Spingarn Research Center, Howard University.

— G. FRANKLIN EDWARDS

FREEMAN, ELIZABETH [MUMBET, MUM BETT] (c. 1742–1829), plaintiff in a historic civil rights suit. The daughter of African parents, she was born a slave, probably in Massachusetts. At an early age she and her sister were purchased by Col. John Ashley of Sheffield. When the colonel's wife struck at Mum Bett's sister with a heated shovel, Mum Bett diverted the blow and received on her arm a scar which she bore to her death. She left the Ashley house, refused to return, and appealed to a prominent young lawyer, Theodore Sedgwick of nearby Stockbridge, to prevent reenslavement by Colonel Ashley. She told Sedgwick that while waiting on table she had overheard conversations about the Bill of Rights and the new constitution of Massachusetts. Since she had never heard any exception to the doctrine that all men were born free and equal, she told Sedgwick that she could claim her liberty under the law. Sedgwick argued the case in 1783 before the county court of Great Barrington. When the jury set Elizabeth Freeman free and ordered Colonel Ashley to pay her thirty shillings damages, it was legally established that slavery had been abolished in Massachusetts.

A widow since the death of her husband during the Revolutionary War, and the mother of a young daughter, she refused Colonel Ashley's request that she return to work for him. Instead she worked as a housekeeper and nurse of the Sedgwick children for several years. According to Sidney Kaplan, she eventually left the Sedgwicks and set up house with her daughter. The noted lawyer Zachariah Chaffee, who wrote the article in *DAB* (8, Part 2:549–50), states that she died in Theodore Sedgwick's home.

In a lecture at the Stockbridge Lyceum two years before her death, he urged the abolition of slavery and cited Elizabeth Freeman as a "practical refutation of the imagined superiority of our race to hers." By her extreme industry and economy she supported a large family. While she could neither read nor write, "her conversation was instructive, and her society much sought."

She died surrounded by her grandchildren and great-grandchildren, and was buried in the Sedgwick family plot in the old burial ground in Stockbridge. A plain stone marked her grave with the inscription: "Elizabeth Freeman, known by the name of Mumbet, died Dec. 28, 1829. Her supposed age was 85 years. Born a Slave."

A convenient source is Sidney Kaplan's *The Black Presence in the Era of the American Revolution 1770–1800* (1973, pp. 216–17). A portrait in watercolors (1811) by Susan Sedgwick, in the Massachusetts Historical Society, is Plate 7, following page 84. Kaplan relied on Harriet Martineau's work in 1838 *(Retrospect of Western Travel)* for the early life of Elizabeth Freeman and gives 1781 as the date for the trial. Chaffee, who calls it Sedgwick's "most famous case," gives the date as 1783. Regardless of minor conflicts, Kaplan was right when he wrote that below the inscription on Elizabeth Freeman's gravestone there might be added: "She struck the death blow of slavery in Massachusetts." According to W. E. B. Du Bois, his family tradition believed that Mum Bett's husband, Jacob Burghardt, took part in suppressing Shay's Rebellion (1786). One of Jacob Burghardt's sons was his grandfather (*Dusk of Dawn* . . . [1940], p. 112). — RAYFORD W. LOGAN

FREEMAN, HARRY LAWRENCE (1869–1954), composer. Born in Cleveland, Ohio, on Oct. 9, 1869, the son of Sylvester and Agnes Sims Freeman, a noted singer, Harry Freeman exhibited interest in music at an early age and was appointed organist to the family's church in his early teens. After graduation from high school he spent some time in Denver where in 1892 he attended a performance of Wagner's *Tannhäuser* presented by the Emma Juch Grand Opera Company. "When I retired that night, I could not sleep, as the music had been a revelation and I was stirred by strange emotions. At five o'clock in the morning I arose and, seating myself at the piano, composed my first piece. On each of the next two hundred days I composed a new song." About 1899 he began formal study of music under several teachers in Cleveland, particularly the composer-conductor Johann Heinrich Beck, although Freeman had already composed and produced his first two operas. From 1902 to 1904 he taught at Wilberforce University, then at the Salem School of Music (1910–1913), his own Freeman School of Music (1914–1922), and the Freeman School of Grand Opera (after 1923). It was probably after his stay at Wilberforce that he served as music director for the Pekin Theater Company in Chicago, and then for the Cole and Johnson Brothers' Company in New York. The remainder of his life was spent in teaching, composition, and performance. His best known student was Noble Sissle. His operas, *Voodoo* and *The Octoroon,* secured the Harmon Award in 1930. Excerpts from nine of his operas were given at a special Steinway Hall concert on March

30, 1930, and he was engaged to direct the pageant *O Sing a New Song* at the Century of Progress International Exposition in Chicago in 1934. Among those frequently performing major roles in his operas were his wife Carlotta (a soprano), of Charleston, S.C., whom he had married in 1898, and their son Valdo L. (a baritone). She was said to be the first member of her race to do an emotional role in a legitimate theater, first at the old Lincoln Theater in Harlem and later at the Lafayette. She was prima donna of the John Larkin Company and a principal performer in both the Pekin Stock Company and the Ernest Hogan Company.

His operas (plots and other data are provided by Hipsher) include *The Martyr* (1893), *Zuluki* (1898; only portions of which were performed in Cleveland in 1900), *An African Kraal* (1903; unperformed), *The Octoroon* (1904; unperformed), *Valdo* (1905), *The Tryst* (1909), *The Prophecy* (1911; unperformed), *Voodoo* (1914; first performed in 1928), *The Plantation* (1915; unperformed), *Athalia* (1916; unperformed), *Vendetta* (1923), *An American Romance* (1927), *The Flapper* (1929), *Leah Kleschna* (1931), *Uzziah* (1934), and *Zululand* (a tetrology composed from 1932 to 1947, consisting of *Nada, Allah, The Zulu King,* and *The Slave*). Freeman, who always wrote his own librettos, secured several probable firsts in opera: *The Martyr* appears to have been the first opera by an American Negro (those of the eighteenth-century Chevalier de Saint-Georges would be the first by any Negro composer) and this was the first all-Negro opera production (Deutsches Theater in Denver, Sept. 1893). Although *The Tryst* ran for a week in New York's Crescent Theater (May 1911), *Voodoo* was the first Negro opera to be given in the Broadway district (52nd Street Theater, Sept. 10–11, 1928). *An American Romance* and *The Flapper* are among the first operas to be composed in the jazz idiom, and *The Martyr* might be the first opera by a Negro composer to be performed in Carnegie Hall (1947 revival).

Among his other works is a ballet, *The Slave Ballet from Salome* (1923). His symphonic poem *The Slave,* a description of a day in the life of a slave, was composed in 1925 but has never been performed. He also wrote two cantatas, many songs (including "Whiter" and "If Thou Did'st Love"), and a cycle of four works for undetermined medium: *Chaka, The Ghost Wolves, The Storm Witch,* and *Nada*.

Freeman died of a heart ailment on March 24, 1954, at his home 214 W. 127th St., New York City. His funeral was on March 28 at St. Phillips Episcopal Church, the Rev. Shelton Hale Bishop officiating. He was buried in Mount Hope Cemetery, Yonkers, N.Y. He was survived by his widow and son (*New York Times,* March 26, 1954; *New York Age-Defender,* April 3, pp. 1–2).

A very short biographical sketch of Freeman is included in Eileen Southern's *The Music of Black Americans* (1971). The most extensive coverage of Freeman's music appears in *American Opera and its Composers* by Edward E. Hipsher (1927, 1934). Several works by Freeman are in the Music Department, Moorland-Spingarn Research Center, Howard University.

— DOMINIQUE-RENÉ DE LERMA

FULLER, META VAUX WARRICK (1877–1968), sculptor. She was born in Philadelphia on June 9, 1877, the youngest of four children of William H. and Emma (Jones) Warrick. Henry Jones, her maternal grandfather, was a well-known caterer for the affluent white society of Philadelphia. Meta was educated in the Philadelphia public schools and spent her summers in Atlantic City, where her father owned barbershops. Her mother ran a hairdressing parlor and named her after one of her clients, Meta Vaux, the daughter of Sen. Richard Vaux.

As a child she showed talent in the performing arts. Her mother provided private dancing lessons and her father, loving art, often took her to the Philadelphia Academy of Fine Arts, where he explained painting and sculpture to her. During her school days in Philadelphia one student from each class was selected once a week to study at an industrial art school. Meta Warrick was one of those selected for special training. Upon completing high school in 1894 she won a three-year scholarship to the J. Liberty Tadd's Industrial Art School at the Pennsylvania Museum of Fine Arts (now the Philadelphia College of Industrial Art). Winning a prize for the best work—a bas-relief frieze of thirty-seven medieval costumed figures in procession—she was determined to become a sculptor.

She received a postgraduate scholarship to specialize in sculpture for a year. When she graduated in 1898 she won a prize for a metalwork piece, *Crucifixion of Christ in Agony,* and an honorable mention for her modeling. Teachers and friends suggested that she go to Paris to study art and develop her talent.

In September 1899 young Meta Warrick sailed for Paris. She arrived on October 26 and was to have been met by the artist from Philadelphia, Henry O. Tanner, a friend of her uncle's. For some reason Tanner did not appear at the Paris station and so the young sculptor boarded a cab to the American Girls Club, a residence for American girls studying in Paris. "Why didn't you tell me you were not a white girl?" said the director of the club, upon seeing the young art student. She was not allowed to remain, and with the urging of Henry Tanner she found a room in a small hotel.

Warrick's inadequate financial resources made finding qualified teachers difficult. During the first year she studied drawing, attended lectures on anatomy, modeled in wax and clay at the École des Beaux-Arts, and visited museums to study sculpture and painting. In the summer of 1900 she began sculpting from live models. In the fall she entered Colarossi Academy where she studied modeling under French artists.

During her third and last year in Paris Warrick was invited to visit the great sculptor Auguste Rodin at his studio in Meudon. She brought with her a plaster model of her work, *Man Eating His Heart.* Rodin, after examining the little statue, remarked, "Mademoiselle, you are a sculptor. You have the sense of flow in your fingers." Rodin was greatly impressed with her work and offered to become her master. Often he visited Paris to view and criticize her work.

The young sculptor became bold in the conception and execution of her work. Through a friend she gained a showing of her works at a Paris exhibit. Her head of *John the Baptist* and *The Thief on the Cross* were shown and she began to sell her work. A Mr. Bing, an art dealer, invited her to exhibit at his gallery, L'Art Nouveau. In 1903 three of her works, *The Impenitent Thief, The Wretched,* and *Man Carrying a Dead Comrade,* were exhibited in Paris at Bing's gallery.

After three years in Paris Meta Warrick returned to Philadelphia and opened a studio. She continued to do new work but found American art dealers uninterested in her pieces. Dealers claimed they did not buy domestic sculpture. She felt that if she had been white she would have been accepted. Her works executed while in Paris also were not recognized.

In 1907 she was commissioned to produce 150 Negro figures for the Jamestown Tercentennial Exposition—commemorating the landing of English settlers at Jamestown in 1607. Her work for the Negro exhibit, which illustrated the progress of the Negro since the Jamestown settlement, won a gold medal.

On Feb. 3, 1909, Meta Warrick married Solomon C. Fuller of Boston and Framingham, Mass. A Liberian by birth, he was a graduate of the Boston University School of Medicine, a director of the pathology lab at Westborough State Hospital (Mass.) and a neurologist at Massachusetts State Hospital. Dr. and Mrs. Fuller moved to 31 Warren Rd., Framingham, a house that Dr. Fuller had had built and in which they lived the remainder of their lives.

Upon moving to Framingham Mrs. Fuller had left works done in France and Philadelphia, and her tools, in Philadelphia. They were to have been shipped to her but they were stored in a warehouse. A fire at the storage site in 1910 destroyed almost all of her sixteen years of artwork. The loss temporarily dampened her urge to resume her art. Between 1910 and 1916 the Fullers became the parents of three sons, Solomon Carter Jr., William Thomas, and Perry J.

In 1913 she received a letter from William E. B. Du Bois, then editor of *The Crisis* in New York, asking that she produce a piece symbolic of the spirit of the emancipation. Du Bois's request reawakened her creative spirit and she molded a statue depicting a black boy and girl for New York's fiftieth anniversary celebration of the Emancipation Proclamation. This piece was the real beginning of her move toward using the Negro as a subject.

During the next fifty years Fuller was prolific. At first the top floor of her house became her studio. In 1929 she built her own studio on the shore of Larneds Pond, a short walk from her home in Framingham. It was here that she created some of her finest works, guided other young artists, and annually exhibited her sculpture. During the 1930s she exhibited at local libraries, the Boston Art Club, and at churches. Her works and popularity continued to grow during the 1930s and 1940s. She strove to keep her sculpted figures of people friendly and intimate. Sculpture, she felt, should be for the home.

In 1950 Meta Fuller gave her studio to a former pupil so she could care for her ailing husband, who had lost his sight. Dr. Fuller died in 1953 and shortly after his death she contracted tuberculosis. For two years she was confined to a sanitarium. She returned to her home on Warren Road in 1955 and soon resumed her sculpt-

ing. In 1956 she completed a bust of Charlotte Hawkins Brown, founder of Palmer Memorial Institute in Sedalia, N.C. In 1957 she received a commission from the Afro-American Women's Council in Washington, D.C., to produce doll models of ten famous American Negro women.

In the early 1960s she was commissioned to do a bronze plaque showing a doctor and two nurses for the Framingham Union Hospital where her husband had practiced. A bronze piece, *Storytime* (depicting a mother reading to her three children) was done for the Framingham Center Library and unveiled in 1964. At Howard University in March 1961 Meta Fuller was one of three sculptors whose works received special honor. The occasion was "New Vistas in American Art," an exhibit marking the opening of the new Fine Arts Building at Howard. One of her last pieces was *The Crucifixion,* with the head of Christ raised, done in memory of the four Negro girls killed in the church bombing in Birmingham, Ala., in 1963.

Acquaintance with the works of Meta Warrick Fuller is possible today in public and private places. Her life-size statue *Awakening Ethiopia,* done in 1921 for the "Making of America Exhibit" in New York, is in the New York Public Library's Schomburg Research Center. It shows a standing Negro woman emerging from the wrappings of a mummy. *The Talking Skull* is at the Museum of Afro-American History in Boston. *The Wretched* (done in Paris) is held by a museum in San Francisco built by Mrs. Adolph B. Spreckles, which features the works of Rodin and those he inspired. Her statuette of Richard B. Harrison as "De Lawd" in *Green Pastures* is in the art gallery at Howard University. A bas-relief showing a black youth rising from a kneeling position to meet the morning sun was acquired by the YMCA in Atlanta. At Boston University's School of Medicine is a bronze bust of her husband, Dr. Solomon C. Fuller. *The Dancing Girl* is in the Cleveland Museum of Art.

Meta Warrick Fuller died in 1968 of natural causes; her funeral was held in Framingham. Her body was cremated and her ashes dispersed in Vineyard Haven Sound, Mass. She was survived by sons Solomon C. Jr., Perry James, and William Thomas.

Meta W. Fuller was a productive sculptor for over seventy years. Her sculpture may be divided into distinct phases. Early works dealt with the grotesque, probably emerging from an interest in the Gothic tales of Edgar Allen Poe. Next her interest turned to Afro-American types and more realism. Later she turned to religious subjects. Portraiture and mythological figures were also the focus of a number of her works. Her sculpture captured the human spirit and exhibits remarkable universality.

The best brief critical evaluation is in James A. Porter's *Modern Negro Art* (1943), pp. 62, 77, 86–87, 92, 94). Sylvia G. L. Dannett's "Meta Warrick Fuller" (*Profiles of Negro Womanhood,* 1966, 2:31–46) is a later biographical sketch. See also Elwin Greene's "Profile: Sculptress Meta Warrick Fuller" (*Worcester* [Mass.] *Sunday Telegram,* May 18, 1958, sect. F), Mary White Ovington's *Portraits in Color* (1927, pp. 216–26); and *The Crisis* (Jan. 1918, p. 133; Jan. 1919,

p. 135; Nov. 1919, p. 350; April 1920, p. 337). Personal information was supplied by Solomon C. Fuller, Jr.
— ROBERT C. HAYDEN

FULLER, SOLOMON CARTER (1872–1953), clinician, researcher, and educator, best known for expanding medical knowledge in neuropathology and psychiatry, and one of America's first Negro psychiatrists. His research on degenerative diseases of the brain was pioneering. Born in Monrovia, Liberia, to parents who were state officials, he spent the first seventeen years there before coming to the United States in 1889 to attend Livingstone College, Salisbury, N.C., receiving his bachelor's degree in 1893. He first studied medicine at Long Island College Hospital, Brooklyn, N.Y., and later at the Boston University School of Medicine where he was awarded an M.D. degree in 1897. Fuller completed a two-year internship at Westborough State Hospital in Massachusetts and in 1899 was appointed a pathologist at Westborough State as well as a faculty member of the Boston University School of Medicine. For nearly forty years he taught pathology, neurology, and psychiatry at Boston University. He practiced medicine in both Boston and at his home in Framingham, Mass. His wife, Meta Warrick Fuller, whom he married in 1909, was an internationally known sculptor. He retired as professor emeritus from Boston University in 1937.

Fuller's postgraduate training was outstanding. He studied under leading psychiatrists at the Carnegie Laboratory in New York and at the Psychiatric Clinic and the Pathological Institute of the University of Munich. In 1909 he participated in a symposium occasioned by Sigmund Freud's visit to Clark College in Worcester, Mass. He is pictured in a famous group photograph with Freud and other eminent American psychiatrists of the time. In 1913 Fuller became the editor of the *Westborough State Hospital Papers,* a publication specializing in mental diseases. His own writings on pathologic, neurologic, and psychiatric topics appeared widely in medical journals and books. His research and writing on dementias and a brain disorder known as Alzheimer's disease were well known. His theory that Alzheimer's disease was caused by something other than arteriosclerosis was supported by medical researchers in 1953, the year of Fuller's death. During his professional life he was a member of the New England Society of Psychiatry and the Association of Neuropathologists, and an associate of the American Medical-Psychological Association.

During the early 1970s Fuller's legacy to American psychiatry and to Negro psychiatrists practicing in the United States was given recognition. In May 1971, the Black Psychiatrists of America presented a portrait of Fuller to the American Psychiatric Association in Washington, D.C. In October 1973 the Boston University School of Medicine, as part of its centennial year celebration, memorialized Fuller in an all-day conference. During the commemorative activities a bust of Fuller was presented to the library of his alma mater.

Fuller died of natural causes; funeral services were held in the Wadsworth Funeral Home, Framingham. His body was cremated and his ashes dispersed in Vineyard Haven Sound, Mass. He was survived by his widow and sons Solomon C. Jr., William Thomas, and Perry James.

W. Montague Cobb, "Solomon Carter Fuller" (*JNMA,* 1954, pp. 370–71), is the principal source. Fuller's "A Testimonial to George Smith Adams" (*New England Medical Gazette* 57 [1912]: 467–686) was published in 1912. Information on his later life was based on interviews with surviving members of the family. — ROBERT C. HAYDEN

FULLER, THOMAS (1710–1790), calculator. Fuller was brought from Africa as a slave at the age of fourteen. Although he could neither read nor write, he possessed, according to the best available evidence, extraordinary powers in arithmetic when he was seventy years old. In reply to questions he answered in about two minutes that there are 47,304,000 seconds in a year. In a minute and a half he stated that a man seventy years, seventeen days, and twelve hours old had lived 2,210,500,800 seconds. One of his questioners said that Fuller was in error. The old man replied "top [stop?], massa, you forget de leap year[s]." Recalculation showed Fuller to be correct. If a farmer had six sows, and each sow had six female pigs the first year, and all increased in the same proportion, how many sows would the farmer have at the end of eight years? It took him a little longer to answer this question than the preceding ones, ten minutes, because he had not at first clearly understood, but he gave the correct answer, 34,588,806 sows. He also gave the result of nine figures multiplied by nine.

The basis for acceptance of these phenomenal calculations is an article by Benjamin Rush, friend of Richard Allen, Absalom Jones, and Benjamin Banneker in the *American Museum or Repository of Ancient and Modern Fugitive Pieces, etc., Prose and Poetical* (Jan. 1789, pp. 62–63). Rush stated that Fuller was the property of Elizabeth Coxe of Alexandria, Va. Two travelers from Pennsylvania, William Hawthorne and Samuel Coates, "men of probity and respectable characters," had asked the first three questions and heard the answers. Two other "respectable citizens" of Philadelphia, Thomas Wistar and Benjamin W. Morris, vouched for the nine by nines.

Rush added that Fuller had stated that his memory had begun to fail him and exhibited other evidences of his old age, that he had worked hard but had never been intemperate in the use of spiritous liquors, and that he was grateful to Mrs. Coxe for not having sold him, despite offers of large sums of money.

When Coates remarked that it was a pity Fuller had not had an education equal to genius, the old man replied: "no massa—it is best I got no learning; for many learned men be great fools."

Henri Grégoire, a French humanitarian democrat and revolutionist, accepted the validity of Rush's account and summarized it in *An Enquiry Concerning the Intellectual and Moral Faculties and Literature of Negroes, Followed with an Account of the Life and Works of Fifteen Negroes and Mulattoes Distinguished in Science, Literature, and the Arts,* translated by by D. B. Warden (1810, reprinted 1967, pp. 183–85).

Fuller's obituary in the *Columbia Centinel* (Dec. 29, 1790), on file in the Library of Congress, stated that "Negro Tom, the famous African Calculator," had died at the age of eighty years. "The man was a prodigy." The obituary gave some evidence of his phenomenal ability not included in Rush's article: the number of poles, yards, feet, inches, and barleycorns in any given distance, as well as the diameter of the earth and the number of hairs in the tails of the cows and horses which he looked after. The obituary ended: "Had his opportunities of improvement been equal to those of thousands of his fellow-men, neither the Royal Society of London, the Academy of Sciences at Paris, nor even a *Newton* himself, need have been ashamed to acknowledge him a Brother in Science."

Rush's article and the obituary are in Sidney Kaplan's *The Black Presence in the Era of the American Revolution 1770–1800* (1973, pp. 148–49).

— RAYFORD W. LOGAN

FULLER, THOMAS OSCAR (1867–1942), clergyman, educator, author, and publisher. Born in Franklinton, Franklin County, N.C., he was the youngest of fourteen children of former slaves, J. Henderson and Mary Eliza Fuller. His father, a carpenter and wheelwright, who built many homes in Franklin and other counties, had bought his freedom and that of his wife who had worked in the fields and as a house servant. After the Civil War his father, who had learned to read and write during slavery, bought property and moved his family to his own home. The father died in February 1886 and the mother in November 1892.

Thomas began studying at the age of five, finished the normal school at Franklinton, and graduated from Shaw University in 1890. (The degree of Doctor of Philosophy, awarded by A&M College at Normal, Ala., was honorary.) He received his M.A. degree in 1893. In April of the same year he was ordained a minister. He taught in public schools, pastored churches, organized the Girls' Training School in Franklin by special legislative act, and became principal of Shiloh Institute, Warrenton, N.C. (1895–1898). After serving one year as the only Negro senator in the North Carolina legislature (1899) he conducted a private academy near Warrenton and in 1900 became pastor of the First Baptist Church in Memphis, Tenn. He was principal of Howe Institute in Memphis for some thirty years, one of the secretaries of the National Baptist Convention of the U.S.A. for twenty-five years, and its director of publicity and a member of the Executive Committee of the Baptist World Alliance.

His *Banks and Banking* (1920), a pamphlet of forty-one pages, was designed as a textbook on such subjects as how to start a bank, promissory notes, drafts, checks, travelers checks, and letters of credit, with questions at the end of each chapter. *Flashes and Gems of Thought and Eloquence* (1920), another pamphlet of forty-nine pages, recorded statements he had heard during twenty years at the National Baptist Convention. *History of the Negro Baptists of Tennessee* (1936), a book of 346 pages, was a compendium about the churches and individuals, including Mordecai W. Johnson (later president of Howard University).

Twenty Years in Public Life: 1890–1910, North Carolina–Tennessee (1910), a book of 270 pages, contained biographical information, notable for his laudatory appraisal of his service as a senator in the North Carolina legislature. During the campaign of 1898 he advised, when the election was over, that the people let unnecessary agitation cease and shun "anarchy, intimidation, and riot." When the senators were seated alphabetically, his name was the last called. He was not appointed to any committee, but during his one term he helped obtain the passage of four measures: one gave the superior court of North Carolina a concurrent criminal jurisdiction with county courts; the second abolished an open bar in Warrenton and substituted a state dispensary; a third incorporated the North Carolina Mutual and Provident Association in Durham, which later became the North Carolina Mutual Life Insurance Company; the fourth resulted in the repeal of an act which prohibited outside labor agents from recruiting Negro labor in the state. After the Wilmington Riot (1898), he vigorously opposed a state constitutional amendment which, however, was approved and which effectively disfranchised Negroes. He believed that his plea for ending violence had ended the bitterness following the Wilmington Riot. When the legislature elected Democrats to offices held by Fusionists (who generally supported Negroes), Fuller protested in vain.

Fuller's *Pictorial History of the American Negro . . . ; a Story of Progress and Development along Social, Economic, Educational and Spiritual Lines* (1933) deserves wider recognition than is now generally accorded it. Profusely illustrated, it contains not only substantive discussion (some of it valuable as reflecting conservative thought of the period) but also thumbnail biographies of well-known Negroes in virtually every aspect of life. It is in some respects a popular rather than a scholarly book. The Introduction was written by the commander of the Confederate Veterans, Gen. C. A. De Saussure. An appendix included a biography of Benjamin Banneker by John H. B. Latrobe, and "The Confessions of Nat Turner." His optimistic assessment of the future concluded: "With faith in God, loyalty to the state, and love for our fellow men, let us go forward for another half century of our racial life." The bibliography included many of the well-known books about Negroes.

"Bridging the Racial Chasms": A Brief Survey of Inter-racial Attitudes and Relations (1937), a pamphlet of seventy-three pages, urged equality in the courts, good neighborly relations, human brotherhood, better relations between employer and worker, merchants and customers, landlords and tenants, better treatment of Negroes by government and the press. But it relied on such organizations as the Commission on Interracial Co-operation and the Federal Council of Churches of Christ to achieve his goals. In it Fuller praised the accommodationist philosophy of Booker T. Washington and took pride in the fact that a former Confederate general had written the Introduction to his *Pictorial History*. He inveighed against lynching and peonage, denounced such demeaning terms as "George" (for a colored college president), "boy," and "nigger," and strongly denounced a wage differential for Negro and

white workers. He also praised W. E. B. Du Bois, along with other leaders who did not always see eye-to-eye with Booker T. Washington.

There is no full-length biography of Thomas Oscar Fuller. Assessment of his career is based largely on his own works, published by himself and the National Baptist Publishing Company. For background information about his career as a state senator, see Helen G. Edmonds's *The Negro and Fusion Politics in North Carolina, 1894–1901* (1951). — RAYFORD W. LOGAN

FURNISS, HENRY W[ATSON] (1868–1955), physician and diplomat. He was born on Feb. 14, 1868, in Brooklyn, N.Y., the son of William Henry and Mary Elizabeth (Williams) Furniss. A younger brother, Summer Furniss, also became a prominent physician (Frank Mather, *Who's Who of the Colored Race,* 1915). In 1877 the family moved to Indianapolis where the father became employed in the post office. After graduating from public schools in Indianapolis, Furniss enrolled in the Medical Department of the University of Indianapolis from 1887 to 1889. In 1890 he transferred to Howard University Medical College and received the M.D. degree in 1891. He took postgraduate courses at Harvard Medical School in 1892 and at the New York Post-Graduate School and Hospital in 1894. Then in 1894–1895 he entered the College of Pharmacy at Howard University and received the pharmaceutical doctorate in 1895. To finance his education he had worked as a clerk in the U.S. Census Office (1890–1892). This job entailed study of the wealth, debt, and taxation of foreign governments. In the process Furniss acquired a knowledge of commercial relations and consular forms, since he obtained most of the information from correspondence with U.S. consuls abroad. During 1895–1896 he was an intern at Freedmen's Hospital in Washington, D.C. In 1896 he joined his brother in practice as a physician and surgeon in Indianapolis.

With endorsement from Indiana's Republican congressmen, churchmen, and other civic leaders, Furniss applied for the position of U.S. consul at Bahia, Brazil, in 1897. He was appointed on Jan. 14, 1898, after passing the State Department's examination, and served at Bahia until 1905 (Consular Despatches, U.S. State Department, National Archives, Washington, D.C.). In 1904, in London he married Anna Wichmann, who joined him at his post and accompanied him for the rest of his life. On Nov. 23, 1905, he was promoted to the post of envoy extraordinary and minister plenipotentiary to Haiti. Accompanying him at his formal presentation to the president of Haiti were two other Negro Americans: John Terres, the U.S. consul at Port-au-Prince, and Capt. Charles Young, military attaché. Furniss served at Port-au-Prince until 1913. He was minister during the crucial years preceding the United States' occupation of Haiti in 1915. When Roger L. Farnham, vice-president of the National City Bank of New York City, tried in 1911 to force the Haitian government to accept a United States receivership, Furniss repeatedly opposed him and in turn was denounced by the Bank as being hostile to American interests (Hans Schmidt, *The United States Occupation of Haiti, 1915–1934,* [1971], pp. 49–50). Following his resignation in Sep-

tember 1913, according to established custom when a new president (Woodrow Wilson) took office, he was replaced by a white man, Arthur Bailly-Blanchard of Louisiana, who was more sympathetic to U.S. designs on Haiti. Furniss returned to medical practice, initially in Brooklyn and other places in New York State. He settled in Hartford, Conn., in 1917 and continued practice there for thirty-five years. Retiring in 1952, he moved to live with his son in Bristol, Conn., where he died of pneumonia on Dec. 20, 1955.

Before his foreign service career Furniss had already earned a good reputation as a physician and had read papers before the Indiana state medical society. In the foreign service his performance won high praise from such demanding State Department critics as Elihu Root and Alvey Adee (U.S. State Department, Applications and Recommendations File). Furniss took special pride in the fact that while a loyal Republican, his tenure, touching four presidential administrations, rested more on merit than on the political influence which usually determined such posts (Furniss to Booker T. Washington, Jan. 21, 1909, Washington Papers, Library of Congress). By the time of his assignment to Haiti he was fluent in Portuguese, Spanish, and French, and his knowledge of the local international economic rivalries led the State Department to consider him indispensable until 1913 (Recommendations File). After returning to his medical career he repeatedly declined invitations to use his special knowledge for business ventures in Haiti (Furniss to Whitefield McKinlay, Sept. 21, 1920, McKinlay Papers, C. G. Woodson Collection, Library of Congress). He stayed out of public life to such an extent that when he died he was remembered only as a physician (*Hartford Times,* Dec. 20, 1955).

His survivors included his widow, Anna Wichmann Furniss, a son William R. Furniss, a daughter Mrs. E. Narbert Prouix, and nine grandchildren.

— ALLISON BLAKELY

GANDY, JOHN M[ANUEL] (1870–1947), educator and college president. Born Oct. 31, 1870, on a farm in Oktibbeha County, Miss., six miles south of Starkville, he was the fifth of thirteen children born to Horace and Mary (Goodwin) Gandy, freed slaves and tenant farmers. His paternal grandfather, Ed Gandy, had come to the United States from Ireland following the potato famine of the 1830s, settling first in South Carolina, later in Alabama, and finally in Mississippi. His maternal grandmother was of mixed French, Indian, and Negro extraction. As a young boy he wondered at the wide variety of colors among his relatives. Given the middle name "Mumphis" which he disliked, he later changed it to Manuel. His mother, whose gentle nature contrasted with his father's, exerted a great influence on him.

Like so many other Negroes during this period Horace and Mary Gandy were trapped by the economic servitude imposed on them by the tenant-farmer system. In an effort to escape the unending cycle of debt they, along with several other Negro families in the community, migrated to Sallisaw, Okla., while young John was in school in Jackson College (1886–1888). Because of a lack of money young Gandy's pursuit of an education had been fraught with hardships. The man who was later to become recognized as one of Virginia's outstanding Negro educational leaders secured his early education in one-room rural schools in Mississippi, as he himself said, "going from one rural community to another," Chapel Hill, Ebernizer, and Sand Creek. An avid desire for education, however, caused him to seek funds to attend Jackson College. Admitted to the eighth grade, he completed the course of study two years later when he was eighteen. In 1892 he entered Oberlin Academy and remained nearly two years, leaving because of insufficient funds. An attempt to enter Colgate University also failed because of a lack of funds, but the students there collected enough money to enable him to reach Nashville where he entered Fisk University. Graduating from Fisk with a B.A. degree in 1898, he reenrolled as a nonresident student for courses leading to the M.A. degree in 1901. He studied at Columbia University in the summers of 1903 and 1911, took nonresident graduate courses at Illinois Wesleyan leading to the Ph.D. degree from 1903 to 1913 or 1914 when the program was discontinued. He declined an M.A. degree from the University in lieu of the doctorate because of the cost and the fact that he already had an M.A. In the summer of 1934 when he was sixty-four, he studied at Cornell University. At Virginia State College he was the active sponsor of the Faculty Study Club, a group devoted to continuing study of all facets of education. It is fair to say that he never stopped studying.

His teaching career began at the age of fifteen at a school in Stone County, Miss., south of Hattiesburg, following the receipt of a third-grade teaching certificate (at this time he had the equivalent of only a seventh-grade education). After finishing Jackson College he taught school in Hanson, Indiana Territory. He withdrew briefly from Fisk in the spring of 1894 or 1895 and taught from March to September in Hickman Lake County, Ky. He continued to teach there for four consecutive summers while still a student at Fisk. Appointed professor of Greek and Latin at Virginia Normal and Collegiate Institute, Petersburg, in 1898 at a salary of $900 a year, he taught these courses until they were dropped from the curriculum in 1901 when the college degree program was terminated by the state. He continued, however, as professor of education until his appointment to the presidency in 1914.

Three years after joining the Virginia Normal faculty he married Carrie Senora Brown. Four children were born of this union: Theodore, Horace, Marian, and John Jr. All the surviving children were well educated: Theodore, an M.D.; Marian, two master's degrees; and John Jr., a Ph.D.

On Jan. 29, 1914, the executive committee of the Board of Visitors of the Virginia Normal and Industrial Institute appointed him acting president because of the continuing illness of James Hugo Johnston. Following the death of Dr. Johnston that same year, he was elected to the presidency of the institute at an annual salary of $1000. This appointment occasioned no surprise in the commonwealth because he had developed a statewide reputation as an organizer and leader through his work as executive secretary of the Negro Organization Society. He had become well known also for his advocacy of improved health facilities, schools, homes, and farms for the Negroes of Virginia. He served as president until his retirement as president emeritus in 1943, and continued to live on the campus until his death on Oct. 5, 1947.

As an educator Gandy was progressive. In his valedictory address as president to the Forty-fifth Annual Convention of the Virginia Teachers Association he said: "We are living in a changing world, and it is easy to cling to habits and practices that the world has long ago outgrown. The Association must grow with the changing needs of the schools." "He was also a progressive in his policies and practices," stated Edna Meade Colson, retired dean of the School of Education at Virginia State College and a longtime colleague. "He carried his faculty with him as far as he could at every step, in curriculum development, building programs, class-room facilities, provisions for in-service growth through scholarship grants, committee organization and improved living conditions for students, staff and faculty families" (Colson to T.D.P., Feb. 19, 1974).

Assuming the presidency at a time when Virginia was still recovering from the Civil War, he espoused the cause of higher education for Negroes: "We believe and declare that the educational salvation of the Negro rests more in his own interests and efforts than in [that] of others" (V.N.&I.I. Gazette, July 1908, pp. 5–6). He was determined to see collegiate education, which one of the governors of Virginia had dropped from the curricula, reestablished. Not only was he successful in this but also in having the institute's name changed to Virginia State College for Negroes (1930).

In his recruitment of faculty it was his policy "to contact all of the leading colleges that colored students were allowed to attend." This, according to Richard Jeffreys in "A History of Virginia State College for Negroes" (1937, pp. 173–74), "has brought to the college . . . [a faculty] representing the most outstanding institutions of the country." He believed in the highest standards of excellence. "The college," he said, "should attempt to promote a higher and more rigid scholastic record. This is necessary for the turning out of capable and thoroughly trained students."

Under his leadership Virginia State College grew rapidly. Among the highlights of his administration were the establishment of V.N.&I.I. as the land-grant college for Negro youth of Virginia (1920), a class A rating by the American Medical Association (1929), a standard college accreditation by the Virginia State Board of Education (1930), approval as a class A college by the Southern Association of Colleges and Secondary Schools (1933), election as a member of the Association of American Colleges (1934), approval by the State University of New York as a class A college (1937). A senior ROTC unit (Quartermaster Corps) was established on the campus on July 1, 1947. In addition, by 1936 the college's physical plant comprised 110 acres and thirty-one permanent buildings.

In assessing this development of Virginia State, Jeffreys attributed the success to Gandy's leadership and to his uncanny ability to secure the support of the State of Virginia and outside agencies. Colson concluded:

"No one would claim that John Manuel Gandy secured all these achievements single handedly. On the administrative side, he was supported by strong college personalities; in the teaching field he valued and utilized the assistance of faculty members graduated from the best American colleges and universities; as an educator he associated with national leaders in many fields."

Recognition of his efforts came first in 1928 when he was awarded the bronze medal and $100 second prize by the Harmon Foundation "for developing his institution from a non-accredited school to one offering . . . a two year normal course and a four year college course with A rating in Virginia." He was also the recipient of honorary degrees from Morgan State College (Ped.D., 1920) and from Howard University (LL.D., 1937). Gandy Hall at Virginia State College is named for him.

He served as third president of the Virginia State Teachers Association (1905–1906), president of the National Association of Teachers in Colored Schools (1919–1920), and president of the Association of Presidents of Negro Land Grant Colleges (1923–1926). He was a member of the National Board of Directors of the YMCA and the Board of Trustees of Virginia Union University. He also held membership on numerous commissions, committees, and professional and social organizations.

Among his personal friends were the outstanding educational and political leaders of the era: Booker T. Washington, Robert R. Moton, Mary McLeod Bethune, Mary Church Terrell, E. R. Embree of the Rosenwald Fund, Jackson Davis of the General Education Board, Maggie L. Walker, and many more.

He died of natural causes and was buried in Blandford Cemetery. He was survived by his wife, two sons, and a daughter.

Two unpublished manuscripts by Gandy in the Johnston Memorial Library at Virginia State College—"The Life and Works of John M. Gandy," edited by Edna M. Colson, and a "History of Virginia State College"—are excellent primary sources. Two publications, "Present Day Needs in American Life" (V.S.C. Gazette, Jan. 1933) and "The Virginia State Teachers Association—An Historical Sketch" (Virginia Teachers Bulletin, Jan. 1933), present his own views on education. "A History of Virginia State College for Negroes, Ettrick, Virginia" by Richard Jeffreys (M.A. Thesis, University of Michigan, Feb. 1937) places the educator's achievements in historical context. Basic biographical information is in Who's Who in America, 1936–1937 (p. 950).

— THOMAS D. PAWLEY

GANS, JOE [JOE GANT] (1874–1910), boxer. Gans was born on Nov. 25, 1874, in Baltimore. When he was eleven years old, Al Herford, a white businessman, was so impressed by Joe's fighting with a larger boy that he hired a professional fighter to give him boxing lessons. The lad fought in battle royals in and around Baltimore; during one fight an announcer called him "Gans," a name by which he was thereafter known. In 1899 Gans defeated George McFadden in twenty-five rounds at the Broadway Athletic Club in New York City. This fight earned him a match with Frank Erne for the lightweight

title (133 pounds limitation, 1876–1909, when it was changed to 135 pounds). Gans won the title by knocking him out in the first round at Fort Erie, Ontario, on May 12, 1901. He won and lost several fights (some of them said to have been fixed) and was fairly defeated by Sam Langford on Dec. 8, 1903, with the latter weighing 140 pounds while Gans weighed 135½. A match with Joe Walcott (not to be confused with the later "Jersey Joe" Walcott) in San Francisco on Sept. 30, 1904, was declared a draw.

Gans's most memorable fights were with the Danish-born Oscar Matthew "Battling Nelson." Although ill with incipient tuberculosis, Gans was awarded the first fight in Goldfield, Nev., on Sept. 3, 1906, in the forty-second round when the referee belatedly declared Nelson guilty of committing an obvious foul. Gans lost his title to Nelson by a knockout in the seventeenth round in San Francisco on July 4, 1908. Although increasingly weakened by tuberculosis, he fought Nelson again on Sept. 9, 1908, and was knocked out in the twenty-first round. Even though he said he was "all in" and had broken his right hand in the eighth round, Gans gave Nelson full credit for the victory. Nelson, however, then declared that he would draw the color line against Negro boxers.

Gans's victory over Nelson brought rejoicing to the colored community while his defeats were looked upon as setbacks to the race.

After the third fight with Nelson, Gans went to Arizona in the vain hope of regaining his health. He died of tuberculosis on Aug. 10, 1910, in Baltimore. At his bedside were his wife, mother, and two children. He was buried in Mount Auburn Cemetery, Baltimore, on Aug. 13.

Unlike many boxers he did not die destitute. His will, which turned over his property to his wife Martha and made provision for his mother, included a debt-free, profit-making hotel. In a letter to the New York Age two days before his death, Mrs. Gans stated: "Joe is no millionaire, but he has . . . saved enough so that his family need not want after his days are ended."

The standard sources are A. S. Young's Negro Firsts in Sports (1963), Nat Fleischer's Black Dynamite, vol. 3, The Three Colored Aces . . . (1938), and Ocania Chalk's Pioneers of Black Sport (1975, with photographs on pp. 135–37, 139). — RAYFORD W. LOGAN

GARDINER, LEON (1892–1945), photographer, bibliophile, and researcher. The third in a family of eight children, he was born in Atlantic City, N.J., on Nov. 25, 1892. His parents, Jacob and Martha Gardiner, detected Leon's early interest in reading and encouraged it. His interest in reading was complemented by an interest in athletics. Leon ran cross-country, was an avid bicyclist (having entered and won several competitions), and frequently engaged in long-distance hiking and camping. In 1902 he moved with his family to Philadelphia. Although Leon maintained his earlier interests, two additional areas attracted him: music and photography. In 1909 he began singing in the St. Simon Episcopal Church choir and sought all the reading materials and individual photographers he could find. An attempt to attend a well-known Philadelphia school of photography resulted in overt racial discrimination which greatly distressed him.

Fortunately Gardiner grew up in a stable, racially proud community known for its reservoir of strength. During his youth he began clipping articles pertaining to racial achievements, lynching, and building of institutions, which helped to sharpen his focus. He also attended (1908–1923) public meetings sponsored by the Afro-American Historical Society, founded by Robert Mara Adger. Gardiner's association with this organization gave him an opportunity to report his findings on Negro history, exchange ideas with others, and assist in establishing a nucleus of Negro bibliophiles. He was greatly concerned with the preservation of books, manuscripts, and memorabilia. Some of his contemporaries thought this strange in light of their belief in the "melting-pot theory." Gardiner's unrelenting determination to preserve and make known the history of Negroes was demanding. Working nights in the post office, he spent part of the day researching, consulting rare-book dealers, collecting oral history, and preparing articles for publication. During the 1930s and 1940s Gardiner wrote articles simultaneously for the *Philadelphia Tribune* and *Philadelphia Independent*. Several articles were co-authored with his friend Arthur Huff Fauset (brother of the noted novelist Jessie Fauset), and author of several books. One well-informed article by Gardiner, "One Hundred Years Have Passed Since Garrison Handed This Promise to the World," appeared in the *Philadelphia Tribune* (Dec. 7, 1933). This capsule of the National Anti-Slavery Society generated a lively interest its centennial celebration.

Gardiner's research ability was widely recognized. He received letters from historians and other researchers from many parts of the United States. He often verified obscure facts and suggested unfamiliar sources. In an interview (Sept. 21, 1974), Charles H. Wesley, a professional historian, called Gardiner "a solid and diligent type of researcher." He seemed never to be too busy to assist a fellow worker in Negro history. Gardiner felt that research and publication were not enough; there would have to be a permanent collection of materials on which future generations might build. In 1933 he began assembling the data he had collected over the years, in addition to the Afro-American Historical Society's collection which he had acquired and maintained. In December of that year he deposited these materials in the Historical Society of Pennsylvania and the Berean Institute. This historical collection, rich in eighteenth- and nineteenth-century materials, included letters from Benjamin Banneker, Frederick Douglass, Sojourner Truth, Henry Highland Garnet, Booker T. Washington, W. E. B. Du Bois, Frances E. W. Harper, and others. Information in it abounds on early literary groups, churches, beneficial societies, baseball clubs, political and business history.

Gardiner's work was facilitated by the interest of his two wives, children, and friends. He married first Bernice Modeste who became the mother of their three children, Louise, Leon, and Walter. His second wife Beatrice, whom he married in 1940, was the niece of the novelist Charles W. Chesnutt. Gardiner's strenuous schedule had debilitating effects on his health. When

advised to slow the pace, Gardiner replied six months before his death: "If a man can not do what he enjoys and that which is necessary he is better off dead." On March 5, 1945, he died of a heart attack only a few hours after he had attended a requiem mass for a fellow worker. Funeral services were held in St. Simon Episcopal Church with burial in Mount Lawn Cemetery, Sharon Hill, Pa.

James G. Spady's "The Afro-American Historical Society: The Nucleus of Black Bibliophiles, 1897–1923" (*NHB*, June-July 1974, pp. 255–56) is the principal published source. Gardiner's valuable collection is housed in the Moorland-Spingarn Research Center, Howard University, the Historical Society of Pennsylvania, and the Berean Institute. — JAMES G. SPADY

GARNET, HENRY HIGHLAND (1815–1882), clergyman, abolitionist, editor, temperance leader, and diplomat. He was born on a slave plantation in New Market, Kent County, Md. His grandfather was said to have been a ruler of a tribe in the once-powerful Mandingo Empire of West Africa. When Henry was nine years old, his father George, with the aid of Quaker abolitionists, escaped to New York City. The father, a shoemaker, found employment and enrolled his son in the African Free School No. 1. After graduation, Garnet, Alexander Crummell, and two other colored students enrolled in Noyes Academy, New Canaan, N.H., 1834. After some 300 men with ninety to one hundred oxen dragged the building away, leaving it in ruins in the summer of 1835, young Garnet began in 1836 the study of the ministry at Oneida Theological Institute, Whitesboro, near Utica, N.Y., which had opened in 1826. Completing his studies in 1840, he took up residence in Troy, N.Y., where he was licensed to preach in 1842 as the pastor of the town's only colored Presbyterian church. In the same year he married Julia Williams. From then until 1860 he was one of the most prominent Negro abolitionists and activists. In August 1850 he was a delegate to the World Peace Congress, Frankfurt, Germany, and in 1851 addressed numerous antislavery societies, notably in England and Scotland. He impressed the United Presbyterian church of Scotland so favorably that it sent him (1853) to Jamaica as pastor of the Stirling Presbyterian Church. After three years there he returned to the United States and was elected president of the African Civilization Society (1858). He was among the first to demand that President Lincoln authorize the enlistment of colored troops, and continued to do so despite the draft riots in New York City (1863), which threatened his own safety. While pastor of the fashionable 15th Street Presbyterian Church in Washington, D.C. (March 1864–Oct. 1866), he was the first Negro to deliver a sermon before the House of Representatives (1865), listened to also by some senators. He served briefly with the Freedmen's Bureau, continued his advocacy of justice for Negroes, and lived for a number of years in semiretirement in New York City. About 1879 he married Sarah J. (Smith) Thompson, a widow and a sister of Susan Maria Smith Steward, one of the earliest women physicians. Appointed minister to Liberia, Garnet was given a gala dinner (Jan. 1882) by Edward Wilmot Blyden, minister of the interior, and attended by most of the high-ranking authorities. Garnet praised the nation-building achievements of the Liberian people, though they were far from reaching the heights he described. He died in Liberia on Feb. 12, 1882, and after a funeral attended, it is said, by every Liberian official, was given a state burial in a cemetery overlooking the Atlantic Ocean. Garnet apparently had no children by either wife. His second wife, who survived him until 1911, had had two children by her first marriage, both of whom died quite young.

The expulsion from Noyes Academy (1835) and his association with other abolitionists were important factors in Garnet's social gospel: he opposed not only slavery but also political and economic exploitation. As co-editor with Richard Allen of the *Troy National Watchman* (1842) and as editor (1843) of the equally ephemeral *Troy United States Clarion,* he emphasized the moral and religious uplift of his congregation. Soon thereafter, however, he worked with the Liberty party for enfranchisement and with Gerrit Smith for land reform. Garnet preached against the ''unholy system of landlordism and the labor monopolists,'' devoted much time and energy to women's rights, temperance, religious reform, and the world peace movement. At the landmark National Negro Convention of 1843 held in Buffalo, N.Y., Garnet delivered his famous ''Call to Rebellion'' speech. He demanded that Negroes, both slave and free, adopt a ''motto of resistance'' to slavery. This included actual armed rebellion, if necessary, to overthrow slavery. Although the speech shook the more conservative Negro leadership, many Negroes supported his appeal. The speech failed by only one vote of being approved as the official resolution of the convention. Even so, the Negro mood underwent a sharp shift toward more militant action against slavery. In fact, a similar National Negro Convention held in 1847 in Troy unanimously approved a similar speech given at the convention by Garnet. The convention also adopted another Garnet-sponsored resolution calling for the establishment of a national Negro press.

His Jamaica experience strengthened Garnet's conviction that Negro organizations and self-help provided a partial key to Negro liberation as well as the need for a strong and independent Africa, especially through cotton production. As early as Jan. 21, 1848, he wrote: ''I hesitate not to say that my mind of late has greatly changed in regard to the American colonization scheme. . . . I would rather see a man free in Liberia than a slave in the United States.'' In the same year, however, he wrote that miscegenation was a dead issue, for ''It is too late to make a successful attempt to separate the black and white people in the Western World. This western world is destined to be filled with a mixed race'' (*The Past and the Present Condition and the Destiny of the Colored Race . . .* [1848], p. 25). A year later he favored colonization in any country that promised freedom and enfranchisement to the Negro (Benjamin Quarles, *Black Abolitionists* [1969], p. 216). Frederick Douglass and others charged that Garnet's interest in Africa was an attempt to soft-peddle the abolitionist movement. But Garnet maintained that this was a tactic to weaken slavery by undermining southern monopoly of cotton production. Garnet's militancy was

further shown by his participation in a meeting expressing support and sympathy for John Brown (1859).

His interest in political rights and land reform continued during the Civil War. He wrote in the *Liberator* (Sept. 6, 1864): ''Sound morality must be encouraged; education must be promoted; temperance and frugality must be exemplified, and industry, and thrift, and everything that pertains to a well-ordered and dignified life, must be exhibited to the nation and the world.'' The failure of the federal government to promote these aims during Reconstruction probably contributed to his semiretirement and to his acceptance of the post of U.S. resident minister and consul-general in Liberia (1882).

The principal source for Garnet's career is Earl Ofari's *Let Your Motto Be Resistance* (1972). *The Sketch of the Life and Labors of Rev. Henry Highland Garnet* (1865), by James McCune Smith, is based in large measure on Garnet's *The Past and Present Condition and the Destiny of the Colored Race . . .* (1848). Indispensable for background and interpretation are Benjamin Quarles's *Black Abolitionists* (1969), as well as Jane H. Pease's and William H. Pease's *They Who Would Be Free, Blacks' Search for Freedom, 1830–1861* (1974). There is a very brief sketch by Carter G. Woodson in *DAB* (4, Part 1:154–55). — EARL OFARI

GARNET, SARAH J. (SMITH) THOMPSON (1831– 1911), school principal, civic worker, and suffragette. Born in Queens County, Long Island, N.Y., she was the first of eleven children of Sylvanus and Annie (Springfield) Smith, both of mixed Indian and Negro ancestry, landholders and successful farmers. Although during her childhood there were public schools in New York City (George Washington Williams, *History of the Negro Race in America* [1883], 2:168–69), there seem to have been none on Long Island. Sarah therefore received her early education from her paternal grandmother, Sylvia Hobbs. At the age of fourteen she began studying at normal schools in and around New York City (the first seems to have been established in 1853; ibid., p. 169) and taught in an African Free School, established by the Manumission Society in Williamsburgh (later a part of Brooklyn). In 1930 James Weldon Johnson wrote: ''It would be difficult to over-estimate the value of the African free schools to the Negroes of New York'' (*Black Manhattan,* p. 23). On April 30, 1863, she became the first colored woman to be appointed principal in the New York public school system. Among the notable graduates of the school of which she was principal was the violinist Walter F. Craig. Until her retirement (Sept. 10, 1900) she successfully combined literary and vocational education and was considered a very able administrator.

She was married first to the Rev. James Thompson, an Episcopal minister who became the rector of St. Matthew Free Church in Brooklyn. He died in the late 1860s leaving her with two children, both of whom died young. About 1879 she married Henry Highland Garnet, a prominent minister and abolitionist who left her a widow in 1882.

In her later years she took part in several important organizations. She was a founder and leader of the Equal Suffrage Club, a small organization of Negro women which met in her seamstress shop on Hancock Street, then the home of many well-to-do Negroes, in Brooklyn. An early member of the National Association of Colored Women, founded in 1895, she opposed discrimination against teachers in public schools. She attended the first Universal Races Congress in London (July 1911), "a great and inspiring occasion, bringing together representatives of numerous ethnic and cultural groups, and new and frank conceptions of the scientific bases of racial and social relations of people" (W. E. B. Du Bois, *Dusk of Dawn . . .* [1940], p. 230). Mrs. Garnet brought home literature on women's suffrage which she distributed to her Equal Suffrage Club. She died on Sept. 17, 1911, of arteriosclerosis, and was buried in Greenwood Cemetery, Brooklyn.

A younger sister of Mrs. Garnet, Susan Maria (Smith) McKinney Steward (1847–1918), graduated in 1870 from the New York Medical College for Women, one of the first colored female medical college graduates. She also attended the Universal Races Congress in London (July 1911).

The principal source is Hallie Q. Brown's *Homespun Heroines, and Other Women of Distinction* (1926). The biographical sketch by Leedell W. Neyland in *NAW* (1971, 2:18–19) is based primarily on Brown's book. — RAYFORD W. LOGAN

GARVEY, MARCUS [MOSIAH] (1887–1940), orator, organizer, and black nationalist. Garvey was born in humble circumstances in St. Ann's Bay, on Jamaica's northern coast, on Aug. 17, 1887, the youngest of eleven children of Marcus and Sarah Garvey. Both parents were of unmixed African descent, and the father, a stone mason, was said to be descended from the Maroons, the escaped African slaves whose successful defense of their freedom against the Spanish and British in the seventeenth century gave them a distinctive place in Jamaican history. (Garvey's later insistence on racial purity probably was derived as much from pride in his Maroon heritage as from resentment of the Jamaican three-color caste system in which mulattoes had higher social status than full-blooded blacks like Garvey.) Young Marcus attended the elementary school in St. Ann's Bay and may have had some additional schooling at the local Anglican grammar school, although he was brought up in the Roman Catholic faith. Bright and gifted in the use of language, he read avidly whatever books he could lay his hands on. At the age of fourteen, family financial difficulties obliged him to leave school to become a printer's apprentice, useful training that sharpened the journalistic skills so important in the later development of his movement. In 1904 he began practicing his trade in Kingston, the island's capital, where he began attending street meetings and developed an impressive talent for powerful impromptu oratory.

After participating in an unsuccessful printers' strike in 1907, an experience that left him skeptical of the value of trade unions for black workers, Garvey worked for a time on a United Fruit banana plantation in Costa Rica and on newspapers in Port Limón and Colón, Panamá. He grew increasingly concerned about the humiliating discrimination and exploitation of black people. When he complained to British consular officials about the mistreatment of Jamaicans who had emigrated in search of work elsewhere in the Caribbean, he found them indifferent and concluded bitterly that blacks would never be able to count on justice from whites. In 1912 he went to London where he apparently studied briefly at Birkbeck College and became acquainted with Africans for the first time. One of these, Duse Mohammed Ali, an Egyptian nationalist, fired Garvey's interest in the cause of African independence and gave him a chance to write for his *Africa Times and Orient Review.* While in England Garvey also came across a copy of Booker T. Washington's autobiographical *Up from Slavery* and was profoundly stirred by Washington's philosophy of Negro self-help.

Shortly after Garvey returned to Jamaica, he enlisted the support of a small group of friends and on Aug. 1, 1914, launched the organization that would henceforth occupy all his time and energy, the Universal Negro Improvement and Conservation Association and African Communities League (usually shortened and abbreviated as U.N.I.A.). The association aimed at "drawing the peoples of the race together" through education, the promotion of race pride, worldwide commercial activity, and the development of Africa. Garvey's first project, a Jamaican trades school modeled after Tuskegee Institute, failed to get off the ground, and he decided to seek support in the United States, where he had received a perfunctory invitation from Booker T. Washington to visit Tuskegee. Washington died before Garvey could complete his travel plans, however, and he thus was without even the prospect of an influential American sponsor when he arrived unknown and unheralded in New York on March 23, 1916.

During the next several years he traveled throughout the United States speaking to Negro churches and other groups about the need for unity to advance the race. The initial support for his Harlem branch of the Universal Negro Improvement Association came from the sizable West Indian community, but gradually some American Negroes also came under the spell of his magnetic personality and compelling oratory. In January 1918 he began publishing a newspaper, the *Negro World,* which quickly became one of the leading American Negro weeklies and a highly effective vehicle for the advancement of his black nationalist ideas. Within a short time it achieved a circulation of at least 50,000, with French and Spanish sections carrying the U.N.I.A. message to subscribers in the West Indies, Latin America, and even Africa. The response to Garvey's vivid exhortations for racial pride and solidarity was almost electric; by 1920 he had many thousands of followers and there were scores of U.N.I.A. divisions chartered throughout the United States and abroad. His Liberty Hall, a large auditorium at 114 W. 138th St. in Harlem, which the U.N.I.A. purchased in 1919, almost overnight became the headquarters of a genuine mass movement of international scope.

Undoubtedly a major reason for the astonishing growth of Garvey's movement was his launching of the Black Star Line in mid-1919, a daring scheme that fired the imagination of Negroes. Garvey declared that the time had come for black people to create their own economic opportunities, and as a first step promised a fleet of black-owned steamships to link the black diaspora of the New World with the African "motherland." Its stock limited to Negroes and priced inexpensively at $5.00 a share, in the first year of operation the Black Star Line raised $610,860 and purchased three ships, the small freighter *Yarmouth,* the Hudson River excursion boat *Shadyside,* and a former yacht converted to light passenger service, the *Kanawha.* No matter that Garvey and his Black Star Line associates paid exorbitant prices for small, antiquated ships in poor repair, or that they lacked the experience and resources needed to operate a steamship line successfully—in the eyes of an admiring black world, this daring Jamaican had accomplished something unique in race history with his fleet of ships, operated by a black company and manned by black crews, to link the scattered black peoples of the world. It was a daring dream, and it understandably buoyed the hopes of discouraged American Negroes following the bloody race riots of the "Red Summer" of 1919.

Another part of Garvey's program for Negro economic independence was the Negro Factories Corporation, established in 1919 to provide loans and technical assistance to blacks who needed help in developing their own small businesses. As with the Black Star Line, the corporation's stock was sold to Negroes at $5.00 a share. The venture was less successful than the Black Star Line in raising adequate working capital, but it helped to develop a chain of cooperative grocery stores, a restaurant, laundry, tailor and dressmaking shop, millinery store, and a publishing house.

In August 1920 in New York Garvey presided over the first international convention of his flourishing Universal Negro Improvement Association, a spectacular affair that more than lived up to the *Negro World*'s promise that it would be the largest gathering of its kind in the history of the race. The several thousand delegates came from all forty-eight American states and more than a score of foreign countries on three continents. Even though by this time the British and French had banned Garvey's newspaper from their colonial possessions in Africa, there were a number of Africans in attendance, including a prince, several chiefs, and the mayor of Monrovia, Liberia. A mood of exhilarating race pride accompanied the fervent black nationalism that pervaded every aspect of the month-long convention, the working sessions of the delegates as well as the frequent mass meetings and parades of U.N.I.A. divisions and auxiliaries such as the paramilitary African Legion and the Black Cross Nurses. The convention adopted a sweeping Declaration of the Rights of the Negro Peoples of the World, at once a powerful protest and a comprehensive program of action. The delegates also called for the liberation of Africa and named Garvey the provisional president of the Republic of Africa, a kind of government in exile. When the convention adjourned it was clear that Marcus Garvey, as no other black leader before him, had captured the attention of masses of Negroes throughout the United States and the world, inspiring them to glory in their distinctive color, their proud past, and their bright future. Garveyism—a

heady amalgam of racial chauvinism and black nationalism—was a potent new force in race relations.

The actions of the 1920 convention reflected Garvey's growing interest in Africa, for he believed that the redemption of the Negro motherland would have great symbolic and practical value for the blacks of the New World. Even before the convention he had sent a delegation to Liberia, one of the two independent Negro states in Africa at the time, to explore the possibilities of a U.N.I.A. development project there. Receiving quiet encouragement from the Liberian government, late in 1920 he announced a campaign for a $2-million Liberian construction loan. Within a few months he raised $137,000 for this purpose and dispatched a group of technicians to staff what amounted to a U.N.I.A. mission in Monrovia to develop plans for a Back-to-Africa colonization project.

Like other U.N.I.A. projects, however, the Liberian venture languished as Garvey found himself increasingly obliged to pour all available resources into the foundering Black Star Line, which had become a financial disaster. Whatever its initial value as a promotional tool, the mounting expenses and frequent mechanical breakdowns of the line's fleet gave rise to increasing criticism. By late 1921 the line had abandoned two of its small ships for lack of repair funds and had lost the third at a court-ordered auction which brought only a tiny fraction of its purchase price. And despite Garvey's frantic efforts to reorganize the line and acquire another ship, early in 1922 he and several associates were arrested by U.S. authorities and charged with fraudulent use of the mails in promoting the sale of Black Star stock, an action initiated by some of his Negro critics, of whom W. E. B. Du Bois of the NAACP was the most prominent. Serving as his own attorney, Garvey used his trial in the summer of 1923 as a forum for his race redemption philosophy. Perhaps influenced by his sometimes arrogant courtroom behavior, the jury convicted Garvey while acquitting his co-defendants, and he was sentenced to a maximum term of five years in prison and a fine of $1000.

Even in adversity Garvey retained an impressive following among the black masses. The U.N.I.A. quickly raised funds for his $25,000 bail while he appealed his conviction. Thousands of his followers bought stock in his new steamship line, the Black Cross Navigation and Trading Company, which in 1924 purchased yet another ship, the *General G. W. Goethals,* renamed the *Booker T. Washington.* At the same time the irrepressible Garvey dispatched an advance party of experts and shipped supplies and machinery to Liberia for the construction of four U.N.I.A. settlements on lands earlier promised by the Liberian government. But time was now running out on Garvey's African redemption plan. Pressured by the British and French, the Liberian government abruptly cancelled its agreement, arrested the Garvey delegation, and confiscated the U.N.I.A. supplies, thus ending his Back-to-Africa program. Worse yet, early in 1925 the U.S. Supreme Court declined to review Garvey's mail fraud conviction, and on Feb. 8, 1925, he entered the Atlanta Penitentiary to begin serving his sentence.

Garvey's lieutenants and his devoted second wife,

Amy Jacques Garvey (in December 1919 Garvey had married his secretary, Amy Ashwood; he won an uncontested divorce on June 15, 1922, and a month later married Amy Jacques, who had replaced Amy Ashwood as his secretary), tried with mixed success to keep the U.N.I.A. alive while working for his release. Their campaign was aided by a growing belief among American Negroes, including some former critics, that Garvey had been treated unfairly and that his imprisonment proved his assertion that blacks could not expect justice in a land controlled by whites. Late in 1927 President Coolidge commuted the U.N.I.A. leader's sentence and ordered him deported to Jamaica. Seeking to revive the shattered movement, Garvey presided over another giant convention in Kingston in August 1929 and launched a short-lived Jamaican Peoples Party that advocated home rule and a broad program of social and economic reform for the island. His following dwindled during the Depression, however, as hard times forced Negroes to look to their own survival rather than to grandiose plans for the redemption of the race or of Africa. In 1935 Garvey moved to London where he intermittently published a small magazine, the *Black Man,* and offered correspondence courses in his School of African Philosophy. The decline of his once mighty organization was painfully evident when he presided over small U.N.I.A. gatherings in Toronto in 1936, 1937, and 1938. Twice stricken with pneumonia in the late 1930s and weakened by chronic asthma, in January 1940 he suffered a severe stroke that left him badly paralyzed on the right side. Following a second stroke, he died in obscurity in London on June 10, 1940, at the age of fifty-two, survived by his widow, Amy Jacques Garvey, and two sons, Marcus Jr., and Junius.

Garvey's legacy was largely intangible, for the U.N.I.A. was moribund at the time of his death. His significance lay in creating the first real mass movement among Negroes in the United States and elsewhere, and in demonstrating the powerful appeal for blacks of a philosophy of race pride and black nationalism. Although his last years were anticlimactic, within a generation Garvey's importance as an early spokesman for black power and African independence was universally acknowledged, and a number of governments, including his native Jamaica and several newly independent African states, had honored his achievements as a race leader.

Garvey wrote prolifically about his movement and race philosophy, but little about himself. The closest thing to an autobiography was his article "The Negro's Greatest Enemy" (*Current History Magazine,* Sept. 1923). His widow, Amy Jacques Garvey, edited two volumes of his early writings, *Philosophy and Opinions of Marcus Garvey* (1923 and 1926). Long out of print and rare, both volumes were subsequently reprinted in London in 1967 and New York in 1968–1969. Mrs. Garvey wrote or edited a number of other works about her husband, of which the most important is *Garvey and Garveyism* (1963). See also E. David Cronon's *Black Moses: The Story of Marcus Garvey and the Universal Negro Improvement Association* (1955). A shorter version is in the *DAB, Supplement 2* (Part 2: 221–22). Later useful accounts of the Garvey move-

ment include Theodore G. Vincent's *Black Power and the Garvey Movement* (1971), Elton C. Fax's *Garvey: The Story of a Pioneer Black Nationalist* (1972), and *Marcus Garvey and the Vision of Africa,* edited with introduction and commentaries by John Henrik Clarke with the assistance of Amy Jacques Garvey (1974). See the obituary in the *New York Times* (June 12, 1940, p. 25). — E. DAVID CRONON

GARVIN, CHARLES HERBERT (1891–1968), physician, army officer, and civic leader. Born in Jacksonville, Fla., the son of Edward and Theresa (Decorse) Garvin, he studied at Atlanta University and graduated from Howard University (B.A., 1911; M.D., 1915). Garvin started his private practice of medicine and genitourinary surgery in 1916 in Cleveland, after his internship at Freedmen's Hospital, Washington, D.C. He remained in continual practice in Cleveland with the exception of the time of his service in the armed forces. He was the first Negro physician commissioned in the United States Army in World War I. He served eleven months in France as commanding officer of an ambulance company, 92nd Division. Following his army service Garvin was invited to join the staff of Lakeside Hospital (a part of University Hospitals) and the faculty of Western Reserve University Medical School in 1920, and on his retirement from the school because of age he was an associate professor of urology.

Garvin was an active supporter of Negro business enterprises in Cleveland and was one of the founders of the Dunbar Life Insurance Company and the Quincy Savings and Loan Company. He served the latter as chairman of the board for several years.

In 1927 Garvin built and occupied a home in a then-exclusive neighborhood in Cleveland. Threats of violence were followed by two bombings of the residence. Firm in his belief in the Negro's right to live where he pleased, Garvin courageously refused to yield to these tactics and thus became a symbol to the Negroes in Cleveland and the rest of the nation.

In spite of a busy work schedule and an active life he contributed original articles to medical journals. These technical writings were supplemented by publication of popular articles on related subjects such as "White Plague and Black Folks," "Immunity to Disease Among Dark Skinned People," and "Pioneer in Cleveland," the last concerned with the progress of Negro doctors. He also recorded the experiences of the Negro soldier and officer in the discriminatory atmosphere that prevailed in the American Expeditionary Forces in World War I.

Garvin's interest in community affairs led to his service on the trustee board of Karamu House, a settlement house founded on the principle that solution of racial problems was in the release of the total potential of all people, including the Negro. He served on the board of the Cleveland Urban League and the local branch of the NAACP, and was a life member of the latter. He was national president of the Alpha Phi Alpha fraternity (1912–1914) and was a charter member of Tau Boulé of Sigma Pi Phi fraternity. The Cleveland Board of Education selected him as a trustee of the Cleveland Public Library in 1938 and his service to this nationally famous library was responsible for his election as president of the board in 1940 and 1941 and its secretary for many years prior to his retirement in 1963.

Because of his distinguished service in the field of medicine he was selected as the fourth recipient of the William Alonzo Warfield Award by the Association of Former Interns and Residents of Freedmen's Hospital in 1963. He also served for many years as a trustee of Howard University, rendering effective service particularly as a member of the executive and other committees (1932–1964). Garvin was a fellow of the International College of Surgeons, a member of the Cleveland Urological Society, Cleveland Academy of Medicine, Ohio State Medical Association, American Medical Association, Editorial Board of the *Journal of the National Medical Association,* the John Andrew Clinical Society, American Venereal Society, and president of the Cleveland Medical Association and of Former Interns and Residents of Freedmen's Hospital.

In 1920 Garvin married Rosalind West of Charlottesville, Va., and was the father of two sons, West of Chicago and Harry C., with whom he practiced.

In addition to Russell H. Davis's *Black Americans in Cleveland* (1972), see Rayford W. Logan's *Howard University: The First Hundred Years, 1867–1967* (1969, passim), and Kenneth L. Kusmer's *A Ghetto Takes Shape: Black Cleveland, 1870–1930* (1976). The *Pittsburgh Courier* published articles about his experiences in World War I. — RUSSELL H. DAVIS

GEORGE, DAVID (c. 1742–1810), clergyman. He was born a slave in Essex County, Va., sixty miles from Williamsburg. His parents, John and Judith, both born in Africa, had nine children. He and his family were owned by the Chapels, for whom his mother was cook. Chapel was an excessively abusive master, and George's most painful memories of slavery were seeing his mother and brothers severely beaten. On reaching manhood George, because of his master's cruelty, escaped. He went south, first to the Pedee River region in South Carolina and then to the Savannah River. Here he worked two years for John Green, a white man. Chapel pursued George relentlessly. Again he fled, but was captured by the Creek Indians and became a servant to Blue Salt, their chief. Chapel's son found George with the Creeks and bought him back. However, he escaped and took refuge among the Natchez Indians and lived with their chief, Jack.

George Gaulfin, a planter and merchant who carried on a vigorous trade with the Indians, heard about David George and arranged his purchase from Chapel. For three years George worked for John Miller, Gaulfin's agent among the Indians. At his own request, he went to live on Gaulfin's estate at Silver Bluff in South Carolina, twelve miles from Augusta, Ga. Here he was employed as Gaulfin's personal servant. Four years later he married.

George's religious awareness was first aroused by Cyrus, a Negro from Charleston, S.C. Cyrus advised George, who "lived a bad life," that if he continued it he would never attain salvation. His conversion came with the aid of the Rev. George Liele, and the Rev. Wait Palmer of Augusta, Ga., who came to preach at a mill that George Gaulfin provided his slaves for a church.

Palmer baptized George and the eight persons who constituted the Silver Bluff congregation. Soon after, George began to exhort and pray with them. When it became impossible for ministers to visit the plantation, George, with the permission of his master and instruction from Liele and Palmer as to proper ministerial conduct, became the sole pastor of the Silver Bluff Negroes. Still illiterate, he acquired a spelling book and, with the aid of white children, learned to read the Scripture. He continued as pastor to the Silver Bluff congregation, now thirty-five in number, until the outbreak of the American Revolution.

When the British took Savannah in 1779, Gaulfin, a patriot frightened by their advance, left Silver Bluff, deserting his slaves. David George, his wife and two children, along with fifty others, were forced to leave Silver Bluff, taking refuge behind British lines.

When the British evacuated Charleston on Dec. 14, 1782, David George and his family were among the Loyalists, almost 500 whites and a few Negroes who sailed to Nova Scotia, Canada. There he continued his religious mission, preaching and baptizing people of color and establishing Negro Baptist congregations in both Nova Scotia and New Brunswick.

In 1792 he and his entire congregation at Shelburne, Nova Scotia, with the exception of two Canadian Indians, were recruited by John Clarkson to settle in Sierra Leone, where George established a Baptist church with a following of almost 200.

George died in Sierra Leone in 1810, after a life dedicated to spreading the Gospel. His church at Silver Bluff, S.C., is believed to have been the earliest Negro Baptist church in America. For this and for his ministry in Canada and in Africa, he is best remembered.

The source for the life of David George most widely used is his autobiography, "An Account of the Life of Mr. David George (as told to Brother John Rippon)" (*Baptist Annual Register,* 1792). A chapter on George is included in David Benedict's *A History of the Baptist Denomination in America and other Parts of the World* (1813). Benedict, however, used George's autobiography extensively. For George's work with the Silver Bluff church, see Walter H. Brooks's "The Priority of the Silver Bluff Church and Its Promoters" (*JNH,* 1922, pp. 172–96). For his work in Nova Scotia and Sierra Leone, consult Anthony Kirk-Green's "David George: The Nova Scotia Experience" (*Sierra Leone Studies,* 1960, pp. 93–120). — JUDITH N. KERR

GIBBS, JONATHAN C. (1827?–1874), clergyman and state government official. Gibbs was born in Philadelphia of free parents, Jonathan C. and Maria Gibbs. His father, a Wesleyan Methodist minister, died in 1831, leaving an invalid wife to raise four children. Jonathan was apprenticed to learn carpentry, as was his brother, Mifflin W. Gibbs. Jonathan was converted to Presbyterianism and received enough schooling to enroll at the age of twenty-one in Dartmouth College, with aid from the Presbyterian Assembly. One of two Negro students at Dartmouth, he graduated in 1852. After nearly two years of study with Drs. Hodge and Alexander at Princeton Theological Seminary, Gibbs became a Presbyterian minister. He first went to a colored congregation in Troy, N.Y., with Nathan Lord, president of Dartmouth College, preaching his installation sermon. He moved to a Philadelphia church in the late 1850s. During the Civil War, Gibbs became active in the Negro Convention Movement and attended the National Convention of Colored Citizens of the United States in October 1864 at Syracuse, N.Y., which gave birth to the National Equal Rights League.

Toward the end of the Civil War, the Old Style Presbyterian church sent Gibbs to the South to open churches and schools. He attended the Colored People's Convention of the State of South Carolina which met in Charleston in November 1865, and worked with freedmen in North and South Carolina until 1867 when he moved to Florida to establish schools there. Arriving at the time when freedmen were soon to be enfranchised, Gibbs further expanded his activity from the religious to the political sphere. Elected to Florida's 1868 Constitutional Convention, he served in the reconstructed state government as secretary of state (1868–1873) and as superintendent of public instruction (1873–1874).

His death on Aug. 14, 1874, in the midst of a strong campaign to win him the Republican nomination for Congress, brought to a sudden end a full and promising career of public service. Some mystery surrounds his death. As the outstanding Negro Republican in Florida politics, he had earned the enmity of the Ku Klux Klan as well as some elements of the Republican party. The official cause of his death was apoplexy, but the repeated threats by the Klan and the criticism that he had heaped upon some Republican opponents led many contemporaries to attribute his death to poisoning, as in the case of Oscar James Dunn. Whatever the cause of death, it was widely regretted. White as well as black, conservative as well as Republican, praised his contributions to Florida.

Jonathan C. Gibbs testifies with such men as Francis L. Cardozo and Oscar J. Dunn to the strengths of some Negro leaders in Reconstruction. During the Florida Constitutional Convention (1868) his education and oratorical talent persuaded many observers that there was, in the words of the *New York Tribune* correspondent, "no fitter man in [the convention] white or black." The Florida Republican party was an uneasy coalition, but Gibbs's ability and support among Negro Floridians kept him in positions of prominence. Appointed secretary of state (1868) by the Republican governor, Harrison Reed, as a bid for Negro support, Gibbs became a trusted adviser and acting governor in Reed's absence. His appointment as superintendent of public instruction (1873) followed the election of a native Floridian Republican, Ossian B. Hart, as governor. This new position carried the responsibility for all public education, including the planned agricultural college. W. E. B. Du Bois attributed the establishment of an orderly system of public schools in Florida to Gibbs. In contrast to the 1860 school system that enrolled 4486 pupils at the expense of $75,412, Florida public schools under Gibbs's direction enrolled 21,196 students and expended $139,870.60. This expansion and the establishment of a standardized curriculum came in the face of considerable white opposition to any Negro educa-

tion, especially the integrated schools that Gibbs advocated.

Joe M. Richardson's "Jonathan C. Gibbs: Florida's Only Negro Cabinet Member" (*Florida Historical Quarterly,* April 1964, pp. 363–68) gives a succinct account, as does his *The Negro in the Reconstruction of Florida* (1965). See also Mifflin W. Gibbs's *Shadow and Light: An Autobiography* (1902, 1969), and W. E. B. Du Bois's *Black Reconstruction in America* (1935, pp. 233, 513, 516–17, 520, 617, 643, 655).

— WILBERT H. AHERN

GIBBS, MIFFLIN W[ISTAR] (1823–1915), entrepreneur, lawyer, politician, and consul. One of four children of free parents, Jonathan C. and Maria Gibbs, he was born in Philadelphia. His father, a Wesleyan Methodist minister, died in 1831, leaving an invalid wife to raise the four children. Like his brother Jonathan C. Gibbs, Mifflin became a carpenter's apprentice (at sixteen) and subsequently a journeyman contractor on his own. At the same time he furthered his command of letters through the Philomathean Institute, a colored men's literary society. He was also active in the Underground Railroad with William Still and others. By 1849 he had become prominent enough in the abolitionist movement to accompany Frederick Douglass on a dangerous speaking tour for that cause in western New York. While on the tour, his life abruptly took a new course after talks with prospectors convinced him to go to California to seek his fortune. He arrived in San Francisco in September 1850, having sailed as a steerage passenger. After racial prejudice forced him to quit carpentry work, he used his earnings to become a partner in a clothing firm which specialized in fine imported clothing. The store prospered and Gibbs was soon a prominent citizen: a member of the state Negro conventions in 1854, 1855, and 1857; and in 1855 he was one of the proprietors and an editor of *The Mirror of the Times,* an abolitionist newspaper (I. Garland Penn, *The Afro-American Press and Its Editors* [1891], p. 76). Gibbs was one of a group of prominent Negroes who in 1851 published a list of civil rights resolutions in the *Alto California,* the leading Negro newspaper in the area. He later claimed that this was the first such expression of protest by Negroes in California.

In 1858 he set out to explore another frontier region, British Columbia, where gold had just been discovered. He brought with him outfittings for prospectors and set up a new store for his firm, said to be the first mercantile house there outside the Hudson's Bay Company's fort. He quickly made a small fortune through combining sale of his wares and purchase of real estate. In 1859 he returned to the United States briefly to marry Maria A. Alexander, who was to become the mother of their five children. By 1866 they became well established in Victoria, and Gibbs was elected to the first of two successive terms on the city's Common Council. He was also a director of the Queen Charlotte Island Coal Company.

Then in 1869, unhappy with the course of developments in the local politics in which he had been very active, he moved back to the United States. Having read law with an English barrister in Victoria, he completed formal training in law at a business college in Oberlin, Ohio, where his wife had attended Oberlin College, as would three of their children subsequently (Oberlin College Archives). In 1871 Gibbs set up law practice in Little Rock, Ark., again immediately achieving great success. In 1873 he was appointed county attorney, but had to resign after only a few months because he was elected municipal judge of Little Rock, the first Negro elected to such office in the United States. In 1876 he was elected a presidential elector for Arkansas, receiving the highest vote on the Republican ticket. In 1877 President Hayes appointed him receiver of the U.S. Land Office for the Little Rock District of Arkansas. He served in this bureau for twelve years, and for the final four was receiver of public monies. He was a delegate to all but one of the Republican national conventions from 1868 to 1896. In 1897 he received his last public appointment, U.S. consul at Tamatave, Madagascar. He served there from February 1898 to August 1901, when he resigned for reasons of ill health (General Records of the Department of State).

Returning to Little Rock, Gibbs published his autobiography in 1902; Booker T. Washington wrote the introduction. In 1903 Gibbs became president of the newly organized Capital City Savings Bank in Little Rock (Abram L. Harris, *The Negro as Capitalist,* 1936). He was also a partner in the Little Rock Electric Light Company, a large shareholder in several other companies, an owner of a substantial amount of local real estate. He subsequently devoted much of his time to travel and speaking engagements, and died on July 11, 1915, at his home 1518 Chester St., Little Rock, after an illness of several months. He was ninety-three years old. Funeral services were held on July 13 at First Baptist Church, Seventh and Gaines Streets. He was survived by three children, two of whom became noted in their own right: Harriet Gibbs Marshall, founder of the Washington Conservatory of Music, and Ida Gibbs Hunt, who married Gibbs's successor at Tamatave, William Henry Hunt, thereafter a U.S. consul for thirty years at various posts. The third survivor was his son, Horace Gibbs, a businessman of Aurora, Ill.

The common thread linking all the diverse facets of Gibbs's long career was his intense interest in what he termed "the progress of the race," hence his abolitionist activities and moves to frontier regions where there was greater equality of opportunity. He chose Little Rock for his home after touring the South to determine which city seemed most promising for Negro residents. Over the decades he was prominent at national Negro conventions assembled to discuss the advancement of the race.

Gibbs asserted that wealth and education are the universal keys to race progress. More specifically, he advocated that Negroes build a skilled middle class by acquiring property and excelling in agriculture and industry. As one of three men appointed in 1879 by the Republican National Executive Committee to appraise the suitability of Kansas and other western states for migration of Negroes from the South, he concluded that such migration was a desirable alternative. And while receiver in the Land Office he encouraged thousands of immigrants and others to homestead virgin Arkansas land, and helped them to establish schools. He favored emphasis on trade schools. In 1885, while commissioner of colored exhibits for Arkansas at the World's Exposition in New Orleans, he financed an unsuccessful conference aimed at establishment of industrial schools for the colored race. The signers of the call to the conference included Frederick Douglass, Archibald Grimké, and Benjamin Tanner. Gibbs remained optimistic throughout his career about race progress based on such measures, while expressing full awareness that too little progress was being made.

The most complete presentation of his ideas on the progress of the race, as well as the most detailed account of his life up to 1900, is his *Shadow and Light, an Autobiography with Reminiscences of the Last and Present Century* (1902, reprinted 1968). There is also an autobiographical sketch in the *National Cyclopedia of American Biography* (1900). An account of his activities in Canada is in Robin W. Winks's *The Blacks in Canada* (1972). An obituary was published in the *New York Age* (July 12, 1915, p. 15) and the *Arkansas Gazette* (July 12, p. 5, and July 13, 1915 p. 10).

— ALLISON BLAKELY

GIBSON, JOSHUA [JOSH] (1911–1947), baseball player. Gibson was born in Buena Vista, Ga., the first of three children of Mark and Nancey (Woodlock) Gibson. In 1923 Mark Gibson gave up farming and went to work as a laborer for the Carnegie-Illinois Steel Company in Pittsburgh. Josh and the rest of the family joined him the following year on the city's North Side. Although Pittsburgh was not the "promised Land" that many Negro migrants from the South expected to find, the "Steel City" had many advantages over rural Georgia. The schools were superior; Negro professional and businessmen and the *Pittsburgh Courier* encouraged a spirit of optimism and innovation. There were a few Negro stars on the Pittsburgh public school athletic teams and at the University of Pittsburgh. But other athletic teams, amateur and professional, excluded players identifiable as American Negroes. One of the separate Negro teams was the Gimbels A.C., an amateur club. Josh, who had dropped out of the ninth grade in Allegheny Pre-Vocational School and had taken a job as an apprentice in an air-brake manufacturing company, began playing on the Gimbels team when he was sixteen. Natural baseball ability probably prompted his decision. His prowess as a slugger with the semiprofessional Crawford Colored Giants of Pittsburgh in 1929 and 1930 attracted the attention of the (Pittsburgh) Homestead Grays, one of the best all-Negro professional baseball teams. On July 25, 1930, in what is said to be the first night game in Pittsburgh, he was called out of the stands in Forbes Field to substitute for the injured regular catcher of the Grays. He began a career which during more than fifteen years established him as one of baseball's best sluggers.

He played with the Grays until 1932, when he, Oscar Charleston, and most of the other Grays jumped to the rival Pittsburgh Crawfords (named for the earlier Crawford Giants). During the winters of 1933–1945 Gibson played with teams in Puerto Rico, Cuba, Mexico, or Venezuela. After he deserted the "Craws" in 1937 to play in the Dominican Republic, he was sold back to the Grays for $2500, plus two players. Although hospitalized with a brain tumor in 1943, he continued to play with the Grays until 1947.

As a nineteen-year-old rookie in 1930 Gibson came within inches of hitting the only fair ball ever knocked out of Yankee Stadium, "the House that Ruth Built." The ball left the field between the third deck and the roof at deepest left-center and came down against the back of the bullpen wall. Another few inches and it would have been out. The Grays were a powerhouse. They starred Oscar Charleston and Smokey Joe Williams, Judy Johnson, George Scales, and Vic Harris. In the Negro world series in 1930 against the New York Lincoln Giants, young Gibson hit the first home run ever struck over Forbes Field's centerfield wall, as the Grays won the championship. The next year (1931) was Josh's first full season. He is credited with seventy-five home runs that year. Although most of them came against semipro teams, two of them were hit against big-league pitcher George Uhle in an 18–0 postseason exhibition victory. On the rival Pittsburgh Crawfords, Josh teamed with a skinny Alabama pitcher named Satchel Paige in perhaps the greatest battery in baseball history (although Josh was not the most polished catcher). Owner Gus Greenlee advertised that Josh would hit a home run and Satch would strike out the first nine men. Gibson was as good as advertised: he knocked sixty-seven home runs that year, according to sports writer Ric Roberts of the *Pittsburgh Courier.* The Craws were so strong that they challenged Casey Stengel's all-stars to seven barnstorming games that fall and won five of them.

Gibson hit over sixty home runs in each of six years, and over seventy twice, in 1931 and 1933. How many would he have hit in the major leagues? Playing with a lively ball in a cozy park such as Brooklyn's, some authorities say, seventy-five would not be too high an estimate. Hank Aaron, the all-time big-league leader, averaged one home run every 15.9 times a bat. Babe Ruth averaged one every 11.7. Gibson, counting Negro league games only, hit a homer every 6.8 times up. He also excelled in yearly averages, topping .400 in league games no fewer than thirteen times, according to Roberts. Three times he went over the .500 mark, and once —1932—he soared to .608. His lifetime mark: .423 against Negro leaguers.

Gibson was hitting against good pitching. In sixty years (1887–1947) Negro teams beat barnstorming white big-leaguers 268 games to 168. Josh played major leaguers in eighteen postseason games and hit them at a .412 clip. Dizzy Dean said Gibson hit the longest home run off him, in 1934. When Josh hit two in one game against him that fall, Dean trotted by the Crawfords' dugout, mopped his face, and grinned, "Josh, if you and Satchel played with me on the Cardinals, we'd win the pennant by July 4 and go fishin' the rest of the yar." Teaming with Buck Leonard on the Grays as baseball's greatest home run duo between Ruth–Gehrig and Mantle–Maris, he brought nine straight pennants to the team (1937–1945), probably a record unequalled by any other professional team in any sport. Especially during World War II, they filled spacious Griffith Sta-

dium in Washington, outdrawing even the American League Senators. In one year alone Gibson pumped seven balls into the distant leftfield bleachers, more than all American League hitters combined could do in a single season. When the *New York Daily Worker* began agitating to admit Negroes to the major leagues, the Senators' owner Clark Griffith called Gibson and Leonard into his office for an interview; nothing came of it, however. During the winter of 1941 in Puerto Rico, he hit .480, a record which has withstood more than thirty years of challenge from such later stars as Roberto Clemente, Willie Mays, and Tony Oliva.

Gibson's top pay for the Grays was $1200 a month for four and a half months. Offered an inadequate raise, he jumped to the Mexican league for 1940 and 1941. "Josh was one of the happiest persons in the world until about the 1940's," says Ted Page, another famous player. "Then he began to realize that he was perhaps the greatest hitter in the world and yet was deprived of a chance to make $20,000–$40,000, while Babe Ruth had pulled down $80,000. He realized that he was just as good as Ruth."

It is this realization that may have driven Gibson to drink excessively (and according to some reports, to use drugs). Nevertheless in 1945 Gibson could still lead the Negro National League, organized by Andrew (Rube) Foster in 1920, with .393, compared later to .365 for Roy Campanella and .345 for Robinson. When the two younger men got big-league contracts, says a friend, Gibson didn't know what to do: "He was a frustrated man."

In his late teens Josh Gibson married Helen Mason, who died in August 1930 at the age of eighteen while giving birth to Gibson's only children, twins Helen and Joshua Jr. His second marriage, in 1940, soon resulted in a separation.

On a freezing night in Pittsburgh in January 1947 Josh Gibson came home, apparently half drunk. He died of a cerebral hemorrhage at his widowed mother's home in Pittsburgh, just three months before Jackie Robinson broke the color bar in the major baseball leagues. Josh Gibson and the Negro leagues died together. Ted Page commented: "Some people say Josh Gibson died of a brain hemmorhage. I say he died of a broken heart." Funeral services were held at Macedonian Baptist Church, Bedford Avenue, Pittsburgh, and he was buried in Allegheny Cemetery.

Gibson may have been the most powerful slugger in the annals of baseball. As nearly as can be counted, he slammed 962 home runs in a seventeen-year career that ended with his untimely death at thirty-five. He set long-distance records in Yankee Stadium, Forbes Field, Shibe Park, and others. He fully deserved his election to baseball's Hall of Fame in 1972.

The most recent work is John Holway's *Voices from the Great Black Baseball Leagues* (1975). See also Robert W. Peterson's *Only the Ball Was White* (1970). An article in *Time* (July 19, 1943) and items in the *Pittsburgh Courier* and *Chicago Defender,* (1930–1947) provide contemporary information. The article by Robert W. Peterson in the *DAB, Supplement 4, 1946–1950* (1974) is a factual, warm tribute, with bibliography. Obituaries in the *Pittsburgh Post-Gazette* (Jan. 21,

1947), the *Pittsburgh Press* (Jan. 21, 1947), and the *Pittsburgh Courier* (Jan. 25, 1947) mention two children, Josh Jr. and Helen, a brother and sister, but not the name of his widow. — JOHN HOLWAY

GILPIN, CHARLES S[IDNEY] (1878–1930), singer and actor. The youngest of fourteen children of Peter and Caroline (White) Gilpin, he was born in Richmond, Va. His father was a laborer in a steel-rolling mill and his mother was a trained nurse in the Richmond City Hospital. Charles attended St. Francis, a Roman Catholic school for colored children, until he was twelve. He learned the printing trade in the *Richmond Planet*. His appearances as an actor in theaters and restaurants won him recognition as a promising singer before he left Richmond in 1896 to join his first professional group, Brown's Big Spectacular Log Cabin Company, a minstrel show. After playing only two towns the company was stranded, but Gilpin was picked up immediately by Perkus and Davis's Great Southern Minstrel Barnstorming Aggregation, which after a few months also became insolvent. Abandoning the entertainment business, he took on printing jobs in the Philadelphia area and when necessary turned to barbering and even training prize-fighters for Vernon Campbell. The Carey and Carter Canadian Jubilee Singers engaged Gilpin in 1903 and he performed with them for two years before joining his first really theatrical team, Bert Williams and George Walker, who advertised him as the "baritone soloist" in their Abyssinia Company. This engagement lasted over a year when he left to join Gus Hill's Original Smart Set for a season. In 1907 he joined the Pekin Stock Company of Chicago, the first legitimate theater to be operated by Negroes, which offered him his first opportunity as a dramatic actor. He quickly became a leading man in both drama and opera (the repertory was very extensive) and won acclaim for his performance in *The Mayor of Dixie* (1907), the first play by Irvin C. Miller and Aubrey Lyles. This production, which toured and played New York City, was revised and revived in 1921 under the title of *Shuffle Along*.

From 1911 to 1913 Gilpin made a transcontinental tour with the Pan American Octette, then went to New York and played in Rogers and Creamers's *Old Man's Boy* Company until 1914. After a stint in vaudeville he returned to acting with the Anita Bush Players at the Lincoln Theater, New York. In 1915 Lester Walton, co-manager of the Lafayette Theater Company, Harlem, the first Negro dramatic stock company in New York City, persuaded Anita Bush to bring her players into the Lafayette. Gilpin was definitely the star of the company, which mounted a new play weekly. *Across the Footlights* was the first production of the new resident company. The *New York Age* said of Gilpin: "as good as he has been hailed in other plays, he is at his very best in this." January 1916 opened with an adaptation of Dion Boucicault's *The Octoroon* in which Gilpin played the villain overseer, Jacob McCloskey. His white character makeup was reported to be so effective that audiences applauded this subtle turning of the tables on "blackface." The advertisements for the March 1916 opening of *Southern Life* gave top billing to Gilpin, and said, "supported by the Lafayette Stock Company."

This was the beginning of the Lafayette Players title. The next play, announced as a "race play," *For His Daughter's Honor,* was a great Gilpin success. Gilpin resigned in April 1916 because of a disagreement about salary and bonuses.

When John Drinkwater's *Abraham Lincoln* opened at the Cort Theater in New York City (Dec. 15, 1919) Gilpin played his first Broadway role, William Custis, the Negro preacher. After *The Emperor Jones* by Eugene O'Neill opened at the Provincetown Theater on MacDougal Street on Nov. 1, 1920, Gilpin was an overnight star. He was probably the first Negro actor to play a major role in an American tragedy. The production was moved from the small Provincetown Theater to the Princess Theater, on Broadway (Jan. 29, 1921), where it played 204 performances before going on a two-year road tour.

That *The Emperor Jones* won the Pulitzer Prize in 1921 attests to the happy marriage between script and actor. Montgomery Gregory commented in *The New Negro: An Interpretation,* edited by Alain Locke (1925, p. 157), that "Then by a *tour-de-force* of genius —for the histrionic ability of Charles Gilpin has been as effective as the dramatic genius of Eugene O'Neill—the serious play of Negro life broke through to public favor and critical recognition. . . . In any further development of Negro drama, *The Emperor Jones . . .* will tower as a beacon-light of inspiration. It marks the break-water plunge of Negro drama into the mainstream of American drama." Alexander Woolcott wrote in the *New York Times* after the opening of *The Emperor Jones:* "They have acquired an actor, one who has it in him to invoke the pity and terror and the indescribable foreboding which are a part of the secret of *The Emperor Jones.*"

In February 1921 the Drama League elected Gilpin as one of the ten persons who had contributed most to the American theater. The subsequent invitation to the presentation banquet created some white opposition, but the Drama League held its ground and the affair proceeded without incident. On June 30, 1921, the NAACP awarded Gilpin the Spingarn Medal for "his notable performance in the title role of Eugene O'Neill's *The Emperor Jones.*" While in Cleveland to play in *Emperor Jones,* he contributed fifty dollars to the Karamu Players, who changed their name to the Gilpin Players and inspired dramatic productions in Cleveland. *Emperor Jones* climaxed his career in the theater. In the early part of 1924 he and Rose McClendon starred in the all-Negro cast of *Roseanne,* a play about Negro life in the South.

While playing in Woodstock, N.J., in June 1929, he suffered a breakdown. He died in Eldridge Park, a suburb of Trenton, on May 6, 1930. He was survived by his widow, Alma Benjamin Gilpin (his second wife), and a twenty-seven-year-old son. After a private funeral in Lambertville, his friends conducted lavish rites on June 1, 1930, and provided burial in Woodlawn Cemetery.

There is a brief sketch on Gilpin by Catherine Palmer Mitchell in *DAB* (4, Part 1:314). The controversy over the Drama League Award was reported by the *New York Times* (Feb. 17, 18, 19, 21, 22, and March 7, 1921). An excellent contemporary evaluation is in

James Weldon Johnson's *Black Manhattan* (1930, pp. 182–85, 192, 193). Later significant interpretations are in Edith J. R. Isaacs's *The Negro in the American Theater* (1947, passim) and Loften Mitchell's *Black Drama: The Story of the American Negro in the Theater* (1967, pp. 50, 69, 75, 76, 84–85).

— ANNE COOKE REID

GLASS, CHARLIE (c. 1872?–1937), cowboy and ranch foreman. Glass was born probably in Indian Territory and came to Colorado in 1907 when it is believed he shot the man who killed his father. In 1909 he moved to a ranch in western Colorado and in 1917 to the Turner ranch north of the Colorado River near Cisco and Thompson, Utah, where he spent the rest of his life. Soon he was made foreman of the Lazy Y ranch and became a much-respected cowboy of that range country. He was a large man, very dark in color although he was thought to be one-quarter Cherokee, handsome, and wore his Levis outside his boots instead of inside as was the custom in the Utah-Colorado borderland. Frequently he came into Grand Junction, Colo., where he kept a room, and made the "rounds" on the Barbary Coast where he was a favorite of the Mexican-American girls. At the annual rodeo in Fruita, Colo., he was a great favorite of the crowds as he rode broncos and roped and bulldogged steers. Cattlemen always faced problems of rustlers, claiming that a rancher "had to have a cow with seven calves in order to have veal for Christmas." But the greatest problem in Glass's day was the invasion of transient sheep from the Colorado high country in the winter months.

Although the range was mostly federal and Indian land, cattlemen had divided it up by custom and in 1917 had the added protection of a quarantine line to keep sheep out. Whether Glass was brought to the Lazy Y ranch for the purpose of keeping sheep out is unknown, but it became his principal task and thrust fame upon him in the cattle country. After numerous encounters, he exchanged shots on Feb. 21, 1921, with a Basque herder, Felix Jesui, killing him. This might have triggered a range war had not Glass surrendered to authorities. At the trial in Moab, Utah, beginning on Nov. 18, 1921, Glass testified that Jesui fired the first shot and "that by the time he got his gun into play Felix shot at him two more times with his pistol; that both men fired at each other several times simultaneously before the herder fell." The "not guilty" verdict pleased the people in the crowded courtroom, for any cowboy who would stand up against transient sheepmen was not guilty of murder. The wounds healed as the years passed and Glass often played poker and drank with both cowboys and sheepherders. On the night of Feb. 22, 1937, he was in a game at Thompson, Utah, and after the bottle had been passed many times, someone suggested that they drive to Cisco to play in the big card game there. Two Basques and Glass drove away with spirits high. Soon they were back but in the back of the truck was Glass's dead body. The sheepherders reported that the truck had turned over three times, killing Glass but only scratching them. The body was buried in the Fruita cemetery on the Turner family plot. The *Grand Junction Sentinel* noted: "Cattlemen, former

employees and acquaintances of Glass, all agree that fiction could produce no more colorful nor picturesque a character than Glass. . . . As a cowpuncher, those who worked with him declare he was an expert as any in the game—a good rider, and a top-notch man with the lariat. The fact that he was one of the very few Negro cowboys in the west aided his notoriety. . . ." The legend of Charlie Glass lingers in the Colorado-Utah range country since his death was regarded as a vengence killing. As the "Ballad of Charlie Glass" says, he "Was a cowpoke, boys, who had a lot of class/ Though he's passed the Great Divide/ All the cowmen speak with pride/ 'Bout the cowpoke that they knew as Charlie Glass."

See Walker D. Wyman's and John D. Hart's *The Legend of Charlie Glass, Negro Cowboy on the Colorado-Utah Range* (1970). — WALKER D. WYMAN

GLASS, DICK (fl. c. 1878–1885), frontier outlaw. He was a product of the generally lawless conditions and the intertribal and interracial conflicts in the postbellum Indian Territory.

Both the Creek and Cherokee nations were divided into half-breed and full-blood factions: the former, generally speaking, tending to follow the cultural patterns of the southern whites, including support of slavery and the Confederacy; the latter, less interested in slavery, tending to support the Union, and with more relaxed racial attitudes. The Negro element in both nations had strongly supported the full-blood, pro-Union faction and had emerged from the conflict not only free but with full citizenship. However, their political and social position in the Creek nation was considerably higher than in the Cherokee, and bitter hostility existed between the mixed-blood Cherokee aristocrats and their Creek Negro neighbors, the former resenting the equality asserted by the Negroes, the latter equally resenting the mixed-blood's arrogant airs of superiority.

By 1878 at the latest the Creek-Cherokee border was the scene of undeclared warfare, with young Cherokee riding across the boundary to defy the authority of the Creek Negro lighthorsemen, or mounted police, and to fire into Negro-occupied houses, and with Creek Negroes running off Cherokee livestock. On Feb. 23, 1880, Creek Negro spokesmen claimed that the Cherokee had recently killed four Negroes and wounded six. The headquarters of Negro hositlity and resistance was Marshalltown, in the "Point" between the Arkansas and the Verdigris Rivers, largely inhabited, it was claimed, by Negro horse and cattle thieves who "plied their vocation unmolested, protected by the close-knit racial consciousness of the Creek Negroes" (Debo) and whose principal leader was Dick Glass, concerning whose origins and previous history virtually nothing is known. An informant of no particular authority claims that Dick was much more Indian than Negro, but whatever his ethnic origins he was thoroughly identified with and loyal to the Creek Negro group.

On the night of July 26, 1880, Cherokee possemen took two suspected Negro horse thieves from their homes, carried them into Cherokee territory, and lynched them. When next morning a number of Negroes rode into Cherokee country to look for their missing friends, a party under Dick Glass encountered two young Cherokee, Willie Cobb and Alex Cowan. Insults developed into an exchange of shots, and in a gunfight which crossed and recrossed the Cherokee-Creek boundary, both youths were wounded, Cobb mortally. Several Negroes were also wounded, and Dick Glass himself had his horse killed under him and was shot through the cheekbone—a wound so severe that it was reported as mortal. The enraged Cherokee were unable to capture Dick, but reward-seekers killed two Negro suspects and Douglas Murrell and Dan Coaker were kidnapped, tried in a Cherokee court, and sentenced to death, but were pardoned by the principal Cherokee chief, Dennis Bushyhead. The two chief suspects in the lynching of the Creek Negroes were tried, but triumphantly acquitted.

Dick Glass in the meantime resumed his professional activities. Although he found it advisable to avoid Marshalltown, and also the Cherokee country, he and his band of Negroes otherwise roamed widely through the territory. They specialized in stealing horses, which they sold in Texas for whiskey, bringing it in by the wagonload for illicit sale in the territory. Early in June 1882, Glass, Ben Doaker, and Douglass Murrell were driving a herd of stolen horses near Okmulgee when Creek lighthorsemen attacked, killing Doaker and wounding Glass so badly that he was again reported killed. In the fall the sheriff of Cowley County, southern Kansas, somehow succeeded in apprehending Dick, but on his way to claim the Cherokee nation's proffered reward, mysteriously "lost" his prisoner—allegedly for a payment from Dick's friends which exceeded the Cherokee offer.

Still later in 1882 Dick Glass temporarily abandoned horsestealing and bootlegging in order to command a Negro contingent in the "Green Peach War," a conflict within the Creek nation between full-bloods and half-breeds in which the Negroes naturally supported the old full-blood leader Isparhecher.

The "war" had petered out by the summer of 1883, but between then and the spring of 1885 Dick Glass did not come to public attention. He may have been attempting—or simulating—a more law-abiding way of life. In a long letter of April 24, 1885, to the commissioner of Indian affairs, he claimed that because of his participation in the 1880 gunfight he had been treated as an outlaw and blamed for crimes he had never committed, denied that he was the head of a gang or engaged in theft, and requested the commissioner to obtain for him "a fair trial" in the Creek courts.

But early in June 1885 a party of U.S. deputy marshals, northwest of Colbert in the Chickasaw nation, unexpectedly ran into Glass and several of his band escorting a wagonload of whiskey. When the brief gunfight was over Glass and one of his comrades were dead and the others were prisoners.

Despite Dick's protestations, he was with little doubt a professional horsethief and bootlegger. But, unlike the James boys, Billy the Kid, Crawford Goldsby, and other desperadoes of the period, he was not a bloodthirsty killer and he undoubtedly regarded himself—and was regarded by other Creek Negroes—as a champion of his people in the border warfare against the arrogant mix-

ed-blood Cherokee and in the internal struggles of the Creek nation. (If Robin Hood, legendary outlaw-champion of the Saxon peasantry, ever existed as a historical character, he probably resembled Dick Glass rather more than he did the Robin Hoods of ballads, novels, and movies.)

The chief authority on Dick Glass and the interracial feuding in which he was involved is Angie Debo's *The Road to Disappearance* (1941); she also generously made her voluminous notes, newspaper extracts, etc., available. Kaye M. Teall (ed.), *Black History in Oklahoma* (1971), presents numerous documents, emphasizing the fight of July 27, 1880.

— KENNETH WIGGINS PORTER

GOLDSBY, CRAWFORD [CHEROKEE BILL] (1876–1896), Oklahoma bandit. He was born on Feb. 8, 1876, at Fort Concho, Tex. His father, Sgt. George Goldsby of the 10th Cavalry, although a native of Selma, Ala., and a soldier in a Negro regiment, is said, with doubtful validity, to have been "of Mexican extraction, mixed with white and Sioux Indian"(!), but his mother, Ellen Beck, was half Negro, one-quarter white, and one-quarter Cherokee. When Crawford was only two years old, his father absconded to avoid trial for involvement in a fatal saloon shootout between white civilians and Negro troopers, and his mother took her children to Fort Gibson, in the lawless Indian Territory. Consequently, from infancy Crawford was without parental guidance. However, he spent three years at school in Cherokee, Kans., and two more at the Carlisle, Pa., Indian school, returning to the territory at the age of twelve. His mother had married a white man, William Lynch, but he and the boy did not get along, and even after the short-lived marriage's dissolution, the mother, although passionately devoted to young Crawford, did not attempt to subject him to any discipline or give him any guidance for his conduct except always to stand up for his rights and not to let anyone impose on him.

Crawford developed into a burly youth, who prided himself on his Cherokee heritage, learned the "Cherokee gobble"—an imitation of the call of the wild turkey signifying a death threat—and used it and his powerful physique to lord it over his youthful companions. However, he eschewed intoxicants and did not get into any serious difficulty until the age of eighteen. Then, after being beaten up by a Negro at a dance, he shot the man twice and fled to the hill country where he joined the band of Bill and Jim Cock, Cherokee mixed-blood outlaws. When in June 1894 a posse attacked their hideout near Tahlequah, a posseman was killed and Cherokee Bill—as young Goldsby was now known—was blamed for the murder; in the Lincoln County bank robbery on July 31 he killed a barber. Late in October he formed his own gang, killed his brother-in-law—allegedly for ill-treating his sister—then killed the station agent at Nowata and a conductor on a train near Fort Gibson, and on Nov. 9, during a robbery at Lenapah, he wantonly shot down an unarmed onlooker. Tipped off by a spy, a posse rode against him and his gang, but although his horse was shot out from under him, Bill escaped.

Bill's pursuers, however, learned that he was enamored of Maggie Glass, half Negro and half Cherokee, who was related to Ike Rogers, a former U.S. deputy marshal. Ike, tempted by a share of the $1500 reward for Bill's capture, invited Maggie to spend an evening at his home and also got word to Bill. However, the outlaw stuck so close to his rifle that Ike saw no opportunity to seize him until the following morning when, as Bill bent to the fireplace to light a cigarette, Rogers hit him over the head with a stick of firewood and, assisted by his hired hand, after a desperate struggle managed to subdue the half-dazed desperado.

Cherokee Bill was brought under heavy guard to Fort Smith, tried before the famous "hanging judge," Isaac C. Parker, and sentenced to death for the Lenapah killing. However, his able lawyer J. Warren Reed lodged an appeal to the U.S. Supreme Court, and while awaiting its outcome Bill, with a smuggled revolver, attempted a jail break, killing one guard and engaging in a desperate gun battle with the others. He was promptly tried, convicted, and again sentenced to be hanged, but in the meantime his appeal was rejected and it was for the Lenapah murder that on March 17, 1896, before a vast throng, he finally mounted the scaffold, insouciant almost to the last. When asked if he had anything to say, his classic reply was: "No. I came here to die, not to make a speech." Afterward, however, he asked a priest who had converted him to Catholicism to pray. Then the black cap was adjusted and the lever pulled. (Cherokee Bill was barely twenty years old and during his last two years had killed at least half a dozen men.)

Cherokee Bill became almost as much a part of the legend of the West as Billy the Kid—whose career, indeed, his own somewhat resembled—and his story was told and retold in almost countless publications. He was not, however, a "black hero," but simply an unusually courageous and cold-blooded desperado of a type common in the West of his day; he never displayed the slightest sense of being the champion of any race or people such as was manifested by the Creek Negro outlaw Dick Glass.

The basic published account is S. W. Harman's *Hell on the Border* (1st ed., 1898; 3rd ed., 1953), a book sponsored and partly written by the lawyer J. Warren Reed. Kaye M. Teall (ed.), *Black History in Oklahoma* (1971), provides some further reminiscences. William H. Leckie's *The Buffalo Soldiers* (1967) tells about Sgt. George Goldsby—but does not identify him as the outlaw's father. Numerous other writers have told and retold Cherokee Bill's story, in the main following Harman and Reed. Among the most detailed accounts are Homer Croy's *He Hanged Them High* (1952), Glenn Shirley's *The Law West of Fort Smith* (1957), and Harry Sinclair Drago's *Outlaws on Horseback* (1964).

— KENNETH WIGGINS PORTER

GOURDIN, EDWARD ORVAL [NED] (1897–1966), scholar, athlete, soldier, and judge. Born on Aug. 10, 1897, in Jacksonville, Fla., the son of Walter Holmes and Felicia Garvin Gourdin, he demonstrated early such athletic and scholarly prowess that his family sacrificed and took him to Massachusetts to realize his potential. He prepared at Stanton and Cambridge Latin High Schools for Harvard College, and graduated (1921), B.A.; Harvard Law School (1924), LL.B.

He gained fame as an athlete during his college and university career, passed the bar, practiced law in Boston, and joined the National Guard in 1925. During World War II he served as lieutenant-colonel and later as colonel, commanding the 372nd Infantry Regiment at home and overseas. After the end of the war he held high offices in the Massachusetts National Guard until his retirement in 1959 with the rank of brigadier-general. He also served as a U.S. district attorney and judge in Massachusetts. On May 10, 1923, he married Amalia Ponce of Cambridge, Mass., who became the mother of their four children: Elizabeth, Ann Robinson, Amalia Lindal, and Edward O. Jr.

He died of cancer on July 22, 1966, in the City Hospital, Quincy, Mass., and was buried in Cotuit, Barnstable County, Cape Cod, Mass.

While at Harvard, Ned Gourdin was a member of the varsity track, baseball, and basketball teams (1919, 1920, 1921). He was crowned National Amateur Athletic Union junior 100-yard dash champion (1920), and National Pentathlon champion (1921 and 1922). In a revival of the postwar (1921) Harvard-Yale versus Oxford-Cambridge track meet, Gourdin won the 100-yard dash, and then jumped to a new world's record in the running broad jump, twenty-five feet, three inches, the first human to leap beyond twenty-five feet. In spite of final law exams, lack of training, and leg injuries, he won the silver medal and added points to the American team victory in the broad jump at the Olympic Games (1924) in Paris. The winner of the gold medal was De-Hart Hubbard, another Negro athlete. The next day, in a noncompetitive exhibition demonstration outside Paris, Ned Gourdin soared twenty-five feet, eight inches—fourteen inches beyond the winning Olympic jump. He also was a member of the National Championship Rifle Team.

Returning to Boston, Gourdin had a successful law practice, was appointed assistant district attorney by Pres. Franklin D. Roosevelt, and rose to chief of the legal division until the outbreak of World War II. He was then assigned to a unit that was part of the 372nd Infantry Regiment (which during World War I had been decorated with the Croix de Guerre with Palm for service in the Meuse-Argonne offensive, 1918). After the war the unit had been split among several states and corps areas. It had no commander and no true headquarters. It was inducted into active service on March 10, 1941, and given seven months of training. It made little progress, however, until the sixty-two-year-old colonel was persuaded to retire from active duty and other changes were made in the command (Ulysses Lee, *The Employment of Negro Troops* [1966], pp. 127, 198, 200–1).

Meanwhile, Gourdin, keenly aware of the tradition of participation by Negro troops in all the nation's wars, had used his experience in the Harvard Student Army Training Corps to be commissioned a second lieutenant in October 1925, after refresher drills and courses. He "bucked"—applied himself vigorously—for promotions until on March 3, 1941, he became commanding officer of the Third Battalion of the 372nd with the rank of lieutenant-colonel. In December 1941 he assumed command of the regiment with the rank of colonel.

For several months the regiment was assigned to guard duty in New York City, its metropolitan area, Long Island, and Jersey City. A training battalion was rotated at Fort Dix, N.J., where not only basic military training was taught (1941–1944) but also literacy, basic education, and citizenship to some 1200 troops. Colonel Gourdin took an active part in these programs and under orientation, information, and education (1943–1944), participated in postcollege workshops and seminars in counseling, law, communications, and Negro history.

To raise the morale and military training demanded by field commanders, the chief of army ground forces assigned the regiment for retraining at Camp Breckenridge, Ky. (April 23 to Nov. 8, 1944). Swollen to nearly twice its size by soldiers from other units, discipline deteriorated. But the line between this deterioration and "racially based violence was often vague, especially in the minds of those involved as participants or as immediately responsible commanders" (ibid., pp. 375–76).

Reenforced by men from other army units, the 372nd was assigned to Fort Huachucha, Ariz., in November 1944. As a part of the Fourth Army, the regiment left this staging area and embarked from Fort Lawton, Wash., in April 1945, for the Pacific Theater. V-E Day, May 8, 1945 when the war in Europe officially came to an end, was celebrated aboard transports bound for Honolulu. The Middle Pacific Command retested the 372nd for the "Jungle Training Combat Command" and assigned it to ground defense of Oahu and other Hawaiian islands (May 1945). V-J Day (Sept. 2, 1945), when the Japanese officially surrendered, changed the nature of the assignment to one of rehabilitation, education, and return of eligible personnel to civilian life. Colonel Gourdin became a member of the Mid Pacific Sociology and Psychiatry Board. The 372nd reassembled at Schofield Barracks, was deactivated, and returned to National Guard status. In February 1946 Colonel Gourdin, as assistant executive officer, became a member of the assistant secretary of war's Discharge and Review Board.

Colonel Gourdin returned to the United States on Feb. 11, 1946 and until 1947 served on the Discharge and Review Board under the assistant secretary of war. When he returned to the Massachusetts National Guard, he served as acting chief of staff, acting judge advocate general, and as plans and training general staff officer for defense of the Boston area, and aide to the governor of Massachusetts. When he retired in 1959, he was a brigadier-general.

Simultaneously he resumed his law position as assistant U.S. district attorney. As chief of the Civil Division, he handled such cases as immigration, taxation, leases, and contracts. Active with the state Judicial Council, he was appointed (1952) to be a special justice of the Roxbury District Court, the third Negro to serve on the state bench. In 1958, Gov. Foster Furcolo appointed him to the Massachusetts Superior Court.

Ned Gourdin received several posthumous awards. The National Olympic Athletes Association elected him president in 1965. The Harvard Varsity Club placed in its Hall of Fame (1969) a plaque, the Edward O. "Ned" Gourdin Memorial Award, honoring him as a track jumper, for exemplary character and Harvard community contributions. The Col. Edward O. Gourdin Post 5298, Veterans of Foreign Wars of the United States, was chartered in Springfield Gardens, Queens County, N.Y., in 1968. A handsome clubhouse and memorial were dedicated there (Sept. 1975 and June 1980), with his widow and other family members present.

Ned Gourdin left a legacy of inspiration to younger athletes, officers, and members of the bar and bench. This sketch is based primarily on three publications by Edward Morrow: *History of the 372nd Infantry Regiment,* a pamphlet and broadcast strip for Regimental Day Celebration (1944); *On Guard, The 372nd Infantry, A Marching Tradition,* edited by LeRoy Clay, Edward Morrow, and others, illustrated (1944); and, *A Factual History of the 372nd Infantry Regiment, National Guard of the United States . . . in World War II* (1945). Personal reminiscences of Edward Morrow and those of Colonel Gourdin's family and friends, especially his widow, Mrs. Amalia Ponce Gourdin, were also used. See also "America's Most Democratic Army Post," by Simeon Booker, Herman Burrell, and others (*Ebony,* Dec. 1947). There is a photograph of Gourdin jumping in the Paris Olympics in Edwin B. Henderson's *The Negro in Sports* (1949, p. 48). See also the obituary in the *New York Times* (July 22, 1966, p. 26).

— EDWARD MORROW

GREEN, JOHN PATTERSON (1845–1940) attorney, politician, and civil servant. Green was born at Newbern, N.C., the son of John and Temperance Green, free Negroes of mixed ancestry. John's father was reputed to be the son of John Stanley, a Yankee privateer during the Revolutionary War. His grandmother, Sarah Rice, from Africa, was employed as a servant by North Carolina governor Speight. The elder Green, a tailor by trade, died while John was quite young, leaving the sole support of three children to John's mother. Young John obtained the rudiments of an elementary education at a school maintained by John Stuart Stanley. The Green family left North Carolina in June 1857, traveling by ship to the port of New York, and then by railroad to Cleveland, Ohio. Shortly after arrival, John was sent to Oberlin, Ohio, an abolitionist stronghold, where he lived at the home of John Patterson, a local bricklayer and plasterer. Green subsequently was apprenticed to John Scott, a harnessmaker. Not liking Oberlin, he returned to Cleveland.

Green entered Mayflower School in Cleveland, leaving in 1859 because of financial difficulties. He worked for a time caning chairs and performing odd jobs. In 1862 he found employment with the East Cleveland Street Railway, as a tailor, his father's trade, and as a waiter. During his free time Green studied on his own. The first hint of his many talents surfaced in 1866 with the publication of *Essays on Miscellaneous Subjects by a Self-Educated Colored Youth,* sold in Ohio, New York, New Jersey, Pennsylvania, Delaware, Maryland, and the District of Columbia. After participating in a lecture tour, selling pamphlets, and promoting his essays during the year, he entered Cleveland Central High School in 1866. Following graduation in 1869, he enrolled at the Union Law School in Cleveland, graduating in 1870.

In 1870 he and his wife moved to North Carolina where John clerked in a grocery store. He then ran his own grocery business in South Carolina, was admitted to the South Carolina bar in 1870, and embarked on a career halted only by death. He was elected a delegate to the 1872 South Carolina State Republican Convention and an alternate delegate to the 1872 Republican National Convention at Philadelphia.

Late in 1872 Green returned to Cleveland, began a lecture tour, and obtained the Republican party nomination for justice of the peace in Cuyahoga County. He won the election by over 3000 votes, marking him as one of the early Negro officeholders in the North. The office, comprising a part of the Court of Common Pleas and including among its duties jurisdiction to hear and decide certain civil actions, constituted the first level in the judicial system of the day. Reelected and serving for nine years, his popularity at the polls brought nomination to the Ohio House of Representatives in 1877. Although elected by a sixty-two-vote margin, Green lost to his Democratic opponent in a subsequent recount. He continued in the justice of the peace post and his law practice; renominated for the Ohio House in 1881, Green emerged victorious.

During his first term he served on both the corporations and library committees, and offered a resolution condemning the contract-labor system in operation at the Ohio Penitentiary and other penal institutions in the state. Amid myriad activities he found time to write *Recollections of the Carolinas* (1881). Defeated for renomination in 1884, he served as an alternate delegate-at-large at the 1884 Republican National Convention in Chicago, and spoke on behalf of Republican candidates, sharing the platform on one occasion with Frederick Douglass.

Green maintained his private law practice after the campaign and continued to deliver addresses on behalf of Republican candidates for office. He again won election to the Ohio House of Representatives in 1890, by over a 3000-vote margin. Green's most significant legislative achievement was a bill establishing "Labor Day" in Ohio. When the federal government followed suit, many called Green the "Father of Labor Day" in the United States. He served on the turnpike committee and supported legislation on behalf of civil rights and veterans benefits.

The early 1890s found Green establishing a close friendship with such prominent Republican leaders of Ohio as Marcus A. Hanna and George A. Myers. Hanna was a national Republican leader, and Myers, a barber and confidant of Hanna, was the most influential Negro in Ohio Republican politics. Green began an acquaintance also with John D. Rockefeller, and won election to the Ohio Senate in 1892. Its first Negro member, he won an appropriation for an Industrial Department at Wilberforce University. During the presidential campaign of 1892 he supported Benjamin Harrison in lectures in Ohio. Following expiration of his Senate term, Green toured Europe, served as an alternate delegate-at-large from Ohio at the 1896 Republican National Convention in St. Louis, and spoke throughout Ohio in

support of William McKinley. In addition to Green's forensic abilities, his articles for the Afro-American News Syndicate, which supplied materials to over two hundred newspapers, and his party loyalty further gained the attention of President McKinley. Numbered among the leading contenders for the post of recorder of deeds in the District of Columbia, he was supported by most of the leading Negro newspapers and John D. Rockefeller, his old Cleveland friend. Although the post of recorder of deeds eluded Green, he was chosen the U.S. postage stamp agent in 1897, with a salary of $2200 a year. The general responsibilities of the position involved supervision of the printing and distribution of postage stamps for the entire nation. He served in that position until 1905 when he became acting superintendent of finance for the Post Office Department. A year later he left government employment and returned to his Cleveland law practice.

The last three decades of Green's life found his national activity fairly limited. He devoted a major portion of his time to his law practice, and in 1920 he published his autobiography. Advancing age curtailed any intensive involvement in national Republican politics. He addressed a Chicago audience in 1928 on the subject of "The Relation of Negroes to the Republican Party." Four years later he spoke in New York City on behalf of Herbert Hoover. A staunch Republican, Green became a vocal critic of Pres. Franklin D. Roosevelt's attempted packing of the Supreme Court during the late 1930s. Even in his nineties, Green was a frequent visitor to both the Municipal and Common Pleas Court. At the time of his death he had a case pending in court and easily ranked as the oldest practicing lawyer in Ohio. He died on Aug. 30, 1940, in Cleveland, after being hit by an automobile while alighting from a trolley.

He was married first on Dec. 23, 1869, to Annie Walker, who became the mother of their six children. Following her death on Jan. 15, 1912, he married on Sept. 6, 1912, a widow, Mrs. Lottie Mitchell Richardson. Buried in Woodlawn Cemetery, Cleveland, he was survived by his wife, a son, Jesse B., and a daughter, Mrs. C. C. Johnson.

The most complete account of Green's life is his autobiography, *Fact Stranger Than Fiction: Seventy-Five Years of a Busy Life with Reminiscences of Many Great Men and Women* (1920). Russell H. Davis's *Black Americans in Cleveland* (1972) focuses on Green's Republican party activity. Kenneth L. Kusmer, in his *A Ghetto Takes Shape: Black Cleveland, 1930–1970* (1976), discusses him at greater length and concludes that "Although discrimination was increasing in the prewar period, Green failed to speak out against it, much less lead a fight to reverse the trend" (pp. 120–21). The John P. Green Papers at the Western Reserve Historical Society in Cleveland provide details on Green's law practice, speech subjects, and role in the Republican party. The Green correspondence in the George A. Myers Papers at the Ohio Historical Society in Columbus center on Republican party matters and the personal friendships of the two families. His legislative activity was reported in the *Ohio House and Senate Journals*. The *Cleveland Gazette* and *Cleveland Plain*

Dealer provide extended coverage of Green's public career. — FRANK R. LEVSTIK

GREEN, SHIELDS (c. 1825–1859), one of John Brown's men at Harpers Ferry. Green was born a slave in South Carolina and spent most of his life there. As a young man he escaped and fled north with the help of the Underground Railroad. In Rochester, N.Y., Green found shelter in the home of Frederick Douglass, who has given a detailed description of Green and especially of Green's relationship to John Brown. Green first met Brown at Douglass's home. Douglass wrote that Shields Green, or "Emperor" as he was sometimes called, was "a man of few words, and his speech was singularly broken; but his courage and self-respect made him quite a dignified character. John Brown saw at once what 'stuff' Green 'was made of,' and confided to him his plans and purposes." Green believed in Brown and trusted him. He promised to go with Brown whenever Brown might call him.

Two months before the raid Green accompanied Douglass to southern Pennsylvania to meet with John Brown. Brown did his best to get Douglass to join him in the planned attack. Since Douglass could foresee only failure, he used all his persuasive powers to get Brown to give up the idea. For nearly two days Green heard the two men in their arguments, with Brown presenting the call to action and Douglass forecasting failure and death. Douglass at last saw that Brown could not be turned from his course of action. He later wrote: "I turned to Shields Green and told him he heard what Captain Brown had said, his old plan was changed and that I should return home and if he wished to go with me he could do so. . . . When about to leave, I asked Green what he had decided to do, and was surprised by his coolly saying, in his broken way, 'I b'lieve I'll go wid de ole man'."

Green started south with John Brown's son, Owen. Slave catchers who were patrolling the roads tried to catch them. Only by swimming a river did Shields and Brown escape to make their way to a farm John Brown had rented five miles from Harpers Ferry. Here he assembled his supplies and men. Shields and the other Negroes of the party were kept hidden until Brown was ready to strike on Sunday night, Oct. 16, 1859. Green stayed close to Brown during the attack and throughout the two days of fighting. On Monday afternoon Brown had withdrawn to the well-built engine house, leaving Green with two other men to guard an outer wall. When the engine house came under heavy attack, it seemed that Brown and the men with him were surely doomed. Those at the wall saw that they could escape, but Green again said he would "go with the old man." He went to Brown in the engine house where he fought until the next morning, when the soldiers overran the small party who were out of ammunition.

Green and Brown were captured. Like Brown and the others, Green was charged with treason, murder, and leading slaves to rebel. At his trial Green's lawyer pointed out that because Green was a slave, a noncitizen, he owed no loyalty to the state of Virginia and therefore he could not be guilty of treason. Also as a slave, said the lawyer, Green had the right and indeed the duty to fight for his freedom. The court dropped the charge of treason but Green was convicted on the other two charges. He was hanged on Dec. 16, 1859. He died with John Anthony Copeland on the scaffold which had been built for John Brown and his men. Witnesses said that he obeyed John Brown's last order, that he go to his death like a man.

Frederick Douglass's *Life and Times of Frederick Douglass* (1962 ed., pp. 317–21) tells of his meeting with Green. Osborne P. Anderson's *A Voice From Harpers Ferry* (1861) is the only eyewitness account by one of the participants. See also W. E. B. Du Bois's *John Brown* (1909). — LORENZ GRAHAM

GREENER, RICHARD T[HEODORE] (1844–1922), educator, lawyer, consular officer, and leader of reform movements. Born in Philadelphia to Richard Wesley and Mary Ann (Le Brune) Greener, and raised in Cambridge, Mass., Greener engaged in college preparatory work at Oberlin College in Ohio and at Phillips Academy in Andover, Mass. He achieved his first major distinction when in 1870 he became the first Negro to receive a degree from Harvard College, where he won top prizes for oratory and dissertation writing. He wanted to become a lawyer, but for ten years following graduation he pursued an academic career, first taking two consecutive positions as a school principal: at the Institute for Colored Youth in Philadelphia and the Preparatory High School for Colored Youth in the District of Columbia. In 1873 he accepted the chair of metaphysics and logic at the University of South Carolina. In 1874 he married Genevieve Ida Fleet, by whom he was to have seven children. While teaching Latin, Greek, international law, and U.S. constitutional history, he completed a law degree and was admitted to the bar in South Carolina in 1876 and in the District of Columbia the following year. When, with the "end of Reconstruction," Negroes were again excluded from the University of South Carolina, he became an instructor in the Law Department of Howard University, beginning in 1877 and serving as dean from January 1879 to July 1880. During this period he gained a reputation as a spokesman for Negroes when he advocated migration of the freedmen to western states such as Kansas to settle fertile land and escape oppression. He and Frederick Douglass presented opposing papers on this subject at a congress of the American Social Science Association held at Saratoga Springs, N.Y., in September 1877.

In 1880 the executive committee of the board of trustees temporarily disbanded the Howard University Law Department, ostensibly for lack of students. Greener remained in Washington, serving for two years as a law clerk and then practicing law. In the next several years he campaigned prominently for the Republican party, traveling widely through the near-western and near-southern states. His service was rewarded in 1885 by appointment as secretary of the Grant Monument Association in New York state, until 1892, and as chief examiner of the municipal civil-service board for New York City, until 1889. In the 1890s, at times in desperate financial straits and with his marriage dissolving, Greener sought a foreign service post, hoping to advance to high rank. In January 1898 he was appointed consul to Bombay, India, but declined to go after discovering through British despatches that there was a severe epidemic of bubonic plague in Bombay. While on indefinite delay from that assignment he unsuccessfully sought a naval commission to serve in the Spanish-American war. Then in July 1898 he accepted appointment as the first U.S. consul to Vladivostok, Russia. Reappointed, at the rank of commercial agent at the prerogative of the Russian government, he served in that capacity until 1905. Vladivostok suddenly gained new strategic significance during his term owing to the United States' growing interest in the Far East and the major international conflicts there. Greener was decorated by the Chinese government for his role in famine relief in North China in the wake of the Boxer Rebellion; and during the Russo-Japanese War he looked after the interests in Vladivostok of both the Japanese and British governments, whose representatives were forced to leave temporarily for diplomatic reasons. He was dismissed from his post and from the foreign service on the basis of charges, never substantiated, of improper conduct. When subsequent efforts failed to gain him a formal hearing on this matter and a new government job, he retired to Chicago where he made his home after 1906.

Greener continued to enjoy the respect he had earned through his many public speeches and the writings he had contributed to various periodicals. As late as 1917, Carter G. Woodson sent him a copy of an issue of his new *Journal of Negro History* to critique. Greener's thought reflected the liberal element of the Boston and Harvard intellectual milieu from which he came. He admired Thoreau, Garrison, and Phillips, especially for their independence of thought. The main theme in his writings and his life was individualism, which he viewed as basic to the solution of the political, social, and economic problems of the day. Hence his stand on migration of freedmen, since he saw this as the best way to ensure them a means of competing in a free-enterprise economic system and of securing political liberty. His individualism also determined the nature of his personal role as a reformer. While regarded by many of his contemporaries as one of the most brilliant Negro intellectuals of his generation, and himself often noting the need for Negro leaders, he never filled that role. He was as firm in his advocacy of women's rights and as conspicuous in support of Irish liberation as he was in promoting the Negro cause. He attended the second meeting of the Niagara Movement in 1906, but did not actively support either this movement led by W. E. B. Du Bois or the opposing doctrine of Booker T. Washington, for whom Greener did serve as an informant at the meeting. (It should be added that both men distrusted him.) Rather than join such organizations, he strove to "advance the race" through his writings and by the example of his own success. However, his career revealed the severe limitations of this approach. Controversy surrounded his removal from most of the positions he held; and at the root invariably was his independence of mind, his color, or both. Like some other well-educated American Negroes he discovered that his best chance to utilize and develop his abilities lay abroad. Realization of this made his bitterness and disil-

lusionment all the more intense when his public career ended in Vladivostok after it became a more important post. Thus his optimism about individualism and American society was permanently shaken when he was ultimately unable to attain a status he believed commensurate with his talents and dedication. At the same time his chosen stance isolated him from most other Negroes to such a degree that few of them have viewed him as the champion of their cause.

Although he devoted most of his retirement years to writing, Greener did not publish a major work. There is a brief autobiographical sketch by him, covering his life up to 1870, in the Harvard University Archives. He died of a cerebral hemorrhage at his home, 5237 Ellis Ave., Chicago, on May 2, 1922.

Many biographical sketches of him contain numerous errors and must be used with caution. The most complete is in Frank L. Mather's *Who's Who of the Colored Race.* Carter G. Woodson contributed the brief sketch in the *DAB* (1932, 4:578–79). There is also an article on Greener by Allison Blakely in *JNH* (October 1974). Other materials are in the records of the State Department in the National Archives and the Booker T. Washington and Woodson Papers in the Library of Congress.

— ALLISON BLAKELY

GREENFIELD, ELIZABETH TAYLOR (1809–1876), vocal artist, called the "Black Swan." Born in slavery and educated in freedom, she was possessed of the remarkable vocal range from baritone G, first line in the bass clef, to high C above the treble clef, and the sensitivity and musical intelligence to use that capacity artistically. She was probably the first American Negro musician to gain recognition in England and Canada as well as the United States.

Elizabeth Greenfield was born in Natchez, Miss. (According to her court testimony in 1847, she was born in 1817.) Her family name was Taylor, but through circumstances not recorded, she was taken at the age of one to Philadelphia by a white Quaker named Mrs. Greenfield, who reared her and treated her as a daughter, giving her the family name of Greenfield.

While still a young woman, her unusual voice and personality attracted the attention of a Miss Price, the musically educated daughter of a local physician who gave her instruction on the guitar and piano, and taught her new songs. When Dr. Price entered his household as they were listening to the remarkable singing of the young colored girl, he was delighted. Soon the event was told to Mrs. Greenfield, who had not been informed for fear the secular songs might have offended her. Mrs. Greenfield, however, was pleased, and she encouraged and supported Greenfield in the study of vocal repertory, so that she soon was in demand as a soloist at private parties in the Philadelphia area.

Mrs. Greenfield died in 1844, leaving a substantial bequest to the young artist. The will was contested and soon Miss Greenfield was thrown on her own resources. She decided to go to Buffalo, N.Y., where friends of her patron resided. En route, while on a steamer on Lake Seneca, she made the acquaintance of the wife of General Potter and other philanthropic ladies who were returning to their homes in Buffalo.

Mrs. Potter was so struck with the artistic quality of the young singer that she invited her to stay at her mansion upon their arrival in Buffalo. Her new friends gave a party for prominent citizens of that city, and invited Miss Greenfield to sing. The impression made at that party resulted in an invitation through the press, under the auspices of that group of citizens, to sing a series of concerts.

In October 1851 she sang her first concert before the Buffalo Musical Association. The effect was sensational. Some people had attended through curiosity that a colored woman should be giving a concert. From the press notices the unanimous impression was one of astonishment at the richness, power, compass, and artistry of this remarkable singer. She was given the sobriquet "The Black Swan." The *Buffalo Express* wrote that Jenny Lind, the famous white singer, had never had a better audience than the one "which listened with evident satisfaction to this unheralded and almost unknown African nightingale." With instruction she would "rank among the very first vocalists of the age. She has a voice of great sweetness and power, with a wider range, from the lowest to the highest notes, than we have ever listened to."

The *Daily State Register of Albany* (Jan. 19, 1852) reported that "The Black Swan" possessed "a truly wonderful voice. . . . In sweetness, power, compass, and flexibility, it nearly equals any of the foreign vocalists who have visited this country." It needed only the training and education they had received "to outstrip them all. Among the audience were Governor Hunt and his family, members of both houses of the legislature, other state officials, and a large number of leading citizens. "All came away astonished and delighted."

When Col. J. H. Wood was her "Gentlemanly manager," Greenfield gave concerts in New York City, Boston, Columbus, Milwaukee, Brattleboro (Vt.), and Toronto, all before the end of June 1852. The *Toronto Globe* (May 12–15, 1852) praised the great power of her soprano voice, her piano playing, and her "deep and very clear bass or baritone voice, which she maintained throughout, without any very great appearance of effort, or without any breaking."

According to a comment from Brattleboro, she was "not pretty but plain"; she was, however, gifted "with a beauty of soul which makes her countenance agreeable in conversation." Her singing, especially "when her social nature is called into activity," revealed a "grace and beauty in her manner which soon make those unaccustomed to her race forget all but the melody. Nature has done more for Miss Greenfield than any musical prodigy we have met." A New York City newspaper commented on her "ladylike manners, elegant form, and not unpleasing, though decidedly African features. Of her marvelous powers, she owes none to any tincture of European blood."

Before leaving for Europe after singing in all the free states, citizens of Buffalo organized a very successful testimonial and benefit concert on March 7, 1853. She also gave two successful concerts in New York City, the first of which was attended by an audience of 4000, and the second, on request by a group of citizens, equally

successful. She embarked on a British steamer (April 6, 1853) and arrived in Liverpool (April 16), proceeding to London on April 18.

When failure of promised arrangements left Greenfield stranded, providence once again took a hand: Harriet Beecher Stowe was in London. Her *Uncle Tom's Cabin* (1852) had sold 300,000 copies, been staged, and been widely read in England and on the continent in translation; she was well acquainted with the English nobility in London. In her book *Sunny Memories of Foreign Lands* (Boston, 1854) she reports that Greenfield visited her on May 6, 1853. "The (so called) Black Swan," Mrs. Stowe wrote, "appears to be a gentle, amiable, and interesting young person. . . . She has a most astonishing voice . . . a compass of three octaves and a fourth." Like others, Stowe was so astounded by the breadth and volume of sound that if the listener's back were turned, it would be difficult to imagine that a woman was singing. Mrs. S. C. Hall, in the *Irish Sketches,* was amazed and delighted by Greenfield's rendition of "Old Folks at Home," first in soprano, then in a tenor or baritone. When Mrs. Hall took Greenfield to the home of Sir George Smart, the head of the Queen's establishment and the acknowledged leader of London musical judgment, "he was really astonished and charmed at the wonderful weight, compass and power of her voice. He was also well pleased with the mind in her singing, and her quickness in doing and catching all he told her."

Smart presided at Greenfield's concert at Stafford House on May 27, 1853. Mrs. Stowe noted that in the brilliant and picturesque hall, "the choicest of the *elite* were there. Ladies in demi-toilet and bonneted." Greenfield, who stood among the singers on the staircase, excited a sympathetic murmur among the audience. "She has a pleasing dark face, wore a black velvet hair dress and white carnelian earings, a black mohr antique silk, made high in the neck, with white lace falling sleeves and white gloves." The audience listened with profound attention to "her voice [which] with its keen, searching fire, penetrating vibrant quality, its 'timbre' as the French call it, cuts its way like a Damascus blade to the heart." Sir George escorted her to the piano "and tried her voice by skips, striking notes here and there at random, without connection, from D in alto to A first space in bass clef." When unerringly she struck the sound at nearly the same instant his finger touched the key, the audience burst into applause.

Mrs. Stowe also reported Greenfield's first public morning concert in the Queen's Concert Rooms, Hanover Square, on May 31, 1853. Since the concert was under the patronage of the Duchess of Sutherland, the Duchess of Norfolk, and the Earl and Countess of Shaftesbury, the singer's future was assured. According to the (London) *Times:* "Miss Greenfield sings 'I know that my Redeemer Liveth' with as much pathos, power and effect as does the 'Swedish Nightingale,' Jenny Lind." Her concerts were reviewed with enthusiasm by the *London Morning Post, London Observer, London Advertiser,* and others, culminating in a command performance before the queen at Buckingham Palace, May 10, 1854.

Greenfield returned to New York City in July 1854 on

the steamer *Indiana*. The *New York Herald* said of her concert, " 'The Swan' sings now in true artistic style, and the wonderful powers of her voice have been developed by good training." Greenfield returned to Philadelphia and spent the remaining years of her life teaching voice and giving an occasional concert. "Enjoying the warm love of many friends in those private circles where she was always an ornament and a blessing, this wonderfully gifted lady of the age of sixty-eight years died deeply mourned by all." She died suddenly of paralysis at her home in Philadelphia on March 31, 1876.

The source for much of Greenfield's life is the autobiographical pamphlet *The Black Swan at Home and Abroad* (1855). The account in James Monroe Trotter's *Music and Some Highly Musical People* (1878; with portrait, reprinted 1969) relies in some measure on *The Black Swan*. A recent sketch is that by Samuel R. Spencer in *NAW* (1971, 2:87–89). Obituaries were published in the *New York Times* (April 2, 1876) and the *Philadelphia Public Ledger* (April 3, 1876).

— RAYMOND LEMIEUX

GREGG, JOHN ANDREW (1877–1953), forty-ninth bishop of the African Methodist Episcopal church. Born in Eureka, Kans., on Feb. 18, 1877, the son of Alexander and Eliza F. Gregg, he attended the public and high schools of Eureka; after graduation from high school he matriculated at the University of Kansas at Lawrence, from which he received the B.A. degree in 1902.

Gregg was licensed to preach at Eureka in September 1898, became a part of the Kansas Annual Conference at Emporia in September 1902, and was ordained a deacon in 1903 and an elder at Hutchinson in 1906. He served in several capacities: as pastor of Mount Olive A.M.E. Church, Emporia (1903); as missionary to South Africa (1903–1906) and presiding elder of the Cape Annual Conference (1904); pastor of Bethel A.M.E. Church, Leavenworth, Kans. (1906–1908), and the Ebenezer A.M.E. Church, St. Joseph, Mo. (1908–1913). He was president of Edward Waters College, Jacksonville, Fla. (1913–1920); of Wilberforce University, Wilberforce, Ohio (1920 to May 1924). During the General Conference held at Louisville, Ky., in May 1924, he was elected bishop after a bitter contest that continued far into the night. He was immediately assigned to South Africa for four years. During his assignment he purchased in 1925 an Episcopal residence in Cape Town, built Bethel Chapel in 1927 at a cost of $38,000, and built Eliza Gregg Hall at Wilberforce Institute in South Africa.

In 1926 Gregg was appointed president of Howard University, the first Negro so honored. He declined, believing he could serve humanity more effectively through the A.M.E. church.

After returning from South Africa, Gregg served the Fifth Episcopal District (1928–1936); the Fourth Episcopal District (1936–1948), and the Eleventh Episcopal District (1948–1953). He was a trustee of Wilberforce University (1911–1953) and president of the Trustee Board of Payne Theological Seminary and chairman of its Building Committee (1920–1953). He raised $40,-000 to help reduce the mortgage on Wilberforce University.

In 1943, during the administration of Franklin D. Roosevelt, Gregg was appointed by the Fraternal Council of Negro Churches and President Roosevelt to visit the war areas of the Pacific, North Africa, England, and the Near East. Gregg traveled 56,217 miles by airplane to these areas and ordained forty deacons and elders of the church. "Upon his return to the United States he was welcomed by large crowds in Memphis, Chicago, Kansas City and many other communities where the people were anxiously awaiting word from the troops serving abroad."

Gregg was a member of several organizations: a Thirty-second Degree Mason, the Knights of Pythias lodge, the Elks, Alpha Phi Alpha fraternity, Sigma Pi Phi fraternity (an organization of prominent men), and the National Council of Churches of Christ and co-chairman of its Race Relations Department. An interesting speaker, he delivered the keynote address at the World's Christian Endeavor Convention in Berlin, Germany (1930) and the episcopal address in 1940.

His publications dealt mainly with church literature and philosophy. His articles appeared in many church periodicals, and he was the author of two books: *Christian Brotherhood* (1930) and *Of Men and of Arms* (1945).

Bishop Gregg was very imposing in appearance, almost six feet tall, weighing over 200 pounds, and wearing a goatee. On Aug. 21, 1900, he was married to Celia Nelson of Lexington, Mo. She had attended the public schools of Lawrence and at the time of their marriage was a fellow student at the University of Kansas. During their assignment in South Africa she taught at Bethel Institute and at Chatsworth near Kalabas Kraal. Mrs. Gregg was particularly helpful in educational work during her husband's assignment to the two schools. Until her death she supervised the missionary branches of the Fourth Episcopal District. She died in 1941, after forty-one years of travel and devoted service to Christianity and education.

The second Mrs. Gregg was Melferta McFarland (Dec. 31, 1945). She was the widow of August McFarland who had died in 1937. Both unions were childless.

Gregg is remembered for his popularity with all classes, his devoted service to humanity and the African Methodist Episcopal church. Named for him are churches located in Miami, Tampa, Fort Myers, and Sanford, Florida, and Kansas City, Mo.

He died on Feb. 17, 1953, at Jacksonville and was buried in Kansas City, Kans. He bequeathed $1000 to Edward Waters College to be invested and the interest given annually as a scholarship to a worthy student; he left the rest of his estate to relatives and friends.

The principal sources are Richard R. Wright, Jr.'s *The Bishops of the African Methodist Episcopal Church* (1963, pp. 199–202), Reverdy C. Ransom's *The Pilgrimage of Harriet Ransom's Son* (n.d., passim), Dorothy E. Hoover's *A Layman Looks with Love at Her Church* (1930), and Frederick A. McGinnis's *A History and Interpretation of Wilberforce University* (1941). For his election to and declining the presidency of Howard University, see Rayford W. Logan's *Howard Uni-*

versity: *The First Hundred Years, 1867–1967* (1969, pp. 242–43). Also see the obituary in the *New York Times* (Feb. 19, 1953, p. 22). — MARY M. FISHER

GRIGGS, SUTTON E[LBERT] (1872–1933), novelist, clergyman, social and political moralist. Born in Chatfield, Tex., the son of Baptist minister Allen R. Griggs, he was educated in the Dallas public schools and Bishop College in Marshall, Tex., from which he graduated in 1890. Griggs trained for the Baptist ministry at the Richmond Theological Seminary (later Virginia Union University) between 1890 and 1893. His first pastorate was at Berkley, Va.; two years later he moved to Tennessee to begin some thirty years of ministry there, initially at the First Baptist Church of East Nashville, then for nineteen consecutive years at the Tabernacle Baptist Church of Memphis. On May 10, 1897, Griggs married Emma J. Williams of Portsmouth, Va., a childless union which lasted until his death.

Griggs's young manhood coincided with the sweep of segregationist legislation across the South and the publication of fiction and quasi-scientific works openly questioning the humanity of colored Americans. Like Charles W. Chesnutt, Paul Laurence Dunbar, W. E. B. Du Bois, and Booker T. Washington, Griggs responded with a body of literature of his own making. Published and distributed almost entirely through his personal efforts and at his expense, Griggs's several books and pamphlets were bought by the people whose welfare concerned him the most—the aspiring classes of the black South. In the ten years beginning with his first work, *Imperium in Imperio* (1899), he published all of his five novels and his more significant political treatises, notably *Wisdom's Call* (1909). Thereafter, he abandoned fiction in favor of tracts and handbooks urging spiritual and social uplift.

Almost always the long-suffering victims of southern racism, the heroes and heroines (all Negro) of Griggs's novels do not sacrifice ethical values for personal or political ends. In *Imperium in Imperio*, Belton Piedmont dies rather than support a plan for national violence to solve racial problems. In *Overshadowed* (1901), Astral Herndon prefers voluntary exile to life in the shadow of segregation; he becomes a "citizen of the ocean." In *Unfettered* (1902), Dorlan Warthell wins the hand of lovely, intense Morlene only by submitting a rational, nonviolent plan to solve racial problems in the South. In *The Hindered Hand* (1905), Ensall Smallwood denounces the proposal of a Slavic leader to destroy Anglo-Saxons in America through germ warfare. Baug Pepper of *Pointing the Way* (1908) relies on legal training and racial cooperation to advance his race in America.

Sensational details in these works, however, reinforced Griggs's reputation for near-radicalism and exposed him to later charges of political vacillation and reaction. He believed in the South as the ideal setting of an interracial democracy governed by laws equally applied, but he frowned on racial assimilation as a denial of black pride. A severe critic of both the white South and his own people, he wished to eliminate all forms of delinquency through such established institutions as the church and the law. He became increas-

ingly conservative in later years, when he was sometimes referred to as the "Negro Apostle to the White Race." In general, though, his novels are of a piece thematically and technically. His limitations as a craftsman were considerable, betraying most of the weaknesses of popular sentimental melodrama.

Griggs's reputation was founded on his obvious learning, his prolific writing, and his lifelong devotion to the church. His gentle demeanor, enlivened by an easy eloquence and personal warmth, made him a popular, influential figure at various meetings of the National Baptist Convention. Recognized by his peers as a persuasive intellectual force, Griggs served in its Educational Department for many years. He was especially interested in the training of ministers, and eventually became president of the American Baptist Theological Seminary (1925–1926). In all, he wrote almost three dozen works, many of which are only slender pamphlets. His *Life's Demands, or According to Law* (1916) reveals his wide reading in post-Darwinian theories of social growth, although his "laws" of success derive as much from common sense as from any scientific evidence. Two companion books intended for Sunday school use, *Guide to Racial Greatness* (1923) and a collection of biblical verses, *Kingdom Builders' Manual* (1924), show how closely Griggs identified his concern for his race with that for his religious calling. However, tracts such as *Stepping Stones to Higher Things* and *Paths to Progress,* as well as a flattering biographical pamphlet of a Negro Masonic leader (*Triumph of the Simple Virtues, or The Life Story of John L. Webb,* 1926), did little to revive his reputation—by that time moribund—as a racial spokesman.

Near the end of his life and almost exhausted financially by his publications, Griggs was forced to abandon an ambitious project to rebuild his church in Memphis. He left that city to return to his native Texas, serving as pastor of the Hopewell Baptist Church at Denison, where his father had previously been minister. He resigned to start a Baptist-sponsored institute for religious and civic affairs in Houston, but died within a month of his arrival there.

For Griggs's political and social ideas, see his *Wisdom's Call* (1909) and *Life's Demands, or According to Law* (1916). See also Hugh M. Gloster's "Sutton E. Griggs: Novelist of the New Negro" (*Phylon,* Fourth Quarter 1943, pp. 335–45) for a summary of all the novels and Griggs's career as a novelist; and Robert E. Fleming's "Sutton E. Griggs: Militant Black Novelist" (*Phylon,* March 1973, pp. 73–77).

— ARNOLD RAMPERSAD

GRIMKÉ, ARCHIBALD H[ENRY] (1849–1930), lawyer, editor, author, consul, and civil rights leader. He was born on Aug. 17, 1849, to Henry Grimké, a white lawyer, and Nancy Weston, a slave, on the plantation called "Caneacres," about ten miles from Charleston, S.C. The Grimké family was distinguished, stemming from Judge John Grimké. Archibald's father had two famous sisters in the abolition cause, Sarah Moore and Angelina, who married Theodore Weld, another famous abolitionist. The father acknowledged the paternity of three sons, one of whom became the Rev. Francis J. Grimké of Washington, D.C. In the early 1850s the family moved into Charleston, living on Cummings Street, where the three brothers, Archibald (the oldest), Francis, and John grew up. They attended a private school conducted by liberal white men and run by Simeon Beard for the children of free Negroes.

Henry Grimké had left instructions in his will (1852) that his son, E. Montague Grimké, should free the three slave sons, but Francis was temporarily enslaved. During the Civil War the colored part of the family became legally free but remained in Charleston. The brothers were able to get a secondary education there just following the close of the Civil War, when the wife of the mayor, Gilbert Pillsbury, opened the Morris Street School. All three brothers were good students, and they impressed Mrs. Pillsbury, who had former abolitionist friends and relatives in Massachusetts, where the Grimké sisters had also settled. She sent Archibald and Francis north to continue their education, but they were unable to make any satisfactory arrangements to go to school, even though they were offered menial jobs. Mrs. Pillsbury then had them admitted to Lincoln University (1867) in Pennsylvania. Both received two degrees, B.A. in 1870 (Archibald graduating as Latin salutatorian) and M.A. in 1872.

Archibald Grimké served as the only Negro librarian at Lincoln of that time. He and his brother received aid from their white aunts although they had not met them. Archibald helped organize the Ashmun Presbyterian Church in 1867 and kept the Minutes of church meetings until he graduated. He was so deeply religious that at the age of eighteen he was ordained an elder in the Presbyterian church, and his friends and classmates expected him to become a minister.

Instead he entered Harvard Law School in 1872. Financially supported by his aunts in Massachusetts, he received his LL.B. degree on June 28, 1874. He was the second Negro to receive this degree from Harvard (the first was George Lewis Ruffin, who graduated in 1869). Following graduation from law school, Grimké settled in Boston, gaining admittance to the Suffolk County Bar in 1875 and entering into law practice with James H. Wolff in 1876. For the first few years, business was not very good, despite his family connection, for he was not well-known in the area. Moreover there were not many Negroes in Boston who would turn to Negro lawyers; he was young and some of his clients were too poor to pay.

In the course of establishing his legal practice, Grimké met and married in 1879 Sarah Stanley, the daughter of a white minister who had advocated racial equality and emancipation of slaves, but did not favor interracial marriage. They had only one child, Angelina Weld Grimké, born Feb. 27, 1880. By 1882 Grimké and his family were living in Hyde Park, a suburb of Boston and the residence of the white Grimké sisters. Mrs. Sarah Grimké died in the early 1890s.

Since the practice of law was not very lucrative, Grimké turned in the early 1880s to journalism and politics hoping to make a name for himself and help others in need. In 1883 he set up the first Negro newspaper in the New England area, *The Hub*, a weekly, with the monetary backing of the Republican party in Massachusetts and the personal backing of Henry Cabot Lodge, scion of a famous Boston family. In editing the journal Grimké enlisted the aid of Butler R. Wilson, a graduate of the Boston University Law School in 1884, and also his new law partner. The newspaper, which tried to serve as the voice of protest of the Negroes of New England, operated until early 1886; unfortunately not many issues of the paper survive. The law practice began to prosper, however.

One of the firm's cases involved discrimination against Negroes at a skating rink in Boston. The case was won in a lower court but was dismissed on the owners' appeal to the higher court. However, sentiment in the state over this and other similar episodes helped enact a civil rights bill in the state in 1885. Grimké, as president of the Massachusetts Suffrage League, began to serve as the leader of the Boston "radicals," a group of well-educated Negroes who protested all forms of segregation and discrimination.

He also became a leader of the Negro "independents" in politics. At first, like most Negroes of the era, Grimké was a Republican, and attended the Republican National Convention in 1884 as the alternate delegate to Henry Cabot Lodge. But after the election of Grover Cleveland in 1884, a group of Negro Democrats and some Independents who had supported him emerged in New York and Boston. Moreover in October 1883 the "Republican" Supreme Court of the United States had declared unconstitutional the Civil Rights Bill of 1875. In a long article in the *New York Age* on Nov. 13, 1886 (originally published in the *Boston Daily Globe*), Grimké called for Negroes to think more of themselves than of the Republican party and to vote for Democrats. Grimké did not, however, stop calling himself a Republican, but his basic premise was that "The Republican party is no longer devoted to the colored man."

The demise of *The Hub* in 1886 led Grimké to turn to writing articles for two white newspapers, the *Herald* and the *Traveler* in Boston. He wrote numerous articles and pamphlets published in the first quarter of the twentieth century. One of the most significant articles was "Why Disfranchisement Is Bad" (*Atlantic Monthly*, July 1904, pp. 72–81). In the last decade of the nineteenth century Grimké was awarded contracts for the publication of two books in the American Reformer Series. Both were popular accounts: the first (1891) was *William Lloyd Garrison, the Abolitionist;* the second (1892) was *The Life of Charles Sumner, the Scholar in Politics.* In the first he made no mention of the support Negroes had given to the work of Garrison, and mentioned only briefly the attorney Robert Morris. Grimké viewed Garrison and Sumner as among those chiefly responsible for the downfall of the slave power, and victors in the battle of "Right and Wrong." Despite the shortcomings of these books, they made a name for Grimké in some literary circles and earned him some income.

The participation of Grimké in politics also had its rewards. From 1884 to 1894 he was appointed and reappointed by governors of Massachusetts as a trustee and secretary of the board of the Westborough Insane Asylum. Most significant was his appointment by Grover Cleveland in 1894 to be the consul at Santo

Domingo in the Dominican Republic, where he served from Nov. 16, 1894, to June 30, 1898. His duties included the supervision of the other consular posts, the protection and the encouragement of American economic interests, and balanced reports on the strained relations between France and the Dominican Republic. As a lawyer he became involved in a long dispute over the question of tolls over a bridge built and owned by American interests across the Ozama River. He even went aboard a U.S. warship allowed to practice gunnery in the area. He was so capable that Pres.-Gen. Ulises Heureaux publicly praised him. But like many other American Negroes, he did not receive promotion in the consular service or appointment to a diplomatic post.

When Grimké returned to the Negro struggle in late 1898, Booker T. Washington, spokesman of racial accommodation, was increasing his influence. Grimké was still a believer in racial integration and a leader of the Boston "radicals." He helped draft an open letter to President McKinley in 1899 condemning McKinley's silence on the growing racial oppression against Negroes. He was elected a member and served as president (1903 to 1916) of the American Negro Academy. He wrote numerous pamphlets and articles during these years, some for the academy, on the need for Negroes to use the vote wisely. In 1904 he served as treasurer of the Committee of Twelve, an organization of Negroes designed to end the growing rivalries in racial ideologies. Yet he refused to break completely with Booker T. Washington. Even after he was one of the early supporters of the Niagara Movement of W. E. B. Du Bois, founded in 1905 to oppose the conservative policies of Washington, it was not until the unwarranted dismissal by Pres. Theodore Roosevelt of the Negro soldiers in the Brownsville (Tex.) riot of 1906 that Grimké became, on the whole, a follower of the protest ideology of Du Bois. (Booker T. Washington had agreed with the action of President Roosevelt in the Brownsville riot).

For a short while in the early twentieth century Grimké lived part of the year in Washington and the other part in Hyde Park. But around 1905 he moved with his daughter into the home of his brother Francis, at 1415 Corcoran St. in Washington, D.C. He had saved enough money to enable him to devote most of his time to civil rights. As president of the Washington branch of the NAACP, he participated vigorously in the opposition to Pres. Woodrow Wilson's racist policies. When Wilson extended segregation in the federal department buildings in Washington, Grimké protested to him in a letter (Oct. 29, 1913) against these "reactionary and undemocratic practices." In a spirited exchange (1914) with Rep. Martin Dies (D–Tex.) before the House Committee on Reform in the Civil Service, Grimké argued: "Separation always means inferiority and these people [Negroes] are going to be your equal if God made them your equal. You are not going to deport them; they are valuable workers." Grimké was one of a group of notable Negroes who wrote to the House District Committee (Feb. 11, 1916) that laws forbidding intermarriage would permit a white man to "do what he wants with impunity." The NAACP hailed Grimké's testimony as a

decisive factor in the defeat of bills providing for segregation in the Civil Service. None of the bills introduced during Wilson's two administrations was approved by Congress (Rayford W. Logan, *The Betrayal of the Negro from Rutherford B. Hayes to Woodrow Wilson* [1965], pp. 361–62, 364–67).

On the national level he was a member of the original Committee of Forty (1909), which helped pave the way for the formation of the NAACP (1909–1910); as a member of ten citizens of Washington, D.C., he presented, in vain, a petition against lynching to President Taft (1911). He attended the Amenia Conference (1916) where, following the death of Booker T. Washington in 1915, a temporary accommodation between "conservativees" and "radicals" was achieved. As a member of the Board of Directors of the NAACP he at first opposed, but later supported, the establishment of a separate Colored Officers Training Camp in Fort Des Moines, Iowa. He also vigorously opposed an appropriation by the NAACP to support Dr. Du Bois and the First Pan-African Congress in Paris (1919). Grimké continued this opposition for a number of years. He received the Spingarn Medal in 1919 for his notable achievements in behalf of Negro rights. He retired from active work with the NAACP in 1925, when he was seventy-five and ailing.

He lived in retirement with his daughter Angelina, a teacher in Dunbar High School, and his brother Francis, in Washington. He died at his home on Feb. 25, 1930, leaving an estate valued at over $30,000, a considerable sum at that time. He was eulogized by his brother, Kelly Miller of Howard University, and Du Bois in *The Crisis*. He had been one of the most significant Negro leaders of his time, spanning the era from slavery to the eve of the Great Depression.

There is no comprehensive biography of Grimké. The brief sketch by Edward M. Hinton in *DAB* (1931, 4: 632–33) was written before the publication of such indispensable books as Charles Flint Kellogg's *A History of the National Association for the Advancement of Colored People,* volume I, *1909–1920* (1967), August Meier's *Negro Thought in America, 1880–1915* . . . (1963), and Logan's *Betrayal,* cited in the text. The basic primary sources available are the Archibald H. Grimké Papers in the Moorland-Spingarn Research Center, Howard University, Consular Dispatches in the National Archives, Boston newspapers, and Grimké's writings. — CLARENCE G. CONTEE, SR.

GRIMKÉ, FRANCIS JAMES (1850–1937), clergyman, civil rights advocate, author, and diarist. He was born at "Caneacres," a plantation near Charleston, S.C., the son of Henry Grimké, a gentleman farmer, sometime lawyer, and scion of an aristocratic white family. His mother, Nancy Weston, was Grimké's slave, and served successively as maid for his wife, Selina; nurse to their children after Selina's death (1843); and finally as mistress of "Caneacres." To Henry and Nancy were born two other sons, Archibald (1849) and John (1853). After the father died of yellow fever in September 1852, ownership of Nancy and her children passed to E. Montague Grimké, Henry's eldest son by Selina. Nancy and her boys lived as de facto free persons of color until

1860, when Montague Grimké attempted to enslave his half-brothers. In the process Francis experienced many of the physical horrors of slavery and the psychic trauma of being sold as chattel property.

To avoid enslavement, Francis escaped to the Confederate Army in 1861 and served as valet to an officer for two years. On a visit to Charleston, Montague Grimké had placed him in prison where he became dangerously ill for several months. Restored to his home, his mother nursed him back to good health. His guardian, Montague, sold him to another Confederate officer, and Francis worked as a servant until the end of the Civil War.

Emancipation brought an end to Montague's claims on his slaves. Francis and his brother Archibald briefly attended the Morris Street School in Charleston, taught by Mrs. Parker Pillsbury, a white northern abolitionist. Under the sponsorship of abolitionists, Francis went to Stoneham, Mass., with the intent to study medicine. Frustrated in this desire by race prejudice, he welcomed the assistance of Mrs. Pillsbury to enter (1866) Lincoln University (Pennsylvania) with Archibald. Both pursued a classical undergraduate program, with the moral and material support from two white aunts, Sarah M. Grimké and Angelina Grimké Weld, who had publicly acknowledged the boys as their brother Henry's sons. Francis Grimké was graduated in 1870 at the head of his class and began to study law at Lincoln (1871). The next year he acted as financial agent of the university and in 1873 resumed his legal studies there. In 1874 he enrolled in the Law Department of Howard University. After a year he decided to enter the ministry and in the fall of 1875 enrolled at Princeton Theological Seminary. There he came under the tutelage of A. A. Hodge, the foremost American Presbyterian theologian of the nineteenth century, and of James McCosh, president of Princeton College, with whom he studied in a postgraduate course in philosophy.

Upon graduation from the seminary in 1878, Grimké accepted a call to the 15th Street Presbyterian Church in Washington, D.C., and was ordained in 1878 by the Presbytery of Washington City. In the same year he married Charlotte L. Forten of Philadelphia. Their only child, Theodora Cornelia, was born, and died, in 1880. Grimké left Washington in 1885 to serve the Laura Street Presbyterian Church of Jacksonville, Fla. In 1891 he was elected professor of Christian evidence and mental and moral philosophy at Biddle University, Charlotte, N.C., but did not serve. In 1889 he returned to his first church, there to remain as pastor and pastor emeritus (1928) until his death. When he became pastor, the church was located at 15th Street between I and K Streets NW; after 1918 at 15th and R Streets NW. Among the members of the congregation were some of the most distinguished Negroes in Washington.

Grimké's pastorates spanned the decades of betrayal which subverted the ideals of the Reconstruction era and thrust him into the role of social prophet. In scores of sermons (widely circulated as pamphlets), from *God and the Race Problem* (1903) to *Jim Crow Christianity and the Negro* (1934), Grimké condemned the hypocrisy of American life, especially that of the churches. Targets for his criticism included the American Bible Society; the evangelists, Dwight L. Moody and Billy Sunday; and his own denomination, the Presbyterian Church in the U.S.A. The failure of the northern white Presbyterians to appreciate the feelings and needs of Negro members led to the formation of the Afro-Presbyterian Council (1893). Grimké was a charter member and often the featured speaker at its annual meetings, using this forum to encourage the development of the race through the strengthening of character. Similarly, as chairman of the Committee of Religion and Ethics (1898–1902) of the Hampton Negro Conference, he used its annual report to urge moral excellence as the way to social, as well as spiritual, salvation.

Nevertheless, as the debate over strategy developed between Booker T. Washington and W. E. B. Du Bois, Grimké felt the inadequacy of his own self-help emphasis and grew increasingly at odds with the accommodationist tactics of Washington. Grimké regularly preached on the political conditions of the race, and one of his ten quadrennial messages (1901–1937) is representative of his affiliation with the Du Bois camp; in *The Negro and His Citizenship* (1905), Grimké identified himself with the "radical wing of the race," and urged his audience not "to forget that we have also rights under the Constitution, and to see to it that we stand up for them. . . ." In his "race messages" he emerged as one of the new architects of agitation, perpetuating the tradition of his militant predecessor, Henry Highland Garnet. At the crucial meeting of the Afro-American Council called by Washington in early October 1906 in New York City, Du Bois, Francis Grimké, and Archibald Grimké led a movement that accentuated the schism between the "radicals" and the "conservatives."

Although he advocated agitation, Grimké was not an activist outside the church; the shape of his ministry conformed to his perception of the pastor as moral exemplar, and preaching as the major means of edifying the people. However, the lynching and race riots rampant in the southern states provoked Grimké beyond the role of exhortation. He had warned that such barbarism "begets contempt for law and encourages a spirit which is subversive to all governments." His sermon *Some Lessons from the Assassination of President William McKinley* (1901) referred to the "gangrene in the nation's life" which needed immediate treatment, and the national duty to effect a cure. When violence erupted in Atlanta on Sept. 22, 1906, Grimké urged that it was the duty of Negroes "to be prepared to defend themselves against such organized and murderous assaults as were made upon them in Atlanta" (*Works,* 1:417). In the aftermath of the Springfield, Ill., riot on Aug. 14, 1908, he joined other concerned leaders in signing the call for a meeting from which emerged the NAACP. To this organization and its program he gave strong support from his pulpit and pen, writing, for instance, in 1931: "The conviction, deep, vivid, abiding, as to the righteousness of the cause, should be back of every effort put forth by the Association or any of its officers" (*Works,* 3:613).

With Du Bois and others, Grimké felt the responsibility to provide organized leadership for the Negro community. To this end he joined Alexander Crummell in founding the American Negro Academy in 1897. He fostered opportunities for higher education for Negro youth through his gifts to Lincoln and Howard. He was elected to Howard's Board of Trustees in 1880 and served until 1925 as an effective member of the Executive Committee. He was also briefly a trustee of the public schools of the District of Columbia. He brought to this area of concern the same high moral commitment he took into the pulpit; he was convinced that education, wealth, and political power would be a curse to Negroes unless possessed by men and women who had high ethical ideals. Many contemporaries found his standards of conduct too strict, his lifestyle too austere; they referred to him as the "Negro Puritan." Yet Grimké would not have been offended. Kelly Miller, writing in his *Afro-American* column about Grimké's retirement from Howard's board in 1925, voiced the majority opinion about the cleric: "He has kept the faith. Behold, a man of God in an age of gold."

Francis Grimké idolized his wife, "Lottie," whom he praised as "one of the dearest, sweetest, loveliest spirits that ever graced this planet." Heartbroken after her death on July 23, 1914, he did not marry again.

His repeated criticisms of white churches reached a climax when he delivered an address, "What Is the Trouble with Christianity Today?" at the annual convocation of the School of Religion, Howard University, on Nov. 20, 1923. He denounced the "federation of white churches" in Washington, "which shows that the churches, consciously or unconsciously, are standing for a Christianity that lays greater emphasis upon the color of a man's skin than upon his Christian character." In like manner he excoriated the exclusionary practices of the white YMCA and the specious professions of Christian faith by former Pres. Woodrow Wilson and William Jennings Bryan.

These acerbic remarks provoked the ire of Rep. James F. Byrnes of South Carolina and others who opposed the usual federal appropriations for Howard University. Byrnes did not hold the university responsible for Grimké's address, but did complain that he was a member of the Board of Trustees. Pres. J. Stanley Durkee hedged on the question of academic freedom by pointing out that the School of Religion received no federal appropriations. Grimké had been supported by some well-known Americans, including the sociologist Edward L. Parks and Bishop John Hurst, a member of Howard's Board of Trustees.

Grimké retired in 1925 because of his age and gave some of his books to Lincoln University and the others to Howard University, where they were set apart as the Francis J. Grimké Collection. In his will he bequeathed $4000 to Lincoln University and $4500 to the Board of Pensions of the Presbyterian Church in America.

The Works of Francis James Grimké, in four volumes, edited by Carter G. Woodson (1942), contain most of the important sermons and addresses, a small sample of Grimké's diary writings, and a collection of his correspondence. Woodson has provided a short perceptive biographical introduction. Also valuable is a chapter by Clifton E. Olmsted in *Sons of the Prophets,* edited by Hugh T. Kerr (1963). Henry J. Ferry's doctoral dissertation "Francis J. Grimké: Portrait of a Black Puri-

tan" (Yale University, 1970) is a full-length biography. The Francis J. Grimké Papers are in the Moorland-Spingarn Research Center, Howard University.

— HENRY J. FERRY

HACKLEY, [EMMA] AZALIA [SMITH] (1867–1922), singer, choir director, and music teacher. She was born in Murfreesboro, Tenn., the older of the two daughters of Henry and Corilla (Beard) Smith. Her mother was the daughter of Wilson Beard, an ex-slave who had established in the 1830s a profitable laundry business in Detroit. Corilla Smith received an unusually good education and following her marriage opened a school for children of freed slaves in Murfreesboro. Forced by white hostility to close the school, the family moved to Detroit. There, Azalia graduated from the Washington Normal School in 1886 and taught in elementary schools (1886–1894). A prodigy, she had learned at age three to play the piano and later took private lessons in voice, violin, and French. Married on Jan. 29, 1894, to Edwin Henry Hackley, Denver lawyer and newspaper editor, she earned a Bachelor of Music degree in 1900 from the University of Denver. She studied voice in Paris (1905–1906) under Jean de Reszke (1850–1925), a Polish singer who developed into one of the greatest tenors of the nineteenth century and from 1891 to his retirement in 1901 had been the leading tenor at the Metropolitan Opera House, New York City. She died in Detroit on Dec. 13, 1922, after suffering a cerebral hemorrhage, and was buried in Elmwood Cemetery.

After receiving her degree from the University of Denver, she did more to promote musical work among the colored people in Denver than in any other city in the West (*Denver Post,* 1899). A founder and executive secretary of the local branch of the Colored Women's League, she promoted its goals in the *Denver Statesman,* her husband's newspaper. They founded a fraternal group, the Imperial Order of Libyans, to combat racial discrimination and promote patriotism.

Since the marriage was unhappy, Mrs. Hackley moved to Philadelphia, where she became music director of the Episcopal Church of the Crucifixion. In October 1905 she featured herself and several talented protégés of the People's Chorus (later the Hackley Choral Society) at Philadelphia's Academy of Music. The popular and critical acclaim, and the funds raised, had enabled her to study under de Reszke in Paris in 1905–1906.

Despite her fame and the ease with which she could have "passed," as a "voluntary Negro" she spent much of the rest of her life to developing talented Negroes, notably Marian Anderson, Roland Hayes, and R. Nathaniel Dett. She gave concerts and obtained private support for them and for other colored musicians and teachers of music. Following a third European trip (1909), preceded by her final separation from her husband, she gave lectures, particularly in the South, to Negro schools and organizations, accompanied sometimes by brief recitals or demonstrations. After a brief Canadian tour in 1911, she founded in Chicago the Vocal Normal Institute. Its financial failure in 1915 led her to undertake new lecture tours and to publish in 1916 the *Colored Girl Beautiful,* a collection of her talks designed to promote race pride. Her most significant activity after 1916 was the organization of "Folk Song Festivals" in Negro churches and schools. Maud Cuney-Hare gave this evaluation in her *Negro Musicians and Their Music* (1936, p. 242): " 'The Folk Song Festival' of Mrs. Hackley not only drew attention to the melodic beauty of the music, but also gave the youth of the race a new respect for racial folk material, and an incentive to interpret it. A typical review of her work said, 'An admirable musician herself, the chorus under Mrs. Hackley's leadership sang with a purity of tone, a precision and control that did not lessen the fervor and abandon which gave color to these Spirituals.' "

Despite recurrent illness which resulted in impairment of her hearing and fits of dizziness, she introduced Negro folk songs at an international Sunday school convention in Tokyo (1920). During 1921 she began a tour of California, where failure of plans for a concert in San Diego brought on a severe emotional collapse. Brought back to Detroit, she died there on Dec. 13, 1922.

Since Negro folk songs have not received the scholarly attention given to other forms of music and folklore, Mrs. Hackley is less well known than she deserves to be. The full-length biography *Azalia,* by M. Marguerite Davenport (1947), is inadequate. The best easily available source is the biographical sketch by Josephine Harreld Love in *NAW* (1971, 2:106–8).

— RAYFORD W. LOGAN

HALE, WILLIAM JASPER (1876–1944), educator, businessman, and founding president of Tennessee Agricultural and Industrial State Normal School (later Tennessee State College and State University). Born on Sept. 26, 1876, in the tiny east Tennessee hamlet of Retro, Hale spent his formative years in close association with white paternalism. Because there was no public education for rural Negroes, he obtained the basic essentials of learning in the Quaker and northern Presbyterian-supported schools in Maryville, Tenn. Although his training was limited, Hale had influential white contacts in Chattanooga and they not only ensured him initial employment, but also served as the ever-present foundation upon which he continued to build his career. After starting in a small Negro elementary school, Hale soon parlayed his outstanding administrative talents and his white connections into the most important Negro post in the Chattanooga system —principal of the Negro St. Elmo secondary school. And yet neither his ambitions nor his talents had been fully extended.

When the 1909 state legislature provided for the founding of an "Agricultural and Industrial State Normal School for Negroes," Hale led an unsuccessful active political and financial campaign to locate the new school in Chattanooga. The state superintendent of education, who was a close white associate from Chattanooga, appointed Hale in 1911—despite his very modest formal education—principal (later president) of Tennessee's first and only Negro state college, Tennessee Agricultural and Industrial State Normal School.

When Hale took charge of the few frame buildings on a former farm one mile beyond the limits of Nashville, Tennessee A&I's future was not at all certain. A less-than-generous legislature and a resentful Negro community whose loyalty centered on the liberal arts–oriented Fisk University complicated Hale's task. His conviction, determination, and white support, however, pulled him (and the school) through the critical early years. Hale courted the legislature, became a vital part of the Negro community (hiring Fisk graduates and marrying in October 1912 Harriet Hodgkins, that school's 1912 valedictorian), and was active in interracial work and the sale of war bonds during the tense years of World War I. Despite war, depression, and an often inadequate physical plant, Tennessee A&I gained fully accredited four-year status during the 1920s and the student body grew from 200 to 3000 during Hale's thirty-one years as president.

Hale's greatest contribution at A&I, however, was probably more subtle than the number of graduates or the quality of their education. Although his own methods were often heavy-handed or unorthodox, Tennessee A&I furnished a high percentage of the state's Negro leadership, especially in the rural regions—as Jeanes supervisors and farm and home demonstration agents, as well as classroom teachers. Graduates remained intensely loyal to the school and to Hale. This gave him considerable political influence throughout the state (since school jobs were closely tied to state and local politics), but the spread of his philosophy of work and service was equally noticeable.

Hale's career did not rest entirely on his own credentials, but also on his personal and political connections and his ability to sell his product—conservative, but solid education. Like Booker T. Washington, Hale noted the necessity for favorable publicity in the Negro press and used this influence to project a positive image for his school. His keen business sense promoted the valuable (if controversial) growth of Tennessee A&I and of his own financial resources. Early in his adult career Hale had received valuable investment advice from white banking friends in Chattanooga who rated highly the role of the Negro capitalist and entrepreneur. Hale owned several pieces of business and residential property in Chattanooga, enough stock to be elected vice-president of the Citizens Savings Bank and Trust Company in Nashville, and served as vice-president of the National Negro Business League.

Hale gained considerable state and national recognition. He served as president of the Conference of the Negro Land Grant Colleges, was a founder and president of the Tennessee Inter-Racial League, a member of the Nashville Board of Trade and of President Hoover's Negro Housing Committee. In 1930 he was awarded the Harmon Foundation Medal in recognition of his services to Negro education in the South. But his greatest impact was on Negro Tennesseeans. His school became a vital part of the life of the state, and it was unquestionably Hale's presence and skill which enabled Tennessee A&I to survive a rather perilous beginning.

He died on Oct. 5, 1944, in New York City, and was survived by his widow and three children, William Jr., Gwendolyn, and Edward.

The principal sources are Lester C. Lamon's "The Tennessee Agricultural and Industrial Normal School;

Public Higher Education for Black Tennesseeans" (*Tennessee Historical Quarterly* 32 [Spring 1973]:42–58), and Samuel Henry Shannon's "Agricultural and Industrial Education at Tennessee State University During the Normal School Period: A Case Study" (Ph.D. dissertation, George Peabody College for Teachers, 1974). An obituary is in *JNH* (Jan. 1945, pp. 111–12).

— LESTER C. LAMON

HALL, CHARLES WINSLOW (18??–19??), journalist. One of the significant but little-known journalists in the early twentieth century, between June 1900 and March 1902 Hall contributed eighteen articles to the *Colored American Magazine,* the most important predecessor of *The Crisis*. Fourteen, under the rubric of "Fascinating Bible Stories," narrated in popular language, without profound philosophy or explicit moralizing, the stories of Adam and Eve, Noah and the Flood, Abraham and Isaac, Hagar and Ishmael, Esau and Jacob, Joseph and Benjamin, Joseph and Moses, Moses and Aaron (in two parts), Joshua's defeat of the Amalekites, the Giving of the Law, the Christmas Tale of the Three Magi, the Defeat of Hormah and the Rebellion of Korah, and the Death of Moses.

The other four revealed a perceptive grasp of domestic and international affairs, explained in precise, forceful language, that warrant him a place commensurate with that of John E. Bruce, for example. The first, "The Eighth Illinois, U.S.V.," in the June 1900 issue (pp. 94–103), briefly recalled the "military efficiency" of the "black and tawny warriors" of Africa from the remotest past to the then recent defeat of the Italians in Abyssinia; he referred briefly also to the patriotic participation of Negroes in the wars of the Thirteen Colonies and subsequently. But in the Spanish-American War (1898–1899), "the negro [*sic*] citizen received little recognition. . . . Illinois alone, of all the states, sent into the field a full regiment of infantry, whose every man and officer, from colonel to bugler, was an Afro-American." Originating in the 9th Battalion of Infantry of the Illinois National Guard, the 8th Illinois, U.S. Volunteers, was mustered into the United States service under President McKinley's second call on May 25, 1898. It sailed from Jersey City on Aug. 11, 1898, landed and camped outside Santiago on Aug. 16. Commanded by Col. John R. Marshall, it occupied and policed the city and port of San Luís until March 11, 1899, when it sailed from Santiago to Newport News, Va. On arrival in Chicago on March 18, it was greeted with a splendid ovation, followed by a banquet and mammoth reception. Hall wrote (p. 98) that on April 3, 1899, "The Eighth Illinois had ceased to exist." It was, however, later reorganized and became the 370th Regiment, 93rd Division, in World War I. Hall's article contains a valuable contemporary account of the regiment's record and biographical sketches of some of its officers. It is one of the few contemporary narratives of colored National Guard organizations.

His second article, "The Old or the New Faith: Which?" in the August 1900 issue, perceptively denounced the Republican party for its "shameful surrender and miscarriage of justice, its failure to effectually vindicate its great amendments to the Federal Constitu-

tion [and] adequately protect or avenge its Afro-American allies who have suffered or fallen in its service." He denounced "such advanced thinkers as Charles Dudley Warner and hosts of favorable critics [who] have declared that the Negro is so innately inferior to the white man, and so handicapped by centuries of oppression and degradation as to be unfitted to receive equal privileges, which they must be made to earn and secure by generations of struggle and education." He criticized the belief that the United States was decreed by Divine Providence to become "a colonizing, conquering world-power like Great Britain, to be like her impoverished by immense expenditures, and feared and hated by every other nation." He forcefully condemned the fact that "the leaders and directors of Republican policy teach that the concentration of transportation, manufacturing, financial and commercial enterprises into the hands of a few concerns is best adapted to make men in the mass intelligent, enterprising, and truly free and happy." On the other hand new leaders in the Democratic party, even in the South but especially in the North, fought for justice and truth in domestic affairs; in addition it repudiated exploitation of colonies and dependencies by the United States. He concluded this article as follows: "We may send myriads to fertilize Asiatic islands and deserts with their bones, and expend millions to extend the operations of a few trusts and financiers; but the people, white and black, will do the fighting and the dying, pay the taxes and profits of politician and monopolist, and see themselves and their children ever becoming more dependent upon a greedy and arrogant plutocracy."

The third article, "Queen Victoria and Her Colored Proteges" (Oct. 1900, pp. 312–14), contrasted the cordial reception she gave to a slave girl and the high esteem in which distinguished colored men were held in France and Spain. Referring to the incident of the slave girl, the *New York Journal* headlined its article "All Coons Look Alike to Her Gracious Majesty, Victoria Imperatrix" with a subhead "My Gal is a High-Born Lady."

The fourth article, "Racial Hatred" (Sept. 1900, pp. 246–52), might well, *mutatis mutandis,* have been written decades later. It castigated the press for stirring up race hatred and pointed out that New York City was hardly better than the South. "Long centuries ago, when our Northern white race was shivering in rocky caves, the Negro was carving his heavy lips and other features on the face of the Sphinx, and founding the basic religions whence our beliefs are derived. His turn may come again." He was optimistic: "The greater part of the American people prefer that the Negro should have all the rights and privileges that any other American citizen is entitled to under the law."

Research in the Library of Congress and the Moorland-Spingarn Research Center, Howard University, failed to find biographical information about Hall.

— RAYFORD W. LOGAN

HALL, JUANITA (1901–1968), mezzo-soprano. She was celebrated for her characterization and singing as "Bloody Mary" in *South Pacific,* and one the first Negro performers to play an outstanding role in an otherwise all-white cast. Richard Rodgers wrote, "I loved Juanita. I think everyone who had anything to do with her loved her. . . . Everything she did on stage came across with such zestful spontaneity that many were surprised to learn of her classical vocal training at Julliard or her career as a concert singer. . . . I recall that when I first played her the song 'Bali Ha'i,' she was so overcome that she wept" (*New York Times,* March 10, 1968).

Juanita Hall was born in Keyport, N.J., on Nov. 6, 1901, the daughter of Abram and Mary Richardson Long, and was educated in the public schools of Keyport. She sang in the local Catholic church choir, where she also played the organ although she had not yet learned to read music. At the Julliard School of Music she developed her vocal powers in classical study that was to be the basis of her success. In her teens she married an actor, Clement Hall, who died in the 1920s. They had no children, and she never remarried.

Hall's first major stage role was in Ziegfeld's *Show Boat* (March 1928). In 1930 she sang in *Green Pastures* with Hall Johnson's Choir, and worked with them as soloist and assistant conductor from 1931 to 1936. From 1936 to 1941 she conducted a Works Progress Administration chorus in New York City, and in 1941–1942 she conducted the Westchester Choral and Dramatic Association in the White Plains County Center, taking a chorus of 300 to the World's Fair in 1941 in celebration of Negro History Week. In 1942 she organized and conducted the Juanita Hall Choir, which sang frequently for some years thereafter in concert and on the radio. Meantime she sang in radio broadcasts with Horman Corwin, Kate Smith, Rudy Vallee, and the Theatre Guild of the Air. She sang with the Lunt-Fontaines in *The Pirate* (1942); in *Sing Out, Sweet Land* (1943); in *St. Louis Woman* (1945); *Deep in the Roots* (1946); and *Street Scene* (1947). In 1950 *Look* magazine rated her setting of Langston Hughes's lyric "Love Can Hurt You" "the best blues song of the season—maybe the best one of many seasons." It was recorded on disc by RCA Victor. Other recordings included "Don't Cry, Joe" and "Love Is a Precious Thing."

In 1948 Hall made her debut as "a nightclub song stylist" in the Old Knickerbocker Music Hall, the popular theater café, singing the blues song "Lament Over Love," Langston Hughes's moving lyric set to music by Herbert Kingsley, composer of *The Pirate,* with Kingsley at the piano. She was hailed as the "find" of the year.

Oscar Hammerstein and Richard Rodgers wrote of their discovery of Hall in a talent show sponsored by the Stage Managers Club, "Talent '48." "Oscar and I knew that at least one part in 'South Pacific' had been filled. There was our Bloody Mary—high spirited, graceful, mischievous, proud, a gloriously gifted voice projected with all the skills of one who knew exactly how to take over a song and make it hers" (*New York Times,* March 10, 1968).

On April 7, 1949, *South Pacific* opened at the Majestic Theater on Broadway, and "the mezzo-soprano virtually stole the show from its stars, Mary Martin and Ezio Pinza." Brooks Atkinson, *New York Times* music critic, reviewed the opening night: "She plays a brassy, greedy, ugly Tonkinese woman with harsh, vigorous authentic accuracy, and she sings one of Mr. Rodger's finest songs 'Bali Ha'i' with rousing artistry." James Michener, the author of the book, told her, "you just look as though you belong out there in Bali Ha'i." She won the Donaldson Award voted annually for the "best supporting actress of the season" as a result of her performance in *South Pacific.*

The *Boston Post* (Oct. 18, 1949) offered a description of Hall as a person; "Bloody Mary is a rowdy, dowdy, old part. Juanita Hall is a pleasant, beautifully groomed, soft spoken lady with a quick sense of humour, one of the theater's best character actors and singers."

Although Juanita Hall is best remembered as Bloody Mary, her later career was also filled with honors. In 1952 she was awarded a plaque for her sale of bonds in the Bonds for Israel drive. In 1958 she sang in the operetta *The Flower Drum Song.* She sang a one-woman show, *A Woman and the Blues,* at the East 74th Street Theater (March 28, 1966). Meanwhile she sang extended engagements in Cafe Society and other nightclubs and cafés across the country, and was a successful concert artist.

In the last years of her life she suffered from failing eyesight. She died on Feb. 28, 1968, in Southside Hospital, Bay Shore, Long Island, of diabetic complications. A funeral Mass was offered at St. Malachy's Roman Catholic Church, the "Actor's Church," 239 W. 49th St. in New York City. Burial was in Keyport, N. J. She was survived by her sister, Mrs. Hilda Creed, and a brother, Horace Long.

The vertical files of the Schomburg Center for Research in Black Culture furnished much of the source material quoted in this sketch. For general background, Langston Hughes's and Milton Meltzer's *Black Magic* (1967) is recommended. — RAYMOND LEMIEUX

HALL, PRINCE (1735?–1807), Masonic organizer and abolitionist. Generally accepted accounts about the place of his birth, parentage, early life and career have been found unreliable, especially by Sidney Kaplan's *The Black Presence in the Era of the American Revolution, 1770–1780* (1974, pp. 181–92), and in more detail by Charles H. Wesley's *Prince Hall, Life and Legacy* (1977). This account is based largely on these revisionist interpretations.

Both Kaplan and Wesley rejected the widely accepted statement that Prince Hall was born in Bridge Town, Barbados; that his father was an Englishman and his mother a woman of African descent; and that Prince Hall came to the United States in 1765. There is no convincing evidence about the place of his birth or his parentage. Since his death certificate states that he was seventy-two years old at the time of his death in 1807, it is not unlikely that he was born in 1735. The first documented statement indicates that during the late 1740s Prince Hall was the slave of William Hall, a leather-dresser, in Boston, where he became a member of the Congregational Church on School Street in 1762. On Nov. 2, 1763, he married Sarah Ritchie, a slave. He was manumitted by William Hall on April 9, 1770, as a reward for twenty-one years of faithful service. On

Aug. 22, 1770, Prince Hall married Flora Gibbs of Gloucester, Mass. Their son, Prince Africanus, was baptized on Nov. 14, 1784, at the New North Church, Boston. Wesley concluded that the famous Prince Hall was married once more, to a third wife, Sylvia (or Zilpha) Ward, on June 28, 1798. Wesley accepted the sworn statement that Primus Hall was the son of Delia and Prince Hall. Prince Hall's military record is also uncertain because of several other contemporaneous soldiers named Prince Hall.

On March 6, 1775, a British army lodge of Freemasons attached to the 38th Foot Regiment near Boston initiated fifteen Negroes, one of whom was Prince Hall. Sgt. John Batt, who was in charge of the initiation, issued a limited "permet" on March 17, 1775, for them to meet as a lodge, to "walk on St. John's Day" and "to bury their dead" in the prescribed manner and form. They formed on July 3, 1775, African Lodge No. 1. John Rowe, provincial grand master of North America, granted African Lodge No. 1 a second limited permet. In order to obtain full recognition, Prince Hall as master of the lodge wrote on March 2, 1784, to William Moody, most worshipful master of Brotherly Love Lodge No. 55, London. Since Prince Hall received no reply, he wrote, again as master of African Lodge No. 1, a second letter on June 30, 1784. The resultant charter for the establishment of a lodge of American Negroes was issued under date of Sept. 29, 1784, but did not reach Boston until April 29, 1787. It authorized the organization in Boston of African Lodge No. 459, a "regular Lodge of Free and accepted Masons, under the title or denomination of the African Lodge" with Prince Hall as master, Boston Smith as senior warden, and Thomas Sanderson as junior warden. Prince Hall was to take special care that the lodge followed all the rules and orders of the "Book of Constitution" and to keep a regular account of the lodge's proceedings. Hiram Lodge No. 4, in Providence, R.I., which had received a copy of Prince Hall's African Lodge No. 459, became the second American Negro Masonic lodge on June 24, 1797. In 1798 the third lodge was established with Absalom Jones as worshipful master and Richard Allen as treasurer. These three lodges constituted the Prince Hall Solidarity. In 1977 there were forty grand lodges, including more than 5500 lodges with over 500,000 members. "There were United Supreme Councils of the Northern and Southern Jurisdictions, the Shrine [The Ancient Egyptian Arabic Order of Nobles of the Mystic Shrine] and the auxiliary bodies, all of which carried the name and title of the Prince Hall designation" (Wesley, p. 181).

Although there is no firm evidence that this Prince Hall served at Bunker Hill or as a soldier elsewhere during the American Revolutionary War, he did, however, serve as a skilled craftsman, having made five leather drumheads.

Prince Hall was not only the organizer of Negro Masonry in the United States; he was also an abolitionist and spokesman. He and three other Masons were among eight Negro signers of a petition (Jan. 13, 1777) requesting the Massachusetts state legislature to abolish slavery as incompatible with the patriot cause. Despite support from white allies, the legislature referred the

matter to the Congress of the Confederation. It took no action, and abolition in Massachusetts had to await a state judicial decision in 1783. He was more successful in his efforts to have Massachusetts end the slave trade. In early February 1788 three Boston Negroes, one of them a Mason, were kidnapped. He wrote on Feb. 27, 1788, a petition to the legislature signed by twenty-one other members, protesting the seizure. In addition they denounced the slave trade. Their petition buttressed that of the Quakers in the previous year and of the Boston clergy in 1788. On March 26 of that year the state legislature passed an act "to prevent the slave trade, and for granting relief to the families of such unhappy persons as may be kidnapped or destroyed from this Commonwealth." Letters from Gov. John Hancock and the French consul in Boston obtained the releases of the three Negroes from the French island of St. Bartholomew. Prince Hall and members of the African Lodge organized the festivities celebrating their return to Boston in July 1788.

Meanwhile, at the time of Shay's Rebellion Prince Hall had written Gov. James Bowdoin of Massachusetts (Nov. 26, 1786) that Negro Masons were "peaceable subjects to the Civil powers where we reside [who would not] participate in any plot or conspiracies against the state." They were willing, however, to help to the extent that their "weak and feeble activities" might commend them to the governor. Kaplan's conjecture that Prince Hall was seeking to absolve Negroes from suspicion in Shay's Rebellion may be correct.

The "very disagreeable and disadvantageous circumstances" of Negroes led Prince Hall as grand master and eleven other members of his lodge to propose to the legislature (Jan. 4, 1787) what amounted to a separate state abroad with its own Negro pastors or bishops. With the assistance of money from congregations or otherwise for passage to Africa, the purchase of land, provisions, and utensils, the colonizers would enlighten and civilize "those nations who are now sunk in ignorance and barbarity." This was the first major statement on colonization in Africa, antedating Paul Cuffe's first voyage to Africa by twenty-three years. The House received the petition and buried it in committee (Kaplan, pp. 86–88).

Failing to obtain support for his colonization scheme, Prince Hall sought to ameliorate the plight of Negroes by his participation in politics and his campaign against racial discrimination in education. He voted regularly and paid his taxes. He was only slightly successful in his efforts to obtain state or local support for public schools. On Oct. 17, 1787, he petitioned the Massachusetts legislature that "means be provided for the education of colored people" since they were taxed as were white people. The appeal was fruitless. In 1796 Prince Hall requested the Selectmen of Boston to establish a separate school for colored children. The Selectmen approved his request but stated that no building could be found for them. After a second request in 1800 the school was started in his home, since once again the school committee provided no other place for it. Two students at Harvard College served as teachers until 1806 when increased enrollment led to a move to larger quarters at the African Society House on Belknap Street.

In his address on the centenary of the charter of African Lodge No. 1 (Sept. 29, 1884), George Washington Williams stated: "His chirography and composition show that he must have been a man of more than ordinary talents" (Wesley, p. 9). And Wesley added, "Although there were no schools for negroes [sic] until 1796, Prince Hall, by dint of industry, secured enough of knowledge to read, write, and cipher with considerable ease and accuracy" (p. 10). On the other hand Jeremy Belknap (1744–1798), a Congregational clergyman, historian, and one of the founders of the Massachusetts Historical Society (1790), wrote on March 9, 1788: "I now enclose you the negroes' petition. It is Prince Hall's own composition and hand-writing given me by himself." Support for the idea that Hall wrote the documents attributed to him may result from the listing in the inventory of his possessions after his death of "sundry old books."

Was it from these sundry old books that Prince Hall gained the skill and style of his various petitions and letters and the erudition of his two major "Charges" of June 25, 1792, in Charlestown and June 24, 1794, at Menotomy (West Cambridge), Mass. (quoted in Wesley, pp. 54–61, 109–119)? In the 1792 Charge, Hall wrote in masterly prose about Tertullian's defense of Christians against "heathen false accusations" before his death in Carthage "Anno Christi 202" and about the careers of Cyprian, Titus Vespasian and the "Sanctum Sanctorum" in Jerusalem, the "Cyrean city of Ptolemy" and the Knights of Malta. The 1797 Charge did not include similar evidences of erudition, but was based largely on a profound knowledge of biblical passages. This second Charge, however, referred to an eclipse of the sun and the "bloody wars" of "our African kings and princes." Both closed with unidentified poems, one of which Prince Hall had "found among some papers."

The admonitions to Masons in these Charges might easily have been based on the writings of other Masons. The 1792 Charge urged belief in "one Supreme Being," "love and benevolence to all the whole family of mankind," the good deeds of Samaritans, regular attendance at stated meetings of the lodge, abstinence from "a feast of Bacchus"; in general, good behavior at home and abroad. The 1797 Charge excoriated slave merchants and "low-lived, envious, spiteful persons, some of them not long since, servants in gentlemen's kitchens" who inflicted daily insults upon Negroes in the streets of Boston. He urged his listeners to remember how God had rescued "our African brethren" from even worse treatment in the French West Indies. Although deprived of education, many Negroes advanced themselves through meditation, observation, and repeating psalms, hymns, and sermons. He warned against "slavish fear, pride, envy," perjury, and urged helping those in distress. This credo has guided Prince Hall Masons since his death.

He died of "old age" in Boston on Dec. 4, 1807. His funeral rites on Dec. 11 from his home in Lendell's Lane were in accord with Masonic rites. "A very large procession of blacks" followed him to the grave in the 59th Street Mathews Cemetery, apparently on March 24, 1808. According to Wesley (p. 142) his tombstone (reproduced in Wesley, p. 143), gives, erroneously, Dec.

7, 1807, as the date of his death. He died intestate and his widow, Sylvia Ward Hall, administered his estate valued at $47.22.

In an era when Negroes were denied most of their rights they almost inevitably sought to ameliorate their plight by building their own churches and free schools. A fraternal order like the separate Masonic lodge was a natural aspect of this self-help. Prince Hall ranks among the most significant leaders of these organizations, whose influence grew and became valuable in the quest for a better life.

The best brief treatment of Prince Hall is Sidney Kaplan's *The Black Presence in the Era of the American Revolution, 1770–1800* (1973, pp. 181–92). Lewis Hayden published in 1871 a pamphlet, *Masonry among Colored Men in Massachusetts*. Harry E. Davis's *A History of Masonry among Negroes in America* (1946) and George Williamson Crawford's *Prince Hall and His Followers: Being a Monograph on the Legitimacy of Negro Masonry* (1914) are the most comprehensive studies. The most recent biography, Charles H. Wesley's *Prince Hall, Life and Legacy* (1977), corrects the mistakes notably of William H. Grimshaw's *Official History of Freemasonry Among the Colored People in North America* (1903). It has a comprehensive bibliography, a photograph of the Prince Hall Monument in Boston (p. 178), and of the Prince Hall School, Philadelphia (p. 185). The Charge of June 25, 1792, and that of June 24, 1794, are in *Early Negro Writing 1760–1837*, selected and introduced by Dorothy Porter (1971, pp. 60–78).

— RAYFORD W. LOGAN

HAMLIN, ALBERT COMSTOCK (1881–1912), Oklahoma state legislator. Hamlin was born on Feb. 10, 1881, at Topeka, Kans., to which his slave-born parents, Andrew Jackson and Fanny Hamlin, had come from Tennessee in 1880, as participants in the great "Exoduster" movement of Negroes from southern states; in 1890, however, they joined the new "exodus" to Oklahoma Territory, instigated by Edward P. McCabe. They settled on a farm in Logan County, where the father died the following year. Young Hamlin continued the education he had begun in Topeka and helped his mother on the farm until 1899, when he was married to Katie Weaver, by whom he had four sons and a daughter. He was a devout member of the African Methodist Episcopal church, which he had joined in 1898, and was active in local politics, serving for ten years on the school board and for nine as a trustee of Springvale township. In 1908 he received the Republican nomination for representative to the state legislature from the Third District, and although Negroes were no more than a strong minority, was elected, becoming the first Negro in the Oklahoma State legislature. (Green I. Currin had been elected in 1890 to the territorial legislature.)

Hamlin introduced bills on a variety of subjects. Although a member of the minority party, he obtained the passage of bills appropriating funds for a state school for deaf, blind, and orphan colored children and providing for stricter Sabbath observance. He also obtained passage of a resolution calling for equal facilities for colored passengers on Oklahoma's segregated railroads. In 1910 he was defeated for reelection and was also unsuccessful in contesting the results. As a result of a constitutional amendment (1910) which his original election may have helped to trigger, and which was so unfairly administered as to disfranchise most Negroes, Hamlin was the only Negro elected to the Oklahoma legislature until 1964.

Hamlin died on his farm on Aug. 29, 1912, at the age of less than thirty-two.

Kaye M. Teall (ed.), *Black History in Oklahoma* (1971), has brought together the principal references to Hamlin's brief life. — KENNETH WIGGINS PORTER

HAMMON, BRITON (? – ?), autobiographer. All that is known about Briton Hammon—and that is very little —is gleaned from his fourteen-page publication, *A Narrative of the Uncommon Sufferings and Surprising Deliverance of BRITON HAMMON, A Negro Man,—Servant to General Winslow, of Marshfield in New England; Who Returned to Boston, after Having Been Absent almost Thirteen Years . . . Boston, . . . 1760.* The author is important for one reason only: he was the first known American Negro to publish a prose work. Coincidentally the first generally recognized American Negro to publish a poetical work, one that was also composed in 1760, was named Hammon, Jupiter Hammon. The two, however, were not related. Briton Hammon's *Narrative* is the first of a long and significant line of Negro autobiographical writing that has led from his simple pamphlet through Richard Wright's *Black Boy.*

The *Narrative* begins with the customary eighteenth-century apology "To the Reader," in which Briton Hammon admits that his "Capacities" and "Conditions of Life are very low," and therefore requests the reader to make allowance for them. His purpose, he states, is to "relate matters of Fact" concerning his "Sufferings" as they "occur to my mind." Unfortunately, Briton Hammon wrote so scantily and economically the reader finds only a skeletal account of his experiences.

According to the *Narrative,* Briton Hammon on Dec. 25, 1747, left Marshfield, Mass., went to Plymouth, and took passage on a sloop bound for Jamaica. He had his master's permission, but nowhere in the account does he state the purpose of his journey. Coming back from Jamaica, the ship was caught on a reef about "5 leagues from the shore" of Cape Florida. Hostile Indians came out, burnt the ship, and killed all of the men aboard except Briton Hammon, whom they held captive. Although the Indians threatened to roast him alive, Hammon was spared. He attributes his good fortune to the "Providence of God." Briton Hammon, like Olaudah Equiano (Gustavus Vassa), Jupiter Hammon, John Marrant, and other early Negro writers, believed strongly in "blessed" or "divine providences."

The rest of the work tells without elaboration of any sort the bare facts of Briton Hammon's escape from the Indians, a second escape from the Spaniards who had helped him to get away from his Indian captors, and his eventual landing in England. From there he signed on a ship bound for Boston and discovered with great joy that his master, General Winslow, was also on board.

A Narrative ends with a short homily on the goodness of God and His blessed providence.

We learn from the account that Briton Hammon was a cook, but he gives no details of his work on any of the several ships on which he sailed. He also leaves us somewhat puzzled concerning his status. The word "servant" is used in the title. Was he a servant in the modern sense or an actual slave? We have no way of knowing from what he tells us.

Briton Hammon could have written a fascinating account of his life on board an English man-of-war in actual battle, of his captivity among the Indians, of his imprisonment in a Spanish dungeon, of the treatment of slaves in the West Indies and in America, and of other extraordinary experiences, but he was evidently a very limited man; his "capacities" were indeed low. He was probably far more interested in having *A Narrative* edify and improve as a witness to God's providence than entertain or inform as a travel account. The *Narrative* has been published in *Early Negro Writing, 1760–1837,* selected and introduced by Dorothy Porter (1971, pp. 522–28). — ARTHUR P. DAVIS

HAMMON, JUPITER (1711–1806?), "the first published American Negro poet." He was born on Oct. 17, 1711, and lived and died a favored slave to three generations of the Lloyd family of Lloyd's Neck, Long Island, N. Y. Owned first by Henry Lloyd (who died in 1763), Hammon then served a son, Joseph Lloyd until 1780, then a grandson, John Lloyd, Jr. Each of his masters was helpful in Hammon's publishing efforts. He probably received his early education, "along with other children living on the Lloyd Manor," in a small school privately erected on the premises, instruction being offered by the pious Lloyd family. It is certain that Jupiter Hammon received more education and regard, however paternalistically religious, than other slaves. This is evidenced from his own published remarks, and from a letter dated "May 19, 1730," written by "G. Muirson" to Lloyd; a diagnosis and an equally detailed prescription for Hammon's afflictions of "pains in his Leggs [sic], Knees and thighs ascending to his bowels" are the entire concern.

Early results of his special education are manifest in his 88-line poem, "An Evening Thought. Salvation by Christ, with Penetential Cries: Composed by Jupiter Hammon, a Negro belonging to Mr. Lloyd of Queen's Village, on Long Island, the 25th of December, 1760" (1761), his first known publication. When British troops swarmed over Long Island, Joseph Lloyd, a zealous American Patriot, fled with his family and servants to Hartford, Conn., where, believing a rumor of the fall of Charlestown and fearing the collapse of the American cause, he committed suicide in 1780. With his next master, John Lloyd, Jr., Hammon remained in Hartford throughout the war, probably preaching to local whites and Negroes, and publishing the bulk of his known works. His poetry includes the aforementioned "Evening Thought"; *An Address to Miss Phillis Wheatly [sic] Ethiopian Poetess, in Boston . . .* (1778), *An Essay on Ten Virgins* (1779; presumably verse, this work has not been traced, but was advertised "To be sold" in the *Connecticut Courant* (Dec. 14, 1779); "A Poem for Children" (1782); and "The Kind Master and Dutiful

Servant" (1782), published as part of a prose work, *An Evening's Improvement,* in the text of which he stated: "I am advanced to the age of seventy-one years." His prose pieces published at Hartford include two lengthy evangelical tracts, *A Winter Piece* (1782) and *An Evening's Improvement.* He was back on Long Island later in 1782 when he composed more verses, not yet found, to celebrate the visit to Lloyd Manor of young Prince William Henry, later King William IV of England. For "Members of the African Society in New York," he composed in 1786 another prose work, *Address to the Negroes, in the State of New-York.* A third, posthumous printing of his *Address* (1806) is subsigned by three residents of Oyster Bay who attested to his character and the authenticity of his writing ability, and while they spoke of him in the past tense, they did so as though he could not have been very long dead. Exactly when Jupiter Hammon died and where he is buried are unknown.

At times, Hammon seemed settled in his Calvinist notions of human helplessness and utter reliance on the exclusive will of an abstract God for any kind of justifiable earthly change; at other times he was compassionately aware of and even solicitous for less fortunate slaves, and especially younger Negroes who agitated for freedom in a country that had recently waged a bloody war for freedom. To an attack on his ambivalent position by contemporary Negroes, Jupiter wrote, "my answer hath always been that I am a stranger here and I do not care to be concerned or to meddle with public affairs." His mostly mechanical verses show obvious influences from popular Wesleyan hymnal poetics; all of his verses use the same rime scheme *(abab),* and metrical patterns (alternating iambic tetrameters and trimeters); all are exhortatory. His prose works, equally pious, are self-consciously structured sermons, all displaying predictable deferentiality and biblical allusions and quotations, but these pieces are valuable for their occasional autobiographical comments. Never a powerful writer, but important for historical, social, and literary reasons, Hammon justifies growing attention.

Largely ignored throughout the nineteenth century, he was put before the public by his first biographer, Oscar Wegelin, in his *Jupiter Hammon, American Negro Poet, Selections from His Writings, and a Bibliography* (1915). The most comprehensive biography is Stanley A. Ransom, Jr.'s *America's First Negro Poet, The Complete Works of Jupiter Hammon of Long Island* (1970), which includes a full bibliography of recent notices of Hammon. His "Evening Thought" has been published in *Early Negro Writing, 1760–1837,* selected and introduced by Dorothy Porter (1971, pp. 529–31). There is a brief biography by Benjamin Brawley in *DAB* (4, Part 2:201–2). — WILLIAM H. ROBINSON

HANDY, W[ILLIAM] C[HRISTOPHER] (1873–1958), composer, cornetist, band leader, and publisher. Born in a log cabin in Florence, Ala., the grandson of slaves, he was the son of a Methodist minister, Charles Bernard, and Elizabeth (Brewer) Handy, emancipated slaves. He attended the Florence District School where he studied music with a graduate of Fisk University, Y. A. Wallace. In 1893 he organized a quartet which at-

tracted favorable attention at the Chicago Columbian Exposition in the same year. Subsequently he toured throughout the South with various brass bands as cornetist, primarily in minstrel shows. In 1896 he led his own band as part of the Mahara Minstrels Troup, which toured the United States, Cuba, and Mexico. His activities began increasingly to center in Memphis, Tenn. There in 1909 a song he had written for the political campaign of the legendary "Boss" Edward H. Crump, mayor of Memphis, achieved wide popularity. In 1912 Handy published this song as "Memphis Blues" (originally titled "Mr. Crump" and as much a ragtime piece as a blues). Stimulated by its success, Handy began to collect blues and other Afro-American folk materials and published them as his own compositions, mostly in "properly" harmonized versions. The most famous of these compositions is "St. Louis Blues," published in 1914. Other blues and popular songs followed through the years, but in the meantime he frequently directed bands, with one of which he came to New York in 1918 and made his first recordings. Handy remained in New York and, with his Memphis publishing partner, Harry Pace, started a highly successful music-publishing firm. During the peak of the blues craze and the beginnings of the "race record" market in the early 1920s, many of Handy's compositions ("Aunt Hagar's Blues," "A Good Man Is Hard to Find," and "Careless Love," in particular) became national hits and strong moneymakers.

In 1898 Handy married his boyhood sweetheart, Elizabeth V. Price. She bore him six children and died in 1937. Handy had lost his sight after World War I but partially regained it. In 1943 he fell from a subway station and became totally blind. Nevertheless he continued to be active in his publishing business and in 1941 published his autobiography, *Father of the Blues,* edited by Arna Bontemps. He died on March 28, 1958, at Sydenham Hospital, Harlem, of acute bronchial pneumonia. He had suffered a stroke three years before and traveled only in a wheelchair thereafter. His last public appearance had been on Nov. 17, 1957, at a birthday party at the Waldorf-Astoria Hotel attended by more than 800 persons. Mayor Robert Wagner proclaimed W. C. Handy Week. Special funeral services were held at the Prince Hall Masonic Temple in New York City on April 1 and regular services at Abyssinian Baptist Church the next day. Among the notables who attended were Oscar Hammerstein II, Marian Anderson, and the mayor of Memphis, who offered a W. C. Handy Memorial Park as his last resting place. New York police estimated that 150,000 people lined the funeral route. He was buried in Woodlawn Cemetery, Bronx, N.Y. Among his survivors were his second wife, Irma Louise Logan Handy, whom he had married in 1954 when he was eighty; two sons, William C. Jr. and Wyer; a daughter, Mrs. Katherine Lewis; a brother, Charles; and a grandson, William C. III (*New York Times,* March 29, 1958, p. 17; March 30, 1958, p. 88; April 3, 1958, p. 33). The Handy Heights Housing Development and Museum in Florence, his birthplace, includes a restored cabin in which are housed his piano, trumpet, and other mementoes. The W. C. Handy Park at the foot of Beale Street in Memphis has a bronze statue of heroic size showing him poised to play his horn.

Handy's fame rests on the blues he composed and the traditional tunes he collected, wrote down, and published. Although Handy's family did not want him to become a musician, they acquiesced as long as he did not get involved with what they regarded as "low down" music: ragtime and the blues. The music he played and came to know in the minstrel shows was mostly written-down music, and included marches, particularly those of John Phillip Sousa, and the songs of Stephen Foster.

It was around the turn of the century that Handy, crisscrossing the South in his travels, became aware of the rich musical heritage perpetuated by guitar-picking itinerant blues singers, more often than not playing on homemade instruments. It was this music with its "primitive" beauty which began to haunt Handy. It was a fortunate circumstance of considerable significance in the history of Afro-American music that Handy's previous formal training in music—particularly his work in solfège and dictation with Y. A. Wallace—enabled him to record in notation the folk music he heard in his travels. Like Bartok and Kodaly, who began to collect Balkan folk music early in our century, Handy decided to try to capture in written form the essence of this handed-down, improvised folk music.

Like all such transcriptions, they were bound to be approximations, since the subtleties of intonation, of timbre and rhythm cannot be captured with absolute fidelity in European notation. But Handy felt that publication of these folk materials would not only lend them respectability, but would help make the Western world aware of the riches of this American musical heritage. It is significant that Handy called himself an *"American composer"* (the italics are his). Although his view of the Afro-American musical traditions may have been somewhat influenced by his formal musical education, Handy still performed a valuable service to music and to Negro music in particular. He could be forgiven for wanting to "polish" the "primitive music" he collected in the rural regions of the South, because that was a current attitude maintained by most people then, including most Negroes. Handy's assimilation into the white culture and the commercial music marketplace enabled him to promulgate a music which might otherwise have remained un- or little-known as mere regional obscurities.

This, then, constitutes a significant part of the legacy: a documentation of the black folk heritage of the southern United States, with particular emphasis on the blues. His collections include *Blues: An Anthology* (1926), and in addition to his biography he published *Negro Authors and Composers of the United States* (1935) and *Unsung Americans Sung* (1944). His best known compositions include, in addition to works already mentioned, "Joe Turner Blues" (1915), "Beale Street Blues" and "Old Miss Rag" (both 1916), "Make Me a Pallet on the Floor" (also known as "Atlanta Blues," 1923). He was also the composer of much sacred music, including many anthems and hymns, as well as spirituals.

There are brief biographical sketches in Maud Cuney-Hare's *Negro Musicians and Their Music* (1936, pp. 140–45) and Eileen Southern's *The Music of Black Musicians, A History* (1971, pp. 336–39, 354–55). His autobiography, *Father of the Blues* (1941), is the best source. — GUNTHER SCHULLER

HANSBERRY, LORRAINE VIVIAN (1930–1965), playwright. Born in Chicago on May 19, 1930, the daughter of Carl A. and Nannie (Perry) Hansberry, who had both migrated from the South to Chicago's Southside, and educated in the city's public schools, Miss Hansberry graduated in 1948 and enrolled for two years at the University of Wisconsin. When she moved to New York in 1950, she worked at a variety of jobs, including waitress at a Greenwich Village restaurant owned by the family of Robert Nemiroff, a music publisher. In 1953 she and Nemiroff were married, and the playwright settled down to the work that resulted in *A Raisin in the Sun* (1959), a Broadway production which won the New York Drama Critics Circle Award for the best play of the 1958–1959 season. In 1964 her second Broadway effort—*The Sign in Sidney Brustein's Window*—opened. By this time Hansberry, who had suffered bouts of illness since 1963, was seriously ill. The play was still running when she died of cancer.

The playwright's father was a relatively well-to-do businessman who had migrated from Glaston, Miss., as a young man, worked hard, and succeeded in founding a lucrative real estate firm and one of Chicago's early Negro banks. A race-conscious man, he instilled in his two sons and daughters a mixture of pride in their heritage and faith in the bourgeois tenets of self-help. His philosophy seems to have been that "life was not a struggle—it was something that one *did.*"

When Lorraine was eight years old, he found this view unequivocally contradicted. His attempt to move his family into a white neighborhood was blocked by Illinois state law. While he carried the *Hansberry v. Lee* case to the U.S. Supreme Court and won (1940), his wife, a native of Columbia, Tenn., guarded their new home against white violence. After his victory, which exacted an enormous financial and psychological toll, the father purchased a home in Polanco, Mexico, and made plans to expatriate. But he died of a cerebral hemorrhage in Mexico in 1945.

The family remained in Chicago where the playwright received her early education in half-day schools such as Felsenthal and Betsy Ross. Her elementary education was supplemented by her own voracious reading. She became acquainted with the verse of Langston Hughes, Countee Cullen, and Waring Cuney, and by the age of fourteen had read the seminal works of Carter G. Woodson, co-founder in 1915 of the Association for the Study of Negro Life and History and author of several books on Negro history.

She graduated from Englewood High School in 1948 and enrolled for two years at the University of Wisconsin. While studying stage design and art, she was impressed by the university's productions of O'Casey, Ibsen, and Strindberg. At the end of her second year she moved to New York. Her efforts in painting at the Chicago Art Institute were not extended at the New School for Social Research, and she soon grew discontented with academic life. Between 1950 and 1953 she worked as a sales clerk, journalist, and theatrical producer's assistant. She was first a reporter then an associate editor of Paul Robeson's Harlem-based monthly *Freedom.*

By 1951 she had begun working in Nemiroff's Greenwich Village restaurant, and after she and Robert Nemiroff were married, they took up residence in a "ramshackle Village walkup apartment." The back workroom of this small apartment was the scene of the playwright's apprenticeship. During the next three years she wrote short stories, poetry, and plays. Between her twenty-sixth and twenty-seventh birthdays, she worked almost exclusively on *A Raisin in the Sun,* a three-act drama dealing with the conflicts and aspirations of a Negro Southside family. The play premiered in New Haven and opened at Broadway's Ethel Barrymore Theater on March 11, 1959. Success was instantaneous and sure. The play ran for nineteen months and was eventually made into a full-length motion picture starring the original cast, which included such notables as Sidney Poitier, Claudia McNeil, Ruby Dee, and Diana Sands.

Having awakened to find herself famous, the playwright entered a whirl of social activities while she continued to write. One of her newly found (or "designated," as the case may be) roles was that of spokeswoman for American Negroes in life and art. She participated in conferences like "The First Conference of Negro Writers" (1959) and in symposia such as "The Black Revolution and the White Backlash" (1964). In 1962 she and her husband purchased a home north of New York City in Croton-on-Hudson.

April of the following year brought the first attack of the illness which was to prove fatal. From 1963 until her death, Hansberry was in and out of hospitals, carrying always her manuscripts and unanswered correspondence. In 1964 she wrote the text for a collection of photographs entitled *The Movement,* and on Oct. 15 her second Broadway play, *The Sign in Sidney Brustein's Window,* opened at the Longacre Theater. The play, which was to continue for 101 performances, was running when the playwright died at New York's University Hospital on Jan. 12, 1965. Funeral services were held on Jan. 16 at the Presbyterian Church of the Master, Morningside Avenue and 122nd Street, Harlem. Because of her illness, her divorce from Nemiroff had been kept secret, but he, Shelly Winters, Ossie Davis, Paddy Chayefsky, and Malcolm X were among the mourners. She was buried in Beth El Cemetery, Croton-on-Hudson, N.Y. Nemiroff, who was named executor, received her estate valued at $115,000 and personal items. She was also survived by her mother, two brothers (Perry of Los Angeles and Carl of Chicago), and a sister Mrs. Mamie Tubbs of Los Angeles (*New York Times,* Jan. 13, 1965, p. 1; Jan. 17, 1965, p. 88; Jan. 29, 1965, p. 25; and Feb. 5, 1965, p. 36).

Coming of age during what might be described as the "great thaw" in contemporary race relations, Miss Hansberry's artistic and social vision was far-reaching and optimistic. Not only American Negroes, but colored peoples throughout the world were on the move, and she doubtless had this in mind when she pro-

claimed herself part of a "world majority, and a very assertive one." The chief characters in her plays share this feeling. They are insistent, committed, and enduring because they wish to impose a purpose, a *raison d'être,* on life.

Although Hansberry has been labeled old-fashioned, bourgeois, and assimilationist by various critics, it seems more accurate to say that she worked in the best tradition of American realistic drama. And as a Negro Broadway playwright, she had fewer than a dozen forerunners (none of them women). Efforts by writers like Garland Anderson, Wallace Thurman, and Langston Hughes created little of the stir occasioned by *A Raisin in the Sun.* True, the Black Nationalistic plays of the 1960s and 1970s seemed to render her works passé. Cut off before she had completed a remarkable apprenticeship, Lorraine Hansberry left striking accounts of life's rigorous possibilities and splended dramatic demonstrations that "there are no simple men." But it is well to remember that she was one of the first to assert that the black ghetto was "no place to be somebody" (the title of Charles Gordone's Pulitzer Prize-winning play of 1969–1970) and that "the River Niger" (James Walker's later sensation) flowed with a black and stately heritage.

The most important autobiographical statements are found in *To Be Young, Gifted and Black* (1969), compiled and edited by Robert Nemiroff. The material contained in this volume formed the basis of a play which opened under the same title on Jan. 2, 1969, at the Cherry Lane Theater. The show was filmed for National Educational Television and appeared in 1972. "The Talk of the Town" column of *The New Yorker* (May 9, 1959) also contains a detailed autobiographical account. Nemiroff's and Julius Lester's introductory and critical comments in *Les Blancs: The Collected Last Plays of Lorraine Hansberry* (1972) are quite serviceable. The playwright's own view of the role of the black dramatist are found in " 'Me Tink me hear sounds in de night' " (*Theater Arts,* Oct. 1960). James Baldwin's assessment of Miss Hansberry appears as "Sweet Lorraine" (*Esquire,* Nov. 1969), and William Edward Farrison's review of the collected last plays appears in the *CLA Journal* (Dec. 1972). Harold R. Isaac's "Five Writers and Their African Ancestors" (*Phylon,* 1960) contains some useful critical and autobiographical statements. *Les Blancs,* one of the last plays, opened at the Longacre Theater on Nov. 15, 1970, and had a short run. — HOUSTON A. BAKER JR.

HANSBERRY, WILLIAM LEO (1894–1965), historian and pioneer Africanist. The son of Eldon Hayes and Harriet Pauline (Bailey) Hansberry, he was born in Gloster, Miss., where his father was professor of history at Alcorn College. He attended Atlanta University (1914–1916), then Harvard, where he received his B.S. degree in 1922. The same year he joined the faculty of Howard University, an affiliation that lasted until his retirement in 1959. In the intervening years he earned his M.A. in anthropology from Harvard (1931) and did postgraduate research at the Oriental Institute, University of Chicago (1936–1937), the School of Anthropology and Archaeology, Oxford University (1937–1938), and Cairo University (1953). As a Fulbright scholar in Africa (1953–1954) he studied over 100 archeological sites. Hansberry was the first American Negro to devote his life exclusively to the study of Africa and its ancient civilizations. Forty years before the idea gained wide acceptance, his research led him to the conclusion that Africa's past constituted a unique and highly developed cultural heritage.

Hansberry's father died while he was three, leaving a large historical library of which his son took full advantage. In 1916 he read *The Negro* by W. E. B. Du Bois. This prompted him to leave Atlanta for Harvard, where he could pursue an interest in Africa. He came under the influence of Earnest A. Hooton, chairman of the Department of Anthropology and member of the Peabody Museum Faculty. They remained friends until Hooton's death in 1954. Hansberry resembled his mentor in many respects: among colleagues, both men were known for their subtle humor, and for their heterodoxy; among students, they were beloved for their devotion to teaching and their availability. On the other hand the insistence by the distinguished Egyptologist George Andrew Reisner that Negroes had not played any significant role in the ancient Nile Valley civilizations led him to devote the remainder of his life to discovering the facts. Before graduation from Harvard, Hansberry taught history, African archeology, psychology, and sociology at Straight College in New Orleans (Feb. 1921 to Feb. 1922). He lectured to many groups, including a YMCA conference at King's Mountain, N.C. He so impressed Jesse E. Moorland, Howard University alumnus and trustee, that he was eager to secure his employment at Howard. After Hansberry graduated from Harvard in 1922, he rejected offers of employment from Marcus Garvey and Atlanta University, and accepted an appointment at Howard. He believed that the university could support the ambitious program of teaching and research that he had already begun; in addition, Washington, D.C., offered better opportunities for research than did any other city in which a Negro university was located.

Appointed in 1922 "Special and Part-time Lecturer on Ancient African Civilizations" at $150 per month, Hansberry offered, it was stated, the first courses of their kind in any American university. They were History 12, "Negro Peoples in the Civilizations of the Prehistoric and Ancient World"; History 13, "Negro Civilizations in East Central Africa from the Eighth Century B.C. until the End of the Sixteenth Century"; and History 14, "Negro Civilizations in West Central Africa from A.D. 900 to the End of the Nineteenth Century." Some 800 students were enrolled in the courses. In June 1925 a two-day symposium entitled "Cultures and Civilizations of Negro Peoples in Africa" was held under his chairmanship, with twenty-eight papers delivered by his advanced students.

Hansberry's teachings on African history were, in the 1920s, unorthodox. He taught, for example, that the cradle of civilization was not in the Fertile Crescent, but in Africa, that Egypt had derived its early culture from Kushite and Ethiopian kingdoms to the south. He also taught the more accepted view that a primary destructive agent of Africa's past was the slave traders—Arabs, Europeans, and Americans—who not only destroyed African civilizations but suppressed knowledge of them to support the contention that slavery was a civilizing factor.

These lectures, backed by careful data from his research, endeared him to students but alienated him from many professional colleagues. His views were not only counter to the prevailing scholarship of the period, but came at a time when most American Negroes rejected any association with Africa.

Yet he pressed on in his independent course, generously supported by Howard University and assisted by his wife Myrtle, documenting Africa's past and its greatness with meticulous research. To appreciate his position, one must bear in mind that during the first third of this century there was little popular interest in Africa.

Hansberry found support from some scholars in his field. Charles H. Wesley quoted a letter from Hooton which said that Hansberry "has been unable to take the Ph.D. degree in his chosen subject here or anywhere else because there is no university or institution, so far as I know, that has manifested a really profound interest on this subject." A well-known Africanist, William M. Steen, quoted another letter from Hooton, this one in 1947: "I am quite confident that no present day scholar has developed anything like the knowledge of this field that Hansberry has developed." Du Bois, in *The World and Africa* (1947), wrote: "I have read Eduard Meyer's *Geschichte des Altertums* (1910–1913); but of greatest help to me has been Leo Hansberry. Mr. Hansberry, a professor at Howard University, is the one modern scholar who has tried to study the Negro in Egypt and Africa. I regret that he has not published more of his work. The overwhelming weight of conventional scientific opinion on Africa have overawed him, but his work in manuscript is outstanding" (Foreword, p. x).

After publishing three magazine articles (1921, 1923, and 1930), by 1939, with some financial support from the university, Hansberry had prepared a detailed outline of a five-volume work on the proto-history of Africa, but prior to World War II there was no publisher interested in such an extensive study. In the postwar years he turned to counseling African students, who were attending Howard in large numbers. In 1953 he co-founded the African-American Institute. He helped to establish Africa House, a student hostel in Washington, and to found the All-African Students Union of the Americas.

After his retirement from Howard as associate professor of history in 1959, a number of unexpected events occurred which caused the last five years in his life to be his most rewarding. In that year the eminent Nigerian historian Kenneth O. Diké visited Hansberry, examined his accumulated research, and observed that it *must* be published, to stimulate the new field of African history. This was a turning point, for while his American detractors were prepared to disregard Hansberry, few felt qualified to question Diké's judgment. Later, Thomas Hodgkin of the Universities of Ghana and Oxford met Hansberry and came to the same conclusion as Diké. This was followed in mid-1960 by an offer from Hansberry's former student, Nnamdi Azikiwe, then president of the Nigerian Senate, to underwrite the publication of his projected study. Appealing as this offer was, Hansberry wanted it brought out under American auspices because he felt it to be a uniquely American contribution.

In the same year Kwame Nkrumah, then president of Ghana, offered him a professorship at the University of Ghana and invited him to publish his works there. In late 1961 Dr. Azikiwe, by then governor-general of the country and chancellor of the University of Nigeria, conferred on Hansberry the university's second honorary degree. Two years later the Hansberry College of African Studies at Nsukka was inaugurated by the university with Hansberry in attendance. On the occasion of the formal opening of the new college, Hansberry delivered an inaugural address, "Africana at Nsukka." From Oct. 17 to Nov. 28, 1963, he delivered six public lectures on problems in African history that had occupied him for forty years. In 1964 he was the first recipient of the Haile Selassie I Prize Trust for pioneering work in African history, archeology, and anthropology. Morgan State College conferred upon him the honorary degree of LL.D. in 1965.

By 1960 American Negro awareness, coupled with the emergence of a number of independent African states, had led to a growing American interest in the continent, and with it came the need for scholarly publications. Bennett Cerf of Random House contracted with Hansberry for half a million words on African history, based on an updated version of the 1939 outline. Hansberry was engaged in this project when he died in Chicago in 1965. While he never completed the planned five volumes, his other published works have been collected in the Moorland-Spingarn Research Center, Howard University. Four essays on the origins and development of ancient and medieval Ethiopian history, taken from his private papers, were published in 1975 under the title *Pillars of Ethiopian History: The William Leo Hansberry History Notebook, Volume I,* edited by Joseph E. Harris.

Hansberry's most enduring legacy is the inspiration he gave to thousands of students. Some of his rejected views of fifty years ago are now widely accepted, and although his chief recognition came from Africa rather than from the land of his birth, one feels he rather enjoyed the role of pioneering African Studies in the United States. In a 1961 interview in *Ebony,* he said, "If I had it to do all over again, I would change nothing. It has been an intensely rewarding life and I would live it as I have." The Department of History at Howard University named a classroom for him on Nov. 20, 1972.

Hansberry died of a cerebral hemorrhage in Chicago on Oct. 17, 1965. Funeral services were held on Nov. 6, 1965, in Andrew Rankin Memorial Chapel, Howard University, with interment in Lincoln Memorial Cemetery, Suitland, Md. He was survived by his widow, Myrtle Kelso Hansberry; their daughters, Gail Adelle and Myrtle Kay; and two sisters, Mrs. Carrie Fitchett and Mrs. Mamie Martin (Mrs. Myrtle Kelso Hansberry to Rayford W. Logan, Nov. 30, 1976).

See "William Leo Hansberry," in Michael R. Winston's *Howard University Department of History 1913–1973* (1973, pp. 46–54). The quotations by Wesley and Steen are in Lorraine A. Williams (ed.), *A Trib-*

ute to the Memory of Professor William Leo Hansberry (1972, pp. 19 and 25, respectively).

— RAYMOND SMYKE

HARALSON, JEREMIAH (1846–1916?), congressman. He was born of slave parents on April 1, 1846, near Columbus, Ga. From 1859 to 1865 he was a slave and servant on the plantation of John Haralson in Alabama. Largely self-taught and a self-made man, he was an aggressive, "natural politician," who capitalized on the fact that he was a "pure-blooded" Negro. He ran for Congress in 1868 and campaigned for the Democratic candidates for president while privately supporting the Republican. Running as an independent, he was elected to the Alabama House of Representatives against the Republican candidate. As presiding officer of the district convention which nominated Benjamin S. Turner for Congress, he displayed skill as presiding officer and considerable oratorical ability. In 1870 he was elected state senator from the Twenty-first District. Between 1872 and 1874 he contended with P. B. S. Pinchback of Louisiana and James T. Rapier of Alabama for recognition as a leading Republican in the South, alternately opposing and supporting Ulysses Grant and Charles Sumner for the presidency. He emerged as perhaps the most feared Negro in the state legislature.

He won election to Congress in 1874 by staunchly supporting a strong and controversial civil rights proposal. The *Mobile Register* (June 18, 1874) gave this appraisal: "Jere, black as the ace of spades and with the brogue of the cornfield, ascended the rostrum. A burly Negro, shrewd and fully aware of the strength of his people, insolent to his opponents and always advancing his line of battle while professing to desire nothing but the rights of his race, uncompromising, irritating and bold—Jere struck consternation to the scalawag soul." The *Register* added a few days later that Haralson was "by far the most prominent Negro in the state," and suggested him for a vacancy in President Grant's cabinet. It may be surmised that the suggestion indicated the low esteem in which Grant and his cabinet were held by the newspaper.

After Congress convened in December 1875, he was named to the Committee on Public Education. When his election was contested, the House, in which Democrats had a majority, accepted a unanimous committee report which confirmed his election: although there were some illegal votes in the campaign, Haralson still had a majority. He introduced six bills, resolutions, and petitions, but delivered no speeches. He kept a distant seat in the House rather than one up front which he received by lot.

Although he capitalized on his blackness against light-complexioned Negroes, he became an apostle of reconciliation between blacks and whites in Alabama. He favored general amnesty, was a friend of Jefferson Davis and the influential congressman Lucius Q. C. Lamar. He opposed the use of federal troops in the election of 1876. In a letter published in the *Mobile Register* (Jan. 29, 1876), he asked: "Is it not better for us in general, especially in the South, that there be good feeling between white and black? We must drive out these hell hounds and go for peace between the two races." At the same time he favored universal male suffrage, a program unlikely to create goodwill among Alabama white voters.

He was defeated for reelection in 1876. The Fourth District, the only remaining predominantly black district, had been gerrymandered so that Haralson running as an independent and Rapier as a Republican were defeated by a white Democrat. Haralson then worked as a clerk in the U.S. Customs House in Baltimore, the Internal Revenue Department and the Pension Bureau in Washington. Defeated for reelection to Congress in 1878 and 1884, he became a farmer in Louisiana and a pension agent in Arkansas (1904). He drifted to Selma, Ala., Texas, Oklahoma, and Colorado, where he was a coal miner. He died about 1916, having been reportedly killed by wild beasts. However, no death certificate is on file at Denver in the Colorado Health Department's Bureau of Vital Statistics.

Some essential facts are in *Biographical Congressional Directory, 1774–1927.* Samuel Denny Smith's *The Negro in Congress, 1870–1901* (1940, reprint 1966) is less hostile to Haralson than to many other Negroes. Maurine Christopher's *America's Black Congressmen* (1971), more detailed than Smith but without footnotes, is less laudatory than for some others.

— RAYFORD W. LOGAN

HARDIN, WILLIAM JEFFERSON (c. 1830–1890?), legislator and mayor. Born in Russellville, Logan County, Ky., of unknown parents, he was reared and educated by a Shaker group at South Union, Ky., until he was able to teach school to free Negro children. Hardin migrated to California during the Gold Rush of 1849, and remained there for four years. He then lived for brief periods in Canada, Wisconsin, Iowa, and Nebraska, before moving to Colorado in 1863. He operated a Denver barbershop for ten years, and established a reputation as a Republican politician and public speaker. During his years in Denver he was a close associate and friend of Barney Ford in the struggle for political rights for Negro Coloradoans, and sat as a delegate at several Republican conventions in Colorado Territory. Hardin left Denver in 1873 after a short stint as gold-weigher and clerk in the gold room of the Denver mint, and established a new barbershop in Cheyenne, Wyo. He won election to that territory's Legislative Assembly twice, and became the only Afro-American to do so. After about twelve years in Cheyenne, he went to Park City, east of Salt Lake City, Utah, and won annual mayoral elections in 1885 and 1886. After his second term he returned to Colorado and served two terms as mayor of Leadville, a mining town in the mountains west of Denver. He died in either 1889 or 1890 at Leadville.

Hardin was elected to Wyoming's Sixth Territorial Legislature in 1879 as a Republican. Laramie County had nine delegates and only two of the successful candidates received more votes than Hardin. He served on the Committee on Indian and Military Affairs, took a turn in the speaker's chair, and led a losing fight against a reapportionment bill which reduced Laramie County's representation. His efforts in opposition to this bill earned Hardin a reputation as an eloquent and forceful speaker, bearing out the *Cheyenne Daily Leader*'s prediction that he would prove "the best orator" in the Assembly. Indeed, when he left to become mayor of Park City, he carried a reputation as "the finest speaker in the [Wyoming] House of Representatives" (*Cleveland Gazette,* May 16, 1885). His fame persisted well into the twentieth century. One Wyoming historian, C. G. Coutant, referred to Hardin in a 1942 article *(Annals of Wyoming)* as "the colored orator."

Hardin won reelection to the Seventh Legislature in 1882, although this time he was seventh among the eight winners. He served on the Elections Committee and chaired the Committee on Credentials and Engrossments. In addition, he sponsored three successful pieces of legislation, the most important of which was the 1882 repeal of the prohibition on interracial marriages in Wyoming. This reversed a policy as old as Wyoming Territory. Hardin's bill remained law until replaced with another miscegenation law thirty years later.

Hardin's personal life is not well documented. Forbes Parkhill, Barney Ford's biographer (*Mister Barney Ford,* 1963), claims Hardin married a white Denver milliner while still married to a black woman who lived in Kentucky. Parkhill says the scandal surrounding this affair, coupled with anonymous rumors published by the *Denver News* which claimed that Hardin had dodged the draft during the Civil War, forced him to leave his job at the mint and to quit Denver with his white wife in 1873. The stories may well have been the fabrications of political enemies. Presumably the milliner was his wife Catherine, who died about 1926 at the age of ninety-six. Hardin had at least one child, Mary Elizabeth.

Cheyenne newspapers, particularly the *Daily Leader*'s biographical sketch of Nov. 9, 1879, provide much useful information on Hardin. In addition, Marie Erwin's *Wyoming Historical Blue Book* (1942) and the *Journals* of the Sixth and Seventh Legislative Assemblies contain substantial data on his legislative career. A letter from a son of Hardin's daughter, which is in the collections of the Wyoming State Historical Society in Cheyenne, contains information about Hardin and his family which is not found elsewhere. — FRANK N. SCHUBERT

HARLAN, ROBERT JAMES (1816–1897), businessman, army officer, and civil rights leader. He was born in Harrodsburg, Ky., on Dec. 12, 1816, the son of Judge James Harlan and a mulatto mother. Judge Harlan, father of Associate Justice of the U.S. Supreme Court John Marshall Harlan, who wrote the classic dissent in *Plessy v. Ferguson* (1896), kept Robert in his home and had his two older sons tutor him. Robert saved enough money to open, when he was eighteen, a barbershop and later a grocery store. "Black Indians" forced him out of business. He then began trading in animal skins brought in by hunters. When he was thirty-two, in 1849, he and a party of white men followed by way of the Isthmus of Panama the Gold Rush to California. Within a year and a half he had accumulated gold worth $90,000 (*Cincinnati Union,* Dec. 13, 1934) which he invested in real estate in Cincinnati. He also purchased a large house on the northeast corner of Fifth and

Broadway for his home. In 1851 he visited the first "World's Fair," in the Crystal Palace, Sydenham, England, and remained abroad nearly a year. On his return in 1852 he married Josephine Floyd, the daughter of John B. Floyd, who served as governor of Virginia, secretary of war in the cabinet of James C. Buchanan, and a major-general in the Confederate Army. Their son, Robert James Jr., was born in 1853; Mrs. Harlan died when he was six months old. According to William J. Simmons's *Men of Mark* . . . (1887, p. 614), Harlan returned voluntarily to Kentucky and paid $500 for formal acknowledgment of his freedom.

Before his marriage to Josephine Floyd, Harlan had built and presented to his bride two stonefront houses on the north side of Fifth Street between Broadway and Pike Street. After her death the family moved to the house on Fifth and Broadway. His real estate investments included homes in Cincinnati, two acres of land in Walnut Hills, and the finest photograph gallery in Cincinnati which he bought from James Preston Ball. Harlan also owned a stable of race horses and was said to be the only colored owner allowed to enter horses in races in Louisville, New Orleans, and other southern cities. With the aid of Nicholas Longworth, he built on East Seventh Street the first school in Cincinnati for colored children.

To escape prejudice in the United States, he sailed in March 1859 on board the *City of Manchester* for England. Accompanying him were his son, three daughters by a first marriage, seven race horses, a trotting horse, a trainer and a jockey. Said to be the second American owner to race horses in England, he found the climate unfavorable for them. After the outbreak of the Civil War, his American sources of income were depleted. He returned to the United States in 1868 with only a remnant of his once-considerable fortune.

He devoted most of the rest of his life to civic activities and politics. He gave an oration on the ratification of the Fifteenth Amendment in 1870. He became a trustee of the Cincinnati public schools, working with Peter Humphries Clark, and was a trustee of the Colored Orphan Asylum. In 1872 he was a delegate-at-large to the Republican National Convention that nominated Gen. Ulysses Grant for president. Narrowly defeated for the state legislature in 1880, he was an alternate delegate-at-large to the Republican National Convention in Chicago in 1884. In 1872 he had been appointed by President Grant as special agent-at-large in the Post Office Department. In 1881 he had been appointed a special agent of the Treasury Department by Pres. Chester A. Arthur but was removed by Pres. Grover Cleveland as "an offensive partisan" (Simmons, p. 615). According to the Cincinnati city directories he held the position again from 1890 to 1892.

Two of Harlan's activities are particularly significant. In 1875 he raised a battalion of 400 colored men and was commissioned a colonel by Pres. Rutherford B. Hayes. This was the forerunner of the 9th Ohio Battalion, a part of the 372nd Infantry Regiment in World War I. As a member of the state legislature in 1886 Harlan with William Howard Day and Bishop Benja- in obtaining the repeal of the Black Laws. ing years Harlan lived with his son, Rob-

ert Jr., who was a license deputy in the city auditor's office. He died on Sept. 24, 1897, at his son's home, 1048 Baymiller St., Cincinnati. His death was attributed to his age, eighty-one. Impressive funeral services were held on Sept. 24 at St. Paul's Episcopal Church, Seventh and Plum Streets, with interment in the Colored Cemetery at Warsaw. He was survived by his son and three grandchildren. His contemporaries believed that Harlan was a defender of the rights of Negroes of whom the race could be proud.

The chapter in Simmons's *Men of Mark* . . . (1887, pp. 613–16) differs on factual statements especially from the long article in the *Cincinnati Union* (Dec. 13, 1934), a copy of which is in the Moorland-Spingarn Research Center, Howard University. See also Wendell Phillips Dabney's *Cincinnati's Colored Citizens, Historical, Sociological and Biographical* (1926); *Cincinnati Directories* (1880–1898); the *Cincinnati Commercial Gazette,* the *Cincinnati Daily Star,* the *Cincinnati Gazette,* the *Cincinnati Enquirer,* and the *Dayton Journal Herald,* all for 1870–1897. Obituary notices were published in the *Cincinnati Enquirer* (Sept. 22, 1897, p. 6, and Sept. 25, p. 16).

— PAUL McSTALLWORTH

HARLESTON, EDWIN A[GUSTUS] (1882–1931), portrait painter. He was born in Charleston, S.C., the son of a seaman, Capt. Edwin Guillard Harleston, who became one of Charleston's leading undertakers and died at age seventy-six on April 21, 1931, shortly before his son's death (*New York Age,* May 9, 1931, p. 1). Edwin A.'s early education did not prepare him for the career of an artist even though he expressed interest in art at an early age. Instead he had graduated B.A. (1904) from Atlanta University where he excelled in several sports. From Atlanta, he went to Harvard University with the blessings of his family, hoping to become a physician. The urge to gain creative expression in the visual arts outweighed his interest in medicine, however, and he spent seven years studying at the Boston Museum School of Fine Arts. During his stay in Boston he pursued with distinction the study of anatomy and portrait painting. It was in the latter that he was to excel and be singled out as one of America's most gifted limners of persons of African ancestry. While at the Boston Museum School he received several scholarships and awards. Help from his father, who had retired from his work at sea, came more often after the elder Harleston became the operator of a prosperous funeral parlor in Charleston.

By the time Harleston was forty he was one of the most widely sought after portrait artists living in the South. In 1924 he was called upon by "the colored citizens" of the State of Delaware and the well-known DuPont family of Wilmington to paint the portrait of philanthropist Pierre S. DuPont. The portrait, commissioned by a group of Negro and white citizens in appreciation of his upgrading the quality of education in the schools for Negroes in Delaware, was hung in the State House in Wilmington. In 1925 the portrait won the Amy E. Spingarn Prize given by *The Crisis*.

Also noteworthy were *Portrait of Dr. Ware* (Edmund Asa Ware, former president of Atlanta University, 1924), *Portrait of Dr. Gus Hinton* (William Augustus Hinton, ca. 1926), and *Dancing Girl* (ca. 1930). During the summer of 1930, while he assisted Aaron Douglas in the execution of murals at Fisk University, Harleston commmpleted the *Portrait of Aaron Douglas*. Douglas is pictured standing between two of the large support pillars of the Fisk University Library, with a small portion of the Fisk murals in the background. This portrait, the *Portrait of Miss Sue Bailey* [later Mrs. Howard Thurman] *with the African Shawl*, and *The Old Servant* were included in Harleston's first paintings (1931) in the Harmon Foundation Exhibitions. *The Old Servant*, the most famous of Harleston's paintings, received the Locke Portrait Award of $100 "in appreciation of his quiet and effective services in the advancement of the Negro race." *The Old Bible Student* and the *Negro Soldier* were in the collection of Earl Grant of Los Angeles; those of Douglas and Bailey in the collection of the artist's niece, Edwina Harleston Whitlock of Inglewood, Calif.

Harleston felt a keen obligation to share his knowledge of art with young aspiring artists. This he did by making himself available for lecture engagements at schools such as Talladega College, Tuskegee Institute, and Fisk University. His wife had been trained as a professional photographer at Tuskegee Institute. He was thus able to take along on his lecture tours excellent photographic examples of his own works. Their joint studio was located at 121 Calhoun St. in Charleston, only a few steps away from the house where Harleston was born.

Death came to Harleston, whose life had been divided between that of a professional mortician, civil rights advocate, and artist, on May 9, 1931, just as he was about to embark on another tour of southern colleges where he was scheduled to deliver several lectures on art. His father's sudden death may have contributed to his own death (*Chicago Defender*, May 16, 1931, p. 1).

Accounts of the superb artistry of Edwin A. Harleston are in the Nov. 13, 1924, edition of the *Wilmington* (Delaware) *Evening Journal;* the Harmon Foundation catalogues of 1931 and 1933; "Who is E. A. Harleston?" by Madeline G. Allison (*Opportunity 2*, no. 13, Jan. 1924); "The Bible Student" (*Chicago Art Institute Scrapbook*, Vol. 54, Aug. 1927); James A. Porter's *The Negro in Modern Art*, (1943); and Cedric Dover's *American Negro Art* (1960). Exhibitions in which his work has appeared since his death have been arranged at the Texas Exposition (1940); the Downtown Gallery, New York City (1942); the Barnett-Aden Gallery, Washington, D.C. (1948); and the Howard University Gallery of Art (1952). — DAVID C. DRISKELL

HARPER, FRANCES ELLEN WATKINS (1825–1911), lecturer, author, and reformer. The only child of free parents in Baltimore, she received her first schooling at home but later, orphaned, attended a school for free Negroes run by her uncle, the Rev. William Watkins. About 1838 she went to work for a Mr. Armstrong who apparently encouraged her reading after her chores were done. In 1845, according to William Still, she published a collection of poetry and prose, *Forest Leaves;* apparently no copy exists. From 1850 to 1852 she taught sewing at the A.M.E. church's Union Seminary near Columbus, Ohio, leaving for a better teaching position in Little York, Pa. In 1854, after a Maryland law made free Negroes entering the state from the North liable to sale as slaves, she pledged herself to the antislavery movement. Her success as an orator led to her employment by the Maine antislavery cause. In a passage quoted by Still, "She speaks without notes, with gestures few and fitting. Her manner is marked by dignity and composure." When she married Fenton Harper, a widower, in 1860, however, she settled down on a farm near Columbus. They had one child, Mary, who died at an early age. After her husband's death four years later, she again took up her antislavery crusade and in addition toured the South for the Women's Christian Temperance Union, advocating the need for education and a higher standard of domestic morality. She also took part in at least two conventions (1875 and 1887) of the American Woman Suffrage Association, although in 1869 she had given priority to Negro suffrage as against women's suffrage. In her last decades she worked strenuously for the WCTU, dying at age eighty-five in Philadelphia. Funeral services were held at the Unitarian Church in that city, and she was buried in Eden Cemetery.

Frances Ellen Watkins Harper was a popular poet, speaker, and novelist. Because her poems were published in inexpensive paperback booklets, very few copies have survived. But her popularity is undoubted. *Poems on Miscellaneous Subjects* (1854), subsequently enlarged (1857), was reprinted many times; by 1871, with an introduction by William Lloyd Garrison, it was in its twentieth edition. *Moses: A Story of the Nile* (1869) was expanded in 1889 and became the major part of *Idylls of the Bible* (1901). *Poems* (1871), originally a small book, had grown to ninety pages by 1895. *Sketches of Southern Life* (1872) was enlarged in 1896. As for sales appeal, according to William Still who worked with Harper on the Underground Railroad, *Poems on Miscellaneous Subjects* and *Poems* had sold 50,000 copies by 1878. *Iola Leroy* (1892) went into three editions.

In her longer narrative poems Harper showed considerable ability. Certainly in the long, flowing lines from "Bury Me in a Free Land" there are reasons for the praise and the popularity she enjoyed: "Make me a grave wher'er you will, / In a lowly plain or a lofty hill; / Make it among earth's humblest graves, / But not in a land where men are slaves." Similarly, in *Sketches of Southern Life*, a story of Aunt Chloe and Uncle Jacob, the agricultural folk Negro is heard describing the slaves' reaction to freedom: "We just laughed, and danced, and shouted, / And prayed, and sang, and cried, / And we thought dear Uncle Jacob / Would fairly crack his side."

Vernon Loggins has written that however popular her poems were, they were sentimental and full of feeble echoes of those from whom she borrowed, particularly Henry Wadsworth Longfellow. Moreover, although she undoubtedly got closer to the reality of folk Negro life than any poet before Paul Laurence Dunbar, her *Sketches* were very uneven; in her attempt to mirror

Reconstruction life her lyrics narrated by Uncle Jacob were not as well constructed as those given to Aunt Chloe. On the other hand in *Moses* (1869), probably intended to be read aloud, she reached her peak. After an opening scene in which Moses tells the princess who has raised him that he must leave to lead his people out of Egypt, what seems to be a pseudo-dramatic form gives way to narrative—and the poem's form and content improve. In her most original verse Harper narrates the life of Moses. It is one of the few poems she wrote that did not deal with American Negroes. Note this description of the burial: "And when the grave was finished, / They trod with golden sandals / Above the sacred spot, / And the brightest, fairest flowers / Sprang up beneath their tread. / Nor broken turf, nor hillock, / Did e'er reveal that grave, / And truthful lips have never said, / 'We know where he is laid.' " And compare it with these imitative lines from the *Fifteenth Amendment*. "Ring out! ring out! your sweetest chimes, / Ye bells, that call to prayer and praise; / Let every heart with gladness thrill, / And songs of joyful triumph raise."

In 1892 she wrote for Negro Sunday School Youth *Iola Leroy, or Shadows Uplifted,* almost wholly the product of her reading *Clotelle* by William Wells Brown (1853), the first published novel by an American Negro after the Civil War and the first to deal with Reconstruction. Essentially a defense of the race, even an uplifting novel, *Iola Leroy* was concerned with an octoroon educated in the North who is sold as a slave after her white father dies and her mother's marriage to him is declared illegal. Sold into slavery in South Carolina, she finds her uncle, returns to the North with the help of black friends, becomes a nurse, and after refusing a serious white suitor, she marries a physician who could "pass" but chooses not to. According to Benjamin Brawley, "The book throbs with human interest" but is not well constructed and assumes a didactic tone near the end: for example, Harper writes, "From threads of fact and fiction I have woven a story whose mission will not be in vain if it awaken in the hearts of our countrymen a stronger sense of justice and a more Christlike humanity in behalf of those whom the fortunes of war threw, homeless, ignorant and poor, upon the threshold of a new era." The book, Hugh Gloster concludes, "is historically significant as an attempt to counteract stereotypes and as a transitional novel showing the shift from the slavery background to the Reconstruction setting." Sterling Brown adds that Iola "is another of the octoroon heroines too angelic for acceptance." In short, as a reflection of the period *Iola Leroy* is a valuable source, but it is not first-class literature.

In addition to William Still's *The Underground Railroad* (1872), see Hallie Q. Brown's *Homespun Heroines* (1926), Vernon Loggins's *The Negro Author* (1931), Benjamin Brawley's *Early Negro American Writers* (1935), pp. 290–92), Sterling Brown's *The Negro in American Fiction* (1937, pp. 76–77), and Hugh Gloster's *Negro Voices in American Fiction* (1948, pp. 30–31). There is also an excellent account with a comprehensive bibliography by Louis Filler in *NAW* (1971), pp. 137–38). — DANIEL WALDEN

HARRINGTON, HAMTREE [professional name for **JAMES CARL HARRINGTON**] (1889–1956), comedian, actor, and art enthusiast. His father, James Carl Harrington, Sr., was a rigid fundamentalist preacher. Of his mother little is known other than that she was an attractive woman of Indian origin. Young James, born in Columbia, S.C., was a spirited and imaginative boy who found the strict discipline of home and school more than he could bear. When barely fourteen he ran away from home to join a traveling carnival. Working as a roustabout he earned his keep by helping pitch tents and performing other assorted menial jobs. The work was hard but exciting, for there were always performers he could watch. In spare moments he would also sketch for his own amusement. With his natural aptitudes it was not difficult for James to learn the barber's trade, and although quite able thereafter to earn more as a barber than as a roustabout, the youth never abandoned his fascination for show business. During the early 1900s he carried both his trade and his love of the stage to New York City.

Small of stature, neat, and handsome, the personable young barber soon captured the heart of shapely Edna Murray, a chorus girl. She could outdance all the others on her chorus line and became an onstage showpiece in much the same way as her close chorus friend Josephine Baker. In James Carl Harrington, Edna Murray saw the makings of a good comic. The large eyes he used so naturally and effectively were made to order for the burnt cork pantomime artistry made popular by the great Bert Williams. As the first Negro to be featured in the legendary *Ziegfeld Follies,* Williams's superb stagecraft evoked the accolades of theater-goers. Edna wrote the script for Harrington, most of it pantomime. It featured the quaking, eye-rolling terror of the black comic figure walking alone through a graveyard in the dead of night. The theme delighted white Americans, and many Negroes also found it screamingly funny. Young Harrington's show business career was on its way up. Shortly thereafter Harrington won acclaim in another skit in which he stole a ham, hid it in a tree, and thereby earned the name by which he became so well known.

It was in June 1922 that Creamor and Layton's musical, *Strut Miss Lizzie,* reached New York via Chicago with Hamtree Harrington in the role of the blackface comedian. That same year Lew Leslie's *Plantation Revue,* starring Florence Mills, moved from a New York nightclub to the 48th Street Theatre. Again the comedy was handled by Harrington, who working under cork, was the perfect foil for the lady-like dancing and singing of Miss Mills. At the close of the show, vaudeville awaited the Harrington talents. He teamed with Cora Green, a stately, honey-colored singer from Baltimore. Again the exquisitely groomed loveliness of the singer against Hamtree Harrington's raucous blackface antics established the team of Harrington and Green as one of vaudeville's favorites. They captivated audiences in Europe and they worked this nation's foremost vaudeville houses along with Harlem's famed Cotton Club and Connie's Inn where the orchestras of Duke Ellington and Cab Calloway provided music.

For more than a decade fame and a measure of fortune came to Hamtree Harrington. But he was not completely happy. He found it degrading to work under cork as an eye-rolling, razor-wielding caricature of a black man. To offset the torment of his discomfort he turned to drawing and painting, which he did backstage between shows. He haunted the art galleries of every major city he worked in, and he cultivated friends among the gifted artists of Harlem where he lived. Among the latter was Archie Joseph Jones, a fellow comedian, whose exceptional talent for painting enabled him to exhibit with the Negro professional artists in a 1933 national show presented by the Harlem Foundation. Hamtree boosted Jones's ability and took pride in their close association.

During the early 1930s while in Baltimore, Harrington saw an exhibition of the then young local painter Elton Fax. The two met, liked each other, and Hamtree invited the younger man to visit with him and his family in New York. There they introduced the Baltimorean to Augusta Savage and her circle of friends in the arts.

Meanwhile the autumn of 1933 opened a memorable theater season for Hamtree Harrington. He and Ethel Waters were paired to do a satirical skit in *As Thousands Cheer,* one of America's all-time great musicals. Irving Berlin and Moss Hart wrote it and Marilyn Miller, Clifton Webb, Helen Broderick, and Ethel Waters were its stars. Opening at New York's Music Box Theater on Oct. 2, it enjoyed a long run. Hamtree performed his comedy in *Cheer* without cork, greasepaint lips, and all the other demeaning props he had been required to use in the past. He had finally emerged from his hated cocoon. Subsequent appearances in *You Can't Take It With You* and in a film *His Woman,* starring Gary Cooper and Claudette Colbert, gave him straight comedy to do. Just as he seemed to be finally free of the old tradition he fell victim to one of the ironies of progress.

Radio and budding television were replacing live shows. Vaudeville was dead and Hamtree read the signs accurately. Work fell off and he grew desperate. But vanity induced him to scorn and to refuse to seek work in the Works Progress Administration federally supported theater of the 1930s because he believed the low pay would ruin his reputation as a high-priced comedian. Hamtree therefore "retired" from show business in 1938 to open a photography studio in Harlem just above the famed Apollo Theater upon whose stage he had so often performed. But Hamtree was no businessman and he soon abandoned photography to return to the bit parts that were infrequently offered him. Younger black comics were on the rise and Harrington's star was descending. A copy of *Playbill* for *Shuffle Along* for May 8, 1952, lists him in the cast of this vain attempt to resurrect the bones of a long-dead and dated musical hit of the 1920s.

In 1956 Harrington, then past his middle sixties, made one more effort to rise to prominence. The U.S. government had signed him to travel with a unit booked to entertain troops in Europe and Asia. Every detail was completed except his medical approval. In New York City the examining doctor had shocking news: arteriosclerosis had reached an advanced stage and he could not approve Hamtree's joining the troupe. The aging performer was stunned. According to his son, Hamtree,

living in obscurity in Harlem, was dead in a matter of weeks.

The New York City Department of Health has no record of the death of James Carl "Hamtree" Harrington. Could it be that the proud little comic, down on his luck, had deliberately concealed his once well-known name behind a pseudonym until he could once again "lay-'em in the aisles" with a spectacular comeback? It is entirely possible.

There is no comprehensive biography of Harrington. The principal sources are *Variety* (June 29, 1938), *Playbill* (Feb. 6, 1939, for *Lew Leslie's Blackbirds of 1939;* Oct. 2, 1933, for *As Thousands Cheer*), *New York Herald Tribune* (Feb. 12, 1939), *Flash, Newspicture Magazine* (Feb. 15, 1939), *New York World-Telegram* (July 20, 1932). Hamtree's son, James Carl Harrington III, provided information about his father's work as a barber, his meeting with Edna Murray (the mother of James Carl Harrington III), and his breaking into show business. Young Harrington and Dick Campbell, prominent theater manager, verified "Hamtree's death." The collection on the Performing Arts in Lincoln Center Branch of the New York Public Library furnished the published materials. This contributor relied also upon his personal papers and reminiscences. — ELTON C. FAX

HARRIS, ABRAM LINCOLN (1899–1963), economist. The son of Abram Lincoln and Mary E. Harris, descendants of slaves freed before the Civil War, he was born in Richmond, Va. He earned his B.S. degree at Virginia Union University in 1922, his M.A. degree at the University of Pittsburgh in 1924, and his Ph.D. degree in economics at Columbia University in 1931 with a dissertation on "The Black Worker." His academic career included appointments to the faculties of West Virginia State College (1924–1925), at Howard University (1927–1945) where from 1936 to 1945 he was chairman of the department of economics, and the University of Chicago (1946–1963) where he was professor in the Department of Philosophy and the College. His academic career was interrupted only by service as executive secretary of the Urban League in Minneapolis (1925–1926). His research was supported by the Guggenheim and Charles Walgreen Foundations; he was awarded the LL.D. degree by Virginia Union University and the Quantrell Award for excellence in undergraduate teaching at the University of Chicago in 1961. He served on the Consumer Advisory Board of the National Recovery Administration in 1934 and on the Executive Committee of the American Economic Association (1959–1962).

Harris's early writings deal with problems of achieving social and economic equality, and in his two books, *The Black Worker, The Negro and the Labor Movement* (with Sterling D. Spero, 1931) and *The Negro as Capitalist* (1936), he provided an incisive analysis of alternative programs of reform. These were considered in the light of the new circumstances of massive migration from the rural South to urban industrial centers of the North during the First World War, the race riots that followed, the decline in Negro employment in industry that was gradual after the war, and then precipitous after the Crash in 1929.

Observing the election campaign of 1924 in which no party was committed to legislate programs of reform, he was skeptical of the first alternative, action for civil and political rights. He was particularly disaffected with the Progressives whose strength rested on unions that practiced discrimination in their own membership. His view of the futility of agitation for civil rights rested on the Marxian analysis of political power requiring a basis in economic status. But in any case Harris saw the Negro community, both the masses and the leaders, as very conservative in their political orientation and not susceptible to radical programs.

Second, he rejected the old economic program of Booker T. Washington on the ground that it was ill-suited to the emerging industrial economy where independent small businessmen and craftsmen were to play declining roles and where industrial training was futile in the face of hostility from white trade unions controlling access to jobs.

A third program for action looked to Negro business enterprise and the use of the consumer boycott as a device for bargaining with white merchants selling to the Negro community ("Don't Buy Where You Can't Work"). Harris rejected this strategy, arguing that since most of the white stores were family enterprises and hired no outside help, organized pressure might create more hostility than benefit, particularly among the whites displaced. "What would be more natural than a retaliatory movement of whites demanding that Negroes be employed only by those white capitalists whose income is mainly derived from Negro patronage. . . ? Nationalism, whether racial or otherwise, has never found, nor has it ever sought, validity in sheer economics." Black capitalism was an equally poor solution because, by and large, Negro enterprises were on too small a scale to compete efficiently (he studied Negro banks in detail in *The Negro as Capitalist*) and the cost of inefficiency was a heavy burden on the Negro masses who paid higher prices or lost their savings. The argument developed the concept of "racial tariff" levied by the Negro consumer on white products and merchants, and anticipated by twenty years its important introduction into economic theory.

It was the fourth program that Harris supported, a strong labor movement for practical goals, uniting black and white labor. His conclusion rests on the interests of both, and on the possibility that the white trade union leadership could be persuaded to act on these interests. This solution bore elements of Harris's early Marxist commitment and his lifetime commitment to universal goals.

After he received his Ph.D. degree he embarked on the first of a series of studies of economic philosophy that engaged his interest for the remainder of his career. Starting with institutionalism, Harris published articles on Veblen, Sombart, Commons, and Marx. Rejecting the reforms proposed by each, he turned to the liberalism of John Stuart Mill and found in it the program to which he could commit himself (*Economics and Social Reform,* 1958). There he wrote of Mill: "Progress consists not primarily in material improvement but in moral-aesthetic cultivation . . . innovations and social reform must . . . be effected within a framework of common

moral principles, loyalties and political obligations. . . . His philosophy upholds the ideal of a kind of classless society, that is, one in which all divisions except those of taste, interest, and ability are nonexistent." These words might as suitably be applied to Harris's philosophy.

In his last years he studied Mill's system where it could be tested, in the day-to-day recommendations and reports Mill made in his work for the East India Company. Harris published several articles on aspects of this study ("John Stuart Mill," *Canadian Journal of Economics,* 1964), but the book he was preparing was left unfinished when he died on Nov. 16, 1963, in Billings Hospital, Chicago. Funeral services were held in the University of Chicago's Bond Chapel on Nov. 19. He was survived by his widow, the former Callie McGuinn of Oakland, Calif., whom he had married June 6, 1925, a brother Jonathan, and a sister Madelyn.

Basic information is in *Who's Who in America.* There is an obituary in the *Chicago Tribune* (Nov. 17, 1963, p. 26). — ROGER WEISS

HARRISON, HUBERT HENRY (1883–1927), labor leader, editor, teacher, and author. He was born at Concordia, Danish West Indies (now St. Croix, U.S. Virgin Islands) on April 27, 1883, the son of William Adolphus and Elizabeth (Haynes) Harrison, both of Concordia. When he was sixteen he made a world tour as a cabin boy. The next year he settled in New York City and worked as a hotel bellman and telephone operator. He attended an evening school where his principal instructor, Hendrick Karr, noted that he passed the examination for the diploma at 100 percent, the only student of his class to achieve this mark. He worked for four years as a clerk in the post office, spending his leisure time studying history, science, sociology, psychology, and literature. Concluding that color prejudice was based on economic foundations, he became a Socialist and a contributor to "radical" magazines. From 1912 to 1927 he lectured to large crowds in downtown New York and in Harlem. In 1917, when he left the Socialists, he founded the Liberty League of Afro-Americans and established *The Voice* as its organ. He joined A. Philip Randolph and Chandler Owen, editors of the *Messenger,* in denouncing World War I. For a period Harrison was chief editor of the *Negro World* after W. A. Domingo had served in that capacity. (By that time Owen had become a virulent opponent of Garvey.) Appointed a staff lecturer by the Board of Education of New York City, he also gave several lectures at the City College of New York, at New York University, and was professor of comparative religion at the Modern School, later moved to Stelton, N.J. He gave a notable lecture on education in a chamber of the New York City Hall. He also gave a series of lectures on "World Problems of Race" for the Institute for Social Study in Harlem. He died at the Bellevue Hospital, New York City, where he had been taken for treatment of appendicitis.

Hubert Harrison was one of the more prominent "radical" leaders of the first quarter of the twentieth century. With such generally unpopular leaders as Bill Haywood, one of the organizers of the International Workers of the World, and Elizabeth Gurley Flynn he participated in leading a strike of silk workers in Paterson, N.J. (1912–1913). In a famous meeting at Bethel African Methodist Episcopal Church, New York City, on June 12, 1917, he introduced Garvey when the Liberty League was publicly launched. A resolution written by Harrison and adopted by an assembly of some 2000 people included the following significant statements: "a. We therefore ask, first that the similar rights of the 250,000,000 Negroes of Africa be conceded. . . . b. We invite the government's attention . . . to the continued violation of the 13th, 14th and 15th amendments, which is a denial of justice and the existence of mob-law for Negroes from Florida to New York."

Even as a supporter of Garvey and an editor of his *Negro World,* Harrison did not concur in the extreme views expressed at times by Garvey. Harrison emphasized the cultural interest in Africa and a limited return of skilled scientists and technologists who could contribute to African development. He finally urged deportation of Garvey.

A pioneer in nonconformist thought, Harrison wrote for such publications as the *Truth-Seeker,* the *Call,* the *Modern Quarterly,* the *International Socialist Review,* and was assistant editor of *Masses.* His editorials in *Negro World* were published in *The Negro and the Nation* (1917). A later and larger collection of his writings was entitled *When Africa Awakes: The Inside Story of the Stirrings and Strivings of the New Negro in the Western World* (1920).

Harrison's major influence, however, stemmed from his street orations during lunch hour in Wall Street, in Madison Square, and espeically evenings, first at West 96th Street off Broadway and later on Lenox Avenue. His critical views on religion, birth control, evolution, and social progress sometimes evoked hostility from hearers, when he and his supporters were compelled courageously to defend themselves. However, his ability to make complex subjects clear and simple, and the power of his logic and presentation gained him a hearing in some very difficult situations. It was race prejudice which Harrison encountered and perceived to be growing among several Socialist and labor leaders which caused him to decide that the Afro-American people could not depend on such leaders but must develop leaders of their own. His slogan of "Class First" and then of "Race First" did not give clear direction to his views, however.

Joel A. Rogers considered Harrison "one of America's greatest minds." William Pickens, winner of the Ten Eyck Prize for oratory at Yale University, wrote: "Here is a plain black man who can speak more easily, effectively, and interestingly on a greater variety of subjects than any other man I have ever met even in the great universities. . . . I know nothing better than to say than that he is a walking encyclopedia of current human facts."

He married Irene Horton who was born in Puerto Rico of English-speaking parents from elsewhere in the Caribbean. They had one son and four daughters: William Frances, Marion, Alice Genevieve, Aida Mae, and I'lua Henrietta, all born in New York City.

Of dark hue and medium height, with full lips, an ample nose, and a high rounded forehead, Hubert H. Harrison was not prepossessing but quite impressive. His sparse hair covered his head lightly and his high forehead seemed to make his head taller and add to his stature. His keen black eyes could almost transfix an opponent; when they opened slightly and his lips pulled up somewhat, then a withering blast was on its way. Although generally amiable and never pompous, he bore a reserved but pleasant mien, always bearing himself with conscious dignity.

There is no full-length biography of Hubert Henry Harrison. Biographical information is found in Joel A. Roger's *World's Great Men of Color* (1946, vol. 2). The statement of Harrison's views is based on his publications and on the reminiscences of R. B. Moore who frequently heard him lecture. Additional information was furnished by his children. — RICHARD B. MOORE

HARRISON, RICHARD B[ERRY] (1864–1935), actor. The eldest son of runaway slaves, Thomas and Isabella (Benton) Harrison, he was born in London, Ontario, Canada. Just before his seventeenth birthday his father died and Richard had to help support the family. His favorite employment was selling newspapers near the theater, where he made the acquaintance of visiting actors and devised ways to get into a gallery seat to watch performances. He won many school and church prizes for oratory and dramatic readings and gained some small local reputation for his impersonations of visiting actors.

His desire for theater training forced him to move to Detroit where he studied acting both in classes and privately. He was fortunate in having Edward Weitzel from the Henry Irving Dramatic School, London, England, as a private coach for over a year. Harrison developed a recital program of dramatic readings from Shakespeare and other English and American poets. In 1891 he had his first comprehensive one-man tour of the United States. Financial needs forced him to begin working on the railroad dining car service and he later became superintendent of mails for the Santa Fe Railroad in Los Angeles. In 1892 he was booked with the L. E. Behymer Lyceum Bureau (which later merged with the Great Western Lyceum Bureau) through 1896, playing schools, clubs, and the great Chautauqua circuit. He married Gertrude J. Washington, the first Negro graduate of Chicago Musical College, on Dec. 11, 1895. Paul Laurence Dunbar was his best man. The Harrison-Dunbar friendship had begun in 1893 when Harrison toured with Dunbar to promote Dunbar's book, *Oak and Ivy.*

By the end of the first decade of the twentieth century Harrison had gained a nationwide reputation in the Negro community as a dramatic reader and a skillful interpreter of Shakespeare. In connection with his Lyceum recitals, Harrison began to offer short training courses in the dramatic arts. Soon he came to see that the Negro college was the place to provide such training, and in 1922 he succeeded in persuading North Carolina Agricultural and Technical College at Greensboro to inaugurate a summer session for North Carolina teachers in the theater arts. In the early 1920s he had moved his family to New York where he continued his recitals, taught private students, and later spent part of each year at Greensboro. He was a full-time faculty member there when he went on leave in 1929 to accept the role of "de Lawd" in *Green Pastures,* after the Right Rev. Herbert Shipman, suffragan bishop of New York, convinced him that the role was not sacrilegious.

Green Pastures by Marc Connelly opened at the Mansfield Theater, New York City, on Feb. 26, 1930, played 557 performances there, and enjoyed a long road tour. All told, Harrison gave 1650 performances. One scene was particularly memorable. The Angel Gabriel announced: "Gangway! Gangway for de Lawd God Jehovah!" Harrison appeared dressed in the simple black suit of a Negro preacher. The distinguished critic Sterling Brown wrote that *Green Pastures* "was a miracle in the medieval sense of a biblical story presented upon the stage, and in several more important ways. . . . The frock-coat, fedora, and ten cent cigars are probably Marc Connelly's version of what Roark Bradford said was a Negro preacher's version of God, but the kindly, perplexed father of his people is like the God of the spirituals. If the play is not accurate truth about the religion of the folk-Negro, it is movingly true to folk life" *Negro Poetry and Drama* (1937, p. 119). *Green Pastures* won the Pulitzer Prize in 1930 and Richard Harrison was awarded the NAACP Spingarn Medal in 1931.

Exhausted, he died of heart failure at Fifth Avenue Hospital, New York City, on March 14, 1935. He was survived by his widow, a son Lawrence Gilbert, and a daughter Marian Ysobel.

For almost fifty years Harrison had been a reader of Shakespeare on the Lyceum circuit, a drama coach, a teacher, looking forward to the day he would play Shylock in a fully staged production of *The Merchant of Venice.* His only complete role came when he was sixty-six years old. W. E. B. Du Bois's citation for the Spingarn Medal stated: "The medal is given to Mr. Harrison not simply for his crowning accomplishment, but for the long years of his work as dramatic reader and entertainer, interpreting to the mass of colored people in church and school the first specimens of English drama from Shakespeare down. It is fitting that in the sixty-seventh year of his life he should receive widespread acclaim for a role that typifies and completes his work." Harrison's response expressed the hope that "all aspiring Negro youth [would] know that there is success for them in their own field if they will become prepared, have patience and determination to make their way."

In the May 1931 issue of *The Crisis,* Du Bois attributed the success of *Green Pastures* especially to its interpretation by Negro actors, and above all the high and delicate genius of Richard Harrison. Du Bois praised him for facing up without complaining to long years of "hunger and poverty. He has the high African gift of laughter. He, too, has looked at death and smiled."

Basic information is in *Who's Who in America* (1934–1935). Notable tributes were paid by Brooks Atkinson, "Quite a Proposition" (*Ladies Home Journal,* Sept. 1935) and in the *New York Times* (March 24, 1935). There is a sympathetic sketch by Edwin Francis Edgett in *DAB, Supplement One* (11, Part1:374).

— ANNE COOKE REID

HART, WILLIAM HENRY HARRISON (1857–1934), lawyer, civil rights leader, and founder of a farm for colored boys. He was born in Eufaula, Ala., the son of Henry Clay Hart and of Jennie (Dunn) Hart. His wife Mary and he had two daughters and a son. After walking to Washington, D.C., in the late 1870s as a poor youth, he received from Howard University a Preparatory Department Certificate (1880), his B.A. (1885), LL.B. (1887), M.A. (1889 with a thesis on the "Christian Tendency of International Law"), and LL.M. (1891). Hart served as a private secretary to Sen. William M. Evarts of New York from 1888 to 1891. He was appointed special assistant U. S. district attorney for Washington, D.C., in 1889. He was a member of the bar of all courts of the District of Columbia and the Supreme Court of the United States. From 1890 to 1922 he was a professor of law at Howard University where he taught criminal law, torts, corporations, and criminal procedure. Hart was an extremely bright and creative student as well as lawyer. In 1890 he was appointed to the Chair of Criminal Law. Walter Dyson referred to him in 1941 as "probably the most brilliant" alumnus of the Howard Law School (*Howard University . . .* [1940], p. 234). Hart also served as assistant librarian of Congress from 1893 to 1897, when he was appointed dean of the Department of Agriculture at Howard.

In addition to his legal career, Hart was a humanitarian, loyal alumnus, and musician. For example, in 1897 he founded on the banks of the Potomac River the Hart Farm School for Colored Boys and Junior Republic for Dependent Children, where some 200 wards learned the basics of rural education and farming. He was also instrumental in raising a considerable amount of the total cost of constructing a new Law Department Building for Howard in 1892–1893. His versatility is further demonstrated by his active part in producing theatrical plays in Washington, D.C., in the middle 1880s.

Graduates of the Howard Law School and the members of its faculty have been from its inception in the forefront of the fight to protect the constitutional rights of Negroes. Hart was one of the almost forgotten early activists in the civil rights movement. In *Hart v. the State of Maryland* (1905; 100 Md. 595, 60 Atl. 457), he won an important but little-known case against segregation in interstate travel. In that case Hart was indicted under a Maryland law requiring segregation on trains for refusing to occupy a car and compartment to which he had been assigned by the conductor of the train. He was an interstate passenger, having purchased a railroad ticket for an entire, continuous, and uninterrupted passage from New York City through the states of New Jersey, Pennsylvania, Delaware, and Maryland to the city of Washington. Hart was tried, convicted, and fined five dollars. From that judgment he appealed; on appeal the judgment was reversed in his favor and the conviction set aside. Since Congress had exclusive jurisdiction over interstate commerce, the Maryland segregation statute was invalid as to interstate passengers and had to be construed as not applying to them. This case was decided nine years after *Plessy v. Ferguson* in which the Supreme Court had for the first time enunciated the doctrine of "separate but equal." However, segregation was still legally permitted in railroad cars which were in intrastate travel, and in practice maintained in interstate travel.

On the other hand his rather violent temper got him into many quarrels, one of which led to his separation from Howard University. He ended his contract with the district government for the maintenance of his farm school over a trivial technicality, and entered an unsuccessful suit for several million dollars, declining, it was reported, an offer of $100,000 for settlement.

The encomium of Charles H. Houston is therefore all the more significant: "Professor Hart left the law school before my time, but I have always heard that he was a teacher of great force and ability, and had more influence with the students than any teacher of his day. . . . Professor Hart was a colorful figure, a man of great courage and determination. He was widely read, a gifted conversationalist, and, in his prime, a forceful orator. He is one of the cornerstones upon which the work of the Howard University Law School is built."

Lonely and almost forgotten, he died in Brooklyn, N.Y., on Jan. 17, 1934, and was buried without religious ceremony in Harmony Cemetery, Washington, D.C.

Some of the basic facts about Hart are in *Who's Who in America* (1912–1913). His career at Howard University is discussed briefly in Walter Dyson's *Howard University . . .* (1940) and Rayford W. Logan's *Howard University . . .* (1969). See also *The Afro-American* (Jan. 13 and 20, 1934), and the obituary in the *JNH* (April 1934, pp. 211–13). — CHARLES EDWARD DONEGAN

HAWKINS, JOHN R[USSELL] (1862–1939), educator, church administrator, and university trustee. He was born in Warrenton, N.C., the son of Ossian and Christiana (Eaton) Hawkins, who were lifelong members of the African Methodist Episcopal church. His wife Lillian M. Kennedy, who predeceased him, was the granddaughter of Richard Allen, one of the founders of the African Methodist Episcopal church. He was educated at the high school in Warrenton, Hampton Institute, and Howard University (LL.B., 1915). He taught in the public schools of Warren County, N.C. (1878–1880), and served as principal of the Warrenton graded school (1880–1882). From 1882 to 1884 he was a railway mail service clerk. In 1887 he was appointed business manager and instructor at Kittrell College, N.C., becoming president of the college (1890–1896). Like many other college presidents of the era, he had to travel extensively, accompanied by his wife, to obtain financial support for the college. In 1896 he was elected at the General Conference of the A.M.E. church as commissioner of education, later designated secretary of education. In 1912 he was elected financial secretary of the A.M.E. church, a position he held until his death in 1939. During these years he was also a trustee and fiscal agent of Wilberforce University, Wilberforce, Ohio; a trustee (1925–1939) and member of the Executive Committee of the Board of Trustees, Howard University; and an associate trustee of all the schools of the African Methodist Episcopal church. He was a life member of the Association for the Study of Negro Life and History, its president from 1921 to 1932, and presi-

dent of the Prudential Bank, Washington, D.C. (later the Industrial Bank of Washington). A staunch Republican, he was chairman of the Colored Voters Division of the National Republican Committee in 1928.

His office as financial secretary of the A.M.E. church, at 1541 14th St. NW, was a hub of activity in promoting civil rights for Negroes. Sometime after 1918 he presented to the Washington branch of the NAACP fourteen points, paralleling President Wilson's fourteen points for world peace, which alone could give meaning to the word "democracy" in the United States.

He was one of the Executive Committee of Howard University who voted unanimously to recommend (June 30, 1926) for the presidency of Howard Bishop John A. Gregg of the A.M.E. church, former president of Edward Waters College in Jacksonville, Fla. He had previously stated, at the board meeting of March 25, 1926, that "all his life" he had hoped that he would never have to consider the question of the presidency of Howard University on the basis of race, creed, or color. He hoped that the board would not commit itself to a decision that the next president had to be colored. "But under the circumstances, the most inspirational act on the part of the Trustee board . . . should be to find a colored man who would fit into this place. It would be a source of inspiration to the students to aspire to leadership." He preferred a "composite type" of trained educator and inspirational leader for the presidency. After Bishop Gregg declined the presidency, the board voted unanimously on June 30, 1926, that Mordecai W. Johnson be elected president.

In 1925 Howard University conferred upon Hawkins the honorary degree of Master of Arts.

There is no comprehensive biography of Hawkins. Basic facts are in *Who's Who in Colored America, 1933–1937*, and an obituary in *JNH* (Oct. 1939, pp. 489–91), probably written by Carter G. Woodson. For his activities as a member of the Board of Trustees of Howard University and its Executive Committee, see Rayford W. Logan's *Howard University: The First Hundred Years, 1867–1967* (1969). Hawkins was a joint editor with Richard Robert Wright of the valuable *Centennial Encyclopedia of the A.M.E. Church* (1916). He was the author of a pamphlet, *What Does the Negro Want? Fourteen Articles as a Basis for Democracy at Home* (n.d.). — RAYFORD W. LOGAN

HAYDEN, LEWIS (1815?–1889), Underground Railroad operator, abolitionist, state legislator, and Boston race leader. He was born about 1815 (John Daniels, *In Freedom's Birthplace*, 1914) in Lexington, Ky., the slave of a Presbyterian minister. His mother was "of mixed blood, white and Indian"; his father worked in a bagging factory. When Lewis was quite small his father's master moved away and his mother was bought by a man who wanted her for a mistress; when she refused him, he so ill-treated her that she became intermittently insane, attempted suicide, and in one of her fits threatened Lewis's life. Lewis's owner eventually sold all his brothers and sisters at auction and traded Lewis for a pair of carriage horses.

Probably in his late teens Lewis married fourteen-year-old Harriet, who belonged to another master, and by her had three children, one of whom died in infancy while another was sold off "nobody knows where." He early developed a longing for freedom but rejected an opportunity to escape to Ohio because he saw no way of taking his family along. In September 1844, however, Lewis, Harriet, and their ten-year-old son escaped with the aid of the recklessly daring abolitionists Calvin Fairbank and Delia Webster, teachers in Lexington, who conveyed them by hack and ferry to an Underground Railroad station in Ohio, from which they were forwarded to Canada. Fairbank and Webster, on their indiscreet return to Lexington, were arrested for slave stealing but Fairbank agreed to plead guilty on condition that his associate be pardoned and was sentenced to fifteen years' imprisonment.

The Haydens lived in Canada for about four years and then in Detroit, where Lewis established a school for colored children, raised funds to build a colored Methodist church, and engaged in antislavery preaching. He also raised $650 to pay the Haydens' owners, on condition that they would petition the governor of Kentucky to pardon Fairbank, who was released on Aug. 23, 1849. Probably during this period he also acquired something of an education, but that he also found time for "stirring up a slave insurrection in Louisiana" is unconfirmed and doubtful.

Late in 1849 or early in 1850 the Haydens moved to Boston; the Boston directory for 1849–1850 listed Hayden as "lecturer." However, the 1850–1856 directories showed him as operating a clothing store on Cambridge Street. His native intelligence and forceful, daring character speedily won him a position of leadership among the 2000 Negroes who constituted 1½ percent of Boston's population, while white abolitionists soon came to regard him as the colored community's principal spokesman. Although his appearance, temperament, and behavior were calculated to inspire respect rather than affection—he has been described as "a tall, austere, dark man, rather grim and silent"—he was well liked. He was one of the five Negro members of the 207-man Boston Vigilance Committee, organized on Oct. 14, 1850, to resist the new severe Fugitive Slave Act. His house at 8 (later 66) Southac St. (afterward 1865 Phillips St.) was the chief Boston "station" of the Underground Railroad, where during the 1850s hundreds of fugitives found refuge.

The earliest and most famous of those fugitives were William Craft and Ellen Craft. When they learned that their owner was sending agents to arrest them, William Craft put his "white" wife with a white family and took refuge in the Hayden house, which Lewis not only barricaded but also mined with two kegs of gunpowder so that as a last resort he could blow up both house and assailants. Before leaving for England the Crafts were formally married in the Hayden home by the Rev. Theodore Parker, before a distinguished company.

The following year Hayden demonstrated his capacity for daring, decisive action. When on Feb. 15 a fugitive known as Shadrach was arrested and rushed to the courthouse, a crowd of Negroes, headed by Hayden and Robert Morris, an attorney, stormed into the building, swept up Shadrach, and carried him away. Hayden then got the fugitive to a friendly house, obtained a carriage, and with a friend drove him to Concord, from which he was safely forwarded to Canada.

Hayden, Morris, and several others were arrested but were released on bail, while many other participants fled to avoid prosecution. Consequently, when on April 3, 1851, Thomas Sims, another fugitive, was arrested and put under such heavy guard that he could not possibly be freed save by an attack in force, a sufficiently large body of militant Negroes was unavailable—as Hayden informed the Rev. Thomas Wentworth Higginson, who was one of the few white members of the Vigilance Committee then prepared for such overt and violent action. Nothing was done on Sims's behalf and he was duly returned to slavery. However, when the accused in the Shadrach case came to trial, they were ably defended by John P. Hale and Richard H. Dana, Jr., and none was convicted. On June 16, 1851, the Hayden jury, despite very strong evidence against him, declared that it could not reach a verdict and the case was dropped.

Later in 1851 Hayden and several other Negroes petitioned the Massachusetts legislature to erect a monument in memory of Crispus Attucks, the Negro (probably also part Indian) who was one of the victims of the so-called Boston Massacre of 1770. Hayden and other "operators" also continued quietly with their work, and when Harriet Beecher Stowe visited the Hayden home in 1853 she found thirteen fugitives under its roof.

The comparative peace on the Boston front was broken on May 25, 1854, when the fugitive slave Anthony Burns was arrested and confined in the courthouse. This time the more militant members of the Vigilance Committee, headed by Higginson, were quietly permitted to take over and decided on a mass attack on the courthouse, spearheaded by a select contingent of fifteen whites and ten Negroes recruited by Hayden. The affair, however, was mismanaged and Higginson, Hayden, and only a few others found themselves confronting the locked doors of the courthouse. Nevertheless they battered a door partly ajar with a beam and thrust themselves inside. A wild and confused melee ensued during which Higginson was severely clubbed; Hayden, in his defense, fired a shot which narrowly missed Marshal Freeman, and one of the deputies fell fatally stabbed. The would-be rescuers—outnumbered—were forced out of the building and Burns, like Sims, was eventually shipped South. Curiously, although several other leaders of the attack were arrested—but eventually discharged because of a faulty indictment—Hayden was not one of them.

The Burns tragedy was, however, in retrospect, the darkness preceding the dawn. Although Hayden and others continued to protect and forward refugees, Burns was the last fugitive arrested in Massachusetts. Moreover, the following year the Boston schools were desegregated—an event celebrated on Dec. 17 by a meeting at which Hayden was a speaker.

Hayden's personal fortunes experienced similar fluctuations. During 1850–1856 he had a clothing store on Cambridge Street but in 1857 and 1858 was operating out of his residence. On July 1, 1858, however, the new Republican state administration appointed him a "messenger" in the office of the secretary of state—a position which although humble afforded him a better income and more security.

Hayden's relations with John Brown are confused and obscure. He later claimed to have enlisted half a dozen colored men for Brown's mysterious enterprise but none of them actually participated. He did, however, indirectly make a decisive contribution. Early in October 1859 he somehow learned that Brown was in or near Chambersburg, Pa., desperately in need of money for his "war chest," and so informed the idealistic young abolitionist Francis Jackson Meriam, who hastened south with several hundred dollars in gold, which induced Brown to attack immediately. Without Meriam's contribution the enterprise would have been delayed indefinitely and might have been entirely abandoned—with incalculable but certainly important effects.

The election to the governorship of Massachusetts in 1860 of the staunchly antislavery John A. Andrew meant a great deal to Hayden and the Negroes of Massachusetts. The "poor man's lawyer" and the humble Statehouse employee had somehow become close friends. Hayden, it is alleged, had first suggested that Andrew—then a legislator in his first term—run for governor. After the outbreak of war Hayden, according to Andrew himself, suggested that slaves should be considered "contraband of war," sometime before Gen. Benjamin E. Butler made the expression well known. And Hayden always claimed credit for having urged the governor to organize a regiment of colored volunteers. At the Thanksgiving dinner which the governor ate with the Haydens in 1862, the raising of such a regiment was probably a principal subject of discussion.

Governor Andrew immediately after the Emancipation Proclamation obtained permission to raise colored troops in Massachusetts but encountered unwillingness among Boston Negroes because of the provision that the commissioned officers should be white. Andrew consequently authorized the abolitionist George Luther Stearns to recruit in the West and in Canada. He was accompanied by Hayden, who was of great service—as were other Negro recruiting agents—in bringing the Massachusetts colored regiments up to fighting strength. But the son who had escaped with his parents from Kentucky slavery enlisted in the navy and died fighting under Admiral Farragut.

Immediately after the war his great interest was in the advancement of Freemasonry among Negroes. He visited Virginia and South Carolina for the purpose of establishing lodges, and in several speeches, published 1868–1871, he defended Masonry, attacked the principle of restricting membership to whites or the freeborn, and in particular asserted the validity of the Prince Hall Lodge, the Negro Masonic lodge in Boston of which he was the grand master for a good many years. He was also concerned with temperance and women's rights. In 1873 he was elected to the Massachusetts legislature. Another source of satisfaction was the appropriation in 1888 by the city and state of funds for the monument to Crispus Attucks which he and other Negroes had urged thirty-seven years earlier.

In 1889 Hayden became ill and for months stoically suffered great pain. His principal concern, as his wife revealed to the veteran abolitionist Dr. Henry I. Bowditch, was the mortgage which still hung over his house. The physician immediately formed a committee which raised enough money to liquidate all his debts and leave $1500 for investment. Hayden was thus relieved of anxiety; relief from pain came on April 7. An immense crowd was present at Lewis Hayden's funeral. The secretary of state represented Massachusetts as one of the pall bearers. The secretary of state in whose office Hayden had worked declared: "If he had had an opportunity for early educational advantages, he would have been one of the foremost statesmen of America. He never did anything for policy or from selfish motives." His widow survived him until Dec. 24, 1893. In her will she left some $5000 to Harvard College for a scholarship for poor and deserving colored students, preferably in medicine.

Hayden left no autobiography and no complete, documented life is available, although N. P. Hallowell's *The Lewis and Harriet Hayden Scholarship* (1893), and Henry I. Bowditch's *Life and Correspondence* (vol. 2, 1902), attempted brief, reminiscent sketches which are not always trustworthy. For his early life to his arrival in Boston the principal contemporary authorities are Harriet Beecher Stowe's *A Key to Uncle Tom's Cabin* (1853) and Calvin Fairbank's *How the Way Was Prepared* (1890); for Underground Railroad days, see Thomas Wentworth Higginson's *Cheerful Yesterdays* (1898), Austin Bearse's *Reminiscences of Fugitive Slave Days in Boston* (1880), Archibald H. Grimké's "Anti-Slavery Boston" (*The New England Magazine* 3 (Dec. 1890); for his connection with John Brown, see Frank B. Sanborn's "The Virginia Campaign of John Brown" (*Atlantic Monthly* 36 (Dec. 1875); for his recruiting activities, see Frank Preston Stearns's *George Luther Stearns* (1907). Lewis Hayden's publications on Freemasonry were *Caste among Masons* (1866); *Grand Lodge Jurisdictional Claims; or, War of Races* (1868); *Masonry among Colored Men in Massachusetts* (1871).

Secondary works which sometimes include details not found in the above are Wilbur H. Siebert's *The Underground Railroad* (1898), John Daniels's *In Freedom's Birthplace* (1914), Benjamin Quarles's *Black Abolitionists* (1969) and *The Negro in the Civil War* (1953), and Walter J. Stevens's *Chip on My Shoulder* (1946). — KENNETH WIGGINS PORTER

HAYNES, GEORGE EDMUND (1880–1960), social scientist and leader in religious programs and social work education for Negroes. The older of two children of Louis and Mattie (Sloan) Haynes, he was born in Pine Bluff, Ark. His hardworking, poorly educated, but devout parents shared the lot of the majority of Negroes of the day, being supported by the mother's low wages in domestic service and the father's income as an occasional laborer. Haynes's early elementary education was acquired in the environs of Pine Bluff at a time when education, especially for Negroes in their segregated schools, was rudimentary. After exhausting the educational resources there, Haynes and his sister Birdye were taken by their mother to Hot Springs, Ark. The education he received in this larger, more cosmopolitan city was probably an improvement over that available in Pine Bluff, but perhaps a larger gain was the opportunity for contact with a more structured Negro community which afforded some leadership in education, religion, and other professional fields.

Young Haynes was inspired and supported by his mother who imparted to her children strong religious and moral ideals, and urged upon them the attainment of as much education as possible as the best avenue of escape from poverty and discrimination. With his own innate and strong ambition, and his inquiring mind, he responded eagerly to suggestions for self-improvement. Consequently when one of his employers in Hot Springs, a white physician, told him of institutions where Negro youth could pursue higher education, he set such a goal for himself. Still another inspiration to young Haynes was an opportunity to visit the Chicago World's Fair in 1893. During this experience Haynes observed his first example of racial solidarity and heard discussions on contemporary issues affecting Negro life, especially the questions of migration and emigration. Even at this early age when he was hearing arguments that the best solution to the "Negro problem" was emigration to Africa where the Negro could build his own society unhampered by the roadblocks of prejudice and discrimination, he determined that such was not the path for him. He believed firmly that equity and justice could be achieved by interracial cooperation in America. This belief was to be demonstrated in his later writings and activities.

Exposure to the stimulating social and intellectual life of Negro Chicago in the late nineteenth century intensified his ambition for further education. On return to Arkansas, aided and encouraged by his mother, he was admitted to the Agriculture and Mechanical College at Normal, Ala. Here he had a year of courses in Latin, geography, general history, bookkeeping and arithmetic review, and the Old and New Testaments. After the year at the Alabama school, he transferred to the academy at Fisk University where he completed preparation for college. His college years at Fisk, where he received his B.A. degree (1903), reinforced even more firmly the strong moral force which his mother had supplied all his life. At Fisk he was greatly impressed also by the selfless dedication of the white New Englanders on the faculty. Haynes achieved an outstanding academic record at Fisk, on the basis of which he was admitted to Yale Graduate School where he earned an M.A. degree (1904).

In 1905 Haynes began what was to become a remarkable career in promoting sound race relations and interracial social work. As he entered upon his first professional employment, as secretary of the Colored Men's Department of the International YMCA, Haynes saw an opportunity to bring moral and spiritual leadership to young college students while at the same time encouraging attainment of superior educational records and commitment to betterment of social and economic conditions among Negroes. During 1905–1908 he traveled through the South, visiting virtually all of the Negro colleges.

It was during these years of college work that Haynes met Elizabeth Ross, whom he married on Dec. 14, 1910. Elizabeth Ross was engaged at a somewhat later period in similar work with Negro college youth as the first Negro national secretary of the YWCA, assigned to work largely among the Negro colleges and with Negroes in cities. An energetic, highly intelligent, and talented woman, she had earned a B.A. degree at Fisk in 1903, and had studied at the same professional schools as her husband. Her activities in social welfare were very compatible with those of her husband.

As Haynes worked with Negro youth in the YMCA, he felt a need for broader knowledge, especially in economics and sociology. In 1906 and 1907 he enrolled in summer sessions at the University of Chicago. After moving to New York City, he entered the New York School of Philanthropy (later the New York School of Social Work of Columbia University) from which he graduated in 1910 as the school's first Negro graduate. In 1912 Haynes became the first of his race to be awarded the Ph.D. degree (in economics) from Columbia University. In his continued pursuit of advanced education, Haynes was fortunate in the quality of educational and social leadership to which he was exposed. In Chicago he had come into contact with, among other prominent social reformers, Sophonisba Breckinridge and Jane Addams; at Columbia he was under the tutelage of Edward T. Devine, director of the School of Philanthropy, and Edwin R. A. Seligman, noted economist at the university.

Haynes's years at Columbia coincided with a period of marked concern about problems of rapidly increasing urbanization, emigration, and migration. During the first decade of the twentieth century Negro migration to the cities, especially in the North, were matters of major importance to Negro and white social scientists, social workers, and social reformers. Among agencies seeking to combat the adverse effect of the overwhelming movement of population to New York City were three in which Haynes soon became involved: the Association for the Protection of Colored Women (1905), the Committee for Improving the Industrial Conditions of Negroes in New York (1906), and the Committee on Urban Conditions among Negroes (1910). The first of these, the Association for the Protection of Colored Women, was an organization stimulated by the outrage of intelligent and educated women (both black and white) over the exploitation of uneducated, poor Negro women seeking better wages and working conditions in northern cities. They were easy prey for unscrupulous white and black "agents" of questionable employment agencies. Living conditions for these women were indescribable and they were often led into houses of prostitution. An instigator and active participant in the association was Frances Kellor, a lawyer who had also studied sociology and economics at the University of Chicago, and social work at the New York School of Philanthropy. In New York she became a close associate of Mrs. William H. Baldwin, Jr., co-founder with Haynes of the National Urban League. Prominent Negro women, among them Victoria Earle Matthews (a founder) of New York and Mrs. Willie S. Layten of Philadelphia, were leaders in organizing branches of the association and expanding its work to other port cities. Especially through Kellor and Baldwin, Haynes was drawn into this movement, contributing scholarly studies and proposing improved methods of carrying on the activities.

The second of the forerunners of the National Urban League, the Committee for Improving the Industrial Conditions of Negroes in New York (CIICNNY), found many of the same people involved and included more Negro men. Activities of the committee did not cease with attempts to secure employment but included investigations into the numbers of skilled Negro workers in the city, attitudes of white employers and labor unions toward providing jobs for them, similar duties with regard to Negro women, survey of pertinent laws, and plans for protection of the legal rights of workers. In addition there was recognition of concerns such as need for trade schools and social centers. The committee developed a close working relationship with the Association for the Protection of Colored Women.

These developments occurred during the days of Haynes's graduate study in New York. He had met with Ruth Standish Baldwin (Mrs. William H. Baldwin, Jr.) and Frances Kellor for discussions of the urgent need for social work among Negroes in New York. At the same time Haynes held a research fellowship at the Bureau of Social Research of the Charity Organization Society. Out of his work in these two assignments Haynes conceived the theme for his doctoral dissertation, "The Negro at Work in New York City," which was published in 1912 by Columbia University Press. The study probed the mass migration of Negroes to New York and its causes and effects. Haynes later made similar studies in other parts of the country. Haynes therefore became a ready and eager collaborator when Baldwin and other members of the CIICNNY began to consider the need for expansion of the committee's program beyond industrial concerns and into other geographic areas. Faced with rejection of their first proposal for expansion of CIICNNY, Baldwin and Haynes created a new committee called the Committee on Urban Conditions Among Negroes, which at first centered its attention on conditions of Negroes in New York. In 1910 it became the National League on Urban Conditions among Negroes.

About the same time that Haynes undertook the work of executive secretary of the new committee, he was offered an appointment at his alma mater, Fisk University. Encouraged by Dr. Devine of the New York School of Philanthropy, Haynes developed a creative program to combine the objectives of serving the masses of disadvantaged Negroes and training Negro social workers to meet their needs. To this end he established the educational and training program at Fisk and included a carefully structured component of practice which was to be carried out in the offices and branches of the Committee on Urban Conditions among Negroes. Thus in 1910–1911 the National Urban League was born. From the first the organization had active leadership and assistance of an outstanding group of both Negroes and whites. Although there were others who lent strong support, Haynes and Baldwin are credited with actually bringing the Urban League into being.

As the work of the National Urban League expanded rapidly and financial support did not keep pace, it was increasingly difficult for Haynes to carry effectively the dual responsibilities of leadership of the league and development of his department at Fisk. He was succeeded in 1917 as executive secretary by Eugene Kinckle Jones, and his major role with the league was terminated in 1918 when he moved into an important post in the U.S. Department of Labor. Technically on leave of absence from Fisk University (1918–1921), Haynes became a special assistant—with the title of director of Negro economics—to the secretary of labor. Critical labor shortages during and immediately following World War I resulted in recruitment of Negro workers in unprecedented numbers. Such activity accelerated the migration of Negroes to industrial centers, especially in the North, and led to intensified racial conflict, particularly in employment, housing, and recreation. Branches of the National Urban League (which had expanded greatly during this period) were frequently called upon to help resolve conflicts and to supply support and leadership to the migrants in their adjustment to new living conditions. Many of the personnel responding to this demand were social workers trained by Haynes at Fisk.

During his service in the Department of Labor, Haynes applied his scholarly talents to surveys, analyses, and recommendations for improving the conditions of Negroes in the cities. One of these studies was *The Negro at Work During the World War and During Reconstruction* (1921). This and other studies had such significant impact on the activities of the government that Haynes was invited to membership on the President's Unemployment Conference. Haynes also continued his active concern with churches and their obligation to promote interracial cooperation. In 1921 he directed a survey of Negro churches which included examination of religious life in the Interchurch World Movement. That same year he became one of the organizers and the first executive secretary of the Department of Race Relations of the Federal Council of the Churches of Christ in America. He continued in that capacity until 1947. Searching for the appropriate vehicle to combine moral or religious commitment with practical implementation, Haynes developed the concept of the Interracial Clinic. He conceived of this as a mechanism to deal with racial tensions and other conflict situations arising after World War II. His Interracial Clinics, forerunners of some later community organization techniques, were used successfully in many American cities. During his service with the Department of Race Relations, Haynes also originated Race Relations Sunday.

While on leave from his position with the Federal Council of Churches in 1930, Haynes conducted a survey of the work of the YMCA in South Africa. This was followed in 1947 by another survey of programs in other African countries and proposed programs for the activities of the YMCA. These undertakings brought him into international prominence and from 1948 to 1955 he served as a consultant on Africa for the World Committee of YMCAs. Even in these retirement years Haynes remained actively involved in academic pursuits and efforts for improvement of race relations. He served as a member of the Temporary Commission to Study the Need for a State University in New York, and became a member of the Board of Trustees when the university was established in 1948, continuing to serve through 1953. For approximately nine years prior to his death in 1960 Haynes taught courses at City College of the City University of New York, including "Negroes in American History and Culture," "Principles and Methods of Interracial Adjustment," and "Africa in World Affairs."

Haynes served on numerous boards, commissions, committees, and in many conference groups at national, state, and local levels. Haynes was also a prolific and convincing writer. In addition to the publication of his doctoral dissertation, *The Negro at Work in New York City* (1912), he was the author of *The Negro at Work during the World War* (1921), *The Trend of the Races* (1929), and *Africa, Continent of the Future* (1950). He twice co-authored the article on the American Negro in the *Encyclopedia Britannica* (1929 and 1941–1942). He was also a contributor to the *Social Work Yearbook* and many professional journals in the fields of sociology and social work. Moreover he was also an active member, often among the founders or charter members, of emerging organizations in social work, education for Negroes, and promotion of understanding and advancement of opportunities for the race. In recognition of his exceptional career Fisk University conferred upon him its Alumni Award in 1959.

After the death of his first wife Elizabeth Ross Haynes in 1953, Haynes married in 1955 Olyve Love Jeter, daughter of a Newport, R.I., clergyman. One child, George Edmund Jr., was born of the first marriage. In both marriages Haynes was fortunate to find mates who shared his interests and helped further his work. The second Mrs. Haynes was indefatigable in collecting and preserving his manuscripts and other works, and established the George Edmund Haynes Collection at Yale University. Other Papers are in the Erastus Milo Cravath Library, Fisk University.

Two comprehensive, scholarly, and well-documented books contain excellent accounts of Haynes's career: Nancy J. Weiss's *The National Urban League, 1910–1940* (1974), and Guichard Parris's and Lester Brooks's *Blacks in the City: A History of the National Urban League* (1971). See also Daniel Perlman's "Stirring the White Conscience: The Life of George Edmund Haynes" (doctoral dissertation, New York University, 1972). The National Urban League Archives (1910–1965), consisting of correspondence, files, papers, board meeting minutes, and memoranda, donated by the NUL, are in the Manuscript Division of the Library of Congress. — INABEL BURNS LINDSAY

HAYNES, LEMUEL (1753–1833), soldier, Congregational minister, and first Negro recipient of an honorary M.A. degree. Born in West Hartford, Conn., Haynes believed that his father, whom he never knew, was of "unmingled African extraction"; his mother was a white woman of respectable ancestry in New England who later refused to recognize him. He did not know who gave him his name. When he was five months old he was bound out in Granville, Mass., as a servant until he was twenty-one. His master, Deacon Hill, a man of great piety, taught him the principles of religion; his

mistress treated him as if he were their child. While working on Deacon Hill's farm, Lemuel attended public school and remained an avid reader the rest of his life, especially of the Bible and other religious books. Since the parish lacked a minister, he was called upon to conduct church services and read a sermon; and so he read one of his own.

When his period of indentureship ended in 1774, he enlisted as a Minute Man, joined the army at the siege of Boston, and in 1776 marched to Ticonderoga where he fought under Ethan Allen and the Green Mountain Boys in capturing the fort from the British. Returning to Granville, he declined an offer to study at Dartmouth College. In 1779, however, he began studying Latin and then Greek under white pastors. He translated the New Testament in the original and taught school after hours. In the fall of 1780 several ministers, after a rigid examination, recommended him as qualified to preach. He delivered his first sermon to a white congregation in Granville and in 1883 married Elizabeth Babbit, a young white schoolteacher of the town. Of their ten children three sons were known to be living—one a farmer, one a physician, and the third a law student in Massachusetts. In 1785 Lemuel Haynes was officially ordained a minister in Litchfield County, and filled a pulpit in Torrington, Conn. From then until his death in 1833 he preached to white congregations, notably in Rutland, Vt. (1788–1818), later in Manchester, Vt., and during his last eleven years as an itinerant pastor from Granville in New York City, Albany, and Troy, N.Y.

He became one of the more widely known Congregational ministers of his era. His fame derived in part from his color. A member of his congregation in Torrington deliberately kept his hat on when Haynes first began to preach and then removed it because the sermon made Haynes appear the *"whitest* man" he had ever seen. Some members of that congregation remained, however, unconverted. Later, his biographer recalled, other constituents accepted the "inspired expression, 'I am black, but comely.'" While he did not flaunt his color, he seems to have spoken only once on race and in condemnation of slavery. In *The Nature and Importance of True Republicanism* (1801) he addressed the question of the "pitiful, abject state" of the "poor Africans among us." The "God of nature" was not responsible. He argued that "Nay—but being subjected to slavery, by the cruel hands of oppressors, they have been taught to view themselves as a rank of beings, far below others, which has suppressed in a degree, every principle of manhood, and so they become despised, ignorant, and licentious."

He became more widely known because of his fervent advocacy of other causes. For instance he favored a strong national government under Pres. George Washington. He attacked the Jeffersonian defense of the quasi-war (1798–1800) with "atheistical France." He opposed the War of 1812, but denounced the secession of New England, which had wide support and which led to the end of his pastorate at Rutland.

His involvement in the case of Russell Colvin (1820) reads almost like a modern detective story. In 1813 Colvin disappeared from Manchester, Vt., and years later two brothers of his wife were sentenced to be hanged for the "murder." Haynes became convinced of their innocence, but apparently to no avail. Thirty-seven days before the alleged murderers were to be hanged, Colvin showed up. Haynes's sermon *Mystery Developed* discussed religion and prison conditions along with a review of the case. The pamphlet is said to have been a bestseller for a decade.

His international fame rested on his disputation with Hosea Ballou, a famous champion of the doctrine of universal salvation. Haynes's rejoinder, *Universal Salvation, A Very Ancient Doctrine,* accused Ballou of falsely believing in heaven for all and hell for none. On the other hand Haynes opposed such freethinkers as Thomas Paine and supported such conservatives as Jonathan Edwards.

He reaped several honors. In 1804 Middlebury College, Vt., conferred upon him the first honorary degree of Master of Arts bestowed on a colored American. As a delegate of the General Convention of Ministers in Vermont, he attended the meeting of the General Association of Connecticut at Fairfield. He preached in the Blue Church of New Haven, where Pres. Timothy Dwight of Yale University and others were greatly impressed by his learning and eloquence.

The epitaph on his tombstone reads: "Here lies the dust of a poor hell-deserving sinner, who ventured into eternity trusting wholly on the merits of Christ for salvation. In the full belief of the great doctrines he preached while on earth, he invites his children, and all who read this, to trust their eternal interest on the same foundation."

Carter G. Woodson wrote about Haynes: "Of illegitimate birth, and of no advantageous circumstances of family, rank or station, he became one of the choicest instruments of Christ. His face betrayed his race and blood, and his life revealed his Lord" (*The History of the Negro Church* [1921], p. 65).

The fundamental biography of Haynes is Timothy Mather Cooley's *Sketches of the Life and Character of the Rev. Lemuel Haynes . . .* (1837). There is an excellent brief summary in Sidney Kaplan's *The Black Presence in the Era of the American Revolution, 1770–1800* (1973, pp. 102–8). On page 84 there is a reproduction of a painting of Haynes in the pulpit by an unidentified artist (ca. 1800–1820) in the Museum of Art, Rhode Island School of Design. The honorary degree of Master of Arts was confirmed by a letter from Marion E. Holmes (registrar, Middlebury College, March 10, 1977). His sermon *Universal Salvation* is in *Early Negro Writing, 1760–1837,* edited and introduced by Dorothy Porter (1971, pp. 448–54).

— RAYFORD W. LOGAN

HEALY, ELIZA [SISTER MARY MAGDALEN] (1846–1918), teacher and convent superior. She was born of a white father, Michael Morris Healy, and his mulatto slave Eliza Smith, on a Georgia plantation near Macon on Dec. 23, 1846. Like her brothers, later Bishop James Healy, Fr. Patrick Healy, and Capt. Michael Healy, and her oldest sister Martha, she spent her early childhood years in Georgia. Her father, conscious of the state law prohibiting his emancipation of any children of a slave mother, planned to sell the plantation in 1850 and

move north where he had already sent six of his ten children. Eliza's mother died suddenly in May 1850; her father died in August, leaving three children orphaned in Georgia, Eliza, her year-old sister, Amanda Josephine, and the youngest brother, Eugene. The executors of the estate sent the children to New York. There they were cared for by their older brother Hugh, who had graduated from Holy Cross College in Worcester, Mass., in 1849. He was working for the New York executor, John Manning.

Eliza, her brother Eugene, and Amanda Josephine were baptized as Catholics in the Church of St. Francis Xavier in New York on June 13, 1851. They were kept for a while by the family with whom Hugh boarded. In September 1851 Hugh transferred the girls to the care of the Notre Dame sisters in St. Johns, Québec. Martha Healy had joined the sisterhood as a novice in the same summer. After finishing her elementary education, Eliza enrolled in Villa Maria, Montréal, where she graduated just before the outbreak of the Civil War. In 1861 both Eliza and Amanda Josephine, returning from Montréal, joined Eugene in the foster family of Thomas Hodges and his wife in their home on East Springfield Street in Boston. In 1864, shortly after Martha left the convent to rejoin the family, Fr. James Healy bought a home for the family in West Newton, nine miles from the heart of the city. There Eliza stayed for a dozen years.

During the years in Boston and Newton, Eliza Healy watched the developing career of her brother, Fr. James Healy, as he moved from his initial position as assistant to Father Haskins in the Boys Home to become the secretary to the bishop, first chancellor of the diocese, rector of the cathedral, and pastor of St. James Church, the largest in Boston.

Father James, in turn, took care of all the family matters. He managed the settlement of the estate in Georgia in which Eliza shared. He handled the buying of his Aunt Nancy out of slavery for $1400, to which Eliza contributed part of her share of the estate.

In January 1868 Eliza Healy accompanied Father James together with Amanda Josephine and their foster mother, Mrs. Hodges, on a trip to Europe and Asia Minor. They saw Gibraltar and the Sierra Nevada mountains in Spain as well as the beauties of the Mediterranean. They spent two weeks in Smyrna, visited Messina in Sicily and Naples, saw Vesuvius in eruption, and visited Palermo before returning home.

Family fortunes were heavily damaged by the Panic of 1873. Many of the investments which Father James had held for the family vanished in the crash. In 1874, shortly before her brother became bishop of Portland, Me., Eliza entered the novitiate of the Congregation of Notre Dame in Montréal to pursue her career as a religious nun and teacher. Entering at the age of twenty-eight, she received the habit of the Sisters of Notre Dame on Dec. 22. After two years in the novitiate she made her profession in 1876, taking her vows of poverty, chastity, and obedience. Her final vows were taken in 1882.

Having completed her college and normal school work in preparation for a teaching career, Eliza, now called Sister Mary Magdalen, was assigned to teach at St. Patrick's School in Montréal. Later she taught at St.

Anthony's School and at other Catholic schools in Brookville and Ottawa in Ontario, and at Sherbrooke and Huntington in Québec (1895–1897). At Huntington she was appointed superior of the community of French Canadian nuns. She rescued the school from debt and restored its operation to normalcy. In 1898 she was transferred to the Mother House in Montréal where she served as directress of English studies. From 1900 to 1903 she taught in the congregation's Normal School in Montréal.

In 1900 Sister Mary Magdalen made two trips, one joyful, one sad, from Montréal to Portland, where her brother was winding up a brilliant career as bishop of the diocese that comprised the entire state of Maine. He celebrated his twenty-fifth anniversary as bishop in June 1900, where he shared the honors with his sister Eliza and her brother, Fr. Patrick Healy. In August 1900 Bishop Healy died of a heart attack. Sister Mary Magdalen returned for the funeral.

Sister Magdalen's longest term of service and most significant achievements were during the period 1903–1918 when she was superior of Villa Barlow at St. Albans in Vermont. This distinguished finishing school, named after the Hon. Bradley Barlow of St. Albans, was attended by the daughters of upper-class New England families. The convent and the school were in somewhat straitened circumstances when she assumed responsibility. As the principal or headmistress of the school and superior of the convent, she manifested a remarkably energetic leadership akin to that which her brothers had exerted in Boston and in Washington. She restored the religious vigor of her community of nuns, revitalized the school, and remodeled and refurbished the buildings.

Her strength and skill earned the respect of both the parish and the diocesan officials as well as her community and her pupils. Sisters of the congregation who worked beside her were impressed by her long hours of prayer in the chapel, her ability to move from that into vigorous work at the many tasks that had to be done, and her strict observance of the discipline and good manners which she required of sisters and pupils alike.

After fifteen years as superior of Villa Barlow, Sister Mary Magdalen was missioned to the College of Notre Dame on Staten Island where she served as superior for the last year of her life. Her final illness was brought on by an injury she sustained when her arm was caught in a laundry room wringer at the start of the school year. She had twenty-eight stitches taken in the arm. An infection set in, causing a malignancy for which she was treated unsuccessfully. She finally succumbed to cancer in 1918, at the age of seventy-two.

Sister Mary Magdalen is mentioned as a minor character in the biography of her brother, *Bishop Healy: Beloved Outcaste,* by Albert S. Foley, S.J. (1954, 1969). She is treated at greater length in "Slavery and the Vermont Clergy" by Henry G. Fairbanks (*Vermont History* 27 [Oct. 1959]: 305–12). — ALBERT S. FOLEY, S.J.

HEALY, JAMES AUGUSTINE (1830–1900), the first Negro Catholic priest and bishop in the United States. He was born on a Jones County, Ga., plantation between Macon and Atlanta on April 6, 1830. He was the first son of an Irish father, Michael Morris Healy, and a mulatto slave mother Mary Eliza Smith, related to Ellen Smith Craft, the wife of the famous abolitionist ex-slave William Craft. The first of a family of ten children born of this common-law union, James Healy was deemed by Georgia law to be a slave, whose freedom could be granted only by an act of the legislature. To emancipate his son, his father took young James to Flushing, Long Island, in 1837 for enrollment in a Quaker school. In 1844 he and his brothers were transferred to the Jesuit College of the Holy Cross in Worcester, Mass. There he received his bachelor's degree in 1849 and his master's degree in 1851.

Deciding to become a Catholic priest, James Healy enrolled in the Grand Seminary in Montréal in 1849. He transferred to the Sulpician Seminary in Paris in 1852, and was ordained to the Catholic priesthood there in the Cathedral of Notre Dame on June 10, 1854.

Incorporated into the diocese of Boston by Bishop John Fitzpatrick, James Healy served as his secretary and chancellor. He was pastor of the Cathedral of the Holy Cross during the Civil War. In 1866 he was appointed pastor of the largest church in Boston, St. James, where he served for nine years. He built the large basilica-type church on Harrison Street, a monument to his resourcefulness and impeccable taste. He ruled the Irish congregation by the persuasiveness of his eloquence and the sincerity of his holiness.

In the wider arena of civic life, Father Healy became the bishop's deputy for social action. He played a decisive role in the development of the Home for Destitute Catholic Children, in the establishment of the House of the Good Shepherd, and in promoting and financing the St. Ann's Foundling Home, which grew out of the children's ward of Carney Hospital.

Active also in the organization of the first Catholic Union of Boston, Father Healy worked closely in conjunction with the leaders of that militant group to secure redress of the grievances of immigrants whose rights were violated by public officials. Boys ensnared by the law for petty delinquencies, poor folks sent to the state institutions on Boston Harbor's Long Island and elsewhere, orphans assigned by the court to non-Catholic families, even to farmers far out in the western states, and sick persons immured behind hospital walls that excluded priests and church ministrations, were all objects of Father Healy's solicitude. He appeared before the boards of directors of the public institutions, pleading that the clergy be allowed to minister to their inmates. His persistence finally won out when, in 1875, the first breaches were made in the Protestant strongholds and Catholic religious services were allowed in public institutions.

Father Healy achieved fame as an orator for the special occasions in church life in Boston. He spoke at church dedications and assemblies, such as that of the first great Catholic Festival in the Boston Music Hall in 1874. He also appeared before a special committee in the Statehouse, to champion the immunity of the church from taxation. He vindicated the right of the church to be considered a public benefactor by reason of the social welfare works which it undertook, thus saving the state hundreds of thousands of dollars each year.

In 1875 Pius IX named James Healy bishop of Portland, Me., to head a diocese comprising Maine and New Hampshire. For twenty-five years he administered the diocese, building more than sixty churches, eighteen schools, an equal number of convents and welfare institutions, and caring for a Catholic population of approximately 96,000. He became the most outstanding Catholic orator of New England. Because of his social work on behalf of the widows and children of the Civil War dead, his building of orphanages and foundling homes, and battling against the abuse of child labor, he became known as "The Children's Bishop."

To the other poor, Bishop Healy was also a benign patriach. He was remembered as a friendly prelate whose activity bore more resemblance to that of a busy parish priest than to that of an aloof bishop. He came to know most of his cathedral parishioners by name. They brought to him their complaints and woes. Many of the faithful were recent Irish immigrants who worked along the docks as longshoremen, or in the small industries and shops of the port city as day laborers, toiling from seven to seven every day for nine dollars a week. Healy often paid the overdue taxes of the poor, took care of doctor bills for the sick, and hurried to the aid of widows in their distress. He was pictured as riding through their neighborhoods on his spirited horse with his saddlebags filled with provisions for the destitute.

On the national scene Healy ranked high among the Catholic prelates of the last quarter of the nineteenth century. At the Third Plenary Council of Baltimore in 1884 he made an important series of contributions to the settling of some of the issues that confronted the Catholic church in the United States. He moved with ease and equality among his fellow bishops. He proposed at least three major pieces of church legislation which won approval by the assembly. He was appointed to the commission that planned and carried through the establishment of the Catholic University of America in Washington, D.C. He also served actively as a member of the permanent commission for Negro and Indian Missions set up by the council.

Because of his mixed racial ancestry his way was not easy in a southern city like Baltimore, or in Washington, Norfolk, and New Orleans which he visited on occasion. He encountered racial slurs and discrimination. He was opposed often as a Catholic prelate operating in a predominantly Protestant state. His records show, however, that he was accepted loyally by the hundreds of white priests who served under him without regard for his color. They respected him as one of the outstanding churchmen of New England who had successfully directed the destinies of the larger diocese of Boston for a score of years before becoming their bishop. They knew of his high standing among the other bishops, his close friendship with Archbishop John Williams of Boston, Bishop Matthew Harkins of Providence, and James Cardinal Gibbons, the archbishop of Baltimore who often came to Portland as Healy's guest.

Internationally he was a personal friend of both Pope Pius IX and Pope Leo XIII. The latter appointed him an assistant at the papal throne, just one step below the cardinalate. At his alma mater, Holy Cross, one of the buildings was named in his honor, as were other institutions in Maine. In more recent years schools as far away as St. Louis, Mo., were named for him.

Healy died of a heart attack in Portland, Me., on Aug. 5, 1900. Funeral exercises were conducted in the cathedral church in Portland with interment at the Catholic cemetery just outside of Portland. He was survived by his brothers Capt. Michael A. Healy and Fr. Patrick Healy, S.J., as well as by Sister Mary Magdalen (Eliza Healy), and Eugene Healy.

His biography, *Bishop Healy: Beloved Outcaste* (1954), has been reprinted in the New York Times–Arno Press series *The American Negro: His History and His Literature* (1969). A shorter summary is entitled "Pioneer Priest and Prelate: James Augustine Healy" in the first chapter of *God's Men of Color* by the same author, Albert S. Foley (1955; also reprinted in the Arno Press series). He is also mentioned in William L. Lucey's *The Catholic Church in Maine* (1957).

— ALBERT S. FOLEY, S.J.

HEALY, MICHAEL AUGUSTINE (1839–1904), naval officer and author. He was born on Sept. 22, 1839, the sixth child and fifth son of an Irish immigrant father Michael Morris Healy, and Mary Eliza Smith, a slave on his plantation in Jones County, Ga., seven miles north of Macon on the east bank of the Ocmulgee River. In order to emancipate the nine-year-old Michael, the father sent him in 1848 to join his older brothers, James and Patrick, at Holy Cross College, Worcester Mass. In 1854, reaching the restless age of fifteen, Michael Healy ran away from school to become a cabin boy. His brothers brought him back in 1855 and sent him to school in Montréal. A year later he ran away a second time. Returned to his family, he was sent to school in Douai, Belgium, where he again took French leave. The older brothers, in charge of the family since the death in 1850 of both the parents, decided to let Michael follow his attraction to a seafaring career.

When the Civil War broke out, Michael Healy was in Australia. In 1865 he entered the U.S. Revenue Cutter Service, the forerunner of the present Coast Guard. He saw duty as a junior officer and commander aboard the cutters *Reliance, Vigilant, Moccasin, Active,* and *Rush.* His first major command was the *Thomas Corwin* in which he cruised up and down the North Pacific, the Arctic, engaging in spectacular rescue operations and in pioneer explorations of hitherto unknown territory in Alaska. In 1884 and 1885 he published *The Cruise of the Corwin* reporting these explorations.

In 1886 Healy was assigned to command the famous cutter *Bear,* which had participated in the rescue of the Greeley party marooned near the North Pole two years previously. Healy took command of the *Bear* in New York and sailed it to San Francisco. Thus began the most impressive phase of his career as the main federal law enforcement officer in the waters around the new territory of Alaska. He was federal marshal, revenue officer, grand jury, judge, and chief warden for law-breakers in the remote costal villages of Alaska and on the high seas. In association with Sheldon Jackson, a Presbyterian missionary, Healy engineered the transportation of many herds of reindeer from Siberia to Alaskan shores to help the native Eskimo faced with starvation because of the loss of their seal hunting and other sources of food supply.

His career was as stormy as the Arctic seas. Because of the ruthlessness of his suppression of mutinies against other captains whose crews rebelled against them, Healy was court-martialed for excessive cruelty to seamen in a widely publicized series of trials in 1889, 1891, and 1896. He was convicted and broken to the bottom of the list of captains for conduct unbecoming an officer.

Healy was later called back into service to rescue shipwrecked whalers in the frozen north where no other captains would venture during the fogbound and icebound winter months. For his courage and fearlessness above and beyond the call of duty, Healy won citations from the federal government and from many private organizations.

He was given subsequent command of other Revenue Cutter vessels, including the *McCulloch,* the *Seminole,* the *Thetis,* and the *Chandler.* He was retired from active service on account of age on Sept. 22, 1903. He died of a heart attack at San Francisco on Aug. 30, 1904, and was buried in the Holy Cross Cemetery there. He was survived by his widow, Mary Jane Roach Healy, and by the only son surviving of the eighteen children born to the couple.

Michael Healy was a flamboyant, "Sea-Wolf" type who earned the soubriquet "Hell Roaring Mike" for his achievements in the Barbary Coast bars when his vessel returned to San Francisco after a hard tour of sea duty in the frozen north. He was generous with his wealth and with the profusion of his sailor-type language. He was remembered in Coast Guard circles as one of the most colorful of the captains in that service.

At the end of his life Healy was ranked seventh on the list of captains in the U.S. Revenue Cutter Service. He was regarded as a typical seadog captain of the old school—rough, gruff, fearless, pitilessly stern in discipline, with an impeccable and rigid sense of justice. To the native Eskimo he was a legend. In their villages when they were asked "Who is the greatest man in America?" their answer was "Why, Mike Healy. He is the United States. He holds the power here for the whole country."

In his personal life Healy was a self-made, self-educated man who read voraciously and wrote voluminously. His four-volume diary would probably have been a classic if it had not been destroyed by fire. He was bigger than life aboard his ship, towering above his crew only when he stood on the poop and gave orders. He was of medium height with a strong military figure, well built but not portly. He could display the most uncommonly agreeable manners. He ordinarily carried his grog with the agility of a Parisian dance master. Notable exceptions occurred when his seventy-five-hour tours of duty in the crow's nest navigating his ship through the ice packs of the north gave him occasion to thaw out too rapidly with the brandies he fancied.

He diverged quite noticeably from the religious tradition of his family and especially from his brothers in the Catholic clergy, Bishop James Healy, Jesuit Father Patrick, and Fr. Sherwood Healy, a Boston pastor, as well as from his two sisters who were nuns. He nevertheless

took his brother Patrick on a therapeutic summer vacation tour aboard the cutter *Bear* in 1883. He even took his wife on these summer tours, with the permission of the department.

Tradition has it that he was one of the sea captains used as a model by Jack London in his famous novel *The Sea Wolf.* Some of the fictional Captain Larsen's complications were observable in Healy and led to the bizarre and complicated court-martial that marred his otherwise impressive career.

He is featured prominently in histories of the Coast Guard such as that by Stephen H. Evans, *The United States Coast Guard, 1790–1915: A Definitive History, With a Postscript 1915–1949* (1949); in William Bixby's *Track of the Bear* (1965); and in Polly Burrough's popular book *The Great Ice Ship Bear: Eighty-Nine Years in Polar Seas* (1970). — ALBERT S. FOLEY, S.J.

HEALY, PATRICK FRANCIS (1834–1910), the first Negro Jesuit and the first Negro to earn a doctorate and to become president of a Catholic institution of higher education (Georgetown University, Washington, D.C.). He was born, like his brothers, on a Jones County, Ga., plantation of an Irish father, Michael Morris Healy, and a mulatto slave mother, Mary Eliza Smith. For seven years after his birth on Feb. 27, 1834, he was reared in the family loghouse. He was then sent to join his brothers in a Quaker school at Flushing, Long Island, N.Y. Along with his three other brothers, James, Hugh, and Sherwood, Patrick was transferred to Holy Cross College, Worcester, Mass., in 1844. He received his bachelor's degree in 1850. Upon deciding to enter the Jesuit order that same summer, he enrolled in the novitiate at Frederick, Md., for the two years of training. He taught at St. Joseph's College in Philadelphia and at Holy Cross College for the next six years.

In 1858 he was sent to Rome to continue his ecclesiastical studies, but before the end of the school year he was transferred to Louvain, Belgium, where he completed his course of philosophy and theology. He was ordained to the Catholic priesthood by Bishop Lamont in Liège, Belgium, on Sept. 3, 1864. He stayed on another year at Louvain studying for a doctorate in philosophy, which was awarded him after his final examination on July 26, 1865. The next ten months were spent as a final period of prayer and spiritual training at the tertianship in Laôn, France.

In 1866 Healy returned to the United States to assume the post of professor of philosophy at Georgetown University. There he pronounced his final vows as a Jesuit on Feb. 2, 1867. In 1868 he was made dean of the college; in 1869 he became vice-president of the university. Four years later, on May 24, 1873, Healy was appointed vice-rector of Georgetown upon the death of his predecessor, Fr. John Early. He served as acting president for ten months. He was officially confirmed by Rome, and inaugurated as president on July 31, 1874.

Upon completion of his six-year term as president, Healy was given a two-year extension, resigning his post for reasons of health in 1882. He subsequently served as assistant pastor at St. Joseph's Chruch in Providence, R.I. (1891–1894), and at St. Lawrence Church (later St. Ignatius Church) on Park Avenue and 85th Street in New York (1895–1906). He was spiritual father at St. Joseph's College in Philadelphia (1906–1908), when he was transferred back to Georgetown for the final two years of his life in the infirmary. He passed away peacefully and was buried almost within the shadow of his great monument on the campus, the Healy Building, on Jan. 10, 1910. He was survived by his sister, Eliza Healy (Sister Mary Magdalen).

Healy's greatest achievements are associated with Georgetown University and with the imposing structure on the heights above Georgetown that is visible up and down the Potomac River. He set out to transform the small, antiquated Georgetown College into a modern university housed in splendid Belgian Gothic like that of his alma mater, the University of Louvain. His first three years were spent in planning the big main building at Georgetown, linking Old North, the original brick building which George Washington had visited, and Old South, which faced the Potomac. The Healy Building was begun in 1877 and was substantially completed before the end of his term as president.

In the modernization of the university Healy added academic achievements to match his construction of the physical plant. He was instrumental in establishing closer ties with Georgetown Law School and Medical School to constitute them as corporate parts of the expanding university. He regularly presided both at the college commencement exercises and at the Law School exercises and at those of the Medical School until he arranged for a joint graduation ceremony for all three schools as integral parts of the university.

During these years Healy was also well known for other activities. He was on terms of close friendship with Presidents Andrew Johnson, Rutherford B. Hayes, and Ulysses S. Grant, and other prominent Washingtonians who visited or sent their sons to Georgetown University. He knew the chief justice and associate justices of the U.S. Supreme Court, as well as other prominent jurists in metropolitan Washington. He invited them to the university for lectures, formal appearances, and as judges for oratorical contests. He assisted in negotiating treaties concerning Indians. As head of the Catholic Commission on Indian Affairs he aided Bishop Elloy of the Navigator Islands and conferred with officials of the federal Bureau of Indian Affairs on behalf of missionaries working among Catholic Indians. In addition Healy was on friendly terms with prominent ecclesiastics, among them James Cardinal Gibbons when the prelate was archbishop of Baltimore.

In these public relations activities, he possessed many assets, especially a commanding presence. Besides his officiating and his regular assignments within the college, Healy was constantly on the go to fulfill speaking engagements in the city. He often preached at Trinity Church in Georgetown, at St. Ann's in Tennalytown, St. Stephen's, St. Matthews, St. Peter's, Immaculate Conception Church, and also the Negro Catholic Church of St. Augustine's near the White House, at 15th and L Streets. Both for the laying of the cornerstone of the New St. Augustine's Church on June 14, 1874, and for the dedication of the same church on June 11, 1876,

Healy was invited and accepted the position as assistant to the archbishop.

In academic circles in the District of Columbia, Healy also moved with ease and ready acceptance. Although there is no record that he visited Howard University, he worked closely with the president of Columbian College, the future George Washington University. When some congressmen introduced bills to tax religious and educational institutions in Washington, Healy personally went to Capitol Hill and lobbied successfully against the measures.

Healy is the subject of a full-length unpublished biography by Albert S. Foley, "Dream of an Outcaste." A summary is in his *God's Men of Color* (1955, 1970), Chapter 3, "Georgetown's Second Founder."

— ALBERT S. FOLEY, S.J.

HEMINGS, SALLY (1773–1835), alleged slave mistress of Thomas Jefferson.

Sally was the youngest daughter of John Wayles, Jefferson's father-in-law. Her mother was Elizabeth Hemings, daughter of an African slave and a British sea captain named Hemings. "Betty" Hemings, who became Wayles's mistress after the death of his third wife, and who had already borne six children by a slave, bore Wayles six more. When Wayles died in 1773 the entire Hemings family became the property of Martha Wayles Jefferson, and moved to Monticello in 1775. Nothing is known of Sally's childhood. As a young adult she was called "Dashing Sally," and was described by one slave as "mighty near white," "very handsome," with "long straight hair down her back."

When Jefferson went to France in 1785 he took only his eldest daughter Martha. When the youngest, Lucy, died in Virginia, Jefferson requested that his second daughter, Mary (Polly), be sent to Paris with a middle-aged slave woman who had had smallpox. Instead she was accompanied by Sally Hemings. She was given a modest salary and apparently tutored in French along with her brother James, Jefferson's valet. There is subtle evidence in Jefferson's journals, letters, and account books to indicate that in 1788 the forty-five-year-old widower, lonely after the return to London of his intimate artist friend Maria Cosway, fell in love with the blooming young quadroon, half-sister to his dead wife. Madison Hemings, Sally's third son, in an important but long-neglected memoir, reported that his mother became Jefferson's "concubine" in Paris, and that when he was called home, Sally was *"enceinte* by him." Since by French law she was free, Sally refused to return until Jefferson promised that he would free all her children at twenty-one. A son was born shortly after her return to Monticello in December 1789.

When the scandalmonger journalist James Thomson Callender learned from Jefferson's neighbors about Sally Hemings, and exposed the story in the *Richmond Recorder* of Sept. 1, 1802, he said that the slave mistress by then had had five children by Jefferson. Her oldest son, "Tom," he said, was "ten or twelve years of age," and had features bearing "a striking resemblance to those of the president himself." Jefferson's *Farm Book* (published in 1953) indicates that Sally had borne two daughters, Harriet and Edy, in 1795 and

1796, during Jefferson's temporary retirement. Both had died in infancy. A second son, Beverly, had been born on April 1, 1798, and a daughter, also named Harriet, in May 1801.

Although Jefferson's friends denied Callender's exposé, Federalist editors, hoping to discredit Jefferson with the electorate, republished it widely, along with bawdy ballads lampooning "Long Tom" and "Dusky Sally." Despite anguished requests from Republican editors, Jefferson never specifically repudiated the story, although he did complain privately about the venality of the Federalist press, which was also accusing him, falsely, of atheism, mishandling of funds, and cowardice during the Revolution.

The scandal did not damage him in the election of 1804; he won all but two states. He did not send Sally Hemings away from Monticello, but there is some evidence that the eldest son, Tom, left Monticello about this time. He seems to have been one of the four Monticello slaves described by Jefferson's white granddaughter, Ellen Randolph Coolidge, as "white enough to pass for white," who were permitted to leave under the euphemism of "running away." Sally Hemings bore two more sons, Madison, on Jan. 19, 1805, and Eston, on May 21, 1808. Madison Hemings wrote that Jefferson, although "uniformly kind to all about him," was "not in the habit of showing partiality or fatherly affection to us children. . . . We were," he said, "the only children of his by a slave woman. He was affectionate toward his white grandchildren, of whom he had fourteen."

Sally's children lived in "the great house," and did only light work such as running errands till age fourteen, when they learned a trade. "We were free from the dread of having to be slaves all our lives long," Madison wrote, "and were measurably happy. We were always permitted to be with our mother, who was well used. It was her duty, all her life which I can remember, up to the time of our father's death, to take care of his chamber and wardrobe, look after us children and do such light work as sewing, &c."

Madison also wrote that his brother Beverly and sister Harriet passed into white society and married whites "in good circumstances." This would hardly have been possible without some education and financial aid. Edmund Bacon, white overseer at Monticello, related that Jefferson ordered him to pay Harriet's stage fare to Philadelphia and give her $50. "There was a great deal of talk about it," he wrote. "She was nearly as white as anybody and very beautiful. People said he freed her because she was his own daughter." Bacon blamed an unknown white man for Harriet's paternity, but one should note that he did not become overseer till 1806, five years after Harriet's birth, and never lived in "the great house."

Jefferson's early zeal for emancipation changed to apathy, and it is possible that his entrapment in the Virginia slave society, which severely penalized public acknowledgment of miscegenation, contributed to his ever-deepening certainty that the problem would have to be solved by a generation after his own. Virginia slave laws became so repressive that Jefferson could not free Sally Hemings without seeing her banished from the state unless he specifically petitioned the Virginia legislature. He arranged to free their two remaining sons, Madison and Eston, in his will, but left Sally's emancipation to be discreetly arranged by his daughter Martha Randolph after his death in 1826.

In 1827 Sally Hemings appeared on the official slave inventory as worth $50. Freed in 1828, she moved into a small house near Monticello with her son, who, although listed as white on the Albemarle County Census of 1830, chose to marry mulatto women and stay in the Negro community. The census describes his family by age and sex only. Under his name is listed a woman, fifty to sixty years old, described as white. This is Sally Hemings. So the census taker, in making this small descriptive decision, underlined the irony and tragedy in her life.

Sally Hemings died in 1835 at sixty-two. No sketch or portrait remains, and the place of her burial is unknown. If she wrote letters, they have disappeared, although letters from her brothers to Jefferson are extant. Madison Hemings moved to Ohio, remaining in the Negro community. Two of his sons fought on the Union side in the Civil War, one dying in a Confederate prison. His youngest daughter, Ellen Wayles, moved to California. Her oldest son, Frederick Madison Roberts, became the first Negro elected to the California state Assembly, serving from 1918 to 1934. Eston Hemings moved to Wisconsin in 1852, where he assumed the name Jefferson. His two sons fought in the Union Army as whites; John Wayles Jefferson became a lieutenant-colonel, and later a banker and cotton broker in Memphis, Tenn. Beverly Jefferson became a prominent hotel owner in Madison, Wisc.

For the first detailed account of Jefferson and Sally Hemings see the *Richmond* (Va.) *Recorder* (Sept. 1, 1802). Articles and ballads thereafter peppered the press until 1805. Fawn M. Brodie's *Thomas Jefferson, an Intimate History* (1974) gives the most comprehensive account of Sally Hemings's life. Her Appendix I reproduces the important memoir by Madison Hemings, and a corroborating memoir by another former Monticello slave, Israel Jefferson, both of which had appeared originally in the *Pike County* (Ohio) *Republican* (March 13, Dec. 25, 1873). Appendix III reproduces Henry S. Randall's description of an interview with Thomas Jefferson Randolph concerning Sally Hemings and her children, first published in Milton E. Flower's *James Parton, the Father of Modern Biography* (1951, pp. 236–39). See also Ellen Wayles Randolph Coolidge to Joseph Coolidge (Oct. 24, 1858), published for the first time in the *New York Times* (May 18, 1974), and later in Brodie's *Jefferson* (pp. 498–500).

Letters mentioning Sally Hemings in the *Papers of Thomas Jefferson* (edited by Julian Boyd and others, 1950) include descriptions by Abigail Adams, (11:502, 503, 551, 574), also mention of her in a letter by Mary Jefferson (16:xxi) and by Thomas Jefferson (15:433 and 18:29). Expenditures for Sally Hemings's clothes and other items appear in Jefferson's Paris account books. There are many references to "Sally" in his *Farm Book* (1953). Martha Jefferson Randolph reported the death of Sally's daughter Harriet, and the illness of her son

Tom (Jan. 22, 1798) in a letter to Jefferson; see *Family Letters,* edited by Edwin M. Betts and James A. Bear, Jr. (1966, p. 153). Scrapbooks compiled by Eston Hemings's sons, Beverly Jefferson and John Wayles Jefferson, in the library of the University of California at Los Angeles, give important data about Jefferson's descendants through this son.

For a discussion of the view that Sally Hemings never was a mistress of Thomas Jefferson, see Dumas Malone's "Appendix II, The Miscegenation Legend," *Jefferson the President, First Term, 1801–1805* (1970).

— FAWN M. BRODIE

HENSON, JOSIAH (1789–1883), clergyman, conductor of fugitive slaves, abolitionist, businessman, soldier, and the "Uncle Tom" of Harriet Beecher Stowe's *Uncle Tom's Cabin.* Henson was born a slave, one of six children, on a farm in Charles County, Md. His intractable father, sold to a planter in Alabama when Josiah was young, was not heard of again. His mother was owned by a Dr. Josiah McPherson, a kindly man who gave the lad his first name and the surname of McPherson's uncle who had served in the Revolutionary War. Shunted from one master to another, Josiah was so efficient in his own work and in inducing other slaves to work hard that he was made "manager" of the Isaac Riley plantation in Montgomery County, Md. As a salesman of produce in Georgetown and Washington, Josiah came under the influence of an antislavery white man, whose devout Christianity influenced Josiah to become a preacher to the slaves. In protecting his owner, given to excessive drinking, he was once so brutally beaten that he could not thereafter raise his hands to his head. In 1825 he led a group of slaves to the plantation of his master's brother in Davies County, Ky. There he served as "superintendent" for three years, became a successful preacher, and was recognized by the conference of the Methodist Episcopal church.

After many vicissitudes he escaped with his wife (a slave girl whom he had married when he was twenty-two and who became the mother of their twelve children) and four young children to Canada (Oct. 1830).

During the Canadian Rebellion (1837–1838) Henson served as a captain in the second Essex Company of Colored Volunteers, particulary in the defense of Fort Malden.

One of his sons, Tom, taught him to read. He became a conductor on the Underground Railroad and helped found (1842) a manual labor school in Dawn, Canada, near the Detroit River. He also established a sawmill which shipped walnut lumber to Boston. When the mill became heavily indebted, Henson went to England and raised enough money to cancel the debt. While in England he was awarded a bronze medal, a picture of Queen Victoria and the royal family, as well as other objects in recognition of his polished walnut lumber exhibited at the Crystal Palace Exhibition. He challenged statements about the good treatment of slaves in receiving religious instruction, and was received by some of England's leading statesmen, including the archbishop of Canterbury and Lord John Russell, then prime minister. Despite his appeals for funds, the Brit-

ish-American Manual Labor Institute and the sawmill failed.

On another trip to England, near the end of his life, he visited also Scotland; he and his wife were presented to Queen Victoria at Windsor Castle, where she again gave him a photograph, this time in an easel frame of gold. On his return to the United States he and his wife were received by Pres. Rutherford B. Hayes. He left again for Canada, where he died in Dresden on May 5, 1883, in the ninety-fourth year of his life.

Josiah Henson is best known as the prototype of Uncle Tom in Harriet Beecher Stowe's *Uncle Tom's Cabin.* Published in 1852, this novel, which dramatized the abject cruelty inflicted upon slaves by masters and overseers so increased intersectional relations that some historians listed it among the causes of the Civil War; 300,000 copies were sold within a year, and several dramas were produced. Mrs. Stowe had read his autobiography, *The Life of Josiah Henson, Formerly a Slave, Now an Inhabitant of Canada, as Narrated by Himself,* a pamphlet of seventy-six pages, dictated to an editorial helper and published in 1849. She also had talked with Henson.

One of the important consequences of *Uncle Tom's Cabin* is the continued usage of the term to describe an unctuous, nonaggressive Negro. Francis Butler Simkins, not one of the more stalwart defenders of the role of the American Negro, wrote, for example: Mrs. Stowe's "Uncle Tom was a man of unctuous piety subjected to painful servitude; how the supposedly vile slave system could produce such a spotless character did not trouble Mrs. Stowe's sentimental readers. The answer is obvious, Uncle Tom is untrue to Negro character and environment" (*The South Old and New* . . . [1947], p. 119). What is more important is the question of whether her Uncle Tom accurately reflected Henson's own account of his life.

The fact that he served as manager and superintendent—in other words, overseer—of other slaves supports the stereotype. Even more impressive is his own account that he spurned the efforts of free Negroes in Cincinnati to liberate the slaves he was conducting in 1825 to Davies County, Ky. When he was later tempted to kill his master with an axe, the thought came to him: "What! Commit murder, and you a Christian?"

On the other hand, he finally persuaded his wife to risk the dangerous journey to Buffalo, N.Y., and Canada. And he did conduct two groups of slaves from Kentucky to Canada and did serve as a captain during the Canadian Rebellion. In brief, Henson was neither a constant "Sambo" nor a hero. He himself wrote that slavery turned "the slave into the cringing, treacherous, false, and thieving victim of tyranny." Most of the biographical sketches of Henson are based on his own recollections.

In addition to his 1849 pamphlet *The Life of Josiah Henson . . .,* an enlarged work, *Truth Stranger than Fiction: Father Henson's Story of His Own Life* (1858) has an introduction by Mrs. Stowe. Another version was published in London as an *Autobiography of Josiah Henson (Mrs. Harriet Beecher Stowe's "Uncle Tom")* (1876), and an enlarged version of this edition was published in 1878. Revisionist interpretations are Jessie

Louise Beattie's *Black Moses: The Real Uncle Tom* (1957) and Brian Gysin's *To Master—a Long Goodnight: The Story of Uncle Tom* (1946). There is a short sketch in *DAB* (4, Part 2:564–65), by Benjamin Brawley; a longer one by W. B. Hartgrove, "The Story of Josiah Henson" (*JNH,* Jan. 1918, pp. 1–21). An engraving is on page 202 of John Blassingame's *The Slave Community, Plantation Life in the Antebellum South* (1972). An obituary was published in the *New York Herald Tribune,* (May 6, 1883). — RAYFORD W. LOGAN

HENSON, MATTHEW ALEXANDER [MATT] (1866–1955) co-discoverer of the North Pole. The son of freeborn parents whom he did not name in his autobiography, Henson was born in Charles County, Md. His account of his youth in his autobiography *A Negro Explorer at the North Pole* (1912) differs in significant details from the versions in *Dark Companion* (1947) by Bradley Robinson and *Ahdoolo! The Biography of Matthew Henson* by Floyd Miller (1963). There is general agreement that Henson, orphaned at an early age, lived with an uncle for several years in Washington, D.C., where he worked in a restaurant, and attended school (the N Street School) for some six years. In Baltimore in 1879 he went to sea as a cabin boy on the merchant vessel *Katie Hinds* commanded by a Captain Childs, became an able-bodied seaman, read widely, and served with him for six years through the Straits of Magellan across the Pacific to the China Sea and across the Atlantic and into the Baltic Sea until Henson was eighteen. He worked in Boston as a stevedore, in Providence as a bellhop, in Buffalo as a laborer, and in New York City as a coachman before returning to Washington when he was nineteen.

Chance led to his meeting (1887) in a store with Lt. Robert Peary in either Washington or Baltimore (Herbert L. Frisby in the *Washington Post,* April 10, 1976, p. 3). The store owner, Steinmetz, recommended Henson as a valet to accompany Peary on his trip to survey a canal route through Nicaragua. Peary soon found that Henson's ability to help chart a path through the jungles and his experiences as a seaman made him more valuable as a colleague than as a valet. Peary took Henson with him on all his trips to the Arctic except his first in 1886: 1891–1892, 1893–1895, 1896, 1897, 1898–1902, 1905–1906, and the final dash to the pole 1908–1909.

It is now generally agreed that the claim of Frederick Cook that he reached the North Pole on April 21, 1908, was a hoax. It is certain that Peary was the only white man, along with Henson and four Eskimos, who reached the North Pole on April 6, 1909. Commander Donald B. MacMillan, one of the white men sent back before the final dash, recalled in 1934 that "Henson, the colored man went with Peary because he was a better man than any of his white assistants" *(How Peary Reached the North Pole).* Peary lauded Henson's "adaptability and fitness for the work" and his "loyalty. He is a better dog driver and can handle a sledge better than any man living except some of the best Eskimo hunters. I couldn't get along without him."

Although Peary's friendship with Henson ended at the North Pole and Peary had Henson promise not to

lecture about the trip (a promise he kept for twelve years until financial need caused him to break it), Henson told Herbert M. Frisby that Peary "was a great man. 'No doubt about it. Personally, he was a little on the cold side, but we always got along well except . . . well, we liked each other as far as it went' " (as told by Frisby to Joel Dreyfus in the *Washington Post,* April 10, 1976, p. 3)

There is little question that Henson's race was the predominant factor in denying him due recognition. The article in the *Encyclopedia Britannica* (1959, 7: 425) lists Henson as one of Peary's companions on April 6, 1909. But H. A. Marmer, who contributed the article in the *Dictionary of American Biography* (7: 62–67), did not mention Henson by name, referring to him once as "one negro" and twice as Peary's "negro servant."

Recognition was accorded Henson much later. From 1913 to 1936 by order of President Taft he was employed as a clerk in the New York Customs House. In 1937 the Explorers Club made him a member. Howard University awarded him an honorary M.S. degree in 1939. On Jan. 28, 1944, Congress awarded him one of the joint medals honoring also the five whites of the 1908–1909 expedition. In 1948 he was given the Gold Medal of the Geographical Society of Chicago. President Truman saluted him in ceremonies at the Pentagon in 1950; President Eisenhower honored him at the White House in 1954. And in 1961, six years after his death, Maryland passed a bill providing for a bronze plaque in the State House, Annapolis, as co-discoverer of the North Pole. In the Decatur House, 740 Jackson Pl. NW, Washington, D.C., is also a plaque honoring Henson. Dr. Herbert L. Frisby of Baltimore made his home a memorial to Henson, with pictures of Peary and Henson and a small museum of Eskimo artifacts.

Henson died of a cerebral hemorrhage in St. Claire's Hospital, New York City. Funeral services were held at the Abyssinian Baptist Church and he was buried in an unmarked grave. He was survived by his widow, Lucy, of 246 W. 150 St., and a sister, Eliza Carter of Washington, D.C.

In addition to the references in the text, see the obituary in the *New York Times* (March 10, 1955, p. 27). — RAYFORD W. LOGAN

HILL, LESLIE PINCKNEY (1880–1960), educator and author. He was born in the small town of Lynchburg, Va., on May 14, 1880, the son of Samuel H. and Sarah E. (Brown) Hill. Early in life, he and his family moved to Orange, N.J., where he spent his boyhood. In the public schools there he pursued his high school education with great success. He was later recommended by his teachers for admission to Harvard University, where his academic achievement was also superior. At Harvard he received both his bachelor's (1903) and master's degrees (1904). An education for Hill was not an easy accomplishment, for he had to work many hours as a waiter in one of the fraternity houses and in one of the campus dining halls. His scholarship was not affected, however; he graduated *cum laude,* Phi Beta Kappa. He was also a member of the debating team.

He began his career in the South as director of the

Department of Education at Tuskegee Institute for three years. From there he moved to Manassas, Va., where he served from 1907 through 1913 reorganizing and aiding in the financial development of the Manassas Institute. In 1913 he became principal of the Institute for Colored Youth, and its president in 1933, when the name was changed to Cheyney Training School for Teachers in Cheyney, Pa. Hill served this growing institution with pride and distinction from 1913 to 1951 when he was named president emeritus. The library of this college bears his name. He died of a stroke in Mercy-Douglass Hospital, Philadelphia, and was buried beside his wife in Kennett Square, Philadelphia.

During his presidency Hill directed the Cheyney Chorus which toured colleges throughout the country (he was a talented musician), gained funds, and served as a medium for the advancement of interracial goodwill. He worked in close cooperation with the Quakers, especially. He reorganized the curriculum along then-modern lines and made Cheyney Training School for Teachers (later Cheyney State College) one of the better schools of its kind. In 1913 there were six buildings and twenty high school or college preparatory students. In 1951 there were sixteen buildings and the school was an accredited state-supported teachers college which graduated eighty-nine students.

Before and after retiring in 1951, Dr. Hill (he held four honorary doctorates) led a very active life. He served as a lecturing professor for two summers at the University of California at Los Angeles. For almost three years he was administrator of the Mercy-Douglass Hospital in Philadelphia, guiding it through a difficult period, and received the Seltzer Award for distinguished service. In 1944 he founded Camp Hope, Delaware County, for underprivileged children. He founded the Association of Pennsylvania Teachers and was a member of the National Education Association Commission on the Defense of Democracy Through Education. These are only a few of the organizations in which he was an active and effective leader.

Hill was the author of *Wings of Oppression* (1927), a book of poems, and *Jethro,* a biblical drama first performed in 1931. His poem "The Teacher" has been translated into several languages and set to music; another well-known poem, "Christmas at Melrose," expressed his love for his wife Jane E. Clark, whom he had married in 1907, and their six daughters. His most important work is *Toussaint L'Ouverture, A Dramatic History* (1928), written in five parts and thirty-five scenes. The artistry of the work lies in the intermingling of choice bits of prose and flowing lyricism, both with strong thematic unity.

His views were perhaps best stated in his essay "What the Negro Wants and How to Get It," in *What the Negro Wants,* edited by Rayford W. Logan (1944). A Republican, he endorsed six immediate aims of Negro effort: (1) Protection under the law and no discrimination in the administration of the law; (2) Equality of education; (3) Equality of expenditure for health and hospitalization; (4) Elimination of all inhibiting restrictions in voting—through taxes or otherwise; (5) Equal work opportunity and equal pay; and (6) The right to fight in any branch of the services.

In order to achieve these goals, responsible Negro leaders throughout the nation wanted the same freedom for which the "democracies" were fighting. He added: "The common foe of the whole human race is war, because war is a heinous and blasphemous negation of all human relations. . . . In every emergency, the Negro race in America must give to the nation its unreserved allegiance. Wrongs will remain, but increasing opportunities and obligations will surpass them. Our democracy is not yet a satisfying reality, but Negores are still free to live, strive and die to make it come in God's unhurried time. All else by comparison is trivial."

Essential information is in Charline H. Conyers's, *A History of Cheyney State College, 1837–1951* (doctoral dissertation, New York University, 1960). See also Milton M. James's "Leslie Pinckney Hill" (*NHB,* March 1961, pp. 135–37). An interview with Estella Scott Johnson, administrative assistant to Dr. Hill (1941–1951) was also helpful. See also the obituary in the *New York Times* (Feb. 16, 1960). — GLENDA DIANE SMITH

HILL, MOZELL C[LARENCE] (1911–1969), sociologist and educator. Born in Anniston, Ala., on March 27, 1911, the youngest of seven children of Humphrey and Annie (Williamson) Hill, he left Alabama at the age of five and spent the remainder of his youth in Kansas City, Kans. He received his B.A. (1933) and M.A. (1937) degrees at the University of Kansas, and his Ph.D. degree from the University of Chicago (1946), all in sociology.

It was during his graduate study at the University of Kansas that all-Negro communities captured his attention, and he wrote his master's thesis on one of these, Boley, Okla. At the University of Chicago it was suggested that he expand his study to include an examination and comparison of six of these communities in Oklahoma. The expanded study was his doctoral dissertation. His research was a critical analysis of social organization, social stratification, personality development, and racial attitudes in all-Negro communities. Prior to his research there was a general knowledge of the existence of these communities in Oklahoma and elsewhere; however, none had been the object of empirical sociological study. Each of these communities was settled originally by Negroes who had migrated from other southern communities in an effort to escape the segregation, discrimination, and racial conflict which they had experienced. In a bid to establish a distinct community, they became separatists. In separatism, which was never total, they found a kind of freedom. The organized life in these communities—economic organization, social stratification, the socialization process, religious expression, political participation, and racial attitudes—while similar in form to that found in biracial communities, was also characterized by important differences. One, that between the all-Negro community and the biracial community was the more limited economic base of the former. Second, racial attitudes toward whites, at least as they were articulated, were polarized and strongly negative (Hill, "Basic Racial Attitudes Toward Whites in the Oklahoma All-Negro Community," *American Journal of Sociology* 49 [May 1944]: 519–22).

The establishment of all-Negro communities in Oklahoma met with considerable resistance from both whites and Indians. The hostility was intensified following the efforts of Edwin P. McCabe to make Oklahoma an all-Negro state. According to newspaper and magazine articles of the period, the Indians appeared to be especially hostile to the movement. Hill collected over 200 of these articles describing the clashes between the two races.

Although Hill understood only too well the mainsprings of the ideal of the self-sufficient all-Negro community in the United States, he had serious misgivings about its future economic growth or political influence. Its isolation, although initially self-imposed, precluded any significant broadening of the economic base or increase in occupational opportunities for future generations because of white hostility.

During the course of his professional career Hill's scholarly interests broadened. In his early years the focus of his research was the Negro community and race relations, especially in the Southeast. His treatment of "Cracker Culture," and of race and class stratification in the southeastern region resulted in important extensions of sociological theory and in innovations in methodology. In his later years his major interest was the sociology of education.

On May 5, 1935, he married Marnesba Davis. To this union were born four daughters.

He began his teaching career at Langston University (Okla.) in 1937, where he remained until 1946. In 1946 he went to Atlanta University as a visiting professor of sociology, where he was a colleague of Ira de A. Reid. In 1947 he was appointed professor of sociology and chairman of the department at Atlanta University, a position he held until 1958. He later held posts at Columbia University, the University of Nigeria at Nsukka, Washington University (St. Louis), and New York University, and was visiting lecturer (1952–1953) at the following British universities: Cambridge, Edinburgh, and Manchester. He was an inspiring and demanding teacher. A considerable number of his students who later earned their doctorates attributed much of their success to his teaching.

The twelve years he spent in Atlanta were productive. In 1948 he succeeded Reid as editor of *Phylon: The Atlanta University Review of Race and Culture.* One of the more important marks he left during his stay was the leadership he provided in the development of the Hungry Club. This organization, the brain-child of Reid, was a forum for local leaders in business, politics, and in the academic community. At the club's weekly meetings many plans for social and political change in the Atlanta community were initiated. Among Hill's associates in this venture were men and women who later were leaders of both local and national importance, including the Rev. Martin Luther King, Sr., Whitney Young, Jr., Jesse B. Blayton, M. Carl Holman (later president of the National Urban Coalition), and Grace Townes Hamilton, later a member of the Georgia legislature.

Mozell Hill was not only a traditional scholar. He was also committed to social action, not unusual for Negro sociologists of his generation. Most had a special knowledge of the Negro community, for practically all of them had written their dissertations on some aspect of the subject. Moreover they were often requested to serve as consultants to government agencies and private organizations dealing with community problems. Hill was either consultant to or a member of the board of a number of organizations whose major purpose was the resolution of race conflict and the promotion of community welfare. Several of his assignments deserve special mention. He was co-director of the Georgia Council on Human Relations (1955–1957); special research consultant to the Ashmore Project, headed by Harry Ashmore, sponsored by the Fund for the Advancement of Education, the Ford Foundation, to examine the probable course and impact of school desegregation (1953–1955); with Alexander Miller of the Anti-Defamation League, he planned and conducted pioneering studies in southern race relations; with Mrs. Dudley Moore of the Unitarian Service Committee he helped plan and set up in Knoxville, Tenn., one of the early efforts of a national organization to facilitate school desegregation (1955–1956); he was a consulting sociologist to Norwalk, Conn. (1964–1965), and a number of communities in the New York area, helping them to develop and implement school integration plans; and he was invited by the government of Israel to evaluate that country's entire educational system.

Hill was the recipient of many awards and citations, both for his scholarly achievements and for his public service. At the time of his death he was professor of educational sociology and anthropology, Center for Human Relations and Community Studies, Department of Administration and Supervision, School of Education, New York University. He suffered a stroke in 1967 from which he never recovered. He died on March 26, 1969, and was buried in New York.

Following is a selected list of his more important publications: *Culture of a Contemporary Negro Community* (1943); "Basic Racial Attitudes Toward Whites in the Oklahoma All-Negro Community" (*American Journal of Sociology* 49 [May 1944]: 519–22); "The All-Negro Communities of Oklahoma: The Natural History of a Social Movement" (*JNH* 31 [July 1946]: 254–68); with Albert N. Whiting, "Theoretical and Methodological Approaches to Community Studies" (*Social Forces* 29 [Dec. 1950]: 117–24); with Bevode C. McCall, "Social Stratification in 'Georgia Town' " (*American Sociological Review* 15 [Dec. 1950]: 721–29).

Basic information is in *Who's Who in America, 1969–1970.* The contributor drew upon his personal reminiscences, especially for 1952–1953.

— CLIFTON R. JONES

HILL, PETER (1767–1820), clockmaker. Born on July 19, 1767, presumably a son of slaves owned by the Quaker clockmaker Joseph Hollinshead, Jr., of Burlington Township, N.J., Hill lived as a boy and youth in the Hollinshead household. As he grew older he was trained by his master in the craft of clockmaking so that he could assist in his shop. When he reached the age of twenty-seven in 1794, Hill was manumitted by his master. His freedom was certified in the following spring when he was presented before a committee consisting of two overseers of the poor of the township and two justices of the peace of the county. In a document dated May 1, 1795, they certified that Hill "on view and examination appears to us to be sound in mind and not under any bodily incapacity of obtaining a support and also is not under twenty one years of age nor above thirty five." This manumission document was in accord with the prevailing law relating to the liberation of slaves having achieved legal age.

One of Hill's first acts as a free man was to marry. Four months after his manumission became effective, on Sept. 9, 1795, he was married to Tina Lewis by Thomas Adams, one of the justiices of the peace who had served on his manumission board. He described the groom and his bride in the official records as "Peter Hill of the City of Burlington Clock & Watch Maker and Tina Lewis of the same place Spinster (being free people of color)." Tina Lewis had been noted three years earlier in the records of the Society of Friends of Burlington, which was making a strong effort to provide free schooling to Negroes in their community. In a communication to the Friends' Society for Free Instruction in Philadelphia, the Burlington Society forwarded an example of the writing of one of its pupils, Tina Lewis, as a demonstration of the remarkable progress she had made in four months.

The exact date and location of Hill's first clockmaking shop are not known, but in due course he maintained his shop in his home in Burlington, on the east side of High Street, below Broad Street, directly opposite the residence of Rowland Jones and nearly opposite the Friends' Meeting House. Several doors south of his shop was the cabinetmaking shop of George Deacon, who constructed the cases for many of Hill's clocks.

Hill's name first appeared in the Burlington tax list in 1795, as a householder with a tax levy of six shillings. For comparative purposes, it is useful to note that the tax levy for his former master in the same period was two pounds, one shilling, and fourpence. Hill's estate developed gradually; in the following year he had acquired one head of cattle. In an indenture dated March 3, 1801, Hill purchased a lot of two and one-half acres of land for $500, and in the same year he acquired a horse as well. By 1805 he was taxed for two acres of land, in addition to a house and lot valued at $20, one horse, and two head of cattle. By 1808 he had acquired a second horse and two more acres of land.

After 1814 Hill pursued his craft as a clockmaker also in nearby Mount Holly, while retaining his property in Burlington. Mount Holly is a village in Northampton Township, N.J., seven miles from Burlington. It was first settled by members of the Society of Friends emigrating from England and developed as a farming community with an iron works and later a paper-making mill. Late in the eighteenth century many flocked to the town from Philadelphia to escape the yellow fever epidemic, at approximately the same period that an uprising of slaves developed into a massacre in Saint-Domingue, which resulted in an influx of French refugees and others who came to settle in Mount Holly.

Hill established his clockmaking shop in Mount Holly on Main Street "Next to the premises of Daniel Love. . . . Rev. Gamaliel Bailey lived here about the year 1815

or 1816, he was a silversmith. After him Peter Hill a colored man lived here, and carried on the Clock and Watch business." Hill may have conducted an established clockmaking business for the first few years, because he appeared in the Mount Holly records as a property owner for the first time in 1820. His color appears to have become a consideration for the first time, for he was listed then in a separate section of the tax ratables under "Blacks," as the head of a household and the owner of a sulky. On Feb. 20, 1820, he purchased a brick dwelling house and a lot containing 4466 square links of land on the south side of New Street. He died late in December of the same year, leaving no will. When an accounting was made of his business affairs, it was discovered that he was deeply in debt and that his personal estate was inadequate to pay what he owed. His new house and lot and the remainder of his properties were sold to discharge his obligations.

Hill was buried in the Friends' Burial Ground adjacent to the Meeting House in Burlington, in a plot almost directly across the street from his former residence and shop. Nearby was the grave of Caroline Loango, a young African girl brought from Loango after having been kidnapped by slave traders in the African interior. Hill's grave, however, was unmarked and its location designated only in the records of the burial ground.

Two clocks made by Peter Hill are known. One tall case clock which he made for his neighbor, Rowland Jones, in 1812, is in the Westtown School at Westtown, Pa. The case housing the movement was made by Hill's neighboring cabinetmaker, George Deacon. Another tall case clock made by Hill is in the National Museum of History and Technology of the Smithsonian Institution in Washington, D.C. A clock which Hill repaired and so noted behind the dial is also known.

Brief references to Hill are found in Maj. E. M. Woodward's and John E. Hageman's *History of Burlington and Mercer Counties, New Jersey . . .* (1883, p. 182), Carl E. Drepperd's *American Clocks and Clockmakers* (1947, p. 235), and Carl M. Williams's *Silversmiths of New Jersey 1770–1825* (1949, p. 72). The indispensable manuscript, "Annals of Mount Holly" (1859) by Zacharias Read, is in the Burlington County Historical Society. Other valuable documents are in the Burlington County, N.J., Courthouse, County Clerk's Records 1795–1840, Marriage Book A, p. 5; and the Department of Records, Society of Friends, Philadelphia. Papers Relating to a School for Adult Colored Persons deposited for Joseph W. Lippincott, Burlington Township, Burlington County: Tax Records, 1796–1814; Records of the Deeds, Book I, Book A-2, Book I-2; Burlington County Land Records, Book S, Northampton Township, Burlington County: Tax Records, volume 286; Wills and Inventories, 1821; Records of the Surrogate's Office, 1821. — SILVIO A. BEDINI

HILL, T[HOMAS] ARNOLD (1888–1947), Urban League executive. He was born in Richmond, Va., on Aug. 23, 1888, the son of Reuben and Irene (Robinson) Hill. He married Sara Orlene Henderson on Sept. 26, 1917, and had two children, T. Arnold Jr. and Charles Pinyon. He attended Wayland Academy (1902–1906), Richmond Business College (1907), and graduated from

Virginia Union University (B.A., 1911). He worked for more than twenty years in the Urban League: National Urban League (1914–1916), as assistant to the executive secretary; Chicago Urban League (1917–1925), as executive secretary; National Urban League (1925–1940), as director of industrial relations, and also as acting executive secretary (Nov. 1933 to March 1936). He was a member of the President's Emergency Committee for Employment (1930), a member of the President's Conference on Home Building and Home Ownership (1932), and a vice-president of the National Conference of Social Work (1937). He was also the author of *The Negro and Economic Reconstruction* (1937).

T. Arnold Hill went to the National Urban League in April 1914, a young man of twenty-six. Eugene Kinckle Jones, the league's executive secretary, was searching for an assistant "to publicize public meetings, prepare for meetings of local and national League committees, write all releases, reports, appeals, carry out occasional fund-raising among colored people, oversee the office work . . . and also act as (my) secretary" (Parris and Brooks, *Blacks in the City, A History of the National Urban League* [1971], p. 65). The logical person for the job was Hill—his boyhood friend from Richmond.

Soon the job expanded and Hill was sharing responsibility for organizing local leagues. In the winter of 1916, after several visits to Chicago, Jones realized that a local affiliate was needed there. Negroes were migrating in large numbers from the Deep South. Hill was sent to Chicago to do the organizing. It was a difficult task, despite the backing of influential Negroes and wealthy white business and civic leaders; it took three months to establish the Chicago league. Because of the success of Hill's effort and the groundwork he had laid, Jones and the national trustees agreed to leave Hill in Chicago to become its first executive secretary; Hill was also placed in charge of the newly established national Western Field Office.

In July 1919 this dual job was interrupted by the Chicago race riots. The Chicago Urban League office became an emergency center, helping to restore and maintain order, distributing relief, and disseminating information. Hill was one of six citizens who appealed to the governor of Illinois for an emergency committee to determine the causes of the riot and to recommend remedies to prevent a repetition. The Chicago Commission on Race Relations and its famous report, *The Negro in Chicago* (1922), were the result.

In 1923 Hill entered politics and ran as a candidate for alderman from Chicago's South Side. He was endorsed by some of the league's influential supporters and by the *Chicago Daily News.* Although the *Chicago Defender* and its publisher Robert S. Abbott had previously been strong supporters of the Urban League, it helped defeat Hill. Some attributed Hill's defeat to the fact that he did not have the support of the bulk of the Negro population; others to the fact that his entrance into politics, according to a competent observer, "violated one of the cardinal principles of the Urban League movement. References to politics were scrupulously avoided in League philosophy and in statements

on policy" (Strickland, *History of the Chicago Urban League* [1966], p. 81).

After this setback he continued at the league, but much of the vigor and effectiveness that characterized his first seven years in Chicago began to diminish. By 1925 national league officials realized that Hill would be more useful to the movement if he were moved out of Chicago and given the opportunity to make use of his many skills on the national scene.

The time was ripe, it seemed. Eugene Kinckle Jones had appealed for grants from the Carnegie Corporation and John D. Rockefeller, Jr., to establish a formal industrial program. Money was pledged with the stipulation that the league secure matching funds. On the strength of this pledge, and Hill's recognized effectiveness in Chicago, Jones made an appeal to a Chicago league supporter, Julius Rosenwald, who gave the required financial backing and matching funds. On March 15, 1925, at the age of thirty-nine, Hill was brought back to New York in charge of the new operation as national director of industrial relations.

His experience and personality augured for success. He was of medium height, stocky, and smooth-skinned; had an assured manner; and was immaculate in dress. His nearsighted, large dark brown eyes peered out clearly and with confidence from heavy-rimmed glasses. He was diplomatic and tactful, yet had a sense of humor that often carried him over difficult spots and negotiations. Thrown at once into the task of seeking larger opportunities for Negro workers, he moved swiftly to prepare a favorable climate among employers, the general public, and Negroes themselves. Sensing the need to give special attention to the relationship between Negroes and labor, he urged league support of the efforts of A. Philip Randolph and the Brotherhood of Sleeping Car Porters in their struggle for union recognition. Tenacious and aggressive, Hill would not relinquish his hold on an idea or a position if he felt he was right. This determination aided him in negotiations with leaders of the American Federation of Labor to secure the recognition of black workers. The fight was not fully won, but Hill did not give up.

Hill's forecasts of what Negroes might expect in the foreseeable future in jobs, education, organized labor, and politics were remarkably accurate. Published in his "Labor" column in *Opportunity: Journal of Negro Life,* the official organ of the National Urban League, some forecasts pointing to methods by which Negroes might gain a meaningful place in the nation's economic life were translated into effective action programs which the league pioneered. One of the most far-reaching was born in the fall of 1929. Recognizing that a whole new approach to the problem of unemployment among Negroes was needed, Hill summoned a national conference of local league executives. This meeting developed the basic principle that Negro youth must be prepared for any occupation for which they had aptitude and interest, whether or not there was job opportunity available. The idea was first expressed in the March 1930 issue of *Opportunity.* It urged the necessity for Negroes to place more serious emphasis on vocational training and guidance. A vocational Opportunity Campaign (VOC) espousing this principle was launched in the spring and continued each year for twenty years.

In 1933, during the Depression, President Roosevelt signed the National Industrial Recovery Act (NIRA). Hill moved to ensure benefits for Negroes resulting from the new legislation. Emergency Advisory Councils (EAC) were established in hundreds of communities in both league and nonleague cities. They were designed to inform Negroes about their rights and how to channel their complaints of discrimination to the proper officials, and to motivate them in improving their economic condition. An *EAC Handbook* was published for this purpose.

Quietly persistent yet persuasive, Hill's many trips to Washington were effective behind the scenes, especially during the early days of President Roosevelt's "New Deal." His "aide-mémoires" on the economic conditions and employment needs of Negroes, prepared at the request of federal officials, bore fruit, although not always immediately. "Madame Secretary" Frances Perkins of the Labor Department, and Sen. Robert F. Wagner, the architect of the National Labor Relations Act (1935), studied his facts and suggestions, and many Urban League recommendations were incorporated into administrative regulations. Secretary of the Interior Harold L. Ickes, a friend from Chicago days, was among the officials with whom Hill made frequent contact, because that department was important for the welfare of Negroes. Hill also served as a consultant to NYA Director Aubrey Williams in the planning of the National Youth Administration. Through NUL Vice-President Mary McLeod Bethune, the NYA national director of Negro affairs, the league had a pathway to Eleanor Roosevelt, and Hill tread that path often in the interests of black youth and adults.

The industrial activities of the league were making progress since the department was established in 1925. Therefore in 1939 it came as a shock to the league movement when a conflict arose between T. Arnold Hill and Eugene Kinckle Jones. It developed into a clean break between the two friends, leading to Hill's resignation and to the end of his league career. The conflict had been slowly building up. It was further aggravated during 1933–1936 when Hill's popularity as the league's acting executive secretary increased with local league executives while Jones was on leave. In June 1939 on Hill's twenty-fifth anniversary with the organization, an editorial in *Opportunity* noted: "For over a decade . . . [the Department of Industrial Relations] has striven to focus the attention of the Negro on the importance of participation in America's industrial life as the *sine qua non* of economic progress and of racial advancement. Its work had comprehended the stimulation of education of Negro workers, vocational guidance and placement of Negro youth, and unceasing attack on the color line in industry and organized labor."

In the spring of 1939 Jones became seriously ill and was given a leave of absence. "A replacement was urgently needed and the logical candidate—experienced, seasoned, vigorous and with great prestige among other League executives, government, industry and the social work profession—was T. Arnold Hill" (*Blacks in the City,* p. 266). But the southern field director—Jesse O. Thomas—was placed in the job. Hill was

stunned. He stayed on, however, and continued his industrial relations work. Jones returned to duty early in 1940, and in March Hill abruptly resigned. He was invited to join the executive staff of the National Youth Administration under the supervision of Mary McLeod Bethune, Negro affairs director, where he served for several years.

Making use of his skills and abilities, and the experience he had gained, Hill later served as a consultant to schools, colleges, and other institutions. He concentrated his efforts on the advancement of educational and employment opportunities for youth and adults alike. The work was stimulating and rewarding, but it was not the Urban League which had been close to his heart for so long. Hill never became bitter, as those who knew him intimately during those years attested. His health soon failed, and he died at the age of fifty-nine in Cleveland, Ohio. Funeral services were held in Richmond, Va., and he was buried in the Evergreen Cemetery. He was survived by his widow and his two children.

Essential information is found in Arvrah Strickland's *History of the Chicago Urban League* (1966), Guichard Parris's and Lester Brooks's *Blacks in the City . . .* (1971), and Nancy J. Weiss's *The National Urban League, 1910–1940* (1974). — GUICHARD PARRIS

HILYER, AMANDA V[ICTORIA] GRAY (1870–1957), businesswoman and civil rights leader. Born in Atchison, Kans., on March 24, 1870, she was educated in the public schools there, married Arthur S. Gray in 1893, and came to Washington, D.C., around 1897. Shortly after her arrival she attended the Hunter School of Kindergarten, then attended Howard University and received the Pharmaceutical Graduate degree in 1903. Both Grays, who operated a pharmacy at 12th and U Streets NW, in the heart of the Negro commercial district of that day, became deeply involved in the social and civic activities of the city. Mrs. Gray was the secretary of the Treble Clef Club, and as a member of the Booklovers Club she took part in the organization of the Phyllis Wheatley YWCA in Washington and became its first recording secretary upon its incorporation in 1905. In addition to establishing facilities for young colored women, the group of organizers also attempted to make their political views felt. In 1911 they protested to President Taft against the hanging of a woman, Mattie Lomax; in March 1913 they passed a resolution opposing the opening of five-cent theaters on Sunday; and later in the year they agitated for the appointment of a matron to oversee the activities of colored youth at the public beach in Washington.

At the time of her husband's death in 1917 Mrs. Gray closed the pharmacy and joined a number of other Negro women who participated in the war effort. She was involved in Hostess House activities for Negro soldiers, and was sent to Camp Sherman in Chillicothe, Ohio, by the War Work Council. After the war she served as president of the Phyllis Wheatley YWCA in St. Louis.

In 1923 she married Andrew F. Hilyer, a Washington resident who with his late wife had been involved in many civic and social activities with the Grays. Two years after their marriage Mr. Hilyer died. Mrs. Hilyer remained active in the affairs of the Washington Negro community. She was president and member of the board for many years of the Ionia Whipper Home for Unwed Mothers (Hilyer and Whipper had graduated from Howard University in the same year). She was the president of the Peace Circle, a group formed to rehabilitate the Frederick Douglass home, was president of the Howard University Women's Club, a member of the Citizen's Committee for Freedmen's Hospital Nurses, the Board of Trustees of Berean Baptist Church, and the Association for the Study of Negro Life and History. Her community service earned her awards from the Community Chest, the Afro-American Newspapers, and the NAACP.

Hilyer's activity in cultural, social, business, and political affairs in Washington's Negro community from her arrival in the city until her death in 1957 brought her in touch with the most active individuals in the Washington community of that era, and typifies the commitment and depth of involvement of Negroes like herself who had attained an education and had achieved professional or financial success.

A week after suffering a stroke, she died at her home on June 29, 1957. Funeral services were held at the Berean Baptist Church, 11th and V Streets NW, and she was buried in Harmony Cemetery, Washington, D.C. She was survived by a step-daughter, Kathleen Hilyer Bingham of Gary, Ind., and three nieces. Her will stipulated that her body was to be buried beside that of her first husband. Bequests included $3000 for the Ionia Whipper Home for application on a building loan; $500 to the Howard University Student Aid Fund and $500 to the Art Department; $50 each to the Phillis Wheatley YWCA, the 12th Street Branch of the YMCA and the Stoddard Baptist Home. All of her books were bequeathed to the Moorland Collection, Howard University, and the property where she resided at 1833 Vermont Ave. NW to the Association for the Study of Negro Life and History following the death of one of her nieces, Courtney Davis Scott.

Written information about Mrs. Hilyer is limited. Primary materials on Negro social and civic associations in Washington during the early part of the century (which can be found in vertical files in the Moorland-Spingarn Research Center at Howard University, and the Washingtoniana section of the Martin Luther King Memorial Library) contain references to her and to her husbands. Other information was gathered from recollections of Washingtonians. Most valuable were obituaries in the *Washington Evening Star* (July 2, 1957) and the *Washington Afro-American* (July 16, 1957). — ROBERT G. MCGUIRE III

HILYER, ANDREW F[RANKLIN] (1858–1925), author, inventor, and civil rights leader. Born a slave in Georgia on Aug. 14, 1858, as a child he was taken by his mother to Nebraska, but at her death he moved to Minneapolis, where he was befriended by the wealthy Gale and Pillsbury families. In 1882 he graduated from the University of Minnesota. He then moved to Washington, D.C., where he received his LL.B. in 1884 and his LL.M. in 1885 from Howard University. In 1886 he

was married to Mamie Elizabeth Nichols (1863–1916), a descendant of free Negroes who had lived in the Washington area for several generations. They had two sons, Gale P. and Franklin, and one daughter, Kathleen. Hilyer served as a class II clerk in the Treasury Department and later as a member of the Interior Department, Division of the General Accounting Office. Seven years after the death of his first wife, he married Amanda Victoria Gray (1870–1957), a 1903 graduate of the Howard School of Pharmacy, the widow of Arthur S. Gray who had been active with the Hilyers in Washington civic affairs. Hilyer died at his home at 1833 Vermont Ave. NW on Jan. 13, 1925. Funeral services were held on Jan. 16 in Rankin Memorial Chapel, Howard University, and he was buried in Harmony Cemetery, Washington, D.C. He was survived by his widow; a daughter, Kathleen H. Bingham; a son, Gale P. Hilyer, an attorney in Minneapolis; and a sister, Jennie V. Hilyer, director of nurse training at Florida State Normal School, Tallahassee.

Although he was notable for his educational preparation, his government jobs, his affluence derived from real estate, and his inventions of a hot-air register and a water evaporator attachment for hot-air registers, patented in 1900, Hilyer's real significance lies in his innovative organizational activities aimed at the economic, cultural, political, and educational development of the Negro community. At a time when segments of this community debated the merits of industrial versus liberal education, the priorities of political versus economic development, and the strategies of internal Negro development versus agitation for entrance into the mainstream of American life, Hilyer did not restrict the options for Negro development. For instance, as a law graduate and as a member of the Board of Trustees of Howard University from 1913 until his death, he was committed to liberal and professional education. At the same time he spoke in favor of industrial education, participated in Hampton Institute conferences, and sent his son Franklin to Armstrong, the industrial high school in Washington, D.C. Although he devoted much of his activity to stimulating Negro business development and attended the first meeting of Booker T. Washington's National Negro Business League (1900), he believed equally in the value of the ballot. In addition he believed in developing unity and economic strength within the Negro community. He also urged Negroes to seek jobs with white businesses, and urged Negroes to patronize those white establishments which hired them. If, as some historians have suggested, the Washington–Du Bois controversy polarized Negro leadership at this period, the activities and words of Andrew Hilyer do not reflect such a polarization. Nor does Hilyer betray ambiguity or opportunism, as some writers have imputed to other Negro leaders of the period. He had a comprehensive and balanced approach to Negro development.

Some of his organizational activities illustrate this point. Hilyer was one of the founders and the first president of the Union League of the District of Columbia, which was organized in 1892 "to advance the moral, material and financial interests of the colored people; to inaugurate and maintain a more fraternal feeling and a closer union among them; to foster such a spirit of cooperation that mechanical, industrial and professional enterprises may be established and maintained; and to collect and disseminate among the people such data and information as will best tend to promote these ends." The Union League published directories of Negro businesspeople in 1892, 1894, and 1895, and in 1901 published *A Historical, Biographical and Statistical Study of Colored Washington.* This latter publication, a major effort, was directed and coordinated by Hilyer. In addition the Union League attempted to convince white employers to hire Negroes, and to educate them to use their buying power to bring more economic resources into the Negro community.

In connection with his interest in business development and industrial education he traveled through the South in the winter of 1899, as an expert agent of the U.S. Commission for the Paris Exposition of 1900. He organized an exhibit at the exposition entitled "Collective Exhibit of Negroes in Merchandise, Factories and Allied Occupations."

Hilyer and his first wife were also active in organizing (1901) the Coleridge-Taylor Society, a group of colored musicians dedicated to performing and popularizing the music of the English Negro composer Samuel Coleridge-Taylor, of London. Mrs. Hilyer, an accomplished pianist and a founder of the Treble Clef Club, a Washington women's music group, had met Coleridge-Taylor in London as she was returning from the Paris Exposition. The society brought the composer to the United States in 1904 and 1906 to conduct his works. A contemporary biographer of Coleridge-Taylor made the following statement about the society: "A chorus of two-hundred voices, brought together by Negro initiative and sustained by Negro resources and devoted to the study of the choral masterpieces of the world was a new and significant institution." This activity of the Hilyers is indicative of their pride in Negro achievement, and their ability to mobilize Negro and white support for such an organization. Hilyer also belonged to the Mu-So-Lit Club and to the Bethel Literary and Historical Association, Negro organizations devoted to the discussion of the cultural and social issues of the day. He was also a member of Epsilon Boulé of Sigma Pi Phi, a national fraternity of prominent Negroes.

Because he was a civil servant Hilyer was not able to participate in politics overtly. He was, however, the founder of the Correspondence Club which was designed to influence public opinion, media representation, and public policy as they affected Negroes. The membership of the club was limited to twelve and its existence was never publicized. The members took it upon themselves to write letters to protest injustices to the race and to commend fair treatment, with each member being a watchdog for a specific area (literature, politics, or the media), and each member pledging to mobilize letter writers from outside the club. In essence the Correspondence Club was a secret lobbying organization for the race. As a member of the NAACP, Hilyer also lent his efforts to the struggle against racial injustices.

Supplementary to his activities with Negro organizations Hilyer made studies, delivered speeches, and wrote articles devoted to various aspects of the struggle for racial advancement. While a student at Howard he was the Washington correspondent of the *Northwest Review.* He wrote manuscripts on the following topics: a compilation of commendable achievements of the Negro race in Washington, D.C.; an analysis of American color prejudice; a collection of data about thirty-five Negroes possessing estates valued at over $10,000; and an article on the function of the colored scholar.

There is no adequate biography of Andrew Hilyer. Information was gathered from materials in the Moorland-Spingarn Research Center, Howard University; interviews with the Hilyer family and friends; various Howard University publications; newspapers and burial records. See also the obituaries in the *Washington Tribune* (Jan. 17, 1925, p. 1) and the *Washington Evening Star* (Jan. 15, 1925, p. 7). A letter from the Office of Admissions and Records (Oct. 24, 1975) establishes June 1882 as the date of Hilyer's graduation from college, but does not respond to the question of whether he was the first Negro graduate of the University of Minnesota. — ROBERT G. MCGUIRE III

HINTON, WILLIAM AUGUSTUS (1883–1959), physician, educator, and author. He was born in Chicago, the son of Augustus and Marie (Clark) Hinton. After two years at the University of Kansas (1900–1902), he received his B.S. degree from Harvard College in 1905. Lacking the funds for medical school, he taught at Walden University, Nashville, Tenn., and in Langston, Okla., for the next four years. During the summers he continued his studies in bacteriology and physiology at the University of Chicago. In 1909 Hinton entered Harvard Medical School. Despite the long interval since his premed studies, Hinton maintained a fine scholastic record and completed the course in only three years. The Medical School offered him a scholarship for Negro students, but Hinton refused the offer. In competition with the entire student body he won the Wigglesworth Scholarship and the Hayden Scholarship. After graduating from Harvard Medical School in 1912 Hinton had hoped to obtain an internship in Boston and then to practice medicine among the poor in the southern part of the United States.

Because of his race, he was unable to get an internship in any Boston hospital. Hinton did, however, find a job in the Wasserman Laboratory, which was at that time part of Harvard Medical School. In the mornings he was a volunteer assistant in the Department of Pathology of the Massachusetts General Hospital. At the Wasserman Laboratory, Hinton began teaching serological techniques. In 1915, when the Wasserman Laboratory was transferred from Harvard to the Massachusetts Department of Public Health, Hinton was appointed assistant director of the Division of Biologic Laboratories and chief of the Wasserman Laboratory. In 1918 he was appointed as instructor in preventive medicine and hygiene at the Harvard Medical School, continuing his work as chief of Wasserman Laboratory.

From 1921 to 1946 Hinton served as instructor in bacteriology and immunology at Harvard and as lecturer until 1949 when he was promoted to the rank of clinical professor, the first Negro professor in the university's 313 years. He was retired in 1950 with the status of professor emeritus.

His signal contribution to medical science and practice was in syphilology. Within two years of his graduation from medical school he had published the first of many scientific papers on the serology of syphilis in Rosenau's well-known *Textbook of Preventive Medicine.* Later, during the 1920s, Hinton developed and perfected his world-renowned serological test for syphilis. Because the treatment of syphilis was long, painful, and dangerous, and because the Wasserman and other early tests often resulted in false diagnosis of syphilis, an accurate test was of the utmost importance. Hinton's test, based on flocculation, sharply reduced the percentage of false positives. It also met the requirements of mass screening, quick results, simplicity, replicability, and unambiguity. In 1934 the U.S. Public Health Service reported that its evaluation of the most widely used tests for syphilis showed the Hinton Test to be the best, using sensitivity and specificity as evaluative standards. In 1936 the Macmillan Company published his classic textbook *Syphilis and Its Treatment.* Pointing out that "syphilis is a needlessly common occurrence," he sought to provide a "clear, simple, relatively complete account of syphilis and its treatment for physicians, public health workers, and medical students."

Even after his retirement from Harvard in 1950 he taught there for some time (*Boston Daily Globe,* Sept. 15, 1952), and served until 1953 as physician-in-chief of the Department of Clinical Laboratories of the Boston Dispensary. He also taught at the Harvard School of Public Health, Tufts University Schools of Medicine and Dentistry, and for many years after 1919 was a lecturer at Simmons College, Boston. He was also special consultant to the U.S. Public Health Service and a consultant (1946–1949) at the Massachusetts School for Crippled Children, Boston.

Hinton was a member of the American Society of Clinical Pathologists, the Society of American Bacteriologists, the American Medical Association, the American Association for the Advancement of Science, and a fellow of the Massachusetts Medical Society. In 1948 he was elected a life member of the American Social Science Association in recognition of his achievements as a "distinguished scientist, leading serologist and public health bacteriologist." He lectured frequently to constituent societies of the National Medical Association. Among the more than 4000 of his students was Louis Tompkins Wright, who also gained fame as a physician. W. Montague Cobb listed in 1957 twenty-one of his publications in scientific journals. Hinton declined the award of the NAACP Spingarn Medal for significant contributions on the ground that he wanted to wait until he had achieved a great deal more.

In 1919 Hinton married Ada Hawes, who became the mother of their two daughters, Ann and Jane. After he lost a leg in an automobile accident in 1940, he later "developed such compensatory skill in control of the foot pedals that a drive with him was a thrilling experience. He is very skilled in handicrafts of many kinds, particularly woodworking, and is an accomplished gardener, so that his home in Canton, Massachusetts, where he lives with Mrs. Hinton, is a place of rare and very individual beauty" (W. Montague Cobb, *JNMA,* Nov. 1957, p. 427).

Upon his death in 1959 Hinton's will stipulated that his savings of some $75,000 were to be used to set up a scholarship fund for graduate students at Harvard, with the fund being a memorial to his parents, Augustus and Maria Hinton "who, although born in slavery and without formal education, nevertheless recognized and practiced not only the highest ideals in their personal conduct, but also the true democratic principle of equal opportunity for all, without regard to racial or religious origin or to economic or political status." The fund was to be called the Eisenhower Scholarship Fund "in recognition of the steps toward acceptance of equal opportunity during [his] administration."

Hinton, who survived his wife and devoted companion Ada Hawes Hinton by one year, died of diabetes at his home in Canton. He was survived by his two daughters, Dr. Jane Hinton and Anne Hinton Jones.

The fullest accounts of Hinton's career are James E. Teele's "Three Black Scientists: George Grant, Solomon Fuller and William A. Hinton" (*Conference Proceedings: Candidate for Re-discovery,* 1976) and W. Montague Cobb's "William Augustus Hinton, M.D., 1883–1959" (*JNMA,* Nov. 1957, pp. 427–28). See also "Fiftieth Anniversary Report, Class of 1912" (Harvard Medical School, 1962, pp. 12–13); *Harvard Alumni Bulletin* (July 1959, p. 11); William Worthy's "Letter" in the *New England Journal of Medicine* (Sept. 18, 1952, p. 12); and Barbara Nabrit's "A Question of Merit: A study of William A. Hinton" (Honors Thesis, Radcliffe College, 1972). — JAMES E. TEELE

HODGES, BEN (? –1929), cowboy, cattle rustler, forger, and card cheat. Hodges was the son of a Negro father and a Mexican mother. Little is known about him until he arrived in Dodge City, Kans., with one of the first herds of cattle from Texas. Laying claim to descent from an old Spanish family, he presented apparently legitimate documents to support legal action for recognition of his right to a large land grant in Kansas. While his case was pending in court, he also obtained a letter of credit showing him to be the owner of thirty-two sections of Kansas land. Armed with this evidence, he contracted for the delivery of thousands of cattle from ranges near the Beaver and Cimarron Rivers. Unable to secure the necessary financial banking for the purchase, he obtained free railroad passes and used forged receipts in an attempt to swindle two cattlemen. When his forgery was discovered, he settled for a small sum of money. Accused of stealing a whole herd of milk cattle, he pleaded his own case and won an acquittal. He failed, however, in his attempt to gain appointment as a livestock inspector of Dodge City. His petition was rejected in part because it was supported by local saloon keepers, cowboys, gamblers, and dance-hall girls. More important was his reputation as a notorious cattle thief. He retired to private life, and on his death in 1929 he was buried in the Maple Grove Cemetery. His career was not unlike that, on a smaller canvas, of such other confidence men as Wyatt Earp and Bat Masterson.

One of the few remaining evidences of his successful rascality is a part of his two-hour plea that won his acquittal from the charge of stealing the herd of milk cows. He complained: "What me, the descendant of old grandees of Spain, the owner of a land grant embracing millions of acres, the owner of gold mines and villages and towns situated on that grant of which I am sole owner, to steal a miserable, miserly lot of old cows? Why, the idea is absurd. No, gentlemen, I think too much of the race of men from which I sprang, to disgrace their memory."

The best brief biography of Ben Hodges is in Philip Durham's and Everett L. Jones's *The Negro Cowboys* (1965, pp. 71–78). See also Harry E. Chrisman's *Lost Trails of the Cimarron* (1961). There is a photograph of Hodges on page 156 of William Loren Katz's *The Black West* (1971). — RAYFORD W. LOGAN

HOGAN, ERNEST [REUBEN CROWDERS] (1860?– 1909), actor, producer, singer, and composer. He was born in Bowling Green, Ky., but some facts of his parentage, exact date of birth, and early life are confused and sparse. It is known, however, that this exceptionally talented and versatile man began his career as a comic singer and dancer in the then-popular "medicine shows" of his youth. And it is believed that he took the name Hogan from one of those nomadic vendors of patent medicine for whom he had worked. Hogan was in his mid-twenties when he arrived in New York City about 1885. Minstrelsy was in vogue and Hogan's medicine-show experience had equipped him well to fill the requirements of the medium. At the same time the resourceful young Hogan recognized the limitations of the minstrel show and the caricature of Negro life and thought it projected. He entertained opposing ideas. One of them was to write, produce, and perform in his own shows.

Hogan's inventiveness as a comedian began to assert itself when he left the minstrel shows to go into vaudeville. Although virtually all Negro vaudeville comics of the era following the minstrel tradition, blackened their faces with burnt cork and used greasepaint to create the illusion of huge lips, Hogan spurned the custom. He relied instead on old attire and an uncanny ability to distort his mobile features to a hilarious degree. Moreover, as an actor and singer of consummate skill he was able to shift instantly the mood of his audience from raucous laughter to copious tears.

During the late 1880s Hogan toured with one of the many Negro road companies presenting *Uncle Tom's Cabin.* He also began to apply his musicianship in a new way. Until then the music forms called "coon songs" and "ragtime," forerunners of jazz, were performed primarily by musicians who could not read music. Ernest Hogan was one of the first to put that early popular music on paper, initiating thereby the songwriting aspect of his varied career. His greatest hit song, the one that brought fame and money to Hogan, was, ironically, to haunt him for the remainder of his life. More deeply immersed in creation than conscious of its psychological impact, Hogan had titled his song, published in 1896, "All Coons Look Alike to Me." The song's immense popularity, especially among racist whites who used it to insult Negroes more, profoundly distressed the sensitive Hogan. Yet the prophecy of his

lyrics became clear during the August 1900 race riot of New York City. Stampeding white mobs madly shrieked for the deaths of the only Negroes whose names they were familiar with. Ernest Hogan's was one of them, but he was kept for safety at the Winter Garden, Times Square, where he was playing.

The theater community, however, remained steadfast in its recognition of Hogan's genius. When Paul Laurence Dunbar and Will Marion Cook were seeking a comic star for their 1898 production of *Clorindy,* they chose Hogan. His success in that show enabled Hogan to begin forming and writing his own productions. A musical company that toured New England, Hawaii, and Australia was Hogan's initial attempt. Returning to America he formed The Smart Set whose hit song was his "Watermelon Time," which he sang with telling artistry. Other musicians fell under the Hogan influence. Not the least of them was the younger Will Marion Cook whose "Who Dat Say Chicken in Dis Crowd" was patterned on the Hogan style.

Hogan was at his peak in 1900. He had traveled extensively and had written not only for his own shows but for white companies as well. In 1902 Hogan and producer Gus Hill worked closely together. Then, three years later came Hogan's great show, *Rufus Rastus.* Collaborating with musician Joe Jordan, Hogan wrote the book and starred in *Rastus.* Its lyrics were the work of Lester A. Walton and Frank Williams. But the "show stopper" was a song written by Hogan and Jordan. It was called "Oh Say, Wouldn't That Be a Dream." Those who saw and heard Hogan do that song declared that his rendition of it was one of the great events in the history of the American theater. *Rufus Rastus* ran successfully for two years (1904–1906).

The Oyster Man was another great vehicle for Hogan —and his last. It was written by musician Will H. Vodery and lyricists Flournoy Miller and Aubrey Lyles. Hogan starred in it between 1907 and 1908, and its run would have continued had he not fallen ill of tuberculosis. The brilliant entertainer and writer never recovered. He died in New York City on May 20, 1909, at his home, 1002 Brook Ave., the Bronx, surrounded by relatives and friends. Funeral services were held on May 23 at the Church of St. Benedict the Moor, New York City; among the pall bearers were Bert Williams, Robert (Bob) Cole, and J. Rosamond Johnson. He was buried in the family plot in Bowling Green, Ky., on March 25. Survivors included his mother Louise Crowders, a niece, Maggie Warfield, and a nephew, Richard Van Neter.

There are brief sketches in Maud Cuney-Hare's *Negro Musicians and Their Music* (1937, pp. 157–58), Tom Fletcher's *100 Years of the Negro in Show Business* (1954), James Weldon Johnson's *Black Manhattan* (1930, pp. 102–27, passim), and Eileen Southern's *The Music of Black Americans: A History* (1971, pp. 269, 314–16, 352). An obituary was published in the *Baltimore Afro-American* (May 29, 1909) and the *New York Age* (May 27, 1909, p. 6). — ELTON C. FAX

HOLIDAY, BILLIE ["LADY DAY"] (1915–1959), singer. She was born Eleanor Fagan on April 7, 1915, in Baltimore, Md., the daughter of unwed teenage parents, Clarence Holiday and Sadie Fagan. They married three years later but were separated when Eleanor was still a baby. Mrs. Holiday left her with relatives and went north to work. Eleanor grew up in Baltimore where she suffered the first of many traumatic experiences: when she was ten years old, she was raped by a forty-year-old man who lived in the neighborhood. He was sent to prison and she to a Catholic "correctional" home. It was during these early years that she got her nickname of Billie. Her father had called her "Bill" because of her tomboy ways, and she changed it to Billie after Billie Dove, her silent-film idol.

When she was thirteen she joined her mother who was working as a domestic in New York City. Billie's life became progressively seamier: she smoked marijuana and was in and out of jail as a teenage prostitute. She recalled in her autobiography, *Lady Sings the Blues* (1956), written in collaboration with William Dufty, that when she was thirteen she ran errands for the "madam" in a house of prostitution.

At the same time, however, she developed a consuming interest in music. She was allowed to listen on the parlor phonograph to records by Bessie Smith and Louis Armstrong, who formed a lasting influence on her art. When she was eighteen she made her professional singing debut in Lower Manhattan at $10 a week. One of her biggest fans, John Hammond, the well-known jazz impresario, arranged for her to make her recording debut with Benny Goodman in November 1933. She continued singing in Harlem nightspots but was little known outside these circles.

Her thrust toward international renown began with the series of recording dates that Hammond set up with small bands, usually led by pianist Teddy Wilson. The formula was simple. Some of the best musicians were chosen from the bands of Count Basie, Duke Ellington, Fletcher Henderson, and Benny Goodman. The material recorded was invariably the popular songs of the day. And what resulted was some of the most outstanding jazz singing of all time. Holiday was unusual in that she did not perform songs in a "straight" fashion, that is, sing a composition as it was written. But she would approach it as a jazz instrumentalist. She altered melody, harmony, and rhythm, sometimes more radically than the horn players accompanying her.

During these years she was also a vocalist with the orchestras of Count Basie (1937) and Artie Shaw (1938). In the 1940s and 1950s she toured as a single performer. While Holiday was enjoying international recognition, she was falling into deeper personal tragedy. She found no long-standing happiness in her relationships with men, and her narcotics problem had become more serious with her addiction to heroin. Despite her addiction she still produced great artistic and commercial successes in her recordings of *Fine and Mellow* (1939), and *Strange Fruit* (1939). The latter was a powerful protest song against southern lynching and racial discrimination. She also appeared as a maid in the feature film *New Orleans* (1947).

An arrest for heroin addiction on May 2, 1947, led to commitment in the Federal Rehabilitation Establishment at Alderson, W.Va., for a year and a day. Ten days after leaving Alderson, she played before a packed house at Carnegie Hall, New York City. Deserted except for a few friends, she was denied a cabaret performer's license. This severely restricted her performances in the city that had the most sophisticated jazz listeners. Thereafter her life became even more of a shambles. She was acquitted in San Francisco (1949) of possessing opium. Her voice failed, along with the rest of her capacities. But she had several successful tours in Europe, notably Copenhagen. In 1958 she was reduced to singing for a percentage of the take at the Mars Club in the Rue St. Benoit near the Rue Marbeuf between the Champs-Élysées and Avenue George V in Paris. She made her final appearance in a benefit concert at the Phoenix Theater, New York City, in 1959. She collapsed in her small apartment at 26 W. 57th St. on May 31, 1959, and lapsed into a coma. A police ambulance took her to a private hospital where she lay on a stretcher without attention for an hour. Shunted as a drug addict and alcoholic to Metropolitan Hospital in Harlem, she again lay unattended until her physician, Dr. Eric Caminer, located her and placed her in an oxygen tent. Her serious heart, lung, and liver diseases ended her tempestuous career at 3:10 A.M. on July 17, 1959, in Room 6A12, Metropolitan Hospital.

Billie Holiday had been married three times: to musicians Jimmie Monroe and Joe Guy, and to a businessman, Louis McKay, from whom she was estranged at the time of her death. Funeral services, attended by 3000 mourners, were held in St. Paul the Apostle Roman Catholic Church, near Columbus Circle, New York City, and she was buried in Raymond's Cemetery, the Bronx. She was survived by Louis McKay and a half-sister, Kay Kelly. Her estate was reported as seventy cents in a bank account and $750 taped to her leg, the advance payment for a magazine article that she had agreed to write.

Basic information is in her autobiography, *Lady Sings the Blues,* written with William F. Dufty (1956, paperback reprint 1969). See also Marshall Stearns's *The Story of Jazz* (rev. ed. 1962). The movie *Lady Sings the Blues* (1972) has been criticized for its overemphasis on her addiction. Obituary and other notices were published in the *New York Times* (July 18, 20, 22, and 23, 1959). — HOLLIE I. WEST

HOLLAND, WILLIAM H. (1841–1907), soldier, politician, and educator. He was born a slave in Marshall, Tex., the son of Capt. Byrd (Bird) Holland, who later became secretary of state of Texas. While living in Panola County, Bird purchased William and his two brothers, Milton and James, in the late 1850s, and just prior to the Civil War sent them to Ohio to attend school. William and Milton attended the Albany Enterprise Academy, one of the early educational institutions in the northern United States conceived, owned, and operated by Negroes.

On Oct. 22, 1864, Holland enlisted in the 16th U.S. Colored Troops, a regiment organized at Nashville, Tenn., which included enlistees sent from Ohio. During the war the regiment participated in the battles of Nashville and Overton Hill, the pursuit of Hood to the Tennessee River, and garrison duty in Chattanooga, eastern and middle Tennessee. William's brothers en-

listed in the 5th U.S. Colored Troops, a regiment orga-
nized in Ohio. Milton received the Congressional
Medal of Honor for his role in the Battle of New Market
Heights on Sept. 29, 1864.

In 1867 Holland entered Oberlin College in the preparatory department. Although college records do not
record his graduation, he attended the institution for
two years before returning to Texas to teach school in
Austin and surrounding counties. A staunch Republican, Holland soon gained an appointment in the post
office. When the Fifteenth Texas Legislature convened
in April 1876, he served as the representative from
Waller County. During his term of office Holland fathered the bill which created Prairie View Normal
School for the colored students of the state. Largely
through the efforts of Norris Wright Cuney and Holland,
the Texas legislature passed a bill on April 5, 1887,
creating the Texas Institute for Deaf, Dumb, and Blind
Colored Youth. Edward Fay relates an interesting episode concerning Holland's role in the passage of the
bill. After passing the Texas House in the waning days
of the session, the bill awaited action in the Senate.
Thirty minutes prior to final adjournment, Holland approached Senator Armstead of Smith County in the Senate lobby and persuaded him to move for the passage
of the bill.

Six months later the institute opened on a 100-acre
site, two and one-half miles outside Austin. On Aug. 15,
1887, Democratic Gov. L. S. Ross appointed Holland
superintendent of the institution. For the next eleven
years he remained as head of the institution, becoming
perhaps the first Negro in the nation to direct a public
institution for the instruction of deaf, dumb, and blind
Negroes. The trustees of the institute were white, yet
placed complete confidence in Holland's administrative abilities. His wife Eliza joined the staff in 1890 as
an instructor of the deaf. In 1898 Holland was succeeded by S. J. Jenkins, a Negro Democrat who remained in the superintendency until his death on April
21, 1904. Holland was subsequently reappointed and
served until his death on May 27, 1907, of paralysis of
the heart, at his home in Wells, Tex.

Holland's interest extended beyond public philanthrophy to the private sector, where he started an organization in the Negro community known as the "Friend
in Need" which supplied financial aid to Negro students
unable to meet educational expenses.

The Holland obituary in the *Annals of the Deaf* (Nov.
1907, p. 490) noted: "While he labored under the
disadvantage of having no previous experience with the
deaf, he was a man of education and intelligence and
a good executive officer." A former board member said
of him: "Holland never praised Holland; and every time
I came in contact with him I saw a new and noble
quality, that I had not before observed. Many of us have
lost our truest and best friend. We pray God that the
many good deeds he has done, may prove to be bread
cast upon the waters."

There is no adequate biography of Holland, but a
general account of his life is found in J. Mason Brewer's
Negro Legislators of Texas (1970, pp. 73–74). A brief
sketch is Frank R. Levstik's "William H. Holland: Black
Soldier, Politician and Educator" (*NHB,* May 1973, pp.

110–11). Additional data on his institution and accomplishments are mentioned in Edward Fay's *Histories of
the American Schools for the Deaf 1817–1893* (1893).
— FRANK R. LEVSTIK

HOLLY, JAMES THEODORE (1829–1911), emigrationist, missionary, and bishop. He was born free in
Washington, D.C., according to his own account. At
fourteen he moved with his family to Brooklyn, where
he engaged in shoemaking with his father. By 1848
when he began working as a clerk for the abolitionist
Lewis Tappan, James had developed an active interest
in the antislavery movement in New York. In 1850
James and his brother Joseph opened their own bootmaking shop in Burlington, Vt., where both were drawn
into the burgeoning debate over the emigration of
Negroes. James championed the American Colonization Society while Joseph argued that free Negroes
should remain in the United States. In 1851 James Holly
moved with his bride Charlotte to Windsor, Canada
West, to co-edit Henry Bibb's newspaper *Voice of the
Fugitive.* Holly remained in the Windsor-Detroit area
for three years and endorsed the ill-fated Refugee
Home Society, organized the Amherstburg Convention in 1851, and through his newspaper continuously
espoused emigration as the only solution for American
Negroes. Although he was raised as a Roman Catholic, he joined the Protestant Episcopal church at this
time, becoming a deacon in 1855 and the next year a
priest.

Holly was a delegate to the first National Emigration
Convention in 1854 in Cleveland and in the following
year he represented the National Emigration Board as
commissioner, traveling to Haiti to negotiate an emigration treaty. On that trip he also explored the island as
a possible site for an Episcopal mission. But talks proved
inconclusive and the Board of Missions of the Protestant
Episcopal church denied his application as a missionary
to Haiti. In 1856 he moved to New Haven, Conn.,
where he served until 1861 as priest of St. Luke's
Church and as a teacher in public and private schools.
After attending the 1856 National Emigration Convention, Holly traveled through the eastern states to promote the idea of emigration to Haiti. His lecture *Vindication of the Capacity of the Negro Race for Self
Government and Civilized Progress* was published in
book form in 1857. He denounced the vilification of
Negroes as a "brood of inferior beings" and urged emigration to "monarchical" Haiti, where there was, he
claimed, "far more security for the personal liberty and
the general welfare of the governed . . . than exists in
this bastard democracy [the United States]" (especially
p. 168). He also co-founded, with William Charles
Munroe, the Convocation of the Protestant Episcopal
Society for Promoting the Extension of the Work
Among Colored People, an organization to recruit
Negroes into the church and the emigration movement.

Holly became convinced that free Negroes, working
strictly on their own, could not successfully accomplish
a mass emigration project to Haiti. In 1859 he therefore
corresponded with Rep. Francis P. Blair, Jr., about government aid for emigration. He also badgered the Board
of Missions of the Episcopal church to finance him as

a missionary to Haiti. Not mentioned to the church was his intention to take a group of emigrants with him to Haiti. The fall of 1860 saw Holly working for James Redpath, the official Haitian commissioner of emigration. As a recruiting agent of the Haitian government, Holly lectured widely in Pennsylvania, New Jersey, and New England. In May 1861 Holly took his own 110-member New Haven Colony to Haiti. While other emigration leaders of the 1850s talked of leaving the United States but stayed, Holly talked of leaving and left.

The first year in Haiti was disastrous for Holly's colony. His mother, wife, two children, and thirty-nine other members of his group died of yellow fever and malaria. Other members returned to the United States. Only Holly and a handful of followers remained in Haiti. In autumn 1862 Holly, by then a Haitian citizen, returned to the United States to seek financial support from the General Convention of the Protestant Episcopal church to establish a mission station. His request was denied, but the American Church Missionary Society agreed to underwrite Holly's salary in Haiti. In 1865 the Board of Missions of the Protestant Episcopal church accepted sponsorship of Holly's mission in Haiti, a support, however meager, which lasted until 1911.

Holly dreamed of establishing a national Episcopal church in Haiti—a church to replace the dominant Roman Catholicism on the island. In 1874 he was consecrated missionary bishop of Haiti at Grace Church, New York City, the first Negro Bishop in the Episcopal Church. As the head of his national Episcopal church, Holly attended the Lambeth Conference in London in 1878. He was also recognized as bishop of the Orthodox Apostolic church of Haiti.

Although he rarely visited America after 1861—only seven times in half a century—Holly never lost interest in his black brethren in the United States. He and his second wife Sarah Henley educated nine sons in America. Holly also conducted an extensive correspondence with American Negroes and published many articles on social, political, and religious subjects in the *A.M.E. Church Review*. He never abandoned his belief that emigration was the only way for American blacks to better their lot.

Because he recognized that education and good health were important facets of the church's concern, Holly worked hard to establish schools and medical facilities in Haiti. But the impact of his Orthodox Apostolic church remained slight in all areas of Haitian life. Fires and recurrent revolutions impeded his several activities. When he died of old age on March 13, 1911, his church numbered only a few thousand members. Funeral services were held in the capital and he was buried in Holy Trinity Church, Port-au-Prince.

Of nine children, Theodore Faustin, Augustine, and Alfred were deceased; Alonzo P. B. Holly, M.D., author and specialist for women and children, was living in West Palm Beach, Fla.; Arthur Holly, M.D., eye, ear, and throat specialist, resided in Port-au-Prince; Sabourin Holly, M.D., was practicing optometry in Port-au-Prince; Louis Holly was a civil engineer in Port-au-Prince; Ambroise Holly was a chemist and pharmacist in Haiti; Melle Theodora Holly, a writer and former

lecturer at Tuskegee Institute, was also in Haiti. The following grandchildren were living in or near New York: William G. Holly, an industrial chemist; Louis S. Holly, a commercial artist; Blanche M. Holly, a former teacher at Bethune-Cookman College, Daytona, Fla.; James Theodore Holly, a chemist and pharmacist; Lydia E. Holly, a French interpreter; Mrs. Walter Wilson, Mrs. Joseph Ingram, and Dr. Rudolph Holly, an intern at Harlem Hospital.

For a detailed study of Holly, see David Dean's unpublished dissertation "James Theodore Holly" (University of Texas at Austin, 1972). Holly's role in the emigration movement of the 1850s is evaluated in Floyd J. Miller's *The Search for a Black Nationality* (1975). A commemoration of the centenary of the consecration of Bishop Holly, held at the Washington (D.C.) Cathedral (Feb. 7 and 8, 1975), included a brief biographical sketch by Nancy Gordon [Heinl], *Cathedral Age* (summer 1975, p. 8). His *Vindication . . .* may be conveniently consulted in *Negro Social and Political Thought, 1850–1920, Representative Texts,* edited by Howard Brotz (1968). There is a brief sketch by Benjamin Brawley in *DAB* (5, part 1:156–57).

— DAVID W. DEAN

HOLMES, DWIGHT [OLIVER WENDELL] (1877–1963), teacher, university administrator, and college president. Born in Lewisburg, W.Va., he was the son of John Alexander Holmes, a Methodist minister, and Sarah (Bollin) Holmes. After completing the preparatory and college departments of Howard University, he was granted his B.A. (1901) as valedictorian of his class. As an undergraduate he was active in college life: captain of both the football and basketball teams, president of the Athletic Association, organizer and first president of the tennis club, leader of the first college debate participated in by Howard University students, and leader of the mandolin and glee club. He took graduate work at Howard University, the Johns Hopkins University, and Teachers College, Columbia University, where he earned his M.A. (1915) and Ph.D. (1934), specializing in teacher education and higher education. He was awarded honorary degrees by Howard University (M.A., 1912; LL.D., 1938) and Morgan State College (LL.D., 1953).

In an educational career covering forty-six years, Holmes was a teacher of English at the Sumner High School, St. Louis (1902); teacher, mainly of sciences, at the Colored High School, Baltimore, Md. (1902–1917), where he was also head of the Department of Sciences and vice-principal; instructor in psychology and biology, the Myrtilla Miner Normal School, Washington, D.C. (1917–1919); professor of education and administrator, Howard University, Washington, D.C. (1919–1937), where, in addition to his teaching, he was successively registrar (1919–1921), dean of the College of Education (1921–1934), dean of the Graduate School (1934–1937), and in the summer of 1930, acting president. In 1937 he became the president of Morgan College (later Morgan State University), Baltimore, where he served until his retirement in 1948.

Holmes's career reflects the rigid racial segregation of his era. All of his education, except at the graduate level, and all his teaching and administrative experiences, were in Negro schools and colleges; and all his research and writing was concerned with Negro education. His influence therefore was largely on Negro education. During the early part of his career in higher education, only a handful of Negro colleges were conducting work of actual college level, and among these Howard University was preeminent. He was in a position, consequently, to make significant contributions to the developing system of Negro higher education.

Holmes's outstanding achievements were as a scholar, as a university administrator, and as a college president. His publications include one book and twenty-eight articles in various journals, an excellent record for his times. His book, *The Evolution of the Negro College* (1934), the publication of his doctoral dissertation, constituted the most comprehensive historical treatment of the subject up to then. Its purpose was "to present the circumstances surrounding the establishment and development of the Negro college, in order to furnish an integrated background upon which to project the problems that arise from an inquiry into the present place and function of this group of schools in the scheme of higher education in America." His most significant articles were "Fifty years of Howard University" (*JNH*, July and Oct. 1918); "The Present Status of College Education Among Negroes" (*Bulletin of the American Teachers Association*, 1931), and the following articles in the *Journal of Negro Education:* "The Beginnings of the Negro College" (July 1934), "Does Negro Education Need Reorganization and Re-direction. A Statement of the Problem" (July 1936), "The Future Possibilities of Graduate Work in Negro Colleges and Universities" (Jan. 1938), and "Twenty-five Years of Thomas Jesse Jones and the Phelps-Stokes Fund" (1938); and "The Present Problems Involved in Graduate and Professional Training for Negroes in the South" (*Proceedings of the Association of Colleges and Secondary Schools*, 1939). He also contributed a number of book reviews in various issues of the *Journal of Negro Education.*

At Howard University (1919–1937) Holmes distinguished himself as an organizer and administrator when he was dean of the College of Education and subsequently the first dean of the Graduate School. His pioneer administrative work gains added significance because during his tenure, and with his assistance, Howard University began to assemble a university faculty with research interests in a wide range of fields. While at Howard he was also active in many professional organizations. He was president of the Association of Colleges for Negro Youth for two years and chairman of the Committee on Rating of Negro Colleges, which was instrumental in leading to the decision of the Southern Association of Colleges and Secondary Schools to assume the function of rating the Negro institutions of higher education in its jurisdiction.

In 1937 Holmes became the sixth president, and the first Negro president, of Morgan College, which in 1939 was designated Morgan State College. He guided the transition of the institution from the control of the Methodist church to the State of Maryland. During his ten-year administration the college made substantial gains in financial support, enrollment, size and quality of faculty, range of curriculum, and physical plant. He accepted the role of Morgan State College as a racially separate institution; his thrust in the development of the college was in accordance with the "separate but equal" doctrine, with a very literal interpretation of "equal." His basic philosophy, which guided the development of the college both during and after his administration, is expressed by the following excerpts from his inaugural address: "The Negro needs higher education in the same amount and to the same degree as does the white man. . . . I believe a liberal education should be an experience where one intellectually reaches an appreciation of spiritual values. I am convinced, therefore, that a group of college people should be easily distinguished from a group of non-college people by their superior taste, by their broader comprehension of the meaning of life, by their greater respect for personality, by their heightened sensitivity to social need, by the clearness of their vision and the broadness of their love for humanity, by their ability to think things through and to do things well. This is just another way of saying that colleges should produce the choicest people when judged by those qualities that indicate fineness and usefulness in human beings."

Dwight Holmes married Lucy C. Messer in 1907. She became the mother of their son, Dwight O. W. Jr. In 1957 he married Alverta Morsell Jones in Baltimore. Holmes died in 1963; funeral services were held in Baltimore and, at his request, his ashes were scattered on the waters of the Chesapeake Bay. He was survived by his widow, Dwight O. W. Jr., and one grandchild.

Essential biographical information is in *Who's Who in America, 1946–1947.* Holmes's papers are a special collection in the Soper Library, Morgan State University, Baltimore. — MARTIN D. JENKINS

HOPE, JOHN (1868–1936), teacher, college and university president, member of numerous committees and commissions. He was born on June 2, 1868, in Augusta, Ga. His grandmother, Alethea, was one of several slaves of Judge Hugh Taylor, a large plantation owner. Alethea, whose father was white, was the acknowledged mistress of a white man named Butt, who emancipated her sometime before 1860. Of the seven children of this union, Mary Frances (Fanny) was the mother of John Hope. James Hope, his father, was born in Langholm, Scotland, in 1805. He acquired considerable wealth and lived openly with Fanny in a home frequented by some of the best known white citizens of Augusta. After John's father's death in October 1876, executors of his estate deprived Fanny of all except a pittance left in trust to her. John Hope became aware that he was "only another colored boy."

He completed the eighth year in the Augusta public schools (1881), where one of his teachers was Lucy Laney, and worked as a clerk in a fashionable Negro-owned restaurant. In 1886 he entered Worcester Academy, Worcester, Mass. Although he could easily have passed for white, he insisted upon being recognized as a Negro. He joined the debating society, was editor-in-chief of the school's newspaper, and participated in sports. After graduating with honors and delivering one of the class orations in June 1890, he enrolled with the aid of a scholarship at Brown University in September. He was a member of the editorial board of the *Brown Daily Herald* and founded an off-campus literary club. In 1894 he was class orator at commencement exercises and received the degree of Bachelor of Arts.

From 1894 to 1898 he taught at Roger Williams University, Nashville, Tenn., and then joined the faculty of Atlanta Baptist College. In addition to teaching classics, he served as bookkeeper, introduced football in 1899, and coached for a few years. In June 1906 he became the first Negro president of Atlanta Baptist College (Morehouse College in 1913). On July 1, 1929, he became president of the (new) Atlanta University, the first institution for Negroes offering only graduate work. Following an attack of pneumonia, he died in McVicar Hospital on the campus of Spelman College on Feb. 20, 1936. He was buried beneath his office on the Atlanta University campus.

Although deprived of his inheritance, Hope was not embittered against white people. Like Channing H. Tobias, fourteen years his junior, he lived as a youth in Augusta, a kind of oasis in the Old South. He did not feel isolated at either Worcester or Brown. At Brown, however, he began to associate with the colored people of Providence, including the fellow colored waiters in a large catering establishment. His growing awareness of what W. E. B. Du Bois called "Negro-ness" resulted largely from a visit to Providence of John M. Langston in 1890. Hope was a member of the committee on arrangements which organized a public meeting and banquet. He sat on the platform and attended the banquet. Langston's speech, Hope later wrote, "stamped him as a Negro, an American citizen and a scholar." Du Bois, who like Hope was born in 1868, wrote in 1944 that at Fisk University in 1885, "A new loyalty and allegiance replaced my Americanism; henceforward I was a Negro." Of course, it was not this simple. Like Langston and Du Bois, Hope confronted the problem of being both a Negro and an American citizen. When Langston, on the invitation of Pres. E. Benjamin Andrews, spoke the next day at Brown, Hope "rejoiced that the time had come when, in one institution of learning, culture and ability were recognized, regardless of their color." With some limitations, he nurtured this creed for the rest of his life.

Offered a position on the *Providence Journal,* for which he had already done some reporting, he decided to cast his lot with the colored people of the South. Spurning an offer by Booker T. Washington to teach at Tuskegee Institute, he preferred the liberal arts college, Roger Williams University, in Nashville. The faculty consisted of Negroes and whites, men and women. Hope taught natural sciences, Latin, and Greek.

He heard Washington's famous Atlanta Speech (Sept. 18, 1895), and became more convinced that he did not share Washington's views. On George Washington's birthday, 1896, he told a colored debating society in Nashville: "If we are not striving for equality, in heaven's name for what are we living? . . . Now catch your breath, for I am going to use an adjective: I am going to say we demand social equality." Also in the spring of 1896 in an address on "The Need of a Liberal

Education for Us," he declared: "The Negro must enter the higher fields of learning. He must be prepared for advanced and original investigation. . . . Mere honesty, mere wealth will not give us rank among the other peoples of the civilized world; and, what is more we ourselves will never be possessed of conscious self-respect, until we can point to men in our own ranks who are easily the equal of any race" (quoted by Ridgely Torrence, *The Story of John Hope* [1948], pp. 115–16). Hope thus publicly challenged the views of Washington while Du Bois was still under the spell of the Atlanta Speech.

During his Christmas vacation, Hope married in Chicago Lugenia Burns whom he had met while working there in 1893. Born in St. Louis, she had lived most of her life in Chicago and done social work there. After their marriage she became friendly with the girls at Roger Williams and started a class in physical education. They became the parents of two sons, Edward Swain, born in August 1901, and John Jr. (II), born on Dec. 25, 1909.

Atlanta, the Hopes' home except for travel, from 1898 to 1936, helped mold Hope as he and his wife helped mold the city. It was, in a sense, the "Athens" of Negroes in the South: in addition to Atlanta Baptist College there were also the original Atlanta University, Spelman College for girls, Morris Brown University, Clark College, and Gammon Theological Seminary. Du Bois had joined the faculty of Atlanta University in 1897, the year before Hope did at Atlanta Baptist College. Their friendship ripened during the next thirteen years (Du Bois left in 1910 to join the NAACP). Their intellectual views brought them closer together, and Hope was the only college president who dared attend the Harpers Ferry meeting of the Niagara Movement (Aug. 1906). And he was the only college president, white or Negro, to attend the protest meeting in New York City (May 1909) which resulted in the founding of the NAACP (Clarence A. Bacote, *The Story of Atlanta University* . . . [1969], p. 275). Mrs. Hope was one of the first to do volunteer social work in Atlanta, beginning in 1898 and resulting in the organization ten years later of the Neighborhood Union.

A month after his return from Harpers Ferry, Hope calmly met the fury of the Atlanta race riot and began his active administration of Atlanta Baptist College. In accordance with the policy of the Baptist Home Mission Society, he at first had the title of "acting president." He nevertheless began actively to increase the enrollment on the college level and to seek financial support from northern philanthropic foundations. He secured aid only after Robert Russa Moton, with whom he had had friendly association since 1893, prevailed upon Booker T. Washington to support Hope's pleas. He showed even during these early years his ability to attract to his faculty some of the leading Negro scholars, notably Benjamin Brawley (M.A., Harvard), Clement Richardson, another Harvard graduate, John Brown Watson, a graduate of Brown University, and William J. Bauduit, a graduate of the University of Chicago. For several years he continued to teach, not only the classics but also logic, psychology, and ethics, when no other teacher was available.

In the spring and summer of 1912 he went abroad for the first time: to Scotland, England, France, Switzerland, Italy, and on his return, to Langholm, Scotland, his father's birthplace. He never returned to Langholm (Torrence, *John Hope*, p. 181).

In 1913, when Atlanta Baptist College was renamed Morehouse College, Hope remained as president. He and Brawley, whom he had lured as dean back from Howard University, organized the curriculum which laid the foundation for Morehouse's later reputation as "The College of Presidents" because of the number of graduates who became heads of colleges. Carter G. Woodson, who knew Hope well, rightly called him "a maker of men." Two of the earliest were Mordecai W. Johnson who became president of Howard University and John W. Davis who became president of West Virginia Collegiate Institute (later West Virginia State College). Davis said that Hope exercised his greatest influence on students by his chapel talks, and that as a teacher he talked less about Greek than about life. Morehouse was known also for its early participation in student government.

Hope's activities continued to extend beyond the college campus. He was president of the National Association of Teachers of Colored Schools, a member of the advisory board of the NAACP, of the executive committee of the National Urban League, president of the Association for the Study of Negro Life and History at the time of his death, member of the board of managers of the Atlanta YMCA and the city's antituberculosis association.

Like Du Bois, Moton, and Addie W. Hunton, he observed the treatment of colored soldiers in France during most of the period from Sept. 11, 1918, to July 1919. Among his important recommendations was the substitution of colored for white YMCA secretaries who were generally disliked and distrusted by colored soldiers and officers. After a brief return because of urgent duties at Morehouse, he went back to France in May "with full oversight of the work among Negro soldiers with colored secretaries." He accepted the establishment of separate rest areas at Chambéry and Challes-les-Eaux as tolerable because they were manned by colored YMCA secretaries. He spent some time during his first visit at the front in the Argonne Forest and praised the courage of both the soldiers and the secretaries under fire. Before he left France in July 1919, he had been appointed a member of the field staff of the YMCA and was known as the field secretary for work among colored troops. He continued his interest in the YMCA until his death, giving support particularly to his friend Channing H. Tobias.

World War I left Hope so disillusioned that he hesitated to join the Commission on Interracial Cooperation then being organized by Will W. Alexander, a white southerner and former Methodist minister. After the commission exacted the fulfillment of a promise to commit use of some of the funds from a bond issue for the construction of a public high school for Negroes, Hope accepted appointment on June 25, 1920. Mrs. Hope became a member later and in 1932 Hope was elected president of the commission. The many activities of the commission helped improve race relations.

With the aid of substantial funds from the General Education Board and the American Baptist Home Mission Society, as well as contributions from Negroes, Hope from 1920 to 1929 built the "Greater Morehouse." The Atlanta School of Social Work, later headed by E. Franklin Frazier, opened in September 1920. He retained as dean Samuel Howard Archer, a graduate of Colgate who together with Hope and Brawley had earlier been known as the "triumvirate" which developed Morehouse, and who had acted as president while Hope was in Europe. He brought to Morehouse notably Benjamin Mays who later became president of the college, Nathaniel Tillman as professor of English, and Samuel M. Nabrit as professor of biology. The enrollment more than trebled and new buildings were erected. He employed as his secretary Constance Crocker, who later married Professor Nabrit and remained his indispensable aide until his death. He established cordial relations with Florence M. Read, the new white president of Spelman College who was to play a significant role in the establishment of the new Atlanta University.

Meanwhile he resumed his travels abroad: in 1924 to England and the continent; in 1926 with his wife to several European conferences. In Sweden he and Tobias attended the meeting of the World's Alliance of the YMCA. At a conference in Le Zoute, Belgium, he urged colonial governments to grant wider opportunities for Negroes to work in Africa. In the summer of 1927 he attended the Geneva meeting of the World Committee of the YMCA, of which he was a member. The following spring, as a member of the Commission on Interracial Cooperation, he participated in the conference of the International Missionary Council whose aim was to prevent future international conflict. As a member of a committee on racial policy, he obtained the adoption of a strong antidiscriminatory resolution. Perhaps his most significant voyage was his visit to the Soviet Union in the summer of 1932. In Moscow, Stalingrad, and Rostov, he talked with officials and reported after his return in September, "I was uplifted by what I saw in Russia." A "real vacation" in 1934 took him, accompanied by Mrs. Nabrit, to England, France, Switzerland, and Italy. In December 1935 he visited Haiti ("a beautiful country, a noble, courageous, self-respecting people, poor but carrying their heads high even when in rags"), Jamaica, Colombia, and the Canal Zone ("a painful place racially"). He had perhaps a broader grasp of international relations than did most contemporary Negroes, a valuable asset in his concept of the goals of a university.

On April 1, 1929, the Board of Trustees of the new Atlanta University unanimously elected him president, and he took office on July 1. He outlined a plan for the university, in cooperation with Spelman College and Morehouse College, to offer senior-graduate courses. On April 1, 1930, he submitted "The Six Year Plan," which proposed a graduate school of liberal arts, a library school, a school of business administration, a graduate school of social work through affiliation with the Atlanta School of Social Work, a department of music and fine arts, and more distant goals. The plan included recommendations regarding the architectural redesign of the three campuses, involving a new library, a president's house, a joint administration building, and two graduate dormitories. It declared the intention of the three schools "during this period to develop enough unity and solidarity of both purpose and machinery to make it feasible to invite the affiliation of other colleges [Morris Brown, Clark College, and Gammon Theological Seminary]." It envisioned the offering of the master's degree, and later the Ph.D. Despite recognized deficiencies of the colleges in "culture and scholarship," the university would "insist on the highest standing in the United States" (Bacote, *Atlanta University,* p. 279).

Hope in large measure achieved these goals. He assembled the largest number of well-trained teachers in any predominantly Negro university except Howard. Among the most notable of these were Clarence A. Bacote, history; Helen T. Albro of Spelman, biology; Tillman of Morehouse, English; Mercer Cook of Atlanta, (Miss) William Bryan Geter of Spelman, and Edward A. Jones of Morehouse, French; Brailsford R. Brazeal of Morehouse, economics; Lorimer D. Milton, Jesse B. Blayton, and William H. Dean, Jr., in the Department of Economics and Business Administration; Samuel M. Nabrit of Morehouse, biology; Ira de A. Reid, sociology; and William Stanley Braithwaite, English.

The most distinguished appointment was that of W. E. B. Du Bois as guest professor in the Departments of Economics and Sociology for the second semester 1932–1933. In the fall of 1933 Du Bois became professor of sociology.

These teachers and others less well known but equally capable in many respects provided a high quality of work for ninety-three students who received the master's degree between 1931 and 1936; eighty-one were M.A. and twelve M.S. Summer school (six weeks) was too short to enable students to complete requirements for the degree, but it enabled a sizable number of public school teachers to expand their knowledge and teaching skills. In the summer of 1934 there emerged the Atlanta University Summer Theater under the direction of Anne Cooke (who later married Ira Reid), the first of its kind in Atlanta.

Atlanta University's influence extended beyond the campus. The Department of Education sponsored an annual conference of Negro Secondary School Principals and Teachers of Fulton and De Kalb Counties. One of the most significant activities was directed by Mrs. Hope, Bacote, and Rayford W. Logan (who served on the faculty from 1933 to 1938). Mrs. Hope conceived the idea of a citizenship school, sponsored by the NAACP, to encourage Negroes of Atlanta to vote. In 1932 Bacote was appointed director of the Citizenship School. While he was on leave (1933–1934), Logan expanded the program by the establishment of schools in different parts of the city. As director of the Educational Program of the Alpha Phi Alpha fraternity he initiated registration and voting procedures, which were conducted throughout the South with the slogan "A Voteless People Is a Hopeless People."

Hope supported Mrs. Hope and this project. He also encouraged or permitted members of the faculty to serve on such boards as the Atlanta Urban League. But

during a virtual "reign of terror" in the mid-1930s when the Ku Klux Klan revived its activities, he deemed it prudent for the more aggressive younger members of the faculty to reduce their visibility. On the other hand he used the power of the purse to compel respect from white businessmen. During the construction of the graduate dormitories, for instance, when telephone calls came for "John Hope," he politely but firmly made it clear that continuation of their contracts depended on their addressing him as "Mr. Hope." He also broke new ground when in January 1935 he delivered at the Biltmore Hotel in Atlanta the address of welcome to representatives of more than 480 colleges at the Twenty-first Annual Meeting of the Association of American Colleges.

One of the most dramatic and significant events was the beginning of the first low-rent housing project in the United States. As early as October 1933 Hope had begun urging the Public Works Administration in Washington to appropriate funds for a slum clearance project near the university. On Sept. 29, 1934, Secretary of the Interior Harold L. Ickes set off the fuse that dynamited the first house on the eighteen-acre tract known as Beaver Slide.

Views about Hope as an administrator naturally are conflicting. His biographer, Ridgely Torrence, for instance, did not reveal the autocratic way in which Hope administered Atlanta University. Rayford W. Logan recalls that he held two faculty meetings a year: at the opening of school to greet the members of the faculty and to urge them to come to see him (there was no dean) whenever they had problems; and near the end of the school year when we approved the list of graduates. He brooked no familiarity, although he and Mrs. Hope entertained graciously and elegantly in the president's magnificent home. "Aristocrat and autocrat of the Breakfast Table" is Logan's considered evaluation of Hope who, in his latter years, was a handsome, curly-haired voluntary Negro, proud of his Scottish ancestry but dedicated to the quest of Negroes for equality and justice.

Of the many honors conferred upon him, he probably most appreciated three: the 1929 Harmon Award for Distinguished Achievement in Education among Negroes, election as an Alumni Member of Phi Beta Kappa (Brown University, 1919), and the LL.D. degree (Brown, 1935).

Funeral services were held in Morehouse Chapel and he was carried by students to a simple grave below what had been his office. The most fitting tribute was that of Trevor Arnett, president of the General Education Board: "The extraordinary development which Atlanta University has had under Dr. Hope's guidance and direction has astonished and gratified his friends and has far surpassed their highest expectations. He has laid secure foundations of an institution in the South, on which can be built an edifice at which the Negro can obtain higher education comparable to that obtainable in any other part of the country. His accomplishments entitle him to a foremost place among educational statesmen."

The principal source for this sketch is Ridgely Torrence's *The Story of John Hope* (1948), which, though slightly adulatory, is essential for basic facts. Hope's career as president of Atlanta University is documented in Clarence A. Bacote's authoritative *The Story of Atlanta University, A Century of Service 1865–1965* (1969, especially pp. 273–315). The contributor has, as indicated, also drawn upon his personal reminiscences. See also the sketch in *DAB, Supplement Two* (9, Part 2 [1958]: 314–15). The John Hope Papers are in two locations: those relating to his YMCA activities are at the Moorland-Spingarn Research Center, Howard University; those pertaining to his administration at Morehouse College and Atlanta University are at Atlanta University.

— RAYFORD W. LOGAN

HOPKINS, PAULINE ELIZABETH (1856–1930), musician, stenographer, editor, journalist, author, and publisher. Born in Portland, Me., she was the daughter of Northrup and Sarah (Allen) Hopkins. Pauline's father and stepfather, William A. Hopkins, a Civil War veteran, were Virginians; the latter, a barber and laborer, died on Feb. 19, 1906. Her mother, born in Exeter, N.H., in 1837, was a direct descendant of a well-known New England family which included the clergymen Nathaniel Paul and Thomas Paul; she was also the grandniece of the poet James Whitefield. In her early childhood she lived with her family in Boston, one of the principal centers of abolitionist activities and home of several prominent Negroes. Educated in the Boston public schools, at the age of fifteen she won a prize of ten dollars in gold for her essay on "The Evils of Intemperance and Their Remedies." The contest was sponsored during several years by the noted historian William Wells Brown. Pauline's award encouraged her to seek a career as an author after she graduated from Girls High School.

It was not until 1880, however, that her next literary effort was published. The *Sunday Boston Herald* of July 4, 1880, advertised her production of "Hopkins' Colored Troubadors in the Great Musical Drama, Escape from Slavery," including such well-known troubadors as Sam Lucas and the Hyers Sisters, with a chorus of more than sixty. William A. Hopkins was a mulatto overseer, Sarah A. Hopkins, the "mammy," and Pauline, "the pet of the plantation," and referred to as "Boston's Colored Soprano, a favorite wherever she sings."

The musical drama had five performances, and twelve years later (1892) Hopkins won additional acclaim for her memorial address to the Robert A. Bell Boston Post of the Grand Army of the Republic. Her illustrated lecture on Toussaint L'Ouverture in Tremont Temple and elsewhere also received favorable notices.

In order to earn a living, Hopkins studied stenography and began working in 1892 with wealthy Republicans. After four years she passed the civil service examination and was appointed stenographer in the Bureau of Statistics for the Census of 1895. She held this position for four years.

In 1900 her first novel *Contending Forces, A Romance Illustrative of Negro Life North and South,* was published in Boston by the Colored Co-Operative Publishing Company, 5 Park Square. She declared that "Fiction is of great value to any people as a preserver of manners and customs—religious, political and social. It

is a record of growth and development from generation to generation. No one will do this for us." During much of her life she sought to "faithfully portray the inmost thoughts and feelings of the Negro with all the fire and romance which lie dormant in our history, and, as yet, unrecognized by writers of the Anglo-Saxon race." Although in her introductory note Hopkins stated that she "tried to tell an impartial story, leaving the reader to draw conclusions," Hugh Morris Gloster observed: "Perhaps the best comment that may be made about the book is that it provides interesting sidelights on the struggles of a middle-class Negro family for education, employment, and social betterment in post-bellum Boston" (*Negro Voices in American Fiction* [1948], pp. 33–34). It may be added, however, that in her emphasis on the role of Negroes in writing their own history, Hopkins was one of the neglected precursors of Carter G. Woodson. She promoted the sale of *Contending Forces* by reading sections from the book to women's clubs in many parts of the nation.

Contending Forces led to her serving as editor and frequent contributor to the *Colored American Magazine,* also published by the Colored Co-Operative Company. Appearing initially in May 1900, it was the first Negro journal established in the early twentieth century. Hopkins and her associates stressed the need for the periodical because no other monthly magazine was "distinctly devoted" to the interests of Afro-Americans or to "the development of Afro-American art and literature." (They were in error, for the *A.M.E. Church Review* was similarly devoted.) In this first issue Hopkins contributed a short story, "The Mystery Within Us." During her editorship—the exact date for its beginning is unclear—the illustrated *Colored American Magazine* is a major source for the literature, science, music, art, religions, facts, and traditions of the Negro race during four years.

Pauline Hopkins was one of the major contributors. She wrote three lengthy serials: "Hagar's Daughters, A Story of Southern Caste Prejudice" under the pseudonym of her mother's name (March 1901 to March 1902); "Winona, A Tale of Negro Life in the South and Southwest" (May 1902 to Oct. 1902); and "Of One Blood; or, the Hidden Self" (Nov. 1902 to Nov. 1903). These and her short stories, numbering at least eight, dealt with the then largely taboo topic of interracial relationships, which led to the cancelation of subscriptions by some white readers. Repeatedly declaring that "history is biography," she wrote twenty-one valuable sketches about "Famous Men of the Negro Race" and "Famous Women of the Negro Race." Among the more important dealt with the careers of Williams Wells Brown, Frederick Douglass, Toussaint L'Ouverture, Harriet Tubman, Sojourner Truth, Booker T. Washington, Robert Brown Elliott, Lewis Hayden, and Charles Lenox Remond. She included biographies also of prominent white men. Although not documented, these biographies were carefully written after much research. All were well illustrated with engravings from paintings and photographs.

After she was relieved of her position as editor in September 1904, the November issue expressed appreciation for her services and voiced the hope that she would soon recover from the ill health that made it necessary for her to "sever her relations with this Magazine." The real reason was probably the purchase in 1904 of the *Colored American Magazine* by Fred R. Moore, secretly subsidized by Booker T. Washington as a part of his maneuvers to influence or control Negro-owned newspapers. In a 1912 issue of *The Crisis,* W. E. B. Du Bois asserted that Hopkins had not been conciliatory enough for the new management.

She continued briefly as a contributor to the other early twentieth-century monthly magazine, *Voice of the Negro,* founded in January 1904. She wrote for the December 1904 issue of this first Negro journal in the South a commissioned illustrated article "The New York Subway," giving detailed information about the building of the tunnel and the construction of trains. From February to July 1905 she wrote four articles on "The Dark Races of the Twentieth Century." Edited by J. Max Barber, *Voice of the Negro,* later *Voice,* the magazine, like the *Colored American Magazine,* opposed Washington's conciliatory policies and practices and was a significant precursor of Du Bois's *Moon, Horizon* and *The Crisis.*

Hopkins's literary career virtually ceased with her contributions to *Voice of the Negro.* She founded her own publishing firm, P. E. Hopkins and Company, and in 1905 published in Cambridge *A Primer of Facts Pertaining to the Early Greatness of the African Race and the Possibility of Restoration by Its Descendants, with Epilogue,* a booklet of thirty-one pages. Also, she contributed two articles (Feb. and March 1916) to *New Era* magazine. Published by the New Era Publishing Company in Boston and edited by her, its format was similar to that of the *Colored American Magazine.* This effort to renew the goal of a "monthly devoted to world-wide interests of the Negro race" was unsuccessful, probably because *The Crisis* had preempted the market. Hopkins's first article, "Topsy Templeton," dealt with the efforts of individuals to solve the race question; the second consisted of biographies of two prominent clergymen, Leonard Grimes and Henry Highland Garnet.

She probably had written also the biographical sketch of William Lloyd Garrison in the sixteen-page illustrated souvenir program commemorating (Dec. 10–11, 1904) the 100th anniversary of his birth. She also delivered a short address at this meeting sponsored by the Suffrage League of Boston and Vicinity.

She realized as early as April 6, 1906, the probability that her career would not be duly recognized. In a letter to the *Boston Guardian,* she observed: "I have argued the union of the Negro and labor for a number of years, but being only a woman have received very little notice."

Living in obscurity after 1916, she died on Aug. 13, 1930, at the Cambridge Relief Hospital after suffering on the previous day burns on her entire body when her dress caught fire. She was buried on Aug. 17 in the Hopkins family plot on Lilac Path, in the Garden Cemetery, Chelsea, Mass. One of the few remaining entries in the burial record books in the Town Hall of Chelsea gives Hopkins's place of burial.

Present-day historians accord to Pauline Hopkins greater significance as an editor and journalist than did her contemporaries. Her biographical articles are particularly valuable and her emphasis in her fiction on the attributes of middle-class Negroes deserves comparison with that of Charles Waddell Chesnutt, Sutton Griggs, and Jessie Fauset.

An excellent brief evaluation is in Abby A. Johnson's and Ronald M. Johnson's "Away from Accommodation: Radical Editors and Protest Journalism, 1900–1910" (*JNH,* Oct. 1977, pp. 325–29). Also valuable are Ann Allen Schockley's "Pauline Elizabeth Hopkins: A Biographical Excursion into Obscurity" (*Phylon, The Atlanta University Review of Race and Culture,* Spring 1972, pp. 22–26) and August Meier's "Booker T. Washington and the Negro Press with Special Reference to the *Colored American Magazine*" (*JNH,* Jan. 1953, pp. 67–90). There is a brief biography in the *Colored American Magazine* (Jan. 1901, pp. 218–19), with an excellent photograph signed "Yours for humanity" (p. 201). — DOROTHY B. PORTER

HORSE, JOHN [other forms of surname: Cavallo, Cowaya, Coheia, among others; nicknames: Gopher John, John Nikla—Burnt John; Mexican names: Juan Caballo, Juan de Divos Vidaurri] (c. 1812–1882), Seminole Negro chief, interpreter, military colonist, and Indian fighter. He was born in Florida (probably on the Alachua savannah), a "slave" to chief Charles Cavallo; his father—who may have been his "master"—was a Seminole Indian and his mother a Negro. He presumably experienced the dislocations caused by the American invasions of Florida in 1812–1813 and in 1818. In 1826, while living in Thlonotosassa, he won the nickname of "Gopher John" by selling a brace of "gopher" terrapins over and over again to an officer at Fort Brooke, Tampa Bay (Porter, *Florida Anthropologist,* Dec. 1960; *American Literature,* March 1943).

At maturity Horse was a tall, slim, "ginger-colored" man, with long wavy or "crinkled" hair and a proud carriage and walk, noted both for his tact and diplomacy and his deadly accuracy with a rifle. The Seminole War gave him the opportunity for rapid advancement, and on March 6, 1837, as "John Ca-Wy-Ya," he was a signer of the Treaty of Fort Dade. When this treaty was violated by the reenslavement of Negroes who had surrendered, he joined on June 2 with Osceola, Wild Cat, and others in carrying away the Seminole hostages and renewing the war. On Oct. 21, while on a mission from the Seminole head chief Micanopy to the St. Johns River Indians, he was captured under a flag of truce with Osceola and others and imprisoned in Fort Marion, St. Augustine, but on Nov. 29–30 he escaped with Wild Cat and others (Porter, *Florida Historical Quarterly,* Jan. 1944) and on Dec. 25 was a commander, with Wild Cat, Alligator, and Sam Jones, at the hard-fought Battle of Okeechobee. However, he surrendered the following April, with Alligator, on a promise of freedom to the Negroes who would "come in," and was promptly shipped to the Indian Territory (later Oklahoma).

In the fall of 1838 Horse volunteered to return to Florida to help persuade the Seminole holdouts to surrender and during 1839–1842 served with great success as a United States guide and interpreter, even participating (April 19, 1842) in a daring mounted attack on Halleck Tustenuggee's Mikasuki.

However, after being finally sent west in August 1842, he allied himself with Wild Cat, Alligator, and other militants in striving for Seminole independence and greater protection for the Negroes. He went to Washington in the spring of 1844 as interpreter to a delegation headed by Wild Cat, and on his return narrowly escaped assassination by a member of a rival Seminole faction. He went to Washington again a year later and remained for nearly a year, pleading the cause of himself and his relatives in particular and that of the Seminole Negroes in general. After the attorney-general of the United States announced the illegality of the wartime promise of freedom to Seminole Negroes, Horse early in 1849 founded Wewoka, later the Seminole capital and county seat of Seminole County, as a "city of refuge" where Negroes could keep together and defend themselves against seizure, and in the fall led an exodus of Seminole Negroes to Mexico, in association with a similar movement of Indians under Wild Cat (Grant Foreman, *The Five Civilized Tribes* [1934], pp. 226, 228, 231, 258–59, 262).

The Mexican government settled the Indians and Negroes on the border of Coahuila as military colonists, recognizing Wild Cat as head of both bands and "Juan Caballo" as commander of the Negroes. As such, although often leading his people in battle against *indios bravos* and Texas filibusters, he absolutely refused to participate in Mexican civil wars. The proximity of a large body of free Negroes aroused hostility in Texas. On Sept. 19, 1851, on a visit to Eagle Pass, Horse was seized as a slave and Wild Cat was forced to pay a large ransom for his release. This episode was a factor in the Mexican government's decision to move the Seminole to the less exposed location of Nacimiento, at the headwaters of the Sabina. But even in Mexico Horse was not entirely safe, and in November 1852, at a *fandango* in Piedras Negras, he was shot and wounded by a visiting Texan.

After Wild Cat's death from smallpox early in 1857, the Indians gradually drifted back to the territory and in 1859 Gov. Santiago Vidaurri moved the Negroes to the Laguna de Parras, where under Horse's command they operated effectively against the Apache. The Imperialist invasion, however, scattered the Negroes; some of them returned to the United States and, beginning in 1870, served with distinction as enlisted scouts. John Horse himself was too old for active scouting, and after being badly wounded at Fort Clark on May 19, 1876, in an assassination attempt, he returned with other disillusioned Negroes to Mexico. Although in his later years he is remembered chiefly as a "doctor," philanthropist, and "father of his people," rather than as a warrior, he was sufficiently active and alert, according to a tradition current as late as 1943, to take a leading part in the destruction of a band of dangerous marauders near San Carlos, Chihuahua.

When in 1882 claimants to the Seminole Negroes' land at Nacimiento, backed by the local *caudillo,* José Maria Garza Galan, ordered their removal, John Horse went to Mexico City (Porter, *Phylon,* Autumn 1947) where he obtained from the federal government confirmation of the Seminole claims. Although many conflicting accounts of his death were long current, it is virtually certain that he was the "Juan Caballo" who died of pneumonia in a Mexico City hospital on Aug. 9, 1882. The Seminole Negroes of the John Horse band maintained ownership of the Nacimiento land grant.

Although in 1838 Horse was reportedly married, with one or two children, little definite is known of this family. By his wife Susan July, who survived him, he had only one known child, Joe Coon, although they brought up several other young people. Joe Coon's son John Jefferson and John Horse II (c. 1878–1954) provided valuable information.

Kenneth Wiggins Porter's "O Freedom Over Me!" a detailed account of John Horse and his people, is still in manuscript. Numerous references to John Horse appear in Porter's *The Negro on the American Frontier* (1971, pp. 249–61 passim, 281–86, 319–21, 326–27, 333, 424–60 passim, 474–76, 481–82, 485–86).

— KENNETH WIGGINS PORTER

HORTON, GEORGE MOSES (1797–1883?), poet. Born a slave on the plantation of William Horton in Northampton County, N.C., and later owned by his master's son James and grandson Hall in succession, in Chatham County, he bargained with each—paying the doubled price of fifty cents per day demanded by the latter—for the privilege of earning money on the Chapel Hill campus of the University of North Carolina. His love poems for students who wrote them down and paid prices determined by their need had been nurtured in his youth by revival-meeting hymns heard and read, and by biblical passages that he often creatively versified before he knew how to write. His career thus began with many works either forgotten or attributed to others.

Taught to write at Chapel Hill mainly by Carolina Hentz, an author, abolitionist, and professor's wife, Horton in the 1820s widened his reading (in books given him by students) in the poetry of Homer, Vergil, Milton, James Thomson, and Edward Young, and in the prose of Samuel Johnson and Plutarch. In 1828 three of his poems appeared in the *Lancaster* (Mass.) *Gazette,* Mrs. Hentz's hometown paper. More were printed in *Freedom's Journal,* America's first Negro newspaper (1828); *The Liberator* (1834); and the *Southern Literary Messenger* (1843).

Horton published three volumes of poetry: *The Hope of Liberty* (1829), *The Poetical Works of George M. Horton, the Colored Bard of North Carolina* (1845), and *Naked Genius* (1865). Possibly a fourth, *The Museum,* was printed before 1845 and another, *The Black Poet,* published. *The Hope of Liberty* did not earn enough to buy its author's freedom, as desired, but its twenty-two pages won him local fame and helped abolitionism in two reprintings as *Poems by a Slave* (1837, 1838). Regional proslavery activity probably necessitated the diminished aggressiveness of the ninety-six-page second book, for which Horton wrote an autobiographical preface. (Arthur P. Davis and Saunders Redding speculate that Horton became an unhappy husband and father of two children before 1845.) His letter writing and other continual attempts to gain freedom ended when he reached Sherman's army in Raleigh (April 1865). There he was befriended by Capt. Will H. S. Banks of the 9th Michigan Cavalry Volunteers. Under his guidance Horton published that summer his last work *Naked Genius,* with 42 of its 132 poems reprinted from his *The Poetical Works.* In it he sought dual recognition: as a poet and as a Negro destined by God to escape what his Sept. 1, 1852, letter to Horace Greeley calls his "loathsome fetters." In *Naked Genius* his comic, satirical bent is evident, especially in his treatment of women. He died, probably in Philadelphia, in 1883.

Determined early to master poetry, Horton became its Negro exemplar for his generation. Well read in the light of his sixty-eight years in slavery, he experimentally mingles hymnal patterns with odes, blank verse, and heroic couplets in treating slavery, heroism, poetry, and marriage, among other subjects. His overuse of abstractions, mythology, and stilted diction is attributable in part to his era; but that is more than redeemed when he resorts to a humor, realism, and folk insight that vitalize his language and affirm his sincerity.

For a book-length treatment of Horton, see Richard Walser's *The Black Poet* (1967). W. Edward Farrison's "George Moses Horton: Poet for Freedom" (*CLA* [*College Language Association*] *Journal,* March 1971) is corrective and enlightening. The Sept. 11, 1852, letter to Horace Greeley and some of Horton's poems are in *Cavalcade, Negro American Writing from 1760 to the Present,* edited by Arthur P. Davis and Saunders Redding (1971, pp. 35–41), with a valuable critique (pp. 33–35). — JAMES A. EMANUEL

HOUSTON, CHARLES H[AMILTON] (1895–1950), lawyer and educator. He was born on Sept. 3, 1895, in Washington, D.C., the only child of William and Mary Houston. His father, a graduate of Howard University Law School and a member of the District of Columbia Bar, combined teaching at the Law School with legal practice. His mother abandoned her public school teaching career for hairdressing and sewing in order to provide additional funds for the family.

Charles Houston was graduated at fifteen from Washington's M Street High School (Dunbar High School after 1916) in 1911 and in the fall of the same year he entered Amherst College from which he graduated with a Phi Beta Kappa key and as one of six valedictorians in 1915. During the academic year 1915–1916, Houston was supply instructor in English in the College of Arts and Sciences at Howard and in 1916–1917 he was an instructor on Howard's Commercial College faculty. In 1917 he enlisted in the U.S. Army and was sent to the Colored Officers' Training Camp at Fort Des Moines, Iowa, where he was commissioned a first lieutenant in infantry. He successfully applied for a transfer to field artillery, relinquished his original commission, and was thereafter recommissioned a second lieutenant in artillery. He served with the 351st Field Artillery in France and Germany during World War I.

Following his discharge in early April 1919 Houston taught English until the end of the academic year at Dunbar. In September 1919 he entered Harvard Law School where, during his third year, he was the first Negro elected an editor of the *Harvard Law Review.* He graduated *cum laude* in 1922, in the top 5 percent of his class, with an LL.B. degree. The following year he was the first Negro to be awarded the Doctor of Juridical Science degree at Harvard. He also received a Sheldon Fellowship, providing a one-year stipend for study at the University of Madrid where he attended civil law courses during 1923–1924. He was admitted to the District of Columbia Bar in 1924.

With occasional interruptions, he practiced law with his father in the Houston firm (later with William H. Hastie in Houston and Hastie, and finally in Houston, Bryant and Gardner) from 1924 until 1950.

In 1927–1928, under a grant from the Laura Spelman Rockefeller Memorial, Houston prepared a report entitled "The Negro and His Contact with the Administration of Law." This report formed much of the basis for discussion of Negro lawyers in Carter G. Woodson's, *The Negro Professional Man and the Community with Special Emphasis on the Physician and the Lawyer* (1934) and Charles S. Johnson's *The Negro College Graduate* (1938).

In 1929 Houston was appointed resident vice-dean, and in 1930 vice-dean, in charge of the Howard Law School three-year day program and with general supervision over the Law School Library. Houston also became an associate professor of law but was granted a leave of absence from both positions in 1935 to work for the NAACP. During his six years at the Law School he was in large part responsible for significant improvement in curriculum and for the school's securing accreditation from the American Bar Association and the Association of American Law Schools.

On Oct. 26, 1934, Houston was retained by a joint committee established by the American Fund for Public Service and the NAACP to direct a campaign of legal action and public education against racially unequal apportionment of public education funds and discrimination in public transportation. The ultimate goal was complete elimination of segregation. Houston's appointment was part-time through June 30, 1935; from July 1, 1935 until 1940 he was the NAACP's first full-time paid special counsel. Thurgood Marshall, his former student at Howard, served as assistant special counsel during 1936–1938 and was appointed special counsel in 1938.

Houston argued, in whole or in part, several civil rights cases before the U.S. Supreme Court. He also aided in preparing many other civil rights cases in that Court and in lower federal and state courts.

Houston's first major Supreme Court case was *Missouri ex rel. Gaines v. Canada* (305 U.S. 337, 1938), in which he shared oral argument with Sidney R. Redmond. The Supreme Court held that Missouri could not constitutionally exclude a Negro from the white state university law school in the absence of other and proper provision for the legal education of Negroes. The decisive importance of this case resided in the Supreme Court's determination carefully to scrutinize the good faith of the states in providing separate but allegedly equal facilities. Missouri had provided scholarships for Negroes wishing to study law out of state. The Supreme Court rejected this scheme as a way of avoiding the expense of maintaining a Negro law school. Houston had the major burden of trying this case in the Missouri trial court and he participated as counsel in the Missouri Supreme Court in proceedings prior and subsequent to the U.S. Supreme Court decision (i.e., *State ex rel. Gaines v. Canada,* 342 Mo. 121, 113 S.W.2d 783 [1938]; 344 Mo. 1238, 131 S.W.2d 217 [1939]).

Throughout the 1940s Houston served as general counsel of the Association of Colored Railway Trainmen and Locomotive Firemen and of the International Association of Railway Employees. He pressed, with notable results, for fair representation of minority workers by unions. His second major Supreme Court victory came six years after the *Gaines* case in *Steele v. Louisville & Nashville R.R.* (323 U.S. 192, 1944), where the Court required a white labor union, which was the bargaining representative of railroad firemen under the Railway Labor Act, fairly to represent without racial discrimination Negro firemen excluded from union membership. Houston was also involved in the preparation of legal papers in the Alabama courts leading to the Supreme Court ruling (see 245 Ala. 113, 16 So.2d 416, 1944).

On the same day that he began his oral argument in the *Steele* case, Houston also argued the companion case of *Tunstall v. Brotherhood of Locomotive Firemen & Enginemen* (323 U.S. 210, 1944). *Tunstall,* decided the same day as *Steele,* involved similar issues and was explicitly decided on the same basis as *Steele.* Houston was involved in the preparation of legal papers and presentation of oral argument in the lower federal courts in *Tunstall* both before and after the Supreme Court decision. (See 140 F.2d 35 [4th Cir. 1944]; 148 F.2d 403 [4th Cir. 1945]; 69 F. Supp. 826 [E.D. Va. 1946], *aff'd,* 163 F.2d 289 [4th Cir.], *cert. denied,* 332 U.S. 841, 1947.) The *Tunstall* litigation resulted in an injunction barring a white labor union from discriminating against Negro firemen's seniority and other employment rights as well as a jury award of $1000 in damages.

By deciding in *Steele* and *Tunstall* that the Railway Labor Act forbade racial discrimination in union representation, the Supreme Court did not need to pass judgment on Houston's creative alternative argument, namely that the act violated the Fifth Amendment's due process clause by authorizing collective bargaining on behalf of Negroes excluded from union membership and denied procedural guarantees such as notice of union agreements and an opportunity to be heard. (See 323 U.S. at 195–96, 198–99; 323 U.S. at 212.)

In *Hurd v. Hodge* (334 U.S. 24, 1948), a companion case to *Shelley v. Kraemer* (334 U.S. 1, 1948), Houston shared oral argument before the Supreme Court with Phineas Indritz, who volunteered his services when not at his regular position in the Solicitor's Office of the Department of Interior. Houston also aided in preparing the successful brief in *Shelley.* *Hurd* and *Shelley* barred racially restrictive covenants on real estate in Washington, D.C., and in the states, respectively. Houston carried most of the burden of trial in *Hurd* and argued the case in the U.S. Court of Appeals for the District of Columbia Circuit (i.e., *Hurd v. Hodge,* 162 F.2d 233 [D.C. Cir. 1947]). *Hurd,* in which Houston's richly

comprehensive presentation drew on constitutional, statutory, common law, public policy, and social science materials, was his most extensively prepared case.

Two of Houston's early Supreme Court cases overturned the convictions of Negro defendants sentenced to death by juries from which Negroes had been systematically and arbitrarily excluded solely because of race. These cases were *Hollins v. Oklahoma* (295 U.S. 394, 1935) and *Hale v. Kentucky* (303 U.S. 613, 1938). In neither case was any novel constitutional doctrine involved and in neither had Houston participated as counsel in the proceedings prior to Supreme Court adjudication. Some years later Houston unsuccessfully argued for a rule of criminal law in the District of Columbia recognizing mental deficiency short of insanity. In that case Houston's client was a Negro defendant sentenced to death for murdering a white woman whose racial epithets had infuriated him. (See *Fisher v. United States,* 328 U.S. 463, 1946.)

In addition to these Supreme Court cases, Houston was intimately involved in two other important civil rights cases. In *University of Maryland v. Murray* (169 Md. 478, 182 A. 590, 1936), Houston shared oral argument with Thurgood Marshall before Maryland's highest court and bore the major burden of trial. *Murray* affirmed the Baltimore City Court's order requiring the admission of Negroes to the University of Maryland Law School. (Years earlier the same law school had denied Marshall's admission, leading to his enrollment at Howard.) Houston was also principal trial counsel and successfully argued the appeal in *Kerr v. Enoch Pratt Free Library of Baltimore City* (54 F. Supp. 514 [D. Md. 1944], *rev'd,* 149 F.2d 212 [4th Cir.]; *cert. denied,* 326 U.S. 721, 1945), where the U.S. Court of Appeals for the Fourth Circuit held unconstitutional the racial exclusion of a Negro woman from a library training class operated by a city-supported public library.

Like other Negro lawyers practicing in the South, Houston displayed physical courage, notably in Leesburg, Va. (1933), where he defended George Crawford, a Negro found guilty of murdering a white woman, and in his investigation (1938) of brutalities and racial discrimination at Chicamauga Dam, Tennessee.

He was a member of the District of Columbia Board of Education (1933–1935), an acerbic critic of racial discrimination in the U.S. Army, and a picket against other kinds of discrimination. From 1940 to 1948 he was a member of the NAACP National Legal Committee and was its chairman from 1948 to 1950. He was vice-president of the National Lawyers Guild and vice-president of the American Council on Race Relations. He was an adviser to the Negro activist Consolidated Parents Group, Inc., of Washington, D.C., which spearheaded the drive to desegregate the district's public schools, and he aided the National Committee on Segregation in the Nation's Capital. After serving on the Fair Employment Practice Committee in 1944, he resigned on Dec. 3, 1945, because he could not persuade President Truman to prevent discrimination against Negro employees by the (Washington) Capital Transit Company.

Houston was slightly over six feet tall, well proportioned, and strikingly handsome. His first marriage to Margaret Gladys Moran of Washington, D.C., on Aug.

23, 1924, ended in divorce (September 1937). On Sept. 14, 1937, he married Henrietta Williams, also of Washington. They had one son, Charles Jr., who was six years old when his father died. Houston attended the church of his parents, 19th Street Baptist, but did not find religion a strong motivating force.

A relapse from a heart ailment from which he had suffered for two years led to his death from coronary occlusion in his fifty-fifth year, at Freedmen's Hospital, Washington, D.C. Shortly before his death he requested that George E. C. Hayes take full charge of his unfinished cases and that Hayes, James M. Nabrit, Jr., and others continue the fight for full educational opportunities for all Negro children in the District of Columbia. Funeral services, at which the mourners included five Supreme Court justices, were held on April 26, 1950, in Howard University's Andrew Rankin Memorial Chapel, with interment on the same day in Lincoln Memorial Cemetery, Suitland, Md. He was survived by his wife, son, and father.

Houston's principal significance lies not in his civic activities nor as a columnist for the *Afro-American,* important though these roles were, but in his strengthening of the Howard Law School and his stature as a constitutional lawyer and key strategist in the assault against racial discrimination. As counsel for litigants and as an adviser to other lawyers, Houston helped shape many of the indispensable legal precedents leading to the Supreme Court decisions four years after his death outlawing compulsory racial segregation in public schools (*Brown v. Board of Education,* 347 U.S. 483, 1954; and *Bolling v. Sharpe,* 347 U.S. 497, 1954). Since those decisions spurred other court rulings and federal civil rights laws barring various racially discriminatory practices, Houston had a leading part in overthrowing the entire legal regime of stigmatized racial differences.

Due recognition of Houston's achievements was largely posthumous. On June 25, 1950, the NAACP selected Houston for the Spingarn Medal, awarded annually for "the highest achievement" by a Negro in "any honorable field of human endeavor." Dean Erwin N. Griswold of the Harvard Law School, who presented the medal to his widow and son, read the citation which said in part: "In memory of a lifetime of gallant championship of equal rights for all Americans, of unselfish devotion to democratic ideals, of unwavering fidelity to the American dream of equal opportunity." Public schools in Washington, D.C., Alexandria, Va., Baltimore, Md., and other cities have been named for him. At the formal opening of a new Howard University Law School building (May 1, 1958), Thurgood Marshall stated that not he but Houston deserved the encomium of "The First Mr. Civil Rights." The principal building of the Howard Law School at the University's West Campus has been named in his honor, as well as a law professorship, and numerous bar and law student groups bear his name. Houston wrote his own epitaph in his admonition to his students: "No tea for the weak, no crepe for the dead."

There is no full-length published biography of Houston; the fullest discussion of his life and career is in Genna Rae McNeil's unpublished doctoral dissertation

"Charles Hamilton Houston (1895–1950) and the Struggle for Civil Rights" (University of Chicago, 1976). Geraldine R. Segal has published a short study of his life under the title, taken from a Houston aphorism, *In Any Fight Some Fall* (1975, with photograph, p. 4, and Foreword by William H. Hastie). Essential facts are in *Who's Who in America* (1950–1951). Detailed background, with much attention to Houston's career, is in Richard Kluger's *Simple Justice: The History of* Brown v. Board of Education *and Black America's Struggle for Equality* (1976). Illuminating discussion of Houston's Rockefeller report and of his appointment as NAACP special counsel, against a background of rising Negro demands to supplant whites as principal NAACP legal strategists, is contained in August Meier's and Elliott Rudwick's "Attorneys Black and White: A Case Study of Race Relations Within the NAACP" (*Journal of American History* 62 [1976]; 913–46). Information about his career at Howard University is in Rayford W. Logan's *Howard University: The First Hundred Years, 1867–1967* (1969). Some of the atmosphere, including quotations from Houston, of a 1945 NAACP conference on planning the restrictive covenant cases is in Clement E. Vose's "N.A.A.C.P. Strategy in the Covenant Cases" (*Western Reserve Law Review* 6 [1955]: 101–45, esp. pp. 105–9, 131). Houston's role in various restrictive covenant cases is also discussed in Clement E. Vose's *Caucasians Only: The Supreme Court, the NAACP, and the Restrictive Covenant Cases* (1959, with a photograph of Houston following p. 44). The NAACP strategy against racial segregation and the initial appointment of Houston are treated in Jack Greenberg's *Race Relations and American Law* (1959). Two warm personal tributes are by William H. Hastie ("Charles Hamilton Houston," *NHB,* June 1950, pp. 207–8, with photographs, pp. 208–9), and Erwin N. Griswold ("Charles Hamilton Houston," *NHB,* June 1950, pp. 206, 210, 212–13). General information is in Genna Rae McNeil's "Charles Hamilton Houston" (*Black Law Journal* 3 [1974]: 123–31, with photograph, p. 122). See also the vertical file, Moorland-Spingarn Research Center, Howard University. Other information was obtained from interviews by Rayford W. Logan with Margaret Gladys Moran Houston (March 17, 1969), Robert G. McGuire Funeral Service (March 28, 1969), and Logan's personal reminiscences. Additional data were provided in discussion with Jack Greenberg (Oct. 1, 1975) and in correspondence from Henrietta Williams Houston (May 10, 1976), the Hon. William H. Hastie (Oct. 10, 1975), the Hon. Joseph C. Waddy (Dec. 16, 1975), Geraldine R. (Mrs. Bernard G.) Segal (Nov. 7, 1975), Phineas Indritz (Dec. 11, 1975, and Jan. 7, 1976), and Genna Rae McNeil (June 10, 1977). The Houston Papers are in the Moorland-Spingarn Research Center, Howard University. — CONRAD K. HARPER

HOWARD, PERRY WILSON (1877–1961), lawyer, politician, and Republican national committeeman. He was born on June 14, 1877, to Perry and Sallie Howard in Ebenezer, Miss., a town which his father and a white man founded. Howard was one of the six children in the family. His father made a name for himself as a Republican in Mississippi Reconstruction politics. It was in this political atmosphere and Republican household that the young Howard grew to maturity. In 1898 he graduated from Rust College in Mississippi with an A.B. degree. After one year at Fisk (1899–1900) and the University of Chicago he received his LL.B. from the University of Illinois (1905).

During the time he was pursuing a law degree Howard worked as a mathematics teacher at Alcorn A&M College in Mississippi from 1901 to 1905. In 1905 he left the teaching profession and set up his legal practice in Mississippi. Two years after he began his law practice, he married (Aug. 15, 1907) Wilhelmina L. Lucas, who died in an automobile accident in 1957. They were the parents of three children.

Having been brought up in a politically conscious household, Howard soon entered Republican politics in his state and was a delegate to the Republican National Convention in 1912; he was to attend each convention thereafter until 1960. In 1924 he became chairman of the Mississippi State Republican Committee and held that post until 1932. Although he relinquished it to his friend and trusted ally S. D. Redmond, a dentist, he remained Republican national committeeman for the state from 1924 to 1960. In fact these thirty-six years in this position gave him more seniority than any other Republican, Negro or white, and led to his serving as chairman of committees at several national conventions.

His unswerving Republican loyalty was rewarded in 1921 when President Harding appointed him special assistant to the U.S. attorney-general. During that year he moved to Washington, D.C., and held that position until 1928. He was suspended from that post in 1929 when he was indicted on charges of selling federal jobs. An ensuing trial where many white Mississippians spoke in his behalf ended in his acquittal. He received letters of endorsement from the chief justice, an associate justice, and the clerk of the Mississippi Supreme Court. Southern politicians and newspapers rejoiced because, according to Gov. Theodore Bilbo, they preferred the "Black and Tan" organization to white committeemen whom President Hoover would probably support (George B. Tindall, *The Emergence of the New South, 1913–1945* [1967], p. 170).

After the acquittal he resigned from the post and practiced law as a member of the prestigious firm of (James A.) Cobb, Howard, and (George E. C.) Hayes, at 613 F St. NW, maintaining this practice until his death.

Every four years, however, Howard led the "Mississippi Black and Tan Grand Ole Party" to the Republican National Convention although he lived and worked in the District of Columbia, and each time, with one or two exceptions, was challenged by the "lily White" delegation. But each time the Howard delegation was seated intact until 1956. (In 1960 the Perry Howard–led Black and Tan Republicans were not seated but given "guest" courtesies and honorary delegate status. Howard himself was honored by the convention for being the oldest continuous delegate. He had been a delegate to thirteen conventions.) Many Negroes believed that he, like the other Negro Republican state committeeman, Benjamin J. Davis, Sr., did little to advance their cause.

As legal advisor for the Negro Elks (IBPOEW) Howard attended the San Francisco Conference which organized the United Nations, and urged all Negroes to wire their senators and representatives to insist that the charter include safeguards for the civil rights of all peoples (*Pittsburgh Courier,* May 19, 1945, p. 11).

He resided at 1829 S St. NW, and died in his sleep on Feb. 2, 1961. The week before his death, he had just returned to his office following eye surgery at Freedmen's Hospital. Funeral services were held in Asbury Methodist Church, 11th and K Streets NW, Washington, D.C., and he was buried in Harmony Cemetery, Washington, D.C. He was survived by his son, Perry W. Jr., a sister Sarah E. Howard, both of Washington, and several nieces and nephews, including Washington Municipal Court Judge Andrew J. Howard.

Many of the basic facts are in *Who's Who in Colored America* (1950). His later life is traced in metropolitan newspapers. Obituaries were published by the *New York Times* (Feb. 2, 1961, p. 29), the *Afro-American* (Feb. 11, 1961, pp. 1, 2), the *Pittsburgh Courier* (Feb. 11, 1961, p. 4), and the *Washington Post* (Feb. 2, 1961, p. B4). See also Hanes Walton, Jr.'s *Black Republicans: The Politics of the Black & Tans* (1975), Hanes Walton, Jr.'s and C. Vernon Gray's "Black Politics at National Republican and Democratic Conventions: 1868–1972" (*Phylon,* Sept. 1975, pp. 269–78).

— HANES WALTON, JR.

HUGHES, [JAMES] LANGSTON (1902–1967), author, anthologist, librettist, songwriter, columnist, translator, founder of theaters, and poetical innovator in jazz techniques. He was born in Joplin, Mo., on Feb. 1, 1902, the son of James Nathaniel and Carrie Mercer (Langston) Hughes. His maternal grandfather was Charles Langston, the Ohio abolitionist and half-brother of the better known John Mercer Langston. Between 1902 and 1914 the young Hughes lived in Buffalo, N.Y., Cleveland, Lawrence, Kans., Mexico City, Topeka, Kans., Colorado Springs, and Kansas City, Kans. By 1914 Hughes's parents had separated and in that year he joined his mother and stepfather, Homer Clarke, in Lincoln, Ill. In 1916 he finished grammar school in Lincoln. Elected class poet, he read his first poem at the graduation exercises. Moving to Cleveland the same year, he entered Central High School. As a senior there, he was elected editor of the class yearbook.

The year 1921 was crucial for Langston Hughes. While with Clarke in Mexico he taught English to the "best families" in two Mexican schools; published his first prose piece, "Mexican Games," in *The Brownies Book,* and his now-classic "The Negro Speaks of Rivers" in *The Crisis.* In 1921 he also entered Columbia University but remained there only a year.

In 1922 he went to the Azores, the Canary Islands, and Africa as a mess steward. The next year he went abroad on a freighter, and worked and loafed in Paris, Genoa, and other places. Returning to the United States in 1924, he joined his mother in Washington, D.C., and in the following year was "discovered" there by Vachel Lindsay as a "bus boy poet." Also in 1925, he won first prize for poetry in the *Opportunity* contest, second prize for poetry and third prize for the essay in *The*

Crisis contest. Hughes entered Lincoln University (Pa.) in 1926. He published his first volume of poems, *The Weary Blues,* the same year.

In 1931–1932 Hughes, encouraged by Mary McLeod Bethune, took a poetry-reading tour through the South and West. During the same period he made a trip to Haiti and subsequently went on an abortive trip to the Soviet Union with a movie-making group. In 1937 he went to Spain as a correspondent for the *Baltimore Afro-American,* reporting the civil war then in progress. From 1938 to 1940 Hughes, having returned from Spain, became interested in the Negro theater and founded three important theater groups in Harlem, Los Angeles, and Chicago.

In 1943 he began his column in the *Chicago Defender* in which the life and thoughts of "Simple" were first presented. During 1947–1948 he was visiting professor of creative writing at Atlanta University, and during 1949–1950 was poet in residence at the Laboratory School, University of Chicago. During the 1950s Langston Hughes had a brief and unpleasant but harmless encounter with Senator McCarthy's witch hunt over certain of his alleged leftist activities and writings.

Hughes received many national honors, among them the Anisfeld-Wolfe Award in 1953 for the year's best book on race relations, the Spingarn Medal in 1960, and election to the National Institute of Arts and Letters in 1961.

During the 1950s and 1960s Hughes traveled less and published more, turning out a tremendous volume of edited and creative work of all types. In 1965 he lectured in Europe for the U.S. Information Agency. In 1966 he attended the First World Festival of Negro Art in Dakar. He died on May 22, 1967, of congestive heart failure in Polyclinic Hospital, New York City. Funeral services were private. He was survived by his brother, Gwyn Clark Hughes, and an uncle and aunt, Mr. and Mrs. W. E. Harper.

Poet, fiction writer, dramatist, anthologist, songwriter, autobiographer and biographer, author of children's works, librettist, translator, writer of radio and TV scripts, Langston Hughes was the most innovative and many-sided author of the Negro Renaissance of the 1920s. Hughes was, however, primarily a poet and his ultimate position as an American writer may rest on his work in this field. The most significant portion of Hughes's poetry is found in the following publications: *The Weary Blues* (1926), *Fine Clothes to the Jew* (1927), *The Dream Keeper and Other Poems* (1932), *Shakespeare in Harlem* (1942), *Fields of Wonder* (1947), *One-Way Ticket* (1949), *Montage of a Dream Deferred* (1951), *Ask Your Mama: 12 Moods for Jazz* (1961), and *The Panther and the Lash* (1967).

Hughes wrote a prodigious amount of verse. Working in the field for over forty years, he touched on many subjects and experimented with various styles and techniques. Certain themes, however, tend to recur: poems inspired by Harlem, poems of social commentary and social protest, poems based on or influenced by folk material, and poems concerning the African heritage. There are other pieces which do not fit into these categories—his few religious poems and his nonracial verse,

for example—but in the main his poetry may be classified under them.

Hughes was called the "Poet-Laureate of Harlem," and fittingly so. He wrote more fully about and with more understanding of the Black Metropolis than any other writer. In every major collection of his poems except one, he has verses inspired by Harlem. His best treatment of Harlem, and many believe his best volume of verse, is *Montage of a Dream Deferred,* a work in which the poet depicts all the varying moods of a city on the verge of exploding.

The protest-and-social-commentary theme, like that of Harlem, runs through all of Hughes's poetical works. It is interesting to compare Hughes's attitude toward racial and protest poems with that of Countee Cullen. "To make a poet black and bid him sing" struck Cullen as a peculiar kind of malevolence on the part of God. Hughes, on the other hand, appeared to accept and glory in his mission as a Negro writer. He seemed to consider his poetry a weapon in the arsenal of democracy, and he used it as such. In his two earliest works the protest-and-social-commentary theme is a trickle, but after *One-Way Ticket* (1949) the trickle becomes a full-sized stream, and it continues to grow as it rolls down to the last poetic volume in 1967, the year of Hughes's death. During his mid-career, Hughes wrote many leftist poems, but he was never a Communist. In his protest poems Hughes is often ironic, but seldom bitter. Usually the objective observer, he seems surprised and saddened at America's stupidity and blindness in its treatment of the Negro. Evidently Hughes felt that America did not improve sufficiently because he republished in his last work, *The Panther and the Lash* (1967), several of his earlier protest poems.

Hughes's poems influenced by folk material constitute one of his most important contributions to American letters. Although Paul Laurence Dunbar, Charles W. Chesnutt, and a few others had made limited use of folk material, it was not until the Harlem Renaissance that really broad use of the folk reservoir was made, and the most dedicated experimenter with this great material was Langston Hughes. In his early works he emphasized the blues form; for example, in *Fine Clothes to the Jew* there are seventeen poems in this form (and spirit). Hughes also used the ballad form, dance rhythms, the rhythms of folk speech, and jazz forms and techniques. His experimentation with this material reached its highest peaks in *Montage of a Dream Deferred* (1951) and *Ask Your Mama: 12 Moods for Jazz* (1961). In the first, the poet tried to capture "the conflicting changes, sudden nuances, sharp and impudent interjections, broken rhythms, and passages sometimes in the manner of the jam session, sometimes the popular song. . . ." In the second work Hughes experiments with the fusion of poetry and jazz. In the margins of this poem (or series of poems) are elaborate directions for musical accompaniment to the reading of the verses. Hughes was a pioneer in the poetry-to-jazz movement, perhaps the "father" of it.

The poems of Hughes on the African heritage theme changed and matured over the years. At first he like other New Negro poets made use of the alien-and-exile concept, best represented in Cullen's "Heritage." This theme represented an effort on the part of Negro poets to find in Africa a literary homeland. Probably influenced by the Marcus Garvey Movement, it portrayed the American Negro as a perpetual alien-and-exile from his idyllic African home, whose loss he unconvincingly bemoaned. Hughes never took the alien-and-exile concept too seriously (none of the New Negro poets did). Although he was always interested in Africa, Hughes never put on a "literary dashiki"; he insisted always that he was an American. His later poems on Africa, based not on fantasy as were his earlier, comment on the *real* Africa of emerging nations. Léopold Senghor and other West African and West Indian poets (see the *Negro Digest,* May 1967) look upon Langston Hughes as one of the "fathers" of the Négritude Movement, although Hughes in his earlier years did not know the term (see *African Forum,* Spring 1966).

The fiction of Langston Hughes was published in six novels: *Not Without Laughter* (1930), *Simple Speaks His Mind* (1950), *Simple Takes a Wife* (1953), *Simple Stakes a Claim* (1957), *Tambourines to Glory* (1958), and *Simple's Uncle Sam* (1965); and three volumes of short stories: *The Ways of White Folks* (1934), *Laughing to Keep from Crying* (1952), and *Something in Common and Other Stories* (1963). Most critics agree that the best of Hughes's fiction is found not in his two conventional novels, not in his many short stories, but in the "Simple" series.

Originally conceived in 1943 and appearing weekly as a column in the *Chicago Defender,* Simple grew to become a nationally recognized character and symbol. Representing the folk wisdom and humor as well as the race consciousness of the Negro working class, Simple in these sketches is pitted against a needling "narrator," an educated "straightman" who represents liberal Negro middle-class thinking on racial matters. The scene is Paddy's Bar, and the cast of characters includes Simple's charming and middle-class-oriented girlfriend Joyce, his Harlem landlady, his wife (whom he is finally able to divorce), the fun-loving barfly Zarita, and a host of other Harlem characters. As we read these encounters between Simple and the "liberal" unnamed narrator, we recognize the ambivalent thinking which segregation produces among Negroes. The Simple series illustrates Hughes's deep understanding of Harlem, of the Negro "man in the street," and of Negro life in general. These sketches do what good novels have always done; they give a deep insight into the times, the customs, and the human strengths and weaknesses of a certain people at a certain time. And they do it with a rich humor.

If one thinks of autobiography as principally self-revelation, Hughes's two works—*The Big Sea* (1940) and *I Wonder as I Wander* (1956)—are not outstanding examples of the genre. Evidently Hughes was not given to much soul-searching, or if he was he elected not to share his findings with the reader. He subtitles the first volume *An Autobiography* and the second, with more honesty, *An Autobiographical Journey.* Frankly, both are inclined to be autobiographical journeys and not "pure" autobiography. The two works, however, are fascinating because Hughes traveled to many interesting parts of the world, knew many kinds of people, and had more than his share of unusual experiences. He went to the Soviet Union during the early days of the new regime, was in Spain during the civil war there, lived and taught in Mexico, was a member of the inner group of New Negro writers, and visited many Negro groups and schools in the South. He writes about these experiences as a journalist would write about them. The two works are really a series of vignettes, sketches, and essays. There is not the kind of continuity and fusion that one finds in the conventional autobiography. But the two works are valuable source material for the historian and literary historian of the first five or six decades of the twentieth century. (Unfortunately, neither volume has an index.) Hughes was a keen observer with a great knowledge of human nature.

Langston Hughes was a prolific playwright, but not all of his plays have been published. The list which follows gives, therefore, not the publication dates but the dates on which the works were first staged. Those plays with an asterisk before them appear in Webster Smalley's *Five Plays by Langston Hughes* (1963); the list itself also comes from Professor Smalley's work: *Mulatto* (1935), three-act tragedy; *Little Ham* (1935), three-act comedy; *Troubled Island* (1935–1936), three-act tragedy; *When the Jack Hollers* (1936), three-act comedy; *Joy to My Soul* (1937), three-act comedy; *Front Porch* (1938), three-act comedy-drama; *The Sun Do Move* (1942), full-length music drama; *Simply Heavenly* (1957), two-act comedy with music; *Tambourines to Glory* (1963), two-act gospel singing play; *Soul Gone Home* (1937?), one-act fantasy; and *Don't You Want to Be Free* (1936–1937), a long one-act play, historical drama-panorama.

Hughes was interested in drama from his earliest years. One of his first publications was a dramatic sketch, "The Gold Piece," which appeared in *The Brownies Book* (July 1921). He never lost this interest in the theater and dramatic writing. Hughes contributed much to Negro drama. When the Negro theater barely existed during the 1930s, he gave it a great boost by organizing two groups to encourage Negro dramatists: the Suitcase Theater in Harlem and the Negro Art Theater in Los Angeles. In 1940 he started a third group, the Skyloft Players in Chicago. In addition Hughes himself experimented with several kinds of people's drama, using the blues, gospel songs, spirituals, and other folk material. He wrote for the man in the street; his works, therefore, tend to use simple language and uncomplicated plots; but what they lack in subtlety, they make up for in understanding and compassion.

Langston Hughes's most successful drama, and the first to be staged professionally, was *Mulatto.* Starting in 1935 this tragedy ran a year on Broadway and then toured for eight months. *Mulatto* deals with a theme which appears often in Hughes's works, that of rejection by one's father. He was morbidly interested in the theme because he felt that he had been rejected by his own father. In *Mulatto* he joined the personal rejection by a white father of a Negro son to the theme of racial rejection. It is interesting to note that the genesis of *Mulatto* is a twelve-line poem, "Cross," in *The Weary Blues* (1926). It appears in other poems and short stories and as an opera, *The Barrier,* with music by Jan

Meyerowitz, first produced in 1950 at Columbia University.

Little Ham is probably Hughes's best comedy. It reflects most convincingly and with great humor the life of Harlem's ordinary black citizens—their financial insecurity, their high spirits, and their indomitable courage and will to survive. Based on the local numbers racket, the play takes place on a background of shoeshine and beauty parlors with a stirring Charleston contest finale at the Savoy. It is excellent entertainment in the folk manner.

The play of Hughes which has been most popular with Negro audiences is *Don't You Want to Be Free?*, a long one-act play he wrote for the Suitcase Theater. It ran for 135 performances in Harlem and thirty more in Los Angeles. More of a pageant than a play, it uses blues, spirituals, and a considerable number of Hughes's poems; it also has "Singing, Music, and Dancing" to show the progress of Negroes from oppression by slaveowners and overseers down to Harlem merchants and landlords. It ends, however, on a positive note (one that was typical of the 1930s)—the high note of black and white workers organizing to overcome oppression.

For material on Langston Hughes's life, publications, and criticisms of his many works, see: Donald C. Dickinson's *A Bio-bibliography of Langston Hughes, 1902–1967* (1967), James A. Emanuel's *Langston Hughes* (1967) in Twayne's United States Authors series, and *CLA* (College Language Association) *Journal* (Special Langston Hughes number, June 1968). In addition to articles on Hughes, this issue contains an excellent "Selected Classified Bibliography." Obituary notices appeared in the *New York Times* (May 23, 1967, p. 1, and May 24, 1967, p. 32). — ARTHUR P. DAVIS

HULL, AGRIPPA (1759–1848), soldier of the American Revolution. Born free in Northampton, Mass., he is said to have been brought to Stockbridge, Mass., when he was six by a black man named Joab, a former servant of Jonathan Edwards. Described as being five feet seven inches tall, with black complexion and wooly hair, he enlisted on May 1, 1777, for the duration of the war as a private in the brigade of the Massachusetts Line. After serving for two years, he was for four years and two months an orderly for the Polish patriot, Gen. Tadeusz Kosciusko, in battles ranging from Saratoga, N.Y., to Eutaw Springs, S.C. Assigned to assist surgeons, he always remembered with horror the bloody amputations. In July 1783 at West Point he received his discharge, signed by General Washington. He farmed a small plot of land in Stockbridge, and worked as a butler and major domo. He married a fugitive slave, adopted as a daughter another fugitive, and gained a reputation as the village seer. When Kosciusko made a triumphal tour of the United States in 1797, Hull met him in New York. (It was on this visit that Kosciusko was awarded a grant of land in Ohio which he directed to be sold to found a school for Negroes.)

On June 12, 1828, when Hull was seeking to have his soldier's pension mailed directly to his home, his friend Charles Sedgwick wrote to Acting Secretary of State Richard Rush, enclosing Hull's discharge supporting the request and asking that the discharge be returned since Hull would rather forgo the pension than lose the discharge. Catharine Maria Sedgwick (1789–1867), of Stockbridge and Lenox, generally recognized as the most popular female author in the country before Harriet Beecher Stowe, wrote that Hull had a fund of humor and mother-wit, and was a sort of Sancho Panza in the village, "always trimming other men's follies with a keen perception, and the biting wit of wisdom." Francis Parkman, the eminent historian, after a visit to Stockbridge during the summer of 1844, recorded in his journal on July 7 that Hull had been a soldier in Washington's army. "He had four children in the churchyard, he said with a solemn countenance, but 'these are my children' he added, stretching his cane over a host of little boys. 'Ah, how much we are consarned to fetch them up well and vigorous' etc." Both Parkman and Electa Jones, historian of the village of Stockbridge who wrote shortly after Hull's death at the age of eighty-nine, depicted him as had Sedgwick. A portrait (1848) by an unidentified artist after a daguerreotype of 1844 shows him holding a cane.

The best brief account is in Sidney Kaplan's *The Black Presence in the Era of the American Revolution, 1770–1800* (1973, pp. 36, 38–39). The portrait is reproduced as Plate 3, following page 84.

— RAYFORD W. LOGAN

HUNT, HENRY ALEXANDER (1866–1938), college president and government official. The youngest of eight children, Hunt was born on Oct. 10, 1866, near Sparta, in Hancock County, Ga. His father, a white man, H. A. Hunt, was said to have been a judge. His mother, a Negro, went by the name of Moteat Hunt. Apparently deserted by their father, the four boys and four girls made their living from farming and lived in a "weather-stained cabin on a red hillside," Hunt remembered. Hunt spent his early boyhood chopping cotton, hoeing potatoes, dropping corn, and shelling peanuts and peas for planting. After getting the education which was available to him in his community, Hunt at age sixteen had been prepared for the college department of Atlanta University by Richard Carter, an 1876 graduate. Hunt entered the school when it was adding industrial studies to its academic programs and learned the builder's trade. To earn money for his education, he worked during vacations as a journeyman carpenter. He helped with repairs at the university, the construction of schoolhouses in Georgia and Alabama, and the Georgia state capitol building. As a student Hunt had traits which he continued to exhibit as an educator and leader. George Towns, a collegemate and longtime friend, remarked that Hunt, the most popular member of his class, was captain of the baseball team, judge in the moot court, and president of the Phi Kappa Society. He shared his "goodies" with his friends, and the "preps" below him sought his friendship and advice.

In 1890 Hunt, a tall, slim, almost white young man, earned the B.A. degree from Atlanta University and began his educational career in Charlotte, N.C., as principal of the main public grammar school for Negroes. The following year he was appointed superintendent of the Industrial Department and business manager of Biddle University (later Johnson C. Smith University). Serving also as proctor of boys, Hunt was "idolized . . . because of his virile mind and youthful spirit." His influence over the boys was so great that they began to take more pride in their personal appearance and were stimulated to earn money for additional clothes to supplement their gifts from northern charity.

While in North Carolina, Hunt on June 14, 1893, married Florence S. Johnson, his college sweetheart and sister of Edward A. Johnson, one of the first graduates of Atlanta University. A native of Raleigh, N.C., Miss Johnson graduated from the normal department of Atlanta University. Dorothy, Hal, and Adele were born to the union. Mrs. Hunt labored, with extreme sacrifice and unstinted devotion, side by side with her husband until his death.

After thirteen and one-half years at Biddle University, Hunt accepted the principalship of the Fort Valley High and Industrial School in the Black Belt of his native Georgia. In 1903 Wallace Buttrick and George Foster Peabody of the General Education Board had influenced Hunt "to leave a circle of congenial companions and friends, a comfortable home and a good position . . . to undertake the building up of an institution [of the Hampton-Tuskegee type] to serve a sadly underprivileged group." The school, which Hunt headed from 1904 to 1938, had been founded in 1890 and incorporated in 1895 by a group of black and white leaders. According to its charter it had been intended to be "a school for the higher mental and manual education of the youths and children of Georgia." The combined elementary and high school, which became the Fort Valley State College in 1939, had started in a lodge hall. When the Hunts arrived in the middle Georgia town in February 1904, they found a barren "campus" with four wooden buildings and one under construction, "suspicious white neighbors," and "indifferent Negroes." The foundation for the state-supported college which grew out of the 1890 educational experiment was firmly laid between 1904 and 1938. Until Hunt's death the school, as Bishop H. J. Mikell of the Protestant Episcopal Diocese of Atlanta and chairman of the school's Board of Trustees in 1919, remarked in 1939, "was largely [Hunt's] creation and he served it with the greatest and most unselfish devotion."

Hunt's early life and education in Georgia and experience in North Carolina had equipped him with skills to inspire "young men and women to do practical work of high character." He firmly believed that "the members of his race should be taught those things that have a close relation to the life they will live." Reflecting his Atlanta University background and his philosophy of education, in 1909 Hunt recommended to the school's Board of Trustees that students be awarded "prizes for proficiency in both academic and industrial work in all classes above the 3rd grade."

As John Hope of the Atlanta University system became a leader of the urban Negroes of Georgia, Henry A. Hunt became the patriarch of the rural masses, developing a school which remained in close touch with the community. With extension programs, summer institutes for teachers, community services, health campaigns, and a vigorous crusade for social and economic uplift, Hunt and his school ("A Light in the Valley," as it was known in the state) at Fort Valley became symbols of the potential power of Negroes. He was presented the Spingarn Medal by the NAACP in 1930 because of his "modest, faithful, unselfish and devoted service in the education of Negroes of rural Georgia [and because] in the face of great difficulties he has built up an excellent school and has at all times advanced the cause of his race with tact, skill and integrity." In 1931 the William E. Harmon Foundation honored Hunt for his contributions in education and to the economic security of Negroes. As the *Atlanta Constitution* pointed out on Jan. 26, 1931, the school served as a center "for the preservation of a racial culture for a whole district."

In 1913 the institution became affiliated with the American Church Institute for Negroes of the Episcopal church. It was formally taken over as a church institution by the Protestant Episcopal Diocese of Atlanta in 1918, and the church gave financial support from then until the state took over its operation in 1939. Nevertheless Hunt had to rely largely on voluntary contributions from northern philanthropists and fees from students who could afford to pay. Small sums of money, however, came from local, state, and federal governments. Although Hunt built up the school primarily from northern charity, it was not "at the terrible expense of racial, 'hat in hand,' humiliation."

At the time of his death the school had thirteen well-designed modern buildings, and a campus with shrubbery and lawns. In spite of perennial financial difficulties, the school continued to grow in enrollment and recognition under Hunt's guidance. The enrollment increased from 262 students in 1904 to about 1000 in 1938, including 103 junior college students; the school had gained junior college status by 1928, and the name had changed to the Fort Valley Normal and Industrial School in 1932. Even local whites, who were at first doubtful of his motives, grew to respect Hunt.

Hunt also had a deep interest in farmers. While in North Carolina he had organized a farmers conference, which aided agricultural progress among Negro farmers. In Georgia he continued his work among Negro farmers, organizing in 1907 the first of many annual farmers conferences which were held at the school. Agricultural education was a major part of the school's program during Hunt's era. Because of his concern for those who earned their livings primarily from the soil, the Julius Rosenwald Foundation awarded Hunt a fellowship to journey to Denmark in 1931 to study cooperatives. Because of Hunt's knowledge of the plight of southern Negro farmers, Pres. Franklin D. Roosevelt appointed him in November 1933 as assistant to the governor of the Farm Credit Administration and adviser on special problems of Negroes. He informed Negroes of their opportunities to secure government credit and assisted them in their complaints against injustices on the part of local administrators of the New Deal's farm credit program. He helped some Negro farmers obtain their share of loans, established a farm cooperative near Montezuma in Macon County, Ga., and had considerable success in urging Negroes to establish credit unions.

Although Hunt was no militant social activist, he was a twentieth-century pioneer of social reform. He was a dedicated participant in the work of the NAACP, and he was a delegate to the 1919 Pan-African Congress in Paris. His major contribution, however, was his success in bringing about helpful changes in the "southern way of life" for large numbers of Negroes in the rural South. When Hunt died in the nation's capital in October 1938 of a heart ailment, while still in the service of the government, the *Pittsburgh Courier* appropriately entitled its obituary article "Henry Hunt, Farmer's Friend, Veteran Educator, Succumbs." Funeral services were held in the Fort Valley school's chapel on Oct. 5, 1938, and he was entombed on the campus that he had built. He was survived by his wife and three children.

See the *Fort Valley Message,* a funds-soliciting newsletter edited by Hunt, and articles about the school and the man in the *Crimson and Gray,* the *Atlanta University Alumni Bulletin, The Crisis,* and *Southern Workman* during his life and upon his death. His papers are in the Henry Alexander Hunt Memorial Library at the Fort Valley State College. See also Donnie D. Bellamy's "Henry A. Hunt and Black Agricultural Leadership in the New South" (*JNH,* Oct. 1975, pp. 464–79).

— DONNIE D. BELLAMY

HUNT, IDA ALEXANDER GIBBS (1862–1957), teacher, Pan-Africanist, and civil rights leader. She was born Ida Alexander Gibbs on Nov. 16, 1862, in Victoria, British Columbia. Her father, Mifflin Wistar Gibbs, was a native of Philadelphia, Pa., who had achieved great success as an entrepreneur in California and then in British Columbia. In the late 1860s, while he continued business ventures in Canada, he sent the family to live in Oberlin, Ohio, where Ida's mother, the former Maria Alexander, had attended college. There Ida subsequently completed two degrees at Oberlin College, specializing in English. She received a B.A. in 1884 and an M.A. in 1892. A classmate and friend of hers in the class of 1884 was Mary Church (later Mrs.) Terrell, the noted civil rights leader. Ida's younger sister, Harriet Gibbs Marshall, likewise later became well known as the founder of the Washington, D.C., Conservatory of Music. After college, Gibbs taught for a number of years at the M Street High School in Washington, D.C., and at Florida A&M College in Tallahassee. Meanwhile the final public post in her father's career, his appointment in 1897 as U.S. consul at Tamatave, Madagascar, proved to be very important for Ida Gibbs's future. In 1904 she retired from teaching in Washington to marry William Henry Hunt, who had succeeded her father as consul at Tamatave after having initially accompanied him there as his clerk. For the following twenty-seven years she accompanied Hunt on the remainder of his assignments as a U.S. consul. These included two more years at Tamatave, twenty years at St. Étienne, France, two years in Guadeloupe, a year in the Azores, and two years at Monrovia, Liberia. Hunt retired in Washington in 1932 after a brief assignment at the State Department. He and his wife lived in Washington for the remainder of their lives. He died on Dec. 19, 1951, and she on Dec. 19, 1957.

Over the years, Ida Gibbs Hunt's continued interest in literature led her to publish several articles and reviews on literary and general cultural themes. She also employed her writing and public speaking to support organizations, especially international ones, which promoted peace, women's suffrage, and civil rights for Negroes. She served as assistant secretary of the First Pan-African Congress, in Paris, Feb. 19–21, 1919 (*The Crisis,* April 1919), attended the Paris session of the Second Pan-African Congress, September 5–6, 1921 (*The Crisis,* Dec. 1921, p. 68), and read a paper "The Coloured Races and the League of Nations" at the London session of the Third Congress, 1923 (program from the meeting is in the Hunt Papers). She was referred to as co-chairman with W. E. B. Du Bois of the Executive Committee which planned the London session.

The Hunt Papers, in the Moorland-Spingarn Research Center, Howard University, are the principal source of information. — ALLISON BLAKELY

HUNT, WILLIAM H[ENRY] (1869–1951), career foreign service officer. Born on June 29, 1869, in the village of Hunts' Station, Tenn., he began his formal education in a public school when his family moved to Nashville several years later, but found it necessary to quit school after only a few months to help his mother support the family. For the following fifteen years his primary occupations were custodian, bellhop, and Pullman porter, in various types of establishments and in different parts of the United States and Canada. Having become acquainted with the head master of Lawrence Academy, a preparatory school in Groton, Mass., he gained admittance there in the fall of 1890. He graduated from Lawrence Academy with a scholarship which he used to enter Williams College with the class of 1898. However, he remained at Williams for only one year. From Williamstown he moved to New York City in 1895 and found work as an assistant in a chemical laboratory and later as a messenger for a Wall Street brokerage firm.

Hunt's chance to enter the foreign service came unexpectedly when Mifflin W. Gibbs was appointed U.S. consul at Tamatave, Madagascar, in 1897. Hunt had met one of Gibbs's daughters, Ida, a few years earlier and now jokingly suggested that she ask her father to take him along to Madagascar. To his surprise she complied, and her father agreed. With the aid of a loan from the brokerage firm which employed him, he set out with Gibbs for Madagascar at the end of 1897.

In early 1898 Hunt became Gibbs's consular clerk at Tamatave. He became vice-consul in March 1899 and consul in August 1901, when Gibbs resigned because of illness and advanced age. Thus began Hunt's career of thirty-one years at the rank of U.S. consul. He served at Tamatave until 1906. On his first leave of absence to the United States in 1904 he married Ida Gibbs, who thereafter accompanied him at all his posts. In November 1906 he was appointed consul at St. Étienne, France, where he remained until 1926, rising from the rank of consul of class eight in 1915 to class six in 1920. With the reorganization of the foreign service, in 1924 he was given the rank of foreign service officer class seven. When the State Department closed the St. Étienne post Hunt was transferred to Guadeloupe, West Indies. In late 1929 he moved to St. Michaels, the Azores. This was followed by his final foreign post, as consul and second secretary of the legation at Monrovia, Liberia, from January 1931 to late 1932. In August of that year he was assigned to the State Department in Washington and in December he retired (General Records of Department of State). He played no public role during the final two decades of his life and died on Dec. 19, 1951, in Wshington.

Hunt's long career included excitement, danger, and some quite bizarre experiences. An example of the latter is the assignment he and M. W. Gibbs carried out in Madagascar of collecting specimens of all the wild animals on the island for shipment to the National Zoo in Washington, D.C., only to have to release all of them again after the naval commander assigned to transport the animals refused to do so (Records of the State Department). Hunt fit very comfortably into the role of consul in both its social and administrative aspects. The reports he submitted to the State Department on the economics of the areas where he served were especially meticulous and drew praise from his superiors. At times his reports also received wider circulation, both in government publications and the general press. For instance, he published a number of articles in the *Bulletin of the American Geographical Society of New York,* of which he became a corresponding member.

However, it was probably not Hunt's skill as a reporter, but his success socially that was the decisive factor in his career, that is, his diplomatic skill in dealing with people. He demonstrated this from the outset when he and Gibbs were able to establish amicable relations with the French officials in Madagascar at a time when the French were still bitter about the controversial affair involving John L. Waller, the U.S. consul at Tamatave from 1891 to 1894 who had remained and opposed the French takeover of the island in 1895 and 1896 *(Foreign Relations of the United States 1895, 1896).* At the same time Hunt, an accomplished horseman, reportedly taught the Malagasy Queen Ranavalona III to ride. The close friendship Hunt developed with Gen. J. S. Gallieni, who served for a time as governor-general in Madagascar and was later famous as a World War I hero, continued after Hunt was transferred to St. Étienne. During his twenty years there he enjoyed high popularity, becoming an integral part of the community, as is attested by his election as head of numerous social and cultural organizations. During World War I he promoted a number of relief activities.

The St. Étienne post was the high point of Hunt's career and was particularly remarkable because during most of that period he was the only Negro consul serving in Europe, an area generally considered inaccessible for Negro consuls because of their color. Hunt was not unaware of the peculiarity of his status. Although while in Madagascar he apparently shared the French colonialist attitude which viewed the Malagasy peoples as backward and uncivilized, he did not attempt to forget his origins nor lose his racial identity. Over the years he kept in touch through correspondence and short visits home. Among his collected papers are materials relating to several of the main organizations for advancement of the Negro, including the Niagara Movement, the NAACP, Pan-African activities, and the Association for the Study of Negro Life and History. His wife Ida took special interest in these and in the world peace movement. She and W. E. B. Du Bois were co-chairmen of the executive committee which planned the Third Pan-African Congress, held in London in 1923.

Hunt made few public statements in regard to social or political developments. However, it must be kept in mind that his public statements were restricted by State Department regulations, which applied even after his retirement. A strong case might be made for the view, expressed by Du Bois in a 1924 *Crisis* article, that Hunt's service seemed to merit higher rank than that granted by the State Department. Hunt did not echo this sentiment, even in those letters to his superiors that are available in State Department records, although he was disappointed with the assignments which followed St. Étienne. In any case, given the status of the Negro in American society during the time spanned by Hunt's career, it might be more appropriate to measure his achievement in terms of his professional survival instead of rank attained.

There is no published biography of Hunt. See the W. H. Hunt Papers, Moorland-Spingarn Research Center, Howard University. — ALLISON BLAKELY

HUNTON, ADDIE D. WAITES (1875–1943), civic leader and YWCA official. She was born in Norfolk, Va., on June 11, 1875, the eldest of the three children of Jesse and Adelina (Lawton) Waites. Her father had a substantial wholesale oyster and shipping business and was co-owner of an amusement park for Negroes. He was a founder of the Negro Elks (IBPOEW) and prominent in the African Methodist Episcopal church. Her mother died when Addie was very young, and she was reared by a maternal aunt in Boston. After attending the Boston Girls Latin School and a Spencerian business college in Philadelphia, she went to Normal, Ala., to teach in a vocational school which later became the Alabama Agricultural and Mechanical College. In 1893, in Norfolk, she was married to William Alphaeus Hunton of Chatham, Ontario. The descendant of a Virginia slave who had emigrated to Canada, Hunton had come to Norfolk in 1888 to become secretary of a colored YMCA. The Huntons moved in 1899 to Atlanta. Of their four children, only the two younger, Eunice and William Alphaeus Jr., survived infancy. In 1906 the family moved to Brooklyn, N.Y., which remained Mrs. Hunton's home for the rest of her life.

Addie Hunton had assisted her husband in his work and had frequently traveled with him to YMCA conferences. Thus she had already acquired considerable experience when in 1907 the National Board of the YWCA appointed her secretary for work among Negro students. She spent the winter of 1907–1908 touring the South and Middle West. In 1909 Mrs. Hunton went with her children to Switzerland and Strasbourg where she took classes at the Kaiser Wilhelm University. Upon her return to America in 1910 she resumed an active round of YWCA work, but her husband was now seriously ill with tuberculosis. In 1914 the family moved to Saranac Lake, N.Y., where they remained until Hunton's death in 1916.

America's entry into the First World War found Mrs. Hunton a widow with her children nearly grown, and she volunteered for YMCA service. When she reached France in June 1918 she was one of three Negro women permitted to work among the 200,000 Negro troops. Her first assignment was at the supply and transport center of St. Nazaire. Here she added a literacy course and a popular Sunday evening discussion program to the usual canteen, movies, and other services offered at YMCA huts. In January 1919 she was transferred to a leave area near Aix-les-Bains in southern France. She helped organize a full program of educational, religious, athletic, and cultural activities for more than a thousand Negro troops who arrived each week for a brief interval of rest and relaxation. Her most arduous assignment began in May, when she was assigned to the military cemetery at Romagne, near Verdun, where Negro soldiers were engaged in reburying other Americans killed in the Meuse-Argonne battle. Living in a tent under most trying conditions, she tried to allay the seething resentment of the soldiers forced to endure indignities and discrimination because of their race. In the autumn of 1919, after a final six weeks of YMCA work in Brest among troops awaiting transport home, Hunton returned to America and wrote *Two Colored Women with the American Expeditionary Forces* (1920) with Katheryn M. Johnson.

She served on the Council on Colored Work of the National Board of the YWCA, was president of the International Council of the Women of Darker Races and of the Empire State Federation of Women's Clubs, and was a vice-president and field secretary of the NAACP. She was also a pillar of the National Association of Colored Women, whose founding convention she had attended in Boston in 1895 (as a delegate from the Woman's League of Richmond, Va.) and which she had served for a time (1906–1910) as national organizer. A member of the Women's International League for Peace and Freedom, she was also a member of the league committee which visited Haiti in 1926 to observe the United States occupation at first hand. The committee's report, *Occupied Haiti* (1927), contained a chapter on race relations by Hunton. She was one of the principal organizers of the Fourth Pan-African Congress (New York City, 1927).

Her last public activity came at the 1939 New York World's Fair when she presided over a ceremony honoring outstanding Negro women. She died in Brooklyn of diabetes on June 21, 1943, and was buried in Cypress Hills Cemetery there.

Addie W. Hunton's *William Alphaeus Hunton* (1938) is the principal published source for much of her career. Anna V. Rice's *History of the World's Y.W.C.A.* (1948) is useful for the organization's activities. The records and reports on work with Negro women, National Board of the YWCA, New York City, contain much valuable information. Interviews with Eunice Hunton Carter provided many personal details. Her death certificate is on file in the New York City Department of Public Health. See also the article in *NAW* (1971, 2:240–41). — JEAN BLACKWELL HUTSON

HUNTON, WILLIAM ALPHAEUS (1863–1916), YMCA secretary. The sixth son of Stanton and Mary Ann (Cooper) Hunton, he was born in Chatham, Ontario. Since his mother died when he was four years old, he was reared largely by his father. After finishing high school in Chatham, he graduated from the Wilberforce Institute of Ontario (1884). He taught public school in the little town of Dresden, Canada, and in May 1885 was appointed a probationary clerk in the Department of Indian Affairs, Ottawa. There he was perhaps the only colored member of the YMCA. In 1888 he went to Norfolk, Va.—the first Negro employed by the YMCA. Three years later he became the first colored secretary of the International YMCA. In 1893 he married Addie D. Waites of Norfolk, Va. Of their four children, only the two younger, Eunice and William Alphaeus Jr., survived. Hunton was recognized as the most prominent and influential colored YMCA secretary until 1914 when he was stricken by tuberculosis. Several months at Saranac Lake, N.Y., arrested but did not cure the disease. He died at his home in Brooklyn, N.Y.; after a quiet service there he was interred in Cyprus Hills, Brooklyn.

Hunton's career is significant for several reasons. It was in some respects similar to the life of other Negroes who came to the United States after their parents had settled in Chatham to escape slavery in the United States. His activities as a colored YMCA secretary provides one of the better perceptions of this organization during the latter part of the nineteenth and early twentieth century. He personified the type of Christian-oriented leadership that helped shape the lives of many other prominent Negroes.

His father, Stanton Hunton, had been born a slave in Virginia. His owner, a humane, aristocratic maiden in Virginia, helped his early education but required him to purchase his freedom (about 1840). Probably aided by the Underground Railroad, he made his way in 1843 to Chatham, a refuge for runaway slaves. He instilled in his son Christian ideals, attended his son's Bible class in Sunday school, and helped him gain an education. Stanton Hunton's home was one of those visited by John Brown (1858) in preparation for his raid on Harpers Ferry. The Christian ideals and an identification with British loyalties influenced much of the son's life.

When he was invited to go to Norfolk as the first colored YMCA secretary, he accepted because "It was God's leading and I could but follow" (Addie W. Hunton, *William Alphaeus Hunton, A Pioneer Prophet of Young Men* [1938], p. 17). He carried on such usual activities as literary and debating societies, educational work, and athletics; he established a small library and choral club. His greatest interest lay, however, in his Bible Study Class, of which there was a Women's Auxiliary.

After 1891, when he became the first colored secretary of the International YMCA, he traveled extensively to organize or, in his words, to "disorganize" groups that were establishing potential YMCA branches. In 1893 he wrote a pamphlet, *The First Step,* which prescribed the methods for groups to seek the organization of such local branches.

He faced squarely the question of the admission of colored applicants to white branches. In the South, no colored men were admitted. In the Middle States and "a Northern state," the white associations "pigeonholed" applications until the colored applicant ceased pushing the matter. "The third method of treatment, and, I believe, the only one endorsed by the International Committee, is that which accords to colored applicants the very same treatment given to white." This meant in practice that a very small number of "the best element among young colored men" were admitted (ibid., p. 35). In other words, Hunton accepted the pragmatic policy of establishing separate colored YMCA branches.

In 1896 he helped organize the Colored Men's Department of the YMCA. During 1898 he visited several camps in the United States where Negro troops were stationed, and became a fervent advocate of peace. By 1898 he had concluded that he should devote most of his time to work among college students. The appointment in that year of Jesse E. Moorland as the second colored YMCA secretary permitted him to focus his major work on college campuses, while Moorland engaged particularly in organizing branches in cities. In 1905 Hunton helped obtain the appointment of George Edmund Haynes for work among students during the summer. Haynes served only a short time. Among Hunton's other most notable recruits was Channing H. Tobias, in 1911.

The first colored student association had been organized at Howard University in 1876, followed by those at Fisk University and Walden College in 1877. By 1911 there were more than 100 student associations with a membership approaching 7000 in twenty states and the District of Columbia. Hampton Institute had the first student building.

Because of malaria contracted during a long trip in the South, followed by a debilitating illness, Hunton did not live long enough to see much of the expansion of YMCA buildings, begun by George Foster Peabody in Columbus, Ga., and by John D. Rockefeller in Washington, D.C., and continued by Julius Rosenwald in 1910. The Chicago philanthropist announced that he would give $25,000 toward the cost of a building in any city that would raise $75,000 by popular subscription.

Another problem that confronted Hunton was the participation by Negroes at the annual meetings of the International Convention of the YMCA. In 1906 he mentioned the "growth of inter-racial problems of the work," and frequently regretted the fact that he was the only colored man at these meetings. He rejoiced, however, that at Mobile, Ala., in 1907 there was "not a ripple of unpleasantness observed on account of our presence." An address by J. W. E. Bowen and Hunton's reading of the Scriptures and prayer were most heartily received (ibid., p. 92). In 1910 he addressed the nonsegregated Tennessee State Convention, whereas in 1906 at a meeting of the Student Volunteer Association in Nashville, colored students had to sit in the gallery.

The best known of the conferences for colored students was held at King's Mountain, N.C., in the summer of 1912. Hunton, as the senior secretary of the Colored Men's Department, presided. Others present were David Jones, then secretary of the Colored YMCA in St. Louis, and Channing H. Tobias. Max Yergan, later executive secretary of the Council on African Affairs, was inspired to give up the study of law and to enter YMCA

work. Emory Smith, who was already a divinity student at Howard University, was reenforced in his commitment.

The 1913 meeting of the World's Student Federation Conference at Lake Mohonk, N.Y., was, on the other hand, unsegregated. Prior to it, Hunton had escorted three foreign delegates in visits to Negro schools. He led the colored delegates at a garden party given by Mr. and Mrs. Cleveland Dodge at their estate, Greystone, in Riverdale-on-the-Hudson. He and Mrs. Hunton were permanent hosts at the tables for eight or ten other guests at Lake Mohonk. It was there that Hunton delivered his last public address.

Hunton's illness was aggravated by the 1906 riot in Atlanta, Ga., where the family had lived after 1899. He suffered a severe attack of colitis, and the family moved to Brooklyn.

Hunton's activities included two trips abroad. In 1894 he was a member of the American delegation to the Golden Jubilee of the YMCA in London. Before returning to the United States he visited famous sites there and in Eton, Stratford-upon-Avon, Oxford, northern England, Glasgow, and Edinburgh. He basked in his "Britishness," a residue of his life in Canada. He also toured Paris, Brussels, and Antwerp.

On his second trip he sailed from San Francisco in 1907 to attend the World's Student Christian Federation Conference in Tokyo, where he received many compliments about his address. He then traveled to Kyoto and Shanghai, where he was greatly distressed by the poverty of large numbers of Chinese. From Shanghai he went on to Hankow, Peking, Tientsin, and Korea, where he wrote in his diary one of his most interesting observations: "The Koreans impress me as being a faible [sic] people, unless it is their broken spirits I see under the unwelcome domination of the Japanese" (ibid., p. 113).

His wife, who always referred to him as "Mr. Hunton," wrote that "he was handsome, cultured, and very definitely earnest." He could relax occasionally, as when he took her to see a Wild West show in which Buffalo Bill was the main attraction. "He was always conservative in opinion and expression and never dogmatic" (ibid., pp. 13, 38, 39–40).

At the King's Mountain Conference (1912), Tobias later recalled that Hunton was a "man who knew God intimately—I should say who knows God intimately, for now his knowledge of Him is perfect" (Tobias Papers, Box 1, X970.4, in the library of the National Council of the YMCA in the USA, New York City). John Hope wrote that "In the early days of my administration as president of Morehouse College, no man was more helpful to me than Hunton in giving good advice" (Addie Hunton, p. 168). It was W. E. B. Du Bois who referred to him as a "Pioneer Prophet of Young Men" (ibid., p. x).

At the closing meeting of the Lake Mohonk Conference in 1913, Hunton urged: "Pray with us that there shall come to the heart of the world not only the intellectual interpretation of the brotherhood of man, but a spiritual acceptance of it, so that speedily there may dawn a glorious morning when man shall not judge his fellow-man by color, race, tradition or any of the other accidents of life but righteousness and truth and unselfish service to humanity" (ibid., p. 120).

The major source is the loving memoir by his wife, Addie W. Hunton, *William Alphaeus Hunton, A Pioneer Prophet of Young Men* (1938).

— RAYFORD W. LOGAN

HURSTON, ZORA NEALE (1901?–1960), writer, anthropologist, and folklorist. Hurston was the most widely published Negro woman writer of her era, whose talents surfaced with the "Harlem Renaissance," and yet one of the least known and least understood artists of that period. Between 1920 and 1950 Hurston wrote short stories, plays, novels, articles, essays, critiques for newspapers, journals, and magazines; she wrote and produced a musical review for the theater, conducted field research in the southern United States, the Caribbean, and Central America; and produced two major publications based on her folkloric research.

Zora Neale Hurston was an "outrageous woman" who shattered all concepts of what women were supposed to do. A complex, controversial, flamboyant individual, she put her multifaceted career as an artist before all else. It was probably the effort to maintain this defiant stance that eventually led to Hurston's decline. Her last writings were confused and angry, and she died destitute. Despite this tragic ending which cast a negative image over her, upon closer review Hurston's life and work break through with brilliance.

Hurston was born in the all-Negro town of Eatonville, Fla., on Jan. 7, probably in 1901 although there are no birth records to substantiate the year. Hurston herself used dates from 1898 to 1903. She was one of eight children of John and Lucy Ann Hurston. Her father was mayor, minister, and carpenter in Eatonville. Growing up in a community governed by Negroes and rich in Negro oral tradition provided Hurston with a repertoire of experiences and a perspective on black people that shaped much of her work in later years.

After the death of her mother and the remarriage of her father, Hurston left Eatonville. She was shifted from relative to relative until at the age of fourteen she began working as a maid and wardrobe girl for a Gilbert and Sullivan traveling troupe which eventually brought her to Baltimore, Md. There she entered the preparatory school of Morgan College from which she graduated in 1918. She moved to Howard University to study from 1919 to 1924 under Lorenzo Dow Turner. It was at Howard University, under the tutelage of Turner and Alain Locke, that Hurston began to develop her talents as a writer.

Her first short story, "John Redding Goes to Sea," was published in *The Stylus* in May 1921. In December 1924 "Drenched in Light" was published in *Opportunity* (edited by Charles S. Johnson). For this early work and for much of her creative experience, Hurston drew on the culture of her hometown of Eatonville. Although she had left Eatonville and was in the midst of a Negro middle-class environment, her writings show she had taken Eatonville with her. Eatonville was more than subject matter; it provided a cocoon from which she dealt with the world she entered during the 1920s and 1930s, the Harlem Renaissance.

The response to "Drenched in Light" brought Hurston to the attention of the supporters of the Renaissance. It also drew from her peers some of the criticisms that would follow her throughout her career. The key character, Isie Watts, is a happy-go-lucky, devilish, secure southern child. Watts represents a strand which runs throughout Hurston's writings—Negroes sitting on porches, telling stories, joking and carefree. Her critics charged that this view fed stereotypes held by whites without showing the brutality suffered by Negroes in southern society. The Eatonville cloak Hurston wrapped around herself permitted her to project the view of an all-Negro community having only the slightest contact with whites.

With the publication of "Spunk" in *Opportunity* (1925), and with the help of her mentors Locke and Johnson, Hurston propelled herself into the ever-widening circles being created for Negro artists. Upon receiving an award for "Spunk," she moved to New York City and obtained a scholarship to Barnard College. From 1925 to 1927 she studied anthropology under Franz Boas. Continuing to write, Hurston joined with Langston Hughes and Wallace Thurmond in the summer of 1926 to found the short-lived avant-garde magazine *Fire!* These young writers saw themselves as rebels, writing for art's sake in defiance of those like Locke and W. E. B. Du Bois who urged Negro artists to reflect a consciousness about the race in all their work. Hurston and her colleagues took the position that their first responsibility was as creative artists and that to describe Negroes only in relation to their white oppression was in fact exploitive. From her Eatonville perspective Hurston knew that there was a well of black experience, a black community, and a life within that community that had managed to extract an independence from many of the racial pressures of the larger society.

Urged by Boas, whom she called "Papa Franz," Hurston undertook her first field research. She went to Alabama for Carter G. Woodson and the Association for the Study of Negro Life and History to interview Cudjo Lewis, an ex-slave. The results were published in the *Journal of Negro History* as "Cudjo's Own Story of the Last African Slaves" (1927). This was a low point in Hurston's work for it has since been revealed that much of the work was plagarized from *Historic Sketches of the Old South,* a book published thirteen years earlier by Emma Langdon Roache. As the article included material not previously uncovered, it appears that Hurston did interview Lewis. She returned to interview him again and in 1931 wrote a full-length unpublished work based on his life.

After this faulty start, Hurston's folkloric research broke new ground. Supported from 1927 to 1932 by Mrs. Rufus Osgood Mason, Hurston went again to Eatonville and to Louisiana. Mason insisted on owning Hurston's material and on approving all uses of it. These severe restrictions reveal the pressures Hurston and some other artists of the period faced as they attempted to carry out their work.

Hurston received a Rosenwald fellowship in 1934 and Guggenheim field research fellowships in 1935 and 1936. *Mules and Men,* published in 1935, was the result of this period of investigation. It includes a report on Hurston's work in Louisiana, perhaps the first investigation of voodoo practices among American Negro communities in the United States. Hurston's methods for collecting material on voodoo reveal the techniques she used in the field: she learned the ceremonies and rituals by apprenticing herself and going through the various stages of initiation. Her second work in folklore, *Tell My Horse* (1938), was on Jamaica and Haiti. Again, as far as possible Hurston included herself as part of the culture from which she was collecting data. In spite of the movement between scientific reporting and creative writing, *Mules and Men* and *Tell My Horse* remain vanguard works, making major contributions to our knowledge of black American, African, and Caribbean folklore.

The period of Hurston's folklore research also covers her most creative output as a writer. Between March and June 1930, again supported by Mason, Hurston worked with Langston Hughes on a play, *Mule Bone,* only the third act of which was published. Hurston and Hughes quarreled in February 1931 when Hughes charged Hurston with attempting to take full credit for the creation of the play. The dispute was never clearly resolved. Hurston countered that the stories and jokes were hers and indeed they appear in much of her folkloric work. Hughes acknowledged this but considered Hurston as the folkloric subject and himself as the creative writer.

In her first published novel, *Jonah's Gourd Vine* (1934), Hurston fully used her knowledge of folklore. Jonah, a minister, seems to be drawn from Hurston's father, and his sermons are among the richest parts of the book. The novel was praised for its use of folklore and criticized for its lack of a statement on the effects of racism on Negroes in the South.

Hurston's most artistically successful novel, *Their Eyes Were Watching God* (1937), is a love story written in eight weeks as she struggled to clear a deep and intense love affair. The story was unique in its presentation of the heroine, Janie, and in the warmth of the statement it made about black women and romantic and sensual love in Negro relationships.

Moses, Man of the Mountain appeared two years later. In it Hurston endowed the biblical Moses with a twentieth-century Negro personality. *Dust Tracks on the Road,* Hurston's autobiography published in 1942, was her most commercially successful publication. It is not, however, an accurate representation of her life. This was the picture of Zora Neale Hurston that she wanted the world to see. The careful reader can sense Hurston weaving the story to shape the desired personality, a vague image of an ambitious, driving, fantasizing woman.

The next several years were dominated by Hurston's largely unsuccessful attempts to obtain funding for her work. She wanted to do research among Negro communities in Central America, and after several attempts in 1945 and 1946 finally sailed for British Honduras in May 1947. Her trip was partially financed by an advance for a novel on which she was working, and during her stay she completed *Seraph on the Suwanee* (1948). Unlike her earlier writings, this story is about Florida whites; for the first time Hurston left the Eaton-

ville experience. The book does, however, paint a poignant picture of Arvay Henson Meserve, a woman entrapped in marriage.

In her personal life Hurston had rejected such entrapment. She was married twice, to Herbert Sheen in May 1927 for four months after a relationship of six years, and to Albert Price III, a man several years her junior, in June 1939. They filed for divorce after eight months. Although attempts were made at reconciliation, the divorce was finalized in November 1943. Hurston wrote that her personal relationships failed at the point that she was expected to give up her work and identity as a creative person to maintain the expected role of a wife.

Seraph on the Suwanee was Hurston's last major publication. The decline of financial support for field research and lack of opportunities for publishing seemed to coincide with a devastating personal experience, Hurston's arrest on a morals charge involving an emotionally retarded sixteen-year-old boy. Although the charges were dropped and she was cleared, the press, especially the Negro press, played up the most distorted aspects of the charges and the impact on Hurston was overwhelming. She returned south, working for a short time as a drama instructor at North Carolina College in Durham and as a script writer for Paramount Pictures.

Hurston's occasional publications during the 1950s added greatly to the controversy revolving around her as a writer and a political person. It may have been the Eatonville perspective that motivated her to write articles opposing the 1954 Supreme Court desegregation decision because she felt that black people did not need to be integrated in order to learn. But this does not explain articles against the right to vote such as "Negro Votes Bought," published in 1950. Her articles in ultra-conservative publications such as the *American Legion Magazine* indicate Hurston's willingness to allow her views to be used by forces opposing the struggle of Negroes for equality and justice.

Zora Neale Hurston was mystical, impulsive, restless, and driven. One of the more creative spirits of her day, Hurston pioneered in the investigation of Negro folk culture with an enthusiasm that has rarely been matched.

The most comprehensive work on Hurston is Robert Hemenway's *Zora Neale Hurston, A Literary Biography* (1977). This revisionist and sympathetic work contains a complete list of Hurston's published and unpublished writings, numerous photographs, and reveals new data and a number of new primary sources. Important also is a Hurston reader edited by Alice Walker with an introduction by Mary Helen Washington, *I Love Myself When I Am Laughing and Then Again When I Am Looking Mean and Impressive* (1979). Brief biographical sketches reflecting much of the negative interpretation of Hurston, along with comments on her productive work, can be found in Arthur P. Davis's *From the Dark Tower, Afro-American Writers 1900–1960* (1974) and Darwin T. Turner's *In a Minor Chord, Three Afro-American Writers and Their Search for Identity* (1971). Hurston's obituary appeared in the *New York Times* (Feb. 5, 1960). — BERNICE JOHNSON REAGON

JACKSON, LUTHER P[ORTER] (1892–1950), educator, historian, and Virginia civic leader. He was born in Lexington, Ky., the ninth of twelve children of ex-slave parents Edward W. and Delilah Culberson Jackson. There is evidence which suggests that his paternal grandfather, Jordan Jackson, was the son of a slave (Mary Jackson) and one of Mary Todd Lincoln's brothers. Luther's mother was formally educated following the Emancipation and became a schoolteacher. His father was a self-educated dairy farmer. Two years after her husband's death in 1909, Delilah Jackson moved her family to Kansas City, Kans., where some of the children had already migrated, and remained there until her death in 1943. Luther, whose aspirations for education came from his mother, received his elementary and high school education at Chandler Normal School in Lexington, Ky., graduating in 1910. He entered Fisk University where in 1914 he received the B.A. degree. He continued as a graduate student for one semester during 1914–1915 and was awarded his M.A. in 1916. He then took correspondence courses and in the summer of 1919 enrolled at the University of Kansas. He was a student in history and education at the City College of New York in 1920–1921, and of Columbia University Teachers College in 1921–1922. He reenrolled in Columbia in the summer of 1923, but five years later transferred to the University of Chicago where he studied in 1928–1929 and 1932–1933. He was awarded the Ph.D. degree in history on Aug. 27, 1937.

In 1915 Jackson began his teaching career as director of the Academic Department and teacher in the Voorhees Industrial School, Denmark, S.C., remaining there until 1918. His South Carolina experience led to two studies published later in the *Journal of Negro History:* "Educational Efforts of the Freedmen's Bureau and Freedmen's Aid Societies in South Carolina, 1862–1872" (Jan. 1923) and "Religious Instruction of Negroes, 1830–1860, with Special Reference to South Carolina" (Jan. 1930). In 1913 he joined the staff of the Topeka Industrial Institute in Topeka, Kans., remaining there until 1920. In 1922 he was appointed director of the High School Department and teacher of history at Virginia Normal and Industrial Institute, which became Virginia State College in 1930. In 1925 he was promoted to associate professor of history. Upon his return from graduate study at the University of Chicago in 1929, he was promoted to professor of history and chairman of the history and social science unit. He held this position until his death.

In September 1922 he married Johnella Frazer, a 1914 graduate of the Fisk University Department of Music and daughter of P. T. Frazer, principal of Male and Female College, Hopkinsville, Ky., and became the father of four children: Laura Frances, Luther Jr., Edward Frazer, and John Tevis.

Jackson was an authority on the Negro in Virginia. His method of research emphasized the study of records in courthouses—wills, property lists, tax records, marriage records. By the time of his death he had, according to Dorothy B. Porter, published at least sixty-one books, articles, pamphlets, news articles, and brochures covering a broad spectrum of history, biography, education,

civic and community activities. He also wrote a weekly column "Rights and Duties in a Democracy" for the *Norfolk Journal and Guide* (1942–1948). His scholarly studies won for him the unstinting praise of Carter G. Woodson: "He knows more about Negro families in Virginia than any other man living" (Annual Report of the Director, *JNH,* Oct. 1947, p. 410). His studies and publications, especially those relating to the participation of Negroes in the American Revolution, resulted in his appointment to the Virginia World War II Historical Commission by the governor of Virginia.

His principal work, *Free Negro Labor and Property Holding in Virginia, 1830–1860,* originally the subject of his doctoral dissertation, was first printed in 1942 by D. Appleton Century in association with the American Historical Association and the American Council of Learned Societies. Subsequently published as a paperback by Atheneum in 1969, it was republished in 1970 by Russell and Russell, and reissued in 1971. Other scholarly works include *Virginia Negro Soldiers and Seamen in the Revolutionary War* (1944) and an article on the same subject in the *Journal of Negro History* (July 1942, pp. 247–87), and *Negro Office Holders in Virginia, 1860–1895* (1945). Rayford W. Logan completed the editorial work on *Memoirs of a Monticello Slave,* which Jackson was working on at the time of his death.

About 1929 he conceived the idea that "the most effective way to educate one's self and to educate others is to mingle with the people beyond the college campus, and to promote among [them] such organizations as will lead to their advancement" (typed resumé, April 25, 1943). As a result Jackson organized, led, and worked zealously in four areas of civic and community activity: voting, Negro business enterprise, community singing, and financial drives in behalf of the ASNLH and the NAACP. Three of these activities, begun locally in Petersburg, Va., expanded into statewide movements.

Closest to his heart was voting. To this end he organized and directed the Petersburg League of Negro Voters which became the Virginia Voters League. He compiled and published annually *The Voting Status of Negroes in Virginia.* His rallying cry was "A voteless people is a hopeless people," coined by the Alpha Phi Alpha fraternity. His efforts in Virginia received national recognition when the Southern Regional Council requested him to make a comprehensive study of Negro suffrage in the South in 1947, which was published in pamphlet form as a special issue of *New South* (June–July 1948) under the title *Race and Suffrage in the South since 1940.*

In Petersburg he was well known for his work in behalf of the Petersburg Negro Business Association (which later became the Virginia Trade Association). A good musician on the cornet who, according to his brother Wilbur, "could transpose on sight" (biographical notes in manuscript by Wilbur Jackson), he organized the Petersburg Community Chorus of one hundred voices and conducted it in annual concerts beginning in 1933 and continuing to 1941.

Jackson's local campaigns to raise funds for the ASNLH and the NAACP were also expanded into statewide campaigns under his direction. His enthusiasm caused students of Virginia State College to refer to him as "Mr. N.A.C.C.P." A grateful Virginia Conference of Branches of the NAACP cited him "For unselfish and devoted services in enhancing the voting status of Negroes" on Oct. 2, 1948.

As one study indicates: "Jackson had his hand in almost every area concerning the betterment of the Negro." He served on at least nine boards, associations, and councils in furtherance of his belief that "the highly educated" should become involved in the activities of the masses of people. These included the Negro Organization Society, Southern Regional Council, Southern Conference Educational Fund, the Virginia Teachers Association, and the Virginia Association of Elks. As a consequence, he drove himself constantly. He never took vacations. An early riser, he walked at such a fast pace that his eldest son recalled that he had difficulty keeping up with him. A nap at midday revived him. When he was home he remained at his office on the campus until eleven and twelve o'clock at night. The killing pace he set for himself undoubtedly caused the heart condition—a condition which, according to his son, he kept from his wife—and the heart attack which led to his death on April 20, 1950. Funeral services were held in the College Chapel, and he was buried in Blandford Cemetery, Petersburg, Va. He was survived by his wife Johnella, his daughter Laura Fulcher, and three sons: Luther Jr., Edward, and John Tevis.

Politically, Jackson was regarded as a moderate, even a conservative who believed in and practiced interracial goodwill. He was a congenial man with "hearty and spontaneous laughter" (L. F. Palmer, *NHB*, June 1950, p. 198). An accident while carrying a trunk during his student days at Fisk University caused the loss of his right index finger, but apparently this never affected his genial disposition or outlook on life.

Perhaps the best estimate of Jackson was the tribute paid to him three years before his death by Arthur P. Davis: "The most valuable leader in Virginia, Dr. Jackson is that rare combination of scholar and man of the people. . . . Luther Jackson has a profound faith and love for the people and he has never allowed his academic interests to take him away from them." On April 17, 1955, Luther Jackson High School was dedicated in his memory at Merrifield, Fairfax County, Va.

A valuable source concerning Jackson and his work is *Black Historians, A Critique* by Earl E. Thorpe (1969), which summarizes an article by Jackson evaluating the *JNH* and places him in the new school of black historians (see also "With a Grain of Salt," *Norfolk Journal and Guide,* Oct. 4, 1947). The Jackson Collection in the Johnston Memorial Library of Virginia State College, catalogued by James Brewer, contains a great deal of primary source material used in Jackson's research. "Luther Porter Jackson, Bibliographical Notes" by Dorothy Porter (*Negro History Bulletin,* June 1950, pp. 213–15) is the most complete bibliography, listing sixty-one items. "Luther Porter Jackson" by J. H. Johnston, in the same issue of the *NHB,* and the obituary also by Johnston in the *JNH* (Oct. 1950, pp. 352–55), are evaluations of his life and work by a longtime colleague.

John Hope Franklin's prize-winning review of *Free Negro Labor and Property Holding in Virginia, 1830–1860,* published in the *JNH* (Jan. 1943, pp. 86–88), is a thorough evaluation of Jackson's principal work. *Who's Who in Colored America* (1950) provides basic biographical information. — THOMAS D. PAWLEY

JASPER, JOHN (1812–1901), preacher. He was born a slave on a plantation in Fluvanna County, Va., the youngest of several children of Philip Jasper, a slave preacher, and his wife Nina. After the death of his father his mother, who had become the head servant in a rich family, sought to give him "righteous guidance." While still a young man he worked first in Williamsburg, Va., and then in the Richmond tobacco factory of Samuel Hargrove. His conversion, like that of many other mystics, was dramatic. Shortly after viewing a Fourth of July parade in 1837 he wondered about the value of such demonstrations. According to his own account, on July 25 he realized his sinful ways, thought he would die, and cried to heaven for mercy. The clouds vanished and he was so exalted that his feet felt as though they were on mountains and he could blow off the factory roofs. He was able to restrain himself, however, until the noon hour when he encountered an old man and an old woman who had been seeking to convert him. When his exaltation aroused the curiosity of an overseer, he was told that Jasper had "got religion." Hargrove, a devout member of the First Baptist Church of Richmond, urged Jasper to spread the good news to the factory workers, his family, and the community.

He became a member of the First African Baptist Church, and began to preach and to study the Bible with another slave, William Jackson. He won fame in many parts of Virginia; he consoled Confederate prisoners, and after the Civil War preached to small groups on Mayo Island in the James River between North and South Richmond. As pastor of the First African Baptist Church and of the Sixth Mount Zion Baptist Church in Richmond, he attracted increasingly large crowds and, about 1880, won renown for his sermon "De Sun do Move," which he is said to have delivered 250 times.

He died peacefully on March 30, 1901, almost ninety years old, at his home at 1112 St. James St., Richmond, surrounded by his family and many friends. His body lay in state at the Sixth Mount Zion Baptist Church, where thousands viewed his remains. The church, where a section was reserved for white people, was packed to "suffocation," with thousands more outside, for the funeral on April 4. He was buried in Ham Cemetery, and a tall monument was erected over his grave.

His fame was based largely on his simple, ungrammatical language, imagery, and emotionalism which appealed to the great mass of uneducated freedmen. A portion of one of his sermons is reported as follows: "Ef dere is any of dem pherloserphers whar's been takin' so many cracks at my ol' haid 'bout here, he is corjully invited to step for'ard an' squar up dis vexin' business. I here tell yer dat yer carn't squar a circle, but it looks lak dese great scholers done learn how to circle de squar. Ef dey kin do it, let 'em step to de front an' do de trick. But, mer brutherin, in my po' judgment, dey carn't do it 'tain't in 'em to do it. Dey is on de wrong side of de Bible, dat's on de outside of de Bible, an' dere's whar de trouble comes in wid 'em. Dey done got out of de bres'wuks of de truf, an' ez long ez dey stay dere, de light of de Lord will not shine on deir path. I ain't keerin' so much 'bout de sun, tho' it's mighty convenient to have it, but my trus' is in de Word of de Lord. Long ez my feet is flat on de solid rock, no man kin move me. I's gettin' my orders f'om de Gawd of my salvation.''

There is a belief also that his tall, ungainly appearance and sex life won favor with especially the female members of his audiences, white as well as black. He married first Elvy Weaden in Williamsburg; then, after his conversion in 1837, Candus Jordan, who bore him several children. Divorcing her, he married Mary Anne Cole, shortly after the Civil War. After her death, he married for the fourth time a ''godly woman of maturity and discretion, who survived him.'' Even in modern times some preachers, white and black, male and female, have used their sex appeal to attract large audiences.

Jasper's career is in sharp contrast with that of the erudite minister Walter H. Brooks, who was a member and pastor of the First African Baptist Church before Jasper's pastorate and in 1877 pastor of the Second African Baptist Church of Richmond.

An obituary about Jasper in the *Richmond Times* (March 31, 1901, p. 13), reveals the high esteem in which he was held by some segments of the white community: ''Some people have the impression that John Jasper was famous simply because he flew in the face of the scientists and declared that the sun moved. In one sense that is true, but it is also true that his fame was due, in great measure, to a strong personality, to a deep, earnest conviction, as well as to a devout Christian character. Some preachers might have made this assertion about the sun's motion without having attracted any special attention. The people would have laughed over it, and the incident would have passed by as a summer breeze. But John Jasper made an impression on his generation because he was sincerely and deeply in earnest in all that he said.''

Information about Jasper is based largely on William E. Hatcher's *John Jasper: The Unmatched Negro Philosopher and Preacher* (1908). There is a laudatory abridgement in Benjamin Brawley's *Negro Builders and Heroes* (1937, pp. 80–87). See also Edwin A. Randolph's *The Life of Rev. John Jasper* (1884). Long obituaries were published in the *Richmond Times* (March 31, 1901, p. 13; April 4, 1901, p. 2; April 5, 1901, p. 6, and the *Richmond Dispatch* (April 5, 1901, p. 6).

— RAYFORD W. LOGAN

JEFFERSON, ISAAC (1775–c. 1853), slave of Thomas Jefferson and narrator of valuable memoirs. Born at Monticello in December 1775 and taken to Yorktown by the British, he apparently lived at Monticello after his release at the end of the Revolutionary War. He accompanied Jefferson to Philadelphia in 1790, and returned to Monticello for about nine years with Jefferson's son-in-law, Thomas Mann Randolph. He helped nurse Jef-

ferson in his old age (Jefferson died in 1826). Little is known about his subsequent life except that in 1847 he was a blacksmith in Petersburg, Va., with a shop not far from Pocahontas Bridge.

His reminiscences, published as *Memoirs of a Monticello Slave, As Dictated to Charles Campbell in the 1840's by Isaac, one of Thomas Jefferson's Slaves* (1951), was edited with an introduction by Rayford W. Logan. The editor, who examined Campbell's manuscript in the McGregor Library, University of Virginia, was convinced that Campbell faithfully recorded what Isaac Jefferson said. Campbell, a scholar of considerable note, a teacher, and principal of Anderson Seminary in Petersburg (1855–1870), died in the Staunton Lunatic Asylum on July 11, 1876, after some years of invalidism, but the manuscript was written in the late 1840s. One of the least known of the slave narratives, it is one of the most authentic and valuable for the information about Thomas Jefferson.

Isaac Jefferson's mother was named Usler or Ursula but nicknamed Queen, because her husband George was commonly called King George. As a boy Isaac toted wood and made the fires for his mother, who was a pastry cook and washerwoman. When Jefferson went to Williamsburg to attend the House of Burgesses, Isaac and the other slaves stayed in the Assembly House. A year after the seat of the state government was moved to Richmond in 1779 because of fear of British invasion, Isaac and other slaves accompanied him. Isaac made fires for baking bread and ginger cakes. When the British were close to Richmond in 1781 Isaac learned to beat a drum as a signal that the enemy was approaching. Jefferson left for the mountains and ''Isaac never see his old master arter dat for six months.'' After the British captured Richmond they took the slaves to Yorktown, one of the officers giving Isaac the name of Sambo. The British treated the slaves well, but Isaac did not mention whether any defected. After the surrender of Cornwallis, General Washington brought the slaves back to Richmond, Jefferson returned, and Isaac resumed his life as a slave.

When Jefferson went to Philadelphia as secretary of state in 1790 (not as president; *Memoirs*, p. 24), Isaac accompanied him on horseback. In Philadelphia Isaac learned the tinner's trade, making cups and tin, copper, and sheet iron. He was the only ''black boy'' in the tin shop of a man named Bringhouse. Jefferson was so pleased with Isaac's new skill that he sent him, after four years, to carry on the tin business at Monticello. But the business failed after two years. ''He then carred [*sic*] on the nail-business at Monticello seven years; made money at that'' (*Memoirs,* p. 27). This brief entry does not state whether Isaac shared in the profits. It does assert, however, that Jefferson reportedly had the first nail-cutting machine in Virginia, imported from England.

The *Memoirs* tell us little about Isaac after, presumably, 1803. When Jefferson had a swelling in his legs about 1822 (Fawn M. Brodie, *Thomas Jefferson: An Intimate History* [1974], p. 460), the *Memoirs* states that Isaac and John Hemings, another slave, ''nursed him two months: had to car [*sic*] him about on a han-barrow. John Hemings went to the carpenter's trade same year and Isaac went to the blacksmiths'' (p. 31). Campbell closed the *Memoirs* with a reference to Isaac and his blacksmith shop in Petersburg in 1847: ''Isaac is rather tall of strong frame, stoops a little, in color ebony:—sensible, intelligent [and] pleasant: wears large circular iron-bound spectacles & a leather apron. . . . P.S. Isaac died a few years after these recollections were taken down. He bore a good character'' (p. 36).

Evidence is lacking that Jefferson freed Isaac—there is no discussion of Jefferson's views on slavery in the *Memoirs*. Mrs. Brodie, who analyzed at length Jefferson's ambivalence about slavery, listed five slaves freed by his will (p. 466), but Isaac Jefferson was not one of them. Brodie raised the question why Jefferson did not free Sally Hemings, concerning whom an entry in Chapter 2 of the *Memoirs* provides basic information about the origins of the Hemings but not about Jefferson's alleged relationship with Sally Hemings. Campbell recalled Isaac's recollection that ''Folks said these Hemings'es was old Mr. Wayles' children.''

The manuscript used for the *Memoirs of a Monticello Slave* is in the McGregor Library, University of Virginia, Charlottesville. An incomplete manuscript at William and Mary College goes as far as Chapter 7 and omits the passage about Sally Hemings and ''old Mr. Wayles'' children.'' The *William and Mary Quarterly* . . . (Oct. 1951, pp. 561–82) reprinted the *Memoirs,* with an introduction by R.W.L. There are brief references in *The Papers of Thomas Jefferson,* edited by Julian P. Boyd et al. (3:334n, 5:244n, 17:242n; 1951, 1952, 1967).

— RAYFORD W. LOGAN

JENKINS, DAVID (1811–1877), editor, abolitionist, Mason, and politician. Jenkins was born in Lynchburg, Va. His early education came at the hands of a private tutor hired by his father. In 1837 he moved to Columbus, Ohio, working as a painter and glazier. By virtue of his thrift and industry, Jenkins was able to amass a goodly sum of money and several pieces of real estate.

On Dec. 27, 1843, he established and edited in Columbus *The Palladium of Liberty,* a weekly newspaper dedicated to the abolition of slavery and the advancement of the Negro in the United States. The idea of the newspaper came as a result of the State Convention of Colored People held in August 1843. In addition to its strong antislavery stance, the *Palladium* gave editorial support to the education of colored children, temperance, moral reform, and the elective franchise. The paper maintained a distribution throughout Ohio and the eastern states. Numbered among the local and traveling agents were Charles Langston, Henry Highland Garnet, and William Wells Brown. The *Palladium*'s life was relatively short, for by the winter of 1844 it had ceased publication. Nevertheless the paper had served as one of the early Negro-operated newspapers in the Midwest.

Jenkins firmly believed in constant agitation against slavery. From the time of his arrival in Columbus until the end of the Civil War, he actively pursued this position with numerous speeches and writings. Jenkins's zeal for the antislavery cause is demonstrated by the handbills he carried with blank spaces which could be filled in to advertise his meetings to denounce slavery. In 1848, in association with Frederick Douglass, Henry Bibb, and William H. Day, Jenkins signed an Address to the Colored People asking them to ''act with white anti-slavery societies whenever they could and where they could not set up societies for themselves without exclusiveness.''

During the 1840s and 1850s Jenkins regularly attended the sessions of the Ohio General Assembly, often presenting petitions and memorials on behalf of the rights of Negroes. His frequent appearances in the Ohio legislative chambers earned Jenkins the nickname of the ''Member at Large.'' In 1856 he petitioned the legislature for changes in the school law regarding Negroes.

Jenkins's antislavery activities were not limited to speeches or writings, but included active participation in the Underground Railroad, with special emphasis on the central Ohio region. He also maintained an interest in the Masonic order, serving as worshipful master of St. Marks Lodge No. 7 in Cincinnati from 1858 to 1860, and holding a variety of other offices during the 1860s and 1870s.

In the decade preceding the Civil War Jenkins became active in the many Negro conventions in Ohio. He was instrumental in the formation of the Ohio State Anti-Slavery Society, begun after the State Convention of Colored Men of Ohio in 1858. His Ohio associates in this work included Negroes of national reputation such as Charles H. and John Mercer Langston of Oberlin, Ohio, and Peter H. Clark of Cincinnati.

During the Civil War, Jenkins was a staunch supporter of the Union and the enlistment of colored troops. In August 1863 he was elected president of a statewide committee promoting appeals of funds for colored troops and support for the Union cause.

In 1873 Jenkins left Columbus to take up residence in Canton, Miss., where he began teaching. His move to Mississippi came through an appointment from the Freedman's Bureau, the appointment being his recompense for enlistment efforts in Ohio during the Civil War. Two years later he was elected to the Mississippi legislature, serving one full term. On Sept. 5, 1877, after an illness of five days, Jenkins died.

The most complete biographical data on David Jenkins are in William H. Parham's and Jeremiah A. Brown's *An Official History of the Most Worshipful Grand Lodge Free and Accepted Masons for the State of Ohio* (1906). The files of *The Palladium of Liberty* in the Ohio Historical Society provide a glimpse at Jenkin's attitudes toward slavery and other issues of the day. Scattered through copies of the *Ohio House* and *Senate Journals* are indications of Jenkins's presence at legislative sessions. — FRANK R. LEVSTIK

JOHNSON, CAMPBELL CARRINGTON (1895–1968), army officer and social worker. He was born in Washington, D.C., on Sept. 30, 1895, the son of the Rev. William Henry and Ellen Berry (Lee) Johnson. His father served at different periods as pastor of Israel Baptist Church in Washington, and Beulah and Liberty Baptist Churches in Alexandria, Va. The young Johnson received his education in those cities. Following his graduation from Washington's M Street High School in 1913, he worked at various jobs to earn college tuition, enrolling in Howard University in the fall of that year. When he was forced by lack of funds to withdraw before the school year was over, he returned to work, but reentered Howard in 1915. His education was interrupted once again in 1917 by World War I. He volunteered, and entered the Officers Training Corps at Fort Des Moines, Iowa, receiving his commission as first lieutenant of infantry on Oct. 15, 1917. He was assigned to the 350th Field Artillery at Camp Dix, N.J., where he organized and commanded Battery A, the war's first battery of field artillery composed of Negro troops. He served as commander until 1918 when all Negro officers in the regiment were relieved of command. The organization left for overseas duty under white officers who had been attached to the regiment for several weeks and had trained under its Negro officers. He was transferred to Washington to assist in the organization of the Student Army Training Corps Instructors' Camp at Howard University, where he served as senior military instructor until the unit's demobilization on Dec. 21, 1918. In November of that year he married Ruby Etta Murray, of Alexandria, Va., by whom he had one son, Campbell Carrington Jr. After the Armistice he received orders to assist in the organization of the Reserve Officers' Training Corps unit at Howard University. The organization was completed on Feb. 3, 1919, and with the rank of captain he taught military science and tactics there. Following his discharge from the service later that year, he was appointed to the section in the Bureau of War Risk Insurance (now the Veterans Administration) which handled insurance and compensation claims of Negro veterans. He was later made chief of this section and served until he resigned in 1923.

In 1920 he received a B.S. degree from Howard University's College of Liberal Arts and in 1922 an LL.B. degree *cum laude* from its School of Law. He was admitted to practice before the North Carolina and District of Columbia bars in 1922, and during the years 1922 to 1926 he maintained a limited law practice in the District of Columbia.

In 1923 he became executive secretary of the Twelfth Street (later the Anthony Bowen) Branch of the YMCA of Washington, a position he held for seventeen years. It was during his administration that this institution showed steadily increasing progress in every department. His success resulted in his being made director of a training institute for Negro YMCA secretaries held at Bordentown, N.J. During this period he was also active in community organization and race relations in Washington. He was one of the first to see the advantages of the Community Chest method of fundraising campaigns. He assisted in the organization of the district's Community Chest, and as a member of its original Board of Trustees, obtained from this body a formal statement of policy that it would operate without discrimination as to race or color. He helped organize neighborhood settlement houses sustained by the chest in the southeast, southwest, and northwest sections of the city. Concerned about their lack of recreational facilities, in the summer of 1932 he established a camp for Negro boys of Washington. He operated it for one season with voluntary contributions. The following year he persuaded A. E. Lichtman, a Washington theater owner, to donate funds to establish an improved facility to be known as Camp Lichtman. Through his efforts this camp was later moved to a more desirable site provided by the Interior Department. He spoke throughout the city advocating the admission of Negro churches to the Washington Federation of Churches (later the Council of Churches). After first turning down the proposal, the federation not only agreed to admit them, but later became one of the strongest factors in desegregation in the city. From 1939 to 1960 he was a member of the Board of Parole of the District of Columbia, serving as chairman for the last fourteen years. From 1932 to 1947 he served as instructor in social science in the School of Religion at Howard University. Although interested in many phases of social welfare, housing was his principal and continuing interest. He considered adequate housing basic to the solution of some of the most serious social problems. He was one of the organizers of the Washington Housing Association which dealt, in an advisory capacity, with problems of public housing in the district.

In 1940 Pres. Franklin D. Roosevelt appointed him executive assistant to Gen. Lewis B. Hershey, the director of Selective Service, National Headquarters, Washington. He was assigned to this civilian Selective Service job as a member of the army since he had remained active in the U.S. Army Reserve from the time of his discharge in 1919 until this recall to duty. By 1943 he had attained the rank of colonel. His duties with Selective Service included interpreting the system to persons affected by it. His many speeches and public statements directed to Negro veterans showed his concern for their successful readjustment to civilian life. He was an effective member of the Committee on the Participation of Negroes in the National Defense Program (1940–1942), which persuaded President Roosevelt to assign eligible Negro reserve officers to new Negro regiments and to give Negroes an opportunity to earn reserve commissions, if officer candidate schools were established for selectees (Franklin D. Roosevelt to Rayford W. Logan, chairman, Nov. 7, 1940, Roosevelt Papers, Hyde Park, N.Y.).

In March 1946 he was awarded the Army Commendation Ribbon; in May of that year he was awarded the Army Distinguished Service Medal for exceptionally meritorious service in carrying out his military assignment. In the citation accompanying the award, he was declared responsible for the solution of problems pertaining to the rights, privileges, and obligations of minority racial groups affected by the Selective Training and Service Act, approved Sept. 16, 1940. In 1947 he was assigned as executive assistant to the director, Office of Selective Service Records. In 1948, at the time of the reorganization of the National Headquarters, he was assigned as assistant to the director, Selective Service System.

In June 1950 he was appointed by President Truman as a member of the National Capital Housing Authority and later was elected its vice-chairman. He secured from this body the passage of a resolution ending official segregation in public housing in the District of Columbia.

In 1964 he was assigned as assistant director of the Selective Service System. His duties consisted of supervision of the administrative functions of the system, including organization, management, personnel, incentive awards, supplies, printing, statistics, and race relations. At the time of his death he held this position with the rank of a senior colonel on active duty in the U.S. Army. His death at his home in Washington on Aug. 22, 1968, followed a heart attack. Buried with full military honors at Arlington National Cemetery, he was survived by his widow, his son, Campbell Jr., his sister Eudora H. Winters, five grandchildren, and other relatives.

In 1968 a posthumous Legion of Merit and Distinguished Service Award was presented to his widow and son. He was cited for inspiring leadership, for contributing significantly to the successful mission of the Selective Service System, and was lauded as a pioneer in equal opportunity for minorities.

His papers contain a wealth of information and his personal views on a large number of vital issues. For instance, he stated on June 7, 1950, with respect to the Negroes at the Officers Training Camp, Fort Des Moines, Iowa (1917), that "the Government was still undecided whether to commission those Negroes who had now fulfilled all the necessary training requirements." If the trainees desired to remain another month, by that time the army would have made up its mind. Some good men, many of whom had left jobs and families, quit in disgust. By the end of the additional month the War Department "did determine that it would use a certain number of Negro officers in a separate division." In a memorandum of March 4, 1941, he had suggested that specially trained Negro reserve officers might be utilized in the new Negro units. A few weeks later (March 21, 1941) he criticized the lack of opportunities for Negroes to attend West Point and Annapolis—none had graduated from the Naval Academy and none between Charles Young in 1889 and Benjamin O. Davis, Jr., in 1936, from West Point.

Johnson pointed out on Aug. 28, 1942, that the high degree of illiteracy among Negro selectees could be reduced by utilizing Negro educators in the South—yet he was the only Negro present at a meeting to discuss the subject. He further emphasized that federal funds would have to be used since states could not be depended on to help reduce illiteracy.

At least as early as February 1944 he was concerned about the postwar world. Young people did not want to be subjected to a "way of life where honor, decency and fair play are unknown." A year later he stated that discrimination by manufacturers, labor unions, and individuals had not disappeared "as though by magic." Even so, "we must not let this fact deter us from our duty, nor weaken our loyalty" but should "continue to press for the removal of all" disabilities. Achievement

of this goal "may be one of the significant factors in determining whether America actually won the war!" He pointed out in November 1944 that Negroes in service units had learned skills which would be helpful after the war was over, whereas those in combat training had "been taught skills in killing and maiming which, it is hoped, they will speedily forget upon their return."

Two of Johnson's other major interests included housing and home rule for the District of Columbia. With respect to housing, he stated on Feb. 1, 1951, as a member of the National Capital Housing Authority, that the question in Washington was not whether there should be integration, but how it should be done. On Nov. 14, 1952, he wrote that "there are no sound reasons against permitting the residents of the District of Columbia to govern themselves."

Johnson was a man of great intellectual integrity, with high standards of conduct for all, himself included. In his personal relations he was invariably charming and amiable. The functions he performed were both difficult and controversial because he stood between those too slow to change and those who seemed too much in a hurry for change. From both groups he gained respect and concessions which brought change where there had been little before. He was a man of dynamic energy whose activities within his community were numerous and varied. Forty-eight civic, social welfare, educational, and religious organizations with which he had been affiliated presented him with a scroll in recognition of twenty-five years of distinguished service to the Washington community.

Sources of information include materials provided by his son and his sister, Eudora H. Winters. A major portion of his voluminous papers is in the Moorland-Spingarn Research Center, Howard University, and contains an informal, unfinished autobiography, copies of his speeches, published articles, and numerous clippings about his career. See also *Who's Who in America* (1966–1967), Rayford W. Logan's *Howard University: The First Hundred Years, 1867–1967* (1969), and the *Howard University Record* (vol. 13, May 1919).

— CHARLOTTE S. PRICE

JOHNSON, CHARLES SPURGEON (1893–1956), social scientist, editor, and educational statesman. He was born in Bristol, Va., on the Tennessee border, the eldest of six children of Charles Henry and Winifred (Branch) Johnson. His father was a Baptist minister who took great pride in the quality of his own education, and at an early age Charles Johnson was exposed to the classics of Western literature, theology, and history. This early literary exposure was reflected in Johnson's own later writings as well as in his encouragement as an editor of creative writings by others. It was perhaps also by virtue of his family background and his educational training that an incident during his early years was to make a strong impression on him which he never forgot and helped to sensitize his later training in the field of human relations. After becoming president of Fisk University, he recalled how he and his mother customarily stopped at a soda fountain for refreshments after shopping in town. On one day, however, the owner of the drugstore told his mother that he could not serve them anymore at the counter. Johnson never forgot his sense of dismay and the humiliating embarrassment of his mother when she was unable to explain this incident to him.

Johnson left home at the age of fourteen to attend Wayland Academy and Virginia Union University in Richmond, Va. He finished the university in three years, graduating with a B.A. in 1916, greatly influenced by a teacher of Greek, Joshua Simpson, who he felt prepared him to understand the nature of human relations in modern society. From Virginia Union, Johnson went to the University of Chicago where he formed a close association with sociologist Robert E. Park from whom he developed an objective, scientific attitude toward race relations. While studying at the University of Chicago, where he received the Ph.B. degree in 1918, Johnson served as director of research and records (1917–1919) of the Chicago Urban League, of which Park was the president. Johnson's studies were interrupted by his service as a regimental sergeant major in France, where he participated in the Meuse-Argonne offensive. He returned to Chicago in 1919 to continue his work under Park. After the Chicago race riot of 1919, Johnson was named associate executive director of the Chicago Commission on Race Relations, which developed the classic study *The Negro in Chicago: A Study of Race Relations and a Race Riot.*

Johnson moved to New York in 1921 to become the director of the Department of Research and Investigations for the National Urban League. In 1923 he assumed also the editorship of the National Urban League's new magazine *Opportunity: A Journal of Negro Life. Opportunity* became an outlet for the research and investigations of the Urban League as well as a fountainhead of the "Harlem Renaissance" of the 1920s. Negro literary figures and artists of the time, Alain L. Locke, Claude McKay, Langston Hughes, Countee Cullen, Aaron Douglas, Arna Bontemps, and many others were presented in its pages. A series of articles on African art helped to reveal to America the artistic heritage of the Negro race.

In 1928 Johnson left the National Urban League to become chairman of the Social Science Department at Fisk University, and it was here that he did most of his social science writing. An interesting bridge between his work at the National Urban League and his beginning at Fisk University was his position as research secretary for the National Interracial Conference, Washington, D.C., in the fall of 1928. The data from this conference became Johnson's book, *The Negro in American Civilization: A Study of Negro Life and Race Relations in the Light of Social Research* (1930).

Johnson was a prolific writer. After his inauguration as president of Fisk University (1946), a bibliography compiled by the Fisk University Library (1947) listed seventeen books of which he was the author or co-author, fourteen other books to which he had contributed chapters, and more than sixty articles. In addition to *The Negro in Chicago* and *The Negro in American Civilization,* several other books are worthy of mention. *Shadow of the Plantation* (1934) related the racial and cultural influences of the plantation to the social patterns and personality changes of Negroes in this type of economic organization. *The Negro College Graduate* (1938) attempted to synthesize his social and educational philosophy. *A Statistical Atlas of Southern Counties* (1941) listed social and economic data for 1104 southern counties, classified according to major crop types and urbanization. *Growing Up in the Black Belt* (1941) dealt with the personality development of southern rural Negro youth and criticized the caste theory of race relations in the South. In *Patterns of Negro Segregation* (1943), a result of Johnson's participation in Gunnar Myrdal's *The American Dilemma* (1944), Johnson delineated the class structure of the Negro community and described the differential behavioral responses of the various classes.

Johnson's skills in marshalling facts, forged during his *Opportunity* days, served him well from 1943 to 1948 when he edited *A Monthly Summary of Events and Trends in Race Relations,* a magazine that grew out of a confidential request from Pres. Franklin D. Roosevelt. Johnson served every president from Hoover to Eisenhower, beginning as the American member of the commission appointed by the League of Nations to investigate forced labor in Liberia in 1930. In 1946 he went to Japan as one of the advisers on the reorganization of the Japanese school system. He was a member of the U.S. delegation to the First UNESCO Conference, (Paris, 1946; Mexico City, 1947), a delegate to the World Council of Churches (Amsterdam, 1948), and to the Conference on Indian-American Relations (New Delhi, 1949). He was awarded several honorary degrees, including D.H.L. (Howard University, 1941), Litt.D. (Columbia University, 1947), and LL.D. (Harvard University, 1948; the University of Glasgow, 1952). He was one of the most influential Negroes in the nation, and many foundations and philanthropic enterprises such as the General Education Board, the Rosenwald Fund, the Carnegie Foundation, the Ford Foundation, and others, relied on his counsel.

In 1946 Johnson became the first Negro president of Fisk University, where he assembled an outstanding faculty and made it a strong research center. He also developed one of the strongest social science departments in the country in the field of race relations. Johnson provided a training laboratory for young social scientists, both black and white, who were interested in empirical research in race relations. Sociologist Edgar Thompson of Duke University wrote in the 1940s that there were only two strong sociology departments in the South, one at the University of North Carolina and the other at Fisk University.

During his presidency, Fisk University added several major buildings and doubled its educational budget. Over a million dollars was added to its endowment. A closed-circuit television system was developed to train students in this new communications medium and an early-admissions program was begun for exceptional high school students. As a result of its strong faculty and program, chapters of Phi Beta Kappa and the American Association of University Women were established.

Among the social scientists whom he helped develop were Lewis Wade Jones, G. Franklin Edwards, Clifton Jones, and Harry Walker, the last three having served on the faculty at Howard University. Many other social scientists spent a year or more at Fisk as "Senior Fellows," including Herman Long, Hugh Smythe, August Meier, and Bernard and Rhoda Goldstein. Johnson's former sociology students and senior fellows included U.S. Ambassador Samuel C. Adams, Judge L. Howard Bennett, and college presidents Albert N. Whiting, Lionel H. Newsom, and Stanley H. Smith.

Johnson married Marie Antoinette Burgette in 1920. They had four children: Charles Jr., Robert Burgette, Patricia Marie, and John Vincent. He died of a heart attack on Oct. 27, 1956, in the railroad station at Louisville, Ky., while on his way to attend a meeting of the Fisk University Board of Trustees in New York City. He was buried in Nashville, Tenn. He was survived by his wife, four children, and three sisters, Lily Epps, Sarah Hawks, and Julia Johnson.

A full-length biography of Charles S. Johnson was completed by Patrick J. Gilpin as a doctoral dissertation at Vanderbilt University (1973). Published biographical materials include James Blackwell and Morris Janowitz (eds.), *Black Sociologists, Historical and Contemporary Perspectives* (1974); three articles by Ernest W. Burgess, Elmer A. Carter, and Clarence H. Faust in *Phylon* (vol. 17, Fourth Quarter 1956), on "Charles S. Johnson: Social Scientist, Editor, and Educational Statesman." Other articles include "Charles S. Johnson: A Scholar and a Gentleman," in *Thirteen Against the Odds* by Edwin R. Embree (1944), and Preston Valien's "Charles S. Johnson" in *International Encyclopedia of the Social Sciences* (1968) and "Sociological Contributions of Charles S. Johnson" (*Sociology and Social Research* 42, March–April 1958). He was regularly included in *Who's Who in America. See also* the obituary in the *New York Times* (Oct. 28, 1956, p. 88).

— PRESTON VALIEN *and* BONITA H. VALIEN

JOHNSON, EDWARD A[USTIN] (1860–1944), teacher, lawyer, historian, businessman, and politician. He was born a slave in the Sylvester Smith mansion in Raleigh, N.C., on Nov. 23, 1860, one of eleven children of Columbus and Eliza A. (Smith) Johnson, both slaves. As a child he watched the Union soldiers march through Raleigh. His early education was given to him by a free Negro woman, Nancy Walton, who also taught many young white aristocrats. At about the age of ten he entered what later became the Washington High School for Negroes, which had been founded by a brother of Justice David Brewer of the U.S. Supreme Court. Johnson and Brewer had long walks and talks together about geology and botany. In 1877 he was so impressed by one of the first two graduates of Atlanta University that he changed his plans to attend Oberlin, enrolled in Atlanta University in 1879, and spent one year in the Collegiate Division (1882–1883). While at Atlanta he taught in the rural areas of Georgia, read the Bible regularly, and became a lifelong Congregationalist. He was also a close friend of Butler R. Wilson (Class of 1881), who became one of the first Negroes admitted to the American Bar Association. For a short period after he left Atlanta University, Johnson taught and served as a principal in the Atlanta public schools. In 1885 he left Atlanta permanently and lived in Raleigh

until 1907. He taught and served as principal of Washington High School (1885–1891), which had a large school population for that time of about 1200. He also maintained a small barbershop, as he had done while a student in Atlanta. As early as 1886 Johnson participated in the convention of the North Carolina Negro Teachers Association, which demanded adequate but separate high schools and normal schools for Negroes. Among those present at the meeting was Anna J. Cooper, later an educator and a leader in the club movement for Negro women.

It was through his teaching in Raleigh and, apparently, the urging of the white superintendent of the Raleigh schools that he came to see the great need for a history of Negro achievements in the United States, written on a level for school children. In 1890 he published his widely used *A School History of the Negro Race in America from 1619 to 1890,* seven years after George Washington Williams had published his two-volume *History of the Negro Race in America,* which was for the adult reader. Published to mark twenty-five years of Negro freedom and dedicated to other Negro teachers, it revealed his Bible-reading days by tracing the origins of Negroes to the "Great Flood." The book, which was used as a school text in North Carolina and Virginia, made Johnson well known. But it was not a carefully documented study; it contained little that was new and was replete with errors. The book, however, went through at least four editions (1890, 1896, 1899, and 1911).

Johnson began the study of law at the newly founded (1888) Law Department of Shaw University in Raleigh, and in 1891 he graduated with an LL.B. degree as the school's first law graduate. He was such an excellent student that he joined the Law Department in 1893 as an instructor in law, stenography, and typewriting, and served as dean of the Law Department until 1907, when he left Raleigh to live permanently in New York City. In 1894 he had married Lena Allen Kennedy, the great-granddaughter of the Rev. Richard Allen, the founder of the African Methodist Episcopal church. They had one daughter, Adelaide.

Johnson's interest in the practical aspects of the law led him into politics. A staunch Republican all his life, he served from 1897 to 1899 as an elected alderman in Raleigh. In 1897 he was appointed a clerk of the federal district attorney for the Eastern District of North Carolina, and stayed at this post until 1907 at a salary of $900 per annum. He was also chairman of the Republican party in the 4th Congressional District, a delegate to the Republican National Conventions in Minneapolis (1892), St. Louis (1896), and Philadelphia (1900). In 1904 Pres. Theodore Roosevelt made him an honorary brigadier-general in his inaugural parade.

Like many other Negro attorneys of his day, Johnson did not find the practice of law very lucrative. Yet he became one of the largest property owners in the city of Raleigh, owning as many as 100 houses, and was one of the founders, along with Booker T. Washington, of the National Negro Business League (1900). He continued to write: in 1899, a popular treatment of the *History of the Negro Soldiers in the Spanish-American*

War and Other Items of Interest, which was later included in a reissue of his *School History;* in 1904 a utopian novel, *Light Ahead for the Negro,* predicting that Negroes would overcome their caste status and persecution in a century. W. E. B. Du Bois reviewed the book favorably in *The Dial* in 1905.

Despite his relative affluence, Johnson suffered such harsh racial discrimination that he left Raleigh for New York in 1907. He won admittance to the New York bar and settled in Harlem at 17 W. 132nd St. to practice law and pursue a successful business. He did not, however, neglect his Republican party activities. In 1917, with the support of the United Civic League, he was the first Negro elected to the New York State legislature, representing the 19th Assembly District. Although Johnson served only one term (from Jan. 1, 1917, to Dec. 31, 1918) he was credited with aiding the enactment of significant legislation. One law sought to ban discrimination in public accommodations; another created free state employment bureaus to help reduce discrimination in employment. A third sought to prevent discrimination in publicly supported hospitals. These laws were praised in many places, including England. Ten years later, Johnson, although blind since 1920, made, as he expected, an unsuccessful attempt to win the Republican nomination in the 21st Congressional District. He did not expect that a sufficiently large number of Negroes would vote. In 1928, however, Oscar de Priest was the first Negro to win election to Congress in a northern city, Chicago.

Johnson's last book, *Adam vs. Ape-Man in Ethiopia,* was published in 1931. In it he upheld the biblical version of creation and he also maintained that Ethiopia was one of the centers of creation. Just prior to his death he was at work on a history of the Negro in Raleigh during Reconstruction.

In his will he bequeathed two-thirds of his estate of $75,000 to institutions in Raleigh, among which were the Negro blind, the Congregational church, and a music scholarship at Shaw. He also left $1000 to the NAACP. He died after surgery on July 25, 1944, in Sydenham Hospital, New York City, and was buried in Woodlawn Cemetery, New York City.

Raleigh newspapers contain some information on the aldermanic and legal activities and charitable acts of Johnson. The *Journal of the New York Legislature* for 1918 is the best source on his year as legislator. See *The Crisis* (April 1929, April 1933), and the obituaries in the *Journal of Negro History* (Oct. 1944, pp. 505–07); the *New York Times* (July 25, 1944); *New York Herald Tribune* (July 26, 1944), and the New York *Amsterdam News* (July 29, 1944). The sketch by Edwin R. Lewison in *DAB, Supplement Three, 1941–1945* (1973, pp. 390–91), is an excellent critical evaluation.

— CLARENCE G. CONTEE, SR.

JOHNSON, FENTON (1888–1958), playwright, poet, short-story writer, editor, and social reformer. Born on May 7, 1888, in Chicago, he attended the University of Chicago, Northwestern University, and the School of Journalism at Columbia University. During 1906–1907 he went south to teach, but poverty and literary ambitions drove him back to Chicago. While only nineteen years old, he had several plays performed in Chicago's old Pekin Theater. The listing of *The Cabaret Girl* (1925) in James V. Hatch's *Black Image on the American Stage* (1970) suggests his continued interest in drama during the "Harlem Renaissance."

But Johnson's major achievements were in poetry. *A Little Dreaming* (1913), his first collection, reveals the influence of both English and American romanticism, including the plantation tradition. More promising than the sentimental dialect poems and the melancholic lines to "Swinburne" and "Dunbar," however, is the realism of "The Plaint of the Factory Child." In *Visions of the Dusk* (1915) and *Songs of the Soil* (1916) Johnson rejected Victorian modes of expression for the language of the plantation and levee. "The Georgian poets and writers are seeking romance out of their environment," he writes. "I feel that the true artist can go no further than the American Negro for romantic inspiration." Thus in the lyrical portraits of fiddling Zeke in "Eulogy," the hairless sage in "Uncle Rufus," and the holy man of God in "De Elduh," we witness a big-city poet unearthing the wealth of the Negro folk tradition and demonstrating that even dialect can rise above caricature in the hands of a talented artist. Affirming the religious core of Negro life, Johnson discarded dialect in his adaptations of the spirituals, and in "Shout, My Brother, Shout" anticipates the free-verse experiments of Jean Toomer and James Weldon Johnson. Levee songs like "Shuffle 'Long" and "The Song of the Fish Market" provide a sharp contrast to the plaintive note of the plantation songs and are a harbinger of the phenomenal success of the musical *Shuffle Along* (1921). Fenton Johnson's reputation is not based on these early privately published volumes, however, but on the later naturalistic poems influenced by Sandburg and Masters. Although it was probably the free-verse spirituals in Harriet Monroe's *Poetry* (1918) and William Stanley Braithwaite's *Anthology of Magazine Verse* (1918) that first introduced Alfred Kreymborg and other modernists to the young poet's work, it was the radical disillusionment and use of language in "The Scarlet Woman" and "Tired," his two most frequently anthologized poems, that impressed them most. Together with "The Minister" and "The Banjo Player," poems selected from an unpublished fourth volume entitled "African Nights," these sardonic portraits were hailed as the best examples of a new attitude by many Negroes toward white American civilization. A fifth volume of forty poems, written in a racy, stark, realistic idiom while the poet was working with the Federal Writers Project, also remained unpublished.

Between 1912 and 1917 Johnson saw three of his short stories appear in *The Crisis.* Characteristic of his cultural and social commitment at the time is "The Black Fairy," (Oct. 1913, pp. 292–94), the story of a black member of "the world council of fairies" who shows a young girl her glorious African past but defers revealing the future until the race has been redeemed and "there is no longer a white civilization or a black civilization, but the civilization of all men." In 1920 he published *Tales of Darkest America,* a collection of unimaginative, unpolished stories written for *The Favorite Magazine.*

Contrary to his popular image as poet, Fenton Johnson was not an inveterate pessimist but a crusading journalist, editor, and social reformer. In 1916 he founded *The Champion Magazine,* a monthly survey of Negro achievement in music, sports, and the theater. The magazine's mission was to reconcile the races and "to impress upon the world that it is not a disgrace to be a Negro, but a privilege." *The Champion Magazine* folded in 1917. A year later Johnson founded *The Favorite Magazine.* But like its predecessor, "the world's greatest monthly" was, after a fitful three-year struggle, another losing venture. James Moody, a friend, assisted in soliciting advertisements and subscriptions, while Johnson wrote all the material for the magazine under different pseudonyms. Convinced by 1920 that the "solution of the race problem" would come only through a vigorous system of propaganda and social settlement workers of both races, Johnson launched "The Reconciliation Movement." In the January 1921 issue of *The Favorite Magazine,* he explains the proud tradition to which his organization subscribed. "The Reconciliation Movement," he writes, "is not a movement of submission. It is a movement of love, that love that reconstructs life through gentle but firm methods. . . . We are materialists, such materialists as Jesus of Nazareth was, as Abraham Lincoln was and as Toussaint L'Ouverture was."

During the Depression, the failure to realize his literary and social dreams inspired poems like "Others" in which the poet bitterly declares: "We are Others, the great Forgotten, the scoffed at, the scum of the publishing houses." The tremendous power of these later poems overshadowed Johnson's early optimistic vision and won him the misleading image as the poet of utter despair. Johnson died in Chicago on Sept. 17, 1958.

The fullest account of Fenton Johnson is "The Story of Myself" in *Tales of Darkest America* (1920, pp. 5–8). — BERNARD W. BELL

JOHNSON, HENRY (1897?–1929), soldier. Johnson was born around the turn of the century in Winston-Salem, N.C. After briefly residing there, his family moved to Albany, N.Y., where he had various jobs ranging from delivery boy in a drugstore to a Red Cap at Albany's train station. He also earned the reputation of being a fighter and a troublemaker, a "cracker hater," but paradoxically was also described as a "boy who knew his place." On Sept. 17, 1917, he married Georgia Edna Jackson, formerly of Great Barrington, Mass., and they resided at 23 Monroe St. Albany. They had no children. After his army career, he returned to Albany and toured the country to promote the sale of Liberty Bonds. Discharged, despite his wounds, with zero disability, he was unable to find gainful employment. He died in poverty at Walter Reed Army Hospital on July 2, 1929, and was buried with full military honors in Arlington National Cemetery.

Discontented with his life, Johnson enlisted in the army on June 5, 1917, and was mustered in on July 25 as a private in Company C, 15th New York National Guard.

After his unit became nationalized, it was shipped to Camp Wadsworth, Spartanburg, S.C., for its basic training. While the regiment was stationed there, many local whites became resentful of the "disrespectful Northern Negroes." After racial tensions flared, the War Department ordered the regiment shipped to Europe in order to avoid another racial clash, as had occurred in Houston, Tex., in August 1917. Johnson's outfit landed at Brest, France, on Jan. 1, 1918, and entrained within half an hour for St. Nazaire. The troops were first used in such tasks as laborers, stevedores, and the engineer services at Montoire, some six miles down the Loire River, although some were sent to French training schools to learn to use French weapons. Because of racial tension, the 15th, renamed the 369th Infantry Regiment, was sent to the front in March and attached to the 16th Division of the French army, thus making it the first American military unit to reach the war zone.

On May 1, 1918, Johnson was, according to his muster roll, promoted to the rank of sergeant. Shortly after the Americans took command of a bridge near the Aisne River, Johnson and Pvt. Needham Roberts were on sentry duty (May 13–14, 1918) when the Germans decided to recapture the bridge and perhaps overrun the inexperienced American troops. In the early morning hours a force of about thirty-two Germans surprised Johnson and Roberts and cut them off from their regimental headquarters, leaving them with only their pistols, knives, and a few hand grenades. During the ensuing attack, Johnson was wounded three times and Roberts twice. After the Germans realized that the Americans' ammunition was exhausted, they rushed to seize them. Johnson and Roberts became separated and Roberts was taken prisoner. Johnson, using the butt of his revolver and his bolo knife, rushed the Germans. As the hand-to-hand battle raged, Johnson managed to rescue Roberts and the startled Germans retreated. When the battle subsided, Johnson was credited with killing at least four Germans and wounding perhaps ten or more. Because Johnson and Roberts held their ground, they prevented the regiment from suffering heavy casualties. Johnson and Roberts were taken to a French hospital where Johnson was treated for serious wounds on both feet, bayonet wounds of the back, stabs on the left arm, and knife cuts on the face and lips. This skirmish was later to be dubbed the "Battle of Henry Johnson." Both men were awarded the Croix de Guerre, France's highest military honor, Johnson's with the Gold Leaf, and both men were cited by General Pershing and General Foch.

On Feb. 14, 1919, Johnson was discharged from the army and returned to the United States where the regiment received a tumultuous welcome up New York's Fifth Avenue. Later New York Gov. Alfred E. Smith and a delegation of other officials met Johnson at Albany's train station, where he received a homecoming reception and later attended a chicken dinner in his honor. There were other honors, including a proposal to name a street after him, offers of movie contracts and vaudeville acts, as well as proposed collections from different parts of the country to assist him until he recovered sufficiently to work.

The hero's welcome for Johnson was short-lived. The proposed street dedication and monetary gifts never materialized. Johnson decided to leave Albany to go on tour of the country with Col. William Hayward in the promotion of Liberty Bonds. He was forced to leave Texas for talking about "crackers." No monuments were erected for Johnson, but a bridge was erected for a George Dunn who was the first white enlistee from Albany in the American Expeditionary Force. Totally disabled, Johnson was unable to do any meaningful work. While France awarded him its highest military honor, Johnson's muster roll indicated that the United States awarded him no military honors, not even the Purple Heart. As a result of his inability to find employment, the lack of promised money, and denial of disability pay, Johnson died in Washington almost in poverty.

Information about Johnson leaves many unanswered questions. Both the United States and the French military records centers for World War I were destroyed by fire. The most comprehensive account is the chapter "The Battle of Henry Johnson," in Arthur W. Little's *From Harlem to the Rhine* (1936, pp. 192–201). The citation for the Croix de Guerre for Johnson and Roberts, with photographs and a translation, is on page 369. The contributor talked with men who knew Johnson and was thus able to collect valuable information that otherwise could not be acquired. Among them were Harold Ceasar, James Johnson, and James Hinder, in Albany, N.Y. — ROBERT LEE BAKER

JOHNSON, JACK [JOHN ARTHUR, LIL' ARTHUR]

(1878–1946), heavyweight boxing champion. Born in Galveston, Tex., the son of a devout school janitor, and one of at least seven children, Johnson quit school after the fifth grade and worked as a milkwagon helper, a livery stable boy, and a baker's apprentice. The booming port of Galveston gave him an opportunity to work as a longshoreman on the docks and perhaps contributed to his growing prowess which enabled him to beat a local bully. Despite the objections of his parents, he began to practice in a gym as a boxer. He traveled widely in the United States, hopping freight trains, working at odd jobs, begging and gambling. Returning to Galveston, he resumed work on the docks and fought several semiprofessional bouts. He worked on a Florida fishing boat, went north, and became a professional boxer by 1897. In 1898 he married his childhood sweetheart, Mary Austin (his only colored wife).

Jack Johnson learned some of his boxing skills from Joe Walcott, "The Barbados Demon" (not to be confused with the later "Jersey Joe" Walcott), who won the welterweight (147-pound limitation) in 1901, and from Joe Choyinski (a Polish Jew) who fought James J. Jeffries to a draw in a heavyweight (over 175 pounds) bout on Feb. 23, 1900. Choyinski knocked out Johnson in a match in Galveston that landed them briefly in jail since professional fighting was then illegal in Texas. From 1902 to 1907 Johnson won fifty-seven bouts, some of them against other leading Negro heavy-weights such as Joe Jeannette to whom he lost on a foul in the second round in Philadelphia on Nov. 25, 1905, and Sam Langford ("Boston Tar Baby") whom he defeated in fifteen rounds in Chelsea, Mass., on April 26, 1906. Johnson by this time weighed 194 pounds and Langford only 158. In 1906 Johnson knocked out Bob Fitzsimmons, who had been heavyweight champion from 1897 to 1899 but was in his mid-forties when Johnson defeated him. James J. Jeffries, who succeeded Fitzsimmons and retired as undefeated heavyweight champion in 1905, refused to fight Johnson because of his race. When Tommy Burns beat Marvin Hart, Jeffries awarded Burns the "title."

Johnson taunted Burns until the latter agreed to a title bout at Rushcutter Bay, near Sydney, New South Wales, Australia, on Christmas Day 1908. Carrying on a running conversation Johnson pummeled Burns so severely that police stopped the bout in the fourteenth round. Johnson had been compelled to agree to accept a small share of the purse and to permit Burns's manager to serve as referee.

The new champion encountered greater difficulty in having his title fully accepted. He fought a number of mediocre contenders and in 1909 knocked out in the twelfth round Stanley Ketchell, the middleweight (160-pound limitation) champion. Ketchell weighed 160 and Johnson 209. The search for "the great white hope" began at a time when racial tension was mounting—the Springfield, Ill., riots (Aug. 14 and 15, 1908) had provoked the consternation that led to the organization of the NAACP in 1910.

The champions of "white supremacy" found their hope in Jim Jeffries, who challenged Johnson although Jeffries was grossly overweight and had to lose pounds to get into condition after five years without a major fight. In a memorable bout under a blazing sun in Reno, Nev., on July 4, 1910, Johnson scored a knockout in the fifteenth round. The fights between Negroes and whites were worse than those following the Joe Gans–Battling Nelson matches—eight persons were reported killed and many more injured, especially in small towns. The search for a successful "white hope" continued and racial tension increased.

Johnson's wife had left him and he became known as a womanizer. On Jan. 18, 1911, he secretly married Etta Terry Duryea, the recently divorced wife of Clarence E. Duryea, a wealthy turfman of Hempstead, Long Island. The marriage became known in February 1912. On Sept. 11, 1912, Mrs. Johnson shot herself, reportedly because of remorse over her marriage, aggravated by ostracism by her white friends. On Nov. 7, 1912, Jack Johnson was arrested on the charge of having violated the Mann Act, commonly known as the White Slave Law, which made it a crime to transport women across state lines for unlawful purposes. About a month later Johnson, who had been released on bail after incarceration for four days, married his former "business secretary," Lucille Cameron, an eighteen-year-old white woman. After an hour's deliberation by a jury, Johnson was found guilty (May 13, 1913) of violating the Mann Act, which had become law on June 25, 1910, after the acts for which he was found guilty. On June 4, 1913, Johnson was sentenced to a year and a day in the penitentiary and fined $1000. Taking advantage of time allowed to put his affairs in order, Johnson and his new wife fled to Canada and then to France.

There he became widely known for his flamboyant style of living and carousing.

Meanwhile, Johnson's first marriage had so infuriated many white Americans that Rep. Seaborn A. Roddenbery of Georgia introduced (Dec. 11, 1912) a constitutional amendment to ban racial intermarriage. Roddenbery declared that "No brutality, no infamy, no degradation in all the years of southern slavery possessed such villainous character and such atrocious qualities as the provisions of [state] laws . . . which allow the marriage of the negro Jack Johnson to a woman of the caucasian strain." The bill died, nevertheless, in the Committee on the Judiciary (Logan, *The Betrayal of the Negro . . .* [1968], p. 364).

Johnson lost his title as heavyweight champion of the world to Jess Willard in Havana, Cuba, on April 5, 1915. The preponderance of evidence indicates that Johnson allowed Willard to knock him out in the twenty-sixth round—photographs show Johnson shielding his eyes from the sun while lying on his back and waiting for the count of ten. It was rumored that Johnson allowed Willard to win the fight in return for promises that the Mann Act conviction would be dropped when Johnson returned to the United States. For the next five years Johnson remained in exile, living most of the time in Spain, where he gave exhibition fights, acted in a film, and even performed as a professional matador. He returned to the United States in 1920 and served ten months in Leavenworth Prison. He was divorced by his third wife in 1924 and in the summer of the next year he married Irene Marie Pineau, a divorcée, who remained with him until he died. Johnson fought almost until then, but eked out a living as a guest lecturer in evangelical churches, selling stocks, as a nightclub master of ceremonies and movie extra. After the mid-1930s he worked principally as a lecturer at Hubert's Museum, a combination sideshow, penny arcade, and flea circus on New York City's 42nd Street.

One of his many joys was driving big automobiles—he raced the world-famous Barney Oldfield, for example. This sport, almost a mania, led to his death. He lost control of his car while driving at more than eighty miles an hour near Franklinton, N.C., about twenty miles north of Raleigh, on June 11, 1946. He died of internal injuries later the same day at St. Agnes Hospital, Raleigh. Funeral services were held at Pilgrim Baptist Church in Chicago and he was buried in Chicago's Graceland Cemetery. He was survived by his wife and a brother Henry (*Chicago Defender*, June 22, 1946, p. 2).

Despite his tempestuous life, Jack Johnson was one of the greatest fighters of all time. Nat Fleischer, longtime editor of "boxing's Bible," *Ring Magazine,* ranked him in 1949 as the greatest heavyweight, listing Jack Dempsey fourth and Joe Louis sixth. Johnson was elected in the first group chosen for Boxing's Hall of Fame when it opened in 1954.

In forty-seven years of fighting, Johnson had been knocked out only three times.

One study, *Bad Nigger! The National Impact of Jack Johnson* (1975), by Al-Tony Gilmore, was criticized for its alleged undue emphasis on racism, for example, in the *Journal of American History* (Dec. 1975, pp. 732–

33). Ocania Chalk's *Pioneers of Black Sport* (1975, pp. 144–61) is a useful summary, with photographs on pages 144, 147, 149, 155, 157, 158, and 160. Johnson wrote an autobiography, *Mes Combats,* in 1914 while in exile in France; a second, *Jack Johnson in the Ring and Out* (1927); and *Jack Johnson Is a Dandy, An Autobiography,* edited by Dick Schapp (1970). Probably the most authoritative work is Finis Farr's *Black Champion: The Life and Times of Jack Johnson* (1964). Farr also contributed an excellent summary with a brief annotated bibliography in *DAB, Supplement Four, 1946–1950* (1974, pp. 432–34). Al-Tony Gilmore's "Jack Johnson and White Women: The National Impact, 1972–1973" (*JNH,* Jan. 1973, pp. 18–38), gave a detailed analysis, showing especially white denunciations and the mixed reactions of Negro newspapers and of such leaders as Booker T. Washington and W. E. B. Du Bois. Howard D. Sacklek's play *The Great White Hope* (1968) dramatized the search for a white boxer to defeat Johnson. An obituary was published in the *New York Times* (June 11, 1946).

— RAYFORD W. LOGAN

JOHNSON, JAMES WELDON (1871–1938), teacher, lyricist, consul, author, editor, poet, and civil rights activist. He was born in Jacksonville, Fla., the second of three children of James and Helen Louise (Dillet) Johnson. James Johnson was born a freeman of mixed ancestry in Richmond, Va., in 1830. His wife, of French and Haitian Negro ancestry, was born in Nassau and received her early education in New York City. They were married in April 1864 in Nassau and moved in 1869 to Jacksonville where James Johnson worked as a headwaiter in a fashionable hotel (as he had done in New York City and Nassau). Mrs. Johnson taught at the Stanton School, the city's largest grammar school for Negroes. Their first-born, a daughter, died soon after the arrival. Their first son, named James William, was born on June 17, 1871, and their second son John Rosamond was born in 1873. (In 1913 James changed his middle name to Weldon.) Like T. Thomas Fortune, he looked back upon Jacksonville as one of the most liberal towns in the nation for colored people. This not-altogether roseate view probably accounts in some measure for Johnson's lack of extreme bitterness that characterized Richard Wright, who had grown up in Jackson, Miss. In addition, Johnson's mother aroused his early interest in music, drawing, and books. In church he heard Negro spirituals and folk sermons, bases for some of his later fame. He himself was not deeply religious. He met Booker T. Washington, Joseph C. Price, Fortune, and other Negroes who inspired a broader outlook on life in the United States. In 1884 he made the first of several trips to New York City.

Since there was no high school open to Negroes in Jacksonville, his parents sent him in 1887 to Atlanta University for his secondary and college education. During the summers of 1891 and 1892 Johnson taught in rural Henry County, Ga., where the crudity of life led him to identify with the problems of Negroes in general. He worked as a carpenter during the World's Columbian Exposition in Chicago in 1893, where he heard Frederick Douglass deliver an oration and Paul Laurence Dunbar read one of his poems. During his college days Johnson wrote about thirty poems, some in dialect but most dealing with the race question. He so improved his public speaking that he delivered the graduation oration in 1894. He was an outstanding student, a baseball player, and a member of the university's quartet that toured New England during summers. He left Atlanta University convinced that Negroes had the major responsibility for removing their inferior status in order to prove their mental, moral, and physical equality. Until his death in 1938 he devoted most of his life to developing the knowledge and skills he had learned at the university to achieve this goal.

As principal at Stanton School in Jacksonville (1894–1901), he instituted courses in 1895 that led to a high school diploma. In 1895 he founded the *Daily American* and wrote editorials reflecting the difficulty of developing a consistent and effective policy in race relations. For instance, he endorsed a separate Negro exhibit at the Atlanta Cotton States Exposition (1895) but opposed the extension of separation in public schools to private schools. The *Daily American* supported the Republican party in national elections and the Democratic in local. Lack of support by the Negro community led to the demise of the paper in early 1896. He met W. E. B. Du Bois probably for the first time in 1896 when he served as secretary at the first Atlanta University Conference on Negro Life. He read law with a white lawyer, and in the spring of 1898 became the first Negro lawyer admitted to the bar in Duval County. He formed a partnership with Douglas Wetmore, a friend from his Atlanta University days who "passed for white" during his one year at the University of Michigan Law School and who helped inspire Johnson's novel *The Autobiography of an Ex-Colored Man* (1912, reprinted 1927). On Jan. 1, 1898, Johnson introduced Booker T. Washington as the Emancipation Day orator, calling him "the inspiration of the race," and emphasizing the need to study Negro history to develop pride. In 1901 he wrote an essay advocating both industrial and academic education as well as racial assimilation. In 1900 he wrote the words of "Lift Every Voice and Sing" and his brother wrote the music of this song that came to be known as "The Negro National Anthem." It bespoke "the gloomy past" and "the white gleam of our bright star," It ended: "Shadowed beneath Thy hand,/ May we forever stand./ True to our God,/ True to our native land."

The increasing racial subjection of Jacksonville Negroes led the two brothers to leave Jacksonville in 1902. They had already teamed with Robert (Bob) Cole in producing several successful songs. Unlike Bert Williams and George Walker, the trio did not include minstrelsy, but generally Negro themes. In 1901 Cole and the Johnson brothers signed a contract with Joseph W. Stern and Company that guaranteed monthly payments. Their big break came when in 1902 Marie Cahill added "Under the Bamboo Tree" to her musical comedy *Sally in Our Alley*. By 1903 Stern and Company had sold more than 400,000 copies. The trio, dubbed "Those Ebony Offenbachs," May Irwin, Anna Held, Fay Templeton, and Lillian Russell also popularized such tunes as "The Old Flag Never Touched the Ground" and

"Didn't He Ramble." They also wrote music for exclusive Klaw and Erlarger productions—*The Sleeping Beauty* and *Humpty Dumpty*. Some songs were published in the *Ladies' Home Journal*. In 1903 the team produced *The Evolution of Ragtime: A Musical Suite of Six Songs Tracing and Illustrating Negro Music*. James Weldon Johnson's collaboration ended when he was appointed consul in Venezuela in 1906.

In addition to his musical career Johnson studied literature, especially the literature of the theater, with Brander Matthews, the authoritative professor of dramatic literature at Columbia University. In 1904 Johnson had become treasurer of the Colored Republican Club, headed by Charles W. Anderson, a confidant of Booker T. Washington who helped Anderson win (1905) appointment as collector of internal revenue for the Second District of New York (which included Wall Street). James Weldon Johnson, his brother, and Bob Cole wrote two songs for Theodore Roosevelt's presidential campaign of 1904: "You're All Right, Teddy" and "The Old Flag Never Touched the Ground."

Johnson's association with Anderson and Booker T. Washington led him to refrain from participation in the Niagara Movement, organized by Du Bois in 1905 to oppose the conservative policies of Booker T. Washington. This stance contributed to a recommendation by Washington that Johnson be given a consular appointment. After passing an examination, he was offered the post of U.S. consul at Puerto Cabello, Venezuela. Recovering from illness, he sailed on March 16, 1906. Despite continued requests by Anderson and Washington for an appointment in Europe, Johnson was assigned in 1908 as consul to Corinto, Nicaragua, with promotion to Class VII, two steps above his rank in Puerto Cabello. He assumed his post in April 1909, left in early October to marry in New York City (Feb. 10, 1910) Grace Nail, the daughter of well-to-do real estate entrepreneur John B. Nail. They arrived in Corinto in the spring during the revolution which enabled the United States to gain virtual control of Nicaragua. The Johnsons returned to the United States on leave in the summer of 1911, when he was promised a transfer to a European post. Johnson returned alone in March 1912 and soon found Corinto the chief entrepôt for American armed forces and a stronghold of Pres. Adolfo Diaz, whom the United States supported. Johnson stalled attacks by the rebels on Corinto until the arrival of U.S. forces that ended the threat to Corinto in September. He again took leave and joined his bride in New York in Dec. 10, 1912. The election in November of Woodrow Wilson as president made it clear that he, like other Negroes and Republicans in general, could not expect appointments or reappointments. He resigned on Sept. 1, 1913, and Secretary of State William Jennings Bryan accepted his resignation on Sept. 9.

Although his consular service did not win him his cherished European post, it provided him enough leisure to devote considerable time to writing. In 1912 the small firm, Sherman, French, and Company published his anonymous *The Autobiography of an Ex-Colored Man*. Mixed reviews limited sales until the "Harlem Renaissance" of the 1920s increased its popularity. The distinguished critic Sterling A. Brown wrote in 1958:

"This narrative of a fair-skinned Negro who passed for white depicted a cross-section of Negro experience in America with authenticity and insight" (*DAB, Supplement Two*, p. 345). Johnson's friend Brander Matthews paved the way for the publication in the *New York Times* on Jan. 1, 1913, of his poem, "Fifty Years." An inspirational poem, commemorating the fiftieth anniversary of the Emancipation Proclamation, its theme is expressed in the lines: "This land is ours by right of birth,/ This land is ours by right of toil;/ We helped to turn its virgin earth,/ Our sweat is in its fruitful soil." It won the praise of Matthews, Theodore Roosevelt, Booker T. Washington, Charles Waddell Chesnutt, and W. E. B. Du Bois.

Neither the *Autobiography* nor "Fifty Years" won sufficient acclaim to assure a livelihood in literature. After a visit to Jacksonville to settle the estate of his father, who had died in 1912, in the fall of 1914 he became editor of Fred R. Moore's *New York Age*. Moore wrote Washington, "He is a good friend of ours." His editorials, "Views and Reviews," won the praise of a wide spectrum of critics from Emmett Jay Scott, Washington's secretary, to Oswald Garrison Villard, editor of the *New York Evening Post* and at that time an occasional critic of Washington. By rarely mentioning the names of either Washington or Du Bois, Johnson alienated neither. By insisting that Negroes should use the press as a means of fighting militantly for their rights, he appeared to be intellectually on the side of Du Bois. He continued to emphasize race pride. He pragmatically supported a separate YMCA in Harlem (as he did also in 1917 in acceding to a separate training camp for colored officers), and criticizing "hyphenated" Americans, except Jews. He revealed an innate conservatism by condemning the "utopian" concept of a League of Nations, "modern" ideas of education, and an eight-hour day for railroad workers. He increased his insufficient income slightly by collaborating (for the last time) with his brother in writing two songs and translating from Spanish into English the libretto of Enrique Granados's opera *Goyescas*, which was presented at the Metropolitan Opera House in 1916. He helped promote the sale of the few remaining copies of his *The Autobiography*. In the Nov. 16, 1916, issue of the *Age* he voiced his pessimism about the effects on Negroes of Woodrow Wilson's election.

Meanwhile he was verging toward the most important aspect of his activist career, as an organizer and field secretary (Sept. 1920 to Jan. 1931) of the NAACP. His reasons for his joining are still debatable. In 1914 Du Bois had begun cultivating his friendship, and Johnson had joined the NAACP in early 1915. But he maintained his close ties with Tuskegee even after the death of Booker T. Washington on Nov. 14, 1915. Washington's death helped facilitate the First Amenia Conference in August 1916, which attempted to achieve an accommodation between the "radicals" and the "conservatives." Although Johnson wrote in the *Age* (Sept. 14, 1916) that the conference was "one of the most remarkable gatherings that has taken place in this country," it failed to reconcile the two opposing groups. One of its more significant achievements was Johnson's recognition that the NAACP was emerging as the organiza-

tion most likely to promote some of the goals which he sought. Joel Spingarn considered Johnson's participation at Amenia a "coup d'état."

On Nov. 1, 1916, Du Bois wrote Johnson urging him to consider favorably the offer made by Spingarn, chairman of the board of the NAACP, to become a "candidate for organizer and hoping that Johnson's field correspondence might be an interesting feature of the *Crisis.*" Johnson accepted in mid-December 1916.

His field work in the South in early 1917 led to the organization of the Dixie District, which added thirteen branches and 738 members of the association. The entry of the United States into World War I caused a reduction in staff, Johnson's appointment as acting secretary, and the need to find a capable assistant for Johnson in the national office. Johnson chose Walter White of Atlanta, Ga., who joined the association in February 1915. Adopting an idea of Oswald Garrison Villard (chairman of the board before Joel Spingarn), Johnson organized the famous silent march protest in New York City of July 28, 1917, against lynching. A memorable photograph shows Du Bois and Johnson marching behind the lead row of muffled drums. Silent protest turned to anger when thirteen soldiers of the Negro 24th Infantry were executed for their alleged participation in the Houston riot (Aug. 1917). In one of his most eloquent speeches Johnson told a Carnegie Hall audience several months later that "the strains of Disfranchisement, of Jim Crowism, of Mob Violence, and of Lynching" should be washed out from the American flag in the war "to save the world for democracy." The war would give colored peoples freedom from their colonial masters and migration of American Negroes from the South to the North would help in their struggle for equality.

He resumed his work of organizing new branches when the board of directors in February 1918 employed a white man, John R. Shillady, as secretary. With the able assistance of Shillady, White, and Du Bois, Johnson mounted a highly successful campaign to organize new branches from among the large number of Negroes gainfully employed in war industries and from sympathetic whites. Two of the most able assistants were Robert Bagnall and Johnson's classmate at Atlanta University, George Towns. Towns was particularly successful in implementing in Atlanta (1919) a suggestion of Shillady's and Johnson's to encourage Negroes to vote (a campaign resumed in the 1930s by Austin T. Walden, Mrs. John Hope, and Rayford W. Logan). Although some of the branches lost their vitality after the war and most of the members were middle-class and upper-middle-class Negroes, the branches helped make the NAACP the strongest organization engaged in the battle for equal rights for Negroes.

The results of World War I caused disillusionment to Johnson and many other Negroes who believed their participation in the war would improve their condition. The determination of some whites to subject Negroes, including recently returned veterans, to prewar racial restrictions led to a series of race riots. A riot in Washington, D.C., on July 21, 1919, precipitated in part by inflamatory articles in the *Washington Post* and the *Washington Star,* prompted Johnson and Herbert Seligmann, publicity director of the NAACP, to make an on-site investigation. Johnson's visit induced the *Star* to run a series of articles acknowledging some responsibility for the riot. Riots in Chicago, East St. Louis, and other cities provoked Johnson's graphic term, "Red Summer."

His on-site investigation in 1920 of the American occupation of Haiti was a most effective revelation of the brutalities of the U.S. Marines, financial control by the National City Bank of New York, political control of government by the marines, censorship of the press and imprisonment without trial of those opposing U.S. domination. Johnson's four articles, "Self-Determining Haiti," published in Villard's *The Nation* between late August and the end of September 1920, were used by the Republicans in their defeat of Wilson and his imperialist policies. Johnson's articles, his agitation and that of Ernest Gruening, managing editor of *The Nation,* and others, as well as desire of the Harding administration to discredit Wilson, led to a full-scale Senate inquiry in late 1921 and early 1922. The final report recommended some minor changes but further extended U.S. political, military, and financial control. It was in effect a "white wash." Even after the marines were withdrawn in 1934, U.S. control continued.

In November 1920, after serving briefly as acting secretary, Johnson succeeded Shilladay as secretary of the NAACP. Shilladay had resigned in June 1920 following a vicious beating in Austin, Tex., in August 1919 while investigating an attempt by the Texas attorney-general to examine the membership books of the NAACP.

From November 1920 to December 1930, except for leaves of absence, Johnson was one of the most effective champions of equal rights for Negroes. He maintained, in general, cordial relations with members of the board, the professional staff, and even with White and Du Bois who did not work together harmoniously. He wisely rejected in 1920 a proposal that the NAACP take over the publication of Carter G. Woodson's *Journal of Negro History* because the NAACP did not have the necessary funds; in like manner he opposed the proposal of William Pickens, field director, that the NAACP undertake the organization of a labor movement—this was rather a task for the National Urban League. Like most leaders, he was at times ambivalent in his basic philosophy. In order to preserve the concept of interracial cooperation, he opposed in 1921 moving the headquarters of the NAACP from downtown Fifth Avenue to Harlem. On the other hand he supported the "Negro Sanhedrin," the short-lived proposal of Kelly Miller for an organization of Negroes of all varieties of opinion. While sympathetic to the emphasis of Marcus Garvey on race pride, Johnson opposed his willingness to abandon the fight for racial equality, his Back-to-Africa Movement, and his fomenting hostility between West Indian and American-born Negroes. He was a leader in the fight (1921–1924) which resulted in the establishment of a veterans hospital in Tuskegee, with a Negro director and staff. Reversing his antilabor stance of 1916, he supported the efforts of A. Philip Randolph and others in the mid-1920s to organize the Brotherhood of Sleeping Car Porters and Maids, and favored

using Negroes as strikebreakers against exclusionary white trade unions.

In politics also he shifted allegiance. At first a Republican like most Negro leaders, he became disillusioned by Harding's and Coolidge's do-nothing policies. He called for the organization in 1922 of a "Liberty Party," supported Robert La Follette, and the Progressive party in 1924 until its platform omitted planks in support of the demands of American Negroes. He urged a break with the Republican party, doubted the possibility of gaining political power in the largely Democratic-controlled South, and urged Negroes to attempt to exercise the balance of power in the rapidly expanding northern urban communities.

He and Walter White raised funds for the sensational Sweet case in 1925, and Johnson drew up the request by the NAACP's board for a contribution from the American Fund, established by Charles Garland. This led to a bitter attack (Oct. 9, 1926) in the *Pittsburgh Courier,* edited by Robert L. Vann, which accused Johnson, Du Bois, and the NAACP of using the funds for the NAACP. Johnson pointed out that only about 5 percent of the fund had been used for Negro organizations and enterprises. On Sept. 14, 1929, Vann wrote that he had not seen the editorial and would not have approved it if he had seen it. Johnson also coordinated the work of the NAACP in the landmark Texas white primary cases (1927 and 1929).

Suffering from overwork, Johnson in 1926 bought an old farm in Great Barrington, Mass., the birthplace of Du Bois, where the Johnsons had spent parts of the summer at Mary White Ovington's home. He and his wife restored the old barn into a cottage and hoped for some respite from his multitudinous activities. Instead, he attended many interracial conferences, participated in an "unprecedented" seminar on the Negro at the University of North Carolina, Chapel Hill, in 1927, and in 1929 helped organize the cooperative consortium of Atlanta University with Spelman College and Morehouse College. During White's leave of absence (1927–1928) Johnson again overworked himself and had to take leave in the spring of 1929. The recipient of a Rosenwald Fellowship (1929–1930), Johnson attended the third biennial conference of the Institute of Pacific Relations in the fall of 1929 in Kyoto, Japan. Refreshed by the change of scene and the long ocean voyages, he returned to New York and finished the manuscript of *Black Manhattan,* which was published in 1930, and a long satirical poem "Saint Peter Relates an Incident of the Resurrection Day."

Instead of returning to his post at the NAACP, he accepted in October 1930 the Adam K. Spence Chair of Creative Literature and Writing, a post established for him at Fisk University. On Dec. 17, 1930, he submitted his resignation which the NAACP board accepted with "deep regret" on Dec. 29. At the same time it elected Johnson a member of the board and a vice-president of the association. At a testimonial dinner attended by some 300 in New York City in May 1931, several speakers, notably Du Bois, extolled his contributions to the NAACP, his race and country.

Johnson's appointment at Fisk was in recognition of a notable literary career. He had written several magazine articles and pamphlets; his *The Autobiography,* published in 1912, had been reprinted in 1927. *The Book of American Negro Spirituals* (1925) and *The Second Book of American Negro Spirituals* (1926) had been enthusiastically praised. His poem, "The Creation: A Negro Sermon," published in *The Freeman* in 1920, had been incorporated into the collection of sermons published in 1927 under the title *God's Trombones, Seven Negro Sermons in Verse.* Prof. Sterling Brown wrote in 1937: "Material which usually made ludicrous, is here invested with dignity and power. . . . The rhythms of these chants have true poetic quality" (*Negro Poetry and Drama,* p. 68). *Black Manhattan* (1930) is an indispensable source for Negro Life, theater, and biography from 1626 to 1930.

Fisk provided an opportunity for Johnson to lecture, to help develop outstanding students like John Hope Franklin, and to work with such scholars as Horace Mann Bond, Alrutheus Taylor, and E. Franklin Frazier. Since he had to be in residence only from January to June, he had time to write and to speak at such colleges and universities as Northwestern, the University of Chicago, Oberlin College, Swarthmore, Yale, and the University of North Carolina. He again overworked himself and underwent surgery in 1934 for a peritonsillar abcess. After relaxing with his wife in Great Barrington, he began in 1934 a series of fall lectures (until 1937) at New York University on Negro literature and and the contributions of Negroes to American culture. In the late 1930s the Johnsons spent some of their vacations at Dark Island off the Maine coast. They enjoyed their life so much that Johnson declined consideration to succeed John Hope as president of Atlanta University after his death in 1936. Johnson gave Walter White sage advice and other help. He urged the new secretary to accept the fact that the International Labor Defense had taken over from the NAACP the defense of the Scottsboro Boys, and at White's request, persuaded Spingarn to withdraw his resignation as president of the NAACP. And he supported White in the controversy over "voluntary segregation" which led to Du Bois's resignation as editor of *The Crisis* in 1934. Johnson elaborated his own views and that of the NAACP in favor of integration in *Negro Americans, What Now?* (1934). Du Bois, in a carefully reasoned review in the *New York Herald Tribune Book Review* (Nov. 18, 1934, pp. 23–24), restated his reasons against the possibilities of integration.

Johnson considered his autobiography, *Along This Way* (1933), as perhaps "one of the standard American autobiographies." Its value lies particularly in its account of the rise of Jim Crow, the migration of Negroes to the North, the emergence of the NAACP and of the "Harlem Renaissance." Like many other autobiographies, however, it generally placed the author in a favorable light.

James Weldon Johnson met a tragic death. On the way from Great Barrington to their summer home in Maine, his wife was driving through a blinding rainstorm on June 17, 1938, when a train struck them at an unguarded railroad crossing. Johnson died almost immediately and his wife was confined to a hospital for several weeks. Over 2000 persons attended the funeral, on June 30, in Salem Methodist Church, Harlem, with the Rev. Frederick Cullen, father of Countee Cullen, officiating. The principal eulogy was delivered by Gene Buck, president of the American Society of Composers, Authors, and Publishers, of which Johnson was a charter member. Among the mourners were Fred Moore, Claude McKay, Langston Hughes, Carl Van Vechten, Arthur and Joel Spingarn, Walter White, and Du Bois. Johnson was buried, at his request, in his lounging robe and formal trousers, with a copy of *God's Trombones* in his hand, in Brooklyn's Greenwood Cemetery. He was survived by his widow and his brother. Eulogies expressed more sympathy and praise than any Negro had received since the death of Booker T. Washington in 1915. Kelly Miller, one of the few who voiced reservations, pointed out that Johnson was "conservative, cautious and courteous." Sterling Brown wrote in *Supplement Two* of the *DAB* in 1958: "A man of poise and dignity, of warm friendliness, of ironic humor in spite of fundamental seriousness, he refused to allow racial affronts to break his spirit. To him the purpose of the N.A.A.C.P. was to 'vindicate the American idea of' opportunity and recognition of merit. His own career is such a vindication."

Among the many honors bestowed upon Johnson was the Spingarn Medal (1925), the annual award for "the highest or noblest achievement by an American Negro." He received honorary degrees from Atlanta University, Howard University, and Talladega College.

See Eugene Levy's *James Weldon Johnson: Black Leader, Black Voice* (1973). Thoroughly researched and balanced, it relied in some measure on Johnson's *The Autobiography of an Ex-Colored Man* and *Along This Way,* but also on the NAACP Papers, in the Library of Congress, and the James Weldon Johnson Papers in Yale University's Rare Book and Manuscript Library, and at Fisk University; other papers are listed in the bibliography. There are several letters in Herbert Aptheker (ed.), *The Correspondence of W. E. B. Du Bois* (vols. 1 and 2, 1975, 1976). The best brief account is by Sterling Brown in *DAB, Supplement Two* (1958, pp. 345–47). Obituaries appeared in the *New York Times* (June 28, 1938, p. 18; and July 1); and *The Crisis* (1938, pp. 295–98). — RAYFORD W. LOGAN

JOHNSON, J[OHN] ROSAMOND (1873–1954), composer, actor, and director of plays. One of three children of James and Helen Louise (Dillette) Johnson, he was born in Jacksonville, Fla., on Aug. 11, 1873. He was two years younger than his famous brother, James Weldon Johnson. Early in their lives James expressed astonishment at the volume of Rosamond's voice. Rosamond left Jacksonville in 1890 and did not return until the spring of 1897; during six years of this time he studied music, mainly at the New England Conservatory in Boston but at least briefly in Europe.

Returning home, Rosamond set himself up as a private music teacher, advancing the tuition rates considerably above what had been customary but still attracting many students. Besides a broad teaching program, he became choirmaster and organist for a large Baptist church and teacher of music at the Baptist academy. The concerts of his students attracted music lovers from all over the city, including whites, in a highly segregated community. One of his earliest compositions was the setting to music of a poem by his brother; he used the resulting anthem for an Easter service. He and James also wrote an operetta for the graduation exercises of the high school.

The summer of 1899 he and James spent in New York, meeting such key figures in the music business as Isadore Witnaeck, Harry B. Smith, and Reginal de Koven. They played their opera *Toloso* (which was never produced) for Oscar Hammerstein. *Toloso* had taken the sting and shame from minstrel and ragtime and given dignity to Negro music. But because it lampooned the imperialistic ambitious of Uncle Sam so soon after the Spanish-American War, it was anathema to the Broadway producers. Many of its songs, however, found their way into later musicals and into the repertories of such famous stars as May Irwin, Fay Templeton, Anna Held, and Marie Cahill. In later songs also, Rosamond Johnson won the reputation of being a new force in syncopated Negro music, remaining whimsical, but departing decisively from the stage caricatures of crap-shooting, chicken-stealing, and razor-wielding. He retained the unique flavor and the boldness of authentic Negro character and won respect for his sincere and honest approach.

For a Lincoln's Birthday celebration (Feb. 12, 1900) James and Rosamond wrote "Lift Every Voice and Sing," later recognized by many (partly through the impetus of the NAACP) as the "Negro National Anthem." Since its first performance by the schoolchildren of Jacksonville, it has been sung by millions.

Rosamond had made his professional debut in Boston in 1894. From 1896 to 1908 he was supervisor of music for the Jacksonville public schools. In 1900 the Johnson brothers established a partnership with Bob Cole; after 1908 Rosamond spent most of his time in New York. His musical personality was so original and his activities so forceful and comprehensive that he broke down barriers against the Negro and against "the Negro's place" in the world. Personally, musically, and racially he earned and maintained the title of "pioneer."

His impact on Europe was at least as strong as it was on the United States. As early as 1912, when Bob Cole's health failed, Rosamond became director of Oscar Hammerstein's Grand Opera House in London. In 1927 he was writing letters to his brother from King's Commercial Hotel, Oxford Road, Manchester, expressing great enthusiasm for his "African Drum Dance"—far above, he said, anything he had so far attempted—and great pleasure at its being published by Curwen and Son, Ltd., in London. Songs from the *Czar of Zam*, a light opera he had done with Bob Cole, were played in Drury Lane pantomimes, and later imported to the United States by Klaw and Erlanger. In London he also produced for Charles B. Cochrane several editions of Lew Leslie's *Blackbirds*. On July 13, 1913, he had married one of his former music students, Nora Ethel Floyd. From this union came two children, a daughter Mildred, and a son Donald.

As a creator of expressive and colorful music, Rosamond Johnson was phenomenal. His arrangements of spirituals included dozens of individual songs and all the music in five books—*The Book of American Negro Spirituals* (1925), *The Second Book of American Negro Spirituals* (1926), *Rolling Along in Song* (1937), *Sixteen New Negro Spirituals* (1939), and *The Album of Negro Spirituals* (1940). The total number of spirituals he arranged exceeded 150. In *Rolling Along in Song*, which he called "a chronological survey of American Negro music," are eighty-seven arrangements; besides the thirteen spirituals, he classified the songs as jubilees, plantation ballads, plantation and levee pastimes, minstrel songs, jail-house songs, work songs, ragtime, street cries, and "blues and 'de chain gang.' "

Beginning early in the 1930s he contracted with the Handy Brothers Music Company, Inc., to publish spirituals for the *Library of Negro Music for Mixed Voices* and some remarkable arrangements were brought out under this imprint. His *Sixteen Negro Spirituals* were dedicated to a famous radio and concert group of the time, the Southernaires.

His output in music for show business was even more extensive than his folklore contribution. Counting individual numbers and songs he wrote for musicals between 1897 and 1940, one can be sure of 160 items. One can be equally sure that he kept writing after 1940, that he contributed songs without getting credit, that he wrote songs he did not publish, and that he put his special touch on twenty or more songs which had been lyricized and basically composed by others. He contributed songs to such song books as *The Evolution of Rag-Time* (1903), *Cole & Johnson Vocal Folio* (1904), *Sing-along Album of Musical Readings and Children's Songs of the Vaughn de Leath Junior Melody Circle* (1932), and *Fond Song Memories of the 90's* (1936). Besides this mountain of songs, Rosamond Johnson did compositions exclusively for the piano. The "African Drum Dance No. 1," of which he was inordinately proud, was published in 1928. Before this had appeared "The Merango" (a Cuban dance) in 1905, "The Siberian Dip" in 1911, and "Tango Dreams" in 1914.

His gifts to the musical theater were great in quantity and quality. From one to six or seven of his creations were sung in each of the following stage musicals: *The Belle of Bridgeport* and *Central-Park* (1900); *The Alabama Blossom, Champagne Charlie, The Little Duchess,* and *The Sleeping Beauty and the Beast* (1901); *Huckleberry Finn, In Dahomey,* and *Sally in Our Alley* (1902); *In Newport* and *Whoop-Dee-Doo* (1903); *Humpty Dumpty,* originating in London (1904); *The Shoo-Fly Regiment* (1906); *The Red Moon,* in which Rosamund Johnson starred with Bob Cole (1908); *Mr. Lode of Kole,* written in collaboration with Bert Williams (1909); *Hello Paris* and *A Lucky Hoodoo* (1911); *Little Miss Fix-It* (1912); *Come Over Here,* a London Opera House revue (1913); and *Brown Buddies* (1930).

He contributed "Big Indian Chief" to the Sixteenth Annual Production of the Mask and Wig Club of the University of Pennsylvania in 1904 and "My Lulu San" to the Seventeenth Annual Production in 1905. Besides Bob Cole and his brother, he collaborated with James Reese Europe and Andy Razaf. In addition to these famous stars, the following sparkling stage personalities introduced or sang Rosamond Johnson's songs in a variety of popular shows: Peter F. Dailey, Virginia Earle, Henry French, Marie George, Mabelle Gilman, Eddie Leonard, Alice Lloyd, Trixie McCoy, Lillian Russell, Billy A. Van and the Beaumont Sisters, and Weber and Fields.

As an actor he was equally at the top of his profession. He made his acting debut in John W. Isham's *In Oriental America* in 1897. This was the first Negro show to play Broadway. Thereafter, among numerous other engagements, he played leading roles in the original casts of *Porgy and Bess* (1935), *Mamba's Daughters* (1939), and *Cabin in the Sky* (1940). He also acted in *Americana Revue* (1928) and *Little Show* (1929).

On many occasions he served as director and play doctor, beginning in 1896 with his direction of *Black Patti's Troubadours,* which had been built around the sensational singer Sisseretta Jones.

His fame came and went, as did his money. "Lift Every Voice and Sing" brought him much fame and honor. "Lil' Gal" (from Dunbar's famous poem) shone gloriously for a few years early in the century and was given a fine recording by Paul Robeson and Lawrence Brown. Robeson also recorded "Since You Went Away." In *Along This Way,* James Weldon Johnson reports that Rosamond earned a substantial sum from it after John McCormack, the Irish tenor, put it in his concert repertory. The "African Drum Dance" was played by the Omaha Symphony Orchestra, under the baton of Joseph Littau, in 1930.

Rosamond Johnson was proud of founding the New York Music School Settlement for Colored People in Harlem in 1918. The year before he had been awarded an honorary master's degree by Atlanta University. He was also made a subchief of the Iroquois because his *The Red Moon* dignified the American Indian. A Republican and a Methodist, he was also a member during most of his long life of the American Society of Composers, Authors, and Publishers.

He died in his sleep of a cardiac condition on Nov. 11, 1954, at his home, 437 W. 162nd St., New York City. His funeral was held at St. Philips Church, and he was survived by his widow, Mrs. Nora E. Johnson, their son Donald, and daughter, Mildred L. (*New York Herald-Tribune,* Nov. 12, 1954, p. 10; *Pittsburgh Courier* [Washington ed.], Nov. 20, 1954, p. 1).

The best sources on his life include James Weldon Johnson's *Along This Way* (1933)—and his *Black Manhattan* (1930); Jack Burton's "The Honor Roll of Popular Songwriters," Part 12, no. 20 (*Billboard* 61, no. 21 [May 21, 1949]: 38–39); the obituary in the *New York Times* (Nov. 12, 1954); and letters, clippings, and card files in the James Weldon Johnson Collection of the Beinecke Rare Book and Manuscript Library, Yale University. — JOHN LOVELL, JR.

JOHNSON, LUCY BAGBY (1834–1906), considered to be the last fugitive slave returned to the South from the North under the Fugitive Slave Act of 1850. Her capture, detention, and trial in Cleveland, Ohio, created great excitement in the city in January 1861 and for a time threatened serious consequences. There had been other attempts to remove fugitive slaves from the city

between 1850 and 1860, but the case of Lucy Bagby overshadowed them all in the interest and indignation it aroused.

On the morning of Jan. 19, 1861, a group of law officers led by a deputy marshal forcibly entered the home where Lucy Bagby was employed, removed her, and placed her in the county jail on a charge, filed by her owner, of being a runaway slave. A mob gathered about the jail and made threats of removing her from the custody of the sheriff. Three of Cleveland's prominent white lawyers volunteered to act as her counsel and made an immediate application for a writ of habeas corpus, contending that she had lived in a free state before coming to Cleveland. The court decided that the sheriff had no right to hold Bagby in prison and ordered her release. However, she was immediately arrested by U.S. marshals who found it necessary to swear in 150 special deputies to prevent her release by force by an aroused mob. While the prisoner was being transferred to the government building, it was evident that only a slight incident could have precipitated major violence. The federal commissioner who heard the case decided there was no doubt that Bagby was a fugitive and he was compelled to enforce the law even though he found the duty distasteful. The commissioner offered to contribute to a fund to purchase her from her master, but the owner refused to sell her.

When Bagby was taken to a train bound for the South she had to be surrounded by special marshals to prevent her release by irate citizens. Attempts to rescue Lucy from the train were foiled when the suspicious actions of the would-be rescuers were noted and protective measures were instituted.

Lucy Bagby was taken back to her West Virginia home, but when her owner tried to take her farther south after the Civil War broke out, she was rescued by a Union Army officer. Freed by the Emancipation Proclamation, she went to Athens, Ohio, and then to Pittsburgh. There she married George Johnson who had been a soldier in the Union Army.

Later Lucy Johnson returned to Cleveland, established a residence, and died there in 1906. As an aftermath of the case, a Negro man was charged with complicity in securing her capture. After investigation by a mixed committee of white and Negro members of the Fugitive Aid Society, he was exonerated when he was able to prove that he had warned her of her impending capture but that she had ignored his warning. Her case was illustrative of the aid provided openly to fugitive slaves in some northern cities.

In addition to Russell H. Davis's *Black Americans in Cleveland* (1972), see Elroy M. Avery's *History of Cleveland and Its Environs* (1918) and *Annals of the Early Settlers Association of Cuyahoga County,* published by the Executive Committee, Cleveland (vol. 5., no. 1., pp. 31–33, and no. 2, p. 142, 1904).

— RUSSELL H. DAVIS

JOHNSON, SARGENT C[LAUDE] (1887–1967), sculptor and printmaker. He was born in Boston on Oct. 7, 1887, the third of six children of Anderson Johnson of Swedish ancestry and Lizzie Jackson of Cherokee and African ancestry. His father died in 1897, his mother in

1902. An uncle, Sherman William Jackson of Washington, D.C., and maternal grandparents in Alexandria, Va., cared for Johnson and his siblings during their early years. One of the most important sculptors and printmakers during the second quarter of the twentieth century, his works in terracotta, copper, wood, cast ceramic, cast stone, and black clay, and his lithographs and etchings were especially prominent during the 1930s and 1940s in the San Francisco Bay Area. Between 1925 and 1970 his works appeared in twenty-nine different exhibitions.

In 1902 Johnson was orphaned to the Sisters of Charity in Worcester, Mass., where he attended the public schools and specialized in music and mechanical drawing. He studied music in Boston before going to Chicago to live briefly with relatives and to pursue his interest in art. Johnson arrived in San Francisco in 1915 and in the same year married Pearl Lawson. In 1920 he was working as an artist painting photographs and in 1921 as a framer. His daughter (and only child) Pearl Adele was born in 1923.

Shortly after his arrival in San Francisco he attended the A. W. Best School of Art. From 1919 to 1923 and from 1940 to 1942 he attended the California School of Fine Arts. In 1921 and 1922 he received first-prize awards for his work as a student at the California School of Fine Arts. From 1925 to 1933 Johnson maintained a studio in his backyard in Berkeley; he worked there evenings and in his spare time, using wood, ceramics, oils, watercolors, and graphics.

Johnson's early works were portraits and busts of his close friends and art associates, or works inspired by ideas affecting his own life. *Elizabeth Gee,* a ceramic bust of a Chinese girl, his neighbor's daughter, gained recognition in a local exhibit in 1925. From 1926 to 1935 the Harmon Foundation of New York exhibited Johnson's sculpture. A favorite among the active Negro artists, he won a number of awards in the Harmon shows for the force and strength of his sculpture and his artistry in combining materials. In 1935 the Harmon Foundation presented Sargent Johnson in a three-man exhibition in New York. His featured piece was *Forever Free,* a redwood sculpture of a black mother and her child with several coats of gesso and fine linen, sanded between layers and painted black and white. The flesh areas are a rich copper brown. Judged by many to be his greatest work, Johnson used the most prominent physical characteristics of the Negro to create a powerful American black image. There is a relationship to sculpture of African origin found in this work through the static position of the head, arms, and feet, as well as the quality of inner tension.

Johnson was at his peak stylistically during the "Harlem Renaissance" period, which coincided with the Harmon Foundation exhibitions. His works became nationally and internationally known through the shows and sales of this foundation. Most of his work during this period reflected ideas of the Renaissance. Portraits, masks, and mother-and-child themes were repeated often in his sculpture and drawings. In 1935 Johnson stated that he was producing "strictly a Negro Art," especially the more primitive slave type, which few

artists had done. He aimed to show "the pure American Negro, . . . the natural beauty and dignity in that characteristic lip and that characteristic hair, bearing and manner" and to show "that beauty not so much to the white man as to the Negro himself." Otherwise, although he was not easily discouraged, he would have failed. He was concerned with color not solely as a technical problem but also as a means of heightening the racial character of his work. "The Negroes are a colorful race; they call for an art as colorful as they can be made" (*San Francisco Chronicle,* Oct. 6, 1935).

Johnson was employed as an artist, senior sculptor, and supervisor with the Federal Arts Project in San Francisco in the late 1930s. In 1937 his carved redwood relief panel (eight feet by twenty-two feet) was placed at the California School for the Blind. He created two cast stone eight-foot-high sculptures for the Golden Gate International Exhibition, which were permanently installed. Johnson taught art classes for the Junior Workshop program of the San Francisco Housing Authority and sculpture at Mills College in 1947. In 1944 and 1949 he received the Abraham Rosenberg Scholarship which allowed him to travel to study sculpture and ceramics. From 1945 through 1965 he made numerous trips to southern Mexico to study clay and ceramic materials from archeological sites.

Always interested in trying new and advanced techniques, between 1947 and 1967 he produced nearly a hundred plates and panels, using porcelain on steel panels. The scenes were abstract, surrealistic, and impressionistic. They included animals, multiracial subjects, children, and geometric designs—all in vivid bright colors and exciting in movement. He received several commissions to produce porcelain enamel panels, one in 1949 a mural which covered a wall in the Richmond, Calif., City Hall Chambers.

In the late 1950s and 1960s Johnson continued to work on polychrome wood pieces and focused on universal themes boldly stylized. He used totempole effects and multiracial themes. Shaped diorite rocks and cast rock for animals and abstract forms became favorite materials during his later years. He also studied metal sculpture in the late 1950s and produced a small number of cast bronze works and welded sculptures of forged enameled wire forms.

Johnson was concerned with quality of workmanship, viewing the world and its art, absorbing all that he saw and read, and applying the ideas and techniques in a unique and fresh way. There is a relationship in his work to West African tribal art (Dan, Ife, Benin), Mexican, and synthetic cubism. His approach to the use of materials as well as design was unique. As James A. Porter wrote: "It may be a merit of Johnson's art that it transcends racial interests; indeed it gives the double impression of uniqueness and audacity that one frequently gathers from the apt elliptical expressions of Negro folk poetry" (*Modern Negro Art,* 1969, p. 118).

During the last twenty years of his life Johnson was afflicted with severe angina pectoris. He died of a heart attack on Oct. 10, 1967, in Mount Zion Hospital, San Francisco. Funeral services were held on Oct. 14 in the

Estrelleta Mortuary, 1115 Valencia St. He was survived by his daughter, Pearl Johnson of Cleveland, and a sister of Chicago (*San Francisco Examiner,* Oct. 12, 1967, p. 47; *San Francisco Chronicle,* Oct. 12, 1967, p. 36).

Biographical information is in Yvonne Greer Theil's *Artists and People* (1959, pp. 109–15), and *Afro-American Artists, A Bio-bibliographical Directory,* edited by Theresa D. Cederholm (1973, pp. 150–52). His works are listed in the Oakland Museum's Art Division Special Gallery, *Sargent Johnson: Retrospective* (Feb. 1971), and *Harmon Foundation Catalogue* (1926–1934), which reproduces *Two Sculptures* (1935, pp. 10–11). There are reproductions of *Copper Mask* and *Forever Free* in Porter's *Modern Negro Art* (1969, pp. 252 and 259, respectively). His works have been represented in the Fine Arts Gallery, San Diego; the Art Gallery, Howard University; the Oakland Museum, the San Francisco Maritime Union and Museum of Art; the Golden State International Exhibition; and the Richmond, Calif., City Hall Chambers. — ROBERT C. HAYDEN

JOHNSON, WILLIAM (1809–1851), businessman and diarist. Johnson's thirteen-volume journal of antebellum Natchez, Miss., is one of the more remarkable documents in American historiography and caused historian Allan Nevins to call him "one of the most . . . interesting of American diarists."

Johnson, who was born and died in Natchez, was freed by his white master, William Johnson of Adams County, Miss. (who had previously manumitted his mother and sister), in 1820, through an eloquent petition to and a special act of the Mississippi General Assembly. He was apprenticed to his free brother-in-law, Philadelphia-born, Natchez barbershop proprietor and businessman James Miller, who became a surrogate father in teaching him the ethical principles which became a lasting part of his character. Miller initiated him into the ways of free Negro existence, and indicated many of the vaguely marked boundaries of his economic and social status in relation to the Natchez white community.

At the age of nineteen, Johnson acquired a barbershop in Port Gibson, Miss., but two years later sold out and purchased Miller's Natchez barbershop when Miller moved to New Orleans. In 1833 he purchased a brick building on Main Street, paying off the note within two years. By the middle 1830s he had become the most enterprising young businessman in Natchez. He owned several rental properties, and rented rooms, offices to professional men, and retail store rooms to small shopkeepers. For a while he ran a toyshop and retailed wallpaper. He rented carts and other vehicles. He sold coal and sand, and conducted a street-watering business. He loaned money in small amounts and for short terms to whites and Negroes alike, speculated in farmland, and owned three or four slaves.

During those years Johnson became one of the most respected free Negroes of the Natchez area. He dressed fashionably, regularly purchased books, newspapers, and magazines, and engaged in political and other discussions with the white patrons of his barbershop, many of whom were leading citizens of Natchez and the surrounding countryside. He made several trips to New Orleans and to other lower Mississippi River towns, and in 1833 spent two months traveling in the North, visiting New York, Philadelphia, and other cities. Two years later, twenty-year-old Ann Battles, who had been freed by her Natchez master in Cincinnati, married the most eligible Negro bachelor in Natchez. Their tenth child was born only a month before the father's death.

After 1835 Johnson built several business structures, including the "Fancy Store on Main Street," enlarged his money-lending business, completed a new three-story brick home only half a block from the Adams County Courthouse, and increased his agricultural operations. At the time of his death he owned more than 350 acres of general farming and timber land, several rental buildings and small businesses, and fifteen slaves.

Johnson was assassinated in 1851 as a result of a land-boundary dispute with a Virginia-born free Negro, Baylor Winn who, although "supposed to be a Negro," had voted and had given testimony in court. Despite two trials, including a change of venue, Winn was acquitted, and his murder of Johnson "was avenged by law no more than if he had been a common slave." Johnson was eulogized by the Natchez press as "an esteemed Citizen," and as a man who held "a respected position on account of his character, intelligence and deportment."

There were times during the early years when Johnson undoubtedly believed that if he achieved economic success, if he maintained high standards of rectitude, the day might come when he would be more completely accepted by the Natchez white community. That day never came. Although he had access to the courts, he failed to secure the right to serve on a jury, to vote, or to join one of the city's militia companies. Although he contributed his time and money to numerous causes, attended public meetings and the theater, and went to church, he was seldom permitted to sit with his white neighbors on the ground floor. He was buried, however, along with his mother and one of his daughters, in the cemetery of the Natchez Cemetery Association. They were the only Negroes buried in the white section.

Johnson's sixteen-year diary (1835–1851), the only known complete chronological journal kept by an antebellum free Negro, was discovered by Edwin Adams Davis in 1938, one of the most significant southern historical findings of that period. While the diary is uneven, its merits far outweigh its deficiencies, for it was written by a man who was intelligent, observant, curious about many things, even in temperament, well informed about his community, and largely unimaginative —all characteristics of a good witness.

Few occurrences in the Natchez vicinity escaped the diarist—births and deaths, weddings and elopements, political meetings and campaigns, horse races and cockfights, concerts and trials, balls and epidemics, land deals and speculations. He revealed important phases of general southern life and particularly free-Negro–white relationships. He mirrored, on a few occasions with considerable intensity, the economic and social position of one individual, as well as his daily activities, attitudes toward the slavery regime, and thoughts and opinions on local, state, national, and international affairs. Hodding Carter III concluded that "it is no over-statement to say that this is the most unusual personal record ever kept in the United States."

See William Ransom Hogan's and Edwin Adams Davis's *William Johnson's Natchez, the Ante-Bellum Diary of a Free Negro* (1951) and Edwin Adams Davis's and William Ransom Hogan's *The Barber of Natchez* (1954). — EDWIN ADAMS DAVIS

JOHNSTON, JOSHUA (? – ?), painter. Born a slave, probably in the latter part of the eighteenth century, Johnston lived in the vicinity of Baltimore until the 1830s. He had three masters, all of Baltimore: Gen. Samuel Smith, Revolutionary War hero who served in Pres. Thomas Jeffersons' Cabinet as secretary of the navy and later as U.S. senator from Maryland; Gen. John Stricker, a hero of the War of 1812; and Col. John Moale, one of the leading military figures in the regiment that defended Baltimore against the British during the Revolutionary War, a wealthy landlord, judge, and prosperous merchant. One of the three owners encouraged young Johnston to master "doing likenesses," or portrait painting. A portrait of Mrs. John Moale (Ellin North) sitting in the company of her granddaughter, Ellin North Moale, painted by Johnston, attests to the fact that the artist enjoyed a very close and trusted relationship with the Moale family as early as 1800. Even at this time Johnston had already established himself in the city of Baltimore as a "Free Householder of Colour."

As early as Dec. 19, 1798, Johnston was the recipient of the kind of patronage which enabled him to post this advertisement in the *Baltimore Intelligencer:* "Portrait painting . . . as a self-taught genius deriving from nature and industry his knowledge of Art . . . experienced many unsuperable obstacles in the pursuit of his studies, it is highly gratifying to him to make assurances of his ability to execute all commands, with an effect, and in a style, which must give satisfaction. Apply at his House, in the alley leading from Charles to Hanover Street, back of Sear's Tavern."

The house referred to by Johnston was a stone's throw from the residence of Col. and Mrs. John Moale. Their town house occupied the block severed by Redwood, Hanover, Lombard, and Sharp Streets. Johnston's studio was on German Street two years prior to the time of the advertisement in the *Intelligencer.* These circumstances suggest his association with the Moale family, but also support the idea that Johnston was an artist of accepted status in the late eighteenth century. Between 1800 and 1824, notices of Johnston's desire to "create a likeness" of prominent citizens of Baltimore and environs appeared from time to time in the Baltimore City directories. The last record of Johnston's occupancy of a studio appears in the City Directory of 1824, listing him as residing in Old Town on Sleigh's Lane near Spring Street.

He adopted the general practice of masters of American portraiture of his day, completing detailed costume work on a subject prior to engaging a sitter. Johnston may have been a student of Charles Peale Polk, a nephew of Charles Willson Peale, a Baltimore artist whose major works were executed in Philadelphia. The style which Johnston employed in all of his paintings shows a love for the same kind of details that are characteristic of Polk's work. All his subjects seem to have been wealthy persons from the coastal regions of Maryland and Virginia. The stiff manner in which all of his subjects are represented shows that he had settled on a particular style of expression bound in the colonial tradition. Almost always, with the exception of a few canvasses where desolate dark space is broken by the use of a curtain, there is a solid background, usually in dark umbers and black, which propels the subject forward as though partially lighted by a tenebrous effect. He sought to give clarity to his compositions by painting only the essential elements of the subject. A few brass tacks are often seen in the design of a Sheraton chair on which his subjects sat, but this form of decoration was an actual part of the sitter's environment. It is obvious from the many examples of his work that he understood the mechanics of structural painting as advocated by the academicians of his day. Many prominent families praised his work and he became the favorite limner of polite society in Baltimore during thirty or more years.

Numerous works by Johnston have been located since J. Hall Pleasants first brought his name to the attention of the American public in 1939. Works of note other than the portrait of *Mrs. Moale and Her Granddaughter* that are attributed to Joshua Johnston are *Portrait of a Cleric* (which to this writer's knowledge is the only existing subject by the artist of a black person), portraits of *Mr. Andrew Bedford Bankston* (1804), *Mrs. Thomas Kell and Daughter* (c. 1789–1790), *The Kennedy Long Family* (c. 1805), *The James McCormick Family* (c. 1810), *Man of the Shure Family* (c. 1810), *Bennett Sollers* (c. 1810), *Mrs. Abraham White Jr. and Daughter,* and numerous other works in private collections in the East and Midwest. Johnston executed all of his works in oil, painting on canvasses which ranged from eighteen by twenty-four inches to fifty by seventy inches.

For valuable accounts of his artistry, see especially J. Hall Pleasants's "Joshua Johnston, the First American Negro Painter" (*Maryland Historical Magazine,* June 1942), and Romare Bearden's and Harry Henderson's *Six Black Masters of American Painting* (1972, pp. 1–19). Exhibitions in which his work has appeared since his discovery have been arranged, among many places, at the Baltimore Museum of Art, the National Gallery of Art, the Howard University Gallery of Art, the City College of New York, Bowdoin College Museum of Art, and Fisk University Gallery of Art. There is no accurate record of the exact place or date of Joshua Johnston's birth or death. — DAVID C. DRISKELL

JONES, ABSALOM (1746–1818), first Negro priest of the Protestant Episcopal church, abolitionist, and Masonic leader. Born a slave in Sussex, Del., but always zealous to learn, Jones taught himself to read. At sixteen he was brought to Philadelphia where he worked in his master's store as a handyman and clerk. In the evenings Jones worked for himself and attended Anthony Benezet's school. According to his own account he married a fellow slave in 1770. His father-in-law, John Thomas, and Friends (Quakers) in Philadelphia helped purchase his wife, paying £30 and being "forgiven" for £10. He bought a house in his wife's name, and purchased his freedom in 1784. He purchased a lot, on which he built two houses that he rented. In 1786, in Philadelphia, he met Richard Allen. Together they became lay preachers among the colored members of St. George's Methodist Episcopal Church. At first they had seating on the main floor of the church. As a result of active evangelistic and pastoral work by Jones and Allen, the Negro members increased tenfold. The church officials became alarmed and, without notifying them, decided to segregate them in an upstairs gallery. After a scuffle during a Sunday service in November 1786, in which ushers attempted to remove Jones and others, the Negro members walked out of the church in a body. On April 12, 1787, they organized themselves into the independent Free African Society, the first such body in the United States. Both benevolent and religious but without denominational affiliation, it denounced slavery. Members met monthly and paid dues which were applied to burial expenses, sick relief, and care of widows and fatherless children. Members who gambled, drank, or disregarded marriage vows were warned, fined, and finally expelled. Absalom Jones and Richard Allen acted as "overseers" of the beneficial and mutual aid society, and encouraged the organization of other Free African Societies in Newport, Boston, and New York.

On Jan. 1, 1791, Jones and Allen began to hold regular Sunday services. With the aid of Benjamin Rush, "The African Church" was organized on July 7, 1791. Toward the end of 1792 the Free African Society decided to erect a church building, but construction was interrupted in 1793 by a severe yellow fever epidemic, when the two co-workers organized the Negro community to serve as nurses and undertakers. In the next year Jones and Allen refuted allegations of exorbitant rates and cheating, a refutation which was endorsed by the mayor of Philadelphia.

Both Jones and Allen favored affiliation with the Methodist church but an overwhelming majority of their followers did not, since they had been "so violently persecuted" by the Methodists, and voted to unite themselves with the Episcopal church. Allen, who believed that Methodism was more appropriate to Negroes, withdrew from the African Church with a few followers. Jones reluctantly remained as sole leader. The African Church was dedicated by two Episcopal rectors on July 17, 1794, and formally received into the Diocese of Pennsylvania on Oct. 17, 1794. Jones was licensed as lay reader and the Negroes were granted "control over their local affairs forever." The African Church became St. Thomas African Episcopal Church.

The diocesan convention in 1795 agreed to dispense Absalom Jones from Greek and Latin as requirements for ordination, but stipulated that no Negro could attend the annual convention or "interfere with the general government of the Episcopal Church." On Aug. 16, 1794, Bishop White ordained him deacon. After ordination, Jones, a man of medium height, stout frame, and dark complexion, appeared habitually in public in black clerical attire and powdered wig. Although he is said to have been very earnest and impressive as a preacher, his forte was constant parish visiting. He was widely esteemed for his mild manner and even temper. Under his leadership, St. Thomas Church increased in membership from 246 in 1794 to 427 the next year. As rector, he baptized 1195 persons; however, only 274 of these were confirmed. When he was ordained to the priesthood in 1804, he became, at the age of fifty-eight, the first priest of African descent in the United States.

For Absalom Jones, the church was not only for worship and religious instruction but for education, mutual relief, and protest. Since there was in Pennsylvania no state-supported education for Negroes, they had to provide it. In 1804 Jones founded at St. Thomas his second school; he also established the Female Benevolent Society and the African Friendly Society.

Jones and Richard Allen continued to be co-workers. Usually associated with them in community enterprises was James Forten, the sailmaker, a member of the St. Thomas vestry. In 1798 the African Masonic Lodge was founded in Philadelphia. Jones was elected worshipful master and Allen treasurer. In 1799 and 1800 the two men led the Negro community in petitioning the state legislature for the immediate abolition of slavery. In 1800 they sent a similar unsuccessful petition to Congress. In 1808 Jones published a sermon on the abolition of the slave trade. In 1809 Jones and Allen founded the Society for the Suppression of Vice and Immorality. They also began a short-lived insurance company. During the war of 1812 Forten joined the two in recruiting 3000 blacks to form a "Black Legion."

On April 11, 1816, Absalom Jones helped consecrate Richard Allen as the first bishop of the African Methodist Episcopal church. In January 1817 Jones worked with Forten and Allen to organize a convention of 3000 Negroes who vigorously condemned the newly formed American Colonization Society. Jones died at his home, 32 Powell St., Philadelphia, on Feb. 13, 1818. His funeral at his home on Feb. 16 was "attended by a considerable number of the clergy, and other respectable white inhabitants and by an immense concourse of people of colour" (the [Philadelphia] *American Daily Advertiser,* Feb. 19, 1818, p. 3). He was buried in the shadow of St. Thomas Church.

A valuable early source is William Douglass's *Annals of the First African Church, in the U.S.A., now styled The African Episcopal Church of St. Thomas, Philadelphia* (1862). George Freeman Bragg's *The Story of the First of the Blacks, The Pathfinder Absalom Jones* (1929) is the most complete biography. Scattered references and bibliography are in Carol V. R. George's *Segregated Sabbaths: Richard Allen and the Rise of Independent Black Churches, 1760–1840* (1973). The "Petition of Absalom Jones and Seventy-Three Others to the President, Senate and House of Representatives" (Dec. 30, 1799), and Jones's "A Thanksgiving Sermon, Preached January 1, 1808" are in *Early Negro Writing,*

1760–1837, selected and introduced by Dorothy Porter (1971, pp. 330–32 and 335–92, respectively).

—J. CARLETON HAYDEN

JONES, EDWARD (1808?–1864), missionary to Sierra Leone. He was the son of Jehu Jones (1767?–1833) and his wife Abigail, "free persons of color" and residents of Charleston, S.C. The father owned the most prestigious hotel in Charleston, where he belonged to the exclusive Brown Fellowship Society. While Edward was a student at Amherst College, Mass. (1822–1826), part of his family, including his mother, moved to New York. At college he remained unconverted despite the revivalistic atmosphere and was not among those receiving academic honors at graduation, but it was recalled that he was treated as "a brother student." Jones graduated from Amherst two weeks before John Brown Russwurm, long considered the first Afro-American college graduate in the United States, received his degree at Bowdoin. (Recent research has shown, however, that Alexander Twilight received his B.A. degree from Middlebury College in 1823.)

From 1828 to 1830 Jones studied at Andover Theological Seminary; then, after further work at the African Mission School, Hartford, Conn., he was ordained a priest of the Episcopal church (1830) and simultaneously awarded an honorary M.A. by Trinity College, Hartford. Arriving in Sierra Leone in 1831, he served as a schoolmaster first in Kent, then in the Banana Islands. Suspended because of alleged negligence, he worked under the colonial chaplain in Freetown until reinstated as a schoolmaster in 1838.

In January 1841 Jones became principal of Fourah Bay Christian Institution, a school founded in 1827 by the British Church Missionary Society. Jones made trips to England to raise money, supervised the erection of a much-needed building, and helped free the institution from elementary work, which was shifted to a new grammar school. The institution took the name "college" in 1848, offering a unique program in African languages.

The first naturalization ordinance in Sierra Leone was passed in 1845 to allow Jones to be a British subject while in the colony. In 1853 he participated in an expedition that sought vainly to establish a mission among the Ibos. A leading figure in the colony and even rumored to be under consideration for a bishopric, Jones faced mounting troubles during his later years. He was called to England in 1858 "to tender explanations on matters of a personal character," and the activities of the college, where enrollment had dwindled, were suspended. Returning to Sierra Leone, he shifted his labors to a pastorate in Freetown and assisted in editing the *African and Sierra Leone Weekly Advertiser,* published under missionary auspices. He became editor of the *Sierra Leone Weekly Times and West African* in 1861, but was shortly thereafter dismissed, having provoked the wrath of Gov. Stephen John Hill by siding against him in disputes with the bishop.

Jones married Hannah, a daughter of Gustavus Reinhold Nyländer, and after her death the daughter (possibly sister) of another German missionary to Sierra Leone, Frederick Bultmann. He had several children by his first wife and at least two by his second. His third marriage, in 1862, was to a Miss Shuff (Keith, p. 94, 105). In failing health, he went to England, where he died at Chatham.

See Stephen Keith's "The Life and Times of Edward Jones" (Amherst College honors thesis, 1973, chaps. 1–2), Hugh Hawkins's "Edward Jones: First American Negro College Graduate?" (*School and Society,* Nov. 4, 1961, pp. 375–76), and Thomas J. Thompson (ed.), *The Jubilee and Centenary Volume of Fourah Bay College, Freetown, Sierra Leone* (1930, pp. 16–25, 97).

—HUGH HAWKINS

JONES, EUGENE KINCKLE (1885–1954), Urban League executive. Born in Richmond, Va., on July 30, 1885, the son of Joseph Endom and Rosa Daniel (Kinckle) Jones, he married Blanche Ruby Watson in 1909 and had two children, Eugene Kinckle Jr., and Adele R. He received his B.A. degree from Virginia Union University in 1906, and his M.A. degree from Cornell University in 1908. He served as an instructor in social science at State University, Louisville, Ky. (1908–1909), and a teacher at Central High School, Louisville (1909–1911). He devoted almost four decades to the Urban League: field secretary (1911), associate chief executive (1912–1917) of the National League on Urban Conditions among Negroes; executive secretary (1917–1941); and general secretary of the National Urban League (NUL) (1941–1950). He died after a brief illness on Jan. 11, 1954, in New York. His funeral was held in New York City at Mount Olivet Baptist Church and he was buried in Flushing, Long Island. He was survived by his widow, two children, and two grandchildren.

Jones's father, a former slave, was one of the early Negroes in Virginia to become a college graduate; his mother was born free. Both parents were teachers, and he was brought up in the campus atmosphere of Virginia Union, with its biracial faculty. This early environment made a deep impression on young Jones, which he later recognized as having a lasting influence on his life. He wrote in his unpublished autobiography, "I had seen my mother and father on mixed faculties of white and colored teachers where equality was recognized within the group. This contributed to my growing belief in the essential equality of men, and in the capacity of the Negro, with opportunity, to measure up, man to man, with any other racial variety."

This concept inspired his character and leadership during four decades in the National League on Urban Conditions among Negroes, and the National Urban League. So closely did the man and the organizations become interwoven that it is impossible to portray his life without telling their story.

In 1910, George Edmund Haynes, director of the Committee on Urban Conditions among Negroes, one of three New York agencies concerned with the problems of Negroes in the city, looked for an assistant to become field secretary. He tapped Jones for the job when Jones was teaching high school in Louisville. Taking a leave of absence for a year, Jones began work on April 10, 1911. Six months later when the three agencies merged to form the National League on Urban

Conditions among Negroes, Jones became field secretary. He cast his lot with the fledgling agency, made his first social study, a report on "The Negro Community of New York," and began what proved to be a lifetime career devoted to helping improve the social and economic conditions of Negroes.

His appointment in 1917 as executive secretary of the NUL resulted in part because Haynes had accepted an appointment at Fisk University in 1910 to train Negro social workers. Not only did Haynes spend much of his time there, to the detriment of the League's work, but he and Jones disagreed about its priorities. Haynes deemed the training of social workers necessary to the programs of the League, while Jones emphasized the expansion of the League's affiliates and "interracial teamwork" to gain "equal opportunity." Under Jones's direction the characteristic thrust of the League, as he repeatedly emphasized, was to approach a racial problem through documented social research. "We hope to work ourselves out of a job," Jones frequently said, "and I look forward to the day when Urban League services are no longer needed." Wherever there was need to help Negroes, Jones found some way for the League to enter the situation and do something constructive about it. When he felt that the League's program demonstration had proved a need—such as in the areas of probation and parole, juvenile delinquency, recreation, and travelers aid—then he turned aside to find some other agency, either public or private, to take over the program into a larger arena, thus "working the League out of a job."

Tall and handsome, lean and energetic, confident and optimistic, he inspired others. His own self-confidence spurred him on, as he acknowledged in his unpublished autobiography: "The one important factor in my life which I consider primarily responsible for whatever success I have attained is self-confidence. I believe that no man can succeed in any undertaking unless he has confidence in his own capacity and believes sincerely in the principles underlying the policies formulated for the work he is doing."

Whether leading a delegation to confront trade-union representatives to demand fair treatment for Negro workers or sitting in conference with heads of corporations to seek wider employment opportunities, Jones held to Urban League demands—often his own agenda —with bulldog tenacity. Equally courageous and determined before the boards of America's great foundations and philanthropies, such as Rosenwald, Carnegie, and Rockefeller, his skill in negotiation netted hundreds of thousands of dollars in support of "the vital work of the Urban League," as he so earnestly described it. Undaunted by rebuffs, he would return another year with stronger appeals and more facts and figures to buttress his requests for fair treatment, for jobs, or for finances to support his work.

There were many "firsts" in the Jones career. Alpha Phi Alpha, the first Negro college fraternity, was organized at Cornell University (1906) when he was a graduate student. Jones was one of its first initiates and founders. The next year he became the second president of Alpha chapter there, and was a member of the committee that selected the design for the fraternity's pin. During the Christmas holidays in 1907, assisted by two other founders, he organized Beta chapter at Howard University, and singly, Gamma chapter at Virginia Union University. He was one of the trustees who secured the incorporation of the fraternity by the state of New York (Feb. 2, 1908).

There are other milestone achievements credited to the fertile mind of Jones. *Opportunity: Journal of Negro Life* (1923–1948) was an idea developed jointly with Charles S. Johnson, its first editor. It was established to meet the unfilled need of Negro artists and writers who had no publication outlet for their talents. Through *Opportunity,* the Urban League encouraged them and brought their work before a nationwide audience. Countee Cullen, Langston Hughes, Claude McKay, and Aaron Douglass were only a few so recognized. The magazine was the official organ of the league, and most of its factfinding studies and the speeches and articles of Jones were published in its pages.

With uncanny acumen he was able to develop a situation that later would rebound to benefit many. By 1926 Arthur A. Schomburg of New York had amassed an impressive collection of books, documents, manuscripts, art, and artifacts by and about Negroes. Schomburg offered the collection to his friend for the National Urban League. Unable to handle such an acquisition, Jones approached the Carnegie Corporation and persuaded its directors to purchase the entire collection for $10,000 and give it to the New York Public Library. The Schomburg Collection, expanded a hundredfold, became priceless and an outstanding repository of information on Negroes. It was later called the Schomburg Center for Research in Black Culture.

A program of fellowships for graduate study in social work was also kept alive by Jones's determination. He encouraged and motivated many young men and women to enter the field of social work, and found the money to finance fellowships at leading graduate schools. Several were trained under the Urban League fellowship program to become executive directors of local Urban Leagues; others, such as Abram L. Harris, William Lloyd Imes, Benjamin E. Mays, Alonzo Moron, Ira De A. Reid, and Forrester B. Washington, made outstanding contributions as educators and social scientists.

Called upon repeatedly to represent the interests of American Negroes in discussions of the social and economic welfare of the nation's citizens, Jones had the intelligence and wisdom to make important contributions to the discussion of problems, and he had the strength of an important national organization behind him. He served on many factfinding commissions, and on boards and committees, often the first Negro to do so. The Urban League and its executive had access to local, state, and federal officials for discussions of conditions affecting black citizens, and the chance to make recommendations for improvement of those conditions.

By 1940 Jones was recognized as an honored elder statesman in race relations. With waning strength after years of strenuous activity and a serious illness, he was no longer able to keep up the steady pace that was required to maintain a solid financial base for the

League, and to provide executive leadership to an enlarged and still growing national organization and fifty-eight local leagues with a budget in 1939 of over half a million dollars. He reluctantly turned to Lester B. Granger, one of the young men he had brought into League service, and handed over the reins. He served as general secretary, however, until 1950, sharing his wisdom and experience as needed.

Two comprehensive, scholarly, and well-documented books contain excellent summaries of Jones's career: Nancy J. Weiss's *The National Urban League, 1910–1940* (1974) and Guichard Parris's and Lester Brooks's *Blacks in the City: A History of the National Urban League* (1971). For his activities as a member of Alpha Phi Alpha, see Charles H. Wesley's *The History of Alpha Phi Alpha: A Development in Negro College Life* (1929). An "Abridged Autobiography," an unpublished manuscript in the possession of Mrs. Adele Jones Penn, provided much valuable material. Many of Jones's speeches and articles, as well as information about him, are in numerous issues of *Opportunity*. The National Urban League Archives (1910–1965), consisting of correspondence, files, papers, board meeting minutes, and memoranda, donated by the NUL, are in the Manuscript Division of the Library of Congress.

— VERNON E. JORDAN, JR.

JONES, FREDERICK MCKINLEY (1893–1961), inventor of the first practical refrigeration system for trucks and railroad cars, which completely changed the food transport industry. Jones was born in Cincinnati, Ohio. His mother died when he was an infant, and his father about nine years later. An orphan at nine years of age, he went to Kentucky where he lived with a Catholic priest, Father Ryan. He did odd jobs in the priest's church and rectory, and attended school through grade six. At sixteen he returned to his birthplace in search of a job. He was inclined toward auto mechanics and managed to secure a position as an apprentice mechanic. His natural ability to deal with machinery was supplemented by his independent reading and study of books on auto mechanics. Three years later he was foreman of the automobile shop. Moving to Chicago in 1912, he worked as a pipefitter before moving to Hallock, Minn., in the same year to work as a mechanic in a garage that repaired farm machinery. Jones enlisted in the U.S. Army during World War I, served in France as an electrician, and earned the rank of sergeant. At the end of the war he returned to Hallock and took employment as a mechanic of farm machinery. During the 1920s he mastered electronics through self-study and gained local recognition for building a radio station transmitter for Hallock and a device for combining sound with motion-picture film. His work came to the attention of Joseph A. Numero in Minneapolis who owned a company that manufactured motion picture equipment.

In 1930 Jones accepted a job with Cinema Supplies, Inc., in Minneapolis. Sound equipment made by Cinema Supplies was used in movie houses throughout the northern Midwest and in eighty-five more houses in Chicago. On June 27, 1939, Jones received his first patent, No. 2,163,754, for a ticket-dispensing machine for movie-house tickets. During the late 1930s he worked behind the scenes designing an air-cooling unit for food transported to market by trucks. His invention led to the formation of a new business by Joseph Numero and Jones. Numero sold his movie sound equipment business to Radio Corporation of America and switched from making movie-house equipment to manufacturing air conditioners for trucks. By 1949 the U.S. Thermo Control Co., founded jointly by Jones and Numero, had boomed to a $3-million-a-year business. They manufactured air coolers for trains, ships, and airplanes to keep foodstuffs from perishing. Jones's invention made it possible for the first time to transport meat, fruit, vegetables, eggs, butter, and other produce that needed refrigeration over long distances during any season of the year. Jones received a patent on his refrigerating unit on July 12, 1940 (Patent No. 2,475,841). Portable cooling units designed by Jones were used in U.S. Army hospitals and on the battlefield during World War II to keep blood, medicines, and food at exact cool temperatures.

Jones was awarded more than sixty patents, forty for refrigeration equipment alone. In 1944 he was elected to membership in the American Society of Refrigeration Engineers. During the 1950s he served as a consultant on refrigeration problems to both the U.S. Defense Department and the Bureau of Standards. Later, trucks transporting perishable foods throughout the United States were equipped with refrigeration units above the truck cab manufactured by Thermo King Corporation (formerly U.S. Thermol Control Co.) of Minneapolis. On June 10, 1977, Jones was inducted into the Minnesota Inventors Hall of Fame, Redwood Falls, Minn. Survived by his widow, Mrs. Lucille Jones, he had died in Minneapolis of lung cancer on Feb. 21, 1961, and was interred at Fort Snelling National Cemetery, Minn. Funeral services were conducted by Rabbi Albert Minda of Numero's congregation.

The most comprehensive biography is *Man with A Million Ideas* by Ott and Swanson (1977). See also Robert C. Hayden's *Eight Black American Inventors* (1972, pp. 44–59), *Gopher Historian* (Fall 1969), published by the Minnesota Historical Society, and Steven M. Spencer's "Born Handy" (*Saturday Evening Post*, May 7, 1949, pp. 22–31). — ROBERT C. HAYDEN

JONES, JOHN (1816–1879), businessman, civil rights leader, and philanthropist. Jones was born free in Greene County, N.C. His mother was a free mulatto and his father a German named Bromfield. His mother, fearing that Bromfield or his relatives might seek to enslave John, apprenticed him to a man named Sheppard, who taught the boy a trade. Sheppard moved to Tennessee and bound him over to work near Memphis as a tailor for Richard Clere. Fearing that the heirs of Clere might sell him into slavery, John obtained permission to return to North Carolina where (Jan. 16, 1838) Judge V. D. Barry of the Eleventh Judicial District ordered his release from apprenticeship. He returned to Memphis, where he worked until 1841. He moved to Alton, Ill., and married Mary Richardson, the comely daughter of a free Negro blacksmith whom he had met in Memphis before returning to North Carolina. They participated actively in the abolitionist movement until 1845 when they moved to Chicago. They had one daughter, Lavinia. Jones prospered as a tailor, taught himself to read and write, and continued his abolitionist activities. He died on May 27, 1879, after a long illness, and was buried in Graceland Cemetery.

His prosperous merchant tailoring establishment at 119 Dearborn St. enabled him to expand the abolitionist and civil rights activities he had begun in Alton. His home was a station on the Underground Railroad through which scores of runaway slaves escaped to Canada. In 1856 John Brown stayed with Jones on several occasions, and brought Allan Pinkerton, the famous detective and abolitionist, to visit him. Beginning in 1853 Jones campaigned against an Illinois law prohibiting the migration of free Negroes into the state. Frederick Douglass generally stayed in the Jones home when he visited Chicago. Douglass, who called Jones "my old friend," wrote about an incident that happened to them when they were on an antislavery tour in the West. Douglass remarked that he had made a remarkable discovery in the stables. When Jones inquired about the discovery, Douglass stated that he had seen black and white horses eating from the same trough. Douglass and Jones were then served at table with other guests (Frederick Douglass, *Life and Times,* reprinted from the revised edition of 1892, 1962, p. 454). Jones was an active participant in a convention (1856) at Springfield, Ill., to petition for the rights of Negroes. In 1857 it was ruled that the laws of other states recognizing slavery could not affect the condition of fugitives in Illinois. In 1864 Jones published his pamphlet of sixteen pages, *The Black Laws of Illinois and a Few Reasons Why They Should Be Repealed,* printed by the *Chicago Tribune.* These Black Laws prohibited a Negro from testifying in court against a white man. Jones pointed out also that he was paying taxes on property worth $30,000 but could not vote. Jones made speeches, wrote articles, circulated his pamphlet, and lobbied until the state legislature, in late January 1865, repealed these provisions of the Black Laws. He was active also in obtaining the ratification of the Thirteenth Amendment (Illinois was the first to ratify), and of the Fourteenth and Fifteenth Amendments to the U.S. Constitution. Jones, along with George T. Downing, was in the delegation headed by Douglass which on Feb. 7, 1866, objected to Pres. Andrew Johnson's opposition to Negro suffrage and his favoring Negro colonization. According to Douglass, "from this time onward the question of suffrage for the freedmen was not allowed to rest" (ibid., pp. 382–87).

Jones served a short term and a full term (1872–1875) as a member of the Cook County (Chicago) Board of Commissioners, one of the first Negroes in the North to win an important elective office, and perhaps the first in Illinois. During his full term he fought actively against separate schools, a fight won in 1874. Along with some other commissioners he was defeated in 1875, but he was acquitted, for lack of evidence, of alleged participation in a conspiracy.

Although he lost some of his fortune (estimated at close to $100,000) in the Great Fire in Chicago (1871), he remained one of the city's more prominent citizens.

When the family celebrated in 1875 thirty years of residence in Chicago, many prominent citizens honored him, and the *Chicago Tribune* spoke glowingly of his career. Their home was known for its gracious hospitality. Jones contributed generously to charitable institutions and other philanthropies. His funeral was attended by "an immense course of friends and well-known citizens." His career exemplified the unusual success of rising from obscurity to fame.

There is an excellent account of Jones's career in Arna Bontemps's and Jack Conroy's *Anyplace But Here* (1946, pp. 45–52). See also F. H. H. Robb's *Negro in Chicago, 1779–1929 . . .* (1927 [?]). William Loren Katz's *The Black West* (1971) reproduced the free papers of John Jones and photographs of Jones and his wife (pp. 66, 68, 69). — RAYFORD W. LOGAN

JONES, [MATILDA] SISSIERETTA [JOYNER] [called **BLACK PATTI**] (1869–1933), dramatic soprano. She was born in Portsmouth, Va., one of two children of the Rev. Jeremiah Malachi Joyner and Henrietta B. Joyner. Her father was a former slave and her mother was said to have a fine soprano voice. Matilda moved to Providence, R.I., probably in 1876, where her father preached and supplemented his income by taking odd jobs. She began her formal training in music when she was about fourteen or fifteen with Ada, Baroness Lacombe, and others at the Providence Academy of Music. On Sept. 4, 1883, she married David Richard Jones, who handled some of her business affairs and whom she divorced in 1898 for drunkenness and nonsupport.

Evidence concerning her professional training after 1883 is unclear: she may have studied voice with a private teacher at the New England Conservatory of Music and with other trained vocalists. She made her professional debut in New York City in 1888 and received critical praise during a six-month tour of the West Indies with the Tennessee Jubilee Singers. She first gained wide publicity by her singing at a jubilee spectacle and cake-walk, for which she was specially engaged, at Madison Square Garden, New York, on April 26–28, 1892. A critic for the *New York Clipper* dubbed her "Black Patti," a term she disliked for its apparently condescending comparison with the famous Adelina Patti but which her manager and the press used thereafter. Her success was so great that efforts were made to have her sing the dark roles in *Aïda* and *L'Africaine* at the Metropolitan Opera House. Although she was signed by the managers, racial prejudice prevented her appearance (not until 1955 did the first Negro, Marian Anderson, sing at the Met). Booked for the concert stage, she sang, on the invitation of Pres. Benjamin Harrison, at a White House reception in September 1892, at the Pittsburgh Exposition later that month with Levy's Band, toured the country as a soloist with the band, and sang again the next year at the Pittsburgh Exposition with Gilmore's Band. During an almost year-long concert tour of Europe, she reportedly gave a command performance for the Prince of Wales.

Upon her return to the United States, Voelckel and Nolan presented her in an all-Negro show, *Oriental America,* written by Robert (Bob) Cole. In 1893, also, she starred in *Black Patti's Troubadours,* the music for which was written by Cole. The first part followed the minstrel tradition; in the finale, "The Operatic Kaleidoscope," "Black Patti" appeared in songs and operatic selections with the chorus. During a nationwide tour until 1916, she expanded her role to include selections from such operas as *Lucia de Lammermoor, Il Trovatore, Martha,* and Sousa's *El Capitán.* After public interest in this contrived production waned, the star retired to her home in Providence in 1916. There, largely forgotten, she died of cancer on June 24, 1933. Funeral services were held at the Congdon Street Baptist Church, and she was buried in Grace Church Cemetery.

William Lichtenwanger, the well-known musicologist at the Library of Congress, praised "the first Negro prima donna" for her "natural soprano voice of great richness, with considerable range and power. . . . She seems to have been weakest in florid passages, excelling in broadly lyric rather than in brilliantly dramatic roles; almost invariably she impressed her white listeners with [a hint of condescension?] her impeccable enunciation." She "forced the musical and theatrical worlds in the United States to accept the Negro in a new image." Although she sang neither spirituals nor *Lieder,* "she paved the way for Roland Hayes and Marian Anderson who did" (*NAW* 2 [1971]:288–90). Lichtenwanger also has an excellent critical bibliography. A contemporary, James Weldon Johnson, wrote that "She had most of the qualities essential in a great singer: the natural voice, the physical figure, the grand air, and the engaging personality" (*Black Manhattan,* 1930, p. 99).

— RAYFORD W. LOGAN

JONES, SCIPIO A[FRICANUS] (1863?–1943), Arkansas politician, attorney, fraternal order leader, and judge. Jones was born of a slave mother and a white father about 1863. His mother was Jemmima Jones, a slave of Dr. Sanford Reamey, a landowner and physician of Tulip, Dallas County, Ark. After emancipation, he lived with his mother and her husband, Horace Jones, in Tulip. Sometime before his twentieth birthday Jones moved to Little Rock and entered Bethel University, where he completed the preparatory course. He next entered the newly established Shorter College in North Little Rock, where he took a teacher training course and received a bachelor's degree (c. 1885). After graduation from college, Jones taught in the public school at Sweet Home near Little Rock. While teaching he began the study of law, and in 1889 he was admitted to practice before the lower, and later the higher, courts of Arkansas. He was admitted to practice before the U.S. Supreme Court on Dec. 10, 1914. He was elected special judge of the Municipal Court in Little Rock, April 8, 1915. Besides the practice of law, Jones was active in financial endeavors. In 1908 he established the Arkansas Realty and Investment Company. He was also a stockholder in the People's Ice and Fuel Company of Little Rock and national attorney general of the Mosaic Templars of America. He was considered for appointments as the U.S. minister to Haiti during the Taft administration, but the appointment was never made.

Jones's first wife was Carrie Edwards, whom he married in 1896. They had one child, a daughter named Hazel. His wife died at an early age and Jones married for a second time, in 1917, Lillie M. Jackson of Pine Bluff, Ark. This second marriage produced no children. Scipio A. Jones died of arteriosclerosis at his home in Little Rock on March 28, 1943, and was buried in the Haven-of-Rest Cemetery there.

The most noteworthy contribution of Scipio Jones was his defense of the legal and political rights of Negroes. He defended the right of Negro Shriners (Ancient Egyptian Arabic Order of Nobles of the Mystic Shrine of North and South America) to use the name "Shriners" and Shrine paraphernalia. Discriminatory penal systems, the "grandfather clause," and the exclusion of Negroes from grand and petit juries were all subjects of Jones's legal crusading. He was also instrumental in securing a state appropriation to finance the training of Negro professionals in out-of-state schools. His most famous civil rights case came in the defense of twelve Negroes sentenced to death in the aftermath of the bloody Elaine, Ark., race riot of October 1919. Jones, working with a prominent white Little Rock attorney, George W. Murphy, appealed the death sentences through the Arkansas courts. When the case, *Moore v. Dempsey* (261 U.S. 1923), finally reached the U.S. Supreme Court, Jones prepared the legal briefs that the famous white lawyer Moorfield Storey used in not only freeing the twelve convicted Negroes, but also in indicting the entire economic and racial climate of the east Arkansas "black belt."

A more perplexing problem to Jones than the protection of the Elaine defendants was the guarding of the political rights of Negro Republicans. From the late 1880s until the 1930s there was constant conflict between those who wanted an all-white party (the "Lily Whites") and those who sought an open party (the "Black and Tans"). In 1902 Jones helped organize a slate of Negro Republicans to challenge the Lily Whites and Democrats in the general election in Little Rock. The struggle reached a breaking point in 1920 when the Negroes took the unprecedented course of nominating a Negro candidate, J. H. Blount, for governor. In that year Jones was selected as the Black and Tan contender for Republican national committeeman from Arkansas. Four years later he helped organize a Black and Tan protest meeting in Little Rock in which a list of demands for equal political treatment was drawn up and presented to the Lily Whites. Eventually a compromise was effected which guaranteed Negro representation on the State Republican Central Committee. Symbolic of the compromise was Jones's 1908 and 1912 election as a delegate to the Republican National Convention.

As national general attorney of the Mosaic Templars, Jones purchased $50,000 of Liberty Bonds during World War I. He was general counsel also for several other similar organizations of men and women. Among his many civic activities was his service as chairman of the Board of Managers of the Aged and Orphans' Industrial Home, Dexter, Ark.

See Tom Dillard's "Scipio A. Jones" (*Arkansas Historical Quarterly* 31 [Autumn 1972]: 201–19). Highly laudatory sketches of Jones may be found in Octavius Coke's *The Scrapbook of Arkansas Literature* (1939) and A. E. Bush and P. L. Dorman (eds.), *History of the Mosaic Templars of America, Its Founders, and Officials* (1924). For Jones's role in the defense of the Elaine riot defendants, see Arthur I. Waskow's *From Race Riot to Sit-In, 1919 and the 1960s* (1967). A photograph is in *Mosaic Templars,* facing page 237.

— TOM W. DILLARD

JOPLIN, SCOTT (1868?–1917), composer and pianist. Joplin was born in Texarkana, Tex., where he and his three brothers and two sisters grew up and went to school. Inheriting their parents' musical gifts, all but one of the Joplin children sang and played a variety of instruments. Their father, Giles Joplin, as a former slave had fiddled dance music at his master's parties; their free-born mother Florence Givens Joplin, a Kentuckian, sang and played the banjo. Despite poverty and the other hardships of Negro life in the Reconstruction South, the Joplin home rang with music. Growing up in this atmosphere, music was as natural to Scott as breathing, but he recognized it as his predestined vocation when as a small child he had an opportunity to experiment with a keyboard. Gaining access to a neighbor's piano, he displayed so remarkable an instinct for improvisation that he soon excited the wonder of the Negro community of Texarkana.

The interest of white Texarkanians may be attributed to Joplin's courageous and resourceful mother, whom he later movingly commemorated in his opera *Treemonisha.* Forced by Giles Joplin's desertion to support her six small children—but at the same time determined that her talented son receive the lessons that she was unable to provide—Florence Joplin took Scott along to the houses where she worked as a domestic, and she prevailed on her employers to allow him to practice on the parlor piano while she went about her household chores. Inevitably, talk of the talented black child spread throughout white Texarkana, and a legendary German music teacher is reported to have heard Scott and volunteered to instruct him in piano and harmony. This teacher has been credited with having opened up to Joplin the fascinating vistas of European music and to have implanted in him the consuming desire for musical education that became his lifelong commitment.

Among the great mass of Joplin apocrypha that has sprung up—perhaps because factual information concerning his life is sparse—it is often difficult to sift fact from fiction. Much has been made of this German teacher, but efforts to identify him have been vain. It is known, however, that a number of teachers in the Texarkana area did offer to give Joplin lessons, and he apparently received a creditable training in basic music theory as well as piano playing, as his later admittance to advanced harmony and composition courses at the George R. Smith College for Negroes in Sedalia, Mo., would indicate.

By the time Joplin reached his teens he expanded his already busy playing schedule at churches and "socials" to include more questionable localities, thereby rounding out the full scope of professional activity permitted to a black musician in late-nineteenth-century America. The situation was wryly summed up by Eubie Blake, the great Negro composer and pianist (born in 1883), who as a boy had come along the same hard route. He said, "There were only two places where a Negro musician could play in those days: in church or in a bordello. And you know you couldn't make a living in a church!"

It might have been Joplin's early entrance into the world of the honky-tonks—a world that he was to inhabit for a number of years—that triggered his bitter disagreement with his estranged father. Giles Joplin demanded that his son exchange the uncertainty of a career in music for the security of a job on the railroad. Scott hotly refused, and the ensuing controversy is believed to have hastened his departure from Texarkana; he left when he was in his middle teens to become an itinerant pianist. Continuing to perform in disreputable places, he probably also appeared more respectably as accompanist for the Texas Medley Quartette, a male singing group he had organized, which unaccountably included five members, two of whom were his younger brothers, Robert and Willie.

Exactly when Scott Joplin left Texarkana or precisely where he roamed is not clear, but it may be assumed that he followed the typical pattern of Negro itinerant pianists of the period, playing in saloons and brothels in red-light districts of towns and villages along the Mississippi Valley. During his wanderings Joplin undoubtedly absorbed great quantities of native music, black and white, as well as the new, rapidly evolving ragtime (then called "jig piano"), that would ferment in his creative subconscious and later yield the materials from which he fashioned his highly distinctive compositions.

By 1885 Joplin came to St. Louis, then a raw, successful trading town in the most flamboyant American nineteenth-century tradition. Commerce was enormous, money plentiful, and "sporting life" activities went on at a furious pace, day and night. Establishing himself as a pianist at "Honest" John Turpin's popular Silver Dollar Saloon, Joplin joined the febrile sporting world in which Negro pianists were indispensable.

In 1893 Joplin joined the great musicians' migration to Chicago for the World's Columbian Exposition, where, on the periphery of the fairgrounds, rival "jig piano" practitioners from all over competed in exploiting the intoxicating new music.

In 1894, after the close of the fair, Joplin migrated to Sedalia, a smaller version of St. Louis—but no less spirited—where he resumed his honky-tonk employment, taking a job at the Maple Leaf Club. But he also took up the threads of his education, going to the George R. Smith College for advanced musical studies. Joplin participated in a number of other non-honky-tonk activities: he mingled in respectable society (where he was warmly received); he played cornet in the Queen City Concert Band, a Negro organization reputed to have been the first band to play ragtime; he reorganized the Texas Medley Quartette (increased to eight members), with whom he toured in vaudeville until 1896; he began formally to compose and in 1895 to be published.

Although he might already have composed ragtime pieces, Joplin's first published compositions were in no way related to ragtime, nor did they hint at the beautiful, meticulously wrought ragtime pieces that were to follow. ''Please Say You Will'' and ''A Picture of Her Face,'' the first two of his songs that were published in Syracuse, N.Y., while Joplin was touring with the Quartette, exemplify period sentimentality at its most banal. Although they may be excused as having been written for the Quartette's vaudeville repertory, it is true that these first songs, together with the first three piano pieces, ''The Crush Collision March,'' ''Combination March,'' and ''Harmony Club Waltz,'' published the following year in Temple, Tex., while the Quartette was again on tour, might have been concocted by any uninspired hack of the period.

All the more dramatic, then, that Joplin's next published work *Original Rags,* composed in 1897 and issued in 1899 by the Kansas City publisher Carl Hoffman, suddenly revealed the full-fledged artist, expressing with a sure hand the originality and richness of invention and the painstaking craftsmanship which distinguished Joplin's music. Joplin found his native language in ragtime; as a gifted creative artist, he fashioned from its essentially commonplace elements an appealing music of high and enduring quality.

The year 1899 marked the crucial turning point in Joplin's life. Shortly after the publication of *Original Rags,* another rag he had composed in 1897 was issued after having been rejected by two publishers. The publication of ''Maple Leaf Rag'' by the Sedalia music dealer John Stark not only changed the course of Joplin's life (and Stark's), but influenced the future direction of American popular music as well. Creating an unprecedented sensation—more than a million copies of the sheet music were reported to have been sold—''Maple Leaf Rag'' to a great extent precipitated the worldwide ''ragtime madness'' that was to last until about the time of Joplin's death in 1917.

''Maple Leaf Rag'' earned for Joplin the title ''King of Ragtime.'' More significantly, it liberated him from the dives and saloons in which he had cut his musical teeth. Benefiting from an unusual business agreement with John Stark, a white man of liberal principles for his time, Joplin was paid royalties on the sales of ''Maple Leaf Rag,'' and with his newfound financial security he turned his back on his stereotyped career as a honkytonk pianist. In 1900 he married Belle Hayden, the widowed sister-in-law of his young protégé and musical collaborator Scott Hayden. The couple moved to St. Louis in the footsteps of John Stark, whose publishing business had outgrown Sedalia with the success of ''Maple Leaf Rag.'' In St. Louis the Joplins set up housekeeping, and Joplin—essentially a quiet and serious man—devoted himself to a life of teaching, study, and composition.

During his St. Louis years (until 1905, when his marriage came to an unhappy termination) Joplin produced no fewer than nineteen piano pieces—rags, marches, waltzes—outstanding for their melodic beauty and careful workmanship. Although he was primarily a composer for the piano (few of Joplin's sparse output of songs equalled the quality of his piano compositions), he seems always to have been preoccupied with the desire to write works in larger forms for the music theater. As early as 1899, while still in Sedalia, Joplin had produced a staged version of his extended choreo-

graphic song *The Ragtime Dance* in an effort to persuade Stark to publish it. Stark was timid about bringing out an unconventional work, and it was not until 1902, after much controversy, that he grudgingly consented to issue a voice and piano version of *The Ragtime Dance* (the performance in Sedalia had been accompanied by a small orchestra conducted by Joplin).

The Ragtime Dance acted as a kind of preliminary sketch for the ill-fated ragtime opera *A Guest of Honor,* which soon followed. Stark again refused to risk publication of a long work of limited and uncertain appeal, so Joplin secured his own copyright of the unpublished opera in 1903; he might have considered the possibility of publishing it himself, having already in 1901 brought out his rag ''The Easy Winners'' under his own imprint. *A Guest of Honor*—still unpublished—was performed in 1903 in St. Louis by a group billed as Scott Joplin's Ragtime Opera Company, and presumably it was the chief attraction of their projected tour of towns in Missouri, Nebraska, Iowa, Illinois, and Kentucky, announced in the *New York Dramatic Mirror.* At some undisclosed time, all traces of the score of *A Guest of Honor* unaccountably vanished. This unsolved mystery has tantalized successive generations of Joplin's admirers who persist in believing that it will someday be found. On the basis of Joplin's known perfectionist standards, it is not entirely unlikely that he might have had second thoughts about his unpublished score and destroyed it himself.

Mystery, too, surrounds Joplin's wanderings from the time he left St. Louis in 1905 until he arrived in New York in 1907. He was rumored to have visited Texarkana, to have gone to Chicago, even to have traveled to Europe. In all likelihood he was off in some out-of-the-way place working on *Treemonisha,* for it was later reported (*New York Age,* March 5, 1908, quoted in Charters and Kinstadt, *Jazz: A History of the New York Scene,* 1962) that the ragtime world had been set agog by Joplin's announcement that he had come to New York to find a publisher and a producer for the grand opera that he had been composing. The opera was, of course, *Treemonisha,* and this heartbreaking quest was to dominate the remaining decade of Joplin's life.

Despite Joplin's preeminent position as ragtime's greatest composer, the audacious concept of a serious grand opera by a black composer—particularly a black ragtime composer—was rejected. In addition the opera, despite its folk-fable trappings, conveyed a social message: that through education Negroes would find their own road to true freedom. Far ahead of his time, Joplin further provided in *Treemonisha* an exemplary young woman, who had not only the education but the other necessary qualities of leadership. Nothing like it had ever been known in music.

Although willing enough to accept Joplin's ragtime compositions—ten of his best piano pieces were issued between 1907 and 1910—publisher after publisher (John Stark included) rejected *Treemonisha.* After four years of trying, Joplin realized that he had come to a dead end. Fearful for the survival of his opera, in 1911 he needlessly overextended himself and undertook the enormous responsibility of publishing it himself. This gigantic undertaking initiated the final series of disastrous frustrations and tragic failures that culminated in Joplin's breakdown and death.

After publishing *Treemonisha* Joplin intensified his efforts to have it produced on the stage. Although the *New York Age* of Aug. 7, 1913, announced a production of *Treemonisha* for the following fall at the Lafayette Theater and Joplin advertised for singers in the next week's issue, nothing more was heard of the production.

With each successive disappointment Joplin's obsession with *Treemonisha* intensified. Ultimately, his monomania devoured his entire existence: he gave up playing in public, he dismissed (or lost) all his students, and he even sacrificed his composing—only three more piano pieces were published after 1911. Joplin plunged feverishly into the task of orchestrating the opera, with his friend Sam Patterson standing by to copy out the parts as each page of the full score was completed. Ironically repeating the pattern of loss that seems to have haunted Joplin, every trace of this orchestration disappeared as utterly as *A Guest of Honor*—indeed it is not known if it was ever completed.

In 1915 Joplin staked everything on a last desperate effort to interest backers and presented an informal, unstaged audition of *Treemonisha* for an invited audience at a small hall in Harlem. Lacking the appurtenances of a stage production, and with Joplin at the piano substituting for the orchestra, the effort, although painstakingly prepared, was received with bored indifference by an uncomprehending audience. Joplin was crushed. From then on his mental deterioration, probably already far advanced, rapidly progressed. Joplin was afflicted with syphilis.

By the autumn of 1916 Joplin's second wife, Lottie Stokes Joplin, whom he had married in 1909, and who had resolutely and devotedly supported him throughout the terrible years of his anguish, realized that his condition was hopeless and committed him to the Manhattan State Hospital, where he died the following April.

The phenomenal rebirth of Joplin's music in the 1970s after more than half a century of virtual silence is perhaps without parallel in the history of American music. Completely vindicating Joplin's belief in the validity of his art, his rags, at one time stigmatized by the musical establishment because of their disreputable origins, were respectfully performed by celebrated musicians and symphony orchestras. His collected works have been published in a hardbound, scholarly edition, and was also issued in Braille.

In the continued absence of a documented biography of Joplin, the information found in Addison Walker Reed's "The Life and Times of Scott Joplin," unpublished, is more factual than the preponderance of Joplin writings. Facts on his early life are found in Jerry L. Atkins's "Scott Joplin and Texarkana," unpublished; other biographical material is contained in William J. Shafer's and Johannes Riedel's *The Art of Ragtime* (1973), also Rudi Blesh's and Harriet Janis's *They All Played Ragtime* (1950), a much quoted but undocumented and highly romanticized treatment of the subject. Innumerable articles include Roy Carew's and Don E. Fowler's "Scott Joplin, Overlooked Genius," in three installments (*The Record Changer,* unnumbered

volumes, Sept. and Oct. 1944); S. Brunson Campbell's "Ragtime Begins" (*The Record Changer,* March 1948); and Martin Williams's "Scott Joplin, the Ragtime King, Rules Once More" (*Smithsonian,* Oct. 1974). Critical essays on *Treemonisha* include "A Musical Novelty" (*American Musician,* June 24, 1911); Harold Schonberg's "Treemonisha" (*New York Times,* Jan. 30, 1972); Harold Schonberg's "The Scott Joplin Renaissance Grows" (*New York Times,* Feb. 13, 1972); Alan M. Kriegsman's "Treemonisha: Cheers and Contagious Zest" (*Washington Post,* Aug. 11, 1972); Robert Jones's "Jumpin' Joplin" (*New York Daily News,* May 26, 1975); Peter Davis's " 'Treemonisha'—An Innocent Dream Come True" (*New York Times,* June 1, 1975). Comprehensive information is found in Vera Brodsky Lawrence (ed.), *The Collected Works of Scott Joplin* (1971). On May 3, 1976, Joplin was awarded a special posthumous Pulitzer Prize for his compositions.

— VERA BRODSKY LAWRENCE

JORDAN, GEORGE (1847–1904), soldier. Born in Williamson County, Ky., he left farming to enlist in the newly formed 9th Cavalry at Nashville, Tenn., on Dec. 25, 1866. In his thirty years of service, he participated in several Indian campaigns including the grueling Victorio War of 1879–1880. He won a Congressional Medal of Honor for his heroic leadership against the Apaches, served twelve years as first sergeant of K Troop, 9th Cavalry, and, retired in the West, he helped open it for settlement. Jordan died after a long illness at his home in Crawford, Neb., on Oct. 25, 1904, and was interred at nearby Fort Robinson on the following day.

Jordan's adulthood and the history of the 9th Cavalry on the Indian frontier are components of the same story. He joined the regiment at New Orleans when it was less than four months old and served with it at six different Texas posts during 1867–1875. During these years he participated in conflicts with Indians, Mexican raiders, and American outlaws. In 1876 he and the regiment were transferred to New Mexico, where he spent five years, until reassigned to Fort Supply, Indian Territory.

While in New Mexico, Jordan saw action in one of the most brutal frontier wars, the campaign against Victorio. This White Mountain Apache fled the Mescalero reservation near Fort Station with about 100 warriors in the fall of 1879 and terrorized whites in Arizona and New Mexico for a year. Jordan's heroic deed occurred when the campaign's outcome was still in doubt. He and a detachment of twenty-five Negro troopers were alerted by a messenger on the night of May 13, 1880, that the small white settlement near abandoned Fort Tularosa, west of the Mescalero reserve, was in grave danger. Jordan and his men rode all night to reach the community. As soon as they arrived, he had his men erect a stockade, into which he moved the panic-stricken settlers. He organized his small force for defense and waited for the attack. At dusk 100 Apaches struck the improvised fortress but Jordan and his detachment drove them back. The Indians attacked a second time but were again repulsed; then they rode off. Jordan's prompt and capable leadership prevented a massacre and brought him the Medal of Honor.

Jordan spent his last twelve years of active duty at Fort Robinson, Neb. He was with Maj. Guy Henry's battalion of the 9th Cavalry during their rescue of the 7th Cavalry from a Sioux ambush on the Pine Ridge reservation, S. D., the day after the famous Wounded Knee massacre of Dec. 29, 1890. Here, at at Tularosa ten years before, the Negro troopers rescued whites in extremely precarious positions from attacking Indians.

Jordan retired on March 30, 1897. He spent his last years at Crawford, only three miles from Fort Robinson, and was generally recognized as the leader of the small Negro community, made up largely of former soldiers and their families. In the fall of 1904 a local physician advised him to seek hospitalization at Fort Robinson, but the post surgeon rejected his application. Jordan died a few days later. The surgeon's explanation—that he did not have room for Jordan—was accepted in Washington. This does not diminish the tragedy of the death of Jordan, a career soldier and Medal of Honor winner denied care by the service to which he had devoted his life.

There are no published biographies of Jordan. Enlistment Registers and the reports of Chaplain William T. Anderson (in the National Archives), Col. George F. Hamilton's "History of the Ninth Regiment U.S. Cavalry" (undated manuscript, U. S. Military Academy library), and William H. Leckie's *The Buffalo Soldiers* (1967) all contain useful information on his career.

— FRANK N. SCHUBERT

JUST, ERNEST EVERETT (1883–1941), research scientist. He was born on Aug. 14, 1883, in Charleston, S.C., the eldest of three children of Charles Frazier Just and Mary (Matthews) Just. His father and paternal grandfather were wharf builders who had erected some of the largest docks in Charleston harbor. Charles Just died when Ernest was four years old. His widowed mother supported the family by teaching school in Charleston and at the phosphate fields three miles from the city, where she established a cooperative farming and industrial settlement, later named Maryville in her honor. Receiving his early education in his mother's school, Just entered the Academy of South Carolina State College in Orangeburg, where he studied from 1894 to 1900. Encouraged by his mother to continue his education in the North, Just left South Carolina in 1900, working his way to New York on the Clyde Line. In New York, while reading the *Christian Endeavor World,* he learned about a preparatory school in Meriden, N.H., the Kimball Union Academy, which he entered in the fall of 1900. At Kimball he studied the classical course, was president of the debating society, editor of the school newspaper, and the highest ranking student at graduation in 1903. Just then matriculated at Dartmouth College, where he continued his outstanding academic performance. Although he excelled in Greek, Just decided to major in history and biology as a student of the historian Herbert D. Foster and the biologist William Patten. A Rufus Choate Scholar for two years, Just was elected to Phi Beta Kappa in his junior year, earned highest departmental honors in both history and biology, and was awarded the B.A. degree in 1907, *magna cum laude.*

In the fall of 1907 Just joined the faculty of Howard University's College of Arts and Sciences as an instructor in English. He also served as instructor in English and rhetoric in the Commercial College at Howard. In 1908 he organized the first drama group at Howard, the College Dramatic Club. Directed by Just, Benjamin G. Brawley, and Marie Moore-Forrest, the successful productions of these years were the foundation for the later development of professional instruction in drama at Howard. While he was a teacher of English, Just met Ethel Highwarden of Columbus, Ohio, an instructor in German in the Teachers College at the university from 1906 to 1910. They were married on June 26, 1912, and had three children, Margaret, Highwarden, and Maribel.

Just was appointed to the faculty of Howard University at a time of its rapid expansion under the leadership of Pres. Wilbur Patterson Thirkield (1906–1912). His development program included "modernization" of the traditional classical curriculum by addition of technical subjects such as engineering and by increased emphasis on the natural sciences. Because of Just's outstanding work in biology at Dartmouth, Thirkield persuaded him in 1908 to abandon English, begin graduate work in biology, and thereafter develop this field in the science laboratories then under construction. In the summer of 1909 Just began his graduate training at the Marine Biological Laboratory, Woods Hole, Mass., as a student in the course on the marine invertebrates, followed in the summer of 1910 by the course in embryology. (During the summers of 1911, 1912, 1913, 1914, and 1915, he attended the University of Chicago in addition to his work at Woods Hole.) At the Marine Biological Laboratory he met Prof. Frank R. Lillie of the University of Chicago, who became his mentor and lifelong friend. During the summers of 1911 and 1912 Just served as Lillie's research assistant on a project investigating fertilization and the breeding habits of *Nereis,* a marine worm, and the sea-urchin *Arbacia.* In these early years at Woods Hole, Just identified the fields which were the focus of his research for the remainder of his career: fertilization, cellular physiology, and experimental embryology. During the academic year 1915–1916 Just was granted a leave from Howard, permitting him to attend the University of Chicago, which awarded him the Ph.D in zoology on June 6, 1916.

Just achieved distinction as a scientist remarkably early in his career. In 1912 he published his first paper, "The Relation of the First Cleavage Plane to the Entrance Point of the Sperm" in the *Biological Bulletin,* which was followed by five others in three years. These won for him recognition, in Lillie's words, as "the best investigator in the field of biology that his people has produced in America." The high opinion of Just's work held by the small circle of marine biologists reached a broader national public when he was presented on Feb. 12, 1915, in Ethical Culture Hall, New York, the first Spingarn Medal, awarded by the NAACP "to the man or woman of African descent and American citizenship, who shall have made the highest achievement during the preceding year or years in any honorable field of human endeavor."

The Spingarn Medal brought attention not only to

Just's research, but also to his vital role in the improvement of instruction in the Howard Univerrsity Medical School, where he served also as professor and head of the Department of Physiology from 1912 to 1920. During this period Just divided his time equally between the Medical School and the College of Arts and Sciences, teaching physiology in separate classes to medical, dental, and pharmaceutical students from 9:00 A.M. to noon, Monday through Saturday, and zoology to students in the College of Arts and Sciences from 1:00 to 5:00 P.M. daily. Just taught in the Medical School without compensation. He was probably the first member of the Howard medical faculty to emphasize research as part of instruction, particularly notable because the majority of medical faculties in this period were part-time practitioners; medical schools accordingly gave a low priority to research.

The decisive turning point in Just's career as a teacher at Howard, and as a research scientist, came in the winter of 1920. His friend, Professor Lillie, introduced him to Julius Rosenwald at the Shoreham Hotel in Washington, D.C. Well known for his philanthropic support of Tuskegee Institute, YMCA buildings for Negroes, and school buildings for Negroes in the rural South, Rosenwald was struck by the juxtaposition of Just's brilliance as a scientist and racial discrimination in America which barred Just from the research facilities and graduate students of white universities. Rosenwald decided to create for Just a special situation at Howard that would remove some of the formidable obstacles to his career. For the period 1920–1925 Rosenwald made a grant to Howard University of $80,000 for use by Just. The grant was made on the condition that Just remain head of the Department of Zoology, that he cease the double load of teaching by abandoning instruction in the Medical School, and that he be granted each year a six-month leave of absence so that he could pursue his research without interruption. This arrangement permitted Just to conduct research at Woods Hole from April to September each year. His research was also supported during 1920–1933 by the National Research Council. With this unprecedented support, the 1920s were a golden age of research for Just. From 1912 until 1920 Just produced nine research papers on fertilization; from 1920 to 1930, his research yielded thirty-eight. He was also co-author in 1924 (with Frank R. Lillie, T. H. Morgan, and others) of *General Cytology,* published by the University of Chicago Press. From 1912 to 1928 Just's research was in the field of experimental embryology, particularly the investigation of fertilization, experimental parthenogenesis, cell division, and mutation. During this period his experiments on the detection of electrochemical reactions within living cells were revolutionary. He was able in 1925 to "reproduce all the histological characteristics of human cancer cells" in a series of experiments on the effects of ultraviolet radiation on cells. He also said that he was "the first person to have increased the number of chromosomes in an animal." The medical implications of Just's investigations in cellular physiology were particularly clear in his twelve years of research on hydration and dehydration, for the treatment of edema and nephritis. In the late 1920s Just began to synthesize his research findings in an effort that aimed at no less than a "definitive analysis" of the chemistry and physics of protoplasm. This was the crucial transition to the final phase of his research career. After 1928 Just undertook the development of a theoretical system that would integrate conceptually his basic laboratory research findings from 1912 to 1928 with the more general and fundamental problems of biology. Just considered this theoretical work the crowning achievement of his career. The conceptual elements of the theory were presented to the scientific community for the first time in September 1930 when Just was one of twelve zoologists invited to address the General Session of the Eleventh International Congress of Zoologists in Padua, Italy. The theory was later published in three articles, initially in German ("Die Rolle des Kortikalen Cytoplasmas bei vitalen Erscheinungen" [*Naturwissenschaft,* 1931]; "On the Origin of Mutations," [*American Naturalist,* 1932]; and "Cortical Cytoplasm and Evolution" [*American Naturalist,* 1933]). Building on his experimental observations, Just exphasized the role of the ectoplasm in cellular development, and postulated that a fundamental understanding of life itself and evolution would be derived from an analysis of the physiochemical processes of the ectoplasm, and its systemic interaction with the inner cellular substance and the external environment. Just believed that his theory was "nothing short of a revolution in our biological thinking" because it was a "new basis for the understanding of vital phenomena" (Just's report to the Julius Rosenwald Fund, 1933). The decade of the 1930s was a period of growing recognition of Just's contributions to science. In 1930 he was elected vice-president of the American Society of Zoologists, and six years later a member of the Washington Academy of Sciences. Equally significant was his appointment to the editorial boards of the leading journals in his field: *Biological Bulletin* (Woods Hole, Mass.), *Physiological Zoology* (Chicago), *Protoplasma: Zeitschrift fuer physikalische Chemie* (Berlin), *Cytologia* (Tokyo), and the *Journal of Morphology* (Philadelphia).

Just's increasing research productivity during the late 1920s and early 1930s had a paradoxical effect on his relation to Howard University. A grant from the Rockefeller Foundation (1925–1930) and a second grant of $80,000 from the Rosenwald Fund (1928–1933) encouraged Just to regard himself as primarily a research scientist. He found teaching more burdensome, despite the generous annual leave policy that had been established in 1920. On the other hand the university's president, Mordecai W. Johnson, and the officials of the Rosenwald Fund insisted that the grants were to support, in addition to Just's research, the development of a strong department of zoology, as well as young Negro zoologists trained by Just. Initially this difference between Just and Johnson was muted because of the friendship between the two men during the first four years of Johnson's administration (1926–1930). After Just's enunciation of his new theory, he argued that he be permitted to devote himself entirely to research. The president maintained that graduate instruction and the development of Negro biologists were not inconsistent with research. The struggle between Just and Johnson, which gradually intensified, cast a shadow over Just's later years at Howard. Graduate instruction in zoology at Howard began in 1929, one year after the second Rosenwald Grant. It is clear that the Rosenwald Fund expected Just to devote a significant part of his time to graduate training. Just later rejected this view and did not encourage graduate work in zoology at Howard. From 1929 to 1933 there were fifteen graduate students, eight of whom completed work for the M.S. degree. But in 1933–1934 there were no graduate students, and only one in 1934–1935. Just taught only graduate students in this period. Just's problems with Howard also intensified after 1929 because of his wish to work in European laboratories. A deeply sensitive and cultivated man, Just felt plagued by American race prejudice. In Europe, particularly Germany, he felt free in a way that was impossible in the United States. Apart from a few of his colleagues at Howard, like his close friends Alain Locke and Kelly Miller, Just did not find intellectual companionship there, and he was cut off from most of his white colleagues by institutionalized segregation. He felt "trapped by color" at Howard; he believed science should be "color-blind" and was offended by the appellation "Negro scientist." European scientists were more receptive to his later work than Americans, and Just thought they were more interested in his research than in his racial identity. Moreover, unlike Washington, where restaurants, the theater, academic and other cultural institutions were segregated, work in Europe permitted him amplitude for his nonscientific interests.

On Sept. 18, 1929, Just was invited by Max Hartmann to be a guest researcher at the Kaiser Wilhelm Institut für Biologie, Berlin-Dahlem. Considered by many scientists of the time as "the world's greatest research laboratory," Just wrote to Edwin Embree of the Rosenwald Fund tht the invitation to work in Berlin was "the most flattering recognition which I have yet received." He was the first American to be invited to this laboratory where the staff included winners of the Nobel Prize. For six months during 1930, 1931, and 1932, Just was at the Kaiser Wilhelm Institut and a fellow at the Harnack-Haus der Kaiser Wilhelm Gesellschaft zur Förderung der Wissenschaften. When Hitler came to power in 1933, Just's work in Berlin ceased. He then shifted his work to Naples, where he worked at the Stazione Zoologica (April to July 1933 and Jan. 1934 to Jan. 1935) supported by a grant of $10,000 from the Carnegie Institution of Washington while on leave from Howard. At Naples, where he had first conducted research from January to August 1929, Just undertook pioneering research on sex reversal, and succeeded in changing the sex of *Platynereis* by experimental methods. During these years in Europe, Just began to lose contact with his American colleagues. He also attempted to persuade foundations to provide him with financial assistance that would permit him to abandon permanently his university association and remain in Europe.

In Germany and Italy Just worked on two books. The first was a synthesis of his laboratory research and new theoretical perspective, published in 1939 as *The Biology of the Cell Surface*. The second, published in the same year, was a handbook that summed up Just's world-famous techniques for handling living marine eggs, *Basic Methods for Experiments in Eggs of Marine Animals*. Increasingly alienated from Howard University, and stymied by the refusal of white American universities to offer him a position, Just returned to Europe. He was on leave from Howard from January 1938 until September 1940. During this period Just made the claim that Howard should give him "back pay" for those years that his salary was provided by the Rosenwald Fund, and further that the university should provide him with a pension despite the fact that he had refused to participate in the university's retirement system and was too young in the absence of disability to be eligible.

In March 1938 Just began to work, without salary or official responsibility, at the Laboratoire d'Anatomie et d'Histologie Comparées of the University of Paris during the fall and winter months. In the spring and summer he conducted research at the Sorbonne's Station Biologique at Roscoff, Finistère. In the experiments conducted in France from 1938 to 1939 Just hoped to develop proof for his position that the correct approach to the study of life was neither mechanistic nor vitalistic, but rather holistic and interactive. Simultaneously he worked on the philosophical implications of his research, writing that "the philosophical aspect of my work is based on study of Hegel, Kant and Mach and the study of modern physics—Heisenberg, Schroedinger, Planck, von Laue, Jeans and Eddington." Just believed that there was a pressing need for the integration of biological science and social philosophy. He was bitter about what he regarded as rejection of his efforts. He wrote that the source of his problem was that "most people, however generous in point of view, start with the postulate that a black one cannot and should not deal with such problems. As a black, I am supposed to keep within a certain sphere of activity. This for thirty odd years I have done, more or less. Now I am for the first time in my almost fifty-three years sure that I have something of value for the human race. I want a chance to do my work. And I do not want to be told over and over again that my place is with my people; that only as a black in the circumscribed arena of the black world must I work" (Just to Max Wolf, Jan. 21, 1936). Just rejected the view of Lillie and other American zoologists that he should return to the United States. Arguing that only in Europe could he develop "the basis for a new biology," Just insisted that he "felt freer in Europe and have only there a sense of dignity" that he "never had before." In a letter to Lillie (Aug. 12, 1936), Just wrote that "the value of my ideas for biology is such that it puts me out of place in a make-believe university. And since it appears to be no chance that I get a place in a real university or research institution in America, I must use the years before me in every way possible to keep aglow the flame within me, which in my particular circumstances and as a Negro I am not allowed to nourish in America."

In Paris during the summer of 1939 Just was married to Hedwig Schnetzler, a German biologist from Heidelberg who had been his research assistant in Berlin. When war between Germany and France was declared in September 1939, the French military authorities barred Just from the laboratories where he had worked. The Justs left France in September 1940, and he was reappointed to his position as professor and head of the Department of Zoology. On May 5, 1941, he was elected to membership in the New York Academy of Sciences. Just died of cancer on Oct. 27, 1941, at the Washington home of his sister Inez. He was buried in Lincoln Cemetery, Washington, D.C. In an obituary tribute to Just (*Science,* Jan. 2, 1942), Frank R. Lillie wrote that "in the twenty summer sessions that Just spent at the Marine Biological Laboratory at Woods Hole he became more widely acquainted with the embryological resources of the marine fauna than probably any other person." Lillie was constrained to say that, despite this achievement, "an element of tragedy ran through all Just's scientific career due to the limitations imposed by being a Negro in America, to which he could make no lasting psychological adjustment in spite of earnest efforts on his part. . . . That a man of his ability, scientific devotion, and of such strong personal loyalties as he gave and received, should have been warped in the land of his birth must remain a matter for regret."

There is no adequate biography of Just. Among the more useful obituary statements are those by Frank R. Lillie (*Science,* Jan. 2, 1942) and by Benjamin Karpman (*Journal of Nervous and Mental Disease,* Feb. 1943). Evaluations of Just's contributions to science include the sketch by M. Wharton Young prepared for the dedication of the E. E. Just Laboratory of Cell Biology at the Howard University College of Medicine, May 18, 1972 (in the Moorland-Spingarn Research Center); W. Montague Cobb, "Ernest Everett Just, 1883–1941" (*JNMA,* Sept. 1957, pp. 349–51); and W. T. Fontaine, "Philosophical Implications of the Biology of Dr. Ernest E. Just" (*JNH,* July 1939, pp. 281–90). See also the profiles by Kelly Miller (*Howard University Record,* April 1925), Mary White Ovington (*Portraits in Color,* 1927), S. M. Nabrit (*Phylon,* Second Quarter 1946), and Fred D. Miller (*DAB, Supplement 3,* 1941–1945). For Just's relations with Howard University (1938–1940), see Rayford W. Logan's *Howard University, The First Hundred Years 1867–1967* (1969, pp. 348–50). The Ernest E. Just Papers are deposited in the Manuscript Division, Moorland-Spingarn Research Center, Howard University. — MICHAEL R. WINSTON

KECKLEY, ELIZABETH (c. 1818–1907), dressmaker, White House modiste, and confidante of Mary Todd Lincoln. Born in Dinwiddie, Va., one of the slaves belonging to the Burwell family, in her teens she was taken to St. Louis by Anne Burwell Garland and her husband. As a seamstress and dressmaker, she helped support the Garlands, their five children, and her own son George, whose father was white. She married James Keckley who asserted he was a free Negro. She left him when she found out that he was not only a slave but a ne'er-do-well. Through loans from her customers, on Nov. 15, 1855, she purchased her freedom and that of her son. She repaid the loan, learned to read and write, spent a few weeks in Baltimore, and settled in Washington. Among her customers was Varina Howell Davis, wife of Jefferson Davis. From early 1861 to 1868 she

was the dressmaker, personal maid, and confidante of Mrs. Lincoln. After the publication in 1868 of her book *Behind the Scenes or Thirty Years a Slave, and Four Years in the White House,* the friendship with Mrs. Lincoln ended and Keckley's dressmaking business declined. Except for a brief career (1892–1893) as a teacher of domestic science and a regular attendance at the 15th Street Presbyterian Church in Washington, she lingered in virtual obscurity until her death of a paralytic stroke in Washington on May 26, 1907, at the Home for Destitute Women and Children. Her principal support came from a small pension paid to her as the mother of George, killed as a Union soldier at Wilson's Creek, Mo., on Aug. 10, 1861.

Keckley's influence on Mrs. Lincoln in part stemmed from Keckley's devotion to eleven-year-old William Wallace ("Willie") Lincoln. She washed and dressed him when he died in February 1862. Mrs. Lincoln "felt a rare loyalty and spirit of service in Elizabeth Keckley, giving her trust and confidence not offered to others" (Carl Sandburg, *Abraham Lincoln, The Prairie Years and the War Years* [1954], pp. 248, 333). This influence increased the sympathies of the president's wife toward the Negro. In the fall of 1862 she gave $200 to the Contraband Relief Association, a group of Negro women founded and headed by Keckley to assist former slaves who had come to the District of Columbia.

Keckley, a handsome, almost white woman with straight black hair, is one of the many controversial personalities of the Lincoln presidency, especially after the publication of *Behind the Scenes.* The preface sought to embellish the image of the plump, flighty Mary Todd Lincoln. It provoked a storm of criticism because of its statements about Mrs. Lincoln's private opinions of highly placed officials, of the Lincolns' family life, and of Mrs. Lincoln's attempts in 1867 to sell some of her personal effects. Some of its validity seemed beyond question, for it included two score letters from Mrs. Lincoln to "My dear Lizzie" (Keckley).

The authorship of *Behind the Scenes* is also a subject of considerable debate. Benjamin Quarles, in his biographical sketch in *NAW,* stated that it was ghostwritten by James Redpath or Hamilton Busbey, "both skilled penmen" (2: 311). An article in the *Washington Star* (Nov. 11, 1935), stating that Jane Swisshelm was the true author, provoked a little-noticed discussion. John E. Washington replied in the Nov. 15 issue that Keckley was the author. Francis J. Grimké, pastor of the 15th Street Presbyterian Church, which Keckley attended for over thirty years, stated in the January 1936 issue of the *JNH* that Keckley gave the impression that she was capable of writing it. Carter G. Woodson, commenting on Grimké's article, wrote of "Persons who were personally acquainted with Mrs. Keckley and knew this book as being the product of her own pen." Albert J. Lanen, who signed himself as an "Employe of The Minnesota Historical Society" and who had edited a volume of letters written by Mrs. Swisshelm, concluded that it was not "impossible that Mrs. Keckley should write such a book. At the same time it would not be impossible for Mrs. Swisshelm, or any other person of literary training, to have assisted her in the editorial work." Lanen asked Grimké for any information he might provide. Grimké asked Mrs. Carrie Syphax Watson for the requested information. Mrs. Watson, who stated that she had known Keckley for several years, and referred to her as Aunt Keckley, wrote to him on March 19, 1936: "I gleaned from her conversations with me that the chapters were of her own assembling. The Carleton Co. [publishers of the book] may have, in their review made corrections in construction of phrases and grammatical errors" (Francis J. Grimké, *The Works of Francis J. Grimké*, edited by Carter G. Woodson [1942], 4:545–49).

The most comprehensive account of Elizabeth Keckley, with photographs, is in John E. Washington's *They Knew Lincoln* (1942). The best brief sketch is that by Benjamin Quarles in *NAW* (1971, 2:310–11).

— RAYFORD W. LOGAN

KING, MARTIN LUTHER, JR. (1929–1968), civil rights leader, minister, and author. Born on Jan. 15, 1929, at 501 Auburn Ave. NE, in Atlanta, Ga., the second of three children of the Rev. Michael (later Martin) and Mrs. Alberta (Williams) King, he attended public elementary and high schools as well as the private Laboratory High School of Atlanta University, and entered Morehouse College at age fifteen in September 1944 as a special student. Recipient of a bachelor's degree in sociology (1948), young King enrolled in September 1948 at Crozer Theological Seminary, Chester, Pa., receiving his B.D. degree three years later with highest honors and winner of the J. Lewis Crozer postgraduate fellowship. At Boston University King prepared a dissertation in philosophy entitled "A Comparison of the Conceptions of God in the Thinking of Paul Tillich and Henry Nelson Wieman." He was awarded the Ph.D. degree in systematic theology at the end of 1955. For two years he had taken parallel courses in philosophy at Harvard University.

In early 1954 King accepted his first pastorate at the Dexter Avenue Baptist Church in Montgomery, Ala., assuming full responsibility on Sept. 1. He and his wife Coretta, whom he had met and married in June 1953 while still at Boston University, had been residents in Montgomery less than one year when Mrs. Rosa Parks defied the ordinance regulating segregated seating on municipal transportation (Dec. 1, 1955). King's successful leadership of the Montgomery Bus Boycott, ably assisted by Edward Nixon and the Rev. Ralph Abernathy, catapulted him into national prominence.

In the aftermath of the boycott, King traveled, mediated, wrote, and delivered speeches. Travel took him and Mrs. King to Ghana and India where, on the former trip in March 1957, they celebrated Ghanaian independence with Vice-President Richard M. Nixon and met Prime Minister Kwame Nkrumah; and on the latter in February 1959, learned firsthand of the nonviolent doctrine of *Satyagraha* (Truth Force) and spoke with Prime Minister Nehru and the spiritual leader, Vinoba Bhave. Meditations inspired by the life and teachings of Gandhi, by pacifist counsels of friends in the Fellowship of Reconciliation (FOR), and especially by the personal demands of his emerging stature resulted in King's first book, *Stride Toward Freedom* (1958), a vivid and reflective account of the Montgomery struggle. While

autographing *Stride Toward Freedom* on Sept. 20, King was stabbed and seriously wounded by a deranged Negro woman in a Harlem department store. Writing was accompanied by action. On May 17, 1957, he participated with labor leader A. Philip Randolph, Rep. Adam Clayton Powell, Jr., civil rights leader Roy Wilkins, and others in the Prayer Pilgrimage at the Lincoln Memorial, Washington, D.C. Urged by prominent Negro Baptist ministers in the South to assume a more regional role, King accepted the presidency of the Southern Christian Leadership Conference (SCLC), resigning his Montgomery pastorate and moving immediately to Atlanta in January 1960 where the SCLC had its headquarters.

Intensifying his activities, King lent moral and financial support to the newly formed Student Nonviolent Coordinating Committee (SNCC), also based in Atlanta; attended the Democratic National Convention in Los Angeles in July 1960, where with Congressman Powell and NAACP executive director Roy Wilkins, he attempted to elicit firm civil rights commitments from leading contenders for the presidential nomination. He compelled the Atlanta police to arrest him and some thirty students who insisted on service at a department store lunch counter. Three days later, on Oct. 25, 1960, with his probated sentence for a recent traffic offense revoked, and unknown to his attorney, King was spirited to Georgia's Reidsville State Prison. National outrage was instantaneous and overwhelming. King's Reidsville incarceration probably influenced the outcome of the 1960 presidential election because of President Eisenhower's and candidate Nixon's refusal to intervene while John F. Kennedy expressed publicly his concern by telephoning Mrs. King on Oct. 26.

Although he traveled and spoke widely and committed the SCLC to southern voter registration, King's major energies were absorbed from December 1961 to August 1962 in the Albany, Ga., desegregation movement. After Albany came Birmingham, Ala. (April-May 1963), with its combat literature—Birmingham Manifesto, "Letter from Birmingham Jail," and *Why We Can't Wait* (1964)—Danville, Va. (July 1963), and the March on Washington (Aug. 28, 1963). In January 1964 *Time* magazine chose King as Man of the Year, the first American Negro so honored. During the spring, SCLC supported the desegregation efforts of the Negro citizens of Saint Augustine, Fla. At the end of the year, in recognition of his nonviolent civil rights leadership, King was invited to Sweden to receive the Nobel Peace Prize (Dec. 10, 1963), the second American Negro so honored (Ralph Bunche was the first, in 1950).

The Selma, Ala., demonstration and the harrowing Selma–Montgomery March (Jan.-March 1965) were dramatic undertakings whose limited achievements could not obscure the serious rifts in the Civil Rights Movement. The younger militants of the Congress of Racial Equality (CORE) and SNCC began to lose confidence in nonviolent tactics if not in the charisma of King. SCLC's assault on conditions of economic and social discrimination in Chicago. (Jan.-Aug. 1966) was more abortive than Selma. While King's efforts in Chicago encountered solid opposition from the mayor and fanatic hostility from the city's white working-class population, his several trips to Mississippi (June 1966) in response to the statewide civil rights Freedom March, organized in the wake of the shooting of James Meredith, Negro graduate of the University of Mississippi, underscored the growing doubts about nonviolent passive resistance. He was upstaged in Mississippi by Stokely Carmichael's Black Power enthusiasts and constrained in Chicago to accept a spurious compromise, the Summit Agreement (Aug. 26), because of a white and black backlash there. This agreement between the groups led by Dr. King and representatives of the city of Chicago, countersigned by an impressive array of civic, civil libertarian, labor, religious, banking, and real estate institutions, was an affirmative-action program without enforcement machinery. On April 4, 1967, at New York's Riverside Church and on April 15 at United Nations Plaza with Harry Belafonte, CORE's Floyd McKissick, SNCC's Stokely Carmichael, and Dr. Benjamin Spock, King unequivocally denounced the Vietnam War.

A year of profound stocktaking ensued, characterized by spiritual disillusionment, intellectual growth, and tactical radicalism, much of it reflected in his book *Where Do We Go from Here: Chaos or Community?* (1967). In the midst of organizing his Poor People's Campaign, King hurried to Memphis, Tenn., to assist striking municipal sanitation workers. A few minutes after 6:00 P.M. on April 4, 1968, standing on the balcony of Memphis's Lorraine Motel, Martin Luther King, Jr., was shot to death. James Earl Ray, a white man he had never met, was later convicted of the crime.

King's assassination deprived America of a towering symbol of moral and social progress. The calamity was compounded because it aborted the third and potentially most seminal phase of his career, nonviolent populism. Nonviolent populism was the consequence of both the successes and the failures of antecedent strategies. First had come the early direct-action phase, commencing with the Montgomery Bus Boycott and ending with the Selma–Montgomery March (1955–1965). Listening to her husband's speech on that latter occasion, Coretta King stated: "I realized we had really come a long way from our start in the bus protest." Public accommodation barriers had begun to fall throughout the South; public schools were gradually becoming integrated; an improved climate for minority job opportunities was manifest; and an unprecedented sense of black dignity had emerged. The institutional climax of these achievements came with the signing of the 1964 Civil Rights Act (July) and the 1965 Voting Rights Act (Aug. 6).

The immediate causes of enactment of the 1964 legislation were its association with a martyred president, John F. Kennedy, and the unique political prowess of Lyndon Johnson, the new president. The proximate cause, however, was to be found in the national civil rights preoccupation engendered to a large extent by the appalling violence of Birmingham whites against peaceful demonstrations orchestrated by King and his assistants. With its brutal police chief, Eugene "Bull" Connor, its fire hoses and police dogs, and its flayed women and church-bombed children, Birmingham became the racial cynosure of America. President Kennedy deplored Birmingham publicly shortly before his death and moved cautiously to persuade Congress to enact legislation to end the worst abuses in race relations.

Martin Luther King did more: he electrified an audience of nearly 200,000 in Washington, D.C., where on Aug. 28, 1963, he proclaimed: "There will be neither rest nor tranquility in America until the Negro is granted his citizenship rights. The whirlwinds of revolt will continue to shake the foundations of our nation until the bright day of justice emerges." That day of the March on Washington for Jobs and Freedom, he shared his dream with America that the "bright day of justice" was forthcoming. "I have a dream that one day every valley shall be exalted," he intoned, "every hill and mountain shall be made low, the rough places will be made plain, and the crooked places will be made straight, and the glory of the Lord shall be revealed, and all flesh shall see it together." The grand oratory, visionary mystique, moral presence, and charisma which had welded the traditionally cautious Negro citizens of the South into an increasingly effective force were supremely manifest in this speech.

The second phase, the "northern phase," was largely determined by the equivocal performance of the SCLC in Selma, Ala. After the cavalry charge on civil rights marchers by Sheriff James "Jim" Clark's deputies at Selma's Edward Pettus Bridge on March 7, 1965, King returned from Atlanta to lead a second march from Selma to Montgomery. Hundreds of outsiders arrived to participate, including such prominent figures as Methodist Bishop John Wesley Lord, Msgr. George L. Gingras of the Washington, D.C., Roman Catholic archdiocese, Rabbi Richard G. Hirsch of the Union of American Hebrew Congregations, the Rev. David K. Hunter of the National Council of Churches, James Farmer of CORE, James Forman of SNCC, and the Rev. Fred Shuttlesworth of Birmingham. The fact that a federal court had enjoined the march at the request of the Justice Department, and that King vowed to defy it, encouraged many Civil Rights advocates to hope that the SCLC president was becoming more radical.

At Brown Chapel African Methodist Episcopal Church just before the march, King proclaimed, "We have the right to walk the highways, and we have the right to walk to Montgomery if our feet will get us there. I have no alternative but to lead a march from this spot to carry our grievances to the seat of government. I have made my choice. I have got to march. I do not know what lies ahead of us. There may be beatings, jailings, tear gas. But I would rather die on the highways of Alabama than make a butchery of my conscience."

None of the rank-and-file marchers nor any of the leaders of other organizations (SNCC, CORE) knew that President Johnson's special emissary, Leroy Collins (former governor of Florida and then head of the Justice Department's Community Relations Service), had been instrumental a few hours earlier in persuading SCLC to accept a compromise. The march was to halt after crossing the Pettus Bridge and reaching the barrier of Alabama state troopers. Having secretly accepted this compromise, the SCLC was astonished when the state police stood aside, opening the Selma–Montgomery highway. Nevertheless, after a few minutes kneeling in prayer, King led the marchers back to Brown Chapel. This Selma Bridge Compromise on March 9, despite the federally authorized and successful march to Montgomery twelve days later, marked the beginning of the decline of his authority over the Civil Rights Movement. "If the police had turned them back by force," Eldridge Cleaver wrote later, ". . . the violence and brutality of the system would have been ruthlessly exposed." King's decision at Pettus Bridge made him suspect by those who saw in him the racial moderate whose hopes for progress depended on the goodwill of liberal whites and the federal establishment.

On Jan. 22, 1966, the "northern phase" opened with King installing himself and, several days later, his family in a slum apartment at 1550 South Hamlin Ave., in Chicago's Lawndale section. Henceforth, housing and jobs were SCLC's main themes. On Feb. 23, SCLC and CCCO (Coordinated Council of Community Organizations), comprised of local branches of CORE, NAACP, SNCC, Urban League, the West Side Federation, and the Woodlawn Organization, dramatically seized a delapidated tenement; rent receipts were to be placed in "trusteeship" until the landlord agreed to repair the property. As in the case of Birmingham (and unlike Albany and Selma), extensive preliminary contacts with local leadership and careful planning and mobilization characterized what soon became known as the Chicago Movement. Circumstances permitting, SCLC's and CCCO's Chicago scenario would have unfolded at a deliberate pace—intensive community voter registration and civic campaigning, increasing fair housing and fair employment propaganda combined with viable boycott stratagems, marshalling of progressive civic and federal pressure against City Hall, and finally, well-organized massive rallies and marches. Counselled by the Agenda Committee (the Catholic Interracial Council, Chicago Renewal Society, the Packing House Workers Union, American Friends Service Committee, the Urban League's William Berry, and the Revs. Arthur Brazier and Al Raby, and others, King intended to prove by success in Chicago that he possessed a "strategy for change, a tactical program that will bring the Negro into the mainstream of American life as quickly as possible."

Before the Chicago Movement was well underway, however, James Meredith was wounded by gunfire, on June 6, while on a solitary march to Jackson, Miss. King was immediately diverted from Chicago by a month of intermittent but intense and dangerous activity in Mississippi, joining forces with civil rights activist Charles Evers, Floyd McKissick of CORE, and Stokely Carmichael of SNCC. Despite the proclaimed truce between SCLC and its critics, King was shocked by the favorable reception given to Carmichael's shouted slogan "Black Power!" at a rally in Greenwood, Miss. The Mississippi experience made King realize that "for twelve years I, and others like me, had held out radiant promise of progress. I had preached to them about my dreams. . . . Their hopes had soared. They were now booing because they felt we were unable to deliver on our promises." Thus success in Chicago was more crucial than ever.

"We have got to deliver results—nonviolent results in a Northern city—to protect the Nonviolent Movement," said the Rev. Andrew Young of SCLC's general staff. The original blueprint was revised. In early July, King opted for giant rallies and demonstrations in Chicago's business district and marches into blue-collar white residential enclaves such as Bogan Park and Cicero. On July 10, at Soldiers Field, he warned: "This day we must decide to fill up the jails of Chicago, if necessary in order to end slums. This day we must decide that our votes will determine who will be the next mayor of Chicago. We must make it clear that we will purge Chicago of every politician, whether he be Negro or white, who feels that he owns the Negro vote." He then went to City Hall to nail to the door a list of specifics concerning housing, hiring, and wage demands. Two days later Chicago was engulfed by a three-day race riot. Then, despite superficially cordial meetings with Mayor Richard Daley, came a hardening of the city's position, followed by invasions by civil rights marchers into white neighborhoods and violent white reaction. Ultimately, the prospect of escalating violence, and the rapid loss by the SCLC of liberal white and federal support, resulted in the hurried and virtually meaningless compromise, the Summit Agreement of Aug. 26, 1966.

The Chicago stalemate was more serious than the standoff at the Selma bridge, and for the same reasons. Inflamed by the nostrums of Black Power, many young urban Negroes were increasingly attracted to the violent examples of Watts and Harlem. The signals from liberal whites and the Johnson administration were equally distressing. With an eye on the public opinion polls, the White House resisted demands for the strengthening of civil and voting rights legislation and totally ignored pleas from King and A. Philip Randolph for a ten-year poverty budget of $100 billion. King's diminished influence in Washington had already been patently manifest during the June 1966 White House Conference on Civil Rights where, excluded from the agenda committee, he was also prevented from speaking, while spokesmen for other civil rights organizations or for more conservative positions monopolized the sessions. He found himself blamed by some blacks for being too moderate and by many whites for being immoderate.

Although discouraged by SCLC's board of directors from doing so, King found it increasingly difficult to refrain from condemning the Vietnam War. "It is worthless to talk about integrating if there is no world to integrate in," he had admonished SCLC officers in July 1965; "There must be a negotiated settlement even with the Vietcong." Prominent Negro leaders warned him to keep silent. He did, although he warned them in an article in the *Chicago Defender* (Jan. 1, 1966): "The Negro must not allow himself to become a victim of the self-serving philosophy of those who manufacture war that the survival of the world is the white man's business alone."

After Chicago there were pressing political reasons for SCLC to alter its tactics, but the final phase, the "nonviolent populism phase" (1967–1968), was not motivated solely by politics. King had begun to grasp the deeper relationships of economics and poverty, to understand that racism was also a function of national fiscal priorities. "For years I labored with the idea of reforming the existing institutions of the society, a little change here, a little change there," he confessed soon after Chicago. "Now I feel quite differently. I think you've got to have a reconstruction of the entire society, a revolution of values."

To bring about this "revolution of values" he overrode the counsels of intimates and well-wishers and spoke out unequivocally against the Vietnam War at New York's Riverside Church (April 4, 1967). "The Great Society has been shot down on the battlefields of Vietnam," he told the audience. Before 125,000 people massed in United Nations Plaza (April 15), and later at churches and on campuses, King aided pacifists such as Benjamin Spock and Yale's chaplain, William Sloane Coffin, to galvanize protest against the war. In February 1968 he took another controversial step; against overwhelming advice to the contrary (even within SCLC) he inaugurated the Poor People's Campaign which envisaged a trek to Washington of 3,000 disadvantaged blacks, browns, reds, and whites to demand an end to all forms of discrimination and the funding of a $12-billion "Economic Bill of Rights." "We will place the problems of the poor at the seat of government of the wealthiest nation in the history of mankind," King announced. "If that power refuses to acknowledge its debt to the poor, it will have failed to live up to its promise to insure 'life, liberty and the pursuit of happiness' to its citizens."

The stratagem of King's last months was imaginative and bold. He hoped to create a movement "powerful enough, dramatic enough, morally appealing enough, so that people of goodwill, the churches, labor, liberals, intellectuals, students, poor people themselves [would] begin to put pressure on congressmen." A national movement—a coalition of poverty and pacifism—consecrated to stopping a $30-billion-a-year war in order to start a domestic program of intrinsic social and economic reform might have had great impact if King had survived the summer of 1968. Death liquidated the leader but his legacy has been enriched through the years. That legacy is contained in his first civil rights speech, delivered on the eve of the Montgomery Bus Boycott (Dec. 6, 1955): "For many years we have shown amazing patience. We have sometimes given our white brothers the feeling that we liked the way we were being treated. But we come here tonight to be saved from that patience that makes us patient with anything less than freedom and justice."

Impatience with the denial of freedom and justice was King's special legacy. It was not diminished by allegations about his private life, resulting from vindictive electronic surveillance by the FBI under then director J. Edgar Hoover. Among the many memorials are the Martin Luther King, Jr., Public Library in Washington, D.C., and the Martin Luther King, Jr., Center for Social Change in Atlanta. His permanent resting place is on a site adjoining the Ebenezer Baptist Church on Auburn Avenue in Atlanta. He was survived by his mother, father, widow, and their three children. On July 4, 1977, Pres. Jimmy Carter conferred on him posthumously the Medal of Freedom, the nation's highest civilian award.

Lerone Bennett, Jr., in *What Manner of Man?* (1968),

has written a useful history of the early years. Jim Bishop's *Days of Martin Luther King, Jr.* (1971), is exciting, gossipy, and unanalytical. Coretta Scott King's *My Life with Martin Luther King, Jr.* (1969), is indispensable but disappointing. David L. Lewis's *King: A Critical Biography* (1970–1978) is the fullest account to date. Lionel Lokos's *House Divided* (1968) is steadfastly biased against King, but useful if read with care. William Robert Miller's *Martin Luther King, Jr.: His Life, Martyrdom, & Meaning for the World* (1968) is somewhat hagiographic but profitable in tracing King's philosophical and theological formation. Lawrence Reddick's *Crusader Without Violence* (1959) is a very good analysis of the King of the Montgomery Era.

Among the volume of articles and studies on Martin Luther King, Jr., the following are particularly informative: Renata Adler's "Letter from Selma" (*New Yorker,* April 10, 1965, pp. 121–57), James Baldwin's "The Dangerous Road Before Martin Luther King" (*Harper's,* Feb. 1961), David Halberstam's "The Second Coming of Martin Luther King" (*Harper's,* Aug. 1967, pp. 39–51), Julius Lester's "The Martin Luther King I Remember" (*Evergreen,* Jan. 1970), and August Meier's "On the Role of Martin Luther King" (*New Politics,* Winter 1965). — DAVID LEVERING LEWIS

LAFON, THOMY (1810–1893), businessman and philanthropist. He was born in New Orleans, the son of free persons of color. Like many others of his class at that time, much information about his parentage and early life is scanty and conjectural. His mother, Modest Foucher, was probably of Haitian descent; his father was Pierre Laralde, who was either a Frenchman or of French and Negro extraction. Laralde may have deserted Lafon in his childhood; it is not known how he acquired the surname Lafon. He spent his early life in poverty, but managed to acquire enough education to become a schoolteacher. About 1850 he began to operate a small store on Orleans Street. He made loans at advantageous rates and invested in real estate before the Civil War. After the Civil War, he became one of the wealthiest Negro brokers in New Orleans: Lafon, Aristide Mary, and Drosin Macarthy among them owned $253,800 in property. When Lafon died in 1893, his estate was worth almost half a million dollars (John W. Blassingame, *Black New Orleans 1860–1880* [1973], p. 76). His wealth resulted from his shrewd investments, the rapid expansion of New Orleans, especially after 1880, and his frugal style of living.

Although Lafon is best known for his philanthropies, he worked before and during the Civil War with Louis Charles Roudanez, Oscar Dunn, and others in demanding political equality for free people of color in New Orleans (Donald Everett, "Demands of the New Orleans Free Colored Population for Political Equality, 1852–1865," *Louisiana Historical Quarterly,* April 1955, pp. 60–61).

He is said to have donated large sums to the American Anti-Slavery Society and to the Underground Railroad. He contributed to the Catholic Indigent Orphans Institute founded by Madame Bernard Couvent in the early 1830s, and in 1866 gave two lots as a site for the first orphanage of the Louisiana Association for the Benefit of Colored Orphans. His will made provision for his aged sister (he never married) and some friends, but left the bulk of his estate to charitable, educational, and religious institutions in New Orleans. Among them were the Charity Hospital, the Lafon Old Folks Home, the Society of the Holy Family, the Shakespeare Alms House, Straight University, and the Eye, Ear, Nose and Throat Hospital.

A devout Catholic, fluent in French and Spanish, frequently mistaken for a European, a devotee of the arts and music, he cast his lot with his own people, and gave financial aid to the deserving, regardless of race, sex, color, or religion. He died at his home (on the corner of Ursuline and Robertson Streets) and was buried in St. Louis Cemetery on Esplanade Avenue.

His career has not been unrecognized. When the state legislature voted to have his bust executed and placed in New Orleans, Grace King wrote: "It will be the first public testimonial by a state to a man of colour, in recognition of his broad humanitarianism and true-hearted philanthropy" (Grace King, *New Orleans: The Place and the People* [1895], pp. 352–53). Rodolphe Desdunes ended his ode "Thomy Lafon" with the lines "Merci, car en mariant le principe et le bien,/ Aucun nom ne vivra, Lafon, plus que le tien." Ferdinand Rousseve gave this prose translation: "We give thee thanks, for, because thou didst wed principle and good works, no name, Lafon, shall live longer than thine" (*The Negro in Louisiana, Aspects of His History and His Literature,* 1937, pp. 145–46 and ns. 26 and 27). New Orleans has named one of its public schools for him.

There is a brief sketch by J. M. Murphy, "Thomy Lafon," in *NHB* (Oct. 1943, pp. 6, 20). A longer sketch, a warm tribute listing documentary sources, is by Melvin J. White in *DAB* (1932, 1933, 5:546–47).

— RAYFORD W. LOGAN

LANEY, LUCY CRAFT (1854–1933), educator. She was born in Macon, Ga., the seventh of ten children of David and Louisa Laney. David, born a slave in South Carolina, learned the carpenter's trade, purchased his freedom, and in 1836 went to Macon where he was employed to teach his trade to slaves. He was formally ordained a minister in the "Old School" Northern Presbyterian Church, spurning the Southern Presbyterian synod which would have limited his ministry to Negroes. However, he was pastor of a colored church in Savannah, where Lucy spent her early years. Her mother, a slave of the Campbells, a prominent Macon family, married David Laney, who purchased her freedom, thus assuring the freedom of the children.

Lucy received her early training from a daughter of the Campbells, and graduated from the Lewis High School in Macon, later Ballard Normal School. With the aid of the American Missionary Association, she entered the original Atlanta University, graduating in 1873 as one of the four members of its first Higher Normal Department class. From 1873 to 1883 she taught in the public schools of Macon, Milledgeville, Augusta, and Savannah. In the last year, aided by the Presbyterian Board of Missions, she opened a school in a lecture room of the Christ Presbyterian Church, Augusta.

Chartered by the state on Jan. 6, 1886, the school expanded and moved to new quarters, where it encountered numerous difficulties. A trip to the General Assembly of the Presbyterian Church in Minneapolis (1887) led to some financial assistance and a meeting with Francina E. H. Haines, who persuaded others to give financial assistance. Laney named her school the Haines Normal and Industrial Institute. With a contribution of $10,000 from Mrs. Marshall, she constructed the first brick building in 1889. Contributions by other northern benefactors, including Mrs. Anson Phelps Stokes, and institutional support by the Board of the Presbyterian church were inadequate, and Laney had to continue her trips to gain additional financial assistance. Despite many difficulties the school in 1931 had twenty-seven teachers, 300 high school students, and 413 elementary school students, and an income of $25,000. When she died of nephritis and hypertension on Oct. 23, 1933, the *Augusta Chronicle* wrote: "Lucy Laney was great because she loved people. She believed that all God's children had wings, though some of the wings are weak and have never been tried. She could see in the most backward that divine personality which she endeavored to coax into flame." Five thousand Augustans are said to have filed past her bier.

Haines Institute was essentially the "lengthened shadow" of Lucy Laney. Since Negro public high schools were few even in large southern cities until after World War I, she set high standards for teachers, which enabled pupils to continue their higher education. She herself took summer courses at the University of Chicago. She is credited with opening Augusta's first kindergarten and a nurse training department which evolved into the school of nursing at Augusta's University Hospital. She urged Negro writers to go to the Sea Islands of Georgia and South Carolina to "study the Negro in his original purity, with a culture close to the African."

Her greatest contribution consisted of the influence on her students and teachers. One of her later most distinguished students was John Hope; she was "the inspirer of John with his first love of the classics." Mary McLeod Bethune began her teaching career at Haines Institute. Graduates sent their children to Haines and made contributions for its support.

The institute began to decline during the Great Depression: the Presbyterian church withdrew its support and private contributions dwindled. It is also possible that the development of public schools in Augusta was a factor in its demise: the institute was closed in 1949 and its building razed.

Appreciation of her stature as an educator and a spokesman for the dignity of Negroes is seen in the Lucy C. Laney High School, on the site of the institute, and a painting in the State House in Atlanta.

Three of the principal sources for her career are Mary White Ovington's *Portraits in Color* (1927, pp. 53–63), Sadie I. Daniel's *Women Builders* (1931, pp. 1–27, with photograph), and Benjamin Brawley's *Negro Builders and Heroes* (1937, pp. 279–82). The most convenient recent scholarly treatment is Sadie Daniel St. Clair's biographical sketch in *NAW* (1971, 2:365–67). — RAYFORD W. LOGAN

LANGSTON, CHARLES (1817–1892), abolitionist, educator, and reformer. Langston was born in Louisa County, Va., the second son of Capt. Ralph Quarles, a white plantation owner, and a part-Indian, part-Negro freedwoman, Lucy Langston. The other children born of this union were brothers Gideon Quarles Langston and John Mercer Langston, and a sister Maria. Charles was also half-brother of William, Harriet, and Mary Langston, born to his mother Lucy before her move into Captain Quarles's home. In his early life he was educated by his father. He and his brother Gideon were the first Negroes enrolled in the preparatory department of Oberlin College (1835–1836), defraying a part of their expenses by performing manual labor for the college. He taught school for several years and again attended the preparatory department of Oberlin College (1841–1844). From then until 1858 he participated in abolitionist and political activities. In 1858 he gained national prominence by his participation in the rescue of a fugitive slave. He helped recruit colored soldiers during the Civil War, but his age prevented him from enlisting. After the war he married Mary Sampson Leary, the widow of Lewis S. Leary who had been killed in John Brown's raid on Harpers Ferry in 1859. (Their daughter, Carolina Langston Hughes, was the mother of Langston Hughes.) Langston participated actively in politics, education, and business in Kansas until his death of chronic stomach trouble in Lawrence. Funeral services were held at the Lawrence A.M.E. Church.

After the death of his parents when he was a teenager, young Langston received a generous inheritance and in 1834 his freedom papers, along with those of his brothers Gideon and John. Arriving in Chillicothe, Ohio, in the late fall of 1834, Charles and Gideon found accommodations for themselves and took John to live with Col. William D. Gooch, who had been appointed an executor of the Quarles estate and legal guardian for the children. After his year at Oberlin (1835–1836), he helped establish and taught in a school for Negro children in Chillicothe. He began his civil rights activities as a member of the executive committee which edited the *Palladium of Liberty* in Columbus, Ohio, established and published (1842–1843) by David Jenkins. Langston served also as a sales agent for the paper. At the State Colored Convention in Columbus in September 1844 he proposed repeal of Ohio's Black Laws, to provide equal education for Negro children in public schools, prohibition, and increased opportunities for home ownership. (The laws were not finally repealed until 1887.) In politics he supported the Liberty party. Although he did not receive a degree from Oberlin, he urged his brother to graduate from the college and the theological school. In the mid-1840s Charles and Martin R. Delany, abolitionist and author, barely escaped with their lives in Marseilles, Ohio, from a white mob which shouted "Kill the niggers."

At the Colored National Convention in Cleveland (1848), Langston served on the Business and Organization Committee and was appointed to the National Central Committee. During the same year he was appointed deputy most worthy patriarch for the West of the national organization the Sons of Temperance. The following year he played a key role in the organization of the convention movement in Ohio, the "most continuous, energetic and aggressive of black state convention movements" in the United States. In 1850 Langston aided in the formation of the Ohio Colored American League. His proposal for a Negro newspaper, for which he was chosen editor, had to wait several years. At the Ohio Constitutional Convention of 1851 he urged delegates to strike the word "white" from its constitution and at the State Colored Convention he denounced the Fugitive Slave Act of 1850 and suggested that slaves arise and claim their liberties.

He taught school and became principal of the Columbus Colored Schools in 1856. He and David Jenkins also operated a hotel. Langston organized the St. Marks Masonic Lodge in 1852, served as its first worshipful master until 1855, and later became deputy grand master in the statewide organization. In July 1853, Langston, George B. Vashon, and Charles L. Reason, as members of the Manual Labor Committee of the Colored National Convention in Rochester, N.Y., suggested the establishment of an institution with emphasis on agriculture, mathematics, and training in various trades. Although there was no immediate response to the suggestion, Wilberforce University, Wilberforce, Ohio, was established in 1856 by the Methodist Episcopal church as a response to such a suggestion.

He became increasingly active in the abolition movement, serving as recording secretary and business agent of the Ohio Anti-Slavery Society in 1853. Long a conductor on the Underground Railroad in Lorain County, Ohio, he was one of two men convicted in the rescue of a fugitive slave, John Price (Sept. 1858). The Oberlin-Wellington Rescue, which became one of the best known of similar efforts, won widespread acclaim and sympathy for Langston. Among the courtroom observers was John Brown, who attempted for several months to enlist Langston for the planned raid on Harpers Ferry. Langston successfully denied charges of complicity in the raid. Brown's martyrdom led Langston to declare in a memorial speech: "I never thought that I should ever join in doing honor [to] or to mourning any white man."

In Kansas, where Langston and his family resided after the Civil War, he advocated Negro suffrage, and to a lesser degree, votes for women. In 1872 he became principal of the Colored Normal School at Quindaro, the successor to Freedmans University, founded by the A.M.E. church. After less than a year he became a farmer and owner of a grocery store in Kansas. In September 1872 the Republican State Congressional Convention at Lawrence nominated him as a presidential elector. He ran third in a field of five, receiving 66,805 votes. He continued his connections with the Masonic order, addressing a state reunion at Topeka in 1875.

During April 1880 Langston presided over a Convention of Colored Men held in Topeka which advocated changes in the Refugee Relief Board that dispensed aid to Negro migrants to Kansas. The convention also urged support of the national Republican party. In September another Convention of Colored Men demanded the presence of Negro candidates on the Republican ticket. A long and heated debate at the convention led to a proposal for the nomination of Langston for lieutenant-governor. However, the convention reconsidered their position and withdrew Langston's name. Another Convention of Colored Men at Topeka in 1882 appointed Langston to the committee on order of business and repeated the demand for Negro candidates. Four years later he switched from the Republican to the Prohibition party and received the party nomination for state auditor. In 1892, at the age of seventy-three, Langston died at Lawrence, Kans. He was survived by his brother, John M., who died in 1897, and several nephews and nieces.

The most complete account of Charles Langston's youth is found in John Mercer Langston's *From Virginia Plantation to the National Capitol* (1894). Langston's support of Negro rights is most completely documented in *Minutes of the State Conventions of Colored Citizens of Ohio;* in *Minutes of the Proceedings of the National Negro Conventions: 1830–1864,* edited by Howard H. Bell (1969); and in Jacob R. Shipherd's *History of the Oberlin-Wellington Rescue* (1859). His relationship with the Masonic order is detailed in William H. Parham's *An Official History of the Most Worshipful Grand Lodge Free and Accepted Masons* (1906). His collegiate background is found in the *General Catalogue of Oberlin College, 1833–1908* (1909). The Oberlin College Archives provide data on Langston's academic, marital, and genealogical background. William E. Bigglestone's "Straightening a Fold in the Record" (*Oberlin Alumni Magazine,* May-June 1972) asserts that the Langston brothers were the first Negro students to enter Oberlin rather than James Bradley. The *Cleveland Plain Dealer* and *Cleveland Leader* provide comprehensive coverage of the Oberlin-Wellington rescue and Langston's role in the antislavery movement. Summary information on Langston's involvement in Kansas politics and education is available in several editions of Daniel W. Wilders's *The Annals of Kansas* (1886). — FRANK R. LEVSTIK

LANGSTON, JOHN MERCER (1829–1897), educator, diplomat, and politician. He was born in Louisa Court House, Louisa County, Va., the son of Capt. Ralph Quarles, a white plantation owner, and Lucy Langston, of both Indian and Negro descent. The youngest of four children (sister Mary, brothers Gideon and Charles), he also had a half-brother William and a half-sister Harriet, born to Lucy Langston before she moved into Captain Quarles's plantation house. After both parents died in 1834 he was taken to the home of Col. William D. Gooch, a special friend of his late father who had promised to look after and educate him. Gooch's daughter Victoria began his education, which was continued in the public schools of Chillicothe, Ohio, at the Baker Street Baptist Church in Cincinnati, again in Chillicothe under George B. Vashon, the first colored graduate (1844) of Oberlin College. Encouraged by Vashon, young Langston entered the college preparatory department in 1844; he received his B.A. degree in 1849 and his M.A. degree in 1852. He entered the Theology Department in that year, thus becoming, according to his own account, the first Negro student to enter a theological school in the United States. His real desire, however, was to practice law. Unable to gain admission to a law school, he read law under Judge Philemon Bliss

in Elyria, Ohio, and was admitted to the bar in September 1854. On Oct. 25, 1854, he married Caroline M. Wall, then a senior in the Literary Department of Oberlin College. He practiced law in Brownhelm (where he was elected town clerk in 1855, perhaps the first such position held by an American Negro) and Oberlin, and continued his activities in the Conventions of Colored Citizens and antislavery societies. He declined an offer of John Brown in 1859 to accompany him on his journey to Harpers Ferry. He served as town clerk, secretary of the Board of Education, and visitor of schools in Oberlin, and was elected to the Board of Education in 1860. During the Civil War he helped recruit colored soldiers, especially for the 54th and 55th Massachusetts and 5th Ohio Regiments. During 1868–1869 as an inspector-general of the Freedmen's Bureau, he was favorably received in many sections of the South by both whites and Negroes.

He took charge of the newly opened Law Department of Howard University on Jan. 6, 1869, served as its dean (1870–1873), and vice-president and acting president of the University (1873–1875). For seven years he was a member of the Board of Health of the District of Columbia, and its attorney. From 1877 to 1885 he was resident minister and consul-general in Haiti and chargé d'affaires in the Dominican Republic. He was president of Virginia Normal and Collegiate Institute, Petersburg, Va. (1885–1887). In 1890 he won a contested election to the House of Representatives, the only Negro to date elected from Virginia. Defeated for reelection, he returned to his home, Hillside Cottage, Fourth and Bryant Streets NW, Washington, where he died of apoplexy on Nov. 15, 1897, and was buried in Woodlawn Cemetery, Washington, D.C. He was survived by one daughter, Nettie (Mrs. James C. Napier), three sons, Arthur, Ralph E., Frank Mercer, and several grandchildren.

In the late fall of 1840 an antiabolitionist mob seized and destroyed the press of the *Philanthropist,* an antislavery newspaper published in Cincinnati. While young Langston escaped harm, the violence made "a lasting impression on him." On the other hand he was befriended not only by Colonel Gooch but also by the family of Prof. George Whipple, in whose home he boarded while a student at Oberlin. He was reminded, however, that outside the favorable atmosphere of Oberlin he was "only another Negro": on March 1, 1845, he was denied lodging in the Neil House, the major hotel in Columbus, because "We do not entertain *niggers!*" Denied admission to a law school at Ballston Spa, N.Y., and one in Cincinnati, he read law with Judge Philemon Bliss and lived in the family home. Judge Bliss helped Langston pass the bar examination in 1854 by pointing out that under Ohio law, Langston was a "white man" and thus not denied the right to practice law by the Black Laws of the state. Four years later Langston witnessed the famous Oberlin-Wellington Rescue case for which his brother Charles, one of two men convicted of participation in the rescue, served a sentence of twenty days in jail and paid a fine of $100.

Meanwhile his participation as speaker and official in the State Convention of Colored Citizens of Ohio, the

Colored National Convention at Rochester, N.Y., in July 1853, the Ohio Anti-Slavery League, and the American Anti-Slavery Society, which he addressed in May 1854, helped to gain him wider recognition not only in the antislavery cause, but also as an advocate of colored schools with colored teachers in Ohio and the importance of engaging in commerce. He changed from espousing emigration as late as 1852, because of the "natural repelancy" between the races, to opposition in 1854 and belief in an integrated society in the United States.

At the same time he continued his practice of law which became increasingly extensive and lucrative. His most famous case resulted in the acquittal, for lack of evidence, of Edmonia Lewis, a Negro student at Oberlin College who had been accused of poisoning one of her white roommates (1862). Miss Lewis later won international renown for her sculpture.

Langston's increased stature was recognized in 1864 when he was elected president of the National Equal Rights League, an early forerunner of the Niagara Movement, (organized by W. E. B. Du Bois in 1905 to oppose the conservative policies of Booker T. Washington) and the NAACP. From 1865 to 1867 one of the themes of his addresses was "Citizenship and the Ballot," supporting Negro suffrage on the grounds of loyalty and devotion to the Union. As inspector-general of the Freedmen's Bureau beginning in 1867, he visited North Carolina, South Carolina, Louisiana, Alabama, and Georgia, advocating wider educational and occupational opportunities for freedmen. He was enthusiastically welcomed by colored residents of his birthplace, Louisa Court House, Va., and entertained by some of the leading white citizens. But a few days earlier the proprietor of the only Republican hotel in Leesburg, Va., refused to serve him and his white friends in the public dining room for fear that the hotel would be destroyed by fire as soon as Langston and his friends left town. For one of the few times, Langston accepted dinner service in his room with only one of his white friends.

In October 1868 Langston founded and organized the Law Department of Howard University and took charge of it when classes formally began on Jan. 6, 1869. He terminated his connection with the Freedmen's Bureau but continued other interests. He addressed the Colored National Labor Convention, called by Isaac Myers in Washington (Dec. 1869). His criticism of Democrats for hurting the chances of the Republican party led to his being denied admittance to the 1870 meeting of the Colored National Labor Union, but he did address its 1871 meeting, dwelling mainly on politics. He accepted appointment by General Grant in 1871 to the Board of Health of the District of Columbia, a post he held until October 1877. In 1872 he was elected a member of the Board of Trustees of the Freedmen's Savings and Trust Company and of its Finance Committee. He opposed in vain the appointment of commissioners to replace the trustees when the bank was forced to close in June 1874. Langston presided at the unveiling of the monument to Abraham Lincoln in Lincoln Square, Washington, D.C. (April 14, 1876).

Langston's tenure as dean of the Law Department of Howard University marked the graduation of the first law class (Feb. 3, 1871) and the second (July 30, 1871). In 1872 Charlotte E. Ray received her diploma and is traditionally referred to as the first woman in the United States to graduate from a regular nonprofit law school, and also the first woman admitted to practice law before the U.S. Supreme Court. Several of the male graduates achieved recognition as lawyers and government officials.

Langston's tenure as vice-president and acting president of Howard University, and the circumstances leading to his forced resignation on July 2, 1875, have been a source of controversy, due in part to Langston's account. The following summary is based on the Minutes of the Board of Trustees and of its Executive Committee. After he was elected vice-president of the university on Dec. 1, 1873, he encountered opposition to the definition of his authority and responsibility. This opposition was spearheaded by Amzi L. Barber, a white member of the board who aspired to be vice-president and who was involved in some shady real estate operations that were costly to the university. In response to Langston's request for clarification of his authority, the board voted on Dec. 27, 1873, that he possessed the same authority as did Pres. Oliver O. Howard whose frequent absences necessitated a vice-president. When General Howard resigned, the board on Dec. 25, 1874, considered five nominees to succeed him, one of whom was Langston. At this meeting the resignation of Langston was received. He refused to accede to requests that he withdraw his resignation, and the board was notified on Jan. 12, 1875, that he had consented to serve as acting president for the rest of the school year.

On June 16, 1875, he renewed his resignation as vice-president and dean of the Law Department (on Dec. 25, 1874, he had resigned only as vice-president). The board voted to lay Langston's resignation on the table and to proceed to the election of a president. Frederick Douglass received one vote, Langston four, and George Whipple, who had befriended Langston at Oberlin College and who had received ten votes, was declared elected president of the university. Langston wrote in his autobiography: "It is due to all concerned that it be stated that every colored trustee voted for Mr. Langston, while every white one voted for Mr. Whipple."

On July 2, 1875, the Executive Committee voted unanimously: "Resolved, That the resignation of J. M. Langston, LL.D, as Vice President of the University and Dean of the Law Department tendered December 25, 1874, and renewed verbally on the 16th day of June, 1875, be and is hereby accepted." Only three members of the Executive Committee, all white, were present. One of them, Edward P. Smith, on Dec. 16, 1875, was elected president, since Whipple had resigned on July 12, 1875.

While Langston's praise of his administration showed his usual lack of modesty, he did not deserve the shabby treatment inflicted upon him. "His leadership enabled the University to survive its most severe financial crisis" and he "ably guided the University through retrenchments and fund-raising and also managed its real estate and investments."

After leaving Howard University, Langston delivered addresses in several cities, emphasizing the value of Negro support for the Republican party, and the importance of educational and intellectual activities. In September 1887 Pres. Rutherford B. Hayes, whose candidacy he had supported, nominated him resident minister and consul-general to Haiti, and chargé d'affaires to the Dominican Republic. His dispatches, many of them summarized in his autobiography, revealed his disillusionment about economic conditions in Haiti, the recurrent revolutions, the problem of asylum in the residences of diplomats, and the unsuccessful offer of Pres. Étienne Félicité Salomon of the Bay and a part of Môle St. Nicolas to the United States in 1883. At the same time he reported the potential designs of France, Britain, and Italy on the independence of Haiti.

He served also as the West Indies attorney for John Wanamaker and Company of Philadelphia. According to established practice, he submitted his resignation following the election of Pres. Grover Cleveland in 1884. After its acceptance in July 1885, he returned to the United States and brought suit against the United States for back pay, which was approved by the U.S. Supreme Court.

Virginia Normal and Collegiate Institute experienced great growth, improvement, and interracial goodwill under his presidency from December 1885 to Dec. 23, 1887, according to Langston's account. When Democrats gained control of Virginia and the institute's Board of Visitors, Langston resigned and soon began his campaign for the U.S. House of Representatives from the 4th Congressional District. Despite opposition from Gen. William Mahone, head of the Republican party in Virginia, and from Frederick Douglass, Langston won the nomination. He also attended the Republican National Convention as a delegate from Virginia, throwing his support to the nomination of John Sherman as a presidential candidate. On Election Day in November 1888, he faced a Democratic opponent and a candidate of the Mahone faction of the Republican party. By the means of ballot-box chicanery, Langston's Democratic opponent won by a plurality of 641 votes. Langston persisted in his efforts to gain the seat to which he had been elected, his seating being decided by a vote of the U.S. House of Representatives on Sept. 23, 1890. He retained his seat until March 3, 1891. While in the House, he served on the Education Committee, drawing up legislation calling for a National Industrial University for Colored Youth, but the session ended before action was taken on it. He made speeches to provide for the observance of February 12 and April 27 as national holidays to commemorate the anniversaries of Presidents Lincoln and Grant. He denounced the harassment of Negro voters in the South and requested information about action on the Voting Enforcement Act of May 31, 1870. Although he urged restricting the vote for federal office to those citizens who could read and write English, he was one of the very few members of Congress who called for the enforcement of Section 2 of the Fourteenth Amendment which required reduction in the number of representatives in proportion to those denied the right to vote. He was also disappointed in his effort to make two appointments to the U.S. Naval Academy. Although barren of results, he revealed during his very short term an understanding of some of the basic flaws in American society as far as Negroes were concerned.

Renominated for the Fifty-Second Congress, he failed of reelection. He did serve, however, as a delegate to the 1892 Republican National Convention. Nominated for the Fifty-Third Congress, he refused the candidacy.

It is difficult to evaluate the legacy of Langston. One of his significant intellectual legatees was John Hope, who heard him deliver the speech at Brown University in 1890 and perhaps received "a kindling of the flame which he was to carry forward to another generation" as president of Atlanta Baptist College, Morehouse College, and the new Atlanta University (Ridgely Torrence, *The Story of John Hope* [1948], pp. 92–93). The Colored and Normal University in Oklahoma Territory, founded in 1897, was later named Langston University in his honor.

The principal source is his self-serving autobiography, *From the Virginia Plantation to the Nation's Capitol,* written in the third person (1894, reprint 1969). His career at Howard University is developed in Rayford W. Logan's *Howard University: The First Hundred Years, 1867–1967* (1969, esp. pp. 48, 62–81); his career in Haiti is in Logan's *The Diplomatic Relations of the United States with Haiti, 1776–1891* (1941, esp. pp. 370–80). The brief sketch by Raymond C. Miller in *DAB* (Part 2, 5:597–98), asserts that in his autobiography Langston "told with real charm the story of his dramatic and useful life." Samuel Denny Smith wrote an extraordinary *non-sequitur* when he asserted that Langston's bitterness, "in the opinion of some, . . . was directly responsible for a great increase" after 1888 in the number of "Negro rapes of white women with resultant lynchings" (*The Negro in Congress, 1870–1901,* 1940, p. 117). *Freedom and Citizenship: Selected Lectures of Hon. John Mercer Langston* (1883), compiled by the Rev. J. E. Rankin, presents an excellent survey of Langston's position on issues of importance to Negroes in nineteenth-century America. Other articles of Langston's authorship can be found in Julia Griffith's *Autographs For Freedom* (1854), and the January 1859 issue of *The Anglo-African Magazine. Minutes of the Proceedings of the National Negro Conventions 1830–1864* (1969), edited by Howard H. Bell, documents Langston's role in this particular movement. For his activities in Ohio's convention movements, *Minutes of the State Convention of the Colored Citizens of Ohio* (1849–1860) should be consulted. The Oberlin College years are surveyed in Robert S. Fletcher's multivolume *A History of Oberlin College* (1943). Files of the *Cleveland Leader* and the *Lorain County News* provide a broad coverage of his pre-Reconstruction years. A comprehensive account of Langston's life is William F. Cheek's unpublished dissertation, "Forgotten Prophet: The Life of John Mercer Langston" (University of Virginia, 1961). — FRANK R. LEVSTIK

LANUSSE, ARMAND (1812–1867), soldier, poet, author, and educator. He was born and died in New

Orleans. According to Rodolphe Lucien Desdunes in his work *Nos Hommes et Notre Histoire* (1911), Lanusse was educated in his native city and not in Paris as asserted by Edward Larocque Tinker. The only view Lanusse had of France, stated Desdunes, was through the prism of his imagination. He was the first elected principal of the Bernard Couvent Institute for Indigent Catholic Orphans when it opened in New Orleans in 1852, and he remained on the faculty until 1866, the year prior to his death. The orphans school was located at Grands Hommes and Union Streets. He was assisted in the early years by Joanni Questy, Constant Reynes, and Joseph Vigneaux-Lavigne. Lanusse so resented slavery and racial injustice that he directed this school for colored children in the deep South despite the hostility of whites, with his life in jeopardy for promoting Negro education.

One of New Orleans's most intelligent Creoles of Color, a lover of the classics and an excellent teacher, Lanusse exposed his students to the writings of La Fontaine, Boileau, Fénelon, Racine, and Corneille, making them true inheritors of the best French literature. Lanusse was loved and revered by both his co-workers and his pupils for his efforts. He was not only a true gentleman but an outstanding leader and patriot. Easily capable of passing as a white person, of distinguished demeanor and handsome bearing, Lanusse preferred to remain true to his origin, namely, a Creole of Color. His origin was more important to him than the fact that he was an American and a Louisianian.

To Lanusse all men were equal, all men deserved equal respect and equal recognition. There was no partisanship in his philosophy of man. And Lanusse expected this same recognition for his compatriots. Therefore, he stressed in his writings the necessity and the importance of peaceful living, of kind relationships, and the recognition of the dignity of the individual. Lanusse was an idealist more than a realist and suffered at times when his aspirations fell short of full realization. On the other hand Lanusse inherited a violent temper against flagrant wrongs.

Lanusse endeavored to identify himself with the underprivileged. Shunning luxury even though he could have enjoyed to some degree a life of affluence, he preferred simplicity of living, in demeanor and in dress.

The antebellum decades from 1820 to 1861 constituted a golden age of Louisiana literature, and during this period a large number of Creoles of color had amassed wealth and had enjoyed the benefits of a splendid education in France. Charles Testut so appreciated the writings of the *gens de couleur libres,* such as Armand Lanusse, that he included him and Joanni Questy, as well as Camille Thierry, in his *Portraits Littéraires* (1850), along with fifty-two other authors. As the Rev. Charles E. O'Neill, S.J., points out in his introduction to *Our People and Our History,* many French-language writers of nineteenth-century Louisiana were partly of African ancestry. Among them were poets, journalists, and dramatists.

In 1845 Lanusse launched *Les Cenelles,* the first anthology of Negro verse published in America. In this work of 215 pages there are eighty-two poems, the

work of seventeen Creoles of Color. In addition *Les Cenelles* contains several selections by Victor Hugo, Lamennais, and Lamartine. Among the seventeen poets featured are Joanni Questy, Victor Séjour, Monsieur A. P. (presumably A. P. Desdunes, brother of Rodolphe L. Desdunes), Armand Lanusse himself, and his brother Numa Lanusse. Edward Maceo Coleman in his *Creole Voices* (centenary edition, 1945, p. xiii) asserts that these poets had as their chief guides Lamartine and Béranger. Lanusse declared in his poem ''Besoin d'écrire'' that he had early turned to Lamartine's ''pure and lively flame.'' The title of the little volume, *Les Cenelles,* is symbolic of the modesty and the beauty of the small pink and white blossoms that grace the thorny hawthorn shrub which bears a fruit of sparkling white berries. The book includes subjects that depict nature, love, the sea, life, death, joy, optimism, sadness, and topics of local interest. Lanusse wrote its dedication and its introduction and he contributed eighteen poems. As editor he commended his compatriots for their talent, ambition, fervor, and persevering effort that yielded such a remarkable harvest.

Lanusse likewise contributed columns to the newspapers *L'Union* and *La Tribune* of New Orleans, particularly during the Civil War when he wrote in defense of his people. Possibly he was somewhat rash when, as a conscripted soldier in the Confederate Army, he refused to fly the Union flag over the Bernard Couvent School. But this action was most probably prompted by resentment over any public action at a time when political matters were in such a state of flux. Later he recanted these ideas and gave full loyalty to the Union cause and to freedom of the slaves. Lanusse contributed likewise to *L'Album Littéraire,* whose first appearance in 1843 was the first recorded literary publication issued by Louisiana free people of color. This short-lived review, published by J. L. Marciacq with the assistance of Armand Lanusse, was the springboard for future and greater ventures by the *gens de couleur libres* in literary endeavors.

Through his own efforts and study, Lanusse acquired a vast store of knowledge. His poems reflect a singular charm; his prose indicates especially the influence of such scholars as Noel, Chapsal, Poitevin, Lefranc, and Bescherelles.

Principal sources for the life of Lanusse are Rodolphe Lucien Desdunes's *Nos Hommes et Notre Histoire* (1911), translated by Dorothea Olga McCants, D.C., as *Our People and Our History* (1973, pp. ix, 6, 10, 11, 13, 14–25, 53); and Charles Barthelemy Rousséve's *The Negro in Louisiana: Aspects of His History and His Literature* (1937, pp. 43, 56–58, 63–70), with two of his poems (pp. 178–179).

— DOROTHEA OLGA MCCANTS, D.C.

LATIMER, LEWIS H[OWARD] (1848–1928), inventor, poet, musician, author, artist, and civil rights activist. He was born in Chelsea, Mass., on Sept. 4, 1848, the son of a slave who had escaped from Virginia and gone to Boston. William Lloyd Garrison, Frederick Douglass, and other abolitionists secured the funds to purchase his father's freedom. When Lewis was ten years old, his father disappeared, leaving his mother with four children. Lewis was sent to a farm school for boys and was later joined by his brother William. Escaping, they went to Boston and helped support the family, Lewis selling copies of Garrison's paper *The Liberator*. Lewis enlisted in the Union Navy and saw action on the James River aboard the U.S.S. *Massasoit*.

Honorably discharged in 1865, he found after many disappointments a job as office boy in the firm of Crosby and Gould, patent solicitors. Purchasing a set of secondhand drafting tools and reading available books, Latimer asked his employers to permit him to do some drawings. The request was grudgingly granted and he was given a desk with an increase in pay. The office where he was employed was located near the school where Alexander Graham Bell was conducting experiments on a telephone. They became friends and Bell, according to contemporaries of Latimer, asked him to draw each part of the telephone that Bell was perfecting, to illustrate how it worked. When the drawing and the machine were completed, Bell was granted a patent in 1876.

In 1880 Latimer was employed by the United States Electric Lighting Company, Bridgeport, Conn., where he worked with Hiram S. Maxim. Latimer invented carbon filaments for the Maxim electric incandescent lamp and obtained a patent for it in 1881; he also invented a cheap method for making the filaments. Maxim and an associate raised money to set up factories to manufacture Latimer's inventions, which were used in railroad stations in the United States, Canada, and other countries.

He began his association with Thomas A. Edison in 1883, serving as engineer, chief draftsman, and expert witness on the Board of Patent Control in gathering evidence against the infringement of patents held by Westinghouse and General Electric. Latimer was one of those who responded in 1918 to the initial call that led to the formation of the Edison Pioneers; he was the only colored member. A "Statement of the Edison Pioneers" on the occasion of his death ended: "Broad-mindedness, versatility in the accomplishment of things intellectual and cultural, a linguist, a devoted husband and father, all were characteristics of him, and his genial presence will be missed from our gatherings" (Dec. 11, 1928).

Latimer's *Poems of Love and Life,* a booklet of twenty-five pages, was privately printed and published by his friends and admirers on the seventy-seventh anniversary of his birthday in 1925. More important was his book of 140 pages, *Incandescent Electric Lighting: A Practical Description of the Edison System. . . .* Published, with illustrations, in 1890, it was a pioneer work on the subject.

In 1895 a letter by Latimer stated that colored Americans were looking to the best interests of their country when they protested against crime and injustice inflicted upon any class or condition of citizenship. In 1906 he taught mechanical drawing to immigrants at the Henry Street Settlement in New York City.

On Dec. 10, 1873, he married Mary Wilson, who became the mother of their two children, Louise Rebecca and Emma Jeanette. He died in Flushing, N.Y., on Dec. 11, 1928. On May 10, 1968, the Lewis H.

Latimer public school in Brooklyn was named in his honor.

Brief biographies are *The Story of Louis Latimer: Manual and Study Guide,* by Negro History Associates (1964); *Eight Black American Inventors,* by Robert C. Hayden (1972, pp. 78–92); *Black Pioneers of Science and Invention,* by Louis Haber (1970, pp. 49–60); and *The Hidden Contributors: Black Scientists and Inventors in America,* by Aaron E. Klein (1971, pp. 97–108).

— JOHN HENRIK CLARKE

LAWSON, RAYMOND AUGUSTUS (1875–1959), concert pianist and teacher. He was born on March 23, 1875, in Shelbyville, Ky., one of two children of Lewis and Mary Lawson. He began the study of music at an early age; at ten he was organist in a Baptist church. With the encouragement of George McClellan, who was responsible for sending over 500 young men to Fisk University, Lawson's family transferred the young pianist to the Fisk Academy. He remained at Fisk to complete the college course in music (1895) and to receive his B.A. degree (1896), the first person in the history of the university to complete both courses of study. He was greatly inspired by his piano teacher Mary Chamberlin, who was also to teach his gifted son Warner many years later. In the summer of 1895 McClellan arranged several concerts for Lawson in New England. Mrs. Charles Dudley Warner, wife of the writer and herself a musician, heard him and was so impressed by his talent that she offered him scholarship aid to attend the Hartford Conservatory of Music.

Lawson began his long teaching career in 1896 with a studio in the old Hartford Life Insurance Building; at the same time he entered upon three years of study with Edward Noyes, head of the piano department at the Conservatory. Upon completion of this study (1899) Lawson was presented by Hartford's Memnon Club in a joint recital with Harry T. Burleigh, baritone soloist of St. George's Episcopal Church of New York City. In June 1902 Lawson married Ida Napier, niece of James Carroll Napier, who was register of the United States Treasury during the Taft administration. Ida Lawson continued her musical activities in joint concerts with her husband and as director of the Open Door Community Chorus. She was also soprano soloist at Talcott Congregational Church where Lawson was organist and choir director for over thirty years. Four children were born to them: Warner (1903), Grace (1904), Rosalind (1906), and Elizabeth (1909).

Lawson had a distinguished career as a concert pianist. He chose, however, to devote most of his energy to building what was considered to be one of the finest piano studios in New England. He died on Feb. 8, 1959, a much honored and revered citizen of Hartford.

Lawson's success as a concert pianist was not simply unusual for one of his race but outstanding by any standard. His training included tutoring in Munich (1911) by the pianist Ossip Gabrilowitsch, who provided a letter of introduction to another famous pianist, Theodor Leschetizky. Upon hearing Lawson play in Vienna, Leschetizky is quoted as saying "Americans generally have technique; Mr. Lawson has poetry." In 1911 and again in 1918 Lawson was soloist in the G-minor piano concerto of Saint-Saens with the Hartford Philharmonic Society, Howard N. Prutting conductor. Both times he was received with enthusiasm by sell-out houses and with overwhelmingly favorable reviews by music critics.

Lawson gave recitals in many cities, including Springfield, New Haven, Boston, New York, Philadelphia, Washington, D.C., Indianapolis, Memphis, and Louisville; there were also joint appearances with Roland Hayes, Marian Anderson, William Richardson, Harry T. Burleigh, and others. He performed frequently on Negro college campuses, favoring, of course, Fisk University. Music critics such as Phillip Hale *(Boston Herald)* and Olin Downes *(Boston Post)* praised his sensitive, poetic, and technically outstanding performances. Very important to him were the Monday-morning musicales sponsored by Mrs. C. D. Warner, who had become his close friend and musical collaborator. On these occasions Lawson and Mrs. Warner played piano concertos together for invited guests, a practice which continued until her death. Through several joint recitals the two collected considerable sums of money for war-devastated France and Poland. Paderewski, upon hearing of this, arranged to meet Lawson and became his friend.

Lawson taught thousands of students, most of them white. Ironically, he prepared some to fill positions in leading conservatories from which he would have been barred because of his race. The recitals of his students, which constituted a significant part of the musical life of Hartford, were given regular press coverage and drew capacity audiences. Most notable were those at which a single advanced student was presented annually in Unity Hall before an audience of 500. His students organized the Pianoforte Club in 1928 and instituted a remarkable series of recitals in which Lawson himself performed with his students until the early 1950s. Among his students were his daughter Rosalind, later an associate professor of sociology at the University of Hartford, and his son Warner, who became a concert pianist, and as dean of the School of Music at Howard University, conductor of its internationally famous choir.

Endowed with an extraordinary capacity for loyalty, friendship, and kindness, Lawson retained strong ties with many of his students and with all who befriended him as a young pianist. He enjoyed association with Clarence Cameron White, Samuel Colendge-Taylor, Nathaniel Dett (whose *Enchantment Suite* he gave its first performance for the National Association of Negro Musicians in 1922), Harry T. Burleigh, and Roland Hayes.

Lawson was honored not only by Hartford but also across the nation. In Hartford he was elected to the honorary board of the Philharmonic Society; was invited to be a judge for the instrumental scholarship competition of the Hartford School of Music; was a charter member and later president of the Hartford Instrumental Music Foundation, Inc. (a group interested in the redevelopment of the instrumental program in the public schools). The citizens of Hartford referred to him as the "Dean of Hartford Teachers of Piano" in recognition of the great stimulus he provided to music in that city. He served as a judge of musicians selected to compete for the Harmon awards (1926–1928). Howard University conferred upon him the honorary degree of Doctor of Music in 1930; later the chapter of Pi Kappa Lambda (honorary music fraternity) of that university made him an honorary member. Fisk University featured his achievements in its exhibit at the 1940 American Negro Exposition in Chicago; in 1951 Lawson also received the alumni award from his alma mater. The National Association of Negro Musicians elected him to its board of directors in 1922 and honored him in 1939, along with H. T. Burleigh, Lulu V. Childers, and Harriet Gibbs Marshall, for his exceptional achievement in the field of music over a period of forty years and for his role as a teacher of young musicians.

Short biographical statements on Lawson are included in *Famous Modern Negro Musicians* by Penman Lovingood (1921) and in *The Negro's Contribution to Music* by Maude W. Layne (1942). Numerous references to Lawson and his students may be found in issues of the Hartford newspapers from 1900 to 1959.
— DORIS E. MCGINTY

LAYTON, JOHN TURNER (1849–1916), music educator and hymn composer. Little is known of his early life, except that he was born in New Jersey. He studied music at the Cardiff and Collins Institute, Round Lake Conservatory, Martha's Vineyard, the New England Conservatory, and privately in Washington, D.C. During the Civil War, Layton served in the armed services. After the war he went to Washington, D.C., where he was a policeman for a few years before he began teaching music in the public schools in 1883. Later he was appointed the first male director of music for the colored schools. In 1873 Layton became the choir director at the Metropolitan A.M.E. Church, a post he retained for forty-three years. In 1902 he helped to organize the (Samuel) Coleridge-Taylor Choral Society and served as its director until his death.

One of Layton's significant accomplishments was his contribution to the 1897 Hymnal of the A.M.E. church, which was the eleventh edition since 1818 but the first to include music. In 1895 Layton had proposed to the Bishops' Council at Wilberforce University that a music hymnal be published. The proposal was accepted and he was appointed to the three-man committee. As the sole musician on the committee, he was totally responsible for its musical aspect. The hymnal included a dozen or more of his compositions, four of which have been retained through the 1941 and 1954 revisions: "We'll Praise the Lord," "O God, We Lift Our Hearts to Thee," "Savior, Hear Us Through Thy Merit," and the music of "Jesus, Lover of My Soul."

Layton was notable also for his leadership in bringing the Afro-English composer Samuel Coleridge-Taylor to the United States on two occasions. In June 1903 the composer was invited to Washington, D.C., to conduct the Choral Society in a program of his music, and the festival took place on Nov. 16. The second Coleridge-Taylor Music Festival took place at the Metropolitan A.M.E. Church in Washington: "The Atonement of the Quadroon Girl" on Nov. 22, 1906, and "Hiawatha" on

Nov. 22. Coleridge-Taylor personally directed a chorus of 180 voices and the Symphony Orchestra from Philadelphia. Among the soloists was Harry T. Burleigh (*Washington Bee* advertisement, Nov. 17, 1906, p. 5). Layton exerted a strong influence on the musical life of Washington, D.C., over a long period, and encouraged the musical development of many talented persons, among them the composer and violinist Clarence Cameron White.

In March 1906 Wilberforce University conferred upon him the honorary degree of Doctor of Music. After a long illness Layton died on Feb. 14, 1916, in Washington, D.C. Funeral services were held at Metropolitan A.M.E. Church on Feb. 18. He was survived by his widow Julia Mason Layton and two sons, J. Turner, who later achieved recognition as a musician, and Alfred Mason, a student at M Street High School, Washington, D.C.

Sources included Frank Metcalf's *American Writers and Compilers of Sacred Music* (1925), and the obituaries in the *Washington Bee* (Feb. 19, 1916, p. 1) and the *Indianapolis Freeman* (Feb. 22, 1916).

— EILEEN SOUTHERN

LEACH, ROBERT BOYD (1822–1863), physician and civil rights leader. He was probably the first Negro doctor in the city of Cleveland, Ohio, starting his practice there in 1868. In addition to his professional services he was frequently mentioned in connection with the struggle of Negroes to gain their full rights as citizens. Born in Virginia but taken by his parents to Jackson County, Ohio, when he was five years old, Leach came to Cleveland as a young man in 1844 and worked on the lake steamships during the navigation season. His kind and genial disposition led to his being assigned to nurse the sick on the ships when necessary. The medical book in the ship's medicine chest was his guide. This assignment developed his interst in science and he read whatever medical books he could secure during the off-season from navigation. Malaria was the scourge of his day, and he was credited with compounding a specific remedy which met with some success in the treatment of this disease.

After he completed the two-year course of study at the Western Homeopathic College in Cleveland in 1858, the editor of the *Cleveland Leader* commented, "Dr. Leach not only secured a fair reputation and acquired an honorable profession during his residence in the city but he has an intelligent, interesting family and a home with all the pleasant surroundings which well directed industry and economy so usually bring with competence directed by good taste." Leach was in the Cuyahoga County (Cleveland) delegation to the Ohio State Convention of Colored Men in 1853 held in Columbus, in which William Howard Day and Charles H. Langston played prominent parts. This convention claimed for Negro Americans the rights of citizens which existed under the constitution of the nation and the state. At the first annual meeting (Jan. 1860) of the Ohio State Anti-Slavery Society, Leach was placed on a committee to present the grievances of the Negro people to the state legislature and was also elected to the executive board of the society for the following year.

With the outbreak of the Civil War, Leach assisted with the recruitment of Negro soldiers. In 1863 he planned a trip to the national capital to enlist, but while visiting friends in Philadelphia, he died of a liver ailment on July 29.

The major source is Russell H. Davis's *Black Americans in Cleveland* (1972). — RUSSELL H. DAVIS

LEARY, LEWIS [SHERIDAN] (c. 1836–1859), one of John Brown's men at Harpers Ferry. He was born of a slave mother in North Carolina. His father reportedly was Jeremiah O'Leary, an Irishman who freed her and the children she had borne him. Lewis grew up in Ohio, where he worked as a harness maker and dropped the "O" from his name. He had some schooling at Oberlin College, and married Mary Sampson Patterson, the grandmother of Langston Hughes; she also attended Oberlin College. Leary was one of Brown's first recruits committed directly to the raid at Harpers Ferry. He was the uncle of John Copeland, with whom he departed for Virginia in September 1859. He left a six-month-old baby and his wife without saying that he was going away to fight to free slaves.

Leary and Copeland joined Brown's small band on a farm near Harpers Ferry. They received about three weeks of training and indoctrination. The company was made up of twenty-two men, including John Brown and three of Brown's sons. Seventeen of them were white. Five were Negroes and one of these, Shields Green, was a fugitive slave.

Near midnight on Sunday, Oct. 16, 1859, Leary and the others under Brown's leadership entered the town of Harpers Ferry and seized the federal rifle factory, the armory where heavy military equipment was made, and the arsenal where guns and ammunition were stored. On the following day, Monday, Leary was in a detail holding the rifle factory. The militia, with support of local citizens, attacked; in the fighting Leary was killed. His widow received the torn and blood-stained cape in which he died.

In 1899 the body of Leary was disinterred at Harpers Ferry. It was reburied at North Elba, N.Y., near the grave of John Brown.

Osborne P. Anderson's *A Voice from Harper's Ferry* (1861) is the only eyewitness account by one of the participants. W. E. B. Du Bois's *John Brown* (1909) gives details about the raid. Jules Abels's *Man on Fire: John Brown and the Cause of Liberty* (1971) is the source for the reburial of Leary's body.

— LORENZ GRAHAM

LEDBETTER, HUDDIE [called **LEADBELLY**] (1885–1949), singer and composer. He was born near Mooringsport, La. The Cherokee ancestry of his maternal grandmother was later a source of pride. He was the only natural child of Wess and Sallie (Pugh) Ledbetter, originally from Mississippi, who farmed together sixty-five acres. His mother, who led the church choir, gave him his first music lessons. Two uncles, Bob and Terrell Ledbetter, taught him to play the accordion. In 1900 he had a daughter, Arthur Mae, by a childhood sweetheart, Margaret. His refusal to marry her created resentment. He dropped out of school and worked on the family farm, carrying a pistol in a holster under his coat. When he was sixteen and known as the best guitar player and singer in Louisiana, he adopted the style and verses of accomplished blues singers on Fannin Street, the red-light district of nearby Shreveport. He and his wife Lethe worked during summers on farms near New Boston, Tex. In the winter he played his guitar and sang in the red-light district of Dallas, where he learned many songs from bluesman Lemon Jefferson. After hearing a musician play a twelve-string guitar, he bought one the next morning. His powerful bass voice earned him the nickname "Lead Belly" or "Leadbelly."

A handsome, strongly built young man, his womanizing led to his initial sentence of one year on the chain gang for attacking a woman who resisted him. Escaping after three days and hidden by his father, he was convicted on May 24, 1918, for murder, and assault to murder another woman. Escaping again, he was sentenced under the alias of Walter Boyd to thirty years on the Shaw State Prison Farm. Escaping a third time, and recaptured, he was transferred in 1920 to the Central State Farm near Houston. His strength made him the lead man on the fastest working chain gang, and his musicianship attracted the favorable attention of visitors to the prison. A plea in song for mercy won a pardon from Gov. Pat M. Neff on Jan. 15, 1925. Returning to his home in Mooringsport in 1926, he worked with the Gulf Refining Company and continued to develop as a blues singer. In 1930 he was sentenced to ten years at hard labor for assault with intent to murder five men who had demanded whiskey. As on the Texas chain gang, he became the lead man. A plea for mercy to Gov. O. K. Allen of Louisiana and a recording by John and Alan Lomax of his song "Irene, Good Night," won him a reprieve on Aug. 7, 1934. He joined Alan Lomax, who was recording folk songs in southern prisons, and sang to encourage the inmates to record for Lomax. At night he played his guitar and sang in local bars. After traveling some 6000 miles, Lomax and Ledbetter went to New York City, where Ledbetter, introduced as the "bad nigger," won the acclaim of many, including the kind of whites whose outlook would later be called "radical chic." He performed before the Poetry Society of Cambridge and at Harvard, where Prof. George Lyman Kittredge told Lomax that Ledbetter was a "demon." While singing and playing the guitar with a skill and intensity that swayed audiences which could not understand the words, he often introduced talks before songs and during verses which explained his music.

On Jan. 21, 1935, Lomax arranged for Martha Promise, Ledbetter's common-law wife to come north for a widely publicized wedding in Wilmot, Conn. Marriage did not put an end to his womanizing, but he went back to Shreveport on March 26, 1935, with his wife. Returning to New York, he resumed his career as a folk singer, but large music studios refused to issue his recordings because of doubt that they would sell. In Hollywood he was an entertainer at parties given by celebrities and was the butt of a cruel joke to take a screen test at "45 to 9 at Hollywood and Vine." The experience led to one of his popular songs, "4, 5, and 9." Back in New York, he did a series of half-hour programs

for radio station WNYC. He died of amytrophic lateral sclerosis ("Lou Gehrig's Disease") in Bellevue Hospital, New York City. He was survived by his widow, Martha Promise Ledbetter, of 414 E. 10th St., New York City; a daughter, A. Mae Richardson of Kansas City, Mo.; a sister and two nieces.

Conflicting interpretations of Ledbelly's career as a musician and a man revived after the production in 1976 of the Paramount Pictures film *Leadbelly*, directed by the well-known Negro photographer N. Gordon Parks. Mixed reviews confirmed previous evaluations of Ledbetter's comprehensive repertoire of traditional folk and children's songs, blues, and topical numbers, and his influence on Paul McCartney, Pete Seeger, and Bob Dylan. "Rock Island Line," "Midnight Special," and "Goodnight, Irene" were advertised as his more memorable compositions. As in the case of many other artists, critics differed about the relative impact of Ledbetter as a criminal and a "champion of the proletariat."

John and Alan Lomax wrote two authoritative biographies of Ledbetter and his music: *Negro Folk Songs as Sung by Lead Belly* (1936) and *The Leadbelly Legend* (1965). The influence of Leadbelly on the white folksong movement is best discussed by Bob Groom in *The Blues Revival* (1971). There is an excellent article by William R. Ferris, Jr., in *DAB, Supplement 4* (1974, pp. 475–77). The Recording Division of the Library of Congress has made available extensive recordings of interviews and music made by John and Alan Lomax.

— RAYFORD W. LOGAN

LEE, ARCHY (1840–1873), subject in a famous fugitive slave case. Born a slave in Carroll County, Miss., he lived there until he was eighteen when he was taken by Charles Stovall, the son of his master, to Sacramento, Calif., in the winter of 1857. By early 1858 Stovall feared that Sacramento Negroes would persuade Archy to strike for freedom and prepared to return him to Mississippi. Archy realized his master's intentions and fled, but was apprehended in a Sacramento hotel managed by free Negroes. Upon his being jailed, Archy's cause was taken up by the leaders of the Sacramento Negro community. The subsequent legal moves resulted in an absurd state Supreme Court decision which denied freedom to Archy while granting the justice of his claim. Archy's young master then brought Archy to a ship in San Francisco Bay in an attempt to carry him back to slavery. By this time the Negro leadership of San Francisco was alerted and they rallied white legal talent and raised funds to continue the fight for Archy's freedom. After a dramatic scene on board ship in the middle of San Francisco Bay, Archy was rescued and a long series of legal moves on his behalf was begun.

In a chain of court appearances, beginning with a petition for a writ of habeas corpus (Jan. 8, 1858), the argument was made by Archy's lawyers that the state Supreme Court's decision was too ridiculous to be taken seriously. Also, under state law Archy was not a fugitive since he made his strike for freedom within the state's boundaries and was therefore not a fugitive under federal law. Legal maneuvers brought the case ultimately out of the local courts and before the U.S. commissioner in San Francisco (a southerner), who agreed that the case was not a federal one and set Archy free on April 14, 1858. In that nine-week period the case went from the Sacramento courts to the state Supreme Court where a final decision to put Archy back into slavery seemed to have been reached. Then Archy was taken to a hideout near San Francisco from which he was to have been spirited onto a boat enroute to the South. This was frustrated, however, and the case started over in the sympathetic San Francisco courts.

In a desperate move the proslavery defense succeeded in getting the case back to the unhappy southern-born commissioner. He then again ruled that it was not his case and the San Francisco court decision to set Archy free was sustained.

This victory resulted in a number of celebrations by the San Francisco Negro community in which Archy Lee was the center of attention. A large-scale exodus of California Negroes to Victoria, British Columbia, was under way because of the Fraser River gold rush and the apparent imminence of additional racist legislation in California. Within days of Archy's victory, ships were leaving with hundreds of Negroes for Victoria, and Archy joined them. He probably remained in British Columbia through the Civil War years. He was reported to be in Nevada in the Washoe silver region in 1862, but this was probably an error. A more accurate source related that he became a drayman in Victoria in the 1860s and accumulated some property. There is no firm information about him until 1873, when he was found ill in the sands along the Sacramento River. He was taken to a Sacramento hospital where he died of pneumonia in that year. Although otherwise insignificant, he carved a niche in the history of California as the victor in the state's most important fugitive-slave case.

Rudolph M. Lapp's *Archy Lee, A California Fugitive Slave Case* (1969) gives the fullest account. See also William E. Franklin's "The Archy Case: The California Supreme Court Refuses to Free a Slave" (*Pacific Historical Review*, May 1963, pp. 137–54). The case is in *California Reports* (1858, esp. p. 171) and in Helen Honor Tunnicliff Caterall (ed.), *Judicial Cases Concerning American Slavery and the Negro* (vol. 5, 1937).

— RUDOLPH M. LAPP

LEE, CANADA [adopted name of **LIONEL CORNELIUS CANEGATA**] (1907–1952), jockey, boxer, and actor. He was born on May 3, 1907, in New York City's San Juan Hill district, and attended Public School 5 in Harlem. His parents, James Cornelius and Lydia (Whaley) Canegata, started his musical education when he was seven. He began studying violin under the composer J. Rosamond Johnson, and in his early teens he played in a student concert at Aeolian Hall. At the age of fourteen he ran away to the races at Saratoga to become a jockey. After two years as a jockey on the racetracks at Saratoga, Belmont, Aqueduct, Jamaica, and on the Canadian circuit, plus two more years of exercising horses for prominent owners, he returned home penniless and overweight. A chance meeting with a friend, Willie Powell, who had turned prize-

fighter and trainer, helped him enter the ring. From the basement of a Methodist church near his parents' home, he put on boxing gloves for the first time, acquired a manager, Jim Buckley, and soon entered the amateur ring. In rapid succession he emerged the victor in 90 of 100 bouts and won the Metropolitan Inter-City and Junior National Championships, and the national amateur lightweight title.

In 1926 he turned professional, and in a few years moved from a lightweight to a leading contender for the welterweight championship. He fought more than 200 professional bouts, losing only 25. It was as a professional prizefighter that he acquired the name Canada Lee. In 1933 a detached retina ended his ring career, and he returned to music.

In 1934, leading his own band, he was a struggling musician. He decided to audition at the Harlem YMCA for a Works Progress Administration theatrical production which led to a role in *Brother Mose*. Unable to support himself, however, through work in the theater, he became a stevedore at age twenty-eight. Although acting was to become his profession, he never lost his love for boxing. Despite the fact that he had lost his sight in one eye, and sustained cauliflower ears and a broken nose from boxing, he loved the game, and believed it helped him in his acting. "Boxing, that's like hot music. You have to think. In the ring I learned balance and fluidity of movement."

In 1936 Lee first won critical acclaim as Banquo in the Federal Theater's Negro *Macbeth*, produced by Orson Wells. He played Jean Christophe in *Haiti* with Rex Ingram. For the Theater Union revival of *Stevedore* he played the part of Blacksnake. In 1939 he had a featured role of Draylon in *Mamba's Daughters*, starring Ethel Waters. That same year he narrated the CBS program, "Flow Gently, Sweet Rhythm," featuring John Kirby and Maxine Sullivan.

In 1941 Lee's role as Bigger Thomas in Richard Wright's *Native Son* brought him his greatest acclaim. According to the *New York Times* (March 30, 1941), his portrayal of Bigger Thomas was hailed as "the most vital piece of acting on the current stage." Richard Watts, Jr., wrote in the *New York Herald Tribune* (March 30, 1941): "A fine actor, giving one of the season's best performances." Brooks Atkinson said of Lee's performance in the revival of the play the following year: "A superbly imaginative player. . . . When he is on the stage, he inhabits it. . . . The quality of life Mr. Lee imparts to a scene is overwhelming—partly physical, partly magnetic" (ibid., Dec. 26, 1943).

Lee appeared as Thomas Piper in Saroyan's *Across the Board Tomorrow Morning* (1942) and as a Negro sailor in *South Pacific* (1943). In 1944 he played a Negro steward in the film *Lifeboat* and Dannie in *Anna Lucasta* on Broadway. He narrated a radio series, "New World A Coming" on WMCA, starred in and produced *On Whitman Avenue* (1944), and was featured in the *Dutchess of Malfi* (1944), in which he played Daniel de Bosola in "whiteface," and he played Caliban in Margaret Webster's *The Tempest* (1945). In 1947 he was a prizefighter in the film *Body and Soul*.

Lee died of a heart attack on May 9, 1952. He had been in failing health for two years and had collapsed in Africa at the end of the film *Cry the Beloved Country,* in which he played the lead. He was survived by his widow, the former Juanita Waller, and their children Frances and Carl Vincent, an actor. Funeral services were held in Salem Methodist Church, 128th Street and Lenox Avenue, New York City, and he was buried in Woodlawn Cemetery.

Basic facts are in *Current Biography* (1944), *Who's Who in Colored America* (1950), the obituary in the *New York Times* (May 10, 1952), and Evelyn Mack Truitt's *Who Was Who on Screen* (1974). See also the Canada Lee file in the Schomburg Center for Research in Black Culture, New York City, and the Hallie Flanegan Papers in the New York Theater Library (Performing Arts Research), Lincoln Center, New York City. Reminiscences of J. Scott Kennedy were also used.

— J. SCOTT KENNEDY

LEE, ULYSSES [GRANT, JR.] (1913–1969), college professor, editor, army officer, and historian. He was born in Washington, D.C., Dec. 4, 1913, the son of Ulysses Grant and Mattie (Spriggs) Lee. His father, a businessman, owned a grocery store in Fairmount Heights, Md. The junior Ulysses was the oldest of seven children. On Dec. 24, 1942, he married Vivian Gill, a social worker and the daughter of a well-known Washington physician.

Ulysses Lee received his secondary education at Dunbar High School, graduating in 1931. From 1931 to 1935 he attended Howard University, earning his B.A. degree *summa cum laude.* In 1936 he received an M.A. in English, also from Howard, and then studied for a year at the University of Pennsylvania. In 1953 Lee was awarded his Ph.D. "with honors" at the University of Chicago. His major field was the history of culture, with a concentration in American literature, history, church history, philosophy, and art.

Lee's professional career was rich and varied. Beginning as a graduate assistant at Howard (1935–1936), he subsequently taught as instructor and assistant professor at Lincoln University (Pennsylvania) from 1936 to 1948. (During this period, he had two leaves, one academic, the other military.) In 1940 he was a visiting professor at Virginia Union University; in 1953 he joined the English faculty at Lincoln University (Missouri), remaining there until 1956 when he joined the faculty of Morgan State College. During the year of his death, Lee taught concurrently at Morgan and the University of Pennsylvania.

An important part of Lee's professional career involved several important editing assignments. Exceptionally able in this field, Lee began this phase of his career with the Federal Writers' Project. From 1936 to 1939 he worked with the project as research assistant, consultant, and editor. According to Sterling A. Brown, who was Lee's immediate supervisor, Ulysses Lee was "most helpful" on two of the project's important publications: *Washington: City and Capital* and *The Negro in Virginia.* He was associate editor of the *Midwest Journal,* an editor of the Arno Press (which published a series of reprints of Negro material), a member of the editorial board of *CLA* (College Language Association) *Journal,* and associate editor of the *Journal of Negro*

History. At the time of his death, Lee was editor designate of the latter periodical.

Lee actually had two careers, one in the academic world, the other in the military. It is interesting to note that Ulysses Lee was a second-generation army man. His father, before becoming a grocer, had been a cavalry sergeant stationed first in the Indian territory and later in the Philippines. Lee's military career began with the ROTC program at Howard. As a commissioned graduate of that program and as a reservist, he was called up in 1942. He was one of the first officers assigned to the Information and Education Division of the army. A first lieutenant in 1942, Lee was a major ten years later. During World War II he served as an education officer and editorial analyst in the field, and at headquarters of Army Service Forces. From 1946 to 1952, he was staff historian in the Office of the Chief of Military History, Department of the Army. His career in this office was productive and outstanding. As a specialist on all phases and aspects of the Negro's connection with the U.S. Army, Lee wrote not only his major study, *The Employment of Negro Troops* (1966), but also contributed to other works in the series of which his study is a part.

In addition to his academic interests—which took him to many campuses and cities as lecturer and radio-TV speaker, and in 1965 to Nigeria and Sierra Leone to participate in seminars of the American Society of African Culture—Lee always found time to work on a national as well as on a local level with his church, the Protestant Episcopal church, and with his veterans group, the American Veterans Committee of World War II. He was deeply loyal to both of these commitments.

From his high school years, when he won the Harvard Club Award (1930–1931), throughout his entire academic career, Ulysses Lee was the recipient of many distinguished honors and awards for high intellectual achievement. Among the outstanding examples of this recognition given him were the Rosenwald, the Alvia K. Brown (University of Chicago), and the Rockefeller fellowships. He received the Army Commendation Ribbon (Medal) in 1946. Lee was elected in 1958 an alumni member of Howard University's chapter of Phi Beta Kappa.

Ulysses Lee produced two major works. The first of these, *The Negro Caravan* (1941), he edited in collaboration with Sterling A. Brown and Arthur P. Davis. *The Negro Caravan* is a pioneering and seminal anthology of Negro American writings. The second, Lee's more important work, *The Employment of Negro Troops (United States Army in World War II),* is a scholarly, comprehensive, and history-making study of the army's policies and practices toward the Negro soldier. It is a massive and impressive work.

In addition to these two volumes, Lee wrote a good number of scholarly reviews, monographs, and articles, including the following: "Frank Norris: A Definition" (unpublished master's thesis, Howard University, 1936); the 1944 Army Service Forces manual, *Leadership and the Negro Soldier* (Lee was editor-author of this work); "The ASNLH, The Journal of Negro History, and American Scholarly Interest in Africa" (*Présence*

Africaine, 1958); and "The Draft and the Negro" (*Current History,* July 1968).

Ulysses Lee was a great and inspiring teacher. Restrained, precise, patient, he did not resort to the kind of dramatic presentation that some teachers—good and bad—often use to impress their students. He did not need such devices, and he was too modest to think in terms of impressing anyone. His students *and* his colleagues, however, *were* impressed, by the encyclopedic fullness of his mind, by his far-ranging intellect that seemed to take all knowledge for its province. Lee could talk charmingly and with authority, not only on literature and history, his two major fields, but also on music (he had a good knowledge of both classical and jazz music), the history of cocker spaniels, American railroads, cookery, and many other fascinating subjects.

Lee's students expressed their appreciation of him in different ways. Those at the University of Pennsylvania gave him standing ovations; those at Morgan State voted him the Distinguished Teacher Award in 1963.

Lee was in some respects a scholar's scholar, the kind of academician who was often asked by his friends and colleagues, because of their great respect for his ability, to read and criticize *their* manuscripts. He was always willing to undertake this kind of chore. Lee was a scholar's scholar in yet another way. Never a prolific writer, he was most interested in the acquisition of knowledge for the simple pleasure of knowing.

Ulysses Lee suffered a fatal heart attack on Jan. 7, 1969, as he was returning from Morgan State to his home in Washington, D.C. His funeral was held on Jan. 11, 1969, in the Bethlehem Chapel of the National Cathedral in Washington. The Very Rev. Francis B. Sayre, dean of the cathedral, officiated at the service. The eulogy was read by Sterling A. Brown, Lee's teacher and friend. He was interred in Lincoln Memorial Cemetery, Suitland, Md. He was survived by his widow, Vivian (Gill) Lee, four sisters (Edmonia Francis of Washington; Dorothy Amos of Washington; Aramenta Anduze, St. Croix, Virgin Islands; and Lois Killings, Akron, Ohio); and two brothers, William and Ira, both of Washington (*Washington Post,* Jan. 9, 1969, p. B6, and Jan. 11, p. E4; *Washington Afro-American* [Red Star ed.], Jan. 14, 1969).

As very little biographical material on Lee has been published to date, his career is best reflected in his own writings. Robert Ewell Greene's *Black Defenders of America, 1775–1973: A Reference and Pictorial History* (1974) has a brief sketch of Lee. Obituaries appeared in the *Washington Evening Star* (Jan. 9, 1969), the *Washington Post* (Jan. 9, 1969), and the *New York Times* (Jan. 11, 1969). *On Being Black: Writings by Afro-Americans from Frederick Douglass to the Present,* edited by Charles T. Davis and Daniel Walden, is dedicated "To Ulysses Lee Distinguished scholar and teacher in Afro-American literature and culture." The Lee Papers are in the Moorland-Spingarn Research Center, Howard University. — ARTHUR P. DAVIS

LEIDESDORFF, WILLIAM ALEXANDER (1810–1848), pioneer settler in California, entrepreneur, vice-consul, and government official. Born in St. Croix, Danish West Indies, the son of a Danish planter and a

mulatto mother, he came to the United States as a boy with his two brothers to work in their father's cotton business. He became master of vessels sailing between New York and New Orleans, and came to California, then under Mexican rule, in 1841 as manager of the 160-ton schooner *Julia Anna,* on which he made trips to the West Indies until 1845. Meanwhile, engaging in trade in San Francisco, he secured in 1843 a Mexican land grant for two large lots on the corner of Clay and Kearney Streets. In 1844 he became a Mexican citizen in order to acquire the 35,000-acre Rancho Rio de los Americanos near Sutter's sawmill on the banks of the American River. Despite his Mexican citizenship, he was named vice-consul in October 1845 by Thomas O. Larkin, the U.S. consul in Monterey, Calif. His letters to Larkin in 1846 are a valuable source of information about intrigues in San Francisco. He also met with the explorer John C. Frémont and other Americans, apparently to discuss the seizure of California by the United States. He nonetheless continued to obtain land from the Mexican government: in 1846 he was given a lot on the corner of California and what became later Leidesdorff Street, on which he built a warehouse.

When Capt. John Montgomery landed with seventy marines in July 1846 and raised the American flag over the plaza, Leidesdorff is said to have translated the night before the proclamation read by Montgomery. In 1846 he built a hotel on his first lot and in 1847 bought a cottage at the corner of California and Montgomery Streets where he lived the rest of his life.

Hubert Howe Bancroft, the principal author of *History of the Pacific States* (1882–1890), stated that in 1847 Leidesdorff "launched the first steamer that ever sailed into San Francisco Bay" (5:577–78). Bancroft added that Leidesdorff was not only one of the town's most prominent businessmen but a member of the City Council, treasurer and a member of the school committee, and took an active part in local politics. He spoke several languages, was honorable for the most part in his transactions, but jealous and hot tempered.

He was chairman of the San Francisco school board which opened California's first public school in April 1848. In May he became a victim of typhus and was buried beneath the floor of Mission Dolores. He died about two months after the *San Francisco Californian* reported on March 15, 1848: "Gold Mine Found" at Sutter's sawmill. After many years of litigation his estate was awarded to army Capt. Joseph Folsom for $70,000. Bancroft wrote: "Vice-Consul Leidesdorff died in 1848, leaving property then regarded as inadequate to pay his liabilities of over $40,000, but a year later its value had so advanced as to give to the heirs an amount larger than the debts, while agents managed to make fortunes by administering the estate." It is thus an exaggeration to call Leidesdorff a "millionaire." The value of the estate grew after the gold strike in 1848 at Sutter's sawmill, not far from Leidesdorff's claim on the American River.

In 1851 George McKinsty, Jr., who had worked for Sutter at the outset, sent a letter to an old friend, Edward Kern of Philadelphia, in which he gave "a lugubrious recital of disaster, sudden death and disappearance." In his list was " 'William A. Leidesdorff, dead.' " Few visitors or even old inhabitants of San Francisco know that Leidesdorff Street, parallel to Montgomery Street in the heart of the San Francisco business district, is named for him.

The best published account is William Sherman Savage's "The Influence of William Alexander Leidesdorff on the History of California" (*NHB*, July 1953, pp. 322–31). The map on pages 34–35 of *The Old West: The Forty-Niners,* by William Weber Johnson (Time-Life Books, 1974), shows the close proximity of Leidesdorff's claim to the sawmill in 1848. Delilah L. Beasley has a brief account in *The Negro Trail Blazers of California* (1919, reprinted in 1969, pp. 107–8). Both Savage and Beasley relied largely on Hubert Howe Bancroft's *The History of the Pacific States of North America* (vols. 4, 5, and 6, 1882–1890). Other useful references are in *Blacks and Their Contributions to the American West: A Bibliography and Union List of Library Holdings Through 1970,* compiled by James deT. Abajian (1974). — RAYFORD W. LOGAN

LEMUS, RIENZI BROCK (1881–1945), soldier and labor leader. Lemus was born in Richmond, Va., on Jan. 8, 1881. His parents were Charles H. and Mamie L. (Brock) Lemus. He attended that city's public schools prior to his enlistment in the army at the age of eighteen. He served briefly in the 8th Volunteer Infantry Regiment, shortly after the Cuban Campaign of the Spanish-American War. When the regiment was disbanded, he enlisted in the 25th Infantry, a regular regiment manned by Negro enlisted personnel. He served with K Company through the active years of the Philippine Insurrection, saw action at several stations in Luzon, and was honorably discharged on March 18, 1902. Lemus then worked for about two and a half years as a Pullman porter, and the next twenty years as a dining car waiter. On April 11, 1917, he wrote to Joel E. Spingarn, chairman of the board of the NAACP, strongly endorsing a separate training camp for colored officers as an opportunity for young southern Negroes to escape from the harsh conditions imposed by the "cracker convict guards and landlord farmer." He led in the movement to establish a labor union among dining car cooks and waiters, which culminated in the Brotherhood of Dining Car Employees of 1919. He served that organization as grand president continuously until 1941.

Lemus established his union among the cooks and waiters of various New England railroads and the New York Central. A similar organization, the Dining Car Cooks and Waiters Association, emerged among workers on the Baltimore & Ohio and other eastern Pennsylvania lines at the same time. In the spring of 1920, under the auspices of the New York Urban League, the two unions negotiated a merger under the name of the Brotherhood of Dining Car Employees. Lemus, who remained president, called the new organization "a successful all-Negro protective trades-union . . . of ten locals and a Grand Lodge." The Brotherhood's headquarters was in New York City, where Lemus moved from his Washington, D.C., residence sometime after 1925.

The new organization proved a potent bargaining unit in its early years. Of its many victories, perhaps the most notable was the awarding by the director-general of railroads of the eight-hour day and overtime pay for its members in 1919. This award was preserved after the end of federal control of railroads negotiated with the Atlantic Coast Line, the Boston & Albany, the New York Central (East), the Pennsylvania, the Southern, and the Seaboard Air Line Railroads. Lemus and the union also won the first formal agreement on rules governing the employment of dining car men, from the New York, New Haven & Hartford in 1921. After a decade of growth, the union had about 2700 members, or half the Negro dining car workers on lines east of the Mississippi. By the mid-1930s the Brotherhood began to lose its vitality and aggressiveness, while the Hotel and Restaurant Workers of the powerful American Federation of Labor cut into its strength with an organization drive. Finally, in 1941 Lemus was voted out of office, and the Brotherhood was absorbed into the larger United Transport Services Employees.

During his years with the Brotherhood, Lemus wrote occasional articles on labor matters for newspapers such as the *Boston Chronicle* and the *New York Age.* However, his more obscure contributions to the *Colored American Magazine* and the *Richmond Planet* at the turn of the century are much more important. The series of about thirty *Planet* letters (1899–1902), all written while in the Philippines, describe vividly the military campaigns of the 25th Infantry and the terrain over which they were fought. The letters also depict the off-duty life of the soldiers, particularly the YMCA. His articles in the *Colored American Magazine* (March and May 1902, and March 1903) vigorously opposed a proposal to colonize American Negroes in the Philippines. Filipinos, he wrote, were suspicious of outsiders, and expropriation of their land would lead to wholesale slaughter of the colonists. His articles, along with T. Thomas Fortune's article in the *Independent* (Sept. 24, 1903), constitute two of the best firsthand accounts of the attitude of Filipinos toward American Negroes at the time.

There are few good sources on Lemus's life. The biography in *Who's Who in Colored America 1941–1944* provides some basic information. Lionel Franklin's *The Negro Labor Unionist of New York . . .* (1936) has some valuable references based in part on interviews with Lemus. Sterling D. Spero's and Abram L. Harris's *The Black Worker* (1931), Herbert R. Northrup's *Organized Labor and the Negro* (1944), and William B. Gatewood, Jr.'s *Black Americans and the White Man's Burden, 1898–1903* (1975) are among the best sources of background information. See also Hal S. Chase's unpublished manuscript "The Struggle for Negro Officers: The Fort Des Moines Training Camp, 1917" (1976, in the files of Rayford W. Logan). — FRANK N. SCHUBERT

LEWIS, [MARY] EDMONIA (1845– ?), sculptor. The daughter of a Chippewa Indian and a Negro father, she was born in Greenwich, N.Y. After her mother died in 1848, her father in 1849 left Edmonia in the care of two Indian aunts. She sold mocassins, bead baskets, and pin-cushions at Niagara Falls, Genesee Falls, and Watkins Glen, N.Y. With financial aid sent by her only brother Sunrise, who had been a successful gold miner in California, she attended school in Albany, N.Y., until 1859 when her brother returned east and enrolled her in the preparatory department of Oberlin College. From 1860 to 1862 she studied in the college department, and changed her Indian name (Wildfire) to Mary Edmonia Lewis. Accused of poisoning two of her white schoolmates in January 1862, John Mercer Langston won acquittal of the charge on the ground of insufficient evidence, and she left for Boston. There she began a career as a sculptor which she continued abroad, particularly in Italy. She gained recognition as one of the prominent sculptors of her time, but little is known about her after 1911. No record has been found of the date or place of her death. She married Dr. D. J. (or D. G.) Peck of Philadelphia about 1869.

In Boston, her brother hired rooms for her in the Studio Building, 89 Tremont St. As she told Lydia Maria Child, a prominent author and abolitionist, in the summer of 1862, "I had always wanted to make the forms of things; and while I was at school [Oberlin?] I tried to make drawings of people and things." She also recalled that her mother was well known for inventing new patterns for embroidery and "perhaps the same thing is coming out in me in a more civilized form ("Edmonia Lewis," Broken Fetter, March 3, 1865). Recommended by her Oberlin teachers, in Boston she met William Lloyd Garrison, who introduced her to his friend Edmund Brackett, a local sculptor. Pleased with her execution of models he had given her, he became her teacher. She benefited also from the criticism of several other Boston artists, especially Anne Whitney. Lewis began to be well known after she offered for sale at the Studio Building a number of medallions of John Brown (advertised in the Liberator, Jan. 29, 1864, and subsequent issues). Plaster casts of the medallion which she had copied from the Brackett bust were put on sale at the Soldiers' Relief Fair held in Boston to raise money for the Sanitary Commission. Also on exhibition were busts of Col. Robert Gould Shaw which she made from photographs after his death, having seen him only once as he passed through a crowded street riding at the head of the 54th Massachusetts Regiment. The success of this sculpture was due largely to her intense feeling of gratitude and reverence for Colonel Shaw. Garrison helped to sell these first works, and sufficient money was raised by their sale and from contributions of friends to enable her to go abroad for study.

Lewis left on Aug. 26, 1865, visiting briefly London and Paris. She crossed the Alps, then stopped in Florence where she met Hiram Powers, one of the best known and most financially successful American sculptors in Italy at that time. She was received by the U.S. minister to Italy, George Perkins Marsh, and his wife. In Florence, Powers gave Edmonia Lewis a molding block and Thomas Ball, a sculptor and friend of Powers, gave her tools. After a brief stay in Florence she went to Rome, where she became acquainted with sculptors Anne Whitney (then living in Rome), Charlotte Cushman, and Harriet Hosmer. The most successful of the group, Harriet Hosmer, who had admired Edmonia's bust of Colonel Shaw which she had seen while visiting in Boston, gave her criticism and help.

In Rome, Lewis studied and worked hard. She occupied the former studio of Antonio Canova (1757–1822), the influential Italian sculptor.

Probably the most important of her early work was Forever Free, a composition in marble completed in 1867 showing a man and a woman overcome with emotion on hearing the news of their emancipation from slavery. This sculpture was sent to the United States in 1868 for exhibition at the National Testimonial in honor of William Lloyd Garrison. It is owned by the Howard University Gallery of Art. A second important marble statue was a figure of Hagar in Her Despair in the Wilderness (1868). She took it to Chicago in August or September of 1870 where she exhibited it. The statue was reported to have been raffled off for $3000 (The Revolution, Nov. 24, 1870, p. 634). Another reference claimed that Hagar was sold in 1870, for $6000 (Anne Whitney to Sarah Whitney, Feb. 21, 1869; Jan. 14, 1871). The New National Era (Sept. 15, 1870) stated that a gentleman in Chicago had purchased the sculpture. Hagar is owned by the Frederick Douglass Institute of Afro-American Art in Washington, D.C.

Lewis's portrait busts were of her heroes: Sumner, Lincoln, Longfellow, Wendell Phillips, Jesse Peck Thomas, Dionysus Lewis, Maria Chapman, and others. Her sympathy for women who had struggled and suffered are seen in her Hagar and in the Death of Cleopatra. Contemporary critics found that the "effects of death are represented with such skill as to be absolutely repellent," yet "a very original and striking one" that "could only have been produced by a sculptor of very genuine endowments." The Death of Cleopatra was first exhibited at the Philadelphia Centennial Exposition of 1876. Considered "the grandest statue in the exposition," it weighed two tons, was twelve feet high, and took over four years to execute. Purchased by the International Art Association of Chicago sometime after 1876, it is among the lost works of Edmonia Lewis. She earned money to defray her expenses through sales of her work at exhibitions in California and Minnesota.

Early in her career, her studio in Rome became a fashionable place for tourists to visit. Calling cards on her table represented a number of European and American names and many titled persons. Charlotte Cushman and American friends in Rome presented in May 1867 The Wooing of Hiawatha to the YMCA in Boston. The young Marquis of Bute, it is said, purchased for $3000 her Madonna with the Infant Christ in her Arms, and built a shrine especially for the piece on the Isle of Bute. A wealthy merchant named Sandbatch, who resided in Liverpool, ordered a colossal bust of Longfellow, then the most popular American author in Europe. A copy of this bust, later placed in the Harvard College Library, is in the Schlesinger Library, Radcliffe College. Terracotta models were said to have been presented to each subscriber for the marble figure. Lady Ashburton purchased the Old Indian Arrow Maker and his Daughter, which was exhibited at the Philadelphia Centennial Exposition of 1876. A marble copy is in the George Washington Carver Museum at Tuskegee Institute, Ala.

Edmonia Lewis returned to the United States several times, first in 1869, for the purpose of exhibiting and selling her sculpture. While she received many commissions, the cost of shipping these works from Rome to the United States and from the East to the West Coast was an expensive task. While in Chicago with her statue of *Hagar* in September 1870, she received a commission to chisel a life-size statue of a seated figure of John Brown which she was asked to complete in the spring of 1871, for the Union League Club of New York City. *The Revolution* (May 4, 1871), reported that she was "just putting up the clay" for the figure. It is not known if the statue was completed.

Edmonia Lewis proudly stated during an interview in Indianapolis (*American Register,* undated clipping in the writer's files, but after January 1875) that she was the only woman who had monuments in two cemeteries—one to Lynch Blair at the Graceland Cemetery in Chicago and the other, *Hygeia,* in Mount Auburn Cemetery in Cambridge, Mass. (commissioned in 1875) by Harriot K. Hunt, one of the first American women physicians, shortly before Jan. 2, 1875).

On Sept. 1, 1873, Lewis opened an exhibition of several pieces at the Art Association Gallery in San Francisco. Among them were *Hiawatha's Marriage,* a life-size bust of Abraham Lincoln, *Cupid Caught,* and her group of infants, *Asleep* and *Awake.* For *Asleep* and *Awake* Lewis had received a gold medal and a diploma from the Academy of Art and Sciences in Naples. A month later she exhibited at the San Jose Fair. *Hiawatha's Marriage* was purchased by Mrs. C. L. Low in San Francisco; the groups *Asleep* and *Awake* were presented to the San Jose Library in July 1924. It is not known who purchased them at the time of the exhibit. The Library Association of San Jose purchased the bust of Lincoln for the library. *Cupid Caught* was sold to an unknown purchaser. While in San Francisco at a reception planned for her, Lewis told the committee that while she appreciated their kindness, it would "do her more honor to take the cost of the reception and purchase the bust of Lincoln." Her sculptures not sold at private exhibition were usually auctioned off.

On the eve of her second departure for Rome (Jan. 13, 1874), a fine reception was given her by the ladies of the Grant and Wilson Club, at the residence of Peter S. Porter in New York City. The Rev. Henry Highland Garnet and George Petterson were among those attending. It was reported on this occasion that she had twenty men at work in her Rome studio.

It is not known whether or not Lewis was present when her statue of *Hygeia* was erected in the Auburn Cemetery, but she did unveil her bust of the late Charles Sumner on the occasion of its presentation to William H. Johnson (Aug. 24, 1875). The program was held in the Hamilton Street Church, Albany, N.Y.

Edmonia Lewis received many orders for her sculptures from eminent and wealthy persons in the United States. Several published reports in 1879 mentioned that busts, probably terracotta of Lincoln, John Brown, and Sumner, were to be seen on mantelpieces in homes. It is not known how many copies she executed of her single works; few are known to have been preserved. *The Old Arrow Maker and His Daughter* is owned by James H. Ricau of Piermont, N.Y. The Carver Museum at Tuskegee also owns a copy. *Awake* is also

in the Carver Museum and at the San Jose Library. *Minnehaha* and *Hiawatha* are part of the permanent collection of the Howard University Museum, in the Moorland-Spingarn Research Center.

Contemporaries of Edmonia Lewis describe her as small, below medium height, with a complexion and features that showed her African origin. From her Indian mother she inherited her straight, black, abundant hair and "proud spirit." In business matters she was straightforward and intelligent. Of her early struggles, she is said to have spoken frankly. A fluent talker when aroused, she nonetheless had something of "habitual quietude and stocism." In spite of her artistic success, she usually maintained in her manner a trace of the "sadness of African and Indian races."

Patience, courage, and a strong will were characteristics needed to fight color prejudice which she encountered on her road to success. Without great physical strength she would have been unable to master the fatiguing process she endured to bring her models to a completed form. One visitor to her studio described her countenance as "bright, intelligent and expressive," and picturesque in the red cap she wore while in her studio.

Little is known about her life after 1885. Scannell O'Neil wrote in "The Catholic Who's Who" (*Rosary Magazine,* Jan. 1909, pp. 322–23) that though well-nigh forgotten and advanced in years, "she is still with us." *The American Catholic Who's Who* for 1911 gave her address as Rome, Italy.

For Langston's defense of Lewis, see Geoffrey Blodget's "John Mercer Langston and the Case of Edmonia Lewis: Oberlin, 1862" (*JNH,* July 1968, pp. 201–18). Two scholarly evaluations are James A. Porter's "Edmonia Lewis" (*NAW,* 1971, 2:397–99) and his *Modern Negro Art* (1943, reprinted 1969, pp. 57–63), with reproductions of marble busts, *Awake* and *Asleep,* and of Jesse Peck Thomas and Abraham Lincoln (pp. 214–15). Contemporary magazines and newspapers published many articles about Lewis. In addition to manuscript sources listed in James Porter's *NAW* article, there are valuable letters in the Dorothy B. Porter Papers in the Moorland-Spingarn Research Center, Howard University. — DOROTHY B. PORTER

LEWIS, OLIVER (? – ?), winning jockey of the first Kentucky Derby (1875). Little is known about him except that he was one of fourteen Negro jockeys out of fifteen, that he rode Aristides, that the distance was a mile and a half instead of the present mile and a quarter, that he later became a trainer in Lexington, Ky., and that attended the Derby in 1907. It may be assumed that Lewis, like Isaac Murphy and other Negroes, learned to ride at an early age in Kentucky and had an almost uncanny skill in handling horses.

Lewis is mentioned in many books, sometimes without his racial identity, as the jockey on Aristides, winner of the first Kentucky Derby. Not even the principal researcher of Negro jockeys, the late Marjorie Rieser Weber, found additional information about Lewis (Mrs. King Buckley, Librarian of the Keenland Library, Lexington, Ky., to R.W.L., Aug. 12, 1976).

— RAYFORD W. LOGAN

LEWIS, WILLIAM H[ENRY] (1868–1949), football player and coach, lawyer, and public official. He was born in Berkeley (later part of Norfolk), Va., the first of four children of Ashley Henry and Josephine (Baker) Lewis, former slaves who had been manumitted several years before the Emancipation Proclamation. His father became a Baptist minister in Portsmouth, Va., where young Lewis attended public schools. He worked at odd jobs to pay his way through Virginia Normal and Industrial Institute in Petersburg, Va., and at Amherst College where he had an excellent record, graduating with a B.A. degree in 1892, in the same class as Calvin Coolidge. He received his LL.B. degree in 1895 from the Harvard Law School. He won renown as center on the football team, began to practice law in Boston, and became the senior partner in the firm of Lewis, Fox and Andrews. On Sept. 23, 1896, Lewis married Elizabeth Baker of Cambridge, a student at Wellesley College. From 1893 until about 1900 he was a "radical" activist in support of civil rights for Negroes. Opposition by his wife and recognition of the need for support by Booker T. Washington for his political ambitions led to Lewis's ambivalence until 1903 when Washington used his influence with Pres. Theodore Roosevelt to secure Lewis's appointment as assistant U.S. attorney for Massachusetts (1903–1906). Lewis also served as assistant U.S. attorney for the six New England states (1907–1911). In 1911 President Taft appointed him assistant attorney-general of the United States, the first subcabinet post held by a Negro. In 1913, when Woodrow Wilson became president, Lewis formed a new law firm in Boston with Matthew L. McGarth and won fame for his success in several court cases. After his wife's death in 1943, Lewis moved from his home in Dedham, Mass., to Boston. He died of a heart attack on New Year's Day, 1949. He had become a convert to Roman Catholicism, and the high requiem mass was attended by Gov. Robert F. Bradford, former mayor of Boston James M. Curley, Charles Francis Adams, and other Boston notables. He was buried in Mount Auburn Cemetery in Cambridge. He was survived by his first daughter Dorothy, who had married a Frenchman in France, and by his only son William H. Jr., a lawyer who had joined his father's firm.

Lewis won recognition at Amherst not only as a scholar, but also as a debater and football player. In his senior year (1891–1892) he was the team's captain, probably the first known Negro to win this distinction in the Ivy League. Although weighing only 170 pounds, he played center on the Harvard team with a line that averaged 200 pounds. During his second year at Harvard he served as temporary captain, and in 1892 and in 1893 he was the first Negro named to Walter Camp's All-America team. He wrote a *Primer of College Football* in 1896, one of the early books on the subject, and assisted in coaching the Harvard team for several years. Although he turned down an offer in 1898 to become football coach at Cornell University, he continued his interest in the game throughout his life.

His major interests, however, were civil rights, the practice of law, and government service. While at Harvard he was denied service in a local barbershop. He and Butler R. Wilson, another capable lawyer, suc-

ceeded in having the state legislature amend its 1885 statute so as to forbid racial discrimination in a wider area of public accommodations, whether the facility was licensed or not. In 1899 he was elected to the first of three one-year terms on the Cambridge Common Council, and in 1902 he won a seat in the Massachusetts House of Representatives but was defeated for reelection in the following year.

By that time Lewis had recognized the need for Booker T. Washington's friendship for advancement of his ambitions. In 1898 he had delivered a memorable attack on Washington in his presence. After W. E. B. Du Bois arranged a meeting between Lewis and Washington, Lewis began to swing from the camp of the "radicals" to that of the "conservatives." During 1902 he did some legal work for Washington, and after his defeat for reelection to the state legislature Lewis found that Pres. Theodore Roosevelt also was pleased with his new views. With Washington's help, he was appointed an assistant district attorney in Boston. In public he continued to oppose any "compromise of human rights." He joined William Monroe Trotter, George W. Forbes, William H. Ferris, and others in an unsuccessful attempt (Louisville, Ky., July 1903) to gain control of the Afro-American Council. Soundly defeated by Washington and his supporters, Lewis presided at the famous meeting of the Boston branch of the National Negro Business League (July 30, 1903) which came to be known by the hyperbolic title the "Boston Riot." When hecklers sought to prevent Washington from speaking, Lewis made a plea for free speech and introduced Washington. But it was in vain; he had to call policemen to arrest a persistent heckler. Trotter and his sister Maude were arrested, and Washington was able to complete his speech. Lewis was one of the Boston "Bookerites" (supporters of Washington) who testified for the prosecution. Trotter, who served a brief jail sentence, called Lewis "the dirtiest cur in this case." Lewis, veering closer to the Bookerites, helped persuade Forbes to leave Trotter's paper, *The Guardian of Boston,* shortly after the trial.

Booker T. Washington continued to support Lewis for public office, as assistant district attorney for Boston (1903), and most important, assistant attorney-general of the United States.

He appeared, with others, before President Wilson to support a loan to Liberia in 1918, served on the policy committee of the Republican party in 1920, and in 1923 helped secure from Coolidge the appointment of Du Bois as special minister to the 1924 inauguration of Pres. C. D. B. King of Liberia. Two years later he supported the appointment of James A. Cobb as a municipal judge of Washington to replace Judge Robert Terrell. Lewis, Butler R. Wilson, and others tried in vain to prevent the showing in Boston of the movie *The Birth of a Nation* (1915). The death of Booker T. Washington in November 1915 released Lewis from domination by Washington. He became less hostile to Trotter and the *Guardian.* But Lewis was considered one of the Bookerites at the (First) Amenia conference, called by Joel E. Spingarn in the summer of 1916 which seemed to effect an uneasy understanding between the rival groups. Thereafter his role in politics was not very significant.

Meanwhile, however, he gained fame in several legal cases. In 1926 he won life imprisonment for a Providence, R.I., Negro accused of murdering a white physician at a time when the death penalty was common. He earned large fees for defending accused bootleggers. One especially important civil rights case was *Corrigan v. Buckley* (1926), in which he and counsel for the NAACP argued against restrictive racial covenants. The Supreme Court ruled that they did not violate the Fourteenth Amendment since they were acts of individuals and not of a state. Even more widely known was his defense in 1941 in the impeachment trial of his old friend Daniel H. Coakley, a member of the executive council of the governor of Massachusetts, who was found guilty of using the influence of his office to obtain paroles for criminals.

The career of William H. Lewis encouraged many young Negroes to seek excellence at Amherst, Harvard, and other Ivy League schools, to practice law, and to enter government service. Although his ambivalence as a "radical" and a "conservative" was well known during his life, he was later perceived as a stalwart defender of equal rights for Negroes and of legal rights in unpopular cases.

There is an excellent sketch, with a comprehensive bibliography, by Peter Shiver, Jr., in the *DAB, Supplement Four* (1974, pp. 492–94). See, in addition, particularly Stephen R. Fox's *The Guardian of Boston: William Monroe Trotter* (1970, esp. pp. 18, 26, 44–57, 83–84, 108, 158–60, 192–97, 200–1, 267–68). Useful manuscript collections are the Papers of Theodore Roosevelt, of Calvin Coolidge, and most important, of Booker T. Washington, all in the Library of Congress.

— CLARENCE G. CONTEE, SR.

LIELE, GEORGE (c. 1750–1820), said to be the first ordained Negro preacher. He was born in Virginia of slave parents, Liele and Nancy, and held by the family of a Baptist deacon, Henry Sharp. The Sharp family took him to Burke County, Ga., prior to 1770, where a white minister brought him into the Baptist fold. He preached to slaves on the plantations along the Savannah River from Silver Bluff to the suburbs of Savannah. Sometime before the American Revolution, Sharp manumitted Liele. After Sharp's death, his heirs tried to reenslave Liele, but British officers whom he had served prevented the attempt.

During the three years of the British occupation of Savannah (1779–1782), he preached to Negro Baptists, slave and free, in Savannah. Among those who listened to him were David George and Andrew Bryan. When the British sailed from Savannah for Jamaica, Liele accompanied them, paying his passage as an indentured servant. During a layover of several weeks, Liele went to Savannah and baptized Bryan, his wife, and a few others who became the founders of the African Baptist Church in Savannah. The governor of Jamaica allowed Liele to work out his indentureship. Obtaining his free papers in 1784, he preached first in a private home. After the Jamaica assembly permitted him to preach, despite opposition from members of the Anglican church, he expanded his ministry to rural areas, gained a large number of communicants, built a church, taught

a free school, and gained a living as a farmer and hauler of goods. He died in Jamaica and was buried there. He was survived by his wife and four children.

A pioneer in Baptist churches for Negroes in America, Liele's church in Savannah was not the first (the oldest was the Silver Bluff Church, 1773). Carter G. Woodson attributed Liele's success to his "unusual tact." He did not accept as communicants slaves who did not have the permission of their masters or overseers. "Instead of directing attention to their wrongs, [he] conveyed to them the message of Christ" (*The History of the Negro Church,* 1921, p. 47).

This view is not supported by contemporary evidence. While in Jamaica, Liele was jailed on a charge of preaching sedition. Loaded with irons and his feet in stocks, he was not permitted to have visits from his wife and children. Tried on a capital charge, he was acquitted for lack of evidence. Jailed again for failure to pay an indebtedness on the chapel he was building, he remained in prison until he had paid his debt in full.

Liele reportedly gave this account of the nature of his religious experience: "I always had a natural fear of God from my youth, and was often checked in conscience with thoughts of death, which barred me from many sins and bad company. I knew no other way at that time to hope for salvation but only in good works" (John Rippon, *Baptist Register* [1791]; Liele to John Rippon, Dec. 18, 1791).

In addition to Rippon and Woodson, see John Clarke et al., *The Voice of Jubilee, A Narrative of the Baptist Mission, Jamaica, from the Commencement* (1865). There is an excellent brief account in Sidney Kaplan's *The Black Presence in the Era of The American Revolution, 1770–1800* (1973, pp. 76–77).

— SAMUEL L. GANDY

LLOYD, JOHN HENRY (1884–1965), baseball player. One of the finest baseball players of all time, Lloyd was called "the black Honus Wagner," after the great white shortstop of the Pittsburgh Pirates. Curious, Wagner went to see Lloyd play and declared that he was honored "that they should name such a great ball player after me."

Lloyd was born in Palatka, Fla., near Jacksonville. His father died when he was an infant, and after his mother remarried he was given over to the care of a grandmother. He left school before completing the elementary grades and became a delivery boy in a store. He broke in with the Macon Ga. Acmes in 1905. Waiting tables and playing ball in Florida resort hotels over the winter, he was picked up by the Cuban X-Giants, a misnamed team of American Negroes who played out of Philadelphia and claimed to be the best Negro team in the world. They were good enough to play the Philadelphia Athletics in 1906, and although they lost, the young Lloyd got four hits in five at-bats. The following year, with the rival Philadelphia Giants, Lloyd played the As again, cracking out two more hits. Journeying to Cuba for the winter of 1909–1910, Lloyd joined the Havana Reds for a series against the American League champion Detroit Tigers. Although Lloyd had a disappointing series at bat, the Reds won four and lost two. Even the Reach official baseball guide called it "disastrous'' for the champs. In three games against a strong all-star squad of big-leaguers, Lloyd got three hits in nine at-bats against the great Addie Joss, as the Reds won two of the three games. The next winter Lloyd returned to Cuba to meet the Tigers again. This time Ty Cobb, the American League batting and base-stealing champ, also played. Lloyd wore cast-iron shin guards under his stockings to protect himself against Cobb's notorious spikes, and tagged Ty out on three straight attempts to steal. Even more satisfying, Lloyd outhit the fiery Georgian as well: an even .500 for twenty-two games against Cobb's mark of .369. Cobb was so furious he vowed never to play against Negroes again. The Tigers were followed to Havana by Connie Mack's world-champion A's. Lloyd hit .300 against the best A's pitchers as the Reds swept the three-game series.

From Havana, Lloyd joined the New York Lincoln Giants, along with Spottswood Poles (another "black Cobb''), Jimmy Lyons, Louis Santop, Cyclone (Smokey) Joe Williams, and Cannonball Dick Redding. It was one of the finest teams of all time, and Lloyd led it at bat with an average of .475. In 1913, with Lloyd as manager, the Lincoln Giants won 101 games and lost only 60. In the autumn they won four out of five against big-league opposition. Williams beat the great Grover Cleveland Alexander in the final game 9–2, as Lloyd collected two hits and stole four bases.

After managing the Brooklyn Royals, the Atlantic City Bacharachs, and the Columbus Buckeyes, Lloyd joined the Philadelphia Hilldales in the new Eastern Colored League in 1923. With Lloyd, Santop, Raleigh "Biz" Mackey, Jesse "Nip" Winters, and William "Judy" Johnson, the Hilldales won the pennant with ease. Lloyd managed and batted .410. Jumping to the Bacharachs the next year, Lloyd did even better. He teamed with the great Dick Lundy on double plays and slugged a league-leading .444 at the age of forty.

Lloyd moved back to the Lincolns in 1926, and in 1930 was instrumental in opening Yankee Stadium to Negro teams. A benefit for A. Phillip Randolph's Brotherhood of Sleeping Car Porters, it drew 19,000 fans. Pop Lloyd was remembered as a gentleman in an era of roughneck baseball. His strongest oath was "Dad gum it." And he was a patient teacher of young players. Was Pop Lloyd born too soon? "No," he once said, "I don't feel that I was born at the wrong time. I feel it was the right time. I had a chance to prove the ability of our race in this sport, and because many of us did our best for the game, we've given the Negro a greater opportunity now to be accepted into the major leagues with other Americans." In 1938 a St. Louis sports writer, Ted Harlow, called Lloyd the greatest player of all time, including Cobb and Babe Ruth. The Babe himself was once asked whom he regarded as the best player he ever saw. "You mean major leaguers?" he asked. "No," was the reply, "the greatest player anywhere." "In that case," Ruth reportedly replied, "I'd pick John [Henry] Lloyd" (*Esquire*, Sept. 1938). Lloyd died on March 19, 1965, of arteriosclerosis after a two-year illness. His wife was his only close survivor, but he left a host of friends in and out of baseball with dimming memories of his grace at shortstop and his picture swing. He was inducted into the Hall of Fame on Aug. 8, 1977.

See John Holway's illustrated *Voices from the Great Black Baseball Leagues* (1975), based in large measure on interviews with former players, journalists, and contemporary newspapers. The book also contains valuable photographs. Robert W. Peterson's *Only the Ball Was White* (1970), likewise based on interviews and newspapers, has a photograph of Lloyd in uniform in 1918. — JOHN HOLWAY

LOCKE, ALAIN LEROY (1885–1954) philosopher, educator, and critic. He was born on Sept. 13, 1885, in Philadelphia, Pa., the only child of Pliny Ishmael Locke and Mary (Hawkins) Locke. She was a descendant of Charles Shorter, a free Negro who had been a soldier in the War of 1812 and established a tradition of education in the family. Pliny Locke was the son of Ishmael Locke (1820–1852), a free Negro whose career as a teacher in Salem, N.J., attracted the support of the Society of Friends. Under its auspices, Ishmael Locke attended Cambridge University in Britain, and then worked in Liberia for four years, establishing schools. While in Africa he married an Afro-American educator from Kentucky who was also engaged in establishing African schools. He later served as headmaster of a school in Providence, R.I., and principal of the Institute for Colored Youth in Philadelphia.

Pliny Ishmael Locke graduated from the institute in 1867, taught mathematics there for two years, and then taught freedmen in North Carolina during the early years of Reconstruction. He matriculated in the Howard University Law Department in 1872, worked as an accountant in the Freedmen's Bureau and the Freedmen's Bank, and for a time served as Gen. O. O. Howard's private secretary. After he completed law school in 1874 he returned to Philadelphia, where he became a clerk in the U.S. Post Office.

As a child, Alain Locke was nurtured in a genteel and cultivated environment that shaped his interests and choice of career. Because of the sixteen-year engagement of his parents before marriage, they were already middle-aged when he was born; he was six years old when his father died. Mary Locke, supporting the family by teaching, was a disciple of Felix Adler, and sent her son to one of the pioneer Ethical Culture schools. This was the beginning of Alain Locke's educational preparation, unusual when compared to the general population, but quite rare for Negroes before the turn of the century. A serious early illness, rheumatic fever, permanently damaged his heart. Locke's reaction to the physical restrictions imposed by his heart condition was to seek "compensatory satisfactions" in the cloistered world of books and in his study of the piano and violin. He attended the Central High School of Philadelphia from 1898 to 1902, graduated second in his class, and was awarded a B.A. degree with honors. From 1902 to 1904 he studied at the Philadelphia School of Pedagogy, where he was first in his class when he received a second bachelor's degree. He then entered Harvard College where he made a remarkable record. Completing the four-year course in three years, Locke won the college's most prestigious prize, the Bowdoin Prize for an essay in English (1907), was elected to Phi Beta Kappa, and awarded the Bachelor of Arts degree *magna cum laude*.

It had been a particularly fortunate period to study philosophy there, during "the golden age of philosophy at Harvard," when Josiah Royce, Hugo Muensterberg, George Herbert Palmer. Ralph Barton Perry and William James were on the faculty. In his senior year Locke passed the qualifying examination in Latin, Greek, and mathematics for the Rhodes Scholarship, which had been established in 1904. When he was selected, after oral examination in Philadelphia, as a Rhodes Scholar from Pennsylvania, Locke achieved a distinction that was to set him apart for the remainder of his life. In addition to the intrinsic prestige associated with the Rhodes Scholarship was the honor of being the first Negro selected; during his lifetime he remained the only American Negro Rhodes Scholar. The impact of his selection in 1907 was particularly dramatic because of the efforts of many white American scholars, especially psychologists, to "prove" the intellectual inferiority of Negroes as a rational basis for segregation. Locke thus became a symbol of youthful Negro intellectual achievement, justifying those who urged that Negroes be given an equal opportunity to enter white educational institutions and intellectually demanding professions.

Rebuffed by five Oxford colleges, which under the agreement establishing the Rhodes Scholarship retained the right of admission, Locke was admitted to Hertford College where he studied philosophy, Greek, and *Literae Humaniores* from 1907 to 1910. He then attended the University of Berlin from 1910 to 1911. Although these years in Europe were not entirely free of racial prejudice (indeed he encountered it at Oxford), they opened to Locke new perspectives for viewing American society and culture. Intellectually, his experience at Oxford and Berlin was also the foundation for much of his later interest in aspects of "modernism" in literature, architecture, music, dance, painting, and sculpture. Equally important, Locke developed in Europe a global conception of the race problem and a corresponding interest in Africa and the problems of nonwhite colonies elsewhere. While at Oxford he met many Africans, and was a founder (and secretary) of the African Union Society. The society's constitution said that it was to be a medium for cultivating "thought and social intercourse between its members as prospective leaders of the African Race," and to encourage "a wide interest in such matters as affect the welfare of the Race in Africa and in all other parts of the world." Nurturing the contacts he made with Africans at Oxford and in London, Locke's extensive correspondence in later years broadened his intellectual influence on the emerging leadership of Africa and the Caribbean.

When Locke returned to the United States in early 1912 he was fortified by an unusual intellectual and cultural experience, but still in search of a vocation and an accommodation with American racial conditions. Thrust by race outside the circle of opportunities shared by whites of similar education, he was also an oddity, or at least a stranger, among most American Negroes. Teaching in the increasingly segregated public schools was the only realistic chance he had for employment in Philadelphia, and his relatively sheltered experience scarcely prepared him for the Negro world elsewhere.

An unusually introspective and perceptive person, Locke recognized these limitations, and decided to take a six-month tour of the South. There, he said later, he came to a new understanding of "the Negro problem" and also concluded that his vocation was to be a college teacher.

On Sept. 3, 1912, Locke was appointed to the faculty of the Teachers College at Howard University as assistant professor of the teaching of English. At that time the dean of the Teachers College, Lewis Baxter Moore, a Ph.D. in Greek from the University of Pennsylvania (1896), was serving simultaneously as professor of philosophy in the College of Arts and Sciences. Probably because of Moore's seniority, Locke did not have the opportunity to teach philosophy at Howard until 1915. Locke began his career in philosophy at Howard teaching logic and ethics in the College of Arts and Sciences, while continuing to teach philosophy, education, English, and literature in the Teachers College.

Locke had come to Howard at a fortunate time. Wilbur P. Thirkield, its energetic white president from 1906 to 1912, had successfully reformed the curriculum in arts and sciences, creating a new emphasis on the social and natural sciences, and fostering the "university" idea over the older "collegiate" traditions rooted in the study of Latin, Greek, and mathematics. Enthusiastic about the transformation of the university, Locke believed that Howard should become a center for research on problems related to race, "culture contact," and colonialism. Additionally, he conceived of Howard as the best place in the United States to develop a Negro cultural center and "incubator of Negro intellectuals." His views, quite close to those of Kelly Miller, who was dean of the College of Arts and Sciences, were also a logical extension of lectures delivered at Howard in 1911 and 1913 by W. E. B. Du Bois, Arthur A. Schomburg, and Carter G. Woodson.

In 1915, one year after Jesse E. Moorland donated his large library on the Negro in America and Africa to Howard, Locke petitioned the university's Board of Trustees for approval of a systematic course on race and race relations. When the board, adhering to the nineteenth-century conception of Howard as a "nonracial" institution, refused to approve the course, the Howard chapter of the NAACP and the Social Science Club sponsored for two years an "Extension Course of Lectures" by Locke. The series was entitled "Race Contacts and Inter-Racial Relations: A Study in the Theory and Practice of Race." In the lectures Locke maintained that "racial differences and race inequalities [are] undeniable, [and] traceable invariably . . . to historical economic and social causes." A pioneer among American scholars in the field of comparative race studies, Locke observed as early as 1915 that "a study of race contacts [is] the only scientific basis for the comprehension of race relations." Although the faculty of the College of Arts and Sciences in 1916 endorsed a course on the Negro, the university trustees again rejected the proposal, with the comment that it was "inexpedient to establish a course in Negro problems at this time."

Thwarted, for the time being, in his efforts to foster the formal study of race at Howard, Locke again focused his energies on philosophy. In 1916 he was appointed an Austin Teaching Fellow at Harvard for one year. His doctoral dissertation, an extension of a long essay he had written at Oxford, was in the field of axiology, "The Problem of Classification in Theory of Value." He was awarded the Ph.D. from Harvard in 1918.

During the First World War, Locke was general secretary of the Central Committee of Negro College Men at Howard, and served as an instructor in the Student Army Training Camp established there in 1918 to train Negro students from more than seventy colleges.

In the period 1918 to 1924 Locke emerged as one of the faculty leaders at Howard and according to contemporary evidence, a major source of intellectual inspiration to students and the growing Negro youth movement. In 1924 he was granted sabbatical leave to work "in collaboration with" the French Oriental Archeological Society of Cairo. The university trustees also appointed him the "official head of the Howard University Mission." Representing the Negro Society for Historical Research as well, Locke went to the Sudan and Egypt. At Luxor he was present at the reopening of the tomb of Tutankamen. Justifying the excursion of a philosopher into the apparently remote field of archeology, upon his return from Egypt Locke wrote an article on Luxor in which he said that "the problems of Egyptian archaeology are now not so much those of discovery as those of interpretation; . . . the burden of scholarship is on the verge of turning to those interpretive problems which are in the fields of comparative art, comparative religion and comparative sociology." Reflecting a strong American Negro interest in Egypt of long standing, Locke also said that one significant point was that the ancient world's first great "cultural renaissance" was "focalized here in an African setting and in a polyglot civilization that must have included more African and possibly even Negro components than will ordinarily be admitted. . . ." Locke lectured widely on his experiences in Egypt, and presented a paper on Luxor at the Twenty-seventh Annual Meeting of the American Negro Academy (Dec. 28, 1928).

When Locke returned from Egypt he found Howard in upheaval because of a student strike protesting the administrative arbitrariness of its white president, J. Stanley Durkee. In the administration's effort to gain control of the situation, and perhaps also put an end to faculty protests about salary and academic rank inequities, several professors including Locke were fired in June 1925 on the alleged grounds of university reorganization, consolidation, and efficiency.

Locke's dismissal after thirteen years of service proved to be a major blunder, as strenuous protests by alumni and others erupted. The Howard Welfare League's charge that President Durkee was destroying scholarship at Howard was typical: "The best evidence of this is the dismissal of Alain LeRoy Locke, Rhodes Scholar. . . . If such a man of ripe scholarship as that of Dr. Locke cannot teach at Howard University, the administration cannot be endeavoring to run Howard as an institution of learning." From June 1925 to June 1928 Locke did not teach at Howard, although the trustees agreed in December 1925 to pay his salary for the academic year 1925–1926, after persistent protests in

the Negro press and in "mass meetings" in various cities. Characteristically it was Locke himself who made the best statement of the issues underlying the student unrest at Hampton, Fisk, Lincoln, and Howard. In a brilliant article in the September 1925 *Survey Graphic,* "Negro Education Bids for Par," Locke wrote that Negro education, "to the extent that it is separate, ought to be free to develop its own racial interests and special aims for both positive and compensatory reasons."

Ironically, this interlude of uncertainty about his future in the academic world was intellectually one of Locke's most productive periods. Although he lectured frequently and wrote book reviews, Locke had published only seven articles prior to 1923, notably on ethics in education (*The Teacher,* 1904), a critique of Oxford (*The Independent,* 1909), and an analysis of "the American temperament" (*North American Review,* 1911). In 1923 he became a prolific contributor of articles and reviews to the Urban League's new magazine, *Opportunity: Journal of Negro Life,* founded that year and edited by Charles S. Johnson. The next year Locke became associated with *Survey Graphic,* edited by Paul Kellogg, which for six years had been featuring articles on nationalism in the "New Ireland" and the "New Russia." In March 1925 Alain Locke was organizer and editor of the *Survey Graphic* issue devoted to the "New Negro," entitled "Harlem, Mecca of the New Negro." Contributors included Charles S. Johnson, James Weldon Johnson, W. E. B. Du Bois, Arthur A. Schomburg, Kelly Miller, Walter White, and a number of the "younger poets" whose talent Charles S. Johnson had been promoting in the literary contests sponsored by *Opportunity.* The lead essay, "Enter the New Negro," by Locke, asserted that a transformation of Negro life had occurred in which "social disillusionment" had been replaced by a "deep feeling of race" which had become "the mainspring of Negro life." Locke maintained that the "New Negro," frustrated by the economic and political barriers of segregation, was conscious of "acting as the advance-guard of the African peoples in their contact with Twentieth Century civilization." He also believed that the "pulse of the Negro has begun to beat in Harlem."

Released from his academic routine at Howard, Locke edited a book expanding the scope of the *Survey Graphic* issue, shifting the focus from Harlem to contemporary Negro cultural life. Published in December 1925 by Albert and Charles Boni, *The New Negro* was an instant success. One of the most handsomely produced books of its era, it included graphics by Winold Reiss and Aaron Douglas, a rich selection of fiction, poetry, music and drama criticism, and penetrating essays on the changing social environment of race relations. In his Foreword, Locke said that Negro life was "not only establishing new contacts and founding new centers, it is finding a new soul." Asserting that there was a "renewed race-spirit that consciously and proudly sets itself apart," Locke thought his book was representative of the "first fruits of the Negro Renaissance."

When *The New Negro* not only received excellent reviews, but also became a symbol of a "new era," Locke emerged as the principal spokesman of what he called "The New Negro Movement." He began to enjoy a unique position. His numerous critical essays and reviews on contemporary Negro literature and art established him as the leading academic authority in these fields. In addition, his many contacts with influential white editors, scholars, philanthropists, cultural leaders, and "patrons of the arts" gave him an unusual opportunity to foster the careers of young writers and artists. His enthusiasm for these writers was reflected in his hyperbolic statement in the *Annals of the American Academy of Political and Social Science* (November 1928) that it was "safe to assert that more worthwhile artistic output and recognition have been achieved in less than a decade than in all the range of time since 1619."

The most important "patron" for Locke was Mrs. R. Osgood (Charlotte) Mason (1854–1946), a wealthy, eccentric widow whom he met in February 1926. Convinced that Western civilization was collapsing because of "artificial values" and technological excess, she was committed to the preservation and propagation of the values of "primitive peoples"—at one stage of her patronage the American Indians, later American Negroes. Locke became her "talent scout" and coordinator, doling out funds and instructions to many of the leading Negro writers and artists of the period, notably Zora Neale Hurston, Langston Hughes, Aaron Douglas, and Richmond Barthé. In return for her patronage "Godmother," as she was called, acted as editor and censor, editing Hughes's *Not Without Laughter* and directing Hurston in her collection of southern folklore. For thirteen years she subsidized Locke's annual travels to Europe, and urged upon him the exotic primitivism which threatened to turn the "New Negro Movement" into a cult, isolated from the social and political realities of American Negro life. Under "Godmother's" influence Locke began to lecture Negro artists on the inspiration they ought to derive from African art. Locke even asserted in the late 1920s that there was a "racial temperament" derived from Africa. In 1928, for example, he wrote that although the American Negro was thoroughly assimilated in American *culture* with respect to language, religion, and mores, there was an "African or racial temperament, creeping back in the overtones of his half-articulate speech and action, which gave his life and ways the characteristic qualities instantly recognized as peculiarly and representatively his."

In the same period Charlotte Mason also subsidized Locke's development of one of the best African art collections in the United States. Locke's role as a pioneer collector and critic of African art has been relatively neglected, compared with his better known influence on "the New Negro Movement." Influenced by some of the French artists and collectors whom he met during his almost annual visits to Paris in the decades between the World Wars, Locke was one of the earliest Americans to write perceptively about the importance of African art, pointing out that its significance went far beyond its influence on the cubists and other avant-garde European artists. In May 1924 Locke wrote: "African art has two aspects, which . . . must be kept rigidly apart. It has an aesthetic meaning and a cultural

significance. What it is as a thing of beauty ranges it with the absolute standards of art and makes it a pure art form capable of universal appreciation and comparison; what it is as an expression of African life and thought makes it an equally precious cultural document, perhaps the ultimate key for the interpretation of the African mind." Locke organized numerous exhibitions of African art for three decades, and wrote the introductions to several landmark catalogues of African art.

Although Hughes and Hurston eventually broke their relationship with Mrs. Mason, Locke remained personally loyal to her through her thirteen-year hospitalization prior to her death. By the mid-1930s, however, he had gradually abandoned the primitivist aesthetics of his patron and the quasi-mystical or atavistic concept of a "racial temperament" which was not only increasingly rejected by modern social science, but had been contrary to Locke's own conception of race before he encountered Mrs. Mason, as is evident in his *Howard Review* article "The Concept of Race as Applied to Social Culture" (1924).

In an *Opportunity* article, "The Negro: New or Newer" (1939), Locke indicated his disillusionment with much of the earlier "New Negro" writing when he wrote that the phrase "New Negro" had become "a slogan for cheap race demagogues who wouldn't know a 'cultural movement' if they could see one, a handy megaphone for petty exhibitionists who were only posing as 'racialists' when in fact they were the rankest kind of egotists, and a gilded fetish for race idolators who were at heart still sentimentalists seeking consolation for inferiority."

Although Locke thus repudiated much of what was called the "Negro Renaissance," his intellectual role had been perhaps even more important than his personal promotion of some of the younger writers like Countée Cullen and Langston Hughes. William Stanley Braithwaite wrote later that just as Erasmus was "the propelling spirit of the Northern Renaissance of the early sixteenth century," Locke was "the propelling spirit" of the Negro renaissance of the 1920s, whose "humanistic philosophy" served as a broad base for the specific encouragement of Negro cultural expression.

When the Great Depression abruptly destroyed the conditions that had made possible the brief vogue in publishing creative writing by Negroes, Locke became less a promoter of young writers and more a critic. In the late 1930s Locke developed a concept that "racial art" was not genuinely separate from "mainstream" or "universal art," as then commonly supposed, requiring an artist to make a choice. As in the case of the art of Marian Anderson, Locke wrote in *Opportunity*, "the more deeply representative it is racially, the broader and more universal it is in appeal and scope, there being for truly great art no essential conflict between racial or national traits and universal human values."

As he would for the remainder of his life, Locke shuttled between multiple roles and was a cultivated insider in many spheres of life, working, he said, on "the cleavage planes" of racial and cultural divisions in the United States. He was, for example, a pioneer in the Negro theater movement, helping to produce in 1916 *Rachel* by Angelina Grimké, and to establish in 1921, with T.

Montgomery Gregory and Marie Moore-Forrest, the Howard University Players as the hopeful forerunner of a national Negro theater. Locke and Gregory believed that Negro drama could become an integral part of the evolving American theater, creating new opportunities for "the dormant dramatic gifts of the Negro folk temperament" while also representing distinctively American themes. In 1927 Harper & Brothers published Locke and Gregory's landmark book *Plays of Negro Life: A Source-Book of Native American Drama*, with illustrations and cover decorations by Aaron Douglas.

In June 1927 Locke was reappointed to the faculty of Howard University, but did not actually return until the following year. In the summer of 1927 he was commissioned by the Foreign Policy Association to study the League of Nations's mandate system, the problem of "native labor" in Africa, and the development of African education since the war. Locke worked in Geneva, and although his report was not published by the FPA (perhaps because of the "political sensitivity" then of the forced-labor issue and the well-financed campaign of the Phelps-Stokes Fund to shape African education) he gained new insight into the limitations on independent Negro research when sponsored by whites. In the academic year 1927–1928 he served as exchange professor at Fisk University.

He returned to Howard in 1928 during a major reorganization of the university, under the leadership of its first Negro president, Mordecai W. Johnson. At this time Locke was a close advisor of the new president, and urged the development of Howard as a Negro institution, in contrast to its earlier equivocations as a "nonracial" institution. In June 1928 Locke wrote Johnson that the "main justification for a Negro university, entirely apart from its origin out of a dual system of race education, is the possibility of its developing on the basis of a standard university special work as a center for the research study of the problems of Negro group life."

Locke not only revived his earlier proposals for the systematic study of race, but also recommended the adoption of his plan for an African Studies Program, which he had first proposed to President Durkee in 1924. "It is my opinion," Locke wrote, "that no greater incentive could be given in the promotion of real independent and original scholarship among Negroes than that of [the] development of interest in the broader and more intellectual aspects of the race problem." He wrote to Johnson on June 8, 1928, that Howard could become "the clearing house in America for information and counsel about the Negro people and their situation in the world." Moreover the African Studies program could be "the base for re-establishing the broken contacts of the American Negro, and for re-educating him to a knowledge of his past and a realization of his duty and mission with respect to Africa." Locke's detailed proposal for the study of African history, anthropology, ethnology, colonial history and administration, education, art, and culture, was not implemented during his lifetime; an African Studies Program was organized at Howard in 1954.

In reviewing his career at Howard, Locke concluded in this period that his "main objectives" had been "to

use philosophy as an agent for stimulating critical mindedness in Negro youth, to help transform segregated educational missions into centers of cultural and social leadership, and to organize an advance-guard of creative talent for cultural inspiration and prestige." In addition to these strategic objectives, he had worked to link "the discussion of colonial problems with the American race situation, toward the internationalization of American Negro thought and action" (private memorandum, Locke Papers).

The failure of Howard University to establish an African Studies Program in the late 1920s as Locke advocated did not deter him from his efforts to create at Howard some forum for focusing its intellectual energy on problems related to Negro life. In 1935 he was an organizer of the university's Division of the Social Sciences, in which he included the Department of Philosophy because of his conviction that in the twentieth century philosophy would be most important as a critical and synthesizing discipline for the social sciences as it had been historically, first for the humanities and then for the natural sciences.

The Social Science Division at Howard sponsored annual conferences for more than forty years which in a measure carried out the role Locke had projected for the university as an intellectual "clearing house" on questions of race, domestically and internationally. Soon after his successful efforts to create the Social Science Division, in cooperation with E. Franklin Frazier, Abram Harris, Ralph J. Bunche, and others, Locke embarked on what may have been his most important contribution to Howard as a teacher (as distinct from those he made as scholar and exemplar of the academic life). In 1935 he began his association with the reform of the liberal arts curriculum, which resulted in a coherent integration of the major disciplines in a general education program, influenced by similar reforms at the University of Chicago and Columbia University. The new curriculum, which endured for four decades, reflected Locke's emphases on critical analysis in the framework of humanistic values, and the need a democratic society has for learning to be linked to "responsible intelligent action" by its members. Locke's national stature as a reformer in American higher education from the 1930s until his retirement was recognized by his selection as a contributor to the volume *Goals for American Education* (1950), the Ninth Symposium of the Conference on Science, Philosophy, and Religion, for which he wrote "The Need for a New Organon in Education."

Almost concurrently with his work on the reform of Howard's liberal arts curriculum, Locke became more deeply involved in the adult education movement, in which he had first participated in 1924 as a delegate to the first Adult Education Conference sponsored by the Carnegie Foundation. In 1933 the Carnegie Corporation granted funds to the American Association for Adult Education for Locke to evaluate experimental adult education centers in Atlanta and Harlem. The same year he compiled *The Negro in America* for the American Library Association as a venture in adult education and "intergroup relations."

The success of these efforts led to the establishment

in 1935 of the Associates in Negro Folk Education, sponsored by the American Association for Adult Education, the Rosenwald Fund, and the Carnegie Corporation. Locke served as secretary and editor, while Lyman Bryson of Columbia University served as "advisory editor" representing the AAAE and holding veto power over publications of the Associates in Negro Folk Education, which was exercised in the case of a manuscript by W. E. B. Du Bois it commissioned but never published. Between 1936 and 1942 the ANFE published a series of nine "Bronze Booklets" by leading Negro scholars, including Ira De A. Reid, Sterling A. Brown, Ralph J. Bunche, and Eric Williams. The series, Locke said, was planned "to bring within reach of the average reader basic facts and progressive views about Negro life." Locke wrote two works in the series, *The Negro and His Music* and *Negro Art: Past and Present.* In 1940 the ANFE also published Locke's *The Negro in Art: A Pictorial Record of the Negro Artist and the Negro Theme in Art,* the most significant in its field and Locke's best known work after *The New Negro.* Reviews emphasized Locke's "excellent taste, his keen distinction, his broad human sympathy and appreciation," in addition to the industry and learning required to produce such a book.

Locke's philosophical work in the decades of the 1930s and 1940s was concerned primarily with value theory, aesthetics, and social philosophy, culminating in a coherent view of "cultural pluralism." Despite his prolific book and art reviewing, including annual retrospective review articles in *Opportunity,* and later in *Phylon,* Locke maintained his earlier interest in formal philosophy both as teacher and writer. His major publications in value theory were "Values and Imperatives" in *American Philosophy, Today and Tomorrow,* edited by Horace M. Kallen and Sidney Hook (1935), and "Pluralism and Ideological Peace" in *Freedom and Experience,* edited by Sidney Hook and Milton Konvitz (1947).

Locke's mature conviction that cultural pluralism, based on a social science understanding of race, culture, and social evolution, was a key to producing a new and humane world order led to the development of his pioneering anthology, co-edited with Bernhard J. Stern, *When Peoples Meet: A Study in Race and Culture Contacts* (1942). In November 1942 *Survey Graphic* published a special issue *Color: Unfinished Business of Democracy,* with Locke as special editor. Emphasizing the importance of the elimination of segregation and racial discrimination in the United States, Locke placed the American race problem in the larger context of the war aims of "the democracies" and their implications for European colonies in Africa and Asia. The issue sold out in a month; a second edition was published to meet the demand for what leading newspapers regarded as an inevitably influential publication in shaping public opinion and policy. A year later, while he served as inter-American exchange professor in Haiti, he wrote *Le rôle du Nègre dans la culture américaine,* which became the nucleus of a much larger project he believed would be his magnum opus.

By the end of World War II, Locke was one of the best known Negro scholars in the United States. A founding member of the prestigious Conference on Science, Philosophy and Religion (chairman in 1945), he was also a member of the editorial board of the *American Scholar,* philosophy editor for the *Key Reporter* of Phi Beta Kappa, and a regular contributor to national journals and magazines. In 1945 he was also elected president of the American Association for Adult Education, the first Negro to serve as president of a predominantly white, national education association.

As American higher education began to grope toward a voluntary and tentative desegregation in the North and West, Locke was besieged for lecture dates because of his credentials and reputation. In the academic year 1945–1946 Locke was visiting professor of philosophy at the University of Wisconsin. In 1947 he was visiting professor at the New School for Social Research, followed in 1948 by a visiting professorship at the City College of New York. After 1948 he continued to teach concurrently at C.C.N.Y. and Howard, continuing his practice of many years of commuting each week to New York, which had been his "second home" since the early 1920s. In 1950 he served on the faculty of the Salzburg Seminar in American Studies. Among Locke's important activities in the years before his retirement from Howard were his efforts, which extended over a period of fifteen years, to secure a chapter of Phi Beta Kappa at Howard, which was achieved in 1953, a major milestone in the history of Negro higher education.

In the last years of his life Locke was working on a book, *The Negro in American Culture,* which he did not live to complete.

One of the high points of Locke's life was his retirement from Howard University. In a rare gesture of esteem for a member of its faculty, the university awarded Locke on June 5, 1953, the honorary degree of Doctor of Humane Letters. On that occasion Pres. Mordecai W. Johnson's citation stated appropriately that Locke's "intellectual interests have been as broad as life itself. You have been a valuable critic of dogmatic ideology, a creator of free-moving ideas, an appreciator of the great cultural diversity in American life and a gentle but persuasive apostle of that unity of America and the world which thrives upon the coexistence and cooperation of individual and cultural differences." A particularly important part of the citation emphasized that Locke had been "a nucleus around whom an increasingly large group of scholars have been brought together in the College of Liberal Arts, whose work has won and received the approval of our sister universities, the confidence of Phi Beta Kappa, and a rapidly growing group of other learned societies."

In July 1953 Locke moved to New York, which had long been his goal, to enjoy the greater freedom there and to escape the segregation of Washington and its meagre cultural life. His recurrent heart trouble struck him in the spring of 1954 and he died on June 9, 1954, in Mount Sinai Hospital. He had never married. Funeral services were held at Benta's Chapel, Brooklyn, N.Y., on June 11, Dr. Channing Tobias officiating. Cremation took place at the Fresh Pond Crematory, Little Village, Long Island. His extensive collection of African art was bequeathed to the Howard University Gallery of Art, and his papers to the university's Moorland-Spingarn Collection. His manuscript on *The Negro in American Culture* was completed by the daughter of his close friend Ernest E. Just, Margaret Just Butcher, a colleague at Howard.

Although Locke's numerous essays would fill several volumes if collected for publication, he wrote no sustained analysis of the many cultural and racial problems that occupied him from the 1920s to the 1950s. His influence, though difficult to assess precisely, was probably greater than indicated by the residue of his writing, and he was clearly one of the most important spokesmen for an independent Negro intellectual tradition. With the dramatic rise of racial consciousness in the former European colonies, Locke's influence became internationalized.

There is no full-length biography of Locke, but a growing body of scholarly research has emerged since the 1960s which traces his diverse contributions to education, philosophy, and the arts.

See the obituary in the *New York Times* (June 10, 1954); John W. Cromwell's "Alain LeRoy Locke" (*African Times and Orient Review,* April 1913, pp. 313–14); Stanley J. Kunitz and Howard Haycraft (eds.), *Twentieth Century Authors* (1942, p. 837); *Current Biography* (1944); *Who's Who in America* (1954–1955); Rayford W. Logan (ed.), *The New Negro Thirty Years Afterward* (1955); Eugene C. Holmes's "Alain Locke: Philosopher, Critic, and Spokesman" (*Journal of Philosophy,* Feb. 28, 1957, pp. 113–18); H. M. Kallen's "Alain Locke and Cultural Pluralism" (*Journal of Philosophy,* Feb. 28, 1957, pp. 119–27); Ralph J. Bunche, W. E. B. Du Bois et al., "The Passing of Alain LeRoy Locke" (*Phylon,* Third Quarter 1954, pp. 243–52); Douglas K. Stafford's "Alain Locke: The Child, the Man, and the People" (*June,* Winter 1961, pp. 25–34); Lillian Avon Midgette's "A Bio-Bibliography of Alain LeRoy Locke" (M.S.L.S. thesis, Atlanta University, 1963); Eugene C. Holmes's "Alain L. Locke and the Adult Education Movement" (*JNE,* Winter 1965, pp. 5–10); and Arthur P. Davis's *From the Dark Tower: Afro-American Writers, 1900–1960* (1974, pp. 51–60, 240–44). Excellent guides to Locke's published and unpublished work in his voluminous papers have been prepared by Esme Bhan of the Manuscript Division, Moorland-Spingarn Research Center, Howard University.

— MICHAEL R. WINSTON

LOGUEN, JERMAIN WESLEY ["JARM"] (1813–1872), "conductor" on the Underground Railroad, author of an autobiographical slave narrative, and thirteenth bishop of the African Methodist Episcopal (A.M.E.) Zion church. Loguen was born about sixteen miles from Nashville in Davidson County, Tenn. His slave mother Cherry had been born free in Ohio, where she was kidnapped and sold to David Logue who became the father of Jermain. Logue sold Jermain and his mother to an owner who treated them brutally. The constant whipping of his mother, the murder of a slave, and the sale of his sister led to his determination to seek freedom. Although the Underground Railroad was not yet as efficient as it was later to become, Quakers helped Jermain flee through Kentucky and southern In-

diana (c. 1834–1835) to Detroit and Hamilton, Ontario, Canada. There he learned to read, worked as a lumberjack and farmer, and recrossed to central New York, studied at Oneida Institute in Whitesboro for three years and opened a school for Negro children in Utica. In November 1840 at Busti he married Caroline Storum. They moved to Syracuse, where he opened another school for Negroes and managed the Underground Railroad station there.

He started his ministry in 1841, joined the New York Conference of the African Methodist Episcopal Zion church, and was ordained in 1842. He established some half dozen churches (1843–1850), the most important of which was the Abolition Church in Syracuse. He changed "Jarm," the name Logue had given him, to Jermain, Logue to Loguen, and added Wesley as his middle name for the great Methodist minister, John Wesley. He and Frederick Douglass worked closely together on the Underground Railroad, and Loguen contributed articles to Douglass's *North Star* and *Frederick Douglass' Paper* in 1847. One of Loguen's daughters, Amelia, married Douglass's son Lewis. Another daughter, Sarah Marinda, was an 1876 graduate of the Syracuse Medical School. She married Charles Alexander Fraser in 1882 and remained in the Dominican Republic until ca. 1902. Their daughter, Gregoria Fraser Goins, a friend of Madame Evanti, lived in Washington for many years. (Gregoria Fraser Goins Papers, "Biographical Notes," Moorland-Spingarn Research Center, Howard University).

The Fugitive Slave Act of 1850 imperiled his liberty as it did that of other runaway slaves. Indicted for participation in the rescue of a fugitive slave, Jerry McHenry, on Oct. 1, 1851, Loguen, Samuel Ringgold Ward, and others escaped to Canada. Returning to Syracuse, he resumed his activities as manager of the Underground Railroad station there. In the decade before the outbreak of the Civil War he is credited with helping some 1500 slaves to escape. The most famous, Harriet Tubman, found refuge in his home. Frederick Douglass was inspired by Loguen and Henry Highland Garnett to meet John Brown in Ontario in 1858. But Jane H. Pease and William H. Pease concluded that "there is no evidence to indicate that Loguen was actively involved either in the planning or the execution of the Harpers Ferry Raid" (p. 248). In the summer of 1859 Loguen returned to Syracuse to help Negroes in campaigning for the Liberty League.

He was one of the outstanding preachers of the Southern Conference of the A.M.E. Zion church organized in Washington, D.C., on May 2, 1859. Elected bishop in 1864, he resigned from the Southern District to which he was assigned, fearing that it was too soon for a fugitive slave to go to a slaveholding area. He was reelected in 1868 and assigned to the Fifth District, including the Allegheny and Kentucky Conferences and adjacent mission fields. After two years he was transferred to the Second District (Genesee, Philadelphia, and Baltimore Conferences). In 1872 he was reelected bishop to take charge of mission work on the Pacific Coast. He died in Saratoga Springs, N.Y., before he could leave.

The principal source of information is *The Rev. J. W.*

Loguen, as a Slave and as a Freeman, a Narrative of Real Life (title page 1859, with a few letters dated 1860). John W. Blassingame concludes that the book, written in the third person, was Loguen's autobiography (*The Slave Community, Plantation Life in the Ante-Bellum South* [1872], p. 232). Additional details are in Bishop William J. Walls's *The African Methodist Episcopal Zion Church: Reality of the Black Church* (1974), J. W. Hood's *One Hundred Years of the African Methodist Episcopal Zion Church* (1895), and Jane H. Pease's and William H. Pease's *They Who Would Be Free: Blacks' Search for Freedom, 1830–1861* (1974). The best brief account is by William H. Allison in *DAB* (6, Part 1:368–69). An obituary was published in the *New York Tribune* (Oct. 1, 1872). Portraits in oil of Loguen and his wife by William Simpson are owned by the Howard University Gallery of Art.

— RAYFORD W. LOGAN

LONG, JEFFERSON FRANKLIN (1836–1900), congressman. Born on March 3, 1836, near Knoxville, Crawford County, Ga., the son of a white man and a slave mother, he was self-educated and a merchant tailor in Macon, Ga., by the end of the Civil War. In January 1871 he became the second Negro (Joseph Hayne Rainey of South Carolina was the first), and the only one from Georgia, elected to the U.S. House of Representatives during Reconstruction. On Feb. 1, 1871, he was the first Negro to deliver a speech in the House. He served only until March 3, 1871, when the 41st Congress expired. He resumed his business in Macon, participated in a southern Republican convention at Chattanooga, Tenn. (1874), and was a delegate to the Republican National Convention in 1880. He died in Macon on Feb. 5, 1900.

Despite his brief term in the House, his name was frequently mentioned when in the late 1960s and the early 1970s Negroes in Georgia again sought seats in the Georgia legislature and the House of Representatives. During Long's campaign for the House he spoke out vigorously against lynching and other forms of violence. He especially urged Negroes to vote for the Republican party. On Dec. 20, 1870, when the election was held, a serious race riot in Macon resulted in the death of several persons. Samuel Denny Smith, the adversely critical biographer of Negroes during Reconstruction, attributed the riot and Long's election, to "plural" voting and to ballots by Negroes from Alabama and South Carolina (*The Negro in Congress, 1870–1901* [1940], p. 73). Smith did not give the background of Georgia politics, without which the election of 1870 is difficult to understand. In September 1868 the Georgia state legislature had declared all colored members ineligible and replaced them by candidates who had received the next highest number of votes. This action encouraged the Ku Klux Klan to increase its violence against Negroes. Under the leadership of Henry McNeal Turner, they met in convention in Macon in 1869, and reported their findings to the Joint Committee on Reconstruction. Congress voted in December 1869 to exclude members from Georgia until the state ratified the Fourteenth and Fifteenth Amendments and placed it again under military rule. After ratification of

these amendments, Georgia members were readmitted and took their seats on Jan. 10, 1870.

This background helps understand not only Long's appeal to Negro voters in December of that year, and the determination of whites to exclude Negroes from election to Congress, but also Long's only speech in Congress, on Feb. 1, 1871. He opposed removing Confederate disabilities because their leaders publicly stated that they would then again assume control. In his own state, he said, 500 loyal men had been shot down by disloyal men, not one of whom had been brought to justice. Disloyal men hated the government and loyal men did not dare to carry the Stars and Stripes through the streets for fear of being deprived of their jobs or their votes by men who had committed Ku Klux Klan outrages. Despite his appeal, Congress enacted a bill permitting most ex-Confederates to qualify for voting without first establishing their allegiance to the Union; it became law without President Grant's signature. During his brief term in Congress, Long also supported the enforcement of the Fifteenth Amendment and advocated universal suffrage in the District of Columbia.

A photograph in the Schomburg Center for Research in Black Culture, New York City, portrays Long with a strong profile, close-cut black hair, moustache attached to cheek sideburns. He and his wife, Lucinda, had six children.

When Andrew Young was elected to the House in 1972, frequent mention was made of the fact that he was the first such Negro since Jefferson Long.

Basic information about Long is in *Biographical Congressional Directory, 1774–1927*. Brief sketches are in Samuel Denny Smith's *The Negro in Congress, 1870–1901* (1940) and Maurine Christopher's *America's Black Congressmen* (1971), which reproduces (following p. 115) the photograph from the Schomburg Center. For the background of Georgia politics, see W. E. B. Du Bois's *Black Reconstruction* . . . (1935, pp. 495–511).

— RAYFORD W. LOGAN

LOVE, NAT ["DEADWOOD DICK"] (1854–1921), cowboy. Born a slave in a log cabin in Davidson County, Tenn., Love was the youngest of three children. He worked as a cowboy for twenty years, excelling in roping, shooting, and the other skills of his trade, earning the title of champion in 1876 in contests at Deadwood, S. Dak. Despite the laws of slavery he obtained a modest ability to read and write at his father's knee. These lessons and whatever educational experiences he may have had were sufficient to enable him to write a presentable autobiography in 1907: *The Life and Adventures of Nat Love: Better Known in the Cattle Country as "Deadwood Dick."* After 1890 he worked in the Pullman service until his death in Los Angeles in 1921.

Love's father Sampson worked as a foreman in the fields; his mother was a cook. When his father returned from service as a laborer in support of the Confederate forces, the destitution of a sharecropper followed the distress of slavery and the deprivation of war. At the age of fourteen, upon his father's death, Nat became head of the family and supported his mother and his widowed sister and her two children. Their precarious living came from sharecropping and an off-season job at $1.50 a month. He earned additional income by breaking horses to ride, and acquired a skill that would later be of great importance to him.

A lucky raffle ticket brought him enough money so that, after dividing it with his mother, he was able to clothe himself and to seek greater opportunities. He started on foot for the West in February 1869. Upon his arrival in Dodge City, Kans., he found work as a cowboy. At once he earned admiration for his unsuspected ability to ride a bucking bronco which his new companions had furnished him for his initiation. By this unusual feat, the "tenderfoot" was accepted by the Duval outfit at $30 a month. An Indian attack soon followed. "At the first blood curdling yell, I lost all courage and thought my time had come to die." While under attack, his companions taught him how to use a handgun.

In 1872 Love was employed by the Pete Gallinger Company on the Gila River in southern Arizona. He found the cowboy's life agreeable, with its long days in the saddle, its hair-breadth escapes, risky rescues, mustang hunts, roundups, long cattle and horse drives with the "wild sons of the plains whose home was in the saddle and their couch, mother earth, with the sky for a covering." His superior physique, his keen eye, quick wit, alert mind, carried him successfully through an early cowboy's life on the open range, with its attendant adventures. He eagerly accepted the hardships of extremes of weather and geography, wild animals, stampedes, outlaws, and Indians.

Recognizing the need for proficiency with the tools of his trade, he set himself goals to excel. As a result he had the trust, confidence, and acclaim of his peers and employers. He became the Gallinger "chief brand reader," a position important in roundups on the open range in the identification and care of his employer's property.

At a Fourth of July celebration in 1876, after a cattle drive to Deadwood, S. Dak., Love found himself in competition with the best cowboys in the West. He won the contest to rope, throw, tie, bridle, saddle, and mount an untamed bronco, a feat he did in nine minutes, a record. He won the shooting contests with a rifle at 100 and 250 yards and with the Colt .45 at 150 yards. He entered and finished these matches with the confidence of a man who declared that "if a man can hit a running buffalo at 200 yards, he can hit pretty much of anything he shoots at." He was given the name "Deadwood Dick" by his admiring fans.

Love was captured by Indians, and was unwillingly adopted by the tribe. He escaped after an incredible ride of a hundred miles in twelve hours of darkness, carrying with him two new bullet holes, part of the total of "the marks of fourteen bullet wounds on different parts of my body."

As the high tide of the cowboy's world began to pass with the coming of trains, Love quit the fading wave and joined the crest of the new. He rode the iron horses with unreduced enthusiasm. His ambition remained the same: to earn a place in the community and to occupy it proudly and happily.

The major source is Harold Felton's *Nat Love, Negro Cowboy* (1967). Nat Love's *The Life and Adventures of Nat Love* . . . was reprinted in 1968 with an introduction by William Loren Katz. Katz stated in his *The Black West* (1971, pp. 150–152) that Love was "the self-made frontier hero." There is a full-page illustration. A revisionist interpretation of cowboys is the anthology edited by William Savage, Jr., *Cowboy Life: Reconstructing an American Myth* (1975).

— HAROLD W. FELTON

LUCA, ALEXANDER (1805– ?), musician and founder of the famous musical Luca Family quartet. Born on a farm near Milford, Conn., at age twenty-one he apprenticed himself to a shoemaker in Milford. His association with other apprentices resulted in a growing interest in the local singing school where he was welcomed and undertook the study of music in which he excelled. He later moved to New Haven, where he met and married a Miss Lewis, of a musical family. His excellent voice and musical training earned him a position as chorister in the Congregational church. He organized a quartet including Dinah Lewis, his wife's sister, a gifted singer, and his two first sons, with whom he gave concerts in New Haven and nearby towns. He taught his sons the shoemaker trade, and with the help of Dinah, they were educated in music. All members were highly gifted, and the youngest son, Cleveland, was a piano prodigy who at the age of ten had a repertory of masterpieces and the ability to play difficult music at sight, a talent he frequently proved in public performance.

The Luca Family performed as a vocal quartet or as an instrumental group. Simeon sang first tenor; Alexander Jr., second tenor; Cleveland, soprano; and John, bass-baritone. Simeon played first violin; Alexander Jr., second violin; John, cello or bass; and Cleveland, piano. Alexander Sr. was musical director and manager, as well as vocalist. Wherever they went they earned a reputation of refinement, intelligence, and superb musicianship. In their debut in the Old Tabernacle on Broadway (May 1853), as guests of the New York Anti-slavery Society, they thrilled an audience of 5000 people. "In witnessing the display of genius by the wonderful pianist, and listening to the sweet strains of classical harmony formed by the tuneful voices and skilfully played instruments of this troupe of colored artists, they found their claims for the race so fully sustained" (James Monroe Trotter, *Music and Some Highly Musical People* [1880], p. 96).

The press was almost unanimous in praise of their concerts. An extensive review in the *Niagara Courier* of Lockport, N.Y. (Sept. 2, 1857), on Cleveland's performance stated: "With the exception of the celebrated [William] Mason, [an outstanding American pianist], we have never had his superior as a pianist in Lockport. . . . The Luca Family, in the quiet and unostentatious display of their musical powers, are doing more to secure position for the colored man than all the theorists and speculators about the rights of man have yet accomplished in America."

In Ohio in 1859 the Luca Family met and joined in frequent concerts with the famous (white) Hutchinson Family. Again the press was enthusiastic, but one review, from Fremont, Ohio (Feb. 25, 1859), is worth quoting: "We have, perhaps, a stronger feeling of prejudice than we should have felt under other circumstances, had their abolition proclivities been less startling; but to see respectable white persons (we presume they are such) traveling hand in hand with a party of negroes, and eating at the same table with them, is rather too strong a pill to be gulped down by a democratic community.''

The Luca Family disbanded as a troupe when Cleveland decided to go to Africa in 1860. He composed the national anthem of Liberia, where he later caught a fever and died on March 27, 1872.

James Monroe Trotter quotes press notices extensively and describes at firsthand the performances of this remarkable family. He also notes that at the date of publication of his *Music and Some Highly Musical People* in 1880, Alexander Luca Sr. still resided in Zanesville, Ohio, where he sang in a church.

— RAYMOND LEMIEUX

LYLES, AUBREY (1884–1932), comedian. He was born in Jackson, Tenn. He and Flournoy Miller formed a partnership that remained unbroken until Lyles died in New York City on Aug. 4, 1932. Miller and Lyles toured Tennessee in a comedy act. Lured by northern big-city promises of fame and wealth, they went to Chicago where they were hired by Robert Motts to write for his Pekin Stock Company, a well-known Negro theater group. Their first play, *The Mayor of Dixie,* was such a hit that Motts decided to send it to New York City. Since he did not include the two young Tennessee writers in his plans, Miller followed the show as its property man and Lyles as valet for the star, Harrison Stewart.

In New York Lyles met the great comedian Ernest Hogan, who engaged him and Miller to write Hogan's biggest hit, *The Oyster Man* (1907–1908). With the closing of both the Pekin Company and *The Oyster Man,* Miller and Lyles sought vainly to write material for big-name vaudeville performers before returning to writing comedy material for themselves. Success was instantaneous when the major vaudeville circuits presented them as feature attractions. One skit, the boxing burlesque, was especially uproarious. Scarcely more than five feet tall, Lyles's frantic efforts to cope with his rangier partner convulsed audiences throughout the nation. Indeed Lyles, onstage, was the constant victim of Miller's verbal barbs and put-downs. And in their ''interrupted-conversation'' routine in which neither permitted the other to complete a sentence, Lyles usually got the worst of it.

They made their debut in Europe in 1915, touring London and the British Isles in André Charlot's *This And That.* Back in America, Lyles and his partner left vaudeville to appear in *Darkydom* and later in *Shuffle Along.* The latter was Broadway's first all-Negro hit musical. Miller and Lyles wrote the book while Noble Sissle and Eubie Blake wrote the lyrics and music, respectively. Opening in 1921, *Shuffle Along* ran for three years, touring the United States, Canada, and London. Its producers, owners, and star performers were Sissle, Blake, Miller, and Lyles.

Later shows in which Lyles appeared and/or to which he contributed his writing talents were *Runnin'*

Wild (1924), *Rang Tang* (1927), *Keep Shufflin'* (1928), and *George White's Scandals.*

Runnin' Wild had a successful run of eight months at the Colonial Theater, where it introduced to wider audiences the ''Charleston,'' a dance that had been known almost exclusively to Negroes. *Rang Tang* at the Majestic Theater did not draw well despite a droll scene in which an airplane finished its flight at sea before Miller and Lyles were able to reach Africa. *Keep Shufflin'* seemed to indicate the need for a new type of Negro musical. Offstage, Lyles was known for his free-spending, flamboyant, and daring lifestyle.

For further information, see James Weldon Johnson's *Black Manhattan* (1930, pp. 187–90, 209, 216, 224, 229), Edith Isaacs's *The Negro in the American Theater* (1947, p. 66), Tom Fletcher's *100 Years of the Negro in Show Business* (1954, pp. 201–5), and Loften Mitchell's *Black Drama* (1967, pp. 76–77, 85–86). The statement that Lyles and Flournoy Miller attended Fisk University is not confirmed by available university records (letter from Mrs. Aline Rivers to Rayford W. Logan, Jan. 13, 1977). — ELTON C. FAX

LYNCH, JOHN ROY (1847–1939), speaker of the Mississippi House of Representatives, member of Congress, army officer, and lawyer. The third son of Patrick Lynch, a native of Dublin, Ireland, and Catherine White, a slave, he was born on Sept. 10, 1847, on Tacony Plantation near Vidalia, Concordia Parish, La. After purchasing his wife and family with a view to moving them to New Orleans, Patrick Lynch suddenly became ill. Before his death he transferred title in them to a friend who promised to treat them as free persons, since manumission required their removal from the state. The friend did not keep his promise; instead he sold the Lynch family to another planter who removed them to Natchez, Miss., John Roy Lynch remained a slave until 1863, when Union forces occupied Natchez.

After working at odd jobs for several years, Lynch secured employment in 1866 in a studio where he learned the trade of a photographer. Soon he became the manager of a thriving photographic business in Natchez. Meanwhile he learned the value of an education, although his own training was meager. When the whites began to establish schools in 1865 they made no provisions for educating Negroes, and Lynch had to wait until a group of northern teachers established an evening school for Negroes in 1866. It remained open only four months, but Lynch was in regular attendance the entire time. Thereafter his education was informal—reading books and newspapers, and listening to the recitations in the white school across the alley from the studio. Within a few years he had not only become quite literate but had also developed a capacity for oral expression that made a favorable impression on his listeners.

Lynch was scarcely twenty years old when new political opportunities came to him and the other freedmen by the Reconstruction Acts of 1867. He became active in one of the local Republican clubs in Natchez and wrote and spoke in support of the new state constitution. His activities came to the attention of Gov. Adelbert Ames, who in 1869 appointed him to the office of justice of the peace. Before the end of his first year in that office, he ran successfully for a seat in the House of Representatives of the Mississippi legislature. In his first term he became a member of two important standing committees, military affairs and elections, and soon proved to be one of the most active members of that body. In the second session, the speaker, H. W. Warren of Leake County, recognized the talents of the young Negro from Adams County by appointing him to several special committees and entrusting much of the Republican party's legislative program to his care.

On the first day of his second term, beginning in January 1872, Lynch gained a seat on the Committee on Credentials, and on the second day he was elected speaker of the House. In that position he wielded enormous power, including his single-handed redistricting of the state, which gave the Republicans five safe districts out of six. In the same year his party sent him as a delegate to the Republican National Convention, where he served on the Committee on Resolutions. When he returned from the convention, he and his friends decided that he should run for the lower house of the U.S. Congress against the white incumbent Republican, L. W. Perce. It was not because Perce was white that Lynch opposed him. Lynch described Perce as a "strong and able man" who had made a "creditable and satisfactory record." It was simply that Lynch wanted the seat for himself. When he defeated Perce for the nomination, most of Perce's supporters worked for Lynch, and he went on to defeat handily the Democratic candidate, Judge Hiram Cassidy.

It was as a congressman-elect that Lynch presided over the 1873 session of the lower house of the Mississippi legislature. It was a busy and productive session, and Lynch's firm hold on the proceedings was evident from beginning to end. At the close of the session the house unanimously adopted a resolution complimenting and thanking the speaker for the manner in which he presided, "with becoming dignity, with uniform courtesy and impartiality, and with marked ability." On behalf of the members of the house, J. H. Piles of Panola presented Lynch with a gold watch and chain, "as a memento of our high admiration for you as a gentleman, citizen, and Speaker."

Lynch was twenty-six years old, the youngest member of the 43rd Congress, when he took his seat in December 1873. He drew two committee assignments, Mines and Mining, and Expenditures in the Interior Department. His maiden speech (Dec. 9, 1873) in connection with the bill to repeal the increase of salaries of the members of Congress was marked by grace and good humor and made a favorable impression on the members. His membership in that body ran through several terms. He was reelected in 1874 but was defeated in 1876. He ran again in 1880, and when the Democrats certified returns indicating that his opponent, Gen. James R. Chalmers, was the winner, Lynch successfully contested the election and took his seat in April 1882. After losing his bid in the election of 1882, he retired to his home in Adams County to manage the plantation he had acquired.

As a member of Congress Lynch was careful to attend to the needs of his constituents. He introduced bills for the relief of private persons, to donate the Natchez marine hospital to the state, and to provide for an additional term of the U.S. District Court for the Southern District of Mississippi, but they did not become law. Perhaps the bill that took his greatest attention was the Civil Rights Bill. In 1874 he argued for its passage "not only because it is an act of simple justice, but because it will be instrumental in placing the colored people in a more independent position. . . ." In February 1875 he chided Republicans who had not supported the bill and appealed to all members of the House, "republicans and democrats, conservatives and liberals—to join with us in the passage of this bill, which has for its object the protection of human rights." Since he could claim some credit for the bill's passage in March 1875, many of his white constituents could not forgive him and worked hard for his defeat the following year.

By the time that Lynch left Congress he had become prominent in the national councils of the Republican party. He served as chairman of the Republican state executive committee from 1881 to 1892. He was a delegate to the party's national conventions in 1884, 1888, 1892, and 1900. In 1884 a group of young Republicans led by Theodore Roosevelt and Henry Cabot Lodge successfully engineered the election of Lynch to the position of temporary chairman, over Powell Clayton of Arkansas, the choice of the Blaine forces that had expected to control the convention. As temporary chairman Lynch became the first Negro to deliver the keynote address before a national political convention. Having no time to prepare an address, Lynch spoke briefly. He was satisfied, he said, that the people of the United States were too loyal to allow a man to be inaugurated president whose title to the position was brought forth by fraud and whose garments "may be saturated with the innocent blood of hundreds of his countrymen." Obviously, only Democrats wore bloody shirts!

From the time of Lynch's retirement from Congress in 1883 to his death in 1939 he was engaged in a variety of public and private activities. Declining positions offered him by Democrats, Pres. Grover Cleveland and Secretary of the Interior, L. Q. C. Lamar, he did accept an appointment by Pres. Benjamin Harrison as fourth auditor of the treasury, a position he held from 1889 to 1893. In 1898 he accepted President McKinley's appointment as paymaster of volunteers in the Spanish-American War with the rank of major in the army. In 1901 he took the same post in the Regular Army. His tours of duty took him to Cuba, Omaha, San Francisco, and the Philippines, and he retired from the army in 1911.

Meanwhile Lynch had become quite active in the plantation and city real estate market in Adams County, Miss. In 1869 he purchased two lots in Natchez, and by 1898 he had purchased eleven more parcels of Natchez property, ranging from one to four lots, and four plantations in Adams County containing more than 1800 acres. Having done well in the real estate business, Lynch disposed of all of his Mississippi holdings by 1905.

In the early 1890s Lynch began to study law on his own, and in 1896 he passed the Mississippi bar on the second attempt. Shortly thereafter he became a partner in the Washington law firm of Robert H. Terrell. He practiced law in the nation's capital and in Mississippi until he entered the army in 1898. His marriage in 1884 to Ella Somerville, by whom he had one daughter, ended in divorce. In 1911 he married Cora Williams, and after his retirement from the army they moved to Chicago where he entered the practice of law and engaged in real estate operations. From time to time he participated in various efforts by Negroes to find solutions to their problems. In 1879 he attended the National Conference of Colored Men of the United States held in Nashville, Tenn. In 1886 he supported Negro membership in labor unions that did not "resort to lawlessness and violence." In 1913 he published his *Facts of Reconstruction,* in an effort to set the record straight about the part played by Negroes in that tragic era. It is easily the best account of Reconstruction by a Negro participant. In 1917 and 1918 he published two papers in the *Journal of Negro History,* challenging the assertions of historian James Ford Rhodes, branding the latter's history a work of errors.

A man of slight build and almost ascetic mien, Lynch was widely recognized as an eloquent speaker, an able advocate in politics and law, and a charming, amiable associate in personal relations. He spent his final years writing his autobiography, a generally accurate work that is concerned primarily with his political career. He died from the infirmities of old age on Nov. 2, 1939, at his Chicago home he shared with his wife, who survived him. He was buried with full military honors at Arlington National Cemetery.

Lynch's writings include *The Facts of Reconstruction* (1913); "Some Historical Errors of James Ford Rhodes" (*JNH,* Oct. 1917); "More About the Historical Errors of James F. Rhodes" (*JNH,* April 1918); *Reminiscences of an Active Life: The Autobiography of John Roy Lynch,* edited by John Hope Franklin (1970), and *DAB, Supplement 2* (1958, pp. 395–96); See also the *Biographical Directory of the American Congress* (1950); *Who's Who in America, 1934–1935; New York Times* (Nov. 3, 1939); Samuel Denny Smith's *The Negro in Congress, 1870–1901* (1940); and Vernon L. Wharton's *The Negro in Mississippi, 1865–1890* (1947).

— JOHN HOPE FRANKLIN

MACARTY, VICTOR-EUGÈNE (1821–c. 1890), New Orleans–born pianist, composer, orator, politician, and civil rights leader. The son of Eulalie de Mandeville and an unknown father, he was a member of the free colored family group of that name, many of whom were persons of education, wealth, and refinement. These free colored people were the descendants of a Spanish-Irish family named McCarthy which changed the spelling to Macarty. Most of the white men of this prominent Creole family showed a distinct preference for stable connections with free women of color. As in the case of Eulalie de Mandeville, the common-law bride of Eugène Macarty, these free colored women were frequently the natural daughters of some of the most prominent white Creole families, and these families recognized them with substantial marriage dowries and personal gifts. When the extremely wealthy Marigny de Mandeville family placed their colored daughter Eulalie

in the hands of Eugène Macarty, she had chosen this white man of wealth and family position as her life mate; after his death in 1845 she received property amounting to $12,000. Through judicious and energetic management she amassed a fortune of $155,000. She educated her sons and daughters and helped to launch them in their careers.

In his early youth Macarty studied the piano under Prof. J. Norres. His brilliant versatility included a rich and resonant baritone voice; an ability as a first-rate amateur actor and orator; and a leading politician of the Reconstruction era. In 1840 Macarty attracted the attention of Pierre Soulé, one of the most prominent whites in the public life of New Orleans. Through Soulé's intervention, and that of the French ambassador to the United States, Macarty was admitted to the Imperial Conservatoire in Paris although he was then past the age prescribed for admission. There he studied music, harmony, and composition.

On his return to New Orleans Macarty gained fame as a pianist, able amateur actor and comedian, composer, and Negro leader. In the theatrical productions of the free colored group the leading role in any play was "bestowed upon him by common consent." His best known roles as an actor were those of Anthony in the play of the same name and that of Buridan in *La Tour de Nesle,* both by Alexandre Dumas.

Macarty was drawn into the vortex of popular issues of the Reconstruction era, and being an excellent speaker he soon became a familiar and highly esteemed spokesman in the interest of civil rights. He was the first to bring suit against the St. Charles Theater because of seating discrimination. Being white enough to "pass" easily, he took a seat in the "white" section of the theater in January 1869, when he attended the opera *Figaro Bravo.* When he was "discovered" and ordered to leave, he threatened to slap the manager's face and kick him for good measure. Since the manager continued to segregate Negroes, they boycotted the theater until the national civil rights act was passed in 1875. In 1869 he was appointed city administrator of assessments by Gov. Henry Clay Warmoth. He also held other positions of trust under Republican administrations. As a leading businessman he acquired a sizable income equal to his status as a Negro leader. By common consent Macarty was placed with the heads of the Republican party's radical wing that for a short time exerted a powerful influence in behalf of civil rights. The militant *La Tribune de la Nouvelle-Orléans* described him (June 20, 1865) as "One of the most talented men who are an honor for our population and one of whom we are proud," and then added: "his literacy acquirements and his enlightened taste secure him a place of distinction in our community."

Macarty was a friend and admirer of Natalie Populus, granddaughter of Maj. Joseph Savary, hero of the Battle of New Orleans. Macarty's poem "La Fleur Indiscrète," published in the *Tribune* of July 22, 1866, was dedicated to her. Probably because of his varied activities, his musical compositions were far less numerous than those of his contemporaries; only a few of them have been preserved. Among these are *Fleurs de Salon* (1854), containing two separate compositions, "La Caprifolia" and "L'Azalea." *Fleurs de Salon* contains this statement beneath the author's misspelled name: "Pianist of the fashionable Soirees of New Orleans." Grace King, author of *New Orleans, the Place and the People* (1896), voiced serious doubts whether anyone "has ever known the full poetry and inspiration of the dance who has not danced to the original music of a Macarty or a Basile Barès." She also declared that "It is a pleasure to own the conviction . . . that America will one day do homage for music of a fine and original type, to some representative of Louisiana's coloured population."

See especially various issues of *La Tribune de la Nouvelle-Orléans*. See also James Monroe Trotter's *Music and Some Highly Musical People* (1878, reprint 1969). For background, see Herbert Sterkx's *The Free Negro in Ante-Bellum Louisiana* (1972) and John W. Blassingame's *Black New Orleans, 1660–1880* (1973). Original scores are in the Howard-Tilton Library at Tulane University and the Marcus B. Christian Collection of the Earl Long Library, University of New Orleans. Information about the decisions on the Mandevilles and their Macarty descendants is in Helen Catterall (ed.), *Judicial Cases Concerning Slavery and the Negro* (1932, 3:-392, 589, 611–12) — MARCUS B. CHRISTIAN

McCABE, E. P. [first name probably **Edward,** although frequently printed as **Edwin,** and middle name probably **Preston**] (1850–1920), politician. McCabe was born on Oct. 10, 1850, "of humble parents," in Troy, N.Y., the second son and youngest child of three. His mother Elizabeth, a mulatto, was born in Delaware, c. 1822 (U.S. Census, 1860: Newport, R.I.); his father's name is unknown and his identity obscure. Soon after McCabe's birth his parents moved to Fall River, Mass., and in a short time to Newport, R.I., but while in grammar school he was sent to Bangor, Me., to continue his education in "that liberal State." Soon, however, according to one authority, the family removed to San Francisco where after a year his father died. The family then returned to Newport, and McCabe himself went to New York City where he worked as a clerk and porter for the Wall Street firm of Shreve, Kendrick & Co. In 1872 he went to Chicago where he had a clerkship with the hotel firm of Potter Palmer until his intelligence and skill in penmanship won him a position in the treasurer's office of the Cook County courthouse, where he worked for about two years.

When the "Exoduster" movement to Kansas got under way, he and his friend Abraham T. Hall, Jr., city editor of *The Conservator,* a Negro newspaper, decided to join a Hodgeman County colony, but at Leavenworth, Kans., Hall heard about the Nicodemus colony, Graham County, northwest Kansas, and he and McCabe decided to join it. When in April 1878 the friends arrived in Nicodemus they set themselves up as "Attorneys and Land Agents," assisting new arrivals to get settled. McCabe was elected secretary of the Nicodemus Town Company and served until its disbanding in April 1879. On April 1, 1880, he was appointed temporary county clerk and served until June 1; in November 1881 he was regularly elected to the position, principally by white voters.

Sometime in late 1880 McCabe was married in Chicago to Sarah J. Bryant, who had been born in 1860 in Cincinnati, Ohio.

McCabe was of distinguished presence—according to an old acquaintance—"a handsome man of Indian complexion," while others described him as "almost a white man in appearance." Photographs show him as aggressively but neatly mustached, nattily dressed, and well groomed. He was undoubtedly highly intelligent, well educated for the time and place, possibly with a good deal of office experience. For whatever combination of reasons, he rapidly attained recognition as the principal leader in a Negro population which had increased from 17,000 in 1870 to 43,000 a decade later; although less than 5 percent of the state's total population, it was worthy of political consideration, and in 1882 the Kansas Republicans elected McCabe state auditor.

McCabe received wide publicity and acclaim as having probably attained the highest state office of any northern Negro, and in 1884 was reelected, but in 1886 the Republicans nominated "an Irishman" for McCabe's position. After the end of his term of office he went to California, for a vacation and perhaps to do some prospecting. However, he was soon back in Topeka, where he operated as a real estate agent, gave loyal support to the Republican party in the election of 1888, and again offered himself, this time unsuccessfully, for state office.

McCabe by early 1889 was naturally discouraged in regard to his Kansas prospects. He had told a friend that he was looking forward to the election in 1888 of a Republican president, in which case he expected an important appointment in Washington, D.C. After Benjamin Harrison's inauguration he accordingly went to the national capital, hoping with the support of Kansas Sens. James J. Ingalls and Preston B. Plumb to press his claims successfully for such an appointment—probably as register of the treasury, a plum which sometimes fell to Negro political leaders. However, during the late 1880s would-be landseekers and ambitious politicos were showing increasing interest in the ceded portions of the Indian Territory which were soon to be opened to settlement and become Oklahoma Territory. In July 1889 Kansas Negroes formed in Topeka the Oklahoma Immigration Association for colonizing the territory with "industrious colored farmers and others," with H. W. Rolfe, editor of the *Kansas Citizen,* as president and William L. Eagleson, the pioneer editor, as corresponding secretary and manager. McCabe, appointed Washington representative, conceived the grandiose ambition of obtaining the territorial governorship, and received strong Negro support. Since the widespread assumption was that such an appointment would be a step toward making Oklahoma a Negro, or Negro-dominated territory and state, threats of assassination were rife. Although some of his more ardent supporters certainly advocated such a state, McCabe himself was probably too intelligent to believe in its feasibility. Early in March 1890 he declared—he could hardly have said less: "If I should be appointed governor I would administer the laws . . . without fear or favor to white and black alike." But before the end of the month he had given up his gubernatorial ambitions and became an unsuccessful candidate for territorial secretary.

Despite these disappointments McCabe—although he is said to have been offered, and declined, the meagre consolation prize of immigration inspector at Key West, Fla., in April 1890—moved to Guthrie, Oklahoma Territory, where he opened a real estate office. He soon was appointed first treasurer of Logan County, and when the first Oklahoma council, or upper house, was organized, he was chosen for the post of the "temporary secretary."

Late in 1890 or early in 1891 McCabe became heavily involved in the establishment and development of the all-Negro town of Langston—named for John M. Langston, Virginia's first Negro congressman (1889–1891)—twelve miles northeast of Guthrie, then the capital. According to a widely accepted account, McCabe purchased 320 acres for this purpose, but more probably operated as principal promoter and sales agent for the owner, Charles H. Robbins, a white man. He sold contracts for Langston lots throughout the South, each contract also entitling the purchaser to a railroad ticket to Langston. Perhaps also remembering that within a few years of Nicodemus's founding its principal businesses were owned by whites, McCabe's contracts provided that the title to lots in Langston "could never pass to any white man, and upon them no white man could ever reside or conduct a business." By April 1891 Langston had a population of 200, including a doctor, preacher, and schoolteacher.

McCabe was also interested in the *Langston City Herald,* which began publication on May 2, 1891, with "the old war horse" W. L. Eagleson as editor, and which devoted itself to publicizing both the community and the territory to southern Negroes. Although the 1890 census revealed that the nearly 22,000 Negroes in the territory (including the Indian Territory) constituted only 8.4 percent of the population, they were sufficiently numerous and well organized in some counties to constitute a significant political factor, as indicated by the election of Green J. Curran, McCabe supporter and former Topeka policeman, to the legislature from Kingfisher County and McCabe's own appointment as treasurer of Logan County. McCabe's objective was to build up the Negro population, and consequent political strength, in other counties. The *Langston Herald* campaigned zealously for the Negro colonization of the Cimarron Valley, which was to be opened to settlement on Sept. 22, 1891, and McCabe was reportedly endeavoring to collect 15,000 Negroes at Langston as a staging point for the "rush." Racial feelings rose high, and on the day of the rush two Negroes were badly wounded. McCabe, going out unarmed to investigate, was fired on by three whites but was rescued by Negroes armed with Winchesters. In spite of all difficulties, several hundred—perhaps nearly a thousand—Negro families obtained homesteads.

McCabe, through the *Herald,* for a time continued to promote Negro colonization, but by September 1892 he had sold out his interest in the paper to a group of Guthrie Negroes, to whom he also apparently turned over his agency for the sale of lots in Langston. However, a few days after the rush of Sept. 16, 1893, into

the Cherokee Strip, McCabe established there a new town, Liberty, southwest of Langston and three miles north of Perry, and for several months devoted himself to its development and promotion. Any hopes he may have had for political preferment had again been dashed when the newly inaugurated Democratic president, Grover Cleveland, appointed a Confederate veteran as governor of the territory, but McCabe, taking the long view, increasingly concentrated on strengthening the Republican party among Oklahoma Negroes and his own position in the party. In 1894 the Republican Territorial League elected him secretary, and when the Territorial Assembly met early in 1895 he was appointed assistant chief clerk. Although his claim that, through his efforts, the territory was "safely Republican" was a gross exaggeration, he had achieved recognition as its Negro political leader, the position which a dozen years earlier he had attained in Kansas.

In 1897 McCabe achieved two triumphs: the legislature finally established the Colored Normal and Agricultural University, and located it at Langston, the community which McCabe had done so much to develop and which, after having once achieved a population of nearly 2000, had declined to perhaps 250; and the new Republican governor conferred upon him the office of assistant, or deputy, territorial auditor—which, although a comedown from his state auditorship of Kansas (1883–1887), was nevertheless the highest office then held by any Negro in Oklahoma or in the West in general. But having achieved this appointment, McCabe's activity declined, although he served with sufficient acceptability and retained enough political reputation that a series of Republican governors regularly reappointed him, so that he continued in office for a decade, until Nov. 15, 1907, the day before Oklahoma became a state.

With statehood—which Negroes generally opposed—ended McCabe's dream of an Oklahoma in which Negroes, even if not dominant, would be able to exercise political influence, win their share of offices, and protect their rights, as they had in Graham County, Kans., and even in such Oklahoma Territory counties as Logan and Kingfisher. The first bill introduced into the state legislature, and duly passed, provided for racially separate railroad coaches and waiting rooms, and although in 1908 a young Logan County Negro, Oscar C. Hamlin, was elected to the legislature, in 1910 a constitutional amendment in effect disfranchised Oklahoma's Negroes for half a century.

McCabe did not yield to Jim Crow without a struggle. In February 1908, with reviving energy, he took the lead in challenging the enforcement of railroad segregation, but court after court sustained the law and in 1914 the U.S. Supreme Court affirmed Oklahoma's constitutional right to legislate "separate but equal" accommodations. However, long before this decision McCabe, in the fall of 1908, had sold his Oklahoma holdings and left a state in which, after nearly a score of years, he no longer had a satisfactory place. Nor, indeed, did he really have a place anywhere, for, now in his late fifties and confronting an era in which the Negro's political and social status had either reached or was rapidly approaching its nadir, he had no prospect of resuming the political career to which he had devoted over a quarter century in one state and in another territory and which, indeed, had virtually become his life.

After the Supreme Court's decision in *E. P. McCabe et al. v. Atchison Topeka and Santa Fe Railroad Company et al.,* McCabe's name passed out of public view. He had returned to Chicago, where he lived in obscurity and on March 12, 1920, died in extreme poverty, of myocarditis. His wife brought the body to Topeka, the scene of his greatest triumph, where on March 15 it was interred in the presence only of his widow, a white undertaker, and a gravedigger. Two children—Edwina (1881–1907) and Eddie (Sept. 18–19, 1885)—had long predeceased him.

McCabe had been largely responsible for encouraging thousands of southern Negroes to settle in Oklahoma Territory, where many had obtained government land; even though they encountered separate schools and under statehood were unsparingly segregated and disfranchised, they were at least better off than the landless sharecropper kinsmen they had left behind. When in 1964 four Negroes were elected to the legislature and the following year the "Jim Crow" law of 1907 was repealed, McCabe's long-deferred dream began to move toward reality.

No biography of McCabe exists, although Glen Schwendemann has generously supplied numerous references to Kansas and Oklahoma newspapers. Alene Simpson, librarian of the Oklahoma Historical Society, Oklahoma City, has also investigated his career and has furnished references to census reports and to Oklahoma biographical collections. Some information about his career to 1887 is in William J. Simmons's *Men of Mark . . .* (1887). Marion Tuttle Rock's *Illustrated History of Oklahoma* (1890) deals briefly with his life up to his settlement in Oklahoma Territory, differing from Simmons in several details, while the *Business and Resident Directory of Guthrie and Logan County, OK., for the Year Commencing Sept. 1st, 1892* (1893) presents an even briefer eulogy. Glen Schwendemann's "Nicodemus: Negro Haven on the Solomon" (*Kansas Historical Quarterly* 34, Spring 1968), a scholarly study, is authoritative for the Kansas years. The principal sources for his Oklahoma career are Kaye M. Teall (ed.), *Black History in Oklahoma* (1971), a documentary collection; Daniel F. Littlefield, Jr., and Lonnie E. Underhill's "Black Dreams and 'Free' Homes: The Oklahoma Territory, 1891–1894" (*Phylon*, Dec. 1973); and Jere W. Robertson's "Edward P. McCabe and the Langston Experiment" (*Chronicles of Oklahoma* 51, Fall 1973); these last two heavily documented studies largely supersede Mozell C. Hill's "The All-Negro Communities of Oklahoma" (*JNH*, July 1946, pp. 254–68). The information about McCabe in Roy Garvin's "Benjamin, or 'Pap,' Singleton and his Followers" (*JNH*, Jan. 1948) is full of obvious errors, but a few bits are worth salvaging. Information about McCabe's wife, family, death, and funeral comes from the Oklahoma census of 1890, newspaper items supplied by Glen Schwendemann, and cemetery records, newspaper stories, and the Luther P. Jackson, Jr., Notes furnished by the Kansas Historical Society. — KENNETH WIGGINS PORTER

McCLENDON, ROSE [ROSALIE VIRGINIA SCOTT] (1884–1936), actress. She was born in Greenville, S.C., the daughter of Sandy and Tena (Jenkins) Scott. About 1890 she moved with her parents, an older brother, and a sister to New York City, where her parents worked as coachman and housekeeper for a wealthy family. Later her family moved to West 53rd Street, then in the principal center of Negroes in Manhattan. On Oct. 27, 1904, she was married to Henry Pruden McClendon, a licensed chiropractor. He, like some other Negroes of his profession, worked most of the time as a Pullman porter. The family moved to 138th Street in Harlem, where such real estate dealers as Philip H. Payton and John B. Nail had made it possible for Negroes to rent or purchase homes and apartments. Along with the former inhabitants of the downtown area, churches, including St. Mark's African Methodist Episcopal Church, moved to Harlem. Rosalie performed in and directed plays and cantatas in the church. After winning a scholarship at the American Academy of Dramatic Art in Carnegie Hall (c. 1916) she played her first theatrical role in *Justice* (1919–1920). From then until December 1935 she was one of the most famous colored actresses of the period. She contracted pleurisy, died of pneumonia at her home on July 12, 1936, and was buried in Mount Hope Cemetery, Westchester, N.Y.

McClendon did not win instant fame as did Florence Mills, for example, probably because recognition as an actress was more difficult to achieve than as a singer and dancer. In fact she first gained prominence in *Deep River* (1926), a "native opera with jazz" by Laurence Stallings and Frank Harling. Her bit part as Octavie, "the proudly withered madam" of a house of quadroon women, won for her "rave" notices. In December 1926 she had the role of Goldie McAllister in Paul Green's Pulitzer Prize–winning folk tragedy *In Abraham's Bosom,* in which Bledsoe had the leading role. Her reputation grew with her role of Serena, the wife of Robbins, a young stevedore, in *Porgy* another folk play by Dorothy and DuBose Heyward (1927), presented by the Theater Guild. After a long run in New York, she toured the United States and abroad. In two of the plays, *House of Connelly* (1931) and the all-Negro cast of *Never No More* (1932), the story of a lynching, she had the roles of Big Sue and Mammy, respectively. She had one of the lead roles in the radio series "John Henry, Black River Giant." As Cora Lewis, she starred in Langston Hughes's *Mulatto,* a protest play which opened on Oct. 24, 1935, at the Vanderbilt Theater in New York City. The theme is that of rejection by one's father, a topic in which Hughes had a morbid interest because he had been rejected by his own father. In *Mulatto* he joined the personal rejection by a white father of a Negro son to the theme of racial rejection. Cora Lewis was the colored wife in *Mulatto,* which ran for 375 performances, the second-longest run by a Negro playwright. Rose McClendon died before the play closed. Brooks Atkinson, the famous critic, wrote in the *New York Times*: "*Mulatto* is flaming with sincerity. . . . [A]fter a season devoted chiefly to trash, it is a sobering sensation to sit in the presence of a playwright who is trying his best to tell what is on his mind."

Rose McClendon and Dick Campbell organized the Negro People's Theater, and Campbell and Muriel Rahn organized the Rose McClendon Players. The latter, housed in the 124th Street Library auditorium, presented two plays. It was in *Deep River* that she gave her best performance. In the *New York World* Alexander Woolcott paid her this tribute: "In the third act of *Deep River* when, for a moment, the vast stage was emptied and one heard only the murmur of unseen choruses, saw only the lazy tracery of the tree shadows upon the gray-green Jalousies of the old New Orleans house, the door opened on the high balcony and down the winding stone steps came an aging mulatto actress who played, in black taffeta and diamonds, the procuress of the quadroon ball. She stood there for a moment, serene, silent, queenly, and I could think only of the lost loveliness that was Duse's. The noble head carved with pain, was Duse's."

When *Deep River* was having its trial performances in Philadelphia, Ethel Barrymore slipped into snatch what moments of it she could. "Stay till the last act if you can," Arthur Hopkins whispered to her, "and watch Rose McClendon come down those stairs. She can teach some of our most hoity-toity actresses distinction." It was Barrymore who hunted him up after the performance to say "She can teach them all distinction."

There is a brief biography by Lillian W. Vorhees in *NAW* (1971, 2:449–50). A photograph of McClendon as Cora Lewis in *Mulatto* on page 58 of Lindsay Patterson (ed.), *Anthology of the American Negro in the Theater: A Critical Approach* (1967). James Weldon Johnson's *Black Manhattan* (1930) is one of the best sources for the evaluation of the plays. In 1946 Carl Van Vechten established the Rose McClendon Memorial Collection of photographs of distinguished Negroes at Howard and Yale Universities.

— RAYFORD W. LOGAN

McCOY, ELIJAH (1843–1929), inventor. He was born in Colchester, Ontario, Canada, the third of twelve children born to George and Mildred (Goins) McCoy, both fugitive slaves who had escaped from Kentucky into Canada prior to his birth. His father served in the Canadian army. McCoy attended grammar school near his home but subsequently went to Edinburgh, Scotland, where as an apprentice he learned to be a mechanical engineer. Later he went to Detroit to practice his trade, but he was unable at first to secure employment because of racial discrimination. He obtained employment, however, as a fireman on the Michigan Central Railroad, where from time to time one of his cumbersome duties was oiling the engine. When the train stopped, McCoy dismounted; with a can in hand, he would walk around and pour oil on the cylinders, screws, and levers of the machinery where the friction tended to heat and wear out engine parts. At Ypsilanti after two years of experimenting he received on June 23, 1872, patent no. 129,843 for his lubricator for steam engines, the first of his inventions. To obtain additional funds for his experiments he assigned the patent to William and S. C. Hamlin of Ypsilanti. Although this was the first device of its kind, the patent office used the

term "improvement" to designate that the method ameliorated the difficulties of the existing device, which in this case was oiling by hand.

The next three McCoy patents, issued in 1872, 1873, and 1874, also pertained to lubricators for engines. In order to finance his own experimental machine shop, McCoy assigned 50 percent of these to Sullivan M. McCutchen and Edward P. Allen, both of Ypsilanti. In 1875, McCoy had two patents issued pertaining to lubricators for steam cylinders, both assigned to others. For the next seven years no patents were issued to McCoy; however, in 1882 he was issued two for lubricators, both of which were assigned to Charles B. and Henry C. Hodge of Detroit.

The McCoy 1883 patent designated a lubricator was designed for specific use with air-brake pumps. Prior to this invention, there was considerable difficulty with the lubricators that were constructed for the purpose of supplying steam cylinders and valves of air-brake pumps. This was owing to the fact that when the steam was cut off from the cylinders, the pump created a vacuum and by so doing raised the check-valve from its position, thus sucking oil or other lubricants out of the oil reservoir unless the attendant remembered to close the valve in the brake pump. Usually this was not done and oil was wasted and the supply became exhausted. This invention attempted to correct the difficulty by placing an additional lubricator on top of the cylinder or removing the top and extravagantly pouring oil to prevent friction and groaning. This patent was also assigned to the Hodges of Detroit. From 1884 through 1888 McCoy had a total of eight patents issued, assigned for the most part to the Hodges. These included various types of lubricators and attachments such as a steam dome for locomotives, lubricants for slide valves and locomotive cylinders, a lubricant attachment with air-brake cylinders, and a lubricator for improving engines where steam was used to aid in feeding oil to the cylinders. McCoy's lubricating devices were used for years on stationary engines and locomotives, steamships on the Great Lakes, on transatlantic liners, and machinery in many factories.

From 1889 through the end of the century, McCoy was issued a total of nine patents, including a dope cup lubricator, a sight-feed chamber connected with the lubricator, a lubricant for heavy oils, a lubricator for locomotive engines, and an oil cup with a support and sight-feed arm. One attachment was constructed to ensure the regular delivery of the lubricant to the working parts of the cylinder in quantities that varied with the speed of the engine. Another in this series pertained to a method of cleaning the sight-feed glass and oil nozzle without removing either or the oil that controlled the valve. These patents were assigned to the Detroit Sheet Metal and Brass Works of Detroit, and the Penberthy Injector Company.

From 1905 through 1915 McCoy had fifteen lubricator patents, assigned for the most part to Penberthy, individuals, and the Detroit Lubricator Company. One sought to improve cleansing the oil on its way from the storage to the journal; here the engineer could use either oil as a lubricant or water when desired. Another concerned alleviating difficulties of lubrication in cold weather. The remainder pertained to sight-feed lubrication, independent lubrication for a two-piston cylinder, air brakes, and other such devices, also a method for protecting the valves from dust and dirt so that fewer accidents would be caused owing to displacement of parts. Patents issued in 1914 and 1915 pertained to lubricators that introduced graphite or other solids that would not produce clogging. This last lubricator patent, issued in 1920, was assigned to McCoy's own company and pertained to the use of graphite.

McCoy had four patents and two designs that were not related to lubrication. These included a folding ironing table, a folding scaffold support, a buggy top support, and a tread for tires. The two designs, issued in 1899 and 1923, respectively, included a lawn sprinkler and a vehicle wheel tire. All of these were assigned in whole or in part to other individuals.

In spite of the forty-two patents and two designs, McCoy died a comparatively poor man since it was difficult for him to capitalize on his own inventions which yielded millions of dollars to others. Yet the story has become legend that the expression "The Real McCoy" was associated with his ingenious work. A person who desired a lubricator was prone to ask "is this a McCoy?" The dealer would say, "Yes, it's the real McCoy." Today the expression is used to mean that a product is genuine, whatever it may be.

In failing health after 1926, and widowed for several years, he lived for about a year in the Eloise Infirmary, Eloise, Mich., where he died of senile dementia caused by hypertension. He was buried in Detroit.

The *Official Gazette of the U.S. Patent Office* lists his inventions. Robert C. Hayden's *Eight Black American Inventors* (1972, pp. 93–103), a book for juveniles, has a photograph of McCoy (p. 93) and drawings of the 1872 and 1915 lubricators (pp. 95 and 100, respectively). There is a brief sketch by Carl W. Mitman in *DAB* (6, Part 1:617). — MAE P. CLAYTOR

McDANIEL, HATTIE (c. 1895–1952), singer, vaudeville performer, and actress. She was born in Wichita, Kans., the thirteenth child of a Baptist minister, Henry, and his wife, Susan (Holbert) McDaniel. The McDaniel family soon moved to Denver where the young McDaniel was brought up and educated in primary school and at East Denver High School. It was in Denver that, perhaps influenced by her mother who sang in church, she began her early career as singer, vaudeville performer and actress. But it was not until 1932 when she was approximately thirty-seven years old that she made her debut in motion pictures, the medium which brought her controversy, fame, and one of the highest awards of the film industry. In 1916 although she had never formally studied acting, she was awarded a gold medal for excellence in "the dramatic art" by the Women's Christian Temperance Union in Denver for her recital of a reading called "Convict Joe." Just prior to that time, or immediately thereafter, she joined her oldest brother Otis, who wrote his own songs and shows which he performed with his own company in small-town tent shows. The experience of writing her own material and singing on the road prepared her for her radio debut with Prof. George Morrison's Negro

Orchestra in Denver. She is reputed to be the first Negro woman to sing for radio; her subsequent radio appearances include the Eddie Cantor and Amos 'n Andy shows.

Between 1924 and 1930 McDaniel's career developed new dimensions. She was a headline singer on the Pantages and Orpheum Vaudeville circuits; at one time she formed her own act in Kansas City, and performed before conventions of the Elks and the Shriners throughout the South. During one particularly lean period between vaudeville engagements in Milwaukee, she found a job as a rest-room maid at Sam Pick's Suburban Inn. One night, responding to a call for volunteers from the service attendants to fill out the stage show, she sang "St. Louis Blues" and that was the end of her maid's job. Subsequently she created the "mammy-maid" character for the silver screen and played it with such strength, subtlety, irony, and hilarity as to earn her both rigorous criticism and "household word" fame. But before her movie debut of 1932 in Twentieth Century Fox's *The Golden West,* she established a substantial reputation on the legitimate stage touring every important city in the United States in Edna Ferber's and Jerome Kern's operetta *Showboat.* When she went to Hollywood in 1931, she was featured on a variety show on Los Angeles radio station KNX, sponsored by a bakery that manufactured "Optimistic Donuts." The show ran for one year and earned McDaniel the title, "Hi-Hat Hattie." In the next year McDaniel's movie career began. She appeared in some seventy movies until 1949. She fell ill in 1951 and died of cancer on Oct. 25, 1952, at the Motion Picture Country House in San Fernando Valley. Funeral services were held in People's Independent Church of Christ and she was buried in Rosedale Cemetery. Widowed once, McDaniel had married and divorced Nym Langford, James Lloyd Crawford, and Larry Williams. She was survived by one brother, Sam (Deacon) McDaniel, a film actor who died in 1963, a niece, and a nephew, Elzey Emanuel, also a film actor.

Between 1932 and 1949 she had featured roles in one production by Eagle Lion, one by World Wide, one by Republic, seven by Paramount, eight by Metro Goldwyn Mayer, ten by RKO, thirteen by Universal Artists, fifteen by Twentieth Century Fox, and fifteen by Warner Brothers. She was acclaimed for her roles, notably in *Blonde Venus* (Paramount, 1932); *Babbit* (Warner Brothers, 1934); *The Little Colonel* (Fox, 1935); *Music Is Magic* (Fox, 1935); *They Died with Their Boots On* (Warner Brothers, 1941); *Reap the Wild Wind* (Paramount, 1942); *Since You Went Away* (Universal Artists, 1944); and most particularly as Mammy in the 1936 Universal production of *Show Boat,* starring Paul Robeson.

Even though McDaniel worked in motion pictures for most of her life, she was perhaps known to an even wider audience for her starring role as Beulah on the CBS radio show by that name. Originally the role had been played by two white men: first by Marlin Hurt, and on his death by Bob Corley; each respectively had impersonated the Negro domestic about whom the series revolved. McDaniel took over the role in the fall of 1947 and continued it until she fell ill in 1951. Praised by some, maligned by others for the "mammy" housekeeper roles which she inevitably played, her answer was "I portray the type of Negro woman who has worked honestly and proudly to give our nation the Marian Andersons, Roland Hayeses and Ralph Bunches." A favorable comment by an editor of *Our World Magazine* (March 1948) pointed out that the magazine did not condone the caricatures made of Negroes on stage, screen, and radio, but it should not be forgotten that McDaniel, Eddie Rochester, and others had a living to make. The fault lay with Negroes' real enemies, "the producers and directors who give the characters the slant. . . . With a so-called 'handkerchief head' role, Miss McDaniel won an Academy Award [for her supporting role in *Gone With the Wind*]." She was paid $1500 a week as "housekeeper" in Proctor and Gambel's million-dollar radio show "Beulah." If in personifying a role in Negro life which existed, she made "a couple of thousand a week, good. Especially when she takes the money to fight pressures which cause Negroes to find most of their employment in White folks' kitchens." McDaniel donated the Oscar for the role in *Gone With the Wind* to Howard University.

The best published sources are Peter Nobel's *The Negro in Films: Literature of the Cinema* (1970) and Donald Bogle's *Toms, Coons, Mulattoes, Mammies and Bucks: An Interpretive History of Blacks in American Films* (1973). Obituaries appeared in the *New York Times* (Oct. 27, 1952), the *Amsterdam News* (Nov. 1, 1952), and *Our World Magazine* (Feb. 1952). The vertical files on Hattie McDaniel at the Schomburg Center for Research in Black Culture and the Lincoln Center Library and Museum of Performing Arts of the New York Public Library contain valuable information. See also the obituary in the *New York Times* (Oct. 27, 1952, p. 27; Nov. 2, 1952, p. 88; Nov. 5, 1952, p. 17).
— ELEANOR W. TRAYLOR

McGHEE, FREDERICK L[AMAR] (1861–1912), lawyer and civil rights leader. He was born in Aberdeen, Monroe County, Miss. His parents, Abraham and Sarah (Walker) McGhee, were slaves; his maternal grandmother had been a native African. His father, a blacksmith who had learned how to read and became a Baptist preacher, continued to preach after emancipation. He taught his children, including Frederick, how to read and write. After emancipation, the family moved to Knoxville, Tenn., where young Frederick was left an orphan in 1873. Disheartened but not discouraged, Frederick continued his education under Presbyterian missionaries and also at Knoxville College. In 1879 he went to Chicago where he worked as a waiter, he began the study of law in 1882, and won his licence in 1885.

After practicing law in Chicago for three years, where one of his partners was Illinois state legislator Edward H. Morris, McGhee migrated to St. Paul, where his admission to the bar at that time made him, it is said, the first Afro-American to be licensed in what was then largely a frontier state, and permitted to practice before the Minnesota Supreme Court. He became well known for his oratorical ability, his keen mind, his courtroom abilities, and his success with difficult criminal cases, including murder. He had an interracial clientele. Several of his cases made front-page news in Minnesota. When he died in 1912, W. E. B. Du Bois, in a glowing obituary in *The Crisis,* wrote that McGhee had been the "most famous criminal lawyer at the St. Paul bar, and with a predominantly white clientele, he literally worked himself to death." Du Bois described McGhee as "tall, thin, dark, with a hawk-like physiognomy, piercing eyes, and intense and eloquent in speech." While in St. Paul, McGhee did not suffer much discrimination, but he deeply resented even that little. A prominent Catholic layman, he had as his friend there Archbishop Ireland, who spoke at the 1902 meeting of the National Afro-American Council in St. Paul. Several years before his death in 1912 he had become one of the major Negro leaders in Minnesota.

McGhee was also prominent in national race causes. He was one of the signers of the "call" issued by Bishop Alexander Walters (March 10, 1898) for a meeting of the National Afro-American League, which became the National Afro-American Council later in the year. He served as the head of its legal bureau and was program chairman at its meeting in St. Paul in 1902. The following year he was elected financial secretary. Even though McGhee said in 1904 that he did not believe in complete social equality, he would not accept racial discrimination. In the same year he worked with Booker T. Washington and James Cardinal Gibbons of Maryland in their unsuccessful efforts to prevent the disfranchisement of Negro voters of Maryland. He also assisted Washington in lobbying for the appointment by the U.S. Senate (1905) of William D. Crum as collector of customs at Charleston, S. C.

But McGhee had difficulties also with Booker T. Washington. In 1903 McGhee had been one of the leaders of efforts to make the National Afro-American Council adopt more radical attitudes and actions. In 1904 he wrote Washington that although he could support Theodore Roosevelt as a national Republican, the state and local political scene in St. Paul forced him to remain a Democrat, which was unusual for Negroes of the day. This may explain why he never got a major appointment or held office. Du Bois gives full credit to McGhee for originating the idea of the Niagara Movement to oppose the conservative policies of Washington ("The Niagara Movement," *Voice of the Negro,* Sept. 1905, pp. 619–22). The two men became good friends. Within the Niagara Movement, McGhee worked on the legal branch, notably in 1907 when he brought an unsuccessful case against the Pullman Company for discrimination.

When the NAACP began having its meetings in 1910, McGhee was among the regular participants. In 1912 he and his good friend Valdo D. Butler founded the St. Paul branch of the NAACP. But McGhee died on Sept. 9, 1912, from pleurisy before he could see the branch well established. His wife, Mattie B. Crane, whom he had married in 1886 in Kentucky, and who had worked closely with him in his organization work, survived him. There was also a daughter, Ruth. The *Minneapolis Journal* carried only a short notice of his death, while Du Bois wrote an obituary in *The Crisis* (Nov. 1912, p. 15), and one when his wife died in 1933.

Brief biographies are in William B. Hennessey's *Past and Present of St. Paul, Minnesota* (1906) and his *Gopher Historian* (1968–1969), Earl Spangler's *The Negro in Minnesota* (1961), and August Meier's *Negro Thought in America* (1966). *The Western Appeal,* a Negro newspaper, and the *Minneapolis Journal,* a white paper, both of St. Paul, contain additional evidence. Some of McGhee's letters are in the Booker T. Washington Papers, Library of Congress.

— CLARENCE G. CONTEE, SR.

McGIRT, JAMES E[PHRAIM] (1874–1930), poet, editor, and publisher. He was born in Robeson County, N.C., near the town of Lumberton. He spent his early years on farms near Greensboro, N.C., with his parents, Madison and Ellen (Townsend) McGirt. In 1892 McGirt enrolled in Bennett College, a Methodist-affiliated institution then just outside Greensboro, graduating with a bachelor's degree in 1895. In the preface to his first book, *Avenging the Maine, A Drunken A.B., and Other Poems* (1899), McGirt blames exhausting manual labor and a lack of leisure time for the slimness of the volume and the feebleness of its verse. McGirt's employment situation did not prevent him from revising and enlarging the first edition of *Avenging the Maine* in 1900 and adding in the next year a new collection of poems entitled *Some Simple Songs and a Few More Ambitious Attempts.* After briefly residing in Hampton, Va., he established himself in Philadelphia where, in September 1903, he issued the first number of *McGirt's Magazine,* an illustrated monthly dealing with the activities of American Negroes in art, literature, science, and public affairs. Although his duties as editor and publisher consumed most of his time and all of his savings, McGirt continued to write music and poetry. In 1906 he published his third book, *For Your Sweet Sake: Poems.* The paucity of critical notice his poetry received probably contributed to McGirt's decision to bring out his only book of short stories, *The Triumphs of Ephraim,* in 1907.

In 1909 *McGirt's Magazine,* reflecting declining sales, changed from a monthly to a quarterly. A year later it ceased publication when McGirt decided to return to Greensboro. With his sister he took control of the Star Hair Grower Manufacturing Company and turned it into a successful business. After accumulating a considerable amount of property in and around Greensboro, he became a realtor. He died in Greensboro on June 13, 1930. Funeral services were held on June 15 at St. Matthew's Episcopal Church and he was buried in Maplewood Cemetery, Greensboro. He was survived by his mother.

McGirt's contribution to literature was small. His first book of verse is, as he admitted, amateurish and undistinguished. Although his technical skill increased with each volume of poetry, he was never a sure metrist or a skilled rhymer. At his best, McGirt wrote conventional lyrics suitable for the pages of popular magazines. McGirt's fiction displays an equally unsophisticated understanding of the art of the short story. The eight stories in *The Triumphs of Ephraim* usually deal with problems of romantic love encountered by youthful and largely unindividualized Negro heroes and heroines. Unlike his poems, which despite their lack of polish often give evidence of deep personal feelings at work, McGirt's short stories reveal both a lack of experience and an uncertainty of purpose which together account for McGirt's brief and unsuccessful literary career.

The most useful biographical, bibliographical, and critical studies are John W. Parker's "James Ephraim McGirt: Poet of 'Hope Deferred' " (*North Carolina Historical Review,* July 1954, pp. 321–35); "McGirt, James Ephraim" (*North Carolina Authors: A Selective Handbook,* 1952, pp. 79–80); and "James E. McGirt: Tar Heel Poet" (*The Crisis,* May 1953, pp. 286–89). *The Triumphs of Ephraim* was reprinted in 1972 by Books for Libraries Press, Freeport, N.Y. Hugh Gloster gave a brief critique of *The Triumphs* in his *Negro Voices in American Fiction* (1948, pp. 70–71). Some issues of his magazine are in the Moorland-Spingarn Research Center at Howard University, the Library of Congress, Atlanta University Library, and the Schomburg Center for Research in Black Culture, in New York.

— WILLIAM L. ANDREWS

McGUIRE, GEORGE ALEXANDER (1866–1934), founder and bishop of the African Orthodox church. He was born on March 26, 1866 at Sweets, Antigua, and educated at the local school, at the Antigua branch of the Mico College for teachers, and at the Moravian Miskey Seminary in the Danish West Indies. From about 1888 he pastored at Fredericksted a Moravian church made up of British West Indians. He then emigrated to the United States and entered the ministry of the A.M.E. church. He became an Episcopalian on Jan. 2, 1895, and was ordained deacon in 1896 and priest the next year by the bishop of southern Ohio who placed him in charge of a Negro congregation in Cincinnati. He served St. Philip's Church in Richmond, Va., and St. Thomas African Church in Philadelphia where he also studied medicine. He quickly gained a reputation as a leading Negro Episcopal clergyman. Appointed archdeacon for colored work in Arkansas sometime after May 1905, in three years he increased the missions from one to nine. He also came into spirited conflict with his bishop, a pronounced racist who believed that the Episcopal church should segregate Negroes into a separate national jurisdiction.

McGuire resigned to establish St. Bartholomew's Church for West Indians in Cambridge, Mass. In 1909 he presented the largest confirmation class to the bishop. While serving in Cambridge he completed his medical studies and was awarded the M.D. degree in 1910 from the Boston College of Physicians and Surgeons. He resigned in February 1911 when St. Bartholomew's experienced racial discrimination in gaining representation in the diocesan convention. He then worked for two years as field secretary of the American Church Institute for Negroes. As he traveled throughout the country he became even more discouraged by the status of Negro Episcopalians.

He returned to Antigua to visit his sick mother in 1913 and volunteered to serve a local parish. He also practiced medicine and became widely known on the island. He collided with colonial officials when he supported striking sugarcane workers. McGuire returned to the United States in 1918 to join forces with Marcus Garvey, who made him chaplain-general of the Universal Negro Improvement Association and "titular archbishop of Ethiopia." McGuire broke with the Episcopal church in 1919 to organize a Catholic church under Negro control. He established a congregation in New York City known as the Good Sheperd Independent Episcopal Church. As he traveled lecturing for the UNIA, he formed similar churches in Brooklyn, Pittsburgh, Sydney, Australia, Nova Scotia, Cuba, and the Dominican Republic.

A general convention of the churches he had established in New York City, which he called on Sept. 2, 1921, organized the African Orthodox church and elected McGuire as bishop. It adopted a declaration of faith and constitution which affirmed traditional Catholic doctrines such as the seven sacraments, the apostolic succession, and the invocation of saints, and provided a hierarchical government of bishops, archbishops, primates, and patriarch. Membership was open to all, but the church was to be "controlled by Negroes." Thus McGuire realized his vision of an independent Catholic communion under Negro leadership. After unsuccessful attempts to obtain episcopal ordination from the Reformed Episcopal church, the Roman Catholic church, the Protestant Episcopal church, and the Russian Orthodox church, he was consecrated by an "episcopus vagans," Joseph Rene Vilatte, exarch of the American Catholic church. Race pride was a cornerstone of the African Orthodox church. In August 1924 he urged blacks at the UNIA convention to burn representations "of a white Madonna and a white Christ" and to worship "a Black Christ" and a "Black Madonna."

Shortly thereafter he broke with Garvey, who wanted to locate the UNIA headquarters in the West Indies, and devoted himself to the development and extension of his church, founding the Endick Theological Seminary, an order of deaconesses, and the *Negro Churchman,* which he edited. The African Orthodox church attracted mostly Anglican West Indian immigrants. It spread to the South in 1925 when McGuire started a parish in West Palm Beach, Fla. Two years later he consecrated an African as primate of the central and southern African province. At the same time McGuire was elected as patriarch with the title of Alexander I. His church then spread to Uganda where it grew to about 10,000. Its greatest strength, however, was in New York City where on Nov. 8, 1931, he dedicated Holy Cross Pro-Cathedral, a remodeled house purchased by McGuire from funds obtained by mortgaging his own home. In 1934 the church had about 30,000 members, about fifty clergy, and thirty churches located in the United States, Africa, Cuba, Antigua, and Venezuela.

McGuire died on Nov. 10, 1934. He was survived by his wife, Ada Robert McGuire, a native of Antigua, and a daughter.

See Arthur C. Thompson's *The History of the African Orthodox Church* (1956), Byron Rushing's "A Note on the Origin of the African Orthodox Church" (*JNH,* Jan. 1972), and Gavin White's "Patriarch McGuire and the Episcopal Church" (*Historical Magazine of the Protestant Episcopal Church,* June 1969). There are brief valuable references in *Black Moses . . .* by Edmund David Cronon (1955, pp. 69, 103, 178–80, 189).

— J. CARLETON HAYDEN

McJUNKIN, GEORGE (1851–1922) ranch foreman and discoverer of significantly ancient bison bones near Folsom, N. Mex. McJunkin was born in rural Texas. His father, a blacksmith, became free before the Civil War. On the horse-raising ranch where he grew up, the boy acquired ranch skills and—remarkably, for a rural child of that time—four years of schooling. As a boy he worked as a freighter's helper and buffalo skinner. However, it was his knowledge of horses and cows that led to his unique place in the annals of prehistory.

At twenty-one he helped push several hundred horses up Texas trails to the Colorado–New Mexico borderlands. On those high plains he remained to work almost fifty years as a bronco-buster, top hand, and ranch foreman. While foreman at the Crowfoot Ranch near Folsom, he also homesteaded. Later he traded his land for cattle that, under his brand, were run with those of his employer. As foreman at the Crowfoot he not only conducted the usual ranch operations, but supervised crews—including Anglo-Americans and Mexican-Americans—in laying pipe, making boundary surveys, and in the techniques of horse-breaking.

He did not marry and left no children of record.

About 1908 while riding along Wild Horse Arroyo, a tributary of the Dry Cimarron River, McJunkin spotted odd-looking bones protruding from the arroyo's banks. He observed they were markedly different from cow and buffalo bones—larger and with extraordinary horn formations. An avid reader and nature observer, McJunkin realized the bones called for examination by experts. For years he talked of these strange bones, hoping to attract to the site students of such phenomena. But it was not to happen in his lifetime.

McJunkin died in the Folsom Hotel, Folsom, in January 1922, and was buried in the Folsom cemetery.

A few months after McJunkin's death a party of amateur naturalists, including his friends Fred Howarth and Carl Schwachheim, took steps further to study the extraordinary bones he had talked of. They visited the site and extracted bone specimens for study at home. It was 1926, however, before Howarth and Schwachheim delivered bone samples to J. W. Figgins and Harold Cook, scientists at the Colorado Museum of Natural History in Denver, whose interest was immediately aroused.

Figgins and Cook visited the northern New Mexico site of the bone bed, and were convinced the site held materials of paleontological interest. In 1926, under their direction, excavations began at the Folsom site, and the field study implicitly confirmed McJunkin's surmise that the bones were indeed unusual, for eventually these scientists were to analyze the specimens and pronounce them skeletal material from bison extinct for about 10,000 years. But even greater meaning was to attach to the discovery of spearpoints embedded in the ribs of faunal fossils because such weapons connoted the existence of humans contemporaneous with the ancient bison. When these weapons were found clearly associated with the bones, Figgins began a campaign to attract archeologists to view *in situ* the artifacts that eloquently revealed man had existed in the Americas several millennia earlier than archeologists had estimated. Finally responding to Figgins's summons were Barnum Brown of the American Museum of Natural History, Frank H. H. Roberts, Jr., of the Smithsonian Institution, and A. V. Kidder of Phillips Academy at Andover, Mass. Convinced of the authenticity of the points, field studies at Folsom continued a third year with the support of the American Museum added to the Colorado Museum's well-established studies, and by the end of the third field year a total of nineteen projectile points had been discovered.

The findings at Folsom were to cause a revolution in archeological doctrine. Overthrown was the estimate that ancient man had lived on this continent only since about the time of Christ. McJunkin had come upon the kill site of Stone Age hunters gone more than 100 centuries.

In the literature about McJunkin there is controversy about whether he found spear points. Acceptable records indicate, however, that he did not find the crucial spear points—artifacts which clearly associated the bison bones with correspondingly ancient humans. McJunkin's importance rests on his recognizing the extraordinary nature of the bones and persuading people more knowledgeable than he to study them. Doubtless, his efforts resulted in earlier study of the bone bed than would have happened otherwise.

The Life and Legend of George McJunkin by Franklin Folsom (1973) is the most comprehensive volume about McJunkin. Magazine articles about him include "George McJunkin's Pile of Bones" by Mildred Mayhall (*Old West,* Winter 1973, p. 19); "The Bookish Black at Wild Horse Arroyo" by Jaxon Hewitt (*New Mexico Magazine* 49, nos. 1/2 [Jan.-Feb. 1971]: 22); "The McJunkin Controversy" by George Agogino (*New Mexico Magazine* 49, nos. 5/6 [May-June 1971]: 41). Among the many reports of the scientific research at Folsom, journal articles by J. D. Figgins written soon after discoveries are illuminating; two of his articles are "The Antiquity of Man in America" (*Natural History* 27, no. 3 [1927]: 229–39) and "An Additional Discovery of the Association of a 'Folsom' Artifact and Fossil Mammal Remains" (*Proceedings,* Colorado Museum of Natural History, 10, no. 2, 1931).

Also valuable were interviews and correspondence with a dozen individuals who knew George McJunkin, men and women who graciously provided access to their memories as well as to their pictures, letters, and documents; professional consultants also made themselves available for supplying and correcting data related to the scientific aspects of the Folsom inquiries. M. L. Doherty made available a copy of Thomas Owen's "George McJunkin," a speech to the Kiwanis Club, Raton, N.Mex. (June 26, 1951). — MARY F. GERMOND

McKAY, CLAUDE (1889–1948), poet, novelist, and short story writer. He was born in Clarendon Hills, a parish in central Jamaica, the son of prosperous and highly respected peasant parents. When six years old, he moved into the home of his free-thinking schoolteacher brother, who lived near Montego Bay. Under his brother's tutelage, the young McKay was introduced to literature, science, socialism, and free-thinking. At sixteen McKay moved to Kingston to learn a trade, but abandoned the idea after a short stint as an apprentice. He then joined the island constabulary. In Jamaica he met the first of several white persons destined to influence his life. This was Edward Jekyll, an Englishman who had come to the island to study Jamaican culture. Jekyll taught McKay French, introduced him to many authors of classic world literature, and persuaded him to write dialect poetry. Before he left his native land, McKay had published two volumes of verse: *Songs of Jamaica* and *Constab Ballads,* both in 1912.

In the same year McKay went to Tuskegee Institute to study agriculture. Rebelling against the regimentation he found there, McKay left after a year and went to Kansas State College, where he remained for two years. Inheriting a small legacy at the time, McKay decided to give up agriculture and pursue a writing career in New York City. He soon lost most of his legacy in an unsuccessful business venture; after that, still trying to write, McKay supported himself through menial work.

McKay was married briefly. In his autobiography, he cavalierly dismisses this episode in two brief paragraphs. He does not even bother to give his wife's name.

During his early New York years, McKay met two men who encouraged and helped him in his writing. One was Frank Harris, editor of *Pearson's Magazine,* who published several of McKay's poems; the other was Max Eastman, the leftist editor of *The Liberator.* Later on the poet became associate editor of *The Liberator* under Eastman.

The year 1919 found McKay in England. While there he came to know and work with Sylvia Pankhurst on the radical *Workers Dreadnaught.* He also published in London a volume of verse, *Spring in New Hampshire* (1920). Returning to New York, he brought out his first American volume, *Harlem Shadows* (1922), which is now considered a landmark in New Negro Renaissance publications. In the same year McKay left the States to make a triumphal tour of Russia. Although he never joined the party, the poet met many of the Communist leaders and was lionized by them and by the people of the Soviet Union. McKay left Russia in 1923 and spent several years living in France, Spain, Morocco, and other countries. He was away from America from 1922 to 1934, but during this interim he published his three novels: *Home to Harlem* (1928), *Banjo* (1929), and *Banana Bottom* (1933).

After his return to America McKay wrote articles on the Harlem labor movement for *American Mercury* and *The Nation;* published *A Long Way from Home* (1937), his autobiography; and brought out a journalistic work, *Harlem: Negro Metropolis* (1940). During the winter of 1941–1942 he became quite ill. In 1944 he was converted to Roman Catholicism, and the man who had been a free-thinker and a radical for most of his life spent his last years attacking the liberal causes he had earlier espoused. He had had a stroke in 1943 and died in a Chicago hospital on May 23, 1948. Interment was in Calvary Cemetery, Woodside, N.Y.

The poetry of Claude McKay is found in three major

publications: *Spring in New Hampshire* (1920), *Harlem Shadows* (1922), and a posthumous volume, *The Selected Poems of Claude McKay* (1953). Like other poets, Claude McKay had his favorite themes, to which he returned again and again. His most popular subject is not racial protest, as one would imagine, but nostalgia, a longing for the poet's tropical home and his youth spent there. Several of these poems are well written and show the author's great skill as a nature poet. The best known, and probably the best, of these nostalgic pieces is the superbly executed "Flame-Heart."

The second most popular theme in McKay's verse is the city. As a peasant from the rural section of Jamaica, the young West Indian was alternately attracted and repelled by the bigness, the frenzied pace, the impersonality, and the challenge of New York. In "The City's Love" and "The White City," he gives, respectively, the two sides of his love-hatred attitude (he also does it most explicitly in his autobiography). McKay's hatred of the city is not always racial. In part it is the reaction of a nature-loving romantic against the ugliness of an industrialized society.

McKay's poetry also shows an ambivalent attitude toward America. He is both attracted and repelled (and challenged) by the "titanic strength" of this brute country. In his sonnet "America," he tells us: "Although she feeds me bread of bitterness. . . . I love this cultured hell that tests my youth!"

Two minor themes in McKay's poetry became quite popular among later New Negro poets. The first is found in his sonnet "The Harlem Dancer," the mother of many subsequent cabaret-dancing-black-girl poems of Langston Hughes and other poets. The second is Africa. McKay has several poems on the "black homeland," but he is far more realistic about Africa than were those U.S.-born New Negro poets who followed him. They tended to romanticize and fantasize the "Dark Continent."

The poems of McKay which appear most often in anthologies are racial protest poems, even though a few have no racial tags. "If We Must Die" is a good example of this type. As is commonly known, Sir Winston Churchill used it during the darkest days of World War II to bolster British morale, and yet it was a rallying cry of young Negro writers during the 1925 Renaissance. White America considered the piece incendiary in 1919, and Henry Cabot Lodge had it entered in the *Congressional Record* that year under that rubric. Among the other poems in this racial protest group are "Baptism," "White Houses," and "The Lynching," all three brilliantly written sonnets.

The poetry of Claude McKay is classic poetry—clear, restrained, well structured. Much of it is written in the sonnet form, a form he handled superbly. It is ironic to note that McKay, although acknowledged as a strong influence on the New Negro Renaissance, did not experiment with modern verse forms and did not make use of American Negro folk materials, two practices characteristic of the movement. It is equally ironic to learn that this writer, who is so definitely a "classicist" in his verse, is one of very few New Negro authors who emphasized "primitivism" and the seamier side of Negro life in his novels.

In several ways Claude McKay was decidedly an ambivalent character, both as man and artist. In his autobiography he makes the revealing statement: "My damned white education has robbed me of much of the primitive vitality, the pure stamina, the simple unswaggering strength . . . of the Negro race." This conflict between his "white education" and his alleged belief in the value of primitivism is emphasized in most of his fiction; in fact it is the overriding thesis of his three novels.

McKay's first and most popular novel, *Home to Harlem,* came out in 1928. Although McKay denied the connection, it was seemingly influenced by Carl Van Vechten's *Nigger Heaven,* published three years earlier. The work tells in episodic fashion the adventures of Jake, a charming, easy-going, black "noble savage" who finds and loses Felice, a lovely, brown-skinned Harlem girl—he forgets her address. The rest of the book tells of Jake's search for his lost love, a search which takes the reader to bars, rent parties, cabarets, drinking joints, and ballrooms. Jake's associates include pimps, hustlers, "sweet" (kept) men, and all of the other inhabitants of Harlem's lower world. Throughout the novel, particularly when he allows his protagonist to "philosophize," the author strongly suggests that Jake's life is somehow more genuine, more satisfying than the lives of ordinary church-going, respectable Harlemites.

Most white critics liked *Home to Harlem;* most Negro critics damned it. W. E. B. Du Bois's attitude was typical. He felt that, among other things, the novel catered to those prurient demands on the part of whites who liked to see Negroes depicted as basically licentious. Measured by modern standards *Home to Harlem* is almost shockingly clean. Its major fault is not licentiousness, but weakness as a novel.

The second novel, *Banjo: A Story Without a Plot* (1929), is essentially *Home to Harlem* moved to "the Ditch," a section of Marseille in which one finds all of the lowest elements. The primitive hero here is Banjo, an American Negro musician, whose way of life is far more elemental, far more hippie-like than that of Jake, and incidentally, not quite as interesting. One gets the impression that the author, using the same pattern, tried to write another *Home to Harlem,* but did not quite succeed.

McKay's last novel, *Banana Bottom* (1933), is for most critics his best fictional work. Although it too exaggerates the primitive thesis, it is artistically a better work than either of the first two. The scene, well depicted, is the author's homeland in the islands. The central character is Bita, in some ways a female counterpart of the noble savage, Jake. Rebelling against the straitlaced missionary education in which she had been reared, Bita "goes primitive" and finds a satisfaction she had not known before. This novel implies and suggests the same criticism of the Establishment found in the first two, but somehow does it better.

In addition to the three novels, McKay published *Gingertown* (1932), a collection of twelve short stories, six with a Harlem background. Many of these stories concern color differences among Negroes. McKay was seemingly obsessed with the problem of color. He speaks on occasion of "the keen ecstatic joy a man feels in the romance of being black,'' and when he uses the word *black,* he uses it literally. Several of the short stories in *Gingertown* emphasize the cruelty inherent in color-consciousness.

In 1937 McKay's *A Long Way from Home,* a full-length autobiography, was published. Although fascinating in some respects, the book has serious faults. The author ignores or glosses over certain aspects in his life which the reader has a right to know; he is guilty of name-dropping; he has very decided prejudices which he often shows unwittingly; and he is occasionally inconsistent in his attitude toward whites. For some readers, McKay emerges from his autobiography a clever but slightly dishonest chronicler.

As one examines the whole body of McKay's works, he is not as impressed as were McKay's contemporaries. Of his fiction, *Banana Bottom* has the best chance to survive. Claude McKay's finest work, many critics now believe, is his poetry, particularly certain of his nostalgic pieces *and* those brilliant, ironic protest poems which set the tone for the protest writing of the "Harlem Renaissance."

Although six or more of Claude McKay's major works have been reprinted, there is still no full-length study of the author. Stephen H. Bronz's *Roots of Negro Racial Consciousness* (1964) gives a short account of the life and works of McKay which is very useful. In addition, critics who have written commentaries on Negro fiction —among them Sterling A. Brown's *The Negro in American Fiction* (1937, 1969), Hugh M. Gloster's *Negro Voices in American Fiction* (1948), Robert A. Bone's *The Negro Novel in America* (1965), and Edward Margolies's *Native Sons* (1968)—have all devoted sizable sections of their works to McKay's novels. See the critical commentary in Arthur P. Davis's *From the Dark Tower: Afro-American Writers, 1900 to 1960* (1974). See also the obituary in the *New York Times* (May 24, 1948, p. 19). — ARTHUR P. DAVIS

MAHONEY, MARY [ELIZA] (1845–1926), pioneer trained nurse. She was born in Roxbury, now a part of Boston. Her parents, Charles and Mary Jane Stewart Mahoney, originally from North Carolina, lived with their two other children, Ellen and Frank, at 31 Westminster St. She graduated as a trained nurse from the New England Hospital for Women and Children in 1879 and devoted more than forty years to professional nursing and improving the status of graduate nurses. Suffering from cancer since 1923, she died at the New England Hospital in Boston on Jan. 4, 1926, and was buried in Woodlawn Cemetery, Everett, Mass.

It is not known why Mahoney chose, when she was almost thirty-three years old, the career of a trained nurse. Perhaps the graduation of Linda Richards from the New England Hospital for Women and Children in 1873, as America's first trained nurse, inspired her. Nor is it definitely known whether Mahoney's race was an obstacle to her acceptance at the hospital. If it is true that she cooked, washed, and scrubbed before and/or during her training, such employment was not uncommon. Completing the period of training of sixteen months was no small achievement. Of the forty who applied with her in 1878, only eighteen were accepted

on trial for training, nine continued, and four received the diploma after completion of a rigorous program. In addition to twelve hours of lectures Mahoney, like the other students, spent twelve months in the hospital's medical, surgical, and maternity wards, gaining experience in such subjects as "position and manner of nursing in families, physiological subjects, food for the sick, surgical nursing, child-bed nursing, disinfectants, and general nursing" during all hours of the day and night. She spent the last four months on widely praised private duty in homes in the community. She was paid three dollars a week to purchase "slippers and simple calico dresses."

Her record probably helped overcome the prevailing practice of racial discrimination in most nursing schools; by 1899 the New England Hospital had five Negro alumnae. One unsuccessful student was her younger sister Ellen Mahoney, who enrolled when she was twenty-seven. She completed the eighteen-month course, but the hospital records reveal that while she gave satisfaction in many ways, "her answers on examination were twenty unsatisfactory, so she was refused the diploma." Ellen Mahoney, who lived to be ninety, was in poor health during many years and was cared for by her sister Mary.

She seems to have been employed almost entirely as a nurse in private homes, perhaps because of refusal of hospitals to employ Negro trained nurses. Although she was one of the few early Negro members of the American Nurses Association, she must have believed that a separate organization could better advance the professional status of trained Negro nurses. In 1908 she enthusiastically supported the organization in New York City of the National Association of Colored Graduate Nurses (NACGN). When John B. Hall, a Boston friend who was a prominent Negro physician and leader of the separate National Medical Association, suggested that the NACGN hold its first national meeting in Boston, Mahoney gave the welcoming address and was elected chaplain. She seldom missed a national meeting of the NACGN and recruited new members. Her last attendance was in Washington, D.C., in 1921, as a guest of the Freedmen's Hospital Alumnae Association. The nurses presented a large basket of beautiful roses to Pres. and Mrs. Warren G. Harding with the request that the NACGN be placed on record as a body of 2000 trained women ready when needed for world service. The organization was dissolved in 1951 when Negro nurses were admitted to the American Nurses Association.

A strong supporter of women's suffrage, she is said to have been one of the first women to register and vote in Boston after the ratification of the Nineteenth Amendment in 1920.

She is best known, however, for her contributions to nursing. Several local affiliates of the NACGN were named in her honor. In 1936 the NACGN established the Mary Mahoney Medal, to be awarded to one of its members for distinguished service to nursing. The first recipient was Adah B. Samuels Thoms, who had described Mahoney as having "an unusual personality and a great deal of personal charm." A pioneer trained graduate nurse, her graduation and almost forty years of nursing inspired other Negro women to pursue successful careers. Even after the merger of the NACGN with the American Nurses Association in 1951, the Mary Mahoney Medal continued to be awarded in recognition of significant contributions to intergroup relations.

Adah B. Thoms's *Pathfinders: A History of the Progress of Colored Graduate Nurses* (1929) contains essential facts, as does Mable K. Staupers's *No Time for Prejudice: A Story of the Integration of Negroes in Nursing in the U.S.* (1961). Mary Ella Chayer's "Mary Eliza Mahoney" (*American Journal of Nursing,* April 1954), and her sketch in *NAW* (1971, 2:486–87) are the most recent publications. — ANNA B. COLES

MAJORS, MONROE ALPHEUS (1864–1960), physician, author, editor, civil rights leader, and poet. Born in Waco, Tex., the youngest of three children of Andrew Jackson and Jane Barringer Majors, and educated in the public schools of Austin, he studied at West Texas College, Tillotson Normal and Collegiate Institute, Central Tennessee College, and in 1886 graduated from Meharry Medical College, Nashville, Tenn. He practiced medicine in Brenham, Calvert (the first Negro to do so), and Dallas, Tex., and moved to Los Angeles, where in 1889 he was the first Negro to pass the California Board of Examiners, becoming certified on Jan. 26, 1889 ("New Licentiates," *Southern California Practitioner* 4[1889]: 78). From 1890 to 1895 he practiced medicine in Waco, where he established the first Negro drugstore in the Southwest, and in Decatur, Ill., until 1899, in Waco again until 1901, in Chicago until 1923, and in California until perhaps 1955. On May 22, 1889, he had married Georgia A. Green, who became the mother of Grace Majors (Boswell). In 1908 he divorced his wife and in September 1909 married Estelle C. Bond, a noted Chicago musician. A duaghter, Margaret Jeannette Bonds Majors (Richardson), was born of this union. Majors, who had been in poor health since 1956, died in Los Angeles of natural causes on Dec. 10, 1960. He was survived by his daughter by the first marriage, Grace L. Majors Boswell, and her daughter and three sons, all of Los Angeles; also by his daughter by his second marriage, Margaret Bonds Majors Richardson.

Although the practice of medicine was his profession, Majors was remarkably versatile. He helped earn his expenses by working at the age of ten as a page in the state legislature in Austin, at the Raymond House, and as a post office clerk there while he was in college. At Meharry he reported public functions for the Nashville daily newspapers. His political activities, inspired by witnessing the seating of forty-seven Negro members of the state House of Representatives and four in the Senate (1874–1877), caused him repeated difficulties. In Brenham he and thirteen colleagues, because of the exclusionary policies of the American Medical Association, organized in 1886 the Lone Star State Medical Association (later the Lone Star State Medical, Dental, and Pharmaceutical Association). In the 1880s white opposition to a resurgence of Negro political activities led to such violence that Majors moved to Los Angeles in 1888 and passed the medical examination in 1889. There he participated in the meetings of medical soci-

eties and gave lectures at the Los Angeles Medical College. As editor of the *Los Angeles Western News,* he helped secure for the first time the appointment of Negroes to the police force, in the city public works, and in the office of the assessor and collectors of taxes. Encouraged by Robert Charles O'Hara Benjamin, the first Negro editor of the *Los Angeles Daily Sun,* Majors began the compilation of *Noted Negro Women: Their Triumphs and Activities.* Published in Chicago in 1893, it is an indispensable biographical dictionary.

After his return to Waco in 1890 Majors practiced medicine, lectured at Paul Quinn College (1891–1894), and edited the *Texas Searchlight* (1893–1895). In 1894 he was elected president of the Lone Star State Medical, Dental and Pharmaceutical Society. He was also appointed chairman of the Board of Directors of the Texas Cotton Palace Exposition, an exposition so well organized that a number of white citizens wanted him elected mayor of Waco.

After he moved to Decatur, Ill., in 1898, he practiced medicine and politics so successfully that ill feelings developed between him and white physicians. His life was threatened after he was interviewed by a newspaper reporter concerning a lynching which had occurred in Decatur three months before his arrival there. On the advice of friends he moved to Indianapolis where he was appointed to the staff of the *Indianapolis Freeman* (1898–1899) as its associate editor.

Between 1896 and 1899 numerous articles on many subjects appeared in the *Indianapolis Freeman* by Majors. He also published some poems. His weekly column, "Majors Melange," contained much homely advice and philosophy. Another valuable article was "White Caps in Texas" (Aug. 29, 1896), about the organization that had terrorized Negroes. He urged his race to become thinkers in an article entitled "The Beauty of Thought" (Dec. 25, 1897). His article "Negro Leaders Not Needed, but Great Men Can Become of Yeomen Service to the Race" (March 20, 1897), is an example of his urging the Negro to help his race, to study and be thrifty. He also wrote articles on blindness among Negroes, the power of the press, colored physicians, reminiscences of slavery days, crime and criminals.

Majors returned to Waco in 1899 where he served from 1899 to 1900 as superintendent of the hospital he had built between 1893 and 1895, by then a city hospital. His political involvements again forced him in 1901 to leave Texas for Chicago, never to return to the South. From 1901 until about 1923 Majors practiced medicine in Chicago. He continued his writing career, and at the request of Booker T. Washington accepted in 1908 the editorship for three years of the *Chicago Conservator.* His editorials appeared in the *Broad Ax* (Chicago) and the *Chicago Defender.* In 1917 Majors published "Ode to Frederick Douglass," and in 1921 *First Steps to Nursery Rhymes,* described as one of the very early books for colored children. His poems appeared in the *Washington Bee,* the *Peoples Advocate,* the *Colored American,* and other newspapers.

He was a prominent leader for many years in other activities. In 1908 he served as a commissioner of the Lincoln Day Centennial, and in 1915 the governor of Illinois appointed him commissioner for the Negro Half

Century of Freedom and Progress. After 1925 as Majors gradually lost his eyesight these activities were restricted. After two ophthalmic operations, one in 1926 and the other in 1933, his vision remained extremely poor. On March 4, 1933, he returned to Los Angeles where he lived with relatives for approximately three years, practicing medicine for two of them. He may have practiced medicine in Monrovia, Calif., until 1955. Here his health failed and his family moved him back to Los Angeles in 1956.

Monroe Majors was a member of many medical organizations, social and fraternal clubs, including the United Order of Odd Fellows, the Knights of Pythias, United Brothers of Friendship. A Thirty-second Degree Mason, a Republican, and a Methodist, he was also a member of the National Business League and the NAACP.

Majors's principal claims to distinction reside in his major profession of medicine. He is credited with having added the term "paralysis diabetes" to the medical literature. Surviving members of his family recall that despite a rather disagreeable personality, he was quite a "ladies man," was widely known as "big daddy," and had four wives.

An almost complete, although brief biographical sketch is W. Montague Cobb's "Monroe Alpheus Majors, 1864–" (*JNMA*, 1955, pp. 139–41). An earlier, longer sketch is Hightower J. Kealing's Introduction to Majors's *Noted Negro Women* (1893). Later information is found in J. A. Chatman's *Lone Star State Medical, Dental, and Pharmaceutical History* (1959?); "Dr. Monroe A. Majors: First Native Black Texan to Practice Medicine" (*Texas Informer,* Dec. 6, 1969, supplement, p. 12); and "Wacoan's Art Exhibit Features Texas M.D.'s" (*Waco Tribune Herald,* Nov. 27, 1969, p. 10A). The reminiscences of some of his survivors were shared with the contributor.

— CONSTANCE PORTER UZELAC

MALCOLM X [born Malcolm Little; also known by his adopted religious name **El-Hajj Malik El-Shabazz**] (1925–1965), Muslim minister and political leader. Malcolm was born in Omaha, Neb., on May 19, 1925, the seventh of eleven children of the Rev. Earl Little, a Baptist minister and an organizer for Marcus Garvey's Universal Negro Improvement Association. The family was harried out of Omaha by white vigilantes, and when Malcolm was six years old his father was murdered in Lansing, Mich., apparently by a Ku Klux Klan–style terrorist group. In the years thereafter the family began to disintegrate; Malcolm dropped out of school after the eighth grade, moved first to Boston and later to Harlem, and drifted through a succession of "hustles"—running numbers, pushing (and using) drugs, steering customers to brothels, finally organizing a burglary ring in the Boston suburbs. In 1946 at age twenty-one he was arrested there and sentenced to eight to ten years in prison for burglary and larceny; he served nearly six and a half years before his parole in 1952.

In prison Malcolm was introduced by his younger brother Reginald to the teachings of the Lost-Found Nation of Islam, the sect led until 1975 by Elijah Muhammad and known popularly as the Black Mus-lims. Malcolm quickly became a convert, took the Muslim "X" in place of the "slave name" Little, shed his past, and entered upon his own reeducation, beginning by copying words out of a dictionary from A to Z. He was ordained a minister after his release, and over the next twelve years he became the best known and most effective evangelist of the Nation of Islam, heading its Harlem mosque, organizing dozens more temples from Connecticut to California, building its following from 400 to perhaps 10,000 registered members and countless additional sympathizers. But Malcolm's growing celebrity excited jealousies within the movement's hierarchy, and his own increasing worldliness drew him away from its more cultish beliefs. After months of quickening tension, Muhammad suspended him in December 1963, officially for having referred publicly to President Kennedy's assassination as a case of "chickens coming home to roost." Three months later, in March 1964, Malcolm quit the Nation of Islam.

In the months that followed he organized two new groups of his own—first, in March, the Muslim Mosque, Inc., in Harlem; later, in June, the Organization of Afro-American Unity, with chapters in the United States, Europe, and Africa. At first Malcolm proclaimed his continuing allegiance to Muhammad's Black Muslim theology. But beginning with a *hajj,* or pilgrimage, to Mecca that spring, and continuing on a long sojourn in the Middle East and Africa that summer and fall, he converted to orthodox Islam, denounced Muhammad as a "racist" and a "religious faker," and came into increasingly open and bitter conflict with him. The Muslim newspaper *Muhammad Speaks* called Malcolm a hypocrite and pronounced him "worthy of death"; there were in fact several threats against and attempts on his life by assailants he believed to be Muslims, and on Feb. 14, 1965, unidentified attackers firebombed his home while Malcolm, his wife Betty, and his four daughters were asleep inside. A week later, on Feb. 21, Malcolm was shot and killed just as he began a speech to 400 followers at a rally in the Audubon Ballroom in New York. The Nation of Islam denied any complicity in his death. Three Black Muslims—Norman 3X Butler, Thomas 15X Johnson, and Talmadge X Hayer—were nevertheless convicted of the murder in March 1966. More than a decade later Hayer gave sworn testimony —supported by circumstantial evidence—that the assassination was indeed an act of Muslim vengeance against Malcolm, but that Butler and Johnson were innocent.

Malcolm's life had been an extraordinary series of personal transformations—"a chronology of changes," he wrote in his *Autobiography,* that brought him out of the degradation of the street to a catalytic place in the black struggle of the 1950s and 1960s. His role in that struggle was to be witness for the prosecution against white America for what he saw as three and a half centuries of crimes against Negroes; he called himself "a field Negro," and he used every forum available to him—the pulpit, the radio and television "talk shows" —to give voice to the discontents of the grandsons and granddaughters of field slaves in the ghettos of the urban North and West. Offstage and off-camera, he was a man of enormous charm, priestly in his bearing and his private life, warm and witty in company, gallant toward white people even in the days when he considered them universally and irremediably evil. But given a platform and a microphone, he became a pitiless scold. He denounced integration as degrading to those Negroes who sought it; he derided nonviolence as unmanly; he ridiculed the orthodox civil rights movement of the day, Martin Luther King, Jr., most of all; he identified whites as the enemy of blacks and cheered at tornadoes, hurricanes, earthquakes, airplane crashes, even the Kennedy assassination—anything that might cause them anguish or pain. "When I'm talking," he said without apology, "I use everything that's around." That he was widely called a demagogue as a result did not trouble him, at least not until the last months of his life; he saw himself as a shock therapist, speaking, as he often said, "as a victim of America's so-called democracy" and therefore willing to say quite literally anything to be heard.

Malcolm spent nearly all of his public career in the service of Elijah Muhammad, as a minister and ultimately as Muhammad's national representative to the outside world. During those dozen years Malcolm accepted and preached as literal truth that white people were a race of devils created by a treasonous black scientist for the torment of the "so-called American Negro"; that Allah had granted this satanic race 6000 years hegemony over the world but now was prepared to visit a terrible vengeance upon them; that He had raised up Muhammad as His Last Messenger and "missioned" him to lead the blacks to safety in a separate state, either in Africa or in a partitioned-off sector of the United States. But Malcolm gave Muhammad's fundamentalism a contemporary political edge and brought it out of the backstreet mosques into full public view in the mass media and on the university lecture circuit. He became in the process a kind of threatening counterpoint to the nonviolent, assimilationist movement then reaching its flowering in the ministry of King. Malcolm scoffed remorselessly both at the means of the orthodox movement ("This mealy-mouth, wait-in, beg-in, plead-in kind of action") and at its headlined successes in breaking down the structure of segregation in the American South. "Coffee with a cracker," Malcolm snorted. "That's *success?*"

Because of his personal and spiritual bond with Muhammad, Malcolm's break with the Nation of Islam was painful. But it was an emancipation as well; the breach, and Malcolm's travels to Mecca and Africa thereafter, liberated his free-running intelligence from the black-and-white simplicities of the gospel according to Elijah Muhammad. His last year was itself a kind of pilgrimage, from the certitudes of the Black Muslims through a conventional street corner black nationalism to an ideology of more subtle weave—a shifting and uncompleted blend of orthodox Islam, African socialism, Third World anticolonialism, and that doctrine of racial solidarity that blossomed after his death under the name "Black Power." Malcolm softened his attitudes toward individual whites but not toward white America, which he continued to the end to regard as irredeemably racist. "There might be some good [whites]," he conceded at his most brotherly, "but we don't have

time to look for them. Not nowadays." His responses to this first premise became the commonplaces of the generation of militant young blacks who followed him —his insistence on the legitimacy of violence in self-defense; his advocacy of black control of the institutions and the politics of the black community; his unremitting stress on the beauty and worth of blackness and the African past; his argument for the identity of interest of the dark-skinned majority of mankind against what he saw as a common white oppressor. But his more enduring legacy was his accusation. He saw black Americans as the victims of a historic wrong that could not be redeemed by a few token concessions to a few acculturated and therefore "acceptable" blacks. "You don't stick a knife in a man's back nine inches," he said, "and then pull it out six inches and say you're making progress."

Malcolm failed by many of the conventional measures of leadership. Neither the MMI nor the OAAU attracted large followings, and both languished after his death. He was brilliantly received on his travels in the Middle East and Africa, but was unable to achieve his first political goal there—persuading the Africans to bring charges against the United States in the United Nations for having violated the human rights of American Negroes. He tried without success in his last months to effect a liaison with the civil rights leaders he had so roundly attacked; Malcolm, for them, remained until his death a kind of outlaw figure—a man defined by his mass-media reputation as an apostle of violence and hate.

His real place in the history of his time began to be seen clearly only after his death and the publication of the *Autobiography* nine months later. In life he had been the surrogate for the anger of the urban black poor, for whom the civil rights movement in the South was a distant abstraction as against their own daily struggle for survival; long before the ghetto rioting of 1964–1968, Malcolm laid their explosive grievances before the nation with unrelenting and in the end prophetic fury. In death he became widely recognized as the harbinger of the great black upheaval of the middle and latter 1960s, that time of rising race consciousness and race pride embodied in the slogans "Black Is Beautiful" and "Black Power." Malcolm was considerably sentimentalized after his assassination, by both blacks and whites who only posthumously saw past his media reputation as a common hatemonger. Neither image, sinner or saint, entirely suits him: the historic Malcolm X was instead a prophetic figure in a tumultuous time, a dissonant voice who cried out at the flood tide of the civil rights movement that nonviolence was crippling, integration a sham, and progress an illusion for just so long as an underclass of the black poor was growing up neglected in the inner cities. "America's problem is *us,*" Malcolm said; the object of his uncompleted ministry was to make America realize that in time.

The most important primary sources on Malcolm's life and thought are *The Autobiography of Malcolm X* (1965); several anthologies of speeches, notably George Breitman (ed.), *Malcolm X Speaks* (1965), and *By Any Means Necessary* (1970); and a number of recorded speeches, of which *Message to the Grass*

Roots, (1965) is the best example. Among biographies, Peter Goldman's *The Death and Life of Malcolm X* (1973, rev. ed. 1979) focuses on Malcolm's last years, his assassination, and his place in history; Breitman's *The Last Year of Malcolm X* (1967) is a shorter Marxist analysis proposing that Malcolm was moving toward revolutionary socialism. A public school in Harlem was named for him in 1976. — PETER GOLDMAN

MALVIN, JOHN (1795–1880), abolitionist, educator, and businessman. Born free in Dumfries, Prince William County, Va., he was the son of a free mother, Dalcus Malvin, and a slave father. In 1802 he was an apprentice to the clerk of his owner. Upon the latter's death in 1813 he learned carpentry from his father. Taught to read and spell by an old slave who used the Bible for the lessons, he joined the Baptist church and solemnized slave marriages with the permission of the owners. To ensure his free status he moved in 1827 to Cincinnati, agitated against Ohio's Black Laws, and became a leader in community activities, as well as in the Underground Railroad in several Ohio cities and in Louisville, Ky. On March 8, 1829, he married Harriet Dorsey in Cincinnati. Seeking to migrate to Canada, the Malvins moved to Buffalo, N.Y., but John Malvin acceded to the wishes of his wife who did not want to leave behind her slave father in Kentucky. From 1832 to 1880 Malvin was one of the most prominent Negro leaders in Ohio. On July 30, 1880, he died in Cleveland and was buried in the Erie Cemetery there.

Although the Black Laws were not strictly enforced, they prevented Negroes from attending schools and entrance to benevolent institutions, and imposed a $500 security bond on Negroes entering the state. Malvin continued his agitation against them and espoused emigration to Canada and migration to the West as a refuge. His arrest and brief imprisonment as a "fugitive slave" in the fall of 1831 spurred his interest in emigration and migration. After his aborted plan to migrate from Buffalo to Canada, he settled in Cleveland, where he worked for three months as a cook on the schooner *Aurora* which plied the Great Lakes.

In 1832 he organized in Cleveland the School Education Society which operated a school for Negro children. Since the Ohio legislature did not authorize schools for Negroes or appropriate funds for their support, the costs of operation were borne by subscription and private appeals. In 1833 Malvin purchased the freedom of his father-in-law, Caleb Dorsey, and organized and occasionally preached in the First Baptist Church in Cleveland. Needing more remunerative means of support after the purchase of his father-in-law, he bought, with the assistance of a local white businessman, *The Grampus* which transported limestone and lumber to Cleveland from islands in Lake Erie. After paying the debt on the vessel, he sold it and worked on the construction of the First Baptist Church. He maintained his connection with it until his death in 1880.

In 1835 Malvin called a meeting in Columbus of a State Convention of Colored Men which established a School Fund Society to provide educational funds for Negroes. Its immediate achievement was the opening of schools in Columbus, Cleveland, Cincinnati, and Springfield. Malvin was elected president of the society in 1839.

Meanwhile he worked as a hand on the steamboat *Rochester* plying between Buffalo and Chicago, and in 1840 purchased the canal boat *Auburn* which transported wheat and other merchandise on the Ohio Canal. After selling it back to its previous owners, he remained as its captain. He acted as an agent for *The Colored American,* a weekly published in New York (1837–1842) by Charles Bennett Ray. In 1843 he became the agent of David Jenkins's *Palladium of Liberty.* He became more widely known when he was a delegate to the National Convention of Colored Citizens in Buffalo in August 1843, and by his organization of an Ohio State Convention of Colored Citizens in Columbus in September 1844.

His campaign for the repeal of some of Ohio's Black Laws won him additional recognition. He advocated the employment of speakers to canvass the state and lobby the legislature, and during 1846 participated in a number of debates in Cleveland on the subject. It was at this time that he proposed migration to the West and a petition to Congress for a grant of land. He served as a delegate to the National Convention of Colored Freemen in Cleveland in 1848, and served on the Business Committee which filed an eloquent "Declaration of Sentiments" in favor of repeal. He was one of the speakers at celebrations when the prohibitions against Negroes entering the state, Negro education, and Negro court testimony were repealed in 1849 (the provisions prohibiting interracial marriage, integrated schools, and a penalty for judges solemizing interracial marriage were repealed in 1887). During the 1850s Malvin regularly attended the Ohio State Conventions of Colored Citizens, one of the most influential in the nation. He was an active conductor on the Underground Railroad, was elected vice-president of the Ohio Anti-Slavery Society in 1858, and served as one of its general lecturers from 1858 to 1860. Throughout the decade Malvin appeared as an orator at the annual August celebrations of emancipation in the British West Indies.

During the early months of the Civil War, Malvin called a meeting of Cleveland Negroes to urge the organization of Negro troops. Gov. William Dennison denied the request on the grounds that white troops could win the war, and colored troops were not organized until 1863. Malvin attended the last National Convention of Colored Men, held in 1864 in Syracuse, N.Y. He was a member of the Committee on Public Speaking and one of the convention's vice-presidents. In the same year he was also elected president of a Negro Citizens group in Cleveland.

After the war he actively supported "Radical Reconstruction," gave orations on the Fifteenth Amendment, and prepared a public memorial on the death in 1868 of Thaddeus Stevens, one of the most prominent leaders of "Radical Reconstruction." Malvin was chosen chairman of the Colored Republican Club in Cleveland in 1870, and in 1877 his friends sponsored a testimonial dinner in honor of his long struggle for the uplift of Negroes. In 1879, a year before his death, the *Cleveland Leader* published his *Autobiography,* a forty-two page booklet.

The *Autobiography* is the principal source for his career. His involvement in promoting civil rights and community activities are mirrored in the pages of the *Cleveland Daily Herald* and *Leader.* The *Minutes of the State Conventions of Colored Citizens* for the decade of the 1850s and the *Minutes of the Proceedings of the National Negro Conventions: 1830–1864,* edited by Howard H. Bell (1969), document his important participation. Wilbur Siebert's *The Underground Railroad from Slavery to Freedom* (1898) notes his involvement in abolitionist activity. An excellent brief summary is "John Malvin, A Western Reserve Pioneer," by Harry E. Davis (*JNH,* Oct. 1938, pp. 426–34).

— FRANK R. LEVSTIK

MARRANT, JOHN (1755–1791), author, preacher, missionary, and Masonic lodge chaplain. The facts that are known about John Marrant's life come almost entirely from his published works. They tell us that he was born in New York in 1755; that he lived in several communities in the South, including St. Augustine, Fla., and Charleston, S.C.; that like several other eighteenth-century Negro writers, he met and was influenced by the Rev. George Whitefield, the great English preacher and co-founder with John Wesley of the Methodist Movement; that after a traumatic religious experience, he was captured by Cherokee Indians, lived among them for some time, learned their language, and converted a few of them to Christianity; that he served with the British Royal Navy and saw bloody action against the Dutch in 1781; that in London he was sponsored by the famous Countess of Huntington, who persuaded him to go to Nova Scotia as a Methodist missionary; that for about four years he preached and saved souls in and around Halifax, Nova Scotia; that he was brought into the Masons by Prince Hall in 1784 and by 1789 was the chaplain of the African Lodge of Masons in Boston. Arthur A. Schomburg, who reprinted Marrant's Masonic Sermon (1789), claims that "John Marrant was undoubtedly one of the first, if not the first, Negro minister of the gospel in North America." Schomburg also claims: "He was the first man to carry the word of God and the teaching of Jesus Christ to the Cherokees, Creeks, Catawar, and Housaw Indians. . . ."

Marrant seldom called attention to the fact that he was a Negro or wrote about racial matters. One of the rare references to color in his works is found on the title page of the *Narrative,* where he is designated as "A Black." Marrant's reticence on this score probably accounts for his being left out of the early collected Negro biographies; he is mentioned in none of them. It also accounts for his neglect by the abolitionists. And yet Marrant was a popular author. His *Narrative* ran to at least seven editions, the seventh appearing in London in 1802. But the number of editions does not tell the full publication story. Dorothy Porter's *Preliminary Checklist of the Published Writings of American Negroes, 1760–1835* (1945) lists nineteen different printed versions of the *Narrative,* the latest in 1835. The work obviously owed its popularity not to the appeal of John Marrant as a Negro writer, but to the religious nature of the book, to its delineation of God's "wonderful dealings" with the author. John Marrant actually belongs

more to the history of early Methodism than to that of Negro letters.

In addition to a few miscellaneous sermons, Marrant published the following significant works: *A Narrative of the Lord's Wonderful Dealings with John Marrant, A Black . . . Taken down from his own Relation, Arranged, Corrected, and Published by the Rev. Mr. Aldridge. . . . London: . . . 1785; A Journal of the Rev. John Marrant, From August the 18th, 1785, to the 16th of March, 1790. To which are added, TWO SERMONS; . . . London: . . . 1790; A Sermon Preached on the 24th Day of June 1789 Being the Festival of St. John the Baptist at the Request of the Right Worshipful Grand Master Prince Hall and the rest of the Brethren of the African Lodge of the Honorable Society of Free and Accepted Masons in Boston . . . Boston: . . . 1789.*

Of these three publications, the *Narrative* is not only the most popular but the most readable as well. The *Journal* is largely a monotonous recital of Marrant's preaching and missionary engagements in and around Halifax. It presents a seemingly endless series of biblical texts for sermons, of accounts of "love feasts," and of the author's other activities in the campaign to spread the Christian message. *A Sermon,* again, is not a spectacular work. Since he was preaching to Masons, he develops the theme of God as the Grand Architect of the Universe. After stating that Cain was the first Mason or builder, he discusses all of the other great builders in the Bible. Interestingly, there is only one specific reference—and that a brief phrase—in the sermon which lets the reader know that the speaker and audience are Negroes.

The *Narrative,* however, is quite a different story. It is a fascinating and, one must in fairness add, an incredible work. Marrant either suffered from religious hallucinations when he wrote the book, or was a consummate fabler. The *Narrative* has several hard-to-believe examples of God's "wonderful dealings" with the writer, the most spectacular being the latter's "singular deliverance" from a raging sea: "We were overtaken by a violent storm; I was washed overboard, and thrown on again; dashed into the sea a second time, and tossed upon deck again. . . . I was in the sea the third time about eight minutes, and the sharks came around me in great numbers; one of an enormous size, that could easily have taken me in his mouth at once, passed and rubbed against my side. I then cried more earnestly to the Lord than I had done for some time; and he who heard Jonah's prayer, did not shut out mine, for I was thrown aboard again; these were the means the Lord used to revive me, and I began now to set out afresh."

It is regrettable that John Marrant elected not to write also about his own people. If he had not been so blindly intent on bearing witness to the Christian Word, he could have left us a great deal of valuable information about the eighteenth-century Negroes that he, as chaplain of the African Lodge of Masons in Boston, must have known.

A Narrative of the Lord's Wonderful Dealings with John Marrant is conveniently found in *Early Negro Writing, 1760–1837,* selected and introduced by Dorothy Porter (1971, pp. 427–47). — ARTHUR P. DAVIS

MARSHALL, HARRIET [HATTIE] GIBBS

MARSHALL, HARRIET [HATTIE] GIBBS (1868–1941), founder of music conservatories. She was born on Feb. 18, 1868, in Victoria, British Columbia, to Mifflin Wistar Gibbs and Maria Ann (Alexander) Gibbs of Kentucky. Her father, a native of Philadelphia, was at the time a prominent local businessman and had been elected to two terms of the Victoria City Council. In 1869 the Gibbs family moved to Oberlin, Ohio, and Harriet subsequently attended Oberlin College, as had her mother, brother, and sister. In 1889 she became the first Negro to complete the full course at Oberlin's Conservatory of Music. At the time the conservatory did not grant degrees, but it granted her the Mus.B. degree in 1906 (Oberlin College Records). After a year of postgraduate training, including some in Europe, she returned to the United States in 1890 and founded a music conservatory at Eckstein-Norton University, an industrial school at Cane Spring, Ky. Her aim was to help preserve the rich heritage of Negro music and to develop the musical talent of Negroes. In 1900 she was appointed director of music for the colored public schools of Washington, D.C. While still holding that post in October 1903 she founded the Washington Conservatory of Music and School of Expression, located in the True Reformer Building, 902 U St. NW, a gift from her father, and became its president.

On June 23, 1906, Harriet Gibbs married Napoleon Bonaparte Marshall, a Harvard graduate who had practiced law in Massachusetts and New York. He had helped her in promoting her conservatory before their marriage and continued to do so. However, his subsequent career drew her away from the conservatory for extended periods. After his reputation and prospects were enhanced through service in the First World War as an infantry captain wounded in combat, in 1922 he was given a position with the U.S. legation in Haiti, with the promise of an eventual diplomatic post. As early as 1913 his father-in-law, who had served as a consul and had brought about the appointment of his other son-in-law as his successor, had attempted to obtain a consular post for Marshall. Marshall had been led to believe that his initial assignment in Haiti would be as special attaché for improving race relations between Haitians and Americans. However, as it turned out, Marshall was appointed only as a clerk in the legation and although he and Mrs. Marshall spent six years in Port-au-Prince they were unable to improve his situation significantly.

Their years in Haiti were nevertheless eventful; both were active in aiding Haitians working to improve the living conditions of the people, and they supported demands for removal of the U.S. Marines occupation force from Haiti. Mrs. Marshall was especially active with various charities and collaborated with a Haitian friend in founding the Jean Joseph Industrial School in 1926 in Port-au-Prince. Another direct result of the stay in Haiti was Harriet Marshall's slim volume *The Story of Haiti,* published in 1930.

After Napoleon Marshall died in 1933 Mrs. Marshall again concentrated her attention on the conservatory. In 1937 she expanded it by creating the National Negro Music Center. The new center featured a library and departments specializing in research, creative work, and teaching young people. Mrs. Marshall died suddenly on Feb. 25, 1941, in Burrell's Private Hospital, Washington. Her funeral was held on Feb. 28 at the conservatory and she was buried in Arlington Cemetery, next to her husband. She was survived by her sister, Ida Gibbs Hunt, her brother Horace E. Gibbs, and her brother-in-law, William H. Hunt (*Washington Tribune,* March 1, 1941). Her conservatory survived until 1960.

There is no adequate biography of Harriet Marshall; the best sources are the Washington Conservatory of Music Records, and the William H. Hunt Papers, both in the Moorland-Spingarn Research Center, Howard University. — ALLISON BLAKELY

MARSHALL, JOHN R.

MARSHALL, JOHN R. (1858– ?), army officer. Born in Alexandria, Va., on March 15, 1858, where he attended public school and also in Washington, D.C., he became a deputy clerk in the county clerk's office of Cook County, Ill. He was active in organizing (1891) the 9th Battalion of Infantry of the Illinois National Guard. It was the nucleus of the 8th Illinois Volunteer Regiment, colored, which he commanded with the rank of colonel and sailed from Jersey City on Aug. 11, 1898, arriving in Santiago, Cuba, on Aug. 16. Shortly thereafter he was made governor of the province of San Luís and governor of the port. During several months he kept the 8th Regiment encamped on a hill outside San Luís, but later occupied the old Spanish barracks and arsenal, placing them as well as the city in excellent sanitary condition. His policy of allowing Cubans to buy and sell within the lines established good relations between the inhabitants and the regiment. A nearby fight between Cubans and the 9th U.S. Volunteers of Negro Immunes, commanded by white officers, was later quelled by Marshall. His wife was one of a ladies committee in Chicago that raised $600 for hospital supplies and supplementary delicacies for the post hospital at San Luís. In February 1899 Inspector-General Brekenridge, after reviewing the regiment and the camp at San Luís, wrote that the 8th Illinois was "as fine a volunteer regiment as ever entered the service."

On March 11, 1899, the 8th Illinois sailed from Santiago on the S.S. *Sedgwick* for Newport News, Va. Arriving in Chicago on March 18, it was honored by a mammoth reception. Charles Winslow Hall, a frequent contributor to the *Colored American Magazine,* wrote in June 1900 that on April 3, 1899, the last private of Company M was paid off and mustered out of service. "The Eighth Illinois had ceased to exist." It did so only temporarily, for a new 8th Illinois became the 370th Regiment of Infantry, 93rd Division, in World War I. Its commander was a son of Maj. Franklin A. Denison who, according to Hall, was born at San Antonio, Tex., in 1862.

The major source is Charles Winslow Hall's "The Eighth Illinois, U.S.A." (*Colored American Magazine* 1 no. 3 [Aug. 1900]: 94–103). — RAYFORD W. LOGAN

MARSHALL, ROBERT ["BOBBY"] WELLS

MARSHALL, ROBERT ["BOBBY"] WELLS (1880–1958), pioneer Negro professional football player. He was born in Milwaukee, Wis., on March 4, 1880. His parents were Richard C. Marshall, a train porter, and

Samantha Jane (Gillespie) Marshall. They had five other children—Louis, Ida, Margareth, Sadie, and Alice.

A natural athlete, Robert Marshall starred in track, baseball, and especially football at Minneapolis Central High School (1899–1902). In the latter year he enrolled in the University of Minnesota, graduating in 1907. In 1911 he began working for the state Grain Weighing Department, mostly in Minneapolis but also in Duluth. While working, he played semipro football and baseball until 1920 when, at the age of forty, he played in the National Football League with the Rock Island (Ill.) Independents. He played with the Collegiate All Stars in 1922, with the semipro Minnesota "Liberty-Snyders," and in 1923 against the Minnesota Marines of the NFL. In 1925 he played with the Duluth Kelleys of the NFL. When he retired from the Grain Department on March 31, 1950—after thirty-nine years—Gov. Luther Younghal headed the list of more than 600 friends who honored him in the Grand Ballroom of one of the large Minneapolis hotels.

He died in Minneapolis on Aug. 27, 1958, and was survived by his wife Irene (who died in 1979), three children (Robert W. Jr., Donald J., and Betty J. Session), a sister (Margareth Lee), and his brother Louis. Another son, William W., had won the Golden Gloves Welterweight Championship in 1942 and died on the Keller Golf Course a month before his father.

In 1907 Robert W. "Bobby" Marshall was elected to the National Football Foundation Hall of Fame in recognition of his college seasons of 1905 and 1906. Walter Camp selected him for All-America Second Team End in 1905 and 1906. Marshall was the first Negro to be chosen for the team by Camp since he had selected William Henry Lewis as center on the first team (1893 and 1894).

Like many other Negro pioneers, Marshall is virtually unknown but he helped pave the way for subsequent stars.

This article is based primarily on Ocania Chalk's *Pioneers in Black Sport . . .* (1975) and information supplied by Marshall's daughter, Betty J. Session.

— OCANIA CHALK

MARTIN, JOHN SELLA (1832– ?), clergyman, abolitionist, editor, and civil rights leader. Born a slave in Charlotte, N.C., he escaped in 1856, went to Chicago, studied for the ministry in Detroit, and took charge of a church in Buffalo, N.Y. He preached on several occasions at Tremont Temple, Boston, and in Lawrence, Mass., became pastor of the Joy Street Baptist Church in Boston (c. 1859), and held pastorates in New York. He traveled abroad several times and volunteered for the Union Army in 1861. With Frederick Douglass and others he addressed the famous meeting at Tremont Temple (Jan. 1, 1863) when news arrived of Lincoln's Emancipation Proclamation. He joined George T. Downing and others in urging Douglass to become editor-in-chief of the *New Era,* of which he was an editor. He served as pastor of the fashionable 15th Street Presbyterian Church in Washington, D.C., delivered memorable addresses before the Paris Anti-Slavery Conference (Aug. 27, 1867) and the Republican National Convention, Cincinnati (1872).

In the aftermath of John Brown's raid on Harpers Ferry in 1859 there was widespread debate about the willingness of slaves to fight for their freedom. Martin, then pastor of Joy Street Church in Boston, drew large audiences for his addresses on Nat Turner. He also pointed out: "They [slaves] have learned this much from the treachery of white men at the North, and the cruelty of white men at the South, that they cannot trust the white man even when he comes to deliver them" (*Liberator,* Dec. 9, 1859). But after the attack on Fort Sumter (April 12, 1861) Martin, who had just returned to Boston after a lecturing tour in England, wrote to President Lincoln: "If I can be of any manner of service here, should your excellency ever think it best to employ my people, I am ready to work or preach or fight to put down this rebellion" (quoted by Benjamin Quarles, *Lincoln and the Negro* [1962], p. 67). Shortly before this he was one of the delegation, including William C. Nell, Robert Morris, and William Wells Brown, which told Lincoln of their vigorous opposition to colonization.

His views were comprehensively revealed in his address as a delegate of the American Missionary Association before the Paris Anti-Slavery Conference (Aug. 27, 1867). He refuted many accusations made then and later about the freedmen. There was a popular notion that the Negro "is a coward. Yet he has proved that he will fight, though for one I have no eulogy to pass upon him for doing that which is the last resort of a cur that cannot run away." As long as the Negro slave behaved like a Christian waiting for civilization to free him, "the whites called him a brute, too degraded to wish for freedom or try to win it." But when he began to act really like a brute and fight, whites called him a man. Martin exaggerated when he agreed with Wendell Phillips that "the Negro race is the only one in history which, unaided, broke its chains of bondage."

In one of his more pungent statements he declared: "The Negro, too, is a man that will work." In words that seemed to anticipate the false accusations made by E. Merton Coulter in his *The South During Reconstruction, 1865–1877* (1947), Martin believed that "whenever they [the freedmen] could get work the majority have remained to do it. When they could get paid for their work they have worked to profit, and when they have made money, they have learned to save it." He did not deny that there was a large number of lazy Negroes; if there had not been, it would have been necessary to send them abroad lest they be corrupted by the bad example of white vagabonds.

"The Negro will learn" was the next theme in this carefully organized address. Proof lay in the fact that in New York, Boston, New Orleans, and Mobile "there are to be found some of the most accomplished men and women to be found anywhere, some of them of such unmixed African blood that they cannot be robbed of their virtues and attainments by that Anglo-Saxon pride of race which believes in no blood it has not corrupted by the vices of amalgamation."

The work of the American Missionary Association gave evidence of the eagerness of the freedmen to learn, and that "The Negro can be elevated." In another refutation of a frequently accepted belief, Martin declared that "The Negro is a lover of family and home and some of the most touching records of this transition state [from slavery to freedom] are to be found in the efforts of husbands to find their wives, and wives their husbands, that slavery tore from them, and for parents to find their children, and children their parents." He attributed these virtues to the Negro's "love of religion."

The educated Negro would be "the main link of binding the South to the North." More important, "a civilized and converted population of Africans in America means the civilization, in no very distant day, of Africa itself."

Like J. Sella Martin, this oration is not widely known. Carter G. Woodson, who included it in his *Negro Orators and Their Orations* (1925, pp. 256–61), listed it among "The Oratory of Defiance." It should be listed instead among "Optimistic Oratory."

Information about Martin is scanty. There are brief references in Frederick Douglass's *The Life and Times . . .*, edited by Rayford W. Logan (1962); *The Works of Francis J. Grimké,* edited by Carter G. Woodson (vol. 4, 1942); Floyd Miller's *The Search for a Black Nationality* (1975); Benjamin Quarles's *Black Abolitionists* (1969); *The Black Press,* edited by Martin Dann (1971); and Jane H. Pease's and William H. Pease's *They Who Would Be Free* (1974). Research by the staff of John W. Blassingame, editor of *The Frederick Douglass Papers,* has uncovered a wealth of material in American and English journals (report dated March 25, 1976).

— RAYFORD W. LOGAN

MATTHEWS, VICTORIA EARLE (1861–1907), journalist, author, clubwoman, and social worker. She was born a slave in Fort Valley, Ga. Her mother, Caroline Smith, was said to have been a Virginian. Her white father was so cruel that her mother fled to New York, leaving her nine children with an old nurse. After emancipation Caroline Smith returned to Georgia, where she found Victoria and three other of her children being reared in their white father's household. After "considerable legal trouble, she succeeded in gaining possession of her children, and returned with them to New York, stopping on the way at Richmond and Norfolk."

She attended Grammar School 48 in New York City, but was soon forced to seek employment as a domestic worker. She was thereafter largely self-taught, using the library of the house in which she worked. She was first a "sub" for reporters on the large dailies of New York City, later for other newspapers and magazines. In 1879 she married William Matthews, a coachman, and settled in Brooklyn with their one son, Lamartine. In 1892 Mrs. Matthews became the first president of the Woman's Loyal Union of New York, and in 1895, with Josephine St. Pierre Ruffin and others, helped found in Boston the National Federation of Afro-American Women. She was the principal planner of the meeting in Washington, D.C., when the federation merged with the National Colored Women's League, organized by Mary Church Terrell, to become the National Association of Colored Women. Under Terrell, its first president, Matthews served (1897–1899) as national organizer.

Meanwhile, after the death of her son at age sixteen and with her growing concern for colored girls who were lured into becoming prostitutes, she shifted her interest to social welfare. She attended the Congress of Colored Women of the United States at the Atlanta Exposition (Dec. 1895) and toured the South, especially New Orleans, to investigate the "red-light" districts and the "employment agencies" which found "jobs" for colored girls in the North. In 1897 she founded the White Rose Industrial Association and opened the White Rose Mission as a social center for Negro female migrants who settled in the tenements of New York's Upper East Side. The mission trained the newcomers and found employment for them as domestic servants. White Rose agents watched the piers in New York and Norfolk, Va., to prevent colored girls from becoming victims of a "white slave" racket. After T. Thomas Fortune persuaded Booker T. Washington to visit the ramshackle mission, Washington spoke at a fundraising dinner which helped make possible the opening of a larger mission on 86th Street. This was similar to other settlement houses of the era with mothers' clubs, recreational facilities, and a kindergarten. Matthews was a pioneer there in teaching a class in Negro history and establishing a large library of books by and about Negroes. When her health began to fail, her duties were taken over by able assistants.

She died in New York City of tuberculosis at the age of forty-five, and was buried in Maple Grove Cemetery, Kew Gardens, Long Island City. The White Rose Mission later moved to 136th Street in Harlem, where a plaque commemorates her life and work.

Matthews was the "most popular" of the lady writers when I. Garland Penn published his *The Afro-American Press . . .* in 1891. The pages about her, probably based on information which she supplied, stated that she had been a "sub" reporter for the *New York Times, Herald, Mail and Express,* as well as *Sunday Mercury, The Earth,* and *The Phonographic World.* She was also a New York correspondent for the *National Leader, Detroit Plaindealer,* and the *Southern Christian Recorder,* and contributed to the *A.M.E. Church Review.* She wrote articles also for the leading Negro newspapers: the *Boston Advocate, Washington Bee, Richmond Planet, Catholic Tribune, Cleveland Gazette, New York Globe, New York Age,* and the *New York Enterprise.* Her stories were published in the *Waverley Magazine, New York Weekly,* and the *Family Story Paper.*

Emma Lou Thornbrough, in her *T. Thomas Fortune: Militant Journalist* (1972), wrote that Matthews was a reporter for the *Globe* and the *Age.* She assisted Fortune in editing the short-lived *Atlanta Southern Age* during her 1895–1896 tour of the South. She prepared, at Fortune's request (1896), an article that Booker T. Washington was writing. Matthews selected and edited for Fortune Washington's speeches in *Black-Belt Diamonds . . .* (1898) (Thornbrough, pp. 126, 127, 153, 165, 167). In addition she had written a slim volume, *Aunt Lindy* (1893), the tale of an ex-slave in postwar Georgia who resisted temptation to murder her former master.

For the early life of Matthews, see I. Garland Penn's *The Afro-American Press . . .* (1891); for her later career, Hallie Q. Brown's *Homespun Heroines and Other Women of Distinction* (1926). See also Jean Blackwell Hutson's article in *NAW* (1971, 3:510–11).

— RAYFORD W. LOGAN

MATZELIGER, JAN EARNST (1852–1889), inventor. He was born on Sept. 15, 1852, in Paramaribo, Surinam (South America), the son of a Holland-born engineer and a native Negro mother. In 1855 Jan moved to the home of a paternal aunt. At the age of ten he began an apprenticeship in the machine shops superintended by his father. His experience and observations sparked young Matzeliger's interests and talents in mechanics.

Matzeliger left Surinam in 1871 to become a sailor aboard an East Indian vessel. Two years later at the end of the cruise he disembarked at Philadelphia. For the next few years Matzeliger worked in odd jobs around the Philadelphia area. In 1876 he left for the New England states, living in Boston, and eventually settling in Lynn, Mass.

Shortly after settling in Lynn, Matzeliger found employment in a shoe factory operating a McKay sole-sewing machine. He also spent time on the heel-burnisher and the button-hole machine. Matzeliger's facility with the English language was limited during his first days in Lynn. He quickly made up for the shortcoming by attending evening school and studying during his free time. His spare hours soon became absorbed in self-education, and he maintained a personal library emphasizing scientific and practical works. Matzeliger's abilities ranged beyond the mechanical, for he possessed a marked talent in painting. He presented a number of paintings to friends and gave lessons in oil painting.

By September 1880, after years of observation and practical experience, Matzeliger over a period of six months assembled his first machine. The device, constructed of wire, wood, and cigar boxes, was the first crude step toward perfecting a mechanical laster for the manufacture of shoes. The new model, built from assorted castings and iron parts, took four years to construct. The assembly process took place in a vacant corner of the plant where Matzeliger worked. Adequate financing for the invention soon presented a major problem. To secure a patent, arrange demonstrations, and complete finishing touches, Matzeliger knocked on doors to obtain the needed capital. Financial support was soon obtained from C. H. Delnow and M. S. Nichols of Lynn at the cost of two-thirds ownership of the device.

With sufficient capital in hand, Matzeliger was granted patent no. 274,207 on March 20, 1883, for the "Lasting Machine." The drawings sent to the Patent Office so confused the patent officials that one had to be sent to Lynn to personally observe the machine. In the following year Matzeliger joined the Christian Endeavor Society at the North Congregational Church. Although never a formal member of the church, he attended services quite regularly and participated in a number of church functions. Matzeliger's affiliation came about only after suffering a number of rebuffs from other churches in the community because of his race.

Indefatigable in his zeal for work, the inventor continued to perfect his "Lasting Machine" for its first factory test. On May 29, 1885, during the first public operation of the machine it made a record run of lasting seventy-five pairs of shoes. In subsequent days the machine came to be termed the "Niggerhead Laster."

Finding themselves unable properly to finance the production of Matzeliger's invention, Delnow and Nichols sought additional capital from George A. Brown and Disney W. Winslow. The result was the creation of the Consolidated Lasting Machine Company which began to manufacture Matzeliger's device. The "Lasting Machine" was indeed "revolutionary," for it could turn out from 150 to 700 pairs of shoes a day compared to a top of 50 by the manual method. Unfortunately, proper recognition for the machine came only posthumously with the awarding of the Gold Medal and Diploma at the Pan-American Exposition of 1901. The Consolidated Lasting Machine Company which purchased Matzeliger's patents quickly expanded and by the late 1890s merged a number of smaller companies to form the United Shoe Machinery Corporation. The corporation soon came to dominate the shoe machinery industry in the United States with a capitalization of millions.

Matzeliger's mechanical genius was not limited to a single "Lasting Machine." He patented a number of items prior to his death and had several granted thereafter. The patents included no. 415, 726, "Mechanism for Distributing Tacks, Nails, etc." (Oct. 12, 1888); no. 421,954, "Nailing Machine" (Feb. 25, 1890); no. 423,-937, "Tack Separating and Distributing Mechanism" (March 25, 1890); and no. 459,899, "Lasting Machine" (Sept. 22, 1891).

In the summer of 1886 Matzeliger contracted what appeared to be a cold, but when properly diagnosed turned out to be tuberculosis. Although bedridden, he continued to paint and work on his experiments. His health continued to worsen and he died in Lynn Hospital on Aug. 24, 1889, less than a month before his thirty-seventh birthday, and was buried in the Pine Grove Cemetery, Lynn. He did not marry. He did not live to see the profound impact of his invention on the shoe industry or to reap the benefit of the financial legacy of the invention. He willed the North Church a substantial portion of his holdings in the shoe machinery companies.

Jan Matzeliger has not been the subject of a full biographical study. Sidney Kaplan's "Jan Earnst Matzeliger and the Making of the Shoe" (*JNH*, Jan. 1955, pp. 8–33) provides the most complete account of the inventor's life and impact on the shoe industry. There is a brief sketch by Carl W. Mitman in *DAB* (1961, 6:426–27). The *Official Gazette of the U.S. Patent Office* lists the various patents granted to Matzeliger. The importance of Matzeliger and his interests in Lynn, Mass., are frequently covered in such newspapers as the *Lynn Item* and the *Lynn News*. The standard history of the American shoe industry is F. J. Allen's *The Shoe Industry* (1922). The paintings and papers willed by Matzeliger to his foster son, Perrie Lee, fell into the hands of a neighbor, Ernest Rideout. Some remained in Rideout's family; others were sold to antique dealers (Roger C. Storms, Lee Historical Society, Lee, Me., to Rayford W. Logan, Aug. 30, 1975).

— FRANK R. LEVSTIK

MERRICK, JOHN (1859–1919), businessman. Born a slave in Clinton, N.C., he did not know his father; however, his mother Martha seemed to have compensated for the absence of the father. When John was twelve, he and his mother moved to Chapel Hill, N.C., where he worked as a brickyard helper to support his mother and younger brother Richard. There is no available information on John's life between his birth and the time he started working at the brickyard. When he was eighteen, he, his mother, and his brother moved to Raleigh, N.C., where John became a hod carrier. Later, as a brickmason, he helped build the first building on the campus of Shaw University. He then worked as a shoe shiner in a barbershop, and learned and practiced the trade of barbering. In 1880 he joined John Wright, a fellow barber who had established a shop in Durham. Between 1880 and his death in 1919, Merrick became one of the leading Negro businessmen of the South.

By 1918 Merrick had become seriously ill, suffering from cancer or a similar disease. He died on Aug. 6, 1919, in Durham and was buried on Aug. 8 after funeral services at St. Joseph's A.M.E. Church. He had married Martha Hunter, and they had five children, Geneva, Mabel, Edward, John Jr., and Martha, four of whom survived.

About 1881 Merrick bought a lot and built homes for his and Wright's families on Pettigrew Street. By 1892 Merrick had become owner of the barbershop; within four years, the owner of five barbershops, two for Negroes and three for whites. In 1887 he and his family had bought and moved to a six-room house on Fayetteville Street, which at the turn of the century was the location of the homes of the city's prominent Negroes.

In the barbering business, Merrick was best known for his dandruff cure, on which he had been working since 1890. Advertisements, written by Merrick, were found after his death in 1919. One advertisement read: "Something ought to be done and must be if you save your self [sic] from baldness. No dandruff cure has ever been put upon the market that has found such favor with the Tonsorial profession as Merricks Dandruff Cure. No greece [sic] no fussy odor it is quick its cooling and cleaning power make it wonderful."

Among his customers and personal friends were some of the prominent white business families of Durham, notably James B. Duke, the philanthropist and pioneer in the production of cigarette-making machinery. According to tradition, after Merrick had shaved him in 1895 William Jennings Bryan gave Merrick a silver dollar, dated 1882, and told him not to spend it until after Bryan became president of the United States.

In 1883 Merrick and other Negro businessmen purchased from a Reverend Morrison of Georgia the fraternal order of the Royal Knights of King David. The order, built around the biblical story of David and Goliath, also had insurance features for its members. In 1918 the organization had 21,000 members, $22,000 in bonds and securities, and owned $40,000 in property. Merrick bought the interest of most of the members and was supreme grand treasurer from the time of his purchase until his death in 1919.

Merrick, meanwhile, had persuaded the Duke family to provide funds in 1901 for Lincoln Hospital, founded by Aaron W. Moore. After an initial gift of $13,000 by Washington Duke, the father of James B. Duke, the family contributed an additional $20,000 for the hospital, located on Fayetteville Street. Merrick was elected president of the trustee board and helped develop it as one of the better private hospitals for Negroes in the South.

John Merrick was best known for founding the North Carolina Mutual Life Insurance Company (Oct. 1898). The seven men who invested fifty dollars each were John Merrick, Aaron McDuffie Moore, P. W. Dawkins, D. T. Watson, W. G. Pearson, E. A. Johnson, and James E. Shepard. Merrick was elected president of the organization, which began operations in April 1899. In late 1899 when the business venture was a complete failure, Merrick and Moore called a meeting and bought the interest of the other five investors. The firm was reorganized with John Merrick as its president, Aaron M. Moore as treasurer and medical director, and Charles C. Spaulding as vice-president and general manager. During the first six years the organization met so many obstacles that they thought many times about dissolving it. Spaulding made frequent trips across North Carolina soliciting buyers for the company's policies. This effort at first was a failure. Not until the company began advertising in the *Blade,* a Negro newspaper of Raleigh, did business grow. The company's assets at Merrick's death are evidence of its growth: in 1899 Mutual's total income was $840; in 1919 it was $1,662,527.28. In 1918, the company had over $16 million of insurance in force.

In 1910 Booker T. Washington visited the city of Durham on one of his "Educational Pilgrimages," and described it as the most progressive city in the South for Negroes, and Merrick as the leader of Negro business in Durham. Washington, Merrick, Moore, and Spaulding were close friends and shared similar economic ideologies. Shortly before his death Merrick visited Tuskegee Institute and was invited by Washington to accompany him on his tour through Florida.

Merrick's next business venture was the development of a bank in Durham. Although he was not solely responsible in the preliminary stages for the founding of the Mechanics and Farmers Bank, he later made extensive efforts to help establish it and became its first vice-president. R. B. Fitzgerald and W. G. Pearson were initially the most active. Pearson talked with Merrick, but he did not think the time was quite ripe to launch a bank. Pearson and Fitzgerald subscribed $1000 each, and after approaching Merrick again, he too subscribed. The bank was organized when $10,000 in subscriptions had been secured.

In an effort to develop more businesses for Negro citizens in Durham, Merrick founded the Bull City Drug Company in 1908. The Fitzgerald Drug Company, which had grown out of the Durham Drug Company, organized in 1895, was not located in the Negro section of Durham, but on Parrish Street; later a store was opened on Pettigrew Street in the Negro section.

In 1910 Merrick also founded the Merrick-Moore-Spaulding Real Estate Company, in which he often found profitable investments. When there was property that the insurance company could not handle because of insurance regulations, he handled it to his personal advantage.

The Durham Textile Mill, founded in 1914, is regarded as the only business started by Merrick that failed. The mill manufactured socks and was probably the only one of its kind in the world operated by Negroes. Factors which caused its failure were the inability of its founders (Merrick, Moore, and Spaulding) to find the time to commit themselves fully to its development, inexperience of the manager, C. C. Amey, in the hoisery business, and lack of trained and experienced personnel.

The legacy of John Merrick was given perspective in E. Franklin Frazier's "Durham: Capital of the Black Middle Class" (*The New Negro: An Interpretation,* edited by Alain Locke [1925], pp. 333–40). Frazier compared the careers of the Negro leaders to those of the nation's other fortune builders. "Their lives are as free from the Negro's native love of leisure and enjoyment of life as [Benjamin] Franklin's life. . . . When we trace the history of this development we must begin with the late John Merrick." Negro businesses, especially the Mechanics and Farmers Bank and the North Carolina Mutual Insurance Company, located in the heart of downtown Durham, were the culmination of the successful struggle of these pioneers.

The only full-length biography is R. McCants Andrews's *John Merrick: A Biographical Sketch* (1920). There is much valuable information in William J. Kennedy's *The North Carolina Mutual Story* (1970) and Walter B. Weare's *Black Business in the New South: A Social History of the North Carolina Mutual Life Insurance Company* (1973). Contemporary magazine articles include Booker T. Washington's "Durham, North Carolina: A City of Negro Enterprise" (*Independent,* March 30, 1911, pp. 642–50), and Clement Richardson's "What are Negroes Doing in Durham?" (*Southern Workman,* July 1913, pp. 614–19). See also C. C. Spaulding's "Business in Durham" (*Southern Workman,* Dec. 1937, pp. 364–65).

— GEORGE W. REID AND FREDDIE L. PARKER

MERRITT, EMMA F[RANCES] G[RAYSON] (1860–1933), educator, lecturer, and welfare worker. She was born at Dumfries, Prince William County, Va., the daughter of John and Sophie (Cook) Merritt, who brought her to Washington, D.C., at the age of three. Her early education was acquired in the public schools of the District of Columbia. She received four years of normal school training at Howard University from 1883 to 1887 and later specialized in mathematics there. She took collegiate training at George Washington University, then known as the Columbian University, from 1887 to 1889 and again from 1895 to 1898 when she studied child psychology and sociology. She also studied at the Cook County Normal School in Chicago (1898–1901) and the Berlitz School of Languages, Paris, (1913 and 1914). She graduated from the Phoebe Hearst Training School in Washington, D.C., in 1901. In 1925 she received an honorary M.A. degree from Howard University.

For fifty-four years (1876–1930), Merritt was an active and successful educator in the public schools of the District of Columbia. She began her career as a first-grade teacher and went on to become principal of the Banneker School in 1887, principal of the Garnet School in 1890, director of Primary Instruction in 1898 and supervising principal, Divisions 10–13, in 1927, a position she held until her retirement from the public schools of the District of Columbia in 1930.

Merritt made lasting contributions to public education by modernizing instruction at the elementary school level. She was recognized as one of the few well-trained teachers of her time who had knowledge of modern educational methods and how to apply them. She established and equipped the first kindergarten at the Garnet School in 1896 (and personally raised funds for teachers' salaries), and also started the first summer school at Stevens School. She also organized and developed a primary department. It was as its director that she was most creative. She organized demonstration and observation schools to assist in improving instruction. She established homogeneous groupings of children for teaching purposes, initiated on-the-spot learning methods through visits to places of educational significance, and introduced the silent reading technique before provision for it had been made in the course of study.

Her influence as an educator extended beyond Washington, as she introduced new concepts and methods of teaching to many eastern and southern states, from Dover, Del., to Dallas, Tex., through her demonstrations, lectures, and summer school teaching. This influence was extended through the "multiplier effect" of the contacts she maintained with her former students as she communicated new educational concepts and techniques to them.

Carter G. Woodson noted the impact of Merritt's work on the educational system of the District of Columbia when he described her as a significant factor in the successful education of the many Negroes of local and national prominence who received their early training in the public schools of Washington.

In civic life Merritt was actively involved in social and welfare work. She organized in 1898 and directed the local Teachers' Benefit and Annuity Association until 1933, and the Prudence Crandall Association for Needy Children. She was president of the Washington branch of the NAACP (1930–1933), director and member of the executive board of the Southwest Social Settlement House (1910–1925), and for twenty-eight years (1905–1933) served the Phyllis Wheatley YWCA as Chairman of the Finance Committee. She was treasurer of the Banneker Boys Club (1931–1933), director of Mother-Child Center (1929–1933), treasurer of the Lend-a-Hand Club, and associated with the Ionia R. Whipper Home for Unwed Mothers.

She died at her residence, 1630 Tenth St. NW, Washington, D.C. Among her closest survivors were a niece, a nephew, and two great-nieces, three of whom became teachers.

On Nov. 10, 1944, the Emma F. Merritt School in the

District of Columbia was dedicated to her memory.

Some information about Emma Merritt may be found in Minutes of the Washington, D.C., Board of Education (vol. 21), and Carter G. Woodson's "Emma Frances Grayson Merritt" (*Opportunity,* Aug. 1930). Other sources are *Who's Who in Colored America* (4th ed., 1933); *The Crisis* (Sept. 1930); *JNH* (April 1932, pp. 351–54); *Colored Y.W.C.A. Annual Reports* (1907–1909); Sylvia G. L. Dannett's *Negro Heritage Library; Profiles in Negro Womanhood,* vol. 1, *1619–1900* (1964). — HELEN M. BLACKBURN

MICHAUX, ELDER SOLOMON LIGHTFOOT (c. 1885–1968), charismatic and dynamic evangelist, founder of the Church of God Movement, and entrepreneur. He was born around 1885 in Buckroe Beach, Va., into a devout Baptist family. The family established residence in Newport News, Va., where he was educated in the public schools and aided in the family's seafood business. During his youth he was self-employed as a fishpeddler, selling wares particularly to military men at Camp Lee near Petersburg, Va. From this experience Michaux learned the power of persuasion, which aided him in his career as a religious leader.

In 1917 Michaux established the first black Church of God in Hopewell, Va. Since this church did not prosper, he organized a Church of God Movement in Newport News (1919), where he began to broadcast his services over a local radio station. He continued his work in Hampton, Va., which gained new converts and spread throughout the state. In 1928 in Washington, D.C., he erected the Church of God under the Gospel Spreading Association, at 2030 Georgia Ave. NW, across the street from what was then the Griffith Stadium. There he achieved national acclaim by his broadcasts on radio (and later television), colorful religious exercises, aid to the poor, and as entrepreneur.

He married Mary Eliza Pauline of the Eastern Shore of Virginia in 1906. They had no children. Elder Michaux died on Oct. 20, 1968, at Freedmen's Hospital, Washington, D.C., almost two months after a stroke. Funeral services were held at the Church of God, 19th and Jefferson Streets, Newport News, Va., with more than 3000 people attending. FBI director J. Edgar Hoover stated in a telegram that Michaux's contribution to human understanding is "one that will never be forgotten." He was buried in Pleasant Shade Cemetery, Hampton, Va. (his wife had died in October 1967). He was survived by three sisters and two brothers.

In 1922 Michaux was arrested in Newport News, for holding racially integrated baptismal services. He appeared in court as his own counsel, successfully argued his case in biblical language, and was acquitted.

The philosophy of his movement was based on two principles: (1) the sacred word of the Supreme Being which makes no reference to class, division or race; (2) the belief that the Church of God is the only institution that could correct what he regarded as the iniquitous practices of Western religion. It was Michaux's belief that Negroes should create a religion of their own which would not encompass the evils of other religions.

Michaux used radio time on WJSV in Alexandria, Va., daily and CBS radio on Saturday to broadcast his message. He was known as the "Happy Am I Evangelist" and the "Colored Billy Sunday." Every morning at seven o'clock he explained that W stood for willingly, J for Jesus, S for suffered, and V for victory over the grave. It was popularly believed in Washington that he used the two-fingered symbol, "V for Victory" before Winston Churchill did. He organized the "Cross Choir" of 156 trained singers to stage elaborately executed programs at churches and marches, usually at the Griffith Stadium. Until 1938 he baptized large numbers of followers in the Potomac River. In that year Clark Griffith, principal owner of the Washington baseball team, provided a large tank in the ball park, where Elder Michaux, clad in a black robe, high rubber boots, and a black skullcap, baptized his "sheep" in water reported to have been imported from the River Jordan. His baptismals were preceded by a parade through the streets of Washington that drew enormous crowds.

His fame and influence induced Griffith, President Eisenhower, District Commissioner George E. Allen, "Steve" Early, personal secretary to Franklin D. Roosevelt, and Harry Butcher, vice-president of the Columbia Broadcasting Company, to become honorary deacons of the Church of God.

Michaux's influence stemmed not only from his religious exercises but also the official monthly paper *Happy News,* with a circulation of approximately 8000. He believed that people were losing respect for the church because the church was not responsive in times of distress. It therefore became the policy of the Church of God to provide shelter and food for evicted persons. The church also accepted the responsibility of collecting evictees' furniture and personal articles from the street and placing them in dwellings provided by the church. The church established an employment agency for church members and community people. It sponsored additional programs such as projects for the aged and disabled, farms, orphanages, schools, and hotels.

One of his more important enterprises was his participation with Albert Irvin Cassell in the development of one of the largest privately owned housing developments for Negroes in the United States, Mayfair Mansions and the Mayfair Extension First Commercial Site, completed on July 4, 1946, on the site of the old Benning Race Track in Washington, D.C. This complex of 594 garden-type apartments served the housing needs of middle- and lower-income Negroes.

Like other evangelists Michaux has been praised and criticized. He gave solace to those poor Negroes who found little solace in established churches. On the other hand he was condemned as an old-style camp meeting preacher who fought the devil rather than racism. His Church of God remained after his death a landmark for evangelistic services.

Some basic facts about Michaux are in *Who's Who in Colored America,* edited by G. James Fleming and Christian E. Burckel (1950, p. 372). For a detailed discussion of Elder Michaux and the Church of God Movement, see Chancellor Williams's "The Socio-Economic Significance of the Store-Front Church Movement in the United States since 1920" (Ph.D. dissertation, American University, 1949) and James D. Tyms's "A Study of Four Religious Cults Operating Among Negroes" (M.A.

thesis, Howard University, 1938). To gain an insight into the programs of the church, see *Happy News* (March 1938). General information regarding Elder Michaux may be obtained from the Federal Writers Project's *Washington City and Capital* (1937). An excellent brief evaluation is in Constance McLaughlin Green's *Washington: Capital City, 1879–1950* (1963, pp. 403–5). A pamphlet by E. F. Lark, *Presenting a Pictorial Review of Elder Solomon Michaux . . .* (1941), describes his famous cross and radio choirs and civic activities. See also Lightfoot Solomon Michaux (comp.), *Spiritual Happiness Making Songs* (n.d.), which contains 160 songs. Obituaries are in the *Washington Evening Star* (Oct. 21, 1968, p. B5), and the *Norfolk Journal and Guide* (Nov. 2, 1968, p. 2.

— JANETTE HOSTON HARRIS

MICHEAUX, OSCAR (1884–1951), producer of all-Negro movies. He was born on a small farm near the Ohio River, about forty miles above Cairo, Ill., the fourth son and fifth child in a family of thirteen, born to parents who were former slaves. He disliked the drudgery of farm life but enjoyed school and salesmanship; he early developed a strong distaste for the colored clergy. At seventeen he left home, and after working at a variety of jobs, became a Pullman porter on a Chicago–Portland run, gaining a knowledge of the West which influenced him toward a "life on the land," and in 1904 he purchased "a relinquishment on a homestead" in Gregory County, southern S. Dak., just north of Dallas. A hardworking, bookish, somewhat priggish young man, a great admirer of Booker T. Washington, he was successful as a farmer, got along well with his exclusively white neighbors, and was scornful of Negroes unwilling to leave the bright lights of the cities for the agricultural opportunities of the West.

Micheaux turned to writing fiction partly to publicize these opportunities but principally because of a frustrated romance and an unhappy marriage; to his early semiautobiographical narratives we owe almost all our knowledge of his life to 1918. In 1913 he published anonymously, at his own expense, *The Conquest: The Story of a Negro Pioneer,* which deals with the experiences of "Oscar Devereaux" and seems to be pretty straightforward autobiography, fictional principally in the suppression or change of proper names. After achieving success as a farmer, "Devereaux" falls in love with a Scottish girl but, because opposed on principle to interracial marriage (and perhaps also because in 1909 South Dakota passed an antimiscegenation law) he decides to forget her and marries the daughter of a lecherous, dishonest, and hypocritical Methodist minister, who breaks up the marriage.

The Conquest and subsequent works probably would have perished stillborn had not the author undertaken aggressive promotional tours, especially through the principal colored communities of the South, holding meetings in churches, schools, and homes, and selling directly to the people. On his experiences during a book-selling tour he based *The Forged Note: A Romance of the Darker Races* (1915). His third book, *The Homesteader* (1917), is a melodramatization of the latter part of *The Conquest,* but is geographically specific.

The "homesteader," Jean Baptiste, goes through the same experiences with a Scottish girl and the daughter of a villainous colored minister as the hero of *The Conquest,* but the wife, while insane, kills her father and herself, and the Scottish girl's mother proves to have been "of Ethiopian extraction," which leaves her and Jean Baptiste free to find happiness together. One is more inclined to believe in the unhappy marriage which appears in both books than in the "happy ending" of *The Homesteader.* While the style of *The Conquest,* which Micheaux had revised by semiprofessionals, is dull and pedestrian, *The Homesteader* is a literary disaster, with an unbelievably complicated plot, long-winded, pretentiously awkward writing, stilted conversations, and the grotesque misuse of words. Nevertheless, the author's promotional methods won for it considerable circulation.

In 1918 Micheaux abandoned South Dakota and the autobiographical "novel" for a new location and a new form of expression. When the Nebraska-based Lincoln Motion Picture Company, one of the independent Negro companies inspired by the ultraracist classic *The Birth of a Nation* (1915), approached Micheaux for film rights to *The Homesteader,* he insisted on directing the film version, and when the company declined, he raised funds among Oklahoma farmers to whom he had previously sold his novels and organized in New York City the Oscar Micheaux Corporation; its first production was *The Homesteader* (1919).

Micheaux's productions, about thirty of which appeared from 1919 to 1937, were typically "quickies" and "cheapies," which, operating on a shoestring, he wrote, directed, and produced, using existing buildings instead of special sets, eschewing retakes—even when the actor stumbled in his lines—and usually completing a picture in six weeks. Lighting and editing tended to be poor and "the acting could be dreadful." His plots were mostly of a standard, melodramatic character, employing as heroes and heroines light-skinned Negroes in roles which could as well have been filled by whites and publicizing them through such sobriquets as the "black Valentino," the "sepia Mae West," the "colored Cagney," and the "Negro Harlow." *Birthright* (1924), however, was based on a pioneer novel of southern racial relations by T. S. Stribling, later a Pulitzer Prize winner, and Micheaux introduced Paul Robeson to the screen in the otherwise undistinguished *Body and Soul* (1924).

Micheaux survived as a producer for nearly a score of years primarily because of his promotional skill. He employed the same methods in distributing his films as he had with his novels, traveling from community to community to whip up a demand for his current release and raise funds for the next. "A hefty six-footer, given to wearing long Russian coats and extravagant wide-brimmed hats," he would step into a meeting hall with the air of "God about to deliver a sermon" and was able to "talk the shirt off your back." He was even able to persuade white southern movie-house owners to put on all-Negro matinee performances, and sometimes also special midnight showings for all-white audiences who were titillated by his frequent "raunchy cabaret scenes."

Although in 1928 the Micheaux Film Corporation went into bankruptcy—after he allegedly had put most of his films into his wife's name—his productions continued without interruption, and in 1931, moreover, "when most Negro independents were closing up shop, he released *The Exile,* the first all-talking motion picture by a black company." Of a dozen subsequent movies, *Veiled Aristocrats* (1932) was presumably based on a 1923 novel by Gertrude Sanborn, a well-meaning but inept white author whose title referred to Chicago's intelligent, well-educated, and refined mulatto community, "aristocrats" because they were descended from the white aristocarts of the Old South and Europe but "veiled" from due recognition by their color. (The black proletariat was discreetly kept offstage.) The dénouement, reminiscent of *The Homesteader,* is the revelation that the wealthy "white" heroine is herself colored so that nothing bars her marriage to the talented mulatto hero. Micheaux, however, suspended his cinematic activities after Communist-led pickets forced RKO to drop the showing of *God's Stepchildren,* a movie of "passing."

For several years Micheaux's life was obscure. Then, through the Book Supply Co., of New York, he published *The Wind from Nowhere* (1941), a reworking of *The Homesteader,* with a hero named Martin Eden—with no apologies to Jack London—*The Case of Mrs. Wingate* (1944), *The Story of Dorothy Stansfield* (1946), and *The Masquerade.* In 1948 he reemerged as a cinematist with his most ambitious production, *The Betrayal,* the "first all-Negro motion picture to have a Broadway premiere"—which was also a cinematic reworking of a theme which had become an obsession, being immediately based on *The Wind from Nowhere.* The *New York Times* (June 26, 1948) described it as presenting "in painful detail" for something over three hours "the marital woes of an enterprising young Negro who develops an agricultural empire in South Dakota"; other comments were: "often confusing . . . so gauche as to provoke embarrassed laughter. . . . sporadically poor photography and consistently amateurish performance and direction."

This ambitious failure was Micheaux's last cinematic effort. He had probably overextended himself financially, and in any case a more sophisticated audience now preferred the superior artistry of the major studio films which during the 1940s were making at least a feeble beginning toward presenting Negro characters in relatively dignified roles compared to Micheaux's old-fashioned melodrama.

Micheaux died in Charlotte, N.C., on April 1, 1951, while on a promotional tour. His films aimed primarily at the "black bourgeoisie" and at creating a fantasy world in which Negroes were as educated, cultured, and prosperous as whites, had ignored the difficulties of the black peasantry and proletariat to emphasize such middle-class problems as "passing," but they had at least, however, moved sharply away from the traditional stereotypes of servant and clown and presented Negroes in roles with which his audiences could "identify."

Whether or not Micheaux was himself ever actually involved in one or both of the marriages described in *The Conquest, The Homesteader,* and *The Wind from Nowhere,* his widow was Alice B. Russell, an actress whom he had married c. 1925, and who after his death "lived for years in virtual seclusion . . . refusing to comment on her husband's life or work."

The principal authority for Micheaux's most significant years and activities is Donald Bogle's *Toms, Coons, Mulattoes, Mammies, and Bucks: An Interpretive History of Blacks in American Films* (1973). Daniel J. Leab's *From Sambo to Superspade: The Black Experience in Motion Pictures* (1975) is also helpful. Hugh M. Gloster's *Negro Voices in American Fiction* (1948) analyzes his first three novels; and Merritt Hull, in a letter to *Frontier Times* (Oct.-Nov. 1966), remembers an unnamed Negro farmer in South Dakota whom his parents "knew and liked" and who sent them a copy of a book he had written, entitled *The Conquest.*

— KENNETH WIGGINS PORTER

MILLER, DORIE (1919–1943), winner of the Navy Cross. Miller was born on Oct. 12, 1919, on a small farm near Waco, Tex. His parents, Connery and Henrietta Miller, earned a meager living as sharecroppers on a twenty-eight-acre farm. At an early age Dorie worked with them. The work, fresh air, and wholesome food made him in his teens a strong man, five feet ten inches tall and weighing over 200 pounds. Although his knowledge of the world was limited by his few years of schooling and trips to Waco for the sale of the farm produce, he had a yearning for wider horizons. His reasons are unknown, but when he was nineteen, he harkened to the slogans of a navy recruiting officer in Waco and joined the navy. Since Waco was an inland city, Dorie may have listened to anyone who promised him an opportunity to leave the farm and Waco's restricted opportunities for Negroes.

At that time the messman branch was the only one officially open to Negro enlistment (until June 1, 1942). Even after the Selective Service Act was passed in September 1940 providing for the induction and training of selectees without discrimination based on race or color, the navy continued to rely on volunteers until February 1943, in order not to comply with the law. Consequently, when Miller enlisted, and for some time thereafter, he had no opportunity to rise above the rank of messman.

After the unusual indoctrination, brief training ashore, and then sea duty, he was on board the battleship *Arizona* when it was anchored at Pearl Harbor on Dec. 7, 1941. The *Arizona* was the battleship "most devastatingly bombed. . . . The forward part of the ship was a mass of flames and shattered, twisting metal. Bodies lay thick on the deck. Men were running out of the fire, falling on the deck, jumping over the side. Japanese planes were flying low over the ship, strafing the fleeing seamen."

As a messman Miller had never been instructed to fire a gun. Knocked down by the explosion of Japanese bombs, he might have leaped overboard as did many other members of the crew. Instead he moved the ship's captain, who had been mortally wounded, to a place of greater safety and tinkered with the gun until it fired. The Japanese plane that was his target burst into flames and crashed into the sea. He was credited with downing three more planes before he was ordered to leave the ship.

Twelve weeks after Pearl Harbor, and in response to insistent pressure, Dorie Miller was awarded the Navy Cross, and advanced to mess attendant first class. He received a hero's celebration in Waco and Dallas. He was asked to address a graduating class of noncommissioned officers at the navy's Great Lakes Training School (Dorie Miller was not considered eligible for such training). He was sent to Bremerton, Wash., to qualify as a cook.

In November 1943 he boarded a small carrier, *Liscome Bay,* at Astoria, Ore., sailed to San Francisco, and then toward Makin Island in the Central Pacific, where it was to join an attack force. On Nov. 24, 1943, a Japanese submarine sank the *Liscome Bay,* with most of her officers and crew, including Dorie Miller.

It may be doubted that Miller's heroism significantly altered navy policy with respect to Negroes. Segregation continued; not until June 1949 did the naval academy graduate its first Negro, Ens. Wesley A. Brown. Dorie Miller was commemorated by a navy recruiting poster and by the Dorie Miller Trophy, awarded on Oct. 3, 1950, by the secretary of the navy. A housing development in Corona, N.Y., was also named in his honor in the 1950s.

See Dennis D. Nelson's *The Integration of the Negro into the U.S. Navy* (1951). A good account is also in Langston Hughes's *Famous Negro Heroes of America* (1958, pp. 183–86). See also Ben Richardson's *Great American Negroes,* revised by William A. Fahey (1956, pp. 317–24). — RAYFORD W. LOGAN

MILLER, KELLY (1863–1939) educator, essayist, and intellectual leader. Miller was born on July 18, 1863, in Winnsboro, S.C., the sixth of ten children of Kelly Miller, a free Negro who served in the Confederate Army, and Elizabeth (Roberts) Miller, a slave. He began his education in the first local school established during Reconstruction. A missionary, the Rev. Willard Richardson, recognized Miller's special aptitude for mathematics and arranged for his admission in 1878 to the Fairfield Institute, founded in Winnsboro by the Northern Presbyterian church. In 1880 he was awarded a scholarship to Howard University, where he attended the Preparatory Department, completing in two years the three-year cirriculum which emphasized Latin, Greek, and mathematics.

While attending the College Department of Howard University (1882–1886), he worked as a clerk for two years in the U.S. Pension Office. He had been appointed to the position after taking the examination prescribed by the Civil Service Act passed during the first administration of Grover Cleveland. The greatest influences on him at Howard were his professor of Latin and history, James Monroe Gregory, and Pres. William Weston Patton, who taught philosophy and preached at weekly vesper services required of all students. Miller said in later years that it was "difficult to overestimate the advantage of such cultural contact to a country boy of the crude surroundings and contacts such as I sustained prior to my entrance to Howard University."

From his savings he purchased a farm for his parents in 1886 as a graduation gift.

Miller continued work at the Pension Office after graduation. Upon the advice of Simon Newcomb, a famous astronomer in charge of the Nautical Almanac at the U.S. Naval Observatory and a professor of mathematics at Johns Hopkins, Miller studied advanced mathematics from 1886 to 1887 with Newcomb's assistant Capt. Edgar Frisby, an English mathematician at the Naval Observatory. At the end of this year Miller asked Newcomb to recommend his admission to Pres. Daniel Coit Gilman of Johns Hopkins University. Since Miller was to be the first Negro student admitted to the university, the matter was taken to the Board of Trustees, which decided in favor of admitting him because of the university founder's well-known Quaker beliefs. After this decision Gilman personally received Miller to inform him that "all the opportunities and facilities of the university" would be open to him. Miller later said that during his two years there he "met with no classroom embarrassment on the part of students or professors" and added that he was treated with "cool, calculated civility." From 1887 to 1889 he studied mathematics, physics, and astronomy at Johns Hopkins. An increase in tuition in 1889 prevented Miller from continuing his graduate studies. After teaching for a few months at the M Street High School in Washington, D.C. (1889–1890), where Francis L. Cardozo was principal, Miller was appointed professor of mathematics at Howard University.

On July 17, 1894, Miller married Annie May Butler, a teacher at the Baltimore Normal School whom he had met while he was as student at Johns Hopkins. The Millers had five children—Isaac Newton, Paul Butler, Irene, May, and Kelly Jr.

Kelly Miller's career had several distinct aspects: as a teacher and university administrator; intellectual advocate and "philosopher on the race question"; and journalist.

Miller was at Howard University from 1890 to 1934. He occupied a unique position in the university because of the national reputation derived from his lecturing and writing during the period 1895–1925. Although a mathematician by training, Miller recognized the importance of the new discipline of sociology for an objective understanding of the race problem in the United States, and in 1895 he was responsible for adding sociology to the college curriculum at Howard. From 1895 to 1907 he was professor of mathematics and sociology. His increasing interest in sociology resulted in a decision to teach that subject exclusively. For ten years (1915–1925) he was professor and head of the Department of Sociology. He taught sociology from 1925 until his retirement in 1934.

Miller's impact at Howard was most clearly demonstrated during his tenure as dean of the College of Arts and Sciences (1907–1919). A dramatic expansion of Howard University was encouraged by Wilbur P. Thirkield, president from 1906 to 1912. In order to accomplish this, the old classical curriculum was modernized, expanding the natural science and social science offerings. More students were recruited to the college largely through Miller's efforts. He traveled extensively throughout the South and Middle Atlantic states, lecturing at high schools and churches about the educational opportunities offered by Howard University. During his deanship the enrollment increased at an annual rate of 40 percent; an enrollment of 75 undergraduates and 8 graduate students in 1907 grew to 243 undergraduate and 31 graduates in 1911. According to Dwight O. W. Holmes, Dean of the College of Education at Howard from 1920 to 1934, through Miller's travels and his reputation as a writer "the claims of the University and the College of Arts and Sciences were brought to the attention of aspiring youth throughout the country." The policy of curriculum modernization was controversial because some critics believed that President Thirkield was lowering the intellectual standards of the institution in his attempt to steer a middle course between the educational, political, and social opinions of the "radical" Negro intellectuals associated with the Niagara Movement and the "conservative" views of Booker T. Washington.

Miller's reaction to the ideas and leadership of Booker T. Washington evolved from forceful opposition to reserved approval of most of his programs, with the significant exception of education. At a meeting in 1896 of the Bethel Literary and Historical Association of the Metropolitan A.M.E. Church in Washington, Miller was one of the speakers critical of Washington's widely acclaimed "compromise" address a year earlier at the Cotton States Exposition in Atlanta. Later Miller praised Washington's emphasis on self-help and initiative. As he gradually became a major figure in the controversy about Washington's leadership, he was critical of both camps, insisting that each side defined the issues too narrowly. The bases for one of Miller's best essays were two anonymous articles on "radicals" and "conservatives" in the *Boston Transcript* (Sept. 18 and 19, 1903). Six years later it was, with some alterations, the lead essay in his book *Race Adjustment.* Observing that "no thoughtful Negro is satisfied with the present status of his race" burdened by an "unfriendly public opinion . . . which is being rapidly crystallized into a rigid caste system and enacted into unrighteous law," Miller asked how can the Negro be expected "to contemplate such oppressive conditions with satisfaction and composure." Protest was natural although its manner "may be mild or pronounced, according to the dictates of prudence."

Miller mercilessly analyzed the character and programs of the contending camps. William Monroe Trotter, the editor of the *Boston Guardian,* who had served a jail term for heckling Washington in the so-called Boston Riot, was characterized as a man who although he made "great sacrifices for the cause," and was "as uncompromising as William Lloyd Garrison," lacked "moral sanity and poise." For Trotter, Miller wrote, "agitation is not so much the outgrowth of an intellectual or moral comprehension of right and reprehension of wrong, as it is a temperamental necessity. Endowed with a narrow, intolerant intensity of spirit, he pursues his ends with a Jesuitical justification of untoward means." While praising W. E. B. Du Bois as a "painstaking investigator and a writer of remarkable lucidity and keenness," Miller pointed out that "the men who are

now extolling him as the peerless leader of the radicals were a few years ago denouncing him bitterly for his restrained and reasoned conclusions. It is almost impossible to conceive how the author of *The Philadelphia Negro* could have penned the *Second Niagara Movement Manifesto,* without mental and moral metamorphosis. When Du Bois essays the role of the agitator . . . it is apt to result, as did his 'Atlanta Tragedy' in an extravaganza of feeling and a fiasco of thought. . . . Du Bois is passionately devoted to the welfare of his race, but he is allowing himself to be exploited in a function for which he is by nature unfit."

Of the Niagara Movement, composed in Miller's words of "some of the ablest and most earnest men of the Negro race," he was critical because of what he regarded as its intemperate manifestoes issued from picturesque settings with historical or melodramatic associations such as Niagara Falls and Harpers Ferry. "Verbal vehemence void of practical power to enforce demands," he wrote, "is an ineffectual missile to be hurled against the stronghold of prejudice." He was no less sharp in his criticism of Washington. Noting the contrasts between the character of Frederick Douglass and Washington, he said the former was "like a lion, bold and fearless"; the latter, "lamblike, meek, and submissive." He developed the contrast: "Douglass escaped from personal bondage, which his soul abhorred; but for Lincoln's proclamation, Washington would probably have arisen to esteem and favor in the eyes of his master as a good and faithful servant. Douglass insisted upon rights; Washington insists upon duty." On the positive side of his evaluation of Washington he said that "he urged his race to do the things possible rather than whine and pine over things prohibited. According to his philosophy, it is better to build even upon the shifting sands of expediency than not to build at all because you cannot secure a granite foundation."

More important than Miller's analysis of the two contending groups was his appraisal of the conflicting claims made for industrial and collegiate education for Negroes. He lectured widely on the subject, and wrote numerous articles and pamphlets, insisting that "the subject of industrial and higher education is merely one of ratio and proportion, and not one of fundamental controversy," and that both forms of education were needed for the "symmetrical development" of any race. In the face of the extended campaign by Washington to make manual training the dominant, if not exclusive, form of education available to Negroes, Miller became the advocate of a comprehensive system of education.

His most extended analysis of this question was "The Education of the Negro," published in 1902 as Chapter 16 (pp. 731–859) of *The Report for 1900–1901* of the U.S. Bureau of Education. It is also his most technical treatment of the impact of economic and social conditions on the education of Negroes, and reveals his understanding of the significance of social science data for comprehending the complex nature of the problem. As a background to those sections of his report entitled "The Intellectual Capacity of the Negro," "The Need of the Higher Education," "Objections to the Higher Education of the Negro Answered," "The Relative Claims of Industrial and Higher Education," and "The Higher Education of Colored Women," he wrote comprehensively on the economic conditions of Negroes, the impact of urbanization, the type of occupational differentiation that had emerged since emancipation, and the impact of discrimination by white labor unions and employers. An analysis of this study reveals that virtually all of Miller's later essays and newspaper articles on education were derived from the ample mine of data and argument he had compiled in 1902.

In such leading journals as the *Journal of Social Science, Dial, Education, The Educational Review, Forum,* and others, Miller ably refuted the extravagant claims of the industrial education lobby and defended the colleges. He concluded that the "fundamental aims of education should be manhood not mechanism. The ideal is not a working man but a man working." By 1905 he was clearly one of the most influential Negro educators in the nation, whose allegiance was sought by both camps. He was distrusted by each of them because of his refusal to adopt their dogmatic arguments. In reply to critics of his middle-of-the-road position he said, "effective horsemanship is accomplished by straddling" ("Come Let Us Reason Together," *Voice of the Negro,* 3 [1906]:67).

Evaluations of Miller's career tend to overlook his contributions to sociology as a discipline because of the emphasis given to his well-deserved reputation as a controversialist and commentator on major public issues. While there can be no doubt that his greatest impact was as an educator and popular essayist, his more technical sociological articles should not be ignored. His earliest contribution in this field was an analysis of Frederick L. Hoffman's *Race Traits and Tendencies of the American Negro,* a work published in 1896 under the auspices of the American Economic Association which attempted to demonstrate that the alleged genetic inferiority of Negroes was the cause of their social disorganization and that the high mortality rate of the Negro population would cause its disappearance in the United States. Miller's critique of Hoffman, a statistician of the Prudential Insurance Company of America, was published in 1897 as the first Occasional Paper of the American Negro Academy, founded earlier that year by Alexander Crummell. His critique of Hoffman is based on a technical analysis of census data and presented in a style far different from his better known essays. Other selected examples of Miller's important sociological articles are "The Ultimate Race Problem" (*Atlantic Monthly,* April 1909), "Eugenics of the Negro Race" (*Scientific Monthly,* July 1917), "Education of the Negro in the North" (*Educational Review,* Oct. 1921), and "Enumeration Errors in Negro Population" (*Scientific Monthly,* Feb. 1922). Although he devoted more of his time to educational administration, lecturing, and writing essays mainly for a general rather than an academic audience, Miller was nevertheless a pioneer in the attempt to study race relations from an objective point of view.

A major turning point in Miller's career was his appointment as acting dean of the College of Arts and Sciences at Howard in October 1907, not long after Booker T. Washington was elected a member of the university's Board of Trustees (May 28, 1907). The *Boston Guardian* said that President Thirkield had "betrayed" the Negro race by this action since Howard was the most significant example of the type of education advocated by the Niagara Movement radicals. In July 1907 the *Horizon* magazine regarded the Miller appointment as an indication that he had made "a deal" with Washington. Evidence is lacking to confirm or reject these speculations. Miller was clearly the most respected and prolific Negro on the Howard undergraduate faculty at that time, and was a logical choice for dean. He was also close to Thirkield and did not disagree in principle with the president's expansion plans or attempts to attract private philanthropy to Howard by some accommodation with the trend toward applied sciences. When Thirkield persuaded the trustees in 1908 to abandon the use of the university's seal which had as its motto "Equal Rights and Knowledge for All," Miller suggested as its Latin replacement "Veritas et Utilitas," a typical Miller compromise through fusion of the Harvard motto and the philosophy of Tuskegee. He was appointed dean of the College of Arts and Sciences on Jan. 21, 1908. Miller's influence at Howard grew under Thirkield, and was even greater during the administration of his unassertive successor, Stephen M. Newman (1912–1918).

In addition to his role in modernizing the curriculum in the College of Arts and Sciences, Miller was a leader in the effort to introduce the systematic study of the Negro at Howard. As early as 1901 he proposed to the Board of Trustees that Howard support the publications of the American Negro Academy. While the board did not support this proposal, it permitted the academy to hold some of its meetings on the campus. Miller believed that Howard should become a center for studies of the American Negro and Africa, and continued to urge the inclusion of such courses in the curriculum. He envisioned the establishment of a "Negro-Americana Museum and Library." In 1914 he persuaded Jesse E. Moorland, a Howard trustee and alumnus, to donate to Howard his large private library on the Negro in Africa and the United States as a first step in the development of the proposed museum and research library. Miller claimed that the board's reluctance to enter this field was so pronounced that it decided to call the library "The Moorland Foundation" and referred to "the squeamishness of certain members who at that time did not wish to perpetuate any racial terminology in the archives of the University." Initially little progress was made in realizing Miller's dream for the expansion of the Moorland Foundation, but eventually it became an important resource for the increasing number of scholarly studies on the Negro in the decades following the First World War.

Miller's remaining sixteen years at Howard were largely anticlimactic. He was often mentioned as the inevitable choice to be the university's first Negro president. He was so closely identified with the institution at the time that it was not uncommon for it to be called "Kelly Miller's University." He was the most persistent advocate of the view that since Negro professors were excluded from white universities, they ought to have the opportunity to exercise leadership in Negro institutions. Moreover, he believed that the first generation of white missionaries in Negro schools, whom he admired greatly, had not been succeeded by men of the same caliber or high moral convictions.

Miller played a decisive role in exposing the inadequacies and hostile racial views of Howard's last white president, J. Stanley Durkee (1918–1926), who demoted Miller to dean of the Junior College (1919–1925) before he abolished that college entirely in 1925. Miller never recovered his former power within the university, although he remained a figure revered by older faculty and alumni. His influence outside the university was unaffected by his reverses at Howard. He engaged in an especially bitter controversy with the first Negro president of Howard, Mordecai W. Johnson. Miller became alarmed by what he regarded as an influx of "radical" members of the faculty, particularly in the social sciences. When the Social Science Division of Howard University and the Joint Committee on National Recovery jointly sponsored a national conference on "The Economic Crisis and the Negro" at Howard in May 1935, which included Socialists and Communists on the program, Miller joined with his friend, Rep. Arthur Mitchell of Illinois, and Sen. Joseph Tydings of Maryland in urging a congressional investigation of "communistic teaching at Howard University." When Johnson defended the university's right to sponsor the conference, and declared that if Negroes had to surrender academic freedom they "might as well go back to the cornfield," Miller said that it was more than "his patriotism could stand" and that Johnson's "defiance of Congressmen constituted a dangerous influence to the young minds of students in a Government-supported institution" (Washington Post, Aug. 30, 1935, p. 1).

By the 1930s Miller was clearly dismayed by the trend of race relations and politics. He had deplored the pessimism of youth after the First World War, the so-called lost generation, and was alarmed by the declining influence of religion on education and other aspects of American life. Opposed to the mass migration of Negroes from rural to urban areas, he warned of the destructive impact of city life on Negroes unprepared for the harsh competition for employment and the continuing discrimination of white employers and labor unions. In the 1920s and 1930s, when many of the younger Negro intellectuals regarded labor unions as a "progressive" force, Miller remained skeptical, pointing out the discrepancy between the labor movement's promises and its performance. Miller published statistics indicating the Negro's rapid loss of agricultural land in the South, and urged the encouragement of agriculture as one way to stem the tide of deterioration in the social conditions of Negroes.

Kelly Miller contributed articles to leading newspapers from an early period in his life, but did not become a major figure in the Negro press until the 1920s and 1930s. His weekly column, appearing in various papers as "Kelly Miller Says," "Kelly Miller Writes," and "From the Pen of Kelly Miller," was published in more than one hundred newspapers, including the Afro-American (Baltimore), the Washington American, the New York Age, and the Richmond Planet. He also wrote for the Washington Post, the Boston Transcript,

the Springfield Republican, the New York Herald, the New York Times, and the New York Tribune. In 1923 it was estimated that his columns reached half a million readers. His role as newspaper pundit rather naturally followed his earlier activity as pamphleteer and essayist in magazines.

Miller's first major success with a pamphlet was As to the Leopard's Spots: An Open Letter to Thomas Dixon, published in September 1905. George Washington Cable considered Miller's reply to Dixon as the "ablest, soundest and most important document that has appeared on this subject in many years." An Appeal to Reason on the Race Problem: An Open Letter to John Temple Graves followed a year later as a response to the Atlanta race riot. Miller countered demagogic race baiting with a style that combined compelling logic, irony, and wit to devastating effect. Some of the articles Miller had published in magazines were later issued as pamphlets. An especially popular essay was "The Political Plight of the Negro" in The Nineteenth Century (Aug. 1911). In the London Review of Reviews, W. T. Stead said that this article was "the most intrepid and thoroughgoing defense of the political capacity of the Negro" that he had seen. As a result of this response Miller began publishing his "Race Statesmanship Series" which included in addition to the "Political Plight" essay, "Education for Manhood," "The Negro's Place in the New Reconstruction," and others. By far the most popular essay in this series, and his most widely distributed pamphlet, was The Disgrace of Democracy: An Open Letter to President Woodrow Wilson, published on Aug. 4, 1917, in reaction to the riots in Memphis and East St. Louis. Arguing that a "democracy of race or class is no democracy at all," Miller cited the spreading white lawlessness and victimization of Negroes as undermining the basis for genuine democracy. "It is but hollow mockery of the Negro," he wrote to Wilson, "when he is beaten and bruised in all parts of the nation and flees to the national government for asylum, to be denied relief on the ground of doubtful jurisdiction. The black man asks for protection and is given a theory of government." Miller's Disgrace of Democracy sold over 250,000 copies. The military authorities prohibited it on army posts and attempts were made by the government to silence Miller. He recalled later that despite these attempts to suppress the pamphlet he found that it had been read by many colored officer candidates at Fort Des Moines when he visited there.

In 1913 Miller also began publishing Kelly Miller's Monographic Magazine, which reproduced essays related to race and national affairs. The popularity of the pamphlets and essays led to their compilation and publication as books. The most important of these were Race Adjustment (1908), Out of the House of Bondage (1914), and The Everlasting Stain (1924). In his later years Miller was sometimes referred to as "the Sage of the Potomac," and "Philosopher of the Race Question."

After his retirement from Howard in 1934 Miller revived his plan for the development of a research center and museum at the university devoted to the documentation and preservation of Negro history and culture. Despite failing eyesight from cataracts, he began an autobiography, and continued his habit of fifty years of maintaining a large vegetable and flower garden. A man of simplicity who retained "the common touch," Miller never owned a watch or fountain pen, and delighted in the wide circle of his friendship which embraced alike the illiterate as well as the learned. He died of a heart attack at his home on Dec. 29, 1939. His funeral was held at Andrew Rankin Memorial Chapel, Howard University, on Jan. 2, 1940, and he was interred at Lincoln Memorial Cemetery, Washington, D.C. He was survived by his wife and four of his children.

There is no adequate biography of Kelly Miller. The Kelly Miller Papers in the Manuscript Division of the Moorland-Spingarn Research Center at Howard University are limited to correspondence related to his museum and research library project, his partially completed autobiography, and a scrapbook. Useful biographical sketches include one by E. Franklin Frazier in *DAB, Supplement 2* (1958, pp. 456–57); D. O. W. Holmes's "Kelly Miller" (*Phylon,* Second Quarter 1945, pp. 121–25); Carter G. Woodson's "Kelly Miller" (*JNH,* Jan. 1940, pp. 137–38); and George Frazier Miller's "The Great Kelly—Kelly Miller as I Knew Him" (*Baltimore Afro-American,* Sept. 7 to Oct. 19, 1940). Useful interpretations of Miller's career are August Meier's "The Racial and Educational Philosophy of Kelly Miller, 1895–1915" (*JNE,* Spring 1960, pp. 121–27); Bernard Eisenberg's "Kelly Miller: The Negro Leader as a Marginal Man" (*JNH,* July 1960, pp. 182–97). A perceptive contemporary evaluation is found in William H. Ferris's *The African Abroad* (1913, vol. 1, Chapter 21, "Professor Kelly Miller's Philosophy of the Race Question," pp. 383–89). An unpublished bibliographic guide to works by and about Miller prepared by Marieta L. Harper is in the Reference Department, Moorland-Spingarn Research Center, Howard University. — MICHAEL R. WINSTON

MILLER, THOMAS EZEKIEL (1849–1938), lawyer, congressman, and college president. He was born in Ferrebeeville, S.C., on June 17, 1849, of free parents. Extremely light in complexion, he was indistinguishable from a white man. Although he refused to pass for white and recognized Richard Miller and Mary Ferrebee as his parents, he was plagued throughout his life by rumors that he was actually the illegitimate child of a white couple.

While he was still an infant, Miller's parents moved to Charleston where he attended schools for free Negroes despite laws which prohibited them. After the Civil War, Miller went to Hudson, N.Y., and later to Lincoln University (Pennsylvania) to complete his education. After graduating from Lincoln in 1872 he returned to Columbia, S.C., where he took a law course at the recently integrated University of South Carolina. He read law under two of the most prominent members of the South Carolina bar, State Solicitor P. L. Wiggins and Chief Justice Franklin Moses, Sr., of the state Supreme Court. Admitted to the state bar in December 1875, Miller began practicing law in Beaufort.

While studying for the bar Miller became active in the

Beaufort County Republican party. He was elected school commissioner in 1872 and became a representative in the South Carolina General Assembly in 1874. He held on to this post despite the Republican disaster in the election of 1876 and was sent to the state Senate in 1880. He was the Republican nominee for lieutenant-governor in 1880, but party leaders decided not to field a state ticket that year because of the determined and violent opposition of the Democrats. Although he left the state Senate in 1882, Miller continued to be active in political affairs, serving as the Republican state chairman in 1884 and returning to the state House of Representatives in 1886. In 1888 he won the Republican nomination for the 7th Congressional District seat on the first ballot. Having apparently lost the general election to Democrat William E. Elliott by more than a thousand votes, Miller protested to the Republican-controlled House of Representatives that the vote count was fraudulent. Miller's case came to a vote just after that of John M. Langston, congressman from Virginia. Several Democratic members walked out in protest at Langston's successful challenge, and Miller's opponents contended that there was no longer a quorum. After Speaker Thomas Reed of Maine ruled that there was a quorum and that a roll-call was in order, Miller won the contest by a vote of 157 to 1.

However, Miller's victory came on Sept. 24, 1890, almost two years after his election and just at the beginning of his campaign for reelection. In the 1890 election the situation was almost exactly reversed; for although Miller defeated both Democrat William E. Elliott and a former Republican, E. M. Brayton, at the polls, the South Carolina Supreme Court declared Elliott the victor on the pretext that Miller's ballots were the wrong size and color. This time Miller's challenge was rejected by the House Elections Committee.

Miller returned to Beaufort which he represented again in the state House of Representatives from 1894 to 1896 and in the state constitutional convention of 1895, where he and Robert Smalls unsuccessfully opposed a clause to disfranchise Negroes. When federal funds for Claflin College were cut off because of its Methodist affiliation, Miller played a leading role in the campaign to establish a state-supported Negro college at Orangeburg. He was appointed the college's first president in March 1896, a position he held until 1911. He was credited with helping introduce the policy of employing Negro teachers in Negro schools. After his retirement from the presidency, he lived in Charleston for several years and then in Philadelphia from 1923 to 1934. In an address before the Association for the Study of Negro Life and History, (Washington, Feb. 1930), he castigated Pres. Rutherford B. Hayes for his role in reducing the participation of southern Negroes in politics. A few years after returning to Charleston, he died on April 8, 1938. He was buried there, and his epitaph, "Not having loved the white man less, but having felt the Negro needed me more," is carved on his tombstone.

Miller's period of service in the Congress was very limited as a result of his extended contest and unsuccessful reelection campaign. Indeed his first major speech was as a lame-duck member on Jan. 12, 1891.

In that speech he replied to critics of the so-called Force Law, which was designed to provide federal supervision and protection of voters in federal elections. Miller condemned the South for its "lynch law," the injustices of its courts to northern whites as well as to blacks, and economic oppression. It was the prejudiced attitudes of white southerners that discouraged the investment of northern and western capital in the South, he insisted. He pointed out the inconsistencies in the charges that Negroes sold their votes on the one hand, and that they were slaves of the Republican party on the other. He maintained his faith that it was the admixture of different peoples and cultures that had always led to the progress of civilization. He made this speech in spite of threats that this action would imperil his chances of regaining his seat. This was Miller's only major speech in Congress, but it indicated a great deal about his character and political courage.

There is no full-length biography of Thomas Miller, but brief sketches of his life are in *The Biographical Directory of the American Congress* (1971), Samuel Denny Smith's *The Negro in Congress, 1870–1901* (1940), Maurine Christopher's *America's Black Congressmen* (1971), and George B. Tindall's *South Carolina Negroes, 1877–1900* (1952). See also the obituary in the *JNH* (July 1938, pp. 400–2). — THOMAS HOLT

MILLS, FLORENCE (1895–1927), singer and dancer. She was the youngest of three daughters of John and Nellie (Simon) Winfrey. Many of the facts about her early life are uncertain. Writing in 1930, James Weldon Johnson stated that she was born in Washington, D.C. According to other accounts she was born in Virginia and moved at an early age to Washington. There is general agreement that she was a child prodigy on the stage, billed before she was six as "Baby Florence Mills," expert in cakewalking and buck dancing. She and her two sisters, Olivia and Maude, made their debut as "The Mills Trio" in vaudeville (1910). Florence appears to have begun to sing and dance without her sisters some time thereafter. Until she was twenty-five she played in vaudeville from coast to coast, increasing her salary from nine dollars a week to several times that amount and polishing her act. In traditional theater history she won stardom when she replaced Gertrude Samuels, one of the leads in the popular Negro revue *Shuffle Along,* who had become ill, at the 63rd Street Music Hall in New York City in September 1921. From then almost until her death on Nov. 1, 1927, she won fame at home, in London, and Paris.

She left *Shuffle Along* to star in Lew Leslie's *Plantation Revue* (1922) at the New York Plantation Club. She was the star in Leslie's *From Dover to Dixie* (also known as *Dover Street to Dixie*) in London (1923), and one critic called her "by far the most artistic person London has had the good fortune to see." The production under the name of *Dixie to Broadway,* which opened in New York on Oct. 29, 1924, at Schuberts' Broadhurst Theater on Broadway, added to her fame, and Leslie starred her in *Blackbirds of 1926.* After playing six weeks to packed houses at the Alhambra Theater in Harlem, *Blackbirds* ran for six months in London, where the Prince of Wales is said to have seen it sixteen

times, and had a long run in Paris. Returning to New York City on Oct. 12, 1927, for a delayed appendectomy, she died in a hospital on Nov. 1 of paralytic ileus and general peritonitis.

Her funeral was one of the most spectacular of the era. Five thousand persons were said to have been packed in Mother Zion A.M.E. Church in Harlem for highly emotional services, and more than 100,000 mourners were reported to have jammed the streets outside the theater. As the funeral procession neared 145th Street, a low-flying airplane released a symbolic flock of blackbirds. She was buried in Woodlawn Cemetery in the Bronx.

Obituaries echoed the praise of the London critic in 1923. In a perceptive critique, James Weldon Johnson, a noted lyricist, wrote in *Black Manhattan* (1930, pp. 199–200) that she could be "whimsical" and almost "grotesque" but never "coarse"; "risquée" and "seductive," but not "vulgar," for she possessed a naïveté that was alchemic. "As a pantominist and a singing and dancing comedienne she had no superior in any place or any race." But Johnson doubted that she could really sing, for her upper range was "bird-like in tones." Nevertheless, with her small voice, she sang her favorite song, "I'm a Little Blackbird Looking for a Bluebird" with "such poignancy as always to raise a lump in your throat."

Rudolph Fisher, an active participant in the "Harlem Renaissance," included Florence Mills with Roland Hayes and Paul Robeson as great musicians during the 1920s. Lester Walton in the *New York World* (Nov. 23, 1924) emphasized another facet of her significance. Her impressive success demonstrated that a colored musical show could be a financial and artistic success on Broadway, provided that "it measured up to the high standards set with respect to class, cleanliness and merit."

There is an excellent brief biography, with bibliography, by Anne Cooke Reid in *NAW* (1971, 2:545–46). In *Black Manhattan,* facing page 198, are photographs of Mills's head and full length in a striking pose.

— RAYFORD W. LOGAN

MINTON, HENRY McKEE (1870–1946), physician, founder and superintendent of a hospital. He was born on Dec. 25, 1870, in Columbia, S.C. His parents were Theophilus J. and Virginia Jennie (McKee) Minton of Philadelphia, who had taken temporary residence in Columbia. His parents, who moved to Washington in the early 1870s, sent him to public schools in that city and later to the academy at Howard University. In 1887 Minton entered Phillips Exeter Academy in New Hampshire from which he graduated in 1891. He excelled in both academic and extracurricular work, particularly literary activities. He was elected assistant managing editor of the school newspaper *The Exonian,* later the managing editor of the *Literary Monthly,* president of Golden Branch (the debating society), and co-editor of the class book, *The Peau.* He participated in athletics, and was class orator at commencement.

Following graduation Henry Minton returned to his home in Philadelphia, where his family urged him to enter the University of Pennsylvania Law School. He lost interest in these studies, however, and withdrew after his first year. He was interested in science and entered the Philadelphia College of Pharmacy and Science in the fall of 1892, and graduated with the degree of Ph.G. in 1895. On the fiftieth anniversary of his graduation (June 5, 1945), he was honored for "fifty years of post graduate extra-mural service to his fellow-men" and presented with an embossed plaque before a large assembly.

In the fall of 1897 Minton opened what may have been the first pharmacy owned by Negroes in Pennsylvania. The nature of this work strengthened his continuing desire to enter the field of medicine. In 1902 he registered in Jefferson Medical College and was awarded the M.D. degree in 1906, becoming, as far as records reveal, the first Negro graduate of that institution.

Minton's contribution to the advancement of the Negro in America lies in two widely different areas: medicine and the founding of a hospital. He was a thoroughly trained, patient, and methodical physician, warm and friendly in manner. He was among the early Negro physicians to recognize the need for a modern, efficient, hospital in Philadelphia where young Negro physicians could serve their internships and become better qualified to practice their profession. He was shocked that young Negro doctors were denied, as was he, the right to intern in the hospitals of the same medical schools from which they graduated. It was equally important for these young doctors to have a hospital where their patients could be sent for study, treatment, and when necessary, surgery.

In the summer of 1907 Minton, in company with a Negro graduate of the University of Pennsylvania Medical School, Eugene T. Hinson (whose ancestors owned the land on which Lincoln University stands) and Algernon B. Jackson (later professor of public health at Howard University), joined to establish Mercy Hospital in Philadelphia. (The first Negro Hospital to be established in Philadelphia was the Douglass Hospital, founded by Nathan Francis Mossell in 1895.) Minton became superintendent of Mercy in 1910 and retained this post for twenty-four years, and his staff membership until his death in 1946. Mercy Hospital and the founding fathers, Minton, Hinson, Jackson, and a few others, gave more than 200 young Negro graduates of medical schools, half of whom were from white universities, the others from Howard and Meharry Medical Schools, the opportunity denied them by the score or more white hospitals in Philadelphia and the hundreds in America, to complete their medical training as internes and later as residents, so they could be accepted as fully trained physicians. Many of these men and women later became skilled surgeons, specialists, and professors of medicine in many parts of the United States.

Minton served for many years, beginning in 1910, as a clinician in the Henry Phipps Institute of the University of Pennsylvania and as a specialist in tuberculosis, and from 1923 as supervisor of the Negro Tuberculosis Bureau in Philadelphia. He was the author of two pamphlets: *Early Negroes in Business in Philadelphia* (1913) and *Causes and Prevention of Tuberculosis* (1915). He also contributed articles to *Opportunity,*

the *New York Medical Journal,* the *Hospital Social Service Magazine,* and the *Journal of the National Medical Association.* He served on the Board of Directors of Mercy Hospital, Downingtown Industrial School, the Armstrong Association, and Whittier Center.

At the turn of the century distinguished Negroes lived in an atmosphere of physical, spiritual, and intellectual isolation. They therefore desired an association of men of like training and culture. Minton called a meeting at his home (May 4, 1904) at which he discussed the many social problems faced by Negro professional and business leaders. He and five other physicians founded America's first Negro Greek-letter fraternity, Sigma Pi Phi. This nationwide fraternity is not only a social organization of leading citizens but also one concerned with public issues. Minton established several subordinate boulés (chapters) and served as grand sire archon.

On Dec. 24, 1902, he married Edith G. Wormley. He died in Philadelphia of a heart attack during Christmas week, 1946, and was buried in Merion Cemetery. He was survived by his nephew Russell F. Minton, and the latter's son Russell Jr.

The best brief source is William Montague Cobb's article "Henry McKee Minton, M.D., 1870–1946" (*JNMA,* July 1955, pp. 285–86). Charles H. Wesley's *History of Sigma Pi Phi . . .* (1954) narrates the founding of the organization and Minton's later activities.

— RAYMOND PACE ALEXANDER

MITCHELL, ABBIE (1884–1960), dramatic and concert soprano, actress, and teacher. She was born on the Lower East Side in New York City. Her mother, the former Miss Holliday, was of Afro-American descent, and her father was of German-Jewish origin. Both parents were musical. At an early age Abbie gave evidence of being a musical prodigy.

After schooling in Baltimore she returned to New York City in 1897 to audition for a part in the musical comedy *Clorindy, the Origin of the Cakewalk,* with lyrics by Paul Laurence Dunbar and music by Will Marion Cook whom she married the following year. At age fourteen she took over the lead part in that musical, which created a sensation on Broadway. There is an excellent picture of her at that age in Edith Isaacs's *The Negro in the American Theater* (1947, 1968). *Clorindy* was the first musical to explore the possibilities of syncopated Negro music, written by a brilliant Negro composer who had also studied composition with Anton Dvořak. Mitchell also toured for several years with Black Patti's Troubadors. Throughout her life, Black Patti (Mme. Sissieretta Jones) remained one of her idols. During these years Mitchell also studied voice and music theory with Harry T. Burleigh. Taught many songs by her husband, and his settings of Dunbar's poems, she sang them in a series of Sunday-evening concerts on Broadway, and at parties given by such socialites as the Astors, Goulds, Morgans, and Vanderbilts. She also studied voice with Emilia Serrano, and later in Paris with Jean de Reske for two years.

The following summer Cook wrote another musical, *Jes Lak White Folks,* which was produced at the New York Winter Garden, in which Mitchell was one of the principals. About 1900 she sang for Calvé who told her: "You have a glorious voice but voice is only one tenth of the battle."

In 1902 Dunbar and Cook collaborated again in a musical *In Dahomey,* book by Jesse Shipp, produced by Bert Williams and George Walker. It made Negro theatrical history by being staged in the New York Theater in Times Square, the center of the theatrical district. Abbie Mitchell played and sang "Brownskin Baby Mine." Williams and Walker took the play to London where it was produced at the Shaftsbury Theatre beginning in May 1903. In June, to celebrate the birthday of the young Prince of Wales, later Edward VIII, the royal family invited the company to Buckingham Palace for a command performance. For some reason the producers left Mitchell in the hotel, thinking she would not be missed. Noting her absence, the king, who had seen the show, asked: "Where's 'She ain't no violet'?" (That was the nickname Londoners had given her: the first line in a song by Will Marion Cook, "Brownskin Baby Mine," Mitchell's featured number.) The king sent his royal coach to fetch her before permitting the performance to go on. *In Dahomey* toured Europe and created a dance craze: "the cakewalk of 1903 broke up the patterns of turns and glides that dominated the European round dances" (Curt Sachs).

Mitchell, upon her return to New York, became part of Negro theatrical life on 53rd Street, in the Marshall Hotel, frequented by such well-known actors, musicians, composers, writers, and better paid vaudevillians as Bob Cole, J. Rosamond Johnson, Bert Williams and George Walker, Ernest Hogan, Will Marion Cook, James Reese Europe, Ada Overton (Mrs. George Walker), Theodore Drury, Will Dixon, and Ford Dabney. They were the nucleus and mainspring of her life as an artist. They also became the first Negro concert group, twenty entertainers, to sing and play music written in the Negro style with all Negro participants. They called themselves the Nashville Students and had their debut in the spring of 1905 at the Proctor 23rd Street Theater, featuring Ernest Hogan (comedian), Mitchell (soprano), and Ida Forsyne (dancer). They made such a smash hit that they were booked at Hammerstein's Victoria Theater on Broadway daily, and in the Roof Garden nights, and later toured Europe for eight months as the Memphis Students in the Olympia in Paris, the Palace Theatre in London, the Schumann Circus in Berlin, and many other cities.

In 1908 Abbie Mitchell starred as lead soprano in the Cole and Johnson musical *Red Moon,* which later toured Europe and in which she sang a command performance for Czar Nicholas II of Russia.

Beginning about 1915 Mitchell played leading roles in Harlem's Lafayette Theater at 132nd Street and Seventh Avenue, where "coloured performers in New York experienced for the first time release from the restraining fears of what a white audience would stand for; for the first time they felt free to do on the stage whatever they were able to do" (*Black Manhattan,* pp. 171–72). Even at this early age, Mitchell was not exactly a newcomer to dramatic roles; for a year or so she had been a member of the talented stock company at the old Pekin Theater in Chicago. She was ideal for the lead in

plays for the next five years in the standard repertory presented at the Lafayette, Howard, and other Negro theaters.

Of her performance as Madame X in the play by that name in New York, produced by the Lafayette Stock Players, a critic wrote in the *New York Amsterdam News* (Sept. 21, 1927) that her career in drama was accidental. She had minor parts for seven months, learned overnight the part consisting of long speeches in 104 pages so successfully that she was handed the lead.

During 1910–1917, when Negroes were excluded from theaters in downtown New York, there developed in Harlem a real Negro theater, headed by the Lafayette Players. Mitchell, a gifted and magnetic personality, was a part of the Lafayette Players who brought to the Harlem community such plays as *The Servant in the House, On Trial, The Love of Choo Chin, Within the Law, Dr. Jekyll and Mr. Hyde, Raffles, The Count of Monte Cristo, Charley's Aunt, Othello, The Chocolate Soldier,* and many others. These players broke the stereotype that "there should never be any romantic love-making in a Negro play." They opened up avenues toward full acceptance in the Broadway legitimate theater for Negro actors, which culminated in 1917 in the performance of three plays done by Negro players in the Garden Theater, and led to the inclusion of Negroes in such plays as Eugene O'Neill's *The Moon of the Caribbees* and *The Emperor Jones,* and to her own performances in *In Abraham's Bosom* (1926), *Porgy and Bess* (1935), *The Little Foxes* (1939), and others.

In 1920 Jean de Reszke had declared that she had a perfect mezzosoprano voice. She became more and more famous as a recitalist in every major city of America and Europe; she was probably the first American to be invited to sing in the Soviet Union. When she went to Paris she studied voice with Szbrilla, teacher of Reszke, and repertory with Reszke himself. She became famous as a singer of the French repertory and of German *Lieder.* Her programs always included Negro folk and art songs. While playing with Helen Hayes in *Coquette* in Chicago (1929) after a Broadway season, Mitchell said: "All my work as an actress has been done with my singing in mind. I learned that a singer must know dramatics, but I could not stop for a long course." Instead she accepted in 1931 the offer of Tuskegee Institute to head the vocal department.

During the next three years she also continued singing on tour. The *New York Age* (May 2, 1931) praised "the infinite variety of Abbie Mitchell's charm" and "vocalistic artistry," in recital at A.M.E. Zion church. She had been kept in Chicago by a radio contract which had her singing over a national hookup. In that concert she sang a group of French songs by Duparc, Fauré, Hahn, Foudrain, and Debussy, a suite of German songs by Pahlen, translations of poems by Langston Hughes and Countee Cullen, a group of American and English songs by Bantock, Nevin, and La Forge, and a group of spirituals by Will Marion Cook, William L. Dawson, and Hall Johnson. On Nov. 22, 1931, when she sang a recital in Town Hall, it was announced that "The Greatest Singer of the Present Day will appear in an all-Negro Song Recital." The *St. Louis Argus* (Nov. 27, 1931) reported: "Abbie Mitchell, who has given convincing evidence in the past as a singer of German lieder, chose to devote her gifts Friday afternoon at the Town Hall to a program of songs by and of Negroes. Miss Mitchell was no less the artist in this type of music. She understands it as few other singers even of her race do." Reviewing an earlier recital, Charles D. Isaacson of the *New York Morning Telegraph* wrote: "Her diction and handling of the German group of songs was a feat: *Die Lorelei* of Liszt was memorable. Her diction was a model of her white rivals. Followed the Ritorno Vincitor from *Aïda*. What an *Aïda* this woman would make!"

While Mitchell was at Tuskegee her career as a concert artist continued to be reviewed with growing enthusiasm in various cities: The *Pittsburgh Courier* (Sept. 23, 1933): "Abbie Mitchell is the greatest singer of songs that the Negro has." The *Washington Tribune* (Oct. 26, 1933): "Prolonged applause greeted her rendition of Schubert's *Erlkoenig, Lied der Mignon* (Schubert) was well received, as was Chausson's *Apaisement.* But the enthusiasm of the audience knew no bounds when she gave the impressively beautiful interpretation of the Aria Ritorna Vincitor from *Aïda* (Verdi)."

Her return to the stage in 1934 was motivated by a dream that she expressed in an interview printed in the *Pittsburgh Courier.* After praising the Negro's superior personality, soul, deep-rooted emotions, and beautiful art of expression, she asserted that there was a goal not yet reached: a "Negro opera," produced by "a race man. . . . But I'm so afraid it will eventually be a white person. The Metropolitan Opera House is a goal. The gates of that place must be crashed yet by a Negro. . . . I had hoped Roland Hayes would make it."

Abbie Mitchell succeeded in opera, although not at the Metropolitan. In July 1934 she sang in *Cavalleria Rusticana* at the Mecca Temple in New York, and again with the Aeolian Opera Company on Aug. 4, 1934. She also continued in the theater, first as Binnie in *Stevedore* (1934), as Clara in *Porgy and Bess* (1935), and as Addie in *The Little Foxes* (1939). The last program in the possession of her son, Mercer Cook, lists her appearance in the summer of 1947 at Westport, Conn., in *The Skull Boat,* starring Fay Bainter. Poor eyesight prevented her from considering the role of the mother in Lorraine Hansberry's *A Raisin in the Sun* (1959).

Mitchell, whose life was filled with glamorous success and hard work, said of herself: "I have come from the dinge of smoke and heat, tired and worn from singing, and lit the oil lamp. In quietude while my loved ones slept, I dug down to the roots of French, German, Italian, theory, harmony and counterpoint.—I have always studied and I still am studying." That was in 1933. Her life epitomized the paradox that beset Negro artists who knew the glamour of the early 1900s and were idolized by European audiences, sovereigns, and Harlem theater-goers, but denied total American acceptance.

Abbie Mitchell died in Harlem Hospital on March 16, 1960. Her husband Will Marion Cook had died in 1944. Her daughter Marion had died in New York City in 1950. She was survived by her son, Mercer Cook, a professor at Howard University, and three grandchildren.

Loften Mitchell's *Black Drama: The Story of the American Negro in the Theater* (1967), Tom Fletcher's *100 Years of the Negro in Show Business* (1954), Edith Isaacs's *The Negro in the American Theater* (1947), and Maud Cuney-Hare's *Negro Musicians and Their Music* (1936), contain valuable information. Important for background is James Weldon Johnson's *Black Manhattan* (1930). Additional information was provided by Mercer Cook to Rayford W. Logan.

— RAYMOND LEMIEUX

MITCHELL, CHARLES L[EWIS] (1829–1912), printer, soldier, and government official. He was born in Hartford, Conn., on Nov. 10, 1829, to a well-known family of free Negroes. His ability to read and write enabled him to learn how to set type as a printer. But he was not unaware of the struggle slaves were having. When he migrated to Boston from Hartford in 1853, he used his knowledge as a printer on *The Liberator,* edited by William Lloyd Garrison. Inspired by his work with Garrison and by the belief that the Civil War would end slavery, Mitchell enlisted on July 14, 1863, at the age of thirty-three at Readville, Mass., as a private in the 55th Massachusetts Infantry Regiment. Stationed at Morris Head, S.C., by November 1864 he was put on temporary duty with the First Brigade headquarters to serve as the sergeant in charge of printing. He was described in army records as about five feet ten inches tall, with light brown complexion, black hair, and hazel eyes. Shortly after his printing duty was over he went back to his old company (F) of the 55th Regiment. On Nov. 30, 1864, he lost his right foot in combat at Honey Hill, S.C., and spent the rest of his army time in hospitals in New York City and Worcester, Mass. He received a disability discharge on Oct. 20, 1865; For the rest of his life Mitchell received a pension of about thirty dollars monthly.

With the Civil War over, Mitchell entered Boston politics as a Republican, and as a wounded veteran had the "Stateliest step of the soldier." In November 1866 he won election from his ward to the Massachusetts General Court, the state legislature's lower house, thus becoming one of the early Negroes elected to a state legislature. On the same day that he was elected, Edward Garrison Walker, a son of David Walker and an attorney, was also elected. For years the two men had a friendly debate over who had been elected the first Negro legislator.

After the end of his one-year term in 1867 Mitchell remained interested in the affairs of Boston. In April 1869, at the age of thirty-nine, he was appointed the first Negro to be an inspector of customs in Boston. From 1871 to 1899 he served as clerk at an annual salary of $1400, and thereafter at $1600 per annum. Mitchell worked at the customshouse for forty years, retiring in 1909.

He participated in the activities of the Grand Army of the Republic in Massachusetts and movements for improved race relations in Boston. He served as one of the pallbearers in 1879 at the funeral of William Lloyd Garrison. During the Spanish-American War he helped organize Company L, the Negro company in Massachusetts. He died of apoplexy on April 13, 1912, at his home, 24 Sherman St., Roxbury. His wife Nellis Brown Mitchell, a music teacher and local singer whom he had married in Dover, N.H., in 1877, was his only immediate survivor. He was buried in Dover.

Published information is in the *Boston Globe, Boston Evening Transcript,* the *New York Age,* and *The Crisis* (July 1912). His army record is in Military and Pension Records, National Archives. — CLARENCE G. CONTEE, SR.

MITCHELL, JOHN R., JR. (1863–1929), journalist, politician, and banker. Born on the northern outskirts of Richmond, Va., to John and Rebecca Mitchell, who were described as "exceptional slave parents," he worked as a child as a carriage boy for his former master, but also managed to acquire an education, graduating in 1881 as valedictorian of the Richmond Normal and High School. After a brief teaching career and a stint as correspondent for the *New York Globe,* he assumed control in 1884 of the *Richmond Planet,* a weekly newspaper which had been founded the previous year by E. A. Randolph. He quickly transformed the *Planet* into one of the nation's leading Negro newspapers.

Mitchell's initial fame came from his crusade against lynching and his militant opposition to discrimination. At a time when Negroes were being lynched on the flimsiest of pretexts, he urged his fellow Negroes to purchase arms for their self-defense. "The best remedy for a lyncher or a cursed mid-night rider," he wrote in 1890, "is a 16-shot Winchester rifle in the hands of a Negro who has nerve enough to pull the trigger." He constantly sought to foster race pride, often ending his editorials with the refrain "Great is the Negro!" "Don't cringe and cower," he admonished. "Stand up for your rights with manly dignity." His attacks on lynching, Jim Crow, and "ruinous race-legislation" put him in the forefront of the protest of the period, while his skill as a journalist made the *Planet* distinctive. Over the masthead he placed a drawing of a strong black arm, with flexed muscles and clenched, upraised fist. According to one contemporary, his "pen seemed dipped in vitriol." His success with the *Planet* won him the presidency of the Afro-American Press Association (1890–1894).

Although Mitchell believed that the right to vote was the "badge of the freeman," his own political ambitions were frustrated by powerful whites. He served on the Richmond City Council from 1888 to 1896, but lost his seat in an election marked by open fraud. When he ran again in 1900 he was once more defeated as the Democrats stuffed the ballot boxes and stole the votes of "respectable colored men." White Republicans meanwhile relegated him to the lowest positions within the party hierarchy. They rebuked him for "raising the color line" and refused to let him run for Congress in 1890. His disenchantment with Republicans grew acute at the time of the Spanish-American War, when he emerged as one of the nation's most outspoken Negro opponents of imperialism. He discouraged Negro participation in the war on the ground that a "man who is not good enough to vote and hold office in a country is not good enough to fight and shed blood for it."

After the disfranchisement of Negroes in Virginia

ended his political career, Mitchell focused his attention on business. In 1902, in an event which marked a turning point in his life, he founded the Mechanics Savings Bank of Richmond. Previously he had pinned his hopes for the race on agitation and political power; now he looked to economic betterment as a means of advancing his cause. Using funds available to him as grand chancellor of the Virginia Knights of Pythias, he began to invest heavily in real estate, buying a movie theater, a cemetery, and other business property in Richmond. The assets of his bank always remained small by white standards, but the four-story brick bank building which he erected in 1910 in downtown Richmond became a symbol of what a Negro might accomplish in the twentieth-century South.

As a prosperous businessman Mitchell discovered that he had little choice but to mute the tone of his protest. The leading bankers of Richmond counseled him in financial matters and in return expected him to conform to their image of a Negro leader. These businessmen, whom he came to think of as typical of the "better class of Southern whites," arranged for his admission in 1904 as the first, and for many years the only, Negro member of the American Bankers Association. As he once admitted, at the annual meetings of the association southern whites exhibited him as a "ringing testimonial of their kindness, forbearance, and ability to make something out of nothing, so to speak." Nonetheless he was heartened by the reception he received from millionaires, and he began to identify his own progress with that of the race. One casualty of his success was the *Planet,* which grew staid and respectable and began to rely heavily on syndicated materials.

Although his protest was no longer strident, Mitchell continued to speak out against racial injustice. During Virginia's constitutional convention (1901–1902) he wrote dozens of editorials attacking disfranchisement, and in 1904 led a boycott of Richmond's newly segregated streetcars. In 1911, when the city sought to legislate against the movement of Negroes into white neighborhoods, he lobbied against the ordinance requiring residential segregation. The passage of the measure that year profoundly depressed him, since it indicated that the "better class of whites" were unwilling or unable to protect Negroes in moments of crisis; never again would he be quite so sanguine about the future of southern race relations. During World War I his articles about the mistreatment of Negro soldiers led to the confiscation of the *Planet* by postal authorities. In 1921 he made one final, and unsuccessful, venture into politics: he ran for governor of Virginia on what Negroes called a "lily-black ticket." The campaign was waged not so much against the Democrats as against those white Republicans who sought to revive the South's two-party system at the expense of the Negro.

In 1922 the Mechanics Savings Bank went into receivership and Mitchell was indicted for mismanagement. Although he was never convicted, scores of depositors blamed him for the loss of their savings, and the bank's failure became his personal Waterloo. Some local Negroes speculated that the "white people were out to get him," but Abram L. Harris, an economist who studied the bank's collapse, came to different conclusions. The state banking commissioners had known for years that the bank was in trouble, he wrote, but they failed to intervene either because "they respected Mitchell and therefore gave him as much latitude as they could . . . or because they felt it did not matter what a Negro banker did." The white bankers were willing to "wink at the errors of the child race." Mitchell vowed he would save his bank and regain his good name, but he died on Dec. 3, 1929, after a brief illness at his home, 515 N. Third St., Richmond, "virtually a poor man." Funeral services were held at Fifth Street Baptist Church and he was buried in Evergreen Cemetery.

The best source for a study of Mitchell's life is the *Planet;* a nearly complete file exists for the period 1890–1929. For accounts of his youth, almost all borrow from the sketch in William J. Simmons's *Men of Mark . . .* (1887). Abram L. Harris in *The Negro as Capitalist* (1936) analyzes the collapse of the bank, while several articles focus on Mitchell: James H. Brewer's "Editorials from the Damned" (*Journal of Southern History* 28 [1962]: 225–33); Willard B. Gatewood, Jr.'s "A Negro Editor on Imperialism: John Mitchell, 1898–1901" (*Journalism Quarterly* 49 [1972]: 43–50, 60); August Meier's and Elliot Rudwick's "Negro Boycotts of Segregated Streetcars in Virginia, 1904–1907" (*Virginia Magazine of History and Biography* 81 [1973]: 470–87). See also Ann F. Alexander's "Black Protest in the New South: John Mitchell, Jr., and the Richmond *Planet*" (Ph.D. dissertation, Duke University, 1973). A study of Mitchell by James Wesley Smith, *The Strange Way of Truth* (1968), relies almost entirely on the *Planet,* 1900–1904. See, too, the obituary in the *Richmond Times-Dispatch* (Dec. 4, 1929, p. 2; Dec. 5, 1929, p. 11). — ANN ALEXANDER

MOLINEAUX, [MOLYNEUX] TOM (1784–1818), boxer. He was born a slave, probably in Georgetown, District of Columbia, on March 23, 1784. Molineaux was the name of the family for which the father and mother of Tom and four other brothers were also slaves. Strongly influenced by his father, Zachary, who is credited as the founder of boxing in the United States, Tom took up the sport at an early age. At the age of fourteen, after Tom's father had died, the youngster took his place as the chief handyman around his master's estate. Several years later his owner promised him the sum of $100 and his freedom if he were successful in defeating the slave of a neighboring planter in a pugilistic contest. Intent on winning his freedom, Tom accepted the match and won.

With the prize money and his newly gained freedom, Molineaux headed for London where, he had been told, fame and fortune were to be won in boxing. Arriving in London at the age of twenty-four, Molineaux fought several matches and earned the distinction of being the first American to fight in an international bout. With strength, confidence, and determination as his chief assets, he soon became known to boxing enthusiasts as the "Negro challenger to British heavyweight supremacy."

The highlight of Molineaux's ring career came in his two matches with Tom Cribbs, the British champion.

The first match took place on Dec. 18, 1810, on Copthall Commons, near East Grimstead. Cribbs held little respect for Molineaux and boasted that he would roundly beat him so that he would never again challenge an Englishman. The fight was hard fought and appeared to be an even match before Molineaux accidentally fell and badly injured himself in the last round. He bravely attempted to rise but his legs gave way and he signaled to the referee that he could not go on. Thus Cribbs was awarded the victory and retained his title. Molineaux was granted a rematch in 1811, but this time he proved to be no match for the British champion and was easily defeated.

Molineaux's ring career plunged steadily downward following the second defeat by Cribbs. Frequently engaging in street brawls, drinking beyond his capacity, and failing to keep in proper fighting condition, Molineaux quickly lost the bulk of his ring earnings. Hoping to regain his financial status he decided on another boxing tour of England. Having twice fought Cribbs his reputation made him a favorite. He knew how to wrestle well and when he struck a spot where wrestling was more lucrative than boxing, he engaged in active competition. However, as a top-flight wrestler he failed miserably.

During the tour Molineaux drank excessively and soon found himself in deplorable physical condition. He was still able to defeat several mediocre opponents. By reason of his showings in these bouts a match was made for him with George Cooper, a famous British boxer. They met on March 11, 1815, at Corset Hill, Lanarkshire, Scotland, and in less than twenty minutes Molineaux had lost his last big fight.

After the Cooper bout Molineaux embarked on a tour through Ireland, and at the end of 1817 he was teaching the art of boxing as he watched his meager savings dwindle into poverty. The sun of the once great fighter's prosperity had set. During the last ten months of his life he was dependent on the sympathy of his black friends in the 77th Regiment, stationed at Galway, for his sustenance. He died in the band room of that regiment on Aug. 4, 1818, a wasted skeleton, a penniless beggar, a shell of his former self.

Mainly because Molineaux was illiterate, he was plagued throughout his career with less than honest managers, trainers, and promoters. His chief weakness was his habit of giving away money with such generosity that he could never shake hangers-on. However, in spite of his handicaps he holds the distinction of being America's first great boxer.

An early reference is R. K. Fox's *The Black Champions of the Prize Ring from Molineaux to Jackson* (1890). Later accounts, based in large part on Fox, are in the standard books: Edwin Bancroft Henderson's *The Negro in Sports* (1949) and N. S. Fleischer's *Black Dynamite . . . from 1782 to 1938* (1938).
— AL-TONY GILMORE

MONTGOMERY, ISAIAH T[HORNTON] (1841–1924), planter, congressman, founder of an all-Negro town, and conservative politician. His mother, Mary Lewis, was the daughter of Virginia slaves. His father, Benjamin Thornton Montgomery, was born in Loudon

County, Va., in 1819. In 1837 he was sold to Joseph Davis (brother of Jefferson Davis), an unusually enlightened owner of Hurricane, a plantation at Davis Bend, south of Vicksburg, Miss. Encouraged by Joseph Davis, Benjamin Montgomery learned to read and write; he established a store on the plantation and became manager of Hurricane as well as of Brierfield during the absence of Jefferson Davis. On Nov. 19, 1866, Joseph Davis sold both plantations to Benjamin Montgomery and his two sons, William and Isaiah, for $300,000. By 1876, "Poor crops, the declining price of cotton, severe credit losses among their tenants, and the large interest payments on Hurricane and Brierfield combined to push them to the edge of bankruptcy" (Hermann, p. 204). Worn out by these difficulties, Benjamin Montgomery died, intestate, on May 12, 1877. In 1879 the mercantile firm of Montgomery and Sons was foreclosed for failure to pay mortgage indebtedness, and in 1881 Hurricane and Brierfield were auctioned to the Jefferson Davis family and the grandchildren of Joseph Davis.

Isaiah Montgomery attributed the failure in large measure to the fact that it did not provide for land ownership by the former slaves. He revived Davis's dream by founding in early 1888 the all-Negro town of Mound Bayou, Miss. Many of the early settlers were freedmen who had become landowners after the Civil War. By 1907 "the village had become the center of a thriving agricultural colony of some 800 families with a total population of about 4,000 blacks. . . . The government of the colony also was kept under black control." But during and after World War I some colonists migrated to northern cities; the price of cotton fell from a dollar to fifteen or twenty cents; women landowners were forced to seek employment as domestic servants and male landowners became sharecroppers. The death of Isaiah Montgomery on March 4, 1924, effectively ended the dream. "By 1940 a visitor described Mound Bayou as a dilapidated, depopulated town with little left to excite race pride" (Hermann, pp. 223, 225, 241, 243).

Isaiah Montgomery is better known for the support he gave the Mississippi constitutional amendment in 1890 which effectively disfranchised most Negroes while permitting equally unqualified whites to vote. Montgomery, a Republican and the only Negro member of the constitutional convention, made a speech that lasted almost an hour. In it he expressed his conviction that the best interests of both races required the Negro vote to be reduced to a total well below that of the whites. He supported a committee report which, according to his estimate, would disfranchise 123,000 Negroes and 12,000 whites, leaving a total Negro vote of about 66,000 and a white majority of more than 40,000. He justified the proposed amendment by stating his belief that it would result in better race relations, because Negroes would turn from politics to increasing their knowledge and property; they would then gradually be permitted to reenter politics. His speech won the approval of the Democratic press in Mississippi and in the nation as a whole, and President Cleveland praised it. Vernon Wharton believed that Montgomery's speech "did more than anything else to allay suspicion and opposition in the North" (p. 212). Both Wharton and John R. Lynch called Montgomery's role in the convention a "mystery." Although he was an honorable and intelligent man, he must have known that the amendment would mean, as it did, the virtual elimination of Negroes from politics in Mississippi.

The 1890 constitutional amendment imposed a poll tax of two dollars as a requirement for voting, excluded voters convicted of certain crimes, and barred from voting all those who could not read a section of the state constitution, or understand it when read. Few Negroes paid the poll tax; they were more likely to be convicted than were whites; registration officials generally applied the "understanding clause" to certify whites and disqualify Negroes.

Mississippi was the first southern state to adopt a constitutional amendment that disfranchised Negroes while permitting equally unqualified whites to vote. By 1915 all the states of the former Confederacy and Oklahoma had by various means accomplished the same aim.

Janet Sharp Hermann, who has written the best biography of Montgomery, concluded that he "thought he was acting in the best interests of his [Mound Bayou] colony and their example would benefit all Mississippi blacks. Given local conditions at the time, his judgment was not implausible" (p. 232).

One significant result of Montgomery's speech was his friendship with Booker T. Washington. Montgomery served as one of the Negro commissioners at the Atlanta Exposition in 1895, where Washington made his famous accommodationist speech. In 1900 Montgomery joined Washington in founding the National Negro Business League. On Washington's recommendation, Pres. Theodore Roosevelt appointed Montgomery collector of government monies in Jackson, Miss. He was asked to resign when a surprise investigation found that Montgomery had deposited $5000 of government funds in his personal account. Montgomery immediately made restitution.

In the vain hope of gaining goodwill for his Mound Bayou colony, Montgomery continued his role of accommodationist in public while privately expressing doubt about the behavior of whites toward Negroes.

No son survived Isaiah Montgomery. Two of the four daughters had moved from Mound Bayou. One daughter, Lillian Belle, was severely handicapped. The other daughter, Mary Booze, became a Republican national committeewoman. His brother, William Thornton, had died in 1909. Martha Robb Montgomery, whom he had married in 1871, had been not only a loyal wife and mother of their twelve children but also a business partner of considerable ability. She died in 1923, seven months before the death of Isaiah Montgomery.

Janet Sharp Hermann's scholarly *The Pursuit of a Dream* (1981) is the principal source. Vernon Lane Wharton's *The Negro in Mississippi, 1865–1890* (1947) and John Hope Franklin (ed.), *The Autobiography of John Ray Lynch* (1970), give additional valuable information. — RAYFORD W. LOGAN

MOORE, FRED[ERICK RANDOLPH] (1857–1943), journalist and political activist. Moore was born in Virginia to a slave mother and white father. While still an infant, his family moved to Washington, D.C., where he attended public schools and sold newspapers on the streets. Moore later rose in the messenger ranks in the U.S. Treasury Department to serve seven secretaries as personal messenger and confidential aide. He was with President Garfield when he was assassinated in 1881, and in 1887 Moore accompanied Secretary Daniel Manning to Europe on departmental business for three months. Upon his return to the United States, Moore took a job as vault and delivery clerk in a New York bank headed by Manning. In this capacity he had charge of all shipments of money for eighteen years. He married Ida Lawrence, a Washington, D.C., native, in April 1879. Only six of their eighteen children lived to adulthood. Three of them later worked on Moore's newspaper staff while Gladys, one of four surviving daughters, married Lester Walton, a journalist who later became U.S. minister to Liberia. While holding the bank job Moore committed himself to the principles of racial solidarity and capital investment by helping form an abortive Negro protective league in 1892 and joining in the league's offshoot, the Afro-American Building and Loan Association, later in the year. The company returned only minimal dividends. In 1905 Moore became an investor and officer of the Afro-American Realty Company, an ambitious enterprise conceived by Philip A. Payton, Jr., to buy white properties in Harlem to rent and sell to in-coming Negro residents. The company's failure to fill its expanding properties with renters led to its collapse in 1908, despite Moore's last-minute efforts to help save valuable acquisitions.

During the first decade of the twentieth century Moore integrated several facets of a career that would establish his prominence in racial and national affairs. He became actively involved in Republican state and national politics, beginning as a district captain. In 1902 he made a strong but unsuccessful bid for a Brooklyn seat in the state Assembly. Two years later he was appointed a deputy collector of internal revenue, a post he resigned a few months later when Booker T. Washington asked him to become an organizer for the National Negro Business League. Moore's penchant for journalism also led him to part-time work for the *New York Age*. In 1905, with funds secretly supplied by Washington, he became editor and part-owner of the Boston-based *Colored American Magazine,* whose headquarters then moved to New York. Two years later in a complicated financial maneuver worked out by Washington, Moore took over the *Age,* the most widely read Negro newspaper of its time. His political importance grew with his national journalistic influence. He was elected an alternate delegate to the Republican National Convention in 1908 and attended every subsequent state and national convention. From 1908 to 1920 Moore also served on every National Negro Republican Committee during presidential campaigns. The *Age* also did extensive publicity for the party during this period. In the 1920s Moore promoted black capitalism and political candidates in Harlem, and won election as a New York City alderman in 1927 and 1929. He was also actively involved in interracial efforts which led to the formation of the National Urban League in 1910–

1911 and served on the league board for three decades. After long service to the Negro community he died of pneumonia on March 1, 1943, at his home, 228 W. 135th St., New York City. His wife had died on July 14, 1939; he was survived by two sons and three daughters.

While it was Moore's business association with Booker T. Washington which enabled him to make his mark, it was his unflagging adherence to the principles of self-help, racial solidarity and pride, black capitalism, and racial justice which made this association and his enduring prominence possible. Moore practiced what he preached, sometimes at considerable personal sacrifice and economic risk. In 1904 he spent weekends away from home organizing business leagues in northern cities. Then he mortgaged his home and life insurance policy and resigned his bank job to invest in the *Colored American Magazine.* Under Moore's leadership the magazine continued to stress economic advancement and character building, but it also attacked racial injustice in the South, noting not only the horrors of lynching but also the psychologically destructive effect of segregation. As the magazine's debts grew, Moore accepted financial backing from Washington for the purchase of the *Age* from T. Thomas Fortune. What Moore lacked in brilliance, wide-ranging interests, and the fine details of journalism, he made up for in hard work, determination, and an abiding commitment to Washington's economic philosophy and to a fair deal for the Negro. His political partisanship tempered his criticism of Republican administrations during the Progressive Era, but not to the point where principles were sacrificed.

Under Moore's management the *Age* continued its prominence as a race advocate. His early limitations as an editorial writer and his small, inexperienced staff restricted the scope of the weekly's views and coverage, prompting criticism that the quality of the weekly deteriorated. Nevertheless its circulation increased from 5000 a week in 1907 to 14,000 in 1910. The *Age* not only retained its primacy among Negro New York papers for another two decades, but also extended its reach through Moore's personal circulation drives in the Deep South and the employment of such distinguished editors as James Weldon Johnson. In 1919 the *Age* followed the Negro migration to Harlem where Moore established a modern printing plant and expanded the newspaper's coverage of racial affairs. It dramatically exposed the aims and methods of the Ku Klux Klan after World War I, promoted Negro political power in the 1920s, and reported the cultural achievements of the race.

Moore's increasing support by the Harlem community capped his long career as organizer, political activist, and journalist. After the war he was in the forefront of the unsuccessful effort to remove racial discrimination in the American Federation of Labor. In 1924 he helped nominate a Negro congressional candidate, and five years later he was instrumental in electing a Negro ticket to the state Assembly. Although the ascendancy of the Democratic party, economic liberalism, and the emergence of the *New York Amsterdam News* decreased Moore's influence in the 1930s, he was one of the early sponsors of Harlem's "Don't Buy Where You Can't Work" campaign. While his dream of black capitalism lay in ruins and racial discrimination was still powerful at his death on March 1, 1943, Moore had helped sow the seeds of change.

For Moore's early journalism career and association with Booker T. Washington, see Emma Lou Thornbrough's *T. Thomas Fortune: Militant Journalist* (1972) and August Meier's "Booker T. Washington and the Negro Press: With Special Reference to the *Colored American Magazine*" (*JNH*, Jan. 1953). Moore's role in the Urban League can be traced in Guichard Parris's and Lester Brooks's *Blacks in the City: A History of the National Urban League* (1971). Valuable information was found in the Booker T. Washington Papers, Library of Congress; the Emmett J. Scott Papers, Soper Library, Morgan State University, Baltimore; the Robert R. Moton Papers, Tuskegee Institute. His obituary and portrait appeared in the *New York Times* (March 3, 1943, p. 24). — JOHN B. WISEMAN

MOORLAND, JESSE EDWARD (1863–1940), clergyman and YMCA executive. He was born on Sept. 10, 1863, in Coldwater, Ohio, the only child of Nancy Jane Moore and William Edward Mooreland. The family traced its ancestry in the United States back to the eighteenth century when John Moore, a free Negro, married an Irish woman, Nancy Mollie Moorland, in 1717. John Moore took his wife's surname but spelled it Mooreland. Branches of the family were known variously as Moore or Mooreland. (When an adolescent, Jesse Edward decided to drop the "e" from his surname.) The family was particularly proud of its free status during the slave era, and the prominent role some members had played in local community affairs. Joseph Johnson, the brother of Jesse Moorland's great-grandmother, Massa Johnson, had fought in the Black Hawk War at the Battle of Horse Shoe Bend. A great-grandfather was a Baptist minister with an interracial congregation in North Carolina; an uncle, William D. Moorland, M.D., had a lucrative practice in Stewart County, Tenn., and was a member of the Nashville Institute; a grandfather had been a schoolteacher in Tennessee in the 1830s. Other members of the family (the Moore branch), such as Furnie Moore, were active participants in the Underground Railroad, and some, like Amos Moore, settled in Liberia in the 1840s. Jesse Moorland's grandparents on both sides were born near New Bern, N.C. In 1807 the Moores left North Carolina, traveling by oxcart across the mountains to settle near Clarksville in Stewart County, Tenn., where they became substantial landowners who exercised the right to vote. His maternal grandfather moved to Ohio in 1858 because of the imposition of new restrictions on free Negroes in Tennessee, including disfranchisement and the requirement that bonds be posted to guarantee good behavior. In Coldwater, Ohio, the Moores became successful farmers.

Jesse's mother died at the age of nineteen, when he was fifteen months old. His father, who died ten years later, left the farm in Coldwater and Jesse was reared by his maternal grandparents. His early education was in a small county school near the farm. In an autobio-

graphical fragment written in later life, Moorland recalled that an important part of his education as a boy came from his grandfather, whose daily routine at the end of the day included reading aloud Bunyan's *Pilgrim's Progress* and *My Bondage and My Freedom* by Frederick Douglass. "What I know of these books," he said, "I remember from those precious winter evenings by the cheerful fire." He later attended the Northwestern Normal University in Ada, Ohio, where he met his future wife, Lucy Corbin Woodson of Berlin Crossroads, Ohio. The Moorlands were married in 1886. The couple taught briefly in the public schools of Urbana, Ohio, before moving to Washington to attend Howard University. Mrs. Moorland enrolled in the Normal Department, graduating in 1893, and her husband in the Theological Department, where he graduated as salutatorian of his class in 1891.

After graduation from Howard, Moorland was ordained a Congregational minister. In 1891 he organized a church in South Boston, Va., and the same year was appointed secretary of the colored YMCA in Washington, where, he later said, he "learned the hardships and difficulties in a pioneer field." He served in this post two years, resigning to become pastor of Howard Chapel in Nashville, Tenn., a Congregational church supported by the American Missionary Association in New York. He remained in Nashville from 1893 to 1896, when he succeeded the Rev. Sterling N. Brown as pastor of the Mount Zion Congregational Church of Cleveland, Ohio.

A widely read man in English and American literature, history, geography, and current social and political affairs, Moorland was in the vanguard of progressive American Protestant clergymen of the 1890s who wanted to adapt Christian theology to the practical needs of their congregations. The surviving manuscripts of his public lectures and sermons, as well as the notebooks from his daily study sessions from this period, reveal the intellectual sources of his later efforts to develop a "practical, muscular Christianity" responsive to changing social conditions.

In his first sermon, delivered in 1890 while still a Howard student, Moorland said that the "great need of today is a Gospel incarnate, a Gospel applied to human needs, to both soul and body." He held to these principles for the remainder of his career. His fullest exposition of these views is found in his essay *The Demand and the Supply of Increased Efficiency in the Negro Ministry,* published as Occasional Paper no. 13 by the American Negro Academy in 1909. Arguing that "no other single class of individuals has had, and still has, so large and far reaching an influence as our ministers," Moorland maintained that in the training of ministers less emphasis should be placed on traditional theological studies and more on modern subjects such as sociology, where students would "get some practical knowledge of human relations and conditions of the present time." Moorland's concept of an "efficient" minister was that he would work to have parishioners "own their own homes . . . take proper care of their children," and become a community leader capable of lifting "the burdens of the poor" and "to get our people out of crowded alleys . . . that they may be where their little children may have a chance for true development."

Moorland pursued this type of practical ministry in Cleveland for two years. It was a logical extension of his views to accept the offer of William Alphaeus Hunton in October 1898 to become a member of the Colored Men's Department of the YMCA, which had been created in 1890 as one of fifteen departments of the International Committee of the YMCA.

From 1888 to 1898 Hunton had worked alone, developing YMCAs on Negro college campuses and in cities with sizable Negro populations. By 1898 the burdens of travel, organization, and maintenance of this increasingly national enterprise had become obviously too great for one man. After 1898 Hunton specialized in campus work and Moorland in what was called "city work." Moorland's religious background and social work interests were excellent preparation for the career he began in 1898.

As Moorland conceived the YMCA, it could be developed as a vehicle for meeting some of the social needs of colored youth, and also serve significantly as a means for "constructive cooperation" between representatives of the "better element" of the white and Negro communities. In an unpublished essay on "The Young Men's Christian Association Among Colored Men" written in 1901, Moorland depicted some of the problems encountered by Negro youth in cities that he believed the YMCA was called upon to combat. Noting that in other areas of life Negroes always received less than a full share of society's benefits and opportunities, he added that "the young colored man unfortunately comes in for a full share of that which is demoralizing in our cities. Because of caste he is debarred from many places of helpful influence, but is amply provided with every form of vice that other men have and thus is often trained in sin."

In a speech from the same period, Moorland similarly combined the religious and social objectives of his work. "Give men a good social environment," he said, "and you have certainly done a great deal to start them upward. . . . The social element is one of the potent factors in destroying men. Here is the highway for the saloon, club and many times the house of ill-fame." As a result of this conception of the problem, Moorland emphasized in his city work the development of facilities that would be a "positive community environment" in microcosm, so that the colored YMCA could be a refuge from the social disorganization that was apparent among the growing numbers of migrants to cities that became a flood with the advent of World War I. Moorland designed programs that included lectures, debates, Bible classes, workshops on job skills, literacy classes, and "wholesome recreation" with a heavy emphasis on athletics. The major obstacle was resources. Not a single colored YMCA had a building adequate for such a program.

Most of the Negro associations did not own the often rundown row house or over-the-store walk-up in which they held meetings. Moorland therefore resolved to emphasize the erection of buildings designed specifically for YMCA purposes. This project was to be his greatest success and the one which revealed the gifts of organization, persuasive enthusiasm, and business sense for which his contemporaries honored him. His first major

success was in Washington, D.C., where the oldest colored YMCA had been organized by Anthony Bowen in 1853. Moorland's plan had four elements: (1) presentation of an activities program far more ambitious than previously imagined possible; (2) organization of the leading colored men in Washington to give substance to the expectation that the plan could be realized; (3) presentation of the fundraising drive as a challenge to the race pride of Negroes; and (4) solicitation of funds from white philanthropists who would find the Washington colored YMCA building fund an opportunity to support an effort of Negroes who wanted "to help themselves." Moorland said to his audiences, "Save your young men and save your race. Save your young men and you save your country. Save your young men and you save the world." This formula proved to be highly successful. For the new building on Twelfth Street NW, Moorland raised $26,000 from Washington Negroes, $25,000 from John D. Rockefeller, $25,000 from Julius Rosenwald, and $25,000 from the National Council of the YMCA. This became a model for the nation, and the basis for the later program to erect $100,000 YMCA buildings for Negroes. When the Twelfth Street YMCA building (the terminology adopted to avoid racial identification) was completed, Dean Kelly Miller of Howard University said that it was "the most imposing and complete structure in the world occupied by Negroes for purposes of purely social and moral uplift."

While Moorland was at work on the Washington YMCA building project in 1910 he was called to Chicago to supervise a fundraising drive for construction of a YMCA building projected at a cost of $150,000. During his first week in Chicago Moorland was invited to a meeting by Julius Rosenwald to discuss the campaign to which he had already donated $25,000. Moorland convinced Rosenwald that the Chicago and Washington campaigns could be models for the nation, and in a bold stroke persuaded him to make a "challenge to the Negro citizens of America." Rosenwald agreed to donate $25,000 to any Negro YMCA that raised a minimum of $75,000 on its own, so that a building costing no less than $100,000 could be constructed. The offer was to be valid for five years. Rosenwald said seven years later that he made the decision "then and there," without further deliberation, because he was "so favorably impressed with Dr. Moorland," who would, under the agreement, be responsible for "arousing the interests of the people in the larger cities" and managing the campaigns for the five-year period. By the standards of 1910 these sums were commonly thought to be far beyond what generally poor Negroes could raise for YMCA buildings.

After the 1910 meeting with Rosenwald, Moorland nevertheless conducted successful building campaigns in nineteen cities, raising a total of more than $2 million. Moorland's fund drives were highly sophisticated campaigns that emphasized careful planning, organization of "blue ribbon" committees, "monster rallies" in large churches or stadiums, attracting the support of the white political and voluntary organization leadership, and the "challenge" to the Negro community to demonstrate its pride and sense of civic responsibility. A premium was placed on "crash campaign" tactics, with most public aspects of the fund drive lasting for no more than ten days. In Chicago he raised $67,000 in less than ten days, in Atlanta $50,000 in the same period. In the Atlanta campaign, as in others, Moorland's publicity emphasized large contributions by Negroes of modest means who were prepared to give their savings "for the boys' future." A number of former slaves gave $1000 or more, in one case "all of his savings earned in freedom." Kelly Miller observed that the campaigns were successful because the "Negro was assigned a task that assumed citizenship, manhood and the possibilities inhering in both." Moorland himself echoed this view some years later when he wrote to George Arthur (March 3, 1934) that "Mr. Rosenwald's gift challenged colored people to self-respect through self-support."

As it became clear that the effort to build new YMCA facilities for Negroes in the larger cities was going to succeed, Moorland recognized the need to attract and develop the best possible full-time local staff. In the earlier years most cities had volunteer or part-time secretaries; after 1910 the pattern was to have full-time secretaries who had received special training and exhibited the management and community-organizing skills necessary to direct an institution. In 1911 the Kings Mountain Conference was organized in North Carolina for training secretaries. This training center supplemented the Summer School Association for the Training and Development of Employed Officers at the YMCA. Organized at Hampton Institute in 1907 by Hunton and Moorland, it was first called the Secretarial Institute. By 1911 the institute was held at a camping ground at Arundel on the Chesapeake Bay in Maryland and was renamed the Chesapeake Summer School Association. In 1924 it was moved to the New Jersey Manual Training School for Colored Youth at Bordentown after a fire destroyed the Arundel camp. Through these training institutions Hunton and Moorland created a remarkable cadre of young leaders, many of whom later became college presidents, social workers, and voluntary association executives. Faculty at the institutes included William Stuart Nelson, David Dallas Jones, Channing H. Tobias, Mordecai W. Johnson, John Hope, John W. Davis, Charles H. Wesley, R. R. Moton, William J. Trent, Sr., W. E. B. Du Bois, and Campbell C. Johnson.

By the outbreak of the First World War, when Moorland had succeeded Hunton as senior secretary, the Colored Men's Department of the YMCA was a significant national institution which included 107 student associations on college campuses, 39 city associations, 14 industrial associations, and 2 railroad associations; its assets included twenty-nine buildings, and it maintained, in addition to the local secretaries, two state secretaries and eight international secretaries. During the war it provided staff to U.S. Army camps where Negro officers and soldiers were trained, and sent fifty secretaries to Europe to provide programs for Negro troops stationed there. By 1920 the department was able to send Max Yergan, who had been appointed student secretary in 1915 and served in India during the war, to South Africa where he developed YMCA programs and facilities for the black and colored population.

Moorland retired as senior secretary of the Colored

Men's Department in 1923, when he had reached the YMCA's mandatory retirement age of sixty. He had moved from Washington to New York four years earlier to work at the national headquarters, and lived in Brooklyn. He was at the height of his influence because of the continued success of the programs he had developed. He left the YMCA reluctantly. He had established an important network across the nation of able community leaders, had supervised the planning and construction of an impressive number of buildings in most of the large cities of the United States, was highly regarded as a fundraiser, and was affectionately known as "The Dean" by the hundreds of YMCA workers who had been trained during his tenure. After retirement he gave some of his time to national civic organizations and local New York charities. In 1926 he served as president of the National Health Circle for Colored People (formerly the Circle for Negro Relief), whose object was "to organize opinion and support for public health work among colored people."

Moorland's greatest interest after retirement was Howard University where, because of his continued vigor and the amount of time he had available, he could become virtually a "professional trustee." Appointed to the university's Board of Trustees in 1907 Moorland had distinguished himself on the board as a man who could compose differences between various contending factions. His thorough preparation for board meetings, mastery of minute administrative detail, and the wide range of contacts he had made through his travels for the YMCA, made him one of the most knowledgeable and influential trustees. Recognized as a brisk and capable administrator, Moorland's engaging manner, combined with a gift for understatement and good timing in committee meetings, made him an unusually effective member of the board. He was also successful as an intermediary between the white and Negro members of the board which became polarized at times, notably in the 1920s when there was growing sentiment among alumni and faculty that Howard should have a Negro president. Moorland's role was critical during the 1920s because of his support of J. Stanley Durkee, a white Congregational minister whose peremptory manner and policies of administrative centralization and curricular reorganization caused widespread opposition from students, alumni, and faculty. Moorland frequently attempted to mollify alumni and faculty opposed to the president, and emphasized a "constructive approach" to the crisis that simmered until Durkee's resignation in 1926. His successor, Mordecai W. Johnson, had been associated briefly with Moorland in the YMCA during the war, and after his widely reported success as a commencement speaker at Harvard in 1922, had been urged repeatedly by Moorland to come to Howard to direct an institute for the training of ministers.

During the stormiest years of the Johnson administration in the 1930s Moorland was chairman of the Executive Committee of the Board of Trustees. In this capacity he used his considerable influence, as much as the often volatile situation permitted, to steer the university clear of fruitless controversy and also encourage cooperation within the board. Albert Bushnell Hart, Harvard historian who had served on the board since 1919, wrote to Moorland on March 6, 1935, that "your fellow members of the Board look upon you as one of the hard-headed, experienced and cautious members of the Board. I greatly admire the style in which you lead the business of the Executive Committee."

Moorland's concern for Howard went far beyond the usual trustee interest in finance, improved management, and general educational policy formulation. He had long believed the university had a distinctive intellectual role to play in the general field of Negro studies, particularly in the specialized areas of history and sociology. As early as 1912 he had supported the proposals of Kelly Miller and Alain Locke that instruction and research on Africa and the American Negro be encouraged by the board. His first major step in support of this idea was his decision in 1914 to donate to Howard his private library on the Negro. In his letter of Dec. 18 to the president of the university, Moorland noted that his collection "has been regarded by many experts as probably the largest and most complete yet gathered by a single individual. . . . I am giving this collection to the University because it is the one place in America where the largest and best library on the subject should be constructively established." In recognition of the significance of this gift, the university's trustees established the collection as "The Moorland Foundation," creating the first research library in an American university devoted exclusively to materials on the Negro. Moorland added to the foundation annually, secured space for it in the new Founders Library, planned in 1930 and opened in 1939, as well as financial support. His interest extended also to the university's Department of History, which he hoped would take special advantage of the resources of his collection. He was responsible for the addition in 1919 of Carter G. Woodson, and William Leo Hansberry in 1922 to the history faculty.

Moorland's friendship with Woodson had developed from the early years of the Association for the Study of Negro Life and History. He was an incorporator, a member of the Executive Council of the association, and served as secretary-treasurer until a break between Woodson and Moorland in 1921. Brewing as early as 1920, when Moorland urged Woodson to adopt a more "diplomatic" or conciliatory tone toward President Durkee, the serious rupture developed in 1921 when Moorland urged Woodson to cooperate with a plan suggested by representatives of the Carnegie Corporation and the Rockefeller Foundation that the ASNLH and the Department of Records and Research at Tuskegee Institute, under the direction of Monroe Work, cooperate in a comprehensive research program in historical and contemporary studies of the Negro. Moorland believed that "constructive cooperation" was superior to competition between the two research organizations, and doubted that the foundations would support either adequately on a separate basis because of duplication of costs and staff. Woodson not only rejected Moorland's advice, but impugned his intelligence and motives. On Feb. 24, 1921, Woodson wrote Moorland, ". . . I am not by myself in feeling that your race leadership is unsound because of your slavish attachment to the incompetent poor whites who are ex-

ploiting the Negro race under the pretext that the time has not yet come when the Negro can dispense with these ignorant traducers, who in trying to fortify themselves in the midst of a changing order, have veered around to the position of the southern white man." Without the courtesy of direct notification, Moorland was replaced as secretary-treasurer of the ASNLH. The reaction in some philanthropic circles was predictable. Thomas Jesse Jones wrote to Moorland on March 2, 1922, that he noted the "important changes" made in the Executive Council, and stated that the support granted the ASNLH by the Phelps-Stokes Fund was "made largely because of the interest you and Dr. Robert E. Park had in the Association. We felt that Dr. Woodson, with your backing, would carry on research according to scientific principles."

Moorland's relations with Jones, who had been appointed to the Howard Board of Trustees in 1915, was indicative of his belief in "constructive cooperation" between "representative" Negroes and whites. He was one of a small circle of Negroes who served as intermediaries in race relations at a time when segregation was thoroughly institutionalized. In this context it was believed that "statesmanship" was required to secure assistance from powerful whites representing foundations such as the General Education Board, the Phelps-Stokes Fund, and the Rosenwald Fund, which supported Negro higher education and interracial projects designed to improve race relations. In this group Moorland was a pioneer, who had to tread a treacherously thin line between the traditional "conservatism" of certain Negroes, the "radicalism" of others, and the need to be on good terms with whites capable of providing needed assistance for improving the worsening plight of Negroes after the acceleration of urban migration during World War I.

As Moorland conceptualized the issue, the race problem in the United States was "not a Negro's problem, neither is it a white man's problem. It belongs to both and we are all here in this fair land and it is our duty and business to make it a fit place where we all can live happily and where we can be conscious that justice is blind and knows no race, no color . . ." (Moorland to Dr. Charles H. Bough, Feb. 24, 1915). At various times in his career the concept of "color blind justice" was regarded as either "radical" or "conservative" as social and political conditions changed. Kelly Miller had said on Dec. 15, 1917, on the occasion of the twenty-fifth anniversary of Moorland's first appointment in the YMCA, that he was "not a conservative, neither is he a radical, but he is a progressive . . . indeed a statesman." That is probably the estimate that best fits Moorland's entire career. Not a man of party, faction, or ideology, he bent his efforts toward practical cooperation guided by an optimistic faith in the ability of "sensible men of goodwill" to solve difficult social problems.

Moorland was active in numerous organizations. A Thirty-third Degree Mason, he was also a member of the Alpha Phi Alpha fraternity, a trustee of the Frederick Douglass Home Association, and various other civic groups in Brooklyn and Washington. He was awarded an honorary Doctor of Divinity degree by Howard University in 1906 and by Oberlin College in 1924. Lucy

Moorland died on March 20, 1939, at the home, 183 S. Oxford St., Brooklyn. Moorland died on April 30, 1940, at the Flower Fifth Avenue Hospital in New York following a heart attack two weeks earlier. His only survivor was a cousin, Louise Lane, a public school teacher in New York City. Funeral services were held on May 3, 1940, at the Nazarene Congregational Church in Brooklyn, where he had been a trustee, and later on the same day at the Andrew Rankin Memorial Chapel at Howard University. He was interred at the Lincoln Memorial Cemetery, Suitland, Md.

There is no biography of Jesse E. Moorland. Useful sources include the obituary notice, presumably written by Carter G. Woodson, in *JNH* (July 1940, pp. 401–3); "A Tribute to the Memory of Jesse E. Moorland" (*Howard University Bulletin,* July 1940, p. 12); "University Community Mourns Death of Dr. Jesse Moorland" (*The Hilltop,* Howard University, May 14, 1940, p. 2). Among Moorland's publications the most useful summary of his career is found in "The Young Men's Christian Association Among Negroes" (*JNH,* April 1924, pp. 127–38). There are useful clippings in the vertical file of the Moorland-Spingarn Research Center, and a biographical fragment in the Research Department prepared in 1974 by Diane G. Dillon. The richest source for study of his career as clergyman, YMCA executive, and university trustee is the Jesse Moorland Papers, Manuscript Division, Moorland-Spingarn Research Center. Included in the papers are several autobiographical fragments, voluminous correspondence, reading and lecture notes, sermons, photographs, and materials collected for a projected history of the Colored Men's Department of the YMCA.

— MICHAEL R. WINSTON

MORGAN, CLEMENT G[ARNETT] (1859–1929), lawyer and civil rights leader. A son of slaves, Clement and Elizabeth Garnett Morgan, he was born in Stafford County, Va. Just after the Emancipation, the family moved to Washington, D.C., where the son completed the Preparatory High School for Colored Youth (later the M Street High School). But since there seemed no opportunity for Clement to put to use his high school education, he became a barber. Unsatisfied with barbering, Morgan traveled to St. Louis, Mo., where he taught school for four years. Still unsatisfied, Morgan arrived in Boston about 1885, enrolling in and graduating with distinction from the Boston Latin School in 1886. He attended Harvard College the same year, working as a barber to support himself. Other funds were raised by giving readings at summer resorts, including one summer with W. E. B. Du Bois, a fellow student at Harvard. Morgan was such a brilliant student that he won scholarships worth $1200, almost enough to meet all of his college costs. In his junior year he won the prestigious Boylston Prize for oratory; in his senior year (1890) Morgan was also selected as the class orator. Many newspapers praised and others derogated his selection. Morgan based his philosophy on patience, earnestness, sincerity, and unselfishness, and he believed fervently that every human being must have the opportunity to develop his intellectual faculties. Such attitudes formed the roots of Morgan's later vehement

opposition to Booker T. Washington and his strong support of the views of Du Bois.

After graduation Morgan spent the next three years in the Harvard Law School, from which he received his LL.B. degree in 1893. One of his classmates was William H. Lewis, first Negro All-America football player (1892 and 1893), and later assistant attorney-general of the United States. Morgan was the third Negro to get a law degree from Harvard and the first Negro to obtain degrees from both the college and the law school. Admitted to the Suffolk bar on Aug. 8, 1893, he practiced law in Cambridge in the same office for the rest of his life. He joined the Negro "radicals," who included Butler R. Wilson, Archibald H. Grimké, George Forbes, William Monroe Trotter, and for a short period, William H. Lewis. In 1895 and 1896 Morgan served as the first Negro elected to the Common Council of Cambridge from Ward 2, a predominantly white area. He served in 1898 and 1899 as an alderman in Cambridge. His campaigns in 1899, 1900, and 1908 for election to the state legislature were unsuccessful. As a politician, Morgan was consistently Republican.

In the late 1890s Boston was the major center for opposition to the accommodationist leadership of Booker T. Washington. Forbes and Trotter, as editors of the *Guardian,* and Morgan were courageous in their trenchant criticisms of Washington. Morgan was one of the attorneys for Trotter at his trial for causing the so-called Boston Riot of July 1903. In 1904 Morgan was one of the Committee of Twelve, formed with Booker T. Washington and Du Bois, an unsuccessful effort to reconcile these opposing leaders and their racial ideologies. The failure of reconciliation led Morgan to join as a key member of the Niagara Movement, founded in 1905 by Du Bois, who stressed an ideology of racial equality and protest. Morgan headed the Massachusetts branch of the Niagara Movement. But he was involved in the split between Trotter and Du Bois in 1907, over a disputed sponsorship of a Niagara Movement fund-raising activity in Boston. The split hastened the demise of the Niagara Movement. Morgan followed his friend Du Bois into the NAACP in 1909. Morgan served from 1912 to 1914 as one of the few Negro members on the executive committee of the Boston branch of the NAACP. For the rest of his life in Cambridge Morgan was active in his profession and in protest activities, especially against the showing in Boston of the film *The Birth of a Nation* (1915 and 1921).

On June 1, 1929, Morgan died at Massachusetts Homeopathic Hospital, Cambridge. Funeral services were held at the Harvard Street Methodist Church on June 4. His wife, Gertrude Wright Morgan, from Springfield, Ill., whom he had married in 1897, survived him.

The best published sources are Emory J. West's "Harvard's First Black Graduates; 1865–1890" (*Harvard Bulletin,* 1972, pp. 24–28); Elliott M. Rudwick's *W. E. B. Du Bois: Propagandist of the Negro Protest* (1969, pp. 94–119); and Stephen R. Fox's *The Guardian of Boston, William Monroe Trotter* (1970). Additional information is in the Du Bois Papers at the University of Massachusetts. Obituaries appeared in the *Boston Globe* (June 3, 1929, p. 18) and the *New York Age* (June 8, 1929, p. 9. — CLARENCE G. CONTEE, SR.

MORGAN, GARRETT A. (1875–1963), inventor and editor. The seventh of eleven children of Sidney and Elizabeth (Reed) Morgan, he was born and reared on a farm in Paris, Ky. His slave mother had been freed in 1863 by the Emancipation Proclamation. At the age of fourteen, with six years of schooling, he went to Cincinnati where he worked as a handyman for a wealthy landowner and hired a tutor to help him with his grammar. In 1895 he moved to Cleveland where he remained the rest of his life and patented his inventions. In 1908 he married Mary Anne Hassek, who lived with him at 5202 Harlem Ave. NW for most of the next fifty-five years.

His first job in Cleveland, as a sewing machine adjuster for a clothing manufacturer, sparked his lifelong interest and skill with things mechanical. In 1907 Morgan started the first of his several business enterprises—repairing and selling sewing machines. His sewing machine business prospered and in 1909 he opened his own tailoring shop with thirty-two employees to manufacture coats, suits, and dresses. The versatility and creativity of Morgan was further exhibited by the G. A. Morgan Hair Refining Company that he started in 1913 with a human hair-straightening process that he discovered and perfected.

On July 25, 1916, an explosion ripped through a Cleveland waterworks tunnel 250 feet below Lake Erie. Workmen trapped in the gas- and smoke-filled tunnel were carried out to safety by Morgan and rescuers wearing a safety hood (now known as a gas mask) invented by Morgan. He had first appeared with his safety hood and smoke protector in 1912. During 1913 and 1914 he improved his original mask. His safety helmet, as it was sometimes called, was designed for speedy work. It contained no valves to adjust, no bindings about the neck, no straps to buckle, and no heavy tanks of air. It could be put on and taken off almost as easily as tipping one's hat. This helmet could be donned in seven seconds and taken off in three. Clean air was supplied to the wearer from a bag of air suspended in the rear by two tubes leading from the hood. There was enough air in the bag to permit a man to stay in the midst of suffocating gases and smoke from fifteen to twenty minutes. This helmet was specially designed to work in the midst of heavy smoke that rested on the floor of a burning room or on elevations in dense clouds of smoke. It was also useful when one was spraying trees or shrubbery with chemicals that produced dangerous and offensive fumes. In his patent application he called his safety helmet a "Breathing Device." He was awarded a U.S. Patent in 1914, no. 1,113,675.

After the 1916 life-saving performance of his perfected mask, manufacturers produced and fire departments used Morgan's invention. He traveled from state to state demonstrating his gas mask. In many southern states he had to hire a white man to demonstrate his device while he passed as an Indian. When it became widely known that the gas mask's inventor was a Negro, production and use of the mask was curtailed. His mask, however, protected American soldiers in the battlefield from deadly chlorine gas fumes during World War I.

On Nov. 20, 1923, Morgan was awarded U.S. Patent no. 1,475,024 for his invention of a three-way automatic traffic signal. The G. A. Morgan Safety System advertised the traffic-regulation device as "A better protection for the pedestrian, school children and R.R. crossing." He also received patents for the traffic device in Canada and England. The "Go-Stop" signals used before Morgan's invention had no intermediate or neutral signal. In other words, there was no "yellow light" as it was later known. So without a traffic officer present, the signals "go" and "stop" could be completely ignored, thus leading to serious accidents. Morgan's signal was designed so that the stop and go signs could be left in a half-mast position that enabled automobiles to move in all directions without an attending traffic officer. He sold his rights to the traffic signal to General Electric for $40,000.

As well as being an astute businessman with his inventions, he was also civic minded. Because of inadequate news coverage concerning Afro-American affairs in the local newspapers of Cleveland, he established in 1920, and published until 1923, a weekly newspaper, the *Cleveland Call,* which advertised his hair treatment products. He served as treasurer of the Cleveland Association of Colored Men until it merged with the NAACP and he became a lifelong active member. In 1931 he ran as an independent candidate for the City Council in Cleveland. His platform included: (1) relief for the unemployed, and a more economic and efficient administration of public affairs; (2) improved housing conditions; (3) better lighting and policing, and improved sanitation; (4) improved city-owned hospital accommodations. He was unsuccessful in his first and only bid for public office.

Morgan received several awards and citations for his inventions: First Grand Prize Golden Medal by the National Safety Device Company at the Second International Exposition of Safety and Sanitation in 1914; honorary membership in the International Association of Fire Engineers; a U.S. government citation for his traffic signal; and national recognition at the Emancipation Centennial Celebration in Chicago, September 1963, a month after his death. A public school in Harlem was named for him in 1976.

In 1943 he had contracted glaucoma which gradually left him almost blind for the rest of his life, despite yearly visits to the Mayo Clinic in Rochester, Minn., until 1959. He died in Cleveland. Funeral services were held at the Antioch Baptist Church and he was buried in Lake View Cemetery, Cleveland. He was survived by John P., Garrett A. Jr., Cosmo H., and seven grandchildren.

The principal printed sources are Henry E. Baker's *The Colored Inventor* (1913) and Robert C. Hayden's *Eight Black American Inventors* (1972, pp. 18–29), with photographs (pp. 16, 24) and drawings of his safety helmet (p. 20) and of his traffic signals (pp. 26, 27). — ROBERT C. HAYDEN

MORRIS, EDWARD H. (1858–1943), lawyer and fraternal leader. He was born on May 30, 1858, in Flemingsburg, Ky., the son of Hezekiah and Elizabeth (Hopkins) Morris. His family moved to Cincinnati and then to Chicago before Morris was three years old. He was educated in St. Anne's and St. Patrick's College

(1864–1874), and read law in the office of Edward A. Fisher, a white Chicago attorney. He was admitted to the Illinois bar in 1879. In 1896 Morris and Jessica D. Montgomery, a legal secretary for the city of Chicago, were married. They had no children.

He early gained a substantial reputation as a brilliant lawyer. While serving as an attorney for Cook County in charge of taxes, Morris sustained the right of the county to tax insurance companies, and before the Illinois Supreme Court he was successful in causing the first Civil Rights Law of Illinois in the case of *Baylies v. Curry* in 1889 to be upheld. It was said that he never lost a case before the Supreme Court of Illinois or the United States. He served two terms as a member of the Illinois General Assembly (1890–1892 and 1902–1904). He introduced a bill for schoolteachers' pensions, and a bill to legalize slave marriages for the purpose of rights of inheritance, both of which were enacted.

In private practice after 1904 Morris served as consulting attorney for railroad and corporate interests, and used his office to give talented and able young Negro lawyers experience in corporate law. One of his protégés, Edward E. Wilson, served for over thirty years as chief attorney in the office of the Cook County state attorney in the preparation of briefs to be used before the Appellate Court. Morris's legal briefs were such models of thoroughness that they were given to the Howard University Law School. Following the Chicago Race Riot of 1919, he was appointed by Gov. Frank O. Lowden to the Chicago Commission on Race Relations. The report of the commission, *The Negro in Chicago,* is a classic study of urban problems and race relations. Morris also served in 1920–1921 as a member of the Illinois Constitutional Convention. He was named receiver for the State of Illinois in 1930 when the Jesse Binga State Bank became bankrupt.

Morris joined the United Grand Order of Odd Fellows in 1882, and became the deputy grand master in 1884. He served as grand master from 1888 to 1903, and was again elected grand master in 1910 and served in that post until his death in Washington, D.C., on Feb. 3, 1943. Under his leadership the lodge, which was founded in 1843, became one of the strongest fraternal orders in the country. He had traveled to Australia and to Great Britain as an Odd Fellows representative.

Although retired from active practice six years prior to his death, he retained the title of senior partner in the law firm of Morris and (James E.) Cashin. He died of a heart attack in the home of Henry P. Slaughter, editor of the *Odd Fellows Journal,* in Washington, D.C. Funeral services were held in Chicago and he was interred in Oakwoods Cemetery, Chicago. He had one heir, Denise Denison Morris, an adopted daughter.

See the obituaries in the *Chicago Defender,* city and national editions (Feb. 6, 1943); the reminiscences of Dorothy B. Porter added information about his death.

— DORIS E. SAUNDERS

MORRIS, ROBERT, SR. (1823–1882), lawyer civil rights leader. He was born free on June 8, 1823, the son of York Morris, a prosperous waiter in Salem, Mass. York's father had come from Africa to Massachusetts as a very young man. Robert received some formal education at Master Dodge's School in Salem. When about thirteen years old, while working as a table boy, Robert met Ellis Gray Loring, a well-known Boston abolitionist and lawyer, and his wife. Loring persuaded the Morris family to allow Robert to go to Boston, live at the Lorings, and work in their home. From servant in the Loring family, Morris became a clerk and a student in Loring's law offices. As early as 1844 Morris began the serious study of law under the tutelage of Loring. A very persevering student, Morris, with the aid of Loring, was admitted to the Suffolk bar on Feb. 2, 1847, thus becoming one of the first Negro lawyers in the United States.

Boston in the mid-nineteenth century was one of the centers of liberalism and abolitionism. However, the city of Boston had a segregated primary school for Negro children. Morris and other Negro leaders fought this practice by boycott and Morris helped represent colored parents in the unsuccessful suit in 1849 against this system, *Roberts v. the City of Boston* (5 Cush. 198, 59 Mass. 158, 1849). Attorneys for the plaintiffs argued that a unified school system would alleviate the great distances Negro children were forced to travel, and that the dual system was contrary to the state constitution, and detrimental to both races. The main lawyer was Charles Sumner, soon to be U.S. senator. Morris moved out of Boston to Chelsea to protest this type of segregation. He won wide support and recognition for his efforts against other forms of segregation in Boston and Massachusetts, including streetcars, eating facilities, and other public places.

Morris became best known for his activities against slavery. He worked with William Lloyd Garrison, Ellis Loring, Wendell Phillips, and other abolitionists in Boston. He was a member of the integrated Vigilance Committee, a group of abolitionists against the enforcement of the Fugitive Slave Act of 1850. He opposed efforts by Boston Negroes to set up a separate Vigilance Committee. Morris was also one of the conductors on the Underground Railroad, helping to spirit runaways to Canada. His opposition to the Fugitive Slave Act led him to aid in the rescue in 1851 of Shadrach, a runaway slave recaptured in Boston. For his part in the release of Shadrach, Morris was tried and acquitted, for lack of evidence. His brave acts increased his popularity, and his carefully prepared defense and cross examinations increased his law practice.

By the early 1850s he had become a justice of the peace, and had been admitted to practice before U.S. district courts. He sometimes served as judge of a magistrate court in Boston and in Chelsea. Although this was not a high judicial office, it appears to have afforded Morris the distinction of being the first American Negro to have exercised some judicial power.

As the Civil War approached Morris and Charles Lenox Remond urged, unsuccessfully, the creation in 1852 in Massachusetts of a Negro military unit with Negro officers. Morris was one of the speakers in 1855 at a celebration when the segregation in the schools of Boston were declared unconstitutional. In 1858, after the Dred Scott decision, he asserted that the doctrine of states rights did not require Massachusetts to enforce it. During the Civil War, Morris hailed Lincoln's call for volunteers, but he was opposed to the enlistment of Negroes in the army unless they received equal treatment and the right to have Negro officers. As he had before the war, he also opposed vehemently any plan to colonize the free Negro population.

Morris was described as being of unmixed Negro descent, small in size, and impeccably dressed. He married Catherine Mason; she bore him a son, Robert Jr., who was admitted to the bar in September 1874. Robert Jr. had studied in Europe and at the Harvard Law School.

By the time of the death of Robert Sr. on Dec. 12, 1882, he had built up a practice of over $3000 annually among both the Negroes and the Irish of Boston. He was one of the most famous Negro attorneys in the United States. When Morris died, George Lewis Ruffin, the first Negro graduate of the Harvard Law School, and Edward Garrison Walker, the son of David Walker, praised him as one of the Negro pioneers in the abolition movement and in the legal profession.

He died after a protracted illness at his home on West Newton Street, Boston. Funeral services were held on Dec. 15 at the Church of the Immaculate Conception, Harrison Avenue, Boston. Among the pallbearers were Ruffin, Lewis Hayden, and George T. Downing. Buried in Holywood Cemetery, Brookline, he was survived by his widow and his son.

There are general biographical details in Pauline E. Hopkins's "Robert Morris" (*Colored American Magazine,* Sept. 1901) and in Charles Sumner Brown's "The Genesis of the Negro Lawyer in New England, Part I" (*NHB,* April 1959). Additional information is in Benjamin Quarles's *Black Abolitionists* (1969). Obituaries appeared in the *Boston Evening Transcript* and the *Boston Daily Advertiser* (Dec. 13, 1882) and the *Boston Evening Journal* (Dec. 13 and 15, 1882). The major source is *The Liberator.* — CLARENCE G. CONTEE, SR.

MORTON, "JELLY ROLL" [FERDINAND JOSEPH LA MENTHE] (1885–1941), composer and pianist. He was born in Gulfport, Miss., the son of E. P. ("Ed") La Menthe. His early life there, in Biloxi, Meridian, and New Orleans, left an indelible mark on his career. In 1902 he began composing, wandered to Tulsa, Chicago, and Mobile (1904–1905), and later to other cities, as a pianist, "professor," pool shark, gambler, vaudeville comedian, and composer. In 1927 he met Mabel Bertrand of New Orleans. She later married him, exercised a wholesome influence on his stormy life, and remained his wife, living in Harlem until his death in Los Angeles on July 10, 1941. A requiem high mass was said at St. Patrick's Church. Several of his fellow musicians accompanied his remains to Calvary Cemetery. He was survived by his widow and two sisters.

His father, a handsome light-brown-skinned "very wild" Creole carpenter and owner of properties, who soon deserted his wife, launched his son on a musical career. A trombone player himself, he took young Ferdinand (he was not known as "Jelly Roll" until later) to the French Opera House in New Orleans.

His musicianship and his bohemian lifestyle were products of his age: the casual but kindly guidance of relatives, and the peculiarities of race relations in the South. After his father disappeared, his mother married Willie Morton, of whom little is known. His mother died when he was fourteen, and he was raised largely by his godmother, Eulalie Echo, and his Aunt Lallie. Eulalie Echo proudly took him to saloons and to jail when she was confined. There he heard the inmates singing, his "first inspiration" (after his father's trombone playing?). His first instrument, made of two chair legs and a tin pan, "sounded like a symphony to him."

At age five he played the harmonica. At age six he tried the jew's-harp, and later the guitar, violin, drums, trombone, and finally piano. He studied guitar with a Spaniard. At age seven he was already an accomplished guitarist, and had been playing in street bands. His family respected the musicians at the opera, but any other musician was considered a tramp. He began to play the piano after hearing a concert at the opera house. His aunt sent him to St. John's University, and later he studied with a colored teacher, a Professor Nickerson.

Another influence that became a thread throughout his life was voodoo as practiced by his Aunt Lallie. She kept glasses of water around the house and "voices came out of them." At night chains rattled and sewing machines ran. Jelly Roll kept holy water all around his bed.

After the death of his mother when he was fourteen, he earned three dollars a week in a cooperage. By that time he had developed a reputation as a pianist among his young friends, and they helped him become a "professor" in a house in the tenderloin, which was a legal district at that time, with streets filled with men, policemen everywhere, women of all kinds and levels standing in doorways, music in every house, any kind of drug easily available; there he made twenty dollars in tips the first night.

His aunt soon recognized the source of his new flashy clothes and told him to move out of her house, because she would not permit him to corrupt his young sisters who had been placed in her care. Jelly Roll, heartbroken, traced his ambition to build his own life, to meet the world by himself with his talent, from that moment of rejection by his aunt. He walked the streets till morning and took the train to Biloxi where his godmother had a summer place. He played in small clubs there and in Meridian, Miss. Returning ill to Biloxi he played piano in a white sporting house until, threatened with lynching by the townsmen, he returned to New Orleans.

In 1902 Jelly Roll met Tony Jackson, who also had a great influence upon the seventeen-year-old pianist. "There was no tune that come up from any opera or any of any kind or anything that was wrote on paper that Tony couldn't play." Tony was a master of all styles. He could sing opera like an operatic star, or could play blues or stomps on the piano, or do a fast-paced dance to accompany a nude girl in a swank honky-tonk. All the great New Orleans pianists assembled after 4:00 A.M. at The Frenchman's, in the back room after all the nightspots were closed, there to play until midafternoon the next day. Here jazz was born, Jelly Roll said, and here he began to analyze the differences between ragtime, blues, and jazz. He claimed that he invented the word *jazz.* Here too, at age seventeen, Jelly Roll wrote "New

Orleans Blues," followed by "King Porter Stomp," "Alabama Bound," and other songs.

Shortly thereafter (c. 1904) Jelly Roll was in Tulsa and in Chicago. In 1905 he was in Mobile. He traveled extensively in the following years as pianist, "professor," pool shark, gambler, as vaudeville comedian. In 1911 he was in New York, playing "Jelly Roll Blues." He began writing orchestral arrangements of his works in 1912. "Jelly Roll Blues" was published for orchestra in Chicago in 1915, "making it one of the first if not the first jazz orchestration ever published" (Schuller, p. 317). Melrose published more than a dozen Morton orchestrations in the 1920s.

Jelly Roll traveled with Benbow's show to Louisville, Winston-Salem, Richmond, Chicago, Washington, Baltimore, Kansas City, St. Louis, Jacksonville, and many other cities. While he was in New York in 1911, James P. Johnson described him as wearing a diamond set in his front tooth and having two girls with him. Johnson said: "Jelly Roll wasn't a piano player like some of us down here. We bordered more on the classical theory of music."

In Chicago in 1917 Jelly Roll was offered a job in Los Angeles. While there he got in touch with a girlfriend from New Orleans, Anita Gonzales, who had a saloon in Las Vegas. She soon moved to Los Angeles and bought a small hotel. Jelly Roll, who had several small businesses, a dance hall and others, moved to Watts County so they could stay open all night. He sent to New Orleans for a "real band," and they arrived dressed in boxback coats and skin-tight trousers. They were very successful playing New Orleans music, but did not stay long because Jelly Roll would not let them cook their own food on the job as they did in the "low-down honky-tonks on Perdido Street." They packed up and went back to New Orleans. Jelly Roll made money in the business, which has been described as made up of musicians, "entertainers," and "waitresses." Jelly Roll used to show his friends his trunk full of money. He wore diamond-studded garters.

Always, however, Jelly Roll played piano and traveled up and down the coast with bands under his leadership. Anita always traveled with him. He was so jealous of her that she had no friends, and although he wanted to sing with the band and was a good singer, he refused to let her sing. In 1922 he left Los Angeles and returned to Chicago.

In 1927 he first met Mabel Bertrand, in the Plantation Club in Chicago. An "octoroon" dancer who had been an entertainer with wide experience in Europe and in the United States, she had been raised in a convent in New Orleans after her parents, Dr. Bertrand and her Shawnee mother, died. Jelly Roll tried various tricks to win her, and finally married her. In 1929 and 1930 she traveled with him in his big Lincoln. For the men he had a bus with a sign: "Jelly Roll Morton and His Red Hot Peppers."

Jelly Roll's real drive was music. The other activities were an expression of his rich personality: a pool shark, fast with his hands; a gambler, a showman and a fancy dresser (on the job the musicians wore tuxedos, but Jelly Roll frequently wore a wine-colored jacket, white trousers, white shoes, diamond-studded tie, and dia-

monds on his socks). Mabel put it succinctly: "I have been loved by a great man, I have watched a genius at work in the cold lonely hours." He worked incessantly. In the middle of the night he got up to jot down ideas, and when he gave the "dots" to the musicians, he insisted that they play exactly what he wrote. He told them in rehearsal what the sequence of solos was to be, and they played their improvisations exactly as he had directed. For that reason Gunther Schuller devotes a chapter of his *Early Jazz* to "Jelly Roll Morton, the First Great Composer."

Perhaps no early jazz musician has been so completely recorded on discs, to say nothing of piano rolls. He said that his first record was cut in 1918. His complete discography covers twenty-two pages, and ranges from 1922 to 1930, with nearly a dozen companies, the most frequent being Victor. The climax came in 1938 with the invitation by Alan Lomax to record the history of jazz for the Library of Congress. They are a historical document revealing the piano virtuosity of the unique personality that was Jelly Roll Morton.

The story of his death is typical of his life, and it might have happened many times before when, as a pool shark, gambler, or flashy hotel owner, he had defied desperate gamblers and won. One night in 1939 in the Jungle Inn in Washington, D.C., Jelly Roll told some rowdies to shut up and slapped one of them. As he turned back to the piano the fellow knifed him in the head and then above the heart. Jelly Roll never fully recovered.

In the last two years of his life Jelly Roll found a new role as an important historical figure. French writers discovered him, his recordings in the Library of Congress (1938) were reissued, and his early records became collector's items. Victor recorded some of his early works and tunes from the Library of Congress sessions. He recorded with a band of the best New Orleans men available. But his strength was waning and he had difficulty breathing.

He died on July 10, 1941, in Los Angeles, in the arms of Anita Gonzales. She said that he had to die because his Aunt Lallie, the voodoo witch, had died, and because she had "sold his soul to Satan" when he was a boy.

Morton was the first great composer of jazz, in contradistinction to rags and blues, whose style as composer equaled his unique style as pianist, band leader, and recording artist. He insisted that "if music was going to be 'loud and blatant' and if it was going to lack contrast and variety," it was "simply bad music and poor jazz no matter how advanced in style" (Gunther Schuller, *Early Jazz* [1968], p. 143). Moreover, "Jelly Roll was an intellectual and a wit as well as a fine (perhaps our first good) composer" (Alan Lomax, *Mister Jelly Roll . . .* [1973], p. x).

Alan Lomax's *Mister Jelly Roll: The Fortunes of Jelly Roll Morton, New Orleans Creole and Inventor of Jazz* (1973), a sensitive and informed biography, has a valuable discography and appendix. Gunther Schuller's *Early Jazz* (1968) is the best scholarly analysis of Jelly Roll's music. See also his obituary in the *Chicago Defender* (national ed., July 26, 1941, p. 20).

— RAYMOND LEMIEUX

MOSSELL, GERTRUDE E. H. BUSTILL (1855–1948), teacher, journalist, and author. She was born on July 3, 1855, in Philadelphia, the daughter of Charles H. and Emily (Robinson) Bustill of Philadelphia, originally members of the Society of Friends who later joined the Old School Presbyterian Church. Gertrude was educated in the public elementary schools of Philadelphia, the Institute for Colored Youth, and the Robert Vaux Consolidated Grammar School. Her writing ability was developed with care during her years at Vaux Grammar School; as a graduating student she delivered the class oration, "Influence," which brought her to the attention of Bishop Henry McNeal Turner, editor of the *Christian Recorder.* He secured the essay for publication in the magazine and invited the young writer to contribute future articles; several articles appeared in the *Recorder* and the *Standard Echo.* For seven years she taught in the public schools of Camden, N.J., Philadelphia, and Frankfort, Ky. From 1880 to 1887 she wrote for the *Philadelphia Press, Times,* and *Inquirer.*

She married Nathaniel F. Mossell of Lockport, N.Y., in 1893. A leading physician in Philadelphia, Mossell was the founder of the Frederick Douglass Memorial Hospital and Training School in Philadelphia. Marriage and the birth of two children curtailed her dual careers as teacher and journalist for a time.

Meanwhile, in 1891 she was on the staff of the *Indianapolis Freeman, Richmond Rankin Institute,* and *Our Women and Children.* Two articles of particular interest to the reading public of the 1890s were "Power of the Press" (n.d.) and "Women in Journalism" (n.d.). Throughout Mossell's career she urged the expansion in Negro newspapers of all news pertinent to Negroes. These papers had a special mission, she stated, which called for diligence and constant struggle to excel in news reporting. In a letter to the editor of the *New York Age,* Mossell also suggested that the papers had not done all they could to become known or to use other means of distribution, such as sales by youth. She noted: "I have never yet seen a colored newspaper sold on the streets by a newsboy." She further suggested the use of other means than subscriptions, such as news dealers and agents.

Her writing career continued with syndicated columns and articles in leading Philadelphia newspapers—the *Philadelphia Echo,* the *Philadelphia Times,* the *Independent,* and the *Press Republican*—on issues of "race literature and women's questions." She also edited the Women's Department of the *New York Age,* the *Indianapolis World,* and the *New York Freeman,* assisted in editing the *Lincoln Alumni Magazine,* and contributed to the *A.M.E. Church Review* and other journals.

She was the author of two books: *Little Dansie's One Day at Sabbath School* (1902) and *The Work of the Afro-American Women* (1894). *The Work* related the story of the rise of Afro-American women during the nineteenth century which she called the "Women's Century." It witnessed abolitionist and temperance movements, the emergence of coeducational institutions of higher learning, the struggle for suffrage and women's place in the larger world of men in journalism, literature, medicine and science, business, scientific inventions, and education. The intelligence and diligence of Negro women made them a valuable asset in securing rights and privileges for colored people. While half the book presented Afro-American women in historical perspective, most of the other half presented poems written by women like Phyllis Wheatley, Sarah Forten, Frances Ellen Watkins Harper, and Josephine Heard. Negro institutions such as Livingstone College, Tuskegee Institute, and Howard University were briefly discussed.

Mossell engaged in numerous social welfare activities. After 1895 she was collector for the charity fund of the Frederick Douglass Hospital; she organized a fundraising project of $30,000 for the hospital building, and served as president of its Social Service Auxiliary. She published two postcards, Emancipation and Dear Old Philadelphia, founded the Bustill Family Association, and organized the Philadelphia branch of the National Afro-American Council.

Monroe A. Majors's *Noted Negro Women: Their Triumphs and Activities* (1971 reprint) is an important source. See also *The Black Press, 1827–1890: The Quest for National Identity* (1971), edited by Martin Dann. Mossell's *The Work of the Afro-American Women* (1894) reveals her civil rights activism and feminist leanings.

Mossell died on Jan. 21, 1948, at the Frederick Douglass Memorial Hospital at the age of ninety-two after an illness of some three months. Private funeral services were held at the Morris Funeral Home, 717 S. 19th St., Philadelphia, and she was buried in Eden Cemetery. She was survived by two daughters, four grandchildren, a niece, and two nephews, Paul Robeson and the Rev. Benjamin O. Robeson. Her obituary appeared in the *Philadelphia Tribune* (Jan. 24, 1948, pp. 1, 2).

— CLAUDETTE BROWN

MOSSELL, NATHAN FRANCIS (1856–1946), physician and hospital superintendent. He was born in Hamilton, Ontario, Canada, on July 27, 1856, of freeborn Negro parents, Aaron and Eliza Bowers Mossell, originally of Baltimore. His parents, like other free-born Negroes living in northern cities, faced great hardships. Early one morning they had packed their children and all their household belongings they could safely carry, and by horse, carriage, and cart, fled to Canada. Mrs. Mossell's sister was Louise Bustill, who married William Robeson. They had four sons, one of whom was Paul Robeson. Aaron Mossell was a successful brick manufacturer in Hamilton. In later years the title to some of the land which he had purchased for his business became involved in litigation, and upon settlement in 1865 he moved his family to Lockport, in northern New York. At this time there were five children, Charles, Mary, Nathan, Alvaretta, and Aaron Jr.

Nathan came to Philadelphia in 1873 and at the age of nineteen entered Lincoln University where he and his older brother Charles worked. He graduated in 1879 with a B.A. degree. When the American Colonization Society approached him at a time when he wanted to study medicine but had not the requisite money, he wrote: "The fact that the presence of the free colored people increased the slaves' restlessness and dissatisfaction, had more to do with the American Colonization Society's interest in the deportation of free colored people to Liberia, than any interest on the Society's part in Liberia *itself.* This accounts for the disfavor of the colored people as a whole for the American Colonization Society. I decline your offer of assistance." Instead he applied for admission to the Medical School of the University of Pennsylvania, which he entered in 1872 and from which he graduated with highest honors in June 1882. He was the first Negro graduate from any of its departments. His younger brother, Aaron Jr., in 1888 was the first colored graduate of the Law School of the University of Pennsylvania. Sadie Tanner Mossell (Mrs. Raymond Pace Alexander), the daughter of Aaron Mossell, Jr., was one of the first three Negro women to earn the Ph.D. degree (1921), the first colored woman graduate of the University of Pennsylvania Law School (1927), and the first colored woman lawyer in the state of Pennsylvania.

After his graduation, Mossell soon encountered trouble in many areas. He was refused membership in the Philadelphia County Medical Society. After a bitter fight and the support of the University of Pennsylvania professors of medicine, he was admitted. It was about this time (1885) that Mossell, desiring to increase his knowledge in special medical fields, studied abroad in two famous British hospitals, Guy's and St. Thomas, in London. Upon his return he learned that nearly thirty hospitals in the Philadelphia area continued to deny admission to Negroes for internships or nurses training. The various medical colleges in Philadelphia offered to help him establish a hospital if he agreed to open it on a segregated basis. This was refused by Negro leaders who sought instead to get the state legislature to appropriate funds for the opening of a hospital to be managed by Negro doctors for patients of all races and colors. After this failed, through his own meager funds and monies raised by public appeals, church donations, and through the efforts of Negro women, led by his hardworking wife, a three-story building at 1512 Lombard St. was purchased and on Oct. 31, 1895, the Frederick Douglass Memorial Hospital and Training School for Nurses was born. Of the funds necessary to purchase the property, equip it with beds and linens, and manage it for the first year, 86 percent was contributed by Negroes and 14 percent by white friends. The state also appropriated $6000 annually. In 1908 a building four times the size of the first building was purchased and completely outfitted as a modern hospital with a 100-bed capacity.

Mossell's superintendency of Douglass Hospital was not a "bed of roses." He attracted a proficient staff of Negro physicians, and many white specialists came to Douglass to aid in their training. There was, however, constant friction between Mercy Hospital, founded by Henry McKee Minton and others in 1907, and Douglass; and litigation sought to oust Mossell. Realizing that one hospital would better serve the growing Negro population of Philadelphia, he agreed to the proposed merger of Mercy-Douglass Hospital in 1948. In 1954 the modern building of this merged institution at 50th and Woodland Avenue was one of the more imposing in Philadelphia.

Mossell was an uncompromising champion of human rights and equal justice for the Negro citizens of Philadelphia. He journeyed to Niagara Falls with W. E. B. Du Bois in 1905 as one of the organizers of the Niagara Movement, a forerunner of the NAACP. He was among the first to demand Negro professors at his alma mater, Lincoln University. He was the organizer of one of the first protests against the showing of *The Clansmen* and *The Birth of a Nation,* and led hundreds of Negro marchers down Broad Street in protest. He organized the annual pilgrimage to the burial place of the Pennsylvania abolitionist Thaddeus Stevens. He retired in 1944 from the practice of medicine at age eighty-eight but despite his age he began a drive to open the doors of Girard College to Negro boys. (After many years of litigation, it was finally opened.)

Mossell died on Oct. 27, 1946, of natural causes after an illness of two months, at his home, 1432 Lombard St., Philadelphia. Funeral services were held on Oct. 31 at the Tindley A.M.E. Church, Broad and Fitzwater Streets, with interment in Eden Cemetery. He was survived by his widow, two daughters (Mazie Griffin and Florence Holmes of Philadelphia), and a brother (Aaron Mossell of England).

W. Montague Cobb's "Nathan Francis Mossell, M.D., 1856–1946" (*JNMA,* March 1954), is the indispensable source. One of Mossell's granddaughters, Gertrude Cunningham, a retired Philadelphia public schoolteacher, made available from her private collection letters, pamphlets, and memorabilia. Obituaries appeared in the *Philadelphia Inquirer* (Oct. 28, 1946, p. 3), the *Philadelphia Evening Bulletin* (Oct. 28, 1946, p. 16B), and the *Pittsburgh Courier* (Nov. 2, 1949, p. 5).

— RAYMOND PACE ALEXANDER

MOTEN, LUCY ELLEN (1851–1933), educator. Born to Benjamin and Julia Moten in Fauquier County, Va., near White Sulphur Springs, she attended the preparatory and normal departments of Howard University (1868–1870) and graduated from the Salem (Mass.) State Normal School in 1876. She was appointed in 1870 a teacher in the District of Columbia public schools and was assigned to the O Street School. In 1883 she was appointed principal of the Miner Normal School, 17th and Church Streets NW, Washington, D.C., and remained in this position until her retirement in 1920. During this period she also enrolled in the Howard University College of Medicine and received the M.D. degree in 1897, but never practiced medicine so far as can be established. She was fatally injured in a New York traffic accident and died on Aug. 24, 1933.

Moten's principal contribution lay in her thirty-seven years of service as head of the Miner Normal School (Miner Teachers College after 1933), which supplied teachers for the Negro division of the District of Columbia public schools. Assistant Superintendent Garnet C. Wilkinson remarked at a Founders Day exercise honoring Lucy Moten in 1934 that "the entire elementary school personnel of the colored public schools . . . with but few exceptions, in the period 1883–1920 received their . . . training . . . under . . . Dr. Moten."

Moten's chief influence on her pupils lay in the development of culture and character, qualities which she viewed as ranking equal in importance with technical competence. Various personal reminiscences emphasize this point. One former student recalled that she presented "a rare combination of culture, refinement, good taste, and intelligence. . . . There was elegance; there was dignity; there was savoir-faire." A colleague in the normal school recalled the daily assemblies during which Moten gave talks on character and occasionally brought public attention to any young lady whose attire was not considered proper.

The annual reports Moten prepared for the District of Columbia school board also reflect this emphasis upon character. In the 1893–1894 report she argued for standards of admission which would include "morals and manners as exhibited in regularity, punctuality, personal talk, purity of thought . . . genuine self respect" (p. 186). In the report for 1910–1911 she indicated that the primary aim of the normal school should be to train "strong moral character" (p. 264).

Another characteristic aspect of Moten's views on teacher education was the importance of health and physiology. She interpreted this as applying both to the teacher's fund of professional knowledge and to her own physical well-being. She stated that "without acquaintance with the physiological and hygienic laws, no teacher is prepared to enter upon her work." At the same time she urged greater selectivity in admitting students to the school so as to guarantee that each student possessed the "physical as well as moral qualifications." She began giving lectures on hygiene, physiology, and anatomy to the prospective teachers as early as 1894, and by 1902 she had brought in an additional physician to lecture on the diseases of children, disinfectants, personal hygiene, and emergency treatment. In 1903 regular visits by an outside doctor were begun for the purpose of checking on the health status of the students.

Aside from her service to the Miner Normal School, Lucy Moten is remembered for a bequest of approximately $50,000 to Howard University. The income from this fund has been used to provide opportunities for travel abroad by Howard University students. (She had become convinced of the educational value of travel through her own frequent summer trips to Europe.)

Principal published materials respecting Lucy Moten include a biographical sketch by Thomasine Carrothers, "Lucy Ellen Moten, 1851–1933" (*JNH* 19 [Jan. 1934]: 102–6). A shorter sketch is included by G. Smith Wormley in a series of short biographies, "Educators of the First Half Century of Public Schools of the District of Columbia" (*JNH* 17 [Jan. 1932]: 124–40). The typescript of a biography by Gladys T. Peterson is in the library of the University of the District of Columbia. This library also has a small collection of papers relating to Lucy Moten. There are references to Lucy Moten in various studies of education in the District of Columbia, Howard University, and the Miner Teachers College. The most extensive is Henrietta R. Hatter's "History of Miner Teachers College" (master's thesis, Howard University, 1939). None of these biographical materials is critical or analytical. Apparently no substantial body of Moten papers survives. The main source of primary material is the series of annual reports on Miner Teachers College written by Lucy Moten and published in the annual reports of the Board of Trustees of the District of Columbia public schools. — EARLE H. WEST

MOTON, ROBERT RUSSA (1867–1940), educator. Born on Aug. 26, 1867, to Booker and Emily (Brown) Moton in Amelia County, Va., he soon moved with his family to Prince Edward County where they worked on the plantation of Samuel Vaughn near Farmville, and Robert was taught by Vaughn's youngest daughter. He engaged in hunting and fishing with both white and Negro playmates. Robert left home in 1880 to work at a lumber camp in Surry County, Va. Having a strong desire for an education, he enrolled in Hampton Institute in 1885. After completing the junior year, he began teaching in Cottontown, Cumberland County, Va. During this year he also read law in the office of the superintendent of schools in Farmville, and received a license to practice law. He returned to Hampton in 1889, completed the senior year, and became assistant commandant in charge of the male student cadet corps. In 1891 he was appointed commandant, with the title of "major," a position he held for twenty-five years. He retained the title throughout his life.

During his tenure at Hampton Institute Moton came to be recognized as a leader in a wide range of activities associated with racial advancement. In 1900 he was elected president of the National Negro Business League and was reelected for more than twenty years. In 1908 he was made a trustee of the Jeanes Fund and secretary of the board. The same year he made the first of several tours through the southern states as an associate of Booker T. Washington. The 1908 tour carried them through Mississippi, in 1909 through Tennessee and South Carolina, and North Carolina in 1910. Their last tour was through Louisiana in 1915. On these trips Moton usually led the audience in singing "Negro melodies," and Washington would speak. The two men cooperated closely to promote the Hampton-Tuskegee idea of vocational education and biracial cooperation as the best means of advancement. They also participated in joint fundraising meetings in the northern states.

Upon the death of Washington in 1915 Moton was appointed principal of Tuskegee Institute and held this position until his retirement in 1935. In this position it was natural that he would be viewed not merely as Washington's successor at Tuskegee, but as his successor in other aspects of racial leadership. These included his role as advisor to the federal government on racial policies and in the appointment of Negroes to federal positions, advisor to philanthropists in the distribution of educational funds, and guiding spirit in a variety of organizations devoted to racial advancement.

According to Alvin J. Neely, Moton supported the establishment of the Colored Officers Training Camp at Fort Des Moines, Iowa (1917), and secured the appointment of Emmett J. Scott who had been secretary to Booker T. Washington, as special assistant to the secretary of war. Claude A. Barnett emphasized Moton's role as advisor on federal appointees to Presidents Wilson, Harding, Coolidge, Hoover, and Franklin D. Roosevelt. In 1918 Moton toured France and the war zone to investigate the treatment of Negro troops. Throughout the war years he also toured the United States and spoke on War Savings Stamps and for Liberty Loan drives.

Following the war Moton exercised a leadership role that resulted in the building of a veterans hospital for Negroes in 1923 on land donated by Tuskegee Institute, and in the adoption of a policy giving opportunity for Negroes to staff the hospital. He participated in the formation of the Commission on Interracial Cooperation (1918), and secured a gift from George Eastman to aid in underwriting the commission. In 1927 Moton served as a member of the Hoover Commission on the Mississippi Valley Flood Disaster. In 1930 he went to Haiti as chairman of the U.S. Commission on Education in Haiti.

During his tenure as principal at Tuskegee, Moton was responsible for several developments. The endowment of the school increased from $2,312,149 at the beginning of his tenure to $7,772,106 at his retirement. Most of the increase was accomplished during a combined campaign for Hampton and Tuskegee in 1926. Shortly after taking office at Tuskegee, Moton arranged for an extensive independent study of the curriculum at the school. One further result of his efforts was the upgrading of the program of study. The first announcement of college-level work appeared in the catalogue for 1925–1926, with a B.S. degree being offered in both agriculture and education.

On June 7, 1905, Moton married Elizabeth Hunt Harris of Williamsburg, Va. She died childless in 1906. In 1908 he married Jennie Dee Booth, a graduate of Hampton Institute and a teacher in the Whittier Training Institute at Hampton. To them were born three girls (Catherine, Charlotte, and Jennie), and two boys (Robert and Allen). Moton received honorary degrees from Oberlin College, Williams College, Harvard University, Virginia Union University, Wilberforce University, and Howard University. In 1930 he received the Harmon Award for contributions to better race relations, and the NAACP Spingarn Medal in 1932 for distinguished service. Moton was a Baptist, and an Independent Republican. He died on May 31, 1940, at his home, Holly Knoll, Capahosic, Va., and was buried at Hampton Institute.

An assessment of Moton's influence and contributions requires that he be viewed primarily in relationship to Booker T. Washington. Prior to Washington's death Moton was a loyal supporter, joint fundraiser, companion on tours, and a defender who could be counted on to say the right thing in a speech or to place an appropriate article or letter in a newspaper or magazine according to the strategic needs of the moment. After 1915 Moton occupied Washington's position at Tuskegee and in national racial leadership. He was able to leave as his own contribution an improved administrative structure, greater responsiveness in the Tuskegee vocational curriculum to the changing requirements of business and industry, elevation of academic standards, and above all, greatly increased and more stable financial support for the institution.

Both before and after 1915 Moton's educational ideas as well as his views on racial progress were essentially Washington's. He preached the same doctrine of optimism and hope, of hard work, self-improvement, and patience. He may have been somewhat more forthright and direct than Washington in expressing the anger and frustration of Negroes at racial injustice (especially in *What the Negro Thinks,* 1931), but even these expressions were made in the same predominantly white or interracial forums that had been available to Washington.

Like Booker T. Washington, Moton is a controversial figure. W. E. B. Du Bois asserted that Moton was able through powerful white influence to obtain hotel accommodations in the North by refraining from use of public dining rooms and lobbies (*The Crisis,* April 1934, p. 115). He had been accused of urging Negro troops in France during World War I to refrain from protest against the indignities heaped upon them, especially by American officers and soldiers. Perhaps the best example of Moton's views is expressed in his parting words to a group of Negro soldiers. He urged them to "go back to America as heroes, as you really are"; to continue to conduct themselves "in a straightforward, manly, and modest way." Upon returning, they should find a job as soon as possible, acquire land and a home, marry and settle down. He hoped they would do nothing in peace that would spoil their magnificent record in war. He told a group of white officers and soldiers that it was their duty and sacred obligation to see that Negroes who had demonstrated their loyalty should have "a fair and absolutely equal chance with every other American citizen, along every line." Du Bois reported that one Negro who had heard Major Moton accused him of telling jokes by a colored preacher and of not seeking information about their grievances. Du Bois added that Moton did not attend the First Pan African Congress in Paris in February 1919.

On the other hand Du Bois warmly congratulated Moton for refusing in 1923–1924, despite pressure and intimidation by the Ku Klux Klan, to staff the newly established Veterans Hospital on the campus of Tuskegee Institute with white doctors, white nurses, and colored nursemaids. "He [Moton] and the Negro world demanded that the government hospital at Tuskegee be under Negro control. Today, at last, it is" (*The Crisis,* Sept. 1924).

As chairman of the commission appointed by President Hoover to study educational conditions in Haiti, Moton submitted a sound, critical report. It recommended the restoration of a unified educational program under the direction of the minister of public instruction in place of the dual system which provided for a grossly underpaid liberal arts program under the Haitian government and generously supported vocational schools under American control. The normal school for girls should be enlarged; teachers should be paid on the basis of merit and their salaries should enable them to devote full time to their duties. The budget for education should be increased. That the recommendations bore little fruit was due to the limited resources of Haiti and some continued American control. Moton considered the refusal of the U.S. government to provide transportation to and from Haiti on U.S. Navy ships a "humiliation" to Haiti and the colored people of the United States.

There is no adequate biography of Moton. Brief laudatory sketches are in Mary White Ovington's *Portraits in Color* (1927, pp. 64–77) and Ralph W. Bullock's *In Spite of Handicaps,* (1927, pp. 15–21). Albert L. Turner's brief sketch in *DAB, Supplement 2* (1958, pp. 476–77) has little interpretation except for Moton as a "disciple of [Booker T.] Washington." *Robert Russa Moton of Hampton and Tuskegee* (1956), edited by William Hardin Hughes and Frederick D. Patterson (the latter Moton's son-in-law and successor at Tuskegee), consists of chapters by authors who emphasized specific aspects of Moton's life based primarily on personal recollections. The book must be regarded as more of an appreciation or memorial to Moton than as a scholarly, historical treatment. Moton's autobiography, *Finding a Way Out* (1920), is valuable for his own interpretation of his investigations of the army and its services.

Materials on Moton's tenure at Hampton are in the Hampton Archives, Collis P. Huntington Memorial Library, Hampton Institute; on his Tuskegee tenure, in the Robert Russa Moton Papers (1916–1935) in the Hollis Burke Frissell Library, Tuskegee Institute. Smaller collections of materials are located as follows: National Negro Business League materials in the Albon L. Holsey Correspondence (1904–1947), Hollis Burke Frissell Library, Tuskegee Institute; correspondence relating to the southern tours and other matters in the Booker T. Washington Papers (1882–1942), Library of Congress; Records Collection, Southern Regional Office, National Urban League (1912–1946), Library of Congress; the John Hope Papers (1868–1936), in the Trevor Arnett Library, Atlanta University; Papers of the Negro Rural School Fund, in the Anna T. Jeanes Foundation Collection, Harvey S. Firestone Library, Princeton University.

— EARLE H. WEST

MURPHY, CARL (1889–1967), journalist, publisher, civil rights leader, and educator. He was born in Baltimore, Md., on Jan. 17, 1889, the son of John Henry Murphy, Sr., and Martha (Howard) Murphy. His father, born a slave, served in the 30th Regiment, U.S. Colored Maryland Volunteers, during the Civil War. He saw action under Grant in the Wilderness Campaign and under Sherman in North Carolina. Impressed by the changes in his life that had made him a free man, John Murphy continued to believe in the possibilities for black advancement despite the formidable obstacles to that goal in late-nineteenth-century American society. He founded the *Baltimore Afro-American* in 1892 and continued to publish it until his death in 1922. His insistence on education as a vital attainment for blacks in their struggle for equality encouraged his son Carl to go on from his Howard University graduation in 1911 to earn an M.S. at Harvard in 1913 and continue his studies at the University of Jena in Germany the following summer.

Carl Murphy enjoyed his return to scholarly life at Howard, serving as professor of German and chairman of the department from 1913 to 1918. Those years marked the great migration of blacks to northern cities;

Baltimore, which had had a stable black population, experienced a 27 percent growth in the 1910–1920 decade and comparable increases in succeeding decades. Negro publishers in the North such as Robert Abbott of the *Chicago Defender,* Robert L. Vann of the *Pittsburgh Courier,* and John Murphy of the *Baltimore Afro-American* were able to expand greatly their modest operations in behalf of a rapidly increasing, hard-pressed colored community. Impelled by the urgings of his father and by his own sense of new opportunity, Murphy reluctantly left college teaching and joined his father on the staff of the *Afro-American* in 1918. After his father's death in 1922 he served as editor until his own retirement in 1961. His astute direction made the *Afro-American* one of the largest Negro newspapers in the nation, published twice weekly in Baltimore and Washington, D.C., and weekly in Philadelphia, Richmond, and Newark. He served as president of the National Newspaper Publishers Association in 1954–1955 and was a member of the Board of Directors of the NNPA and its news service.

The growing circulation of the *Afro-American* provided a fine forum for Murphy's consistent advocacy of Negro equality in the years after World War I. He helped develop the NAACP into an effective arm of this struggle. After 1930 the NAACP, primarily under Charles Houston's and Thurgood Marshall's legal direction, maintained its painstaking and methodical campaign for the enlargement of the areas of equality through legal action. Murphy became a member of the Board of Directors in 1931, and in 1935 joined the coalition that built the Baltimore branch into one of the largest in the nation. He also became chairman of the legal redress and administration committee. Aided by his foresight and patience, Maryland became the focal point for many of the cases that the NAACP pursued to pathbreaking legal victories. One of the groundwork cases for the Supreme Court's public school desegregation decision of 1954 was the Donald Murray case of 1935, which opened the University of Maryland Law School to all citizens. This was followed by victories in the first teachers' equal pay case, the first segregated public recreation case, the first public employment case.

Murphy not only gave freely of his writing talent, using the *Afro-American* as a weapon to carry on the fight, but he also contributed funds generously. Thurgood Marshall, a mainstay of the NAACP Legal Department, stressed, "He supported this legal fight, lock, stock, and barrel. I can't think of a single case that I, along with the NAACP, argued in the Supreme Court [when he] wasn't there. . . . I can't remember any time when I asked Carl for money that I didn't get it. . . . When I needed money to get lawyers Carl was always there. That was when it wasn't so fashionable, in the 1930's and 1940's. There were some who believed and some who didn't; but Carl always believed."

The Supreme Court decision in 1954 outlawing public school segregation was a fitting capstone to these efforts. Murphy was honored by the National Urban League in that year, receiving its American Teamwork Award. The following year he was the fortieth recipient of the Spingarn Medal from the NAACP. By then a new generation of civil rights leaders was forging new tactics in the continuing struggle. Murphy supported Martin Luther King and the men of his generation even as he maintained the necessity for continuing the careful codification of legal rights.

Like his father, Carl Murphy believed in the transcendent importance of education for Negroes in their struggle for equality. Although he left teaching for journalism, he maintained his educational concerns, most notably with Morgan State College in Baltimore. He led the effort in 1939 to transfer control of the college from the Methodist Church to the state of Maryland. A charter member of the new board of trustees of Morgan State College, he became chairman in 1953, and for the rest of his life used this position to encourage expansion and modernization. The Fine Arts Auditorium building was named for him, and in 1963 the Carl Murphy Scholarship Fund was created to honor him by encouraging African students to attend Morgan State.

In his private life Murphy was a participant in fraternal and educational institutions, including Alpha Phi Alpha fraternity, and was a recipient of honorary degrees from Central State University in Wilberforce, Ohio, and from Lincoln University in Pennsylvania. At the center of his life was his family, where he impressed upon his six daughters the moral and religious values he had learned from his father. His first marriage to Vashti Turley of Washington, D.C., lasted for forty-two years until her death on March 17, 1960.

The scrappy, five-foot-two, 130-pound man took great pride in his athletic accomplishments, with particular delight in recalling his football playing as a bantamweight while at Howard. He also prided himself on his collection of rare books, his writing of poetry and books of prayers, and his gardening. After a long day at the *Afro* he would remark, "I'm going home to my garden, to my flowers, to restore my soul."

He died on Feb. 26, 1967. He was survived by his second wife, Lillian Parrot Murphy, and by his daughters: Dr. Elizabeth Murphy Moss, Ida Murphy Peters, Carlita Murphy Jones, Vashti Murphy Matthews, Frances Murphy Campbell, and Jeanne Murphy Davis.

The best source for Murphy is the *Baltimore Afro-American,* available on microfilm from April 1893 to date. That newspaper published a memorial-obituary issue on March 4, 1967. The bulk of Murphy's personal papers are still held by family, but fragments are in the Soper Library, Morgan State College, the Pratt Library in Baltimore, and the NAACP Collection at the Library of Congress. Additional information is contained in the commemorative booklet, "Fortieth Spingarn Medal, Awarded to Dr. Carl Murphy . . . June 24, 1955," and in the book of prayers written by Murphy and compiled by his daughter, Elizabeth Moss, on the first anniversary of his death, "In Memoriam, Carl Murphy, January 17, 1889–February 25, 1967." Interviews for this article were given by Charles H. Wesley, historian, educator, and longtime friend of Murphy, and by his daughter, Dr. Moss. — ANDREW BUNI

MURPHY, ISAAC [ISAAC BURNS] (1861?–1896), jockey. Murphy was born in Lexington, Ky., perhaps on Jan. 1, 1861, the date designated as the birthday of all thoroughbred horses. His mother's name was Burns, a daughter of Green Murphy. It was at her request that in the fall of 1876 Isaac took the name Murphy. Growing up in the heartland of Kentucky, he had ridden his first race in Louisville on May 22, 1875. His first winning mount was Glentina, at the Crab Orchard Park in Lexington on Sept. 15, 1876. His records were in most respects not topped. He won 44 percent of all the races in which he rode: 1412 mounts, 628 winners. He was the only jockey to have won the Derby, the Kentucky Oaks, and the Clark Stakes, all three at one meeting (1884), and the first rider to have back-to-back Derbies (1890 and 1891). His three Derby wins were unequaled for thirty-nine years (by Earl Sande in 1930) and not exceeded for fifty-seven years (Eddie Arcaro won his fourth Derby in 1948 and his fifth in 1952). Murphy was the first jockey to be voted into the Jockey Hall of Fame (1955) at the National Museum of Racing, Saratoga Springs, N.Y. He died of pneumonia on Feb. 12, 1896, in Lexington, leaving an estate of $30,000 to his only heir, his wife Lucy.

Although largely forgotten today, Negro jockeys were prominent until the early twentieth century. Many Negroes had worked on farms in Kentucky and throughout the South and gained a reputation for being particularly adept with horses. Many learned to ride when they were young enough to toddle in a stall. They grew up in the saddle, worked their horses in the mornings, rode the same mounts in the afternoons, and were willing to accept a nominal fee for their efforts. In the inaugural Derby on May 17, 1875, fourteen of the fifteen jockeys in the race were Negroes. The winner was Oliver Lewis, aboard Aristides.

Isaac Murphy was thus following in the footsteps of other Negro jockeys when he began his virtually unmatched career. He won three runnings of the Hindoo Stakes (1883, 1885, and 1886) the Latonia Derby in Kentucky, (May 23, 1887), and four of the first five runnings of the American Derby at Washington Park, Chicago (1884, 1885, 1886, and 1888). At Saratoga, N.Y., in 1882 he won an incredible forty-nine victories in fifty-one starts. It is reported that a few weeks before Murphy's 1884 Kentucky Derby victory on Buchanan, the horse had nearly unseated Murphy at the post in Nashville and then bolted over the track. Only the owners' threat of suspension induced him to ride Buchanan at the Derby. He won his second Kentucky Derby in 1890 on Riley and his third on Kingman in 1891. Meanwhile, at the Coney Island Jockey Club, Sheepshead Bay, New York City, on June 25, 1890, he had won by a head one of his most memorable races: a match with Snapper Garrison, whose final surges came to be known as a "Garrison finish" not only in horseracing but also in other sports.

Murphy inspired other Negro jockeys to follow in his footsteps: they won the Kentucky Derby in 1876, 1887, 1880, 1882, and 1883. Murphy's career virtually ended in 1891. He had a weight problem and during the off-season winter months it would reach 140 pounds. He dieted strenuously prior to the spring race meetings, and his body was weakened and subject to infection—which led to pneumonia and death on Feb. 12, 1896.

A recently erected marker and gravesite in Man o' War Memorial Park, Fayette County, Ky., inscribed Isaac Burns Murphy, gives 1860 as the year of his birth.

The late Marjorie Rieser Weber, a principal researcher of Murphy and other Negro jockeys, concluded that "he was considered the greatest judge of pace the country had ever seen, the near-perfect jockey who rode with his hands and heels and only drew his whip to satisfy the crowd. His integrity and honor were the pride of the turf" (enclosure with letter from Mrs. King Buckley, Librarian, Keenland Library, Lexington, Ky., to R.W.L., Aug. 12, 1976). Additional valuable information was in a letter from Mrs. Buckley to R.W.L. (Sept. 9, 1976). A brief published sketch is in Jack Orr's *The Black Athlete: His Story in American History* (1969). — RAYFORD W. LOGAN

MURPHY, JOHN H[ENRY], SR. (1840–1922), editor-publisher of the *Baltimore Afro-American* newspaper. Born on Christmas Day, 1840, in Baltimore, the only child of Benjamin Murphy, Jr., and Susan Ann (Coby) Murphy, he was born a slave and was freed by the Maryland Emancipation Act of 1863. His parents were married in Baltimore in 1838. Young Murphy followed in the footsteps of his father and grandfather and became a whitewasher and home decorator. During the Civil War he was a sergeant in the infantry for nearly two years. In 1868 he married Martha Elizabeth Howard, the daughter of a successful farmer of Montgomery County, Md. They met at church where his father directed the choir; he played the organ and she sang in the choir. The couple had eleven children, five sons and six daughters.

As superintendent of the Sunday school of Bethel A.M.E. Church in the late 1880s, Murphy became interested in uniting the A.M.E. Sunday schools into a state convention similar to the Methodist Epworth League and the Baptist Christian Endeavor. To do this he conceived the idea of establishing a Sunday school newspaper, bought an old manually operated press and a few fonts of type, and began printing the *Sunday School Helper* in his basement. Two years later, in 1892, the pastor of a local Baptist church, the Rev. William M. Alexander, started the *Afro-American* to promote his church and his new provision store. Murphy became business manager of the four-page paper, and gradually his interest in publishing increased. In 1896 he bought the *Afro-American* for $200 and merged it with his *Sunday School Helper*. By this time his older boys were growing up. His son Daniel took over the printing of the paper, his older brother worked on circulation, and their sisters wrote stories, set type, and helped with the folding and mailing.

It was nearly a decade before the two younger sons, Carl and Arnett, were old enough to be assigned chores on the paper. But they came up through the ranks as folders, newsboys, and printer's devils. Later Arnett was to become advertising director, and Carl, who taught German at Howard University (1913–1918), resigned to become editor of the paper. Three years later their father retired.

Although the elder Murphy did not know one font of type from another until he was fifty, and had not seen a modern press even of that day, in the 1890s he turned over to his family's management a well-equipped newspaper printing plant with typesetting machines and a three-color thirty-two-page rotary press. And the *Baltimore Afro-American* which he purchased for $200 had become the largest Negro newspaper along the Atlantic seaboard. Starting out with only unpaid family workers in 1896, Murphy saw his staff increase to nearly 100. In 1922 the *Afro-American* had a circulation of 14,000. John Henry Murphy, Sr., died at his home, 1616 McCulloch St., Baltimore, on April 5, 1922, after a short illness following the shock caused by the death of his son Daniel H. in Florida a few weeks before. His funeral was held on April 8 at Bethel A.M.E. Church, Druid Hill Avenue and Lanvale, with burial in Auburn Cemetery, Baltimore. His wife had predeceased him by seven years. He was survived by four sons and four daughters.

On his eightieth birthday, Dec. 25, 1920, he wrote a letter to his sons setting forth what he considered the measure of a newspaper. This has become the paper's credo. It reads in part: "I measure a newspaper not in buildings, equipment and employees—those are trimmings. A newspaper succeeds because its management believes in itself, in God and in the present generation. It must always ask itself 'Whether it has kept faith with the common people; Whether it has no other goal except to see that their liberties are preserved and their future assured; Whether it is fighting to get rid of slums, to provide jobs for everybody; Whether it stays out of politics except to expose corruption and condemn injustice, race prejudice and the cowardice of compromise.'"

Still valuable is *The Negro Press in the United States* by Frederick G. Detweiler (1922, reprint 1968). See also *Good News for You* (1969, pp. 5–7). Obituaries appeared in the *New York Age* (April 8, 1922), the *Baltimore American* (April 6, 1922), the *New York Times* (April 6, 1922, p. 17). Indispensable were the Murphy family Papers, made available by John H. Murphy III, chairman of the board of the Afro-American Newspapers. Information about the circulation in 1922 was obtained by William J. Scott, Supervisor, Photographic Laboratory, Moorland-Spingarn Research Center. — SHERMAN BRISCOE

MURRAY, DANIEL [ALEXANDER PAYNE] (1852–1925), librarian, bibliographer, and biographical researcher. The youngest child of George and Eliza Murray, he was born on March 3, 1852, in Baltimore and was named after Daniel Alexander Payne, the African Methodist Episcopal bishop who pastored Baltimore's Bethel Church from 1845 to 1850. Shortly after 1861 he left home for Washington, D.C., where his brother managed the U.S. Senate restaurant. In 1871 he became a personal assistant to the librarian of Congress, Ainsworth R. Spofford, and under his tutelage Murray broadened his knowledge, became proficient in several foreign languages, and acquired invaluable research skills. He married in 1879 the attractive Anna Evans, an Oberlin College graduate whose uncle (Lewis Sheridan Leary) and cousin (John Anthony Copeland, Jr.) participated in John Brown's raid on Harpers Ferry. Advancing to assistant librarian in 1881, he held this position until his retirement from the Library of Congress in 1923, after fifty-two years of service. In 1899 he was asked to prepare a special display on "Negro Literature" for the American Exhibit at the 1900 Paris Exposition. The search for materials by Negro authors and the drive to document their lives absorbed Murray in a lifelong project. Initially he labored on a "Bibliographia-Africana" and later on an "Encyclopedia of the Colored Race," an undertaking which occupied him until his death on Dec. 31, 1925.

Murray's work on the "Negro Literature" display for the Paris Exposition helped to establish him as an authority on Negro bibliography. Because he planned to secure as many volumes as possible for the Paris exhibit and future preservation in the Library of Congress, he sought the title of every book and pamphlet written by persons of African ancestry. In January 1900 he published an eight-page preliminary list of 270 titles with an appeal for additional citations. Responses to this list led to identification of 1100 works, 500 of which became the "Negro Literature" display. Seven years later he catalogued 5000 titles for the Jamestown, Va., Tercentenary and assembled a list of more than 12,000 books and pamphlets by Negro authors. Murray also developed a personal library of 1488 volumes which he bequeathed to the Library of Congress. Together with the works shown in Paris, this material for some time constituted the Library of Congress's "Colored Author Collection."

As he accumulated more titles, Murray felt compelled to document the authors' lives. Endeavoring to authenticate their ancestry, he began to write his "Bibliographia-Africana" to include all known literature by Negro writers, with biographical data about them. Convinced that the record of Negro progress and achievement was in their literature, he designed his book to dispel notions of racial inferiority and to prove that color was not an impediment to intellectual accomplishment.

Murray published some of his research in a column for the *Voice of the Negro.* Because of his bibliographic knowledge and background in the Library of Congress, he was frequently called upon for information on Negro history and literature, lectures before historical and literary societies, and testimony before the U.S. Congress. At the Library of Congress he had developed a reputation for his remarkable memory, whereby he often directed patrons to the precise location for their book requests without consulting the serial lists. Among his chief concerns were civil rights and a rigorous education for Negro youth. He often testified before Congress against segregation laws. He believed that Afro-Americans, even with equal opportunity, could achieve only limited success in life because their education did not prepare them for industrial employment. Despite his endorsement of industrial education, Murray maintained the need for quality instruction in all subjects, whether vocational or academic.

The rich vein of material which he unearthed, one of the first among Afro-Americans seeking knowledge about their past, and the desire to provide emulable images for Negro youngsters, influenced Murray in 1910 to expand his efforts into a "Historical and Biographical Encyclopedia of the Colored Race Throughout the World." For this project he solicited some of the most prominent and knowledgeable Negroes in Africa, America, and the Caribbean to serve as assistant editors. Among those who consented were John E. Bruce, John W. Cromwell, William S. Scarborough, Arthur A. Schomburg, and Richard R. Wright, Jr. The fact that sources used to vindicate Negro people were in large measure written solely by whites disturbed him. What would have been the nature of history for Greek posterity, he mused, if it had been written exclusively by Romans? His six-volume encyclopedia composed by Negroes would survey the "Colored Race's Progress and Achievements" from antiquity to the twentieth century.

He encountered considerable difficulty in securing a publisher for his encyclopedia, discovering that several firms would print the work but none would market it. He soon devised a plan of advance subscriptions similar to the *Jewish Cyclopedia* which was published with a guarantee of 8000 subscribers. Receiving an enthusiastic but limited response, Murray continued his quest for a publisher. When he died he left a book-length manuscript, "Bibliography of Negro Literature and Historical Sketch of Negro Authors and Authorship," almost 500 biographical portraits of Negro historical figures, and more than 250,000 index cards with book titles, background material, and information on events significant to Negro people worldwide. He bequeathed the manuscripts to the State Historical Society, Madison, Wisc.

He was a member of Philadelphia's American Negro Historical Society of which his cousin, William Carl Bolivar, was a founding member in 1897; of the Bethel Literary and Historical Society, and of the Benjamin Banneker Association, both in Washington; and a corresponding member of the Negro Library Association of New York City, of which Arthur A. Schomburg, John E. Bruce, and James Weldon Johnson were also members. He wrote several articles for the *Voice of the Negro* between September 1904 and July 1906.

Daniel Murray's vision of a Negro encyclopedia was similar to that of W. E. B. Du Bois and Carter G. Woodson, who also made ill-fated attempts to produce a multivolume reference work on the heritage of Negroes. Although his prodigious research was never published, his role as a bibliographer of Negro literature makes him a pioneer in the Negro history movement.

Daniel Murray died of natural causes at his residence, 924 S St. NW, Washington, D.C., and was buried in Woodlawn Cemetery, Washington. He was survived by his widow Anna and seven children.

There are brief references to Murray in Frank L. Mather's *Who's Who of the Colored Race* (1915, pp. 203–4); *History of the American Negro,* edited by Arthur Bunyan Caldwell (1922, 6: 25–27); *The Negro in the United States: A Selected Bibliography,* compiled by Dorothy B. Porter (1970, pp. v–vi); and Wallace Van Jackson's "Some Pioneer Negro Library Workers" (*The Library Journal,* March 15, 1939, pp. 215–17). An obituary appeared in *The Crisis* (June 1926). There are pictures of Murray in the *Library Journal* and *The Crisis;*

of his wife and most of their children in *NHB* (Nov. 1946). Information about his testimony before Congress is in *How to Solve the Race Problem: The Proceedings of the Washington Conference on the Race Problem in the United States,* edited by James Lawson (1904), and in the Murray Papers. Information on other aspects of Murray's life are in these papers, most of them in the State Historical Society, Madison, Wisc.; and a few in the Moorland-Spingarn Research Center, Howard University, and the Manuscript Division, Library of Congress. See also Robert L. Harris, Jr.'s "Daniel Murray and the Encyclopedia of the Colored Race" (*Phylon,* Sept. 1976, pp. 270–82). — ROBERT L. HARRIS, JR.

MURRAY, GEORGE WASHINGTON (1853–1926), congressman. Born a slave in Sumter County near Rembert, S.C., on Sept. 24, 1853, he attended the University of South Carolina (1874–1876), which had been opened to Negro students by the Republican state government. In 1876 he began teaching in the public schools and operated a small farm in Sumter County until February 1890 when he was appointed inspector of customs in the Charleston Customs House.

Although active in local politics prior to his Customs House appointment, Murray's political ambitions appear to have been focused on the national stage by this politically important position. A few months after his appointment he became a candidate for the Republican congressional nomination. Running against the veteran politician Thomas E. Miller, and the white collector of internal revenue E. M. Brayton, Murray failed to get the nomination. However, his visibility as a prominent candidate and as chairman of the state Republican convention may have helped him win the nomination two years later. Again he was pitted against Miller and Brayton, along with Robert Smalls, but this time Murray won as a compromise candidate on the fourth ballot. After a closely contested general election, he defeated the Democrat E. W. Moise by fifty votes after the Democratic State Returning Board decided several key precincts in his favor. The board's surprising decision was probably the result of internal divisions between competing Democratic factions.

Although officially elected to two terms in Congress (1893–1895 and 1895–1897) Murray actually spent little time in his seat. During the second and third sessions of his first term (Aug. 7, 1893–March 3, 1895) he was absent for extended periods. He was apparently defeated by Democrat William Elliott in his campaign for reelection in 1894, but Murray successfully contested Elliott's election and won back his seat. However, the final vote on the contest did not come until June 1896, during the final months of the 54th Congress. Murray won the Republican nomination again, but lost to William Elliott by more than 2000 votes in the 1896 campaign. His second challenge failed, and he retired to his real estate enterprises in Sumter County. In 1905 Murray moved to Chicago where he wrote two rather turgid books on race relations which were privately printed, *Race Ideals* (1914) and *Light in Dark Places* (1925). He remained an active platform speaker and political figure until his death on April 21, 1926. He was buried in

Lincoln Cemetery in Chicago after a large, well-attended funeral service at which John Roy Lynch was the principal speaker. Murray was survived by his wife Cornelia, and two children.

As a congressman Murray's independence of thought and action were perhaps his most striking features. His supreme self-confidence and oratorical ability were demonstrated when as a freshman congressman he rose to speak on the deeply divisive free-silver coinage issue. He won loud applause from free-silver advocates when he drew a witty and deft analogy between the condition of the devalued silver certificates and the discrimination and prejudices against Negroes. He noted playfully that the usual order of things was reversed with metals in that the "little yellow, gold man" was considered superior to the "white man" silver. Refusing to play the usual role of the reticent freshman member, he spoke in vain against the repeal of the last provisions of the Reconstruction Acts, and introduced, again in vain, bills to establish normal and industrial schools, to exempt the YMCA from taxes, and to provide funds for aged and needy Negroes. During his second term (June 4, 1896–March 3, 1897) he repeatedly and unsuccessfully called for an investigation of fraud and intimidation in South Carolina. He frequently engaged in floor debates and heckled opposition speakers with sharp questions.

Murray was not only a good debater but a resourceful leader. To help counter Democratic attempts to disenfranchise Negroes by imposing property requirements for voting, he purchased 10,000 acres of land, subdivided it into tracts of 25, 50, and 100 acres, and resold them to Negroes. A dark-horse victor for the congressional nomination in 1892, he was practically cut off financially by the major Republican contributors. Yet he managed a successful congressional campaign after several years of political drought for Republicans. When he ran for reelection in 1896 he found the party split between so-called "Black and Tan" and "Lily White" Republican factions. Murray joined the Lily Whites and worked toward a reunification of the two groups. The party names were actually misnomers, for prominent Negroes and white Republicans participated in both factions and both conventions nominated all-white state tickets for the 1896 elections. The reunification efforts failed and the Republican party went down to a defeat, ending Murray's political career.

Since there is no full-length biography, the major source for Murray's life is his own account in *The Biographical Directory of the American Congress* (1971). The sketch in Samuel Denny Smith's *The Negro in Congress, 1870–1901* (1940) relies largely on racially and politically biased sources. Maurine Christopher's *America's Black Congressmen* (1971) adds new information but fails to document its sources. The best secondary source is George B. Tindall's *South Carolina Negroes, 1877–1900* (1952). — THOMAS HOLT

MURRAY, PETER M[ARSHALL] (1888–1969), surgeon, hospital administrator, author, leader of struggle for equal rights for Negroes within the medical profession, and university trustee. He was born in Houma, La., one of four children of John L. and Louvinia (Smith)

Murray. Economic and educational opportunities in the rural South were limited. His parents therefore moved to New Orleans, where his father worked as a stevedore, but young Peter remained with his grandparents on the farm until at age twelve he joined his parents and enrolled in New Orleans University (later Dillard University) to continue his elementary education, in 1900. He continued his studies until he received his B.A. degree in 1910. His mother had worked as a practical nurse in a local hospital and was so impressed with what she had learned about medicine that she was determined to have her son become a physician as the best means for him to serve himself and his fellowman.

Shortly after his college graduation he went to Washington, D.C., obtained a civil service job, and entered the College of Medicine at Howard University in the fall of 1910. He continued to work and pay for his own education as well as send money home to his ailing mother. In 1914 he graduated with honors in surgery and obstetrics, which were destined to become his lifetime specialties. His performance in the College of Medicine led to his appointment as an assistant and instructor in surgery; in 1918 he became assistant surgeon-in-chief of Freedmen's Hospital. His clinical experience was unusual since there were no residency programs in operation until over two decades later in the middle 1930s. Murray established his private practice in Washington in 1915 and became a medical inspector for the District of Columbia Public Schools (1917–1918). Charlotte Wallace, a music teacher in this system and a concert singer, became his bride in 1917. After three years the young couple forsook the capital city for the broader opportunities of New York City, where he began his medical practice in 1921 and became an active participant in the cultural and professional life of Manhattan. Favored with the unusual clinical and surgical experience he had obtained in Washington, he soon became affiliated with several hospitals and sanitoria in New York and New Jersey.

Starting in the lowest rank of the Harlem Hospital clinic in 1928, he advanced through all the intermediate ranks to become director of the gynecological service and retired in 1953 after twenty-five years of exemplary service, but continued to serve as president of the Medical Board and director of obstetrics and gynecology at the Sydenham Hospital. In 1958 the mayor of New York appointed him to the local Board of Hospitals. In 1954 the governor of New York selected him for the Board of Trustees of the State University of New York, where he served as chairman of its Committee on Medical Education which secured large appropriations for expanding the state's educational facilities. He was also a member of the President's National Medical Advisory Committee on Health Resources.

Murray organized the Howard alumni of New York City and was active in both the National Medical Association and the American Medical Association. He served as president of the NMA in 1932, was chairman of its Publication Committee from 1942 to 1957, and was awarded the NMA's Distinguished Service Medal in 1954. In 1955, when Dillard University built its new chapel, he donated the carillon and clock as a memorial to his mother "whose great faith and strong Christian character inspired him to dedicate his life to the Ministry of Medicine and whose labors made his education possible."

The Medical Society of the County of New York, with some 7000 members, was the largest in the nation, and Murray's twelve years of service in its House of Delegates led to a similar position in the national organization, the American Medical Association, in 1950. He was the first Negro to attain this position in the AMA's history of over 100 years and was a catalyst for the desegregation of the organization's local chapters. In 1954 Murray was elected president of the Medical Society of the County of New York.

He also served as vice-president of the Hospital Council of Greater New York (1954–1961). For over a decade Murray was a trustee of the National Medical Fellowships (Chicago) and also served as president. He was a member of the New York Academy of Medicine and served on its Committee on Medical Education. In 1926, twelve years after his graduation, Howard University elected him to its Board of Trustees where he served until retired as an emeritus trustee in 1961. His most valuable service was as chairman of the Committee on the "Report of the Dean and Faculty of the College of Medicine Licensure Examination," in 1952. Its recommendations included the appointment of additional teachers, improved salary scales, additional supplies, equipment, and research funds, increased facilities, closer integration of Freedmen's Hospital and the College of Medicine, consideration of requiring medical students to take the National Board Examination at the end of their sophomore year, and continuing efforts to secure entering students with better academic preparation. On Oct. 27, 1953, the Board of Trustees approved new procedures for determining the entrance requirements and selection of applicants. Subsequent implementation of other recommendations also improved the performance of students.

He was certified by the American Board of Obstetrics and Gynecology in 1931, and was a fellow of the American College of Surgeons and the International College of Surgeons. His wider clinical experience led to the publication of a series of original scientific articles in medical journals, beginning the year after he started his New York practice: "Gastric & Duodenal Ulcers, with Report of Two Cases" (*JNMA* 14 [1922]: 143–46).

In 1969 the plaque for distinguished service of the New York Academy of Medicine was presented to Murray for over thirty years of membership and distinguished contributions to the medical community and public service. As the first Negro member of the AMA's House of Delegates, he worked diligently for the elimination of restrictive racial provisions in all of its component societies, even in the Deep South. Upon retiring from this legislative body of the AMA after twelve years, he stated in his farewell address at the Denver meeting in 1962: "While I retire from the House, I shall not retire from the fight. I'll be found on the frontline trenches fighting for the ideals of the A.M.A." He was an active participant in the staff integration of Harlem Hospital in the 1930s and Sydenham Hospital during the 1950s.

A dignified man with a forceful personality, modest and soft-spoken, Murray combined a career in clinical and surgical practice with civic responsibilities that made him an elder statesman in medicine.

Murray died on Dec. 19, 1969, in St. Clair's Hospital, New York City. Funeral services were held at St. Mark's Methodist Church, New York City, where he had been a member of the Stewards Board. He was survived by his widow Charlotte, a son John, and a grandson John Jr.

Principal sources are the Peter Marshall Murray Papers, Moorland-Spingarn Research Center, Howard University, and the articles by W. Montague Cobb (*JNMA,* 1922, pp. 143–46; *JNMA,* Jan. 1970, p. 67). M. W. Young drew also upon his personal reminiscences. See also Rayford W. Logan, *Howard University, The First Hundred Years, 1867–1967* (1969), and the obituary in the *New York Times* (Dec. 21, 1969, p. 63). — M. WHARTON YOUNG

MYERS, GEORGE A. (1859–1930), politician, barber, and civic leader. He was born in Baltimore on March 5, 1859, the eldest of three children of Isaac and Emma V. Myers. In May 1868 he lost his mother. Two years later Myers enrolled in the preparatory department of Lincoln University in Chester County, Pa. When his father married Sarah E. Deaver, he returned to Baltimore and graduated from the first grammar school for colored children. Because of the racial practices in that city, Myers was denied admission to the Baltimore City College.

Myers left Baltimore in 1875 and worked as an apprentice to Thomas James, a veteran painter in Washington. Not liking the trade, he returned to Baltimore and studied the barber trade under Thomas Gamble and George S. Ridgeway. He accepted this trade against his father's will, who wanted him to enroll in Cornell Medical School. In 1879 he settled in Cleveland and served for nine years as the foreman for James E. Benson's Waddell House Barber Shop. Because he was an affable person, he made many friends and opened the famous Hollenden Barber Shop at the Hollenden Hotel in 1888. Elbert Hubbard, author of *A Message to Garcia,* styled his shop "the best barber shop in America." With such a reputation, Myers's shop became a recruiting station for Negro political leaders.

His father, an influential labor leader who fought for equal rights, influenced his son's career. Although his father urged him to stay out of politics, Myers's environment and background led him to it. His contacts with famous politicians and the wide acquaintance he developed within his race motivated his decision. Myers first sprang into political prominence when he served as a delegate to the Republican National Convention at Minneapolis in 1892. It was his vote that elected William M. Hahn national committeeman from Ohio and brought "the McKinley-Hanna Organization into being." Later William McKinley and Marcus A. Hanna played important roles in supporting Myers's political endorsements.

During the campaign of 1896 Hanna chose Myers to organize the Negro delegates from Ohio. He not only organized these delegates but had almost the entire control of McKinley's interests in Louisiana and Mississippi. Before the convention in St. Louis, Myers informed the delegates of their specific duties and pro-

cured the money for their expenditures. After the convention McKinley personally thanked Myers for his aid and promised him a political appointment in the event of his election. Myers refused to accept any office. But through his recommendations, Maj. William T. Anderson served as chaplain of the 10th U.S. Cavalry; John R. Lynch became paymaster in the U.S. Army; and Blanche K. Bruce was appointed register of the U.S. Treasury. Later he secured the appointment of Charles A. Cottrell as collector of internal revenue at Honolulu. Moreover, Myers served as Hanna's personal representative on the Republican State Executive Committee for 1897–1898. The committee eventually proved to be the most important state committee in the history of the Republican party of Ohio.

The men Myers recommended were usually representative Negroes, because if Myers found a person unworthy of serving, he refused to grant his endorsement. To Myers, a man evinced his importance as "a race man" by having a profound interest in his people, by helping the members of his race whenever possible, and by defending them against unjust imputation.

In 1900 the Republican State Convention elected Myers its alternate delegate-at-large to the Republican National Convention in Philadelphia. Through his efforts Sen. Matthew S. Quay's resolution, reducing southern representation, which Hannah controlled, was defeated. After serving three terms as a member of the Republican State Executive Committee, and after the deaths of President McKinley and Senator Hanna, Myers retired from politics and devoted his entire time to his family, business, and civic activities. In 1896 Myers took as his second wife Maude E. Stewart.

In 1912, through the recommendation of Booker T. Washington, Myers was offered the management of the entire Republican organization among Negro voters of the country by Charles D. Hilles, chairman of the Republican National Committee. Again, because of his family and business, he refused to accept the offer. This was the first time that conducting a national campaign among Negroes was offered to a single individual.

Although conservative in politics, in any matter which concerned Negroes Myers was "an uncompromising reformer." Despite his friendship with James Ford Rhodes, he had no qualms about criticizing the treatment in Rhodes's *History* of the so-called black control of the Reconstruction governments. According to Myers, Rhodes made his mistake when he did not talk "with prominent Negro participants." He expected Rhodes, who he felt was fair and free of anti-Negro prejudice, to aid in dissipating "this damnable prejudice . . . that we as people have to contend with." In Myers's view the Negro desired only basic political and civil rights.

Since he was respected in Cleveland, Myers was able to do much to alleviate anti-Negro prejudice in that city. He called the attention of Elliot H. Baker, editor of the *Plain Dealer,* to the objectionable use of the terms "negroes" in lowercase and "darky" in that paper, and had the practice stopped. A few years later, when the *Plain Dealer* retrogressed in this matter, he obtained from editor Paul Bellamy a clear-cut promise that these terms would not be used again. He had two Negro policemen placed in the area around the Woodlawn Hill municipal swimming pool to prevent threatened trouble over its use by Negroes.

In the last few years of his life Myers did not change his philosophy. He continued to manage his shop and maintained his interest in civic matters. After serving almost half a century as a barber, he was financially secure and ready to retire. After years of hard work, he had developed a chronic heart condition. Nevertheless, when the management of the hotel informed him that after his retirement his thirty Negro employees would be replaced by white manicurists and barbers, he remained in his shop until his death on Jan. 17, 1930.

He died at the New York Central ticket office in Cleveland just after purchasing transportation to Hot Springs, Ark., where he intended spending a month in an effort to improve his heart condition. His funeral was held at his home in Cleveland on Jan. 21 and he was buried in Lake View Cemetery. He was survived by his first wife, Sarah E. Myers of Baltimore, and their son Herbert D.; his widow Maude, and their daughter Dorothy Virginia. Both children taught in the Cleveland public schools (*Cleveland Gazette,* Jan. 25, 1930, p. 1).

John A. Garraty's introduction to the *Correspondence of George A. Myers and James Ford Rhodes, 1910–1923* (1965), contains valuable information. Russell H. Davis's *Black Americans in Cleveland* (1972) is a convenient source. Felix James's article "The Civil and Political Activities of George A. Myers" (*JNH,* April 1973, pp. 166–78) is a brief summary, based in large measure on the George A. Myers Papers in the Ohio Historical Society and the John P. Green Papers in the Western Reserve Historical Society. — FELIX JAMES

MYERS, ISSAC (1835–1891), pioneer labor leader and Mason. Born in Baltimore on Jan. 13, 1835, the son of poor free parents, he grew up in a slave state that afforded no public school education for Negro children, but received a common school education in the private day school of the Rev. John Fortie. At sixteen he was apprenticed to James Jackson, a prominent colored ship caulker. By 1860 young Myers was a skilled worker, superintending the caulking of clean-line clipper ships.

Even before the Civil War whites had resorted to violence to eliminate Negroes from the caulking trade. In October 1865 the white caulkers of Baltimore, joined by the ship carpenters, went on strike, insisting that Negroes be discharged as caulkers and longshoremen. Supported by the local government and the police, the strikers succeeded in driving the Negroes from the shipyards. Thrown suddenly out of employment, the colored workers held a meeting to decide what to do next. Myers proposed that they form a union of Negro caulkers to sponsor a cooperative company that would purchase a shipyard and railway and carry on business cooperatively. The proposal caught fire; the caulkers issued stock and quickly raised $10,000 among Negroes in Baltimore. They borrowed $30,000 more from a ship captain, secured a six-year mortgage, purchased an extensive shipyard and railway, and took possession on Feb. 12, 1866.

Within six months after beginning operations the Cheseapeake Marine Railway and Dry Dock Company employed 300 Negroes at an average wage of three dollars a day. It obtained a number of government contracts and paid off its debt within five years. As it expanded, it employed white mechanics as well as Negroes. "The organization of the ship company," noted W. E. B. Du Bois, "saved the colored caulkers," and the failure of the whites to drive out "the colored caulkers put an end to their efforts to drive colored labor out of other fields" (*Economic Cooperation among Negro Americans,* Atlanta University Publications no. 10, 1907, p. 153).

By the fall of 1868 colored workers in a number of cities were organizing unions to improve their condition. In Baltimore there were several such unions, among them the Colored Caulkers' Trades Union Society of Baltimore, with Isaac Myers as president. The white and colored caulkers' unions cooperated and even met to discuss common problems. As a result of this experience Myers began to think of the possibility of organizing a colored labor movement on a national scale which would work in unison with white labor organizations. His vision was enhanced by an unprecedented action on the part of the leading organization of white labor, the National Labor Union. In December 1868 the NLU Executive Committee extended a formal invitation to all persons interested in the labor movement, regardless of color or sex, to attend the annual convention in Philadelphia on Aug. 16, 1869.

Myers, representing the Colored Caulkers' Trade Union Society of Baltimore, was one of nine colored delegates at the 1869 NLU convention. A highlight of the gathering was Myers's address, in which he voiced the sentiments and aspirations of colored workers. He paid tribute to the white delegates for their awareness of the need for unity between Negro and white workers. As for the former, they too stood for unity. "We carry no prejudices. We are willing to forget the wrongs of yesterday and let the dead past bury its dead." Myers announced that Negro labor leaders had issued a call for a National Labor Convention to meet in Washington, D.C., in December. Delegates would be admitted without regard to color, and he would be happy to have the cooperation of the NLU at the meeting, "as you have ours now" (*New York Times,* Aug. 19, 1869).

Myers was elected president of the (Colored) National Labor Union, the first such national organization in American history. In February 1870 he undertook an organizing tour for the new colored labor federation. In his speeches to racially mixed audiences he insisted that for both races to triumph they had to unite and act together, but that before that could happen Negroes had to unite among themselves. If they failed to do so, he warned, they would find themselves pushed out of the trades, to become "the servants, the sweepers of shavings, the scrapers of pitch, and the carriers of mortar." Myers therefore appealed to colored workers to join trade unions and also to establish cooperative associations (*New National Era,* April 27, 1870).

In August 1870 Myers once again attended the convention of the National Labor Union, one of five Negroes present. A bitter battle broke out when white delegates insisted that Negro workers abandon the Republican party and support an independent party of labor reform. Myers warned that there could be no unity between white and black labor if the former demanded that Negroes abandon the Republicans. "While the Republican Party is not the *beau idéal* of our notion of a party," he declared, "the interests of workingmen demand that they shall not hazard its success either by the organization of a new party or by an affiliation with the Democratic Party." The resolution in favor of a Labor Reform party was overwhelmingly passed, sixty to five, with all the Negro delegates opposed. The 1870 NLU convention was the last one Negro delegates attended.

At the second annual meeting of the (Colored) National Labor Union on Jan. 9, 1871, Myers delivered his swan song as president. He was able to report progress: unions established during the year were "in a flourishing condition." However, he conceded that the (C) NLU, hampered by financial difficulties, had not been "as successful as many friends of our race and cause anticipated" in reaching colored workers. He urged that conventions be held in every state, North and South, to form more labor unions, but stressed that "politics . . . be left entirely out of these conventions, and the business interests of the people considered." In conclusion he once again emphasized that unity of black and white labor was essential to the success of both, but that first it was necessary for Negro labor to organize and achieve its own power before such unity could become a meaningful reality (*New National Era,* Jan. 19, 1871).

After he stepped down as (C)NLU president, Myers continued to be active in the organization until its demise soon after the third annual convention in the fall of 1871. From 1872 to 1879 he worked as a detective in the Post Office Department. Following his retirement he opened a coal yard in Baltimore, but left that in 1882 to become a United States gauger, a position he held until February 1887. In the years following, Myers successfully organized and was president of the Maryland Colored State Industrial Fair Association, the Colored Business Men's Association of Baltimore, the Colored Building and Loan Association of Baltimore, and the Aged Ministers Home of the A.M.E. church. Active in the A.M.E. church, he was for fifteen years superintendent of the Bethel A.M.E. School of Baltimore. He was also a grand master of Maryland Masons and author of a *Mason's Digest,* and a sacred drama. He was twice married; one of his sons, George A. Myers, became a leading political figure in Ohio. He died on Jan. 26, 1891, at his home, 1218 Jefferson St., Baltimore, from paralysis. Funeral services, said to have been the largest for a colored person in Baltimore, were held on Jan. 29 at Bethel A.M.E. Church on Saratoga Street, and he was buried in Laurel Cemetery. He was survived by his second wife, the former Sarah E. Deaver, and his son George.

There is no biography of Myers. The article "The Late Isaac Myers of Baltimore, Md." (*A.M.E. Church Review* 7 [April 1891]: 351–56), incorporating much material originally published in the *Indianapolis Freeman* (Oct. 12, 1889), is the best source for his life. However, it must be used with caution; the material relating to Myers's role in the (Colored) National Labor Union is inaccurate. Philip S. Foner's *History of the Labor Movement in the United States,* vol. 1 (1947), is the standard reference work. See also Foner's *Organized Labor and the Black Worker, 1619–1973* (1974, pp. 21–22, 24–26, 37–40, 43), and Philip S. Foner and Ronald L. Lewis (eds.), *The Black Worker: A Documentary History from Colonial Times to the Present* (1978, 1: 416–29, 2:3, 20–28, 43–47, 57, 69, 71–74, 77, 82, 83, 88, 90, 94, 95, 100, 106, 110, 112, 113); *Cleveland Gazette* (June 1, 1895), and Felix James's "The Civil and Political Activities of George A. Myers" (*JNH,* April 1973, pp. 166–78). Obituaries appeared in the *Baltimore American* (Jan. 27, 1891, p. 5; and Jan. 30, 1891, p. 6). — PHILIP S. FONER

NAIL, JOHN [JACK] E. (1883–1947), businessman. He was born in New London, Conn., the first of two children of Elizabeth and John B. Nail, and sister of Grace Nail. The Nails, however, made their home in New York City, having migrated there from Baltimore in 1863. Securing employment in a gambling house, the senior Nail saved enough money to open a tavern and expand his business into a restaurant, hotel, and billiard parlor. In the early twentieth century he purchased a few apartments in Harlem, thus giving his son an awareness of the profits awaiting energetic and aggressive Negro entrepreneurs. After graduating from a New York City public high school and working briefly in his father's tavern, young John worked as a salesman for the Afro-American Realty Company. But in 1907, when the financial and internal problems of the company surfaced, Nail and Henry G. Parker, another of the firm's ambitious salesmen, opened their own realty firm in Harlem. In aims and goals this company was a carbon copy of the Afro-American Realty Company of Philip A. Payton, and both Nail and Parker seemed propelled by the same business and personal ambitions that had characterized Payton's earlier career, to provide housing for Negroes in Harlem and garner the handsome profits that would reward their efforts. Nail was the driving force in this new business partnership and surpassed his former boss Payton in both his determination to house Negroes in Harlem and make it a profitable venture for his company. He no doubt absorbed some of his dedication to the social, political, and economic uplift of Negroes from his brother-in-law James Weldon Johnson, who had married Grace E. Nail on Feb. 10, 1910. Both families purchased summer homes in Great Barrington, Mass., where Johnson did much of his writing.

In 1911 Nail predicted that the value of real estate in Harlem would soar as the population of Manhattan shifted farther north. In the formative years of Harlem's transition into a Negro community, he repeatedly advised Negroes to acquire property in Harlem and hold on to it at all cost. In this nascent period of "black capitalism" Nail's strategy was designed to produce profits for his company and concomitantly aid Negroes in securing modern living quarters. In 1911 Nail and his pastor, the Rev. Hutchens C. Bishop of St. Philip's Episcopal Church, who had passed for white on several occasions and purchased real estate in Harlem as early as 1906, engineered a real estate deal in Harlem involving property totaling $1,070,000. This deal included land for the building of the new St. Philip's Church and several apartment buildings to be rented by the church. Consumating this deal and facilitating the movement of Negroes into Harlem, Nail and Parker were off to an auspicious beginning. As whites moved out of Harlem and Negroes moved in, Nail and Parker rapidly acquired more property to manage and deals to negotiate. The firm became the agent for the colored branch of the YMCA as it moved from its downtown location to Harlem and also handled the sales and renting of the apartments designed by the architect Stanford White (these apartment complexes were turned over to Nail and Parker by the Equitable Life Insurance Company). The firm also transacted deals for Negro businesses such as the Wage Earners' Savings Bank and the Copeland Realty Company. The firm's most well-known client was Madam C. J. Walker, who purchased property in Irvington-on-Hudson. As the firm expanded in 1916 Nail persuaded James Weldon Johnson to invest in the company and to encourage his influential friends to support it. By 1925 the firm managed approximately fifty apartment complexes and its annual income amounted to $1 million. For their roles in facilitating the movement of Negroes into Harlem, Nail and Parker later became known as the "Little Fathers" of Negro Harlem.

Nail was also emerging as one of the most influential Negro realtors in New York City. He became the first Negro member of the Real Estate Board of New York, the only Negro member of the Housing Committee of New York, a member of the Harlem Board of Commerce and the Uptown Chamber of Commerce. Later, when reform codes were needed in the housing industry during the Depression, Nail was brought in as a consultant for Pres. Herbert Hoover's Commission on Housing. As he continued to rise to greater influence in the real estate world, Nail increased his activities in charitable, political, and Negro uplift organizations, working for the YMCA, the Republican Business Men's Club of New York, the NAACP, and the New York Urban League.

Nail also sought to make Harlem a prestigious community for Negroes by encouraging Negro businesses and ownership. But the Depression began the deterioration of Harlem and the simultaneous undermining of the financial stability of firms such as Nail and Parker. In 1933 the firm went bankrupt and was dissolved. The same year, however, Nail opened his own firm at 249 W. 135th St. His first commissioned job was to lease six apartments for the also financially troubled St. Philip's Church. The following year Nail attempted to secure $8 million of some $25 million of federal New Deal funds earmarked for the renovation of deteriorating urban communities like Harlem. Nail asked James Weldon Johnson for help in persuading the federal government to provide the funds. Included in these plans was a proposal to get the Mexican painter, Miguel Covarrubias, a friend of Johnson, to sketch the deteriorating conditions in Harlem as part of a massive campaign. The plan never materialized and Harlem continued to decline, especially after the race riot of August 1943. When Nail died in 1947 public housing had replaced

Nail's dream of a middle-class Negro Harlem of individually owned homes promoted by Negro entrepreneurs. This disillusionment was expressed in a poem found in Nail's scrapbooks (p. 4): "The realtor stood at the pearly gates;/ His face was worn and old/ He merely asked of the man of fate/ admission to the fold./ 'What have you done,' St. Peter asked,/ 'to seek admission here?'/ 'Why I was selling real estate/ on Earth for many a year!'/ The gate swung open sharply/ as St. Peter touched the bell./ 'Come in,' he said, 'and take a harp./ You had enough of Hell.' "

Nail died during the night of March 5–6, 1947, at Lenox Hill Hospital. His funeral was held at St. Philips Episcopal Church, 214 W. 134th St., on March 8, with interment in Greenwood Cemetery, Brooklyn. He was survived by his widow, his sister, an aunt Josephine Miller, and a cousin Gertrude Berry (*New York Herald-Tribune,* March 6, 1947, p. 26; *New York Age,* March 15, 1947, p. 1).

Published works about Nail and his Harlem include James Weldon Johnson's *Along This Way* (1933) and *Black Manhattan* (1930); Gilbert Osofsky's *Harlem: The Making of a Ghetto* (1966); and excerpts from newspapers in *Harlem on My Mind, Cultural Capital of Black America 1900–1968,* edited by Allon Schoener (1968). A photograph of Nail's "Big Deal" on West 135th Street, c. 1915, is on page 141. The James Weldon Johnson Papers in Yale University's Beinecke Rare Book and Manuscript Library contain valuable information, as do the Papers of the Works Progress Administration in the Schomburg Center for Research in Black Culture, New York City. — MACEO CRENSHAW DAILEY, JR.

NAPIER, JAMES CARROLL (1845–1940), lawyer, politician, government official, banker, and civic leader. Born near Nashville, Tenn., on June 9, 1845, one of four children of free parents, William C. and Jane E. Napier, James attended a private school for free colored children in Nashville, where his father operated a livery stable. In 1859 James and his brother Elias were enrolled first in Wilberforce University and then in Oberlin College. Attracted by Reconstruction patronage opportunities, James Napier left college in 1867 and returned to Tennessee. He served as Davidson County commissioner of refugees and abandoned lands under the Freedmen's Bureau for a year, and then obtained a State Department clerkship in Washington, said to be the first Negro to hold such a position. Encouraged by John Mercer Langston, Napier received his LL.B. degree from Howard University in 1872. He immediately returned to Nashville to set up practice. In 1878 Napier married Langston's only surviving daughter, Nettie. She died in 1938 without leaving any children.

While developing a respectable law practice, Napier's political connections greatly influenced the course of his lengthy career. He held patronage appointments under the Grant, Hayes, Garfield, and Arthur administrations, and from 1878 until 1885 served on Nashville's City Council. Napier became Tennessee's ranking Negro Republican and remained in this position until early in the twentieth century. He served on the state Republican Executive Committee almost continuously for thirty-five years, representing the state at six Republican National Conventions, and once ran as the party's unsuccessful candidate for Congress from the 5th Congressional District (1898). Shortly after the turn of the century, however, Tennessee's political system became increasingly influenced by "lily whitism" within the Republican party and by Negro disfranchisement in electoral politics. New conditions dictated new Negro leadership, and the quiet, connections-oriented Napier gave way to the younger and more aggressive Robert R. Church, Jr., of Memphis. Napier's active political career, however, had ended with a flourish. Especially utilizing a longtime friendship with Booker T. Washington, Napier repeatedly sought the position of register of the treasury, the most prestigious patronage job open to colored Americans. After turning down consolation offers as consul in Bahia, Brazil, (1906) and consul-general for Liberia (1910), Napier was finally named to the Treasury post by Pres. William Howard Taft in 1911. He served as register until resigning in 1913 as a protest against the Wilson administration's segregation policies. Napier returned to Nashville and retired from politics.

Napier's philosophy of racial improvement emphasized economic self-help and education. He held a firm commitment to the development of Negro businesses, and took a special interest in banking. Disturbed by the demoralizing impact of the failure of the Freedmen's Bank, Napier invested in the ill-fated Penny Savings Bank of Chattanooga, and then, in 1903, pledged his own estate as security for the first year's operation of the One-Cent Savings Bank in Nashville. Napier served as the nonsalaried cashier of this bank (later the Citizens Savings Bank) from its founding until his death. He was not a speculative person, and along with Richard Henry Boyd, the bank's founding president, he influenced the institution's conservative and careful path through the perils of early-twentieth-century black business enterprise. The Citizens Bank never grew rapidly or contributed much to the economic growth in Nashville, but these had not been Napier's goals. His main consideration was to encourage thrift and restore confidence in race businesses. Not unexpectedly, Napier was an early supporter of the National Negro Business League, bringing the national meeting to Nashville in 1903 and becoming its president after Booker T. Washington's death in November 1915. Napier continued to endorse the conservative approach to race relations. He represented this leadership faction at the first Amenia conference in 1916 and frequently spoke against the more aggressive methods of W. E. B. Du Bois.

Napier participated actively in civic affairs, concentrating his efforts as Nashville city councilman upon expanding public services in the Negro community. As his contacts with white politicians and philanthropists widened, Napier became a valued member of such boards of trustees as those of the Anna T. Jeanes Fund, Meharry Medical College, and Fisk and Howard universities. Napier took these appointments seriously and also played a major role in the founding of the Tennessee Agricultural and Industrial State Normal School for Negroes (later Tennessee State University) in Nashville. For many years he also lectured on medical jurisprudence at Meharry.

He died on April 21, 1940, at his home, 120 15th Ave., Nashville. His funeral was held on April 24 in Fisk Memorial Chapel, the Rev. Henry Allen Boyd officiating, and he was buried in Greenwood Cemetery. He was survived by two nephews, (Charles N. Langston and John Mercer Langston) and three nieces.

James Carroll Napier belonged to an elite social and economic class of colored Americans. He never identified with nor moved easily among the masses. Nevertheless, this small, quiet, dignified, and light-skinned patriarch was a source of pride and continuity in Negro Nashville. He represented success, made direct contact with the dominant forces in society, and in his own paternalistic way, worked diligently for the advancement of his race.

See Cordell Hull Williams's "The Life of James Carroll Napier from 1845 to 1940" (M.A. thesis, Tennessee State University, 1954) and Lester Crawford Lamon's "Negroes in Tennessee, 1900–1930" (Ph.D. dissertation, University of North Carolina, 1971). See also the obituary in *JNH* (July 1940, pp. 400–1) and the *Nashville Banner* (April 23, 1940, p. 14).

— LESTER C. LAMON

NASH, CHARLES EDMUND (1844–1913), soldier and congressman. He was born in Opelousas, La., of free parents, Richard and Masie Cecile Nash, on May 23, 1844. As a young man Charles moved to New Orleans, where he was employed as a bricklayer. In July 1863 he enlisted in the 10th Regiment of the Corps d'Afrique at Port Hudson, La., and was promoted to first sergeant in the 82nd U.S. Colored Infantry. Ten days before his discharge he received a field promotion to first lieutenant, which appears not to have been approved.

Military service was tragic for Nash, for he lost the lower third of his right leg as a result of wounds received in an attack on Fort Blakely, Ala., during the closing days of the war. These wounds caused him a great deal of discomfort and pain in later years, and often impaired his ability to earn a living. However, it was probably his military service and affiliation with the Republican party that won him an appointment as night inspector in the large and politically powerful New Orleans Customs House in the late summer of 1869. His political associations at the Customs House provided the basis for his successful nomination as the Republican candidate from the 6th Congressional District of Louisiana in 1874.

Although two other Negroes were also nominated and elected to Congress from Louisiana, J. Willis Menard in 1868 and P. B. S. Pinchback in 1876, neither was seated. In contrast, Nash's admission to the 44th Congress was undramatic and uncontested. He was assigned to the Committee on Education and Labor, but during his single term of service in a Democratic Congress he had little opportunity to make a significant impact. The lone bill he introduced, a measure providing a survey of a bayou in his district, died in the Commerce Committee. Like most freshman congressmen he was not active in floor debates. Indeed, when he attempted to speak on the Louisiana elections he could not get the floor. Insisting that he had come to speak on the issue, Nash declined the offer to have his remarks published in the *Congressional Record.* On June 7, 1876, he gained the floor to make a major address on political affairs in his home state. His speech was both an attack against southern Democrats for their unfairness to white native Republicans and an appeal for racial and political peace. He began by defending the ex-Confederate Gen. James Longstreet for his conversion to Republicanism from attacks by Rep. Jesse Yeates of North Carolina. The social ostracism of native white Republicans and such unfair attacks by Democrats on their motives might force his party into the hands of "ruffian" whites and "ignorant" Negroes who would plunder the South, Nash warned. The race issue was simply a matter of ignorance, and education would dispel "narrow prejudices as the sun dispels the noxious vapors of the night." He insisted that blacks and whites were not enemies but brothers. His impassioned peroration, "Over brothers' graves let brothers' quarrels die," won warm applause from his colleagues. The usually critical Samuel Denny Smith called the speech "excellent."

Evidently the applause back home was less enthusiastic, for Nash lost a bid for reelection to Democrat Edward Robertson by more than 5000 votes. The faction-ridden Louisiana Republicans gave him something less than full support in this critical election, and Nash did not bother to contest the result. He returned instead to his former occupation as a bricklayer in New Orleans, interrupted briefly by a stint as postmaster in Washington, La., from Feb. 15 to May 1, 1882. Two years later his first wife, Martha Ann Wycoff Thomas, whom he had married after his election to Congress, died in Opelousas. On March 8, 1905, Nash married Julia Lucy Montplaisir, a white native of New Orleans of French extraction. Nash was sixty years old at the time and his wife was forty. He had long since ceased to be active in politics, and his disability and age had forced his retirement from any strenuous manual labor several years earlier. However, he was employed as a cigar maker until his death on June 21, 1913. He was buried at St. Louis Cemetery in New Orleans.

Ironically, although Charles Nash was the only successful Negro candidate for Congress from Louisiana, he was the least distinguished, having neither the education and polish of Menard nor the political acumen of Pinchback. He was largely a product of the Customs House machine in New Orleans and his brief congressional tenure did not allow him time to develop independence or make a significant political impact.

The major sources on Nash's life are *The Biographical Directory of the American Congress* (1971), Samuel Denny Smith's *The Negro in Congress, 1870–1901* (1940), and Maurine Christopher's *America's Black Congressmen* (1971). — THOMAS HOLT

NELL, WILLIAM COOPER (1816–1874), abolitionist, lecturer, journalist, and historian. Born in Boston, the son of William G., an associate of David Walker, and Louisa, a native of Brookline, Mass., he attended a local colored grammar school and graduated from a mixed school. Although he was an honor student, he did not, because of his color, receive a prize. This discrimination

led him to campaign for equal rights for colored children; he briefly studied law, and in 1831, inspired by Garrison's *Liberator,* immersed himself in the antislavery cause. Nine years later he joined prominent white abolitionists in petitioning Boston for desegregated schools. Subsequently rejected, it marked the beginning of Nell's fight to end separate schools.

In the early 1840s he began his lengthy association with the *Liberator,* writing articles, supervising its Negro Employment Office, and representing Garrison at various antislavery functions. When Frederick Douglass returned from Europe in 1847, Nell presided over the welcoming home ceremonies, and then accompanied Douglass to Troy, N.Y., where they attended the National Colored Convention. Both, however, looked on "complexional" organizations as obsolete, serving only to alienate white organizations. That winter Nell became publisher of Douglass's *North Star;* he also became active in New York State antislavery organizations. On occasion he rebuked those who failed to support the abolitionist press more enthusiastically. He reserved his most heated reproofs, however, for the American Colonization Society, which he denounced in the press.

In 1850 he ran unsuccessfully for the Massachusetts legislature on the Free Soil party platform. Also that year, Nell united with other Negroes and whites in forming a Committee of Vigilance to undermine the Fugitive Slave Act. He also took an active role in the Underground Railroad, until a serious illness forced his temporary retirement.

Undaunted, he continued to write, and in 1851 issued a twenty-three-page pamphlet, *The Services of Colored Americans in the Wars of 1776 and 1812.* In conjunction with its publication he sent the first of many petitions to the Massachusetts legislature for a Crispus Attucks Memorial. That same year, when Douglass formally broke with Garrison, Nell left the *North Star,* and two years later formed a Garrisonian Association in support of his editor. Shortly thereafter he attended the Rochester (N.Y.) National Convention of Colored Men, where he and Douglass came into direct and heated conflict. Douglass accused Nell of conspiring against him. Nell denied the accusation, but Douglass remained unconvinced and the breach widened.

In 1855 Nell published a more comprehensive history, *The Colored Patriots of the American Revolution.* On April 28 of that year the Massachusetts legislature abolished segregated schools. In recognition of his efforts, Massachusetts Negroes and leading whites held a presentation dinner honoring Nell.

Three years later, in opposition to the Dred Scott decision, Nell staged the first Crispus Attucks celebration in America. He abhorred the fact that both the federal and state governments were "shaping their legislation to practically enforce the atrocious" decision, and he unsuccessfully petitioned the Massachusetts legislature to declare the decision unconstitutional.

Despite the many setbacks delivered the Negro, Nell strongly criticized those Negroes who preached despair. Instead he advised them to "take counsel of their hopes, rather than be depressed by their fears." When the Civil War erupted, Nell took up the cause of colored

America's equal participation in the war effort. That spring he claimed the honor of being one of the first Negroes appointed to a federal post. The postmaster of Boston, John G. Palfrey, had nominated him for postal clerk, a position he held until his death, caused by "paralysis of the brain." He was survived by his widow whom he had married in April 1869. Appropriately, his mentor and friend William Lloyd Garrison delivered the eulogy.

Nell's two books are among the more valuable sources for later historians. He wrote also "Lewis Sherrard [*sic*] Leary" (*Pine and Palm,* July 27, 1861). See also Carleton Mabee's "A Negro Boycott to Integrate Boston Schools" (*New England Quarterly,* Sept. 1968) and especially Robert P. Smith's "William Cooper Nell: Crusading Black Abolitionist" (*JNH,* July 1970). The brief sketch by Harold G. Villard in *DAB* ([1937] 1962, 7:413) contains many of the essential facts and available bibliography. — ROBERT P. SMITH

NEWBY, DANGERFIELD (c. 1815–1859), one of John Brown's men at Harpers Ferry. Newby was born in Virginia. His mother was a slave but his father, a Scotsman, granted freedom to his children when he died. Newby lived on a farm near Harpers Ferry. He was known as a quiet man, strong, sensible, and devoted to his wife and their seven children, all of whom were slaves. They lived near Warrenton, Va., on the farm of their master. His wife had written a letter to Newby saying that her master was planning to sell her "down river." Newby, willing to do anything he thought might help to free members of his family, participated in John Brown's raid.

John Brown arrived in Harpers Ferry six months before his planned attack. During that time Newby served Brown as a spy in the community. He did not join the John Brown group until the eve of the raid. He was first among them to die when the fighting started on Oct. 17, 1859. After he was killed, angry citizens fired into his body repeatedly and those without guns beat it with clubs. His ears were cut off as souvenirs. Later, hogs rooted and tugged at the torn body, consuming its parts.

An eyewitness, Joseph Barry, later wrote in his book *The Strange Story of Harpers Ferry* (1903) that "none of the good people of Harpers Ferry appeared to be at all squeamish about the quality or flavor of their pork that winter."

Newby's body, or what remained of it, was buried in a shallow grave at Harpers Ferry. In 1899 it was disinterred and taken to North Elba, N.Y., where it was laid in a grave near that of John Brown.

After the raid Newby's wife and his children were sold to a trader who took them to the Deep South.

Osborne P. Anderson's *A Voice from Harper's Ferry* (1861) is the only eyewitness account by one of the participants. W. E. B. Du Bois's *John Brown* (1909) gives details about the raid. Jules Abels's *Man on Fire: John Brown and the Cause of Liberty* (1971) is the source for the reburial of Newby. — LORENZ GRAHAM

NICKENS, JAMES (? –c. 1838), seaman and soldier of the American Revolution. A free-born descendant of Edward Nickens, a well-to-do Negro landowner of Lan-caster County, Va., Nickens and several brothers and cousins fought on land and at sea. James Nickens enlisted in the naval service in the early days of the war for a period of three years. He served on three or four vessels, notably for two years and three months on the *Norfolk Revenge,* an armed galley propelled by sails. After his discharge from the navy he enlisted at the Lancaster Court House for land service for the remainder of the war. He joined troops under Baron von Steuben in Cumberland County, and served in an artillery regiment in South Carolina under Gen. Nathaniel Greene. At the battle of Eutaw Springs, it is reported that officers prevented him from fighting, stationing him in the rear to take charge of the baggage.

After three years of service in the army he returned to Virginia and in 1818 began to receive the regular veterans' federal pension of $96 a year. His son, James Jr., received a grant of 200 acres of land in Ohio from the state government for his father's service. Like many other Virginia veterans and their descendants he sold his claim and perhaps purchased land in Virginia. As late as the 1940s descendants of Nickens were well-known residents of Stafford, Fauquier, Culpeper, and Warren counties, Va.

This sketch is based on *Virginia Negro Soldiers and Seamen in the Revolutionary War* by Luther Porter Jackson (1944, pp. 24–28). — RAYFORD W. LOGAN

NORTHUP, SOLOMON (1808?–1863), author of a slave narrative. He was born free in Minerva, N.Y., the son of a former Rhode Island slave, Mintus Northup, who had moved to New York with his owner at the beginning of the nineteenth century. Several years before Solomon was born his father was freed by his owner's will and became a landowning farmer who could meet the $250 property qualification required of colored voters in New York. Befriended in this environment, Northup followed in his father's footsteps. Until the age of thirty-three, he lived a simple uneventful life with his wife Ann Hamptom and their three children, farming and working as a violinist and semiskilled laborer in and around the small towns of upstate New York. Then, suddenly, in March 1841 he fell victim to a series of bizarre events that make his one of the more amazing autobiographies.

Northup accepted an offer from two strangers in Saratoga, N.Y., to catch up with their traveling circus and play in its band. But when the chase ended, Northup had been drugged, beaten, and sold to the major slave traders, Price, Birch and Company of Washington, D.C. Subsequently he was shipped to New Orleans via the costal trade from Hampton Roads, Va., on board the brig *Orleans.* This was a sister ship of the *Creole* which was seized by its slave passengers in October 1841, several months after Northup's departure from the same port. Northup and several of his compatriots had also tried to commandeer their ship but failed when smallpox struck his chief co-conspirator.

When Northup arrived in New Orleans he was purchased by a planter in the Red River region of Louisiana near Alexandria. For the next twelve years Northup lived in that area as a chattel slave under several masters. He tried on several occasions to escape but each effort failed. Except for another set of bizarre circumstances which enabled him to get word to his friends and family in New York, he might have died a slave.

Samuel Bass, an itinerant Canadian carpenter and perhaps an adventuresome abolitionist, plotted with Northup in 1852 to arrange his escape. A letter was dispatched to two white businessmen and former acquaintances of Northup in Saratoga. The letter eventually brought Henry B. Northup to the rescue as an official agent of the governor of the State of New York. A scion of the family that had once owned Northup's father, Henry B. Northup secured the necessary legal arrangements to free Northup. Bass, fearing the local slaveholders' wrath, went into hiding after assisting the rescuer and died eight months later in the home of a free black woman, Justine Tounier. Northup never again communicated with Bass and never learned of his final outcome.

Soon after Northup returned to his family in Glens Falls, N.Y., in January 1853, he set out to write the narrative of his enslavement. The demand for such literature was evident after the amazing success of Harriet Beecher Stowe's antislavery novel Uncle Tom's Cabin, which was released only a year before Northup's escape and was just then sweeping the Western world in many editions and translations. The remarkable similarity between the setting of that novel and the location of Northup's captivity in the Red River region of Louisiana was instantly noted by newspaper reporters who heralded Northup's sensational story. Mrs. Stowe herself grasped at those first newspaper accounts for use in The Key to Uncle Tom's Cabin, a sequel designed to prove the authenticity of her earlier novel.

Educated as a youngster in New York, Northup was literate but not a trained writer. He therefore turned for assistance to an acquaintance, David Wilson, who had served as superintendent of the area's public schools. Wilson was not an antislavery activist like most amanuenses of slave narratives. Instead he was a local author and poet who before and after Northup's narrative wrote other popularized accounts based on local events. Working together very closely, the two men finished their project within three months. By July 1853 the book, Twelve Years a Slave, was in the hands of reviewers.

The narrative won immediate success. It sold over 30,000 copies in American and European editions during Northup's lifetime and was reprinted several times in the nineteenth century after his death. He sold the copyright to the original publisher for $3000 and used the money to purchase a home in Glens Falls, where he lived with his wife and the family of his oldest daughter until about 1863 when he died.

The greatest personal satisfaction from the publication of the autobiography probably came when it led to the identity and capture of his kidnappers in 1854. The book caused one of its readers, Thaddeus St. John, to recall his meeting with two New York acquaintances, Alexander Merrill and Joseph Russell, in the company of an unknown black man while he was traveling to Washington in 1841. When a conference between St. John and Northup drew instant recognition, charges

were pressed by New York authorities against Russell and Merrill. Although their guilt was never questioned during several complicated trials and appeals, legal technicalities eventually led to the release of the two kidnappers.

No contemporaries, even in the South, ever questioned Northup's truthfulness. In fact, copies of his narrative purchased by Louisiana slaveholders remained within their families, inscribed with notations that attest to its accuracy. Even the cruelest owner of Northup, Edwin Epps, who was portrayed in the book as a "Simon Legree," confessed its truthfulness to a curious Union soldier from New York who had searched him out during a Civil War campaign in Louisiana in 1863.

The value of the narrative has been recognized by the leading students of slavery, whatever their differences of interpretation about the institution. Ulrich Phillips, Kenneth Stampp, Stanley Elkins, and John Blassingame have all either attested to the credibility of the narrative or used it extensively in their studies of American slavery. For an evaluation of Northup's narrative and its place within the genre of slave narratives, see John Blassingame's The Slave Community . . . (1972); Solomon Northup, Twelve Years a Slave (1965), edited by Sue Eakin and Joseph Logsdon; and Gilbert Osofsky's Puttin' on Ole Massa (1969). — JOSEPH LOGSDON

O'HARA, JAMES EDWARD (1844–1905), congressman. O'Hara was born in New York City on Feb. 26, 1844. According to Maurine Christopher's America's Black Congressmen (1971), his father was an Irish seaman and his mother a West Indian Negro. The family moved to the West Indies in 1850, but some time before the Civil War James O'Hara settled in North Carolina to work as a schoolteacher. He was employed as an engrossing clerk at the constitutional convention of 1868. After serving in the state House of Representatives from 1868 to 1869, he studied law at Howard University but did not graduate. He completed his studies in North Carolina and was admitted to the bar in 1873. Settling in Enfield, N.C., O'Hara served as chairman of the Halifax County Board of Commissioners and county attorney from 1872 to 1876. He was also one of only six Negroes elected to the state constitutional convention of 1875.

O'Hara made three unsuccessful campaigns for a congressional seat before his practically uncontested election to the 48th Congress (Dec. 3, 1883). He had lost a bid for the Republican congressional nomination in 1874 to John A. Hyman. In 1876 white Republicans threw out enough delegates to defeat O'Hara. After winning the nomination on the twenty-ninth ballot in 1878, he lost the election to William Kitchin, a white Democrat. O'Hara's attempt to contest the election was thwarted when a fire destroyed his home and the evidence for his challenge. This tragedy caused a delay which led Congress to reject his challenge. In the 1878 defeat O'Hara had had to contend not only with the Democrat Kitchin, but a dissident Negro Republican as well. But in the 1882 election he was unopposed and won by more than 17,000 votes. In 1884 he was reelected to the 49th Congress by a 6700-vote majority, but in the 1886 election he again was opposed by a white Democrat, Furnifold M. Simmons, and a Negro Republican, Israel Abbott. O'Hara lost the election to Simmons by a 2000-vote margin. Retiring from the national scene, O'Hara resumed his law practice in New Bern, N.C., and remained active in local politics until his death from a stroke on Sept. 15, 1905.

As a congressman O'Hara was an active legislator and an aggressive spokesman for several local and national causes. In the first session of the 48th Congress he introduced legislation to reimburse depositors of the Freedmen's Savings Bank and Trust Company for losses resulting from its failure a decade earlier. Although this bill died in the Committee on Claims, the persistent O'Hara reintroduced it during the first session of the 49th Congress. The second attempt, however, was no more successful than the first. Also unsuccessful was his attempt to have the value of the *Planter,* a vessel captured by Robert Smalls during the Civil War, reappraised and the benefits for Smalls and his crew increased. O'Hara's dogged determination did pay off, however, when after numerous attempts he succeeded in amending the Rivers and Harbors Appropriation Bill to secure greater funding for North Carolina projects.

While O'Hara's legislative efforts were diverse, including a bill introduced to benefit the Cherokee Indians of North Carolina, the issue he gave his most persistent attention to was civil rights legislation. In the state constitutional convention of 1875 he had advocated unsuccessful amendments designed to weaken and ridicule a Democratic proposition to outlaw interracial marriages. During his first year in Congress (1883–1884) he offered a constitutional amendment to guarantee the Negro's civil rights, evidently in response to the U.S. Supreme Court's decision in 1883 overturning the Civil Rights Act of 1875. This proposal died in committee, as did his effort to ensure equal accommodations in the restaurants and other public places of the District of Columbia. He did succeed, however, in amending the District of Columbia Appropriations Bill of 1887 to forbid discrimination in the pay of male and female schoolteachers.

O'Hara, a sharp and clever debater, succeeded in inserting a provision into the Interstate Commerce Bill of 1884 to require nondiscrimination in interstate railroad travel. In support of this provision he pointed out that Congress had already provided protection for animals in transit and was by this bill attempting to regulate freight rates. Therefore it was high time the national government acted to "also throw a shield around the citizen's rights." Unfortunately, Democratic opponents succeeded in weakening his amendment before final passage.

O'Hara was one of the outstanding Negro legislators to serve during the nineteenth century. He spoke frequently and articulately on a wide variety of issues and he won some legislative victories through sheer persistence. In a Congress with a different racial and political climate he might have been even more effective.

There are no full-length biographies of James O'Hara, but brief sketches of his life are in *The Biographical Directory of the American Congress* (1971), Samuel Denny Smith's *The Negro in Congress, 1870–1901* (1940), Maurine Christopher's *America's Black Con-*

gressmen (1971), and Elizabeth Balanoff's "Negro Legislators in the North Carolina General Assembly, July 1868–February 1872" (*North Carolina Historical Review,* Jan. 1972, pp. 22–55). — THOMAS HOLT

OLIVER, JOSEPH "KING" (1885–1938), jazz cornetist and bandleader. He was born near Abend, La., but grew up in New Orleans. After his mother, Jennie Davis, died in 1900, his half-sister, Victoria Davis Johnson, cared for him. He took employment as a butler at the age of seventeen and retained the job for nine years. As a child he performed in a children's brass band and probably received his first music instruction from the band's leader, Walter Kinchin. Early in life he lost the sight of one eye. He first studied the trombone, then later changed to the cornet. He began playing professionally about 1907 and during the next decade played with several brass bands: Olympia, Onward, Magnolia, Eagle, and Allen's Brass Band. He played also in cabarets with Richard Jones's Four Hot Hounds, Kid Ory's band, and his own group. It was Kid Ory who first billed him as "King Oliver" in 1917. During this period Oliver befriended the young Louis Armstrong, giving him free cornet lessons and finding music jobs for him.

The music played by Oliver and his contemporaries was racy, hot, and ragged; it incorporated elements of folk, blues, and ragtime in its brass-band style. In addition to playing for parades and dances the bands engaged in impromptu competitions on the streets. Armstrong tells how Oliver and Kid Ory "would give with all that good mad music they had under their belts and the crowd would go wild." New Orleans rated Oliver the best cornetist in the city; his playing was increasingly in demand everywhere, including college dances at Tulane University. Even then he had begun to innovate, such as putting a kazoo in the bell of his instrument, which gave it a distinctive tone.

During 1900–1917 the French Quarter red-light area called Storyville or "the District" provided good-paying, steady employment for Negro purveyors of hot music. After the United States entered World War I, New Orleans was filled with servicemen who found the attractions of Storyville irresistible, and the federal government forced its closing on Nov. 12, 1917. Oliver was among the hundreds of Negro musicians left stranded with the closing of their major source of income. He departed for Chicago in the summer of 1918, where he first played with the bands of Lawrence Duhé and Bill Johnson, then later formed his own. He played at the Pekin cabaret and the Dreamland dance hall and in 1921 toured in California.

When he returned to Chicago in 1922 Oliver organized his seven-piece "King Oliver's Creole Jazz Band," which was to make music history. He sent to New Orleans for Louis Armstrong and used others who had earlier migrated to Chicago: clarinetist Johnny Dodds, drummer Baby Dodds, and trombonist Honoré Dutrey. Pianist Lil Hardin and banjoist-guitarist Bud Scott completed the band. In April 1933 Oliver's band became the first Negro group to make a series of recordings, for Paramount, Gennett, Okeh, and Columbia. The recordings represent a landmark in the history of jazz, the first time that the rich store of Negro music was made available to the public. Oliver made arrangements for his group and composed some pieces, of which the best known are "High Society," "West End Blues," "Dixieland Blues," "Mr. Jazz," "Canal Street," and "Sugar Foot Stomp," also known as "Dippermouth Blues." In 1924 Armstrong left the band and it ceased to exist. Oliver started a new group, the Dixie Syncopators, with which he recorded, toured, and went to New York's Savoy Ballroom in 1927. This group was disbanded in the fall of 1927.

After 1928 Oliver's career took a downward turn, although he continued to tour and record. He lived for a while in Nashville, Tenn., and although misfortune dogged his steps, he continued to lead bands until 1937. After 1935 pyorrhea prevented him from playing with his old fire. In 1937 he settled in Savannah, Ga., where he spent the last year of his life in penury and obscurity, first as a fruitstall worker and then a poolroom attendant. After his death of a cerebral hemorrhage on April 8, 1938, his body was shipped to New York for burial by his half-sister Victoria in Woodlawn Cemetery.

Two biographical studies are Walter C. Allen's and Brian A. L. Rust's *King Joe Oliver* (1957) and Martin T. Williams's *King Oliver* (1960). Letters written by Oliver are published in Frederic Ramsey, Jr., and Charles Edward Smith's *Jazzmen* (1939). See also Louis Armstrong's *Satchmo* (1954), John Chilton's *Who's Who of Jazz* (1970), Gunther Schuller's *Early Jazz* (1968), and Eileen Southern's *The Music of Black Americans: A History* (1971). Valuable information was also provided by Oliver's nephew, Ulysses Kay. — EILEEN SOUTHERN

OWEN, CHANDLER (1889–1967), journalist, publicist, Socialist and Republican party functionary. Although born in Warrenton, N.C., and graduated from Virginia Union University in 1913, Owen was a northerner for most of his life. He came to New York City when the National Urban League made him one of its first fellows, and paid for his graduate work at the New York School of Philanthropy and Columbia University. In that city he met another young migrant, A. Philip Randolph, and the two studied Marx and Lester Frank Ward, listened to radical speakers of both races, and joined the Socialist party in late 1916, when Owen severed his Urban League connection. The two campaigned for Morris Hillquit in 1917, ran an employment bureau, and edited a Negro hotel-workers' newsletter until they began publishing their own Marxist-oriented monthly, the *Messenger* (1917–1928).

Through 1920 the two militants' writing focused on their admiration for the social aspects of the Russian Revolution, their pacifist objections to the First World War, their inclinations toward radical industrial unionism (both the International Workers of the World and Negro imitations of it), and their own participation in the Socialist party. Owen ran for New York assemblyman in 1920. The two were jailed briefly for allegedly violating the Espionage Act, and the Post Office Department and other governmental agencies considered them so subversive that their second-class mailing permit was lifted; their offices were ransacked more than once during the Red Scare hysteria.

Owen played a major role in the magazine's crusade to get Marcus Garvey deported in the early 1920s, but by 1923 he grew disillusioned with Socialist radicalism and moved to Chicago. He became managing editor of Anthony Overton's *Chicago Bee* in the mid-1920s, using it to support Randolph's efforts to unionize the Pullman car porters; at the same time he entered Republican politics, unsuccessfully seeking the House seat held by Rep. Martin Madden in 1928. This was to be Owen's last attempt at elected office, and he thereafter played a more significant, and behind-the-scenes, role in the party. He also continued newspaper work, and so impressed Frank Knox of the *Chicago Daily News* that he was a paid columnist for several years on that paper.

The occupation which provided Owen with his greatest success after the 1920s was public relations. Before and during the Second World War he worked for the Anti-Defamation League of B'nai B'rith and wrote on black anti-Semitism. During the war he was employed by the Office of War Information as its consultant on race relations, and wrote its pamphlet *Negroes and the War* (1942). Over five million copies were distributed to both soldiers and civilians. This tabloid-format booklet stressed the losses in liberties that Negroes would suffer if Hitler were victorious, while emphasizing the social gains that had been made under the New Deal. (Privately, Owen was not so enthusiastic about the Roosevelt record.) Also during this period he reached the zenith of his influence in the Republican party as a personal acquaintance and major speechwriter for Wendell Willkie and the publicity chairman of the Negro division of Willkie's 1940 campaign. His official title did not limit his activities to reaching Negro voters; he wrote important speeches for other audiences.

From 1945 to his death Owen continued promotional activities, both within and without the Republican party, as well as occasional journalism. He wrote speeches for Thomas Dewey in 1948, campaigned first for Robert Taft and then for Dwight Eisenhower in 1952, and did similar behind-the-scenes tasks for Gov. William Stratton, Sen. Everett Dirksen, and various local Illinois politicians. The only break in his longstanding Republicanism came in 1964 when he could not support Barry Goldwater and worked briefly to elect Lyndon Johnson. His private activities included promotional schemes, not all of which found buyers (for example, a proposal to encourage American corporate investment in Nigeria and another to write company propaganda for General Motors during a strike).

Chandler Owen was the type of individual who left different impressions on those who met him. To his close associates in the *Messenger* period he possessed a finely honed wit, not without cynicism and sarcasm. An iconoclast on nearly every subject, he found the *Messenger* a perfect outlet for his biting attacks on society. To those who knew him in later years he could be either a promoter and schemer, an influence-peddler trying overly hard to capitalize on his contacts with rich whites, or a writer and speaker of great intelligence and dynamism. Those who remember him with affection describe him as a sought-after speaker and writer who impressed many with the cogency of his argument and the breadth of his knowledge. It should be added that Owen could on occasion adjust his principles: he (infrequently) wrote political materials for Democrats, on a fee basis, and justified supporting Lyndon Johnson by claiming that his past civil rights record was of no relevance for, like Saul of Tarsus, Johnson had been converted and was now a St. Paul.

Owen's most important contributions came in his first thirty-five years, particularly during his co-editorship of the *Messenger,* as he wrote and spoke on the very cutting edge of racial militancy. The magazine's criticism of other Negro figures and analysis of the racial status quo was among the more perceptive analyses of World War I–era America. After this period Owen was less involved in purely racial affairs, and his direct impact on the black community, at least from 1945 to his death, was negligible.

There is no full-length biography of Owen. He is best revealed in the *Messenger.* There are valuable references in *A. Philip Randolph: A Biographical Portrait* by Jervis Anderson (1972). Theodore Kornweibel, Jr., who also interviewed numerous contemporaries of Owen, has charted his early career in *"No Crystal Stair": Black Life and the MESSENGER, 1917–1928* (1975).

— THEODORE KORNWEIBEL, JR.

PACHECO [FATIO], LUÍS, or LOUIS, LEWIS (1800–1895), Florida interpreter and central figure in a congressional *cause célèbre.* Louis owes his fame principally to Rep. Joshua R. Giddings's semifictional antislavery work *The Exiles of Florida* (1858). Louis was born on Dec. 26, 1800, in Spanish Florida, at New Switzerland, a plantation on the St. Johns River, the slave of Francis Philip Fatio. His parents were "pure-blooded negroes," and his father, Adam, was a "remarkably intelligent and ambitious negro," a "carpenter, boat-builder, and driver." Louis early became acquainted with the neighboring Indians, among whom he had a sister; a brother had been captured as a child but had returned some twenty years later and from him Louis "picked up a great deal of the language." During his boyhood his master's daughter, Susan Philippa Fatio, taught him to read and write. "He was ambitious to learn, and of quick perception" and acquired "a good deal . . . of book learning." But he was also of "a roving disposition" and "hated restraint." His knowledge of the free-and-easy life of the Seminole Indians and the Negroes who lived among them encouraged these tendencies, and as he grew older he occasionally ran away to live with the Indians. He early married a girl belonging to Ramón Sanchez of St. Augustine, who subsequently purchased her freedom, and the contrast between her position and his own probably contributed to his restlessness.

Louis's last flight from New Switzerland occurred shortly before Christmas 1824, when he is said to have run away to St. Augustine to visit his wife and decided not to return. After several months he was located at the Spanish fisheries on the Gulf Coast and taken to Tampa where, at his own request, he was sold to Col. George Mercer Brooke, commanding the fort there, who employed him as an interpreter, since he spoke four languages—English, Spanish, and probably, the two Musk-

hogean languages of the Seminole, i.e., Hitchiti and Muskogi. Louis was subsequently sold from officer to officer until Maj. James McIntosh in 1830 sold him to Antonio Pacheco, a Cuban with a trading post at Sarasota. After Don Antonio's death, Louis continued in the service of his widow. During the decade after his last unauthorized departure from the Fatio plantation Louis had shown none of his previous restlessness; his duties were not onerous and his position as interpreter was one of responsibility and prestige.

However, on Dec. 23, 1835, Louis was hired at $25 per month to accompany as guide and interpreter the command of Maj. F. L. Dade which, in anticipation of the outbreak of war with the Seminole Indians, was being sent from Fort Brooke, Tampa Bay, to reinforce the garrison at Fort King (Ocala). En route, on Dec. 28, the Seminole Indians and Negroes attacked the detachment and killed the entire command save two, who escaped terribly wounded. The assumption was that Louis was among the slain, but when, after the Treaty of Fort Dade (March 6, 1837) numerous Seminole chiefs began to "come in" with their people for shipment to the West, Louis in April or May appeared in the entourage of Chief Jumper, who claimed to have saved his life and therefore to be "entitled to him."

Louis thereupon entered a twilight zone of controversy and legend. As a Negro survivor of a detachment of U.S. soldiers which had been annihilated by an enemy force in which Negroes were conspicuous, particularly, it was alleged, in finishing off the wounded, he was a convenient scapegoat. A widely circulated 1837 publication described him as a free Negro who had joined the enemy and read to them the papers found on the dead (John Lee Williams, *The Territory of Florida,* 1837). Maj. Gen. T. S. Jesup, commanding in Florida, not only, as he later declared, found "the evidence . . . almost conclusive that he had been in constant communication with the Indians from the time the [Dade] command marched from Tampa Bay to that of its defeat" but also "abundant evidence that he had, on several occasions . . . taken part with the hostiles in their depredations upon the frontier inhabitants of Florida." If the general had not been so busy "he would have had him tried upon a criminal charge," and probably executed. As an alternative, after keeping him under confinement at Tampa Bay until the spring of 1838, he had him shipped to Fort Pike, La., en route to the Indian country. But Jesup never presented any of this "abundant" and "almost conclusive" evidence, and not until many years later was Louis able to reply to these charges.

At Fort Pike a white slave trader claimed Louis and thirty-one other Negroes on the basis of claims, purchased from Creek mercenaries, to Negroes they had captured. Louis, whether legally slave or free—and he was listed as "Said to be Free"—had certainly not been captured by the Creeks, so the claimant probably singled him out because he looked valuable. However, after the civil authorities had retained these Negroes in New Orleans (May 21 to June 28, 1838) the courts refused to sustain the claim, and Louis by September had reached the Indian country—after which he vanished from more than local notice for well over half a century. However, during the next score of years he gained *in absentia* a stature and notoriety as a *cause célèbre,* a symbol, and a character in fictional history which he has never entirely lost.

Mrs. Pacheco had moved to Cuba not long after the destruction of Dade's command, but a representative of the Pacheco estate had claimed Louis as soon as he surrendered, only to have the claim rejected on the grounds that he was too dangerous to be left in or even near Florida. It is not known exactly what action was taken during the subsequent decade except that in January 1842 General Jesup defended his shipment of Louis to the West and that Capt. John C. Casey, who had hired Louis as guide and interpreter, strongly supported the general's action. Although describing Louis as "very intelligent—speaking four languages . . . able to read and write . . . an able-bodied, likely negro, in the prime of life," he added that he "would be very valuable"— probably worth $1000—"where [sic] he not as bad as he is bright. It would be far better to pay any price for such a man and leave him in Arkansas, or hang him, than to return him to his owners, and let him return to the borders of Florida."

In 1847 Mrs. Pacheco's representative petitioned Congress for compensation on the grounds that her slave, while in the service of the United States, had been captured by Indians and that, when these Indians surrendered him, Major-General Jesup, instead of returning him, had shipped him west, beyond her ability to recover him, as admitted in the general's own statement. A majority of the House Committee on Military Affairs agreed to recommend a bill for fair compensation, but four antislavery members drew up a minority report, opposing the bill on the grounds that it recognized slavery. After protracted discussion and parliamentary maneuvering, during which the bill was both narrowly passed and narrowly defeated, on Jan. 19, 1849, it finally again passed the House but was never brought before the Senate, so the widow Pacheco remained uncompensated, to the great satisfaction of Joshua R. Giddings of Ohio and other antislavery congressmen. A more important result was that although Giddings was already aware of the Seminole Indians and their Negro allies whose history about a decade later he treated so romantically and imaginatively, the Pacheco case was responsible for his decision to make Louis a principal hero.

Giddings achieved this objective by accepting as valid General Jesup's most extreme accusations and charges as to Louis's involvement in the Seminole War —but treating them as greatly redounding to his credit —and also by elaborating considerably upon them, even deliberately distorting well-known facts to produce a more dramatic and tightly knit narrative.

Louis's own story was that after being hired as guide and interpreter, he was sent after the Dade detachment and found it on the Little Hillsborough. At the time of the attack he was with the advance guard, in "perfectly open country, and . . . had just looked carefully for Indians," when he "heard a rifle shot, and looked back . . . just in time to see Major Dade fall . . . shot in the breast." The country, a little before apparently empty, was now filled with charging Indians and Louis, much

frightened, threw down his gun and lay down behind a tree. As each Indian came up and leveled his gun at him he pled for his life, saying that he was a slave who was only doing as he was bidden. Chief Jumper finally intervened to protect him, but when the next day he asked permission to go back to his people, since he was "Spanish property," the chief angrily refused. Louis consequently "remained with the Indians," although once he stole a canoe and, traveling by night, reached the mouth of Peace (Pease) Creek, only to be captured and returned. Eventually he came to Tampa with the Indians and at Major-General Jesup's order was sent "in irons" to the Indian country near Fort Gibson.

Louis's life thereafter was far less romantic than the one imagined by Giddings, but more tragic. After living for a decade with the Seminole as a free man, he was in 1849 arbitrarily "sold," along with about thirty other Negroes, at $50 a head, to Marcellus DuVal, the corrupt Seminole subagent (probably by the new head chief Jim Jumper, Old Jumper's despicable son), and was put to work on the large DuVal farm south of Van Buren, Ark. (Thomas Elton Brown, "Seminole Indian Agents, 1842–1874," *Chronicles of Oklahoma* 52, Spring, 1973). In 1852 Louis and the other Negroes were "carried" to the vicinity of Austin, Tex., where they were living in 1861.

In 1892 a silvery-bearded Negro with deeply lined features appeared in Jacksonville, Fla., and identified himself so convincingly to Mrs. John L'Engle (the former Susan Philippa Fatio) as her former pupil Louis, that she supported him during the remaining two years or so of his life. During this period his "thoughts were fixed on the beyond" and his time was largely devoted to church attendance. "He said many times that he did not care to live now as he had set himself right before the world" —in an interview of October 1892 in which he presented one of the most vivid accounts on record of the destruction of Dade's command and exonerated himself, to general satisfaction, from the old charges of "betrayal." He died on Jan. 5, 1895, and after a funeral "attended by many representatives of the old families of Jacksonville," was buried at his birthplace of New Switzerland.

Louis Pacheco was a man of remarkable intelligence and energy who in a free society would probably have achieved distinction, but the frontier slave communities in which he spent his active life gave no proper scope for these qualities. His fate was to be remembered principally in the roles imposed on him from without—as the scapegoat for the military in the Dade debacle and as the symbol of the rebellious, red-handed slave in Giddings's semifictitious *Exiles.*

The only important authorities for Louis Pacheco's early life, prior to December 1835, and for his later life, after his arrival in the Indian country, are two interview statements and an obituary. "The Dade Massacre" (*Florida Times-Union* [Jacksonville], Oct. 30, 1892) was called to public attention by Minnie Moore-Wilson in *The Seminoles of Florida* (1896), and Kenneth Wiggins Porter used it and an obituary published Jan. 8, 1895, in "The Early Life of Luis Pacheco Né Fatio" (*NHB,* Dec. 1943). Volume 2 of *Pioneer Florida* (1959), edited by D. B. McKay, brought to light a statement allegedly published in the *Austin* (Tex.) *Commercial Journal* (Aug. 1861), which agrees in numerous respects with the 1892 interview but adds important details. Unfortunately, however, the *Commercial Journal* was published only 1877–1881, so that August 1861 could not have been the date of publication. Probably an interview of that date was published subsequently, and a copy of the issue, whatever it was, fell into the hands of McKay.

A principal authority for Louis's career from the "Dade massacre" to his arrival in the Indian country is "Report of the Committee of Military Affairs on the Petition of Joseph Elzaurdi, the Legal Representative of Antonio Pacheco, Praying Compensation for a Slave" (*House Report,* 30th Cong., 1st sess. [1847–1848], vol. 1, no. 187, serial no. 524). The National Archives, Department of the Interior, Florida Emigration Files, May–July 1838, contains lists and letters mentioning Louis.

Kirk Munroe's *Through Swamp and Glade: A Tale of the Seminole War* (1896), a "boys' novel," uses a character named Louis Pacheco who is, however, a youthful mulatto, Wild Cat's companion, rather than a mature Negro, and has a sister Louisa who is Wild Cat's *inamorata.* — KENNETH WIGGINS PORTER

PARKER, CHARLIE ["YARDBIRD," or "BIRD"] (1920–1955), musician. Born in Kansas City, Kans., on Aug. 29, 1920, he was the only child of Addie Boyley and Charles Parker Sr. Charles Sr. was a vaudeville singer, dancer, and pianist, railroad chef, and drunkard, who separated from his wife in 1929 and was knifed to death by a woman in 1937. She earned the family income in those early years as a domestic. She later became a nurse. From this humble and violent origin, Parker developed into an outstanding jazz alto saxophonist and innovator, an artist who "effected a total change not merely in the approach to the alto but to the entire concept of jazz improvisation. Parker spoke through his horn like a consumer of basic English who had suddenly swallowed the whole dictionary yet miraculously managed to digest every page" (Leonard Feather, *The Book of Jazz,* 1965).

In 1927 the family moved across the river to Kansas City, Mo., the larger city of nearly 400,000. Parker graduated from Crispus Attucks Public School at age eleven, and entered Lincoln High School where he played tuba, according to his mother, who bought him an alto saxophone (1933) because the tuba "was so funny coiled around him with just his head sticking out." He developed slowly as a performer, but he spent his nights in the alleys near speakeasies listening to the jazz musicians inside. The legend is that he earned his nickname "Yardbird," later shortened to "Bird," from his habit of sitting in the yard back of speakeasies fingering his saxophone. He was also called "Yard." Late at night he returned home with his sax in a brown bag, put it under his pillow, and went to sleep.

Parker later wrote about himself: "I began dissipating . . . when I was 12 years old; three years later a *friend* of the family introduced me to heroin. I woke up one morning very soon after that feeling very sick . . . the panic was on." He spent his life fighting addiction, warning young people against it, especially in broadcasts. Still later he said: "Any musician who says he is playing better on tea, the needle, or when he is juiced is a plain, straight liar" (Ira Gitler, *Jazz Masters of the Forties* [1966], p. 17).

After one year of study on saxophone Parker played in the band of Lawrence Keyes with other high school musicians. Gene Ramey said of him, "he was the saddest thing in the band." In 1935 he played his first professional job, Thanksgiving Day, at $1.25 for the evening. He quit school in 1935 and played at Greenleaf Gardens.

In 1936 he married Rebecca Ruffin, who bore a son Leon Francis Parker in 1937; they divorced in 1941. He then married Geraldine Margaret Scott on April 10, 1943.

The influences that first matured Parker musically were the jam sessions in Kansas City. "I tried doing double tempo on *Body and Soul.* Everybody fell out laughing. I went home and cried." When jamming with Count Basie's musicians in the spring of 1937, Jo Jones threw his cymbal across the room to express his opinion of Parker's playing; Parker packed up and left. He kept trying, and during the summer of 1937 joined the band of George E. Lee and played at a resort in the Ozarks. He took all the records of Count Basie with him and memorized Lester Young's solos. Efferge Ware, the guitarist, taught him how to play chord changes on the saxophone. In September Parker played in Jay McShann's band for a short time, then with Buster Smith, from whom he learned a more mature alto style, then back with McShann. Parker rode the rails to Chicago, where he went in baggy clothes directly from the freight train to Club 65. Billy Eckstine tells how Parker asked Goon Gardner to let him blow his alto, and "upset everybody in the joint" with his flamboyant style and technique. Parker was only eighteen.

Parker went to New York and for some months washed dishes in Jimmy's Chicken Shack where Art Tatum was the featured musician. Later he got a job with a group at Monroe's Uptown House. He went back to Kansas City where he played with Harlan Leonard's band and with Jay McShann again.

In 1939 Bird met Dizzy Gillespie in the Booker T. Hotel in Kansas City. McShann said of Gillespie, "he played in the same style as Bird—only on the trumpet" (Gitler, p. 19). Bird discovered his real style while jamming with guitarist Biddy Fleet. He "came alive" when he discovered that "what he had been hearing but couldn't play" was the high tones of the chords used as a melody. The piece was "Cherokee" (Sounds 1206, *Charlie Parker Bird on the Air,* recorded 1944–1945).

McShann had a great influence on Bird by putting him in charge of the reeds, which gave him the opportunity to write and to lead other musicians. Bird played his first records with McShann in 1940, and in 1941 the record *Confessin the Blues* (Decca) sold 81,000 copies. In 1941 McShann was playing at the Savoy Ballroom in New York, and Dizzy Gillespie, Chubby Jackson, Sid Catlett, and others came to sit in. These experiences and the jam sessions with Gillespie, Thelonious Monk, and others at Minton's Play House were so rewarding to Bird that he gave up touring with McShann and stayed in New York. In 1942 he played with Noble

Sissle's Band, doubling on clarinet. He also doubled on tenor with Earl "Fatha" Hines, and Gillespie said, "He played superbly. The whole band would be turned to look at him. Nobody was playing like that."

Parker toured with Billy Eckstine in a big band including Dizzy, and earned rave notices. His roots were now in 52nd Street where the new sounds were being heard. He returned to New York and formed his own trio, with Joe Albany on piano and Stan Levey on drums. Levey said: "I'd never heard anything like it."

Guitarists had a strong influence on Parker. In 1944 he recorded with Tiny Grimes for Savoy. In May 1945 Parker and Gillespie played with their own quintet at the Three Deuces on 52nd Street. Gillespie said later, "I was more for chord variations and he was more for melody, but when we got together, we influenced each other."

Nov. 26, 1945, is a date remembered by jazz experts. Savoy MG-12079, *The Charlie Parker Story,* is a record of a jam session in its entirety. Of "Ko Ko," one of the musical selections in the recording, Martin Williams wrote: "It has been a source book of ideas for fifteen years and no wonder; now that its basic innovations are more familiar, it seems even more a great performance in itself." "Ko Ko" has been called a condensed history of bop. These were great years, in which Parker and Gillespie led in the development of the style that is known as bop or bebop, a revolt against the comfortable lazy rhythms, harmonies, and melodies of commercialized music of the previous period.

Parker joined Gillespie in Hollywood at Billy Berg's. In 1946 they had their own group at the Finale Club in Los Angeles with Joe Albany and Miles Davis. The reception at Berg's was not cordial. With the exception of musicians, most Californians were not ready for the new music. Heroin was more expensive and money was scarce. Now Parker's excesses and addiction caught up with him. On July 29 he played a recording of "Lover Man" for Dial; in bad condition, he collapsed with a nervous breakdown. He was sent to Camarillo State Hospital and confined for six months. In February 1947 he made the record *Relaxin at Camarillo.* During these months he recorded with Granz's Jazz at the Philharmonic in Los Angeles. In April he returned to New York, amid great acclaim.

The year 1947–1948 was Parker's greatest period. His music perhaps reflects the love he felt for his new wife Doris Sydnor, whom he had known since 1944 and who had followed him to California and returned with him to New York. They were married in Tijuana, Mexico, in 1948.

Parker participated in the International Jazz Festival in Paris (1949). André Hodeir described Charlie Parker in *Jazz, Its Evolution and Essence* (1956), as "the real leader of the be-bop movement . . . just as Louis Armstrong around 1930 dominated his period . . . by creating new masterpieces that gave it a new reason for surviving . . . by boldly paraphrasing the melodies either in whole or in part." One French musician expressed surprise that there was no statue to Charlie Parker on Fifth Avenue.

Upon his return to New York, Parker found a new nightclub, Birdland, named in his honor. He played

there frequently until March 1955, a few days before his death.

The last years were chaotic. He married Chan Richardson in July 1950 and they had two children, Pree (b. 1951) and Baird (b. 1952). Pree died in 1953. Parker, depressed, took codeine in 1954. He was discovered by Chan at 5:00 A.M., treated, and cured at Bellevue. Discharged on Sept. 10, he recommitted himself Sept. 28. He was nevertheless featured in a Town Hall concert on Oct. 30.

Meantime he had returned to Europe in 1950: Sweden, Paris, and London. Back in Los Angeles in 1952 and 1953, he played and recorded some of his greatest works such as "In the Still of the Night," with rich orchestral background and vocals (*The Genius of Charlie Parker # 7,* V6-8009).

Drugs and alcohol finally took their toll in 1955. In Rochester, N.Y., he called for one number and came in playing another one. Fights with the men in Birdland were frequent, and other jobs were intermittent between sparks of the old genius when he played his best. He had given up heroin but was drinking heavily, as many as eight manhattans in a half hour. Peptic ulcers, liver trouble, and a heart that he had abused all his life finally downed him. He had gone to the apartment of his friend the Jazz Baroness, the Baroness Nica de Koeningswarter, the sister of Lord Victor Rothschild, in the Hotel Stanhope. Attended by a physician, he lasted five days, and succumbed while laughing at a juggling act on television, on March 12, 1955. He was buried in Kansas City, Mo.

The years have enhanced his reputation. André Hodeir wrote: "Charlie Parker was unquestionably jazz's greatest saxophonist and probably, with Louis Armstrong, its greatest improviser. . . . Parker's art contains musical and emotional potentialities which have not been fully exploited by younger musicians" (*Toward Jazz,* 1962).

Ross Russell's *Bird Lives! The High Life and Hard Times of Charlie (Yardbird) Parker* (1973) and Ira Gitler's *Jazz Masters of the Forties* (1966) are excellent biographies. In the Schomburg Collection is Bird's manager Robert Reisner's sensitive and affectionate *Bird: The Legend of Charlie Parker* (1962), which was adapted into a play in 1965 at the Café Au Go, 152 Bleecker St. Two novels have central characters based on Parker: Russell Ross's *The Sound* (1961) and John A. Williams's *Night Song* (1961), which was made into a film version in 1965, with Dick Gregory playing the part of Eagle.

Parker's awards include the New Star Award (1946 Esquire Poll) Downbeat Poll (1950–1954), Metropolitan Poll (1948–1953), Downbeat Hall of Fame (1955), Downbeat Critic's Poll (1953–1954), EOJ Poll as "Greatest Ever" (1956). His discography was done by Guy Kopelowicz, "Discographie de Charlie Parker" (*Jazz Hot,* Année 24, no. 133, June 1958, 40 pp.).

— RAYMOND LEMIEUX

PARKER, JOHN P. (1827–1900), abolitionist, inventor, army recruiter, and entrepreneur. He was born in Norfolk, Va., the son of a white father and a slave mother. At the age of eight Parker was sold to a slave agent in

Richmond, who in turn sold him to a slave caravan headed for Mobile, Ala. While on the auction block in Richmond, he was chained to an aged slave who was subsequently whipped to death. In Mobile, Parker was purchased by a physician who employed him as a household servant. While serving in the physician's home he learned to read and write. In 1843 he accompanied his owner's sons who were sent north to attend college. However, his owner feared he might escape in the North and soon requested Parker's return to Mobile.

While in Mobile, Parker worked in furnaces and iron manufactures, and as an apprentice acquired a rudimentary knowledge of the trade of plasterer. The plasterer, however, became dissatisfied with Parker's work and used a lathe with a nail attached to beat him. While hospitalized he was able to flee from Mobile to New Orleans where he stowed away aboard a riverboat bound for the North. He foolishly went above deck, was discovered, and was returned to his physician owner at Mobile. Apprenticed to a molder at a local iron foundry, he soon became a competent molder. Rigging up his own bench Parker quickly outpaced the production of other workers in the shop. The resulting ill-will among fellow workers brought a transfer to a New Orleans foundry, where his productive zeal alienated his co-workers and brought about his dismissal. Fearing that he would soon become a fieldhand, Parker worked during the next two years at a foundry and as a stevedore, purchasing his freedom for $1800 from his earnings.

In 1845, having paid the full amount for his freedom, Parker obtained a pass for Indiana, where he hoped to find employment at foundries near New Albany or Jeffersonville. On his northward journey Parker first began his career as a "conductor" on the Underground Railroad. Near Cincinnati, in concert with a local Negro barber, he was able to remove two young girls from slavery.

On May 12, 1848, Parker married Miranda Boulden, a native of Cincinnati. Eight children were born to this union, most of whom were to gain some success in the teaching profession across the country.

Around 1848 Parker left the Cincinnati area where he had worked in the molder's trade, and opened a small general store at Beachwood Factory, Ohio. Two years later he moved to Ripley, Ohio, the residence of the Rev. John Rankin, abolitionist and operator on the Underground Railroad. In Ripley, Parker worked independently of Rankin and prior to the Emancipation Proclamation took an active role in removing, reportedly, over 1000 slaves from bondage. Unlike many abolitionists Parker remained aloof from the organized church, which he viewed as an "enemy of the people."

Although devoted to the abolitionist cause Parker did not allow his inventive mind or entrepreneurial talents to lie fallow. In 1854 he erected a small foundry near Ripley, where he produced both special and general castings. Numbered among Parker's employees was a white Kentuckian, James Shrofe, whose family owned slaves. Much to Shrofe's annoyance Parker hid the slaves from the family and sent them to Canada.

Following federal approval of colored troops for service in the summer of 1863, Parker became a recruiter for the 27th Regiment, U.S. Colored Troops, one of two Ohio units. He was largely responsible for the enlistments the regiment gained from Kentucky. Parker's foundry also furnished castings to the war effort.

Parker's business, which came to be named the Ripley Foundry and Machine Company, manufactured among other things slide valve engines and reapers. At its peak the foundry employed twenty-five men full time. The foundry was still operating in 1981, although no longer under family ownership. In addition to his entrepreneurial talents Parker possessed an inventive mind, perhaps his most significant claim to recognition. He is among a limited number of Negro inventors who obtained patents in the United States before 1900. In September 1884 he patented a "screw for tobacco presses" and less than a year later, in May 1885, obtained one on another similar device. He is also reputed to have invented the "Parker Pulverizer," a type of harrow. Parker remained in the foundry business until his death on Jan. 30, 1900.

The "Autobiography of a Slave, John Parker, Brown County, Ohio, circa 1880," a typescript in the possession of the Flowers Collection of Southern Americana at the Duke University Library provides the most complete account of Parker's life. Louis Weeks's "John P. Parker: Black Abolitionist Entrepreneur, 1827–1900" (*Ohio History,* Spring 1971) places Parker in proper historical perspective and presents the most comprehensive published account. Henry Edwin Baker's *The Colored Inventor: A Record of Fifty Years* (1913) documents Parker's inventions. — FRANK R. LEVSTIK

PAUL, NATHANIEL (1793?–1839), clergyman and abolitionist. Paul was born free in 1792 or 1793 in Exeter, N.H., to a Negro veteran of the Revolutionary War. With his brothers Thomas, Benjamin, and Shadrach, he entered the ministry of the Baptist church. In Albany, N.Y., in 1820 he helped organize the Albany African Church Association. In 1822 he became the first pastor of the African Baptist Church, the only Negro church in Albany. Paul became an outstanding leader among Albany Negroes and his church became the gathering place for community activities. He began the Adult African Sunday School on May 12, 1822. Described as "ardently devoted to the education of the young and rising generation," Paul was instrumental in establishing the Wilberforce School, Albany's only school for Negro youth until 1873, which met weekdays in his church. Although the first two teachers were white, the third was his nephew, Thomas Paul, Jr., one of the first Negro graduates of Dartmouth. Nathaniel Paul was also founder and first president of the Union Society of Albany for the Improvement of the Colored People in Morals, Education, and Mechanic Arts.

Paul, "a solemn and persuasive" preacher, was one of the earliest prominent Negro abolitionists. In his oration celebrating the abolition of slavery in New York on July 5, 1827, he castigated slavery as "a hateful monster, the very demon of avarice" and urged "Africa's sons" to acquire education and to prepare for a new dispensation. Slavery, he argued, was destined to be overthrown and equal rights established due to the overruling providence of a "God of justice." He declared: "Did I believe that it [slavery] would always continue, and that man to the end of time would be permitted with impunity to usurp the same undue authority over his fellow, I would disallow any allegiance or obligation I was under to my fellow creatures, or any submission that I owed to the laws of my country; I would deny the superintending power of divine Providence in the affairs of this life; I would ridicule the religion of the Savior of the world, and treat as the worst of men the ministers of the everlasting gospel; I would consider my Bible as a book of false and delusive fables, and commit it to the flames; nay, I would still go farther; I would at once confess myself an atheist, and deny the existence of a holy God."

In the columns of *Freedom's Journal* and its successor *Rights for All,* he denounced the American Colonization Society and the Christian churches which, he maintained, supported colonization because of their control by rich pewholders.

He and his brother Benjamin, a pastor in Rochester, N.Y., in 1830 joined the Wilberforce Community in Upper Canada (Ontario) which had been established by Cincinnati refugees fleeing the fierce anti-Negro riot of 1829. Paul organized a Baptist church and a school which was taught by a daughter of Benjamin, who was elected to the board of managers. Austin Steward, a former grocer of Rochester, was president.

When the project to establish a Negro manual-labor school on the collegiate level at New Haven was thwarted by local white opposition, Wilberforce, Canada, was selected as the new site. Paul was commissioned in 1831 to spend two years in England collecting funds for the school and to remit them to Arthur Tappan, project treasurer. After borrowing passage money in Albany and Rochester, Paul, armed with a strong letter of commendation from John Colbourme, lieutenant-governor of Upper Canada, sailed from New York on Dec. 31, 1831.

Paul, the first of many American Negroes to carry the cause of abolition to England, was successful in his public appearances. British antislavery leaders, such as John Scobie, George Thompson, and Thomas Clarkson, welcomed him. In 1832 he gave evidence before a Parliamentary committee investigating slavery. William Lloyd Garrison joined him in the summer of 1833. At a great meeting held at Exeter Hall in London on July 13, 1833, Paul, sharing the platform with Garrison and Irish patriot Daniel O'Connell, charged the American Colonization Society with being American Negroes' "most bitter enemy" whose purpose was to perpetuate slavery. When Garrison left England in the autumn, Paul advanced him $200 to cover his transportation, a loan that was to lead to considerable misunderstanding among Paul, Garrison, and Tappan.

After the abolition of slavery in the British West Indies on Aug. 1, 1833, Paul decided to remain in England, since British abolitionists, having succeeded in the West Indies, were beginning to form societies for worldwide abolition. When Steward received Paul's letter in December 1833 he anxiously dispatched William Nell, a young Canadian Negro, to persuade Paul to return with the collected funds. Nell conveyed the message but, like Paul, did not return from England.

Free to remarry following the death of his first wife, Eliza, on Dec. 2, 1827, Paul married an Englishwoman and did not return until April 1835. Empty-handed, he reported that he had collected $8,015.80, expended $7,019.80 for expenses, loaned Garrison $200, and that he was owed $1600 in back salary. Disappointment and indignation in Wilberforce were so great that his life was threatened with lynching.

He returned to Albany and resumed his pastorate in 1838. Suffering from dropsy of the chest and an enlarged heart, he died on July 17, 1839. His last public act had been to attend a meeting convened by the Rev. Charles Bennett Ray to secure support from Albany Negroes for his newspaper, the *Colored American.* Paul was survived by his widow, Ann.

The import of his life was indicated by the *Colored American* which called him "a patron of everything, which tends to the emancipation of the enslaved and the enfranchisement of his aggrieved country men, and the promotion of the Redeemer's Kingdom." Paul was typical of the antebellum ministers who used their independence and influence to work for the abolition of slavery and the uplift of the Negro community.

Paul was the author of four tracts cited in Dorothy B. Porter (ed.), *Early American Negro Writings, Papers of the Bibliographical Society of America* (1945). His 1827 oration is in Carter G. Woodson (ed.), *Negro Orators and Their Orations* (1925), the 1833 speech in Dorothy B. Porter (ed.), *Early Negro Writing, 1760–1837* (1971). For aspects of Paul's life, see William H. Pease's and Jane H. Pease's *Black Utopias: Negro Communal Experiments in America* (1963); Austin Steward's *Twenty-Five Years a Slave and Forty Years a Freeman* (1861); Carter G. Woodson (ed.), *The Mind of the Negro as Reflected in Letters During the Crisis, 1800–1860* (1926); and George R. Howell's *History of Albany County* (1886). — J. CARLETON HAYDEN

PAUL, THOMAS SR. (1773–1831), clergyman, Masonic leader, and missionary. Paul was born free in Exeter, N.H., on Sept. 3, 1773. His father fought in the Revolutionary War. Three of his six brothers, Benjamin, Nathaniel, and Shadrach, also became Baptist ministers. Educated at a Baptist school in Hollis, N.H., he began preaching in 1801 and was ordained at West Nottingham, N.H., on May 1, 1805. Paul then moved to Boston at a time when the Negro community was organizing its own social institutions in response to Negro population growth, increased discrimination on the part of whites, and the desire for Negro leadership. Already in existence were the African Masonic Lodge, the African Society, and the African School, all of which met in private homes. Paul organized Negroes, indignant at the "Negro Pew," into a congregation on Aug. 8, 1805. He formed a committee on Feb. 26, 1806, to raise funds for purchasing a lot and to build thereon a meeting house with a schoolroom for the purpose of instructing "Africans in the principles of religion and education." Cato Gardiner, a native of Africa, single-handedly collected $1500. A group of white businessmen advanced sizable loans to the project, supervised the finances, and held title to the property until the mortgage was fully paid. The sale of pews was limited to "Africans and people of color." The African Meeting House, built on Beacon Hill in Belknap (later Joy) Street, was an imposing brick structure, three stories high, and costing $7230. It was Boston's first building to be constructed entirely by Negro craftsmen. When Paul was installed as pastor on Dec. 4, 1806, he reserved the first floor for white guests and the galleries for blacks.

After the death of Prince Hall in 1807, Paul, the only Negro pastor in Boston, emerged as the major leader. He was chaplain of the influential African Grand Lodge No. 459. His church, the only building in Boston controlled by Negroes, naturally became the focal point and meeting place for communal activities. The first floor was occupied by the African School taught by Prince Saunders. As Boston Negroes migrated to the neighborhood of the church, Beacon Hill became known derisively as "Nigger Hill."

Paul was respected by the white community and apparently experienced minimal discrimination. As a minister he participated regularly in the Boston Baptist Association, serving in 1820 as its representative to a nearby New Hampshire association. He was one of the few Negroes listed without racial designation in the white section of Boston city directories; however, after 1821 he too was relegated to the "Colored" section.

Such was his prestige as a pastor that some Negroes in New York City who desired a separation from a white Baptist church invited him to establish there a Negro Baptist church. This he did by founding the Abyssinian Baptist Church on July 5, 1809. Paul then returned to his pastorate in Boston. In 1815 he was lionized by abolitionists in England when he traveled there under the auspices of the Baptist Missionary Society of Massachusetts.

Paul persuaded the missionary society to commission him "to introduce the Protestant religion" in Haiti. With his passage paid by William Gray, Boston shipping magnate, and accompanied by Prince Saunders, he sailed from Boston on May 31, 1823, carrying a supply of Bibles and letters from prominent New York merchants. He arrived on July 4, 1823, at Port-au-Prince, where he was warmly received by Pres. Jean Pierre Boyer who was actively encouraging American Negro migration. Boyer, however, warned him that indiscreet Protestant preaching could easily cause rioting by the uneducated Roman Catholic population. Paul, therefore, prudently limited his evangelistic efforts to private homes and halls. His ignorance of French greatly hindered his efforts, and he returned to Boston shortly after September 1823. Thus Paul shares with Lott Cary the distinction of being a pioneer Negro Baptist missionary.

Although Paul praised Haiti as "the best and most suitable place offered to emancipated people of colour, for the enjoyment of liberty and equality," and carefully noted its geography and social and economic conditions for the benefit of prospective emigrants, he believed that conditions were not yet auspicious for black Americans to migrate to "the delightful island." Accordingly he continued his work for the abolition of slavery and the uplift of the American Negro community. Toward the end of 1827 he joined other Negroes

at the Belknap Street home of David C. Walker, where they promised their support to the newspaper *Freedom's Journal,* about to be published by John B. Russwurm, who had been teaching at the African School, and Samuel Cornish. Paul and Walker became general agents for the paper. Paul heartily encouraged William Lloyd Garrison, who founded New England's first abolitionist society at Paul's church. Paul resigned his pulpit in 1829 and died on April 13, 1831, after a painful illness.

Thomas Paul was married on Dec. 5, 1805, to Catherine Waterhouse by whom he had three children, Anne Catherine, Thomas Jr., and Susan. Anne Catherine married Elijah Smith, a headwaiter and poet. Thomas Jr. served a printing apprenticeship with Garrison, attended Noyes Academy with Alexander Crummell and Henry Highland Garnet, was one of the first Negro graduates of Dartmouth, and became a teacher. Susan Paul became a teacher and abolitionist.

The African Baptist Church, which served as a Jewish synagogue from 1904 to 1972, later housed the Museum of Afro-American History.

See J. Marcus Mitchell's "The Paul Family" (*Old Time New England,* Winter 1973) and Donald Martin Jacobs's "A History of the Boston Negro from the Revolution to the Civil War" (Ph.D. dissertation, Boston University, 1968). — J. CARLETON HAYDEN

PAYNE, CHRISTOPHER H[ARRISON] (1848–1925), clergyman, editor, and government official. He was born of free parents near Red Sulphur Springs, Monroe County, Va. (now W.Va.). His mother was the slave daughter of James Ellison, who instructed her and set her free. When Christopher was two years old, his father Thomas Payne, a cattle drover, was stricken with smallpox and died while taking a herd over the mountains to market. The boy's mother taught him to read so early he could not remember when he had not read. By the age of ten he had read through the New Testament. During the Civil War he was compelled to serve in the Confederate Army as a valet, but in 1864 returned to Monroe County to work on a farm. In 1866 he married Delilah Ann Hargrove (also given as Hargo), by whom he had six children. He worked on an Ohio River steamboat, settled in Charleston, W.Va., and went to school at night, beginning an intensive career of work and study which made him the leading figure of his race in the state. By 1868 he had gained his teaching certificate and gone to teach school in the mountains, while farming during the summer months. In 1875 he was converted and the next year licensed to preach. In 1877 he was ordained for full work in the ministry and entered the senior class of the Preparatory Department of Richmond Institute (later Virginia Union University). He preached in West Virginia (1878–1880), returned to Richmond, pastored the Moore Street Baptist Church, and studied at Richmond Theological Institute for three years while working to support his wife, children, and mother. He graduated in 1883 from the academy and the Theological Department of Richmond Institute.

A man of dignity, Payne impressed those he met with his earnestness and competence. He was appointed by the American Baptist Publications Society as a Sunday school missionary, and traveled for it from Norfolk, where for a while he held a pastorate, through West Virginia. He later estimated that as a minister he had delivered some 1500 sermons, converted 500 people, and founded nine churches and two Sunday schools while aiding dozens of others. Ill health forced him to give up evangelizing in 1884 and to assume duties as pastor of the First Baptist Church of Coal Valley, W. Va., but he had established a reputation impressive to white and Negro leaders alike. It enabled him to wield influence throughout the area.

Payne edited several weekly newspapers intended to strengthen the Negro community and neutralize prejudice among its foes. The *West Virginia Enterprise, The Pioneer,* and *Mountain Eagle* reflected his clear, forceful writing and speech; in addition he provided correspondence for the *Virginia Star* and the *Richmond Planet.* Payne emphasized education for his people: one of his projects was for a school with an industrial department.

He entered vigorously into politics. In 1884 he was an alternate delegate to the Republican National Convention. Four years later he represented the 3rd Congressional District of West Virginia at the convention which nominated Benjamin Harrison for president. Leaders of his state credited Payne's influence among the Negro voters with their having won their state campaign, and endorsed him for minister to Liberia in 1889. That year, however, he was appointed deputy collector of internal revenue at Charleston. In 1891 his efforts for improved educational opportunities for youth helped obtain passage of state legislation (1891) for a land-grant college, West Virginia Colored Institute (later West Virginia State College) at Farm, eight miles northwest of Charleston.

Payne had turned to the study of law, and in 1896 was admitted to practice in West Virginia. That year he was the first of his race to become a member of the state legislature. In 1903 he was appointed U.S. consul to St. Thomas, Danish West Indies. When the United States purchased these islands in 1917, Payne's services as consul ended. After the death of his first wife he stayed on with his second wife, A. G. Viney of Gallipolis, Ohio, practicing law, and acting as prosecuting attorney and police judge until his death at St. Thomas on Dec. 5, 1925.

Payne was not a spectacular figure and he did not attain national prominence, but his career was significant in West Virginia. I. Garland Penn saw him as "unquestionably, the most representative [N]egro in the state of W. Va., both in religion and politics" (*The Afro-American Press and Its Editors,* 1891, p. 569). Information about Payne's early life is based primarily on the sketch, probably autobiographical, in William J. Simmons's *Men of Mark . . .* (1887, pp. 368–73). He was listed in *Who's Who in America* (1916–1917). There are a few additional details in the article by Harrison G. Villard in *DAB* ([1934] 1962, 7, Part 2:324–25). The dates for his graduation from Richmond Institute are in the *General Catalog* (pp. 20, 21). The obituary, probably written by Carter G. Woodson, in the *JNH* (Jan. 1926, pp. 225–27) described him as "this useful man."

— LOUIS FILLER

PAYNE, DANIEL A. (1811–1893), clergyman, educator, church historian, and civic leader. Payne was born in Charleston, S.C., of free parents. His father, London Payne, was of English and African forebears; his mother Martha, of light-brown complexion and delicate frame, was of Indian and African heritage. Both parents left a deep impression on Daniel. "Often their morning prayers and hymns aroused me from my infant sleep and slumbers" and their concern for education was early passed on to him. After their death when he was nine and a half years old, he was raised by a great-aunt. For two years he attended the Minor's Moralist Society School maintained by free Negroes, where he studied the Bible and literature, one of a number of youth who were "ranked by some as economically and intellectually superior to any other such persons in the United States." Daniel was then apprenticed to a succession of artisans. His hunger for learning kept him reading into the night. He was also tutored privately by Thomas S. Conneau, who not only aided him in English and mathematics, but in French, Latin, and Greek.

In 1826 he joined the Methodist Episcopal church, and in 1828 he began a small school with three pupils, and during the evenings also instructed adult slaves. His success was immediate. The next year he built a school in which he taught a constantly expanding course of studies, from history—his "great delight"—to the sciences. On Dec. 17, 1834, the South Carolina legislature made such studies illegal and their teachers subject to a fine and whipping. Payne closed his school sadly, and on May 9, 1835, left the state, resolving not to return until slavery was ended.

In New York he was advised that the best field for him was the ministry. He studied at the Lutheran Theological Seminary, Gettysburg, Pa., from 1835 to 1837 when poor eyesight caused him to discontinue. He supported himself by blacking boots, working at table, and doing other menial jobs. He was licensed to preach in 1837 and in 1839 was ordained by the Franckean Synod of the Lutheran church, an antislavery advance guard of the denomination. He served briefly as pastor of a Presbyterian church in East Troy, N.Y., where his exhortatory style of speaking caused him to lose his voice for a year. Declining an invitation to become a traveling agent of the American Anti-Slavery Society as inappropriate to his ministry, he opened a school in Philadelphia in 1840, which grew rapidly. He joined the African Methodist Episcopal church in 1841, was received as a preacher by its Philadelphia Conference (1842), and appointed the following year to its traveling ministry. In Washington, D.C., he helped build the pews in Israel Bethel Church, organized perhaps the first colored pastors association, and founded a school for young preachers. He also worked to organize a Home and Foreign Mission Society. Such measures were taken in the face of prejudice against an educated ministry. In 1845 he was transferred to Bethel Church in Baltimore.

In 1846 Payne was delegated to represent his church at a conference of the Evangelical Alliance in London, but a stormy voyage threatened the ship and he returned to the Washington area. A turning point in his career was the antagonism he met from the Ebenezer A.M.E. Church in Baltimore, which rejected him as a pastor for being too genteel and as one who "Won't let them sing the cornfield ditties." The rebuff set him off on one of his most important projects, which was approved by the General Conference of 1848: to prepare a history of their church. In pursuing this work Payne encountered indifference as well as careless disregard for documents and details. But his persistent inquiries and visits, which took him from New Orleans to Canada, enabled Payne to preserve materials and information which are an indispensable source for the history of the denomination.

At the General Conference of 1852 Payne was elected a bishop, an event which Benjamin Brawley called "the most important event in the history of the African Methodist Episcopal Church since the election of Richard Allen to similar office in 1816." For the next twelve years he traveled widely, sometimes in slave territory where his safety was not ensured. He continued his efforts to set up schools, organize mothers for home training and education, and preach the need for literary and historical societies. He published in 1850 *Pleasures and Other Miscellaneous Poems.* He wrote, in the *Anglo-African Magazine,* "I admit that gold is a *great power.* But I also *contend,* that *knowledge* is a *greater.* In a country like this, where gold is an *idol* to be worshipped, who fears a 'rich negro?' " (April 1859, p. 120). His own experience in the South had shown him that the ability to impart knowledge was "indeed a power dreadful and dreaded."

The deepening social crisis found Payne continuing to be concerned for his own charges as well as the nation's policies. His program for his own people was unreservedly moral. At the same time he sought funds for practical needs, as in his appeal to the abolitionist Gerrit Smith in December 1860 in behalf of six worthy young men who were preparing for the ministry. As he wrote, he did all he could, but "you know I am myself poor; and I find it difficult to provide for my own family." He was also among those who importuned Pres. Abraham Lincoln to announce the emancipation of the slaves, and worked with Charles Sumner and Carl Schurz to that end.

On March 10, 1863 he purchased for $10,000 Wilberforce University, founded by the Methodist Episcopal church in Xenia, Ohio, in 1856. Payne became the first president of a Negro institution of higher learning in the country. Under his direction Wilberforce survived a severe fire in 1865 and attained solvency by his acquisition of $92,000 during his presidency. His educational methods and discipline permitted Wilberforce to attract responsible students and educators. His return to Charleston following the end of the Civil War was a personal triumph. He founded the South Carolina Conference (May 15, 1865), which became the center for A.M.E. church expansion throughout the South.

In 1866 Payne published his *Semi-Centenary and the Retrospection of the AME Church in the United States of America.* The next year he visited Europe, where he was received as a distinguished American. Very thin, keen-eyed, and highly dignified, somewhat under average size but impressive with ample forehead and a voice expressing consecration, he was chosen to be president at the organization of the Methodist Pastors Association in Paris in 1868. A delegate to the first Ecumenical Conference of the Methodist Episcopal Church (London), he read a paper (Sept. 13, 1881) on Methodism and temperance. In the same year he founded the Bethel Literary and Historical Association in Washington, D.C.

He resigned active management of Wilberforce in 1876, but became chancellor of the university and dean of its theological seminary. His duties as a bishop were diminished to give him time for literary work. His *Treatise on Domestic Education* (1885) summed up many of his views and experiences. His *Recollections of Seventy Years* (1888) was one of the important memoirs of his time. Payne's interest in maintaining standards and projects of value to his people never flagged. For instance, in 1892 Payne offered W. E. B. Du Bois a position at Wilberforce University.

At the World Parliament of Religions in Chicago in 1893, as part of the World's Columbian Exposition, Payne was a conspicuous figure, and on Sept. 22 presided at a session commemorating American liberties. He later prepared, as usual, to spend his winter in Jacksonville, Fla., but died at Wilberforce on Nov. 21, 1893. His remains were taken to Baltimore for burial.

Payne was married in 1847 to Julia A. Ferris, who died within a year. He was married in 1853 to Eliza J. Clark.

The principal sources are Payne's *Recollections of Seventy Years,* with an Introduction by the Rev. Francis J. Grimke . . . edited by the Rev. C. S. Smith (1888); *History of the African Methodist Episcopal Church,* edited by the Rev. C. S. Smith (1891); *The Life of Daniel Alexander Payne LL.D.,* by the Rev. C. S. Smith (1894); and Josephus Roosevelt Coan's *Daniel Alexander Payne, Christian Educator* (1935). The brief sketch by Harrison G. Villard in *DAB* ([1934] 1962, 7, Part 2:-324–25) offers a few more details. — LOUIS FILLER

PEAKE, GEORGE (1722–1827), inventor. Peake, whose name was variantly spelled Peek and Peak, was a native of Maryland but had lived in Pennsylvania before becoming the first permanent Negro settler in Cleveland. He was a British soldier in the French and Indian War and served at the battle of Québec under Gen. James Wolfe. He was later reported to be a deserter from the British army with money entrusted to him to pay the soldiers.

Peake's residence in Cleveland dates from 1809 when he arrived with his family. He bought a 100-acre farm on the western outskirts of the city. Along with his four sons he was remembered because he gave to the community a highly prized labor-saving device, a new type of hand mill which he invented. Prior to this mill, grain was processed with a rather crude instrument called a "stump mortar and spring pestle" which the pioneer settlers adapted from the Indians. Peake's mill was also superior to the Indian device because it produced a better quality of ground meal by the use of stones eighteen to twenty inches in diameter.

Peake's wife was evidently a woman of some means, for she was reputed to have possession of a half bushel of silver dollars, a mark of distinction when the commercial medium was barter and trade. Peake's ability to purchase a 100-acre tract of land was evidence that he compared favorably with other pioneers.

Peake died in September 1827 at the patriarchal age of 105; the place of his interment is unknown.

The major source is Russell H. Davis's *Black Americans in Cleveland* (1972). Gertrude V. R. Wickham's *Memorial to Pioneer Women of the Western Reserve* (1896) is the principal source for Peake's wife. Earlier sources are John D. Taylor's *History of Rockport, Ohio* (1858) and the *Cleveland Leader* (Nov. 8, 1858). No patent for his hand mill was recorded (Davis to Rayford W. Logan, Oct. 10, 1974). — RUSSELL H. DAVIS

PEAKE, MARY S[MITH] [KELSICK], (1823– ?), pioneer schoolteacher. Born free in Norfolk County, Va., for several years she lived in Alexandria with her aunt, Mrs. John Paine, where she acquired a good education. When Alexandria was retroceded to Virginia in 1846 and its schools closed to Negroes, Mary Peake moved to Norfolk with her mother. A period of religious mysticism, stemming perhaps from her vision of service to the poor, led her to participate actively in aiding the poor and the helpless, assisted by the First Baptist Church of Norfolk. When her mother married Thompson Walker, the family moved to Hampton. There Mary Peake founded the Daughters of Zion to look after the ill and the needy, and to teach children and adults in her home. In 1851 she married Thomas D. Peake, who had been manumitted some years before, served in the Mexican War, and gone to sea. Their daughter Daisy was born some five years later. When the town of Hampton was burned by Confederates the night of Aug. 7, 1861, the Peakes escaped to Brown Cottage on the grounds of Chesapeake Female College, downstream and across the Hampton River. On Sept. 17, 1861, she opened on the first floor of Brown Cottage the first of the schools sponsored by the American Missionary Association. Already in the terminal stages of tuberculosis, she died some time thereafter.

Peake is frequently referred to as the "first Negro teacher in a day school after the beginning of the Civil War." In fact, others had preceded her in teaching in the settlements under Union control. She was, however, the first to teach in the American Missionary Association schools. And "she was the first of the teachers who brought to her work manifest excellence along with dedication, and whose school served as an inspired example for those who followed her." The legend that she taught her first classes under the beautiful "Emancipation Oak" on the outskirts of the present Hampton Institute is unfounded. (Peake was too weak to walk from Brown Cottage to the tree; Negroes under the protection of Fortress Monroe had been freed by the Confiscation Acts of Aug. 6, 1861, and July 17, 1862; the Emancipation Proclamation of Jan. 1, 1863 did not cover these areas.)

Most accounts are based on the Rev. Lewis C. Lockwood's *Mary S. Peake, the Colored Teacher at Fortress Monroe* (1862). He had talked with her, her mother, and contemporaries. Edward Graham of Hampton Institute obtained information about her family in an interview (Sept. 7, 1967) with Gertrude Peake Anderson,

daughter of Thomas D. Peake by his second marriage.
— RAYFORD W. LOGAN

PELHAM, BENJAMIN B. (1862–1948), editor, politician, and municipal official. He was born in Detroit, the third son and sixth child of Robert and Frances (Butcher) Pelham. The Pelhams, free Negroes, had moved to Detroit in 1862 with their five children from the farm they owned in Petersburg, Va., to escape persecution by local whites envious of Pelham's prosperity as a mason and builder. Benjamin Pelham attended Detroit public schools, and while still in school became a newsboy for the *Detroit Post* (later the *Post-Tribune*). Upon graduation from Detroit High School he obtained a job as an apprentice typesetter at that newspaper, Michigan's leading Republican daily. The industrious youth came to the attention of *Post-Tribune* owner James H. Stone, who paid for a course in accounting for young Pelham at a local business college. In 1879 while still in the *Post-Tribune*'s employ seventeen-year-old Benjamin Pelham began his own "amateur" eight-page paper *The Venture,* as an offshoot of a small printing firm he also owned with his brother, Robert Jr. In 1883 the Pelhams and two Negro associates founded the weekly *Plaindealer,* successor to the *Venture,* operating out of offices in the *Detroit Post-Tribune* building with a staff of five in addition to the principals. The Pelhams continued to work for the *Post-Tribune* company while publishing their own newspaper.

The *Plaindealer* became widely known throughout Michigan and the entire Midwest for its strong political views and comprehensive coverage of Negro affairs. In 1884 the *Plaindealer*'s editorials successfully promoted a Colored Men's State Convention which provided a vehicle for colored political expression in the Midwest and was the impetus for a subsequent national colored convention. Benjamin Pelham also led a successful campaign for the election of a Negro as delegate-at-large to the Republican National Convention held in Chicago later that year.

In addition to news of weddings, births, parties, and other social notes, the *Plaindealer* carried articles by the leading Negro figures of the day, including Frederick Douglass, Blanche K. Bruce, John E. Bruce, Ida B. Wells (Barnett), John R. Lynch, and others, and printed dispatches taken from other important newspapers on events in their areas affecting Negroes.

In 1893, after ten years of publication, the *Plaindealer* ceased publication in the midst of financial difficulties. Ben Pelham had been appointed a clerk in the Internal Revenue Office. The head of that office, Collector James H. Stone, was the same man who had taken an interest in him as a child and had interested him in business. In 1895 Pelham became a clerk in the Detroit treasurer's office. Detroit then had a population of 200,000 of which 3500 were Negroes. Pelham then moved to the office of the registrar of deeds where he worked until 1906. In that year Charles Buhrer, who had been the printer for the *Detroit Post-Tribune,* was elected county auditor and he appointed Ben Pelham county accountant, the highest nonelective office in Wayne County (Detroit) government.

A few years later Pelham was also named clerk to the

Board of Auditors, a seemingly minor job in which he became influential because of his responsibility for shaping the agenda for the board, Detroit's governing body. Ben Pelham became known in Detroit political circles as a shrewd politician and able administrator whose help was sought by knowledgeable men who had important business to do with municipal government in that city. When Democrats won city hall in 1934, Republican Pelham retained his post because of his encyclopedic knowledge of the city's administrative maze. When he retired as county accountant in 1942 after forty-seven years of continuous public service, Wayne County had become the fourth largest in the nation with a budget of $40 million. Pelham, who was then eighty, had married in 1895 Laura Montgomery of Sandwich, Ontario, and they had two children, Frances and Alfred M. The latter subsequently became budget director of Wayne County. Benjamin Pelham died in Detroit on Oct. 7, 1948.

Although brief, *Forty Years in Politics: The Story of Ben Pelham* (1957), by Aris A. Mallas, Jr., and others, is the best printed source. I Garland Penn's *The Afro-American Press and Its Editors* (1891, pp. 158–61) is valuable for its comments about the *Plaindealer*.

— ERNEST DUNBAR

PELHAM, ROBERT A., JR. (1859–1943), politician, journalist, government official, and inventor. He was born on a farm near Petersburg, Va., the second son and fifth child of free Negro parents, Robert A. and Frances (Butcher) Pelham. After harassment by local whites envious of the Pelhams' relative prosperity, the family sold its farm and moved briefly to Columbus, Ohio, and Philadelphia, before settling in Detroit around 1862. In Detroit Pelham's father worked as a mason, plasterer, and independent builder. The senior Pelham entered politics after Negroes received the vote in 1870 and served regularly in city, county, and state Republican conventions. He was also a trustee of Detroit's Bethel African Methodist Episcopal church. Robert Pelham, Jr., attended Detroit public schools (which were segregated until 1872), and while still in school became a newsboy for the *Detroit Post*.

After his graduation from high school in 1877, with three years of military training, young Pelham took a full-time job at the *Post* (later the *Post-Tribune*), then Detroit's leading Republican daily newspaper, eventually heading its subscription department. From 1884 to 1891 Pelham and a younger brother Benjamin distributed the *Post* and its successors as independent contractors. While still employed at the *Post*, Robert joined his brother Benjamin in editing and publishing a short-lived "amateur" newspaper, *The Venture* (1879); then the Pelham brothers and two Negro associates (William H. Anderson and Walter H. Stowers) started the weekly *Plaindealer* (1883–1893). The *Plaindealer*'s mission was "to set an example that there is no field of labor which cannot be successfully explored and cultivated by the Afro-American who is energetic and painstaking; to provide a medium for the encouragement of literary work, for the creation of a distinctive and favorable Afro-American sentiment, for the dislodgement of prejudice and for the encouragement of patriotism."

As the newspaper's managing editor and business manager for eight years, Pelham was the major force that helped make that publication the leading Negro newspaper in the Midwest. Among its contributors were Frederick Douglass, John R. Lynch, Blanche K. Bruce, John E. Bruce, and Ida B. Wells (Barnett). (The *Plaindealer* was the second newspaper in Michigan to own and operate the Rogers Typography Press, and the Pelhams continued to do job printing as well as printing a small newspaper for its white publishers.)

Robert Pelham propelled himself into a position of prominence in local, state, and national Negro affairs by drawing on his family's influence, his editorship at the *Plaindealer*, and his own considerable political skills. He attended state colored conventions and represented Detroit at the 1884 National Colored Men's Convention in Pittsburgh, after the *Plaindealer* had campaigned editorially for the creation of these conventions, and he served as temporary chairman of the Michigan Colored Convention. In 1889 Pelham was one of the colored leaders responsible for the creation of the short-lived Negro protest organization, the Afro-American League, and the *Plaindealer* became its Michigan voice.

Sharing his father's conviction that the road to Negro progress lay through political participation, Pelham worked diligently in the 1880s organizing political clubs in the Negro community while gaining increasing prominence in the Republican party organization. In 1884 he was a founder of the political-social Michigan Club and a member of the Young Men's League, both overwhelmingly white organizations. In the same year (1884) Pelham was appointed a clerk in the office of Detroit's collector of internal revenue. In 1887 he was also given a state appointment as deputy oil inspector for Detroit. Pelham was a delegate to the 1888 Republican National Convention, a sergeant-at-arms at the 1896 convention (after declining a nomination as delegate that went to an influential white politician), and was a member of the Afro-American bureau of the Republican National Committee.

As the leading Negro politician in Detroit in the 1880s and 1890s, Pelham was a key figure in bringing that city's Negroes into the Republican fold while at the same time obtaining a measure of political leverage.

In 1891 Pelham was appointed a special agent of the U.S. Land Office and left the *Plaindealer*, but he lost his federal post when Democrats won the presidency in 1893. The Republicans regained the White House in 1897 and Pelham was reinstalled in the job as land office agent the following year.

In 1900 he moved to Washington, D.C., and won an appointment as a clerk in the U.S. Census Bureau. He attended Howard University while working at the bureau and received his LL.B. degree in 1904. During a thirty-seven-year career with the Census Bureau, Pelham received patents for a tabulation machine (1905) and a tallying device (1913) for use in the bureau's work. After his retirement from the bureau in 1937 he published and edited the Negro weekly *Washington Tribune* from 1939 to 1941, and was founder of a Negro news agency, the Capital News Services, Inc.

Pelham married Gabrielle S. Lewis of Adrian, Mich., in 1893. Mrs. Pelham, a noted pianist, was director of music at Howard University from 1905 to 1906, and also operated a school of music in the capital. The Pelhams had four children: Dorothy, Sarah, Benjamin, and Frederick. Pelham died of a coronary occlusion at his home in Washington on June 12, 1943, and was buried in Lincoln Memorial Cemetery.

He was an important architect of Negro political strategies in the last two decades of the nineteenth century.

The essential facts are in Aris A. Mallas, Jr., and others' *Forty Years in Politics: The Story of Ben Pelham* (1957). See the sketch, with a critical bibliography, by David M. Katzman in *DAB, Supplement 3, 1941–1945* (pp. 595–96). I. Garland Penn's *The Afro-American Press and Its Editors* (1891, pp. 158–61) is valuable for its comments about the *Plaindealer*. A longer sketch with biographical information, comments about the *Plaindealer,* and an engraving, is in William J. Simmons's *Men of Mark . . .* (1887, pp. 1022–26).

— ERNEST DUNBAR

PENN, I[RVINE] GARLAND (1867–1930), teacher, editor, and author. Penn was born in New Glasgow, a small village in Amherst County, Va. When he was five years old his parents, Isham and Maria Penn, moved to Lynchburg, Va., where there were better schools. In 1882 he entered the junior class of the high school. Needing funds, he taught in a school in Bedford County for one year and graduated from the Lynchburg high school in 1886. During 1886–1887 he was superintendent of a school in Amherst County; in the latter year he became a teacher in the Lynchburg public schools and rose to the position of principal.

Meanwhile he had begun his career as an editor. Before his graduation from high school, he was on the editorial staff of the *Lynchburg Laborer.* His discussion of the material, intellectual, moral, and religious welfare of Negroes and of Virginia won the praise of the editors of the white newspapers, the *Spirit of the Valley* and the *Lynchburg Daily Advance.* Lack of support, however, soon forced the *Laborer* to suspend publication. He then wrote for the *Richmond Planet* of John Mitchell, Jr., and the *Virginia Lancet.* In 1889 he was a correspondent for the *Knoxville Negro World* and the *New York Age.* Daniel B. Williams, on the faculty of Virginia Normal and Collegiate Institute, Ettrick, Va., mentioned among Penn's more important public speeches an address at the annual conference of the colored Methodist Episcopal church in Charlottesville (1889) which advocated the establishment of a theological and normal school in Virginia. Penn was twice appointed commissioner at Lynchburg for the Petersburg Industrial Association, and was secretary of the Board of Directors of the Lynchburg Real Estate Loan and Trust Company.

Penn is best known for his *The Afro-American Press and Its Editors,* published by Willey & Co., Springfield, Mass., in 1891. The title page lists "Contributions By" twenty well-known Negro men and one woman, Mrs. N. F. (Gertrude Bustill) Mossell. Part I, consisting of seventeen chapters and 105 pages, gives brief accounts of newspapers and magazines published and edited by Negroes, from *Freedom's Journal* and *Rights of All* (1827) to 1891. Part II devotes 199 pages to short bio-

graphical sketches of seventy-four editors. Most of them are short—shorter, for example, than those in *Men of Mark . . .* (1887) by William J. Simmons. Like those in Simmons, they are usually laudatory. Penn did, however, mention about twenty significant individuals not included in *Men of Mark,* notably John B. Russwurm, Nathaniel Paul, Thomas Paul, Charles Ray, David Ruggles, and T. McCants Stewart. Among those to whom Penn expressed appreciation for assistance were Richard T. Greener, T. Thomas Fortune, Alexander Crummell, Frederick Douglass, and Benjamin W. Arnett for loans of books and information.

The Afro-American Press and Its Editors has served as a valuable point of departure for subsequent relevant works.

In 1893 Penn wrote an eighty-one-page brochure, *The Reasons Why the Colored Man Is Not in the World's Columbian Exposition, The Afro-American's Contribution to Columbian Literature,* with an introduction by Frederick Douglass. He was head of Negro exhibits at the Cotton States and International Exposition in Atlanta (Sept. 18, 1895) and is said to have asked Booker T. Washington to speak.

He was a joint editor with Henry Davenport Northrop and contributor to *The College Life; Or Practical Self-Educator; a Manual of Self-Improvement for the Colored Race . . . Giving Examples and Achievements of Successful Men and Women of the Race . . . Including Afro-American Progress.* Published in 1895, this little-known volume of almost 700 pages (and "hundreds of superb engravings") typified the attempt to counter white-supremacist sentiment near the end of the twentieth century. Penn was also co-editor (with J. W. E. Bowen) in 1902 of a somewhat similar volume of 600 pages, *The United Negro: His Problems and His Progress, Containing the Addresses and Proceedings* (of) *The Young People's Christian and Educational Congress, held* (at Atlanta), *August 6, 1902* (reprinted 1969).

From 1897 until 1912 Penn was assistant general secretary of the Methodist Episcopal church. In 1912 he was elected corresponding secretary of the M.E. Board of Education for Negroes, and held the position until 1925, when he became secretary of endowments and field activities in the same department. He was a trustee of many educational institutions and a member of the Joint Commission on Unification of the M.E. Church.

At the time of his death on July 22, 1930, he had been married for forty-one years. His wife predeceased him on June 19, 1930.

Much of the factual information about Penn is in his *The Afro-American Press and Its Editors* (1891, with an introduction by Daniel D. Williams). For his career after that date, see *The Crisis* (Feb. 1931, p. 56). See also *The Booker T. Washington Papers,* edited by Louis R. Harlan et al., vol. 3, *1889–1895* (1974).

— RAYFORD W. LOGAN

PENNINGTON, J[AMES] W[ILLIAM] C[HARLES] (1807–1870), teacher, clergyman, author, and abolitionist. He was born a slave on the Eastern Shore of Maryland. Accounts of much of his life are based on his autobiography, *The Fugitive Blacksmith, or, Events in* the History of James W. C. Pennington . . . formerly a Slave in the State of Maryland, United States. Generally accepted as his own work (not ghost written as were many other slave narratives), it was published, with a preface, in London in 1849 and quickly went through three editions. His infant years were marked by brutality; when he was four his mother, an older brother, and he were given to his first master's son, Frisbie Tilghman of Hagerstown, Md., and taken to live in Washington County. He was hired out as a stone mason, learned blacksmithing on the home plantation, and worked at the trade until he ran away when he was about twenty-one. After a perilous flight he arrived at the home of a friendly Pennsylvania Quaker. A Quaker taught him the fundamentals of a beginner's education, which he continued in evening school and under private tutoring on the western part of Long Island. In the early 1830s he taught in colored schools in Newtown, Long Island, and New Haven, Conn. He studied theology and held pastorates in African Congregational churches at Newtown (1838–1840) and at Hartford (1840–1847). In the latter city he served twice as president of the otherwise all-white Hartford Central Association of Congregational Ministers. Meanwhile in 1841 he had been named president of the Union Missionary Society (a forerunner of the American Missionary Association), which urged its members not to buy slave-produced goods. The society denounced colonization but favored participation by American Negroes in carrying the Christian Gospel to Africa. Pennington was launched on a career which continued until alcoholism caused his death on Oct. 20 or 22, 1870, in Jacksonville, Fla.

In 1843 he represented Connecticut at the World's Anti-Slavery Convention and was a delegate of the American Peace Convention to the World's Peace Society meeting in London. He was given a tea at Surrey in June, attended by 500 guests. In July he delivered two impressive sermons at the Queen's Street Chapel in London. He also lectured and preached in Paris and Brussels. During much of the period 1847–1855 he was pastor of the First (Shiloh) Presbyterian Church on Prince Street in New York City. One of the more memorable events during his pastorate was the two-day meeting in April 1849 where speakers refuted the charge allegedly made in England that American Negroes supported the American Colonization Society. In addition to Pennington, the speakers included Charles B. Ray, Henry Bibb, Charles Reason, George T. Downing, Charles Lenox Remond, and Frederick Douglass. Pennington was one of the few, however, who later emphasized the little concern by France and England for the evangelization and conversion of the indigenous peoples of Africa. At about the same time (1850) he made in The Fugitive Blacksmith one of his most caustic criticisms of slavery in the United States. In 1852 Pennington, along with Reason and Samuel E. Cornish, argued against an appropriation by the New York state legislature to assist emigration.

After the passage of the Fugitive Slave Act (1850) Pennington, fearing recapture as a runaway slave (a fact which he had not made known to his wife), went abroad until a payment of $150 was made to the estate of his former master and he was manumitted at Hartford on June 5, 1851. During this trip abroad he was, according to some historians, awarded the degree of Doctor of Divinity by the University of Heidelberg. The original source of the statement seems to be in the sketch of Pennington in William J. Simmons's Men of Mark . . . (1887, p. 914).

During this second trip Pennington, sponsored by the Glasgow Female Anti-Slavery Society, gave impassioned denunciations of slavery throughout Scotland, attended the World Peace Conference at Frankfurt-am-Main, returned to England with Henry Highland Garnet, and after an enthusiastic welcome in the United States resumed his active career.

Pennington, Ray, and James McCune Smith helped raise money for the successful defense of the "Christiana Sufferers," including thirty-five Negroes, who had been charged with treason for preventing the capture of runaway slaves.

Pennington helped organize in 1855 one of the early civil rights groups, the New York Legal Rights Association, and brought suit against the Sixth Avenue Railroad Company for the right to use public conveyances. Although his suit was unsuccessful, Jane H. Pease and William H. Pease conclude that the organization "achieved within four years considerable equality of treatment in the city's transportation system" (p. 167).

On the eve of the Civil War, Pennington became increasingly militant. During the imprisonment of John Brown, Pennington urged in a guest editorial in the Anglo-African Magazine (Nov. 5, 1859): "Pray for John Brown." He asked, "Shall all these abominations be done and ratified among men on earth, and the Mighty and Holy God remain inactive upon His Throne?" Pennington clearly expected the answer to be no.

In addition to The Fugitive Blacksmith, Pennington wrote A Text Book of the Origin and History, &c. &c of Colored People (1841). Proud of his allegedly "unadulterated African Blood," he attributed racial characteristics such as color to environment rather than race. He asserted that American race prejudice glorified neither God nor man, and denied that Negroes were the descendants of Cain. A few of his sermons and addresses survive, including Covenants Involving Moral Wrong Are Not Obligatory Upon Man: A Sermon (1842) and The Reasonableness of the Abolition of Slavery (1856). He also contributed articles to the Anglo-African Magazine. During some of his later years he was listed in the Minutes of the Presbyterian General Assembly as a member of the Third New York Presbytery, without a pastorate, his address appearing as New York, Hartford, or vaguely, Maine.

Little is known about Pennington's private life. Frederick Douglass and his wife "were married by Rev. J. W. C. Pennington, then a well-known and respected Presbyterian minister. I had no money with which to pay the marriage fee, but he seemed well pleased with our thanks" (Douglass, Life and Times of Frederick Douglass, Written by Himself . . . reprinted in 1962 from the revised edition of 1892, p. 205). Increasingly debilitated by his alcoholism, Pennington went to Jacksonville, Fla., in 1869 or 1870 hoping to regain his health.

He founded a small colored Presbyterian church but died on Oct. 20, 1870, according to the *Minutes of the General Assembly, Presbyterian Church in the U.S.A.* (1871, p. 601), or Oct. 22, according to the *New York Observer* (Nov. 10, 1870).The rather short but favorable article by A. Everett Peterson in *DAB* (7, Part 2:-441–42) makes no mention of the degree from Heidelberg.

The best interpretations of Pennington's career, supported by specific footnotes, are in Benjamin Quarles's *Black Abolitionists* (1969) and Jane H. Pease's and William H. Pease's *They Who Would Be Free . . .* (1974).

— RAYFORD W. LOGAN

PETIONI, CHARLES A[UGUSTIN] (1885–1951), physician, editor, businessman, and spokesman for West Indian independence. The son of Charles E. and Alicia (Martin) Petioni, he was born in Trinidad on Aug. 27, 1885, where he was educated and began a career in business and journalism. In 1913 he married Rosa Alling and became the father of two daughters, Margaret (who died before 1950) and Muriel. In 1918 the colonial government of Trinidad sent word to him that his outspoken views about local political and economic conditions had permanently damaged future career opportunities for himself and his family. He therefore departed for New York, where he worked as a manual laborer during the day and attended the City College of New York at night. Upon completion of the premedical course at City College, he entered Howard University School of Medicine from which he graduated in 1925. After an internship at St. Agnes Hospital in Raleigh, N.C., he returned to New York where he began medical practice. He devoted much of his subsequent life, however, to numerous Afro-American and West Indian social, political, economic, and medical organizations. He died on Oct. 15, 1951.

He acquired some knowledge of business as a clerk and manager (1901–1908) of the Trinidad branch of the famous Paris firm, Félix Potin and Company. He gained experience as a journalist by serving as chief reporter and subeditor of newspapers in Trinidad (1908–1918), associate editor of the *New Negro* in New York (1918), Washington representative of *Business World* (1921–1922), and most important as a reporter (1921–1925) while a student at Howard University for *Negro World,* the organ of Marcus Garvey and his Universal Negro Improvement Association.

When he began to practice medicine in New York he became part of a complex struggle for better medical conditions for Negroes in Harlem. Serving a neighborhood which had become predominantly Negro, Harlem Hospital had only recently admitted Negro doctors to practice. In addition Negro graduates of white medical schools were considered to be, and sometimes considered themselves to be, superior to graduates of Negro medical schools. Petioni fought for equal status for the graduates of Howard and Meharry, and later helped to unite the warring factions of Negro physicians when they came together to found the Central Harlem Medical Society. At a later period, because conditions in public hospitals had not improved satisfactorily, Petioni helped to organize a group which bought Mount Morris Park Hospital as a private institution for Negroes.

His views on the economic development of what he called "our group" required emancipation from "economic slavery and dependence . . . without any assistance on the part of others." To this end he founded the Metropolitan Benefit Insurance Society, Ltd., in Trinidad and the Trinidad Co-operative Bank, Ltd. In New York City he founded the Trinidad Benevolent Society and the Lupetner Finance Corporation. This experience led the founders of the Carver Federal Savings and Loan Association to consult him about their proposed institution, and at the time of his death he was vice-chairman of the board of that organization.

Petioni's most significant activities sprang from the needs of the West Indian community in Harlem and also embraced activities of Afro-Americans, West Indians in the Caribbean, and Africans. The Trinidad Benevolent Association, an organization similar to many in New York, provided social and economic support for West Indian immigrants from the respective islands. However, Petioni's vision extended beyond a parochial identification with one island.

In 1930 he founded the West India Committee of America, which became the Caribbean Union. The purposes of this organization were to stimulate the development of West Indian business enterprises, give charity to West Indians in need, find employment for immigrants, encourage naturalization, lobby for better treatment of West Indians under British rule, and foster better relations between native and foreign-born Negroes in New York. In 1936 the organization raised money and supplies to aid the defense of Ethiopia against Italy and registered strong protests against Britain's lifting of sanctions against Italy. Later that year Petioni, as president of the Caribbean Union, led a coalition of Negro groups to Mayor Fiorello LaGuardia to protest general conditions in Harlem, and specifically the policies of the Police Department and the Board of Education. This united effort, for which Petioni was the spokesman, included organizations as diverse as the Communist party, the Urban League and the Peace Mission Kingdom (Father Divine).

The activities of the Caribbean Union demonstrate that although Petioni retained a strong identification with the West Indies, he did not believe in divisions among Negroes in their struggle against white oppression. In 1936 he wrote an article "The Intra-racial Problem" in which he expressed great concern about a growing rift between native and foreign-born residents of Harlem, saying that whites who sought to control blacks were the only ones who benefited from this division. He also urged support for a resolution of the National Negro Congress in February 1946 to create an International Negro Congress in order to establish better relationships among Negroes throughout the world. He also worked with Adam Clayton Powell, Jr., in the successful effort to obtain jobs for Negroes in white-owned Harlem businesses.

Petioni was actively involved in events which ultimately led to the independence of some of the British West Indies. In the late 1930s a group of West Indians in New York formed the West Indies National Emergency Committee to discuss the implications of World

War II and of United States interests in the Caribbean on the future of the West Indies. This group became the West Indies National Council of which Petioni was the second president. Through the active financial support of the West Indian community in the United States it held mass meetings, sought allies among Latin American governments, established contacts with leaders in the West Indies, and attempted to influence the British and United States governments in order to assert the right of West Indians for self-determination, self-government, and independence. Petioni, as representative of the council, went to the 1945 United Nations San Francisco Conference to lobby for this right. His activities earned him a place on the U.S. attorney-general's subversive list.

Some basic facts are in *Who's Who in Colored America* (1950). Most helpful were the manuscripts of the Works Progress Administration study "The Negro in New York," in the Schomburg Center for Research in Black Culture, New York City, and interviews with members of the Petioni family, friends, and associates.
— ROBERT G. MCGUIRE III

PICKENS, WILLIAM (1881–1954), educator, orator, editor, and civil rights leader. He was born in Anderson County, S.C., on Jan. 15, 1881, the sixth of ten children and the first son of Jacob and Fannie Pickens. Jacob, who was a strong influence on William, managed a white hotel in Pendleton, S.C. In 1888 the Pickens family moved to Arkansas, where William graduated first in his class from Little Rock's Negro high school. In 1902, after three years at Talladega College in Alabama, he transferred to Yale University. He completed a degree in classics in 1904 and was the second Negro elected to Yale's Phi Beta Kappa chapter. For the next sixteen years Pickens taught classics and sociology at Negro colleges: Talladega (1904–1914), Wiley University in Marshall, Tex., (1914–1915), and Morgan College in Baltimore (1915–1920), where he became the college's first Negro dean (thereafter he was best known as "Dean" Pickens) and later vice-president.

Pickens left Morgan College in 1920, moving with his wife (the former Minnie Cooper McAlpine whom he had married in 1905) and three children to New York City to become field secretary of the National Association for the Advancement of Colored People (NAACP). A member of the Committee of One Hundred of the association in 1910, Pickens, while teaching at Talladega and Morgan, was one of the NAACP's most successful recruiters. He worked closely with NAACP Board Chairman Joel E. Spingarn in establishing the Louisville branch (1914), challenging "Jim Crow" in Memphis (1915), and advocating the colored officers' training camp at Fort Des Moines, Iowa, during World War I. Pickens delivered major addresses at the NAACP's 1915 convention and its National Conference on Lynching in 1919, and by 1920 was recognized, in Langston Hughes's words, as "one of the most popular platform orators in America." As a contributing editor (1919–1940) of the Associated Negro Press, the largest Afro-American news-distributing service, Pickens, in addition to writing about national and international affairs, publicized the NAACP's activities in his weekly

articles, which appeared in more than 100 Negro newspapers.

As field secretary (and later director of branches) of the NAACP from 1920 to 1940, Pickens's responsibilities included recruiting new members, helping establish new branches, acting as liaison between the national office and the branches, participating in fundraising campaigns, and handling special assignments. He investigated several notorious lynchings and collected firsthand evidence of racial discrimination at public facilities in the South. In 1930 he initiated the NAACP's campaign against Senate supporters of Supreme Court nominee John J. Parker. Pickens rallied Kansas Negro voters against Henry Allen (R-Kan.), who had been floor leader for Parker's nomination.

Throughout his career Pickens was at the center of controversy. At first identified by William Monroe Trotter as a "Bookerite," Pickens joined the "radicals" in 1905 in attacking Booker T. Washington's accommodationist policy. He wrote for the Niagara Movement's organ, *Voice of the Negro,* and in 1910 signed W. E. B. Du Bois's anti-Washington "Appeal to England and Europe." Pickens briefly considered working for Marcus Garvey's Universal Negro Improvement Association, but in 1922 he denounced Garvey's Back-to-Africa scheme and alliance with the Ku Klux Klan, and joined the "Committee of Eight" in demanding Garvey's imprisonment. Pickens worked with Earl Browder and other American Communists on the "Hands Off China" Committee and other anti-imperialism and anti-war organizations, and following his Russian visit in 1927, he wrote favorably about the Soviet experiment. But he rejected their overtures and in the 1930s he was the NAACP's leading critic of the Communists' handling of the Scottsboro Case. Although generally popular with NAACP branch leaders, Pickens often clashed with executive staff members, especially National Secretary Walter White.

In 1937 Pickens took a year's leave from the NAACP to lecture for the Federal Forum Project, a national network of adult education centers. He spoke to racially mixed audiences about Negro history, culture, and contemporary racial issues. In May 1941 he took another leave to serve as director of the Interracial Section of the Treasury Department's Savings (later War) Bonds Division. Although he was a lifelong Republican and outspoken critic of President Roosevelt's failure to support civil rights legislation, Pickens was chosen because before Pearl Harbor he was one of the most prominent Negro leaders who advocated American intervention against Germany and Italy.

As he had in World War I, Pickens preferred reserving criticism of armed forces segregation policies until after the war was over. The NAACP, led by Walter White, advocated a "Two Front" policy, opposing discrimination while supporting the war effort. Pickens's public criticism of the "Two Front" approach led to his dismissal as NAACP field secretary in June 1942. The following year Martin Dies (D-Tex.), chairman of the House Committee on Un-American Activities, accused Pickens of being a Communist and tried to remove him from his Treasury post. House leaders, fearing adverse reaction among Negroes during wartime, came to Pickens's defense. He remained at his job, and by 1945 his staff had sold an estimated $1 billion worth of bonds to Afro-Americans. Pickens retired from the Treasury Department in 1950. In his last year he and his wife traveled in Europe, the Middle East, and the West Indies. On April 6, 1954 he died aboard ship off the Jamaica coast and was buried at sea.

Pickens's autobiography, *Bursting Bonds* (1923), ends with his becoming NAACP field secretary. Pickens's political and social views are most clearly expressed in his *The New Negro* (1916). *The Crisis* (Sept. 1937, pp. 276, 285) describes four lectures in Seattle for the Federal Forum Project. There is an obituary, probably written by William M. Brewer, in the *JNH* (July 1954, pp. 242–44). An unpublished dissertation based on the comprehensive Pickens Papers at the Schomburg Center for Research in Black Culture is Sheldon Avery's "Up From Washington: William Pickens and the Negro Struggle for Equality, 1900–1954" (1970).

— SHELDON AVERY

PICKETT, BILL [professional nicknames: The Dusky Demon; The Modern Ursus] (1870–1932), internationally famed rodeo performer and the originator of "bulldogging." He was born on Dec. 5, 1870, in Williamson County, Tex., the second child of thirteen born to Thomas Jefferson Pickett, a former slave said to have been of "mixed Negro, Caucasian, and Cherokee Indian blood," and his wife Mary (Janie) Virginia Elizabeth Gilbert, a small, very dark, woman of "Negro, Mexican, Caucasian, and Indian extraction."

After going through the fifth grade Bill became a ranch hand, developed his roping and riding skills, and invented a type of steer wrestling known as "bulldogging." Wrestling steers or bulls down by hand, sometimes popularly called bulldogging, goes back to the Roman arena, but "bulldogging proper" involved the performer's riding up alongside an animal, throwing himself onto its back, gripping its horns, and twisting its neck until he could sink his teeth into its upper lip or nose, and then throwing his hands wide and toppling off its back, his weight and the painful grip of his teeth bringing the animal over on its side.

The various accounts of how and when Pickett originated this technique agree only that he got the idea from seeing a cattle dog holding a "cow critter" by the nose or upper lip. According to one account Pickett developed this feat out of the exigencies of working cattle in the Texas brush country, where roping was often impossible and the cowboy sometimes had to throw an animal by wrapping its tail around his saddle horn or wrestling it to the ground by its horns. Pickett was grappling ineffectually with an unusually stiff-necked longhorn cow when he remembered a big mastiff which could bring rebellious steers to the ground by gripping their noses in his teeth, in the manner of the bulldogs which thus "baited" English bulls. Pickett accordingly sank his teeth into the animal's nostrils or lip and immediately brought her down. (But another story says that when he was only ten he discovered that he could throw a calf by this method and also hold calves with his teeth during branding.) He eventually began regularly to use his bulldogging skills both in catching

wild cattle in the brush and in putting on exhibitions at various stockyards. Sometime in the late 1880s Pickett became at least a semiprofessional, appearing at county fairs and on similar occasions.

On Dec. 2, 1890, Pickett had married Maggie Turner, by whom he had nine children, and the responsibilities of a growing family may have stimulated greater professionalism. Under a series of white managers (c. 1898–1906) he bulldogged at first in various Texas cowtowns and then—sometimes in association with some of his brothers—in other western states, Canada, and Mexico. In 1905 he received national attention (*Leslie's Illustrated Weekly*, Aug. 10, 1905) as "a man who outdoes the fiercest dog in utter brutality."

Pickett stood five feet seven inches tall and weighed only 145 pounds, but was "hard and tough as whalebone, with . . . powerful shoulders and arms." He wore a small moustache and for exhibition purposes "dressed as a Spanish bullfighter." In 1907 he was signed to a contract with the Miller brothers' famous 101 Ranch Wild West Show, with headquarters in Oklahoma's Cherokee Strip. He became one of its principal attractions, perhaps its star performer, and under its auspices attained national and international fame, appearing for a decade all over the United States, in Canada, Mexico, Argentina, and England. During this period the exploit which he had invented was accepted as a regular and leading rodeo event, although soon considerably modified. Few if any of Pickett's imitators were willing, at least for long, to follow the original technique of "taking a mouthful" of a steer's upper lip or nostrils and depending on the grip of the teeth and the weight of the body to throw the animal. Some so-called bulldoggers were simply "twisting them down" by hand. Objections by humane societies may also have contributed to abandonment of the true bulldog style. Advancing years and their concomitant dental deficiencies forced even Pickett to depend on the leverage of his powerful hands rather than the grip of strong jaws and teeth, although for some time he continued at least to simulate his old bulldog stunt and for publicity purposes he was sometimes fined for "cruelty to animals." But bulldogging for some time survived vestigially, with the "bulldogger," after throwing a steer by hand, holding it briefly by its upper lip with his teeth.

Pickett became a legendary figure and was credited with such fabulous feats as throwing a buffalo bull and a fully antlered bull elk. Although at various times "nearly every bone in his body was broken," he so thoroughly "dominated" the animals that no steer or bull ever tried to gore him after a bulldogging. His most grueling experience was undoubtedly in the Mexico City bullring (Dec. 23, 1908), after Joe Miller for publicity purposes had callously bet that Pickett could "stay with" a Mexican fighting bull for fifteen minutes, during five minutes of which he must actually be grappling with the animal—unless he threw it earlier. But the Mexican audience, enraged at this "insult" to their national sport, showered him and his horse with missiles ranging from fruit and cushions to bottles, brickbats, and knives, his horse was badly gored, he was severely gashed and had three ribs broken, and although he won the bet by staying on the bull's back for seven and a half minutes, he never succeeded in throwing the animal and he and his horse narrowly escaped with their lives.

Pickett retired from rodeo shortly after 1916. He went back to the 101 Ranch, where he worked until near the end of the 1920s, then settling on a little ranch he had bought near Chandler, Okla. However, when in 1931 the 101 Ranch was in serious financial difficulties, he returned to help out. On April 2, 1932, while roping a stallion on foot, the animal turned on him and smashed in his head. He was buried at White Eagle Monument, Marland, Okla.; the Cherokee Strip Cowboy Association erected a marker and Col. Zack Miller, who declared that he was "the greatest sweat-and-dirt cowhand that ever lived," wrote a poem in his honor which long adorned bunkhouse walls. His principal memorial, however, is the rodeo event without which, although in drastically modified form, no rodeo is complete. Homer Croy's verdict is that he "contributed more to rodeos than any other one person."

The only full-length account is Col. Bailey C. Haines's *Bill Pickett, Bulldogger: The Biography of a Black Cowboy* (1977), but innumerable books and articles about the 101 Ranch and Wild West Show, rodeo, and the Western cattle country give significant attention to this fabulous character. — KENNETH WIGGINS PORTER

PINCHBACK, P[INCKNEY] B[ENTON] S[TEWART] (1837–1921), Negro leader of the Reconstruction era. He was born on May 10, 1837, probably in Macon, Ga., the son of a white Mississippi planter, William Pinchback (who later moved to Virginia), and Eliza Stewart, a woman of mixed African, Indian, and Caucasian ancestry. She had been Pinchback's slave but was taken by him to Philadelphia and emancipated before the birth of Pinckney. Hence Pinckney, who was the eighth of ten children whom she bore to Pinchback, was free-born.

In 1846 or 1847 young Pinckney and his older brother Napoleon were sent to Cincinnati to attend school. In 1848, following the death of William Pinchback, Eliza and the rest of her children moved to Cincinnati to forestall an attempt by white relatives of the elder Pinchback to reenslave them. Denied any part in the inheritance of Pinchback's estate, the family was in severe financial straits. Pinckney went to work as a cabin boy on canal boats in Ohio and later on Mississippi riverboats. By 1861 he had attained the position of steward.

In May 1862 he jumped ship at Yazoo City, evaded the Confederate blockade, and made his way to New Orleans, already controlled by Union forces. After volunteering for service to the Union he was assigned the duty of recruiting colored volunteers, later known as the Corps d'Afrique. However, he resigned his commission as captain after a short time in protest against discriminatory treatment of colored officers and troops. After Gen. Nathaniel Banks decided to expand Negro forces, Pinchback was authorized to raise a company of colored cavalry.

As early as 1863 he began to urge political rights for Negroes, declaring that if they were not allowed to vote they should not be drafted. He asserted that his troops "did not ask for social equality and did not expect it, but they demanded political rights—they wanted to be men." Pinchback played a prominent part in the founding and organization of the Republican party in Louisiana, and became a member of the state central committee in 1867. As a member of the Louisiana constitutional convention of 1867 he worked for free tax-supported schools, universal suffrage, and an article guaranteeing the civil rights of all persons. In 1868 he was elected to the state Senate, where he fought for the adoption of a law prohibiting discrimination in public accommodations, and was a delegate to the 1868 Republican National Convention. In 1870 he founded the *New Orleans Louisianian,* a newspaper which continued publication until 1881.

In 1871 he was elected president *pro tempore* of the state Senate and as a consequence succeeded to the position of lieutenant-governor when the incumbent, Oscar J. Dunn, died. From Dec. 9, 1872, to Jan. 13, 1873, he was acting governor during the interval when the white carpetbag governor, Henry Clay Warmoth, was suspended because of impeachment proceedings.

During this stormy and confused period when rival factions fought for control of the Republican party, Pinchback was at first allied with Warmoth. But as Warmoth made overtures to the liberal Republican movement and Democrats, Pinchback became increasingly alienated from him. In 1871 he announced his support for the reelection of President Grant. In 1872 there was strong support for the nomination of Pinchback as governor, but he withdrew from the contest and acquiesced in the nomination of W. P. Kellogg, whom he had formerly opposed. In return Pinchback was named as candidate for congressman-at-large and was declared elected. While he was serving as acting governor, the state legislature also elected him to a six-year term in the U.S. Senate. Both elections were contested and in each case Pinchback's opponent was ultimately seated. However, the Senate voted him a sum of money equal to his senatorial pay during the prolonged period when the contest was being decided.

In 1877, after the Democratic claimant to the governorship, F. T. Nicholls, was installed in office, Pinchback promised him his support after Nicholls gave assurances he intended to protect the rights of Negroes. Nicholls appointed Pinchback to the State Board of Education. In 1879 Pinchback served as delegate to the state constitutional convention, where he sponsored a provision which resulted in the establishment of Southern University. In spite of his temporary support of the Democratic governor, Pinchback continued active in Republican politics. In the *Louisianian* he expressed growing disillusionment over the prospects of Negroes in post-Reconstruction Louisiana. From 1882 to 1885 he held the post of surveyor of customs at the port of New Orleans, his last political appointment of consequence.

In addition to his political activities Pinchback was an astute and successful businessman. Among his business enterprises were a cotton factorage in which he was a partner and the Mississippi River Packet Co., established in 1870. He received more than $16,000 from the U.S. Senate in lieu of the salary denied him. From successful investments he was able to live comfortably.

In 1885 he began the study of law at Straight University and was admitted to the bar the following year, although he does not appear to have engaged in actual practice.

For a short period between 1892 and 1895 Pinchback was a U.S. marshal in New York City. He later moved to Washington, D.C., where he received several honors and was active in politics. In 1898 he participated in the unveiling of the Frederick Douglass Monument in Rochester, N.Y. At first an ardent advocate of civil rights, he recognized in the early twentieth century the power of Booker T. Washington. In January 1904, when Edward H. Morris attacked Washington at a meeting of the Bethel Literary and Historical Association in Washington, D.C., Pinchback defended the "Sage of Tuskegee." In the same year he joined Washington in supporting the confirmation of William D. Crum for the position of collector of customs of the Port of Charleston, S.C. After the death of Washington in 1915, Pinchback's political influence declined.

W. E. B. Du Bois said of Pinchback: "To all intents and purposes he was an educated, well-to-do, congenial white man, with but a few drops of Negro blood, which he did not stoop to deny, as so many of his fellow whites did" (*Black Reconstruction in America* . . . [1935], p. 469). He dressed elegantly, was urbane in manner, and an eloquent speaker. In 1860 he was married to Nina Hawethorne. The couple had six children, of whom two died in infancy. A grandson was Jean Toomer, who arranged for Pinchback to be buried in the family vault at the Metairie Ridge Cemetery, New Orleans.

The first full-length biography of Pinchback, *Pinckney Benton Stewart Pinchback* by James Haskins (1973), while based largely on secondary sources, included research in the Pinchback Papers in the Moorland-Spingarn Research Center, Howard University. There is a short article by Ella Lonn in *DAB* ([1934], 7, Part 2: 611). An obituary was published in the *Washington Post* (Dec. 22, 1921) and in the *Baltimore Afro-American* (Dec. 30, 1921).

— EMMA LOU THORNBROUGH

PIPPIN, HORACE (1888–1946), soldier and painter. The first child of Christine and Daniel W. Pippin, he was born in West Chester, Pa., on Feb. 22, 1888. When he was three his parents, who were the offspring of ex-slaves, moved to Goshen, N.Y., where they found work as domestic laborers. Horace went to the segregated ("colored") school, where he continually got into trouble for drawing when he should have been doing his schoolwork. At ten Horace left school and drifted from one menial job to another until the outbreak of World War I, when he hastened to join the New York State 15th National Guard. This Negro unit was shipped to France and renamed the 369th Infantry Regiment after arrival in France in early 1918. There, in the Argonne Forest, Pippin experienced the most traumatic moments of his life. His unit was in the thick of the battle, once under fire for several days without relief, and Pippin was ultimately wounded in the right shoulder. He received the Purple Heart and an army disability pension, but his right arm—his painting arm—was severely crippled. He once wrote that the war "brought out all the art in me.

I came home with all of it in my mind and I paint from it today."

On Nov. 21, 1920, Pippin married Ora Jennie Featherstone Wade, a widow four years his senior, and went to live in West Chester, the town of his birth. He helped his wife to deliver her laundry, worked at times as a junk man, sang in the Methodist choir, and became active in the American Legion. Nine years passed before he began to paint.

Holding the wrist of his injured right arm in the fist of his left hand, he controlled the movement of the tiny brushes. He worked for three years on his first painting, *The End of the War, Starting Home,* adding layer after layer of paint to convey the bitter struggle in the mud, and no doubt to purge his memory of it.

In 1937 when the West Chester County Art Association held its annual show, Pippin entered two pictures. They were so enthusiastically received by N. C. Wyeth, the famous illustrator who lived in nearby Chadds Ford, that Christian Brinton, the association's president, decided to give Pippin a one-man show. It opened on June 9, 1937, at the West Chester Community Center, containing ten paintings and seven burnt wood panels— designs Pippin executed by holding a hot poker against a flat piece of wood. Although only one painting was sold, the work was seen by Holger Cahill, a New York art critic, and Hudson Walker, a dealer, who borrowed four pictures for the Museum of Modern Art's Masters of Popular Painting show which opened in New York in 1938. Robert Carlen, owner of a Philadelphia gallery, then offered Pippin his first important one-man show. It opened in January 1940 and made Pippin instantly famous.

The philanthropist Albert C. Barnes, one of the first to buy Pippin's work, invited the artist to see his collection of French impressionists and post-impressionist works. Whether inspired by these paintings or by joy at his own success, Pippin's work, which had formerly been somber, now took on a bright staccato of color and design. He embarked upon a series of *Victorian Interiors*—his own versions of the wealthy drawing rooms he began to frequent, a John Brown trilogy, and the three *Holy Mountain* pictures, statements of fervid faith that wars must end. His work sold rapidly both at Carlen's and at New York's prestigious Downtown Gallery; he was collected by museums and movie stars and offered commissions. But even as his reputation soared, his personal life clouded. His wife suffered a breakdown and had to be confined in Norristown State Mental Hospital, while his stepson Richard Wade went off to face in World War II the horrors Pippin knew so much about.

Alone, Pippin took solace at the local bar. After one particularly late evening, his housekeeper went to rouse him and found him dead in bed. His death certificate records only that on July 6, 1946, at age of fifty-eight, his heart stopped. He was buried in Chestnut Grove Annex Cemetery, West Chester.

Pippin can properly take his place among the few great "naive" painters of the world. His art conveys a vision of the American scene—its history and folklore, its exterior splendor and interior pathos—that was uniquely his own.

Some of the museums and galleries of art which own Pippin paintings are the Philadelphia Academy of Fine

Arts, the Philadelphia Museum of Art, the Phillips Collection (Washington, D.C.), the Joseph H. Hirshhorn Museum (Washington, D.C.), the Albert Knox Art Gallery (Buffalo, N.Y.), the Baltimore Museum of Art, the Metropolitan Museum of Art (New York City), the Los Angeles County Museum of Art, the Carnegie Institute (Pittsburgh), Bryn Mawr College, and Howard University.

The first book to celebrate Pippin's work, *Horace Pippin, a Negro Painter in America,* was written by Selden Rodman in 1947. Rodman and his wife Carole Cleaver later wrote a biography, *Horace Pippin, The Artist as a Black American,* published in 1972. *From Harlem to the Rhine, The Story of New York's Colored Volunteers,* by Arthur W. Little (1936), gives a chronology of the 369th Regiment in France. See also Mark Stevens's "Pippin's Folk Heroes" (*Newsweek,* Aug. 22, 1977, pp. 54–60). — CAROLE CLEAVER RODMAN

PLANCIANCOIS, ANSELMAS (1822–1863), soldier. Born free in Louisiana, he enlisted on Sept. 10, 1862, in the 96th Regiment, U.S. Colored Infantry, and was assigned on Sept. 27 to Company E of the 1st Louisiana Regiment of Native Guards (Free Colored) with the rank of sergeant. The 1st and 3rd Louisiana Native Guards had been organized on May 2, 1861, by Gov. Thomas Moore, who feared an attack by Union forces. When a Union attack on April 28, 1862, compelled the Confederate soldiers to evacuate New Orleans, the Native Guards remained to protect their families and property. Gen. Nathaniel P. Banks, commanding the Department of the Gulf, retained the two regiments for service in the Union Army and changed the name of the 1st Louisiana to the 1st Infantry Regiment, Corps d'Afrique. When the Bureau of Colored Troops was organized in 1863, the Corps d'Afrique was renamed the 73rd Regiment, U.S. Colored Troops.

Planciancois's regiment was ordered to participate in the attack upon Port Hudson, the last remaining Confederate fortification on the lower Mississippi. Located approximately thirty miles north of Baton Rouge, La., it had been built by slave labor and presented a formidable obstacle along the river. Stretching over three miles along an eighty-foot bluff and protected by twenty mounted siege guns and thirty pieces of field artillery, Port Hudson was further protected on land by a semicircle of abatis—piles of trees in front of ramparts—which was buttressed by a series of rifle pits and outworks.

The Union forces subjected the stronghold to four hours of bombardment and rushed simultaneously all along the assault line. The Native Guards, with 1080 men, were formed into four lines on the right flank. Capt. André Cailloux of Company E led his men into battle with Planciancois carrying the colors. Cailloux was fatally wounded prior to his company's reaching a ditch the men had to swim in order to attain the objective. Disorganized, the regiments were reassembled and made a second assault four hours later, likewise repulsed by the Confederates. Unknown to the Native Guards, they were the only soldiers assaulting Port Hudson and therefore were the undivided attention of the rebel artillery. Incredibly, the Union forces in the center and left flank had failed to mount their offen-

sives during the two operations of the Native Guard. Their lack of activity undoubtedly contributed significantly to the casualties sustained by the colored soldiers. In addition to the Native Guards, the 1st Regiment of Louisiana Engineers engaged in combat on the right flank.

In the final assault against Port Hudson on May 27, 1863, Planciancois carried the flag to the front of the enemy's fortifications. He is reported to have said: "I'll bring back the flag or know the reason why." While waving his company forward, the top of his head was lifted off by a six-pound artillery round and he fell with the flag clutched in his hands. Two colored corporals struggled for possession of the flag in order to have the honor of bearing it in battle. Before the assault was terminated, six men who had carried the flag were killed. Port Hudson was one of the first major battles in which colored regiments participated.

Planciancois was survived by his wife, Margaret Walts. Born free in 1829, she had married Planciancois on July 5, 1851, in New Orleans. Of their three sons—Louis (born April 21, 1851), Joseph (born Feb. 4, 1853), and Anselmo (born June 9, 1863)—the oldest two died relatively young, in 1871 and 1877, respectively. Margaret Planciancois lived with her youngest son and received a pension for the military service of Anselmas Planciancois.

Relatively few records exist pertaining to the career of Planciancois. The best of these are his pension records in the National Archives and the Records of the Adjutant-General's Office, Record Group 94. Narratives with information concerning his military career and the battle of Port Hudson are contained in Benjamin Quarles's *The Negro in the Civil War* (1953) and the unpublished master's thesis of Mary F. Berry, "The History of the 73rd and 75th United States Colored Infantry Regiments" (Howard University, Washington, D.C., 1962). — CHARLES JOHNSON

PLEASANT, MARY ELLEN [MAMMY PLEASANT] (c. 1814–1904), abolitionist, entrepreneur, civil rights leader, and "boarding house" keeper. Where she was born is very difficult to determine. Some claim she was born on a Georgia cotton plantation and showed so much promise that she was purchased by a slave master who sent her to Boston to be educated. Another account states that she was born on a Virginia plantation but does not explain how she got to Boston. In an interview with Samuel Post Davis, printed in the *Pandex of the Press* (San Francisco, Jan. 1902), she said she was born in Philadelphia on Aug. 19, 1814, that her name was Mary Ellen William, her father a rich merchant from the Sandwich Islands, and her mother a free colored woman. She was sent to Nantucket to live and be educated by a family named Hussey. Most of those who have written about her in later years have insisted that her mother was a slave and her father perhaps a Cherokee Indian.

According to Delilah L. Beasley (*The Negro Trail Blazers of California,* 1919, pp. 95–97), a planter named Price bought her freedom and sent her to Boston to be educated. There she met Garrison and other abolitionists and married Alexander Smith, reputedly a Cuban planter, who is said to have left her a legacy of some $45,000 to assist the abolitionist cause. Presumably shortly thereafter, she married John P. Pleasant (Pleasants?), a former overseer on the Smith plantation, about whom little is known.

They came to San Francisco in 1849 during the gold rush. It seems that her reputation as a cook had preceded her, and she was offered $500 a month for her services. In spite of the very attractive offer, she refused and instead opened a restaurant and boarding house of her own. Here boarded many of those who became prominent in the history of California, among them David Broderick, William Sharon, David S. Terry, and Thomas Bell. She continued in this business until 1858. Her activities are said to have included houses of assignation. She also managed estates and made loans (at 10 percent a month), but in spite of success she closed her business and moved back east. Some say she went back to Boston, others that she went to Canada. Whether she met John Brown in Canada is not certain; she was there at one time, and she and John Pleasant bought a house in Chatham. The deed to this property was in the collection of Boyd B. Stutter, who was secretary of the American Legion, San Francisco, for a time (letter to W.S.S.).

For many years it was said that Mary Ellen Pleasant gave John Brown $30,000 to help him finance the attack on Harpers Ferry. In this she was supposed to be complying with the desire of her first husband, who had insisted she spend a part of her inheritance for the freedom of slaves. The available records do not reveal that John Brown ever had any large sums of money. One of the largest amounts, $600, was given by one Frances Jackson; others gave smaller amounts. It would seem that the important problem is not whether Mary Ellen Pleasant gave $30,000, but whether she was in Canada and contributed to John Brown's raid in any way. He had probably left Canada before she arrived; in her own account she did not say she went directly to Canada, but rather indicated she went to Boston. This remarkable and mysterious woman probably did give something to the undertaking, but how much is an open question. She claimed that, disguised as a jockey, she went to Virginia to stir up the slaves but could do little, for John Brown struck too soon. She was, however, able to escape to New York and return to California.

She did not open another restaurant, but entered the employment of a banker, Thomas Bell, as a housekeeper, because she could get large sums of money from him for almost any reason. She managed the household, spent money as she saw fit, and indeed is supposed to have planned as well as controlled the "House of Mystery," a three-story mansard-roofed mansion on Octavia Street.

Mary Ellen Pleasant was involved in many events in San Francisco, especially the famous case of *Sharon v. Sharon* (1881). William Sharon had made a fortune in Nevada mining and several other projects; he was a former senator from Nevada and belonged to the group of young men who had boarded at the Pleasant house. He met Sarah Althea Hill, it is said, through Mary Ellen Pleasant. Hill lived in an apartment provided by Sharon, but when he tired of her he had her removed. She, however, claimed to be his wife and produced a certificate of marriage which he insisted was not authentic. She then sued for divorce on the ground of infidelity and demanded a division of the property. During the protracted proceedings, she confessed that she had acted under instructions from Pleasant, and the latter admitted that she had advanced more than $5000 to Hill. A federal judge ruled that the contract was a forgery and that the whole scheme had originated in the mind of "this scheming, trafficking, crafty old woman," Pleasant.

Her notorious reputation as a keeper of houses of assignation and her involvement in *Sharon v. Sharon* have obscured her earlier civil rights activities in California. According to tradition, during the 1850s and 1860s she rescued slaves in rural areas where they were illegally held. She aided Negroes in their fight to secure the passage of a state law (1863) giving Negroes the right of testimony in courts. Contemporary newspapers and court records validate the claim that through her, Negroes were able to ride on the city's street cars.

After the death of Thomas Bell, Pleasant stayed in the "House of Mystery" until 1899 when she was ordered out. In 1902 she became ill and was found by Mrs. L. M. Sherwood of San Francisco, moved to the Sherwood residence, and remained under their care until her death. The end came on Jan. 11, 1904, and closed the career of one of the most controversial figures in the history of San Francisco. There was a fight over the property she was reputed to own. On Dec. 20, 1902, Mary Ellen Pleasant had made a will leaving everything to the Bell children. Seven days before her death she made a second will leaving all her property to the Sherwoods. The courts honored the first will. On her tombstone in Napa, where she was buried, is the inscription, "She was a Friend of John Brown Mary Ellen Pleasant." Memorial services were held on Feb. 12, 1905.

See the biographical sketch by W. Sherman Savage in *NAW* (1971, 3:75–77). Helen O'Donnell Holdredge's undocumented *Mammy Pleasant* (1953) gives no evidence of the existence of any memoirs or autobiography. The three-page insert in *Pandex of the Press* (Jan. 1902) described the extensive nature of the "Memoirs," but the February 1902 issue stated they had been discontinued because of a misunderstanding between the author and the editor. Holdredge's *Mammy Pleasant's Partner* (1954) narrates particularly Pleasant's connections with Thomas Bell. For the streetcar case, see *Pleasants* (John J. and Mary E.) *respondents v. the North Beach and Mission Railroad Company, appellant,* a broadside (1868), in the California State Archives, Sacramento.

— W. SHERMAN SAVAGE *and* RAYFORD W. LOGAN

PLEDGER, WILLIAM A[NDERSON] (1851?–1904), editor, lawyer, civil rights leader, and politician. Born a slave on a Georgia plantation, he became the state's leading Negro politician before he was thirty, and remained a power in the Georgia Republican party throughout the late nineteenth century. The son of a slaveowner, Pledger grew up near Jonesboro, just south of Atlanta, and moved to the capital city after the Civil War. There he did odd jobs while cultivating the friendship of important Reconstruction politicians. Pledger taught school in Athens during the 1870s, then moved back to Atlanta with his wife and two children to continue his own education at Atlanta University. He left college during his senior year and returned to Athens, where he began publication of the *Athens Blade,* the first of his three successive weekly newspapers. During the 1880s and 1890s Pledger held several minor federal appointments. Admitted to the bar in 1894, he spent the rest of his life practicing law, editing the *Atlanta News* and later the *Atlanta Age,* and immersing himself in the affairs of the Republican party.

A self-made man and proud of it, Pledger was a fluent orator and skilled debater, a man of strong will and quick intelligence. Above all, he was an activist. Once, when an Athens mob was preparing to lynch two Negro prisoners, Pledger led armed Negroes to the jail, defied the mob, and prevented the lynchings. On another occasion, after unsuccessful efforts to prevent a caucus of his white Republican opponents, Pledger and a crowd of supporters barged in to take control of the meeting. In the ensuing row Pledger was arrested and thrown in jail on a disorderly conduct charge, later dismissed.

The Georgia politician first achieved success by engineering a Negro takeover of the Republican state executive committee in 1880. Whites usually filled the party's top leadership posts, although the overwhelming majority of rank-and-file members were Negroes, an arrangement preferred by the national party. Through a series of adept political moves Pledger emerged as party chairman in 1880, the first Negro to hold that position. Along with other Negro Republican spokesmen he tried to protect race interests while contending with paternalistic white Republicans, who attempted to dominate Negroes, and a lilly-white faction which wanted to expel them. Pledger was in the thick of party in-fighting, which usually centered on control of federal patronage and delegate selection to the Republican National Convention. After a two-year tenure as state chairman, Pledger lost his fight to keep party control in the hands of Negroes, but received as compensation a federal appointment as surveyor of customs in Atlanta.

Pledger's reputation was that of a party maverick. He unsuccessfully urged the white Republican leadership to field candidates on both state and local levels, and opposed Republican efforts to fuse with the Populists in the 1890s. There Pledger rejected Tom Watson and his radical agrarians in favor of the "wealth and intelligence" of paternalistic white Democrats. The Georgia lawyer and editor remained steadfast to the national party, and was a delegate to every Republican National Convention between 1880 and 1900. His only attempt to win elective office was an unsuccessful contest for state representative in 1888.

Philosophically, Pledger occupied the middle ground between accommodation and protest. His newspaper editorials vigorously denounced lynching and disfranchisement, views he maintained in the face of threatened violence. Active in forming the Afro-American League in 1890, Pledger condemned the racism of southern whites in a speech to league delegates. Yet he managed to stay in the good graces of conservative Georgia Democrats, and he cultivated a friendship with

Booker T. Washington which eventually led him into the camp of the Tuskegeean. Pledger was both a militant crusader for equal rights and a political realist, always with an eye to his personal advancement.

During his last years Pledger became nominal head of the Georgia Republican party, served as vice-president of the Afro-American Council, and vied unsuccessfully for a diplomatic post. Active to the end, Pledger spent his final days attending the executive committee meeting of the Afro-American Council and lobbying against a move to reduce southern representation to the Republican National Convention.

There is no full-length study of William A. Pledger. His political career receives attention in Clarence A. Bacote's doctoral dissertation, "The Negro in Georgia Politics, 1880–1908" (University of Chicago, 1955), and in Olive Hall Shadgett's *The Republican Party in Georgia from Reconstruction Through 1900* (1964). A flattering contemporary account is Cyrus Field Adams's "Col. William Pledger, The Forceful Orator and Fearless Editor" (*Colored American Magazine* 5 [June 1902]: 146–49). The *Atlanta Constitution* followed Pledger's career in the 1880s and 1890s. His correspondence with Booker T. Washington and Emmett J. Scott in the Washington Papers in the Library of Congress sheds light on Pledger's behind-the-scenes political activities.

— JOHN A. DITTMER

PLESSY, HOMER ADOLPH (? – ?), plaintiff in landmark Supreme Court decision. The literature contains little biographical data concerning Plessy. Exhaustive investigation discloses no known living close survivors. However, a distant living relative stated that he believed Plessy was probably born in New Orleans, and was employed as a carpenter like most male members of his family at that time. With the aid of the Comité des Citoyens, an organization of Negroes in New Orleans, Plessy was the plaintiff in *Plessy v. Ferguson* (163 U.S. 537, 1896), decided by the U.S. Supreme Court on May 18, 1896. Justice John Marshall Harlan cast the only dissenting vote. The decision established the "separate but equal" doctrine which was to remain the law of the land for nearly sixty years. Plessy's petition to the U.S. Supreme Court set forth the following arguments: Plessy was a citizen of the United States and a resident of the state of Louisiana, of mixed descent, in the proportion of seven-eighths Caucasian and one-eighth African blood; the "colored blood" was not discernible in him and he was entitled to every right, privilege, and immunity secured by the Constitution and laws to citizens of the United States of the white race.

The background of the case was this. On June 7, 1892, Plessy paid for a first-class passage on the East Louisiana Railway from New Orleans to Covington in Louisiana, entered a passenger train, and took a vacant seat in a coach reserved for white passengers. Plessy disobeyed the conductor's order to vacate the seat and to occupy a seat in a coach reserved for colored people. A police officer helped to eject Plessy from the train and take him to the parish jail of New Orleans, where he was charged with having criminally violated a Louisiana statute of 1890 requiring white and colored persons to be furnished with separate accommodations. Plessy, contending the law violated the Thirteenth and Fourteenth Amendments, petitioned for a writ of prohibition and certiorari against John H. Ferguson, judge of the criminal district court for the Parish of Orleans, to the Louisiana state Supreme Court, and asked the higher courts to prohibit Judge Ferguson from holding the trial. The state Supreme Court held that the law was constitutional and denied the relief sought by Plessy, but allowed his writ of error to the U.S. Supreme Court.

Plessy was represented by lawyers A. W. Tourgée and S. F. Phillips. Justice Brown delivered the majority opinion of the Court, holding that the Louisiana statute requiring segregation by race on trains did not violate the Thirteenth and Fourteenth Amendments to the U.S. Constitution by abridging the privileges or immunities of United States citizens or deprive persons of liberty or property without due process of the laws. He stated: "We consider the underlying fallacy of the plaintiff's argument to consist in the assumption that the enforced separation of the two races stamps the colored race with a badge of inferiority. If this be so, it is not by reason of anything found in the act, but solely because the colored race chooses to put that construction on it." Justice John Marshall Harlan, dissented: "The arbitrary separation of citizens, on the basis of race, while they are on a public highway, is a badge of servitude wholly inconsistent with the civil freedom and the equality before the law established by the constitution. It cannot be justified on legal grounds." The *Plessy* decision opened the door for additional oppressive segregation laws.

The landmark case of *Brown v. Board of Education* (347 U.S. 483, 1954) overruled *Plessy v. Ferguson*. In *Brown* the U.S. Supreme Court in a unanimous decision in essence adopted Justice Harlan's dissenting opinion in the *Plessy* case and rejected the "separate but equal" doctrine established in *Plessy*.

The Thin Disguise: Turning Point in Negro History, Plessy v. Ferguson (1896), edited by Otto H. Olsen (1967), is the most comprehensive published treatment. See also C. Vann Woodward's "The Birth of Jim Crow: Plessy v. Ferguson" (*American Heritage,* April 1964, pp. 52–55, 100), and two articles by Barton J. Bernstein, "Plessy v. Ferguson, Conservative Sociological Jurisprudence" (*JNH,* July 1963, pp. 196–205) and "Case Law in Plessy v. Ferguson" (*JNH,* July 1962, pp. 192–98).
                                                                       — OTTO H. OLSEN

PLUMMER, HENRY VINTON (1844–1905), chaplain, temperance leader, and Baptist clergyman. Born a slave on the Calvert plantation in Prince George's County, Md., he was sold first to owners in Washington, D.C., and then in Howard County, Md. He escaped in late 1862 and enlisted in the navy in 1864. During sixteen months of honorable service, much of it on the gunboat *Cordelion* of the Potomac flotilla, he taught himself to read. After his discharge he prepared for Wayland Seminary in Washington, D.C., from which he graduated in 1879. Meanwhile he worked as a night watchman at the Washington post office and as minister to congregations in Charles and Prince George's Counties. Following ordination, he was a missionary for Mount Carmel Baptist Church in Washington. On July 8, 1884, Pres. Chester A. Arthur appointed him chaplain of the 9th Cavalry, on the recommendation of Frederick Douglass and several white Maryland Republicans. Plummer thus became perhaps the first Negro chaplain in the post-Civil War army. After ten years of service in Kansas, Wyoming, and Nebraska, he was dismissed from the army for conduct unbecoming an officer in the autumn of 1894. He returned to Kansas, where he served the Rose Hill Baptist Church in Kansas City and the Second Baptist Church in Wichita. He died in Kansas City, Kans., on Feb. 8, 1905, after a long illness.

While chaplain of the 9th Cavalry he persistently and aggressively advocated temperance, which placed him in direct conflict with the army's canteen system. His efforts, which included creation of a Loyal Temperance Legion among the children of the Negro troops at Fort Robinson, Neb., played a major part in bringing on his trial. Moreover his widespread popularity among the soldiers, which he established through the legion, represented a threat to an all-white command structure. While these tensions grew, he boldly proposed to the War Department a plan for the colonization of central Africa. He asked for a leave of absence to command an expedition of fifty to one hundred Negro soldiers, who Plummer expected would accompany him voluntarily. He believed the soldiers would make excellent pioneers, as they were disciplined and trained for frontier service. In justifying the plan, Plummer wrote that central Africa would provide an excellent outlet for the talents of future generations of Afro-Americans and thus reduce racial tensions at home. The United States could also meet the challenges of European imperial powers, while helping Negroes "secure a slice of the African 'turkey.'" The proposal stimulated the interest of A.M.E. bishop Henry M. Turner, the leading emigrationist at that time, who wrote the government in support of Plummer's scheme. The War Department rejected the plan.

Court-martial charges against the chaplain were pressed just three months after he submitted the plan. The army accused him of drunkenness. Sgt. Robert Benjamin, the only witness who supported the allegation, acknowledged a ten-year-old grudge against Plummer, which grew out of a dispute at Fort Riley. Benjamin was promoted shortly after the trial at Fort Robinson. Plummer was convicted and dismissed in spite of eyewitness testimony and the protests of Bishop Turner and former Rep. John M. Langston. Plummer then moved to Kansas and tried vainly for several years to obtain restoration to the service. Meanwhile he served his churches and won election to the executive board of the Kansas Baptist Convention in 1902.

He married Julia Lomax at Hyattsville, Md., in 1867. They had six sons and two daughters. Four of the sons bore the names of men who were prominent in the final phases of the struggle against slavery: Thaddeus Stevens, Charles Sumner, Ulysses Grant, and Hannibal Lincoln. His wife survived him and moved to Washington, D.C., where she lived with her son Henry Vinton Jr., until her death in 1915.

Plummer's sister, Nellie Arnold Plummer, wrote a collective biography of the family, *Out of the Depths* (1927), which focuses on their father, Adam Francis

Plummer, but contains substantial information on the chaplain as well. The most useful manuscript materials on his career are in the records of the Adjutant General and Judge Advocate General, National Archives. Two weekly newspapers, the *Kansas City* (Kansas) *American Citizen* and the *Wichita Searchlight,* and the Kansas State Historical Society's collection of minutes of Kansas Baptist conventions also contain useful data.

— FRANK N. SCHUBERT

POINDEXTER, JAMES P. (1819–1907), clergyman, abolitionist, politician, and civil rights advocate. He was born in Richmond, Va., the son of Evelina Atkinson, a woman of Negro and Cherokee descent, and Joseph Poindexter, a white journalist for the *Richmond Enquirer.* Poindexter attended school in Richmond until his tenth year when he began an apprenticeship as a barber, an occupation which he was to practice for many years. In 1837 he married Adelia Atkinson, who died in November 1876. During 1837 the Poindexters moved to Dublin, Ohio, a village ten miles north of Columbus. Dissatisfied with life in this farming community, they moved to Columbus the following year, residing there for the remainder of their lives.

Soon after settling in Columbus, Poindexter joined the Second Baptist Church, preaching and officiating when there was no regular minister. In 1847 a Negro family that had previously owned slaves in Virginia joined the church. Although the family had sold the slaves before leaving for Ohio, forty members of the congregation led by Poindexter left Second Baptist to found the Anti-Slavery Baptist Church. This church remained in existence until 1858, when Poindexter returned to the Second Baptist Church as pastor. He remained there until his resignation in 1898.

Poindexter's barber business served as his livelihood for many years, and it was through this work that he came to know the leading statesmen, lawyers, doctors, and educators of Ohio. Acquaintance with them served him well later in securing gubernatorial appointments.

Soon after his arrival in Columbus, Poindexter personally made teams and wagons to convey escaping slaves northward over the Underground Railroad. His comrades in this work included members of the Negro and white communities in Columbus. For nearly three decades he actively agitated against slavery, and in the decades after the Civil War frequently delivered eloquent addresses at August Emancipation Day celebrations in the Negro community.

During the Civil War he and his wife formed the Colored Soldiers Relief Society in Columbus. The society dispensed material and financial aid to colored soldiers and their families, since the state had failed to appropriate funds for this purpose.

The Fifteenth Amendment, declared in effect on March 30, 1870, led to the emergence of Poindexter as a political figure. In January 1871 he helped head a call for a mass Convention of Colored Men in Columbus to encourage their voting "for securing and maintaining . . . the legitimate benefits resulting from our newly acquired rights under the Constitution." The convention pledged allegiance to the Republican party and its candidates. Although Poindexter promoted the Repub-

lican party among Negroes in the state of Ohio, he based his support on issues and withdrew it when he felt party actions were mistaken.

In the summer of 1873, after his nomination by the Republican Central Committee for a seat in the Ohio House of Representatives, the first such nominee, he was defeated though a qualified and able candidate. He was again defeated in the next election. In 1876, however, he served as an Ohio delegate to the Republican National Convention which nominated Rutherford B. Hayes of Ohio for president. During the winter of 1876–1877, while the seating of the president was still in question, Hayes conferred with Poindexter and Frederick Douglass in Columbus on the "southern question." Hayes recorded in his diary for Feb. 18, 1877: "I talked yesterday with Fred Douglass and Mr. Poindexter, both colored on the Southern question. I told them my views. They approved." The approval by Douglass is not in accord with his statements (*Life and Times* . . . [1962], pp. 536–37). For his support and counsel to Hayes during the campaign, Poindexter received consideration for appointment as U.S. minister to Haiti.

Although unsuccessful in his bid for national office, Poindexter was successful on the local and state levels. In 1880 he was elected to the Columbus City Council, the first colored man in the city to serve on that body. His competence gained him reelection in 1882 and vice-presidency and membership on the Poor Committee. The City Infirmary director noted in his annual report for 1882 that Poindexter was the only one who had taken any marked interest in his duties. In December 1884 he was appointed to the Columbus Board of Education. Reelected four times, he served for ten years, the period of his greatest personal impact on Columbus society. Poindexter chaired the following committees: schoolhouse sites, rules and regulations, textbooks and course of study, and discipline. He also served as a member of eight other board committees. When Roman Catholic school officials requested the use of an unoccupied room in a public school while awaiting the completion of construction on a school of their own, Poindexter gave his support to the use of the quarters and a potentially touchy problem was solved. He vigorously continued his twenty-year agitation for integration of the public schools and adequate physical facilities for schools in Negro neighborhoods.

Poindexter received his first state appointment in 1880 when Gov. Charles Foster named him to the Board of Trustees of the Ohio School for the Blind. He remained on the board until 1883. Two years later, however, when Democratic Gov. George Hoadley nominated him to the Board of Trustees at Ohio University, his appointment was defeated by two votes on the grounds that he was too partisan. Early in 1887 he was named to the Board of Directors of the State Forestry Bureau, a position which he held for three consecutive terms until the bureau went out of existence in 1900. In April 1896 he was also named to the Board of Trustees at Wilberforce University.

Poindexter maintained an active interest in other civic affairs, heading the Columbus Pastors Union, serving in the Columbus and Ohio Centennial Celebration, and participating in the Sons of Protection, a Negro burial and benefit association. He was an indefatigable letter writer and the pages of the *Ohio State Journal* often contained the entire texts of his sermons as well as position statements on public affairs.

On Feb. 7, 1907, Poindexter died following a prolonged bout with pneumonia. During the period of his illness, the Rev. Washington Gladden was a daily visitor to his bedside. His memorial service was attended by nearly 2000 mourners, marking it as one of Columbus's largest to that date.

There is no adequate biography of Poindexter. The most comprehensive account is Richard C. Minor's "James Preston Poindexter, Elder Statesman of Ohio" (*Ohio History,* 1947). Documentation regarding the Hayes meeting is in Charles R. Williams (ed.), *Diary and Letters of Rutherford B. Hayes* (1922–1926). Information about his local and state posts is in the published annual reports of each governmental agency; about his theological and political beliefs in the files of the *Ohio State Journal,* to which he was a frequent contributor.

— FRANK R. LEVSTIK

POOR, SALEM (1758– ?), soldier of the American Revolution. Poor was born free in Massachusetts. Leaving his wife, he enlisted in a Massachusetts militia company under Capt. Benjamin Ames. Like Peter Salem he served with valor and intrepidness at the Battle of Bunker Hill (it was really fought at Breed's Hill) on June 17, 1775. Like Salem, who was credited, perhaps mistakenly, with killing Maj. John Pitcairn, Poor was perhaps responsible for picking off Lt.-Col. James Abercrombie. In any event, Col. William Prescott and thirteen other officers petitioned the General Court of Massachusetts a few weeks later, suggesting that the Continental Congress itself bestow "The Reward due to so great and Distinguisht a Caracter." The petition read: "The Subscribers begg leave to Report to your Honble. House (Which Wee do in justice to the Caracter of so Brave a Man) that under Our Own observation, Wee declare that A Negro Man Called Salem Poor of Col. Fryes Regiment. Capt. Ames. Company in the late Battle at Charleston, behaved like an Experienced Officer, as Well as an Excellent Soldier, to Set forth Particulars of his Conduct would be Tedious, Wee Would Only begg leave to say in the Person of this sd. Negro Centers a Brave & gallant Soldier—"

There is no record that Poor received a reward.

Gen. George Washington on July 10, 1775, issued instructions that no more Negroes were to be recruited but those already serving, like Salem Poor, could complete their terms. On Nov. 12, 1775, Washington issued orders prohibiting Negroes from serving whether new volunteers or those seeking to reenlist. After he learned that Lord Dunmore, governor of Virginia, on Nov. 7 had proclaimed free all Negroes willing to serve under the British flag, Washington on Dec. 30 ordered recruiting officers to enlist free Negroes and the Continental Congress approved on Jan. 16, 1776, the reenlistment of free Negroes. Poor served at Valley Forge and White Plains.

There are brief accounts in Benjamin Quarles's *The Negro in the American Revolution* (1962, p. 11) and Sidney Kaplan's *The Black Presence in the Era of the American Revolution, 1770–1800* (1973, pp. 19–20). Both are based on Revolutionary Rolls (Massachusetts Archives, State House, Boston; 180:241).

— RAYFORD W. LOGAN

POSEY, CUMBERLAND [CUM] (1890–1946), baseball team organizer and manager. For thirty-six years Cum Posey was the guiding genius who built one of the finest baseball teams put together, the Homestead Grays. Led by Josh Gibson and Buck Leonard, they won nine straight pennants in the Negro National league (1937–1945), a record perhaps unequalled in any professional sport. And many insist that these were not the best Gray teams. Some prefer the 1926 club that won forty-three straight games; others, the 1930 squad that swept eleven out of twelve from the proud Kansas City Monarchs; still others, the 1931 Grays that won 136 games while losing only seventeen.

The man who built them all was Cum Posey. Posey was born in Homestead (then Harding Station), Pa., the son of Angelina (Stevens) Posey and Cumberland Willis Posey, Sr., a riverboat pilot, said to be the first Negro to build a boat on the Monongahela River, and an early investor in the *Pittsburgh Courier.* Cum attended the University of Pittsburgh, Duquesne University, and Pennsylvania State University, where he is said to have played football and basketball (Sept. 1909 to Feb. 1911). He also helped organize the famous Loendi basketball club in Pittsburgh and was considered one of the best colored guards in the country. In 1910 Posey joined the semipro Homestead Grays baseball team, a team of steel workers who played other steel mill teams around Pittsburgh. In addition to playing outfield, he booked their games and in 1917 was promoted to manager. By 1922 the Grays were a full-fledged professional club and Posey negotiated rights to play in Pittsburgh's Forbes Field when the National League Pirates were on the road. With such stars as Sam Streeter, Vic Harris, and George Scales, the Grays refused to join the new Eastern Colored League, finding independent barnstorming more profitable. In 1926 Posey enticed the great pitcher, Smokey Joe Williams, to join the Grays, and that fall felt strong enough to challenge Lefty Grove and a big-league all-star team to a series of four games. The Grays won three of them.

Posey claimed the Negro championship of the world in 1930 for the Homestead Grays. His power-packed team starred Williams, Oscar Charleston, and nineteen-year-old Josh Gibson. They beat the New York Lincoln Giants of John Henry Lloyd to clinch the title. The following year they challenged the big-leaguers again and won two games 10–7 and 18–0. Then disaster hit. A rival team, the Pittsburgh Crawfords, appeared and lured away Charleston, Gibson, and most of the other Grays' stars. With Satchel Paige pitching, the "Craws" were indeed a formidable club; Posey challenged them to a city series and beat them three games out of four.

But 1938 was a low year for the Grays. Posey needed money and found it in a partnership with Rufus "Sonnyman" Jackson. He began rebuilding, starting with husky first baseman Buck Leonard. The team paid Depression salaries and traveled by bus to save money, but, says Leonard, "I played with the Grays 17 years and never missed a payday. You were always booked to play somewhere every day," sometimes two or three games a day. Gate receipts were small, except for the big Sunday double-headers. Those, Leonard says, were "getting-out-of-the-hole days." Pitcher Wilmer Fields added: "Posey'd have a fit if he thought they were going to rain us out. Back in the 'bus' leagues, if you had 20,000 people, we were going to play four and a half innings somehow."

In 1937 it was the Crawfords who needed money. They sold Gibson back to Posey for what was then a high price, $2,500 plus two players. The Grays promptly won the pennant, the first of nine straight. Even the Pirates refused Posey's challenge for a series. Posey moved the team to Washington, D.C., and wartime crowds swelled attendance. With Satchel Paige in town to pitch, crowds often reached 30,000, more than the American League Senators could draw.

In January 1946 Josh Gibson died suddenly. Posey himself was dead only two months later. If he had lived just three more weeks he would have seen Jackie Robinson make his historic debut into organized baseball. An era had ended; a new one was about to be born.

Posey married Ethel Truman in 1913. He died on March 28, 1946, and was buried in Homestead Cemetery. He was survived by his wife and three of their five daughters.

See John Holway's illustrated *Voices from the Great Black Baseball Leagues* (1975), based in large measure on interviews with former players, journalists, and contemporary newspapers. The book also contains valuable statistics. Robert W. Peterson's *Only the Ball Was White* (1970) is likewise based on interviews and newspapers. — JOHN HOLWAY

POWELL, A[DAM] CLAYTON, SR. (1865–1953), clergyman, author, and reformer. Powell was born in a log cabin in Soak Creek, Franklin County, Va., on May 5, 1865. His maternal grandmother was an Indian and his maternal grandfather was said to be a German. His parents, Anthony and Sally Dunning Powell, had been slaves. He began his early education in October 1871, moved with his stepfather and mother to West Virginia in 1875, attended Rendville Academy (Perry, Ohio), and in 1892 graduated from Wayland Seminary and College, Washington, D.C. (later merged with Virginia Union University, Richmond, Va.). On July 30, 1889, he had married Mattie Fletcher Schaefer of West Virginia; they were the parents of two children, Blanche and Adam Clayton Jr. Adam Sr. was a special student at Yale University Divinity School (1895–1896). He was pastor of Immanuel Baptist Church, New Haven, Conn. (1893–1908). On Dec. 31, 1908, he began his pastorate at the Abyssinian Baptist Church located on West 40th Street, New York City; in 1937 he resigned and was pastor emeritus until his death on June 12, 1953. His son succeeded him as pastor. In 1946 he had married Inez Means of Clifton, S.C. Funeral services were held in Abyssinian Baptist Church.

In early life Adam gave indication of his determination and capacity for learning and hard work. He walked five miles each day to his first school. Under a friendly white teacher he is said to have learned the alphabet in one day; a year later he could read passages in the Bible. In West Virginia he earned fifty dollars a year doing chores on a farm. In 1887, when he sought unsuccessfully to enroll in the Law Department of Howard University, he secured a job at Howard House, a hotel. While studying at Wayland Seminary and College, he worked as a janitor and waiter.

His choice of the ministry, begun with encouragement from his stepfather, continued under J. B. Scott, owner of Howard House, who gave him the opportunity to read the entire Bible. He was most influenced by G. M. P. King, president of Wayland. His personal appearance was an asset: tall and straight, he walked with pride. By nature he was gentle and considerate.

After a brief pastorate at Ebenezer Baptist Church in Philadelphia (1893), Powell was called to Immanuel Baptist Church New Haven. Many Yale students began attending Immanuel Church and helped the pastor shape his destiny. The Powells' home was a place of social ease for these students. Many of them encouraged and helped him as a special student at Yale Divinity School during 1895–1896. On Dec. 31, 1908, when Dr. Powell (he had been awarded an honorary D.D., Virginia Union University, 1904) began his pastorate at the Abyssinian Baptist Church, established by Thomas Paul and others in 1808, he and his family were given a cold-water flat in an area notorious for its many prostitutes. Powell did not rest until the area was cleaned up and the houses of prostitution closed.

Recognizing the population trend toward Harlem, the church in the spring of 1920 purchased lots at West 138th Street. Summer tent meetings were held but interest was waning and Powell threatened to resign. On April 9, 1922, ground was broken and construction began. The dedication of the Abyssinian Baptist Church and Community House, costing in excess of $334,000, began on May 20 and terminated June 17, 1923. Powell was responsible for building the first adequate community house or recreational center in the most congested Negro area in the United States. A social and religious education program was launched, including Powell's fondest dream—to purchase a home for aged members. On July 4, 1926, the church dedicated a home for the aged at 732 St. Nicholas Ave. and named it after the pastor, the A. Clayton Powell Home of the Abyssinian Baptist Church. It could accommodate seventeen persons and was successfully operated for twelve years, although not half the persons who entered were able to pay. As an expression of appreciation for his leadership, the congregation sent him on a three-month trip to Europe, Egypt, and the Holy Land. In 1929 he was honored by the Harmon Foundation for his work in developing Abyssinian Baptist Church. By the mid-1930s the church had 14,000 members, the largest Protestant congregation in America. During the Depression Powell and the church helped feed the poor, regardless of color, and campaigned for better jobs and city services. He lectured on race relations at Colgate University for three years and at other institutions of higher learning, including the College of the City of New York and Union Theological Seminary. He was an editorial writer for the *Christian Review* and a vice-president of the NAACP. He visited and studied social and other conditions in England, France, Germany, Switzerland, and Central America. He was the author of several books, including *Saints in Caesar's Household* (1939), *Picketing Hell* (1942), and *Riots and Ruins* (1945). When Powell died in 1953 he was hailed as one of the great preachers and leaders of his time.

The principal sources for his life are his autobiography, *Against the Tide* (1938), and Neil Hickey's and Ed Edwin's *Adam Clayton Powell and the Politics of Race* (1955). See also the obituaries in the (New York) *Amsterdam News* (June 13, 1953, p. 1; June 20, 1953, p. 38). — SAMUEL DEWITT PROCTOR

POWELL, WILLIAM FRANK (1848–1920), educator and diplomat. He was born in Troy, N.Y., on June 26, 1848, to William and Julia (Crawford) Powell. His father's ancestors were Indians. In spite of the difficulty that a Negro boy faced at this time in getting an education, the youth attended public schools in Brooklyn and Jersey City. He studied further at the New York School of Pharmacy, at Lincoln University (Pa.), and later graduated from the New Jersey Collegiate Institute in 1865 at the age of seventeen.

Powell's first significant job after his college graduation was an appointment by the Presbyterian Board of Home Mission to teach in a school for Negroes in 1869 at Leesburg, Va. In 1870 he opened perhaps the first state school for Negro children in Alexandria, Va., and directed its operations for five years. He then became principal of a school at Bordentown, N.J., from 1875 until 1881. That year Powell moved to Washington, D.C., and became a bookkeeper at the fourth auditor's office in the U.S. Treasury Department. In 1881 he declined a consular appointment to Cap-Haïtien, Haiti.

During 1884 the thirty-six-year-old educator was elected superintendent of schools in the fourth district of Camden, N.J. He implemented plans for the introduction of manual skills and training in schools, and was also instrumental in the erection of a building specifically for industrial training. In 1886 he returned to the classroom and taught at the predominantly white Camden High and Training School until 1894. He became also a very prominent voice in the school system of Camden and throughout New Jersey.

On June 17, 1897, Powell became the first American appointed to the new title of envoy extraordinary and minister plenipotentiary to Haiti (and also chargé d'affaires to the Dominican Republic) by President McKinley. Powell aimed at improving the deteriorating attitude of the Haitian government toward the United States and encouraging American commercial interests in the Caribbean. Within months, he met the first of many crises. A Haitian act effective on Oct. 1, 1897, required an additional tax on American merchants and clerks in Haiti. A controversy soon centered on the firm of Weyman and Company, and Secretary of State John Sherman viewed the law as a violation of treaty rights with the United States. Within weeks Powell influenced the Haitian government to waive this "discriminatory tax," beginning May 8, 1898.

During Powell's second year in Haiti (1899) his correspondence reflects four issues: the arrest of the American vice-consul-general, the removal of a Haitian who moved into the U.S. legation in Port-au-Prince, a Haitian decree that required all refugees in legations to leave Haiti at the very earliest opportunity, and a new law requiring all foreigners in Haiti on business to obtain a license. Each problem was subsequently settled in favor of the United States.

The following year (1900) the Haitian courts played a leading role in Haitian diplomacy. They contended that they had no judicial right over foreigners. Secretary of State John Hay pointed to article six of the treaty of 1864 which guaranteed American citizens the right to use the courts of Haiti in disputes between American and German citizens, but the courts maintained their decision. Meanwhile the German minister decided to create special courts to try foreigners. In spite of the implications for the United States nonacceptance of the Calvo Doctrine (forbidding intervention by one nation in the domestic affairs of another) at the first Pan-American Conference in 1889, Powell fought successfully against the special courts since he felt that they would be a violation of Haiti's sovereignty.

During 1901 Powell's letters to Washington centered mostly on international topics, and life appeared to be less hectic. However, by mid-1902 Haiti faced virtual civil war. Powell's letters announced the resignation of the president, requested the help of a United States naval ship, described the cities under provisional government, inquired about recognition and relations with the "de facto" government (he was directed to adopt the "de jure principle"), informed the State Department about Haitian permission to allow the U.S. consulate to protect Cuban interests in Haiti, and described the election of a new congress and president.

In early 1903 the Haitian government proposed the restriction of Syrian immigration and Powell unsuccessfully tried to discourage such a law. Between Sept. 12, 1903, and Aug. 8, 1904, there was increased diplomatic correspondence. The subjects ranged from the license tax on Americans and their ships to the Naturalization Treaty and the safety of naturalized American Syrians, and even (1905) to claims from Puerto Rican citizens in Haiti. Powell's willingness to help the distressed seemed to be unpopular in the State Department. He finally resigned on Oct. 12, 1905, after eight hard years. After returning to his home in Camden, N.J., Lincoln University in 1907 conferred on him the LL.D. degree. Two years later he became an editorial writer for the *Philadelphia Tribune*.

Powell married twice, first in 1868 to Elizabeth M. Hughes of Burlington, N.J., and then in 1899 to Jane B. Shepard of Camden. The best approximate date of his death is Jan. 23, 1920.

Basic facts about Powell's life are in *Who's Who in America* (1912–1913, 1920–1921). Ludwell Lee Montague's *Haiti and the United States, 1714–1938* (1940) has scattered comments. There is a brief reference in James A. Padgett's "Diplomats to Haiti and Their Diplomacy" (*JNH*, July 1940, pp. 303–5). Indispensable are the List of United States Consular Officers (1789–1939), Diplomatic Records, National Archives, and *Register of the United States Department of State to January 18, 1902* (1902). — GLENN O. I. PHILLIPS

PRICE, JOSEPH CHARLES (1854–1893), clergyman, educator, editor, orator, and civil rights advocate. Born on Feb. 10, 1854, in Elizabeth City, N.C., he was the son of a slave, Charles Dozier, who had married a free woman, hoping thereby to ensure the freedom of his children. After Dozier, an illiterate but skilled ship's carpenter, was sold and sent away, his mother, whose name is not recorded, married David Price from whom the boy took his surname. During the Civil War the family moved to New Bern, N.C., "the rendezvous of large numbers of free Negroes."

In 1862 Price favorably impressed the Rev. Thomas M. Battle, superintendent of the Sunday school of St. Andrew's Chapel (also referred to as St. Peter's A.M.E. Zion Church), later a Miss Merrick who taught a day school, and about 1866, James Walter Hood, who became in 1872 the seventeenth bishop of the A.M.E. Zion church. Price attended in 1866 the St. Cyprian Episcopal School, supported by a Boston philanthropic Society. He taught for four years (1871–1875) in Wilson, N.C., attended Shaw University in Raleigh for a brief period, and transferred to Lincoln University, Oxford, Pa. He won oratorical prizes in his freshman and junior years and was valedictorian of his class in 1879. During his senior year he began studying in the junior theological department and graduated in 1881. He was licensed to preach in 1876, ordained a deacon, and elected a delegate to the 1880 General Conference of the A.M.E. Zion church in Montgomery, where his oratory and education led to his ordination as an elder. He became an agent for Zion Wesley Institute, founded in Concord, N.C., in 1879 and designated in 1880 as the chief educational institution of the church.

Chosen a delegate to the Ecumenical Conference of Methodism in London (1881) he attracted favorable attention by his oratory and lectured in the British Isles on the condition of Negroes in the United States. He particularly advocated support of such institutions as Zion Wesley Institute to train American Negroes for service in Africa. He raised a net sum of $10,000 which, added to $1000 contributed by white citizens of Salisbury, N.C., led to the establishment there of Zion Wesley College in October 1882. He devoted the next years of his life to making Livingstone (named in 1885 at his suggestion for the famous explorer and missionary in Africa) one of the important liberal arts colleges for Negroes in the South. It was incorporated in 1885.

Beginning in October 1882 Livingstone had five students in one two-story building on forty acres. Supported by the A.M.E. Zion church, it also received substantial aid after Price's visit to the Pacific Coast in 1885 from such philanthropists as William E. Dodge, Collis P. Huntington, and Leland Stanford. W. E. B. Du Bois, rarely given to hyperbole, wrote in *The Crisis* (March 1922, pp. 1–3) that had Price lived, Livingstone College would have become a "black Harvard."

Some historians believe that if Price had not died in his fortieth year on Oct. 25, 1893, he would have become one of the more influential Negroes of the latter part of the nineteenth century. Described as a "full-blooded Negro, six-feet-two inches tall and weighing almost three hundred pounds," he ranked with Frederick Douglass as a powerful orator. While he refused to

be considered for the bishopric, Memorial A.M.E. Zion Church, erected in Rochester, N.Y., in 1907, included a memorial window to Price along with those to Douglass, Harriet Tubman, and Susan B. Anthony. Price was one of the signers of the appeal by T. Thomas Fortune for a national convention to be held in Chicago on Jan. 15, 1890. Price was elected president of the National Afro-American League and also of the National Equal Rights Convention.

Price's leadership was of short duration. In February 1890 he was named chairman by acclamation of a group of 445 Negroes in Washington, D.C. The group established a Citizens' Equal Rights Association of the United States and issued a pamphlet stressing the view that good conduct, education, and the acquisition of wealth would help gain full citizenship rights. Price urged a merger of this group with the National Afro-American League, but P. B. S. Pinchback was elected president of the American Citizens' Equal Rights Association of the United States. Pinchback, Douglass, John Mercer Langston, and Blanche K. Bruce refused to attend the second convention of the National Afro-American League in Knoxville, Tenn., in July 1890. Their opposition and lack of financial support led Fortune not to hold a meeting in 1891, and in 1892 he announced the demise of the league. The Citizens' Equal Rights Association also became inactive. Except for an unsuccessful meeting called by Bishop Henry McNeal Turner in 1893, the Washington meeting of 1890 marked the end of the Convention Movement which had begun with the first National Convention of the Free People of Color in Philadelphia in 1830.

Neither Fortune, nor Price, could establish leadership in the early 1890s. A careful comparison of a speech that Price frequently made in the late 1880s with Booker T. Washington's much better known address in Atlanta on Sept. 18, 1895, may provide an explanation as to why Price was not catapulted into the role of the "leader of his race." First, his speech was longer than Washington's. Second, and more important, Price did not go as far as Washington did in propitiating the "New South." Price stated that "The southern question is simply this,—How long can we deny to men their inalienable and constitutional rights, the denial of which they most keenly feel?" The Negro was "ready and willing to make any terms that are reasonable, just and fair; but a compromise that reverses the Declaration of Independence, nullifies the national constitution, and is contrary to the genius of this republic, ought not to be asked of any race living under the stars and stripes; and if asked, ought not to be granted." Washington was to declare: "Ignorant and inexperienced, it is not strange that in the first years of our new life we began at the top instead of at the bottom." Price contended that the criticism that the Negro, "intoxicated with freedom and blinded by ignorance, was not prepared for the exercise of his franchise twenty-five years afterward," was unreasonable to say the least, in view of the race's rapid progress during that period. Washington asserted: "It is important and right that all privileges of the law be ours, but it is vastly more important that we be prepared for the exercise of those privileges." Washington electrified his audience when he dramatically assured: "In all things that are purely social we can be as separate as the fingers, yet one as the hand in all things essential to mutual progress." Price categorically stated that "The Negro does not desire and does not seek social equality with whites." Social equality did not obtain among Negroes: Negroes had the "rare privilege of choosing any color" in their own race, "from the snowy white to the ebony black." Colored men and women did not seek nonsegregated accommodations on trains because they desired the society of whites, but because they desired "comfort, protection, and nourishment." There were a great many whites whom Negroes refused to accept on terms of social equality as "quickly and even more quickly than those whites would hesitate to accept them." Unlike Washington, Price did not glorify the faithful slave nor did he promise that Negroes would further demonstrate their loyalty by working "without strikes and labor wars." Both orators were optimistic about the future. But Washington's peroration was more mellifluous in his belief that with a prayer to God there would be a "blotting out of sectional animosities and suspicions." Price had confidence "not only in the better element, progressive, humane, and patriotic of the South," but he also believed that "as the South has seen some of the errors of the past . . . it will come to discover the aggravating and retarding delusions of the present." Price closed his peroration: "For the work which those [Reconstruction] ideas started will never be completed, and the whole duty of the North never fully done until the last vestige of the peculiar institution is destroyed, and the smoking and dying embers of that fire which its hands have kindled shall have been forever extinguished" (*Negro Orators and Their Orations,* edited by Carter G. Woodson [1925], pp. 488–501). A potential Negro leader could not prescribe northern intervention which by the 1880s had become anathema to the South.

Price went further when he wrote in the *New York Age* (Oct. 11, 1890): "If we do not possess the manhood and patriotism to stand up in the defense of these constitutional rights, and protest long, loud and unitedly against their continual infringements, we are unworthy of our heritage as American citizens and deserve to have fastened on us the wrongs of which many of us are disposed to complain" (quoted by Meier, p. 81).

In that same year (1890) Price espoused literacy qualifications for voting applied equally to both races. At the Mississippi Constitutional Convention in August 1890, Isaiah T. Montgomery had proposed literacy, property, and other qualifications for voting for the express purpose of disfranchising most Negroes while permitting equally unqualified whites to vote. It seems, however, that Price, Langston, and Fortune in 1893 believed that the application of such literacy qualifications would not prevent full and equal citizenship rights for Negroes. In 1891 Price had praised Grover Cleveland and believed that Negroes should support Democrats who were dominant in the South "even at the sacrifice of nonessentials" (*Independent,* Jan. 1, 1891).

Price died of Bright's disease on Oct. 25, 1893, in Salisbury, and was buried in front of Huntington Hall at Livingstone College. Four of the leading white lawyers of Salisbury were pallbearers and the mayor and the city council attended. He was survived by his widow and four small children.

The fullest account is in William J. Walls's *Joseph Charles Price, Educator and Race Leader* (1943); references are in Walls's *The African Methodist Episcopal Zion Church, Reality of the Black Church* (1974, esp. pp. 309–14, with a photograph of Price on p. 311). An earlier, laudatory chapter, "Joseph C. Price," is in John W. Cromwell's *The Negro in American History . . .* (1914, pp. 171–78). Price's career is evaluated by August Meier in *Negro Thought in America, 1880–1915, Racial Ideologies in the Age of Booker T. Washington* (1963), and Emma Lou Thornbrough in *T. Thomas Fortune, Militant Journalist* (1972). In his chapter "Of Mr. Booker T. Washington and Others" in *The Souls of Black Folk* (1903), W. E. B. Du Bois wrote: "Price and others had sought a way of honorable alliance with the best of the Southerners" (p. 42); "for a time Price arose as a new leader, destined, it seemed, not to give up, but to restate the old ideals in a form less repugnant to the white South. But he passed away in his prime. Then came the new leader [Booker T. Washington]" (p. 49).

— RAYFORD W. LOGAN

PRINCE, LUCY TERRY (1733–1821), poet and civil rights advocate. Prince was born in Africa, kidnapped, and brought to Deerfield, Mass., where as a slave of Ebenezer Wells she was baptized when she was five. When she was sixteen she wrote a ballad "The Bar's Fight" about an Indian attack on Deerfield. On May 17, 1756, she married Abijah Prince, who had served during the French and Indian War (1744–1748). A free man at the time he married Lucy, he purchased her freedom. Then and later he owned land in Northfield, Mass., and in Guilford and Sunderland, Vt. By 1785 they had six children, two of whom served in the American Revolution. Abijah Prince died in 1794 and his widow settled in Sunderland in 1803. During her last eighteen years she rode horseback over the mountains to her husband's grave on their old Sunderland farm. She died in Sunderland in 1821.

Lucy Terry is frequently referred to as the first American Negro woman poet; her "The Bar's Fight" was published for the first time by Josiah Gilbert Holland in his *History of Western Massachusetts* (1855). (The first published poem by a Negro woman in the United States, by Phyllis Wheatley, appeared in 1776.) Seven of the twenty-nine lines of "The Bar's Fight" reveal the tone and substance of what has been called "the most accurate picture of the event on record" (William Loren Katz, *The Black West* [1971], p. 60): "August 'twas the twenty-fifth/ Seventeen hundred forty-six/ The Indians did in ambush lay/ Some very valient men to slay/ 'Twas nigh unto Sam Dickinson's mill,/ The Indians there five men did kill/ The names of whom I'll not leave out. . . ."

Lucy Terry Prince was a remarkable woman. In 1785, after the Princes' fence had been torn down by their white neighbors in Guilford, she persuaded the governor's council to order the Guilford selectmen to protect her family. She was unsuccessful, however, in a personal appeal she is said to have made to have one of her sons enrolled in Williams College. There is no convincing evidence to show that she won, by her own pleading, a civil case before the Vermont Supreme Court.

The brief biography of "Lucy Terry Prince: Vermont Advocate and Poet" by Sidney Kaplan in *The Black Presence in the Era of the American Revolution, 1770–1800* (1973, pp. 209–11), includes her only poem.

The principal sources are Josiah Gilbert Holland's *History of Western Massachusetts* (1895), George Sheldon's "Negro Slavery in Old Deerfield" (*New England Magazine,* March 1893), and Sheldon's *History of Deerfield, Massachusetts* (1896).

— RAYFORD W. LOGAN

PRIOLEAU, GEORGE W. (1856–1927), clergyman and chaplain. Born in Charleston, S.C., to slave parents, L. S. and Susan Prioleau, he graduated from Claflin University, Orangeburg, in 1875, and taught in the public primary schools of Lyons Township, Orangeburg County. He joined the Columbia, S.C., Conference of the African Methodist Episcopal church, of which his father was a pastor at St. Mathews, just north of Orangeburg, in 1879. His first pastorate was at Double Springs Mission, Lawrence County. In 1880 the Columbia Conference sent him to Wilberforce University, where he enrolled in the Theological Department. After his 1884 graduation he served churches in Hamilton and Troy, Ohio. In 1888 he was appointed professor of theology and homiletics at Wilberforce. After the Theological Department became Payne Theological Seminary he occupied the chair of historical and pastoral theology (1890–1894). In 1890 he also became presiding elder of the Springfield District of the Northern Ohio Conference. In 1892 he served as the district's delegate to the General Conference in Philadelphia. From that year until 1895 he was also secretary of the Northern Ohio Conference.

In the spring of 1895 he accepted a commission as chaplain of the 9th Cavalry, which he joined at Fort Robinson, Neb. He contracted malaria just prior to departure for the Cuban campaign of the Spanish-American War and spent the summer of 1898 on recruiting duty in his native Charleston. He served two lengthy tours of duty in the Philippines before his transfer to the 10th Cavalry on the Mexican border in 1915. Two years later, as senior chaplain in the army, he was promoted to major and was transferred to the 25th Infantry at Schofield Barracks near Honolulu. He retired to his home in Los Angeles in 1920, and organized the Bethel A.M.E. Church in that city.

Prioleau's first wife, Anna L. Scovell of New Orleans, held two degrees from Wilberforce. She died at the age of forty at Fort Walla Walla, Wash., in February 1903. He married Ethel G. Stafford of Emporia, Kans., in 1905, while he was stationed at Fort Riley. Prioleau and his second wife had four children: Mary S., Ethel Susanna, George Wesley, and Lois Emma.

Prioleau was a vocal advocate of military careers for Negro men. The low military pay still surpassed the income most Afro-Americans could expect and the army provided some measure of security and dignity. In his only published work, "Is the Chaplain's Work A Necessity?" in Theophilus G. Steward's *Active Service or Gospel Work among the U.S. Soldiers* (1897), he explained his own role as that of a shield against the corrupting influences which abounded in the towns near military posts. His actions suggest a more complex responsibility. In 1917 his efforts to raise funds from 25th Infantry soldiers yielded $3200 for the NAACP and the Negro victims of the East St. Louis, Ill., riot.

After his long ministry in Ohio and tenure at Wilberforce, he corresponded regularly with the *Cleveland Gazette.* His letters and the news articles in that paper provide substantial information regarding his career. Other biographical data are in Delilah Beasley's *The Negro Trail Blazers of California* (1919), and articles in *The Crisis* (Dec. 1917 and April 1918), and *The Colored American Magazine* (April 1909).

— FRANK N. SCHUBERT

PROCTOR, HENRY HUGH (1868–1933), Congregational clergyman, author, and lecturer. Proctor was born on a farm near Fayetteville, Tenn., on Dec. 8, 1868. His parents, Richard and Hannah (Murray) Proctor, had been slaves. He first attended a rural school and then completed the common course in the public schools of Fayetteville, after which he became a teacher at Pea Ridge, Tenn., and later at Fayetteville, where he served also as principal. In 1884 he enrolled at Central Tennessee College at Nashville, but after one term moved to Fisk University from which he received the B.A. degree in 1891. He regarded the six years at Fisk as the formative period of his life. His philosophy and character were shaped to a large extent by Helen C. Morgan, professor of Latin, who had come as one of the school's first teachers and "builded her life into the walls of Fisk"; Anna Cahill, who brought "a thoroughness, a culture and refinement that was [*sic*] rare indeed"; her husband, Henry S. Bennett, "whose great sermons . . . laid in my heart the foundations of the desire to be a preacher of the gospel"; Adam K. Spence, "an enthusiast in missions, a passionate lover of Negro music, and our beloved teacher in Greek and French"; and President Erastus Milo Cravath, of whom there was "no man his equal in poise, dignity and magnanimity . . . a real Christian." In 1893 he married Adeline L. Davis, who had been a fellow student and had become a member of the Fisk faculty after her graduation. In 1894 he graduated from Yale Divinity School, was ordained into the Congregational ministry, and received an invitation to serve as pastor of the First Congregational Church in Atlanta, Ga.

Proctor remained in Atlanta until 1920, when the membership of his church grew from 100 to 1000, and an impressive new house of worship was erected. This church had been founded by the American Missionary Association during Reconstruction and had continued to receive support from the association until Proctor's arrival. From the beginning of his pastorate it was self-supporting, and began its own missionary activities among the poor and in the Atlanta jails.

In 1903 Proctor and George W. Henderson, president of Straight University in New Orleans, took the lead in founding the National Convention of Congregational Workers among Colored People, of which Proctor became the first president. This organization aimed at making the Negro Congregational churches of the South self-supporting, the establishment of a department of church extension for the promotion of Negro Congregationalism, the improvement of the theological department of the schools of the American Missionary Association, and the employment by these schools of more of their graduates as teachers. Proctor was chosen in 1904 as assistant moderator of the National Council of Congregational Churches, and that year Atlanta's Clark University conferred on him the Doctor of Divinity degree. But it was his activities following the Atlanta race riot of 1906 that were to bring him to national attention.

While the terror of the riot still gripped the city, Proctor and Charles T. Hopkins, a white attorney, brought together forty persons—twenty Negroes and twenty whites—to form the Interracial Committee of Atlanta for the purpose of quieting tensions and alleviating the conditions which had produced racial conflict. Convinced that one of the major problems was the absence of recreational and cultural activities for the city's Afro-American population, Proctor determined to make First Congregational an institutional church, offering social, welfare, and cultural programs to the entire Negro community. Through his leadership the church established a gymnasium, a library, an employment bureau, a counseling service, a home for working girls, a kindergarten, a model kitchen and sewing room for domestic science instruction, a ladies' parlor for reading and relaxation, and an auditorium with a seating capacity of 1000. In 1910 Proctor organized the Atlanta Colored Music Festival Association, which presented "the best musical talent of the race." Proctor also served as chairman of the Carrie Steele Orphanage, which was supported by his congregation.

At the request of the War Department, Proctor went to Europe in 1919 to improve the morale of the Negro troops of occupation. He said that he traveled 4000 miles and spoke to 100,000 Negro troops. In 1920 he accepted a call to the Nazarene Congregational Church in Brooklyn. Here he continued to promote interracial cooperation and worked to establish another institutional church. In 1926 he was elected moderator of the New York City Congregational Church Association, an honor bestowed by 400 delegates representing sixty-five churches with 26,000 white and 5000 Negro members.

Proctor was a noted lecturer, particularly famous for an oration, "The Burden of the Negro," which he delivered before hundreds of audiences across the nation. He was a frequent contributor to the *American Missionary* and the *Congregationalist*. He wrote a series in 1931 on "Negro Migration from the South" for the *New York Herald Tribune,* and wrote two books, *Sermons in Melody* (1916) and *Between Black and White* (1925). He founded the *Georgia Congregationalist,* which later became the *Congregational Worker,* the national organ for Negro Congregationalists.

Proctor was a lifelong Republican and a conservative in many respects. Pres. William Howard Taft and former Pres. Theodore Roosevelt spoke at his Atlanta church on separate occasions. He was a close friend of Booker T. Washington, whom he first met in 1895 when he was part of the official escort for Washington at the Atlanta Exposition. Washington spoke at the ground-breaking ceremonies in 1908 for the new church building in Atlanta. Some years after Washington's death, Proctor said that in philosophy he was between Washington and W. E. B. Du Bois, since both men and their programs were necessary. His conservatism was more the brand of his white missionary teachers at Fisk than it was that of Washington. He was no accommodationist. He was an outspoken advocate for equal rights for Negroes and he openly and courageously fought disfranchisement in Georgia. On the other hand he was a strong believer in self-improvement by Afro-Americans as a road to better race relations, and he was fiercely proud of his race and heritage. He hailed the spiritual as the Negro's greatest gift to the world, and he said the ultimate leader of the race would not be a Booker T. Washington but a Roland Hayes. One of his famous sermons, "Why I Am Glad I Am Colored," was published in the *Southern News* in 1924.

Proctor died of blood poisoning at St. John's Hospital in Brooklyn and was buried in Southview Cemetery in Atlanta. He was survived by his widow (1870–1945) and five of their six children, three daughters and two sons.

The Henry Hugh Proctor Papers are in the Amistad Research Center, New Orleans. See also Henry Hugh Proctor's *Between Black and White* (1925) and Altona Trent Johns's "Henry Hugh Proctor" (*The Black Perspective in Music* 3 [Spring 1975]: 25–32).

— CLIFTON H. JOHNSON

PROSSER, GABRIEL (c. 1775–1800), leader of a slave insurrection. Gabriel and his brothers Martin and Solomon were slaves on the estate of Thomas H. Prosser in Henrico County just outside Richmond, Va. The wife of his master taught him to read and write. Very little is known about his physical appearance except that he had lost two front teeth and had several scars on his head. Gabriel was a careful student of the Bible, especially the Old Testament, where he believed he found his prototype in the picturesque and legendary figure of Samson, in imitation of whom he wore his hair long. He believed that he was a child of destiny, raised up by Jehovah to bring a great deliverance to his people.

Gabriel planned an audacious, although unsuccessful, slave uprising. He organized over 1000 slaves and oversaw the making of weapons and bullets. On Saturday night, Aug. 30, 1800, the insurrectionists assembled at a brook on the Prosser estate and divided into three columns under previously selected leaders to converge on Richmond, about six miles away. They were to sieze the penitentiary, recently converted into an arsenal, and the powder house, and seal off the bridges around the city. Their plan to kill as many whites as possible could have succeeded in a surprise attack because the city could not have mustered more than four or five hundred men and thirty muskets in its defense.

The insurrection, however elaborate and detailed the plans for it, failed almost before it started. That day two slaves of the Sheppard family told of the plot which was to be executed that night. Gov. James Monroe was informed and he immediately dispatched troops to strategic points in the city and in pursuit of the insurgents. That night a heavy rain caused the streams to rise and virtually isolate the Prosser estate. Because roads and bridges became impassable and because many insurrectionists interpreted the storm as a prophetic sign, the assembled group disbanded and only a small number were eventually apprehended.

Gabriel went into hiding. On Sept. 21 he hailed the schooner *Mary,* which had run aground four miles below Richmond, and was secreted aboard. But his presence became known, and when the schooner put in at Norfolk two constables boarded the ship and captured him. He was committed to the Richmond penitentiary on Sept. 27, was tried on Oct. 3, and together with some other insurrectionists, was hanged on Oct. 7. In all, forty-one men were hanged.

The fullest accounts of Gabriel and the Gabriel Insurrection are found in the *Journal of the Senate of the Commonwealth of Virginia, December 1, 1800–February 2, 1802* and *Calendar of Virginia State Papers and Other Manuscripts* (vol. 9, 1890). Joseph Cephas Carroll includes the insurrection in his *Slave Insurrections in the United States, 1800–1865,* (1938), as does Herbert Aptheker in his *American Negro Slave Revolts* (1943). Accounts of the insurrection appear in the *Commercial Advertiser* (New York; Oct. 13, 1800), the *Virginia Herald* (Fredericksburg; Sept. 10, 1800), the *Richmond Recorder* (April 3, 1800), the *Boston Gazette* (Oct. 6, 1800), and the *Norfolk Herald* (Oct. 9, 1800). — WILLIAM J. KIMBALL

PURVIS, CHARLES BURLEIGH (1842–1929), physician, medical educator, and hospital administrator. Born in Philadelphia on April 14, 1842, he was one of eight children of Harriet (Forten) and Robert Purvis, Sr. His parents moved from Philadelphia in 1844 to a country estate in Byberry, Pa. Although Charles attended Quaker schools for his elementary education, perhaps the most important educational influences were his parents. His mother, the daughter of James Forten, the wealthy Philadelphia sailmaker and civic leader, was a founder in 1833 of the Female Anti-Slavery Society. His affluent father's abolitionist activities brought Charles into contact with many of the movement's leaders, and for the remainder of his life he embodied their commitment to civic equality and social reform.

From 1860 to 1863 Purvis attended Oberlin College. Two years later he graduated from Wooster Medical College (later Western Reserve Medical School) in Cleveland. During the summer of 1864 he had worked as a military nurse at the large contraband relief center in Washington, in the barracks of Camp Barker near 13th and R Streets, a forerunner of Freedmen's Hospital. His experience there, where he contracted typhoid fever, may have influenced his decision to join the philanthropic crusade to provide health care and other assistance to the desperately impoverished ex-slaves. In 1865 he enlisted in the Union Army as acting assistant surgeon, was assigned to duty in Washington, D.C., and served until 1869. In these years immediately after the Civil War there were only six Negro physicians in Washington. Meanwhile a new medical facility had been built on the grounds of Howard University for the Freedmen's Hospital, to meet the needs of the large number of former slaves who had migrated to the capital. The Negro population had increased from 14,316 in 1860 to 38,663 in 1867.

In 1869 Purvis was appointed assistant surgeon of Freedmen's Hospital, serving until his promotion as surgeon-in-chief in 1881. On March 15, 1869, he was also appointed to the medical faculty of Howard University, becoming the second Negro teacher of medicine in an American university. From 1869 to 1873 he taught courses on materia medica, therapeutics, botany, and medical jurisprudence, and held the Thaddeus Stevens Chair (1871–1872). From 1873 to 1888 he was professor of obstetrics and the diseases of women and children, and from 1889 to his retirement from the faculty in 1907 he was professor of obstetrics and gynecology.

From 1869 to 1926 Purvis was a major influence in the development of Howard University and its medical school. As a result of the national financial crisis of 1873 the university's trustees informed the medical faculty that since their salaries could no longer be provided by the university, each teacher was obliged to resign, but could be reappointed with no guarantee of salary. Thereafter the medical faculty would be on a "self-supporting" basis. Only three members of the medical faculty remained at Howard under these conditions, Alexander T. Augusta, Gideon S. Palmer, and C. B. Purvis. Because of his leadership during the ensuing crisis (when the law school closed, for example), Purvis was credited with saving medical education at Howard. To General Howard he wrote on June 16, 1873: "While I regret the University will not be able to pay me for my services, I feel the importance of every effort being made to carry forward the Institution and to make it a success." Purvis was elected secretary of the virtually independent and unpaid medical faculty, serving in that critical post until 1896. From 1873 to 1906 Purvis taught medicine with virtually no compensation; a year after his retirement the university resumed limited responsibility for medical faculty salaries. It was therefore literally true that the personal sacrifice of Purvis and his colleagues made medical education possible for more than half the Negro physicians of that era.

Purvis also participated in the unsuccessful effort of Negro physicians in 1869–1870 to gain admission to the Medical Society of the District of Columbia, affiliated with the American Medical Association. Although the three physicians proposed for membership were well qualified, and two, Purvis and A. T. Augusta, were professors of medicine, they were refused because of their race. The U.S. Senate did not act on Charles Sumner's bill to repeal the charter of the medical society, which defended its racial policies on the ground that membership was personal and social rather than professional. Purvis and others then established in January 1870 the interracial National Medical Society of the District of Columbia. This organization declared that the United States was the only country, and medicine "the only profession in which such a distinction is made. Science knows no race, color, or condition; and we protest against the Medical Society of the District of Columbia maintaining such a distinction." At its 1870 annual meeting the American Medical Association firmly established racial caste in American medicine by voting to bar Negro delegates and refusing to recognize the National Medical Society.

When Pres. James A. Garfield was shot at the Washington railroad station by Charles J. Guiteau on July 2, 1881, Purvis was the first physician to treat the president. Appointed surgeon-in-chief of Freedmen's Hospital several months later by Pres. Chester A. Arthur, in recognition of his treatment of Garfield, Purvis was the first Negro to be in charge of a civilian hospital (Augusta had been in charge of military hospitals). Despite any distinction that might be attached to that fact, Purvis objected to such racial classifications. "I have always resented," he said, "the expression 'leading colored doctor or lawyer.' A colored doctor means half a doctor." He insisted that "American manhood must know of no color." He was uncompromising on segregation and the attempt by whites to qualify citizenship or membership in professions by race. "We are all Americans, white, black, and colored. . . . As Negroes nothing is demanded, as American citizens every enjoyment and opportunity is demanded."

Despite the restrictions imposed on him, Purvis was a successful physician, educator, and hospital administrator. Known as a stern taskmaster as a teacher, he was the only colored member of Howard's medical faculty from 1877 to 1885. He was also the only member of the original medical faculty assembled by General Howard to serve the university throughout the nineteenth century. He provided a continuing link with the interracial ideals of the founders, and steered the school away from racial provincialism. He served as president of the medical faculty from 1899 to 1900, and was elected dean in 1900, but declined the position.

During his administration, Freedmen's Hospital not only grew rapidly, serving in 1886 as many as 5000 patients, for example, but also improved its standards. It became a national institution, serving as the teaching hospital of Howard University (though technically under federal rather than university auspices). Moreover Freedmen's provided medical care to a substantial and growing number of patients from southern states who were denied admission to local hospitals on racial grounds. Purvis was removed as surgeon-in-chief in 1894 after the election of Grover Cleveland, whose secretary of the interior, Hoke Smith of Georgia, for the first time politicized the position. A Democrat, Daniel Hale Williams of Chicago, succeeded Purvis. For some years thereafter Purvis worked to remove the hospital from politics. When District of Columbia officials sought in 1903 to close Freedmen's and build a city hospital unaffiliated with Howard, Purvis fought the proposal. Through his network of friends in Congress, the proposal was defeated. If he had failed it was probable that continued medical education at Howard would have been impossible, since its students would have been barred from the new municipal hospital. He also lobbied, successfully, for an appropriation from Congress for a new $600,000 building for Freedmen's, which was under construction from 1904 to 1906. In

1908 the university's trustees stated that the new hospital was "a monument to his personal energy."

Purvis was also a leader in other civic affairs in Washington. He served on the Board of Education, and the Board of Health in the District of Columbia. From 1897 to 1904 he was a member of the Board of Medical Examiners. He was also one of the few Negroes on the influential Washington Board of Trade.

Licensed to practice medicine in Massachusetts in 1904 and admitted to the Massachusetts Medical Society, Purvis moved to Boston in 1905 where he resided the remainder of his life. He resigned from the medical school on May 28, 1907. On May 24, 1908, he was elected to the Howard Board of Trustees, and was an active and influential member until his retirement from the board on June 1, 1926.

A handsome and imposing man, respected professionally and socially, Purvis was one of the most effective leaders of the effort to prove, in his words, that "brain development knows no race, or complexion." A convinced cosmopolitan, he was early interested in international relations. After World War I he said that Japan not only sought to be "a second Germany," but predicted it would "challenge the white nations of the world," and that European colonialism would end in Asia and Africa.

Purvis had married Ann Hathaway of Maine, who was white, on April 13, 1871. They had two children, Alice, who became a physician, and Robert, a dentist. He died on Jan. 30, 1929, in Los Angeles, Calif.

See W. Montague Cobb's "Charles Burleigh Purvis, 1842–1929" (*JNMA*, Jan. 1953, pp. 79–82); Rayford W. Logan's *Howard University, The First Hundred Years, 1867–1967* (1969); Walter Dyson's *Howard University, the Capstone of Negro Education* (1941); Daniel Smith Lamb's *Howard University Medical Department* (1900); W. Montague Cobb's *The First Negro Medical Society* (1939); and Herbert M. Morais's *History of the Negro in Medicine* (1967). Brief sketches are in William Wells Brown's *The Rising Son* (1874) and William J. Simmons's *Men of Mark . . .* (1881). For his career at Freedmen's Hospital, see Thomas Holt et al., *A Special Mission: The Story of Freedmen's Hospital, 1862–1962* (1975). Particularly illuminating about his racial attitudes is his extensive correspondence with Francis J. Grimké, available in the Manuscript Division, Moorland-Spingarn Research Center, Howard University. — MICHAEL R. WINSTON

PURVIS, ROBERT, SR. (1810–1898), abolitionist and civil rights leader. Purvis was born in Charleston, S.C., on Aug. 4, 1810, of mixed parentage. His father, William Purvis, a cotton broker, had left England around 1790, and became a naturalized American. Robert's mother, Harriet Judah, was free-born, although the daughter of a slave, Dido Badaraka, who had been kidnapped from her native Morocco at the age of twelve and sold into bondage. Given her freedom when she was nineteen, Dido had married a German, Baron Judah. Their daughter, Harriet, and William Purvis had three sons, one of them Robert. At the age of nine, Robert was brought to Philadelphia and placed in a private school. Seven years later, in 1826, his father died, leaving him $120,000. With an academy-level education and ample means, Purvis was ready for a career by the time he reached manhood.

Although his wealth might have made him a defender of the status quo rather than a reformer, Purvis had shown an early interest in the crusade against slavery. His father had given him antislavery books, and the young man's inclination to join the movement was confirmed in 1830 when he made the acquaintance of the revered Benjamin Lundy and William Lloyd Garrison. It was the latter, rather than Lundy, who personified the new school of abolitionism with its strong denunciation of the slaveholders and its demand for immediate, uncompensated emancipation. Garrison and Purvis formed an early and lasting friendship. While in Philadelphia during the first week of June 1832 Garrison stopped for a few days at the residence of Purvis. In a thank-you letter written later that month, Garrison referred to his host as "one to whom I am so deeply indebted, and whose friendship I prize at a high rate."

Purvis and Garrison were both prominent participants in the formation of the American Anti-Slavery Society at Philadelphia in December 1833; Purvis publicly praised Garrison on that historic occasion. Traveling to England the following summer, Purvis bore letters of introduction from Garrison to a score of British reformers, among them Daniel O'Connell, the Irish patriot, and Sir Thomas Foxwell Buxton, parliamentary leader of the antislavery forces. Purvis was greeted warmly by both.

Although Purvis worked with the national antislavery group, he gave far more time to the work in his own state. Late in 1836 he was chosen by the Negroes in Philadelphia to deliver the formal eulogy at a memorial observance for Thomas Shipley, whose appearance before the courts had saved hundreds of Negroes in Pennsylvania from slavery. Until 1859 Purvis was the only colored member of the old-line Pennsylvania Society for Promoting the Abolition of Slavery. From 1845 to 1850 he was president of the far more active Pennsylvania Anti-Slavery Society, declining a sixth term. Earlier he had been the president of the Vigilance Committee of Philadelphia during its six-year existence (1839–1844), the group often meeting at his house to plan ways to assist runaway slaves. Purvis was also the only chairman of the General Vigilance Committee, the successor to the pioneer organization, holding that post from 1852 to 1857. Interracial in composition, both vigilance groups extended assistance to an average of 100 fugitives a year.

Some of these runaways were housed overnight, or longer if necessary, at the home of Purvis, where a skillful carpenter had constructed a secret room reached by a trapdoor. Fellow abolitionists likewise found a warm welcome awaiting them at the Purvis home, one of them dubbing it "Saints' Rest," where "the wicked ceased from troubling and the weary are at rest." Guests who dined at the Purvis home could be sure that they were served food not produced by slave labor, Purvis being an exponent of the "free produce" movement. Abolitionist guests found a kindred spirit in Purvis's wife Harriet, daughter of sailmaker James Forten. She was one of the founders, in 1833, of the

Female Anti-Slavery Society of Philadelphia, had attended the second antislavery convention of American women in Philadelphia five years later, and was a faithful worker in the annual money-raising fairs held by the Pennsylvania Anti-Slavery Society.

Slavery was not the only target that drew the Purvis fire. In 1833 he opposed a legislative proposal that would have prevented out-of-state free Negroes from settling in Pennsylvania. In 1838 he fought vigorously, if unsuccessfully, to defeat the adoption of a new state constitution which would bar Negroes from voting. He was chairman of the seven-man committee which drew up a lengthy protest, an "Appeal of Forty Thousand Citizens Threatened with Disfranchisement, to the People of Pennsylvania." When in 1853 colored children were excluded from the public schools in Byberry, the township in which he lived, Purvis refused to pay taxes, asserting that such nonpayment was "a vindication of his rights and personal dignity, against an encroachment upon them as contemptibly mean as it was infamously despotic." Since he was a large taxpayer, the directors of the public schools decided to rescind their exclusionary edict. In 1857 Purvis denounced the Dred Scott decision, stating that he owed no allegiance to a government founded on the proposition that a black man had "no rights a white man was bound to respect."

Purvis was interested in racial uplift as well as in racial reform. In 1831 he joined in an appeal to establish a manual labor school for Negroes. Two years later he was one of the founders of the Philadelphia Library Company of Colored Persons. He was active in the annual Colored Conventions, which began in 1830 and embraced colored leaders from the northern states. In the convention of 1833 he served as the vice-president and corresponding secretary from Pennsylvania. Purvis also supported such racially neutral reforms as the temperance crusade, women's rights, and prison improvement. He believed in racially integrated reform groups, rather than racially separated ones.

Like many other Negro leaders Purvis welcomed the coming of the Civil War. A longtime opponent of colonization, he criticized President Lincoln for his early recommendations that Negroes voluntarily leave the country. He promoted colored enlistments in the Union Army, although bitterly condemning the War Department for its ruling that the commissioned officers in colored troops be white. But with the Emancipation Proclamation and the eroding of slavery in the Confederacy, Purvis became much more hopeful for the future. "I am proud to be an American Citizen," he said in May 1863 at the thirtieth annual meeting of the American Anti-Slavery Society.

With the end of the Civil War Purvis's public activities diminished greatly. For a period he took an interest in municipal reform in Philadelphia, but the great bulk of his time was spent in tending to his tree-lined lawn, his fine orchard, and his prize-winning livestock. His greatest pride was his son, Charles B. Purvis, surgeon-in-chief at the Freedmen's Hospital, and for more than thirty years (1868–1907) a professor in the medical school of Howard University. A highlight of Purvis's later years was his attendance at the fiftieth anniversary meeting of the American Anti-Slavery Society, held on

Dec. 4, 1883, in Philadelphia. Purvis, who presided, was one of the society's three surviving founders, and he would outlive the other two—Elizur Wright, Jr., and John Greenleaf Whittier.

Purvis died on April 15, 1898, a victim of apoplexy. The funeral was held in Philadelphia, with interment at the Fair Hill Friends' burial ground in that city. He was survived by his second wife, Tacy Townsend, and his son Charles. The *New York Times* carried a eulogistic notice of his death, the American Negro Historical Society passed a series of resolutions praising him, and the *Washington Bee* editorialized that he was one of the few men who deserved to have a monument to his memory.

In 1883 Purvis wrote a three-page sketch of his parentage and early abolitionist activities, which appears in R. C. Smedley's *History of the Underground Railroad in Chester and the Neighboring Counties of Pennsylvania* (1883). Joseph A. Borome's "Robert Purvis and His Early Challenge to American Racism" (*NHB,* May 1967) deals primarily with his trip abroad. The abolitionist weeklies, particularly the Garrison-edited *Liberator,* carried notices of Purvis's activities. Benjamin Quarles's *Black Abolitionists* (1969) contains numerous references. — BENJAMIN QUARLES

RAINEY, JOSEPH HAYNE (1832–1887), congressman and the first Negro seated in the U.S. House of Representatives. Rainey was born on June 21, 1832, in Georgetown, S.C., to slave parents, Edward L. and Gracey Rainey. Edward Rainey was able to purchase his and his family's freedom sometime between 1840 and 1850 and establish himself as a relatively prosperous barber in Georgetown. Joseph Rainey apparently lived in Philadelphia for sometime during the early 1850s and there he married a woman named Susan. Rainey followed his father's vocation and had established himself as a barber in Charleston. He was drafted by the Confederacy to work on military fortifications in Charleston harbor and from there managed to escape to Bermuda in 1862 together with his wife.

He returned to South Carolina at the end of the war to become active in the Republican party, serving as Republican county chairman and as a member of the Republican state executive committee from 1868 to 1876. In 1868 he was elected as a delegate to the state constitutional convention from Georgetown. He seldom spoke in the constitutional convention, but strongly supported measures such as amnesty and debt relief that were favorable to the ex-Confederates and white planters. On the other hand, he opposed radical land-reform measures and argued unsuccessfully for the disfranchisement of persons who failed to pay the poll tax. Under the new reconstructed government he was elected to the state Senate, serving there as chairman of the important Finance Committee. Rainey was elected to Congress in 1870 to fill the unexpired term of Benjamin F. Whittemore, a white Republican and native of Massachusetts, who had been forced to resign because he had sold West Point cadet appointments.

Rainey was reelected to four consecutive terms from the 1st Congressional District, but was defeated by Democrat John S. Richardson in the 1878 election.

Georgetown, Rainey's home district, had a Republican electoral majority of well over two to one, and there he was practically unchallenged. He had faced tough competition at the polls in only two of five successful campaigns. Samuel Lee, a Negro Republican, led a revolt against the regulars in 1874, and John S. Richardson, a white Democrat, attempted to profit from the violent and fradulent campaign in 1876. In both cases Rainey successfully parried legal challenges by his defeated opponents. Lee's contest was dismissed unanimously by the House Committee on Elections, and although Richardson's challenge was upheld by the Elections Committee in 1876, the House recommitted its report, thereby effectively allowing Rainey to retain his seat.

In Congress, Rainey astutely linked his continued support of general amnesty legislation to Democratic support for the Civil Rights Bill of 1875. He made effective speeches in favor of legislation to enforce the Fourteenth Amendment and the Ku Klux Klan Act. Having been a victim of discrimination in public accommodations on numerous occasions, the olive-complexioned congressman was a very active proponent of civil rights legislation, including the integration of public schools.

After leaving Congress, Rainey was appointed a special agent of the Treasury Department and served until July 15, 1881. After failing in the attempt to become the first Negro clerk of the U.S. House of Representatives, he began a note brokerage and banking business in Washington, D.C. This business failed and by 1886 he had joined William H. Chew in operating a coal and wood yard. In the spring of 1887 Rainey returned to Georgetown in ill health with little money. He died of congestive fever on Aug. 1, 1887, leaving a widow and five children.

Joseph Rainey's career was something of an anomaly. Although he held several prominent political offices, he does not appear to have exercised a commensurate influence in his party. He was neither a forceful personality and orator like Robert B. Elliott, nor a quiet, effective politician like Robert Smalls. He was a staunchly loyal party man, and basically conservative in both his demeanor and political positions. Nevertheless, quiet and reserved, Rainey was well liked by his colleagues and respected by his political enemies for undisputed integrity. His most notable speech was a eulogy of Sen. Charles Sumner of Massachusetts on March 11, 1874. Rainey's application for an IRS appointment in 1879 was supported by eighty-four of his fellow congressmen, including the future Pres. James A. Garfield. He resigned after serving two years. During an absence of the speaker in May 1874, Rainey became the first Negro to preside over the U.S. House of Representatives.

Since there is no full-length biography, the major source for Rainey's life is his own account in *The Biographical Directory of the American Congress* (1971). The sketch in Samuel Denny Smith's *The Negro in Congress, 1870–1901* (1940) relies on racially and politically biased sources; Maurine Christopher's *America's Black Congressmen* (1971) adds new information but fails to document its sources. — THOMAS HOLT

RAINEY, "MA" [professional name of **GERTRUDE PRIDGETT RAINEY**] (1886–1939), entertainer, usually called the "Mother of the Blues." She was born on April 26, 1886 in Columbus, Ga. Little is known about her parents, Thomas and Ella Allen Pridgett, who lived originally in Alabama. The family included two other children, Melissa and Thomas Jr.

Rainey's interest in the stage developed early. She made her debut in 1900 at the Columbus Opera House in a talent show called *The Bunch of Blackberries.* Four years later she married William "Pa" Rainey, who came through Columbus in a traveling show; thereafter she was known as "Ma" Rainey. For several years they toured with various minstrel shows. Between 1914 and 1916 they traveled with Tolliver's Circus and Musical Extravaganza under the name of "Rainey and Rainey, the Assassinators of the Blues." The act combined comedy, dancing, and singing. Eventually the couple separated and Ma Rainey toured on her own with the celebrated Rabbit Foot Minstrels. Through the 1920s and 1930s she appeared mostly in the rural South, performing on the T.O.B.A. (Theater Owners Booking Association) circuit.

She made her first record in December 1923 at age thirty-seven and recorded until 1928, making about ninety recordings. Ma Rainey was not the first singer to record the blues (Mamie Smith preceded her by two years), but it was Rainey, along with Bessie Smith, who introduced the earthy sounds of the South, the raw blues of field workers, to the general record-buying public. Negroes all over the country eagerly bought her records.

Rainey usually sang in a moaning, poignant style, but she could also perform with lusty vigor. She recorded with many of the top musicians of her day, including Louis Armstrong, Fletcher Henderson, Coleman Hawkins, Thomas Dorsey, and Tampa Red. Her themes were frequently those of a woman lamenting an unrequited love, and the titles of songs she recorded bear this out. They include "Jealous Hearted Blues," "Trust No Man," "Gone Daddy Blues," and "Sweet Rough Man."

Sterling Brown's poem "Ma Rainey" (*Southern Road, Poems by Sterling Brown* [1932], pp. 62–64) told how folks flocked to hear her sing: "Sing us 'bout de hard luck/ Roun' our do'./ Sing us 'bout de lonesome road/ We mus' go. . . .'"

In personal appearance Rainey was gaudy, and inspired ambivalent reactions. Heavy featured, squat, usually attired in striking gowns and sparkling jewelry, and flashing a mouthful of gold teeth, she could captivate an audience with her electrifying manner and powerful voice. Blues singer Champion Jack Dupree, who saw her frequently, told British critic Derrick Stewart-Baxter: "She was really an ugly woman, but when she opened her mouth—that was it! You forgot everything. She knew how to sing those blues, and she got right into your heart."

After only five years of successful recording Rainey was told that her rural southern blues had gone out of fashion, and she made her last recordings on Dec. 28, 1928. However, she continued performing and touring until 1935, when she returned home to Columbus to live after the death of her sister Melissa, and her mother. In her last years she operated two theaters she owned in Rome, Ga. She died on Dec. 22, 1939, and was buried in the family plot in Porterdale Cemetery.

The principal sources are Thomas Pridgett, Jr.'s "The Life of 'Ma' Rainey" (*Jazz, Information,* Sept. 6, 1940, reprinted as liner notes to *The Voice of "Ma" Rainey,* Paramount record album P-1); Derrick Stewart-Baxter's *Ma Rainey and the Classic Blues Singers* (1970). The article by Marshall W. Stearns in *DAB, Supplement 2* (1958, pp. 547–48), includes a perceptive analysis of the blues as an art form, and a bibliography.

— HOLLIE I. WEST

RANGER, JOSEPH (c. 1760– ?), able seaman. Born perhaps in Northumberland County, Va., living later in Elizabeth City County, he is said to have served longer and on more warships than any of the other seventy-five Negroes from Virginia: on four vessels during the American Revolution and for six years thereafter. He began his career on the *Hero,* was transferred first to the *Dragon,* then to the *Jefferson,* and finally to the *Patriot,* all vessels of the state of Virginia. He probably was engaged in combat, for he was on the *Jefferson* when it was blown up by the British on the James River; also on the *Patriot* when its entire crew was captured and held by the British until after they surrendered at Yorktown. After the war he served on the Virginia vessels *Patriot* and *Liberator* until 1787. Under the Federal Pension Act of 1832 Ranger received an annual sum of $96 and 100 acres of land, possibly in the Virginia Military Reserve of the Northwest Territory.

Information about Ranger and most other seamen, Negro and white, during the American Revolution is sketchy. The source of this sketch is *Virginia Negro Soldiers and Sailors in the Revolutionary War* (1944, pp. 13–15), by Luther P. Jackson, Sr., the pioneer Negro researcher in the state's archives.

— RAYFORD W. LOGAN

RANSIER, ALONZO JACOB (1834–1882), congressman. One of four Negro congressmen elected from South Carolina during the Reconstruction period, he was born free in Charleston on Jan. 3, 1834. Little is known about Ransier's childhood except that his parents may have been Haitian immigrants. At the age of sixteen Alonzo was employed as a shipping clerk in Charleston. Since this was one of the occupations from which free Negroes were excluded by law, his employer was fined one cent and costs of court for the violation. This incident illustrates the ambiguous position free Negroes occupied in Charleston society during the antebellum period. Special restrictive laws regulated their activities, but often these laws were either ignored or lightly enforced. Thus Ransier, like many other free Negroes, was able to secure a livelihood and a measure of education generally denied to other Negroes.

Given these advantages Ransier played a leading role in the founding of the state's Republican party after the Civil War. In 1865 he was one of the first Negroes appointed by Gen. Daniel Sickles to serve as a registrar of elections. He represented Charleston in the Constitutional Convention of 1868 and in the state House of

Representatives from 1868 to 1870. In 1870 he became the state's first Negro lieutenant-governor after defeating ex-Confederate Gen. M. C. Butler by 33,000 votes. In 1872 he was elected to represent South Carolina's second district in the U.S. Congress, defeating ex-Union Gen. William Gurney, a candidate of the Independent Republican faction, by 13,000 votes.

Ransier was seated on Dec. 1, 1873, because he had been elected to fill for the few remaining months of the 42nd Congress the vacancy caused by the expulsion of Robert C. DeLarge, as well as to a full term in the 43rd Congress. Ransier was appointed to the Committee on Manufactures and was a very active legislator despite his brief service. He introduced a bill to provide federal funds to rebuild the west wing of the Citadel Academy, but the proposal died in the Appropriations Committee. He was prominent in the debates on national issues, speaking forcefully for the Civil Rights Bill of 1875, favoring proposals for a six-year presidential term and higher tariffs, and opposing wage increases for federal officials.

The faction-ridden South Carolina Republicans showed scant appreciation for Ransier's performance, however. Although he had strongly opposed the Liberal Republican movement in 1872 and had campaigned nationally to hold Negroes in line for President Grant, he returned from Washington in 1874, insisting that the state party must clean house and rid itself of the corrupt Gov. Franklin Moses, Jr. Although Moses was indeed rebuffed at the Republican convention, Ransier lost the congressional nomination to Charles W. Buttz, a white Republican.

Deprived of an opportunity to continue the work he had begun in Congress, Ransier sought and received an appointment as collector of internal revenue for the second district of South Carolina in May 1875. Within that same year, however, Ransier's wife Louisa died, shortly after the birth of their eleventh child, Charles Sumner. Although he was left with a respectable amount of real estate and municipal and railroad stocks, Ransier soon became impoverished after his wife's death. His last employment before his death on Aug. 17, 1882, was as a day laborer for the Charleston city government.

Although he was not among the dominant personalities in the South Carolina Republican party, Ransier was one of its more prominent and popular leaders. He was only the second Negro to hold the position of chairman of the Republican State Central Committee, after the death of B. F. Randolph in 1868. He was also a vice-president of the convention which nominated Grant and Wilson in 1872. His own nomination for collector of internal revenue in 1875 was supported by the entire South Carolina congressional delegation.

Ransier was generally considered a conservative in both his manner and on most of the political issues he faced as a delegate to the Constitutional Convention of 1868 and as a state representative. One issue on which he took a strong stance, however, was civil rights legislation. In the 1868 Constitutional Convention he had advocated striking the word "white" from every state law. As a congressman he proposed a similar amendment to the Civil Rights Bill of 1875. Indeed in his maiden speech before Congress he opposed attempts to sacrifice the provisions integrating public schools and warned Republicans that the Negro vote was crucial to their national margin of victory. In this speech Ransier expressed what was probably the major element of his political philosophy, the faith that equal rights would enable the Negro to become a better citizen and reduce the nation's prejudices against him. He cited the good records of Negro students at such mixed schools as Yale, Harvard, Oberlin, Cornell, and Berea, to validate his point.

The major sources on Ransier's life are *The Biographical Directory of the American Congress* (1971), Samuel Denny Smith's *The Negro in Congress, 1870–1901* (1940), and Maurine Christopher's *America's Black Congressmen* (1971). — THOMAS HOLT

RANSOM, REVERDY CASSIUS (1861–1959), forty-eighth bishop of the African Methodist Episcopal church, civil rights leader, and editor. The son of George and Harriet (Johnson) Ransom, he was born in an Ohio town mainly populated by the Society of Friends (Quakers), Flushing, to which his parents had migrated from Virginia before the Civil War. His maternal grandmother Lucinda, who had been a slave in Virginia, was already living in Flushing and it was in her log cabin that Reverdy was born. Four years after his birth he went to live with his paternal grandfather, Louis Ransom, in Washington, Guerney County, Ohio. In the school for colored children held in the A.M.E. church building Reverdy learned to read and write. When his family moved to Cambridge, Ohio, in 1869, he spent several years in the Negro public school. Since he could not be enrolled in the white public schools, his mother had him tutored by some members of the families where she was employed as a domestic servant. Reverdy visited these homes almost daily and acquired some of the culture, manners, and conversation of wealthy whites. Since many of them sent their sons to college, Reverdy's mother was determined that her son should also go to college. Encouraged further by Samuel J. McMahon, in whose bank Reverdy worked, he continued his self-education, attended a summer normal school, and taught a short-term county school for two years. His savings and the funds from a mortgage his mother placed on her home enabled him to enter Wilberforce University in the fall of 1881.

During one year at Wilberforce he had the good fortune to fall under the influence of some of the notable Negro scholars of that era. Benjamin F. Lee was president; William S. Scarborough, a graduate of Oberlin College (1875) and author of a widely used Greek textbook (1881), was on the faculty. Hallie Quinn Brown, a teacher, elocutionist, and civil rights leader who had graduated from Wilberforce in 1873, was living in the town. The religious influence which was to shape Reverdy's life was enriched by Bishops Daniel A. Payne, James A. Shorter, and Benjamin W. Arnett.

Seeking to broaden his education, young Ransom transferred in 1882 to Oberlin College. Although Oberlin was the first college in the state to accept Negro students for degree courses and was famous for its "liberalism," Ransom found that despite the apparent friendship of white students, colored students were not included in the college's social and recreational activities. He lost his scholarship when he addressed a meeting and voiced strong objection to a new regulation segregating colored girls in the Ladies Dining Hall. He enjoyed, however, the lasting friendship of Mary Church, who as Mrs. Terrell was to become one of the notable women of the twentieth century. Another friend was John Alexander, later a cadet at West Point whose expulsion became a minor *cause célèbre.*

Returning to Wilberforce he was able to enroll by using funds his mother supplied by selling her cow. Supporting himself with various chores in Xenia and Wilberforce, he overcame hunger and ill-fitting clothes and received his B.D. degree from Wilberforce in 1886. Meanwhile he had been licensed to preach in October 1883, and in 1885 joined the Annual Conference of the A.M.E. church in Zanesville, Ohio. He was ordained a deacon in 1886 at Meadville, Pa., and an elder in 1888 by Bishop Payne at Cannonburgh, Pa. Elected the forty-eighth Bishop of the A.M.E. church at Louisville, Ky., in 1924, he served as an active bishop until 1952.

From 1886 to 1952 he had a distinguished career in the A.M.E. church, as an orator, editor, and author; he was also a participant in political and civic affairs. He served his first pastorate (1886) in Altoona, Pa., where the church had thirteen members and paid him a salary of about five dollars a Sunday. Two years later he was appointed pastor to Manchester Mission, Allegheny, Pa., later called North Pittsburgh. White neighbors stoned the house he had purchased, breaking twenty-seven windows. He nevertheless served there from 1888 to 1890, and Allen Chapel, a continuation of Manchester Mission, was later a testimony to the steadfastness inculcated by Ransom. In September 1890 Bishop Payne transferred him to North Street Church, Springfield, Ohio. Many members of this congregation were intelligent and prosperous; each Sunday the streets in front of the church were lined with carriages and buggies.

Transferred by Bishop Payne to the pastorate of St. John's Church in Cleveland, he paid off the mortgage on the church with the aid of a substantial contribution by the powerful businessman and Republican leader, Mark Hanna. In 1894 the first Board of Deaconesses in the A.M.E. church was organized by Ransom.

In Chicago, where he took charge of Bethel Church in 1896, he expanded his social and political activities. To meet the needs of large numbers of Negro migrants from the South, he established a Men's Sunday Club and worked with Jane Addams in her pioneer social settlement, Hull House. With her support and that of other settlement workers, he bought in 1900 the A.M.E.–connected Institutional Church and Social Settlement on Dearborn Street near 39th Street. The large building had a gymnasium for young men, clubs for boys, reading rooms, a kindergarten, and a men's forum. Although the building was bombed after he spoke against policy gambling (later called "playing the numbers"), he remained there for four years. He also helped organize the 8th Illinois Regiment under colored officers, which fought during the Spanish-American War.

He continued his civic activities after his transfer in June 1905 to the Charles Street A.M.E. Church, Boston, one of the oldest examples of colonial architecture in the city. On Nov. 11, 1905, in historic Faneuil Hall, in an address in honor of William Lloyd Garrison, he declared: "The Negro is here 10,000,000 strong, and, for weal or woe, he is here to stay—he is here to remain forever." He joined the Niagara Movement organized by W. E. B. Du Bois and others in opposition to the conservative policies of Booker T. Washington. At the second meeting, in Harpers Ferry in August 1906, Ransom voiced his militant view: "There are two views of the Negro question. One is that the Negro should stoop to conquer; that he should accept in silence the denial of his political rights; that he should not brave the displeasure of white men by protesting when he is segregated in humiliating ways. . . . There are others who believe that the Negro owes this nation no apology for his presence. . . ; that being black he is still no less a man; that he should refuse to be assigned to an inferior place by his fellow-countrymen."

He continued his militancy after his appointment in 1907 to Bethel A.M.E. Church in New York City. Although Booker T. Washington sought to preserve his conservative influence by addressing the A.M.E. Quadrennial Conference at Kansas City, Kans., in 1912, the convention confirmed the success of the radicals by electing the Niagara Movement's Reverdy Ransom, editor of the *A.M.E. Church Review.* Under his editorship (1912–1924) this journal continued to include significant articles on a wide range of subjects.

In 1913 he established in the part of Manhattan known as "New York's Black Tenderloin" a mission, the Church of Simon of Cyrene. Here he ministered to the poor. In 1918 he was nominated by the United Civic League of New York as a candidate for the 21st Congressional District of New York. He was defeated because of a discrepancy in filing the petition for the candidacy; his name was not allowed to appear on the ballot and he had to run as a write-in candidate in the election.

Among the many young men aided and influenced by Ransom were Paul Laurence Dunbar, Monroe N. Work, and Richard R. Wright, Jr. When Dunbar's first book of poems, *Oak and Ivy,* was published in 1893, he had no money to pay the printer. Dunbar brought 100 copies to Ransom's church in Springfield at the pastor's request. After an introduction of Dunbar to the congregation, all copies were sold. Monroe Work went on to become the noted bibliophile and editor of the *Bibliography of the Negro in Africa and America* (1928), while Wright rose to the bishopric in the A.M.E. church.

Six feet two inches tall and of dignified mien, Ransom ably represented the A.M.E. church at the Ecumenical Conference of Methodism (London, 1901; Toronto, 1911; and London, 1921). He was the first Negro appointed (1936) a commissioner of the Ohio Board of Pardon and Parole, a position he held until 1940. Pres. Franklin D. Roosevelt appointed him in 1941 a member of the Volunteer Participation Committee in the Office of Civil Defense. He also served as president of the Board of Trustees at Wilberforce (1932–1948) and as historigrapher of the A.M.E. church for several years.

Reverdy Ransom was married three times. His first wife, Leanna Watkins of Cambridge, Ohio, bore him one son, Harold George. His second wife, Emma Sarah Conner of Salem, Ohio, whom he married in 1886, was a teacher, a leader in the missionary field, and her husband's assistant in his social and civic work. Reverdy C. Jr. was born of this union. After fifty-five years of marriage she died in 1941 and was buried near Wilberforce. In 1943 Ransom married Georgia Myrtle Teal Hayes, a graduate of Cheyney Training School and Cornell University. She was dean of women at Wilberforce University (1934–1943) and supervisor of the Third District Missionary Society of the A.M.E. church (1943–1956).

Ransom died at his home, Tawawa Chimney Corner in Wilberforce, in 1959 at the age of ninety-eight, and was buried in Wilberforce.

His long career is revealed in some of his own publications: *School Days at Wilberforce* (1890), *Duty and Destiny* (1893), *The Future of Christianity and the Negro* (1925), *The Pilgrimage of Harriet Ransom's Son* (1949?). He edited the *Year Book of Negro Churches . . .* (1935/36). His oration in Faneuil Hall is in Carter G. Woodson (ed.), *Negro Orators and Their Orations* (1925, pp. 531–41). He also wrote a poem, "The New Negro," included in Alice Dunbar-Nelson's *Paul Laurence Dunbar,* reprinted from the *A.M.E. Church Review. The Bishops of the African Methodist Episcopal Church* by Richard R. Wright (1963, pp. 287–93) is the standard reference. Frederick A. McGinnis covers part of Ransom's career in *A History and Interpretation of Wilberforce University* (1941). — MARY M. FISHER

RAPIER, JAMES THOMAS (1837–1883), cotton planter, government official, labor leader, and congressman. He was born in Florence, Lauderdale County, Ala., on Nov. 13, 1837, the fourth son of a free Negro barber John H. Rapier, Sr., and his free Negro wife Susan. At the age of five he was sent to live with his slave grandmother Sally and slave uncle James P. Thomas (for whom he was named), and attend school in Nashville, Tenn. He spent a number of years in Tennessee, and in 1856 he traveled to Canada to further his education. Living with another uncle, Henry K. Thomas (also a brother of John Rapier), he studied Latin, Greek, mathematics, and the Bible at the King School in Buxton, Canada West, and later attended a normal school in Toronto. Besides securing an education he also experienced a religious conversion. "My coming to Canada is worth all the world to me," he wrote in 1862. "I have a tolerable good education and I am at peace with my Savior." He is also said to have attended the University of Glasgow and Franklin College in Nashville.

Returning to the South about 1863 he took up residence in Maury County, Tenn., and in 1865 began a campaign to secure the franchise for Negroes. At the Tennessee Negro Suffrage Convention in 1865 he delivered the keynote address: "We know the burdens of citizenship and are ready to perform them," he asserted. But the ballot for Negroes was not forthcoming in 1865–1866, and Rapier went home to Florence,

rented part of Seven Mile Island (a fertile stretch of land in the Tennessee River), hired twenty-one Negro tenant farmers, and put in a crop of cotton. Within a year the *Alabama State Sentinel,* a leading Republican newspaper, ranked him "among the most extensive planters in the Tennessee Valley."

When the long-awaited opportunity to accept "the burdens of citizenship" came with the passage of the Congressional Reconstruction Acts (March 1867), Rapier again entered the political arena. Presiding over the first meeting of freedmen in northwestern Alabama, he advised Negroes, who now had the vote, "to proceed with calmness, moderation and intelligence"; elected a delegate to the first Republican state convention in Montgomery, he served as chairman of the platform committee. Along with two others, Rapier drafted the party's platform, which among other things asked for "free speech, free press, free schools and equal rights to all men and the full enjoyment of the rights of citizenship without distinctions on account of color." Rapier's moderate stance in the early days of Reconstruction prompted an opposition Democrat to say: "He is, in every particular, except that of race, a superior man."

But race was important. Shortly before the presidential election of 1868 Rapier was driven from politics as well as his home by the Ku Klux Klan. Fleeing from Florence to Montgomery, he remained in seclusion for nearly a year. In 1870 he emerged as the Republican nominee for secretary of state, but the continued violence of the Klan, the virulent attacks of conservatives, and strong dissatisfaction among white Republicans caused his defeat.

The next year he was appointed assessor of internal revenue (Montgomery District), the first Negro to attain such a high patronage position in the state. Attacked by Democrats as a token Negro, Rapier retorted: "Make no allowances whatever for my color. If I prove an inefficient officer my color should be no shield." Despite continued conservative attacks, he served capably for two years.

Meanwhile he also became involved in the Negro labor movement. Attending three national Negro labor conventions (1869–1872), he spoke out against the deplorable economic conditions of Negro tenant farmers in the South. In 1870 he was elected a vice-president of the National Negro Labor Union, and representing the union discussed a federal land bureau for Negroes with President Grant. He also organized the first affiliate of the NNLU in the South (the Alabama Negro Labor Union), and became its president and executive chairman. In 1872, however, realizing that Republican indifference, the opposition of white landowners, and a lack of federal initiative had doomed the Negro labor movement, he again turned his attention to politics.

Receiving the congressional nomination of the Republican party (Second District), he launched a vigorous campaign for office. He made speeches in thirty-six southeastern Alabama towns and stations in thirty-six days, founded a campaign newspaper, the *Republican State Sentinel,* and wrote a number of editorials against the highly respected, one-armed ex-Confederate candidate William Oates, as well as Horace Greeley and the

Liberal Republicans. By concentrating on the issues (and with a peaceful election made possible by the KKK prosecutions under the federal Enforcement Acts), Rapier won a resounding victory (19,000 to 16,000). Before leaving for Washington he commented rather immodestly: "No man in the state wields more influence than I."

Shortly after the election he was appointed state commissioner to the Fifth International Exhibition in Vienna, Austria, and in 1873 he spent five months abroad. "The moment I put my foot upon the deck of a ship that unfurled a foreign flag," he later said, "distinctions on account of my color ceased." In Congress he pushed through a bill to make Montgomery a port of delivery, which proved to be a great economic boon to the "Black Belt," and also supported legislation to improve the common school systems of the South, to curb violence in Alabama, and secure civil rights for Negroes. He played also an important role in the final passage of the 1875 civil rights law.

Despite these efforts most white Alabamans were outraged at the thought of Negroes representing the capital of the former Confederacy in Congress. No sooner had Rapier won his seat than conservatives launched a violent campaign to drive him from office. In 1874 through race riots, intimidation of Negro voters, and fraudulent discounting of Republican ballots, they "redeemed" the state for the Democrats. Although Rapier contested the election, he later withdrew from the contest and left Washington. He ran, again unsuccessfully, in 1876 in the newly gerrymandered 4th Congressional District.

After Reconstruction he remained active in politics, attending the 1880 Republican national convention in Chicago (where he supported Treasury Secretary John Sherman for the presidency), and working hard for the 1882 state Republican ticket. He also served as collector of internal revenue for the Second Alabama District (1877 to 1883), and again manifested outstanding abilities as an administrator. "The excellent condition of your office," the revenue commissioner reported in 1882, "indicates a gratifying degree of energy and zeal on the part of yourself and your assistants. Your grade is first class." At the same time he became a leader in the Negro emigration movement. Acting as chairman of the emigration committee at the Southern States Negro Convention in Nashville (May 1879), Rapier urged Negroes to leave the South. "It is my opinion," he said, "that a black can not develop mentally or morally [in the South], for at every branch and cross road he will find something to remind him that he is a Negro." He later purchased land in Kansas (along the Kansas and Pacific Railroad) for the settlement of Negroes, and toured the state (at the behest of Minnesota Sen. William Windom), reporting to the U.S. Senate Committee on Emigration. But before his dreams of emigration could be realized, and after a long illness, Rapier died of pulmonary tuberculosis (May 31, 1883) at the age of forty-five. He was buried in Cavalry Cemetery in St. Louis where no memorial of any kind marked his grave. A notice in the Democratic newspaper (the *Montgomery Daily Advertiser*) that had most consistently opposed Rapier acclaimed him as "a conspicuous instance of official integrity, and fidelity in the discharge of his public duties." It is paradoxical that James Rapier, who began Reconstruction calling for "calmness, moderation and intelligence," ended his career demanding that Negroes leave the South.

Brief published accounts include *The Biographical Directory of Congress* (1971), Samuel Denny Smith's *The Negro in Congress, 1870–1901* (1940), Maurine Christopher's *America's Black Congressmen* (1971), Eugene Feldman's "James T. Rapier, 1839–1884" (*NHB*, Dec. 1956, pp. 62–66), and his "James T. Rapier, Negro Congressman from Alabama" (*Phylon* 19 [Winter 1958]: 417–23). See also Loren Schweninger's unpublished doctoral dissertation, "James Rapier and Reconstruction" (University of Chicago, 1972). — LOREN SCHWENINGER

RAY, CHARLES B[ENNETT] (1807–1886), journalist, clergyman, and abolitionist. The eldest of seven children of Joseph Aspinwall and Annie (Harrington) Ray, he was born in Falmouth, Mass., on Christmas Day 1807. He received his early education at the schools in his hometown. In the early 1830s abolitionists enabled him to study theology at Wesleyan Seminary in Wilbraham, Mass. He later studied for a brief period at Wesleyan University in Middletown, Conn., leaving there because of racial prejudice. Between the years that he attended schools in his hometown and enrolled in the theological seminary, Ray held several odd jobs such as working on his grandfather's farm in Westerly, R.I., for approximately five years. Later he learned the trade of bootmaking, working at this for a while at Vineyard Haven, Mass. When he first went to New York City in 1832 he opened a boot and shoe store.

Ray married Henrietta Green Regulus in 1834. She died in childbirth on Oct. 27, 1836, as did the infant child. In 1840 Charlotte Augusta Burroughs of Savannah, Ga., became his second wife. Seven children were born of this union, two boys and five girls. Three of the girls survived their father: Florence T. Ray and Charlotte E. Ray were both lawyers, the latter having graduated from the Law Department of Howard University in 1872 and became, reportedly, the first woman lawyer admitted to practice in the District of Columbia; Henrietta Cordelia Ray received her education in the School of Pedagogy, a department of New York University, and became a poet.

Ray, ordained a Methodist minister in 1837, later became a Congregational minister, associating himself with the Crosby Congregational Church in New York City. Beginning in 1845 he served as the pastor of the Bethesda Congregational Church in that city for more than twenty years. Since his congregation was small, Ray devoted much time to the abolition movement and to journalism, activities for which he was best known. In 1833 he joined the American Anti-Slavery Society and was a "conductor" on the Underground Railroad. In 1843 he joined the New York Vigilance Committee which consisted of thirteen men of both races to assist runaway slaves. In 1848 Ray became the corresponding secretary for this organization, remaining an active member for fifteen years. He was a paid member of the American Missionary Association, a fervent missionary worker, a strong believer in the temperance movement, and a member of the New York Society for the Promotion of Education Among Colored Children. He was also a member of other organizations such as the African Society for Mutual Relief, the Congregational Clerical Union (an organization established to discuss issues concerning the church and the clergy), and the Manhattan Congregational Association, an organization composed of Congregational clergy. From 1846 to his death he was a city missionary in New York. At the annual meeting of the American and Foreign Anti-Slavery Society in New York in May 1853, he and George T. Downing regretted Harriet Beecher Stowe's support of colonization, and Ray hoped that something could be done to counteract her influence.

Meanwhile in 1837 he was appointed general agent of *The Colored American,* the fourth weekly published by Negroes. He became part owner with Phillip A. Bell in 1838 and later sole owner, and sole editor from 1839 to its demise, after a short suspension, in April 1842. It was published at 9 Spruce St., New York City, and cost two dollars a year, payable in advance. Its objects were "the *moral, social* and *political* elevation of the free colored people; and the peaceful emancipation of the slaves." It would "advocate all lawful and peaceful measures to accomplish its objects." Ray traveled and lectured in many cities and contributed articles condemning the prejudice from which Negroes suffered. *The Colored American* supported the Liberty party, founded in 1839 because of its belief that neither the Whigs nor the Democrats could strongly oppose slavery, inasmuch as many of its members were slaveholders. Ray served as one of the convention secretaries at the party's Buffalo convention in August 1843.

Ray died in New York City on Aug. 15, 1886, and was buried in Cypress Hills Cemetery, Brooklyn.

The principal source is in the memoir by two of his daughters, Florence T. Ray's and Henrietta Cordelia Ray's *Sketch of the Life of Rev. Charles B. Ray* (1887). The brief sketch by Harrison G. Villard in the *DAB* ([1963], 8, Part 1:403–4) is based largely on the memoir and Penn. Benjamin Quarles's *Black Abolitionists* (1969) is indispensable for Ray's abolitionist activities. See also Gerald Soren's *The New York Abolitionists* (1971). — DOLORES LEFFALL

RAYNER, JOHN B. (1850–1918), educator and Populist leader. He was born a slave in Raleigh, N.C., the son of Kenneth Rayner, a prominent white plantation owner, and Mary Ricks, a slave. With the aid of his father, Rayner pursued his education after the Civil War at both Shaw University and St. Augustine's Collegiate Institute in Raleigh, although he did not graduate from either. Later Rayner taught in rural schools near Raleigh. He was first elected to public office in Tarboro, N.C., where he served as deputy sheriff. In 1874 Rayner married Susan Clark Staten, their union producing two children, Mary and Ivan Edward. Following his religious conversion Rayner worked for a time in North Carolina as a Baptist minister.

Rayner moved his family to Robertson County, Tex., in 1881. There he taught school and preached; an advocate of Booker T. Washington's insistence on self-help, Rayner became associated with R. L. Smith's Farmers Improvement Society. After the death of his first wife, he married Clarissa S. Clark who bore him three children, Ahmed Arabi, Loris Melikoff, and Susie. By 1892 Rayner exchanged his original Republican sympathies for Populism and became a highly regarded stump speaker and organizer, credited with bringing thousands of Negroes into the Populist party. He was reported as being the best Populist orator or organizer among Texas Negroes. As a member of the party's state executive committee in 1895 and 1896, Rayner wrote two articles for its organ, the *Southern Mercury:* "Political Imbroglio in Texas" (Aug. 1, 5 and Sept. 19, 1895) and "Modern Political Methods" (April 9 and June 26, 1896). In the latter he urged: "If you want the negro to vote a straight people's party ticket you must put men on the precinct or county tickets whom he likes. Kind words and just treatment go further with the negro than money or promises."

With the gradual absorption of many Texas Populists into the Democratic party after the election of 1896, Rayner also became more active in self-help and vocational education programs for Negroes in Texas. In 1902 or 1903 he helped to found the Texas Law and Order League, an organization designed to promote employment and greater conformity to law among Negroes. By the fall of 1904 he had accepted a position as financial agent for developing Conroe-Porter Industrial College of Conroe, Tex. Rayner remained in this position for two years. During this time he also began to align himself once again with the Republican party. In August 1911 he was appointed by R. L. Smith to serve as financial agent and fundraiser for the Farmers Improvement Society School at Ladonia, Tex. Retiring in 1913, Rayner spent the last five years of his life in Calvert, Tex., writing solicited letters to the editors of several newspapers in Texas and working to a limited extent for local Republican candidates. He died in Calvert on July 14, 1918.

The John B. Rayner Papers are housed in the Schomburg Center for Research in Black Culture, New York City. The most complete sources of information about Rayner are Jack Abramowitz's "John B. Rayner—A Grass Roots Leader" (*JNH,* April 1951) and Roscoe C. Martin's *The People's Party in Texas* (1933).
— WILLIAM L. ANDREWS

REASON, CHARLES LEWIS (1818–1893), educator, reformer, and writer. Born in New York City on July 21, 1818, the eldest son of Michiel and Elizabeth Reason who had emigrated from the West Indies, he attended the New York African Free School where at the age of fourteen he became an instructor; then he studied to prepare for the General Theological Seminary of the Protestant Episcopal church in New York City, but was denied admission because of his race. In 1849–1850 he served as professor of belle-lettres, Greek, Latin, and French, and adjunct professor of mathematics at New York Central College, McGrawville, N.Y. Subsequently, as principal of the Institute for Colored Youth in Philadelphia from 1852 to 1855, Reason increased enrollment from 6 to 118 students and developed a good library and a popular public lecture series. For the next thirty-seven years he was a teacher and principal at several schools in New York City where, with Charles B. Ray, he founded the Society for the Promotion of Education Among Colored Children. Although partially paralyzed in his later years, Reason continued teaching until the age of seventy-two, when he retired with the longest service in the city school system.

From the 1830s Reason worked alongside the most distinguished activists of his day for the abolition of slavery, for civil rights, suffrage, and industrial education; and he opposed African colonization plans. He aided fugitive slaves with the General Vigilance Committee of Philadelphia and later served many political societies in New York state as secretary, lecturer, and writer of convention calls and position papers. His poem, "The Spirit Voice" (1841), an eighty-six-line ode, is a stirring summons to disfranchised Negroes of New York militantly to seek full manhood and freedom; and the forty-eight-stanza poem "Freedom" (1846) commemorates Thomas Clarkson and eloquently bids liberty triumph over church and state-supported slavery. Reason's essays "Caste Schools" (1850) and "The Colored People's Industrial College" (1854) appeal for equality of educational opportunities.

Nothing is known about Reason's private life except that he married three times, the last to Clorice Esteve whom he survived. A handsome man of light complexion, Reason won the respect and admiration of contemporaries for his superior intelligence and learning, generosity, modesty, teaching ability, and selfless dedication to race advancement. He died in New York City of kidney and heart failure on Aug. 16, 1893, and was buried in Greenwood Cemetery, Brooklyn.

J. R. Sherman's *Invisible Poets* (1974) documents Reason's life and known writings and includes a bibliography. A personal appraisal is in Daniel A. Payne's *Recollections of Seventy Years* (1888) and William J. Simmons's *Men of Mark . . .* (1887), pp. 1105–12) contains a brief biography and two poems.

— JOAN R. SHERMAN

REASON, PATRICK HENRY (1816–1898), engraver, lithographer, abolitionist, and fraternal order leader. He was born in New York City, one of four children of Michel and Elizabeth Melville Reason. Patrick was baptized on April 17, 1816, as Patrice Rison. His father Michel Rison was from St. Anne Island, Guadeloupe, and his mother Elizabeth Melville from Saint-Domingue. Patrick's young sister Policarpe died in 1818 at age four. His brother Elver (or Elwer) did not attain the prominence that Patrick or his brother Charles Lewis did. All three brothers received their early education at the New York African Free School, established on Mulberry Street by the New York Manumission Society. Patrick's ability as an engraver was recognized at age thirteen when he made an engraving of the New York African Free School which was printed as a frontispiece for Charles C. Andrews's *History of the New York African Free Schools . . .* (1830).

In 1833 Patrick Reason, with the consent of his mother (his father having died), was apprenticed for four years to Stephen Henry Gimber "to learn the art, trade and mystery of an engraver." Gimber was to pay

Patrick's mother three dollars a week. Two years later Patrick designed a stipple engraving of a kneeling slave in an attitude of prayer with chains hanging from her wrists and the inscription "Am I not a woman and a sister?" It was widely used by abolitionists as frontispieces to their publications, on antislavery broadsides, stationery, and commemorative coins. This design was not original with Reason. A figure of a chained kneeling slave, in similar position and attitude with the motto "Am I not a man and a brother?" was designed in October 1787 for a seal used by the English Committee for the Abolition of the Slave Trade. It was influential in kindling antislavery sentiment in Great Britain, and with its direct and pathetic appeal was no less an inspiration to American abolitionists.

Reason's interest in portraiture began in 1835 when he made a stipple engraving of the likeness of Granville Sharp which was printed as a frontispiece for *A Memoir of Granville Sharp* (1836) by Charles Stuart. Reason based his engraving on an engraved portrait of Sharp by T. B. Lord of London.

For the next fifteen years Reason's portraits and designs appeared as frontispieces in slave narratives, in books such as Lydia M. Child's *The Fountain for Everyday in the Year* (1836), *Thoughts on Slavery Written in 1774* by John Wesley (reprinted in 1839 by the American Anti-Slavery Society), and in periodicals. An excellent engraving of a slave, James Williams, was published in 1838. On April 12 of that year Reason's business card in the *Colored American* (p. 47) advertised that he was a "portrait and landscape Engraver, Draughtsman and lithographer." The *U.S. Magazine and Democratic Review* printed three excellent engravings by Reason to accompany biographies in the periodical. One, his well-executed portrait of Benjamin Tappan, an antislavery Ohio senator, appeared in the issue of June 1840 (p. 540). The editor noted that it was "a faithful representation of the strongly marked and intellectual countenance of one who has been styled by a contemporary—'the venerable patriarch of the Ohio democracy.' It presents him to the eye as he now daily appears amid the exciting scenes of the American Senate, calm, collected and attentive with the apparent self-possession of one not unconscious of superior strength." Reason had used a painting of Tappan by Washington Blanchard as a model. A copy was published in the *Dictionary of American Portraits* (1967, p. 609). Reason engraved another portrait of a younger Benjamin Tappan, made from a daguerreotype. Lewis Tappan paid Reason $70 to make a steel engraving of his brother Benjamin and on July 11, 1840, Tappan wrote to Reason that the Tappan family was pleased with the portrait and that the "anti-slavery cause would be advanced if it were known that a Negro was capable of such craftsmanship." He added that "perhaps it will be best to wait until you have engraved two or three more before the secret is out."

Reason's line and stipple engraving of the prominent lawyer and diplomat George Mifflin Dallas appeared in the February 1842 issue of the *U.S. Magazine and Democratic Review*. Since no statement indicates it was engraved after a portrait, Reason may have both drawn and engraved it. Another portrait by Reason published in the June 1844 issue contained an engraving of Robert Adrian, the mathematician, after a painting by Ingraham. It carried the statement that it was engraved by Patrick Henry Reason and signed by Adrian.

Other engravings by Reason include a portrait of the Rev. Peter Williams, Jr., rector of St. Phillips Church in New York City, deposited for copyright on Aug. 28, 1841.

While he lived in New York Reason completed a line and stipple engraving of the Rev. Baptist Noel, member of the London Emancipation Society, and of the Rev. Thomas Baldwin made for the *Baptist Memorial*, the portrait of Henry Bibb used as a frontispiece for the *Narrative of the Life and Adventure of Henry Bibb* (1850), and the engraved copper nameplate for the coffin of Daniel Webster, who died on Oct. 24, 1852.

Reason's treatment of groups is seen in his copper-plate engraving of a certificate of membership in the Masonic order, an original conception of the Faith, Hope, and Charity composition showing Charity surrounded by her children, and a certificate of membership in the Grand United Order of Odd Fellows. The New York Public Library also has a copper-plate engraving of a mountainous landscape after a drawing by W. H. Bartlett, supposed to represent Balboa ascending the mountains. James A. Porter stated that this "meticulous work shows Patrick Henry Reason attained great skill in representation of minute gradations of value" (unpublished notes).

During the New York draft riots in 1863 the merchants organized a committee for the relief of colored victims. The Rev. Henry Highland Garnet, who had been asked to aid in the work, wrote an "address to the Executive Committee of merchants for the Relief of Colored People," which was presented to them on Aug. 22, 1863. This acknowledgment was "elaborately engrossed on parchment and tastefully framed by Patrick Reason, one of their own people."

At one time Reason worked for the New York publishers, Harpers, as an engraver preparing map plates, and for a New York firm as engraver of plates for printing banknotes. According to Martin R. Delany, he also frequently did government engraving.

Since white engravers refused to work with him, firms often refused to hire him and his name appeared in the New York City directories from 1846 to 1866 as a "col'd" engraver.

Reason married Esther Cunningham of Leeds, England, on June 22, 1862. In 1869 he left New York with his wife and young son Charles and went to Cleveland, where he had been invited to work as an engraver with several firms. For more than fifteen years Reason worked with the jewelry firm of Sylvester Hogan, a wholesale and retail dealer in fine jewelry and silver plate. The Cleveland Directories listed Reason as an engraver until 1899.

Reason was a member of the New York Philomathean Society, organized in 1830 for literary improvement and social pleasure. He, James Fields, and other members, feeling the need of an organization for mutual protection in case of sickness and death, decided to form their society into an Odd Fellows Lodge. They petitioned the International Order of Odd Fellows for a

dispensation on behalf of the Philomathean Society, but their application was refused. The were, however, granted a dispensation from Victoria Lodge No. 448 in Liverpool of which Peter Ogden, a New York Negro, was a past grand master, and it became on March 1, 1843, Philomathean Lodge No. 646, New York. On Feb. 29, 1844, Philomathean Lodge No. 646 was formally authorized to institute Hamilton Lodge No. 710, New York, with which Reason was affiliated. He designed and engraved the first certificate of membership for the Odd Fellows. Reason was the composer of the Ruth degree, the first "degree to be conferred under certain conditions on Females" by Hamilton Lodge No. 710, New York, and he was the first person invested with this honor. A subcommittee conferred the degree on him as the founder on Aug. 23, 1858. Reason did much to develop the secret ritual of the order, devising a better system of signs, grips, and words. As past grand master he was the orator at some of the order's annual meetings. At the meeting of Sept. 4, 1856, in Broadway Tabernacle, New York, his speech was said to have been the finest given up to that time (*Odd Fellows Journal*, Oct. 21, 1920; Nov. 18, 1921).

The souvenir program and Jubilee Celebration Booklet contain facsimile reproductions from the minutes of Hamilton Lodge No. 710; dated Feb. 25, 1847, and March 9, 1848, they are all in the painstaking and beautiful handwriting of Patrick Reason whose name appears subscribed as permanent secretary.

Reason was also active in the New York Masons. He was grand master from 1862 to 1868, and grand secretary from 1859 to 1860. In 1862 Baron de Bulow of France on his visit to the United States conferred the Thirty-third Degree of Masonry on Reason. On Bulow's second visit to America in 1864 he organized a Supreme Council of Colored Americans whom he had earlier created Thirty-third Degree Masons under a Commission as sovereign grand inspector general of the Supreme Council of France. Upon learning that colored brothers were refused recognition by the white brothers, he obtained a special patent and organized a Supreme Council for the States, Territories, and Dependencies with Reason, then most worshipful grand master of Masons for the State of New York, as the presiding officer. Reason was grand master in New York from 1861 to 1867.

As a youth Reason was interested in the educational, social, and economic situation of the Negro. He was an intelligent and able lecturer on behalf of his people. At the age of twenty-two Reason, as president of the Phoenixian Literary Society of New York City, addressed its anniversary meeting on "The Philosophy of the Fine Arts" (July 4, 1837). His speech was reported in newspapers "as well-delivered and showing a talent and research and a thorough knowledge of the subjects full of sound reasoning and historical references." In the fall of the same year he was an active member of a committee appointed to arrange a public meeting to honor James McCune Smith on his return from a successful educational trip in Europe. During this time Reason also gave evening instruction to individuals and groups in "scientific methods of drawing." In 1838 he was awarded the first premium (prize) for india ink drawing at the Mechanics Institute Fair. At the annual meeting of the American Anti-Slavery Society in 1839, Reason signed a protest "against the principle, assumed by a majority of persons representing said Society at its present meeting that women have the right of originating, debating and voting on questions that come before said Society and are eligible to its various officers" (*Weekly Advocate,* Feb. and Sept. 1837; *Emancipator,* May 23 and Sept. 26, 1839, p. 87).

Interested in education, Reason served as secretary of the New York Society for the Promotion of Education Among Colored Children, organized and incorporated on Dec. 7, 1847, because separate colored schools were neglected and in some instances closed. Subject to the supervision of the city's board of education, the society had authority to open and manage nonsectarian schools for colored children; two were opened in 1848. Reason participated in the Albany Convention of Colored Citizens in 1840, serving on six important committees. On perhaps one of the most important, he served with Charles B. Ray, James McCune Smith, Theodore S. Wright, and Phillip Bell to draft a reply to derogatory remarks concerning Negroes made by Secretary of State John C. Calhoun to the British minister to the U.S. in April 1844 relative to the revolt of slaves on board the *Creole.* At a mass meeting in New York Negroes empowered a committee to draft a reply, which was written by Smith and forwarded as a memorial to the U.S. Senate.

Patrick Henry Reason died in Cleveland on Aug. 12, 1898, after a long illness of carcinoma of the rectum. Funeral services were held at his home, 162 Dunbam St., with burial at Lakeview Cemetery, Cleveland. His wife Esther and a son Charles L. Reason survived him (*Cleveland Gazette,* Aug. 20, 1898, p. 2).

The most useful sources about Patrick Reason were "Indenture, Patrick Reason" (1833); Charles C. Andrews's *History of the New York African Free Schools in the City of New York* (1830); Charles Brooks's *The Official History and Manual of the Grand United Order of Odd Fellows in America* (1871); the Cleveland City Directories (1869–1898); New York City Directories (1846–1866); Henry Highland Garnet's *A Memorial Discourse Delivered in the Hall of the House of Representatives* (1865, p. 59); William H. Grimshaw's *Official History of Masonry Among the Colored People of America* (1908, pp. 130, 348); James A. Porter's *Modern Negro Art* (1945, pp. 35–38, 156, 175); *The Colored American* (April 12, 1838, p. 47; Sept. 22, 1838, p. 123); *Emancipator* (May 23, 1839, p. 14; Sept. 26, 1839, p. 87). The indenture is in the Moorland-Spingarn Research Center, Howard University, and the record from Register of Baptism and Record of Marriages, Church of St. Peter, N.Y., is in the Schomburg Center for Research in Black Culture, New York City. — DOROTHY B. PORTER

REID, IRA DE AUGUSTINE (1901–1968), sociologist and author. The son of Daniel Augustine and Willie Robertha (James) Reid, and born in Clifton Forge, Va., on July 2, 1901, he spent his early boyhood in Harrisburg and Philadelphia, attending the public schools in Germantown, a suburb of Philadelphia, until his father,

a Baptist minister, accepted a pastorate in Savannah, Ga. Because there was no public high school for Negroes in Georgia, Ira attended Morehouse Academy, and at sixteen entered Morehouse College. His father died the year he entered Morehouse and the family moved to his mother's home in West Virginia. During World War I Reid tried unsuccessfully to attend the Colored Officers Training Camp at Fort Des Moines, Iowa. Exempted from the draft in West Virginia, he was conscripted for service in Georgia. When the war was over Reid stayed out of school for a year and a half but later made up a half year, and received his B.A. degree from Morehouse in 1922.

Reid was director of the high school at Texas College, Tyler, Tex. (1922–1923); he spent the summer of 1923 studying at the University of Chicago and was an instructor (1923–1924) at Douglass High School in Huntington, W.Va. A fellow of the Pittsburgh Urban League (1924–1925), Reid was awarded his M.A. degree from the University of Pittsburgh in 1925. While working as industrial secretary of the New York Urban League (1924–1928), he made a study of Harlem churches and wrote the article "Let Us Pray," published in *Opportunity,* in Sept. 1926.

In 1928 he succeeded Charles S. Johnson as director of research of the NUL and editor of *Opportunity,* and held these positions until 1934. He received his Ph.D. degree in sociology at Columbia University in 1939. His dissertation was published as *The Negro Immigrant, His Background, Characteristics and Social Adjustment, 1899–1937* (1939). Reid's *In a Minor Key: Negro Youth in Story and Fact,* written under the auspices of the American Youth Commission, was published in 1940. *Sharecroppers All,* written in collaboration with Arthur Raper, was published in 1941. He also made surveys of community racial problems in Albany and Troy (1928), Denver (1929), New Jersey (1930–1931), Pittsburgh (1932), Baltimore (1934), and special studies for the National Commission on Law Observance and Enforcement ("A Study of 200 Negro Prisoners in Western Penitentiary, Pennsylvania"), and the White House Conference on Child Care. As a fellow of the Julius Rosenwald Fund, Reid studied at the London School of Economics during the 1939 Lent term.

From 1934 to 1946 Reid was professor of sociology at Atlanta University, but during some years made almost weekly trips to Washington: in 1937 he directed a federal survey of white-collar and skilled workers; from 1937 to 1941 he was consulting social scientist and 1941–1942 consultant on minorities for the Social Security Board; and consultant on Minorities, War Manpower Commission, (1940–1942).

In 1942 Reid helped establish and became director of the People's College, an adult education program of Atlanta University. With the retirement of W. E. B. Du Bois, he became chairman of the Department of Sociology in 1943 and editor of *Phylon* (1943–1946). He was visiting professor of educational sociology, School of Education, New York University (1946–1947). During 1946, as visiting professor, he taught three days a week at Harverford College, Pa., where at the request of the students he was appointed professor and chairman of the Department of Sociology and Anthropology in

1947; he became professor emeritus at Haverford in 1966. He was assistant editor of the *American Sociological Review* (1947–1949); member, Advisory Commission, U.S. Department of Labor (1946–1948); consultant on Higher Education, Trusteeship Division, United Nations (1949); visiting professor, New York School of Social Work, Columbia University (1951–1954); editor, *Racial Desegregation and Integration* (1956); member, Governor's Commission on Higher Education, Pennsylvania (1956); and member, Commission on Higher Education, Philadelphia (1958). During the summer of 1958 Reid was visiting professor at Pennsylvania State University; in 1962, visiting director, Department of Extra-Mural Studies, University College of Ibadan, Nigeria; Danforth Distinguished Visiting Professor of Sociology, International Christian University, Tokyo, Japan (1962–1963); and visiting professor, Harvard (summer of 1963).

Other publications by Reid are *The Negro Population of Denver, Colorado* (1929); *Social Conditions of the Negro in the Hill District of Pittsburgh, Pennsylvania* (1930); *Negro Membership in American Labor Unions* (1930); *The Negro's Relation to Work and Law Observance* (1931); *The Negro in New Jersey* (5 vols., 1932); *The Problem of Child Dependency Among Negroes* (1933); *The Negro Community of Baltimore* (1935); *Adult Education Among Negroes* (1936); *The Urban Negro Worker in the United States: 1925–1936* (1938); "The Church and Education for Negroes" (a chapter in Trevor Bowen's *Divine White Right,* 1934). Reid also contributed articles to *Social Forces,* the *Virginia Quarterly, Opportunity, The Nation,* and *Survey Graphic.*

He was a member of Phi Beta Kappa (hon., Haverford); a fellow of the American Association for the Advancement of Science; a fellow and member of the Executive Committee, American Sociological Association (1948), and vice-president (1954); president of the Eastern Sociological Society (1955). He was associate director of the Division of Race Relations, American Missionary Association (1943); associate executive director of the Southern Regional Council (1944–1945); consultant to the American Council on Education (1965); and a member of the Governor's Commission on Police Brutality (1964). He held positions on the executive or directing boards of the Southern Sociological Society, the Southern Conference for Human Welfare, the Committee on Mass Education in Race Relations, the National Sharecroppers Fund (of which he was a founding member). He served as senior consultant, Study of the Aged, Pennsylvania Department of Welfare; co-director, Study of Social and Medical Services for the Elderly, Philadelphia Geriatric Center; member, Advisory Council on Teacher Grants, Danforth Foundation. In an attempt to make "the social sciences effective in community life," Reid was a member of the Board of Directors of the American Cancer Society; on the Board of Overseers, William Penn Charter School, Philadelphia; a trustee of the National Urban League; president, Urban League of Philadelphia; and a trustee of the National Child Labor Commission. Reid was a member of the Society of Friends.

On Oct. 15, 1925, he married Gladys Russell Scott.

The mother of his child Enid Harriet, she died in June 1956. Reid married Dr. Anne M. Cooke on Aug. 12, 1958. He died of emphysema in Haverford and was survived by his widow and daughter.

There is no full-length biography of Reid. The sketch in *Current Biography* (1946, pp. 503–5) is useful. He was regularly listed in *Who's Who in America* and *American Men of Science.* Brief valuable references are in Nancy J. Weiss's *The National Urban League, 1900–1940* (1974) and Clarence A. Bacote's *The Story of Atlanta University: A Century of Service, 1865–1965* (1969). See also the obituary in *NHB* (Nov. 1968, p. 8). — IRENE DIGGS

REMOND, CHARLES LENOX (1810–1873), abolitionist, orator, and equal rights advocate. The eldest son of John and Nancy (Lenox) Remond, he was born in Salem, Mass., where he received his education. His father, a well-known Salem hairdresser, merchant, and caterer, was a native of Curaçao. Charles Remond became an active member of the Massachusetts Anti-Slavery Society in 1838 when he was appointed its first Negro lecturer. On speaking tours with other agents throughout Massachusetts, Rhode Island, Maine, New York, Pennsylvania, and the Midwest, he lectured every day, sometimes twice a day for three-week periods, often out-of-doors when halls and houses were closed to him. In spite of numerous mobs and rumors of mob activities, he persistently demanded "immediate, unconditional emancipation for every human regardless of tongue or color." As a Garrisonian he urged moral suasion as the only method to end slavery. His fiery eloquence and strong appeals to reason made him much in demand as a speaker. Parker Pillsbury called Remond the most forceful abolitionist of his day, whose "power of speech, argument and eloquence rarely if ever" failed to thrill a House of Congress or legislative hall.

At age thirty Remond, then a resident of Rhode Island, was chosen by the American Anti-Slavery Society one of the four delegates to attend the 1840 World's Anti-Slavery Convention meeting in London on June 12, a highlight of his career. He was forced to travel in the steerage of the *Columbus* because of his color. Upon arrival at the Convention hall, Remond also learned that the London convention had forced the American female delegation, because of their sex, to sit in the rear gallery of the auditorium. Remond, along with William Lloyd Garrison and the two other delegates, refused to occupy their seats on the floor and seated themselves in the gallery with the women. Lady Byron conspicuously took a seat in the small gallery with Garrison and Remond, conversing freely with the latter.

At a public anniversary meeting of the British and Foreign Anti-Slavery Society in Exeter Hall on June 23, the day after the close of the World's Anti-Slavery Convention, Remond, in his first speech in England, said that for the first time in his life, he "stood upon soil which a slave had but to tread to become free." Relating pertinent facts concerning both the slave and the free man of color, he condemned the slave system "which was driving to misery and death thousands every year." Eager to inform the people of England, Scotland, and Ireland on the subject of American slavery, Remond remained abroad for eighteen months. Wherever he went he was received with great enthusiasm by large audiences. Glowing accounts of his speeches appeared in the local newspapers, and he was treated with courtesy and respect by leaders in British society.

When Remond sailed for home on the *Caledonia,* a Halifax packet, on Dec. 4, 1841, he brought with him an "Address from the People of Ireland" containing 60,000 signatures, urging Irish residents in the United States to "oppose slavery by peaceful means and to insist upon liberty for all regardless of color, creed, or country." He also brought a number of boxes, the contents of which were to be sold at the Boston Anti-Slavery Bazaar in December 1841. Henry Thompson and eminent merchants in Liverpool saw to it that Remond had a comfortable berth and was given the best attention during his voyage home.

Remond arrived in Boston exhausted from continuous illness during the rough voyage, only to face immediately the Jim Crow car from Boston to Salem. Eager to be present at the opening of the bazaar he met at the depot two white friends who seated themselves in the compartment for persons of color. Immediately the conductor forced Remond's friends out of it, no new experience to Remond. On Feb. 22, 1842, when Remond became the first Negro to address the legislative committee in the Massachusetts House of Representatives, his speech on "Rights of Colored Persons in Travelling" was one of the great orations of the day. He was beseiged with requests to lecture at antislavery meetings, Negro conventions, anniversary and protest meetings. For instance, at the Jan. 28, 1842, meeting held in Boston urging the abolition of slavery in the District of Columbia, Remond presented to the audience of 4000 the "Address from the People of Ireland" in a speech that was "brief, but energetic and eloquent." The hostility of many Irish-Americans to Negroes and to abolition led many American Negro leaders to manifest little interest in the plight of the Irish in England (Gilbert Osofsky, "Abolitionists, Irish Immigrants, and the Dilemma of Romantic Nationalism" (*American Historical Review,* Oct. 1975, pp. 889–912).

At the testimonial meeting of colored citizens of Boston (Dec. 17, 1855) to honor William Cooper Nell for his efforts in opening the public schools of Boston to all children, regardless of color, Remond stated that he regarded the occasion as an indication that colored people were beginning to understand "the necessity for adhesiveness and consistency," but he wished it to be clear that they were dissatisfied "as long as they were excluded from the jury box," especially when colored men were to be tried. He urged his people to withhold taxes when legal rights were denied them. "Their motto should be 'no privilege, no pay.'" The Negro should have been more radical, not afraid of martyrdom, not too slow in their movements or too indefinite in their views and sentiments.

Regardless of the indignities Remond suffered because of his color he opposed designation by color. At the May 9, 1867, National Convention of the American Equal Rights Association, where he was elected one of the vice-presidents and served on its finance committee, he opposed the word *colored* in one of the resolutions. In a letter dated April 5, 1869, Remond "objected to colored schools, colored Churches with colored ministers and colored teachers—also to a black minister to black Hayti." During the great debates which took place as to who should obtain citizenship first, women or the Negro man, Remond stated at the May 9, 1867, meeting: "All I ask for myself, I claim for my wife and sister. . . . No class of citizens in this country can be deprived of the ballot without injuring every other class."

Remond was in poor health most of his life. His salary as an antislavery lecturer was irregular. To supplement his income, he opened in June 1856 a Ladies and Gentlemen's Dining Room, "conducted on strictly temperance principles." Remond evidently did not spend much time serving customers, for in the fall and winter there were inaugurated the "100 Conventions" which were held in New England, New York, Pennsylvania, Ohio, Michigan, Indiana, Illinois, and Wisconsin. His heavy lecture schedule and the death of his first wife Amy Matilda, the daughter of Peter Williams, on Aug. 15, 1856, at age forty-seven, further undermined his health.

When recruitment of Negro troops for the Civil War began on Feb. 16, 1863, Remond was appointed one of the agents to enlist men for the 54th Massachusetts Regiment, the first colored regiment from the northern states to see action. In 1865 he was appointed a Boston street light inspector. Six years later he became a clerk in the Boston Custom House, a position he held until his death.

Early in 1866 Remond moved to South Reading, Mass., renamed Wakefield in 1868, where he paid taxes from 1866 to 1873. In Greenwood, a subdivision of Wakefield, he owned land, a house, livestock, a barn, and a carriage house. Shortly after he settled in Wakefield his son, Wendell P., died on March 29, 1866, at the age of two and a half. His last son, Albert Ernest, was born in Wakefield on July 31, 1866. Both of these children were by Remond's second wife Elizabeth Thayer Magee, who died on Feb. 3, 1872. Remond's young daughter died two and a half months later at age twelve. The death of Charles L. Jr., a student, occurred on July 7, 1881, at the age of twenty. Tuberculosis, which afflicted the entire family, caused the death of Charles Lenox Remond on Dec. 22, 1873, at the age of sixty-three. The *New York Times* and the *Boston Transcript* noted his death.

Charles Lenox Remond, advocate of equal school rights, universal suffrage, and abolition, achieved distinction in his own country and abroad despite prejudice. Faced constantly with poverty, he nonetheless contributed financially to the support of the abolitionist movement. His speeches between 1842 and 1862 leave no doubt that he was one of the leading Negro orators of his day, often compared to Wendell Phillips. Remond lived and worked with friends who knew little of the hardships imposed on him because of color prejudice. His fight was not for the slave alone but for the freedom of all regardless of color.

For information about Remond, see especially Miriam L. Usery's "Charles Lenox Remond, Garrison's Ebony Echo" (*Essex Institute Historical Collections,* April 1, 1970); Benjamin Quarles's *Black Abolitionists* (1969); Carter G. Woodson (ed.), *The Mind of the Negro as Reflected in Letters Written during the Crisis, 1800–1860* (1926), and his *Negro Orators and Their Orations* (1925); "Letters of Charles Lenox Remond" (*JNH,* 1925). The brief article by Harrison G. Villard in *DAB* (8, Part 1:499–500) is sympathetic. Records in Wakefield, Salem, and Boston, were also useful.

— DOROTHY B. PORTER

REMOND, SARAH PARKER (1826–1894), abolitionist and physician. She was born in Salem, Mass., one of the eight children (six girls and two boys) of John and Nancy (Lenox) Remond. Her father, who had been born in Curaçao, had been since 1798 one of the best known citizens of Salem. She received her early education in the public schools of Salem, where she and her sisters encountered much racial prejudice. Early parental training instilled in Sarah a love for humanity and a belief in equal rights for all. In 1835 Sarah's father became a life member of the Massachusetts Anti-Slavery Society. Other members of the Remond family were also active abolitionists. Sarah Remond served on committees of the Salem Anti-Slavery Society, which had been formed as early as 1832, the New England Anti-Slavery Convention, and was at one time corresponding secretary of the annual meeting of the Essex County Anti-Slavery Society. She gave financial support to these organizations and numbered their leading members among her friends.

Sarah Remond began lecturing with her brother Charles in Groton, Mass., in July 1842. In July 1846, at the onset of the war with Mexico, she was one of the signers of the Anti-War Pledge. She protested segregation in churches, theaters, and other public places. She purchased in May 1853 three tickets for the dress circle for a performance of Madame Henriette Sontag who was appearing in Mozart's *Don Giovanni,* at the Howard Athenaeum in Boston, which advertised that for all performances colored people would be admitted only to the gallery. When Sarah Remond and her friends were forcibly ejected from the seats for which they had tickets, Remond had the agent for Madame Sontag arrested and immediately brought civil suit, for damages, in the First District Court of Essex. She won her case, collecting damages in the sum of $500. A few months later, Remond was involved in a similar episode at the Franklin Exhibition in Philadelphia. In 1856 she was appointed a lecturing agent of the American Anti-Slavery Society. Usually accompanying her brother, she spoke in various towns in New York, Rhode Island, Massachusetts, and as far west as Alliance, Ohio.

Weary of discriminatory practices in the United States, Remond decided late in 1858 to go to England to further the cause of abolition, to "breathe free air," as well as "to further her education." She believed she could convince the English public not to buy slave-grown American cotton. Her family had purchased only free produce for many years. Carrying letters of reference from American and English abolitionists, and accompanied by the Rev. Samuel J. May, Remond arrived on Jan. 9, 1859, in Liverpool where she addressed her first English audience on Jan. 21. For an hour and a half she eloquently depicted the sufferings of the slaves, especially women in bondage. She expressed "her unbounded indignation at the apathy which the professing Christians throughout the whole of the United States as a body manifested on this subject; and concluded with an earnest appeal for the moral and religious sympathy and influence of free England in the abolition movement." During the next few days she gave five lectures in Warrington, and she was presented with an inscribed silver watch. As a result of Remond's visit, the Warrington Anti-Slavery Society contributed $100 to the American Anti-Slavery Society, accompanying the donation with an address signed by the mayor, the members of Parliament for the borough, the rector of the parish, and by 3522 other persons of various ranks and classes.

In the next three years Sarah Remond lectured in approximately twenty cities and towns to thousands of factory workers as well as to influential townspeople in England, Scotland, and Ireland. In many localities she was listened to "with breathless attention" and was regarded as the "living refutation of the theory of Negro inferiority." The *Scotsman* reported that her work had been so effective that five years after speaking at a meeting she was still recalled as "a perfect rhetorician who had made the finest and most touching appeal on behalf of the Negro the writer had ever heard" (Dec. 12, 1865).

From October 1859 to 1861 she attended the Bedford College for Ladies (later part of the University of London). On June 13, 1862, she presented a paper at the fifth session of the Congrès International de Bienfaisance de Londres entitled "Les Nègres aux États-Unis d'Amérique."

Remond protested discrimination abroad as well as at home. She, her sister (Caroline Putnam), and friends were not permitted to use first-class accommodations they had bought for a trip aboard a Cunard steamer from Boston to Liverpool in November 1859. After a series of letters to the Cunard line and newspaper publicity, Mrs. Putnam later informed the press that on her return passage on the same Cunard ship she and her party during the entire passage were admitted to "all the rights and privileges of first class passengers" even though slaveholders were aboard. In London a disagreeable situation arose when Remond and her sister visited the legation of the United States in early December 1859 to request a visa for travel to Paris. Their request was denied on the grounds that "they were not citizens of the United States . . . [and] it was not the practice of this legation either to grant passports to persons of color or to *visé* them." Remond was further told by Benjamin Moran, assistant secretary of the legation, that her passport "undoubtedly had been obtained by fraud, and did not truthfully describe her." An appeal to the American minister to Great Britain, George Mifflin Dallas, was fruitless. The English and the Scottish press condemned the incident for its incivility "as well as for the course adopted here of refusing to recognize Negroes as citizens."

In 1864, while serving on the Executive Committee of the Ladies London Emancipation Society, Remond published a pamphlet in London, *The Negroes and Anglo-Africans as Freedmen and Soldiers.* After the Civil War she lectured on behalf of the freedmen and solicited clothing and funds for them. Her letter to the *London Daily News* in 1865 protested attacks on Negroes in the London press after an insurrection in Jamaica, and a statement in *The Freedman* revealed her continued opposition to colonization (Feb. 1, 1866).

Remond established residence in Florence in late 1866. She attended the Santa Maria Nuova Hospital between 1866 and 1868. After a regular course of study and hospital practice, she obtained a diploma certifying her for "professional medical practice" in 1868 (*The Revolution* 2 [Oct. 22, 1868]: 250; *National Anti-Slavery Standard,* Oct. 10, 1868). Elizabeth Buffom Chace on a visit to Florence in 1873 reported that Remond was "winning a fine position in Florence as a physician."

Little is known about her subsequent life. In a letter from Rome (Feb. 11, 1887) Frederick Douglass referred to a visit he had made to his "old friends the Remonds," probably Sarah and her sister Caroline, who had gone to live with her. Remond married Lazzaro Pintor on April 25, 1877. According to manuscript records in the Protestant Cemetery in Rome, Sarah Parker Remond, who was buried there, died on Dec. 13, 1894.

This article updates two previous publications by Dorothy B. Porter: "Sarah Parker Remond, Abolitionist and Physician" (*JNH,* July 1935), and the sketch and bibliography in *NAW, 1607–1950* (1971, pp. 136–37). Additional information is based on later research in Europe. — DOROTHY B. PORTER

REVELS, HIRAM RHOADES [RHODES] (1822–1901), clergyman, army recruiter, U.S. senator, and college president. He was born free in Fayetteville, Cumberland County, N.C. Little is known about his parentage, and some statements concerning his career until 1863 are conflicting. He is said to have been part Croatan Indian, which is not implausible. According to what may be the best evidence, he received his early education in a school run by a free colored woman in Fayetteville, later taught school, worked as a barber, and continued his education at a Quaker Seminary in Liberty, Union County, Ind., and Darke County (Ohio) Seminary for Negroes. In 1845 he was ordained a minister in the African Methodist Episcopal church in Baltimore. He taught, lectured, and served A.M.E. congregations in Ohio, Indiana, Illinois, Missouri, Maryland, Tennessee, Kentucky, and Kansas. He completed his formal education as a scholarship student at Knox Academy, Galesburg, Ill. (1856–1857). From 1858 to 1863 he was the first Negro pastor of the Madison Street Presbyterian Church in Baltimore. In the latter year he helped organize the first two colored regiments in Maryland and later one in Missouri, where he founded a large school for freedmen in St. Louis. He served briefly as a chaplain in the Union Army, helped the Freedmen's Bureau set up schools in Mississippi, and assisted the provost marshal in managing the affairs of the freedmen in Vicksburg. His health failing him, he recuperated during two years in Kansas and Missouri. After a brief sojourn in New Orleans, he was appointed presiding elder of the African Methodist Episcopal church in Natchez, Miss.

He began his political career as an alderman in Natchez in 1868 and was elected to the Mississippi state Senate in 1869. The state legislature in January 1870 elected him to the U.S. Senate, the first Negro chosen to become a member of either House of Congress. After acrimonious debate, the Senate seated him by a vote of forty-eight to eight on Feb. 25. He served only until the end of the short term, March 3, 1871.

He returned to Mississippi and was named the first president of Alcorn College, in Rodney, on the site of what until the Civil War had been Oakland College. In 1875 he campaigned for the white conservatives in their successful attempt to overthrow the Republican-dominated state government and was rewarded for his efforts by the new governor, John M. Stone, by again being appointed in 1876 to the presidency of Alcorn. Before resuming work at Alcorn he preached in New Orleans and was named by the General Conference of the A.M.E. church to edit the *Southwestern Advocate.* The paper was not then successful and he returned to Alcorn. After his retirement in 1882 he lived in Holly Springs, Miss., as district superintendent of his church.

He died after a paralytic stroke on Jan. 16, 1901, while attending the Upper Mississippi Conference of the A.M.E. church at Aberdeen, Miss. He was survived by his wife, Phoebe Bass of Zanesville, Ohio, who died of a lingering illness one month later. His income during his various careers, especially the presidency of Alcorn College, left only the family home in Holly Springs and a small sum for three surviving daughters and a grandchild.

Revels's career as a politician and a college president reflected the precarious position of Negroes during Reconstruction, particularly in Mississippi. Since Negroes constituted a majority of the voters after the Reconstruction Acts of March 2 and 3, 1867, the white minority in this bastion of the Confederacy used violence, economic coercion, and political maneuvers to regain effective control. Mississippi refused to ratify the Fourteenth Amendment and remained under federal control until Feb. 23, 1870, when it was readmitted to the Union. Since most Negroes supported the Republican party, most whites were Democrats. They did not, however, restore white rule until 1875. Revels, recognizing this shift in power, supported white conservatives in overthrowing the Republican-dominated state government. Mississippi became increasingly a "closed society" and adopted a constitutional amendment in 1890 which disfranchised practically all Negroes while permitting unqualified whites to vote. Meanwhile state appropriations in support of Alcorn University steadily declined despite general acceptance of Revels as a favorite of the white leaders of the state.

When the Republican leadership in the Senate moved on Feb. 23, 1870, to approve the seating of Revels to fill the expired term of Jefferson Davis, opposition was typified by the argument of Sen. Willard Saulsbury, Democrat from Delaware, that "the advent of a negro or mulatto or octoroon in the Senate of the United States" left him "but little hope for my country. I would avert if possible this great great calamity." Other senators, however, such as Henry Wilson and Charles

Sumner of Massachusetts, led the fight which won the seat for Revels.

As a freshman senator he was named to what was then the insignificant Committee on Education and Labor and in 1871 to the Committee for the District of Columbia. Essentially a cautious person, Revels did not press vigorously for rights for Negroes, although in his maiden speech on March 16, 1870, he strongly opposed the proposed readmission of Georgia unless certain safeguards were added to the bill which would protect the rights of freedmen. On the other hand, in his first major address on May 17 he advocated amnesty for all former Confederates, providing that they pledge their loyalty to the government of the United States. He indicated that such a policy was unanimously endorsed by the Republican party in Mississippi and that harmony between the races prevailed in his home state. Later, however, he changed his mind about the idea of general amnesty, feeling that "too much amnesty has led to the murderous activities of the disloyal after they had reached the point of acquiescing." During his short tenure in office, which expired on March 3, 1871, Revels voted for the readmission of Texas under a Republican government, for naturalization to be extended to Negroes by striking out the word "white," and for the enforcement of the Fifteenth Amendment. He also introduced bills to repair and construct levees in Mississippi, to grant lands and right of way to aid the New Orleans and Northeastern Railroad, to abolish the franking privilege, and to enforce a federal elections law. In his swan song (Feb. 8, 1871) he favored desegregating public schools in the District of Columbia. None of these bills was approved.

Revels' career reached its peak before and during his brief term as the first Negro elected to either House of Congress. Shortly before taking his seat, he was entertained by such members of Washington's Negro elite as George T. Downing, who ran the Capitol Restaurant, and Dr. Charles B. Purvis, a professor in the Medical Department of Howard University. He delivered lectures in a number of cities and in the summer of 1870 nominated a Negro, Michael Howard, to West Point. Although Howard soon dropped out, his appointment reveals efforts on Revels's part that offset some of his accommodationist views and practices.

After the expiration of his term Revels lapsed into relative obscurity except for his presidency of Alcorn. During those years his seeking the favor of the white leadership in the state is evident in his refusal to testify in 1875 before a Senate committee investigating charges of murder and intimidation during the election of Democrats, supported by Revels, to the state legislature.

Under his leadership Alcorn University, the infant institution, granted a number of scholarships to ambitious young Negroes. However, the former senator was evidently not an adept administrator and became caught between the demands of a white-dominated legislature and some members of the faculty and student body who wanted him to be a more aggressive leader. Revels resigned the presidency in 1873 to become secretary of state *ad interim* of Mississippi. He returned to the Alcorn presidency later that same year, but was removed from office in 1874 by the Republican governor, Adelbert Ames. Revels's dismissal did not sit well with the student body; they revolted and about sixty of them withdrew from the school. His tenure from 1876 to 1882 was quiet, probably because of Revels's accommodating posture and the increasing acceptance of white domination by faculty, students, and most other Negroes. His most notable faculty appointment was that of George B. Vashon, an 1844 graduate of Oberlin College and the first Negro on the faculty of Howard University.

His career in national politics is well summarized by Samuel Denny Smith, a generally hostile interpreter of Negroes during and after Reconstruction: "He blazed the way, and it was easier for others to follow. Revels was not as intelligent as [Robert Brown] Elliott, nor as shrewd as [Robert] Smalls, but no later Negro was received any better by the whites of both parties and sections. At the same time he had not neglected the interests of his own people" (*The Negro in Congress, 1870–1901* [1940], p. 25).

The short article by J. G. de Roulhac Hamilton in *DAB* ([1935], 8, Part 1:513) represents the faint praise characteristic of that era. More sympathetic are Elizabeth Lawson's *The Gentleman from Mississippi . . .* (1960), Maurine Christopher's *America's Black Congressmen* (1971, pp. 1–14), and Samuel Denny Smith's *The Negro in Congress, 1870–1901* (1940, pp. 13–25). Valuable background material is in Vernon Lane Wharton's *The Negro in Mississippi, 1865–1890* (1947, pp. 159–60, 253–54). Wharton based his research in part on Revels's "Autobiography" in the Carter G. Woodson Papers, Library of Congress. For a short study of the debate and seating of Revels, see Donald L. Singer's "For Whites Only: The Seating of Hiram Revels in the United States Senate" (*NHB*, March 1972, pp. 60–63).

— DONALD L. SINGER

RICHARDS, FANNIE MOORE (1841–1922), pioneer teacher and civil rights activist. Richards was born on Oct. 1, 1841, to a family of prosperous free Negroes in Fredericksburg, Va. Her father, Adolph Richards, a Guadeloupe native of mixed ancestry who had been educated in London, operated a carpentry shop in Fredericksburg. Her mother, Marie Louise Moore, a native of Fredericksburg, was the daughter of Edwin Moore, a Scotsman, and his wife, a free colored woman from Toronto, Ontario. Her earliest education was most likely received in the clandestine school maintained by free Negroes and taught by a Scots-Irishman in the home of Richard De Baptiste.

When her father died in 1851, her mother sold the family property and moved to Detroit where other free Virginia families congregated (such as the De Baptistes and the Pelhams). She studied English, history, drawing, and needlework in Toronto where her sister and brother-in-law lived. Then she attended the Teachers Training School in Detroit.

After operating a private school for three years, she was appointed the teacher at Colored School No. 2 in September 1865, thereby becoming Detroit's first Negro public school teacher. In 1867 she, her brother John D. Richards, a businessman and Republican politician, and other relatives led the fight against the segregated Detroit public schools which provided twelve years of education for whites but only six for Negroes. In 1870, after organized Negro political agitation had led to two acts of the state legislature and a decision by the state Supreme Court, the school board reluctantly abolished the separate schools for Negroes.

Richards was then assigned to the Everett School where she remained until her retirement on June 6, 1915. During her fifty years of teaching she became widely esteemed for her continuous study of modern pedagogic methods, her high standard of scholarship, her knowledge of literature, and especially her sympathy with children of all races. Most of her students were of German, Jewish, or Negro extraction. They were accustomed to surrounding and clinging to her as she walked to and from school. She visited the homes of her pupils and invited them to her home. In 1872 she was selected to inaugurate the first kindergarten in Detroit. She was honored in 1910 by the daily papers which published testimonials by influential white citizens.

Although she was the sole Negro teacher in a predominantly white school, she stated that she had never "felt the least discrimination" from either teachers or pupils. She accompanied other teachers on their annual excursions to Washington, "just to lend a little color," as she put it. She was devoted to her race and considered her career an example of what Negroes could accomplish, given the opportunity. She wrote that "no race has advanced more rapidly than ours, and Negroes have not shown all they can do yet." A close associate of Booker T. Washington, she believed that it was through education that Negroes were "going to make their mark."

She was a faithful member of the Second Baptist Church, Detroit's oldest Negro congregation, where she taught Sunday school for over fifty years. She saved nearly half her meager salary which she used to found the Phyllis Wheatley Home for aged Negro women on Nov. 12, 1897. Richards served as its first president, and after its incorporation in 1901, as chairman of the board of trustees. When the Freedmen's Progress Commission was organized by the state legislature on April 21, 1915, she was chosen as an honorary vice-president. She died on Feb. 13, 1922.

Fannie Richards was honored by the city of Detroit in December 1970 when her portrait was placed in the Detroit Historical Museum.

See W. B. Hartgrove's "The Story of Marie Louise Moore and Fannie M. Richards" (*JNH*, Jan. 1916), Harvey C. Jackson's "Pioneers and Builders in Michigan: Fannie M. Richards" (*NHB*, May 1942), and "Tea at Museum Honors First Negro Teacher" (*Detroit Historical Society Bulletin*, Jan. 1971). — J. CARLETON HAYDEN

RILLIEUX, NORBERT (1806–1894), chemical inventor, engineer, and Egyptologist. His birth record on file in the City Hall of New Orleans states: "Norbert Rillieux, quadroon libre, natural son of Vincent Rillieux and Constance Vivant. Born March 17, 1806. Baptized in St. Louis Cathedral by Père Antoine." It is not known whether he was specifically freed or whether his mother was already free. The elder Rillieux, an engineer

and inventor, adopted his son and gave him his name, a practice not unusual at the time. As the son of a wealthy French planter, young Rillieux was given the material and educational advantages of the colored Creole "Cordons Bleus," an allusion to a blue cord or sash worn by pre-Revolutionary French nobility. Although the situation of the colored Creoles deteriorated after the purchase of Louisiana by the United States in 1803, Rillieux attended Catholic schools in New Orleans and went to Paris to be educated. He studied engineering at L'École Centrale in Paris and at the age of twenty-four, after graduation, was an instructor in applied mechanics at L'École Centrale, the youngest instructor at the school up to that time. He contributed many papers on steam technology to engineering journals.

Rillieux's first inventive efforts were directed toward developing more efficient methods of refining sugar. He had developed an interest in sugar refining when he was a boy on his father's plantation. The method then in use for refining sugar was called the "Jamaica Train." This was a series of open kettles in which the cane juice was heated. The juice was poured from one kettle to the next in the series with long-handled ladles. In the last and smallest kettle the juice was heated to crystallization. The "Jamaica Train" was slow and inefficient and the quality of the sugar could not be well controlled.

Rillieux's Multiple Effect Vacuum Pan Evaporator, patented in 1843 (patent no. 3237), utilized a number of physical principles to increase the efficiency of sugar refining. The cane juice was heated in enclosed vacuum pans. The existence of a partial vacuum in the enclosed pans reduced the boiling point of the liquid with a consequent improvement in fuel economy. Pipes led the steam and heated juice from one pan to another in such a way that the steam could be utilized for further heating, thereby achieving even greater fuel efficiency.

Rillieux returned to New Orleans in 1840 to perfect his invention and to arrange for testing. He made arrangements to construct prototypes of the evaporator on a sugar plantation. The tests revealed various problems and Rillieux made several design modifications. Patent no. 4879 for the improved evaporator was awarded on Dec. 10, 1846. The evaporator was a large, bulky apparatus that looked somewhat like a stationary locomotive. Installation of the device was a major construction job and Rillieux personally supervised many installations. The patent application for the 1846 version of the evaporator included the following: "The first improvement is in the manner of connecting a steam engine with the evaporating pan or pans in such a manner that the engine shall be operated by the steam in its passage to the evaporating pan or pans at the temperature required for the process."

The 1846 version of the evaporator was very successful and thousands were erected on plantations in Louisiana and the West Indies. It had a revolutionary effect on the sugar industry. The rate of sugar production was dramatically increased and the price significantly reduced. Until Rillieux's invention was available, white crystalline sugar was a relative luxury and generally used only on special occasions. Rillieux's invention made sugar so abundant and cheap that sugar refiners had to create new markets for the product. It soon became a common household item. Rillieux had to contend with legions of imitators and patent pirates. Some of his plans were stolen and taken to Europe. Thousands were manufactured by the pirates and sold as genuine Rillieux evaporators.

Since the evaporator increased the production capabilities of sugar plantations, it increased the demand for field slaves. Following the invention of the evaporator the price of field hands strong enough to work in the cane fields often rose to as much as $5000, a formidable sum in the 1850s. It is not known if Rillieux, who could have himself been a slave at his father's whim, expressed any concern over this situation which served to strengthen the economic incentive to defend slavery.

Rillieux, however, did suffer from the prevailing racism that increased in Louisiana following the 1803 Louisiana Purchase. After 1803 thousands of white southerners poured into Louisiana and their attitudes soon became a fact of life in New Orleans. When Rillieux returned to New Orleans from Paris in 1840 he found that he could not stay at certain hotels that he had patronized earlier. Colored veterans of the Battle of New Orleans were no longer allowed to participate in the Victory Day parade and celebration.

Following the success of the evaporator Rillieux turned his attention to developing a sewage-disposal system for New Orleans. Sewage disposal had always been a problem in low-lying, marshy New Orleans. Rillieux submitted his plans to the New Orleans authorities and was turned down. The basis of the rejection was racial. At the time abolitionists were quite active and the New Orleans city fathers were afraid that accepting a civil engineering project designed by a Negro might strengthen the abolitionist cause. Several years later a sewage disposal plant almost exactly like Rillieux's was adopted by New Orleans. He left New Orleans in 1854 in reaction to the passing of a law which required all Negroes to carry identification passes.

Upon his return to Paris he resumed teaching at L'École Central and was soon made headmaster. He was very active in engineering research, and engineering journals of the period are filled with his articles. Rillieux developed an interest in Egyptology and made significant contributions to the deciphering of hieroglyphics. He continued an active career until his death in 1894.

Following the Civil War, Rillieux's evaporator played a significant role in the economic recovery of the Louisiana region. The multiple-effect evaporator principle is now basic in the chemical industry. It is widely used in other applications such as the production of soap, gelatin, glue, and in waste-recycling processes in paper mills and other industries. Rillieux's ideas have been summed up in three basic principles which are axiomatic to all students of sugar refining and chemical engineering. As stated by Charles Brown, a chemist in the U.S. Department of Agriculture, "I have held that Rillieux's invention is the greatest in the history of American chemical engineering, and I know of no other invention that has brought so great a saving to all branches of chemical engineering." In 1934 a plaque honoring Rillieux's contribution to Louisiana's sugar industry was placed in the Louisiana State Museum in New Orleans. It states that it was dedicated "by Corporations representing the Sugar Industry all over the world."

According to P. Horsin-Devon who knew Rillieux for many years, Rillieux, at the age of eighty-five, lost a French patent for a combined process of juice heating, vapor boiling to grain, and multiple-effect evaporation because "experts were unwilling to recognize its invention." It was, however, widely used later. The lack of recognition was such a blow to Rillieux that he died in his eighty-ninth year "more from a broken heart than from the weight of years." He was buried in the churchyard of Père La Chaise Cemetery, Paris. The inscription reads: "Ici reposent/ Norbert Rillieux/ ingénieur civil à la Nouvelle Orléans/ 18 Mars 1806/ décédé à Paris le 8 Ocbre 1894/ Emily Cuckow, Veuve Rillieux/ 1827–1912." Little more is known of his wife Emily except that she was in comfortable circumstances during the final years of her life.

The best source is "A Negro Scientist of Slavery Days" by George P. Meade (*NHB,* April 1957, pp. 159–63, reprinted from *Scientific Monthly,* 1946, pp. 317–26). Meade's article is based largely on an article by P. Horsin-Devon in the *Louisiana Planter and Sugar Manufacturer* (Nov. 24, 1894). It is all the more valuable because of well-documented footnotes by Sidney Kaplan. See also Aaron E. Klein's *The Hidden Contributions: Black Scientists and Inventors in America* (1971) and Louis Haber's *Black Pioneers of Science and Invention* (1970). — AARON E. KLEIN

ROBERTS, FREDERICK MADISON (1880–1952), mortician, newspaper publisher, and California state legislator. Although Roberts is principally known for his long service as the first Negro state legislator in California, less well known is the fact that he was the great-grandson of Sally Hemings, Thomas Jefferson's alleged mistress. One of the sons, Madison Hemings, born on Jan. 19, 1805, moved to Ohio. His youngest daughter, Ellen Wayles Hemings, was the mother of Frederick Madison Roberts.

He was born in Chillicothe, Ohio, in 1880 and was taken at the age of six to Los Angeles where his father was a pioneer undertaker. He graduated from Los Angeles High School, attended the University of Southern California, and worked his way through Colorado College, Colorado Springs, and a school of mortuary science. In 1910 he was deputy assessor of El Paso County, Colo. After returning to Los Angeles he began his long career as a mortician and also purchased the weekly the *New Age,* which he edited (c. 1912–1948). He was for several years principal of the public schools in the all-Negro town of Mound Bayou, Miss., after which he returned to Los Angeles and resumed his editorship of the *New Age* and his undertaking business. He also edited the weekly *Colorado Springs Light* (1908–1912[?]).

In 1918 Roberts was elected on the Republican ticket to the California state legislature from the 74th District (later the 62nd), in which two-thirds of the voters were white, although the proportionate number of Negroes was increasing, and was repeatedly reelected. In his campaigns and legislative service he was noted as emphasizing Republicanism rather than race. However, as a result of the New Deal surge he was defeated in 1934 by Augustus F. Hawkins, a Negro Democrat. He continued a strong interest in politics, and in 1946 was a Republican candidate for the House from the 14th Congressional District but was defeated by Helen Gahagan Douglas.

He had just returned from the Republican National Convention of 1952 when he was fatally injured in an automobile accident and died on July 19. He was survived by his widow, Pearl, and two daughters, Gloria and Patricia.

An obituary in the *Los Angeles Times* (July 20, 1952) gives the main facts of Roberts's life, while further details through 1918 appear in Delilah L. Beasley's *The Negro Trail Blazers of California* (1919). The *California Blue Books* and W. N. Davis, Jr., Chief of Archives, furnished further information.

— KENNETH WIGGINS PORTER

ROBESON, ESLANDA CARDOZO GOODE (1896–1965),

civil rights and Pan African activist, anthropologist, author, and business manager of Paul Robeson. She was the only daughter and one of three children of John and Eslanda Cardozo Goode. Her father, born in Chicago, was a clerk in the War Department and her mother was the daughter of Francis Louis Cardozo, prominent Reconstruction official in South Carolina and educator. Eslanda was born in Washington, D.C., and spent her early years with the Cardozos and the Goodes. Her father died when she was six; her mother moved to New York City where she could earn a better living and educate Eslanda and her two brothers in nonsegregated schools. Eslanda joined the Episcopal church, attended the University of Chicago and Teachers College of Columbia University, where she earned a B.S. degree in chemistry in 1923. She is said to have been the first Negro analytical chemist at Columbia Medical Center.

In 1920 she urged Paul Robeson to take a role in a YMCA production of *Simon the Cyrenian*. In 1921 Robeson became associated with Eugene O'Neill's Provincetown Players and married Eslanda. She became and remained his manager, except during a period of separation for a few years after 1932, until her death. Despite a marriage that was difficult at times, she wrote in 1951 that she had married a "super-duper husband." She died on Dec. 13 in Beth Israel Hospital, New York City, after an illness of several months. "The cause of the death was not announced." P. L. Prattis, a friend of many years, wrote that she had her first operation for cancer in Moscow. She was survived by her husband, their son Paul Jr. (born on Nov. 12, 1927), and other relatives. Funeral services and interment were private, attended only by her immediate family.

Despite her difficult role as the wife and business manager of one of the outstanding and controversial Americans of the twentieth century, and the mother of their son, Eslanda Robeson won deserved recognition in her own right. She accompanied him on most of his travels abroad (1927–1939). She stood with him when in the 1940s he refused to tell U.S. House and Senate committees whether he was a member of the Communist party (although in 1946 he had sworn to a California state legislative committee that he was not a member). When he was refused a passport in 1952 because he would not, on grounds of conscience, take the required oath that he was not a Communist, and his income dropped from $104,000 in 1947 to about $2000 a year in the early 1950s, the Robesons had to sell their cherished home, The Beeches, in Enfield, Conn. When she was called before a Senate subcommittee in the 1950s she stated that she was a "very loyal American," but like her husband would not sign the affidavit that she was not a Communist. She pointed out to the senators: "You're white and I'm a Negro, and this is a very white committee."

Although she had told an audience in New Haven, Conn., where she was accompanied by Henry A. Wallace, candidate for president on the Progressive party ticket in 1948 that, while she had spent some time in Russia but would not live there, she, her husband, and their son spent their self-imposed exile in the Soviet Union (1958–1963).

Meanwhile she continued her studies, wrote two books, became an acerbic critic of U.S. foreign policy, a dedicated civil rights activist, and Pan-Africanist. She studied anthropology at the University of London and the London School of Economics (1936–1937). She also studied in the Soviet Union at the National Minorities Institute, Leningrad, and at the Hartford Seminary Foundation, Hartford, Conn., where she received her Ph.D. degree in anthropology in 1945.

Her interest in Africa began when, as she was growing up, she had heard a great deal about the "Yellow Peril," the "Black Menace," and the *Rising Tide of Color* (Lothrop Stoddard's book by that title had predicted that white civilization would be overwhelmed by the darker races). In 1936 she and her son traveled through southern, central, and eastern Africa from Cape Town to Cairo, praising the Soviet Union's "ideals of human equality." Her book *African Journey* (1945), based on her diary, discussed the spiritual and material cultures of African intellectuals, leaders of the national liberation movements, tribal chiefs, and ordinary tribesmen. The book is enhanced by the observations of her son and the knowledge of their travel companions, Max Yergan (an American Negro YMCA secretary) and Akikiki Nyabongo, a Ugandan prince. The sixty-four pages of photographs of villages and people give the reader an understanding of some of the continuing basic problems. In 1944 she had written that as a result of World War II, the interest and attention of the world were directed toward Africa and statesmen would have to consider the freedom of all peoples. She had missed the five Pan-African Congresses (1919, 1921, 1923, 1927, and 1945) as well as the Afro-Asian Conference at Bandung, Indonesia, in 1955. She did, however, attend the All African Peoples Conference at Accra, Ghana (Dec. 5–12, 1958), where she deplored the absence of women delegates. Instead of white colonialists speaking for Africans, "Africans plan, for all of Africa, government of, and by the African people."

Perhaps her most effective work was done as a member, with her husband, of the Council on African affairs, one of the best informed private organizations on the subject. In 1945 the council sent her as an observer to the San Francisco Conference which founded the United Nations. In 1946 she again went to Africa, this time traveling by foot, on horseback, car, boat, steamship, and plane in the Congo, Ruanda-Urundi, and French Equatorial Africa. She was thus able to discuss knowledgeably problems of Africa and Africans before the United Nations Trusteeship Council. It was the support given by the delegates of the Soviet Union to the emerging self-governing and independent nations of Africa that reenforced her sympathies for the Soviet Union.

In 1950, when support of the People's Republic of China was considered subversive, Mrs. Robeson declared after a visit (1949–1950) that the government would not crack up. Land had been divided among rich and poor alike; everyone had a home, a school, a job, and a chance to go to school. Women were on a basis of equality with men. This roseate picture was an exaggeration that represented the goals she desired.

Three years later, in an open letter to President Eisenhower (Daily Worker [New York], March 19, 1953), she criticized the U.S. foreign policy that urged friendship with the former enemies, Germans and Japanese, but opposition to former allies, the Russians and Chinese. Like the "majority" of Americans she opposed the war in Korea. She objected to the huge expenditure on arms that might become obsolete and wanted to visit her friends without fear of a visit by the FBI.

Her concern about foreign affairs did not preempt her criticism of injustices inflicted on Negroes in America. She was particularly outraged by the assassination of Harry T. Moore and his wife Harriet on Christmas night 1951—"not on Heartbreak Ridge on the distant battlefield of Korea, but on Heartbreak Ridge here in Mims, Florida, U.S.A." They were killed by a bomb that destroyed their home. Their only "offense" was their attempt through the local branch of the NAACP to improve, through lawful means, the conditions of their fellow citizens. Their assassination proved, she wrote, that real democracy and the world prestige of the United States were threatened by "a few vicious, powerful active UnAmericans."

She had earlier praised the Soviet Union for the "absence" of racial discrimination while condemning particularly England for its racial prejudices, and discrimination in France as a result primarily of racist white Americans. She had not spent enough time in Germany to determine the extent to which Hitler's propaganda affected the treatment of American Negroes (Afro-American, June 15, 1940).

Understandably, she contrasted East Germany with Hitlerian Germany. In East Berlin in September 1963 she recalled that in 1934 she and her husband had felt during a day stopover in Berlin "the vicious racist atmosphere of the place." On a previous trip to East Germany she had visited the Nazi concentration camp at Ravensbruck and had helped dedicate a memorial to the 92,000 women killed there. In an address celebrating the annual Memorial Day for the Victims of Fascism, Mrs. Robeson declared that she and her husband would "continue to fight fascism in all its forms." During this visit she was awarded both the German Peace Medal and the Clara

Zetkin Medal, an East German decoration for women who had distinguished themselves in the fight for peace and a better world. This seems to be the only such recognition during her life. Since her death and especially since the death of Paul Robeson in Philadelphia on Jan. 23, 1976, many Americans have praised them for their unselfish dedication to their concept of equal rights for all. In one of her last published statements—from Selma, Ala., in March 1965, nine months before her death—she hurled her defiance: "History shows that when a Government cannot, or will not protect its citizens, then the citizens must protect themselves as best they can. And they will, too." Freedomways devoted its Fourth Quarter 1966 issue to a "Tribute to Eslanda Robeson." The first section consisted of "Remembrances of Eslanda" from friends and associates; the second section, of selections from her writings.

Additional information is based on The Worker, (Dec. 19, 1965, p. 3) and other newspaper articles in the vertical file, Moorland-Spingarn Research Center, Howard University. Her book, Paul Robeson, Negro, written in 1930, has been widely summarized for the ancestry and career of her husband. The book also provides valuable insights about her personality and intimate relationship with him. Some of the more valuable parts of the book vividly describe Harlem and London after World War I. — RAYFORD W. LOGAN

ROBINSON, LUTHER [BILL "BOJANGLES"] (1878–1949), dancer. He was born in Richmond, Va., the grandson of a slave and the son of Maxwell Robinson, a machine-shop worker, and his wife Maria, who sang in a local church. Orphaned while a baby, Luther, his brother and sister were reared by their grandmother. Luther's formal education ended before his eighth birthday when he quit school and ran away to Washington, D.C., where he worked as a stable boy at the Benning Race Track. In Washington he was exposed to the traveling minstrel groups, then in great vogue, which made their way in and out of the city. After a fight with his brother William, Luther assumed the name Bill. Fascinated by the entertainers and their exuberant, sometimes outlandish performances, he studied the drawling, shuffling routines and the dances of the Negro performers doing the "buck and wing" or the "clog," an American variation on the Irish jig. Captivated with dancing by then, Robinson was able to use the basics of the minstrel tradition to begin the development of his own intricate, complexly syncopated, and energetically rhythmic dance style, and was soon performing on the streets.

His early professional appearances were with Eddie Leonard's minstrel show, The South Before the War, which had opened in New York City in 1892. After a successful run Robinson worked for some ten years as a waiter in Richmond. In 1908 in Chicago he met Marty Forkins, who became his lifelong manager and tutor. He continued to develop his elaborate routines. Soon he was a headline performer on the vaudeville circuit and was billed as the "Dark Cloud of Joy" and touted as "The King of Tap Dancers." One critic wrote that he "restores for his audience the primal freshness of their own lost rhythmic powers."

In 1926 Robinson, just reaching the peak of his talents, appeared in London. "This captivating step dancer is a veritable bundle of joy," a *Daily Express* reviewer wrote, heralding the dancer's triumphant engagement. Robinson returned to the States and had one of his greatest successes in the now historic revue Lew Leslie's *Blackbirds of 1928*. In 1933 he worked in another *Blackbirds* revue, and in *Brown Buddies*. By this time he had emerged as a legendary entertainer. He was so successful that reviewers called him everything from "incomparable" to "inimitable" to "a great artist of the modern stage." After 1934 he had so captured the American popular imagination that he was referred to as the "Mayor of Harlem." He was known to all as Bojangles, a nickname that seemed to sum up the ebullient vitality of his personality.

Perhaps the essence of the Robinson dancing style was the way in which he comingled his remarkable sense of rhythm, physical dexterity, and easy-going naturalness to convey an optimistic—a "copasetic," as he might have said—air. He had refined the basic folk rhythms and dance patterns of "black America" into a new art form. With his light, breezy, carefree style, he also introduced and perfected the staircase dance, in which he tapped his way "to glory" up a row of steps. This routine of Robinson's was widely imitated, but no performer did it with quite the buoyancy, confidence, and urbane *savoir-faire* of the master.

With all his success, however, he was also a controversial figure, criticized for mugging, grinning, and "tomming" as he performed, all of which seem to cater to crass white tastes to see "nigger antics." Some of the criticism may have stemmed from his motion picture appearances. From 1929 to 1943 he worked in ten Hollywood features as well as in some independently produced all-black movies made outside the film capital. His first screen appearance, dancing in *Dixiana* (1930), was greeted with wild, enthusiastic cheers and applause from the audience. But the movies that brought him the most attention and criticism were the popular features he made with Shirley Temple: *The Little Colonel* (1935), *The Littlest Rebel* (1935), *Rebecca of Sunnybrook Farm* (1938), and *Just Around the Corner* (1938). In all these films, as well as in *In Old Kentucky* (1935) with Will Rogers, Robinson was the congenial, ever-smiling, kowtowing, happy-go-lucky, childlike servant. Despite the criticism it was generally thought, however, that Robinson's performances had more dignity and less self-demeanment (also less artistry) than those of an actor like Stepin Fetchit, who worked in films at the same time. Robinson had trouble speaking his lines convincingly, but he was a master once he dropped the script and went into his dance. One of the finest moments in the history of musical American movies remains the one in which Bill Robinson teaches Shirley Temple how to dance up the magic staircase in *The Little Colonel.*

Robinson left Hollywood to return to Broadway to star in Michael Todd's *Hot Mikado* in 1939, a jazz version of the Gilbert and Sullivan operetta performed at the New York World's Fair. The play was a rousing, success. His next appearance, in *All in Fun* (1940) was, however, not well received. His last performance was

as a romantic lead opposite Lena Horne in the all-Negro musical *Stormy Weather* (1943).

His marriage to Fannie S. Clay in Chicago shortly after World War I ended in divorce in 1943. He married Elaine Plaines on Jan. 27, 1944. Little is known about their private lives. Robinson died of a chronic heart condition at Columbia Presbyterian Medical Center in New York City on Nov. 25, 1949. His body lay in state at an armory in Harlem, schools were closed, and thousands watched the funeral procession to the Cemetery of the Evergreens in New York City.

He was eulogized as a great American folk hero. During half a century he worked his way up from performances that brought him $5 a week to those that earned him $6500 a night before international audiences that included kings, queens, statesmen, literary figures, and as he would say, "plenty of us common colored folks." He was an "honorary mayor of Harlem," a lifetime member of policemen's associations, fraternal orders, and a mascot of the New York Giant's baseball team.

See Donald Bogle's *Toms, Coons, Mulattoes, Mammies, and Bucks: An Interpretive History of Blacks in American Films* (1973). Perceptive critiques were written by St. Clair McKelway ("Profiles—Bojangles," *The New Yorker,* Oct. 6 and 13, 1934) and Joe Laurie, Jr. ("Bill 'Bojangles' Robinson," *Variety,* Nov. 30, 1949). The *New York Times* published articles after his death (Nov. 26, 28, and 29, 1949) and an obituary was published in *Variety* (Nov. 30, 1949). The informative article by Thomas Cripps in *DAB, Supplement 4* (pp. 695–96), has a comprehensive bibliography.

— DONALD BOGLE

ROCK, JOHN SWEAT (1825–1866), physician, dentist, lawyer, and abolitionist. Rock was born probably in Salem, N.J. His free parents were able to support his education in Salem public schools until he was nineteen. From 1844 to 1848 he taught in a one-room school, gave private lessons, and studied medicine with two white physicians. Denied admission because of his race to a medical school in Philadelphia, he studied dentistry under a white dentist and opened an office in Philadelphia in 1850. He received an M.D. degree in 1852, probably from the short-lived American Medical College in Philadelphia, and practiced the profession of both dentistry and medicine. He was admitted into the Massachusetts Medical Society, sometime after John De Grasse had been admitted in 1854.

He seems to have first gained prominence as an abolitionist in the 1850s. A vigilance committee, meeting frequently in the home of Lewis Hayden, harbored an increasing number of slaves after the Fugitive Slave Act of 1850. Rock received compensation from the committee for his services to sick fugitives. He participated in the campaign which resulted (1855) in the legal desegregation of public schools in Boston. He, George T. Downing, Robert Purvis, and Charles Lenox Remond were members of a delegation from the Colored National Convention meeting in Philadelphia (1855) who visited a Quaker held in jail on the false charge of refusing to reveal the whereabouts of three fugitive slaves.

Experiencing difficulty in speaking, he had a throat

operation and decided to seek relief in France. When Secretary of State Lewis Cass ruled that since Negroes were not citizens they could not receive U.S. passports, the Massachusetts legislature granted him a state passport which was recognized by French officials. Sailing on the *Vanderbilt* in late May 1858 he spent eight months in France studying the French language and literature. In Paris Dr. Auguste Nélaton, a member of the French Academy, operated on Rock's throat and advised him to curtail his speaking and his medical practice. Rock gave an account of this visit and operation in the *Liberator* (Feb. 1859).

After his return to the United States Rock curtailed his medical practice but continued his speaking. Along with Downing, Purvis, Remond, and William C. Nell he vigorously opposed the American Colonization Society. He was one of the speakers at the Faneuil Hall meeting (March 5, 1858) held to commemorate Crispus Attucks Day. He predicted that "sooner or later the clashing of arms will be heard in this country and the black man's services will be needed." He was one of the first to develop the theme that "black is beautiful," contrasting "the fine tough muscular system, the beautiful, rich color, the full broad features, and the gracefully frizzled hair of the negro [*sic*], with the delicate physical organization, wan color, sharp features and lank hair" of the white man.

This emphasis was symbolic of efforts to combat the concept of racial inferiority. In 1860 he addressed the Committee on Federal Relations of the Massachusetts House of Representatives, urging unsuccessfully the deletion of the word "white" from the state's militia law. Expanding his Crispus Attucks Day Address of March 5, 1858, he pointed out that "It is not difficult to see that [this idea of Negro inferiority] is a mere subterfuge to bolster up the infamous treatment which greets the colored man in this slavery-cursed land, where to us patriotism produces no honor, goodness[,] no merit and intellectual industry[,] no reward. . . . I believe in the equality of my race." And, he asserted, Negroes in the United States were making more progress than similarly oppressed whites in South Carolina, Ireland, the two Sicilies, Hungary, and Russia.

At the twenty-ninth anniversary meeting of the Massachusetts Anti-Slavery Society in 1862, Rock emphasized that "We are colonized in Boston" because, despite some progress, discrimination in employment, public accommodations, some churches, and even graveyards, made him wonder how significant the gains were. He added, perhaps sarcastically: "If we are never to derive the benefits of education, it would be a misfortune for us to see inside of a school-house." He asked whether colonization schemes resulted from the fear that after 250 years of enslaving Negroes the nation would soon no longer enslave them and hence would want to banish them. He implied that Chief Justice Roger B. Taney was continuing to live so that Rock would not be admitted to practice before the U.S. Supreme Court. Taney died in 1864 and in the following year "An old order was passing. Now in the Supreme Court chambers for the first time a Negro was admitted to practice before that high tribunal: John S. Rock, an attorney of ability and good name in the city of Boston"

(Carl Sandburg, *Abraham Lincoln: The Prairie Years and the War Years* [1954], p. 538).

Rock was the first speaker at the famous Tremont Temple Meeting in Boston (Jan. 1, 1863), while the audience anxiously awaited confirmation that Lincoln had signed the Emancipation Proclamation. He compared the great moment to that of the old maid who said on the eve of her marriage: "This is the day I long have sought/ And mourned because I found it was not." When the audience disliked this comparison with Lincoln's delay in signing the Emancipation Proclamation, Rock shifted his emphasis and brought the spectators to their feet when he noted that "we must acknowledge that he has exceeded our most sanguine expectations."

When Congress in 1863 authorized the raising of colored troops, Rock became one of the main recruiters for the 54th and 55th Massachusetts Infantry Regiments. In August 1864 he was also one of the vehement critics who helped gain equal pay for colored troops. As a delegate from Massachusetts to the National Convention of Colored Men held at the Wesleyan Methodist Church in Boston, he demanded on Oct. 6, 1864, the "equal opportunities and equal rights" that "our brave men are fighting for." He praised Lincoln and the Republicans as the party of freedom and unity, and condemned the Democrats as advocates of slavery, despotism, and disunity. Elected one of the vice-presidents of the convention, the last of those of that era which had begun in Philadelphia in 1830, Rock and George L. Ruffin were publishers of an account of the convention.

Following his admission to practice law before the U.S. Supreme Court, Rock was received on the floor of the House of Representatives, perhaps the first Negro lawyer to be accorded this distinction. Preparing to return to Boston, he was arrested at the Washington railroad station for not having his pass. Rep. James A. Garfield (later president) introduced a bill that abolished passes for Negroes.

On Jan. 31, 1865, Rock attended services at the 15th Street Presbyterian Church in Washington, where the Rev. Henry Highland Garnett was pastor. While in Washington he contracted a cold but attended several meetings honoring him in Boston. His health deteriorated rapidly and he died of tuberculosis on Dec. 3, 1866, at 83 Phillips St., where he had lived with his mother and son. Masonic funeral services were held in the Twelfth Baptist Church, Boston, and he was buried in Woodlawn Cemetery, Boston. His tombstone bore the inscription that he was the first Negro lawyer admitted to practice before the U.S. Supreme Court. A Masonic lodge in Cambridge was named the John S. Rock Tabernacle. His major contribution was not in his professions of medicine, dentistry, or law, but in the advocacy of equal rights for Negroes before and during the Civil War.

Among the easily accessible publications, valuable for their background interpretations, are Jane H. Pease's and William H. Pease's *They Who Would Be Free: Blacks' Search for Freedom, 1830–1861* (1974) and three books by Benjamin Quarles: *Black Abolitionists* (1969), *Lincoln and the Negro* (1962), and *The Negro in the Civil War* (1953). The best book by a contemporary is William Wells Brown's *The Black Man, His Antecedents, His Genius, and His Achievements* (1863). Specific sources are Eugene P. Link's "The Civil Rights Activities of Three Great Negro Physicians (1840–1940)" (*JNH,* July 1967, pp. 169–84); George W. Forbes's "John S. Rock" (unpublished typescript biography in the Rare Books and Manuscripts Room, Boston Public Library); and Donald Martin Jacobs's "A History of the Boston Negro from the Revolution to the Civil War" (Ph.D. dissertation, Boston University, 1968). *Harper's Weekly,* (Feb. 25, 1865) had an engraving of Rock. Recent publications are Clarence G. Contee, Sr.'s "Teacher, Healer, Lawyer, The Supreme Court Bar's First Black Member" (*Yearbook 1976, Supreme Court Historical Society,* pp. 82–85), and "John Sweat Rock, M.D., Esq., 1825–1866" (*JNMA,* May 1976, pp. 237–42). — RAYFORD W. LOGAN

ROGERS, ELYMAS PAYSON (1815–1861), clergyman, missionary, and poet. He was born on Feb. 10, 1815, in Madison, Conn., the son of Abel and Chloe (Ladue) Rogers. As a third-generation American, Rogers traced his ancestry to an African great-grandmother, Old Tamar, whose slave ship was wrecked off the coast of Connecticut in the early eighteenth century. The Rev. Jonathan Todd, pastor of the East Guilford church, purchased Tamar and raised her from childhood with his family; her descendants Cesar and Abel worked as farmers for the Todds. In the early 1830s Rogers left the farm of his impoverished parents to work and attend school in Hartford.

Determined to be a minister and preach the gospel in Africa, he enrolled in 1835 at Gerrit Smith's school in Peterboro, N.Y. In the winter of 1836–1837, needing money to continue his education, he taught in a public school for Negro children in Rochester, N.Y., and that spring he matriculated at Oneida Institute in Whitesboro, N.Y., to prepare for the ministry. For the next five years, as the seasons changed, he alternated teaching in Rochester and studying in Whitesboro until his graduation from Oneida in the spring of 1841. As a teacher in Rochester, Rogers befriended an illiterate fugitive slave, Jermain Wesley Loguen, and secured his admission to Oneida Institute.

Rogers settled in Trenton, N.J., where he served as principal of a public school, married Harriet E. Sherman of Rochester in August 1841, and studied theology until, on Feb. 7, 1844, he was licensed by the New Brunswick Presbytery. He took charge of the Witherspoon Street Church in Princeton (1844–1846) and received full ordination to the ministry in 1845. Rogers then joined the Newark Presbytery on Oct. 20, 1846, and for the next fourteen years was pastor of Plane Street Church in Newark, which grew and prospered under his care. The Presbyterian and Congregational Convention of 1857 in Philadelphia, where Rogers delivered the opening sermon, supported his motion to denounce the Dred Scott decision as "a sin against God and a crime against humanity." His two verse satires of the 1850s also incisively express such political protest. Rogers joined the African Civilization Society, and after many years of labor in its behalf, on Nov. 5, 1860,

sailed from New York to Sierra Leone. Deeply moved by Old Tamar's homeland, he lamented the fact that Africa had for so long been the hunting ground of merciless slave traders. He sailed the West African coast, visiting Monrovia, Bassa, Sinoe, and Cape Palmas, seeking land for a colony of black Americans and expressing the hope, in letters home, that many more missionaries would come to bring the "arts of civilization" and the gospel of Christ to Africa. In mid-January 1861 Rogers fell ill and died, after only fifty days on African soil, on Jan. 20, 1861.

His 925-line poem, "The Repeal of the Missouri Compromise Considered" (1854–1856), and the shorter "A Poem on the Fugitive Slave Law" (1855) are erudite topical satires, courageous ventures for a poet of the 1850s. "The Repeal" condemns white America, North and South, the church, and politicians for sacrificing honor to greed and expediency with the Compromise of 1820 and the Kansas-Nebraska Bill of 1854; and "A Poem" insists that man-made laws which violate God-given rights must be subservient to the Higher Law. Rogers's moral indignation, neatly balanced by wit and logic, gives power to these significant satires.

Joseph M. Wilson's *The Presbyterian Historical Almanac . . . for 1862* (vol. 4, 1862) gives biographical data. Manuscript letters from Rogers and his colleagues (1860–1861) in the American Missionary Association Archives, Amistad Research Center, New Orleans, relate his experiences in Africa. A biography, discussion of the poetry, and a bibliography are in Joan R. Sherman's *Invisible Poets* (1974). — JOAN R. SHERMAN

ROGERS, J[OEL] A[UGUSTUS] (1883–1965), historian and journalist. He was born in Jamaica on Sept. 6, 1883, the son of Samuel and Emily (Johnstone) Rogers. After serving four years in the Royal Army, Royal Garrison, Heavy Artillery, he came to the United States in 1906 and was naturalized in 1917. Largely self-educated, he mastered several foreign languages, traveled extensively in Europe and Africa, and became one of the most prolific writers of his time. In 1930 he attended the coronation of Emperor Haile Selassie of Abyssinia, and after the Italian invasion, covered the conflict (1935–1936) for the *Pittsburgh Courier.* For many years he lived at 37 Morningside Ave. in the heart of Harlem, where he had a voluminous library and entertained interested and interesting guests. Most of his books were published by J. A. Rogers Publications.

He contributed articles to the *Journal of Negro History, The Crisis, The Messenger, Survey Graphic, American Mercury,* and was for many years writer of an illustrated feature "Your History" for the *Pittsburgh Courier.* In 1917 his first book, *From Superman to Man,* was published by M. A. Donohue & Co. in Chicago. Rogers later encountered difficulty in securing publication of his historical books because he lacked formal education and challenged generally accepted views about race and the identity of Negroes. On the other hand Rogers possessed a knowledge of Spanish, French, Portuguese, and German, so Rogers also did research in European and African libraries and museums.

In addition to his major works, discussed below,

some of his other books were *As Nature Leads* (1919), *The Ku Klux Spirit* (1923), *World's Greatest Men of African Descent* (1936), *World's Greatest Men and Women of African Descent* (1936), *The Real Facts About Ethiopia* (1936), *Nature Knows No Color Line* (1952), and *Africa's Gift to America* (1951).

An evaluation of Rogers's books is difficult. Concerning *From Superman to Man* (first published in 1917, a fifth edition of which was published by Rogers c. 1941), Du Bois wrote on the jacket of Rogers's *Sex and Race* (3 vols., 1940–1944): "The person who wants in small compass in good English and in attractive form the arguments for the present Negro position should buy and read and recommend to his friends 'From Superman to Man.'" Another significant comment on the inside jacket of *Sex and Race* was that of the Catholic Board for Mission Work Among the Colored People, New York City: "There are more objections against the colored race answered in this book more satisfactorily and convincingly than in any book we have read upon the question." A short book of some fifty pages, illustrated, by Rogers, *100 Amazing Facts About the Negro, with Complete Proof; a Short Cut to the World History of the Negro,* first published in 1934(?), had reached its twenty-fourth revised edition in 1963. The third and enlarged illustrated *The Real Facts about Ethiopia* was published c. 1936.

Sex and Race is the most comprehensive of his books and includes much of the material in his earlier books as well as in his *World's Great Men of Color.* In the Foreword of volume 1 (1940), Rogers wrote: "This book is dedicated to a better understanding among all the varieties of the human race," and added in Chapter 1: "We shall show in these pages that sex relations between so-called whites and blacks go back to prehistoric times on all the continents." All three volumes contain numerous photographs and have many footnotes and appendices.

Whether one agrees with some of Rogers's conclusions about "The Oldest Race" or his racial identification of individuals, the reader must bear the burden to prove the contrary. To be sure, the controversy concerning the first *Homo sapiens* continues; on the basis of knowledge available in 1940–1944, Rogers presented conclusions difficult to deny. His documented accounts of "les amours" of well-known personalities from ancient times to Shakespeare and Baudelaire, for example, through the 1930s and early 1940s shocked more readers then than later.

On a different level, his paragraphs about a speech by Marcus Garvey in Paris (Oct. 1928) are all the more valuable because this period of Garvey's life is relatively unknown.

It was Part II of volume 2, "Anglo-Saxon America," that probably led some historians and other writers to label Rogers a propagandist. This section, however, is as well documented and in most instances as cautious in its conclusions as are the other sections of the three volumes. Rogers was one of the very few historians of his period who mentioned, for example, Elleanor Aldridge (2:202) and Sally Hemings (2:221).

It is perhaps not surprising that no institution of higher learning in the United States conferred an honorary degree upon Rogers. In 1930, however, Rogers was elected to membership in the Paris Society of Anthropology and in the same year he was one of the speakers at the International Congress of Anthropology which was opened by Paul Doumer, president of France. He was also a member of the American Geographical Society and the Academy of Political Science.

Probably no competent critic of Rogers gave a more accurate evaluation than did Du Bois in *The World and Africa* (1947, p. xi): "I have learned much from James [i.e., Joel] A. Rogers. Rogers is an untrained American Negro writer who has done his work under great difficulty without funds and at much personal sacrifice. But no man living has revealed as many important facts about the Negro race as has Rogers. His mistakes are many and his background narrow but he is a true historical student." "A Proud West Indian," he was read more widely than either Du Bois or Woodson, for many barbershops and other popular places provided his books for customers.

He died at the St. Clare's Hospital, New York City, on March 26, 1965, after a few days' illness following a stroke. His funeral was kept secret at his request. He was survived by his widow, Helga Bresenthal Rogers; a half brother Jan H. Rogers, and a half sister Constance Hall (*The Crisis,* April 1966, p. 201).

Rogers deserves a full-length biography. He probably merits a higher rank among American historians than he has received. The sparse facts in *Who's Who in Colored America* (1950) are inadequate. He was, for example, one of the few columnists who publicly defended Du Bois when he was indicted (1951) for "failure to register as agent for a foreign principal." The best brief study is W. Burghardt Turner's "Joel Augustus Rogers: An Afro-American Historian" (*NHB,* Jan. 1972, pp. 34–38); it has a photograph and a comprehensive bibliography. — RAYFORD W. LOGAN

ROMAN, CHARLES VICTOR (1864–1934), physician, teacher, editor, and historian. He was born in Williamsport, Pa., the son of James Williams and Anne Walker (McGuin) Roman. His father, a canal boat owner, moved to Canada where he married and settled in Dundas, Ontario. Charles, one of five brothers, worked in a cotton mill and studied in a night school established for the mill boys by the Rev. Feathersome Osler, the father of the famous Sir William Osler (1849–1919), one of the greatest physicians and teachers of his era. After an injury to his right knee that required amputation, Charles entered the Hamilton Collegiate Institute, Ontario, and completed the four-year course in three years. He taught in the public schools of Kentucky and Tennessee, studied at Fisk University, and received his M.D. degree from Meharry Medical College, Nashville, Tenn. (1890). He practiced medicine briefly in Clarksville, Tenn., and in Dallas, Tex. (1890–1904). In 1904 he studied at the Royal Ophthalmic Hospital and Central Nose and Throat, and Ear Hospital, London. In that same year he was appointed to teach these subjects at Meharry; from 1919 to 1933 he was also director of health at Fisk University. He served as the fifth president of the National Medical Association (1904–1905), and was the first editor of the *Journal of the National Medi-*

cal Association (1909), serving until 1919. During World War I he was an official medical lecturer in the army (1918–1919). In 1891 he had married a schoolteacher, Margaret Vorhees of Dallas. They had no children.

Roman was not only well known as a teacher, physician, editor, and president of the National Medical Association, but was also the author of important books and addresses, notably A Knowledge of History Is Conducive to Racial Solidarity (1911), American Civilization and the Negro (1916), and "Racial Self-Respect and Racial Antagonism" (delivered before the Southern Sociological Congress, Atlanta, 1913).

Roman's A Knowledge of History Conducive to Racial Solidarity was published in 1911, and frequently delivered as an oration. Roman's interpretations of the subject were also clearly revealed in this publication and oration. He referred to the wars between Russia and Japan, and Abyssinia and Italy, as refutation of the canard that "only a white nation could defeat a white nation in battle." He derided the canard that "the Negro never made any history," pointing out that "because if anybody ever made any history he was not a Negro. Thus by circular reasoning they make their position logically invincible." He drove home his basic point by writing that "Racial solidarity and not amalgamation is the desired and desirable goal of the American Negro."

He favored Negro support of Negro institutions, labeling as an "ethnological curiosity . . . the Negro who does not wish to attend a Negro church, buy from a Negro merchant, consult a Negro lawyer or doctor, deposit in a Negro bank, or live in a Negro neighborhood, or send his children to a Negro school."

His conception of Negro history was unequivocal: "Oh! for a Negro pen to record the lives of our great men and women! I would not circumscribe the fields of learning nor rob white children of their pride of lineage; but I would teach Negro children the glorious deeds of Negro men and Negro women FIRST." A history of Methodism was as incomplete without Richard Allen as without John Wesley. At a time when their names were little known, he urged that Sissieretta Jones and Flora Batson should not be forgotten. And he added: "How could the story of the adaptation of popular education to the needs of the people be told without the name of [Booker T.] Washington; or the history of polemic protest against race prejudice be written without mentioning Du Bois?" Finally, he voiced the "hope that Negro scholarship will become self-luminous with a brilliancy that will give our race correct historical perspective, and lead us to that ethnological respectability and racial solidarity which the floods of prejudice have so persistently washed beyond our grasp." Rarely has a physician so ably healed the sick and so urgently urged the need for Negro history.

He died of a heart attack at his home, 130 14th Ave. North, Nashville, on Aug. 25, 1934. His funeral was held on Aug. 27 at St. Paul's A.M.E. Church, and he was buried in the family square, Greenwood Cemetery. He was survived by his widow, a sister, an adopted daughter, and a nephew, C. Lightfoot Roman of Mayfield, Canada (Nashville Banner, Aug. 26, 1934, p. 14).

The basic facts of Roman's career are in Who's Who in Colored America, edited by Thomas Yenser (1937). See also the obituary in JNH (Jan. 1935, pp. 116–17), probably written by Carter G. Woodson, and an article by William Montague Cobb in JNMA (July 1953, pp. 301–4. A Knowledge of History . . . may be conveniently found in Carter G. Woodson (ed.), Negro Orators and Their Orations (1925, pp. 643–52). There are reproductions of the cover of the first issue of the Journal of the National Medical Association (Jan.-March 1909), and an individual photograph of Roman and as a member of a group in Herbert M. Morais's The History of the Negro in Medicine (1967, pp. 69, 70).

— RAYFORD W. LOGAN

ROSE, EDWARD (? – ?), guide, hunter, and interpreter. Said to be an escaped slave, of Negro, Caucasian, and Cherokee ancestry, he was during the early nineteenth century a guide and interpreter for the better known, younger men who followed him. He was involved in most of the early ventures into the unknown West, toward the Rocky Mountains. He was one of the first of the "Mountain Men" and one of the most durable. There are several conflicting stories of his death. Hiram M. Chittenden in The American Fur Trade of the Far West (1954) says that Rose's grave was opposite the mouth of the Milk River. Rose was in the Manuel Lisa trapping expedition that left St. Louis in 1807 and established a trading post at the mouth of the Big Horn River. He was one of the Ezekiel Williams group of 1809 assigned to the sensitive task of escorting Big White, the Mandan chief, back to his home after he had come down the river with the returning explorers Lewis and Clark. It was the first all-land journey to the area around the mouth of the Little Missouri.

In 1811 Rose was guide and interpreter for the "Astorians" led by Wilson Price Hunt. The party met with disaster within a few days after Rose was relieved of his responsibility at the Big Horn River, a circumstance caused by Hunt's unfortunate distrust of Rose.

After another season with Lisa in 1812 Rose, as a trapper and chief of the Crow Indians, faded from view until 1823 when he joined the second William H. Ashley trapping venture. He distinguished himself in a battle with the Arikara Indians and was appointed a temporary officer, leading a mixed group of white soldiers and Indians in the "Missouri Legion" under the command of Col. Henry Leavenworth. It was Rose who, alone, entered the Arikara village to negotiate successfully an end to the hostilities. After the battle, which assured an open Missouri River toward the Rockies, Rose saved a group led by Jedediah Strong Smith which was traveling overland through the Badlands from the Missouri to the Rockies. This group has been described by Harrison Clifford Dale in The Ashley-Smith Explorations (1941) as "the most significant group of continental explorers ever brought together." In 1825 Rose was guide, hunter, and interpreter with a large treaty-making expedition to the Upper Missouri commanded by Gen. Henry Atkinson and Maj. Benjamin O'Fallon, where, single-handedly, Rose brought an angry band of 600 Crow braves under control.

In an era as adventurous as any the United States has

known, Rose was described by Colonel Leavenworth as a "brave and enterprising man." To Washington Irving he was "powerful in frame and fearless in spirit." He has been characterized by LeRoy Hafen and W. J. Ghent as a "daredevil adventurer," and Charles L. Camp wrote that he "displayed gallantry which brought high praise from his commanders." Hiram M. Chittenden observes that Rose bore a bad reputation, but adds that "everything definite that is known of him is entirely to his credit," and that "he would stand as high as any character in the history of the fur trade."

Ed Rose was invaluable as guide and interpreter. He knew the topography of the Upper Missouri region. He knew the languages and customs of the Indian tribes and was respected by them. He was one of the first men who blazed the trails that led to the great days of the fur trade and extension of the sovereignty of the United States.

A biography by Harold W. Felton, *Edward Rose, Negro Trail Blazer* (1967), contains a selected bibliography. See also Kenneth W. Porter's "Negroes and the Fur Trade" (*Minnesota History,* Dec. 1934, pp. 421–33) and J. Norman Heard's *The Black Frontiersmen; Adventures Among American Indians, 1528–1928* (1969). — HAROLD W. FELTON

ROUDANEZ, LOUIS CHARLES (1823–1890), physician, editor, and civil rights leader. He was born in St. James Parish, La., on June 2, 1823, the son of Louis Roudanez, a French merchant and Aimée Potens, a woman of color. His baptismal records register him as white, but by personal choice throughout his life he was considered colored. He received his early education in New Orleans, worked as a clerk at Hill and Cooley's notion store, and invested his savings in municipal bonds, later sold at a great profit. As a youth of twenty-one Roudanez enrolled at the University of Paris in 1844 to study medicine under the famous Dr. Phillipe Ricord. Within seven years he completed the required courses for his degree in medicine and returned to the United States. He then entered Cornell University for further studies and graduated four years later with a second degree in medicine. In 1857 he returned to New Orleans, opened his office for practice, and at once began to earn a lucrative income. In 1858 he married Celie Sauley, who bore him eight children, three of them sons who likewise became doctors of medicine.

In 1862 when New Orleans was taken by federal troops, and there were some 10,000 free men of color in the Crescent City, Roudanez believed it was time for his people to demand equality. He used newspapers to further this goal. The militant Republican journal *L'Union,* launched with his help in 1862, was the first Negro newspaper published in Louisiana. In it he published columns which stressed economic equality and abolition of slavery. In 1864 when *L'Union* was about to close for lack of sufficient support, Roudanez bought its rights and equipment, and with the assistance of his two brothers established *La Tribune de la Nouvelle Orléans* which became the first triweekly published in both English and French. Its first edition appeared on July 21, 1864. After Oct. 4, 1864, *La Tribune* became a daily newspaper, the first Negro daily to be published in the United States.

Under the editorship of a Belgian, Charles Houzeau, and a Negro, Charles Dallas of Texas, with Paul Trévigne as assistant editor, the *Tribune* was the organ of the Radical Republicans in Louisiana for four years. As early as Jan. 17, 1865, it declared: "We assert that the sons and grandsons of the colored men who were recognized French citizens, under the French rule, and whose rights were reserved in the treaty of cession—taken away from them since 1803—are not savages and uncivilized inhabitants of the wild swamps of Louisiana. We contend that the freedmen, who proved intelligent enough to shed their blood in defense of freedom and the National Flag, are competent to cast their votes into the ballotbox."

The *Tribune* supported (Feb. 22, 1865) the Freedmen's Aid Association, of which Roudanez was an officer, in its ambitious attempt to establish cooperatives among the recently emancipated slaves. It championed universal suffrage, weekly wages for the former slaves, and the denial of congressional seats to ex-Confederates. It also attacked white leaders in the Republican party who sought the colored vote by giving positions to tractable Negroes. Roudanez regularly wrote editorials staunchly championing Negro political rights but not social equality. During these four years the *Tribune* was one of the most influential Negro newspapers of the period (the *New Orleans Black Republican* was published only in 1865); it is an indispensable source for a study of Reconstruction politics in Louisiana.

Ironically Roudanez and the *Tribune* lost much of their influence after Negroes began to vote in large numbers (1867). Conflicting evidence suggests that Roudanez at first supported for lieutenant-governor in 1868 Francis E. Dumas, who had been one of the largest slaveholders. His defeat was attributed to Roudanez, and the *Tribune* temporarily closed during 1868. It was reactivated briefly in 1869 and then ceased publication. Its place was taken by the *New Orleans Louisianan,* founded by P. B. S. Pinchback in 1870.

Roudanez did not renew his political activities until 1873 when he supported the Unification Movement, a reform group that sought harmony between the races by fusing Negroes, Democrats, and conservatives. By that time, however, the tide had begun to turn against the Negroes' quest for equal rights. The struggle for power in Louisiana, "with the Negro as a pawn between the two forces of Northern and Southern capitalists" (Du Bois, *Black Reconstruction,* p. 482), probably further led Roudanez to confine his activities largely to the practice of medicine.

From 1873 until his death in 1890 Roudanez had less and less to do with politics. He devoted his life to his family and to his medical practice. He regained part of the fortune he lost in closing *La Tribune,* he visited his children at school in Paris, and he endeavored to live out his years in peaceful service to his community.

The principal printed sources are Rodolphe L. Desdunes's *Nos Hommes et Notre Histoire* (1911), translated and edited by Sister Dorothea Olga McCants as *Our People and Our History* (1973), Charles B. Roussève's *The Negro in Louisiana, Aspects of His History and His Literature* (1937), and A. E. Perkins's "James Henri Burch and Oscar James Dunn in Louisiana" (*JNH,* July 1937, pp. 321–34).

— DOROTHEA OLGA MCCANTS, D.C.

RUFFIN, GEORGE L[EWIS] (1834–1886), lawyer and judge. He was born in Richmond, Va., the first son of George W. and Nancy (Lewis) Ruffin, free Negroes who had little property but some education. The family of eight children moved in 1853 to Boston, where young Ruffin attended the Chapman Hall School and began his long association with the Republican party. He graduated from Chapman Hall and in 1858 married Josephine St. Pierre of Boston. Disheartened by the Dred Scott decision in 1857, they sailed for Liverpool in 1858 but returned six months later to Boston, where Ruffin earned his living as a barber. Because of nearsightedness, he was unable to enlist in the 55th Massachusetts Colored Regiment. While he and his wife were active in the Home Guard and the Sanitary Commission, Ruffin began to earn a reputation. His review (1863) in the *Anglo-African,* a Negro weekly published in New York City, cited serious omissions and an excess of misinformation in *The Black Man, His Antecedents, His Achievements,* by William Wells Brown. As a delegate to the National Negro Convention (Oct. 1864) in Syracuse, N.Y., which demanded Negro suffrage and supported Lincoln for reelection, Ruffin was described as a "great man."

Continuing his barbering, he read law with the firm of Jewell Gaston and was admitted to the Harvard Law School, which did not then require a college degree. He graduated in 1869, the first Negro to earn the LL.B. degree from Harvard, and perhaps the first American Negro to graduate from a university law school and obtain a law degree. He was admitted to the Suffolk County bar on Sept. 18, 1869. One of the first Negroes admitted to practice law in Boston, he joined the firm of Harvey Jewell. He and Jewell won seats in 1869 and 1870 from the Old Ward 6 in the state legislature, where Ruffin focused his attention on the violence in the South and was known as an able speaker and debater. In 1876 and 1877 he was elected to the Boston Common Council and continued his attendance at Negro conventions, presiding over the New Orleans meeting in 1872. He developed a thriving law practice, and at the request of his friend Frederick Douglass, wrote the introduction to the 1881 revision of his *The Life and Times of Frederick Douglass.* In November 1883 he was appointed by Benjamin Butler, the Democratic governor of Massachusetts, a judge of a municipal court in Charlestown (some ten years after Mifflin W. Gibbs had been elected a judge in Little Rock, Ark.). In 1883 he was also appointed consul resident in Boston for the Dominican Republic.

On Nov. 20, 1886, he died in Boston of Bright's disease, after several weeks of illness. He had contributed so much money to charities and racial uplift that he died almost impecunious. He was survived by his widow, three sons, and a daughter.

He and his wife were among the more prominent colored citizens of Boston. A son and Butler R. Wilson, another prominent lawyer, were partners in his law firm. Among those who sent congratulations to Ruffin on his appointment as judge were the historian, George Washington Williams, then residing in Boston, T. Thomas Fortune, editor of the *New York Freeman,* and Douglass.

Ruffin did not mute his insistence on equality after his appointment. He wrote Douglass a note of congratulation after his marriage—the second—to a white woman, Helen Pitts, which created a stormy controversy. His article, "A Look Forward," in the prominent *A.M.E. Church Review* (July 1885), defended the marriage and asserted that racial amalgamation, however unpopular, was the "final" and "inevitable" solution of the race problem. He attended the first meeting of the Massachusetts Colored League in 1883, which urged Negroes to vote as independents.

Ruffin had been the first president of the Wendell Phillips Club of Boston, and a member and one-time president of the Banneker Literary Club of Boston. For twelve years he was superintendent and an important officer of the Twelfth Baptist Church of Boston, one of the most influential in the city.

The brief laudatory sketch in William J. Simmons's *Men of Mark . . .* (1887) was probably written by Ruffin. His personality is delineated in William Wells Brown's *The Rising Sun* (1874) and in the brief references to Mrs. Ruffin in Hallie Q. Brown's *Homespun Heroines and Other Women of Distinction* (1926, pp. 151–53). A brief summary is Emory L. West's "Harvard's Black Graduates" (*Harvard Bulletin,* May 1972). A major portion of the Ruffin Papers are in the Moorland-Spingarn Research Center, Howard University.

— CLARENCE G. CONTEE, SR.

RUFFIN, JOSEPHINE ST. PIERRE (1842–1924), clubwoman and civil rights leader. Ruffin was born in Boston, the fifth daughter and last of six children of John and Eliza Matilda (Menhenick) St. Pierre. Her mother was born in Cornwall, England. Her father, the son of a Frenchman from Martinique and of Betsey Hill of Negro, French, and Indian descent, was a clothes dealer in Boston and a founder of Zion Baptist Church. Because the schools were segregated in Boston until 1855, Ruffin attended public schools in Salem, continuing her education in Boston after 1855. In 1858, at a time when young women married early, she became the wife of George Lewis Ruffin. They lived for several months in Liverpool, England, hoping to find refuge from the racial discrimination in the United States, but soon returned to Boston. During the Civil War they were active members of the Home Guard and, through the Sanitary Commission, mended and made clothes at the Twelfth Baptist Church.

The Ruffins, friends of Frederick Douglass and William Lloyd Garrison, were active in furthering the advancement of Negroes. Mrs. Ruffin participated in civil rights causes, local welfare work, and the women's suffrage movement. In 1879, when southern Negroes no longer found a welcome in Boston, she helped organize the Boston Kansas Relief Association to aid those who chose to move to Kansas. She served for many years as a visitor for the Associated Charities of Boston, worked with Julia Ward Howe and Lucy Stanton on the Massachusetts Moral Education Association and the Massachusetts School Suffrage Association, of which she was a charter member.

When her husband died in 1886 almost impecunious because of his gifts to charity and welfare causes, Ruffin expanded her own career. Her children became well-respected members of the Boston community. Hubert practiced law and served in the Boston Common Council and state legislature; Stanley became an inventor and organist, and George was also an organist. Florida Ruffin (Mrs. Ridley) taught in the Boston public schools and, with her mother, was a member of women's organizations. Despite the responsibilities of rearing her children, Ruffin gained recognition for herself.

She is best known for her concern for the rights of women. In early 1889 she expressed to white women of the Georgia Educational League her pleasure that they were willing to help uplift Negro children in the South, and added that Negro women in the North were ready to assist them. In the early 1890s she served as one of the editors of the Negro weekly, *Boston Courant,* and was a member of the New England Women's Press Association until the early twentieth century.

It was her interest in the Women's Club Movement that gained her national prominence. In 1894 with her daughter, Florida Ridley, and Maria Baldwin, a Boston school principal, she organized the Women's Era Club, which soon included sixty prominent Negroes in Boston. Its aim was to further the welfare of Negroes in general and Negro women in particular. At the same time she continued her friendship with Mrs. Howe, Susan B. Anthony, and Elizabeth Cady Stanton, and participated in the white women's club movement in Massachusetts.

In August 1895 she called a convention of Negro women at the Charles Street A.M.E. Church in Boston and expressed the hope of demonstrating the existence of a "large and growing class" of intelligent and cultured Negro women. She believed in integration and blamed southern white women for forcing Negroes to establish separate organizations. A National Federation of Afro-American Women, with Ruffin as president, was formed. In 1896 her organization was merged in Washington with a rival organization, headed by Mary Church Terrell, to become the National Association of Colored Women. Terrell was president and Ruffin one of the vice-presidents. Ruffin was also instrumental in developing in 1896 the Northeastern Federation of Women's Clubs.

The most dramatic incident of her career resulted from her attempt to gain recognition by white women for her Women's New Era Club, whose monthly *Woman's Era* she edited. It was affiliated with the Massachusetts State Federation of Women's Clubs of which she was a member of the executive board. She also served on the executive committee of the General Federation of Women's Clubs, which had accepted the Women's New Era Club for membership. But at the Milwaukee Convention of the General Federation (1900), where she was a delegate for three groups, two white and one Negro, opposition by southern white women prevented representation of the New Era Club.

The convention was willing to accept her as a representative of the two white clubs but not of the New Era Club. Ruffin refused to accept the evasion, and the General Federation of Women's Clubs continued its color bar for many years.

Although the New Era Club ceased to exist, Ruffin aided in the establishment of the Association for the Promotion of Child Training in the South, of the lively Boston branch of the NAACP, and with Maria Baldwin, of the League of Women for Community Service. She helped found in 1902 the American Mount Coffee School Association for the enlargement of the school in Liberia and served as its vice-president.

Ruffin died of nephritis in Boston on March 13, 1924. Funeral services were held in Trinity Episcopal Church where she had been a member. She was buried in Mount Auburn Cemetery, Cambridge.

The best brief account of Ruffin's life is the sketch by Adelaide Cromwell Hill in *NAW* (1970, 3:206–8), with a comprehensive bibliography. Emma L. Fields's "The Women's Club Movement in the United States, 1870–1900" (master's thesis, Howard University, 1958, esp. p. 62–86) is valuable notably for the Milwaukee Convention, which is summarized in Rayford W. Logan's *The Betrayal of the Negro from Rutherford B. Hayes to Woodrow Wilson* (1965, pp. 238–41). Some of the Ruffin Papers and incomplete files of the New Era Club are in the Moorland-Spingarn Research Center, Howard University, and the Amistad Research Center, New Orleans. See also "Josephine St. Pierre Ruffin at Milwaukee, 1900," by Pauline Hopkins (*Colored American Magazine,* July 1902, pp. 210–13), and "Some Famous Women" (Aug. 1902, pp. 273–77).

— CLARENCE G. CONTEE, SR.

RUGGLES, DAVID (1810–1849), businessman, abolitionist, journalist, and hydropathist. Born in Norwich, Conn., the eldest of four sons and one daughter of David and Nancy Ruggles, both free-born, young David may have received his early education in the Sabbath School for the Poor in Norwich, which admitted free people of color as early as 1815. In 1827 he went to New York City where from 1829 to 1833 he was in the grocery business. His shop was on the same street where young James Hope, the white father of John Hope, had opened a successful grocery store in 1827. In early 1834 he left the grocery business and opened a bookshop at 67 Lispenard St. near Broadway, where he circulated abolitionist, anticolonization, and other publications and prints. He was thus "the earliest known American Negro bookseller." He also did job printing, letterpress work, picture framing, bookbinding, and composed letters on "such subjects as his abilities are capable of comprehending on moderate terms." In September 1835, his bookstore was burned by a white mob.

Beginning in 1833 as a traveling agent for the *Emancipator and Journal of Public Morals,* an abolitionist weekly, Ruggles wrote articles and pamphlets, edited a newspaper, and gave lectures denouncing slavery and colonization. Financial difficulties, ill health, and temporary virtual blindness in 1842 ended his career as one of the better known abolitionists. He then began a career as a hydropathist until the recurrence of an in-flamed optic nerve in his left eye in September 1849. With his mother and sister at his side, he died on Dec. 26, 1849, of a severe case of inflamation of the bowels. His remains were interred in the Norwich cemetery, not far from the house in which he was born.

In his lectures as traveling agent in various eastern cities for the *Emancipator,* he secured subscriptions for the paper and emphasized the importance of the press as a means of promoting the economic, cultural, and social progress of colored citizens. Six essays in the *Emancipator* (Jan. 13–Feb. 17, 1835) stressed the need for a free press, condemned the American Colonization Society, urged immediate emancipation as the only remedy for slavery, and made a special plea for support of the paper by women. "Our hope for victory, under God, is in the power of the *press*" (emphasis in the article, Feb. 10, 1835).

His stature as a journalist grew with a renewed attack on colonization in his first pamphlet, *Extinguisher, Extinguished . . .* (1834). A year later in his *Abrogation of the Seventh Commandment, by the American Churches* he attacked the proslavery hypocrites who sought to use the prestige of the church to keep the Negro in a status quo, and boldly cited the condition of the Negro female slaves who could not offer any resistance to the "incessant licentiousness of the white slave holding population." Numerous published letters and editorials and other printed pamphlets mark Ruggles as one of the best of the early Negro writers. Another journalistic effort was the *Mirror of Liberty,* which he edited and published in New York from 1838 to 1841. His strong arguments protesting colonization, segregation, disfranchisement, and slavery established him as a "critical, witty and logical writer."

Ruggles, an active and daring "conductor" on the Underground Railroad from 1835 to 1838, received fugitives in New York sent to him by William Still in Philadelphia. He cared for them before sending them on to Albany and other cities in the North. As secretary of the New York Vigilance Committee, organized in 1835, Ruggles led a dangerous existence, often seeking in court to prove the free status of kidnapped Negroes. He urged that fugitives be brought into court by a writ of habeas corpus and be given a jury trial in order that the status of the so-called slave be determined. Ruggles's hatred of the slaveholder and his love of freedom made him a thorn in the side of many southern slave-holders. The New York Vigilance Committee, with the aid of Ruggles, handled some 300 cases of fugitive slaves during the first year of its existence. The most famous, in September 1838, was Frederick Washington Bailey (who later changed his name to Frederick Douglass).

Ruggles was annoyed by personal feuds with his associates and the lack of their support. He became involved in court cases and libel suits. In one instance on Dec. 28, 1835, he was arrested and sent to jail. From 1837 to 1842 Ruggles had been under the care of several physicians in New York, one of whom in 1839 had urged him to discontinue work. Early in 1842, almost completely blind and with no financial resources, Ruggles was in such poor health that his physician gave him only a few weeks to live. In the fall of 1842, Lydia Maria Child, a prominent white abolitionist, learned of Ruggles's condition and made it possible for him to visit Florence, a suburb of Northampton, Mass., and her home. The Northampton Association of Education and Industry accepted Ruggles as a member. This community organization was composed of "practical abolitionists" who worked and lived together under a principle of "equal brotherhood."

While Ruggles was recuperating in this "paradise" he learned of the successful treatment of disease through hydrotherapy. Since drugs and various treatments had not helped Ruggles, he decided to treat himself by the natural remedy of water, diet, and rest. After eighteen months of treatment with the aid of a medical practitioner, his health was restored and his eyesight improved to the extent that he was able to see enough to walk without help. His case convinced acquaintances who were sick that a water treatment had advantages. Since Ruggles had equipment for bathing which he had constructed for his own use, he began to treat a few persons. Ruggles had remarkable ability to diagnose ailments by his acute sense of touch. He believed that the skin was the "organ through which the symptoms and characters of diseases" were indicated, a theory which he called "cutaneous electricity" (*North Star,* Feb. 23, 1849).

His first patients were members of the Northampton Association of Education and Industry. Success with them secured for him the patronage of wealthy friends who advanced him $2000 for the erection of a building. On Jan. 1, 1846, Ruggles purchased "the oilmill house" on the picturesque bank of the Mill River which furnished him with an abundant supply of water. Here he erected the first new building exclusively for hydropathic purposes in the United States. The building contained twenty rooms and had separate parlors, bathing, and dressing rooms for men and women. Ruggles's advertisement in newspapers stated that he could cure "headache, bronchitis, general and nervous debility, pulmonary affections, liver complaints, jaundice, acute and chronic inflammatory rheumatism, neuralgia, sciatica, lame limbs, paralysis, fevers, salt rheum, scrofulous and erysipelas humors." At the same time he said that hydropathy was not a cure for every disease. His first case to attract attention was reported in the *Northampton Democrat* of June 1844. His numerous cures were reported in the water-cure journals and in the newspapers. The water-cure journals and the antislavery newspapers carried many editorials and letters describing the successful treatments of cases by Ruggles at Northampton. They spoke of his "skill, acute perception, energy, perseverance and his pure carbon waters."

Soon many persons came seeking relief and cure. Sojourner Truth, at age forty-nine suffering from several illnesses for which her physician had told her there was no cure, found relief after one week of treatment by Ruggles. At the end of her tenth week she left the establishment cured of scrofulous humors and dyspepsia. Her case was reported in the press on Dec. 31, 1845. William Lloyd Garrison, the abolitionist, was one of the best known patients at the Northampton water-cure establishment. Several supposedly incurable women taking the treatment published statements concerning their cures. One, the wife of a slaveholder, stated that the "doctor" was destined to become so "extensively known as to secure for himself that wide reputation as a skilfull diagnostist and hydropathist." She further wrote that there had been a change in public opinion during the last five years toward Ruggles's theory of "cutaneous electricity." "Now, almost every acknowledged scientific psychological writer in this country or Europe who has investigated the subject from Baron Liebig, to Dr. J. B. Dodd, sustains Dr. Ruggles' theory and he is justly regarded as the discoverer of cutaneous electricity. . . ."

Ruggles had from the beginning emphasized the dependence of cure on the electrical action present in the skin. In a long letter dated March 30, 1846, to a friend, Ruggles described in detail his method of diagnosis and cure. From January 1846 to March 1849 he purchased and leased approximately 112 acres of land and erected several fine buildings.

Acquaintances described Ruggles as a man of "ordinary size, with an athletic form and dark complexion," and noted that he had "an intelligent and benevolent countenance." He encountered perils with the courage of a martyr and commanded the respect of all who knew him. Many persons owed their life to him. He literally wore himself out in support of his causes.

For documentation about Ruggles, see four articles by Dorothy B. Porter: "David Ruggles, An Apostle of Human Rights" (*JNH*, Jan. 1943, pp. 23–50); "David Ruggles, 1810–1849: Hydropathic Pioneer" (*JNMA*, Jan. 1957, pp. 67–72, and March 1957, pp. 130–34); and "The Water Cure" (with the collaboration of Edwin C. Rozueni), in *The Northampton Book* (1954, pp. 121–26). In addition to several articles in the *Liberator, Green Mountain Spring, Hampshire Gazette* and the *North Star,* contemporary evidence of Ruggles's established reputation in *Water Cure Journal* (Feb. and Nov. 15, 1847; April 15, 1847) is particularly valuable. Some of Ruggles's most significant writings are in *Early Negro Writing 1760–1837,* selected and introduced by Dorothy Porter (1971). Vital statistics are in MSS Records, Office of Registry of Deeds, Northampton, Massachusetts. — DOROTHY B. PORTER

RUSSWURM, JOHN BROWN (1799–1851), early college graduate, editor, abolitionist, colonizationist, and government official in Liberia. He was born a slave in Port Antonio, Jamaica, of the union between a white American merchant bachelor, John Russwurm, and one of his female slaves whose name is not known. For the next eight years the boy was treated as free and stayed in Jamaica with his father. As was the custom of the day, some mulatto children were often sent elsewhere to be educated. The father sent John Brown, as he was then known, to Québec in 1807 to receive good formal schooling. In 1812 the father left Jamaica to settle as a merchant in Portland, Me., then a part of Massachusetts. There he married the next year Susan Blanchard, who insisted that the father give the boy the family name and treat him as a member of the family. Even after the death of the father in 1815, John Brown Russ-

wurm stayed with his new mother. In 1819 he left home to go to school at Hebron Academy, Hebron, Me., as preparation for going to college to be a minister or doctor. In September 1824 he entered Bowdoin College in Brunswick, Me. He graduated on Sept. 6, 1826, as one of the very early Negro graduates of an American college. (Although Russwurm was thought to be the "first" Negro graduate of an American college, he was probably the third. Edward Jones received his B.A. degree from Amherst College two weeks before Russwurm's graduation, and Alexander L. Twilight graduated from Middlebury College [Vt.] in 1823.) Russwurm, in his commencement speech, hinted that he wanted to migrate to Haiti, then the only independent Negro Latin American nation. Instead he settled in Liberia, where he was an editor and government official. He died and was buried in Liberia in 1851.

Russwurm's principal historical significance was his effort to found the Negro press in the United States. When he graduated from Bowdoin in 1826, he migrated to New York City, then one of the centers of the free Negro population. The press of the city was pro-slavery and scurrilous in its attacks on the free Negro in the United States. As a consequence there emerged the idea that Negroes needed their own voice, a press, to answer these attacks and to work for the abolition of slavery. In the winter of 1826–1827 a group of Negro leaders in New York City met at the home of M. Boston Crummell and agreed to launch a newspaper. On March 16, 1827, the first issue of the first Negro newspaper in the United States, *Freedom's Journal,* appeared. Samuel E. Cornish, a Presbyterian minister, was the senior editor, and Russwurm was the other editor. Agents for the paper worked in Canada, the United States, Haiti, and England. Among the agents was David Walker of Boston, who published his provocative "Walker's Appeal" first in the pages of *Freedom's Journal.* In the first issue the editors noted that the chief reason for the paper was that it was going to plead "our own cause." At first the newspaper was an active voice in the abolition struggle and in the fight against the efforts to colonize free American Negroes in Africa. Its ultimate aim was full and equal citizenship. The weekly newspaper at first sustained itself by subscriptions and by ads.

On Sept. 14, 1827, the partnership between Cornish and Russwurm came to an end. Since Cornish wanted to devote full time to his ministry, Russwurm became sole editor. In the same issue (Sept. 14, 1827) Russwurm said that *Freedom's Journal* was going to examine carefully the problem of colonization. The issue also stated that it was fostering a "national solidarity race movement." Russwurm had indicated that he was a Negro nationalist. On Feb. 14, 1829, however, Russwurm told his astonished readers that he had been converted to colonization in Africa. Shortly thereafter, in March 1829, Russwurm ceased his role as editor. He had decided to move to Liberia as the only place where Negroes could develop themselves since, he believed, they could never enjoy full citizenship in the United States. Cornish resumed the editorship and continued the paper for a year under a new name, *The Rights of All.*

In November 1829 Russwurm arrived in Monrovia, Liberia. He spent the rest of his life in Liberia as an editor, educator, and public official. He edited the *Liberia Herald* from 1830 to 1835, when he resigned in protest against the efforts of the American Colonization Society to control it. From 1830 to 1836 he was the superintendent of education in the Monrovia colony. In both capacities he advocated the migration of Afro-Americans to Liberia. He became one of the first Negro colonial agents for the American Colonization Society from about 1834 to 1836. By this time he had begun to master several of the African languages in Liberia. In 1836, after working for a few years as an advisor, Russwurm was appointed as governor of the Maryland in Liberia Settlement, which had been founded by the Maryland Colonization Society in 1834 at Cape Palmas. The first Negro to hold rank as a governor in Negro Africa, his appointment was considered a test of the political abilities of Negroes. An able administrator, he worked cooperatively with Africans, with emigrants, and with whites. He encouraged agriculture and trade, built a stone jail that could also be used as a fort, took a census in 1843, and established a court with presiding justices. He and Joseph Jenkins Roberts, the Negro governor of the ACS colony, paved the way for the annexation of the Maryland in Liberia Settlement, which took place five years after Russwurm's death on June 9, 1851.

At his death he was highly praised for his gubernatorial skills. He was survived by his wife, Sarah McGill Russwurm, a daughter of Lieutenant-Governor McGill, and four of their five children. A monument was erected to him in Harper, Cape Palmas, where he was buried; Russwurm Island off the promontory of Cape Palmas was named for him. He had left his mark as one of the founders of the Negro press in the United States and as a colonizationist who wanted to see Liberia become a demonstration of the abilities of the Negro people.

There is no satisfactory full-length biography of Russwurm. Mary Sagarin's *John Brown Russwurm, The Story of Freedom's Journal* (1970) is for juveniles. A brief sketch by W. E. B. Du Bois is in *DAB* ([1935] 1963, 8, Part 2:253). See also William M. Brewer's "John Brown Russwurm" (*JNH,* Oct. 1928, pp. 413–22) and Philip S. Foner (ed.), "John Brown Russwurm, A Document" (*JNH,* Oct. 1969, pp. 393–97). His career in Liberia and a biographical sketch (inaccurate in some details) are in Charles Henry Huberich's *The Political and Legislative History of Liberia . . .* (2 vols., 1947, passim). His views are expressed in *Freedom's Journal* and in *African Repository,* the organ of the American Colonization Society. Major primary sources are the papers of the American Colonization Society and the Maryland Colonization Society, deposited in the Library of Congress and the Maryland Historical Society, respectively. — CLARENCE G. CONTEE, SR.

SALEM, PETER (1750–1816), American Revolutionary War soldier. He was born in Framingham, Mass., the slave of Jeremiah Belknap, who came from Salem (hence Peter's last name). Belknap sold Salem to Maj. Lawson Buckminster. Negroes had been excluded from militia service in Massachusetts since 1656 because of fear that they might participate in slave insurrections. Sheer need for soldiers during the French and Indian Wars, however, was greater than the fear, and the service of Negroes during these wars facilitated their enrollment during the early days of the American Revolution. The Committee on Safety in May 1775 permitted free Negroes, but not slaves, to be used. Some slaves were used but, more significantly, some were freed. Among them was Peter Salem, one of the Minutemen who had fought at Concord on April 19, 1775. On April 24, 1775, Salem enlisted in Capt. Thomas Drury's company of Col. John Nixon's 5th Massachusetts Regiment, and served with it in the Battle of Bunker Hill (it was really fought at Breed's Hill).

According to a widely accepted belief, Salem fired the shot that killed British Maj. John Pitcairn at the Battle of Bunker Hill on June 17, 1775. Twelve years later Dr. Jeremy Belknap recorded in his diary that someone who was present at the battle had told him that "A negro man belonging to Groton, took aim at Major Pitcairne [*sic*], as he was rallying the dispersed British troops shot him thro' the head." Samuel Swett, whose eighteenth-century chronicle is the first published account, wrote: "Among the foremost of the [British] leaders was the gallant Maj. Pitcairn, who exultingly cried 'the day is ours,' when Salem, a black soldier, and a number of others shot him through and he fell." Even in a small engagement of this kind participants frequently differ about a particular event; second- or thirdhand accounts necessarily vary. It is clear, however, that Peter Salem did fight in the battle and *may* have been one of those who killed Major Pitcairn.

John Trumbull, who witnessed the battle from Roxbury across the harbor, may have talked with Salem but Trumbull was in London in 1786 when he painted the Battle of Bunker Hill. In that painting, now in the Yale University Art Gallery, Salem is a Negro servant of Lieutenant Grosvenor, and the likeness may have been based on a model in Trumbull's London studio. The musket which Salem holds in his hand was of the French Charleville type, preserved in the National Museum of History and Technology, Division of Military History, Smithsonian Institution. The 1801 engraving by John Mitan of Trumbull's painting gives the same prominence to Salem, but according to William C. Nell's *The Colored Patriots of the American Revolution* (1855), later engravings omitted Salem.

Although best known for his role at Bunker Hill, Salem reenlisted in the Massachusetts regiment in January 1776 and fought also at Saratoga and Stony Point. Gen. George Washington on July 10, 1775, issued instructions that no more Negroes were to be recruited but those already serving, like Peter Salem, could complete their terms. On Nov. 12, 1775, Washington issued orders prohibiting Negroes from serving, whether new volunteers or those seeking to reenlist. After he learned that Lord Dunmore, governor of Virginia, on Nov. 7 had proclaimed free all Negroes willing to serve under the British flag, Washington on Dec. 30 ordered recruiting officers to enlist free Negroes and the Continental Congress approved (Jan. 16, 1776) the reenlistment of free Negroes. Salem reenlisted in January and served until the end of the war. After the war he built a cabin near Leicester, Mass., and wove cane for a living. In 1816 he died in the poorhouse in Framingham, whose citizens in 1882 erected a monument to his memory, with the inscription: "Peter Salem/ A Soldier of the Revolution/ Concord/ Bunker Hill/ Saratoga/ Died, August 16th, 1816."

Sidney Kaplan summarizes Belknap and Swett, adds some additional details, and has photographs of the Charleville musket, Mitan's rendering of Trumbull's painting, and a detail of Lieutenant Grosvenor and Salem in the original (*The Black Presence in the Era of the American Revolution 1770–1800* [1973], pp. 18–19, frontispiece and p. 19, Plate 1, following p. 84, respectively). Benjamin Quarles's *The Negro in the American Revolution* (1961) and John Hope Franklin's *From Slavery to Freedom* (4th ed., 1974) do not give Salem sole credit for the slaying of Major Pitcairn.

— RAYFORD W. LOGAN

SANDERSON, JEREMIAH BURKE (1821–1875), abolitionist, California civil rights leader, educator, and clergyman. Sanderson was born in New Bedford, Mass., on Aug. 10, 1821. His father, Daniel, was of Scottish descent and his mother, Sarah, of African and Gay-Head Indian descent. He attended elementary schools for Negro children in New Bedford. As a young man he earned the reputation as one of the best read Negroes in New England. He became a barber and practiced his trade in New Bedford and Wareham, Mass. He made his first reported public address as an active abolitionist in 1841 in Nantucket at an antislavery meeting, at which Frederick Douglass also made his debut. Throughout the 1840s Sanderson lectured in Massachusetts and upper New York State. In 1853 he became a member of the National Council of the National Colored Convention that met in Rochester, N.Y. In 1854 Sanderson left for California, leaving behind his wife Catherine and five children. One of the children joined him in California in 1860.

During his New England years he was an active abolitionist. He grew up in an atmosphere dominated by the militant abolitionism of William Lloyd Garrison. During the growing schism between Garrison and Frederick Douglass in the early 1850s Sanderson seemed to avoid taking sides, although there is evidence that he quietly leaned toward Douglass. Douglass spoke and wrote flatteringly of Sanderson. But the internecine warfare between abolitionists was anathema to the gentle nature of the man. It may have been one of the reasons why he left for California shortly after a New Bedford conference of Negroes rejected emigrationism abroad but endorsed going to California. On Nov. 20, 1855, he was one of the signers of a petition for civil rights, especially the right to give testimony in court.

He was a secretary and delegate to the 1855 and 1856 Colored Conventions of California. He taught school in Sacramento for several months while attempting to influence the local board of education to grant financial support to the school for Negro children. In 1859 he took charge of the public school for colored children in San Francisco. He remained in this position as a teacher and principal until 1865. During his years

as a teacher he was also a pastor in the African Methodist Episcopal church. He was the organizer and first president in San Francisco of the Young Men's Union Beneficial Society, a Negro cultural and self-education organization. He was also one of the organizers of the Franchise League (Aug. 12, 1862), one of the trustees of the Ladies' Union Beneficial Society and of the Ladies Pacific Accumulating and Benevolent Association, both of San Francisco. From 1868 to 1874 he was in charge of the Stockton school for colored children. It was here that he established his statewide reputation as a fine teacher. Sanderson, with other leading Negroes in California, organized a statewide conference in 1871 to work for integrated education. Another prominent lobbyist was Mifflin W. Gibbs. He also entered the political arena and was elected to the Republican State Judicial Convention in 1873. In 1874 he moved to Oakland to assume pastoral duties and to take the leadership in the Equal Rights League of Oakland, where a rapidly growing Negro community was emerging. On Aug. 19, 1875, he was killed in a train accident in Oakland.

Sanderson was a staunch antimigrationist and in public matters he stood for civil rights for the Negro. His public statements also reflected pride in his African ancestry and a deep involvement in his church work. In 1875 he was elected secretary of the state conference of the A.M.E. churches of California and the state delegate to the A.M.E. national conference in Atlanta. He died before he could fulfill this charge.

Rudolph M. Lapp's "Jeremiah B. Sanderson: Early California Leader" (*JNH*, Oct. 1968) and references in Delilah Beasley's *The Negro Trail Blazers of California . . .* (1919) are the principal sources, the latter containing a passage from his diary. The Papers of the beneficial society are in the California State Archives, Sacramento. — RUDOLPH M. LAPP

SASH, MOSES (1755– ?), farmer and laborer. Sash appears to have been a leading participant in Shays Rebellion which took place in Massachusetts in the winter of 1786–1787. His grandparents may have been Robbin Freeman and Ann Sash, whose marriage was recorded in the Unitarian Church of Bridgewater, Plymouth County, as occurring in 1737 or 1738. It cannot be established definitely whether Ann Sash was white or Negro; Freeman, a common surname taken by free Negroes (free man), was probably exchanged for Sash as the family name. The same record discloses the marriage of their two children: Mary Sash, a "Negro woman," and Tom Drew, a "Negro man," were married in 1755; Moses Sash and Sarah Colly, "molatoes," in 1752. (Stoughton town records reveal a second marriage of Sarah Sash to Samson Dunbar of Braintree in 1765.) To them, in nearby Stoughton, were born a daughter, Hulda (1753), and a son, Moses (1755). In 1770 the authorities, for reasons not ascertainable, warned Hulda Sash to depart the town. Whether Moses left with her is uncertain. There is, however, a record in 1777 of his residence in Cummington, a town adjacent to Worthington in Hampshire County.

The rebellion was in large part caused by the economic instability of Massachusetts after the Revolutionary War. The state had incurred a large debt; special taxes were imposed, soldiers were not paid, debtors were jailed, and mortgages foreclosed. Using many of the methods of organization employed during the Revolutionary War the encumbered farmers arose to demand paper money and to protest taxes. The rebellion indicated that the popular control of government was still strong and was a forerunner of the Whiskey Rebellion. Sash, thirty-two at the time of the rebellion, was described in the documents as five feet, eight inches tall with a black complexion and woolly hair.

He had enlisted in August 1777 as a private in Col. Ruggles Woodbridge's Regiment and spent three and one half years in the Northern Department. In May 1781 he reenlisted for a three-year term in Cummington as a private in Lt.-Col. John Brooks's 7th Regiment, but the war ended before the end of his term.

Evidence of his participation in Shays Rebellion is on the back of Document 159060 in the Office of the Clerk, Suffolk County Courthouse, Boston. This document refers to Sash as "a Captain and one of Saises Councill." The indictment charges in part that on Jan. 20, 1787, he "did advise persuade invite incourage and procure divers persons citizens of this Commonwealth by force of arms to oppose this Commonwealth and the government thereof." Forced to flee from Arsenal Hill in Springfield by government troops, the rebels were chased through Chicopee and South Hadley and were rallied by Shays in Pelham, where they dispersed to find food and guns. The second indictment, Document 159059 (also in the Office of the Clerk, Suffolk County Courthouse, Boston), states that on Jan. 30 in South Hadley, Sash "fraudulently, unlawfully and feloniously two gun . . . with force of arms did steal, take and carry away." According to Sidney Kaplan, members of Shays' council of war and directors of the rebel strategy were expressly excluded from indemnity. The fact that Sash was indicted rather than indemnified further indicates that he was probably among the leaders of the rebellion. No court action was taken on the indictments against Sash because John Hancock, the incoming governor, pardoned almost all of the participants in the uprising. Among those indicted, according to Kaplan, Sash was the only Negro, the only laborer, and the only subject of two indictments. Although virtually unknown to most historians, Moses Sash deserves mention with Crispus Attucks as a rebel in the early history of the United States. There is no information about his later life.

The best published source is the article by Sidney Kaplan, "A Negro Veteran in Shays' Rebellion" (*JNH*, April 1948, pp. 123–29). The information about Sash's ancestry and early life is in footnote 4, page 126, of Kaplan's article. The transcription of the indictments against Sash was made by Susan Mentser.

— JEWEL H. BELL

SAUNDERS [SANDERS], PRINCE (? –1839), educator, author, Mason, and colonizationist. Born in either Lebanon, Conn., or Thetford, Vt., the son of African-born Cuff and Phyllis Saunders, and baptized on July 25, 1784, at Lebanon, he had his early schooling in Thetford, taught a colored school in Colchester, Conn., and studied in Moor's Charity School at Dartmouth College

in 1807 and 1808. On the recommendation of Pres. John Wheelock of Dartmouth, he began teaching in Boston in November 1808 at Boston's African School. He favorably impressed influential Bostonians, notably the Unitarian minister William Ellery Channing. In 1811 Saunders became secretary of the African Masonic Lodge and founded and administered the Belles Lettres Society, a literary group of young white men. He was a friend of Thomas Paul, founder of the Negro Baptist church in Boston (1806) in which Saunders taught. He became engaged to the daughter of Paul Cuffe, but for reasons unknown the engagement was broken. It was his friendship with Cuffe that perhaps awakened or increased his interest in the colonization of American Negroes abroad.

In 1815 he accompanied Thomas Paul to England as a delegate of the Masonic Lodge of Africans, with letters of recommendation to prominent Englishmen, to further education and missionary work in Africa. He became acquainted with royalty and nobility and, more important, with William Wilberforce and Thomas Clarkson.

These English abolitionists shifted Saunders's interest from Africa to Haiti, to which Wilberforce in particular had been requested by King Henri Christophe to send teachers. The English reformers also wanted to change Haiti's official language from French to English and the people's religion from Catholic to Protestant—long-run objectives of Christophe's vision. Arriving in Haiti in early 1816 Saunders was received with enthusiasm by the king, became intimately connected with the royal family and the nobility, and started instructing the Lancastrian system of teaching ("teach one to teach one" on a large scale). In 1816 he introduced vaccination into Haiti under the direction of Wilberforce and vaccinated Christophe's children. Sent back to England around April 1816 to carry important letters from Christophe to his English friends and to return with additional teachers, Saunders published while in London *Haytian Papers*, a translation of the laws of Haiti and the Code Henri (laws regulating the kingdom's agriculture, commerce, police, and sociopolitical organization). The frontispiece is a striking engraving of Saunders, showing his pronounced African features and self-assurance.

Returning to Haiti in December 1816 Saunders fell into disgrace from his role of adviser to King Christophe, who blamed him for having "presumptuously" published the *Papers* without his authorization. Perhaps because of the success of the Lancastrian schools and the introduction of vaccination, Christophe allowed Saunders, his warm admirer, to continue his work until 1818, when he sailed for Boston.

In that year Saunders published in Boston a second edition of the *Haytian Papers*. Settling in Philadelphia, a center of free Negro activists, he served as a lay reader in St. Thomas African Episcopal Church, founded by Absalom Jones. He joined the Pennsylvania Society for Abolition, and in opposition to such anticolonizationists as James Forten, stressed the colonization of free Negroes in the Caribbean, especially Haiti. In an address to the American Convention of Abolition Societies he portrayed Haiti as "the paradise of the New World" and urged colonization there to prevent southern

Negroes from seeking refuge in the North. He published his views in *An Address Delivered . . . before the Pennsylvania Augustine Society for the Education of People of Color* and *A Memoir Presented to the American Convention for Promoting the Abolition of Slavery,* both in 1818. Clarkson and Wilberforce praised Saunders but Christophe denounced him for his tendency to exploit the king's name.

In August 1820 Saunders returned to Haiti with letters from Philadelphia leaders said to represent thousands of free Negroes who wanted to migrate to Haiti, if Christophe and President Boyer (his rival in Haiti's Southern Republic) agreed. Since Christophe had had an attack of apoplexy, Saunders had to wait until early October before King Henri promised him a ship and $25,000 for transporting American Negroes to Haiti. Before the king could sign the agreement his army rebelled, Christophe's regime collapsed, and the crippled and demoralized king committed suicide on Oct. 8, 1820. Saunders's scheme likewise collapsed and robbers seized his property, including his clothes.

Shortly thereafter, Boyer triumphantly entered Christophe's capital, Cap-Henri renamed Cap-Haitien. Completely depressed, Saunders asked to see the president who courteously received him. But Boyer, predisposed against anyone who was associated with Christophe, refused all his requests, whether his migration scheme proposal or reimbursement of Haiti-related personal expenses. After this and another fruitless attempt during a fourth trip to Haiti in 1822–1823, Saunders's aversion increased toward Boyer and his less autocratic if not democratic regime. His letters to Clarkson were filled with defense of Christophe and attacks on Boyer's permissiveness which, he said, was leading Haiti to destruction. On May 2, 1823, he went even further, asking Clarkson for England's and Russia's intervention against Boyer.

Saunders's career from 1823 to his death in 1839 is a subject of controversy. An article by Arthur D. White in the *Journal of Negro History* (Oct. 1975, pp. 534–35) accepted what he considered valid evidence that Saunders served as Boyer's attorney-general until 1839. Given the antecedents, however, it is doubtful that Saunders, even assuming a reconciliation, would have received such a high position under Boyer. Haitian historians have not recorded such a reconciliation and cabinet appointment. Saunders died in Port-au-Prince, Haiti.

Regardless of whether Saunders was Boyer's attorney-general, and despite his weaknesses and passions (self-assertive nature, extremely accommodative approach to Negro progress, justification of extreme authoritarianism), Saunders ranks among remarkable men of his time, having been an educator, abolitionist, lecturer, and writer. His particular distinction, shared by few, comes from the international dimension he gave to the Negro problem. Moreover he was exceptional because he pioneered in the role of foreign development advisor to emerging nations.

There are frequent references and background information in Earl Leslie Griggs and Clifford H. Prator (eds.), *Henri Christophe and Thomas Clarkson: A Correspondence* (1968); Hubert Cole's *Christophe: King of Haiti*

(1967); Vergniaud Leconte's *Henri Christophe devant l'Histoire* (1931). The sketch by Marion Phipps Sanders in *DAB* ([1963], 8, Part 2:382) deals almost exclusively with Saunders's career to 1820. See also William Douglas's *Annals of the First African Church in the United States of America now Styled the African Episcopal Church of St. Thomas* (1862) and Maxwell Whiteman's "Prince Saunders . . . A Bibliographical Note" (*Historic Publications* no. 238, 1969), and *Calendar of the Manuscripts in the Schomburg Collection of Negro Literature* (1942, p. 143).

See also the article by Arthur D. White, "Prince Saunders: An Instance of Social Mobility Among Antebellum New England Blacks" (*JNH,* Oct. 1975, pp. 526–35).
— FRANCK BAYARD

SAVAGE, AUGUSTA (1892–1962), sculptor and teacher. She was born on Feb. 29, 1892, a native of Green Cove Springs, Fla., the seventh in a poor family of fourteen children of Cornelia and Edward Fells. Five of those children never reached their maturity. As a child Augusta gave evidence of her proclivity for sculpture. "At the mud pie age," she once stated, "I began to make *things* instead of mud pies. I had very little schooling and most of my school hours were spent in playing hookey in order to go to the clay pit—we had a brick yard in our town—and made ducks out of clay." Her creative efforts intrigued everyone who saw them —except her father. Edward Fells, a fundamentalist preacher, did not take kindly to the thought that a child of his would dare to "fashion graven images" under his roof. He forbade Augusta, under threat of corporal punishment, to continue with "this work of the devil."

In 1907 Augusta Fells married John T. Moore and they had one daughter, Irene, born in 1908. After John Moore's death a few years later, she was married to James Savage, a carpenter (the marriage ended in divorce in the early 1920s). In 1915 Savage had moved to West Palm Beach where clay soil was not abundant, and Augusta suspended her modeling—until she chanced upon a pottery on the city's outskirts.

Begging twenty-five pounds of clay from the potter she eagerly resumed her sculptor's efforts. The result yielded several pieces, including an eighteen-inch figure of the Virgin Mary which came to the attention of George Graham Currie, superintendent of the county fair. When Currie entered Augusta's work in the fair, he also saw to it that a special prize of $25 was awarded to her unique exhibit. Additional donations swelled the young artist's resources to $175. She set out for Jacksonville, confident that well-to-do Negroes there would support her with commissions. Jacksonville's affluent Negro community was not cordial to Savage and after foundering there for a while she continued north to New York City. Her capital upon arrival was $4.60. She also had a letter of introduction from George Currie to the well-known sculptor Solon Borglum.

Through Borglum, Savage was enrolled as a student of sculpture at Cooper Union (1921) and studied under George Brewster until 1923. Because of her maturity she was not only able to work after school hours to support herself but she was able also to "skip" much of the preliminary instruction. In 1923 she was granted a scholarship for study at Fontainebleau, France. But when the American Committee of seven white men discovered that she was colored, they withdrew the scholarship. Angry and hurt, but by no means crushed, Augusta Savage sought (and found) solace and compensation in her sculpture. It was more than mere coincidence that the subject matter she chose would reflect her sense of having been humiliated and outraged. Three of the sculptures she completed were particularly strong. The first was of W. E. B. Du Bois. Her handling of the planes of Du Bois's finely formed head clearly expressed the resolute militancy and intelligence of the great scholar. And her sculpture became not only a tribute to Du Bois but also a tribute to her own controlled response to the meanness that had driven her to do it.

Her sculpture of Marcus Garvey became her response to the hero-image of the black nationalist. But it was in *Gamin,* the third exercise, that the young artist brought her earliest experiences to full flower. This saucy, Negro boy of the city's streets is at once quizzical and scornful as he looks askance at a world he has come to know far too early and too intimately. *Gamin* was an instantaneous hit. It won a Rosenwald Grant for her and with that aid she embarked for Europe for further study and work (1929–1931).

In the decade following her return to New York in 1931 she produced several strong sculptures. Among them were *Martiniquaise,* a carving in black Belgian marble; *After the Glory,* a powerful condemnation of war which, like all her major works in plaster, was never cast in bronze; and *Envy,* a particularly fine woodcarving. Meanwhile she had for a number of years helped and encouraged younger artists. By letting them work in her various studios and by providing them with employment during the Depression years she became a legendary figure in Harlem. Her position as a supervisor on the Works Progress Administration Art Projects enabled her to give a start to many artists. Jacob Lawrence, William Artis, Norman Lewis, and Elton Fax are but four who were the recipients of her generous aid.

Her studio was open to the famous and the obscure alike. Poet and scholar James Weldon Johnson was a frequent visitor and friend. When in 1937 the New York World's Fair Board of Design chose Augusta Savage to make a sculpture for the court of the Community Arts Building, it was natural that her contribution would be inspired by Johnson's great poem "Lift Every Voice and Sing." Although not her greatest achievement in art it became her most publicized work.

She opened the Salon of Contemporary Negro Art in Harlem, a tastefully appointed gallery, the first of its kind there. But a sudden collapse of its funding closed the Salon before it had a chance to function. Weary and discouraged, the gifted and moody woman retired to a small plot of land in New York's Catskill region in 1945. Abandoning her art and her former associates, she became an assistant to a commercial mushroom grower. For the next seventeen years she made infrequent trips to New York City, where she occasionally did minor repairs on a few of her plaster sculptures owned by close friends.

She died of cancer in virtual obscurity in Abraham Jacobi Hospital, New York City, on March 26, 1962, following a lingering illness. Her third husband, Robert Lincoln Poston, a lawyer, had predeceased her in March 1924. She was survived by her daughter, Irene Allen, two brothers, Herbert and Arthur Fells, and three sisters (*New York Times,* March 27, 1962, p. 37; *New York Herald-Tribune,* March 27, 1962, p. 16; *Pittsburgh Courier* [national ed.], April 7, 1962, sec. 2, p. 4; Tony Martin, *Race First* . . . [1976], pp. 207–8).

Elton Fax drew on his reminiscences for the later years of Augusta Savage's life. There are valuable references, especially in Benjamin Brawley's *The Negro Genius* (1937), Alain L. Locke's *The Negro in Art* (1943), Cedric Dover's *American Negro Art* (1960), and especially Romare Bearden's and Harry Henderson's *Five Black Masters of American Art* (1973, pp. 76–98). There is also an excellent sketch by De Witt S. Dykes in *NAW* (1980, pp. 627–29). — ELTON C. FAX

SAVARY, JOSEPH (? –c. 1822), Saint-Domingue–born patriot, soldier of fortune, and hero of the Battle of New Orleans. He was the close associate of whites and generally referred to as a mulatto Creole of Santo Domingo (Saint-Dominique). The names of his parents can only be conjectured. Since he was believed to have been the brother of Belton Savary, another hero of the Battle of New Orleans, he was probably the son of Charles Savary and Charlotte Lajoie. He was an officer in the Saint-Domingue army under the French Republic and rendered outstanding services to the whites during the slave uprising in that colony. He and his family were among the whites, free people of color, and slaves who fled their native land and finally landed in New Orleans in 1809. When he reached the United States he brought with him a reputation as an able officer and a man of great courage. A. Lacarrière Latour, the historian, admiringly stressed the fact that prior to his admittance to the United States, Savary had already "occupied an honorable and distinguished reputation in the wars of St. Domingo."

In the meager accounts concerning Savary's early days in Louisiana he is first mentioned as a member of the Lafitte brothers' privateer-pirate group operating at Barataria prior to the Battle of New Orleans. In fact Gov. W. C. C. Claiborne had already described the Negro element of that group as "Santo Domingo negroes of the most desperate character, and no worse than most of their white associates." It was Claiborne who suggested to Gen. Andrew Jackson the enlistment of the Saint-Dominguans in the American cause; the general admired Savary and his men to the end of hostilities. Despite the fact that the Saint-Dominguans were generally admired for their bravery and heroism on the battlefield, they were never fully trusted by the dominant whites.

Historians generally accord to Savary titles such as captain, major, and colonel. Latour, in a single paragraph, refers to him as both captain and colonel. In dispatches General Jackson referred to him as "Colonel Savary" and only rarely as "Captain Savary." According to one record Jackson appointed him again as a major sometime before Dec. 19, 1814. It was before this date, however, that Savary began to organize the

2nd Battalion of the free men of color. With the exception of a small number of men from Martinique, the 2nd Battalion was composed almost entirely of Saint-Dominguans. This group went to Savary's home and was there enlisted, but remained without arms until only a short time before entering the fight.

Savary's 2nd Battalion of men of color was mustered into service on Dec. 19; the next day Governor Claiborne reported to General Jackson that the battalion was now organized and wished to be put into action. Three days later, having been supplied with repaired muskets that formerly had been regarded as "unfit for use," this battalion played a leading role in the battle of the night of Dec. 23. It was in this night's engagement that Savary lifted his voice in Saint-Dominguan French, translated as "March on! March on, my friends, march on against the enemies of the country!"

On the decisive day of Jan. 8, 1815, both battalions of free colored men were far removed from contact with the British lines. This "Line Jackson" was where General Jackson himself had taken his stand during the engagement. Yet it was in this area that some of Savary's men made an "unauthorized sortie" in order to reach the British lines where Gen. Sir Edward Pakenham was desperately using his plumed hat to beat his wavering men back into action. Vincent Nolté, Hervey Allen's original *Anthony Adverse,* was a participant in that day's fighting. Famed in the drawing rooms and financial exchanges of two hemispheres, Nolté described the action that followed in a letter to the *Niles Register:* "New Orleans colored regiment were so anxious for glory that they could not be prevented from advancing from over our breast works and exposing themselves." They fought like desperadoes, he added, and deserved distinguished praise.

In this "unauthorized sortie" a man whose name went down in army records as "Sergeant Belton Savourie" returned to Line Jackson in such a mortally wounded condition that he died two days later. All was well, however, with the American forces. General Pakenham had been shot twice and the utter rout of his forces soon followed. This was probably the day when —according to white tradition—General Jackson, in a moment of wild exultation, hugged Colonel Savary to his breast on the field of battle. It is a matter of record that Charles Savary, Belton's father, was awarded a sum of money for the death of his son by an act of the Louisiana legislature (Feb. 6, 1815). When Charles died his wife, Charlotte Lajoie, was awarded a pension (March 22, 1831). Oral traditions among the descendants of the free colored people maintain that it was "Bowie Savourie of Attakapas" who shot General Pakenham and they spell out the name "Savourie" in the same erroneous manner as it is entered on army rolls. Years later General Jackson, in describing Pakenham's death in a letter to his former secretary of war, called no name, but simply wrote: "I have always believed he fell from the bullet of a free man of color, who was a famous rifle shot and came from the Attakapas region of Louisiana."

The warm admiration that had persisted between General Jackson and Savary suffered a change after hostilities when the latter apparently defied an order to command his men to march out of the city they had defended. A highly dramatic impact is couched in the general's statement of the refusal of "Captain Savary's corps to march out of the city agreeable to my order." This unrealistic demand that the men should quit the city after hostilities was based on the dominant white group's distrust of armed Negroes in their midst. Most of the free men of color who fought in the Battle of New Orleans became disillusioned and regarded themselves as *"objets de mépris"* (objects of scorn) in the eyes of their former white comrades. This view was more naturally felt by the heroic Savary. Unlike him, one of his closest white associates, Pierre Lafitte, seems to have made no effort to hide his "hatred . . . of the ungrateful Americans." And it was to the warm embrace of the Lafitte brothers at Galveston that Savary and a large number of his countrymen returned after the Battle of New Orleans.

The Galveston to which Savary returned was the almost undisputed domain of the legendary Lafittes, Pierre and Jean. They and their associates were so involved in international intrigue that it was difficult to unravel the ties of patriotism, smuggling, privateering, filibustering, revolution, and—most probably—outright piracy. Savary had gone to Galveston around August 1816. His rendezvous at that time was with Commodore Louis Aury, "the daring South American naval commander," who was then collecting a fleet of vessels to converge at Matagorda, Tex. The number of men he had brought with him is not stated, but it is recorded that some 200 Negroes in Aury's little fleet mutinied, took possession of three vessels, and sailed away. Savary then returned to New Orleans, raised forty more Negroes, and in company with José Manuel de Herrara, representing the revolutionary Mexican Congress and other soldiers of fortune, landed at Aury's Galveston post and then proceeded to Matagorda.

Savary and his Saint-Dominguans were admired by both royalists and rebels; one royalist, writing to the Spanish Minister at Philadelphia, included "the Santo Domingan free colored people of New Orleans" among those who "will be easily able to ruin the projects that our enemies are forming in the Gulf." Gen. José Alvarez Toledo, the Mexican rebel turncoat, in his plan of July 1816 for the suppression of the Mexican revolution, referred to Col. Joseph Savary as an intelligence agent to evaluate an alleged offer by President Pétion of Haiti to aid Herrara.

More and more Savary aligned himself with the Mexican insurgents against Spanish rule. By 1816 a group of Mexicans, free Negroes, free men of color, whites, and South Americans began to use Galveston, Mexico, Santo Domingo, and Haiti as bases to launch revolutionary activities and privateering expeditions against Spain and Spanish commerce. Savary, Herrara, Alexandre Pétion, Aury, Simón Bolívar, the Lafitte brothers— and even the New Orleans Associates—not only began to threaten, but also weakened Spanish rule in South America.

No record has been found of Savary's death. In 1819 he addressed a petition to the Louisiana House of Representatives, requesting a pension for five years. That body reported that "the said Joseph Savary deserves a reward for the services by him rendered to this state under command of major general Jackson during the invasion of the British.'' Since he was once described as "Colonel Savary, a man in whom Mr. Aury has much confidence,'' the question naturally arises as to whether he remained with Aury at Galveston and later returned to New Orleans, or whether he continued on to Vera Cruz with Herrara, and in a later contact with Pétion agreed to serve as his emissary to the Mexican rebels. Stanley Faye is certain that after Savary left Galveston he returned to New Orleans to live and offers as proof this brief listing in *Paxton's New Orleans Directory of 1822*: "Savary Col. Joseph, 158 Burgundy, cor. Hospital.''

The principal sources are Roland B. McConnell's *Negro Troops of Antebellum Louisiana: A History of the Battalion of Free Men of Color* (1968); A. Lacarrière Latour's *Historical Memoirs of the War in West Florida and Louisiana in 1814–1815* (1816); Harris G. Warren's "The Firebrand Affair: A Forgotten Incident of the Mexican Revolution'' and "Documents Relating to George Graham's Proposal to Jean Lafitte for the Occupation of the Texas Coast'' (*Louisiana Historical Quarterly,* vol. 21), and his "Toledo's Reconciliation with Spain'' (ibid., vol. 23); Stanley Faye's "Privateersmen of the Gulf and Their Prizes'' (ibid., vol. 22) and "The Great Stroke of Pierre Lafitte'' (ibid., vol. 23).

— MARCUS B. CHRISTIAN

SCARBOROUGH, WILLIAM SANDERS (1852–1926), philologist and university president. He was born in Macon, Ga. Scarborough's father Jeremiah, born near Augusta, Ga., had been freed in 1846 by his master. His father was said to have been the great-grandson of an African chief with a strain of Anglo-Saxon ancestry. His mother, Frances Gwynn, was a slave of mixed ancestry, one of her grandfathers a Spaniard and the other an Indian. His mother was born in Savannah. Scarborough's parents lived in Savannah in their early years, but his mother went to Macon when about twenty years of age, where they were married. The son took his mother's slave status, as the law required, but her servitude was only nominal. After her marriage she lived in her own home and the family seldom felt the burdensome restrictions of the slave system. Two other children died in early childhood.

Both parents, despite prohibitions of the slave codes, learned to read and write. Jeremiah Scarborough secured a responsible position, instructing new employees of the Central Railroad of Georgia. Profoundly religious, he was an earnest member of the Methodist Episcopal church and later of the African Methodist Episcopal church. Frances Scarborough was nominally the slave of Col. William de Graffenried, an aristocrat of humane views who enabled the Scarboroughs to enjoy a home of their own in Macon. The youthful Scarborough learned basic studies with the help of a neighboring free Negro family and a white man, J. C. Thomas. As the Civil War began he was already schooled in carpentry but was apprenticed to a master shoemaker. Emancipated after the Civil War, he attended various schools, including Lewis High School in Macon, and joined his mother's church, the Presbyte-

rian, but later became a member of his father's church, the African Methodist Episcopal church.

In 1869 he entered Atlanta University, an American Missionary Association school, where he spent two years, studying geometry, Latin, Greek, advanced arithmetic, and other subjects. The school was permeated by a disciplined Christian atmosphere. He had planned to study law at Yale, but circumstances led him to Oberlin where he lived with the family of a deceased professor, Henry E. Peck. The family entertained distinguished visitors, and he drew inspiration from members of the Oberlin Negro community. Scarborough continued to develop systematic habits of study and participated in literary and debating activities. During one long winter vacation he taught in an academy in Athens County, Ohio, and later in one near Washington Court House, Ohio.

Graduating from Oberlin College in 1875 he returned south for a visit with his parents. He secured a position at Lewis High School, but it was burned down during the bitter Hayes-Tilden campaign in 1876. He later took charge of a Negro school, Payne Institute at Cokesbury, S.C. As southern whites pursued repressive measures against Negroes, he studied briefly at Oberlin Theological Seminary and received an M.A. degree in 1878 from Oberlin College. He then visited friends in Philadelphia where he learned that he had been appointed professor of Latin and Greek at Wilberforce University, founded in 1853 and incorporated in 1856. The main building was destroyed by fire in 1865, but when Scarborough arrived in 1876 the new building was still unfinished.

In 1881 Scarborough married a white woman, Sarah C. Bierce of Danby, N.Y., a graduate of Oswego Normal School, in New York State, who taught at Wilberforce (1877–1914). Although childless their marriage proved a rewarding one. Scarborough had a decided interest in the classics but lost his position in 1892 because of the demand for utilitarian subjects. Then as professor in Payne Seminary he was supposed to raise his own salary. During this period Mrs. Scarborough's salary in the normal department, by then supported by state funds, was a real boon. Frederick A. McGinnis, a historian of Wilberforce, states that he was "the greatest scholar to be connected with the institution in half a century." In 1897 he was reappointed to his former professorship at Wilberforce and made vice-president. As president of Wilberforce after 1908 he found leadership to be very difficult as the institution was burdened with a heavy debt. Increased funds, however, came from the African Methodist Episcopal church and from friends of the institution. A badly needed women's dormitory was erected, partly through gifts from Andrew Carnegie and E. J. Emery, formerly of Cincinnati.

The university took an active part in training for military service in World War I, when a unit of the Student Army Training Corps was established on the campus. But in spite of Scarborough's constructive achievements, tensions continued to develop. In 1920 John Andrew Gregg, president of Edward Waters College, Jacksonville, Fla., succeeded Scarborough at Wilberforce.

During the years in which Scarborough was professor and then president at Wilberforce he was active and even aggressive in scholarly pursuits in linguistics, particularly in relation to classical philology. He had published a widely used textbook, *First Lessons in Greek* (1881), and in 1882 was elected to membership in the American Philological Association, the third Negro to be so recognized. In 1886 his *Birds of Aristophanes* was published. In spite of financial problems and some racial discrimination he endeavored to carry on research and to attend national meetings of the Philological Association. Sometimes he read a paper or presented one for publication in the *Transactions* of the association. Often these contacts were very rewarding to him, opening, as he said, "a new world of thought and endeavor."

Scarborough's influence helped secure the enactment by the Ohio legislature of the Ely-Arnett Law of 1887, which eliminated statutory segregation in the public schools of Ohio.

He contributed numerous articles to national magazines, including *Forum* and *Arena,* which emphasized aspects of controversial subjects: "The Future of the Negro" (*Forum,* March 1889) and "The Negro Question from the Negro's Point of View" (*Arena,* 1891). His article in *Forum,* "The Educated Negro and Menial Pursuits" (December 1898), raised the question of why the educated Negro should be given "a pick instead of Greek and Latin," for the classics would open to him considerations of life's higher aspects. Thus he presented a different public emphasis toward Negro education than that offered by Booker T. Washington. Scarborough continued his interest in linguistics, especially in relation to the Negro, contributing to *Arena* in 1897 "Negro Folk-Lore and Dialect." In 1903 his *The Educated Negro and His Mission* was published in the *American Negro Academy Occasional Papers.* For many years he spoke at numerous gatherings concerned with educational, religious, and racial problems, and he made three trips to Europe. During and after his Wilberforce presidency he continued to be a vigorous leader in the African Methodist Episcopal church.

For several decades he was a leading spokesman for the Negro constituency in the Republican party in Ohio. He regretted the rather indifferent attitude of the Republicans toward Negro rights, but saw no hope for the Negro in supporting Independents or the Democrats. His activities brought him in close contact with such Ohio Republican leaders as Joseph B. Foraker (governor and senator) and Warren G. Harding. When he left the presidency of Wilberforce, Scarborough sought a government appointment in Washington. One practical difficulty was the intolerance of white government workers toward Negro co-workers, but late in 1921 he received a minor appointment as assistant in farm studies in the Department of Agriculture. He personally went to Southampton County, Va., to study the situation of the Negro farmers in that rich area, and he gained some reputation as an authority on the Negro farmer in the South. The death of Pres. Warren G. Harding, who had been his patron, led to Scarborough's retirement on Dec. 31, 1924. He returned to his Ohio home, where he died on Sept. 9, 1926.

See Francis P. Weisenburger's "William Sanders Scarborough: Early Life and Years at Wilberforce"

(*Ohio History* 71 [Oct. 1962]: 203–26) and "Scarborough, Scholarship, The Negro, Religion, and Politics" (*Ohio History* 72 [Jan. 1963]: 25–50). A collection of Scarborough Papers is in the Wilberforce University Library. The brief article by Harrison G. Villard in *DAB* (8, Part 2:409–10) omits many important details about his presidency of Wilberforce and his political activities. *Who's Who in America, 1924–1925,* gives the birth date as 1854. An obituary was published in the *New York Times* (Sept. 12, 1926).

— FRANCIS P. WEISENBURGER

SCHOMBURG, ARTHUR ALFONSO (1874–1938), bibliophile, curator, writer, and Mason. He was born in San Juan, Puerto Rico, on Jan. 24, 1874. His parents were Carlos and Mary (Joseph) Schomburg. He was educated in the public schools of Puerto Rico, graduating from the Instituto de Instrucción and the Instituto de Enseñanza Popular. He attended St. Thomas College in the Virgin Islands and began to collect books and photographs about the Negro's past in Puerto Rico. He taught Spanish and for five years was secretary of the Las Dos Antillas Cuban Revolutionary party in New York City, trying to free Cuba and Puerto Rico from Spain.

Schomburg came to New York City in April 1891 and worked for five years in the law office of (Gen. Roger A.) Pryor, Mellis and Harris. During this period he was also a member of the Porto Rico Revolutionary party in New York. After Cuba won its independence from Spain in 1898, he went on an expedition to Central America, also visiting Haiti and other Caribbean countries. He married Elizabeth Hatcher of Staunton, Va., on June 30, 1895, and there were two children: Arthur Alfonso Jr., and Kingsley. In 1896 he began teaching Spanish and wrote two pamphlets about Haiti and the Cuban poet Plácido in the early 1900s. On March 17, 1902, after the death of his first wife, Schomburg married Elizabeth Morrow Taylor of Williamsburg, N.C., and there were two children: Reginald S. and Nathaniel T. His second wife died in 1909. About 1914 he married Elizabeth Green and there were three children: Dolores Marie (Thomas), Carlos, and Fernando. In 1906 he began working for the Bankers Trust Company on Wall Street, where he remained for twenty-three years. He rose from messenger to head of the mailing department, supervising a staff of eleven.

Harry A. Williamson, Schomburg's longtime friend, stated that he did not know when Schomburg became a Mason (it was in 1892) but he knew that Schomburg was master of his Lodge El Sol de Cuba No. 38 (later the English-speaking Prince Hall No. 38) in 1911. Schomburg remembered Williamson from the time he had participated in 1908 in the centenary of Prince Hall Masonry in Boston. He was elected as grand secretary of the Grand Lodge in 1918, serving until 1926. In this office he dedicated pages of the *Transactions of the Grand Lodge for 1920* to outstanding Negroes in Masonic history such as Prince Hall, Lewis Hayden, Bishop J. W. Hood, William T. Boyd, and also to William Henry Upton, a white man who wrote on Negro Masonry. Schomburg served on the committee that revised the constitution and statutes of the Grand Lodge in 1919, wrote several magazine articles and brochures on Masonry, some defending Negro Masons in the 1920s, and became a Thirty-third Degree Mason in 1925. In 1936, he persuaded Harry A. Williamson to place his collection on Negro Masonry (over 800 books, pamphlets, periodicals, photographs, manuscripts, scrapbooks) in the New York Public Library's Division of Negro Literature, History, and Prints. Williamson continued to add to his collection until his death in 1965.

During Schomburg's first thirty-odd years in the United States the ground-breaking Atlanta University *Studies* under the direction of W. E. B. Du Bois were published (1896 to 1914); the American Negro Historical Society of Philadelphia was formed in 1897 to collect documentation of Afro-American progress and development; the American Negro Academy was founded also in 1897 by Alexander Crummell to help the Negro's struggle through scholarly research and writing; the Paris Exposition of 1900 included Daniel Murray's eight-page *Preliminary List of Books and Pamphlets by Negro Authors* and an eleven-page *List of Colored Inventors in the United States;* the Negro Society for Historical Research was formed in 1911 by John E. Bruce and Arthur Schomburg, and published three occasional papers, one of which was Schomburg's important *Racial Integrity: A Plea for the Establishment of a Chair of Negro History in Our Schools, Colleges, etc.* (1913); and the Association for the Study of Negro Life and History was founded by Carter G. Woodson, George C. Hall, and others in 1915 to collect historical and sociological documents and to promote studies of the Negro. Schomburg stated in his essay "The Negro Digs Up His Past" (in Alain Locke's *The New Negro: An Interpretation* [1925], p. 231) that "a group tradition must supply compensation for persecution, and pride of race the antidote for prejudice. History must restore what slavery took away."

There were several early Negro bibliophiles and collectors of books and documents: Schomburg, Jesse E. Moorland, Henry P. Slaughter, John E. Bruce, Wendell P. Dabney, and William Carl Bolivar. Some of their collections were later acquired by the libraries of Negro colleges as they began in earnest to build up Negro collections. Schomburg compiled a catalogue of the exhibition of books, manuscripts, paintings, engravings, and sculpture by the Negro Library Association at the Carlton Avenue YMCA, Brooklyn (Aug. 7–16, 1918). He was elected president of the American Negro Academy in 1922. Over the years he searched indefatigably the book marts of Europe, Latin America, and the United States, and by 1926 had a collection of over 5000 books, 3000 manuscripts, 2000 etchings, and several thousand pamphlets, the highlights of which he described in "The Negro Digs Up His Past." The New York Public Library opened in May 1925 a new Division of Negro Literature, History, and Prints, better to serve the growing Negro community of Harlem. In 1926 the Carnegie Corporation made a grant of $10,000 to the New York Public Library for the acquisition of Schomburg's collection.

Schomburg began to travel in Europe and add to his collection at the library. In 1927 he received the William E. Harmon Award (a bronze medal and $100) for outstanding work in the field of education. He retired from Bankers Trust Company on a pension in 1929 and from 1930 to 1932 was curator of the Negro Collection in the Fisk University Library. Another gift from the Carnegie Corporation in 1932 enabled the New York Public Library to hire Schomburg as curator of the Division of Negro Literature, History, and Prints, a position he held until his death on June 10, 1938, in New York City at the age of sixty-four. The division was named in 1940 the Schomburg Collection of Negro Literature and History, and in 1973 the Schomburg Center for Research in Black Culture. He was survived by his widow Elizabeth Green Schomburg, a daughter Dolores Marie Thomas, and seven sons: Carlos, Fernando, Nathaniel T., Arthur Alfonzo Jr., Reginald S., and Kingsley.

Schomburg was a generous person. He allowed many writers of the Harlem Renaissance period to use his private collection. Kenneth B. Clark has written about the time Schomburg spent talking with him as a boy and the great influence he had on Clark's life (*Wilson Library Bulletin,* Sept. 1965). John Henrik Clarke has also attested to the impact of his early discussions of African history with Schomburg upon his life work as an Africanist. Schomburg was a popular lecturer to Negro groups on Negro history and a writer of columns and articles for the *New York Amsterdam News,* the *Pittsburgh Courier, A.M.E. Church Review, Opportunity, The Crisis, Forum Quarterly, The Messenger, Champion Magazine, Interracial Review,* and others.

Some of his other writings are *A Bibliographical Checklist of American Negro Poetry* (1916); "Economic Contribution by the Negro to America" (1915) in *The American Negro Academy Occasional Papers;* an appreciation in the first collected edition of Phillis Wheatley's *Poems and Letters* (1915) edited by Charles P. Heartman; a new edition of John Marrant's *A Sermon Preached on the 24th Day of June 1789* [i.e., 1784] at the African Lodge of Free and Accepted Masons in Boston (192?) and "African Exploration" in *Negro: An Anthology* (1934, 1970), edited by Nancy Cunard. Schomburg worked on *Negro History in Outline* (Bronze Booklet no. 8), scheduled for publication in 1937, but it was not completed before his death and was never published. Schomburg felt that his research had established three main conclusions: (1) that Negroes had been for centuries active pioneers and collaborators in the struggle for their own freedom and advancement; (2) that Negroes of attainment and genius have been regarded as exceptional even by friends and have been unfairly dissociated from Negroes so that they got no credit; and (3) that the remote racial origins of Negroes, contrary to what is generally believed, show a record of believable achievement when scientifically viewed and, more important, are of vital general interest because of their bearing on the beginnings and early development of culture.

The Schomburg Center for Research in Black Culture, Schomburg's great memorial, had grown by the late 1970s to 80,000 volumes, art objects, musical recordings, photographs, prints, sheet music, manuscripts, scrapbooks, pamphlets, playbills, programs, newspaper clippings, magazine articles, and Negro newspapers (mostly on microfilm) and periodicals. With the flood-tide of thousands of books published (reprints and new books) in the 1960s and 1970s on practically all aspects of Negro life and thought, the center had long outgrown its old quarters and an ample building to house it was constructed.

Another memorial was Pastor Argudin y Pedroso's portrait of Schomburg, presented to the Division of Negro Literature, History, and Prints of the New York Public Library by his son Fernando Schomburg in 1931. Other evidences of recognition are Intermediate School 201 in Manhattan, named Arthur A. Schomburg Intermediate School 201 in 1968; the Arthur A. Schomburg Plaza (110th Street and 5th Avenue, New York City); a housing project whose cornerstone ceremony was laid in May 1973; and the sheet music in his honor "The Curator" (1942), by Jean Stor (music) and La Verne Barber (lyrics), part of seven songs from "Unsung Americans Sung" (*Negro History in Song,* edited by W. C. Handy and published by Handy Brothers Music Co., New York City). His daughter, Dolores Thomas, has the bulk of his papers, but some are in the Schomburg Center for Research in Black Culture.

Biographical publications include Donald Franklin Joyce's "Arthur Alonzo [*sic*] Schomburg: A Pioneering Black Bibliophile" (*Journal of Library History,* April 1975); "The Saint That Moves Us: A Profile of Arthur Schomburg" (*Schomburg Center for Research in Black Culture Journal,* Fall 1977); "Arthur Alonzo [*sic*] Schomburg" (*Black Heritage,* Sept.-Oct. 1977); Elinor Desverney Sinnette's "Arthur A. Schomburg, Black Bibliophile and Curator: His Contribution to the Collection and Dissemination of Materials About Africans and Peoples of African Descent" (doctoral dissertation, Columbia University's School of Library Science, 1977); and the entry in the *Dictionary of American Library Biographies* (1978). See also Jean Blackwell Hutson's "The Schomburg Collection" in *Harlem: A Community in Transition* (1964), edited by John Henrik Clarke (1969); Stanton F. Biddle's "The Schomburg Center for Research in Black Culture: Documenting the Black Experience" (*Bulletin of the New York Public Library,* vol. 76, 1972); Ernest Kaiser's "Library Holdings on Afro-Americans," in *Handbook of Black Librarianship,* edited by E. J. Josey and Ann Allen Schockley (1977).

— ERNEST KAISER

SCOTT, DRED (c. 1795–1858), plaintiff in the famous case *Scott v. Sanford.* Scott was born a slave in Southampton County, Va. Tax Lists of 1818 stated that Scott, then more than sixteen years of age, was owned by Capt. Peter Blow and John Moore. At that time Dred Scott was known as Sam. He was moved to Madison County near Huntsville, Ala., in 1818. After twelve years the Blow family and Sam moved to St. Louis. Upon the death of Peter Blow in 1831 his son Charles, as administrator of his estate, sold Sam in 1833 for $500 as a valet to John Emerson, a surgeon in the U. S. Army stationed at Jefferson Barracks, Mo.

Sam [Blow] or Dred was of pure African ancestry in which he took great pride. Approximately four feet, nine inches tall, he was of stocky build with a dusky skin and woolly hair. Some contend that prior to his first marriage he was careless in dress but had a swaggering walk and a tendency to gamble. This latter trait caused difficulties with his new master, who whipped him for it. He ran away to the Lucas Swamp near St. Louis but was caught and returned. In 1834 Emerson was transferred to Fort Armstrong at Rock Island, Ill., where under the Northwest Ordinance, slavery was prohibited. However, since military personnel did not regard themselves as citizens of the states, many of them brought along slaves.

In 1836 Emerson was moved to the Wisconsin Territory where slavery was barred by the Missouri Compromise. With Emerson's consent Scott married a slave girl Harriet, bought from Major Taliaferro, an Indian agent from Virginia. This was his second marriage, since his first wife had been sold. The following year, with Emerson's transfer to Fort Gibson, the Scotts were hired out as servants until 1838 when they returned to Jefferson Barracks. Between 1834 and 1848 Sam took the name Dred Scott. Two conjectures have been proposed. John A. Bryan contended that the name resulted from the ironic humor of soldiers; in their teasing they bestowed the nickname of "Great Scott" upon him, contrasting his small stature with the tall Gen. Winfield Scott. Also, southern Negro dialect pronounced "great" as "dret," and allegedly newspaper reports unfamiliar with the dialect mispronounced it "Dred." In 1839 aboard the steamer *Gypsy* en route to St. Louis, in the vicinity of the Mason-Dixon Line, the Scott's first daughter was born. Her name was Eliza, perhaps in honor of Mrs. Emerson, the former Eliza Irene Sanford. Their second daughter, Lizzie, was born at Jefferson Barracks, and it was reported that two sons of the Scotts had died in infancy.

Emerson died in 1843, leaving all of his property in trust to Mrs. Emerson for the benefit of their minor daughter. No slaves were specifically mentioned in his will. Meanwhile Dred was hired out to Captain Bainbridge, who released him in Texas in 1846. Scott returned to St. Louis and tried to purchase freedom for himself and his family. While no satisfactory explanation can be given for Mrs. Emerson's refusal, it was common knowledge that her father was proslavery and head of a committee to protect slavery interests. Her father was named the administrator of the estate left to her, rather than her brother, as was erroneously stated. Approached by two attorneys, Burd and Risk, called "nigger lawyers" for taking slave cases, the Scotts sued for their freedom in county court. They charged assault and false imprisonment and sought damages of $10, the customary legal procedure. When they lost and moved for a new trial, the verdict was set aside and another trial granted on Dec. 2, 1847. Mrs. Emerson appealed to the Missouri Supreme Court but her appeal was dismissed since the case was pending in the lower court. The second trial of Dred Scott was held on Jan. 12, 1850, under Judge Alexander Hamilton. The Scotts won, based on the fact that Dred had been carried into a free state and territory.

While the case was pending in the state court, Mrs. Emerson in 1850 moved to Massachusetts and married Dr. C. C. Chaffee, a strong opponent of slavery. Her brother, John F. A. Sanford, agreed to handle all her legal matters. The Scotts were left in St. Louis and hired out by the circuit court under jurisdictional control of the sheriff. The wealthy sons of Captain Blow and friends were still assisting Scott with funds and counsel in the effort to obtain his freedom. Mrs. Emerson allegedly did not want to own slaves, but could not sell or free Scott and his family because she considered them property left in trust. Moreover in view of the long hiring-out period, there were damages of about $1000 which she did not want to pay. In 1852 the state Supreme Court reversed the judgment of the circuit court and remanded the Scotts to slavery. Her brother Sanford, who had moved to Missouri prior to her departure, arranged for her former lawyers to remain on the continuing case.

Urged by his new lawyer friends for whom he worked as a janitor, Scott in 1853 brought a new suit against Sanford. Prior to this, to facilitate the case in court, an agreed-to statement was concocted between the two sides. Part of it alleged erroneously that Scott was sold to Sanford. Since the matter was said to be between two "citizens," *Scott v. Emerson* (which became *Dred Scott v. Sandford*) was a case for the federal district court. (It was then that the clerk misspelled Sanford as Sandford.) Losing the case and their motion to overrule the findings, Scott's attorneys appealed to the U.S. Supreme Court on a writ of error. Neither party appeared in Washington before the Supreme Court, but Scott was represented by Montgomery Blair, a former resident of St. Louis, then living in Washington. Montgomery Blair was the son of Francis P. Blair who threw in his lot with the young Republican party. Gamaliel Bailey, abolitionist editor of the *New Era* and a friend of Scott's, agreed to finance the case. On March 6, 1857, with two dissenting votes, the U.S. Supreme Court held that Scott was not free by reason of his removal to the free state of Illinois or the free Wisconsin Territory. His status was determined by the courts of Missouri which had decided he was not free. Since he was not a citizen of Missouri he could not bring suit against Sanford, a citizen of another state. Mrs. Chaffee, immediately following the decision, transferred title to the Scotts to Taylor Blow.

Throughout the litigation reporters stated that Scott was "lazy," "shiftless," "unreliable," "frequently unemployed," and was forced to rely on the generosity of the sons of the former owner. Revisionists assumed that Scott was portraying the slave psychology among those employers who were short of human kindness. Apparently the Blow family, his lawyers, and his employers saw some good in him and his family. His last employers, Mr. and Mrs. Theron Barnum, owners of the famous Barnum Hotel in St. Louis where he was employed as a porter, contended he gave them satisfactory service. Although Scott was a man without training and void of ambition, James Milton Turner ("Dred Scott Eulogized," *St. Louis Dispatch,* April 18, 1882), held that he was an affectionate father and faithful husband who longed for freedom with his family. Certainly not a roustabout, he was a member in good standing of the Second Baptist Church. Scott neither fully comprehended the "fuss in Washington" over him, nor did he live long enough to see his case as a partial cause for the Civil War. Through white friends he realized that he had become a person of extraordinary importance. However, the long struggle for livelihood and freedom bore too heavily upon him, and he died of tuberculosis in St. Louis on Sept. 17, 1858, and was buried in an unmarked grave in Wesleyan Cemetery. He was later reburied by the Blows in section 1, lot 177, of the Calvary Cemetery. Mrs. Charles C. Harrison, Jr., a granddaughter of Taylor Blow, donated a marker in September 1957.

On the ninety-ninth anniversary of the famous Dred Scott decision, at least nine or more direct descendants were estimated living in St. Louis and the Midwest. Dred Scott Madison of Grand Rapids was a policeman; a great-grandson, John A. Madison, practiced law in the same court which denied his forebear the right to sue. This courthouse at Broadway and Market became a museum.

The "Dred Scott Collection" in the Missouri Historical Society at the Jefferson Memorial in St. Louis includes, among others, the Blow Manuscripts, the legal reports of the county, state, and federal governments, and various newspapers of 1857 and 1858. Some valuable monographs are Thomas Benton's *History and Legal Exam, the Supreme Court, and Dred Scott* (1909); E. S. Corwin's "The Dred Scott Decision in the Light of Contemporary Legal Doctrines" (*American Historical Review,* Oct. 1911). Walter Erlich concluded in "Was the Dred Scott Decision Valid?" (*Journal of American History,* Sept. 1968) that it was. The brief sketch by Thomas S. Barclay in *DAB* (8, Part 2:488–89) perpetuated the image of Scott as unaware of the significance of his case and a "good-natured and lazy porter at Barnum's Hotel, St. Louis, where he was an object of interest and curiosity to the guests."

— PAUL MCSTALLWORTH

SCOTT, EMMETT J[AY] (1873–1957), editor, Republican politician, author, and university administrator. Scott was Booker T. Washington's private secretary from 1897 until the latter's death in 1915, and this identification with the Negro leader was the principal shaping force of Scott's long and varied career. He was born in Houston, Tex., on Feb. 13, 1873, the son of Horace L. and Emma Kyle Scott. He was persuaded by the Rev. (later bishop) Isaiah B. Scott to attend college. He spent three years at Wiley College in Marshall, Tex., from 1887 to 1890 but did not graduate, although years later Wiley awarded him an honorary degree for his achievements. He left college to become a journalist, first as a reporter for the white daily *Houston Post* for three years, and then in 1894 he founded his own Negro weekly newspaper, the *Houston Freeman.*

Scott was an admirer of Booker T. Washington from the beginning of his career, writing a favorable editorial on the Atlanta "Compromise Address" in 1895. He managed so well the publicity and promotion for Washington's speech in Houston in June 1897 to a large audience that a few days later Washington offered him a position as his private secretary. After some indecision and some haggling over salary, Scott accepted the position and arrived at Tuskegee with his recent bride, the former Eleanora Baker of Houston, on Sept. 10, 1897. She became the mother of their five children.

Scott described many years later his first day at work at Tuskegee. Washington treated him in a brusque, matter-of-fact way he had not expected. "With but short preliminaries," Scott remembered, "he began to advise me of what he would expect, and then pushed toward me a huge pile of diversified correspondence, and remarked most casually, without even going into it with me, 'I wish you would dispose of these letters as rapidly as possible,' and walked from the office." Washington assigned Scott two stenographers, but Scott had never dictated before. By late afternoon, however, he presented Washington with the sheaf of completed letters. Washington promptly signed all but two, which he sent back for redictation. "Naturally, I was a very happy young man that I had seemed to translate his thoughts and ideas in the replies made," Scott later recalled (Emmett J. Scott, "Twenty Years After: An Appraisal of Booker T. Washington," *JNE*, Oct. 1936, pp. 545–46).

Scott quickly became part of Booker T. Washington's inner circle, his friend, confidant, and agent. He scanned the white and black newspapers for information important to his chief, and served as his emissary on confidential missions to confer with politicians, editors, and others. He was Washington's chief deputy at Tuskegee when Washington had to be away, and subordinated his own ideas and interests to those of his superior so completely that it was almost impossible to tell which of Washington's communications was written by him and which by Scott. Washington said of Scott in one of his autobiographies: "Without his constant and painstaking care it would be impossible for me to perform even a very small part of the labor that I now do. Mr. Scott understands so thoroughly my motives, plans and ambitions that he puts himself into my own position as nearly as it is possible for one individual to put himself into the place of another, and in this way makes himself invaluable not only to me personally but to the institution" (Booker T. Washington, *The Story of My Life and Work,* 1901).

Scott took a leading part in the detailed work of maintaining what came to be called the "Tuskegee Machine," the elaborate web of influence and power that Booker T. Washington exerted over Negro men and institutions—the press, the churches, schools and colleges, political officeholders, and others. In 1909 Scott was one of three U. S. commissioners sent to Liberia during that country's diplomatic and economic difficulties, and the report he helped to write strongly influenced the decision to establish, in effect, a protectorate over Liberia. In 1912 the Tuskegee trustees elected Scott the secretary of Tuskegee Institute. As Scott's influence increased, many Negroes believed that he went beyond Booker T. Washington in attacking the Tuskegeean's enemies and interfering unduly in the affairs of Negro newspapers and Negro rights organizations. The evidence suggests, however, that the two men were in full agreement. It was in his personal business ventures that Scott's independent ambitions came to the surface. Among his business investments were the Afro-American Realty Company of Harlem, the *Voice of the Negro* magazine, the African Union Company

for trade with West Africa, the Bank of Mound Bayou in Mississippi, the Standard Life Insurance Company, and several small automobile companies.

After Washington died in 1915 Scott was seriously considered as his successor, but he was passed over and Robert R. Moton was chosen in his stead. Perhaps this was because Scott seemed to prefer to remain in the shadow of Washington's dominant personality. After the United States entered the First World War, Scott escaped from any rivalry with Moton when he became special Assistant to the secretary of war in charge of Negro affairs. (This assignment enabled him to write his informative illustrated *Scott's Official History of the American Negro in the World War,* 1919, reprint 1969.) At a time when race relations were exacerbated by race riots, discrimination against Negro soldiers, and low morale, Scott was an effective go-between but not a leader, conveying the thinking of the War Department to Negroes and their thinking to the War Department. He also wrote *Negro Migration During the War,* a volume in the series "Preliminary Economic Studies of the War" sponsored by the Carnegie Endowment for International Peace (1920, reprint 1969).

He was secretary-treasurer and business manager of Howard University from 1919 to 1932, and secretary until his retirement in 1938. Before the election in 1926 of the university's first Negro president, Mordecai W. Johnson, Scott was the university's most important Negro administrator. In 1920 he was a member of a committee to develop a retirement system that became effective during the administration of President Johnson. In 1922 he was a member of a committee which made recommendations resulting in salary increases for members of the faculties and administration. In 1923 he was member of a committee which recommended the procedure for electing the first alumni trustee. A capable and suave administrator, he survived conflicts with Johnson until his retirement (Rayford W. Logan, *Howard University: The First Hundred Years, 1867–1967* [1969], passim).

Scott dreamed of personifying the beliefs and goals of Booker T. Washington. With Lyman Beecher Stowe he wrote a laudatory biography, *Booker T. Washington: Builder of a Civilization* (1916). He tried without much success to raise money for the Booker T. Washington Memorial Fund at Tuskegee. For several years he participated in an ill-starred movie-making venture, a production entitled *The Birth of a Race,* to be based on *Up from Slavery* and also designed to rebut D. W. Griffith's racist movie *The Birth of a Nation.*

It was in his business activities that Scott most nearly approximated Booker T. Washington's philosophy. He shared Washington's belief that the Negro who struggled for and achieved business success and property ownership would be respected by whites and eventually would be given political and civil rights. Scott knew the Negro business community intimately, for throughout its first fifteen years he was secretary and principal organizer of the National Negro Business League, founded in 1900. His principal business ventures in the 1920s and afterward were in real estate, insurance, and banking, all under Negro management and primarily serving Negro customers and clients.

Scott was also an active Republican politician. In the 1890s, before moving to Tuskegee, Scott was for a time the secretary of Norris Wright Cuney, the leading colored politician in Texas for several decades in the late nineteenth century. Scott's political involvement during the Tuskegee years was in subordination to Booker T. Washington's role as the chief Negro political boss of the time. Nevertheless Scott was an active political operator, not only in the "Black and Tan" political faction in Alabama but on the national level. He went many times to see Theodore Roosevelt and Taft at the White House as Washington's emissary, and he watched the interests of the Tuskegee Machine at the Republican National Conventions and in the deliberations of national Negro organizations.

After Washington's death in 1915, the influence of the Tuskegee Machine declined but Scott continued as a Republican in every election from 1916 to the 1940s. In response to Woodrow Wilson's federal segregation policies, Scott worked to enlist Negroes to support Charles Evans Hughes, and similarly Harding, Coolidge, and Hoover, despite their lukewarmness and even hostility to Negro interests. Throughout the 1920s and 1930s Scott was on the Republican Colored Advisory Committee. In 1941 the Republican party "loaned" Scott to one of its largest financial backers, John G. Pew, president of the Sun Shipbuilding Company at Chester, Pa. This nonunion company established the all-Negro Yard No. 4 with Scott in charge, which built a number of ships under government contracts. As he directed this work, Scott organized Negroes in the yard and in the area for the Republican party, also under Pew family direction. While the yard provided employment opportunities for Negroes, it made it easier for the unit to be dismantled after the war.

When the yard was closed in 1945 Scott retired to Washington, D.C., where he did occasional work in public relations. After a long illness in a Freedmen's Hospital ward, he died on Dec. 12, 1957. He was survived by two sons, Emmett J. Jr., and Horace L., and two daughters, Mrs. Aaron H. Payne and Mrs. Maurice Garland.

The principal sources of information are the Emmett Jay Scott Papers at Morgan State University, Baltimore, and the Booker T. Washington Papers at the Library of Congress. Many of Scott's letters also appear in the published *Booker T. Washington Papers,* edited by Louis R. Harlan and others (1972–). James E. Waller wrote a detailed study, "Emmett Jay Scott: The Public Life of a Private Secretary" (M.A. thesis, University of Maryland, 1971). See also the obituary in the *Washington Afro-American* (Dec. 14, 1957, pp. 1–2, 8).

— LOUIS R. HARLAN

SÉJOUR, VICTOR (1817–1874), dramatist. He was born in New Orleans, La., on June 2, 1817, the son of Louis Victor Séjour Marou, a free man of color from Saint-Marc, Saint-Domingue, and Héloise Philippe Ferrand, a quadroon of New Orleans. His parents were married at St. Louis Cathedral in January 1825, thus legitimating the birth of Victor and his older brother Roujes-Louis, born in 1811. A sister, Marie-Françoise-Amelie, was born in 1826. His father, who had served in D'Aquin's Battalion of Free Men of Color in the defense of New Orleans in December 1814 and January 1815, owned and operated a tailor shop on Chartres Street. He was apparently sufficiently well off to have Victor instructed by Michel Seligny in his Saint-Barbe Academy.

About the time of his seventeenth birthday Victor Séjour went to France. Within two years the first of his works to appear in print was accepted by the *Revue des Colonies* (1837), published by "a society of men of color." "Le Mulatre," a short story or novelette set in Saint-Marc, tells the tragedy of Georges, a young mulatto. The author's narrative conveys anguish over the suffering arising from slavery and racism. Style and theme were different in Séjour's next publication, an ode expressing his intense French feelings when the remains of Napoleon were brought from St. Helena to be interred in Paris. "Le Retour de Napoléon" formed part of the collection *Les Cenelles* (1845), edited by Armand Lanusse after initial publication in Paris (1841).

In 1844 Séjour's first play was accepted for production by the national theater (later known as the Comédie Française). *Diegarias* is a stirring historical drama in verse set in fifteenth-century Spain. His next play (1849), *La Chute de Séjan (The Fall of Séjanus),* also in verse, was presented by the same prestigious theater.

For *Richard III* (1852) Séjour preferred prose; never again did he return to verse. A nineteenth-century romantic, the author drew on Shakespeare whom he admired deeply, but gave his own sentimental touches and interpretation. A box-office hit, the play enjoyed a long run. Séjour was hailed as "among the most beloved of the young literary generation."

L'Argent du Diable (The Devil's Money; 1854), also a success, was a happier play than most by Séjour. After *Les Noces Venitiennes* (Venetian Wedding; 1855), with cloak and dagger, romance and intrigue, came *Le Fils de la Nuit* (Son of Night) in 1856, dedicated to Alexandre Dumas, friend and fellow man of color. The staging was spectacular for this story of a kidnapped infant who grew up to win finally his ducal heritage and save Naples. Full-house audiences applauded the play through an extraordinary six-month run. Then came a tour *en province.* Séjour was at the pinnacle of popularity, but a warning critic judged that Séjour "stirred" his audience more than he "moved" them. For a long time friends ignored such criticisms; Séjour saw three of his plays staged in the following three years.

Twice he brought contemporary events to the stage. In *La Tireuse de Cartes* (The Fortune Teller; 1859) he interpreted the Mortara Affair; co-author with him was J.-F.-C. Mocquard, secretary of Napoléon III. The following year in *Les Massacres de la Syrie* he hailed Napoléon III's expeditionary intervention to halt the Druses' killing of Christians in Syria. The emperor himself attended both these plays.

Séjour's only one-act comedy *Le Paletôt Brun (The Brown Overcoat)* was first played in 1859. From 1860 to 1870 a series of nine swashbuckling adventure plays with historical settings kept his name before the public, but without fulfilling his high promise. In 1870 *Henri de Lorraine* received such cold treatment from the critics that Séjour withdrew it from the printers.

By then he was tired and in failing health. The Franco-Prussian War and the Commune were hard to bear for this lover of France and of Paris. His thoughts and feelings flowed out in a novel *Le Comte de Haag,* published as a newspaper serial in the spring of 1872. The villain is a Prussian member of the International, sent with false papers into France to spy for Prussia and to plot social upheaval. In this novel Séjour editorially pressed the bourgeoisie for needed social reforms while he censured the incendiary violence of the revolutionaries. Ill health prevented the completed publication of the serial.

Contrary to what several authors have said, the Volunteers of 1814 *(Les Volontaires de 1814)*—subject and title of Séjour's next play—served not in New Orleans (like Louis Séjour) under Jackson against the British, but rather in eastern France under Napoléon I against the Coalition. This play was one more expression of Séjour's devotion to France and admiration for Bonaparte.

Along with idealistic devotion to his adopted France, Séjour in his writing reveals his thoughts on faith in God, fidelity to promises, dignity of labor, and courage in adversity. He dwells on love of parents and their children, and on the beauty of romantic and marital love. Amid his successes he dutifully and devotedly brought his parents to Paris, where they lived out their last years. In spite of his plays' high appreciation for marriage and their attractive portrayal of fidelity, Séjour fathered three sons of three mothers out of wedlock.

Although after *Le Mulatre* he did not produce any publications on a racial theme, he did work on a five-act drama entitled "L'Esclave" (The Slave), but, never staged or printed, the play has not come to light. In *Le Martyre du Coeur (The Martyrdom of the Heart;* 1858), the one who undoes every plot and trick of the villain is Placide, a Negro from Jamaica, executor of the will of a late French emigré.

Tuberculosis brought him to the Municipal Hospital about Sept. 11, 1874. Unable to pay the modest costs, he was assisted by the Société des Auteurs et Compositeurs Dramatiques. He breathed his last on Sunday, Sept. 20, 1874, and was buried in Père-Lachaise Cemetery. Paul Feval, speaking at the graveside in the name of the Société, recalled "the youthful creole, with brow of bronze, with energetic lips, with eyes afire." The eulogist told also of the later sensitive Séjour, wounded by the drama critics, "walking the boulevards, wan, sombre, nervous, poor, a distant reflection of himself."

Although this native of the United States achieved fame in Paris, it is noteworthy that his early education was received in New Orleans. Mid-nineteenth-century Louisiana newspapers carried reviews of his dramas, and at least one of his plays was staged in New Orleans in the antebellum era. Moreover he was hailed by twentieth-century writers like Rodolphe L. Desdunes and Charles Roussève as an enduring reminder to white and black alike of the highly talented Louisiana free Negroes, who in spite of obstacles succeeded in science, music, literature, business, and philanthrophy. In 1974 the centenary of the death of one of the great playwrights of Louisiana's past history was commemorated in his native city in a variety of ways: Loyola University staged a Séjour play and provided a panel discussion of his career. *Les Comediens Français* produced a play in French, and Southern University included Séjour in a mural of great Negroes of Louisiana.

The articles on Séjour by Edward Larocque Tinker in *DAB* (8, Part 2:565–66) and in *Les Écrits de Langue Française en Louisiane au XIXe Siècle* (1922) have, in spite of weaknesses, been the often-copied source of information on the dramatist. The Reuter dispatch announcing his death was printed in French, British, and American newspapers. Lengthy notices appeared in the Paris press. For a recent evaluation, see Charles Edwards O'Neill's "Theatrical Censorship in France, 1844–1875: The Experience of Victor Séjour" (*Harvard Library Bulletin* 26 [1978]: 417–41).

— CHARLES EDWARDS O'NEILL

SHADD [CARY], MARY ANN (1823–1893), outspoken champion of the fugitive slave and free Negro settlers who went to Canada West (Ontario, Canada) in the 1850s. Born on Oct. 9, 1823, in Wilmington, Del., the oldest of thirteen children of Abraham Doros and Harriet (Parnell) Schad, Mary Ann's prominence in history rests in part upon the approximately twelve years she spent in Canada, where she was editor of the best of the fugitive slave newspapers, the *Provincial Freeman,* worked as a colleague of the redoubtable Samuel Ringgold Ward, and may have been party to John Brown's insurrectionist plans at the Chatham Convention. In 1856 she married Thomas G. F. Cary and had a daughter, Sally. In 1862 Mrs. Cary became a naturalized British subject, but in 1863 she returned to the United States to be an active writer and suffragette, and died in Washington on June 5, 1893.

Mary Ann (or as sometimes spelled, Anne) Shadd (on occasion spelled Shad) spent much of her early life in search of an effective religion, only to conclude that all organized religious institutions compromised with slavery and should be avoided. As a child she was a Roman Catholic, yet she was educated by Quakers at Price's Boarding School in West Chester, Pa. She strongly felt that colored Americans need not assimilate with predominantly white groups, and at one time she espoused African Methodism. She gave up teaching in Wilmington, West Chester, New York City, and Norristown, Pa., to go to Canada West with her brother Isaac shortly after the passage of the Fugitive Slave Act (1850). She wrote one of the first of the descriptive pamphlets on that British colony, *Notes on Canada West* (1852), in order to inform fugitives of what they might expect to find there. In the same year she and Isaac became schoolteachers in Windsor, opposite Detroit, to which the greatest number of fugitives initially were going, and were supported by the American Missionary Association. On the whole, white A.M.A. teachers did not do well in Canada West, and in later years she tried to conceal the fact that she had been supported by the nondenominational American-based body. In any event, the A.M.A. found itself overextended in its Canada Mission and in 1853 it suspended the Windsor school.

By this time Mary Ann Shadd had found her true calling, journalism. In March 1853 Samuel Ringgold

Ward launched the *Provincial Freeman,* an outspoken and well-edited journal intended largely for the fugitive slave community; Mary Ann Shadd was listed as its publishing agent for the first number, issued from Windsor. A year lapsed before a second issue followed, in March 1854, from Toronto. In the summer of 1855 the paper moved again, to Chatham, in the heart of the fugitive settlements. (By this time her family, led by her father Abraham, had also come to Canada). Ward and Shadd brought their printing press with them and won the contract to be the official printers for the Chatham Town Council. Since Ward was now fully engaged in lecture tours throughout the province and in Britain for the Anti-Slavery Society of Canada, founded four years before, the actual editorial chores fell increasingly to Miss Shadd. For a short time William P. Newman was the nominal editor (although William Still, agent for the *Provincial Freeman* in Philadelphia, recognized her authority), but in the spring of 1856 she, together with H. Ford Douglass and Isaac Shadd (then married to Amelia Freeman) became the formal editors. At the end of 1858 the paper ceased publication, although Isaac Shadd apparently revived it briefly during the Civil War before moving to Mississippi.

In the meantime, Mary Ann Shadd made herself a spokesman for those fugitives who did not think of themselves as exiles awaiting return to the United States but had chosen to take up permanent residence under the British flag. In the newspaper, and on lecture tours throughout the Midwest in 1855–1856, she attacked Negroes and whites who sought to compromise in any way with slavery, or who were prepared to accept temporary second-class status. She opposed begging ministers—those who sought to support their congregations by soliciting funds throughout the province—as well as drunkenness. Above all she lashed out at self-segregated Negro settlements, of which there were three of significance in Canada West: Wilberforce, Elgin, and the Refugee Home Society's holdings near Amherstburg. Feeling that all such settlements inevitably led to discrimination, she urged fugitives to take an active part in the life of the broader community. She supported the True Band Society of Amherstburg, a militant group opposed to begging and in favor of settling the many internecine colored quarrels through colored arbitration boards rather than airing the fractiousness of fugitive leadership in the public press. She therefore opposed the Refugee Home Society in particular, since it was self-segregated, legally based in Michigan, and led by white men and a Negro, Henry Bibb; ultimately she publicly accused all of the society's agents of malfeasance, asserting that Detroit whites were cheating the fugitives in granting them five acres of land conditional upon the purchase of twenty more—clearly beyond the financial capability of most fugitives—and in keeping for administrative expenses between 20 and 25 percent of all funds solicited.

She also made war upon a competing newspaper, the *Voice of the Fugitive,* because it encouraged Negroes to think of themselves as impermanently in Canada West, and she singled out Josiah Henson, Hiram Wilson, and Bibb (the last partially because he revealed that she had accepted support from the A.M.A. despite her

more recent attacks on that body) for special scorn, warning Negroes that all their "caucuses, conventions, [and] resolutions" would be fruitless, since their "pretended leaders" returned to such meetings for ego satisfaction "like a dog to his vomit." And as a Garrisonian she had no use for John Scoble or the British and Foreign Anti-Slavery Society. At times her anger could be misdirected, as when she denounced the Anti-Slavery Society of Canada for not sponsoring a bazaar on behalf of her newspaper, under the mistaken impression that it had done so for *Frederick Douglass' Paper,* and she ultimately broke with both Ward and the society's secretary, Thomas Henning, weakening her position with moderate readers. Nonetheless her views were consistent throughout in advocating a sense of black pride at a time when few spoke in such terms.

In time Mary Ann Shadd made her peace with the A.M.A., for after teaching in Michigan briefly (1862), she again became a schoolteacher for the missionary group, in Chatham. In August of 1863 she was appointed a recruiting officer for colored volunteers to the federal armies, working in Indiana. At the end of the war she moved to Washington, where she was principal of a public school and wrote for Frederick Douglass's *New National Era* and John W. Cromwell's *The People's Advocate.* She had in the meantime applied her journalistic talents to another task: she helped Osborne P. Anderson, one of John Brown's assistants during his meeting in Chatham in May 1858, to prepare his notes for the publication of *A Voice from Harpers Ferry* in 1861. Thereafter she pursued a law degree at Howard University (awarded in 1883) and joined the National Women's Suffrage Association. In 1881 she returned briefly to Canada to help stage a suffragette rally. She would, however, continue to be best known for the *Provincial Freeman.*

Mary Ann Shadd is the subject of essays by S. C. Evans in Hallie Q. Brown (ed.), *Homespun Heroines and Other Women of Distinction* (1926, pp. 92–96), and by Sylvia G. L. Dannett in *Profiles of Negro Womanhood,* vol. 1, *1619–1900* (1964). The essays contain contradictions. She is discussed by Robin W. Winks in *The Blacks in Canada* (1971) and in " 'A Sacred Animosity': Abolition in Canada," in Martin Duberman (ed.), *The Antislavery Vanguard: New Essays on the Abolitionists* (1965, pp. 301–42). Most material on her comes from the pages of her newspaper the *Provincial Freeman* (original copies of which—to 1858—are at the University of Pennsylvania), from the *Voice of the Fugitive,* and the *Toronto Globe.* In 1977 Jim Bearden and Linda Jean Butler published a sound biography, *Shadd: The Life and Times of Mary Shadd Cary.* The Mary Ann Shadd Cary Papers are in the Moorland-Spingarn Research Center, Howard University.

— ROBIN W. WINKS

SHEPARD, JAMES EDWARD (1875–1947), educator. The oldest of twelve children of the Rev. Augustus and Harriet E. (Whitted) Shepard, he was born in Raleigh, N.C., and educated in the public schools of that city. In 1894 he received a Ph.G. degree (Graduate Pharmacist) from Shaw University in Raleigh, and worked for a year as a registered pharmacist in Damill,

Va. In 1898 he founded in Durham with John Merrick and others an insurance company later called the North Carolina Mutual Insurance Company. Some years later he founded and became a trustee of the Mechanics and Farmers Bank of Durham. He served as a clerk in the recorder of deeds office in Washington, D.C. (1899–1900).

From 1899 to 1905 Shepard traveled extensively as field superintendent for the International Sunday School Association. Also during the same years he was deputy collector of U.S. revenue in Raleigh. In 1910 he was the only Negro speaker at the World Sunday School Convention in Rome. He also traveled in Africa and Asia as a Sunday school leader. An early leader of the Republican party in North Carolina, he supported many of the Republican presidents in the early twentieth century, especially as one of Theodore Roosevelt's advisors on Negro appointments. He corresponded with Thomas E. Dewey, former governor of New York and Republican presidential candidate, former Under Secretary of State Sumner Welles, former Secretary of State James Byrnes, and former Senate Minority Leader Alben Barkley of Kentucky. Although neither Byrnes nor Barkley was overtly favorable to the Negro, both were powerful men on whom Shepard relied to secure federal assistance for North Carolina College.

Shepard was one of the most respected Negro leaders in North Carolina between 1910 and 1945, one of the state's ten most valued citizens ("Dr. Shepard," *High Point Enterprise,* July 9, 1945), and a "national leader" of his race (*Durham Morning Herald,* March 18, 1945). In 1944 Negroes in Durham renamed their public school the James E. Shepard School for Negroes. In 1949 Shepard was commemorated by the North Carolina General Assembly through a resolution sponsored by Rep. Robert M. Gantt of Durham.

Despite these encomiums he was subjected to severe criticism for his policy of seeking accommodation with white citizens. For instance he was dubbed "Minister of Apology in the Department of Propaganda for the Southern States and Their Sympathizers Who Believe in Racial Discrimination Predicated on the Legal and Systematic Repression of Negroes" ("We Ain't Ready Department," *Peoples Voice* [New York], Feb. 26, 1944). In 1930 Shepard supported Pres. Herbert Hoover's nomination for the U.S. Supreme Court of John J. Parker of Charlotte, N.C., although many Negro leaders denounced him because of his widely reported racist views. Shepard stated that Parker had changed his position and should not be blamed for his earlier comments. U.S. Rep. Oscar De Priest of Chicago denounced Shepard's position and vowed never to appear in public with Shepard. Parker's defeat was hailed as a major victory by friends of Negroes and organized labor.

On the other hand such outspoken champions of the race as W. E. B. Du Bois and Benjamin E. Mays pointed out that "he was, while seeming to capitulate, a supreme strategist, sabotaging the arrogations of whites and forcing them to pay a stiff price for segregation." He urged all Negroes in the nation to master the English language because English-speaking people would prevail in the Western world. He also urged students at

North Carolina College to study the sciences and prepare for "racial leadership" by taking advantage of every opportunity and by being "fair and friendly."

Perhaps Shepard's greatest contribution was the founding of the institution that later became North Carolina Central University at Durham. Highly involved in religious activities in the Baptist church of North Carolina, Shephard had chartered in 1910 a private institution known as the National Religious Training School and Chatauqua "for the colored race" to give six-week courses to ministers and teachers. It was established on a twenty-five-acre lot which was formerly one of the city's trash piles; the land was primarily a gift to Shepard from some of the prominent citizens of Durham. In 1915 the school was so indebted that it was sold at auction and purchased by Mrs. Russell Sage and then reorganized to become a National Training School. In 1923 the General Assembly of North Carolina took under its auspices the National Training School, renamed it the Durham State Normal School, and began to support it. Renamed again in 1925 as the North Carolina College for Negroes, the college included courses in liberal arts and the preparation of teachers and principals of secondary schools. By 1927 the General Assembly began to expand the physical plant of the college with help from private donations by B. N. Duke and others. In 1929 the college graduated its first full four-year class. The North Carolina College for Negroes was the first state-supported liberal arts college for Negroes in the United States. Shepard sponsored many circulars and broadcasts on the radio for public and financial support. By 1947 he had developed a modern college for Negroes with an estimated annual budget of $3.5 million. The school had progressed from a training school for the religiously oriented to a four-year liberal arts institution offering by 1941 graduate and undergraduate work in the arts and sciences, a law degree in 1940, and a degree in library science in 1941.

On Nov. 7, 1895, Shepard married Annie Day Robinson; they had two children, Marjorie Augusta and Annie Day.

Stricken by a stroke in his office, Shepard died on Oct. 6, 1947, and was interred in Beechwood Cemetery, Durham. He was grand master of Prince Hall Masons in North Carolina, grand patron of the Eastern Star of North Carolina, finance secretary of the Knights of Pythias of North Carolina, director of the Mechanics and Farmers Bank of Durham, president of the North Carolina Teachers Association, and trustee of Lincoln Hospital and Lincoln School for Nurses in Durham.

There is no full-length biography of Shepard. Basic facts are in *Who's Who in America* (1942–1943). Useful sources are "The Story of North Carolina College, Its Founder" (*Campus Echo,* Nov. 11, 1960); "Last Rites Held for Noted Educator Here; Many Notables Pay Tribute" (*Carolina Times,* Oct. 11, 1947); "Good Sense Beats It All" (*Greensboro Daily News,* Nov. 5, 1945). Background information is in "History" (*North Carolina Central University Annual Bulletin 1972–1973,* June 1972) and Helen G. Edmonds's *The Negro and Fusion Politics in North Carolina, 1899–1901* (1951, reprinted 1973). The sketch by David O. Van Tassell in

DAB, Supplement 4 (1974, pp. 742–73), characterized Shepard as " 'A master of human relations.' "

— GEORGE W. REID

SHOREY, WILLIAM T. (1859–1919), whaling master. Shorey was described by the *San Francisco Chronicle* in 1907 as "the only colored captain on the Pacific Coast." He was born on the island of Barbados in 1859 and spent his childhood there. His father was a Scottish sugar planter on the Caribbean island, and his mother, Rosa Frazier—called by Delilah Beasley in *The Negro Trail Blazers of California* (1919) an unusually "beautiful creole lady"—was a native Barbadian.

As the oldest of his mother's eight children it was necessary for Shorey to begin working at an early age. Although slavery had been abolished in Barbados several decades earlier (1834), the opportunities for a young man like Shorey were still quite limited, and he was apprenticed in his early teens to a plumber. Finding the drudgery of this occupation uncongenial, and strongly attracted by the sea, as were many young men reared on the island, Shorey bade farewell to his family in 1875 and shipped on a British vessel bound for Boston. The English captain of the ship "took a fancy" to his eager and alert neophyte crew member and taught Shorey the rudiments of navigation, a vital subject which the aspiring mariner continued to study avidly under the aegis of Capt. Whiffer D. Leach, a noted whaling captain of Provincetown, Mass.

E. Keble Chatterton states in *Whalers and Whaling* (1926) that the whaler's difficult life "was likely to appeal only to three classes of men: those who had been compelled to leave the land to avoid gaol or starvation, those who thought they were going to see the world and gain adventures, and those who were determined to work their way up until they owned a whaling ship of their own." All three factors were operative in Shorey's case. First, as a Negro in an age in which racial prejudice and discrimination were very prevalent, the number of occupations in which he might hope to find acceptance and success was limited. However, there had always been a rough sort of democracy on board a whaling ship, where a man was accepted for what he could do, rather than on the color of his skin or national origin. Second, for a young man who had grown up in the sequestered confines of the island of Barbados the chance to travel widely must have had a strong appeal. Third, Shorey did have a real determination to work his way up, and he was highly successful in this endeavor.

Shorey shipped on his first whaling voyage in 1876 from Provincetown. He sailed as a "greenhand" but returned as a "boat steerer"—a considerably more important member of the crew. On one of his early voyages Shorey almost lost his life while pursuing a sperm whale. "Evidently enraged," he related years later, "the whale attacked first one boat, smashing it, and then a second one, and then attacked the one I was in. By good fortune we were able to fire a bomb into him, which, exploding, killed him and saved us."

Undaunted by such harrowing experiences at sea Shorey pursued his career in whaling assiduously. His rise through the ranks was rapid—attesting to his intelli-gence, skill, and determination. After only four years on whaling ships, by 1880 he had become an officer. He sailed from Boston in November of that year as third mate on the *Emma F. Herriman* on a trip which took him around the world. By the end of this exciting three-year voyage, he had been promoted to first officer. This particular voyage was memorable for another reason, since it took him to San Francisco, which was to be his home port for the remainder of his lengthy career.

Shorey shipped again on the *Herriman* in 1884 and 1885, sailing as second and then as first officer on ten-month voyages, which were typical of West Coast whaling. Then in 1886, only a decade after beginning his whaling career, he made the great step to the coveted position of command—thus becoming the only Negro captain of major vessels on the West Coast in his era. This was a great tribute to Shorey's ability and stature among his fellow seamen, for the whaling captain had to be a man of many and varied talents. He had to be an experienced and skilled sailor, an excellent navigator, a shrewd trader, an intelligent and forceful leader, and able to assume all kinds of responsibility. "During the course of an average voyage," Elmo Hohman wrote in *The American Whaleman* (1928), the whaling master "was almost certain to act as physician, surgeon, lawyer, diplomat, financial agent, entrepreneur, judge, and peacemaker." Shorey possessed all the requisite qualifications and was to prove himself one of the most able practitioners of this demanding profession.

In 1887 Shorey married Julia Ann Shelton, the talented daughter of one of the leading Negro families of San Francisco, and they cruised to the Hawaiian Islands aboard the *Herriman* on their honeymoon. Two years later, in 1889, Shorey took command of the recently built brig *Alexander*. He made two successful voyages as captain of the *Alexander* in 1889 and 1890, but disaster struck in 1891 and the *Alexander* was sunk in the Arctic ice pack in the Bering Sea. Shorey's skill, courage, and resourcefulness, however, managed to save the entire crew. The loss of the *Alexander* did not affect his career adversely, and upon his return to San Francisco he was immediately placed in command of another vessel, the *Andrew Hicks*. The *Hicks* was already an old vessel when Shorey took command and had been described by her previous captain as "mighty shaky." It is a further tribute to Shorey's skillful seamanship that he completed eight successful voyages with the *Hicks* between 1892 and 1902.

After serving as captain of the *Hicks* and *Gay Head*—one of the most famous of the San Francisco whalers—Shorey took command of his last vessel, the *John and Winthrop*. Built at Bath, Me., in 1876—the year Shorey began his whaling career—this sturdy bark sailed under Shorey on five whaling expeditions between 1903 and 1908, with the most exciting voyage occurring in 1907. While in the Okhotsk Sea the ship experienced two fierce typhoons which badly damaged the vessel, carrying away several of the ship's longboats and all of the sails, and threatened to sink the vessel. Upon returning to port the crew testified that "nothing but Captain Shorey's coolness and clever seamanship saved a wreck."

By the end of the first decade of the twentieth century

the whaling bark had become an anachronism and whaling a moribund industry in the United States. William Shorey accordingly retired in 1908 and spent the remaining decade of his life ashore in Oakland, Calif., where he was a respected member of the community, much sought after as a raconteur of thrilling tales of his exciting profession, and where he died and was buried in 1919.

The only work devoted to Shorey is E. Berkeley Tompkins's "Black Ahab: William T. Shorey, Whaling Master" (*California Historical Quarterly,* Spring 1972), which contains extensive footnote references to a variety of unusual sources, including a number of personal interviews with Shorey's daughter, Victoria G. Francis of Berkeley, Calif. — E. BERKELEY TOMPKINS

SIMMONS, WILLIAM J. (1849–1890), soldier, clergyman, educator, and biographer. He was born on June 26, 1849, in Charleston, S.C., the son of slaves, Edward and Esther Simmons. While he was still a young child his mother fled with him and her two other children to the North. In order to evade slave catchers they lived successively in Philadelphia, Roxbury, Mass., and Chester, Pa., before finally settling in Bordentown, N.J. An uncle, Alexander Tardieu, helped to support the family during these years and personally provided the children with their basic education.

At the age of twelve Simmons began an apprenticeship with a white dentist and learned the profession well enough to treat several of his employer's patients. Rebuffed in an attempt to enroll in a dental school in Philadelphia, and becoming disaffected with his employer, he enlisted in the Union Army at the age of fifteen. During his year of military service he participated in several engagements in the vicinity of Petersburg, Va., and was present at Appomattox when Lee surrendered to Grant in April 1865. Upon returning to civilian life he resumed his occupation as a dentist's assistant. A turning point in his life came, however, when he joined a white Baptist church in Bordentown and subsequently decided to become a minister. Encouraged and assisted by members of the church to continue his education, he first attended Madison (later Colgate) University and then Rochester University, in New York State. Forced by difficulties with his eyes to leave the latter institution after his first year, he enrolled in Howard University in Washington, D.C., in 1871 and graduated two years later with his B.A. degree; in 1881 he received an M.A. degree.

During his senior year at Howard, Simmons helped to defray his expenses by teaching at two public schools, becoming the principal of Hillsdale Public School. After teaching for a brief period in Arkansas following his graduation, he returned to the District of Columbia and resumed teaching at Hillsdale. On Aug. 25, 1874, he married Josephine A. Silence of Washington, who bore him seven children. After the marriage the Simmonses moved to Florida where they lived for the next five years. After unsuccessfully trying his hand at land investments and growing oranges, Simmons returned to teaching, serving as the principal of Howard Academy. He also became an ordained minister, pastored a small church, and held such public offices as

deputy county clerk and county commissioner. About 1877 the family returned to Washington where Simmons again taught school until 1879 before going to Lexington, Ky., to become the pastor of the First Baptist Church.

In Kentucky, where he spent the rest of his life, Simmons became a prominent leader in Negro educational and religious circles. In 1880 he assumed the presidency of the virtually defunct Normal and Theological Institution, a Baptist school in Louisville, and eventually transformed it into the State University of Kentucky, Louisville. Two years later he became the editor of the *American Baptist.* These twin positions provided him with excellent platforms from which to promote his social views and programs. Like many of his contemporaries he advocated industrial training for Negro youth; however, he argued simultaneously for the separate training of the academically talented in "literary institutions" in order to provide Negroes in the South with a pool of talent from which to staff their high schools, colleges, and universities. In keeping with his dual educational perspective he not only administered the State University of Kentucky but also founded, shortly before he died, what was presumably a school for industrial training at Cane Spring, Ky. As editor of the *American Baptist* he sponsored the organization (1886) at St. Louis of the American National Baptist Convention and became its first president.

Although he campaigned in Florida in 1876 for Rutherford B. Hayes, the Republican candidate for president, Simmons was politically independent. In subsequent years he admonished Negro voters against becoming "a slave to party." He advised them to support instead only those candidates and political factions on the state and local levels who were willing to promote their interests. An outspoken critic of Jim Crow practices in general, he singled out for special condemnation the mistreatment of Negroes in southern courts and their exclusion from state and municipal jobs. He was also an active participant in several Negro conventions held in Kentucky and other states for the purpose of devising programs for the improvement of social conditions in the South.

Simmons is best known to posterity as the author of the biographical dictionary *Men of Mark: Eminent, Progressive, and Rising* (1887), most of whom were born in slavery. Attempting to counter the growing tendency within white academic and lay circles to portray the Negro as inherently inferior, Simmons sought to show both friends and oppressors of Negroes that they had survived the ordeal of slavery with "their spirituality and love of offspring" undiminished and "that the Negro race is still alive, and must possess more intellectual vigor than any other section of the human family." He was especially hopeful that his volume would inspire young Negroes to seek an education. Since most of the biographical sketches were written by the biographees, modern scholars use it with great caution.

His plan to write a companion volume on Negro women was aborted by his premature death at the age of forty-one, at Cane Spring, Bullit County, Ky. Ill since May 1890 of heart failure and "dropsical diseases," he died on Oct. 30, 1890, surrounded by his wife and seven children. His funeral was held at the Fifth Street Baptist Church, Louisville, on Nov. 3, under the auspices of the Masonic Unity Lodge No. 12. Members of the lodge escorted his body to Cane Spring where he was buried (*Courier-Journal,* Oct. 31, 1890, p. 4; Nov. 3, 1890, p. 2). The *New York Age* (Nov. 8, 1890, p. 2) stated that his death was "a calamity to the race."

Information about Simmons is based on Henry McNeal Turner's introduction to *Men of Mark.*

— ARNOLD H. TAYLOR

SIMMS, WILLIE (1870–1927), jockey and trainer. He was born in Augusta, Ga., on Jan. 16, 1870. As a little fellow he was greatly attracted by the gay colors of the jockeys' silks at the county fairs. Without his parents' consent he went to New York, where at first he was able to find only a few mounts. His ability to handle a particularly obstinate horse, however, attracted the attention of "Coe" Leighton, a trainer for Rep. W. L. Scott. Simms established himself as an accomplished jockey when (1889) he defeated the idol of the East, "Snapper" Garrison in the rich Expectation Stakes. It was Garrison's surges in the last strides that led to the term "Garrison finish" not only in horseracing but in other sports. Simms in the final strides won by a nose. Four years later he was noticed by the Dwyer brothers, Michael (Mike) and P. J., whose astuteness was generally recognized. At Sheepshead Bay in New York Simms rode five winners in six mounts on June 23, 1893. On Aug. 24, 1894, he repeated the feat. Two years later he won the Kentucky Derby on Ben Brush and in 1896 on Plauduit. Michael Dwyer and Richard Crocker took him to England, where he rode with very short stirrups and an extra-long wrap on his mount's head. This was perhaps the introduction to the British of a new style of racing, later to be emphasized and adopted by the American jockey Ted Sloan. According to Edwin B. Henderson, Simms "became the first American jockey to win an event on an English course with an American horse, owner, trainer and equipment—the first all-American victory." After his return to the United States he trained horses as late as 1924.

One of the wealthiest jockeys of his time—his fees for winning mounts and his salary came to $20,000, and he invested his money wisely—he remained a bachelor and lived with his widowed mother in Asbury Park, N.J. He died there of pneumonia on Feb. 26, 1927.

The major source of information is the biographical sketch by the late Marjorie Rieser Weber, a principal researcher of Simms and other Negro jockeys, in the Keenland Library, Lexington, Ky. Additional brief information is in Edwin B. Henderson's *The Negro in Sports* (1949). — RAYFORD W. LOGAN

SINGLETON, BENJAMIN ["Pap"] (1809–1892), millennarian and migrationist. Born in Nashville, Tenn., he was sold to slaveowners in the Gulf States several times but each time he escaped back to Nashville. After fleeing to Canada, he settled in Detroit until the end of the Civil War. He worked as a scavenger in Detroit and ran a boarding house which often harbored other fugitive slaves. After the Civil War, Singleton returned to Nashville where he became a cabinetmaker and began

to fulfill his "God-given mission" of assuring his race safety and security, whether in Tennessee or elsewhere.

W. A. Sizemore, Columbus Johnson, and several other Negroes worked with Singleton in the 1870s. They had urged Negroes to acquire farmland in Tennessee in the late 1860s, but whites refused to sell productive land to Negroes at any but prohibitive prices. In the early 1870s several Negro families from Nashville migrated to Kansas on the recommendation of a scouting team which had visited the state. A few years later Singleton began conducting parties of central Tennessee Negroes to Kansas in cooperation with Columbus Johnson. Johnson had remained in Topeka in 1877, after he and Singleton had sought out the best locations for Afro-American settlement.

In 1874 Singleton and his associates had formed the Edgefield Real Estate and Homestead Association (Edgefield lies just across the Cumberland River from Nashville proper), and between 1877 and 1879 they steered hundreds of Negro migrants to Kansas. When the millennarian ("Salvationist") Exodus engulfed and overshadowed their movement of planned migration, the Exodusters (as the millennarians were called) filled the two already established Singleton colonies. One lay in Dunlap, Morris, and Lyon Counties, the other in Cherokee County. Exodusters also flocked to Nicodemus, on the western prairie, a hamlet settled in 1877–1878 by two groups of Negro Kentuckians. Singleton, Sizemore, and a young man from Nashville, Alonzo DeFranz, lived in the Dunlap colony until the middle of 1880, when Singleton testified before the Senate committee on the Exodus.

Benjamin Singleton came to nationwide attention in 1880 as he claimed to be *"the whole cause of the Kansas immigration"* in testimony before a U. S. Senate committee on the Exodus to Kansas. Singleton claimed authorship of that millennarian movement which had abruptly taken some 20,000 Afro-Americans from Mississippi, Louisiana, and Texas in the spring of 1879, and which in fact had no one central leader. Nonetheless, in the years following the Exodus Singleton was accorded the title "Father of the Exodus."

Singleton took credit for the Exodus for two cogent reasons. He had printed and circulated hundreds of posters and fliers advertising his and the Edgefield Read Estate and Homestead Association's Kansas activities. Although many of these fliers appeared to be of interest only to residents of Nashville, Singleton's circulars may well have encouraged other migrants to depart from their southern homes. He sent them into the very states from which the Exodus of 1879 flowed, Mississippi, Louisiana, and Texas. However, he also distributed his fliers in other states which did not contribute to the Exodus to any perceptible degree, such as Alabama, North and South Carolina, Georgia, and Virginia. Whatever their actual influence, the circulars were secondary to Singleton's sense of mission.

Appropriating the spontaneous Exodus, Singleton proclaimed that God had worked through him: "Right emphatically, I tell you to-day," he declared, "I woke up the millions right through me! The great God of glory has worked in me. I have had open air interviews with the living spirit of God for my people; and we are going to leave the South." Two years after the Exodus this same sense of divine appointment led him to found a new organization.

After a brief consideration of retirement and a political trip into Indiana in 1880, Singleton formed the United Colored Links in Tennessee Town, Topeka, early in 1881. Tennessee Town took its name from the large number of Negro Tennesseeans settled in that quarter of the city. During the Links' brief life, it attempted coalition with the white workingmen's Greenbacker party, but its central goal was race unity, in order to "build manufactories and other institutions of industries, which will enable us to make men and women of our sons and daughters" (Singleton Scrapbook, p. 33). The meager means at the United Links' disposal fell far short of underwriting the alternate economy Singleton envisioned, and the group did not last past 1881. Undaunted, Singleton returned to the public arena two years later.

Sensing a renewed interest in migration among Negroes, in 1883 Singleton formed a "Chief League" for emigration to the Mediterranean island of Cyprus. The Cyprus bubble soon burst, but its emigrationist impulse grew into the Trans-Atlantic Society, which Singleton organized in 1885. In sharp contrast to his conciliatory stance in the 1870s, the Trans-Atlantic Society spoke of repatriation of the "African" people to their "Fatherland" in apocalyptic terms. "We shall! We will!, bridge the ocean," thundered the Trans-Atlantic, "that the sons and daughters of Ham may return to their God-given inheritance, and Ethiopia regain her ancient renown, and be enhanced with modern splendor. We shall not die out! We shall not wear out" (Singleton Scrapbook, p. 56). In 1887 the Trans-Atlantic took the unequivocal position that "nothing short of a separate national existence will ever meet the wants and necessities of our people."

The Trans-Atlantic Society disappeared from record in 1887 and proved to be Singleton's last contribution to racial betterment. After several years of ill health, he died in St. Louis in 1892 with a long record of concern for the welfare of his people in the United States and in foreign countries. Like others wrestling with American racial discrimination, Singleton was not able to realize his vision of real freedom for lack of large-scale organization and sufficient money.

Printed sources on Benjamin Singleton include Arna Bontemps's and Jack Conroy's *Anyplace But Here* (1966, chap. 5); Walter L. Fleming's " 'Pap' Singleton, the Moses of the Colored Exodus" (*American Journal of Sociology,* July 1909, pp. 61–82); Roy Garvin's "Benjamin, or 'Pap" Singleton and his Followers" (*JNH,* Jan. 1948, pp. 7–23); Nell Irvin Painter's *Exodusters: Black Migration to Kansas Following Reconstruction* (1977); U. S. Senate, *Report and Testimony of the Select Committee of the United States Senate to Investigate the Causes of the Removal of the Negroes . . .* 46th Cong., 2d sess., Senate Report 693 (Washington, 1880, 3:379–91). The Singleton Scrapbook is in the Kansas Historical Society. — NELL IRVIN PAINTER

SISSON, JACK [TACK, GUY WATSON, PRINCE] (c. 1743–1821), soldier of the Revolutionary War. Sisson was a leader of the troops who captured British Maj.-Gen. Richard Prescott at his headquarters near Newport, R.I., in July 1777. Colonel Barton, who commanded the detachment, went ahead with Sisson close behind him. They quickly got rid of the single sentry at the door. Then, according to an early newspaper report, with "the rest of the men surrounding the house, the Negro, with his head, at the second stroke, forced a passage into it, and [into] the general's chamber." Colonel Barton gave General Prescott only time to put on his breeches. A ballad, reported to have been composed by a Newport sailor, popularized the capture by "Cufee," a common name for any Negro, who told the general: "Your breeches, massa, I will take,/ For dress we cannot stay."

Catherine Williams, the biographer of Colonel Barton, treated with "genteel racism" Sisson's exploit and later life. A "black servant" of the colonel, he had an exaggerated opinion of his role and regretted that his name had not appeared in accounts of the capture. Made a drummer, he later appeared on holidays in his uniform while urchins listened to his stories and his cracked voice singing an old ballad. The *Providence Gazette* (Nov. 3, 1821) published his obituary: "In Plymouth (Mass.) . . . a negro man, aged about 78 years. He was one of the forty brave volunteers."

Sidney Kaplan's *The Black Presence in the Era of the American Revolution 1770–1800* (1973) summarizes the little that is known about Sisson and characterizes Catherine Williams's treatment as indicative of "genteel racism." — RAYFORD W. LOGAN

SLAUGHTER, HENRY PROCTOR (1871–1958), typographer, journalist, leader of fraternal organizations, and book collector. He was born in Louisville, Ky., the son of Sarah Jane Smith and Charles Henry Slaughter. When he was six years old his father died, leaving his mother with two boys and a girl. He sold newspapers to help support his mother, and as he worked his way through school, became the main support of his family. After graduating as salutatorian from Central High School, he served his apprenticeship as a printer on the *Louisville Champion* where he became associate editor with Horace Morris, who in 1894 was deputy grand master of the Prince Hall Masons of Kentucky. Slaughter also began to write feature articles for local dailies. By 1893 Slaughter was foreman of Champion Publishing Co., and in 1894 he became associate editor of the *Lexington Standard.* Shortly afterward, as manager of the *Standard* he was described as making "logical speeches, having a trenchant pen and strong hand at the helm of the *Standard."* He studied at Livingstone College, Salisbury, N.C., where he also instructed a printing class, and became manager-foreman of the A.M.E. Zion Publishing House. The Rev. George W. Clinton, editor of the *Star of Zion,* praised Slaughter for his "excellent contributions" during his absence.

The only Negro who took the examination for the position of compositor at the Government Printing Office, in 1896 Slaughter accepted an appointment, which he held until 1937. He was certified for appointment the day after his standing was made known to the public, and was assigned to the Agricultural Division.

While employed in the printing trade he served as proof-reader, monotypist, linotype operator, compositor, and machinist. He received his Bachelor of Laws degree in 1899 and his Master of Laws degree in 1900 from Howard University, but never practiced law.

Slaughter's interest in the Odd Fellows developed early, and for many years he was a member of the board of directors, as well as presiding officer, of the lodge of the Grand United Order of Odd Fellows. He was a Thirty-third Degree Mason and editor of the *Odd Fellows Journal* from 1910 until it discontinued publication in 1937. Slaughter served as permanent secretary of the Corinthian Lodge 3859 of Odd Fellows. For a number of years he was a member of the Jonathan Davis Consistory No. 1, Prince Hall Masonry; the Past Grand Master's Conference No. 4, Odd Fellows; and Eudora Household of Ruth No. 1267, Odd Fellows. For several years at the annual meetings of the stockholders of the Odd Fellows Hall Association (Washington, D.C.), he was elected to the Board of Directors. He was also at one time director of the Odd Fellows Hall Association, as well as of the Peoples Savings Bank at Staunton, Va.

Slaughter took pride in his membership in the American Negro Academy, preparing elaborate suppers and luncheons for the members when they met in Washington. He was known to them, to members of the Mu-So-Lit Club, the Labor Day Bunch, and the Pen and Pencil Club as a gourmet and one of Washington's most liberal entertainers and hosts.

Slaughter had a long interest in politics. He was a committeeman at the inauguration of Presidents McKinley, Roosevelt, Taft, and Wilson. For several years he was secretary of the Kentucky Republican Club in Washington. He was also staff correspondent of the *Kentucky Standard* in Louisville and special contributor to the *Philadelphia Tribune,* the *American Baptist,* and the *A.M.E. Church Review.*

Slaughter was for many years superintendent of St. Luke's Episcopal Sunday School, Washington, D.C., and vestryman of the church. He was also secretary of the St. Luke's chapter of the Brotherhood of St. Andrew.

In any area where he thought he could be useful, Slaughter associated with men of both races—bishops, ministers, and political figures. He was one of the pall-bearers at the funeral of P. B. S. Pinchback of Louisiana, who died on Dec. 20, 1921. Slaughter was reliable, tactful, and made friends easily. His relations with whites were unusual. He was the only Negro elected as chairman of a "Chapel," one of the sections of the Typographical Union of the Government Printing Office which at that time had 1600 members of whom about twenty were colored. At age eighty-six Henry Slaughter was honored as the Sixty-Year Man in the Typographical Union.

Slaughter's lifelong hobby was collecting books, pamphlets, music, photographs, prints, and manuscripts relating to the history of the Negro. He became a well-known authority on the subject. His ten-room residence contained more than 10,000 volumes, many of them rare. "My books are my best friends and I would rather furnish a house with books than with furniture," he often said. In addition to his books he had a file of 100,000 newspaper clippings concerning important events and persons. He attempted to collect books of all types and on every phase of the slavery question, the Civil War, and the African background. He also aimed to acquire all works by individual Negro authors. He took great pride in his collection of autograph signatures of the men in Abraham Lincoln's cabinet, the presidents of the United States, and well-known Negroes, and in his rare engravings, broadsides, manuscript letters, slave papers, and a few museum pieces. He purchased many of his books from the valuable William Carl Bolivar collection in Philadelphia, from firms in England and Ireland, and from auction houses in Philadelphia and New York City. In 1946 Atlanta University purchased his private library.

Slaughter married Ella M. Russell of Jonesboro, Tenn., on April 27, 1904. She died on Nov. 2, 1914. On Nov. 24, 1925, he married Alma R. Level of Chicago; they later divorced. After a brief illness, Slaughter died in Washington, D.C., on Feb. 14, 1958, and his body was cremated on Feb. 18. Slaughter was survived by a sister, Ida S. Gray of Louisville, and three nephews: Frank H. Gray of Louisville, Columbus Gray of Philadelphia, and Charles R. Gray of Washington, D.C.

From the time he was a newspaper boy Slaughter learned to save a part of every dollar he earned. His prudent handling of his finances enabled him to build one of the nation's finest private collections of books on Negro history and culture. His lifelong motto was "learn to know the value of socks and you will learn the value of stocks."

There is no biography of Slaughter. His views are best found in the *Odd Fellows Journal* (1910–1937); the *Journal* has biographical information in the Jan. 5, 1922, Jan. 1, 1925, March 5, 1925, and Dec. 3, 1925, issues. Other biographical information is in *Colored American* (May 10, 1902); *Pen and Pencil Club Program, Commemoration of the 85th Anniversary of Birth of Frederick Douglass* (Feb. 14, 1902, and 1903); *Pen and Pencil Pointers* (Feb. 14, 1907); *Who's Who of the Colored Race* (1915, pp. 245–46); *Washington Times* (May 30, 1936); *Afro-American* (July 8, 1939); obituary in the *Washington Afro-American* (Feb. 22, 1958). — DOROTHY B. PORTER

SLOWE, LUCY DIGGS (1885–1937), teacher, school administrator, and college dean. She was born in Berryville, Va., the third daughter and youngest of seven children of Henry and Fannie (Porter) Slowe. Her father died when she was nine months old, her mother when she was six. She lived with a paternal aunt, Martha Slowe Price, until 1898 in Lexington, Va., when they moved to Baltimore. She graduated as salutatorian from the colored high school there, and with the aid of a scholarship received her B.A. degree from the College of Arts and Sciences, Howard University, in 1908. After teaching English in high schools in Baltimore and Washington, and receiving an M.A. degree in English from Columbia University (1915), she became principal of Shaw Junior High School in Washington (1919). Three years later she was appointed the first dean of women at Howard University, a position she held until her death from influenza and a kidney disease, on Oct. 21,

1937. She had served also as associate professor of English. She was buried in Lincoln Cemetery, Suitland, Md., just outside Washington.

Slowe was an innovator. While a student at Howard she was one of the founders and a vice-president of Alpha Kappa Alpha, the first Greek-letter sorority among Negro college women. She was the first principal of a junior high school, Shaw, for Negroes in the District of Columbia. Slowe began one of the early steps toward integration in the district's public schools when she initiated an in-training service extension course on education by Columbia University, which was attended also by teachers from the white junior high school. As dean of women at Howard University she began to change the functions of that position from the traditional role of a matron to that of a participant in the formulation of educational policies. She extended this concept from Howard to other Negro institutions of higher learning as well as to the concept of the role of dean of men.

Slowe was also a pragmatist, working to strengthen Negro organizations and promoting "interracial" goodwill in predominantly white organizations. With Mary McLeod Bethune she helped found the National Council of Negro Women (1935) and served as its first secretary. In an era when most Negroes were barred from many professional organizations, she was the first president of the National Association of College Women, patterned after the American Association of University Women, of which she was also a member. The National YWCA presented an especially difficult problem, since it in principle approved steps toward participation in policy making while continuing to maintain separate colored branches. Eva D(el) Vakia Bowles resigned in 1932 from the staff of the National Board of the YWCA because of her opposition to the board's reorganization plan which, she believed, would diminish the "participation of Negroes in policy making." Slowe continued to work with the National YWCA. On the other hand, like Mary Church Terrell, she was a member of the integrated Women's International League for Peace and Freedom.

Slowe won seventeen tennis cups at a time when Negroes were not permitted to compete with white players. She sang contralto in St. Francis Catholic Church and in her own Madison Street Presbyterian Church in Baltimore.

This interest in music led to her management of a "Cultural Series" at Howard University beginning in 1929, which presented Tourgee DeBose (concert pianist), Countée Cullen, the Howard Players (founded in 1907), the Men's Glee Club (founded in 1873), the Women's Glee Club, Marian Anderson, and Abbie Mitchell. In 1932–1933 musicians from Howard University participated in a concert by the National Symphony Orchestra (Washington, D.C.).

Like other strong personalities Slowe had difficulties with Mordecai W. Johnson, president of Howard University. The university's trustees on Oct. 26, 1937, five days after her death, adopted a glowing resolution praising her valuable contribution "to the development of Negro Womanhood both within and without the University." In 1943 women of the university donated a stained-glass window in her honor to the University Chapel.

The principal sources for Slowe's career are in the article by Marion Thompson Wright in *NAW* (1971, 3:299–300), which has a good bibliography, and the obituary in *JNH* (Jan. 1938, pp. 136–37). Information about the "Cultural Series" and the difficulties with Mordecai W. Johnson is in Rayford W. Logan's *Howard University* . . . (1969, esp. pp. 199, 200, 231, 292, 336–338), with a photograph facing page 196.

— RAYFORD W. LOGAN

SMALLS, ROBERT (1839–1915), Civil War maritime hero and congressman. Born a slave in Beaufort, S.C., he was the son of a slave mother, Lydia, born in 1790. According to tradition his father was Moses Goldsmith, a wealthy Jewish merchant of Charleston, but his and his mother's owners were John and Henry McKee. In 1851 young Smalls was hired out on various jobs in Charleston and was permitted to keep a small fraction of his wages. In 1856 he married a slave, Hannah Jones, who bore a daughter, Elizabeth Lydia, on Feb. 12, 1858. A son, Robert Jr., born in 1861, died of smallpox in his third year. Sarah Vorhees was born on Dec. 1, 1863.

Hannah Smalls died in 1883. Smalls was married again, in 1890, to Annie Wigg, a teacher and a graduate of Avery Institute, Charleston. Their son William Robert was born in 1892. Annie Smalls died in 1895.

During the years preceding the Confederate attack on Fort Sumter on April 12, 1861, Smalls had become a skilled seaman and an expert coastal pilot. Employed on the Confederate dispatch boat *Planter,* Smalls and eight Negro crewmen stole the vessel from its dock. With his wife, his two children, and five other passengers aboard, Smalls sailed past the shore batteries encircling Charleston Bay and surrendered the ship to a flotilla of the Union blockade on May 13, 1862. His feat helped convince Secretary of War Edwin Stanton to authorize the recruitment in South Carolina of 5000 volunteers of African descent. The *Planter* was assigned to transport duty for the U.S. Army with Smalls officially designated as its pilot. It was subsequently refitted as a gunboat and Smalls was appointed its captain after leading the vessel safely through Confederate fire on Dec. 1, 1863. While the *Planter* underwent extensive repairs in Philadelphia, Smalls hired tutors to teach him to read and write. His seafaring service ended when the *Planter* was decommissioned in 1866.

Returning to Beaufort, center of a predominantly Negro congressional district, he continued his informal education, acquired property, launched his political career, and served in the state militia until 1877, rising to the rank of brigadier general. His acts of generosity toward the family of his former owners won the support of some whites and his ability to speak the Gullah dialect of the Sea Islands helped establish his leadership.

Elected by the newly enfranchised freedmen to South Carolina's Constitutional Convention of 1868, he drafted a resolution which gave the state its first system of free education. As a member of the state legislature's lower house (1868–1870) and of the Senate (1870–1874), he helped obtain legislation for local improvements. Both houses, however, rejected his proposals that the state government demand the return of lands seized by federal tax commissioners during the war. His opposition to wasteful spending and corruption also won support from some whites.

Elected to Congress in 1874, he won passage of a $50,000 appropriation for the development of navy facilities at Port Royal, S.C., and of a bill to return the Citadel, Charleston's military college, to the city or pay a fair rent for its use. He successfully opposed sending troops to police Texas on the ground that they were needed to preserve law and order in the southern states. On the other hand he failed to win support for an amendment that "in the enlistment of men in the army . . . no distinction whatever shall be made on account of race or color."

Despite the turbulent campaign of 1876 as a result of which Wade Hampton's "Red Shirts" and the Democrats "redeemed" South Carolina from the Republicans, Smalls won a contested election which was confirmed by the Democratic-controlled House of Representatives. But under the South Carolina "Redeemer" government, he was one of several subjects of investigation. Accused in 1877 of having accepted a bribe of $5000 while a state senator, he was assumed by the Redeemers to be guilty before his trial. Sentenced by the state court to a three-year term in the state penitentiary, he served only three days. The state agreed to drop its charges if the federal courts, to which Smalls had appealed, would drop their charges against South Carolina for alleged violation of election laws, a compromise made without Smalls's knowledge. The governor of South Carolina granted Smalls a full pardon, and the case was not carried to the U. S. Supreme Court since it had already been settled.

Defeated in 1878 largely through intimidation and fraud, Smalls was reelected in 1880 but the House did not confirm his election until the session was almost ended. He was able, however, to win passage of a bill for the erection of a custom house, a post office, and other government buildings in Beaufort. In 1882 Smalls helped to assure the election of E. M. Mackey, a white man married to a colored woman, by withdrawing his own bid for the nomination to ensure party unity. When Mackey died on Jan. 28, 1884, Smalls was elected without opposition to fill the vacancy.

In the 1884 campaign Smalls was elected for a full term. During this, his last term, he was appointed to the War Claims Commission and submitted fifteen claims to it; he also introduced thirteen private bills and seven public ones. His unsuccessful plea to override President Cleveland's veto of a pension for the widow of former Union general David Hunter provided Smalls with an opportunity to pay tribute to Hunter's concern for the freedmen—the real reason, Smalls said, for Cleveland's veto. He opposed reform of the Civil Service and repeal of the Tenure of Office Act of 1867, which declared that the president could not remove federal officers who had been approved with the consent of the Senate without first getting the Senate's consent to their removal. (It was this act which formed the legal basis for the impeachment proceedings brought against Pres. Andrew Johnson.) His effort to secure passage of a law requiring all eating places in the District of Columbia to serve everyone regardless of color was voted down.

Smalls was defeated in 1886 by dissension between dark-skinned and light-skinned Negroes on the Republican side and by a massive Democratic party campaign. His effort to invalidate the election failed; the House seated his opponent, William Elliott. In 1888 Smalls was persuaded not to compete for the nomination against a younger congressional aspirant, Thomas E. Miller. At the state Constitutional Convention of 1895, Smalls waged a gallant but foredoomed fight to prevent Negro disfranchisement, the announced aim of the white-dominated assemblage.

Smalls completed his long career by becoming customs collector of the still active port of Beaufort (1889–1912). He declined both the colonelcy of a Negro regiment in the Spanish-American War and the post of minister to Liberia, probably because he suffered from diabetes. His last public action, in 1913, prevented the lynching of two Negroes held in the Beaufort jail. After he informed the sheriff that armed Negro citizens were ready to burn white homes unless a lynch mob was turned away, the sheriff and a quickly deputized posse maintained effective control until the threat subsided.

During his last three years Smalls was increasingly incapacitated by ill health. He died in his home on Prince Street in Beaufort on Feb. 23, 1915. His funeral was held on Feb. 26 at the First Avenue Baptist Church. Members of the Masonic Lodge Sons of Beaufort no. 36, and Odd Fellows Lodge no. 2211 accompanied his body to Tabernacle Baptist Church Cemetery. He was survived by his two daughters, Sarah and Elizabeth, a son William Robert, and several grandchildren.

See Dorothy Sterling's *Captain of the Planter* (1958) and Okon Edet Uya's *From Slavery to Public Service: Robert Smalls* (1971). The sketch by Francis Butler Simkins in *DAB* ([1963], 9, Part 1:224–25), which has a comprehensive bibliography, emphasizes his "moderate views, modesty and lack of education." For a longer and more favorable view, see Maurine Christopher's *America's Black Congressmen* (1971, pp. 38–54). *The Biographical Directory of the American Congress* (1929, p. 1708) gives the date of his death as Feb. 22, 1915; see the obituaries in the *New York Age* (March 4, 1915, p. 1) and the *Savannah Tribune* (March 6, 1915, p. 1) which give Feb. 23. — PHILIP STERLING

SMITH, BESSIE (1894–1937), entertainer and blues singer. She was born in poverty in Chattanooga, Tenn., one of a family of seven children, including two brothers who died in childhood. Her father, William Smith, died shortly after her birth, and her mother, Laura Smith, died before Bessie was nine. She was raised by her eldest sister, Viola. At the age of nine she began singing on the Chattanooga streets for nickels and dimes. In 1912 she joined a traveling show which included Gertrude "Ma" Rainey and her husband. That job and others with the Raineys contributed to the myth that "Ma" Rainey had kidnapped the young Bessie and taught her the art of blues singing.

Bessie Smith spent much of her life traveling with show groups in which she sang, danced, and played comic sketches. Such groups usually played to Negro audiences. About 1920 she married Earl Love, who died shortly afterward. Three years later she married John Gee, a Philadelphia nightwatchman, and thereafter she made Philadelphia her home. Bessie loved children and in 1926 the Gees adopted a relative of one of the women in her entourage, naming him Jack Gee, Jr. The marriage was stormy, complicated by Bessie's constant travels and heavy drinking, and by John's jealous nature, which frequently led to fights and public scenes. In 1930 the couple separated.

After several unsuccessful auditions Bessie Smith began her recording career in 1923 with her first record, coupling "Down Hearted Blues" and "Gulf Coast Blues." All of her released recordings were made for Columbia, and they proved so popular that proceeds from their sales helped keep the company financially solvent. Some of her recordings sold 100,000 copies within a week. Billed as the "Empress of the Blues," she became the highest paid Negro performer in the country. She toured many of the larger cities with her own tent show, traveling in a custom-built railroad car. Special performances for white audiences in southern cities played to packed houses and stimulated the demand for more of her recordings.

In her youth Bessie Smith was tall and slender. Although she became much heavier, sometimes weighing more than two hundred pounds, she remained attractive, with a dynamic personality and marked dramatic ability. In her stage show she sometimes simulated a recording session, and used a variety of striking costumes which emphasized her natural beauty. Her propensity for acting is evident in the two-reel motion picture *The St. Louis Blues,* made in 1929. Shortly afterward the popular craze for the blues declined, and long years of travel and drinking began to take their toll. A last recording session in 1933 combined her talents with some of the best swing musicians and resulted in four fine selections.

Bessie Smith is sometimes described as a rough, violent person who drank excessively, recklessly squandered her money, became involved in numerous fights, and made unreasonable demands on her employers. Yet those who knew her also recalled a kindly and generous Bessie Smith who once canceled her engagements to personally nurse the seriously ill infant son of Frank Walker, her business manager. Both sides of her nature have sufficient basis in recollection to establish her as a complex, changeable personality.

Bessie Smith died as a result of an automobile accident near Clarksdale, Miss. Musicians and jazz fans circulated a legendary account which held that her life could have been saved had not a white hospital refused to accept her. Edward Albee strengthened the legend with his play *The Death of Bessie Smith.* The facts are that a Memphis physician happened upon the accident, provided emergency treatment, and called an ambulance which took her directly to the Negro Hospital in Clarksdale. There her injured arm was amputated and she died shortly afterward, apparently from internal injuries. Her body was taken to Mount Lawn Cemetery in Sharon Hill, near Philadelphia. Seven thousand people attended her funeral, but her grave remained unmarked for more than thirty years. Finally, a letter to a Philadel-

phia newspaper sparked a campaign to purchase and place a headstone over her grave.

Bessie Smith was an artist of first-rate talent and lasting influence. Some of the best musicians of the 1920s, including Louis Armstrong, James P. Johnson, Charlie Green, and Joe Smith, accompanied her on records. She possessed a rich contralto voice and a marvelous control on blues and jazz numbers, some of which she wrote herself. "She was the best blues singer there was," commented Sidney Bechet, "but that trouble was inside her and it wouldn't let her rest." Louis Armstrong said: "She used to thrill me at all times, the way she could phrase a note with a certain something in her voice no other blues singer could get. She had music in her soul and felt everything she did." She profoundly influenced such other great singers as Billie Holiday and Mahalia Jackson. All of her available recordings, reissued from 1970 to 1973, preserve for posterity her voice and musical expression.

Chris Albertson's biography, *Bessie* (1972), corrects many erroneous facts repeated by earlier writers. It is thoroughly researched and based in part on material from Ruby Walker, Bessie's niece by marriage, and Jack Gee, Jr., and it is highly critical of John Gee. Paul Oliver's *Bessie Smith* (1961) is a brief interpretive work, as is Carman Moore's *Somebody's Angel Child* (1969), which leans heavily on material from John Gee. Gunther Schuller's *Early Jazz* (1968) contains an excellent analysis of Bessie Smith's music. George Avakian's fine notes for an early four-record Bessie Smith reissue set are condensed and reprinted in Martin T. Williams (ed.), *The Art of Jazz* (1959). See also Larry Gara's sketch in *NAW* (1971, 3:306–7) and Marshall W. Stearns's in *DAB, Supplement 2* ([1958], 11, Part 1:616–17).

— LARRY GARA

SMITH, FERDINAND C[HRISTOPHER] (1894–1961), union leader and journalist. Smith was born in Jamaica, British West Indies, but facts about his parentage and early life are not known. He started going to sea in 1918, came to the United States legally in that year, filed his intention two years later of becoming a U.S. citizen, and joined the International Seamen's Union. Meanwhile he had gone to sea and neglected to complete the necessary legal steps for becoming a citizen. He had nineteen years of sea service, putting into almost every port in the world. In 1936 he had risen to the rank of chief steward. He was a member of the Strategy Committee and chairman of the Food Committee in the 1936–1937 seamen's strike against the "gloryholes"—dirty, crowded living quarters aboard ship—bad food, fink books, blacklists, and employment that averaged six months a year, with earnings about $500 a year. He accepted membership on the nine-man Strategy Committee on one condition: "If we win, the new union will not tolerate segregation or discrimination of any sort." The seamen voted that plank into the constitution of the new National Maritime Union. From that time until 1945 he was one of the more powerful, albeit little-known Negro labor union leaders. He also served on boards of several important organizations. Smith died in Kingston, Jamaica, in mid-August 1961.

Smith served as trustee of the Stewards Division of the NMU (1937–1938) and in 1938 was chosen vice-president in general elections. At the 1939 convention, when the office of vice-president was abolished he was elected national secretary, and reelected to the position in the general elections of 1940, 1942, and 1944. He was a member of the Executive Board, New York Industrial Union Council, from its inception in 1943, when the Philadelphia convention of the National CIO elected him a member of its Executive Board, serving until 1947. At the Boston Convention (Nov. 1942) he was elected a member of the CIO Committee to Abolish Racial Discrimination, serving until November 1944. He was also a member of the New York State Executive Board of the CIO for several years after 1942.

The National Maritime Union, under its president Joseph Curran and national secretary Ferdinand Smith, was one of the more radical unions. Wilson Record believed that Smith owed much of his success to the support of Communist party factions in the NMU (*The Negro and the Communist Party,* 1951, p. 180).

The exclusionary policies of most of the trade unions led Smith and a few other Negro leaders (but not Willard S. Townsend) to accept Communist support. Nevertheless, Pres. Franklin D. Roosevelt wrote Curran in 1942: "Questions of race, creed and color have no place in determining who are to man our ships. The sole qualifications for a worker in the maritime industry, as well as in any other industry, should be his loyalty and his professional or technical ability and training" (*Steering to Victory,* a pamphlet of the NMU, 1944, unnumbered page 2).

This statement reiterated the substance of Roosevelt's Executive Order 8802 (June 25, 1941) prohibiting discrimination against workers in defense industries or government because of race, creed, color, or national origin, and declaring it the duty of employers and labor organizations "to provide for the full and equitable participation of all workers in defense industries, without discrimination because of race, creed, color, or national origin." The executive order also established in the Office of Production Management a Committee on Fair Employment Practices to receive and investigate complaints of discrimination in violation of the provisions of the order and to take appropriate steps to redress grievances which it found to be valid.

Convinced of Roosevelt's sincerity, the National Council of the NMU at its semiannual meeting in New York (July 1944) adopted a resolution to send Smith on a tour of the country to support the reelection of Roosevelt and a "progressive Congress." The resolution lauded Smith as "one of the ablest leaders . . . who can help the Negro people forward in their struggle for economic, political and social freedom."

In pursuance of its nondiscrimination policy the NMU recruited a mixed crew for the new Liberty freighter *Booker T. Washington,* which set sail on Oct. 20, 1942, under the command of a Negro captain, Hugh Mulzac.

Smith fought racial discrimination in several cities. He was credited with helping prevent the Harlem disorder in 1943 from developing into a full-scale riot. He made appeals over radio and soundtruck to stop the outbreak,

and rushed to Syndenham Hospital to have his picture taken with a colored soldier who urged: "Tell them to stop." This proof that the soldier had not, as rumor stated, been killed helped calm the angry protesters. During a wildcat transit strike in Philadelphia, he helped organize a committee of labor, church, and civic leaders to alleviate racial tension until the army took over by order of President Roosevelt. At the invitation of several organizations Smith conferred with city officials and civic leaders in Los Angeles, San Francisco, and Seattle to promote interracial harmony and support of the war effort.

In 1935 the International Seamen's Union of America, affiliated with the AFL, had a total membership of 20,400 of whom 5030 or 24.7 percent were Negroes. In 1944 the CIO-afiliated NMU was the bargaining agent for "more than 90,000 men of every race, color and creed." According to the *New York Herald Tribune* (Aug. 25, 1944) Smith as national secretary of the NMU reported that colored and white members of the union awaited jobs in the same NMU hiring places in southern port cities. They used the same mess halls and the same sleeping compartments aboard ship. The NMU contract prohibiting discrimination "because of race, creed, color or national origin" had been accepted, Smith reported, by 124 ship companies.

Ferdinand Smith, along with Joseph Curran, helped develop one of the best integrated labor unions during a period of hostility by many white leaders and workers. Robert Weaver wrote in 1946: "The aggressive action of NMU to secure ship command for qualified Negroes, the union's outstanding educational program for intergroup understanding, and its fight for the Negro's right to work have given Negroes a new concept of the role of labor unions in the Negro's economic struggle" (*Negro Labor, A National Problem,* 1946, p. 234).

Smith was influential in many civic activities. He served as a member of the Board of Trustees of Syndenham Hospital, where Negro and white patients, Negro and white interns, nurses, and physicians, shared facilities and worked in an experiment that attracted favorable nationwide attention. He was also a member of the Board of Directors of the Council of Pan American Democracy, the Council on African Affairs, and of the *People's Voice.* He contributed a weekly column to the *Voice* and articles in *Opportunity.*

His decline from power began in 1945 when it was revealed that as an alien he was ineligible under the constitution of the NMU to hold office. He and Curran began clashing in 1945 and at the NMU's biennial convention in the fall of 1947 Curran specifically charged that Smith had held his office fraudulently for seven years. In February 1948, when the Justice Department launched its drive to deport aliens accused of Communist activity, Smith was arrested at his home, detained at Ellis Island, and deported to Kingston, Jamaica, under a class order classifying him as undesirable and subversive. The warrant of arrest further stated that he had not had a valid immigration visa at the time of his last entry into the country in 1946, from Mexico.

Much of the information is based on *Steering to Victory* (1944) and *1946 Election Supplement* (Bernard Raskin, director of publications of the National Maritime Union of America to R.W.L., Sept. 9, 1975). Charles Lionel Franklin's *The Negro Labor Unionist of New York . . .* (1936) contains valuable background information. Information about Smith's age, arrest, deportation, and death is in newspaper clippings in the vertical file of the Moorland-Spingarn Research Center, Howard University, especially the obituary in the *New York Times* (Aug. 16, 1961, p. 31).

— RAYFORD W. LOGAN

SMITH, HARRY C[LAY] (1863–1941), newspaper editor and politician. Born in Clarksburg, W. Va., he moved to Cleveland, Ohio, at an early age and remained there the rest of his life. In 1882, one year after graduating from Central High School, he established the *Cleveland Gazette,* and for almost sixty years he devoted most of his time to publishing and editing that militant newspaper. Prior to about 1895 Smith was also a musician and composer of popular songs. The *Gazette,* an eight-page weekly, was one of the better Negro journals of its day. It published news of Negro activities in Cleveland and reports from correspondents in many other Ohio cities as well. The paper circulated throughout the state and, to a lesser extent, the Midwest. At the beginning of the twentieth century its circulation probably was close to 10,000, but readership declined steadily after World War I with increasing competition from other Negro newspapers in Cleveland.

Early in his career Smith became involved in Republican politics. In return for his support of Joseph Foraker for governor in 1885, Smith was named a deputy state inspector of oils, a post he held for four years. A persuasive orator, Smith won election three times to the Ohio General Assembly, serving during 1894–1898 and 1900–1902. During this period Smith was a prominent ally of Albion W. Tourgée in the fight to outlaw Jim Crow railroad facilities, and as a legislator he helped enact the Ohio Civil Rights Act of 1894 and the Anti-Mob Violence Act of 1896. Unfortunately, Smith picked the wrong side in the political battle that was shaping up in the Ohio Republican party in the 1890s. Supporting the Foraker faction, he outspokenly criticized the Marcus A. Hanna machine and as a result found himself increasingly alienated from the main sources of political power in the state as well as from the many colored politicians who supported Hanna. Smith became more politically independent after 1902. By 1908 he had become disenchanted with the GOP's racial policies, and he was particularly infuriated by Theodore Roosevelt's dismissal without honor of three companies of the Negro 25th Infantry after the Brownsville riot in August 1906. Smith urged Negroes to register their protest by voting against Taft.

Smith returned to the Republican fold during the Wilson administration, but beginning in 1920 he again became openly critical of the GOP. He sharply rebuked the Harding and Coolidge administrations for the military occupation of Haiti and the continued segregation of Negroes in departments of the federal government. In 1924 Smith supported Robert La Follette's Progressive party and in 1928 backed Herbert Hoover only as "the lesser of two evils." More significant was Smith's

opposition to Republican leadership at the local and state level. Complaining of declining Negro patronage and the failure of GOP leaders to support more Negroes for political office, Smith ran as an independent for City Council in 1921 against the Negro "machine" candidate; he also entered the GOP primary race for secretary of state in 1920 and for governor in 1922, 1924, 1926, and 1928. He won none of these contests, but his involvement aided the growth of Negro insurgency in the Ohio Republican party and helped lay the groundwork for the Negro exodus from the GOP in the 1930s. Ironically, Smith himself chose not to participate in that exodus. Citing the power of southern Democrats and Franklin Roosevelt's failure to deal with lynching and segregation, the *Gazette* editor swung back to support the Republicans after 1932.

Smith was an outspoken foe of segregation and one of the most consistently militant race spokesmen of his day. From the very first issue of the *Gazette* he attacked segregation and racial discrimination in all its forms, and he was equally critical of Negroes who practiced self-segregation in the name of racial solidarity. Smith was active in the successful struggle to desegregate Ohio schools in 1887. In Cleveland he led the fight against the creation of a colored Phillis Wheatley home for girls and opposed movements for separate recreational facilities, hospitals, and social welfare facilities for Negroes. Smith advocated three methods of fighting discrimination: political pressure, legal action, and the boycott. In the 1890s he favored the study of Negro history to give "a proper pride of race and self" and vigorously opposed colonization schemes. During the tense World War I period he urged Negroes to defend themselves and retaliate against white mobs if attacked.

Except for his advocacy of Negro support of Negro businesses, Smith opposed the doctrines of self-help, racial solidarity, and separatism that became popular with the rise to power of Booker T. Washington after 1895. Smith was one of the earliest and most vociferous critics of Washington, and he readily joined with William Monroe Trotter and other "radicals" in attempting to undermine the prestige of the Tuskegeean. Smith found Washington's accommodating posture on race issues both futile and unmanly. Instead he advocated agitation and protest. Smith was one of the founders of the Afro-American League in 1890 and took an active part in the militant Niagara Movement founded in 1905 by W. E. B. Du Bois and others to oppose Washington. In 1910 he was named a member of the NAACP's Select Committee of One Hundred, although he later criticized that organization for not being diligent enough in combating racism.

Unfortunately, Smith's difficult personality limited his capacity for leadership. He revealed his contentiousness in the pages of the *Gazette* by carrying on personal vendettas against individuals whom he disliked. Like Trotter and Chicago newspaper editor John G. Jones, Smith too often personalized the struggle for racial equality. He was quick to criticize and slow to cooperate with other Negro leaders, even those who agreed with him. Although on many occasions Smith's criticisms were warranted, at other times they created unnecessary disunity and injured the cause of racial advancement. Paradoxically, the same maverick qualities that made Smith outspoken in the pursuit of racial justice also limited his ability to further the principles he believed in.

Smith's career is discussed briefly in August Meier's *Negro Thought in America, 1880–1915* (1963), and more extensively in Kenneth L. Kusmer's *A Ghetto Takes Shape: Black Cleveland, 1870–1930* (1976).

— KENNETH L. KUSMER

SMITH, JOSHUA BOWEN (1813–1879), caterer, abolitionist, and state senator. He was born in Coatesville, Pa., but little is known of his childhood other than that a wealthy Quaker sent him to public school. In 1836 he went to Boston where he obtained a job as headwaiter at the Mt. Washington House. While serving at the table of Robert Gould Shaw he met Charles Sumner who became his lifelong friend. Smith worked for a short time in the family of Shaw and for Thacker, the leading colored Boston caterer. In 1849 Smith opened his own catering establishment and for more than twenty-five years had a thriving business for private individuals and abolitionist organizations as well as for troops during the Civil War, some of which he recruited. A staunch abolitionist, he and Lewis Hayden vigorously opposed the 1850 Fugitive Slave Act. He was the first Negro member (Oct. 1867) of the St. Andrew's Lodge of Freemasons of Massachusetts, serving later as junior warden of Adelphi Lodge of South Boston. Smith represented Cambridge as a senator in the state legislature during 1873 and 1874, and is said to have been the only Negro from Massachusetts to attend a national convention at that time. Ill for several months, he died on July 5, 1879. Many notables attended an impressive funeral at his residence, 37 Norfolk St., Cambridgeport. Burial services were conducted at Mount Auburn Cemetery. He was survived by his widow Emiline (a daughter had predeceased him).

He gained a sizable fortune by providing class-day entertainments at Harvard College. The sums paid him for similar occasions enabled him to provide lavish catering services for national antislavery bazaars, the Massachusetts Female Anti-Slavery Society, the Twentieth Anniversary (Jan. 24, 1851) of the *Liberator,* and the issuance of the Emancipation Proclamation. On this last occasion, Wendell Phillips unveiled William H. Brackett's bust of John Brown. Smith was so moved that he reluctantly accepted a check for $100, much less than the cost of the large reception. Smith's catering service won him the friendship of such notable abolitionists as William Lloyd Garrison, George Luther Stearns, Robert Gould Shaw, Theodore Parker, and Charles Sumner. His catering service also enabled him to employ fugitive slaves, while he kept a watchful eye on the movements of slave-hunters who searched for their prey in Boston restaurants. Among the most famous refugees were Ellen and William Craft. Smith refused, however, to permit William Craft to use his name in a book or to help him collect money because it was not possible for Craft, while living in Massachusetts, to conduct a school in Georgia.

During the Civil War, Smith lost most of his fortune as caterer for the 12th Massachusetts Regiment of Volunteers. The first volunteer regiment raised in Massachusetts, it was named the Webster Regiment for the son of Daniel Webster. Gov. John Andrew selected Smith because he was the only caterer in Boston who had the means, pluck, and patriotism to undertake the job. Andrew agreed to pay Smith an amount less than that charged by other caterers. Over a ninety-three-day period when Smith furnished rations for officers and men while the regiment was in Boston and moving to Harpers Ferry, his expenditures amounted to $40,378. In addition he performed many other costly services for which he did not ask to be refunded. When he presented the bill on July 26, 1861, Governor Andrew informed the Executive Committee of the Webster Regiment that he had refused to pay the bill because "no funds had been appropriated by the legislature with which he could legally pay" it. All other catering bills for service to regiments in Massachusetts were assumed and paid for by the state, and Congress reimbursed it. The federal government did pay the Executive Committee of the regiment at the rate of thirty cents a ration, the amount fixed after the first several months of the war, when a more economical mode of rationing had been adopted. Smith finally received $23,760.80, leaving $16,617.20 unpaid. On May 24, 1879, Smith filed in the office of the clerk of the Superior Court for the County of Suffolk, asking for payment of the balance plus interest since July 26, 1861. When he died on July 5, 1876, he bequeathed to his wife his personal estate of $750 and debts amounting to $22,596.99. These resulted in part from his expenditures for the Webster Regiment and his contributions to the abolitionist cause.

Although his widow petitioned the commonwealth in 1879, after the death of her husband, for the sum due him, she received nothing. A small allowance from his estate made by the judge of probate was insufficient for her livelihood. At age fifty-five, she was obliged to work as a domestic to support herself. Since the administrator of Smith's estate did not have the means for proving the claim against the commonwealth, Smith's widow abandoned the case. It is not known whether or not she received a suitable allowance from the treasury of the commonwealth which she had requested in consideration of her husband's services.

In July 1849 Smith, as vice-chairman of a Boston committee, had presented a silver pitcher to William Lloyd Garrison. Two of his other activities were not consummated until several years after his death. On March 5, 1851, Smith was one of seven Boston citizens who petitioned the state legislature for an appropriation of $1500 for the erection of a monument in honor of Crispus Attucks. The request was not granted until 1888. In the fall of 1865 Smith promoted the collection of private subscriptions for a monument to Robert Gould Shaw and the 54th Massachusetts Regiment which he had commanded. It was not until 1897 that $23,000 was raised for the erection of the memorial on Boston Common.

One incident illustrates Smith's magnanimity. As chairman of the Committee on Federal Relations of the state legislature he was called upon, on very short notice (March 10, 1874) to report resolutions on the death of former Pres. Millard Fillmore. As President Fillmore had signed the Fugitive Slave Act of 1850, Smith stated: "All the winter I have been trying to make you see that my friend Charles Sumner was right in urging that we forget past difficulties and now, in regard to the ex-president who has deceased, I have only to say, 'Father, forgive him, for he knew not what he did.' "

Sumner died the next day, March 11, 1874. He bequeathed his valuable painting *Miracles of the Slave,* which he had purchased in Venice, to Joshua Smith.

For information about Smith, see *Vital Records to 1850, Cambridge Births;* Lucius R. Page's *History of Cambridge, Massachusetts, 1630–1877, with a Genealogical Register* (1877); *Statement of the Claim of the Late Joshua B. Smith against the Commonwealth for Subsistence Furnished the 12th Regiment of Massachusetts Volunteers,* petition (May 14, 1879); Benjamin F. Cook's *History of the 12th Massachusetts Volunteers (Webster Regiment;* 1882); Boston Directories (1849–1873); *Boston Daily Advertiser* (June 7, 1878); *Boston Morning Journal* (June 7, 14, 1878); *Boston Evening Transcript* (July 7, 8, 1879); *Boston Evening Traveler* (July 8, 1879). In addition there are important documents in the Boston Public Library.

— DOROTHY B. PORTER

SMITH, STEPHEN (1797?–1873), businessman, clergyman, philanthropist, and abolitionist. He was born in Paxtang, Dauphin County, Pa., the son of an enslaved mother, Nancy Smith. On July 10, 1801, when but five years of age he was indentured to Gen. Thomas Boude, a Revolutionary patriot, and before maturity assumed the management of Boude's lumber interests in Columbia, Pa. With a loan of fifty dollars, Smith purchased his freedom on Jan. 3, 1816. He also purchased release from his indenture in 1816, and on Nov. 17, 1816, married Harriet Lee, sister of Isaac Harford Lee. He soon established his own prosperous lumber business and also engaged extensively in real estate operations. His wife kept an oyster and refreshment house.

Smith was one of the initial subscribers to, and agent for, *Freedom's Journal* and subsequently the *Emancipator.* In 1831 he presided at a meeting of the free colored people of Columbia to protest against the policies of the American Colonization Society. In 1832 he purchased, at his own expense, a frame church building for use of the Mount Zion African Methodist Episcopal congregation. In August 1834 his office was attacked by a mob during the severe anti-Negro riots in Columbia, and after a second riot on Oct. 2, 1834, he was publicly warned (Oct. 27, 1835) to leave the community by those who were resentful of his business success. But with support from some prominent white citizens he resolved to remain. In 1836 he became a member of the General Conference of the African Methodist Episcopal church and about 1838 was ordained to preach. He was actively involved in the operations of the Underground Railroad, both in Columbia and in Philadelphia.

Smith attended the national conventions of the free people of color in New York (1834) and Philadelphia (1835) and participated in the organization of the American Moral Reform Society. He attended the first meeting of the Pennsylvania Anti-Slavery Society (1837) and was an active participant in the Pennsylvania State Convention of Colored Citizens (1848) and the national conventions held at Rochester, N.Y. (1853), and Philadelphia (1855). He was a charter member of the Social, Civil, and Statistical Association (1860) and an ardent supporter of the Republican party.

In 1842 Smith moved to Philadelphia where he resided at 921 Lombard St. in a house purchased from his friend Robert Purvis. He operated a large coal and lumber yard at Broad and Willow Streets while his longtime associate, William Whipper, managed his interests in Columbia. A partner in his Philadelphia enterprises was Ulysses B. Vidal, who had married Smith's wife's niece. During his first decade in the city Smith acquired thirty-six properties and held substantial investments in securities. In 1849 Smith and Whipper had on hand several thousand bushels of coal, 2.25 million feet of lumber, and twenty-two of the finest merchantmen cars running on the railroad from Columbia to Philadelphia and Baltimore. The firm owned $9000 worth of stock in the Columbia Bridge Company and $18,000 worth of stock in the Columbia Bank. Stephen Smith was the reputed owner of fifty-two good brick houses of various dimensions in Philadelphia, besides a large number of houses and lots in Columbia, and a few in Lancaster. The paper of the firm of Smith and Whipper was good for any amount wherever they were known. The principal active business, attended to by Smith in person, was that of buying good negotiable paper and speculating in real estate. He was described by Martin R. Delany as "decidedly the most wealthy colored man in the United States." On March 15, 1858, John Brown conferred at Smith's house with a group of prominent Negro leaders on his plan for freeing the slaves.

Smith was a generous benefactor of the Institute for Colored Youth, the Home for Destitute Colored Children, the House of Refuge, and the Olive Cemetery. One of the incorporators of the House for Aged and Infirm Colored Persons (later the Stephen Smith Home for the Aged) he contributed the ground and $28,000 for a building and made the home the principal beneficiary of his substantial estate. He built the Zion Mission at Seventh and Lombard Streets in Philadelphia, a church at Chester, and another at Cape May, N.J., where he maintained a summer home. A member of Bethel African Methodist (Mother Bethel) Church in Philadelphia, he preached at all the churches of his communion in Philadelphia.

Smith was "a mulatto, of medium size, strongly built, fascinating countenance, with indelibly marked features." He was greatly respected for his wealth, his religious commitment, and his manifold contributions to the welfare of his people. He died in Philadelphia on Nov. 4, 1873, and was buried in Olive Cemetery, which he had saved from "the sheriff's hammer." His widow, who died on Aug. 17, 1880, was buried beside him and his mother.

The most substantial account of Smith is in William Frederic Worner's "The Columbia Race Riots" (*Lancaster County Historical Society Papers* 26 [Oct. 1922]: 175–87). — RICHARD P. McCORMICK

SNAËR, SAMUEL, JR. (1835–c. 1900), New Orleans–born musician, composer, and conductor of his own orchestra. His father was an organist in one of the white churches of the city; the younger Snaër also served in a similar position as organist for St. Mary's Italian Church for many years. A teacher of violin and piano, he played with talent a dozen different musical instruments, among them the violin, violoncello, piano, and organ. He was unexcelled as a violoncellist. A *littérateur* whose advice was eagerly sought by the writers and poets of his day, Snaër, according to Rodolphe Desdunes, "was perhaps a greater musical savant than was Macarty," one of his leading contemporaries.

Snaër, like many men of genius, had a rather contradictory nature, and for this reason confused many persons who witnessed his actions in different situations. He was of an easy-going, amiable disposition, careless with his manuscripts, not very energetic in seeking publishers for his music, and those manuscripts that were returned to him after careless hand-to-hand journeys among friends were later consigned to the bottom of his trunk, to oblivion and insects. Both of his biographers, James Monroe Trotter and Desdunes, bemoaned his extreme modesty and his lack of caution in lending his manuscripts, but Desdunes, while admitting his musical genius, says that he never became prominent in his profession, and that long before his death his indolence made him forgotten as the musical genius that he really was. On the other hand, Trotter, who wrote while Snaër was still living, spoke of him as a brilliant pianist, a skillful performer on the violin and violoncello, and an esteemed teacher of violin and piano. Both of these biographers, however, seemed to sense the fact that racial difficulties had hurt this man who had a beautiful tenor voice but would not sing, and was too indifferent to court the attention of music publishers. His very environment produced in him a resignation to apathy and indifference during his later years.

In 1853, when only eighteen years of age, Snaër composed his "Soussa Fenêtre, paroles de L. P. Canonge," published by Louis Grunewald in 1866; during that same year Grunewald also published his "Le Chant du Départ, paroles de A. Garreau," of which two editions were issued. His "Rappele-Toi, paroles de A. Musset," was published by Grunewald in 1865. (The words to all of these songs seem to have been written by white men; Canonge was a prominent theatrical manager of his day, and Armand Garreau was a prominent writer and beloved tutor of many of the young people of color.) Then followed *Grazielle,* for full orchestra, "Le Bohémien, and "Le Chant des Canotiers"—the last probably of folk origin. These compositions were followed by a large number of polkas, mazurkas, quadrilles, and waltzes. Like most of the popular compositions of that day, Snaër's were based on love, carnival, and other romantic themes, but his close connection as church organist introduced the more solemn note found in many of his masses. Lengthy excerpts from his *Gloria* and *Agnus Dei,* each composed for three voices, are reproduced in Trotter's *Music and Some Highly Musical People.*

Despite his timidity and retiring disposition, Snaër

sometimes blazed forth like a star of the first magnitude. One of these occasions was during a benefit concert for Mrs. Louise De Mortié's orphanage, when he led his own orchestra in the opening number on the program, an overture which he had composed. Some of the finest free Negroes that the city had produced were in attendance. The Orleans Theater was filled and a group of prominent white northern "adventurers" were present in imposing array. On this night of May 10, 1865, before a vast audience, Snaër returned to the stage to conduct his orchestra in Dédé's *Quasimodo Symphony.* It was a galaxy of musical stars: when Victor-Eugène Macarty appeared at the piano, it was later described as a musical triumph. When it was Basile Barès's turn to take the stage, he literally "held the house in rapture" with the playing of two of his own compositions—"The Magic Belles" and "The Fusées Musicales." In 1877, on the night of Oct. 14 when a "Grand Vocal and Insturmental Concert" was presented at the Masonic Hall, St. Peter and St. Claude Streets, Snaër's "Le Bohémien" was included in the program. Said Trotter: " 'Le Bohémien' is one of several of Professor Snaër's pieces that show him to be a writer of fine abilities." Snaër's facility in composing was matched by his facility in remembering his scores. Twenty-six years after he had composed his "Sous sa Fenêtre," and without having seen the score for many years, he could sit down and write it out, note for note. He could recall equally well each of his compositions —even those of an elaborate and difficult character. He once wrote from memory a great solemn mass that he had composed several years past. In later years he became interested in chess playing and left a reputation as a player of merit.

Principal sources are Maud Cuney-Hare, *Negro Musicians and Their Music* (1936); Rodolphe Desdunes, *Nos Hommes et Notre Histoire* (1911); Charles B. Rousséve, *The Negro in Louisiana* (1937); various issues of *La Tribune de la Nouvelle-Orléans.* For original scores of New Orleans Negro music, see the Howard-Tilton Library of Tulane University and the Marcus Christian Collection of the Earl Long Library, University of New Orleans. Six pieces, some abbreviated, are in James Monroe Trotter's *Music and Some Highly Musical People* (1878). For background, see John W. Blassingame's *Black New Orleans, 1660–1880* (1973), and Herbert Sterkx's *The Free Negro in Ante-Bellum Louisiana* (1972). — MARCUS B. CHRISTIAN

SPAULDING, CHARLES CLINTON (1874–1952), businessman. He was born in Columbus County, N.C., on Aug. 1, 1874, to Benjamin McIver and Margaret Moore Spaulding. During his early years he attended the local school and worked on his father's farm. In 1894, at the age of twenty, Spaulding left his father's farm and moved to Durham, N.C., where he resided for the remainder of his life. In 1898 he graduated from Whitted School with what was then considered a high school education. Immediately after graduation Spaulding became the manager of a local cooperative Negro grocery store, a position that started him on his lifelong career as a business leader.

In 1899 John Merrick and Dr. Aaron Moore, who had organized the North Carolina Mutual and Provident Association the year before, impressed by Spaulding's reputation for honesty and reliability, hired Spaulding to put life into their struggling enterprise. In 1900 Spaulding was promoted from part-time agent to general manager on a full-time basis. He was also chosen at the same time as a member of the Board of Directors and the third member of the management team. This began the famous Merrick–Moore–Spaulding triumvirate that was to have an influence on the firm for the next fifty-two years. A later president of the firm, William Jessie Kennedy, Jr., has stated that it was Spaulding's initiative and efforts which enabled the firm to achieve its foremost position among Negro life insurance companies in America (The North Carolina Mutual Story). It was also in 1900, on Sept. 26, that Spaulding married his first wife, Fannie Jones, a clerk in the Home Office. They were the parents of four children: Margaret, C. C. Jr., John A., and Booker B. Spaulding. Following the death of Fannie Spaulding, on Aug. 19, 1919, he married Charlotte Garner of Newark, N.J., on Jan. 3, 1920.

In the initial years Spaulding served the association in many capacities, including agent, clerk, janitor, and general manager. As general manager Spaulding developed a market for the association and hired a new group of agents. The company went through many critical periods during its early years, but Spaulding's optimism and zeal helped the association survive these stages. Many writers dealing with this period have stated that the triumvirate was governed by an overriding sense of trusteeship and a special mission for the "economic salvation of the Negro race."

After 1905 the firm expanded rapidly. Between 1903 and 1911 it launched two newspapers, a drugstore, the Mechanics and Farmers Bank, the Merrick-Moore-Spaulding Real Estate Company, and a short-lived hosiery mill. By 1915 the association had branches in twelve other states and the District of Columbia.

In 1919 the name of the association was officially changed to the North Carolina Mutual Life Insurance Company. In this same year, after the death of Pres. John Merrick, Spaulding was elected secretary-treasurer of the company. Four years later, in 1923, upon the death of President Moore, Spaulding was elected president of the company and remained in this office until his death in 1952.

Under Spaulding's leadership as president the company became the largest Negro business in the United States. Spaulding's management allowed the company to survive the Great Crash and the Depression. Spaulding wrote to W. E. B. Du Bois that "the depression has made all of us better businessmen, it has taught us how to manage more efficiently." Spaulding reiterated this idea of development in 1932 in an address delivered at the annual meeting of the Association for the Study of Negro Life and History. He stated that the business world offered many opportunities for economic advancement for Negroes and that a successful business was the most efficient weapon with which to fight segregation and discrimination.

President of North Carolina Mutual and "Mr. Negro Business," Spaulding served as president of the National Negro Business League and helped to reorganize the league in 1938 when it faced dissolution. Spaulding also helped to organize the not-so-successful National Negro Insurance Association in 1921, the first Negro organization of its kind. Another important aspect of Spaulding's life interests was in the development of Negro colleges. Although not a college-trained man himself, Spaulding campaigned to save many financially imperiled Negro colleges and served as trustee for Howard University, Shaw University, and North Carolina College in Durham. He was also active in church and community affairs in Durham. By the time of his death Spaulding had addressed many conferences and conventions, served on many boards and committees, and received many awards, honors, and degrees.

His death on Aug. 1, 1952, his seventy-eighth birthday, ended an era in the development of the North Carolina Mutual. The company had grown from an initial investment of $350 to assets of more than $43 million.

He died of bronchial pneumonia at his home, 1006 Fayetteville St., Durham. His funeral was held on Aug. 4 at White Rock Baptist Church, where he had been a deacon and a trustee, the Rev. Miles Mark Fisher officiating. Large crowds followed from the church to Beechwood Cemetery.

A discussion of Spaulding's life and work is in William J. Kennedy, Jr.'s The North Carolina Mutual Story, A Symbol of Progress, 1898–1970 (1970) and in An Economic Detour, A History of Insurance in the Lives of American Negroes (1940) by Merah S. Stuart. The most comprehensive study of Spaulding's impact on insurance and Negroes is Walter Weare's Black Business in New South, A Social History of North Carolina Mutual Life Insurance Company (1973). These books include extensive bibliographies. See also the obituary in the Norfolk Journal and Guide (Aug. 9, 1952, pp. 1, 2).

— SYLVIA M. JACOBS

STANCE, EMANUEL (c. 1848–1887), soldier. Born in Charleston, S.C., he enlisted in F Troop of the 9th Cavalry in 1867 and rose to the rank of first sergeant in less than three years. He served with the same unit in many Indian campaigns during twenty years and became the first Negro soldier to win the Congressional Medal of Honor during the Indian Wars. Stance was murdered just outside the Fort Robinson, Neb., military reservation on Christmas morning 1887.

Stance, who was barely five feet tall, won his Medal of Honor against the Kickapoos in May 1870. On the morning of May 20 he led a scouting party from Fort McKavett, in central Texas, northward to Kickapoo Spring. After covering ten miles he discovered a party of Indians leading a herd of horses. He and his patrol surprised and drove off the warriors and captured several horses before camping for the night. On his way back to McKavett the next morning he drove off a party of Indians attacking a small wagon train and captured additional horses. The Kickapoos reappeared later but Stance repelled their attack. In still another encounter he attacked a small village and rescued two white prisoners. Stance received his award at Fort McKavett on July 20, 1870, and thanked the adjutant-general in a letter he wrote the same day: "I will cherish the gift as a thing of priceless value and endeavor by my future conduct to merit the high honor conferred upon me.''

He remained at Fort McKavett over the next three years. In 1874 he served in Gen. Ronald Mackenzie's expedition against the Comanches and Kiowas, after which he was stationed at Fort Concho, Tex. He fought in the Apache wars of New Mexico from 1877 to 1881, and served at Fort Reno, Indian Territory, from 1882 to 1885, when he moved to Fort Robinson. During his years at Reno, Stance was involved in frequent efforts to restrain or expel homesteaders who sought to claim lands in the unopened Indian Territory (Oklahoma).

Stance was a rigid disciplinarian who tended to treat his men with excessive harshness. After an officer found him dead outside Robinson from four bullet wounds, officers and enlisted men believed he had been murdered by one of his own men. One soldier was tried but not convicted. Stance was buried with military honors at Fort Robinson on Dec. 28, 1887. Investigations continued for several months but the army finally abandoned efforts to find his killer.

Stance was said to have left an autobiographical manuscript but it has never been located. His only other writings are the few letters in military files of the National Archives. Aspects of his career are recounted in Theodore F. Rodenbough and William L. Haskins (eds.) *The Army of the United States* (1896); Col. George F. Hamilton's ''History of the Ninth Regiment of Cavalry'' (undated manuscript, U.S. Military Academy Library); William H. Leckie's *The Buffalo Soldiers* (1967); and Irvin H. Lee's *Negro Medal of Honor Men* (1967). — FRANK N. SCHUBERT

STEWARD, FRANK RUDOLPH (1872–1931), lawyer and army officer. He was born at Wilmington, Del., one of eight children of Theophilus Gould Steward and Elizabeth (Gadsden) Steward. His father was a prominent clergyman, chaplain, author, and educator. Steward prepared for college at Phillips Exeter Academy, Exeter, N.H., and received his B.A. degree from Harvard College in 1896. He graduated from Harvard Law School in 1899. In the same year he was appointed captain, 49th Infantry, U.S. Volunteers, and served with the regiment in the Philippines (1899–1901) where his father also served as government superintendent of schools for the province of Luzon. According to an article in the *Colored American Magazine* (Jan. 1901, pp. 201–2), Steward was provost judge in San Pablo. He was admitted to the bar in Pittsburgh and practiced law there until his death. A general practitioner, with an office at 413 Fourth Ave. and a home at 3313 Milwaukee St., he believed that he had tried more than the average number of homicide cases. He took a more or less active interest in politics, and was a member of the Electoral College of Pennsylvania, casting his vote for Harding and Coolidge. On Oct. 27, 1910, he married Adah M. Captain; there is no record of children. A year later he received the LL.D. degree from Wilberforce University, where his father after 1907 had served as vice-president, chaplain, and teacher.

Steward was a contemporary at Harvard of William Monroe Trotter, W. E. B. Du Bois, and William H. Lewis. Although Steward appears not to have received honors upon graduating from Harvard College, he had some of the same professors as did Du Bois and Trotter, notably George Herbert Palmer and George Santayana (philosophy), Francis Peabody (social ethics), and Albert Bushnell Hart (history). He did not have courses with Josiah Royce and William James, who greatly influenced Du Bois and Trotter. The records furnished by the Harvard University Archives do not list the courses he pursued in law school. The requirements for graduation, however, were rigorous.

This sketch is based primarily on information furnished by Harvard University Archives: *25th Annual Report—Class of 1896* (p. 553); *Obituaries: 40th Anniversary Report—Class of 1896;* his courses and teachers as an undergraduate; and *Catalogue, 1897–98, The Law School* (p. 522). The brief sketch in the *Colored American Magazine* (Jan. 1901) has a photograph (p. 201). See also William Steward's and Theophilus Steward's *Gouldtown* (1913). For his service in the Philippines, see William B. Gatewood, Jr.'s ''Smoked Yankees'' and the Struggle for Empire: Letters from Negro Soldiers, 1898–1902 (1971, pp. 294–96). — RAYFORD W. LOGAN

STEWARD, SUSAN MARIA SMITH MCKINNEY (1847–1918), pioneer woman physician. Born in Brooklyn, one of eleven children of Sylvanus and Annie (Springstead) Smith, both of mixed Negro and Indian ancestry, Steward was believed by some historians to have been the first colored female medical college graduate (relatively recent research, however, has placed her as first in New York State, and third in America). She graduated in 1870 from the New York Medical College for Women, and was the valedictorian of her class, under her maiden name of Susan Maria Smith. In 1888 she completed a postgraduate course at the Long Island Medical College Hospital, the only woman in the class, and in the entire college.

As a teenager she had been a serious student of the organ, studying under two famous Brooklyn teachers, John Zundel of Plymouth Church, and Henry Eyre Browne of the Brooklyn Tabernacle. This preparation qualified her to serve as church organist and choir director of Brooklyn's Bridge Street Church for the quarter century that she practiced medicine in Brooklyn.

In 1874 she married the Rev. William G. McKinney, an Episcopal minister of Charleston, S.C., and practiced under the name of Dr. Susan Smith McKinney until his death in 1896, when she married Chaplain Theophilus Gould Steward, whose first wife had died in 1893. She moved to Wilberforce University in Ohio, where she became its resident physician while her husband was serving as a chaplain in the Philippines.

Meanwhile in 1881 McKinney co-founded the Women's Hospital & Dispensary at Myrtle and Grand Avenues in Brooklyn, and was a member of the staff until she left Brooklyn in 1896. This later became the Memorial Hospital for Women and Children. By a strange coincidence this hospital closed its doors permanently in 1918, the same year that Steward died in Wilberforce. She also (as Dr. McKinney) served on the staff of the New York Medical College and Hospital for Women, at 213 W. 54th St., in Manhattan, and from

1892 to 1896 as a manager and one of two female members of the medical staff of the Brooklyn Home for Aged Colored People. She was a member of the Kings County Homeopathic Society and the New York State Medical Society.

In 1911 Steward addressed an interracial congress in London on "Colored Women in America." This was probably the first Universal Races Congress, which her older sister Sarah, the second wife of Henry Highland Garnet, also attended. Steward also read a paper on "Women in Medicine" before the National Association of Colored Women's Clubs at Wilberforce, Ohio, on Aug. 16, 1914. A reprint of this paper gives probably the most nearly complete list of colored women who became pioneers in the study and practice of medicine.

In 1975 the Dr. Susan Smith McKinney Jr. High School at 101 Park Ave., Brooklyn, commemorated the area in which her offices and the hospital which she co-founded were located.

McKinney had two children by her first marriage: Anna who married Louis Holly, son of Bishop James T. Holly; and William Sylvanus McKinney, an Episcopal priest. McKinney and her second husband, Theophilus Gould Steward, had no children. She died at Wilberforce and was buried on March 10, 1918, in the family plot at Greenwood Cemetery, Brooklyn.

Sources include *Announcements of the New York Medical College for Women* (1870, 1882); *Medical & Surgical Register of the United States* (1890); Stiles's *History of Kings County; Transactions of the Homeopathic Medical Society of the State of New York* (vol. 31); *Catalogue* of the Long Island College Hospital (1888); the *New York World-Telegram and Sun* (May 9, 1960); Brooklyn Directories (1870–1896). The descendants of Susan Steward also provided valuable information. — WILLIAM S. MCKINNEY, JR.

STEWARD, THEOPHILUS GOULD (1843–1924), clergyman, chaplain, author, and educator. Steward was born in Gouldtown, an old community of free Negroes in Cumberland County, N.J. His parents were James Steward, a mechanic who fled to Gouldtown as a nine-year-old indentured servant, and Rebecca (Gould) Steward, who was descended from John Fenwick, a seventeenth-century proprietor of West Jersey. Theophilus Steward became a minister in the African Methodist Episcopal church in 1861. Four years later he accompanied Bishop Daniel Payne to Charleston, S.C., where he participated in the reestablishment of the denomination in that state (South Carolina had prohibited all Negro churches). He also organized the first Negro school in Marion, Ga., served a Macon, Ga., congregation from 1868 to 1871, helped write the Georgia Republican platform in 1868, led a successful protest by Americus (Ga.) freedmen against compulsory labor contracts, worked as a cashier of the Freedmen's Bank in Macon, and speculated in cotton. In the next twenty-five years he served congregations in Brooklyn, Philadelphia, Wilmington, and Washington, D.C. He also undertook a missionary journey to Haiti in 1873, where he established a church in Port-au-Prince. In 1884 he nearly achieved election to the presidency of Wilberforce University, where he had received the degree of

Doctor of Divinity three years previously. In 1891 he accepted a commission as chaplain of the 25th Infantry Regiment. Steward served in Cuba and the Philippines as well as several western posts before he retired in 1907 to become vice-president, chaplain, and professor of history, French, and logic at Wilberforce.

He wrote several books, the first of which was *Memoirs of Mrs. Rebecca Steward* (1877). His next volume, *Genesis Re-read* (1885), dealt with the then highly controversial issue of Darwinian theory and its relation to the Genesis version of creation. Steward's position of evolutionary theism, which placed the evolutionary process within the context of a divine plan, was far in advance of most other Methodist ministers and established his reputation as a theologian. *Genesis Re-read* was used as a text at Payne Theological Seminary, a branch of Wilberforce, for several years. While serving as chaplain he wrote *The Colored Regulars in the U.S. Army* (1899, reprinted 1969), perhaps the best of several efforts to commemorate the heroic service of the Negro regulars during the Spanish-American War.

Steward also wrote two pamphlets, *Active Service or Gospel Work Among the U.S. Soldiers* (1897) and *How the Black St. Domingo Legion Saved the Patriot Army in the Siege of Savannah in 1779* (1899), which was followed much later by *The Haitian Revolution 1791 to 1804 or Sidelights on the French Revolution* (1914). This important illustrated book was used as a text at Wilberforce, probably by Steward himself; it is frequently cited by later historians. He also wrote a personal memoir, *Fifty Years in the Gospel Ministry* (1920) and a family history (with his brother William), *Gouldtown, A Very Remarkable Settlement of Ancient Date* (1913). His lesser writings cover as wide a range as his books, and include *Colored American Magazine* articles on conditions in the Philippines and a poem, "The Aged Patriot's Lament," which appeared in the *Manila Times* (Feb. 6, 1901).

Steward's military career began at Fort Missoula, Mont. He went from there to Chickamauga and Cuba with his regiment. He returned to the United States for only a short time, and was the featured speaker at a Brooklyn peace jubilee sponsored by the Montauk Soldiers Relief Association in September 1898. He then returned to war, this time in the Philippines. While stationed in Manila he served as government superintendent of schools for the province of Luzon. In the summer of 1902 he and the 25th Infantry were transferred to Fort Niobrara, Neb. He finished his career at Fort Reno, Okla., where he was retired for age.

His years at Wilberforce were occupied largely with teaching and writing. He also found time to lead Wilberforce fundraising drives in many midwestern cities. He and his wife, Dr. Susan Steward, went to the First Universal Races Congress at the University of London (July 26–29, 1911) as delegates of the A.M.E. church. He wrote his study of the Haitian revolution during this period. Preparation for this book probably combined with his own military experience to produce a theory of education for black Americans which partially dissented from the industrial training advocated by Booker T. Washington's job-oriented and W. E. B. Du Bois's academic emphasis. In a letter published in the *In-*

dianapolis Freeman (Aug. 19, 1905) he urged that all schools for Negroes employ ex-soldiers to teach drill and military tactics to all male students. "Soft men," he argued, "cannot carry on a hard fight." His analysis of the Haitian revolution gave support to this position: in Haiti, only the reality of Negroes as victorious soldiers forced whites to shed their disdain. There, as elsewhere when oppressed peoples struggled for liberty, "swords precede plowshares and . . . the spear goes before the pruning hook" (*Haitian Revolution,* p. vi). Steward's views of education have been generally ignored in the continuing emphasis on the debate between Du Bois and Washington. However, he probably contributed a rationale of particular relevance to the development of military programs, which were instituted at some Negro high schools and colleges at the turn of the century.

Steward married Elizabeth Gadsden in Charleston, S.C., in 1866. She bore him eight children and died in 1893. Three years later he married Susan Maria (Smith) McKinney, the widow of the Rev. William G. McKinney, an Episcopal minister of Charleston, and one of the earliest female medical college graduates.

Several of Steward's sons (by his first wife) achieved considerable professional success. Frank, a Harvard graduate and the author of several magazine articles, served as a captain of the 49th Infantry during the Philippine Insurrection. He later practiced law in Pittsburgh. Charles, also a Harvard graduate, was a Boston dentist. Theophilus B. taught English in the Kansas City, Mo., colored high school, and Gustavus was cashier of the Supreme Life and Casualty Company of Columbus, Ohio, after teaching in the Philippines and at Tuskegee Institute. Steward had no children by his second wife.

Steward's own books, articles, and letters to newspapers contain the best data on his career. Two Negro newspapers, the *Indianapolis Freeman* and the *Cleveland Gazette,* frequently reported his activities. These papers and the biographical sketch in M. A. Broadstone (ed.), *History of Greene County, Ohio* (1918), contain useful supplementary information.

— FRANK N. SCHUBERT

STEWART, [STEWARD] JOHN (1786–1823), missionary to the Wyandott Indians. He was born in Powhatan County, Va., the son of free Negro parents of mixed Indian ancestry. While he was very young, Stewart's parents moved west to Tennessee, leaving him behind. Steward remained in Virginia until he was twenty-one, when he began to drift westward in an attempt to ascertain the whereabouts of his parents. His travels brought him to Marietta, Ohio, around 1811, where he fell victim to a gang of robbers. Soon after his arrival in Marietta Stewart went on a drinking spree, causing him at one point to contemplate suicide. He was able to recover his senses and apprenticed himself to a sugar mapler in Washington County, Ohio, where he was given the opportunity to engage in reading, prayer, and meditation during his free time. This cloistered existence was only temporary. Upon returning to Marietta Stewart again took to drink. Quickly realizing the futility of constant drunkenness, he rented a house in Marietta, where he set himself up in the blue-dying business. During this period he underwent a religious conversion

bringing him to join the Methodist Episcopal church in Marietta.

In the spring of 1815, following a near-fatal bout with tuberculosis, Stewart decided to spread the Gospel among the Indians. Leaving Marietta, he began a northerly trek, first stopping at Goshen, Ohio, on the Tuscawaras River, the site of the Moravian mission among the Delawares. From November 1816 until the following spring Stewart labored among the Wyandott Indians in the Sandusky, Ohio, area. Acting as his interpreter was Jonathan Pointer, a Negro taken prisoner by the Wyandotts during his youth who was fluent in their language. During the winter months Stewart was successful in converting his interpreter, a number of Wyandott chieftains, and some tribal members to Christianity. Stewart's activities marked the first really successful and continuing Methodist mission among the Indians in the United States.

From the summer of 1817 until the latter part of 1818 Stewart returned to the Marietta area. Relatively little is known of his activities during these months. In the fall of 1818 he returned to northern Ohio, continuing his missionary activities. In March 1819, while attending the quarterly meeting of the Mad River Circuit, he was regularly licensed to preach the Gospel. Rumors, begun by denominational rivals implying that Stewart had no real authority to preach, were somewhat allayed by this licensing and his status among the Indians was restored.

On Aug. 7, 1819, the Ohio Annual Conference of the Methodist Episcopal church established the first official Methodist mission to the Indians, based on the groundwork laid by Stewart. From 1819 through 1822 he continued work among the Wyandotts, aiding the Rev. James B. Finley in his missionary school at Big Springs. About 1820 Stewart married a mulatto girl named Polly. Largely through the efforts of Bishop William McKendree, money was raised to purchase a tract of fifty-three acres near Sandusky for Stewart and his bride.

During the summer of 1822 Stewart was visited by a group of supporters of Richard Allen, who had separated from the Methodist Episcopal church to form the African Methodist Episcopal church. Stewart joined with them, "believing he could be more useful among his own people than among the whites." In the fall of 1823 his health grew worse, confining him to house and bed. He died on Dec. 17, 1823, at his home.

The only biography of Stewart is Joseph Mitchell's *The Missionary Pioneer or A Brief Memoir of The Life, Labours, and Death of John Stewart, Man of Colour* (1827). Further details of Stewart's activities are in James B. Finley's *History of the Wyandott Mission* (1840). Scattered references to Stewart and his work among the Wyandotts are in the *Methodist Magazine* and *Minutes of the Annual Conferences of the Methodist Episcopal Church* for the years of his ministry. His address to the Wyandott Indians and letter to William Walker (May 25, 1817) are in *Early Negro Writing, 1760–1837, Selected and Introduced by Dorothy Porter* (1971). — FRANK R. LEVSTIK

STEWART, T. McCANTS (1854–1923), lawyer, pastor, author, editor, and educator. Born free in Charleston, S.C., the son of George Gilchrist and Anna (Morris)

Stewart, he attended school there and entered the academy at Howard University (1869), remaining there until 1873. He entered the University of South Carolina and received the B.A. degree in 1875 as valedictorian and the LL.B. degree in the same year. In that year he became a partner with Robert Brown Elliott and D. Augustus Straker in their Charleston law firm. At the same time he was professor of mathematics in the State Agricultural College, Orangeburg. According to his own account he then studied theology and philosophy at Princeton Theological Seminary.

Ordained a minister in the A.M.E. church on Oct. 13, 1877, he was pastor of Bethel A.M.E. Church in New York City, where at the same time he practiced law. In 1883 he and his wife, in the company of Hugh M. Browne, went to Liberia as Charles Sumner Professor of Belles Lettres, History and Law at the College of Liberia. En route they visited Scotland, England, France, and Germany, and he wrote a series of letters, published in the *New York Globe* (1884), some describing West Africa. Somewhat disillusioned by the prospects for liberal arts education in Liberia, he returned to the United States to observe vocational education at Hampton Institute. In 1886 he resumed the practice of law in New York City. He gained widespread attention in 1890 when, as counsel for T. Thomas Fortune, the fiery editor was awarded $1,016.23 from the proprietor of a saloon who refused to serve him because of his race and used force to have him ejected. He also wrote editorials for Fortune's paper, the *New York Freeman.* He and Fortune lobbied (1891) to get New York State to adopt a law which prohibited insurance companies from "making any distinction between white and colored persons . . . as to the premium or rates charged for policies."

When a group of destitute Negroes from Oklahoma arrived in New York City in 1892, Stewart and Fortune sought to provide relief for them so that they could return to Oklahoma rather than continue to Liberia. From 1891 to 1895 he was a member of the Brooklyn Board of Education. In 1898 Stewart moved to Honolulu, and his glowing reports stimulated Fortune to go there. In 1903 he established the weekly *Portland* (Ore.) *Advocate,* then returned to Liberia in 1906 and became associate justice of its Supreme Court. In an *Address to the Executive Committee of the Liberia Bar Association* (1909) he sharply criticized the administration of justice. He was removed from his position in 1915.

He lived in England from 1915 to 1921 as the respected "Judge McCants Stewart" and continued his interest in Africa, particularly Liberia. He founded in October 1918 the African Progress Union to promote the solidarity of Afro-Americans and Africans. It became a key organization for Pan-Africanism in Great Britain (1918–1931) when, after his death in 1923, the League of Colored Peoples was formed. The cold and damp winters of England forced the Stewarts to move to St. Thomas, Virgin Islands, in 1921, where he practiced law and became a prominent citizen. He was a member of a delegation from the Virgin Islands to the United States in 1922. Becoming ill, he returned to St. Thomas, died on Jan. 7, 1923, and was buried there. He was survived by his second wife, Alice (his first wife,

Charlotte, the mother of their three children, had died some years earlier).

His son Gilchrist Stewart, an attorney whose report on the Brownsville Riot in August 1906 helped spur the Senate investigation, was active in the Constitution League, a bridge between the Niagara Movement (organized in 1905 by W. E. B. Du Bois and others to oppose the conservative policies of Booker T. Washington) and the NAACP.

T. McCants Stewart generally placed greater emphasis on economic improvement than on political action. Along with Straker and Fortune, and members of the Colored Farmers' Alliance, he was influenced to some extent in the 1880s by Henry George's single-tax views and the exploitation of the poor by the rich. This economic approach led him to encourage the development of commercial relations with Liberia rather than large-scale colonization. In addition he advocated a stay-at-home policy for American Negroes as a distinct ethnic group who would help "build up a new Christian Negro Nationality in the 'Fatherland.'" He also urged industrial education in 1889 so that Negroes could win recognition in organized labor and in racial business cooperation ("The Afro-American as a Factor in the Labor Problem," *A.M.E. Church Review,* July 1889, p. 38). It is not known whether the exclusionist policies of trade unions or his life in Hawaii led him to modify his views about colonization. When he returned with his family to Liberia in 1906, he was quoted as saying: "I watch with great interest the fight which you are making in the United States for equality of opportunity. But I regard it as a hopeless struggle, and am not surprised that many Afro-Americans turn their faces toward Liberia" (*Liberia,* Bulletin no. 31 [1907], pp. 30–32). Encouraging Afro-Americans to migrate to Africa was a continuing problem during the rest of Stewart's life. It is probable that his removal from office as a justice of the Supreme Court of Liberia in 1915 made him less enthusiastic about this part of the "Fatherland."

As a member of the Brooklyn Board of Education he is said to have won the fight to have the word "colored" removed from the school system and in having colored teachers teach classes of white and colored students. A one-time Democrat, he became a Republican in 1895, partly because of disillusionment with the policies of Pres. Grover Cleveland but also because Stewart, like some other prominent Negroes, was being "frozen out of a job" by objections from Democrats.

There is no comprehensive biography of Stewart. The brief sketch in William J. Simmons's *Men of Mark* . . . (1887, pp. 1052–54) goes only to the resumption of his practice of law (1886), after his return from Liberia. The slightly longer sketch in Fitzhugh Lee Styles's *Negroes and the Law* (1937, pp. 128–31) adds little and leaves the impression that Stewart (who died in 1923) was still living in Liberia. Stewart's views on Liberia after his first trip are expressed in his *Liberia: The Americo-African Republic* (1886). The best sources are August Meier's *Negro Thought in America, 1880–1915* . . . (1963, passim), and Emma Lou Thornbrough's *T. Thomas Fortune, Militant Journalist* (1972, passim). For Stewart's criticism of Liberian courts and his dismissal as associate justice of the Supreme Court, see Raymond Leslie Buell's *The Native Problem in Africa* (1928, 2:717, and n.35a). His Papers in the Moorland-Spingarn Research Center, Howard University, contain valuable material concerning his career as an attorney in Hawaii (1898–1905). — CLARENCE G. CONTEE, SR.

STILL, WILLIAM (1821–1902), abolitionist, writer, and businessman. Still was born near Medford, in Burlington County, N.J. His father, Levin Steel, was a former slave who had purchased his own freedom and changed his name to Still to protect his wife Sidney, who had escaped from slavery in Maryland. After her first escape attempt had failed she ran to her husband with two of their four children and changed her name to Charity. Their son William was the youngest of eighteen children. From early boyhood he worked on his father's farm and as a woodcutter. He had little formal schooling, but read what was available and studied grammar on his own. He left home when he was twenty, finding employment with neighboring farmers. In 1844 he went to Philadelphia, where he worked at various jobs, including handyman in several households.

In 1847 he married Letitia George, who became the mother of his four children. The year of his marriage, Still found employment in the office of the Pennsylvania Society for the Abolition of Slavery. His duties were janitorial and clerical, but he soon became involved with aiding fugitives from slavery. He was in a unique position to provide board and room for many of the fugitives who rested in Philadelphia before resuming their journey to Canada. One of those former slaves turned out to be his own brother, Peter Still, left in bondage by his mother when she had escaped forty years earlier. William Still later reported that finding his brother led him to preserve the careful records concerning former slaves which provided valuable source material for his book *The Underground Railroad* (1872).

When Philadelphia abolitionists organized a vigilance committee to assist the large numbers of fugitives going through the city after the Fugitive Slave Act of 1850, they named William Still chairman. John Brown's wife stayed with the Still family for a time following the Harpers Ferry raid, and several of Brown's accomplices received aid from Still. Although he concluded his work in the antislavery office in 1861, Still continued his association with the society, serving for eight years as vice-president and president from 1896 to 1901.

While working for the abolition society Still began purchasing real estate. During the Civil War he opened a store handling new and used stoves, and later established a very successful coal business. In 1864 he became post sutler at Camp William Penn, where Negro soldiers were stationed.

William Still's book on the Underground Railroad was an important addition to the literature of the antislavery movement. One of the small number of postwar accounts written or compiled by Negro authors, it provided a much-needed corrective to the memoirs of white abolitionists. Still recognized the many contributions of white abolitionists, but he also pictured the fugitives themselves as courageous individuals, struggling for their own freedom, rather than as helpless or passive passengers on a white Underground Railroad. His journals were the only day-to-day record of vigilance committee activity covering a prolonged period. In addition to the accounts of the fugitives, he included excerpts from newspapers, legal documents, letters from abolitionists and former slaves, and biographical sketches.

Although the executive committee of the Pennsylvania Society for the Abolition of Slavery had asked Still to write his book, the work and its publication and distribution were a product of his own effort. His stated purpose was to "encourage the race in efforts of self-elevation." He believed that the most eloquent advocates of Negroes were Frederick Douglass, William Wells Brown, and other self-emancipated champions. It was his mission as a Negro to record their heroic deeds, and he hoped the book would serve as additional testimony to the intellectual capacity of his race. "We very much need works on various topics from the pens of colored men to represent the race intellectually," he told one of his sales agents. Still's book went into three editions and became the most widely circulated work on the Underground Railroad. He proudly exhibited it at the Philadelphia Centennial Exposition in 1876, a powerful reminder of the condition of Negroes during slavery.

Still worked in other ways to improve the status of Negroes. In 1855 he traveled to Canada to visit communities where refugees from United States slavery had settled. His positive reports counteracted some of the criticism of Negroes in Canada then in circulation. Five years later he cited the examples of successful Negroes in Canada to argue for the emancipation of all slaves. In 1859 he started a campaign to end racial discrimination on Philadelphia railroad cars by exposing the injustice in a letter to the press. Eight years later the campaign ended successfully when the Pennsylvania legislature passed a law forbidding such discrimination. In 1861 Still helped organize and finance a social, civil, and statistical association to collect data about Negroes. When some Philadelphia colored citizens opposed Still's crusade for equal service on the streetcars, he wrote *A Brief Narrative of the Struggle for the Rights of the Colored People of Philadelphia in the City Railway Cars* (1867).

In 1874 Still was again involved in controversy when he openly supported a reform candidate for mayor of Philadelphia. To explain his repudiation of the Republican candidate, Still spoke to a public meeting and later published a pamphlet entitled *An Address on Voting and Laboring* (1874). As an active member of the Presbyterian church he helped found a Mission Sabbath School in North Philadelphia. He also organized in 1880 one of the early YMCAs for Negro youth, served on the Freedmen's Aid Commission, and was a member of the Philadelphia Board of Trade. He helped manage homes for aged Negroes and destitute Negro children, as well as an orphan asylum for the children of Negro soldiers and sailors.

He died of heart trouble caused by Bright's disease, and was survived by his widow, two daughters, and a son.

William Still's book *The Underground Railroad*

(1872) contains a biographical sketch written by James P. Boyd. Alberta S. Norwood's unpublished University of Pennsylvania master's thesis, "Negro Welfare Work in Philadelphia Especially as Illustrated by the Career of William Still, 1775–1930" (1931), provides useful information and some correspondence. Parts of Still's manuscript journal of the Philadelphia Vigilance Committee as well as personal letters are in the William Still Papers in the Historical Society of Pennsylvania. His obituary appeared in the *Philadelphia Public Ledger* (July 15, 1902). The brief sketch by Harold G. Villard in *DAB* ([1935, 1936], 9, Part 2:22–23) gives most essential facts. See also Lurey Khan's *One Day, Levin . . . He Be Free, William Still and the Underground Railroad* (1972). — LARRY GARA

STRAKER, DAVID AUGUSTUS (1842–1908), lawyer, politician, educator, judge, lecturer, author, and newspaper publisher. He was the son of John and Margaret Straker of Bridgetown, Barbados. After graduating from Codrington, the island's college, he taught school and became principal of one of the island's high schools, St. Mary's Public School. In 1868 he came to the United States to assist in educating the former slaves. From 1868 to 1869 he taught school in Louisville, Ky. In 1869 he entered the Law Department of Howard University and received his law degree in 1871. In the same year he married Annie M. Carey and obtained employment as a clerk in the U.S. Post Office. He left this post in 1875 and moved to South Carolina, where he became a member of the law firm of (Robert Brown) Elliott, Dunbar, (T. McCants) Stewart and Straker.

In 1876 he began his political career. In addition to making speeches in support of the Republican ticket, headed by the gubernatorial candidate D. H. Chamberlain, Straker won a seat representing Orangeburg County in the state's House of Representatives on Nov. 28, 1876. Because the state election results were disputed, the Democrats and Republicans of South Carolina formed separate Houses, each contending that it was the legal body. After the Compromise of 1877, Pres. Rutherford B. Hayes recognized Wade Hampton, the Democratic claimant, as governor of the state. When the latter took office, the state House excluded those members who had sat with the Republican House after the election of 1876 and had refused to purge themselves of contempt as required by the representatives. Straker, a rock-ribbed Republican, refused to purge himself, and was unseated in favor of his Democratic opponent. Orangeburg County was just as steadfast as Straker, however, for it reelected him for two more consecutive terms, although he was rejected by the House each time. In a letter to the secretary of the treasury in 1880, Robert Brown Elliott urged that his partner be appointed inspector of customs, since his "professional prospects" had been "ruined and his business destroyed by the proscription of the Democrats on account of his steadfast devotion to his party and its principles." Appointed in July 1880, Straker was stationed in Charleston. He held this post until March 1882 when he was appointed dean and professor of the new law school at Allen University in Columbia, where he also taught French. Under Straker's guidance the first class from the law school graduated in May 1884. The class consisted of four young men who, according to the *South Carolina Daily Register* (June 12, 1885), when they were examined by the Supreme Court of the state, were "highly complimented for their fitness, and admitted to practice."

While dean of the law school Straker continued to practice law and received wide recognition for his work as the defense counsel in a murder case, *Coleman v. State,* which is reported in 20 S.C. 442 (1884). James Coleman, a Negro in his mid-twenties, had confessed to murdering his sister-in-law, Sarah Willis, with an axe. When Coleman was brought to trial in April 1883 Straker relied on the defense of transitory insanity, which was a relatively new defense in criminal cases. The insanity defense was debated by lawyers and doctors at the end of the nineteenth century. In spite of Straker's novel and untiring efforts, Coleman was found guilty. Straker then appealed the case to the state Supreme Court, which refused to overturn the judgment of the circuit court. As a last resort Straker petitioned the governor to commute Coleman's sentence to imprisonment for life on the ground of his "impulsive insanity." His plea was in vain, and Coleman was hanged on May 9, 1884. Straker had built a strong case in support of Coleman's "temporary insanity," and he believed that if Coleman had been white he would not have been hanged. Straker later wrote that "this inequality in the administration of justice lies deep in the social condition of the South." He was further disheartened because his political ambitions were thwarted by the growing strength of the Democrats in the state. Increasing political impotence, racial discrimination, and personal intimidation convinced Straker that he should leave South Carolina.

In 1887 he moved to Detroit. After he was admitted to the bar of the state, he opened a law office. He became very popular among both races as a lawyer and lecturer on the "New South." Many commendatory references were made to his court work by the daily papers. He reportedly enjoyed a "lucrative" mixed practice, which increased after his handling of *Ferguson v. Gies,* a civil rights case that he appealed to the Michigan Supreme Court. The case, reported in 82 Mich. 358 (1890), served as a precedent for civil rights cases from the turn of the twentieth century. The case was initiated by William W. Ferguson, a Detroit Negro who was publisher of Straker's *The New South Investigated* (1888), and later realtor, lawyer, and state legislator. On Aug. 15, 1889, Ferguson took a friend to George H. Gies's restaurant for dinner. Although whites could sit anywhere in the restaurant, Negroes were permitted to sit on one side only. After Ferguson and his friend had sat on the side reserved for whites, a waiter informed them that they could not be served until they moved to the other side. Irate, Ferguson then questioned Gies, the owner, who confirmed the statement made by the waiter. Ferguson insisted that he be served where he sat, but the equally obstinate owner refused. After some words were passed between the men, Ferguson and his friend left the restaurant without being served. Shortly after the incident Ferguson retained Straker to represent him in a suit against Gies.

Straker argued that Gies had violated a Michigan statute of 1885 which made it illegal to discriminate in public places on account of race. In addition he contended that the Thirteenth, Fourteenth, and Fifteenth Amendments had been enacted to prohibit discrimination in legal rights among citizens. Therefore Gies had no right, in law, to discriminate between patrons on account of color, and could not justify racial discrimination by saying that it was a regulation of business. Although Straker's arguments were well founded in law, the "separate but equal" concept was gaining strength throughout the country during the post-Reconstruction period. When the jury trial ended in defeat, Ferguson and Straker appealed to the Michigan Supreme Court. The *Detroit Plaindealer* reported of Straker's appellate argument that "it was the prevailing opinion of those who were present that the Supreme Court of the state of Michigan has not heard for many years a stronger or more forcible plea that justice should be meted out." This time Straker and Ferguson won by a unanimous decision. Judge J. Morse, in writing the decision for the court, declared that "the man who goes either by himself or with his family to a public place must expect to meet and mingle with all classes of people. He cannot ask, to suit his caprice or prejudice or social views, that this or that man shall be excluded because he does not wish to associate with them. He may draw his social line as closely as he chooses at home, or in other private places, but he cannot in public places carry the privacy of his home with him."

Despite this decision, racial discrimination in public places began to increase notably after 1896 when the U.S. Supreme Court sanctioned the "separate but equal" doctrine in the *Plessy v. Ferguson* decision. Jim Crow practices, however, were continually challenged, and *Ferguson v. Gies* served as a precedent for some of these attacks. Examples of decisions in which *Ferguson v. Gies* was cited include *Bolden v. Grand Rapid Operating Corporation* (239 Mich. 320, 1927), *Bell v. State of Maryland* (378 U.S. 226, 1964), and *Beech Grove Investment Co. v. Civil Rights Commission* (380 Mich. 405, 1968).

The *Ferguson v. Gies* case increased Straker's popularity, and in 1893 he became the first Negro elected a circuit court commissioner for Wayne County. He compiled *The Circuit Court Commissioner's Guide, Law and Practice* after a brief trip to Barbados. He was reelected for a second term in 1895, but his militant support of equal rights for Negroes virtually ensured defeat for a third term.

As a political activist, Straker was associated with some of the most eminent men of his time, including Oliver O. Howard, Charles Sumner, Frederick Douglass, Booker T. Washington, and W. E. B. Du Bois. Straker shared some of Washington's views but he did not adhere to Washington's public philosophy of accommodation. Straker argued eloquently for the right of every citizen to vote, to hold public office if he so desired and was qualified, to obtain an education in keeping with his abilities, to live wherever he pleased, to work at whatever job suited his talents, and to have equal access to all public facilities. Straker agreed with Washington, however, that racial discrimination

would ultimately cease as Negroes became more educated and their economic status improved. Like Washington he also promoted industrial education. He thought that it would provide the average Negro youth with some marketable skills, but he insisted that training in the professions was equally important, for he believed with Du Bois that the progress of the Negro race depended on the leadership of talented Negro professionals.

Straker also supported Negro unity, in America and elsewhere. He was one of the organizers and the first president of the National Federation of Colored Men, a forerunner of the NAACP founded in Detroit in December 1895. The organization divided the United States into districts where subordinate branches would be established. It sought remedies against lynching, fraudulent elections, and disfranchisement. In addition it pledged to work for equal employment opportunities, to fight discrimination in public facilities and to seek equal enforcement of the law for all citizens. Nonpartisan, it proposed to achieve its objectives through political pressure and agitation. One of the political achievements of the federation was the adoption by the National Republican Executive Committee in 1896 of an antilynching plank in the Republican platform. Henry Sylvester Williams, who organized the Pan-African Conference in London (1900), consulted with Straker prior to the conference.

Straker expounded his philosophy in many books and articles and in his newspaper, the *Detroit Advocate* (1901–1908). Among the many articles he wrote for the *A.M.E. Church Review* were "Are We Now Influenced More by Opinion than Fact?" (vol. 1, April 1885); "The Congo Valley: Its Redemption" (vol. 2, Jan. 1886); "Law and Law Reforms" (vol. 5, Oct. 1889); "Civil Rights" (vol. 8, March 1890); "The Negro in the Profession of the Law" (vol. 8, Oct. 1891); "Lynch Law in the South" (vol. 11, Oct. 1894); "The Organization, Object and Aim of the National Federation of Colored Men of the United States" (vol. 11, Dec. 1895); and "How the Anti-Lynching Plank Was Put Into the Republican Platform" (vol. 13, Oct. 1896).

He died after a week's illness, of pneumonia, on Feb. 14, 1908, at his home, 230 Bagg St., Detroit. His wife of thirty-six years had died also in 1908. His funeral was held on Feb. 17 at St. Matthew's Church and he was buried in Woodmere Cemetery. He was survived by an adopted daughter, Anna Glover (*Detroit Free Press*, Feb. 15, 18, 1908, pp. 5, 9).

His books include: *Reflection on the Life and Times of Toussaint L'Overture* (1885); *The New South Investigated* (1888); *A Trip to the Windward Islands* (1896); *Circuit Court Commissioner's Guide: Law and Practice* (1897); and *Compendium of Evidence* (1899).

At the turn of the twentieth century Straker exercised a great deal of political influence and enjoyed wide public recognition. Shortly before he died on Feb. 14, 1908, he had been nominated as a delegate to the State Constitutional Convention of 1908. "The passing of Augustus Straker," commented Du Bois in the *Horizon*, "calls for some tribute of respect. He represented the rapidly dwindling number of Reconstruction actors, and one, too, who never gave up his ideas and never crawled and kow-towed to the 'New South' " (March 1908, p. 3).

See Dorothy Drinkard-Hawkshawe's doctoral dissertation, "David Augustus Straker, Black Lawyer and Reconstruction Politician, 1842–1908" (Catholic University of America, 1974). Also valuable is "A West Indian's Response to Post Civil War American Society, D. Augustus Straker, 1842–1908," by Glenn O. I. Phillips (1978). The most valuable published source (for his South Carolina career) is Peggy Lamson's *The Glorious Failure: Black Congressman Robert Brown Elliott and the Reconstruction in South Carolina* (1973).

— DOROTHY DRINKARD-HAWKSHAWE

SUMNER, FRANCIS CECIL (1895–1954), psychologist. Born on Dec. 7, 1895, in Pine Bluff, Ark., the son of David A. and Ellen L. (Jarvis) Sumner, he attended elementary schools in Plainfield, N.J., Washington, D.C., and Norfolk, Va. His father apparently was dissatisfied with the quality of secondary education available to a Negro youth in the segregated schools. Sumner's application form for employment at Howard states "private instruction in secondary subjects by father." Sumner was admitted to Lincoln University (Pa.) "by examination" in 1911, when he was fifteen. He received a B.A. degree in 1915 *magna cum laude,* with special honors in English, modern languages, Greek, Latin, and philosophy. He was awarded an M.A. degree at Lincoln in 1917.

Sumner entered Clark University, Worcester, Mass., in 1917 and received his Ph.D. degree in 1920. He was a university fellow in psychology at Clark in 1917–1918 and 1919–1920. (He spent 1918–1919 in the U.S. infantry in France.) His dissertation was "The Psychoanalysis of Freud and Adler"; G. Stanley Hall was his major professor and his minor professors were E. G. Boring, J. W. Baird, S. W. Fernberger, and K. Karlson.

After teacing at Wilberforce University (1920–1921) and West Virginia State College (1921–1928) he went to Howard where he was chairman of the department from 1930 until his death in 1954. He had married Nettie M. Booker in 1946; there were no children.

Sumner produced at least forty-five publications. Some dealt with "pure" psychology, such as actual brightness and distance of colors when apparent distance is held constant, and affective tone of actual impressions. He also had an interest in applied psychology and published papers on measuring the relevance of picture to copy in advertising and the influence of color on the legibility of copy. Especially interested in the psychology of religion, he gave a paper in 1931 at the International Congress of Religious Psychology, Vienna, on "The Mental Hygiene of Religion."

One of the most unusual aspects of Sumner's interest in psychology was the work he did for *Psychological Abstracts.* Beginning in 1946 he wrote approximately 2000 abstracts for that journal, mostly from foreign-language sources. In the academic year 1948–1949, alone, he contributed 505 abstracts. Nearly all of these were from French and German sources; the remainder were from Russian, Spanish, and English sources.

Throughout his career, however, Sumner was also concerned with psychology as it applied to aspects of Negro life. This was demonstrated in his own work and in graduate theses done by students working under his supervision. Just one illustration of this is seen in 1940 when students of his completed M.S. theses on attitudes toward the administration of justice affecting Negroes. During that same period there was work on the mental health status of Negro college freshmen and environment as a factor inhibiting creative scholarship among Negroes.

He was a fellow of the American Psychological Association and of the American Association for the Advancement of Science; a member of the Eastern Psychological Association, the Southern Society for Philosophy and Psychology, and the District of Columbia Psychological Association.

Sumner was head of the Psychology Department of Howard University from 1930 until his death in 1954. This department has been the main source of Negroes who have gone on to the Ph.D. degree in psychology. Of the approximately 300 Negro holders of the Ph.D. degree in psychology in the mid-1970s, sixty received their B.S. and/or M.S. degrees in psychology at Howard. There were about two hundred additional individuals with a terminal M.S. degree in psychology from Howard, most of whom were employed as psychologists. Sumner was the principal influence in the development of this department of psychology.

He died of a heart attack on Jan. 11, 1954, in Washington, D.C. After funeral services in Andrew Rankin Memorial Chapel, Howard University, on Jan. 15, he was buried in Arlington National Cemetery. He was survived by his widow and a brother, Eugene (*Washington Evening Star,* Jan. 12, 1954, p. A10).

There is no comprehensive biography of Sumner. This sketch is based on the Annual Reports of the dean of the College of Liberal Arts, interviews with Max Meenes, a member of the Department of Psychology, and personal reminiscences. — JAMES A. BAYTON

TALBERT, MARY BURNETT (1866–1923), educator and civil rights advocate. Born in Oberlin, Ohio, she graduated from Oberlin High School and Oberlin College at the age of nineteen in 1886. After serving as assistant principal of Bethel University in Little Rock, Ark., she resigned to become principal in the Union High School there. She married William A. Talbert and moved to Buffalo where she remained the rest of her life. The statement that she earned a Ph.D. degree from the University of Buffalo at an unspecified date can not be substantiated.

She served as treasurer of the Michigan Avenue Baptist Church and founded the Christian Culture Congress, of which she was president for twenty years. A charter member of the Empire State Federation of Colored Women, she was president of the National Association of Colored Women from 1916 to 1921 and a director of the NAACP. During World War I she sold thousands of dollars of Liberty bonds and served as a Red Cross nurse in France. In one of her more significant activities, she started the crusade for the passage of the Dyer antilynching bill (1921), and raised $12,000. She traveled thousands of miles, speaking to mixed audiences, in a vain effort to obtain its passage. Talbert represented the NACW at the sixth quinquennial meeting of the International Council of Women in Christiana, Norway (1920), and lectured on race relations and women's rights in many European countries. She was largely responsible for the restoration of the Frederick Douglass home in Anacostia, D.C., in 1922. In that year she became the first Negro woman to win the NAACP Spingarn Medal for "notable achievement."

Less well known than Mary Church Terrell or Mary McLeod Bethune, she deserves a full-length biography. There is a brief sketch in Sylvia G. Dannett's *Profiles of Negro Womanhood* (1964). Several notices were published in *The Crisis* (Feb. 1917, pp. 174–76; Aug. 1917, pp. 167–68; July 1921, p. 130; July 1922, p. 125; Aug. 1922, p. 171; Dec. 1923, pp. 56–57).

— RAYFORD W. LOGAN

TANNER, BENJAMIN TUCKER (1835–1923), editor and eighteenth bishop of the African Methodist Episcopal church. Born in Pittsburgh, Pa., the son of Hugh S. and Isabel H. Tanner, he attended Avery College in Allegheny, Pa. (1852–1857), working as a barber to pay expenses. He studied at Western Theological Seminary, (1858–1860), was ordained a deacon and then an elder in the AME Church (1860). Following his ordination as elder he served for a time as minister of a Presbyterian church in Washington, D.C. He retained his affiliation with the AME church, however, and in April 1862 became the head of the Alexander Mission, said to be the first of its kind established in Washington by that church. He was pastor of churches in Georgetown and Baltimore (1863–1866) and principal of the AME Conference school in Frederick, Md., before being appointed to Bethel Church in Philadelphia, Pa.

From 1868 to 1884 Tanner was editor of the *Christian Recorder,* a church publication. Through Tanner's leadership the *Recorder,* which had been published erratically in the past, emerged as an important weekly newspaper, containing news about national political events as well as church affairs. In 1884, with the endorsement of the AME General Conference, he launched the *A.M.E. Church Review,* a quarterly, which quickly became a leading Negro magazine of high literary quality.

During the years that Tanner served as editor a racially repressive climate was growing in the U.S. that gradually came to manifest itself in Jim Crow legislation. He was convinced that racial solidarity offered the most effective means to combat racial injustice, and he encouraged Negroes to support businesses owned by Negroes and the Negro press. Both the *Recorder* and the *Review* editorially reaffirmed this position, as well as urging equal educational opportunity. However, Tanner never adopted the form of black nationalism advocated by his contemporary, Bishop Henry McNeal Turner. His views coincided more closely with those of another AME bishop, Daniel A. Payne.

Tanner was consecrated a bishop in 1888. He gave up his work on the magazine because of the additional responsibilities of his new office, but remained interested in the education of those preparing for the ministry as well as education for the community at large. For a brief period, in 1901, he served as dean of Payne

Theological Seminary of Wilberforce University in Ohio.

Interested in promoting ecumenical relations, in 1881 Tanner attended the Ecumenical Conference in London. In September 1901 as a delegate to the Third Ecumenical Conference of Methodism, also in London, he read a paper, "Elements of Pulpit Effectiveness." In 1908 he served as one of the AME delegates to the first Tri-Council of Colored Methodist Bishops, which also included representatives from the AME Zion church and the Colored Methodist Episcopal church. At the General Conference of the AME church (1908) he was relieved at his own request and retired on half pay, the first to receive this pension. After retirement, he continued relatively active in religious affairs until his death.

Tanner married Sarah Elizabeth Miller on Aug. 14, 1858, and they had seven children: Henry Ossawa, Carlton, Sadie, Mary, Bertha, Belle, and Hallie. His son Henry Ossawa became a painter, and his daughter Hallie, became the first woman physician to practice medicine in Alabama. Carlton, his other son, became an AME minister and missionary to South Africa. Tanner died of natural causes on Jan. 15, 1923, at his home in Philadelphia.

Tanner's most widely circulated book was a history of African Methodism, *An Apology for African Methodism* (1867). He also wrote on other ecclesiastical topics as well as on matters that related to the general history of the race. In addition to the *Apology,* he wrote *The Negro's Origin: and Is the Negro Cursed?* (1869); *An Outline of Our History and Government for African Methodist Churchmen* (1884); *The Color of Solomon, What?* (1895); *Dispensations in the History of the Church* (1899); *The Negro in Holy Writ* (1900); and *Hints to Ministers, Especially of the AME Church* (1900).

Brief biographical accounts of Tanner are in the following: Harold G. Villard's sketch in *DAB* (9, Part 2: 296); Richard R. Wright, Jr.'s *Encyclopedia of African Methodism* (1948) and his *The Bishops of the AME Church* (1963); and Charles Spencer Smith's *A History of the African Methodist Episcopal Church* (1922). The date Wright gives for Tanner's death, 1915, is incorrect; according to the *New York Times* obituary, Tanner died on Jan. 15, 1923. For a discussion of the *Christian Recorder,* and the *A.M.E. Church Review,* see August Meier's *Negro Thought in America, 1880–1915* (1963). — CAROL V. R. GEORGE

TANNER, HENRY OSSAWA (1859–1937), expatriate painter of biblical, landscape, and genre subjects, and the first American Negro artist to win international recognition. He was born on June 21, 1859, in Pittsburgh, Pa., the eldest of seven children of Benjamin Tucker Tanner and Sarah Elizabeth (Miller) Tanner. On his father's side he was the descendant of several generations of free Negroes. His paternal grandparents, Hugh S. and Isabel H. Tanner, were early Negro leaders in Pittsburgh. His father was a graduate of Avery College and Western Theological Seminary in Allegheny, Pa. His mother was the daughter of Charles Jefferson Miller, the mulatto son of a white plantation owner in Winchester, Va., who moved to the free state of Pennsylvania with his family in 1846. Sarah Miller married Benjamin Tanner in 1858 and their son Henry Ossawa's birth the next year came shortly before his father was ordained deacon and elder in the African Methodist Episcopal church.

The first six years of the artist's life were spent in Washington, D.C., and nearby towns, where his father served as minister and organizer of schools for freedmen during the Civil War. In 1866 Benjamin Tanner was appointed pastor of Bethel Church in Philadelphia and moved his family to their home. At the age of thirteen Henry Tanner realized his interest in art, a subject that submerged all other interests and, with his parents' encouragement, began to develop his natural talent for drawing and painting. An attempt to study with a professional artist, Isaac L. Williams, failed when his teacher insisted that Tanner learn mechanical drawing. At seventeen he left school and wished to become a professional artist, but his father was opposed to the idea, knowing the racial obstacles he would confront in this profession. Bowing to parental wishes, he worked in the flour business for a while, but after a bout of illness finally won his father's consent to pursue art as a career. From 1876 to 1880 he followed a solitary course, painting portraits, landscapes, and seascapes, and sketching and modeling clay figures of animals in the Philadelphia Zoo. At the age of eighteen he made a trip to the Adirondacks where he painted realistic landscapes, two of which were later exhibited at the Pennsylvania Academy of the Fine Arts. He also went to Florida, but nothing is known of this trip. He sold a few pictures, largely to his parents' friends, but received no recognition otherwise.

In 1880 he enrolled as a student at the Pennsylvania Academy of the Fine Arts, the oldest, and at that time the best, art school in the United States. His teacher was Thomas Eakins, admired by his pupils but a controversial figure in Philadelphia because of his progressive method of teaching anatomy from the living model instead of plaster casts. From Eakins, whose esteem for Tanner is evident in the portrait he painted of him in 1900, he acquired a better knowledge of anatomy, a feeling for the third dimension and the importance of light in his pictures, as well as a subsidiary interest in photography. By inclination a romantic-realist, however, Tanner shared neither his teacher's scientific zeal nor his objective vision. He remained only two years at the academy, then left in the hope of making enough money to go abroad. He was motivated on two counts: he wanted to follow the example of countless American artists, including Eakins, and study art in Europe, and he wished to experience a world relatively free of racial prejudice. For the next seven years his pictures were shown at the Pennsylvania Academy of the Fine Arts and the National Academy of Design in New York, and a few were sold. He also did black-and-white illustrations for *Harper's Young People* and other periodicals, but these sales were not encouraging.

Disappointed by his lack of success, Tanner left Philadelphia in 1888 to try his hand as a professional photographer in Atlanta, Ga. The venture was a financial mistake. He had no business ability, but through his friendship with Bishop Joseph Crane Hartzell, a trustee

of Clark University in Atlanta, he was offered a teaching position there. Before his classes began he spent several months in the North Carolina mountains near Highlands, where he painted and sketched the scenery and people. One of the most perceptive of these studies of Negro life, all of which belong to his early career, is *The Banjo Lesson,* painted around 1893 from a sketch made at this time. Returning to Atlanta, he taught art for nine months at Clark University and simultaneously worked at his own painting and modeling. The next fall Dr. and Mrs. Hartzell arranged an exhibition of his work in Cincinnati, and when no picture was sold they bought them all. With this money and assurance of additional support from his father, he sailed for Europe on Jan. 4, 1891.

It was Tanner's intention to study in Rome, but on his way to Italy he visited London and Paris and, attracted by the latter's opportunities for art study and its friendly atmosphere, he decided to remain. He enrolled at the Académie Julien, where for five years he worked under two well-known academic artists, Benjamin-Constant and Jean-Paul Laurens, the first of whom became a personal friend. He also studied the Old Masters at the Louvre and in his spare time sketched the animals at the Jardin des Plantes. During his first two summers in France he painted at Pont-Aven and Concarneau in Brittany. In 1893 he returned to Philadelphia but found the racial restrictions of life in America no longer tolerable. After a few months at home he sold all his available pictures at auction, and with his father's promise of further help returned to Paris. In 1894 he achieved his first success when a genre painting, *The Music Lesson,* was accepted by the Société des Artistes Français for their yearly salon. This was followed the next year by another, *The Sabot Maker,* that attracted favorable criticism in the American as well as the French press.

For the salon of 1896 Tanner turned from genre to a biblical subject and exhibited *Daniel in the Lions' Den,* which received Honorable Mention and brought his name to the attention of a wider public on both sides of the Atlantic. As a result of this success and the promise of another in a new biblical picture, *The Raising of Lazarus,* Rodman Wannamaker, who knew Tanner through his membership in the American Art Club, sponsored Tanner's first trip to the Holy Land. From January to May 1897, Tanner visited Egypt, Palestine, and Italy, and was in Venice, on his way home, when he learned of the French government's desire to purchase his *Raising of Lazarus* (which had won a medal of the third class at the Paris Exhibition in 1897) for their collection of foreign paintings in the Luxembourg Galleries. The following year *Annunciation,* subsequently acquired by the Philadelphia Museum, continued his series of salon successes. In the fall of 1898 Wannamaker sponsored a second and longer trip to Palestine. A result of this six-months' visit was his painting of *Christ and Nicodemus,* exhibited in Paris in 1899 and in 1900, which was awarded the Lippincott prize and purchased for the permanent collection of the Pennsylvania Academy of Fine Arts.

In 1900 Tanner was awarded a silver medal at the Exposition Universelle held in Paris. By this time his position as one of the leading American expatriate artists in Paris was assured. His reputation was based on his religious paintings, which conveyed through tonal harmonies the poetry and mystery of the Bible, although his landscape and genre pictures are of equal merit.

On Dec. 14, 1899, Henry Tanner was married in London to Jessie Macauley Olssen, a talented young white singer from San Francisco who had posed as "Mary" for his *Annunciation* the year before and who, after marriage, continued to be his model. The first year of their marriage they spent in Paris, then (1901 to 1904) made several changes of residence, living briefly at Mt. Kisco, N.Y., Granada, Spain, and for a longer period, again at Mt. Kisco in a small artists' community planned by Atherton Curtis, a wealthy art connoisseur and collector whom Tanner had known in Paris and who remained his life-long friend and patron. Some months after the birth of their son and only child, Jesse Ossawa, in New York on Sept. 25, 1903, the Tanners again left the United States, this time for permanent residence in France. From 1904 to 1906 they lived at Sceaux, then moved to an apartment in Paris. In 1912 Tanner bought a house at Trépied, a picturesque village in the Pas de Calais, and from then until the last years of his life he divided his time between Trépied and his studio-apartment at 51 Boulevard St.-Jacques in Paris. He did, however, make infrequent visits to the U.S. and brief trips to England and the Near East.

The years 1900–1914 were the happiest and most productive of his life. He enjoyed a quiet social life in the "American Colony" in Paris and was prominent in the activities of the American Art Club and the Society of American Artists. His pictures appeared regularly at the Salon of the Société des Artistes Français, and in 1906 another of his paintings, *Christ at Emmaus,* was bought by the French government. In 1908 his *Wise and Foolish Virgins* was given a place in the Salon d'Honneur, second only to that accorded Détaille's *Chant de Départ.* During the summer months he was active in Trépied with the Société Artistique de Picardie, and in 1913 was elected its president. In the United States, honors followed in succession.

In 1901 Tanner was awarded a silver medal at the Pan-American Exposition in Buffalo and in 1904 a silver medal at the St. Louis Exposition. In 1905 he was the first American Negro artist to be included in the annual exhibition of the Carnegie Institute. In 1906 his painting, *The Two Disciples at the Tomb,* was awarded the Harris prize and purchased by the Art Institute of Chicago. In 1908 he had his first one-man show in New York at the American Art Galleries, and in 1909 he was elected an associate member of the National Academy, along with Mary Cassatt and Frederick Waugh. In 1911 and 1913 his pictures were exhibited at Thurber's Gallery in Chicago and at Knoedler's in New York, and in 1914 were included in the Anglo-American exhibition at Shepherd's Bush in London. It was during this period that he developed his unique pictorial style. The realistic details seen in his early landscapes, genre, and biblical pictures gave way to broad, simple forms and his rich brown tones to a vibrant tonality, developed by the use of white underpainting covered with a series of colored oil glazes in which blues and blue-greens predominate.

He favored moonlight scenes, in which the contrast of light and shade heightened the poetic or mystical effect.

This tranquil and successful period of his life came to an end with the First World War. At the outbreak of hostilities most of his American artist friends left for the United States, but except for a brief stay with his family in England in August and September 1914, when Trépied was temporarily occupied by the Germans, he stayed in France. He spent most of 1914 and 1915 in Trépied and Paris, and in 1916 at Vittel, a health resort in the Vosges mountains. In 1917, depressed by the war and unable to paint, he joined the American Red Cross as lieutenant in the Farm Service Bureau to work on a rehabilitation program he had devised for convalescent soldiers. In June 1918 he was transferred to the Bureau of Publicity as artist, and for a year he sketched and painted in the war zone. War was not a congenial subject for his art, however, and his night scenes of the interiors and exteriors of Red Cross canteens done in 1918 (and owned by the American Red Cross Museum in Washington, D.C.) are notable only for their harmonious colors.

After 1919, conditions in France were changed for Tanner. He had lost some of his physical vigor during the war years. Few of his artist friends returned to their old homes, and new art forms, with which he was not sympathetic, were assuming greater importance in Paris exhibitions. He continued to paint in the same poetic style but on smaller canvases, with ghost-like forms that seem to express a sense of brooding mysticism. In 1923, in spite of waning public interest in traditional art, he was named chevalier of the Legion of Honor by the French government, an honor he considered the greatest of his career. In America, less affected by the war, he continued to enjoy popularity. In 1915 he was one of four American painters to win a gold medal at the Panama-Pacific Exposition in San Francisco, and during the postwar years his pictures were well received in exhibitions throughout the East and Midwest. In 1925 one of his *Sodom and Gomorrah*s was presented to the Metropolitan Museum in New York, where it hung for many years. In 1927 he was elected to full membership in the National Academy, and in the same year was awarded the Bronze Medal at the exhibition of the National Arts Club in New York. In 1930 he was given the Walter L. Clark prize by the Grand Central Art Galleries.

In 1924 he made his last trip to the United States. His wife died in 1925, bringing to an end a marriage that had been unusually happy, and shortly after this his son, a graduate of Cambridge University and the London School of Mines, began to suffer a breakdown in health that lasted many years. These personal tragedies, added to by the financial depression of the 1930s, made him disinclined to travel. He remained in Paris, occasionally going to Trépied and the Dordogne to see his son, and continued to be active in the American Artists' Professional League and the Société Internationale de Peinture et Sculpture. In 1933 he moved from his old apartment to a small studio in the rue de Fleurus, and in spite of increasing frailty, painted on a restricted scale until his death on May 25, 1937.

Tanner's success by way of the traditional salon, his lack of sympathy with new trends in art, and his long years of expatriation in France led to the steady decline of his reputation during the years following his death. In America how much the fact of race contributed to his growing obscurity cannot be gauged, for many representational artists of his generation fell into the same artistic limbo. Even in his lifetime, however, many critics had overlooked his importance in the mainstream of American art by placing him within the subcategory of "Negro artist," and it would be unrealistic to assume that this bias ended with his death. For thirty years his name was kept alive largely through the writings on American Negro art of Alain Locke and James A. Porter. In 1945 an exhibition of his work was sponsored by the Philadelphia Alliance, but it was not until the 1960s, when interest was renewed in representational art and public attention was focused on the artistic achievements of American Negroes, that the full range of his talent was seen in a series of important exhibitions. The most comprehensive of these was the large one-man show held at the Smithsonian Institution (July 22 to Sept. 9, 1969).

Tanner's contribution to the history of American art is twofold. It lies not only in the high quality of his art, in which narrative appeal is secondary to a skillful and subjective use of color and chiaroscuro, but in the fact that at the turn of the century he was one of a handful of American artists whose individual efforts established American art as an independent force instead of a peripheral aspect of European art. His contribution to American Negro history is no less notable, for his success in Paris was unprecedented for a Negro artist and gave hope and confidence to younger, less privileged Negroes seeking recognition in art. Tanner often regretted the reasons for his long exile in France, for in spite of his happy life abroad in a society that accepted him, he never ceased to identify as a member of the Negro race or to have concern for racial problems in America. As the years passed his connections with the United States inevitably became more tenuous, but he viewed with gratification the race consciousness growing among American Negro artists. He was represented in the first large all-Negro art show in 1921, held at the 135th Street Branch of the New York Public Library, and was flattered when, in 1922, a group of Negro artists in Washington, D.C., formed the "Tanner Art League." Race, nevertheless, was secondary to art in his thinking, and he persistently refused to help young artists who came to see him except on the basis of talent.

His ideals were as high for himself as for others, and he labored long on each of his pictures. His output was consequently small in relationship to his years of work, but few artists have expressed more effectively the mystery of the Bible or the poetry of nature.

He died in his sleep on May 25, 1937, in his apartment on the rue de Fleurus, Paris. He was survived by his only son, Jesse Ossawa Tanner. Tanner was buried in the cemetery at Sceaux, near Paris, beside his wife and a stone's throw from the resting place of Marie Curie.

Marcia M. Matthews's *Henry Ossawa Tanner, American Artist* (1969) is based on his personal papers and other primary materials. Henry O. Tanner's "The Story of an Artist's Life, I" (in *World's Work*, 1909), is a relatively brief but valuable autobiographical account of the artist's youth and early career. A. E. Taylor's "The American Colony of Artists in Paris" (*International Studio*, 1912) describes the artists Tanner knew and the milieu in which he lived. Clara T. MacChesney's "Poet-Painter of Palestine" (*International Studio*, 1913) describes Tanner's studio, his method of working, and his technique. Jessie Fauset's "Henry Ossawa Tanner" (*The Crisis*, 1924) is based on an interview with the artist during his last visit to the United States. Alain Locke's *The Negro in Art* (1940) includes a study of Tanner within the context of American Negro Art. James A. Porter's *Modern Negro Art* (1943, reprint 1969, pp. 28, 64–77, 83, 94) is a valuable critique, with contemporary quotations. Carroll Greene, Jr.'s "Afro-American Artists: Yesterday and Today" (*The Humble Way*, 1968) is a more recent study of Tanner's place in American Negro art history. Marcia M. Matthews's "The Art of Henry O. Tanner" (*Records*, Columbia Historical Society of Washington, D.C., 1969–1970) is a critical assessment of Tanner's art relative to his retrospective exhibition at the Smithsonian Institution, July-Sept. 1969. Patricia Read's sketch in the *DAB, Supplement 2* (1958, pp. 648–49), is in error in stating that Tanner died childless. — MARCIA M. MATHEWS

TARRANT, CAESAR (? –1798?), pilot during the American Revolution. He was born a slave, probably in Hampton, Va. His master, Carter Tarrant, from whom Caesar took his name, trained him to pilot ships in Virginia waters. Serving throughout the Revolution, he piloted ships in battle in the vicinity of Hampton and Elizabeth City County. He distinguished himself particularly as pilot of the schooner *Patriot* when it captured the British brig *Fanny* laden with supplies for the forces at Boston. In 1789 the Virginia legislature set Caesar Tarrant free because he had "entered very early into the service of his country and continued to pilot the armed vessels of the state during the late war." Earning his living probably as an artisan, he bought several pieces of property in Hampton. He bequeathed to his "loving wife" his houses, lot, and household furniture, as well as all money due him from his creditors. He further provided that after the death of his wife the property should be sold, with his free daughter, Nancy, receiving half the income and his slave daughter, Liddy, her freedom and the remaining half. On March 4, 1833, the federal government granted Nancy 2666⅔ acres of land in Ohio, the maximum amount given to Virginia Negro veterans of the Revolution. She probably did not move to Ohio, but purchased additional land in Hampton, perhaps with proceeds from the sale of a portion of the Ohio tract.

The principal recent sources are Luther Porter Jackson's *Virginia Negro Soldiers and Sailors in the Revolutionary War* (1944, pp. 20, 22–23), and Sidney Kaplan's *The Black Presence in the Era of the American Revolution* (1973, p. 53). — RAYFORD W. LOGAN

TAYLOR, ALRUTHEUS A[MBUSH] (1893–1954), teacher and historian. Born in Washington, D.C., the son of Lewis and Lucy (Johnson) Taylor, and educated in the city's public schools, he attended the University of Michigan where he majored in mathematics. Before he obtained a degree, however, the completed a one-year teaching appointment in 1915 as an English instructor at Tuskegee Institute. After he received his B.A. degree from Michigan (1916), he became a social worker for the New York Urban League (1917 to 1918). The League attempted to improve employment opportunities for Negroes, particularly those who had recently migrated to the North. In 1919 Taylor married Harriet Wilson of Fowler, Ind., and later that same year he accepted a position as a mathematics teacher at West Virginia Collegiate Institute where he remained until 1922. There he became closely associated with Carter G. Woodson, who stimulated Taylor's interest in history and encouraged him to pursue this discipline in graduate study. Taylor was admitted to Harvard in 1922, and in 1923 had earned his M.A. degree. Taught by Edward Channing, Arthur M. Schlesinger, Sr., and Samuel Eliot Morison, he received excellent training as a historian. Taylor was awarded a Ph.D. degree in history from Harvard in 1935. He had joined the faculty of Fisk University in 1926 as professor of history and chairman of the department. From 1930 until 1951 he served as dean of the College of Arts and Sciences. Taylor's first wife died in 1941; two years later he married Catherine Buchanan. Taylor died of a cerebral hemorrhage at Hubbard Memorial Hospital, Nashville, Tenn., on June 4, 1954. Funeral exercises were held in Fowler on June 7, preceded by brief services in Fisk Memorial Chapel on June 5. He was survived by his widow, her children (four sons and a daughter) by a former marriage, two sisters, and a brother.

Taylor's reputation as a historian rests on his studies of the Negro in Reconstruction, published over a period of two decades. While pursuing his master's degree, Taylor was appointed the first full-time investigator for the Association for the Study of Negro Life and History (founded in 1915) and the fruits of his research soon began to appear in print. His first work dealing with the Negro in the Reconstruction period, "Negro Congressmen: A Generation After," appeared in the *JNH* in 1922. In this essay Taylor demonstrated that the lack of specific bills in Congress in behalf of Negroes was not due to the fact that the Negro representatives were irresponsible or slovenly, but because they were a minority and were regarded with scepticism even by the members of their own party.

While working toward his Ph.D. degree, Taylor published in 1924 his first monograph, *The Negro in South Carolina during the Reconstruction*. In this and two subsequent works, *The Negro in the Reconstruction of Virginia* (1926) and *The Negro in Tennessee, 1865–1880* (1941), Taylor aimed at destroying the stereotype of "Sambo," the ignorant or corrupt tool of the carpetbaggers. Taylor carefully marshalled evidence to show that Negroes served well as state and local officials in the majority of cases, and were often outstanding public servants. In all his works Taylor's research and documentation were prodigious and his viewpoint reasonable and detached, although reviewers often criticized him for his reluctance to venture into interpretation.

Although Taylor's two books published in the 1920s were among the first monographs setting forth a revi-

sionist view on Reconstruction, he was writing when Negro historians virtually went unread beyond the small circle of Negro scholars. It became obvious that his studies had made little impression on historical interpretations of the Reconstruction period when, three years after the publication of his second book, Claude Bowers's *The Tragic Era* appeared and was enthusiastically received by most readers as the true picture of the period.

For three decades at Fisk University Taylor continued his part in the campaign to establish the revisionist interpretation. In 1938 he wrote a scholarly survey of the historiography of Reconstruction, "Historians of the Reconstruction" (published in the *JNH*). After dispassionately analyzing the interpretations set forth by James Ford Rhodes, William A. Dunning, and others, Taylor lauded W. E. B. Du Bois's *Black Reconstruction in America* (1935) as the most accurate treatment of the subject, although his own fine state studies were not even mentioned. One of the first revisionists, Taylor was fortunate enough to live to see his views accepted and shared by many leading scholars.

Taylor was also concerned with other aspects of the Negro experience in America. In 1941 he co-authored *A Study of the Community Life of the Negro Youth,* and he wrote an unpublished labor of love, "Fisk University: A History, 1896–1951."

Taylor was a beloved teacher, respected scholar, able administrator, and prominent community leader in Nashville. While he was dean at Fisk, it became the first Negro school to receive full accreditation by the Southern Association of American Universities. Also at Fisk, Taylor founded the Harriet Wilson Taylor Scholarship in memory of his first wife, and for the last four years of his life was president of the Board of Trustees of Nashville Kent College of Law.

No full-length biography of Alrutheus A. Taylor has been written. Basic biographical information is available in the 1955 edition of *Who Was Who in America* as well as in Harry W. Greene's *Holders of Doctorates Among American Negroes* (1946). Taylor's contributions to historical scholarship are briefly described by Earl E. Thorpe in *Black Historians: A Critique* (1971), while additional information on his life and work appears in the lengthy obituary notices in the *JNH* (July 1954) and the *American Historical Review* (July 1954). Other obituaries appeared in the *Nashville Banner* (June 5, 1954, p. 14) and the *Pittsburgh Courier,* Washington Edition (June 12, 1954, p. 2).

— DANIEL SAVAGE GRAY

TAYLOR, SUSIE KING (1848–19?), Civil War nurse. The first of nine children of Hagar Ann Reed and Raymond Baker, she was born a slave on the Grest Farm, Isle of Wight, off the coast of Georgia. When she was seven her owners permitted her to live with her grandmother in Savannah, where she was taught to read and write by a Mrs. Woodhouse, a free colored woman who ran a clandestine school for Negro youth. Susie continued her studies under Mary Beasley, a Negro nun. She also studied for a few months under a young white friend, Kate O'Connor, and then under James Blois, a high school student, until the middle of 1861.

She often wrote passes for her grandmother, forging the name of her mother's employer, to evade curfew restrictions. When the Civil War began, Georgians attempted to discourage Negroes from "going over" to the Yankees by telling frightening stories of Yankee atrocities. Nevertheless, at the age of fourteen she joined her uncle's family when they fled to St. Catherine Island, which was then under Union control. She later traveled to St. Simon's Island where she established a school for approximately forty children and any interested adults.

In August 1862 Capt. C. T. Trowbridge came to St. Simon's Island for the purpose of obtaining men to complete the ranks of the South Carolina Volunteers (later the 33rd U. S. Colored Infantry), the earliest Negro regiment organized by the Union Army (March 1862). In October the island residents were evacuated to Beaufort, S.C. The exact date of her marriage to Sgt. Edward King is not known, but by the time of the evacuation they were married and the new Mrs. King followed her husband when he joined the Volunteers. She was enlisted as a laundress. Neither she nor her fellow Negro volunteers received any payment for the first eighteen months of service.

The Volunteers first gained news of their freedom when the Emancipation Proclamation was read to them on Jan. 1, 1863. On that occasion Mrs. King declared that "They sang or shouted 'Hurrah!' all through the camp, and seemed overflowing with fun and frolic." A number of oxen were roasted whole to celebrate the event.

As the regiment moved up and down the southeastern seacoast, Mrs. King spent much of her time teaching members of Company E to read and write. She also learned how to handle a musket, and claimed to be an accurate shooter. While in Beaufort, in the summer of 1863, she met Clara Barton at Camp Shaw hospital, and frequently accompanied her in her work with the Red Cross, caring for the sick and wounded soldiers.

The South Carolina Volunteers fought bravely as they made expeditions into Georgia and Florida. After capturing the city of Jacksonville, they were ordered back to South Carolina for picket duty. In June 1864 they were ordered to Folly Island, and later to Morris Island where the Massachusetts 54th, another colored regiment, bravely attacked Fort Sumter. In July the Volunteers were the vanguard of an attack on Fort Gregg. The attack was prematurely discovered by Confederate forces who inflicted severe casualties on the Union detachments, yet the soldiers could take some comfort in the knowledge that Mrs. King was there to care for the wounded.

On Feb. 28, 1865, the regiment was ordered to take Charleston as the rebels evacuated the city. It was an odd sight to see colored troops attempt to extinguish the fires set by the rebels while Confederate citizens jeered them. Mrs. King continued to care for the sick and injured in a mansion on South Battery Street.

After brief skirmishes in Georgia and southern South Carolina, the troops returned to Charleston in November 1865. On Feb. 9, 1866, orders were received to "muster out" the 33rd U.S. Colored Troops. Altogether Mrs. King spent four years and three months in the service of colored troops without receiving so much as a dollar for her work. Of this work she said: "I was glad, however, to be allowed to go with the regiment to care for the sick and afflicted comrades."

Having risked their lives in service to their country, Mrs. King and her fellow citizens were rewarded with discriminatory treatment as they attempted to use a steamer from Savannah to Darian. Undaunted, she and her husband returned to Savannah where they settled, and she opened a school for Negro children on South Broad Street. Sergeant King, an excellent carpenter, was prevented from working at his craft because of racial prejudice. On Sept. 16, 1866, he died, leaving his pregnant wife. In 1872 Mrs. King received $100, paid as bounty to the widows of Union soldiers.

Following the birth of her baby boy, Mrs. King opened a night school for adults, but was forced to close when her students began attending a newly opened free night school. In the fall of 1872 she obtained employment as a laundress for a wealthy couple, Mr. and Mrs. Charles Green. In the spring of the following year, Mrs. King traveled North with them as their cook. In 1874 she again returned North where she sought employment in Boston. In 1879 she married Russell L. Taylor, about whom she wrote little, but it seems she no longer had to work.

True to her devotion to the "boys in blue," in 1886 she helped organize Corps 67 of the Boston branch of the Women's Relief Corps, the auxiliary to the Grand Army of the Republic, assuming the presidency in 1893. In 1896 she identified many veterans living in Boston.

In February 1898 she went to Shreveport, La., where her son, an actor, lay desperately ill. Since she could not get a berth on a train to take him to Boston, she was forced to leave him to die in Shreveport and return to Boston.

In later years when Mrs. Taylor was asked if the Civil War had been fought in vain because of the treatment her race was receiving in the twentieth century, in both North and South, she said: "We cannot sing, 'My Country, 'tis of thee, Sweet land of Liberty'! It is hollow mockery." On another occasion, however, she urged that Negroes should not condemn all whites and wrote, mistakenly, "here [in Massachusetts] is found liberty in the full sense of the word . . . irrespective of race or creed, liberty and justice for all."

Her compassion for the wounded during the Civil War led her to express concern for the plight of Cubans during the Spanish-American War. She died sometime after the appearance of her autobiography, *Reminiscences of My Life in Camp: With the 33d United States Colored Troops, Late 1st S. C. Volunteers,* published in 1902. A reprint (1968) is more easily available. There is a summary in Sylvia G. L. Dannett's *Profiles of Negro Womanhood* (1964–1966, 1:166–73).

— JOHN E. FLEMING

TEMPLE, LEWIS (1800–1854), inventor of a whaling harpoon, variously known as Temple's Toggle, the Temple Iron, and Temple's Iron, that revolutionized and became the standard harpoon of the whaling industry in the middle of the nineteenth century. He was born in Richmond, Va. There is little information about his early life. He arrived in New Bedford, Mass., in 1829 and that same year married Mary Clark from Maryland. They had a son, Lewis Jr. (b. 1830), a daughter Nancy (b. 1832), and several years later Mary, who died at the age of six. By 1836 Temple operated a whalecraft shop on Coppin's Wharf, while also active in the abolitionist movement. In 1845 he opened a blacksmith shop on Walnut Street. Whalers from New Bedford, a center of the whaling industry, often talked of the whales that struggled free from the arrowhead-shaped harpoons no larger than the jaws of the whales. In a barbershop while Temple was listening to the reason for the loss of some whales, the barber's scissors gave Temple his idea for his first toggle harpoon, which he invented in 1848. It had a movable head or barb. The barbed head of Temple's harpoon pivoted at right angles to the shaft and held fast once it penetrated the whale's flesh. When Temple's Toggle Iron entered the whale, the barb was parallel with the shank. To hold the barbed head parallel until it cut through the blubber, a wooden pin about the size of a matchstick was used. It was placed in the hole that ran through the shank and the barb of the harpoon. Under the pull of the whale in its desperate attempt to escape, the wooden pin holding the barbed head in a fixed position was broken. This allowed it to toggle or turn across the end of the shank and become firmly anchored. The head in this position was not likely to slip out of the blubber and was more secure than in any other form of harpoon, "the single most important invention in the whole history of whaling." Other whalecraft makers quickly copied the toggle harpoon (Clifford W. Ashley, *The Yankee Whaler,* 1926).

Temple never secured a patent on his invention; another whalecraft maker produced 13,000 Temple irons between 1848 and 1868. Temple did, however, become more prosperous from the manufacturing and sales of his iron, and in 1852 moved to a larger blacksmith shop next to his home. He remained active in civic affairs and in 1853 he and other citizens of New Bedford signed and presented a temperance petition to the mayor of New Bedford. In January 1854 he contracted with a construction firm to build a new and bigger brick blacksmith shop near Steamboat Wharf. This shop was never finished because Temple died in May 1854 from injuries suffered in a fall during the autumn of 1853. He had been walking at night near the site for his new shop when he was tripped by a plank carelessly left by city workers constructing a sewer. He sued the City of New Bedford for $2000 for the injury and the loss of time from his business. The $2000 was awarded in March 1854, but at the time of his death it had not been paid. For some reason it was withheld from his wife, so his home and shop on Walnut Street and the half-finished shop on School Street, together worth $700, and $300 for his stock, were used to pay debts. Temple died a poor man and little of his estate was left for his wife and family. He was buried in Rural Cemetery, New Bedford, and was survived by his widow and Lewis Jr.

An early reference to Temple is "Fastening Irons" (*New Bedford Evening Standard,* Feb. 20, 1904). Sidney Kaplan's "Lewis Temple and the Hunting of the Whale" (*New England Quarterly,* March 1953) contains basic information. See also Robert C. Hayden's *Eight Black American Inventors* (1972, pp. 32–43); a photograph is on page 30 and drawings of the harpoons on page 38. — ROBERT C. HAYDEN

TERRELL, MARY CHURCH (1863–1954), teacher, author, and civil rights leader. She was born in Memphis, Tenn., the daughter of Robert R. Sr., and Louisa (Ayers) Church. Her father, a self-educated former slave, had become quite prosperous after Reconstruction when he shrewdly invested his money in real estate during the yellow fever epidemic in Memphis in 1878–1879. In order to escape the segregated system of education in the South, Mary was sent to Yellow Springs, Ohio, to attend Antioch College's "Model School," the forerunner of the kindergarten program in the United States. Upon completing her elementary and secondary education in Ohio, she pursued the classical curriculum of Oberlin College from which she received her B.A. degree in 1884 and her A.M. degree in 1888.

She was an instructor at Wilberforce University between 1885 and 1887. In 1887 she obtained employment in the public school system of Washington, D.C., as a Latin teacher in the Preparatory School for Colored Youth, (named the M Street High School in 1891). The years 1888 through 1890 offered interesting and enriching experiences when she toured Europe, studying languages.

Perhaps the first Negro woman known to have been offered the position of registrar of a white college, she declined the appointment at Oberlin in 1891 in order to marry Robert Herberton Terrell, later judge of the Municipal Court of the District of Columbia. In 1892 and 1893 she served as the first woman president of the Bethel Literary and Historical Association. Founded in Washington in 1881, its membership had included Daniel Alexander Payne, Lewis Douglass, John W. Cromwell, and Kelly Miller.

Mrs. Terrell was appointed to the Board of Education in Washington, D.C., in 1895, probably the first colored woman to hold this type of position in the United States. After resigning in 1901, she was reappointed in 1906 and held the post until 1911.

An activist in the women's rights struggle, she worked ardently organizing colored women in their fight against racism and sexism. After forming the Colored Women's League of Washington, D.C., she played an instrumental role in the merger of the Washington group with other Negro women's organizations to establish the National Association of Colored Women in 1896. Elected its first president, she served the organization in various capacities for many years, to the extent that the membership acclaimed her honorary president for life. During the first half of the 1920s Mrs. Terrell also held the position of second vice-president of the International Council of Women of the Darker Races. The president of the council was Mrs. Booker T. Washington and its programs centered on promoting greater understanding and knowledge of people of color throughout the world.

To Mrs. Terrell, however, the subordinate status of women in society was not solely a matter of race. She worked closely with such allies as Susan B. Anthony,

Jane Addams, Carrie Chapman Catt, and Inez Milholland. Throughout the 1890s, and in fact until the Nineteenth Amendment was ratified in 1920 granting women the right to vote, she was an active member in the National American Woman Suffrage Association. She was a speaker at the 1898 and 1900 biennial sessions of the association. The two conventions were held in Washington, and Mrs. Terrell addressed in 1898 the specific problems of colored women and in 1900 the issue of "The Justice of Woman Suffrage."

She was also an important figure within the international women's movement. Representing colored women in the American delegation to the International Congress of Women (Berlin, 1904), she was the only American to deliver her address in English, German, and French. On June 27, 1904, a *Washington Post* article, "Need To Be Polyglot," praised her great success in communicating with the largely German-speaking audience. In 1919 she received international recognition at the Quinquennial International Peace Congress in Zurich. Under the presidency of Jane Addams, pioneer social worker, the United States branch of the Women's International League for Peace and Freedom unanimously selected Mrs. Terrell to be on the program of the conference. The third event marking her representation of colored women abroad occurred when she addressed the International Assembly of World Fellowship of Faith in London.

Like her husband, she found herself torn between her "Talented Tenth" ideals and the pervasive influence of Booker T. Washington. She worked with him to prevent W. E. B. Du Bois from securing the position of assistant superintendent of public schools in the nation's capital. On the other hand, she criticized Washington for his dialect stories and accommodationist policies. Her work with the NAACP especially drew fire from Washington upon both her and her husband, who owed his appointment (1910) as a municipal court judge in the nation's capital to Washington. While Washington refused to accept Du Bois's invitation to attend the 1909 meeting which laid the foundation for the organization of the NAACP, Mrs. Terrell was one of two colored women who signed the "Call" for that meeting and served as a member of the Committee of Forty set up by the 1909 Conference, which her husband did not attend. She was also a member of the Committee on Membership and Credentials for the 1910 meeting which formalized the organization of the NAACP. She spoke at the Second Annual Conference of the National Negro Committee (May 12–14, 1910) which condemned disfranchisement in the South. And for many years she was vice-president of the Washington branch of the NAACP.

Immediately after World War I she worked with the War Camp Community Service in an effort to establish recreational centers for demobilized soldiers.

The enfranchisement of women created new opportunities. During the presidential campaign of 1920, the National Republican Committee appointed Mrs. Terrell director of work among colored women in the East. In 1932 the Republican party again assigned her the job of organizing colored women in that area. Her talents as a political organizer also won respect from Ruth Hannah McCormick who employed her in her senatorial campaign during the 1930 Illinois election.

Oberlin College honored her in 1929 by including her in *The Book of Achievement,* recognizing 100 of Oberlin's most influential graduates. In 1933 she was a speaker at the 100th anniversary of the college's founding. In 1948 Oberlin bestowed upon her the honorary doctorate in humane letters. She was awarded two other honorary doctorates: by Wilberforce University in 1946 and by Howard University in 1948.

In 1949, after a three-year battle, Mrs. Terrell gained membership in the Washington chapter of the American Association of University Women and brought an end to its policy of excluding Negroes. In that same year she assumed leadership of the Co-Ordinating Committee for the Enforcement of the District of Columbia Anti-Discrimination Laws.

The story of her life is a narrative of struggle against injustice. Amid the affluent surroundings of the Memphis suburb in which she spent her early years, Mary Church received her initial knowledge of the cruel and exploitive nature of slavery from stories recounted by her maternal grandmother. As she matured, she grew increasingly sensitive to the plight of her people, who although recently freed from the "peculiar institution" were still chained by the shackles of racial discrimination, illiteracy, and poverty. Early experiences in the relatively liberal Oberlin community, and later activities in the District of Columbia, throughout the nation, and abroad, widened her perspective of social movements to include not only the freedom struggle of her race, but also women's rights, temperance, and pacifism. Thus she won the respect and friendship of Frederick Douglass, Samuel Coleridge-Taylor, and H. G. Wells. In 1906 she interceded in behalf of the colored soldiers involved in the Brownsville, Tex., Riot by appealing to then-Secretary of War William Taft to investigate the matter before an order of dismissal. She actively protested the court decision which ultimately found the Negro soldiers guilty and affirmed a sentence of discharge without honor.

Injustice perpetrated on even seemingly insignificant individuals did not go unnoticed by her. Among her several outstanding battles in 1949 was her effort to free a family of Georgia sharecroppers from imprisonment. Charged with murder, Rosa Lee Ingram and her two sons maintained a plea of innocence, inasmuch as the homicide had been clearly one of self-defense. Mrs. Terrell, as chairman of the national committee to free the Ingram family, appealed to both the United Nations and the governor of Georgia in their behalf. Instead of the death sentence, they were given life imprisonment (they were finally freed in 1959).

Two of her most decisive victories occurred in the later years of her life. At eighty-six years of age she sought admittance to the American Association of University Women. During the early part of the century, between 1905 and 1910, she had held membership in the Washington branch of this organization (then known as the Association of Collegiate Alumnae, but changed to the AAUW in 1921). Having withdrawn her membership for personal reasons, Mary Church Terrell did not seek readmittance until 1946.

During these decades the city of Washington, like most of the United States, had become increasingly segregated, establishing Jim Crow laws to cover most aspects of life from government employment to restaurant service, from public education to recreation centers. The Washington chapter of the American Association of University Women likewise reflected this trend and refused to reinstate her, although the parent body had no official racial qualification and even accepted her on the national level. The New York branch of the AAUW also solicited her membership. However, to Mary Church Terrell and a few members of the Washington branch, especially old classmates from Oberlin, the principle was not merely a matter of individual membership but rather one of establishing a policy that respected educational qualifications without regard to race.

A three-year battle ensued which witnessed, on the one hand, adverse rulings from both the District and U.S. Appellate Courts, and on the other, the national body's attempted expulsion of the Washington chapter in support of her. By July 1949 public opinion had risen to such a peak that the Washington branch officially seceded to form the University Women's Club, with those remaining members committed to a policy of racial equality and becoming the newly official chapter of the AAUW.

The crowning achievement of her long and fruitful life was the desegregation of restaurants in the nation's capital. In 1949 she became chairman of the newly organized Coordinating Committee for the Enforcement of the District of Columbia Anti-Discrimination Laws. Commonly called the "Lost Laws of 1872–1873," these statutes required restaurants and other eating places to serve any "respectable, well-behaved person." As one of the principals in the test case against the Thompson Restaurant, she endeavored to have the validity of these laws reinterpreted by the courts. She and the Coordinating Committee waged their fight on several fronts, through the press, negotiation, boycott, and picketing. For almost a year she also led an economic boycott of those department stores in Washington refusing to serve Negroes in their restaurants. Picketing was not a new activity to her. Before the passage of the Nineteenth Amendment she had demonstrated in front of the White House with the National Women's party led by Alice Paul. At ninety years of age Mary Church Terrell was even more formidable as she marched, supported by a cane, at the head of picket lines. Several stores yielded under this pressure; however, the determining factor was the U.S. Supreme Court's decision in 1953 to uphold the applicability of the 1872 and 1873 laws in Washington, D.C. (*District of Columbia v. John R. Thompson Co.,* 346 U.S. 100, 1953).

Besides lecturing throughout the country at Chautauqua gatherings, American Missionary Association forums, women's rights meetings, and university campuses, she wrote articles for many outstanding journals and newspapers. Some of these include "Lynching from a Negro's Point of View" (*North American Review,* June 1904), "Peonage in the United States" (*Nineteenth Century,* Aug. 1907), "Taft and the Negro Soldiers" (*Independent,* July 1908), "Woman Suffrage and the Fifteenth Amendment" (*The Crisis,* Aug. 1915), and "The History of the High School for Negroes in Washington" (*JNH,* July 1917).

Inspired by the life of Harriet Beecher Stowe, Mary Church Terrell honored the abolitionist author on the centennial of her birth by writing a short biography, *Harriet Beecher Stowe: An Appreciation* (1911). Her commitment to developing positive racial images among colored youth motivated her to produce a pageant for the D.C. public schools in honor of Phillis Wheatley in 1932. While on the Executive Committee of the Women's International League for Peace and Freedom, she wrote the pamphlet *Colored Women and World Peace* (1932). Her major work was her autobiography, *A Colored Woman in a White World* (1940).

Mrs. Terrell died at the age of ninety in Anne Arundel General Hospital, Annapolis, Md., on July 24, 1954. Funeral services were held at Lincoln Congregational Temple, 11th and R Streets NW, Washington, D.C., on July 29, with interment in Lincoln Memorial Cemetery, Suitland, Md. She was survived by her adopted daughter Mary Terrell Tancil Beaupreu, her daughter Phyllis Langston, a sister Annette Church, a niece Roberta Church, and a nephew Thomas Church.

Because her life spanned more than a decade beyond the publishing of the autobiography, some of her most outstanding achievements are not covered in this work. Constance Daniel discussed Mrs. Terrell's efforts to integrate the American Association of University Women in her article "Together—Across New Frontiers" (*Women United,* Oct. 1949). This was also described by Janet McKelvey Swift, member of the Washington branch during the controversy and fellow classmate of Mrs. Terrell, in "Oberlin's Share" (*Oberlin Alumni Magazine,* Sept. 1949). Gladys B. Shepperd's *Mary Church Terrell—Respectable Person* (1959) relates her final victory in desegregating the restaurants in the District of Columbia.

Sylvia Lyons Render's "Afro-American Women: The Outstanding and the Obscure" (*Quarterly Journal of the Library of Congress,* Oct. 1975, pp. 310–15, 319–21) presents a useful summary with transcripts from her diary, photographs, and references. Obituaries appeared in the *Washington Sunday Star* (July 25, 1954, p. C-5), *Evening Star* (July 27, 1954, p. A-12), and *Washington Post and Times Herald* (July 25, 1954, p. 16). Additional valuable information is in the Mary Church Terrell Collection in the Moorland-Spingarn Research Center, Howard University (Containers 1, 2, and 3), and the Mary Church Terrell Papers, located in the Library of Congress. — EVELYN BROOKS BARNETT

TERRELL, ROBERT HERBERTON (1857–1925), municipal court judge. He was born in Charlottesville, Va., on Nov. 27, 1857, the son of Harris and Louisa Ann Terrell. He received his early education in the public schools of the District of Columbia and at Groton Academy, Groton, Mass. He worked to help finance his college education at Harvard College from which he graduated as one of seven *magna cum laude* scholars in June 1884. He later studied at Howard University Law School from which he received an LL.B. in 1889 and an LL.M. in 1893. After teaching five years in the District of Columbia public schools (Sept. 1, 1884, to Aug. 30, 1889), he resigned to work as a chief clerk in the office of the auditor of the U.S. Treasury.

On Oct. 28, 1891, he married Mary E. Church of Memphis, Tenn., an Oberlin College graduate. From 1892 until 1898 he practiced law in Washington, D.C. He left his practice to become a teacher, and later the principal of the M Street High School in Washington, D.C. In the 1890s he was elected to the Board of Trade.

Terrell's later career revealed the ambivalence of many other Negro leaders, including his wife, who were torn between their belief in civil rights and the conservative views of Booker T. Washington. Terrell owed to Washington his appointment as a justice of the peace in the District of Columbia in December 1901. Nevertheless he criticized Washington for condoning Pres. Theodore Roosevelt's summary discharge without honor of colored soldiers of the 25th Infantry after the Brownsville (Tex.) Riot in August 1906. This criticism led another "Bookerite," Charles W. Anderson, to comment that "Judge Terrell had better take a stitch in his tongue." William Monroe Trotter charged, with respect to officeholders who like Terrell and Anderson owed their appointments to Washington: "The Colored people understand they are talking for pay and not for truth, and so pay little heed to their orations." Through Washington's influence President Taft nominated Terrell for the position as judge of the Municipal Court of the District of Columbia on Jan. 15, 1910, and signed the appointment despite bitter protests on racial grounds in the Senate. Terrell continued to serve under Republican presidents until his death on Dec. 20, 1925.

As early as 1896 he had regretted the general ignorance of Negroes about their own history. In 1903 he delivered an address, *A Glance at the Past and Present of the Negro,* in (Robert R.) Church's Auditorium before the Citizen's Industrial League of Memphis on Sept. 22, 1903.

During his tenure as judge Terrell also served on the faculty of the Howard University Law School (1910–1925). He was also for many years grand master of the Grand United Order of Odd Fellows of the District of Columbia. In February 1911 he was one of the charter members of Epsilon Boulé in Washington of Sigma Pi Phi fraternity, which included some of the most distinguished Negroes in the nation. The Robert H. Terrell Law School existed in the District of Columbia from Aug. 12, 1931, to 1950, and an elementary school, at First and Pierce Streets NW, Washington, D.C., was named for him. He and his wife were among the most prominent members of Washington's colored elite.

Terrell had suffered a stroke about four years before his death. A second a year later left him paralyzed on one side. In early December 1925 asthma had aggravated his condition. He died at his home, 1615 S St. NW. Funeral services were held in Metropolitan Baptist Church and he was buried in Harmony Cemetery, Washington, D.C. He was survived by his wife, an adopted daughter Mary Terrell Tancil of Chicago, a natural daughter Phyllis Terrell Goines (Langston) of Washington, a half-brother William H. H. Terrell of Washington, and a half-sister Laura Terrell Jones of Tus-

kegee, Ala. (*Washington Tribune,* Dec. 26, 1925, p. 1).

There is no comprehensive biography of Terrell. The best source of information is Mary Church Terrell's *A Colored Woman in a White World* (1940). Information about the law school is available in the *Catalogue of the Robert H. Terrell Law School, 1949–1950* (vertical file, Moorland-Spingarn Research Center, Howard University). See also the obituary, probably written by Carter G. Woodson, in the *JNH* (Jan. 1926, pp. 223–25).
                                                    — AUBREY ROBINSON, JR.

THIERRY, CAMILLE (1814–1875), poet. He was born in New Orleans. His father had come from Bordeaux and his mother was an octoroon. The family amassed a sizable fortune as wholesale liquor merchants in New Orleans, and Camille was thus able to devote himself largely to his own interests. Like many other colored Créoles, he sought escape from race prejudice in New Orleans by going, at an undetermined date, to France. He spent the rest of his life in Paris and Bordeaux, except for a brief return to consult with the manager of his considerable property. He died in Bordeaux, shortly after receiving news of the virtual loss of his property.

One of the earliest and most prolific of the colored poets of New Orleans, Thierry published his first poem, "Les Idées," in *L'Album Littéraire,* a review that included poems, stories, fables, and articles by writers eager to arouse in young readers a stronger determination to stand firm against discrimination among races. *L'Album Littéraire* had a brief life of but three or four years (1843–1847[?]) and then ceased publication. With the appearance of Thierry's "Les Idées," his talent was quickly recognized. Armand Lanusse immediately contacted him and urged that his writing be included in a new project, the publication of America's first Negro anthology of verse, *Les Cenelles.* This little book of some 215 pages made its appearance in 1845.

Of the eighty-two poems in *Les Cenelles* (some dated as early as 1828), fourteen are by Thierry. Their titles, translated, are "The Damned," "The Past," "The Mariner," "The Suicide," "You," "Adieu," "The Awakening," "To Mademoiselle," "To the One I Love," "Ideas," "The Ghost of Eugene B.," "Speak Always," "Jealousy," and "The Corsair's Sweetheart." The last, composed by Thierry in his youth, was probably the most popular of the group. Thierry's charming lyric "To the One I Love," expressive of tender sentiment and filled with exquisite imagery, illustrates in graphic form the simple artistry of the poet.

Several of his other poems were published in *La Chronique* (April 16, 1848) and in *L'Orléanais.* One of the more famous of these latter, which generally reflect the influence of Lamartine, is "Mariquita La Calentura," a description of the joys and tragedies of a Spanish family in New Orleans. *Les Vagabonds,* published in Paris and Bordeaux (1874), has been lost. It is generally believed to have been a portrayal of three typical colored boys who wandered the streets of New Orleans during the poet's boyhood.

Paul Trévigne wrote about Thierry in the *New Orleans Louisianan,* (Dec. 25, 1875): "His poems are composed with peculiar care, and comprise all the various rhythms of French prosody. Some of them are to be classed among the finest poetical efforts of Louisiana's most gifted writers" (quoted in John Blassingame, *Black New Orleans, 1860–1880* [1973], p. 135).

The career and evaluation of Thierry are based on Rodolphe L. Desdunes's *Nos Hommes et Notre Histoire* (1911), translated and edited as *Our People and Our History* (1973) by Sister Dorothea Olga McCants, D.C. See also Charles B. Rousséve's *The Negro in Louisiana . . .* (1937). — DOROTHEA OLGA MCCANTS, D.C.

THOMAS, JAMES P. (1827–1913), barber and businessman. Thomas was born in Nashville (Davidson County), Tenn., the son of Judge John Catron (one of the justices in the Dred Scott case), and a black slave, Sally. While Catron neglected his son, Sally earned enough money as a cleaning woman to purchase his freedom in 1834. Under Tennessee law, however, he was a slave as long as he remained in the state. He performed chores for his mother, mastered the basics of reading, writing, and arithmetic in a drafty one-room school, and became an apprentice (1841) in the barbershop of another slave, Frank Parrish. In 1846 he opened his own shop in the house where he was born and his mother was still operating a laundry. Located at 10 Deaderick St., within a few blocks of several banking houses, the courthouse, and the Capitol, it attracted many well-known customers and was advertised in the city's first business directory (1853).

He accompanied Andrew Jackson Polk through Louisville, Cincinnati, Buffalo, and Albany to New York City in 1848. They stayed at the Hotel Astor but Thomas was denied a seat on a bus and rudely ejected from a theater. After a second trip to the North in 1851, Thomas's master, Ephraim Foster, petitioned the Davidson County Court for his freedom. Foster praised Thomas's "exemplary character" and the court ordered him to be emancipated. Thomas petitioned the court to grant him immunity from the law which required free Negroes to leave the state. The court granted his petition and James Thomas became the first Negro in the county (and perhaps in the state) to gain both freedom and residency.

Learning that William Walker, a boyhood playmate, was organizing a confederation of states in Central America and that a quadroon had been appointed secretary of state, Thomas and his nephew John H. Rapier, Jr., joined Walker in Granada, Nicaragua. When they learned that Walker was planning to establish a dictatorship and restore slavery, they returned to Nashville by way of several midwestern states. Despite requests that he reopen his barbershop, Thomas left Nashville for the last time in 1856. After another trip through the Midwest, he settled in St. Louis and found employment on the Mississippi steamer *William Morrison.* He courted the beautiful, wealthy, free mulatto Antoinette Rutger, whose grandfather had been one of the first slaves brought to Missouri. Antoinette's mother opposed her marriage to an ex-slave, but Thomas's persistent courtship won him acceptance among upper-class Negroes and recognition in the directory, *The Colored Aristocracy of St. Louis,* in 1857.

During the Civil War, Thomas opened a barbershop in the city, began speculating in real estate, and like some other affluent free Negroes, supported the Confederacy, although late in his life he severely criticized the racial attitudes of white southerners. In 1868, after a ten-year courtship, he finally married Antoinette Rutger. "It was a most imposing affair. The elite of the city were present," noted the conservative *St. Louis Dispatch* under a headline: "Rich Nigs Wed." "The bride has property and money to the value of $400,000. The husband is worth nearly the same amount. The bridal veil [alone] cost $750. The Rev. Mr. Thomas Berk performed the ceremony at St. Vincent's [Catholic] Church."

Although the *Dispatch* overestimated his wealth, during the next quarter of a century Thomas became one of the richest men in St. Louis, white or black. Buying and selling real estate, building and improving a number of rental apartments (mostly on Rutger Street, between Sixth and Seventh Streets), overseeing a ten-chair barbering business (in the central business district), and speculating in the stock market (mostly on railroad and insurance company stock), he accumulated an estate worth at least $250,000. At the height of his financial career, he rented 48 apartments (38 on Rutger Street and 10 on Jefferson Avenue), controlled real estate in various sections of the city, and owned two mansions: one in the city, and one in Alton, Ill. (across the Mississippi and twenty miles north of St. Louis). In a single city block (#301), as conservatively estimated by city tax officials, Thomas owned property valued at $98,430. One business transaction, typical of many others, illustrated his business acumen. In 1870 he purchased thirteen acres of city property for $7000. Only three years later, he sold the same real estate for $28,000.

Late in 1873, seemingly unaffected by the worst depression the United States had known, Thomas set out for Europe. Traveling to England, France, Italy, Austria, Germany, and the Low Countries, he was greatly impressed with the style of life on the continent: "In Paris, I saw people who could pass for colored in America without trying, but [judging] from their general demeanor and bearing, [they] had never worn the yoke." In Rome, "a most interesting place, where visitors of all colors, from all clims [*sic*] visit," and in Berlin, with its "patient, plodding, hard working set of people," he enjoyed extended stays. Upon his return, Thomas said bitterly: "Every colored man ought to know, although he has been treated as a companion [in Europe], on American soil, all that comes to an end. [Negroes] are supposed to take [their] regular place. Custome [*sic*] has so ordered it."

During the depression of 1893–1896 Thomas was forced to mortgage much of his property, and he never really recovered from the economic downturn, which caught many businessmen by surprise. He devoted the last years of his life to his family (although Antoinette died in 1897, his children James, Pelagie, John, Joseph, Anthony, and Thomas were a continual source of satisfaction) and to writing some autobiographical reminiscences (unpublished) about life in the antebellum South. In a collage of memories about slaves and free blacks, "poor whites" and planters, and some of the excitement in the decade before the Civil War, Thomas recalled that "slaves had no fair conception of time nor money." They belonged to no unions, but simply did what they were told to do, "whether it required one or fifteen hours." Significantly, he placed poor whites at the bottom of the social ladder, below free blacks. They had neither land nor slaves, and were something of an anomaly in the South.

After a lingering illness, James Thomas died on Dec. 17, 1913. Although still owning a few apartments, he had lost most of his wealth. His personal estate (which had once included such items as a $2000 piano) was valued at only $1.45. Despite having so little at the end of his life, Thomas had achieved a great deal, and at a time when Negroes were relegated to the lowest caste in American society, his accomplishments were remarkable.

A copy of his manuscript autobiography is in the Moorland-Spingarn Research Center, Howard University. This is the only known source.

— LOREN SCHWENINGER

THOMPSON, JOHN EDWARD WEST (1855–1918), physician and diplomat. Thompson was born in Brooklyn. When he was only ten years old, his parents moved to Providence, R.I. He received his early education in public schools in Massachusetts, Connecticut, and Rhode Island, and graduated with "high honors" from Yale Medical School in 1883. Weeks later he married Miss McLinn, a New Haven "colored lady of good position." Her father was a carpenter at Yale but she had received a good education. With his new bride, Thompson spent eighteen months in France, where he studied various medical techniques in Paris.

In late 1884 he returned to New York, began a lively medical practice, and quickly attained prominence in social and professional circles. This achievement led the *National Cyclopedia of Biography* in 1904 to comment that "He is a noted illustration of the capacity of the colored race to rise to excellence and prominence under the influence of social advantages and suitable education" (p. 478).

In New York social circles, Thompson became known as an excellent French scholar and informed in international law. After the Democratic administration of Grover Cleveland refused to permit the Republican historian George Washington Williams, who had been confirmed by the Senate in 1885 as U.S. minister to Haiti, to take up his duties, Thompson became interested in the position. He was highly recommended by Noah Porter, president of Yale College, the medical faculty of the college, the Catholic bishops of New York and Delaware, and A. S. Hewitt, mayor of New York City. All declared Thompson "the best fitted colored man" for the position.

On May 7, 1885, Thompson was nominated by President Cleveland minister resident and consul-general to Haiti. The Negro newspaper *The New York Freeman*, commenting on his Senate confirmation (Sept. 16, 1885), acclaimed it an achievement and described him as "a gentleman of culture and refinement and remarkably pleasant in manner." He succeeded John M. Langston.

After Thompson arrived in Haiti on June 24, 1885, he found many of the problems that had retarded the development of Haiti and caused conflict with the United States. He was fortunate in having as the U.S. secretary of state Thomas F. Bayard. Bayard took the position that if the United States could not "honorably" press a claim against a foreign government, the claim should be dropped. In response to a despatch from Thompson, Bayard informed him (Nov. 7, 1885) that the United States did not claim extraterritorial rights in Haiti and discouraged the use of American ships in Haitian waters by Haitians asserting the right of asylum. On the other hand, when the State Department in 1886 threatened reprisals against Haitian ships in American waters because of Haitian legislation imposing new obligations on American ships in Haitian waters, Thompson had to point out that Haiti had no merchant ships. In 1887, however, Bayard refused to compel Haiti to pay to two American merchants claims that had previously been awarded. Thompson aided Stephen Preston, the Haitian chargé d'affaires in Washington, in presenting evidence to Bayard that led to his decision.

Bayard's and Thompson's most crucial problem arose during the struggle between François Légitime and Florvil Hyppolite for the presidency of Haiti. Bayard adopted a policy of strict neutrality. On Oct. 16, 1888, Légitime's gunboat seized an American liner, *Haytian Republic*, for violating a blockade that he had proclaimed and took it as a prize to Port-au-Prince. In accordance with instructions from Bayard, Thompson protested vigorously and after Légitime's "prize court" justified the seizure, Thompson recommended the sending of the American warship *Yantic* to enforce Bayard's demand for release. Bayard sent two ships and in December the ship was released. Thompson's despatches vividly portray the struggle within Légitime's government and accurately forecast a continuation of the civil war between Légitime and Hyppolite. The despatches also give a vivid picture of such internal problems as the debt and sanitary conditions in Port-au-Prince and other cities.

In accordance with established custom, Thompson resigned on Feb. 18, 1889, after Benjamin Harrison had been elected president. When some American interests requested that Thompson be retained to relieve "any anxiety for the future," Harrison kept him in Port-au-Prince with instructions to maintain strict neutrality. He remained at his post until Oct. 15, 1889, almost two months after Légitime resigned and more than a month after Hyppolite was elected president. Thompson thus eased the transition for the appointment of Frederick Douglass.

Thompson returned to the United States with his wife and their three-year-old son, Reed McLinn. He practiced medicine in New York City until 1913. During Cleveland's second administration, Thompson applied for a diplomatic post, preferably in France. Cleveland stated that "a colored man would be looked down upon if stationed in a European city," probably a reflection of Cleveland's views. Thompson rejected the president's luke-warm offer to appoint him "surgeon-general" at Freedmen's Hospital. It is not known whether the rebuff was responsible for Thompson's arrest and conviction shortly thereafter on a charge of "disorderly conduct."

Thompson then established his medical practice in Bridgeport, Conn., where he worked among the poorer people until his death on Oct. 6, 1918. He had been stabbed in the hallway of his office, 966 Main St., Bridgeport, by a disgruntled patient, Thomas Saloway, who accused Thompson of having accepted $300 for medical services that left him in poorer health than before his treatment. Thompson died in an ambulance on the way to a hospital and Saloway committed suicide. The former diplomat was survived by his sons, Lt. Ernest Thompson and Pvt. Elliot Thompson, U.S. Army (*New York Age*, Oct. 12, 1918, p. 1).

Thompson's mission to Haiti is discussed in Rayford W. Logan's *The Diplomatic Relations of the United States with Haiti, 1776–1891* (1941). Basic information about his life is in the New York City Directories of the 1890s and the Bridgeport City Directories (1913–1920). The principal unpublished source is the two-volume *The List and Register of the United States Consular Officers, 1789–1939,* which includes diplomatic records, application forms, and personal letters.

— GLENN O. I. PHILLIPS

THOMS, ADAH B. SAMUELS (1863?–1943), registered nurse, pioneer in public health nursing, administrator, and civil rights leader. Born in Virginia, the daughter of Harry and Melvina Samuels, she received her elementary and secondary education in Richmond, was married briefly (hence her name of Thoms), and studied elocution at the Cooper Union, New York City, in the 1890s. In 1900 she graduated, the only Negro in a class of thirty, from the Woman's Infirmary and School of Therapeutic Massage. She worked in New York City and North Carolina, where she became head nurse at St. Agnes Hospital in Raleigh. In 1903 she entered the new school of nursing at the Lincoln Hospital and Home in New York City. In her second year she was made head nurse on a surgical ward. After her graduation in 1905 she became supervisor of the surgical division; from 1906 to 1923 she was assistant director of nurses, serving occasionally as acting director of the training school. In that capacity she added (1917) a course in the new field of public health service which she herself took. She also took special courses at the New York School of Philanthropy (later the New York School of Social Work), Hunter College, and the New School for Social Research. After retirement from the Lincoln Hospital in 1923, she was active in several organizations in Harlem. A diabetic, her sight began to fail. In 1943 she died from arteriosclerotic heart disease, and was buried in Woodlawn Cemetery.

Like many other Negroes during the first half of the twentieth century Mrs. Thoms (who was married briefly to Henry Smith) was a leader in improving conditions within segregated health delivery systems and in combating segregation. In August 1908 as president of the Alumnae Association of Lincoln Hospital she helped, along with Martha Franklin of New Haven, organize the National Association of Colored Graduate Nurses, at St. Mark's Methodist Church, New York City. As its first treasurer and president (1916–1923) she campaigned for better employment opportunities for qualified Negro nurses in hospitals and public health agencies as well as raising admission standards in nursing schools. After the ratification of the Nineteenth Amendment (Aug. 18, 1920) she urged colored nurses to vote and to encourage their patients to follow their example.

Like Mary Church Terrell, for example, she was a pioneer in the participation of colored women in international organizations. In 1912 she was one of the first three Negro delegates to the International Council of Nurses at Cologne, Germany. As a consequence, later meetings of the council included Negro nurses from Africa, South America, and the Caribbean. Mrs. Thoms also broadened her knowledge of nursing and hospital administration by visiting hospitals in Europe.

Beginning with 1917, as president of the National Association of Colored Graduate Nurses, she achieved only limited success in obtaining the utilization of Negro nurses in the Nursing Service of the American Red Cross. The surgeon-general of the United States refused to authorize this service even though it was approved by the chairman of the Committee on Red Cross Nursing Service. Not until December 1918, during the great influenza epidemic, were eighteen qualified Negro nurses assigned to the Army Nurse Corps. Although they received equal pay and rank, and although the patients were not segregated, the nurses were forced to live in separate quarters.

Mrs. Thoms was more successful in working toward the integration of colored graduate nurses with the American Nurses Association, of which she had been an early member, and of the National Organization for Public Health Nursing. As president of the Association of Colored Graduate Nurses, she opposed a merger with the National Medical Association. This opposition facilitated the integration of the Colored Graduate Nurses Association with the other two organizations in 1951, eight years after her death. Her many activities made her the logical choice for the first award (1936) by the association which she had helped found and directed, the Mary Mahoney Medal, named for the first Negro to become a trained nurse.

The principal source for much of Mrs. Thoms's career is her *Pathfinders: A History of the Progress of Colored Graduate Nurses* (1929). A biographical sketch is in *NAW* (1971, 3:454–57). The sketch, written by Mabel Keaton Staupers, was based on her *No Time for Prejudice: A Story of the Integration of Negroes in Nursing in the U.S.* (1961) and other sources. See also Mrs. Thoms's "President's Address, National Association of Colored Graduate Nurses" (*JNMA* Oct.–Dec. 1920, pp. 73–74). — RAYFORD W. LOGAN

JACK THORNE [DAVID BRYANT FULTON] (1861?–1941), polemicist. He was born in Fayetteville, N.C., to Benjamin and Lavinia Robinson Fulton. After spending his early childhood in the Fayetteville area, he went in 1867 to live with his mother in Wilmington, N.C. There he was educated in schools established by the American Missionary Association. Later, he took his first step toward a literary career, contributing articles under the pen name of "Jack Thorne" to the *Record,* a Negro-owned Wilmington newspaper.

In the spring of 1887 Jack Thorne went to New York City, joining the Pullman Palace Car Company as a porter in 1888. With his earnings he brought his wife to Brooklyn, where he lived for the rest of his life. In addition to his work in the Pullman service, he was employed for several years by the Central Branch of the YMCA of Brooklyn. He worked at other times for a music publishing house in New York and for Sears, Roebuck. He died in Brooklyn on Nov. 14, 1941.

Jack Thorne's first independently published work was *Recollections of a Sleeping Car Porter* (1892), a forty-five-page description of the "many things that suggest the humorous as well as the tragic and ridiculous" in the "checkered life of the porter." His second book, a novel, *Hanover, or the Persecution of the Lowly* (1900), focused on violent racial conflict in the South. Part exposé, part tract, and part fiction, *Hanover,* according to its author, was designed to provide "a truthful statement of the causes" that led to the "massacre" that took place in Wilmington, N.C., in November 1898. However, in the course of returning an indictment against a group of white conspirators and reviewing a few incidents of black heroism during the massacre, *Hanover* became less a novel than a somewhat diffuse group of stories centered on a historical event.

Between 1903 and 1906 Jack Thorne gained prominence in Brooklyn for his letters and articles published in a number of New York newspapers. Bits of verse, autobiographical sketches, and a number of "Pullman Porter Stories" testify to the varied purposes to which Jack Thorne turned his pen. But the bulk of his writing in these years consisted, as he said in his introduction to a collection of his newspaper writings, of "answering traducers and endeavoring to ward off the blows aimed at my people by the enemy." Most of the pieces in *Eagle Clippings* (1907) show Jack Thorne attacking race slander in books and periodicals and criticizing political and social developments which he judged hostile to Negroes. Some of his short stories include "The Great White Way," a sketch of New York City at the turn of the century; "A Tale of the Reconstruction Period," concerning the exploits of Henry Berry Lowery, a mulatto outlaw in North Carolina; and "The Cap'n," a character sketch of a railroad train inspector.

After 1907 Jack Thorne divided his attention among poetry, essays, pamphlets, and short stories. His short stories rarely found a publisher. One, a celebration of the life of Abraham Lincoln, he read to a large gathering in Brooklyn on the centennial anniversary of Lincoln's birth. In July 1923 he presented "Mother of Mine; Ode to the Negro Woman" to the annual convention of New York Colored Women's Clubs. The condition of the Afro-American woman had also been the theme for his *Plea for Social Justice for the Negro Woman* (1912). This pamphlet pointed out the threat to the purity and dignity of Negro womanhood caused by black concubinage in the South before emancipation and the persistence of black prostitution for white patrons in the North. But the most direct statement of Jack Thorne's racial views appeared in the *African Times and Orient Review* for December 1913. Discussing "Race Unification; How It May Be Accomplished," he rejected the idea that the future of Negroes rested on amalgamation with or reliance on whites and emphasized the need for a knowledge of "race history," "race achievement,"

and "race literature" as a stimulus to "race pride" and advancement. This anticipation of some of the ideals of the Garvey movement is typical of the work of Jack Thorne, a writer whose literary career was built on pride in race and a commitment to the defense of his people.

The Arno Press has reprinted *Hanover* (1969), edited by Thomas R. Cripps, but there are no critical studies of Jack Thorne. The biographical information is based in part on the reminiscences of his ninety-three-year-old second wife, Katie Gummer, a widow whom he had married in 1917 when he was a widower.

— WILLIAM L. ANDREWS

THURMAN, WALLACE (1902–1934), journalist, novelist, playwright, and ghostwriter. He was born in Salt Lake City, Utah, but information about his early life is scanty. It is said that he had an Indian grandmother who married a Jewish peddler. An obituary stated that he was survived by a grandmother, Mrs. A. L. Jackson, his mother, Mrs. Beulah Dewey, and an uncle, Arthur Jackson, all of Salt Lake City. Contemporaries described Wallace Thurman vaguely as "dark skinned." He finished high school in Salt Lake City, was a medical student during the winter and spring quarters (1919–1920) at the University of Utah, achieving good grades in chemistry and pharmacy.

After a few years in California he came to New York in 1925, at the beginning of the "Harlem Renaissance." This "New Negro Movement," Sterling Brown wrote, "had temporal roots in the past and spatial roots elsewhere in America, and the term has validity, it seems to me, only when considered to be a continuing tradition" ("The New Negro in Literature, 1920–1955," in *The New Negro Thirty Years Afterward,* edited by Rayford W. Logan [1955], pp. 47–58). Thurman met many of the writers and artists who illuminated the Harlem Renaissance and became one of its central personalities. His hectic, bohemian life led to his death of tuberculosis in a charity hospital on Welfare Island, New York, Dec. 22, 1934.

During the early 1920s in Los Angeles he wrote a column, "Inklings," for a local Negro newspaper, read about the New Negro Movement, and met Arna Bontemps, who became one of its best known participants. Thurman's attempt to promote the Movement on the West Coast in his own magazine, *The Outlet,* failed after six months and he came to New York in 1925. He gained experience as a reporter and editor on another short-lived publication, *The Looking Glass.* Theophilus Lewis, a kind of mentor who knew him well throughout the Harlem years, had helped him find the job with *The Looking Glass* and then with the "radical" monthly magazine the *Messenger.* As editor of the latter he published not only his own work but that of Bontemps, Langston Hughes, and Zora Neale Hurston. In the fall of 1926 he left the *Messenger* and became circulation manager of the liberal white monthly, *The World Tomorrow.*

In the summer of 1926, with Hurston, the painter Aaron Douglas, Hughes, and others, he founded *Fire,* "a new experimental quarterly devoted to and published by younger Negro artists," according to his article, "Negro Artists and the Negro" (*New Republic,*

Aug. 31, 1927). Benjamin Brawley (*The Negro Genius* [1937]) said that "its flame was so intense that it burnt itself up immediately." Its idea, as Hughes wrote in his autobiography, *The Big Sea* (1940), was that "it would burn up a lot of the old, dead conventional Negro-white ideas of the past, épater [flabbergast] le bourgeois" into the realization of the existence of the younger Negro writers and artists." The hope that it would provide a wider outlet than that afforded by *The Crisis, Opportunity,* and the *Messenger* expired after the first issue. Only a few bookstores in Greenwich Village put it on display; white critics generally ignored it; W. E. B. Du Bois and other writers in the Negro press harshly criticized it. Thurman, who had advanced most of the money for publication, spent the next three or four years paying the printer. *Harlem, A Forum of Negro Life,* which he published two years after the cessation of *Fire,* folded after two issues.

Harassed by debt and jobless during much of the time, he had boils, a swollen thyroid gland, and infected glands which required surgery. In 1927, however, his articles were published in the *New Republic,* the *Independent, The World Tomorrow, The Bookman,* and *Dance Magazine.* These publications and his adverse criticism in *The Looking Glass* of *The New Negro* (1925), edited by Alain Leroy Locke, established Thurman as a kind of *enfant terrible* of the Harlem Renaissance.

He found a job on the editorial staff of McFadden Publications, and in 1929 Macaulay Company published his first novel, *The Blacker the Berry,* a title borrowed from an old Negro folk saying, "the blacker the berry, the sweeter the juice." Its main theme, "interracial schisms based on skin color," was in part autobiographical. The principal character, Emma Lou, born of a middle-class family in a small midwestern town, went to Los Angeles, then to New York in a vain effort to escape the scorn and discrimination of light-skinned Negroes. But Emma Lou, like some others, used skin bleachers and hair straighteners to appear more like those who scorned her. This theme of self-hatred later became popular with some authors and sociologists.

He became a ghostwriter for *True Story* and other publications, as well as of books. It was his play *Harlem,* which opened in February 1929 at the Apollo Theater on Broadway, that won Thurman overnight fame. Although a white writer (William) Jourdan Rapp collaborated on the play, Thurman wrote the plot and dialog of this startlingly realistic drama of Harlem life and of its evils as faced by a mother in an uptown flat. Based on a short story, "Cordelia the Crude," which Thurman had written and published in *Fire,* the highly melodramatic story recounted the disillusionment of a family that sought escape from harsh conditions in the South only to find that New York was not a "city of refuge" but a "city of refuse." Like *Blacker the Berry, Harlem* also developed the theme of prejudice against West Indians. The play ran for over ninety performances in New York City and was also received warmly in Los Angeles and Chicago. Of the favorable and unfavorable reviews, a comment by Edith J. R. Isaacs in *The Negro in the American Theatre* (1947, p. 86) is one of the more significant: "[*Harlem*] showed a simple

Southern mother, terrified and helpless as she sees her family caught in the eddies of life in a Harlem railroad flat, with its by-products of rent parties, of the 'sweetback,' of the 'hot-stuff man,' of lotteries and vice. . . . Violent and undisciplined as the play was, it left a sense of photographic reality."

The publication of *Blacker the Berry* by Macaulay led to several years of Thurman's association with the company: as reader (the only Negro Langston Hughes knew to hold this position with a major publisher) and as editor-in-chief, beginning the summer of 1932. Macaulay published Thurman's second and third novels in 1932.

The title *Infants of the Spring* comes from Shakespeare's *Hamlet:* "The canker galls the infants of the spring/ Too oft before their buttons be disclosed" (I, iii, 39). The novel deals with the impact of bohemian tendencies ("the canker") upon the literati (the "infant") of the Harlem Renaissance (springtime). In debunking the "Negro Renaissance," Thurman spoke of the artists and writers who exploited the white people who supported it as the "Niggeratti." "Being a Negro writer in these days," in the words of one of his minor characters, "is a racket and I'm going to make the most of it while it lasts. I find queer places for whites to go in Harlem . . . out-of-the-way primitive churches, side-street speakeasies, and they fall for it. About twice a year I manage to sell a story. It is acclaimed. I am a genius in the making. Thank God for this Negro Literary Renaissance! Long may it flourish!" *Infants* is clearly autobiographical. Raymond (Thurman) is a victim of his own self-hatred. It is Paul, however, an artist who had lived with Raymond at Niggerati Manor who committed suicide. Thurman's description of the debauched life in the manor is one of the best literary etchings of the life of the "Niggerati" for which many whites condemned Carl Van Vechten's *Nigger Heaven.* Thurman is generally credited with coining the word "Niggerati."

Another aspect of Thurman's pessimism is evident in an unpublished three-act play, "Jeremiah, the Magnificent," written in collaboration with Jourdan Rapp, probably about 1930. After exploring the problems of Marcus Garvey in his Back-to-Africa Movement, the authors wrote: "Africa is for the Africans and the native sons and daughters of Africa shall return to their native shores. You must gird up your loins my children; invest your souls with the Holy Spirit."

Langston Hughes described in memorable words his prodigious capacity for reading, and drinking gin, which he did not like. He liked being a Negro but felt it a great handicap; he adored bohemianism, but thought it wrong to be a bohemian. "He liked to waste a lot of time, but he always felt guilty wasting time. He loathed crowds, but he hated to be alone" (*The Big Sea*).

Mae Gwendolyn Henderson's evaluation is probably as accurate as any: "In terms of his literary contributions, Wallace Thurman has been regarded as one of the minor figures of the Renaissance. His significance, however, far exceeds the work he left behind. Not only was he tremendously influential upon the younger and perhaps more successful writers of the period, but his life itself became a symbol of the New Negro Movement."

In 1934 Thurman had signed a contract with Foy Productions Ltd. to do the scenario of *High School Girl* and *Tomorrow's Children,* the latter a film on sterilization which was censored in New York. This took him to Hollywood, where his earnings enabled him to follow an even more destructive life than in New York. Despite a previous attempt to regain his physical and mental health in Florida and Jamaica before going to California, Hollywood was the prelude to his last days. When he went back to New York in May 1934, his despondency led to a drinking binge until he passed out. Ironically he was taken to City Hospital, on Welfare Island, New York, the institution he had described in *The Interne* (1932). After six months in the ward for incurables, he died of tuberculosis on Dec. 22, 1934.

Funeral services were held in New York City on Christmas Eve. In addition to his relatives, among those present were Countée Cullen, Rose McClendon, Walter White, and Louise Thompson, his former wife. Interment was in Silver Mount Cemetery on Staten Island.

Two of the best sources for Thurman's life and work are Hughes's *The Big Sea: An Autobiography* (1940, esp. pp. 233–38) and Mae Gwendolyn Henderson's "Portrait of Wallace Thurman" (*The Harlem Renaissance Remembered,* edited by Arna Bontemps [1972], pp. 147–70, with footnotes and bibliography, pp. 290–91). See also Doris E. Abramson's *Negro Playwrights in the American Theatre, 1929–1959* (1969, pp. 32–43). The Wallace Thurman Folder in the James Weldon Johnson Collection, Yale University, contains correspondence, other unpublished materials, and *Fire.* "Cordelia the Crude" appears in *Black American Literature Fiction,* edited by Darwin T. Turner (1969). A typescript (carbon copy) of the play "Jeremiah the Magnificent" is in the Schomburg Center for Research in Black Culture, New York City. A valuable obituary, "Death Claims Noted Writer," by Theophilus Lewis, was published in the *New York Amsterdam News* (Dec. 29, 1934, pp. 1–2). — ERNEST B. BOYNTON, JR.

TILLMAN, NATHANIEL PATRICK, SR. (1898–1965), educator and philologist. The only son of Nathan and Catherine Tillman, he was born on Jan. 17, 1898, in Birmingham, Ala. His parents died when he was still a boy, and he was reared by his grandmother. He received his B. A. degree in 1920 from Morehouse College, Atlanta, Ga. After spending two years as a teacher at Alcorn College in Mississippi, he returned to Atlanta in 1924 where he spent the remainder of his academic career. He was an eminently successful debating coach and won acclaim as a director of Shakespearean productions.

He earned both his M.A. and Ph.D. degrees from the University of Wisconsin, in 1927 and 1940, respectively. He also studied at Oxford in the summer of 1934 and at the University of Chicago. The recipient of numerous fellowships, he was a University Scholar (1926–1927), a General Education Board Fellow (1931–1932), and held a Rosenwald Travel Fellowship in 1934. He was co-editor with Hugh M. Gloster of *My Life, My Country, My World: College Readings for Modern Living,* a reader-composition text for college freshmen, published in 1952. This publication was widely enough

adopted to warrant a second edition. His most important scholarly work was done on the medieval English poet John Lydgate, *Lydgate's Rhyme as Evidence of His Pronunciation.* The handbook which governed the format and style of theses produced at Atlanta University in the 1940s and 1950s was co-authored by G. Lewis Chandler and Tillman. He contributed scholarly articles to such journals as *American Speech, Phylon: The Atlanta University Review of Race and Culture,* and the *Quarterly Journal of Higher Education Among Negroes.*

He was the Morehouse College registrar from 1924 to 1932, serving also as professor of English and chairman of the college's English Department after 1927. Acting academic dean of the school, (1932–1934), he continued to serve as chairman and teacher until 1957. During these years he taught courses at Atlanta University and in 1942 became professor and chairman of the English Department of the university. Between 1955 and 1961 he was first acting and later dean of the School of Arts and Sciences of Atlanta University. He combined the duties and responsibilities of chairman and dean with those of a stimulating classroom teacher until physical disabilities forced his resignation as department chairman and dean in 1961. From then until his death he was professor of English.

He was married on Sept. 13, 1920, to Mattie V. Reynolds. Two children were born from that union: Nathaniel P. Jr., who later became a well-known educator, and Virginia, later Mrs. Whatley. A diabetic who had lost both his legs, he died on Oct. 17, 1965, a few hours after he had been presented, in absentia, a plaque by the trustees of Atlanta University in appreciation of twenty-five years of devoted service to the university. Funeral services were held in the Dean Sage Auditorium on the Atlanta University campus, with interment in Atlanta's South View Cemetery. He was survived by his widow and two children.

Active in the national councils and associations in his academic field, he was in demand as a speaker and consultant for such national groups as the National Council of Teachers of English and the College Language Association, which awarded him its Distinguished Contributor's Award. It was as a teacher, however, that he had his greatest and most lasting impact, and made his most significant contribution. Admired for his scholarship, wit, and compassion by generations of students, as early as the 1930s he was regarded by Arthur D. Wright, president of the John F. Slater Fund, as "one of the best teachers of English in the South." A tribute paid to him in 1963 by former students for his "sincere interest in guiding and teaching" and for the "high standards" he exemplified in his profession is reflective of his ability to both teach and inspire youth. He was regarded by his colleagues as "a great teacher, an excellent scholar, a skilled administrator, a wise counselor and a true friend," who represented "a rare combination of talents, skills, and capacities in a single individual."

This sketch is based on the records of Morehouse College, Atlanta University, interviews, personal reminiscences, and Clarence A. Bacote's *The Story of Atlanta University: A Century of Service, 1865–1965* (1969). — EDWARD F. SWEAT

TOBIAS, CHANNING H[EGGIE] (1882–1961), YMCA secretary, and religious and civic leader. The son of Fair and Belle Robinson Tobias, he was born in Augusta, Ga., on Feb. 1, 1882. His father was a coach-man and his mother, who died when he was twelve, a domestic servant. He received his early education at the Lucy Laney's school, Haines Institute, a B.A. degree from Paine Institute (1902), both in Augusta, and a B.D. degree from Drew University, Madison, N.J. (1905). He taught biblical literature at Paine College (1905–1911). In 1911 he began one of the most significant activities of his career, his work with the YMCA. From 1911 to 1923 he was secretary of the National Council of the YMCA, with headquarters in Washington, D.C.; from 1923 to 1946 he was senior secretary of the Colored Department of the National Council, with headquarters in New York City. In the latter year he became the first Negro director of the Phelps-Stokes Fund, New York City, a foundation devoted to the improvement of edu-cational opportunities for Negroes. He was elected a member of the Board of Trustees of the NAACP in 1943. Ten years later he left the Phelps-Stokes Fund to become chairman of the board of the association, a position which he held until he retired in 1959 as chair-man emeritus.

In addition to these major responsibilities, Tobias held several significant governmental positions: mem-ber of the National Advisory Committee on Selective Service and the Joint Army and Navy Committee on Welfare and Recreation during World War II and, in 1946, of the Civilian Committee of the U.S. Navy, member of President Truman's Committee on Civil Rights (1946 and 1947), and of the Mayor's Committee on Survey Management of New York City. In 1951–1952 he was an alternate U.S. delegate to the Sixth General Assembly of the United Nations in Paris, with the special assignment as representative on the Com-mittee on Trust and Non-Self Governing Territories. His interests encompassed many other activities. He at-tended the Paris session of the Second Pan-African Congress (Sept. 1921). During 1926 he was a delegate and speaker at the World Conference of the YMCAs at Helsingfors, Finland; he lectured at Riga, Latvia, and visited YMCA centers there and in Estonia, Poland, and Czechoslovakia. He and Benjamin E. Mays, dean of the School of Religion at Howard University, were the two Negro members of the twelve-party U.S. delegation to the World Conference of the YMCAs in Mysore, India (1936–1937). Before and after the conference Tobias traveled in the Near East and Far East. He vigorously supported the implementation of the U.S. Supreme Court decisions (1954–1955) which declared segrega-tion in public schools unconstitutional. At various times he was a director of the Marshall Field Foundation, Jessie Smith Noyes Foundation, trustee of Palmer Me-morial Institute, Sedalia, N.C., and Hampton Institute, serving as chairman of the board in 1946. In that year also he was a trustee of the New School for Social Research, New York City. He was also an influential member of the Board of Trustees of Howard University (1931–1953). A life-long Republican until the early 1940s, he campaigned vigorously for Pres. Franklin D. Roosevelt in 1944 and supported Henry A. Wallace for

president in 1948. He contributed articles to various magazines, was a member of the board of editorial advisers of the *Protestant Digest,* and served on the editorial board of the *Protestant Voice.*

One of the best sources for an evaluation of Tobias is his autobiography in *Thirteen Americans: Their Spiritual Biographies* (1953). Augusta, where he was born and spent his early years, had what "was com-monly known as good relationship between the races, but of course all within the framework of segregation." Its lack of cultural provincialism spilled over into the Negro community. "The fact that I was born and grew up in such a city, accounts in part for the lack of bitter-ness with which I have been able to approach consider-ation of racial relationships in the South" (p. 179). But a quiet persistence and an uncanny ability to "calm ruffled waters" made Tobias an effective leader during half a century. For instance, on March 7, 1934, he wrote to Will Rogers protesting his use of "As the old 'nigger' said." Rogers replied that there was no better friend of the Negro than he was.

In early October 1930, in a report on his visit to YMCA branches in the central, western, and southern states, Tobias favored separate branches as a means of wielding leadership Negroes could not possibly achieve as long as they constituted only a negligible minority in a branch controlled and operated by white people. In 1944, on the other hand, he denounced segregation in schools, on trains, streetcars, and buses, in the use of blood plasma by the Red Cross, the treat-ment of Negro nurses, separate units in the armed forces, denial of equal opportunity for employment by industry and organized labor. He also made an oblique attack on segregation in Protestant churches by praising the more liberal practices of the Roman Catholic church and the activities of outstanding Jew-ish leaders ("Negro Thinking Today," *Religion in Life,* Spring 1944). Nor did he hesitate to attack the YMCA at the YMCA World Conference in Mysore, India (1936–1937): "America and South Africa are practi-cally the only countries in the world where racial ex-clusion is practiced in YMCA's."

Although a minister of the Methodist church, his Christian belief was independent and not sectarian. Two men outside the Christian faith who greatly in-fluenced his religious beliefs were a Jewish philanthro-pist, Julius Rosenwald, and a Hindu, Mahatma Gandhi. While a delegate to a conference of the World's Com-mittee of Young Men's Christian Associations at Mysore, India (1937), he discussed for an hour and a half on a train with Gandhi a number of written ques-tions. The first was: "Negroes in the United States (12,-000,000) are struggling to obtain such fundamental rights as freedom from mob violence, unrestricted use of the ballot, freedom from segregation in all forms and an opportunity to find employment in skilled, as well as unskilled forms of labor. Have you out of your struggles in India a word of advice or encouragement? I ask this fully appreciating how differently situated the two peo-ples are."

Gandhi replied: "I had to contend against some such thing, though on a smaller scale, in South Africa. The difficulties are by no means yet over. All I can say is that there is no other way than the way of non-violence—not of the weak and the ignorant but of the strong and the wise." But in 1945 he did not believe that Gandhi's pacifism was the proper course in all circumstances. Instead he favored the more aggressive attitude of Nehru who "does believe that we cannot get social change by waiting for it. We must stand for the right and make it come" (interview with Henry Beckett, Sept. 20, 1945 "Closeup").

In this same interview, his attack on imperialism and colonialism presaged his stance at the Sixth General Assembly of the United Nations: "We are concerned that this war bring to an end imperialism and colonial exploitation. We believe that political and economic democracy must displace the present system of exploitation in Africa, the West Indies, India, and all other colonial areas."

He stated emphatically his own position on race relationships in his autobiography (1953): "*I am unalterably opposed to segregation based on race, creed, or color. . . .* [emphasis in the original]. First, it cheapens human personality and leads to crime against the group affected by it. . . . Second, segregation is un-American in spirit and practice. . . . Third, and most important of all, I object to racial segregation, because it is an insult to the Creator" (pp. 180–81). He did not hold Negroes entirely blameless. One group considered every problem from the viewpoint of its own personal advantage. In the second group was the so-called "Uncle Tom type." Then there was the ultraradical type who believed in agitation for the sake of agitation. Tobias counted it a privilege to be identified with "the Negro who will not bow or bend obsequiously before other people in order to gain something for himself, who will not lie about conditions, or about what is in his own heart, who is willing to cooperate, but only on terms of mutual respect. This is the group with which all who are interested in true democracy for America will have to deal."

He strongly supported President Truman's comprehensive special message to Congress (Feb. 2, 1948). In a telegram to Walter White, secretary of the NAACP, Tobias stated: "One strong motive back of this message was a conviction on the part of the President that America was handicapped in its international relations by the existence of a double standard of citizenship affecting a tenth of the American population." Tobias urged White and heads of other organizations to send telegrams supporting President Truman to senators and congressmen.

Tobias's imposing stature and convincing delivery made a favorable impression at the Sixth General Assembly of the United Nations. On Nov. 21, 1951, in a prepared speech to the Committee on Trusteeship, he stated that his own observation in various non-self-governing territories, particularly in West Africa, led him to believe that the "old colonialism is dead." The United States had made great strides toward promoting self-government in Puerto Rico, Alaska, and Hawaii. The U.S. delegation believed that "territories should be encouraged and assisted to become self-governing as rapidly as possible and we would not wish such development delayed as a result of laying down so many complex factors to be met that the people might become discouraged in their onward progress toward self-government."

On Jan. 30, 1952, he supported in Committee III a resolution that strongly urged that personal restraints on bona fide correspondents be removed, that sentences imposing arbitrary restraints on such persons be revoked, and that appeals be made to governments to do all in their power to safeguard the rights of correspondents "freely and faithfully to gather and transmit news." The resolution involved the case of William N. Oatis, a U.S. citizen held in prison in Czechoslovakia.

In a third prepared release (Jan. 2, 1952) he presented the view of the United States on land reform to Committee II: "This problem, as the Economic and Social Council has stated, is a *necessary part of any effective and comprehensive program of economic development"* (emphasis in the release).

Like many other outspoken leaders, he was accused of being a Communist. After his appearance before the McCarran Committee, following his nomination by President Truman as an alternate delegate on the U.S. delegation to the Sixth General Assembly, Westbrook Pegler had written that Tobias "has a record of connections with flagrant Communist fronts exceeded by few other individuals in the files of the House Committee on un-American activities."

In one of his last important public statements as chairman of the board of the NAACP, he stated in his Fiftieth Anniversary Keynote Address (New York City, July 13, 1959): "The philosophy of the NAACP is deeply rooted in Americanism, and particularly in the humane and egalitarian principles of the Abolition movement. The spiritual progenitor of our movement was William Lloyd Garrison and not his contemporary, Karl Marx. . . . From the outset the NAACP recognized first, that its objectives could be secured through orderly, democratic processes and second, that equality of citizenship was *unattainable* [my emphasis] within the framework of racial segregation. . . . There is, I am convinced, ample ground for optimism."

His selection as the speaker on this occasion is evidence of the high esteem in which he was held by the board of the NAACP. Conversations with other members of the board of the Phelps-Stokes Fund, especially Emory Ross, chairman, and trustees Claude Barnett, Ralph Bunche, Guy Johnson, and Frederick D. Patterson, give further evidence of the stature of the man whom *Ebony* (Feb. 1951) had described as "the elder statesman of Negro America." Not the least of his achievements was the substantial, though incomplete progress toward the goal he had stated in Hartford, Conn. (June 6, 1944) at the Second Century of the founding of the YMCA: "The Association of tomorrow must remove all bars to membership based upon race and color alone."

In what may be considered his "goals," he left a manuscript copy of "The Task Ahead." He wrote, probably in 1957: "The Task Ahead Must Take the World View. The World Picture: Russia, China, India, Africa, Europe, America:

"I. We must give wholehearted support to U.N. in fight against totalitarianism wherever found—*not pas-*

sive but aggressive support. At same time must insist that U.S. *not* sacrifice principle to expediency in dealing with colonial powers.

II. Must continue to oppose vicious apartheid practice of Malan Government in S.A. No difference in principle between S.A. and Russia.

"III. Must encourage self-government in Gold Coast and Nigeria.

"IV. We must insist that the covenant of Human Rights be ratified.

"V. On the Home Front continue Relentless Warfare against all Segregation—Morally, Religiously, Constitutionally wrong, Legally indefensible. Government—No gradualism. Rights not to be conferred upon you—They belong to you—[illustrations].

"VI. Pursue more vigorously than ever our Registration Campaign.

"VII. Promote a campaign of Education to bring about mutual trust and understanding across racial lines."

Channing Tobias received many honors in recognition of his effective leadership. In 1928 he received the Harmon Award for Religious Services, in 1943 he was named on the Arthur Schomburg Honor Roll, and in 1948 the Spingarn Medal for Distinguished Achievement. Gammon Theological Seminary awarded him an honorary D.D. degree in 1924 and Morehouse College an honorary LL.D. degree in 1942. He also received the first honorary degree (LL.D.) conferred upon a Negro by New York University, at its 118th Commencement Exercises, 1950.

He married first in Milledgeville, Ga., the former Mary Pritchard on Nov. 10, 1908. Their older daughter Belle, a Phi Beta Kappa graduate of Barnard College with an M.A. from Wellesley College, married Austin Curtis, a chemist at the George Washington Carver Institute, Tuskegee, Ala. She died in October 1936. Their younger daughter Mary, a graduate of New York University with an M.S. degree from Columbia University, married William H. Dean, Jr., on Thanksgiving Day 1936, and was the mother of their two children, Channing and Joyce. After his death on Jan. 8, 1952, she married Sherwood A. Messner, national program director of the United Cerebral Palsy Association. Tobias, after the death of his first wife in 1949, married (on March 31, 1951) Eva Gassett Arnold, the widow of James Arnold, a YMCA secretary.

After a long illness, Tobias died in Harkness Pavilion on Nov. 5, 1961. The funeral was held at Riverside Church, New York City, on Nov. 8, 1961, where Benjamin E. Mays (who had been president of Morehouse College since 1940) delivered the eulogy before a large assembly of notable mourners.

In addition to the sources mentioned in the biography, the article (with photograph) in *Current Biography, Who's News and Why* (July 1945), gives essential details. Indispensable were materials provided by his daughter, Mary Tobias Messner, and the Tobias Papers in the library of the National Council of the Young Men's Christian Associations of the United States of America, 291 Broadway, New York City. These have been supplemented by the author's personal reminiscences. — RAYFORD W. LOGAN

TOLSON, MELVIN B[EAUNORUS] (1900–1966), educator and author. He was born on Feb. 6, 1900, in Moberly, Mo., a son of the Rev. Alonzo Tolson, a Methodist Episcopal minister of Negro, Irish, and Indian ancestry, whose largely self-taught scholarship (Latin, Hebrew, and Greek) gave his oldest son a lifelong example. His mother Lera Hurt Tolson was a Cherokee of mixed ancestry, musically talented, who encouraged the artistic interests of all her four children, but particularly of Melvin.

Tolson's education in the public schools of the various towns in Missouri and Iowa where his father's ministry took the family, was effective and marked particularly, according to his own later testimony, by an eighth-grade teacher in Mason City, Iowa, "who was white and who trained him to be a perfectionist" in public speaking. He finished high school in Kansas City, Mo., where he "was captain of the football team, class poet, and both director and actor in the Greek Club's Little Theatre." He enrolled in Fisk University in 1919 and transferred to Lincoln University (Oxford, Pa.) in 1920, where he graduated with honors in 1923.

At Lincoln he courted and married talented Ruth Southall, of Virginia. Their four children received advanced degrees and pursued academic and professional careers.

Tolson stated repeatedly that his years in public school were marked by a relative absence of the racism he encountered in later life, particularly in the South as a teacher in a Texas college (Wiley College, 1924–1947) whose students he taught to take their equality seriously, and to develop their talents to the utmost. His students, some of whom later became well known in their own right, included James Farmer, Frederick Douglass Weaver, Thomas Cole, and others. In 1930 he entered graduate school at Columbia University but did not complete all requirements for his M.A. until 1940.

During this depression decade, although his principal energy went into teaching, he wrote widely: poetry, fiction, drama, and for a brief time a column ("Caviar and Cabbage") for the *Washington Tribune*. Most of his writing during this period remained unpublished, however, until his poem "Dark Symphony" appeared in *Atlantic Monthly* (1941). The repeated rejection of his most ambitious manuscript, "A Gallery of Harlem Portraits" (a 350-page free-verse poem somewhat in the style of Edgar Lee Masters's *Spoon River Anthology,* completed in 1932) was so discouraging that he virtually abandoned verse for several years.

In 1944 publication of his collection of poems *Rendezvous with America* received considerable critical acclaim. It was certainly a strong first book, although it gave little evidence of the mature style which would a decade later mark *Libretto for the Republic of Liberia* (1953). Awards and honors (Omega Psi Phi Award, 1945; Poet Laureate of Liberia, 1947; *Poetry* magazine's Bess Hokim Award, 1951) began to accumulate, but he still remained little known in wider literary circles until he received national and international acclaim following publication in 1965 of *Harlem Gallery: Book I, the Curator.*

In 1947 Tolson was appointed professor of creative literature in Langston University (Oklahoma) and in

1965 was appointed as first holder of the Avalon Chair in Humanities at Tuskegee Institute. He died at the height of his literary powers, after numerous operations for cancer, on Aug. 29, 1966, and was buried on Sept. 3, 1966, at Guthrie, Okla.

An excellent critical biography with complete bibliography is Joy Flasch's *Melvin B. Tolson* (1972). The Melvin B. Tolson Papers, Manuscript Division, Library of Congress, contain his manuscripts and correspondence. — ROY P. BASLER

TOLTON, AUGUSTINE (1854–1897), Catholic priest. He was born on April 1, 1854, to two Catholic slaves in a humble slave cabin on a plantation near Brush Creek, Ralls County, in northeastern Missouri, not far from Mark Twain's city of Hannibal on the Mississippi. Augustine was the second son in a family of four, two boys and two girls. His father, Peter Paul Tolton, a slave of the Hager family, married an Elliot plantation slave, Martha Jane Chisley, in St. Peter's Church in Brush Creek. She had been baptized a Catholic in infancy in her native Meade County in the Catholic section of Kentucky. Raised as a slave of the Manning family, Martha was given as part of the dowry when one of the Manning girls married a Missourian named Stephen Elliot. All during the years before the Civil War, the young couple prayed for freedom. The Dred Scott Decision, whereby the famed Missouri slave was returned to bondage by the U.S. Supreme Court in 1857, had seemed a fatal blow to their hopes. But with the fall of Fort Sumter (1861), it seemed time for his parents to make a break for freedom. Peter Tolton decamped to join the Union Army, but his life in freedom was a short one. He died in a hospital in St. Louis during the war. His mother also determined to reach the promised land of freedom across the Mississippi in Illinois. One night she took her four children, one a babe in arms, and fled hurriedly through Ralls and Marion Counties until she reached the river. There she was challenged by some Missourians who tried to apprehend her as a runaway slave. Federal soldiers who happened along at the time rescued her, and with their aid she crossed the river that same night, some miles south of Quincy, Ill.

Young seven-year-old Augustine never forgot that thrilling escape. Years later he recalled how, together with his older brother and his younger sister, he ran out of breath to keep up with his frightened but determined mother. She had her heart set on Quincy and freedom. She attained both. The family settled down in the comparative peace of Quincy, free at last. Martha Jane Tolton went to work to support the family. In time the two older boys joined her at the large Harris Tobacco Factory at Fifth and Ohio Streets to help earn enough for the family. For twelve years young Augustine worked there as a tobacco stemmer and factory hand. Owing to the seasonal nature of the work, the factory was idle for more than three months a year. It was during this time that Augustine attended "winter" classes at the public Lincoln School. Attending Mass at St. Peter's Church along with the white Catholics of the parish, young Augustine and his brother came to the attention of the pastor, Fr. P. B. McGirr. He decided to admit the Toltons to his parish school, notwithstanding the disapproval and the threats of some segregationists. For six years Augustine attended school and the church, while tending the furnace at St. Peter's.

In 1875 his mother secured a position as a housekeeper for a priest in one of the northeastern Missouri parishes. She took her small family with her, Augustine going along in the hope of keeping up his studies under the new priest who promised to tutor him. For eleven months they stayed in Missouri. The atmosphere was very unsuitable to Mrs. Tolton—Negroes were still being kidnapped and sold as slaves in Missouri, notwithstanding emancipation.

Back in Quincy, Augustine went to work again, first in a horsecollar factory and later with a soda firm. The Franciscans of the local Catholic high school tutored him in Latin, Greek, German, English, and history before work in the morning and later in the evening. He continued to be deeply religious and to aspire to the priesthood. He joined the Temperance Society at St. Peter's Church, and kept the teetotaler pledge.

In later years, Father Tolton gave credit to the German Franciscans for opening the way to his career. Fr. Michael Richardt was impressed with Tolton's intelligence, liveliness of mind, piety, and modesty. He spoke to Bishop Peter J. Baltes about Tolton's desire to be a priest, and as the bishop was then on his way to Rome he promised to secure admission for the young man to the College of the Propagation of the Faith there. With the help of the Franciscan Father General, Tolton was admitted, and on Feb. 15, 1880, left Quincy for Rome. He sailed from Jersey City on the *Westlicher* the following Saturday (Feb. 21), accompanied by three Franciscans who were also on their way to Rome. Tolton first saw the Eternal City on March 10. He matriculated at the College of the Propagation of the Faith two days later, studying there for five years.

In 1885, there was some question as to whether he would be ordained for foreign missions or for the United States. He told of the incident thus: "When on the eve of going to St. John Lateran to be ordained the word came expressing doubt whether I would be sent here. It was said that I would be the only priest of my race in America, and would not be likely to succeed. All at once Cardinal Simeoni said: 'America has been called the most enlightened nation; we will see if it deserves that honor. If America has never seen a black priest, it has to see one now. Come and take an oath to spend your whole days in your own country.' "

On April 24, 1886, Tolton was ordained to the priesthood by Cardinal Parocchi, in the Basilica of St. John Lateran. On Easter Sunday the newly ordained priest offered his first Mass on the high altar of St. Peter's, usually reserved for the pope.

On June 13, 1886, Cardinal Simeoni missioned him to America, and he arrived in New York on July 6. His first Mass in the country was said at St. Mary's Hospital in Hoboken, where he had been sheltered before sailing to Rome. The following Sunday, St. Benedict the Moor Church, at Bleecker and Downing Streets in New York City, was the scene of his first solemn High Mass. He sang at ease with his powerful voice, standing erect in the full six feet of his height, and making an impressive figure flanked by the two white priests who assisted him as deacon and subdeacon.

Homecoming to Quincy was a gala day for Martha Jane Tolton and her son. On July 18 Father Tolton offered a solemn High Mass in St. Boniface Church. Toward the end of the month, on July 25, Father Tolton was named pastor of St. Joseph's Catholic Church for Negroes. The congregation occupied a former Protestant church which belonged to St. Boniface's parish. This was turned over to the parishioners for their use as a church upstairs and a school in the basement. There were eighty members in the congregation. They were poor, desperately so, and the total annual collections did not amount to more than a hundred dollars. Although the parish did not prosper, there were external compensations to offset the frustrating work of the depressed parish. Father Tolton was often invited away from Quincy to lecture and preach. He spoke at the First Catholic Colored Congress in Washington in 1889. He addressed assemblies of Catholics in Boston and New York. Cardinal Gibbons invited him to Baltimore to preach and minister to Negro Catholics.

Unafraid, Father Tolton ventured even into the deep South. In 1890, at the invitation of Bishop Gallagher of Galveston, Tex., Father "Gus" preached in the cathedral to a predominantly white congregation. He made a striking figure in the pulpit, his red cincture contrasting with his black cassock just as did the red pompon of his biretta. The wearing of the special red colors made the altar boys believe he was a bishop. But that privilege was merely the sign that he had been trained in the College of the Propagation of the Faith in Rome.

In 1889 an opportunity opened for Father Tolton in Chicago. A wealthy philanthropist, Anne O'Neill, donated $10,000 toward the establishment of St. Monica's Church for Negro Catholics. The archbishop offered the new post to Father Tolton, who secured authorization from his bishop for a transfer. In 1889 he took up his residence at St. Augustine's Church on Prairie Avenue in Chicago. The next year he opened St. Monica's Chapel in the 2200 block of South Indiana, in the heart of the Negro neighborhood. It was no reflection on Father Tolton that his work was not marked with spectacular achievements. He was personally a solid man of integrity, well versed in his clerical matters, fully capable of delivering sermons that were sound in theology, useful in application, and forcefully presented. He was proud of his color, aglow with devotion to his race and his people, affectionate toward his mother, and faithful to his parish duties and his priestly vows. His one relaxation was a pinch of snuff now and then.

Father Tolton fitted easily into the clerical life in Chicago. He made friends with the more than one hundred priests who served the expanding metropolis. It was with them that he journeyed to Kankakee during the first week of July 1897 to make the diocesan retreat. It was an excessively hot summer, and on the way home, on Friday, July 9, he was stricken by the heat. Rushed to Mercy Hospital, he lingered throughout the day, but died that night. He was only forty-three.

As he requested, his body was taken back to Quincy for burial. His mother accompanied the sad cortege, together with her daughter Anna, now Mrs. Pettes, and her other son. Representatives of Catholic Negro organizations from Chicago also journeyed to the last rites. Twelve priests of Quincy met the body at the station, and a large crowd filled St. Peter's Church to overflowing for the funeral. One of the largest crowds ever to form a procession to the cemetery trailed after the hearse and the carriage bearing the clergy and the family. Father Tolton's body was laid to rest in St. Peter's Cemetery.

Father Tolton's life is summarized in many articles. A full-length biography has been published by Sister Caroline Hemesath, *From Slave to Priest* (1973). A shorter sketch is available in Albert S. Foley's *God's Men of Color* (1955, 1970, Chapter IV, "Good Father Gus," pp. 32–41). — ALBERT S. FOLEY, S.J.

TOOMER, [NATHAN] JEAN (1894–1967), poet, playwright and fiction writer. Born in Washington, D.C., the son of Nathan and Nina Toomer, he was still an infant when his father deserted his mother and she returned to the family home in Washington, ruled by his grandfather, Pinckney Benton Stewart Pinchback. His earliest memories were of bitter quarrels between his mother and his grandfather who had opposed her marriage. When his mother moved to New York in 1904, young Toomer blamed his grandfather for her moving. But soon after she married again, the Pinchbacks joined her. They were accompanied by "Eugene Pinchback," as the family called him to obliterate all memory of his father. When his mother died following an appendectomy in 1909, Eugene returned to Washington with his grandfather and his grandmother, Nina Emily. After attending public schools in Washington, D.C., he studied agriculture for a semester at the University of Wisconsin, attended the Massachusetts College of Agriculture for one week, and then enrolled in a physical training college in Chicago. Rejected for the draft in World War I because of poor eyesight and a hernia, he took odd jobs—selling cars in Chicago, teaching physical education in Milwaukee, and working as a ship fitter in New Jersey. In 1921 he served as temporary superintendent of a small Negro industrial school in rural Georgia, an experience that inspired much of *Cane.*

His career began and reached its peak in the 1920s when he produced sketches and poems for such magazines as *The Double Dealer, Broom, The Dial, Opportunity, The Crisis,* and *The Little Review.* In 1923 he published *Cane,* his one full-length work. *Cane* did not go into a second printing, but it made Toomer a major celebrity of the "Harlem Renaissance." His work directly influenced Langston Hughes, Countée Cullen, and Zora Neale Hurston, among others. William Stanley Braithwaite called him "the very first artist of the race." Charles S. Johnson correctly noted that Toomer had "the most astonishingly brilliant beginning of any Negro writer of this generation."

After the publication of *Cane,* Toomer traveled in France where he spent the summer of 1926 at the Gurdjieff Institute in Fontainbleau (he had possibly spent the summer of 1924 there as well). He had become absorbed in Gurdjieff, in Ouspensky (author of *In Search of the Miraculous*), who had worked with Gurdjieff, and in mysticism generally. This interest is reflected in

Toomer's shorter pieces such as "Mr. Costyve Duditch" (1928), "Winter on Earth" (1928), and "York Beach" (1929), as well as *Essentials* (1931), his book of aphorisms. During the 1920s also Toomer had formed friendships in a literary coterie that included Hart Crane, Kenneth Burke, and Waldo Frank. In the 1930s, however, he became increasingly withdrawn personally and abstract in his work. "We do not have states of being," he said; "we have states of dreaming" (*Essentials*).

On Aug. 22, 1931, Toomer married the novelist Margery Latimer, a descendant of Anne Bradstreet, in Portage, Wis. The couple lived in Carmel, Calif., and Chicago until Margery Latimer died in childbirth one year later. In November of the following year (1934), according to Darwin Turner, Toomer married Margery Content, daughter of Harry Content, a prominent Wall Street stock broker. With this second marriage he virtually disappeared from American literary life. He moved to Bucks County, Pa., lived within the Quaker community, and wrote occasional pieces for the *Friends Intelligencer*. Except for a tour of India with his wife in 1939, Toomer remained in Pennsylvania the rest of his life. His final publication was "The Flavor of Man" (1949), a lecture delivered to the Society of Friends. His autobiographical journal, "Earth-Breath," awaits publication.

Both of Toomer's marriages were to white women, and Toomer himself was nearly white in appearance. He often expressed resentment or dismay at being identified solely as a "black writer." Late in his life when asked about his color he responded, "I would consider it libelous for anyone to refer to me as a colored man. . . . I have not lived as one, nor do I really know whether there is any colored blood in me or not." In 1922, when Max Eastman and Claude McKay, as editors of *The Liberator,* requested a brief biography of Toomer, Toomer cited his decendance from Pinchback, the acting governor of Louisiana during Reconstruction. But Toomer added, "I seem to have (who knows for sure) seven blood mixtures: French, Dutch, Welsh, Negro, German, Jewish, and Indian." His quandary about his racial identification was authentic. It contributed strongly to those questions of human identity and place at the center of Toomer's work.

"I am of no particular race," Toomer wrote in *Essentials:* "I am of the human race, a man at large in the human world, preparing a new world." This is the contention of Nathan Antrum, the meditative central figure of "York Beach." Antrum, speaking for his author, observes that man "is a nerve of the cosmos, dislocated, trying to quiver into place." He passes the summer at a vacation resort where various encounters help him only to determine that the sense of his own place is elusive and uncertain. Similarly, "Mr. Costyve Duditch," the eternal world traveler, returns home briefly to Chicago to rediscover that the meaning and definition of his life depend on his constant wanderings. For Toomer, who spent most of his life in spiritual travel, the search for place seemed perpetual. He was disgusted with a civilization whose two emblems were "the machinegun and the contraceptive" (*Essentials*), but appeared never to enjoy that "sense of unity with all creation" ("The Flavor of Man") he consistently advocated.

This search for unity, for roots, is at the heart of *Cane,* as well as Toomer's other work, but *Cane* ought not to be classified with Toomer's later and more philosophic pieces. *Cane* is specifically about being "black in America." All of the novel's characters are homeless in one way or another, and the underlying, and understated, truth of the novel is that the home which the characters know they can never reach, but in whose existence they nevertheless wholeheartedly believe, does not exist. *Cane* is not a novel in the formal sense; it consists of sketches, poems, and a play, "Kabnis," which Toomer wrote at different times and then organized for purposes of the book. The organization is deliberate, however, and conveys the unity of Toomer's thesis.

The structural unity of *Cane* is radial. It centers on the story "Box-Seat," which tells of Dan Moore's love for a schoolteacher named Muriel. Muriel rebuffs Dan's love because Dan seeks personal freedom, which Muriel fears. Separately they attend a theater performance of boxing dwarfs. The victorious dwarf holds up a mirror to the audience, to reflect its own brutality, and offers a white rose, now red with his blood, to Muriel. Muriel falters, then reluctantly accepts the offering. Dan stands and shouts, "Jesus was once a leper," and runs from the theater and Muriel, perhaps toward his self-respect.

Everything in the story links up with or suggests something else in the novel at large. Houses such as the theater "house" are symbols of constriction, of a peopled housed and boxed in. The association of innocence with sugarcane—Dan says, "I was born in a canefield"—is repeated in two early sketches, "Karintha" and "Fern." Time is a destructive force in "Box-Seat," as it is in the main story, "Kabnis." There is an old man in the audience whom Dan invests with prophetic powers, and the same kind of ancient figure appears in "Kabnis" (as well as in Toomer's play *Balo*). Dan takes his name from King Daniel, as other characters in *Cane* also take their names from biblical associations, always ironic: Becky from Rebekah; her two sons from Jacob and Esau; Dan is related to Paul and John. Muriel is akin to all of the women in *Cane,* who have lost their natures and are trapped in civilization. Dan is like all of the men of the novel, out to find or prove something which perpetually seems to fly out of reach.

As "Box-Seat" is the core of *Cane,* "Kabnis," the long final section, served as the outer rim. Ralph Kabnis is an ex-schoolteacher with "a lemon face" (p. 158), full of self-disgust, boredom, and hatred who spends his days cursing his fate and wishing for "an ugly world." He seeks to pull himself together, but he can neither pull himself together in terms of his personal momentary well-being, nor culturally or historically in the name of his people. Through Kabnis, as through Dan Moore and Muriel, Toomer is pointing to the cultural and spiritual dislocation of American Negroes. In an early sketch, "Carma," Toomer said that "the Dixie Pike has grown from a goat path in Africa." In "Kabnis" he proves that the goat path is long overgrown and hidden.

The "action" of "Kabnis" is the revelation of an old man, Father John, who has been living in a local basement, silent for years. When at last Father John speaks, he says, "O th sin th white folks 'mitted when they made the Bible lie." This comes as no revelation to Kabnis whose life has been in a sense a demonstration of that sin. The story ends with a Saturday night party which degenerates into an orgy, after which the drunken Kabnis has to be led upstairs from the basement, essentially to nowhere.

The title *Cane* refers to roots, and to the idea of support as well. All of the characters in *Cane* vainly seek something to lean on. But there may be a deeper pun here, too. Cain and Abel were the sons of Eve, equal at their births, except that by divine caprice or mystery Cain was automatically rejected by God and Abel was the favored boy. Abel could converse with God, but Cain did not even have Abel to talk with, and when Cain finally killed his brother, after his own offerings to God had been refused, God placed a mark on Cain so that he might be known to suffer eternal punishment. The book of Genesis then says that "Cain went out of the presence of the Lord," but even while Abel had lived, Cain had not enjoyed that presence. For no reason but an accident of birth, Cain, like Kabnis and Dan Moore, had always been a fugitive.

Toomer accomplished most of his creative writing at a period in modern literature when fragmentation was coming to the fore both as a method of presentation and as an expression of the fundamental disunity of modern thought and experience. One attempts to piece Toomer himself together through his own fragmented writings, but the task is formidable. In "The Flavor of Man," he said that "A man's roots must go down into what is deeper than himself, his crown touch what is higher, his heart open to the beyond, and the whole move forward. Then he will be connected with the great heart and power of life." The special tension in Toomer's life and work derives from the distance between wishing and achieving such a connection.

There is no full-scale biography of Toomer. Biographical sketches have been provided by Arna Bontemps and Waldo Frank in their introductions to editions of *Cane* (both in 1969); Bontemps has another essay on Toomer in *Anger and Beyond* (edited by Herbert Hill, 1968), "The Negro Renaissance: Jean Toomer and the Harlem Writers of the 1920's." Langston Hughes briefly discusses Toomer and his "great dilemma" about race in his autobiography, *The Big Sea* (1940, pp. 241–43). Criticism of *Cane* may be found in Robert Bone's *The Negro Novel in America* (1965) and in Roger Rosenblatt's *Black Fiction* (1974). Darwin Turner has a critical biographical essay on Toomer in his *In a Minor Chord: Three Afro-American Writers in Their Search for Identity* (1971) and Arthur P. Davis in *From the Dark Tower, Afro-American Writers 1900 to 1960* (1974, pp. 44–51), with a photograph (from the Moorland-Spingarn Research Center, Howard University, p. 50). *The Wayward and the Seeking: A Collection of Writings by Jean Toomer,* edited by Darwin T. Turner, was published in 1980. On the question of Toomer's alleged denial that he was a Negro, Kenneth W. Porter pointed out that Toomer is in *The Negro Caravan,* edited by Sterling A. Brown, Arthur P. Davis, and Ulysses Lee (1941, pp. 41–54, 355–56), and that in the 1940s when

he knew Toomer, he had not sought to deny his Negro "race" (Porter to Rayford W. Logan, Sept. 14, 1975). Toomer's unpublished works are in the Toomer Collection, Fisk University. — ROGER ROSENBLATT

TOTTEN, ASHLEY L. (1884–1963), labor union executive. Born in St. Croix, Danish West Indies, the son of Richard W. and Camilla Totten, he was educated at the Christiansted Boys High School, came to the United States in 1905, and was naturalized in 1911. From 1915 to 1925 he worked as a Pullman sleeping car porter. By 1925, influenced by the *Messenger* and the soap-box forums of A. Philip Randolph, he had gained the reputation of being one of the leading Negro radicals in Harlem. He helped organize the Brotherhood of Sleeping Car Porters and served for many years after 1932 as its international secretary-treasurer. During that same period he was also president of the American Virgin Islands Civic Association. Later he was reporting officer for the Railroad Retirement Board, an executive of the League for Industrial Democracy, a member of the American-China Policy Association and of the Welfare Defense League.

The organization of the Brotherhood of Sleeping Car Porters is one of the significant developments in trade unionism and the quest of Negroes for economic improvement and dignity. From 1867 when the Pullman Company was incorporated as the manufacturer and operator of railroad sleeping cars, Negroes had almost a monopoly as porters. Some of them were leaders in their community.

Attempts to organize a union of the Pullman car porters began in 1909 but the brotherhood was not organized until Aug. 25, 1925. Totten is given credit for helping persuade Randolph to assume leadership in the movement that led to its organization. It was not until Aug. 25, 1937, however, that the Pullman Company recognized the brotherhood as the bargaining agency for the porters and maids employed by the company, and granted a substantial wage increase as well as a reduction in the work month from 400 to 240 hours. It was the first agreement signed between a union of Negro workers and a major American corporation.

This victory was achieved despite the opposition of the company, some leading daily and Negro newspapers, support of the company by some Negro politicians such as Perry Howard, national committeeman from Mississippi and a special assistant to the U. S. attorney-general. Like some other opponents of the brotherhood, Howard branded it as an "agent of Communism." Kelly Miller of Howard University, a foe of unionism, was another critic of the brotherhood. Still another obstacle was the use of stool pigeons who informed the company about the leaders of the movement to organize. Totten defined a stool pigeon as "a male or female employed as a decoy to spy on others; a confidence man for the dirty work of the employer; a seller of souls; a traitor to little children. In the Pullman service, a Negro stool pigeon is a low, degraded human being akin to a contemptible skunk."

After Totten was discharged as a porter for pretending he was ill when he really planned to attend a meeting of Chicago porters, he was a leader in the abortive effort (1924) to organize a bona fide union. When the Pullman Company refused the demands to reduce working hours and to increase wages, the defeat was said to be "the beginning of the Brotherhood of Sleeping Car Porters."

During the twelve years between organization in 1925 and recognition in 1937, Totten was effectively active in organizing divisions of the brotherhood. During the organizing activities Randolph on one occasion had to prevent Totten from collecting weapons for use against strikebreakers. In 1929 Totten was so severely beaten that he suffered for the rest of his life. Transferred to New York, he was appointed one of the vice-presidents of the brotherhood. He was in such dire financial difficulty that on one Christmas he did not have carfare to visit his wife and children in Queens. Until shortly before his sudden death in Frederiksted, St. Croix, on Jan. 26, 1963, he served as secretary-treasurer of the brotherhood. He was survived by his widow, Mrs. Violet Victoria Totten (*Daily News,* Charlotte Amalie, V.I., Jan. 29, 1963, pp. 1–2).

There is no comprehensive biography of Totten. His career in the brotherhood is best revealed in Jervis Anderson's *A. Philip Randolph: A Biographical Portrait* (1972). There are brief references to him in Brailsford R. Brazeal's *The Brotherhood of Sleeping Car Porters: Its Origin and Development* (1946). The usual basic facts are in *Who's Who in Colored America* (1950), edited by G. James Fleming and Christian E. Burckel. The following articles by Totten in the *Messenger* reveal his thinking: "Pullman's Soothing Valve" (Jan. 1926), "An Exposé of the Employee Representation Plan" (April 1926), and "Robbing the Porter" (June 1926). See also his account of the 1924 wage conference in his four-part series "Why the Plan is a Fraud" (*Black Worker,* Feb. 15 to April 1, 1930). There are excellent group photographs, including Totten, in Anderson's *A. Philip Randolph,* between pages 146 and 147.

— RAYFORD W. LOGAN

TOWNSEND, WILLARD S[AXBY] (1895–1957), labor leader. Townsend was born in Cincinnati, Ohio, and following graduation from high school took his first railroad job as a "red cap." After his military service in World War I he resumed his railroad employment as a dining car waiter out of Chicago. In an attempt to escape the closed employment system for Negroes on the railroad, he entered the University of Toronto to pursue a premedical course, later transferring to the Royal Academy of Science from which he received a degree in chemistry. Although armed with formal training, he was forced in 1932 to reenter industry where he was destined to remain as a worker and as a labor leader the rest of his life. He was determined that the Negro railroad workers, many educated as he was, would receive the respect and opportunities they deserved.

His career as a labor leader actually began in 1936 when he was elected vice-president and later president of an AFL red cap local. He had organized red caps at five Chicago train stations. His action was prompted by the long history of opposition of AFL railroad unions to Negro workers. Townsend, faced not only with the practice of barring Negro workers from the unions but also with the attempts to remove them completely from the industry, dreamed of and was determined to organize all Negro railroad workers into one union. By 1937 he had become the president of the International Brotherhood of Red Caps, an outgrowth of the 1936 move in Chicago.

In 1938 Townsend faced a major crisis involving his union. The white exclusive-membership railroad unions did not consider his workers employees of the industry because they worked largely for tips. When the Fair Labor Standards Act of 1937 was implemented, these unions sought to have Townsend's members declared independent contractors and not eligible for union organizations or qualified to bargain for their rights after the Interstate Commerce Commission declared his union members employees. However, his battles with the railroad unions, the insensitive Railway Adjustment Board, and a recalcitrant railroad management still hampered his effort to gain full recognition and bargaining rights for his union. Townsend continued to pursue his struggle to widen the coverage of his union, organizing train porters and Pullman laundry workers as well as red caps. In 1940 the International Brotherhood of Red Caps became the United Transport Service Employees of America (UTSEA) and Townsend remained as president. In 1942 he led his union out of the AFL into the CIO, where he became a member of that organization's executive board. Townsend then faced a second crisis as to whether or not his members were "essential workers" under war conditions. Most railroads, however, had begun to pay UTSEA wages, but this protection was watered down by continued efforts by the railway clerks belatedly to absorb UTSEA. Townsend plunged into this new struggle and his union survived.

Although he failed to pursue his original chosen career, he realized the value of education and despite his union activities found time to earn LL.B. and J.D. degrees through correspondence school and night classes from the Blackstone College of Law in Chicago. His civic and community involvement was substantial as he believed the working man should be part of the total struggle for human dignity. He also found time to serve as a lecturer on human and industrial relations at Seabury Western Theological Seminary at Evanston, Ill. In 1942 he received the Race Relation Leadership Award from the Arthur Schomburg Collection of the New York Public Library.

At the end of World War II Townsend faced the last big crisis of his union leadership career. Revolutionary economic and technological changes were taking place in the railroad industry. Competitive modes of transportation and lack of interest in railroad service employment resulted in the steady decline of UTSEA. In 1955 the CIO merged with the AFL and Townsend became a vice-president of the merged organization.

He had suffered from a stomach disorder and kidney ailment, and died on Feb. 3, 1957, at Provident Hospital, Chicago. Funeral services were held in Grace Presbyterian Church on Feb. 6, and he was buried in Cincinnati, Ohio. He had been briefly married to the famous singer, Alberta Hunter. In 1978 she said that she had left him when she heard that he had applied for a job as a waiter in a club where she was singing. She "wanted him to do something on his own'' (*Washington Post,* Jan. 9, 1978, p. B-6). He was survived by his widow, Consuelo Townsend, and a son, Willard Jr.

He would have been saddened but not discouraged had he lived to see UTSEA, reduced to a membership of less than 2000, merged in 1972 with his former arch enemy, the railway clerks.

The biographical sketch in Rayford W. Logan (ed.), *What the Negro Wants* (1944, pp. 350–51), was written by Townsend. His essay (p. 183) stated: ''Today the CIO stands as a national bulwark in the struggle to extend the democratic process into every phase of American life.'' The obituary in the *New York Times* (Feb. 5, 1957, p. 23) contains a brief biography. See also the *Chicago Defender* (Feb. 9, 1957, p. 2).

— M. BRENT OLDHAM

TRENT, WILLIAM JOHNSON, SR. (1873–1963), religious educator and college president. Born in Charlotte, N.C., on Dec. 30, 1873, the son of Edward and Malinda Johnson Trent, he received his B.A. degree from Livingstone College (Salisbury, N.C.) in 1898, and his M.A. degree in 1910. At Livingstone, Trent was an outstanding student and a star athlete who played in the first Negro college football game, against Biddle (later Johnson C. Smith) in 1892. During his student days he sang in the first musical group which toured to raise money for the college. They performed at the Atlanta Exposition in 1895 when Booker T. Washington made his famous ''Exposition Address.'' Like many of his contemporaries he worked summers on railroad dining cars or in resort restaurants to finance his education. Following service in 1898 as religious advisor in the United States with the 3rd North Carolina Regiment during the Spanish-American War, Trent was for a year president of Greenville Junior College in Tennessee (1899–1900). He then moved to Asheville, N.C., to begin twenty-five years with the YMCA (Asheville, 1900–1911; Atlanta, 1911–1925). During fourteen years in racially segregated Georgia his deep interest in human relations led him to help establish the Atlanta Urban League and the Atlanta School of Social Work (1925). He was also an organizer of the first national NAACP meeting held in the South.

A dedicated lay leader in the African Methodist Episcopal Zion church, Trent returned to Salisbury in 1925 to become Livingstone's fourth president. He studied during summers at the University of Chicago (1926–1928). In the course of a thirty-two-year administration he guided church-supported Livingstone from heavy debt and academic deficiency to a solid position as a solvent, fully accredited, liberal arts college and theological seminary. His deep interest in young people and in community affairs was recognized in 1951 when he became the Salisbury City School Board's first Negro member, appointed by the mayor to a six-year term. He was also a member of the Southern Inter-racial Commission.

After retiring from Livingstone in 1957, Trent remained in Salisbury and maintained an active interest in the AME Zion church. He was considered by many as the church's best oral historian. He spent his last years among the close friends and colleagues he had known

as Livingstone's president, and died of natural causes in 1963, a few months short of his ninetieth birthday.

He left a legacy in the careers of his children. In 1904 he had married Annie Bell Mitchell of Asheville; their daughter, Altona Trent Johns, became a well-known composer of children's songs and visiting professor at Southern University, Baton Rouge, La. In 1909 Trent married Maggie Tate of Charlotte. Born of that union were a son, William J. Jr. (educator, first executive director of the United Negro College Fund and assistant personnel director of Time, Inc.), and a daughter, Mary Estelle Trent Stewart (a Red Cross worker in Europe during World War II and later in Japan). Trent married Hattie Covington after his second wife died. Following Hattie Trent's death, he married the former Cleota Collins. Trent had a great sense of family and profound faith in the ability of Negroes to make their mark in the world.

Basic information is in *Who's Who in America* (1956–1957). The contributor drew also upon his personal reminiscences. — O. RUDOLPH AGGREY

TRÉVIGNE, PAUL (1825–1908), editor and historian. A mulatto born in New Orleans, he was the son of a veteran of the Battle of New Orleans. For some forty years he taught in his native city at the Catholic Indigent Orphan School. Later he served as editor of the militant Republican journal *L'Union* (1862–1864) and then of its successor *La Tribune de la Nouvelle-Orléans* (1864–1868 and 1869), owned and published by the New Orleans physician and editor, Louis Charles Roudanez. These papers so aroused the animosity of white southerners that there were threats to kill Trévigne and burn *La Tribune*. The editor then chose to use a more easy-going style, laughing as he chastised and using satire to put his points across. This role most probably spared him disagreeable reprisals and rebuttals, particularly at a time when white people were little accustomed to accepting the opinions of a man of color. Trévigne's newspapers, published in French and English, reflected prose and poetry written in the florid style of correspondents well read in Pascal, Voltaire, Rousseau, Montesquieu, Abbé Grégoire, and Plato. Since the articles were not signed, it is virtually impossible to determine those written by Trévigne. Even the fact that Roudanez was the senior editor does not provide a satisfactory answer.

The closing of *La Tribune* hampered severely the efforts of the Créoles of Color to continue the enrichment of their already highly advanced ethnic society in New Orleans. *L'Union,* from its inception in 1862, revealed perhaps the first true attempt of Louisiana Negroes to mold their energies into a political force. Charles Vincent asserts that Negroes, chiefly brokers, realtors, and planters, claimed ownership of some $15 million of taxable property in New Orleans and exercised a decided influence there. They reiterated the fact they were educated, refined, and cultured, and they pleaded for an end to hypocritical democracy and asked for rank as human beings with full civil and economic equality.

Trévigne's ''Centennial History of the Louisiana Negro,'' serialized in 1875 and 1876 in the *Louisianian,* a newspaper of former Governor P. B. S. Pinchback, is still a valuable source. In this tribute, which was part of the commemoration of the 100th anniversary of American Independence, Trévigne dealt with the literary, artistic, and scientific contributions of Negroes in Louisiana. Apparently Rodolphe L. Desdunes, then a young man, received inspiration and some material for his *Nos Hommes et Notre Histoire* (1911) from the pioneering venture of Trévigne.

Trévigne died at the advanced age of eighty-three in his native city. Trévigne was a valuable observer of his era. He manifested courage and daring even at the risk of his life. He was an instrument toward bringing about a closer bond and a degree of appreciation between his constituents and their white neighbors. He prepared the way for writers such as Rodolphe L. Desdunes, Alice Dunbar-Nelson, and later Charles B. Rousseve and Marcus Christian.

The career and evaluation of Trévigne are based on Rodolphe L. Desdunes's *Nos Hommes et Notre Histoire* (1911), translated and edited as *Our People and Our History* (1973) by Sister Dorothea Olga McCants, D.C. See also Charles B. Rousseve's *The Negro in Louisiana . . .* (1937); Finnian Patrick Leaven's "*L'Union* and the *New Orleans Tribune* and Louisiana Reconstruction" (master's thesis, Louisiana State University, 1966); and Charles Vincent's "Negro Leadership in Louisiana" (master's thesis, Louisiana State University, 1968). — DOROTHEA OLGA MCCANTS, D.C.

TROTTER, JAMES MONROE (1842–1892), army officer, politician author, and amateur musician. He was born on Feb. 7, 1842, in Grand Gulf, Miss., the son of a white man, Richard S. Trotter, and his slave Letitia. When Richard Trotter was married in 1854, Letitia, her son, and two younger daughters from the union were sent to live in the free city of Cincinnati. Here James Trotter attended the Gilmore school for freed slaves and worked as a hotel bellboy and as cabin boy on a riverboat. Later he briefly attended academies in Hamilton and Athens, Ohio, but according to his son was largely "self-educated." When the Civil War came, he was a schoolteacher in Pike County, southwestern Ohio.

In 1863 he was recruited by John Mercer Langston and traveled to Boston to join the 55th Massachusetts Regiment, a Negro unit with mostly white officers. Trotter rose through the ranks to become a second lieutenant and one of the regiment's four Negro commissioned officers. He was slightly wounded leading his men in battle near Honey Hill, S.C., in November 1864. In camp he held classes in reading and writing, and helped organize a regimental band which, he later wrote, gave "a certain refinement to what would have been without it but a life of much coarseness."

On racial issues he displayed the genteel militancy that marked his entire life. His commission as a second lieutenant was delayed for several months, to the satisfaction of some of the regiment's white officers. "O how discouraging!" Trotter wrote, "How maddening, almost! . . . An officer told me that it was 'too soon,' that time should be granted white officers to *get rid of their prejudices* so that a white Lieutenant would not refuse to sleep in a tent with a colored one. Of course he *supposed* that an objection of this kind would be made always by the white Lieut., and that an educated decent colored officer would never object to sleeping with the former whatever might be his character."

When Negro troops received a laborer's wage of ten dollars a month instead of the soldier's pay of thirteen, Trotter took a leading role in persuading his regiment to decline remuneration until the scale was equalized by Congress. For over a year, then, the regiment served without pay. At one point the Massachusetts legislature voted to make up the difference in pay, and sent two men with the funds to the regiment's encampment in South Carolina. But Trotter made a stirring speech arguing that the principle of equality was more important than the money in question. As he later wrote to one of the men from Massachusetts, it was "a great Principle, that for the attainment of which we gladly peril our lives —Manhood and Equality." The soldier's wage was finally granted to the Negro troops, and Trotter finished his military service with the Commission on Labor in South Carolina. "The duties are quite arduous," he noted, "but I am very glad to be here, as I have ample opportunity to be of service to the freedmen."

In August 1865 he was mustered out in Boston and decided to settle there, as he and several other Negro officers were rewarded with appointments in the Boston Post Office. He was married in 1868 to Virginia Isaacs of Chillicothe, Ohio, whom he had known since his schoolteaching days. According to family tradition, she was a great-granddaughter of Thomas Jefferson, descended from the liaison between Jefferson and his slave Sally Hemings. In any case, the family of James and Virginia Trotter was a model of Victorian rectitude. "In the home is *safety,*" wrote Trotter; "over its members are extended the protecting wings of guardian angels; while without are often snares and danger, either in palpable forms, or in those hidden by the glittering, the alluring disguises which are so often thrown over vice." Three children were born: William Monroe in 1872, Maude in 1874, and Bessie in 1883.

Trotter's racial pride and lifelong interest in music combined in 1878 to produce a book, *Music and Some Highly Musical People,* published by Lee and Shepard in Boston and by the firm of Charles W. Dillingham in New York. It was racially ambivalent, proud of black achievements but leaning toward the "higher" forms of white culture. The preface disavowed "all motives of a distinctively clannish nature," yet declared that the book, a record of Negro musicians in the United States, was "a much-needed service" to some of music's "noblest devotees and the race to which the latter belong." Sharpening the point, Trotter hoped his book would inspire "the people most concerned (if that be necessary) with a greater pride in their own achievements, and confidence in their own resources."

The volume included a general, nonracial discussion of music, with quotations from English poets such as Dryden, Milton, Pope, Wordsworth, and Byron. But there was also a firm indictment of "the hateful, terrible spirit of *color-prejudice.*" The blind pianist Thomas Greene Bethune, "Blind Tom," was praised without reservation: "unquestionably and conspicuously the most wonderful musician the world has ever known.'' The slave spirituals, as performed by the Fisk Jubilee Singers, were described as ''our only distinctively *American* music; all other kinds in use being merely the echo, more or less perfect, of music that originated in the Old World.'' Trotter was still the Victorian gentleman, however, and hoped that the Jubilee Singers would reach ''a higher aim'' in their music while keeping ''the heartiness, the soulfulness, of their style of rendition.'' Similarly, he liked the music played by the Georgia Minstrels but ''was not pleased, of course, with that portion of the performance (a part of which he was compelled to witness) devoted to burlesque.''

He resigned his post office job in 1882 as a protest when a white man was promoted over him. With the federal bureaucracy controlled by Republicans, he extended his protest by switching allegiance to the Democrats, thus joining a small group of Negro mugwumps in the North. In 1883 he worked for Benjamin F. Butler's campaign to be governor of Massachusetts, and after Butler's victory, called on Negroes to stop selling their votes for money: ''Our race is yet so far 'in the woods' that it cannot afford to imitate these Caucasian vices. Let us not contaminate our holy cause by baseness of any kind.'' Three years later he served as chairman of a meeting, held in Boston, of Negro ''Independents'' from the New England states.

Ultimately his prominence among Negro Democrats brought him nomination by Pres. Grover Cleveland to be recorder of deeds in Washington, D.C., at the time the highest federal job held by Negroes of the majority political party. Democrats opposed him because of his color and Republicans because of his politics. Trotter owed his confirmation by the Senate (32–10, March 3, 1887) to endorsement by the two Republican Massachusetts senators and votes of other Republicans who constituted two-thirds of the majority. The position, previously held by Frederick Douglass, was highly lucrative during Trotter's tenure from 1887 to 1889 because a real estate boom in Washington increased his salary which was based on a percentage of the transactions. While in office he refused to participate in any protest activities.

He returned to Boston when the Republicans won the election of 1889, and started a real estate business. He died of tuberculosis on Feb. 26, 1892, and was survived by his widow, his son, and two daughters.

Trotter's *Music and Some Highly Musical People* (1878) contains valuable biographical information and is a major source for the subject. See especially Stephen R. Fox's *The Guardian of Boston: William Monroe Trotter* (1970) and Jack Abramowitz's ''A Civil War Letter: James M. Trotter to Francis J. Garrison'' (*Midwest Journal,* 1952, pp. 113–22). Trotter's Civil War Letters are in the Edward W. Kingsley Papers, Duke University, and a manuscript sketch of Trotter is in the George W. Forbes Papers, Boston Public Library.

— STEPHEN R. FOX

TROTTER, [WILLIAM] MONROE (1872–1934), businessman, editor, and militant civil rights leader. He was born on April 7, 1872, at his grandparents' farm outside Chillicothe, Ohio, one of three children of James Monroe Trotter and Virginia Isaacs Trotter. He grew up in comfortable circumstances in Hyde Park, a white suburb of Boston, in the bosom of his loving family and steeped in abolitionist tradition. In this atmosphere of relative tolerance in Massachusetts, he was touched by the color line but not scarred by it. The greatest influence on his early life, and his constant inspiration later, was his father, James Monroe Trotter. As late as 1907 when Ray Stannard Baker asked William Trotter for biographical information to be included in *Following the Color Line,* he responded with a letter that was mostly about his father. He was raised on stories of abolitionism and the Civil War, and all his life took his cues from the antislavery ''Old Guard'' he reverently listed in 1921: ''Garrison, Phillips, Sumner, Weld, Downing, Nell, Trotter.''

While James Trotter pursued his career at the Boston Post Office, and later in real estate and politics, young Monroe grew to be a bustling, moralistic, well-liked youth, the favored child and only son among three children. The only Negro in his high school class, he led in scholarship and was elected class president. He also showed an early interest in religion, his mother's influence perhaps dominant in this area. He was so active at the white Baptist church in Hyde Park that he was urged to enter the ministry. But his father disapproved strongly because it would have meant eventually serving a segregated congregation. Monroe (as he was called) finished high school, took a job as a shipping clerk in Boston for a year, then entered Harvard College in the fall of 1891.

He thrived at Harvard, encountering no major discriminations. He worked hard at his courses and made Phi Beta Kappa in his junior year, the first Negro to be so honored at the College. Following the custom of the day, he took a great variety of courses, concentrating finally in politics and history. After the death of his father during his freshman year, he won scholarships that paid for most of his expenses; during his last two years the family was also supporting a daughter at Wellesley College. His best friends at Harvard were three white students, including a Jew and a southerner from Florida. He wheeled around town on his bicycle, hyperactive and somewhat disorganized, and took up the new sport of tennis, introducing it to his country cousins back in Ohio during a family sojourn there in the summer of 1892. Still very active in church work, and pursuing a separate life in Boston's polite Negro society, he enjoyed a four-year idyll in Cambridge.

The idyll continued for about five years after his graduation. Settling on a career as a negotiator of real estate mortgages, he learned the business by working in a white firm, in a job he obtained through Civil War associates of his father's. He went into business on his own in 1899 and, by his own later testimony, was soon ''starting to rise.'' Given his business prospects, family background, and prestigious education, he reveled in another role among Boston's Negroes as the highly eligible bachelor-about-town. ''I have furnished my room at home somewhat like my college room,'' he told a friend, ''and any young woman who comes into it is supposed to make a decoration for it. I have secured only three decorations on that plea so far.''

Such diversions presumably ended in 1899 with his marriage to Geraldine Pindell, who came from an old Boston family with its own tradition of racial militancy. Trained as a bookkeeper, she was a lively, independent woman. W. E. B. Du Bois knew her while he was at Harvard in the early 1890s and remembered her in his *Autobiography* as "a fine forthright woman, blonde, blue-eyed and fragile."

Trotter later tended to regard these years as a golden interlude, self-indulgent and perhaps complacent, and contrasting starkly with the harsh and self-sacrificing *Guardian* years. Although essentially true, this contrast should not be drawn too sharply. Even right out of college, he had no illusions about the personal obstacles presented by his color in the business world where he hoped to make his fortune. In Boston, and more obviously in the South, conditions for the race were worsening. These weighed heavily on his highly sensitized racial conscience. "The growth of caste feeling and caste laws," as he called it, combined with what he described as "Booker Washington's betrayal of the colored people," were pushing him toward a life that he had not anticipated.

The great decision of his life, to start the *Guardian* and plunge into racial agitation and organizing, was not made quickly. It crept up on him for years and derived in part from frustrations in his real estate business. At the turn of the century Jim Crow customs were spreading even to Boston, historically regarded (as Trotter said) as "the most liberal city on the color line." "I have had my ups and downs in business," he wrote in June 1902, "having been obliged to move once in January and again in February." By then he had launched the *Guardian* and could boast that it enjoyed a circulation of 2500 after only eight months.

The newspaper, in contrast to his business troubles, was an overnight success. For the first two years it was co-edited by another well-educated young Negro, George Washington Forbes. Forbes was a native of Mississippi who had worked his way through Amherst College. Cynical about politics, he was basically a literary man, earning his living as a librarian at the West End branch of the Boston Public Library. His position as a city employee left him vulnerable and contributed to his withdrawal from the *Guardian* after two years.

By then Trotter was committed to the great crusade of his youth, a vendetta against Booker T. Washington. The *Guardian* appeared when Washington's reputation among Negroes was at its height. Crying in the wilderness at first, the *Guardian* revived the old opposition against him, including such leaders as Du Bois. It started the process that led to the Niagara Movement (founded in 1905 by Du Bois and others), the NAACP, and the resurgence of the protest tradition among Afro-Americans. "The Tuskegee Machine" and "the opposition," as the two camps came to refer to each other, locked in a mortal struggle that did not entirely abate even with Washington's death in 1915.

The *Guardian* indicted Washington on three major points: first, that he was responding to increasingly intolerable racial conditions with an unreal, complacent optimism that things were actually improving. Living in Alabama, Washington had a need to be circumspect;

living in Boston, Trotter called for "the spirit of protest, of independence, of revolt."

Second, that he led a hypocritical political life. On the one hand, Washington would demean political rights in favor of economic development and the acquisition of bourgeois habits. On the other hand, he was proud of being able to vote himself, and was Pres. Theodore Roosevelt's trusted first-term advisor on southern and racial politics. Trotter, a political independent, distrusted such an alliance between the White House and the race's most public figure.

Third, that he was building his own monument at Tuskegee Institute and trampling on the rights of Negroes who aspired to other forms of education. Trotter, the Harvard graduate, was insulted by Washington's self-serving promotion of manual and industrial training, and by his denigration of classical forms of education.

Thus joined, the battle became bitter as both sides resorted to personal attacks and underhanded methods. These came to light over the so-called Boston Riot of July 1903, the most famous episode of Trotter's career, as he served a month in jail for his part in disrupting a speech by Washington. Trotter had gone to the meeting, held at a Negro church on Columbus Avenue in Boston, to ask Washington some embarrassing questions. Other parties, perhaps without Trotter's consent, were more disruptive, and Trotter as the known leader of the opposition was made the scapegoat. Washington's associates in Boston hired lawyers and pursued the case to its conclusion.

That month he spent in the Charles Street Jail was a benchmark in his life. In his absence, Geraldine Pindell Trotter took on a greater role with the *Guardian*. She partly made up for the loss of co-editor Forbes who— with a separate libel suit hanging over him, also brought by the Washington forces—broke with Trotter and retired to his job at the library. And most significantly, the jail term was the final push that brought the brilliant talents of Du Bois into the "radical" camp and established, albeit temporarily, friendly relations between him and Trotter. Two weeks after the Boston Riot, when a white friend had questioned his actions, Trotter told the friend to read Du Bois's *The Souls of Black Folk*, published the previous spring. "I am serious and in earnest," said Trotter. "Read the book."

The two most able champions of the anti-Washington persuasion worked together for only a few years, however, notably in the Niagara Movement from 1905 to 1907. Trotter's bulldog traits of tenacity and independence that served him so well in his fearless journalism hamstrung his organizing efforts. The Niagara Movement was beset by other problems, notably opposition from Tuskegee and the fact that Trotter, in Boston, and Du Bois, in Atlanta, could give it only such time as they could snatch from their other work. But it really foundered on personal quarrels and the forbidding personalities of its two leaders. "It is impossible," one Niagara member finally decided, "for a man with ideas and opinions of his own, for a man with personality and individuality, to get along with Trotter." Over the years, many of his other associates would come to similar conclusions.

Trotter attended the founding conference of the NAACP in New York in 1909, but aside from occasional contacts over the next few years, never joined forces with the new organization. He could not be reconciled with the two main leaders of the early NAACP, Oswald Garrison Villard and his nemesis Du Bois. He was also estranged from the group's local leadership in Boston. More to the point, he could not abide the white money and leadership that ran the NAACP at least until the 1920s. His own group, the National Equal Rights League, which grew out of the 1908 presidential campaign, was always (as he described it in 1920) "an organization of the colored people and for the colored people and led by the colored people." As the NAACP's influence grew, Trotter's leadership became increasingly idiosyncratic and isolated on the left wing of the race's leadership.

His effectiveness as a leader was also diminished by his shifting support of political parties. Because of Roosevelt's summary discharge without honor of three companies of the Negro 25th Infantry following the Brownsville Riot of August 1906, Trotter supported Sen. Joseph B. Foraker, who had opposed their action, for the Republican nomination for president in 1908. With the support of such Regular Republicans as Charles Anderson and Ralph Tyler, Taft was overwhelmingly nominated. Taft's appointment of William H. Lewis as U.S. assistant attorney-general did not prevent Trotter from accusing Taft of fostering and encouraging "race prejudice and race antagonism [more] than any man in the history of the country." Like Du Bois and Bishop Alexander Walters, Trotter supported Woodrow Wilson for president in 1912, largely because of the desire to keep Roosevelt, and to a lesser extent Taft, out of the White House.

In taking this action, so reflective of his mugwump tendencies—his National Independent Political League campaigned under the slogan, "We Stand for Men and Measures Rather than for Party"—Trotter found a dubious race champion in Woodrow Wilson. As president, Wilson approved the increased segregation of federal office buildings, failed to appoint Negroes even to their "traditional" positions in the civil service, and otherwise embarrassed his Negro campaign supporters. When Trotter brought a delegation to the White House in November 1914, Wilson and Trotter engaged in an intemperate argument for forty-five minutes that ended when Wilson ordered the group from his office.

In his later years Trotter seemed a picturesque anachronism. He was arrested again in 1915 for his part in trying to have the film *The Birth of a Nation* closed in Boston. He made a quixotic journey to the peace conference at Versailles in 1919, aiming to have a racial equality clause adopted in the treaty. But essentially he confined himself to Boston as his national reputation declined inexorably. His wife's death in the influenza epidemic of 1918 removed his life's partner and most important supporter. With her loss the *Guardian* and its editor grew ever more isolated. He hung on into the early years of the Depression, still putting out his paper, and died, an apparent suicide, on his sixty-second birthday in 1934.

His early militancy made him attractive to some later

viewpoints. But fundamentally, Monroe Trotter was an old-fashioned Christian gentleman, imbued with concepts of duty and service, secure in the simple moralism of the nineteenth century, concerned above all to set an example for his race to follow. "I must say to you John," he lectured a college friend seven years after their graduation, "that you showed poor staying powers to get into the use of tobacco and of beer. It is strange to me how you fellows change your principles. Tobacco is not important, but it is important to set a good example in the matter of liquor." More than anything else, he would want this final judgment: that he did not change his principles.

Trotter was one of the twentieth century's first important Negro leaders in the militant tradition. He made his greatest impression as the spearhead of the race's internal struggle against the conservative leadership of Booker T. Washington. Later, during the early years of the NAACP, Trotter's National Equal Rights League was the main organizational alternative for Negroes who liked the NAACP's relative militancy but disliked the white money and leadership behind it. Personally, Trotter epitomized Richard Hofstadter's embattled mugwump: the patrician at bay, displaced by the vulgar currents of a new era.

See Stephen R. Fox's *The Guardian of Boston: William Monroe Trotter* (1970). Aside from the scattered files of the *Guardian,* major manuscript sources are the Trotter correspondence in the papers of W. E. B. Du Bois at the University of Massachusetts, of J. A. Fairlie at the University of Illinois, of Archibald H. Grimké, Joel E. Spingarn, and Freeman H. M. Murray in the Moorland-Spingarn Research Center, Howard University, and of George A. Towns at Atlanta University. There is a small collection of Trotter papers at Boston University.

— STEPHEN R. FOX

TRUTH, SOJOURNER (1797?–1883), evangelist, abolitionist, reformer, and women's rights activist. Next to the youngest of the several children of James and Elizabeth, slaves of a wealthy Dutch-speaking farmer, she was born in Hurley, Ulster County, N.Y. The facts about her early life are obscure. Her original name is variously given as Belle, Isabelle, and Isabella, and her first language was Dutch. From a very young age she spoke to God and believed that He spoke to her. Inspired by her mother, from whom she was separated when she was eleven, her religious beliefs were intensified by the cruelty of her slavery experiences. Sold four times, she was tormented from 1810 to 1826 by the wife of John Dumont, her master in New Paltz, N.Y. She bore at least five children to a fellow slave, Thomas. Her son Peter was sold and sent to Alabama despite a state law forbidding such a sale, and became emotionally disturbed for the rest of life as a result of beatings by an insane master.

Belle seems to have been protected against a loss of faith by an early decision that God's seeming indifference was rooted in her own failure to ask His help soon enough or earn His goodwill by struggling to do a better job herself. For years she sought her image of God in a man, twice believing she had found him. Twice deceived, she came at last to trust only the voices in her own head which, as she matured, articulated *her* conscience and *her* personal vision of truth and justice. But her independent nature had asserted itself even in slavery. She had run away from Dumont in 1826 when he broke his promise to free her a year before state law would require, and found refuge with Isaac and Maria Van Wagenen.

Newly emancipated but still barefoot and penniless, she had confronted the local court with the aid of other Quaker friends and obtained the return of her son from Alabama. About 1829, as a domestic servant and evangelist in New York City, she searched for fourteen years for her particular idea of justice among the churches and religious sects of the corrupt and fast-growing port. From 1829 to 1834 she was particularly influenced by a wealthy fanatic, Elijah Pierson and his wife (until her death in 1830), and through him the self-styled prophet Matthias whose "Kingdom" was at Sing Sing. When the "Kingdom" fell apart in 1834, she lost her savings and furniture. Meanwhile she attended from time to time the African Zion Church in New York City. One day in 1843 her voice told her to leave the city and testify to the sins committed against her people.

She assumed the name "Truth" for God, but "Sojourner" because she was to "travel up and down the land" testifying and showing the people their sins. The forty-six-year-old pilgrim wandered through New England until she reached the utopian colony called the Northampton Association of Education and Industry. There she became an enthusiastic convert to abolition, working with William Lloyd Garrison, Wendell Phillips, Frederick Douglass, David Ruggles, and other famous abolitionists. While Douglass was speaking at an antislavery convention in Boston, he expressed his apprehension that "slavery could only be destroyed by bloodshed, when I was suddenly and sharply interrupted by my good old friend Sojourner Truth with the question, 'Frederick, is God dead?' 'No,' I answered, 'and because God is not dead slavery can only end in blood.' My quaint old sister was of the Garrison school of non-resistants, and was shocked at my sanguinary doctrine, but she too became an advocate of the sword, when the war for the maintenance of the Union was declared" (*Life and Times of Frederick Douglass . . .* edited with a new introduction by Rayford W. Logan [1962], p. 275).

In 1850 Sojourner Truth discovered the new women's rights movement at a conference in Worcester, Mass., and began her long friendship with Lucretia Mott, Elizabeth Cady Stanton, and other leaders.

With her six-foot frame, black skin, and deep, resonant voice, Sojourner Truth aroused curiosity wherever she appeared. She became famous for her quick wit, remarkable singing, and pithy genius for illuminating controversial issues in her own unschooled language. In 1851 she headed west to attend a women's rights conference in Akron, Ohio, and stayed to testify in other western states, settling in the mid-1850s in Battle Creek, Mich. There her three daughters and grandsons joined her, and she solicited gifts and food for the volunteer colored regiments after the outbreak of the Civil War.

In 1864 she went to Washington, where she met President Lincoln. She taught housekeeping skills to former female field hands at Freedmen's Village in Arlington, Va., nursed colored soldiers at Freedmen's Hospital, and helped distribute relief supplies to the jobless ex-slaves who crowded the camps of the capital city. Distressed at the suffering and enforced idleness of the destitute refugees, she conceived the idea of a "Negro State" in the West. She presented a petition to some senators in 1870 to settle Negroes on public land in the West. But it had too few names, she felt, so she worked for several years to get many more names in order to impress Congress. Although her campaign failed, it is believed that the exodus of many Negro families from farther south in 1879 may have been inspired in part by her idea. According to available evidence, she visited some of the refugees in Kansas.

She died on Nov. 26, 1883, at her home in Battle Creek. She was, as far as can be determined, eighty-six years old. Her funeral at the Congregational Church was said to have been the largest ever held in the town. She was buried in Oak Hill Cemetery, Battle Creek.

See Jacqueline Bernard's *Journey Toward Freedom: The Story of Sojourner Truth* (1967). Olive Gilbert published several editions of the original *Narrative of Sojourner Truth . . . Drawn from Her Book of Life,* originally printed in 1850. The 1878 edition was reprinted by Arno Press in 1968. Hertha Pauli's *Her Name was Sojourner Truth* (1962) was the first effort to piece out Sojourner Truth's life beyond the materials offered in the Gilbert book. Arthur Huff Fauset's *Sojourner Truth: God's Faithful Pilgrim* (1938) was the first modern biography that restored her to public attention. There is no sketch in the *DAB,* but *NAW* (1971, 3:479–81) has an illuminating article by Saunders Redding.

— JACQUELINE DE S. BERNARD

TUBMAN, HARRIET (c. 1821–1913), fugitive slave, abolitionist, nurse, spy, and social reformer. Born in Dorchester County on the Eastern Shore of Maryland, she was the daughter of slaves, Benjamin Ross and Harriet Green, and was originally named Araminta by her master. Defying slave custom, she later used her mother's first name. During childhood Harriet sustained a serious head injury which caused her to suffer sleeping spells periodically for the rest of her life. Slavery offered Harriet no opportunity to attend school; however, she possessed innate intelligence and creativity as well as extraordinary foresight and judgment. She acquired unusual physical strength as she worked in the fields, and within her small but muscular ebony frame swelled a growing determination to be free. In 1844 her mother forced her to marry John Tubman, a free man. When her master died in 1849 and the rumor spread that the slaves were to be sold to the Deep South, she and her two brothers decided to escape to the North. They returned, but she continued to Philadelphia. Two years later she went back to Maryland for her husband, who had married another woman.

On her journey to freedom Harriet Tubman was guided by the North Star and aided also by conductors of the Underground Railroad, such as Ezekiel Hunn and Thomas Garrett of Delaware. But while the masses of her race remained enslaved she could find no true solace in her newly won liberty. She made approximately nineteen trips into the South and rescued some 300

Negroes from slavery. "She preferred to start the journey on Saturday night, so that she could be well on her way before the owners had an opportunity the following Monday to advertise the escape of their slaves." Once started, there was no turning back for squeamish passengers whom she fearlessly admonished at gunpoint: "Live North or die here."

After delivering her precious cargo at the planned destination, Harriet Tubman often worked at such jobs as laundress, cook, or seamstress in order to sustain many fugitives. Both black and white abolitionists hailed Harriet Tubman as the "Moses" of her race. She was respected and honored by such leaders as Frederick Douglass, Susan B. Anthony, and Ralph Waldo Emerson. To the southern slaveholder and other proslavery advocates, however, her name became anathema. She was unpopular among antiabolitionists in the North, also. They attacked and severely beat her when, in April 1860, she led a group that took from the police and marshals in Troy, N.Y., Charles Nalle, a runaway slave, and assisted him in his escape to Canada. Although her efforts seldom resulted in material reward, a strong faith in God and what she believed to be "inner vision" (i.e., clairvoyance) inspired her with the courage and confidence needed to successfully plot dangerous escape routes and still avoid capture. Neither the harsh Fugitive Slave Act of 1850 nor a $40,000 bounty for her arrest, dead or alive, could outmatch the cunning and daring of Harriet Tubman, who in 1857 performed the incredible mission of emancipating both of her aged parents and finally resettling them in Auburn, N.Y., on land purchased from William H. Seward.

While in Canada in April 1858, Harriet Tubman had the opportunity to meet John Brown, who referred to her at times as "General Tubman." A sincere friendship was established between them. She approved his plan to seize the government arsenal in Harpers Ferry, W. Va., and offered her support. However, by uncontrollable circumstances, she was unable to recruit fighters or even join the ranks of Brown's band. She was deeply grieved by his defeat and his subsequent hanging; she forever regarded him as the true "Savior of our people."

With the outbreak of the Civil War, Harriet Tubman immediately asserted her right to participate. With a letter from the governor of Massachusetts, John Andrew, she reported to Gen. David Hunter at Hilton Head, S.C., where she worked effectively in the Union Army as a cook, nurse, scout, and spy. In the spring and summer of 1865 she worked briefly at a freedmen's hospital in Fortress Monroe, Va.

The ending of the war did not signal the culmination of her unselfish concern and devotion for the welfare of the Negro masses. In North Carolina she endured hard times in attempting to establish schools for the freedmen. Later in 1869 she married Nelson Davis, a Negro Civil War veteran. Moreover she was successful in paying off the mortgage on her home in Auburn with the royalties from a short book, *Scenes in the Life of Harriet Tubman* (1869), written for her by Sarah H. Bradford and printed and circulated by Gerrit Smith, Wendell Phillips, and some Auburn neighbors. The federal government showed less gratitude for her services. Only after some thirty years of effort, supported at one time

by Secretary of State William H. Seward, did Congress award her a pittance of twenty dollars a month for her wartime services. Private citizens contributed to the support of the Harriet Tubman Home for Indigent and Aged Negroes in Auburn. The Harriet Tubman Home building was constructed in 1952 at a cost of $23,000 and an additional $7000 for equipment by the A.M.E. Zion church. After its dedication as a national shrine (April 1953) it was managed by officials of the church.

In the twilight of her years Harriet Tubman was active in the temperance and women's rights movement. Black and white people mourned her death of pneumonia in March 1913. She had a full military service for her funeral and was buried in Fort Hill, Auburn. A year later the Cayuga County Historical Society Association erected a tablet in memory of her work and Booker T. Washington delivered the tribute. The greatness of her life represented almost a century of struggle, beginning with the Negro's fight against slavery and ending in efforts toward social justice. On Feb. 1, 1978, the U.S. Postal Service issued in Washington, D.C., a thirteen-cent Harriet Tubman stamp, the first in a new "Black Heritage U.S.A." series.

Sarah H. Bradford's expanded *Harriet Tubman, The Moses of Her People* (1886, reprinted in 1961 with a valuable introduction by Butler A. Jones), is the basic source for her early life. Earl Conrad's *Harriet Tubman* (1943) gives a fuller and better documented account of her entire life. Dorothy Sterling's *Freedom Train, The Story of Harriet Tubman* (1954), recreates the essence of her life and personality. There is an excellent short biography by Dorothy B. Porter in the *DAB* (1936 [1964], 10:27) and a longer one by John Hope Franklin in *NAW* (1971, 3:481–83). — LORRAINE A. WILLIAMS

TURNER, BENJAMIN S. (1825–1894), congressman and politician. Born near Weldon, N.C., and taken to Alabama at the age of five, he was the first ex-slave in that state to win national recognition. Information about his early life is meager. In Selma, he ran a thriving livery stable and was a prosperous merchant. In 1867 he was named tax collector of Dallas County and two years later became a Selma city councilman. According to one report he could write nothing more than his name, but the Washington correspondent of the *New York Globe* wrote that Turner had become educated. Elected in 1870 to the House from the 1st Congressional District of Alabama, he introduced three bills in the brief session which began March 4, 1871. None of them, notably to restore political and legal rights to ex-Confederates generally and to one of his Dallas County constituents, received consideration.

In the second session he is best known for his two speeches, which were printed in the Appendix. His speech favoring the refund of a cotton tax of $250 million which the federal government had collected from southern states (1866–1868) was based on the arguments that it had handicapped those states, inflicted dire hardship on the Negroes who worked in the fields, and was unconstitutional. In his second speech he addressed the vital issue of land for the freedmen. He pointed out that "While we pay gratuitously to Chinese, Japanese, and Indians millions of dollars annually, we hesitate to even lend to the landless but peaceable and industrious citizens of the South $1,000,000 annually to help them aid themselves and at the same time greatly develop the resources of the country. Nor can this loan be attended with the least risk to the Government, for it is secured by the best of security, placing a small portion of the surplus money of the Treasury to profitable use, and at the same time paying the Government large interest." Like most speeches printed in the Appendix, it also received no consideration. He did, however, secure the passage of two private pension bills.

In the 1872 election he was defeated because another Negro, Philip Joseph, ran as an independent, split the Negro vote, and ensured the election of a white candidate. In the short session from December 1872 to March 3, 1873, Turner introduced no bills, but out of party loyalty supported the test oath, mixed schools, civil rights, and the franking privilege, while opposing civil service reform and the removal of names of battles on war flags.

Returning to Alabama, he remained active in county politics while James T. Rapier and Jeremiah Haralson became Negro leaders in national politics. He resumed his farming until his death on March 21, 1894.

The essential facts about Turner are in *Biographical Congressional Directory* (1929). The two speeches are in *Congressional Globe* (42d Cong., 1st sess., Appendix, pp. 530, 540). Maurine Christopher quotes portions of them in *America's Black Congressmen* (1971), and Samuel Denny Smith summarizes them, calling them "very able speeches," in *The Negro in Congress, 1870–1901* (1940). There is a photograph of Turner in a composite photograph of the first seven Negroes in Congress, reproduced from the Schomburg Center, on the second page after page 115 in Christopher.

— RAYFORD W. LOGAN

TURNER, CHARLES H. (1867–1923), biologist and educator. He was born in Cincinnati where he graduated from high school. His father, Thomas Turner from Alberta, Canada, was employed as a church custodian and his mother, Addie Campbell Turner from Lexington, Ky., was a practical nurse. In 1891 he earned a B.S. degree and in 1892 an M.S. degree, both in biology, from the University of Cincinnati. During 1892–1893 he served as an assistant instructor in the Biology Laboratory at the University of Cincinnati. He could have devoted his professional lifetime to scientific research but instead he chose to teach full time and to conduct his research when free from classroom duties.

From 1893 to 1895 Turner was a professor of biology at Clark College, Atlanta, Ga. He taught briefly in the public schools of Evansville, Ind., and in his hometown of Cincinnati. During 1906 he was principal of College Hill High School in Cleveland, Tenn. In 1907–1908 he became professor of biology at Haines Normal and Industrial Institute which had been founded by Lucy Craft Laney in Augusta, Ga. In 1908 he moved to St. Louis, Mo., as a biology teacher at Sumner High School, the position he held until the time of his death. Between 1892 and 1923 Turner carried out original scientific experiments on ants, bees, moths, spiders, cockroaches, and several other insects. Most of his research

was done alone and unaided. For his pioneering works and discoveries and contributions to knowledge of the field of animal behavior he was awarded the Ph.D. degree in 1907 by the University of Chicago.

It is significant that with a Ph.D. degree in biology he remained a high school biology teacher from 1908 to 1923. However, he was known among scientists for his animal behavior research, especially for his more than fifty research reports published on neurology, invertebrate ecology, and animal behavior. His published research appeared in such journals as the *Biological Bulletin*, the *Journal of Comparative Neurology*, *Zoological Bulletin*, the *Journal of Animal Behavior*, and the *Psychological Bulletin*. His studies included "Psychological Notes on the Gallery Spider," "Habits of Mound-Building Ants," "Experiments on the Color Vision of the Honey Bee," "Behavior of a Parasitic Bee," "Hunting Habits of an American Sand Wasp," and "Do Ants Form Practical Judgments?" He discovered that a species of moth which responds only to the high pitch of a whistle can be taught to respond to low pitches when the low tones mean danger to this insect. His scientific work was studied by other scientists in America and Europe. Quotations from his published articles were found in important books of the time on animal behavior such as *The Animal Mind*, *Wheeler's Ant Book*, and *The Psychic Life of Insects*. Three years in succession he was chosen to write the annual article outlining and weighing the advances made in the science of biology during the previous year. In the animal behavior literature of France a certain characteristic ant movement (toward the nest) was given the name of its discoverer. The movement was called "Turner's circling," which referred to a peculiar turning movement, observed and described by Turner, taken by some species of ants as they found their way back to a nest.

Turner was an outstanding and inspiring teacher. He brought a wealth of firsthand information about the behavior of living things into his high school classrooms. After his death the St. Louis Board of Education erected a school for the physically handicapped and named it the Charles H. Turner School. In 1954 the school became the Turner Middle School. Turner's interests were not restricted to science. He wrote nature stories for children and thirty-two unpublished poems. He worked in civil rights movements in St. Louis and was a leader in developing social service for Negroes.

Basic information about Turner is on pages 70–91 of Robert C. Hayden's *Seven Black American Scientists* (1970). See also "Dr. Charles H. Turner" (*Transactions of the Academy of Science of St. Louis*, a paper read at the memorial to Turner at Sumner High School, St. Louis, May 25, 1923). — ROBERT C. HAYDEN

TURNER, HENRY McNEAL (1834–1915), chaplain, agent of the Freedmen's Bureau, politician, editor, bishop, college president, and colonizationist. He was born near Abbeville, S.C., the son of free parents, Hardy and Sarah (Green) Turner. His father died while he was young, and he worked in the cotton fields and as an apprentice to a blacksmith. By the time he was fifteen, through his ingenuity and the aid of liberal whites he had learned to read. Employed by a law firm, he also learned to write and do simple arithmetic. More important was his belief that his mother was descended from African royalty, a belief that accounted in large measure for his later interest in Africa.

In 1851 he joined the Methodist Episcopal church, South. Licensed to preach in 1853, he became an itinerant minister in most of the southern states until 1857 when he settled in St. Louis. The next year he severed his ties with the white M.E. church, South, and joined the Negro-controlled African Methodist Episcopal church. He was ordained a deacon in Baltimore in 1860 after he had improved his grammar and studied Latin, Greek, and Hebrew. Two years later he became an elder and pastor of Israel Church in Washington, D.C. His sermons urging his parishioners to join the Union Army were brought to the attention of President Lincoln who in 1863 appointed him a chaplain in the army—probably the first Negro to hold this position—attached to the 1st Regiment, U.S. Colored Troops.

Mustered in 1865, he was appointed chaplain by Pres. Andrew Johnson in the Regular Army and assigned as an agent of the Freedmen's Bureau in Georgia. He soon resigned and established a number of churches as a base to help the freed Negroes participate in politics. Elected a Republican member of the Georgia Constitutional Convention of 1867, he successfully sponsored measures which prevented the sale of property whose owners were unable to pay their taxes, and to provide relief for banks. On the other hand, he favored a pardon for Jefferson Davis and an educational qualification for voting. Despite these concessions, he was vilified by whites and tried "on the wildest and most groundless accusations ever distilled from the laboratory of hell." He was acquitted, however, in every case (W. E. B. Du Bois, *Black Reconstruction . . .* [1935], p. 499). The harassment forced him to resign as postmaster in Macon, Ga., and as a Customs inspector. Meanwhile, white supremacy was being restored in Georgia. In September 1868 the Georgia legislature formally declared all Negro members ineligible to hold seats. Turner, "the most antiwhite—and most disliked—Negro member," circulated throughout the state an eloquent assertion of their right to their seats. After the state rejected the Fifteenth Amendment in March 1869, Congress placed Georgia under military rule for the second time and required ratification of the amendment. The state legislature ratified, restored Negro members to their seats, and on Jan. 10, 1870, Georgia was admitted to the Union for the second time. Turner served only one term in the state legislature, from 1868 to 1870, and turned his attention to the A.M.E. church and other activities.

In 1876 he was made manager of the AME Book Concern in Philadelphia, served as bishop (1880–1892), was president of Morris Brown College in Atlanta for twelve years, wrote *The Genius and Theory of Methodist Policy* (1885), and compiled a cathechism and a hymnbook. He founded the *Southern Christian Recorder* (1889), the *Voice of Missions* (1892), and the *Voice of the People* (1901). He was president of several boards and historiographer of the AME church.

Turner was best known, however, as the leading advocate of African colonization during the late nineteenth and early twentieth centuries. He became an advocate at least as early as 1874, and felt deeply honored when he was elected a vice-president of the American Colonization Society in 1876. His support stemmed largely from his conviction that Negroes had no worthwhile future in the United States. God had brought Negroes from Africa so that they could be Christianized and acquire skills which would enable them to "redeem" Africa. Slavery, he contended, was a "providential" institution and "training school" in this development. But Negroes had been betrayed by Reconstruction and by the Civil Rights decision of 1883 which declared unconstitutional the Civil Rights Act of 1875. It was the duty of the federal government to aid the return of Negroes to Africa by paying them reparations for their labor as slaves. Africans and Western Negroes would build a nation in Africa which would hold its own against Europe or America. The AME church was the rightful body to establish an "African" church which would transcend ethnic, cultural, and local ties in creating one African people.

He made four trips to Africa between 1891 and 1898, lectured widely in Europe, West and South Africa, and wrote scorching editorials in the *Voice of Missions* and *Voice of the People,* excoriating the United States and urging support for colonization in Africa. Serfs in Russia were lords as compared with Negroes in the United States. His enthusiasm led him to write a roseate picture of Liberia in 1892: "One thing the black man is here, that is manhood, freedom, and the fullest liberty." He hoped to live to see the United States have its memory blotted from the pages of history. "A man who loves a country that hates him is a human dog and not a man." But as Bishop Benjamin F. Lee said in 1893, Turner "speaks of the United States as Hades and of Africa as Eden; yet even he still holds his residence in Hades, only paying Eden a brief visit once a year."

Colonization abroad, advocated earlier by Martin R. Delany and Edward Blyden, among others, was condemned by Frederick Douglass and at least temporarily by T. Thomas Fortune. Probably not more than 25,000 American Negroes sought refuge in foreign lands.

A tall, handsome man, Turner was an eloquent, fiery, and even vituperative orator and writer. He married four times: in 1856, 1893, 1900, and some time later. He had several children, only two of whom survived him. True to his vow not to die on the soil of the United States, he died in Windsor, Ontario, on May 8, 1915, and was buried in Atlanta, Ga. In 1973 he was chosen one of three Negroes whose portraits are displayed in the state Capitol in Atlanta (the other two are Lucy Laney and Martin Luther King, Jr.).

For partial biographical data, consult Mongo Ponton's *Life and Times of Henry McNeal Turner* (1917), John T. Jenifer's *Centennial Retrospect History of the African Methodist Episcopal Church* (1916), and Robert R. Wright, Jr.'s *The Bishops of the A.M.E. Church* (1963). For insight into his domestic emigration activities and his general political philosophy, Edwin Redkey's *Black Exodus, Black Nationalist and Back-to-Africa Movements 1890–1910* (1969) and *Respect Black: The Writings and Speeches of Henry McNeal*

Turner (1971) are valuable. Josephus R. Coan gives a detailed account of Turner's involvement in the Independent Church Movement in South Africa in his unpublished dissertation "The Expansion of Missions of the African Methodist Episcopal Church in South Africa, 1896–1908" (Hartford Seminary, 1961). And Carol Page's unpublished M.A. thesis, "Bishop Henry McNeal Turner and the 'Ethiopian Movement' in South Africa, 1896–1904" (Roosevelt University, 1973) gives a political view of Turner's visits to West and South Africa. The brief article by Harold G. Villard in the *DAB* ([1936], 10, Part 1:65–66) devotes one sentence to his trips to Africa and advocacy of the return of Negroes to Africa. Basic facts are in *Who's Who in America, 1914–1915.* — CAROL PAGE

TURNER, JACK (c. 1840–1882), political activist and martyr. Born a slave in Alabama about 1840, he became the property of Beloved Love Turner, a wealthy planter of Choctaw County (one of a tier of counties in the state's south-central area known as the Black Belt). Although uneducated—Jack ultimately learned the basics of reading and writing—he was imposing: tall, powerfully built, with black skin. As a chattel he and his master developed close ties of friendship, and Jack became an important part of the plantation's work force.

After the Civil War, Jack was set free and took his former owner's surname. He married a light-skinned Negro woman named Chloe (they had four children), and remained in Choctaw County earning a living as a tenant farmer. Despite his lack of formal education, Turner was highly intelligent, a persuasive orator, and a natural leader. During Reconstruction the Republican party was organized in Alabama, as in other southern states, and came to political power. In Alabama, the bastion of Republican strength was in the Black Belt, predominantly populated by Negroes. Jack Turner helped organize the Republican party in Choctaw County. Its components included Negroes, a few local whites (among them Beloved Love Turner) contemptuously dismissed as scalawags, and a scattering of newly arrived northerners derisively labeled carpetbaggers. Negroes constituted a large majority of of the coalition, and it was Turner, along with other Negro leaders, who persuaded the former slaves to articulate their freedom by voting. The results were success at the polls in local, state, and national elections.

Because of his conspicuous political role, Turner became the inevitable target of reprisal by local whites, for he was a symbol to many whites of the bitterness of defeat and a constant reminder of the new social, economic, and political order. Hoping to minimize Turner's influence, county officials and town magistrates in the county seat of Butler began lodging various charges against him. During and after Reconstruction Jack was arrested, tried, and occasionally convicted of drunkenness, stealing, fighting, and adultery. Most of the charges were petty and deliberately contrived to control Jack Turner. Found innocent as often as guilty, Jack refused to be intimidated. Despite various brief periods in jail he continued to farm, even managing to buy eighty acres, care for his family, and keep Choctaw County Negroes active politically.

In 1874 Alabama was "redeemed" as the factionalized Republicans were defeated, and the state settled down to decades of rule by the "Bourbons," the conservative Democrats. They were not seriously threatened until the Populist challenge of the 1890s. Although Democrats proclaimed the doctrine of white supremacy, they used the votes of Negroes—obtained by fraud and economic and physical coercion—to maintain themselves in power.

Jack Turner and the Negroes of Choctaw County continued to support the Republican party. In the late 1870s and early 1880s they cooperated with the rising Independent and Greenback parties. In several elections the new coalition made respectable showings, and in the governor's election of August 1882 Choctaw County actually gave the Greenback candidate a majority of its votes. Although the state went Democratic by a large margin, local Democrats, embarrassed and humiliated, blamed their defeat on the activities of Jack Turner.

A few days after the election, a bundle of papers was found on a country road. Supposedly the secret minutes of a revolutionary organization of Negroes headed by Jack Turner, the packet was turned over to county authorities. Claiming that he and his followers had a plan to massacre all of the whites in the country, officials effected the arrest of Turner and six of his followers on Aug. 16 on charges of conspiracy. Two of the accused were taken from the jail and tortured into making confessions. On Aug. 19, a mass gathering of whites and a few Negroes assembled on the courthouse square of Butler and went through the motions of a trial. The mob decreed that Turner was guilty and sentenced him to death. He was taken from the jail and hanged from an oak tree on the courthouse lawn.

The lynch mob's act set off repercussions in the upcoming November elections, and for a brief time Turner gained national as well as regional attention. The Republicans claimed the lynching was an act of political murder, and the Democrats countered with the argument that Jack Turner was guilty and deserved to die. In the elections the Democrats emerged triumphant, but in Choctaw County the vote was extremely close as Turner's followers demonstrated their loyalty to his martyrdom.

Close inspection of the incriminating documents makes clear that they were forged and, as it was pointed out at the time, no stretch of logic could explain why an "army" of Negroes intent on murder would keep notes on their plans or be so careless with them. The final proof of Turner's innocence was the disposition of the conspiracy charges against his lieutenants. After interminable continuances, the charges against the men were dropped and they were released. Jack had been eliminated by a group of men who framed him and cruelly manipulated the emotions of white citizens into believing him guilty. Their fears were translated into the gory work of a lynch mob and the death of an innocent man.

Jack Turner had refused to accept the world around him. Mercurial, hot tempered, imperfect, he was always the activist. He declined to accept a society that relegated him and his family to an inferior status, and he fought to change the existing order. Even his enemies admitted his bravery and courage. That he made a philosophical analysis of his condition is doubtful, but his commitment and the price he paid are a part of the historical record.

Published sources are William Warren Rogers's and Robert David Ward's *August Reckoning: Jack Turner and Racism in Post-Civil War Alabama* (1973), and " 'Jack Turnerism': A Political Phenomenon of the Deep South" (*JNH,* Oct. 1972, pp. 313–32); also valuable is Gerald Lee Roush's "Aftermath of Reconstruction: Race, Violence, and Politics in Alabama, 1874–1884" (M.A. thesis, Auburn University, 1973).

— WILLIAM WARREN ROGERS

TURNER, JAMES M[ILTON] (1840–1915), educator, diplomat, and spokesman for Negro claims in the Indian Territory. He was born a slave in St. Louis County, Mo., on May 16, 1840. His father, John Turner, purchased his wife Hannah and son when the boy was four. He learned to read at a secret slave children's school conducted by nuns at the St. Louis Catholic Cathedral, and attended a school headed by the Rev. John Berry Meachum, located in the basement of the First Baptist Church on Almond Street. In his early teens he went to a day tuition school in Brooklyn, Ill., and in his fourteenth year studied at the preparatory school at Oberlin College.

During the Civil War he was a valet to a northern officer, and reportedly was wounded in the hip at the Battle of Shiloh. He limped for the rest of his life. After the war he championed the cause of Negro education and in 1866 was appointed by the Kansas City school board to teach in Missouri's first tax-supported school for Negroes. That fall he took charge of schools in Boonville, Mo. Turner helped to solicit about $5000 from Negro soldiers in the South for a new Negro school in Missouri. This amount, along with the funds collected by the 62nd and 65th Colored Infantry, became the basis for Lincoln Institute, Jefferson City, Mo. (Lincoln University after 1921).

Also active in politics, Turner's matchless oratory helped win an appropriation from the state legislature, almost without a dissenting vote. In 1868 he became a member of Lincoln's board of trustees. In 1870 he urged the state legislature, in view of the voluntary contributions of the colored soldiers, to appropriate funds based on the number of students without regard to color. He was appointed assistant state superintendent of schools, charged with the responsibility of establishing free public schools for Negroes.

He emerged as the state's leading radical politician, chiefly because of his extensive tours on behalf of Lincoln Institute and the Equal Rights League. The American Equal Rights Association, founded in May 1866 with the aim of securing suffrage for Negro men and all women, had as one of its vice-presidents Frederick Douglass.

In 1870 Turner swung 20,000 Negro votes for Governor McClurg. His support of Ulysses S. Grant resulted in an appointment as minister resident and consul-general at Monrovia, Liberia, on March 1, 1871. (Although frequently referred to as the first Negro to enter the diplomatic corps, he was not; Ebenezer Bassett had

been appointed to Haiti in 1869.) During his seven years in Liberia, frequent tribal uprisings and changes of government led him to oppose settlement by American Negroes, especially because of the equatorial climate.

After receptions in Europe, Turner returned home triumphantly in 1878; enthusiastic Negroes hauled his carriage through the streets of St. Louis. Shortly thereafter he married Ella de Burton of St. Joseph's Parish, La. She died on March 2, 1908; there were no children.

During the "Great Exodus" movement of 1879, Turner helped establish a refuge depot in St. Louis for Negroes on the way to Kansas. As president of the "Freedmen's Oklahoma Association" of St. Louis he sent the secretary of the interior a circular promising 160 acres of land to every freedman who would occupy the public lands of Oklahoma.

His eulogy of Dred Scott before the Missouri Historical Society (St. Louis, April 18, 1882), praised the Negroes' contributions in developing the United States, emphasized the significance of Scott in the history of Missouri, and commended the Missouri Historical Society for being the "first" in any state to include a Negro among its records of the history of its state. He also presented an oil painting of Scott to the widow of Theron Bainum, for whom Scott had worked.

In 1886, as attorney for Negro members of the Cherokee nation who had denied them a proportionate share of the $300,000 granted to that nation by Congress for lands taken from them at the end of the Civil War, Turner helped bring the claims to the attention of President Cleveland. In 1889 Congress awarded $75,-000 to be divided among the Cherokee, Delaware, and Shawnee freedmen. He also interested himself in claims for Choctaw and Chickasaw freedmen.

A mishap caused Turner's death on Nov. 1, 1915. While in Ardmore, Okla., he was caught in the debris of a railroad tank car explosion which wrecked half the town. According to the *St. Louis Argus,* his funeral, conducted by Missouri Negro Masons, was the largest in St. Louis for a Negro. Glowing tributes were paid him and he was buried in Father Dickson Cemetery near his birthplace. The *St. Louis Argus* praised particularly his successful fight for Negroes in the Indian Territory.

Irving Dilliard's publications are valuable: "James Milton Turner: A Little Known Benefactor of His People" (*JNH,* Oct. 1934, pp. 372–411); "Dred Scott Eulogized by James Milton Turner, A Historical Observance of the Turner Centenary, 1840–1940" (*JNH,* Jan. 1941, pp. 1–6); and his brief article in the *DAB* (10, Part 1: 66–67). See also N. Webster Moore's "James Milton Turner: Diplomat, Educator, and Defender of Rights" (*Missouri Historical Society Bulletin,* Oct. 1970, pp. 194–201). Primary sources are the *Journal* of the Missouri House and Senate, Catalogues and Minutes of the Lincoln University Board of Trustees (1871–1879), and the Indian Archives, Oklahoma Historical Society, Oklahoma City, Okla. — GOSSIE HAROLD HUDSON

TURNER, NAT (1800–1831), insurrectionary leader. The child of slave parents and the property of Benjamin Turner, he was born in Southampton County, Va., in 1800, probably in October.

The following seems well established: he worked as a field hand in cotton and tobacco production. He was mechanically gifted and deeply religious; as a result of the latter fact he served as a kind of exhorter, preaching on Sundays to slaves and some white people; at least one of these, Ethelred T. Brantley, was baptized by Nat Turner.

Sometime in his childhood his father ran away. This occurred after infancy certainly, for Turner stated that he had a somewhat vague memory of his father. His father was never retaken; it is likely that he became one of the large number of fugitive slaves in the Great Dismal Swamp (which lies in southern Virginia and in northern North Carolina) and who lived there as maroons.

Turner himself fled in 1821 and managed to remain away for one month. He stated that religious compunctions troubled him—perhaps he owed service to his earthly master—and that he therefore returned. He added that other slaves criticized him for returning and told him this had been a foolish thing. In 1822 his owner, Samuel Turner, died and Turner was sold to a neighboring planter, Thomas Moore. It was in 1825 that Turner baptized Brantley and in 1828 that he had a vision telling him it was his duty to struggle against the enslavement of his people. In 1830 Nat Turner was moved to the home of Joseph Travis, whom Mrs. Moore had married. In February 1831 an eclipse of the sun occurred; newspapers of the time reported that it had a marked effect on many people in the United States. Nat Turner considered the phenomenon as a sign to him to commence an uprising against slavery. He seemed then, for the first time, to have mentioned the idea to a few others and they selected July 4—for obvious reasons—as the day to begin the rebellion. Nat, however, stated that he was ill on that day and that therefore the action was postponed.

On Aug. 13, 1831, another "sign" appeared; this was the peculiar bluish-green cast to the sun. The time was at hand and on Saturday evening, Aug. 20, Turner met with two trusted fellow slaves—Hark and Henry—and they planned to have an enlarged meeting the next day, Sunday, Aug. 21. Sometime around noon five slaves, Hark, Henry, Nelson, Jack, and Will, met in accordance with this proposal; at about 2 P.M., Nat joined them. He had not seen Will before concerning the uprising and asked him why he was there. Will replied that freedom was as dear to him as to other men; with this answer Nat was satisfied and bade him welcome.

It was then decided that after midnight on Aug. 21 the uprising would start. Accordingly, at about 2 A.M. on Aug. 22, 1831, these six slaves moved to the attack, beginning at the home of Joseph Travis. There they were joined by another slave, Austin. The uprising began at the Travis home with the killing of five people —three men, a woman, and a child. Thereafter for some forty hours insurrection ravaged Southampton County. Somewhere between sixty and eighty slaves, most of them mounted, participated in the rebellion. The killing of whites was not indiscriminate; in at least one case the home of poor whites—no better off than slaves, in Turner's view—was bypassed. A total of at least fifty-seven white people and perhaps as many as

sixty-five were killed by the rebelling slaves; the victims included men, women, and children.

The slaves met some early minor resistance in the effort and suffered slight casualties, but when news of the uprising reached authorities, state patrols, volunteer military companies, U.S. forces, and the state militia were pressed into service. The rebels, who had never been well armed, having been up and fighting for some forty hours, were exhausted. The military and police forces terminated the outbreak before Turner could really get started for the county seat, Jerusalem (later called Courtland), where arms and ammunition abounded.

Turner managed to hide in a cave in Southampton County; his presence was reported a dozen times in various sections of the country. He never left Southampton and was captured, by accident, on Oct. 30, 1831, by Benjamin Phipps. On Oct. 31 he was turned over to the sheriff of the county and held in prison. From Nov. 1 to Nov. 3 he was interviewed by the court-appointed attorney, Thomas Gray; the text of that interview, as transcribed by Gray, was published as his so-called *Confessions*—a main source for the data on Turner and the rebellion.

On Nov. 5 Turner was tried, found guilty, and sentenced to death by hanging. On Nov. 11, 1831, at about noon, Nat Turner was hanged by Edward Butts, deputy sheriff, in the county. The manner of the disposal of the body is in doubt; where it was interred was kept a secret.

Nat Turner was able to read and write; precisely how he learned is not clear. He lived with a woman he considered his wife—legal marriage, of course, was banned for slaves—and they had children, although exactly how many is not certain. His wife was tormented and beaten while Nat Turner was being sought; after his execution she seems to have been sold south. Descendants of Nat Turner were known to be living in the Midwest in the 1950s.

The contemporary press stated that Nat Turner went to his execution bravely and with head up. His interrogator himself stated that when he tried to get Nat Turner to admit that what he had done was wrong and foolish, Nat arose from his prison cot and stated: "Was not Christ crucified?" After the suppression of the rebels, perhaps as many as 200 Negroes were killed in Southampton.

Turner was described in the offer of $500 reward made by Governor John Floyd of Virginia for his capture: "Nat is between 30 and 35 years old, 5 feet 6 or 8 inches high, weighs between 150 and 160 pounds, rather bright complexion, but not a mulatto, broad shoulders, large flat nose, large eyes, broad flat feet, rather knock-kneed, walks brisk and active, hair on top of head very thin, no beard, except on the upper lip and the top of the chin, a scar on one of his temples, also on the back of his neck, a large knot on one of his bones of right arm, near the wrist, produced by a blow."

The Turner rebellion came at the tail-end of a depression. It was a culmination also of a period of marked slave unrest and agitation—from Denmark Vesey's plot in 1822, David Walker's pamphlet in 1829, to the Virginia Constitutional Convention (1829–1830) and the appearance of Garrison's *Liberator* in January 1831. This period was marked, *prior* to Turner, by the extreme tightening of slave control measures throughout the South and by the reinforcing of United States forts in Virginia and in Louisiana, because of signs of slave unrest.

Although the evidence indicates that Turner acted without outside confederates, it is clear that many other uprisings and plots, and reported plots, occurred immediately after the Turner effort. This was true in literally every slave state and especially throughout Virginia and North Carolina. Hundreds of slaves were arrested and dozens were executed throughout the South until early 1833. In the period after the revolt, slave control measures and laws aimed against free Negroes were further intensified.

In Virginia the uprising led to intensive debate about the wisdom of slavery, but legends that the rulers of Virginia seriously considered emancipation are exactly that—legends. The uprising came as a kind of climax of a whole decade of slave agitation in the United States, and indeed in the Western Hemisphere, and it served as a catalyst for the ensuing generation of heightened antislavery agitation and intensified proslavery defense —the latter exemplified in Thomas R. Dew's defense of slavery, published in 1832 and directly provoked by the Turner outbreak and the discussion it induced.

The literature on Nat Turner is extensive. A fairly full bibliography up to 1936 will be found in Herbert Aptheker's master's thesis, published in 1966 as *Nat Turner's Slave Rebellion.* The historical novel by William Styron, *The Confessions of Nat Turner* (1967), was a bestseller and Pulitzer Prize winner. It provoked *Ten Black Writers Respond* edited by John Henrik Clarke (1968) and the detailed critique in Aptheker's *Afro-American History: The Modern Era* (1971, pp. 80–95). A massive study is Henry Irving Tragle (ed.), *The Southampton Slave Revolt of 1831: A Compilation of Source Material* (1971). See also *The Fires of Jubilee: Nat Turner's Fierce Rebellion,* by Stephen B. Oates (1975). The article by James G. deRoulhac Hamilton in the *DAB* ([1936], 10, Part 1:69–70) is representative of accepted scholarship at the time of its publication. — HERBERT APTHEKER

TWILIGHT, ALEXANDER L[UCIUS] (1795–1857), educator, preacher, and legislator. Born in Bradford, Vt., the third of six children of Mary and Ichabod Twilight, free Negroes, Alexander was indentured to a neighboring farmer at an early age. He saved enough to purchase the last year of his indentureship in 1815. It is not known how he obtained enough education to be admitted in the same year to Randolph Academy, where he completed by 1821 his secondary education and the first two years of the college curriculum. In the latter year he entered Middlebury College and received his B.A. degree in 1823. Twilight was thus the first known Negro college graduate, having preceded Edward Jones at Amherst College and John Brown Russwurm at Bowdoin College, both in 1826.

Twilight spent most of the next thirty-one years (1826–1857) in Vermont. He began his teaching career in Peru, N.Y., studied theology, and was granted a li-

cense to preach by the Champlain Presbytery in Plattsburgh, N.Y. At the age of thirty-four he accepted an invitation to take over the preceptorship of the Orleans County Grammar School at Brownington, Vt. From 1829 to 1834 he was not only the principal of the school but also minister of the local church, whose members worshipped on the second floor of the school. The increased enrollment necessitated the construction, under his direction, of a new building, "Athenian Hall." A three-story granite building, perhaps the largest academy building in the northernmost part of the state, constructed "without financial backing from the county or even much support from within the village itself—[it] testified to the raw power, physical and spiritual, of the man." He retired from the school in 1847 and taught in nearby villages until 1852, when he returned as headmaster of Brownington Academy and local minister. After one year he resigned from both positions but continued to direct the grammar school until October 1855, when a stroke left him paralyzed. He died in June 1857, and was buried close to the church, the grammar school, and the granite academy he had built. He was survived by his widow, Mary Ladd Merrill Twilight, whom he had married in 1826. She lived until 1878 and was buried beside the remains of her husband. It is not known whether they had children.

In addition to Alexander Twilight's remarkable career as educator and minister, he had the distinction of being one of the first American Negroes elected to a state legislature, serving at Montpelier, Vt. (1836–1837).

This sketch is based on the only known published account of Twilight's life: "The Iron-willed Black Schoolmaster and his Granite Academy," by Gregor Hileman (*Middlebury College News Letter,* Spring 1974, pp. 6–26). The article contains footnotes, photographs of Alexander Twilight and his wife, their gravestones, Athenian Hall, and other buildings.

— CLARENCE G. CONTEE, SR.

TYLER, RALPH WALDO (1859–1921), reporter, editor, and government official. He was born in Columbus, Ohio, one of eight children of James S. and Maria McAfee Tyler. While a young man, Tyler held a number of jobs—teacher, janitor, clerk, postal carrier, and stenographer. In 1888 he joined the staff of the *Columbus* (Ohio) *Dispatch* first as a stenographer; as the editor's secretary, he became acquainted with all aspects of newspaper work. Tyler also ran a barbershop for a few years to supplement his newspaper income. While on the *Dispatch* staff, he began to take an interest in Ohio political affairs, especially legislation about and appointments for Negroes. Through Jeremiah "Jere" Brown, a Negro state legislator from Cuyahoga County, he channeled information concerning appointments and legislation. Active in the Republican party, Tyler did not at first seek or allow himself to be considered for office. In 1893 he began a correspondence with George A. Myers, owner of the Hollenden Barber Shop in Cleveland and a power in Negro Republican politics in Ohio through his friendship with Marcus A. Hanna. Over the next three decades Myers often served as confidant, advisor, and backer of Tyler. In 1896 Tyler's attendance at the Republican National Convention in St. Louis provided his first real journalistic break. When the regular *Dispatch* reporter became intoxicated and was unable to report the proceedings, Tyler's articles were published, although under the byline of the regular reporter. Through his friendship with Myers, who was delegate at the convention, Tyler became a supporter of the Hanna faction of the Republican party.

The journalistic experience served Tyler well, for in the ensuing years offers came from Negro newspapers in the North for his contributions. When in 1905 the *Columbus Dispatch* came under new ownership, Tyler left to work on the *Ohio State Journal* (Columbus), and he continued his extracurricular writings. During December 1905, for example, he wrote a pamphlet on race relations using the pseudonym of Olga Louise Cadijah.

During the early years of the twentieth century Tyler began to seek a political appointment. In 1906 he actively campaigned for an appointment as consul in a South American country, garnering letters of support from the Rev. Washington Gladden, the Rev. James Poindexter, George A. Myers, and Sen. Charles Dick. In the spring of 1907 Pres. Theodore Roosevelt, on the advice of Booker T. Washington, appointed Tyler auditor of the Navy Department. His duties were to settle all accounts of the department, including those of the secretary of the navy. He retained the post through the remainder of the Roosevelt and the Taft administrations, and the early days of the Wilson administration. His abilities in the office brought Judge Robert H. Terrell of Washington, D.C., to remark that his observations during thirty years led him to believe that Tyler's performance compared favorably with that of white and colored officeholders.

Shortly after leaving office in 1913 Tyler served widely as the national organizer for Booker T. Washington's National Negro Business League. In 1914 the American Press Association syndicated Tyler's columns documenting his observations of conditions in the South. While in the post of organizer for the league, he worked closely with Emmett J. Scott, Booker T. Washington's personal secretary. Tyler returned to active political participation in February 1916, when he filed petitions for delegate-at-large to the Republican National Convention from Ohio. Although unsuccessful in his candidacy, he made a respectable showing at the polls, receiving over 30,000 votes. Tyler's work with the Business League, especially in the South, supplied him with an opportunity to undertake a personal study of Negro migration to the North, which he reported in magazines, newspapers, and publications of social service organizations.

Following the United States declaration of war against Germany in April 1917, Tyler returned to Washington, D.C., where he became secretary of the National Colored Soldiers Comfort Committee. In June 1918 Emmett J. Scott, special assistant to the secretary of war, convened a conference of Negro editors which called for the sending of a Negro newspaperman to Europe to report on the activities of Negro troops. On Sept. 16, 1918, the Committee on Public Information announced Tyler's appointment as the first and only official Negro war correspondent in the war. Assigned

to Gen. John J. Pershing's staff, for the next four months he wrote from the Metz region. His reports from the front were sent to the Committee on Public Information, which turned them over to Scott for editing and distribution to Negro newspapers throughout the nation. Tyler's firsthand enthusiastic reports of the gallantry and heroism of Negro units contributed to the morale of Stateside Negroes. Although he was a civilian correspondent, Tyler's job was not without hazard, for in a letter home he mentioned: "shells flying about him . . . got a lacerated hand, run over by a truck, and lost my eyeglasses." His three sons—Waldo, Ralph Jr., and Harold—were also at the front.

Upon his return to Ohio, Tyler was given a dinner by the Employers League of Columbus. During much of 1919, in speaking engagements throughout the North he defended and extolled the role of the Negro soldier in the First World War. In April 1919 he became editor of the *Cleveland Advocate,* a leading Negro newspaper in the North, and contributed articles to Chicago and New York newspapers. The speaking tour also presented him with an opportunity to test a newly passed Ohio civil rights law. During the spring of 1919 he was refused service by a Springfield, Ohio, restaurant owner on account of color. Tyler brought suit against the owner through Sully James, an NAACP lawyer, and was awarded $100 in damages. Tyler further added to his editorial duties at this time by taking an associate editorship with the *Columbus Ohio State Monitor.*

At 1 A.M. on June 2, 1921, Tyler died of apoplexy. An obituary in a Cincinnati paper stated: "He was strongest in leadership and it is a matter of regret that his race has not more conservative thoughtful men in their directing groups. Always he preferred reasonableness to force."

He had died at his home, 175 South Champion Ave., Columbus. His funeral was held there on June 4, and he was buried in Greenlawn Cemetery. He was survived by his widow, three sons, two brothers, and two sisters (*Columbus Dispatch,* June 2, 1921, p. 2; *Cleveland Gazette,* June 11, 1921, p. 1).

The fullest published account is in Emmett J. Scott's *The American Negro in the World War* (1919). Tyler's private and political views are best documented in his correspondence with George A. Myers, preserved in the George A. Myers Papers at the Ohio Historical Society, Columbus. His talents as a reporter, editor, and essayist are evident in the files of the *Columbus Dispatch, Ohio State Journal, Cleveland Advocate,* and the leading Negro newspapers of the early twentieth century. — FRANK R. LEVSTIK

VANN, ROBERT LEE (1879–1940), newspaper publisher, lawyer, entrepreneur, politician, civil rights leader, and government official. Vann was born on Aug. 27, 1879, in Ahoskie, Hertford County, N.C. His mother, Lucy Peoples, was the daughter of Fletcher and Martilla (Holloman) Peoples, ex-slaves who eked out a living by operating a general store in Ahoskie. His mother, who worked as a cook for the Albert Vann family, called her son Robert Lee in honor of his great-grandfather and Vann, the name of the family for which she worked. Robert's father is unknown.

Robert enjoyed playing with boys of prominent white

families in nearby Harrellsville, finished Springfield Colored High School in 1892, worked as a waiter in Boston and graduated as valedictorian of Baptist-run Waters Training School in Winton, N.C., in 1901. While a student at Wayland Academy, Richmond, Va. (1901–1903), he was influenced by John T. Mitchell, editor of the *Richmond Planet,* who opposed disfranchisement and virulent Jim Crowism. With the aid of a $100 Charles Avery scholarship, he entered Western University of Pennsylvania in Pittsburgh as a sophomore in 1903. He worked during summers, gained a reputation as an orator and debater, and served for two years as a regular contributor to the school newspaper; in his senior year he was its editor-in-chief, the first Negro to achieve this position. He graduated as class poet in 1906, graduated from the Law School in June 1909, and passed the bar examination on Dec. 18, 1909. On Feb. 17, 1910, he married Jessie E. Matthews. To supplement his income, he served as counsel for the *Pittsburgh Courier,* organized by a small group of Negroes in March 1910 and incorporated on May 10, 1910. In the fall he became editor, treasurer, and legal counsel, positions which he held until his death in 1940.

With Ira Lewis as business manager, he developed the *Courier* into one of the leading Negro newspapers of his era. Its crusades against segregation and discrimination, and for fuller recognition of Negroes in the white press, increased circulation as did the migration of sizable numbers of Negroes from the South during World War I to the rapidly growing city of Pittsburgh.

Meanwhile Vann used his influence among Negro voters to win appointment in March 1918 as fourth assistant city solicitor, the highest position held by a Negro in the municipal government. His wholehearted support of Negro participation in the war probably accounts for the fact that he, unlike A. Philip Randolph, Chandler Owen, W. E. B. Du Bois, and Robert S. Abbott, among others, escaped government scrutiny and criticism.

Otherwise, Vann's editorial policies were frequently inconsistent. He opposed and supported a boycott against Kaufmann's, the oldest department store in Pittsburgh. From 1919 to 1922 he opposed strikes by AFL and other unions seeking recognition and reduction of the twelve-hour day. In 1925 he supported Randolph's attempt to gain recognition of the Brotherhood of Sleeping Car Porters. Then in 1928 Vann demanded Randolph's resignation, asserting that his Socialist past impeded his achieving an agreement with the Pullman Company. Andrew Buni, the authoritative biographer of Vann, suggested that the change in policies may have resulted in a loss of circulation while at the same time Abbott's *Defender* had begun to support the porters' cause. Whereas in 1917 Vann had condemned the Houston rioters, he later demanded full pardon, not merely commutation of sentence.

The decade of the 1920s laid the foundation for the *Courier*'s leadership among Negro newspapers in the 1930s. From 1925 to 1929 Vann devoted most of his time to the paper, published columns by George Schuyler, Joel A. Rogers, and Walter White. Knowledgeable writers reported on the rising participation of Negroes in sports. The *Courier* joined the Associated Negro

Press in 1925 and used the services of a promising reporter, Louis Lautier, the syndicate's Washington correspondent. Wilburt Holloway's cartoons and photographs of beauty queens and socialites, suggested by Ira Lewis, attracted many readers.

Not all of Vann's crusading was productive. In 1924, for example, he futilely advocated enforcement of the second section of the Fourteenth Amendment. In the early 1930s his vigorous denunciation of the "Amos 'n Andy" radio program was weakened by some Negro leaders' enjoyment of this lampooning of Negro life. Support of Marcus Garvey and his exclusive articles in "America's Best Weekly" during 1930 brought few additional readers because of greater interest in the Depression. The *Courier*'s policy on the "Scottsboro Boys" in the early 1930s alienated many readers: Vann and Schuyler insisted that participation by the "Communist-led" International Labor Defense jeopardized efforts to save the accused from execution.

The increased circulation (nearly 55,000 in city and national editions in 1926) required a larger plant, costing over $100,000, which opened in 1929 at 2628 Centre Ave. Vann's enthusiastic support of Ethiopia after the Italian invasion of Oct. 26, 1935, of Joe Louis, and his reporting of Jesse Owens's four gold medals and Hitler's contempt for Negroes at the 1936 Olympic games helped increase circulation to a quarter of a million in 1938. An outside audit certified sales of almost 150,000 during the ensuing years. In 1936, the year before the *Courier*'s silver anniversary, holders of its common stock received the first dividend in seven years.

The gathering storm of World War II prompted Vann to fight vigorously in the *Courier* for better treatment of Negroes in the armed services, a struggle he had begun as early as World War I. He protested against the demeaning duties assigned to Negroes in the four Regular Army regiments, the small number of Negro officers, and the widespread publicity given to the alleged failure of Negro combat officers in World War I. He assigned Percival L. Prattis, then city editor of the *Courier* and a veteran of World War I, to publicize these protests. Vann also engaged the cooperation of attorneys Charles H. Houston and Louis R. Mehlinger (both veterans of World War I), and Louis Lautier, the *Courier*'s capable Washington-based correspondent, to advocate a separate Negro division. Vann and Prattis further supported the Committee on Participation of Negroes in the National Defense Program, of which Rayford W. Logan was chairman and which Vann's biographer, Buni, erroneously calls "Vann's Committee." This publicity, continued after Vann's death, helped the *Courier* maintain a leading position among Negro newspapers.

In politics Vann was a pragmatist. At first a Republican, in 1921 he was not reappointed assistant solicitor and was defeated for judge of the Allegheny Court of Common Pleas. Further disenchanted by the policies of Presidents Harding, Coolidge, and Hoover, he supported Franklin D. Roosevelt in the 1932 election; Roosevelt rewarded him with the position of special assistant to the U.S. attorney-general. But the attorney-general assigned him to insignificant duties, and Vann perceived earlier than did some members of the "Black

Cabinet'' and some historians the limited achievements of the New Deal for Negroes. He devoted instead more time to supporting Democrats in Pennsylvania, where in 1935 he helped obtain the enactment of a state equal rights law he had sponsored as early as 1918. He resigned from the Department of Justice as of January 1936. In 1940 he supported the Republican candidate Wendell Willkie for president.

The financial success of the *Courier* was due in large measure to Vann's editorship and Ira Lewis's business management. Vann was less successful in his own business enterprises. A firm believer in the ''American Dream,'' for Negroes as well as for whites, and a staunch supporter of Booker T. Washington's self-help programs and National Negro Business League, Vann had neither training nor sufficient capital. His monthly magazine *The Competitor: The National Magazine,* founded in January 1920, failed after eighteen months. He lost additional sums in other business enterprises before and during the Great Depression.

As with most other Negro lawyers of his era, his practice was confined largely to unremunerative criminal cases. He did make, however, a not insignificant contribution: in 1921 he advanced the then relatively novel argument that pretrial newspaper accounts prejudiced a murder trial for which he sought commutation of the sentence of death. Although he lost the case, extensive coverage in the *Courier* substantially increased sales.

In January 1940 Vann was operated on for abdominal cancer and he died of cancer in Shadyside Hospital, Philadelphia, on Oct. 24, 1940. He was buried in Homewood Cemetery, and survived by his widow, Mrs. Jessie Vann.

A bronze plaque was placed on the wall in the entranceway of the *Pittsburgh Courier:* ''In Loving Memory of Robert L. Vann: Publisher, Lawyer, Statesman, Brilliant Editor, Loyal Friend, Fearless Champion of Rights. Erected by His Admiring Employees Who Profited Greatly by His Precepts and Example.''

Public schools were named for him in Ahoskie, N.C., and the Hill District of Pittsburgh. Scholarships were established at Virginia Union University and the University of Pittsburgh in his name, from bequests Vann left to the schools. At Virginia Union University, the Robert L. Vann Memorial Tower was erected. And on Oct. 10, 1943, the Liberty Ship *Robert L. Vann* was launched in Portland, Me., taking its place alongside two other vessels named after prominent Negroes, the *Booker T. Washington* and the *George Washington Carver.*

It was as a newspaper editor and publisher that Vann made his most important contribution. Along with T. Thomas Fortune, William Monroe Trotter, Robert S. Abbott, Carl Murphy, Roscoe Dungee, and P. B. Young, Sr., he was among the foremost Negro newspaper editors of the first half of the twentieth century. Like them, he used his paper as a vehicle generally to support the advancement of worthwhile causes. They contributed in no small measure to changing despondency at the nadir—the turn of the century—to the hopes that preceded the rising expectations after mid-century. They were, of course, aided by dramatic changes resulting primarily from the two World Wars. The Negro press held an honored place in the struggle for equal rights.

The authoritative biography is Andrew Buni's *Robert L. Vann of the Pittsburgh Courier: Politics and Black Journalism* (1974). — RAYFORD W. LOGAN

VARICK, JAMES (1750–1827), founder and first bishop of the African Methodist Episcopal Zion church. He was born in Orange County, near Newburgh, N.Y. His mother was a slave in the household of the Varicks (Van Varcks), but later manumitted. His father, Richard Varick, was born and baptized in the Dutch Church of Hackensack, N.J., in 1720. James grew up with his parents in New York City, where he may have attended the Free School for Negroes near what became Nassau Street between Cedar and Liberty Streets. By the close of the American Revolutionary War, James had learned the trade of shoemaking and was operating his own shop. When Varick was about sixteen he joined the famous (white) John Street Methodist Episcopal Church, where he was licensed to preach. Racial prejudice in New York City, which compelled Negroes to sit in the galleries or rear seats of churches, in 1796 led James Varick with some thirty Negroes to withdraw from John Street and form the first colored church in New York City. Meanwhile, around 1790, he had married Aurelia Jones, who became the mother of their seven children, four sons and three daughters, four of whom survived.

On Sept. 7, 1800, James Varick and his followers dedicated a church, ''Zion,'' at the corner of Church and Leonard Streets, a few minutes' walk from Wall Street. He and two others became the first three colored deacons ordained in New York State (1806). Varick, meanwhile, supported his family by working as a shoemaker and tobacco cutter. He also ran a classroom in the family home, 42 Orange (later Baxter) St., and in Zion Church. It was in Zion Church that Varick preached the ''Sermon of Thanksgiving on the Occasion of the Abolition of the African Slave Trade'' (Jan. 1, 1808). He was the first chaplain of the New York African Society for Mutual Relief, organized in 1810; probably active in Boyer Lodge No. 1, the first African Masonic lodge in New York State, established in 1812.

He was also one of the vice-presidents of the New York African Bible Society, established on Jan. 17, 1817, and worked to establish the African Methodist Episcopal (Zion) Church, New Haven, Conn., in 1818. He was a member of a committee of Negro businessmen and preachers who petitioned the New York State Constitutional Convention (1821) to grant Negroes the right to vote. Along with Alexander Crummell, Samuel Cornish, John B. Russwurm, Richard Allen, and others, he helped establish (March 1827) *Freedom's Journal,* the first Negro newspaper in the United States. It operated from facilities in Zion Church. Varick and Cornish were among early Negro leaders who opposed the colonization movement. Varick was elected the first bishop of the AME Zion church at its first annual conference, and consecrated on July 30, 1822; he was reelected at the second annual conference in 1824. It was at his Zion Church that thanksgiving was celebrated on July 4, 1827, after New York enacted final emancipation of Negro slaves in the state.

Two weeks later, on July 22, 1827, Varick died in his home. After funeral services in Zion Church, he was buried in the Colored Union Cemetery (later Woodlawn Cemetery) in New Windsor, a mile from Newburgh. His ashes were later transferred to the crypt of Mother Zion Church, Harlem.

The full name, African Methodist Episcopal Zion church, was not adopted until the General Conference of 1848. Both the organization and the name Zion resulted in large measure from the activities of James Varick. The first church, organized in 1796 and built in 1800, was called Zion. When incorporated in 1801, the organization bore the name of "The African Methodist Episcopal Church in New York." Varick was one of the principal proponents of separation from the (white) Methodist Episcopal church and the African Methodist Episcopal church founded by Richard Allen, Absalom Jones, and others. Partly because the AME church is better known than the AME Zion church, Varick is less well known than are Allen and Jones, for example. It was, however, like many other Negro church organizations, "after emancipation the center of Negro social life" (W. E. B. Du Bois, *The Negro American Family* [1908], p. 130). "For the Negro masses, in their social and moral isolation in American society, the Negro church community has been a nation within a nation" (E. Franklin Frazier, *The Negro Church in America* [1963], pp. 44–45). It was also "the meeting place for business organizations . . . the platform of our first teachers . . . the only classroom that black children ever knew in a number of cities and towns," and the advertising place for "black businessmen and professionals" (William J. Walls, *The African Methodist Episcopal Zion Church: Reality of the Black Church* [1974], p. 536).

The best source for the career of James Varick is Walls's *The African Methodist Episcopal Zion Church . . .* (1974, esp. pp. 43–95). An engraving of Varick is reproduced on the front of the jacket and page 8. See also the short sketch by Harris Elwood Starr in the *DAB* ([1936], 10, Part 1:225–26). — RAYFORD W. LOGAN

VASHON, GEORGE BOYER (1824–1878), attorney, educator, and writer. He was born on July 25, 1824, in Carlisle, Pa., the third child and only son of the abolitionist John Bethune Vashon. The family moved to Pittsburgh, Pa., where in 1838 George Vashon was secretary of the first Juvenile Anti-Slavery Society in America. He entered Oberlin College at age sixteen and in 1844 earned the first bachelor of arts degree conferred by Oberlin on a Negro. While in college, Vashon taught school in Chillicothe, Ohio, where he won the community's admiration and the gratitude of John Mercer Langston, his pupil, whom Vashon personally enrolled at Oberlin in March 1844. Returning to Pittsburgh, he studied law under Judge Walter Forward until 1847 when he applied to take the bar examination. This application was denied and his subsequent "show cause" order rejected on the grounds that colored people were not citizens. Discouraged by such discrimination, Vashon left for Haiti, but stopping in New York City, he took the bar examination and on Jan. 11, 1848, he became the first lawyer of his race in the state of New

York. Vashon spent thirty months teaching at the Collège Faustin in Port-au-Prince, Haiti, returning in the late summer of 1850 to practice law for four years in Syracuse, N.Y., where he wrote his remarkable epic poem "Vincent Ogé" (1853).

From the fall of 1854 until 1857 he was professor of belle-lettres and mathematics at New York Central College in McGrawville, N.Y. He then moved back to Pittsburgh, and in 1857 married Susan Paul Smith of Boston, a teacher who was fourteen years his junior. They had seven children. Vashon did not reapply for admission to the Pennsylvania bar, but served as a principal and teacher in Pittsburgh in the colored public schools (1858–1863) and at Avery College (1864–1867). He was the first Negro teacher at Howard University, serving during the one year (1867–1868) that the evening school existed at that time. Instead of a fixed salary he received as compensation the tuition paid by the nine students in his class. According to the *Oberlin Review* (Nov. 20, 1878), Vashon was a solicitor for the Freedmen's Bureau in Washington, D.C., in the fall of 1867 and held other responsible positions there. In 1869 he was delegate from Rhode Island and chairman of the committee on credentials at the national convention of Colored Men of America in the capital, and he joined the national executive committee of this group in 1870. He taught at Alcorn University, Rodney, Miss. (1874–1878), and died there of yellow fever, Oct. 5, during the epidemic of 1878. He was buried somewhere on the campus of Alcorn University in an unmarked grave.

Vashon was a brilliant scholar, skillful in Greek, Latin, Hebrew, German, and French, and a fine essayist and poet. His writings include learned disquisitions on the history, geography, and mythology of the Nile River; on the legal and historical grounds for Negro citizenship; on the advances of astronomy; and on the civilizing benefits of literature and position papers arguing eloquently for universal suffrage and against compulsory Negro emigration. His poems are "A Life-Day" (1864), an allegory of southern history denouncing race prejudice; a commemorative "Ode on the Proclamation of the Fifteenth Amendment" (1870); and his masterpiece, the 139-line "Vincent Ogé," which treats the Haitian insurrection of 1790–1791 as a symbolic universal racial conflict in a perpetually chaotic world. Vashon High School in St. Louis was named in recognition of his many achievements, notably in education.

Joan R. Sherman's *Invisible Poets* (1974) offers a documented biography, criticism of poetry, and a bibliography. Benjamin Brawley's *Early Negro American Writers* (1935) reprints "A Life-Day" and "Vincent Ogé." See also Rayford W. Logan's *Howard University, The First Hundred Years, 1867–1967* (1969), and Walter Dyson's *Howard University . . . A History, 1867–1940* (1941). — JOAN R. SHERMAN

VENTURE, [BROTEER], [SMITH] (1729?–1805), "black Bunyan." He was born a slave in Guinea, West Africa, the eldest son of Saungm Furro, prince of the tribe of Dukandarra. At the age of eight Broteer was renamed Venture by a speculating slaver from the New England colonies. Venture toiled for James Mumford, Fisher's Island, N.Y., and Thomas Stanton, Stonington,

Conn., marrying when he was twenty-two another slave, Meg, about his own age. When he was thirty-one, he was sold to Col. Oliver Smith, also of Stonington, from whom he took his surname. Five years later he purchased his freedom for £71, two shillings. Moving to Long Island, income from feats of his prodigious labor enabled him to purchase his wife for £40, his daughter Hannah for £44, his sons Solomon and Cuff for $400; he also redeemed three other slaves. When he was forty-seven he sold his holdings and moved back to Connecticut, where he again achieved renown for his labor. In 1798, when he was sixty-nine, his *A Narrative of the Life and Adventures of Venture . . . Related by Himself* was printed. A few insignificant details of his life until his death from infirmities and old age on Sept. 19, 1805, are based on tradition. He was buried in the cemetery adjoining the First Congregational Church, East Haddam, Conn. He was survived by his wife, who died on Dec. 17, 1809. Stone slabs marked their graves.

As in the case of most slave narratives, Venture's autobiography must be read with considerable caution. Venture's feats were indeed prodigious, according to his account, first published in 1798. When he was nine years old he had, he wrote, successfully defended himself from attack by one of his master's sons and three assistants. After he voluntarily surrendered, he was suspended from a gallows for an hour during which he was whipped by three dozen whips from a peach orchard. He betrayed a confederate with whom he had planned an escape by boat down the Mississippi. By cleaning shoes and boots, catching muskrats and minks, raising potatoes and fishing at night, "and odd spells," he accumulated "currency including 2,000 coppers" which he carried, along with £5 of his wife's money to his master at Stonington Point. He carried a barrel of molasses on his shoulders for two miles, seven bushels of salt on his knees for two or three rods. After an altercation of his wife and himself with the master's wife, his master hit him on the head with a club two feet long and as large as a chair post. Venture was "badly wounded"; he still bore the scar in 1796. He complained to a justice of the peace; his master and his master's brother attempted to beat him again. Venture "immediately stamped them both under me, laid one of them across the other, and stamped them both with my feet what I would." During six months he cut and corded 400 cords of wood and threshed out seventy-five bushels of grain. On a whaling voyage of seven months with Colonel Smith, the vessel returned laden with 400 barrels of oil. Eleven weeks of work at East Haddam enabled him to purchase ten acres of land at Haddam Neck. He continued to acquire land, some seventy acres, and the sale of his farm gave him enough money to build his own house. He owned no fewer than twenty boats, canoes, and sail vessels. Despite being cheated by white men, he owned in 1796 more than 100 acres of land and three habitable houses.

Regardless of Venture's veracity about his prodigious feats, his *Narrative* is valuable for its portrayal of the life of slave and free Negroes in Connecticut during much of the eighteenth century.

Venture's *Narrative* is available in *Five Black Lives*

. . . with an Introduction by Arna Bontemps (1971, pp. 4–25), followed by "Traditions of Venture Known as Venture Smith," compiled by H. M. Selden (pp. 26–34), and in *Early Negro Writing 1760–1837, Selected and Introduced by Dorothy Porter* (1971, pp. 538–58). There is an abridged version in Sidney Kaplan's *The Black Presence in the Era of the American Revolution 1770–1800* (1973, pp. 220–23). — RAYFORD W. LOGAN

VESEY, DENMARK (c. 1767–1822), insurrection leader. A free Negro, Vesey's birthplace is unknown: some writers suggest Africa; others, St. Thomas, Danish West Indies. In 1781 he was among 390 St. Thomas slaves delivered to St-Domingue by Capt. Joseph Vesey. Impressed by the lad's intelligence and appearance, Vesey made a pet of him, but sold him. Probably feigning epilepsy in the sugar fields, Denmark was returned as "unsound" on Vesey's next stopover at St-Domingue. For two years as the captain's personal servant he experienced the slave trade on voyages to Africa and among the West Indies. In 1783 Captain Vesey settled in Charleston, gave up the slave trade, and became active in civic affairs. Following the great 1791 uprising, many of St.-Domingue's slaveowners found refuge in Charleston, and Vesey's home was a center of relief activity. Here Denmark absorbed details of the revolt which was to become his model and rallying cry.

Thanks to a winning 1799 lottery ticket of $1500 he purchased his liberty and opened a carpentry shop. A master at his craft, he gradually acquired wealth and prestige; still, his wives and children were slaves. The idea of a liberation war, stimulated by the insurrection in St-Domingue which had led to the independence of Haiti (1804), obsessed him, and he had the freedom of movement to implement his dream among plantation slaves over a vast area. In the city itself he often engaged whites in argument while Negroes were present, and exhorted the slaves to claim their equality, stressing incendiary verses from the Bible in casual street encounters. An increasingly charismatic figure, he galvanized the congregation of the African Methodist church with his impassioned sermons. Eventually he was regarded with messianic awe. He read antislavery pamphlets aloud, interpreted the 1819 congressional debate over the admission of Missouri, and quoted from the fiery addresses of Sen. Rufus King to show that Negroes were illegally held as slaves.

By the end of 1821 he had worked out his battle plan in his home, 20 Bull St., and selected his leaders: Ned and Rolla Bennett, slaves of the governor; Peter Poyas, a ship carpenter; and Gullah Jack, "a man of magic" whose followers believed him bulletproof. The uprising was set for July 14: Charleston's whites would be vacationing, there would be no moon, and plantation hands —in town on a Sunday—would arouse no suspicion. At midnight the secret army would move, striking at all key points, seizing arsenals and blocking bridges. Vesey himself would lead a unit to the main guardhouse while others galloped through town killing whites to keep them from giving the alarm. During May the slave conspiracy grew to 9000—embracing a wide territory.

When one of his followers forgot Vesey's injunction

against approaching any household slaves, the plot began to unfold. The authorities moved swiftly, but Vesey countered by pushing the date forward to June 16. Then a second house slave informed. At once Charleston bristled. Governor Bennett created a new regiment; troops covered every point that might be attacked. Even so, only two blocks from the center of military preparations, Vesey tried to summon his army from the countryside. When his messenger was turned back by a patrol unit, it was clear that nothing could be attempted on the sixteenth. All lists were burned, and all who had gathered were sent home to await orders. The next night ten were arrested, including Ned and Rolla Bennett and Peter Poyas. Vesey went into hiding. On June 19 the trials began, in a courthouse ringed by troops. No Negro could get within two blocks of it. No whites except the owners and lawyers of the accused were allowed inside. The prisoners could not see all their accusers.

On June 20, under torture, one man broke and the hunt for Vesey was on. Police searched Charleston inch by inch. On the night of June 22 they arrested him at the home of a former wife. Admitting nothing, he insisted on challenging the witnesses himself. On June 28 the chief judge delivered the verdict. "It is difficult," he declared, "to imagine what *infatuation* could have prompted you to attempt an enterprise so wild and visionary. You were a free man; were comparatively wealthy; and enjoyed every comfort. . . . You had, therefore, much to risk, and little to gain." At 6 A.M. on the July 2, 1822, composed and silent, Vesey and five associates were hanged before an immense crowd. Gullah Jack had planned to liberate the condemned as they were led to the gallows, but he was thwarted by a series of new arrests. A few days later he himself was taken. As a lesson to other slaves, his execution was staged on "The Lines," a high rise of ground.

Suspecting all its Negroes, not knowing where or how many weapons Vesey had hidden, Charleston asked for and received federal troops. On July 26, twenty-two Negroes were hanged at "The Lines." Four more died on July 30, another on Aug. 9. A total of thirty-eight were released for lack of evidence, fifteen acquitted and discharged, forty-three sentenced to be deported, and thirty-five hanged. The informers received their freedom plus a lifetime annual stipend. Early that winter the South Carolina Assembly adopted severe measures aimed at preventing future outbreaks. The Negro Seamen Act, forbidding free Negroes to enter South Carolina ports, was soon declared unconstitutional, yet it continued to be enforced and brought South Carolina's sectionalist mood to a boil. In the years that followed, some key figures in the 1822 drive against Vesey became prominent among the South's most violent secessionists: James Hamilton, chief prosecutor of Vesey; Robert Trumbull and Nathaniel Heyward, members of the Vesey tribunal; Robert Hayne, commander of the special June 16 regiment; and John L. Wilson, whose slave betrayed the June 16 plot.

At first various official versions of the insurrection were widely circulated; afterward news of the inflammatory event was suppressed. Elsewhere, however, Vesey became a symbol of martyrdom in the cause of liberty. His plot is said to have inspired John Brown; Frederick Douglass filled the ranks of Lincoln's first colored regiment with the battle cry: "Remember Denmark Vesey of Charleston."

The "oratorio" by Waldemar Hille and Aaron Kramer, *Denmark Vesey,* has been widely performed. *The Trial Record of Denmark Vesey* is available, with an introduction by John O. Killens (1970), who has also written a fictionalized biography, *Great Gettin' Up Morning* (1972). The standard work is John Lofton's *Insurrection in South Carolina, The Turbulent World of Denmark Vesey* (1964). See also Richard C. Wade's "The Vesey Plot: A Reconsideration" (*Negro Digest* 15 [Feb. 1966]: 28–41). The sketch by Anne King Gregoire in the *DAB* ([1936], 10, Part 1:258–59) makes the odd comment that "In the face of the intense excitement that prevailed, it was considered remarkable that the customary machinery of the law functioned and that no unusual punishments were inflicted." — AARON KRAMER

VODERY, WILL [HENRY BENNETT] (1884–1951), composer and arranger. Vodery was a native of Philadelphia. His father, Will Vodery, was an instructor of Greek at Pennsylvania's Lincoln University. Young Will, who is said to have inherited his talent from his mother, played piano for his Sunday School when he was nine years old. Four years later he was his church's organist, in the interim having composed his first song, "My Country, I Love Thee." Upon graduation from Philadelphia's Central High School in 1902, young Vodery entered the Hugh A. Clark University in Pennsylvania to study music. There, working with the German-trained Louis Koemmennich, he began the serious study of the rudiments of his profession. Two years later he was in New York City embarking on a professional career. His first job was making arrangements for the M. Whitmark & Sons musical *A Trip to Africa*. The introduction to Whitmark had come through comedian Bert Williams, who had become aware of Vodery's ability during his frequent stays at the Philadelphia boarding house run by the Vodery family.

In 1905 Vodery worked as custodian of the Theodore Thomas Chicago Symphony Orchestra. When not discharging his duties he studied symphony under the concert manager, Frederick Stock. It was also while in Chicago that Vodery wrote one of the most popular hit songs of the day, "After the Ball Was Over." Returning to New York in 1907, he wrote the title song for *The Oyster Man,* starring Ernest Hogan, arranged the music for Williams's and George Walker's *Bandana Land,* and traveled abroad as music director with the production. More songwriting and the management of a stock company in Washington, D.C., brought Vodery into partnership with J. Lubrie Hill, another great Negro showman of the Williams and Walker company.

The partners worked together on Hill's hit show *My Friend from Dixie,* which was seen in New York by Florenz Ziegfeld. Impressed, the celebrated impressario bought the finale and incorporated it into his *Follies* (1911). Vodery also wrote the music for *Dr. Beans from Boston,* starring comedian S. H. Dudley. Then further musical work with the vaudeville show featuring Ada Overton and George Walker again drew Ziegfeld's attention to Will Vodery. This time Ziegfeld hired the composer-arranger to do a complete show in which Bert Williams was featured (1915). One of Vodery's songs written especially for Williams, "Dark Town Poker Club," was popularized by singer-comedian Phil Harris.

With the entry of America into World War I, Will Vodery received a commission of lieutenant and bandmaster of the 807th Infantry Band. Perhaps the only Negro in the French school for bandmasters at Fort Beteu, France, after the war he graduated with highest honors. At war's end he returned to New York. Back with Ziegfeld and in the milieu of Broadway, he prepared the music for such postwar shows as *Whoopee, Miss 1917,* and *Show Boat.* It was during the rehearsal of *Miss 1917* that Vodery introduced young George Gershwin to Clifford Goldmark, who became Gershwin's teacher. Vodery was also the first to bring a Negro band to a Broadway nightclub. In 1921 he not only introduced the band to the Plantation Club but he brought in a Negro chorus line as well.

Vodery's subsequent work with *Show Boat* starring Jules Bledsoe, and with *Shuffle Along* brought him in close touch during the 1920s with Florence Mills, Josephine Baker, Eubie Blake, Noble Sissle, Flournoy Miller, Aubrey Lyles, and Ethel Waters, to mention but a few. Later editions of *Whoopee* and *Kid Boots* starring Eddie Cantor, *Show Boat* starring Paul Robeson, and *Pony Boy* with Will Rogers, used his music. Hollywood beckoned to Vodery in 1929. There he supervised the music for Fox Films and provided direction for several studio orchestras.

An often-overlooked Vodery contribution to the development of jazz was his work with bandmaster and orchestra leader James Reese Europe. Together the two pioneered in consolidating the "sweet" music of the reed instruments with the "hot" music of the brasses. Unhappily, Vodery, in being loosely labeled an "arranger" (along with other similarly trained and motivated Negro musicians of the 1920s), was denied the rank of the creative composer that he actually was. Vodery could not have worked for twenty-three years for the Ziegfeld Productions, as well as those of the British producer Charles Cochran, had he not possessed exceptional skills.

A victim for many years of diabetes and kidney trouble, he died in the Kingsbridge Veterans Hospital, the Bronx, on Nov. 18, 1951, at age sixty-seven. His funeral was held on Nov. 23 at the Rodney Dade Funeral Home, 2232 Seventh Ave., New York City, and he was buried with full military honors in Pinelawn Cemetery (*Chicago Defender,* Dec. 11, 1951, p. 2).

For his early life, see Bart Kennett's *Colored Actors' Union Theatrical Guide* (1920), John Jacob Niles's *Singing Soldiers* (1926), and James Weldon Johnson's *Black Manhattan* (1930). Later details are in Loften Mitchell's *Black Drama: The Story of the American Negro in the Theater* (1967) and Eileen Southern's *The Music of Black Americans, A History* (1971).

— ELTON C. FAX

WALDEN, AUSTIN T[HOMAS] (1885–1965), army officer, lawyer, civil rights leader, and judge. Walden was born in Fort Valley, Ga., on April 12, 1885. His parents, Jeff Walden and Jennie Tomlin Walden, were born in slavery. After completing his public school education in Fort Valley, in 1907 he received a B.A. degree from Atlanta University, where he played on the baseball team, and an LL.B. in 1911 from the University of Michigan School of Law, where he received several prizes for his oratorical ability. He began the practice of law in Macon, Ga., in 1912. He was commissioned a captain in the Officers Reserve Corps at Fort Des Moines, Iowa (Oct. 15, 1919), and was assigned to Fort Dix, N.J. He commanded Company I, 365th Infantry, in France and served as a trial judge advocate of the 92nd Division. On May 18, 1918, he married a Baltimore public school teacher, Mary Ellen Denny, whom he had known while in attendance at Atlanta University. To this union were born two daughters, Jenelsie W. (Holloway) of Atlanta and Austella W. (Colley) of Chicago.

Following his return from army service he practiced law for a time in Macon and moved to Atlanta in 1919. His firm prospered. Although his work in the courts was varied, it was civil rights that drew the headlines and the hostility of many southern politicians. Through his unflinching devotion to equal justice, he participated in several significant cases. Three were the unsuccessful Horace Ward effort to enter the University of Georgia, his assistance in prosecuting white men in Ku Klux Klan trials, and his aid in the prosecution of a group called the Blackshirts, who allegedly attempted to keep Negroes from voting. In this case he helped the Fulton County prosecutor obtain the conviction of two men for killing a Negro student near the campus of Clark College in Atlanta. It was said to be the first time a Negro attorney had helped prosecute white men in the state.

Other noted cases included the six-year court fight that gained equal pay for Negro public school teachers, and suits which forced voter registrars to allow Negroes to qualify for Democratic primaries after the "white primary" was outlawed. He was chief negotiator when Negroes won peaceful desegregation of Atlanta lunch counters in the fall of 1961.

In 1964 he received a special outstanding achievement award from the University of Michigan. The certificate said, in part: "As he built up a successful practice [in Atlanta] he also involved himself deeply with the drive of his race for equal rights under the law. He has lent direction and spirit to the National Association for the Advancement of Colored People and to local groups, has become the beloved elder statesman of the Negro Community in Atlanta and has won the confidence of the city as a whole."

His contribution to the economic, business, political, and social development of the Negro in Atlanta and Georgia is shown by the positions of leadership he held. He was founder and first president of the Gate City Bar Association. He also served as chairman for many years of the Executive Board of the YMCA and the Atlanta Urban League. He was president of the Alumni Association of Atlanta University, a national vice-president of the NAACP, a member of its National Legal Committee for forty years, chairman of the trustee board of Wheat Street Baptist Church, and a teacher of the Bryant Bible class he organized. For twelve years he was counsel for the National Baptist Convention, U.S.A. He was founder and first co-chairman of the Atlanta Negro Voters

League. His appointment in 1964 by Mayor Ivan Allen as an alternate judge of the Municipal Courts of Atlanta was perhaps the first such appointment in Georgia and the South since Reconstruction.

He retired from his twenty-nine years of active law practice in 1963. He then acted as civil counselor, taking charity cases free. During the last twenty-five years of his life Walden was an ardent Democrat. He was elected in 1962 to membership on the State Democratic Committee of Georgia and was appointed by Gov. Carl E. Sanders a delegate to the Democratic National Convention. This was the first time Negroes had been included in a Georgia Democratic Convention delegation. He campaigned actively for former presidents Harry Truman and John Kennedy, and Democratic presidential candidate Adlai Stevenson. Pres. John F. Kennedy appointed him to the American Battle Monuments Commission.

He died in Atlanta on July 2, 1965. The mayor of Atlanta paid tribute to him by stating that "Much of Atlanta's outstanding pioneer progress and better race relations was due to the effective leadership of 'Colonel' Walden. His leadership laid the groundwork for much that is now an accepted fact."

This sketch is based on articles in the *New York Times, Atlanta Constitution, Atlanta Journal, Atlanta Daily World,* records in the possession of the Walden family, and interviews with his widow.

— GRACE TOWNS HAMILTON

WALKER, MADAME C. J. [SARAH BREEDLOVE]

(1867–1919), businesswoman. Born near Delta in northeast Louisiana, the daughter of poor farmers, Owen and Minerva Breedlove, she was orphaned in childhood and reared by her married sister. While living in Vicksburg, Miss., when she was fourteen she married a man by the name of McWilliams and bore him a daughter, A'Lelia. After her husband's death in 1887 she moved to St. Louis where she supported herself and her daughter by working as a washerwoman. In 1905 she began to perfect a formula and using a hot iron for straightening the hair of Negro women, as well as a cream for "improving" the complexion. The following year she moved to Denver, Colo., where she married Charles Walker, a newspaperman. She demonstrated her methods by door-to-door salesmanship, trained agents who established their own businesses, and expanded her business by travels, demonstration, and lectures in the South and East. In 1908 she organized a second office in Pittsburgh, Pa., managed by her daughter A'Lelia. In 1910 she moved both offices to Indianapolis, where she built a plant to manufacture her products. Her business expanded to such an extent that before her death she was a millionaire. Although warned by physicians at the Kellogg Clinic, Battle Creek, Mich., that her hectic life increased her hypertension, she continued her activities, became ill in St. Louis, and died of chronic nephritis at her country home, Villa Lewaro, Irvington-on-Hudson, N.Y. After funeral services held in her church, Mother Zion African Methodist Episcopal Zion Church, New York, she was buried at Woodlawn Cemetery in the Bronx.

Madame C. J. Walker's Hair Grower, pomade, and other products made her one of the more successful businesswomen of the early twentieth century. Her extensive advertising, mostly in Negro newspapers, skillful use of agents, and establishing of a fashion made straight hair "good hair." Moreover she gave employment to some 3000 persons, mostly women who, naturally, set the example for potential clients. Her success was so phenomenal that others are said to have imitated her, notably Annie M. Turnbo Malone with her "Poro System" and her "Poro Colleges" in St. Louis and Chicago, and Madame Sarah Spencer Washington with her "Apex System" in Atlantic City. Her fame spread to the Caribbean, later to Paris, where her style was adopted in the 1920s by the famous dancer Josephine Baker, and inspired a French company to manufacture a similar pomade known as the "Baker-Fix."

Madame Walker, who invested some of her wealth in real estate, lived in lavish, almost regal style. In 1914 she built a town house in Harlem at 108–110 W. 136th St. and at no. 110 a completely equipped beauty parlor (Negroes had begun to move from the West 53rd Street center to Harlem at the beginning of the twentieth century). In 1917 Madame Walker, at Irvington-on-Hudson, built Villa Lewaro, an Italianate country house designed by the Negro architect Vertner Tandy, one of the founders of the Alpha Phi Alpha fraternity.

Not all of Madame Walker's fortune was spent in "conspicuous consumption." She was a liberal contributor to the NAACP, homes for the aged in St. Louis and Indianapolis, the Colored YMCA of Indianapolis, and the needy of Indianapolis. She maintained scholarships for young women at Tuskegee Institute and contributed to Palmer Memorial Institute in Sedalia, N.C., founded by her friend Charlotte Hawkins Brown. She gave cash prizes to her agents, whom she organized as "Walker Clubs," for their philanthropic community work. Her contracts bound the agents to personal hygiene which preceded state cosmetology laws. She advocated "cleanliness and loveliness" to advance self-respect and racial pride. While she bequeathed most of her estate and business to her daughter A'Lelia, her will also established a trust fund for an industrial and mission school in West Africa and provided bequests for Negro orphans and old folks' homes, colored YWCA branches, and private secondary and collegiate institutions.

An editorial in the July 1919 issue of *The Crisis* observed that Madame Walker "revolutionized the personal habits and appearance of millions of human beings." James Weldon Johnson likewise extolled her for teaching colored women the "secret of the enhancement of feminine beauty." He added: "Notwithstanding, it is idle to expect the Negro in Harlem or anywhere else to build business in general upon a strictly racial foundation or to develop it to any considerable proportions strictly within the limits of the patronage, credit, and financial resources of the race" (*Black Manhattan* [1930], p. 283). To a considerable measure, Negro-owned beauty parlors and other Negro-owned businesses and professions cast doubt upon this categorical conclusion.

The best easily available biographical sketches with bibliographies are those by Martha Gruening in the *DAB* ([1936], 10, Part 1:358–59), and by Walter Fisher in *NAW* (1971, 3:533–35). — RAYFORD W. LOGAN

WALKER, DAVID (1785–1830), dealer in old clothes, agent for *Freedom's Journal,* militant abolitionist, and theoretician of total African revolt. Walker was born of a free mother and slave father in Wilmington, N.C. In accordance with law in the antebellum South, he took the status of his mother. His father's life as a chattel slave, his mother's defenselessness as a black woman in the era of slavery, and his sufferings in a slave society greatly influenced the life of the sensitive, bright young man. Walker determined to leave the South, but before doing so traveled widely there, studying the miserable conditions of slaves.

Walker settled in Boston, began teaching himself to read and write, and in 1827 entered the clothing business on Brattle Street. It was said that had he not been so generous with his possessions he would have acquired wealth. Instead he spent a great deal of time, when not helping others, reading the literature of slavery from the time of Egyptian bondage to the slave systems of Greece and Rome and beyond, the history of Africa, Asia, the Americas, and European peoples from early to more recent times. In 1828 he married "Miss Eliza ——.'' Their only child, Edwin G. Walker, was born posthumously.

Henry Highland Garnet, who talked to Walker's widow, described Walker's personal appearance as "prepossessing, being six feet in height, slender and well-proportioned. His hair was loose and his complexion was dark." When one adds to that his ascetic's fire, Walker's appearance on the platform and elsewhere are better imagined. Walker's "Address Delivered Before the General Colored Association" in Boston, reproduced in *Freedom's Journal* (Dec. 1828), bore the mark of a disaffected spirit which, although turbulent, had not quite found its outlet. He urged his audience to follow a direct path toward freedom, provided it did not infringe on the U.S. constitution, called for unity, and denounced slaveholders and their collaborators.

He abandoned all such reserve in his best known work, *David Walker's Appeal in four articles together with a Preamble to the Colored Citizens of the World, but in particular and very expressly, to those of The United States of America,* which appeared in 1829. Walker described Negroes in the United States as the most oppressed and degraded set of beings since the world began—made so by disobedience to God, and more tangibly by cruel and heartless white overlords. Walker ascribed the wretchedness of Negroes to their enslavement, ignorance engendered largely by the slave system, white preachers of the religion of Jesus Christ, and the plans of the American Colonization Society. He concluded, after a survey of history, that while Africans had some white friends in the world, especially in England and even in America, the great majority of whites were the "natural enemies" of Negroes and of people of color generally.

In his *Appeal,* Walker appealed to Negroes the world over to revolt against their oppressors. To achieve this end, he overestimated the power of Africans, contending that even those in the United States were capable of routing the oppressor. Pointing to various countries in the Caribbean, he noted African numerical superiority and seemed incredulous that some Negroes had not risen to strike their white foe.

Despite the strength which he ascribed to Negroes, Walker recognized that in the United States and elsewhere they had been so crippled by oppression that only by taking their destiny in hand could they win freedom and come into their heritage. This perception courses through the *Appeal* with a strength that should merit Walker consideration as perhaps the first major ideologist of black nationalism to emerge in the U.S. In fact he posited nearly all aspects of black nationalist thought, including a messianic role for Negroes, concern for peoples of color everywhere, recognition that Negroes must provide their own defenses, approval of their command of leadership in all areas of endeavor, insistence that they one day dwell in a nation—presumably after the destruction of "natural enemies." Meanwhile there was no need to spurn white allies.

In not eschewing assistance from whites, Walker gave his support to a fundamental tenet of antebellum black nationalist thought. Beyond that, he believed there was at least a slight chance that blacks and whites might one day live in freedom in America. He made a sincere gesture of Christian forgiveness, promising peace and harmony if whites would make a national acknowledgment of their crimes against black people. Still, the nature of the freedom Walker had in mind dictated that Negroes in the United States, even if free among whites, continue to struggle for the liberation of African peoples everywhere. "Your full glory and happiness, as well as all other coloured people under Heaven," he wrote, "shall never be fully consummated, but with the entire emancipation of your enslaved brethren all over the world." Thus Walker broke beyond the constraints of nationalism to frame Pan-African theory—no mean feat considering attacks on African humanity during slavery. In this regard he helped establish a conception of black nationalism which was upheld by major nationalist theoreticians of the slave era and later, the indivisibility of freedom for those of African descent.

Walker repeatedly accused the persecutors of Negroes of being avaricious seekers after power. His references to white Americans dragging blacks around the country to dig up gold, to the riches in the land arising from the sweat of slaves, indicate an incipient but determined class orientation. Walker, Garnet tells us, deliberately turned his back on wealth in the interest of helping the oppressed and died poor. In a revealing tribute to Samuel Cornish, the outstanding divine and co-editor of *Freedom's Journal* and editor of *Rights of All,* Walker remarked, "I believe he is not seeking to fill his pockets with money, but has the welfare of his brethren truly at heart. Such men, brethren, ought to be supported by us."

Pointing to fragmented "Afro-America," Walker severely criticized traitors among people of color, urging unity behind objectives to be determined by black leaders. Unlike Robert Alexander Young, whose *Ethiopian Manifesto* appeared shortly before Walker's *Appeal,* he did not suggest that God be primarily responsible for the freedom of his people. Urging the appropriateness of killing a man trying to kill you as you would drink a glass of water when thirsty, he noted that while Negroes should await the proper opportunity before attacking, they must be prepared to offer their souls for those of the whites, "to kill or be killed." Walker predicted that colored peoples would one day eliminate some whites from the face of the earth.

The *Appeal* helped create such insecurity in the white South that legislative sessions were convened, secretly, to pass laws suppressing the seditious tract and preventing the circulation of similar pamphlets. The actions of the Georgia legislature, symbolic of aims in the North Carolina, Virginia, Mississippi, and Louisiana legislatures, made it a crime punishable by death to introduce or circulate literature inciting servile attempts to overthrow the system of slavery. In addition Georgia legislation made it a punishable crime, by jail or fine, to teach slaves to read or write. Legislation directed exclusively at Negroes ranged from Georgia's barring black sailors from setting foot on shore—for fear they would introduce inflammatory literature—to Virginia's barring Negro ministers from preaching to their own people because some were said to have read the *Appeal* from their pulpits.

A company of Georgia men, offering a reward of $1000 for Walker dead and $10,000 for him alive, vowed to fast until one of the two objectives was realized. "It was the opinion of many," Garnet wrote, following Walker's mysterious death in 1830, "that he was hurried out of life by means of poison." Walker was survived by his wife, probably a fugitive slave protecting her identity through omission of her maiden name, and their son, Edward G., who in 1866 became the first Negro to be elected to the Massachusetts legislature.

The complete text of David Walker's *Appeal* is conveniently found in Sterling Stuckey's *The Ideological Origins of Black Nationalism* (1972). Illuminating analyses of the *Appeal* and its effects are in Herbert Aptheker's *One Continual Cry* (1965) and Clement Eaton's *Freedom of Thought in the Old South* (1940). The *Appeal,* with information about David Walker, is also in Henry Highland Garnet's *Walker's Appeal with a Brief Sketch of His Life* (1848). See also the brief sketch by Martha Gruening in the *DAB* (10, Part 1:340).

— STERLING STUCKEY

WALKER, EDWARD [EDWIN] G[ARRISON] (1831?–1901), businessman, lawyer, legislator, and politician. The only child of Eliza and David Walker he was born in Boston after his father's death. His mother, "Miss Eliza ——," was probably a fugitive slave. His father was author of the "subversive" *David Walker's Appeal* . . . published in Boston in 1829. The exact birth date of the son is uncertain. An obituary, which called him Edwin, listed the date as Sept. 28, 1835. But since the father is said to have died in 1830, Edward must have been born in either 1830 or 1831.

Young Walker attended public schools in Boston and earned his living as a leather worker and owner of his own shop with as many as fifteen workers. The heritage of his father and the Boston abolition atmosphere led young Walker to aid in the release of the slave "Shadrach" from capture in 1851. Among others in the party were Lewis Hayden and Robert Morris, well-known abolitionists in Boston. Such an episode may have been the key to the fact that Walker later acquired a copy of *Blackstone's Commentaries* and while in the leather business began to read law. He devoured other law books, and studied law in the offices of John Q. A. Griffin and Charles A. Tweed in Charlestown, a part of Boston. In May 1861, after easily passing his law examination, he became probably the third Negro to be admitted to the Suffolk bar. A tall dark man of imposing figure, he had argumentative skills and fine oratorical ability. Since his practice thrived, he gave up his leather business.

It was an easy step from law practice to politics. He was at first a Republican. In 1866 the Democrats and the Republicans split in his electoral district when he ran and surprisingly won a seat for a one-year term from Ward 3, in which there were only three colored voters, to the Massachusetts General Court (legislature). Since the polls in Ward 3 closed a few hours earlier than did those in Ward 6 where Charles L. Mitchell was elected, Walker was probably the first Negro elected to a state legislature in the United States. An independent thinker, Walker opposed the Republicans and was not nominated in 1867. He then became a Democrat, and was said to have brought more Negroes of Massachusetts into the Democratic party than other Negro politicians.

Meanwhile his growing law practice made him one of the prominent lawyers in Boston. Many of his clients were Irish. He kept pictures of Irish resistance leaders in his office, and was the only Negro member of their secret order. He saw in the Irish a lesson on how to rise in America through politics. Robert Morris and Walker were among the best known and most successful Negro lawyers who served Irish clients.

Walker never lost his interest in politics. He was a staunch follower and a defender of Benjamin F. Butler, both as a Republican and a Democrat. Walker took to the stump every time Butler ran. It was only natural that in 1883 when Butler, as governor, wished to appoint a Negro as a judge, he nominated Walker. But the Republicans in control of the approval machinery rejected Walker three times. The position went instead to George L. Ruffin, the first Negro graduate of the Harvard Law School and a consistent Republican. Walker remained bitter about this the rest of his life. In 1885 and 1886 he and George T. Downing of Rhode Island helped start the Negro political independence movement in New England. In the 1890s Walker served as president of the Colored National League, and in 1896 was proposed for president of the United States on a Negro party ticket.

Walker attended the Charles Street AME Church, although he was not a member. His funeral was there after he died on Jan. 13, 1901, a well-honored pioneer of Boston Negro attorneys.

Full, but somewhat inaccurate, obituaries were published in the *Boston Globe* and the *Boston Evening Transcript.* See also the article on him by Pauline E. Hopkins, "Edwin Garrison Walker" (*The Colored American Magazine* 2 [March 1901]: 358–66, 372). A few more references to Walker are in William Ferris's *The African Abroad* . . . (1913, vol. 2).

— CLARENCE G. CONTEE, SR.

WALKER, GEORGE (1873–1911), comedian, dancer, singer, actor, producer, and promoter. Born in Lawrence, Kans., the son of a policeman, Walker left home at an early age to join a traveling medicine-man show that took him to California. On the road, Walker rattled bones, shook tambourines, mugged, and grinned to win laughs and applause. By the time he arrived in San Francisco he disliked the traveling show and searched for theater work.

In the early 1890s on a city sidewalk in San Francisco, the sprightly twenty-year-old entertainer, down on his luck, met another who was in search of a partner for a new comedy routine. Neither knew anything about the other, yet they decided to cast their lots together and casually exchanged names. And then without further fanfare George Walker and Bert Williams embarked on one of the most successful and celebrated stage careers in the annals of American theatrical history, a partnership that endured for sixteen years.

In recent years more attention has been paid to Bert Williams than to George Walker. But the latter was a remarkable figure in his own right. Williams tended to be withdrawn and melancholic. Walker, however, was all razzle-dazzle, back-slapping extrovert, and it was his fiercely ambitious drive that helped get their act on the road.

They called themselves Walker and Williams at first. Then they flipped a coin and changed the billing. In the beginning their act failed. In the tough, frenetic honky-tonks and grease joints of San Francisco they were ignored. On a tour through the South they were booed and jeered. In their first big Chicago engagement with John Isham's Octoroons (1895), which was one of the first Negro companies that attempted to transcend the rigidity of minstrel-man humor and give its performance a chance for discovering new forms of self-expression, Williams and Walker "bombed" their first week and were promptly fired. Later the two reworked some of their old material and changed roles, with Williams becoming the comic and Walker something of a flamboyant straight man, and then billed themselves as "Two Real Coons" so tht audiences, accustomed to the old-style white minstrel performers who went in blackface and cruelly parodied and burlesqued the antics of Negroes, might know they were seeing a new kind of genuine black humor. The billing change worked, and the two had their first bona fide success.

Shortly afterward they made their New York debut in 1896 in *The Gold Bug*, produced at the Casino Theater by Canary and Leder. The show failed, but a few months later the team was booked into Koster and Bial's Music Hall, then the city's most important vaudeville house. Shrewdly, the pair ended their act on a spectacular note. Dressed "to kill," and ready for action with two lush "coppertone" beauties by their side, they threw themselves into an exuberant, uninhibited, high-steppin' rendition of a dance long popular in the Negro community, the cake walk. Audiences had never seen it done quite that way before. And soon the cake walk, in the hands of Williams and Walker, became the ultimate city sensation. White socialities were taking it up, and Williams and Walker, who had been booked into

the music hall for a one trial week, stayed on for forty and became the rage of a craze-hungry nation.

In 1898 the two took over important roles in the Will Marion Cook–Paul Laurence Dunbar musical *Clorindy*. In 1899 they appeared in *A Lucky Coon* and in *The Policy Players* (1900). By then the two men had developed their own company of stock performers and situations. Eventually, with shows such as *Sons of Ham* (1900), *In Dahomey* (1902), *In Abyssinia* (1908), and *Bandana Land* (1908), they further extended Negro theater. *In Dahomey* emerged as a historic event, the first Negro show to open downtown in the heart of Manhattan's theater district, at the prestigious New York Theater. On stage, too, another historic event took place. No longer were audiences seeing simply a skillful rehash of minstrel or medicine-man-show antics. Nor was there the crude disjointedness of typical vaudeville fare. Instead there was musical theater, a fully worked-out plot and carefully defined characters as well as music, comedy, and dance, all incorporated to flow rhythmically with the mood of the script. American musical comedy was in its brilliant infancy. And two Negroes with the first important all-Negro company, had helped father it.

Later the comedy of Williams and Walker may have appeared to be merely that of the city slicker in heated contest with the country bumpkin. Yet beneath the surface something else was at work, the theme of survival. On the one hand the plots of *Sons of Ham* and *In Dahomey* reveal the black man (usually played by Walker) compelled to live by his wits and ingenuity. Walker was always the wise guy who couldn't be told anything because he already knew it all, the flashy, outrageously extravagant dresser, the loudmouth dude who was always at odds with the civilized world, the system, the almighty self-righteous Establishment itself. He was the Negro man of ambition forced into being a sharpster because at heart, as surely the Negro audience knew, there was no other outlet for a Negro so strongly aggressive and energetic. The plays never spelled out America's racism. But then they didn't have to, because the audience filled in the gaps in the scripts.

Yet curiously (and perhaps as an outgrowth of the Edwardian age of which it was a part), the comedy of Williams and Walker also had as its winners the simple ordinary black folks. The plot outlines maintain that virtue triumphs; deceit fails. But Negro virtue was different from white virtue. The Negro winners were never simply innocents lent a helping hand by a kind fate. Generally they were realists dramatically aware of life's shady adversities. They used their mother wit to outslick the slicker. Many of the howling, hooting, hollering routines of Williams and Walker, in which absurdity was piled upon absurdity, looked dated later. And, frankly, the humor was of the "coon" variety, where watermelon-stealing and chicken-eating caricatures of Negroes were perpetuated by blacks themselves. But their work, wild and untempered, apparently struck a nerve and delighted white audiences, but also pleased colored ones, too.

Generally the planning, staging, and promoting were left to Walker. In the later productions he vehemently sought to incorporate an African theme, although that theme was never fully thought out. He was as well the man who fought with the white producers reluctant to back a full-scale Negro extravaganza. For *In Dahomey* he got a budget of $15,000, then almost unheard of. Later the show made four times that amount. Afterward, his ambition growing, Walker pushed for a $30,000 budget for *In Abyssinia.* He envisioned an elaborate, "totally African" production with live tigers and giraffes, a mountain pass with a real waterfall, and a cast of 125 performers. He was turned down repeatedly. During negotiations Williams was ready to give in to the producers' cutbacks, but Walker tirelessly muscled his way ahead. In the end he had to settle for some compromises, including mere live camels instead of the tigers and giraffes. But more important, he got his waterfall —*and* his $30,000 budget. And the show was a hit.

Onstage Walker was an expert dancer and a charismatic singing comedian who popularized the song "Bon Bon Buddy." Offstage his life was a further exercise in showmanship and an unadulterated celebration of his own stardom. In 1899 he married the talented showgirl Ada Overton. But the marriage did little to change his private life. An inveterate clotheshorse given to the latest fads, he was said to have spent more time at his tailor's than at home. He continued frequenting the bars, cafés, and nightspots he loved and where he was surrounded by adoring fans. His love affairs were reportedly legion.

Walker's last stage appearance before a lingering and painful death from syphillis in 1911 was in *Bandana Land.* Afterward the company fell apart. Unfortunately, no one, not even Bert Williams (who was to go on to a spectacular career alone), seemed possessed with the stamina and administrative industriousness to keep such a big troupe going.

The comedy of the two (as well as the kind of showmanship and promotion Walker was so fond of) had an incalculable influence on American entertainment. The team's distinct brand of comedy was the precursor of such Broadway shows as *Shuffle Along, The Chocolate Dandies, Don't Play Us Cheap,* and later *The Wiz* and *Bubblin' Brown Sugar,* not to mention movies such as *Cabin in the Sky, Stormy Weather, Uptown Saturday Night,* and *Let's Do It Again.*

Walker's career is described in Donald Bogle's *Toms, Coons, Mulattoes, Mammies and Bucks, An Interpretive History of Blacks in Films* (1973). There are also valuable comments in James Weldon Johnson's *Black Manhattan* (1940). — DONALD BOGLE

WALKER, JAMES EDWARD (1874–1918), teacher, school administrator, and army officer. He was born in Albermarle County, Va., one of two children of slave parents, Peter and Lucy Ella Walker. The family moved to Washington, D.C., about 1881, where his father obtained employment which enabled James to attend the Preparatory High School for Colored Youth (renamed the M Street High School in 1891). Completing the requirements at M Street in 1893, he graduated a year later from Miner Normal School and began teaching in Division Thirteen of the Washington public school sys-

tem. As teacher, principal of the Syphax and Banneker Schools, and supervising principal of the division, he spent twenty-four years in the public schools. In 1906 he married Beatrice Louise Johnson, who had attended the same schools and also taught at the Banneker School. Two children were born of this union: James E. Jr. (April 24, 1907), who became a successful physician in Washington, and Beatrice L. (Sept. 22, 1909), who taught at the Monroe Laboratory School of Miner Teachers College.

Walker is best known for his service in the army. Originally enlisted as a noncommissioned staff officer, he was commissioned a first lieutenant (May 1, 1896) in the 1st Separate Battalion, District of Columbia National Guards, and assigned the duties of adjutant. Promoted to captain on July 3, 1909, following competitive examination he succeeded Maj. Arthur Brooks (Aug. 10, 1912) as major and commanding officer of the battalion. He commanded it when it was mustered into federal service (June 27, 1916) and sent to guard waterworks near Naco, Ariz., during the Mexican campaign. He also served as an intelligence officer. After engaging in several field exercises, the battalion returned to Fort Myer, Va., and was mustered out of service on Oct. 23, 1916. Belief that there was no uncertainty about the loyalty of the 1st Battalion led Pres. Woodrow Wilson and Secretary of War Newton D. Baker to activate the 1st Separate on March 25, 1917, to guard the facilities and structures in Washington and its the vicinity. In the summer and fall of 1917 the 1st Separate also guarded railroads and bridges east of Harpers Ferry, W.Va. On Jan. 1, 1918, the 1st Separate became the first battalion of the 372nd Infantry Regiment organized at Camp Stuart, Newport News, Va. The regiment was on the high seas when it learned that Walker had died at Fort Bayard, N.M., of tuberculosis on April 4, 1918. He was buried in Arlington National Cemetery.

Like Maj. Arthur Brooks, Walker inspired many young men to seek a military career. A notable example was Arthur C. Newman, who had married Walker's sister-in-law, served as a captain in World War I and later commanded the 1st Separate Battalion. American Legion Post 26 was named in honor of Walker, and a tree was planted in his memory at the main entrance of the Hamline United Methodist Church, 16th and Hamline Streets NW in Washington. In 1938 the Board of Education renamed the Benjamin Banneker Elementary School (at Third and K Streets NW) the James E. Walker School "because of his educational and patriotic contributions to his community and nation." A new school, Walker-Jones, at First and K Streets NW, perpetuates his memory.

Details concerning Walker's military career are in Record Groups 94 and 407, the Records of the Adjutant-General; Record Group 120, Records of the American Expeditionary Forces; and Record Group 165, Records of the War Department General and Special Staffs, located in the National Archives, Washington. For his educational career, see the records of the Board of Education of the District of Columbia as well as the contemporary issues of the *Washington Bee.* A brief mimeographed biographical sketch by Paul E. Sluby, Jr.

(in the Moorland-Spingarn Research Center at Howard University, 1973), contains valuable information, especially about his parents and his life in Washington. Information about his wife's father, Solomon James Johnson, is in *The Collected Papers of Solomon James Johnson,* edited and introduced by Paul E. Sluby, Sr. (1973). The reminiscences of Rayford W. Logan, who served in the 1st Separate Battalion and the 372nd Infantry Regiment, added some details. — CHARLES JOHNSON, JR.

WALKER, MAGGIE LENA (1867–1934), businesswoman. She was born in Richmond, Va. Her mother, Elizabeth Draper, a former slave, worked as assistant cook in the household of an Elizabeth Van Lew of Richmond, who had opposed slavery, supported the Union cause during the Civil War, and was postmistress of Richmond when Elizabeth Draper worked for her. According to family tradition Maggie's father was a northern abolitionist author. The early death of her stepfather William Mitchell, a butler for Miss Van Lew, left his widow as the breadwinner. She took in washing; Maggie delivered the clothes, did the marketing, and looked after her brother John.

Maggie graduated from the Armstrong Normal School (in reality a high school), taught in a public school for three years, became an agent for the Woman's Union (an insurance company), and took business courses in accounting and salesmanship. On Sept. 14, 1886, she married Armistead Walker, Jr., a building contractor several years her senior, and they had three children. In May 1899 she became executive secretary-treasurer of the Independent Order of St. Luke, a fraternal business organization, and in 1902 began publishing the *St. Luke Herald.* A year later she founded and served as president of the St. Luke Penny Savings Bank; she also started the short-lived St. Luke Emporium, a department store. On the other hand the Penny Savings Bank flourished, absorbing the other Negro banks in Richmond into the Consolidated Bank and Trust Company (1929–1930). She served as chairman of its board of directors until her death in 1934.

It is difficult to determine the forces that motivate an individual's career. The responsibilities of doing the marketing for her mother and looking after her brother may have laid the foundation for Maggie Walker's business career and the concept of self-help. While Richmond cherished its image as the one-time capital of the Confederacy, the sympathetic views of Miss Van Lew and two white teachers in the Lancaster public school, where Walker later taught, probably encouraged hope. Other contemporary Richmond Negroes, notably John Mitchell, Jr., who became editor of the *Richmond Planet* in 1884, and Wendell Phillips Dabney, who founded the *Union* in Cincinnati (1907), typified successful struggle against almost insuperable obstacles. Virginia Union University, founded in 1867, encouraged ambition. Churches, especially the Baptist, not only preached the gospel but promoted education through Sunday schools.

More decisive was the concept of self-help among Negroes soon after the Civil War. One of the earliest organizations was the Grand United Order of St. Luke, a fraternal and cooperative insurance venture founded in Baltimore (1867) by an ex-slave, Mary Prout, to ensure sick care and proper burial for its members. Maggie Walker joined the order when she was a girl, was promoted to a minor position when she was seventeen, and became its executive secretary-treasurer in 1899. By that time the concept of self-help urged by Booker T. Washington, Alexander Crummell, Andrew Hilyer, and others had won widespread support. In 1899 W. E. B. Du Bois held the Atlanta Business Conference and discussed (in his Atlanta University Publication No. 4) *The Negro in Business.* In 1900 Booker T. Washington organized the National Negro Business League. When Walker changed the name from the Grand United Order of St. Luke to the Independent Order of St. Luke and moved its headquarters to Richmond in 1899, many Negroes supported such orders, partly because many white insurance companies refused to sell them policies. Under Walker's management and inspirational leadership, the order, with no reserve fund or head office, had 3408 members. Her salary is reported to have been eight dollars a month, for which she collected dues, verified claims, kept books, and paid out claims as they became due. When the order gave her a testimonial on Nov. 30, 1924 in the City Auditorium, the order had 100,000 members, a building costing $100,000, an emergency fund of $70,000, and an organ, the *St. Luke Herald.* There were fifty-five clerks employed in the home office and 145 field workers; 15,000 children were enrolled in thrift clubs she had started. Much of her success was due to her appeal to churches.

Although the St. Luke Penny Savings Bank had the name of the order, it was legally a separate institution. As the St. Luke Bank and Trust Company, later the Consolidated Bank and Trust Company, it was a depository for gas and water accounts in Richmond, and for city taxes.

Maggie Walker did not confine her activities to these institutions. In 1912 she organized the Richmond Council of Negro Women with 1400 members and raised the first $5000 which enabled Janie Porter Barrett to purchase a farm at Peake, not far from Richmond, for training "delinquent" Negro girls. She also contributed generously to the needs of the school and farm. As president of the council, she raised funds for the Negro tuberculosis sanatorium at Burkeville, Va., and a Negro community center and a nursing home in Richmond. She became president of the state branch of the NAACP and served on other boards and councils.

She carried on many of these activities despite personal tragedies. Her son Russell accidentally killed her husband in 1915. Her mother died in 1922 and Russell in 1923 (a younger son had died in infancy). Walker herself was increasingly incapacitated after a fall in 1907, which necessitated an elevator in her home and the use of a wheelchair. She died of diabetic gangrene in 1934; funeral services were held at the First African Baptist Church and she was buried in Evergreen Cemetery, Richmond.

Virginia Union University awarded her an honorary degree in 1925; a street, a theater, and a school have been named for her. Despite the decline of small-scale fraternal cooperatives concomitant with the rise of Negro-owned actuarial insurance companies, the Independent Order of St. Luke continued its existence on a reduced scale.

Most of the career of Mrs. Walker was described in Wendell P. Dabney's *Maggie L. Walker and the I. O. of St. Luke* (1927) and Sadie I. Daniel's *Women Builders* (1931). She was eulogized in Benjamin G. Brawley's *Negro Builders and Heroes* (1937), with a portrait facing page 268. The fullest brief account is by Sadie Daniel St. Clair in *NAW* (1971, 3:530–31). An obituary was published in the *JNH* (Jan. 1935, pp. 122–23).

— RAYFORD W. LOGAN

WALLER, JOHN L[OUIS] (1850–1907), lawyer, politician, journalist, consul, entrepreneur, and army officer. He was born a slave in New Madrid County, Mo., on Jan. 12, 1850. In December 1862 his family was relocated to Inka (later named Tama City), Iowa, by Union troops. He began his formal education in 1863 in Toledo, Iowa, and graduated from Toledo High School. In 1874, given free access to the personal library of Judge N. M. Hubbard of Cedar Rapids, he studied law for three years and was admitted to the Iowa bar in 1877. He went to Leavenworth, Kans., presumably to take advantage of the opportunities offered by the migration of Negroes, and was admitted to the Kansas bar. As the first Negro to practice law in Leavenworth, he encountered a good deal of prejudice in that Missouri-oriented community. He moved to Lawrence, Kans., where in May 1879 he married Susan T. D. Bray, the former Susan Boyd, a widow with two children who was to bear Waller four more. Waller had been previously married to Amelia Lewis, who died without children in 1884.

He won a reputation as an orator, and by 1880 was a member of the Douglas County Republican central committee and of the state central committee. But he was narrowly defeated as a candidate for the state legislature. On March 10, 1882, assisted by his wife, Waller began publishing a weekly newspaper, *The Western Recorder,* which staunchly supported the Republicans and civil rights for Negroes, while continuing his law practice and his political activities. He also strongly supported Edwin P. McCabe in his successful campaign for state auditor, and in 1883 was elected to the Lawrence Board of Education. In 1885, because of illness, he sold his newspaper. By early 1887 he had sufficiently recovered to be elected assistant sergeant-at-arms at the state House of Representatives. He moved to Topeka where in 1888 he joined his cousin, Anthony Morton, in founding *The American Citizen,* with his brother L. J. Waller as managing editor. Failing to achieve the Republican nomination for state auditor, he sold his interest in the paper and moved to Kansas City, Kans. In early 1890 he wrote to the *Topeka Daily Capital* in support of McCabe's project of "opening up the Cherokee Strip and Oklahoma for a Negro state." After another unsuccessful attempt to gain the Republican nomination for state auditor, he was in 1888 a Republican elector for Kansas and in 1889 deputy sheriff (county attorney) for Shawnee County.

During the same period he began communicating to prominent Republicans his desire for appointment as U.S. consul to Haiti. In 1891, aided by strong endorsements from leading Kansas politicians such as Gov. L. U. Humphrey and Sen. P. B. Plumb, Waller's efforts resulted in his appointment (Feb. 1891) as consul at Tamatave, Madagascar. Waller served at this post until January 1894. Then began a series of developments which in 1895 and 1896 made him the accused in a criminal case which became an international *cause célèbre* and cost him eleven months of solitary confinement in a French prison. This chain of events began when Waller exploited close ties he had established with the Malagasy government to obtain a large land concession worth millions in products such as mahogany, teak, and rubber. He intended to create a new colony there through leasing the land. However, this plan was bitterly opposed by France, which claimed to hold a protectorate over the island and had for many years been in the process of taking control.

In December of 1894 the French launched the invasion which resulted in their gaining control in 1896. In March 1895 French authorities arrested Waller. He was tried by a military court on charges of breaking French postal regulations and transmitting military intelligence to the Malagasy. He was sentenced to twenty years of solitary confinement and shipped to France. The letter from Waller used as evidence in the case was to his wife, and while it did discuss the war situation, it was not demonstrated at his trial nor since that France had any legal jurisdiction over him at the time. The real motive of the French officials appears to have been to establish specific grounds for their refusal to recognize Waller's land concession, which posed a threat to their complete control of the island.

Spurred by public pressure expressed through the press and by resolutions from both houses of Congress, the U.S. State Department arranged for Waller's release in February 1896. John M. Langston was one of Waller's attorneys during this period. As a condition of his release, however, the U.S. government agreed not to pursue further a damages claim Waller made against the French government for imprisoning him. Waller continued for years, without success, to gain redress on his own from the French government for those damages and for loss of his land concession.

Upon his return from prison he again became active in Kansas politics, primarily through public speaking for the Republican party. He was also editor-in-chief of the *American Citizen,* from June 27, 1896, to March 19, 1897. In July 1898 he helped organize Company C of the 23rd Kansas volunteer infantry regiment, was elected its captain, and commanded the company through its training and during its service in Cuba, where it arrived in September 1898. Waller was honorably discharged from the army on April 10, 1899. He returned to Cuba for a time, having noted a great potential for economic development there. In July 1899 he published a letter through the Associated Press calling for emigration of 3,000,000 Negroes from the southern United States to Cuba, Puerto Rico, and the Philippines. He proposed that Congress appropriate $20,000,000 which would be repaid by duties on exports once the emigrants were resettled and productive (*The [Indianapolis] Recorder,* July 8, 1899). In late 1899 he announced formation of the Afro-American Cuban Emigration Society. However, nothing came of this venture. By 1904 he had moved to New York City. He died of pneumonia on Oct. 13, 1907, in Mamaroneck, N.Y. Among his survivors was Paul Andreamentania Rezaf-kerifo, the son of his daughter Jennie and a Malagasy nobleman, and later famous as a composer of American popular music under the name Andy Razaf.

Waller very consciously promoted his own advancement and that of the Negro in general. He moved to Kansas to take advantage of the opportunities presented by the surge of Negro migration there in the 1870s. In his writings and speeches he devoted much attention to Negro colonization experiments, and it is clear that he hoped to promote his own through his land concession in Madagascar and the proposal concerning Cuba. In rising from slavery to acquire advanced professional training and prominent social and political status, he came to believe that there was no limit to the kind of personal achievement possible for a man with ambition and ability. In the end, however, he concluded that race prejudice restricted him from entry into the higher levels of economic enterprise, as in his experience in Madagascar. This case and the absence of recognition for the contribution of Negro troops in the war against Spain caused him to become disenchanted with the Republican party, which had been the main vehicle of his rise to prominence. This culminated in his supporting the Democratic presidential candidate, William Jennings Bryan, in 1900.

A sizable collection of documents concerning Waller is included in *Foreign Relations of the United States 1895* (Pt. I, pp. 251–396) and in *House Document No. 225* (Ser. No. 3425; 94th Cong., 1st sess., 1895–1896). See also the *New York Times* (April 2, 1894 to Feb. 25, 1896, passim). There is also an article by Allison Blakely, "The John L. Waller Affair," in the *NHB* (Feb.–March 1974). — ALLISON BLAKELY

WALLER, THOMAS WRIGHT

WALLER, THOMAS WRIGHT (1904–1943), jazz pianist, organist, composer, and entertainer. He gained fame as "Fats" Waller, and was one of the most gifted, popular and riotous "characters" of the first half of the twentieth century. His alcoholic escapades were as legendary as his recognition as an outstanding contributor to the enjoyment by a vast number of lovers of music in the United States, the British Isles, and the European continent.

The youngest son and seventh in a family of twelve children, six of whom died in infancy, he was the son of Edward Martin Waller and Edeline (Lockett) Waller of Virginia. They had moved about 1889 to New York City, and Thomas was born on 134th Street on May 21, 1904. His father became a deacon in the Abyssinian Baptist Church and his mother sang in the choir and played the organ. Well fed at home, Thomas was called "Fats" in his boyhood. By 1915 he began frequenting Harlem nightspots where he heard various styles of famous pianists. But it was the organ which most inspired his genius, nurtured in early years by his mother. During the war years he also began his drinking, which

later became the acute alcoholism that periodically incapacitated him and resulted in his death at the age of thirty-nine.

The years immediately after 1918 significantly influenced his later life. He played his first band engagement as a pianist and met Edith Hatchett (whom he married shortly after his mother's death in 1920). James P. Johnson became his mentor and, after his father's opposition to a career in music, his surrogate father. Thomas Jr. was born shortly after Fats's marriage, which soon resulted in separation and divorce. Waller was twice imprisoned briefly for failure to pay alimony; continued alimony difficulties further increased his drinking and led to absences from his professional engagements. In 1927 he married Anita Rutherford, whom he later praised as "the greatest contributing factor" to his success. This was probably an exaggeration, for while his second wife was more congenial than his first, he continued his excessive drinking. His success was due rather to his genius, to his associations with such musicians as Johnson, Willie "The Lion" Smith, Duke Ellington, and the white cornetist Bix Biederbecke. Two other white men, Phil Ponce in the early 1930s and Wallace T. (Ed) Kirkeby in his later years, booked some of Waller's most successful performances.

Perhaps the most important factor in his success, however, was the growing popularity of radio. Although he made his first radio broadcast in 1923 and recorded several hundred titles, he was little known outside New York City until 1931. On his first trip abroad in 1932 on the *Île de France,* Waller won fame in Paris not only for his piano playing but also for his gargantuan appetite for booze and women. After his return, Phil Ponce booked him for an appearance over a radio station in Cincinnati. Waller's "Fats Rhythm Club" was so successful that he spent more than a year in the Midwest.

After an impromptu piano performance at a private party in New York City in 1934, William S. Paley, head of the Columbia Broadcasting System, arranged for several guest performances by Waller. At the same time Ponce obtained such a lucrative contract for Waller and the Rhythm Club that between 1934 and 1942 he found it difficult to spend most of his income in riotous living and alimony. His own composing steadily declined and his performances became more irregular and unpredictable. When Kirkeby succeeded Ponce in 1938, he temporarily helped Waller recover by arranging a trip, accompanied by his wife, to Scotland, England, and Denmark. The trip was so successful that the Wallers bought a house in the St. Albans section of Queens, New York City.

The last three years of his life were filled with triumph and disaster. On a tour through southern states in 1941 he and his orchestra suffered the racial discrimination and segregation typical of most of the region at that time. In January 1942 he gave his first jazz solo recital at Carnegie Hall, New York City; his performance on the piano and organ, however, grievously disappointed most of the audience and provoked denunciation by critics. Later in 1942 he won acclaim for the large number of performances, without pay, to entertain hundreds of Negro and white servicemen. For a brief period he followed the ominous warning of physicians and abstained from drinking. But on July 13, 1942, wartime restrictions banned new recordings. He enjoyed a brief moment of fame in 1943 for his role in *Stormy Weather,* which featured "Bojangles" Robinson and Lena Horne. He wrote the score for a successful musical, *Early to Bed,* and in solo tours for servicemen and on radio programs sang and played some of the musical's songs, as well as other popular pieces such as "Sometimes I Feel Like a Motherless Child" and Duke Ellington's "Solitude." After a two-week run at the Zanzibar Room in Los Angeles he was so exhausted, especially after a flu attack, that during the last three nights he was only semiconscious. On the way back to New York, he died of bronchial pneumonia on Dec. 15, 1943.

His personal and professional friends attended the funeral services at Abyssinian Baptist Church, with the pastor (later congressman) Adam Clayton Powell, Jr., delivering the eulogy. Outside the church several thousands jammed the streets. His body was taken to Fresh Pond Crematory. Lengthy obituaries and funeral notices paid eloquent tributes to his brilliant professional career and his ebullient personality.

Eileen Southern's *The Music of Black Musicians: A History* (1971) mentions Waller's influence on Duke Ellington and Count Basie (pp. 386, 388) and quotes the evaluation (p. 409) by Gunther Schuller: "His real service lay in taking the still somewhat disjunctive elements of [James P.] Johnson's style and unifying them into a single, cohesive jazz conception in which ragtime was still discernible beneath the surface as a source, but no longer overtly active as a separate formative element." Southern added: "Waller made yet another contribution to the history of jazz: he was the first person to successfully adapt the style of jazz pianism to the pipe organ and the Hammond organ. And yet he played standard concert music equally as well as he played jazz."

The best biography is Joel Yance's *Fats Waller: His Life and Times* (1977). It lists representative biographies and linear notes to some of Waller's record albums. In 1980 performances of *Ain't Misbehavin'* engendered a revival of interest in and appreciation of his career.

— RAYFORD W. LOGAN

WALLS, JOSIAH T[HOMAS] (1842–1905?), soldier, congressman, and farmer. Born free in Winchester, Va., on Dec. 20, 1842, and pressed into serving as a valet in a Confederate artillery battery, he was captured at Yorktown, Va., in the spring of 1862. After attending school for a year in Harrisburg, Pa., he enlisted as a private in a colored infantry regiment then being organized at Camp Penn, near Philadelphia. His regiment took part in the bloody assault on Fort Wagner, S.C., (July 1863) and in the Florida campaign (February and March 1864). He was appointed heavy and light artillery instructor to the troops defending Jacksonville and the St. John's River. After his discharge in 1865 he became a successful farmer in Alachua County, Fla. He attended the Republican party state convention in Tallahassee in 1867, and was elected a member of the state constitutional convention and legislature in 1868.

He served in Congress as the state's only representative from March 1871 to Jan. 29, 1873, and as one of two representatives from December 1873 to March 1875 and from December 1875 to April 19, 1876.

Little is known of Walls's personal life. He has been referred to as a teacher and as a lawyer, but meager evidence of formal education is available. After his years in Congress, he owned and operated a large, prosperous farm near Gainesville until a freeze destroyed most of his orange grove. Then he moved to Tallahassee to become assistant to the superintendent of farms of the State Normal and Industrial College for Colored Students (later Florida Agricultural and Mechanical University). *The Biographical Directory of the American Congress, 1774–1961* reports that Walls died in Tallahassee on May 5, 1905, and was buried in that city. Evidence still under examination, however, casts doubt on this report which can be substantiated by neither a gravestone nor by local burial records since they were destroyed by fire.

Walls's congressional record indicates he was a man whose ideas were ahead of his time in many instances. Serving in an era of confusion, hatred, and narrow political alignments, he called for support for the Cubans' struggle for freedom more than twenty years before the United States sent military aid. Furthermore, Walls foresaw the possibilities of Florida as a tourists' paradise, extolling its sunshine, climate, and other resources in eloquence similar to that of the Florida Development Commission in the 1950s and 1960s. Walls even favored a Florida ship canal. He also advocated a National Educational Fund, for "education is the panacea for all our social evils, injustices and oppressions." While this may have shown "his naïve faith" in education as Samuel Denny Smith charges in *The Negro in Congress, 1870–1901* (1940), his fears concerning education for Negroes' being neglected if left to the southern states were prophetic. Many of the fifty-one bills Walls introduced during his five years in Congress were for private pensions, internal improvements of waterways and harbors, establishing mail routes, relief for men who had served in the Seminole Wars and for Florida citizens who had lost property during the Civil War, and general amnesty. He abstained from the final vote on the Civil Rights Bill (Feb. 5, 1875) because it omitted reference to public schools.

While it is relatively easy to discover what Walls tried to do for Florida, the justice or injustice of the two unseatings of the thrice-seated congressman is far from clear. First seated as a Republican member of the House of Representatives (March 4, 1871), Walls suffered the indignity and insecurity of a congressional announcement five days later that his right to serve was being contested by Democrat Silas Niblack of Lake City. Extensions of time permitted the parties to gather evidence; a leave of absence granted to Walls and the delayed decision by the Committee on Elections left the case unsettled until Jan. 21, 1873. On Jan. 29 the House, without a record vote, declared Niblack, not Walls, entitled to represent Florida. Walls had served almost twenty-three months in the 42nd Congress before being ousted.

In November 1872 Walls was reelected, defeating

the same Silas L. Niblack by a clear majority of over 1700 votes, and served the full term without contest. Walls was destined, however, to be unseated again in the 44th Congress after serving approximately one year and six weeks (March 4, 1875, to April 19, 1876) when Democrat Jesse Johnson Finley of Jacksonville successfully contested his election. Deprived of party support, Walls lost the nomination for Congress in 1876. He served one term in the state legislature and returned to farming.

Basic information is in the *Biographical Directory of the American Congress, 1774–1961* (1961); his speeches are in the *Congressional Globe* (42nd Cong.) and the *Congressional Record* (43rd and 44th Congs.) Maurine Christopher's *America's Black Congressmen* (1971) is more satisfactory than is Samuel Denny Smith's *The Negro in Congress, 1870–1901* (1940). Joe M. Richardson's *The Negro in the Reconstruction of Florida, 1865–1877* (1965) and Peter D. Klingman's *Josiah T. Walls: Florida's Black Congressman of Reconstruction* (1976) supplant earlier books.

— GRACE RUSHINGS MAXWELL

WALTERS, ALEXANDER (1858–1917), twenty-fourth bishop of the African Methodist Episcopal Zion church, president of the Afro-American Council, and Pan-Africanist. He was born in a room in the rear of the Donohue (Donahoe) Hotel in Bardstown, Ky. His father, Henry Walters, was a slave. His mother, Harriet (Mathers) Walters, who was born a slave in Virginia, became the property of Michael Donohue of Bardstown. A tall, commanding light-brown woman, weighing over 200 pounds, she gained respect for her honesty, industry, and defiance of ill treatment. Alexander was the sixth of eight children, four of whom died in infancy. He studied at private schools and was educated for the ministry in the AME Zion church. When he graduated (1875) as valedictorian of this school five miles from his home, he completed his formal education. In 1876 he and his brother Isaac worked as waiters in the Bates House, Indianapolis; both became members of the Masons, Odd Fellows, and the United Brethren of Friendship.

In March 1877 Walters was licensed to preach by the Quarterly Conference of the AME Zion church and appointed pastor of a newly organized church in Indianapolis. On Aug. 28, 1877, he married Katie Knox of Louisville, Ky., by whom he had five children. The following year Walters was admitted to the Kentucky Conference, appointed to the impoverished Corydon Circuit, and ordained a deacon on July 8, 1879. Elected assistant secretary of the Kentucky Conference in 1881, he began a rapid rise in the AME Zion church. He held successful pastorates in Louisville (1881–1883), San Francisco, and Portland, Ore. (1883–1886). While serving as presiding elder in San Francisco, he was elected to represent California at the General Conference held in May 1884 at the historic "Mother Zion" Church, New York City. Mary E. ("Mammy") Pleasant contributed $200 in gold toward his travel. Early in Walters's career, Bishop James Walker Hood had recognized his potential for growth in the church. The General Conference concurred with Hood's opinion

when it elected Walters first assistant secretary for the conference.

After pastoring briefly in Chattanooga (1886) and in Knoxville (1886–1888), he returned to New York where he was pastor at Mother Zion. During his first year at the church, the Board of Bishops appointed him to represent the Zion church at the World's Sunday School Convention in London. Among the passengers on the *Bothnia* was Walter H. Brooks, pastor of the 19th Street Baptist Church, Washington, D.C. On boarding ship and in England, Walters experienced the hostility of white southerners who resented the presence of colored delegates. This trip to the continent resulted in interesting observations, particularly about cathedrals, Egypt, and the Holy Land. In the fall of 1889 he succeeded the Rev. Jacob Thomas as general agent of the denomination's book concern. At the age of thirty-four Walters was elected bishop of the Seventh District by the General Conference meeting in Pittsburgh on May 4, 1892.

As bishop, Walters was concerned with the secular and spiritual well-being of his district. He was well aware that the Republican party after 1877 sacrificed the Negro on the altar of goodwill between the North and the South. To give some measure of protection to Negroes, T. Thomas Fortune, editor of the *New York Age*, issued a call (Nov. 4, 1889) for the organization of a National Afro-American League. At the head of the list of those concurring was Walters. The organization existed for only two years before it died from what Fortune described as a general lack of interest. During the 1890s Congress continued to retreat from its commitment to provide civil rights for Negroes; state legislatures passed laws barring the Negro from the polls; and on Sept. 18, 1895, Booker T. Washington made his famous Atlanta speech in which he sanctioned separate development while ignoring the latest lynchings. Within a year the Supreme Court gave its approval to the doctrine of "separate but equal" in the *Plessy v. Ferguson* decision. Having taken note of these events, Walters asked Fortune to call a meeting of race leaders. On Sept. 15, 1898, in Rochester, N.Y., they organized the National Afro-American Council, with Walters as president. At the second meeting of the council in Washington, D.C. (Dec. 29, 1898), the members drew up what was probably the most comprehensive program up to that time to address the problems of Negroes.

In his address to the council Walters outlined the struggle for freedom by the Afro-American and his contributions to American society. Opposed to the stand taken by Booker T. Washington, Walters said that he was against the Negro's withdrawing from politics and that "the real question which confronts us is, shall the Negro be granted equal rights in the United States?" During the Aug. 18, 1899, national meeting in Chicago, Walters opposed Henry McNeal Turner's idea of Negro emigration to Liberia, and then presented a strong defense for Negro rights in the United States.

By the beginning of the twentieth century W. E. B. Du Bois had labeled Walters as "leaning toward Washington." While efforts were being made in 1905 to organize the Niagara Movement, Walters did seem to lend his support to Washington's efforts to counteract Du

Bois's activities. By 1908, however, Walters had reversed this trend and began to cooperate with the Niagara Movement. In the same year, he joined the District of Columbia branch of the movement.

Like Du Bois and William Monroe Trotter, Walters believed that since the Republican party had abandoned the Negro he would have to split his vote if he was to exercise any influence in politics. All three therefore supported the election of the Democratic candidate, Woodrow Wilson, in the 1912 election. Although not changing their theoretical position, they became disenchanted with Wilson when he approved the expanded segregation of government workers in the capital.

Walters's activity on the national scene was broadened by his trips abroad. After the 1890 trip he attended the Ecumenical Conferences in London (1891), where he rebutted derogatory allegations concerning Afro-Americans made by white American Methodists. At the Pan-African Conference conceived by H. Sylvester Williams and held in London (July 23–25, 1900), Walters was chosen by the delegates to preside and was elected president of the Pan-African Association. He is reported to have served as nonresident bishop to Africa (1904–1908); he went to West Africa in 1910 to reorganize the Cape Coast, West Gold Coast, and Liberia Conferences of the AME Zion church. When he landed in Sierra Leone, he was impressed by the number of black men holding all kinds of governmental positions. When he arrived in Liberia, he said that "a thrill of joy possessed me as I stepped from the boat on to the shores of my fatherland." Walters thought that his church's first priority was to lay the basis for education and then allow the church to become an outgrowth of the schools. The United States had a moral obligation to Liberia and could not afford to see it gobbled up by Great Britain, France, or some other European power. In 1911 he visited churches in Jamaica and Demerara, where Walters Chapel was built by his successor in 1911.

Walters was held in high esteem nationally and internationally. President Wilson offered him the post of minister to Liberia in 1915, but out of concern for his duty at home he declined the offer. At the time of his death on Feb. 2, 1917, from a cardiovascular disease, he was a trustee of the United Society of Christian Endeavors, a member of the Administrative Committee of the Federal Council of Churches of Christ in America, a vice-president of the World Alliance for Promoting International Friendship through the Churches, and a trustee of Livingstone College and Howard University. The Walters Institute in Wilmot, Ark., founded in the late nineteenth century (which on Jan. 20, 1936, became the Walters Southland Institute, near Lexa, Ark.), perpetuated for many years his contributions to education; Walters Memorial Church in Chicago and Walters Memorial Church in New York City, his endeavors in behalf of the AME Zion church.

His first wife died on Dec. 22, 1896; his second wife, the former Emeline Virginia Bird, died on Feb. 27, 1902. He later married Lelia Coleman of Bardstown, Ky. All aided him in his various duties. He was survived by his third wife and six children. He was buried in Mother Zion's Cypress Hill Cemetery in Brooklyn.

Walters's autobiography, *My Life and Work* (1917), is indispensable not only for his career but for perceptive observations about the AME Zion church, its trends and especially the Afro-American Council. *The African Methodist Episcopal Zion Church, Reality of the Black Church* (1974) by William Jacob Walls provides valuable additional details. There is a short sketch by Rufus E. Clement in the *DAB* (1936 [1964], 10, Part 1:398–99). Walters's panegyric, "Abraham Lincoln and Fifty Years of Freedom," is in Carter G. Woodson's *Negro Orators and Their Orations* (1925, pp. 554–67). *Reasons Why the Negro Should Vote the Democratic Ticket in This Campaign,* which resulted in severe criticism, was published in 1912. Owen Charles Mathurin's *Henry Sylvester Williams and the Origins of the Pan-African Movement, 1869–1911* (1976) criticizes Walters's *My Life and Work,* especially for its failure to list some of those present at the London conference of 1900. — JOHN E. FLEMING

WARD, SAMUEL RINGGOLD (1817–1866?), abolitionist, orator, and Underground Railroad worker. He was born of slave parents, William and Anne Ward, on the Eastern Shore of Maryland. His mother would not say where, fearing he might inadvertently make statements which could lead to their recapture. His parents were both dark, as was he, the second of their three children, all boys. His mother "hired her time," working off the estate and paying it an annuity. Her independence offended her owner, who would have sold her but for Samuel's sickliness. Fear that his return to health might result in sale, his parents in 1820 fled north with their children and settled in Greenwich, N.J., among Quakers. In 1826 a rash of slave catchings in the area set the Wards off again, this time for New York City. In the Mulberry Street school for Negro children, young Ward advanced his education along with such talented companions as Henry Highland Garnet and Alexander Crummell. In 1833 Ward was converted and looked forward to becoming a minister, meanwhile teaching in a school for colored children in Newark, N.J. In 1838 he married a Miss Reynolds of New York, with whom he had a number of children, several of whom died in youth.

Ward early interested himself in the antislavery movement. Having grown to a tall, imposing figure with notable eloquence and impassioned gestures, he attracted the attention of such influential abolitionists as Gerrit Smith and Lewis Tappan. Precisely how he pursued his incomplete studies in classics and theology is not certain—he briefly attended Oneida Institute Whitesboro, N.Y.—but they gave him a clear style of speech and writing, apposite references, and a dignity and rhetoric which stirred audiences. During his American career, he and Charles Lenox Remond were acclaimed the most famous spokesmen, after Frederick Douglass, for Negro rights. He was frequently referred to as "the black Daniel Webster."

Ward was appointed traveling agent of the American Anti-Slavery Society in 1839, and in the same year was licensed to preach by the New York Congregationalist (General) Association. He identified himself with the moderate branch of abolitionists in New York, and joined them when the Liberty party was formed in 1840. In April 1841 Ward was invited to become pastor of an all-white Congregationalist church in South Butler, N.Y. He later expressed dissatisfaction with his own inefficiency, yet also noted that the church grew under his direction. He appears to have edited briefly two reform weeklies.

In 1843 Ward resigned his pastorate because of a throat condition which he feared would damage his voice. In December of that year he moved to Geneva, N.Y., where doctors treated him successfully and also tutored him in medicine, another field which Ward regretfully abandoned. In the next year his activities in behalf of the Liberty party in New York State may have helped it take enough votes from Henry Clay to defeat him for the presidency. In 1846 Ward became pastor of another all-white Congregationalist church, this one in Cortland Village, N.Y. One of five vice-presidents in founding the American Missionary Association in 1846, he continued to oppose the admission of new slave states, efforts of New York politicians to disfranchise Negroes, and the unwillingness of churches to disavow slavery proponents. Partly because Martin Van Buren opposed the abolition of slavery in the District of Columbia, in 1848 Ward declined to support Van Buren's Free Soil party.

The passage of the Fugitive Slave Act in 1850 roused Ward to oratorical efforts which took him throughout the North. The next year, living in Syracuse, N.Y., he took an active part in freeing Jerry, a runaway slave, from prison. Fearing that his conspicuous role might lead to his apprehension, he fled to Canada where he was joined by his family several months later. He took up residence in Toronto, and considered himself a British subject. Ward joined his efforts with those of other Canadian Negroes, the majority of them immigrants from the United States. He was involved in attempts to build Negro settlements, aid refugees from the United States, fight anti-Negro prejudices in Canada, and found newspapers. As before, he was employed as an agent and orator. In 1853 he was asked by his society to visit Geat Britain to raise funds, and in April left secretly for New York where he boarded the Cunard ship *Europe*. His ocean trip and long stay in England, Scotland, Wales, and Ireland furnished him with much of the material for his *Autobiography of a Fugitive Negro* . . . (1855).

Ward's experiences perplexed him. He had already noted that his early benefactors had been people of wealth and distinction, and that harassment had come from the poor. Ward struggled to view positively hopes for better understanding, as, for example, between the Irish and his own people. Yet he could not but feel grateful for the cordiality and warmth given him by lords and ladies, and others of "superior" class and education. Ward was firm in asserting the values and qualities of his race, but his *Autobiography* exhibited dissatisfactions which appear to have made unbearable to him a return to the harsher realities of Canada and the neighboring United States, despite the unqualified admiration he received from such a leader as Frederick Douglass.

Ward's dilemmas seemed reduced by a gift of fifty acres in St. George Parish in Jamaica from a wealthy English Friend, John Candler. Ward left, presumably with his family, for Jamaica late in 1855. He apparently did not flourish there, yet he served Baptists as pastor in Kingston, and was said to have wielded political power there. He is also said to have suffered poverty in St. George Parish, where he lived after 1860.

The principal source is Ward's *Autobiography of a Fugitive Negro: His Anti-Slavery Labours in the United States, Canada & England* (1855, reprinted 1968 and 1970). No copies have been found of his *Reflections Upon the Jordon Rebellion* (1866), which might throw light on his life in Jamaica. There is a brief sketch by Fred Landon in the *DAB* ([1936], 10, Part 1:440). Additional valuable details are in Benjamin Quarles's *Black Abolitionists* (1969). — LOUIS FILLER

WARING, LAURA WHEELER (1887–1948), educator and portrait painter. Born in Hartford, Conn., the fourth of six children of the Rev. Robert Foster and Mary (Freeman) Wheeler, she had the advantages of upper-class Negroes and excellent public schools. Her father, the minister of the Talcott Street Congregational Church, received his diploma from the Theology Department of Howard University in 1877. After graduation from Hartford High School, Laura studied for six years (1906–1912) at one of America's finest art schools, the Pennsylvania Academy of the Fine Arts. A William Emlen Cresson Memorial Travel Scholarship (1914) enabled her to study briefly in several European cities. She established the art and music departments at Cheyney Training School for Teachers, near Philadelphia, and directed them for more than thirty years. Meanwhile, in 1924 she made a second trip abroad, this time accompanied by Jessie Redmond Fauset, a teacher, editor, and novelist. After her return her paintings were exhibited in some of the most noted art galleries, and in Paris, during her third trip. She was in charge of Negro art during the Sesquicentennial Exposition (Philadelphia, 1926) and director of Negro exhibits in the Texas Centennial Exposition (1937). She married Walter E. Waring, a professor at Lincoln University, Pennsylvania. After a long and painful illness, she died on Feb. 3, 1948.

Laura Wheeler Waring had the advantages of training unusual for American artists of her era. On her first trip abroad (1914) she spent much time in the Louvre and studied the works of several masters, particular the landscapes of Claude Monet in Luxemburg. During her second trip (1924) she studied at the Academie de la Grande Chaumière, Paris, where she was influenced especially by Boutet de Monvel and Eugène Delecluse. Her visits to France, London, Dublin, Rome, Luxemburg, and North Africa provided subjects for some of her paintings, for instance, *Houses at Semur*, France. A versatile artist, she shared in the painting of a mural for the Pennsylvania Building during the Sesquicentennial Exposition (1926). Her landscapes of Chester and Delaware Counties, Pa., gained wide acclaim.

She was best known, however, for her portraits. One of the best known is that of Ann Washington Derry, for which she received (1927) the second Harmon Award. Some of her portraits are documentary, especially those of James Weldon Johnson, W. E. B. Du Bois, John

Haynes Holmes, Mary White Ovington, and Leslie Pickney Hill. It is understandable that she has been accused of being primarily a painter of upper-class Negroes and whites. Few others could afford the cost of having their portraits painted by a famous artist. Moreover, some of her paintings, like that of Anne Washington Derry, do not fall in this category. Of special sociological significance was a canvas, *Mother and Daughter* (1927), which portrayed a mulatto mother with her quadroon daughter. Other well-known paintings were *The Co-Ed* and *The Musician*.

Waring's work was exhibited in the Pennsylvania Academy of the Fine Arts, the Philadelphia Museum of Art, the Corcoran Gallery (Washington, D.C.), the Brooklyn Museum, and many others. During her third trip abroad she exhibited at a one-man show in the Galerie du Luxembourg, Boulevard Saint-Germain, Paris. In May and June 1949 she was honored by an exhibit of her works in the Howard University Gallery of Art.

Laura Waring died after a long illness at her home, 756 N. 43rd St., Philadelphia, on Feb. 3, 1948. Private funeral services were held on Feb. 7 and she was buried in Eden Cemetery. She was survived by her husband, a sister, and two brothers (*Philadelphia Tribune,* Feb. 7, 1948, pp. 1, 2).

There is an obituary, probably written by Carter G. Woodson, in the *JNH* (July 1948, pp. 385–86). A longer biographical sketch and evaluation is "Laura Wheeler Waring," by Milton M. James, in the *NHB* (March 1956, pp. 126–28), with reproductions of portraits of her husband and an oil painting of Anne Washington Derry. *In Memoriam, Laura Wheeler Waring, 1887– 1948. An Exhibition of Paintings, May and June, 1949. Washington, D.C. Howard University Gallery of Art* (1949) is in the Moorland-Spingarn Research Center, Howard University. — RAYFORD W. LOGAN

WASHINGTON, BOOKER T[ALIAFERRO] (1856– 1915), educator and race leader. Washington was born on April 5, 1856, in Franklin County, Va., His father was an unknown white man; his mother, Jane, was the slave cook of James Burroughs, a small planter. Booker's elder brother John was also the son of a white man. Sometime after Booker's birth his mother was married to Washington Ferguson, a slave. A daughter, Amanda, was born to this marriage. James, Booker's younger half-brother, was adopted. His mother named her child Booker Taliaferro but later dropped the second name. Booker gave himself the surname "Washington" when he first enrolled in school.

Booker spent his first nine years as a slave on the Burroughs farm. In 1865 his mother took her children to Malden, W. Va., to join her husband, who had gone there earlier and found work in the salt mines. At the age of nine Booker was put to work packing salt. Between the ages of ten and twelve he worked in a coal mine. In 1871 he went to work as a houseboy for the wife of Gen. Lewis Ruffner, owner of the mines. Mrs. Ruffner, a strict New Englander, was an important influence in the boy's life, helping to instill in him a regard for cleanliness, orderliness, and satisfaction in a job well-done.

In Malden young Washington acquired some fundamentals of an education, partly through his own efforts and partly by attending school while continuing to work in the mines. In 1872, at the age of sixteen, he took what was probably the most decisive step in his life when he entered Hampton Normal and Agricultural Institute in Virginia. The dominant personality at the school, which had opened in 1868 under the auspices of the American Missionary Association, was the principal, Samuel Chapman Armstrong, the son of American missionaries in Hawaii. Armstrong, who had commanded Negro troops in the Civil War, believed that the progress of the freedmen and their descendants depended on education of a special sort, which would be practical and utilitarian and would at the same time inculcate character and morality.

Washington traveled most of the distance from Malden to Hampton on foot, arriving penniless and dirty. He was given work as a janitor to pay the cost of his room and board. Armstrong arranged for a white benefactor to pay his tuition. At Hampton, Washington studied academic subjects and agriculture, which included work in the fields and pig sties. He also learned lessons in personal cleanliness and good manners. His special interest was public speaking and debate. He was jubilant when he was chosen to speak at his commencement. The most important part of his experience at Hampton was his association with Armstrong, whom he described in his autobiography as "a great man—the noblest rarest human being it has ever been my privilege to meet." From Armstrong, Washington derived much of his educational philosophy. Armstrong, Lewis Adams (a former slave), and others helped Washington establish Tuskegee, and in later years he helped his former student gain access to white philanthropists.

After graduating from Hampton with honors in 1875 Washington returned to Malden to teach school. In 1878 he went to Washington, D.C., where he spent eight months as a student at Wayland Seminary, an institution with a curriculum which was entirely academic and where there was no work program for students. This experience reinforced his belief in an educational system which emphasized practical skills and self-help. In 1879 he returned to Hampton to teach in a program for American Indians.

In 1881 the opportunity of his life came. The Alabama legislature had authorized the establishment of a normal school to train Negro teachers at Tuskegee in Macon County, the heart of the "Black Belt." Armstrong was invited to recommend a white teacher as principal. Instead he recommended Washington, who was accepted. When Washington arrived at Tuskegee he found that no land or buildings had been acquired for the projected school, nor was there any money for these purposes since the legislative appropriation of $2000 for the school was for salaries only.

Undaunted by these inauspicious circumstances, Washington went to work to sell the idea of the school and to recruit students from the Negro families in the county, at the same time seeking the support of local whites. The school opened in a shanty loaned by the Negro church. Soon the youthful principal was able to borrow money from the treasurer of Hampton Institute to purchase an abandoned plantation on the outskirts of Tuskegee as a permanent site. Students went to work to build a kiln to make bricks for buildings. Within a few years a classroom building, a dining hall, a girls' dormitory, and a chapel had been built. The sale of bricks from the kiln raised some of the money for the buildings. By 1888 the school owned 540 acres of land and had an enrollment of more than 400. It offered training in such skilled trades as carpentry, cabinetmaking, printing, shoemaking, and tinsmithing. Boys also studied farming and dairying, while girls learned cooking and sewing and other skills related to homemaking. Through their own labor students supplied a large part of the needs of the school.

In the academic departments Washington insisted that efforts be made to relate the subject matter to the actual experiences of the students. Strong emphasis was placed on personal hygiene, manners, and character building. Students followed a rigid schedule of study and work, arising at five in the morning and retiring at nine-thirty at night. Although Tuskegee was non-denominational, all students were required to attend chapel daily and a series of religious services on Sunday. Washington himself usually spoke to the students on Sunday evenings.

In some respects Tuskegee was a replica of Hampton, and many members of its staff, especially in the early years, were Hampton-trained. But at Tuskegee the staff was always all-Negro, whereas at Hampton the principal and most of the teachers were white. Olivia Davidson, a graduate of Hampton and Framingham State Normal School in Massachusetts, became teacher and assistant principal in 1881. In addition to her academic duties she played an important part in raising money for the school. In 1885 Washington's older brother John, also a Hampton graduate, came to Tuskegee to direct the vocational training program. Other notable additions to the staff were George Washington Carver, who became director of the agricultural program in 1896; Emmett J. Scott, who became Washington's private secretary in 1897; and Nathan Monroe Work, who became head of the Records and Research Department in 1908.

Beginning in 1892 annual Tuskegee Negro Conferences were held to which thousands of rural Negroes came to learn better farming methods. The establishment of the State Agricultural Experiment Station at Tuskegee in 1897 made possible an expansion of extension services. Later the building of a hospital and the inauguration of a nurse's training program supplied additional services to the community. Tuskegee's influence extended far beyond Alabama. Graduates of the school taught in all of the southern states, and by the time of Washington's death in 1915 several similar institutions modeled on Tuskegee had been founded in other states. Tuskegee graduates were found in various places in Africa, engaged in efforts to spread the Tuskegee system of education and improved methods of agriculture. By 1915 Tuskegee had an endowment of $1,945,000 and a staff of almost 200. Nearly 2000 students were enrolled in the regular courses and about the same number in special courses and the extension division. But in spite of the growth in size and functions of the school

and his own multifarious activities, Washington's personality permeated the entire institution and he continued to concern himself with minute details of administration and the conduct of staff and students.

Much of Washington's time was spent in raising money for Tuskegee and in publicizing the school and its philosophy. His success in securing financial aid from northern philanthropists was one of his most remarkable achievements. As Tuskegee grew, many of the new buildings bore the names of white benefactors. In 1898 Washington gained invaluable publicity when President McKinley visited Tuskegee and praised its program. The following year Washington launched a campaign for a permanent endowment at a meeting at Madison Square Garden in New York City. Through his fundraising efforts he became acquainted with such leaders of finance and industry as John Wanamaker, Henry H. Rogers of Standard Oil, Collis P. Huntington, Robert C. Ogden, William H. Baldwin, Jr., and Andrew Carnegie. These men and others of similar circumstances gave money to Tuskegee and served on its board. Carnegie became the largest single donor to Tuskegee. Washington also received aid for Tuskegee and for other educational programs for southern Negroes from such philanthropic foundations as the Peabody Education Fund, the John F. Slater Fund, and the Julius Rosenwald Fund. He played a part in establishing others, such as the Anna T. Jeanes Fund and the Phelps-Stokes Fund.

Although Tuskegee was Washington's most enduring monument, his work as an educator was only one part of his many-faceted career. As early as 1884 he addressed the annual meeting of the National Educational Association in Madison, Wis. But it was his address at the opening of the Cotton States and International Exposition in Atlanta on Sept. 18, 1895, which won him a national reputation. The speech before a racially mixed audience was directed primarily to the whites. Although only about fifteen minutes long, it contained the essence of Washington's racial philosophy. The oration was enthusiastically received by the audience and widely reported in the white press, which began to hail Washington as leader and spokesman for all American Negroes and successor to Frederick Douglass, who had died a few months earlier. Little noticed then and almost unknown later is the observation by James Creelman, a well-known reporter of the *New York World* (Sept. 19, 1895, p. 1), that at the end of the speech "most of the Negroes in the audience were crying, perhaps without knowing just why."

After the Atlanta address Washington was in such demand as a speaker that he spent a substantial part of each year on the lecture circuit. In his speeches he continually reiterated his educational and racial views. To win the attention of his audience and to illustrate points he wished to make he frequently told humorous "darky" stories, which pictured Negroes as lovable, shiftless, ignorant, gullible, yet shrewd. White audiences loved the stories. The lectures, the stories, and other activities of Washington were so widely reported in the press that he became one of the best known Americans of his day.

Washington's fame was also spread by his writings, especially his autobiography, *Up from Slavery,* which

appeared in book form in 1901 after having been serialized in *The Outlook.* The book became a bestseller in
the United States and was ultimately translated into
more than a dozen languages. The account of Washington's struggles and the successes which he achieved
through persistence and self-reliance was influential in
interesting men like Andrew Carnegie and Henry H.
Rogers in Tuskegee. Royalties from the book were also
a source of income for the school.

In 1901 Washington's influence was significantly
widened when Theodore Roosevelt became president.
In his speeches and writings Washington frequently
took a deprecatory attitude toward politics, but during
the Roosevelt and Taft administrations he wielded far
more political power than any other Negro, and probably had more influence at the White House than some
white southerners. That Roosevelt invited the black educator to lunch at the White House was well known; in
fact the incident created a sensation, especially in
southern newspapers. That the president consulted
Washington on appointments and racial and southern
policies was not widely known. Washington's influence
was responsible for the appointment of certain northern
Negroes, notably Charles W. Anderson as collector of
internal revenue in New York and William H. Lewis as
assistant attorney-general. Southern Negro politicians
learned that they needed Washington's endorsement in
seeking appointments. Washington was also responsible for the naming of some southern whites. Best known
was his recommendation of Gold Democrat Thomas G.
Jones to a federal judgeship in Alabama. Washington
worked assiduously, although secretly, to hold the
Negro vote for Taft in 1908. In 1912 he supported Taft,
the regular Republican candidate, instead of Roosevelt,
the Progressive, but with the election of the Democrat,
Wilson, his political influence declined sharply.

While always preserving a facade of humility and
publicly disclaiming any desire to be recognized as
"race leader," Washington did see himself in this role
and worked unceasingly to maintain this image of himself among both whites and Negroes. This is illustrated
by his relationship to the National Afro-American Council (successor to the National Afro-American League,
which had been founded in 1890 by T. Thomas Fortune
and revived under the new name in 1898). At first
Washington worked behind the scenes to ensure the
election of officers friendly to him and the adoption of
policies consistent with his views. Beginning in 1902 he
attended national conventions of the council and
played a conspicuous role although he never was an
officer. Internal dissension between Washington's critics and his supporters weakened the council and was a
factor in its decline.

The National Negro Business League, founded in
1900 largely at Washington's instigation, was completely dominated by him and the Tuskegee philosophy.
He served continuously as its president until his death.
The league paid no attention to questions of civil and
political rights but concentrated on encouraging the development and support of Negro-owned and -operated
businesses.

In maintaining his role of race leader and in shaping
Negro opinion Washington's relations with the Negro

press were important. He publicly denied trying to exert
any influence on the press and flatly asserted that he
had no financial interest in any publication, saying that
it would be improper for him to do so. But in spite of
his denials he was part owner of a few publications and
subsidized numerous others in a small way, and regularly supplied them with news stories and editorials favorable to himself. Most important were his relations
with T. Thomas Fortune's *New York Age,* the most
prestigious Negro newspaper. Although Fortune was
much more militant than Washington the two men were
close friends for many years. Because the *Age,* like
nearly all race papers, was chronically in financial difficulties, Washington loaned money to Fortune and subsidized the *Age* for several years. In 1907 the *Age* was
incorporated with Washington secretly one of the principal stockholders. A few months later, when Fortune
suffered a mental breakdown, Washington clandestinely advanced money to Fred R. Moore to enable him
to buy Fortune's interest in the *Age.*

Much about Washington's ideology and some clues
to his personality may be gleaned from his speeches
and published writings. His basic philosophy appears to
have crystalized early and to have changed little. Although he was a prolific writer and speaker, he constantly reiterated a few ideas. Some of his books and
articles were wholly ghostwritten; in others the research
and part of the writing were done by others. Among the
men who thus assisted Washington were T. Thomas
Fortune, S. Laing Williams, Max Bennett Thrasher, Robert E. Park, and Nathan Monroe Work. But there is no
reason to think that the ideas and opinions expressed
were not Washington's own.

At the outset of his career, he wrote, he realized that
the success of Tuskegee depended on winning the support of three groups—the "best class" of southern
whites, northern whites with a philanthropic interest in
the South, and members of his own race. It is evident
in everything he published or said publicly that he
weighed the effects of his words on these three groups.
At first reading what he said appeared to be simple and
straightforward, but a closer reading reveals a man who
was complex, subtle, and ambiguous. His writings show
little intellectual or scholarly depth, but they reveal an
understanding of psychology, particularly the psychology of the white-dominated society in which he lived
and with which he had to deal. The views which he
expressed on almost all subjects—economic, political,
social, racial—were essentially the prevailing views of
white Americans. On the whole he said what white
Americans wanted to hear. Publicly he was indomitably
optimistic about the future of race relations. He invariably addressed whites in conciliatory terms. He was
always quick to praise any evidence, however slight, of
goodwill and constructive effort by whites. He did not
completely ignore white injustices toward Negroes, but
he mentioned them so delicately and subtly that most
whites were oblivious of any implied criticism. On the
other hand, in speaking to and about members of his
own race he was sometimes sharply critical. He always
laid greater emphasis on the duties and responsibilities
of Negroes than on their rights. Both blacks and whites
gained the impression that he thought that the primary

responsibility for improved race conditions lay with Negroes.

The core of Washington's philosophy was that through hard work, thrift, self-help, and economic progress Negroes would improve their status and be accepted by whites into the American body politic. The opportunity to earn a living and acquire property was more important than the right to vote. But if Negroes made themselves economically indispensable, they would gain political and other rights. "No race that has anything to contribute to the markets of the world is long in any degree ostracized," he said in the Atlanta address. He also advised Negroes: "Cast down your buckets where you are." To the end of his life he insisted that there were better opportunities in the South and less economic discrimination than in the North. Along with emphasis on economic progress he preached the doctrine of thrift and the dignity of labor. The opportunity to earn a dollar in a factory was of more importance to the Negro, he said, than the opportunity to spend a dollar in the opera house.

He organized the National Negro Business League, which emphasized racial solidarity and sought to win respect by developing economic independence from the white community. But he usually stressed the economic interdependence and mutuality of interests of whites and blacks. He tried to persuade southern whites that to help Negroes improve their condition was in their own self-interest. On the subject of labor relations his views were consistent with those of the white industrialists who were Tuskegee's benefactors. He sometimes spoke disparagingly of labor unions and stressed the advantages of employing Negroes who were "loyal" and "unresentful," and not given to strikes and boycotts.

The educational system which he developed at Tuskegee reflected his economic philosophy. Slavery had meant work, and in the early days of freedom, said Washington, Negroes had too often looked upon education as a means of escaping from work. Tuskegee stressed the dignity of labor and the moral value of working with the hands. Above all, the emphasis was on the practical value of education, the preparation of students to be successful farmers, artisans, and teachers. Efforts were made to relate the course of study to the world in which the students lived. Tuskegee sought to enable students to improve their economic condition but not to make them dissatisfied or unable to adjust to the realities of life in the South. Later critics pointed out that the system, although called "industrial education," did not include training in skills related to the technology of industry in the twentieth century.

Washington appeared to have little interest in developing the cultural or intellectual interests of his students. He frequently made disparaging remarks about Negroes who studied French grammar or Latin or Greek but who did not have needed vocational skills. In reply to his critics he admitted that there was a need for Negro colleges to train potential leaders, but he insisted that industrial training best met the needs of most blacks at their stage of economic and political development.

On the subject of political rights Washington's position was ambiguous. As already noted, he himself wielded substantial political power during the Roosevelt and Taft administrations, but his writings gave the impression that he thought that the granting of suffrage to freedmen during Reconstruction had been premature. In *Up from Slavery* he said that it was the duty of the Negro "to deport himself modestly in regard to political claims." On several occasions he asserted that he supported educational and taxpaying requirements for voting, but he asked that they be applied impartially to white and black alike. For instance, he hoped in 1898 that the Louisiana "grandfather clause" would not give one interpretation for the white man and another for the Negro, and repeated his view before the Bethel Literary and Historical Association in Washington, D.C. on May 29, 1900. And in November 1908 he suggested to President-elect Taft that he say in a speech that since only a small proportion of Negroes would be allowed to vote under the new southern state constitutions, "it is important that these constitutions be applied with equal and exact justice to black and white alike." He seemed honestly to believe that once Negroes acquired education and property whites would no longer oppose their participation in politics.

On the sensitive question of the social relations between the races Washington was cautious and circumspect. "The wisest among my race," he said in the Atlanta address, "understand that the agitation of questions of social equality is the extremest folly." He did not publicly protest most Jim Crow laws and practices, although in the last years of his life he wrote several articles in which he criticized the inequities in the school system of the South and expressed opposition to racial residential zoning laws.

In spite of the cautious stance which he maintained publicly, behind the scenes Washington was actively engaged in efforts against disfranchisement and other forms of discrimination. Recent research has shown not only that his ultimate goals were complete racial equality but that he devoted money and effort to challenge increasing racial disabilities. He tried to use his influence against Lily White control of the Republican party in the South. In 1903 and 1904 he secretly financed and employed a lawyer for two Alabama suffrage cases which were unsuccessfully appealed to the U.S. Supreme Court. He financed successful appeals in a case involving exclusion of Negroes from an Alabama jury and in the Alonzo Bailey peonage case. He also assisted in several efforts to challenge Jim Crow transportation practices. But so carefully did he conceal his part in these activities that his white contemporaries were oblivious to them, and few Negroes knew of them. At the time of his death all the southern states had enacted laws and constitutional amendments that effectively disenfranchised Negroes, while permitting equally unqualified whites to vote.

Certainly one of Washington's greatest talents was in the realm of public relations. His success in winning the support and praise of white Americans was remarkable. Andrew Carnegie thought he was "certainly one of the most wonderful men living or who ever has lived." Many other industrial, political, intellectual, and religious leaders were almost as laudatory. A few southern demagogues like Ben Tillman vilified Washington for his

find because it is widely scattered in newspaper articles and manuscript collections. The best set of news clippings is located in the vertical file on the Whipper Home at the Martin Luther King Memorial Library in Washington, D.C. The Leigh R. Whipper Papers in the Moorland-Spingarn Research Center at Howard University contain biographical data about the Whipper family which include the St. Luke's Church obituary notice.

— ROSALYN TERBORG-PENN

WHIPPER, WILLIAM (1804?–1876), moral reformer and businessman. He was born in Little Britain township, Pa. Little is known of his early life and education, but by 1828 he was residing in Philadelphia, engaged in the occupation of steam scouring, a process for cleaning clothing. In 1834 he operated a "free labor and temperance grocery" in the city. His learning and considerable literary skill were displayed in his "Address before the Colored Reading Society of Philadelphia" (1828) and in his "Eulogy on William Wilberforce" (1833), as well as in frequent communications to the press. In 1837 he published in the *Colored American* his notable essay, "Non-Resistance to Offensive Aggression."

Whipper was an active participant in all of the annual conventions of free people of color held between 1830 and 1835, and later participated in the Pennsylvania state convention (1848) and the national conventions held in Rochester, N.Y. (1853), and Philadelphia (1855). At the national convention in 1853 he played a leading role in organizing the American Moral Reform Society (1835–1841). Dedicated to the principles of education, economy, temperance, and universal liberty, and in theory not confined to men of color, the society had its strongest support within Philadelphia. His address "To the American People" at the First Annual Meeting of the society in the Presbyterian church, Seventh Street below Shippen in Philadelphia (Aug. 14–19, 1837), explained these goals and concluded: "We do most cordially hope that a moral fabric may be reared that will promote the cause of righteousness and justice throughout the country." James Forten, Sr., was elected president of the society; John F. Cook, Sr., and Whipper, secretaries. Whipper was editor of the society's journal, the *National Reformer,* the first magazine edited by a Negro, throughout its brief existence from September 1838 to December 1839.

By 1835 Whipper had moved to Columbia, Pa., where on March 10, 1836, he married Harriet L. L. Smith. He became associated with the wealthy Negro lumber merchant Stephen Smith, and they carried on an extensive business based both in Columbia and Philadelphia. Active in the Underground Railroad, Whipper estimated that between 1847 and 1860 he spent $1000 annually aiding hundreds of fugitive slaves who passed through Columbia to freedom.

1853 Whipper visited Canada and purchased land on the Sydenham River, near the Dawn community at Dresden, Ontario. Several of his relatives emigrated to Canada and Whipper was preparing to move there also when the outbreak of the Civil War caused him to remain in the United States. He aided the Union cause financially, and in 1866 was a member of the delegation headed by Frederick Douglass that remonstrated unsuccessfully with Pres. Andrew Johnson on civil rights issues.

After 1865 Whipper conducted his Philadelphia lumber business in partnership with his nephew, James W. Purnell, who had been associated with Martin R. Delany in the latter's Niger River expedition. In 1868 he became a resident of New Brunswick, N.J., where he was recorded in the 1870 census as having a total worth of $108,000. He became cashier of the Philadelphia branch of the Freedmen's Savings Bank in 1870, and although the affairs of the branch were well managed, it closed in 1874 when the parent institution collapsed. Whipper transferred his residence to Philadelphia in 1873. He died there after a long illness on March 9, 1876, and was buried in Olive Cemetery. His wife died in Camden, N.J., on Sept. 23, 1906. Among his descendants were his son William J. Whipper (a delegate to the 1868 South Carolina Constitutional Convention, a municipal judge, and a member of the 1895 Constitutional Convention); a granddaughter Ionia Rollin Whipper (who in 1941 founded a home for unwed mothers in Washington, D.C.), and a grandson Leigh Whipper (a well-known stage and movie actor).

Whipper was "a mulatto of fine personal appearance, above the middle size." Not an effective speaker, he was most frequently called upon at the numerous meetings he attended to draft resolutions and eloquent addresses. Early in his career he viewed the "moral elevation" of his people as a prerequisite to their enjoyment of full freedom, but later he espoused the position that freedom was the inherent right of all men. Although he was often involved in controversy because of his commitment to abstract reform principles and his adamant opposition to institutions based on "complexional distinctions," he was esteemed and respected by his contemporaries for his learning and his business acumen.

There are no reliable biographies, but there is a brief sketch, together with a portrait and an autobiographical memoir, in William Still's *The Underground Railroad* (rev. ed., 1879). The 1828 address and the "Address to the American People" are reproduced in *Early Negro Writing 1760–1837,* selected and introduced by Dorothy Porter (1971). The Leigh Whipper Papers, which contain biographical data about the Whipper family, are in the Moorland-Spingarn Research Center, Howard University. — RICHARD P. McCORMICK

WHIPPLE, PRINCE (? – ?), soldier of the American Revolution. He was born in Amabou, Africa. When he was about ten, he and a cousin were sent by his comparatively well-to-do parents to be educated in colonial America, from which an elder brother had returned four years earlier. The captain of the ship sold Prince Whipple and his cousin into slavery in Baltimore and he was later purchased by General Whipple of Portsmouth, N.H., from whom he took his surname. According to tradition, accepted by the historian William C. Nell, Prince Whipple was with Gen. George Washington when he crossed the Delaware, Christmas 1776. A painting in 1819 by Thomas Sully depicts Washington preparatory to the crossing; he was accompanied by three white officers and a young Negro soldier. There is also one recognizable Negro oarsman in the painting in 1851 of the rowboat by Emanuel Gottlieb Leutze. Nell identified the soldier and the oarsman as Prince Whipple, "body-guard to Gen. Whipple of New Hampshire, who was Aid [sic] to General Washington."

Emancipated during the war, as were other slaves who served in it, Prince Whipple was entrusted by General Whipple to carry a large sum of money from Salem, Mass., to Portsmouth. Attacked by ruffians near Newburyport, he struck one with a loaded whip and shot the other. He was one of nineteen "natives of Africa"—"born free"—of Portsmouth who petitioned the council and House of New Hampshire sitting in Exeter in 1779 to restore their freedom "for the sake of justice, humanity, and the rights of mankind." They argued that "the God of nature gave them life and freedom, upon the terms of the most perfect equality with other men; That freedom is an inherent right of the human species, not to be surrendered but by consent, for the sake of social life; That private or public tyranny and slavery are alike detestable to minds conscious of the equal dignity of human nature." He died in Portsmouth at the age of thirty-two, leaving a widow and children.

See Sidney Kaplan's *The Black Presence in the Era of the American Revolution, 1770–1800* (1973). Kaplan reproduced the Sully painting, which is in the Museum of Fine Arts, Boston, and an undated engraving in the New York Public Library by Paul Girardet of the Leutze painting. — RAYFORD W. LOGAN

WHITE, CLARENCE CAMERON (1879–1960) composer, violinist, educator, and author. He was born in Clarksville, Tenn., the son of James W. White of free Negro-white parentage and the former Jennie Scott of free Negro-Indian parentage. His father, a medical doctor and also principal of the Clarksville High School, died before Clarence had reached the age of two. Clarence lived his early childhood in the home of his mother's parents in Oberlin, Ohio, where he absorbed the musical atmosphere of Oberlin in which his mother had studied the violin and from which she had graduated in 1867. His mother was teaching in the public schools of Chattanooga, Tenn., where she met and married William H. Conner who, Clarence said, "was a true father" to him. His little sister Jamesina died at age four months, leaving him the only child. Clarence began the study of the violin at age eight, with the warning from his grandfather: "If you ever play for a dance, I'll take the violin away from you!" Clarence was also a boy soprano soloist in church choirs.

In 1890 his father accepted a position as medical examiner in the Government Pension Office in Washington, D.C. Clarence studied the violin with Will Marion Cook, a pupil of Joachim. His first violin performance in churches date from age fourteen. His theory studies resulted in his first composition for violin and piano (also at age fourteen), and his piano accompanist was to become his future wife, Beatrice Warrick, then age eight.

In 1896 Clarence entered Oberlin Conservatory where for four years he was the only Negro student, and graduated in violin in 1901. For the next two years he studied and performed in Boston, New York, and New Haven. In 1902 he played a concert in New York City where he had already made the acquaintance of Harry T. Burleigh, Paul Laurence Dunbar, and other Negro artists. Booker T. Washington was present at the concert and invited White to play at Tuskegee. The influence of these men upon the young musician was profound.

In 1903 White was invited by Harriet Gibbs, (first colored graduate of Oberlin Conservatory) to join the new Washington Conservatory of Music faculty as violin teacher, vice-president, and registrar. He later also taught music in the public schools of Washington, D.C. In 1905 he married Beatrice Warrick. Their first son, William, was born that year; they later had a second son, Clarence Cameron Jr.

A turning point in the composer's life was the visit of Samuel Coleridge-Taylor in 1904. White studied composition with the famous Afro-British composer in London in the summer of 1906 and returned to London in 1908–1911 where he also studied with the famous Russian violinist Michael Zacherewitsch. White was first violinist in the distinguished String Players Club of Croydon. He performed throughout Europe and the United States with Coleridge-Taylor during these and the subsequent three years. In 1910 he established a studio in Boston and performed extensively, accompanied by his wife. He also taught in the Boston Public Schools from 1912 to 1923. During 1914–1924 he conducted the Victoria Concert Orchestra of Boston. In 1924 he joined ASCAP.

From 1924 to 1931 he was director of music in West Virginia State College at Institute, W.Va. While there he became interested in Haitian music and history through the professor of romance languages John F. Matheus, for whose play *Tambour* White wrote incidental music, including a ballet number "Meringue" (1928).

They conceived the idea of writing an opera based on the life of Dessalines, first emperor of Haiti. Granted financial aid by the Julius Rosenwald Fund (1930–1931), they visited Haiti to study the music and culture of voodoo. They also received help from the Harmon Foundation. The theme that evolved was based on the struggle by the Christian Dessalines against the voodoo religious practices that held captive his beloved Défilée. The title *Ouanga* is a magic word meaning "voodoo charm." The plot is based on historical incidents, including the assassination of Dessalines.

The opera, completed in 1932 and performed that year in concert in Chicago, won the David Bispham Award. The first stage production of *Ouanga* (1949) was in South Bend, Ind., under the auspices of the Burleigh Musical Association. Joseph Charles, Haitian ambassador to the United States, attended the performance. The *South Bend Tribune* reported: "the rhythmic pattern . . . often sweeps to majestic terrifying heights. His score is a gem of orchestration." In 1950 *Ouanga* was produced in the Academy of Music, Philadelphia, by the Negro Dra-Mu Opera Company in full staging, costumes, and ballet. Reviews in the *New York Times, Musical Courier, Musical America, Philadelphia Bulletin,* and *Amsterdam News* were all enthusiastic. Arthur Farwell, distinguished American composer, wrote that "the music of *Ouanga* is one of beauty, much variety, expressiveness, exquisite lyricism, resourceful in rough dramatic expression on occasion. Too much cannot be said of the beauty and masterfulness of the orchestration." In 1956 there were performances in New York at the Metropolitan Opera House and in Carnegie Hall, both in concert version with ballet by the National Negro Opera Company.

In 1928 White was awarded an honorary M.A. by Atlanta University, and in 1933 the honorary D.Mus. by Wilberforce University.

White also studied composition in Paris with Raoul Laparra in 1930–1931. A String Quartet, *Prelude, Dawn, Jubilee Hallelujah,* was performed by the faculty of L'École Normale de Musique. From 1931 to 1935 White was director of music at Hampton Institute, where from 1933 to 1935 he conducted the Hampton Institute Choir, carrying on what he described as "Dett's sensitive musical achievement." Reviews of his conducting attest the fine musicianship he brought to this group. From 1937 to 1941 White organized community music programs for the National Recreation Association, traveling widely, making his home in Chicago and later in Elizabeth, N.J., where his wife became ill and died. His two sons had already predeceased her.

In 1943 he moved to New York City, where he married Pura Belpré, specialist in Puerto Rican folk stories and children's books. In 1954 he won the "Tranquil Music" Benjamin Award in New Orleans for his orchestral work *Elegy.*

White's music is characterized by lyricism, expressiveness, and a strong sense of folk origins. As Carter Harman wrote in the *New York Times* (1950), he "made little attempt to keep up with the Copelands but it might be said that he is happily in step with the Puccinis." His music has been widely performed by distinguished artists, including Fritz Kreisler, Jascha Heifetz, Albert Spaulding, Camilla Williams, Carol Brice; by leading symphony orchestras including the Boston, National, Vienna; by the Goldman and U.S. Marine Bands; and many other performers. His publishers included Carl Fischer, Sam Fox, Elkan, Boston Music, Theodore Presser, G. Ricordi, Birchard, and others. His compositions include "Bandanna Sketches" (1918), later arranged by him for orchestra and also for band, among them "Nobody Knows the Trouble I've Seen," played by Kreisler and published in the *Kreisler Folio;* works for orchestra such as *Tambour, Kutamba, Elegy;* works for piano, voice and piano, chorus; and the opera *Ouanga.*

He also wrote many articles, among them "Negro Music: A Contribution to the National Music of America" (*Musical Observer,* Nov. 1919 to March 1920).

During his last years he lived at 409 Edgecombe Ave., New York City. He died in Sydenham Hospital on June 30, 1960, and was survived by his widow, Pura.

Basic facts are in *Who's Who in America, 1952–1953.* Useful are Hildred Roach's *Black American Music, Past and Present* (1973), and Eileen Southern's *The Music of Black Musicians: A History* (1971). His obituary appeared in the *New York Times* (July 2, 1960, p. 17). Mrs. Pura White had extensive materials which she generously made available for this brief study. — RAYMOND LEMIEUX

WHITE, GEORGE H[ENRY] (1852–1918), teacher, lawyer, member of Congress, real estate dealer, banker, and founder of an all-Negro town. White was born in Rosindale, N.C., on Dec. 18, 1852, of Negro, Irish, and Indian parentage. He was the last former slave to serve in Congress and the last "Post-Reconstruction" Negro member of the House of Representatives. After attending public schools, while aiding the family in farming and making casks, he studied at Howard University (1873–1877), receiving a certificate from the Normal Department. During the summers he taught in North Carolina and continued teaching after graduation. He passed the bar examination, opened an office in New Bern, and practiced there and in other parts of the state. In 1880 he was elected to the state House of Representatives from the 8th District, in the "Black Belt." One of his significant achievements was the passage of a bill for four normal schools for Negroes, and he served as principal of the school in New Bern. Elected in 1884 to the state Senate with the support of Populists, he continued, with limited success, his interest in public schools. He served on the committees for the insane asylum, insurance, and judiciary. In 1885 he was elected solicitor and prosecutor for the 2nd Judicial District, serving until 1894. Meanwhile he practiced law in New Bern and Tarboro.

These activities plus his ability as an orator, organizer of Negro Republicans, and local grand master of the Masons, contributed to his election to Congress in 1896, to which he was reelected in 1898. The only Negro member of the House of Representatives, he considered himself a spokesman for all Negroes. But President McKinley's inaugural address in 1897 promised that he would do all he could to achieve the "revival of esteem and affiliation" between the North and the South. During this period of euphoria White could accomplish little except the transfer of $100,000 unclaimed by Negro veterans of the Civil War. His unsuccessful measures reveal, however, the wide range of his interests on vital issues. He urged the formation of federal artillery regiments of Negroes and the enforcement of the second section of the Fourteenth Amendment to reduce the representation in the House from those states which denied Negroes the right to vote. His most important proposal was a bill (Jan. 20, 1901), the first of its kind, to make the lynching of American citizens a federal crime. Although 109 persons, including eighty-seven Negroes, had been lynched in 1899, White's proposal that any person participating actively in or acting as accessory in a lynching should be convicted of treason, doomed his bill to defeat.

One of his little-noted significant addresses (Feb. 23, 1900) was a reply to vicious attacks upon Negroes "as savages, as aliens, as brutes, as vile and vicious and worthless." White retorted: "It is easy for these gentlemen to taunt us with our inferiority, at the same time not mentioning the cause of this inferiority. It is rather hard to be accused of shiftlessness and idleness when the accuser closes the avenue of labor and industrial pursuits to us. It is hardly fair to accuse us of ignorance when it was made a crime under the former order of things to learn enough about letters to even read the Word of God."

On the other hand, his "valedictory" (Jan. 29, 1901), in which he called attention to the achievements of American Negroes despite job discrimination, Jim Crow, and lynching, and again asked for action on his antilynching bill, has been frequently quoted. White predicted: "This, Mr. Chairman, is perhaps the Negroes' temporary farewell to the American Congress; but let me say, Phoenix-like he will rise up some day and come again. These parting words are in behalf of an outraged, heart-broken bruised and bleeding, but God-fearing people, faithful, industrious, loyal, rising people—full of potential force." His prediction was not fulfilled until Oscar DePriest was elected (1928) as a representative from Illinois.

Most biographical sketches of White include only brief references to White's career after 1901. An unpublished doctoral dissertation by George W. Reid (Howard University, 1974) concluded that the years 1901–1918 were more significant. He had moved with his family to Washington, D.C., where he had opened a law office at 609 F St. NW, in the downtown section. Little is known about his law practice, but he began his interest in establishing an all-Negro town. In 1899 he went to Whitesboro, Cape May County, N.J., and with five associates bought 1700 acres of a large plantation. Members of his land improvement company included George F. T. Cook and John F. Cook, Jr., two of the most highly respected men in Washington. By 1903 a small number of southern Negroes seeking a better life had begun to migrate to Whitesboro.

In 1905 White moved to Philadelphia, where he successfully practiced law and incorporated (Sept. 26, 1907) the People's Savings Bank. First located at 1428 Lombard St. and then at 1508 Lombard St., in the heart of the Philadelphia business district, it enabled some Negroes to purchase homes and engage in business. It was liquidated in 1918, partly because White's ill health prevented him from devoting the necessary time to his business.

White served on the boards of *Who's Who in Philadelphia,* the Frederick Douglass Hospital, the Home for the Protection of Colored Women, and the Berean Schools. He worked with the Constitution League on the Brownsville case (1906), and became a member of the executive committee of the NAACP's Philadelphia Branch.

Like many other Negro leaders of his period, White was torn between his tendency to support W. E. B. Du Bois and recognition of the value of Booker T. Washington's pragmatic program.

Whitesboro was probably White's most enduring achievement. In 1906 the town had a population of more than 800, with 300 families living in single-family houses. They earned a fairly substantial income from farming, a sawmill, and fishing. Many had purchased their farms and homes through the relatively easy terms provided by White and his bank. At the time of his death in 1918, the outlook for Whitesboro was favorable.

White was buried in Eden Cemetery, Philadelphia.

There are brief biographical sketches in Samuel Denny Smith's *The Negro in Congress, 1870–1901* (1940), mostly unfavorable, and Maurine Christopher's *Black Americans in Congress* (1971), more detailed and commendatory. — GEORGE W. REID

WHITE, WALTER [FRANCIS] (1893–1955), author, and chief executive of the NAACP from 1929 to 1955. He was born in Atlanta, Ga., to George and Madeline (Harrison) White. The son of a mailman, White was blue-eyed and blond-haired, and possessed a complexion fair enough to enable him to "pass" for white. At the age of thirteen he witnessed the Atlanta race riot and saw his home almost invaded by a blood-thirsty white mob. White always recalled that night when "I discovered what it meant to be a Negro." Subsequently as a student at Atlanta University he met a different kind of Caucasian, and throughout his life he retained warm recollections of a number of his white professors.

White graduated from Atlanta University in 1916. Quickly becoming active in the civic life of Atlanta's Negro community, he helped lead the campaign against the mounting racial discrimination practiced by the city Board of Education. When the board, which offered whites a high school education, planned to end schooling for Negroes after the sixth grade, aroused Negroes protested. In order to carry out the fight, an NAACP branch was formed late in 1916 with White as secretary. The board modified its policy; more important for White's career was the fact that his speaking abilities and flair for organization had impressed the NAACP's field secretary, James Weldon Johnson. At Johnson's suggestion the NAACP national board of directors invited White to join the staff as assistant secretary. White began his new duties in New York at the beginning of 1918.

At the time the NAACP was a small organization. It was originally intended that White would handle routine chores for the secretary, a white social worker, John R. Shillady. But the able and aggressive young Atlantan quickly proved himself extremely valuable. An excellent speaker, he was helpful in developing NAACP branches and became adept at representing the NAACP in negotiations with high government officials. Perhaps White's most outstanding contribution to the organization in this period was his work in the struggle against mob violence. White volunteered to undertake the dangerous task of investigating some of the most outrageous lynchings, and because he could pass for white he was able to secure valuable information—although on at least one occasion he only narrowly escaped being lynched himself. When the Chicago race riot erupted in 1919, White was sent there to organize the defense of innocent Negroes charged with attacking whites.

In 1920 James Weldon Johnson became the NAACP's first Negro secretary, and during the next decade he and White were a remarkably successful team. Under their administration the association grew rapidly, sank deep roots into the Negro community, and clearly became the dominant racial advancement organization. Moreover, the rise of Johnson and White marked the advent of a Negro staff within the NAACP which not only gave Negroes a key voice in policy making, but also tied the national office more closely to the branches and to local Negro communities throughout the country. The two men complemented each other exceedingly well. Johnson brought to the NAACP a wide range of political, civic, and literary contacts, possessed an extraordinary tact and diplomacy in working with people, and while not lacking in administrative talents, functioned primarily as the Association's ambassador to white and black America. Walter White, on the other hand, at the time a virtually unknown young man, proved to be an administrator par excellence. Possessed of a quick mind and a passion for detail, as well as enormous ambition, he quickly made himself invaluable to Johnson and the board of directors. Although the NAACP spent a great deal of effort agitating for the enactment of a federal antilynching law, it was evident by the 1920s that the organization's most important work would lie in the courts. And Walter White's major arena of operations was in the legal program. Although not a lawyer, he mastered complex legal matters and acted as administrator for the NAACP's legal committee. Working closely with the chairman of this committee, Arthur B. Spingarn, he handled negotiations with local lawyers and carried out much of the committee's routine business. His influence grew steadily and by the mid-1920s all important decisions regarding legal work were in practice made jointly by the two men. Having become indispensable to the board, he was the obvious choice to succeed Johnson as secretary of the NAACP in 1931.

White was a zealous crusader for the Negro's rights, but he had other extensive interests as well. During the "Harlem Renaissance" White aspired to follow in Johnson's footsteps and become a successful writer. He was awarded a Guggenheim Fellowship for creative writing and wrote two novels—The Fire in the Flint (1924), centering on lynching, and Flight (1926), which dealt with the theme of passing—as well as one nonfiction work, Rope and Faggot (1920), a major indictment of lynching.

In 1929, with Johnson ill and on leave, White served as acting secretary and the following year spearheaded one of the NAACP's most publicized and successful campaigns, the fight against the confirmation of Judge John J. Parker for a seat on the U.S. Supreme Court. Parker, a North Carolina judge, had publicly supported Negro disfranchisement, and the NAACP, whose legal strategy depended on enforcement of the Fourteenth and Fifteenth Amendments, through Supreme Court decisions, was deeply disturbed. The association mounted an intense struggle to influence senators to vote against Parker. White skillfully marshalled the NAACP branches, and thousands of letters and telegrams poured into the Senate Office Building; at the same time the secretary utilized contacts and friendships he had developed with prominent politicians to put further pressure on certain senators. Parker was finally defeated by a vote of 41 to 39. Although much of the credit for this must go to the AFL which opposed him for his antiunion record, the NAACP exulted in its victory. White and the NAACP, anxious to demonstrate further the potential of the Negro vote, followed up this achievement by leading a campaign in the autumn elections against several senators who had backed Parker; at least two of these Republicans were defeated, in large part because of Negro opposition.

The onset of the Depression was presenting the NAACP with the most serious crisis it had faced since its founding. Income plummeted, and simultaneously the association had to grapple with the catastrophic economic problems of Negroes. As a result of several internal developments which will be discussed below, Walter White was able to bring the NAACP through these critical years; indeed, it emerged with greater prestige and a more solid record of achievement than before. He presided over modifications in the organization's structure and program, with the local branches gaining greater influence at the national policy level, and the association paying greater attention to the economic problems of Negro workers. White emerged with unprecedented personal control of the organizational machinery and a degree of power in the NAACP's affairs that no single person had ever before exercised.

The NAACP's first response to the Depression was to try to keep solvent. With income from memberships declining disastrously, White spent considerable time raising money among white philanthropists. On his recommendation the board of directors cut staff substantially. This action led to an unprecedented staff rebellion with most department heads, from The Crisis editor W. E. B. Du Bois down, criticizing White in a sharply worded complaint to the board. Never before in the organization's history had staff thus challenged the secretary. The board sided with White, and most of the staff backed down. A few were dismissed, and White emerged with undisputed control over all staff except Du Bois.

From the beginning Du Bois had run The Crisis as an autonomous unit within the NAACP. More than once his editorial independence had brought him into conflict with the board, but his personal prestige and eminence had prevented an open break. Both White and Du Bois were men of strong ego, but they probably would have tolerated each other and their sharp differences of opinion if the Depression had not produced serious differences about strategy. The Crisis, which had been virtually self-supporting, had become a deficit operation draining badly needed funds from an organization already fighting for financial survival. In this context, Du Bois's espousal of an editorial position, "nondiscriminatory segregation," that ran counter to the NAACP's basic ideology, precipitated a head-on clash with White that ended in Du Bois's resignation from the association in 1934. Management of The Crisis came under White's jurisdiction, with the appointment of Roy Wilkins, the new assistant secretary, as editor.

White's relationship with Wilkins was quite different from the one that White had sustained with Johnson. Whereas Johnson had delegated authority freely, White exercised a tight grip over the organization's staff and did not permit the assistant secretary to have a virtually independent sphere of operations. Thus, for example, while Wilkins took over much of White's earlier task of handling the routine administration of the legal work, White continued to involve himself directly in the important litigation undertaken by the association and to make the key decisions with Arthur Spingarn.

Throughout Walter White's administration the NAACP remained basically committed to fighting for enforcement of the Negro's constitutional rights. However, the Depression and the New Deal provided the association and White with new challenges and opportunities. The Roosevelt administration, despite its limited commitment regarding the needs of Negroes, proved more responsive to those needs than had its predecessors. Negroes were included in the emergency relief and job programs, and subsequently in other federal programs such as public housing. The Roosevelt administration appointed an unprecedented number of Negroes to prominent positions in the federal bureaucracy. These policies raised the hopes of Negroes, who now demanded additional gains. For example, in 1933 upon the initiative of White and the NAACP, various Negro organizations established the Joint Committee on National Recovery (JCNR) to fight discrimination in the administration of New Deal programs. The JCNR was especially effective in exposing the unequal wage rates provided by the National Industrial Recovery Act codes.

Although the NAACP had thus somewhat broadened the scope of its efforts, critics complained that White and the association were dominated by a concern for the Negro middle class that prevented the development of meaningful projects addressed to alleviating the desperate plight of the Negro masses. Pressures came most importantly from a group of young Negro intellectuals that included Howard University professors Abram Harris and Ralph Bunche. They wanted the NAACP to encourage the unionization of Negro workers and to build a close alliance with progressive elements of the labor movement, which would shortly achieve prominence through the rise of the CIO with its explicit policy of organizing workers without regard to race. Harris, Bunche, and others also denounced the oligarchic character of the NAACP's self-perpetuating national board of directors in whose selection the branches had no voice.

The critics were essentially accurate in their assessment that White as well as the most influential board members wanted the NAACP to maintain its emphasis on securing enforcement of constitutional rights. And they were also essentially correct about the oligarchic nature of the association. Although their criticism, centering on the board, failed to take into account the role of Secretary White himself, in actual fact beginning with Johnson's administration there had been a steady trend toward a shift of power from the board to the secretariat. Because whites were the most influential figures on the board, even though that body was half Negro in membership, this change also marked the ascendancy of Negro influence within the association. There were several reasons for the board's new deference to the salaried Negro officers. The very growth in size and complexity of operations under Johnson and White during the 1920s made it increasingly difficult for volunteer board members to exercise close supervision. The most they could do was to help formulate board policy, and since there was a basic consensus on this matter it was easy for the board to follow the secretary's leadership. Second, the effectiveness with which Johnson and White ran the organization encouraged the board to rely on their judgment.

White's relationship with the board during the first half decade of his own administration largely revolved around Arthur Spingarn and his brother Joel, both of whom had been leading figures in the organization al-

most since its inception. Because White refused to consult her, Mary White Ovington, one of the NAACP's founders, resigned as chairman of the board at the end of 1931. Joel Spingarn, who succeeded her, shared with White a basic consensus about the association's direction, but at times forcefully injected himself into the running of the organization, clamping down on what he regarded as unnecessary expenditures, and encouraging White to broaden the association's program to cope with the economic catastrophe of the 1930s. Where in matters of broad policy White worked closely with Joel Spingarn, more important for the day-to-day running of the association was the fact that White exerted great weight with the board through his warm relationship with Arthur Spingarn. Arthur Spingarn, besides continuing to perform his legal functions, also served in other key roles, including membership on the nominating and budget committees. The other busy board members found it easy to ratify the recommendations of the able and increasingly celebrated Walter White and his conscientious ally Arthur Spingarn.

With the younger Negro intellectuals vigorously pressing the association to change its direction, Joel Spingarn successfully pushed a reluctant White to hold a conference with a cross section of these critics. Subsequently both White, the astute administrator, and Joel Spingarn, the skillful interpersonal leader, realizing that the organization would have to respond to the agitation, encouraged the board to appoint a Committee on Future Plans chaired by Abram Harris. The Harris Committee's report urged the association to democratize board elections and to encourage Negroes "to view their special grievances as a natural part of the larger issues of American labor as a whole." White lauded the report but doubted that funds could be obtained to carry out its recommendation that the association create workers' councils to educate the masses for economic and political action. Certainly implementation of this proposal would have drastically altered the organization and curtailed the struggle against disfranchisement and segregation.

Both the organizational structure and the association's program remained in most basic respects unaltered. The legal campaign against segregation and disfranchisement was intensified and White spent a major portion of his time for two years (1937 and 1938) in an unsuccessful campaign to secure passage of an antilynching bill. Yet changes in the NAACP did come about. The branches received some voice in electing board members. And in the following years the NAACP gradually forged an alliance with the new CIO unions. The turning point came in 1941. Requested by the United Automobile Workers to help get Negro scabs out of the Ford automobile plants, White secured assurances that the union would cease discriminatory policies against Negro members. He personally went to Detroit and successfully urged many Negro strikebreakers to leave the factories.

Meanwhile, hurt by all the criticism, Joel Spingarn had quit as board chairman in 1935 and was succeeded by White's close friend, the distinguished Negro surgeon Louis T. Wright. Although there had been no pressure on Spingarn to resign, his withdrawal symbolized the weakening of the crucial role white leaders had played in the association since its founding, and served further to consolidate Walter White's control. Spingarn and White had always been in basic agreement about goals and strategies, but Wright deferred to the secretary's judgment even more. White's relationship with Wright reveals the way in which the organization's informal structure was changing, so that while the board was still the legal governing body, the chief locus of power now shifted decisively to the secretary. White's influence became so pervasive that he frequently suggested to the nominating committee candidates which it chose for board membership, and he regularly attended meetings of the nominating committee himself. Through his friendship with Wright he was able largely to decide on appointments to key board committees. And prior to the monthly meetings of the national board of directors White and an inner circle of key members would meet at Wright's apartment to plan strategy for the next day.

Moreover, in the same year that Wright became chairman, the work of the association and the role of the staff were strengthened by the creation of a legal department headed by the brilliant Negro lawyer Charles Houston. In its early years the NAACP had usually employed prestigious white lawyers who offered their services without remuneration to conduct its most important cases, a policy to which Walter White fully subscribed. Because of the extreme racism of the period, Negro lawyers were frequently at a disadvantage in the courts. During the early 1930s, after pressure from Negro lawyers who wanted to lead the legal struggle for the race's freedom, White moved in this direction. He secured both Houston and his law partner, William H. Hastie, for key NAACP cases in 1933 and 1934, and was finally successful in arranging for a foundation grant to enable the NAACP to hire Houston in 1935. This appointment, coming almost simultaneously with Joel Spingarn's withdrawal, marked the final consolidation of Negro dominance in the NAACP. And even though the legal staff exhibited greater autonomy than any other department, its establishment was another step in enhancing the power of White and the organization's bureaucracy, since it greatly diminished the significance of the legal committee chairman. Arthur Spingarn welcomed these developments, and after his brother's death in 1939 gracefully assumed in 1940 the largely ceremonial post of association president.

Thus by the mid-1930s the NAACP was increasingly influenced by Negroes, and the secretary had emerged as the dominant figure. The consolidation of the association's administrative structure in a sense marked the end of the era. Walter White had built the structure that provided the basis for the NAACP's wartime and postwar growth and legal victories that culminated in *Brown v. Board of Education* in 1954. In the twenty years following the creation of the legal department the NAACP had successfully fought the legal battle against the white primary, restrictive covenants in housing, segregation in transportation and publicly owned places of recreation, inequities in the segregated southern educational system from the graduate level down to the primary school, and ultimately achieved the overturning of the "separate but equal" doctrine itself.

In addition to his work as assistant secretary, acting secretary, and secretary of the NAACP, White participated in many other activities. He was a delegate to the Second Pan-African Congress (London, Brussels, and Paris, 1921), consultant to the U.S. delegation at the San Francisco Conference which organized the United Nations (1945), and consultant to the U.S. delegation at the U.N. General Assembly (Paris, 1948). As a war correspondent for the *New York Post,* he wrote excellent firsthand reports about the European, Mediterranean, Middle East, and Pacific war zones (1943–1945), and wrote *A Rising Wind* (1945). During his year's leave of absence from the NAACP (1949–1950) he participated in Round the World Town Meeting of the Air, visiting European countries, Israel, Egypt, India, Japan, and the Caribbean. He contributed articles to *Harper's, The Nation, The Crisis, American Mercury, Saturday Review of Literature, Negro Digest, Collier's, Saturday Evening Post, New Republic, Reader's Digest,* and *Annals of the Academy of Political and Social Science.* He also wrote a syndicated column for the *New York Herald-Tribune,* and was a regular columnist for the *Chicago Defender.* In 1937 he received the Spingarn Medal for investigating lynchings and lobbying for the antilynching bill.

Yet, ironically, White ultimately lost control of the superb administrative mechanism he had built. Through the years there were always a few dissident board members who were hostile toward him and critical of the concentration of power in his hands. They charged him with operating a "one-man show." As he became more and more of a celebrity, he spent increasingly less time in the office, lecturing for pay to other organizations. To some extent he lost his close grip on the handling of administrative detail at the same time that he made himself vulnerable to charges that he was using his position as NAACP secretary for personal gain. To his opponents both on the board and in several of the NAACP branches, Walter White appeared to be a self-centered publicity seeker. When he divorced his Negro wife of over twenty-seven years, the former Gladys Powell, mother of his two children, Jane and Walter Jr., in order to marry a white woman, Poppy Cannon, his critics, exploiting his domestic problems, claimed that he embarrassed the association. When he returned from a year's leave in 1950, he found the board polarized over whether to keep him in office or replace him with Roy Wilkins, who had been acting secretary in his absence. After an acrimonious debate the board voted to retain White with the title of executive secretary but delegated authority to Wilkins over all internal matters, and made him responsible directly to the board. White, however, continued to formulate broad organizational policy and to act as the association's spokesman. Yet in reality his power had been substantially reduced. He died of a heart attack in 1955, just after the NAACP had achieved its victory in the school desegregation cases. Survived by his widow and his two children, he was cremated at the Ferncliff Cemetery, Hartsdale, N.Y.

White's importance lies not in the originality of his program and ideology, which had basically been set for the NAACP by Du Bois and its other founders, but flowed from his organizational talents. White was primarily a builder. With his industriousness and drive, his flair for public relations, his ability to popularize the NAACP's message through the spoken and written word, and his knack for establishing valuable contacts with people like Eleanor Roosevelt, Wendell Willkie, and a host of journalists, politicians, and civic leaders, White brought the NAACP to the point where it was increasingly recognized as a major force in American society.

The principal printed sources are Walter White's *A Man Called White* (1948), Poppy Cannon's *A Gentle Knight* (1956), and B. Joyce Ross's *J. E. Spingarn and the Rise of the NAACP* (1972). Much other valuable information is in Nathaniel P. Tillman, Jr.'s "Walter Francis White, A Study in Intergroup Leadership" (unpublished Ph.D. dissertation, University of Wisconsin, 1961); the Papers of the D.C. Branch of the NAACP in the Moorland-Spingarn Research Center, Howard University; and the Papers of the National Office in the Library of Congress. There is a brief obituary in the *JNH* (July 1955, pp. 296–98).

— AUGUST MEIER *and* ELLIOTT RUDWICK

WHITFIELD, JAMES MONROE (1822–1871), poet, colonizationist, and Mason. He was born on April 10, 1822, in New Hampshire. A barber, he was a poet and political activist whose genius and potential for race leadership were praised by Frederick Douglass, William Wells Brown, and Martin R. Delany. Whitfield was a descendant of Ann Paul, sister of Thomas Paul, an Exeter, N.H., clergyman; and he was the brother of Elizabeth P. Allen, whose daughter was Annie Pauline Pindell. Nothing is known about Whitfield's early life; at the age of sixteen, he prepared a paper for a Cleveland convention urging Negro settlement on the borders of California (1838), and for the next twenty years he participated in emigration and colonization activities, working alongside James T. Holly and Delany in the 1850s. At the same time he lived and worked as a barber in Buffalo, N.Y. (1839–1859). From Buffalo, he contributed dozens of poems to the *North Star* and *Frederick Douglass' Paper* (1849–1856); he published *America and Other Poems* (1853), dedicated to Delany, and a series of letters brilliantly advocating colonization against arguments of Douglass and William J. Watkins (*North Star*, Sept. 25, Nov. 15, Dec. 30, 1853).

Whitfield's work for the National Emigration Conventions in Cleveland (1854, 1856) brought him national recognition; he promoted publication of a periodical, the *Afric-American Repository*, to support emigration; he supported the proposal of Rep. Frank P. Blair, Jr., of Missouri to acquire land for colonization in Central America (1858); and in 1859 Whitfield was sent as fact-finding commissioner to Central America, where it is assumed he traveled for the next two years.

In August 1861 he returned to San Francisco. Abandoning his emigrationist interests, he lived and worked as a barber in California for most of the ten years until his death. From June 1863 to 1865, he was a barber in Portland, Ore., and in Placerville and Centerville, Idaho; from May 1869 to July 1870 he lived in Elko,

Nev., where he participated in literary and political projects of the Elko Republican Club and became, with three other men, the first of his race to sit on a jury in Nevada (Elko County).

Whitfield was grand master for California of the Prince Hall Masons (1864–1869). In August 1868 he installed the Masonic Ashlar Lodge of Virginia City, Nev., and returned there in April 1870 to read his 152-line "Poem" commemorating ratification of the Fifteenth Amendment. During his years in the West, Whitfield published a major 400-line work, "A Poem Written for the Celebration of President Lincoln's Emancipation Proclamation" (1867); and he contributed many poems and letters to the *San Francisco Elevator* and *Pacific Appeal* (1863–1870), papers which frequently reported his travels. Whitfield died of heart disease on April 23, 1871, and was buried in the Masonic cemetery, San Francisco.

Although he had no formal education and, as Douglass wrote, "the malignant arrangements of society" chained him to the barbershop (*Anti-Slavery Bugle*, Aug. 24, 1850), Whitfield became a major propagandist for black independence and racial retributive justice. His poems, cynical, bitterly pessimistic, and angry, denounced an America corrupted by slavery, the "land of blood, and crime, and wrong"; and his finest work dramatizes the estrangement, crippling, and ultimate defeat of creative black men by race prejudice. Whitfield's poetry of protest and despair are among the most robust and convincing of his time.

Vernon Loggins's *The Negro Author* (1931) discusses his poetry. Joan R. Sherman's *Invisible Poets* (1974) offers a documented biography, criticism of poetry, and a bibliography. — JOAN R. SHERMAN

WHITMAN, ALBERRY ALLSON (1851–1901), poet and clergyman. Born a slave in the Green River Country, Hart County, near Mumfordsville, Ky., he became free in 1863, shortly before his mother and father died. He did manual labor in shops and on railroads in Kentucky and Ohio for several years. Although he had only about seven months of schooling, he studied for six months under Bishop Daniel Alexander Payne at Wilberforce University. In 1873 he published his poem, *Leelah Misled* and, in 1877, when he was pastor of an African Methodist Episcopal church in Springfield, Ohio, and a financial agent of Wilberforce University, *Not a Man and Yet a Man. The Rape of Florida* (1884) represented a much more ambitious venture, in Spenserian stanzas. It was reprinted a year later as *Twasinta's Seminoles: Or, The Rape of Florida;* in 1890, along with his first poem, a third edition appeared called *Not a Man Yet a Man*, Second Edition, Completely Revised, with some miscellaneous poems grouped under the title "Drifted Leaves." His last work, an epic poem in two parts, was *An Idyll of the South* (1901). Late in the 1880s, in ill health in Kansas, Whitman had to move to a healthier climate. Sometime in the next decade he went to St. Philip's AME Church in Savannah, Ga. When the church burned down he began the task of rebuilding, only to be transferred to Allen Temple in Atlanta by his bishop. He died in Atlanta in 1901.

In the preface to *Not a Man and Yet a Man* Whitman

recalled that although born in slavery "I was in bondage, [but] *I never was a slave,*—the infamous laws of a savage despotism took my substance—what of that?" As he saw his early days, he had enjoyed the blessings of cabin life and hard work. Thus with all gone "excepting my manhood," he wrote, he realized that "Adversity is the school of heroism, endurance the majesty of man, and hope the torch of high aspirations."

Whitman's early poems were imitative, clearly showing the influence of Walter Scott, Lord Byron, Henry Wadsworth Longfellow, and John Greenleaf Whittier. *Not a Man and Yet a Man,* for example, was a poem of great length, possibly the longest poem ever written by a Negro, but it was made up of too many poetic strains. Writing fervently of the wrongs suffered by Negroes at the hands of whites, he invented a tragic tale of love and romance to clothe the message. In *The Rape of Florida,* however, he was more successful, using Spenserian stanzas more boldly and imaginatively. Again a story of love and adventure, of the expulsion of the Seminoles from Florida, Whitman aimed higher: in the dedication addressed to Bishop Henry McNeal Turner, he wrote, defending himself of the charge of imitation, that "To this view of the matter, I will say by way of defense: some negro is sure to do everything that any one else had ever done, and as none of the race have executed a poem in the 'stately verse,' I simply venture in." Thus, he invoked William Cullen Bryant's memory with "O! shade of our departed sire of song!/ If what to us is dim be clear to thee,/ Hear while my yet rude numbers flow along!" Fortunately, stanzas here and there are excellent, as "Come now, my love, the moon is on the lake,/ Upon the water is my light canoe,/ Come with me, love, and gladsome oars shall make/ A music on the parting wave for you."

In his last major work, *An Idyll of the South,* Whitman, who had continued to experiment and grow, built his two poems on a story of a slave girl who looked white: in "The Octoroon" she is loved by the son of a slaveholder; in "The Southland's Charms and Freedom's Magnitude" he pays tribute to Generals Grant and Lee, moralizes about the Civil War, and ends with a vision of a better day.

Looking back, when he was forty years old, Whitman wrote: "I was 'bred to the plow.' Amid the rugged hills, along the banks of the Green River in Kentucky, I enjoyed the inestimable blessings of cabin life and hard work during the whole of my early days. . . . Adversity is the school of heroism. . . . Acquainted with adversity, I am flattered of hope and comforted by endurance." He also recognized that "Genius, in a right good soul, is the highest impress of the Divine Image of clay." Whitman had too many shortcomings and technical faults to win recognition as a major poet. On the other hand, as Vernon Loggins put it in *The Negro Author* (1931), he had a gift for hearing and reproducing music for words; above all, he was "the most talented Negro poet between Phillis Wheatley and Paul Laurence Dunbar." Benjamin Brawley, in *The Negro Genius* (1937), concurred, saying Whitman was "probably the ablest of the poets of the race before Dunbar." Sterling Brown stated in his perceptive sketch in the *DAB* ([1936], 10,

Part 2:138–39): "He was the most considerable poet of his race before Paul Lawrence [*sic*] Dunbar . . . in bulk and in familiarity with poetic models, but his distinction is one of ambition rather than achievement."

The best biographical sources are the prefaces, generally autobiographical, of Whitman's publications. Daniel A. Payne's *Recollections of Seventy Years* (1888) is valuable for the Wilberforce connection.

— DANIEL WALDEN

WHITTAKER, JOHNSON CHESNUTT (1858–1931), West Point cadet, lawyer, and educator. He was born a slave on Aug. 23, 1858, the son of a free Negro, James Whitaker, and a slave, Maria J. Whitaker, on the plantation of the senior James Chesnut of Camden, S.C. (In later years he added the second "t" to his middle name.) Between 1874 and 1876 he attended the then-integrated University of South Carolina. In 1876 he received his congressman's appointment to the U.S. Military Academy at West Point. He began his training there on Aug. 23, 1876, but never graduated. He was dismissed for academic deficiency on March 22, 1882.

After his separation Whittaker went on a brief national speaking tour, but soon became a teacher at Avery Institute, Charleston, S.C. On May 26, 1885, he was admitted to the South Carolina bar and shortly thereafter began a law practice in Sumter. About 1890 he married Page E. Harrison and fathered two sons, Miller F., a leading South Carolina educator, and Johnson C. Jr., later a member of the first all-Negro state surveying team in Michigan. Two baby daughters died at birth. In the 1890s he became principal of the first Negro public school in Sumter and in 1900 worked for the Census Bureau. From 1900 to 1908 he was secretary of the college and principal of the Academy of the Colored Normal Industrial, Agricultural and Mechanical College of South Carolina (later South Carolina Agricultural and Mechanical College, then South Carolina State College). Between 1908 and 1925 he was teacher, assistant principal, and then principal of Douglass High School in Oklahoma City (where one of his students was Ralph Ellison). From 1925 to 1931 he was professor of psychology and education and principal of the academy in Savannah. He died on Jan. 14, 1931, from a hemorrhaging gastric ulcer and was buried in the Negro Cemetery in a dilapidated section of Orangeburg. He was survived by his widow, two sons, and a grandson.

It was at West Point that Whittaker became a *cause célèbre.* When he entered the academy in 1876, his roommate was the man destined to become West Point's first Negro graduate, Henry O. Flipper. When Flipper graduated in 1877, and after another colored cadet was dismissed for academic deficiency, Whittaker was alone. He was ostracized by the white cadets and lived a virtually monastic life. On April 6, 1880, his traumatic experience began. He was found unconscious in his room at reveille, with his legs tied to his bed, his arms bound, his earlobes slashed, and his hair cut in several places. He told a story of three masked attackers in the night. The commandant of cadets reported that his investigation convinced him of Whittaker's guilt of self-mutilation. A stunned Whittaker immediately asked for and was granted a court of inquiry. This court met from April to June 1880. The case received front-page coverage in the national press and Congress debated the issue. The inquiry's decision sustained the commandant's opinion. National reaction was unfavorable, particularly since the inquiry had highlighted West Point prejudice toward Whittaker because of his race.

Pres. Rutherford B. Hayes determined the need to meet the rising tide of criticism and replaced Gen. John M. Schofield as West Point superintendent with former Freedmen's Bureau head Oliver O. Howard and granted Whittaker a leave of absence and then a court-martial. The court-martial, requested by Whittaker and his supporters, met in New York City from January to June 1881. Whittaker's defense was handled by Daniel H. Chamberlain, ex-governor of South Carolina, and by Richard T. Greener, Harvard's first Negro graduate and Whittaker's former professor at the University of South Carolina. The government case was presented by Asa Bird Gardiner, probably the foremost army lawyer of the period. The president of the court-martial board was Gen. Nelson A. Miles, the foremost non-West Pointer in the army, while General-in-Chief William T. Sherman looked on closely.

Whittaker was again found guilty. The court, however, recommended leniency. In the fall of 1881 the judge advocate-general of the army, D. G. Swaim, threw out the decision because of improper utilization of the handwriting evidence and because the president had had no power to call a court-martial in the first place. After further consultations Secretary of War Robert T. Lincoln (the former president's son) determined the trial should be invalidated. On March 22, 1882, Pres. Chester A. Arthur so ruled. That same day, however, Lincoln also ordered Whittaker's separation from the academy because of an examination failure in June of 1880.

Although the Whittaker case received wide coverage in the contemporary press and although it is a graphic illustration of the position of the Negro in the late nineteenth century, until recently historians have given it only cursory coverage. Those historians who have discussed it have usually uncritically accepted the West Point version. See John F. Marszalek's "A Black Cadet at West Point" (*American Heritage,* Aug. 1971) and his biography of Whittaker, including a detailed discussion of the West Point events: *Court-Martial: A Black Man in America* (1972). — JOHN F. MARSZALEK

WHITTAKER, MILLER F[ULTON] (1892–1949), architect and college president. The son of Johnson Chesnut and Page (Harrison) Whittaker, he grew up in Sumter and Orangeburg, S.C., and Oklahoma City, Okla. He attended the Colored Normal Industrial, Agricultural, and Mechanical College of South Carolina (later South Carolina Agricultural and Mechanical College, then South Carolina State College) and in 1913 received a B.S. degree in architecture from Kansas State College (later Kansas State University). In 1928 he received a M.S. in architecture from the same institution.

He also studied at Harvard University and Cornell University.

Whittaker joined the faculty of South Carolina Agricultural and Mechanical College in 1913 as a member of both the Drawing and Physics Departments. From 1925 to 1932 he held the position of dean of the Mechanical Arts Department. During this same period he became a registered architect in South Carolina (1918) and Georgia (1928). He superintended the design and construction of all the college buildings erected while he was a faculty member. It is believed that during his lifetime he was the only Negro architect in South Carolina. During World War I Whittaker joined the U.S. Army and served as a second lieutenant with the 368th Infantry for one year in France, where he studied at the Army School at Langres.

Upon the death of the college's president Robert Shaw Wilkinson in 1932, Whittaker was made president of South Carolina Agricultural and Mechanical College. His appointment at the age of thirty-nine prompted *The Crisis* (Aug. 1932) to write that he "had attracted wide attention, brought visitors from over the world to examine, study and appreciate the campus buildings which he had designed."

Whittaker was the third president of the college (Thomas E. Miller and Robert Shaw Wilkinson preceded him). During his seventeen-year tenure the college's existence continued to be a difficult one but it progressed physically and academically. Eight new buildings were added and an additional seventy-five-acre farm was purchased. The college's financial position was strengthened, the student body enlarged, the existing vocational curriculum improved, and new programs, notably a Law Department, added. Whittaker maintained close ties throughout the state and nation by speaking engagements, personal acquaintance, and membership in educational organizations. He was president of the Conference of Land Grant Colleges (1936–1937), and several times was head of the State Association of College Presidents, Deans, and Registrars. In 1933 he was chosen one of the seven outstanding presidents of land-grant colleges and was awarded a summer scholarship to Cornell University. He was listed in *Who's Who in America.*

President Whittaker died of congestive heart failure at the relatively young age of fifty-six. His funeral was attended by leading educators and state officials, including Gov. J. Strom Thurmond and Rep. Hugo S. Simms, Jr. The eulogy was delivered by Benjamin E. Mays, then president of Morehouse College. Burial was at Orangeburg Cemetery. In 1969 South Carolina State College honored his memory by naming its new library the Miller F. Whittaker Library. He was survived by his niece Cecil Whittaker Boykin (later McFadden) and his nephew Peter Whittaker.

Whittaker perhaps best expressed his philosophy when he addressed the 1937 graduating class: "I have an ideal for this College. It is this: That each student shall give evidence of high moral character and personal worth, serious intellectual effort, an understanding of his obligations to society. Things of the spirit, the common virtues of courtesy, honesty, integrity, and tolerance are just as important as the training of the intellect. To this end we would have this College put an indelible stamp of culture and refinement on its students.''

There is no full-length study of Miller F. Whittaker. He is mentioned in the brief history of his college, Nelson C. Nix's *South Carolina State College, A History* (1937). He is also briefly mentioned in his father's biography: John F. Marszalek's *Court-Martial: A Black Man in America* (1972). A eulogy is K. W. Green's ''Miller Fulton Whittaker'' (*Negro Educational Review* 1, April 1950). — JOHN F. MARSZALEK

WILLIAMS, BERT (1873–1922), entertainer. He reportedly made more than the president of the United States. W. C. Fields called him the funniest man he had ever seen, and also the saddest. When he performed, lines formed around the block waiting to catch a glimpse of him. Yet during a tour at the height of his success, he still slept in third-rate segregated hotel rooms. And if chance ever permitted him to stay at one of the better hotels, he had to ride the freight elevator and was forced to eat in his room.

He was born Egbert Austin Williams in Providence, Nassau. His paternal grandfather was the Danish consul whose wife, born there, was said to be one-fourth African and three-fourths Spanish. His father, a papier-mâché maker, also married a colored woman. They lived on a delightful plantation until the father's serious illness led to their moving to California. After attending school in San Francisco, Bert lacked funds to study engineering at Stanford University. Meanwhile he had developed a love of reading and music which he maintained throughout his life. He played many instruments, particularly the banjo, and sang and danced in the streets for coins. He had a natural gift for mimicry and singing, and became an entertainer in cafés and honkytonks along San Francisco's Barbary Coast. In 1895 he met George Nash Walker, another comedian, and began his rise to prominence. For sixteen years, theirs was a remarkable fellowship of two, Walker being the fast-talking, Kingfish slicker type on stage while Williams performed as the bumbling, forever awkward, forever frazzled, forever funny humbug of a dupe. Together the two men discovered in themselves and one another unique comic personalities. In a string of successful shows such as *Sons of Ham* (1900), *In Dahomey* (1902), *In Abyssinia* (1908), and *Bandana Land* (1908), they captivated audiences with their highly charged, rapid-fire brand of hysterics and became the first internationally famous team of black stars in the history of American entertainment. The two formed their own company. With men such as Jesse Shipp, Alex Rogers, and Will Marion Cook, and their talented wives, Ada Overton Walker and Lottie Thompson Williams, their repertory company stretched its talents year by year and showed audiences the possibilities of Negro drama that touched on, if it did not fully elaborate, authentic Negro folk humor.

This amazing team and its company came to a premature end, however, when Walker became ill in 1907. Compelled to carry on alone, Williams's first solo appearance was in a pallid comedy called *Mr. Lode of*

Koal, which had a brief run in 1909. Despite its failure, Bert Williams realized he could perform by himself—and perform well. From there he went on to a series of successful vaudeville performances.

But his great triumph came in 1910 when the most important theatrical producer of the period, Florenz Ziegfeld, signed him to star in the famous *Ziegfeld Follies.* Before Williams went to work for Ziegfeld, there had been no big-name Negro stars. Negro performers frequently lit up otherwise mediocre shows, transforming dull standard routines and skits into high-flung, outlandish one-man carnivals. But they never received featured billing, seldom played the major vaudeville houses, and never made the lucrative salaries they deserved. All that changed because of Williams.

For almost a decade Williams appeared in various editions of the *Follies* as well as in Ziegfeld's other popular revue, *Midnight Frolics.* Usually, this handsome six-footer came on late in the show. The first thing audiences saw under the bright spotlight was a white-gloved hand extending from the wings, with fingers slowly, rhythmically in motion. A long black-suited arm followed, then the other hand and arm. And before he had entered, audiences knew exactly who it was and burst into wild, enthusiastic applause. Onstage Williams's striking good looks were always camouflaged. He was dressed shabbily and always appeared in blackface. According to Williams's own statements, this shy, reclusive man felt freer to shed his own inhibitions when protected by the mask of burnt cork.

In the *Follies,* Williams's rendition of the woefully comic-pathetic song ''Nobody'' and his five-man poker game pantomime continued to delight audiences. The Ziegfled company itself included some of the brightest names in American theatrical history: W. C. Fields, Fannie Brice, Anna Held, Marilyn Miller, Will Rogers, Eddie Cantor, and Ed Wynn. When he worked with other cast members, Williams was equally impressive and spectacular. He appeared opposite Cantor in a blackface father-son routine and opposite the highly acclaimed British comic Leon Errol in a porter-tourist skit. Williams's humor proved fiercely aggressive and competitive, and he stole every scene in which he appeared.

It was this later work with the *Follies* that transformed Williams into a theater legend. He seemed capable of doing a little of everything exceedingly well. His recordings of songs such as ''Nobody,'' ''Jonah Man,'' ''I'm in the Right Church, but the Wrong Pew,'' and ''Come After Breakfast, Bring Along Your Lunch, and Leave Before Supper'' were said to have sold in the hundreds of thousands. He could dance in a slow, leisurely, but distinctly personal fashion. He was as well a master of the doubletake and double entendre. Perhaps more important to the development of black humor, he infused his work with a certain world-weary pathos. While amusing, Bert Williams could also be sad and disturbing, his giant clown's face frowning as much as it smiled. Williams emerged as the common fellow who kept on pushing and pulling, the unlikely but ultimate survivor who did so simply because he kept his eyes open to life's absurdities. Life played jokes on him. And he in turn played jokes on life. Yet, curiously, despite the fact that he always got the last laugh, there was the bruised, tormented side. Williams was the funny, confused, misanthropic black man operating in a world he did not care to understand, the man who survived through some expense to his own private inner recesses. There was a part of Bert Williams that no audience ever seemed to be able to fully figure out. And no doubt this elusive quality added to his appeal.

Some of the Williams elusive pathos may have sprung from his private life. Although the Williams family moved to California while he was yet young, he retained the proud air of the foreign born who cannot fully comprehend the racial codes so prevalent in American society. Yet Williams was acutely sensitive to those codes nonetheless. It has been said that he had it written into his Ziegfeld contract that he would not appear on stage at the same time as any white female cast member. Nor did he want to tour below the Mason-Dixon line. Apparently no one knew better than he the peculiar perils facing the Negro entertainer. Williams was no doubt aware, too, that by going in blackface (and at the same time while appearing on a white stage), he may sometimes have distorted his characters into caricature. Withdrawn, moody, given to chronic depression, he spent much of his time away from the theater. He lived quietly with his wife Lottie in New York City. One of his greatest pleasures was in his diverse book collection.

Toward the end of his career, Williams left the Ziegfeld company and starred in two shows built exclusively around him: Broadway Brevities in 1920 and Under the Bamboo Tree in 1922. It was during a performance of the latter that he collapsed in a Detroit theater, later contracting pneumonia and dying a premature death in 1922. At the request of the South Lodge of Masons, he was buried with Masonic honors by St. Cecilia Lodge No. 568 of New York.

Ann Charters's excellent biography, The Story of Bert Williams (1970), contains documentary photos and reproductions of his most famous songs. See also Donald Bogle's Toms, Coons, Mulattoes, Mammies and Bucks, An Interpretive History of Blacks in American Films (1973). The brief article in the DAB (10:249) by Walter Prichard Eaton gives essential facts. — DONALD BOGLE

WILLIAMS, DANIEL HALE [DR. DAN] (1856–1931), surgeon and educator. He was born in Hollidaysburg, Pa., the fifth child of Daniel Williams, Jr., a barber, and Sarah Price Williams, housewife, both of mixed ancestry. In 1878 he graduated from Haire's Classical Academy in Janesville, Wisc., where he had gone with his sister Sally to work—he as a barber and she in the hair goods industry—after his father died and his mother settled in Rockford, Ill. Considering and then rejecting law as a career, in 1878 he apprenticed himself to Henry Palmer, one of the area's outstanding physicians who had served ten years as surgeon-general of Wisconsin. Palmer helped prepare him to enter Chicago Medical College from which he graduated with an M.D. degree in 1883.

Opening an office in Chicago at 3034 Michigan Ave. in an interracial neighborhood, Williams quickly began to widen his practice and to increase his professional responsibilities. He was appointed attending physician at the Protestant Orphan Asylum and to the surgical staff of the South Side Dispensary. Next came appointments as clinical instructor at the Chicago Medical College and as surgeon to the City Railway Co. Despite his busy schedule he kept abreast of developments in the field of medicine and in 1887 attended the International Medical Congress in Washington, D.C. In 1889 he was appointed to the Illinois State Board of Health, serving four years and sharing the responsibility of drafting major regulations affecting public health. One of his strongest desires was to add another hospital to Chicago's limited number, an institution open to all races but one especially where young Negro doctors could serve internships and Negro nurses could be trained. His efforts culminated in the opening of Provident Hospital in 1891, with a staff of colored and white doctors and a nurses' training school, the first of its kind. It was during this period, because of his concern for those who could afford his services as well as for the underprivileged, that he became known affectionately as Dr. Dan. He was also admired because he was never too busy to address a civic group or play his bass viol—music was his favorite hobby—at a charity affair.

At the Gynecological Society meeting in March 1893 he presented his first major paper, "Appendicitis," advocating the prevailing conservative approach. During May he entertained his mother's cousin, the eminent Negro leader, Frederick Douglass, who was visiting in Chicago as Haitian commissioner to the World's Fair. Douglass presented $50, the entire proceeds from a local church lecture, to Provident Hospital. That same year Williams won acclaim as the first surgeon to perform a successful heart operation. As reported in the Chicago Daily Inter-Ocean (July 22, 1893), he sutured the pericardium of a stabbing victim who survived and regained his health completely. Claims were made that a similar operation had been performed earlier by another surgeon, but the New York Medical Record subsequently reported in the issue of March 27, 1897, that "this case is the first successful or unsuccessful case of suture of the pericardium that has ever been recorded."

In February 1894, feeling that he could be of greater service to his race, Williams accepted an appointment as chief surgeon at Freedmen's Hospital in Washington, D.C. He resigned in February 1898, frustrated with the internal politics and bureaucratic restraints imposed on the federally funded institution.

In April 1898 Williams married Alice Johnson, an attractive Washington schoolteacher. Returning with his bride to Chicago, he established a residence at 3301 Forest Ave., reopened his practice, and rejoined the staff at Provident Hospital, which had moved into a larger building in 1896. In June he was appointed with the rank of colonel to a board of surgeons to examine potential medical officers for service in the war with Spain. Having been accused in absentia of malfeasance during his tenure at Freedmen's Hospital, he returned to Washington to vindicate himself before a congressional investigating committee.

Disappointed by the loss of his only heir during childbirth in 1899, Williams widened his medical activities and research. He presented a major paper to the Chicago Medical Society in December 1900 refuting what he termed the myth that Negro women might develop tumors of other origins, but never an ovarian cyst. Visiting Meharry Medical College in Nashville, Tenn., he served without pay as a professor of clinical surgery. In St. Louis he attended the National Medical Association meeting and demonstrated surgery at the Municipal Hospital. During the next decade he visited twenty states and was instrumental in establishing forty hospitals serving essentially Negroes.

In 1913 he was appointed associate attending surgeon at white St. Luke's Hospital, an honor which caused a group of powerful and jealous Provident associates to turn against him. Again, as at Freedmen's, the bickering and disloyalty were more than he could tolerate, and he resigned from the staff and board of the hospital he had founded twenty-one years earlier. But 1913 was not entirely unrewarding. He was then the only Negro included in a group of one hundred charter members of the American College of Surgeons.

In 1924 his wife died and two years later, suffering from a stroke, he went into semiretirement at his home in Oakmere in Idlewild, Mich., dying there on Aug. 4, 1931. He was survived by his sisters Ann and Alice, and his sister-in-law Mrs. Matilda Price Williams. A bronze plaque honoring him was later hung in the lobby of Provident Hospital, engraved "Daniel H. Williams, 1858 [sic]–1931, Distinguished Surgeon, Founder of Provident Hospital."

Illustrative of his research are: "Several Cases of Inflammation Starting in the Caecum and Vermiform Appendix" (American Journal of Obstetrics 28 [1893]: 260–81); "Stab Wound of the Heart and Pericardium, Suture of the Pericardium. Recovery. Patient Alive Three Years Afterward" (New York Medical Record 51 [March 27, 1897]: 437–39, illustrated); "A Case of Intestinal Obstruction Following Ventro-Fixation" (American Gynecological and Obstetrics Journal 16 [1900]: 573); "The Need of Hospitals and Training Schools for the Colored People of the South," reprint of a paper read before the Phillis Wheatley Club at Nashville, Tenn., Jan. 23, 1900, 5 pages, illustrated (National Hospital Record, Detroit, n.d.); "A Report of Two Cases of Caesarean Section under Positive Indications with Terminations in Recovery" (American Journal of Obstetrics 45 [1901]: 315–22, 400–3, illustrated); "Unusually Large Pyosalpinx" (Surgery, Gynecology, Obstetrics 22 [1916]: 741–42).

A driving force behind every institution he became associated with, Williams contributed significantly to the development of both Provident and Freedmen's Hospitals, but especially the latter. Soon after his arrival at Freedmen's he organized the hospital into seven departments: medical, surgical, gynecological, obstetrical, dermatological, genitourinary, and throat and chest. He further integrated the staff, established four internships, revitalized the nurses' training program, and acquired a serviceable horse-drawn ambulance. In one year under his direction the hospital's 10 percent mortality rate was appreciably reduced. During his first year as chief surgeon he performed or assisted with 533 operations, only eight of which resulted in fatalities.

In January 1895 Williams was instrumental in the formation of the interracial Medico-Chirurgical Society of Washington, and in December went to Atlanta, Ga., to help organize the National Medical Association, declining the presidency but serving as vice-president.

In spite of his brilliant professional achievements, William's personal life was unfulfilled and frequently saddened. His brother, Price, had died suddenly in 1895, his mother in 1900, and his sister Ida in 1902. Personality conflicts with his wife Alice were a source of constant frustration to him until her untimely death. In 1925, at the age of sixty-nine, he invited Leon Tancil to assist him with his office practice. Three years later Tancil left to establish his own practice and a few years afterward, in poor health, Williams closed his office.

At his death he bequeathed his estate to his surviving relatives, the Washington YWCA, Howard and Meharry Medical Schools, and the NAACP. The pioneer surgeon was buried in Chicago's Graceland Cemetery in an unmarked grave.

The standard biography of his life is Helen Buckler's Daniel Hale Williams: Negro Surgeon (1954). Other sources are Lewis H. Fenderson's Daniel Hale Williams: Open Heart Doctor (1971) and Who's Who in America, 1906–1921. — LEWIS H. FENDERSON

WILLIAMS, EDWARD CHRISTOPHER (1871–1929), librarian, teacher, and writer. He was born in Cleveland, Ohio, the only son of Daniel P. Williams, a Negro, and Mary (Kilkary) Williams of Tipperary, Ireland. He was educated in the public schools of Cleveland and in 1892 received his B.A. from Adelbert College of Western Reserve University where he was elected to Phi Beta Kappa and was valedictorian of his class. From 1892 to 1894 Williams was first assistant librarian of Adelbert College, and from 1894 to 1898 the librarian of the Hatch Library of Western Reserve. From 1898 to 1899 he was university librarian of Western Reserve. He remained at Western Reserve until 1900. A brilliant and stimulating teacher, he taught library courses in bibliography, reference work, public documents, and book selection. Williams was granted a leave of absence from Western Reserve in 1899–1900 to study at the New York State Library School in Albany, where he completed the two-year course in one year. Returning to Western Reserve, he was admired by his students for his scholarship in history, literature, and language. They spoke of him as an excellent teacher who "vitalized books by connecting them with human interests and needs," as an individual who had a "keen sense of the picturesque and the humorous" and "from whom one always caught some fire of inspiration." While at Western Reserve, Williams was secretary of the Ohio Library Association and chairman of its college section. He lectured each year at the Ohio Institute of Library workers held at the annual meeting of the Ohio Library Association.

In 1909 Williams left Cleveland and became principal of the M Street High School (in 1916 named Dunbar High School) in Washington, D.C., a position he held until June 1916. A continued interest in library training and organization led him to accept the position of librarian of Howard University in 1916, where during the next several years he developed library training courses, expanded library resources, and increased the staff. In 1921 he was appointed head of the Romance Languages Department, teaching courses in Italian, French, and German. In addition to his teaching and library duties at Howard, Williams engaged in many aspects of campus life, serving on committees, as associate faculty editor of the *Howard University Record* (to which he contributed many articles), and actively supported dramatics. Along with his university duties he found time to address civic, literary, and professional groups, as well as to serve on the staff of the 135th Street Branch of the New York Public Library during his summer vacations.

Had Edward Christopher Williams lived, he might have become a creative writer of note. The Howard University Players performed his classical dramas *The Exile, The Sheriff's Children,* and *The Chasm.* His series on Washington colored society, "Letters of Davy Carr, A True Story of Colored Vanity Fair," was published in 1925 and 1926 in the *Messenger* magazine. Williams published poems and short stories anonymously and under the pseudonym of Bertuccio Dantino.

While on leave from Howard University in December 1929, Williams became ill in New York City where he was attending the School of Library Service at Columbia University working toward a Ph.D. He died on Dec. 24 in Freedmen's Hospital, Washington, D.C., leaving a wife Ethel Chesnutt Williams, a daughter of the well-known author Charles Waddell Chesnutt, a son Charles and a granddaughter Patricia Ann Williams. The funeral of Edward Christopher Williams, who had lived during most of his Washington years at 912 Westminster St. NW, was held on Dec. 27 in Andrew Rankin Memorial Chapel, Howard University, Pres. Mordecai W. Johnson officiating. He was interred at Lincoln Cemetery, Suitland, Md.

Additional information on Williams is in the following: Dorothy B. Porter's "Edward Christopher Williams" (*Phylon* 8, no. 4, 1947), E. L. Josey's "Edward Christopher Williams, Librarian's Librarian" (*NHB* 33, no. 3, March 1970), and Russell H. Davis's *Memorable Negroes in Cleveland's Past* (1969). Obituaries appeared in the *Washington Evening Star* (Dec. 26, 1929, p. 7) and *Washington Tribune* (Dec. 27, 1929, p. 1). — DOROTHY B. PORTER

WILLIAMS, FANNIE BARRIER (1855–1944), lecturer and clubwoman. She was born in Brockport, N.Y., the youngest of three children of Anthony J. and Harriet (Prince) Barrier. Her parents and grandparents, who had been born free, enjoyed friendly contacts with whites in Brockport. She attended the local schools and graduated from the academic and classical course of the State Normal School at Brockport in 1870. She taught school in the South and in Washington, D.C., studied in the New England Conservatory of Music in Boston and the School of Fine Arts in Washington. In 1887 she married in Brockport S. Laing Williams of Georgia, a graduate of the University of Michigan and an honors graduate of the Columbian Law School in Washington (later the George Washington Law School).

They had no children. From 1893 to the late 1920s she was one of the best known and most effective colored lecturers and clubwomen. Largely inactive after 1921, she lived with her only sister (she had also a brother), died of arteriosclerosis in 1944, and was buried in the family plot in Brockport's High Street Cemetery.

Her life after her marriage revealed an ambivalence not unlike that of many other Negro leaders of the late nineteenth and early twentieth century, including for example Robert H. and Mary Church Terrell. Her early lectures and writings supported the militant protest ideology of Frederick Douglass. In Chicago, where she helped her husband in the establishment of his law practice, she delivered in May 1893 one of her best known addresses, "The Intellectual Progress of the Colored Women of the United States since the Emancipation Proclamation." In this speech before the World's Congress of Representative Women at the Columbian Exposition in Chicago, she declared: "The colored people are in no way responsible for the social equality nonsense. . . . Equality before the law . . . is totally different from social equality." She won, however, a victory for "social equality" when after a year-long controversy she was admitted in 1895 as the "only colored member" of the Chicago Woman's Club. Sometime later she used her light skin and assertion "Je suis française" to prevent being moved from the coach for white passengers to a Jim Crow coach while traveling in the South. Whether true or not, she said to herself "that there was quite a strain of French blood in my ancestry, and too that their barbarous laws did not allow a lady to be both comfortable and honest" ("A Northern Negro's Autobiography," *Independent*, July 14, 1904, p. 95). The date of this article is significant because after 1900 she is said to have become a strong champion of the accommodationist views of Booker T. Washington.

Meanwhile she was active in social welfare work in Chicago, credited with assisting Daniel Hale Williams in founding (1891) Provident Hospital with a biracial staff of doctors and a training school for nurses. She helped found the National League of Colored Women (1893), and with Mrs. Terrell, its successor, the National Association of Colored Women (1896). She was also active in the Illinois Woman's Alliance. By 1900 she had achieved considerable success in urging employers to hire qualified Negro women for stenographic and clerical jobs—not many white women held executive or managerial positions in those days.

This interest in job opportunities probably led her to espouse Booker T. Washington's emphasis on practical training, without rejecting the value of a broader education. In 1900, the year that Washington, T. Thomas Fortune, and Emmett J. Scott founded the National Negro Business League, Williams, along with Washington, was a contributor to *A New Negro for a New Century.* At the 1902 convention of the Afro-American Council in Saint Paul, supporters of Washington, Fortune, and Scott maintained control and Williams was elected corresponding secretary, succeeding Ida Wells-Barnett, who along with her husband had joined the opposition. In the same year Williams wrote: "The Negro woman's club of to-day represents the New

Negro with new powers of self-help" ("Club Movement Among Colored Women," in J. W. Gibson and W. H. Crogman [eds.], *Progress of a Race* [1902], p. 203).

Both Williams and her husband assiduously courted Washington, since her husband, like many other suppliants, sought Washington's support for a federal position. When she was told to discontinue writing a column about women's activities for Fortune's *New York Age* (1907), she apologized to Washington for having believed that he had a considerable financial interest in the paper and was allowed to continue her column. Her husband mentioned to Washington allegedly unsavory reports about Fortune's conduct and in 1907 was the ghostwriter of Washington's biography, *Frederick Douglass*. In 1908 S. Laing Williams received his reward with appointment to the post of federal assistant district attorney in Chicago. In that same year, however, he wrote that the New Negro, "unlike his grandfather, is sensitive to wrongs, writhes under injustice and is fretful under discrimination" ("The New Negro," *Alexander's Magazine,* Nov. 1908, pp. 17–22). Woodrow Wilson's election in 1912 started the decline of Booker T. Washington's power in the White House and the president removed from federal office William H. Lewis (assistant U.S. attorney-general), James C. Napier (register of the Treasury), and others, including S. Laing Williams. Then the two Williamses began working with W. E. B. Du Bois and the NAACP. After the death of her husband in 1921, Williams was less active, except for serving on the Library Board of Chicago (1924–1926), reportedly the first woman and the first Negro to hold this appointment.

Her career and views are in her address "The Intellectual Progress of the Colored Women of the U.S. since the Emancipation Proclamation" (in May Wright Sewall [ed.], *The World's Congress of Representative Women* [1894], 2:696–711) and "A Northern Woman's Autobiography" (*Independent,* July 14, 1904). August Meier's *Negro Thought in America, 1880–1915: Racial Ideologies in the Age of Booker T. Washington* (1963), and Emma Lou Thornbrough's *T. Thomas Fortune: Militant Journalist* (1972) are particularly valuable for the relationships of Fannie Barrier Williams and S. Laing Williams with Washington and Fortune. Two perceptive sketches, by Allan H. Spear in the *DAB, Supplement 3* (1973, pp. 827–28) and by Leslie H. Fishel, Jr. in *NAW* (1971, 3:620–22) have comprehensive bibliographies. — RAYFORD W. LOGAN

WILLIAMS, GEORGE WASHINGTON (1849–1891), soldier, clergyman, lawyer, legislator, and historian. The second child of Thomas and Ellen Rouse Williams, he was born on Oct. 16, 1849, in Bedford Springs, Pa. During his early life his father, a common laborer in search of work, took the family successively to Johnstown and Newcastle, Pa. As a lad George Williams had virtually no formal schooling, and at an early age he was placed in a house of refuge in western Pennsylvania where he learned the barbering trade. When Negroes were permitted to enlist in the Union Army in 1863, Williams—only fourteen years of age—assumed the name of an uncle and enrolled. When it was discovered that he was under age he was discharged, but after many entreaties he was permitted to reenlist. He saw service in several battles and was wounded near Fort Harrison, Va., in 1864. Legend has it that after being mustered out at the end of the Civil War Williams entered the Mexican army, saw service in many battles, and rose to the rank of lieutenant-colonel (this has not been confirmed). In August 1867 he enlisted in the 10th Cavalry of the regular U.S. Army and remained in the service until 1868 when he was given a medical discharge at Fort Arbuckle where he had sustained a gunshot wound in the left lung.

Upon leaving the army in September 1868 Williams went to St. Louis, and he later made much of the fact that it was there that he was baptized at the First Baptist Church. In the following year he was in Quincy, Ill., when he heard of Howard University. He applied to Gen. O. O. Howard for admission, and entered that institution in September 1869. After a few months Williams dropped out and took some courses at Wayland Seminary, also in Washington. In his quest for training as a minister, a career upon which he had by this time decided, he presented himself before the faculty of the Newton Theological Institution in Massachusetts in September 1870. While he could not qualify for the program in theological studies, he was admitted to the program of general studies. Two years later he was admitted as a junior in theology, and he was one of the commencement orators at his graduation in 1874 when he spoke on "Early Christianity in Africa."

Shortly after his ordination in June 1875 Williams became the pastor of one of New England's oldest and most important Negro Congregations, the 12th Baptist Church of Boston. At his installation he conceded that in Boston he would have the ears of only a few hundred members, but the field was nevertheless an important one which, if well cultivated, "will furnish the 'one that shall chase a thousand, and the two that shall put ten thousand to flight.'" Williams did not remain long enough to cultivate the field. Fourteen months after his installation he had resigned and moved to Washington. In the nation's capital Williams undertook to edit a journal, *The Commoner.* Although the new venture had the support of such persons as Frederick Douglass and John Mercer Langston, it did not prosper, and Williams was forced to take a job in the Washington Post Office to sustain himself.

Williams was pleased to abandon the venture in journalism in order to accept the postorate of the Union Baptist Church in Cincinnati, where he was installed in March 1876. Within a few months he became involved in a number of secular activities, including the study of law and Republican politics. In 1877 he was an unsuccessful candidate for the state legislature, and a few weeks later he resigned his pastorate. While studying law in the office of Judge Alphonso Taft and at the Cincinnati Law School, Williams had a variety of jobs, such as Internal Revenue storekeeper and secretary in the auditor's office of the Cincinnati Southern Railway. He also contributed articles to the *Cincinnati Commercial* under the pen name of "Aristides." In 1879, with the strong support of the Republican organization in Cincinnati, Williams was elected to the House of Representatives of Ohio.

Although he served only one term in the state legislature, Williams was an active member of considerable influence. He was chairman of the Committee on the State Library as well as a member of the Committee on Universities and Colleges, and several select committees. He introduced many private bills and petitions from his constituents, and a number of public bills in which he gave particular interest to the regulation of the police in the larger cities of the state. None of his public bills passed. One of his more vigorous efforts was his unsuccessful attempt to secure the repeal of the statute prohibiting the intermarriage of whites and blacks in Ohio. Williams did not seek reelection in 1881. The campaign of 1879 had been bitterly fought, and Williams's election was by the smallest margin of any Republican candidate. Some of his constituents, moreover, were very critical of some positions he had taken while in the legislature, especially his support of the removal of a Negro cemetery to make way for a white development. Finally, Williams had become preoccupied with yet another career, and not even politics could stand in the way.

Williams had been interested in the study and writing of history for years. He had written a history of the 12th Baptist Church during his pastorate, and he had delivered many lectures on historical subjects. During the nation's centennial he began to think seriously about the role of Negroes in the history of the country, and began to collect material on that subject systematically. While in the legislature he did research in the state library, and when he finished his term he visited and worked in numerous libraries in the East. By the end of 1881 he had finished a lengthy manuscript, and in the following year G. P. Putnam's Sons brought out his *History of the Negro Race in America from 1619 to 1880* in two volumes and a popular edition of two volumes in one.

The appearance of Williams's history was a major event in publishing and literary circles. No American Negro had ever undertaken so ambitious a task. It was reviewed widely and, in some quarters, favorably. The *Magazine of American History* (April 1883) called it a creditable performance and declared that "No one who fails to become acquainted with the contents of this book can claim to have a full understanding of American history." While the *Atlantic Monthly* (April 1883) lamented Williams's "petty hostility" to Massachusetts by praising Connecticut more than Massachusetts for its early antislavery stance, it conceded that the author had produced a work of great value, "one that will be a treasury of facts for future students." When Harper published his *History of the Negro Troops in the War of the Rebellion* in 1887 the praise was even less reserved. By this time Williams was widely regarded as the historian of his race, for he had written two works that were not only the first of their kind, but compared quite favorably in research and composition with other historical works of the period.

Although Williams continued to write, he also continued to hold political ambitions. He was therefore quite gratified that President Harrison appointed him minister to Haiti in March 1885. Although the Senate confirmed the appointment and the Department of

State issued his commission, the incoming Democratic administration refused to permit him to take up his duties. There ensued a long, bitter, and unsuccessful effort on the part of Williams to force the Department of State to honor the appointment. He finally resorted to the U.S. Court of Claims where he sued for his salary, but this too was without success.

Williams always regarded such experiences as obstacles that were to be overcome, and he serenely went about the task of finding new areas of endeavor. Having been admitted to the Ohio bar in 1881, he moved to Boston in 1883 where he was admitted to the practice of law. After the publication of his history, he was in demand as a lecturer and even began to travel abroad. In 1884 he attended the World Conference on Foreign Missions in London and traveled on the continent. He was back in Europe in the following two years, and on one of these trips he met Leopold, King of the Belgians, and began to formulate plans to assist in the development of the Congo by recruiting American Negroes to work there. In 1884 he had written articles on African geography, and in testimony before the Senate Committee on Foreign Relations, had urged recognition by the United States of the Congo Free State. In 1889 he was commissioned by S. S. McClure to write a series of articles on the Congo, and in the same year Collis P. Huntington asked him to report on the progress of the Congo railroad that was under construction by the Belgians.

When King Leopold sought to discourage him from going to the Congo, Williams was more determined than ever to see that land before attempting to persuade Negro Americans to go there. In January 1890 he sailed from Liverpool, and after visiting various points of interest en route, spent four months exploring the Congo from the mouth of the Congo River to its headwaters at Stanley Falls. The trip was a revelation of Belgium's inhuman exploitation, and in *An Open Letter to His Serene Majesty, Leopold II, King of the Belgians,* Williams excoriated the King for his cruel oppression of the people of the Congo. The published report was widely circulated and discussed in Belgium, France, England, and the United States. He also wrote articles for McClure's Associated Literary Press and in 1890 published two other reports: *A Report Upon the Congo-State and Country to the President of the Republic of the United States* and *A Report on the Proposed Congo Railway.* He then visited Portuguese and British possessions in Africa and spent several weeks in Egypt.

In the late spring of 1891 Williams was back in England, where he worked on a lengthy manuscript in which he planned to make further exposures of the Belgian policy in the Congo. During the summer he became ill, and in early July friends took him to Blackpool where they hoped that the sea air would assist his recovery. This was a vain undertaking. Suffering from tuberculosis and pleurisy, he died on Aug. 2, 1891, in the Palatine Hotel and was buried in Layton Cemetery, where in 1975 an American historian placed a stone on his grave with the following engraving: "George Washington Williams, Afro-American Historian, 1849–1891."

Williams was a man of modest build and light complexion. He was fastidious in his dress and proper in his social manners. In June 1874 he married Sarah A. Sterrett of Chicago with whom he had one son. They both survived him. His death, when announced in the American press, shocked many American Negroes, who just two years earlier had voted in the *Indianapolis Freeman* that Williams was one of the ten greatest Negroes in history.

The few papers of Williams that were conveyed by his widow to Henry P. Slaughter do not survive. There are autobiographical statements in his *History of the Twelfth Baptist Church* (1874) and *History of the Negro Race in America* (1882). There are numerous inaccuracies in the *DAB* (10, Part 2:263–64). See also *The National Cyclopedia of American Biography* (1900, vol. 10), *Biographical Cyclopedia and Portrait Gallery of the State of Ohio* (1884, vol. 3), the *New York Tribune* (Aug. 5, 1891), the London *Times* (Aug. 10, 1891), and two articles by John Hope Franklin, "George Washington Williams, Historian" (*JNH,* Jan. 1946), and "George Washington Williams and Africa" (Department of History, Howard University, 1971).

— JOHN HOPE FRANKLIN

WILLIAMS, JOE [SMOKEY JOE, CYCLONE JOE] (1886?–1946), baseball pitcher.

Williams was born in Seguin, Tex., probably in 1886 (other dates sometimes given are 1874 and 1885). His mother was either Indian or part Indian, his father a Negro. Reminiscences about his career differ only slightly. In 1908 when he was pitching for the San Antonio Broncos, Arthur W. Hardy (another baseball player) later recalled that he must have been six feet, five or six inches tall and that his blazing fastball "looked like a pea" to batters. In 1909 he pitched against the Leland Giants in Birmingham; although he lost (3–2), Andrew (Rube) Foster, "the Father of Black Baseball" and manager of the Leland Giants, asked Williams, "What's your name, boy?" "They call me 'Cyclone,'" the youngster replied simply. Foster took Williams north with him in 1910. In 1912 Joe jumped to the New York Lincoln Giants, which may have been then the best Negro team in the country, possibly the best of any color. They boasted shortstop John Henry Lloyd, outfielder Spottswood Poles, catcher Louis Santop, and pitcher Cannonball Dick Redding.

Williams was so strong many batters swore he could throw a ball through a wall. It reportedly took two catchers to hold him in a nine-inning game. New York Giant infielder Frankie Frisch recalled that hitters didn't dig in against Williams. "You weren't exactly afraid, but you have a little respect when you're facing guys like that." Luckily for the hitters, Williams also had pinpoint control. In 1913 Williams beat Turkey Mike Donlin's big-league all stars 9–1 on a two-hitter. He beat the Philadelphia Phils and the great Grover Cleveland Alexander 9–2, striking out nine men, compared to six for Alexander. He also defeated Bender of the Athletics 2–1 on three hits. The next autumn Williams faced the Phils again. Alexander, a thirty-one-game winner in the National League, gave up one run, and Joe went into the ninth leading 1–0. He walked the bases full, then struck

out the next three men. Alexander was so angry he tore his glove to shreds in the dugout.

Williams's finest performance was a game in 1917 against John McGraw's Giants, who had finished second in the National League. Williams pitched a no-hitter for ten innings, striking out twenty, but losing 1–0 on an error. Giant outfielder Ross Youngs congratulated him: "That was a hell of a game, Smokey," giving him his lifelong nickname. He followed that a year later with a brilliant 1–0 victory over Walter Johnson of the Washington Senators in a duel between the two greatest fastballers in baseball. Against the strong semipro Brooklyn Bushwicks in 1924, Williams struck out twenty-five men in twelve innings.

In 1926 Williams joined Cum Posey's Homestead Grays which played out of Pittsburgh. By 1930 they were perhaps the finest Negro team in the country— Monte Irvin and others say the finest Negro team of all time. A young Samson named Josh Gibson caught. The infield included Oscar Charleston, one of the greatest Negro players in the history of the game, plus Jud Wilson and George Scales. In the outfield were "Cool Papa" Bell, Vic Harris, and Ted Page. The Kansas City Monarchs, the strongest team out west, challenged the Grays to a series under the Monarchs' new-fangled portable lights. In one memorable game (1930) Williams faced Chet Brewer, an emory ball specialist. The lights were not as bright as in later years, and in twelve innings Brewer struck out nineteen men while Williams gave just one hit before he finally won it 1–0.

Williams could still "throw smoke," although he was well over forty. Satchel Paige says he pitched against Joe twice before large crowds in Pittsburgh's Forbes Field, home of the National League Pirates. Paige says he won the first game 2–1; Williams the second, 3–2. But Williams was twenty years older than Paige at the time.

Williams retired in 1934. Posey, an authority on Negro baseball, maintained that only Johnson and perhaps Lefty Grove could match Williams's fastball in his prime. And Ty Cobb declared that Smokey Joe would have been a sure thirty-game winner if he had played in the majors. In twenty-six postseason games against the best white big-league clubs from 1913 through 1932, Williams won nineteen, lost six, and tied one. Among his victims: Walter Johnson, Grover Alexander (twice), Chief Bender, Rube Marquard, and Waite Hoyt, all of whom are in the Hall of Fame. The tie was 1–1 against the New York Giants and Marquard in ten innings. Two of the losses came in 1932 when Joe was forty-six years old. In 1952 a poll of thirty-nine experts in the *Pittsburgh Courier* named Williams first, ahead of Satchel Paige, by a vote of twenty to nineteen.

The principal sources are John Holway's *Voices from the Great Black Baseball Leagues* (1975) and Robert W. Peterson's *Only the Ball Was White* (1970). Holway reproduced on page 173 a photograph of the Homestead Group (1931), which includes Williams. There is an undated individual photograph in Peterson (p. 216). Since both authors relied on the reminiscences of other players, there are some minor differences. Peterson in particular has numerous statistics.

— JOHN HOLWAY

WILLIAMS, PETER, JR. (1780?–1840), clergyman, abolitionist, and opponent of colonization. He was born about 1780 in New Brunswick, N.J. His father, Peter Williams, Sr., was a slave, but his mother, Mary Durham, was an indentured servant from St. Kitts. Both parents were of unmixed African descent. In 1783 his father was bought by the John Street Methodist Church in New York City, where he had moved his family. While working as sexton and undertaker at the church, his father purchased his freedom in 1796. He became a leading member of the free Negro community and a founder of the African Methodist Episcopal Zion church. He operated a tobacco shop and funeral establishment which enabled him to purchase a house and other property.

The younger Williams's first schooling was at the New York African Free School operated by the Manumission Society, on land donated by Trinity Church. He was also taught privately by his pastor, the Rev. Thomas Lyell, of the John Street Church. When Lyell left Methodism for the Episcopal church, Williams seemed to have joined him. In any event he associated himself with the congregation of black Episcopalians who worshipped at Trinity Church on Sunday afternoons led by an aged Negro lay reader. Williams was confirmed about 1798 by John Henry Hobart, who privately tutored him along with other Episcopal clergymen. Hobart also officiated at his wedding held in his father's house. When the lay reader died in 1812, Williams was elected by the congregation as lay reader and licensed by the bishop. Under Williams's leadership the Negroes organized themselves in 1818 as a separate congregation, acquired a lot, and erected a wooden church at a cost of $8000. The small congregation contributed liberally but the largest amounts came from Trinity Church and from a white Episcopalian who gave $2500. The church was consecrated on July 3, 1819, as St. Phillip's African Church.

The church burned down the next year, but as it was fully insured Williams replaced it with a brick structure worth $10,000. The congregation grew and acquired a rectory. On one occasion he presented 115 candidates for confirmation. Among his parishioners were James McCune Smith, Alexander Crummell, Charles L. Reason, Peter Vogelstang, and George Thomas Downing. On July 10, 1826, he was advanced to the priesthood, thus becoming the second American Negro so ordained.

Williams seems to have accepted the racial discrimination he experienced within the Episcopal church. In conversation he was simply called "Peter" by the bishop and other clergy, whereas white clergymen were addressed as "Mister ———." Bishop Hobart counseled him not to attempt to gain representation for himself or St. Phillip's in the diocesan convention, a right enjoyed by all other ministers and parishes.

Although Williams was primarily occupied with his duties as rector of St. Phillip's Church, he was a conspicuous leader in the free Negro community. He believed that Negroes should remain in the United States where they were "entitled to full citizenship rights," and by mutual self-help, education, and cooperation with liberal-minded whites, to improve their status.

Highly regarded for his learning and speaking ability, Williams was selected to give the oration in New York on the abolition of the slave trade on Jan. 1, 1808. In 1817 he preached at the funeral of Paul Cuffe.

Williams was one of the chief co-founders of the first Negro newspaper, *Freedom's Journal,* in 1827. He was also a founder in 1833 of the Phoenix Society, whose tasks were to visit families, provide clothing for poor children, help young men obtain jobs, encourage church attendance, and establish lending libraries and a manual training school. Williams was especially concerned about education for Negro youth, several of whom, such as Crummell, he assisted financially. He was instrumental in establishing a high school, taught by John Peterson, lay reader and later assistant minister at St. Phillip's.

Williams vigorously opposed the American Colonization Society which he denounced for its "unreasonable, unrighteous, and cruel" effort to force free Negroes out of their native land. He was very interested in the emigration of Negroes from Cincinnati after the 1829 riot and helped to raise money for the Wilberforce, Canada, settlement. Along with Richard Allen, James Forten, and others, he proposed the first national convention of colored leaders which met in Philadelphia in September 1830. After the 1831 convention, as chairman of the executive committee, Williams led the abortive attempt to establish a manual training college at New Haven, Conn. At the request of the National Colored Convention of June 1833, he and Forten wrote to the marquis de Lafayette and other European liberals explaining that American Negroes favored immediate abolition and full manhood rights and opposed colonization in Liberia. Williams, however, supported those who voluntarily chose to emigrate. Among those he helped to go to Liberia was John B. Russwurm. He himself went to Haiti for three months to assist colored Americans who had gone there.

Williams threw his full weight into the abolition movement. When the American Anti-Slavery Society was organized in December 1833, he was one of six Negro managers. Agitation for abolition and civil rights, together with competition by Negroes for jobs, provoked a severe riot by white workers in New York City on July 7, 1834. For three days mobs roamed the city, attacking and burning homes and institutions in the Negro sections. Infuriated by a rumor that Williams had performed an interracial marriage, a mob demolished St. Phillip's Church and rectory, forcing Williams to flee. Bishop Benjamin T. Onderdonk admonished Williams to avoid controversial political questions which disturbed the "peace of the community," and to resign publicly from the abolition society. Williams reluctantly complied, but stated that all he had wanted was "to obtain freedom for my brethren." His submission was supported by his congregation but caused him to lose some of his accustomed esteem in the Negro community. However, "he continued as an influential factor among the Negroes until his death in 1849 [*sic*]" (Carter G. Woodson, *Negro Orators and Their Orations* [1925], p. 32, n.2).

The probable date of his death is Oct. 17, 1840. He was survived by his wife and daughter.

The fullest account of Peter Williams's life is B. F. DeCosta's *Three Score and Ten: The Story of St. Phillip's Church* (1889). Two addresses are in *Early Negro Writing, 1760–1834, Selected and Introduced by Dorothy Porter* (1971): "An Oration on the Abolition of the Slave Trade; Delivered in the African Church, in the City of New York" (Jan. 1, 1808, pp. 343–53, with testimonials that he wrote it, pp. 353–54), and "A Discourse Delivered in St. Phillip's Church for the Benefit of the Colored Community of Wilberforce, in Upper Canada, on the Fourth of July" (1830, pp. 294–302). Two of Williams's hymns are on pages 568–70. Information about his early life is in Joseph Beaumont Wakely's *Lost Chapters in the Early History of African Methodism* (1858). — J. CARLETON HAYDEN

WILLIAMS, WILLIAM TAYLOR BURWELL (1869–1947), educator.

The son of Edmund and Louise Williams, he was born in Stonebridge, Va., on July 3, 1869. He attended the public school at Millwood, in Clarke County, Va., and at the age of seventeen became a teacher in one of the county's public schools. From 1886 to 1888 he was enrolled in the Normal Course of Hampton Institute, Hampton, Va., after which he taught for a year in the Whittier School, the elementary department of that institution. In 1893 he graduated from Phillips Academy, Andover, Mass., and in 1897 from Harvard College, receiving the B.A. degree.

After completing his college education Williams was appointed principal of School No. 24, subsequently named the McCoy School, in Indianapolis. He resigned in 1902 to become field agent for Hampton Institute and the Southern Education Board. As field agent his primary duty was to make studies of educational conditions in Virginia and other southern states. He married Emily A. Harper on June 29, 1904. They had no children.

Retaining his connection with Hampton Institute, Williams was appointed in 1904 field agent for the General Education Board. As field agent for the General Education Board, Williams worked among the Negro population of the South, urging local educational activities and providing professional assistance to communities eager to improve their schools. By 1910 he was working concurrently as field agent for Hampton Institute, the General Education Board, and the John F. Slater and Anna T. Jeanes Funds, having been appointed to the latter two in 1906 and 1910, respectively.

As field agent for the Slater Fund, Williams helped establish some 384 county training schools for Negro youth in thirteen southern states. The brainchild of James Hardy Dillard, director of the Slater Fund and president of the Jeanes Fund, the county training school extended elementary (and later, high school) training to thousands of Negro youths for whom the state boards of education had provided little or no educational opportunities. The county training school also relieved many Negro colleges from having to provide elementary and high school facilities.

The purpose of the Jeanes Fund (Negro Rural School Fund) was to establish a competent and systematic plan of supervision of rural schools, by appropriating money to aid the southern counties in employing supervisory teachers. Popularly called the Jeanes teachers, they supervised primary instruction in the Negro schools of the rural South, organized industrial classes in these schools, and organized and continued community clubs to promote activities for general community improvement. As field agent for the Jeanes Fund, Williams was responsible for directing the work of the Jeanes teachers, as well as assessing the need for additional supervisory teachers.

During more than thirty years his work with the Slater and Jeanes Funds and with the General Education Board brought Williams into direct contact with every phase of Negro education in the South, and with leading educators, black and white. He was known throughout the South as one of the best informed persons on Negro education. Through careful observation of school conditions and helpful cooperation with teachers, Williams exerted a constructive influence on Negro education in the South.

His interest in Negro education was not limited to the United States. On two occasions, once in 1922 and again in 1930, Williams was sent to Haiti as a member of United States commissions on education. The purpose of the second commission was to investigate the cause of Haitian complaints against the educational system maintained by American occupation officials. They had established a vocational school system separate from that of the national "classical" system, and had increased appropriations to the former while the national schools were allowed to deteriorate. The 1930 U.S. Commission on Education, headed by Robert Russa Moton, principal of Tuskegee Institute, published a valuable report in 1931 about the discriminatory practices in public education, made recommendations for removing them, and improving the quality of education in a unified system, with an increased budget under Haitian control.

A strong proponent of industrial education, Williams's personal recommendations concerning education in Haiti, as well as the Virgin Islands (to which he was sent in 1928 as a member of another education commission), stressed the need for increased vocational and agricultural training for the island youths in order to develop a self-reliant yeomanry in both populations.

At the invitation of Dr. Moton, who in 1916 had succeeded Booker T. Washington as principal of Tuskegee Institute, Williams in 1919 came to Tuskegee where he served as consultant in the teacher-training program of the institute. When the College Department of the institute was organized in 1927, Williams became its first dean. Under his direction, following in the Washington tradition, the College Department placed emphasis on advancing the program of vocational education to college standards, offering B.S. degrees in agriculture, teacher training, technical arts, and domestic science. In 1936 Williams was elected vice-president of Tuskegee Institute, and served until his death on March 26, 1941.

In 1918 Williams was appointed assistant supervisor of vocational training in colored schools for the Committee on Education and Special Training of the U.S. War Department. In this capacity he aided in establishing vocational units of the Student Army Training Corps.

In 1917, when the Department of Labor initiated a study of the northward migration of Negroes which had intensified during and after World War I, Williams was selected as one of the special investigators to conduct the study. The result of this study was *Negro Migration in 1916–17,* published under the auspices of the U.S. Department of Labor in 1919. Williams, the sole Negro investigator, was one of the five contributors.

Williams was the author of numerous articles on Negro education, most of which appeared in the *Southern Workman* (1904–1924), of which he was an editorial staff member. He helped to organize the Negro Organization Society of Virginia, which worked for better schools, farms, homes, and health. He also assisted in the organization of the National Association of Teachers in Colored Schools, and for two terms served as its president.

In 1923, Morehouse College, Atlanta, Ga., conferred upon him the honorary LL.D. degree; and in 1934 he was awarded the twentieth Spingarn Medal for his distinguished service to Negro education.

The most extensive information on Williams is in the Manuscript Collection, W. T. B. Williams Papers, Tuskegee Institute Archives, Tuskegee Institute, Alabama. Information on the philanthropic organizations with which Williams was affiliated is in *A History of Negro Education in the South* by Henry Allen Bullock (1967). For the 1930 mission to Haiti, see Rayford W. Logan's *Haiti and the Dominican Republic* (1969, esp. p. 140) and U.S. Department of State, *Report of the United States Commission on Education in Haiti* (1931). There is an obituary in the *JNH* (July 1941, pp. 411–12).

— JOELLYN PRYCE EL-BASHIR

WILSON, BUTLER R[OLAND] (1860–1939), lawyer and civil rights leader. The son of Dr. John R. and Mary (Jackson) Wilson, he was born on July 22, 1860, in Greensboro, near Atlanta, Ga. His father was a prominent physician and active leader. After attending the local public schools, young Butler entered Atlanta University. While an undergraduate he became well known as a debater and captain of the varsity baseball team; in the summers he taught school. When he graduated in 1881 he was chosen the class orator. Wilson rejected his parents' desire that he become a minister; forced to pay his own way, he migrated to Boston in 1881 and entered the Boston University School of Law. There he began his close association with Archibald H. Grimké, the second Negro graduate of the Harvard Law School (1874); and in the mid-1880s helped him edit the local Negro weekly, *The Hub.* In 1884 Wilson received his LL.B. degree and began his practice in Boston. His first law partners were Grimké and George L. Ruffin, the first Negro northern municipal judge and the first Negro to receive a Harvard law degree (1869). After 1887 Wilson practiced law independently and built an excellent practice in criminal law, maintaining an office in downtown Boston. In 1898 the governor appointed him a master of chancery in Boston, a signal honor. Wilson became one of the most respected lawyers in New England. He had more whites than Negroes as clients, at times assisting Moorfield Storey, the white Boston lawyer who served as president of the American Bar Association and president of the newly founded NAACP.

Shortly after Wilson began his law practice, he and Grimké were involved in a case of discrimination at a skating rink in Boston (1885). A lower court upheld the Negro plaintiff but the higher court dismissed the case. In 1893, when William Henry Lewis (the Harvard All-America football player and later assistant attorney-general of the United States) was twice refused a haircut in a white barbershop in Cambridge, Wilson and Lewis helped expand the state civil rights law to cover barbershops and other public places.

Wilson was a member of the Boston "radicals," who included Grimké, William Monroe Trotter, George Forbes, and Clement G. Morgan. Thus it is not difficult to understand why Wilson became one of the anti-Booker T. Washington leaders in New England. The *Guardian,* a Negro weekly edited in Boston by Forbes and Trotter, also voiced Wilson's views. In 1905 Wilson was one of the fifty-nine original endorsers of the call for the Niagara Movement, founded in 1905 to oppose Washington, by W. E. B. Du Bois. When the NAACP was founded in 1909–1910, Wilson aided in the development of branches by helping to organize the active Boston branch in 1912. He and his wife, Mary Evans Wilson, whom he married in 1894, were the chief organizers and activists in the branch. He was the executive secretary of the Boston branch from 1912 to 1926, president of the branch from 1926 to 1936, and a member of the National Board of Directors in the 1920s.

It was as a member of the NAACP that Wilson made his mark as a leader. Moorfield Storey and other NAACP officials secured the admission of Wilson and Lewis as the first Negro members of the American Bar Association in 1912. In Boston he protested against the segregated YMCA and the showing of the film *The Birth of a Nation* in 1915 and 1921. He vehemently opposed the segregated army post at Fort Des Moines to train Negro officers in 1917. During these early years he served as an attorney for the NAACP. In the postwar years Wilson refused to support any fundraising activity to aid Du Bois in his Pan-African work as a part of the NAACP, whose activities, he insisted, should be confined to the United States. He was also one of the leaders against an attempt in 1924 in Massachusetts to ban intermarriage. These activities probably explain why he did not seek political office for himself, although as a regular Republican he campaigned for others. In 1917, however, he accepted appointment by the governor to the Massachusetts board of appeals on fire insurance rates, an office he held for the rest of his life.

He was a loyal and prominent alumnus of Atlanta University. He, James Weldon Johnson, and others helped prepare the papers which resulted in the first of the Atlanta University Publications, *Mortality Among Negroes in Cities* (1896). When he addressed a fundraising dinner at Trinity Church in Boston (1894), the *Boston Record* stated that "the capacity of the colored race for education is well illustrated in this brilliant example." At another meeting in Broadway Tabernacle in New York City, presided over by Chauncey M. Depew, president of the New York Central Railroad and later

U.S. senator, Wilson stated that support of schools like Atlanta University would go far toward solving the race problem. He also argued that the Negro problem had to be fought on American soil and "not by a cowardly evasion" such as deportation to Africa. In February 1900, he, Lewis, Trotter, and Forbes delivered addresses at the Lincoln Day Dinner, which was probably the first meeting in that area organized by Negro men "to endorse 'the position taken by the University in regard to the collegiate education of Negroes.' "

In Boston, Wilson lived on Rutland Square, an affluent neighborhood to which some Negroes had moved in the 1890s. In 1928 Mary Evans Wilson died; she had given birth to five children, three boys and two girls. She was buried from the Columbus Avenue African Methodist Episcopal Zion Church. On Oct. 31, 1939, Butler R. Wilson died of pneumonia. Survived by two sons and a daughter, his funeral was held at the New Charles Street Church, Roxbury, and he was buried in the Forest Hills Cemetery.

See Conrad Reno's *Memoirs of the Judiciary and the Bar of New England* (1901, vol. 2). Some useful primary source material is in the Records of the NAACP, Library of Congress; a few details appear in John Daniels's *In Freedom's Birthplace* (1941), Stephen R. Fox's *The Guardian of Boston, William Monroe Trotter* (1970), and Charles Flint Kellog's *NAACP . . .* (1967, vol. 1). See also Clarence G. Contee, Sr.'s "Butler R. Wilson and the Boston NAACP Branch" (*The Crisis,* Dec. 1974, pp. 346–48). — CLARENCE G. CONTEE, SR.

WILSON, J[AMES] FINLEY (1881–1952), editor, fraternal leader, and politician. He was born in Dickson, near Nashville, Tenn., the grandchild of emancipated slaves, and one of several children of the Rev. James L. and Nancy Wiley Wilson. An adventurous youth, he went to Denver when he was thirteen and joined Coxey's Army in the famous march of 1894. An aunt forced him to leave one of its offshoots and sent him home. He graduated from Pearl High School, Nashville, and studied at Fisk University. After roaming in the West, New York City (1894), the Klondike (1898–1899), Utah (1900), working as a miner in Arizona and a cowboy in Wyoming, he returned to the East where he became an editor. On Aug. 28, 1922, on his forty-first birthday, he was elected grand exalted ruler of the Improved Benevolent Protective Order of the Elks of the World (I.B.P.O.E. of W.), a position to which he was annually reelected until shortly before his death, after ailing from diabetes for some three years, in Washington, D.C., on Feb. 18, 1952.

Wilson ("The Grand") made the Elks the largest of the Negro Social Welfare and Fraternal Societies. The I.B.P.O.E. of W. had a membership of only some 30,-000 at the time he was elected grand exalted ruler, over 500,000 members and some 900 lodges at the time of his death. Membership far exceeded that of the Prince Hall Masons or the Odd Fellows, for example. During his twenty-six years, the order gave over $700,000 in grants-in-aid for scholarships to young men and women, some of whom became leaders in their professions and communities.

Wilson understood the manipulation of power; he won support of the masses almost as much as had Marcus Garvey. His parades were gala events, both for the participants and the large number of spectators. He enlarged the location of the Washington lodge from a relatively unpretentious house to a spacious building on the corner of Second Street and Rhode Island Avenue NW. Although the I.B.P.O.E. of W. was ridiculed by many upper-class Negroes, its membership included sizable numbers of doctors, dentists, pharmacists, and lawyers. Some of them laughed at the hi-jinks of initiation and then wondered whether they were much different from those of their "high-class" organizations. Undoubtedly, self-interest led many of them to join, for membership increased their patients or clients. The large membership enabled Wilson to pose as a leader in the Republican party, but he never held a higher position than sanitary inspector in Denver during his early years. His power was increased by his membership in the Masons, the Odd Fellows, the Knights of Pythias, and the Order of St. Luke's.

The John Brown Reader, edited with a foreword by William C. Hueston and J. Finley Wilson (1949), is an illustrated, uncritical tribute. The Elks had purchased the John Brown Farm (sometimes called the Kennedy Farm) of some 250 acres near Harpers Ferry, where John Brown trained and drilled his men. In an address, "The Colored Elks and National Defense," delivered at the Annual Session of the National Baptist Convention (Cleveland, Ohio, Sept. 1941), Wilson stated that Negroes' participation in World War II would be a "stand against Hitlerism." He hoped that democracy would work in America; urged the passage of antilynching and anti-poll tax bills, the building of a healthy morale, the need for education, the raising of living standards, and better job opportunities. Negroes were "proud to serve" in the war. They should buy defense bonds and Elk women should enroll in Purple Cross Nurse Units.

Wilson was survived by his widow, the former Leah Belle Farrar of Richmond, Va., whom he had married on July 28, 1924. At the time of his death, he resided at 1813 Vernon St., NW in Washington. The business address of the I.B.O.P.E. of W. was 1915 14th St. NW.

The principal source is Charles H. Wesley's *History of the Improved Benevolent and Protective Order of Elks of the World, 1898–1954 (1955).* Obituaries were published in the *Washington Post* (Feb. 20, 1952), the *Chicago Defender* (March 1, 1952), *NHB* (May 1952), and *JNH* (July 1952). — RAYFORD W. LOGAN

WOODS, GRANVILLE T. (1856–1910), inventor. Born in Columbus, Ohio, on April 23, 1856, the son of Tailer and Martha Woods, at the age of ten he began work in a machine shop, spending his evenings attending school or receiving private instruction. When he was sixteen he went to Missouri and worked on railroads as a fireman and engineer. In 1876 he worked in a Springfield, Ill. steel mill and then in a machine shop in New York City, while studying electrical and mechanical engineering in the evening. On Feb. 6, 1878, he embarked on a long tour aboard the British steamship *Ironsides.* From 1882 to 1884 he was an engineer on the Danville and Southern Railroad. When he was twenty-eight (1884), he and his brother Lyates opened their own machine shop in Cincinnati. He lived in Cincinnati from 1884 to 1890 and from then in New York City until his death. Between 1884 and 1907 he patented some thirty-five inventions that were vital to the development of electrical and mechanical equipment. He apparently never married; a small newspaper item concerning an affair with an unnamed woman has been generally suppressed. On Jan. 28, 1910, following a stroke, he was admitted to Harlem Hospital in New York City. He died there on Jan. 30, and on Feb. 3, was buried in Grave 144, Range 3, Plot 5, St. Michael's Cemetery, Astoria, Queens, New York.

Granville Woods received his first patent on Jan. 3, 1884 for a steam boiler furnace. This invention promoted a better method of combustion and economized fuel. His second patent (Dec. 2, 1884), was a telephone transmitter, an apparatus for transmitting messages by electricity. Woods's invention, which was assigned to the American Bell Telephone Company of Boston, produced distinct and greater effects than the instruments then in use. His third patent (April 7, 1885) for transmitting messages by electricity was advantageous for domestic use because individuals practicing the Morse alphabet could speak over the same wire with the same instruments that were used for telegraphic practice.

During 1887 Woods patented seven inventions, three of which were assigned to the Woods Electric Company of Cincinnati, and two to himself. These two (June 7 and July 5, 1887) included a relay instrument and a polarized relay. The relay was used in telegraphy and the polarized for communication between moving trains, thus reducing the danger of accidents. The patents assigned to the company also improved communications. The telephone system and apparatus (Oct. 11, 1887) was devised for the transmission of words and other sounds conducted by electricity, with the object of obtaining increased force of the transmitting impulses that controlled the action of the diaphragm and the receiving end in order to obviate effects produced by neighboring lines. Both the railway telegraph and the inductor of the telegraph alarm (Nov. 15 and 29, respectively), likewise improved electrical communication between trains, vehicles, or a fixed station. In addition, two patents on the electromagnetic brake (Aug. 16 and Oct. 18, 1887) promoted safety by the use of electromagnetic force in the operation and control of railway brakes.

In 1888 Woods increased the number of his patents by five, three of which were assigned to the company and two which he retained. The two retained included one for a galvanic battery (Aug. 14, 1888), and one for railroad telegraphy (Aug. 28, 1888). The telegraphy pertained to moving vehicles, particularly trains, and provided an increase from a given dynamic force with a simple permanent conductor. The galvanic battery was a simple instrument which was usable for ordinary purposes where batteries were applicable. Those assigned to the company included those for an overhead conducting system for electric railways, an electromotive railway, and tunnel construction for electric railways (May 29, June 26, and July 8, respectively). The tunnel carried the conductors of electromotive railways below

the surface of the ground in such a position that they could be reached and utilized by the traveling contacts on the car or motors through a slot at the surface of the roadway.

Two patents issued Jan. 1, 1889, and Oct. 14, 1890, pertained to an automatic safety cut-out for electric circuits. Woods had long recognized the dangers from electrical conductors. The first patent pertained to the conductor carried above the earth on supports in which breakage or sagging between the supports brought the wire into contact with people or animals. The second concerned electric lights and power circuits where there was a danger from accidental contact when telephone or telegraph wires or parts of buildings were destroyed.

Woods then moved to New York City where he spent most of his time on his inventions. Here, he had a total of eighteen; of these, four were assigned to himself: for a re-electric railway supply system (Oct. 31, 1893), an amusement apparatus (Dec. 19, 1899), an incubator (Aug. 28, 1900), and an automatic circuit-breaking apparatus (Nov. 20, 1900). The circuit-breaking device was a safety measure since it provided for the automatic interruption of the action of a driving motor when a pickup switch failed to open the circuit after the car had passed the section. By this device the motor driver was compelled to attend to the switch and to the interrupting apparatus of the car. The reelectric supply insulated the mode of connecting circuits. The incubator provided an even temperature for the hatching of chicks and the amusement apparatus included a series of tracks for motor vehicles found at summer and other resorts.

Woods's other patents were assigned as follows: electric railway system (American Engineering Company, 1891), electric railway conduit (Universal Electric Company, 1893), systems of electrical distribution (S. E. Riley, Oct. 13, 1896), electric railway (General Electric Company, Jan. and Nov. 1901, March 1902, and June, 1904), electric railway system (Electro Magnetic Traction Company, 1901), regulating and controlling electrical translating devices (four to Harry Ward Leonard, East Orange, N.J., Sept. 1901 and Jan. 1902), system of electrical control (Henry C. Townsend and Delbert H. Decker, Trustees, 1904). Patents for railway brake apparatus (March 29, 1904, and July 18, 1905) issued to Granville and his brother Lyates were assigned to Westinghouse Electric and Manufacturing Company. Two patents for safety apparatus (Oct. 16 and Nov. 27, 1906) were assigned to the General Electric Company. Woods's last recorded patent was for a vehicle controlling apparatus (Sept. 24, 1907).

Further research is necessary to explain why such a versatile inventor died in virtual poverty. He probably had to pay huge legal fees for defense in a suit for criminal libel in 1892. Woods had charged that his patents for an electric railway had been stolen by the manager of the American Engineering Company. Arrested and held briefly in jail for lack of money to pay his bail, he confronted powerful businessmen and politicians.

Elementary Public School No. 335 in Brooklyn, N.Y., named for him, was dedicated in 1969. Gov. John J.

Gilligan of Ohio on Oct. 11, 1974, issued a proclamation to recognition of the "Black Edison" who had "more than 60 patents to his credit."

The fullest account of Woods is in M. A. Harris's *The Black Book* (1974). Harris also published a eulogistic *Granville T. Woods 1856–1910 Memorial* (1974). It is valuable, however, for its listing of the numbers, brief descriptions, and names of assignees of Woods's patents. The earlier standard references are Henry E. Baker's *The Colored Inventor* (1913) and "The Negro in the Field of Invention" (*JNH,* Jan. 1917, pp. 21–36). Much of the early information is based on the biographical sketch, probably written by Woods, in William J. Simmons's *Men of Mark . . .* (1887, pp. 107–12). Woods wrote a brief article in the *Booklovers* magazine (July 1903), "Possibilities of the Negro, The Advance Guard of the Race." — MAE P. CLAYTOR

WOODSON, CARTER GODWIN (1875–1950), educator, historian, and editor. Born on Dec. 19, 1875, in New Canton (Buckingham County), Va., the oldest of nine children of former slaves, James and Anne Eliza (Riddle) Woodson, he could not attend the five-month school because his parents needed the small wages from his work in the coal mines. Self-educated until he was seventeen, he moved in 1892 with his family to Fayette, W.Va. His work in the coal fields there prevented him from attending full time the Douglass High School in Huntington, W.Va., which he entered in 1895. Despite the severe handicaps of his early education, he completed the course in a year and a half (1896) and was admitted to Berea College, Berea, Ky., shortly thereafter. He received his B.L. degree on June 3, 1903. Meanwhile, on May 18, 1901, he had received his certificate qualifying him to teach in the West Virginia public high schools. He taught in Winona in Fayette County, and was principal of Douglass High School (1900–1903). He studied at the University of Chicago during the summer quarter 1902 and the autumn quarter 1903, took correspondence courses during the summer of 1905, and received his B.A. degree on March 17, 1908. Meanwhile he had spent three years (1903–1906) as supervisor of schools in the Philippines, where he learned to speak Spanish fluently. He had also spent a year of study and travel (1906–1907) in Asia, North Africa, and Europe, including a semester at the University of Paris. On Aug. 28, 1908, he was awarded his M.A. degree from the University of Chicago. He was in residence at the Harvard Graduate School of Arts and Sciences in 1908–1909. From 1909 to 1918 he taught French, Spanish, English, and history at the M Street and Dunbar High Schools, Washington, D.C. He served as principal of Armstrong High School in 1918–1919, and was concurrently on the faculty of the Miner Normal School in Washington.

While teaching in Washington, he did research at the Library of Congress for his doctoral dissertation, "The Disruption of Virginia," which completed his work for his Ph.D. in history, awarded by Harvard University in 1912. A co-founder (with George Cleveland Hall, W. B. Hartgrove, Alexander L. Jackson, and J. E. Stamps) of the Association for the Study of Negro Life and History, he established the *Journal of Negro History* in 1916.

He served as director of the association and editor of the *Journal* until his death.

Appointed dean of the School of Liberal Arts and head of the Graduate Faculty at Howard University from 1919 to 1920, Woodson also served from 1920 to 1922 as dean of West Virginia Collegiate Institute (later West Virginia State College) where he reorganized the curriculum. In 1922 he retired from college teaching and devoted the rest of his life to writing, editing, and promoting popular interest in Negro history.

In 1921 Woodson organized the Associated Publishers, a subsidiary of the ASNLH which became the most important Negro-owned publishing company for the next thirty-five years. He died of a heart attack in his home on April 3, 1950; following funeral services at Shiloh Baptist Church on April 8, he was buried in Lincoln Memorial Cemetery, Suitland, Md. A loner by temperament, he never married.

As a teacher, Woodson was dignified, stern, and demanding, whether in the high school, college, or university. At Howard, Woodson supervised the first M.A. thesis in history approved by the Graduate Faculty. An adherent of the "new history," which went beyond political and military issues, Woodson was particularly interested in the history of the Negro's participation in the economic and social development of the United States. It is difficult to trace precisely the origins of Woodson's interest in Negro history. No courses in the subject were offered at his college or graduate school. A possible indication of his interest was his trip to Egypt in 1907. His doctoral dissertation "The Disruption of Virginia" (1912) is a more definite indication. His interest may have been spurred by the intensification of segregation in Washington, and the increasingly popular distortion of history represented by such films as *The Birth of a Nation* (1915).

Although it is not possible to determine their precise impact on Woodson, there were many developments in the intellectual and social life of Negroes that indicated greater interest in Negro history. These included the Atlanta University Studies of the Negro Problems (1896) and the founding of the American Negro Academy (1897), the American Negro Historical Society of Philadelphia (1897), the Negro Society for Historical Research (1912), and the Moorland Foundation, a Library of Negro Life at Howard University (1914)..

On Sept. 9, 1915, Woodson, along with George Cleveland Hall, W. B. Hartgrove, Alexander L. Jackson, and James E. Stamps, founded in Chicago the Association for the Study of Negro Life and History (later Afro-American). The ASNLH was committed primarily to historical research; publication of books on Negro life and history; promotion of Negro history through schools, colleges, churches, and fraternal groups; and collection of historical manuscripts.

The *Journal of Negro History,* which Woodson edited from Jan. 1, 1916, to his death on April 3, 1950, was one of the better specialized scholarly journals. It contained articles by reputable scholars, Negro and white, men and women. Most of the articles dealt with the Negro in the United States, a sizable number about Africa, and a few about Latin America.

In supporting Woodson's nomination for the Spingarn Medal in 1925, W. E. B. Du Bois wrote that Woodson "has done the most striking piece of scientific work for the Negro race in the last ten years of any man that I know. He has kept an historical journal going almost single-handed, founded a publishing association, and published a series of books with but limited popular appeal. It is a marvelous accomplishment."

"An Evaluation of the First Twenty Volumes of the *Journal of Negro History*" (*JNH,* Oct. 1935, pp. 397–405), by Luther P. Jackson, stated: "The writings in the early issues of this Journal reflect infancy; the later issues show maturity. The early volumes show a low standard of documentation; the later volumes show a high standard of documentation." Arthur M. Schlesinger, Sr., commented that the *Journal* ranked "with the best learned periodicals of the country" (*NHB,* May 1950, p. 172).

In order to popularize the study of Negro history, Woodson in 1926 inaugurated Negro History Week, and in October 1937 the *Negro History Bulletin.* Negro History Week encompassed Lincoln's Birthday and the generally accepted date of Frederick Douglass's Birthday. It became increasingly popular, as branches of the association were established in cities throughout the United States. Woodson spoke at meetings in large cities and mayors proclaimed Negro History Week. Extensive planning, with the participation of prominent community leaders, preceded each NHW campaign. Circulars were distributed to educational institutions and the press, public libraries, labor and fraternal organizations, social welfare and literary societies. There were also book exhibits, lectures, pamphlets, news stories, and editorials. Negro History Week became a nationally recognized observance, and was one of the most significant popular movements in the development of race consciousness and pride among Negroes. It also contributed to increasing knowledge among whites of the contributions made by Negroes to the history of the United States.

The annual meetings of the association, usually in October, were also occasions for promoting scholarly as well as popular interest in Negro history. Among the notable presidents of the association during Woodson's life were John R. Hawkins, John Hope, and Mary McCleod Bethune.

The *Negro History Bulletin* provided historical materials for instruction in elementary and secondary schools. The *Bulletin* enjoyed a large circulation and reached an audience that would not ordinarily be exposed to Negro history, particularly its inspirational aspects.

Woodson wrote and edited more books in the field of Negro history than any other scholar. In addition to his doctoral dissertation, his scholarly works include *The Education of the Negro Prior to 1861* (1915), *The History of the Negro Church* (1921), *A Century of Negro Migration* (1918), *The Negro Professional Man and the Community* (1924), *The Negro Wage Earner* (with Lorenzo Greene; 1930), and *The African Background Outlined* (1936). The works he edited are indispensable sources: *Negro Orators and Their Orations* (1925), *Free Negro Heads of Families in the United States in 1830* (1925), *Free Negro Owners of Slaves in the United States in 1830* (1925), *The Mind of the Negro as Reflected in Letters Written during the Crisis, 1800–1860* (1926), and *The Works of Francis J. Crimké* (4 vols.; 1942).

Among the more valuable of his popular writings are *Negro Makers of History* (1928), for junior high school students; *The Story of the Negro Retold* (1935), for senior high school students; *African Myths* (1928); *The Miseducation of the Negro* (1933); and *African Heroes and Heroines* (1939). *The Negro in Our History,* first published in 1922, was for many years the most widely used Negro history text in high schools, colleges, and universities. One of Woodson's great disappointments was his inability to secure adequate support for his proposed *Encyclopedia Africana.*

Soon after the founding of the ASNLH it received $25,000 from the Carnegie Corporation, $25,000 and $37,500 from the Laura Spelman Memorial, and $32,-500 from the Rockefeller Foundation. Evidence in the Woodson Papers at the Carter G. Woodson Center, Washington, indicates that Thomas Jesse Jones of the Phelps-Stokes Fund had a role in the withdrawal of foundation support of the ASNLH and the research conducted by Woodson and his associates. Despite the praise of Woodson's scholarship in his books and the *Journal of Negro History* by distinguished historians and other scholars, Jones maintained that Woodson had become "a propagandist with a distinct antipathy to movements for racial cooperation." Perhaps the most important source of Jones's animosity was Woodson's criticism of the African Educational Commission headed by Jones, which attempted to establish a system of education in Africa most likely to perpetuate colonial rule. The loss of foundation support greatly hampered Woodson's work. It also convinced him that in order to protect his independence he would have to build the ASNLH as a Negro organization supported primarily by Negroes. Even after Woodson had established himself as a scholar, some white scholarly organizations treated him as an inferior. When the Social Science Research Council made a grant of $4000 to him 1928, it stipulated that expenditure of the funds would be supervised by three white historians.

Woodson impressd his contemporaries and younger persons as a "man with a cause." He lived frugally on the top floor of 1538 9th St. NW, where the lower floors were used as offices and the basement as a warehouse for books. Though usually stern, he had occasional flashes of humor. Wedded to his work and his independence of thought and action, Woodson was distrustful of collaborative enterprises sponsored by whites. In light of his earlier conflicts with Thomas Jesse Jones and their devastating outcome, it is not surprising that Woodson refused to participate in the *Encyclopedia of the Negro* project, sponsored by the Phelps-Stokes Fund.

The impact of Woodson's career has been summarized by John Hope Franklin: "Those of us who look, with deep appreciation, at his many successful undertakings can observe the very salutory effect that they have had on the writing and study of American history and the consequent regard that many have developed for the history of the Negro. . . . One can only be certain of two things: that the contributions of Carter G. Woodson to American historiography have been significant and far reaching and that the program for rehabilitating the place of the Negro in American history has been stimulated immeasurably by his diverse and effective efforts."

Some details in *Current Biography* (Feb. 1944) have been corrected in this sketch. See the entire issue of the May 1950 *Negro History Bulletin.* In addition see Rayford W. Logan's "Carter G. Woodson, A Profile" (*Phylon* 6 [Fourth Quarter 1945]: 315–21) and his article in the *DAB, Supplement Four* (1974, pp. 910–12); L. D. Reddick's "Carter G. Woodson: An Appreciation" (*Phylon* 11 [Second Quarter, 1950]: 177–79); W. E. B. Du Bois's "A Portrait of Carter G. Woodson" (*Masses and Mainstream* 3 [June 1950]: 19–25); and Patricia Watkins Romero's "Carter G. Woodson: A Biography" (Ph.D. dissertation, Ohio State University, 1971). There is no adequate biography of Woodson. His papers are in the Library of Congress, the ASALH (Woodson Center), and the Moorland-Spingarn Research Center, Howard University. — RAYFORD W. LOGAN

WORK, MONROE NATHAN (1866–1945), bibliographer, sociologist, teacher, and writer. He was born in Iredell County, N.C., one of eleven children of slave parents, Alexander and Eliza (Hobbs) Work. In 1876 the family settled in Cairo, Ill., where he began his education. Ten years later the family moved to Kansas where his father obtained a 160-acre farm near Ashton, and young Work continued his education in a small schoolhouse. For a while an invalid father and an ill mother necessitated his operating the family farm, his brothers and sisters having left home.

Work started his high school training at age twenty-three in Arkansas City, Kans., earning a living by working on odd jobs, and graduating in June 1892. Unable to obtain a teaching position and interested in the church, he was ordained and given a pastorate in the African Methodist Church at Wellington, Kans., which he kept for only a few months. In September 1893 Work staked a claim in southern Kansas and on Oct. 15, 1895, deposited it in the General Land Office of the United States. Later he sold his claim in order to raise funds to further his education. He graduated from the Chicago Theological Seminary in 1898, but unsuited for the ministry, he entered the University of Chicago where he received the Bachelor of Philosophy degree in 1902. The M.A. degree in sociology and psychology in the Department of Sociology was awarded to him in 1903 (he was probably the first Negro to receive this degree from the University of Chicago).

From 1903 to 1907 he taught English, history, and pedagogy at Georgia State Industrial College in Savannah. Here he began to write articles on African and Afro-American life and to conduct research that was to be his concern the rest of his life. He taught a course, Introduction to the Bibliography of the Negro, and through grants from the Carnegie Corporation purchased thousands of cards on Africa from the Library of Congress.

Work, who had become aware of the importance of accurate documentation in Negro studies while at the University of Chicago, accepted Booker T. Washington's invitation in 1908 to become director of records and research at Tuskegee Institute. In 1912 Work edited and published *The Negro Year Book, Annual Encyclopedia of the Negro,* which, with some exaggeration, "summarized all the information available in regard to existing conditions." For those who desired additional information, a bibliography of articles and other publications "of various sorts, carefully classified," related almost exclusively to the Negro in the United States, was included. The volume sold for twenty-five cents, plus five cents for postage. Nine editions were edited by Work. The inclusion of a select bibliography of the Negro in the first edition was of such interest to readers that they requested further bibliographical data. In 1921 Carnegie Corporation grants to the Department of Records and Research at Tuskegee enabled Work to devote most of his time to the compilation of what was to become the most comprehensive bibliographical tool for the study of the Negro. He purchased cards from the Library of Congress on the Negro in America and Africa and secured the necessary clerical assistance. In 1926–1927 "the plan of the Bibliography took on its final form as a result of conferences held with Dr. W. A. Slade, Chief Bibliographer of the Library of Congress, Dr. C. T. Loram, Commissioner of Native Affairs of the Union of South Africa, Dr. Diedrich Wassermann, Professor of African Languages at the University of Berlin and others" (Phelps Stokes, p. xii). These latter included authorities on the Negro in Latin America. Aided by grants from Tuskegee Institute and the Phelps-Stokes Fund, Work did research in the most important United States libraries, and abroad, including the British Museum, the British Colonial Office, the Royal Colonial Institute of London, the Colonial Institutes of Brussels and Hamburg, the Bibliothèque Nationale in Paris, the Library of the League of Nations, and other university, public, colonial, and missionary libraries. He also conferred with European authorities on Africa and bibliography. Work expressed in his preface his gratitude to some thirty experts abroad and in the United States (including Charles S. Johnson and Arthur Schomburg) for their helpful criticism.

In 1928 Work's *A Bibliography of the Negro in Africa and America* was published by H. W. Wilson Co., New York City. Its purpose was "to furnish an accurate and comprehensive handbook of the titles and authors of valuable books, pamphlets and articles from periodicals on the Negro in Africa and America." The volume listed a selection of more than 17,000 entries printed prior to 1928, in seventy-four carefully classified chapters. Part One was devoted to "The Negro in Africa," Part Two, Section One to "The Negro in the Settlement of America" (including the Thirteen Colonies, the United States, the West Indies and "South America"), Section Two to "The Negro in the United States," and Section Three to "Present Conditions of the Negro in the West Indies and Latin America." Both parts included a bibliography of bibliographies. Negro authors were indicated by an asterisk. The volume, including an index of authors, totaled 698 pages.

The value of the *Bibliography* cannot be measured. Its significance, in the words of Anson Phelps Stokes, as early as March 1928, was not an exaggeration: "I believe" that it "will prove a valuable book of references for all University, College and public libraries, and that students of social conditions in Africa and the United States, especially those concerned with that most complicated of all social problems, the race problem, will find it absolutely indispensable." Although the well-known philanthropist gratuitously expressed his satisfaction that Work was "an American Negro, with only a trace of white blood," his conclusion was a well-deserved tribute: "It [the *Bibliography*] is a monument of which any race may well be proud." It is more indispensable today than in 1928, partly because no comparable work has been published. A reprint of Work's *Bibliography* was published in 1965.

After the publication of *The Bibliography of the Negro in Africa and America,* Work began "A Bibliography of European Colonization and the Resulting Contacts of Peoples, Races, Nations, and Cultures." The prospectus, dated April 23, 1945, stated that its purpose was to provide a set of references for the study of "Contacts of Peoples, Races, Nations and Cultures." Since he compiled the references from the point of view of European colonization, he was able to place the Negro in a general frame of reference which included "all the peoples and races, who, as the result of colonial enterprise have directly or indirectly come under the influences of European culture." He therefore broadened the scope of his first bibliography, increasing the number from 17,000 to about 100,000 in the new bibliography. It is unfortunate that Work did not live to see this great bibliography in print. The world of scholarship lost what would have been the greatest bibliography published in the field of Afro-American scholarship.

Work's other activities included the promotion of programs for the improvement of rural and urban Negroes in and near Savannah, Ga., working with the Annual Framers Conference and the Georgia Colored State Fair, as well as helping to establish Negro history as a recognized and respectable field of study. While at Tuskegee, Work gave Booker T. Washington help in the writing of his *Story of the Negro.* When Washington established National Negro Health Week in 1915, Work wrote its first *Health Week Bulletin.* Work's meetings with Carter G. Woodson in Washington and Chicago helped stimulate the organization in 1915 of the Association for the Study of Negro Life and History. His initiation of the annual Tuskegee Lynching Records was important to the press, government officials, educators, librarians, and students.

Work published a few poems and over fifty-nine articles in numerous periodicals on folklore, the church, education, community problems, labor, health, business, economics, and African life. He lectured extensively before learned societies and teachers. Work received many honors: the first, in 1929 was the Harmon Foundation Award of $400 and a gold medal, in recognition of his "scholarly research and educational publicity through periodic publication of the *Negro Yearbook* and the compilation of a *Bibliography of the Negro.*" The Alumni Association of the University of Chicago in 1942 gave him its Citation for Public Service at the fiftieth anniversary of the university for "Unselfish and effective service to the community, the nation and hu-

manity," the first Negro thus honored. Howard University conferred upon him the honorary Doctor of Letters on June 4, 1943. He was a member of the American Sociological Society, the American Economic Association, the American Academy of Political and Social Science, the Association for the Study of Negro Life and History, the American Association for the Advancement of Science, and the International Institute of African Languages and Culture; he was also a trustee of the National Association of Teachers in Colored Schools. He was a member of the board of directors of a proposed "Encyclopedia of the Negro" which resulted in the publication of *Encyclopedia of the Negro: Preparatory Volume with Reference Lists and Reports* by W. E. B. Du Bois and Guy B. Johnson with the cooperation of five other scholars.

On Dec. 27, 1904, Work married Florence Evelyn Hendrickson of Savannah, who greatly aided him in his research during the forty-one years of their marriage. They had no children. He died of natural causes after an illness of several months in Tuskegee on May 2, 1945, and was buried in the Tuskegee Cemetery. He was survived by his widow (*Pittsburgh Towner,* May 12, 1945, p. 4).

The principal sources are Jessie P. Guzman's "Monroe Nathan Work and His Contributions" (*JNH,* Oct. 1949, pp. 428–61); Work's "Preface" and Anson Phelps Stokes's "Introduction" to *A Bibliography of the Negro in Africa and America.* — DOROTHY B. PORTER

WORMLEY, JAMES (1819–1884), businessman. Wormley was born in Washington, D.C., on Jan. 16, 1819. Both of his parents were born free and had come to Washington in 1814 from the plantation of a "wealthy Virginia family." His father, Peter Leigh Wormley, was dark while his mother was almost white. They lived on E Street, near 14th Street NW, where James was born. Peter Wormley kept a livery stable and at an early age James began driving his own hack, mostly for visitors to some of the capital's leading hotels, including the Willard. In 1849 he went to California during the gold rush, served later as a steward on a Mississippi River steamer, on ocean-going vessels, and at the Metropolitan Club in Washington, D.C. Shortly before the Civil War he opened his own catering business on I Street near 15th, next door to a candy store operated by Anna Thompson, whom he had married in 1841.

Although a husband and the father of three sons and a daughter, James Wormley accompanied Reverdy Johnson, newly appointed minister to England, as steward. Despite the difficulties of transporting terrapins from the Chesapeake Bay and the Potomac River, Wormley kept them edible and prepared them in such fashion as to win the approval of Johnson's guests—not the first nor the last example of "culinary diplomacy." Wormley went to Paris on his own and then returned to Washington, where he acquired a building on the southwest corner of H and 15th Streets. Using the older property on I Street as an annex, he opened in 1871 the hotel that came to be known as Wormley's Hotel. According to tradition he was unable to pay the mortgages on the new property and transferred it to Rep. Samuel

Hooper of Massachusetts, who rented it to Wormley. Until some years after Wormley's death in 1884 the hotel was noted for its excellent menus and maintenance. Many congressmen and other notables stayed there.

Among his principal friends and supporters were such businessmen as George Riggs, a banker; William Wilson Corcoran, philanthropist and financier; and Sen. Charles Sumner. Shortly before Wormley's death, Lord Coleridge, chief justice of England, reserved nine rooms at the hotel (Frank G. Carpenter, *Carp's Washington* [1960], p. 61).

If Wormley's Hotel were still standing it would probably be listed as a National Historical Landmark for it was there that the conference in February 1877 between representatives of Rutherford B. Hayes and of Samuel Tilden, resulted in the historic "Compromise of 1877." In dispute were twenty electoral votes, nineteen of them from Florida, Louisiana, and South Carolina, and one from Oregon. Tilden, the Democratic candidate, had 184 undisputed votes, leaving only one for his election. Hayes needed all of the twenty. An electoral commission chosen as a result of the Wormley Hotel Bargain or Compromise gave all the disputed votes to Hayes. There is no evidence that James Wormley participated in the compromise (Feb. 26, 1877) that gave the presidency to Hayes and brought about the withdrawal of the last of the federal troops in South Carolina and Louisiana, and "the end of Reconstruction."

The hotel was managed by James T. Wormley, the eldest son, until the financial crisis of the 1890s. In December 1893 it was sold to Charles E. Gibbs, one-time manager of another famous Washington Hotel, the Ebbitt House, who continued to operate it under the name of Wormley's hotel until 1897, when it became the Colonial Hotel. In 1906 the structure was torn down and replaced by the Union Trust Company building.

After Wormley died on Oct. 18, 1884, in Boston where he had gone for treatment of "calculus" (probably gall or kidney stones), his body was returned to Washington and "lay in state" in the summer parlor of his hotel. The *Washington Post* reported that the flags of Washington's principal hotels flew at half-mast. Among the prominent pallbearers were T. E. Roessle, manager of the Arlington Hotel; C. C. Willard of the Ebbitt House; and O. G. Staples, longtime proprietor of the Riggs House, all of whom were white.

Wormley left an estate estimated to be in excess of $100,000. His children and grandchildren were among Washington's colored elite.

There is no full-length biography of James Wormley. This sketch is based in part on an article by Charles E. Wynes, "James Wormley of the Wormley Hotel Agreement" (*The Centennial Review,* Winter 1975, pp. 397–401). For a revisionist interpretation of the "Bargain" or "Compromise," see especially C. Vann Woodward, *Reunion and Reaction: The Compromise of 1877 and the End of Reconstruction* (1951, esp. p. 207). — RAYFORD W. LOGAN

WRIGHT, JONATHAN JASPER (1840–1887), educator, politician, and judge. Wright was born in Luzerne County, Pa., but spent most of his childhood in Sus-

quehanna County, to which his family moved shortly after his birth. His father was a farmer. After attending Lancastrian University in Ithaca, N.Y., Wright read law in law offices in Montrose and Wilkes-Barre, Pa., and taught school at the same time. In 1865 he went to South Carolina, where he attended a colored people's convention in Charleston (November 1865) which protested the attempt of the state legislature to keep the former slaves in their servile status. He also served as an organizer of schools for the freedmen under the auspices of the American Missionary Association. He returned to Pennsylvania where in 1866 he was admitted to the bar, the first Negro to achieve that distinction in the state. Returning again to South Carolina he worked for the next two years for the Freedmen's Bureau as a legal adviser to the former slaves. Like many other bureau employees he also engaged in politics, and helped to organize the Republican party in the state. He played a leading role in the South Carolina Constitutional Convention of 1868, supporting the levying of a poll tax on all adult males to finance the public schools, limited tenure for judges, an elected state judiciary, U.S. appropriations for the purchase of homesteads, and a $10 per diem for members of the convention. He insisted that it was the duty of the convention to "destroy all elements of the institution of slavery." The new constitution was adopted by the convention in April 1868 and by the people: 70,000 for, 27,000 against, and 35,000 abstaining. Even after whites gained control in 1877 the constitution remained largely unchanged until the state Constitutional Convention of 1895, which retained many of the 1868 provisions but virtually disfranchised Negroes. Wright's Beaufort constituents elected him to the state Senate in 1868 and on Feb. 1, 1870 he was elected to fill the unexpired term of one of the justices on the state Supreme Court. In December 1870 he was elected to a full term of six years on the court, probably the first Negro to hold such a position in the United States. His two colleagues were a "scalawag" and a white "carpetbagger" to whom he left many of the important decisions. He was generally respected as a competent and honest judge.

Judicious in temperament and conciliatory in his conduct, Wright was regarded by his contemporaries as a man of integrity. He was also an ardent champion of the rights of Negroes. In 1871 he won $1200 in damages from a southern railroad company for having been evicted from a car reserved for first-class white passengers. On the other hand his role in the contest between Daniel H. Chamberlain and Wade Hampton for governor of South Carolina, (1876–1877) was ambivalent. Since Franklin J. Moses, Sr., the chief justice of the state Supreme Court was ill, Wright and the other associate judge, A. J. Willard, had to resolve the issue. On Feb. 27, 1877, the two associate justices ruled in effect that Hampton was the legal governor. Judge Wright asked that the actual filing be suspended until March 2 and that word of it not be made public until that day. Two days later he changed his mind and asked that his signature to the ruling be revoked. His request was not granted and Hampton was declared governor. Both the Republican and the Democratic press agreed that Wright had acted under duress by both Republicans and Democrats; in addition it was widely reported that Wright was being kept constantly drunk. Since Robert Brown Elliott was a friend who apparently kept watch over Wright during these days and may have written the ancillary opinion on which Wright based his revocation, there may be some basis for the allegation. On March 2, Judge Willard declared the ruling of Feb. 27 effective and Hampton became governor.

After 1877 Wright apparently was no longer active politically. Following the overthrow of the Republican government, he resigned, effective Dec. 1, 1877. Charges of corruption were unsubstantiated and dropped. He lived in comparative obscurity and there is no record that he practiced law. He never married; after a lingering illness of tuberculosis, he died in his rooming house in Charleston.

Two early books, Alrutheus A. Taylor's *The Negro in South Carolina during Reconstruction* (1924) and Francis B. Simkins's and R. H. Woody's *South Carolina during Reconstruction* (1932) were the principal sources until Peggy Lamson's *The Glorious Failure: Black Congressman Robert Brown Elliott and the Reconstruction in South Carolina* (1973), which gave a detailed account of Wright's role in the Chamberlain-Hampton controversy. The brief sketch by Robert H. Weinefeld in the *DAB* ([1936], 10, Part 2:558) gives some essential facts. — ARNOLD H. TAYLOR

WRIGHT, LOUIS TOMPKINS (1891–1952), surgeon, hospital administrator, and civil rights leader. He was born in LaGrange, Ga., the younger of two sons of Dr. Ceah Ketcham and Lula (Tompkins) Wright. His father, who had graduated from Meharry Medical School in 1881, became a clergyman after practicing medicine briefly in Rome, Ga. In 1899 after his father's death in 1895, his mother married Dr. William Fletcher Penn, a brother of I. Gariand Penn. Young Wright was valedictorian of his class in 1911 at Clark University in Atlanta, where he had also received his elementary and secondary education. Encouraged by his stepfather, he gained admission to the Harvard Medical School and graduated in 1915, *cum laude* and fourth in his class. He interned at Freedmen's Hospital (1915–1916) and passed state board examinations that, through reciprocity, made him eligible to practice anywhere in the United States. He practiced in Atlanta with his stepfather, and became treasurer of the local branch of the NAACP, at the same time that Walter White was made secretary.

Commissioned a first lieutenant in the U.S. Army Medical Corps at Fort McPherson, near Atlanta, he served at the Colored Officers Training Camp in Fort Des Moines, Iowa, and at Camp Upton, N.Y., where he was assigned to the 367th Infantry Regiment of the 92nd Division. In France he suffered a phosgene gas attack that permanently damaged his lungs. After hospitalization he was in charge of surgical wards at Field Hospital 366, the triage hospital of the 92nd Division. He received the Purple Heart and was discharged with the rank of captain. By competitive examination he rose to the rank of lieutenant-colonel in the Army Medical Corps, but resigned his commission because of the damage to his lungs.

From 1919 to 1952, except for three years of illness from pulmonary tuberculosis, Wright combined his profession and his civic activities to promote better health assurance and expand equal opportunities for Negroes. He engaged in private practice, became in 1929 the first city public surgeon, and served on the staff and as director of the Department of Surgery of Harlem Hospital. He was active in the local branch of the NAACP, and during his last seventeen years was chairman of its national board of directors. In addition to these activities he engaged in scientific and clinical research and published numerous reports in leading journals.

His work won him significant honors: in 1934 the second Negro admitted to the American College of Surgeons (Daniel Hale Williams had been a founder of the ACS in 1913); a D.Sc. degree from Clark University, Atlanta, in 1938; diplomate of the American Board of Surgery in 1940; the NAACP Spingarn Medal in 1940; founder membership of the American Academy of Compensation Medicine and the presidency of the Medical Board of Harlem Hospital in 1948. In that same year he was a member of the Medical Care Committee of the National Health Assembly. In 1949 he was made a medical adviser to the director of Selective Service for New York City. In 1950 he was appointed to the New York Committee of the American Cancer Society and in 1951 became a member of the Medical Advisory Council of the New York Hotel Trades Council and Hotel Association. He was a fellow of the American Medical Association and the National Medical Association. The Louis T. Wright Library of Harlem Hospital was named for him in 1952, and a public school in Harlem in 1976.

He married Corrine Cooke in 1918. She, their two daughters—Dr. Jane Cooke Wright (Mrs. Jones) and Dr. Barbara Penn Wright (Mrs. Pierce)—and three grandchildren survived him.

Louis Wright's zealous determination precipitated numerous controversies, many of which furthered the achievement of constructive goals. When an assistant professor of obstetrics at the Harvard Medical School told him that he could not do his deliveries in Boston Lying-In Hospital because of his race, his classmates supported him in his insistence that, in accordance with the catalog, he would make deliveries in that hospital. While a senior at Harvard he stayed out of school for three weeks to demonstrate against the showing of *The Birth of a Nation*. Incensed by the allegation that the Schick test for diphtheria was of no value to Negroes because of the heavy pigmentation of their skin, he conducted a study while interning at Freedmen's Hospital which showed that the allegation had no scientific basis.

Through the influence of his friend, Civil Service Commissioner Ferdinand Q. Morton, the Medical Board of Harlem Hospital agreed in 1919 to admit Wright and a few other Negroes as adjunct visiting surgeons and physicians. He was one of the leaders in the successful fight against the establishment of a new Jim Crow hospital in Harlem and of the building in the North of a second Negro Veterans Administration hospital (the first was at Tuskegee). He was unsuccessful during the 1940s in preventing the transfer of a financially burdened hospital in a neighborhood abandoned by whites to new auspices under what was called an interracial plan. Sydenham Hospital was established, but financial difficulties led to its being taken over by the city. He consistently criticized the exclusionary policies and practices of the American Medical Association and advocated national health insurance when it was first proposed.

Wright's role as chairman of the board of the NAACP (1935–1952) is difficult to determine. W. Montague Cobb, who knew him well, has written that "by his strong, firm hand at the helm of the N.A.A.C.P., [he] steered that organization intact through some of the most perilous storms it had ever faced, into some of its most important accomplishments." On the other hand, August Meier and Edwin M. Rudwick concluded, after research in the NAACP Papers in the Library of Congress, that Walter White really controlled the board's policies. "Through his friendship with Wright he was even able to largely decide on appointments to the key board committees. And prior to the monthly meetings of the national board of directors White and an inner circle of key members would meet at Wright's apartment to caucus on strategy for the next day." Walter White, more than Wright, was responsible for the final dismissal as of Dec. 31, 1947, of W. E. B. Du Bois as director of special research. This was all the more surprising to Du Bois because Wright had "willingly taken care of me and my family without charge" (*The Autobiography of W. E. B. Du Bois* . . . edited by Herbert Aptheker [1968], pp. 326–36).

It was as a physician and surgeon that Wright made his most significant contributions. In addition to his criticism of the Schick test for diphtheria, "possibly the first scientific study based on any work carried out in any Negro hospital, Dr. Wright introduced the intradermal method of smallpox vaccination. He devised a splint for cervical fractures and introduced a special plate for the repair of certain types of fractures of the femur. He also developed a plate out of an inactive material, tantalum, for repair of recurrent hernias. He and his team of workers were the first to use the antibiotic, aureomycin, in man." His chapter on "Head Injuries" in *The Treatment of Fractures* by Charles Scudder (1938) was the first contribution by a Negro to an authoritative medical symposium of its kind. In 1948 he established the Harlem Hospital Cancer Research Foundation and secured funds for its support from the U.S. Public Health Service and private sources. He encouraged younger associates to engage in research and publication: eighty-nine of Wright's publications list fifty-one different persons as joint authors. Perhaps his crowning achievement was as director of Harlem Hospital. "With statesman-like maturity he welded into a harmonious whole the various white and Negro groups that comprised the staff of Harlem Hospital. He recognized and faced directly the problems faced by other minorities, particularly Jewish and Italian physicians and dealt with these with characteristic honesty and directness so that shortly before his death he was able to refer to the institution as 'the finest example of racial democracy in the world.' " Although this evaluation was an exaggeration, it expressed the basic philosophy of his goals.

With the exceptions noted in the text, this sketch is based, with the permission of W. Montague Cobb, on his warm tribute, "Louis Tompkins Wright, 1891–1952," in the *JNMA* (March 1953, pp. 130–48).

— RAYFORD W. LOGAN

WRIGHT, RICHARD (1908–1960), author, existentialist, and expatriate. He was born in a sharecropper's cabin in Roxie, near Natchez, Miss., on Sept. 4, 1908. His father, Nathan Wright, was a farmhand who later sought work in the city but deserted his family when Richard was five. His mother, Ella (Wilson) Wright, a rural schoolteacher, then struggled as a housemaid to raise her two sons during their trek from Natchez to Memphis, then to Elaine and West Helena, Ark., until she suffered a series of paralytic strokes that left her disabled and her sons at the mercy of her mother's family for material support. Hunger, destitution, and emotional insecurity were Wright's heritage from the very start, and his mother's brutal illness imbued his perspective on life with dark existential anguish. After a brief stay in an orphanage, he spent most of his childhood and youth in the home of his maternal grandparents in Jackson, Miss. There his grandmother undertook to educate him. Her strict morality and strength of character possibly prevented him from becoming a delinquent, but her religious fanaticism forever estranged him, not only from Seventh-Day Adventism, but from any organized religion. Since his refusal to be baptized was openly interpreted as the reason for God's retribution on his mother, Christianity increased his guilt feelings and came to represent for Wright an unbearable form of oppression. His poverty and ensuing shame, as well as the requirements of the Adventist diet and ritual in a predominantly Baptist neighborhood, limited his full participation in the rich folk culture and street games of his environment. He withdrew into himself, but school and the pleasures of reading and storytelling, the exercise of his own vivid imagination, provided him with the compensations he needed to believe in himself and help explain the early awakening of his literary interests.

A victim of racial discrimination in both its violent and more subtle manifestations, Wright suffered deeply from the frustrations and fears engendered by the Jim Crow system to which his early freedom had not taught him to conform. He realized that going north was the only avenue open to him for physical survival and intellectual development. Accordingly, after graduating from the ninth grade he left for Memphis in 1925. There he worked in an optical company and completed his intellectual awakening through the reading of H. L. Mencken and a few American naturalist writers. Two years later he arrived in Chicago with his family, determined to surmount the barriers of racial prejudice, poverty, and incomplete schooling. After a series of jobs as a dishwasher, porter, insurance salesman, and substitute clerk in the post office, Wright was forced into unemployment and relief by the Depression. Yet the Depression also brought him into contact with Garveyism, then with Marxism and the Communist party, which he joined in 1933. He did so because his sense of personal frustration and despair merged with the unrest of the urban poor, suffering the same kind of economic exploitation, and because his talent won him easy acceptance in the left-wing literary circle of the John Reed Club. Wright's first publications in left-wing magazines such as *Left Front, The Anvil, International Literature,* and *New Masses* were inspired, enthusiastic, but generally crude revolutionary poems.

In the mid-1930s, however, he was encouraged by his success among fellow writers at the Federal Theater Project and the Federal Writers Project and turned to prose and short-story writing. He also led the Southside Writers Club which Frank Marshall Davis, Fenton Johnson, and Margaret Walker attended. By the time he decided to move to New York to further his literary career in the spring of 1937, Wright had already completed a naturalistic novel, *Lawd Today* (later published posthumously), and most of the short stories he gathered in the collection *Uncle Tom's Children.*

Winning the 1938 *Story Magazine* prize for "Fire and Cloud" and with the subsequent publication and success of *Uncle Tom's Children,* Wright was able to devote his efforts to another novel, the material for which he had partly gathered while working in a Boy's Club in the Chicago Southside. He quit his job as a journalist for the *Daily Worker*'s Harlem bureau, then his position in the New York Federal Writers Project, and wrote *Native Son* in 1939. *Uncle Tom's Children* explored racial tensions and drama in the rural South, where conflict culminated in violence and the realization that the black protagonist had to fight as an individual, or better, organize for collective resistance in the face of open repression. *Native Son* was different. It presented a portrait of the rebellious young Negro in the northern ghettos, Bigger Thomas, a product of the racism and oppression of American capitalism. Bigger had potentialities which could be truly revolutionary but which could also explode into fascistic violence. By not depicting his black protagonist as a "blameless champion of the proletariat," Wright was severely criticized by Communist critics while the racist press denounced him as a Red. Yet the success of the book among the liberal audience was tremendous. A Book-of-the-Month Club choice, it catapulted Wright into national fame and relative wealth. More secure, he founded a family and launched into several literary projects: he wrote the stage adaptation of his novel in collaboration with Paul Green; he completed an important poetical folk history of the Negro in the United States, *Twelve Million Black Voices,* with photographs by Edwin Rosskam; he finished *The Man Who Lived Underground,* probably his finest novella.

Then in 1943 Wright wrote his autobiography from his early Mississippi childhood until his departure from Chicago in 1937. The publication of the first sections (i.e., until his move to Chicago in 1927) as *Black Boy,* another Book-of-the-Month Club choice, made him into something of a culture hero. Its sales exceeded those of *Native Son* and the book was discussed all over the country and soon translated in a half dozen languages. By lending his voice to "the average Southern black boy" and exposing with sobriety and naked terseness the workings of the racist social order, Wright probably wrote his best book. The dramatic narrative technique, depth of feeling, and often painful unmask-

ing of the self account for the high rank *Black Boy* enjoys among American classics.

From the moment he had published *Native Son* Wright had been active in interracial cooperation and in the fight against discrimination, but he was also anxious to travel in order to gain a better perspective on the United States. He had spent a couple of months in Mexico in 1940, several vacations in Canada, and had applied unsuccessfully for a trip to Eastern Europe before actually sailing for Paris in the spring of 1946, once the influence of Gertrude Stein and an official invitation from the French government helped him secure a passport. At the time Wright was a controversial figure, widely known as a pro-Communist militant while he had in fact already withdrawn from the CPUSA. The break took place as early as 1942 when Wright realized that the Communists used the Negro cause more than they served it. After reluctantly endorsing the party's propaganda for unconditional American Negro participation in the war against the Nazis, Wright could not countenance their lack of protest against discrimination in the Red Cross blood banks and similar injustices. When he published the last third of his original autobiography as *I Tried to Be a Communist* in mid-1944, Wright was severely attacked by the left wing, while the U.S. government remained wary at the thought of letting him go and speak on the "race question" with his well-known honesty.

In France, Wright was seeking the best of the humanistic tradition in response to the challenge established by American postwar materialism. He was welcomed by the existentialists, especially Jean-Paul Sartre and Simone de Beauvoir. The atmosphere of freedom and the cultured surroundings Wright enjoyed enticed him to go back to France and live there permanently when, after his return to New York in 1947, he experienced several instances of racism in the Greenwich Village neighborhood where he lived. Now that he had become one of the most famous American Negroes, he realized that there were limits and barriers the system would never allow him to cross. Thus he fled. But he was also moving toward something new, toward the discovery of other cultures in Europe, and in Africa which he had already contemplated visiting. A long period of intellectual building, a search for values and traditions, ensued for almost seven years, during which Wright was strongly attracted by existentialist philosophy.

While working on a number of projects, among which was the not-too-fortunate filming of *Native Son* in Buenos Aires, Wright led the life of a celebrity whom writers, artists, and intellectuals from all over would visit and consult. But at the same time he was pushing his philosophical quest far beyond the mere psychoanalytical readings he had attempted in New York, into the metaphysical field of Nietzsche, Kierkegaard, Heidegger, and the German existentialists to whom his early liking for Dostoevsky had led him. The result of this search was *The Outsider,* completed in 1953, about the same time as a minor novel on a psychoanalytical theme, *Savage Holiday.* Because of its artistic flaws, due mostly to the lack of balance between action and philosophical exposé, *The Outsider* has not been recognized for the important treatise on the plight of twentieth-century man it really is. The novel portrays a hero faced with existential choices, often placed in a situation of absolute freedom beyond good and evil, and often yielding to his egotistic impulses and hubris, yet who finally realizes the necessity for common action and dies proclaiming the value of human solidarity.

Wright's early themes had been the urbanization of the Negro American and the fate of the individual in modern mass society. While suffering from the suspicion which surrounded progressives in the McCarthy era and becoming estranged from the American public of the "silent generation," Wright explored the international sociopolitical scene: both the decadent structure of old European countries like Catholic Spain (of which he wrote a nearly psychoanalytical report in *Pagan Spain*), and the problems of the nations newly freed from colonialism. An extended trip to the Gold Coast is the subject of his travel narrative *Black Power,* in which he does not spare British colonists and Protestant missionaries, and in which he criticized some of Nkrumah's policies but strongly advocated a mobilization of all forces in order to foil the attempts of world capitalism against the possibilities of Pan-Africanism in the emerging nations. *The Color Curtain,* a firsthand report on the 1955 Bandung Conference, analyzed the motives and perspectives of the first political meeting from which the "white" Western world was excluded. A series of lectures (notably "Tradition and Industrialization: The Plight of the Tragic Elites in Africa," delivered to the First Congress of Black Writers and Intellectuals, which he helped to organize in 1956) are gathered under the title *White Man, Listen.* They constitute Wright's political testament and ultimate warning to the conscience of the West.

Increasingly involved in combating discrimination in the United States as well as supporting African nationalism through his essays, lectures, and interviews, Wright kept writing poetry in the form of the Japanese haiku and a good deal of fiction. He never completed an intended trilogy on the spiritual pilgrimage of a black youth from a small Deep South town to Paris, then to North Africa and back to the United States, but managed to publish the first volume, *The Long Dream,* which is the account of Fishbelly's childhood and adolescent conditioning by racism. The second volume, "Island of Hallucinations," unpublished, exposes the intrigues within the black colony in Paris and the political espionage over these expatriates in the 1950s. Shortly before he died Wright gathered a second volume of short stories, *Eight Men.* These stories include early works of the 1940s, like "The Man Who Lived Underground" and "The Man Who Killed a Shadow," in Wright's more violent and existential vein, and significantly, a few pieces in which his humor and satire have freer rein, like *Man of All Works* and *Man, God Ain't Like That* (both original plays for German radio), and especially "Big Black Good Man."

When he died an exile in Paris on Nov. 28, 1960, Richard Wright enjoyed international fame as the greatest Negro novelist, although in the United States his reputation had been somewhat eclipsed by that of Ralph Ellison and James Baldwin. Moreover, he remains, possibly second only to W. E. B. Du Bois, the most important Afro-American writer of our century, an example to many both through his commitment as a critical conscience of the modern world and through the scope of his creative endeavors. His pilgrimage from the Deep South to the Middle West, from Chicago to New York, then from the United States to Europe, Africa, and the East reflects an important chapter in Afro-American social and intellectual history. It is symbolic of the transition from a quasi-feudal system to mass society, from the parochialism of the Deep South to the wider vision of the Third World. Wright's attempt to illuminate the reality and meaning of the Afro-American experience roused his concern for the gradual awakening of the colonized and the dispossessed; in turn his quest for a humanistic meaning in modern life led him to participate in the ferment of European thinking, examine the problems of nations freshly independent from colonialism, and finally, criticize the static complacency of anti-Communism in post-World War II America as well as the neocolonialistic policies of the entire Western world.

Wright's death of a heart attack at the age of fifty-two followed a spell of amoebic dysentery which he had contracted in Africa, but was also the result of lifelong tensions and of the more recent attacks during the 1950s that he suffered from those who resented his commitment to the black struggle, to the point that he has been called by several critics "a victim of the Cold War." His works are likely to endure as products of a "representative man" of his times as well as for their intrinsic literary value. *Native Son, The Man Who Lived Underground,* and *Black Boy* are generally regarded as his finest achievements from the standpoint of literary art and depth of vision. Yet *The Outsider,* which has been somewhat discarded for its lack of technical subtlety, remains an impressive thesis novel and the first authentically existentialist American novel. The impact of his writing and of his personal example on Afro-American writers is important, although hard to determine precisely. Only recently has Wright begun to receive the serious critical attention he deserves as a major writer. He had received the Spingarn Medal in 1941, and was regularly listed in *Who's Who in America.*

Wright married Dhinah Meadman in 1939 and Ellen Poplar in 1941. She was the mother of their two children, Julia and Rachel.

See Michel Fabre's *The Unfinished Quest of Richard Wright: A Critical Biography* (1973), which includes an extensive bibliography. *Richard Wright's Native Son* (1970), edited by Richard Abcarian, and *Twentieth Century Interpretations of Native Son* (1972), edited by Houston A. Baker, Jr., are excellent critical handbooks. Dan McCall's *The Example of Richard Wright* (1969) is stimulating and often perceptive. Edward Margolies analyzed particularly *The Art of Richard Wright* (1968), and Kenneth Kinnamon, *The Emergence of Richard Wright* (1973). *Richard Wright: Impressions and Perspectives,* edited by David Ray and Robert Farnsworth (1973), supplements them.

— MICHEL FABRE, *translated by* MELVIN DIXON

WRIGHT, RICHARD ROBERT, SR.

WRIGHT, RICHARD ROBERT, SR. (1855?–1947), educator, politician, editor, and banker. He was born in Dalton, Ga., the only child of Robert and Harriet Waddell. Richard traced his ancestry to his maternal grandmother, Lucy, a Mandingo princess who landed at Havre de Grace, Md., during the latter part of the eighteenth century. His father, of mixed African and Cherokee descent, was the coachman on a plantation where his mother was a house servant.

When Richard was two years old, his father escaped to free territory, and he and his mother were taken to Cuthbert, Ga., where she married Alexander Wright and gave birth to two more children. He escaped during the Civil War and joined the Union Army. After emancipation, Harriet Wright took her children to Atlanta, where Richard in 1866 was among the first Negro children who attended the American Missionary Association's Walton Springs School. Originally called the "Car-Box," it was renamed the Storrs School in recognition of a fund donated by the Rev. Henry Martyn Storrs, pastor of the First Congregational Church of Cincinnati, Ohio. Gen. Oliver Otis Howard, commissioner of the Freedmen's Bureau, visited the Sunday school at the Storrs church in 1868 and asked the students what message he should tell the children of the North about them. Young Wright stood up and said, "Tell them, General, we're rising." This incident inspired the poem "Howard at Atlanta" by the great abolitionist John Greenleaf Whittier. Since the poem contained the word "Massa," Wright wrote Whittier on March 26, 1869, that he had given up using that word. Wright and ten of his classmates were chosen to attend Atlanta University (incorporated on Oct. 16, 1867). He taught school during summers and was graduated B.A. and valedictorian of the university's first collegiate class in 1876. On June 7 of that year he married Lydia E. Howard of Columbus, Ga.,; they became parents of four sons and five daughters.

After graduation Wright became principal of an elementary school in Cuthbert, organized farmers cooperatives, and conducted the state's first Negro county fair. In 1878 he organized the Georgia State Teachers Association, served as its first president, and began publishing its *Weekly Journal of Progress,* later the *Weekly Sentinel,* two of the early post-Reconstruction papers. In 1879 he represented Georgia Negroes at the First National Conference of Colored Men of the United States in Nashville, which sought to ameliorate the plight of Negroes, especially by migration to Kansas. There he gained the favorable attention of John Roy Lynch and Pinckney B. S. Pinchback and laid the foundation for his later participation in Republican politics. Meanwhile in 1880 he founded the first public high school for Negroes in Georgia, Ware High School in Augusta, where he taught, among other students, the younger brother and sister of John Hope.

His political activities may have aided his career in education. He was an alternate delegate in 1880 to the Republican National Convention in Chicago, an important participant at the conference of the Afro-American League in Minneapolis (1881), a member of the Republican state central committee beginning in 1882, a U.S. Department of the Interior special agent for land development in Alabama (1885), and a delegate to Republican National Conventions through 1896. In return for his influence with Negro voters, he was appointed by President McKinley paymaster in the army with the rank of major during the Spanish-American War. In 1897 he declined appointment as minister plenipotentiary to Liberia because of his commitments to his family and college. His appointment to the presidency of the land-grant college in Georgia for Negroes may have been due in part to his political influence.

A conservative tide in Augusta's city politics had forced the closing of Ware High School. About the same time the Georgia state legislature in 1887 discontinued appropriations to Atlanta University because it refused to bar attendance by a few white students, children of officers and faculty. After prolonged discussion of the relative merits of "classical education," which some opponents considered unwise for the "inherently inferior" Negroes, and vocational education, the governor signed (Nov. 26, 1890) a bill for the establishment of a colored land-grant school, the Georgia State College of Agriculture and the Mechanic Arts at Athens, Ga. White citizens protested its location in the same city as the University of Georgia, and in October 1891 the legislature established in Savannah the State College of Industry for Colored Youth. Wright was the logical choice for the presidency, because he had devoted fifteen years to teaching and administering schools. He remained president for thirty years, until 1921. He set an example for research on Negroes by visits to museums and libraries in Europe. One of the members of his faculty was Monroe Nathan Work, who began research for his *Bibliography of the Negro in Africa and America.*

His tenure was troubled by the control of white trustees who objected to Negro higher education, especially Wright's efforts to include classical education in the curriculum. His organization of the Negro Civic Improvement League less than two years after his arrival in Savannah did not increase his popularity with these trustees. The increasing pressures of the time gradually forced Wright to withdraw from politics and to follow the emphasis placed by Booker T. Washington on programs of self-help and cooperative efforts with whites. He still was unable to obtain sufficient support for an adequate curriculum; a Phelps-Stokes report in 1916 and a federal survey in 1921 confirmed this finding and Wright's presidency came to an end.

He began a new career as a banker and elder statesman. Realizing the need to encourage thrift by the large number of postwar Negro migrants from the South, he joined his son Richard R. Wright, Jr., and a daughter Lillian W. Clayton in founding in Philadelphia (1921) the Citizens and Southern Bank and Trust Company. He was motivated, moreover, by a clerk's calling his daughter Julia "nigger" in the Savannah bank where he had maintained an account for many years.

Conscious of the necessity of having a sound business background as a result of his previous experience as board member of a bank in Savannah, Wright recognized that the high attrition rate among Negro businesses generally, and banking specifically, was frequently due to mismanagement, ignorance, and undercapitalization. He therefore enrolled in the Wharton School of Finance, University of Pennsylvania, where his son had received a doctorate in economic history (1911). Another son, Emanuel, was persuaded to transfer from the School of Architecture to the Wharton School. During the same time Wright's former journalistic experience inspired another son, Whittier Wright, to work in that field as well as practice medicine.

Raising the initial capital of $125,000 was largely the responsibility of Wright. He traveled widely and persuaded wealthy and poor Negroes in Texas, Georgia, and Louisiana, among other states, to invest in a solvent institution like a bank. His reputation as an honest and qualified man provided the kind of stability needed to survive such economic crises as the 1929 stock market crash and subsequent depression. The fact that Wright managed to maintain banking operations during the worst depression in the first half of the twentieth century can be credited to both the diversity of his investment portfolio and the conservative policy of the bank.

Following the massive economic depression Wright resumed his outside activities. In 1933 the governor of Pennsylvania, J. S. Fisher, appointed him a member of the commission to erect a statue in memory of Negro soldiers killed in all of the American wars. The death of his wife and the necessity to expand his depositors sparked new activities. Accompanied by his daughter Harriet he went to Haiti, a country in which he had become interested by visits in Philadelphia of Dantès Bellegarde, former minister to the United States. Wright met three ex-presidents, received a warm welcome in many parts of the republic, and discussed the possibility of importing coffee to the United States. In 1935 Wright organized the Haitian Coffee and Products Trading Company, which imported and sold coffee until the outbreak of World War II. In 1939 he sponsored a Goodwill Air Trip to Haiti.

Near the end of his life he attended the conference in San Francisco (1945) that organized the United Nations. At a banquet in his honor organized by some of the city's leading bankers and attended by other notables, he flatly stated that employers would either have to give Negroes jobs or pay for welfare assistance (reminiscences of Rayford W. Logan, one of the guests).

This banquet was a fitting recognition of his long career which included the presidency of the National Association of Presidents of A&M Colleges (1906–19), and of the National Association of Teachers in Colored Schools (1908–1912). He was instrumental in helping secure an appropriation of $250,000 for the Semi-Centennial Emancipation Exhibition (1913), the establishment of the National Freedom Day Association, and a commemorative stamp for Booker T. Washington. He had visited England, France, and Belgium in 1919 to gather information for the Georgia Archives about Negroes in the war.

He died on July 2, 1947, of circulatory failure. Survived by five daughters and three sons, he was buried in Mt. Lawn Cemetery in Sharon Hill, Pa., after funeral services in St. Matthews AME Church, Philadelphia, attended by Charles C. Spaulding, J. Finley Wilson, and some 1200 other mourners.

The longest biography is Elizabeth Ross Haynes's *The Black Boy of Atlanta* (1952). His early career is discussed in Clarence A. Bacote's *The Story of Atlanta University, A Century of Service, 1865–1965* (1969); Ridgely Torrence's *The Story of John Hope* (1948); and August Meier's *Negro Thought in America, 1880–1915* (1963). *The Radio Speeches of Major R. Wright Sr.* were privately printed by Harriet S. B. Lemon in 1949. See also James G. Spady's *Umoja, Afro-American Journal* (1975, pp. 11–17); and the obituaries in the *New York Times* (July 3, 1947) and the *JNH* (Oct. 1947, pp. 529–30). He was regularly included in *Who's Who in America*. There is an excellent sketch by Andrew Buni in the *DAB, Supplement 4, 1946–1950* (1974, pp. 915–16). — JAMES G. SPADY

WRIGHT, THEODORE SEDGWICK (1797–1847), prominent clergyman, antislavery leader, and reformer. He was born probably in New Jersey (*The Liberator*, June 25, 1836), the son of R. P. G. Wright, an early leader in national Negro conventions. He was educated at the New York African Free School, and thanks to support from DeWitt Clinton, Arthur Tappan, and others, at Princeton Theological Seminary (1825–1828), becoming the first Negro graduate of an American theological seminary. (John Mercer Langston is erroneously said to have been the first.) Shortly thereafter he succeeded Samuel Cornish as pastor of the First Colored Presbyterian Church (also called Shiloh Presbyterian Church), New York City, a post he held for the remainder of his life. On temporary leave because of illness, he sent a letter to the church on June 20, 1832, urging the members to "be stedfast [sic], immovable, always abounding in the work of the Lord." On May 29, 1837, Wright married Adaline T. Turpin of New Rochelle, N.Y.; little is known of his family life. He died, it is said as a result of years of overwork, on March 25, 1847.

Although Wright was beloved as a minister, his most significant work was as an abolitionist and champion of Negro rights. He was a founder of the American Anti-Slavery Society in May 1833 and became one of four Negro members of the first board of managers (the others were Peter Williams, Samuel Cornish, and Christopher Rush). He was a member of that organization's executive committee until May 1840, when he joined leading New England abolitionists, including Rush, Cornish, and Henry Highland Garnet, in withdrawing from the American Anti-Slavery Society and forming the American and Foreign Anti-Slavery Society, which opposed Garrisonian radicalism. In the 1830s he was an agent for the New England Anti-Slavery Society, traveling and lecturing extensively on their behalf; he also worked with the New York State Anti-Slavery Society and the Evangelical Union Anti-Slavery Society. At the meeting of the former in Utica (Sept. 1837), he made two dramatic and influential speeches against prejudice and colonization entitled "The Progress of the Antislavery Cause" and "Prejudice Against the Colored Man." These speeches condemned prejudice and expressed the desperate need for its eradication, ideas dominant during the rest of his life.

Wright spared no effort to assist fellow Negroes, both economically and culturally. He was chairman of the

New York Vigilance Committee, formed in November 1835 for the purpose of preventing the kidnapping of Negroes and to aid fugitive slaves; the committee urged trial by jury in all cases involving alleged fugitives. He was vice-president of the Phoenix Society founded in 1833 for the improvement of Negroes "in morals, literature, and the mechanical arts," which was substantially supported by Arthur Tappan. He was president of Phoenix High School, established by New York Negroes in 1836. He presided at a mass meeting in Tabernacle Hall, New York City (Aug. 1, 1838), to celebrate British emancipation in the West Indies (Aug. 1, 1833). He was active in the Negro cooperative movement and was one of Gerrit Smith's agents for the abortive plan to distribute 120,000 acres of land to Negro families. He agitated for Negro suffrage as early as 1838; in August 1840 he signed the call for the New York State Convention of Negroes in Albany, and he was personally active in circulating petitions to the New York legislature for the suspension of property requirements for Negro voters.

Over the years Wright directed his considerable energy into other channels of reform besides abolition and Negro rights. As early as 1831 he was a member of temperance societies and was urging members of his church to sign pledges. In 1841 he was elected treasurer of the Union Missionary Society (James W. C. Pennington was named president) which sent missionaries to Africa; when the society merged into the American Missionary Association he became one of its officers. During his last years he grew increasingly interested in politics. In 1844 he was a member of the Liberty party committee which chose the presidential and vice-presidential nominees. He preferred, however, that Negroes not identify themselves with political parties. Except for Frederick Douglass, few American Negroes of his generation labored more assiduously and more effectively for the freedom and equality of his race than Theodore S. Wright.

Contemporary transcriptions of some of Wright's speeches are in the *Colored American* (July 8 and Oct. 14, 1837, for instance). Material including speeches also appears in *The Liberator* (June 26, Nov. 5, 1836, and Oct. 13, 1837; the April 2, 1847, issue has the most complete obituary).

Wright's Pastoral Letter of June 30, 1832, is in *Early Negro Writing 1760–1837, Selected and Introduced by Dorothy B. Porter* (1971, pp. 472–77); two Utica speeches are in Carter G. Woodson (ed.), *Negro Orators and their Orations* (1925, pp. 86–95). Significant material about Wright's life is in the following: Bella Gross's "Life and Times of Theodore S. Wright, 1797–1847" (*NHB*, June 1940, pp. 133–38, 144); Charles H. Wesley's *Neglected History, Essays in Negro-American History...* (1965); Herbert Aptheker (ed.), *A Documentary History of the Negro People in the United States* (1965–1966); and Benjamin Quarles's *Black Abolitionists* (1969). — WALTER M. MERRILL

YORK (c. 1770–bef. 1832), member of the Lewis and Clark expedition to the Pacific, 1804–1806. York was the son of Old York and, probably, of Rose, his wife in 1799, house slaves of the Clark family. According to a family tradition he was "brought up" with William Clark (1770–1838) in Caroline County, Va., and on the Kentucky plantation near Louisville to which the family moved in 1785. In 1799 Clark inherited York as part of his father's estate, and since York was a large and "remarkably stout, strong negro," he was a natural choice to accompany his master on the expedition as body servant.

Although officially Clark's valet, York frequently accompanied Clark on small side expeditions, and shared in other duties. York had probably acquired some knowledge of woodcraft on the Kentucky frontier; he proved himself a successful hunter. He also sometimes added to the party's usual meat diet by collecting greens and roots.

York's other services were unusual or even unique. During the months the expedition spent in preparation in Missouri (Dec. 1803 to May 1804), he may have picked up a smattering of French for, according to a Nor'wester who visited the party after it had been joined by the French-Canadian Toussaint Charbonneau and his Shoshone wife Sacagawea, "A mulatto, who spoke bad French and worse English, served as interpreter." Apparently the Indians talked to Sacagawea, who passed on what they said to her husband, who conveyed her meaning in Canadian French to York, who turned it into English for the benefit of his master, and so on in reverse. York may also have picked up a smattering of Indian languages, for in the later stages of the expedition he was sometimes assigned the duty of trading with the Indians for food—a responsibility, however, which he may have owed merely to his great popularity with the Indians as both a curiosity and an entertainer.

York revealed his public relations value in October 1804 among the Arikara. They had never seen a black man before and "all flocked around him and examined him from top to toe." York took full advantage of the opportunity, displaying "his powers of Strength, &c. &c.," and informing the Indians that he had once been a "wild animal, and caught and tamed by his master. . . . he carried on the joke and made himself more turribal than we wished him to doe." The Arikara, however, were fascinated rather than repelled. Their women, according to Clark, were "verry fond of carressing our men &c.," and York shared fully in these attentions. He continued to enjoy the favors of the Indian women all the way to the Pacific.

During the expedition's winter sojourn among the Mandans of the Upper Missouri, York improved his performance, adding a dance exhibition which produced astonishment that "So large a man should be active &c. &c.," and established him as "great Medison." (The great Western artist Charles M. Russell immortalized York among the Mandans in a painting in the Montana Museum of History, Helena.) The Shoshone the following summer were as much attracted by "a man . . . who was black and had short curling hair" as by the merchandise offered in exchange for horses. In the fall, on the Clearwater, York danced for the Nez Percé Indians, and a few days later for Indians on the Columbia.

For over two years York had enjoyed a degree of

freedom in an exciting and important enterprise. In November 1805 he and Sacagawea were permitted to vote with the other members of the expedition on the location of their winter quarters.

His displays of strength and his other entertainments undoubtedly contributed to smoothing the expedition's path across the continent, and he ranked as a celebrity among Indian nations from the Missouri to the Columbia. But after the expedition's triumphant return, he had to readjust to a slave society. Several stories, consequently, have provided him with a happier future. In various accounts he abandoned the expedition during its return journey to settle among the Walla Walla (Maude A. Rucker [ed.], *The Oregon Trail* [1930], pp. 146–47), returned to the mountains and became an important man among the Crows (*Adventures of Zenas Leonard,* edited by John C. Ewers; 1959 [1st ed., 1839], pp. 51–52; Thwaites, 1:185, note), and most recent and fantastic, "elected to remain in the Oregon Country, where he soon became the prosperous owner of a successful fleet of freight wagons" (Otto Lindenmeyer, *Black History: Lost, Stolen, or Strayed* [1970], pp. 67–69).

York's actual postexpedition life was more prosaic. Although according to one tradition he merely resumed his position as Clark's valet and continued in that capacity until his death, Clark's own story, as communicated to Washington Irving in 1832, is more probable and more depressing. York returned to Kentucky with his master, but in 1813 when Clark went to St. Louis as governor of the Missouri Territory and superintendent of Indian Affairs, he was hired out near Louisville so that he could be near his wife, the slave of a local family. Clark eventually set him free and set him up with a wagon and six horses as a freighter between Nashville and Richmond, but York, so able as a frontiersman, was much less so as an independent, free Negro businessman. Allegedly he did not take very good care of his horses and when two of them died he sold the others at a loss, hired out as a free servant, and was ill-treated, whereupon he set out to return to St. Louis and Clark, but died of cholera en route.

For the Lewis and Clark expedition, the best source is Reuben Gold Thwaites (ed.), *Original Journals of the Lewis and Clark Expedition, 1804–1806* (7 vols., 1904), but John Bakeless's *Lewis and Clark: Partners in Discovery* (1947), sometimes brings Thwaites up to date. The traditions about York's boyhood and postexpedition life in William Clark Kennerly as told to Elizabeth Russell's *Persimmon Hill: A Narrative of St. Louis and the Far West* (1948), were dictated in extreme old age by a man who was only fourteen when Clark, his uncle by marriage, died. For York's life after 1806, see *The Western Journals of Washington Irving,* edited by John Francis McDermott (1944), which Bakeless also uses in considerable detail. — KENNETH WIGGINS PORTER

YOUNG, CHARLES (1864–1922), army officer, expert mapmaker, and musician. Young was born in a log cabin in Mayslick, Mason County, Ky., on March 12, 1864. His former slave parents (his father was said to have been a private in the Union Army) took him with them when he was nine years old to Ripley, Ohio, a short distance across the Ohio River. He graduated from the Colored High School there in 1880. Gifted in languages and music, Young taught in the high school and was preparing to enter a Jesuit college when he took the competitive examination for West Point. He entered the U.S. Military Academy in 1884, the ninth Negro to be appointed, the third to graduate, and the last until nearly half a century later when Benjamin O. Davis, Jr., graduated with the Class of 1936. The life of a plebe at West Point is never an easy one, but the five years Young spent there (he was turned back after his first year for failure in mathematics) must have been the toughest in Young's life. Only a person of iron will and determination could have stayed the course. Encouraged and assisted by his instructor in engineering, Lt. George Goethals (who later constructed the Panama Canal), Young passed and received his commission as a second lieutenant on Aug. 31, 1889, two months after the regular graduation exercises. In later years classmates spoke admiringly of his fortitude.

After his graduation Young was appointed second lieutenant of 9th Cavalry and had a taste of frontier life at Fort Robinson, Neb., where he served from September 1889 until September 1890. Transferred to Fort Du Chesne, Utah, for four years, in 1894 Young was appointed professor of tactics and military science at Wilberforce University, following the establishment of a military department there during the Cleveland administration. Aside from his military duties at Wilberforce, Young taught French and mathematics. William S. Scarborough, later president of Wilberforce but in Young's time a professor of Greek, remembered him as "Thoroughly loyal to the interests of the college and at no time, when called upon, did he refuse to give service, though not officially bound to do so."

On Dec. 22, 1896, Young was promoted to First lieutenant. With the outbreak of the Spanish-American War in 1898 he wrote to the War Department requesting permission to join his regiment, should it be called to active service. He served as a major (wartime rank) in command of the 9th Ohio Volunteer Infantry from May 1898 to January 1899, in Virginia, Pennsylvania, and South Carolina, when he again joined his 9th Cavalry troop at Fort Du Chesne. In February 1901 Young was promoted to captain and April of that year found him en route to the Philippines where he spent eighteen months commanding troops and had his first taste of real warfare in the tropical jungles of Samar, Blanca Aurora, Duraga, Tobaco, and Rosana, and where he earned from his men the nickname "Follow Me."

Returning to the United States in October 1902, Young served as acting superintendent of Sequoia and General Grant National Parks, Calif., for the better part of 1903. An officer inspecting troops stationed as guard in the parks reported: "The drill of Captain Young's I Company (9th Cav) was excellent. His troop is without doubt the best instructed of any of the four troops on duty in the parks, and he is entitled to credit for keeping it up to proper standard of instruction while attending to his many duties as Park Superintendent." On completion of his tour, the Board of Trade of Visalia, Calif., passed a resolution extending a vote of thanks to Young for his outstanding services. Young's next post was commanding a troop at the Presidio of San Francisco. During this time he was married, on Feb. 18, 1904, to Ada Mills of Xenia, Ohio.

With his bride, Young went to Port-au-Prince, Haiti, as military attaché, in 1904, the first Negro military attaché in the history of the United States. A Haitian newspaper account of the time recorded Young's presentation at the National Palace to Haiti's president, Nord-Alexis, and spoke of him as "A handsome Black with distinguished bearing and charming manners." Young's years in Haiti must have been happy and were certainly productive. Accredited also to the Dominican Republic, he covered most of the island on horseback, mapped many remote and hitherto uncharted sections, and carefully revised existing maps of the principal towns, indicating fortifications in his precise West Point hand. He sent back to the Army War College voluminous reports on the country, its people, the government, agriculture, armed forces, and customs (including voodoo, in which he is said to have been "an initiate by request"). Unfortunately, many of these papers were destroyed by the army in 1925. Parts of Young's monograph on Haiti were used by the U.S. Marine occupation forces in 1915 and a few of his maps are still in the National Archives.

It was during his Haitian tour that Young wrote his book, *Military Morale of Nations and Races* (1912). Dedicated "Homage to Country," the foreword is dated Port-au-Prince, Nov. 23, 1906. Here too he was inspired to write a drama based on the life of Haiti's great hero, Toussaint Louverture. The manuscript of this unpublished work appears to have been lost. The text of his English-French-Créole dictionary, a painstaking work also unpublished, is in the library of the Army War College, Carlisle, Pa.

On Dec. 25, 1906, the Youngs' first child, a son, Charles Noel, was born in Xenia, Ohio (Mrs. Young returned home for the birth). Young was detached from attaché duty in April 1907, but was long and fondly remembered by his Haitian friends. J. F. Geffrard dedicated a book, *Some Historical Points* (1915), to "My Friend Major Charles Young."

From May 1907 to June 1908 Young served with the 2nd Division (Intelligence), War Department, General Staff, Washington, D.C. In August 1908 with his wife and small son he sailed for Camp McGrath in the Philippines where he commanded troop and third squadron. His daughter, Marie Aurelia, was born at Batangas on March 26, 1909.

Returning to the States, from June 1909 until December 1911 Young commanded the 2nd Squadron at Fort D. A. Russell (later Fort Francis E. Warren), Wyo., a tour of duty punctuated by a brief period of maneuvers at San Antonio, Tex. While at Fort Russell Young received a long letter from his friend Booker T. Washington, urging him to accept assignment as military attaché to Liberia. Young replied: "I am always willing to aid in any work for the good of the country in general and our race in particular, whether the race be found in Africa or the United States." In March 1912, after three months in the office of the chief of staff in Washington, Young sailed for Monrovia where he was to spend two years

as military attaché and to help reorganize the Liberian Frontier Force and Constabulary (relieving Lt. [later Brig.-Gen.] Benjamin O. Davis, Sr.). While in Liberia Young traveled all over a country whose only means of transportation were by boat, on foot, or in a hammock. He was again mapmaking. American Minister William D. Crum reported to the secretary of state in August 1912: "Captain Young is at work preparing a map of the Republic." In December of that year he was wounded by a bullet in the right arm on an expedition into the interior to rescue one of his American officers ambushed by Gola tribesmen. In 1913 he suffered a prolonged attack of black water fever which left him greatly weakened and necessitated a leave of absence.

Despite the protests of the president of Liberia and the U.S. State Department, Young was recalled in 1915 under the terms of the "Manchu Law" which required that an army officer must not serve on other than troop duty for more than three years. It was early in his Liberian tour (Aug. 28, 1912) that Young received his promotion to major. When he returned home, the secretary of state of Liberia wrote to the U.S. State Department, expressing "Grateful appreciation for the most valuable services rendered the Republic by Major Young in connection with the reorganization of its Frontier Forces, services which will always stand as a monument to Major Young's name in the annals of the Republic." For his exceptional work in Liberia, Young, on Feb. 22, 1916, was awarded the Spingarn Medal, given annually by the NAACP to a Negro for distinguished achievement. The presentation was made by the governor of Massachusetts at the Tremont Temple, Boston, before a crowd of over 3000.

From February 1916 to March 1917 Young served with the "punitive expedition" in Mexico where he commanded a cavalry squadron and rode to the relief of Major Tompkins and his men, ambushed near Parral. While in Mexico, on July 1, 1916, Young was promoted to lieutenant-colonel. A letter to the adjutant-general of the army from then Brig.-Gen. John J. Pershing at Dublan, Mexico, recommended Young for command duty and spoke of him as "Among those who have shown very high efficiency throughout the campaign." Upon his return from Mexico he established a school for Negro enlisted men at Fort Huachuca, for he foresaw the coming of a war and was determined that men of his race would be prepared to enter an officers' training camp if one should be established.

With the U.S. entrance into World War I, American Negroes visualized Lt.-Col. Young commanding troops in France, an assignment he would have eagerly accepted and ably carried out. Fate, and seemingly the temper of the times, denied him a general's stars. In June 1917, as the army mobilized to go to France, Young took his promotion examination for full colonel. To his dismay he was found physically unfit and sent to Letterman General Hospital in San Francisco for further tests. Supporters have to this day been convinced that the adverse findings were racial rather than clinical. The diagnosis of "high blood pressure" was scoffed at. What the army failed to reveal was that in addition to very serious hypertension (230 mm systolic; 150 mm diastolic), Young was suffering from an advanced case of chronic nephritis (Bright's disease) from which in fact he died less than five years later.

The examining board at Letterman found Young's physical appearance "astonishingly better than his medical examination indicates." Young would not be convinced that he was not as fit as ever. The only avenue for promoting him was to retire him first, then for the army board to recommend his advancement to full colonel on the retired list (where active-duty physical standards need not apply). On June 22, 1917, Young was retired, then promoted to full colonel, for "disability contracted in the line of duty." To prove his physical fitness Young made a journey by horseback from Ohio to Washington, but to no avail. The bitterness felt by his friends was compounded by the army's failure to recall him to active duty until just five days before the armistice.

Young's retirement became a bitterly controversial issue. He himself protested it in vain, as did many prominent Americans both black and white. On Nov. 6, 1918, Young was recalled to active duty with the Ohio National Guard at Camp Grant, Ill.

In 1919, still on active duty, at the special request of the State Department, Young again sailed for Monrovia as advisor to the Liberian government. This was to be his last journey. On Jan. 8, 1922, while on an inspection visit to Nigeria, Charles Young died of nephritis at Grey's Hospital in Lagos. Young's remains were buried in Lagos, by the British military authorities, with full military honors. Later, at the request of his widow, they were returned to the United States. On May 27, 1923, the Colonel Charles Young Post 398 of the American Legion in New York held services in his honor in the great hall of the City College of New York. Assistant Secretary of the Navy Franklin D. Roosevelt, Joel E. Spingarn, and W. E. B. Du Bois were among the speakers. Roosevelt stated: "No man ever more truly deserved the high repute in which he was held, for by sheer force of character, he overcame prejudices which would have discouraged many a lesser man."

On June 1, 1923, Young's body was brought in state to Washington. A military cortege escorted it to its final resting place in Arlington Cemetery. According to the *Washington Evening Star* (June 1, 1923) the funeral services were participated in by the U.S. Army, the Grand Army of the Republic, United Spanish War Veterans, Army and Navy Union, the American Legion, unaffiliated veterans of World War I, and prominent civilians, white and black. Final tribute was paid in the massive marble amphitheater where, according to the *Star,* only three other persons had been given funeral services. They were two Confederate veterans and the unknown soldier. All colored schools in Washington, D.C., were closed out of respect to "the distinguished Negro" and were well represented at the funeral services. Also attending was a delegation representing the state of Ohio, which included Harry E. Davis, a member of the state legislature, and Pres. John A. Gregg of Wilberforce University. The Howard University Choir, under the direction of Lulu Vere Childers, gave musical selections. In his funeral oration Chaplain O. J. W. Scott,

friend and tentmate of Young's during the Mexican campaign, said: "Colonel Young believed a man laughs a thousand times where he weeps but one." In an interview Campbell C. Johnson, secretary of the 12th Street Branch of the YMCA, stated that Young was "the hero of the entire colored race." Young was survived by his widow and two children.

Published information is scarce. The illustrated thirteen-page pamphlet, *A Biography of Colonel Charles Young* by Abraham Chew (1923), a rare copy of which is in the Moorland-Spinarn Research Center, Howard University, is valuable although marred by several errors. One of the most glaring is the statement, accepted by many writers, that Young "was with the men that charged up San Juan Hill" during the Spanish-American War. The falsity of this statement is evident in his military record based on holdings in the National Archives and West Point, and "Colonel Charles Young" by Nancy Gordon Heinl (*Army Magazine,* March 1977). *A Tribute to Colonel Charles Young* by W. S. Scarborough (1922) is in the West Point library. Brevet Maj.-Gen. George W. Cullum's *Biographical Register of the Officers and Graduates of the U.S. Military Academy* (1920) gives a complete list of Young's posts while on active duty. The National Archives (Diplomatic and Modern Military sections) have extensive references to Young's service in Haiti and Liberia. The author of this sketch fortunately researched his record in the Personnel Archives, St. Louis, before they were destroyed by fire on July 12, 1973. — NANCY GORDON HEINL

YOUNG, P[LUMMER] B[ERNARD], SR. (1884–1962), editor and publisher. Born in Littleton, N.C., the son of Winfield and Sally (Adams) Young, he married Eleanor Louise White of Raleigh in 1906. From this union there were two sons: P. B. Young, Jr., and Thomas White Young. In 1950, after the death of his first wife, Young married Josephine F. Moseley of Norfolk, Va.

From 1903 to 1905 he was at St. Augustine's College in Raleigh in a dual role: as a student and also as a printing instructor. Young learned his trade and began his newspaper work as assistant to his father, who founded and published the *True Reformer,* a small newspaper in their hometown.

In 1910 Young moved to Norfolk, and by 1910 had acquired ownership of a fraternal organ published by the Knights of Gideon and known as *The Lodge Journal and Guide.* Dropping "Lodge" from the name, he expanded the paper from a weekly of four pages with a circulation of 500 to a standard thirty-two-page newspaper with the largest circulation of any weekly, white or Negro, published below the Mason and Dixon Line.

From 1910 to 1946 Young served as both editor and publisher of the *Norfolk Journal and Guide,* but in the later years he shifted a large share of the business and editorial responsibilities to his two sons, each excellently trained for his respective function. Under the direction of the three Youngs, the *Guide* became, in the opinion of many critics, the best edited Negro newspaper in America. With a circulation of about 40,000, it was fourth among the "big four" Negro papers at the time of Young's death. The *Guide* received three Wendell Willkie Awards for outstanding performance in journalism. It also won several National Newspaper Publishers Association citations for journalistic excellence.

Although he never graduated from college, P. B. Young, through membership on many educational boards, exerted an appreciable influence on Negro education. From 1930 to 1940 he was a member of the board of trustees of the Anna T. Jeanes Fund. At various times he was a trustee of Hampton Institute (1940–1944), St. Paul's Polytechnic Institute, Lawrenceville, Va. (1940–1944), and Norfolk State College (originally Virginia Union University [Norfolk Unit], subsequently Virginia State College [Norfolk Division]). As a member of the "Founders Group which rendered special and outstanding service," Young was associated with the school from its beginning in 1935 until his death, first as a member of the Advisory Committee, later as a trustee. From 1957 until his death in 1962 he was chairman of Norfolk State's Board of Trustees. Young's connection with Howard University was similar. Joining Howard's Board of Trustees in 1934, he became a member of its Executive Committee in 1939, its chairman in May 1940. On April 13, 1943, he was elected chairman of the board, the first Negro to hold that position. He served until Oct. 16, 1948, when he was succeeded by Lorimer D. Milton, president of the Citizens Trust Company, Atlanta, Ga. He was a wise counselor during most of the "maturing years" of Howard's president Mordecai W. Johnson.

Because of his contributions to education and other fields, Young was the recipient of many awards and distinctions, among them honorary doctorates from Shaw University, Virginia Union University, Virginia State College, Tuskegee Institute, and Morehouse College.

A man of broad interests, Young was interested in movements and activities that concerned the Negro, and this interest was nationally recognized. He was appointed in 1943 to the President's Commission on Fair Employment Practices. He was one of the founders of the Inter-racial Commission and became vice-president of this organization's successor, the Southern Regional Conference. He was cited in 1928 by the Harmon Foundation for distinguished achievement in business. The *Richmond Times-Dispatch* (Dec. 31, 1939) placed him on its annual honor roll of outstanding Virginians for that year; four governors of the state named him to state commissions.

Negro journalists had a deep respect for P. B. Young, and during his later years he was the acknowledged "Dean of the Negro Press" (the NNPA named him "Editor of the Year" in 1960). A surprising number of the nation's top Negro journalists began their careers with "P. B. and the *Guide*." By precept and example, Young exerted a therapeutic influence on the Negro press. A moderate by nature, he felt that one could wage just as effective an attack on prejudice and discrimination with dignity and good taste as through sensational newspaper practices. He refused to allow the *Guide* to become a scandal sheet. Young published a paper that had quiet, factual, well-researched news stories and some of the most solid and constructive editorials of the era.

Although a moderate, perhaps a conservative (in the finest sense of that controversial term), Young was by no means a reactionary. In a symposium on "Negro Editors and Communism" published by *The Crisis* (April–May 1932), Young made this revealing comment: "it has been the policy of the *Journal and Guide* not to view Communism as a thoroughgoing, death-dealing evil but to regard it as just one of the factors in a growing world-wide ideal to improve the conditions of the underprivileged."

P. B. Young, Sr., died of respiratory complications culminating in pneumonia, on Oct. 9, 1962. His funeral was held at Norfolk's Grace Episcopal Church with the Rev. Richard B. Martin, rector, officiating. He was buried in Calvary Cemetery, Norfolk. His survivors were two sons, Bernard Young, Jr., and Thomas W. Young; his widow, Mrs. Josephine M. Young; three grandchildren, Bernard Young III, Davis C. Young, and Millicent Young, all of Norfolk; one great-grandchild, Elizabeth J. Young, Washington, D.C.; his sister-in-law, Anna W. Young; and several nieces and nephews. Obituaries were in the *Norfolk Virginian-Pilot* (Oct. 10, 1962), the *Norfolk Ledger-Star* (Oct. 10, 1962), and the *Washington Post* (Oct. 11, 1962).

Young was regularly included in *Who's Who in America*. For his service at Howard University, see Rayford W. Logan's *Howard University, The First Hundred Years: 1867–1967* (1969). The contributor, who served as correspondent for the *Guide* (1933–1950), based his analysis of the paper largely on this experience, and his knowledge of the Young family on his personal reminiscences and correspondence. Additional information was provided by Undine Davis, women's editor of the *Guide*. — ARTHUR P. DAVIS